Dear West Customer:

West Academic Publishing has changed the look of its American Casebook Series®.

In keeping with our efforts to promote sustainability, we have replaced our former covers with book covers that are more environmentally friendly. Our casebooks will now be covered in a 100% renewable natural fiber. In addition, we have migrated to an ink supplier that favors vegetable-based materials, such as soy.

Using soy inks and natural fibers to print our textbooks reduces VOC emissions. Moreover, our primary paper supplier is certified by the Forest Stewardship Council, which is testament to our commitment to conservation and responsible business management.

The new cover design has migrated from the long-standing brown cover to a contemporary charcoal fabric cover with silver-stamped lettering and black accents. Please know that inside the cover, our books continue to provide the same trusted content that you've come to expect from West.

We've retained the ample margins that you have told us you appreciate in our texts while moving to a new, larger font, improving readability. We hope that you will find these books a pleasing addition to your bookshelf.

Another visible change is that you will no longer see the brand name Thomson West on our print products. With the recent merger of Thomson and Reuters, I am pleased to announce that books published under the West Academic Publishing imprint will once again display the West brand.

It will likely be several years before all of our casebooks are published with the new cover and interior design. We ask for your patience as the new covers are rolled out on new and revised books knowing that behind both the new and old covers, you will find the finest in legal education materials for teaching and learning.

Thank you for your continued patronage of the West brand, which is both rooted in history and forward looking towards future innovations in legal education. We invite you to be a part of our next evolution.

Best regards,

Louis H. Higgins
Editor in Chief, West Academic Publishing

CASES AND MATERIALS ON
CONSTITUTIONAL LAW
THEMES FOR THE CONSTITUTION'S THIRD CENTURY

Fourth Edition

...

By
Daniel A. Farber
Sho Sato Professor of Law
University of California, Berkeley

William N. Eskridge, Jr.
John A. Garver Professor of Jurisprudence
Yale University

Philip P. Frickey
Alexander F. and May T. Morrison Professor of Law
University of California, Berkeley

AMERICAN CASEBOOK SERIES®

WEST®
A Thomson Reuters business

Mat #40641307

COPYRIGHT © 1993 WEST PUBLISHING CO.
© West, a Thomson business, 1998, 2003
© 2009 Thomson Reuters
    610 Opperman Drive
    St. Paul, MN 55123
    1–800–313–9378
Printed in the United States of America

ISBN: 978–0–314–18445–0

TEXT IS PRINTED ON 10% POST CONSUMER RECYCLED PAPER

To Mike, Jackie, and Lisa

D.A.F.

———

In Memory of My Grandfathers

W.N.E., Jr.

———

To Chuck and Mike

P.P.F.

Preface to the Fourth Edition

In preparing this edition, we benefitted from many comments and suggestions from numerous professors and students. Our institutions have provided us again with outstanding support as well. We thank Deans Christopher Edley and Harold Koh. Many research assistants worked on this revision, with Yale students Elizabeth Phelps (Class of 2010) and Baolu Lan (2010) deserving special mention.

Finally, we thank our students for their attention, their patience, and their assistance in improving these materials yet another time around.

Daniel A. Farber
William N. Eskridge, Jr.
Philip P. Frickey

May 2009

Summary of Contents

Appendices and Index

Table of Contents

───────

'You bastard,' said James bitterly. He was upright now, leaning against the doorpost to catch his breath. His face was unmarked except for a graze on his jaw, but he was dusty and dishevelled. 'Don't think you're getting away with it.'

'With what exactly? Selling the firm's secrets, hitting you, or screwing your family?'

'You're welcome to the girl, I wouldn't fancy it,' said James.

Saul turned away, not trusting himself.

The secretary spoke up, full of irony. 'Can I consider it safe to go now?'

'Thank you, my dear, you may,' said James. 'A timely entrance, if I may say so.'

After she had gone the two men still stood, wondering where this latest development placed them. 'I could sack you,' said James.

'You wouldn't get anyone who could do the job half as well,' said Saul.

'I concede that. But I might be prepared to lose efficiency to lose you as well. Have you thought of that?'

'Oh yes,' said Saul.

'Well then.' James was surprisingly rattled, he wanted to sit down and drink a cup of hot sweet tea. 'Let's say I'll keep my own counsel on the Judge affair, for now. I know what I think, whatever you say. But as far as I'm concerned, you're on borrowed time. Understood?'

'I always understand you, James,' said Saul bitterly. 'And you have never once surprised me.'

If the cacophony of present day looms was less than in days gone by, reflected Diana, then in the past it must have deafened within hours. The noise was constant, a steady thrumming that you became used to until you tried to speak to someone and realised that only a bellow inches from the ear would suffice. All the workers should have worn ear muffs or plugs, but the older ones never bothered. If someone enquired about it, they produced the stock excuse. 'Just popped outside for a minute, I haven't had time, sir.' And a lot of comfort fooling the factory inspectorate would be when they were stone deaf at sixty!

Although she was largely unfamiliar with the details of the weaving shed, even Diana could see that things were different. Looms had been moved, and there were three new Sulzers, grouped together. They weren't the latest type but they were revolutionary by Judge's standards, regulated by punched cards fed in on a roller. What was more, there seemed to have been a sudden infusion of colour to the place. Every shunt of the nearest loom produced another half inch of vivid green cloth, the one next to it glaring orange.

Wearied by the noise, Diana slipped out of the side door and up the stairs to what had been Andrew's office. When she reached the top corridor, she paused in surprise. There was a smell of polish in the air, and on one side table a vase of flowers, ineptly arranged but present nonetheless. Rowan was certainly making herself at home, then. Rapping on the door with a peremptory hand, she did not wait for a reply before entering.

'Good heavens, Rowan! What are you doing?'

Her daughter, wearing a superb plum wool dress, her hair a gleaming black cap, was standing before a side table, grinning into thin air, casting down pieces of cloth like a conjuror. Rowan jumped, turned and went pink.

'I was practising. I've got an appointment today.'

'For the Magic Circle, I presume?'

Rowan gathered up her samples almost protectively. 'It's a big firm, I've got to do it right.'

Diana sat herself down in the chair before the desk and surveyed the room. 'You've certainly cleaned this place up. But I need hardly say, Rowan, that this wasn't the idea. You were to wind the business up, remember?'

'It — wasn't possible,' said Rowan airily. 'The bank manager didn't want me to, he was really keen for me to carry on. We wouldn't have got anything if we'd folded it. And, actually, we're making a remarkable recovery.'

'So James tells me,' said Diana meaningfully.

'I don't know how he should know.' Some of Rowan's confidence ebbed away. She hunched one shoulder, all at once vulnerable. 'You won't let him get at Judge's, will you?' she asked worriedly. 'I know he's saying horrid things about us. He told one firm that we can't deliver, they rang up and said so.'

Diana's eyebrows lifted a millimetre. She looked delicious this morning, her auburn hair glowing against her biscuit tan, a gold clip holding a white and tan silk scarf at her throat. 'You've been spying, Rowan,' she said in a sing-song voice.

'No, I haven't! I've just been using my intelligence. And we're doing really well, Mr. Blood at the bank keeps boasting about me at meetings.'

'You're certainly dressing better,' remarked Diana. 'What a superb dress. You look at least twenty-five, and nowhere near as plain as usual.'

'Thank you,' said Rowan grimly. Her mother never paid a real compliment, she was incapable of it. Still, half a loaf was better than no bread.

'Aren't people a little surprised to find that you are in charge of Judge's?' asked Diana with feigned innocence. Rowan was getting far too entrenched here, a position based on a falsehood.

'Nobody knows,' retorted Rowan. 'And I would rather Dirty Jim didn't go around telling them. When I go for orders everyone thinks I'm just the daughter of the family who's gone into selling. If they want a price reduction they think I have to go back and ask someone, some professional, if that's OK.'

'And do you?' asked Diana, amazed.

'I come back, sit in the office for five minutes, and 'phone them,' grinned Rowan. 'It's quite simple really. All I have to do is work out what making something costs us; Mr. Blood helps me with that; and if necessary I sell it at that price. We've got to get in with them, you see. We'll make the profit next year.'

'I see.' Diana folded her gloves.

Suddenly Rowan realised that her need to boast had taken her beyond caution. 'You won't tell James, will you?' she begged. 'Please don't let him get at me.'

'Honestly, Rowan, he is not an ogre!' snapped her mother. 'Anyway, I didn't come to talk business. I came about Sally.'

A grin split Rowan's pale face, paler than usual these days from hours spent indoors. 'He wants her out of the house,' she declared. 'You've only been back a week! Now tell me he isn't an ogre.'

'It's just — Sally isn't very — she doesn't fit in. I feel it myself, she can hardly make a remark without mentioning her father. And of course she is at a difficult age, very moody. I've discussed it with her and she wants to come back to you. I shall take care of her financially, of course. It might be best, Rowan —'

'He's threatening to stop Andy's college fees,' said Rowan shrewdly.

Diana flared. 'He wouldn't dare! Oh, Rowan, you're an adult, you understand about sex! The moment we try to make love, and we've been apart for weeks, she's hammering on the door. If we forget to lock it she walks straight in and stands by the bed, demanding a drink of water or something. I absolutely cannot bear it.'

Rowan felt choked with hot rage, and hotter embarrassment. That her mother should think her the proper recipient for such confidences! Had she no sense of shame at all? But all she said was a prim, 'You're not even married to him.'

'Do be your age!'

Her daughter turned away, tears pricking her eyelids. Why

144

did she have to come here, bringing it all back, bringing with her memories of how it used to be, in a warm, safe childhood when if you went into Mummy's bedroom Daddy was there too, with a hug and a kiss and an invitation to snuggle down between them. Why did she have to smash that mirror, to overlay the image with one of her and James Barton, obscenely linked, in an act of which Rowan knew nothing?

She swung round. 'I'll have Sally back, today, right now. She shouldn't stay with you.'

'Thank goodness! Of course, we can all still go on holiday together -'

'No, thank you,' said Rowan. 'By the way, I'd rather you didn't visit us here. After all, I'm not sure that I can trust you not to tell him more than he should know.'

Diana stared at her. 'Don't forget, Rowan dear, that although you are nominally in charge, the power is mine,' she said thinly.

Rowan was silent. Her gaze was fixed on the floor, where the worn carpet had been taken up and the wood floor polished, even though it was draughty. It was all a front, everything in it was pretend, she wasn't really in charge, the firm wasn't really doing well, the range wasn't original and the new looms were only new to them. But, if it was a lie, it was one she had to live, because one day it might be true.

Diana drifted to the door with that long, cool stride that in Rowan was giraffe ranginess.

''Scuse me.' Joe Partridge barged past her into the room, a navy T-shirt showing his tattoos to advantage, a clutch of dockets in his mechanic's hand. 'Here Rowan,' he said forcefully. 'We can't have them buggers in the warehouse taking delivery without checking. Took one look and I could see they'd got half a load of t'wrong wool! Carpet stuff it is, Herdwick or sommat.'

Rowan sighed. 'I'm going to give him the push, you know, the one that tells you it can't be done before you've finished telling him what you want. He's been working here thirty years too many already .'

'Right,' said Joe. 'OK for a driving lesson tonight?'

''Bout seven? Oh — I can't! My little sister's coming. I could bring her too though, couldn't I?'

Joe looked dubious. 'Thought we might go for a drink after.'

'Well, you come at seven and we'll see what's happening.'

Joe nodded and left, giving Diana a cursory grunt in passing. She came back into the room. 'Rowan dear —'

Rowan looked up from perusing the dockets Joe had brought. 'I thought you'd gone, Mother,' she said distantly.

'Are you taking up with that man?'

Rowan shrugged. Her hackles were even now starting to rise. 'I don't quite know what you mean.'

'He is greasy, he has tattoos, your father would die if he knew you were selling yourself so cheap. I at least gave you credit for some discrimination.'

Her daughter's fingers closed on the dockets, crushing them. 'My father's already dead,' she flamed. 'At least I don't do things in front of people! He's kind, he's energetic, he's considerate and he isn't anyone else's husband. In my book that makes him a thousand times better than bloody James Barton!'

Diana let out her breath in a weary sigh. 'You'll never be told, will you, Rowan?' She turned on her heel and left.

On her own, Rowan seethed. Why had she gone on like that about Joe? He was a good friend, but no more than that. They kissed a bit, he sometimes had to be restrained from putting his hand on the crotch of her jeans, but that was just his idea of a proper end to an evening. What really interested him, both of them, was getting Judge's back on its feet, and with it Partridge Carriers. They wrangled over his rates and the number of trips he did. But now, because of Diana's shocked and hypocritical reaction, she had an urge to take Joe and flaunt him, tattoos and all.

Chapter Fifteen

Driving down the familiar suburban street set up in James a flurry of sensation. He had passed this way at least twice a day for years and years, you couldn't rub out history. He remembered the day he and Marjorie had first taken Richard to boarding school, at the tender age of eight, driving down this road with everyone talking tensely about school and how they would be sure to take care of Richard's rabbit.

There was the day Marjorie's mother had died and he had driven this route with her, sobbing wearily into her handkerchief as he tried to sympathise, and instead fought impatience. And in the last years, the heavy homeward trips to what seemed to him a stifling and joyless house. He spun the wheel and swung automatically into the drive.

The sameness was almost shocking. He could believe that he had only to walk in, as he used to do, and call peremptorily 'Marjorie! Marjorie, I'm home!' for her to emerge from the lounge and set about getting his dinner. She had always been very good about that, he remembered. As soon as he had changed, the dinner would be there, on the table, waiting for him.

At Aspley Manor they often had guests, or were dining out. There were long hungry waits before food, and if he went into the kitchen there weren't any biscuits or anything, just avocados and apples. He went up to his old front door, and there was the key, still on his ring, next to those for the car. He slipped it into the lock.

'Marjorie! Marjorie, it's me.'

The hall was just the same: thick carpet, pictures of

Richard on the walls, revolting floral wallpaper. It had all the hallmarks of suburban affluence from the brass barometer to a dozen limited edition prints of birds. In the past he had regarded Marjorie's lack of taste as a major crime, but standing there, waiting, it seemed familiar and comforting.

She came out of the lounge and said, 'Hello, James.' She was just the same, short and dumpy, wearing one of the endless house cardigans she knitted for herself. 'Fancy a cup of tea?' she asked.

'Wouldn't mind,' said James. They went through to the kitchen, dripping with Georgian oak and latticed windows. He noticed how warm the house was, in stark contrast to Aspley Manor where the wind blew outside the house and inside the carpets lifted in the draught. 'I thought Richard was going to be here,' he said.

Marjorie made a quizzical face. 'He's angry with you still. He might come in later, we'll just have to see.'

'Are you still angry with me?'

She met his eyes. 'I never was, James, or at least not for long. You left me behind. Perhaps I should have tried to keep up, but I didn't. It was both our faults.'

He swallowed. 'That's very decent of you.'

She set a tray with dainty china cups and twee tea spoons and took it through to the gas fire in the lounge. James felt familiar irritation as he sat there, the ghosts of too many leaden evenings rising up to haunt him.

'Diana and I are getting married next month,' he said aggressively.

'I trust you're not giving me an invitation,' said Marjorie.

'Not you, no. Richard though. I would like him to be there and meet Diana. He might understand a bit more.'

Marjorie let out a hoot of laughter. 'See what a classy bit of stuff you got on top of!'

'God, Marjorie, I'd forgotten how vulgar you can be sometimes.' James put down his cup angrily. Suddenly everything about her angered him, but most of all her lack of feeling.

'You didn't give a damn whether I left you or not, did you?' he snapped.

She met his eyes fair and square. 'Not a lot, no. When I did care you were working. Years and years I never saw you, except in bed. Richard hardly knew you at all, I had to show him pictures! I made a life for myself, I had to.'

James said nothing. Marjorie reached down the side of her chair and got out her knitting, clicking up and down the rows as efficiently as a machine.

They heard the front door open. James got to his feet and went out into the hall, smoothing his hair and feeling almost nervous. His son, Richard, was leaning a tennis racquet against the hall stand and stepping out of his trainers. He had James's hair, slightly less red, and a deeper colour to his eyes so that they verged on blue. He lacked the thin skin of the redhead and instead had Saul's skin, smooth and lightly tanned. A vision of the boy in his childhood rose up to choke James.

'You're looking well,' he said thickly.

'Am I?' Clearly Richard was spoiling for a fight.

'Your mother and I have been having a chat. She seems quite happy.'

'Fat lot of consideration you ever gave to it. Look, will you get out of my way? I want to go up and have a shower.'

'Oh, for God's sake, Richard! All right, you're angry, but it's ancient history now. It's two years since I left here.'

'And the first time I've seen you in all that time,' said Richard, giving his father a grimace that could never have been a smile.

They stood, facing each other, James blocking the way through the narrow hall. They had never touched and now they stood at a distance, as if to avoid contamination. James reached into his pocket and drew out a thick square envelope. 'Wedding invitation. Next month. I should like you to come.'

'Get stuffed, Daddy.'

'I imagined you might say that. It's a pity, I think you'd like Diana. She's a very remarkable woman. Her son's going to play the violin at the reception, his college is tipping him for stardom. You needn't bother to reply. If you want to come we'll make room for you.'

'Are you bothered it will look bad if I don't turn up? You can't leave us flat and then demand attendance when it suits you. No, I won't come, you can take that as final. Now, get out of my way.'

He tried to push past his father, but James grabbed his shoulders and held him. They stood, frozen in the contact. James thought, 'I would never have done this before Diana. She awakened me to touch.' 'I love you Richard,' he said gruffly. 'I know I haven't shown it. You're finishing university soon and I want you in the firm. Come and see me, we'll discuss it.'

Richard looked away, screwing up his mouth against emotion. 'I've got a job,' he muttered. 'I'm going to work for International Wools. I'm one of the leg men, they want to send me to South America straight after my finals.'

'There you'll be one of twenty, with me you're the heir apparent. Please, Richard, I need you.'

'No.' The boy put up a hand and grasped his father's wrist, wrenching it from his shoulder. He ran up the stairs, head bowed.

James went back to Marjorie. 'You've done a job on him, haven't you? Really turned him sour.'

'You should have visited him when it happened. He waited and waited for you.'

'I didn't know! Why didn't you tell me?'

She shrugged, with benign malevolence. 'Why did you need telling?'

On the way home he thought, 'Thank God for Diana! Just thank God I've at last got someone with feelings.' When they made love she didn't lie passive beneath him, she demanded, insisted, on satisfaction. It was like a mountain that he climbed often, knowing the thrill would be there on the summit, yet sometimes hardly able to bear the effort of the climb. When they were married, things would be calmer. He looked up and saw that the car had headed unerringly into Lumb Lane.

This time he took a girl he hadn't seen before, a West Indian with a black bush of hair. She had heard of him though, she knew what he wanted — straight sex and a bit of dirty talk about other men. They did it while another couple of girls stood chatting by the wall, only mildly interested. Afterwards the girl said, 'Dangerous this sort of thing. You could get mugged. You ought to set a girl up in a flat. I know a nice place.'

James laughed. 'I bet you do. No, I like it this way. Know who I am, do you?'

She nodded. 'Everyone does.'

'If you want to get on in this world, go ask for a job at Bardsey Mills. I'll put in a good word for you.'

She made a face. 'Why d'you think I'm on the game? They don't take blacks.'

'They will if I tell 'em. Go on, give it a try.'

She got out of the car, grinning. 'You never know, I might at that. Name's Mandy.'

He started the engine. 'I'll remember, Mandy.'

Chapter Sixteen

On the day of the wedding, Rowan stood in the little back bedroom in the mill cottage and cursed. Sally, dressed in smart pink and white, sat on the bed. 'You should wear your lovely wool dress,' she urged.

'Not to this I won't,' declared Rowan. 'The dress would be spoiled forever.'

'You don't have to go,' said Sally.

Rowan sighed. When she had said that to her mother the reply had been uncompromising: 'Come or I take over the firm.'

'I haven't got anything,' she said despairingly. She would not wear her plum, that was her buying outfit and someone might spill something on it. Apart from that her wardrobe was trousers, trousers and more trousers. So, trousers it would have to be when she longed to upstage her mother and amaze James Barton by her charming and elegant appearance. Diana should have threatened her earlier.

She pulled on a pair of black velvet skintight trews. If she wore them with black high heels the bottom half was all right, but the top was extremely difficult. Sally said, 'That skinny white T-shirt and your blue silk blouse.'

'Together?' She tried them. The white top was actually sleeveless and very low cut, it had to be worn without a bra. If she wore the silk blouse with the sleeves rolled to the elbow to disguise the burn mark on the cuff from the iron — a lesson in ironing silk never subsequently forgotten — and she cinched it with Sally's gold chain belt . . . she turned to her sister.

'What do you think?'

'Smashing. Very sexy, when Joe sees that he'll rape you in the back of the van.'

'Sally! Don't be horrible. Have you done your homework?'

'No. And I'm not going to.'

Rowan knew better than to argue with her. Confronting Sally these days meant drilling through her carapace of wordly control into a seething mass of emotion. Hysterics were commonplace, but whenever Rowan steeled herself to talk to Diana about it the only suggestion was to pack her off to a psychiatrist, when anyone could see Sally wasn't mad! Rowan supposed it was inevitable, really. If you took grief and shock and impotent rage and mixed them together with adolescence, you produced an unholy cocktail.

She glanced sideways at her sister. Despite the little girl dress Diana had chosen, Sally was developing into a lovely woman. Her cascade of blonde hair, held back Alice in Wonderland style and falling over her shoulders, could not disguise two plump breasts that put Rowan's skinny figure to shame. Yet she had her mother's long legs and slender waist. Sally, at thirteen, was distinctly toothsome.

Rowan pulled her hair free of its band and bent over to brush it, trying to shake her head free of horrible thoughts. Sally's friends were all boys these days, she picked them up on the way to and from school. Sixteen year olds in leather jackets, shambling along beside Sally in her school uniform. And Sally was becoming a great deal too knowing. Rowan, who knew not very much herself, was daily fighting panic.

Bumping along in Joe's van, the girls were unusually silent. Rowan was conscious of a guilty pleasure in the outing, because it was a party and she hadn't been to one in ages. Her avowed stance of prim outrage was starting to bore her. She wanted to have fun and yet still not let James Barton think he had won her over, a difficult balancing act.

Glancing across at Joe, cheerfully whistling through his teeth and ramming the ancient gear lever up and down the box, she knew she had done right. In his smartest clothes of sharp suit and dark green button-down shirt, his hair over his collar and his nails still ineradicably black with grease, he was in himself an insult to James. The presence of Joe turned Rowan from dutiful daughter into freedom fighter, and left her at liberty to have as good a time as she chose.

Joe turned into the Town Hall car park, expertly carving up a Mercedes Sports and a Jaguar. Sally said, 'Oh, look, I remember them. They used to be Daddy's friends, fuck them.'

Joe glanced at Rowan, but she didn't meet his eye. 'I don't like to hear girls swear, Sally,' said Joe sternly.

'And who the fuck cares what you like?' retorted Sally, flinging out of the van.

Rowan caught Joe's arm. 'Don't get at her, she's in a state. I knew today was going to be bad. Mother insisted she come, I kept trying to tell her Sal wasn't up to it.'

'There's no excuse for that sort of rudeness,' complained Joe. 'She needs a clip round the ear, she does.'

Not for the first time Rowan felt the desire to hit Joe with a brick, to knock some vestige of sensitivity into his brain. Perhaps the Rugby League had knocked it out. More likely that it had never been there, which was why he was such a success at the game, mashing opponents without a qualm.

'You're getting in a state as well, aren't you?' said Joe.

Rowan grinned into his earnest face. He was a simple soul, but he tried.

They followed Sally into the building. It was the usual functional public place, more suited to planning permissions than marriage. Expensively dressed people were everywhere, half of them unknown to Rowan. James and Diana hadn't arrived.

'I hope they come,' complained one woman, her feathered hat wobbling. 'I didn't dress up like this to spend the morning in the Town Hall and get a basket meal at the local pub.'

'Where is the reception?' asked Rowan.

'Why, at the Manor, of course. And who are you, dear, a relative of James's?'

Sally, whose demure dress was somewhat at odds with her

provocative sprawling across the wooden chairs, said: 'Not yet but she soon will be. Won't it be fun to be related to the shit, Rowan?'

'Be quiet, Sally,' said Rowan levelly. As the woman moved away, Rowan asked: 'Are you determined to make a scene, Sal?'

'Yes. No. I don't know. I just hate it here, I hate all of it.'

'I know, I know.' Rowan sat down next to her and took her hand. She could feel Sally shaking, a fundamental shudder that involved her whole body. 'Do you remember when we were little and you had nightmares? I used to sing you a song, didn't I?'

'You can't sing it here,' said Sally miserably. 'What's going to happen, Rowan? Everything's so frightening and horrid.'

Rowan looked at her. 'Nothing's going to happen. We'll be fine, you and me, I won't let anything go wrong. After today we don't have to see him again.'

'I wish I was as brave as you,' said Sally. Rowan almost laughed. If Sally knew how scared she was, how she clung to the one or two constants in her life because of the security they offered, would her sister be reassured? Or would it be the shifting of one of her few rocks?

'When it's all going on, I'm going to think about the song,' she said feebly. 'You think about it too, Sal.'

There was a commotion by the door. Diana and James entered, followed by a morose-looking Andy. A rustle went through the crowd, a gentle chorus of admiration, and Joe said, 'By, she's a stunner, your ma.' Jaundiced as she was, Rowan couldn't disagree. Diana was wearing her hair swept up into a knot, and perched on the top was a ridiculous and flirty piece of green lace. Her jade silk suit had a narrow skirt and flowing jacket, worn over a pale lemon camisole. Her nipples showed through, the only provocative statement in an otherwise prudish rig. James, in a pale grey suit, white shirt and blue tie, wore an unaccustomed heavy gold bracelet. It was as if he was today celebrating more than a

156

marriage; he was showing the world his money, his sex appeal and his power. 'This is my woman,' he was saying, 'any man here must long to have her in his bed. Here is my gold, I can even afford to wear it as jewellery, and soon you will see my magnificent, enviable home.'

They stood together, Diana and James, welcoming their friends. Andy pushed roughly past them, clattering chairs to reach his sisters. The enemy triumvirate stood shoulder to shoulder and glowered.

'You're not really going to play for them, are you?' demanded Rowan.

'Yes, I am actually,' said Andy. 'It's good practice for me. After all, music's got nothing to do with any of this.'

'Yes it has,' said Sally. 'You shouldn't do it, you're betraying Daddy.'

Andy looked away from the girls: he drew imperceptibly apart from them. 'My music's my own,' he said stolidly. 'I won't have it dragged into everything. I have to play when I'm asked, it's vital. I ought to be asked more.'

Everyone was settling down and falling silent, but defiantly Rowan kept on talking. 'Aren't you doing as well as you hoped, then?'

'Yes. No. I want more appearances, they keep saying I'm not ready. But it's them, they don't want the hassle of having me well known, they want to keep me under wraps. My career's got to start soon, I can't play to myself forever. Mother's asked a music critic from the paper to come to the reception. I'll get some publicity for my next competition.'

'Will you win?' asked Sally. He had been placed three times so far.

Andy nodded. 'This time, I must.'

The registrar cleared his throat and at last they subsided. The sunlight was falling through a dusty window, sending speckles of gold splashing across shoulders and faces. Rowan pushed herself out of her body, she sent herself soaring up into the sunshine, away from this horrible place. Her ears closed against the words being spoken, her face

157

took on a look of distant happiness. Saul, sitting grimly by the door and amazed at himself for being there, for a scant second admired her and wondered who she was. He felt a shock of recognition.

Afterwards the throng moved like water out into the car park, trickling away towards Aspley Manor in their smart cars. The van, proclaiming its status to all who wanted to read the name on the side, blasted blue smoke over the legs of people next to it and roared vulgarly out. They were squashed in the front this time, with Andy bumming a ride.

'All right, Sal?' asked Rowan.

The girl nodded. With one of her mood swings she had backed off from the edge and retreated into little girl solemnity. 'She's all right,' Rowan told herself. 'I don't have to worry about her any more today.' She was tired of worrying, her head ached with responsibility. Surely now she could enjoy herself?

Diana and James were greeting guests as they arrived. When James saw them approaching, he put on an act for the benefit of those watching. 'Well, hello you lot! Is this the latest thing, arriving like a parcel?'

'We've been treated like parcels, we thought we'd make the point,' retorted Rowan. James could say nothing without worsening things. He glared at Rowan, a gaze of such venom that she felt herself colour. Diana drew her to one side and said softly, 'Don't you dare make a scene! And why are you dressed like some sort of pop star? And with that vulgar man, why did you bring him?'

'I like him,' said Rowan, because she did. And at that moment she admired him, standing amidst so much unaccustomed wealth in the magnificent hall of the Manor House, looking round as if speculating on how much it would fetch for scrap. Joe had no sense whatsoever of inferiority, he was right up there, tattoos and all.

Diana contented herself with a hissed, 'Just make sure he behaves!' and went back to James's side. Joe wandered off, saying loudly, 'Think we'll get a drink then, Ro?'

158

'Don't mind if I do,' said Sally naughtily, and followed him in search of booze. Rowan caught Andy's arm. 'You keep an eye on her, Andy! It's your turn.'

'All right,' he said vaguely. Rowan wasn't to know that he hadn't heard her, that his mind was totally involved with the pieces he was to play.

She too strolled off, aware that she was attracting stares. It was an unusual sensation, she didn't know if they were admiring or incredulous. Suppose she did look ridiculous, as Diana had said? Very tall, very thin, very flat-chested. A man came towards her carrying two champagne flutes.

'There you are, Rowan,' he said. 'I was looking for you. Here's some champagne.'

She turned a little pink, and took the glass. 'Hello, Saul.'

As she sipped, he stared at her. She looked down, trying to glance surreptitiously at him, because he was so tanned and healthy. All she could see properly from under her lids were his hands, the hairs on them gold from the sun, the fingers squared at the ends. A sudden and unexpected sensation caught at her stomach. She looked up into his face and he was staring right at her.

'You look gorgeous,' he said softly. 'Like the principal boy in a pantomime, the boy prince.'

'My mother said I looked like a pop singer,' said Rowan, trying to laugh.

'Well, so you do. I'll be your first fan, if you like.'

Rowan gulped her champagne. This man was flirting with her, and it was so, so exciting. 'I thought you'd be furious with me,' she said bravely.

'Who, me? Just because you stole our range?' He rolled his eyes in amazement. She wondered if he had drunk more than one glass of champagne. 'I did you a favour. You're the one who ought to be worried, I might call it in.'

'What do you mean?'

'I might ask for something in return, something you don't want to give. I could have lost my job for you.'

'But you didn't have to show me,' said Rowan, backing away a little. 'You know we're so small, we can't hurt Bardsey's. Anyway, what would you want?'

He laughed at her, shaking his head. 'Rowan, you are so young. Come on, let's find some more champagne, let's dance.'

There was no dancing yet, they had first to eat the food Diana had provided. Lobster and salmon, venison and beef, snails *à la grecque* and caviare, centred around an ice sculpture of a heron. 'It should have been a vulture,' said Rowan.

Saul, drinking yet another glass of champagne, said hazily, 'You're too hard on him. He's a great man in his own way. But he's a jealous man, and you and I nibble away at him. I suppose he's childish really, he has a thousand toys but can't lend any one of them, not to me, not to you, not to anyone.'

'I wonder if Mother knows that?' said Rowan, driving her sharp teeth into some really quite tender meat.

'I think he's met his match there, don't you?'

They both turned and stared across at the happy couple. Diana was bending to talk to a man who was a friend of James's, and her breasts were swinging forward into the camisole, lolling unfettered above and against the silk. The man was enjoying it but James was not, he kept trying to persuade Diana to straighten and move on. Easily, deftly, Diana kept him at bay and teased him. When at last she straightened up and moved away with James, he said something fiercely to her and she merely smiled, and lifted one scornful eyebrow.

'She's so sure of herself,' muttered Rowan. 'When I see her look like that, I hate her.'

'You might be like her one day,' said Saul.

The champagne made Rowan reply, 'I haven't got the boobs.'

He laughed and put his hand on her shoulder. 'I bet they're lovely little apples,' he said softly. 'Topped with cherries. Just what I like for a tasty mouthful.'

Rowan cast him a startled look. She moved away hurriedly. 'I'm going to the loo,' she said shortly, and went, almost running. Saul cursed. He really should not have drunk so much.

Rowan went in search of Sally and Joe. There was no trace of Sally, but since Andy was nowhere to be seen either she assumed they were together. Joe was being propositioned by a woman wearing the sort of professional make-up that only looks good in photographs. He was watching her phlegmatically, sitting on a hard wooden Elizabethan chair, her hand stroking his muscled thigh as it bulged against his trousers. He saw Rowan and stood up, discarding the woman with firm kindness, as if she were a cat.

'Hello, Ro,' he said. 'Been wondering where you got to. Fancy some air?'

The woman glared at Rowan, her face falling into grim lines. She mumbled something and began to weave an unsteady path back to the booze.

Rowan and Joe went out into the gardens. It wasn't particularly warm. 'Would you believe it,' he commented. 'That old biddy wanted me to go upstairs with her and — you know — in one of the beds. I was fair took back.'

'She looks the sort,' said Rowan.

The beautiful, windy parkland all around made her feel sad all of a sudden. A peacock, one of James's conceits, was trailing its tail over the lawn as if carrying not some beautiful appendage but a load of trouble. 'I wish I could go home,' said Rowan.

'Party's hardly started,' said Joe. 'Wonder if there's any beer?'

They went back into the house, Rowan determinedly trying to shake off her gloom. Diana was crossing the hall. 'There you are, Rowan. Come along, Andy's going to play.' She looked as strung up as if she were going to play herself. James came out of the dining-room.

161

'Diana! Come along, you can't desert everyone.'

'I have to see to Andy,' she said abstractedly. 'This is important for him.'

'And today is important for me,' said James, every word clipped and pointed. 'For both of us.'

But Diana seemed not to notice. 'Go on, will you, Rowan, see to things,' she murmured, and went off to find Andy.

James reached out and caught Rowan's arm. 'I'll thank you to control your sister,' he said nastily, venting his anger on Diana's daughter. He was gripping her arm to the bone.

'Stop it,' she whimpered.

'Here you, let go of her,' said Joe, and caught James's arm in turn, gripping like a vice.

'For Christ's sake!' said James incredulously, releasing Rowan. Joe slowly released his own grip. Indentations remained in the cloth of James's suit where Joe's fingers had pressed. James flexed his fingers. 'Sally is drunk as a skunk and being sick in one of the bedrooms,' he said furiously, clearly at the end of his tether. 'And your mother is fussing over the future Yehudi Menuhin. Since you, Rowan, are the only one sober and actually present, would you mind coming in and helping me get everyone through for this bloody concert!'

Rowan eyed him nervously. 'Is Sally all right?' she asked.

'Now she's being sick, yes. Before that she appeared to be trying to seduce one of my oldest friends.'

She snapped back, 'If he was a friend of yours, it was probably the other way round.'

She went into the dining-room and began to smile and usher guests through to the chairs set out in the ballroom. James stood and watched her, then glanced back at Joe, standing stolidly in the hall. 'What does she see in you?' he asked.

Joe said, 'Dunno. You got any beer?'

'In the cupboard in the kitchen, ask someone. God, what a day.' He too went to his task of guiding the guests.

Upstairs Andy was tight with nerves, snapping at his

162

mother every time she spoke. 'Just remember, take it steadily,' she insisted.

'Don't be stupid! It's meant to be fast. This isn't a school concert, there are critics out there.'

'Try not to think of them,' she advised.

'Of course I shall think of them! I have to remember they are there, I *want* them there.'

Diana subsided. She tried to straighten his tie and he cursed her, she smoothed his hair from his forehead and he hit her hand away. Then, he turned and picked up his violin. 'Good luck,' she said, but she might not have been in the room. His face settled into smooth, inward-looking lines. Violin and bow in one hand, he pulled his jacket down with the other and went down to play.

Diana's legs felt weak. Suppose it went wrong, suppose he did not play as she knew he could and this opportunity she had given him turned to stone? If the school was right and he wasn't ready, this was the worst thing she could have done. Somehow she couldn't face going downstairs, sitting there while people watched her watching him. She would sit on the bed here and listen.

The babble of conversation was falling away, silence was spreading through the house. The air was heavy with expectation. When it had lasted for long seconds, when she thought her nerves would break waiting for the notes, someone said, 'Why don't you go down?'

She looked up, startled. It was Saul, James's half-brother. He stood in the doorway, tall, brown, swaying slightly. 'Be quiet,' she breathed. 'I want to listen.'

Shrugging, he came into the room and sat on the bed beside her. In her tense, hyper-sensitive state she thought she could hear his heart. They were quite silent. In a matter of seconds Andy began to play.

The notes fell clear and sure and beautiful. The piece was sonorous, almost melancholy, swelling to wild joy and then drifting into tranquillity. Diana's eyes closed as she listened, and then as Andy launched himself upon the central allegro vivace, taking it at a gallop, her eyes flew open and her nails bored into the palms of her hands. Instinctively Saul's hand covered hers, they could hear each other's breathing, they sat together in mutual tension. As the piece moved to its gentle conclusion, they each let out their breath in a long sigh.

Diana said, 'Isn't he wonderful? I knew he could do it, he needs an audience to show what he can do.'

'He's brilliant,' said Saul. 'But the other day I heard someone say you could have been better. They heard you when you were at school.'

Her face relaxed into a smile. 'I was good. I still am, but James doesn't really understand.'

'James never does undertstand,' said Saul throatily.

They looked at each other. He thought how beautiful she was, how luscious, in the ripe bloom of maturity. Downstairs the violin still played, Andy was settling to a popular, merry piece he could play blindfold. 'You really excited me today,' said Saul. 'I was watching you. I thought I would die if I could just make love to you.'

'Would it be so thrilling?' asked Diana slowly. She felt as if the music had caressed her senses, liberating her.

Saul grinned. He reached out and took hold of her breast, loose within her silk top. 'You're my brother's wife. There would be nothing more thrilling. And for you too, this is your wedding day after all. You've got to keep one step ahead of James, you know.'

'Oh, I know,' said Diana. She reached out and touched Saul's crotch where his erection reared hard and tireless. 'You're very young,' she murmured. 'James gets so tired sometimes. He'll be tired tonight.'

'Well then — ' Saul got up and shut the door, turning the key in the lock. 'We'd be doing him a favour then, wouldn't we? Taking the pressure off.'

He unzipped his fly and his erection sprang free, like a blind caged beast. Diana laughed, almost hysterically. 'If you men knew what you looked like!' she said. 'At least take your trousers off.'

He had her over the end of the bed, his feet still on the floor. Either side of him spread her stockinged legs and as he thrust between them, seeing even as he struggled that she was looking at him with contained, judgmental mockery, he felt sudden sympathy for James. It was good, oh it was good and fierce and wonderful, but this was not a woman you could fail. In this one act with her a man could taste the joy of heaven and the torment of hell.

All at once she convulsed about him. He let himself go, bathed in sweat, exhausted, guilty and yet triumphant. 'Never again,' he told himself, watching her dress. James was welcome to her.

In the ballroom Andy was smiling, bowing, acknowledging the applause. He only ever looked truly relaxed, reflected Rowan, in those brief moments following a successful performance. He was tense even when he played, and that was transmitted, sometimes uncomfortably, to the audience. He was wonderfully gifted, but even now there was the sense of potential not quite realised and it had been like that since he first stood up in front of the family and played 'Three Blind Mice'.

Someone James knew, in television, was at her elbow, rather the worse for wear. 'Fantastic, wonderful,' he slurred. 'D'you play? No? Pity, you'd be a sensation, should be a model. Wish your brother was a bit more off the beam, doesn't look mad enough.' He wandered off to tell Andy that he ought to dress like a deranged monk. Rowan felt her spirits starting to rise again, reviving at the compliment like a flower after rain. Did she really look like a model? Perhaps she ought to capitalise on it and take to way-out dressing. It was bound to be more fun.

The chairs were being moved to make room for a disco. Some of the women were going to the cloakroom to repair their make-up and take off their hats, and a press photographer had appeared to snap the local celebrities. Diana came into the room. She had changed into a pale flowing kaftan. She went across to James, took hold of his upper arm in both her hands and kissed his cheek.

'Better now?' he murmured, aware that the photographer was recording the scene.

'Much,' she replied. They exchanged a look and a laugh, in a rare moment of true intimacy. Saul, watching from the doorway, sober now and hardly believing what he had done, thought, 'God, but she's a viper.' 'You poor sod, James,' he murmured.

Diana turned and caught his eye across the room. She gave him a rueful grin and then, as James began to talk business with a fellow wool baron, she drifted casually over. Curtains were being drawn and strobe disco lighting was replacing the sunny afternoon. The first record began to play, 'Love Love Me Do.'

'Why on earth did we do it?' she said softly.

'God knows. I can't really believe we did.'

She eyed him speculatively. 'Don't look so anxious, it wasn't the start of anything. It was a vulnerable moment, that's all. Nothing for you to worry about.'

Saul said, 'It was a shitty thing to do, even to James.'

She shrugged. 'I think James can take it. Oh look, there's Rowan.'

She summoned her daughter with a peremptory wave, and Rowan's face became inscrutable. Nonetheless she came over. 'Did you want something?'

'Darling, thank you for helping James. You must have some fun, I think you should dance with Saul.'

'Not to this, it's too slow. Anyway, no one else is dancing.'

'Don't be difficult.'

Diana left them. Saul said, 'I'm sorry I was rude earlier. I was drunk.'

'Aren't you any more?'

'No.'

They stood in silence. The man running the disco, getting no response with his dirgelike first record, cut it off in midstream and instead put on 'Purple Haze.'

166

'Good God,' said Saul. 'That's a bit wild for the middle of the afternoon.'

'Let's dance,' said Rowan, because she wouldn't when told and would when not.

'I think I'm too sober,' said Saul. Nonetheless he went out onto the floor.

Rowan was a good dancer, and she knew it. Whenever exotic movement was called for in a school play, the consensus had always been 'Ask Rowan Judge'. Long legs and arms twined and twisted, her narrow hips undulated as well as any belly dancer's. Now, with guitar music howling into the atmosphere, with champagne inside her and the lights dimmed, she let herself go. People turned to watch, and Saul, whose normal style of dancing resembled grape treading during the siesta, knew he looked a fool. There was nothing for it but to enter into the spirit of the thing. He took off his jacket and tossed it to the side and then really got down to it, feeling the sweat sticking his shirt to his back.

'That's better,' said Rowan, punctuating the music by clasping her hands together and whirling them round as if throwing the hammer.

'Good God,' said James, watching from the sidelines. 'You have to admit she's fantastic.'

'Which is more than can be said for Saul,' commented Diana. 'I would say energetic and workmanlike, but lacking in anything resembling talent. Oh, my God, look at her now. She can be really embarrassing.'

At that moment Joe came into the room. He fancied himself as a dancer and at Rugby Club dos was often asked to perform. He watched Saul's antics for a moment then sniffed, hitched up his trousers and sauntered on to the floor. 'Get off, mate,' he said sympathetically. 'I'll show you how.'

Saul, who had not realised the extreme length of 'Purple Haze', retreated to the bar. 'Right, Ro,' said Joe. 'Let's motor.'

He caught Rowan by the waist, flung her from arm to

arm, released her and did a handstand, going over on to his feet and gyrating on the floor for a moment or two before getting up. The photographer's flash gun popped and popped again, Joe let out an ear-piercing rebel yell, Diana hid her face in her hands and James stormed on to the dance floor and yelled at Rowan, 'Get that ape out of here!'

In the end Rowan drove the van home while Joe snored beside her and Sally sat by the window, green-faced and silent. She felt absolutely empty, drained of unhappiness, expectation, everything. They had attended not a beginning but an end; she was tonight shutting the door on the past.

The little mill house was in darkness. She left Joe in the van to sleep it off and helped Sally into the house and up to bed. How good it was to be home again. She went out into the yard and stood looking at the dark bulk of the mill, as inefficient and outdated a structure as anyone could wish for. Stone on stone on stone, each tough and creamy piece hacked out of the earth and placed there by hand. Bradford was full of such mills, and the labour required to build them defeated the imagination. City of stone, city of soft, soft wool. Was her mill, was wool itself, doomed to die, as the stonemasons themselves had quietly passed away? There was no place for anything that could not pay its way.

Yet the mill comforted her. Without it there would be choices and decisions to make, about herself and her future. What was going to happen to her? She was eighteen and the years ahead were like the blank pages of an exercise book, waiting to be filled. She wanted so much out of life, she wouldn't settle for half measures, not in anything! Nobody seemed to understand. There was an ache, a long slow ache deep inside that had been with her for years and only today seemed sharp and insistent. It was a longing for someone, something, that was hers and hers alone. She wanted to be loved.

Chapter Seventeen

Diana put down her violin almost roughly. It was not often that music failed her, but today it seemed not to calm her thoughts but to work against them, so that the music jangled and her head whirled and the notes tied themselves into knots that were translated into tangles in her mind. She slammed the case shut, closing her eyes for a desperate second. Perhaps a walk in the garden might help.

One of the cleaners was polishing the hall floor but Diana took no notice and left footprints on it. Normally she would take care to avoid antagonising the help, simply because they tended to leave, which was a nuisance. The woman stood in mute accusation, watching Diana's white set face.

It was cold outside and Diana had not stopped to get her coat. She didn't mind, the discomfort distracted her. Arms folded across her body she walked briskly down a gravel path and through the orchard. The apples were poor this year, it had been cold early on and killed the blossom, and then later there had been no sun to ripen the fruit. Nonetheless she picked one of the hard green knobs and gnawed it, grimacing at the taste. What on earth was she going to do?

Because the answer to that question was not going to come easily, she found her mind drifting back. Didn't it all prove she should never have left Andrew? She had killed him, as surely as if she had put a knife in his ribs, and yet it might have ended like that anyway. The business would have gone down, he was useless at it, and their marriage, their family, could never have survived bankruptcy. More to the point then was that she should never have married him, and the causes of that were lost. It might be now that she should never have married James. She was beginning to think that was the bitter truth.

Why was it that strong men always had chinks in their armour where she was concerned? It made her despise them, just a little. She had loved James most when he had blackmailed her into continuing the affair, when he had outfaced Andrew, brutally disillusioning him. He seemed different now, a middle-aged man hanging on to youth.

Last night, as on so many nights, they had gone to a nightclub with some of James's vulgar textile friends. After some wild dancing in which Diana had been almost assaulted by a man who professed to have known James for years, they had gone on to a gambling club. The croupier had been a small weary girl in a tight black dress. James flirted with her, giving her chips. Diana, not at her best and never a gambler, had bad-temperedly lost fifty pounds. In the car on the way home she and James had had one of those scratchy, nasty arguments.

'What on earth do you want to do in the evenings, damn it?' he had raged. He did not understand her essential puritanism. Left to herself she ate a light supper, practised, read and listened to music.

At least she had ensured that Andy's training was the best, and that was something for which she had cause to thank James. But the girls — well, Rowan was never easy. As for Sally, she was as wild if not wilder. Was it something in the genes perhaps? Rowan had never been so precocious, but Sally was so much prettier. Too pretty, she thought anxiously. If only James wasn't such a pig about the girls.

Annoyance sparked through her. He was a bastard sometimes, an absolute sod, and she didn't trust him. Only last week her so-called friend, Linda, whom she now remembered had shunned her when first she left home, had commented lightly, 'Donald saw your James the other day, in Lumb Lane of all places! You'll have to tell him he'll catch something.'

170

Diana had replied smoothly, 'Don't be silly, Linda. It's a short cut he often uses.'

'He'd stopped the car. Probably buying a paper or something. You'll have to tell him, people will talk.'

'I'm sure they wouldn't be so foolish.'

You didn't forget conversations like that. To hell with him catching something, so might she! If this other thing hadn't been on her mind she'd have challenged him straight out, and even though he denied it he would have known that she knew. The extent of her hurt surprised her. If she lost James what would she have, what would be left to her?

Her breasts were full and aching, they always were in early pregnancy. If only James liked children the whole thing would be simpler. Except − could you foist what could well be another man's child on to your husband? Wouldn't you remember every day that it lived? Again she told herself, as so many times before, it had been just once with Saul that month and many times with James. The odds were that James was the father, she had grown careless and didn't always use her diaphragm even with him. She had got out of the habit of considering pregnancy somehow, she had felt past all that sort of thing. Yet here she was again, sick and weary and aching, and she didn't want a baby, whoever's it was, she was too old for broken nights and nappies.

The decision seemed to be made then. She would make an appointment with a clinic and get herself seen to. She felt better at once and started to walk back to the house, but the logistics of a stay in a clinic rose up to haunt her. What would she say to James?

She made an appointment at the clinic for the very next morning, and set out in the car soon after James left for work. The place was familiar, it was where she attended for her smears and check-ups, she had parked in this self-same place half a dozen times at least. Then as she went in she had an overwhelming sense of unreality. She wasn't really pregnant, none of this was real, the doctor would examine her and tell her to stop imagining things. The routine of the clinic mesmerised her and it was a doctor she had seen before, young and distant. As she undressed and lay on the couch, as the doctor felt her breasts and belly and reached up inside her to feel her womb, she was inexorably reminded of those other times she had experienced this.

The doctor rinsed his hands at the basin and Diana scrambled back into her clothes. He said, 'I think about six weeks. Is that your feeling?'

'Yes,'

'And why do you want a termination, Mrs. Barton?'

'I'm too old. I have three grown-up children, I'm not up to it any more. It's not something I want to think about.'

'Well.'

She pulled her blouse straight and sat down before his desk. All the composure she normally had at her disposal seemed to desert her, she was on the verge of tears.

'Have you discussed it with your husband?' enquired the doctor.

Unwisely she said, 'No, and I'm not going to. I don't want it, he won't want it, not at his age. He doesn't like children.'

In a paternal, soothing voice, the doctor said, 'That may not be the case, Mrs. Barton. He might be thrilled to be a father in middle age, you never know. Now, it seems to me best if you go off and talk to him about it and then, if he agrees, you can both come and see me again.'

Diana stared at him, dumbfounded. 'You mean you won't do it?'

'Not without your husband's agreement.'

'You stupid, pompous sod!'

She left in a rage and it was still burning when James came home that evening. Somehow, when she saw him, it dissolved into tears. 'Oh James, I'm so glad you're home,' she wept. 'It's been such a terrible day.'

'What on earth's the matter?' He was taken aback, but

172

most flattered. The row earlier in the week had lingered, they had been stiff with each other. He patted her shoulder and she leaned against him, a gesture he misinterpreted. He cupped her breast and squeezed but she yelped.

'Don't do that, it hurts.'

'Does it? Why, are you ill?'

She gulped. 'Yes. Yes, I'm ill, and I've got to have an operation and you've got to agree. It's so silly but you will agree, won't you?'

James's face changed. 'What sort of operation?'

Wiping the tears with her fingers, Diana said, 'Just a silly woman's thing. It isn't important. Look, I'll get us both a drink.'

He was watching her with cool grey eyes, she could feel them boring into her, she could almost hear his brain clicking. 'Are you trying to get an abortion?' he demanded. 'Are you pregnant?'

She turned to face him. 'Yes. How did you know?'

'I'm not stupid, Diana. How far gone are you?'

'About six weeks. But it doesn't matter, I'm getting rid of it. We're too old for babies. If the doctor hadn't been such a fool I'd have been done tomorrow. He's got some ridiculous idea that you'd be delighted to have another family. Apparently middle-aged men get a kick out of parading with a pregnant belly beside them, as if they were walking around with an erection on public display.'

James said, 'He's right. I shall like it.'

It was what she least wanted to hear and yet she knew all along she had expected it. The tawny eyes opened wide with rage. 'James! It's my body, I'm the one involved! I won't have it, I absolutely refuse!'

She flung herself down on to the sofa, chewing at her fists. He went and took hold of them saying 'Diana, Diana' but she hit out at him and kicked up at his groin. 'Bitch,' he muttered and pushed her down, forcing her back on to the sofa. She resisted, silent but red-faced with anger, until

173

suddenly he let her go. She gave a cry and lay there, breathing hard.

'You've been going with prostitutes,' she panted. 'Don't deny it, you've been seen. I've probably got some filthy disease.'

He was going to deny it. But somehow he wanted her to know. 'I go quite a bit,' he said casually. 'Tuesdays and Thursdays usually, the girls know me. You won't catch anything, I always use a rubber.'

She looked up at him. 'Oh God,' she said miserably. 'Why on earth did I leave Andrew for you?'

Later in the evening, when they were both very drunk, he said, 'The baby will save us, you know. We'll have something together.'

'Will we?' She lay slumped in a chair, her hair a tangled mass around her face. Already he could see that her waist was thickening, her breasts hanging heavily.

'I'll never go near another scrubber if you have it,' he promised her.

'What did you go for in the first place?' she demanded. 'I never said no to you.'

'Different thing,' he said. 'It's like masturbation, you don't think of the girl. It's quick, they don't care about you. Sometimes the other girls stand about, they don't even bother to watch. They'll do anything if you pay them enough.'

'How much for what I do for you?' hissed Diana.

James reached across and put his hand on her belly. He had the upper hand, he had got his own back on her and it satisfied him. 'I wouldn't do that with them. You've got to understand. You're different, I love you. I want our baby.'

She sat up and stared into his face, hating his slight smile. 'What would you do if I still got rid of it? I could, you know, if I told them what you've been doing. They'd realise what sort of man you are.'

He picked up his whisky glass and drained it. 'I'm your

sort of man,' he said. 'But you know how I'd feel about it, you know what would happen.'

'What? Tell me. Go on, say it.' She had to know that she really couldn't win. She had to know that there was no easy way out.

'I'd leave you.'

Diana felt herself go very, very cold.

Rowan drove her ancient car slowly and carefully through the dismal streets of the Leeds suburb, trying to look for the name of the firm she was visiting and avoid running over a dog, cat or child. Now that she had her own driving licence she found herself thinking far more about the journey to her customers than the customers themselves, she was exhausted by anxiety even before she arrived. Somehow the presence of Joe next to her, however drunk or disinterested he might be, had acted as a tranquilliser and without him she was suffering acute withdrawal symptoms.

When she finally drew up in a parking place, having rejected three others because they would need reversing, she had a headache and found she couldn't quite remember why she was there. It came back to her in a rush of panic. To visit Sylvex, a company she had approached before but hadn't persuaded to buy anything from her. They were one of those large, unobtrusive firms that made up vast ranges of clothing under a bewildering number of labels. Most people had something by Sylvex in their wardrobe and never knew it.

She got out of the car and locked it carefully. She was wearing a long orange skirt, orange beret, boots and a vivid green fitted jacket. The material was Judge's own, run up for her by Mr. Suzman, who was only too delighted to make something 'looking like some fun' as he described it.

Now, out in public wearing the fruits of their combined imaginations, she felt conspicuous and perhaps foolish. A girl of her height shouldn't try to stand out, she should merge into the scenery, play down her long legs, narrow waist, over-sinuous neck.

The tailor hadn't thought so. 'You look so good,' he had chuckled. 'I think you could be in a play. I like that. Now I make for you a tabard, and tight pants. Good cloth this time.'

'Our cloth,' said Rowan firmly, and then, as an after-thought, 'and it is good.'

'It is not worsted,' he retorted.

'That doesn't matter, it's still good. Please, Mr. Suzman, use my cloth and make it look good. Please.'

He gave in to her, perhaps because his fatherly kindness had been so stretched by his own girls that he had plenty over for someone else's. The final outfit had delighted them both. She had swirled out of the shop longing for an occasion to wear it.

Where had all that confidence gone? Sometimes she had it, buckets of it, and other times, times like this, it leaked away as if every bucket was a sieve.

But, you didn't need real confidence if you could fake it. Striding into the lobby, lined with well-dusted plastic palms, she announced, 'I have an appointment. Rowan Judge to see Mr. DeSande.'

She stood in the middle of the floor, swinging on her heel and looking at the clothing samples pinned to the walls all around. Men's voices approached from the hinterland of the building. One of them rang an unpleasant bell. Two men came through the swing doors into the lobby.

'Hello, James,' said Rowan bravely.

He swung round, fixing her with the twin cannon of his grey eyes. 'Good God,' he declared. 'You look like something out of a bargain basement ragbag.'

His escort, the managing director, Mr. DeSande, lifted an eyebrow. Rowan knew she must not respond in kind, it would be tactless. 'I'm sorry you don't like it, James,' she said coolly. 'It's our own cloth, I suppose that would account for it. By the way, how is Mother?'

'Haven't you spoken to her? She was going to ring you.'

'Has something happened?'

James slid his hands into his pockets. This announcement was one he could savour. 'She's pregnant,' he declared. 'Due at the end of April.'

Rowan's response was highly gratifying. The colour drained from her cheeks, she looked shocked to the core. 'Oh,' she said feebly. 'Oh dear.'

Mr. DeSande, who had been observing the exchange with some interest, said, 'My dear, can I get you something? It must be quite a surprise.'

'I'm all right, thank you,' said Rowan. But Mr. DeSande took her arm and led her to a chair. 'I am sorry,' she apologised. 'Could I have a drink of water?'

Casting James a look of deep reproach, DeSande said, 'Of course, my dear,' and went off to fetch it.

'Stop play-acting,' snapped James as soon as he was gone. 'Are you hoping for the sympathy vote?'

'Yes,' she retorted. 'And I'll get it. Mother must be mad, she knows how horrible you are to children.'

'Only other people's children.'

Rowan looked away, her thin fingers playing with the fluffy pile on her skirt. James thought, 'She really is upset, she's white as a ghost, and so thin.' From the heights of his proven potency he looked down and felt sorry for her. 'How's business?' he asked jerkily.

She glanced up. 'All right. Hard work though.'

'Damned hard work I should think, turning that mess round. Are you making much of your own stuff yet?'

She sighed. 'Not a lot, no. Most of it's contracted out.'

'Then if I were you, I'd sell that barn of a mill and get somewhere more sensible,' advised James. 'You'll never get back into proper production, you haven't the capital. And if you try, it'll break you.'

Hearing her own worst fears voiced galvanized Rowan.

She got to her feet, saying shrilly, 'That isn't true! You're always wanting to run us down, you want me to fail! You want me to come begging to you for help, you want us all to be grateful and living on handouts. The only reason you pay for Andy is because it puts him on your side. I won't give you the satisfaction!'

Mr. DeSande, entering with the glass of water, saw her take a step towards him. She reached for the glass but her hand didn't take it. For a long second she hung suspended in the air and then crumpled on to the cold marble tiles.

When James told Diana about it over dinner, she asked, 'Did you leave her there? Was she all right?'

'She was fine,' said James. 'DeSande was fussing over her like a mother hen. The thing that appals me is I'm not sure she didn't stage the whole performance, she might even have got an order out of him. Which is more than I could manage.' He grimaced thoughtfully.

'I thought you said you were making a courtesy call,' said Diana.

'That was the excuse, yes. Hello Bill, just thought I'd pop in and see how you're getting along, been a long time, and so on. The truth is we can't get orders from them and no one knows why. I bet she got something.'

Diana got up and went slowly over to the sideboard to bring the pudding. She was feeling tired tonight, although in general the pregnancy was flourishing. She stifled a yawn. 'I wish Rowan could do something else,' she said wistfully. 'She's leading a terrible life, no fun and only that ghastly Partridge man to go about with. God help us if she's sleeping with him.'

'Probably got tattoos on his balls,' said James absently. As Diana sat down again he reached out and took her hand. 'Look,' he began. 'I've been thinking. Judge's can't possibly make it as it is, they haven't the money, and Rowan's grinding herself into the floor over it. That faint wasn't put on, she'd gone green. I know she and I have been at loggerheads, but I don't hate the girl! She's got guts. Wouldn't it be best if I bought out Andy and Sally's share of Judge's and put in some investment? I'll pay a bit over the odds, to show there's no fiddle going on. When she knows I've got control, she'll sell her share too, there should be enough to buy a little business. Fashion shop or something.'

Diana put his hand to her cheek. 'That is so sweet of you,' she murmured. 'But she'll never agree!'

He shrugged. 'She doesn't have to. You do. It's time the poor girl had some life, or she'll turn into an old maid with a tacky business and nothing else. I don't want our baby growing up asking, "Why didn't you ever do anything for Rowan, Daddy?" I owe her this, and I owe it to you.'

In the candlelight Diana's eyes gleamed like vintage port. 'Sometimes you really surprise me,' she whispered. 'You make me glad about the baby, and I wasn't at all till tonight. I'm grateful to it already for making you kind to Rowan.'

'Didn't I tell you it would make all the difference?' James leaned across and brushed her soft lips with his own. He felt a great, abiding peace.

At first Rowan could make no sense of the letter. She sat trying to understand what it said, half-aware that Sally was using the kitchen shears to cut her long blonde hair into a ragged bob.

'What do you think of it?' asked Sally.

Rowan glanced up. 'It's lopsided. Go to the hairdresser. Has Mother been talking to you? About selling your share of Judge's?'

'I haven't given her the chance. She wanted to meet me in town last week but I didn't go. Is that from her?'

'No. Her solicitors.'

'She can't take me to court for not meeting her in Rackhams!' wailed Sally. Rowan said nothing so she picked up her school bag, in which she kept sweets and pop comics but never homework, and flounced out.

Joe's van roared in as Rowan went out to the mill. It was his day for taking scoured wool to be carded and spun, he had a regular contract now. She went across to talk to him. 'Joe,' she said cautiously, 'have you heard any rumours lately? About Judge's?'

'Nah.' He heaved a bale of wool aboard the van. 'Only rubbish.'

'What sort of rubbish?'

'Someone said he'd heard that Bardsey's were buying you out, but as I said, it's a family firm, they can't.'

Her face flamed. 'Not Bardsey's!' she exploded. 'She couldn't sell it to that man, not even she could do that!'

'Well, she wouldn't, would she?'

Rowan thrust the letter in his face. He stared at it, sometimes his lips moved. 'I don't understand it,' he said at length.

'Oh, give it here!' Rowan snatched it back. 'It says they want to meet me to discuss the agreed disposal of the company. I thought at first it was something left over from Dad dying, but it isn't. It's Mother. She's trying to sell out from under me, and she hasn't breathed a word. God, I hate her!'

'No you don't, Ro,' soothed Joe.

'And I hate you too!' she shrieked.

As soon as she had stopped shaking she drove out to Aspley Manor. It was nearly Christmas but the weather was still mild, the leaves hung on the trees awaiting a gale to send them flying. Rowan stared out at the park and said loudly, 'You've got all this, James Barton, why do you need poor little Judge's as well? Doesn't anything satisfy you?'

When she arrived she got out of her car and tramped round to the back door. She could see her mother, sitting at the kitchen table, still in her dressing gown. It hung open and her swollen belly, a strange protruberance on an otherwise slim figure, bulged out obscenely. As Rowan flung open the door, Diana jumped.

'Rowan! Why, you did startle me.'

'Did I?' She sat down opposite her mother, watching her with fierce green eyes. They gleamed with unshed tears.

'I've been wanting to talk to you,' said Diana awkwardly.

'I bet you have. I'm not going to let you do it, I won't!'

'Well, it's not up to you, is it?' said her mother. 'You can't stop me. I've put a lot of thought into what's best for you, all of you. I can't let you go on treating Andy and Sally's shares in the business as irrelevant, it isn't fair.'

A tremor crossed Rowan's white face. 'I'll never sell him my share,' she said bitterly.

'You might have to,' said Diana. 'Darling, at the price he's paying the others I'd be mad to refuse. I have to act in their best interests!'

'But not in mine,' said Rowan.

'It is in your best interests if you had the sense to see it! You slave away at that place nineteen hours a day, you never go anywhere, never have any fun. If you really won't sell then you can sit tight and reap the profits when James has the firm turned round.'

Rowan flared, it was like someone throwing petrol on the embers of a fire. 'I'm the one that's turning it round! That's the only reason he wants it, now it's doing well! The man's a crook, a shark, you should see that!'

'Darling, that's rubbish,' said Diana patiently.

Rowan half rose to her feet. 'You say it's rubbish. Did he tell you about the other day, about Sylvex? He couldn't get an order, not however much he grovelled. I got one. I got the biggest order we've ever had, and James Bloody Barton knows it! And the reason is that we do what he can do, but we do it cheaper and quicker and without so much paper. We do what people want. He hasn't cornered the market in business ability. He's been so busy sleeping with other men's wives and buying houses and racketing from one nightclub to another that he didn't notice what we were doing, what *I* was doing!'

181

'Have you heard something about James?' demanded Diana. 'If so, you've got to tell me.'

Momentarily diverted, Rowan said, 'What should I have heard? What's he done?'

Her mother swallowed. 'Well. Nothing, I shouldn't wonder. He's working very hard now I'm expecting this baby. It's changed him.'

'Oh yeah,' sneered Rowan. 'All of a sudden he's turned sweet and lovable. Don't you think it's a bit odd? Don't you think what he really wants is Judge's at a bargain price, before we start showing what we can really do? Because we're going places, Mother, we really are!'

'But at what cost?' Diana got up and came round the table, shuffling a little in her silly mules. 'Darling, you're white as a ghost, you're thin, you've got bags under your eyes. I want you to be free of all this, and to please me, because of the baby, James will set you free. I think that's sweet of him, only you can't see it.'

Rowan felt like crying. Why was it that other people always seemed to think they knew what was best for her and never took a blind bit of notice of what she said?

'You don't mind about the baby, do you, Rowan?' asked her mother, almost plaintively.

'You know I do,' said Rowan shortly. 'It's childish, but I do. It seems rather horrible somehow, and the way he gloats about it is even more horrible.'

'That's just the way you see him. In your eyes he does nothing right. Look, will you drive me into town? We'll go and see James and talk about this.'

'No,' said Rowan. 'I won't see him. And I warn you, Mother, that if you sell to him I'll never speak to you again, and I won't let Sally speak to you and I'll try my best to turn Andy against you as well. James doesn't need Judge's and I do.' She spun on her heel and flounced out, sending the door crashing back against the wall. The winter wind, at long last tinged with ice, blew gustily across the floor.

Diana drove herself to see James. These days she had a Porsche, which she did not want but James had chosen. Occasionally he would borrow it because it suited his image sometimes to be the boy racer, screaming through the park and outstripping Rolls-Royces on the road into town. He now considered his own Roller very staid, an old man's car. The novelty had palled, as with so many things. Perhaps with him, everything?

The Porsche's bucket seat didn't suit her back. She wriggled uncomfortably. She wished James would get rid of the damn thing so she could get back to a neat hatchback with room for the shopping and escape being chatted up by other drivers at traffic lights. Her cool, disdainful profile framed in the window of the Porsche seemed to be irresistible.

Today was particularly troublesome. Some guy in a Japanese hotrod chased her all the way into town, grinning and making faces, and had the temerity to follow her into the multi-storey car park. It occurred to her that it might have been wiser to park at Bardsey's, but so often there wasn't a space. The man would go away if she was firm with him. She got out of the car and locked it, her wide tan coat swirling about her, concealing all trace of her pregnancy.

'You certainly do that car a favour, don't you, sweet-heart?'

He was in front of her as she hurried to the exit.

'Go away,' she said distantly and tried to push past him. He caught her arm, the other hand fastening on her hand-bag. For the first time Diana felt scared. 'What a pretty, rich lady,' purred her attacker.

She said nothing but pulled back, holding on to the bag and staring in fixed horror into the man's grinning face. He was in no hurry, he was enjoying tormenting her, frightening her. Suddenly he jerked her forward, pushing her between two cars. He was forcing her to her knees. A short, anguished scream broke from her.

'Diana? Diana, are you all right?'

She tried to pull round, yelling, 'Saul! Saul, come quickly!' and saw that he was getting out of the Aston, a hundred yards away across three lines of cars. The man let go of her, lashing out with a punch that caught her in the belly. She fell with a painful grunt. 'Rich bitch,' said the man and left her.

She lay in a daze, not thinking. After a minute or so Saul picked her up.

'He got away down the stairs,' he told her. 'I thought I'd better come and see to you.'

'He hit me,' muttered Diana. 'I think I'm all right.'

Saul helped her to her feet. She was white and shaking, with dirt on her coat and her face. 'Er — the baby,' said Saul awkwardly. 'Do you think I'd better call an ambulance?'

'No.' she was fierce and emphatic. 'Help me to get to James. I shouldn't have parked here. I don't know why I did.'

They went down in the lift together, Saul supporting her and hating every minute of it. Diana said, 'You don't have to look so pained.'

'I'm sorry,' he said. 'Diana, there's something I've been wanting to ask you.'

The lift doors opened and they stepped out in unison. 'If it's what I think it is,' said Diana, 'then you can rest easy. It isn't yours.'

He let out his breath in relief. 'Thank God for that. It's one thing having a drunken fling, but we can do without results. And James is over the moon, full of untypical love and charity, even to me. I've been choking on guilt.'

'Poor you,' said Diana thinly.

When James saw his wife he went white. 'What in God's name happened?' he asked. Diana shook her head, fighting tears. Saul said, 'She was attacked in the car park. I got there before he could do much but I think he punched her. You'd better call a doctor.'

'I'll do better than that. We'll get the consultant gynae-cologist. See to it, will you? Tell him it's an emergency. Darling, lie down at once, here on the sofa. It's all right, I'm here now.'

Diana clung to him, suddenly shaking violently. 'He was going to rape me,' she whispered. 'He was dragging me off to do it. He might have killed me!'

'But it didn't happen.' James gripped her hands hard. 'And the important thing is to look after this baby.'

'But I was so frightened!'

'Yes, yes, of course you were.' James adored her at that moment. All her hard edges had been knocked away, she was dishevelled, vulnerable and she needed him.

Saul came back into the room. 'He's coming straight over. They're bringing up some tea, I thought Diana could do with it.'

Diana struggled up into a sitting position. She would not be seen like this by Saul of all people. In a tight, high voice she said, 'James, I was coming to tell you. I don't think I can sell Judge's to you, Rowan just won't have it. She was raving at me this morning.'

'That bloody girl!' declared James. 'Take no notice, Diana, she ought to know better than to make scenes. We don't need her consent.'

'But I thought — ' began Diana.

'Darling.' James put his hands either side of her head. 'Don't think. You needn't worry, I'll see to it.'

Saul, absorbing everything about this exchange, said, 'That poor girl. There's no end to what you'll do to her, is there, James?'

'You keep your nose out of it,' snapped James. 'It's none of your business.'

'I like Rowan,' said Saul. 'She's a brave kid. Losing Judge's now, when she's done so well, it would break her heart.'

'But it's *for* Rowan,' said Diana shakily. 'To take away

185

some of the strain. She's having a terrible time working there!'

'She doesn't think it's terrible,' said Saul. 'If she says she wants to keep the firm, then that's probably what she means. It's not up to you to say what's good for her and it certainly isn't up to James. I'm not surprised he wants to get his hands on Judge's, they're proving quite a thorn in his side.'

'Rubbish,' said James automatically. He rested a hand on his wife's belly. 'Good Lord, Diana, it's fluttering. Can you feel it?'

'Yes. Yes, I can. Saul, do you really think Rowan should keep on wearing herself out like that? She looks so tired.'

'Then she probably needs some help. She doesn't need a takeover.'

James, unable to concentrate on what seemed to him a trivial discussion when the life, the welfare, of his unborn child was at stake, snarled: 'Diana! Lie down and rest, you're not doing yourself any good.'

'But James, if Saul thinks — ' began Diana.

'I don't care what Saul thinks,' he declared. 'Look, it isn't important. We'll let her keep the firm for now, we've got a year or two before the children get control, and she'll have it motoring by then. It might cost me a bit more but I can take it any time I want. Now lie down and rest.'

Obediently, thoughtfully, Diana lay down. So much for James's altruism then. The momentary impulse to take the strain from Rowan would not have survived an instant if he had not also wanted to get his hands on a thriving and competitive business. She had been naive, and more than that, stupid. If James owned Judge's it would benefit no one but James, and the exclusion included her. Marriage to James was not like marriage to Andrew, there was no merging of interests. She must watch out for herself, and for Andy, Rowan, all of them, because James was a hunter and they were all his prey. Perversely, the thought lessened the distance between them. When he reached out and touched her cheek she brushed her lips against his hand.

Chapter Eighteen

When Saul wandered into Judge's yard his spirits sank. It was rather worse than he had expected. But then he was used to Bardsey's fleets of wagons, efficient loading bays and neat paintwork, he was not prepared for the ramshackle air of making do that typified this relic of the nineteenth century. Set against the valley side, for half the day it was in shadow, while for the other half it basked in soft Yorkshire sun. Without light the stone was black, charmless; in the sunshine it took on the colour of old honey.

He sauntered towards the mill and was almost immediately intercepted by a young and aggressive warehouseman. 'Can I help you? Looking for Miss Judge?'

'Er – yes I was. Name of Barton. Saul Barton.'

'You come with me.'

It was rather like being put under armed escort. But then, he thought, if James had been as security conscious Rowan would never have got to see the range. Or indeed, if he had been less treacherous. He didn't regret it.

They went upstairs to Rowan's office. She was crouched over her desk, doing sums, rather like a child at school, her tongue at the corner of her mouth and pages of workings out screwed up everywhere.

'Hello, Rowan,' he said.

She looked up and went pink. 'Oh, hello, Saul. Just a minute.' She picked up her papers and put them all carefully into a folder, put the folder in a drawer and locked it.

'You can't be too careful,' said Saul pointedly.

'People are so sneaky.' She grinned at him.

The warehouseman said, 'I've still got them bales waiting,

miss, they've been waiting all week.'

Rowan looked troubled. 'Have you? It's not like Joe to let us down. Can you get on to him?'

'I thought you might want to.'

'No. You do it.'

They waited until he had left. Saul said, 'Have you fallen out with Joe Partridge?'

She shook her head. 'Not really. He's cross with me. He's only left those bales so I'll ring him, and I won't.'

She was wearing a pair of black trousers, gathered at the ankle, and over the top a straight tabard of the same black material, with appliqued green fabric roses dotted around on it. And she had had her hair cut again, into wisps that wandered about her face. She looked wistful and strange.

'I thought you were serious about him,' said Saul.

'It seems he thought that, too,' said Rowan, sighing. 'It annoyed Mother so I led him on a bit. I didn't realise he didn't know, and now he's all upset and hurt and it's my fault.'

She looked rather unhappy and all at once Saul thought of the trail of women he had left behind who had thought he was more serious than he intended. He had never hung around long enough to feel this sort of guilt, and that in itself made him feel guilty. He'd used a lot of women.

He found himself longing to ask if she had slept with Joe. He had an arousing picture in his mind of Rowan's long, thin body beneath the tattooed stockiness of the man, of her white innocence ravaged by an insensitive brute. A fierce erection was making itself felt, he hoped she couldn't see it. He sat down, unasked.

'Did you want something?' asked Rowan innocently. Her green eyes in that white face were like emeralds, he thought. How was it that she had bypassed prettiness and yet become desirable? She was nothing but skin and bone. He tried to speak but his voice croaked. 'Rowan — I wanted you to come on a trip with me.'

'Whatever do you mean?'

He wished she would stop looking at him in that gently enquiring way, he wished her little breasts would make more or less of an impression on her clothes. That pert hint of a presence disturbed him utterly. He got up, startling her, and strode over to the window, putting his back to the room. 'It's like this,' he said loudly. 'James hasn't given up on getting Judge's, he's biding his time. If you're going to keep him at bay you can't rely on your mother. In the end James can make her do anything, it's only her pregnancy keeps him from cracking the whip now. But if you can move the firm on, make a leap into the international market, he won't be able to afford to buy you out. I'm going to Japan on a selling trip. I want you to come with me.'

Rowan stared at his back. 'Is this the favour you said I owed you?' she asked stiffly.

He turned and laughed. 'No, of course not. Separate rooms, I promise. But you can't break into the overseas markets on your own, you need help and I want to help you.'

'Why?'

That was Rowan, direct and uncompromising. He crossed to her desk and sat close to her on the edge. He ran his fingers down the edge of her tabard. 'Because I like you. Because James deserves to be troubled by you. Because I often go to Japan and should love to have you to show around.'

'Who pays for the fare?' she asked, and he thought, 'God, doesn't she ever think of anything except business?'

'I'll pay half,' he promised. 'And we won't tell James what's going on, will we?'

She looked up at him. 'Ought I to trust you?' she demanded.

'To a point,' he said.

When he had gone, Rowan sat at the desk and felt shivers racking her body. That man, that strange man. From the

189

moment he came into the room she had been conscious of heat, moving from him into her, making her aware of a deep inner fire in her belly. At the wedding reception he had called her breasts tasty mouthfuls, she hadn't forgotten.

It was all his fault that things had got out of hand with Joe. She had wanted to know if men really did put their mouths there. When Joe had started his usual late night grope she'd encouraged him to get into her T-shirt. Before she'd got used to his big, clumsy hands he was pushing her down under him, and she was cursing and hitting him and telling him to get off. The whole thing had revolted her, she felt ashamed and guilty and foolish. More than that, she felt – unsatisfied.

It had ended in a fierce and bitter row. Joe thought that after all this time she owed him 'a bit of the other', as he described it. He cared about her. He thought she cared about him. And if she said she did he would be wrongly encouraged, and if she denied it she would be lying. Joe was her friend, her good friend, and she didn't want more than that.

Was Saul Barton a friend? He was acting like one – almost. At least he was no friend of James's, she was sure there was no way he would work with James against her. He was certainly a playboy, letting money cascade into the mouths of endless women, or so she had heard. To her he seemed entirely sincere, surely she wasn't wrong about that? He was such fun; when he was around the world looked different, felt different, quite possibly was different, because he did what he wanted and took nothing at all seriously. Perhaps that included her.

He was right about James, that much was certain. And perhaps she ought to go to Japan. It was the market of the future, everybody said so. She'd never been anywhere.

Suddenly she was bubbling with excitement. It was as if a fairy godmother had waved a wand, transporting her from fluff and dust and drudgery out into the great wide world. And if Saul proved not to look after her, she was sure she could look after herself.

* * *

They were to go in January, and Rowan told no one at all. The secret bolstered her, because it was Christmas and she hated it, because everything about the season recalled how it used to be. Andrew always loved Christmas, he was silly and fun and made them all stand outside in the garden singing carols on Christmas Eve. Sometimes even a tinny rendering of 'The Holly and the Ivy' in the supermarket made Rowan blink back tears.

This year Diana was insisting on a family Christmas at Aspley Manor. Rowan had longed to refuse, but dared not do so and besides, could not face the day in the gloomy little cottage. So she, Sally and Andy all attended and sat round the festive board.

Just as she had known it would, everything about James enraged her. He sat at the head of the table exuding self-satisfaction, and however much Rowan tried to deflate him she couldn't. Diana was almost as bad, presiding over her expanding belly much as James over the turkey, as if between them they had discovered the secret of everlasting life. Determinedly Rowan concentrated on the turkey.

'That's what I like to see, a good appetite,' said James. 'Want some more, Rowan love?' She felt like a rattlesnake kept like a pet in a basket.

She waited until the pudding before dropping her bombshell. 'Mother,' she began casually, 'will it be all right if Sally stays with you after Christmas? I'm going on a selling trip.'

Everybody's spoon paused. She could feel James watching her, but she looked instead at Sally's small, pretty face. She was accusing. 'You didn't tell me you were going anywhere. Why? I'll come, I won't stay here.'

'It's business, you can't come,' said Rowan. 'You wouldn't enjoy it.'

'You don't want to tow me around with you, that's all,' said Sally. 'I won't be dumped here, not with him!' She flicked a contemptuous hand at James.

'Don't be a bore, Sal,' said Andy lazily. 'I'll be here, so he won't have just you to yell at.'

'I wouldn't have to yell at you if you would do your practising at reasonable hours,' stated James forcefully. 'That means before twelve at night and after six in the morning! Good God, can't you three even let Christmas dinner pass without a scene? Rowan, you'd better find somewhere else for Sally, I won't have Diana upset. In case you've forgotten, she is expecting our baby.'

Diana, who had listened to all this with her usual calm, said, 'Do be quiet, James. Of course Sally will come here. Rowan, where are you going?'

'A selling trip,' said Rowan.

James, who quite liked Diana to see him as over-protective, said in a milder tone, 'Do we have to be quite so secretive? You're not in the KGB yet surely?'

'You'd sell your own son if it suited you.'

To her surprise, James winced. He picked up his wine glass and drained it.

'How did you get on with Richard?' asked Diana levelly.

'As you might expect.' James's tone was icy, precluding further questions. The expensive camera, chosen by James after hours of deliberation, had gone out with him in the car that morning and had returned with him, smashed.

Rowan said, 'Please don't snoop around the mill while I'm away, James. They've been told to watch out for you.'

'I see no reason to go and look at half a dozen ancient looms and a lot of empty floorspace,' said James cuttingly. 'Diana, this pudding is excellent.'

Sally put down her spoon. 'I feel sick,' she announced.

James threw down his own spoon. 'I knew that brat would disrupt things somehow! If she wants to throw up, she can do it somewhere else. Rowan, put her in the car and take her home.'

'Darling, do you really feel ill?' asked Diana, ignoring him. 'Come and lie down upstairs.'

In the ensuing disruption Andy wandered off to watch

television and James and Rowan sat before the unfinished pudding and looked at each other.

'And a Happy Christmas to one and all,' said James.

Rowan, knowing she was to escape from them, raised her glass. 'Happy Christmas,' she said.

Rowan felt utterly filthy. She was exhausted and sweaty, hungry and yet sated with plastic airline meals. Her feet felt swollen. She longed for sleep but was too jumpy to rest. On the flight out, Saul had drunk steadily, making her more and more nervous. He had been exuberant, then sleepy, and at last vaguely amorous, sitting very close and resting his hand on her knee. She had been relieved to see him go to his own room, but now she was alone and she felt abandoned in this foreign place, amidst a sea of jabbering Japanese.

In truth, everyone in the hotel spoke English and Saul was only next door, but it wasn't the same, it wasn't home. She had longed to go, and now she longed to go back. Moving with slow deliberation she went into the bathroom and took off her clothes, then almost scalded herself on the taps. The water was nearly boiling, the room was instantly filled with steam. So much better than the lukewarm dribble at the mill cottage, she told herself, where the towels were rough and the bathroom freezing. In Tokyo it was just as cold, but everywhere was properly heated. In a technological world the Japanese had learned to work the switches.

She eased herself gently into the steaming bath. It was wonderfully soothing, she would like to stay there forever. Dimly she heard a knock on her bedroom door. She took no notice, the door was locked and they couldn't get in. Besides, it would only be the chambermaid. She closed her eyes and began to daydream, her favourite saga in which Judge's was filled once again with machinery, all of it high-tech and super-efficient. The Queen was bestowing her award for industry. 'We are proud to know that you, Rowan Judge, have single-handedly revitalised Britain's textiles,' she was announcing.

Saul's voice said, 'So there you are.'

Rowan's eyes flew open. Saul was leaning on the doorpost staring down at her naked body, obscured only by a cloud of steam and some very clear water. He looked very tall and very powerful.

'Get out,' said Rowan flatly.

'I don't think I want to,' said Saul.

'I knew you were drunk on the plane,' said Rowan. 'Go away and sober up.'

He straightened up and took a step towards the bath. In a flurry of movement Rowan pulled her knees to her chin and crouched there. He put out his hand and touched her hot, wet shoulder. 'You are so wonderfully long and smooth,' he murmured. 'Are you like that on the inside?'

'Go away,' repeated Rowan. 'I don't want you here, you're drunk and I don't like it.'

'And to think I only came to see if you were all right.'

'Well, I am.'

'And I'm not,' he said mournfully. 'Why don't I come in that bath with you?'

Rowan turned her head away. She wasn't going to look at him, she wasn't going to think of him. Rapidly, purposefully, she soaped her sponge and started washing herself with brisk, unerotic movements. Saul sighed. After a few moments she heard her bedroom door close.

In the morning, after they had both slept, Saul was apologetic. Rowan sat herself down at the breakfast table, barely glancing at him. He poured her some coffee and she sipped it, gazing into the middle distance. 'I know I made a nuisance of myself,' said Saul. 'Sorry.'

'I thought you were going to rape me,' said Rowan.

He grinned. 'Me? I think I'm a bit too soft-hearted. One squeal and I'd call the St. John's Ambulance. I can't even squash flies.'

'Do they have the St. John's Ambulance out here?' asked Rowan.

'Shouldn't think so. They're a bit bloody bloody, the Japanese, actually. They probably expect you to hobble to hospital with a broken leg. By the way, are you a virgin?'

She spread her napkin brusquely. 'Yes. But I don't think it needs treatment, thank you.'

He picked up the coffee pot and refilled her cup. 'Let me know if it does. I wouldn't hurt you for anything, Rowan.'

She was awash with heat. She couldn't look at him. All through breakfast he made sensible conversation about their visits that day and she could barely reply. Was it so odd still to be a virgin? Was the male body something she ought to experience?

They went upstairs to get their samples and their coats. Rowan sat on her bed, her hands folded in her lap. Sally was on the pill, she had found the packet in her bedside drawer when she was looking for something. There had seemed nothing she could usefully say. It was one of the lads from the brickworks. He and Sally met on the corner most Saturdays, she said they went for walks. What happened in the dark and smelly alleys? Sometimes there was brick dust on the back of her coat... Rowan imagined her pressed up against some wall. Yet if she fought her and kept her in, Sally lay in her bedroom sobbing, frighteningly out of control. To give in to Sally seemed the only way to maintain some precarious balance. And here was Rowan, so much older, supposedly so much more mature, afraid of something even her little sister understood.

The door opened. It was Saul. 'Where did you get the key?' she asked.

'From Reception,' he said. 'They think we're sleeping together, they'd be surprised if they knew we weren't.'

Rowan got up and gathered her things. The sample case was a lead weight, she had probably put in too much but it was no use wanting something in Tokyo that you had left in Bradford.

'Don't be scared,' said Saul. 'I'm not going to be horrible to you.' But it wasn't Saul she was scared of. It was herself.

They went out into a crisp, cold morning, the Japanese sun sparkling down through the winter smog. The crowds were offputting, filling the pavements, surging into and out of buildings with early-morning zeal. Rowan clung to Saul's arm to avoid losing him. 'The Tokyo beehive,' he yelled to her above the row. 'They don't sting.'

'But how can they bear it?' She and Saul towered above the Japanese, she could feel people watching her, hear those closest muttering about her. At least Saul seemed to know where he was going, and so did she in principle. They were to visit an agent who was organising their tour of potential customers. He was a man Saul had worked with before.

Saul, striding peremptorily into the road, flagged down a taxi. He had to drag Rowan out of the way as the door swung open. 'It's automatic,' she said wonderingly, and smiled dubiously at the Japanese driver. He smiled back and bowed his head and for some idiotic reason she was thrilled that even the taxi driver should be Japanese. She felt as if she was in some sort of film set and that the real world was on the other side of the buildings, or the street, or perhaps in the taxis. She kept looking for the exit.

They joined a snail's pace queue of traffic. Rowan gazed out of the window at the hordes of people. 'They're dressed just like us,' she said in disappointment.

Saul said, 'I'll take you to Akasaka one evening and you can see the geishas going to work by rickshaw. They're an odd mixture, the Japanese, they keep the old style going but a bit as if they're acting it.'

'I felt like that,' said Rowan eagerly. 'It's like being in a play.' She felt close to him suddenly, she felt that he understood.

'By the way,' said Saul. 'Don't say much at this meeting.

My agent isn't used to dealing with women, he'll only want to talk to me.'

'I can't have that! I'm here in my own right!'

He put his arm round her and gave her a squeeze. 'Darling Rowan, this is Japan. It isn't the same here, try and remember that.'

No. It wasn't the same. She allowed herself to relax a little against him.

The agent was called Yushida, but whether this was his first or second name Rowan could not establish. He bowed to her formally, putting his hands together, and after a moment's hesitation she repeated the gesture.

'How was your journey?' he asked politely. 'Do you have family at home?' Perhaps she hadn't replied properly. At any rate they were the last words he said to her until she and Saul were being ushered out. 'I am honoured to have met you,' said Yushida, repeating his bow.

'And I am less than honoured to have met him,' said Rowan sourly, once they were safe in the street. 'Will they all be like that?'

'Until you've been here a dozen times or so,' said Saul. 'And then you've got to sort of grovel. "If you'll forgive my presumption, Yushida-san, might I suggest that if it were not too inconvenient for you would it be all right if this trip I made a profit?" It's hard enough for Western men here, let alone a girl.'

'Aren't I lucky to have you looking after me?' purred Rowan. For he *had* taken care of her; after the list of Bardsey appointments he had nudged away at Rowan's side of things. They were to spend three days in Tokyo and then go on to Kyoto for two. There seemed to be nothing arranged for the last three days, though the return date for their ticket was open.

'Do we have to keep time free to go back and see people again?' asked Rowan curiously.

Saul glanced at her. 'I thought we should keep some days

available. Look, with a bit of luck these people we're going to see this afternoon will entertain us tonight. What do you want to see? Puppets, that's Bunraku, or Kabuki, or Noh? For God's sake avoid Takarazuka, it's like one of those thirties films with nothing but girls with feathers on their heads and ballgowns parading down staircases grinning. Terribly proper and terribly boring.'

'I've heard of Noh,' said Rowan. 'But I can't remember what I've heard.'

'Nobody can remember much after a Noh performance,' said Saul ruefully. 'It would be all right if it didn't go on so long. On and on and on. I learned to meditate at a Noh theatre. I recommend the puppets.'

'I don't know why you didn't say the puppets in the first place,' said Rowan. 'Why ask me when you know and I don't?'

'Don't be ratty,' said Saul. 'Or I'll take you to a Noh play.'

'If you know about Noh, say no,' retorted Rowan. 'You'd have to sit through it too, remember.' Saul chuckled.

They lunched at a cafeteria which had plastic replicas of the meals set out in the window. Rowan liked the look of none of it and what she did choose turned out to be excruciating. 'I shall starve to death,' she said miserably, watching Saul munch his way stolidly through something he said was Oyako-don and then proceed to finish her Kitsune Udon.

'We'll stop at a hamburger store,' he assured her. 'You're being very British, Rowan.'

'Only my taste buds,' she said apologetically. 'I really am trying to be cosmopolitan, I'm bowing so often I feel as if my clockwork's running down.'

'I don't suppose you eat much anyway.' He sat back and eyed her wand-like figure. She was wearing a green wool tube that clung to every bone and fleshy protuberance. It extended right down to her white boots.

'Normally I eat like a horse,' she said. 'But horses

198

wouldn't eat this either. Don't stare at me like that. Is the dress all right? I thought it looked a bit staid.'

He cleared his throat. 'You realise when you stand sideways I can see your pubic mound?'

Rowan's face flamed. She said, 'You're just trying to embarrass me. Stop it.'

'I would if I knew how. Oh God, Rowan, but you do turn me on.'

She kept her eyes on the table. All around people chattered away in Japanese, and a Japanese waitress came up to their table, bowed and smiled. 'She wants to clear away,' said Saul. 'Come on, love.'

She got up automatically bowing and smiling at the waitress. 'James calls me love,' she commented. 'It makes me want to savage him.'

'The difference is that I don't do it to annoy,' said Saul obliquely.

They took a taxi to an enormous shiny skyscraper. Just the look of it intimidated Rowan, and she was beginning to feel exhausted. Everything was so difficult when you understood none of the language, could read not one word of the writing and the familiar was so dangerously spiked with the oriental. She was hungry, too, because Saul had forgotten her hamburger. His presence was the one constant in a changed world. She felt a momentary panic if he went to the washroom in case something inscrutable happened to him and he didn't come back.

They fizzed up to some floor or other in a glass lift. The controls were so high-tech Rowan didn't understand them. You appeared to be able to programme the lift to call back for you.

'That really is awfully clever,' said Rowan admiringly.

'Don't be fooled by it,' said Saul. 'It's a bloody silly idea and it doesn't work. People at the top of this building can wait hours to get down because the lift's loyally visiting floors where the people long since took the stairs. The

Japanese are not that brilliant. Remember, we built the empire!'

'And they the transistor radio,' said Rowan.

'The empire didn't need batteries.'

The doors swung open and Saul stepped out. Before Rowan could follow they closed again. 'Saul! Help! Help!' she shrieked, but the lift had kidnapped her. Paralysed with fear she was swept onward and upward. Where was Saul? Where was she? How did you sound the alarm? When the doors again opened she fell out into the midst of a group of small Japanese men.

'I do beg your pardon. Do excuse me,' she burbled. They all grinned, bowed and jabbered at her. Pinning a fixed grin to her own face she blundered away from them, looking desperately for the stairs. One of the men followed her and kept on jabbering, and it was only after a few hectic moments that she realised he was actually talking English. The Japanese accent was thicker than custard.

'I want to get down,' said Rowan slowly. 'I can't find the stairs.'

He bobbed up and down, and eventually Rowan deciphered something on the lines of: 'Please, allow me to accompany you in the lift? What is your destination?'

Explaining that she didn't know was beyond her. She backed away, grinning, and he followed her, grinning and bowing, and every time she opened a door and found it wasn't the stairs, he held it for her as if she wanted to go through and she had to back away again like some demented inmate of a mental hospital. When at last she found the stairs and bolted down them he stood at the top, chattering unintelligibly and bowing.

She met Saul coming up to meet her. 'Thank God!' Rowan flung her arms round his neck in an agony of relief. 'I thought I was going to be trapped here forever with these insane Japanese.'

Saul pulled her to him, and for a minute they stood,

pressed together. Then Rowan pulled back, flushed and awkward. 'Where's your sample case?' asked Saul.

'Oh no! Oh, I can't have! I've left it in the lift!'

Saul put his fist to her head in a mock threat. 'Idiot! Don't you know you lose your life before you lose your samples? Just wait here.' He started past her back up the stairs but she followed like an apologetic puppy. They met her Japanese friend coming down, carrying the sample case.

'I could not allow the lady to be distressed,' he burbled, or something similar.

Rowan, Saul and the Japanese indulged in an orgy of bowing and grinning.

It was late when Saul and Rowan finally made it back to the hotel. They had displayed their samples, Saul had negotiated prices for both of them, and they had found themselves transported from office to restaurant, from restaurant to Bunraku, and just when they were becoming mesmerised by the brilliant half life-size puppetry they were whisked away to a club where hostesses with traditional painted faces served them formally. For Rowan it had all been too much. She was almost sobbing with weariness.

'Come on, I'll put you to bed,' said Saul as she slumped against him in the lift.

'Not that as well.' She tried to pull away from him, but he held on to her.

'It's all right, I'm not that insensitive. This is the exciting glamorous life of the salesman: aching feet, upset stomach and exhaustion.'

'My face aches,' she groaned. 'I never want to smile again.'

'More tomorrow, love,' said Saul remorselessly. 'And you've got to keep on making the sales, so get with it.'

'Brute!'

He unlocked her bedroom door and watched her fall fully clothed on to the bed. He came in after her and pulled off her

201

boots. 'Have a bath, you'll feel better.'

'No! Go away, I'll be all right.'

'Shut up and let me baby you.'

He reached behind her head, found the zip of her dress and peeled it down from her shoulders. Rowan lay on the bed, helplessly languorous. His large brown hands touched the skin at her waist. 'My hands go right round you,' he said wonderingly.

'Do they?'

She had said she didn't want him, but now, in exhaustion, she wanted to be at his mercy. If he had made love to her now she needn't resist, she could blame it on Japan. But he didn't. Instead he put his arm beneath her knees, lifted her and swept the dress away. She lay in her underclothes, watching him beneath shadowed lids, her arms like seaweed spread about her on the bed.

He pulled the quilt across her. 'We'll stop there,' he said shakily. 'Are you all right?'

'Yes,' she murmured. 'Thank you, Saul.'

'Think nothing of it. Look, I'm going downstairs for a drink in the bar. You'll be all right, won't you?'

She felt warm and safe and cherished. 'Goodnight,' she whispered.

On the way downstairs Saul felt lightheaded. The more he was with Rowan the more attuned he became to her long-legged spiky elegance, the more he loved her directness, her moments of gauche embarrassment. His face split into an involuntary smile. How he loved looking after her. He went on down the stairs to assuage his longings with a few glasses of Japanese whisky.

The day they left Tokyo for Kyoto, Rowan felt a great sense of release. She wasn't used to the roar and bustle of a great city, and in Tokyo, that westernised bridge across two cultures, there was a filth that left a dark ring around the nostrils at the end of the day. Nonetheless when you sent your grubby white shirt to the laundry it came back spotless, beautifully folded and wrapped in plastic, with a flower nestling against the collar.

Sitting in the air-conditioned express train, watching Saul slumped easily in the seat opposite, she knew things had changed. They were comfortable with each other, unembarrassed. She didn't ask any more what they were going to do with their last three days in Japan. To ask she felt would be to spoil everything, to label emotions and intentions and put them in cardboard boxes. With Saul even the mundane seemed exciting. She could sit here on this train forever, just watching the way his long legs sprawled, the way his eyes looked out lazily from beneath his hair.

'I started too high,' she said thoughtfully. 'My first trip abroad should have been France or somewhere.'

Saul grunted. 'That would have been a mistake. In France, my sweet, if you want to get decent sales you have to visit hundreds of customers, and in Germany hundreds more. And you have to be fluent in the language. They don't have any patience with some blundering Briton who expects everyone to know English. Now in Japan no one thinks you should know the language, and look at the orders we've been getting. Worth a little trouble, don't you think?'

Rowan sighed. 'What do you think James is getting up to while I'm away?'

Saul shrugged. 'Replacing me, I shouldn't wonder.'

Rowan could tell by his tone that he meant it. She sat up. 'He wouldn't. He knows how valuable you are to the firm.'

'And I happen to think he's got it in for me just now. Well, for a while actually. And just now Diana's gunning for me as well and it isn't healthy. I can sense it in the air.'

'Mother? Whatever for?'

Saul gazed out of the window at the frosty countryside. There was a temple framed against grey-blue sky, and a tractor roaring across a field next to it. 'You know her,' he said vaguely. 'She has her moods.'

Rowan fell silent. Actually she didn't think Diana particularly moody, or at any rate not for inexplicable reasons. In general she was rather cool, infuriatingly so.

In Kyoto Saul taught Rowan how to display her samples. He sat on the bed acting the part of the customer while Rowan practised her geisha girl style of humble, deprecating modesty, putting forward each piece of cloth as if it were almost too unworthy to be noticed. 'I'm too tall for this,' she complained. 'You have to be nearer five foot and Japanese.'

'It's the smirk that counts, not the height you do it at,' said Saul. 'Anyway you can always kneel.'

'I will not!'

Diverted for the moment, Saul picked up two of Rowan's swatches, a grey flannel and a navy with red on the weft. 'These are nice,' he said. 'Did you think these up yourself?'

'Not really. There seemed a lot of that sort of stuff in the Paris fashions. I study all the magazines, you know.'

'I thought you were getting more and more way out.' He twitched the hem of her tunic, a style Rowan was very fond of. He was becoming equally fond of it; sometimes he thought she looked like his squire, young, boyish, eager to do his bidding. He liked the concept enormously.

'I'm going to have one made shorter,' she commented. 'And I shall wear tight trousers with it.'

Saul lay back on the bed. 'Take it off,' he murmured.

She glanced at him. 'I don't think − now?'

Their eyes met. He said, 'Don't you want to know where we're going?'

Rowan wrapped her long arms around herself, walling herself in protectively. 'I'll leave it to you,' she said in a small voice. 'I suppose we'll be − together?'

Saul swallowed. 'Very together. Absolutely together.'

Rowan nodded, dipping her head, half in shame. There could be no end but this.

That night they were taken to see Sumo wrestling. Rowan

found it strangely erotic, watching huge bearlike men waddling around almost naked. It wasn't that they were attractive, except in their confidence and arrogance, it was more that they were so unashamedly physical. It made her aware of her own body, her thinness as opposed to their enormous bulk, her damp skin set against the oil and sweat of their own vast chests. The Japanese next to her was bobbing up and down in excitement, she felt sorry for him. Her presence was inhibiting him terribly. Saul's leg pressed wordlessly against her own. Between them they generated a living sexual charge.

Chapter Nineteen

They had not done as much business in Kyoto. For all Rowan's assumed humility, she seemed to be too much for the provincial city. People stared at her and apologised for doing so, they treated her like an exotic species.

'They'll give you orders next time,' Saul consoled her, lending his weight to her suitcase as she tried to shut it.

'I'm not sure I shall come again,' she said. 'It's such hard work. I keep remembering how much money it's all costing, and if you don't get the orders it's terrible.'

Saul put out a finger and tapped her nose. 'Don't get down. If you get disheartened, you've had it. The one thing you've got when selling is your confidence.'

She let out a long, dismal sigh. 'But it's so hard. I tried so hard!'

'And the world's an unfair place. I remember one week I had, on my own, I ended up standing in a Spanish marketplace after a week selling nothing. I couldn't bear to keep on trying, I thought I wanted to die. I sat on the edge of a fountain and got green slime on my suit, and that does not look good. But I dragged myself up to the next guy and he bought something, and suddenly I was back up there. I was making it.'

'You never seem not to be confident to me. I don't know where you get it from.'

'It helps if you don't mind making a fool of yourself.' She looked away, because they both knew how much she hated to appear ridiculous. He picked up the bags. 'Ready? We'll check out.'

Standing in the lobby while Saul settled up, Rowan let her

207

mind flit nervously over the immediate future. She sidled up to him. 'Where are we going?'

'On the train. Then a hire car.'

'But where to?'

He grinned, white teeth in a brown face, his fair hair falling over his forehead. He smelled faintly of booze, or mouthwash or something. 'You wait and see,' he said. 'It'll be worth it.'

A vendor on the train sold them bento, a beautifully gift-wrapped packed lunch. It was almost too lovely to open, but in the last days Rowan had lived mainly on the American-style hotel breakfasts and little else. She was unfastening the string of her box almost before Saul had paid for it, and when she took off the lid she gasped. Then she said woefully, 'I can't eat it! It's too beautiful!' Exquisite little portions of highly coloured and unidentified foods were rolled and cubed, sliced and decorated, set out with all the care of a jeweller working on a Fabergé egg. Nothing was large, nothing was ugly, it seemed criminal to spoil something so perfect.

Torn between admiration and hunger, Rowan almost moaned. But hunger won the day. She picked up a cube of what appeared to be pressed rice, decorated with a pre-sumably edible green flower. She munched. Her face fell into lines of disappointment. 'It's horrible,' she said dismally. 'Rubbish,' said Saul and took another of the cubes. He chewed vigorously and then his jaws slowed. The food moved in a glutinous lump around his mouth. Eventually he gave a Herculean swallow and got rid of it. 'That lacked a little something,' he confessed. 'Try that dinky little pink thing.'

Rowan picked up the round pink glob and nibbled at it cautiously. 'Some fruit they very sensibly haven't tried out on the rest of the world,' she declared. 'You can have it.'

Eventually Saul consumed most of the contents of both lunchboxes, and Rowan went hungry. 'Health farms ought to send their obstinate cases here,' she muttered. 'One hundred per cent success rate, everyone beanpole thin in days.'

Saul wiped his hands on a tiny tissue from the lunchbox. 'Look,' he began, 'where we're going tonight is very Japanese. You're going to have to eat the food, you'll be ill if you go on like this.'

'Where are we going tonight?' she asked. 'Don't tease, I want to know.'

'Spoilsport. It's a Ryokan, a traditional Japanese hotel: sleep on the floor, beautifully painted paper walls, plum blossom in the gardens, perfect little flower displays. It's out of this world.'

Rowan said glumly, 'Do they do omelettes?'

Saul stared at her in outrage. He couldn't believe she was so plebeian. 'Look, Rowan, you've come half way across the world, you're experiencing a whole new culture! Why in God's name do you want an omelette?'

'Because I'm hungry!' she flared. 'Next time I come abroad I'm bringing a crate of baked beans as well as the samples, I don't see why I have to starve. I hate raw fish. I can't bear pickled octopus. And I don't care how pretty the vegetables are, if they don't taste nice I don't want to eat them!'

She fell silent, hopelessly woebegone. After a moment Saul sighed, delved into his pocket and brought out a chocolate bar. Rowan fell on it, almost gibbering with relief. She didn't stop until she had licked every last crumb off the silver paper. 'You're a saint,' she murmured to Saul. 'How many did you bring?'

'I bought two dozen this morning. Will that last you three days?'

She nodded. 'I should think so. You know, I think I'm human again. I'm not open to reason when I'm hungry.'

'So I noticed.'

After a while she said, 'Did you buy anything else this morning?'

'Like what?' He was watching her with an expression she had learned to recognise, he used it when selling. It welcomed and encouraged, but gave no clue as to his own thoughts.

'If you've only booked one room,' she said doubtfully, 'then really don't you think we ought — don't you think you ought — I'm not on the pill,' she finished bravely.

He cleared his throat. She realised he was actually rather embarrassed. 'That's all right,' he said brusquely. 'I'll take care of it.'

'I don't want anything that needs taking care of,' snapped Rowan. 'That's the whole point!' Their eyes met. Suddenly they were convulsed with laughter.

The Ryokan was set deep in the country. When they drew up in their car, wondering if they had taken a wrong turning because they could see no building, two men appeared, bowed, and ushered them towards a path. The trees, just starting to bud, stood in gentle symmetry. 'Where's the hotel?' asked Rowan.

'We must walk to it,' said Saul. 'They'll bring the luggage.'

He took her hand. Together they strolled down the path, and there was the sound of water and birds singing. It was rather cold. As they rounded a bend they saw before them a long low building, in the ancient style, with a heavily gabled roof that dipped at the eaves. Before it was a small pool and as Rowan passed she saw that it was filled with gleaming golden fish.

'Remember,' said Saul softly, 'we're entering yesterday.'

A woman in a kimono was waiting for them. Silent, but bowing and smiling, she motioned to their feet. 'Slippers,' said Saul. They stepped out of their footwear and the woman covered her mouth in giggling amazement at their huge European shoes. They each put on silken slippers. Rowan's were embroidered with birds. Still silent except for giggles the hostess slid aside a paper door and went through. Saul and Rowan padded after her.

'This is weird,' said Rowan softly. Outside they could hear the water gently falling.

'It's superb,' said Saul. 'What next, do you think?'

'Don't you know?'

He shook his head. 'I've never been to one of these either.'

Their hostess stopped at another sliding paper door and stood aside to let them pass through. They were in a lobby, the floor covered in matting. Another door stood open showing a step up to the bare interior of a tatami-covered room. The only furniture was cushions and a low table. A shelf at floor level carried a vase with a single spray of flowers. As Rowan stood there, the woman fluttering about, she had the feeling that they had stepped through a door and might not be able to step back.

Left to themselves they began to relax. There were cotton robes, yukata, which were to be worn whilst in the Ryokan, and over them a thicker gown. When Rowan peered through the shutter she could see one or two Japanese men strolling around the garden dressed in the same way. She took up her robes and looked for the bathroom.

'Saul,' she said dubiously. 'Come and look at this.'

There was no bathroom. Instead there was a cubicle and in it a ceramic bowl, set in the floor. A pair of slippers stood to one side, and there was even a flower arrangement.

'Where do we wash?' asked Rowan.

'Not in there,' said Saul. 'Do you want a bath?'

'Well — yes,' she said dubiously. She wished she could enjoy this as much as Saul appeared to. The strangeness of everything upset her slightly, she felt she could not get her bearings, and added to which the place was not warm. Draughts whistled under the doors and rattled the paper walls.

They found the bathroom down the hall, a large tiled room with taps and little wooden seats, a huge steaming tub of water in the centre. Saul's face became unreadable.

'Well?' said Rowan. 'Is this it?'

'Looks like it,' said Saul. 'But it's communal. Don't worry, I think this is the women's one.'

'I'll lock the door,' said Rowan. 'I won't be long.'

'Er, what I mean is – ' explained Saul '– everybody uses it – together.'

Rowan gaped. 'At the same time?'

'Well, I think so. It's my first time too, you know.'

Again they started to laugh. They were blundering about this stylized oriental world like a couple of elephants. A little voice broke in on them. 'Please excuse. This is not gentlemen's washplace.'

They turned to see a diminutive Japanese lady, her greying hair drawn back into a bun and spectacles on her button nose. She bowed, and automatically Rowan bowed, and while she was so doing Saul backed out of the room. 'Saul!' squeaked Rowan in a panic.

The Japanese lady advanced on her. 'I help you,' she said determinedly. 'I show you the Japanese way.'

When Rowan at last staggered back to their room she could say nothing for some minutes. She was wearing her robes and sank down on to the cushions in a flurry of fabric. 'Have some sake,' said Saul, holding out a tiny ceramic cup. 'It's hot.'

'I don't need any more heat,' said Rowan. 'She boiled me!'

'The water is hotter in Japan,' he agreed. 'You'd think it would affect fertility or something. I forgot to tell you, you're not supposed to wash in the bath, you do that before you get in.'

Rowan sniffed. 'Actually, I found out the hard way. That woman made me undress and took a scrubbing brush to me. Then she poured hot water all over me and made me get into boiling water in the bath. And she wouldn't let me get out!

212

After a while I lost all feeling, I think my toenails are going to drop off. By the way, she thinks we're on honeymoon.'

Saul settled down beside her. He sipped the sake and then passed her the cup. It was quite pleasant, she decided. In fact, now that she had bathed, it was all quite pleasant. The sound of water gurgling outside, the slow, formal functioning of the place, the austerity of their spotless room. With so little to distract her she found her attention focusing alarmingly on Saul. His legs were brown and covered in thick, golden hair. She could see the inside of one thigh, the muscles like ropes beneath the skin. She sipped some more sake and let out her breath in a long, wanting sigh.

Saul reached out and took the cup away from her. 'Let's put out the bedding,' he said softly.

'Suppose someone comes?' she whispered back. 'Someone might hear us.'

He took hold of her hand, pulling her gently to her feet. 'Let them hear. I agree with the Japanese lady. We're on honeymoon.'

She didn't know what to do. The heat of the bath clung to her and fused with an inner heat, her breasts felt swollen. Fluid seemed to have drained into her groin, the folds of tender flesh at the entrance to her body were heavy and engorged. Saul was laying out the bedding, unfolding it into a smooth and wrinkle-free couch. An embroidered white quilt was spread on the top. 'Will I bleed?' she asked.

He straightened and turned. 'I don't know. You look so young in that robe thing, you hardly seem old enough.'

'Then I'll take it off.' She slipped her arms out of the robe and let it fall to the floor. Saul's face became set.

'You're lovely,' he said throatily. 'Like white marble.'

'Let me see you,' whispered Rowan. Her hands fluttered above her pubic hair, she wanted to hide herself but also show him what was there. She wished she was drunk.

Saul took off his robe. Before he let it fall to the floor he held it in front of his genitals. 'It's such an ugly, brutal thing,

I can't bear to hurt you with it.'

'I want to see,' said Rowan. He let the robe fall. She stared at him, at first unable to believe that his body, so brown and firm and muscled, should come to its focus in that thing. It was blind, and wet, and thrusting. Saul would take care of her, that thing would not.

She turned away, covering herself with her hands, and he came up behind her and put his arms round her. She could feel it against her back, even now pulsing and thrusting. 'Don't be afraid, there's no need, I promise. Let me touch you, please, please!' He was kneeling, turning her towards him, burying his face in her belly, in the rough hair at its base. Disgust rose in her, it was appalling, horrible!

But, like an express train, a feeling surfaced from her primitive soul. It coursed through the fluid in her belly, it set her legs trembling so she could do no other than part them. His mouth sucked at her folds, for long, endless, but so short seconds. Rowan arched herself back from him, her thin fingers clawing at his hair, arched herself till she should have cracked.

Suddenly Saul lifted his head. 'Get on the bed,' he said urgently. 'Hurry.' He was fumbling with plastic, trying to fit a sheath. Staggering, bewildered, Rowan pulled back the quilt and lay down. She was dizzied, disorientated. And he was desperate. He came to the bed and got straight on top of her, she couldn't believe the weight of him. The thing was nudging at her. 'Spread your legs wider,' he urged. 'Wider! God, but you're tight.'

It was hurting her, at first hardly at all and then as he powered it with his haunches, more and more. She let out a cry and he covered her mouth with his, her tongue thrashed against his. She clawed at his buttocks. A sudden, sharp agony as she split. She screamed into his mouth.

He became quite still inside her. Hot blood damped her pain, it was only sore now. Lifting, he said, 'All right?'

She couldn't speak. Gradually her long, slender legs

wrapped themselves around him and they rocked together, he striving to contain himself as instinctively he sought the long thrusts that would satisfy him. She wouldn't let go, he bucked and carried her with him, and suddenly he took hold of her knees and forced them down. The first hard stroke brought a cry but he was beyond caring. Seconds later he was finished.

The quiet of the Ryokan lapped about them once again. Water, the sound of birds. Rowan said softly, 'Nothing will ever be so wonderful again.'

'Don't pretend,' whispered Saul. 'Look at the blood!'

It was everywhere. Rowan rubbed her finger on the sheet and smeared the fluid on to Saul's lips. 'I wanted to bleed, for you. You can do what you like to me, I won't ever say no! I want to please you, and I don't know how, I want you to do that again and again, all the time!'

He fell on her, mouthing her shoulders, her little apple breasts, licking the sweat from her belly. She laughed, already aware of the insistent throbbing of her womb. Why hadn't she let him do this before, why hadn't she known? 'I do love you,' she whispered. 'I do love you so.'

Time passed, measured in sighs and tears and laughter. They played a game, there in the bare little room, exploring each other from tiptoe to crown of head, remarking and caressing each fold of skin. 'I shall never get over your feet,' said Saul, cradling them in his hands. 'You have the only beautiful feet in the world.'

'They're too big,' said Rowan lazily, lying back on the futon.

'Rubbish! They're just long. Everything about you is long, long and narrow. You make me feel like a raw, badly hewn statue.'

She reached up and put her arms around his shoulders. 'Poor you, poor you! A statue turned to stone. What shall I do to turn you back to flesh and blood, to let you know and enjoy the − pleasures − of life?' She ran a long-fingered hand up his thigh.

'That's doing quite well,' he commented. 'But not well enough. A kiss in the right place is what's needed.'

'Which is the right place?' asked Rowan.

He grinned and pulled her head down. 'You can only find that by experiment. Lots and lots of experiment!'

They lay entangled together, and never wished themselves apart.

On the last night, Rowan cried. There was no need to ask why, even the lady who brought the food knew why. She came with three perfect lilies and set them on the floor. 'They remind me of my father's funeral,' wept Rowan.

'You can't think of that here, you can't think anything unpleasant.' For the first time he seemed restless. He got up and wandered about the room, which was too small for such things. Suddenly he turned. 'What clothes have you got?'

'What do you mean? I've got lots of clothes.'

'I mean something special!' He went to the cupboard that housed their suitcases and rummaged through it. At once things spilled out on to the floor, spoiling the spartan symmetry of their clutterless room.

'It's all ended,' sighed Rowan. 'Even before we go.' She got up and extracted a silk dress from the suitcase. 'This is special. I bought it for Christmas, but Aspley Manor was so cold I didn't wear it.'

Saul looked at her sad face above the folds of silk. The dress was lovely, but to him she was lovelier. In the last days her face had lost its childlike look and in its place was a glow. He felt weak with love for her. He knew that if he didn't do it now he never would, but just go on and on, like a rootless plant, feeding on others. He so wanted her, he so wanted what she could give him. He needed walls, he needed purpose. He said, 'Wear your dress and marry me. We can get it done at the Embassy in Tokyo.'

She had known he was going to ask her but not now, not yet. She shook her head, choked with tears.

'Don't say no! You can't mean no!'

'I don't mean no!' she croaked. 'I mean yes. But I'm crying!'

They were glad to go in the end. They wanted to celebrate, to shout and tell the world what had happened, but in the Ryokan all was quiet and calm and inner tranquillity. Once in the hire car they sang sea shanties and recited dirty poems, and Saul said, 'Thank God we can drink something that isn't sake. I wonder how long it takes to get married?'

'Ages, I should think,' said Rowan. 'Whatever will Mother say?'

Saul grimaced. That was something he did not intend to think about.

Chapter Twenty

They asked a professional photographer to take pictures of
the wedding. They loved every one of them, from the stiff,
rather embarrassed officials who had so obviously been
inveigled into posing, to the prints of Saul and Rowan themselves. The photographer had shot them from below, so she
was all legs in a swirling silk dress and he was as tall as a
house in his good dark suit. Their faces were almost distant,
the faces of strangers, caught forever in a moment of joy.

Back in cold and windy England, sleeting with rain that
caused a bad skid on the way back from the airport, it was
hard to remember the exuberance. Saul said, 'I thought we'd
go straight to Aspley Manor and tell them. Best to get it over
with.'

She nodded wearily. A thought struck her. 'Where are we
going to live? I know your flat's nearer to Bardsey's but I'm
not sure I ought to be away from the mill. What do we do?'

He took his eyes off the road to grin at her and the Aston
wagged its tail. Rowan gripped the seat nervously. 'Calm
down, will you?' he said. 'We're not going to crash. Look,
I've been thinking. I know we sort of assumed I'd be
working at Bardsey's and you at Judge's, but when you
think about it that isn't going to work. James won't stand it
for an instant, nor should he. Too damned incestuous for
words. Now, I don't want you to think I'm treading on your
toes but I do feel the most sensible thing would be for me to
come over to Judge's. There's no doubt that you need my
selling skills, is there?'

'We can't afford a full-time salesman,' said Rowan
incredulously. 'It's impossible!'

'Not if you and I work the same way. Right now you take what you need out of the business, and so would I. No fixed salaries, we're both sensible. We'd be partners, running it together, because don't forget James may have chained me up on sales but it's not my only skill, ducky. I know Bardsey's inside out. Think of all that experience I can bring to your very own door.'

Rowan felt bewildered. She hadn't considered any of this. 'It isn't the same sort of thing at all,' she said feebly. 'We might not work well together.'

He gave a slight shrug. 'Always a possibility. Not very likely, is it?' He reached over and put his arm round her and she snuggled up to him, for the moment shelving her doubts. Not for a second had she considered sharing Judge's. She felt as if someone had ambushed her and demanded the donation of some vital organ.

After a few moments she said, 'Where would we live then? At the mill?'

He nodded. 'Best all round really. My flat costs an absolute bomb and I'm hardly ever in it. What's more we could have odd women turning up there for months to come, blowing in from South America or somewhere and wanting to catch up on lost time. You'd be amazed the number of times two arrive together, must be something to do with the phases of the moon. In fact, it's quite possible I married you out of pure self-defence!'

'Have you had lots of women?'

He popped a kiss on to her head. 'Lots. But have I loved lots of women? Well, there it's just one. And I love her quite a lot.'

The anxieties that had crowded in on her since the airport seemed to recede a little. She loved Saul so very much, it was as if all her emotions were sensitised. If she woke in the night she lay looking at him as he slept, adoring the blunt curve of his nose and running her fingers over the stubble of his cheek. If he ignored her or she upset him then she was utterly miserable. For him to love her even a tenth as much seemed miraculous.

Thin snow covered the drive up to the Manor. The car left black tracks in it, which were covered again within minutes. 'We can't stay long,' said Rowan. 'We'll be stuck for the night.'

He hugged her. 'Don't be scared.'

'I'm not scared of James!' she said in crisp amazement. Saul laughed.

Diana opened the door herself. With the lights behind her, and warmth spilling out of the door into the open air, she looked the essence of womanly fertility. Pregnancy softened her, blurring the outline of breast and belly, high forehead and arched nose. She was wearing a dress of soft green velvet and when she saw them she put her hand to the lace at her throat. 'Rowan darling! And Saul! Did you meet on the way here?'

Saul took Rowan's hand and stepped inside. 'Not really. More on the way out. We've been to Japan together.'

There was a slight pause before Diana closed the door with a definite click. 'Good heavens,' she said thinly. 'How interesting for you both. Won't you come through? James has a cold and is home this afternoon.' Rowan went willy nilly into the drawing room. She wished Saul would not hold her hand, it embarrassed her, it lacked dignity. 'Is Sally all right?' she asked tensely. 'She wasn't any trouble?'

'Darling, you know she was,' said Diana. 'It's all right, she's upstairs playing records or something. And I have the feeling that you are about to be just as troublesome. Aren't you, Rowan? James dear – ' She pushed through the heavy oak door. A fire was blazing and a big wing chair was pulled up to it. 'James, we have Rowan and Saul to see us. They've been away together.'

There was a sneeze. A muffled voice said, 'Oh my God!'

James peered round the edge of the chair like a tortoise looking out of its shell. His carrot hair was on end, and was

221

nearly matched for colour by his nostrils. Clearly he had a terrible cold. 'As if I don't feel ill enough,' he said morosely. 'I knew there was something going on, I told you as much, Diana. You're looking bloody pleased with yourself, Saul. How many more secrets have you handed over in pillow talk? I suppose you took her to Japan?'

'He didn't take me anywhere,' said Rowan, dishonestly. 'I went of my own accord.'

'That sounds like the wrong half of a music hall joke,' said Saul. He grinned at James cockily, as if for once and at long last, he had the advantage.

It rattled James. 'I couldn't give a damn about your comings and goings,' he said nastily. 'Good God, Saul, it wasn't supposed to be a pleasure cruise! Is it too much to ask if you did any business?'

Saul moved to sit down on the arm of the sofa. He pulled Rowan with him, and kept her against his leg. The moment was one to savour. 'We got an awful lot done over there actually,' he said. 'Lots of orders, for Bardsey's and Judge's. And Rowan and I got married.'

Into the silence, Diana said, 'I knew she'd done something stupid. Rowan, how could you? You're barely nineteen years of age! Thank God for divorce.'

James sneezed again. He took his time blowing his nose, letting everyone worry about what he was going to say. 'I imagine you've thought of the implications for Bardsey's,' he said at last.

Saul grimaced. 'You could say that. I think that at long last you are going to have to manage without me. I had intended moving on to another company, but we've talked and the best thing is if Rowan and I run Judge's together.'

James sniffed. 'What a very convenient move for you. Do you mind being married for your business potential, Rowan?'

She ducked her head but Saul said sharply, 'Don't be so

bloody silly! Deny it as you might, James, I have acquired some few skills at Bardsey's. I can do a lot for Judge's and you're going to find it very much harder to replace me than you think.'

'I'm calling in the loan on your flat,' declared James triumphantly.

Rowan glanced at Saul, she had not known anything about this. But he only said, 'I thought you might. Put your mind at rest, we're setting up house at Judge's.'

'If you expect that firm to keep you in the manner to which you're accustomed, you'll find they can just about let you have a push-button biro!'

Rowan pulled away from Saul and went to sit down. 'Please don't squabble,' she said wearily. 'There isn't any point.'

'You realise I could still sell Andy and Sally's shares to James?' snapped Diana. She handed round glasses, adding, 'It's whisky. We need more notice for champagne.'

'I'm sure you won't sell,' said Rowan anxiously. 'Please, Mother.'

'Oh, she's a dear little girl when she wants her own way,' said James. 'I swear you don't know what you're taking on, Saul. She's a termagent.'

Diana ignored him. 'I won't sell yet, Rowan, that's all I can promise. I'll have to see how things go. When I've had the baby and things have settled down, we can talk about it.'

Rowan knew it would have to do. She felt rushed and unprepared; all she had volunteered for was marriage, not to change her entire way of life. But if having Saul meant doing just that, she would do it gladly. All the same, she felt the shifting sands of uncertainty.

Diana went to the drinks cabinet and refilled her glass, saying, 'Don't tell me not to drink, James, I need it, we all need it. You hardly know this man, Rowan! Why on earth couldn't you wait until you came home? You're not pregnant, are you?'

'No! No, I'm not.'

Saul said, 'Look, you're upsetting her. You might at least try and be pleased. You and I at least can be friends, can't we, Diana?'

'What else?' said Diana ironically.

Rowan got up and went out, she could not stand a minute more. The house was cold. Between the pockets of warmth, chill air hung lifelessly. She found Sally upstairs, crouched over an electric fire. She was dropping cotton on to the element and watching it flare.

'You'll electrocute yourself,' said Rowan.

Sally spun round. 'Rowan! At last! Why didn't you ring or something? It's been terrible here, purgatory!'

Rowan sat on the bed. 'I couldn't ring, I was in Japan. Sally, I've got married. To Saul.'

Sally gaped. 'You mean — Saul Barton? His brother?'

'Well, half-brother. Yes. We got married in Japan. They're being so odd about it downstairs, Mother especially.'

Sally turned back to the fire. 'Well, what do you expect? So I've got to stay here, have I?'

'I — I don't know. We haven't discussed it. We'll work something out and it'll be better, really it will!' Even to herself it sounded feeble.

A smile struggled on to Sally's face, but soon died. 'Will it? I hope you'll be happy, Ro, I do really. I mean, he's very nice and things. Isn't he? I don't know him very well.'

'Neither do I,' said Rowan, and then clapped a hand over her mouth. 'Isn't that stupid! Of course I know him. He's so kind, he really is.'

Sally began to giggle, the high-pitched beginnings of hysteria. 'Don't, Sal, don't!' begged Rowan. 'Let's go and tell Andy. Is he in the music room? Please!' With a gasp Sally stopped. They went to tell Andy.

Andy took it better than anyone. 'Good idea, I should think,' he said dispassionately. 'He can help you with the business.'

'I didn't think I needed help,' said Rowan. 'At least — yes, I suppose he can do things.'

'You can be so hellish patronising,' remarked her brother. 'You should give the guy a chance. By the way, do you want to hear my new piece? You can tell me if I've improved, you haven't heard me for a bit.'

Rowan shook her head. 'Not today. I'm a bit jet-lagged. I'll go and have a drink.'

'Me, too,' said Sally.

'They're not letting you drink, are they?' asked Rowan anxiously. 'You know how bad it is for you.'

'She can't stop me and neither can you,' said Sally, and there was an edge to her, a rock on which Rowan had foundered before. It was no use crossing Sally when she was in this mood.

Andy caught her arm as she went out, holding her back after Sally had gone. 'She's bound to be upset, Ro,' he murmured. 'I mean, Mum's got him, I've got my music and all of a sudden you've got this bloke. Leaves Sally a bit on her own.'

'And what do you suggest I do about it?' said Rowan tightly. 'There's not only me that has to look after everyone. And anyway I don't know how.'

Andy's bow swung idly between his fingers, it was as if he wasn't involved in all this, as if he was merely observing. 'No one else can do it,' he commented, feeling no breath of criticism.

When Rowan went downstairs, Sally wasn't there. James and Saul were drinking hard while Diana paced the room, turning her wedding ring over and over on her finger.

'There you are, Rowan!' she exclaimed. 'Are you going to stay? It's snowing heavily.'

'I don't know,' said Rowan. 'Saul, what are we going to do about Sally?'

He looked blank. 'What am I supposed to do? Give her some camels and donate her to the owner of some Asian takeaway?'

Diana said crisply, 'The point is that Sally lives with Rowan. She hates being here, she behaves terribly and causes nothing but trouble. I don't want to wish her on you two, I know how important it is to have privacy when you're first married — '

'All that screwing in front of the fire,' said James wistfully. 'My God, Diana, if they do stay tonight we'll be kept awake till dawn by creaking bedsprings!'

Rowan blushed scarlet. Saul, quite unmoved, said: 'Let's have another, James, or are you getting even stingier? Before I left they were saying you even haggle with the tarts.'

'I don't think we need to hear your vulgar tittletattle, Saul,' snarled Diana, and stormed out into the hall. Rowan followed.

Diana, arms folded over her stomach, was pacing up and down the marble flags, her expression one of irritation bordering on rage. 'Mother — ' begged Rowan.

'What?' snapped Diana.

'Mother, you're not letting Sally drink, are you?'

'I have as little control over Sally as over you it seems.' She turned on the girl, saying desperately, 'Oh God, Rowan, how do things get so tangled? What on earth possessed you to marry him?'

Taken aback, Rowan stammered, 'But I thought — you like him. You said so. You told me he was nice.'

'Did I? Well... we'll just have to see, won't we? But you're far, far too young and I never thought you'd be the one to rush off and do something like this! You know nothing about men.'

Sensing something, Rowan said slowly, 'What should I know?'

Diana said breathlessly, 'Nothing, everything! What if I told you James had been going with — women. Paying for it. I mean, what if I told you that? Even Saul, he won't be faithful to you. He could go off with a married woman or anything, even just once.'

Rowan watched her mother's white, tense face. She felt an obligation, however unwelcome, to try and comfort. 'I think James loves you, Mother,' she murmured. 'He's given up an awful lot for you, his son and everything.'

The words took a little time to make an impression. Then, stiffly, Diana smiled. 'Yes. So he has. And you're going to be wonderfully happy, aren't you, my darling? Next time you come we'll have champagne.'

The drive to the mill cottage was cold and slow, the snow falling in soft, handkerchief sized lumps against the windscreen. Rowan had insisted they left, she couldn't bear to spend the night there. Saul sat behind the wheel, despite all he had drunk. Rowan said, 'Would you mind terribly if Sally lived with us? I'd mind if it was your brother.'

'That would be James and we'd both mind.' He was silent, guiding the car smoothly through the snow. 'I'd rather we were on our own. It's a big change for us both, we're bound to make a mess of things to start with.'

Rowan nodded fiercely. 'Did I tell you I can't cook? I mean, I'm useless, I burn fish fingers.'

'Oh Christ! Well, I don't suppose it matters. I'll do the fish fingers, you put up the shelves. They threw me out of woodwork for incompetence.'

'I can't do that either,' sighed Rowan. 'Actually, I don't think there's anything I can do. Nothing at all.'

His hand came off the wheel and ran along her thigh. 'You can do the important things, love,' he murmured, and at that moment the car slid into the gutter. The back wheels churned uselessly. In the end Rowan had to drive while Saul got out and pushed. Snow heaped up under the low-slung bumpers, hampering every yard. 'Much more of this and I'll be glad to see it go,' said Saul, shivering. 'And I love this damned car.'

'Do you love it more than me?' asked Rowan, blowing on her blue fingers.

'Not at the moment, I don't. Look, it's only two hundred yards, let's leave it and walk.'

Obediently she got out. They took a case each and locked up the rest in the car. Then they started trudging. 'I wonder if one day you'll leave me in the snow and walk home,' she said.

'Only if you run out of petrol. You look frozen, lovey, and that house is going to be like an icebox. We should have stayed, you know.'

'Not with James leering.' She slipped and dropped the case. Saul picked it up and carried two, while she struggled along on her own.

'Cheer up,' he said shortly, and she tried to smile at him. At least he understood.

There were lights on in the cottage. 'Someone's there,' said Rowan in a shrill, nervous voice. 'Someone's in my house.'

Saul put down the cases, waving her quiet. He walked stealthily to the door, stood listening, and at the last moment threw it open. There was a cry and a scuffle. Rowan flew into the house. Saul and Joe Partridge were embarrassedly disentangling themselves from the wreckage of her standard lamp. The fire was lit and the little room was warm.

'I − I wasn't expecting it to be you,' said Saul diffidently.

'Lucky you caught me by surprise,' said Joe. 'I mean, I'm handy.'

'I'm sure you are.' Saul picked up three of Joe's shirt buttons and handed them back to him.

Joe said, 'I've been looking after the place for you, Ro. Had to light the fire to stop pipes freezing, you shoulda thought. Can't leave a place empty in middle of winter, not without draining system.'

Rowan twisted her hands together. 'It looks lovely, Joe. Thanks.'

Joe stood looking at Saul, waiting for him to go. For a scant second Rowan considered fleeing herself, running out into the snow and ending these dreadful interviews. The silence lengthened.

'What Rowan means,' said Saul awkwardly, 'is that she and I got married a few days ago. It was a bit unexpected. It was in Japan. And we couldn't have a nicer present than coming back to a warm house. Could we, Ro?'

'No – no,' said Rowan. She went to the fire and rubbed her hands together, not daring to look Joe in the eye. He stared at her, a sad disbelieving gaze. 'We only made up our minds out there,' Rowan burbled. 'We didn't want to wait.'

'You could've written,' said Joe. 'I mean, Ro – you make me feel a right plonker. You're not up the spout, are you?'

'My mother said that too,' said Rowan. 'But I'm not. Saul, there's some sherry in the kitchen, I think.'

'Cupboard by the stove,' said Joe glumly. 'But I'll be off, Ro. This is no place for me, not now.'

He pushed out through the door into the snowy yard, and Rowan had to pick up his jacket and rush after him. The wind stung her face, it might have been that making her eyes water. 'I'm sorry, Joe,' she murmured, pushing the jacket at him. Inexplicably, she added, 'I didn't mean it!'

'I hope you know what you do mean, Ro,' he replied. 'I hope you know what you done.'

She went back into the house. Saul was watching her. 'I didn't think he'd be so upset,' she said mournfully. 'He looked as if I'd slapped him.'

He tipped her chin up and kissed her. 'Can't be helped, love. A woman your age can't have more than one husband at a time, particularly if she can't cook. Have some sherry, I'm off for fish and chips.'

When he came back she was sleepy from warmth and hunger. The smell of food revived her. They sat before the fire and devoured the fish and chips from the paper.

'I always lose pounds of weight on a trip to Japan,' complained Saul. 'And in the States I pile it on. In France the

229

food's good but all that wine gives me the runs and I come back needing milk and Farley's rusks, and in India it's not whether you got a bad gut but whether or not you needed hospitalising for it.'

'I like it best at home,' said Rowan comfortably.

'Coward. Give me somewhere else every time, or at least a large part of the time. Home in large doses is just bloody boring: no revolutions, no weird food, no nutters trying to jump out of the aeroplane.'

'That's what I like about it,' defended Rowan.

He turned his head to give her a deep and lingering kiss. 'My darling, we are totally incompatible.'

They slid together down on to the rug. Rowan said, 'I hate to do this. James knows we're doing it.'

'Bollocks. Oh, Rowan, if there was another plate of fish and chips I'd eat it, but failing that I'll feast on you — '

There was a knock on the door. Saul said, 'If it's Joe Partridge, I'll kill him.'

'Don't you dare touch him,' said Rowan hastily. 'He's got a conviction for savaging someone on the rugby field. They had to gather up pieces to send to hospital.'

Hastily zipping up, Saul went to the door. 'Now look here — ' he began. Then he stood there, absolutely silent. Rowan crept nervously up behind him, peering round to see who it was. Standing dismally in the snow, her bag in her hand and her face blotched with cold and tears, was Sally.

Chapter Twenty-One

Snow fell heavily during the night and by morning the mill yard was a white carpet, only pocked with the tracks of birds. The stone buildings looked magical, almost weightless. Here and there a drift of snow hung down from the gutters, like a joke, like a tipped hat on a drunk. Rowan stepped back from the window.

Saul was still fast asleep, but with new orders to set in train and the mill running itself all the time she was away, she couldn't bear to waste time sleeping. She dressed very quietly, and wondered if from now on she and Saul would have to do everything quietly. Last night they had made love as silently as criminals, in case Sally heard them through the wall. It wasn't fair, she thought miserably, it just wasn't fair.

As a gesture to Saul, and in some measure Sally who had hitch-hiked from the Manor and arrived frozen solid, Rowan lit the fire. The place smelled of fish and chips, a delectable scent last night and revolting this morning. The air freshener had run out. Someone would have to do some shopping, and it ought to be Sally, to make up for all the upset she was causing.

Stamping across to the mill, Rowan felt mean. It wasn't Sally's fault. As a little girl she had been adored and rather spoiled, because she was so pretty and bubbly and fun. Overnight someone had switched off the sunshine. Nowadays everyone thought she was a nuisance.

Rowan had forgotten to put on her boots and by the time she reached the weaving shed her shoes were full of snow. Ignoring the sensation she went rapidly round the looms.

One was standing idle, not set up. Did that mean they had finished the run of black or was there a problem? She went sniffing about the burling and mending department, checking the rolls. It looked as if the black was done, with two weeks in hand. They might be able to fill in with a few sample runs, or do a spec order on the misty blue tweed. She had a feeling that was going to sell really well. She must ask Mr. Suzman to make her a cape with purple frogging...

Her feet left wet prints on the way through to the dye-house. The little spark of optimism within her faded and died. During the night the snow had drifted in through the cracked tiles and skylights. It lay in pristine heaps amidst the squalor. Puddles of dye had leaked out of the battered vats and frozen on the floor, no two puddles the same colour. The dying took so long, it was so hard to get a match. If they didn't modernise, and they couldn't afford to modernise, what would they do?

'Hello, Miss Rowan. You're in early.'

It was the boiler-man. Wasting no time in pleasantries, she said, 'Will you look at this mess? How am I ever going to afford to make it better?'

He tramped through on his way to stoke the boiler. 'Won't seem so cruel when t'snow's cleared away. 'Sides, never thought we'd last this long so you haven't done so bad, lass, never fear.'

Her feet were freezing. Wrapping her arms around herself, she scurried back to the house. Saul was sipping tea. 'Made some for you,' he said. 'Went out and found the milkman, got bread and eggs as well. I was going to do egg on toast.'

Rowan eyed him. 'Do you think I ought to do that? I mean – '

Saul said, 'I don't think poaching an egg is going to make my balls fall off. If watching me makes you grow a beard, then all right, you do it.'

She tilted her head to one side. 'Well, who *is* going to do it? And the shopping and the cleaning and everything. Somebody's got to.'

Saul went into the kitchen and found a saucepan, sloshed some water into it and put it on the gas. Then he cut two doorsteps of bread and shoved them under the grill. 'Having lived alone for a great many years, there are a few things I can cook,' he said cheerfully. 'But I've been thinking. This is a ghastly house, needs pulling down if anything. God knows how you've escaped electrocution, the wiring's lethal. Let's move, get a flat somewhere, a big flat. Then we might at least have a bit of privacy, and if we get a housekeeper we might have some comfort as well.'

'A housekeeper?' Rowan was almost dumbfounded. 'I can't afford that! I can't afford anything! No!'

He waved a knife under her nose. 'Don't get hysterical, love! You're a working woman, you've got to have help. A cleaner then. A new flat and a cleaner.'

She swallowed. 'But this is so convenient. So close to the mill.'

'And so bloody, bloody uncomfortable.'

For a moment she saw it with his eyes. Familiarity had blinded her to the cottage's inherent nastiness, the tiny rooms, the damp, the miserably mean thinness of doors and walls and skirtings. Seventy years ago someone had built it on the cheap and it showed. 'I suppose we could get a mortgage,' she said doubtfully.

'Course we could. I'll ask around, find somewhere.'

She watched him anxiously, nibbling her lip. He wanted to spend money. He wanted to spend *her* money. All at once she was back to the time when she had to beg for money for food. She remembered the panic of it, the feeling of total helplessness. She ate her breakfast, grateful for every mouthful, saying not a word.

They went over to the mill together. As soon as all the workers had arrived she called a meeting in the canteen and introduced Saul to them. He made an attractive little speech about Judge's being a family firm, complimenting Rowan on her achievements thus far. He said they were going to expand into many overseas markets. He said that he and Rowan were going to share responsibility, that he was only too glad to relieve her of some of her heavy burden. Afterwards they went back to Rowan's office.

'Had I better come in here?' asked Saul. 'It could take another desk.'

She hardly seemed to be listening. 'What? Oh yes, fine. Look, use mine for the time being, I've got things to see to in the mill.'

'I'll come,' he said quickly. 'I've got to get the feel of things.'

But Rowan hesitated. 'Look, it's a busy day, I've been away so long. Why don't you look at the post and sort out some selling appointments? You can have my desk. Otherwise we'll both want to use it together.'

He thought of insisting. Years of selling had attuned him to the put-off and he knew at once that Rowan was feeling threatened. Instinctively, he backed off. 'OK, I'll get on here. I know you'll want to talk to everyone on your own. We'll take it gently, I won't try and get involved in everything right away.'

She beamed at him, and rushed over to kiss him. 'I knew you'd understand.'

When she'd gone he sat down in her chair, put his feet on her desk and started reading the mail. There was nothing of great interest and much that was very boring. He put the fire on, hooked the telephone towards him and started ringing round his cronies, having a chat about life and spreading the word about his marriage and his move. After a long time, when Rowan had still not returned, he sauntered across to the house, yelled at a still slumbering Sally to get up and rustled up some lunch.

Rowan appeared at twelve-thirty. 'You left the fire on in my office,' she said at once.

'What of it?' As far as Saul was concerned, it was a cold day and the fire needed to be on.

'Rowan never leaves fires or lights burning,' said Sally. 'She's paranoid.'

'I don't believe that for a minute,' said Saul. But Rowan said, 'I have to watch the bills you know! People just don't think. I mean, if you knew how much one light can cost – it isn't as if it takes much trouble, every penny saved is just so important – ' She trailed into silence. Saul was staring at her as if she had gone bonkers.

'I told you, she's a terrible Scrooge,' declared Sally, by her very presence inhibiting any sensible discussion. Kicking her chair like a child, she went on, 'Mother said to ask what you wanted for a wedding present. James said you could have anything except a new loom.'

'Right then, I'll have a card,' snapped Rowan. She sank her hands into her pockets and spent a pleasant minute blaming James for everything.

Saul went to the fridge and poured himself a glass of milk. 'Tell him we don't need his handouts.'

'I wish it was true,' said Rowan morosely. 'He never gives anything without making you want to throw it back at him. You think he does it on purpose, but thinking it makes you feel horribly ungrateful.'

'At least he's giving you a present,' said Sally. 'I think he quite likes you actually. He thinks you're tough.'

Rowan sniffed expressively.

In the afternoon she let Saul look through the sales ledger, and when he suggested one or two improvements she listened wide-eyed and then forgot about them. The next day, she was in at half-past seven and when he strolled up at around nine she managed to sidetrack him into an unnecessary and unimportant task. She seemed to be rushing around hectically, trying not to notice he was there. It was infuriating and hard to tackle: in the mill they could be overheard and at home there was Sally. Besides, everyone he spoke to seemed to assume he had married Rowan to get in at Judge's and he suspected that she was hearing the same thing. Denials got him nowhere, and anyway, there was an element of truth in it. Why else had he married her so quickly? He would have married her if she had had nothing, of that he was sure, but the haste? He had wanted out of Bardsey's and in at Judge's, because it was right for Rowan as well as himself. And because he had thought that, and because she might now be thinking it, he had to tread carefully.

Saul took her out for a drink in the evening. The snow was almost gone and they drove across dark moors, with sheep leaping out into the headlights and owls swooping low. For some reason the owls moved to the open spaces in winter, although to human eyes there was no shelter, nothing. But on winter nights they could be heard, hunting the heather, calling to each other.

The little pub was warm, smelling of beer and woodsmoke. He bought her a gin and tonic, a double whisky for himself, and said: 'Are you sorry we agreed to work together?'

'No. No, of course not.' She opened her eyes wide in pretended innocence.

Saul said, 'We can stop if you want. I'll look for a job somewhere else and you can keep playing solitaire. Do you want that?'

She swallowed visibly. 'Of course I don't. Everybody would think we'd fallen out over it, wouldn't they?'

'They'd be right.'

She clinked the ice in her drink, her face closed and defensive.

Saul said, 'You're going to have to let me have a piece of the action, Rowan. You're not playing fair.'

Still she said nothing. 'Look,' he said, 'you can't do everything yourself. I know you want to but it's physically impossible. If the firm's going to grow, you have to have help. I can help you. Between us, we can put Judge's on the map!'

The ice clinked again. At last she said, 'I didn't think you wanted Judge's. I thought you wanted me.'

'Oh Christ! I knew that was it.'

He downed his Scotch and went to the bar for another. 'Look,' he said, returning, 'if I'd wanted to marry for money I've had a dozen chances over the last few years. I married you, because you're you. I would have married you if you didn't have a bean. And Judge's isn't the be-all and end-all you think it is, sweetie! It's a little, run-down firm trying to swim in rough seas. And I can help. I'm a bloody good swimmer.'

Her face twisted. 'Everybody thinks I've been stupid.'

'Why do you care what they think? I don't. They don't count, all those people. We're the ones that matter. I love you, Rowan.'

She smiled tearfully. 'And I love you, too. I know I've been a beast, I will try harder, I promise.'

He popped a kiss on her nose. 'Then let's get things straight. I want my name on the cheques, so I can get the things I need. One of those things is a decent desk, and I need it right away.'

'You can use mine,' said Rowan fearfully. 'You don't need a new one!'

'Oh yes I do. And I always give my mother some money each month, otherwise she can't manage. That's a commitment I always made out of my salary but now of course Judge's has to see to it. Will you put my name on the cheques, Rowan?'

She ducked her head and would not look at him. He clasped his hair and said forcefully, 'Rowan, what are you afraid of? I'm not going to bankrupt you!'

'Aren't you?' She turned towards him and her great green eyes were brimming with tears. 'You don't understand! It isn't five minutes since I was so hard up there wasn't

237

anything to eat and they were turning off the electricity! And you want a new desk and a standing order to your bloody mother and a new flat and a cleaner and God knows what else! We can't afford it, Saul.'

He drained his whisky and prepared to get another. 'I've looked at the books. It isn't can't, it's won't. You are hanging on to money as if your life depended on it. I know the firm needs capital, I know you want to get back to where you used to be, but for God's sake, you've got to live.'

He went to get more drinks, though Rowan had barely sipped hers. When he came back, she said, 'I know I'm being silly but I do so want to get everything in-house again, then we can really make it big. We'd worry James something cruel.'

Twirling his glass, Saul said, 'How about worrying James a bit less and pleasing me a bit more?'

'But I do please you! I try to, really I do. Don't I?' She looked young and frightened and vulnerable. When she looked like that, he couldn't persist.

She gave in on the cheque book and the desk and the money for his mother. He went out and bought a beautiful new sofa, in dark red leather, so that they could at last sit down in the evenings without being impaled on springs, and on the same day bought three new typewriters and retired the firm's old ones. 'Can't send out letters looking like ransom demands,' he commented. 'I can't believe anyone would go on using a typewriter that long since lost the letter A.'

Rowan went to the bathroom and sat on the loo, trying to think things out. There was no privacy anywhere any more: Saul was in her office, Sally was in the house and confusion buzzed within her head. Yet she knew there was no real problem, only her own habits. She liked working on her own, she was used to it. Saul did not know how much it cost her to push even crumbs of responsibility his way. It seemed to her that unless she watched everything, all the time, the fabric of the mill would crumble.

Sally banged on the door and yelled, 'Rowan! Are you going to be all day?' and wearily Rowan got up. Sally's intermittent attendance at school nowadays verged on the occasional, but she left in a month's time and was promising to get a job. She was going to work as a beauty consultant in a Bradford store, wearing inch thick make-up on her flawless skin and advising ladies who certainly knew a great deal more about wrinkles than she did. Rowan stared at her own face in the bathroom mirror. No wrinkles, but a wide-eyed haunted look in her great green eyes. With her large bronze hoop ear-rings she looked almost Egyptian.

She went heavily downstairs and left the bathroom to Sally. Saul was sitting at the table, scanning the newspaper.

'I thought you were in the mill,' said Rowan nervously.

'I was. I wanted to talk to you, Rowan.'

'Oh.' It was another of those 'Why won't you involve me?' talks, she could tell. When he said crisply, 'Fashion fair next week, in Germany. I'll be going off on Sunday night, OK?' she blinked in surprise and said meekly, 'Oh, all right then. Fine.'

'Is that all you can say?' He got up and came across to her, taking her by the lapels of her jacket and shaking her gently. 'Don't you want to come? It could be like Japan, selling all day and screwing all night, one endless coupling − Rowan, I could eat you!'

She turned her face up to his and they kissed. He pushed her back against the table and slid his hands beneath her clothes to feel for her breasts.

'Really! Do excuse me,' said Sally. She flounced into the room and began banging about looking for a book. Saul and Rowan disentangled themselves.

'Don't you have any tact?' demanded Saul angrily. 'We wouldn't mind a little privacy once in a while.'

Sally picked up her book. 'I know you don't really want me,' she said, ducking her head.

'But darling, we do!' declared Rowan, lying in her teeth.

239

She couldn't bear to see Sally look so hurt and little girl. 'Don't we, Saul?'

He sighed gustily. 'Yes. Yes, we do. It's just — Sally, you can't just barge in on us whenever you feel like it!'

'I think you should do that sort of thing in the bedroom,' she said primly.

'We've got to move,' declared Saul. 'We'll get her a studio bedroom or something but we have to move!'

They retreated to the mill. Rowan said, 'I can't come to Germany, you know. There's masses of work on and I've got an appointment with the bank manager.'

'Shouldn't I be coming to that?' said Saul.

Rowan flushed. 'Oh, I hadn't thought. I know him so well you see, and — will it be all right if I tell you all about it afterwards?'

He shrugged. 'Looks like it will have to be.'

She knew she had offended him. That night she rushed out to the shops and bought some steak and some wine, she made a salad and put candles in bottles on the table. The steak was overcooked and tough, the candles smoked, and besides, a cosy dinner for two isn't the same when there are three of you. They went to bed at half-past nine. Saul said, 'I rang an estate agent chum this afternoon. There's a penthouse flat going, with a separate bit for granny. Super new block, doorman, everything.'

Rowan groaned but Saul put his arms around her, pulling her head into the hollow of his shoulder. She said, 'Perhaps I should ask Mother to have her.'

'Perhaps you should. But I've got an option on the flat anyway. We'll have a look when I get back, OK?'

'OK.' She stretched out her legs, putting her entire length in contact with him. The hairs on his chest were soft prickles against her breasts, she wanted him to love her. But instead he said, 'Why don't you ever talk to me?'

'But I do. We're talking now.'

'I mean in the mill. As soon as there's a problem you dash

off and deal with it, you don't even tell me when it's over.'

'They just seem like — my problems.'

'Don't you mean "our" problems?'

She nodded unhappily. 'Yes. I suppose I must mean that.'

Beneath the bedclothes their legs entwined. He seemed suddenly to want to dominate. He swung on top of her, his bulk crushing her fragility in a way that made her long for him to crush her almost to death. She let out a cry as he came into her, it was repeated with every hard thrust, but just as the pinpoint of feeling within her threatened to burst, there was a knock on the door. 'Are you all right, Rowan?' called Sally. 'You're making such a noise.'

'Go to hell, Sally,' yelled Saul, and climaxed, gasping.

Rowan chewed at her fists, caught between rage and frustration. 'And we forgot the bloody rubber,' hissed Saul.

She buried her face in his neck. 'I don't think it matters. I've got a pain, I think I'm starting my period.'

He ruffled her hair.

Three days later Saul departed on his German trip. Rowan was ashamed at herself for being so relieved. No more negotiating between Sally and Saul, trying to keep them both happy; no more guilt about the mill; no compulsion to keep the house neat and tidy, or to wash her hair every day of her period because it got so greasy. Reading the paper over a messy breakfast table one morning, she said to Sally, 'Are you going to be nicer when Saul comes back? You've been really horrid lately and it isn't fair, Saul's so kind to you.'

Sally stared from beneath a blonde and shaggy fringe. 'Men are never any use,' she said bitterly. 'Even Daddy left us, he didn't care about me or you or anyone. You think they'll stop you being lonely but they don't, it doesn't last. They only love you while they're getting the best.'

Rowan swallowed. 'Saul's not like that. Please, Sally, try and understand. One day you'll find someone to love you.'

She watched her sister's sullen little face. What was going on in there? Once Sally had been so simple to understand;

compared with herself and Andy she had been an open book. But, ever since their father's death the pages had wrinkled and curled until even her everyday actions held devious and unhappy meanings.

There was nothing more pleasant, reflected Rowan, than an interview with the bank manager when the accounts looked healthy. If she had not suffered those first, frightening encounters she would never have appreciated these cosy little chats.

'You're keeping staff costs well down I see,' said Mr. Blood happily. 'An awful lot of places are letting them race away.'

'I won't give a wage rise,' said Rowan. 'We're not out of the wood yet, not by a long way. I shall need at least a hundred and fifty thousand for my new carding machine.'

Mr. Blood tapped his lip with his finger. 'That doesn't look too unreasonable. We can lend that, I think. When could you let me have some projections, Rowan dear?'

For a brief, delectable second, she closed her eyes. She had started to lose hope of ever getting the machine. 'Tomorrow,' she said breathlessly. 'I shall have to look at absolutely all the machines, to make sure we have the best, but I know what it will cost and I know what it should do. Oh, Mr. Blood, I never thought I'd manage it!'

He beamed at her, inwardly congratulating himself on supporting her so well all this time. 'I always had faith in you, Rowan Judge.'

By the end of the week she had placed the order. She met Saul off the plane at Yeadon, still bubbling with excitement. He saw her running towards him across the marble floor, her burgundy skirt billowing out around her, and he dropped his case, spread wide his arms and hugged her.

'Did you miss me, sweet? I've been longing to get home. The wide world isn't nearly so much fun as it was.'

She slid her fingers up into his hair, by the feel of it

242

reminding herself of delicious hours when she explored every hair he possessed. 'I missed you so much, I never stopped working. That way I didn't have to think about it. Saul, I've got some wonderful news! I've bought the new card.'

She was conscious that somehow she had said the wrong thing. His arms fell away, he picked up his case and began striding towards the exit.

'Saul! Saul, what's the matter? Aren't you pleased for me?'

'What do you want me to say?'

'Well — it's our firm, you ought to be thrilled.'

He stopped then and faced her. '*Our* firm? Are you sure you think that, Rowan? Because you don't act as if it was anything except your own personal toy. And you never did learn to share your playthings, did you?' She was threatened by tears and in a choked voice said, 'I don't understand. I only said I'd bought the card, you knew I wanted to.'

'Just bought the first one that came along, did you?' He folded his arms, not bothering to lower his voice so that people yards away could hear what they were saying.

'I researched it, naturally, as well as I could.'

'What make is this card then?'

'German. They're all German, you ought to know that.'

'I do know that. Rowan — oh God, you must see! I've been in Germany all week. I could have bought direct, we could have gone for a forward contract on the currency, we could have arranged for someone to go across and learn how to work the bloody thing! Instead you buy from a middleman who showed you a few leaflets. You're not stupid, Rowan, you just didn't want me involved.'

'That isn't true!' She began to cry now, in earnest. How did things get so twisted? She had been having such fun talking to people and studying machines, it was the culmination of years of work and he wanted to take that away from her! She tried to explain. 'It was my work that bought it. Judge's means such a lot to me, it can't be the same for you!'

'If it did, you'd soon put a stop to it, wouldn't you, Rowan?' Wearily, he picked up his case and walked on.

All the way home she tried to make it up. He drove along, completely silent, while she burbled. At last he said, 'Do shut up, Rowan.'

She choked off in mid-sentence and sat making patterns in her flesh with her long nails. When they had driven for twenty minutes in total silence, she said, 'I bet you got lots of orders,' in a falsely cheerful voice.

'Quite a few, yes. Mostly short runs.'

Her head came up. 'We do have a minimum order, you know.'

'You might, I don't. Sprats to catch mackerels. You cancel one of them and I shall tear you limb from limb.'

'And you told me you were soft-hearted,' complained Rowan, trying to sweeten him.

'Marriage certainly shows you another side to people, doesn't it?' He shot her a glittering smile. This time Rowan shut up completely.

Chapter Twenty-Two

After dinner that night, Saul went out and didn't come back. Rowan sat up until three, four o'clock, waiting and waiting. The fire went out. The clock ticked loudly. Far away across town she heard a car engine but it went away again.

At last she crept upstairs and into bed. Suppose he was dead, suppose he had left her, suppose he was even now lying injured in some gutter? She felt lost and bewildered, because love had seemed so easy when it began and now was so terribly difficult. There seemed no way in which she could go through her days without trampling on Saul's feelings, not because she wanted to but because she knew nothing of the way he felt! Vast areas of him were unknown to her, and whereas once she had relished the voyage of discovery, now she was almost too timid to put a toe in the pond. Suppose he didn't love her any more?

Next morning when he had still not returned she dragged herself to the breakfast table, loathing Sally for being there and seeing her blotched and puffy face.

'Told you,' said Sally. 'Has he gone for good?'

'If he has, I'll blame you,' said Rowan viciously. 'You want to break us up.'

Sally got up and made coffee, then took some ice out of the fridge. 'You can't go to work looking like that. Try this.'

Rowan took the offering. Sally fluctuated between child and woman with dizzying speed.

She was in her office when Saul came back. She saw his car pull into the yard and when the familiar, tall, long-legged figure got out she thought she would die with joy. She stood at the window until he went into the house, then she flew downstairs and followed him. He was slumped in a chair, eyes closed, shirt unfastened, his tie loose around his neck.

'I thought — I didn't know where you were,' gasped Rowan. She had prepared a dozen speeches in the night for just this moment and had forgotten every one of them.

His eyes opened slightly, he looked at her and then closed them again. Almost hysterical, she screamed, 'Where were you then? At least you can tell me that?'

'Why don't you make some coffee?' said Saul wearily.

Nonplussed, she went and did so. He took the mug from her and sipped it, grimacing. 'Can't you tell me where you went?' she begged, hating herself and him for her subservience.

He shrugged. 'Around. I ended up at my mother's.'

'You could have rung me! I don't even know where she lives.'

He yawned, got up and prepared to go to bed. 'It never seemed to me that you were even remotely interested. But I'll take you to see her, if you want.'

'I do want,' said Rowan, nodding firmly. 'And Saul — I am sorry, I am truly, I didn't mean anything. I'll cancel the carding machine if you like.'

He seemed hardly to be listening. Wearily, not even looking at her, he trudged up to bed.

Because of the row, Rowan fiddled about, putting the superficial things right. They went to see his mother, Mrs. Howarth, a pale, insignificant woman who gave her fruit cake with too few currants. Despite the 'Mrs' she had never married, but at old man Bardsey's suggestion had adopted a new name and pretended widowhood. It was Saul who had thrown off the false surname, insisting on Barton, on his rights.

They were all glad when it was time to go. There was a natural timidity about the woman that Rowan found difficult; she could only liken the conversation to tempting a shy

246

rabbit with a lettuce leaf. One sharp word or gesture and all confidence was gone.

Afterwards she said to Saul, 'There you are then. She seems very nice.'

'We didn't have to go,' said Saul irritably.

'Well, you said you wanted me to,' retorted Rowan. 'What else did you want?'

She stared at him uncomprehendingly. His eyes were so brown sometimes that she could not see into them, she felt excluded from him. Only the day before two men in the dye-house had behaved absolutely stupidly, mixing two lots of cloth and turning the whole lot bottle green, and no sooner had she heard about it than she had gone down and verbally slaughtered them. Then it had turned out Saul had dealt with the matter only that morning, and she hadn't given anyone time to tell her. Since she was the one who looked a fool, why was it he who was offended? Since it was she who had been made to share, why did he behave as if he was losing out? She didn't understand and she felt angry and bewildered.

A few days later, James telephoned. 'Hello, Rowan, it's me.'

'Which me is that?' she asked, knowing perfectly well.

'The me that sends you decent wedding presents. What was it now?'

'A silver coffee set. I'm thinking of flogging it.'

'You would, you mercenary bitch! Rowan, I want you to go and see your mother. I don't know why I have to remind you, but it seems she's spawned three ungrateful brats and I have to do these things. She's feeling very low, and that's not good for her or the baby. It means an awful lot to us.'

'I'm glad to hear you are capable of human feelings, James. 'Bye.'

'Wait! Don't hang up!' His voice cracked with urgency. She waited, because his call was about more than daughterly duty. 'I just wanted to tell you that I'm suing Saul for breach of contract,' he said jovially. 'He owes me at least a year's salary and I'm going to have a crack at getting him for the use of confidential information. That should be an absolute doddle, he's bound to be using what he picked up at Bardsey's. I thought you ought to know.'

'Thank you so much, James,' she said frostily. 'I hope I can do the same for you some day.'

'Well, I don't see why he should walk all over me. By the way, a word in your ear, Rowan. Keep him on his lead. He never did understand the principle of profit, thinks he can spend it first and make it later. Don't let him bankrupt you, love.'

Rowan slammed down the receiver. How dare he say that, on the very day she saw from the statement that Saul's expenses for the German trip were over £2,000? Most of it for small orders that would bring in little or no profit. A familiar, panicky sensation began in the pit of her stomach. She visualised a barren future, her firm crippled by interest charges, dealt a death-blow by a court case and its lifeblood finally drained by extravagance.

Saul came into the room, whistling between his teeth. She didn't dare say anything to him, not until she had calmed down. He watched her forcing her arms into her jacket. 'Where are you going? Is the building on fire or what?'

She picked up her bag and stood hovering, trying to decide what to tell him. 'James rang,' she said at last. 'He wants me to go and see Mother, she's a bit low.'

'Then why the rush?'

'Saul – James is going to sue you for breach of contract. He says he can get you for passing on company secrets.'

He threw back his head and gave a bellow of laughter. 'Well, wouldn't you know! The old bastard. Hang on a minute, let's have a think.' He wagged a finger at her. 'We'll say he fired me because of our marriage. He can't prove he didn't any more than we can he did, but it looks likely. And we'll claim Judge's and Bardsey's are industries so diverse they do not compete, and his sacking me was simply further evidence of his paranoia in that direction. You never know, I might get legal aid. I've got a big enough overdraft.'

'What overdraft?' She goggled at him. 'I didn't know you had one.'

'Good God, Ro, it's only five thousand quid! Bardsey's probably owe me that in back expenses claims. I ran it up because they never settled without a six month argument.' He saw the bleak look of panic in her eyes. 'You don't have to behave as if I've revealed a criminal past,' he said incredulously.

She blushed and picked up her handbag. 'I'm not behaving like anything, I'm going to see my mother.'

'All right. I suppose I should have told you. But I realised the fuss you'd make. Good God, you look sick if I buy three bottles of wine!'

'No I don't. Or at least, I don't mean to. Look, I don't want to talk about it.'

'Well, I do. We have got to talk about it, Rowan.'

'No! I'm going to see Mother.' He put out a hand to stop her but she struck it aside, she wouldn't look at him. He could have held her easily but he couldn't bring himself to clench his fist on that long thin arm. For some reason the sound of her feet running along the corridor filled him with pain and rage. For a minute he wanted to catch her and hit her, smash that closed, watchful look. As her car pulled jerkily out of the gate he went to the cupboard and poured himself a drink.

In the last stages of pregnancy, Diana was looking bloated, tired and old. She waddled through to the sitting room and fell into a chair. 'Don't ever get pregnant,' she told Rowan. 'It goes on forever and it's boring and painful and ugly. I see James looking at me sometimes, wondering where this elephant came from.'

'Did Dad look at you like that?' asked Rowan.

'I don't know. Possibly. I doubt it. I'm too old for all this, that's the trouble. You'll probably sail through without a murmur.'

Rowan grimaced. 'No thanks. How on earth could I manage? I've far too much to do.'

'And I have far too little,' said her mother.

They looked at each other. 'You've still got your music,' ventured Rowan.

'My ankles swell when I stand up. And James only wants to go out to nightclubs, and at the very least I owe this baby more than gin and cigar smoke. He goes without me quite a lot. I remember I was every bit as bored just before I had you, and then afterwards when you screamed twenty-three hours out of the twenty-four, I would have given anything for boredom.'

'Didn't you ever like me?' demanded Rowan. 'It doesn't sound like it.'

Diana laughed. 'My darling, if I hadn't adored you I would have wrung your neck. Did James ask you to come?'

'Yes,' admitted Rowan. 'But I would have anyway. He's trying to wreck us, you know.'

'From what I gather now that Saul is with you, he thinks you're trying to wreck him. Tit for tat, darling, you can't expect anything else. Can you tell me how it's going?'

Launched on her favourite theme, Rowan gave her mother a carefully expurgated account of progress. Almost two-thirds of their cloth was woven at the mill now, and the ancillary processes were steadily being gathered back under their own roof. They were getting a well deserved reputation for quality, colour and style.

'This is Judge's own,' she boasted, picking up her cloak. She had tossed it casually across the back of her chair, taking pleasure in the generous folds of burgundy cloth. 'Can you see, we've woven in a tiny black thread? It gives the whole thing depth.'

Diana reached out her hand, and even that was puffed up by pregnancy.

'It's lovely,' she said. 'Was that Saul's idea?'

'Good heavens, no! I mean — I'm sure he'd like to get involved but — it's all a bit difficult, really.'

Thoughtfully, Diana let the fabric fall. 'Well,' she said. 'Have you made a mistake?'

'No,' said Rowan quickly. 'We're just taking some time to adjust, that's all. I didn't think it through, I didn't — he seemed different in Japan. But we're both different, it wasn't real life.'

'And what's so awful about real life?'

'Nothing! But he wants to do things his way and he doesn't understand the mill. I don't understand him. I try so hard, I cook him lovely meals and he gets up half an hour later and makes scrambled egg. I can't seem to do anything right.'

Diana's lovely head tilted to one side. 'He must have realised he was marrying a tomboy! If he didn't, he should have. Darling, weren't you surprised when he wanted to marry you all of a sudden, didn't you suspect anything? I don't say it was all avarice but James wouldn't let him get control of Bardsey's, for good reasons I might add, and he saw his chance. God, that man!'

Rowan got up. 'It's no use talking to you, I know you hate him and you'll only tell James.'

'No I won't! And I don't hate him, not exactly — I don't know him. But, darling, you know how stubborn you can be! You'll dig your heels in just for the sake of it. As far as you're concerned there's one way to do a thing and everyone else is insane. If you want to be happy in marriage, you've got to learn to — to see the other person's point of view.'

'Have you learned that?' demanded Rowan. 'As I remember it, Dad always saw *your* point of view.'

'And I see James's,' said Diana. 'You don't want a lapdog, do you? I didn't.'

Rowan swung her cape around her shoulders. She felt a sudden and unexpected urge to hug her mother, to beg her always to be there. Diana was softened by pregnancy, she

251

seemed vulnerable. Underneath her calm Rowan sensed that she was afraid, and fear of that sort was catching. At the door she asked jerkily, 'Will it be all right? The baby?'

Understanding at once, Diana nodded. 'I'm a little old, but it isn't the first. James has hired a great man to attend me. I expect it will hurt rather a lot, but that's all. They might even do a Caesarean, in which case I won't know anything at all about it.' She smiled, and on a rare impulse reached out and hugged her daughter. They clung briefly together and then parted in mutual embarrassment.

Driving home, Rowan was consumed with anxieties. She hunted about for one she could deal with, and thought of James's law-suit. Not stopping to analyse her motives, she drove into the car park of her firm of solicitors. They were a solid, unimaginative body of men who regarded Rowan with the fascination of bullocks teased by a butterfly, and as for her, just listening to legal jargon calmed her. It gave her the feeling that everything in life could be filed under a heading, if only you could decide which one.

It seemed that dismissed or not, Saul was almost certainly in breach of contract. They could well be liable for damages. 'Mr. James Barton can build a very fair case against him,' said the solicitor cordially. 'He could claim that he was justified in dismissing your husband, or that even if he did not dismiss him, he could well have done so. The Japan trip was somewhat risqué under the circumstances. I mean, escorting a competitor and then marrying her in the firm's time – '

Rowan stood up. 'Thank you,' she said crisply. 'I don't need moralising, I can assure you. I should like you to let me have a report of the worst possible case, and also the probable outcome. Get counsel's opinion if you must.'

'Well – yes,' he said doubtfully. She swirled her burgundy cape in his face and was gone.

As expected, the interview made her feel better. She had done something, and by so doing had stilled the gremlins that came out at night and nagged her with horrid possibilities. On the way home she stopped off and bought some fish, because Saul liked it and would be pleased.

To her surprise, when she got in Saul was in the bedroom, in his shirtsleeves, fiddling with his bow tie. 'Where on earth are we going?' she asked.

He grinned at her. 'Sorry, love, you're not included. Customer entertaining, this is. We're going gambling, he insists. There'll be a big order in it, I know him of old.'

'Is it a Bardsey customer? With this thing on with James, we'll have to tread carefully.'

In a dry voice, Saul said, 'I think I know my own business, thank you, Rowan.'

Something in his tone caught her on the raw. 'Talking of your business, I've been to see the solicitor,' she said. 'I think we'd better not pay off your overdraft just yet, a few debts will look much better in court.'

He looked bemused. 'What on earth are you talking about?'

'The court case, James suing you for breach of contract. I've had a long talk with the solicitor and I've decided − '

His expression silenced her. 'Just a minute. You have decided about *my* court case? *My* overdraft? *My* affairs?'

Discomfited, she said, 'Not quite like that, of course. But with James you can't afford to hang about, not if you want to win!'

'And you do, don't you, Rowan? It means more to you than anything I can do, anything I say, Sally, your mother, even God himself. Just so long as *you* keep on winning.'

Her eyes widened angrily. 'That's not fair! Who's going to take care of things if I don't? You don't understand the mill, you just don't! I never wanted you in it, it was never my idea! Can't you see that?'

In a deadly tone, he said, 'We agreed, Rowan. We talked about it and we agreed.'

'You talked and I went along with it. I knew it was a lousy idea.'

'But then every idea that isn't yours is lousy, isn't it, love? That's one of the other things I've learned about you.'

Alight with fury, she blazed at him. 'And what else have you learned, may I ask? Do tell me while we're on the subject.'

His smile glittered. He swept his arm to encompass the bedroom, almost obscured under Rowan's habitual clutter. 'Now that you ask, I wouldn't mind it if you put the odd piece of your clothing away now and then. I wouldn't mind if you cleaned the bath after you, or washed the odd dish, or even mastered the Hoover once in a while. I am bloody sick of living my life picking up after a slut!'

'You said we'd share the work,' she screeched in outrage.

'Who the sodding hell's sharing? When it comes to the house I do it, when it comes to the mill you do it. And I've got this funny foible, Rowan dear, when I get married I prefer it to be to a woman!'

Rowan picked up a cotton wool filled china bowl from the dressing table and hurled it at him. It smashed against the wall. They both stood in silence, as cold as before they were hot.

There was a knock on the door. 'Did somebody break something?' called Sally innocently.

Saul took a deep and shuddering breath. 'Yes, someone did. But don't worry, Sally, Rowan broke it so Rowan will clear it up. Actually she's going to clear up quite a few things, and with a bit of luck we might possibly rediscover the furniture!' He flung open the door, pushed Sally hard to one side and stormed out.

Once in the car he felt calmer. Why in God's name did she have to be so bloody butch? Fighting hard, all the time, elbowing him out of the way so that she could do it her way, have it her way, all the way. And it wasn't her, or at least it wasn't all of her. Inside, beneath the fear and the insecurity and the aggression, there was soft, yielding, feminine Rowan, who needed him. He was too close to her, he thought dismally. At a distance you could see through her toughness but close up her carapace repelled. Reaching down inside the pocket of the door he found a silver hip flask and expertly uncorked it. The liquor hit his throat like hot coals, and he gasped and drank again. He felt, more and more often, that he might just have made the biggest mistake of his life.

The gambling club was one he used to visit quite often. Fringed red lights hung low over the tables and men huddled round intently. Velvet curtains muffled all sound except the high pitched click of chips, the whir of the roulette wheel and the bored voice of the girl dealing vingt-et-un. She looked tired and thin; her low-cut black dress could have done with more filling. Thank God Rowan had the sense not to wear plunge necklines, he thought, instead cultivating skin-tight jersey dresses that showed up her nipples in the cold.

He was dining so he went through to the bar, at once ordering a double Scotch. His customer hadn't arrived as yet, so he spent the time scanning the crowd. As always in Bradford it was cosmopolitan; the croupiers Italian, two or three very tall, very loud Germans speaking accented English, and a sprinkling of Asians. The ethnics were inveterate gamblers given the chance which, as with all things pleasurable, was usually denied them. The vast majority were Moslems for whom it was forbidden to drink or gamble, but the men here were presumably stretching a point. If you spend your days working twelve-hour shifts in a factory, followed by a couple of hours at the mosque, was it any wonder you fancied blueing some money on a flutter? Yet they were nervous punters, risking little.

The customer still had not arrived so he finished his drink and went through to play roulette. He got the chips in twenties, which was unusual for him, he generally chanced a fiver here or there. On the first turn of the wheel his number came up.

The croupier shrugged and smiled, and a girl dealing Black Jack rippled the cards encouragingly. They didn't mind what he won as long as he stayed long enough to give most of it back. He turned to go back to the bar to get another drink. There, in front of him, unavoidable, was James.

'And hello to you,' said James. 'Winning, I see.'

'Just a flutter. I'm waiting for someone, we're dining. Fancy a drink?'

'I'll have a Scotch. Glad to meet you actually, I wanted to talk.'

They went back into the bar and James at once settled himself at a corner table. It was early, the place was thin of people. Saul ordered two doubles and sat down. In the pinkish glow of light James looked healthier than normal. He also looked remarkably cheerful. 'You're going to have to make her sell, you know.'

Saul laughed. 'Not a cat in hell's chance! She lives and breathes the sodding firm.'

'That's what I mean. If you want any sort of life, you'll have to make her get rid of it. Diana won't sell Andy or Sally's shares unless Rowan wants to quit, so you make her. It's not long before Andy's of age, so we can't waste time. I'll give you a bloody good price, you'll be able to start something new. Something you can handle without the little woman's guiding hand. I tell you, it's your only hope.'

'Are you saying I can't handle Judge's?' Saul dribbled water into his Scotch and downed it in one. He raised his finger to the waiter for another.

'She won't let you handle Judge's,' said James. 'I admit, I'm scared of her. She's too damned good, she could go places. I've heard the way she's treating you, like the lackey. My advice to you is get her pregnant and make her sell up.'

Saul chuckled again, this time with real amusement. He looked at James's smooth, outwardly innocent face and for once in his life knew exactly what he was thinking. It was all falling into place. James, with a single call to Rowan, had planted a few seeds of suspicion. Saul was unreliable, Saul needed direction, Saul wasn't a man you could leave in charge. Besides which, Saul was going to cost her money. James knew that Rowan was paranoid about money, it was only Saul who had found it out the hard way. Having driven his wedge, James was now ready to commiserate with one half of the partnership and suggest a suitable way out. It was admirably neat.

'Is Diana enjoying her pregnancy?' he asked as a diversion.

'What? No, not one bit. But it draws their fangs, brother mine, it draws their fangs. They come over all dependent and start treating you as the protector and breadwinner. And wouldn't that be a nice change?'

'I'm surprised you're out tonight, actually. Doesn't Diana mind being left alone?'

James grunted. Oddly enough *he* minded, let alone Diana. He couldn't understand now why he had come. He knew Diana was capable of telephoning the ambulance herself but he had the horrible feeling that if he allowed her to do so, she would not forgive him. In a moment he would go home again. He couldn't relax, his mind refused to free itself of concern.

'I thought it was a bit sneaky trying to get me for breach of contract,' said Saul.

James came back to the present with a start. 'What? Oh that. You certainly asked for it and I'm taking it all the way. I've a feeling I shouldn't have told Rowan though, that girl is too sharp by half. She'll have done some damage limitation by now, I don't doubt.'

'Naturally,' said Saul. He felt a leaden sense of doom weighing him down. Why didn't he have this sharp, fencing mentality, possessed by both Rowan and James, enabling them to seize upon and devour the enemy? He was more fun, he was more witty, he could walk into a room full of squabbling people and charm them all into good humour. But he was so absolutely, totally, unmentionably bored by this continual state of war.

James said, 'That your man? Christ, another one of ours. I warn you, we're turning ourselves on our ear to see you off and we've got the muscle to do it.'

Saul got up and left him. He greeted his guest and ordered more drinks, anything to dull his senses. In a while, after a meal, they would gamble a little. Tonight he wanted to gamble a lot.

Chapter Twenty-Three

James went out to his car. He wouldn't have minded a girl tonight, but it was starting to rain and he was distinctly unhappy about Diana. Aspley Manor was a bleak, desolate sort of place in winter, he didn't like it much. The peacocks trailed about cackling like witches, leaving their infernal droppings on the doorstep. Summer was the time, with the oaks in leaf and bees buzzing in the drowsy air. He turned the car out of town and accelerated hard.

'Diana! Diana!' He was calling almost before he had opened the door. He knew something was wrong, he could feel it. The light was on in the drawing room. He burst in. She was lying on the sofa, her huge belly uppermost and her face contorted. 'For God's sake, Diana! Say something!'

Through gritted teeth she muttered, 'Contraction. Can't. Ambulance coming.'

'Sod the ambulance, I'll take you in the car! Oh, darling, I knew something was wrong.'

The contraction subsided and Diana put up a hand to push damp hair from her forehead. 'Don't panic, James. I started around six, I didn't think much would happen till at least eleven. I took ages with the others. And this is a bit — beastly.'

James leaned down and slipped his arms under her shoulders. 'Car. Quickly. This is no time for stoicism, both you and the baby could be at risk. How long since you called the ambulance?'

'Over half an hour,' grunted Diana.

'Then they've probably got lost. Right, hold on to me. We'll stop whenever we must, but let's hurry.'

They made slow progress. Every contraction drained

Diana a little more, her breath was coming in racking gasps. James had panic on a tight rein, this did not look right at all! At last she was safely in the car, as if that was all that safety asked. He sent the machine howling off into the night.

'I knew I was too old,' she muttered.

'Nonsense. You should have gone into hospital straight away, that's all. God knows what might be happening — '

'That's right, cheer me up!'

He glanced at her. The skin of her face was drawn down in lines of pain.

He said, 'Sorry. I'm anxious, that's all. I couldn't bear to lose you.'

'Suppose we lose the baby?'

At another time he would have decried her pessimism, but as the rain slashed at the windscreen and her body contorted once again, it seemed the most likely outcome. Already there was a ball of sorrow lodged in his guts. He drove harder still.

Another car was leaving the gates of the nursing home as he swung into it. The rear wing of the Mercedes slid away on the wet road, catching the other car, a Jaguar, a glancing blow. James cursed and drove on, screeching to a halt at the door. The driver of the stricken car ran up, exuding fury.

'I say! What the hell do you mean driving off like that?'

'Get out of my way, damn you! My wife's in labour, she's seriously ill.'

'I don't consider that any excuse — '

James ignored him and ran into the hospital. The man turned to Diana, sitting immobile in the car. 'I'm sorry, madam, but I really must insist — ' He was silenced by a long moan. Her head lolled against the seat. Slowly and unhappily the man withdrew, went back to his car and drove away.

Hours later James remembered him. Who on earth had he been? As far as James recalled, the Merc had made a terrible mess of his Jag. A doctor appeared in the corridor and James tensed, but the man walked past. It was at times like these you fervently wished you had never given up smoking, he thought distractedly. When would they tell him what was happening?

A nurse passed in the corridor. It was amazing the activity in this place in the middle of the night. He glanced at his watch, it showed a quarter to six. Nearly morning then. He had been there forever.

The soft footfalls of theatre boots took him by surprise. 'Mr Barton?'

'Yes. Yes.' He couldn't bear to hear and he couldn't bear not to know. The doctor smiled above his green mask, the smile of compassion or congratulation? 'She's fine,' said the doctor. 'Mother and son are doing well. A smashing baby boy.'

James hardly believed him. 'But — the baby was distressed. That's why you operated, you wouldn't even wait for the senior anaesthetist.'

'We had to hurry and we did. Another half hour and he would have been seriously damaged, I've no doubt of that at all. As it is, your wife's going to be rather pulled down for a while, but the baby's just fine. What are you going to call him?'

James didn't know. Perhaps Nicholas? 'I'll have to look at him first,' he said decisively. 'Let's see the little blighter, then.'

The baby was in the special care nursery, but in contrast to two other infants, wired up like robots, he was without impedimenta of any kind.

'You ought to be monitoring him,' said James at once. 'I'll pay for it, I want the best.'

'There's a mattress monitor,' soothed the doctor. 'Tells us if he stops breathing. Like I said, he's a healthy chap. Quite a whopper, in fact.'

To James he looked tiny. Brownish down covered the little head, he had minute slices of mother of pearl for fingernails. 'Nicholas James,' he said softly. 'Two good strong names.'

'Sounds fine to me,' said the doctor. 'Talk it over with your wife.'

James's head came up. Who did this man think he was to

patronise and advise, like some sort of schoolmaster? 'I want to see Diana,' he snapped. 'Now.'

The doctor was nonplussed. What had he done to cause that furious grey-blue stare? 'She'll be very dopy,' he prevaricated.

'Nonetheless I wish to see her. For God's sake, man, I am her husband!'

They passed down corridors full of early morning activity. Cleaners bustled past with mops and buckets, a porter pushed a trolley laden with clean linen. Even this early a florist was delivering baskets of flowers for some new arrival. James determined to demand a feast, a forest of flowers. There was a bubble of elation building within him, he couldn't stop thinking about Nicholas James. How he longed to tell Diana about him, she'd be dying to know.

Yet when he entered her room and saw her lying there, white and still, her tawny eyes mere slits beneath her lids, his heart went cold. 'Diana? Darling?'

Her head turned on the pillow and he moved to take her hand, but it was wired up to a drip. 'So tired,' she whispered. 'It hurts.'

He stroked her head, her forehead was damp and clammy. 'We've got a beautiful boy, darling, he looks wonderful. Nicholas James. Will you like that?'

'Yes.' She licked her lips and at once he reached out for a glass of water. But she didn't want it. He said, 'Better tomorrow, my angel. I'll let you sleep. You know I love you.'

Her eyes gently closed. He stood looking at her until the doctor said, 'As I told you, she had a rough time. Come again this evening, she'll be better then.'

James nodded. It shocked him to see her like this, white and bloodless, her lips bruised from her own teeth. How she must have suffered, and she hadn't wanted the child at all. Yet she had given it to him, so that he could try again, make a fresh start at fatherhood.

He had failed so badly with Richard. Ought he to ring him and tell him what had happened? Richard always found it

262

easy to be cruel over the 'phone. The best thing would be to visit him now, in his flat, it might just be the moment to restore some semblance of a relationship. On this first day of Nicholas James's precious life, James felt an impulse of reconciliation.

Richard's flat was in an expensive suburb of Leeds, close to Roundhay Park. On summer nights he was sometimes treated to the sound of pop concerts in the park, which he liked if it was Genesis or some esoteric jazz band, but loathed if it was teenybopperish. Besides, the younger element invariably parked their heaps in front of his garage door and walked over his Ferrari when he left it outside. Not that they had to stretch their legs much; the car's dark blue shell rose a mere couple of feet from the floor and drove like an elongated skateboard, clinging to the tarmac. But, it was useless in snow and the front end tended to lift if he crested a hill at more than a hundred and ten, so he was deliberating whether to get shot of it. He was engrossed in pleasurable speculation when his father rang the bell.

'One pint, please,' yelled Richard, not bothering to stir from his designer kitchen chair. The bell rang again. Cursing, he put down his toast and shambled over to the door. He was feeling a little the worse for wear, still jetlagged after three days back and struggling with the thought of a day in the office. How nice it would be to be paid that much for not doing the job.

When he saw James his jaw momentarily sagged. They hadn't met in months, they never wrote, 'phoned or communicated in any way. 'Hello,' said James. 'Can I come in?' He pushed his way into the flat, determined to forestall any rejection.

'How did you know where I lived?' asked Richard.

Shrugging, James said, 'I make it my business to know what's important. This is all very flash and expensive. Are you enjoying the job then?'

'Yes — yes.' It wasn't entirely true. Last week he'd been in South America, buying alpaca. One moment he'd been up in the highlands, trading with peasants in flap hats chewing coca to combat altitude sickness, the next in Rio sampling the fleshpots. When he started he'd found nothing more exciting, but nowadays he was bored by the endless waits at airports, unamused by the stomach upsets and tired of the increasing preventative tablets and injections. Sometimes he almost thought it would be easier to catch the disease. But, when he got back home, there was the office and paper and not enough responsibility.

'You must be doing all right,' commented James, eyeing the original modern paintings and exquisitely simple Swedish glass ornaments.

'Bonus. I had a good year last year. And I — well, I do a little on my own account.'

James raised an eyebrow. If the firm found out Richard would be up the creek without a paddle, but the boy knew that, he was old enough. Clearly it was a risk he wanted to run.

'Dad, why are you here in bow tie and dinner jacket? You've obviously been up all night, have you been thrown out or something?'

'Not exactly, no.' James savoured the moment. His bubble of pride swelled and exploded inside him, he felt like singing. 'Diana had our baby last night,' he announced. 'Nicholas James. I thought you should be the first to know.'

Richard swallowed hard. 'I see. Congratulations. Why on earth should you think it has anything to do with me?'

'Well — it's your brother. Isn't that important to you?'

Richard turned away into the bathroom, shedding his towelling robe as he went. 'Actually no, it isn't,' he called, starting to run the shower. 'I don't think there's a lot that happens to you that is of concern to me, as a matter of fact. I thought I'd made that clear.'

James went into the kitchen and made himself some coffee. He took it to the bathroom, leaned against the open door and talked. Richard's body, dimly seen through the opaque shower screen, was covered in reddish blond hair. James wondered if Nicholas would have such hair, it was

264

hard to tell with babies. 'I still see you as heir apparent to Bardsey's,' he yelled, above the noise of the water. 'You can't be entirely free of me. Half your credit rating is because you're my son. They know I won't let you go down.'

'Won't you? I would have thought you capable of anything,' shouted Richard. He turned off the shower and reached out for a towel. James handed one to him, monogrammed he noticed. His son certainly knew how to live the high life. Nonetheless he was lean and fit, not a surplus inch on him.

James thought ruefully of his own body, getting older whether he liked it or not. Was the boy better looking than him? Sometimes when he looked in the mirror he was shocked to see how sparse his carroty hair seemed, how much the colour was dimming.

'Why don't you come into the firm?' he asked jerkily. 'We could do with a younger view. Sometimes I think I'm getting set in my ways.'

'I heard you'd been having a few problems. Loss of market share and so on.'

'All due to Saul,' thought James ruefully. He'd known he was good, but not how good. Nowadays Bardsey's sales team was a headless lizard, unhappy and unco-ordinated. Damn the man.

'We've had the odd hiccup,' said James automatically. Then, remembering that he was trying to tempt his son, he admitted, 'We've expanded a bit too rapidly, as it happens. You need a phenomenal rate of growth when you do that. We've got a comber, a dye-house, several finishing plants, and one or two aren't doing so well. I haven't the time for them, not when Bardsey's own operation is struggling. That's why I need you.'

For a brief second James saw his son waver. Afterwards he knew that with the right word then, he could have swayed him. Like an idiot, he said the wrong thing. 'Just think, one day I might have two sons working for me!'

Richard pulled the towel round him and strode out of the room. 'Thanks, Dad, but I don't see myself as playing nursemaid to the brat. You might not be too old for father-hood, but I'm certainly past playing games with little brother.'

'Don't be so bloody silly, Richard — you know I didn't mean —' but he wasn't sure what he had meant. He might want to give Richard all he desired, but now there was Nicholas to consider. Like it or not, Nicholas had changed things. 'At least come round and have a meal,' he demanded.

Richard sighed. 'OK, OK. Give me a ring sometime, will you?'

Just then the bedroom door opened. In it was framed an exquisitely small, exquisitely pretty Chinese girl. She was stark naked except for her hair, which fell well past her waist. One neat little breast seemed to James to wink at him through the fronds. 'Richard?' she lisped charmingly. 'I did not know we had a visitor.'

Richard glared at the girl, making it plain she was un-wanted. Nonetheless he introduced her. 'Er — Lin Yu, this is my father, James Barton. Dad, this is Lin Yu.'

Still quite naked she extended her little hand. 'So pleased to meet you.'

'Me too,' said James gruffly. 'I was inviting my son to dinner — two weeks, Richard, I should be delighted if you would also come, Lin Yu.'

'How kind.' She inclined her pretty head, causing the breast to pop in and out like a puppet. Fearful for his control, James made for the door.

'I never had it so good,' he said sardonically to Richard. 'Took me years to have any fun.'

'She's a very nice girl,' said Richard weakly.

'I bet she is,' said James.

Outside he wondered where else he could go. It was still so early and the pent-up tension in him cried out for release. He thought of Rowan, and at once turned to his car. There was nothing more natural than that he should tell Diana's children personally.

As he drove he felt an almost uncontrollable urge to head

straight back to the hospital, to stare and stare at the minute scrap of life he had created. The thought of how it would be when at last the boy came home delighted him so much he found himself chuckling out loud.

There was a carrier's wagon blocking the entrance to Judge's, smart dark green with the name 'Partridge' emblazoned on the side. James grimaced. If the satellites were flourishing, what did that tell you about the planet? He parked in the street and walked in, noting that the driver was not Partridge himself, and if that wasn't uncalled for expansion he'd like to know what was. A frisson of insecurity rippled up his spine. Bardsey's was so big, how would it be if the tide was turning towards the little people, leaving people like him washed up on the sand? It was paranoia of course. Bardsey's could crush a firm like Judge's as and when it chose.

There was a light on in the cottage and he went and rapped on the peeling paint of the door. After a moment or two Rowan answered. She stood staring at him, wearing jeans and a sweatshirt, her face white and strained. There was a duster in her hand and her feet were bare.

'You don't do the cleaning, do you?' asked James. 'Why don't you get someone in?'

Rowan stood aside to let him enter. The little house was neat and sweet-smelling, but nothing could do much to redeem a dingy room dominated by one huge sofa. James looked about him distastefully. 'Good God, I shouldn't have thought Saul would put up with this. A great deal too basic for his tastes.'

'We're going to move,' said Rowan shortly. 'Has something happened? Why are you here?'

Hardly able to contain his excitement, James thrust his hands energetically into his pockets. 'Your mother's had the baby. They operated. A boy, Nicholas James.'

He watched Rowan swallow. She said, 'Oh. Oh, I'm glad. How are they both?'

'Diana's tired. But he's such a beautiful baby, quite

267

perfect. You forget how small they are, you know,' he added diffidently.

Suddenly Rowan warmed to him. For once he was letting down his guard and she was in no mood to stab him. 'I'll send flowers,' she promised. 'I'm − I'm really pleased for you, James.'

He nodded. 'Kind of you. Very kind. I went to tell Richard, you know, and it was almost as if he saw the baby as some kind of threat. So ridiculous when you think it's been years since Richard even acknowledged me as his father! I don't understand the boy.'

'You wouldn't,' commented Rowan drily.

She turned away and resumed polishing the table, although nothing could redeem its scratches and the marks of cups. 'It really is about time you let me buy you out,' said James. 'I'm going to insist that Sally and Andy sell their shares to me.'

Rowan's head came up. 'If Mother agrees, and I don't think she will, I'll keep my share regardless. I'll be a thorn in your flesh for ever.'

'And I shall close you down and leave you with nothing.'

'And I shall buy ten Bardsey shares, turn up at the Annual General Meeting and raise hell.'

They glared at each other. James said, 'You don't have to live like this! You could be rich!'

'I'll get rich my own way, thank you.'

Somehow the interview had degenerated into another of their squabbles. He made for the door, feeling beleaguered. He should have left things as they were, he had enough irons in that fire, but Rowan brought out the worst in him every time. 'Where's Saul?' he demanded. 'I think I should at least tell him the good news.'

'He's out' said Rowan flatly. 'Seeing a customer. Don't worry, I'll tell him.'

She stood at the door and watched him stride away, his black coat flapping with that special brand of self-importance James had made his own. The carrier's wagon was reversing out, the yard had been made for horses and was far too small for lorries, even without the Aston Martin parked erratically across one corner. It had been masked from James by the wagon. She felt light-headed from lack of sleep, first because Saul hadn't come home and then because he had. That he had driven home at all was a miracle and she had no idea where he had been. He might remember, but she doubted it.

Her guilt enveloped her, like an itching blanket. She had driven him to it, as surely as if she had poured each drink, because she had been managing and unscrupulous and inconsiderate. If she changed now, at this desperately late stage, surely she could put things right?

James drove into Bradford past the vast, empty Lister's mill that was so much an industrial dinosaur it was judged to be of historical importance.

Everyone had suggestions for it, but there was nothing nowadays that needed floor after floor of space. The mind boggled at the thought of the old days, the people employed in their thousands turning out stuff that was in demand throughout the empire. What had gone wrong? Had the men got fat and careless, had other nations simply got tired of going without? Times had changed, that was all. The men who started these mills were much like himself, they would have understood each other. But in between each driving, thriving generation there were sons who took it for granted and grandsons who frittered it away. He had seen for himself that Richard was hopelessly extravagant – smoked glass coffee tables and silk rugs – he hadn't kept an eye on him, that was the trouble. Nicholas was going to be different. James was never one to overlook a second chance.

He thought of that girl, the Chinese, Lin Yu. She was just – gorgeous. Her lack of modesty made you wonder a little, though. Was she on the game? It was hard to believe something so lovely would have to resort to that, but then everything had its price, he supposed. Did she live there or just stay over? What did she do when Richard was at work? With a sudden grin he swung the car on to the Leeds road. If Richard was still there he'd make up some tale about a date for dinner or something. One thing was certain: if Lin Yu was alone in that flat then he was not going home for breakfast.

She answered the door in a silk robe. 'Hello,' she said politely. 'Richard is at work just now.'

'Oh − oh dear, I didn't think he'd have left. May I come in and scribble him a note?'

'By all means.'

As he brushed past her, he caught the distinctive tang of sex. So, Richard had taken care of her before he left. The thought was exciting. He felt her watching him with those black, hooded eyes. 'Do you have any paper?' he asked, and she wandered about, looking.

'I don't know where he keeps it,' she confessed.

'Perhaps the bedroom,' said James and went through. Black sheets, rumpled into a knot in the centre of the bed, Lin Yu's tiny shoes, and hanging over the back of a chair, a scrap of lace that must be her knickers. He picked them up and held them out. 'You're so tiny,' he said. 'I can hardly believe you fit into these.'

She watched him for a moment. Then she began to open drawers, looking for some paper.

'You don't live here?' said James.

'Oh no. I come to Richard sometimes. I have many friends.'

'Friends?'

She straightened up. Her body was invisible within the robe but her hair, so long and black, intrigued him. He reached out and held the coarse black strands. 'Richard tells me you are very rich,' said Lin Yu. 'Do you want to be my friend?'

James swallowed hard, and let her hair fall. 'That depends. What do you charge your − friends?'

'That is not kind.' She lifted a finger and waggled it at him. 'I am so fond of Richard, I am so happy to spend time with him. He is away so much, I do not see him enough. Richard knows I have other friends who are sometimes kind to me.'

270

'Doesn't he mind? Knowing other men are — '

She smiled at him, revealing tiny white teeth, cat's teeth. 'But they are all so nice, my friends. I am very, very expensive.'

Lifting her skirt she stepped up on to the bed. Neatly and precisely she undid each of the tiny buttons of her robe, letting it fall about her. The long black hair concealed her almost entirely, and with a swing of her head she set it in motion, catching it in her arms and bundling it up to the crown of her head. 'See,' she said. 'Do you want me?'

Her pubic hair was oiled and curled, James put out his hand and touched it. 'I am very small inside,' she confided. 'Feel.'

He knelt on the bed and extended his finger up between her legs. A tiny, wet passageway into which his massive penis would never go. 'Why don't you undress?' she said encouragingly.

James took off his clothes. He expected her to lie down on the bed, but instead she came and stood in front of him. She was so small that his crotch came just above her waist. He pressed obscenely up between her breasts. Suddenly she put her arms around his neck. A monkey wriggle and she was climbing him, arms and legs like wire. Her fingernails dug into his skin and he cried out, and again as she lowered herself on to him. She hung from his neck, her feet off the floor, impaled on him. James started to laugh. 'You're fantastic. Doesn't it hurt you?'

'I like a big man,' she said calmly. 'You're bigger than Richard, you know that?'

He took hold of her buttocks and moved her back and forth, it was incredibly exciting. 'I've got stuff I can give you to make it better,' she murmured, her hair swinging to and fro with every stroke. 'Not here but at my home. I can make a man do it four times, each one better.' She reached out and took up an odd piece of metal from the bedside, shaped like a mushroom. James was thrusting towards climax. As the moment approached, she reached under her own leg and pressed the cold metal against the back of his testicles. He

271

was aware of an explosion of sensation, his legs buckled and he fell forward, the girl beneath him, on to the bed.

His heart was pounding desperately. 'My God, my God,' he murmured. 'You're an expert.'

'Will you buy me a flat, Richard's father?' she asked, tickling his nose with her hair.

'Richard would know,' said James. 'I don't want to upset him that much.'

'He is always away,' purred Lin Yu. 'I tell him I save for the flat. I make sure you come when he is not there, I make it so good for you. Your wife's had a baby, she won't want a man like you bothering her. I like a big strong man, you come to me any time you like.'

James thought for a moment. It was certainly time he stopped picking up girls on the street, it was far too dangerous. And this one was something else again, even now she was licking and caressing his nipple. He rolled off her, mentally reviewing how he could secretly arrange the finance.

'You find the flat,' he instructed. 'I'll come to you there. I don't want you at the house except as Richard's girlfriend.'

'It excites you, that I am Richard's,' she said shrewdly. 'Let me excite you more.'

James lay back on the bed, spreading his legs wide and abandoning himself to utter and delicious pleasure. Her little pink tongue and catlike teeth sucked and nibbled ecstatically and as he lay there, suffused with rising heat, images flashed across his mind: Rowan's face, with her huge green eyes; Saul, Richard, both so much younger, fitter than he; Nicholas James; at the last he thought of Diana, and he pushed the thought away, because he loved Diana and she had no place here, even in his mind.

Chapter Twenty-Four

The penthouse flat was huge, light and airy. It had floor-length windows, beige fitted carpets and an astronomical rent, although they could decide to buy within a year. Rowan both loved and hated it, because it seemed to her the sort of place that sapped resolve, that spent money rather than earned it. Besides, it worried her to be so far from the mill. A mere half-hour certainly, but that was aeons in terms of involvement. On the credit side Sally had her own bedroom and sitting room, as well as a tiny kitchenette, and with two bathrooms there was no need to share.

The very first evening, Rowan and Saul sat with a bottle of wine in their very own sitting room, and listened to the faint murmur of Sally's television through the wall.

'Bliss,' sighed Rowan, sinking down in one of the chairs that had come with the flat. They had some odd items of furniture because of the terms of the tenancy, including a light oak dining room suite, uncomfortable brass bedstead and a cocktail cabinet.

'I'm trying not to say I told you so,' remarked Saul. 'This is how it should have been from the start.'

'I know, I know.' Rowan put out her hand and caught hold of Saul's fingers. She felt like a sailor who has survived a terrible storm, and while she was grateful to be alive she wasn't all that keen on setting sail again. Marriage was so much more difficult than it looked. Because you loved someone it didn't mean you knew what was best for them, or even what they thought was best for them. In marrying Saul she seemed to have learned more about being separate than being together. Holding hands with him then she made a silent resolution to be more understanding, to listen to what he had to say, to adopt his suggestions however half-baked they might seem.

'Why don't we have a baby?' said Saul.

Rowan dropped his hand and sat bolt upright in the chair. 'You don't have to do everything James does,' she squeaked. 'No!'

Saul laughed. 'All right, all right, calm down. It was just a thought. We want to have babies sometime, don't we?'

Rowan considered. It seemed to her she had only just got rid of Sally, she had no desire at all to replace her with someone even less reasoned and a great deal less independent. 'When I'm thirty,' she said. 'I can remember Sally as a baby. They're sick all the time, usually down your front. And I wouldn't be able to work.'

'No.'

Saul got up and wandered across to the stereo. He glanced through the records, finally selecting a violin concerto. It was Rachmaninoff, played with too much technique and not enough emotion.

'I wish Andy would get famous,' mused Rowan. 'Why isn't he? He can do this miles better.'

'Not in public,' said Saul.

Rowan turned to stare at him. 'What do you mean? You haven't heard him.'

'Yes, I have. On my last London trip, he was put on at the last moment in a lunchtime programme at the Festival. He — he was absolutely right, every note was there, every nuance, you couldn't fault him.'

'But?' interposed Rowan.

'But indeed. He lacked magic. He doesn't look interesting enough, he doesn't have anything new to say about the music. I went round afterwards and he was with this appalling wet girlfriend who was telling him all the things he shouldn't be hearing, like how wonderful it was. It's not that he can't do it because we both know he can. But when it comes to the big occasion he just seems to fall short somehow.'

Rowan's first instinct was to jump up and tell Saul that he knew nothing at all about it, that Andy had always been brilliant and would one day be acclaimed. After all, she and Andy had been loyal to each other for years before Saul came on the scene and such loyalties are not easily discarded. In her heart, though, she knew Saul was right. He had put his finger on something she had occasionally suspected, but never dared look at head on. Despite his brilliance and his faultless execution, Andy so often fell just a millimetre short. In practice he could reduce men to tears, but on a stage, in front of thousands, the same notes were powerless. There was no explaining it. Perhaps also there was no curing it.

'Why?' she asked.

Saul shrugged. 'I suspect self-doubt. All his life people have told him he was wonderful, even when he knew he wasn't. If he had some yardstick of criticism that he could trust, he might start to see the difference between really good and just OK. At the moment he doesn't believe his best performances and doesn't recognise his lesser ones.'

Rowan gnawed at her thumb, staring into the sterile coals of the electric fire.

'You didn't mean that about having a baby, did you?' she asked suddenly.

Saul came and sat on the arm of her chair. His hand slipped down the front of her blouse and cupped her little breast. 'You know I did.'

She arched herself against his palm. He had been so warm to her since she agreed to move. 'When I get the mill on its feet.'

He noticed the word 'I' and winced. Moving hadn't changed things. All the time she had been in the flat she had been itching to get back to the mill.

Irritation surged in him, he was damned if he was going to

resign himself to this. Whatever he did Rowan turned like a piece of iron to a magnet, back to the mill. What was it James had said? 'It draws their fangs, brother mine, it draws their fangs.'

Rowan looked up at him, his face was closed and expressionless. 'Saul?'

He glanced down at her. 'Let's go and try out that bed. If we bump up and down on it enough we might get rid of the lumps.'

They went into the bedroom, leaving the record playing. Saul put out the lights although normally he liked them on. She put her arms round his neck. Somehow he seemed apart from her, even now when they touched down the length of breast and belly and thigh. She felt him looking at her face in the dark.

'Do you love me?' he asked.

'You know I do. More than anything.'

'Well then. That's all that matters.'

She heard him fumbling in the drawer for the condom, there was the rustle of paper. She lay back and waited for him, in that half-life of heat and desire that knows no world outside itself. When at last his body came and covered her she felt warm and loved and safe.

The noise of the weaving shed was like the sea, an insidious background roar. It met you when you entered, it rang in your ears after you left, but while you were there, amongst the looms, it went unnoticed. Rowan never noticed it. For her it was built into the fabric of her life, a reassuring and comforting cacophony.

Today they were warping up a new design, a complex mixture of blue and silver and charcoal. The threads on the huge wooden balloon appeared unrelated; even after years of practice you could not look at them and know the appearance of the finished fabric. You had to wait, endlessly, while the ballooned fibres were wound on to a beam, taken bodily to the weaving shed and tied, one at a time, to the shed of a loom. Only then, with the loom itself combining warp and weft, could you see the cloth.

Rowan was impatient. Her feet hurt and it all seemed to be taking too long. What did this piece matter? Suppose after all this trouble it didn't sell? The most pressing problem of the day was the vague stain that had unaccountably appeared on the bulk order of red cloth they had ready for a manufacturer of ladies' jackets. She suspected the finishing, but feared it could be some contaminant from the wool itself. They would have to wash the cloth again and hope for the best, which in any event would be shrinkage and some loss of quality. Was it all worth the bother?

She sank her hands in her pockets and wandered out into the loading bay. Joe Partridge was there, counting lots. 'Hello, Ro. You look a bit peaked.'

'I don't feel too good actually. Perhaps I've got a bug.'

'Been looking a bit rough for a day or two, I think. Get yourself to the doctor, lass, don't hang about.'

To change the subject she put out a finger and tapped a heavy gold bracelet on his wrist. Each square link appeared to have been hacked out wholesale from some ingot. 'We're paying you too much.'

'This? Bit of image. Going up in the world, we are, Ro.'

She supposed it was true. Now they were in the penthouse they had friends in for drinks and glamorous dinner parties at which the cordon bleu daughter of a lord cooked spectactularly. They had chicken stuffed with duck and then with quail, and raspberries frozen into exquisite mounds of puree. The food looked fantastic and everyone was very impressed, but for her part Rowan always felt slightly sick.

At the weekend she had visited Diana and the baby at Aspley Manor, in the big, sunshiny nursery. Diana had decorated it in lemon yellow and white, she lay prettily on a couch while the baby slept in his cradle. Flowers were banked on every table and through the window there was a view of lawns and trees and distant hills. The whole scene, from Diana with her baby to the heart-breaking beauty of the moors, struck a chord in Rowan's soul. There was more to life than the mill. She felt like a mole coming up into daylight after a lifetime of toil, seeing the sun, but too weary to enjoy it. She didn't know what was wrong with her.

They were calling her from the weaving shed. She turned to go. 'You know, I think I will go and see the doctor. I've hardly the energy to care about anything at the moment.'

Joe looked slightly pained, somehow managing to imply that he would have taken better care of her than that Flash Harry she'd taken it into her head to marry. All he said was, 'Then you get yourself off, lass.'

But the appointment never got made. That evening she was content to let Saul drive her home, although they usually took two cars, for convenience sake. She sat wearily next to him and listened to Stevie Wonder on cassette. The energy of the man drained what little spark she had left.

'Not too good, are you?' said Saul sympathetically.

She shook her head and he chuckled. 'Tell you what, why don't we do the Paris shows next week? I can wangle tickets for most of them. Luxury hotel, wonderful food and wild fashions.'

'I don't seem to like food very much at the moment,' said Rowan. 'But I would like to go — I think.'

It was the thought of the packing that depressed her. It was as much as she could do to choose clothes for ordinary days and take them out of the wardrobe. In the back of her mind she thought how sad it was that Saul didn't realise how ill she was. Cancer seemed the most probable cause of her symptoms, and she was probably going to die. Fortunately she was too tired to feel very concerned.

Eventually Sally did the packing. At the last moment Rowan came to life and extracted a meaningless promise from her sister not to have boys in the flat, or girls that smoked, or anyone else unpleasant. Naturally enough no sooner were Rowan and Saul safely across the Channel than Sally threw a party at which two boys smoked pot, one snorted heroin and someone dropped cassis on the beige carpet. Sally spent the rest of the week trying to remove the stain and make the place look less like the scene of a singularly bloody murder.

Rowan had never been to Paris, and Saul had been there many times. He knew his way round the Metro, could summon a taxi out of nowhere, was used to the horrors of Parisian traffic. All Rowan had to do was dress each morning in something exotic and hang on to his arm while he swept her from one show to another, from Karl Lagerfeld classicism to Issey Miyake oddness. They were ushered in almost without comment while other far more important souls had their tickets queried. Everyone simply believed that Rowan was a catwalk model, rushing from one show to the next with a model's usual lack of punctuality.

She looked entirely the part. Mr. Suzman was dressing her in silk these days, or at least what passed for silk. Dresses with high necks and no shape but that imprinted by Rowan's thin frame; camisole tops so brief that it took nerve to wear them. She would stride past in tight black trousers and high heels, her little breasts bouncing behind their thin covering of green or ochre or puce and a jacket loosely hanging on the points of her shoulders. Doormen held doors for her, photographers took pictures, and afterwards shambled Saul, trying to look like her minder.

'We're going to get rumbled soon,' muttered Rowan, trying to efface herself on yet another little gilt chair in another overheated salon. 'Can they throw you out retrospectively?'

'We haven't deceived anyone,' said Saul. 'They chose to deceive themselves. Besides, if things get really tough at Judge's, I'll set you up out here. You're obviously the type.'

'Thin as a rake and tall as a Zulu,' muttered Rowan as the

279

first girl, who looked like a Zulu, set her elongated legs on to the catwalk.

They were there to look at style, and yet to ignore it completely. It was the feel of the thing that counted, whether it was drape or cling or swirl, or perhaps, and most unusually, cloth cut to stand off the body in planklike regimentation. What was shown here would be watered down and copied all over the world, and unless fabrics like these were in Judge's ranges there was no hope of tempting designers into the fold. If you waited for the magazines you waited too long; you became a follower in the train of the more ambitious.

The heat of the room was becoming intense. There was a constant rustle of fanned programmes and even the models' tight-skinned faces were beaded with sweat. Saul watched two girls stride aggressively in time to the heavy funk music, the woman in front applauded and flapped her programme at one and the same time. The smell of her perfume was overpowering in the heat. With no more than a gentle sigh, Rowan slid off her chair and fainted.

The French understand drama. Rowan was extracted and removed with white-coated efficiency, while all around people moved their chairs, kept one eye on the show and muttered imprecations. A woman of icy elegance commented in Spanish, 'The girl's obviously anorexic and probably on drugs,' to which Saul replied, also in Spanish, 'I'll thank you to refrain from insulting my wife!'

'*Anglais, n'est-ce pas?*' queried a matron of her daughter.

'*Japonais,*' interrupted Saul meanly, and vaulted over the last three chairs to get to the stretcher.

It took all his persuasion to make them let her go. They wanted to send her to hospital and immure her at enormous cost in a private room.

'She's perfectly all right,' insisted Saul. 'It was the heat. A doctor will come to our hotel.' He bundled the conscious, but shivering, Rowan into a taxi. She sagged against him. 'OK?' he asked.

'No. I think I'm dying. I think I've got cancer.'

'Oh. Oh, is that it?'

She began to cry. 'I'm sorry, Saul. I didn't mean to die!'

He put his arms round her and held her tight. 'You aren't going to die, sweetheart. You'll be fine soon. We'll call the doctor and get him to tell us what's wrong. Won't we?'

She nodded up at him. He felt a surge of love for his difficult, spiky girl. He would want for nothing if she would always stare at him with just that helpless trust.

'You knew, didn't you? You've known for weeks!' She sat up in the hotel bed, a curlicued affair covered in white and gold leaf. Her cheeks were bright red with rage.

'Er — let's say I suspected. I thought you must too, until this afternoon. Classic symptoms, lovey.'

'I suppose you'd know! How many illegitimate babies have you fathered, may I ask?'

'None, actually.' He lowered himself cautiously on to the end of the bed, and she kicked at him. 'Why are you so upset? It's an accident, that's all. You wanted a baby in the end, why not now?'

She put her hands in her hair and tugged it. If she didn't feel so ill she'd take revenge on him, but as it was it took all her strength to remain angry. 'I wanted to look after my mill,' she wailed. 'And it'll be all nappies and sick and rusks and no sleep! I can't bear it! I can't, I can't, I can't!'

Saul gently pulled her hands out of her hair and held them. He felt as he sometimes did when he played good poker and won, quietly triumphant. At the same time he felt sorry for poor, straightforward Rowan whom he had beguiled so easily. 'Do you really not want it? A soft pink baby, all your own. Do you really not?'

'Yes. No! Oh Saul, I don't know what I want.' She felt trapped. Her body, and fate, had trapped her. Rowan Judge, businesswoman and active member of the human race, was being shackled by her femininity. Warm, unbreakable bonds of love and need that she longed for, even while hating them. Wearily she leaned against her husband. The mistake had been in loving him, and in loving him still.

They went home the next day. The purple stain dominated the sitting room carpet like an egg-laying toad.

'What will the landlord say?' remarked Rowan. 'We'll have to buy the blessed place.'

'We can't bring a baby up here,' said Saul. 'You need a garden and a swing.'

Sally looked at them suspiciously. 'What baby?'

'One that's better behaved than you are,' snapped Rowan waspishly. 'You had a party, didn't you?'

'No,' lied Sally, and Rowan didn't have the strength to argue.

Sally sat down and began to cry, though whether because of the baby or the carpet no one knew. Saul patted her awkwardly on the shoulder, although he always avoided touching her. There was something vaguely incestuous even about shaking hands with Sally, because he couldn't deny the attraction of her small-boned prettiness. She had the habit, when they were alone together, of sitting close to him, her shoulders thrown back to emphasise her breasts. Now though she seemed entirely childlike, caught out in a prank.

'Rowan's not in the least maternal. She'll be horrid to it,' said Sally.

'Mothers always love their children,' said Saul with confidence. He was thrilled with himself, with Rowan, with the entire world. 'It's in the hormones, you can't avoid it.'

Rowan didn't believe in hormones. She fought hard against them, only to find that they had her pinned against the ropes. The canteen made bacon sandwiches for coffee break in the morning, great greasy white baps crammed full of best back, and the smell was enough to make her throw up in the potted palm. Everyone told her she'd be better soon, but in the meantime they got used to seeing her crouched on the stone stairs, white-faced and miserable, fighting to keep her breakfast down. And after lunch she nodded off at her desk, like some eighty year old.

Saul said, 'You can't go on like this. Take some time off, stay in bed. You look like a ghost.'

'A ghost with a beer gut,' said Rowan distastefully, staring down at her rapidly distending belly. It seemed to be growing awfully quickly. She resented it, fiercely; sometimes she lay in bed and wished it away, and afterwards went shopping and bought it bootees to make up. They bought a cot and baby bath, and Diana promised to give them a pram. Even before the baby arrived it was clear that big as the penthouse was, the small bedroom was nowhere near big enough for a nursery. Rowan found herself looking resentfully at Sally, wishing her anywhere but here. She could not be a parent to her sister, not when true parenthood beckoned so insistently.

Gradually, peacefully, her fingers slackened on the reins of the mill. Saul took over this and then that, leaving her free to stay in bed or go to the doctor or visit her mother.

Diana said, 'It suits you. You've stopped wearing those terrible boyish clothes.'

'Saul likes those,' said Rowan. 'Now I've got bulges everywhere.' She looked ruefully down at her odd exterior, clad in a print cotton dress with a Peter Pan collar.

'Actually, in that you look far too young,' said Diana.

Rowan wished she could have returned the compliment. Diana looked lined and ill, lying on the sofa but still looking as if she should have been in bed. The baby was in a Moses basket, swathed in a forest of white lace. Rowan stared in, for once fascinated.

'How do you know he's not dead?' she asked.

Diana levered herself up on her elbow. 'He's fine, darling, look at his lovely colour. And look, he's sucking in his sleep.'

'So he is.' Rowan gazed at the tiny lips, saw the little, wanting movements of the hands and wondered what it would be like to feed such as this, to offer her own body as sustenance. Once it had seemed unthinkable, now it had an almost lascivious charm.

'Does James still like him?' she asked. James's wild enthusiasms often waned, in her experience.

'He dotes,' said Diana. 'In fact, we're a couple of idiots. We can spend an entire evening staring at him telling each other how wonderful he is, and planning his education. We can't decide if he should be Prime Minister or merely revolutionise medical science. By the way, I've heard from Andy.'

Diana got up heavily and fetched Andy's latest letter. 'He's really unhappy at the moment. Even when he won the competition he got bad reviews. They're talking about theatricality in his playing, not enough basic worth. Technically he's brilliant, of course, but he doesn't have the right style.'

Rowan remembered Saul's assessment and grunted. 'Perhaps he needs a bit more − passion!'

'They're always saying his playing sounds Russian, and I hope they mean it as a compliment! He's the least passionate of all of you. Or perhaps he isn't. Boys don't show it as much, we don't encourage it, and then their wives complain. Do you think Andy has a girlfriend?'

Rowan nodded. 'Definitely. The appalling cellist, with the buck teeth and the long frizzy hair. He was very vague when he was up last, I think they're living together.'

'Shock, horror,' said Diana with irony. She put her hands to the sides of her head as if trying to smooth away a headache. Rowan was suddenly assailed by her beauty. That mane of tawny hair against the white bony face, the glow of her eyes, that were somehow enhanced by the shadows that surrounded them. So little of it had been passed on to either of her daughters; they inherited this and that, neither the incomparable whole. Even Sally, with her blonde prettiness, lacked her mother's structure.

And in the midst of it, Rowan had a premonition of death. She saw her mother's lovely face rotted to a skull, she saw Sally gone to dust in the ground. The ghosts of all things horrible reached out with dead fingers, plucking at her, calling to her. Air was denied, her lungs were flat and empty, not even enough for a moan. Before her mother's horrified gaze, she fainted.

Saul came to fetch her. They had called the doctor who put it down to raised blood pressure. Bed rest for at least a fortnight, no excitement, no work, nothing. In front of the others Saul was kind, but matter-of-fact. Alone in the car together, he suddenly pulled over to the side of the road and buried his head in his hands. 'Oh God! I thought something terrible had happened. I thought it was just a faint, but you were so white!'

'I'm sorry. I don't know what happened, I had a sort of dream — I thought — I don't know what I thought.'

He put his arms round her as if to ward off anything and everything. 'There's not enough of you, that's the trouble, you try and do too much on no flesh. You've got to eat more. Just stay in bed and grow that baby.'

'Yes. Yes, I will.' The dream still haunted her, she felt cold and lonely. She snuggled into her husband and he put his hand over the protrusion of her stomach. 'I love you, Rowan,' he muttered. 'I know recently you've thought I — I haven't said it. I was to blame, I rushed you, I didn't try to understand. I never stopped loving you.'

Softly, tenderly, she nestled her face into the hollow of his shoulder. It was warm and human and utterly familiar.

Almost despite himself Saul was developing an affection for Judge's. At first it had seemed entirely Rowan's creature, without frills or extravagances, pared down as puritanically as only Rowan knew how. But then you got to know people,

285

you found out how it all came about, and things looked different. When a firm has teetered on the brink of disaster, nobody fails to take life seriously.

Now that Rowan was tucked up in bed Saul could allow a little relaxation to creep in. Joyless money-grubbing wasn't in him. If people couldn't have fun while they toiled, then where was the point? Besides, a little community spirit never went amiss. He started letting people buy lengths of cloth, heavily discounted. Then he began a snooker club, setting aside one of the large wasted rooms upstairs for use at lunchtime. It became his habit to wander round the mill, chatting to people, sometimes about work but more often about their families. One thing became very clear: most of the women working at Judge's, and there were quite a few, had children at home. Sometimes Grandma helped out; more often it was a hit and miss affair of childminders for the under fives, and for older children, a hazardous and often unsupervised few hours from leaving school to Mum getting home, sometimes not until six.

He thought about it in bed one night, lying awake while Rowan peacefully slept beside him. When finally he drifted off to sleep he found himself suddenly back in his own childhood, alone in the house while his mother cooked and cleaned for the old man. He made them live in their own house, he wouldn't have them with him. Saul was cold. They had a coal fire and his mother didn't like to leave him in the house with a fire, so he sat in his short trousers with his knees to his chin, waiting for her to come home. After a bit he got bored, and he was jolly cold. He had seen his mother light the fire lots of times, he knew exactly how. Yet somehow it wasn't easy when you did it yourself, the paper wouldn't crumple as it should. One sheet hung out of the fireplace and when he lit it, burning his fingers on the matches, it flared up, bright as the sun. In his dream he stood watching it, just as he had that day, watching the paper fall from the fire on to the rug. The same sense of fear, the same immobility, unable

286

even to back away towards the door.

Saul sat up with a yell. Rowan, sleepily waking, said: 'Saul? What is it? Are you all right?'

He passed a hand across his face and found it wet with sweat. 'It's OK,' he said breathlessly. 'I had a dream.'

Rowan turned towards him and stroked his arm. 'What was it? You gave such a yell.'

'Well, I would! When I was six, I set the house on fire. I dreamed about that.'

'Good God!' Rowan sat right up now. 'How on earth did you do it? Were you hurt?'

'No, actually, I wasn't. My mother came back and dragged me out of the blazing room. I was just standing there, watching it. I'd been trying to light the fire. It was winter. I was cold.'

'You could have been killed! Oh, you poor darling, how could your mother let you?'

'It wasn't her fault. She was working for the old man and he didn't like me in the house at that time of day. He liked to bring people back for a drink and a kid my age didn't fit in. So she left me on my own till she got in. And the fire brigade came and put it out, and the insurance paid up, and after my mother had gone on at him for a couple of months the old man allowed me to go there after school. I just had to stay in the kitchen all the time, that's all.'

'Bloody man! James takes after him, exactly.'

As the dream lost its grip Saul leaned back against the pillows. 'He fights against being like him quite a bit, actually. The old man was a sod and a stupid one. But that sort of callousness does rub off, you know. Me first, the rest nowhere. He learned it from the old man.'

Rowan swallowed. 'Do you think I'm like that? Selfish?'

'You?' He laughed. 'You'd walk a hundred miles in bare feet to do something for someone you loved. Your mother, Sally, me, we only have to hint we need you and you're there. But — you're scared, Rowan. You're frightened of being poor, and lonely. Sometimes you think nobody can love you, and that — doesn't make you very lovable.'

She buried her face against him. 'I know, I know. Perhaps it's because mother always loved Andy best.'

'She might love him best, but that doesn't mean she doesn't love you at all. I think it's Sally gets the thin end of the wedge there, actually. If Diana could only be the least bit consistent ... one minute it's off on a fantastic holiday, look how Mummy loves you, the next it's fend for yourself, don't call me.'

'That's her all over. She gets very involved; she's either doing something or she's not. On and off like a light, that's Mother. She can be absolutely singleminded. And Sally — I try to help her, Saul, truly I do.'

He let out his breath, letting go of the dream at the same time. After a bit he said, 'I think she's coming right. Not so many boys hanging round, and she comes home more often, too. When does she start this beauty course?'

'End of the month. I wish we could be on our own though, Saul, especially when the baby comes.'

He put his arms round her. 'Perhaps she'll move in at the college. We must get some reward for being good, we don't need riches in heaven but we do need space down here.' Gently, soothingly, their legs entwined. It was comforting, and he had a vague wish for comfort, because of the dream. It haunted him.

The plan which formed in his head that night was not one he imparted to Rowan. He knew instinctively that she would balk at the cost. But, they had a huge mill, largely unused, and they were demanding quality work at less than the best rates of pay. Fringe benefits were bound to be cost-effective. So he employed two nursery nurses to run a day-long crêche and to supervise school-age children after hours. He signed a cheque for equipment, sent in decorators to transform one of the upstairs galleries and they were off.

In the first week they had ten children all day and forty after school. The babies were paid for, but the nominal charge for the older children barely covered the milk and biscuits they devoured. They were like a starving army falling on a town, intent on pillage, but Saul knew if he charged too much they would simply have to take their chance once again on the streets. The women who worked in the mill simply couldn't afford more.

Looking at the wild and exuberant children he felt an immense sympathy for their mothers. He began to see them not as workers but as needy and deserving cases; he found it harder and harder to insist on time-keeping, quality control and speed. They had to go home and cook and clean, not to mention coping with some member of the mob upstairs! He had always known at Bardsey's that they paid little or no attention to the welfare of the staff, and now at Judge's he had the chance to implement a new and worthwhile system. Naturally people would feel grateful, and gratitude would produce results. He left it at that.

His main interest, as always, was sales. Everything about it intrigued him, from the initial scent of his quarry, through the stalking, the initial flirtation or, if the mood was right, the direct attack, all the way to the final handshake with promises of devotion from all sides. Even when a potential customer was absolutely against everything right from the word go, he would talk and weave a little, trying to sense what it was that had so alienated them from salesmen. Were they too pushy? Saul was so discreet he might have been there to clean the carpet. Did they not understand the problems and difficulties of business today? He was as sympathetic and encouraging as a marriage guidance counsellor. They all fell for him, from nervous girls setting out on a career buying for chainstores, to hard-nosed men who had been in it for more years than he had had hot dinners.

But even Saul had the occasional sticker. Marcus Arnaud,

designer of fabulously chic clothes featured in all the glossies, wouldn't look at English cloth. He bought only from Italy, where they would do what you wanted, where the colours were superb, the runs as short or as long as you liked. What could a designer like him do with bolts of cloth when he only ever made perhaps two or three of something? Yet Saul wanted him, desperately; he wanted photographs of Marcus Arnaud clothes, made up in Judge's cloth, each with the distinctive MA logo, all over his office. What a seller that would be.

'Look, we did this for Marcus Arnaud, exclusive of course. We were very influenced by the Paris shows, were you able to make it this year? Marcus loves this heavy weave. But we do have this very similar and remarkably well-priced fabric you might care to look at? Absolutely right for the moment.'

Picking cherries would be arduous in comparison.

Saul went on a raid. Best suit, handmade shirt, gold cufflinks. 'Where on earth are you going?' demanded Rowan, sitting prettily up in bed and watching him dress. The doctor had extended her bed-rest to at least another week, so she had no choice but to stay in bed reading Mothercare catalogues and baby books.

'London for the day,' said Saul. 'Don't worry, I've left everything shipshape in the mill. They're finishing that blue and grey stuff you saw set up. I like it, I'm taking a sample. You've got taste, my love.' He dropped a kiss on her head.

'You only married me for my colour sense,' grumbled Rowan. 'If I hadn't been togged up in purple tunics, you'd have gone off with someone else.'

Saul grinned. Rowan had it in her to be a brilliant designer of more than just cloth. When she let herself go she was capable of real imagination. But, so often in anything except textiles, her fears kept her creeping round the corners of the room instead of striding out into its centre.

'If it looks like I'm going to be late, I'll ring you,' he said, as he was picking up his sample case.

'You're not taking much,' said Rowan doubtfully.

'Only what counts. Have a good day, love, and don't do anything. Is the doctor coming?'

She nodded. 'He said if my blood pressure hadn't gone down, I had to go into hospital.'

'He only said it to keep you in bed, silly. See you soon.'

He thought about Rowan as he drove to the station. The baby had been a godsend, exactly what they both needed. As James had said, if you wanted femininity then pregnancy was your goal. Rowan was even learning to knit! Not that he wanted her out of the firm forever; today, for instance, he could have done with someone who knew what they were doing minding the shop. Yesterday the washer had broken. A hugely tall machine in which lengths of cloth thrashed about on rollers, it served the dual purpose of cleaning the material after manufacture and fluffing up the fibres to thicken it. It had taken three hours to mend, and without anyone keeping an eye on them they had left the cloth dripping inside it. Wool did not improve with a good long soak. It was as felted as a doormat, simply because no one was thinking. He dared not tell Rowan, it would have dealt the final blow to her blood pressure. The order would go out late, there was no avoiding it.

He travelled first-class on the train, although Rowan would always travel second. It put him in the right frame of mind. He was talking to a man who thought nothing of charging three thousand pounds for a dress, so a few quid on a railway ticket and three whiskies was hardly going to count. Not that he wanted much for the cloth; it was enough for Arnaud to use Judge's own. At King's Cross, Saul stopped to buy a buttonhole, choosing instead of a rather dull carnation in red or white, a small yellow and crimson rose. Then, fortified, confident and determined, he took a taxi to Marcus Arnaud.

'Mr. Arnaud, please. Saul Barton. We're meeting for

lunch.' It was an appointment he had made with the secretary, managing to imply that they met not infrequently and that Marcus had suggested a date round about now.

'Yes — Mr. Barton — do you have a card?' The receptionist was nervous because he was good-looking and very well-dressed, not the sort of man you asked for his credentials. Clearly Arnaud had boggled at his lunch appointment and would not take kindly to being tricked by a salesman.

Saul flicked a card cursorily at the desk. Printed for just such an eventuality it was thick, very white and read in gold letters "Saul Barton — fabric" with a 'phone number. It had got him into any number of places, simply because they did not know who, where from or what for.

'We are acquainted,' said Saul, permitting a shade of irritation to colour his voice. The receptionist scuttled away nervously.

Within two minutes he was going upstairs. Marcus Arnaud was in his studio, a large light room littered with dummies and cloth and drawings. A small, thin man known only to Saul from photographs, he half-hid behind his desk. Saul thrust out a hand. 'Marcus! Good to see you after all this time. How are you? When was it? Paris?'

Arnaud waved a vague hand. 'Might well have been. I travel so much — '

'Don't we all,' agreed Saul. He was mentally trying to gauge the man's sexual standing. Was he gay or merely rather effete? Single, at his age, probably meant gay but you couldn't always be sure. 'Been to Italy recently?' he asked apparently inconsequentially. 'They're losing it, you know. Bloody government as always! I remember you telling me you'd had a bit of a problem with duty before, hadn't you?' That was a safe enough bet, everybody had that problem. 'And now of course they're talking about this tax. The government'll be out in five minutes, but the tax could be on for five years!'

'Er — which tax would that be?' Arnaud was standing transfixed while Saul unpacked his samples as casually as a man looking for his sandwiches.

'The worst. Something to do with the massive salaries the designers have been getting; they're trying to get a rake off. Half the big names are moving on, we'll see the results in a year or two no doubt. You'll have noticed it was all a bit dull at the last show.'

That year the Italians were showing all puce and dark green. 'One can always tell,' said Arnaud. 'Myself, I know what it's like to be unappreciated!' He made an extravagant bow, and they laughed together.

'I've booked a table for one o'clock,' said Saul, glancing at his watch. 'Thought I'd let you see what's new first. This is a little mill, got a fantastic girl in charge there, very innovative. I mean, when did you last see something like this from Yorkshire?' Apparently haphazard, he tossed the blue that Rowan had set up in an aesthetic heap on top of a navy flannel laid out on a table. Turning immediately away, he pulled out a large piece of glowing burgundy. When selling like this you never showed tiny squares of cloth, you gave them yards to look at. He half took out some green and black stripe, very much to Arnaud's taste if his wallpaper was anything to go by, and then put it away. 'No, you won't want the green, it's too different.'

'May I see?' Arnaud was trying to get into the case. Amazing how often that trick worked.

Reluctantly, Saul took out the green. 'As I said she's original. I'm not a designer myself, I don't have the instinct. Perhaps she's done too much with that.'

'On the contrary! It's superb! How much for this? Exclusive.'

Saul looked perturbed. 'I didn't expect to sell that one — I warn you, it's pricey.'

'Please! How much?'

In the end, after much coaxing, Saul quoted a highish

price. He was making it up, because by now Arnaud would have paid anything. He took an order for the green, the blue, and for the burgundy. Arnaud summoned a model to drape it round herself. The girl eyed Saul beneath long black lashes, walking backwards and forwards with her hips thrust out and her bottom undulating. Well, he thought, that was a come-on if ever he saw one. Before Rowan he wouldn't have hesitated.

When she had gone, Arnaud laughed. 'She likes you. Shall I give you her number?'

'Er – no thanks.' Saul grinned deprecatingly.

They lunched at a very expensive restaurant. Saul ate heartily, Arnaud picked at the food. He seemed preoccupied about something, every now and then falling silent and looking down at his plate. Suddenly, with the coffee, Saul felt the toe of a shoe gently against his shin. His blood went cold. Oh God, why on earth had he shied away from saying he was married? Only because he thought the guy was queer and he hadn't wanted to put him off – but then he hadn't wanted to turn him on, either!

In his mind's eye he saw the order crumbling and Arnaud running, screaming and outraged, away. He looked Arnaud full in his soft, rather anxious eyes.

'Marcus – I won't pretend I don't like you a lot. We only met briefly before, I didn't think you'd remember. But – you were someone I felt I had to see. There was an attraction, I won't deny it.'

Arnaud let out his breath in a long sigh. 'I didn't know, I didn't remember. God, I can be so stupid sometimes.'

'I had a few appointments in London and I thought I'd make you one of them. I knew you'd be someone I could talk to. I've got a few problems. A relationship, you know how it is. This guy – he wants more than I've got to give somehow. It's my fault, I'm the one that can't commit myself. And, you know, I really care about him.'

'So – you don't want to go out on a limb with me.' The

foot withdrew. Arnaud's eyes, naturally rather sad, Saul noticed, fell away.

'It isn't that!' Saul caught his hand, and then, as if they might have been seen, dropped it again. He allowed himself to appear confused and embarrassed.

'God, you're in a mess,' said Arnaud. 'Come back and have a drink. We'll talk a little, you need it.'

Back at the studio, they had a couple of brandies. 'Actually I'm in a steady relationship,' confided Arnaud. 'But I wouldn't say it was exclusive, and that goes for both of us. Your guy, he wants it that way, does he?'

'Oh yes. And if I do meet someone else and things get out of hand, well, I hate myself for it. Nine times out of ten I tell him and then the world falls apart. But if I don't tell him it's worse and he suspects anyway. I'm a lousy liar.'

'You're just too damned honest.' Arnaud got up, clearly wanting to close the proceedings. 'Look, you've got the order, and you know where I am. Any time you want to come and talk you're welcome. I mean, I've been there, you know?'

'Yeah. Thanks.'

They shook hands. Saul picked up his sample case and made it out into the street. His head was spinning and if he relaxed for a second he thought his stomach muscles would go into spasm. God, but that had been close! He'd nearly lost the order.

Going back on the train he allowed himself the luxury of a small chuckle, feeling mean about it. Arnaud was a nice guy. As he leaned back in his seat, worn out by the mental demands of the day, he felt a slight dimming of his spirits. Back to the mill and its problems: washers, looms, the noisy kids that enraged the men while delighting the women. It was the continual dashing from one task to the next that he hated, ten balls in the air all at once. Then he thought of Rowan. He thought of how he would tell her about the day, how much she would laugh and enjoy it. Suddenly he couldn't wait to get back.

Chapter Twenty-Five

By the time Saul reached home, Rowan had been in hospital for some hours. She remained there for weeks, emerging every now and then for a few days at home and being bundled back in as soon as her blood pressure rose, which it did almost the moment she stood up. She was bewildered, tearful and anxious. Saul soon discovered that the best thing he could do was to say nothing at all about Judge's beyond a soothing and often repeated, 'Nothing to worry about. Everything's fine.'

Lots of people visited her, since the maternity wing was attached to the main hospital and it seemed that most people at some time or another had a visit to make there. Everyone loved the maternity wing, peering in at the new babies. Only Rowan hated it. She was beginning to believe that she would never have a baby of her own, that it would die and she would be left forever with a paralysing grief.

To begin with she was in the GP wing merely for bedrest, and no one took much notice of her. As time went on and she did not improve, the size of the baby started to give cause for concern. To Rowan they seemed ridiculously anxious, because she had an enormous belly, like a mountain distending her thin body, but nonetheless they transferred her to the ward for difficult cases. The consultant came round every day and listened to her bump, feeling her increasingly podgy ankles and wrists.

'Who would have thought you'd be a problem, at your age?' he said to her. 'Not even twenty-one!'

She felt ashamed of herself for lack of reproductive skill. 'Is there going to be a problem?' she asked humbly.

He lifted his eyebrows at her impudence. 'I really couldn't say, Mother. We may induce you a little early. I shall let you know if it's advisable.'

'Thanks very much,' said Rowan morosely. This wasn't her baby any more, it was barely even her body; they were toys for the professionals to play with.

She complained to Saul. 'Honestly, the man's a clam, he won't say a thing. I don't like him one bit.'

'Does he know what he's doing?' asked Saul.

'Hard to say. I suppose we'll know afterwards. It's all rather frightening really.'

He held her hand tight. Every day, after his visit, he sat in the car and thought about the swollen, ill girl in the bed. The weight of his responsibility crushed him.

Most nights he went home to find Sally waiting up for him, with a casserole or something in the oven. He was grateful, but these days he was increasingly uncomfortable in her company. There was something about the way she behaved towards him that pushed the relationship beyond the place he intended it to be, although there was no convenient niche for brothers and sisters-in-law. Two sexual beings in a proximity closer than would have been acceptable in any other situation, and yet neither was supposed to acknowledge it.

'Look,' said Saul at last, 'you don't have to wait up for me. And you don't have to cook either, I can manage for myself.'

Sally flushed. 'You'd just have some bread or something, you wouldn't eat properly. I like to look after you. I like waiting for you to come in.'

'All the same, I'd rather you didn't.'

She turned quickly away, and he knew she was crying. All his soft-hearted sympathy reproached him. She was a vulnerable little girl.

'Please don't get upset,' he said awkwardly. 'If you really want to stay up, then I suppose it's all right. Sally, please stop crying.'

'Thank you. Thank you!' Her blue eyes, washed with tears, seemed infinitely appealing. Of the two sisters, Sally was by far the more sensual of the two, he thought. Mature breasts thrust out against her jumper, in contrast to her bitten nails. He knew, without a doubt, that they should not be here together like this. But what could he do? Sally had no one's exclusive love and the least he could do was offer her affection. Yet here was a luscious young girl alone in the house with him, and his wife locked up in hospital.

The next night Sally cooked *coq au vin*. She had dressed in a jumper with a low scooped neck, showing two inches of cleavage, and her hair was caught up on either side of her head in diamante clips.

'Are you going somewhere?' asked Saul doubtfully.

She laughed. 'Not at this time of night. I just thought it was about time you saw something more appealing than hospital nighties.'

'I find what's in that hospital nightie very appealing.'

Hoping he had quelled her, he sat down and began to eat the meal.

'Is it all right?' asked Sally, sitting opposite him and leaning forward. 'It's a new recipe and it took me ages.'

'It's all right.' All Saul's natural politeness struggled against such brusque praise. He tried not to look at Sally. In the gentle light of a table lamp she appeared luminous, her body infinitely soft, her hair a cloud around her head. He was too tired for all this. What he needed was not a precociously sexual teenager but his own solitary bed.

'Do you like me, Saul?' asked Sally.

He pushed his plate away and considered. 'Sometimes. Tonight, not a lot.'

Her cheeks flamed. 'How can you say that? I cooked you a lovely meal, I waited hours for you! Don't you even think I look pretty? I tried so hard, Saul.'

There was no tempering of the wind. He said, 'You're trying as hard as you know how. As far as I can work out you

299

are doing your devilish best to seduce me, though why that should please you when your sister's ill and unhappy in hospital is an absolute mystery.'

Sally giggled naughtily. 'But she wouldn't know, would she? We'd have such fun. I'm quite experienced, you know, I'd make it good for you.'

'I have never been interested in the leavings of mangy tomcats, I'm afraid.'

There was a terrible silence. Sally stood up very slowly. 'You don't know what it's like,' she said. 'Nobody cares about you unless they're getting something, and with men it's the same thing every time. And you don't really love Rowan. You married her to get Judge's, and now you've got rid of her to hospital you're as pleased as a dog with two tails. The pathetic thing is that she thinks you love her. Bastard!'

He blinked. What he felt and what she thought he felt were so far apart as to be quite unrelated. 'Things aren't as sour as they look to you,' he managed. 'And nothing's that simple either — give me this and I'll give you that. You don't have to sell yourself to be liked. You're a beautiful girl. If you would just value yourself a bit more you'd start to see we don't have to be animals!'

Sally eyed him assessingly. 'You blackmail Rowan into doing what you want,' she said.

'Oh my God.' Saul put his fist to his forehead. 'Look,' he began, 'our marriage, mine and Rowan's, is our business. We don't need you standing on the sidelines giving a running commentary. To you things look one way; to us, each of us, they aren't like that at all. Your sister is — she's every bit as insecure as you, but a thousand times more determined. That isn't easy to live with.'

Seeing her opening, Sally hunched a shoulder. 'Like I said, what you need is some relaxation.' Quite suddenly Sally pulled off her top. She stood, smiling, her breasts restrained by a minuscule lace bra.

'Put that back on,' said Saul tightly.

She laughed, pulled her bra down and jiggled her breasts at him. 'You know that you want to,' she whispered, in a parody of the seductress.

Saul leaped towards her. As he caught her round the waist and upended her, Sally's triumph turned to fear. 'Stop it! Leave me alone!' she wailed, kicking and screaming like the child she was.

'I'll teach you to play your filthy games,' roared Saul, and walloped her bottom with the flat of his hand, five, six, seven times. Sally screeched and struggled, but he would not let her go. When at last he released her she collapsed sobbing on to the floor, cradling her bottom in her hands.

'I think you'd better move out,' said Saul menacingly.

She looked up at him through strands of tear-soaked hair. 'I wouldn't stay here if you paid me. Pig! I can afford my own flat, you know, I own a quarter of the firm! Then we'll see who I get to come and visit.'

He pointed a parental finger at her. 'You will go to an all-girls hostel and stay there!' he roared. 'I'll not have you setting up as a part-time tart, you'll learn some discipline for once in your life. And if a word of this reaches Rowan, you'll find out what it's like to get a real spanking. In comparison that last little effort was a few light taps!'

'Brute! Bastard!' screamed Sally, but he was gone. She took off her shoe and hurled it viciously against the closed door.

He told Rowan that Sally had left after she had been placed in the care of the hostel matron. It had been instant antagonism. The matron sensed trouble and bristled, causing Sally to salute the enemy by turning her radio on full blast.

'She'll be OK,' said Saul, reassuring himself as much as Rowan.

'Tell her to come and see me,' begged Rowan. 'I worry about her. She hasn't been for over two weeks.'

'Since she started her course. It's much easier for her now she's at the hostel, no buses.'

'Yes.' Rowan felt helpless and out of it. Nobody ever considered her any more, they made decisions and told her afterwards.

They decided to induce the birth at just over eight months. Rowan was seriously unwell, when Saul looked at her he could believe she might die. There had been a light in her that he only remembered when he saw it extinguished, as it was now, as she lay with a drip in her arm and the line of her chin quite lost in swelling.

'Not long,' he said, taking his seat beside her.

'You've had a drink. I can smell it.'

'You bet I have. Wish you could have one too, actually.'

'So do I.' She put out her free hand and he held it. They had taken her wedding ring off weeks ago, when her finger had swollen. Suddenly she started to cry.

Saul smoothed her hair, feeling so close to her, wishing he could pick her up and run far away. 'What is it, lovey? Tell me.'

'I'm so frightened. Suppose it is all wrong, suppose it isn't the right shape? They never tell us anything. I don't want to be here, they treat me like an animal.'

'I think they know what they're doing,' he said helplessly. 'We wouldn't know if they didn't.'

They watched in silence as a nurse came in and adjusted the drip, patting Rowan as she left. 'She thinks I'm a dog,' growled Rowan. 'Pat pat, all day long.'

'They treat me worse than a dog,' said Saul. 'The moment I walk in there's a swishing of curtains, as if they were shutting out some prowling wild beast. I'm beginning to feel like a convicted rapist.'

'It's all your fault, that's why. They blame the men for all this, we women had nothing to do with it.'

Saul did not reply. He knew she had had nothing to do with it.

302

The contractions began about twenty minutes later. Every now and then Rowan was examined to see how she was getting on, and Saul was sent out into the waiting room. He found Diana there.

'Saul, I popped in to see her and they said they'd started her off. Why so early, is she all right?'

He had hardly exchanged a word with her in the last year, he realised. 'I don't know, I think so. She's fed up, of course. It's her blood pressure, they won't leave her any longer.'

'Blasted hospitals! They will interfere so. Ask if I can go in for five minutes, I'd love to see her.'

But they were permitting no visitors except, reluctantly, the father. The consultant swept in occasionally, peered at Rowan, told her to be a good girl, and left. 'Woof woof,' she said loudly but he did not reply, merely raising his eyebrows and leaving. His expression conveyed that he had known all along that he was right about these creatures; the gravid woman was brainless.

Three hours later she was too weary for humour. So many faces, peering down at her. Another three hours, the shift changed and all the nurses were different, but the consultant was there and always, thankfully, Saul. Increase the drip, look at the foetal monitor, listen. They discussed her in huddles in the corner of the room, holding her fate in their hands and presuming their right to keep it to themselves.

As the consultant bent over her yet again, always avoiding her eyes, she demanded, 'What's the matter? Why won't you tell me?'

'Everything's going fine, Mother,' he intoned, not looking up.

'I want my husband back. Why do you keep sending him away? I want him.'

The consultant turned to speak to a nurse. 'Get Mother something to calm her please, Sister.'

'I don't want anything to calm me! I want to know what

303

the hell's going on, I want my husband. I want my baby!'

'Of course you do, dear.' The sister bustled up, it was her duty to protect the doctors from distraught patients. Rowan thought, 'This is a nightmare, they've trapped me here, I shall never escape.' 'I want to go home,' she wailed.

They hustled Saul back in, because Mother was getting herself in a state. 'Are they telling you anything?' she asked pathetically. 'Nobody even looks at me.'

'I think we'll hurry her up,' said the consultant, staring at the monitor, and nurses rushed to adjust the drip.

The room came and went in a recurring wave of pain. Rowan had no sensation of giving birth, the baby was being ejected from her, wrenched too early from the womb. Neither she nor the baby was ready for it. Unable to move because of the wires and tubes, she lay stranded and suffering. 'Can't you give her something?' Saul kept asking. His hands were cut by her nails where she had gripped him.

'Not long now,' intoned the consultant.

'Too many drugs don't help baby,' whispered the sister, explaining. 'They won't let it get too bad.'

'It's too bad already,' muttered Saul. He barely trusted himself to say more. The sight of Rowan lying there, agonised, almost reduced him to tears. Once, and only once, she cried out, but immediately clamped her lips shut on the pain.

'You don't have to be brave in front of me,' whispered Saul.

When she could speak, she said weakly, 'It's not you, it's them. Why don't they go away. I want to be left alone.'

Suddenly the consultant was putting on plastic gloves. 'Forceps please, sister,' he said distantly. 'Tell the husband to leave.'

'Why don't *you* tell the bloody husband?' yelled Saul. 'I'm not leaving, I'm staying here.'

But they hustled him out. 'We have to think of the baby,' said the sister accusingly, and defeated him. He stood outside the door, listening to Rowan's small choked gasps of pain.

They put her legs up in stirrups and gathered in a scrum at the end of the bed. The sister put a mask over her face and told her to breathe. She struck it away because they were suffocating her. It was torture, absolute torture. Pain, between her legs, sharp, raw, but more bearable than the other. The consultant began pulling, it was like having her innards extracted, the sister at one end holding her down, a dozen people at the other disembowelling. She closed her eyes, her teeth clenched to breaking point. She could hear the sister whispering 'All right, dear, all right, this is the worst, soon over.' When, suddenly, it stopped she didn't believe it. Seconds passed before she opened her eyes. Nobody spoke.

'It's a little girl, dear.'

'Can I see her?'

'She's had a rough time. She needs some help, they've taken her straight away to special care.'

'What's she like? Is she all right, has she got everything? She'll be all right, won't she?'

The sister looked down at the exhausted, wrecked girl on the bed. What could she say to her, now, when she had been through so much, with courage that even brought the odd kind word from the consultant? 'You've been a very brave girl, my dear.'

So the sister prevaricated. 'Baby's had a big struggle, but she has all her arms and legs. There's nothing missing at all.'

Rowan's face relaxed. Even so soon after the birth the swelling was subsiding. She looked again like a mischievous, green-eyed cat.

'We'll clean you up, and then hubby can see you,' said the sister. Rowan lay back, letting herself drift into warm half-sleep, believing that, in the end, everything had come right. She had her baby, she had her daughter.

'You've a daughter,' said the nurse to Saul. 'Your wife's fine.'

He felt a wave of joy building inside him, he tried to rush back to Rowan but the nurse blocked his path. 'The consultant wants to talk to you.'

Saul didn't know it wasn't standard procedure. He hung about in the corridor and the consultant strode towards him, stopping at the last moment as if to mention some minor point that had almost slipped his mind. 'Oh yes — baby Barton. Thought we might lose it at one point. Pity we didn't know. Down's Syndrome baby. Acute mental retardation. My advice to you is to institutionalise the child at once. Don't even see her, there isn't any point. The mothers get upset, you know. Sister will see to all the forms.'

He made to move away but Saul caught his arm. 'Say that again,' he said confusedly. 'What's the matter with it?'

The doctor raised his voice as if talking to an imbecile. 'Down's Syndrome,' he said loudly. 'The child's a mongol, a congenital idiot. You've got to put her away.'

He shook off Saul's stunned hand and rushed down the corridor. A nurse said, 'He finds these things very difficult, I'm afraid. Why don't you come and have some tea?'

But Saul blundered sightless away. He found himself in the waiting room and there, still waiting, was Diana. He stared at her in disbelief.

'What's the matter? For God's sake, tell me! Is it Rowan?'

He shook his head. He wiped his hand across his mouth in a bewildered, unconscious gesture. 'That man — the doctor — he says the baby's an idiot. We've got a little girl and she's — it's Down's Syndrome.'

Diana's face barely changed. After a few moments she took an enormous breath, and Saul realised that for long seconds she had stopped breathing. 'Poor Rowan,' she said. Her voice grated as if on coals of fire. 'And poor you. I am so, so sorry.'

Suddenly he had to talk, he couldn't keep it in a moment longer. 'Rowan won't be able to take this, I never meant it to be like this. He says we've got to put it away. I mean, why don't they just knock it on the head and be done with it? They would if they could, damn them! I don't believe it, I just don't believe it. Why to Rowan? Why to us?'

Diana took his arm. 'Sit down. Come on, sit down, people are staring. It doesn't help to get upset, Rowan will see. Do you want me to go in to her and you stay here?'

'No! The whole thing's my fault. I have to stay with her.'

'If there's anything wrong it isn't anybody's fault.'

He turned his head and looked at her. She had flung on an old mac and her hair needed washing, but still she had a raw, long-boned attraction. That he could feel it, now, horrified him, but somehow all his emotions seemed very close to the surface. There were feelings in him now that he had thought lost forever: childlike terror, grief, the rage he had felt when James had everything and he so little.

'Why did you have a perfect baby?' he asked suddenly. 'You didn't deserve it.'

She recoiled. 'God help us if we all got what we deserved.'

They came to take him to Rowan. Diana asked if she could go in and they said they would ask, but no one came to call her. She sat outside, twisting her gloves, wondering if Saul was right and she hadn't deserved Nicholas. God help her daughter. These things always broke up marriages, destroyed people. 'Dear God,' she prayed, 'if it isn't right, let it die.'

When Rowan woke Saul was sitting by the bed. 'Hi. You've been asleep for hours.'

'Have I?' She tried to ease herself up in the bed, but it hurt terribly. She lay back again. 'Have you seen her? They rushed her off and I didn't get a glimpse, but the sister said she was fine.'

'Oh. Oh, did she?' He sat there, immobile. Rowan realised that he must be at least as tired as she.

'You ought to get some sleep,' she said fondly. 'Tell me, what does she look like?'

He took a deep breath. 'She's – a sort of little, yellow Chinese rabbit.'

A vague frown creased her brow, she was so pale, so bloodless. 'Chinese? The poor little thing. Are there any horrid marks? Sometimes they get scars. From the forceps.'

'A bit of a bruise perhaps, over her ear. Nothing much to see.'

She put out her hand, astonished at how much effort the gesture required, and rested it on his sleeve. 'I'm just so relieved it came out right in the end,' she murmured. 'I can't tell you how worried I've been. When can I see her, did they say?'

'No – no, they didn't. She's still pretty sick, Ro. Incubator, oxygen, the lot.'

'I know, it looks terrible, doesn't it? I used to pop in and have a look in special care when they let me get up for a bath. They nearly all get better.'

He stared down at her happy, sleepy face. Exhaustion was dulling his senses, he couldn't think or talk coherently. The last place he wanted to be was here. Without a word he got to his feet and started to leave but Rowan called out in a high, nervous voice: 'Saul? Saul, what's the matter?'

He took two more steps before he realised he had to stop. 'Saul?' she called out again. 'What is it?'

He went back to the bed. There was no easy way of saying it. 'She's got Down's Syndrome,' he said flatly. 'Our baby's a mongol.'

Those eyes, so large and green, in Japan he had thought he could drown in them. They were like hard, impenetrable glass. 'You don't mean that,' she said.

'Yes, I do. There isn't any doubt, even I can see she isn't right. They didn't want me to see her. They want us to put her away.'

She dragged herself up, teeth gritted against the pain. 'I've got to see! Take me there, right now!'

He shook his head, screwing his eyes tight against the tears that would not subside. 'They don't want you to. They — they say the mothers get upset.'

A nurse hurried up with something in a plastic medicine cup. 'Something to soothe you,' she said, trying to tip it willy-nilly down Rowan's throat.

'Go to hell,' said Rowan, hitting it away and spilling it. 'They showed you the wrong baby, they said my baby was fine. I want my baby!'

'I'll have to call the doctor,' said the nurse in a low voice to Saul.

Totally fraught, he shouted, 'Don't be so bloody silly, woman! There isn't a pill to put this right! She's got to realise, now, that we've got the booby prize. Our baby's a — a mongol.'

He thought that if Rowan had not spilled the medicine he would have drunk it. Anything to take away the pain. He thought his head would explode from the pressure of agonised thought. A little, yellow monkey of a child that was to be thrown in the rubbish, and forgotten about.

Rowan said, 'I hurt so much. There isn't a part of me that doesn't hurt.'

Saul thought, if it's bad for me it's ten times worse for her. He took her hand and held it tight. 'We'll come through it, lovey. Tomorrow we'll know what to do.'

'Will we?' She looked at him with such lost desperation, he had to find strength enough for two. He nodded, with false decision. 'We'll work something out. By the way, your mother's here, do you want to see her?'

Rowan's fingers tensed on his. 'I don't think I can see anybody. Ever.'

'She can come back tomorrow, I suppose.'

After a while Rowan drifted into a shocked doze. Saul went to find Diana. She was pacing the corridor with a plastic cup of cold coffee in her hand.

'She won't see anyone,' he told her. 'I don't know if she really believes it yet.'

'She ought to see the child,' said Diana shortly. 'She'd see at once that it wasn't normal, she can't possibly believe something she hasn't seen. You should insist!'

'Rowan's ill in bed, the baby's hooked up in an incubator, if the hospital doesn't agree she can't see it. And they won't agree. They want it packed off to some asylum, as soon as possible.'

Diana's face constricted. 'It might be best, you know. You're both so young –'

'Perhaps it is best, I don't know. I don't like being pushed into something like this. We ought to have time to think.'

'Look.' Diana took hold of his arm and then let go again, moving her hands as if to scrub out the unacceptable gesture. 'Look, I've had four children, all normal. Not one of them has been easy to bring up. They take up time and money and energy; they take all your goodwill and then all your rage on top. If sometimes they bring people together, then more often they drive them apart. It isn't easy. The only thing that makes it worthwhile is the lovely people you hope they're going to be.

'Oh, Saul, I wasn't a natural mother and I don't think Rowan is either, but even if she was I'd still not want her to struggle with a handicapped child. This baby can't ever be anything! The chances are it will hardly know where it is, at home with you or in some institution. Send it away.'

He had been watching her without blinking. She was suddenly aware of the square strength of his face. 'I don't think we can wriggle out of our responsibility,' he said grimly. 'If you want my opinion I think you've been a bloody awful parent, mostly because you put what you wanted before your kids. You haven't given a thought to that poor, unloved little scrap that Rowan and I produced. Nobody wants her, not even her mum and dad. At least we owe her the courtesy of deciding what's in her best interests, not just in ours, or yours, or the bloody hospital's! Everybody but the baby can take care of themselves, and it seems to me that the one person who needs care is the one nobody cares about.'

'Blame me if you want,' retorted Diana. 'Blame whoever you damn well like, but don't make Rowan take that child home! It will finish you both.'

She turned on her heel and went out. Saul stood watching her mac swinging to the rhythm of her long stride, and he was conscious of wild, unreasoning hatred. He wanted it to be Diana's fault, somebody's fault! He wanted a victim that he could hit.

Exhaustion was dulling his brain. He knew if he should do anything, he should go home and sleep. Instead he went back to look at his daughter, pushing his way past the nurse and himself finding the secluded corner where his baby was starting her life as she was to live it, shut off and alone. When he saw her first he could not believe that she was so small, so wizened and so ugly. Now he saw that her skin was dry and flaking, the monkey skull covered with sparse wisps of hair. There was a tube in the child's nose but she was awake. A thin slit of blue eye seemed to watch him. All of a sudden he thought of a name.

'We'll call you Hannah,' he said.

Chapter Twenty-Six

Hannah lay motionless, a little yellow scrap of life. Strangely, although still in the incubator, she was without the tubes and monitors that characterised all the other babies there. Saul, refreshed by a sleep that had been as deep as it was unexpected, said: 'Are you trying to let her die?'

The nurse flushed uncomfortably. 'Of course not. Doctor feels she should be transferred as soon as she's fit.'

'Is she fit?' demanded Saul.

The nurse avoided his eye. 'Doctor would like to send her this afternoon. He says it will be better for your wife.'

Saul ran down the stairs to Rowan's ward. The curtains around her bed remained drawn. From behind them he could hear a considerable commotion.

'Don't you dare touch me with that thing! Don't you dare!' shrieked Rowan.

Saul raced down the ward and burst through the curtains. The sister, a nurse, the consultant and another man were all muttering soothingly while a syringe was produced from a kidney dish like some sort of evil missile.

'Stick that in her and I'll sue you!' declared Saul.

Rowan's expression changed from panicky fury to tearfulness. 'They won't let me see her,' she wailed. 'I tried to go and see and they stopped me, and they keep trying to make me sign forms!'

The consultant said irascibly, 'Good God, woman, we are trying to do what's best for you! Do you want to be saddled with a gibbering idiot all your life? If you take the brat you'll be back here begging us to take her away within six months. I warn you, you'll be too late then! My recommendation counts for something, I can tell you. I have women queuing up to get their great, over-sexed idiot sons taken away from them.'

'We have a little girl,' said Saul grimly. 'And nobody has once tried to explain what we can expect or where she might go or anything. The decision is ours, not yours!'

'I can't make a decision, I haven't even seen her,' wept Rowan.

The other man spoke up. 'As a psychiatrist, I fully understand the emotions you must be feeling . . .' he began.

'I bet you bloody don't!' said Saul.

'. . . and amongst them there is of course bewilderment. You feel you want to blame the hospital, to believe that they were in some way at fault. In reality we have a great deal of experience of this type of child and we can sincerely recommend – '

'Have you ever been to one of these homes?' demanded Rowan.

The psychiatrist paused. 'We – we do know of their excellent reputation – '

'I bet none of you've been,' she interrupted. 'Go on, tell me, is it a nice pretty house or a Victorian barn with stone floors? Is it only for babies or is everyone lumped in together? Well?'

The consultant sighed patiently. 'I am very well acquainted with St. Anselm's.'

'St Anselm's!' chorused Saul and Rowan together. It was the local lunatic asylum, from which inmates occasionally escaped out of locked wards to terrorise the neighbourhood.

'I'm going to take her home,' said Rowan hysterically, trying to swing her legs out of bed. 'I won't stay here a moment longer. You all think you know what's best for me. It's like a police state!'

'Hang on a minute, love.' Saul put a hand on her shoulder and restrained her more effectively than the sister's armlock of a moment ago. He glared at the consultant with loathing. 'I think she should be taken home in an ambulance, with our baby. And I want somebody to come and see her at home. Isn't there a nurse that calls round?'

'Oh, she can have the health visitor,' said the consultant contemptuously. 'See how much use she'll be when there's a sudden haemorrhage.'

'We'll take our chance. We'd like to go now, please.'

The consultant fixed his gaze on the psychiatrist, who advanced reluctantly into the fray. 'You will appreciate that neither of you is in any condition to make a rational choice,' he began. 'Naturally you feel bewildered and angry – '

'You said that before,' complained Rowan. 'We know how we feel. I just can't understand why you won't let us do one single thing that we say we want to do. It's not us that's mentally retarded, it's the baby!'

She flung back her head and stared round at them all. She had said it, she had admitted it out loud. Saul took her hand, she felt strong and calm and positive.

The consultant let out his breath in an angry sigh. 'Oh, very well, sister, get them sent home! It is after all they who will live to regret it.'

The medical staff filed away. On the bed, discarded, lay the committal forms. Saul said softly to Rowan, 'Is this what we really want to do?'

She allowed herself a small, rueful grin. 'I don't know. It might be. Can we do it first and see if we like it later? I just couldn't send her away, not without even a look.'

He kissed her dark, tousled head. He was so full of love and anguish that it almost hurt to breathe.

The ambulance was delayed for hours, and only when Saul prepared to remove wife and child in his car did it miraculously become available. As a concession to them, the baby was to be sent home in a portable incubator, so that she would continue in a constant temperature. When they saw the contraption wheeling towards them, both Saul and Rowan tensed.

'Let me see,' said Rowan, wrapped in blankets in a wheel-chair. They were in the front hall of the hospital, much observed by everyone passing by. There could have been no less private place for a mother first to see her child and because of it Rowan set her face in an expression almost masklike. Saul pushed her towards the plastic box that contained their baby. She put out her hands and rested them on the upper dome, peering between her fingers at what lay within. At last after long minutes she withdrew her hands, folded them in her lap and looked away. They wheeled her into the ambulance.

The doors shut, the engine started, they began to move. In the dim light Saul, Rowan and their baby were together. 'Her name's Hannah,' said Saul. 'I don't want anything else, it seems right.'

Rowan looked at the plastic box. 'Hannah,' she tried. 'Hannah.'

'What do you think of her?'

She shrugged stiffly. 'I don't know. She isn't what I expected. I don't feel I know her. Saul, what do we give her to eat?'

He felt embarrassed. 'I thought — she'll suck from you, won't she?'

'I don't know if I want her to. Not if we're not keeping her.'

He knew without being told that Rowan was rigid with terror. She was frightened of Hannah, of herself, perhaps most of all of her own ignorance. Neither of them had any idea how to take care of a baby, let alone a handicapped one. What would Hannah turn into? Like most of the world, when they had witnessed mental disability they had simply walked the other way, never once exercising their minds on causes and possibilities. They were completely unfitted for this task.

When they reached home the ambulance men helped Rowan out and into the lift, then brought the incubator up too, plugging it into a socket in the flat's sitting room. It seemed out of place in the stark, bare, elegant room. The whole flat was geared to adult living.

'We're not ready,' apologised Saul feebly. 'I wasn't expecting this.'

The ambulance man cast a sage eye over the low shelves with the landlord's collection of delicate ornaments. 'Going to find it tough here,' he advised. 'My advice is to get somewhere a bit less open plan, with a garden. These kids need space.'

'Do you know anything about them?' asked Rowan, grabbing at this one solid piece of information.

'My sister's kiddie's one,' he said casually. 'Nice little chap. Got to watch for colds, weak chests they got. When I send him sommat at Christmas he writes me a letter, just a few words like, but he writes them. You wouldn't have believed that now, would you?'

Rowan's beam of relief was out of all proportion to the snippet of encouragement. Saul saw the men out and came back. 'Perhaps he's exceptional,' he said cautiously.

'And perhaps he isn't! Oh Saul, suppose they're all wrong? I mean, she won't ever be brilliant or anything, but she might be just sort of − average? They don't know how she'll turn out.'

He didn't want to depress her. Hannah was starting to mew, a sound that was more animal than baby. He said, 'Why don't we try feeding her?'

Apprehensively they extracted Hannah from her plastic box. She let out a cry and waved her arms about, not settling even when Rowan brought her inexpertly to the breast. Neither of the two main participants had a clue what to do and Saul could only offer vague advice. Rowan's breasts were sore and hard, the baby chewed on tender nipples without really sucking. After an hour, Rowan was in tears and the baby sucking its fists unhappily.

'She'll die of starvation. I don't know what to do! Why doesn't someone tell me what to do?'

There seemed to be nobody they could ask. The isolation of their position crushed them. They had foundered almost at once in thinking that they could cope with this child. If they asked for help, would they be accused of incompetence and have their baby forcibly taken away? Fear does not breed rational thought.

Saul said, 'Suppose we try her on a bottle? They must have done that in hospital.'

'Do you think so?' Rowan clutched at the suggestion. Within minutes Saul found himself racing out to find a chemist before it closed.

Bottle feeding did seem to be the answer, at first. They could pour milk quite easily from a fat teat into their lethargic infant. But it seemed to come out again just as easily, regurgitated all over everything and going up the baby's nose and making them think she was choking. The night passed in a haze of bottles and sick and anxiety. In her state of weary hysteria Rowan could not handle Hannah calmly, the slightest set-back caused her to panic and multiply disaster. They hadn't enough of anything, either disposable nappies or bottles or baby clothes or bedding. Again and again the baby fed, vomited over everything, and reduced Rowan to tears.

At two in the morning Saul sent Rowan to bed and bathed the baby. It was the only thing to do, although whether it would finish her off or not he could not know. She was so sticky and smelly and miserable, he lowered her into the sink and tenatively wiped at her stick like limbs with cotton wool.

'You're too small to eat much,' he told her. 'We won't feed you so much.'

He was reminded of rearing baby birds when he was young. There had been a sparrow, fallen from the nest just before fledging, which he had brought to adulthood. He dried the child and wrapped her in a towel, putting her, mewing, into the incubator while he made up yet another feed, this time thinning it drastically.

The flat was absolutely silent, except for the baby. He picked up the child and settled into a corner of the old sofa, feeling drained of everything except weariness. He started to feed his daughter, with painful slowness. It took over an hour to give her a very few ounces but at least this time it stayed down. Holding her like a piece of china, he lifted her back into the incubator and closed the top.

He had to go to bed, no power on earth could keep him awake longer. Saul staggered along the hall, cast off his clothes and fell between the sheets. Rowan was very warm and soft, he cuddled close to her to gain some of her heat. If only, if only it hadn't had to be like this! It could have been so wonderfully different. He fell, dreamless, into sleep.

Next day the health visitor came, Nurse Brown. She was a short, motherly soul, steeped in the practicalities of life. She scanned the little household with her bright eyes, taking in the mother's nerves, the father's exhaustion and the baby's sickliness. As a first step she unwrapped Hannah and weighed her.

'A very little chicken,' she said thoughtfully. 'I'm surprised they sent you home with her this small. If you wanted I could send you both to a nursing home for a few days, until you get sorted out.'

'No,' said Rowan shortly. 'It's only feeding that's a problem. I can't seem to feed her myself.'

Nurse Brown nodded. 'You won't, she's too weak. I want you to give her a bottle every two hours, a little amount each time, even if she seems too sleepy to take it. Let's try now.'

She watched as Rowan tried inexpertly to coax food into the baby. The teat was too big and milk flooded out and swamped the child. Rowan tried to mop up, got in a state and wailed.

'Let me,' said Saul, taking the little bundle in his big square hands. 'I got the hang of this last night.' Neatly and efficiently, he settled baby and bottle, tilting the teat only enough to let a gentle flow through.

'Very good,' said Nurse Brown, genuinely relieved. The mother was clearly too upset for competence, but the father seemed to know what he was doing. 'Can your mother come and stay, dear?' she asked Rowan.

They both insisted that no one was coming to stay. So it was up to the father to take care of this baby, it seemed.

On the way out, the nurse said quietly to Saul, 'Has she accepted the child? She seems very distressed.'

He sighed and ran his hands through his hair. 'We neither of us know what we've got, if we're honest. I think Rowan wants to believe it's all a terrible mistake.'

'That's as clear a case as I've seen, I'm afraid,' said the nurse, stomping out to her car in her sensible flat shoes. 'You've got a little girl that may be sweet, and may not. She'll certainly look different. And she'll need a lot of training, years and years of it. Nobody can tell you how much or how little she'll be able to do, Hannah's herself and that's all you can say. Take it as it comes, that's my advice.'

When he went back in Rowan said tensely, 'Did she say anything?'

He shrugged. 'She agrees with the diagnosis, that's all.'

'Huh!' Rowan got up stiffly and went to look down at Hannah. 'She isn't what they think, you know,' she said. 'They're all wrong. Perhaps she might be a bit slow, but if we paid for a good school she'd be all right. We'll have to look for a good one.'

Saul was stunned. 'You know that's silly,' he said gently. 'She can't be normal, Ro, there's no use hoping for it.'

Turning to him, her smile wavered and cracked. 'I know,' she sobbed. 'But I can't live with that, I can't bear it! I have to believe they're wrong.'

He put his arms round her and rested his cheek against her hair. In the hospital she had seemed to face it so bravely, he could not know that she had expected, and still expected, for the cup to pass away. There was a sense of utter desperation welling inside him, he felt that for the first time in his life he was in a situation that was both untenable and inescapable. It was terrifying.

A week later Diana insisted that they come round for lunch. It was to be Hannah's first outing and neither Saul nor Rowan particularly wanted to go. Nonetheless Saul knew that they should, because somehow the longer they hid the harder it was to come out at all.

The health visitor had sent the incubator back to the hospital. She felt it was unnecessary and tended to make the mother treat the child as some sort of freak. 'She's a child like any other,' she told Rowan, fruitlessly. 'You don't need to treat her like a wild animal. Take her out, let people see her.'

'I couldn't bear them to stare.' Rowan shuddered at the thought of it and the health visitor said forcefully, 'There's no point in being over-sensitive. She is what she is and you must love her for it. We can't order our babies like groceries, we have to take what comes. And I think it's about time you got out of that dressing gown, my girl, you should get up and get on. You've a life to lead.'

So Rowan dressed listlessly in one of her purple tunics, leaving the trousers underneath unbuttoned at the waist. Hannah wore some of the pretty baby clothes sent as presents before the birth. Against the pure white wool her face was like a wizened old man's. They packed bottles, nappies and changes of clothing, setting off an hour late for Aspley Manor.

Diana opened the door to them. 'We thought you weren't coming,' she said. 'My goodness, Rowan, you look so thin. Already.'

Rowan looked drawn and anxious, her face nothing but eyes.

Saul said, 'She could do with a good meal. We both could. Hannah takes so much looking after we've hardly time to eat.'

James came down the stairs, looking uncomfortable. He

321

shook Saul's hand and bent down to kiss Rowan on the cheek, a gesture as unprecedented as it was unwelcome. 'Nice to see you both,' he said heartily.

'There's three of us,' said Rowan in a small voice.

'Yes. So there is. Well, doesn't she look tiny!'

He and Diana peered in at the scrap of humanity lying in the basket. They were both horribly aware of the loud and healthy bawling coming from upstairs. 'I must go and see – ' said Diana vaguely, and hurried off.

'You don't have to worry about us seeing him,' said Rowan. 'We won't mind.'

But when they took her at her word and brought Nicholas into the drawing room, to sit in his baby chair and crow and bounce in healthy activity, she minded very much. Suddenly she put her hands up over her eyes. 'Oh God, why don't you take him away!' she said forcefully.

Diana got up at once and did so. James said, 'I'm sorry, Rowan. I did think it might be tactless but Diana felt – these things do take some getting used to. I didn't think you realised what you were taking on.'

Saul cleared his throat. 'I don't think we can go back now. Can we, Rowan?'

She said nothing for a long minute.

'Rowan?' hinted Saul.

'No,' she said finally. 'No, of course not. We're making the best of it, that's all.'

'But this might not be the best,' said James, speaking very loudly and heartily. 'There are a lot of places that take children of this age, small homes where they can be brought up just as if they were in a family.'

'Then why not keep her in the family?' said Saul. His face and tone were equally bleak. 'She's tiny, we don't even know her yet. Of course we're keeping her.'

'It's easy for you,' said Rowan in a low, miserable voice.

Saul got up and went over to the window. 'Any chance of

a drink, James?' he asked, and at once James got up and poured him a Scotch.

'I've dropped the breach of contract case,' he said pityingly.

'Thanks a bloody lot!' retorted Saul. 'That must be proof positive that we're social lepers. We don't need your sympathy. You go on and sue, James. We'll knock you into touch, don't you worry.'

James's expression did not alter. 'I know what a strain this must be,' he soothed.

Saul downed his whisky and went without asking to pour himself another. He glanced at his watch. 'Time to feed the baby, Rowan.'

'It always seems to be time.' She picked up the baby and started to unfasten Hannah's nappy. She glanced at James. 'How's business?'

He shrugged. 'Not bad. Better than for you at the moment, or so I hear. Well, you've both been so preoccupied things are bound to have slipped a bit. You should have let me buy you out while you had the chance.'

Rowan's eyes flicked across to Saul, then back to Hannah's thin little body. The baby kicked her short legs, bicycling with rare energy.

'She'll get cold.' Saul put down his drink, came across and fastened Hannah's clean nappy. Rowan wandered off to heat the bottle in the kitchen.

Diana had mistakenly indulged James in the kitchen, permitting him to stuff the room with custom-built units. Acres of worktop gleamed, enough for a restaurant, redeemed by the flowers, fruit and sculpture that Diana had installed en masse to redeem the place. Rowan couldn't find a pan. She opened and closed cupboards endlessly before she located one.

While she stood waiting at the hob, James came in. 'You ought to watch it, Rowan,' he said. 'I told you Saul would ruin you and he damn nigh has! It's about time you got back to work.'

She glanced at him coolly. 'I never believe anything you tell me, James.'

He came very close to her. 'Well, you should. You and I don't get on, ducky, but we understand each other. You're not suited to spending your days caring for a no-hope child. Get back to work! It's what you're best at.'

Rowan turned to him, the warm bottle clutched in her hands. She looked lovely, thought James suddenly, waif-like and strange. 'Do you know any children like her?' she asked.

He thought for a moment. 'There was a kid when I was young. Short, clumsy, with a big tongue. We used to tease him, make him repeat swear words and so on. And we'd muddle him up about his name and after a bit he'd cry. Someone would always take him home, we weren't that cruel.'

Rowan shuddered visibly. She who hated dependence for herself could not bear it for her child. To be at the mercy of others' charity, for all your days. Hateful, hateful affliction!

Diana came in, determinedly cheerful. 'Saul's waiting for that bottle, Rowan.' With Rowan safely despatched, she hissed at James, 'Do you really have to regale her with these horror stories? The least we can do is let her realise for herself how hopeless it all is.'

'I think somebody ought to tell her the truth!'

'I suppose so.' Diana wrapped her arms around herself, and then as if still not enough comforted, moved to let James hold her also. 'I'm just so glad it wasn't Nicholas. It should have been, you know, I'm the right age.'

Suddenly James was tired of all this emotion. He said petulantly, 'I don't suppose we could have something to eat, could we?'

Diana wasn't a natural cook. She had none of that generosity of spirit that creates rich pies and luscious gravies, cakes heavy with fruit and homeliness. Her meals were well-presented, adequate and somehow disappointing. Saul munched, found nothing he could directly criticise, and felt vaguely depressed. James too was nostalgically drawn to the memory of Marjorie's Sunday lunches, for which he had never thanked her at the time. Airy Yorkshire puddings and crispy roast potatoes, leeks done just so in a spicy white sauce. 'This is very good, dear,' he said to Diana.

'Thank you, James.' Diana turned to Rowan. 'Darling, I have to tell you — Andy's been offered an American tour.'

'Oh. Wonderful.'

'Yes, isn't it? They'll love him over there. If it wasn't for Nicholas, I think I'd go and see him perform. He'll be in New York, Boston, Washington and a couple of places I don't think God has even heard of. They throw those in to pad it out a bit. Carnegie Hall one day, schoolrooms the next.'

'Andy won't like being sold cheap,' said Rowan crisply. There was no one more conscious of his own worth than her brother. 'You ought to go, Mother, you could take Nicholas.'

Diana poked a fork round her plate. 'I don't know. I should so love to go, what do you think, James? Couldn't you come?'

But James had no wish to watch his wife mooning about after Andy and to spend his evenings listening to the endless banshee wailing of the violin. He would much prefer another kind of amusement: Lin Yu; some gambling; a little of the cocaine she had introduced him to, a lot of that stuff that made him come like a volcano. Much as he adored his wife and baby, he'd adore them far more when they got back. 'I can't really spare the time, darling,' he said mournfully. 'But you could go. Hire a nanny over there to help with Nicholas. Enjoy yourself.'

The phone rang and he got up automatically to answer it. The dining room was wood-panelled and the telephone was hidden obscurely in a carved box. As he reached in and extracted it, Saul and Rowan exchanged amused glances. James took everything, even panelling, to impossible lengths.

'Yes,' said James, and listened. He dangled the receiver from a disinterested hand. 'For you, Rowan. That ape who used to shamble around after you.'

'Joe?' She got up and hurried to the phone. 'Joe, what is it?' The line crackled and buzzed, but through it Rowan could hear Joe's voice, tight with adrenaline. 'Get back here, Ro. The place is blazing. The fire brigade's here but, my God, it's got hold!'

She was aware of her heart, thundering erratically. 'Not the mill, Joe. It'll be the cottages, not the mill!'

'It's like to be the whole bloody lot, Ro! I've got to go.'

The line went dead. She stood frozen for a long second and then slowly turned to the others. 'The mill's burning,' she said softly.

Chapter Twenty-Seven

The car squealed through the afternoon, tangling with day-trippers returning from the Dales and making its way aggressively down every twist and byway known to them. Rowan sat in the back holding the baby while Saul wrenched at the wheel. When they got near they could smell smoke, hanging in the windless air. At the end of the street a policeman tried to stop them but Rowan leaped from the car, Hannah still in her arms.

'Let me through. That's my mill burning, that's Judge's!'

'Not with the baby, miss,' protested the policeman, and she turned and thrust Hannah at Saul. She ran down the road like a hare, when this morning she had found it hurt to walk.

Water was everywhere, trickling over the cobbles. She had to climb past a fire engine and its fat, wormlike hoses, stuck like a cork in a bottle in the gateway. The mill had been built for another age, it handled neither lorries nor fire engines well. When she got through and could see the gaunt front of the building, she heard herself whispering, 'Oh my God, oh my God. Thank you, God.' For there was no conflagration, there was almost nothing to see, simply an outpouring of smoke from an upstairs window.

'That's the offices,' said Saul.

She glanced at him. 'What did you do with Hannah?'

'The policeman's got her. I'm going in.'

He ran forward and Rowan went after him. The warehouse was sodden, dripping with water, and when they burst into the weaving shed so was that. A fireman, huge in waders and helmet, his axe held casually in his hand, said, 'Out of here, please. Fire's upstairs, but we're containing it.'

Rowan moved protectively towards her brand new card. 'You can lose everything except this,' she said 'we've only just got it.'

'I'm sure it's insured, madam,' said the fireman disinterestedly and tried to hustle them out.

Saul stood firm, refusing to follow his wife. 'I can't see anything,' he complained. 'It smells like an inferno, but is it just the offices?'

'That and a room that seems to have been used as a nursery. It started upstairs, funnelled through in the roof space and went into the cottages. Quite a sight when it was burning properly but we've just about got it out now, sir. If you'd like to talk to the fire chief, he'll tell you everything.'

Inexorably they were pushed back into the yard. Rowan turned and stared at the row of cottages. She had assumed from Joe's words that they had survived, she didn't even bother to look. But instead of her little house there was a shell, windows empty of glass, the neat white frames black with smoke. The curtains they had not needed at the flat hung like charred rags.

'That was our home,' she said dismally.

'Not any more,' said Saul. He went and sat down on a stone path edging. He could barely think straight, this on top of everything; Hannah, Rowan and barely three hours sleep a night. He felt ill.

'Here, mate.' It was Joe Partridge, and he had a bottle. Saul put it to his lips and drank, deliberately scorching his throat. He coughed hoarsely. 'Thanks.'

'Could see you needed it. Bit of a bad do all round lately.'

'You can say that again. Can't quite take it in, really, but it looks as if the cottages are finished.'

'And the offices. By the way, they think it started in that nursery of yours. Some plonker stuck a nappy over a heater and left it turned on.'

'Oh, Christ!' He reached again for the bottle and drank.

It seemed to be having little or no effect.

He got up and stood staring at the diminishing stream of smoke coming from the offices. All his best schemes came to nothing, the baby, Rowan, even the goddammed nursery. It was as if the world was run by joyless puritans, only happy when they could see people like Saul, fun, amusing people, brought down. If you were James, gave nothing away, used love like tissue paper, betraying and deceiving at every turn, you got what you wanted. It was Saul who lost out, every time.

A long arm stole round him. It was Rowan, snuggling up against him. 'It's not so bad. The mill's still there, nothing important went.'

'I look at the work there is to do and I feel so, so tired.'

'It's not that bad. We'll get through.'

He marvelled at her because, since the baby, she had been lost and helpless. This was the old Rowan, staring clear-eyed into the future.

'What would you have done if the mill had gone?' he asked, because for himself he didn't think he would have cared.

'I'd start it again,' said Rowan, and then as he looked dubious she said fiercely, 'I would, you know! It's important, Judge's. Important to me.'

Word of the fire soon spread. That evening as they sat exhausted in the penthouse flat, the doorbell rang. It was a courier, with an expensive meal for two, a bouquet of flowers and a bottle of champagne, courtesy of some friends of Saul.

'I can't believe this,' said Rowan, confronting creamed quail and a glass of dry champagne. 'The mill almost burned down today and we're celebrating.'

'So we should be,' said Saul, raising his glass and chinking it on hers. With several pre-dinner drinks inside him, he was feeling decidedly optimistic. 'I think that the fire should get us off the hook. I didn't tell you but the bank was cutting up rough. We've got a whacking great overdraft at the moment and you know how short-sighted they are. The insurance money should calm them down a bit. The trouble is, we've expanded so damn quickly, we can't get the orders out as fast as we have to stock up to deal with them.'

'Have we expanded?' asked Rowan in surprise. She had vaguely believed that Judge's was plodding on much as before, because Saul never said anything different.

'We are in demand, my sweet,' admitted Saul. 'I've pulled orders right, left and centre. The problem is filling them.'

'Oh, Saul.'

He waggled his empty glass at her and then picked up the bottle to fill it. 'Don't you "Oh, Saul" me! Plod plod plod, that's you. We're up and running, and thanks to the fire we should run a bit faster. Now that the cottages are ruined, we can pull them down and have one hell of a lot more space.'

The champagne was going to Rowan's head, she felt light-hearted suddenly.

'Shall we get a nanny?' she asked. 'Then I can come back and take care of everything.'

'It doesn't need taking care of,' said Saul irritably. He ate a mouthful of the quail and paused. 'My God,' he said softly, 'real food. Rowan, taste it — quick. I haven't experienced this since I was last in France, it's what food's supposed to be. I'd almost forgotten such things existed.'

Rowan tasted cautiously. 'Bit rich for me.'

'Rich! To a man who lives on frozen pizzas or that appalling leather your mother thinks is roast beef, this is what life ought to be! Here, I'll have yours as well.'

Rowan ate bread while Saul devoured the goodies. When he finished, he put on a record, a quickstep. 'Come on,' he said, putting down his glass. 'Tonight we're letting our hair down.'

She giggled and pushed back some chairs. She had learned to quickstep at school and had never tried it outside a gym.

She was wearing purple pyjamas and felt drunk with champagne and weariness.

'This is turning me on,' said Saul softly. 'Who are you, lovely lady?'

She went on tiptoe to murmur in his ear. 'I am Masha, the Russian spy, and you will come to my room and tell me everything.'

'What do you want to know?' he asked throatily.

'How to get out of Birmingham on the ring road.'

Their footwork dissolved in giggles, and they went hand in hand to sit down. 'Somebody must know how to get out of Birmingham,' said Saul. 'It stands to reason.'

'He's lost his reason,' said Rowan. 'Forty times round the Bullring and we all do. He's fled the country, taking the knowledge with him.'

'And the police are even now trying to extradite him from South America,' added Saul. 'They've got forty Nazi war criminals and still Fred Bloggs eludes them. We ought to break this to the nation, they deserve to know.'

Rowan picked at the concoction they had been sent for pudding. 'Why do these people mess food up so?' she remarked.

'Darling, it's called cooking,' said Saul sardonically. 'One day you might try it.'

She made a face at him. Tomorrow would be different from today. With Hannah asleep and Saul close at hand and her mill miraculously spared, she felt suddenly overwhelmed. Perhaps things could never be as she wished them, but it was a waste of a life to pine always for what you couldn't have. When she heard the mill was burning she had thought it was the end, that she wouldn't be able to go on, and now she found that in fact they were lucky. The tide had turned for them. She had space again.

Undressing in the bedroom, she said, 'We'll get a nanny.'

Saul's head came up. It was he who was bearing the brunt of Hannah's care, he who coaxed the food down and mopped up when she was sick. Rowan couldn't do it, or more to the point, wouldn't do it. Her apparent calm hid something worryingly fundamental.

'You'll get used to her,' he said cautiously.

'Will I? Saul, I meant it. We must have someone to help.' She looked at him pleadingly.

'Do you really not want her?' he asked bluntly. 'We agreed we'd try.'

Rowan brought her knees to her chin and sat on the bed in silence. He said 'Rowan!' insistently and she said in a low, rushed voice, 'I do want to keep her. It would tear me apart not to have her. And it tears me apart to look at her every day and know what she is. I will get used to it, I know I'll get used to it, but I can't do it all at once! I'm going back to work. The mill needs me, especially now. I've got to get back to work.'

He sighed, gustily. 'You know, last time we worked together, it almost broke us up. Do you want me to leave, is that what you're saying?'

'Do you mean Judge's, or me, or both of us?'

There was the small, snuffling sound of Hannah starting to wake. No sleep for them yet, they faced another hour at least of feeding. 'I do love you, Rowan,' said Saul softly. 'You and Hannah.' He went to get the baby out of her cradle. She was such an odd little thing. As he became more accustomed to her he found he preferred her wizened little face to that of the normal variety. There was a certain crushed charm.

Rowan said, 'Judge's does need me. I can run it so well, you don't know.'

'Perhaps I do know. Perhaps that's what I don't like.'

Rowan took the baby and started the feed. Saul couldn't help but notice how often she avoided looking straight into Hannah's face, and when she did she seemed to brace herself, as if suffering a stab of pain. For himself the wound was scabbing over; Hannah was as she was and that was that. Rowan still bled.

332

He said, 'We'll get a nanny and split the work in Judge's. I'll do the selling. I'll have my own staff, do my own trips, have a separate office, separate brief, separate everything. We'll try it and see.'

She put down the baby and flung her arms around his neck, pressing herself into him like a cat. Despite himself she aroused him. Almost against his will he found his hands on her breasts and his knee forcing her legs apart.

'Ow! Don't, Saul. It still hurts.'

Of course it did, he was a brute. He let her go back to the baby.

They found a girl to come and help. Her name was Barbara. Young, eager and tender-hearted to a fault, she was delighted to have a baby whose needs were so great. Decidedly plump, she lived in Sally's little flatlet, an undemanding sort of girl with soft brown hair and breasts that swelled against her hand-knitted jumper. To his own incredulity Saul found himself fantasising about screwing her, and hated himself for it. The girl wasn't even particularly attractive! But he had been months without sex, and the enforced celibacy showed every sign of continuing.

Quite suddenly there was no reason why Rowan should not go back to work. On the first day she hung around the flat, upsetting Barbara. Saul had gone early, saying he had to talk to the insurers, and Rowan had been about to leave for the mill when she thought suddenly, 'I can't.' Suppose the baby forgot her? In a feeble mind there must be a very small reservoir of memory. Rowan was filled with the horror that she might be supplanted.

Barbara said, 'It's all right, Mrs. Barton. Really it is.'

Rowan hated to believe that might be true. Didn't she matter at all to the baby? She went to the cradle and peered in, watching Hannah wave her arms and legs in that odd, slow, swimming motion she had. It was heartbreaking to watch her, heartbreaking to think of her. Rowan picked up her bag and rushed out.

Gradually, as the weeks passed, a sense of order began to seep back into Rowan's life. Every day she worked at the mill and every evening rushed back to be with Hannah and Saul. She loved to watch him with the baby, a big man moved to gentleness, endlessly patient. It was Saul who taught her how to play with the child, because he was so open and unembarrassed. He would sit with Hannah on his lap, her head lolling and her eyes unfocused, and he'd puff out his cheeks into balloons, roll his eyes, gobble like a turkey, whistle like a train.

And the little girl would watch him. It was as if he conjured life out of something only half alive. When Saul played, Hannah emerged from whatever refuge she inhabited and played with him. Once, after twenty minutes of puffing and blowing and tickling, she smiled.

'Did you see that?' Even Saul couldn't believe it.

'Yes. Yes, I saw. Do you think it was wind?'

'Not a bit of it. That was a smile, a proper smile. Do it again, sweetheart, smile for Daddy.'

They waited, Saul jiggled the scrawny body between his square brown hands. The mouth opened, the skin stretched, and Hannah smiled. 'What did I tell you?' He put out his arm and pulled Rowan into his hug. She pressed her face against his chest, forcing back the tears.

They went out to the cinema to celebrate. It was some improbable adventure film with blood everywhere and car chases. After the fifth man had been horribly blasted all over the screen, Saul took Rowan's hand and led her out of the row, pushing past all the avid, popcorn-eating couples.

'Sorry — sorry — I'm blocking your view. Don't worry, it's an act of charity — no, we're not ill, but if we stay much longer we will be.'

Outside in the foyer, Rowan said, 'It wasn't that bad.'

334

'Yes it was. Anyway, you looked bored to tears. I want to talk about our wonderful baby, not sit and feel my brain turn to porridge. Whatever happened to the good films?'

Rowan giggled. 'Daddy said the best film ever was "Casablanca".'

'Man of insight, your dad. They don't make 'em like that any more.' He sucked in his lips, pretending great age and lost teeth.

'Stop it, you fool!' A policeman was watching them stonily, but Saul merely crouched to half his height and did his Quasimodo impersonation. 'The bells, the bells!'

Pink-faced and weak with laughter, Rowan dragged him off round the corner. He straightened up, held her and they kissed, very gently.

'I wish we could go to bed,' murmured Saul.

'Another six weeks, the doctor said.' Rowan's scar tissue had healed painfully. The hospital had removed some and restitched the wound. Saul was beginning to believe they would never touch again!

She put her hand to his cheek, trying to soothe and apologise. 'Let's walk,' she suggested.

He took her hand and squeezed it. 'Yes, let's. It's you with the sore bottom and it's me that's complaining. And on a day when Hannah smiled!'

They set off through Bradford's wide streets. Like many industrial cities, here and there great monolithic blocks of concrete stood in place of older, prettier buildings, but the Wool Exchange remained, and the steep side streets with their shops and warehouses. It was an exotic city too, peopled at night by Asian youths in billowing cotton trousers, here and there an older man shepherding his veiled womenfolk homeward. The dome of the Alhambra Theatre was like the relocation of an eastern temple, a monument to civic self-importance.

They walked hand in hand, for once taking the time to watch the world pass by. When Rowan tired, they sat by the fountain outside the Law Courts, watching the floodlights play upon the water.

'She never smiles for me,' said Rowan wistfully.

'But you never smile for her,' replied Saul.

She nodded. Sometimes the depth of her love for Hannah amazed her, but its shadow was the depth of her pain. 'Why us? Why her?' she burst out, and Saul shook his head.

'I don't know. It seems so cruel to do this to a little one. Life is everywhere: fit, healthy, lively babies. But — it seems to me it's only a tragedy if we make it one. If we love her for what she is, then we've a sweet, smiling little girl. We don't have to make her suffer because we're so greedy we want more.'

Rowan ducked her head into his chest. 'You're so much tougher than me. I'm stupid and practical. I'm always staring at the ground and you never look at it at all.'

He laughed. 'Which is why I keep falling over my feet, sweeting. Love you.'

'And I love you, so very much.'

They walked back, hand in hand, through the swirling river of people emerging from the cinema. In the car Saul played Frank Sinatra love songs on the cassette, while Rowan snuggled down into the cracked leather seats and was happy.

Chapter Twenty-Eight

There was something delicious, thought James, about the smell of a strange woman. Diana had excited him like this once. How long was it before strange became familiar, and ultimately commonplace? Two years perhaps? He had known Lin Yu just eighteen months, although of course he didn't see her all that often. If Richard was home, she would ring him at work and he would know not to call round on Wednesdays. Lately she had been ringing him quite often, he realised, although he hadn't heard a squeak from Richard. They remained, he and Richard, despite all his efforts, on terms of distant politeness.

He rolled over and nuzzled Lin Yu's flat belly. She languidly permitted it. Was he imagining a shade of impatience in her? Young and lovely girls only put up with old men for their money, he thought nastily. In one of those shifts which so alarmed people who knew him well, he lost his temper. 'What the hell's the matter with you? If you don't want to do this you can get out of the damned flat, I'm not paying to be tolerated!'

Lin Yu shrank back up the bed. 'Please, James,' she murmured. 'I think you must be very tired. I too am very tired. It has been a hard day.'

'You should have an easy day if you know I'm coming round. By the way, my wife's going on a trip. I want you to cancel everything, and I mean everything, for the next three weeks. I shall be coming here a lot.'

'But — you can't!' For the first time since he had known her she looked discomfited. Her hair was in a tangle over her shoulders, her knees poked through as angular as a child's.

337

'I can, my sweet,' he said with a purr.

She scrambled towards him, pressing herself against his back and caressing him with her little, sharp-fingered hands. 'But James, it is Richard! He will be here, his flat is being decorated, he will be staying here! I am so sorry, James, I will make it up to you.'

He caught her wrist and pushed it down to the bed. She followed and lay, trying to smile. 'Lin Yu,' he said softly, 'today I rang Richard's firm. He is in South Africa and has been for a month. So what was wrong with Wednesdays?'

Her only concession was a swallow. She tried to laugh. 'You have found me out, James. Good heavens.'

'Would you like to tell me about it?' She tried to wriggle out of his grasp but he gripped her narrow bones tight and she winced. 'That wasn't a request,' he added.

Physical violence frightened her a lot, her smooth saffron skin was tinged with grey. Speaking quickly, she said, 'I have a friend living with me. From Hong Kong, a good friend. He does not like you, James. He wants to marry me, and I should like to marry. So you see – ' Her voice cracked and tailed away.

He let her go and lay back, thinking. He was feeling old, but if he had seen himself then he would have felt better. There was something indestructibly youthful about James's long-boned legs and slim hips, something that not even grey hairs and a sagging belly could entirely destroy. 'Has he any money, this bloke?' he asked.

'He has a job in a supermarket. A manager.'

'Trainee manager, you mean.' James laughed at her. He knew Lin Yu's tastes were not likely to be satisfied by any modest income. It occurred to him that he had no real regard for her at all, he respected nothing except her expertise and that was odd, because he often liked the street girls, he liked their grit.

'Right,' he said at last. 'We can finish this now if you want. Out of the flat by the end of the week.'

'James! Oh, don't be so silly, James.' She began to stroke his foot, to conciliate him.

'Do you still see Richard?' he asked. It was for Richard he felt most aggrieved, because while he did not wish her to love himself, he thought she should love Richard. Although no doubt Richard also treated Lin Yu to this or that trinket, James preferred to think that their relationship was not in the least businesslike. He had a slice of Richard's girlfriend, and left the rest, complete with emotional ties, to his son.

'I see Richard sometimes,' she said cautiously. 'My friend — he does not like Richard.'

'Bit of a pain, this friend of yours,' said James. He visualised Lin Yu and her skinny little Chinese, which admittedly was a much more sensible physical match for her. 'I'm not paying for his little love nest. Look, I'll do this for you. You can keep the flat, for now. I don't want any trouble over when I want to come, though. I ring you and that's that. I come first or you're out. As for Richard, I'll not have you upsetting him. I'm having a shooting weekend while my wife's away, he can bring you. I expect you to make him accept. And I want him looking happy.'

She got off the bed and went to a little box on the dressing table. It was cocaine and she brought it over to the bed, on a beautiful glass tray. James prepared to snort the drug, but then he stopped and tapped the straw on the girl's hand. 'Tell me what you think of me. Honestly.'

For a minute he thought she was going to fob him off with a platitude but she said, 'You are a frightening man, James. You have no care for anyone.'

He thought of Diana, Richard, Nicholas. He said, 'Not true. I just don't care for you much, that's all. But I don't see why that should inconvenience anybody.'

He took up the straw, sniffed hard and felt the sharp burn in his nostrils. The high was immediate, the colours in the room leaped out at him with sudden brilliance. Lin Yu was snorting as well. As she bent he came at her from behind, breaking into her little body like a bull. The feeling of power, the subjugation of this woman, was total pleasure.

When James bought Aspley Manor he also acquired the shooting rights to a considerable area of wood and moor. The woods yielded mainly driven pheasants and a few woodcock, and the moor was grouse with a small flight pond for those who wanted to get up at dawn and freeze while waiting to pot duck. The idea of it pleased him but in reality James was a mediocre shot. He spent a fortune on shooting lessons but was too impatient to listen to what he was told. But, since the moor was keepered and had to be shot, he held weekends. This year he could get at least one out of the way without Diana recording every miss.

It was early in the season and a number of people were still away, so as a last-minute thought he included Saul. That way he felt sure there would be at least one person shooting less well than himself and he could patronise to his heart's content. Besides, he could afford to be sorry for him now, saddled with Hannah. James fingered the photograph of Nicholas he kept on his desk. He thought of the little boy's laugh, his happy chuckle. He had much to be grateful for.

On the day itself, Land Rovers and Range Rovers roared up to the house. Caterers had been called in to provide everything from drinks and bacon sandwiches to a lavish over-the-top lunch, which Diana would have stopped if she had known, since it was a trademark of the nouveau riche. So were James's guns, too new and prettily scrolled all over with pictures of deer and birds. He had once been heard advising the owner of a valuable and well-worn sidelock on how to get one more or less the same, a tale on which that venerable shooting man dined out still.

When Saul stepped out of his Aston, James at once strolled over to him.

'How are you, old fellow? I can lend you a gun if you need one.'

'That's OK, James, I've brought my own,' said Saul. James felt a flicker of annoyance because Saul ought to be a novice, he owed it to his elder brother.

They both stood and watched as Richard's latest sports car chugged up, with that ridiculous pant of a high performance engine trying to crawl.

'Ye Gods, that's a Maserati,' said Saul in wonderment. 'Do you print money for him, James?'

'It's you that's out of step, Saul, old boy,' said James. 'The rest of the family likes making money.'

Saul observed Lin Yu stepping out of the car in a short mink jacket and thigh-high leather boots worn over jeans. 'And he likes spending it, I see. Wow!'

James allowed a smile to cross his face. Lin Yu looked exquisite, her hair in a pony tail that stretched past her waist. She teetered behind Richard like a faithful dog. 'I don't know why you insisted on Lin Yu coming,' said Richard as he approached. 'She hates the outdoors.'

'Does she?' said James disinterestedly. 'Let's have a snifter or two.'

He thought that Saul had probably started already, he smelled of mouthwash. They drank brandy and the conversation got louder and more raucous. The men with dogs began to look at their watches.

'Right then, we'll be off,' said James at last, and began directing people to get in this or that car. It was a muddle because he told Lin Yu to get into a Range Rover with two exuberant Labradors and it was clear she did not like dogs.

'Oh, for God's sake,' said Richard and shoved her into the front seat of a dogless Land Rover. James felt a stab of irritation. He had made a considerable effort to give Richard a pleasant day and he wished he would appreciate it.

Up on the moor they had to walk about half a mile from the track. Lin Yu struggled in Richard's wake; her little voice calling 'Richard! Richard!' could be heard almost continuously. The keeper, a dour man who felt he deserved better things, muttered to Saul, 'Right bloody picnic this is! No decent guns, dogs half-trained and fucking Susie Wong. My poor birds don't deserve it, I don't mind telling.'

'Get me a good spot, will you?' asked Saul, *sotto voce*.

'I should think I will, sir,' said the keeper. 'You're the only chance we've got of hitting a sodding thing.'

Consequently, Saul found himself in the middle of the line. A crack clay pigeon shot, with considerable experience of live game, it amazed him that James thought him a beginner. What more proof did he need that James never exercised his brain for a moment on anyone other than himself? He leaned against the front wall of the butt, setting out his cartridges and checking his gun. The air, still tinged with summer's warmth, smelled of earth and bracken. Bilberry bushes grew amidst the heather, he could see some fat late berries. The grouse would be feeding on bilberry, they would be full of it.

He tried not to think of the grouse who, because of him, had enjoyed their last breakfast. Live shooting was wonderful, difficult and exhilarating, but he hated the birds afterwards, still warm but with sightless eyes. He wouldn't do this any more, he thought to himself. Hannah, and his awareness of her, had altered his perception. He had to consider lives other than his own which, although different, need not be worthless. If he could destroy a bird for the pleasure of it, why not Hannah, for the convenience of it? He often wondered if that was what the hospital had intended.

The birds started to come over, high and fast, difficult shots. He took the first two with a right and left, and despite a fusillade they were the only two that fell.

'Well done,' called James in an affronted voice.

Out of the corner of his eye, Saul could see Lin Yu sitting outside Richard's butt and effectively sending all the birds to the other end of the line. Presumably Richard could not see her and assumed he was getting a thin time purely from chance. He saw three birds rocketing towards that end, but they changed course abruptly and gave him another brace. The way a shot bird would fold its wings and plummet out of the sky, it caught at his soul in triumph and in ecstasy. As he reloaded, he took out his hip flask and sipped at it, smoothly swinging his gun up to meet the next wave of birds. Dimly he heard Richard cursing Lin Yu.

On most shoots they would see lunch off and get back out again, but James's feast was not designed to be eaten or digested quickly. Once back at the house, a good drive and not convenient, the guns started to sink the booze. Saul got himself a whisky.

'You certainly know what you're doing,' said James stiffly. 'I didn't know you shot.'

'I used to do quite a bit,' said Saul. 'Not since I married Rowan, though.'

'Enjoyed making us all look fools, didn't you?'

Saul laughed. 'What I enjoyed most was watching Richard suffer from that girl. Was it your idea to get her here? She's ruining his day.'

James glanced across to where Lin Yu was desperately trying to amuse Richard, although it was clear that he wanted to talk man-talk with the others. It occurred to him that since it had been his, obviously misguided, idea, he ought to help out. He went across to her.

'Why don't I show you round the house, Lin Yu? I'm sure you'll be interested.'

'Oh! Thank you, James!' She beamed at him and rested a tiny hand on his arm. Richard said, 'Good idea,' shortly, and turned away.

James and Lin Yu left the room. The babble of conversation receded to a murmur punctuated by someone's bellowing laugh. The caterers clattered in the kitchen but otherwise all was quiet. James led the way upstairs.

'Why did you make me come?' complained Lin Yu. 'He does not want it, I do not want it. I am cold. I could have spent my day with Chang instead.'

'Don't fuss,' said James. He took her into the bedroom he shared with Diana, half thinking of using the bed, but then he thought what an insult that would be to his wife. Lin Yu said breathlessly, 'Your house is so beautiful. I would give so much for a house like this.'

'You'll not get it with your Chink supermarket manager,' said James. All of a sudden he felt terribly randy. He unzipped his trousers and allowed his penis to rear up. Lin Yu let out her breath in an angry sigh.

'Take off your jacket,' he told her. Beneath the pure silk lining she was naked. Her brown nipples stood up against her pale skin. He half sat himself on the dressing table and beckoned to her. She came, putting her hands on his thighs and kneeling on Diana's low stool. His erection fitted easily into her mouth, he heard himself chuckling as her tongue lapped the tip. Every now and then she held him with her hands and took him into her throat, he turned his palms outward and rubbed her nipples. Instinctively he knew that he was arousing her. The more he rubbed the more sensually she worked on him.

Saul, finding the downstairs cloakroom occupied, came upstairs in search of another bathroom. The door to the bedroom was an inch ajar. He pushed it aside. There, her narrow back arched and her head bent, was the Chinese girl and above her black head James was grinning. In the side mirror of the dressing-table was reflected the girl's face, enraptured by the phallus she was licking. They were so absorbed they noticed nothing. As he stepped away from the door, he heard James groan ecstatically.

Only a few guns went out after lunch, Richard and Saul included. James stayed drinking with his cronies but Lin Yu trailed along after Richard. Saul found himself looking at her, recalling her face, her little breasts pressed into James's palms. He hated himself for his excitement.

For some reason the birds were flying like chickens. The

shots were easy, even though he was squiffy Saul could hardly miss. After half an hour he decided to quit, leaving half a dozen or so men still shooting. He felt in need of a quiet walk back to the cars. In fact, he thought he might walk right to the house. Mist was starting to rise in the valley. From a distance somewhere he heard a train, it was strange how sound carried on to the moor. Close at hand he heard repeated, rhythmic grunting.

He took a step towards a clump of wet bracken. The back of Richard's head appeared, and his backside pumped, up and down. Almost without knowing he crept a step nearer, until he could see the girl's sticklike legs spread wide. The muscles in his gut clamped tight, he gripped his gun hard and turned away.

All the way back to the house he thought of Lin Yu, but not really of her, only of sex. It had been months, he had never known such celibacy. All he wanted was a woman, all he would ever want again. If only, if only he could get in his car, get back to Rowan and die in her.

The impossibility of it choked him. She was still raw and torn, the blasted nanny was there, and besides, to go back to the flat was to take up the burden again. Sex was such a selfish need, it could not be allowed to take precedence over responsibility.

When he got back to the house they were all still drinking. James was well away, smoking cigars and full of self-satisfaction. 'Have a drink,' he said to Saul, waving him towards the row of bottles. 'We've been talking about you. Don here says you're building a house!'

Saul slugged down the whisky and topped himself up. 'I'm thinking about it. On the site of the old cottages. There's nearly an acre all told, even if it is an odd shape. Rowan thinks I'm insane. She thinks we'll go bust.'

'She's damn well right,' said James. 'God, you never could hang on to money.'

'It'll cost a mint,' agreed Saul. 'I want to include a

345

swimming pool for Hannah. Now we've got her, we ought to be closer to the mill, and there it is. The architect's keen as mustard.'

'All they're ever keen on is spending money,' declared James. He turned to encompass the whole gathering. 'Did I tell you about the alterations they wanted me to do to the combing plant? My God, it would have broken me, even me! They even dared to try and swing it on the factory inspectorate, bring in the law to convince me, but of course I knocked that into touch.'

Saul finished his whisky and drifted to the door. He had slipped the half-empty bottle into the pocket of his shooting jacket, where it rested as neatly and secretively as any poacher's bag. His head boiled and his body burned, he hadn't anyone to lend him solace. The evening air made him stagger a little as he walked to his car, but once behind the wheel he felt OK. Only when he began to drive did he realise how much he'd had. The road was coming at him in waves, there was no way he could get home in this state. He saw a wide grassy track leading off into some trees, and the vague thought came to him that he could stop up there and sleep it off. Somehow, while negotiating the ruts of past tractors, the car slithered sideways, putting one rear wheel into the ditch. He was stuck.

Saul got out and stared at the situation. Perhaps he could go back to Aspley Manor, or walk to a telephone. But why did he not for once please only himself? Chances were he'd get booked for drunken driving if he did ask for help. There was a blanket on the back seat of the car. In a moment of rare, selfish pleasure he put it round his shoulders, got back into his seat and opened the bottle of whisky.

Chapter Twenty-Nine

Rowan started to become anxious at around seven in the evening. Saul had promised to be back by then, because it was the nanny's evening off and he knew how difficult Rowan found it alone with Hannah. All the worst things seemed to happen then, all the choking and non-stop crying. But tonight things went fairly well, a feed in three-quarters of an hour and almost instant sleep. Rowan tried to clear up the flat; it was full of baby things. She nibbled on a biscuit, feeling flabby and frumpish, for although she was back to her old weight her shape had changed. Mr. Suzman wouldn't make for another six weeks, he said there was no point until her figure settled down.

She feared it was the end of the old her. She had hips now, and her breasts had taken on definition. If Saul had said he liked the new model she would have felt happier, but some- how there never seemed the time to talk personally. Some- times she and Saul seemed so right together. That night in Bradford, just walking around, remained in her mind as per- fection; but in the midst of the mill, and Hannah, and their increasingly frosty discussions about strategy, romantic time-wasting seemed irrelevant.

The plans for the new house were in a large brown folder on the television, beneath a packet of disposable nappies. Rowan extricated them and settled down to look at the house Saul wanted. A spectacular, wide-roofed bungalow, walled off from the mill, built over a half-cellar that was to be a swimming pool. Glazed doors led from the pool to a garden, intended to grow on what hadn't been earth for hundreds of years. The house itself was designed around a central conservatory, letting light through a glass floor into the pool and, so Saul insisted, trapping sunshine to warm the house.

It was perfect for Hannah. There was only one door, although the windows were all designed so an adult could swivel them, and climb through in an emergency. The pool was inaccessible from the house. The only way in was the sliding, and child-proof, doors from the garden. No stairs, no cars, even the garaging was set outside the enclosing wall. It was a house where a little, retarded child could grow up in sunshine and safety. Even taking into account that they had the site and a large amount of stone, it was costed at over a hundred and fifty thousand pounds.

Rowan chewed her knuckles. Saul was standing firm on the house. He had let her have the nanny, let her back into the firm, but on this he insisted. And on paper she supposed they could afford it, provided absolutely nothing went wrong. They had an order book that could sustain borrowing of this sort; even her carding machine now looked inevitable, whereas before it had seemed gross extravagance. But she wasn't used to believing in luck and hoping for the best, it wasn't her style. She knew, only too well, how narrow was the line between prosperity and ruin, how fickle taste could ruin a business which last month looked good. Saul talked of Bardsey's, but Bardsey's was a case in point. They had expanded into businesses that teetered on the verge of making losses, that cost the parent company time and capital. Yet when James first moved that way no one saw the problems, he had been universally applauded. If they built the house and failed, all the people who were now urging them on would nod sagely and talk about wanton extravagance.

Still, as Saul said, the house was an asset. They could sell that long before the mill, it wasn't money down the drain. Sighing, she put the plans away and looked again at her watch. A quarter past eight and still no Saul.

She rang James. 'Hello? Rowan here. I'm sorry to bother you but Saul's not back and I wondered if he'd left.'

'When I said you were to keep him on a short leash, I didn't mean choke him with it,' said James blearily. In the background there was the sound of men roaring with laughter, and he yelled to them, 'Shut up, you lot! What time did Saul leave, anyone know?' Turning back to the 'phone he said, 'About half-four he left here. He'd had a bit, though.'

'So have you,' said Rowan shortly. 'I'm coming out, he might have crashed or anything.'

In jeans and jumper, and slipping a battered leather jacket over the top, she carefully put Hannah in her travelling basket and went down to her car. She felt scared and shivery, but at least she was doing something. Saul was her rock, she needed him to lean on and his absence unnerved her.

After a crisp day, rain was starting to fall. Her headlights wavered through the drizzle and she realised that even if Saul's car passed her she wouldn't know it. This was a stupid errand, but she went anyway. In the back the baby made sucking noises in her sleep. When she stopped at traffic lights, Rowan turned and looked at her. Such a funny little face in that silly woolly bonnet; such a sweet, defenceless little girl. The wave of almost tearful love, coming from nowhere and swamping her, left Rowan gulping. Someone behind tooted, she fumbled with the gears and nearly stalled. If Saul was dead, killed in some horrible way, there was only her and Hannah, they only had each other.

Soon, though, she was at Aspley Manor, and had seen no crash, nothing. The men had persuaded the caterers to bring them a take-away. The drawing-room was littered with carrier bags and reeked of curry.

'Still not found him?' said James, lurching towards her. 'My God, but you look super! Got a pair of tits at last. Bet Saul knows what to do with those, the dirty bugger!'

'Shut up, James,' said Rowan distantly. 'I don't think Mother will like chicken curry on her Isfahan rug, but you never know.'

'Oh, bloody hell,' said James, following her eyes to where

a carton was leaking in a thick brown pool. He got out his handkerchief and bent down to try and scoop it back in. Rowan sighed meaningfully.

'Does anyone know where Saul might be?' she asked of the company in general. 'Had he had much to drink?' She thought there was no one sober enough to tell her. Men stared at her owlishly, gradually losing the party spirit and starting to feel sleepy or ill.

A tall young man squeezed past her into the room. He was carrying a bottle of wine and a corkscrew. Behind him came a tiny Chinese girl in a mink jacket, carrying a tray. Rowan thought she had never seen anyone look so viciously annoyed in all her life. The girl shot her a glance of white rage. 'Can you help me?' she asked. 'I'm looking for my husband, has he left?'

'I've no idea,' snapped Lin Yu. 'For myself I should like never to have come here, I should like to go!'

The tall man turned on her and said in exasperation, 'Then bloody go! Come on, let's both go, I didn't want the food anyway. I don't know why I let the old man persuade me to come, and I certainly don't know why *you* had to elbow your way in. Excuse me.' He tried to get past Rowan again but she held on to his arm.

'Do you know my husband? Saul Barton.'

'Er — yes, I do. I'm Richard. And you must be —'

'Rowan. Rowan Judge.' She was aware of him looking at her, making connections, remembering about Hannah. She turned away.

The three of them went out to the cars. Rowan said, 'If he's not at the flat when I get back, I'll call the police.'

'I wouldn't, if I were you,' said Richard. 'He'd had quite a bit at lunchtime, and he had a flask in the afternoon. If they find him sleeping it off in the car, that's his licence gone.'

'He could have crashed! He could be hurt!'

'You'd have heard by now.'

Lin Yu, standing by the locked Maserati, said shrilly; 'Richard! I am getting very cold standing here waiting.'

350

'Get stuffed,' said Richard under his breath, and Rowan stared at him. He shrugged. 'Today is the end of the road for me and her. We are what is known as ill-suited, and we know it even if Dad doesn't. He's behaving like a professional matchmaker.'

'Probably fancies her himself,' said Rowan abstractedly, and got into her car.

Richard came to the window and said, 'He might have stopped on a side road. You go ahead, you might see something. I'll keep a look-out, too.'

Rowan drove off slowly, trying to steer and look down tracks and lanes at one and the same time. The Maserati, behind her, seeing the countryside illuminated by her lights, had a better view. Suddenly there was a raucous blast from the horn, almost a donkey's bray. Rowan stamped on the brakes and Hannah woke up. Rowan left her grizzling and jumped out of the car.

'What is it?'

'I saw something up there, your lights just caught it. Probably a courting couple.'

Lin Yu leaned out of the Maserati. 'Richard! I wish to get home at once, please!'

He took no notice and started off up the grassy track. Rowan, about to go after him, remembered Hannah and picked her up out of her basket. Holding the baby tight to her, she followed Richard's dimly-seen shape. Twenty yards up the track he stopped. There was a car all right. She was almost up to it before she realised it was Saul's.

'It's stuck in the ditch,' said Richard. 'He must have left it.'

'Then where is he?' wailed Rowan. Now she was genuinely frightened; she couldn't imagine where Saul might be. Hannah was wingeing in earnest now. She ought to be fed, she ought not to be out in the night, they had weak chests, these babies. Rowan said, 'Here,' and pushed Hannah at Richard. He took hold awkwardly but she gave him no choice. When she opened the car door the internal light came on. In the weak yellow glow they saw him.

'He's dead,' squeaked Rowan. Saul's eyes were half open and turned up in his head, showing the whites. His mouth hung slack and he was sprawled in an unnatural position, half-twisted on the back seat. Hannah's crying was like a wailing cat, adding an eerie dimension to the nightmare.

'For God's sake, take this baby,' said Richard. 'He's only drunk, I think.'

'Nobody can be that drunk,' said Rowan. 'He can't be!' Nonetheless she took hold of Hannah and held her close, closer than ever before. She rocked herself and the child together.

Richard leaned in the back door and shook Saul's shoulders. He shook him hard, and harder still. 'Saul. Saul! Wake up, will you?'

Saul groaned. His eyes moved, the whites swivelled back into his skull. 'Leave me alone,' he mumbled.

'Saul, it's me,' said Rowan, trying to reach in with her free hand and touch him. 'Wake up, please, you're frightening me.'

'He's absolutely out, I'm afraid,' said Richard. He held up the empty whisky bottle. 'Must have decided to make a night of it.'

'He knew I was waiting for him. He knew I needed him.' Rowan felt frantic and tearful.

'Go and sit in your car,' said Richard. 'I'll get him to the road, we can move this in the morning.'

Richard heaved at Saul's loglike body. Once he got him out into the fresh air he seemed to revive a little, enough to groan, stagger briefly on rubber legs, and collapse. Lin Yu tripped down the track.

'Richard! I will not wait any longer.'

'Give me a hand, will you? His wife's got the baby, and she's in tears, poor girl.'

She stepped back, away from Saul. 'He's being sick. He's disgusting.'

Cursing her, Richard wiped Saul's mouth with a clump of grass and resumed his heaving and tugging. It took twenty minutes to negotiate the few yards to Rowan's car, but at least by the time they got there Saul was semi-conscious.

'Where do you live?' asked Richard. 'I'd better help you with him.'

Rowan shook her head. Her brief lapse of control was gone; she was shaken, obviously so, but in command of herself. 'We're in a flat, a penthouse. I'll get the night porter to help, you don't have to bother. Anyway, I think your girlfriend is getting upset.'

He grinned. 'That does not concern me. Are you sure you'll be all right?'

'Yes. Thank you. Thanks a lot.'

She drove off quickly. From the Maserati he heard Lin Yu's shrill voice calling 'Richard. Richard!' and he knew that he didn't care if he never heard her again as long as he lived.

Although it felt terribly late to Rowan, it was still only just eleven. One of the other flat dwellers was holding a party; people in evening dress were coming and going on the stairs and in the lift. Rowan went and whispered confidentially to the doorman.

'I'm afraid my husband's ill. I don't want to bring him through here.'

'Oh. Oh, I see, Mrs. Barton.' Rowan saw from his face that the man saw only too well. The humiliation of it made her flush. She wished she had accepted Richard's offer of help.

'If you take him round to the car park we can put him in the service lift,' said the man wearily. 'He's not being sick, is he?'

'No,' lied Rowan, and went on frantically, stupidly, 'he isn't drunk! It's 'flu, I think. Some kind of bug.'

'Is it?'

Rowan slunk away and drove round to the service entrance, amidst the dustbins and empty bottles. It seemed horribly appropriate.

Between them Rowan and the doorman hauled Saul into the lift. They propped him against the wall but he slid to the floor and sat, his legs splayed apart. He kept mumbling, and at one point said quite lucidly, 'Sorry about this. One too many after dinner.'

'Couple of bottles too many if you ask me,' said the doorman philosophically. 'Does he do this often, love?'

'Of course not! He never drinks normally. It's gone to his head.'

The man gave her a speaking look. At that moment Rowan could willingly have kicked Saul all the way down the lift shaft, she could have killed him for putting her through this shame. Hannah was crying, a truly hungry wail, and the doorman said: 'I suppose having a kiddie like that could drive you to it.'

The lift stopped and Rowan led the way along the hall to the flat. Some people raced up the stairs, round and down again, playing some idiot party game. But at last they were in the flat, at last she could hide him from the world. She gave the doorman a fiver but said no word of thanks. It enraged her to be in the same room as someone who thought Hannah was the cause of things, who wanted to put ordinary human weaknesses at her innocent door.

Later Barbara came back and together they undressed Saul and put him to bed. 'He's been working too hard,' said Barbara. She was a nice girl, kind and sensible. Rowan felt better knowing she was there.

The trouble with the hostel, thought Sally, had nothing to do with the utilitarian nature of the place, or the thin walls, or even the dragon of a matron who ruled like a tyrant queen over her subjects. It was the smell; an amorphous, institutional smell, made up of disinfectant and cabbage and the dust of a thousand impersonal corners. It was supposed to be home and yet it was impossible to mark it with the prints of one's personality.

She got off her narrow bed and went over to the dressing-table, staring at herself in the tarnished mirror. It seemed to her she saw a face that could have been anyone's. She could be anyone, she was faceless in a faceless place. Even her friends were interchangeable; one would do as well as another, to fill the emptiness. She was like a plant in a pond, roots floating aimlessly. No settled home, no settled feeling of being herself.

All her life Sally had seen herself through the eyes of others. She was as she was perceived, a merry little girl, a difficult teenager, a wanton. Since the row with Saul she hadn't known who she was. There was no one to tell her. How she wished he had loved her, taken her to bed and held her, not because of anything she felt for him but because then she would have had her place in his life. He would have owed her something, it would have been a hook to hold her to the family. Almost like being a second wife, a secret wife.

For her, the sex was always a means to an end. She didn't enjoy it particularly. She would lie in the back of a car with some guy up inside her and watch the lights against the sky. The girls here said you shouldn't do it till at least the third date, but why would they see her again if they couldn't have it? Sally always went out without her knickers and if they didn't try she felt stupid and ugly. She was only happy when they were holding her and gasping, saying, 'God, you were wonderful! I love you. I love you.' Anyone could have her, any time, and all she asked was that they liked her, just a little.

There was nothing to do on Sunday afternoons, and it was on that day that her loneliness became unbearable. The other girls were nice enough but she could tell they didn't really like her. Perhaps she was too posh, or too young, or even too generous, because she often bought things for people, even those she hardly knew. They were friendly while she was there but afterwards she was sure they laughed amongst themselves.

She got up quickly and pulled on jeans and a sweater. The ice rink was open on Sundays, she would skate round and round, she might meet someone she knew, some boy. If she bought some coffee and stood drinking it, people would think her friend was still skating. They wouldn't know she was really on her own. You could pretend, skating.

'I am so sorry. Did I hurt you?'

Sally looked up into the dark face. She had fallen heavily and felt dazed, for she had been lost in some fantasy, a mile away from the reality of a crowded ice rink. 'I wasn't looking. It was my fault,' she said jerkily.

'Not at all, I was skating too fast. Come, let me take you to the side.' He helped her up, an Asian of about middle height, with black eyes, blacker hair, and a fierce, warrior face. 'I must find your friends,' he said.

'My — my friends had to go. I was just going, I only stayed for one last round.'

'You like skating?'

She thought. 'Yes. When I'm skating, I don't have to think.'

Her jeans were wet from the ice, the air was heavy with beat music, the rink wild with ice hockey players practising. It was an odd place for meditation. 'Will your parents mind if I buy you some coffee?' asked the man.

'I don't think so,' said Sally. She dropped her eyes to the floor and waited. When he returned with two plastic cups, they stood side by side, sipping. 'I've got to go now,' she said.

'Of course.' He took her cup.

'I have to be back at my hostel. They give me tea on a Sunday.'

'You don't live at home?'

'My parents are divorced.'

He said nothing, but stayed by her side while she went and returned her skates and got her shoes. Sally felt him watching her. She was conscious of each and every movement she made, because he was conscious of it. Her feet, such little feet, slid almost sensuously into her shoes. Her blonde and silky hair, tossed aside, brushed against his face.

'I should like to take you home,' he said.

'Thank you,' said Sally gravely. 'I should like that.'

His name was Mohammed Shafir. He was born in Pakistan, but had come over to England with his parents when he was tiny. 'You see, I am English,' he said, but his language held the distinctive Asian lilt. His mother tongue was Gujerati; he spoke it at home every day of his life until he went to school.

'What do you do?' asked Sally, aware that as they walked he was punctiliously shielding her from the traffic.

He hesitated. 'I am a pattern weaver,' he said at last. 'I would like to be something better someday. But I am the eldest in my family, I could not continue my studies. I should like to be a lawyer.'

'I see.' She made as if to step off the pavement but Mohammed caught her arm. A bus swept round from the right, an inch from Sally's toes. Bradford's wide roads and infamous one-way system required constant vigilance from pedestrians. 'You must be careful,' said Mohammed.

'Thank you. Yes.'

Sally caught the bus back to the hostel and Mohammed came with her. They conversed politely, about his work, about her work, about his family, about hers. 'I'm quite rich,' said Sally suddenly. 'My sister runs a woollen mill. I own a quarter.'

Mohammed's dark eyes stared into the pale depths of her own. 'You must not say such things,' he said gently. 'I might be anybody.'

'But you're not, are you? You're Mohammed. I want to be friends with you.'

The bus jerked to a stop and some white teenage boys got on. When they saw Mohammed and Sally, they nudged each other. 'Take a look at that, then. Wog's doing all right for himself, ain't he? What's the matter, darling, couldn't you get a liquorice stick at the sweet shop?'

When they received no response, the boys went off down the bus. Mohammed said, 'I am so sorry. They have insulted

357

you. I am embarrassed that you should have to tolerate such words.'

'It wasn't your fault. I don't know why people say such things, it's not as if we're doing anyone any harm.'

'Would you like me to go?'

Sally shook her head. 'I want us to be friends.'

At the hostel he shook hands with her formally and took the number of the hostel 'phone. 'Can I lunch with you tomorrow?' he asked. 'I work in the evenings, from seven o'clock.'

'Oh. Oh, I see. I have lunch at twelve, will that be all right?'

'You would please me very much, Sally.'

Alone in her room, she felt light-headed. She had been following the formal steps of a dance, a courtship dance. He was so gentle, so considerate, so wonderfully good-looking! There was something, too, in his very presence that affected her, some mutual charge of sexuality. He had barely touched her and yet she felt more aroused now than ever in her life. Unlike Sally, who flailed about hopelessly in a morass of indecision, Mohammed was firm and set and decided. The attraction of certainty was almost magnetic.

They met every day of that week. They never kissed, but simply held hands under the table at lunch. For the first time in her life Sally began to weave daydreams about someone, imagining what it would be like if he kissed her or held her. When she thought about his face, like something chiselled into the rock of a Maharajah's palace, she experienced shudders of desire. His skin was nothing like the pasty flesh of white men, it even smelled vaguely oriental. Driving a beat-up old station-wagon, he took her to obscure curry houses in distant parts of the city where she sat and watched his hands move as he ate.

He had Saturday nights off. The first Saturday they met at lunchtime and drove out of town, up on to the moors. There was an ice-cream van parked at the side of the road and they bought a cornet each. Mohammed wore a long pale scarf round his neck. Sally wore no knickers.

It was a beautiful day, warm and breezy. White clouds bustled across the sky, and two magpies sat on a rock and squawked at each other. There was an outcrop some distance away, topped by a few scrawny trees. 'Race you!' said Mohammed, and set off, with Sally in hopeless pursuit.

He waited for her behind a tree and jumped out, yelling 'Boo!' Sally shrieked and fell panting against him; he wrestled with her playfully and somehow she was down with Mohammed half on top of her.

'Please! No, please!' He had dreamed of this moment, longed for it, but now it had come he begged her to push him off.

'Don't you love me? Please say you do!'

She lay on the grass, her full breasts pointing up at him and tears in her lovely blue eyes. He had never seen anything so fragile and desirable, so in need of his masculinity.

'I love you more than you can understand,' he said reverently.

Her arms came up around his neck, he was tasting the dizzying sweetness of her kisses. He wasn't a virgin, he had had a woman before, a prostitute. She had been businesslike, he almost revolted. Afterwards he had hated himself but he had lived those few moments again and again since. But Sally! This! He found his hands on her breasts, reaching up under her clothes to find taut nipples. With no intention of asking for more he watched himself lifting her skirt, discovering dark blonde hair, discovering that she cried out in joy when he touched her.

'Stop me!' he begged, pulling his clothes open. But Sally lay back on the ground, waiting for him.

He was very quiet afterwards, and very gentle with her. 'What's the matter?' asked Sally nervously. 'I thought I pleased you.'

'Yes. Yes, you did. But — Sally, you have known men. You have done this before.'

'No, I haven't! No!' She saw his image of her crashing

about them both; he had been entranced by her supposed innocence and cleanliness. Flailing about for some lie that would please him, she said, 'It was my uncle! He did it to me, I couldn't stop him. He'd come to my room at night, I couldn't do anything!'

'Why could you not tell your mother, your father?'

'My father was dead! And my mother wouldn't have done anything. Don't hate me, please don't!'

She flung herself against him, weeping hysterically. He stroked her hair. 'Little bird. Sweet little bird. They take no care of you, your family. From this day, in our hearts, we are married. One day we shall be married in the eyes of the world.'

Sally's sobs choked and died. For all her days there would be Mohammed, loving her, telling her what to do. Once there had been Daddy, and after him a succession of faces, using her, discarding her. But here was Mohammed, taking Daddy's place, loving her and treasuring her. Blood thundered in her ears, she could hear his voice coming from a long way away. 'Sally! My darling, please!' Mohammed would love her forever.

On the day after James's shoot, Rowan paced the flat, taut with unexpressed rage. Saul was still sleeping it off, a loglike figure stinking of booze. Rowan felt she would burst if she didn't talk to someone.

She rang Sally to ask her to meet for lunch. The appalling matron answered and when Rowan gave Sally's name the woman said, 'Are you ringing for him then, is that your game? I told him he's not to call. I don't want him here and I've told madam that as well. She should know better, girl of her upbringing. That's the trouble nowadays. They've got no standards, drop their knickers for any monkey.'

Rowan said, 'I'm her sister. I should like to speak to Sally, please.'

'And I haven't got time to go up and down those stairs, up and down twenty times a day and what thanks do I get? I tell you —'

Rowan replaced the receiver. Either the woman had been half-mad when she took the job, or the girls had driven her to it. She decided to drive round, escaping the flat for half an hour or so. Barbara could look after Hannah.

The hostel was in a once-respectable street. In the past, girls from there had tripped in neat white blouses to office jobs in town, and the hostel rules had been only what any caring parent would expect. Nowadays it was like trying to impose the convent on a tribe of Apaches. The girls saw no reason for coming in at ten, signing in and signing out, meeting their boyfriends in the front hall under the vigilant eye of the matron. The result was a clandestine world of men in the bedrooms, drink under the stairs and a discreet but thriving drug culture. Girls in various wild and wonderful costumes drifted in and out, past the neighbouring doss houses, sleazy pubs and derelict shops.

Rowan parked in the street outside, and went in search of Sally. The place smelled of cheap disinfectant and there were notices everywhere, exhorting girls to come in at ten and refrain from washing dishes in the basins. Rowan ignored the one saying 'All visitors must report to the desk' and ran upstairs to Sally's room. She rapped on the door, calling, 'Sally! Sally, it's me.' From within came the sound of muffled voices and people scrambling furtively. Rowan waited, and after a minute knocked again.

The door opened. Sally's face appeared round it. She seemed to be holding a sheet against herself. 'Have you come to collect me? Don't come in, I'll be out in a minute, Ro.'

'Who've you got in there?' Rowan pushed the door aside and rushed in. Lying in the bed, smoking a cigarette, was an extremely good-looking young man. His hair was thick and black, he had piercing black eyes, and he was Asian.

'Oh, my God!' said Rowan.

'I told you not to come in,' said Sally.

She dropped the sheet and started to get dressed. Rowan looked from Sally's white body, even the pubic hair a dark

361

gold, to the brown man in the bed.

'I think you should leave,' said the man.

'I think you had better go,' said Rowan. 'I don't like people who prey upon my sister.'

He stubbed his cigarette out and pulled himself up in the bed. 'I am so sorry. I did not realise who you were. My clothes, Sally.'

Obediently Sally passed them to him. Their hands touched and held for a brief second. Rowan turned her back while the man got dressed.

'Who is he, Sally?' she asked icily.

'I didn't know you wanted to be introduced. Rowan, meet Mohammed Shafir. Mohammed, this is my sister, Rowan Barton. You can turn round now, he's decent.'

'Not a word I would have used myself,' said Rowan. 'What is he doing here? What are you thinking of, Sally?'

Sally said nothing, instead brushing her hair with fierce strokes.

Mohammed took the brush from her and continued more gently. 'Your sister is right to be upset,' he soothed. 'She thinks I am taking advantage of you.'

'Well? Aren't you?' demanded Rowan.

His liquid brown eyes watched her, giving nothing away. He continued to brush and caress Sally's hair, as if it were the finest silk.

Sally said, 'I'm happy. I'm happier than I've ever been, don't make it dirty.'

'I can't make it anything. It is what it is. Oh God, I wish Mother was here.'

'She wouldn't care,' said Sally.

'That's not true.'

Rowan believed in Diana's care, but not in her expression of it. She gave everything or nothing, devoting herself to a child to the exclusion of all else, only to change seemingly overnight. There was no constant concern, no assurance of continued interest. That had been Andrew's strength, and it had died with him. She said, 'You've got to stop.'

'Why?'

'Oh, for God's sake, Sally, we can't talk in front of him!' Rowan waved a furious hand at Sally's lover.

He was one of the most good-looking men she had ever seen, with a clean, arresting face, white teeth flashing. Only as tall as Rowan herself, he was inches taller than Sally. Although he had finished brushing her hair, he continued to touch her, a gentle, almost reverent touch. 'Your sister is right,' said Mohammed. 'We must explain to her.'

'Don't tell me you were exercising,' said Rowan through her teeth.

Mohammed said, 'But of course not. We were making love.'

Rowan turned on her heel and prepared to go. 'There is absolutely no point in this. Sally can sleep with anyone she wants, I suppose it's stupid of me to want it to be special for her. I suppose you think it *is* special. You know what these people are like, Sally, he'll use you and drop you and go straight back to his people and marry someone else. And you'll be so damned miserable!'

'I understand you thinking that,' said the man. 'I want you to know you are wrong.'

They stood watching her, Sally's head on his shoulder, his arms around her waist. In contrast to the turmoil Rowan felt they were calm, almost serene, buoyed up by the love they felt for one another. It made her want to cry. 'I was going to take you to lunch,' she said gruffly. 'But I'll come next week.'

Out in the car she sat for a moment, her head on the wheel. Suddenly the door flung open and Sally leaped in beside her. There were shouts from inside the hostel, Mohammed was backing away from the matron, laughing and holding up his hands in surrender. The woman was yelling, 'You black bastard! Get out of here, get away from my girls!'

'Come on,' said Sally. 'If I don't get away, she'll throw me out.'

'The woman's appalling,' said Rowan and got out of the

car. 'Why don't you come with us, Mohammed?' she said grittily, and he looked in surprise from the matron to Rowan and back again.

'Thank you,' he said, and got in the back. The matron was left ranting on the pavement.

Rowan took them to an expensive country restaurant. Once a long, low manor house it nestled in a fold of hills. Today the mist hung there, making ghostly swirls out of trees and bushes, touching the skin like a clammy hand. There was a sense of nightmare about the day, the sort of state that results from a fever when people appear where you least expect them and voices come and go out of a miasma. In the bar Rowan ordered gin for herself, orange juice for Sally and Mohammed. She watched her sister. Never had Sally looked so calm and joyous.

'I'm so sorry that we should meet like this,' said Mohammed. 'I have often asked Sally to introduce me to her sister, she speaks a lot about you.'

'And what do you do, Mohammed?' asked Rowan.

'He's a pattern weaver in a mill,' said Sally defiantly.

Rowan realised she had been cherishing the unworthy hope that he might at least be rich, the son of a Maharajah with a fortune in rubies.

'I wish to marry your sister,' said Mohammed.

'Yes. We want to get married,' added Sally.

They sat holding hands and watching her, such bright confidence in their faces that Rowan herself felt a hundred years old. A weight of fear and suspicion descended on her. She took a long gulp of her gin and tonic, hating the man across the table, hating him for making her hate herself.

'He's the wrong colour,' she said flatly.

'Really, Rowan! Don't you think that's just a little ridiculous in this day and age?'

'Yes,' admitted Rowan. 'It ought not to make a difference. But it does and I know it does. I ask you, Sally, why is he a pattern weaver? I know exactly how much they get paid, and a man of his education and intelligence shouldn't put up with

364

it. He wouldn't if he could get anything else,' she added softly.

'We can live on my money,' declared Sally.

'That will not be necessary. I find myself comfortably off, I can assure you,' said Mohammed stiffly.

'You wouldn't with a wife and family,' retorted Rowan. 'And even if you're prepared to live on the breadline, and I can see you are, what about your children? Smut and butter, and however sweet and pretty and clever they are, that's what they'll always be! Out on the edge, nothing nor something.'

'Like Hannah,' said Sally.

Rowan flinched. 'The worst thing about Hannah is knowing what's in store for her. What people will think, what people will say. Watching them leave cafés when we take her in, moving nervously away on trains. They will, you know, everybody does it, I've seen them. *I've* done it. But Hannah's here and I can't do anything about it. You don't have to do that to your children.'

Mohammed shifted in his seat. 'I think Sally spoke out of turn,' he said severely. 'That was a hurtful thing to say, Sally. But Mrs. Barton, Rowan, the world is changing. Perhaps one day your daughter will be loved for what she is, and our children too. We must hope for that day, and work for it. With the goodwill of our friends and families, we shall prevail. And if we do not, our children must, or their children, and beyond. Right will prevail.'

Rowan gazed at him in incomprehension. To her the present was everything, she had no conception of herself as a cog in the wheels of time, working towards a distant future. She could admire the man's philosophy, but she could not live by it. 'Shall we have lunch?' she said feebly.

Rowan wanted, desperately, to tell Sally about Saul, but with Mohammed sitting there, drinking orange juice and looking noble, she dared not. In his presence she felt slightly corrupt, for it was apparent that he was a devout Moslem. 'I shall take the faith,' said Sally.

'Oh.' Rowan's depression deepened. One of her fiercest

dislikes was for fundamentalist religions whose followers claimed, in each and every sect, that they alone had the answers. In her experience they were as misguided and baffled as everyone else, but they committed the cardinal sin of not knowing it.

'I see you do not like that,' said Mohammed seriously. 'Sally will lead the life of a Moslem woman, a good and useful life. It will bring her great happiness.'

'You don't mean — robes, and not seeing visitors and not speaking to people! You don't mean that?' Rowan couldn't believe it.

'A modest and useful life. That is what counts,' said Mohammed.

Sally reached out and took his hand, their fingers intertwining like twigs in the snow. Rowan watched her sister's face; it held an almost religious serenity. In that moment she was truly beautiful. The curve of her cheek was as soft as that of a child. Mohammed's free hand reached out and moved a strand of golden hair from the corner of her mouth and Rowan thought, 'He does love her. For him she is perfection.'

The meal over, Rowan took them back to town and said goodbye to them. They were to spend the afternoon walking together, until it was time for Mohammed to start the evening shift at the mill. 'It pays better,' he confided, as if somehow enhancing his financial credibility. Against her will Rowan liked him, although it would have been so much easier if she had not.

When they were gone, she went back to the flat, and Saul. To her relief he had showered, and was sitting in a chair, white-faced but sensible.

'Did you have lunch?' he asked.

'Yes. I didn't think you'd want any.'

He grinned. 'A fair enough guess. Sorry about last night, love. You know what James's parties are like, booze everywhere. I thought I was OK till I started back.'

'There was a bottle inside the car,' said Rowan. 'A whisky bottle.'

'Was there?' He looked genuinely surprised. 'Someone must have slung it there during the shoot, they were knocking it back all day. You didn't think I'd sat there and emptied it, did you?'

'Of course not.' Though she had thought it, perhaps even now she did think it. What was more, she was almost certain that he had sampled the hair of the dog that very day.

'Don't you think you're drinking rather a lot, Saul?' she asked with feigned lightness. 'I mean, you drink every single day, from lunchtime on.'

'My darling!' He got up and enveloped her in his arms, and even then she found herself sniffing for the booze. Toothpaste defeated her. 'I can handle it,' he whispered. 'OK, I knocked back too many last night, but when have you seen that before? Can't a bloke let his hair down once in a while? I got myself home, didn't I?'

She stared up at him. 'Don't you remember?'

'Of course I do.' But of course he didn't. She couldn't bear to tell him about it; the humiliation did not bear recall.

She pulled away and went to the window. They had a view across the roofs, like the slate backs of whales, and beyond, rising up into the purple distance, were the hills. 'Sally wants to marry an Asian,' she said dismally.

'What?'

She turned round and looked at him. That shock would be registered by everyone she told, she might as well get used to it. 'She wants to marry an Asian, Mohammed Shafir. They are terribly, terribly in love.'

'I don't give a damn! She can't. Not Sally, not pretty Sally.'

'Why not pretty Sally?' asked Rowan.

'Don't tell me you're in favour of it?' Saul went to the cupboard and took out a whisky bottle, pouring himself a small measure. 'She's so young, there'll be decent men a foot deep in a year or so. That girl undervalues herself all the time. And he won't marry her, I'll tell you that. Oh, he'll sleep with her, consider he's made a real conquest, but when it comes to it the family'll whistle up some Pakistani cousin and away he'll go.'

'That's what I said. But he says not, and — well, I believe him.'

'Don't tell me you like the bloke!'

She nodded. 'I do, actually. He's charming, absolutely charming. And as good-looking as anything, a sort of eagle of a man. The trouble is — ' She folded her arms around herself and went back to the window. 'He tells Sally what to do, you see. Fetch this, carry that, don't say that, Sally — and all with such gentle authority. It's just what she needs.'

Saul started to get dressed. 'I'll have to talk to her. She's got to break it off. At her age she doesn't know enough to see where she's going. I won't have Sally turning into one of those timid rabbits of women, hiding in their houses in case they get spoken to, let alone raped. She mustn't get tangled up with all of that.'

Rowan caught his arm. 'Saul — why not?'

Their eyes met. He put out his arms and held her; she let the length of her body lie against him. 'Why not indeed?' he said softly. 'Sad, lost little Sally, if some bloke can give her some happiness, who are we to say he shouldn't? Your parents failed her, we failed her; if this guy can come along with some stability for her, then we should say, "Good on you, son, get on with it!"'

'If it fell apart, then so would she,' said Rowan.

Saul put her away from him to look into her face. 'Would you? If we fell apart? Honestly, Rowan.'

'I'd be in little pieces.'

He pushed her down on to the sofa, gently caressing her. He undid her blouse and licked her breasts, holding one in each hot hand. Rowan's nipples stood up for him, the breasts of a woman. She reached down and felt his penis, swollen to iron rigidity. Saul said, 'I'm sorry. I can't wait, it's been so long.'

She got off the sofa and wriggled out of her trousers and panties. She felt oddly cold and reluctant, although for once there was no need to fiddle with rubbers. The doctor had been only too eager to prescribe the pill and here she was, taking advantage of that much vaunted spontaneity. Yet her crotch felt dry and closed, as it had when the doctors examined it to see how her stitches had healed.

'I'll try not to hurt,' said Saul, and got on top of her. If only, if only she could open to him. Involuntarily her hands went between them, trying to lessen the thing pushing into her. She gave a little yelp of pain.

'You're too dry.' Saul got off and rummaged about, coming up with the vaseline they used for the baby. He made it a game, smearing some on her, letting her smear it on him.

'I love you,' he said, putting a dab on her nose. 'I love the way you are now.'

She lay back again and he covered her, she put her sticky hands on his back and felt his skin slide beneath them. She felt him begin the journey into her body, raking against the scars within, and she clenched her teeth not to let him know how much it hurt. He pushed himself home and the sudden, sharp agony stabbed her. She choked on a scream.

'Darling, are you all right? It's not too bad, is it?'

'No. No.' But the tears were gathering in the corners of her eyes. He said, 'I — I can't stop now. I'll be quick.'

He might not want to hurt her but suddenly he had no choice. Holding her buttocks, he started quick, determined strokes. Her finger nails scored his back, she bit the cushion to stop herself crying out. The knowledge of her pain delayed him, for dreadful seconds he couldn't come. Yet she was so wonderfully tight on him! He thrust again and she groaned, 'Stop it! You're tearing me apart!'

He thought of Lin Yu and James. At last his orgasm swept him on in an explosion of feeling.

She cried, curled up with her hands between her legs.

'I'm so sorry,' said Saul wearily. 'I thought it would be all right.'

'It should be! It's not your fault, I ought to be mended.'

He poured himself another drink. 'It can't have hurt that much.'

'I don't know. It seemed to.'

Rowan felt angry and guilty at one and the same time. He should not have insisted when she didn't want it, and yet did she not owe it to him? They had built a world, once, on this act. Between them they had created paradise. And now he was drinking whisky and she was crying and next door their baby was starting to wake and cry for a feed.

'I'd better go and help Barbara,' she said, getting stiffly off the sofa.

Saul, feeling like a heel, remarked, 'I'm going to fix up a trip this week. The continent.'

'You don't have to go just because of this,' said Rowan coldly. 'It's bound to get better.'

'All the same, I'd better go. We need some time to ourselves, I think. And it's a trip I've been meaning to do. Things should be better when we get into the house, we'll be nearer the mill for one thing.'

'That's months and months,' said Rowan.

She pulled on her clothes and went through to Hannah. It wasn't her fault it hurt to make love, yet he behaved as if she had deliberately held back. And he was going off on a trip, leaving her with the mill, the baby, and their impossible life in the flat – and after last night, when he had inflicted wounds he was too drunk even to remember. Although she tried to put it out, her anger burned.

Chapter Thirty

The sun on the window scattered jewels of light on to the bed. It was one of those rare autumn days when summer seems only yesterday and winter at least a year away. Rowan stood in her nightdress with her hands up to her eyes, blinking at the sky. 'It's a beautiful day.'

Saul looked at her. The nightdress was almost invisible against the sun. He admired this tall, straight, beautiful girl. Then she turned and started getting ready for work. He got out of bed and caught her hand.

'Let's take a day off. Let's go to Blackpool.'

'What for?'

'Nothing. Fun. Because we don't often have fun together. We can take Hannah and have rides at the fair.'

A small grin crept on to her face. 'I've never been to Blackpool. Mother always thought it was vulgar.'

'My darling girl, you've never lived!'

Barbara didn't want them to go. 'This weather won't last,' she said forcefully. 'You don't want Hannah in a damp car all day, do her no end of harm.'

It was becoming clear that the nanny did not trust the parents to take proper care of her charge. 'She wants to come too,' hissed Rowan to Saul.

'Well, she can't. This is our day out. We'll bring you some rock, Barbara.' She gave him another blanket and he added it to the pile of Arctic survival clothing already clutttering the boot.

'I promise we'll take care of her,' said Rowan as at last they were off. 'It's like playing truant from school,' she said, winding down the window and feeling the wind in her hair.

'I used to con my mother into writing me notes about trenchfoot,' said Saul. 'Then they sent me to boarding school.'

'Did you like it?'

''Course not. Nobody ever does. But they brainwash you into thinking you'd have been a vegetable if you hadn't gone, so everyone dutifully sends their sons after them.'

Rowan looked fondly at the baby in her carrycot on the back seat. At least no one was ever going to demand exam passes from that little soul. 'Did you have many friends at school?' she asked, fully expecting a tale of misery and loneliness.

Saul grinned. 'Droves of them. In the holidays I was never at home, I was touring stately homes and Italian villas. On my last report the headmaster wrote, "I should have had no hesitation in making Saul Head Boy were it not for his persistent misconception that life is one long party". And he'd never have made me Head Boy whatever I did, he only chose bores who were going into the church.'

It occurred to Rowan that Saul often presented the face that would be most acceptable to people. 'Perhaps he thought you were.'

He patted her knee. 'An astute comment, my love. I let him think I might be.'

They laughed together, and when Saul stopped for petrol he bought chocolate and four plastic windmills to stand in the open windows and twirl. Hannah blinked at the flashing shapes and Saul said, 'Let's start as we mean to go on! Vulgar as hell.'

It was the end of the season and much of the resort had already been closed down. But there were a few donkeys dozing on the beach, the sun was warm and the smell of fish and chips and rock drifted in the lazy air. Landladies sat at the water's edge in deckchairs and dabbled tired, fat feet in the wavelets. Saul put Hannah in a sling on his back and they wandered along the sands. Rowan took off her

372

shoes and paddled, squeaking at the cold and the fronds of seaweed that tangled round her legs. Saul watched her bright, absorbed face.

'You're so pretty,' he said.

'Thank you, kind sir.' She came out and kissed his cheek, then slid a cold wet foot up his trouserleg and on to his calf.

'Good God, that's freezing! Stop it, you witch. Is this another piece of revenge?'

She looked away. 'What do you mean?'

'Nothing. Nothing to spoil the day. But − Rowan, don't you think I don't know what you feel?'

Gazing out across the blue and shining sea she said, 'At the moment I'm just happy and warm and a bit hungry. When are we going to eat these fish and chips?'

He put his arms round her waist. 'When I think you are good and ready for them. They are absolutely my last penance.'

She turned against him, her hands up at his chest. His breath on her cheek was warm and sweet-scented. 'No more squabbles,' she said softly.

They walked through the town, looking for somewhere to eat. There were pubs everywhere and Saul pretended to be a repentant sinner tempted by the devil. 'No, no! Take away this milk of Satan! I shall not even taste your cheese and onion crisps.'

'They wouldn't let you in anyway,' giggled Rowan. 'We're outcasts now, we've got a baby.'

'Oh God, yes. Doomed to walk the streets looking for a café that has a chair for Hannah and somewhere to change a nappy.'

But the cafés were full of twee oak tables and net curtains, or raucous with pop music and slippery with grease. So they bought fish and chips in the paper and ate them on a bench on the promenade, watching the open buses sail by with their cargo of blank-faced sightseers. Rowan got indigestion laughing because Saul was mimicking their conversation.

'Bit much this sea, in't it, Doris?'

'Aye, you're right there. When I said to Harry I was coming, he said he couldn't do with all that water. Sets him off, you see, at his time of life. We'd have had to stop the coach five times, and it ain't easy on them motorways. No privacy. Will I ever forget the M62 when Harry climbed down the embankment and we had to rescue him with Mildred Greerson's extra-large support hose. . . . '

They went to the fair and Saul won a goldfish and a teddy bear on the shooting gallery. Rowan went in the House of Horrors and came out giggling. 'The skeletons were painted and someone shot me with a water pistol,' she complained, brushing drops off her summer dress. She was tired now and needed a rest; so they, too, went for a ride on an open top bus and ate popcorn. Changing Hannah's nappy, Rowan said, 'She's being very good. Do you think she's happy?'

''Course she is. Because her mum and dad are happy. We're through the worst, you know.'

Rowan believed him. Going home in the car, sticky with rock and sleepy from wind and sun, she was at peace with herself. It seemed to her then that they had weathered storms the like of which would never come again.

Chapter Thirty-One

Richard paced the cold warehouse, his nostrils filled with the unmistakable odour of wool. It was piled everywhere, labelled bales cut open for the buyers to view. Like Richard they walked slowly round, sniffing, touching, making notes. It took years to assess wool properly; most of these men had served an apprenticeship as sorters, standing all day grading fleeces.

The trained eye, and perhaps even more the fingers, could detect the minute difference between sixties and sixty-fours, the tiny variation in fibre that meant absolute softness or a slightly coarser touch. Even a beginner could sort cold country wool, the rough British fleeces grown thick and hard, to distinguish rubbish carpet wool from good stuff badly presented. British farmers took no care, that was the constant complaint. They fed in-wintered sheep by throwing hay on wire racks, and as the animals fed, their fleeces were showered with grass seeds and cut stems. It was hard to get out, and because of it the price was low, which to the farmers meant even less reason to present a good fleece. They came in encrusted with muck, indelibly stained with raddle or dye, and it knocked the price on the head. Richard sniffed contemptuously at some good Hampshire Down that was nonetheless very dirty. He marked it in the list as turbary; the wool was in demand and he might be forced to bid up for it, despite the contamination.

He shivered. These big warehouses were icy cold even on a warm autumn day such as this. Thank God he was off tomorrow, to the Far East, to pick up some silk if he could, and some cashmere. He meant if possible to take up the entire Chinese cashmere stock, and hold it. The price rise would be a few months in coming, but come it would, and Richard fully intended to have some of it on his own account, as well as the firm's. No one could run a Maserati on salary alone.

A friend of his sauntered up. 'Surprised to see you here. Thought you'd given up real work.'

Richard grimaced. 'I've got the wrong name. If you want to get on in this firm, you have to be family. Otherwise they have you sniffing shitty wool for life.'

The other man laughed. 'You're doing all right. Biding your time to get back into your own little empire, I shouldn't wonder. Doesn't Daddy want you in?'

Richard said nothing, and moved on to the next lot of wool. He had been giving that possibility some serious thought lately. The fact was it was time he threw in this job and he would either have to set up on his own account altogether, which was one hell of a risk and would mean investing every penny he possessed, or go into Bardsey's. The decision was made a little easier by his lack of money. Richard spent liberally, and besides, he had taken a tumble on the currency market a few months ago. He'd taken a chance on the dollar and got it rather badly wrong.

His friend said, 'Come for a pint? I've had enough of this for a bit.'

'Yes, I'll join you,' said Richard. He was feeling rather bored with everything. The latest woman in his life had departed the previous week and he was neither sorry nor pleased. It was beginning to seem as if he was going endlessly round the same track, different faces but the same situations. Time to move on.

But the beer was good and the sandwiches better, crisp wholemeal rolls stuffed full of good cheese. Textile gossip washed around him. After a few years in the trade every meeting like this meant a further instalment in a soap opera in which you knew all the characters and most of the plots.

They were talking of Rowan Judge. 'That girl is a bloody phenomenon! There isn't a better mill, design's good, and the organisation's so tight you can hear it twanging. Have you seen the house they're building? Bradford's answer to the Ponderosa.'

'Over-stretching themselves there, if you ask me.' Richard crunched into his roll. His feelings towards Judge's were ambivalent in the extreme. While he had to admire them, he disliked the contrast with Bardsey's. He felt increasingly protective towards that big, sprawling organisation. More and more he considered it his own.

'They've even got their cloth in the London fashion shows. Paris next, and a million Marks and Sparks copies. I mean, that's the way to do it — lean, hard and hungry.'

'She's certainly lean,' said someone, laughing. 'And I bet she's damned hard, too.'

'I don't think she's that,' said Richard, remembering the night of the shoot. 'How much is down to her husband, do you think? My Uncle Saul.'

Everyone considered. 'Quite a bit,' someone conceded. 'He's the one who takes the fliers. But she's the motor, have no doubt about that. Anyway, he's a funny bloke. I was on the 'plane with him going to Zurich, and he was slaughtered. We had to carry him off.'

'Probably so damned relieved to get away from Miss Efficiency.'

They all laughed and ordered more drinks.

Officially, Richard should have gone back to the office, but he was feeling rebellious. When he left the pub, he got in the car and headed up to the moors, intending to walk and blow away the drink. He pulled the car off the road in a lonely and desolate spot, and tramped the late-blooming heather, tasting the cold, cold wind. In the hollows the sun was warm on his face. He put up rabbits from their afternoon doze.

He felt restless and slightly depressed. He had a sense of

futility about his life, that he was grabbing and accruing for no definite purpose. He had the car, he had the flat, he could have this girl, that girl, almost any girl, it seemed, provided he spent enough money — and still it wasn't enough. He wondered if this was a mid-life crisis come rather early. More likely it was delayed adolescence, because the time when he should have been discovering himself had been largely devoted to hating his father. He seemed to have grown out of that lately. When he went back to see his mother, he too felt oppressed. It wasn't hard to understand James, and from that it was a short step to forgiveness.

Well, it was time to go and see the old man. He had fought against it long enough, and if he wasn't careful he would wait too long and find all the cake gone to Nicholas. It was a sobering thought, but Richard was finding himself capable of jealousy, even of a child of barely two. Nicholas received the adoration James had been too busy to give his first son; Nicholas had the Manor House; Nicholas the glamorous mother. He would not also get Bardsey's, not if Richard could help it.

When he got back to the car, a policeman was prowling round it, his patrol vehicle parked at an aggressive angle. 'This yours?' he demanded.

'Yes,' said Richard casually. He was used to police, of all nationalities, at least those in Britain didn't wear guns. 'I've got identification here somewhere.'

He rummaged in his pockets for his driving licence. The policeman said, 'Nice car this. Had it long?'

'Six months or so. Don't worry, it's not nicked. Yet. I had a Ferrari last, it was never at home, you blokes were always finding it next to the canal. Attracted joy-riders like bees to honey.'

'Was that yours?' asked the policeman with real interest. 'I drove that back once. Smashing car.'

'Certainly attracted a better class of criminal. They could turn off the anti-theft locks in less than a minute. This has got a siren you could hear in Italy, touch it and see what happens.'

'I just did,' said the policeman.

Richard sighed. 'Bloody thing never works. Take a good look at it, constable, you could be seeing a lot of this car. I might as well buy a sodding Mini.'

'When they nick those you don't get them back,' said the policeman cheerfully. He walked back towards his car. 'And watch the alcohol intake, won't you, sir?'

Richard stood and watched him go. He put out a casual hand to his car and the siren went off, a banshee wail that sent up a flock of birds a hundred yards away. He swore, fumbled the keys, and at last turned the switch. 'This isn't my day,' he said out loud. The omens were not good for a visit to Bardsey's, but Richard was determinedly unsuperstitious. He sent the car skimming down the hills into Bradford.

It was a while since Richard had visited Bardsey's and he was impressed. There was a fountain outside the main office block, and the doorman was fishing litter out of it with a child's tadpole net. As always the car park was full, so Richard parked across the back of his father's Rolls-Royce and went in.

The doorman shouted after him, 'Here, you can't do that! That's Mr. Barton's car!'

'I know,' said Richard casually and stepped into the lift. He'd like to be Mr. Barton here. He'd been out in the world long enough to appreciate it.

The executive corridor was hushed by thick almond-coloured carpet, with polished oak doors to every room. It had been redecorated since Richard's day in an elegant Regency stripe, and he had no hesitation in attributing that to Diana. Simply by association with her James had lost some of his harsh, aggressive style. It might have done him a lot of good personally, but as far as the business was concerned, James was in danger of losing his edge.

He rapped on James's door and went in. His father was seated at his vast desk, his long-time secretary on the other side, and neither looked as if they were enjoying the experience. Both faces lit up as Richard came into the room. 'Good God! Now what has brought you, Richard? Get him a drink, Margaret, tea, coffee, booze? Come on in, sit down. It's good to see you.'

The effusive welcome verged on the embarrassing. If there was one sure sign that his father was getting old, it was this. In his youth James had no time for emotion, he was leaving all that till later; and later had come.

Richard said, 'I'd love a cup of tea, Margaret. How is everyone, Dad? Diana, Nicholas?'

'Fine, just fine. Nicholas is a grand little chap, I can't see enough of him. I often think, you know, that I missed something when you were young. I worked all the time, never at home really. Such a shame.'

'You weren't happy though, were you? You and Mother.'

James shrugged and put his hands in his pockets. 'Possibly not, I don't know. It didn't matter then, I had my work, I was making good. It was later that things got difficult. How is your mother?'

'Fine.' Richard toyed with the gold paperknife on the desk. To his surprise, next to the pictures of Diana and Nicholas there was one of him, a recent shot, blown up from a snap in one of the trade journals. He was very touched.

Margaret came back with the tea, in an exquisite antique bone china pot. The cups were no attempt at all at a match, except for echoing one of the colours in the flower pattern on the pot. Diana's work again, bringing that touch of style into a business environment. James said hurriedly, 'I know this looks a bit odd but Diana insisted on this pot. I wanted silver, really.'

'She's got tremendous taste,' said Richard. 'You ought to let her have her say on design.'

'I suggested it. She says she leaves all that to Rowan.'

James sipped at his tea, trying not to betray his impatience. If only Richard would come into the firm, if he could see the line stretching on — Richard, Nicholas, their sons — then it was all worthwhile. Suddenly he could wait no longer. 'Are you coming in?' he demanded aggressively. 'It's here for you, waiting.'

Richard picked up a biscuit and broke it gently between his fingers. He tossed one of the pieces at his father and James caught it, like a trout taking a fly. 'I'm coming in,' he said.

They sat for a minute, saying nothing. James started to laugh. He got up, and Richard got up, they shook hands, they held on to each other's forearms, and finally, because nothing else would do, they hugged.

'This is a great day,' said James huskily. 'The greatest day.'

The telephone rang. James picked it up, barking angrily: 'I don't want any calls, I'm with my son.'

'It's urgent, sir.'

The connection clicked. James heard Diana, gulping, gasping. Even before she spoke, he was aware of terror. 'James? Come home. It's Nicholas, it's Nick. The doctor's here.'

'What is it? Diana, tell me.'

'Come home, James. You must come home.'

She hung up and James stood, still holding the receiver, staring into space. 'She says it's Nick. The doctor's there. She didn't say why.'

Their eyes met. Richard thought, 'I knew something terrible would happen today.' There was a judder of relief that it was not to him. He said, 'He must be ill. It might not be bad. Come on, Dad, I'll drive you.'

James automatically took his coat from the cupboard. They walked down the corridor, but then James started to run. The two men sprinted down the stairs, out past the fountain and into the car park. There was the feeling that if they got there quickly, if only they could get there in time, it would be all right. The Maserati, its power unleashed for once, howled mightily. The traffic parted before them, Richard pressed the throttle and the acceleration kicked them in the back. James said, 'Why haven't they taken him to hospital? If he's ill, he should be in hospital.'

'Perhaps he's not that ill.'

James bent his head. In a quick glance sideways Richard saw that his father was crying.

There was nothing lovelier than Aspley Manor that autumn day. The trees were turning, their leaves wonderfully gold and brown and purple, as yet only lightly scattered on the grass. There were cattle in the park, quietly chewing the cud as the Maserati punched a hole through the afternoon quiet. James fell out of the car almost before it had stopped, and staggered up the steps shouting, 'Diana? Diana!'

Richard followed. He carried with him a sense of doom.

Diana was in the drawing-room. She stood before the empty fireplace and her face was utterly white. She just stood there, saying nothing, her hands holding one of Nicholas's little jumpers. The doctor stood by her and as James burst in, and then Richard, he cleared his throat. They all stood, absolutely silent. 'I'm sorry,' said the doctor. 'Nicholas died shortly after lunch today.'

Diana's hands began to knead and twist the jumper, she began to cough, and only after seconds did they realise that she was crying dry, hard sobs.

James said, 'Where is he? You should be working on him, where is he?' He rushed from the room and the doctor followed, and Richard. Only Diana was left, twisting the tiny jumper, and sobbing.

He was in the bedroom, in his cot with the side down, and he bore the marks of all that they had tried to do to him. His little face, that had always been bright-eyed and happy, was empty now and bruised by the masks and tubes, bruised pointlessly. James held his hands and for the first time ever his son's little fat fingers failed to close. It smelled still of Nicholas, of nappies and talcum powder and sleep. He began to howl.

The doctor turned to Richard and said helplessly, 'He'd been dead an hour or more. There was nothing I could do.'

'But what was it? How did it happen?'

'I don't know. I just don't know.'

Downstairs they could hear Diana's harsh, gagging cries, but each sound from James came after long seconds when it seemed his misery was too great to express. For Richard it was unbearable, though he had not loved this or any child, and he knew that what he felt was a shadow of the grief of others. He would have given anything to escape from this, and he knew that so would they all. He put out his hand and held his father's shoulder, James put up his own hand to grasp it, and Richard thought of Diana with no one to comfort her. Richard turned to the doctor. 'We must get her children. She has to have them now.'

An ambulance came, and gently they coaxed James, and then Diana, away from the baby. Such a tiny bundle in such a huge van, they could almost have put him in a box, thought Richard vaguely. For some reason both James and Diana wanted to go to the hospital and they couldn't all get in the Maserati or Diana's Porsche, so he wandered round to the garage and found a little hatchback there, he didn't know whose it was. When he brought it round, Diana said, 'That's the gardener's,' but James just got in and so did she.

'I'll lead,' said the doctor, and Richard followed him, longing to turn on the radio to drown the sounds coming from the back seat. Suddenly James yelled, 'You left him! Why did you leave him alone? What in God's name happened?'

After a moment Diana said weakly, 'Nothing happened.

It was just as usual. He had his breakfast, you were there, you saw him. He didn't want his nap, he was a bit fractious, nothing much. He had his orange juice and I did music with him. He banged on his xylophone, he was so good. I took him out in the park.'

'He was ill, he must have been ill.'

'He wasn't ill! When we came back he had his lunch. He had egg and toast and some yoghurt. And because he hadn't had his sleep, I put him down. He went straight off, as good as gold. I was pleased because he'd been a bit grumpy all morning, and I wrote some letters and made some 'phone calls. I popped in to see him after about an hour, at the most an hour and twenty minutes. And − and − I couldn't wake him up.' She sounded so utterly bewildered.

James said, 'You let him get cold. I was always telling you to wrap him up more.'

She began to whimper horribly and Richard said, 'We can't know what it was, none of us can. There's no sense in blame.'

But Diana burst out, 'It's because I wanted Hannah to die! I did, I did, I wanted her to die! And now God's taken my baby away from me, he's taken my Nicholas. Do you know what, James? Shall I tell you? I hate bloody God!'

Chapter Thirty-Two

At the hospital they stood, grief-stricken, amidst the every-day business of sprains and broken legs. The GP came and shepherded them into a side room and James and Diana sat slumped in chairs, every now and then saying something that they had said before, and would say again, many, many times.

'He was so little.' 'He was so lovely.' 'I only left him for an hour, he was asleep!'

Richard asked Diana for some telephone numbers for the children, and she gave him Andy's and Sally's but couldn't find Rowan's. So Richard went out to the payphone, asking round for money when he found he only had notes and some roubles, finally getting enough to call Andy in London. He rang what seemed to be his flat and a girl answered, he could hear her calling Andy from somewhere. At last he came to the 'phone.

'Yes? What is it?'

'Look, you don't know me, I'm Richard Barton. There's been a — a tragedy. The little boy, Nicholas, he's dead.'

'Which little boy?'

Richard felt unreasoning rage. 'Your mother's son, Nicholas! She needs some help, I thought you might come.'

'Oh. Oh, I see. What do you think I might do then? Are there arrangements?'

'None that I can't see to. She's — beside herself. I think you should come.'

'But I've got a concert tomorrow night!' Richard heard the infuriated sigh, followed by the mental shifting of gears. 'I suppose I'd better come. Tell her I'm coming, tell her —

just say that. God, how I hate these things!'

'None of us is having a ball, as it happens,' said Richard shortly and hung up. 'Self-centred prick,' he thought to himself. After that it was Sally, and a murderous call to some woman who seemed to think he was trying to seduce the girl, over the 'phone, for God's sake! When he was down to his last coin Sally came, and talked to him in a young, breathy voice.

'It's kind of you to ring,' she said. 'I'll come at once. Poor little boy.'

He instinctively knew that Rowan should be there. She was after all the eldest child, though he knew her not at all except by reputation and that one odd night. He reversed the charges on a call to Judge's, and thankfully it was accepted but neither Saul nor Rowan could be found. In the end he left a message, relieved to avoid that same dreadful repetition.

When he went back, James was sitting with his sleeve rolled up.

'We're taking blood samples,' explained the nurse. 'Doctor wants to do an immediate comparison, before – well, as soon as possible. We have to know what happened, you see.'

As she went out, a policeman entered. Richard had a terrible sense of *déjà vu*. It was the same man who had looked at the Maserati that afternoon. But of course they had to make sure about Nicholas, it wasn't usual for a child to die like that. He went out of the room, to get some air, to escape for an instant. He heard the policeman say, 'There were a number of bruises on the body,' and Diana screamed, 'Oh God, he thinks I killed him! He thinks I killed my little boy!'

'Why don't you arrest us and be done with it?' yelled James violently.

The GP began to explain about the resuscitation and Diana sobbed. Richard couldn't stand any more. He walked quickly down the corridor, passing a small blonde girl and

an Asian man. The girl caught at his sleeve. 'Aren't you —
I'm sorry, I thought you might be Richard. I'm Sally.'

'Oh. How did you know who I was?'

'You look like James. Is Mother all right?'

Richard shook his head. 'Apparently the police have to be
in on it. A shambles really, the whole thing.'

Sally hesitated, obviously unsure of what to do, and
Mohammed said gently, 'You must wait, Sally, until everything is finished. We will wait here.'

Obediently the girl moved to one of the chairs and sat
down. Richard sat next to them, though all he wanted was to
get out of there.

Suddenly the swing doors burst open again and Saul
rushed in. His tie was crooked and something about the way
he walked hinted that he might be drunk. Richard got up.
'The police are in there. You can't go in yet, we have to
wait.'

'Sod that! I know how this feels, God, don't I just!
Everything spoiled, everything gone wrong.'

Richard hung on to him. 'Stay here, old man, you're
pissed, you know you are.'

Saul hesitated. His big head swung and he blinked, trying
to focus his eyes. 'I am a bit. But I had to come, I couldn't
not —' He caught sight of Mohammed and Sally. He said
blearily, 'This the wog you're shacking up with, Sally? Oh,
don't get all frosty, it's your life. You might have more luck
with your kids — they could come out all black and white
checks. Look at Hannah, we did something wrong there,
didn't we? And now poor little Nick. He was a nice kid,
Nick. I was jealous of him. He was just what I wanted for
us.'

Mohammed got up and said seriously to Saul, 'I do not
wish you to be offensive to Sally. We are to marry. I am trying to persuade my parents to accept her.'

Saul snorted with laughter. 'Don't tell me they don't
approve! Good God, that's a bit bloody rich. Look at you

people, coming over from some mud village in Pakistan, taking over our town, turning it into Pakistan except for the cows — and you'd introduce those if we let you — and then disapproving of us! Do you wonder you're not welcome here?'

Richard said, 'Shut up, Saul, will you? This doesn't help.'

Mohammed said, 'It doesn't matter. I'm used to this, I understand it. He's drunk, that's all.'

The policeman came out of the room and at once Sally got up to go inside. Saul said, 'Why in God's name did I come? She won't want to see me. If I'm in the same room with the woman, she twitches until I'm gone.'

Richard said, 'I thought Rowan might come.'

'She's out somewhere, I don't know where. Out all day. I wouldn't get this stewed if Rowan was there.' He looked owlish. 'She doesn't like it, you know.'

'Not bloody surprised,' said Richard. He felt no sympathy for Saul, only irritation. There was something sour about a man who waited till his wife was away to get paralysingly drunk.

Saul said, 'I can see you're another bloody puritan. They're all over the place, you know. "Lead a good clean life, lay off the booze, lay off the fags, don't shag the women or your cock'll fall off." Look at our ethnic friend here, even he can't manage all three. Can't get his hands on a black girl so he gets Sally on her back instead. Christ, I didn't mean that!

'What I mean is, old fellow —' he rested a hand on Mohammed's stiff shoulder ' — you just take care of Sally. She's a good girl. Had some rotten luck, needs taking care of.' He turned and blundered away again. Richard knew he ought to stop him because he was in no state to drive, but instead he let him go.

Mohammed said, 'Don't please feel that you must stay with me. I am only waiting for Sally. I don't wish to meet her mother today, it would be wrong.'

'Yes.' Richard ran his hand over his face and through his hair. He felt exhausted, and angry at being involved. He wanted nothing so much as to go home.

James came out of the room, red-eyed, almost shrunken. Richard went to him. 'Are you OK?'

James let out his breath painfully. 'I'll be all right. The medical supremo wants to talk about something. Will you come?'

'OK.'

They went down the corridor to yet another small office. The white-coated man behind the desk barely looked at them, it was amazing how few people could. It was as if grief of such intensity hurt even those who saw it.

The doctor said, 'I know I can say nothing to console you. These deaths are rarely explained. There will be an inquest, of course. On the face of it, we would appear to have a cot death. I understand he was a little under the weather?'

'Yes — yes,' said James feebly.

'There is one unusual factor. The child's blood group is A rhesus negative, and the commonest grouping for this syndrome is O positive. Any statistical phenomenon is important in researching the causes of these appalling events.'

'My blood group's O,' said James vaguely.

'Yes, I'm aware of that. The child was adopted, I take it?'

'What?'

'When did you receive the baby, Mr. Barton? We have to investigate his natural parents, the circumstances of his birth. There may have been damage of some kind, a difficult delivery —'

'But he isn't adopted. My wife had a Caesarean section, in a nursing home!'

The doctor lifted his head fully for the first time. 'Oh, I see.' His lips moved soundlessly as he tried to recover the situation.

Richard said quickly, 'Obviously you haven't got all the facts, we'll come back and talk again when everything's

389

clarified − ' But James dropped a heavy hand on his arm and silenced him.

'What are you saying?' he demanded.

The doctor blustered. 'Genetically, of course, the picture is rather confused, but all things considered − '

'Are you saying I'm not the father? Let me see those notes.' He lunged across the desk and grabbed at the papers. They were blood group slips and he could make no sense of them.

Richard said, 'Leave it, Dad, you're not thinking straight.'

'This pillock says I'm not Nick's father! Do you know anything about these blood groups?'

'No, nothing,' lied Richard.

'I bloody well know who's A negative,' said James wildly. 'Bloody Saul! Damn nigh cut his finger off when he was six. They had to put out an SOS for blood.'

'Mr. Barton, if you would just calm down,' said the doctor desperately. 'Of course you are the father of your child!'

James tossed the papers back on to the desk. 'I can't stand any more of this. I'm taking my wife and going home.'

Richard made as if to go out with him, then turned and went back in to the doctor. The man was sweating. He wiped the corners of his mouth with the back of his hand. Richard said in a low, vicious voice, 'You are not to let any of this come out at the inquest. Understand?'

The doctor said, 'How in God's name was I to know? It could have been artificial insemination, anything.'

'Just shut up about it, will you?'

He went out after James. He found Diana with Sally. They were sitting holding each other and crying. Across the room sat James. He was watching his wife with an odd and dangerous expression.

It was late when Rowan got back to the flat. She had been to

Harrogate, to a small but avant garde fashion show, and afterwards she and the girl designer had sat and talked. The visit had been Saul's suggestion, but when she got home he demanded, 'Where on earth have you been?'

'Harrogate,' she said in surprise. 'You told me to go.'

'Like hell I did!' He got up, staggering a little.

Rowan said, 'Is Hannah all right? I don't know why you have to drink like this when you're on your own, it's silly.'

'I've got to tell you,' he said vaguely. 'There's been an accident.'

Rowan's eyes widened in her pale face. She dropped her bag and flew into the next-door room, frightening Barbara, who was watching television, almost out of her wits. 'Is Hannah all right? Saul said there'd been an accident.'

Barbara put down her packet of crisps. 'Not to Hannah, Mrs. Barton. To Nicholas.'

'Yes,' echoed Saul. 'Nicholas. Cot death baby.'

Rowan went back into their own room and sat on the bed. She put her face in her hands and rocked to and fro. Saul said, 'It's all right, you know. It isn't Hannah.'

Rowan whispered, 'Suppose it was? I used to wish it was, in the beginning. Poor, poor Mother. And poor James. They've got so used to thinking poor us.'

Suddenly Saul picked up a shoe and hurled it across the room. 'I hate this sodding world!' he yelled.

Rowan flinched. 'I'll ring Mother now!' she muttered.

She dialled the number and James answered. He sounded brisk, too brisk.

'I'm so sorry,' said Rowan inadequately.

'Yes. Well. Lot to be sorry about, isn't there? I'll get Diana.'

'James – please, James. You were kind to me about Hannah. Thank you.'

His voice came back, cracking. 'It's easy to sympathise. Not so bloody easy to applaud, I was never good at that. And a bloody sight harder to take it on the chin, I find. Here's your mother.'

'Rowan?' Diana was hoarse with sobbing. 'Darling, Andy's here and his terrible girlfriend. I don't want them in the house, I don't want anyone.'

'Er — why don't you send them here?' asked Rowan.

'Yes. Yes, of course I will. You're always so practical, aren't you, never any emotion. You were like that when your father died, all you thought of was the mill. I wish I was as lucky as you.'

Across the room Saul lurched to a pot plant and was sick. Rowan said, 'I dare say you do, Mother. I'll come tomorrow, shall I?'

'Do you know, they thought I'd killed him? They thought I'd beaten him to death!'

'I don't suppose they did really. They have to think of these things, you know.'

'You would say that. Oh, Rowan, why was it Nicholas? Why did it happen to him?'

Swallowing down her tears, Rowan said levelly, 'I don't think we can know that. Don't forget, Mother, it's not Nick you're crying for. It's you, always you. I cried so much for Hannah till I realised that.'

'I'm sorry for what I thought about Hannah,' wailed Diana. 'I'm sorry, but it doesn't bring him back!' She dissolved into hysterical sobbing.

After a moment Andy came to the 'phone and Rowan gave him directions to the flat. In a low voice, he said, 'I can't wait to get out of here. God, Rowan, it reminds me so much of Father.'

'I'll make up a bed,' said Rowan, and hung up.

Saul was wiping his ashen face with a towel.

'You OK?' she asked bleakly.

'Yes, fine.' Saul was capable of functioning almost normally when still very drunk. It was only when he went an inch over the edge that you realised he hadn't been sober for hours. He said, 'I went to the hospital to see her... Saw Sally's Maharajah instead.'

Rowan grinned at the apt description. 'What did you think?'

'Sort of holy man in mufti, if you ask me. Very eldest son, very authoritarian. Just wish he wasn't black.'

'Well, brownish,' said Rowan. 'I don't want him to take her over, if you know what I mean.' She struggled to articulate what she felt. 'He just seems so terribly foreign!'

Saul shrugged. 'He is foreign. He just happens to live here. It doesn't make them English, whatever it says on the passport.'

He went to the cupboard and poured himself a vodka and Rowan a gin and tonic. She hardly tasted her drink. Nowadays she found herself so sensitive to Saul's intake that she barely enjoyed anything herself. Again she tried to tackle it. 'Don't you think you're drinking a bit much? It can't be doing your liver any good.'

He didn't look at her for a moment. Then he said, 'I'll cut back a bit. I had a bit too much today, I had a lunch out and that started it.'

'But it's most days.'

'Look, Rowan.' He put down his glass and took hold of her hands. 'Look. We've got Hannah, we've got the business, we've got a lot on our plates. You've got your way of dealing with it, you smother yourself in that mill like a mole digging a tunnel. I've got my way. Sometimes I overdo it and take a drop too much, but it isn't often, is it?'

She wanted to say yes, because although she rarely saw him drink she suspected, strongly, that he often did. Instead she said, 'No. But I worry about you, Saul, terribly!'

'And I worry about you, honey.'

They were talking, obliquely, about sex. The weeks clicked by and still it was torture. She trailed to and from the doctor and all he said was, 'give it time'. She was considering giving up taking the pill, there seemed little point when they never made love. Now she put her arms round his neck, planting little kisses all over his face. He responded, urgently, pushing her back with that delicious intent that used to excite her so. In the back of her mind she felt cold fear. Suppose it still hurt?

The telephone rang. Saul cursed and rolled off to lift the receiver. It was the doorman to say Andy had arrived with his girlfriend and couldn't understand why he didn't appear to be expected. Rowan put her hands to her head, feeling a headache starting to throb. She would take an aspirin and rub out the pain, and if she could rub out today also, that would surely be a blessing.

Chapter Thirty-Three

Sometimes even Rowan stood and stared at Judge's and found it hard to remember how it used to be. To Andy it was unrecognisable. The fire had been a blessing. They had at last rid themselves of old, unusable floors, the ancient boiler, even the antiquated and hard to clean canteen. In the midst of the reconstruction the mill was like a mutant, the old severe style contrasting with light, high-tech design.

'We're building a nursery,' said Rowan with pride. 'It was Saul's idea.'

'Can we afford it?' asked Andy.

The 'we' jarred on Rowan's nerves.

'Yes, just,' she admitted. 'That was what I wanted to talk to you about. I want to go public.'

'Don't be so bloody silly!'

He walked away from her, just as he had when they were small and she had hatched some fantastic and impossible plot. Andy was always the one to see the flaws; if anyone was relentless about practicalities, it was he.

'I can do it,' she said, tugging at his sleeve. 'Will you listen, Andy!'

He stopped and folded his arms. 'Rowan, I don't want to talk mills. I accept I've got to stay till the funeral, though God knows why. Mother screams every time she sees Astrid.'

'She has that effect on a lot of us,' said Rowan waspishly. 'You shouldn't have brought her. Andy, this is important!'

'I don't want to waste my time money-grubbing.'

'Thank you,' said Rowan. 'We paid you a handsome dividend last year, I might remind you.'

'Very gratefully received it was. No doubt you'll want a rake-off from my concerts in return.'

'If you made anything, I might,' snapped Rowan. But this bickering was getting them nowhere.

'Look, we can go public. Saul knows this company that's collapsing, it's got a public quotation, everything, but it's bust. We can buy it. We can change the name afterwards, but we've got our quotation. Apparently we then have to make a rights issue and get in lots of lovely money, and with it we can build our new dye-house and everything. The insurance will replace things pretty well, but we want to step up from here. Expand.'

'Who would own Judge's then? It's still me, isn't it?'

'You only have half,' countered Rowan aggressively. 'If you really must have it that way then we can arrange it so you still have control. But you've got to agree, Andy! It really is important.'

They walked on into the mill. Andy mooched round, ignoring the nods and grins of those who had known him when he was a boy. In contrast Rowan stopped and chatted here and there, exchanged the odd joke with someone, chivvied the overlooker about sweeping up. This was her world; within it she felt calm and resourceful and sane. Andy hated it. From a boy he had loathed the noise and turmoil, it was Rowan who stood entranced watching the coarse strands of wool turned into gossamer and on into thick, warm cloth. Yet Andy had been preferred, he was the boy and his it was. It would have been fairer, thought Rowan viciously, if she had been given the talent for music. At least then there would have been some semblance of justice.

This was the first time she had seen Andy alone. His girlfriend, Astrid, trailed about after him like an overfed spaniel, fighting off anyone who wanted to do anything for Andy, even so much as pass him a scone. With Diana she took it upon herself to reinterpret all Andy's conversation:

'I think what Andy means, Diana, is — ' and saying what she thought he ought to mean. It was incredible that Andy tolerated it.

Something about her brother bothered Rowan. He had never been one to show quite what he felt but now he wasn't happy.

'Are you sick of Astrid?' she asked abruptly. 'Do you want to get rid of her?'

He looked surprised. 'No, not particularly. I'm very fond of her. She's on edge, you don't see her as she really is.'

Rowan reflected what a pity it was that you could not veto the people about to be admitted to the family. Astrid at every funeral, christening, wedding, and many Christmas dinners would be almost more depressing than James. The addition of Mohammed would put the lid on it.

'Is it the music?' she asked. 'I thought you were doing OK.'

His faced twisted slightly. He had Diana's bones, theatrically prominent, slightly strange in a man but very photogenic. He said, 'Let's go up to the office. I want to talk.'

Rowan was lodging in a stripped-out anteroom while the building work was taking place. She had draped cloth round the walls, swathes of it hanging like medieval tapestry, emerald against black, against orange, against dark, vibrant blue. Like a cat she had lined her box, and like a cat she lived in it, a home-loving but still independent cat. Her hair was shaggy these days, and she wore dramatic eye make-up. 'I wanted to tell you,' said Andy awkwardly, 'You look great. I mean, really.'

'Mother doesn't think so,' said Rowan ruefully.

'Well, when did she ever? She always wanted you to dress like her, but on you it was a disaster. You looked like a runner bean in a dry year.' He waved at her skintight trousers and over-tunic. 'That's your style. Principal Boy meets Lolita.'

397

She said nothing, but her eyes scanned his sagging cord trousers, worn sports jacket and crumpled cravat. 'You're not getting on, are you?'

'How did you guess?' He sighed and went to the cupboard where Rowan kept the drinks, finding nothing but Perrier water and tonic. 'A temperance campaign, I see. Fewer bottles for Saul to find.'

'Don't be silly. I don't like drink in the office, that's all.'

He poured himself a Perrier and flung himself into a chair. 'If it wasn't for the money from the business, I'd be completely broke. It pays for my flat and the tours, the expenses don't nearly cover it, not for Astrid as well. I don't understand what I'm doing wrong, you see. I won the competition, everybody said I was made, but the agent couldn't arrange much because all the best venues are booked years in advance. Then somehow I didn't get off the ground when he did make the bookings. People had forgotten about me, I got bad reviews.'

'What about the American tour? Mother said that went well.'

Andy snorted. 'She would. Two big concerts at which I played one piece, the rest piddling little affairs with old ladies coming up afterwards and saying, "You were wonderful, Mr. Judge. Can you advise me about my grand-daughter, she's six months old and has a wonderful talent." The whole thing was a fiasco, I was barely mentioned in the papers.'

'Oh. I see.'

Rowan went to the cabinet and poured herself a glass of water. Andy was without doubt a brilliant violinist, but his style was different. He showed to best effect in dramatic pieces, where his technical virtuosity could be given full rein, not in the worthy symphonic works for which his agent seemed intent on booking him. More to the point, perhaps disastrously, on a stage he lacked presence. In her mind's eye she pictured a revised Andy, his hair instead of drooping

398

wearily over his collar permed into energetic curls. A soft black suit, they had just the cloth, a mile distant from ordinary men's suiting, made up in a collarless jacket and baggy, front-pleated trousers. With it he would wear a white silk shirt and a floppy bow tie.

'Stop looking at me like that,' said Andy. He felt better now he had confided in Rowan. A little honesty broke through the mists like sunshine.

'What you need is a fresh start,' said Rowan, still staring at him assessingly. 'It's a good thing you've got to stay for a bit. First stop Mr. Suzman. If I beg, he might get something together in a couple of days. Then the hairdresser, and when you're up to scratch we'll ring up the *Yorkshire Post* ... story about the local boy made international violinist coming back at time of crisis. The television stations often pick up from there, and if we get a spot you've got to give it everything.'

Andy looked dumbfounded. 'What's local television supposed to do for me?'

'Get you noticed. If we can't sell you altogether as a concert violinist, you'll have to be everybody's favourite classicist. The concert career could follow, we'll just have to see.'

Andy watched her over the rim of his glass. Unspoken words hung in the air, both he and Rowan circled round them cautiously. 'Er — this isn't entirely free, is it, Rowan?' he said at last.

'I don't know what you mean.' She wandered about the room, touching the fabric on the walls, feeling it with a professional hand. 'I'd do it for you anyway, you know that. But Andy — I do want to go public. Please, Andy. You've got to agree.'

'If you're sending me up the wrong alley, I'll do you, Rowan.'

'Coward! You never would take a chance.' She picked up a pencil and threw it at him. He caught it and threw it straight back, catching her on the side of the head.

'Ouch! You never had any chivalry either.'

'Good God, if I had you'd have crucified me. I remember you tying me up for hours.'

'Ten minutes,' said Rowan scornfully. 'Anyway, I always saved you in the end. Didn't I?'

He grinned and acknowledged it.

For Diana the inquest passed in a blur. James was there, of course, and she asked Andy to come, though he brought the appalling Astrid with him. Richard arrived just as it was about to start. When he put his hand on James's shoulder, Diana thought her husband was going to cry. She wanted to hold hands, but somehow he evaded her grasp. There was a distance between them, she knew it was there and was too grief-stricken to cross it. When they said the name, Nicholas James Barton, she dropped her face into her gloved hands and wept.

The evidence was straightforward enough. After only an hour the coroner was pronouncing death by unspecified natural causes. 'I offer the parents my deepest sympathy,' he said in a cool voice that precluded any real emotion. 'They should not hold themselves to blame in any way.'

Outside Diana said urgently to them all, 'You see, he said it wasn't my fault. He told me that.'

'Of course it wasn't,' said Andy, and Astrid said, 'What Andy means, Mrs. Barton, is you shouldn't feel any guilt at all.'

'Oh, shut up,' flared Diana. 'Can we go home, James? I can't stand any more.'

'Can't you?' James stared at her with what seemed almost like cold hatred. Diana recoiled, saying, 'James?' and it was left to Richard to save the situation, smoothly moving between them. 'Come on, let's have a pub lunch. Coming, Andy?'

'I have to meet Rowan,' said Andy vaguely, and Diana

said, 'She's always got time for other people, it's only me she neglects,' although it was she who had refused to allow Rowan at the inquest. She might have brought Saul.

Over lunch, with Diana picking distractedly at the food and James, it appeared, barely noticing what he was eating, Diana said, 'Richard, have you seen Sally's black man?'

Richard swallowed down some tasteless steak and kidney. 'Only once. They seem happy together.'

'I can't understand it, I just cannot understand it. Her father would be so ashamed.'

James snorted. 'He was good at that sort of emotion; it was the positive things he couldn't manage. Bloody wimp, that was Andrew, and Andy takes after him.'

'Oh, do shut up,' snarled Diana. 'I wouldn't expect you to have any standards.'

'And what sort of standards do you have, may I ask? Or is that too leading a question at the moment?'

Diana stared at him uncomprehendingly. Richard said, 'I think you got the wrong end of the stick at the hospital, Dad. Why don't we talk about it after the funeral?'

James dug his fork viciously into his food. 'Perhaps we will at that.'

Rowan took Hannah to the funeral. Saul held her as Rowan, Andy and Sally stood at the graveside, watching the tiny coffin go into the earth. A spray of roses went with it, bearing the inscription 'To Darling Nick, with all Mummy's love', and few people noticed the omission of James. But at the last moment he stepped forward and almost defiantly threw in a little bunch of freesias. He bent down and picked up handfuls of earth, sending them rattling fiercely down on to the coffin. He threw more and more, until Richard took hold of him and led him away.

He allowed himself to be led through the crowd, openly weeping. As he passed Saul, he stopped. Softly, very softly, he said, 'I'm going to break you, Saul. Take my word, I am going to finish you.'

Saul said, 'You don't have to feed on this, James. You don't have to let it turn you sour.' He lifted the baby in his arms and turned her face towards him. She let out a tiny cry and he cradled her close. James spat into the earth and walked away.

At the house afterwards neither Diana nor James appeared. Saul had gone back to the penthouse with Hannah. 'Something's upset him,' he told Rowan. 'And that's a bloody silly thing to say on a day like this, but there you are. If it helps him to hate me, then so be it. It doesn't do me any harm.'

'Doesn't it?' She stood watching him, wanting to ask him not to drink. But if she asked him he would yell and do it to spite her, so it was better to say nothing. She went to the Manor alone, and talked to people she hadn't seen since her father died.

Andy came across to her, followed by the faithful Astrid. He was wearing the clothes Rowan had chosen for him, and looked like an exotic prince. 'I've been asked to the television studios,' he said, barely concealing his excitement. 'I did it!'

'Well done,' said Rowan, somewhat ironically. 'You must play, of course, even if they don't ask you to.'

'I've got a piece organised. I wondered if you'd like to hear it, actually.'

'What I think Andy means is, should he play it now?' interrupted Astrid, and Rowan gazed at her in amazement.

'This is a funeral, Astrid,' she said icily. 'We are not here for a concert performance. Andy can play it to me another time.'

She signalled to Sally to come, and made ready to leave. In the hall she could dimly hear the sound of raised voices from upstairs. She grimaced at her sister. 'Hammer and tongs. I suppose he thinks it's Mother's fault.'

'He always wants to blame someone. Let's get out of here, Ro, Mohammed's waiting for me.'

In the car the girls sat in silence, letting the weight of the day fall away from them. At last, Sally said, 'Rowan, what do you really think of Mohammed?'

'You know what I think. He's a very nice man. That doesn't mean you should marry him, Sal.'

'His family's against me, you know. They won't even see me.'

'I suppose they have the same objections as me. It will be very, very difficult, not just for you but for the children.'

'I don't think I care. I want to marry him, Rowan, more than anything in the world. I don't care if we have to live in a hovel!'

Rowan stopped the car on a double yellow line, causing a bus behind to hoot furiously. 'Look, you're not poor, Sally. Up to now, Mother's had control of your share of the firm, but if you married you would get that. We're going to go public, I've persuaded Andy to agree and we're going to do it. You're going to have an awful lot more than you ever expected. And if there's one thing I'm pretty sure about, it's that Mohammed will not like you having all that money. He seems to me to be a very proud man.'

'He is.' Sally put her thumb in her mouth and bit the side of it, a habit she had long grown out of. 'We wouldn't have to use it.'

'That would be absolutely ridiculous!'

'But his family might like me if they thought I was rich.'

Rowan put her head on the steering wheel and groaned. 'I just know this isn't right,' she said wearily. 'Good God, if you knew how hard it is to be married to someone the same as you, let alone someone different! We don't want it for you, his family don't want it for him, we can't all be bonkers!'

Sally took her hands out of her mouth and folded them

403

purposefully in her lap. 'I don't think you understand at all, Rowan. If I didn't have Mohammed, I wouldn't have anything. I only feel happy when he's there.'

That was a feeling Rowan remembered so well. And who was she to advise on marriage? People had to learn for themselves, and there was no saying that Sally would learn the same lessons as her sister. As Rowan well knew, happiness and misery lurked where you least expected them.

Chapter Thirty-Four

Sally was adept at sneaking in and out of the hostel unseen. To get in she loitered on the steps, occasionally withstanding the obscene suggestions of drunks on the way to the doss house. Sooner or later she would hear a gaggle of girls in the hall and in she would go, a short dash up and round the corner, and she was away.

If Mohammed was with her, it was more difficult. Then she sacrificed herself, engaging the matron in long conversations about lost letters while Mohammed sprinted up the stairs. They laughed about it afterwards, and even when he was caught he never seemed upset. 'She is so like my mother,' he told Sally, not without affection. It was one of the many things she did not understand about him, but that was part of his charm. He was different, somehow exotic. When he made love to her she was a precious vessel into which he poured himself.

On the evening of the funeral he found her packet of birth control pills. He sat on the edge of the bed, irritably lighting a cigarette, clicking his fingers for her to bring him an ashtray.

'You must stop taking these,' he said suddenly.

'But — I can't.' She felt nervous of him. When he neglected to indulge her it was like the sun going in and frost descending.

'I wish for a child. My mother will accept you when you are with child, she will take you as her daughter.'

'We ought to get married first,' said Sally doubtfully. 'Suppose she still wouldn't see me? I'd be pregnant and I'd have nothing.'

'Sally, Sally!' He turned and took her face in his hands, the forefingers roughened by work in the mill. 'I shall always take care of you. If I had a house of my own I would take you to it. For now I must persuade my father to let us come to his house, to have a room of our own. If my mother agrees, he will agree.'

'Do you think I ought to come and see them?' asked Sally nervously.

Mohammed drew on his cigarette, thinking about it. In his house there lived his parents, his three sisters and two brothers as well as an uncle and a cousin. That evening his father and uncle would be working. It might be a good time to confront the rest of them with Sally, to let them see that he had truly won a prize. He turned to her. 'Get dressed. A long skirt, trousers perhaps. Let your hair fall down, I like it so.'

Sally dressed before his watchful gaze, putting on dark tights, a long skirt and a high-necked jumper. When she began her make-up, Mohammed came up behind her and took her breasts in his hands. She let him fondle her, leaning her head back against his naked torso. She turned to lick his hot, different skin and after a moment he took her by the hand and led her to the bed. He pulled her clothes down just enough to allow himself entry, Sally knew at once that it was not one of those times when he was prepared to give her satisfaction. He pumped in silence, then ejaculated copiously. When Sally stood up, warm strings of semen hung from her. She had to wipe herself with tissues.

Mohammed washed his penis at the basin. He said, 'My mother knows we do this. You must not mind if she shows some contempt for you.'

Sally stared at him. 'I can't go! She shouldn't know about us, you shouldn't have told her!'

'I do not lie to my mother, Sally. Besides —' he took her hands and held them, lovingly — 'I want her to know that you have only me. It is right that I should look after you.'

Nonetheless, when they walked together down the narrow street of terraced houses, some of the doors painted in violent reds and purples and yellows, she felt odd and out of place.

There were lots of children around, quiet and well-behaved all of them, watching her as if she were a zoo creature stepped outside the cage. They came to a yellow door, and Mohammed went in. Sally followed, almost sick with fright, sampling for the first time the perfumed, spicy aroma of an Asian home.

There seemed to be people everywhere: girls in saris, two young boys in silk suits. Everybody talked and not one word could Sally understand. She found herself hustled through to the kitchen. Word of her arrival had spread instantly throughout the house. Everyone crowded into the passage behind her, longing to see her meeting with Mohammed's mother.

She was small and plump. She wore glasses perched on the end of her nose and she was cooking. The room was spotlessly clean, but quite unlike anything Sally had known in a kitchen. An old gas stove stood against one wall, there was a chipped white sink and a wood table standing on a square of lino. Pots and pans hung everywhere on the walls, great metal things that would have done duty for an army, and there was an old dresser with glass-fronted cupboards crammed full of tins and foodstuffs. Overpowering everything was an astonishing smell of garlic.

'Mother, this is Sally,' said Mohammed formally in English. His mother cast a fulminating glance at Sally and then rocketed off at her son in a fusillade of Gujerati.

'How do you do?' said Sally feebly, when she paused for breath. The woman took no notice. She uttered a few more paragraphs to her son and turned back to her cooking.

A young woman stepped out of the throng in the passage and said something to her mother. She turned to Sally. 'My mother doesn't speak English. I am sorry for your welcome. I am Fadeema.'

'I thought she would be reasonable,' said Mohammed crossly. 'I am an educated man, I have found an educated wife, of good family.'

'Pah!' said his mother.

'I thought she didn't speak English,' whispered Sally nervously.

Mohammed made a face. 'She likes to think she doesn't speak English.'

He rattled away at his mother in Gujerati and Fadeema steered Sally into the front room. It was heavily decorated with flock paper, brass ornaments stood around a gas fire and there was a television showing an Asian video. A beauty was flashing dark eyes pleading with her lover. Fadeema went across and turned it off. 'You are a student? I am a student also, of medicine.'

'Oh.' Sally felt intimidated. She attended her beauty course but did only moderately well, mostly because she had no real wish to give facials and wax legs. She was discovering that the bodies of other women repelled her slightly. 'Don't you find it difficult?' she asked.

'It is difficult at home, yes,' said Fadeema. 'My parents don't approve of the men students. They've got used to it though, as long as I come straight back.'

Mohammed came back into the room, clearly upset. He said something angrily to Fadeema and she turned and smiled awkwardly at Sally. 'My mother is unwell. I am so sorry you cannot share a meal with us. Perhaps another time.' She went out, and for a moment or two Mohammed paced up and down, muttering angrily.

'What did she say?' asked Sally.

'Everything. That you are a prostitute, that you will give me disease, that she will never welcome such a woman into her home, corrupting her children. She doesn't understand the English! I told her, we are in a different world, I lead a different life to my father, I cannot live as he lived. It's no use, none of it.'

Sally rubbed her arms. The very air in the room felt hostile. 'Can we go now?' she asked. 'I don't want to stay here.'

He was instantly there for her. 'Poor Sally, poor little bird. I should never have brought you. We'll go out and have some food, we don't need this rubbish!' He shouted the last words for the benefit of his mother.

Together he and Sally went into the hall. It was empty now but for a young girl solemnly skipping on the threadbare carpet, the youngest sister. With every step her plaits flew up and banged down on her back. 'And you can keep your nose out of it,' said Mohammed unnecessarily and bustled Sally into the street. The girl watched them seriously, and then stuck out her tongue at her brother's back.

All the way down the road Sally could feel eyes watching her, curtains twitching as they assessed the precise length of time she had been in the house. In these cramped streets everyone knew everyone else's business, and the scene in the house would have been of maximum interest to the entire community.

'They don't live as if they were in Britain at all,' said Mohammed viciously. 'They remain just the same, that man said it and it is true. They would live like this on the moon: the same prejudices, the same judgements.'

'What are we going to do, Mohammed?' asked Sally. She felt unutterably weary and depressed.

'I will not give up! My mother will never reject my child.'

A headache was starting to build behind her eyes. She trusted Mohammed totally, but she couldn't bear to think of her mother's face if she was pregnant and unmarrried, of Rowan's patient disappointment. They would all understand, only too well.

They had a meal at a restaurant Mohammed knew, run by men who hailed Mohammed like a long-lost brother and ignored Sally almost totally. Afterwards he took her all the way back to the hostel, although the mill where he worked was miles away and his ancient car sighed and wheezed continuously.

'I'm sorry. I'm sorry,' he said shaking his head.

'It's not your fault.'

He held her hands between his own. 'I promise it will be all right.' She nodded, and waited until he was out of sight before walking incautiously into the hostel. It was a mistake. The matron collared her.

'Him again! I've warned you, don't come crying to me when you're in the family way!'

Sally ran away up the stairs. She was tired and cold, so she got into bed and automatically reached out for the packet of pills. It wasn't there. She got out of bed and looked everywhere, but it was no use. Mohammed had taken them. Crawling back under the covers, that still smelled of his body, she chewed the side of her thumb.

Andy was to appear on the news magazine programme, in the early evening. It was intended that he give a few moments' brief chat about his career, play a tune, and the presenter could then smile, make a joke and say, 'Let's wish Andy Judge all the luck in the world on his forthcoming tour,' before going on to discuss the roadworks on the M62.

Rowan had no intention of letting it go at that. She took Andy to the mill and made him play his piece, a wild peasant dance by a wild peasant composer. He stood bad-temperedly in the warehouse and played it for her. People crept in to listen. Suddenly everyone had some reason to pass through the warehouse.

'Go away, go away all of you!' said Rowan peremptorily. 'The music's fine, Andy, but you're not.'

'It's the music I'm here for,' said Andy. 'I don't like being on show like this.'

'I think that's your trouble,' commented his sister. 'You want to perform, and when you do you're embarrassed. It holds you back.'

'Rubbish,' said Andy, and moved to put his violin away.

Rowan went up to him. 'Andy,' she said softly, 'I'm trying to help. Will you do something for me, just one thing? It's for you as well.'

410

'Stop trying to sweet-talk me, Rowan! I'm your brother, it doesn't work!'

'What does work then? I'll hit you if you like, there!' She clouted him hard on the shoulder. He gave a howl of rage and chased her. She ran like a hare, in and out of the hessian-bound bales of wool. Andy gave up first, unfit and out of breath.

'I win,' said Rowan. 'Stand on this bale here and play. I'm getting everyone in to listen.'

'For God's sake, no!'

She opened her eyes wide at him. 'Why not? There's no point being flamboyant in private if you can't do it in public. Nobody gets anywhere without practice.'

'But I do practise! Night and bloody day!'

She shrugged. 'Then you're practising the wrong thing. Up you get, Andy.'

He stood on the bale, feeling ridiculous, while she summoned the entire workforce. Since she had just chased them away they were a little bemused, but no one resisted. If Miss Rowan was prepared for once in a blue moon to put something before efficiency then who were they to argue? They gathered and stood grinning, looking up at Andy, an unhappy figure, standing on the bale.

'Get on with it,' called Rowan. 'Once more, with feeling!'

'Get stuffed!' said Andy morosely, and everyone cheered. He grinned at them cautiously. Then he gave an extravagant bow, and his black jacket flapped like wings. 'Ladies and gentlemen,' he declared, 'I am about to — excite you!'

Striking a pose, he put the violin to his chin and began. This time he embellished the tune, which rendered it vulgar to the purist but delighted the audience. As he played, he wandered about on his perch, filling Rowan with dread that he would fall off and break his leg, or worse, his violin. He finished with one leg hanging over space, about to take one final, disastrous step. They stayed silent while he hung there, suspended, but as soon as stepped back there was thunderous applause. People shouted 'More! More!' and they meant it.

Rowan waved them back to their work, and stood waiting for Andy to climb down. As people passed him they gripped his arm and said warmly, 'Grand stuff, lad! The old man woulda been proud of yer.'

Rowan bit the inside of her cheek. Andrew would indeed have been proud, more than for anything Rowan could have done. 'Do it like that tomorrow,' she said to Andy crisply.

'I'd get laughed out of town.'

'Don't be so damned British! If you do it dead-pan no one will remember you for a minute. You're a performer, so damn well perform.'

'Don't let her boss you about, Andy.' Saul had come in. Rowan smiled and went across to him, using the pretence of a kiss to smell his breath. There was the usual give-away, mouthwash, and his eyes had that distant look she associated with drink.

'He's got to do as he's told or he won't succeed,' said Rowan gently.

'Do as he's told, eh? Let's all do as we're told so we can get to the top of the fucking ladder. And then fall off.' He staggered abruptly and Rowan clutched his arm. She didn't look at Andy.

'What did you want?' she asked. 'I thought you were lunching out.'

'I shall not lunch — today,' said Saul.

'Have you cancelled? Do you want me to cancel for you?'

'Will you keep your pretty little nose out of — my business,' said Saul. 'Instead you can go back to the flat and pack everything. We're moving.'

'Into the house? It's not finished.'

'Finished or not, we are moving. I'm sick of the fucking flat! Do as you're told, woman.'

Suddenly, Rowan couldn't stand it. She let go of Saul's arm and fled, running to the new house. There were men working on the roof but inside was deserted. There were bare wires and half-laid floors and not a single door.

A few moments later Andy came in after her. 'What does he mean, live here?' said Rowan helplessly. 'We can't bring Hannah here.'

'He won't want to when he's sober.'

Rowan sniffed expressively.

'Is he ever sober?' asked Andy.

She sighed and wrapped her arms around herself. The rooms were huge and cold, although they would one day be beautiful. 'He doesn't drink in the mornings. The early mornings, at least not that I know of. He's — he's always been a drinker. But lately he's so much worse.'

'He's got a problem,' said Andy. 'He might not know it, but he has. You'll have to get help, love.'

'I daren't.' She fixed huge green eyes on her brother. He had never before considered soft emotions in the context of Rowan, his elder sister, but now he felt sad and protective. 'They might take Hannah away,' she said dismally. 'They could say we're not fit parents.'

Andy let out a crack of mirthless laughter. 'I don't think you need worry on that score. Kids like Hannah aren't wanted by anyone, you'd both have to be drunk all day every day before they took her. Oh, I'm sorry, love. I know that sounds brutal.'

'Yes, it does,' agreed Rowan. 'Everyone always feels they should talk straight about Hannah, when I wouldn't mind a bit of hedging. She's sitting up, you know. I bet you didn't know that.'

'No.'

They left the unfinished house. Rowan went to look for Saul, noting that his old Aston was still in the yard. Perhaps he wanted a new car, she thought wildly. When they went public she would buy him a brand new Porsche, or a Rolls-Royce if he wanted, with a personalised number plate. She would give anything for Saul to be as he used to be.

He was in burling and mending, touching the girls on the thigh and making crude jokes. Rowan thought, 'I know what it feels like to want to kill someone.' Tears were an unrelieved pain in her chest. She said, 'Saul, can you come? I want to talk to you.'

'I can come all right,' he leered, and put his arm round one of the younger, prettier women. She giggled nervously and Rowan snapped, 'I don't think they're paid enough to put up with being mauled by you, Saul.'

He came towards her, waggling his head. 'And what a nasty temper you've got today, Mrs. Barton. Nasty, nasty temper!' His hand reached out and he hit her. The blow caught her shoulder. It was so unexpected that she fell back against the wall.

Two of the women got up and stood like sentinels, worn blue overalls wrapped around their bulky bodies. 'Watch him, Miss,' said one. 'I know what the devils are like when they get like this. He'll have you in hospital, he will.'

Incredulous, Saul said, 'I've never hit her in my life! What the hell do you mean?'

'You just *did* hit me,' said Rowan. Her shoulder hurt and try as she might she was crying, in front of the women, where everyone could see. 'Come away, Saul, will you?'

'God, do you never stop giving bloody orders?' He pushed past her and down the stairs. Rowan wanted to follow but her legs felt like jelly and the women gathered round, full of unwanted sympathy.

'He's had too many, that's what it is, love. Overset him, the funeral and everything.'

'It's all right,' said Rowan desperately. 'He'll be sorry later. He isn't a violent man, normally.'

She knew there was no point in asking them not to gossip, they'd agree and gossip anyway. Gathering her composure to her like a pair of crutches, she followed Saul down the stairs. As she reached the yard she saw his car pull out of the gates, fast and erratic. 'Oh God,' she whispered. 'Oh God, Oh God, Oh God.' What was she to do if he killed himself? What if he killed someone else, a child perhaps, or crippled an old lady? If he got to the flat he would be making a scene, trying to get Barbara to

414

drink with him, playing ridiculous games with Hannah. When he was drunk he always seemed on the verge of dropping her, but Hannah loved it, because it was Saul. The little girl adored him. When she saw him in the mornings she would crow with joy. Rowan taught her to hold a spoon and build bricks, and it was to Saul that Hannah showed off. He was her own, personal god.

It wasn't often that Rowan felt completely at a loss, but she stood in the yard then and had no idea which way to go. On every side were problems, in every place. 'We need a holiday,' she whispered to herself. 'If we could get away from here and have a holiday, everything would be all right.'

Someone was coming towards her from the mill and she couldn't face them. Almost running, she rushed to her car, and then as she was driving out she saw that it was Joe Partridge. She stopped and wound down the window.

'You all right, Ro?' he said.

'No. No, I'm not. What's going to happen, Joe? Everything seems so wrong.'

'Knew you was wrong to marry him. What's he given you but pain, that's what I'd like to know.'

'That isn't true.' She hung her head and whispered, 'I wish I wasn't here, I wish it was different.'

Joe squatted down and put his arm on the door edge. 'Chuck him out, Ro. He's a waster, him, you don't want no more to do with the bastard.'

'But I love him!' wailed Rowan in protest. 'He isn't what you think.'

'You'd do a bloody sight better with me, I can tell you,' retorted Joe. 'Wouldn't see me clouting you in public.'

She felt herself getting hot with shame. 'Does everyone know already?'

''Course they do.'

She wound up the window, excluding Joe, and drove away. He stood watching her. She wondered if she should have married him and had a safe, boring practical life. Saul had always been imagination and flair and excitement, and the reverse of the coin was this. It had to get better.

When she got back to the flat, he wasn't there. She waited until early evening, then drove around Bradford wondering where he might be. At eleven she rang the police, but no accident had been reported and when she spoke about a row they lost interest. At three she went to bed, and lay there, fitfully dozing, waiting to hear him come in, but she woke at six-thirty and he wasn't there.

She couldn't bear to go into the mill. She gave Barbara the day off and wheeled Hannah in her pram, round and round the streets. She got in the car and went out of the town, and carried the baby on to sheep-nibbled grass where she could roll and stretch in safety. 'I will give anything if he's there when I get back,' she told herself. 'I will never be unkind to him again, I shall never be rude, and I will never, never refuse sex, however much it hurts.' Weeks had passed since they last made love. She felt within herself a great desperation.

At last she went back to the flat. When she opened the bedroom door and saw Saul there, sprawled across the bed, his clothes wet and stained and his face grey and unshaven, she almost collapsed with relief. Immediately the telephone rang. It was the doorman. Before she had time to do more than say her name, he said crisply, 'I very much regret, Mrs. Barton, that the residents' committee has made a complaint. Your husband urinated in the main hallway this morning, in front of two ladies.'

'Oh God,' muttered Rowan. 'Tell them I'm sorry — he's sorry —'

'The residents feel he should be asked to leave, Mrs. Barton.'

She held the receiver in a white-knuckled hand. Suddenly she was shouting. 'And you can tell the bloody residents we wouldn't stay here if you paid us! You can all get bloody stuffed!'

Chapter Thirty-Five

They decided to go on holiday to Marbella for a month. When they returned, the house would be completed and the stockbrokers intended Judge's to be poised for the rights issue. Barbara was coming with them, to help with Hannah. They had rented a large villa with a swimming pool.

'It's about time we had some fun,' said Rowan nervously. She and Saul lived in a precarious state of mutual caution, walking around each other's sensibilities. When he recovered from his binge, he had gone out and bought her an emerald choker, fantastically beautiful and even more expensive. Rowan hated it. Every time she set eyes on it she thought of that night, that day, of her pathetic pleas to the landlord to let them stay at least until the end of the week.

On the day before their departure, Andy and Astrid took them out to dinner. Her brother looked almost more cheerful than Rowan had ever seen him, contrasting with Astrid in her dreary cotton dress, sandals and flab. She was a most depressing girl, thought Rowan unkindly.

'Did you see it then?' asked Andy.

'What? Oh, the television. No. No, I didn't.'

'Good God, I thought you at least might show some interest! I — er — I thought you should know, they've asked me to appear on a short series. Four programmes. "Andy Judge and His Musical Friends." I play and then invite one or two up-and-coming 'cellists, or pianists or something. Apparently the guy who was to head it has dropped out. I've got to pretend to be lifelong friends with people I've never met.'

Rowan stretched her face into a smile, saying, 'I'm so

pleased for you. Clever old Andy, you did it! Well, you could be going places.'

'So I could.'

Astrid munched her salad like a cow and said, 'I think Andy means that this is a real springboard, everybody will want him for concerts.'

Folding her hands, Rowan snarled, 'Astrid, why do you always tell me what Andy means? Do you know better than him? Do you think he can't speak for himself perhaps?'

'Don't be so aggressive, Rowan,' said Andy. 'You always were jealous of my girlfriends.'

'As I recall, you never had any girlfriends,' retorted Rowan.

Saul chuckled, and patted Rowan's hand. 'Sibling rivalry never dies, I see. What a charming dress, Astrid, like spring flowers.'

Astrid's cheeks went pink, clashing unfortunately with the dress. When at last they left, they could hear her saying querulously, 'She really is the most self-absorbed creature I ever met, Andy. Only ever interested in her, her, her.'

On the morning of their flight to Spain, Rowan dashed out to Aspley Manor to see her mother. After a fruitless conversation with the cleaner, she at last found Diana in one of the vast greenhouses. She was picking grapes from one of the ancient vines, standing on a ladder to reach the purple clusters and putting them into a wicker basket. Rowan stood and watched her. Diana's movements were slow and deliberate, and her hair needed washing.

'Where's James?' asked Rowan.

'I don't know. At work, I suppose. He comes home, he goes to work, we don't talk.' Diana snipped more bunches of grapes.

'What are you going to do with them all?' asked Rowan. 'Make wine or something?'

Her mother shook her head. 'Throw them away mostly. I don't want them, I don't want anything. But I like it in here.

It's warm, it doesn't remind me.' She got off her ladder and said, 'You know, I don't think James cares at all really. He says horrible things about Nicholas, and about me. I don't think he's capable of caring.'

'Actually, Mother, I think he's heartbroken.' Rowan knew it, although she hardly knew why. But she understood James, she always had.

'Well, if you like to think so,' said Diana.

Rowan longed, as so often before, to tell her mother everything. But there wasn't any point, Diana wouldn't understand. It was sex and yet it wasn't, it was Hannah and the mill and everything. Sometimes she and Saul seemed to have it right, to be on the same 'plane, going to the same place, but then, suddenly, it was different. Was it the drink that did that? Or did he drink because of it? If they got on a real 'plane, now, surely they could go back to the beginning.

'We're going on holiday,' she said.

Diana turned on her. 'Oh God, Rowan, you are so tactless! All right, go, leave me. I know people don't want to be close to me, they can't stand grief. People cross the road when they see me coming. I go into shops and tell the assistants all about it, I can see them hating me and thinking I'm mad. But go on, off on your holiday, everything a miserable mess here and you in the sun having fun.'

'You've got James, Mother,' said Rowan feebly.

Diana's face stretched into a rictus of pain and laughter. 'Oh yes! And James hates me, he does, he really hates me! And I don't know why.'

Rowan left as soon as she could.

The villa, when they finally reached it, was hot and remote. A car was essential. They had hired one at the airport and Saul drove them flat out along the main highway, renowned for its death toll. He had drunk quite a bit on the 'plane, but not enough seriously to affect him. On this road, though, with crumpled cars left rotting on the roadside and Spanish boys leaning out of station wagons, yelling challenges, Rowan and Barbara sat petrified.

As soon as they arrived, Rowan took Hannah into the bedroom and undressed her. She blew on the baby's fat tummy and made her laugh. 'This will get rid of your wheezes, won't it, sweet? No more coughs and colds for Hannah.'

The child had typically dry, flaking skin. Rowan spent pounds on creams and lotions. Ordinary children grew out of such things, and so might Hannah, eventually. Six months late sitting up, and now, at almost eighteen months, she was no bigger than babies of a year old. Patience, that was the thing. One day she would walk, one day she would say 'Mummy'.

'God, but this place is in the back of beyond,' said Saul. He went to the window and stared out at sandy hills covered in scrub.

'Peace and quiet,' said Rowan. 'We shall love it. Have you seen the pool?'

'Yes. Just wish I was in Madrid, that's all. I love Madrid.'

Rowan tried to humour him. 'Well, you could go. I mean you could, we're here for a month. You don't have to stay with us if you don't want to.'

'You want me out of the way, I suppose.'

She glanced at him quickly. He looked tired and tense. He walked around the marble floor in quick strides, his hands clenched in his pockets. She went to him and put her arms round his neck. 'I never want you out of the way. I want you to get brown and fat and happy. I want you to get well.'

'Do you think I'm ill, then? Is that it?'

'You've been working too hard.'

She put her lips along his jaw, mouthing him gently. At last he put his arms round her, he found her mouth and his tongue made sensuous coils around her own. His hands were on her cotton T-shirt, moving it up and down, finding the bones beneath her skin and tracing them gently.

'I love you,' whispered Rowan.

'Do you? Let's give Hannah to Barbara.'

Giggling naughtily, Rowan picked up the quiet girl from the bed and went to the door. 'Barbara! I'm just taking a shower. Would you have Hannah for a moment, please?'

'OK.' Barbara wandered into view, wearing a cheesecloth sundress, like a plum pudding wrapped in muslin. The baby safely removed, Rowan closed the door. She and Saul fell on the bed, laughing like children themselves.

He licked her breasts, he pushed his face into their shallow valley and left a trail with his tongue to her belly and beyond. 'I am enjoying this,' she told herself. 'I just wish I knew it wouldn't hurt.' Her mind kept filling with images of long scars raked by an iron pole, but he wasn't a cruel man, he had never been that. It was she who was cruel to deny him so.

At last he was on top of her. 'All right?' he asked.

'Yes. Go on, do it.'

'I − don't think I can.'

For a minute she didn't understand. Then she touched him. 'Oh dear,' she said dismally.

'Must be a bit tired, I think,' said Saul vaguely, and rolled off her.

Rowan tried desperately to think of something to say. Lots of men had this problem from time to time, or so she understood. But she felt so undesirable. 'We'll have to feed you champagne and oysters,' she said with forced humour. 'Get your clockwork oiled.'

'For Christ's sake, it's you that hasn't been able to for months! You don't have to make a fuss when once I can't perform.'

'I wasn't making a fuss. I didn't want you to feel bad about it, that's all.'

'I wouldn't if you weren't so intent on making a big thing of it.'

'We might have a thing but it certainly isn't big.'

When the comment popped into her mind it had been

421

framed as a joke, but on her lips it sounded hard and unkind.

'You bitch!' said Saul and got off the bed. He went to the suitcases and threw one open, tossing clothes right and left till he found his swimming costume. She felt calmer once his genitals were covered, nothing but a nondescript bulge with nothing asked of them.

'I didn't mean to be horrid,' she said.

'Didn't you?'

He went out of the room, and almost as an after-thought his hand closed on one of the bottles of duty-free spirits he had picked up on the 'plane. Rowan's mouth opened to object. She closed it again. There was nothing she could say.

Chapter Thirty-Six

In retrospect the first disastrous day of the holiday seemed like the last of the awful time at home. It was the end of the worst, Rowan told herself, revelling in day after day of sunshine. It suited her, she wore shorts, a bikini, she would have liked to wear nothing at all and laze round the pool nibbling salads and sipping wine. She and Saul were relaxing together, sending Barbara into town to do the shopping and playing with Hannah, discussing her toes and her eyes and her odd, blunt fingers.

'Would we mind more if we had a normal one?' asked Rowan thoughtfully.

Saul gazed at his daughter through half-closed eyes. 'Probably. We'd compare all the time and now we don't. But, this is the easy bit, it's going to get worse. It's OK to do things for a baby, not for a strapping great ten-year-old.'

Rowan wouldn't think of that; at once she rejected it. 'We might not have to do things. She can learn, she'll just be very slow. She could be independent one day.'

Saul said nothing. He regarded Rowan's optimism with suspicion, it was such a very short step to self-delusion. Live for today, he told himself, enjoy her for what she is and don't expect anything. Suddenly he felt very depressed.

'Why don't we go to bed?' said Rowan boldly. 'We've got to try sometime.'

'Not now, damn it.' He went and opened another bottle of wine. At least wine was something Rowan did not complain about, and he kept up an almost continuous consumption. 'Let's go to the beach this afternoon,' he said.

'Oh. All right.' He was bored then, with her, with her

body, with everything about her. Everything had seemed to be going so well. She blinked back tears.

White dry sand, a breeze, the sun glinting on an endless run of wavelets. Wind surfers careered across the sea, fished out by speed boats when they became exhausted and threatening swimmers when they were not.

'Think I'll have a go at that,' said Saul. It took Rowan by surprise; it was the first positively enthusiastic thing he had said since they arrived. Although she too would have liked to try, it seemed sensible to let Saul have it to himself. She put Hannah down on the sand and spread out her towel. Barbara stood hesitating, and Rowan said, 'You can go off if you like, Barbara. Do what you want.' And Barbara thankfully took off to the beach bar, and the boys.

Left alone, Rowan sat in her bikini and felt conspicuous. She was the only woman in the place with her breasts covered, people stared at her with open curiosity. Perhaps they thought she was deformed or something. Plucking up courage she took off her top and rubbed oil decisively into her skin. Her nipples stood up in fright and embarrassed her, but after ten minutes or so she relaxed. She began playing with Hannah, pouring sand from one bucket to another, putting a spade again and again into her hand.

'Hello there! I thought it was you.' She glanced up quickly, and against the sun, dulled by her sunglasses, barely recognised the man standing over her. He squatted down beside her. A tall man, with reddish hair and a sharp, aware face.

'Richard? Richard Barton?'

'Yes. Well, this is a bit of a coincidence.' She was embarrassingly conscious that she was wearing nothing but a tiny scrap of material that only just covered her pubic hair. Trying to appear casual she picked up her bikini top. 'Don't,' said Richard. 'Please. I didn't want to embarrass you.'

'I'm still putting it on. It's all right when I don't know anyone, but with you here I feel shy.'

424

'Then at least let me help.' He reached up her back and fastened the clasp. To fill the silence, she picked up Hannah.

'She's very good,' he said, trying to think of something positive about the child.

Rowan nodded. 'Too good. You have to stimulate her or she doesn't learn. You have to put experience in, and with normal children they absorb it naturally.'

He trickled sand from one palm to the other. 'I'm amazed at how well you take it. I mean, I don't know much about children but I don't think I could be nearly as calm, a tenth as practical.'

Her mouth twisted and she said, 'Oh no, no.'

'Oh yes! You amaze me, you're fantastic.'

She turned on him. 'That's rubbish! I'm sorry but it is. Today I'm taking it well, you can see me taking it well, I'm here, out here for all to see. What you didn't see, what no one sees, are the days I couldn't face anybody. The day I took her to the clinic and came away again because I couldn't bear to sit in there with all the other babies. I've got a nanny, you know. I have to have a nanny, I was going mad sitting indoors thinking about the future. Most of the time I don't think about it, I pretend she's all right. And people say I'm taking it well. It's an absolute load of rubbish.'

She looked away, out to the windsurfers. 'There's Saul. I didn't know he'd done it before.' He was skimming expertly over the sea, catching the wind and easily outstripping beginners all around him.

'How is he?' asked Richard.

Rowan licked her lips. 'Fine. Just fine. And why are you here, Richard? We're on holiday while they finish our house, but what about you?'

'I'm on holiday too. A bit of time off before I start at Bardsey's.'

The words dropped like lead shot into the pool of their conversation. He could sense Rowan arming herself against him, censoring what she would say.

'I'm pleased for you,' she commented. 'It's odd for James to mend fences.'

'He's had one hell of a battering recently. I never thought I'd feel sorry for him, but I do.'

'Let me tell you, it's a mistake,' snapped Rowan forcefully.

Richard moved so that he had Rowan between himself and the sea. He could seem to stare at the sea and concentrate on her. She was so long and slender, even her neck had unusual length, and her small head was balanced on top like a well-placed flower. Those green eyes too, windows that were at one moment cool and distant, at the next bright with emotion. He wondered what sort of passion she knew with that bum of a husband of hers.

'Are you happy?' he asked suddenly.

For a minute he thought she hadn't heard him. Then she put on her sunglasses again. 'You haven't the right to ask me such a question,' she said at length. 'Happiness isn't something you have or don't have, for always. It comes and goes, lots of times a day sometimes.'

'No, it doesn't. A happy person might not always be knowngly happy, but underneath, there's a layer of contentment. They're at peace with themselves.'

'Well, are you? demanded Rowan. 'Are you contented? You're rich, you've got girlfriends, I suppose. No problems.'

'Lots of problems,' said Richard. 'Or at least one big problem.'

'You're gay!' said Rowan decisively. 'Good, that should upset James.'

'Like hell I am! If you must know, I'm — emotionally dead.'

She stared at him. 'You can't be serious.'

'I am. I don't know what happened to me. When I was a teenager and Dad waltzed off with your mother, I was filled with emotions. They were spilling out right left and centre.

Hate, lust, happiness, love, I had them all. Since I've grown up I haven't got them any more. I just have pale copies. A bit of discontent. Mild dislike. A vague sensation of pleasure.'

'What about sex?' asked Rowan. 'That either is or isn't, surely.'

'There speaks an innocent.' He lounged on his side in the sand, amazed and excited by her directness. 'Sex isn't just on or off, even for men. Some orgasms are a quick spout, nothing to it, get up and go to work and some are – symphonies. Delicious, ecstatic whirls of feeling.' He was getting an erection, he saw her eyes behind the sunglasses focus on it and quickly look away.

Rowan was uncomfortably aware that her odd remark had seemed like encouragement. She began to gather up her things. 'What an expert you seem to be, quite a man of the world. I'm going to take Hannah in the water.'

'You can't, you've got to watch all the things.' He caught her hand. 'I seem to be upsetting you and I don't want to. Stay and talk to me.'

Rowan allowed herself to be pulled back on to the sand. 'I'm just in an odd sort of mood,' she apologised.

'Reaction I should think. You work too hard. And I work too hard, what are we doing in this textile business? We should get used to lying on beaches, we should do it all the time.'

'I'd get horribly, hopelessly bored in about five minutes flat.' She dropped her chin in her hands and grinned at him, and he smiled back, tanned, relaxed, his quick expression that seemed to be habitual. He kept staring at her longer than was polite. She felt herself flushing. 'Why are you looking at me like that?'

He kept his eyes fixed on her. 'You know why. Because you look so lovely. Not many women look great with no clothes on, but you're one of them.'

'You're being ridiculously flattering.' She tried to sound cool, but failed. She stretched out on the sand, looking away

427

from him, hoping he could not tell what she was feeling. Somehow he had managed to prise the cork from the bottle of sexual interest, with him she felt uncomfortably alive. An ache was beginning in her belly, a hot and distressing pain.

'We shall go soon,' she said.

'That would be unkind. I'm alone here, I'm lonely. Give me a helping hand.'

His tone made the remark suggestive. He rolled on to his belly in the sand and she waited tensely for what he was going to say next. But again he surprised her. 'Am I right in thinking you're going public? The papers were full of it on Sunday.'

'We were here, I didn't see. I'm not going to tell you anything you can't find out for yourself.'

Richard laughed. 'I'm not my father, for Christ's sake! I haven't got it in for you.'

'If you're Bardsey's, you've got it in for us. It's sort of undeclared war, Saul meets it all the time, selling. Wherever he puts his foot a Bardsey clodhopper is sure to follow, and a nose, sniffing.'

'Don't tell me he's paranoid as well.'

'As well as what?'

They both looked up. Saul stood, wet and panting. He reached down and picked up Hannah, pressing his wet skin to her dry one. The child squirmed like an animal, a stumpy little teddy bear.

For a second or two Richard remained where he was. Then he sat up.

'Why don't you both have dinner with me tonight?' he said.

'You're not really alone, are you?' asked Rowan. 'I thought that was just a sob story.'

Richard confessed. 'I'm half alone. The lady had to go to Paris for a couple of days, I've got nothing to do till she gets back. Pathetic really.'

'Tragic.'

They laughed together and Saul's antennae, sharper than usual due to sobriety induced by cold water, homed in on the vibes. He wasn't surprised Richard was interested. When he really looked at Rowan, he felt a stab of pride. Gone was the gawky, prickly girl and in her place was a woman of assurance. A sexual woman, who needed and could handle a man's desire.

'OK,' said Saul, taking Rowan aback. 'We'll meet you about eight. I'll make it easy for you and insist Rowan puts her clothes on.'

'Spoilsport.' Richard took his leave of them, passing Barbara on her way back along the beach.

Saul said quickly, 'What did he say? Did he ask you to go to bed with him?'

Rowan laughed. 'Of course not. He's all right, like James really but with the corners knocked off.'

'I think it's you he wants to knock off.' Saul wasn't displeased. The knowledge that Rowan was desired by others was stimulating.

She dressed for the evening in a white jersey silk tube, reaching from above her breasts to above her knees. Underneath it she was of necessity naked since underclothes would have shown. As she walked the fabric moved on her, so every now and then she had to hitch it up over her breasts.

'Great,' said Saul appreciatively. 'Just great.' He had drunk quite a bit after the beach. He lounged on the bed, looking dashing in a white jacket and bow tie. Rowan had thought he might make love to her but the drink was calming him. Later, perhaps.

She picked up her bag and said, 'Shall I drive?' and Saul nodded. In the car her skirt rode up towards her crotch but he did nothing. She felt defiant. She knew she looked good tonight, she wanted some acknowledgement.

Richard gave it to her. They dined at his hotel, an exclusive and expensive alabaster palace. The ceilings seemed carved out of spun sugar, and were reflected in the

429

dark marble floors. Instead of the heavy wood of so much of the country's furniture, there were gilded chairs and airy glass tables, everything so light and delicate that it was like fairyland. Saul slumped in one of the chairs like a man in a Wendy house, his head already turning as he looked for the next drink. Rowan clenched her teeth and sat also, aware that the waiters were fawning on her, that Richard was deliberately positioning himself opposite her knees. In consequence she crossed her legs, wondering how much he could see in the dark shadows of her skirt. Let Saul know that this man found her exciting, let him discover what sort of woman he had.

Richard said, 'I brought the papers out with me. I thought you might be interested.' He laid the quality Sundays out on the low coffee table and Rowan immediately picked them up. She scanned the columns.

'Listen, Saul, where do they get this stuff from? "Isaac Judge is about to take the biggest step of its career in buying itself a stockmarket quotation. Billed by some as a leap in the dark, it is in fact another brilliant move by the successful Bradford firm. Ably managed by one of the textile industry's few women, who rescued it from disaster only a few years ago, the company looks like being a certain growth stock." Why don't they mention you, darling? They could have said one of the industry's few married couples. Going public was entirely your idea. I mean, it was my idea, but you worked out how to do it.'

Saul put down his empty whisky glass and signalled a waiter for another. Rowan froze, unaware that her anxiety was immediately obvious to Richard.

He said smoothly, 'Let's make a night of it. Champagne for everyone. Waiter!'

Saul's next whisky was unobtrusively waved away. Rowan felt weak with gratitude, for while Saul could drink champagne all night and remain conscious, if he continued on whisky at that rate they would all suffer for it.

She said to Richard, 'How do you intend to make James let you do anything? It's awfully hard to let go, you know. When Saul first came to Judge's I almost elbowed him out of the office. I couldn't bear it!'

'What's changed?' asked Saul sardonically.

'Don't be silly, darling!' Rowan was starting to hate the evening, to wish she had never come.

Richard said, 'I think we'll work it out, as you two have, I suppose. He's very keen to get me in, I think he'll be sensible.'

Saul laughed. 'I remember when I started there. He was going to let me run things, he was going to involve me. Took me years to realise he'd never intended anything of the kind.'

'So you married me and got a firm of your own,' said Rowan crisply. 'A good move all round, if I may say so.'

Saul grinned suddenly. 'Are you determined I married for money? If you want us to believe that, you're wearing the wrong clothes.'

'She does look delectable,' agreed Richard, nodding.

A sexual charge seemed to run through all three of them. Rowan felt beads of moisture forming in the small of her back, coursing down into the crease of her backside. The two men shifted in their chairs. Saul ran his thick brown finger round the edge of his glass. Rowan's own fingers caressed the long stem of the glass she held, while Richard reached for the champagne bucket and took out the bottle. The moment was heavy with suggestion. 'We'll have some more of this,' said Richard. 'Let's go and eat.'

Throughout the meal, Rowan felt threatened by him. To begin with she was consciously exciting him, which in turn excited Saul. She was waiting until she was alone with Saul; she knew he would be hard and eager. Everything would be all right after that. But Richard seemed to be demanding something for himself. When a small band set up on the dais and started to play, Richard took Rowan's hand. 'Let's dance,' he said, and pulled her close to him. A tall, spare man, his brain clear and sharp.

They were belly to belly, she could feel him pressing against her. 'He doesn't give you any fun, does he?' whispered Richard. 'Always drunk, always miserable.'

'I don't like you,' said Rowan, almost to herself.

'I'm not surprised. I tell you that you're young, and beautiful, and shackled to a drunk who doesn't know what he's got. Look at him now, ordering a whisky to help things along. He thinks you won't see him. And when we get back he'll dance with you himself, only because I have. Watch.'

He led Rowan back to the table. The whisky had gone and Saul said, 'Right, let's dance then, Rowan.' She went out again to the floor and he clutched her to him and used her to hold himself up. He said, 'That guy really fancies you. He'd give anything to have you.'

'Don't talk like that. I want you to make love to me, don't you want to?'

He laughed. 'You needn't worry. I'll be fantastic tonight.'

At the table there was more champagne. Saul ordered brandy. Rowan said, 'I've had enough, I want to go home,' but the two men kept on drinking, keeping pace with one another. She was thirsty but there was only champagne, so she drank another glass, and then another. 'Let's go up to my room for a nightcap,' said Richard.

'We ought to go home,' said Rowan.

'We're on holiday,' said Saul. 'We can let our hair down once in a while. Don't be such a puritan, Rowan.'

So they went upstairs in the lift. The champagne was having its effect, Rowan felt warm and relaxed. She draped her arms round Saul and leaned on him, and he leaned against the wall. In the bedroom there was a huge double bed, covered in a white quilt. There was a sofa, too, and Saul slumped on it, chuckling. 'She looks gorgeous, doesn't she? Just delicious.'

'Yes.'

Richard poured them all drinks and Rowan kicked off her shoes and wandered about on the marble floor, relishing the chill on her feet. She could feel the two men watching her, she felt strung between them, dancing on a wire, on a rope of sexuality. The drink was very strong, she didn't know what it was. Richard stood in front of her. He touched her breast.

Just his fingers released a charge of electricity. The shock of it was sobering. She glanced quickly at Saul and the look on his face revolted her. 'Don't touch me!' She picked up her shoes, fitting them on as she went, but Saul sat there, watching. 'You want him to, don't you?' she said in horror. 'You want to watch!'

Richard was close behind her. He put his hands around her waist and she hit him.

'Leave her alone,' mumbled Saul. 'Rowan doesn't want to play.' He got to his feet and came swaying across. She hid behind him, sheltering from Richard, from the lascivious ideas of the men who saw her as a creature in some fantasy. If she gave a hint of acceptance they would both have her, one after the other, competing.

Richard said, 'Why do you stick with him? You are so, so lovely.'

'He's drunk,' flared Rowan. 'He doesn't know what he's doing, but you do, you know!'

'So did you,' said Richard softly. 'You wanted it.'

Saul reeled back against the wall, in a state of near coma. 'Oh God, I've been here before,' said Rowan bitterly. 'Help me get him down to the car, will you?'

'You should dump the shit in the street and leave him,' said Richard, his frustration crystallising into anger. 'He's no damn use to you.'

'He's my husband and I love him,' replied Rowan. 'He's the father of my child. He won't always be like this, he'll get better.'

Richard pushed her aside and bent to put Saul over his

shoulders. The big man groaned and mumbled, 'Don't drop me, I'm only little.' Bent under the weight, Richard staggered to the lift and threw him in.

'You don't have to half kill him,' snarled Rowan.

'He's doing worse than that to you, he's eating you alive. When he's not there you're bubbly, relaxed. You're so different, you should see yourself. With him, you're always watching.'

When the lift doors closed, she and Richard were crammed together in one corner while Saul lay sprawled across the floor. Suddenly Richard reached up under her skirt, pushed his hand between her legs and touched her. She couldn't get away. She stood immobile and waited for the lift to stop. It was barely a second but it lasted for ever.

'You're wonderful,' whispered Richard. 'I must make love to you.'

When the lift reached the ground she wriggled away from him, fell over Saul and got out of the door. Richard shouldered his burden and staggered into the car park. As he unloaded Saul into the back seat of the car, Rowan said dangerously, 'Don't you think you can do that to me again. Don't you ever think you can touch me again. I didn't believe you when you said you had no feelings but I do now. They're dead. There's nothing left in you but foul perversions.'

He came round to the driver's door, but she was in the car and locking it. He reached through the open window and took her face between his hands.

'You're sending me mad,' he said wildly. 'You're to blame, you drive me to it and then blame me.'

She struck his hand aside. He caught her wrists and they struggled hard. Then she spat at him, full in the face. They froze into a bitter tableau. He saw Rowan's eyes brimming with tears, and let her go. Jerking the car into gear, she drove furiously away.

The next day, of course, Saul was ill and seemed to

remember nothing of the night before. He blamed his malady on seafood eaten at dinner, and Rowan pretended to agree. Inside herself she carried a small furnace of rage and hurt. However many times she swam up and down the pool, it burned on.

In the afternoon she left Hannah and Saul in Barbara's care and took the car. She was going shopping, deliberately going down the coast to avoid all chance of meeting Richard. Her route took her along the main road, although she had avoided it ever since they came. Now she felt she hardly cared if she ended up mangled in some crash, it would at least stop her thinking.

The reality of wild driving, lorries belching smoke and stray dogs lying dead at the roadside, was more than she expected. After five miles she took the first exit, scuttling off down a side road in terror. A lorry had pulled in on her and shaved her bumper, sending her vehicle into a brief skid on the greasy road. The car was hot but she was cold with sweat. She took her hands off the wheel one at a time and tried to relax them. The road was narrow and dusty, a lane leading away into the hills. Clearly it did not lead to any shopping centre, but anything was preferable to the maelstrom she had left.

After half an hour Rowan found herself driving through a small, white village. A tall woman in black was driving four or five goats down the road towards her, urging them on with a long thin stick. The goats were tall and their floppy ears gave them a cute expression that Rowan found endearing. She stopped the car to let them go past. She could hear her heart beating rhythmically. Outside the open window the goats bleated and a gentle Spanish dust settled on her hair. The place smelled of heat and garlic and dung. The woman with the goats was beautiful, thought Rowan; she was like a figure from another age, a grand lady fallen on hard times.

She became aware that she was thirsty. She got out of the

car and wandered down the street, looking in at the dark houses, shuttered against the sun. There was a shop of sorts, although when she first looked into the cavernous interior after the white glare of the sun she could see little. The cool inside struck at her and made her shiver. Sacks of dates and olives stood on the floor, there were tins on the shelf and hessian-wrapped cheeses on the counter. One whole wall was taken up by giant wine barrels.

The shopkeeper, a woman, came in and murmured to her. Rowan pointed to some cheese and the woman cut some, offering also some tough-looking bread. Rowan added dates, some olives, and a tin of something like spam. The woman was gaining an idea of what this meal was to be, and she brought out tomatoes and some apricots, and finally went to the barrels. She drew off some red wine into a small glass and gave it to Rowan to taste. Rowan took it cautiously, because she had already bought some lemon pop. Besides, she had never much liked booze and nowadays she saw it as intrinsically wicked. It was a trap, well baited but lethal.

The wine was rough and sour. There was nothing in it to commend, but somehow it held all that was real about this place, about this day. To eat this food, to drink this wine, was to share the life of the countryside. The woman filled an old green bottle and stoppered it, then used a blunt pencil to do her sums on a pad.

Out in the street once again, Rowan looked for the goats but they had gone. It was so hot, the light seemed to bleach the colour from the earth, from the houses. But the sky was gentian, the shadows beneath the trees more purple than any dye. In a field of olive trees, wild poppies stained the dusty grass like blood. She went back to her car and sat in it with her eyes closed, watching the sun against her eyelids. At last she started the engine and drove slowly on, with no idea of where she headed.

Chapter Thirty-Seven

It was after seven when at last she found her way back. She was very tired and had begun to despair of ever making sense of hazy directions she received from people she passed. Somehow when she drove to the villa and saw another hire car there she was surprised by the intensity of her anger. Richard, incredibly, had dared to come here.

He was sitting by the pool, under the drifts of flowering creeper, talking to Barbara. 'Where's Saul?' asked Rowan crisply, depositing her packages amidst their cosy glasses.

Barbara raised her eyebrows expressively. 'Oh,' said Rowan. 'Much?'

'Enough.'

She went through to look, but he was asleep, sprawled on the bed, snoring. Prudently she removed all bottles, instead bringing a water jug from the kitchen. If he woke in the night and drank water, he would be so much better in the morning.

When she came back, Barbara had taken the food into the kitchen and was preparing it. The bottle of wine stood alone on the table. 'I was worried about you,' said Richard.

'Don't lie.'

He got up and went to the cabinet to find glasses. Uninvited he took the cork from the wine and poured some for both of them, and after a moment Rowan took the proffered glass. She sipped, tasting again the special flavour of the afternoon, absorbing the essence of that Spanish village. When Richard drank too, she felt as if he was sharing her thoughts, invading her privacy. For a moment she felt as if her soul was laid out for him to see.

Richard said, 'I'm sorry. That's what I came to say.'

'What exactly are you sorry for?'

He shrugged. 'You, mostly. Oh God, don't start getting furious! I mean that and I don't. We were all drunk last night, things got out of hand. Some of it was even your fault, for wearing that dress, doing what you did.'

She finished her wine and then poured herself some more. 'You got in the way between me and Saul,' she said distantly. 'We had our own situation, it didn't need you.'

All of a sudden Richard was fierce. 'What you don't realise is that there isn't a situation with him! Do you know, I've never seen him when he hasn't been drinking? It's been a steady progression, every year a little more, and now he's out of control. He isn't going to get better, Rowan. He's a bum. If you stick with him you're on the road to one hell of a lot of misery.'

She put down her glass and went over to the mirror, one of those ornate Spanish affairs hung surprisingly low on the wall. It reflected her dirty bare feet, her sandals kicked off at the door and the marks of the straps showing white in the muck. Long legs in a sweat-dampened cotton skirt, a sleeveless top sodden between her breasts. Even her hair was stuck to her head, but the dust had changed its colour to dull grey.

'Why do you want to spoil my life?' she asked wearily. 'All you want to do is sleep with me for a bit. I haven't got much now. If I did that I'd have even less.'

'You don't know what you might have,' said Richard desperately. He came and stood behind her, knowing that if he touched her, as he longed to do, she would hit him. 'He doesn't even have to know,' he said softly.

Rowan shot him a look of such contempt that he was scorched by it. 'I think you'd better go,' she said clearly, and at that moment Barbara came in with three plates on a tray. 'But I made him some food,' she said.

'He's not staying for it,' retorted Rowan. She went to the

door and held it open but Richard hesitated, knowing what he wanted to say and unable to say it in front of Barbara. Eventually he walked towards the door.

'You're being too hard on yourself,' he said to Rowan. 'There's no need for it, you must see that.'

'If you're staying in Spain, we shall go home.' She was implacable, her eyes like green glass. And yet, and yet – her legs were trembling. When they stood as close as this, the ridiculous happenings of last night were entirely explicable.

'I'll go,' he said suddenly. 'I'll meet my friend in Paris. But – I want you to know how much I admire you, how much I understand.'

She looked away from him, down at her long, bare, dirty feet. 'You don't understand the first thing about me or any woman. Go away.'

When he'd gone, Barbara tentatively offered her a plate of food. Rowan picked at it, dismally. Barbara said, 'He likes you an awful lot.'

'I imagine that's his stock in trade,' replied Rowan. She felt weary to the bone, and the expected relief at getting rid of him was slow in coming. Dismally she thought of the weeks ahead before they could go home. 'We'll have to try and stop him drinking,' she said, voicing her thoughts.

Barbara's soft mouth twisted. 'We can try. I don't suppose – I mean, there are places that do treatment.'

'Is it that bad, do you think? It isn't very often that he's as bad as this, after all.' Yet in the past months it was more and more often. She was deluding herself in thinking that the times in between were coming to be anything more than hungover interludes.

The baby started to cry and Rowan went to her. As she cuddled and soothed, she wondered was it Hannah, or her, or the mill or what? There was no point in sending him for treatment if the problem remained, if the fault was not in him but in the life she had brought him. Every time he got wildly drunk she felt angry, yes, but guilty too because if she

439

had been different, so would he. A happy man has no need to blot out the world, she told herself, and she had brought him trouble, unhappiness – and Hannah.

That night she lay in the hot bed and listened to Saul's snoring. When at last she fell asleep in the cool of the coming dawn, it was to be wakened minutes later. Saul was climbing on top of her, silently pushing her legs apart. Still half-asleep she felt him nudging into her and there was no pain, nothing. Even pleasure had deserted her. She lay beneath him in the bed and felt unloved and unloving, used by a man who wanted to prove himself to himself. Her mind conjured up a picture of Richard. She hated him, she told herself, he would use her just as much, she was deceiving herself to think otherwise. Yet, as her husband subsided on to her, groaning with pleasure, it was the thought of Richard that gave her comfort.

For the rest of the holiday there was a distance between her and Saul, although they made love several times. Once when Saul was starting drinking before ten in the morning, Rowan asked him if he thought he needed to see a doctor. He said sarcastically, 'Darling, it isn't me that's got a problem, it's you. There's something very puritanical about your attitude to life. There isn't anything I enjoy that you don't think should be rationed.'

There seemed to be quite a bit of truth in that. She sat by the pool or at the window, gazing out over the hot landscape, trying to capture the colours in blocks of felt tip on paper. Designs for cloth seemed to multiply in her head, and she worked on them endlessly, defeating her unhappiness. On the edges of her vision Saul played with Hannah, with total patience, total commitment, drinking all day until he fell into bed unconscious at some time in the evening. Locked into a cell of loneliness, Rowan found herself thinking again and again, 'How did we come to this? Where did we go wrong?'

Chapter Thirty-Eight

Mohammed Shafir disliked his work. His metabolism rebelled against activity at night-time; he would often find himself fighting sleep when to lose concentration for even a minute might be to lose a finger or a hand. His was a mill almost entirely staffed by Asians, an apartheid that had developed almost unnoticed by the outside world. Asians mixed hardly at all with the indigenous population. They lived in their own areas, shopped at their own shops, and worked in cliques or whole factories where English was almost never heard. That, too, Mohammed disliked. He was a man of natural intelligence who could see the futility of walling himself into a ghetto. It rendered a situation tolerable, but did nothing to change it into something better.

Nonetheless, acceptance was written into the very fabric of his life. All Moslems learned it, as they learned the Koran, sitting in the mosque for hours after school, chanting screeds of Arabic. Allah must be obeyed, your father must be obeyed, wives must obey husbands, children obeyed everybody. There was a stability about such a life that was lacking in the English. It was as if lack of discipline set you free to crash into the gutter as well as soar to the stars.

But life was about change. The prophet himself had looked at the world and felt moved to transform it. Mohammed felt, in his heart, that this might be his portion also, in however humble a form. After all, he was uniquely placed to take from each system that which was of worth and put it to good use in a new and different lifestyle. Moslem values, British imagination, Moslem discipline and British freedom of thought.

441

His parents rejected such ideas utterly, of course. They felt that any small movement towards the people they lived beside but not amongst, meant a breach in the walls that protected them. Like the dams in Holland, the first leak would be followed by others until in the end they would all be swallowed up in a deluge of misery and godlessness. It was only through Mohammed's insistence and Fadeema's tact that his sister had been allowed to go to university. He, too, had wanted to go, but there had been no one to sponsor him, no one to stand at his side when he argued unforgivably with his father. So here he was, weaving in a mill, swaying with weariness, dreaming of Sally.

Sally. His sweet, pretty, dear, needy girl. Other men, other less educated men, would not understand her, would think she was tainted. He alone knew how much she needed him, and besides, he was realistic. A girl like Sally would not come to such as him quite unsoiled by the world. He had no illusions about his position on the ladder, the distance that separated him from a girl like Sally. But she had been sent to him, and he to her. It was up to him to rescue her from the chaos of her life, and for her to free him from his chains. In marrying Sally he would be climbing away up the ladder, taking with him the harness of his religion. They would stand together, two people that society preferred apart. Together they would reach heights that alone neither could scale.

The next morning, bone weary but past sleep, he waited for Sally outside the hostel as she left for college. She didn't at once see him and he was at liberty to admire her, small, blonde, her hair piled up on her head in an inexact knot from which tendrils fell charmingly. She wore a neat blue dress and, as always, high heels, because she always wanted to be taller. For himself he loved all that was miniature about her, from her little hands to her short round neck. In comparison he felt that Rowan was far too tall, that her height reflected the sort of woman she was. Sally was no tycoon, she would be his wife and the mother of his children.

'You look so pretty today.'

She saw him and turned, smiling. They held hands. He wouldn't kiss her in the street. He noticed her eyes were red beneath heavy make-up. 'You've been crying.'

'Not really, no. Just a bit, perhaps.'

'I must take you away from that woman in there! I shall speak to her, she must not upset you like this.'

'It isn't her.' Sally spoke with deadly weariness. They walked on to the end of the street, and Mohammed remained silent, knowing she would tell him. The doss house was turning out the drunks and the headcases, the men released from mental hospitals and drifting down to the bottom of the pit. Sally sometimes gave them money, the sad, bewildered ones, but today she had no energy for others. At the end of the street, she said, 'I think I'm pregnant.'

'Oh!' He beamed with joy. At last, at last the door was opening. They could get married, no one would stop them now. 'We will go and see my father tonight,' he said enthusiastically. 'I will insist now. Then of course we shall see your sister — and your mother.' He hesitated over Diana. He disliked the woman, he thought her the cause of all Sally's troubles.

'I don't want to live with your mother,' said Sally. 'I've money, we can buy a house.'

He nodded. 'For the moment I should prefer you to stay with my mother. You can help her, she will learn to love you. It is important that you should know each other, respect each other.'

'But I should much rather we lived by ourselves,' said Sally urgently. 'We're not going to live like your parents, you said so yourself. We're going to do things differently.'

'But first they must see that we can live the old life,' advised Mohammed. 'You are tired, you must not go to work today. Come and have ice cream.'

Sick and anxious, Sally made no objection. The thought

of telling everyone weighed on her, she could imagine only too well what they would say. If only, if only she could see their way clear to a life of their own, a house of their own. It was what she wanted more than anything in the world, a great deal more than this baby. She couldn't imagine the baby, almost didn't believe in it. Yet it was there, growing inside her.

In the evening Mohammed took her again to his parents' house. He had snatched a few hours' sleep in Sally's room at the hostel, but it wasn't enough. As he led Sally through the front door, he felt weary and on edge, unfitted for the announcement he was to make. But he undertook much of his life when he was not at his best. He hardly knew what it was to be relaxed, well-fed and well-rested.

His father was watching an Asian video. It was a highly coloured romance, a tale of love and sin, about as far from anything his father had ever experienced as the moon from the sun. Mr. Shafir was a tall grizzled man with a beard and long, stained teeth. He worked in a combing plant, sweeping up because the overlooker thought him incapable of more, and he resented it.

Mohammed's uncle and his young brother were in the room too, all wearing the tunics and trousers that determinedly proclaimed them foreigners in an alien land. Sally took an unhappy, gasping breath.

'Father,' said Mohammed clearly. His father pretended not to hear. His uncle and brother looked uncomfortable. Mohammed went across to the television and turned it off. 'Forgive me, Father,' said Mohammed. 'I have brought Sally to see you. We are to marry.'

His father ignored him and told his brother in Gujerati to turn the television back on. Mohammed stopped him on the way. 'Father, Sally is to have my child,' he said.

The old man seemed to shudder slightly. He turned his head and stared at Sally. She found herself looking into eyes misted with cataracts. Then he erupted into furious Gujerati, railing at his son, getting up to hit at him with big, gnarled hands.

Sally backed out into the hall. Everyone had heard; Fadeema was there, and from the kitchen Sally could hear Mohammed's mother, weeping and wailing. In the front room Mohammed and his father shouted violently at each other, from the kitchen came the sound of smashing crockery. Fadeema said, 'Come upstairs, Sally. It wasn't fair of Mohammed to bring you to this.'

In the cramped little room upstairs that Fadeema shared with her sister, Sally said, 'He wants us to live here. I don't want to.'

Fadeema considered. 'It would be best if you could try, Sally. My mother will accept you if you are here, and help her. You see, she thinks you will steal him away and she will lose her son. And she knows Mohammed will do as he wants. They have found three girls before for him to marry and he wouldn't look at them. You see, your — condition — does make a difference.'

It was hard to believe, when downstairs the arguments raged and the crockery smashed.

Eventually an uneasy peace fell. Fadeema led Sally back downstairs to where Mohammed was confronting his parents in the front room. They stood side by side, rigid with disapproval. Mohammed's mother took one look at Sally and began to cry.

'It is agreed,' said Mohammed stiffly. 'My mother will make you welcome, Sally, when we are married. Otherwise we shall set up home elsewhere.'

Silently, Sally nodded. She was on the verge of tears.

Valley House. A gentle name for a beautiful home. When Saul and Rowan returned from holiday they weren't prepared for the progress that had been made. In place of grey plaster and bare floors there was white paint and acres of pale-green carpet. The doors and skirtings were of light wood, like a house in Scandinavia, light and clean and new. Through the huge double-glazed windows they could see nothing as yet but rubble and heaps of earth, but it was possible to imagine the elegant gardens the architect described, complete with cherry trees and lawns. Harder to visualise was that anyone would ever want to swim in the dirty, half-tiled hole that was to be the pool, but for now Rowan was too pleased with what she had to worry about what she had not.

They had no suitable furniture. The mishmash of pieces they had collected since they married would be a disaster in the clean elegance of Valley House, thought Rowan. There was a need for good wood, leather and glass, and lovely fabrics in striking patterns. Her stomach dropped at the added expense; she would never be able to spend money with the open-handedness of Saul. And she didn't like to think of Saul just at the moment.

She never seemed to act rationally where he was concerned. If she wanted to say something to anyone else, she would pick a time and phrase it as carefully as she could. But on their first evening back, camping in the house on air beds and tables out of the offices, she had said bluntly, 'I think you should see a doctor about your drinking. And Barbara agrees.'

The crime was multiplied because he was not at that moment sober. He swung round on her. He seemed very big and brown, almost leonine. Such dark brown eyes he had, so dark sometimes the pupils were invisible, and when he was drunk he could stare indefinitely without blinking. 'Brown is a frightening colour,' thought Rowan.

'Who the hell are you to discuss my habits with the hired help?'

Barbara shot a scared glance at Rowan, picked up Hannah and got out of the room. Rowan said, 'We didn't discuss you. We sort of agreed it. After all, she's the one that helps me put you to bed.'

'Don't exaggerate.' He always lived with the illusion that it was never as bad as she knew it to be. He always missed the worst bits. Even if he was conscious, he never remembered them.

'It isn't fair on me, or Hannah, or anyone,' Rowan struggled on, though she would have retreated if she could. He was pacing the vast empty room, and she crouched on an office chair, wondering if he was going to hit her. It seemed ridiculous. The Saul she knew once, the Saul she had married, couldn't even squash a fly.

He stopped and stared at her. 'You want me out, don't you? You want to pretend I'm an alcoholic so you can have your precious firm all to yourself and shack up with sodding Richard Barton.'

Her head came up. 'It was you that thought Richard Barton should join in!' she flared. 'I was the one who stopped it, but you won't remember, you were too pissed!'

'I get a bit sloshed once in a while and suddenly I'm an alcoholic.' He stopped in front of her chair, put his hands on either side of her face and pressed. 'I'm warning you, Rowan, I don't like being pushed around. I always knew you were a bossy woman. What you need is a firm hand.'

She remained quite still, feeling him pressing on the sides of her skull. At the moment it seemed as if he could crush her head with just the pressure of his big hands. She reached up, touched his wrists and he let her go. 'Won't you stop for Hannah?' she asked, finding her breath dragging through shrivelled lungs.

'Hannah wants for nothing that I can give her.' He left her suddenly, crossed the floor and wrenched open a holdall. It contained the duty-free allowance. Rowan opened her mouth to protest, then closed it again. As always when she challenged him, she succeeded only in making things worse.

For once she couldn't escape her anxieties, either in the mill or with the stockbrokers who were within days of launching the company on the stock exchange. Before they left, she was entranced by all the manipulating, but now her mind wandered in meetings and she had to be reminded of what they had agreed. To escape it all she and Barbara went furniture shopping and Rowan bought this and that, some of which she liked, and some of which would just about do.

'You'll be sorry you rushed it in the end,' said Barbara sagely, sipping coffee while she rested her substantial ankles on the crossbar of Hannah's pushchair. Barbara was getting extremely fat, she had even put on weight in Spain when to Rowan's mind it was often too hot to eat.

'I don't know what I'd do without you,' said Rowan suddenly. Barbara's sensible, kindly support was always there. She didn't gossip about Saul or Hannah, she didn't comment on the rows. 'If you left, I'd just crumble,' she added.

'Well, I'm not going to leave,' declared Barbara, with solid loyalty. 'You and Hannah need me, and he's not a bad old thing when he's sober.'

'He used to be lovely,' Rowan heard herself say. And in saying that, admitted that he wasn't any more.

Sally and Mohammed called when Rowan and Barbara were trying to arrange some of the lumpish furniture they had bought. There was a wall cabinet for the sitting-room which the man in the shop had declared was ideal for all those little knick-knacks. Rowan had no knick-knacks but thought she perhaps should acquire some, and the cabinet had concealed lighting and mirrored shelves and several other features that, now she thought about it, she intensely disliked.

'I'm going to send it back,' she said wearily to Sally. 'Barbara said I shouldn't have bought it in the first place.'

'Then why did you?' asked Sally. She had never known Rowan impulse buy in all her life.

'I suppose I was thinking about other things.'

Remembering her manners, Rowan sat them down on the

new leather Chesterfield and perched herself on one of the office chairs. 'Would you like a drink?' she asked Mohammed. 'Oh no, you don't, do you? Tea then.' She got up and went through to the kitchen, a beautiful room cleverly designed to exclude Hannah from the cooking area by means of a raised step and gate. Rowan blundered about looking for cups and milk and sugar.

'Is something the matter?' asked Sally. Not even her own preoccupation could entirely blot out her sister's air of anxious distraction.

'What? Oh, it's just the house. The firm's taking off, the house needs attention, everything. Everything.'

Mohammed said, 'We've chosen a poor time. Come, Sally, let's go.'

'Oh, please, no! I'd much rather have someone to talk to.' She tried to smile and seem less pathetic, adding, 'Saul's out, you see. Business.'

They took the tray of tea into the sitting-room and sat down again. The curtainless windows gave the feeling of sitting in a shop window, and one in the process of change at that. 'How's the course?' asked Rowan brightly.

'I'm not finishing it.' Sally took a deep breath, lifting her heavy breasts under her navy jumper. 'I'm pregnant.'

Rowan said nothing. Mohammed said urgently, 'Without this my parents would not agree to the marriage. It was necessary.'

Rowan linked her fingers together. 'I see. Well, then. Congratulations. When's the wedding?'

'It's going to be a Registry Office,' said Sally, looking anything but glad. Rowan felt a pang. She would have loved to see Sally in a puffball dress of white satin, however inappropriate. She would look enchanting, almost a child bride.

'We haven't arranged anything,' said Mohammed. 'We must speak to Sally's mother.'

'Yes.' Rowan hesitated and then said bluntly, 'Come into the kitchen, Sally, I want to talk to you alone.'

In the kitchen, Rowan hissed: 'What's the matter? Don't you want to marry him? Before, it was all you wanted.'

'Yes, of course I do,' moaned Sally, twisting her hands. 'It's just — Rowan, his parents hate me, and he wants us to live with them! With his mother.'

'But you've told him you could have a house, haven't you? We should make a lot of money this year, you'll have a lot of money. He could start a business, anything.'

'He thinks I ought to learn to get along with his mother.'

They went back into the sitting-room. Rowan said, 'She can't live with your mother, Mohammed, it wouldn't be fair.'

Rigidly polite he cast Sally a telling look and said, 'It is for me to decide for my own family, Rowan.'

'Sally is my family at the moment. If you want our blessing you'll do as Sally wishes and get a house of your own; my mother will insist on it.'

'We haven't told her yet,' said Sally dismally.

'Then I suggest we do,' said Rowan. 'Tonight.' She glared at Mohammed. How dare he exploit her sister, how dare he push her around?

'I have no respect for Sally's mother,' said Mohammed grimly.

'And I have no respect for yours,' retorted Rowan.

They marched out to the car. Both Rowan and Mohammed were buoyed up for battle, and between them Sally was crushed.

'I shall be late for work,' said Mohammed distantly. 'My pay will suffer.'

'Allow me to reimburse you,' snapped Rowan.

'I do not need charity!'

Rowan stepped on the accelerator and sent her little car rattling down the road. They could see the lights of the Manor from some distance away, she wondered briefly if they were having a party. But there was only one visiting car. A Maserati.

'Oh,' said Rowan, suddenly discomfited. 'Richard's here.'

'I don't mind,' said Sally. 'Let's get it over with, I can't bear all the hanging around.'

'This is a private matter, Sally,' said Mohammed. 'It is not for strangers to discuss it.'

Rowan rounded on him. 'How dare you tell her what she should and shouldn't do? You're the one who got her into this mess. You're after her money, you're just using Sally to get what you want!'

'It isn't like that,' said Sally miserably.

Rowan got out of the car and went to the front door. The others followed. She knocked on the door and after a while it was opened. By Richard.

He was surprised, Rowan was not. She pushed past him into the house, saying nothing. Chamber music was coming from the sitting-room and when she went in she saw James standing by the stereo. Diana was sitting on the sofa and Andy stood by the fire.

Rowan said, 'What on earth are you doing here, Andy? I thought you were in London.'

He looked embarrassed and Rowan had a cold moment of fear. They hadn't wanted her here tonight. What were they discussing?

James said, 'I see we are to be honoured by one of Sally's friends. Does he speak English, Sally?'

'Thank you, I can also read,' said Mohammed, and extended his hand. James took it, grinning. He had no racial prejudice, but he liked baiting Sally.

Diana, on the other hand, had stiffened visibly. 'What is all this about, Rowan?' she demanded, as if it were all Rowan's fault.

Sally coughed unhappily. 'We just thought — I thought — Mohammed and I are getting married. I'm pregnant.'

'Good God!'

Diana got up, marched to Mohammed, drew back her

451

arm and slapped him hard across the face. He stood quite still, doing nothing, saying nothing. Diana drew back her hand to strike again and Rowan said, 'Don't, Mother. There's nothing to be done but get on with it. He's a nice man, really.'

'And you are such a wonderful judge!' Diana turned on Sally, standing with her head bowed. 'How could you? I just don't know how you could!'

Mohammed spoke and his quiet voice cut across Diana's screeches. 'I shall look after Sally as well as I am able. She will live at my home and be cared for.'

'White slavery, and Sally's paying for it,' retorted Diana.

Rowan went and sat on the sofa and Andy came and sat next to her. 'Have you encouraged this?' he asked softly. 'It's insane, Rowan, you know it is.'

'It has nothing to do with me! But she's pregnant, we can't do anything.'

'She could get rid of it!'

Rowan caught his arm. 'Don't suggest it, please. Not for Sally. It wouldn't be good for her.'

James, who had been watching the action with interest, declared suddenly, 'Let's all have a drink! We can toast the happy couple and their progeny — probably come out in black and white stripes. Let's have champagne.' He went in search of bottles and glasses, Rowan thought she had never felt less like celebrating anything. She could feel Richard watching her.

James brought three bottles and uncorked them expertly. He poured for them all, refusing to take no for an answer, even from Mohammed. The man's dark skin flushed after just half a glass and Rowan knew she must stop this. She should never have brought them, it wasn't doing any good. 'Borrow my car, Andy,' she said urgently. 'Take them back. He's got to go to work, he's on the night-shift at Lester's.'

'Oh, Christ,' said Andy. 'I thought at least he'd be an accountant or something.'

Rowan grimaced and gave him her car keys. They watched Sally diffidently take Mohammed's arm as they left and the cold air met them at the door. Richard said, 'What a pretty girl she is. A doll almost.'

'She was beautiful as a child,' said Diana tightly. 'I don't think I paid her enough attention. You don't, with the third somehow. Why are you still here, Rowan? *You* could have taken them.'

She cleared her throat. 'I thought I'd better find out what you're planning to do with my firm. With Judge's.'

'I don't know why you think we should be doing anything,' said Diana rapidly. 'Besides, it's Andy firm, he is the major shareholder.'

Rowan turned on James. 'Are you trying to buy him out?'

He put up his hands. She thought how old he looked suddenly, how blotched and worn. 'It wasn't my idea.'

'Then whose?'

She turned on Richard and blazed at him. He watched her, his face closed and thoughful. She suddenly remembered how he had looked in the lift, touching her. 'You bastard!' she said softly. 'You're getting your own back. You're going to make me do what you want.'

He shrugged. 'I think you can relax. Andy won't bite. Seems to think you offer the better hope for the future. He seems to think he owes you something.'

'Well, you lot at Bardsey's wouldn't know about that sort of thing,' declared Rowan. 'Thank God Andy's got the sense to avoid you. Just thank God!'

'I would rather thank his television success,' said Diana grimly. 'He can afford to see how you do. But you're over-reaching yourself, Rowan, mark my words, you'll come a cropper one of these days. That man of Sally's will have her share up for sale in no time, and then you might as well resign yourself. Andy will have absolute control.'

'Which is what you've always wanted,' said Rowan.

Diana let out her breath. 'Is it? I don't know any more.

I'm going to bed. Are you coming?' She directed her question to James, but when he shook his head she didn't seem surprised.

After she'd gone he drank another half glass of champagne. 'I'm going out,' he said suddenly. 'I'll take you home, Rowan.'

'I'll take her,' said Richard quickly, and Rowan thought, she didn't want to travel with either. But James's harsh bitterness would be harder to take. She nodded.

When they were alone, Richard made no move to go. 'You won't get my firm,' said Rowan softly.

'I agree, this time I won't. Soon, though.'

She knew she ought to insist they went but suddenly she was tired. The days were so awful now, and when she got home Saul might be there, sprawled on the bed or on the floor. Tonight she hadn't the strength to face it. She sat on the sofa and put her head back, closing her eyes.

Richard said, 'You have the most erotic neck of anyone I have ever seen. It's beautiful.'

'My mother and Sally are far more beautiful than I shall ever be,' said Rowan distantly.

'Not to me.'

She felt the sofa sink as he sat next to her. A finger traced her ear, moving the fine strands of hair out of the way. His mouth was on her neck, hot and lazily wet.

'Stop it,' she murmured. 'You know I won't put up with it.' She felt safe, unthreatened. He couldn't do anything in her mother's house, with her mother upstairs and Andy due back in forty minutes or so. But he didn't stop. His mouth slid to the hollow at the base of her throat, his fingers flicked open a button of her blouse.

'No,' she said more forcefully, pushing at him. It was hard to resist, like fighting through warm treacle. She wasn't aroused, this man hadn't the power to do it, but her limbs felt as if they were in chains. His hand reached into her blouse and took hold of her breast. He rolled her nipple between finger and thumb. She was stabbed with feeling, galvanized by it. She kicked out at him, straight at his groin.

The side of her shoe caught one of his testicles. He let out a strangled moan and fell sideways away from her. She wriggled free and stood up, her flesh burning where he had touched it. She was wearing tight trousers, her groin felt wet with urgent desire. He had nearly seduced her, a minute more and she'd have been incapable of stopping him. She couldn't have borne to stop him.

After a minute, he said thickly, 'I wish you'd get it out of your head that this is all I want from you.'

'I know it isn't,' said Rowan crisply. 'You want Judge's, but you don't mind screwing me on the side.'

'Better me than that drunken prat you married! It makes me sick to think of him on top of you, slobbering over you. Rowan, don't you understand?'

She didn't know what he meant and she didn't care. 'Will you drive me home or shall I ring for a taxi?' she demanded, and he got stiffly to his feet.

They went out to the car together. Richard held on to the bonnet, swaying, and Rowan said, 'I'd better drive.' He handed her the keys and she slid behind the wheel of the Maserati. The engine gave a throaty roar, she couldn't believe the power. Slowly down the drive at first, then up the gears. The night was brilliant with stars. Relaxing a little she let her foot weigh on the throttle and the car leaped forward, punching her in the back and devouring the road. She stamped on the brake and they spun.

Her hands froze on the wheel, the night whirled past her eyes in a rush of trees and confused space. 'Oh my God! Oh my God!' They stopped, still on the road, facing back the way they had come.

'Christ' said Richard. 'Here, let me drive.'

'No. I'll be careful this time.' She waited till her heart ceased its pounding then pulled gently away. The trick was all in gentleness, if she upset this proud beast it would savage her. A grin spread across her face. She was enjoying herself more than for weeks, years, perhaps ever.

'Will you at least slow down?' demanded Richard, almost through clenched teeth. 'We're doing ninety in a thirty mile limit.'

'Oh. I didn't realise. We got back so fast.' She slowed down carefully and began the twisting trail of roads to Judge's.

'Why do you want my mill?' she asked. 'You've got one of your own now.'

Richard laughed. 'Between you and me, it could do with some good red meat in it. Fat and flabby, that's Bardsey's. And this rights issue will bring in such a lot of lovely money. You should have thought of it.'

'I didn't think I'd have to watch Andy. And I was right.'

'So you were.'

She drew up at the mill. Buoyed up with relief at the safety of his car, Richard said, 'Let me kiss you. It doesn't have to mean anything.'

'Kisses don't mean anything, especially to men.' She leaned over to peck his cheek but he caught her shoulders and drew her to him. She had known he would. His lips were warm and slightly moist, where Saul's were always wet and whisky-tasting. The tongue that slid into her mouth now was no intruder, but a soft, gentle, intimate friend that took only what she offered, gave all that she desired. She had forgotten such kisses existed.

'Let's be friends,' whispered Richard.

'We shan't ever be lovers,' said Rowan. 'Good night, Richard.' She slipped out of the car and ran to the house, her long legs teetering a little in her heels. Richard got out and walked round to the driver's side. That girl, that maddening girl! Whenever he saw her she did this to him, upset him. She stole his calm, made him do things he didn't intend, feel what he thought he had outgrown. Feelings. He had had them once, and he had tamed them, locked them away.

Now, that bloody girl aroused desire and frustration and anger.

On the drive back to his flat, his mind strayed to Lin Yu. She had taught him a great deal about loving women; she had taken his youthful bull-at-a-gate enthusiasm and added subtlety and a precise touch. Sometimes when he found himself employing those techniques, as he had tonight, he despised his own calculation. He wanted to love, truly love, to immerse himself in a woman, lose himself and his mind and his bloody, bloody technique. He wanted to unleash his emotions for once instead of keeping them locked up in the box into which he had forced them.

But, he didn't want them out forever. They needed exercise, that was clear, but never again would he be ruled by them. Sometimes, after his father left, he had gone and hidden in the undergrowth behind the football pitch, and howled himself stupid. One afternoon someone heard him, they came looking to see who was making that terrible noise. Cold terror could still engulf him. If he had been found, there would have been no point in living, they would have crucified him.

It occurred to him for the first time that they might not. It had been Reynolds after all, a good sort of chap, he'd been a friend until Richard gave up friends and turned in on himself. If old Reynolds had given him a hand then, listened, he might never have shut himself away like this. A new and sobering thought.

Chapter Thirty-Nine

That night James's thoughts also turned to Lin Yu. He took the Rolls and drove quickly towards town, seeing again pretty little Sally and her out-of-place lover. Whose world did they think they would live in? If they were to have any chance of happiness they would have to lead a halfway-house sort of existence, a painful foot in either camp. He didn't know if either of them realised that.

Lin Yu would be alone when he visited, the boyfriend had despaired and left her. Sometimes he thought that they both focused on these times together; that despite all the odds they each provided more of what the other needed than any other facet of their lives. The relationship was clear and simple and unloving, he would have liked every one of his relationships to be like that. He couldn't bear Diana's red eyes a day longer. He hated her grief, hated, hated her! For she had hurt him so.

The familiar lump formed in his throat and he swallowed it down as he parked. Lin Yu would soothe him. She opened the door wearing a black robe embroidered with dragons and her hair was loose. James said, 'I had to come to you. I need something, I don't know what.'

She led him into the bedroom and took his clothes as he threw them down. When he was naked, he lay on the bed. She knelt and cradled him, stroking his thinning red hair. 'What is it, James? You're very upset.'

'I'm always upset. I can't get rid of it, you see, I can't stop thinking about it!'

'About your little boy? About Nicholas?'

'Yes. Yes.' He sat up and faced her, an ageing, distraught man. She didn't care for him, but he needed her cool thoughts. 'The doctor — he said I wasn't the boy's father. That I couldn't be, the blood group wasn't right. Richard said I'd misunderstood but I didn't, you know. A rhesus negative. The only bloke I know with that group is Saul, and Diana doesn't even like him!'

Lin Yu said, 'Have you spoken to her about this?'

He shook his head. 'I can't trust myself. I think I'd kill her. I wake in the night and look at her, it's almost all I can do not to strangle her there and then! Oh God, what am I going to do? I loved that boy so much, I can't bear to think it was all nothing. That he wasn't mine.'

'Poor James.'

She got off the bed and went to her little herbal cabinet, an antique bought with James's money. She made up a drink of something and gave it to him. He guzzled it desperately, longing to still the madness in his brain. 'Could it be him?' he asked the girl.

She lifted her shoulders delicately. 'Perhaps that's why she doesn't like him. She suspects. Perhaps even she does not know.'

He closed his eyes on tears. 'How could she do that to me? How could he? It all fits, you see; she wanted to get rid of it at first, she wouldn't tell me. She knew it wasn't mine. But him, him! I knew he'd take something from me in the end, whatever I did he'd get it. I kept him out of Bardsey's and look what happened. Now my wife. Now this!'

'James, listen to me, James! Listen to my hands.' She started to massage his shoulders, easing the muscles to his neck and jaw. Gradually he began to relax and she leaned against his back, letting the heat of his body get to her through her thin robe. She took satisfaction from James as and when she could, with a grim fatalism about her life. It seemed to her that James was to be her destiny, and all her struggles against it were to no avail. They were as they were to each other, locked in need and its satisfaction. It was a marriage of sorts.

* * *

460

Sally and Mohammed were married in a civil ceremony, attended by none of his own family and all of hers, if you excluded Andy. Diana was wildly elegant in burgundy silk, but Rowan was simply wild. She had woven some of the designs she had drawn whilst on holiday, and was wearing a dress striped in black and olive and rich green. Mr. Suzman had insisted on a white collar. She looked like a witch masquerading as Little Miss Muffet. And Saul, of course, was drunk.

To everyone's surprise, Richard appeared. James came across to him. 'I didn't think you were even invited.'

'Was it an invitation do? I thought on these occasions it was all hands to the pumps. Poor little kid.'

Somehow the object of their sympathy was not so pitiable today. She looked delectable in cream silk, with a flirty hat perched on top of her blonde bun of hair. Next to Mohammed's severe suit she looked small and fragile. They made a striking couple.

Suddenly the door opened. It was Fadeema, wearing a bright red sari. Both Mohammed and Sally beamed, and the Registrar paused while Diana went to welcome her. The Asian girl stood between Diana and James, an exotic, composed figure.

Saul whispered, 'She's wearing a nose stud.'

'Just as long as Sally doesn't have to wear one,' muttered Rowan.

She felt more and more as if Sally was being sacrificed into some other world, away from them all. Mohammed was a charming, educated man but he was taking Sally from them. She began to cry, and so did Diana, and then, to their surprise, Fadeema joined in.

When it was over, Sally and Mohammed were bubbling with relief. 'Why are you all crying?' demanded Sally. 'He's isn't dragging me off to another country!'

'We cry because you are so pretty and so brave,' said Fadeema. Sally reached out and kissed her. She felt happy

461

when Fadeema was there; if Fadeema could always be in the house, she wouldn't mind Mohammed's mother and her hostility.

They went to Valley House for the reception. Diana eyed the cabinet, still not returned and probably never to be so. 'You have very odd taste, Rowan,' she commented.

'Bloody awful, isn't it?' said Saul. 'I told her to get shot of it. She can't get her finger out.'

'Why don't you go and sleep it off?' said James grimly. He hated to be in the same room as Saul, it was wholly offensive.

'Get stuffed,' said Saul, lurched and fell against the cabinet. One of the shelves slipped and broke.

Rowan tried not to notice. Saul was embarrassing Sally in front of her new family and he really ought to be stopped. Suddenly he went up to Fadeema, breathed fumes on her and demanded to dance.

'Come on, sweetheart, shake a leg,' he yelled.

'How much has he had?' asked James incredulously. 'He must have started last night and kept going. It isn't lunch-time yet.'

Rowan looked for help. She tugged Richard's sleeve. 'Just get him out, will you, please? He can only get worse.'

Their eyes met briefly. He nodded and went to Saul, who was trying to catch Fadeema's hands and boogy. 'Come on, old man, into the kitchen; I'm opening a bottle.' He took less than gentle hold of Saul's arm.

'I want to dance,' said Saul. 'This beautiful lady should dance.'

'There isn't any music yet.' Richard kept it determinedly jovial, masking blatant strong-arm tactics. Saul was hustled blearily away.

'I am so sorry,' said Rowan to Fadeema.

'Sally tells me he has a problem,' commented the girl. 'He is an alcoholic.'

Rowan was taken aback. 'Well, I don't think so —' She

462

began, but Sally added, 'He is, Ro. You know he is.'

'It isn't any of your business,' flared Rowan. 'He isn't always like this. And anyway, he won't have any treatment.'

'That is often the way,' said Fadeema. 'Please, when he does want treatment, let me know. I have a friend who is a specialist.'

Rowan nodded silently, praying that Saul would have passed out by now. When he reached the raucous stage it was only a matter of ten minutes or so.

They lunched on an elaborate buffet ranged on tables around two walls of the dining-room.

'This house must have cost a fortune,' said James. 'Andy ought to see what's being done with his firm.'

'It wouldn't be a firm if it wasn't for me,' said Rowan. 'Why haven't you changed your car, James? You've had that Roller for a good three years.'

'I happen to like it,' he said frostily, and she raised a quizzical eyebrow.

Speaking rather loudly, Richard said, 'We're beyond status symbols, I think, Rowan. Dad's got a good business there, I'm enjoying seeing what's what.'

James said nothing and for some reason Rowan's senses twitched. Like a TB sufferer, now cured, she could recognise the disease in others almost before they caught it. Business problems were just as deadly.

The car arrived to take Sally and Mohammed back home. They were to postpone their honeymoon until Ramadan, when the mill closed, so the first night of their marriage would be spent in his father's house, in the small back bedroom off Carlisle Road. Everyone threw confetti, and Rowan picked up Hannah to encourage her to throw, too.

'Tars,' said Hannah. 'Tars.'

'Yes. Yes, darling, stars,' said Rowan. It was a proper word at last. Her first proper word, when they had begged for 'biscuit' or 'more' or 'mum' or 'dad' or 'no'. Her first word was stars.

She turned away and went back into the house, feeling at once joyful and intolerably lonely. Only Saul knew what it meant, only he would share this moment with her, and he lay snoring and insensible on a bed. Richard had followed her. 'Why did you come in? You looked as if you were going to cry.'

'Did I? Perhaps I was. It was — it was Hannah. She said "stars". Her first word. I threw the confetti and she said "stars", just like that. I know you don't understand. I mean, I know she's more than a year behind other children, but when she was born I hadn't any hope for her at all. I couldn't see anything good in her life, anything good she would bring to us. And then her first word is "stars". I just feel so — humble.'

An odd expression passed over Richard's face. He glanced quickly at Hannah, seeing nothing to hope for, nothing. 'You must love her quite a lot,' he remarked uncomfortably.

Rowan put her cheek against Hannah's. 'That seems a little word for it. When I think they wanted to send her away!'

'You never know, this might be the start of something. One word today; next week, whole conversations!'

She beamed at him. 'Yes! Yes! Saul always thinks I'm silly to hope for too much, but nobody knows what she might do. If she can say "stars", if she knows about stars — well. She could be anything.' She cradled the baby and her impossible hopes at one and the same time.

Richard thought how lovely she looked with her face glowing and her dark lashes making crescents on her cheek. Speaking with false sincerity, he said, 'I'm sure you're right,' and was rewarded with Rowan's shyest, most trusting smile. She thought he understood.

They stood together in the quiet room, amidst the debris of the party, and outside Mohammed and Sally drove away.

* * *

464

Judge's got its stockmarket quotation at a time when the government was trying to prove its record in encouraging business. One day the Prime Minister got up and declared, 'We have been remarkably successful in encouraging growth in manufacturing. Take textiles, for instance, one of the disaster stories of the past; now, have a look at Isaac Judge and tell me that we can't compete, tell me the industry needs mollycoddling. A dynamic company, a company going places, a British company!'

The world and his wife beat a path to the door of Isaac Judge plc. The share price doubled within a month, aided and abetted by the general stockmarket boom, and Rowan couldn't keep up with the work, the orders, the pressure on her poor, decrepit dye house. Valley House was at one and the same time a place of refuge and confusion. She would let no one through that door in the wall; it was her home, her hiding place. No one was going to use Hannah to add human interest to the story, or find Saul drunk and finally destroy him.

Although, actually, Saul was better. After the wedding he seemed to pull himself up a little, drinking nothing at all during the day and only a few whiskies in the evening. He began involving himself again in some of his pet projects, in a rather frenzied way, inviting magazines to write feature articles on the nursery, posting feeler samples to corners of the world as yet unaware of Judge's cloth. It was all hectic and tense, some of it rather pointless, but at least he wasn't drinking. Rowan found the relief exquisite.

Trophy after trophy fell their way, until one day an American company approached them, wanting to manufacture Judge's range under licence in the States. Rowan's gut feel was to reject the idea out of hand, it stank of piracy, but Saul was thoughtful. 'Big market,' he commented. 'We're running at full blast as it is, we can't possibly produce more until we modernise the dye house. And the accounts must go on computer, I've been thinking of it for ages.'

'Bardsey's have got a design computer,' said Rowan morosely, dropping her chin into her hands. 'Apparently you just press buttons and you get a pretty picture of what the design will look like — checks, tartans, you name it.'

'We could have it if you want,' said Saul, snapping a biscuit in half and munching it tensely.

'Yes. But I want better than that. Direct linking to a pattern loom or something. Anything to be better.'

He pushed back his chair and got up. 'Don't be childish.'

She watched him doubtfully. He was itching for a drink, but so far had resisted it. She said, 'Why don't you go to the States and talk to them? At the moment everybody loves us, we ought to take advantage.'

'Yeah. I might.' He didn't seem interested.

Rowan got out the atlas and the diary and began suggesting dates and additional people he could go and see to make the trip worthwhile. 'You could go on Concorde,' she tempted. 'And you could see that designer, the one who always uses our stuff. Hasn't he moved to the States? Marcus Arnaud.'

Saul grinned. 'Oh yes. Marcus. The dear boy. That does seem a long time ago. When we were young and silly, when the world was a fun place.'

Rowan reached up and caught his hand. 'It isn't so bad now, is it?'

Making an effort that was only too apparent, he said, 'No. 'Course not. I'll send a telex and get out and see them.'

Two days before he was due to leave he lunched in town with the directors of Sylvex. Rowan was invited herself but refused; it was one of those occasions when Saul would hunt best alone. She bridled when they suggested price cuts, she lost interest when they waffled on about other firms and other people. It was Saul, the expert angler, who could let his fish run and then land it with hardly a twitch on the line. So she stayed at home and prowled around her mill, and took Hannah to the nursery to sit and watch the other children for a while. Somehow she felt anxious. She couldn't settle to anything.

At half-past four he was still not back, she watched the gate, waiting to see the Aston Martin swing its long nose round the corner. Instead she saw a much newer car, Joe Partridge in his flash Japanese sports.

'You look a bit agitated, Ro,' he commented.

She ran a quizzical eye over his stocky figure, wedged into tight trousers and a jacket in an expensive but vulgar broad stripe. Money had not gone to Joe's head but to his belly. 'You should never have given up rugby,' she remarked, and poked his flab.

'I'll get it off one of these days. Came to talk business, actually.' He looked hopefully in the direction of the house but Rowan turned towards the office. Even her oldest friends were rarely admitted into her home. It was private, so much so that even her cleaning lady was old Elsie from the mill, who could be trusted not to gossip and could be paid far more than the job was worth, for old time's sake.

Nowadays Rowan and Saul inhabited a spectacular office. One wall was glass and looked out over the roofs of Bradford, while low cabinets lined the rest of the room. Saul and Rowan had desks at either end, with 'phones banked on side tables, and above the cabinets hung classic fashion photographs and swathes of Judge's cloth. Joe picked up Rowan's paper knife. It was silver.

'Haven't you got anything better to spend it on, then?'

'That was a present from an anxious supplier. It seems that when I needed help I couldn't get it, but now I don't people are showering me with goodies and offers of co-operation.'

'Well, I'm not.'

Rowan swung round on her heels and went to sit down at her desk. 'What is it then, Joe? Spit it out.'

'Bardsey's want to use me. Exclusive. They're folding their fleet, and they'll pay a third better than you.'

She sniffed. Her chin dropped into her hands and she sniffed again. 'Bugger, bugger, bugger!' she said. 'I thought we were friends.'

'We was, once upon a time. Don't think you're friends with anybody now, though. He's had an effect on you, I knew he would.'

'Life's had an effect on me,' said Rowan shortly. 'We'll increase the rates, Joe, you know that. We've dropped behind, there's been so much to do recently. But don't go.'

'I've pretty well made up my mind.'

His chubby face assumed an aggrieved expression, and she knew he was waiting to be coaxed and cajoled. And she couldn't be bothered. 'Of course you know Bardsey's are in trouble?' she said casually. 'Richard's adopting classic fire-fighting tactics, closing down expensive units and flogging what he can. I just wish I could get my hands on his dye house.'

'They look OK to me,' said Joe. 'Looks like you're jealous, just because you can't push them off their perch. Number one, they are, and you can't stomach it.'

'I won't have to for long,' she remarked and got up. 'They're going to take a tumble all of their own accord. Look, Joe, I'm sorry to rush you but there's something on my mind.'

He got up, hitching his trousers irritably. 'You'll have something on your mind if I leave you in the lurch. You don't know which side your bread's buttered, my girl. I'll let you off this time but I'm damned if I'll have you treating me like a bloody servant.'

'I don't,' objected Rowan.

'You do. You should see yourself these days. You ain't in the human race with the rest of us, you're cold as a bloody ice cube. And it's all his doing, he's done you no good at all.'

Joe stomped out and Rowan wrapped her arms around herself. It wasn't her fault that Joe wanted to be as close to her as before. It wasn't possible, she wasn't even there. She was locked away somewhere deep inside, somewhere she couldn't be hurt. She looked down into the yard, and still the Aston wasn't back. Almost five o'clock, a very long lunch indeed.

The 'phone rang and she hesitated seconds before picking it up. A voice, a man's voice, said: 'Mrs. Barton? I'm sorry to have to tell you there's been an accident.'

It was Joe who drove her to the hospital. She ran after him and banged, screaming, on the window of his car. 'I know he's killed himself. I know he's dead,' she kept saying hysterically, as Joe fished out his bright red handkerchief and gave it to her.

'They said he wasn't dead, didn't they?'

'They'd be bound to lie. They make you come first and then tell you. What am I going to do?'

Joe swung into the hospital grounds. 'Calm down, they'll think they've got a bloody lunatic on their hands! Suppose he's just broken his ankle? You'll have him buried before the plaster's dry.'

Rowan was out of the car before it had completely stopped, running frantically into the hospital. She fell against the enquiries desk. 'My husband. Saul Barton. You told me to come.'

The receptionist leafed casually through a sheaf of papers. 'Barton . . . road accident. Down the corridor, turn left.'

Rowan ran on, aware that Joe was following sedately in her wake. The casualty desk was before her. When she reached it, she couldn't ask. It might be the last moment of ignorance, after this she would have to know.

Someone looked at her. 'Yes?'

'I'm − I'm Mrs. Barton. You called me.'

'Oh yes.' A male nurse took her into a side room, but Saul wasn't there. She sat on a hard plastic chair and waited for them to tell her the worst, wondered which of all these people would do it. A young Asian doctor came in and shut the door. He took another of the chairs and sat down.

'Your husband is unconscious,' he said.

'Oh God! Oh no!'

'I believe his car crashed. Mrs. Barton, he was unconscious before the accident, he'd passed out at the wheel.'

'Is he hurt then? How bad is he?'

'He's been very lucky, he has broken his leg.'

She let the information sink in, closing her eyes against the alien world in which she found herself. 'You seem to be making a dreadful fuss for a broken leg,' she said at last.

'Mrs. Barton, your husband was driving his car with an almost lethal amount of alcohol in his bloodstream. He very nearly killed an entire bus queue, a school bus queue. He missed them by inches. And I believe he's in the habit of such excess.'

'You can't know that,' flared Rowan. 'He doesn't drink often. He'd been out to lunch with some customers, he probably wanted to take a taxi but you never can get them when you want. Something should be done about it.'

'Mrs. Barton — ' The doctor leaned forward and fixed her with his large eyes. 'Fadeema Shafir is a young lady I know well. We have an understanding. I gather that your husband has been drinking heavily for years.'

Rowan shook her head. 'Not for long, no. Not like this. Just since — well, since the baby really.' She put her hands up to hide her face, saying, 'Sorry, sorry! I don't mean to be so foolish. Are the police going to prosecute?'

'I imagine so. And I've made arrangements for your husband to be admitted to an alcohol dependency unit. He has only a small cast on his leg, he'll be able to get about on crutches in a day or so.'

Rowan got up and went to the door, fumbling with the handle. The doctor said, 'You'll want to see your husband.'

'No.' She had seen him unconscious too often, far too often. She ran down the corridor and saw Joe sitting slumped in a chair. When she stopped, her legs shook and

470

her voice shook; she thought she might faint. 'He's all right,' she said vaguely. 'Broken leg, that's all. Let's go.'

Out in the car, she sat shivering. 'They've sent him to be dried out,' she said.

'Take them a good ten years. He'll never give it up, you know he won't.'

'I thought he had, Joe!' She pulled out his lurid handkerchief and stuffed it in her mouth to muffle the sobs. Only real drunks went to these places, only the down and outs. She had wanted him to have treatment, but now she had no faith in it. Suddenly she thought of Saul as a wino, huddled in cardboard boxes in a shop doorway in Bradford, swigging meths round a fire down by the canal. Her sobs froze into icy despair.

Chapter Forty

Visiting hours at the dependency unit were strict, between three and four in the afternoon. It was a difficult time for Rowan, the time when textile men get back from expense account lunches and get down to telephoning. She went on the first day, wearing an expensive emerald green dress and then hiding it under a heavy coat. She felt totally furtive, petrified in case she saw anyone she knew.

The unit was in large grounds, so that the inmates had miles to walk to escape and get a drink. They took heroin addicts as well, who could be distinguished by their methadone-induced spaced out expressions, in stark contrast to the morose twitching of the alcoholics. Saul was still in bed, his leg propped up. There was bruising down one side of his face and his eyes were half closed not, Rowan knew, from any injury, simply a vicious hangover.

'Hello,' she said quietly.

He looked at her from under his lids. 'Terrible headache. Must have got concussion in the accident.'

'Poor you.'

'The brakes failed, you know. I took the corner and the brakes failed. I haven't been looking after the old machine properly.'

'I wouldn't feel too sorry for it, they've carted it off to a scrapyard.'

'Shit!'

They sat in silence. Rowan looked round at the other beds, most of them empty. An old man occupied one at the end. He was badly shaved and muttered to himself, picking invisible pieces off the bedcover. 'That's a real one,' said

Saul, following the direction of her eyes. 'Doctor's a bloody Moslem. They think anyone who has a sherry is an alkie.'

'He's a friend of Fadeema's. He seemed to think you'd had rather a lot.'

'No more than the rest. You know those lunches.' He shifted in the bed and tried to ease his leg. 'How's Hannah?'

'Fine. She's trying to walk. Barbara's wonderful, you know, she spends hours helping her. She suggested something we ought to think about. Apparently they operate on Down's Syndrome children nowadays.'

'What on earth for?'

'Well — to make them look normal. Their eyes, and making their tongues smaller. Things like that.'

She had his interest now. 'Good God. Does it improve their speech or anything?'

'I don't know. But they look better, you see —'

He heaved himself painfully up in the bed. 'I've never heard anything so horrific! You will not inflict pain on Hannah just to stop her embarrassing us, I absolutely forbid it.'

'Suppose it did improve her speech?' said Rowan miserably.

'She'll speak all right. But with a bit of luck she won't ever understand enough to know what's going on.'

'I didn't really mean to do it, it was only a thought,' said Rowan, touching his hand. More softly she added, 'You don't have to be so bitter.'

'You didn't do a bloody thing to stop me being put in here, did you?'

She shrugged. 'I didn't know I could.'

'Why don't you bugger off? You got what you wanted.'

She stood up to go, there was no point in talking to him in this mood. At the last moment, she said, 'I don't know what to do about the American trip. They made an awful fuss when I said we'd cancel at such short notice.'

He looked at her painfully. 'You'll have to cancel. I'll go out later in the year.'

'I wondered if I ought to go.'

He let a pause develop. 'I imagine you intend to go and are just letting me know. OK, go. I'm sure I'll have a fun time in here being talked at and lectured. I hope you fall flat on your face.'

She grinned. 'Pig.'

'Cow.'

Saul gave a morose grunt, she responded with a moo. Rowan quickly bent down and hugged him tight. He put his hand over his eyes. 'Get out of here before I bloody cry. Go on, get out.'

She kissed his thick fair hair and left.

Rowan drove slowly back to Valley House, stretching her neck to ease the crackling tension in her muscles. Barbara was taking Hannah for a walk so she decided to waste a little time for once, and have the house to herself. When she went through the gate she saw the landscape gardeners at work again, enhancing lawns and paths with container grown trees and bushes. An illusion of maturity was being created, somewhat thin now but in a year or two no one would ever know that a scant time before, this had been wasteland.

They were erecting an arbour, to be covered with clematis and honeysuckle. Rowan stepped round the workmen, murmuring apologetically. They eyed her curiously, because nowadays everybody had heard of Rowan Judge. Somehow they hadn't expected someone so slim, so young or so diffident.

It was very quiet in the house. Rowan loved the space and the clean, uncluttered lines. She was even coming to love the nasty cabinet, simply through association. Things didn't have to be beautiful to become familiar, she reflected. From familiarity came affection, and no one cared about flaws in their own dear friends. Saul was right to ban operations on Hannah, she had been cowardly and self-seeking even to think of it.

She made a cup of tea and curled up on the sofa to drink

it.Outside she could hear the faint chatter of the men working in the garden, from the kitchen came the distant hum of the fridge. Perhaps Saul would be cured forever, this could be the day she set out on a new and happier road.

'Rowan! Rowan, are you here?'

Startled, Rowan sat up and pushed the hair out of her eyes. She had been nodding off to sleep. 'Is that you, Sally?' she called.

The girl burst into the room. She was wearing a pink short-sleeved top and a cream sari, swathed across the bulge of her pregnancy. Her hair was caught up in a bun but strands of it tumbled down around her face. Bright spots of angry colour stained her cheeks. 'There you are! At last, I've been right round the mill, in your office, everywhere. I won't have it, Rowan, I won't!'

'I was only taking five minutes off,' said Rowan fearfully.

'I don't mean that. It's her, his mother! Mrs. Bloody Shafir. Do you know what she did? I'm telling you, it's the last straw.'

Rowan got up and went through to the kitchen to put the kettle back on. Sally followed, pacing furiously, like a small enraged kitten. 'We were having chicken and beans,' she declared. 'I'm good at it, I've learned how to cook it and it comes out really well. The whole family likes it, even his father though he wouldn't dare admit it. *She'd* have a go at him. We agreed I'd make it, and she, *she,* went and put two whole chillies in while I wasn't looking! You can imagine what it was like. Everybody's eyes watering, no one eating a thing and me apologising and wondering what I'd done. You can imagine how she smirked. And then this morning I heard her telling one of her friends all about it, they thought I couldn't understand them. They talk the flaming language all day every day, they don't give a damn about it being as rude as hell to do it in front of me! So I got my own back.'

'What did you do?' asked Rowan, wide-eyed at these revelations about kitchen warfare.

'Slung half a pound of whole peppercorns into her vegetable curry. It was like eating badly shot pheasant, pellets in every mouthful. And she had the nerve to tell Mohammed to discipline me! And do you know what?'

'He told you off,' said Rowan, grinning. 'What else did you expect?'

'He should have taken my side,' wailed Sally. 'It wasn't fair! She did it to me first. I just got my own back.'

Rowan kept her own counsel, merely making another pot of tea. When it was brewed she poured two mugs and settled comfortably at the huge pine table.

'Does everyone else like you?' she asked.

Sally nodded. 'They do, quite. I like them. It's just her. If Mohammed needs something, she's there. Let me do it for you, I'll wash it, I'll cook it, I know just how you like it, my son, a mother's touch. If I go to him when he comes in she almost wrestles me out of the way. I won't fight over him. It's damned undignified.'

'I bet he's lapping it up,' said Rowan casually.

Sally considered. 'Actually, he hates it. He can't talk to either of us without the other one getting upset. He keeps saying it's going to get better.'

'Now you can talk to her, it might.'

'It just gives us a wider range of insults, that's all.'

Rowan got up and fetched some chocolate biscuits. 'You must be dying for some English food,' she said sympathetically.

Sally stared at her. 'We do have chocolate biscuits. We don't live at the North Pole. And actually the food's lovely. When you don't have three chillies in it.'

'Or a thousand peppercorns,' added Rowan. 'Well, you'll have to apologise. Then everyone will think how sweet you are and she'll be the baddy. Look at it from Mohammed's point of view — he doesn't want to break his mother's heart. She's old, she hasn't any education, she lives in this semi-purdah they seem to go in for, and she sees her son being dragged into strange, foreign ways.'

Sally put on a sad voice. 'You make her sound so little and pathetic. Poor foreign woman, set down in an alien land. If you knew the way she runs the house! She's about as pathetic and helpless as a barracuda! Everybody thinks these poor women are having a terrible time, and they're not! Great big families, loads of friends and everything happening at home or in the mosque. It's the men who have to go and work in these beastly factories, and then come home for the women to tell them what to do.'

'Does Mohammed do what his mother tells him?' asked Rowan, fascinated.

Her sister grinned. 'No. That's what annoys her.'

Rowan abondoned all thoughts of going back to work that day. She and Sally went through to the sitting room, turned on the television and watched *Blue Peter*.

'Do you remember Mother yelling at us to turn it down?' said Rowan.

'No. No, I don't. I don't remember much about home really. Sunday lunches perhaps. All the silver out and the cut glass fruit bowl. And Dad carving so terribly carefully.'

'The meat was always cold,' admitted Rowan.

'And Mother always got at him for being slow. I think he must have irritated her for years before she ran off, years and years and years.'

There was a sudden thunderous knocking on the front door. The two girls looked at each other. 'Mohammed,' said Rowan and went to let him in.

He was wearing trousers and a tunic, and was stiff with husbandly indignation. He marched past Rowan and into the sitting room. 'Sally. Home.'

She folded her hands in her lap. 'I'm visiting my sister, Mohammed. I'm sure Mother told you that.'

'My mother's taken to her bed. She thinks you have run off for good.'

'Then she must be delighted,' retorted his wife. 'She's

been trying to get rid of me ever since I moved in.'

'But you must not insult her!' yelled Mohammed desperately. 'She is my mother, Sally!'

'And I am your wife.'

Rowan stood between them, looking from one to the other as if at a tennis match. 'I do think this could have been anticipated, Mohammed,' she remarked. 'I did say you oughtn't to live in the same house.'

He shook his head, and said hurriedly, 'It's only till I get promoted! We can't afford a house yet, it isn't possible.'

'I can afford ten houses,' wailed Sally. 'And a new car, everything! You're just being stubborn.'

'I will not have people saying I married you for advancement.' Mohammed looked tortured, a proud man on the rack of duty, tempted by opportunity.

'Why not think of it as a dowry?' asked Rowan sympathetically.

He shook his head. 'If I was in my own country, possibly. Here it is looked down upon. I'm British, I have a British wife. I should not take her money.'

'So you make me miserable instead!' yelled Sally, and threw a cushion at him.

He caught it and threw it back hard. It hit her in the face. She squealed and instantly he was on his knees beside her. 'Darling, darling, are you all right? Oh, Sally, I've hurt you, forgive me!'

Sensibly Sally burst into tears, and Rowan withdrew to the kitchen until they sorted it out. She felt dismal and alone. She and Saul never had rows that ended in kisses and hugs. They were always deeply hurtful, wounding affairs that left lasting scars and were almost never resolved. Half the time Saul seemed unaware that they had had a row; he either didn't remember or found it convenient to forget.

After about twenty minutes Mohammed and Sally came looking for her. They held hands, and Sally was very tear-stained. 'We wanted to ask you something,' she began.

Rowan tried to look encouraging. 'Just don't sell your shares, Sally, or if you do, sell them to me.'

'It isn't that. We want you to give Mohammed a job in the mill.'

Rowan was dumbstruck. Yet when she considered, she couldn't see why she hadn't thought of it before. The mill was as much Sally's as her own, and Rowan's own husband worked there. 'What doing?' she asked confusedly. 'In the office or something? Management?'

'Managing the weaving shed. You don't have a proper manager at the moment, it's all you and Saul. You've said yourself you need one. Please, Rowan.'

'Well,' Rowan chewed the side of her finger. There were no Asians in her mill, or at least none in positions of any seniority. The feeling was that if you let in one, sooner or later there would be hundreds and no room for anyone else. 'Take over anything if you let 'em,' the men said. 'Look what they've done to Bradford.' Yet it was boom and bust that had changed Bradford, and all else evolved from it.

She swallowed. 'We can try,' she said. 'But it's a long way, will the old car stand it?' Mohammed's station wagon was renowned for breaking down at inopportune moments.

'We'll buy a new car,' said Sally urgently. 'We must, Mohammed, it's only fair. And I'll put up with your mother, at least until the baby's born.'

He nodded. 'All right. All right. When should I start?'

Rowan spread her hands. 'Monday, if you like. I'll be in America for ten days or so but that might be best actually. I'm not good at handing over responsibility.'

For a moment he seemed almost overcome. 'I didn't like to ask —'

'I'm sorry that you had to,' broke in Rowan. She felt all the weight of Mohammed's confusion; he felt owed a job, and yet resented any charge of profiting from Sally; he needed Sally's money, but couldn't reconcile taking it with his pride; above all he wanted to leave home, but when it came to it he knew how much hurt it would cause his family. Rowan realised suddenly that if the marriage had caused problems for Sally, they were nothing compared with those facing her husband.

In the evening she lay on the rug and played with Hannah, rolling her over and round like a little ball. Hannah threw her legs in the air and squealed, then struggled into her inaccurate crawl. 'Dad. Dad,' she said. Rowan stared at her. 'Why do you say that now when he isn't here? Not here, Hannah. Dad not here.'

The baby's face fell into a look of vacant incomprehension. Sometimes it was possible almost to see the little cogs turning fruitlessly, making no sense of the complications of life. Hannah didn't understand, Hannah might never understand. The world would go on and Hannah would blunder through it, desperately vulnerable. Sometimes, thought Rowan, it didn't hurt at all, and sometimes it stung as fiercely as on that first awful day. There was such a terrible weight of responsibility. Forever.

The Sunday before she left was a wet, blustery day. When she visited Saul she ran from the car park to the buildings through a hail of twigs and leaves, bursting through the doors pink-cheeked and breathless. Saul was waiting for her, morose on crutches.

'You don't have to look so bloody happy,' he grunted.

'Thanks a lot.'

She took off her coat and scanned the other inmates. They all looked miserable, except for one man, grinning like an idiot. 'He's going out,' said Saul, following her eyes. 'He's getting a drink, that's what he's happy about.'

'What's he been here for then?' asked Rowan. 'I mean, you're supposed to stay off it.'

He said nothing and Rowan dived into her bag and brought out the obligatory goodies; the chocolates and grapes, the books, the transistor radio. 'You look a lot better,' she commented. It wasn't true, he looked ghastly, pale and tense.

'Police came today. I'm going to be banned from driving. Very menacing, they were. If I wasn't in here they'd be putting me in prison, that sort of thing. Can't imagine how I'll manage without the car.'

'Get someone to drive you. Get a chauffeur.'

'That I don't fancy.'

They fell silent. Rowan felt his depression seeping into her. Suddenly he said, 'I know something that should amuse you. We do physical jerks, even me on crutches. This hearty woman, weighs about twenty stone, she parades in front of us in a tracksuit that could double as an army provisions store. We do knee and arm swinging, I have to swing my crutches. Me and the bloke next to me got slung out this morning for obscenity. So they sent the chaplain round and he told us we could be cured by faith in God. I asked if he could give me some personal instruction, and he got all excited till I told him I wanted to turn water into wine. Now I don't even get orange juice, it's a punishment.'

Rowan sighed. She didn't think it at all funny. 'You're supposed to be taking this seriously.'

'I haven't had a drink since I came in here, how much more serious can you get? I don't have to be treated like an infant as well.'

'Do you mean to keep off it? Do you even accept that you should?'

He met her eyes. She knew him so well, she could see straight through the insincerity. He shrugged. 'I'll moderate it a bit. Even I accept I was getting over the top. But I'll not live this life of evangelical purity, not for anyone. I'll do what I bloody like with myself.'

'That's what I thought.'

She got up to go, not even waiting to put on her coat. Saul thumped after her on his crutches and caught her arm. 'I didn't mean that the way it sounded. I love you, Rowan.'

She nodded. 'I know you do. Look, I'm off tomorrow. Ring up Barbara now and then, would you, and the mill. Keep a check on things.'

'You don't mean to say you need me for something.'

The old argument, again. She forced her arms into her coat, shaking off his attempt to help her. 'I don't want you to go like this,' he said.

'Well, you're making me! You're the one that keeps pushing it!'

He struck his fist against his forehead, hard. 'Can't you see what it's like in here! I'm strung out on wires and these bloody people come preaching and taking away the orange juice — ye gods, but people do so love to have a sinner to get at. But — oh, you go, you go, I'm no fun to be with. Be careful, lovey. And have a good time, you deserve it.'

Out in the car park she saw him watching her from the window. She waved, but he didn't wave back.

Chapter Forty-One

From the moment she set foot on United States soil, Rowan revelled in America. It was like the movies, with unexpurgated sound track and the added interest of real danger, from the cars, from the muggers, even from the malevolent customs man who searched her sample case as if every label concealed a secret hoard of drugs, or diamonds, or diseased tomatoes.

'Nice stuff,' he commented, as she struggled to close it again.

'It's my mill, it should be.'

'Don't tell me a pretty lady like you owns a textile mill?'

She became very English and very proper. 'I do indeed.'

'Gee I love that voice! Say it again: "I do indeed." It really turns me on.'

'Look, can I go now? I haven't been to America before, I don't know what to do, you see. Do I find a taxi out here, a cab?'

'You sure do.'

She escaped, breathless with anxiety. Customs men unnerved her; even when totally innocent she felt scarlet with guilt. Her sample case weighed a ton. It took her right back to Japan when she had been so terribly young, so frighteningly innocent. A woman barged in front of her and took her cab, she lost the next to an elderly gentleman and the one after that to an aggressive young man. For the next she pushed and shoved and at last got in. It smelled of air freshener, insecticide and tomato sauce.

Her hotel had been booked by the company she was to visit. When she gave her name the receptionist revealed all thirty-two teeth in a smile and summoned three porters with a lift of the eyebrows. 'Mrs. Barton. The Empress Suite. We do so hope you enjoy your stay.'

'Thank you.' Rowan was propelled to the separate, super-class elevator and whisked away to some distant floor. In her room there was a four-poster bed, two televisions, three telephones, a drinks cabinet the size of a small wardrobe, a bunch of flowers, a bottle of champagne and a complimentary silk dressing gown with a label reading 'To remember us by.' In the bathroom she found a shell-shaped tub with mini jacuzzi, four types of shampoo, enough condoms for the regiment of Welsh Guards and a foot sauna.

No sooner had she thrust bundles of notes at the porters than one of the telephones rang, identifying itself not only by a drunken warble but also a flashing light. 'Hi! Carter Finsbacher here. How was the trip?'

'Fine, fine.'

'Just to tell you we'll be picking you up about six. Wear something a little snazzy. Glad to have you with us, Ms. Judge.'

No sooner had he clicked off than she ran to her suitcase and started looking for something snazzy. She had brought neat business clothes mostly, except for one black silk dress with a scooped neckline and a short, stiff peplum. When she put it on it looked OK, but slightly lacking, although at home she always felt daring in that dress. Here it needed the sort of flashy jewellery she didn't own.

She picked up her bag with its wads of unfamiliar American money and went down to the foyer. Designer shops were clustered round the edge, plush little boxes staffed by elegant women and filled with rich goodies. From a festoon of costume jewellery she bought a very expensive silver and jade pendant, and next door she picked up a long silk scarf in an exotic green print. Safely back in her room she borrowed the hotel's collection of safety pins and made a huge green rosette out of the scarf. Pinned at her waist it echoed the pendant and, more to the point, her eyes.

Rowan scanned herself in the mirror. She was wearing her highest heels, and the heavy pendant round her neck gave her the slightly odd elegance of some African tribes. Saul had once called her a Zulu. When was that? Paris? Three, four years ago, before Hannah was born, before — everything. She let the thought go, she would not let anything spoil her mood. The telephone rang and her heart juddered in excitement. For the first time in ages, perhaps ever, she felt young, rich, at liberty in the world. A dangerous state of mind.

Carter Finsbacher turned out to be short, rather plump and apparently very confident. He had a chauffeur-driven car and made sure she understood it was his and not hired, and what is more it was the best car.

'Nothing's too much trouble for you, little lady,' he confided. 'We've got commitment and we want you to know that. We're high achievers at Bellerphon Textiles, we set our sights high and we score. This your own cloth?'

He fingered the peplum of her dress, quite impersonally. Rowan didn't mind, she was used to textile men shaking you by the hand and feeling your lapel at one and the same time. 'It's wild silk. We're exclusively into woollens, Mr. Finsbacher.'

'Call me Carter. Big market in naturals, it's the way of the future.'

'I think wool's pretty natural,' she said coolly. Then she relented. 'We do a wool and silk mix, actually. It's nice, I'll show you sometime.'

'Great, great.'

He rubbed his palms together as if they were sweating and it suddenly occurred to Rowan that Carter Finsbacher was very nervous. And, since he was alone with her and going to meet his colleagues for dinner, who presumably didn't cause this sort of twitching, she was the cause of the complaint. Inexplicably she found it rubbing off. Her own palms started to sweat.

'I am sorry my husband couldn't come,' she said distractedly. 'He always does the travelling, he knows what to do and things.'

'Leaving you at home to mind the babies,' he said jovially, and then thought it sounded derogatory and started to dig himself out. 'I didn't mean − a worthwhile job, who can say not − but a woman of your standing, I mean, with a textile mill − but bringing up the next generation −'

'I've got a nanny,' interrupted Rowan. 'Our little girl's mentally handicapped.'

Mr. Finsbacher's face stopped twitching. For the first time he looked at her as if she might be a real person. 'How about that? My boy's ten now. Down's Syndrome.'

For a second Rowan wondered if she had somehow known, because she never told people about Hannah. 'Hannah's only three,' she said breathily. 'We don't know any others. Perhaps we'll meet them when she goes to school or something. I don't know.'

Finsbacher stopped rubbing his hands together. 'You should come visit with my wife. We've got four kids, Jimmy's the third. And he's everybody's favourite brother, I'll tell you that, though he's got a temper! Boy, when he gets upset he upsets everybody. But he's a good boy mostly, a real good boy.'

'I'd like to meet him,' said Rowan awkwardly. 'Thank you.'

The restaurant was unimaginably glitzy. A canopy stretched out across the pavement and Mr. Finsbacher marched ahead, a rubber ball of a man pursued by a very tall, very elegant lady. A couple of photographers stationed by the door took flash pictures and then asked each other, 'Who the hell is that?' because this restaurant was the preserve of the rich and the well-known. Broadway stars sat next to television personalities who rubbed shoulders with film stars in town for deals. Round the periphery sat lesser mortals, there to see rather than be seen, amongst which were the men from Bellerphon Textiles.

Four large, sober-suited individuals rose to greet them. Rowan felt hopelessly vulnerable, five of them against one of her. Saul wouldn't have turned a hair. Why, oh why, wasn't Saul here? She shook hands automatically, aware that if she turned her head into the room she would be face to face with more beautiful people than ever in her life before.

When they sat down she couldn't concentrate. One of the heart-throbs of her youth was ten feet away, gazing earnestly at a woman as pale and lovely as any marble statue, and these men wanted to talk textiles! People moved around the room, greeting acquaintances. Rowan could hardly take her eyes off the scene to look at the menu. From what lay on the tables around her, the food was over-processed and done in miniature, baby vegetables next to embryo lamb chops. She ordered abstractedly.

Carter Finsbacher sat back and said, 'Well, how do you feel about our operation?'

Reluctantly, Rowan came back to the task in hand. 'I haven't seen your mill. But the figures look good and so do the samples you sent me. At Judge's we've built up a very good couture range, and while I can see why you'd want to produce it, I can't imagine selling our design skills for anything other than a lot of money. And I don't know how competitive that would make the final product.'

'Very competitive,' said one of the big grey men. 'We'd be selling under the Judge's label with the tag of English quality. We're not aiming for low prices, ma'am, our market segment is way, way up. Judge's Fine English Woollens.'

'Made in America,' said Rowan thoughtfully.

An English actor crossed her line of vision, a man so thin and haggard he seemed to have only months to live, except that he had looked like that for at least the last ten years. 'We'd have to have guarantees,' she murmured. 'I wouldn't want our name on anything scrappy.'

'We run a very tight organisation, ma'am.'

The food arrived and Rowan poked doubtfully at some

unidentifiable seafood. She might be adventurous in many spheres of her life but they did not include food. Neither was she conditioned to the American habit of serving so much of everything, nor to the profligate waste. Wand thin people picked at vast platefuls and then abandoned them. Similarly she gave up on the seafood and ate the bread and butter instead.

A couple came in and all heads turned to see if it was anyone important. The girl Rowan vaguely recognised, a singer who sometimes appeared on British television. Her escort she knew rather better.

'Good God,' she said forcibly. Horrible suspicion filled her mind and she turned bright green eyes on her hosts. 'Do you have anything to do with Bardsey's? I shall find out if you do, you may as well tell me the truth.'

Carter Finsbacher looked trapped, not because of guilt though. 'Er — Bardsey's? Would that be a British firm? I'm afraid — '

Rowan couldn't believe it. 'You must have heard of them! You've heard of us, Bardsey's were the, absolutely *the*, number one firm for years. Worsteds. They supply all the big chain stores.'

'I know them,' one of the others chimed in. 'I had a look at them when we researched your company. Their ratios are not good, not good at all. Too many loss-makers battened on to the main company. Prime meat for a take-over, I should say.'

'Would you?' Rowan sank sharp teeth into her bread, watching Richard exercise visible charm across the table. The girl tossed her hair a lot. It annoyed Rowan even at this distance.

She was well into her steak when Richard spotted her. He seemed taken aback, then threw down his napkin and came straight across.

'Rowan! What the hell are you doing here?'

She chewed and swallowed a piece of steak. 'Hello,

Richard. May I introduce Carter Finsbacher? All these gentlemen are from Bellerphon Textiles. Richard Barton, everyone.'

'Are you treading on my turf?'

She shrugged elegantly. 'I really don't know. Actually I thought you might be stamping all over mine but I'm almost – almost – sure you're not. What are you here for?'

'Er – selling, just selling. And of course it's business *and* pleasure, to some extent. I'm with the lady I met up with in Paris that time. Remember?'

'Too well.'

She looked across and met the over-made-up stare of Richard's girlfriend. Rowan inclined her head very slightly. 'Richard, dear, if you stand there all night our food will go cold. I hate to chase you away.'

He laughed. 'Don't be so damned patronising. Where's Saul?'

'He has a broken leg,' said Rowan. She fixed him with a grim stare, he could so easily destroy her. But all he said was, 'These things will happen.' He started to move away and then came back. 'Look, I want to talk to you about something, strictly business. Where are you staying?'

'I'm committed on this trip,' objected Rowan.

'British to the core, eh, Rowan? Never take a risk.' He knew she couldn't afford to seem timid in front of these textile men.

She pulled a pen and a scrappy envelope out of her purse and scribbled on it. 'Beats me why you couldn't talk business in England. I haven't time to spare, Richard, I warn you.'

'Yeah. So I gather.'

He took the slip of paper and went back to his table. Rowan watched him grimly. 'Bardsey Textiles,' said Carter Finsbacher. 'I knew him when he was a fly boy dealing in alpaca. Took a few too many risks, I thought.'

'A lot of money behind him,' remarked Rowan. 'Gives

people a lot of confidence. Not that he lacked it anyway.'

'The self-made have a sharper edge,' someone commented, and Rowan flushed. She had let them see that she found his affluent background galling. It was British of her to be embarrassed at letting her feelings show, and American of them not to feel anything of the sort.

When Finsbacher dropped her off later that evening, he said, 'Shall I pick you up around half-eight, Rowan? See round the mill early and we can go home and lunch with my wife. The kids are on vacation right now, so it'll be kind of noisy.'

She nodded. 'I'd like that. Thank you very much.'

In her room, restless from too much food and jumpy because of the changes to her internal clock, she ran a hot bath and sat in it. Richard Barton had been just as horrified to see her as she to see him. Why? What was happening at Bardsey's? The storm clouds had been gathering; just scuds on the horizon at first but darker now. She thought of the markets, of the rumours. One of the major chainstores, associated with Bardsey's over a very long time, was importing quite a bit nowadays. Had they junked Bardsey's? As a firm they had pioneered hand in glove manufacture, working so closely with their customers that designs evolved mutually rather than being summoned from one person's brain. The fault, if fault there was, could be said to be the exclusion of truly original thought.

And the wind of change was blowing through the High Street. They were abandoning dull worth for style and flair. For the moment Rowan was playing the right tune, but she had no illusions but that one day the music would change. She could be caught flat-footed. It could be that Bardsey's already had. Were they looking at big losses, trying to grab market share in the US of A to replace that lost in Britain? She didn't know, but it gave her great pleasure to suspect.

On the following day she dressed in boots, an ankle-length

black skirt and a jacket woven to look like purple and green tapestry. She had sweated blood over the design, which had proved much harder to produce than she had ever anticipated. The background purple had killed every other colour until she had chucked in some red before spinning. Only a trained eye could see it, but the effect was to lift the colour dramatically. When Carter Finsbacher saw it, he blinked.

'Now this would be hard for you,' said Rowan offhandedly. 'Our people are very innovative, they have to be.'

He cleared his throat and ushered her to the waiting limo.

As they were pulling away, Rowan saw Richard Barton leap out of a cab. 'Oh God,' she said. 'Do ask the driver to stop.'

She pushed the button to open the window and stuck her head out. 'Are you looking for me, Richard?'

He turned in surprise. 'Hello, Rowan. I was intending to join you for breakfast. Where are you going, it's hardly dawn!'

'Bellerphon Textiles. I think it's quite a way. Look, call me tonight. Better still, take me out to dinner.'

Richard's face was amused and wary. 'Why the sudden affection?' he asked. 'I don't know why, Rowan, but I feel naturally suspicious.'

'Don't be so nervous. Pick me up at seven, OK?'

'OK.' He stepped back and the car swept away from the kerb. He stood watching until it was out of sight.

Rowan had expected the American mill to be way, way ahead of Judge's. She was hanging on the coat-tails of technological advance; somehow she had believed others to be wearing the damn thing. But Bellerphon was a big, old, draughty place with notices everywhere exhorting people to wear ear plugs, smile, have fun and keep their hair tied back, and they had the same mishmash of old and new machines. Rowan saw at once that the layout was inefficient. They had inherited it. America might be young in terms of history but their textile factories had been around long enough to grow old.

'Have you had to shed much labour recently?' she asked.

'Some. Quite a bit over the last few years. We're on the upswing now.'

She nodded. The slump had hit everyone in the West, they had all quailed under the onslaught of foreign goods. She stopped at a loom weaving what looked like blue blazercloth and pointed a long finger. 'One of your warp threads has broken.' Finsbacher went red and hit the stop button. He went into a corner with the man responsible and went even redder. They continued their tour.

Rowan had not expected to be able to make up her mind quickly. Linking up with a company so far away was a leap in the dark for Judge's, and the anxiety level of the Bellerphon men showed that it was a risk for them too. Who would it benefit most? On the face of things Bellerphon, who needed a new image and a new and exciting product. But Rowan indulged her fantasies. Suppose Bellerphon, using her range, hooked just those chainstore people Richard was probably courting? Bellerphon were hungry enough to hunt night and day; they were trying to give her the impression of always playing high but this was certainly their highest yet. Finsbacher was in his mid-forties, he had been through the worst, he knew the score. If they could guarantee quality, she would play ball.

She said as much to Finsbacher as they drove out of town to his house for lunch. He looked dumbfounded. Eventually, he said, 'Don't you have to talk with your husband? With your board?'

Rowan hadn't even contemplated it. 'I do tend to run things my way,' she said vaguely. 'There won't be any objection, I assure you.'

Finsbacher shot her rather an odd look. 'Right. Right.'

His house was a modest, crowded dwelling with a huge tree in the garden. A rubber tyre and a rope ladder hung

494

from it, the grass underneath was worn to bare earth. Rowan followed Finsbacher into the hall.

'Where is everybody?' he yelled, trying to keep his high spirits under wraps. 'I brought our guest home.'

Three unnaturally tidy young people came downstairs, the eldest about eighteen. In their wake careered a squat little boy, arms and legs everywhere and a beam on his flattened face. 'Dad! Dad!' he bellowed. 'I got a clean shirt, Dad! Look!'

He pulled his pink shirt out of his trousers and flapped the tails excitedly. One of his sisters, a girl of about fourteen, said, 'I just did you up, Jimmy!'

'I'll do it,' said Finsbacher. When he put his arms round Jimmy, the boy hugged him.

They went through to the kitchen. Margaret Finsbacher was a little taller than her husband with a smooth, unlined face. She had an air of tranquillity that seemed unaffected by the trauma of entertaining an important guest, or four children, or the large dog trying to batter its way in from outside.

'Dad! Dad!' bellowed Jimmy again. 'See my train, Dad!' He picked up two pieces of wood inexpertly nailed together.

His mother caught his hand. 'Not now, Jimmy,' she said gently. 'Visitors!'

The word had an almost magical effect. Jimmy looked abashed, folded his hands over the train and fell silent. 'Good boy,' said his mother.

They went through to the sitting room for drinks. Finsbacher was different at home, visibly more relaxed. The children made polite and intelligent conversation, with the exception of Jimmy, who sat being ludicrously good. Rowan reached in her bag for a photograph of Hannah.

'I've got a little girl like you,' she said to Jimmy. 'This is her.' He took the photograph and peered at it.

'Do you like your little girl?' he asked.

Rowan nodded. 'Lots and lots. I like you too.'

Jimmy stared again at the picture and then carefully and precisely put it in his pocket.

'I think you've lost that,' said Margaret.

Rowan shrugged. 'I've got more.'

After lunch the adults sat over coffee, watching Jimmy playing on the rope ladder. He was clumsy but careful, making each step with concentration.

'He's terribly good,' said Rowan. 'Very well behaved.'

Margaret Finsbacher nodded. 'It's a mistake to be sorry for them. Like any kid they need discipline, nice clear rules. I worry about him, I worry what's to happen when we're gone.'

'I don't think the others will let Jimmy down,' said Carter.

'But you can't rely on that,' said Rowan. 'You can't expect it.'

'Why not?' said Finsbacher. 'They all love Jimmy. I don't say they've got to live with him but they can take an interest in him and make sure he's set up right. Seems to me it's too easy to take it all on yourself.'

'I'd like to put some money aside for him,' said Margaret, watching her son hang by his arms, bicycling his short legs and roaring with laughter. Rowan thought, 'That is why Carter Finsbacher wants this deal. He needs it for Jimmy.'

She was tired when she got back to the hotel, a whole day of strangers was hard work. If she had known where Richard was staying, she would have rung up and cancelled dinner. Instead she showered and changed into a pair of silk lounging pyjamas. She had never worn them out before but there seemed no reason why she should not. They were cream with huge roses printed all over them. With a belt and high heels they looked oddly stylish. Long dangling earrings in the shape of elephants completed the picture.

The moment Richard saw them, he said, 'Taj Mahal meets Sayonara. Will you change to go to bed or just take off the earrings?'

'Don't be tedious, Richard.' He was wearing a dark suit and red tie. America's businessmen did seem to be boringly conventional in dress, she reflected, any peacock tendencies had been driven out by efficiency and seriousness. Even the women were following suit, in more ways than one. When they sat down to eat, at almost every other table were couples uniformly dressed in dark serge and white shirts.

'I don't want to look like the head waiter,' complained Rowan, aware that people were staring at her. 'It's not my fault the world's gone boring.'

'Talking of bores, how's Saul? I take it he was too smashed to make the trip?'

'He broke his leg,' said Rowan shortly. 'There's no more to it than that.'

'Except the prosecution,' retorted Richard. 'I do read the papers, love.'

She fell silent. Richard found himself studying the thin silk of her pyjama top, which was ever so slightly transparent. He could see the faint shadow of her breasts. 'Don't you ever wear a bra?' he asked.

Rowan started. 'You can't tell, can you? I don't sag or anything?'

He swallowed. 'Quite the opposite. A very pert pair.'

'Just don't get any ideas.'

The waiter came and Rowan ordered egg mayonnaise, which when it came was flavoured with garlic. Richard had mushrooms with garlic and truffles.

'I wish they'd never discovered garlic,' objected Rowan vehemently. 'All restaurants seem to think it's compulsory. Disgusting stuff.'

'Is it?' He hardly seemed to be listening.

She watched him surreptitiously. She could feel that he was angry with her, or possibly he was angry and was venting it on her. 'Bad day?' she asked.

'Could say that.' He met her eyes and she lifted her brows quizzically.

'You don't have to watch what you say,' she offered. 'I'm not going to use it in evidence against you. I think the world's big enough for Bardsey's and Judge's.'

His expression of open scepticism made her blush. 'Anyway, I know what you're doing,' she said defensively. 'One of the big chainstores put you in their pocket and against your better judgement insisted on a useless range. My guess is that the sludge brown was the final straw. If they sold half I'd be surprised. Now they've dumped you for someone more exciting, and that is terribly unfair. And you are left with empty looms and no customers. You're out here trawling.'

Richard put his elbows on the table. 'Since you know so much, I'll add a few titbits. I saw the writing on the wall months ago. Dad told me I didn't understand the business, we had a relationship with our customers, it was mutually beneficial, we mustn't do anything to upset them, et cetera. Now we have a problem, he wants to know why *I* didn't insist on doing things my way. You know what he said to me?' Rowan shook her head. 'That he didn't expect his son to be a yes-man. And it's me breaking stones over here, with the exchange rate against us and a design portfolio that's right out of step. I'm wasting my time.'

'What would you do instead?' asked Rowan.

'Rationalise.'

'You mean, sack everybody and flog off anything that's not tied down?'

'Pretty much, yes.'

Steak arrived and Rowan attacked her inch thick slab with surgeon-like precision. Across the table Richard toyed with his fork and watched her. All those confidences, she thought warily. He was trying to make her believe they were friends, when in fact he was telling her nothing she couldn't work out for herself. He had fine hands, she noticed, tanned, with long palms and mobile fingers. The uninitiated would call them musical, but if you looked at Andy's hands they were almost gnarled with exercise.

'Where's the girlfriend?' she asked. 'Aren't you serious about her?'

'Not now, no. I was once. She can't understand what's changed, we spend a lot of time arguing. I don't know what's changed really. Perhaps – I think I was settling for something that was OK instead of what was really good. I'm setting my sights a bit higher nowadays.'

'Don't be ingenuous.'

Her steak disposed of, or at least as much as she wished it to be, Rowan sat back and sipped her wine, regarding Richard with a cool stare that had in it all the personal interest of a judge at a dog show.

'Why do you pretend to be so sure of yourself?' he asked.

'I don't pretend, I am. Mostly.'

'I'd say it's almost all front. Nervous as anything. Too scared to take risks, any sort of risks. You want to drive a fast car but you don't. You want to spend money but you stop yourself. You want to have fun but you don't know how. You're a cat person, closed, independent and out of it. So sad.'

Saying it made it seem true. Rowan dropped her eyes and gulped at her wine. 'I don't mean to be anything,' she said hastily. 'I just am. I do what I want to do. Anyway, you said we'd talk business.'

He lounged back in his chair. 'I want you to buy our dye-house. Preferential price and a long-term agreement for our cloth to continue going through. Neither of us needs that capacity and you can afford it. We can't.'

'And you want jam on it! We can build one of our own for less than you'd make us pay.'

He grinned. 'We both know you couldn't. Money borrowed for months without return, the whole place disrupted while the building goes on, teething troubles, everything. This is an offer you can't refuse. A ready-made money spinner and a deal to benefit us both. Be sensible, Rowan.'

She looked at him earnestly. 'It does sound sensible. But I hate getting involved with James, it's always a mistake. For him,' she added, letting a smile slide maliciously around her mouth.

A thought struck her. 'Does he know about this?'

Richard grinned. 'Not yet.' He saw her quizzical expression and added, 'As it happens, Dad and I are about to have a fight. One hell of a fight actually. He is going to have to listen to what I say. I am damned if I'm going to be patronized and humoured and bloody well ignored.'

'Told you so,' said Rowan. 'He won't change.'

'He can either change or go bust,' snapped Richard. For a second the rage showed through, fuelled by all James's autocratic tactlessness. Abruptly, Richard came back to the present. 'Let's go on some place.' He cast down his napkin and signalled to the waiter. Caught unawares Rowan wondered why she hadn't had the sense to order a pudding. She liked puddings, they were her reason for dining out.

Once in the street, she said petulantly, 'I hadn't finished.'

'Yes, you had.' Richard waved down a cab and spoke to the driver. 'We're going to a nightclub,' he explained. 'I want to dance.'

'What about what *I* want to do?' demanded Rowan. She felt unconsidered and unappreciated. Before this Richard had always been absolutely focused on her, and here he was giving her minimal consideration.

'Don't be a wet blanket,' he said. She subsided, feeling herself on the verge of feminine acquiescence. Her own servility annoyed her.

Chapter Forty-Two

The nightclub was hot and crowded. Somewhere in the gloom a jazz trumpeter was splitting the smoky air into sharpened pieces of glass, and on the floor a girl danced. Her naked body was painted in blue and gold, her hair was sprayed gold and twisted into snaking ringlets. She lay on the floor, her legs twisted back, supporting herself on one painted arm while she clutched and dragged at nothing. There was sensuality, but also danger. As she knelt, her head thrown back and her body arched in abandoment, many of the women looked away.

When it was over, Richard said, 'Did you like that? Brilliant, isn't she?'

'I don't like that sort of thing. She seemed — evil. I know she was pretending but it was too real.'

Richard reached out and caught her wrist. The danger had excited him, as much as Rowan had been repelled. She couldn't get away, he held her easily. 'Are you frightened of desire?' he said softly. 'You're so innocent. You don't know how good it can be.'

'Let me go,' she whispered. 'I don't like you tonight.'

'You don't like me any night when I let you see what I want from you, because you want it too. You weren't cut out to be Mrs. Faithful, taking the knocks from your sodden block of a husband and opening your legs on the odd occasion when he's not too drunk or too sober. Why be that? It's not what you want.'

She felt off balance, and from that strange standpoint things didn't look normal. Saul was what Richard said, but only sometimes. Or was it always and she pretended not to

501

notice? Time and again when she found herself thinking of Saul she switched at once to business matters. The transition was so smooth nowadays that she did it automatically. Thoughts of Saul meant bad feelings which at once called up something which made her feel safe. Business was safe, it was understandable and depended not at all on emotion. And in those moments when feelings did intrude in that world, for instance when Andy got involved, and Sally and Diana, then she felt her very foundations rocked. There ought to be something solid in the world, something quite unchanging.

'I want to go back to the hotel,' she said to Richard. Her eyes were wide and anxious, he was suddenly aware of her intense vulnerability. He let go of her wrist and took her hand instead, gently. The band was playing a soft, slow blues, a song about love and loss and loneliness.

'Dance with me,' he pleaded. 'I didn't want to frighten you. It's all right, I won't hurt you. You're safe with me.'

Hadn't Saul said that, all that time ago? She allowed herself to be led to the dancefloor. Richard put his arm round her waist, she encircled his neck. In her high heels their faces were almost level. He brushed her lips with a kiss. 'I'm sorry I scared you. I don't know why I do that to you. I get angry at you for not doing what I know we should! And I don't want to seduce you, I want it to be something you want as much as me. We'd do it together.'

The pale lids descended, hiding her sea-green eyes. 'Sometimes I want to. Sometimes some part of me wants to. But it's so selfish, such a mean thing to do.' She looked up at him. They had gone beyond pretence. 'It isn't fair to think only about us.'

'When did Saul ever think about anyone but himself?' said Richard harshly. 'He betrays you every time he takes another drink, a hundred times a day! And I need you, Rowan. It isn't as if I'll go on quite happily on my own, I can't take it like that any more. And there doesn't seem to be anyone else who'll do. I wish there was, really.'

She put her head back and stared at him. 'I don't want this to be serious, you know. I don't intend anything. That isn't what you intend really, is it?'

He had a choice between honesty and dishonesty. He chose, for once, to tell the truth. He sighed. 'If I say it's just a casual thing, you'll like me better, but I won't like me at all.'

Giving up all attempt at dancing he let her go, and they stood facing each other, not touching. The trumpet wailed and howled, and all around them people clung together. They alone stood fiercely apart. Richard said, 'I don't know why it is, but I think about you all the time. I feel angry with you for invading my head like this. You're in my dreams, bothering me. You turn me on when I've better things to do. I think you should come to bed with me because you don't owe your bum of a husband anything. And I should go to bed with you to see if I can get you out of my head! You're a bloody nuisance, Rowan.'

She turned on her heel and went back to the table, picking up her bag and heading for the door. Richard followed, and when they reached the street he found she was walking away. He hurried after her and said, 'Wait for a cab.'

'I want to walk. It's a well-lit street.' She pulled free and went on, and he hung back for a minute, admiring her, watching her pyjamas ripple against her body, her long legs stepping like a giraffe on the Serengeti Plain. Then a hand reached out of a doorway and grabbed her. Richard was running almost before she screamed. When she did it was a muffled shriek against a choking hand. No more than two seconds and Richard was looming over them in the doorway. Rowan wasn't struggling. There was a knife at her thoat.

'Let her go,' said Richard. 'Hurt her and I'll kill you.'

'Give me the money, man.' He was a Puerto Rican, smelling of urine and decay. Drugs, thought Richard, aware of Rowan's huge eyes above the grime-encrusted hand.

'Put down the knife or you get nothing,' he said. He put his hand slowly into his jacket and drew out his wallet. The man's eyes followed it like a snake following the movement of a snake charmer's pipe. 'Take the knife away,' said Richard. The knife moved, a scant three inches. Richard bent down to hand over the wallet and in the same moment kicked hard at the man's wrist. The knife clattered away, the man howled and Rowan bit the hand clamped over her face. Richard had her arm and dragged her to her feet. They ran like hares back to the lights and safety of the club.

'Bastards! Mother fuckers!' screamed the man after them.

There was a cab drawing up, Richard cut in front of the people who had ordered it and thrust Rowan inside. As they drove away the people on the pavement complained angrily, and twenty yards away a scrawny figure still stood, yelling, 'Bastards! Mother fuckers!'

They went back to Richard's hotel. He was in one of the opulent business hotels designed to be that important New York password, the good address. It was comfortable and impersonal, with Richard's briefcase on a chair and a tie draped precisely over a chair. Rowan sat down, shivering, while Richard poured them both stiff drinks.

'I want to clean my teeth,' she said suddenly. 'I can still taste him. God! It makes me feel sick.'

'Use my brush,' said Richard. 'Have a shower if you want.'

She did want. She felt dirty, as if she carried infection. What would she have done if the man had raped her? She would have wanted to kill herself.

The shower made her feel better. She ran the water scalding hot and scrubbed herself all over, even her scalp. Although she didn't lock the door, Richard remained firmly on the other side. His sensitivity surprised her, she hadn't thought him capable of it. In the aftermath of fear she felt tired, in need of warmth and reassurance. She felt, almost as never before, in need of sex, in need of harsh and primitive mating. He had aroused her from the first, she knew that now, and yet as always she'd denied her own emotions. She remembered how he had touched her in the lift and how she had lain awake for hours afterwards. Heat surged in her. Rubbing her hair dry, she wrapped herself in a towel and came out.

Richard was sitting in the chair, sipping his drink. Rowan picked up her own and sat on the bed. The towel was drooping a little around her breasts. She made as if to hitch it up — and then left it. 'Was he an addict?' she asked.

'I expect so. Emaciated little runt.'

'He made me think of Saul. The same desperation. I don't understand it.'

'I don't think there's any point in trying.'

He took off his tie and started to unbutton his shirt. For a moment she watched him, accepting what he dictated for her, letting the sure movements of his fingers tease her senses. Suddenly she thought of James. Those hands were James's hands, that certainty was absolutely his. Her imagination ran the film: James taking off his clothes, her mother lying watching in the bed. Whose bed? The bed of her childhood, the haven of warmth and love and Daddy.

'No!' Her voice came out hoarse and anguished. 'I don't want this.'

'Of course you do.' With victory so close, Richard was beyond persuasion.

'No. I won't do it, ever.'

She got up and went into the bathroom to get her clothes. Richard followed. She tried to push him away. His hands ripped aside the towel. Long white thighs. She turned away from him, bending to put on her pyjamas. He stared into the shadows in the cleft of her buttocks, he put out his hand and tried to penetrate her.

She rounded on him wildly, hitting out hard. 'Get off me, get away!' He felt her fingernails on his cheek and closed with her, holding her wrists high above her head. If only he had taken off his clothes! Jamming her between the washbasin and the bath, he pressed himself against her. She stopped struggling. He looked into eyes like green glass. 'If you rape me,' said Rowan softly, 'I shall call the police. They will put you away for years and years and years.'

He didn't move. 'This isn't rape. It's me making you do what you should.'

She almost spat with anger. 'I know what I want! And it isn't to be screwed in some hotel bathroom by some jerk who thinks he's going to impress me! Let me go, damn you, let me go!' She began to struggle again. Richard held himself against her for a few delicious seconds, and then let go of her wrists. She battered him viciously with her elbows and broke free.

He sat on the edge of the bath as she flung on her clothes. His eyes glittered dangerously. Rowan felt as if she were in the presence of a tiger that might at any moment spring. As she prepared to leave he got up and came over to her, standing between her and the door. He put his hands up under her top and held her naked breasts. In the heat of his palms they seemed to swell, to become pumpkins topped by hard stalks. Feebly she tried to push him away, making no real effort. She closed her eyes to shut him out.

'You want it and I want it,' said Richard. 'But loving scares you, because you don't know how to let go. You don't dare lose control. Get out then! Get out and don't come back.'

He opened the bedroom door and thrust her through it, slamming it after her. She stood in the bare corridor, aflame with heat, her breasts aching and her legs like jelly. Her hand went up to knock on the closed door, to beg him to let her in. At that moment all she wanted in the world was his body. There were voices of people coming up in the elevator. The cold wind of reality rushed into her mind. What was she doing here, about to fawn and beg a man to please, please fill her up? She was in pain, she was wet with desire. She thought of Saul, she thought of Hannah. Her fist fell away. Clutching her bag, she ran to the elevator, to get a cab and get back to her own room, and safety.

The next day she had an appointment with Marcus Arnaud. She felt hungover, not through drink but something very like it. If she had slept with Richard would she have woken refreshed and renewed, or as sour as this, as depressed as this? Sitting at the elaborate dressing table in her room she made up her eyes in great circles of purple, matching her neat purple suit, the shadows echoing her black blouse. The hated emerald choker, Saul's guilt present, went on too. She looked dramatic, very thin and strained.

Arnaud's salon was in a small street of discreet shops. His display window was understated to the point of emptiness, Rowan gazed at the two frocks displayed, beige on beige, and was unimpressed. Pushing the heavy glass door she entered the salon. The atmosphere was more hushed than any funeral parlour. A girl dressed in beige wool with a pure white collar looked up from a desk.

'My name's Barton,' said Rowan, her voice loud in the silent air. 'From Isaac Judge, Bradford. I have an appointment with Mr. Arnaud.'

The girl checked her list. 'I'm sorry, we were expecting a Mr. Barton.'

'My husband, Saul. A broken leg. I'm sorry, I thought my office had informed you.' Mentally she cursed Frances. It was a small slip but in these situations it only took something small to throw Rowan off balance. She was so far from home, so friendless. New York wasn't a friendly town, it gave away nothing at all. You grabbed and took, or went away empty-handed.

The girl got up to lead her to a gilded staircase. Rowan followed her upstairs, past photographs of dresses taken in such odd situations that the clothes themselves were hard to judge. She recognised blue cloth, trimmed with red, both Judge's make. A little surge of relief soothed her nerves.

Marcus Arnaud was in his studio, a small man walking nervously up and down in front of a drawing board. When she entered, he said aggressively, 'I thought it was going to be Saul. He rang personally.'

Rowan swallowed. 'He had an accident, broke his leg. He sends his apologies.'

'Can't he pick up the goddammed 'phone, can't he even do that?'

Rowan didn't understand the note of petulance. 'He's in hospital,' she said vaguely. 'I told him I'd look after everything, he isn't well.'

Arnaud stopped his pacing and looked at her. 'Who are you then? His assistant?'

'I thought they told you. I'm his wife. Rowan, Rowan Barton.'

The man's small, rather pretty mouth dropped open. He caught himself and grinned. 'Oh. Right, right, I see. Er – tell Saul I'm sorry to have missed him. He'd better make a point of looking me up when he's in town next.'

'I'm sure he will. You'd be very welcome to come and visit the mill when you're in England, Mr. Arnaud.'

'That's sweet of you, honey.' He had adopted any number of Americanisms.

Rowan began to unpack her samples, uncomfortable without really knowing why. 'Were you a model girl?' asked Arnaud.

Rowan grimaced. 'Because I'm so tall, you mean? No. I'm a millowner's daughter. And now I own the mill.'

'Just you?'

'And my husband, my brother and sister and a few thousand shareholders. But I was the one that pulled it round. Without me it would have sunk.' It was boasting but she felt she needed it. Although nothing had been said she felt criticised by this man. He seemed to be judging her.

As he looked through the cloth, his eye caught by the couple of Spanish pattern samples she had managed to squeeze in, she babbled: 'It was Saul's idea to sell your end of the market. I didn't think there'd be anything in it for us, but of course there is, indirectly. Why do you have such dull dresses in your window?'

He blinked at her. 'Everybody's got windows like that right now.'

'I thought the idea was to be different.'

He put down the samples. 'You're not a bit like Saul. A more tactful man I never met.'

She sighed unhappily. 'Was that rude? I'm sorry. Look, I can see I'm taking your time. Suppose I pack this lot up and you see Saul when he's better?'

He rested his hand on hers as she started to close her case. His touch was dry and slightly cold. 'Suppose we have lunch. I'd like to talk. About you and Saul.'

Over pasta in an aggressively Italian restaurant, Arnaud said, 'Are you happy, Rowan? In your marriage?'

She stared at him. 'That's not something I like to be asked, thank you. I don't know why you asked it.'

'Then you're not happy. You don't look it, you're all strung up.'

'I just hate travelling, that's all!' snapped Rowan. But to her horror she felt her eyes sting with tears. She fumbled for her handkerchief. 'I'm sorry,' she sniffed. 'Oh, I might as well tell you. Saul broke his leg in a car crash, and he crashed because he was blind drunk. He's in a clinic for alcohol dependency. For God's sake, don't tell everyone. Though everyone knew he was drinking, I don't suppose I should mind now he's being dried out.'

Arnaud poured her some wine. She topped it up with Perrier and drank.

'You don't know about him, do you?' he said.

'About who? Saul? What should I know?'

'He's gay.'

Rowan's eyes, purple-painted, were caverns in her white face. 'That's an absolute bloody lie!'

509

'No, it isn't, lovey. He told me himself. He and I — we understand each other. I met him one time when he was torn up over an affair. I guess he married you soon after.'

'But — I know that's not true. He's normal, he is really!'

'Then why does he drink? He ain't happy, sweetheart. I'm only telling you because I can see things aren't working out. I've been through this with friends of mine. They get married, think they can keep it under wraps, end up leading a double life that makes them and the girl miserable. You need to know. It's the only fair way out.'

As Rowan looked at him, the world tilted on its axis. Arnaud was small, quietly dressed, only so very slightly effeminate, but in her mind he was a drag queen, his lips dripping scarlet, pouting, seducing men into nameless, unimaginable horrors. 'I don't believe you,' she said feebly.

'Not now you don't. Go home and ask him, love. He'll be relieved I told you. Tell him to come and see me. I'd like to help.'

'I bet you would!' Rowan got up and ran. The waiter picked up her sample case from where she had stashed it by the door and struggled after her. She stopped and took it from him, and then couldn't run because it weighed so heavy. That horrible, horrible man!

She caught a cab and sat hunched in the back, listening to her heart thunder against her chest. It wasn't true, there was no way it could be true. But doubts nudged at her. Why did he drink? What did he do on those trips away? What about that time in Spain when he couldn't?

Pacing the hotel room, she tried to think what to do. Her instinct was to get on the first plane home and confront Saul, demand that he confess. Suppose he denied it? He might still be lying. Oughtn't she to keep it to herself, sneak about and find some evidence? Besides, tomorrow was the final meeting with Bellerphon, she should stay for that. But she would burst if she didn't talk to someone.

She rang Richard's hotel with no expectation that he

would be in. When he answered she sat for a moment, holding the receiver in silence. 'Hello? Who is this?' Richard's irritated voice cut through her thoughts.

'It's me. Richard — something's happened. I need you.'

'Are you hurt? Is it someone at home?'

'No, no, nothing like that. I've found out something. Please come, Richard, I'm at the hotel.'

She heard him swallow. 'I've only just calmed down after last night.'

'I know, I know. But this is now and everything's different.'

'Wait there. I'll be fifteen minutes.'

When he arrived she was sitting hunched up on the edge of the bed, surrounded by luxury like a mouse on a sumptuous ship. He sat next to her and put his arm round her shoulders. She was shaking like a leaf.

'What is it? Tell me, quick.'

'It's Saul!' She put her face into his jacket and sobbed, sending rivulets of purple down her cheeks and on to his shirt. 'Oh God, look at the mess I'm making.'

'Never mind that, what the hell is it?'

'A man today — a customer — he says Saul's gay!'

Richard's mouth worked soundlessly. Suddenly he laughed. 'Bloody hell! Do you believe him?'

'It isn't funny! I don't know what I believe. He said that's why Saul drinks, that's why we don't get on. And I thought about all the trips ... and in Spain once, he couldn't, you see. In bed with me, he couldn't!'

'Probably too pissed,' said Richard.

'Well, of course he was! And afterwards it was OK. Except it wasn't OK after Hannah was born, but it was my fault, not his! I was so sore, you see.'

Richard took out his handkerchief and wiped the purple smudges off Rowan's cheeks. 'How did this guy say he knew?'

A shudder went through her. 'I got the impression that he and Saul — that they had — done it. Together.'

'I can't see Saul going in for buggery somehow,' remarked Richard.

'Don't use that word! It's revolting! I don't mind men doing it, but not Saul, please not Saul!'

Richard had never known jealousy before, had never looked at the monster head on. Suddenly he was devoured by it. How dare she prefer that bastard, who cared nothing for her, to him? Not for one minute did he believe Saul was gay, but for that minute he intended that Rowan should believe it. 'He's probably AC DC,' he said lightly. 'A lot of men are. Don't mind who they do it with as long as they can have a change now and then. Probably had a taste of it once or twice, then got into the habit when you weren't in the mood.'

Rowan took a long shuddering breath. 'How could he?' she said softly. 'I don't think I'd care so much if it was another woman, but with that horrible, horrible man!'

'It's all right, my love, it's all right!' He was mouthing her neck, whispering to her. 'God, but you're beautiful, don't ever think you're not. See how you turn me on. There's no need to keep it for him now, is there?'

He pushed her back on the bed and she lay there, letting the tears run from the corners of her eyes. He was undressing her and she let him, submitting to anything he wished to do. Kneeling astride her he stripped off tie, jacket and shirt, then he bent and took her nipple in his mouth in a kiss. 'Oh God. Oh God, no,' she said and pushed him away. Her arousal was suddenly so great that it hurt her to be touched, her whole nervous system tingled. He paused, watching her quizzically. Calming herself with long breaths, she reached up and unzipped his trousers.

Almost desperate, Richard threw off his clothes. He knelt across her and she closed her hand on him, unable to believe that this was happening. He began to peel off her skirt and pants. She wished Saul could see her and know what she was doing! In the midst of her sorrow she shuddered with true and unwavering desire. It had been wrong before, but now it was owed her. He began to kiss and stroke her but she didn't want that. 'Just do it,' she said, and lay back for him, her legs wide. 'Please, do it to me.'

The availability of that black-haired moist opening was too much for him. He got on top of her, his erection searching blindly for long seconds before it plunged home. Rowan clung to his shoulders, her eyes wide and staring. He suddenly felt her tight on him and realised she was in orgasm. He stayed still and waited, forcing himself to hold on. When he began to move again she started to cry out, in exquisite agony. In a room far away he could hear a telephone ringing. Her nails fastened to his buttocks, driving him into her. For a minute he wanted to hurt her as much as she hurt him. He reached the peak and hung there, painfully engorged. Then he flooded into her.

She lay spreadeagled beneath him, they were bonded together with sweat. Richard rolled away, still swollen but aching now as well. He staggered into the bathroom and splashed cold water on to his face. Staring at himself in the mirror, he saw his own shocked expression. For once his excitement had been entirely matched by its release; there was no sense of let-down, only of pressure discharged. Exhausted, he barely knew what he should do.

When he went back, Rowan was curled up on her side. 'Why did you have to wait until you were angry with him?' demanded Richard. 'You should have done it for me, only for me.'

'Yes. Yes, I should.' She rolled on to her back, sprawling wantonly. 'Do it again.'

Just watching her made him stiffen. He lay down beside her and said, 'You do the work.' Slowly and langourously, she straddled him. 'Saul liked this,' she said plaintively.

'To hell with Saul!' Richard caught her round the waist, held her and turned over while still inside. When she was beneath him he thrust at her angrily. 'It's me here, not him,' he hissed. 'Was it ever this good with him?'

Had it been? At the start she had waded through inexperience, there had been none of this wild abandonment. This was, in truth, the most sensual experience of her life. Her breath was coming in gasps. 'You're the best,' she gasped. 'He couldn't do this to me, only you! Just you.'

They stayed together all day, through the evening and on into the night. Usually Richard hated sleeping close to anyone. Now he wanted to die in that huge bed. He wrapped himself round her back, aware of sensations he hadn't even known existed. If only she would forget about that bastard, be his alone. She murmured in her sleep, she murmured, 'Richard?' He dozed, knowing that when he woke she would be there.

The morning was grey and wet. They lay watching the rain splatter the window and it seemed more than enough reason not to get up. 'I fell right down into heaven,' said Rowan lazily. 'I feel so good.'

Richard picked up the 'phone and rang room service for breakfast. While they waited he amused himself tracing the vertebrae so visible beneath Rowan's smooth skin. He buried his face against her. 'You're beautiful. So lovely, so beautiful. What we did was beautiful, wasn't it?'

'Yes. Yes, it was.' She sat up and put her hands against his chest, where the hair was wiry and curled beneath her fingers like coarse wool. 'Fifty-fours,' she thought absently, 'you'd never get it to spin well.'

'What am I going to do?' she asked suddenly.

'Eat your breakfast, read the papers, go to your appointments, come back and have me love you.' He kissed her fingers.

'Suppose that man was lying?'

'Oh, for Christ's sake!' Richard flung himself back down on the bed. 'Whether he was or he wasn't makes no damned difference! Saul's a bum, always has been. Your marriage has had it, Rowan. The sooner you leave him the better.'

'And then what?' She stared at him, challenging him.

'You come to me.'

He had said more than he had intended. Richard got out of bed and went to switch on the television. He lay, changing channels, aware that she was lying absolutely silent beside him.

Suddenly Rowan grabbed his hand. 'Go back a bit. I'm sure I saw — yes! Look, it's Andy!' Instinctively she picked up the sheet and hid herself behind it, in case Andy could see her.

He was standing in some casual breakfast television studio, his violin dangling from one hand. Although his hair was immaculately blow-dried he wore a pair of patched cord jeans and a lumberjack jumper, and over the top a purple waistcoat. He looked relaxed and very handsome.

'What are you going to play for us this morning, Andy?' demanded a ferociously charming girl. 'Something bright for this rainy day. Something to send us all skipping over those puddles.'

'Anything for you, Helene.' He grinned at her and then shot a disparaging wink at the camera. 'Try this for size everyone.' Putting his violin to his chin he began to rattle off gypsy music, weaving in threads from various popular classical tunes. As he played he strolled around in a small circle, grinning into the camera now and then, sometimes closing his eyes and swaying theatrically, as if he was becoming seriously engrossed in the beauty of the music.

'The fake,' muttered Rowan. 'Fake, fake, fake.'

When it came to an end, the presenters gave whoops of delight. 'Thanks a lot, Andy, that was great. Couldn't you just listen to that forever everyone? See you tomorrow, Mr. Wonderful.'

'Look forward to it.' Andy waved his bow and wandered out of camera range.

Helene said, 'Don't forget, everyone, that Andy Judge's fabulous record is available now. I'm certainly buying quite a few as Christmas presents. Now, Jim, what's the latest on the traffic this morning?'

Richard reached out and clicked the set into silence.

Neither Richard nor Rowan said anything for a minute. Then Richard said, 'He's certainly good at it. Very natural.'

'The Pied Piper of Hamelin goes to Hollywood!' exploded Rowan. 'If Mother hears him play like that she'll stab him through the heart with a hatpin. It's rubbish music. And the worst of it is — I encouraged him! I told him to dump his classical principles and get popular. And he has!'

'Then why don't you like it?'

She sniffed. 'I don't know. He played well, didn't he? He's got that, you see, he always did have it. The ability to make you listen, make you think the piece is better than it is. But it never came across in concerts somehow, or at least not properly. I think what I mind is — well, I thought he'd get well known and then go back to being straight. But that didn't look like it, did it?'

'Very profitable though if you ask me. Going to buy the record?'

She nodded. 'Do you think he's dumped the dreadful Astrid?'

'Looks to me as if he's well in with the chrome-plated Helene. Haven't you got an address for him anywhere?'

She shook her head. 'I didn't even know he was in the States.'

Ever since Andy left to go to college he'd been the same. He reserved the right to come back into their lives from time to time, but for himself he demanded privacy. She might have resented it had she not remembered how it used to be. Andy, trying to keep his head together when they all pulled him this way and that. Andy, trying to come to terms with needing James, hating him, his bossy sister taking sides, his father crumbling. Andy, trying not to mind that another man slept with his mother. Yes, he had a lot of reasons for wanting to keep them all at arm's length.

Breakfast arrived at last. Rowan slipped into the bathroom while it was delivered, and while she was there she showered and dressed.

'Where the hell are you going?' asked Richard. He was drinking coffee and scanning the morning papers.

'I've got an appointment in half an hour.'

'So have I. But I don't mind missing it.'

'I don't think I'd better, somehow. It's this franchise thing.'

He put down the paper. 'Look, love, you don't have to feel I'm pressurising you. But I meant what I said. This should be for keeps.'

She stood looking at him, lopsided with one shoe on and one shoe off. 'What about Hannah?'

'Well — she's got a nanny and so on. If she comes in the package, then OK.'

A wry smile crossed her face. She wandered about the suite, picking up things to be put in her bag: lipstick, tissues, a comb. 'You'd be horrified if I took you up on it. Don't worry, I won't.'

'Even if he did screw that queen?'

She hesitated. 'Even if. Probably. But I don't think he did.'

'I do.'

'No, you don't, you just want me to believe it.'

Richard blinked. It was the sort of sharply intuitive comment that surprised him about Rowan. Just when he had decided she always played straight, she headed for an acute and difficult angle. He picked up the newspaper again and flicked it open to the European pages while Rowan picked at a piece of toast and drank some coffee.

The telephone rang. Richard reached out a hand for it and then paused. Rowan grimaced and picked it up. 'Yes? Oh. Hello, Mother. Whatever time is it over there? Er — no, I'm sorry I don't know where Richard is. I may be able to contact him, though. I have seen him around.' She flapped at him hard as he made to take the receiver. 'I see. Yes. That's — that's dreadful. All right, Mother, I'll make sure I find him. And I'll be home tomorrow, I promise. Love to everyone. 'Bye.'

She hung up and stood with her hand still resting on the telephone.

517

'What is it?' asked Richard tensely. 'Tell me!'

'An accident. Bardsey Combers. An Asian got tangled up in one of the conveyor belts. Two men tried to rescue him and one fell into the scouring pans. Impaled on the spikes that push the wool through. He's dead, the others are in intensive care. Everyone's out on strike.'

'Shit, shit, shit!' Richard sat still for a moment. Then with a roar of rage he picked up the breakfast tray and hurled it across the room. Rowan screamed as coffee and toast cascaded everywhere.

'As if I didn't tell him!' raged Richard. 'As if I didn't warn him it would happen! I told him we'd have to modernise or someone would get killed and he said we couldn't afford it. Well, can we afford this, may I ask? We're likely to be prosecuted.'

'Mother didn't say anything about that,' said Rowan, nervously picking toast off the carpet.

'Why in God's name didn't he let me do something? Wanted me in the firm all right, but as sodding decoration! What am I doing here, picking up the pieces from the mess he made, wasting time in bed with you when I should be back there, sorting out that — that shit-house!' He paced around, stark naked.

'Are you going to ring?' asked Rowan.

'What? No. I'm getting on the first plane. He's made a balls of it for the last time. This is where he moves over and lets me do it.'

'He won't let you,' said Rowan. 'I knew he wouldn't in the first place.'

Richard turned on her a look of murderous determination. His eyes were clear as water. She flinched. It was the wolf taking off his woolly disguise.

'I would just like him to try and stand in my way,' murmured Richard. 'I would just love him to try.'

518

Chapter Forty-Three

The huge scouring pans of Bardsey Combers were like enormous bathtubs. The wool entered from a hopper at one end, an avalanche of stinking fibre, matted with dung and straw and grease. The pan itself was filled with constantly circulating water, black with dirt at the start and becoming cleaner and cleaner as the wool progressed on its watery way. Rollers dragged the wool from one pan to another, hooking it on nine-inch metal spikes to let it drop into the next, cleaner bath. It was a hell's kitchen, full of noise and steam and condensation. The men worked half-naked, clambering over the rollers to remove jammed wool, roaring at each other above the rumble of the driers. Nothing was wasted. When the wash water was changed, they piped the greasy sludge away to extract the lanolin. Yet from this maelstrom came soft, clean, sweet-smelling wool.

Richard stood staring at the silent monoliths all around him. Water was dripping somewhere, slow and insistent. Without the swirling clouds of steam the full squalor of the place was evident, torn plastic hanging from the roof, a broken control box held together with wire. Half the problems of the combing plant stemmed from the scouring. The ancient machines were too slow and unreliable. In a rush of demand the wool backed up here and could not be pushed through.

Blinking from lack of sleep, he turned to the man next to him. 'Let's see what happened then.'

The other man swallowed. He it was who had ripped off his white coat to try and staunch the blood, and had stood helpless while it turned red, then black, and the floor all around became slippy with gore. At the time he hadn't considered it but last night, in bed, it had come back to him again and again.

'He was clearing a blockage, sir,' he explained. 'On the belt that feeds the hopper. Some fool had left some twine on a bale and it had tangled in the belt. Wasn't tied up right, you see, he didn't spot it. Not that he's the brightest lad in the world. Well, you don't want that in there, do you?'

'Get on with it,' said Richard.

'Yes, sir. Shan's his name. The man that got caught in the belt. He screamed like, his leg was caught up. Someone pushed the emergency button, but he'd been dragged almost over the hopper. Two blokes ran up straight away to get him out, his leg was a terrible mess, terrible. Couldn't move him, he was caught up, you see. And the hopper wasn't stopped. Before anyone knew, the other two had fallen in. One went straight down on the wool and got pulled out. The other bloke made a grab for the edge of the hopper, missed and went right over. He hit the roller, you see. That one there.'

Richard stared at the huge spikes. He imagined what it must be like to be impaled on them, what it must be like to try and get someone off. 'You got him off, did you?' he asked.

'I helped, sir. We all did. Stuck right through him they did. And he was conscious.'

'I know, I know. No need to give me all the details.'

'Thought you wanted to know, sir. You can see why the men are upset, like.'

Richard resisted the temptation to curse him. 'How about the original casualty?'

'Got a great lump out of his calf. He'll be OK though, won't lose his leg. Bloody lucky.'

'It was his own negligence, though. The accident was entirely his responsibility.'

'The inspector said we should have guarded the belt. He shouldn't have been able to get there, you see.'

Richard saw, only too well. His father had known the safety precautions were substandard and had chosen to do nothing about it. God knows how long it would be before the men could be cajoled back to work, or before they could begin to scour again. There would be claims too, for compensation, and prosecutions for negligence. The accident had been all over the papers. The local daily paper was using it to begin a campaign on factory safety.

He walked swiftly out of the factory and got into the Maserati. There was a small demonstration at the gate, a group of workers with placards reading 'We don't have to die for money' and 'Stop Killing Us'. Hostile faces, both brown and white, in shabby anoraks. He in his Maserati, they in their thin shoes. What possessed a man to put up with working in such a place, he wondered? He couldn't imagine a world of so little opportunity.

His father's car was in its spot in the office car park, the Mercedes. Richard parked next to it and strode past the doorman, ignoring his salute. Too impatient for the lift he went up the stairs two at a time, barged past his father's secretary and into the office.

James looked up, startled, from the papers he had been studying.

'Right,' said Richard menacingly. 'I've come to talk to you.'

'So I see,' said James. He took off the reading glasses he had lately been forced to wear and tossed them on the papers in front of him. 'Never here when you're wanted, are you?'

'It wasn't my idea to go to the States, if you remember. I've been to the combing plant. All we can do is grovel, pay up and modernise. And we've got to do it now, put out a public statement at once. If we co-operate with the factory inspectorate, they might not slam us in court.'

'You're bloody hopeful, aren't you? I'd rather sack the workforce and close down.'

Richard blinked. 'Are you serious? The shareholders would crucify you!'

'Rather that than be held to ransom by a load of lazy fools! The man should never have been on the damned conveyor! I'm not going to give in to them.'

Richard paused for a moment. His father was rattled, perhaps for the first time in his life. He hadn't been the same since Nicholas, of course. 'Time you had a holiday, Dad,' he said.

'Are you trying to tell me I'm past it?' James got to his feet, his hair flopping over his face, glaring at his son. 'If you are trying to push me on to the rubbish heap, then I think you're about twenty years too early! I'm damned if I'll stand here and let you —'

'Have you spoken to the bank?' interrupted Richard. His father's mouth worked.

'Well,' said James at last. 'I see you feel you are in rather a strong position.'

'If we don't get a recovery plan started we are going down the tubes.' Richard strove for reason. 'You've made this firm what it is. Without you there wouldn't be a Bardsey Textiles. But we must, absolutely *must,* sort ourselves out! We can't clothe the looms, we haven't in months! OK, we lost some big customers, but we've got to get back in there. Design, innovation, energy. We've been standing still, and in textiles it may look like you're staying in the same place but it's amazing how fast the scenery changes. We're in big trouble.'

'And you want me out,' retorted James.

'Not especially. I just want me in.'

'Is there a difference?'

The two men stared at each other.

'What if I don't move over?' asked James.

Richard shrugged. 'I'll quit. You know what that could do to confidence — even the boss's son doesn't like it.'

'I could say the crisis is all your fault.'

'Don't think I'm too scrupulous to go to the papers!'

James drew in his breath angrily. Suddenly he burst out, 'God damn it, it *is* your fault! You didn't bring anything to this firm, you've been an expensive luxury! All right, see what you can do. I warn you, if I can't turn it round, you haven't a cat in hell's chance! Not a chance in hell!'

He picked up his reading glasses, made as if to put them in his pocket and then snapped them between his hands. He threw the mangled pieces on the floor at Richard's feet, and with a sweep of his arm cleared the desk. An inkpot rolled on to the carpet, leaving a trail of dark blue.

'You never were any bloody use,' said James. His voice shook, almost with tears. Richard walked to James's chair and sat down.

When James got home, Diana was in the conservatory. He went to find her, which was in itself unusual. He didn't normally concern himself with her whereabouts. She was tending pot plants, wearing rubber gloves and ladling compost from a bag.

'Guess what's happened,' said James ironically.

'I can't. Not another accident?'

'Depends on the way you look at it. He's kicked me out. Richard's kicked me out.'

She put down her trowel and stared at him. 'That's impossible. He couldn't do anything unless you let him.'

He put his hands in his pockets and sat on a corner of the table, careless of the compost on his suit. 'Right prick he's turned into. Right lump of shit.'

'Don't be so vulgar, James!'

'"Don't be so vulgar, James!"' he mimicked her. 'Doesn't matter what you do so long as you do it tastefully, is that it? I used to love your taste, I actually thought it was important. Look what you've brought me. A mausoleum of a home, near bankruptcy, and a son who's prepared to kick me into the grave! He wouldn't have done it if it wasn't for you. You turned him against me.'

Diana turned her head away, her cheeks scalded by sudden tears. 'You don't need to blame me for everything,' she said thickly. 'I know I've made mistakes, some I've regretted over and over again. It wasn't all my doing! I've tried so hard, James, I've tried so hard to make up.'

He got up and went over to a tall plant standing in a huge terracotta pot. He took part of the stem in his hands, cradling it. 'He wasn't mine, was he?' he said.

Diana caught her breath. Was there any point in lying now? She put her gloved hands together, almost in prayer. 'I thought he was,' she said softly. 'There was only such a slight chance he wasn't. It was only the once, you see. And he was yours, really. Nobody else loved him as a father should.'

'You didn't care how much of a fool you made of me.'

'Don't be so bloody stupid! You need never have known. And if you minded that much, why in God's name didn't you let me get rid of him?'

He swung round on her. 'Would you have rather that? Never having had Nick at all? What about never having done it, what about some kind of fidelity?'

She almost sneered at him. 'For you to say that is downright obscene.'

Now that it was at last admitted they experienced relief. Fighting on seemed irrelevant, meaningless, they had done so much of it in the past months. Diana said, 'Will you let Richard push you out?'

James considered. 'I'll have to, for now. I've let things slide so badly these last months. I could do with a rest, perhaps. We could have a holiday. See how things look later on.'

'That's a good idea.'

All of a sudden, James put out his hand. Diana had to pull off her glove, it took seconds. She clutched at him awkwardly. 'He was such a lovely boy,' she whispered.

'He was, wasn't he? He used to laugh when he saw me,

always. Waving his little hands and laughing.'

'You see. It didn't matter, that silliness. Did it?'

For the very first time James wondered if, incredibly, it did not.

That night Richard did not return to his chilly flat until well after nine. He was hungry but there was little to eat except baked beans. He heated some up on the stove, light-headed with weariness and a strange sort of exhilaration. At last, at last! It was as if after years and years of apprenticeship he was now beginning his life.

He thought of Bardsey's, he thought of Rowan. Two twin strands making up the incomparable whole, neither his with any certainty, yet. To keep Bardsey's he had to prove himself; to keep Rowan he had to persist. She had had such a battering from life, poor love. If she wasn't as tough as they come she'd have gone under. And yet, and yet – she was so soft in love, so sweet and tender and young. He laughed at himself. All these years, all that experience, and he was hopelessly, endlessly in love.

The beans were ready. He stirred them neatly with a fork and tipped them on to a plate, putting the pan into the sink for the daily to wash. Before he ate he found pen and paper and settled down to eat and make notes. The press release was done, it should be in every paper that mattered in the morning, and there was a meeting for the combing plant workers at nine. At ten the finance director was coming in, at eleven there was a board meeting, and lunch was with the bank. The only hope, he was certain, was to strip out and sell off anything and everything peripheral to the main organisation. Rowan must take the dye-house. She needed it, she could certainly afford it, and afterwards, when she was with him, she could rent it back to him on favourable terms. A good link, Bardsey's and Judge's. He couldn't fault the old man's judgement there, he'd seen it years ago.

And that was as much as he intended to do tonight. He got

up, slung his plate in the sink too and went into the sitting room to pour himself a small glass of single malt. He reflected on alcoholism. There was something lacking about a man who used this to blank out life, he decided. Perhaps Saul was queer after all, and putting it another way, he was certainly odd. Tremendous potential and not enough grit somehow. James had walked all over him all his life, but all he had done was escape. Would it have taken much for Saul to be where Richard was now, only years earlier? Surely he could have held James to ransom. He just wasn't that sort of guy.

If Rowan was here now, what would they do? Talk, play music, relax together after a hard day. This flat was a cold place, it lacked heart, as he had lacked heart. He hadn't known how much a man could need someone else, a special someone, someone who understood. She was what he had needed all his life. Rowan.

Chapter Forty-Four

On the plane home Rowan sat in silence next to an equally taciturn businessman. The luggage rack was stuffed with presents; a leather case for Saul complete with matching calculator and pocket currency exchanger, and a new desk diary tooled and embossed to within an inch of its life. She was going to give them to him first and question him second, and she wasn't going to believe all that he said either. If he knew that she knew, he might stop — if he had ever started. Suppose he was outraged that she had suspected him even for a second? And suppose even the outrage was a defence? The whole thing was impossible, unbelievable and ridiculous. But wives always thought that, didn't they?

For Hannah she had bought a squashy doll that was programmed to say, 'Hello, Hannah, you're my friend', and an American policeman on wheels. When his hat was depressed he whizzed about making shooting noises. She wondered how many of the goodies on the plane had been bought for much the same reasons as hers.

Where was he now? In Bardsey's glossy offices or amongst the steamy scouring pans of the combing plant? Was he thinking of her? She let her mind dwell on that night, on all the shocking and shameful things they had done. He said she was beautiful and when she was with him she believed it, she loved herself. It was such a relief to be with a man who was in control of himself, instead of at the mercy of a genie in a bottle.

At Heathrow she caught the shuttle to Leeds, and took a taxi home. Jetlag was catching up with her. There was cottonwool between her ears and lead weights on her tongue, anything she had to say fell out in lumps. At least she wouldn't have to talk to Saul until tomorrow, when she would have her wits about her. 'Don't think about it,' she told herself. 'If I pretend to myself it didn't happen, I can pretend to him.' Besides, Richard was right. Saul had committed far greater crimes.

At Valley House she tried to pay off the driver in dollars and eventually wrote him a cheque. 'Can see you don't travel much,' he remarked, and Rowan felt quite offended. Her weary air of what she thought to be cosmopolitan sophistication had been the only thing holding her up. She blundered into the house, calling, 'Hannah! Barbara! It's me!'

They were in the kitchen. The room was warm and bright, there were toys scattered on the floor. There was the smell of coffee. For the first time in years Rowan felt a sense of home, and it had nothing to do with the house, nothing at all. It had all to do with the little squashed figure in denim dungarees that tugged at her heart, and always would. She looked into Hannah's blurred face and was choked by love. She watched the slow dawning of delighted recognition and she wept. Hannah put her palms against the tears and looked at them.

'Mummy's not sad,' said Rowan hastily. 'I'm just so glad to see you, Hannah.'

The baby peered anxiously over her shoulder. 'Dad,' she demanded. 'Dad.'

'She's been missing him a lot,' said Barbara matter-of-factly. 'I thought perhaps she should visit.'

'Not in there,' said Rowan. 'She might never understand, she might think he'd been in prison or something. And actually there isn't much difference.' She thought of Saul suffering his bleak punishment, while she, she —

'There's been a problem,' said Barbara. 'There's been a strike.'

'I know, at Bardsey's.'

'Actually, it was here.'

'Good God!' Rowan swung round on her, peering over Hannah's thin hair.

'At the mill, you mean? At Judge's?'

Barbara nodded. 'They won't work under him, you see. Mohammed.'

Rowan was speechless for a second. Her mouth opened and closed. 'What's happened then?' she asked at last.

'I think he's gone home. They're working again today at any rate.'

Silently Rowan handed Hannah over and went out. In the garden two men were planting bulbs but she ignored them. Nowadays things happened in her world that she knew nothing about, it gave her an odd feeling of helplessness. 'It's all out of control,' she thought, 'I can't cope with it all.' And the cotton wool inside her head seemed to smother even that simple thought.

But in the mill everything seemed normal. One of the looms was standing idle and the weaver was messing about, but the mere sight of her galvanised him into action. She prowled around, letting the noise wash into her, seeing the cloth she had designed and costed born inch by inch into the world. No one met her eye.

Suddenly she started punching stop buttons. The looms shuddered to a halt, one after the other, and the message ran round the shed until at last everything was quiet. People rubbed their hands down their clothes and took off their ear defenders. They all looked guilty as hell.

'Suppose someone tells me what's been going on?' said Rowan loudly. 'Where's Mr. Shafir?'

There was a long pause. Eventually one of the younger men said, 'He's gone home. Seemed best, like.'

'Who for, may I ask? Well?'

'For all of us,' said one of the older men. 'It weren't our fault, Miss Rowan. He didn't understand.'

Rowan looked down at his feet in their big worn shoes. On

Saturday nights he would wear black patent leather lace-ups and when each pair got tatty they were relegated to the mill. This man must have seen out a dozen pairs of shoes in her service.

'You realise we could have the Race Relations Board on us?' she remarked. 'And that's not to mention the trouble with my sister. She owns a sizable share of this company.'

'That's as may be. We couldn't be doing with him.'

'I suggest that a few of you come up to my office at once and explain.' She turned on her heel and went out. Behind her, one by one, looms began to clatter into action once again.

The office was cold, and there was a pile of opened letters on her desk 'Have you been in touch with my husband?' she asked Frances.

'I didn't think, under the circumstances —' said the woman, and Rowan snapped, 'You should have! This was important. And someone should have told me.'

Four men came in. Rowan waved them to chairs and switched on the fan heater. 'Well?' she asked, and forced her eyes to open wide enough to look at them. She would have given anything to sink into sleep, anything.

'We couldn't understand him,' said one. 'He didn't understand Judge's,' said another. 'He's been in some rubbish place where they don't care what it comes out like!'

'And he was trying to bring his bloody friends in! One vacancy we had, and there's a flood of bloody ethnics, some of them don't speak a word of bleeding English! Before you know where we were, we wouldn't have no summer holidays. We'd be closing down for bleeding Ramadan!'

'He don't know how to treat Englishmen, and that's a fact, Miss Rowan. Tret like bloody slaves, we were! There was no standing for it, specially with everyone away. We're sorry it happened like this and we've made up some of the hours, but we're not having a bleeding Paki lording it over us!'

'They've taken over half Bradford as it is! When's it going to stop, that's what I want to know?'

Rowan's patience snapped. 'Oh, don't go on!' she begged. 'All right, I shouldn't have started him while I was away but nothing else seems very important. He speaks very good English, and if you couldn't understand, then you would in time.'

'Why should we have to try?' demanded one. 'It's our mill, Miss Rowan. We was here first.'

'As far as I'm concerned, it's *my* mill! I'll employ who I like. And if he didn't understand how we work then he soon would have! Couldn't you give it just a few weeks? I'm back now, I can help him settle in.'

'No!'

She sighed, feeling the cotton wool in her head turn to barbed wire. 'What was the problem with his attitude then?' she demanded. 'You might as well tell me everything. Was he rude?'

One of the men grimaced. 'To give him his due, I don't think he meant to be. He was nervous like, couldn't give an order straight. It was all, "Get away to your lunch, my man, and let's have no messing. I'm in charge!" Sounds funny now but down there it gets your goat. You see, Miss Rowan, he's just different. And they've got enough of our country, they don't need our jobs as well.'

A sharp buzz of anger at the narrowness of their view made her clench her teeth. They were a tribe, throwing stones at neighbours, convincing themselves that they were the real people, the only people who mattered. But anger was no use to her. She needed tact, gentleness.

'If it was just him,' she said softly, 'you'd get used to him, and he would to you. I promise there won't be any more, at least not without a clear decision from me, and a clear explanation why. I'm not going to throw you out of work in their favour, that's definite.'

'You won't have any choice! Once the Council finds out

we're against them, and he'd be the first to shout, you'll have to have them in. There'll be ten black faces for every job, and up in court if you don't pick one. I don't mind a curry once in a while but I'm damned if I'll have it served up in the bloody canteen every sodding day!'

'Now you're being ridiculous.' She put her hand to her head, shutting her eyes for a second. When she opened them again she saw four stubborn, closed faces. In a lot of ways, she thought, they were right. When different people came in there was no way things could stay the same. She was the one with the liberal principles, but they were the ones who had to make the adjustments. Stupidly she had put everyone into an impossible position.

She moved to the door, indicating that the meeting was over. 'I'll have to talk to Mr. Shafir,' she said distantly. 'And to my husband. I'll let you know what we decide.'

They filed out past her but the last man stopped. He said, 'We want to apologise for having an upset while you was away, Miss Rowan. You've done a lot for us, and for Judge's. The men wanted me to say they wouldn't have let you down if it wasn't important.'

She found her eyes pricking with sudden tears. She nodded, swallowed, and to her embarrassment found her cheeks wet. 'It's just jetlag,' she muttered, scrubbing at them angrily. 'Get on with you.'

She had not been back at the house more than ten minutes when there was a furious hammering on the door. Sally burst in, followed, unhappily, by Mohammed.

'How did you know I was back?' asked Rowan, who had been about to slide off to bed.

Sally, abundantly feminine in a red and gold sari, and hugely pregnant, paused for a moment. 'What? Oh, I told Frances to ring me as soon as you arrived. I take it you've sacked them?'

'Who?' Rowan was playing for time, although an aeon wouldn't be enough to restore her, she felt.

'You know perfectly well. Since you haven't, then I insist that you should. They deliberately flouted Mohammed's authority. I won't stand for it, I'm warning you, Rowan!' She stood, rigid with determination. Against her outrage, Rowan felt totally inadequate.

'What happened, Mohammed?' she yawned. 'Was there one special incident?'

He sniffed. He had a very straight nose, an uncompromising arrow striking down to his lips. She thought distractedly that he would be well suited to leading a warrior band, let alone a bunch of stroppy weavers. 'There were many incidents,' he said distantly. 'It is all the same with these uneducated men. It is race, class, everything. They don't work well, Rowan, and they did not like to be told!'

Rowan cleared her throat. 'I thought they were pretty good on the whole. What I really wanted was for someone to supervise the flow of work through the shed, because that is so important. I didn't need fifty per cent more effort or anything. Perhaps it was my fault. I didn't make myself clear.'

'They don't work hard enough,' said Mohammed.

'Perhaps not by your standards, but they do by ours. Look, I know the sort of conditions your people have to put up with. Endless shifts, the worst jobs and terrible pressure. That isn't what we're about in Judge's. Actually, for our sort of mill I'm not very generous. For your sort of mill, I imagine it looks terribly lax.'

Mohammed nodded. 'I think there should be many changes. They have far too many unearned privileges. The crêche, it is subsidised, a most expensive thing. The canteen food, again it is cheap though terrible quality. I bring my own, and even that is resented! There is smoking, and drinking on Fridays, and time spent in the lavatories that should be spent working. I did nothing that was not justified, even in this mill.'

533

Sally said, 'I think it's most fortunate that Mohammed came and saw what was going on, Rowan. They've been taking you for a ride and you knew nothing at all about it.'

Rowan resisted the temptation to drop her head in her hands and groan. 'But it's about getting the work out on time!' she wailed. 'That's my yardstick, that's what counts! I don't care how many fags they smoke in the loo if they get the cloth made, and made well. These people take a pride in their work, it's up to them to organise their day. Oh God! How on earth am I going to unscramble this?'

Sally moved with unaccustomed dignity to a chair and sat down. 'You can start by supporting Mohammed in his job,' she declared. 'I don't need to remind you that James has a standing offer in for my shares.'

'He couldn't afford them at the moment,' said Rowan absently. 'Look, we'll talk again tomorrow. I've got a splitting headache and I want to see Saul. He'll know what to do.'

'Oh, don't give me that!' flared Sally. 'The only thing he's any good at is getting a drink out of licensing hours. You don't have to pretend he's some sort of prop and support.'

'Sally, that is most rude to your sister,' rebuked Mohammed.

Words trembled visibly on Sally's lips. She and Mohammed exchanged fulminating glances and Rowan realised Mohammed had not intended that Sally should start making threats. He was furious with her.

'I've got to go to bed,' said Rowan miserably. 'I can't stand any more of this.'

'We are going home, Sally,' said Mohammed. 'You are not well.'

'I'm perfectly well,' muttered Sally.

She did indeed look superb. Wisps of blonde hair fell down from her bun and her pregnancy made her stand with her head held regally back to balance her belly. She was flushed with anger, and little beads of sweat stood out on her forehead.

'How long to the baby?' asked Rowan, ushering them out.

'Three weeks or so. Mother's looking forward to it enormously.'

'Is she? I thought she was dreading it!' Rowan couldn't help herself and Sally grimaced patiently. 'Not our mother. Mother. Mrs. Shafir.'

'Oh.' The thought of delivering one's infant direct into the hands of one's mother-in-law turned Rowan's stomach.

'She will help Sally with the baby,' said Mohammed.

Rowan had the sense that he was bored with the conversation, with women in general. It was only his courtesy that allowed him to put up with this feminine chit chat. He wanted Rowan to make a decision, take a firm stand! Although she wanted desperately to go to bed, she said, 'What do you do in the evening then? Do you go out?'

'Mohammed does sometimes,' said Sally thinly. 'I stay with Mother. And Fadeema.'

'Oh. I see.'

When they had gone, Rowan went into the bedroom. She dropped her clothes in a trail from door to bed and fell between the sheets, moaning to herself. Tomorrow she would be able to cope with this, tomorrow she would know what she ought to do. She stretched out her arms, feeling the delicious chill of the sheets against her skin, letting a brief shudder remind her — of what? Rowan slept.

In the car, going home, Mohammed said: 'I will not have you saying these things, Sally! Threatening your sister, demanding things!'

'Somebody had to say it. Rowan never does what she doesn't want if she can get away with it. She just digs her heels in, forever.'

'And so do you. It's time you learned to do as you are told, to obey your husband! Without that, what is there for our children? It is the basis of everything.'

Sally said stiffly, 'I know. I'm sorry. But she made me so angry!'

'Please. Allow me the anger. I know what is best.'

Sally shifted uncomfortably in her seat. 'Are you all right?' asked Mohammed.

'Backache. I don't know — I do feel odd, Mohammed.'

'We shall be home soon.'

They drove rapidly through the dark streets, past the open shops of the Asian quarter with their sacks of beans and their exotic displays of vegetables, set amidst peeling plaster and crumbling brick. By the time they reached the house, Sally was in tears. 'I shall lose the baby,' she whispered. 'It's too early.'

Mohammed leaped from the car and rushed into the house. Fadeema came out, followed by Mrs. Shafir, elbowing people aside to get to Sally. She hauled the girl out of the car and hustled her into the house. 'We shall call an ambulance,' said Fadeema calmly, while Mrs. Shafir berated her daughter-in-law for endangering her child.

The women laid her on the sofa and sent the men out. Mrs. Shafir put expert hands on Sally's belly and said something to Fadeema.

'What was that?' demanded Sally.

'She says you're having twins. Did they say at the hospital? They must have done a scan.'

Sally said nothing. Fadeema caught her shoulders. 'Have you not been going, Sally? You did go, didn't you?'

The girl shook her head. 'They were unkind. They stared at me. All the other women, Asian, white, they all stared. I was different, you see. A white girl in a sari.'

'Yes. I see.'

Fadeema got up and paced around the room. There was the sound of the ambulance siren wailing its way into the street and the men knocked on the door and yelled that it was coming. When they went out, there were faces at every door and window, women clustered around wishing the family good luck. In the ambulance Mohammed was nowhere to be seen. At Sally's side sat his mother and Fadeema.

It seemed to epitomise what had happened to her. Lying there, and again in her hospital bed, Sally kept thinking that her life was a series of rooms. In her childhood she had lived in a huge friendly room, thronged with people. One by one, unaccountably, they had all left. The room had grown cold, terribly cold, she had feared she would freeze to death inside it. But Mohammed had come in to warm her, he had taken her in his arms and lent her the heat of his body. He had taken her from that room to another, which was his own and was to be hers. Then, suddenly, he had pushed her through to another room, entirely filled with women. He visited her often, but he did not live there. He lived apart from her, in the room she had just left. She lived as the women lived, and now they were all that there was to help her.

Her mother-in-law smoothed her hair and continually twitched the blankets down to hide her modesty when the doctor came in. Fadeema sat beside her, cool and intelligent, explaining what was happening. Sally thought she wanted Mohammed but when he did come he was so clearly uncomfortable and so clearly unnecessary that she didn't mind him going. The three women were together, about their own business. It was something Sally found she could accept.

Six hours later she gave birth to twins, a boy and a girl. They were to be called Ali and Shameena.

Chapter Forty-Five

Saul stood at the window and watched his wife get out of her car, glance up and then walk determinedly towards the building. His heart gave a lurch of expectation. How lovely she looked, tall and bright and beautiful. He hadn't known how much he could miss her, a little more each day, a little more each night. It was because he was off the booze, of course. Normally he quenched emotions with a slug of something. He wished that he could now. Oh God, how he wished it!

She smiled when she saw him, her anxious look momentarily gone. 'Hi,' she said breathily. 'Hi, Hi, Hi.'

He stumped across to her. His plaster cast had been reduced by half in the last week and he was almost mobile again. When he took her in his arms there was an ever so slight resistance. 'I missed you,' he croaked, knowing that he was going to betray himself and hating himself for it. Was this what they wanted, all these do-gooders, for him to go around sobbing in public, embarrassing everyone?

'It wasn't so long, was it? You look well. Really well.'

Perhaps by external standards he did. The mirror told him that he looked years younger. He had lost weight, his hair shone, his skin no longer held that doughy, bloated look. Nobody saw beyond that, not even Rowan. Especially not Rowan.

They repaired to a private alcove. He couldn't help himself holding her hand, stroking it. 'Good trip?' he asked, desperately trying to keep himself from the edge.

She nodded, withdrawing her hand to show him the things she had bought. Like a mother, he thought, like a prison visitor. But he dutifully admired the extravagant gifts, none of which he wanted or needed or cared about. In here, in this desperate, terrible place, he was going mad! And she brought him toys to play with. He put down the case and blurted, 'I can't stand it in here. I've got to get out!'

'It is a bit hot.' Rowan chose to misunderstand him. She helped him up and they went out into the garden. Saul stumped round the paths at a furious pace.

'Did I tell you about Mohammed?' said Rowan jerkily, almost running to keep up. 'I started him as a manager in the weaving shed and all the men went on strike. They won't have him back and I don't know what to do. By the way, Sally's had twins.'

It seemed to Saul a string of total irrelevancies. 'What's that got to do with anything? What's that got to do with me?'

Rowan stopped and after a few more strides he did too. 'I wanted your advice,' she said helplessly.

He shrugged. 'Send two rattles.'

Her mouth twisted in pain and she linked her fingers together, forcing herself not to say the bitter and hurtful things that rose to her lips. Forming her words carefully, she said, 'I went to see Marcus Arnaud.'

A brief flicker of interest. 'The dear boy. Actually, he's a nice guy. You know he's gay, don't you?'

'Yes,' she said thinly. She swallowed. 'He said you were, too.'

'Yes. He would.'

She couldn't believe it. Her mouth worked. 'But – not with him! You couldn't!'

Some vague sense of her distress penetrated his self-absorption. 'What? Oh, don't be stupid! I put my foot in it with him the first time we met. He made a pass at me. So, I pretended I was gay but unavailable, saved a lot of hassle and embarrassment.'

'It didn't save *me* any embarrassment! When I went there

540

and said I was your wife, he took me to one side and told me I was married to a queer! I didn't know what to believe!'

'If I may say so, you look remarkably fit on it.'

Total disinterest. He neither knew nor cared what she had suffered. 'You don't give a damn, do you?' she said at last. 'You don't want to hear about America, or Sally, or my little problems. You're in here being waited on hand and foot, nothing to think about but whether to have a bath now or in an hour, and out there I've got a labour crisis and my sister threatening to sell her shares and this American thing and Richard and everything!'

'What about Richard?' asked Saul.

And what about him? She was no liar, and Saul was an expert at seeing what you least wished to reveal. 'Nothing,' she said offhandedly. 'He was in America, sniffing around my deal. It's Mohammed that's the real problem.'

'What possessed you to set him on in the first place? Didn't you think this would happen?'

'No. No, I didn't. He wanted the job, and Sally wanted him to have it, and I didn't think I had the right to refuse.'

'How very diffident of you.'

Saul moved away across the grass and sat down on a wet seat under a tree that was shedding its leaves. Rowan sat beside him, discounting the cost of having her pale green coat cleaned. He reached for her hand and gripped it again, but she couldn't return the pressure. She felt stiff with lies and the need for lies, and furiously angry. She thought he must be able to feel the residue of heat in her veins. 'What am I going to do?' she asked in clipped tones.

Saul sighed. 'Put him in the office. Find him a job, make him a job. If you try and keep him as shed manager at best they'll walk out, at worst they'll string him up. Didn't you see *Zulu*? The men at Judge's think they're at Rorke's Drift, holding out against the invading hordes. At least in the office he won't have much contact with them.'

'But he'll have contact with our suppliers, and our

541

customers. They can't be called models of tolerance either. Suppose he upsets them?'

'So what? About time someone upset the status quo. We can afford it. Do everyone the world of good to have people stepping out of their boxes for once. In ten years' time you might be able to get away with an Asian manager. We have to start somewhere, but God, you can be so clumsy sometimes.'

She withdrew her hand. 'I don't recall that you were in any state to help with the decision at the time. But then you never are in any state, are you? If you're not drunk then you want congratulations for being sober, and sympathy for having to stay that way, and support, and consideration, everything! When do I get some support and consideration? When?'

Both their minds swung back to when Hannah was born. Rowan ducked her head. 'That was stupid of me, I'm sorry. It's jetlag, it takes days to wear off. I didn't mean to sound so –'

'Why don't you go, Rowan? We're not doing any good here, just tearing lumps off each other. Give my regards to Sally. By the way, what colour are they?'

She tried to smile. 'A sort of delicious biscuit. And they're all crumpled and so tiny. They're in the nursery, and when I went Mrs. Shafir was sitting by them on sentry duty. She isn't nearly so fierce as Sally describes. She's small and dignified and she doesn't speak a word of English.'

He wasn't listening. She followed his eyes and saw him gazing out across a ploughed field, to the rising hills beyond. A flock of small birds rose from the field and settled again, then rose and flew in a ragged trail off into the grey distance. She didn't say goodbye. She picked up her bag and walked quickly back, her heels clicking on the path. When she looked at him to wave he was still watching the birds, watching them fly away.

* * *

Depression settled on her like a blanket. She had to go home and talk to people, all of whom would ask well-meaning questions about Saul. She should have married Joe Partridge, she thought, and together they would have built an empire. He was a simple man, wanting simple things, and Saul was the most difficult and complex person she knew. Strange that she hadn't seen any of that when she met him, but then, she had been too young to know much. Now, when she knew what she wanted, she couldn't have it!

She thought of Richard. She conjured up a picture of his face, of how he looked when he was angry, happy, loving her. What did she really owe Saul? Was she honestly intending to spend her life shackled to someone who almost seemed to hate her? Sometimes she hated him, sometimes she wanted to kill him for embarrassing her, hurting her, pointing up every single one of her inadequacies. It seemed a downward spiral into hell.

Back in her office she tried to settle down to work. Her brain fizzed restlessly. Tonight she would go and see Sally and tell her that Mohammed was to come into the offices. It was a capitulation but if Sally was upset she would offer to buy them a little house somewhere, as a gesture of good faith. The firm was awash with money at the moment, the problem was in deciding what to do with it. The dye-house, of course — unless Bardsey's was truly up for sale. She pondered the question. Bardsey's was stuffed full of little goodies that she wouldn't mind in her shopping bag.

The 'phone rang. She picked it up absently, then felt every muscle in her body go rigid. 'It's me,' said Richard.

'Hello me,' she said throatily. 'How are you?'

'Missing you. Needing you. Come to my flat, tonight.'

'I — I can't. I shouldn't. Anyway, I've got to go and see Sally. She's had twins.'

'Christ! Give her my congratulations and come along afterwards.'

'Someone might see me.'

'Wear dark glasses. Darling girl. Darling, darling girl, I can't wait!'

She giggled. 'Stop it. All right, I'll come, just this once. About nine.'

'Great.' He sounded like a snooker player who has potted his last ball. Briskly, he added, 'Must be going, lots to do. See you at nine.'

She grimaced as she replaced the receiver. Presumably on his list of tasks for the day appeared the item 'Rowan — entice to bed'. It was now ticked as completed. But then, he was a thorough man, doing things thoroughly. He knew what he wanted and he was out to get it. The thing was, so was she.

Sally's strained face relaxed only slightly when Rowan appeared at her bedside that evening. The girl was wearing a pink bedjacket, her hair cascading prettily about her shoulders. Seated firmly on one side was Mrs. Shafir, on the other Fadeema and the younger sister. At Rowan's arrival Fadeema got up and tried to persuade Mrs. Shafir to leave, but only after much furious muttering and glaring did she do so.

'Where's Mohammed?' asked Rowan when they were alone.

Sally hunched a shoulder. 'I don't know. He came for about five minutes and said he had to go. He wanted children but now he's not much interested.'

'He will be when they're home,' soothed Rowan.

'If Mother gives either of us a look-in!'

Rowan sat down and cleared her throat. 'I had a talk with Saul,' she began. 'We're going to put Mohammed in the offices. And as a gesture to both of you, I want to buy you a house. The firm will be buying it, of course, but to all intents and purposes it's yours. Choose what you like.'

Her sister's blue eyes fixed on her and beneath that clear gaze Rowan wilted. 'Paying us off. I see.'

'I can't swing it with the workers,' explained Rowan earnestly. 'I would if I could. But if I push it we'll have one of those pointless race rows, with the television cameras in and everyone dredging up their nastiest prejudices, and in the end everyone hating each other more than they did in the first place. There are no winners over these things.'

'But we're certainly the losers.'

'That's rubbish.'

They sat in silence. At length Sally said, 'I'll see what Mohammed says.'

'Good,' said Rowan, glancing at her watch. 'By the way, how are the babies?'

'Very well, I think. Mother's always here. When I go to see them I have to fight my way past her to the incubator.'

'Oh God. But there are two of them. You're going to need help.'

'She thinks Europeans have no idea how to care for children. It's going to be hell.'

Rowan lost her temper. 'Sally, all you have to do is stand up to Mohammed. Get him to move into a house of your own, there's no excuse for this sort of doormat mentality! He might think it's a good idea for wives but I think it's diabolical. And so, in your heart, do you.'

'Do I?' If Sally had ever known exactly what she thought she couldn't remember it now. 'You're so much more independent than me,' she complained. 'I wouldn't mind living there at all if I got on better with Mother. She hates me! She thinks I've made him abandon his culture, she's furious about this job with you.'

Rowan glanced at her watch again and began to gather her things.

'You're not going already, are you?' demanded Sally. 'I wanted to talk.'

'Yes, but Barbara wants to go out – Hannah – I have to go. Back tomorrow, love.' She bent and kissed her sister, rushing away before more could be said. Left alone, without

545

visitors, without her babies, Sally began to pleat the sheet of her bed.

Never had Rowan felt so guilty. The very shadows seemed to harbour friends and acquaintances, all watching her park the car and sneak furtively away. A couple passed her, she dared not look to see if she knew them. She sneaked into the block of flats and crept up the stairs.

When Richard opened the door she fell inside. 'Hide me, quick! I'm sure someone saw me.'

'What if they did?' Richard put his hands under her coat and held her thin, warm body. 'We've got nothing to be ashamed of.'

She relaxed against him, putting her arms round his neck and opening her lips for his kiss. His tongue executed a slow and sensual dance around her mouth, she groaned with pleasure. 'You're so good at this,' she murmured. 'Did you learn it all?'

'I learned what to do, yes. But you taught me why I should do it. Come to bed, delicious girl.'

In bed they revelled in each other. He taught her how to prolong his pleasure, and at the same time made her weak with delight. In the end she begged him to stop. 'I can't take any more. There's nothing left in me.'

Richard rolled away. He was feeling fit, discharging all the adrenaline of the day. Naturally virile, he wanted her again, but later would do. He lay back on the pillow and looked at her.

'How was Saul?'

She put her hands over her eyes. 'Dreadful. The worst. That thing about Arnaud was just stupid, but he didn't care, you see, he didn't mind what I might have thought — he's so wrapped up in himself. No room for anyone but him, it seems to me.'

'He'll be back on the booze the moment he gets out. You know that, don't you?'

'Probably.' She changed the subject, pushing herself up on her elbows and rubbing her fingers through the hairs on his chest. 'Did you have your fight with James?'

'Not only had it, but won. He's letting me turn it round. Ten years ago he could have done it, but not now. We're on the brink, you see. He hasn't realised the way things have changed, the way he's changed! We're going to have to strip out some assets, it's the only hope.'

'Do you have much that's worth anything?'

'Yes, tons. Couple of places with big central offices, worth a packet. Put both on the market and as soon as one's sold we'll be back on course. But if we don't do it or they don't sell or we get some sharp lawyer in about the combing plant accident, then we're going to be iller than ever. We're putting people out of business, of course, but that's what making omelettes is all about.'

'Yes. Nothing else for it.' Rowan leaned back thoughtfully. Mistaking her quiet for arousal Richard swung on top of her. She gasped as he penetrated her, the bed shaking with his robust thrusting. 'You're so good, you're wonderful,' he murmured. Rowan, sated with sex, murmured dutifully. Her eyes gazed unwaveringly up at the ceiling.

She got into her own bed at about three in the morning. Richard had wanted her to stay, he was pushing her faster than she wanted to go. Her body smelled of him, he had taken everything she had to give. His semen, draining out of her, left tell-tale smears on the sheets. How did women having affairs cope with that, she wondered? The smell of adultery, the evidence of it, there in the marital bed. Perhaps they went swimming afterwards, or spent hours in the bath, or wore pyjamas and pretended they were having a three-week period. It was all rather disgusting.

She was offended with herself for thinking that. Nothing she did with Richard could be half as shameful as the things Saul did, on his own, swilling down yet another and another drink. Dear Richard. How little he knew his own father. James would let him have some rope, and Richard would either hang himself or end up trussed like a chicken for the pot. There was no way James was ever giving up Bardsey's. But — just supposing. Supposing while the cat was letting the mice play, someone else came in and stole the tin of pilchards? James deserved it. God knows he had tried to get Judge's often enough.

Would it be a beastly thing to do? She twitched her nose in the dark. It wasn't as if Richard had told her anything she couldn't have guessed really, or found out for herself. He'd be furious, of course. It might be the end of them. But she couldn't bear to let this go, knowing she would forever regret it! If Richard turned against her then so be it, the affair would be decided, but if he didn't — well. Who could know what the future might bring? All you could do was follow your nose and see where it led.

Lying back in her lonely bed, rather chilly in the wide expanse, she knew she ought to feel ashamed of herself. What she was contemplating was certainly betrayal. Instead there was mounting exhilaration, almost a sense that she was putting Richard to the test. Now she would see just exactly what lay beneath that tough skin! And he would know exactly what she was.

Chapter Forty-Six

TAKEOVER!!!

Banner headlines in the financial papers, with pictures of Rowan in all the popular dailies. The bid was so incredibly cheeky. Isaac Judge had enlisted the support of a food and drinks conglomerate, recruited by their stockbrokers, who were lending their considerable muscle to the assault. Bardsey's, so big and so encumbered by hangers-on, wallowed like a liner trying to turn to meet a storm. If this succeeded, so the pundits declared, the door would be open for energetic raiders throughout the business world. Already Judge's had a goodly percentage of Bardsey stock.

But Rowan herself cowered in her office, refusing calls, seeing no one. Thankfully James and Diana were in Barbados, where surely the news would take time to filter. Bardsey's share price climbed and climbed, Judge's fluctuated wildly. No one knew who was going to be left with egg on their face but somehow nobody expected it to be Rowan Judge. She had a habit of falling on her feet.

Day after day Richard called the house, the office, sometimes coming in person to hammer on the door. But she would not see him, because whatever he had to say would hurt her. While she knew she deserved it she could not bear the actual words, not from him.

After a week of reclusive living she started to venture out, visiting Sally in the little house off Carlisle Road, taking some baby clothes and a book on bringing up children she had found helpful with Hannah. The door was opened by Sally herself, red-eyed and distraught.

'You've got to stop her, Rowan,' she demanded tearfully.

'She won't let me near my babies.'

From somewhere upstairs came the sound of wailing children, accompanied by the determined soothing of Mrs. Shafir. It did not seem to be having much effect. 'They're fractious today,' explained Sally. 'She says its my fault with my new-fangled ideas. She thinks I should be ashamed to have produced a girl, and pray about it, when I produced one of each, damn it! It's more than she could do.'

'Where's Mohammed?' asked Rowan. 'It's up to him to sort out his mother.'

'Isn't he working? I mean at Judge's?'

There was an uncomfortable pause. Eventually Rowan shook her head. 'He never came. I thought he'd decided against it.'

'Oh. Oh, I see.'

Sally's hands rose and fell helplessly. Upstairs the wailing grew louder. Suddenly determined, Rowan set foot on the stairs and went to investigate.

Mrs. Shafir was sitting on a bed defiantly trying to rock two babies at once. With a deprecating smile Rowan took one and gave it to Sally. The atmosphere, which had been dense with tension, thinned a little. Out of politeness Mrs. Shafir offered Rowan the other baby, and it was accepted. Gradually, as the sobbing lessened, the occasion became social. They all went downstairs to drink tea together.

'I've suggested that Sally and Mohammed might like their own house,' said Rowan to Mrs. Shafir, speaking loudly as if it might help understanding. Mrs. Shafir said something to Sally.

'She says she does not feel it is for a wife to take a son away from his mother. It is for a son to support his ageing parents in their declining years.'

'A house quite close by,' said Rowan.

Mrs. Shafir gave a glittering smile and spoke again.

'How close can a son be to his mother's heart?' said Sally.

Rowan abandoned all attempt at persuasion. She turned to Sally.

'Suppose I buy the house and put it at your disposal? You could move in when you felt like it.'

Sally rubbed her cheek against her baby's downy head. 'I don't know. Mohammed would have to agree, I don't like to do things unless he does.'

Mrs. Shafir beamed and declaimed.

'How sweet it is for a wife to obey her husband, how true to the will of Allah!' translated Sally dolefully.

'Oh God,' muttered Rowan.

So disturbed was she by Sally's plight within the household that she was halfway down the street before she became aware of the kerb-crawling Maserati. She stared at it, flinched, and started to run towards her own car parked some yards away. In three inch heels she could only teeter helplessly. Richard jumped out of his car and grabbed her.

'Oh no you don't!'

She swallowed. 'Hello, Richard.'

'Don't you "Hello, Richard" me! I've phoned you twenty times in the last week and called round four. Never a convenient time apparently. Too busy stabbing people in the back, I suppose.'

'A very busy time,' she said feebly.

'Busy!'

She couldn't meet his eyes. 'Yes, busy.'

They said nothing and as she did not appear to be about to run away, he let her go. 'Why did you do it?' he asked softly.

She shrugged. 'Don't know really. Seemed like a good idea. It is a good idea, the best. It wasn't anything to do with us.'

'Don't give me that! As soon as my father hears about this he's going to be back on a plane and kicking me out on my arse, and who can blame him? The first thing I do for the company is lose it to the enemy! And I deserve to be kicked out, for being so stupid as to trust you.'

'You didn't tell me anything I didn't know,' she said defiantly. 'You should have realised how vulnerable you were! Anyway, James would never have let you run it for good. And I shall let you stay on, afterwards.'

'Well, thanks very much!' He stepped away from her, the better to express himself. 'She kicks me in the teeth and offers me a set of cut-price dentures! Rowan dear, shall I tell you what galls me about this whole thing? The really difficult bit?'

'What?' she asked, eyeing him warily. She felt he might at any moment hit her.

'It's that I thought I was the one who knew it all. Poor little Rowan, I thought, little inexperienced Rowan. Man of the world that I was, showing her such a good time. I thought, how nice to take care of her. Shall I tell you what I think now, Rowan dear?'

'No,' she said shortly.

'Hard lines, it comes free. I'm not at all surprised that Saul is where he is. I think if I was married to you, I'd be hitting the sauce too. You look like a woman, you sound like a woman, but underneath you're a fucking barracuda!'

She looked round for something to throw at him, but the pavement was bare of missiles. She resorted to words. 'I don't think James would winge like this,' she declared shrilly. 'But then, he always was twice the man you are. I suggest you get back pretty damn quick, Richard, because you're not tough enough to fight me. I shall own you lock, stock and conceit.'

He pointed a shaking finger. 'I'll burn the whole shooting match before I let you get your hands on it.'

'And you'll end up in gaol. That's where all stupid businessmen go, the ones who think they're clever anyway.'

'Anywhere's better than in your pocket. Or in your anything else for that matter.'

She took off her shoe and hurled it at him. It missed, so she took off the other and threw that too. He laughed, caught it and tossed it into a puddle. Rowan was left barefoot and fuming. 'That's how you're going to be at the end of this,' said Richard softly. 'And I won't lend you a penny.' He turned and went back to his car.

That night Rowan sat at home, brooding. She knew she should visit Saul, she hadn't been in days, not since the bid was launched. Presumably he read the papers so he must know about it. But she felt too ill, too miserable and sick. The row with Richard went round and round in her head, she couldn't escape from it! And she knew that all she could have said, should have said, was that she was sorry. She was so, so sorry, not for having launched the bid, but for having hurt him by it. That was life's unfairness, that you could never have anything without paying more than you felt it was worth.

Tonight the sadness would not go away. She turned on the television, watching some inexplicably boring comedy. She felt tearful and jumpy. She went and poured herself a drink, gin and tonic, a large one. After that she had another, and perhaps two more, she lost count. When she was sprawled on the sofa, glass in hand, sniffing tearfully into a handkerchief, Saul came home.

She was so drunk she wasn't at all sure he was really there. She blinked at him owlishly. He had a stick but the plaster cast was gone.

'You are pissed as a newt,' said Saul in amazement.

'I don't get drunk,' she said owlishly. 'Saul gets drunk. My husband, you know.'

'Yes, I have met him. Bit of a prat, don't you think?'

'Only when he's pissed. He's always pissed.' She got up and staggered against the television. Saul fielded her and set her upright.

'Why are you here?' she demanded. 'You've escaped.'

'Actually they were quite glad to get rid of me. I did leave a message asking that you should come and collect, but it seems it didn't get through. Eventually they found a taxi.'

'I don't take messages,' she said vaguely. 'Richard shouts at me all the time.'

'You are trying to pinch his company, sweetheart,' said Saul.

'I'm buying it. You're allowed to do that. And now he doesn't love me any more!' She subsided, wailing, against Saul's shirt front.

Unseen by her, his face went oddly stiff. Already pale from indoor living, he went paler, the colour draining away to leave dead-white skin. Gently he put up a hand and patted Rowan's heaving, drunken shoulder. 'Let's put you to bed, shall we?' he whispered hoarsely.

She rolled half-conscious into bed, weeping miserably. 'It isn't fair, it isn't fair,' she sobbed. 'Everything always goes wrong.'

'Do you want him so much then?' asked Saul. He sounded as if he was breathing broken glass. 'You can tell me. You can always tell me anything.'

'Yes. So I can. I want him more than anything.'

'More than me?' A ridiculous question. She opened a bleary eye and peered into his face. 'I'm glad you're home,' she said. 'It's jolly cold in bed by myself.'

He tucked her carefully in, switching off the light with a shaking hand. When he went back into the sitting room he headed unerringly for the drinks cupboard.

'Where's the point?' he whispered to himself, and there were tears rolling unchecked down his cheeks. 'Where's the sodding point?'

BARDSEY'S WHITE KNIGHT

Rowan swore and crumpled the paper between her hands. Then she swore again and uncrumpled it, smoothing out the rash creases. She read, 'A rescuer has at last appeared to support Bardsey Textiles against the opportunistic depradations of Isaac Judge. Associated Industries, with its

554

huge capital base and diverse interests, should be well able to see off such an impertinent approach. Bardsey's are to be congratulated for persuading AI that they are a company worth such attention, and its shareholders are strongly recommended not to consider acceptance of the Judge offer at this stage. If the bid is to continue there will certainly be an offer of considerably greater magnitude in the near future.'

'Frances!' Rowan bawled furiously for her secretary. The woman came trotting in, flustered as always. It hadn't been like this in Mr. Andrew's day; she couldn't keep up with all this 'phoning to America and London stockbrokers and million pound deals. Besides, she suspected Rowan would have got rid of her long ago if it wasn't for Mr. Saul. He remembered her birthday and bought her bath salts at Christmas, and in return she got rid of the bottles.

'I want a meeting,' snarled Rowan morosely. 'Us, the bank, the stockbrokers and the men from General Foods. I don't care where it is but it must be today or at the latest tomorrow morning.'

'Oh — yes — very well.' Frances made incoherent notes on her pad. 'Will Mr. Saul be coming?'

'What? I shouldn't think so.' Rowan was cool and distant. She didn't know what Saul was doing and she didn't care. The moment he was out of the damned clinic he was drinking again, not even bothering to pretend to be trying. The only limiting factor was his driving ban, but he made do with taxis, and when he was drunk he wouldn't care if he was banned or not. She fully expected to end up visiting him in gaol.

A headache nagged just behind her eyes. They would have to increase the offer substantially, but it was as she had expected. The unexpected factor was the intervention of such a big company on behalf of Bardsey's. The share price would rocket. How had he done it? Richard had no track record. In comparison, hers was impeccable. 'It's because he's a man,' she murmured to herself, feeling beleaguered

555

and feminine. There was no chivalry in the world any more.

But, takeover or no takeover, life had to go on. They had a new showroom now, where customers could see the current range set out in a clear north light. It was a room luxuriant with cloth. She went through to see what was happening to a pale misty tweed that was being considered by a major chain store for a vast range of matching skirts, jackets and trousers. If they took it she would contract out the manufacture; she wasn't turning away other business because of one monolithic order. That had been Bardsey's downfall.

The showroom was untidy. Someone had wandered in and out with a customer and given not a thought to the mess. If you didn't do it yourself nothing ever got done, raged Rowan, and began rolling up cloth and hooking drapes of fabric back on to the pinboard on the wall.

'So there you are.'

She was standing on a table, holding a length of red cloth. Saul took the other end, hopped up beside her and did the job. 'I wanted to talk to you,' he said.

'I'm busy, I'm afraid.' Rowan never wanted to talk nowadays.

'Nonetheless we're going to talk. Rowan, what do you want out of life?'

She almost laughed. 'I'm not standing on a table discussing philosophy!' she said stiffly. 'And I could ask you the same question.'

'But I'm asking you. Will you be happy when you've got Bardsey's? Will you want more and more again?'

'Possibly. I don't know.' Standing on the table, he was too close to her. Now that she and Richard had – well, made love together, she almost felt that if Saul came too near he would sense it. All her instincts were to keep him at a distance.

'Do you want a divorce, Rowan?'

She stepped back and almost fell. He caught her arm and she teetered, at last regaining her footing. 'Why do you have to follow me around saying things like that? I can't cope with that as well! There's a takeover bid on and you want to talk about divorce. You're just cross with me for not involving you.'

His face was unreadable, she couldn't tell what he was thinking. 'I'm not all that interested in what you do or don't cope with. As it happens, Rowan, *I* want a divorce. But I also want Hannah.'

She swung back her hand to hit him, but then closed her fist and put it to her lips instead, gnawing the knuckles. 'No one would give her to you. Not with your record.'

'I know. That's why I'm asking for her.'

She turned and jumped down from the table, twisting her ankle in her high heels. 'You just want to spoil everything for me!' she said hysterically. 'You want to ruin my bid, you don't really want a divorce. You couldn't cope with Hannah.' A thought occurred to her. 'And I wouldn't let you have anything out of the firm, not a penny! I built it myself, all of it!'

'Did you, Rowan? All by yourself?'

She swallowed. 'Everybody thinks it was just me. Oh, why don't you go away? You're only bothering me. I can't think about anything now.'

The door opened and Frances came in. 'What is it?' demanded Rowan.

'The meeting, Mrs. Barton. Two o'clock in Threadneedle Street, it's all arranged.'

'I shall have to get ready then.'

'Am I included in this?' asked Saul.

Rowan barely glanced at him. 'I don't think that would be wise. Under the circumstances, I suggest you keep your nose out altogether! I will do this on my own.'

She staggered out of the room, tottering on her twisted ankle. Her head hurt too, assailed by a thousand mosquitolike thoughts. She felt almost hysterical. It wasn't fair for him to say things like that, she wasn't ready! Oh God, how dare he ask for Hannah? It simply wasn't fair.

The London train was late arriving and when at last she reached the meeting she was last to arrive. Her ankle had swollen and every step was agony, but she fixed a smile on her face and struggled to appear poised and in control. General Foods were ruffled that Bardsey's were making such a fight of it.

'I thought Mr. Barton was coming,' said one man. 'I understand it was his vision that put Judge's on the map.'

'He's been ill,' said Rowan vaguely.

'Is he in support of this bid? I'd like to feel the management team is acting in concert here.'

'Obviously I wouldn't act against his wishes.' The muscles in her jaw were tight.

'We have only your word for that, Mrs. Barton. We want to assure ourselves that continuing with this bid is more than academic. We want to know we can win!'

She could think of nothing to say. She sat in the midst of all these men and felt threatened. Everyone else had brought one or two supporters, she alone was expected to do everything herself.

'I wonder if Judge's has the depth of management to succeed,' said a banker, echoing her own thoughts.

Rowan dredged up some remnants of confidence. 'I assure you we have the determination to win, and we will,' she declared. 'Don't forget my brother and sister are also shareholders in Judge's. I'm not quite alone.'

'And they do fully support the offer?'

'Of course.' It was a blatant lie. She hadn't even considered asking either of them.

As she left she had the feeling that she had escaped by the skin of her teeth. Why had those men thought it would be easy, she wondered? Everyone imagined textile companies

558

to be lodged in the nineteenth century, but Bradford men had always been sharp, and gamblers, and they were still. Scarred by years of battling for their commercial lives, they weren't men to quit at the first crackle of gunfire. This was guerrilla warfare, with every avenue mined. As if in response to her thoughts she suddenly saw James. He was coming out of a merchant bank.

Instinctively she stepped into a doorway and hid. God help her if James was back. He looked well, no less pale than always despite the sun of Barbados, but there was about his step the old vigour and verve. 'Damn him,' thought Rowan dully. 'Damn, damn, damn him!'

At night Bradford streets were cold and in the yellow light of the street lamps greasy pavements glistened. Mohammed walked quickly, making for a cafe where he would meet his friend Fahad. Vague memories of his childhood stirred: running through dry streets with the day's heat still hanging in the air, all around the bustle of people. There it was at night that the world came to life, in the markets and the shops. In contrast with these damp evenings, it seemed like paradise.

Fahad was lounging on a plastic chair, as always surrounded by friends. But he kicked someone out of the circle to make room for Mohammed.

'Have you eaten?'

'Yes.'

Fahad offered a cigarette but Mohammed refused. He said, 'My car's broken down again. Starter motor.'

'You should talk to my uncle. He can get you parts.'

Mohammed was surprised. 'I didn't know he had anything to do with cars.'

Fahad nodded. 'Well then, doesn't that show you? He's got a garage now. Marrying that girl has put you out of touch.'

Fahad punched him playfully and Mohammed cuffed him

in return. They'd known each other a long time, but after school Fahad had gone back to Pakistan for six months and they'd lost touch. He was very successful, importing spices and rugs, and he was married to an educated Asian girl who somehow managed to combine docility with Western charm. In Fahad's household there seemed to be none of the squabbling that characterised his own home, and in Fahad's life there was none of the confusion that Mohammed felt so acutely. Fahad knew who he was and he knew what he wanted to become.

When Mohammed at last got up to leave Fahad came with him, flinging a friendly arm round his shoulders. In the street, privately, he said, 'Thought any more about what I suggested?'

Mohammed nodded. 'I don't know. I'd love to go in with you, but — ' he felt foolish admitting it ' — the money's my wife's.'

'So it's yours! She can't object to you bettering yourself, can she? Look, I can't wait forever. I need a partner and I want it to be you, but if it isn't you I'll find someone else. I'm importing all the time, I can't be there and here as well.'

'My wife's sister wants me in her office — '

'I keep telling you! There's no way she'll give you any responsibility. Look, don't take this wrong. I heard about what happened in the weaving shed. What makes you think it would be any different in the office? This way you can make real money, and without breaking your mother's heart. Get a little respect, for once in your life. Make a few trips back home, did I tell you I've a house there? And what are we here for if not to get on? You want to go back as somebody, don't you?'

Mohammed looked at him. Fahad was so persuasive, Mohammed envied him so much. He had a good car, a big house, a lot of respect, both here and at home. Sally's people had given him nothing. Was it not for his own kind to extend a helping hand? The English failed to understand the ties of religion and family.

The rain was falling again, and in the distance came the wail of a police siren racing to break up a fight in one of the West Indian pubs. After all, he was a father now, it was time to put away dreams and face reality.

Sally was bone weary. Despite the daytime battles over the children, at night she alone was expected to get up and see to them. Mohammed was out most evenings, talking with friends, he came in well after midnight. When she asked what they talked about, he said, 'You wouldn't understand. About Pakistan, and the life there. About the government.'

She knew nothing at all about Pakistan, she could not relate her English picture of primitive, over-crowded living with the scene the family painted, of communities and traditions and ceremonies. For Mohammed to talk about Pakistan seemed to her to make him less and less English.

One night when she had settled the twins at last and Mohammed was not as yet asleep, she asked, 'Why didn't you take the job at Judge's? It was a good job. It would have helped us.'

He grunted, she thought he was going to ignore her. Then he said, 'I used to think that was the way. To become more English, become like the English. I wasn't the first, it's been tried before. My friends, they've all tried. But I am Asian. I shall always be Asian.'

'You didn't have to lose that.'

He sat up, linking his hands round his knees. 'Fahad's made me an offer. He wants me to go into business with him, invest. I shall sell out of Judge's.'

Sally sat frozen. 'But — Rowan was going to get us a house. She promised.'

'That can wait. I visited James Barton today. He would like to buy your shares, we should have a great deal of money. I agreed that you would sell them to him.'

'To James? Mohammed, you can't! Rowan's always been

so good to us, you just can't do this!'

'She has done nothing for me. She did not even dismiss those men. You yourself said you would sell the shares.'

'Yes, but I didn't mean it.'

She went to the cradle and rocked it, although the baby inside was asleep. Little Ali, worshipped by all the family, given the best cradle, the best clothes, the most prayers. Shameena always came second. 'I don't think I want to,' she said nervously.

'I have told him, Sally. It is not for you to disagree.'

The conflict might have come then, she was never sure if she would have capitulated if it had. But a cry rang through the quiet house. 'Fadeema. Fadeema! Salleeee!'

'Mother.' Sally got up and hurried on to the landing. The parents slept downstairs on a couch in the sitting room. They could hear a muffled grunting.

Fadeema came out of her room, her long hair in two plaits on her shoulders. She hurried down, Sally and Mohammed close after her. Mother was moaning, clasping her small brown hands. On the bed her husband sprawled, his eyes turned up in his head, his breath coming after long and agonising pauses.

'Oh no. Oh no.' Fadeema and Mohammed bent over him. They pulled open his clothes, exposing his grizzled chest. Even Sally could see the convulsive spasms of the heart, the unnaturally distended rib cage. Mother let out the beginnings of a wail. Instinctively, Sally put her arms around her. They stood there, watching, while Mr. Shafir died.

He was to be embalmed and sent to Pakistan for burial. The expense was considerable. Again, Mohammed told Sally she must sell her shares. He didn't understand her reluctance. If she wouldn't sell to James, why not approach Rowan and sell to her? Sally would not.

The death of his father had changed him almost overnight. It was as if his association with her had been no more than a flirtation, a brief waltz with her culture, a show of short-lived defiance. Now he seemed different. He went to the mosque more often, for solemn prayers, and in the house when he spoke no one challenged. He was head of the family now, and Sally was in no doubt that if she sold her shares the money would not be hers, or even theirs, but the family's.

He made love to her often, even when she was longing to sleep. Now that he was in his father's place he seemed to have taken on energy and determination. Sometimes he sounded exactly like his father. Again and again he told her to sell her shares, and again and again she prevaricated. In the end she absolutely refused.

Mohammed took her upstairs into their bedroom. Moving deliberately he struck her face, on one side then the other. She screamed and fell on the bed, and he stood over her, quietly purposeful. 'I have decided to sell the shares. You will remain in your room, Sally, until you agree. Mother will take care of the children.'

'I wouldn't mind if you'd buy us a house!' she sobbed. 'But it's just to put a dead man on a plane, there's no point.'

'My father wished it. And I must go back, to see that all is done properly.'

'You didn't want my money when we married. Why do you take it now?'

'Because we have need of it. My father's honour needs it, and I need it for my business. Sally, why are you not obedient to me? I know what is best for us.'

She stared up at him through a curtain of pale hair, the marks of his hands on her cheeks. He could have beaten her far more severely, she knew, and it would only have been considered justice. In his way he loved her, and was trying to spare her pain. He wasn't a cruel man.

'We won't ever have our own house now Father's dead, will we?' she said dully.

'My mother cannot be left alone, Sally. You would not wish it. Now, will you sell the shares?'

'No.'

He turned on his heels, went out and locked the door. She sat on her own in the bedroom, separated from her children, from food, from the life of the household, a disobedient wife who must be brought to heel. He was the husband, she the wife, they weren't Mohammed and Sally any longer. If he wished, in Pakistan he could marry again, a Moslem could have up to four wives. If she agreed to leave her children behind she could be returned to her family, her marriage an unfortunate mistake. When she sacrificed her will to his she hadn't known that one day he would act against her best interests. She felt betrayed, by her own foolish trust.

Late in the evening Fadeema unlocked the door, bringing food. 'He has gone out,' she explained.

'Can I have my babies?' demanded Sally. 'He hasn't the right to keep them from me.'

Fadeema sat down. 'You must do as he says, Sally. You can't be happy if you don't.'

Sally sighed. 'I seem to be so unimportant to him. He puts Mother before me in everything! He talks to her when he won't talk to me.'

'You must understand, Sally. In our tradition we honour the parents. When I marry my friend I shall honour his mother and she will live with us. And one day Ali will have a wife and she will live with you and do the work, and perhaps then you will be kind to her. Will you?'

'Do I have to wait so long?' said Sally dismally.

Fadeema laughed. 'Not so long, no. In all families the mother rules in the end. You will have more children. Perhaps you will be pregnant before Mohammed goes away, and he will come back to see his new baby. Or babies. It could be twins again!' She wagged a finger.

Sally considered the alternatives. In this family at least she had a place, whereas in her own she had none. She was just Sally, difficult wayward girl. In the end where should her loyalty lie but with her husband, the father of her children? Who best to take care of her? And besides, if he turned against her and withdrew his love, she would be helpless and alone.

That night when Mohammed came home he found the cradles again by the bed. He stood in the doorway, framed by the landing light, looking down at his wife. 'Well, Sally?'

'You can have the shares.' She pulled back the sheet and he saw that she was naked. Still she could excite him, still in that pink and willing flesh lay dizzying temptation. He dragged off his clothes and lay down with her, and as they kissed she thought, 'In this at least I am special to him.' She must make it her world, enthral him in it, and be utterly loved.

Rowan could not believe what Sally had done to her. James held a massive tranche of her shares! She felt hopelessly, horribly threatened.

'You could have anticipated it,' said Saul brutally. 'It makes no difference to the bid, he hasn't got control. He's paid over the odds for them but if we win he'll sell them and still make money. If we lose he's got a foothold in the company.'

'I never thought she'd betray me like that.'

Saul almost laughed. 'Some might say you haven't been exactly honest lately. With anyone.'

'What do you mean?' She forced herself to meet his eyes and something about his glazed stare told her he had been drinking.

'It's no use talking to you,' she said angrily. 'You're never even sober!'

Saul came across. She thought he was going to kiss her and she put her hands up to ward him off. He caught her wrists in an iron clasp. 'God help you if I was,' he said softly, and let her go. She felt cold, although his hands had been hot. She rubbed her wrists.

He went out to walk, down the narrow street, wearing only a jumper on a wet and windy day. Imperceptibly, inch by inch, Rowan was floating out of her depth. Was he going to haul her back in, or leave it until she was way over the horizon? Back she would come, eventually, but possibly more dead than alive.

The cold was sobering him. He went into a shop and bought a mobile of clowns for Hannah. Was he going to become a Sunday father? Turning up like a bad penny to take her endlessly to the zoo? He felt the rage beginning, the murderous, burning rage. You couldn't allow anger like that out, you had to swallow it down, quieten it like the wild beast it was. In the off-licence across the road he bought half a bottle of whisky, and felt proud of himself. In days gone by it would have been at least a full bottle, and possibly two.

Rowan drove slowly up the drive to Aspley Manor. Summoned peremptorily by her mother she had considered refusing to go, but somehow she felt so isolated at the moment. The war between the companies was being conducted in the newspapers just now, with articles on both sides telling tales of the other's ineptitude. The latest scare from Bardsey was that a successful takeover would result in multiple sackings, difficult to refute since it would.

James opened the door to her. 'Well, well, well. Don't you look rapacious.'

She had dressed in black leather trousers and tight leather top. Ridiculous clothes, uncomfortable and hugely expensive, but a much needed boost to her ego. Men turned in the street and stared at her. 'I came to see Mother,' said Rowan frostily.

'We await you, my dear.' He waved an arm extravagantly towards the drawing room. Rowan's nerves jangled, James was wildly confident. When she went into the room, her cheeks flamed. Richard was there. So too was Andy.

'Oh no,' said Rowan dully. 'Not you too! Andy, you can't.'

'Did you ever think you should have consulted me?' Andy was draped theatrically over an armchair. He was wearing a cape lined with red silk.

566

'You look like Dracula on an off-day,' she declared.

'And you look like the star attraction at some whore-house,' murmured Richard.

She turned away, putting her hands together and pacing up and down.

'Where's Mother?' she asked jerkily. 'I think she ought to be here while you dismember me.'

They waited in silence. Rowan's heels clicked on the wooden floor each time she came to the end of the rug. She felt irrationally guilty, in trouble with everyone. It didn't seem fair.

At last Diana appeared, carrying a newspaper.

'There you are, Rowan,' she said distantly, and tossed the paper on to the coffee table.

'What's that?' asked Rowan.

'The article you wrote about Bardsey's. The part that particularly caught my attention concerned "ageing management too preoccupied with the pleasures of the flesh to pay much attention to share dividends". Exactly what did you mean, dear?'

'What it says,' flared Rowan. 'I don't have to apologise for telling the truth!'

'And how about if we wrote about your youthful management, too overburdened with an alcoholic husband and a handicapped child to be concerned with profit?'

Rowan recoiled. 'You wouldn't.'

'Why not? It's the same thing.' Andy got up and came over to her. 'You have started playing very dirty, Rowan. The time has come for me to exercise some control. We're pulling out of the bid.'

'You can't!'

For one dreadful moment she thought he too had sold out. She glanced at James, knowing that if he had control she was finished. But of course it wasn't possible. James could no longer afford it.

She swung round on Richard. 'Haven't you anything to

say? I wrote that but you wrote all that stuff about people losing jobs if we took over.'

Richard shrugged. 'True, and impersonal. You could have considered that what you were writing might hurt your mother as well as James.'

Tears pricked against her eyelids. Everybody was against her, no one saw that she had only been doing what was right, for Judge's! She turned to go and Richard caught her arm.

'You're in no state to drive. I'll take you.'

'I'm all right.' She tried to shake him off, but he wouldn't let go. In silence, watched by everyone, they went out to the car.

He drove her through the park. 'Do you remember driving my car here? You nearly crashed it.'

'I remember.'

He spun the wheel and sent her little runabout down a track leading to a copse of trees. Rowan said nothing to stop him. When they were quite concealed he turned off the engine and sat, holding the steering wheel.

'Bit of a bloody mess, isn't it.'

'My backers will want some kind of forfeit.'

'Ours want us to merge with them. Actually I wish you and I had fought it out straight, without all this backdoor stuff. I could still have beaten you.'

She grinned. 'You might. Was it really wrong to say that about James? It is true.'

'But unwise. Your mother was furious when she first read it.' He turned quite suddenly and started to kiss her.

'Don't be angry with me,' whispered Rowan. 'I can't bear it.'

He said against her neck, 'But why did you do it? I don't understand you at all.'

'I know. I know.'

He was trying to unfasten her trousers. All her misery seemed to fuse into white-hot desire. She pulled the zip down and started to wriggle out of the skin-tight leather. When they were just past her knees Richard swung on top of her, pushing Rowan down across the seats. She was kissing him, nuzzling his ears as he tried to get between her tight thighs. 'I love you,' she murmured to him. 'I do, you know.'

'Of course you do. Oh God, I can't wait!'

They lay tangled together. 'Does Saul do it to you?' asked Richard.

She shook her head. 'We're not on good terms. He's drinking.'

'Yes. You'll have to tell him about us, what we mean to do. Now this is all finished, there's no reason not to.'

'No.' She started to pull up her leather trousers, hating the very thought of telling him. 'We'd have won the bid, you know,' she said suddenly. 'Andy's so stupid, it really is absolutely the best thing for Judge's. OK, we were asset stripping but that's what you were going to do too! We'd fit well together.'

'But you are dropping it, aren't you?' Richard's face told her that he would never quite trust her again.

She sighed. 'I haven't any choice.'

At home, Saul was waiting. She stood in the doorway, the leather trousers sticking to her thighs with sour-smelling proof of her adultery.

'What's happened?' asked Saul.

Frostily she said, 'Nothing that should concern you. Andy's at Aspley Manor. He insists we pull out of the bid.'

'Christ. Oh Christ, the stupid shit!'

She flared up at him. 'I don't know why you aren't cheering! You didn't want this in the first place, you ought to be pleased.'

'Was Richard there?'

'Yes.' She went quickly through to the bathroom, started the water running and stripped off her clothes. Saul leaned on the doorpost watching her. Why should he mind? she thought viciously. Once he was prepared to give me to him.

569

'Do you like Richard?' asked Saul.

'That's a stupid question. We're fighting over the bid.'

'All the same, I should have thought he's your type. The hard, driving sort.'

'As opposed to the soft, drinking sort, you mean?' snarled Rowan in return.

He stood there, saying nothing. She knew without being told that he wanted to make love to her. Quickly, almost scalding herself, she got into the bath.

'It isn't fair, is it?' he said. 'You so wanted Bardsey's.'

'You're too drunk to understand,' she retorted, and started to soap her breasts. Suddenly he knelt down beside the bath, nuzzling her slippery foam-covered skin. Barely an hour before Richard had kissed that same flesh, had licked those same nipples.

'Get off me!' she squealed, and hit at her husband, catching him hard over the ear. In that instant she knew it had been a mistake. Brown eyes, like chocolate, like the depths of brown port, lit with sudden rage. He dragged her out of the bath. She squealed, trying to resist. She had never known such strength. He got her down on the mat.

'You're drunk,' she wailed, 'Barbara will hear! Please, Saul, don't!'

But he was past reason. His hands encircled her throat. Half-choked, in terror of her life, she flailed at him with wet arms. Her ears were filled with sound, she opened her mouth to beg him, beg him to stop. Her tongue croaked helplessly. He was killing her!

Suddenly he let her go. She clung to the side of the bath, dragging air into starved lungs, aware of a tumultuous pulse in her throat. Her husband, her enemy, crashed the door aside as he went out.

Chapter Forty-Seven

Saul lay in bed, watching thin sunshine make patterns on the ceiling. In the kitchen he could hear Hannah singing tunelessly while Barbara counted out loud the numbers of bricks, or dolls, or potatoes. All his love, all his longing, centred on that tuneless little voice. 'God,' he thought, 'I hate all of myself except the part that loves her.'

He got up and went to wash. The bathroom showed no trace of last night, although Rowan's throat was black with fingermarks. She had slept in the spare room, and come to the bedroom only for a scarf. He had uttered not one word of apology.

When he went back to the bedroom he debated whether to have a drink now or in an hour. Usually he had no choice but to drink, his hands shook like leaves in the wind, but this morning he was cold and calm and steady. Poor Rowan, he thought, poor poor Rowan, who had to suffer him. And at the same time he wondered if he should have strangled her. Perhaps that was the way out. To kill the thing that tormented him.

Suddenly he decided what to do. He dressed quickly in a pair of shabby shooting trousers and a jumper, and went out to Rowan's car. Only after ten minutes did he remember the driving ban, and by then it was too late. He kept on, because if he got caught it would be fate and would prove that nothing could go right.

Nobody answered the bell at Aspley Manor, so he wandered round the house setting the peacocks to flight and leaving footmarks on soft lawns. A violin was playing, two violins. He looked through a window at the back of the house and saw Diana and Andy, playing together. He stood, listening.

There was something wrong with the tempo, Andy was quick where Diana was slow, and lingered sentimentally where she was strict. At the end Diana flung down her bow.

'You've turned into the sort of hack player that grinds out love songs in cheap restaurants,' she declared.

'Rubbish!' Andy carefully replaced his violin in its expensive polished case. Diana's battered box seemed a mute reminder of the difference between them.

'You ought not to let them do this to you!' said Diana. 'That record you made embarrassed me so much I couldn't listen to it.'

Andy turned on her. 'Look, Mother, when I did it your way I couldn't get a single booking some months. I'd ring up my agent and her assistant would take it, lying in her teeth. "I'm sorry, Mr. Judge, there isn't anything just now but I'll ask her to ring you." No return call, nothing. You sit, waiting, practising, and the bills come in and your shoes wear out. Now my agent rings *me*, twice a day sometimes, and *I* don't take the calls.'

'I didn't think money would ever mean so much to you,' said Diana in disgust.

'God, Mother, can't you see it isn't the money? I just cannot stand what goes with poverty: the contempt, the pity, the powerlessness! If Dad had had the money, don't you think he'd have been different? You would never have despised him as you did.'

Saul stepped forward and rapped on the window. Diana and Andy jumped, and then Diana went and threw up the sash. 'What are you doing here? How dare you snoop around my home?'

'I rang the bell. You didn't hear. I wanted to talk to Andy.'

'If it's to plead about Rowan's idiotic bid, then he doesn't want to hear. She's got a great deal too big for her boots and she cares about nothing except herself.'

'Do shut up, Mother.' Andy sat on the window ledge and swung himself out into the garden. He landed on the grass, dusted his hands and grinned. They strolled away across the park.

Saul said, 'I knew she hadn't told you about the bid. She's a fool sometimes.'

Andy shrugged. 'Always stupid about Judge's, that's Rowan. About anything she cares about, actually.'

'Yes.' Saul sighed, sinking his hands deep into his pockets. There was a hole in one of them, and Rowan would never mend it. Perhaps indeed she should not, except what was care if not an expression of love? They should care for each other, mutually. If they loved.

'Who's the woman in your life?' he asked Andy.

'American television presenter. Very glamorous, and a bit hard. She'd like to get married but on my side it isn't serious.'

'Don't you want kids?'

Andy shrugged. 'Depends. I wondered about the genes, after Hannah.'

Saul swallowed. 'Sally was OK. I think it's just the mix. Me and Rowan. We don't seem to match.'

'No. Well, I've wondered. You can cut your losses, I suppose?'

'Perhaps.'

Saul stopped and faced the other man. In the clear daylight Andy looked tired and strained, less sure of himself than he had seemed with Diana.

'You must let Rowan go ahead with her bid,' said Saul. 'I know she seems power-crazed sometimes. But she has to try. If she loses through her own efforts then she'll live with it, but this way she'll look a fool and lose the firm's money into the bargain. Besides, I don't think you've any right to stop her. She saved Judge's, all by herself.'

'Saved it, yes. But you put it up where it is today.'

Saul shook his head. 'All I'm saying is, don't do this to

her. Let her for once have what she wants.'

They walked on, past the empty stables, part of which had been converted into garages. James's Rolls-Royce had a flat tyre, and Diana's Porsche needed washing. 'You're right, you know,' said Andy suddenly. 'I'm doing what James wants. And I owe Rowan far more than I do him. She's never let me down.'

'Because she loves you.'

It was said in an odd voice, and Andy glanced quickly at the tall, leonine man beside him. But Saul's face betrayed nothing. All the same, Andy was aware of an almost over-powering sadness. 'You tell Rowan,' said Saul. 'Don't tell her you spoke to me.'

Rowan picked up the telephone. Richard's voice said, 'You bitch!'

She said breathily, 'You said you wouldn't have minded fighting it out. So I am.'

'What if I ask you to let it drop? We don't need this, Rowan, you and I don't need it.'

'It won't hurt us. Not if we really care.'

'Do you care?'

'Yes,' she whispered. 'Yes, yes, terribly. Oh Richard, I can't bear to stay here much longer! He's so awful!'

'Then drop the bloody bid and come to me!'

'I − can't.'

She hung up before more could be said, and smoothed her hands across her cheeks, trying to regain her composure. Everybody thought she was going to win this time. Since Andy's surprising capitulation Judge's, backed by their sponsors, had increased their offer for Bardsey shares. The headlines read 'Judge's Holding Its Nerve', and at meetings nowadays she was congratulated on her management style. But although they were now on her side, she knew better than to trust the City men.

The scarf around her neck was slipping and she adjusted

it. Saul kept away from her, they slept in different rooms and inhabited the house at different times. When this was over she would go and see a solicitor, she told herself, and be free of him. But at lunchtime she went to the house to see Hannah and he was there.

They didn't at first notice her and she stood outside the kitchen, watching him play trains with Hannah's food. For him and his chuffings the little girl opened and closed her mouth, and put up her arms and her sticky face for his kiss. 'Daddy's best girl,' said Saul, and rested his cheek against her hair.

'I'm glad to see you can at least have consideration for somebody,' said Rowan tartly. 'Where is Barbara?'

'I gave her the afternoon off.'

'You hadn't any right.'

'Don't be ridiculous.'

She glared at him, but he looked away. He said, 'James has gone very quiet.'

'He's leaving things to Richard,' said Rowan stiffly. 'He knows he can trust him, I suppose.'

'Not what I'd suppose at all,' said Saul. He picked up Hannah and prepared to leave the room. Rowan said quickly, 'Saul!'

'What?'

'You wouldn't – Hannah. You wouldn't take her?'

'No. No, I won't do that.'

'Thank you.' She stood alone in the kitchen, her hands pressed together as if in prayer.

BARDSEY MAN WRITES: JUDGE'S MANAGEMENT APPALLING – AND I SHOULD KNOW!!!

Diana took the paper from James and gaped at it. 'You're saying Richard wrote this?'

'Yes. Didn't think he had it in him. Tough lad, Richard.'

'Downright cruel, if you ask me!' Diana read on.

'"Married to an alcoholic, mother of a handicapped child, Rowan Judge is at the same time to be pitied and feared. A woman with so little to satisfy her in her personal life has to turn to her work. Sadly, she is best pleased when inflating her bank balance, by fair means or foul. Tragedy has pursued Rowan Judge, but we do not have to welcome it into other, more fortunate lives." You put him up to this, James!'

'All his own idea, I'm afraid.'

James went to the cupboard and poured them both a drink. He was feeling energetic and optimistic. 'I can finish her, you know,' he said suddenly. 'I can absolutely bring her down!'

'I think she's bombproof, James, even for you.' Diana was feeling irritable. She wanted to defend Rowan while at the same time thought that she deserved all she got.

'You watch,' said James. 'Just you watch.' He took her drink to her, and watched her thin fingers curl around the glass. Ageing hands, but still the most beautiful he knew.

Once again Rowan stood in Threadneedle Street. Once again ranged about her were the faces of anonymous men. Last week they had praised her, now they smiled with spurious pity. 'I don't believe it,' she said softly. 'I simply don't believe it.'

'James Barton made a very strong case,' purred the senior man from General Foods. 'When we considered the possibility of a merger with Bardsey's, we saw for ourselves the benefits.'

'Getting the goodies and leaving me out,' said Rowan flatly. 'It's betrayal!'

'No, my dear, business.'

They had summoned her down here just to humiliate her. She stood stock still and fought her urge to pick up something, anything, and throw it at them. Typically secretive, James had sneaked off to General Foods and sold himself to them, leaving Judge's without a backer, betrayed and helpless. 'What in God's name are you going to do with a textile firm?' she demanded. 'At least I wasn't going to close everything down!'

'Perhaps we can sell some parts to you?' someone suggested.

And suddenly Rowan could stand no more. She drew herself up to her full height, and glared down at them furiously. 'I never trade with thieves,' she declared.

Waiting for the lift outside, standing stabbing fruitlessly at the button, she heard them laughing.

In Bardsey's board room, across the gleaming table, Richard faced his father.

'You knew what you were doing to me. You meant to do it.'

'Don't be ridiculous, Richard! She was going to win, we had to stop her.'

'*You* had to stop her. Can't you see how stupid this is? If the worst came to the worst, Judge's and Bardsey's make a good fit together. But us and a food company? Are we going to weave fucking napkins or what?'

James strolled to the head of the table, and laid all his long length down in the great chair. 'You should have seen this way out. I waited for you to get on with it, and I could wait no longer.'

A great wave of rage surged up in Richard. 'What was this then?' he said in a low, shaking voice. 'A test of my balls? You wanted to do down not only Rowan but me as well, simply because I challenged you. I might be your son but to you that means nothing.'

'Oh, it does,' said James thoughtfully. 'Without that you wouldn't have lasted this long. It's my company, you see. Mine!'

'You bloody fool, it belongs to General Foods! See what you've got left in six months.'

James laughed. 'I won't have anything. I'm resigning. You see, my boy, I'm prepared to hand over, but I am not prepared to let you kick me out. That's what I don't think you understood.'

Richard started to pace up and down the length of the table, anything to dispel the whirlwind of feeling within him. 'I don't understand you,' he said thickly. 'We're father and son, you don't have to beat me! This isn't some primitive manhood ritual!'

'Isn't it?' James got up and stretched luxuriantly. He was wearing a silk tie, Richard noticed, and into the fabric was woven the picture of a dragon, mouth gaping wide. 'Look at it this way.' James paused before leaving the room. 'With this tie-up with General Foods we're solvent again. I can retire an extremely wealthy man. Admittedly at the end of the day there won't be much of Bardsey's left for you, but one day you'll get my money. Until then you can do what I did, and what Rowan Judge did, to her damnable credit. You can get your finger out and turn a struggling business into something that looks like success!'

Richard stood, in stunned surprise, and said nothing. After his father left he still stood, utterly frozen.

James didn't want to go home to Diana. At a moment such as this he wanted to prove himself, perhaps for the last time. He was tired of his mistress, she had served her purpose and there was nothing now she could do for him that hadn't been done before. He would pay her off, make the flat over to her, and be done with deceit — for the moment.

Lin Yu wasn't expecting him. She was wearing a cream linen tunic and her hair was caught up in a long ponytail. James noticed that her little face looked shadowed and beneath the yellow of her skin was a tinge of grey.

'Are you ill?' he asked shortly.

She shook her head. 'A little tired, that is all, James. Shall I make you a drink, tea? Cocaine perhaps.'

'Yes, I'll have a snort.'

As she bent over to prepare the drug, he thought that she looked remarkably unattractive. Even Lin Yu was growing older, he supposed, even a whore of her class could not defeat time. Perhaps she was an addict at last. For himself he had no trouble in that direction, his only addiction was power.

But the cocaine was good. Lin Yu took nothing. 'Are you on heroin or something?' demanded James.

'Of course not. I don't want anything now, though.' She started to undress, unbuttoning the tunic from her long neck down to the middle of her thighs. He wasn't getting much of an erection, which showed he was bored with her. Time to get rid of a whore when you couldn't get it up, he told himself. Why pay for what you can't enjoy.

When she was naked she wrapped her arms around herself as if cold and ran to get into the bed. James stripped off and followed her. 'I'm going to make the flat over to you,' he said, guiding her hand to his semi-erect penis. The cocaine had had a bad effect on him, and today that was annoying because it would crown everything to be able to do it. 'Give me something to stiffen me up, would you?' he said.

Lin Yu reached into the bedside drawer and drew out a small bottle of pills. James had used one twice before when he was tired; each time he had been a ram.

'Why are you giving me the flat?' asked Lin Yu.

'Because I think you've earned it, my dear,' said James easily. He lay back and waited for the pill to work, and whether it was the pill or the girl's kneading hand he was becoming hugely distended. James felt drunk and happy. 'I'm paying you off,' he remarked casually. 'We've had a good few years together, after all. You're still quite young, you'll get other blokes quite easily. You'll enjoy it, I shouldn't wonder. What you haven't taught me!'

Lin Yu said nothing. Her little face with its greyish-yellow skin gave nothing away. Moving swiftly and neatly she straddled the man and inserted him inside herself, working up and down with a smooth rhythm.

'Haven't you noticed anything, James?' she asked.

'What — what should I notice?' His eyes were half-closed, he could feel his climax gathering way, way off. She put her fingers against his shoulders, her sharp nails pricked him slightly.

'I look different.'

'Do you — oh my God, this is good. In what way different?'

'James — I'm pregnant with your child.'

He climaxed with his eyes wide open. The air whistled in and out of lungs half-paralysed with shock. The girl got off him and crouched at the edge of the bed. James pushed himself up and half-sat, gasping for breath.

'You're lying, you cow — lying!'

'You can see that I am not. I wanted this from you, James. You can't put me aside, not when I have your son! Another Nicholas. I shall call him Nicholas!'

Somehow James found himself on all fours on the bed. His penis, still enlarged, hung beneath him; beads of sweat stood out like marbles on his forehead. 'Not Nicholas — please — not Nick!'

Lin Yu, frightened at last, caught his arm. 'James? James, what is it?'

The pain in his chest was like being stabbed, worse than that. He couldn't speak to her. Dimly he stared up at the girl, his mouth working, and he thought, 'If she doesn't call an ambulance, I shall die!'

Chapter Forty-Eight

Rowan could count on the fingers of one hand the times her mother had visited her at Valley House. Now Diana crouched on the sofa in the large, light sitting room, a diminished and crumpled figure. Fine strands of grey ran through the tawny hair, not unattractively. Even age in Diana was beautiful, thought Rowan ruefully. Her mother was well past fifty.

'If James is ill, Mother,' she said distantly, 'why are you here? Shouldn't you be at the hospital?'

Diana looked up at her daughter. 'He's got some floozy with him. Some whore. It was doing it with her that gave him the heart attack.'

'Oh. Oh, I see.' Rowan was shocked, and that surprised her. 'Did you know he had — women?'

Diana nodded. 'Yes, I knew. But she's — Rowan, she's beautiful! Tiny and Chinese.'

Rowan's heart rose into her throat and down to her guts. That girl of Richard's, it had to be! James would want her because she had been Richard's, he would find nothing more satisfying than that.

'I think he's going to die.' Diana's voice cracked on a sob. 'I want to kill him, but if he dies I'll wish I was dead too! What am I going to do?'

'Does anybody know he's ill? Have you told anyone?'

Diana shook her head. 'I went to the hospital, then straight here. I don't want anyone else to see him! Not with her!'

Rowan went out of the room. Barbara was out with Hannah for a walk, she could not advise. But at that moment the front door opened and Saul came in. They

581

stared at each other uncomfortably.

'I thought you were at the mill,' said Saul.

'I was. My mother's here. Saul —' She had to confide in somebody, anybody. 'Saul, something's happened. James has had a heart attack.'

A shadow crossed his face. 'Bad? I mean, is he still alive?'

She nodded. 'Intensive care. And he's got some girl with him! Mother rushed to the hospital and she was there. Apparently she's some sort of prostitute and James was with her when it happened.'

'Good God.'

He crossed the hall in swift strides and went into the sitting room. Diana glanced up and said in a voice like raked claws, 'Do I have to be exposed to you as well? It seems that you and James share a great many things, but at least he isn't an alcoholic!'

'Just at this moment,' said Saul drily, 'I am stone cold sober. But don't let that worry you. Look, we should be at the hospital. And someone's got to ring Richard.'

'I'll do it,' said Rowan quickly. Saul glanced at her.

'I suppose you will. Be quick, we've got to go.'

He and Diana were alone while Rowan 'phoned. Diana said, 'I wonder if he was revenging himself? All those women. Because of us.'

Saul blinked. 'What about us? One drunken screw doesn't add up to much in my opinion.'

'Except that in this case it did.' She opened her handbag, took out a powder puff and dabbed it energetically over her nose. 'It produced Nicholas. I suspected it, but only knew for sure when he — died. And James found out then, too. I thought you should know.

'Oh my God. Oh — my — God.'

Diana watched the blood draining from his face, then flooding back patchily. She was conscious of an enormous relief, of a burden handed bodily to someone else. Saul wiped a hand stiffly across his mouth.

Rowan came into the room, herself rather pink. 'Let's go,' she said airily. 'I've left a note for Barbara.'

As they drew into the hospital car park they saw Richard's Maserati howling along the road towards them. He parked and leaped out.

'Does he always come so quickly?' asked Saul bitterly, and Rowan threw him a surprised glance. He looked odd, shocked, and she couldn't believe it was only because of James. As Richard ran towards them, dishevelled and smelling uncharacteristically of booze, she felt herself sliding away from certainty into wild confusion.

'Hello,' said Rowan awkwardly.

'What's happened? Have you been in?'

'Not yet.' Diana drew in her breath, braced herself and set off for the building. The others followed, no one knowing who to walk beside. Behind Saul's back Richard put out his hand for Rowan to squeeze, and she took it.

They had to wait in the corridor while a nurse went to see what was happening. Diana went to stand at the door to the unit, her face anguished. A nurse took her into a side room to complete a form.

'Do you mind about your father?' Rowan asked Richard suddenly.

He looked down at her, as if intensely absorbed. 'Today he almost wrecked me,' he said softly, for her alone. 'He and General Foods have stripped out Bardsey's and given me a shell. Told me to copy you and make a go of it. I've no capital, nothing. But I still want him to live.'

'Then I assume you're not in his will,' said Saul, cutting brutally across the moment. He was walking up and down restively, and Richard put an arm round Rowan to draw her away from her husband.

In an instant Saul gripped Richard's shirt, hauled him towards him and head-butted his face. The younger man's nose and lip exploded in blood, it smeared obscenely over Saul's thatch of hair. 'Don't touch my wife,' said Saul softly. 'I don't like it.'

'What in God's name has got into you?' Rowan ran to Richard's aid, pressing tissues against the mashed flesh.

'It's what's not in me!' retorted Saul. 'I haven't had a drop in three days. And the net result is that I am bloody angry!' He picked up a chair and threw it viciously against the wall.

A nurse came bustling towards them. 'What is going on here?'

'Nothing,' said Saul tightly. 'At least, nothing that matters. I was just venting a little spleen on the bloke that's been fucking my wife.'

'Could you help, nurse?' asked Rowan desperately. 'He's broken his teeth.'

'We have people sick in here!' said the nurse. 'This is not the place for domestic squabbles!' Nonetheless she went to see Richard, leading him brusquely away.

'How long have you known?' asked Rowan.

Saul shrugged. 'Since you told me. It's drink, you know, love. Steer clear of it, you don't know what it might do.'

'Not — not that night you came home!'

'The very same.'

She dropped her eyes in chagrin, and suddenly he couldn't bear to look at her. He turned away, sinking his hands deep in his pockets and bowing his head.

'I didn't mean to hurt you,' said Rowan softly.

'Yes you did. Perhaps I deserved it, I don't know. Do you love him, Rowan?'

She hesitated a long time before answering. 'Yes. Yes, I do.'

She heard him take a long, shuddering breath. At last he said, 'Well. That's it then, isn't it? No point in bashing on with something that's dead, is there?'

'Was that why you — in the bathroom? The other day?'

His eyes were almost black. 'For a second I wanted to kill you. We both know what you'd been doing. And I have never been so — hurt and — and angry — in all my life. Not even James could do that to me. Only you.'

'I'm sorry.' It seemed inadequate, but she said it again. 'I'm sorry.'

Diana appeared, white-faced. 'She's still there,' she said desperately. 'The girl. They say she won't leave. I won't see him with her there, I couldn't!'

'I'll talk to her.' Saul strode through the plastic swing doors. Inside he was surrounded by glass cubicles, each crammed with machinery. In one, next to the bed, sat Lin Yu.

'Hello,' said Saul, watching her. She was composed, almost tranquil, in a soft robe of blue silk. Her hair cascaded down her back, held at the temples by flowers. She nodded her head to Saul.

'How is he?' he asked.

'The doctor says he is stable. Very sick, but no worse.'

'Good — good. Why are you here? You know his wife's outside?'

She fluttered a tiny hand towards the bed. 'But it's right for me to stay. We are much to each other. I am to bear his child.'

Because there was no chair, Saul squatted down next to the girl. He looked up into her delicate face, remembering what he had seen her do to James, what he had seen Richard do to her. This was no innocent. 'What are you hoping for?' he asked softly. 'Money?'

She watched him, trying to assess his threat to her. 'He must keep me,' she said at last. 'If not me, then his child. That's why I stay.'

'You can't trust him. You know that, don't you?'

'Yes. But in this I know he will care for me. If he lives. The child is truly his own, you see. As Nicholas was not.'

Saul let out his breath. 'What a lot you know about him,' he remarked.

'He does not love me,' acknowledged Lin Yu. 'But he will do much for his child.'

585

'All right.' Saul got up. 'Go away for now. I give you my word that even if James dies, I'll make sure you're taken care of. If he lives, it's up to you.'

'Why should I trust you?'

He shrugged. 'I can't imagine. I might get drunk and never think of you again. I don't think so, though.'

She got up and prepared to walk past him, out of the cubicle. Her head came barely up to his armpit. When she was next to him, she stopped. 'You are his brother, are you not? James said strange things about you. He said you were frightened of yourself.'

'What on earth do you mean?' Saul stared down at the tiny, small-boned face.

'I think you are a man of great power. But a kind man also. And all your life you have seen James using his own power to damage things, people. Your mother perhaps? Certainly you. Always you have said, "Power is not for me". But there is nothing else for you. Except drink.'

Saul let out his breath. 'I don't think anyone can know the harm he did me,' he said throatily. 'When I was a boy – I had nothing, you see. I was at his mercy.'

She touched his hands. 'Because he was frightened of you. I know James so well, I understand him. You're not a boy now and he is an old man, sick in bed.'

She moved smoothly out of the cubicle and away. Saul called out, loud in the hushed ward, 'I won't forget. I promise.' She raised one small, pointed hand.

Diana came in, and Richard, his face swollen and cut.

'She's leaving you,' said Richard thickly, as Saul went out.

'Not now, for God's sake,' said Diana. She went to the bed and took hold of James's near lifeless hand.

Saul thought, 'She's the only one of us that really cares whether he lives or dies.'

Out in the corridor, Rowan sat. Her hands were in her lap,

clasping tissues stained with Richard's blood.

'I've got something to say to you,' said Saul.

She glanced quickly up at him. 'Don't say it if it's cruel. We don't have to be cruel, do we?'

He said honestly, 'I don't know. When you ignore emotions they don't go away, you know. They turn sour and poison you, poison the air you breathe. Take James, for instance. I hate him. I've always hated him, loathed him, wanted him to suffer more horribly than anyone in the world! And underneath all that I love him too. If I don't let out the hate the love gets locked up with it, and we've done that, you and me.'

'Is that what you wanted me to know?'

'Not exactly.' He put out a finger and ran it down the parting in Rowan's dark hair. 'I fathered Nicholas. I didn't know it but I did.'

She looked up at him. Her eyes flooded with tears that did not fall.

'You — and Mother?'

'Once. Only ever once. On the day they got married. And it was because I was drunk, and because she was his, and she was willing, and when did a randy bloke who fancied himself as a stud ever turn up a chance like that? I didn't enjoy it. Or at least, I never wanted to repeat the experience. Neither did she actually, it was one of those stupid, stupid moments.'

'Did James know?'

'Not till the boy died. I can feel sorry for him, you know. Such a terrible thing for him to live with.'

Rowan said in an anguished voice, 'What about me living with it? Knowing what you did?'

'You said yourself, we don't matter any more.'

If she had indeed said that she couldn't remember when.

Richard came out of the ward and Rowan got up to go to him. He put his hands on her shoulders, daring Saul to object.

'Don't,' said Rowan, and moved away of her own accord.

587

Saul said, 'Is he conscious?'

'Comes and goes, I think.' Richard's voice was muffled by the swelling. 'I'm going to sue you for the dental bills, you bastard.'

Saul crossed the floor in a stride, yelling, 'Try it and I'll knock a few more down your throat!'

The aggression in him had welled up so fast that they were all taken aback. Saul turned away, clearly under the most minimal control.

'Go in and see James,' said Rowan shakily. 'Then we'll go home.'

The ward sister was becoming agitated by the toing and froing. 'One at a time, please,' she insisted, and Diana, who had been clutching James's long freckled hand, said, 'I want him to myself! Be quick all of you, then just go away!'

As she left, Saul leaned over the bed. James opened a pale eye. 'Upset,' he said weakly. 'About the girl.'

'Yes.' Saul looked down at his half-brother. A deep well of feeling seemed to open inside him. Heat, pain, love, longing, all kept too long controlled. 'You were a bastard to me, you know,' he remarked.

'Was I? Little pillock like you. Thought — thought the old man would give everything to you. He didn't like me much.'

'You were the favourite!'

'Seemed to me — he made more of you somehow. Perhaps not. Hard to tell.' He tried to chuckle. 'If I die I'll ask him.'

Saul took a deep breath. 'James — I'm sorry about Nick. I knew nothing until today. I swear I didn't know.'

It was as if he hadn't been heard. There was the soft buzz of machines and the hushing of a ventilator against another bed. James said, 'Thought you were laughing at me. Saw a doting fool, thinking he was dad.'

'You were, in everything that mattered.'

'Diana said that too. Why did you do it, Saul?'

588

There seemed no way to explain it all. 'I suppose —
because she was beautiful.'

Softly, thoughtfully, James said, 'She was, wasn't she? I
had the most beautiful wife in the world.'

Richard took Rowan into the garden. It was getting dark.
They stood shivering on a little used path. 'Pack some things
and come tomorrow,' he said.

'But what about Hannah? She loves her daddy, I can't
take her away from him and home and everything, not all at
once. It's all right, Richard, we don't have to rush!'

'You can leave her with the nanny, it wouldn't be for long.
He could kill you. If he starts drinking again you're as good
as dead. He's half mad now, you can see it!'

'Really!' He saw her teeth flash in a smile. 'I'm not scared
of Saul. He's got a right to be angry. And I'm not leaving
Hannah!'

Richard said, 'You left her quite happily to go to the
States! Look, I'm not having this. I insist you come tonight,
I'm having no argument.

'And I'm not arguing. But I'm not coming either.'

She began to walk back to the hospital but he caught her
arm. 'Rowan — you can't start feeling sorry for him. He's a
drunk, he's violent. You can't bring a child up in a home like
that!'

'If it wasn't for Saul, Hannah would be in some mental
home,' flared Rowan.

Richard couldn't believe his ears. 'You're unbalanced,
Rowan! You said yourself it was hell! You've got no idea of
the man he is, you can't stay with him.'

'I didn't say I was going to. I'm just not leaving yet.'

Richard turned square to face her. In the half-light his
swollen face looked like a caricature of himself, still
handsome but elongated and enlarged. 'I think you should
know something,' he said in a warm, low voice. 'I wanted to
keep it from you but I see now I can't. You don't know the

589

man you married, Rowan. He — he fathered your mother's child. He slept with your mother. Nicholas was his son.'

'What a horrible thing to say.'

'I'm not lying to you, Rowan. It's true.'

'I know it's true! I just think it's foul of you to tell tales to try and persuade me. Leave me alone, Richard, I'm beginning to think it's you I don't know very well!'

'What do you mean by that?'

She glared up at him. 'That horrible article you wrote in the paper. The mess you made of the bid. James has wrecked your firm and you haven't tried to stop him. Why don't you threaten to resign and veto the merger? You can put it to the board and have it thrown out. But you gave in. You're not up to this, Richard, not by a long chalk.'

'Christ, Rowan, you don't decide about people on the basis of their business acumen! Or do you? Is that the way your mind works?'

In the dark, she clasped her hands. 'I don't know. Right now all I know is I'm going home with Saul. I'll talk to you tomorrow.'

He stood, in the half-light, and listened to her heels clacking away along the path. Everything he touched, everything he had thought solid, was turning to dust beneath his hands. Never in his life had he felt so wretched.

The night was dark and rather chilly. Confused, miserable, Rowan went into the silent mill. Saul was in the house, and Hannah, and Barbara's anxious, watchful eyes. It was better in the mill, quite alone.

Somehow, despite the thousands of times she had been there since, her mind went back to the night she had walked there, and asked Elsie for money for food. A few pounds and she had been happy; she distinctly remembered that surge of relief and joy. If only her problems could be resolved so easily today. Yet what was it her mother used to

590

say? 'Rowan always knows what she wants to do.' If it had ever been true, it wasn't now.

Richard had been wonderful in New York. She had loved everything about him, from the reddish-haired knuckles of his toes to the soft bristle on his face in the morning. She had loved his love of her, the freedom, the delicious sense of sin! Back home, understandably, it wasn't the same. She wasn't free any more, and somehow she wasn't sure she wanted to be.

Her thoughts veered to Saul, and she put up her hands, as if physically to shut him out. Why did he hurt her so? Why was it that, with him, everything hurt so much? With him it was all extremes, and she knew instinctively that with Richard, or anyone, if it hurt at all it would be a pale shadow of this. Saul wasn't good for her, that big, strong, difficult man. She could spend a lifetime trying and never understand him.

A noise in the echoing space made her spin round. He was there, watching her. 'How long have you been here?' she asked.

'Not long.' He came towards her, his footsteps eerie on the stone floor. She had said she wasn't scared of him but here, in this lonely place, he frightened her.

Rowan took a nervous step backward. 'Don't,' he said. 'I'm past anger. I don't think − I wanted to thank you. I know how hard I've made it for you. You never let me down.'

'Yes I did. You've forgotten.'

'Have I?' He stood watching her, his hands in his pockets. Suddenly she longed to hold him, and without knowing what she was doing she went to him and put her arms round his neck. He enfolded her and they stood, hugging each other, knowing how vast was the distance between them. After a moment or two Saul realised she was crying.

He took her back to the house. A fire was burning in the hearth and Rowan went and self-consciously sat in a chair by herself. Almost as if he hadn't noticed, Saul lounged back on the sofa. He said, 'If James dies, Richard should be set up.'

She gulped. 'Depends on the will. Saul — I didn't mean that about not letting you have any of Judge's. I would, of course.'

'Why of course? You've bled for this firm, my girl, all your life! You'll never give it up.'

She went a little pink. 'We can all change, you know. Even me.'

He got up and went to the cabinet. Rowan tensed in her chair, gripping the arms, then almost collapsed when he returned with a glass and a bottle of mineral water. 'Beast.'

'Oh ye of little faith.'

'Are you off it for good?'

He shook his head. 'Not likely. Just until tomorrow. Some people get through the whole of their lives waiting for tomorrow.'

She cupped her hands and dropped her chin into them. 'It was my fault, you know. I drove you to it.'

At last she had roused him. He put down the glass with a crash. 'That is the biggest load of bloody rubbish I have ever heard! You know what drove me to it? Being nice. I'm *not* nice. The trouble is I want to be. Being nicer than James was all I ever had over him, it was my stock in trade, everyone liked me so much more than him. God, was I popular! I couldn't face you down over who ran what in this place because I couldn't not be liked. You know the best thing that ever happened to me?'

She watched him, wide-eyed. 'What?'

'Hannah! You needn't look so surprised, she was! For the first time in my life I had to look at someone and decide what was really important. It wasn't their looks, it wasn't what they could do, it wasn't how bleeding nice they were, it was something quite separate. Some essence of them. Something you could love when everything you looked for in a friend wasn't there. When I thought about her — when I was sober enough to think about her — I began to think about me.'

'I haven't thought about you in ages,' said Rowan. 'I haven't let myself.'

He turned his head away. 'I don't need to be told that.'

Picking up his drink again, he wandered over to the window. 'You'll be good for Richard,' he said. 'Sort him out. In years to come people won't remember you used to be married to someone else.'

'Will you find someone else?' asked Rowan.

'Yes, I suppose so.'

There was a long, waiting silence. The shock of it had her thoughts spinning. That he could think about, even *think* about, someone else, tonight, when everything they had ever meant to each other was coming to such an end — it almost choked her. She tried not to care, she tried to think of anything except that, but suddenly she was shaking with rage.

She said in a low, murderous voice, 'You beast! You don't give a bloody damn. You did marry me to get Judge's, and now you're going to get it and you don't care at all. All these weeks you've known about me and Richard and you haven't done a bloody thing. I hate you, Saul, I hate you because you don't love me one tiny little scrap!' She picked up the mineral water bottle and threw it at him. It sailed through the plate glass window with a crash of resounding magnitude.

In the next room Hannah started to wail and they heard Barbara rush in to her. 'It's all right, darling, your father's gone berserk, that's all.'

'It was me!' yelled Rowan back. 'And he bloody deserved it! The faithless swine!' She threw herself on the sofa and sobbed.

Saul sat down on the edge next to her and patted her back. 'Look,' he said gently, 'I thought you loved Richard. I thought you wanted to leave me and live with him.'

She pushed the hair out of her eyes and struggled to say what she felt. 'I never said I wanted to leave you! But you're all ready to pack my suitcase and wave goodbye!'

'For God's sake, Rowan! You said you loved him!' Saul's face, so dear, so utterly familiar, twisted in real anguish.

'I do love him,' she said miserably. 'But − it isn't the way I love you. It's not a real kind of thing. Not the way we are.'

'You slept with him, you told him you cared! Look, I know I deserve it but this is torture, Rowan. You can't tear me apart just for your amusement.'

'I didn't ever want to hurt you! But − oh, it was better in New York! It was like not being married, I didn't feel bad. Here it was all rather horrid really. Too much like James and my mother. Doing things for yourself, and not for anyone else.'

'Even James and Diana care about each other, after a fashion.' He put his big fingers gently on her cheeks and wiped the tears. Her eyes, wide and suddenly fiercely determined, stared up at him.

'I don't want it to be like that. I want our sort of love, the way it should have been, together and honest and Hannah knowing who her daddy is. We got it right sometimes. Didn't we?'

Saul got up, his hands thrust deep into his pockets. Rain was coming in through the broken window and next door Hannah still sobbed. 'You know I love you,' he said harshly. 'I always have. But I want life my way this time, and that might not be your way. I don't know. We can run Judge's together, but only if you let it happen. I want to expand, buy up great chunks of Bardsey's if we can get it. Diversify. Add a bit of capital to Joe Partridge's set-up and get involved in transport. And I want more kids. Lots more kids.'

Rowan swallowed. 'How many more?'

'About three for starters. We can have all the tests, it might be we have to stop at Hannah. But − Rowan, I want to try.'

Her eyes felt gritty with tears, she felt she might sob and sob forever. It was as if all the tears for years past were dammed up inside her, all her past sorrows and failures and disappointments. 'Children hurt you so,' she wept. 'You hurt me so!'

'But that isn't the most of it!' said Saul in surprise.

'But it's the part you remember.'

He went out and got a board and started to block up the window. Rowan helped him, holding the hammer and the tacks. His hands moving so purposefully twisted her stomach in desire, she was shocked at herself. How could you love one man, sleep with him, yet love and desire another?

When the job was finished, almost before it was done, she had her arms round Saul's neck, her thighs pressed into his. Furtively, to avoid alerting Barbara, they sneaked into their bedroom. Making love, wildly in the dark, Rowan held on to his shoulders and moaned; 'I love you! I love you!' But afterwards, when he said, 'Tell me you'll stay. Rowan, please!' she still said, 'I don't know.'

Chapter Forty-Nine

Before nine the next morning Richard arrived. Everyone was still in bed, Rowan answered the door in her dressing gown with Hannah on her hip. Richard came and stood in the kitchen.

'How's James?' asked Rowan awkwardly.

'Out of danger, they think. Diana's gone home anyway. She sat up with him all night.'

'Oh.'

She felt shy for some reason. The memory of Saul last night was too recent. They had made love so often, had woken barely two hours since to do it again! Like teenagers discovering it for the very first time. And here was her lover, and she felt unfaithful.

Hannah winged and she poured out cereal with one hand, then sat the child down and spooned it up for her. Saul came in, wearing only a towel round his waist.

'What the devil are you doing here? Is James dead?'

Rowan was quick to step in. 'He seems better. And Richard thought — '

'I was worried about Rowan,' said Richard.

'How bloody civil of you.' Saul walked precisely into the spot occupied by Richard, forcing him to move out of the way. Richard moved only the barest minimum.

'You're behaving like a couple of dogs,' said Rowan testily.

'I see the window got broken,' said Richard. 'Get packed, Rowan, you're not staying here another minute.'

Unwisely he reached out a hand and Saul punched it hard out of the way. 'Don't you dare touch her!'

'Will you stop it!' Rowan pushed between them. 'I broke the window.' She looked from one to the other. How she wished that Richard had never come! And yet – Saul wanted so much from her. There was no way of knowing if she could ever be strong enough. She said airily, 'I'm not going now. There's things to do. Hannah's got a busy day. There's a problem in the mill.'

Richard turned on her. 'And when do you think might be convenient, may I ask?'

She dropped her head. 'I don't know.'

Suddenly Saul laughed. 'Tell you what, Richard,' he said kindly. 'We'll ring you. When the mill's running smoothly, when Hannah's out of nappies, when Rowan's got the shopping in and the fridge stocked up. It'll take about – oh, twenty years.'

'Don't laugh at him,' said Rowan miserably. 'It isn't fair.'

'I don't think I have to consider fairness just now. I've had enough of this messing about. You're my wife, Rowan! I am not letting you go!'

In a low voice Richard said, 'It's up to you. We'd be happy together, you know we would.'

And she did know. But she looked around her messy kitchen, at her baby, at her home. Saul loved her, and no one knew more of her than he. He knew her insecurities, the raw ambition, the unattractive drive that whipped her on. Yet when she failed, when weakness and weariness beat her, he was there to comfort, never to blame.

What in turn could she give to him? Only, she saw now, what had been her gift to him since the day they met. Through all the drunkenness and doubt, she had reached into a well of love, expecting always for her bucket to come up empty. Never once had it done so. There was always more, and more again. Even if she left him now, and went with Richard to a calmer life, there would be no end of it; she and Saul could no more disentangle themselves from each other than they could from Hannah. Saul needed her more than he knew. Perhaps she needed him more than she had ever understood. Slowly she shook her head. 'No,' she said. 'No. Not now, not ever.'

Later that day Saul and Rowan left the baby with Barbara and took the tram up Shipley Glen, past the wooden cut-outs of nursery rhyme characters that Hannah might never recognise. They bought ice cream and wandered amidst the families and bored teenagers, watching a boy flying a scarlet kite high into the air. A thin mist obscured the sun.

Suddenly Rowan said, 'Poor Richard. Everything's gone wrong for him.'

Saul snorted. 'I find it difficult to feel all that sorry for him, actually. This might be the making of him, a bit of real struggle. And mark my words, in a few years' time he'll be a carbon copy of his father.'

'If that's my fault, I should die of shame,' said Rowan sc ly.

Yet the shame now was in feeling so terribly happy. Richard's face came back to her, white and stricken, and still here she was, holding Saul's thick hard fingers, awash with happiness. Regret tinged the edges of her vision. But if there was one thing she had learned from life it was the futility of looking back, wishing for yesterday. The lesson that Judge's had taught her was one Richard had to learn: you took what you had and made the best of it, and if you were lucky, if you were brave, the best was very good indeed.

'Do you love me, Rowan?'

She looked at him. Some of his tan was returning but his eyes held none of the laughter she loved. She put her hands up and touched his cheeks.

'With all my heart,' she said softly.

And suddenly the sun came out. Saul caught her wrist and started to run, they sprinted hectically across the rocks and rough ground. When at last they stopped and fell gasping on to the grass they looked up and saw the kite, soaring higher and higher into the brilliant summer air.

Sally sat in the plane, watching England pass beneath her. She was going to Pakistan, for a visit that might extend to years. The green expanse of Yorkshire, dotted here and there with the darker bulk of cities, set down amidst the harsh northern moors, was lost in the billows of cloud. Her whole life had been lived there, everything of concern to her had happened in that wide space. How she loved it.

Her mind drifted on, to the frightening days ahead. Yet she was safe, wrapped up in the life of her husband and his family. She was changing, becoming reconciled, acknowledging that she would pay for what she needed with her freedom. She was coming to know happiness.

Below the spread wings of the aircraft, beneath the cloud, the mills clattered on. James lay on the sofa at Aspley Manor, weak and drained. Richard, his son, struggled with the shattered remnants of Bardsey's, while across the valley Saul and Rowan rearranged their lives.

And in a small neat flat, full of silk and strange objects, a Chinese girl laboured with great difficulty. After hours of torment, almost too much for her small body, at last she gave birth. It was a daughter.

Appendices and Index

Table of Cases

The principal cases are in bold type. Cases cited or discussed in the text are in roman type. References are to pages. Cases cited in principal cases and within other quoted materials are not included.

CASES AND MATERIALS ON
CONSTITUTIONAL LAW
THEMES FOR THE CONSTITUTION'S THIRD CENTURY

Fourth Edition

*

Chapter 1

A PROLOGUE ON
CONSTITUTIONAL HISTORY

Like most legal textbooks, this book primarily uses the case method, which means that much of your time in this course will be devoted to the intensive analysis of particular cases. Individual cases cannot be understood, however, without a knowledge of the broader context of American constitutional law. Some students come to this course having already studied the history of the Supreme Court and theories of judicial review. For others, these topics are new. This chapter is designed as a refresher for the first group of students, and a quick introduction for the second.[a]

Additionally, we will emphasize some of the themes of American history that are particularly relevant to the evolution of our constitutionalism. There is a descriptive thesis lurking in this history. Constitutional law has been responsive to larger changes in American society, especially (1) the development of a national market and a vigorous capitalism; (2) the rise of the modern administrative state; and (3) the great *social movements* that have swept through American history like tornadoes across the prairie. A social movement is a normative mass movement: its leaders galvanize large numbers of citizens in support of an idea or ideology.[b] Among the movements that have shaped American constitutional law are the Revolutionary generation that secured our independence and drafted our first constitutions; the abolitionist movement that triumphed in the Civil War, as well as the white supremacy movement that swallowed Reconstruction; the labor movement and its law-and-order backlash; the civil rights and other nationalizing movements of the twentieth century; the movement to abolish the death penalty; the pro-choice as well as pro-life movements arrayed around the abortion issue; and the women's and gay rights

---

a. This chapter is largely drawn from Daniel Farber & Suzanna Sherry, *A History of the American Constitution* (1990), and William Eskridge, Jr., *Some Effects of Identity-Based Social Movements on Constitutional Law in the Twentieth Century*, 100 Mich. L. Rev. 2062 (2002). Useful background materials on many of the cases discussed in this chapter can be found in Louis Fisher & Neal Devins, *Political Dynamics of Constitutional Law* (2d ed. 1996).

b. For an important introduction to the interconnection of social movement theory and the evolution of public law, see *Symposium: Social Movements and Law Reform*, 150 U. Pa. L. Rev. 1-525 (2001).

movements, whose contests with a traditional family values countermovement closed the century.

One way to understand constitutional doctrine is that, in the medium and long term, it has largely reflected the Supreme Court's institutional response to various economic, intellectual, and social movements. Economically, we have seen the industrialization and urbanization, and later suburbanization, of the United States. Intellectually, the dominant trend has been toward modernization: policies once justified on grounds of religious or status categories must be re-evaluated on the basis of science or individual merit. Nonetheless, individual Justices have affected doctrine in important ways not predetermined by such larger historical forces, and so we also include some biographical information about the most noteworthy Justices.[c] We hope that, besides providing a little "human interest," this biographical information will give you a richer perspective on the Court's history.

The Constitution must first be understood as a document, but a text-based understanding of the document will not answer most current issues of constitutional law. Consider the following six simple but important problems. For each problem identify the potentially relevant constitutional provisions and speculate about the correct interpretation of them given the circumstances. Consider first how each claim would be decided under the main body of the Constitution. Then look for relevant amendments.

1. Plaintiff, an African-American child, brings suit contending that a state statute requiring racial segregation of the public school she attends is unconstitutional. (Does the Constitution provide that the Supreme Court will have the authority to declare the requirement of state law unenforceable on the ground that it is inconsistent with the Constitution?)

2. Plaintiff, an African-American child living in the District of Columbia, brings suit contending that the federal statute requiring the racial segregation of the public school she attends is unconstitutional. (Hint: this will have to involve a different constitutional provision from the first question.)

3. Congress enacts a statute creating the United States Bank, which lends funds to state-chartered banks and controls the money supply. The same statute authorizes the Bank to sue the states in federal court for damages or injunctive relief.

4. Congress passes a statute making it a federal crime to criticize a member of Congress. A state legislature passes a statute making it a state crime to criticize a member of the state legislature.

5. After a major terrorist incident in the United States, the President believes the people involved are nationals of the state of Badnikstan and directs the

---

c. In an appendix at the end of this chapter, we provide short descriptions of all of the Justices who have sat on the Court in the past thirty years. Our primary source, for pre-Reagan appointees, is Congressional Quarterly's *Guide to the U.S. Supreme Court* (1979), which contains biographical sketches of the first 100 Justices. Extremely useful for the period before 1969 is *The Justices of the United States Supreme Court, 1789-1969* (Leon Friedman & Fred Israel eds., 1978) (4 vols.).

Secretary of the Treasury to freeze the monetary assets within the jurisdiction of the United States of all persons who are nationals of Badnikstan or who are descended from nationals from Badnikstan.

6. The Department of Justice detains an American citizen whose parents are from Badnikstan but does not charge that citizen with a crime; she brings a habeas corpus lawsuit challenging her detention as unconstitutional. By executive order, the President suspends the writ of habeas corpus.

Jot down your answers in the margin, and return to them as you consider the following mini-history of constitutional law.

SECTION 1. THE FOUNDING GENERATION:
THE CONSTITUTION AND THE BILL OF RIGHTS, 1787-1791

The first great social and political movement in American history was the generational movement of young colonial men who led the American Revolution against British rule, wrote and implemented our nation's first constitution, and then threw over that plan for a new one that remains one of the foundational documents in modern political theory. The generation of George Washington, James Madison, Alexander Hamilton, Thomas Jefferson, John Adams, and John Marshall was the most important in our legal history.[a]

The nation's first constitution, the Articles of Confederation, was adopted in 1778, during the Revolution. The Articles established a unicameral Congress in which each state had one vote. Congress had the authority to manage foreign relations, but needed the consent of the states to obtain revenues and regulate interstate commerce. This weak confederation left the national government unable to respond to the urgent needs of the country in foreign affairs and domestic economic policy, and demands for reform led in 1787 to a "Constitutional Convention" of representatives from each of the states in Philadelphia. What began as a discussion about how to reform the Articles became an effort to draft an entirely new constitutional structure. The Constitution drafted that summer in Philadelphia was submitted to state conventions for ratification, and by 1788 the required nine states had ratified the Constitution. In 1791, the first ten amendments to the Constitution (the "Bill of Rights") were ratified by the states. This period, from 1787 to 1791, is the foundational period in our constitutional history.

1. *Intellectual Background.* The leaders of the American Revolution and the Framers of the Constitution drew on a wide variety of sources, including classical writers, eighteenth century Enlightenment thinkers, and a variety of English political theorists.[b] As to the English theorists, the Framers drew upon two traditions. One was the "social contract" tradition of Thomas Hobbes and John Locke. This tradition assumed that people are rational beings who seek to maximize their prosperity and happiness. Unfortunately, when a number of

---

a. See, e.g., Joseph Ellis, *Founding Brothers: The Revolutionary Generation* (2000).

b. See Bernard Bailyn, *The Ideological Origins of the American Revolution* (1967); Gordon Wood, *The Creation of the American Republic: 1776-1787* (1969).

such people live in the same society, they tend to invade each others' prosperity and happiness in pursuing their own. This brutish "state of nature" was an impediment to the prosperity and happiness of all, and to avoid it people agreed to form governments. The purpose of such consensual governments was to prevent people from infringing upon the interests of others. The danger of such governments was that the state would become the infringer rather than the protector of individual liberty.

This "liberal," contractarian tradition is the one most people associate with the founding period. Recent accounts of eighteenth century thought, however, stress another, less well-known intellectual tradition, the "republican" tradition.[c] While rooted in Italian Renaissance political theory, republicanism was accessible to the colonists through the teachings of the seventeenth century Opposition party in England. James Harrington and others were appalled by the Crown's use of political patronage to expand executive power. These Opposition thinkers decried the destruction of the old order, the rise of corruption, and the loss of civic virtue. Ultimately, they argued, the fate of the republic rested on the renewed willingness of individuals to sacrifice their private interests for the sake of the common good.

Before the Revolution, most Americans were confident of the virtue of the people and satisfied that it provided a sufficient basis for democratic government. Hence, the Articles of Confederation left virtually all governance to local assemblies and popular collective action. The disadvantages of localism became apparent in the 1780s, when local uprisings disrupted public order, the states refused to cooperate in contributing money and consent for needed national ventures, and some states became rife with factions motivated by self-interest rather than the common good. As a result of this experience, many early Americans lost faith in public virtue as a sufficient basis for government, and they found contractarian theories of government more pertinent to the needs of the country. The republican influence remained strong, however, particularly among the Anti-Federalists who opposed the new Constitution, but also to some degree among Federalists such as James Madison.

2. *Drafting the Constitution (1787)*. The Constitutional Convention assembled in 1787 with a mandate to recommend revisions to the Articles of Confederation. Instead, it ultimately proposed an entirely new constitutional structure with three distinctive features: (1) an assumption of *popular sovereignty*, whereby political power rested in "We The People" and not in any governmental organ, like Parliament or even the states that formed the union; (2) a *federalist* layer-cake arrangement for the exercise of authority, whereby states retained their regulatory powers and governmental autonomy even as a new national government was vested with broad powers and assured supremacy over state laws; (3) a *separation of powers* within the national government, whereby each of three departments (legislative, executive, judicial) was vested with specialized duties and was expected to check the abuses of the other

---

c. For an excellent summary of the historical literature, see Suzanna Sherry, *The Intellectual Origins of the Constitution: A Lawyers' Guide to the Historical Scholarship*, 5 Const. Comm. 323 (1988).

departments. Notably missing in the document was an extensive array of individual rights directly protected against infringement by state or national governments. The process by which the Framers came up with the details of this structure was driven by pragmatic negotiations about protecting personal liberty and local autonomy while simultaneously creating an "energetic" national government.[d]

The main question before the Convention was how much to strengthen the federal government. The debates were initially focused on Edmund Randolph's "Virginia Plan," which was strongly nationalist. It gave Congress the power to veto state laws and to legislate "in all cases to which the separate States are incompetent, or in which the harmony of the United States may be interrupted by the exercise of individual Legislation." Anti-nationalists, mostly representing the smaller states, countered with the "New Jersey Plan," which merely augmented the minimal powers of the Congress and added a weak executive. Although the New Jersey Plan was rejected, the delegates remained sharply divided about issues of state prerogatives. Ultimately, the deadlock over states' rights was broken with the "Great Compromise" giving the states equal votes in the Senate but requiring popular representation in the House.

There was relatively little discussion of the specific powers of Congress. Initially, the delegates agreed to give Congress a veto over state laws (as Madison strongly urged), but the provision was rejected after reconsideration. The specific list of congressional powers now found in Article I was written late in the Convention by the Committee on Detail, and there was only brief discussion of the Commerce Clause or other grants of power. See Chapter 7, § 1, for discussion of the Convention's evolving description of national legislative authority.

The other two branches of the federal government received less attention than the legislature. There was lengthy but largely inconclusive debate about the executive branch, with seemingly endless discussions of whether there should be one chief executive or more, how the executive should be chosen, how long the term should be, whether reelection should be allowed, and so on. As soon as one issue seemed resolved, the debate on another issue would prompt delegates to rethink their positions again. The final upshot was the unitary executive established in Article II. As with Congress, there was much discussion about the structure of the office, but little about its specific powers.

The delegates early on agreed to create a Supreme Court whose members would be appointed for life (subject to impeachment) but disagreed as to whether there should be "inferior" federal courts and what matters federal courts should be empowered to adjudicate. Delegates fearing that federal courts would

---

d. See Jack Rakove, *Original Meanings: Politics and Ideas in the Making of the Constitution* (1996); Wood, *Creation*. See also Julius Goebel, Jr., *Antecedents and Beginnings to 1801* (1971) (vol. 1 of the Oliver Wendell Holmes Devise History of the Supreme Court of the United States); Charles Warren, *The Making of the Constitution* (1928). Most of the contemporary notes of the Convention's proceedings are found in *The Records of the Federal Convention of 1787* (Max Farrand ed., rev. ed. 1987) (4 vols.).

invade state prerogatives proposed tightly limited bases for federal court jurisdiction (cases involving admiralty, foreign interests, trade laws). In a series of compromises, the Convention created the expansive heads now found in Article III, § 1, as well as Article VI's Supremacy Clause, but gave Congress discretion as to the establishment and jurisdiction of "inferior" federal courts and some control over the appellate jurisdiction of the U.S. Supreme Court. The delegates were firm as to the matter of judicial independence (life tenure and no salary diminishment) for all federal judges.

A contentious issue that has remained relevant for subsequent constitutional scholarship was James Madison's proposal that a Council of Revision, consisting of the chief executive and several judges, should have the power to veto congressional legislation, subject to a super-majority override. This proposal surfaced on several occasions but was defeated every time it came to a vote. Six arguments were raised against it: (1) judges' power to expound the laws and determine their constitutionality provided them with a sufficient check against the worst laws; (2) prior involvement in legislation weakens the capacity of judges to decide cases later on; (3) judges have no special expertise as regards policy matters; (4) the Council would improperly mix different powers; (5) judicial participation would weaken the accountability of the executive for vetoing measures and would drain the judiciary of its legitimacy; and (6) the security of popular measures belongs to the political branches.[e]

Although the word never appears in the document, slavery was an important source of dissension at the Convention. The slave states feared that both the slave trade and the "peculiar institution" itself might be threatened by a strong national government. They were also concerned about the issue of fugitive slaves. Yet another question was how to count slaves for purposes of allocating representatives; the compromise solution was the infamous "three-fifths" rule, which was also applied to certain taxes. As to this latter issue, Gouverneur Morris gave an impassioned and prophetic speech, as reported in Madison's convention notes:

> Mr. Govr. Morris moved to insert "free" before the word inhabitants. Much he said would depend on this point. He never would concur in upholding domestic slavery. It was a nefarious institution. It was the curse of heaven on the States where it prevailed. * * * Upon what principle is it that slaves shall be computed in the representation? Are they men? Then make them Citizens and let them vote. Are they property? Why then is no other property included? * * * The admission of slaves into the Representation when fairly explained comes to this: that the inhabitant of Georgia and S.C. who goes to the Coast of Africa, and in defiance of the most sacred laws of humanity tears away his fellow creatures from their dearest connections & damns them to the most cruel bondages, shall have more votes in a Govt. instituted for the protection of the rights of mankind, than the Citizen of Pa. or N. Jersey who views with a laudable horror, so nefarious a practice.

Morris's views did not carry the day. The Constitution included the three-fifths rule and two other provisions that assumed the continuing viability of and even buttressed the institution of slavery but left the issue open for future legislation;

---

e. See Rakove, *Original Meanings* 156-60; James Barry III, Comment, *The Council of Revision and the Limits of Judicial Power*, 56 U. Chi. L. Rev. 235 (1989).

this Sectional Compromise may have been just as important in securing general agreement to the Constitution as the Great Compromise that created the House and Senate as complementary bodies.[f]

3. *The Constitution's Ratification Debates (1787-89).* A distinctive feature of the Constitution was its internal requirement that it be ratified by popular conventions in nine states before it would become operative (Article VII). This procedural feature reflected a substantive theory of popular sovereignty.[g] Starting with Delaware and Pennsylvania, each state assembled a popularly chosen convention which debated (and ratified) the Constitution. Thus, there was no single national debate, but rather a series of local debates about the wisdom of adopting the document.[h] Because the document proposed by those assembled at Philadelphia represented a "consolidation" of power in a central government, too closely akin to the kind of centralized authority that the American Revolution and the Declaration of Independence denounced, opposition to the Constitution was fierce, and there was considerable doubt that the plan would be ratified by the requisite number of states.

The Anti-Federalists' primary objection to the Constitution was that its vesting the national government with so much power threatened both individual liberty and the flourishing of state and local republican governance. The Federalist defenders maintained that broad national authority was needed for the energetic governance lacking under the Articles of Confederation and that the Constitution contained enough internal checks and balances to prevent the national government from becoming oppressive. Thus, Congress (the chief organ to be feared) was unlikely to usurp excessive power because of the internal checks of bicameral approval of legislation and presentment of it to the President for approval (Article I, § 7) and the likelihood that the other branches of the national government (Articles II-III) and state governments (federalism) would thwart usurpative congressional enactments with the ample weapons at their disposal.

The most celebrated Federalist arguments were those published in newspapers by Madison and Hamilton in connection with New York's ratification.

---

f. Article I, § 2, cl. 3 defined a slave as three-fifths of a free person for purposes of political representation and taxation. Article I, § 9, cl. 1 prevented any legislative interference with the slave trade until 1808. Article IV, § 2, cl. 3 required the return of fugitive slaves to their masters.

g. Under the Westminster Model of the United Kingdom (against which we had revolted), not only was Parliament *supreme* as against the judiciary and the Crown, but Parliament was *sovereign.* Our Framers modified the idea of legislative supremacy in their separation of powers thinking but decisively rejected the idea of legislative sovereignty. "We The People" are sovereign, not Congress. See generally Martin Flaherty, Note, *The Empire Strikes Back:* Annesley v. Sherlock *and the Triumph of Imperial Parliamentary Sovereignty*, 87 Colum. L. Rev. 593 (1987).

h. For the state-by-state ratification process, see Goebel, *Antecedents* 292-412; Rakove, *Original Meanings* 94-130. See also Larry Kramer, *Madison's Audience*, 112 Harv. L. Rev. 611 (1999). Primary sources are reprinted in *The Documentary History of the Ratification of the Constitution* (John Kaminski & Gaspare Saladino eds.) (multi-volumes, still in progress); *The Debate on the Constitution: Federalist and Antifederalist Speeches, Articles, and Letters During the Struggle Over Ratification* (Bernard Bailyn ed., 1993) (2 vols.).

Their articles (and a few by John Jay) are collectively known as *The Federalist Papers*, some of which we have excerpted in Appendix 2 of this book. The clash of ideas is best captured in *Federalist* No. 10, written by Madison. Inspired by the republican tradition, the Anti-Federalists had argued against a strong central government, on the ground that local government, closer to the people, best fostered public virtue. Madison's response was complex. He denied that small group politics can eliminate the "vices" of faction, whose "latent causes are thus sown in the nature of man." This resonates of Hobbes and Locke. But Madison also invoked the republican concern that government may become nothing more than factional struggle delinked from the common good. The remedy for this concern, Madison argued, was not the faction-ridden localized government of the Articles of Confederation, but instead the large-scale representative national government of the Constitution. To get the full flavor of Madison's argument, read the excerpt of *Federalist* No. 10 found in Appendix 2.

Federalist Nos. 51 by Madison and 78 by Hamilton, both excerpted in Appendix 2, are also important analyses of the Constitution's structural benefits. Number 78 not only provides an influential account of the role of judicial review, but defends the independent judiciary against charges that judges would thwart the will of the people. (It also provides the Framers' most articulate theory of statutory interpretation.) Like Madison in No. 10, Hamilton in No. 78 maintained that the will of temporary majorities should sometimes be thwarted — and added the further point that the risks of life-tenured judges invading the prerogatives of Congress or the states were greatly overstated by opponents.

4. *The Constitution Ratified and the Bill of Rights as Part of the Deal (1789-91).* Another point of controversy in the ratification debates was the Constitution's failure to guarantee a specific bill of individual rights. Federalists argued that a bill of rights was unnecessary (because the federal government had only limited powers) and potentially harmful (because it would preclude whatever rights were left off the specific list). But these arguments were not fully persuasive. New York and Virginia (the tenth and eleventh states to ratify) called for a bill of rights in their ratification resolutions. So the Federalists agreed to a bill of rights as part of the ratification "deal." The Federalists in the first Congress immediately moved to implement the bargain, as Madison introduced a series of constitutional amendments. Most of these were accepted by Congress, with some modifications.[i]

Madison's speech introducing the amendments (Appendix 3 of this book) gives an important view of his perspective on individual rights. He rejected the

---

i. For detailed background materials on the individual amendments, see *The Complete Bill of Rights: The Drafts, Debates, Sources and Origins* (Neil Cogan ed. 1997). The First Amendment has received much historical attention. Compare Leonard Levy, *Freedom of Speech and Press in Early American History: Legacy of Suppression* (1960) (narrow view of the First Amendment's protections), with David Anderson, *The Origins of the Press Clause*, 30 UCLA L. Rev. 455 (1983) (vigorously disputing Levy's reading of the eighteenth century evidence), and David Rabban, *The Ahistorical Historian: Leonard Levy on Freedom of Expression in Early American History*, 37 Stan. L. Rev. 795 (1985) (highly critical review of the 1985 revised edition of Levy's book).

Federalist argument that a bill of rights was unnecessary because the federal government had only limited powers: "It is true, the powers of the General Government are circumscribed, they are directed to particular objects, but even if Government keeps within those limits, it has certain discretionary powers with respect to the means, which may admit of abuse to a certain extent, in the same manner as the powers of the State governments under their constitutions * * *." Madison also argued that a bill of rights would serve important purposes:

> If [guarantees of individual rights] are incorporated in the Constitution, independent tribunals of justice will consider themselves in a peculiar manner the guardians of those rights; they will be an impenetrable bulwark against every assumption of power in the Legislative or Executive; they will be naturally led to resist every encroachment upon rights expressly stipulated for in the Constitution by the declaration of rights. Besides this security, there is a great probability that such a declaration in the federal system would be enforced; because the State Legislatures will jealously and closely watch the operations of this Government, and be able to resist with more effect every assumption of power, than any other power on earth can do; and the greatest opponents to a Federal Government admit the State Legislatures to be sure guardians of the people's liberty.

Madison was actually less sanguine about state governments than this passage might suggest; earlier in the speech, he had spoken about the need to protect individuals not just from the national legislature, but also from "the abuse of the community."

The Bill of Rights, quickly ratified in 1791, consists of the first ten amendments to the Constitution. These amendments were expected to limit only the national government's exercise of power. Madison's original proposal provided that "[n]o State shall infringe the equal rights of conscience, nor the freedom of speech, or of the press, nor of the right of trial by jury in criminal cases." This restriction on the states was rejected, however.

5. *Historians and the Founding Period.* Historians have actively discussed this important period, the formal beginning of our constitutional tradition. Initially, "whiggish" historians treated the period simply as a high-minded and brilliant period of creative political structuring. Challenging this vision, Charles Beard's *An Economic Interpretation of the Constitution of the United States* (1913) argued that the drafters and boosters of the Constitution tended to be moneyed interests alarmed by the instability and redistributions fostered by decentralized government. Beard suggested that the Constitution was itself a result of the very "factional" capture that Madison had warned against in *Federalist* No. 10. A less cynical view of Beard's thesis would be that the Constitution was responsive to the needs of the aborning capitalist economy for stable expectations, especially as to contractual and property arrangements, and for a powerful central government that could protect American shipping and merchant interests against foreign attacks.

Over the years, historians have come to reject the specific Beard thesis, and to acknowledge that support or opposition to the Constitution cut across class and professional lines.[j] To the limited extent that one can differentiate Federalists from Anti-Federalists, the former tended to be "Young Turks" seeking to instill an energetic, forward-looking vision of polity in a strong national government, while the latter tended to be older, more cautious, and less active in national affairs.[k] It is this later scholarship that inspires our understanding of the Founding Period as the culmination of a normative social movement of like-minded revolutionaries. If it is true that the Founding Generation was united more by ideology than by economic interests, it is even more apparent that its members splintered badly in the 1790s, and more tragic that their divisions seem linked to economic disputes and mundane political interests.

6. *Early Constitutional Debates within Congress, the Presidency, and the States (1790-1801).* The great debates of the Constitution's first decade were carried out more often within the Washington Administration, Congress, and the states than in the Supreme Courts headed by Chief Justices John Jay (1789-95) and Oliver Ellsworth (1796-1800). The most famous example was the *Decision of 1789.*[l] An initial draft of the bill creating the Department of Foreign Affairs posited that the secretary would be removable by the President, without the advice and consent of the Senate. An objection was raised that this language might be read to suggest that the President did not *already* have that authority under Article II, and the language was removed from that bill and was revoked from other department-establishing statutes. Although the exact motivations of different representatives was quite heterogeneous, this series of votes was interpreted at the time and afterwards as a congressional acceptance of the President's removal power for executive department officers.

Consider another, and very different, issue. On February 12, 1790, Ben Franklin and other Pennsylvania abolitionists laid before the House of Representatives a petition for Congress to discourage the slave trade and promote the abolition of slavery. This petition provoked a great debate in the House, with southerners objecting that the preservation of slavery as well as the slave trade was part of the original deal that created the Union, and northerners claiming that the ownership and trade in human beings was deeply inconsistent with the Declaration of Independence and the premises of the Constitution (Ellis 81-119). Although Madison hijacked the abolitionist proposal and turned it into

---

j. See, e.g., Robert Brown, *Charles Beard and the Constitution* (1956) (delegate-by-delegate analysis of the economic interests of those at the Convention shows no correlation between support for strong central government and class interests); Forrest McDonald, *We the People: The Economic Origins of the Constitution* 38-92 (1958) (no fundamental antagonism between personalty and realty interests at Convention, contrary to Beard); *The Reinterpretation of the American Revolution 1763-1789* (J. Greene ed. 1968) (collection of essays attacking Beard thesis).

k. See Stanley Elkins & Eric McKitrick, *The Founding Fathers: Young Men of the Revolution,* 76 Pol. Sci. Q. 181 (1961); Cecelia Kenyon, *Men of Little Faith: The Anti-Federalists on the Nature of Representative Government,* 12 Wm. & Mary Q. (3d Ser.) 3 (1955).

l. The Decision of 1789 is discussed in James Hart, *The American Presidency in Action, 1789: A Study in Constitutional History* (1948). See also Steven Calabresi & Christopher Yoo, *The Unitary Executive: Presidential Power from Washington to Bush* (2008).

a House vote in favor of congressional noninterference in the constitutional status quo, it marked the fact that an issue largely submerged during ratification would haunt the American republic for its entire constitutional history.

For another example from the (very busy) first Congress, the House and Senate passed legislation creating a national bank. When the bill arrived on President Washington's desk for signature into law, the President put to his cabinet the question whether Congress had Article I authority to establish a bank.[m] Reflecting a localist and farmer perspective, Secretary of State Thomas Jefferson opined that Congress did not have this authority, because it was not among those specifically enumerated in Article I. Reflecting a pro-capitalist and nationalist agenda, Secretary of Treasury Alexander Hamilton opined that Congress had such authority under the Necessary and Proper Clause of Article I, § 8. The President went with Hamilton and signed into law the bill creating the first United States Bank. This was an important constitutional precedent for the broad powers of Congress to create institutions for the fostering and managing of the emerging capitalist economy.

In 1798, Congress debated and enacted the Adams' Administration proposal of a Sedition Act making it illegal to publish "any false, scandalous and malicious writing or writings against the government" or its officers — or "to excite against them . . . the hatred of the good people of the United States, or to stir up sedition within the United States." In this case, the constitutional debates did not end in Washington. The legislatures of Kentucky and Virginia immediately adopted Resolutions (drafted by Jefferson and Madison, respectively) asserting that the Sedition Act was unconstitutional for a couple of reasons: The federal government had been delegated no authority (in Article I or elsewhere in the Constitution) to regulate private speech or publication, and so the law was outside of Congress's authority; even if within the jurisdiction of Congress to adopt, the Sedition Act was void because inconsistent with the prohibitions of the First Amendment. Additionally, the Kentucky and Virginia Resolutions of 1798 asserted both that each state party to the "compact" of union retained all sovereign powers not granted to the national government *and* that each state "has an equal right to judge for itself" as to whether acts of the national government went beyond the constitutional authorizations. In response, North Carolina adopted a Resolution agreeing that the Act was unconstitutional but denying that individual states could nullify a federal law. Rhode Island adopted a Resolution maintaining that Article III courts had the exclusive and ultimate authority to pass on the constitutionality of the law. (In prosecutions for violations of the law, inferior federal courts, created by the Judiciary Act of 1789, generally ruled that the Sedition Act was constitutional.)

---

m. See David McGowan, *Ethos in Law and History: Alexander Hamilton,* The Federalist, *and the Supreme Court*, 85 Minn. L. Rev. 755 (2001) (account and analysis of the bank debate).

SECTION 2. THE MARSHALL COURT'S
NATIONALIST VISION, 1801-1835

The Constitution's text changed very little between the adoption of the Bill of Rights (amendments one through ten) and of the Reconstruction Amendments (numbers thirteen through fifteen).[a] But the Constitution itself developed quite substantially under the guidance of its greatest Chief Justice, John Marshall of Virginia. We view Marshall's constitutional jurisprudence as a highly sophisticated continuation of the nationalizing work of the Founding Generation, especially as interpreted by Hamilton.[b]

For one who so much shaped American constitutional law, it is striking how accidental was this Chief Justice's appointment. John Marshall was President Adams' Secretary of State when Adams and his followers were swept out of office in the 1800 election by Thomas Jefferson and the Democrat-Republicans. Chief Justice Oliver Ellsworth resigned in December 1800. Adams first offered the job to John Jay, the neglected third author of *The Federalist Papers*, the first Chief Justice of the United States (1789-95), and Governor of New York. Jay turned the job down, citing the hardships of riding circuit. Marshall and others pushed the President to elevate Associate Justice William Paterson to be Chief, but Adams chose Marshall instead, partly to avoid naming a replacement for Paterson. Marshall, the oldest of fifteen children, was born in a log cabin on what was then the Virginia frontier. His formal legal training was limited to a year of study under George Wythe at William and Mary, but he was the most celebrated advocate of his era in Virginia. He was a star participant in the state ratification debate. After serving briefly as a diplomat and in the House, he was appointed as Secretary of State, and effectively ran the government while Adams was on vacation in 1799.

Marshall's appointment as Chief Justice was part of the Federalists' general strategy to extend their influence beyond 1801 through control of the judicial branch. Thus in 1801, before the Jefferson Republicans took over, the Federalists increased the number of judges and hurriedly appointed Federalists

---

a. The Eleventh Amendment, preventing states from being sued by various litigants, was an immediate reaction to the Supreme Court's decision allowing such suits in *Chisholm v. Georgia*, 2 U.S. (2 Dall.) 419 (1793). The presidential election of 1800 generated the Twelfth Amendment, which revamped the electoral college system of electing the President and Vice President. In the election, Thomas Jefferson and Aaron Burr received the same number of votes for President, sending the election into the House of Representatives. There, Burr fought for the office, even though everyone knew that he was the Democrat-Republicans' nominee for Vice President, and that Jefferson was the intended presidential candidate. Alexander Hamilton, Jefferson's rival in President Washington's cabinet, ensured the election of Jefferson because he thought Burr a scoundrel. In any event, the Twelfth Amendment prevents any similar embarrassment by separating the electoral college votes for the two offices. (Burr was, by the way, a scoundrel. But he had a good eye, and he killed Hamilton in a duel over their political and personal differences.)

b. On Marshall's life and public service, the best source is still Albert Beveridge, *The Life of John Marshall* (1919) (4 vols.). On his transformation of the Court, see G. Edward White, *The Marshall Court and Cultural Change, 1815-35* (1988) (vols. 3-4 of the Oliver Wendell Holmes Devise History of the Supreme Court of the United States).

to those positions. Some judges were appointed just before midnight on March 3, the last day of the Adams Administration. Although Marshall himself had been appointed Chief Justice, he stayed up with Adams, in his capacity as Secretary of State, to sign the commissions. These judicial commissions were hurriedly signed, sealed, and delivered, but in the rush, a few commissions for these and other last-minute appointments remained undelivered when Jefferson took office on March 4. President Jefferson and his new Secretary of State, James Madison, refused to deliver the remaining commissions.[c] Some of the disappointed appointees, including one William Marbury (named as a District of Columbia justice of the peace), sued Madison in the Supreme Court for delivery of his commission.

The 1803 decision in *Marbury v. Madison*, 5 U.S. (1 Cranch) 137 (Chapter 2, § 2A), was Chief Justice Marshall's first important opinion, in which he all at once (1) criticized the new Administration, (2) averted a constitutional crisis, and (3) added a permanent fixture to our constitutional system — namely, judicial review. Marshall declared that Marbury was entitled to his commission, but that bringing suit in the Supreme Court was not a constitutionally authorized way of obtaining it. He thus chastised Jefferson and Madison while still avoiding issuance of an order that probably would have been ignored. *Marbury* is the first Supreme Court opinion explicitly asserting the power of judicial review, the power to strike down federal statutes that violate the Constitution.[d] Its larger importance was in setting forth, in a dramatic setting, high aspirations for the rule of law in the new nation: although slippery in its reasoning, the Chief Justice's opinion insisted that everyone — including the Jefferson Administration and the Marshall Court — was bound by the legal rules set forth in statutes and the Constitution, and suggested that those rules would be deployed in a predictable way by strictly impartial federal judges.

Marshall realized that a *national* rule of law brooked no dissent from the states and their courts (contrary to the Kentucky and Virginia Resolutions). A corollary was the authority of the national judiciary to review *state* statutes and other official action. Again, a complicated procedural tangle led to a significant Supreme Court case. This time, the dispute was over land. Lord Fairfax willed some of his vast northern Virginia land holdings to another British citizen, and the property ultimately devolved to an American, Thomas Martin. The state of

---

c. This was the least of their defiant actions. The House voted to impeach Federalist Judge John Pickering and Justice Samuel Chase; the Senate removed Pickering from office but acquitted Chase. More provocatively, Congress abolished the new Article III judges created during the Adams Administration, a move that generated tremendous constitutional debate within Congress. The Marshall Court upheld the abolition against an Article III challenge in *Stuart v. Laird*, 5 U.S. (1 Cranch) 299 (1803).

d. The statute struck down in *Marbury* was part of the Judiciary Act of 1789, interpreted as giving the Supreme Court original jurisdiction to issue mandamus orders against officials such as Madison. The opinion held that this jurisdiction went beyond that authorized by Article III of the Constitution and thus could not be utilized by the Court. For an exploration of the intellectual context of the decision, see Jack Rakove, *The Origins of Judicial Review: A Plea for New Contexts*, 49 Stan. L. Rev. 1031 (1997); William Michael Treanor, *Judicial Review Before* Marbury, 58 Stan. L. Rev. 455 (2005).

Virginia claimed that it owned the land, having confiscated it from Fairfax during the Revolution because he was a British loyalist. Virginia then granted the land to David Hunter, a Virginian. The Peace Treaty of 1783 and the Jay Treaty of 1794 both provided, however, that land owned by British citizens would no longer be confiscated. In its first ruling in the case, the Supreme Court held that Virginia's attempted confiscation violated the 1783 treaty.

The Virginia Supreme Court refused to follow the Supreme Court's ruling, and the Marshall Court responded in *Martin v. Hunter's Lessee*, 14 U.S. (1 Wheat.) 304 (1816). Justice Story wrote a highly nationalistic opinion for the Court, holding that it had the authority to review state court decisions and to determine whether state statutes violated federal law (including the federal Constitution, federal statutes, and treaties).[e] In a sweeping assertion of national and judicial power, *Martin* held that the national Constitution and laws trumped state laws and practice, and that the Supreme Court was the final arbiter over all levels of government. To similar effect was Chief Justice Marshall's opinion in *Cohens v. Virginia*, 19 U.S. (6 Wheat.) 264 (1821).

The Marshall Court rounded out its jurisprudence of activist nationalism in an opinion confirming Hamilton's arguments for a national bank. In 1816, Congress chartered the Second Bank of the United States. The Maryland legislature imposed a punitive tax on all banks not chartered by the state legislature itself. When the Baltimore branch of the Bank of the United States refused to pay the tax, Maryland sued the branch's cashier, James McCulloch. Chief Justice Marshall delivered the unanimous decision of the Court in *M'Culloch v. Maryland*, 17 U.S. (4 Wheat.) 316 (1819) (Chapter 7, § 1), upholding the validity of the Bank and invalidating the state tax as inconsistent with federal supremacy. His eloquent opinion opened with an assertion that — contrary to the Kentucky and Virginia Resolutions — it was the Supreme Court that must ultimately decide whether Congress' exercise of authority was consistent with the Constitution, lest such matters become the source of endless and not "peaceable" contest among the political branches. Echoing arguments for the bank made by Hamilton a generation earlier, Marshall relied on general legal principles, as well as the Necessary and Proper Clause, to find that the Constitution permitted Congress to exercise broad implied powers. In a phrase repeated in cases through today, he found few limits on congressional power:

> Let the end be legitimate, let it be within the scope of the constitution, and all means which are appropriate, which are plainly adapted to that end, which are not prohibited, but consist with the letter and spirit of the constitution, are constitutional.

---

e. Joseph Story was the greatest scholar on the early Court, the author of nine major treatises, including one on constitutional law! With misgivings about Story's ideology, President Madison appointed him to the Court only after two other candidates (one of them John Quincy Adams) declined the honor. Although appointed by a Republican, Story immediately became Marshall's staunch ally in constitutional cases and helped assure Marshall's continued dominance notwithstanding a string of Democrat-Republican Presidents.

Interpreting the Constitution any less expansively, he said, would turn the document into "a splendid bauble."[f] See also *Gibbons v. Ogden*, 22 U.S. (9 Wheat.) 1 (1824) (Chapter 7, § 2) (broad interpretation of Congress' power to regulate interstate commerce and to preempt the states' laws to achieve national goals).

Having established the supremacy of national authority over state authority and the breadth of the national authority of Congress and the Court, the remaining contribution of the Marshall Court was to announce specific constitutional limits on the power of the states. In *Barron v. Baltimore*, 32 U.S. (7 Pet.) 243 (1833), the Chief Justice ruled that the Bill of Rights placed no limitations on the states, though these amendments obviously remained limitations on the national power. The main specific limitation on the states was the Contracts Clause of Article I, §10. In *Dartmouth College v. Woodward*, 17 U.S. (4 Wheat.) 518 (1819), the Chief Justice's opinion for the Court held that the state of New Hampshire could not unilaterally alter the charter of Dartmouth College, whose case was ardently argued by its leading alumnus, Senator Daniel Webster. See also *Sturges v. Crowninshield*, 17 U.S. (4 Wheat.) 122 (1819) (state's retroactive insolvency law violated Contracts Clause and was therefore unenforceable).

In John Marshall, the Federalists found the ideal Justice to cement the nationalizing features of the Constitution, for the Virginian was intelligently loyal to Federalist principles, without taking unnecessary risks with the Court's fragile political capital. In carrying out his agenda, Marshall revealed a brilliant and deeply learned legal mind, mustering unanimous Courts in most of the constitutional cases and writing most of the decisions himself. And, not least, he was long-lived. Marshall outlived all of his contemporary adversaries, including his enemy Jefferson, and was determined to outlive populist President Andrew Jackson as well. Only in this last aspiration did the Chief Justice fail. He stubbornly refused to resign, notwithstanding failing health, and in 1835 became the first Chief Justice to die in office. While it was being tolled on the occasion of his death, the Liberty Bell cracked. (Can you beat that for symbolism?)

---

f. Marshall's "great ends justify expansive means" reasoning had precedent in the actions of his supposed states' rights enemies, Jefferson and Madison, the authors of the Kentucky and Virginia Resolutions. As President in 1816, Madison had cast aside his earlier constitutional difficulties with the Bank and proposed the legislation creating it, because of the nation's fiscal needs. As President in 1803, Jefferson had purchased the Louisiana Territory from France without a congressional authorization or budgetary allocation. Agreeing that he had exceeded his lawful authority, Jefferson defended his actions in 1810: "A strict observance of the written law is doubtless one of the high duties of a good citizen but it is not the highest. The laws of necessity, of self-preservation, of saving our country when in danger, are of higher obligation." Gerald Stourzh, *Alexander Hamilton and the Idea of a Republican Government* 34 (1970) (quoting Jefferson). Acquiring the Louisiana Territory was neither necessary to preserve the nation nor essential to save it from "danger."

SECTION 3. STATES' RIGHTS, SLAVERY, AND THE TANEY COURT, 1836-1864

The United States underwent a number of major changes in the first half of the nineteenth century: dramatic expansion of the franchise to most adult white males; tremendous geographic expansion and economic growth; and a fervent movement to abolish slavery, which in turn stimulated the South to a more intense defense of that institution.[a] All these developments had important consequences for constitutional law under Chief Justice Marshall's successor, Roger Taney of Maryland. The prevailing constitutional philosophy of Taney's period was *instrumentalist* and *pragmatic*, supporting laws and doctrines that fostered economic development and national unity. Challenging that dominant jurisprudence was the *natural rights* philosophy of the abolitionists, who maintained that all human beings enjoy certain inalienable rights and that the state owes every citizen equal treatment under law.[b] The interplay of these two belief systems set the conceptual stage for the Civil War.

Like President Adams in 1801, President Jackson in 1835 drew his nominee for Chief Justice from his cabinet, Attorney General Roger Taney. As Attorney General, Taney did the heavy lifting in Jackson's campaign against the Bank of the United States. When the Secretary of the Treasury refused to pull federal funds out of the Bank, he was fired, and Taney stepped into his shoes to carry out the order. In 1835, Jackson tried to appoint him to the Court but was unable to get Senate approval. Less than a year later, Jackson sent his name up again as a replacement to Marshall. A brilliant lawyer (like his predecessor), Taney was in some respects a distinguished Chief Justice, but his reputation is fatally tainted by the *Dred Scott* decision (discussed below).

Although Taney supported state autonomy, his Court did not so much curtail federal power as encourage the states to exercise their own police powers vigorously to ensure economic flourishing. For example, in *Proprietors of Charles River Bridge v. Proprietors of Warren Bridge*, 36 U.S. (11 Pet.) 420 (1837), Chief Justice Taney permitted the state of Massachusetts to abrogate a bridge monopoly. The aggrieved monopolist argued that his charter, which had been approved by the legislature, was a contract that could not be changed without violating the Contracts Clause (Art. I., § 10, cl. 1), as interpreted in the

---

a. See generally Daniel Walker Howe, *What God Hath Wrought: The Transformation of America, 1815-1848* (2006), as well as Walter McDougall, *Throes of Democracy: The American Civil War Era, 1829-1877* (2005); David Reynolds, *Waking Giant: America in the Age of Jackson* (2008).

b. See Morton Horwitz, *The Transformation of American Law, 1780-1860* (1977) (nineteenth century legal instrumentalism); William Nelson, *The Impact of the Antislavery Movement upon Styles of Judicial Reasoning in Nineteenth Century America*, 87 Harv. L. Rev. 513 (1974) (abolitionist constitutionalism as a challenge to the prevailing instrumentalism); David A.J. Richards, *Public Reason and Abolitionist Dissent*, 69 Chi.-Kent L. Rev. 787 (1994) (anti-racism and anti-sexism as fundamental natural law precepts at foundation of abolitionist constitutionalism); see also Robert Cover, *Justice Accused: Antislavery and the Judicial Process* (1975) (account of Massachusetts Chief Justice Lemuel Shaw, whose instrumentalist judicial philosophy was inconsistent with his political opposition to slavery).

Dartmouth College case. Interpreting the company's charter, Taney's opinion refused to read the grant of monopoly as broadly as the company wanted, since such a reading would contravene community interests. But the reasoning was unmistakably an instrumentalist contrast with the rights-based logic of the Dartmouth case. "[I]n a country like ours, free, active and enterprising, continually advancing in numbers and wealth, new channels of communication are daily found necessary, both for travel and trade" — and the states need regulatory flexibility to respond to and guide such development in the interest of the larger community. The new Court would give the states more leeway to regulate private interests than the Marshall Court had contemplated.

Most of the Taney Court's slavery-related decisions deployed similar instrumentalist reasoning in support of federal power over state resistance. Article IV, § 2, cl. 3 of the Constitution required the return of fugitive slaves to their masters. Congress in 1793 implemented this provision with the Fugitive Slave Act — anathema to the emerging abolitionist movement, which hearkened to the Declaration of Independence to support its principle that all men should enjoy basic freedoms. At various points, non-slave states were no longer willing to go along with this kind of regulation. For example, Pennsylvania authorities actually arrested Edward Prigg for capturing an escaped slave. But the Taney Court reversed his conviction in *Prigg v. Pennsylvania*, 41 U.S. (16 Pet.) 539 (1842), on the ground that the states were bound by the original constitutional deal — and that enforcement of the original deal was needed to preserve the union. See also *Jones v. Van Zandt*, 46 U.S. (5 How.) 215 (1847) (similar).

Abolitionists denounced *Prigg* as inconsistent with people's natural rights, and state judicial resistance persisted. Wisconsin Justice Abram Smith argued that citizens retained their natural right to assist escaped slaves in securing their needed freedoms — and that the states retained the right to resist the Fugitive Slave Act (updated in 1850), which made this rightful activity a crime. See *In re Booth*, 3 Wis. 145 (1854), recalling the stance of the Kentucky and Virginia Resolutions. Abolitionist constitutionalism required that the Constitution be read against the normative baseline of the Declaration of Independence. The Taney Court emphatically disagreed in *Ableman v. Booth*, 62 U.S. (21 How.) 506 (1859), reaffirming both the Marshall Court's insistence that the states were bound by federal law and *Prigg*'s holding that state cooperation in fugitive slave laws was an essential feature of the original constitutional deal and the continuing viability of the union. The latter point was ironic, as Taney and four Brethren had two years earlier handed down a decision that would hasten the break up of that Union.

In the "Missouri Compromise" of 1820, Congress prohibited slavery north and west of Missouri (north of 36° 30′), in return for allowing the rest of the country to follow a local option approach. The odd consequences of this compromise were illustrated in the case of Dred Scott, a slave. Scott was taken from Missouri (a slave state under the 1820 compromise), where he and his owner resided, to Illinois, where slavery was forbidden by the state constitution, and then to Fort Snelling (now in Minnesota), where slavery was forbidden by the 1820 federal statute. After his return to Missouri, Scott sued for his freedom in federal court. He invoked federal jurisdiction by claiming diversity of citizenship (he was a citizen of a different state from the defendant), and his claim for relief rested upon the Illinois Constitution and the 1820 federal statute.[c]

Dred Scott's case reached the Supreme Court, which originally was disposed to decide it on narrow grounds. Justice Samuel Nelson of New York prepared an opinion rejecting Scott's claims on the ground that *Strader v. Graham*, 51 U.S. (10 How.) 82 (1850), had held that a black person's legal status was to be determined by the law of the state in which he resided, and that federal courts were bound by that law. Justice John McLean of Ohio, a devout Methodist layman who considered slavery an abomination, prepared a staunch anti-slavery dissenting opinion, and Justice Benjamin Curtis of Massachusetts was prepared to dissent along similar lines. The five pro-slavery Justices — Chief Justice Taney and Justices John Catron of Tennessee, James Wayne of Georgia, Peter Daniel of Virginia, and John Campbell of Alabama — decided to expand the case to settle once and for all the slavery question. The aged Chief Justice wrote what they hoped would be the opinion for the Court. (As it turned out, each of the nine Justices wrote opinions, but the Taney opinion is widely considered to be the main one, though to this day there is debate about just what portions of his opinion had majority support.)

Taney first ruled that federal courts had no jurisdiction, because Scott was not a "citizen" of Missouri, as he necessarily claimed. The Constitution when adopted did not contemplate citizenship for free blacks, for "they were at that time considered as a subordinate and inferior class of beings, who had been subjugated by the dominant race, * * * [having] no rights or privileges but such as those who held the power and the Government might choose to grant them." Given this "fixed and universal" view shared by the Framers, the Chief Justice concluded that neither slaves nor their descendants, even if freed, could be considered "citizens" of any state for jurisdictional purposes. This part of Taney's *Dred Scott* opinion is a classic deployment of "originalism" as a constitutional methodology. Under this method, the interpreter asks how the Framers expected the Constitution to be applied to the issue at hand (original intent) or what the Constitution would have been understood to mean by We the People (original meaning). Chapter 2, § 3A will explore these and other approaches to and criticisms of originalism.

Next, the Chief Justice ruled that even if the lawsuit were properly in federal court, Scott could obtain no relief under the Illinois constitution, because he was bound by the laws of Missouri. Nor could he obtain relief through the federal statute, for it was unconstitutional. As to the latter point, Taney reasoned as follows: (1) The Fifth Amendment prohibited the federal government from depriving citizens of their property without just compensation and due process of law. (2) Scott's owner had a property interest in Scott; indeed, the "right of property in a slave is distinctly and expressly affirmed in the Constitution"

---

c. For further discussion of the case and its background, see Don Fehrenbacher, *The Dred Scott Case* (1978); Paul Finkelman, *The Dred Scott Case, Slavery, and the Politics of Law*, 20 Hamline L. Rev. 1 (1996).

itself, another deployment of original intent as a legitimating methodology. (3) The federal statute's effort to deprive the owner of his property was "void" and unenforceable, because it violated "the rights and privileges of the citizen [as] regularly and plainly defined by the Constitution itself." Note how the instrumentalist and pro-regulatory reasoning Taney deployed in earlier cases vanished in the face of the author's sectional loyalty.

The Court's decision in *Dred Scott v. Sandford*, 60 U.S. (19 How.) 393 (1857), was the second time in its history that the Court had declared a federal statute unconstitutional (*Marbury* was the first). Far from "settling" the slavery issue once and for all, *Dred Scott* fanned the flames of discord. Before the 1850s, abolitionists were divided between those who believed slavery inconsistent with the Constitution, properly understood, and radicals who believed the Constitution itself was corrupt because of its protection of slavery. After *Dred Scott*, the radicals gained the upper hand, and the issue of slavery forced the nation into a constitutional corner: Half the nation believed the Constitution had gone to Hell, while the other half believed it represented their Salvation. That there seemed less room for compromise and accommodation undermined the incoming administration of James Buchanan (who knew about the decision in advance). From a political as well as moral point of view, *Dred Scott* was the greatest disaster in the history of the Court.

SECTION 4. RECONSTRUCTION AND THE AMBIGUOUS TRIUMPH OF ABOLITION, 1864-1896

The election of Abraham Lincoln as President in 1860 brought forth a sea change in American constitutionalism. First, it precipitated the Civil War (1861-65) and raised numerous questions the Constitution addressed ambiguously if at all: the legality of state secession, presidential authority to wage war and to suspend civil liberties, and the power of the national government to finance railroads and other massive projects. Second, Reconstruction after the defeat of the South generated the Thirteenth, Fourteenth, and Fifteenth Amendments, which instantiated at least some of the abolitionist philosophy of individual rights of liberty and equal protection, directly enforceable against the states. Third, the implementation of the Reconstruction Amendments shifted away from the vigorous enforcement demanded by the abolitionist natural rights philosophy, and toward a pragmatic and instrumentalist approach reminiscent of the Taney Court's pre-*Dred Scott* decisions.

1. *The Civil War and the Exercise of Great Power by the Federal Government.* The Civil War necessitated a rethinking of American constitutionalism. The Constitution, after all, said nothing about secession. States' rights thinkers like President Buchanan believed that the North was powerless to oppose secession: If the Constitution was a compact among the states, then why couldn't some of them depart from the arrangement? President Lincoln responded that the Constitution had created an inviolable national community

and not a loose confederation whose members could depart at will.[a] Over the course of the war, he and the Republican Party became committed to a fundamental rethinking of national citizenship and individual rights as they struggled with the demands of justice for the southern slaves.

Lincoln's conduct of the war meant that the federal government exercised more power than ever before — and often that power was exercised by the President, without prior authorization by Congress. Within a week after the firing on Fort Sumter (April 12, 1861) initiated hostilities, President Lincoln had not only called out the militia, but had issued a proclamation blockading Confederate ports and authorizing the seizure of ships carrying goods to the rebels. Shipowners challenged this exercise of essentially legislative power by the executive. Not only was there no legislation authorizing this action, but Congress did not even declare war until July 13. Without a declaration of war by Congress, the blockade violated international law, as neutral countries were affected. (But note this conundrum: As a matter of U.S. law, Lincoln treated the South's secession as a nullity, but to satisfy international law Lincoln may have needed a declaration of war, which according to Article I could only be accomplished by Congress.)

A bare majority (5-4) of the Supreme Court found sufficient legislative authorization for the President's action in *The Prize Cases*, 67 U.S. (2 Black) 635 (1863) (Chapter 8, § 1B), but Justice Nelson's dissenting opinion demonstrated that the laws cited by the Court only authorized the President to call out the militia and mobilize the federal armed forces and did not authorize him to blockade ports. Justice Grier's opinion for the Court also suggested that the President had inherent authority to "suppress insurrection against the government of a State or of the United States" and seemed to leave it to the political branches to work out the proper response: "Whether the President, in fulfilling his duties as Commander-in-chief, in suppressing an insurrection, has met with such armed hostile resistance, and a civil war of such alarming proportions as will compel him to accord to them the character of belligerents, is a question to be decided by *him*, and this court must be governed by the decisions and acts of the Political Department of the government to which this power was intrusted."

On April 27, 1861, President Lincoln authorized Commanding General Winfield Scott to suspend the writ of habeas corpus. Scott deployed this power to arrest John Merryman for asserted anti-Union activities in Maryland. Merryman applied to Chief Justice Taney for habeas relief, which Taney granted. *Ex parte Merryman*, 17 Fed. Cas. 144 (C.C.D. Md. 1861). Because the Constitution's authorization for suspension of the writ is in Article I, § 9, cl. 2, the article defining the powers of *Congress*, Taney concluded that the President

---

a. For important analyses of constitutional problems arising out of the Civil War, see Daniel Farber, *Lincoln's Constitution* (2005); William Duker, *A Constitutional History of Habeas Corpus* 140-49, 167-70 (1980); James Randall, *Constitutional Problems Under Lincoln* (rev. ed. 1965); John Sharer, *Power, Idealism, and Compromise: The Coordinate Branches and the Writ of Habeas Corpus*, 26 Emory L.J. 149 (1977). See generally Phillip Shaw Paludan, *The Presidency of Abraham Lincoln* (1994).

could not suspend the writ on his own authority. Indeed, by acting outside of legal authorization, the President was violating his Article II duty to "take care that the laws shall be faithfully executed." Taney ruled that any charges against Merryman had to be subject to ordinary judicial process. Although Merryman was then duly indicted for treason, he was never tried. Lincoln later responded to Taney's legal arguments: Article I, § 9, cl. 2 authorized suspension because there was a "Rebellion" and the "public Safety" required it; the provision says nothing about what organ can suspend the writ — a silence that only a knave would construe so stingily. "[A]s the provision was plainly made for a dangerous emergency, it cannot be believed the framers of the instrument intended, that in every case, the danger should run its course, until Congress could be called together; the very assembling of which might be prevented, as was intended in this case, by the rebellion."

President Lincoln's revolutionary Emancipation Proclamation declared that, by virtue of the President's authority as Commander-in-Chief, "all persons held as slaves" within designated rebel states "are, and henceforward [after January 1, 1863] shall be free." The intended legal effect of this order was ambiguous, and it was never litigated in court, but the Proclamation was much debated. Among its critics was former Justice Curtis, one of the abolitionist dissenters in *Dred Scott*. Under the Constitution, Curtis argued, only Congress — and not the President — can override state laws; the military action against the rebel states did not abrogate the applicability of the Constitution to them. Even if the rebels had absolutely no constitutional rights, all Americans had a public right that the President only act according to the duly established laws of the United States, which Lincoln had not done. (Indeed, the slavery-supportive Fugitive Slave Acts of 1793 and 1850 remained in force until Congress repealed them in June 1864.) Lincoln responded to Curtis and other critics that in cases of "Rebellion or Invasion" the President's Commander-in-Chief powers justified the exercise of quasi-legislative authority over enemy or rebel territory and that the remedy for its abuse was the normal channels of the political process. This kind of reasoning was similar to that invoked by Jefferson to justify the Louisiana Purchase.

2. *Reconstruction and Abolitionist Constitutionalism, 1865-77.* The South's defeat in the Civil War meant the formal end of slavery in the United States — and an opportunity for the triumphant abolitionists to reshape constitutional law.[b] In 1865, Congress submitted, and a sufficient number of states ratified,

---

b. Many legal historians maintain that abolitionist thought was the primary influence on the Reconstruction Amendments. See Jacobus tenBroek, *Equal Under Law* (1965) (originally published as *The Antislavery Origins of the Fourteenth Amendment*) (leading work on the contributions of abolitionists to Reconstruction constitutionalism, arguing inter alia for a broad reading of the Thirteenth Amendment), as well as Michael Kent Curtis, *No State Shall Abridge: The Fourteenth Amendment and the Bill of Rights* 26-56 (1986) (abolitionist natural law theories as the basis for congressional debates surrounding Fourteenth Amendment); David A.J. Richards, *Conscience and the Constitution: History, Theory, and the Law of the Reconstruction Amendments* (1993) (arguing that abolitionist thought and activism directly influenced twentieth century theories of individual rights). Some legal historians emphasize that moderate and conservative Republicans, with little connection to the abolition movement, were more important to the Reconstruction

the Thirteenth Amendment, which made slavery and any "involuntary servitude" illegal. (This instantiated the abolitionists' central proposition: no person can have a legal or moral right to "own" any other human being.) Shortly thereafter, Congress created the Freedman's Bureau to provide clothing, medical care, and relocation for white and black refugees; to assist the transition of freedmen to the status of productive citizens with full contractual rights; and to establish schools to improve literacy and computational skills among the new citizens. Several congressional enactments of the period were explicitly limited to helping people of color. In 1866, Congress passed the first Civil Rights Act, which implemented the abolitionists' equal treatment principle, guaranteeing every citizen the right to make and enforce contracts, to sue, to purchase and convey land, and to enjoy the equal benefit of all laws and proceedings for the security of persons and property. This statute survives as 42 U.S.C. §§ 1981, 1982.

The most important Reconstruction Amendment was the Fourteenth, whose drafting history and ratification (1868) are recounted in Chapter 2, § 1A. Section 1 redefined citizenship and rights. Implementing the abolitionists' principle of *national citizenship*, the first sentence overruled what was left of *Dred Scott*, by providing that persons born in the United States are citizens of the country first, and of the states in which they reside second. Tracking the natural rights and equality-before-the-law principles of the abolitionists, the second sentence defined several rights enforceable against the states: "No State shall make or enforce any law which shall abridge the privileges or immunities of citizens of the United States; nor shall any State deprive any person of life, liberty, or property, without due process of law; nor deny to any person within its jurisdiction the equal protection of the laws." Note that the rights protected by § 1 go well beyond the property rights protected in the original Constitution (e.g., the Contracts Clause). Section 5 of the Amendment authorized Congress to enforce the provisions of the Amendment "by appropriate legislation."

The Fourteenth Amendment was immediately followed (in 1870) by the Fifteenth Amendment, which forbade racial discrimination in access to voting. Congress enacted further civil rights statutes in 1870, 1871, and 1875, all assuring equal rights for black citizens in jury service, voting, and access to public accommodations. Although the Reconstruction Amendments and statutes did not have nearly as much impact in the South as the Republicans had hoped, they reflected an important transformation of substantive constitutional

---

Amendments than were the "radical" Republicans who were the heirs to the abolitionists. E.g., Eric Foner, *Reconstruction: America's Unfinished Revolution, 1863-1877* (1988) (rise and fall of the radical Republicans in the 1860s); William Nelson, *The Fourteenth Amendment: From Political Principle to Judicial Doctrine* (1988) (importance of moderates to Congress' proposing the Fourteenth Amendment). But many of these historians believe that abolitionist thought introduced the key ideas for the Reconstruction Amendments — natural right to freedom and to certain liberties from state infringement, the importance of the franchise and other rights of "national citizenship," the state's obligation to provide equal protection of the law to all persons — and have been underappreciated by the post-1877 Supreme Court. E.g., Eric Foner, *The Strange Career of the Reconstruction Amendments*, 108 Yale L.J. 2003 (1999); Robert Kaczorowski, *Revolutionary Constitutionalism in the Era of the Civil War and Reconstruction*, 61 NYU L. Rev. 863 (1986).

law. They also represented an important innovation in constitutional law-making.

President Johnson, the Tennessee Democrat who succeeded Lincoln after his assassination, had been committed to the Thirteenth Amendment and used his military governors to pressure the Southern states into ratifying the Amendment in 1865 (he was successful in all but Mississippi). But Johnson opposed the Fourteenth Amendment, and the southern and border states, one by one, passed resolutions rejecting it. One would have thought that this would have been the end of the matter under Article V. But the Radical Republican Congress was adamant about the proposed Fourteenth Amendment and forced a constitutional showdown, first with the recalcitrant states, and then with the President. The Radicals were buoyed by the fact that they convincingly won the elections of 1866, months after the Fourteenth Amendment was submitted to the states.

Armed with the popular mandate, Congress in 1867 passed the first Reconstruction Act, which reconstructed state governments and guaranteed the freed slaves voting rights. Section 5 of the statute denied the southern states the right to send representatives to Congress until they ratified the Fourteenth Amendment! President Johnson denounced the process and did all he could to impede it. The House of Representatives impeached him, and to save his office the President retreated from his anti-Reconstruction campaign. Reconstructed southern governments fell into line and began to ratify the Fourteenth Amendment. In May 1868, Johnson survived his Senate impeachment trial, albeit by only one vote. In July 1868, Secretary of State Seward proclaimed the Fourteenth Amendment ratified.

This procedural history of the Fourteenth Amendment strengthens the impression gleaned from its substantive message, that (to use Bruce Ackerman's felicitous phrase) this was an important "constitutional moment" in our history, on a par with the original framing of the Constitution, and moving the document well beyond the original vision. The precise direction and extent of this constitutional reformation was, of course, left for later generations to define (and redefine). Return to the problems posed at the beginning of this chapter, especially the ones asking about the constitutionality of state rather than federal actions. How does the Fourteenth Amendment change your analysis?

The equal protection guarantee was the most intensely litigated of the new rights enforceable against the states. The Supreme Court applied it in *Strauder v. West Virginia*, 100 U.S. 303 (1879), to strike down a law excluding any but "white persons" from juries. The exclusion violated the central theme of abolitionist jurisprudence, "that the law in the States shall be the same for the black as for the white." In *Yick Wo v. Hopkins*, 118 U.S. 356 (1886) (Chapter 3, § 1B), the Court struck down a law whose enforcement discriminated on the basis of (Chinese) ethnicity rather than race.

In its early decisions, however, the Court was not inclined to give the Fourteenth Amendment much bite when discrimination was not related to race or color. In *The Slaughter House Cases*, 83 U.S. (16 Wall.) 36 (1873) (Chapter 5, § 1), the Court held that the Privileges or Immunities Clause of the Fourteenth Amendment was inapplicable to a state grant of local economic monopolies.

Economic regulation was a far cry from the central purpose of the amendment, the Court reasoned. The primary protection for individual rights remained state law, and nothing in any of the Reconstruction Amendments meant to "degrade the State governments by subjecting them to the control of Congress," nor to change radically "the whole theory of the relations of the State and Federal governments to each other and both of these governments to the people."

The same basic reasoning informed the Court's application of the P&I Clause to laws discriminating on the basis of sex. The Court refused to strike down laws excluding women from the practice of law, see *Bradwell v. Illinois*, 83 U.S. 130 (1873) (Chapter 4, § 2A), or the franchise, see *Minor v. Happersett*, 88 U.S. 162 (1874) (id.). These results were no more surprising than those in the race and color cases, however. The women's movement, which had been galvanized at Seneca Falls in 1848 and which had supported abolition, had been spurned by the Republicans drafting the Reconstruction Amendments, especially the Fifteenth. Some feminists, in turn, opposed one or more of the Reconstruction Amendments. Most feminists focused on efforts to override *Happersett* with an amendment to the Constitution.

3. *The Nation's Retreat from Reconstruction, 1883-1903.* Reconstruction formally came to an end following a deal made between the Republicans and Democrats in 1877. In return for acquiescing in the contested election of Rutherford Hayes as President, the Democrats won the withdrawal of federal troops from the South — an action which left the newly franchised former slaves at the mercy of white planters eager to reestablish their political, economic, and social hegemony. Although the freed slaves continued to assert political power, they were outnumbered and then outmaneuvered all over the South in the 1880s and 1890s. Southern states adopted laws instantiating apartheid, legally requiring segregation of the races and excluding people of color from the franchise, jury service, and other citizenship rights guaranteed by Reconstruction. Northern Republicans turned a blind eye to a literal reign of terror visited upon the freed slaves and their children.

The Supreme Court more or less followed the emerging political consensus. In *The Civil Rights Cases*, 109 U.S. 3 (1883) (Chapter 7, § 3A), the Court ruled that the Fourteenth Amendment did not reach instances of race discrimination by private actors and that Congress therefore had no § 5 authority to bar public accommodation discrimination. Much of the Civil Rights Act of 1875 was swept away by the decision, and Congress did not enact another civil rights measure until 1957. In *Plessy v. Ferguson*, 163 U.S. 537 (1896) (Chapter 2, § 1), the Court ruled that neither the Thirteenth nor Fourteenth Amendments barred the states from requiring racial segregation in railroad transport. Both cases drew dissenting opinions from Justice John Marshall Harlan, an American original. Although he had been a Kentucky slaveowner, Harlan became an anti-slavery Republican and served in the Union Army. His Supreme Court nomination was the result of his crucial support for Rutherford Hayes at the 1876 Republican convention. As a Justice, Harlan is best remembered for his willingness to view issues from the perspective of the politically marginal. He is also said to have been one of the last Justices to chew tobacco on the bench (though the silver spittoons were still in place late in the twentieth century).

In his dissents in *Plessy* and *The Civil Rights Cases*, Harlan argued, persuasively to modern eyes, that the Court's decisions represented a pragmatic but tragic retreat from the values that gave rise to Reconstruction and urged the Court to stand firmly for the equal citizenship of African Americans. But even Harlan did not dissent when the Court assumed that *Plessy* allowed segregated public schools; indeed, he wrote the opinion for the Court in *Cumming v. Richmond County Bd. of Educ.*, 175 U.S. 528 (1899). Nor did he dissent seven years after *Plessy* when the Court unanimously ruled that a federal judge properly declined to issue an injunction against an Alabama voting official who allegedly refused to register more than 5,000 qualified people of color. *Giles v. Harris*, 189 U.S. 475 (1903).

SECTION 5. THE LABOR MOVEMENT, PROGRESSIVISM, AND RIGHTS FOR WOMEN AND BLACKS, 1896-1937

The period after the Civil War was one of great industrial expansion in the North and Midwest — an expansion that stimulated efforts by workers to improve their lot through collective action (labor unions, strikes, and boycotts) and by the state to regulate "abuses" of the new industrial order, including anti-competitive actions by unions, corporate trusts, and railroads. This was not an era in which the Supreme Court engaged in much productive constitutional leadership. During the tenures of Chief Justices Melville Fuller (1888-1910), Edward White (1910-21), and William Howard Taft (1921-30), the Court was sporadically reactionary but more typically drifted from case to case, with little underlying ideological coherence beyond a mild economic libertarianism and a nostalgia for Jefferson's arcadian republic of farmers and shopkeepers. The socio-economic reality, however, was that the United States was becoming an industrial nation of massive trusts, giant railroads, acrimonious labor disputes, and identity-based social movements.

Notwithstanding the Court, the first third of the twentieth century was a generative period for American constitutionalism — yielding important amendments to the Constitution that provided for a federal income tax (XVI, 1913), the direct election of senators (XVII, 1913), and women's suffrage (XIX, 1920); major advances in the ongoing creation of the modern regulatory state, including the first national antitrust law, a food and drug law, and a federal reserve system to manage the flow of money; and doctrinal innovations (typically by state and lower federal court judges), such as the labor injunction, substantive due process, a broad First Amendment, and national rights of criminal procedure. Many of these developments cut across substantive boundaries, highlighting the big tension between the constitutional liberty of contract jurisprudence favored by many judges and the regulatory state's desire to manage the economy more actively.

1. *The Labor Movement and Liberty of Contract in the* Lochner *Era.* Industrialization generated great hardship for workers, who sought to organize collectively to obtain better wages and working conditions. Beginning in the 1870s, America witnessed often violent strife between labor unions and management, first in the railroads and later across American industries. In this struggle, state and federal judges, like the legal profession generally, were

usually allies of management.[a]   And the Supreme Court interpreted the Fourteenth Amendment to protect "liberty of contract" against private coercion and state regulation.

This was not the Court's original view; recall *The Slaughter House Cases*. But dissenting opinions by Justices Stephen Field and Joseph Bradley there argued that arbitrary state interference with people's economic interests constituted a violation of the Fourteenth Amendment's Due Process Clause. While the Court declined to invalidate state laws on *substantive due process* grounds during the tenure of Chief Justice Morrison Waite (1874-88), the Fuller Court used that theory as a sharp weapon for business interests against state regulatory legislation, especially laws protecting workers. Justice Field, joined by his nephew, Justice David Brewer, was able to assemble Court majorities to invalidate several state statutes as violating freedom of contract.[b]

The leading substantive due process case, and one whose name has identified the era, was *Lochner v. New York*, 198 U.S. 45 (1905) (Chapter 5, § 2B). In *Lochner*, a closely divided (5-4) Court struck down a New York law limiting the hours bakers could work. The ruling rested on the statute's interference with "the right of contract between the employer and employees," which is "part of the liberty of the individual protected by [the Due Process Clause of] the Fourteenth Amendment." The Court recognized, as it had in *Plessy*, that the state had wide leeway to enact statutes for the protection of the public welfare. But statutes "limiting the hours in which grown and intelligent men may labor to earn their living, are mere meddlesome interferences with the rights of the individual, and they are not saved from condemnation by the claim that they are passed in the exercise of the police power and upon the subject of the health of the individual whose rights are interfered with, unless there be some fair ground, * * * to say that there is material danger to the public health or to the health of the employees, if the hours of labor are not curtailed." The Court was not persuaded by the extensive evidence that long and continuous exposure to heat, fumes, and dust did in fact impair the health of bakers. "It is impossible for us to shut our eyes to the fact that many of the laws of this character, while passed under what is claimed to be the police power[,] * * * are, in reality, passed from other motives," the Court concluded. Indeed, like dozens of laws of the period,

---

a. See Arnold Paul, *Conservative Crisis and the Rule of Law: Attitudes of Bar and Bench, 1887-1895* (1960); William Forbath, *Law and the Shaping of the American Labor Movement* (1991); Felix Frankfurter & Nathan Greene, *The Labor Injunction* (1930).

b. Stephen Field was one of the more colorful Justices of the Court. The brother of David Dudley Field (the great codifier) and Cyrus Field (who laid the first transatlantic cable), Stephen Field grew up in the East, but moved to California in 1849. President Lincoln appointed Field to the Court in 1863, where he served for 34 years, a record of Supreme Court service broken by Justice Douglas, who served for 36 years. His career was marked by intrigue and scandal, leading to an unsuccessful assassination attempt while he was on the Court. On his philosophy, see Charles McCurdy, *Justice Field and the Jurisprudence of Government-Business Relations: Some Parameters of Laissez-Faire Constitutionalism, 1863-1897*, 61 J. Am. Hist. 970 (1975). David Brewer was Field's nephew, the pious son of missionaries (Brewer was born in Asia Minor). Although not as colorful, Brewer was equally dogmatic in his insistence that economic rights to free contracting were protected by the Constitution.

the New York bakers' statute was enacted at the behest of unions seeking to impose on nonunionized (smaller) bakeries the same maximum-hour rule that they were obtaining from unionized bakeries.

All but one of the five Justices in the *Lochner* majority had voted to uphold the apartheid statute challenged in *Plessy*. As in *Plessy*, Justice Harlan dissented in *Lochner*. He pointed to the evidence that long hours harmed bakers' health and safety. The statute was invalid only if it bore "no real or substantial relation" to health or safety. "If there be doubt as to the validity of the statute, that doubt must therefore be resolved in favor of its validity, and the courts must keep their hands off, leaving the legislature to meet the responsibility for unwise legislation."

Justice Oliver Wendell Holmes, Jr., who had been nominated for the Court (after *Plessy*) in part because he was skeptical of anti-labor judicial activism, dissented separately. "This case is decided upon an economic theory [laissez-faire] which a large part of the country does not entertain," Holmes contended. Nothing in the Constitution protects "liberty of contract." Sunday closing laws, prohibition on lotteries, and other established regulations, all of which had been upheld, were no less offensive to that "right" than the New York statute. Why should this regulation be struck down while other similar ones have been sustained? As a general matter, Holmes argued for very lenient judicial review under the Due Process Clause:

> * * * [A] constitution is not intended to embody a particular economic theory, whether of paternalism and the organic relation of the citizen to the State or of *laissez-faire*. It is made for people of fundamentally differing views, and the accident of our finding certain opinions natural and familiar or novel and even shocking ought not conclude our judgment upon the question whether statutes embodying them conflict with the Constitution of the United States.

> * * * I think that the word liberty in the Fourteenth Amendment is perverted when it is held to prevent the natural outcome of a dominant opinion, unless it can be said that a rational and fair man necessarily would admit that the statute proposed would infringe fundamental principles as they have been understood by the traditions of our people and our law.

Holmes's philosophy was acquiescent in the overall growth of government regulation during the Progressive era. Railroads fell under increasingly detailed regulation as the Interstate Commerce Act of 1887 was repeatedly expanded. The Sherman Antitrust Act of 1891, expanded by the Clayton Act of 1914, subjected big business to unprecedented administrative and judicial scrutiny. The Pure Food and Drug Act of 1906 created an inspection system for meats and other foodstuffs. All of these statutes, and hundreds of others, limited businesses' freedom to conduct their affairs as they wanted.

In fact, the large majority of the business-restricting statutes survived *Lochner*. Most liberty of contract challenges reaching the Supreme Court were rejected. E.g., *Muller v. Oregon*, 208 U.S. 412 (1908) (Chapter 4, § 2A) (upholding law fixing maximum hours women could work, but for essentially sex-stereotypical, paternalistic reasons). Yet *Lochner* had more than occasional bite, especially when legislatures were perceived to be redistributing wealth or power from entrepreneurs to labor unions, which were viewed with suspicion by hidebound federal judges. For example, in *Coppage v. Kansas*, 236 U.S. 1

(1915), the Court invalidated a state law barring "yellow dog" employment contracts precluding union membership, on the ground that the law prevented willing employers and workers from voluntarily agreeing to such terms. The Court's sporadic activism had little to do with due process, and much to do with fears within the bench and bar that new forms of collective organization — bigger government, labor unions, business trusts and monopolies — threatened the traditional economic rights of individuals to get ahead.

It is hardly surprising that, during the tenures of Chief Justices Fuller, White, and Taft, the Supreme Court sometimes narrowly construed federal power when it compromised the interests of the propertied classes. Thus the Fuller Court struck down the progressive income tax as a violation of Article I, § 9, see *Pollock v. Farmers' Loan and Trust Co.*, 158 U.S. 601 (1895) (overridden by the Sixteenth Amendment), and a federal law prohibiting yellow dog contracts in railroad employment as a violation of the Due Process Clause of the Fifth Amendment, see *Adair v. United States*, 208 U.S. 161 (1908). In contrast, *In re Debs*, 158 U.S. 564 (1895), held that the federal government had direct authority under the Commerce Clause to obtain injunctions to break the Pullman Strike. The Pullman Strike had been the culmination of a decade of labor unrest, especially on the railroads, and the Department of Justice's intervention crushing the strike was a fait accompli that Justice Brewer (who authored the opinion) was determined to uphold. The White Court struck down the federal child labor law as beyond Congress' power to regulate interstate commerce, see *Hammer v. Dagenhart*, 247 U.S. 251 (1918) (Chapter 7, § 2), and the Taft Court invalidated Congress' subsequent effort to discourage child labor under its taxing power, see *Bailey v. Drexel Furniture Co.*, 259 U.S. 20 (1922) (Chapter 7, § 4A). In contrast, the Taft Court authorized federal judges to regulate union-management relations through notorious labor injunctions that were issued by the cartload in the 1920s.

2. *The Progressive Era and the Emerging First Amendment.* While we view this period a rather dreary one in the Court's history, it was brightened by the prescient dissenting opinions of Justices Holmes (1902-32) and Brandeis (1916-39), who defended the rights of labor unions to form and carry on their economic activities, of states and the federal government to experiment with novel forms of market regulation, and of unpopular individuals and groups to speak out and carry on their own activities without persecution. Theirs was the voice of the future, and nowhere was that more apparent than in the Court's First Amendment jurisprudence.[c]

Holmes, the son of a well-known Boston essayist, may have been the most broadly intellectual person ever to serve on the Court; his private correspondence pithily discusses European thinkers of the time, and he was a friend of the philosopher William James. His capacity for reflection was tested in the seditious speech cases arising out of opposition to American involvement in

---

c. See David Rabban, *Free Speech in Its Forgotten Years* (1997); David Bogen, *The Free Speech Metamorphosis of Mr. Justice Holmes*, 11 Hofstra L. Rev. 97 (1982). See also Gerald Gunther, *Learned Hand and the Origins of Modern First Amendment Doctrine: Some Fragments of History*, 27 Stan. L. Rev. 719 (1975).

World War I. A veteran wounded three times while serving in the Union Army during the Civil War, Holmes personally had no use for pacifists, and he warned anti-war protesters in *Schenck v. United States*, 249 U.S. 47 (1919) (Chapter 6, § 2A), that much speech allowable in peacetime was not so during wartime. Upholding the conviction of a man who mailed leaflets objecting to the draft, Holmes announced the requirement that the federal government had to show that, under the circumstances, the assertedly seditious words created a "clear and present danger" of national harm. Although the test was applied harshly to Schenck, it was a doctrinal innovation, for earlier decisions left it unclear whether the First Amendment had any application beyond barring prior restraints. Recall the Sedition Act of 1798, and see also *Patterson v. Colorado*, 205 U.S. 454 (1907) (Holmes, J.); *Fox v. Washington*, 236 U.S. 273 (1915) (nudist art can be censored).

In *Abrams v. United States*, 250 U.S. 616 (1919) (Chapter 6, § 2A), the Court followed *Schenck* to uphold the convictions of Russian-born dissidents for objecting to the Allies' efforts against the Bolsheviks — but over Holmes' objection that the publication of "a silly leaflet by an unknown man" posed no clear and present danger to the American war effort. In his dissent, Holmes endorsed the idea that the First Amendment protects the "free trade in ideas" as the best way to get at "the truth." Holmes's dissent was joined by Brandeis, the brilliant "people's lawyer" whose fact-filled "Brandeis brief" had been persuasive in *Muller*.[d] The latter wrote for himself and Holmes in *Whitney v. California*, 274 U.S. 357 (1927) (Chapter 6, § 2A), which added a different but complementary justification for an aggressive First Amendment: Essential to a vigorous democracy is the "opportunity to discuss freely supposed grievances and proposed remedies," a rationale that demands considerable breathing room for people to say and publish ideas considered false and even dangerous by the majority. Better the citizenry be engaged in rancorous debate than rendered intellectually inert by the censor. The Holmes-Brandeis approach was adopted by Court majorities in *Herndon v. Lowry*, 301 U.S. 242 (1937), and *DeJonge v. Oregon*, 299 U.S. 353 (1937), and has ignited a robust First Amendment tradition in American law. (Note that these later cases involved First Amendment challenges to *state* rather than *federal* actions. The Court in *Gitlow v. New York*, 268 U.S. 652 (1925) (Chapter 6, § 2A), assumed that the First Amendment was applicable to the states under the Due Process Clause of the Fourteenth Amendment.)

The free trade in ideas and democracy arguments for a vigorous First Amendment were hardly unique to Holmes and Brandeis; state and federal judges (especially those in cosmopolitan New York) intervened to protect unpopular speech and press in the 1920s and 1930s. This had broad and

---

d. Brandeis's nomination was the subject of bitter Senate opposition, partly because of his liberal views and partly because of anti-Semitism. His opinions were sometimes eloquent, but often so heavily documented and detailed that they make for tedious reading today. Holmes and he generally voted to uphold regulations of business, but for different reasons: Brandeis thought regulation was a good idea, while Holmes thought regulation was a form of stupidity in which the public was entitled to indulge.

unanticipated socio-political ramifications. The birth control movement initiated by Emma Goldman and Margaret Sanger was hounded by state authorities opposed to dissemination of contraceptive devices and information, and both Goldman and Sanger were chased off to Europe during World War I. Sanger returned in triumph when charges were dismissed against her, in part for First Amendment reasons.[e] Although state authorities harassed early birth control clinics, the movement inexorably gained a foothold in American society and won some important anti-censorship victories in the 1930s. The Second Circuit ruled in *United States v. Dennett*, 39 F.2d 564 (2d Cir. 1930), that the federal government could not censor sex education materials and in *United States v. One Package*, 86 F.2d 737 (2d Cir. 1936), that federal law (properly narrowed) did not bar transportation of diaphragms across state lines. Both Congress and lower courts protected literature seriously discussing issues of sexuality and gender in the 1930s.

3. *The Women's and Civil Rights Movements.* The *Lochner* era saw considerable pressure to recognize individual civil rights, and the social movements seeking the right to vote for women and civil rights for people of color yielded more lasting constitutional legacies than *Lochner* did. The most dramatic constitutional moment was the ratification of the Nineteenth Amendment in 1920, the culmination of two generations of political activism.[f] Women emancipated from coverture during the nineteenth century insisted on the civil rights and equal citizenship that the Reconstruction Amendments (as interpreted in *Bradwell* and *Happensett*) had failed to deliver to them as they theoretically had to people of color. Opponents of the amendment argued that women's interests were sufficiently represented by the votes of their husbands and that giving women the right to vote would undermine marriage and the family, which were the proper spheres for women as wives (the theme of a concurring opinion in *Bradwell* (Chapter 4, § 2A)).

Unlike the Fifteenth Amendment, the Nineteenth Amendment was implemented without fuss, and women voted without impediment for Warren Harding in 1920. The amendment had some immediate constitutional ramifications. In its wake, a number of state courts reinterpreted laws requiring jury service by all voters to include previously excluded women. Justice George Sutherland, who as a Republican senator from Utah had voted for the Nine-

---

e. See Ellen Chesler, *Woman of Valor: Margaret Sanger and the Birth Control Movement in America* 127-29, 138-40 (1992); Rabban, *Forgotten Years* 67-70. The Supreme Court upheld Goldman's deportation in *Goldman v. United States*, 245 U.S. 474 (1918), and dismissed Sanger's appeal of her subsequent conviction for violating New York's obscenity law in *Sanger v. People*, 251 U.S. 537 (1919).

f. See Aileen Kraditor, *The Ideas of the Woman Suffrage Movement, 1890-1920* (1965); Ellen Carol DuBois, *Outgrowing the Compact of the Fathers: Equal Rights, Woman Suffrage, and the United States Constitution, 1820-1878*, 74 J. Am. Hist. 836 (1987); Reva Siegel, *She the People: The Nineteenth Amendment, Sex Equality, and the Family*, 115 Harv. L. Rev. 947 (2002). Another "constitutional moment" engineered by a women's movement was the adoption of the Eighteenth Amendment, which barred the distribution of alcoholic beverages. See Joseph Gusfield, *Symbolic Crusade: Status Politics and the American Temperance Movement* (2d ed. 1986). This was an ill-fated moment, terminated by the Twenty-First Amendment (1933).

teenth Amendment, invoked it in his opinion for the Court in *Adkins v. Children's Hospital*, 261 U.S. 525 (1923), which invalidated a law prescribing minimum wages for female employees. To distinguish *Muller*, where the Court had upheld a maximum hour law needed to protect women and the family, Sutherland suggested that the Nineteenth Amendment put women on an equal footing with men, thereby undermining state arguments that women need to be "protected" against workplace conditions that would be tolerable for men.

Many feminists saw their next constitutional step as full legal equality, and in 1923 supporters introduced an Equal Rights Amendment (ERA) in Congress. Although such a constitutional amendment was introduced in most Congresses after 1923, it went nowhere for decades, in part because women's groups were themselves divided as to the desirability of formal equality.[g] Some feared that the ERA would abrogate labor legislation protecting women, just as *Adkins* had suggested that the Nineteenth Amendment undercut the authority of *Muller*. Others believed that the ERA would undermine women's special position as the glue binding the family together. Still others strongly supported the ERA.

At the same time women were rectifying one of Reconstruction's gaps with the Nineteenth Amendment, African Americans and their allies were organizing to reclaim the lost legacy of Reconstruction. The National Association for the Advancement of Colored People (NAACP) was formed in 1908 and immediately commenced a litigation campaign against southern abuse of black people.[h] The NAACP and other civil rights groups won several landmark Supreme Court decisions which created national rights for criminal defendants through liberal constructions of the Fourteenth Amendment.[i] Relying on the Fifteenth as well as the Fourteenth Amendment, the NAACP successfully challenged voting exclusions, including the notorious system of "whites only" primaries in the South. See *Nixon v. Herndon*, 273 U.S. 536 (1927). Finally, and most important, the NAACP stood opposed to apartheid, resisting its expansion into housing ordinances, *Buchanan v. Warley*, 245 U.S. 60 (1917), and initiating a multifaceted campaign in the 1930s against unequal treatment of blacks in public education (Chapter 2, § 1B).

Unlike women, who had access to an occasionally responsive political process, people of color were blocked from political reform by apartheid in the South and dominance of the U.S. Senate by southern members. (Even such elemental reform as anti-lynching legislation was unobtainable from the

---

g. See Cynthia Harrison, *On Account of Sex: The Politics of Women's Issues, 1945-1968* (1988); Verta Taylor, *Social Movement Continuity: The Women's Movement in Abeyance*, 54 Am. Soc. Rev. 761 (1989).

h. See Charles Flint Kellogg, *NAACP: A History of the National Association for the Advancement of Colored People* (1967); James McPherson, *The Abolitionist Legacy: From Reconstruction to the NAACP* (1975).

i. E.g., *Moore v. Dempsey*, 261 U.S. 86 (1923) (trial influenced by outside mob violates due process); *Powell v. Alabama*, 287 U.S. 45 (1932) (defendant has due process right to counsel in capital cases); *Norris v. Alabama*, 294 U.S. 587 (1935) (exclusion of blacks from jury violates equal protection); *Brown v. Mississippi*, 297 U.S. 278 (1936) (due process forbids the use of confessions obtained by police coercion).

Senate.) Federal courts were the only forum willing to listen to black people's complaints of extraordinary mistreatment. Notably, conservative Justices like William Howard Taft and George Sutherland, as well as moderates like Owen Roberts and Charles Evans Hughes, and progressives like Oliver Wendell Holmes, Louis Brandeis, and Benjamin Cardozo, were all willing to grant relief in cases involving lawless treatment of black criminal defendants. In the 1930s, civil rights cases took on an even greater normative urgency, as many Americans came to realize that apartheid resembled the racist policies of Nazi Germany and that the marginalization of African Americans in the South rendered our contrast between American democracy and Russian and German totalitarianism vulnerable if not hypocritical. Accordingly, the NAACP escalated its litigation campaigns against apartheid and unfair criminal process, to an increasingly receptive Supreme Court.

SECTION 6. THE NEW DEAL, THE COURT-PACKING CONTROVERSY, AND THE *CAROLENE* COURT, 1937-1953

The critical election of 1932 made Franklin Delano Roosevelt President and inaugurated a new era in American politics. The winning political coalition assembled by FDR included labor unions and people of color as well as southerners and (some) businesses. The New Deal's many regulatory experiments expanded the scope of the national government and were irrefutable evidence that the United States was an administrative regulatory state rather than the common law laissez-faire entity presumed by the *Lochner* jurisprudence. World War II, the greatest governmental project of the century, not only confirmed the enormous authority of the central government, but also accelerated social change, stimulating new normative aspirations and then constitutional demands by people of color, women, and gay people. The Supreme Court of Chief Justices Charles Evans Hughes (1930-41), Harlan Fiske Stone (1941-46), and Fred Vinson (1946-53) was swept along by these great changes.

1. *The Four Horsemen and Constitutional Crisis (1934-37).* The New Deal entailed much more substantial federal management of the economy than had been tried before, and some of FDR's innovative programs fell athwart the scrutiny of a Supreme Court consisting of four staunch defenders of the *Lochner* philosophy (McReynolds, VanDevanter, Sutherland, and Butler, collectively dubbed the "Four Horsemen"); three Holmesian liberals (Brandeis, Stone, and Cardozo); and two centrists (Hughes and Roberts).

Perhaps surprisingly, the early returns from the Court were mildly encouraging, as almost all federal and state regulatory legislation survived judicial review in 1934.[a] For example, in *Home Building & Loan Ass'n v. Blaisdell*, 290 U.S.

---

a. E.g., *Nebbia v. New York*, 291 U.S. 502 (1934). The traditional understanding of the Old Court seeking to thwart the New Deal has been challenged by a more subtle understanding of an Old Court accommodating some but not all of the New Deal program. See Barry Cushman, *Rethinking the New Deal Court: The Structure of a Constitutional Revolution* (1998); Barry Friedman, *The History of the Countermajoritarian Difficulty, Part Four: Law's Politics*, 148 U. Pa. L. Rev. 971

398 (1934), the Court rejected a Contracts Clause challenge to a state moratorium on mortgage foreclosures and sales. Although he emphasized that "[e]mergency does not increase granted power or remove or diminish the restrictions imposed upon power," Hughes essentially weighed the "vital public interests" pressed by the state against "temporary and conditional" impositions on creditors' rights, a balance calibrated to favor the state. This was the beginning of the Contracts Clause's slow decline.

The Court was more hostile to federal as well as state regulatory measures in 1935, and the axe fell on parts of the New Deal. Thus, the Court invalidated the Railroad Retirement Act in *Railroad Retirement Board v. Alton Railroad Co.*, 295 U.S. 330 (1935) (statute held unrelated to asserted Commerce Clause justification). A key program, the National Industrial Recovery Act, was the next to fall, and to a unanimous Court in *A.L.A. Schechter Poultry Corp. v. United States*, 295 U.S. 495 (1935) (Chapter 8, § 2A) (excessive delegation of congressional power to private groups). In *Carter v. Carter Coal Co.*, 298 U.S. 238 (1936), a divided Court found insufficient federal Commerce Clause power to regulate local coal production. The Agricultural Adjustment Act fell to the Four Horsemen in *United States v. Butler*, 297 U.S. 1 (1936), and the Horsemen served notice that liberty of contract remained a viable limit on government regulation when they (plus Justice Roberts) struck down state minimum wage legislation in *Morehead v. New York ex rel. Tipaldo*, 298 U.S. 587 (1936). Note that the Court's most divisive decisions came in cases where legislatures were redistributing wealth or power from capital to labor, the essential complaint of the old *Lochner* majority.

FDR fumed while the Court dismantled much of his program in 1935-36. But he did more than fume — he took his case to the people, who in 1936 gave him an electoral vote landslide and returned enormous Democratic majorities in both Houses of Congress. Armed and perhaps inflated with this electoral mandate, FDR stunned the legal establishment in February 1937 with his "Court-packing plan." Essentially, the plan was to add one Justice to the Court for each Justice over 70 years old, in order (the President said) to ameliorate the "heavy burden" faced by the Court "handicapped by insufficient personnel with which to meet a growing and more complex business" (reviewing those long and technical New Deal statutes, to be sure). Since there were six Justices older than 70 in 1937, the Court-packing plan would have allowed FDR to appoint Justices who could have been counted on to protect the New Deal against constitutional challenge. One didn't have to be very clever to see what the President was up to. Many of his staunchest supporters were horrified that FDR would "politicize" the Supreme Court.

2. *The "Switch in Time"? Or a Switch in Personnel?* Although the Court-packing plan stirred up a big controversy, the Justices themselves were probably critical in defeating it. A letter from Chief Justice Hughes and Justices Brandeis and VanDevanter to Senator Wheeler in March 1937 dispelled any conceivable

(2000); Richard Friedman, *Switching Time and Other Thought Experiments: The Hughes Court and Constitutional Transformation*, 142 U. Pa. L. Rev. 1891 (1994).

argument that the Court needed younger Justices to catch up in its work; the letter noted that the Court was already caught up, thank you, and that increasing the size of the Court would only slow things down. More important, the Court handed down two important pro-New Deal decisions during the debate in the spring of 1937 — *NLRB v. Jones & Laughlin Steel Corp.*, 301 U.S. 1 (1937) (Chapter 7, § 2), which sustained the National Labor Relations Act against Commerce Clause challenge, and *West Coast Hotel Co. v. Parrish*, 300 U.S. 379 (1937) (Chapter 5, § 2B), which overruled *Adkins* and deflated substantive due process challenges to state labor legislation. Chief Justice Hughes wrote the opinions in both cases, silently joined by poor Justice Roberts, whose change of heart has been branded by history as "the switch in time that saved nine." The Senate Judiciary Committee officially killed the Court-packing plan in June 1937.

Ironically, the Court-packing plan was ultimately unnecessary. It would have given FDR six immediate appointments, but between 1937 and 1941 he got a chance to appoint seven new Justices because of retirements and deaths. Thus FDR appointed to the Court Senator Hugo Black, one of the New Deal's staunchest allies; Solicitor General Stanley Reed; Professor Felix Frankfurter of the Harvard Law School, a leading member of FDR's brain trust and mentor to many young officials staffing the New Deal; SEC Chair and former Yale Law Professor William O. Douglas; Attorney General Frank Murphy and Senator James Byrnes, both early and ardent political allies of FDR; and Attorney General Robert Jackson. FDR also elevated Justice Harlan Stone, a liberal Republican, to be Chief Justice in 1941. On the whole, the New Deal Justices were young, talented, and loyal to the President who appointed them. They transformed constitutional law.[b]

It is instructive to compare the procedural aspects of the transformation of constitutional law that occurred during the New Deal to those aspects of an earlier transformative "moment," that of Reconstruction, that were examined earlier. Recall that Reconstruction involved a major textual alteration of the constitutional document (the addition of the Thirteenth, Fourteenth, and Fifteenth Amendments) in the aftermath of a civil war, through a federally coerced ratification process that seems hard to square with the original expectations surrounding Article V. The New Deal transformation strayed even further from constitutional formalism, because it involved no formal amendment to the Constitution at all. In the New Deal, the combined pressure of the President and Congress, plus the coincidences of death, disability, and judicial appointments, led to a fundamental change in constitutional law. A reconstituted Supreme Court decisively changed direction.

3. *The Revolution of the New Deal Court:* Carolene Products *Footnote Four.* The New Deal Justices reinterpreted the Commerce Clause precedents

---

b. See generally William Leuchtenburg, *The Supreme Court Reborn: The Constitutional Revolution in the Age of Roosevelt* (1995); Daniel Farber, *Who Killed* Lochner?, 90 Geo. L.J. 985 (2002) (reviewing G. Edward White, *The Constitution and the New Deal* (2000)); Mark Tushnet, *The New Deal Constitutional Revolution: Law, Politics, or What?*, 66 U. Chi. L. Rev. 1061 (1999) (reviewing Barry Cushman, *Rethinking the New Deal Court* (1998)).

to vest Congress with broad power not only to regulate economic activities affecting interstate commerce, e.g., *United States v. Darby*, 312 U.S. 100 (1941) (Chapter 7, § 2), but also to aggregate the effects of those activities as a basis for regulation. *Wickard v. Filburn*, 317 U.S. 111 (1942) (same). The New Deal Court halted any serious judicial review of economic legislation and interpreted regulatory laws, especially regulations of labor-management relations, very broadly. For example, the New Deal Court's interpretation of the Norris-LaGuardia Act in *Milk Wagon Drivers' Union v. Lake Valley Farm Products*, 311 U.S. 91 (1940), took federal courts out of the labor injunction business for the next generation. But at the same time it was giving up its role in protecting economic rights, the Court also cautiously began to assume a more aggressive role in protecting individual civil liberties. As much of this book is devoted to a detailed consideration of the Supreme Court's late twentieth-century decisions following in these traditions, we will give only a brief sketch here.

Many of the aspects of the shift from economic rights to civil liberties are evident in *United States v. Carolene Products Co.*, 304 U.S. 144 (1938). Justice Stone's opinion for the Court upheld the constitutionality of a federal statute prohibiting the interstate shipment of "filled milk" (milk from which the butter fat has been extracted and vegetable oil substituted). The Court deferred to a congressional finding that filled milk was "injurious to the public health" because it was not as nourishing as "pure milk." This congressional "finding" is debatable scientifically and in any event seemingly remediable simply by a labeling requirement (e.g., "Contains Filled Milk — Not as Nourishing as Pure Milk, but Less Expensive"). In addition, powerful economic interests had selfish motives for supporting such a statute. Should the Court provide some meaningful scrutiny of statutes that may simply represent political deals among powerful interests, to the detriment of the less powerful, like consumers? In other words, is this too much abdication of judicial responsibility to review economic regulation?

As *Carolene Products* reduced the degree of judicial scrutiny applicable to economic regulation, it suggested, in its now-famous footnote 4, a new set of roles for the Supreme Court:

> There may be narrower scope for operation of the presumption of constitutionality when legislation appears on its face to be within a specific prohibition of the Constitution, such as those of the first ten amendments, which are deemed equally specific when held to be embraced within the Fourteenth. [Citing First Amendment cases.]

> It is unnecessary to consider now whether legislation which restricts those political processes which can ordinarily be expected to bring about repeal of undesirable legislation, is to be subjected to more exacting judicial scrutiny under the general prohibitions of the Fourteenth Amendment than are most other types of legislation. [Citing cases involving the rights to vote, to disseminate information, to organize politically, and to assemble peaceably.]

> Nor need we enquire whether similar considerations enter into the review of statutes directed at particular religious * * * or national * * * or racial minorities[;] whether prejudice against discrete and insular minorities may be a special condition, which tends seriously to curtail the operation of those political processes ordinarily to be relied upon to protect minorities, and which may call for a correspondingly more searching judicial inquiry * * *.

Justice Stone's new roadmap for judicial review was directly inspired by the civil rights movement's normative claim that the Constitution ought to protect people of color and other minorities against "lawless" or "corrupt" local political processes.[c]

The first paragraph of the footnote (which Stone added at the behest of Chief Justice Hughes) seems uncontroversial after *Marbury*: The Court should apply meaningful scrutiny and strike down legislation that violates express constitutional prohibitions. But *Carolene* assumed that these prohibitions also apply to the states through the Fourteenth Amendment, which was a process the NAACP was steadily advancing in its criminal procedure cases. After *Carolene*, the Supreme Court declined to incorporate all the Bill of Rights into the Due Process Clause, see *Adamson v. California*, 332 U.S. 46 (1947) (Chapter 5, § 1), but nonetheless applied particular Bill of Rights protections to state criminal processes. Thus, the Court followed the NAACP's suggestion that due process guaranteed criminal defendants rights not to be convicted on the basis of involuntary confessions, see *Chambers v. Florida*, 309 U.S. 227 (1940); by juries not representative of the community, *Smith v. Texas*, 311 U.S. 128 (1940); and in complex felony proceedings where they were not represented by counsel, *Betts v. Brady*, 316 U.S. 455 (1942). Additionally, the "specific" prohibitions the footnote had in mind, like the First Amendment's protection of speech, are vague and susceptible of any number of judicial constructions. So in *Thornhill v. Alabama*, 310 U.S. 88 (1940), the Court ruled that peaceful picketing was "speech" fully protected by the First Amendment, but just as plausible a construction (and one supported by precedent) would have considered picketing "conduct" not protected by the amendment. For an even more dramatic example, Justice Black's opinion for the Court in *The Steel Seizure Case*, 343 U.S. 579 (1952) (Chapter 8, § 1A), overrode President Truman's seizure of the steel industry during the Korean War on the ground that he was usurping the "legislative" power completely vested in Congress by Article I — but dissenters supported the President's argument that he was carrying out core "executive" duties (given him by Article II), including those vested by the Commander-in-Chief Clause of Article II, § 2. Recall the similar debate over Lincoln's exercise of lawmaking powers during the Civil War, but contrast the different results reached by the Taney and Vinson Courts in *The Prize Cases* and *The Steel Seizure Case*.

The second paragraph of footnote 4 has been more controversial and no easier to apply in practice. This paragraph suggests that judicial deference to statutes such as the one concerning filled milk is based at least in part on a judicial presumption of a fair political playing field. If there is reason to doubt that presumption then there is also less reason to defer to the political process. This justification for undeferential judicial scrutiny might be traced to Madi-

---

c. See David Bixby, *The Roosevelt Court, Democratic Ideology, and Minority Rights: Another Look at* United States v. Classic, 90 Yale L.J. 741 (1981), which demonstrates from personal archives that the *Carolene* Justices — especially Stone, Frankfurter, Douglas, and Black — were specifically motivated by the national embarrassment of apartheid and the Nazi-like injustices toward people of color in the South.

son's observations about local political lock-ins in *Federalist* No. 10 and was justified in the 1930s by reference to the idea that free and open democratic decisionmaking is important for law's legitimacy. See John Hart Ely, *Democracy and Distrust* (1980) (Chapter 2, § 3B), for a more recent articulation. As Justice Brandeis's opinion in *Whitney* had suggested, this was a rationale for a broad view of "speech" protected by the First Amendment: Because picketing is conduct that is "expressive," and a way that workers (and later civil rights demonstrators) can object to the status quo, *Thornhill*'s liberal view of "speech" is supportable under paragraph 2. For another example, the illegitimacy of local governments entrenched by restricting the franchise was the NAACP's pitch for strict scrutiny of southern white primaries in *Nixon v. Herndon* and subsequent cases, as well as subsequent "one person, one vote" challenges to state legislative apportionment (Chapter 5, § 3A). One controversial aspect of this approach is that neither the text of the Constitution nor its history explicitly supports it, and thus it is subject to the charge of judicial activism. A narrower objection is the difficulty in defining what structural defects in democracy are important enough to warrant higher judicial scrutiny.

The third paragraph of footnote 4 has also been controversial. It suggests that the strategy of the second paragraph is insufficient, standing alone, to promote fair politics. For example, even if the formal political rules about voting and so on are fair, a "discrete and insular minority" against which the majority is prejudiced is still likely to lose. The key to the third paragraph is "prejudice," a distortion of the political process under which certain minorities are rendered politically powerless. Illustratively, even if minority citizens in some communities in the mid-twentieth century were able to vote and organize politically, school segregation by race would continue if racially biased political leaders did not need any political support from the minority community. Hence, paragraph 3 was inspired in part by the NAACP's early litigation campaign against apartheid, and in part by prejudice-based municipal discrimination against minority religious groups such as the Jehovah's Witnesses. As with paragraph 2, paragraph 3's theory supporting stringent judicial scrutiny can find no constitutional text specifically supporting it. Moreover, note the difficult definitional questions posed by paragraph 3 (e.g., what is a "discrete and insular minority," and what is "prejudice"). A related problem is where to draw the line on political fairness: For example, should consumers be heard about their inability to prevent the adoption of self-serving economic regulation, like a filled milk statute?

The *Carolene* Court of the 1940s was one that sometimes enforced human rights to protect minorities, as the Stone Court did in *West Virginia State Board of Education v. Barnette*, 319 U.S. 624 (1943) (protecting religious minorities against being required to recite the Pledge of Allegiance in school), and as the Vinson Court did in *Shelley v. Kraemer*, 334 U.S. 1 (1948) (Chapter 3, § 2) (barring courts from enforcing racially restrictive covenants in property transfers). Justice Jackson's opinion for the Court in *Barnette* was a particularly eloquent statement of the new regime, protective of human rights. Like Brandeis before him, Jackson tied the liberty-protecting First Amendment rule against coerced speech to the intellectual and spiritual diversity of American democracy — the very democratic values the United States was fighting to preserve in World War II. He closed his opinion: "If there is any fixed star in our constitutional constellation, it is that no official, high or petty, can prescribe what shall be orthodox in politics, nationalism, religion, or other matters of opinion or force citizens to confess by word or act their faith therein."

Other times, however, the Court recognized that *Carolene* values were at stake but declined for pragmatic reasons to enforce them. The best (or worst) example of this phenomenon was the Court's response to the federal government's program for regulating Japanese-American citizens during World War II. Citing evidence later revealed to have been incorrect and probably perjured, the Army insisted that the loyalty of such citizens could not be presumed. Based upon such suppositions, the Army imposed a curfew on Japanese Americans and then directed that they be evacuated from their homes and relocated in detention camps. These citizens challenged this racially discriminatory treatment under the Fifth Amendment. In *Hirabayashi v. United States*, 320 U.S. 81 (1943), and *Korematsu v. United States*, 323 U.S. 214 (1944), the Supreme Court recognized that the Due Process Clause of the Fifth Amendment regulates racially discriminatory federal laws and that laws restricting the rights of a single racial group are "immediately suspect" and ought to be subjected to the "most rigid scrutiny." Deferring to the Army's assertions of compelling wartime emergency, however, the Court upheld the federal government's curfew (*Hirabayashi*) and evacuation from their homes (*Korematsu*) of Japanese Americans. In *Ex parte Endo*, 323 U.S. 283 (1944), however, the Court ruled that the Army did *not* have legal authority to detain concededly loyal Japanese-American citizens. Because of the racist motivations for targeting only Japanese Americans for special disability, and the corrupt evidence adduced by the government, *Hirabayashi* and *Korematsu* are two of the most criticized Supreme Court decisions of the twentieth century.

SECTION 7. THE WARREN COURT AND THE TRIUMPH OF THE CIVIL RIGHTS MOVEMENT, 1953-1969

An underlying theme of *Carolene Products* was that centralization of power in the national government (the New Deal, World War II) went hand in glove with advances in the civil rights movement (the NAACP). The apex of these twin developments came after the appointment of Governor Earl Warren of California as Chief Justice in 1953. Warren was a major Republican Party figure (Thomas Dewey's running mate for the White House in 1948), enjoyed virtually unprecedented popularity as Governor of California, and helped Dwight Eisenhower win the Republican nomination for President in 1952. Warren's nomination as Chief Justice was probably President Eisenhower's payback of the marker Warren held for his efforts in 1952. Warren did not come to the position with deep legal erudition, or even unusual analytical ability. But he did bring a sense of justice and a tremendous political ability to lead the Court in new, and sometimes radical and controversial, directions. At oral argument, he was prone to brush aside what he considered legal technicalities and ask lawyers to defend the fairness of their positions.[a]

The Warren Court was committed to the legitimacy of the New Deal and centralization of power in Washington, D.C., as well as protecting individual human rights along the lines suggested in *Carolene*. Within that consensus, there was sometimes fierce debate as to how activist the Court should be; much of the debate was shaped by two New Deal appointees, Justices Hugo Black and Felix Frankfurter. Black grew up in a small town in Alabama and received his law degree from the University of Alabama. He was a part-time police court judge and prosecutor. After serving in the military and practicing law for a few years, he ran for the U.S. Senate. He was a key Roosevelt supporter in Congress. After his appointment to the Court, the public was shocked to learn that he had briefly been a member of the Ku Klux Klan, but Black was a strong supporter of civil rights, at least until near the end of his career. He was famous for carrying a copy of the Constitution with him and consulting it when legal questions arose, giving him the appearance of an unsophisticated rustic, but his library showed that he had also read deeply in American history. Black championed the views that the Bill of Rights applied to the states via the Fourteenth Amendment and that the First Amendment was an "absolute." He defended these clear-cut positions with a stubborn eloquence that eventually moved the Court a long way in his direction. Together with William O. Douglas,[b] Hugo Black was for decades the most outspoken civil libertarian on the Court.

Black and Douglas were often aligned against Felix Frankfurter. Frankfurter was an immigrant who worked his way out of the Lower East Side, through a spectacular career as a law student at Harvard, and rose to become a leading member of the Harvard law faculty. He was a key adviser to FDR, a role he continued even after he was appointed to the Supreme Court in 1939. Frankfurter was a strong believer in doctrines of judicial restraint, such as *stare decisis* (the Court must usually follow its prior interpretations of the Constitution), the rule of law (the Court should normally follow the plain meaning and original intent of statutes), and the avoidance of political questions. His later reputation as an anti-civil libertarian is ironic, since he wrote or joined many libertarian decisions and before his service on the Court was a public supporter of Sacco and Vanzetti, a founder of the American Civil Liberties Union, and an

---

a. See, e.g., Bernard Schwartz, *Super Chief* (1983); G. Edward White, *Earl Warren: A Public Life* (1982). There were limits to Warren's "sense of justice": He was an important figure supporting the evacuation and detention of Japanese-American citizens during World War II, convened a special session of the California legislature to enact the most aggressively antigay legislation in American history, and during his service on the Court was no particular friend of equal rights for women. See William Eskridge, Jr., *Dishonorable Passions: American Sodomy Law, 1861-2003* (2008) (detailed history of Warren's anti-homosexual record as governor).

b. Douglas had been a rising young star as a law professor, first at Columbia and then at Yale. He then became the first chair of the Securities and Exchange Commission, and perhaps more important for his future, a poker-playing buddy of FDR. He was appointed in 1939. Over the course of his career, he earned a reputation for both extraordinary brilliance and exceptional carelessness. He was also the most dedicated environmentalist to serve on the Court.

advisor to the NAACP. Nevertheless, by the end of his career on the bench, he was constantly at war with Black and the Warren Court majority over what he perceived as their undue judicial activism. It was only after Frankfurter left the bench that the Warren Court had a solid majority of activist liberals, but Frankfurter continued his judicial restraint campaign from the grave: His intellectual disciple John Marshall Harlan (grandson of the *Plessy* dissenter) took over as the leading dissenter, and many of his law clerks, such as Alexander Bickel, became leading legal scholars and continued his campaign against the Warren Court majority.

1. *The Triumph of the Civil Rights Movement: The Warren Court vs. Apartheid.* The replacement of Fred Vinson with Earl Warren as Chief Justice reportedly broke the Supreme Court's ambivalence about how to handle the NAACP's massive challenge to segregated public schools in *Brown v. Board of Education*, 347 U.S. 483 (1954) (state segregation), and *Bolling v. Sharpe*, 347 U.S. 497 (1954) (segregation in D.C. schools, challenged under the Fifth Amendment) (Chapter 2, § 1). Warren's unanimous decisions striking down school segregation are, we believe, the most important judicial decisions of the post-World-War II era. They embodied the virtues Warren wanted judicial review to foster: equality of opportunity as the goal, fairness as the guidepost, and public morality as the basis for evaluation. The opinions were also illustrative of the central quandary of judicial review: In a representative democracy, what gives the unelected Court the authority to overturn popular desires? How is *Brown* any more legitimate than *Dred Scott* or *Lochner*? Most of the important constitutional theorizing in the last forty years has been directly or indirectly in response to *Brown*. For that reason, Chapter 2 starts with that case, explores it in some detail, and uses it as an introduction to the "big theories" of judicial review. We then systematically examine the doctrinal and theoretical issues raised by the Equal Protection Clause, first in connection with racial classifications (Chapter 3) and then in connection with gender and other classifications (Chapter 4). This focus on individual rights would have been unlikely before the New Deal, and the focus on equality unthinkable before the Warren Court.

Although Warren's opinion in *Brown* focused on the importance of public education and the baleful effects of *de jure* segregation on black schoolchildren, civil rights attorneys read the case as finally giving bite to the *Hirabayashi* and *Korematsu* dictum that race-based classifications are "odious to a free people." The Warren Court confirmed that interpretation in *Loving v. Virginia*, 388 U.S. 1 (1967) (Chapter 3, § 1A), which struck down a state law barring different-race marriages. The Chief Justice's opinion for the Court recognized what appeared to be a per se rule against race-based classifications rooted in the discredited philosophy of "white supremacy." Implicitly after *Brown* and explicitly after *Loving*, race-based classifications were at least "suspect" in American law and required the most compelling state interest to support them.

Brown had enormous and complicated ramifications for American public law generally. Some historians think that *Brown* encouraged the civil rights movement to ever more aggressive challenges to apartheid.[c] The Montgomery bus boycott of 1955-56 (led by Dr. Martin Luther King and his Southern Christian Leadership Conference) was formally resolved in favor of the opponents of racial segregation when the Supreme Court affirmed a lower court ruling that the challenged regime was unconstitutional. *Gayle v. Browder*, 352 U.S. 903 (1956) (per curiam). As the civil rights movement became a mass social movement, with activism focused outside the courtroom, the Warren Court repeatedly struck down southern efforts to suppress peaceful protests, usually through doctrinal innovation under the First Amendment. Thus, the Court created a "freedom of association" (Chapter 6, § 6) to protect the NAACP against state harassment in *NAACP v. Alabama*, 357 U.S. 449 (1958); extended *Thornhill* to protect mass protest marches in *Edwards v. South Carolina*, 372 U.S. 229 (1963), and *Cox v. Louisiana*, 379 U.S. 559 (1965); and created heightened burdens of proof for convictions of lunch counter sit-in protesters in *Garner v. Louisiana*, 368 U.S. 157 (1961). These cases expanded the First Amendment's reach: Not only was expressive conduct protected by the Speech Clause, but group actions, through associations, sit-ins, and protest marches, were protected as well.

Most scholars believe that, whatever the impact of *Brown*, the greatest payoffs for the civil rights movement were the Civil Rights Act of 1964 and the Voting Rights Act of 1965. These enactments were broad assertions of congressional authority and placed the resources of the federal government behind the anti-segregation principle. The Warren Court upheld these statutes against federalism-based attacks in cases excerpted and discussed in Chapter 7. In the cases upholding the 1964 Act, the Court interpreted the Commerce Clause expansively (Chapter 7, § 2); in the cases upholding the 1965 Act, the Court interpreted congressional power to enforce the Fourteenth and Fifteenth Amendments expansively (id. § 3B). During the 1960s, federalism — which had been the shibboleth for the South's massive resistance to integration — seemed deflated. National policy as well as reformist energy were increasingly focused on the national government.

2. *The Evolving Protection of Individual Rights Against Both State and National Infringement.* Responding to cases brought by civil rights groups, the New Deal Court had imported federal criminal procedure standards into the Due Process Clause's assurances of rights in state proceedings. In the 1960s, the Court engaged in a process of *selective incorporation* of most of the specific criminal procedure protections of the Bill of Rights into the Due Process Clause (Chapter 6, § 1); see Jerrold Israel, *Selective Incorporation Revisited*, 71 Geo. L.J. 253 (1982). The Warren Court responded to the terror often visited on

---

c. David Garrow, *Bearing the Cross: Martin Luther King, Jr., and the Southern Christian Leadership Conference* (1986); Richard Kluger, *Simple Justice: The History of* Brown v. Board of Education *and Black America's Struggle for Equality* (1975). Compare Gerald Rosenberg, *The Hollow Hope: Can Courts Bring About Social Change?* (1991) (no), with Michael Klarman, Brown, *Racial Change, and the Civil Rights Movement*, 80 Va. L. Rev. 7 (1994) (*Brown* brought about change only indirectly, by triggering hysterical southern opposition), with David Garrow, *Hopelessly Hollow History: Revisionist Devaluing of* Brown v. Board of Education, 80 Va. L. Rev. 151 (1994) (vigorously disputing both Rosenberg and Klarman).

people of color by racist police officers (in the North as well as South), and this concern for protecting vulnerable defendants from overbearing police led the Court to expand upon the Bill of Rights' protections in the new due process cases. For example, the Chief Justice ruled in *Miranda v. Arizona*, 384 U.S. 436 (1966), that the police could not interrogate accused persons without telling them of their constitutional rights to remain silent and to speak with an attorney, including an attorney paid for by the state if the accused could not afford one (*Gideon v. Wainwright*, 372 U.S. 335 (1963)). The result of the Court's activism was the creation of a *constitutional code of national criminal procedure* in the 1960s, a code that was trimmed back in the 1970s and 1980s but whose character remains part of American public law to this day. E.g., *Dickerson v. United States*, 530 U.S. 428 (2000) (reaffirming *Miranda* as a constitutional rule binding on federal as well as state law enforcement). Because these cases are usually the subject of a whole course in criminal procedure, this casebook does not treat them in detail.

A second aspect of the Due Process Clause was the void-for-vagueness doctrine. Before 1960, the Court periodically struck down "vague" criminal laws that gave insufficient notice to potential violators. E.g., *Stromberg v. California*, 283 U.S. 359 (1931) (anti-sedition law); *Joseph Burstyn, Inc. v. Wilson*, 343 U.S. 495 (1952) (movie licensing law). After 1960, especially in the civil rights protest cases, the Court emphasized different vices of vague laws: they gave police discretion to go after unpopular persons or groups, thereby chilling their exercise of free speech rights. E.g., *NAACP v. Button*, 371 U.S. 415, 432-33 (1963); *Shuttlesworth v. Birmingham*, 382 U.S. 87, 90-92 (1965); *Cox*, 397 U.S. at 551-52 (Black, J., concurring); see Anthony Amsterdam, Note, *The Void-for-Vagueness Doctrine in the Supreme Court*, 109 U. Pa. L. Rev. 67, 88-90 (1960). Although these protest cases represented the high point of the Court's enforcement of the void-for-vagueness doctrine, it retains bite to this day — primarily for the arbitrary enforcement and chilling effect reasons. See *City of Chicago v. Morales*, 527 U.S. 41 (1999), following *Papachristou v. City of Jacksonville*, 405 U.S. 156 (1972) (Chapter 6, § 5).

Although not always consistent with its general *Carolene* philosophy, the Warren Court was also open to recognizing unenumerated but "fundamental" rights: the right to vote (discussed below); the right to travel, see *Shapiro v. Thompson*, 394 U.S. 618 (1969); and the *right to privacy*. Next to *Brown* and its voting rights decisions, the Warren Court precedent with the greatest legal repercussions may have been *Griswold v. Connecticut*, 381 U.S. 479 (1965) (Chapter 5, § 4A), which struck down a law restricting the use of contraceptives as a violation of a right to personal privacy located within the "penumbras" of the Bill of Rights. The Court as protector of fundamental rights is nothing new (see the Takings Clause of the Fifth Amendment and the *Lochner* era's liberty of contract idea), and the Warren Court argued that the right to privacy had deep roots in American public law. Chapter 5, § 4 explores this issue, focusing on the controversies surrounding *Roe v. Wade*, 410 U.S. 113 (1973) (Chapter 5, § 4B), which provided substantial protection for a woman's right to have an abortion, and *Bowers v. Hardwick*, 478 U.S. 186 (1986) (id. § 4C), which provided no protection for private consensual sex by gay men or lesbians.

Consistent with *Carolene*, the Warren Court expanded the reach of the First Amendment even in non-race cases. For example, the Court gave greater bite to Holmes's "clear and present danger" requirement for state regulation of "seditious" speech. In *Dennis v. United States*, 341 U.S. 494 (1951), the Vinson Court had upheld the Smith Act, which made it illegal for anyone to advocate the overthrow of our form of government. Although the Act was aimed at extinguishing the American Communist Party, the Warren Court held that Smith Act convictions upon the basis of abstract advocacy were inconsistent with the First Amendment. *Yates v. United States*, 354 U.S. 298 (1957); *Scales v. United States*, 367 U.S. 203 (1961) (Chapter 6, § 2A). In these and other cases, the Warren Court repudiated the political tradition that had inspired the Sedition Act of 1798.

The Warren Court's philosophy of the Religion Clauses was similarly aggressive and individualist. Enforcing the "wall of separation" suggested in *Everson v. Board of Education*, 330 U.S. 1 (1947) (Chapter 6, § 7B), the Warren Court applied the Establishment Clause strictly, to invalidate compulsory school prayer in *Engel v. Vitale*, 370 U.S. 421 (1962), and *School District of Abington Township v. Schempp*, 374 U.S. 203 (1963), both reaffirmed in *Lee v. Weisman*, 505 U.S. 577 (1992) (Chapter 6, § 7B). These decisions brought upon the Court more sustained public denunciation than any other Warren Court precedents outside of the race area. On the other hand, the Warren Court also gave strong effect to the Free Exercise Clause, construing it to require states to accommodate religious minorities. See *Sherbert v. Verner*, 374 U.S. 398 (1963), limited by *Employment Div'n v. Smith*, 494 U.S. 872 (1990) (Chapter 6, § 7A).

Prior Courts had assumed that libel and obscenity were outside the protections of the First Amendment. The Warren Court reaffirmed the exclusion of obscene speech in *Roth v. United States*, 354 U.S. 476 (1957), but limited obscenity to materials whose predominant appeal is to a "prurient interest, i.e., a shameful or morbid interest in nudity, sex, or excretion." The next generation saw intellectually helpless Justices struggle to determine what racy literature and erotica were protected under this test and amended versions of it (Chapter 6, § 3A). Perhaps more successfully, the Warren Court limited the ability of state libel laws to penalize published falsehoods. In order to assure the existence of a vigorous and unchilled press, the Court ruled in *New York Times v. Sullivan*, 376 U.S. 254 (1964) (Chapter 6, § 2B), that public figures had to demonstrate "actual malice" to recover for libel. Again, the basic test has been refined through subsequent Supreme Court decisions, but unlike the obscenity cases the libel cases have followed a coherent path. Chapter 6 explores these and other doctrinal and theoretical issues implicated in the First Amendment.

3. *The Supreme Court at the Bar of Politics: The Jurisprudence of Voting.* The primary architect of the Supreme Court's individual rights jurisprudence in the 1960s was not Earl Warren or Hugo Black, but was Warren's lieutenant, Justice William Brennan. Although a liberal Democrat, Brennan had caught the attention of the Eisenhower Administration through favorable reviews of his service on the New Jersey Supreme Court. In an act of bipartisanship he soon regretted, Eisenhower in 1956 named Brennan to the Court, where he served

until 1990. The author of the Court's cautious opinion in *Roth* and the critical fifth vote to refuse to decide the contraception issue in 1961, Brennan did not start out as a constitutional activist. But in the early 1960s he emerged as the political captain of the liberal activist Justices and served that role for almost 30 years. Justice Brennan was the main sponsor of the idea of selective incorporation of specific Bill of Rights protections into the Due Process Clause and pressed Justice Douglas to rest the right of privacy on the emanations of various of the Bill of Rights. His opinions in *Button*, *Sullivan*, and later cases are liberal constitutional classics.

Probably Brennan's most important opinion was *Baker v. Carr*, 369 U.S. 186 (1962) (Chapter 9, § 1), which held that an equal protection challenge to state electoral apportionment is justiciable and is not a *political question*. *Baker* remains important as the leading statement of the current political question doctrine: federal courts will ordinarily adjudicate constitutional claims unless the Constitution commits the issue to the political branches, courts lack the expertise or standards to adjudicate the matter, or pragmatic considerations counsel against an adjudication. Generally, federal courts will rarely dismiss a lawsuit under this doctrine, but may well dismiss for lack of standing, which reflects some of the same underlying policies. One legacy of *Baker* was the one-person, one-vote formula the Court adopted in *Reynolds v. Sims*, 377 U.S. 533 (1964) (Chapter 5, § 3A), and subsequent cases. This formula revolutionized state and federal representation, erasing outdated electoral boundaries and the advantages accruing to rural districts and introducing a new politics of decennial gerrymandering. A broader legacy is that the Court has become pervasively embroiled in the political thicket of federal election law — not only monitoring compliance with *Reynolds*, but also regulating political and racial gerrymanders, the deployment of money in politics, the regulation of lobbying, and even the ability of the Census Bureau to estimate population beyond that revealed by actual head counts. A final legacy of *Baker* is one Justice Brennan surely did not anticipate: *Bush v. Gore*, 531 U.S. 98 (2000) (id.), where the Court essentially picked a President in the teeth of apparent constitutional commitment of Electoral College issues to Congress — yet none of the parties or *amici* suggested that these issues constituted a political question.

SECTION 8. THE NIXON-REAGAN COURT: CONSERVATIVE LEGAL PROCESS AND WOMEN'S RIGHTS, 1969-2001

The election of Richard Nixon as President in 1968 ushered in a sea change in American politics and constitutionalism. The Silent Majority that Nixon claimed to represent did not support the apartheid and massive resistance of the Old South but embraced a pragmatic politics critical of the civil rights agenda. Reflecting a new mood among the American people that was skeptical of the central government, Nixon's Court — Chief Justice Warren Burger (1969) and Justices Harry Blackmun (1970), Lewis Powell (1971), and William Rehnquist (1971) — retreated from none of the formal anti-apartheid decisions of the Warren Court but declined to expand on them either. While *de jure* segregation remained taboo, actual integration took a back seat to other constitutional values: federalism, freedom of association, and the perceived institutional limitations of the federal courts. Although the Burger Court went slowly in race cases and was unreceptive to the rights of lesbians and gay men, it was activist in cases involving states' rights, separation of powers at the national level, and the rights of women.

The Supreme Court continued to move in a more conservative direction after President Nixon was forced from office (1974). The next seven appointments installed Justices more conservative than their predecessors: John Paul Stevens, replacing Justice Douglas in 1975; Sandra Day O'Connor, replacing Justice Stewart in 1981; William Hubbs Rehnquist, replacing Chief Justice Burger in 1986; Antonin Scalia, replacing (Associate) Justice Rehnquist in 1986; Anthony Kennedy, replacing Justice Powell in 1987; David Souter, replacing Justice Brennan in 1990; and Clarence Thomas, replacing Justice Marshall in 1991. Only the Clinton-era appointments of Justices Ruth Bader Ginsburg (1993) and Stephen Breyer (1994) bucked the trend toward conservative appointments. Ironically, the parade of appointments by Presidents promising "strict constructionists" resulted in the most aggressive period of judicial review in the nation's history. The Court has, literally, struck down laws left and right, more often than any previous Court in the nation's history.

1. *The Race Cases and a New Understanding of Equal Protection.* Led by Justice Brennan, the early years of the Burger Court continued the Warren Court's insistence on actual integration of formerly segregated public schools, with the high point being the busing order approved in *Swann v. Charlotte-Mecklenburg Bd. of Educ.*, 402 U.S. 1 (1971) (Chapter 2, § 2C1). The Court's opinion rejected pragmatic arguments by *amicus* counsel Lewis Powell, who maintained that forced busing not only violated white people's rights to neighborhood schools, but also would be ineffective because whites would simply relocate to escape too much integration. In *Swann*'s wake, and once Powell was named a Justice, the Burger Court drew lines beyond which lower courts could not go in crafting remedial *Brown* decrees. E.g., *Milliken v. Bradley*, 418 U.S. 717 (1974) (remedial decree cannot require "interdistrict" busing). If the Warren Court was characterized by vision and a sometimes unrealistic focus on equality above other values, the Burger Court was characterized by a cost-benefit mentality which focused closely on the practical efficacy of judicial decrees.

The turning point in the Court's approach to equality issues can be fixed precisely: *San Antonio Independent School District v. Rodriguez*, 411 U.S. 1 (1973) (Chapter 5, § 3B, but you might read this case in connection with the post-*Swann* cases). Mexican-American plaintiffs claimed that Texas's system of financing public schools effectively denied lower-income families anything close to the level of education afforded students in upper-income school districts and sought a remedy under the Equal Protection Clause. Justice Powell's opinion for the Court started with an astute analysis of the institutional limitations federalism imposed upon equality claims: neither the Constitution nor sound principles of democratic governance countenanced dictation of local education decisions by federal judges. Powell saw no justification for extending the Warren Court's voting and travel cases to recognize a new "fundamental right" (education) that would trigger heightened equal protection scrutiny.

Finally, Powell was skeptical of plaintiffs' claims that they were being discriminated against on the basis of wealth and, in any event, rejected the idea that wealth should be treated as a classification (like race) triggering heightened scrutiny. (Plaintiffs also claimed that the state policy had race-based effects, a claim which Powell dished off on the ground that the state could not be charged with discriminatory effects unless they were "intentional." This aside was to be the basis for a formal holding of the Court in *Washington v. Davis*, 426 U.S. 229 (1976) (Chapter 3, § 1B): State policies having racially discriminatory effects were not subject to strict scrutiny unless those effects were intended.)

Justice Powell's opinion for the Court was met by a dissenting opinion by Justice Thurgood Marshall, not only the Court's first African-American Justice, but also the most successful litigator to have sat on the Court since John Marshall. Thurgood Marshall succeeded Charles Houston as the chief litigating counsel for the NAACP and was the architect of that association's anti-apartheid litigation campaign. Although he is best known for his successful argument in *Brown*, many of his most impressive victories were in the courts of southern and border states, where Marshall represented people of color in venues hostile or at best skeptical toward his claims. During his lengthy service on the Court (1967-91), Marshall's chief interests were equal protection law and civil procedure. The *Rodriguez* dissent was his leading statement in the equal protection area.

Without denigrating the federal arrangement, Marshall emphasized the commitment to equality in educational opportunity that was the formal basis for the Court's decision in *Brown* and argued that plaintiffs ought to be given a chance to make their case. On the merits, Marshall set forth a "sliding scale" theory of equal protection: the level of scrutiny the Court should give to a policy depended on the importance of the right to the people excluded, the historical reliability of the classification deployed, and the quality of the state's justification. Under these criteria, as well as the legacy of *Brown*, plaintiffs had made out a strong case. Although the Supreme Court rejected, by a 5-4 vote, Marshall's arguments, many state supreme courts have accepted them as constructions of their state constitutions (Chapter 5, § 3B).

School desegregation was not the only area of constitutional discourse driven by race. In 1963, the NAACP initiated a litigation campaign against the death penalty, one that bore fruit in *Furman v. Georgia*, 408 U.S. 238 (1972) (per curiam). A bare majority of the Court ruled that broadly discretionary death penalty laws violated the Eighth Amendment; four Justices (Douglas, Brennan, Stewart, Marshall) were influenced by the fact that jury discretion to impose death was disproportionately visited upon defendants of color. *Furman* was not the death knell of capital punishment in the United States, however. Like *Brown*, *Furman* contributed to a fierce death penalty countermovement. States responded with statutes limiting capital punishment to the most serious crimes and providing juries with greater guidance in exercising their judgment. Civil rights groups objected that these new statutes did not solve the problems identified by the *Furman* Justices, but the Supreme Court upheld most of these laws in *Gregg v. Georgia*, 428 U.S. 153 (1976), and its companion cases. *Gregg* by no means ended judicial review of death penalty laws. Because of the high stakes on both sides and the open-textured standards of the Eighth Amendment, the Court has continued to review death sentences for procedural and substantive errors.[a]

As in the public school cases, Justice Powell was the critical voice on the Court when it addressed the contentious issue of affirmative action in *Regents of the University of California v. Bakke*, 438 U.S. 265 (1978) (Chapter 3, § 3A).[b] Bakke, a white man, challenged the admission plan for the medical school of the University of California at Davis, which had reserved for minority students sixteen of the hundred places in its first-year class. Bakke and his *amici* argued that any race-based state classification was suspect under *Loving* and that state affirmative action programs deprived white people of their equality rights while reenforcing stereotypes about black people. The state and its many *amici* (including the ACLU, the ABA, and the NAACP's Inc. Fund) defended the program as needed to assure diversity in and to remedy centuries of black exclusion from higher education.

The Burger Court fractured. Four Justices (Burger, Stewart, Rehnquist, Stevens) maintained that the admissions quota violated federal statutory law and did not reach Bakke's equal protection claim. Four Justices (Brennan, White, Marshall, Blackmun) maintained that the quota violated neither federal statutory nor constitutional law. Justice Powell wrote only for himself but delivered the judgment of the Court: The race-based program was subject to strict scrutiny; such scrutiny could be satisfied by a program narrowly tailored to improve institutional diversity or remedy the ongoing effects of past discrimination; the quota program did not meet that test, but a program where race is a plus factor could do so. Although Powell's Solomonic opinion did not settle the contentious issue of affirmative action, it was (and is) widely hailed as a workable solution. Importantly, Powell demonstrated how deference to the institutional needs of state governments (the bases for his opposition to *Swann* and his majority opinion in *Rodriguez*) could serve liberal as well as conservative institutional needs.

The Burger Court never achieved a stable majority for the Powell or any other test for affirmative action, but a majority of the Rehnquist Court treated even "benign" or "remedial" race-based classifications as "suspect." See *City of Richmond v. J.A. Croson Co.*, 488 U.S. 469 (1989) (state and municipal plans); *Adarand Constructors, Inc. v. Pena*, 515 U.S. 200 (1995) (federal plans) (both in Chapter 3, § 3B). Dissenting in *Adarand*, Justice Stevens objected that

---

a. For some of the Court's busy death penalty jurisprudence, see *Coker v. Georgia*, 433 U.S. 584 (1977) (striking down capital punishment for rape); *McCleskey v. Kemp*, 481 U.S. 279 (1987) (rejecting challenge to regime where crimes against white people were regularly punished by death, but analogous crimes against black people were not); *Atkins v. Virginia*, 122 S.Ct. 2242 (2002) (striking down capital punishment for mentally disabled criminals); *Baze v. Rees*, 128 S.Ct. 1520 (2008) (upholding lethal injection as a permissible method for carrying out the death penalty); *Kennedy v. Louisiana*, 128 S.Ct. 2641 (2008) (striking down death penalty for child rape).

b. See generally John Calvin Jeffries, Jr., *Justice Lewis F. Powell, Jr. and the Era of Judicial Balance* 455-501 (1994) (Powell's role in the case); Bernard Schwartz, *Behind* Bakke: *Affirmative Action and the Supreme Court* (1988).

classifications motivated by remedial motives and benefitting racial minorities ought not receive the same beady-eyed scrutiny as those motivated by white supremacy and racial prejudice (*Loving*).   Justice O'Connor's opinion responded that race has been such an unreliable criterion for state policy that it should be presumed inadmissible. Concurring opinions went further, claiming that any kind of state racial classification perpetuates racial stereotypes and prejudice. Like Powell in *Bakke*, O'Connor in *Adarand* also insisted that strict scrutiny not always be fatal scrutiny: A carefully crafted affirmative action plan might pass such scrutiny.

The Rehnquist Court's affirmative action cases de-emphasized the *anti-subordination* goal that the Framers of the Fourteenth Amendment saw as central to the Equal Protection Clause, in favor of the *rationality* goal. That is, the majority Justices viewed the equal protection project as discouraging the state from relying on irrational classifications, rather than improving the status of subordinated classes. They also rejected the *Carolene* paradigm that the Court should only intervene when the political process is dysfunctional. The minority set-aside challenged in *Adarand* was adopted by an overwhelmingly white Congress for the benefit of people of color — in contrast to apartheid measures which had been adopted by white legislatures to marginalize and suppress people of color. See also *Shaw v. Reno*, 509 U.S. 630 (1993) (Chapter 3, § 3C), another opinion by Justice O'Connor opening up equal protection challenges to electoral districts drawn to make it more likely that racial minorities would be elected.

Just as the Court has moved toward a rationality-based but flexible model, where some race-based classifications survived strict scrutiny, so it showed some willingness to give sharper teeth to the standard rational basis test applicable to most classifications challenged under the Equal Protection Clause. In *City of Cleburne v. Cleburne Living Center*, 473 U.S. 432 (1985) (Chapter 4, § 3C), the Court ruled that disability is not suspect like race or quasi-suspect like sex but nevertheless struck down a municipal prohibition of a group home for the mentally disabled on the ground that it was motivated by a " 'bare . . . desire to harm a politically unpopular group.'" Without addressing the suspect classification issue, the Rehnquist Court applied the rational basis test in a similar way to strike down a state antigay initiative in *Romer v. Evans*, 517 U.S. 620 (1996) (Chapter 4, § 3D).

Romer is more broadly significant. Just as African Americans and women had organized themselves into social movements powerfully objecting to legal rules excluding or segregating them, thousands of lesbians, gay men, and bisexuals in the 1970s "came out" of their "closets" to resist pervasive state discrimination against them. Outside a few censorship cases, the Warren Court had construed statutes and constitutional precedents expansively to *add to* rather than ameliorate legal discriminations against gay people. E.g., *Boutilier v. INS*, 387 U.S. 118 (1967) (ruling that apparent bisexuality was per se evidence of "psychopathic personality" requiring deportation of alien). The sex-squeamish Burger Court had found ways to avoid full briefing and decision in every gay rights case to come before it — until *Bowers v. Hardwick* (Chapter 5, § 4C), which yielded an opinion sustaining the constitutionality of state criminalization of "homosexual sodomy" that gay people and their friends found too dismissive of their claims to dignified treatment.[c] Even when rebuffing lesbian and gay equality claims, the Rehnquist Court has avoided the open disrespect of its predecessor, and *Romer* suggests the possibility that the Constitution provides at least minimal protections for lesbians, gay men, bisexual, and transgendered people.

2. *Women's Equality and Privacy Rights.* Ironically, just as Nixon's Supreme Court was turning down the intensity of civil rights litigation, it was turning it up in cases involving the rights of women. A new wave of feminist activism had swept the 1960s, and women insisting on legal equality consciously followed the civil rights model: Establish litigating institutions such as the ACLU's Women's Rights Project and challenge sex-based discriminations on equal protection grounds.[d] As head of the ACLU's Women's Rights Project, Ruth Bader Ginsburg pressed the race analogy in the early 1970s: Sex ought to be a suspect classification for the same reasons race was — it was a trait that rarely advanced legitimate state policies, and such classifications disadvantaged women, either directly by excluding them from opportunities men had or indirectly by perpetuating stereotypes of women as civilizing domestics and of men as public actors.

While Ginsburg was seeking strict scrutiny for sex classifications, the states were debating the Equal Rights Amendment, which Congress had passed in 1972. Justice Brennan came within one vote of establishing sex as a suspect classification in *Frontiero v. Richardson*, 411 U.S. 677 (1973) (Chapter 4, § 2B1). In *Craig v. Boren*, 429 U.S. 190 (1976) (id.), he obtained a Court majority for what has become known as "intermediate scrutiny": Sex-based classifications "must serve important governmental objectives and must be substantially related to achievement of those objectives." Although a vague test, the Burger Court applied it to strike down most sex-based rules excluding women from opportunities men had, but not to invalidate sex-based classifications the Justices considered remedial. These and later cases are excerpted in § 2B1 of Chapter 4. As in the race cases also decided in the 1970s, the Burger Court was unwilling to apply heightened scrutiny to sex-neutral laws merely because they had discriminatory effects on women, unless it could be shown that the effects were intentional (Chapter 4, § 2B3).

The more conservative Rehnquist Court was, ironically, even more aggressive in enforcing the no sex discrimination norm in cases such as *J.E.B. v. Alabama ex rel. T.B.*, 511 U.S. 127 (1994) (regulating peremptory challenges to prospective jurors based on their sex), and *United States v. Virginia*, 518 U.S. 515 (1996) (state cannot run single-sex college) (both in Chapter 4, § 2B1). Indeed, Justice Ruth Bader Ginsburg wrote the opinion for the Court in the latter

---

c. On the antigay jurisprudence of the Warren and Burger Courts, see William Eskridge, Jr., *Gaylaw: Challenging the Apartheid of the Closet* 98-137, 149-72 (1999).

d. See Harrison, *On Account of Sex*; Susan Hartmann, *The Other Feminists: Activists in the Liberal Establishment* (1998); Serena Mayeri, Note, *"A Common Fate of Discrimination": Race-Gender Analogies in Legal and Historical Perspective*, 110 Yale L.J. 1045 (2001).

case, which invalidated Virginia's system of separate schools for men (the Virginia Military Academy) and women (a leadership institute situated in Mary Baldwin College). Justice Scalia's blistering dissent accused the majority of smuggling strict scrutiny for sex-based classifications into the opinion, but the Court applied the intermediate level of scrutiny in a subsequent naturalization case, *Nguyen v. INS*, 533 U.S. 53 (2001).

At the same time the Court was moving toward heightened scrutiny of sex-based classifications, it expanded the right of privacy to assure women the right to abortion. *Griswold* had served as the constitutional basis for a vigorous women's "pro-choice" movement in the 1960s. Sarah Weddington, the lawyer for the pregnant challenger in *Roe v. Wade* (Chapter 5, § 4B), argued that, for most women, pregnancy is one of the most determinative events in their lives. To enjoy the complete freedom to pursue careers, develop as individuals, and plan their families, women need to be able to choose abortions without interference from the state. Surprisingly, these arguments had a very receptive audience among the all-male U.S. Supreme Court — and Harry Blackmun emerged as their advocate within the Court. This was ironic, as Blackmun was appointed as part of President Nixon's promise to name "strict constructionists" to the Court, and indeed Blackmun had been Chief Justice Burger's "Minnesota Twin" in voting to deny judicial relief in the Texas school funding case, the racially disparate impact cases, the early gay rights cases, and the death penalty cases being adjudicated at about the same time. On the other hand, Blackmun had been General Counsel of the Mayo Clinic and was knowledgeable about the medical professional problems with existing state abortion laws (doctors as a class were more opposed to them than were women).

Ultimately, seven Justices joined Blackmun's opinion in *Roe v. Wade*. The opinion recognized women's interest in abortion as a due process right, thereby dislodging the privacy right from the penumbras of the Bill of Rights and re-situating it in the Due Process Clause. Blackmun also ruled that the fetus was not a "person" under the Fourteenth Amendment. Although he recognized that the state had legitimate interests later in a pregnancy to protect the life of the fetus, the holding that fetuses themselves have no legal rights was immediately and strongly contested by the already-emerging "pro-life" movement — a movement greatly energized by *Roe v. Wade*. The pro-life movement has been just as much a social movement as women's liberation and the pro-choice movement. Indeed, a pro-life stance is just as important for some people's identity as being a feminist or pro-choice is for other people. Since January 1973, when the Court handed down *Roe*, this issue has embroiled the body politic and periodically returns to the Supreme Court, as pro-life states try new forms of regulation, sometimes successfully and sometimes not.

Just as the Burger Court had diluted the Court's commitment to the *Carolene* paradigm in the race cases, the women's rights cases suggested that *Carolene* was no longer the driving model for activist judicial review. The Court was not enforcing clear constitutional texts (*Carolene* ¶ 1); according to the critics of *Roe*, the Court was not enforcing any kind of text in the abortion cases. Moreover, the political process was addressing the same issues that the Court was resolving (¶ 2): at the same time the Court handed down *Frontiero* and

Craig, the states were debating the ERA and repealing sex discriminations from their codes; when *Roe* was decided, many states had reformed their outdated abortion laws (four had repealed them altogether), and others were following. This was hardly surprising: as a majority of the voters, women's concerns were ones to which politicians were attentive. As to *Carolene*'s famous ¶ 3, women are hardly the "discrete and insular minority" that African Americans are; indeed, women are a majority and dispersed throughout the population. Their legal disabilities are less the result of emotional "prejudice" and hatred against them than of "stereotypes" about them.

Other critics of these decisions emphasized their departure from original constitutional text and intent. The most ardent original intent critic of the women's rights decisions, and of the privacy right generally, was Professor Robert Bork, an antitrust expert at the Yale Law School and in the 1980s a judge on the United States Court of Appeals for the D.C. Circuit. When President Reagan nominated Bork to a closely divided Supreme Court in 1987, observers predicted the end of *Roe v. Wade*, a prediction Judge Bork confirmed in his Senate testimony, which roundly condemned the privacy decisions, including *Griswold*. A coalition of women's groups, civil rights associations, and other progressives opposed the nomination in an intense public relations campaign that persuaded a large majority of Americans that Bork should not sit on the Court. The Senate rejected his nomination, 58-42. The eventual nominee, Judge Anthony Kennedy of the Ninth Circuit, was the critical fifth vote to reaffirm (and reinterpret) *Roe* in *Planned Parenthood v. Casey*, 505 U.S. 833 (1992) (Chapter 5, § 4B).

3. *Judicial Activism to Protect Constitutional Structure and Accountability: Separation of Powers and Federalism.* The Burger Court's activism was not limited to the women's rights cases. In some respects, the most sweeping decision of recent times was the Court's near-unanimous decision in *Immigration and Naturalization Service v. Chadha*, 462 U.S. 919 (1983) (Chapter 8, § 2B), which ruled that vetoes of agency rules by the vote of one chamber in Congress violated the bicameralism and presentment requirements of Article I, § 7. Chief Justice Burger's broadly written opinion for the Court effectively invalidated the "legislative veto" provisions found in over 200 federal statutes. The structural themes of *Chadha* can be traced to *The Federalist Papers* but remain more important in the modern regulatory state than ever before. Structural limits on the power of Congress and the President are explored in Chapter 8 of this book.

Chapter 9 treats structural limits on the power of the Supreme Court, and in this arena the Burger Court was particularly innovative. The Court set strict limits on the cases and controversies federal courts could adjudicate. Most of the cases involved questions of *standing*, a requirement the Court found not only in Article III but inherent in the system of separate powers (Chapter 9, § 2). The Court has required plaintiffs to show "actual injury," namely, real harm directly caused by the defendant's conduct and remediable through a judgment. Thus, generalized injuries suffered by all, such as wrongful government action harming all taxpayers or citizens alike, were precisely the ones best dealt with in the political rather than the judicial process (hence, the old political question doctrine sneaked back into constitutional law). And the Court was stingy about allowing public interest plaintiffs to use the federal courts to monitor executive underenforcement of statutory schemes.

The triumph of centralized national authority during the New Deal and Great Society — and with it tremendous advances in the civil rights movement — has been followed by a period when most Americans were concerned with too much central authority and too many restrictions on their liberties emanating from Washington, D.C. Although states' rights arguments took a beating from the New Deal through the Warren Court, federalism made a comeback during the Burger and, especially, Rehnquist Courts. As the introductory materials in Chapter 7 suggest, the federal arrangement whereby states retain independent regulatory authority and the national government is limited to specified areas of regulation was central to the forming of the Constitution — and is an arrangement many consider admirable today as a matter of governance. Although the Burger Court flip-flopped on the issue of direct federal regulation of the states, see *Garcia v. San Antonio Metropolitan Transit Authority*, 469 U.S. 528 (1985), overruling *National League of Cities v. Usery*, 426 U.S. 833 (1976) (Chapter 7, § 5B), a stable majority of the Rehnquist Court concluded that Congress and the Court itself have blurred the lines of *accountability* that are essential to the proper function of local democracy and resolved to enforce federalism-based limits on Congress like no Court had done before.

The accountability theme first showed up in the *Brown II* cases. School boards objecting to extensive remedial orders maintained that the success of public education depended on the intimate involvement of parents in their local schools and the accountability of school boards to those parents. If federal judges made local educational policy, school boards could credibly claim that they were not responsible for ongoing problems. The Supreme Court accepted this argument as a basis for curtailing the authority of federal judges to retain jurisdiction indefinitely to monitor compliance with remedial orders. *Freeman v. Pitts*, 503 U.S. 467 (1992) (Chapter 2, § 2C2). For similar accountability reasons, the Court has ruled that Congress cannot "commandeer" state legislatures, *New York v. United States*, 505 U.S. 144 (1992), or state executive officers, *Printz v. United States*, 521 U.S. 898 (1997) (both in Chapter 7, § 5C). In these cases, the Court was policing the tendency of Congress to take credit for a federal program, while shifting many costs and enforcement responsibilities to the states, thereby distracting state officials from their own primary governance duties.

The accountability idea also animated the Rehnquist Court's Eleventh Amendment jurisprudence. The Court has interpreted Article III's grant of "judicial Power" and the Eleventh Amendment not only to bar any kind of lawsuit against the states in federal courts, but also to bar such lawsuits in state courts, *Alden v. Maine*, 527 U.S. 706 (1999) (Chapter 7, § 3D), and in federal administrative adjudications, *Federal Maritime Comm 'n v. South Carolina State Ports Auth.*, 535 U.S. 743 (2002). In *Seminole Tribe of Florida v. Florida*, 517 U.S. 44 (1996) (id.), the Court ruled that Congress has no authority under the Commerce Clause to abrogate states' Eleventh Amendment immunity. Because Congress does have such authority under the Fourteenth Amendment, this holding has stimulated a series of lawsuits to determine whether specific statutes have been properly adopted pursuant to Congress's authority under § 5 of the Fourteenth Amendment.

In its most dramatic decisions, the same five Justices of the Rehnquist Court who formed the majority in the above-cited cases (Rehnquist, O'Connor, Scalia, Kennedy, Thomas) also set firmer limits on Congress's authority under the Commerce Clause and the Fourteenth Amendment. Thus, in *United States v. Lopez*, 514 U.S. 549 (1995) (Chapter 7, § 2), the Court struck down a regulation of private conduct as exceeding Congress's power under the Commerce Clause, for the first time in sixty years. (The statute prohibited the possession of guns within a thousand feet of a school.) And in *United States v. Morrison*, 529 U.S. 598 (2000) (Chapter 7, § 3E), the Court ruled that the federal government did not have authority to adopt the Violence Against Women Act provision creating a cause of action for gender-motivated violence by private persons. Chief Justice Rehnquist's opinion for a 5-4 Court held that the Commerce Clause gives Congress very limited authority to regulate noneconomic activities and that the Fourteenth Amendment gives it no authority to regulate private activities.

While the Burger and Rehnquist Courts were enforcing federalism guarantees against the federal government, they were also enforcing them against the states, primarily under the Court's assumed authority to enforce the "Dormant" Commerce Clause. Thus, the Burger Court struck down state regulations that either directly trenched upon interstate commerce, e.g., *City of Philadelphia v. New Jersey*, 437 U.S. 617 (1978) (id. § 6B1), or imposed "undue burdens" on commerce. An example of the latter was *Kassel v. Consolidated Freightways Corp.*, 450 U.S. 662 (1981) (id. § 6B2). Iowa imposed stricter limits on truck lengths than its neighbors, and truckers challenged the policy on the ground that it limited their capacity everywhere (it was hard for them to avoid Iowa). Four Justices voted to strike down the Iowa law because the costs to interstate commerce outweighed state safety interests, realistically viewed. Two Justices voted to strike it down because they found Iowa lawmakers motivated by the desire to discourage interstate commerce and shift the costs of big trucks to other states. Objecting that the Court was essentially making a policy rather than a legal determination, three Justices voted to uphold the law. (Note the relevance of *Carolene* to these cases: local political processes are prone to shift costs (like the wear and tear of big trucks) to other jurisdictions, and the federal judiciary is a needed check to prevent races to the bottom, where all states try to shift costs in an escalating series of regulatory moves.)

SECTION 9. THE MILLENNIAL COURT

The new millennium represents a seismic break for the Court in several respects. In the short term, the Court heralded the new millennium with one of the most controversial decisions in its history, *Bush v. Gore*, 531 U.S. 98 (2000) (Chapter 5, § 3A). In a 5-4 per curiam decision, a Court dominated by conservative Republican "nonactivists" applied unprecedented equal protection scrutiny to overturn the Florida Supreme Court's procedures for recounting that state's votes in the closely contested election between Vice President Al Gore and Texas Governor George W. Bush. As a result of the Court's decision, Gore, a liberal Democrat, had to concede Florida, and with it the Presidency, to Bush, a conservative Republican. Because the majority in *Bush v. Gore* was not able to justify its activism by reference to either original meaning or constitutional precedent, it was subjected to withering critique inside and outside the Court. Nonetheless, the Court's intervention was decisive and paved the way for President Bush — rather than President Gore — to name replacements for Chief Justice Rehnquist and Justice O'Connor in 2005. The newest members of the Court — Chief Justice John Roberts and Justice Samuel Alito — were talented lower-court judges whose careers started in the Reagan Administration's Department of Justice; pundits expect both men to support Federalist Society values during their tenures.

We hesitate a bit before announcing traits or trends that distinguish the Millennial Court, for we are still in the early years of the new century, and there is a great deal of continuity between the pre-2000 Court and the post-2000 Court. Generally, the Millennial Court has been mildly activist, supporting conservative values most of the time but progressive constitutional values in a surprising number of cases. On the other hand, the new (post-2005) Roberts Court is fairly precedent-respecting. Consider these further themes, the first of which gets started well before the year 2000.

1. *The Court's Pullback from the Imperial First Amendment?* The First Amendment flourished in the twentieth century, and today limits the state's ability to regulate even highly controversial expressive conduct such as flagburning and cross-burning (Chapter 6, §§ 1, 2A); hate speech, including racist and misogynist expression (§ 3B); monetary contributions to political campaigns (§ 2C); offensive expression in the mass media (§ 3B2); commercial speech (§ 3B); festive as well as protest marches (§ 5); and identity speech, including the right of social groups to exclude people some members don't like (§ 6). As the references suggest, we try to cover the high points of the expanding First Amendment in Chapter 6, but please be aware that you will not be able to dig very deeply in an introductory survey course.

Much of the Court's expansion of the First Amendment came through (or was facilitated by) a giant pluralist logroll. Identity-based social movements (especially the birth control, civil rights, and gay rights movements) found the protections of the First Amendment necessary to protect their voices against suppression by the state as they protested the legal status quo. That judges who did not favor birth control, were dubious about protest marches, and considered "homosexuals" a bad lot were willing to protect their free speech and association helped create a tradition whereby the First Amendment became the symbol of law's neutrality. Once these social movements made normative headway and secured antidiscrimination laws from municipal, state, and national legislatures, their traditionalist opponents and identity-based movements on the right (pro-lifers, traditional family values Americans and their groups) claimed the First Amendment's protections for their expressive activities. So Americans, including judges, of a variety of political persuasions supported a First Amendment that vigorously and neutrally protects speech and association rights of all manner of persons and groups.

For this reason, Chapter 6 gives some emphasis to equality-speech clashes, where the state's equality goal of remedying private discrimination limits the liberty of alleged oppressors. This is the common theme of the cross-burning, feminist pornography, the hate speech, and public accommodations cases. A millennial case that illustrates the imperialism of the First Amendment is *Boy Scouts of America v. Dale*, 530 U.S. 640 (2000) (§ 6). James Dale was an assistant scoutmaster expelled from the Boy Scouts when they learned from a media interview that he was an openly gay man. The New Jersey state courts ruled that the Scouts were a "public accommodation" in violation of the state law barring discrimination on the basis of sexual orientation. The Scouts claimed, and a majority of the Court agreed, that the First Amendment protected it against being required to retain members whose presence sent the "wrong message" to the community.

The pluralist deal suggested by *Dale* is that the First Amendment protects people's right to "come out of the closet" as openly gay, but also protects people who do not want to associate with openly gay persons. The deal may be fraying, however. For example, the Roberts Court has declined to read *Dale* and other First Amendment precedents broadly when pro-gay institutions challenge state censorship. Speaking for a unanimous Court, Chief Justice Roberts rejected a First Amendment challenge by gay-friendly law schools to federal fund cutoffs if the schools did not cooperate *fully* with anti-gay military recruitment efforts. *Rumsfeld v. FAIR*, 547 U.S. 47 (2006) (Chapter 6, § 6). The law schools relied on *Dale* to argue that their associational identity as pro-gay was threatened by a federal statute conditioning federal grants on a requirement that law schools provide their best-efforts access to gay-discriminating military recruiters; the Administration's stated justification (in a letter to the Yale Law School) was that law school policy treating military recruiters differently (as by not associating them with the school's official job fair) would be construed by students as a stamp of disapproval by the school. Notwithstanding the apparent effort by the government to stifle dissent — and within an academic context — the Chief Justice distinguished *Dale* and found that there was no significant First Amendment interest posed by the law schools.

The decline of the First Amendment's potency has sometimes cut in favor of progressive regulations. The same day the Court struck down the application of New Jersey's anti-discrimination law against the Boy Scouts in *Dale*, it upheld a Colorado statute barring close contact with anyone entering a health-care (abortion) clinic. *Hill v. Colorado*, 530 U.S. 703 (2000). More important, the Court in *McConnell v. FEC*, 540 U.S. 93 (2003) (Chapter 6, § 2C), upheld most of the Bipartisan Campaign Reform Act of 2002's limitations on soft money and corporate contributions in federal campaigns. For a generation, the Court had strictly scrutinized campaign finance restrictions upon the premises that "money is speech" in that context and that equalization of access to the political process did not justify such restrictions on speech. In the McCain-Feingold Act Case, the Court accepted Congress's stringent limitations on the ground that they were needed to prevent perceptions of vote-buying by special interests. But cf. *Davis v. FEC*, 128 S.Ct. 2759 (2008) (after retirement of Justice O'Connor, 5-4 Court strikes down BCRA's effort to equalize races where there was a self-funding candidate).

Another case suggesting a fraying of the Imperial First Amendment is *Morse v. Frederick,* 127 S.Ct. 2618 (2007) (Chapter 6, § 4B). The Court has long recognized a First Amendment right of high school students to engage in political expression, even within the school. Students at an Alaskan high school were released from classes so that they could view the Olympic Torch Relay in 2002. One student waived a huge banner reading "BONG HiTS 4 JESUS." The student was disciplined by the principal, who considered the banner to be advocating drug use. Chief Justice Roberts' opinion for the Court held that it was reasonable for schools to censor pro-drug speech, even outside the school premises. In a concurring opinion, Justice Alito suggested that the Court's allowance might not extend beyond the context of high school anti-drug regimes.

2. *Precedent and (Conservative) Pragmatism.* Although the Millennial Court contains some stalwart advocates of original meaning (Justices Scalia and Thomas), it is overall a Court whose methodology is common law in style and pragmatic in philosophy — albeit pragmatism with a Federalist Society tilt. Thus, the Court as a whole does not subscribe to one foundational inquiry; the Justices will consider text, original meaning, purpose, and Supreme Court precedent when interpreting the Constitution — with the last source usually driving most of the analysis. The Court both respects precedent *and* interprets it, giving some play to conservative readings of liberal precedents but trying not to overrule anything. (During the 2007 Term, the Roberts Court did not overrule a single precedent.)

Perhaps the best example is *Gonzales v. Carhart*, 550 U.S. 124 (2007) (Chapter 5, § 4B), where a closely divided (5-4) Court upheld the federal ban on "partial birth abortions" against a constitutional privacy attack. In a previous case, a 5-4 Court had struck down a more vaguely worded state ban, *Stenberg v. Carhart,* 530 U.S. 914 (2000). Although the latter *Carhart* decision carefully distinguished the earlier one, commentators and (apparently) the dissenting Justices believed that the different result owed much to the fact that a pro-life Justice (Alito) had replaced a pro-choice Justice (O'Connor) in the interim. It is also notable that Justice Kennedy's opinion for the Court in *Carhart II* made no noise about overruling *Roe v. Wade,* the super-precedent that President George W. Bush had vowed to overturn through his appointments to the Court. Ironically, although the Court seems disinclined to overrule *Roe v. Wade*, it did overrule precedent to recognize a privacy right to engage in consensual sodomy in *Lawrence v. Texas*, 531 U.S. (2003), overruling *Bowers v. Hardwick* (both in Chapter 5, § 4C).

Perhaps the most contentious *stare decisis* debates have been in cases involving race-based criteria. The grand debate occurred in *Parents Involved in Community Schools v. Seattle School District No. 1,* 127 S.Ct. 2738 (2007) (Chapter 3, § 3D). Chief Justice Roberts' opinion for the Court (speaking for a 5-4 majority as to most issues) ruled that efforts by the Seattle and Louisville school districts to achieve actual integration ran afoul the Equal Protection Clause because they used racial criteria without sufficient justification. (Justice Kennedy wrote a concurring opinion that would allow more liberal use of such criteria.) Justice Breyer's dissenting opinion lambasted the Roberts opinion for minimizing or disregarding bushels of Supreme Court precedent; the Chief Justice responded by parsing most of those precedents more narrowly than Breyer would and relying on the Court's now-established jurisprudence holding that even "remedial" race-based classifications are subject to strict scrutiny. E.g., *Grutter v. Bollinger,* 539 U.S. 306 (2003) (Chapter 3, § 3C).

Another example of the Court's conservative pragmatism is *District of Columbia v. Heller*, 128 S.Ct. 2783 (2008), where the same 5-4 majority as in *Carhart II* invoked the Second Amendment to strike down the District of Columbia's bar to possession of loaded and usable handguns within the home. Although *Heller* read the Second Amendment more broadly than the Court had done in previous cases, it did not overrule any precedent, though it did read them very narrowly. Justice Scalia's *Heller* opinion is the most ambitious deployment of original meaning as the reason to strike down a federal statute in the Court's history and has already sparked enormous controversy, with even conservative commentators claiming that *Heller* is the originalist's version of *Griswold v. Connecticut* (1965) or *Roe v. Wade* (1973). We present the materials debated among the Justices as a Problem at the end of Chapter 2.

3. *National Security and the War on Terror.* Less than a year after *Bush v. Gore,* on 9/11/2001, international terrorists destroyed both towers of the World Trade Center and destroyed part of the Pentagon. This dramatic attack on landmarks within our borders alarmed the nation, triggered a far-reaching response by the Bush Administration, and fueled a national conversation about the acceptable balance between national security and human rights. The Bush 43 Administration's response to international terrorism raised a host of constitutional issues, from the legality of presidentially approved torture to the constitutionality of the NSA's secret wiretap program. The only issues that have thus far reached the Supreme Court for full briefing and decision have involved the Administration's indefinite detention of suspected terrorists; these cases are assembled in Chapter 8, § 3 of the casebook.

The first major case was *Hamdi v. Rumsfeld*, 542 U.S. 507 (2004) (Chapter 8, § 3), where a fractured Court ruled that the President could detain American citizens who fought against their country abroad, but that the Administration was required to justify continued detention before neutral decisionmakers. (The Court applied the balancing approach for procedural due process established in *Mathews v. Eldridge* (Chapter 5, § 6).) Following *Hamdi*, the Administration established administrative tribunals to determine whether there remained good reason to detain persons alleged to be "illegal enemy combatants." (In a statutory decision with constitutional overtones, the Court in *Hamdan v. Rumsfeld*, 548 U.S. 557 (2006), applied the Steel Seizure framework rule that "military commissions" created by the President to try illegal combatants for war crimes was contrary to statute.)

The Administration persuaded Congress to authorize military tribunals, with limited process review in the D.C. Circuit, in exchange for a congressional abrogation of the habeas corpus rights of persons detained in connection with the war on terror. Detainees held at Camp X-Ray in Guantanamo Bay, Cuba (territory occupied by the United States and administered under a long-term lease from Cuba) sought to overturn this deal as inconsistent with the Habeas

Clause of Article I, § 9, cl. 2. Again, a closely divided (5-4) Court agreed with the challengers. In *Boumediene v. Bush*, 128 S.Ct. 2229 (2008) (Chapter 8, § 3), the Court held that these detainees were entitled to habeas corpus hearings before Article III federal judges, and not just the administrative process provided by recent statute. Dissenting Justices warned that the Court was risking American lives under circumstances where the President and the Secretary of Defense were better situated to make judgments.

APPENDIX: RECENT JUSTICES

The Burger Court

We have already discussed Justices Harlan, Douglas, and Black, all of whom served under Chief Justice Burger. After Harlan and Black left the Court, the Burger Court was remarkably stable. Justices marked with an asterisk also served under Chief Justice Rehnquist.

Warren Earl Burger, a Minnesota native, graduated from William Mitchell College of Law in St. Paul, where he attended night school. In 1953, he became an assistant attorney general. He became nationally known after he argued an anti-Communist case in the Supreme Court when the Solicitor General had refused to do so. In 1956, he was appointed to the D.C. Circuit, where he was a conservative voice on what was to become a highly liberal bench. He was appointed Chief Justice by President Nixon in 1969. As Chief Justice, he appears to have been poorly regarded by his colleagues — he seemed to have Earl Warren's uneven legal ability but not his personal charm. He was, however, a very effective administrator. Although he was generally conservative, he was far less consistent than his successor in this regard, and joined (or occasionally even wrote) some liberal decisions.

Lewis Powell* was a corporate lawyer in Richmond, Virginia before joining the Supreme Court. He had also served on the Richmond school board, an experience that helped shape his attitudes toward racial issues. His national reputation was due to a stint as president of the American Bar Association. He was technically a Democrat at the time of his nomination, although there is nothing in his judicial opinions to hint at any great sympathy for the post-1968 Democratic Party. Early in his career on the Court, Powell was flattered by a law review article comparing him to Justice Harlan as a judicial craftsman. He seems to have made a conscious effort to be the moderate "voice of reason" on the Court, with the result that he was often the swing voter on the Burger Court.

Harry Blackmun* was appointed by Nixon. He graduated from Harvard *summa cum laude* in mathematics, went on to Harvard Law School, and then clerked for a judge on the Eighth Circuit. He joined the largest firm in Minneapolis, and then became counsel for the Mayo Clinic until President Eisenhower appointed him to the Eighth Circuit. President Nixon turned to him after he failed to obtain confirmation for Judges Haynsworth (who, in retrospect, would have been a good Justice) and Carswell (who was unqualified). Blackmun and Burger were called the "Minnesota Twins" in their early years on the Court, but Blackmun moved progressively away from Burger and was considered a liberal by the time William Rehnquist became Chief Justice.

William Brennan, Jr.* was appointed to the Court by Eisenhower, but was ultimately to emerge as the liberal spokesman on the Burger Court. He had practiced law in Newark until World War II. After returning to practice after the war, he was appointed as a trial judge, and then ultimately to the state supreme court. On the Warren Court, he played an important but quiet role as a moderate coalition-builder. After Warren left the Court, Brennan found himself increasingly in dissent, but up to the very end, he still enjoyed surprising successes in building majorities for occasional liberal results.

John Paul Stevens* was a prominent Chicago antitrust specialist before he was appointed to the Seventh Circuit. Like Byron White and William Rehnquist, he had served as a Supreme Court law clerk before entering practice. He had come to public attention by leading an investigation into corruption in the Illinois courts. His nomination to the Supreme Court was assisted by his friendship with Attorney General Edward Levi, who had taught an antitrust course with Stevens at the University of Chicago. Justice Stevens quickly obtained a reputation on the Court as a maverick who joined neither ideological camp. During the Rehnquist and Roberts Courts, however, he has been the least conservative Justice, simply because all the newer appointments have been more conservative. As a senior Justice when the Court rules in a more liberal direction, Stevens has assigned himself important opinions for the Court in landmark cases involving campaign finance, presidential power, and constitutional standing. He has been a forceful dissenter in cases where the Court has struck down laws regulating firearms, race-based political gerrymanders, campaign finance regulation, and violence against women.

Thurgood Marshall* played a major role in the *Brown* litigation and is probably the most dramatically successful appellate advocate at the Supreme Court level in our nation's history. We detail his historic role as a civil rights advocate in Chapter 2. He was a Howard Law School graduate and became the head of the NAACP Legal Defense and Education Fund, Inc. in 1940. President Kennedy appointed him to the United States Court of Appeals for the Second Circuit; four years later, he became Solicitor General. In 1967, President Johnson nominated him to the Supreme Court. Because he joined the Court just as Warren was about to leave, Justice Marshall was increasingly at odds with the conservative trend on the Court. He and Brennan were staunch allies. Although Justice Marshall was the Court's leading philosopher of equal protection issues across the board (race, sex, poverty, disability, etc.), he was also the Court's leading expert on issues of civil procedure and wrote leading opinions for the Court establishing and enforcing bright-line rules in this area.

Byron White* was a Rhodes Scholar, top of his class at the Yale Law School, a law clerk to Chief Justice Vinson, and a professional football player. His appointment to the Court resulted from his long-time friendship with John Kennedy, going back to his time as a Rhodes Scholar at Oxford. He was an important member of the Kennedy campaign team, became a deputy attorney general, and then moved up to the Supreme Court. During the Warren Court, he was a moderate swing voter, but he became increasingly conservative as he aged, so that ultimately he was sometimes more conservative than several later Republican nominees. Perhaps as a result of his federal service, he seemed to defer to the position taken by the federal government in important cases.

Sandra Day O'Connor* was, as we assume you know, the first woman ever appointed to the Supreme Court. She grew up on a 160,000-acre family ranch in Arizona. She was a classmate of William Rehnquist at the Stanford Law School, but despite a strong academic record, had trouble finding a job. After becoming a state assistant attorney general, she entered politics and eventually became Republican majority leader in the Arizona Senate, the first woman in the United States to hold such a position, before moving on to become a state judge. Given her career in state politics, it is not surprising that she devoted considerable energy to issues of federalism and has been the primary philosopher of the Court's federalism jurisprudence. As a swing vote on the tightly divided Rehnquist Court, Justice O'Connor's voice was critically important on high-voltage issues of race-based affirmative action, gay rights, sex discrimination, campaign finance regulation, and presidential power.

William Hubbs Rehnquist was the most conservative Justice on the Burger Court, but was outflanked by Antonin Scalia and Clarence Thomas during his own Chief Justiceship. He grew up in Milwaukee, graduated first in his class from Stanford Law School, and clerked for Justice Robert Jackson. (Jackson was a brilliant maverick during the Vinson and early Warren Courts, somewhat like Justice Stevens on the Burger Court.) After his clerkship, Rehnquist moved to Arizona and became a supporter of Barry Goldwater. He became the head of the Office of Legal Counsel in the Nixon Justice Department, before being nominated for the Court in 1971. He was strongly but unsuccessfully opposed by liberal groups when he was nominated for Chief Justice.

Potter Stewart was the son of an old Ohio political family. Like White, he was a Yale law school graduate. Eisenhower appointed him to the Sixth Circuit in 1954 and to the Supreme Court in 1958. As a Justice, he had a reputation for solid competence and moderation.

The Rehnquist Court

We have already discussed Chief Justice Rehnquist and the seven Justices who served under both him and Burger. The following are the new Justices appointed during the tenure of Chief Justice Rehnquist.

Anthony Kennedy was President Reagan's third effort at filling the Powell seat after Robert Bork was defeated and a second nomination was withdrawn. Kennedy graduated from Harvard Law School in 1961 and practiced law in Sacramento until his appointment to the Ninth Circuit in 1975. In his first years on the Court, Justice Kennedy started out as Justice Scalia's shadow, but early on their judicial philosophies diverged. He is a moderate conservative who prides himself as the Court's political philosopher. Justice Kennedy has taken a moderately activist stance in protecting a wide array of constitutional values—from the equal protection and privacy rights of gay people (Chapters 4 and 5); to the First Amendment's protection of speech, even as applied to campaign finance and the internet (Chapter 6); to federalism limitations on congressional power (Chapter 7); to the habeas corpus rights of suspected terrorists held without charges at Camp X-Ray in Guantanamo Bay, Cuba (Chapter 8). As a swing vote on both the Rehnquist and Roberts Courts, Justice Kennedy's nuanced views on the right of a woman to an abortion have shaped that constitutional right in important ways (Chapter 5).

David Souter was a judge on the New Hampshire Supreme Court and (briefly) the United States Court of Appeals for the First Circuit before his Supreme Court nomination. He graduated from Harvard College in 1961 and Harvard Law School in 1966, and was also a Rhodes Scholar. He was known as the "stealth nominee" because so little was known of his positions at the time of his nomination. Although initially seen as conservative, he is now seen as a moderate and sometimes allies himself with Stevens. Justice Souter is a libertarian and evolutionary historicist in the mold of the second Justice Harlan.

Antonin Scalia is, in some ways, a modern and more conservative version of Hugo Black. Like Black, he believes in literalism, favors bright-line rules, and abhors "balancing tests." He also shares Black's penchant for blunt, memorable prose but (very much unlike the genteel Black) tends to lob *ad hominem* barbs at his colleagues when he disagrees with them. Scalia was one of a group of prominent members of the University of Chicago Law School faculty to be appointed to the federal appellate courts. He is more interested in legal theory than most of his colleagues. He was nominated along with Rehnquist's appointment to the Chief Justiceship; liberals made a strategic decision to let Scalia sail through while concentrating their fire on Rehnquist. Scalia is the first of Italian ancestry to serve on the Court. He is a formidable dissenter, whose blunt and colorful prose is usually aimed over the heads of his colleagues and directed to Federalist Society law professors, bloggers, think tanks, and even political leaders.

Clarence Thomas replaced Thurgood Marshall, and is only the second African American to serve on the Court. He graduated from College of the Holy Cross in 1971 and Yale Law School in 1974. His most important pre-judicial experience was as the Chair of the Equal Employment Opportunity Commission. He also served briefly on the D.C. Circuit. Because he disavowed most of his previous statements relating to constitutional issues, and claimed never to have discussed *Roe v. Wade* (the abortion decision) with anyone, his confirmation hearings revolved around issues of character. His supporters stressed his rise from an impoverished background; his detractors were more concerned about allegations of sexual harassment made by Anita Hill, one of his former staff members. The Senate confirmed Thomas by only 52-48, the closest ever for Supreme Court confirmation. He and Scalia almost always voted together during the 1990s, but in the new millennium Justice Thomas has emerged as a more distinctive voice on the Court. More than any other Justice in the Court's history, he is willing to overrule precedent—often whole lines of precedent—he believes inconsistent with original constitutional meaning.

Ruth Bader Ginsburg was a professor at Columbia University Law School when President Carter tapped her for the D.C. Circuit. She was well known for her role in leading the Women's Rights Project of the ACLU. During the 1970s, she participated either as counsel for a party or as *amicus* in the leading gender discrimination cases of the day, including *Reed v. Reed, Frontiero v. Richardson,* and *Craig v. Boren,* all of which are included in Chapter 4. In light of this background, she surprised many observers by her nonactivist, middle-of-the-road record as a D.C. Circuit judge. At the time of her elevation to the Court, she was widely viewed as the least liberal of the four Carter appointees to the D.C. Circuit. On the Supreme Court, Justice Ginsburg has been a pragmatist, for the most part aligning herself with Justices Stevens and Breyer. In sex discrimination cases, she is a forceful voice for liberal feminist positions she pressed at the ACLU, best illustrated by her scholarly opinion in the landmark case that sex-integrated the Virginia Military Institute (Chapter 4, § 2B1).

Stephen Breyer was appointed to the First Circuit by President Carter in 1980. A former Harvard law professor and chief counsel to the Senate Judiciary Committee, Breyer is a respected scholar, primarily in the fields of administrative law and regulated industries. As a First Circuit judge, he had a reputation as a moderate. Reminiscent of Justice Brandeis, Justice Breyer is a fact-oriented pragmatist. He is strongly interested in questions like, How does the challenged rule actually work? What would be the real-world consequences of different courses of action by the Court? Deferential to the political process, Breyer is reluctant to adopt highly activist stances of either a conservative or liberal dimension. Although he usually votes with Justices Stevens, Souter, and Ginsburg in constitutional cases, Justice Breyer's cautious and pragmatic philosophy made him a judicial soul mate for Justice O'Connor, whose departure from the Court deprived him of an important conservative ally.

The Roberts Court

Justice O'Connor announced her intention to leave the Court on July 1, 2005, and President George W. Bush appointed Judge John Roberts to succeed her. When Chief Justice Rehnquist died in September 2005, the President nominated Judge Roberts to be the Chief Justice and ultimately nominated Judge Samuel Alito to replace Justice O'Connor. The Roberts Court, as of January 1, 2009, consists of these jurists plus the Justices we have listed under Rehnquist Court plus Justice Stevens, the only surviving Justice from the Burger Court.

John Glover Roberts, Jr. is the seventeenth Chief Justice of the United States. The son of a Bethlehem Steel plant manager, Roberts graduated in 1979 from the Harvard Law School, where he was Managing Editor of the *Harvard Law Review.* After clerking for then-Justice Rehnquist, Roberts was a special assistant to Attorney General William French Smith and was Associate Counsel to President Reagan in 1982-86. In a highly successful career in private practice, Roberts argued 39 cases before the Supreme Court. He was a judge on the D.C. Circuit for two years before his nomination to the Court. His judicial philosophy, clearly articulated in his confirmation hearings and in his judicial opinions, is pragmatic, with a strong Federalist Society tilt. A distinctive feature of the Chief Justice's jurisprudence is his close attention to precedent, and his Court is (thus far) strongly inclined not to overrule even constitutional precedents, though the Chief is inclined to give a narrow reading to liberal Court decisions from earlier Courts.

Samuel Anthony Alito grew up in New Jersey, the son of an Italian immigrant father and Italian-American mother, both schoolteachers. After graduating from Princeton University, he earned his law degree at the Yale Law School in 1975. After Yale, Alito served in the Army and then the Army Reserves, ultimately reaching the rank of captain. He served as assistant to Solicitor General Rex Lee and then to Attorney General Edwin Meese during the Reagan Administration and was a judge of the Third Circuit from 1990 to 2006. Like the Chief Justice, Justice Alito is a pragmatist with a strong Federalist Society tilt. Within the Court, he has earned respect from liberals as well as conservatives for his judicious approach to decisionmaking and his narrowly reasoned opinions that stick closely to legal materials and that avoid the personal attacks and hyperbole characteristic of the modern Court.

Chapter 2

AN INTRODUCTION TO
CONSTITUTIONAL DECISIONMAKING

What is the source of the Supreme Court's power to declare laws unconstitutional? How should that power be exercised? What are its limits? These three questions are basic to understanding constitutional law. Unfortunately, there are no universally accepted answers. We use *Brown v. Board of Education* as a springboard from which to explore these questions. This chapter introduces you to this great constitutional decision, explores the complex constitutional questions it raises, and relates *Brown* to the theoretical debate over the legitimacy and limits of judicial review. If you have not already done so, it would be useful for you to read Chapter 1, which provides a thumbnail sketch of American constitutional history.

SECTION 1. *BROWN v. BOARD OF EDUCATION*:
A CASE STUDY[a]

Like many other American cities in 1951, most important public and private facilities in Topeka, Kansas were segregated by race. There was one hotel for blacks only; the rest served whites exclusively. Downtown restaurants refused to serve blacks or limited them to a take-out menu. One movie theater was for blacks only; another admitted blacks but restricted them to seats in the balcony; the other five movie houses excluded blacks entirely. The swimming pool at a public park was open to blacks — for all of one day each summer. Banks did not lend money to black-owned businesses, and white-owned businesses hired

---

a. This story is drawn from Richard Kluger, *Simple Justice: The History of* Brown v. Board of Education *and Black America's Struggle for Equality* (rev. ed. 2004); Mark Tushnet, *The NAACP's Legal Strategy Against Segregated Education, 1925-1950* (1987), and *Making Civil Rights Law: Thurgood Marshall and the Supreme Court, 1936-1961* (1994); Michael Klarman, *From Jim Crow to Civil Rights: The Supreme Court and the Struggle for Racial Equality* (2004); Mary Dudziak, *The Limits of Good Faith: Desegregation in Topeka, Kansas, 1950-1956*, 5 Law & Hist. Rev. 351 (1987); Philip Elman, *The Solicitor General's Office, Justice Frankfurter, and Civil Rights Litigation, 1946-1960: An Oral History*, 100 Harv. L. Rev. 817 (1987); Dennis Hutchinson, *Unanimity and Desegregation: Decisionmaking in the Supreme Court, 1948-1958*, 68 Geo. L.J. 1 (1979); Mark Tushnet, with Katya Lezin, *What Really Happened in* Brown v. Board of Education, 91 Colum. L. Rev. 1867 (1991). We appreciate the assistance of Dixon Osburn, Georgetown Class of 1992, in the research and drafting of this account.

blacks for predominantly menial jobs. Although the city's junior high and high schools had been ordered integrated under state law, School Superintendent Kenneth McFarland discouraged racial mixing. [Dudziak 366-68; Kluger 375-76, 380.]

The city's elementary schools were segregated by state law. The black elementary schools had what the city considered to be comparable facilities to those in white elementary schools, except that they were located further away from the homes of black schoolchildren. Linda Brown, for example, had to leave home at 7:40 a.m. and walk through train-switching yards in order to catch a bus that would get her to school by 9:00 a.m. [Kluger 409-10.] Oliver Brown, Linda's father, and other parents objected to Topeka's segregated elementary schools. The National Association for the Advancement of Colored People (NAACP) filed suit in federal court on behalf of Brown and similarly situated black parents on February 28, 1951.

The NAACP was seeking invalidation of Topeka's segregated school system on the ground that it was inconsistent with the Equal Protection Clause of the Fourteenth Amendment to the U.S. Constitution (read § 1 of the Fourteenth Amendment, Appendix 1). The NAACP argued that legal segregation of the races in elementary school was tantamount to legalizing a racial caste system harmful to blacks. The NAACP supported its position by introducing studies of the detrimental impact of segregation on black children. Federal District Judge Huxman was persuaded by this evidence and found as a matter of fact that "[s]egregation with the sanction of law . . . has a tendency to retard the educational and mental development of Negro children and to deprive them of some of the benefits they would receive in a racially integrated school system." But the judge felt constrained by prior decisions of the United States Supreme Court to reject the NAACP's claim for legal relief. *Brown v. Board of Education*, 98 F. Supp. 797 (D. Kan. 1951). Judge Huxman surely felt that his decision was regrettable, perhaps even tragic, as a matter of morality and policy. Was his disposition correct, as a matter of law, in 1951? Consider the following materials.

A. THE FOURTEENTH AMENDMENT AND RACE: 1865–1912

The most important legal development in Reconstruction after the Civil War was the adoption of the Fourteenth Amendment (Chapter 1, §§ 3-4).[b] Congress delegated to a "Joint Committee of Fifteen" the task of drafting a constitutional amendment to protect the slaves freed by the Thirteenth Amendment from

---

b. The story of the Fourteenth Amendment is taken from William Nelson, *The Fourteenth Amendment: From Political Principle to Judicial Doctrine* (1988); Alexander Bickel, *The Original Understanding and the Segregation Decision*, 69 Harv. L. Rev. 1 (1955). On the intellectual background of the Fourteenth Amendment in abolitionist thought, see Eric Foner, *The Strange Career of the Reconstruction Amendments*, 108 Yale L.J. 2003 (1999); Jacobus tenBroek, *The Antislavery Origins of the Fourteenth Amendment* (1951); Robert Kaczorowski, *Revolutionary Constitutionalism in the Era of the Civil War and Reconstruction*, 61 NYU L. Rev. 863 (1986); David A.J. Richards, *Abolitionist Political and Constitutional Theory and the Reconstruction Amendments*, 25 Loy. (L.A.) L. Rev. 1187 (1992).

southern efforts to deprive them of political and civil rights. On January 20, 1866, a subcommittee proposed the following language: "Congress shall have power to make all laws necessary and proper to secure to all citizens of the United States, in every State, the same political rights and privileges; and to all persons in every State equal protection in the enjoyment of life, liberty, and property." After debate, the Joint Committee presented the following language to Congress on February 3:

> The Congress shall have power to make all laws which shall be necessary and proper to secure to the citizens of each State all privileges and immunities of citizens in the several states (Art. 4, Sec. 2); and to all persons in the several states equal protection in the rights of life, liberty and property (5th Amendment).

Note that the February 3 language was inspired by existing constitutional provisions and, further, distinguished between "privileges and immunities" of *citizens* and "rights" of *persons* [Nelson, 52-53]. This proposal died in March, as the House focused on passing the Civil Rights Act of 1866.[c] Opponents claimed that Congress had no constitutional authority to enact such a statute, and that charge revitalized interest in a new amendment.

Within the Joint Committee, Representative Robert Owen proposed a five-section draft that was to form the framework for the Fourteenth Amendment. Section 1 prohibited "discrimination * * * as to the civil rights of persons because of race, color, or previous condition of servitude." Although adopting Owen's framework, the Joint Committee broadened § 1 as follows:

> No state shall make or enforce any law which shall abridge the privileges or immunities of citizens of the United States; nor shall any state deprive any person of life, liberty or property without due process of law; nor deny to any person within its jurisdiction the equal protection of the laws.

Like the February draft of the amendment, new § 1 relied on existing constitutional terms: *privileges and immunities* (Art. IV), which had been broadly defined to include the common law rights embodied in the 1866 statute, as well as rights to carry on a trade or business, *Corfield v. Coryell*, 6 Fed. Cas. 546 (C.C.E.D. Pa. 1823); and *due process* (Amend. V). It is not clear from the committee's deliberations what the term *equal protection* was meant to add. The idea probably originated among prewar abolitionists, who maintained that a truly neutral government owes the humblest person the same equal protection of the laws as it owes the high and mighty. In any event, the House passed the proposed amendment on May 10 by a vote of 128-37.

Senator Jacob Howard introduced the amendment in the Senate. He characterized § 1's equal protection guarantee this way: "This abolishes all class legislation in the States and does away with the injustice of subjecting one caste of persons to a code not applicable to another. * * * It protects the black man in his fundamental rights as a citizen with the same shield which it throws over the white man." Senator Howard also stated that the Privileges and Immunities

---

c. The Civil Rights Act of 1866 assured "citizens of every race and color" the "same right * * * as is enjoyed by white citizens" to make and enforce contracts, to pursue lawsuits, to hold and alienate or receive property, and to be protected in their personal and material security. 14 Stat. 27, now codified at 42 U.S.C. §§ 1981-1982.

Clause of the proposed amendment embodied the protections of the Bill of Rights, as well as other fundamental rights protected by the Privileges and Immunities Clause in Article IV. After a debate generally unilluminating as to § 1, the amendment passed the Senate by a vote of 33-12 and was submitted to the states for ratification on June 16.

The proposed amendment was the central issue in the 1866 congressional elections, and the victory of the pro-amendment Republicans was felt to be a popular endorsement of the amendment. The debates were pitched at a rather general level and rarely focused on the technical meaning of *privileges and immunities* or *equal protection*. Proponents of the amendment emphasized that it would assure former slaves and others their "natural, God-given rights," including an "absolute equality of rights of the whole people, high and low, rich and poor, white and black" [Nelson 67, 73]. In the argot of the times, the amendment was seen as protecting against "class legislation" and "unjust and oppressive state laws" [*id.* at 79]. Most historians have argued that the amendment was meant to assure the same kind of *civil rights* guaranteed by the 1866 statute (described in note *c, supra*) — common law rights to contract, own and transfer property, invoke legal process — but not *political rights* such as voting or *social rights* such as private association.[d]

In any event, the proposed amendment was controversial. It was opposed by President Andrew Johnson, many prominent Republicans, and most leading Democrats. Opponents joined with proponents in favoring the equality idea but opposed the amendment on the grounds that it (1) was adopted by an unrepresentative Congress, *i.e.*, without southern state representation; (2) compelled equal treatment for African Americans, Native Americans, and the "Mongol race" (Chinese), who were in fact not equal to people of European descent; and (3) centralized power by affording national constitutional rights directly against the states and thereby changed the essential federalism of the Constitution [Nelson 91-109]. It took over two years to obtain the approval of three-fourths of the states, and two states tried to revoke their approval. Congress overruled those revocations, and Secretary of State Seward proclaimed the amendment ratified on July 28, 1868 (Chapter 1, § 4). The Fourteenth Amendment was followed by the Fifteenth Amendment (1870), which guaranteed former slaves the right to vote. Congress enacted further civil rights statutes, the most important of which was the 1875 statute, which prohibited racial discrimination by public accommodations such as inns and common carriers such as railroads.

The Reconstruction effort met a discouraging reaction at the state level. When the eleven seceding states rejoined the Union, their constitutions provided

---

d. See Michael Les Benedict, *A Compromise of Principle: Congressional Republicans and Reconstruction 1863-1869* (1974); Earl Maltz, *Civil Rights, the Constitution, and Congress, 1863-1869* (1990). The matter is more complicated, however. Nelson, *Fourteenth Amendment* 126-32 shows that many Republicans supporting the Fourteenth Amendment distinguished between (protected) civil and (unprotected) political rights — but many others did not. By Nelson's account, it is not entirely clear whether the Fifteenth Amendment assuring people of color the right to vote added a new protection to those in the Fourteenth Amendment or confirmed or clarified protections already intended.

equal protection guarantees for former slaves, including assurances of equal educational opportunities in several state constitutions. After federal troops were withdrawn from the South in 1877, however, segregationist whites regained political control. Over time, they adopted laws and practices designed to strip black citizens of their right to vote and to segregate blacks from whites in public schools, accommodations, and transportation. Congress after 1877 did nothing to discourage these "Jim Crow" laws, and the federal courts retreated from the broad rhetoric of the ratification debates.

In *The Slaughter House Cases*, 83 U.S. (16 Wall.) 36 (1873) (Chapter 5, § 1), the Supreme Court read § 1 narrowly. Its limitation of the Privileges or Immunities Clause to rights distinctive to national citizenship such as interstate travel rejected the apparent intent of the amendment's Framers to protect civil rights such as common law rights to hold property and enter contracts. The decision shifted political and constitutional theorizing to the Equal Protection Clause. In *Strauder v. West Virginia*, 100 U.S. 303 (1879), the Court overturned a West Virginia statute excluding any but "white male persons" from juries — arguably contrary to the Framers' intent *not* to regulate political rights. The Court's opinion reasoned from the "true spirit and meaning" of the Fourteenth Amendment, its protect-the-freed-slaves purpose. "It ordains * * * that the law in the States shall be the same for the black as for the white; that all persons, whether colored or white, shall stand equal before the laws of the States, and, in regard to the colored race, for whose protection the amendment was primarily designed, that no discrimination shall be made against them by law because of their color." Given this purpose, the exclusion of blacks from juries was unconstitutional because the exclusion "is practically a brand upon them, affixed by the law, an assertion of their inferiority, and a stimulant to that race prejudice which is an impediment to securing to individuals of the race that equal justice which the law aims to secure to all others."

Strauder suggested a potentially far-reaching vision of the Reconstruction Amendments, but in *The Civil Rights Cases*, 109 U.S. 3 (1883) (Chapter 7, § 3A), the Court invalidated as beyond the power of Congress the 1875 Civil Rights Act's federal remedy for private racial discrimination. The Court held that the Fourteenth Amendment was aimed at discriminatory state laws, not discriminatory private action; hence, § 5 of that amendment did not authorize Congress to regulate private activity. Although the Thirteenth Amendment did empower the federal government to regulate private activity directly, the mere refusal to serve blacks "has nothing to do with slavery or involuntary servitude" prohibited by that amendment.

PLESSY v. FERGUSON
163 U.S. 537, 16 S.Ct. 1138, 41 L.Ed. 256 (1896)

JUSTICE BROWN * * * delivered the opinion of the Court.

[An 1890 Louisiana statute required railway companies to provide "equal but separate accommodations for the white and colored races" and made it a crime for passengers to violate the required segregation. In 1892, the state prosecuted Homer Adolph Plessy, whose ancestry was one-eighth African and seven-eighths European, for refusing to leave the car reserved for whites. Plessy argued that he was entitled to sit in the whites-only car and that the state had deprived him of a "property" interest in his whiteness and of the equal protection of the laws. The Court brushed aside the taking-of-property argument and focused on the constitutionality of the Louisiana statute. Writing for seven Justices, Justice Brown ruled that the Thirteenth Amendment was not violated, because "[a] statute which implies merely a legal distinction between the white and colored races — a distinction which is founded in the color of the two races, and which must always exist so long as white men are distinguished from the other race by color — has no tendency to destroy the legal equality of the two races, or reestablish a state of involuntary servitude." The remainder of the opinion addressed the Fourteenth Amendment claim.]

The object of the amendment was undoubtedly to enforce the absolute equality of the two races before the law, but in the nature of things it could not have been intended to abolish distinctions based upon color, or to enforce social, as distinguished from political equality, or a commingling of the two races upon terms unsatisfactory to either. Laws permitting, and even requiring, their separation in places where they are liable to be brought into contact do not necessarily imply the inferiority of either race to the other, and have been generally, if not universally, recognized as within the competency of the state legislatures in the exercise of their police power. The most common instance of this is connected with the establishment of separate schools for white and colored children, which has been held to be a valid exercise of the legislative power even by courts of States where the political rights of the colored race have been longest and most earnestly enforced.

[Justice Brown distinguished between "laws interfering with the political equality of the negro," such as the jury-exclusion law struck down in *Strauder*, and "those requiring the separation of the two races in schools, theatres and railway carriages."]

So far, then, as a conflict with the Fourteenth Amendment is concerned, the case reduces itself to the question whether the statute of Louisiana is a reasonable regulation, and with respect to this there must necessarily be a large discretion on the part of the legislature. In determining the question of reasonableness it is at liberty to act with reference to the established usages, customs and traditions of the people, and with a view to the promotion of their comfort, and the preservation of the public peace and good order. Gauged by this standard, we cannot say that a law which authorizes or even requires the separation of the two races in public conveyances is unreasonable, or more obnoxious to the Fourteenth Amendment than the acts of Congress requiring separate schools for colored children in the District of Columbia, the constitutionality of which does not seem to have been questioned, or the corresponding acts of state legislatures.

We consider the underlying fallacy of the plaintiff's argument to consist in the assumption that the enforced separation of the two races stamps the colored race with a badge of inferiority. If this be so, it is not by reason of anything found in the act, but solely because the colored race chooses to put that construction upon it. * * * The argument also assumes that social prejudices may be overcome by legislation, and that equal rights cannot be secured to the negro except by an enforced commingling of the two races. We cannot accept this proposition. If the two races are to meet upon terms of social equality, it must be the result of natural affinities, a mutual appreciation of each other's merits and a voluntary consent of individuals. * * *

JUSTICE HARLAN dissenting. * * *

In respect of civil rights, common to all citizens, the Constitution of the United States does not, I think, permit any public authority to know the race of those entitled to be protected in the enjoyment of such rights. Every true man has pride of race, and under appropriate circumstances when the rights of others, his equals before the law, are not be affected, it is his privilege to express such pride and to take such action based upon it as to him seems proper. But I deny that any legislative body or judicial tribunal may have regard to the race of citizens when the civil rights of those citizens are involved. [Justice Harlan construed the Thirteenth Amendment as prohibiting "any burdens or disabilities that constitute badges of slavery or servitude," and the Fourteenth Amendment as confirming all other "civil rights that pertain to freedom and citizenship."]

These notable additions to the fundamental law were welcomed by the friends of liberty throughout the world. They removed the race line from our governmental systems. They had, as this court has said, a common purpose, namely, to secure "to a race recently emancipated, a race that through many generations have been held in slavery, all the civil rights that the superior race enjoy." They declared, in legal effect, this court has further said, "that the law in the States shall be the same for the black as for the white; that all persons, whether colored or white, shall stand equal before the laws of the States, and, in regard to the colored race, for whose protection the amendment was primarily designed, that no discrimination shall be made against them by law because of their color." [*Strauder.*] * * *

* * * Every one knows that the statute in question had its origin in the purpose, not so much to exclude white persons from railroad cars occupied by blacks, as to exclude colored people from coaches occupied by or assigned to white persons. * * * The thing to accomplish was, under the guise of giving equal accommodation for whites and blacks, to compel the latter to keep to themselves while travelling in railroad passenger coaches. No one would be so wanting in candor as to assert to the contrary. The fundamental objection, therefore, to the statute is that it interferes with the personal freedom of citizens. * * * If a white man and a black man choose to occupy the same public conveyance on a public highway, it is their right to do so, and no government, proceeding alone on grounds of race, can prevent it without infringing the personal liberty of each. * * *

The white race deems itself to be the dominant race in this country. And so it is, in prestige, in achievements, in education, in wealth and in power. * * * But in view of the Constitution, in the eye of the law, there is in this country no superior, dominant, ruling class of citizens. There is no caste here. Our Constitution is color-blind, and neither knows nor tolerates classes among citizens. In respect of civil rights, all citizens are equal before the law. * * *

In my opinion, the judgment this day rendered will, in time, prove to be quite as pernicious as the decision made by this tribunal in the *Dred Scott* case. * * * The present decision, it may well be apprehended, will not only stimulate aggressions, more or less brutal and irritating, upon the admitted rights of colored citizens, but will encourage the belief that it is possible, by means of state enactments, to defeat the beneficent purposes which the people of the United States had in view when they adopted the recent amendments of the Constitution[.] * * * Sixty millions of whites are in no danger from the presence here of eight millions of blacks. The destinies of the two races, in this country, are indissolubly linked together, and the interests of both require that the common government of all shall not permit the seeds of race hate to be planted under the sanction of law. What can more certainly arouse race hate, what more certainly create and perpetuate a feeling of distrust between these races, than state enactments, which, in fact, proceed on the ground that colored citizens are so inferior and degraded that they cannot be allowed to sit in public coaches occupied by white citizens? That, as all will admit, is the real meaning of such legislation as was enacted in Louisiana. * * *

There is a race so different from our own that we do not permit those belonging to it to become citizens of the United States. Persons belonging to it are, with few exceptions, absolutely excluded from this country. I allude to the Chinese race. But by the statute in question, a Chinaman can ride in the same passenger coach with white citizens of the United States, while citizens of the black race in Louisiana, * * * who are entitled, by law, to participate in the political control of the State and nation, * * * are yet declared to be criminals, liable to imprisonment, if they ride in a public coach occupied by citizens of the white race. * * *

[**JUSTICE BREWER** did not participate in the decision of this case.]

NOTES ON *PLESSY* AND THE CONSTITUTIONALITY OF STATE-MANDATED RACIAL SEGREGATION

1. *The Role of Judicial Review in Our Federal System.* There are three overall questions regarding judicial review you might consider as you evaluate *Plessy*. (The answers to all these questions were well settled by the time *Plessy* was decided.) First, why should legislative enactments be subject to review for consistency with the Constitution? The standard answer to this question is that of *Federalist* No. 78 (excerpted in Appendix 2 to this casebook):

> There is no position which depends on clearer principles, than that every act of a delegated authority, contrary to the tenor of the commission under which it is exercised, is void. No legislative act, therefore, contrary to the Constitution, can be valid. To deny this, would be to affirm, that the deputy is greater than his principal; that the servant is above his master; that the representatives of the people are superior to the people themselves; that men acting by virtue of powers, may do not only what their powers do not authorize, but what they forbid.

This argument might be considered circular in cases like *Plessy*. The Constitution itself derives its authority from "We the People" (see the Preamble). If a legislative enactment is consistent with the desires of "We the People," as segregation was in the 1890s (the South insisted on it, and the North tolerated it), how can it be said that the legislature is traversing its "delegated authority"?

Why should we want to limit the power of the legislature to enact whatever laws "We the People" desire? See *Federalist* No. 10 (App. 2).

Second, assuming that legislative enactments must be consistent with the Constitution, why should federal courts generally, or the Supreme Court in particular, be charged with enforcing this duty? Why not leave it to the legislature or state courts to police constitutional questions? To be sure, one might be suspicious of allowing the Louisiana legislature or judicial system to police local decisionmaking under the circumstances of the Jim Crow regime, but those are not the only alternatives in *Plessy*. Under the Supremacy Clause of Article VI, Congress can pass statutes preempting, or invalidating, state law, assuming those statutes are within Congress' authority delegated by the Constitution. Section 5 of the Fourteenth Amendment provides that "Congress shall have power to enforce, by appropriate legislation, the provisions of this article." Why shouldn't § 5 be considered the primary, or sole, mechanism for enforcing the Fourteenth Amendment?

Third, assuming that the Supreme Court has authority to invalidate state as well as federal legislation, when should that authority be exercised? Note that there are virtues to the *judicial restraint* shown by *Plessy*: The Justices were not approving of apartheid, but merely saying that the Constitution did not clearly prohibit this form of state action. The most thoughtful constitutional theory of that time was James Bradley Thayer, *The Origin and Scope of the American Doctrine of Constitutional Law*, 7 Harv. L. Rev. 129 (1893), which argued that the power of judicial review is a "remarkable practice" in a democracy, unique to the United States. Conceding the existence of such a power, Thayer maintained that it had traditionally, and properly, been exercised with the greatest restraint:

> [A court] can only disregard the Act when those who have the right to make laws have not merely made a mistake, but have made a very clear one, — so clear that it is not open to rational question. * * * This rule recognizes that * * * much which will seem unconstitutional to one man, or body of men, may reasonably not seem so to another; that the constitution often admits of different interpretations; that there is often a range of choice and judgment; that in such cases the constitution does not impose upon the legislature any one specific opinion, but leaves open this range of choice; and that whatever choice is rational is constitutional.

Id. at 144. Note the similarity of Thayer's standard and *Plessy*'s statement of its inquiry, whether the statute "is a reasonable regulation, and with respect to this there must necessarily be a large discretion on the part of the legislature." Was Louisiana's law such a "reasonable regulation"? Or was it a "clear mistake"?

Plessy's judicial restraint must be contrasted with the Court's activism in *Allgeyer v. Louisiana*, 165 U.S. 578 (1897), which invalidated a Louisiana law prohibiting any person from issuing insurance policies on Louisiana property with companies not licensed to do business in the state. The Court reasoned, in part, that the law infringed upon people's fundamental *freedom of contract*, protected by the Due Process Clause of the Fourteenth Amendment. (*Allgeyer* was the first decision in the *Lochner* line of cases, which are discussed in Chapter 1, § 5 and Chapter 5, § 2B.) Isn't there as much reasonable doubt about the unconstitutionality of the insurance regulation as about the transportation regulation? Indeed, didn't the latter violate both passengers' and railroads' freedom of contract, as well as Plessy's equal protection rights?

2. *The Meaning of "Equality" and "Race."* All the Justices sharply distinguished between *social* and *political* equality; neither Justice Brown nor Justice Harlan defended a statute requiring social equality for African Americans. One way to express the differences between the majority and dissent is that the majority characterized the statute as involving *social* and not *political* rights, while the dissent characterized it as involving *civil* and not *social* rights. Recall that most historians believe § 1 was originally meant to assure *civil*, but neither *social* nor *political*, rights. If so, Justice Harlan at least posed the issue in the correct way. But not all the Reconstruction Republicans viewed the matter that way (note *d* above), and *The Slaughter House Cases* and *Strauder* had rejected such an understanding. In that event, the Court may have been right in believing that § 1 policed only political, and not civil (or common law) rights.

What does *equality* itself mean? Both sides had theories of formal and functional equality. Justice Harlan's dissent is particularly interesting. On the one hand, Harlan asserted that the Constitution is "color blind," suggesting that race is no longer a proper *classification* upon which to base public policy. This might be read to suggest a *rationality principle* animating the Equal Protection Clause. On the other hand, Harlan asserted that the Constitution embodied an anti-caste idea, suggesting that race cannot be used to subordinate a particular *class* of people. This might be read to suggest an *anti-subordination principle*. In the context of *Plessy*, both principles pressed in the same direction, but in later cases they do not; this dichotomy is one way of understanding modern debates about affirmative action (Chapter 3, §§ 3A-B) and efforts to draw electoral lines to facilitate the election of minority representatives (id., § 3E).

Note, finally, the way *race* itself was constructed and deployed. Plessy construed himself as white, but the state insisted he was "colored." Harlan himself invoked the "superiority of the white race" as a *noblesse oblige* reason to be nice to the black race. Although modern conservatives invoke Harlan's color-blindness rhetoric and liberals his anti-caste rhetoric, Harlan seemed to make an explicitly color-conscious and pro-caste argument: Did he not suggest that, in addition to citizenship, what whites and blacks had in common was the fact that they were not yellow?[e]

3. *Transportation and Education.* Note the Court's argument that because segregated schools were apparently constitutional, surely segregated transportation must be as well. On the one hand, this was not a foregone conclusion; the case for segregated transportation was constitutionally weaker than that for segregated education. When the Fourteenth Amendment was ratified, most

---

e. See Gabriel Chin, *The* Plessy *Myth: Justice Harlan and the Chinese Cases*, 82 Iowa L. Rev. 151 (1996). As Chin observes, the Court in this period denied American-born Chinese Americans citizenship, see *United States v. Wong Kim Ark*, 169 U.S. 649 (1898), and upheld many other discriminations against them, with Harlan's support. Only Justice David Brewer, who did not participate in *Plessy*, objected to the country's discrimination against Chinese Americans.

northern states had segregated schools, but none had segregated transportation. The latter did not even enter southern law until 1887; the Louisiana statute dated only from 1890. The 1875 Civil Rights Act, adopted to implement the Fourteenth Amendment, prohibited segregation in transportation but said nothing about schools. The common carrier tradition of public transportation made an apartheid policy much more exceptional for that arena than it was for the educational arena. See also *Railroad Co. v. Brown*, 84 U.S. 445 (1873) (applying an anti-discrimination law to bar railroad from segregating the races).

When the Court directly addressed segregation in education, it simply deferred to the practice. Justice Harlan's opinion for the Court in *Cumming v. Richmond County Board of Education*, 175 U.S. 528 (1899), allowed Richmond County, Georgia to close its "colored" high school (leaving minority students with no school), because "the education of the people in schools maintained by state taxation is a matter belonging to the respective states." In *Gong Lum v. Rice*, 275 U.S. 78 (1927), the Court upheld against equal protection attack the segregation of Chinese students in "colored" schools and treated it as settled that federal courts would not intervene in state and local decisions about how to manage their public schools.

B. THE ROAD TO *BROWN*

The promise of national citizenship for African Americans made in the Reconstruction Amendments was all but a dead letter at the dawn of the new century, and none of the organs of government seemed interested in redeeming the situation. Yet in less than two generations *Plessy* was overruled, and the country embarked upon a "Second Reconstruction."

1. *The NAACP and Howard University.* In 1905, W.E.B. DuBois and 59 other men founded the "Niagara Movement" dedicated to an "organized determination and aggressive action on the part of men who believe in Negro freedom and growth," including the right to equal education. Four years later, DuBois addressed a biracial committee formed to redress African-American inequality. He explained how the South maintained blacks as a permanent underclass through disenfranchisement by poll taxes, literacy tests, and coercion; through segregated and grossly unequal educational opportunities, consigning blacks at best to vocational training; and through curtailment of basic civil rights through threats of economic and physical retaliation. The conference and DuBois' speech stimulated the formation of the National Association for the Advancement of Colored People (NAACP) as a biracial coalition to seek racial justice through education, lobbying, and litigation. From the beginning, the NAACP petitioned the courts to relieve African Americans of their continuing servitude.[f]

---

f. On the founding and early litigation of the NAACP, see Kluger, *Simple Justice*; Charles Flint Kellogg, *NAACP: A History of the National Association for the Advancement of Colored People* (1967); James McPherson, *The Abolitionist Legacy: From Reconstruction to the Founding of the NAACP* (1975).

The NAACP submitted its first brief *amicus curiae* (friend of the court) in *Guinn v. United States*, 238 U.S. 347 (1915). Oklahoma required a literacy test for all voters, except those who were entitled to vote before 1866 (the year Congress assured former slaves the right to vote) or who were descended from persons entitled to vote before 1866 (the so-called "grandfather clause"). The NAACP's brief helped the Court understand the invidious racial thrust of the Oklahoma law, and the Court struck it down as inconsistent with the Fifteenth Amendment. See also *Buchanan v. Warley*, 245 U.S. 60 (1917) (NAACP *amicus* brief helped convince the Court to invalidate a Kentucky law requiring residential segregation to prevent "ill-feeling" and "cross-breeding" between the races).

In the early 1920s, the Garland Fund made a $100,000 grant to the NAACP to enable it to pursue a legal campaign against institutionalized racism in the United States. The NAACP used the money to establish a litigation branch, headed by the Dean of the Howard Law Center, Charles Hamilton Houston. In the 1930s, the NAACP defended hundreds of innocent black men against criminal charges and filed dozens of lawsuits seeking equal pay for black schoolteachers and equal resources for black schools. Houston's litigation strategy did not challenge the constitutionality of segregation per se, but instead focused on the implicit requirement in *Plessy* that facilities be "equal" if they be separate. [Kluger 132-37.] As of 1935, courts had always rejected broad attacks on segregated schools, but were sometimes willing to give relief upon claims of unequal resources and facilities.[g]

2. *Chipping Away at Separate But Equal.* The NAACP won its first Supreme Court victory of the equal-though-separate campaign in *Missouri ex rel. Gaines v. Canada*, 305 U.S. 337 (1938). Missouri denied Lloyd Gaines admission to the state law school; the state argued that he could attend an out-of-state law school and Missouri would provide him financial aid. Houston responded that this was on its face an unequal provision of state education to its black and white citizens, and the Supreme Court agreed. "The basic consideration is not as to what sort of opportunities other States provide, * * * but as to what opportunities Missouri itself furnishes to white students and denies to

---

g. Cf. *McCabe v. Atchison, Topeka & Santa Fe Railway*, 235 U.S. 151 (1914), which struck down an Oklahoma statute requiring trains to maintain separate coach sections for blacks and whites but allowing them to have dining and sleeping cars for whites only. Howard University's *Journal of Negro Education Yearbook* published a report on "The Courts and the Negro Separate School" in 1935. By that time, school segregation had been the subject of litigation 113 times in 29 states and the District of Columbia. In 44 cases plaintiffs attacked the constitutionality of segregation, and in 44 cases they lost on the issue. Other evidence, however, suggested that *Plessy*'s requirement of "equal" in the separate-but-equal formula might be the basis for successful litigation. Statistics indicated that the average white schoolchild's education was supported by two and one-half times as much money as that of the average black schoolchild. In 17 of 19 states segregating public education, the state failed to support equivalent graduate and professional education for blacks. The Journal also published articles by Howard Hale Long (Assistant Superintendent in charge of research for schools in Washington, D.C.) and Charles Thompson (Professor of Sociology at Howard) arguing that segregation established psychological patterns of inferiority in black children. [Kluger 168-72.]

negroes solely upon the ground of color. * * * By the operation of the laws of Missouri a privilege has been created for white law students which is denied to negroes by reason of their race. * * * That is a denial of the equality of legal right to the enjoyment of the privilege which the State has set up, and the provision for the payment of tuition fees in another State does not remove the discrimination." As a remedy, Missouri created a law school for blacks at Lincoln University.

In 1938, Houston returned to private practice and was succeeded by 30-year-old Thurgood Marshall, his star student at Howard and an attorney who had done a brilliant job in Maryland state court litigation to equalize the salaries of black and white schoolteachers. Marshall presided over the creation of a separate litigation organ, the NAACP Education and Defense Fund, Inc. (the "Inc. Fund"), and a change in the organization's constitutional strategy. In 1947-48, Marshall persuaded the NAACP to authorize him to attack segregation as per se unconstitutional. This new strategy did not reap immediate rewards. In *Sipuel v. Board of Regents*, 332 U.S. 631 (1948), the Court struck down Oklahoma's failure to provide legal education for its black citizens, but without addressing Marshall's argument that *Plessy* be overruled. Reflecting a pattern followed by other southern states, Oklahoma complied with the mandate by roping off an area in the state capitol and calling it a law school. Further appeal to the Supreme Court, challenging this continuing inequality, was unavailing. *Fisher v. Hurst*, 333 U.S. 147 (1948). One decade after *Gaines*, the South had built no institution where African Americans could pursue doctoral studies. Excluding Howard University's graduate and professional schools, only one of the 29 medical schools in the South was for blacks, and this was also the pattern for pharmacy (one of the 20 schools), law (one of the 40), and engineering (none of the 36). [Kluger 257.] The South still spent twice as much on education for white children as on black children and paid white teachers 30% more than equally qualified black teachers.

Marshall and the Inc. Fund believed that equalization would never come without actual desegregation. Also, there was some evidence that whatever the quality of the facilities might be, African Americans could not hope for true citizenship and political dignity under an apartheid regime. The most famous study was the "doll tests" of psychologists Kenneth and Mamie Clark. The Clarks showed four dolls (two brown and two white) to black and white children aged three to seven. They asked the children: (1) Give me the white doll. (2) Give me the colored doll. (3) Give me the Negro doll. Three-quarters of the children identified the brown doll with "colored" and "Negro," suggesting to the Clarks that the children were quite aware of racial differences and terminology. The Clarks next asked: (1) Give me the doll you like best. (2) Give me the nice doll. (3) Give me the bad doll. (4) Give me the doll that is a nice color. The Clarks' findings were that 57% of the black children preferred the white doll, as did 89% of the white children. From these results, the Clarks concluded that segregation and its atmosphere were assaults on the self-esteem of black children.[h] The NAACP in the 1940s incorporated studies like these in its litigation documents, and they may have contributed to the Court's ruling in *Shelley v. Kraemer*, 334 U.S. 1 (1948) (Chapter 3, § 2), that the Fourteenth Amendment prohibited the judiciary from enforcing racially restrictive property covenants (agreements not to sell property to non-white persons).

Finally, an increasing number of Americans were questioning the legitimacy of race-based exclusionary laws. On the eve of World War II, several Supreme Court Justices recognized parallels between Nazi and American racism, and the special concern for statutes reflecting prejudice against "discrete and insular minorities" in *United States v. Carolene Products Co.*, 304 U.S. 144, 152 n.4 (1938) (quoted in Chapter 1, § 6) reflected those Justices' openness to constitutional claims by racial minorities.[i] World War II further problematized racial classifications.[j] Upholding a wartime curfew applicable only to Japanese Americans in *Hirabayashi v. United States*, 320 U.S. 81 (1943), the Court for the first time stated that "racial discriminations are in most circumstances irrelevant and therefore prohibited." Upholding the wartime internment of Japanese Americans, *Korematsu v. United States*, 323 U.S. 214 (1944), said that "all legal restrictions which curtail the civil rights of a single racial group are immediately suspect."[k]

Skepticism about racial classifications deepened after the war, which both contributed to the NAACP's new anti-apartheid constitutional stance and to the willingness of federal officials to question apartheid. The Court in *Morgan v. Virginia*, 328 U.S. 373 (1946), held that states could not segregate interstate bus transportation; the NAACP brief stressed that the United States had just emerged from a war against "the apostles of racism." The Presidential Commission on Civil Rights condemned segregation in its report, *To Secure These Rights* (1947). The next year, President Truman directed that the armed forces be desegregated. Given these developments, the time was ripe for a frontal assault on American apartheid.

---

h. See Kenneth Clark and Mamie Clark, *Racial Identification and Preference in Negro Children*, in *Readings in Social Psychology* (T. Newcomb and E. Harley eds. 1947). See also Max Deutscher & Isidor Chein, *The Psychological Effects of Enforced Segregation: A Survey of Social Science Opinion*, 26 J. Psychol. 259 (1948).

i. See David Bixby, *The Roosevelt Court, Democratic Ideology, and Minority Rights: Another Look at* United States v. Classic, 90 Yale L.J. 741, 762-78 (1981). See also Louis Lusky (the law clerk who drafted footnote four), *Minority Rights and the Public Interest*, 52 Yale L.J. 1 (1942); Gunnar Myrdal, *An American Dilemma* (1944) (widely read examination of American racism).

j. In 1941, Philip Randolph organized the March on Washington Movement, petitioning the Roosevelt Administration to end federal discrimination against people of color; FDR issued Executive Order 8802, which barred race discrimination in federal government employment, but not in the armed forces. The hypocrisy of Americans' fighting Nazi racism during World War II, while following racist policies at home, was underlined in Gunnar Myrdal, *An American Dilemma* (1944).

k. *Korematsu* was the last Supreme Court decision to permit overt discrimination against a racial or ethnic minority.

Meanwhile, Latinos were challenging their segregation on grounds of ethnicity. Both segregated school districts and the League of United Latin American Citizens (LULAC) asserted that Latino Americans were racially "white," but LULAC objected that its "white" children were segregated from "white" children of northern European descent and that such segregation was irrational. Indeed, the first successful court challenge to apartheid came in a challenge by Mexican-American families. *Méndez v. Westminster School District*, 64 F.Supp. 544 (C.D. Cal. 1946), aff'd, 161 F.2d 774 (9th Cir. 1947). Responding to *Méndez*, Governor Earl Warren presided over the formal abandonment of the anti-Chicano apartheid regime for California schools.[1]

3. *The United States Joins the Inc. Fund in Questioning Separate But Equal.* As it had done in the *Sipuel* case, the Inc. Fund urged the Court to overrule *Plessy* in *Sweatt v. Painter*, 339 U.S. 629 (1950). Heman Sweatt was denied admission to the University of Texas Law School, on the ground that the hastily assembled Prairie View Law School, a few rented rooms and two adjunct teachers, was a suitably equivalent facility. Marshall argued that racial classifications were per se unreasonable and that a one-person law school was inherently unequal to the University of Texas Law School because of the many intangible benefits and connections accruing from attending the latter. Twelve states submitted briefs supporting Texas' solution. The U.S. Department of Justice, for the first time in a public education case, filed a brief arguing that *Plessy* had been incorrectly decided.

Chief Justice Vinson's opinion in *Sweatt* followed the *Gaines* approach, but with striking differences. To begin with, the Court ordered the University of Texas to admit Sweatt, the first time the Court had been so specific in its remedy for a violation of *Plessy*. More important, the Court recognized the significance of intangible differences in the two schools. "The University of Texas Law School possesses to a far greater degree those qualities which are incapable of objective measurement but which make for greatness in a law school." Hence, the hastily assembled alternative could not hope to be an equal facility. Most important, the Court suggested that segregation itself contributed to these intangible differences. "The law school to which Texas is willing to admit petitioner excludes from its student body members of the racial groups which number 85% of the population of the State and include most of the lawyers, witnesses, jurors, judges and other officials with whom petitioner will inevitably be dealing when he becomes a member of the Texas Bar. With such a substantial and significant segment of society excluded, we cannot conclude that the education offered petitioner is substantially equal to that which he would receive if admitted to the University of Texas Law School." See also *McLaurin v. Oklahoma State Regents*, 339 U.S. 637 (1950) (once admitted to previously all-white University of Oklahoma, petitioner could not then be forced to sit in segregated areas of classroom, cafeteria, and library).

---

1. On the LULAC challenges to segregation of Mexican-American schoolchildren, see Ian Haney-López, *Race and Colorblindness After* Hernandez *and* Brown, 25 Chicano-Latino L. Rev. 61 (2005); Juan Perea, *Buscando América: Why Integration and Equal Protection Fail to Protect Latinos*, 117 Harv. L. Rev. 1420, 1425 (2004).

In both *Sweatt* and *McLaurin*, the United States filed *amicus* briefs urging the Court not to apply *Plessy* or *Cumming* to graduate education. Urging the Court to bar racial discrimination for railroad dining cars, the Solicitor General[m] at oral argument in *Henderson v. United States*, 339 U.S. 816 (1950), asked the Court to overrule *Plessy*: "Segregation of Negroes, as practiced in this country, is universally understood as imposing on them a badge of inferiority. . . . Forbidding this group of American citizens 'to associate with other citizens in the ordinary course of daily living creates inequality by imposing a caste status on the minority group.' " Although most of the Justices privately agreed with the Solicitor General, a majority of them were also fearful that overruling *Plessy* without more warning would trigger a firestorm in the South [Hutchinson 19-30]. Thus, the Court ruled narrowly in *Henderson*, barring railroad segregation on statutory rather than constitutional grounds.

By 1951, both the NAACP and the Justice Department were publicly committed to (and the Supreme Court was privately leaning toward) ending *de jure* segregation, whose existence seemed increasingly bizarre as well as politically and morally embarrassing. Florida did not permit whites and blacks to use the same editions of certain textbooks. Texas did not allow interracial boxing. Alabama prohibited white nurses from tending to blacks. North Carolina maintained segregated washrooms in factories, South Carolina segregated washrooms in cotton mills, and four other states required separate washrooms in mines. In eight states, parks, playgrounds, bathing, boating and fishing facilities, amusement parks, racetracks, pool halls, circuses, and theatres were segregated. Eleven states racially segregated their schools for the blind. Fourteen states segregated railroad passengers for trips within their borders. Seventeen states and the District of Columbia segregated public schools. In 11,173 school districts in the United States, African-American children were prohibited by law from attending school with white children. [Kluger 327.]

If you were litigating the *Brown* case, how would you deal with *Plessy* — its reasoning, its status as a precedent? What post-*Plessy* cases would you find helpful? What kind of evidentiary record could you use in order to attack the factual premises of the *Plessy* doctrine? Before reading about the *Brown* litigation, try drafting a few paragraphs of your own for use in a brief.

C. THE END OF SEPARATE BUT EQUAL

1. *The Lower Court Litigation.* In 1952-53, the Supreme Court accepted for review *Brown* and four other cases in order to reconsider the doctrine of separate-but-equal in public education. After *Brown*, the next case taken on

---

m. The Solicitor General is the chief attorney representing the federal government before the Supreme Court. Among the men who served in that office during the twentieth century were John W. Davis and Thurgood Marshall, the adversaries in *Brown*; Philip Perlman and Simon Sobeloff, both instrumental in the Truman and Eisenhower Department of Justice's effort to press the Court to overrule the segregation decisions; Archibald Cox, the Special Prosecutor who initiated the process that led President Nixon to resign, and Robert Bork, the man who fired Cox; Erwin Griswold, former Dean of the Harvard Law School; and Kenneth Starr, who later gained fame as the Independent Counsel who investigated President Clinton.

writ of certiorari[n] was *Briggs v. Elliott.* When the Rev. Joseph A. DeLaine, a Methodist minister, mobilized a wary black community to seek the assistance of the NAACP in challenging segregation in Clarendon, South Carolina, the white community retaliated. The school board fired Rev. DeLaine from his teaching job. Someone set his house afire; when the firefighters arrived, they stood by as the house burned to the ground. White supervisors fired Harry Briggs, the named plaintiff, from his job at a gas station, and his wife lost her job as a maid at a local motel. Levi Pearson, a plaintiff, watched his crops rot in the fields because banks would not lend him the money to lease harvesters. [Kluger 21-25, 303.]

Unlike the educational facilities for blacks in Topeka, Kansas at issue in *Brown*, those in Clarendon County, South Carolina flunked the *Plessy* equality test cold. The total value of the buildings, grounds, and furnishings of the two white schools (with 276 children) was four times the value of the same in the three black schools (with 808 children). The white school buildings were brick and stucco; the black buildings were rotting wood. The white schools had one teacher for every 28 students, the black schools one for every 47. One of the black schools had no running water, another had no electricity. The white schools had indoor flush toilets; the black schools had outhouses. [Kluger 330.] Although the plaintiffs in *Briggs* had winning facts under *Gaines*, they also attacked school segregation as inherently unconstitutional, invoking psychological and statistical evidence. Nonetheless, the three-judge federal court upheld segregation, over a dissent by Judge J. Waties Waring, but the court did enter an injunction that the facilities for blacks had to be equalized (which did not occur).

The third case accepted for Supreme Court review was *Davis v. County School Board of Prince Edward County (Virginia).* The NAACP's challenge to *Plessy* in this case was supported not only by the Clarks' doll studies, but also by testimony of substantial consensus among psychologists that enforced segregation has detrimental psychological effects on members of both the minority and majority populations. Unlike Clarendon County, Prince Edward County disputed the NAACP's social science data. The defense subjected Clark to keen cross-examination questioning the scientific validity of his doll studies and introduced experts who denied that broad conclusions about legal apartheid could be drawn from such studies. Henry Garret, Professor of Psychology at

---

n. There are two basic routes to the Supreme Court: "appeal" and "certiorari." At the time of *Brown*, a party losing in the lower court could "appeal" from (1) a U.S. court of appeals decision invalidating a state statute or (2) a state court decision upholding a state statute against a claim that it violates federal constitutional or statutory law. Until the federal statute governing the Supreme Court's jurisdiction was amended in 1988, the Court's jurisdiction over appeals was mandatory; in practice, however, the Court usually dismissed such appeals summarily, for want of a substantial federal question. Today, mandatory jurisdiction has been almost entirely eliminated. The Court has wholly discretionary "certiorari" power to review (1) a U.S. court of appeals decision in any civil or criminal case, or (2) a state court decision whenever (a) a challenge to a state or federal law is based upon a federal issue, or (b) a federal right, privilege, or immunity is set up or claimed. It takes only four votes to grant certiorari. This "rule of four" means that the Court will sometimes hear a case even if a majority is not initially persuaded of its significance.

Columbia University, testified that "in terms of heredity, physiology and cultural history, the Negro suffers badly when compared with the white man. * * * Physiologists were finding evidence that the Negro's brain was * * * less fissured, less complex and less thick in the frontal lobes where reasoning and abstract thinking go on." [Kluger 502.] The federal court essentially accepted the school board's evidence in its rejection of the assault on *Plessy*. The court ordered Prince Edward County to equalize the white and black schools, but did not set a timetable. [Kluger 506.]

The Supreme Court "noted probable jurisdiction" in the fourth and fifth cases one month prior to the date it had set to hear oral arguments on the first three cases. The Court, in a rare move, called up *Bolling v. Sharpe* from the lower courts on its own initiative. The plaintiffs had only argued that school segregation in the District of Columbia was per se unconstitutional (although there was plenty of evidence that facilities were also unequal), and the trial court had denied relief because of *Plessy*. The Supreme Court also took the appeal in *Belton v. Gebhart* and *Bulah v. Gebhart*, where Collins Seitz, then a state judge, had not only found that the Wilmington, Delaware school system offered blatantly unequal facilities to black students, but also explicitly accepted the NAACP's social science evidence and ordered the white schools to accept black students.

2. *The First Go-Round in the Desegregation Cases.* Once the Supreme Court accepts a case upon writ of certiorari or by noting probable appellate jurisdiction, the parties are on notice that they must file briefs on the merits with the Court. Given the importance of the issue, and the Court's signal that it might overrule *Plessy*, the case attracted several briefs *amicus curiae*, including a brief from the Department of Justice, which again urged the Court to overrule *Plessy*. The Court heard argument on December 9, 1952. The *Brown* case produced a dull argument, in large part because the Topeka Board of Education was in the process of ending *de jure* segregation in public schools.[o]

In the Clarendon County argument, former Solicitor General John W. Davis argued that the county satisfied *Plessy* by equalizing black and white schools and that there was no basis for overruling the longstanding rule of *Plessy*. In constitutional law, courts are supposed to follow precedent, especially when it has been settled for long periods of time and private persons and public entities have relied on it in their plans and established practices. In the South, *Plessy* was the basis for a whole way of life, and Davis maintained that switching the constitutional rule would have thousands of unpredictable and unsettling effects for everyone, so deeply entrenched was the principle against racial integration in the South. (On reargument the next year, Davis added that there was little reason to believe that overruling *Plessy* would actually help black schoolchil-

---

o. There was enormous embarrassment in Kansas that Topeka was involved in the same issues as the openly racist southern districts, and the school board voted not to defend itself on appeal. The Supreme Court instructed the Kansas Attorney General's Office that it had to defend the case, or else concede the invalidity of Kansas' school segregation statute. Ten days prior to oral argument the Attorney General of Kansas gave the case to his young assistant, Paul Wilson, who had never argued before any appellate court. [Dudziak 370-73.]

dren, so entrenched was that principle. "Would that make the children any happier? * * * Would their lives be more serene?" Davis thought not; "the best is often the enemy of the good.")

Thurgood Marshall, for the appellants, retorted that the time had come for the Court to end legal segregation, for it was at odds with the purpose of the Equal Protection Clause, to "eliminate race distinctions from American law" and to secure equality for people of color. *Plessy* was inconsistent with this purpose — but the Court's twentieth century precedents were not. The Court had already invalidated racial discrimination and segregation in graduate education, by making it impossible to prove equal facilities (*Sweatt*); in housing, by striking down segregationist statutes (*Buchanan*) and by refusing to enforce discriminatory private covenants (*Shelley*); in interstate travel, by striking down state segregationist statutes (*Morgan*); in voting, by removing impediments designed to prevent black suffrage (*Lane v. Wilson*, 307 U.S. 268 (1939)), and *Smith v. Allwright*, 321 U.S. 649 (1944)); in economic and employment relations, by invalidating certain efforts to ruin minority businesses (*Yick Wo v. Hopkins*, 118 U.S. 356 (1886)) and to discriminate against black workers (*Steele v. Louisville & Nashville Railroad*, 323 U.S. 192 (1944)); and in jury service, by striking down whites-only jury laws (*Strauder*). The South had been on notice for some time that their "way of life" had to give way to the Constitution, and now was the time for the Court to deliver what the Fourteenth Amendment had promised: actual and full equality.[p]

The Justices discussed the five cases at their Saturday conference. The Court was fractured — four Justices (Black, Douglas, Burton, and Minton) in favor of overruling *Plessy* immediately, three Justices (Frankfurter, Jackson, Clark) inclined to overrule but uncertain as to how or when the Court should do it, one Justice (Reed) opposed to an overruling, and the Chief Justice (Vinson) uncommitted. [Tushnet, with Lezin 1902-07.] Given the need for a more united front in light of expected southern resistance, such a fractured Court ought not proceed to a hasty decision. At the suggestion of Justice Frankfurter, the Court announced on June 9, 1953, that the five cases would be reargued and that the parties must submit briefs discussing the "original intent" of the Fourteenth Amendment regarding segregation in education.

3. *The Second Go-Round in the Desegregation Cases.* Most of the parties duly filed briefs arguing that the Framers of the Fourteenth Amendment either did (the NAACP's brief) or did not (the defendants' briefs) expect the amendment's equal protection guarantees to disallow race-based segregation in public schools. The Justice Department argued that the original intent was indeterminate but that other considerations favored the overruling of *Plessy*.

---

p. The briefs filed by the NAACP included a further argument, developed in their appendix, "The Effects of Segregation and the Consequences of Desegregation: A Social Science Statement." The central point of the statement was the pervasive and harmful psychological effects of law-endorsed segregation on its objects, people of color. Such laws undermine the dignity of those stigmatized, contribute to rigid and authoritarian personalities among white children, and perpetuate stereotypes and racial animosity among all children. The 32 eminent scientists who signed the statement concluded that race ought not be the basis for legal exclusions or segregations.

When the parties reargued the cases on October 12, they were speaking to a different Supreme Court. Between order and reargument, Chief Justice Vinson died and was succeeded by California Governor Earl Warren, who had led the way toward integrated schools in his state. This was to prove significant. In conference after the second argument, the new Chief Justice forcefully stated his intent to overrule *Plessy*. Together with mounting pressure from the media and intellectuals outside the Court, Warren's leadership tipped an unsteady Court toward decisive action. The Chief's pitch was immediately seconded by Justice Black (who was the senior Justice and spoke immediately after the Chief) and then by Justices Douglas, Burton, and Minton. Justices Frankfurter, Jackson, and Clark expressed concerns about the political nature and ramifications of the decision; Warren gently assuaged their concerns, in part by agreeing to address only the constitutionality of *de jure* segregation and postponing decision of remedy (what the school districts must do to comply with the Court's mandate) for the next Term of the Court. Justice Reed, from Kentucky, remained unpersuaded that the "separate but equal" doctrine should have been abrogated, but Warren talked him out of filing a dissenting opinion, which (Warren argued) would undermine the Court's institutional ability to stand behind its decrees.

On May 17, 1954, Chief Justice Warren read his opinion to a hushed gallery. A few days earlier his Court had ruled that states could not exclude Mexican Americans from juries. Warren's opinion for the Court in *Hernandez v. Texas*, 347 U.S. 475 (1954), emphasized the arbitrary lines drawn in anti-Chicano apartheid and ruled that the state could not enforce or deploy them in constructing jury venires. The Chief Justice followed a similar line of reasoning — also for a unanimous Court — in *Brown*. Given the legal arguments in the case and its political sensitivity, how would you have drafted the Court's opinion? (You might jot down an outline before reading Warren's opinion below.)

BROWN v. BOARD OF EDUCATION
347 U.S. 483, 74 S.Ct. 686, 98 L.Ed. 873 (1954)

CHIEF JUSTICE WARREN delivered the opinion of the Court.

[The Chief Justice described the cases, how they came to the Court, and the claims common to the plaintiffs in all the state cases — that the "separate but equal" doctrine of *Plessy* did not satisfy the Fourteenth Amendment's requirement that black schoolchildren be afforded equal protection of the laws.]

Reargument was largely devoted to the circumstances surrounding the adoption of the Fourteenth Amendment in 1868. It covered exhaustively consideration of the Amendment in Congress, ratification by the states, then existing practices in racial segregation, and the views of proponents and opponents of the Amendment. This discussion and our own investigation convince us that, although these sources cast some light, it is not enough to resolve the problem with which we are faced. At best, they are inconclusive. The most avid proponents of the post-War Amendments undoubtedly intended them to remove all legal distinctions among "all persons born or naturalized in the United States." Their opponents, just as certainly, were antagonistic to both the letter and the spirit of the Amendments and wished them to have the most limited effect. What others in Congress and the state legislatures had in mind cannot be determined with any degree of certainty.

An additional reason for the inconclusive nature of the Amendment's history, with respect to segregated schools, is the status of public education at that time. In the South, the movement toward free common schools, supported by general taxation, had not yet taken hold. Education of white children was largely in the hands of private groups. Education of Negroes was almost nonexistent, and practically all of the race were illiterate. In fact, any education of Negroes was forbidden by law in some states. Today, in contrast, many Negroes have achieved outstanding success in the arts and sciences as well as in the business and professional world. It is true that public school education at the time of the Amendment had advanced further in the North, but the effect of the Amendment on Northern States was generally ignored in the congressional debates. Even in the North, the conditions of public education did not approximate those existing today. The curriculum was usually rudimentary; ungraded schools were common in rural areas; the school term was but three months a year in many states; and compulsory school attendance was virtually unknown. As a consequence, it is not surprising that there should be so little in the history of the Fourteenth Amendment relating to its intended effect on public education.

In the first cases in this Court construing the Fourteenth Amendment, decided shortly after its adoption, the Court interpreted it as proscribing all state-imposed discriminations against the Negro race. *Slaughter House Cases*; *Strauder.* The doctrine of "separate but equal" did not make its appearance in this Court until 1896 in *Plessy*, involving not education but transportation. American courts have since labored with the doctrine for over half a century. In this Court, there have been six cases involving the "separate but equal" doctrine in the field of public education. In [*Cumming*] the validity of the doctrine itself was not challenged. In more recent cases, all on the graduate school level, inequality was found in that specific benefits enjoyed by white students were denied to Negro students of the same educational qualifications. *Gaines*; *Sipuel*; *Sweatt*; *McLaurin.* In none of these cases was it necessary to re-examine the doctrine to grant relief to the Negro plaintiff. And in *Sweatt* the Court expressly reserved decision on the question whether *Plessy* should be held inapplicable to public education.

In the instant cases, that question is directly presented. Here, unlike *Sweatt*, there are findings below that the Negro and white schools involved have been equalized, or are being equalized, with respect to buildings, curricula, qualifications and salaries of teachers, and other "tangible" factors. Our decision, therefore, cannot turn on merely a comparison of these tangible factors in the Negro and white schools involved in each of the cases. We must look instead to the effect of segregation itself on public education.

In approaching this problem, we cannot turn the clock back to 1868 when the Amendment was adopted, or even to 1896 when *Plessy* was written. We must consider public education in the light of its full development and its present place in American life throughout the Nation. Only in this way can it be determined if segregation in public schools deprives these plaintiffs of the equal protection of the laws.

Today, education is perhaps the most important function of state and local governments. Compulsory school attendance laws and the great expenditures for education both demonstrate our recognition of the importance of education to our democratic society. It is required in the performance of our most basic public responsibilities, even service in the armed forces. It is the very foundation of good citizenship. Today it is a principal instrument in awakening the child to cultural values, in preparing him for later professional training, and in helping him to adjust normally to his environment. In these days, it is doubtful that any child may reasonably be expected to succeed in life if he is denied the opportunity of an education. Such an opportunity, where the state has undertaken to provide it, is a right which must be made available to all on equal terms.

We come then to the question presented: Does segregation of children in public schools solely on the basis of race, even though the physical facilities and other "tangible" factors may be equal, deprive the children of the minority group of equal educational opportunities? We believe that it does.

In *Sweatt*, in finding that a segregated law school for Negroes could not provide them equal educational opportunities, this Court relied in large part on "those qualities which are incapable of objective measurement but which make for greatness in a law school." In *McLaurin* the Court, in requiring that a Negro admitted to a white graduate school be treated like all other students, again resorted to intangible considerations: " . . . his ability to study, to engage in discussions and exchange views with other students, and, in general, to learn his profession." Such considerations apply with added force to children in grade and high schools. To separate them from others of similar age and qualifications solely because of their race generates a feeling of inferiority as to their status in the community that may affect their hearts and minds in a way unlikely ever to be undone. The effect of this separation on their educational opportunities was well stated by a finding in the Kansas case by a court which nevertheless felt compelled to rule against the Negro plaintiffs:

> Segregation of white and colored children in public schools has a detrimental effect upon the colored children. The impact is greater when it has the sanction of the law; for the policy of separating the races is usually interpreted as denoting the inferiority of the negro group. A sense of inferiority affects the motivation of a child to learn. Segregation with the sanction of law, therefore, has a tendency to [retard] the educational and mental development of negro children and to deprive them of some of the benefits they would receive in a [racially] integrated school system.

Whatever may have been the extent of psychological knowledge at the time of *Plessy*, this finding is amply supported by modern authority.[11] Any language in *Plessy* contrary to this finding is rejected.

We conclude that in the field of public education the doctrine of "separate but equal" has no place. Separate educational facilities are inherently unequal. Therefore, we hold that the plaintiffs and others similarly situated for whom the actions have been brought are, by reason of the segregation complained of, deprived of the equal protection of the laws guaranteed by the Fourteenth Amendment. This disposition makes unnecessary any discussion whether such segregation also violates the Due Process Clause of the Fourteenth Amendment.

Because these are class actions, because of the wide applicability of this decision, and because of the great variety of local conditions, the formulation of decrees in these cases presents problems of considerable complexity. On reargument, the consideration of appropriate relief was necessarily subordinated to the primary question — the constitutionality of segregation in public education. We have now announced that such segregation is a denial of the equal protection of the laws. In order that we may have the full assistance of the parties in formulating decrees, the cases will be restored to the docket, and the parties are requested to present further argument on Questions 4 and 5 previously propounded by the Court for the reargument this Term.[12] The Attorney General of the United States is again invited to participate. The Attorneys General of the states requiring or permitting segregation in public

---

11.   K.B. Clark, Effect of Prejudice and Discrimination on Personality Development (Midcentury White House Conference on Children and Youth, 1950); Witmer and Kotinsky, Personality in the Making (1952), c. VI; Deutscher and Chein, The Psychological Effects of Enforced Segregation: A Survey of Social Science Opinion, 26 J. Psychol. 259 (1948); Chein, What are the Psychological Effects of Segregation Under Conditions of Equal Facilities?, 3 Int. J. Opinion and Attitude Res. 229 (1949); Brameld, Educational Costs, in Discrimination and National Welfare (MacIver ed. 1949), 44-48; Frazier, The Negro in the United States (1949), 674-681. And see generally Myrdal, An American Dilemma (1944).

12.   "4. Assuming it is decided that segregation in public schools violates the Fourteenth Amendment

"(a) would a decree necessarily follow providing that, within the limits set by normal geographic school districting, Negro children should forthwith be admitted to schools of their choice, or

"(b) may this Court, in the exercise of its equity powers, permit an effective gradual adjustment to be brought about from existing segregated systems to a system not based on color distinctions?

"5. On the assumption on which questions 4 (a) and (b) are based, and assuming further that this Court will exercise its equity powers to the end described in question 4 (b),

"(a) should this Court formulate detailed decrees in these cases;

"(b) if so, what specific issues should the decrees reach;

"(c) should this Court appoint a special master to hear evidence with a view to recommending specific terms for such decrees;

"(d) should this Court remand to the courts of first instance with directions to frame decrees in these cases, and if so what general directions should the decrees of this Court include and what procedures should the courts of first instance follow in arriving at the specific terms of more detailed decrees?"

education will also be permitted to appear as amici curiae upon request to do so by September 15, 1954, and submission of briefs by October 1, 1954. It is so ordered.

———

Bolling v. Sharpe, 347 U.S. 497 (1954). The Court handled the District of Columbia case in a separate opinion. "The Fifth Amendment, which is applicable in the District of Columbia, does not contain an equal protection clause as does the Fourteenth Amendment which applies only to the states. But the concepts of equal protection and due process, both stemming from our American ideal of fairness, are not mutually exclusive. The 'equal protection of the laws' is a more explicit safeguard of prohibited unfairness than 'due process of law,' and, therefore, we do not imply that the two are always interchangeable phrases. But, as this Court has recognized, discrimination may be so unjustifiable as to be violative of due process.

"Classifications based solely upon race must be scrutinized with particular care, since they are contrary to our traditions and hence constitutionally suspect. As long ago as 1896, this Court declared the principle 'that the Constitution of the United States, in its present form, forbids, so far as civil and political rights are concerned, discrimination by the General Government, or by the States, against any citizen because of his race.' And in *Buchanan v. Warley*, the Court held that a statute which limited the right of a property owner to convey his property to a person of another race was, as an unreasonable discrimination, a denial of due process of law.

"Although the Court has not assumed to define 'liberty' with any great precision, that term is not confined to mere freedom from bodily restraint. Liberty under law extends to the full range of conduct which the individual is free to pursue, and it cannot be restricted except for a proper governmental objective. Segregation in public education is not reasonably related to any proper governmental objective, and thus it imposes on Negro children of the District of Columbia a burden that constitutes an arbitrary deprivation of their liberty in violation of the Due Process Clause.

"In view of our decision that the Constitution prohibits the states from maintaining racially segregated public schools, it would be unthinkable that the same Constitution would impose a lesser duty on the Federal Government. We hold that racial segregation in the public schools of the District of Columbia is a denial of the due process of law guaranteed by the Fifth Amendment to the Constitution."

NOTES ON *BROWN, BOLLING,* AND THE
ROLE OF JUDICIAL REVIEW

1. *Stare Decisis in Constitutional Cases.* Under the principle of "stare decisis" (Latin for "let the decisions stand"), once the Supreme Court has made a decision, it will follow that decision in future cases and not overrule it. Thus, in *Federalist* No. 78 (App. 2), Alexander Hamilton also said: "To avoid an arbitrary discretion in the courts, it is indispensable that they should be bound down by strict rules and precedents which serve to define and point out their

duty in every particular case that comes before them." Stare decisis was the main basis for John W. Davis's losing argument in the Clarendon County case.

How can the *Brown* decision be squared with stare decisis? To begin with, one might observe that *Brown* did not quite "overrule" *Plessy*, which was after all a transportation case (its discussion of segregation of schools was "dictum" not necessary to the result of the case). The Court found that de jure segregation has a "detrimental effect" on black children and then "rejected" reasoning in *Plessy* "contrary to this finding." That doesn't provide an escape hatch from stare decisis, however. The Court overruled an assumption of *Cumming*, which rejected a public education race discrimination claim, and an assumption or holding of *Gong Lum*, which upheld the segregation of Chinese students. Moreover, by rejecting reasoning essential to *Plessy*'s result, *Brown* was overruling part of the earlier Court's holding. Citing only *Brown*, the Court issued a series of summary opinions invalidating public segregation in public parks, facilities, and transportation.[q]

A defense of *Brown*'s willingness to overrule prior constitutional precedents is that the rule of stare decisis is not an absolute rule, and in constitutional cases the Court has tended to follow the approach in *Burnet v. Coronado Oil & Gas Co.*, 285 U.S. 393, 406-07 (1932) (Brandeis, J., dissenting):

> Stare decisis is usually the wise policy, because in most matters it is more important that the applicable rule of law be settled than that it be settled right. * * * This is commonly true even where the error is a matter of serious concern, provided correction can be had by legislation. But in cases involving the Federal Constitution, where correction through legislative action is practically impossible, this court has often overruled its earlier decisions.

Does this rationale for relaxed stare decisis in constitutional cases apply to *Brown*? It would not have taken a constitutional amendment to have overruled *Plessy* (the tactic Justice Brandeis described as "practically impossible") if Congress, under its Fourteenth Amendment powers, could have outlawed de jure segregation at the state level. Moreover, Congress certainly could have outlawed segregation in the District of Columbia. See U.S. Const., art. I, § 8, cl. 17 (Congress' plenary authority over the District). Since "correction [could have been] had by legislation," should the Court have decided *Bolling* differently from *Brown*? Even if stare decisis is not absolute, should the Court feel free to overrule established precedent like *Plessy* without special justification? To what extent was it important that decisions prior to *Brown* had already undermined *Plessy*?

2. *The Court's Reasoning in* Brown. Surely, the Supreme Court should have strong justification when it declares a statute unconstitutional, and especially when the Court must overrule its own precedents to do so. Did *Brown* give us such weighty justification? The Court relied on neither the text nor the

---

q. See *Mayor & City Council of Baltimore City v. Dawson*, 350 U.S. 877 (1955) (public bathhouses and beaches); *Holmes v. Atlanta*, 350 U.S. 879 (1955) (municipal golf course); *Gayle v. Browder*, 352 U.S. 903 (1956) (city buses, giving the Southern Christian Leadership Conference a victory in its Montgomery, Alabama bus boycott); *New Orleans City Park Improvement Ass'n v. Detiege*, 358 U.S. 54 (1958) (municipal parks and golf course).

"inconclusive" original intent of the Fourteenth Amendment. What is left for the Court to rely on? The Court stated that segregation of blacks in elementary school "generates a feeling of inferiority as to their status in the community." For support, the Court cited a finding of fact made by the district court in *Brown* but ignored contrary findings made by the district court in *Davis* and, further, invoked the "modern authority" collected in footnote 11. Is this persuasive? Social scientists have been skeptical.[r]

First, many believe that the evidence was not rigorously scientific. The Clarks' doll tests, for example, did not demonstrate that the choice of a white doll by a black child really proved that the child felt inferior, nor did they demonstrate the cause of any feelings of inferiority, which may have been more social than legal. The Clarks used too few children to draw statistically significant results, and they failed to use control groups, as required by rigorous scientific technique. The Department of Justice considered the doll tests frivolous, as did many of the NAACP attorneys. [Kluger 321.]

Second, not all of the extant social science evidence supported the Court's result. One finding of the Clarks' doll studies was this:

Doll Choices of Black Children in Southern (Segregated) and Northern (Integrated) Schools

	"Nice Doll"		"Looks Bad"	
	South	North	South	North
Black Doll	46	30	49	71
White Doll	52	68	16	17
No Choice	2	2	35	12

The Clarks admitted that "the southern children [in segregated schools] are significantly less likely to reject the brown doll (evaluate it negatively), as compared to the strong tendency for the majority of northern children [many of whom attended integrated schools] to do so." What could explain this finding? Does it undermine *Brown*'s proposition that de jure school segregation significantly contributes to feelings of stigma and inferiority?

Third, perhaps it was imprudent to link an important development in the law to preliminary scientific findings, as Kenneth Clark later conceded, *A Personal View of the Background and Developments Since the* Brown *Decision*, in *Brown Plus Thirty: Perspectives on Desegregation* 18 (1986). Consider the possibility that later social scientists might come in with evidence, after several years of

---

r. E.g., Harold Gerard, *School Desegregation: The Social Science Role*, 38 Am. Psychol. 869, 870-72 (1983); Ernest Van den Haag, *Social Science Testimony in the Desegregation Cases — A Reply to Professor Kenneth Clark*, 6 Vill. L. Rev. 69 (1960); Symposium, *The Courts, Social Science and School Desegregation*, 38 L. & Contemp. Probs. (Winter/Spring 1975). See generally John Monahan & Laurens Walker, *Social Science in Law: Cases and Materials* 186-211 (5th ed. 2002).

school integration, that black children had an even more negative self-image than before, perhaps because white teachers and students discourage black students by their attitudes and (more tangibly) by "ghettoizing" black students through tracking programs.[s] Would that justify overruling *Brown* and returning to *Plessy*, at least for school districts where such data could be "scientifically" established? Could a district judge presented with such evidence for a local school district hold that, as a matter of fact, segregation is not harmful there, and then conclude that *Brown* is inapplicable there?

3. *Back to Harlan's Dissent in* Plessy? If the social science evidence in footnote 11 is insufficiently persuasive and original intent is indeterminate (or, according to many scholars, cuts against the Court's interpretation, see Problem 2-1 below), what is the *legal* basis for overruling *Plessy*? Why didn't Warren follow the *Plessy* dissent: Apartheid undermined the general goal of the Reconstruction Amendments, which was to integrate African Americans into the country as equal citizens, and created a politically unhealthy "caste" system? Consider also the arguments made by Thurgood Marshall: Apartheid had been shown to be unworkable, and the Court had backed away from it at every opportunity; the time had come to end that social experiment. Put together a legal argument that would have supported an overruling of *Plessy*.

SECTION 2. THE SUPREME COURT'S ROLE IN OUR POLITICAL SYSTEM

Our notes to *Plessy* and *Brown* have raised issues extending beyond the holding and ramifications of those decisions: Does the Constitution contemplate "judicial review," which effectively nullifies statutes adopted by state legislatures or Congress? If the Constitution does contemplate such a power, what responsibilities does that power suggest for the Supreme Court in constitutional cases? In this Section, we want to pursue these issues more systematically, through analysis of the decision establishing judicial review, *Marbury v. Madison*, and of the modern Court's expansion of *Marbury* to require southern states to implement *Brown* (a decision they believed to be unconstitutional) in *Cooper v. Aaron*. This Section will conclude with what is probably the hardest issue arising under *Brown*: To what extent, and how long, may a federal court monitor the operation of local schools in order to assure desegregation?

A. BASES FOR JUDICIAL REVIEW

Marbury v. Madison is the leading case supporting the Court's power to declare statutes unconstitutional. The plaintiff, William Marbury, had been appointed justice of the peace in the District of Columbia for a five-year term by outgoing Federalist President John Adams and confirmed by the Senate one day before the Democratic-Republicans took power on March 4, 1801. The new administration obtained a repeal of the statute creating the D.C. courts and

---

s. See Jacqueline Jordan Irvine, *Black Students and School Failure: Policies, Practices, and Prescriptions* 9-12 (1990).

refused to deliver Marbury's commission. Marbury sued Secretary of State James Madison in the Supreme Court itself — *not* in some lower court whose decision could then be appealed to the Supreme Court. He asked the Court to order Madison to deliver the commission; this was a request for a writ of mandamus — Latin for "we command." For Marbury to obtain this remedy, he had to show (1) that the Supreme Court had been vested with "jurisdiction" (authority) to adjudicate Marbury's lawsuit; *and* (2) that Madison had in fact violated federal statutory or constitutional rules when he withheld Marbury's commission; *and* (3) that mandamus was an appropriate remedy to redress Marbury's legal injury.

Chief Justice John Marshall's opinion did not address the issues in the order that we have listed them. He first focused on issue 2, ruling that Marbury had a "vested legal right" in the commission for its five-year term; that legal right was not "revocable." Marshall next decided issue 3, ruling that under a "government of laws, and not men," a person whose vested legal right is being injured "has a right to resort to the laws of his country for a remedy." Mandamus was a proper remedy, because Marbury had no remedy at law and the officer at whom it was directed, Madison, was depriving Marbury of an absolute right. Marshall's opinion at this point carefully distinguished cases which today would be called "political questions," namely, matters which have been reserved by the Constitution to the discretion of the executive department or the President (Chapter 9, § 1). "Where the head of a department acts in a case, in which the executive discretion is to be exercised; in which he is the mere organ of executive will; it is again repeated, that any application to a court to control, in any respect, his conduct, would be rejected without hesitation. But where he is directed by law to do a certain act affecting the absolute rights of individuals, in the performance of which he is not placed under the particular discretion of the President, and the performance of which, the President cannot lawfully forbid, and therefore is never presumed to have forbidden * * * in such cases, it is not perceived on what ground the courts of the country are further excused from the duty of giving judgment."

Issue 1, the jurisdictional issue, is the heart of the case, as Marshall posed it, and this is the only portion of the opinion excerpted below. Marshall's opinion dissolved that issue into three questions: (A) Has Congress vested the Supreme Court with "original" (as opposed to appellate) jurisdiction in mandamus cases, pursuant to § 13 of the Judiciary Act of 1789? (B) If so, is that grant of original jurisdiction inconsistent with Article III of the Constitution? (C) If so, what is the responsibility of the Court? May the Court exercise jurisdiction granted by a statute that is inconsistent with the Constitution? Note that these three questions involve (A) an interpretation of a federal statute, (B) an interpretation of a specific constitutional provision, and (C) an interpretation of the constitutional "scheme" or structure.

MARBURY v. MADISON
5 U.S. (1 Cranch) 137 (1803)

CHIEF JUSTICE MARSHALL delivered the Opinion of the Court. * * *

This, then, is a plain case for a mandamus, either to deliver the commission, or a copy of it from the record; and it only remains to be inquired,

Whether it can issue from this court.

The act to establish the judicial courts of the United States authorizes the supreme court "to issue writs of mandamus, in cases warranted by the principles and usages of law, to any courts appointed, or persons holding office, under the authority of the United States."[a]

The secretary of state, being a person holding an office under the authority of the United States, is precisely within the letter of the description; and if this court is not authorized to issue a writ of mandamus to such an officer, it must be because the law is unconstitutional, and therefore absolutely incapable of conferring the authority, and assigning the duties which its words purport to confer and assign.

The constitution vests the whole judicial power of the United States in one supreme court, and such inferior courts as congress shall, from time to time, ordain and establish. This power is expressly extended to all cases arising under the laws of the United States; and, consequently, in some form, may be exercised over the present case; because the right claimed is given by a law of the United States.

In the distribution of this power it is declared that "the supreme court shall have original jurisdiction in all cases affecting ambassadors, other public ministers and consuls, and those in which a state shall be a party. In all other cases, the supreme court shall have appellate jurisdiction."

It has been insisted, at the bar, that as the original grant of jurisdiction, to the supreme and inferior courts, is general, and the clause, assigning original jurisdiction to the supreme court, contains no negative or restrictive words; the

---

a. *Editors' note:* Section 13 of the Judiciary Act provided in its entirety:

And be it further enacted, That the Supreme Court shall have exclusive jurisdiction of all controversies of a civil nature, where the state is a party, except between a state and its citizens; and except also between a state and citizens of other states, or aliens, in which latter case it shall have original but not exclusive jurisdiction. And shall have exclusively all such jurisdiction of suits or proceedings against ambassadors, or other public ministers, or their domestics, or domestic servants, as a court of law can have or exercise consistently with the law of nations; and original, but not exclusive jurisdiction of all suits brought by ambassadors or other public ministers, or in which a consul, or vice consul, shall be a party. And the trial of issues of fact in the Supreme Court, in all actions at law against citizens of the United States, shall be by jury. The Supreme Court shall also have appellate jurisdiction from the circuit courts and courts of the several states, in cases herein after specially provided for; and shall have power to issue writs of prohibition to the district courts, when proceeding as courts in admiralty and maritime jurisdiction, and writs of mandamus, in cases warranted by the principles and usages of law, to any court appointed, or persons holding office, under the authority of the United States.

power remains to the legislature, to assign original jurisdiction to that court in other cases than those specified in the article which has been recited; provided those cases belong to the judicial power of the United States.

If it had been intended to leave it to the discretion of the legislature to apportion the judicial power between the supreme and inferior courts according to the will of that body, it would certainly have been useless to have proceeded further than to have defined the judicial powers, and the tribunals in which it should be vested. The subsequent part of the section is mere surplusage, is entirely without meaning, if such is to be the construction. If congress remains at liberty to give this court appellate jurisdiction, where the constitution has declared their jurisdiction shall be original; and original jurisdiction where the constitution has declared it shall be appellate; the distribution of jurisdiction, made in the constitution, is form without substance.

Affirmative words are often, in their operation, negative of other objects than those affirmed; and in this case, a negative or exclusive sense must be given to them, or they have no operation at all.

It cannot be presumed that any clause in the constitution is intended to be without effect; and, therefore, such a construction is inadmissible, unless the words require it. * * *

It is the essential criterion of appellate jurisdiction, that it revises and corrects the proceedings in a cause already instituted, and does not create that cause. Although, therefore, a mandamus may be directed to courts, yet to issue such a writ to an officer for the delivery of a paper, is in effect the same as to sustain an original action for that paper, and therefore, seems not to belong to appellate, but to original jurisdiction. Neither is it necessary in such a case as this, to enable the court to exercise its appellate jurisdiction.

The authority, therefore, given to the supreme court, by the act establishing the judicial courts of the United States, to issue writs of mandamus to public officers, appears not to be warranted by the constitution; and it becomes necessary to inquire whether a jurisdiction so conferred can be exercised.

The question, whether an act, repugnant to the constitution, can become the law of the land, is a question deeply interesting to the United States; but, happily, not of an intricacy proportioned to its interest. It seems only necessary to recognize certain principles, supposed to have been long and well established, to decide it.

That the people have an original right to establish, for their future government, such principles as, in their opinion, shall most conduce to their own happiness is the basis on which the whole American fabric has been erected. The exercise of this original right is a very great exertion; nor can it, nor ought it to be frequently repeated. The principles, therefore, so established, are deemed fundamental. And as the authority from which they proceed is supreme, and can seldom act, they are designed to be permanent.

This original and supreme will organizes the government, and assigns to different departments, their respective powers. It may either stop here, or establish certain limits not to be transcended by those departments.

The government of the United States is of the latter description. The powers of the legislature are defined and limited; and that those limits may not be mistaken, or forgotten, the constitution is written. To what purpose are powers limited, and to what purpose is that limitation committed to writing, if these limits may, at any time, be passed by those intended to be restrained? The distinction between a government with limited and unlimited powers is abolished, if those limits do not confine the persons on whom they are imposed, and if acts prohibited and acts allowed, are of equal obligation. It is a proposition too plain to be contested, that the constitution controls any legislative act repugnant to it; or, that the legislature may alter the constitution by an ordinary act.

Between these alternatives there is no middle ground. The constitution is either a superior, paramount law, unchangeable by ordinary means, or it is on a level with ordinary legislative acts, and, like other acts, is alterable when the legislature shall please to alter it.

If the former part of the alternative be true, then a legislative act contrary to the constitution is not law: if the latter part be true, then written constitutions are absurd attempts, on the part of the people, to limit a power in its own nature illimitable.

Certainly all those who have framed written constitutions contemplate them as forming the fundamental and paramount law of the nation, and, consequently, the theory of every such government must be, that an act of the legislature, repugnant to the constitution, is void.

This theory is essentially attached to a written constitution, and, is consequently, to be considered, by this court, as one of the fundamental principles of our society. It is not therefore to be lost sight of in the further consideration of this subject.

If an act of the legislature, repugnant to the constitution, is void, does it, notwithstanding its invalidity, bind the courts, and oblige them to give it effect? Or, in other words, though it be not law, does it constitute a rule as operative as if it was a law? This would be to overthrow in fact what was established in theory; and would seem, at first view, an absurdity too gross to be insisted on. It shall, however, receive a more attentive consideration.

It is emphatically the province and duty of the judicial department to say what the law is. Those who apply the rule to particular cases, must of necessity expound and interpret that rule. If two laws conflict with each other, the courts must decide on the operation of each.

So if a law be in opposition to the constitution; if both the law and the constitution apply to a particular case, so that the court must either decide that case conformably to the law, disregarding the constitution; or conformably to the constitution, disregarding the law; the court must determine which of these conflicting rules governs the case. This is of the very essence of judicial duty.

If, then, the courts are to regard the constitution, and the constitution is superior to any ordinary act of the legislature, the constitution, and not such ordinary act, must govern the case to which they both apply.

Those then who controvert the principle that the constitution is to be considered, in court, as a paramount law, are reduced to the necessity of maintaining that courts must close their eyes on the constitution, and see only the law.

This doctrine would subvert the very foundation of all written constitutions. It would declare that an act which, according to the principles and theory of our government, is entirely void, is yet, in practice, completely obligatory. It would declare that if the legislature shall do what is expressly forbidden, such act, notwithstanding the express prohibition, is in reality effectual. It would be giving to the legislature a practical and real omnipotence, with the same breath which professes to restrict their powers within narrow limits. It is prescribing limits, and declaring that those limits may be passed at pleasure.

That it thus reduces to nothing what we have deemed the greatest improvement on political institutions, a written constitution, would of itself be sufficient, in America, where written constitutions have been viewed with so much reverence, for rejecting the construction. But the peculiar expressions of the constitution of the United States furnish additional arguments in favor of its rejection.

The judicial power of the United States is extended to all cases arising under the constitution.

Could it be the intention of those who gave this power, to say that in using it the constitution should not be looked into? That a case arising under the constitution should be decided without examining the instrument under which it arises?

This is too extravagant to be maintained.

In some cases, then, the constitution must be looked into by the judges. And if they can open it at all, what part of it are they forbidden to read, or to obey?

There are many other parts of the constitution which serve to illustrate this subject.

It is declared that "no tax or duty shall be laid on articles exported from any state." Suppose a duty on the export of cotton, of tobacco, or of flour; and a suit instituted to recover it. Ought judgment to be rendered in such a case? Ought the judges to close their eyes on the constitution, and only see the law?

The constitution declares that "no bill of attainder or *ex post facto* law shall be passed."

If, however, such a bill should be passed and a person should be prosecuted under it; must the court condemn to death those victims whom the constitution endeavors to preserve?

"No person," says the constitution, "shall be convicted of treason unless on the testimony of two witnesses to the same overt act, or on confession in open court."

Here the language of the constitution is addressed especially to the courts. It prescribes, directly for them, a rule of evidence not to be departed from. If the legislature should change that rule, and declare *one* witness, or a confession *out* of court, sufficient for conviction, must the constitutional principle yield to the legislative act?

From these, and many other selections which might be made, it is apparent, that the framers of the constitution contemplated that instrument as a rule for the government of *courts*, as well as of the legislature.

Why otherwise does it direct the judges to take an oath to support it? This oath certainly applies, in an especial manner, to their conduct in their official character. How immoral to impose it on them, if they were to be used as the instruments, and the knowing instruments, for violating what they swear to support!

The oath of office, too, imposed by the legislature, is completely demonstrative of the legislative opinion on the subject. It is in these words: "I do solemnly swear that I will administer justice without respect to persons, and do equal right to the poor and to the rich; and that I will faithfully and impartially discharge all the duties incumbent on me as _____ according to the best of my abilities and understanding, agreeably to *the constitution*, and laws of the United States."

Why does a judge swear to discharge his duties agreeably to the constitution of the United States, if that constitution forms no rule for his government? If it is closed upon him, and cannot be inspected by him?

If such be the real state of things, this is worse than solemn mockery. To prescribe, or to take this oath, becomes equally a crime.

It is also not entirely unworthy of observation, that in declaring what shall be the *supreme* law of the land, the *constitution* itself is first mentioned; and not the laws of the United States generally, but those only which shall be made in *pursuance* of the constitution, have that rank.

Thus, the particular phraseology of the constitution of the United States confirms and strengthens the principle, supposed to be essential to all written constitutions, that a law repugnant to the constitution is void; and that *courts*, as well as other departments, are bound by that instrument.

NOTES ON *MARBURY* AND THE POWER OF JUDICIAL REVIEW

1. *The Analytical Structure and Reasoning of* Marbury. The Chief Justice's opinion in *Marbury* has tortured generations of law students, because it raised more questions than it answered. See William Van Alstyne, *A Critical Guide to* Marbury v. Madison, 1969 Duke L.J. 1, for an excellent analysis. Consider some preliminary technical questions raised by the opinion:

(a) *Why Was the Jurisdictional Question Not Answered First?* Marshall's opinion started with the merits of Marbury's claim, before moving to the issue of the Supreme Court's jurisdiction to hear the case. But if the Court does not have the "authority" (jurisdiction) to hear the case in the first place, one might argue that the Court's reaching the merits is inconsistent with the "judicial

Power" vested by Article III. In *Hayburn's Case*, 2 U.S. (2 Dall.) 408 (1792), an annotation indicated that it is beyond the "judicial Power" for the Court to issue "advisory opinions," that is, the Court's interpretation of federal law when not in response to a real and live "case or controversy" before the Court. The situation in *Marbury* was similar: In a sense the first part of the Court's opinion is only "advisory," having no legal effect because the Court lacked jurisdiction to do anything in the case. For this reason, the typical practice of the Court is to ascertain that it has jurisdiction before adjudicating the parties' legal and constitutional claims on their merits.

(b) *Does § 13 Give the Court Original Jurisdiction in Mandamus Cases?* In declaring § 13 unconstitutional (in part), Marshall "interpreted" § 13 to be an affirmative grant of original jurisdiction to the Court to issue a mandamus against Madison. Is his interpretation of the statute justifiable? Note the structure of § 13, quoted in footnote *a* above. Its first two sentences relate to the Court's original, and sometimes its exclusive, jurisdiction. Sentence three assures jury trials. Sentence four, containing the mandamus clause at its end, seems to relate to the Court's appellate jurisdiction. The structure suggests that mandamus is simply a power given to the Court in aid of its appellate jurisdiction. (The last clause on mandamus and writs of prohibition might also be read as ancillary powers for the Court whatever the nature of its jurisdiction.) Assuming this reading of § 13 is correct, the Chief Justice should have dismissed Marbury's lawsuit on the ground that the statute did not provide for it to be brought in the Supreme Court; Marbury might be able to sue in a lower court to enforce his rights under the justice-of-the-peace statute, with appeal to the Supreme Court, which could then issue a mandamus to Madison. Even if § 13 were ambiguous on this issue, courts are supposed to choose the interpretation that avoids rather than invites the constitutional infirmity.[b]

(c) *As Interpreted, Was § 13 Unconstitutional?* Marshall found § 13 inconsistent with Article III, § 2, cl. 2: Congress cannot go beyond the grant of original jurisdiction specifically delineated in the first sentence. Under this reading, clause 2 divides the Court's jurisdiction into two worlds: the two categories where the Court has original jurisdiction, and all other cases, which Congress can assign to the Court's appellate jurisdiction. Any other reading, says the Chief Justice, would render clause 2 "without effect." But there are plausible readings of clause 2 that could give it effect without invalidating § 13. The meaning of clause 2 could be that Congress cannot restrict the Court's original jurisdiction in the two enumerated categories (as to which "the supreme Court shall have original Jurisdiction") but otherwise has a great deal of freedom (to regulate and except from the Court's appellate jurisdiction, which could include adding some appellate matters to the Court's original jurisdic-

---

b. This canon of interpretation is based on a desire to avoid unnecessary friction between the legislative and judicial branches. (This rule is not applicable when the Court reviews state laws, as in the *Brown* litigation, because state courts are the authoritative interpreters of state law.) On the canon to avoid constitutional difficulties, see William Eskridge, Jr., Philip Frickey & Elizabeth Garrett, *Cases and Materials on Legislation: Statutes and the Creation of Public Policy* 907-22 (4th ed. 2007).

tion). In short, clause 2 sets up the starting point, from which Congress can add and subtract under the "Exceptions, and * * * Regulations" language.

As to this and the previous question we posed, note an historical anomaly: The Chief Justice asks us to believe that the first Congress, in 1789, enacted a jurisdictional statute which, for no apparent reason, violated a command of the just-ratified Constitution. But 51 of the 92 Members of the first Congress had been at the Philadelphia Convention or one of the state ratifying conventions. The drafter and sponsor of the Judiciary Act, Senator Oliver Ellsworth, had been a leading figure at the Convention and was the Chief Justice before John Marshall. The Court later upheld another provision in § 13 against constitutional attack, with the observation that it "was passed by the first Congress assembled under the Constitution, many of whose members had taken part in framing that instrument, and is contemporaneous and weighty evidence of its true meaning." *Wisconsin v. Pelican Ins. Co.*, 127 U.S. 265, 297 (1888). See also *Ames v. Kansas*, 111 U.S. 449, 463 (1884).

2. Marbury*'s Justifications for Judicial Review*. The Court's reasoning in support of the authority of Article III courts to review legislation to determine its constitutionality poses its own set of mysteries.

(a) *Wasn't the Power of Judicial Review Already Settled?* Before the Constitution was adopted, state courts had exercised power to declare statutes invalid, and there is every reason to believe that the Framers contemplated some kind of power of judicial review. [c] The Supreme Court had struck down a state law under the Supremacy Clause in *Ware v. Hylton*, 3 U.S. (3 Dall.) 199 (1796). Yet when one reads Marshall's opinion, one has the impression that he was writing on a clean slate, citing none of the prior decisions, or even Hamilton's essay in *Federalist* No. 78 (App. 2), from which the Chief Justice drew some of his arguments.

(b) *Does the Constitution's Structure Contemplate the Power of Judicial Review?* The Chief Justice's argument is simple: The written Constitution is the supreme law of the land; any statute contrary to the supreme law is void; in saying what the law is, courts cannot apply a statute when it is trumped by the supreme law of the land. But other countries with "supreme law" do not have traditions where judges make independent evaluations of statutory validity. [d] Where in our Constitution do courts find the authority to make an *independent* evaluation of a statute's constitutionality?

Marshall posited that specific constitutional provisions contemplate a role for judicial review. But the admonitions that "no tax or duty shall be laid on articles exported from any state," U.S. Const. Art. 1, § 9, cl. 3, are addressed

---

c. See William Michael Treanor, *Judicial Review Before* Marbury, 58 Stan. L. Rev. 455 (2005) (state and federal judges struck down statues in 31 cases in the period between Independence and *Marbury*).

d. See Mario Cappelletti & William Cohen, *Comparative Constitutional Law* 74 (1979). Note that an increasing number of industrialized countries have been adopting judicially-enforceable constitutions along American lines in the last generation. See Vicki Jackson & Mark Tushnet, *Comparative Constitutional Law* (1999).

specifically to legislatures, not to courts. Indeed, the admonitions are found in Article I (legislative power). The admonition in Article III, § 3, cl. 1, that "[n]o person shall be convicted of Treason unless on the Testimony of two Witnesses to the same overt Act, or on Confession in open Court," is addressed to courts, in striking contrast. Hence, one might argue that only the provisions in Article III are directions to courts; the directions in Article I are for legislatures. (*Marbury* of course construed Article III; perhaps its holding could be limited to statutes requiring the Court to violate Article III.) Are there persuasive arguments for the broader position that Marshall takes?

(c) *Does Judicial Review Include Review of Federal Statutes?* There is a structural argument Marshall didn't consider. One problem with the Articles of Confederation was that the national government didn't have the power to enforce uniform national policies on the states, and this led to crippling weakness (in the eyes of some). If the Constitution were to remedy this problem, it had to vest authority in the national legislature to make laws and assess taxes, binding on the whole nation and enforceable through the national executive and courts. This is the best explanation of Article III's "arising under" jurisdiction, especially in light of the Supremacy Clause of Article VI. Judicial review of state laws was thus necessary as part of a coherent scheme to create a unified national government. Indeed, § 25 of the Judiciary Act of 1789 authorized the Supreme Court to review lower court decisions adjudicating the constitutionality of state statutes.[e] Most of the pre-*Marbury* exercises of judicial review saw state or federal judges strike down state laws. See William Michael Treanor, *Judicial Review Before* Marbury, 58 Stan. L. Rev. 455 (2005).

But national uniformity does not require the U.S. Supreme Court to review federal statutes. Uniformity could be better achieved by everyone's deferring to whatever rules Congress laid down; consistent with this idea, § 25 gave the Court jurisdiction to review state court decisions invalidating national statutes or treaties. This kind of argument would support judicial review in *Brown* (state statutes), but not in *Marbury* (federal statute). Most of the important constitutional decisions in this book — particularly in the chapters regarding individual rights — involve state rather than federal statutes. Of course, believers in "states' rights" might question whether Congress should be the sole judge of its own powers. And, as Dean Treanor has shown, judges were before *Marbury* especially keen on striking down federal as well as state statutes that encroached upon judicial authority, as Congress was assertedly doing in the Judiciary Act of 1789 (Treanor, *Review Before* Marbury, 496-97, 508-18, 533-41).

Marshall believed that the Court could strike down federal statutes and that the Court could order the Secretary of State to perform essentially ministerial functions. Note how the odd structure of his opinion allowed him to make both points without getting into overwhelming political trouble. The Democratic-

---

e. Section 25 gave the Supreme Court jurisdiction to review "a final judgment * * * in the highest court of law or equity of a State * * * where is drawn in question the validity of a treaty or statute of * * * the United States, and the decision is against their validity; or where is drawn in question the validity of a statute of * * * any State, on the ground of their being repugnant to the constitution, treaties or laws of the United States."

Republicans were irate at the Federalists' last-minute shenanigans. Not only did they repeal the Circuit Court Act, but they revoked the December 1801 Term of the Court and impeached Federalist Justice Chase in 1802 (he was acquitted by the Senate). President Jefferson's hatred for John Marshall was well-known, and it was an open secret in Washington, D.C. that he had Spencer Roane in mind to replace the Chief Justice. Writing *Marbury* the way he did, Marshall was able to embarrass the President (by showing his Administration to be lawless), to assert judicial power over executive officials in appropriate cases (but without actually risking a Supreme Court order that Secretary of State Madison would probably have ignored), and to establish the authority of the Court to invalidate unconstitutional legislation (and proving the Court's impartiality as well, since it was Federalist legislation being struck down).

B. THE COURT'S SUPREMACY IN CONSTITUTIONAL INTERPRETATION?

Brown I did not decide what "relief" (remedy) was to be afforded plaintiffs. The relief usually granted by the Supreme Court when it reverses lower court judgments (as the Court did in all but the Delaware litigation) is simply to remand to the lower court to enter a new judgment consistent with the Supreme Court's decision. In *Brown v. Board of Education*, 349 U.S. 294 (1955) (*Brown II*), the Court remanded the cases to the lower courts to fashion equitable relief, namely, injunctions requiring the school boards to make a "prompt and reasonable start toward full compliance" with *Brown I.* The lower courts were instructed to retain jurisdiction over the litigation and "enter such orders and decrees * * * as are necessary and proper to admit to public schools on a racially nondiscriminatory basis and with all deliberate speed the parties to the cases." Compare *Florida ex rel. Hawkins v. Board of Control*, 350 U.S. 413 (1956) (blacks were entitled to immediate admission to state-run graduate and professional schools).

Brown II's "all deliberate speed" formula was questioned by integrationists as a retreat from the right recognized in *Brown I* and by segregationists as proof that *Brown I* was an invasion of states' rights. Actual implementation of *Brown* was uneven, to say the least. Topeka, which had already abandoned de jure segregation, confessed to the *Brown II* Court that the formerly segregated black schools generally remained all-black and would probably remain segregated, because they were located in mostly black residential areas and because white families had the option of keeping their children in the previously (and still substantially) all-white schools.[f] Although compliance was imperfect in Kansas, *Bolling* was seriously implemented in the District of Columbia, and *Brown* was implemented in part in the border states.

---

f. See Mary Dudziak, *The Limits of Good Faith: Desegregation in Topeka, Kansas: 1950-1956*, 5 Law & Hist. Rev. 351, 379-80 (1987). Nonetheless, on remand, the three-judge court approved the Topeka plan as meeting the Supreme Court's order. "Desegregation does not mean that there must be intermingling of the races in all school districts. It means only that they may not be prevented from intermingling or going to school together because of race or color." *Brown v. Board of Education*, 139 F. Supp. 468, 470 (D. Kan. 1955).

On the other hand, the South fiercely objected to the decision. In March 1956, southerners in Congress issued a "Southern Manifesto" denouncing *Brown* as a "clear abuse of judicial power." Southern states enacted hundreds of laws seeking to impede the implementation of *Brown II* and to harass people of color and their allies in their efforts to seek integration.[g] There were many ways to evade *Brown II*. Prince Edward County, Virginia closed down its schools rather than comply with the Court's mandate. Some districts agreed to token plans for complying with *Brown*. Most districts, however, simply ignored or defied the decision, and state governments enacted hundreds of statutes encoding the "segregation now, segregation forever" philosophy. One defiant district was Little Rock, Arkansas. Governor Orval Faubus and the Arkansas legislature took the position that *Brown* was inconsistent with fundamental constitutional precepts of federalism, with the original intent of the Framers of the Fourteenth Amendment, and with precedent (*Plessy*). Because its leaders' understanding of the Constitution was different from the Court's, Little Rock asked to stay the judicial order requiring limited school integration pursuant to *Brown*. Were the state leaders bound by the Court's interpretation of the Constitution, even if it was "wrong"? The court of appeals held the local authorities to the original decree. The Supreme Court assembled in a special session to decide an appeal by the local officials; the day after it heard the case, the Court issued its mandate affirming the court of appeals and requiring Little Rock officials to proceed with the original plan for partial integration. The decision below, signed by every Justice to show the Court's solidarity, was issued later.

COOPER v. AARON
358 U.S. 1, 78 S.Ct. 1401, 3 L.Ed.2d 5 (1958)

Opinion of the Court by **THE CHIEF JUSTICE [WARREN], JUSTICE BLACK, JUSTICE FRANKFURTER, JUSTICE DOUGLAS, JUSTICE BURTON, JUSTICE CLARK, JUSTICE HARLAN, JUSTICE BRENNAN,** and **JUSTICE WHITTAKER.**

As this case reaches us it raises questions of the highest importance to the maintenance of our federal system of government. It necessarily involves a claim by the Governor and Legislature of a State that there is no duty on state officials to obey federal court orders resting on this Court's considered interpretation of the United States Constitution. Specifically it involves actions by the Governor and Legislature of Arkansas upon the premise that they are not bound by our holding in *Brown*. That holding was that the Fourteenth Amendment forbids States to use their governmental powers to bar children on racial grounds from attending schools where there is state participation through any arrangement, management, funds or property. We are urged to uphold a suspension of the Little Rock School Board's plan to do away with segregated

---

g. See Numan Bartley, *The Rise of Massive Resistance: Race and Politics in the South During the 1950's* (1969); Francis Wilhoit, *The Politics of Massive Resistance* (1973); J. Harvie Wilkinson, *From* Brown *to Bakke: The Supreme Court and School Integration, 1954-1978*, at 78-102 (1979) (describing transition from massive resistance to token compliance with *Brown II*). See also Neil McMillan, *The Citizens' Council: Organized Resistance to the Second Reconstruction, 1954-1964* (1971).

public schools in Little Rock until state laws and efforts to upset and nullify our holding in *Brown* have been further challenged and tested in the courts. We reject these contentions.

[The Court affirmed the appellate court's decision holding the parties to the original judicial decree. Then the Court added, in what might be considered dictum, the following general discussion.] Article VI of the Constitution makes the Constitution the "supreme Law of the Land." In 1803, Chief Justice Marshall, speaking for a unanimous Court, referring to the Constitution as "the fundamental and paramount law of the nation," declared in the notable case of *Marbury v. Madison* that "It is emphatically the province and duty of the judicial department to say what the law is." This decision declared the basic principle that the federal judiciary is supreme in the exposition of the law of the Constitution, and that principle has ever since been respected by this Court and the Country as a permanent and indispensable feature of our constitutional system. It follows that the interpretation of the Fourteenth Amendment enunciated by this Court in the *Brown* case is the supreme law of the land, and Art. VI of the Constitution makes it of binding effect on the States "any Thing in the Constitution or Laws of any State to the Contrary notwithstanding." Every state legislator and executive and judicial officer is solemnly committed by oath taken pursuant to Art. VI, cl. 3, "to support this Constitution." Chief Justice Taney, speaking for a unanimous Court in 1859, said that this require-ment reflected the Framers' "anxiety to preserve it [the Constitution] in full force, in all its powers, and to guard against resistance to or evasion of its authority, on the part of a State. . . ." *Ableman v. Booth*, 21 How. 506, 524.

No state legislator or executive or judicial officer can war against the Constitution without violating his undertaking to support it. Chief Justice Marshall spoke for a unanimous Court in saying that: "If the legislatures of the several states may, at will, annul the judgments of the courts of the United States, and destroy the rights acquired under those judgments, the constitution itself becomes a solemn mockery. . . ." *United States v. Peters*, 5 Cranch 115, 136. A Governor who asserts a power to nullify a federal court order is similarly restrained. If he had such power, said Chief Justice Hughes, in 1932, also for a unanimous Court, "it is manifest that the fiat of a state Governor, and not the Constitution of the United States, would be the supreme law of the land; that the restrictions of the Federal Constitution upon the exercise of state power would be but impotent phrases. . . ." *Sterling v. Constantin*, 287 U.S. 378, 397-398. * * *

[The concurring opinion of **JUSTICE FRANKFURTER** is omitted.]

Edwin Meese, III, *The Law of the Constitution,* 61 Tul. L. Rev. 979 (1987)[h]. The then-Attorney General of the United States agreed with the essential holding of *Cooper*, that judicial interpretation of the Constitution

---

h. Edwin Meese III, The Law of the Constitution, originally published in 61 TUL. L. REV. 979-90 (1987). Reprinted with the permission of the Tulane Law Review Association, which holds the copyright.

"binds the parties to the case and also the executive branch for whatever enforcement is necessary. But such a decision does not establish a supreme law of the land that is binding on all persons and parts of government henceforth and forevermore." As examples, the Attorney General invoked *Plessy*, which the Court itself had reconsidered in *Brown*, as well as *Dred Scott*, which was debated by Stephen Douglas and Abraham Lincoln in the 1858 Illinois Senate race: the former urged obedience to the decision as supreme law, the latter urged nullification.

"The Supreme Court * * * is not the only interpreter of the Constitution. Each of the three coordinate branches of government created and empowered by the Constitution — the executive and legislative no less than the judicial — has a duty to interpret the Constitution in the performance of its official functions. In fact, every official takes an oath precisely to that effect."

Meese rejected the *Cooper* dictum excerpted above. "[T]he implication of the dictum that everyone would have to accept its judgments uncritically, that they are judgments from which there is no appeal, was astonishing; the language recalled what Stephen Douglas said about *Dred Scott*. In one fell swoop, the Court seemed to reduce the Constitution to the status of ordinary constitutional law, and to equate the judge with the lawgiver. * * * [The] logic of the dictum in *Cooper v. Aaron* was, and is, at war with the Constitution, at war with the basic principles of democratic government, and at war with the very meaning of the rule of law."

ARE OTHER GOVERNMENT OFFICIALS REQUIRED TO FOLLOW THE SUPREME COURT'S INTERPRETATION OF THE CONSTITUTION?

Cooper is an easy case on its facts: The school district was under a direct court order to follow *Brown*. As Meese contended, however, *Cooper*'s dictum raises issues not resolved by *Marbury*. American officials have long asserted a power and a responsibility to make their own determinations as to what the Constitution requires.[i] What is there in the Constitution that should persuade us that this is wrong? The Supremacy Clause, invoked in *Cooper*, only applies to state judges — not state governors, municipal councils, or national legislators or administrators. The best argument for the *Cooper* dictum is one founded in the rule-of-law features of the "judicial Power":[j] A central role for law is the authoritative settlement of what the rules are. Law thereby provides a content-

---

i. Thus, in 1798-99, Kentucky and Virginia passed resolutions objecting to the federal Alien and Sedition Acts (making criticism of the Federalist government a crime) as essentially unconstitutional; in 1812-14, New England states objected to our war against England; in the middle part of the century some state courts refused to follow federal legislative and constitutional fugitive slave provisions; President Lincoln considered *Dred Scott* incorrect and acted consistently with that belief, though he also said it was binding on the parties; President F.D. Roosevelt refused to accept many of the Court's *Lochner*-type decisions.

j. The argument in text is from Larry Alexander & Frederick Schauer, *On Extrajudicial Constitutional Interpretation*, 110 Harv. L. Rev. 1359 (1997). Also see Daniel Farber, *The Supreme Court and the Rule of Law: Cooper v. Aaron Revisited*, 1982 U. Ill. L. Rev. 387.

independent basis for our actions; we will follow the rule because the law requires it. The Supreme Court follows wrongheaded precedent for this reason, too — it is better that things are settled finally than that they are settled correctly. The settlement function of law supports not only *consistency over time*, but also *consistency across institutions*. All other public officials should defer to the Supreme Court's interpretation of the Constitution for the same reason we all defer to the Constitution itself. Is this argument persuasive? Many of the commentators agree with Meese.[k] Here are some of their arguments:

1. *Reductio Arguments*. Some are squeamish with a rule requiring deference to Supreme Court decisions whose wrongness goes to the very foundations of the civilized polity. For example, the pre-Civil War Wisconsin Supreme Court upheld a state writ of habeas corpus for a prisoner convicted of violating federal law making it a crime to assist fugitive slaves. See *In re Booth*, 3 Wis. 145 (1854). Justice Abram Smith, concurring, argued that the states retained the right to protect the civil liberties of their citizens against disagreeable federal laws. Against the federal interest in uniformity, "it should be remembered that where one will rules, there can be no freedom for the many. The imposition of uniformity is but another name or process for usurpation or tyranny." The Supreme Court reversed in *Ableman v. Booth*, 62 U.S. (21 How.) 506 (1859), on the eve of the South's own act of ultimate nullification. Does *Cooper*, which relied on *Ableman*, require deference to *Dred Scott*, which held as a constitutional matter that slaves could never be citizens and could not be freed by federal law? Was Lincoln wrong in urging rejection of *Dred Scott*?

2. *Separation of Powers*. The President and Members of Congress take oaths to uphold and defend the Constitution. Does the Constitution's separation of powers authorize or even require each branch to make its own constitutional determinations? This reading of the Constitution is consistent with *Marbury*: The Court can and should refuse to apply an unconstitutional statute to cases before it, but the President can rely on the statute if she or he has a good faith belief in its constitutionality. Only in cases of a court order directed to the President or an executive branch official is deference required. Can the same argument be made with the same force for state officials under the aegis of federalism?

3. *Ongoing Constitutional Dialogue*. Deference to Supreme Court constitutional law might serve goals of consistency, stability, and reliance, but those goals are less important in public law than goals of justice, public debate, and evolution. Recall that *Brown* itself lacked the virtue of consistency over time and deployed explicitly functional modes of reasoning; *Cooper*'s

---

k. See Larry Kramer, *The People Themselves: Popular Constitutionalism and Judicial Review* (2004); Sanford Levinson, *Could Meese Be Right This Time?*, 61 Tul. L. Rev. 1071 (1987); Robert Nagel, *Name-Calling and the Clear Error Rule*, 88 Nw. U.L. Rev. 193 (1993); Michael Stokes Paulsen, *The Most Dangerous Branch: Executive Power to Say What the Law Is*, 83 Geo. L.J. 217 (1994) (also see the friendly responses by Chris Eisgruber and Sandy Levinson in the same issue); David Strauss, *Presidential Interpretation of the Constitution*, 15 Cardozo L. Rev. 113 (1993); Mark Tushnet, *The Hardest Question in Constitutional Law*, 81 Minn. L. Rev. 1 (1996).

invocation of consistency across institutions and formalistic reasoning is joltingly different, yes? Let Orval Faubus criticize *Brown*, and be confident that the national political system would rally around the Court, not because it was authoritative, but because it was right.[1] Just as federalism is supposed to encourage the states to be laboratories of regulatory ideas, so separation of powers should encourage constitutional disagreement among officials — with the hope of stimulating public debate and engagement on such constitutive issues by We the People.

Do these arguments mean that public officials have no duty to follow judicial rulings, except when directly threatened by contempt of court? How secure would individual rights be under such a regime?

C. AFTER *BROWN*: EVALUATION AND CRITIQUE

1. *From* Brown II *to* Swann

Implementation of the Court's decision in *Brown* involved an unprecedented amount of ongoing remedial activity by the federal judiciary and has yielded effects that can be viewed as encouraging, distressing, or incoherent. Most federal judges initially followed the example of Topeka, where the judge accepted a school board plan that left segregation largely in place, and not of Little Rock, where the judge stirred up a hornet's nest by requiring actual integration. As a result, integration proceeded slowly. In the 1964-65 school year, only 2.3% of the black school children in the South were attending integrated schools. (Because of desegregation in California after *Mendez*, Mexican-American and Puerto Rican students were more integrated into public schools than blacks in the South, but Texas schools remained segregated on grounds of ethnicity.) Pressed by constitutional challenges brought by the NAACP and supported by the Department of Justice, the Supreme Court in the 1960s showed open signs of impatience with local foot-dragging. In *Watson v. Memphis*, 373 U.S. 526 (1963), the Court ordered immediate desegregation of municipal recreation facilities, holding *Brown II*'s formula inapplicable and further warning that "*Brown* never contemplated that the concept of 'deliberate speed' would countenance indefinite delay in elimination of racial barriers in schools." Where the *Brown II* formula did apply, the Court began to give it teeth by invalidating half-hearted plans to desegregate. In *Goss v. Board of Education*, 373 U.S. 683 (1963), the Court held that a one-way transfer plan (students could transfer from schools where they were a minority into ones where they were a majority) lent itself to "perpetuation of segregation" and hence was invalid. In *Griffin v. County School Board*, 377 U.S. 218 (1964), the Court held that Prince Edward County, Virginia's closing of its public schools violated the Equal Protection Clause.

---

1. The reality may fall between these two stools, of course. The key event in the duel between the integrationist Court and the segregationist state was President Eisenhower's willingness to send in federal troops. The President was not a fan of *Brown* (though Attorney General Brownell was) and was probably motivated primarily by the shared national interest in squelching state defiance of the federal government.

At the same time southern whites were dragging their feet, people of color were marching with theirs. Peaceful civil rights protests all over the South, often suppressed by violent white policemen and their attack dogs, culminated in Dr. Martin Luther King's galvanizing 1963 March on Washington. One consequence of civil rights activism was enactment of the Civil Rights Act of 1964, which brought the authority of Congress and the Presidency more directly to bear on resistance to school desegregation. Title IV authorized the Department of Justice to bring desegregation lawsuits, and Title VI prohibited racial discrimination in any program receiving federal financial assistance. The Elementary and Secondary Education Act of 1965 linked federal educational funding to compliance with *Brown*. As implemented by tough guidelines promulgated by the Department of Health, Education and Welfare ("HEW"), the link between federal money and school desegregation pushed toward greater compliance. By the 1968-69 school year, 32% of southern black school children were in integrated schools, a fifteen-fold increase from 1964.

Encouraged by political support, the Supreme Court pressed compliance more aggressively; the Court read the *Brown II* mandate to require actual *integration*, and not just *desegregation*. (The distinction may not have been merely remedial and may have reflected a stronger understanding of the substantive right in anti-subordination and not just colorblindness terms.) In *Green v. New Kent County School Board*, 391 U.S. 430 (1968), the local school board adopted a plan allowing pupils to choose which of two schools they would enter; under this plan, the district's schools remained essentially segregated. Supported by Solicitor General Erwin Griswold, the NAACP's Inc. Fund challenged this plan. The Supreme Court, in an opinion by Justice Brennan, held that this plan was not "a sufficient step to 'effectuate a transition' to a unitary school system." The Court cast upon the school board the burden of coming "forward with a plan that promises realistically to work, and promises realistically to work *now*." The test for an acceptable plan was whether it would convert the school system to one "without a 'white' school and a 'Negro' school, but just schools." Federal judges took *Green* as a signal to require more affirmative local action to eliminate school segregation "root and branch," as *Green* suggested. Thus, after *Green*, the Fifth Circuit struck down continuing segregation of Mexican-American students in Texas schools.

Swann v. Charlotte-Mecklenburg Board of Education, 402 U.S. 1 (1971). A large majority of the African-American students in the Charlotte-Mecklenburg school system attended schools that were 99-100% black, and a plaintiff class successfully sued. Invoking *Green*, District Judge McMillan rejected plans offered by the school board, in favor of a plan developed by the court-appointed expert, Dr. John Finger. The Finger Plan rezoned high school districts in ways that distributed black students to previously white schools, and required in addition that 300 African-American students be bused to nearly all-white Independence High School. The Finger plan for junior high schools created nine "satellite" zones, whereby inner-city black students were assigned by attendance zones to nine outlying predominately white junior high schools; this would substantially desegregate every junior high school in the system. For elementary schools, the Finger plan relied on rezoning school districts and grouping two or three outlying white schools with one black inner-city school, resulting in extensive busing of grade school students, but also in substantial integration. Most schools would have student bodies with 9% to 38% minority populations. The issue on appeal was whether Judge McMillan had erred in adopting the Finger Plan, which not only rezoned school districts and created racial pairings and groups of schools, but required the extensive busing of schoolchildren, sometimes far from their homes. **Chief Justice Burger**'s opinion for a unanimous Court affirmed McMillan's decree.

"The objective today remains to eliminate from the public schools all vestiges of state-imposed segregation. Segregation was the evil struck down by *Brown I* as contrary to the equal protection guarantees of the Constitution. That was the violation sought to be corrected by the remedial measures of *Brown II*. That was the basis for the holding in *Green* that school authorities are 'clearly charged with the affirmative duty to take whatever steps might be necessary to convert to a unitary system in which racial discrimination would be eliminated root and branch.'

"If school authorities fail in their affirmative obligations under these holdings, judicial authority may be invoked. Once a right and a violation have been shown, the scope of a district court's equitable powers to remedy past wrongs is broad, for breadth and flexibility are inherent in equitable remedies." See *Hecht Co. v. Bowles*, 321 U.S. 321, 329-330 (1944), cited in *Brown II*. The Chief Justice considered various challenges to the district court's plan. Judge McMillan sought approximately a 71%/29% white/black balance in as many schools as possible. "If we were to read the holding of the District Court to require, as a matter of substantive constitutional right, any particular degree of racial balance or mixing, that approach would be disapproved and we would be obliged to reverse. The constitutional command to desegregate schools does not mean that every school in every community must always reflect the racial composition of the school system as a whole." The Court found, however, that the 71/29 ratio "was no more than a starting point in the process of shaping a remedy, rather than an inflexible requirement." Important in the Court's toleration of such a ratio was the finding of fact that Charlotte-Mecklenburg had operated a dual school system and then had not responded in good faith to the court's request for a remedy effective in the *Green* sense.

"[I]n a system with a history of segregation the need for remedial criteria of sufficient specificity to assure a school authority's compliance with its constitutional duty warrants a presumption against schools that are substantially disproportionate in their racial composition. Where the school authority's proposed plan for conversion from a dual to a unitary system contemplates the continued existence of some schools that are all or predominately of one race, they have the burden of showing that such school assignments are genuinely nondiscriminatory. * * *

"Absent a constitutional violation there would be no basis for judicially ordering assignment of students on a racial basis. All things being equal, with no history of discrimination, it might well be desirable to assign pupils to schools nearest their homes. But all things are not equal in a system that has been deliberately constructed and maintained to enforce racial segregation. The remedy for such segregation may be administratively awkward, inconvenient, and even bizarre in some situations and may impose burdens on some; but all awkwardness and inconvenience cannot be avoided in the interim period when remedial adjustments are being made to eliminate the dual school systems." Based upon this reasoning, the Court accepted Judge McMillan's order to the school system to rezone, pair inner-city and outlying schools, and bus students.

IN *SWANN*'S WAKE: NOTES ON AFFIRMATIVE REMEDIES IN PUBLIC RIGHTS LITIGATION

1. *The Significance of Affirmative Remedies.* The most important point to be drawn from *Swann* is its least controversial: The district court judge has substantial discretion to fashion a remedy. Hence, one judge might order busing to achieve a unitary school system, while another in a similar situation might accept the school board's proposal to build a new school that would draw from both black and white neighborhoods. If both judges make plausible findings that her particular remedy is a sufficient step toward creating a unitary school system and the overall order is not an "abuse of discretion," they should both be upheld on appeal. What is more controversial about *Swann* is how far the Court would permit district judges to go in imposing equity-based remedies on a school system that is moving too slowly.

For example, the Court upheld Judge McMillan's use of racial quotas as a starting point for evaluating the school board's progress and his assignment of students to schools on a racial basis. In a companion case, *North Carolina State Board of Education v. Swann*, 402 U.S. 43 (1971), the Court invalidated a state statute prohibiting assignment on the basis of race in order to create a racial balance in the schools. This is anomalous: *Brown*'s mandate to end a classification based upon race (segregation) has begotten an array of classifications based upon race (racial quotas and assignments). How does Chief Justice Burger defend this apparent anomaly?

2. *A Public Rights Model for Constitutional Adjudication and Rights.* The litigation implementing *Brown* gave new prominence to public law litigation:[m] The traditional understanding of constitutional litigation — the *Marbury* understanding, not questioned in *Brown* — is that an aggrieved plaintiff sues the government to redress her particular constitutional injury, through damages or a prohibitory injunction. The post-*Brown* understanding — reflected in *Swann* — is that a minority group sues to redress an ongoing, pervasive constitutional injury, through an affirmative or even structural injunction. Consider the ways constitutional litigation changes:

---

m. See Owen Fiss, *The Civil Rights Injunction* (1978); Abram Chayes, *The Role of the Judge in Public Law Litigation*, 89 Harv. L. Rev. 1281 (1976); Frank Coffin, *The Frontier of Remedies: A Call for Exploration*, 67 Cal. L. Rev. 983 (1979); Owen Fiss, *The Fate of an Idea Whose Time Has Come: Antidiscrimination Law in the Second Decade after* Brown v. Board of Education, 41 U. Chi. L. Rev. 742 (1974); Paul Gewirtz, *Choice in the Transition: School Desegregation and the Corrective Ideal*, 86 Colum. L. Rev. 728, 751 (1986).

Marbury Litigation	*Swann* Litigation
Litigation arises out of isolated violation of *individual rights*, and is needed to restore the status quo. Relief would be a prohibitory injunction.	Litigation arises out of systematic violation of *group rights*, and is needed to transform the unjust status quo. Relief would be an affirmative or structural injunction.
Operation of law is bipolar, with limited impact on others; court's involvement ends with the issuance of the injunction.	Operation of law is polycentric, with direct impact on nonparties; court retains jurisdiction after issuance of the injunction.
Role of the judge is umpireal; law is neutral and external; litigation reinforces the rule of law.	Role of judge is managerial; law is generated internally among parties, public, and judge; litigation generates public values.

3. *Structural Constitutional Issues in* Swann. Was the intrusiveness of Judge McMillan's remedy consistent with the structure of the Constitution? (For a more elaborate discussion and critique of this new public rights model, see Chapter 9.) First, was it appropriate for a *federal* official to dictate the details of local school zones, pupil assignment, and clustering of schools? Federalism might be offended by the detailed remedy — micromanagement? — imposed on the local authority. In an *amicus* brief filed in *Swann*, the Commonwealth of Virginia (through its counsel, Lewis Powell) argued that, for public schools, the values of localism trumped the values of immediate integration. Specifically, Judge McMillan's plan would undermine the institution of neighborhood schools. Because parental involvement in their children's education (an important variable in student achievement) was most keen when the children attended schools close to their homes, this development would hurt public education for everyone.

Second, should a federal *court* be making essentially legislative or executive judgments in its remedial order? Key to the constitutional design is the separation of legislative, executive, and judicial powers, see, *e.g., Federalist* No. 47 (App. 2) (applying Montesquieu's defense of separate powers to support the Constitution). A danger of the structural injunction and ongoing judicial involvement in the remedy phase of *Brown* litigation is that the judge might be drawn into rulemaking and policymaking — essentially legislative judgments. Under this critique, Judge McMillan's decree went beyond traditional adjudication (barring the school district from unconstitutional practices) and crossed the line into policymaking (such as reconfiguring student and teacher placement rules and setting racial goals).

Third, is it within the "judicial power" for a court to involve itself in "polycentric" problems, such as social restructuring? *Marbury* and *Federalist* No. 78 (App. 2), the leading defenses of judicial review, assume a reactive rather than "proactive" court, one that solves particular "Cases or Controversies," a requirement reflected in the Supreme Court's justiciability case law (see

Chapter 9, § 2). Powell's *amicus* brief in *Swann* made this point: Judge McMillan's busing order was at best a short-term fix for the problem of ongoing segregation; once a busing order was in place, there would be "white flight" to private schools and to suburbs not reached by the busing order. Because a federal judge could not control important variables — parental decisions about where to live and whether to send their children to private schools — judicial efforts to instantiate good social policy were doomed to failure.[n]

2. *Drawing the Line: From* Swann *to* Pitts

Green and *Swann* emboldened federal judges in the South to enter strong remedial orders, which contributed to desegregation in that region. According to the U.S. Commission on Civil Rights, 38% of the nation's black schoolchildren (44% in the South) were attending majority-white schools by 1978 — compared with 23% (18% in the South) ten years before.[o] Dr. Jay Robinson, the Superintendent of the Charlotte-Mecklenburg School System, told Congress in 1981 that *Swann* had not only established an integrated school system, but had been a very positive experience for students and parents of all races.[p]

The Court extended the principles of *Brown* and *Green* to northern schools in *Keyes v. School District No.1*, 413 U.S. 189 (1973), a development that also contributed to the higher level of integration in 1978. Justice Brennan's opinion for the Court held that *de facto* racial segregation (segregation resulting from purely private decisionmaking) in public schools does not violate the Equal Protection Clause; only *de jure* racial segregation (that attributable to the state) is actionable. This holding was of momentous but ambiguous importance to the application of *Brown I* outside the South. On the one hand, because most northern school districts had not been segregated as a matter of law, it might be difficult or at least complicated to establish the state action required by the Court's ruling. On the other hand, state action could be shown by evidence short of a formal apartheid regime. The trial court in *Keyes* had found that Denver had manipulated part of its school system to maintain racially segregated schools, which the Court held was sufficient to satisfy the state action requirement. Indeed, once some state action was found to have contributed to segregation in part of the Denver school district, the Court ruled that the trial court could consider city-wide remedies and remanded to the trial

---

n. One response in the context of *Swann* is that Charlotte (big city) and Mecklenburg (surrounding county) were combined for public school jurisdictional purposes; hence, it would have been harder for white flight to occur. Most big cities with large minority populations are not part of the same school district as their surrounding suburbs, however. How should the Inc. Fund respond to this kind of argument? Is it appropriate in a constitutional case?

o. School Desegregation: Hearings Before the Subcomm. on Civil and Constitutional Rights of the House Comm. on the Judiciary, 97th Cong., 1st Sess. 255 (1981) (testimony of Dr. Flemming).

p. Id. at 17-21; see id. at 382 (testimony of Robert Crain, Johns Hopkins Univ.) (empirical studies suggest that school integration is very helpful for children of color and helpful or neutral for white children); id. at 159 (Prof. Gary Orfield, Univ. of Illinois) (similar).

court to consider whether a city-wide busing plan would be appropriate under *Swann*.

After *Swann* and *Keyes*, popular interest in, and disapproval of, *Green* decrees increased; many white parents were unwilling to have their children bused outside their neighborhood and into integrated schools. Their concerns, moreover, had a new audience within the Court — the four Justices named by President Nixon, especially Justice Lewis Powell, who had headed the Richmond, Virginia School Board and authored the anti-busing *amicus* brief in *Swann*. Rejecting equal protection claims by Mexican Americans that Texas's system of school financing had the effect of discriminating against the poor and people of color (Latinos as well as blacks), Powell's opinion for the Court in *San Antonio Indep. Sch. Dist. v. Rodriguez*, 411 U.S. 1 (1973) (Chapter 5, § 3B, but you might read this case now), set forth a legal process rationale for judicial restraint in public education cases. According to Powell, the constitutional baseline in such cases is that the local democratic process must be the primary decisionmaker; intervention from the judiciary can only be justified by "extraordinary" circumstances; and when the judiciary does intervene it ought not intrude too deeply into local governance. Principles of federalism limited the capacity of the courts to address inequalities in local education. In *Rodriguez*, the Court declined to recognize a constitutional cause of action; in the next case, the Court applied similar principles to limit *Brown II* remedies.

———

Milliken v. Bradley, 418 U.S. 717 (1974). The federal district judge found that the Detroit Board of Education had created and perpetuated a system of racially segregated schools; as an entity created by Michigan, the Board's unconstitutional acts were attributable to the state, ruled the trial judge. Under *Keyes* and *Swann*, the judge rejected the Board's proposed remedy, which would have integrated the city's schools, on the ground that there would still have been "racially identifiable" schools (e.g., inner-city schools 75-90% black). The court determined that there was no effective remedy without busing schoolchildren from inner city (largely black) neighborhoods into the (largely white) Detroit suburbs, and vice-versa. The Supreme Court, in an opinion by **Chief Justice Burger** (joined by the other three Nixon Justices and Justice Stewart, the same majority as in *Rodriguez*), overturned the district court's decree. The Court held that busing between separate school districts is only justified when "racially discriminatory acts of the state or local school districts, or of a single school district have been a substantial cause of interdistrict segregation."

The Chief Justice rebuked the lower court for reading *Swann* to require fairly precise racial balance in a unitary school system, but the court's primary error was its disregard of school district boundaries. "Boundary lines may be bridged where there has been a constitutional violation calling for interdistrict relief, but the notion that school district lines may be casually ignored or treated as a mere administrative convenience is contrary to the history of public education in our country. No single tradition in public education is more deeply rooted than local control over the operation of schools; local autonomy has long been thought essential both to the maintenance of community concern and support for public schools and to quality of the educational process. Thus, in *San Antonio School District v. Rodriguez*, we observed that local control over the educational process affords citizens an opportunity to participate in decision-making, permits the structuring of school programs to fit local needs, and encourages 'experimentation, innovation, and a healthy competition for educational excellence.' "

The Chief Justice concluded that the district court's remedy would violate the integrity of this local structure. The decree's requirement that 54 independent school districts be consolidated into a "super district" would generate a host of operational problems that the court would be ill-equipped to resolve — and any resolution would undermine the local electorate's governance of their own school system. Because *Keyes, Swann*, and *Green* had involved single school districts, they did not justify the lower court's activism, and Chief Justice Burger set forth guidance for future judges. "Before the boundaries of separate and autonomous school districts may be set aside by consolidating the separate units for remedial purposes or by imposing a cross-district remedy, it must first be shown that there has been a constitutional violation within one district that produces a significant segregative effect in another district. Specifically, it must be shown that racially discriminatory acts of the state or local school districts, or of a single school district have been a substantial cause of interdistrict segregation. Thus an interdistrict remedy might be in order where the racially discriminatory acts of one or more school districts caused racial segregation in an adjacent district, or where district lines have been deliberately drawn on the basis of race."

Dissenting opinions by **Justices White** and **Marshall** (and joined by **Justices Douglas** and **Brennan**, the four dissenters in *Rodriguez*) maintained that the trial court's finding of fact that state agencies participated in Detroit's scheme to create and perpetuate a racially segregated school system justified interdistrict relief even under the Court's assumptions. More fundamentally, the dissenters argued that the Court's view of judges' equity powers was at odds with the strongly purposive opinions in *Brown, Green*, and *Swann*. See also *Wright v. Council of the City of Emporia*, 407 U.S. 451 (1972) (refusing to allow the creation of a new school district that would "impede the process of dismantling a dual system"); *Reynolds v. Sims*, 377 U.S. 533 (1964) (requiring state to redraw legislative districts to meet the equal protection one-person, one-vote standard). "Until today," Justice White objected, "the permissible contours of the equitable authority of the district courts to remedy the unlawful establishment of a dual school system have been extensive, adaptable, and fully responsive to the ultimate goal of achieving 'the greatest possible degree of actual desegregation.' "

The Chief Justice responded that all of the precedents — from *Brown* to *Keyes* — involved single school districts and delineated the rights of black students in that specific context; *Green*'s remedial goal of a "unitary" school system cannot be understood without reference to that narrow understanding of what the right is. Concluded Burger: "The constitutional right of the Negro respondents residing in Detroit is to attend a unitary school system in that district. Unless petitioners drew the district lines in a discriminatory fashion, or arranged for white students residing in the Detroit District to attend schools in Oakland and Macomb Counties, they were under no constitutional duty to make provisions for Negro students to do so." The dissenters had a completely different view of the underlying constitutional rights and their violation. "The Court's remedy, in the end, is essentially arbitrary and will leave serious violations of the Constitution essentially unremedied." For a continuation of this debate within the Court, see *Pasadena Board of Education v. Spangler*, 427 U.S. 424 (1976) (overturning lower court order periodically adjusting geographic boundaries for schools to take account of "white flight").

On remand, the district judge in *Milliken* abandoned his effort to produce an integrated school system within Detroit; instead, he ordered massive reform of the inner-city system, including remedial programs, counseling and career guidance, and other measures to be paid for by the state. The Supreme Court affirmed this order in *Milliken v. Bradley (II)*, 433 U.S. 267 (1977), holding that remedial orders may include expenditure of state funds. After *Milliken II*, the Inc. Fund shifted its focus from interdistrict remedies to state and local funding to make urban schools attractive enough to generate integrated student bodies as a matter of choice. E.g., *Missouri v. Jenkins*, 495 U.S. 33 (1990) (Chapter 9, § 3) (district judge may order state and local governments to raise taxes in order to fund programs that remedy *Brown* violations by creating magnet schools attracting students of all races). Neo-federalists of the Reagan era opposed these measures, on the ground that they unduly infringed the principle of local control of public schools.

The *Milliken* decisions rested upon the principle that equitable remedies must be tailored to the violation. The Court required a nexus between the violation and the remedy. Besides the geographic dimension featured in *Milliken*, the tailoring principle might have a temporal dimension. The original nexus between violation and remedy may erode over time, so much that continued remedial intervention would become unjustified. In 1986 the Norfolk, Virginia school district was the first to be given permission by a federal court to end its desegregation plan, and other districts clamored to escape the regulation under *Green/Swann* decrees. In *Board of Education v. Dowell*, 498 U.S. 237 (1991), Bush I Administration Solicitor General Kenneth Starr and former (Reagan Administration) Solicitor General Rex Lee filed *amicus* briefs arguing that school districts in the 1990s were no longer accountable for segregationist policies that ended in the 1960s. Substantially agreeing with Starr and Lee, the Court held that the principle of local control of education requires a district court to dissolve a remedial decree "after the local authorities have operated in [good faith] compliance with it for a reasonable period of time." (In *Dowell*, the original finding of de jure segregation had been made in 1961, the remedial order entered in 1972, and the order dissolved in 1985.) Dissenting, Justice Thurgood Marshall — the advocate who won *Brown* — argued that *Brown* remedial orders should not be dissolved until *Green*'s unitary school system has been achieved.

Freeman v. Pitts, 503 U.S. 467 (1992). The DeKalb County School System (DCSS), located outside Atlanta, was under a *Brown II* consent decree starting in 1969. The district court found in 1981 that student reassignments, magnet schools, and active recruitment of minority faculty pursuant to the decree had disestablished the prior dual school system, but that teacher assignments and funding still reflected the dual system. The court also found that continued segregation, with identifiably black and white schools, was "caused" by changing residential patterns (white flight) and not by anything the local government had done. Hence, the court directed DCSS to deal with remaining teacher-assignment problems but relinquished jurisdiction over student assignment and other issues. Emphasizing the continued existence of racial segregation, the court of appeals reversed and directed the district court to consider the aggressive remedies found effective in *Swann* (pairing of schools, gerrymandering school zones, busing). The Supreme Court, in an opinion by **Justice Kennedy**, reversed the court of appeals. As it had done in *Dowell*, the Court in *Pitts* remanded to the district court, to determine whether the school district had shown a "good faith commitment to the entirety of a desegregation plan," including a plan to remedy ongoing violations.

"A federal court in a school desegregation case has the discretion to order an incremental or partial withdrawal of its supervision and control." This ruling was grounded on the tailoring principle for equitable relief, on *Swann*'s premise that "judicial powers may be exercised only on the basis of a constitutional violation" and that "the nature of the violation determines the scope of the remedy," and on the "vital national tradition" favoring "local autonomy of school districts." In an important passage embracing the neo-federalist emphasis on *local accountability*, Justice Kennedy said: "Returning schools to the control of local authorities at the earliest practicable date is essential to restore their true accountability in our governmental system. When the school district and all state entities participating with it in operating the schools make decisions in the absence of judicial supervision, they can be held accountable to the citizenry, to the political process, and to the courts in the ordinary course. * * * [O]ne of the prerequisites to relinquishment of control in whole or in part is that a school district has demonstrated its commitment to a course of action that gives full respect to the equal protection guarantees of the Constitution. Yet it must be acknowledged that the potential for discrimination and racial hostility is still present in our country, and its manifestations may emerge in new and subtle forms after the effects of *de jure* desegregation have been eliminated. It is the duty of the State and its subdivisions to ensure that such forces do not shape or control the policies of its school systems. Where control lies, so too does responsibility. * * *

"The Court of Appeals was mistaken in ruling that our opinion in *Swann* requires 'awkward,' 'inconvenient,' and 'even bizarre' measures to achieve racial balance in student assignments in the late phases of carrying out a decree, when the imbalance is attributable neither to the prior *de jure* system nor to a later violation by the school district but rather to independent demographic forces. In *Swann* we undertook to discuss the objectives of a comprehensive desegregation plan and the powers and techniques available to a district court in designing it at the outset. We confirmed that racial balance in school assignments was a necessary part of the remedy in the circumstances there presented. In the case before us the District Court designed a comprehensive plan for desegregation of DCSS in 1969, one that included racial balance in student assignments. The desegregation decree was designed to achieve maximum practicable desegregation. Its central remedy was the closing of black schools and the reassignment of pupils to neighborhood schools, with attendance zones that achieved racial balance. The plan accomplished its objective in the first year of operation, before dramatic demographic changes altered residential patterns. * * *

"That there was racial imbalance in student attendance zones was not tantamount to a showing that the school district was in noncompliance with the decree or with its duties under the law. Racial balance is not to be achieved for its own sake. It is to be pursued when racial imbalance has been caused by a constitutional violation. Once the racial imbalance due to the *de jure* violation has been remedied, the school district is under no duty to remedy imbalance that is caused by demographic factors. If the unlawful *de jure* policy of a school system has been the cause of the racial imbalance in student attendance, that condition must be remedied. The school district bears the burden of showing that any current imbalance is not traceable, in a proximate way, to the prior violation." Justice Kennedy credited the district court's factual findings that resegregation occurred because of population shifts (white flight) that could not be attributed to the state.

"Where resegregation is a product not of state action but of private choices, it does not have constitutional implications. It is beyond the authority and beyond the practical ability of the federal courts to try to counteract these kinds of continuous and massive demographic shifts. To attempt such results would require ongoing and never-ending supervision by the courts of school districts simply because they were once *de jure* segregated. * * * As the *de jure* violation becomes more remote in time and these demographic changes intervene, it becomes less likely that a current racial imbalance in a school district is a vestige of the prior *de jure* system. The causal link between current conditions and the prior violation is even more attenuated if the school district has demonstrated its good faith." Although upholding the district court's authority to divest jurisdiction over some features of the school system, Justice Kennedy ruled that the district court must first assure itself that the area of continuing violation (teacher assignment) does not require attention to other areas (student assignment) that are related. The Court also directed the lower court to make sure that the school district "has an affirmative commitment to comply in good faith with the entirety of a desegregation plan."

Justice Scalia concurred with the observation that the Court "should consider laying aside the extraordinary, and increasingly counterfactual, presumption of *Green*" that school districts bear some responsibility for continuing patterns of segregation. In contrast, concurring **Justices Souter, Blackmun, Stevens**, and **O'Connor** interpreted *Green* as requiring district courts in *Brown II* cases to consider whether previous de jure segregation or other school policies contributed to ongoing segregated residential patterns and, before relinquishing jurisdiction over part of the case, to consider whether schools are racially identifiable and therefore vulnerable to resegregation.

Justices Blackmun, Stevens, and O'Connor concurred only in the judgment, because they felt the Court paid insufficient attention to *Swann* and the connection between schools and housing. "This interactive effect between schools and housing choices may occur because many families are concerned about the racial composition of a prospective school and will make residential decisions accordingly. Thus, schools that are demonstrably black or white provide a signal to these families, perpetuating and intensifying the residential movement." The district court left this issue unexamined: DCSS might have encouraged white flight "by assigning faculty and principals so as to identify some schools as intended respectively for black students or white students. Nor did the court consider how the placement of schools, the attendance zone boundaries, or the use of mobile classrooms might have affected residential movement."

NOTE ON THE FUTURE OF *BROWN I & II*

Pitts reflects a duel between state and private responsibility that has bedeviled the Court since *Brown II*. See also Chapter 9, § 3. *Pitts'* premise is consistent with constitutional doctrine prominent since *The Civil Rights Cases* (Chapter 3, § 2): The Constitution generally applies just to state and not private action. In order to find a constitutional violation, therefore, courts have been forced to look backwards to earlier acts of intentional state discrimination. The basic rationale, as in *Pitts*, is that a history of state discrimination has had continuing effects, which the court must now remedy under the tailoring principle. This rationale places a serious, far-reaching judicial remedy on an increasingly tenuous empirical foundation. Even twenty years ago, sympathetic critics questioned whether the causal linkage was strong enough to carry this load, see, *e.g.*, Owen Fiss, *The Jurisprudence of Busing*, 39 L. & Contemp. Prob. 194, 207 (1975). Time has only compounded this uncertainty. But Justice Kennedy's *Pitts* opinion is not the only way to understand the meaning of *Brown I* and the future of *Brown II*. Consider some different approaches:

1. *Everything is connected with state (educational and housing) policies.* Another approach would understand "private" decisions about where to live as pervasively connected with "public" policies, including housing as well as educational policies.[q] Accordingly, the persistence of a dual school system (with identifiably black and white schools) reinforces white people's obsession with the racial composition of schools and thereby facilitates white flight (*Pitts* concurring opinions). Something like this approach recognizes the central role of education in either perpetuating or dealing with racism, and possibly in both.[r]

---

q. This has long been the view of the NAACP's Inc. Fund and many social scientists. See "School Segregation and Residential Segregation: A Social Science Statement," appendix to Brief for Respondents, *Columbus Bd. of Educ. v. Penick* (No. 78-610); "School Desegregation: A Social Science Statement," appendix to Brief of the NAACP [et al.] as *Amicus Curiae* in Support of Respondents, *Freeman v. Pitts* (No. 89-1290).

r. See James Liebman, *Desegregating Politics: "All-Out" School Desegregation Explained*, 90 Colum. L. Rev. 1463 (1990). "[O]ne of the most important lessons that the American public schools teach is that the diverse ethnic, cultural, and national backgrounds that have been brought

Against this approach is the argument that ongoing judicial control of local school systems is inconsistent with federalism and separation of powers and, partly for that reason, a sisyphesian task for courts. Another counterargument is that white flight was caused by court-ordered busing rather than by the school system's decisions, but this link is subject to dispute, as we will see.

2. *Integration as a constitutional mandate*? Maybe the problem is not with the remedy but with the basic definition of the right, a point made by the Burger opinion in *Milliken I*. Rather than conducting a speculative hunt for historical violations and their continuing effects, perhaps we should just say that schools are under an affirmative duty to use reasonable efforts to achieve and maintain racial integration. Although the Court has never taken this position, it was endorsed by Justice Powell in his separate opinion in *Keyes*. Moreover, although the Court has always demanded a causal link, it has allowed use of evidentiary presumptions to establish the link, see Fiss, *supra*, at 207, so the practical effect of the Court's current theory may not be vastly different from the alternative.

The most prominent critic of the foregoing understanding is Justice Clarence Thomas. He did not participate in *Pitts* but did participate in *United States v. Fordice*, 505 U.S. 717 (1992), where the Court ruled that Mississippi could not leave in place "policies rooted in its prior officially-segregated system that serve to maintain the racial identifiability of its universities if those policies can practicably be eliminated without eroding sound educational policies." Concurring, Justice Thomas argued that the Court's opinion did not compel "the elimination of all observed racial imbalance," and thereby allowed traditionally black colleges to survive. He seemed to endorse the idea that the state could "operate a diverse assortment of institutions — including historically black institutions — open to all on a race-neutral basis, but with traditions and programs that might disproportionately appeal to one race or another."

In *Missouri v. Jenkins (III)*, 515 U.S. 70 (1995) (Chapter 9, § 3), Thomas went further. Invoking *Milliken I*, the Court overturned the trial court's order requiring the state to fund inner-city schools in order to attract white students from the suburbs. In a concurring opinion, Justice Thomas charged the lower court (and perhaps the four Justices in dissent) with stereotyped thinking in its efforts to attract white students to black schools. "It never ceases to amaze me that the courts are so willing to assume that anything that is predominantly black must be inferior," Thomas objected. He then rejected the social science basis for *Brown*: "Segregation was not unconstitutional because it might have caused psychological feelings of inferiority." It was unconstitutional because the state classified the students based on race. So long as the state is neutral, there is nothing constitutionally or pedagogically wrong with single-race public schools; "there is no reason to believe that black students cannot learn as well when

---

together in our famous 'melting pot' do not identify essential differences among the human beings that inhabit our land. It is one thing for a white child to be taught by a white teacher that color, like beauty, is only 'skin deep'; it is far more convincing to experience that truth on a day-to-day basis during the routine, ongoing learning process." *Wygant v. Jackson Board of Education*, 476 U.S. 267, 315 (1986) (Stevens, J., dissenting).

surrounded by members of their own race as when they are in an integrated environment." This new voice of color decidedly rejects an integrationist reading of the Equal Protection Clause as both illiberal and disrespectful to black culture.

3. *Nearing the End of the* Brown *Regime?* Consistent with Justice Thomas's later stance, Justice Scalia's *Pitts* concurrence suggested that *Brown*'s time has come and gone and that actual desegregation is a goal beyond the power of courts to require and school districts to attain. During the 1990s, many large school districts, including Denver, Savannah, Buffalo, Dallas, and Wilmington (one of the *Brown* cases), were granted unitary status. Busing ended in the school district where it had first begun — Charlotte-Mecklenburg (*Swann*) — when the Supreme Court refused to hear an appeal from parents who wanted to keep the district under a desegregation order. In September 2002, the Little Rock school district (*Cooper*) was held to be a unitary system freed from judicial supervision.

Consider the subsequent history of the Topeka school system. In the 1980s, African-American parents (including Linda Brown Smith) moved to reopen the original *Brown* litigation, over which the district court had retained jurisdiction. At trial in the new litigation, it was established that the Topeka school system was substantially segregated (eight schools were overwhelmingly nonwhite, five overwhelmingly white). The district court found in *Brown v. Board of Education*, 671 F. Supp. 1290 (D. Kan. 1987), that these racial imbalances were the result of residential patterns rather than actions by the state. The Tenth Circuit reversed, holding that the district had not proved its compliance with *Brown* by demonstrating a unitary school system. *Brown v. Board of Education*, 892 F.2d 851 (10th Cir. 1989). After *Pitts*, the Supreme Court vacated the judgment and remanded the case back to the district court. *Board of Education v. Brown*, 503 U.S. 978 (1992). The Tenth Circuit reinstated its earlier opinion rejecting unitary status, however. See *Brown v. Board of Education*, 978 F.2d 585 (10th Cir. 1992), *cert. denied*, 509 U.S. 903 (1993). It was not until 1999 that the district court concluded that unitary status had been achieved. See *Brown v. Unified School District No. 501*, 56 F. Supp. 2d 1212 (D. Kan. 1999). Meanwhile, over a generation of students have made their way through the Topeka schools.

Pitts has hardly been the swan song for *Brown II* remedial orders, however. Many districts continue to operate pursuant to desegregation plans.[s] But those plans have come under increasing fire, as Justice Thomas's opinions have reflected. Some object that *Swann*-type remedies (especially busing) are

---

s. See Stephan Thernstrom & Abigail Thernstrom, *America in Black and White: One Nation, Indivisible* 315-16 (1997) (1995 survey of 103 school districts found that 45% were under court-ordered desegregation plans, and several more had voluntary plans); Wendy Parker, *The Future of School Desegregation*, 94 Nw. U.L. Rev. 1157, 2007 (2000) (only 13% of the school desegregation cases in the Fifth and Eleventh Circuits had been granted unitary status; many of the cases, however, suffered from "extreme dormancy").

coercive against the victim class.[t] For example, a group of eighteen black parents sought to intervene in *Pitts* to oppose busing. These parents "believe there's nothing wrong with schools that are nearly all black as long as the quality of education is high."[u] Would a *Plessy* regime where "separate but equal" really meant *equal* be preferable to a *Brown* regime where resegregation occurs because of private choices and resegregated black schools are substantially inferior to white schools? Consider Michael Seidman, Brown *and* Miranda, 80 Cal. L. Rev. 673 (1992) (arguing that a *Plessy* regime might be better), and the following materials.

3. *Has* Brown *Made a Difference? A Good Difference?*[v]

By many accounts, *Brown* has been a success. It has been vindicated over time by a near-consensus rejection of de jure segregation and a fair amount of actual integration. By 1981, almost half of the African-American school children in the South attended majority-white schools. Numerous empirical studies have evaluated the effect of school desegregation on schoolchildren: None showed any harm to the educational experience of white schoolchildren, and many showed a statistically significant and positive effect on the educational experience of black schoolchildren.[w] Gains for black schoolchildren were usually significant when there was substantial racial integration from the beginning of the children's education (*i.e.*, in first grade and thereafter). Also during this period of steady desegregation, standardized test scores for black students rose much faster than test scores for white students, substantially narrowing the "achievement gap" between the races.[x] It remains unclear whether school integration played a big role in this narrowing, but most scholars believe it played some role.

Although the evidence is provisional, some studies have found that racial prejudice can be ameliorated by school integration. The U.S. Commission on Civil Rights in *Racial Isolation in the Public Schools* (1967) analyzed data for over 75,000 students in grades nine through twelve in the Northeast. It found a preference by students for desegregated schools and interracial friendships to be positively correlated with *both* the number of years such students had attended desegregated schools *and* the degree of desegregation in their current classrooms. Other experts, however, came to more ambiguous conclusions.

---

t. See, e.g., Charles Cooper, *The Coercive Remedies Paradox*, 9 Harv. J.L. & Pub. Pol. 77, 81 (1986).

u. See Robert Anthony, "Stakes High in DeKalb School Desegregation Case," *Atlanta Const.*, Oct. 6, 1991, at A18. (The intervention was too late to allow them to participate at the Supreme Court level.)

v. Lisa Mahle, Yale Law School, Class of 2004, updated and rewrote the materials that follow.

w. See generally Janet Ward Schofield, *Review of Research on School Desegregation's Impact on Elementary and Secondary School Students*, in *Handbook of Research on Multicultural Education* 597-617 (James Banks & Cherry McGee Banks eds. 1995).

x. See David Grissmer et al., *Why Did the Black-White Score Gap Narrow in the 1970s and 1980s?*, in *The Black-White Test Score Gap* 182-226 (Christopher Jencks & Meredith Philips eds. 1998).

Summarizing various studies, Nancy St. John, *School Desegregation Outcomes for Children* 64-86 (1975), concluded that desegregation sometimes reduced prejudice and promoted interracial friendships but sometimes promoted stereotyping and interracial conflict.

Empirical studies for this period (1950-80) provide some further evidence that *Brown* and allied legal developments yielded beneficial economic as well as educational consequences for African Americans. Consider the following information:[y]

	1940	1950	1960	1970	1980
Average years in school:					
white men	9.38	9.99	10.65	11.51	12.47
black men	4.70	6.83	8.00	9.47	10.96
Average differential years in school (white-black)	3.68	3.16	2.65	2.04	1.51
Black male wages as a % of white male wages	43.3	55.2	57.5	64.4	72.6
Black-white weekly wage ratios by education:					
0-7 years	54.5	63.6	67.0	73.9	82.5
8-11 years	59.7	70.9	70.1	76.8	74.8
12 years	56.5	66.5	66.2	72.2	78.8
13-15 years	47.4	55.8	62.9	75.0	79.8
16+ years	48.7	50.4	60.2	73.0	76.2

These data do not directly support the proposition that *Brown* itself improved the economic position of African Americans, but they do show that the number of years in school for African Americans was slowly catching up to that of whites; the payoff for the same schooling as whites was rising for African Americans (in the 1940s, a black man with a college degree received only about half the wage of a white man with the same degree, but by 1980 the college-educated black man would get three-fourths of a white man's wages); and the wage differential between African Americans and white Americans had been reduced, albeit not nearly eliminated. Researchers conclude that educational levels have overwhelmingly dominated the rise in black wages relative to white wages. It might be argued that to the extent that *Brown* contributed to more and

---

y. See James Smith & Finis Welch, *Black Economic Progress After Myrdal,* 27 J. Econ. Lit. 519 (1989).

better educational opportunities for African Americans, *Brown* contributed directly to the improvement of their relative economic position.[z]

Other studies, including recent ones, suggest a stronger causal link. Students of color educated in desegregated schools have been significantly more likely to attend desegregated colleges, to work in integrated workplaces, and to enjoy racially mixed social and professional networks.[aa] Such "integration" of people of color into mainstream society was arguably the very point of *Brown*, and on that score the decision has enjoyed some success. A handful of in-depth studies examining programs that provide minority students access to primarily white suburban schools provide a class twist on earlier analyses: The best results for students of color have come when they attend schools that are not only racially integrated, but predominantly middle class. Amy Stuart Wells and Robert Crain's case study of the St. Louis consent decree found that students of color who traveled to suburban schools had significantly higher test scores and graduation rates, were much more likely to attend college, and were (qualitatively) more confident and goal-oriented than students who attended city schools, including magnet schools.[a] Susan Eaton's analysis of a voluntary cross-district transfer program in Boston found that almost all past participants (88% of them) believed the program (inaugurated in 1966) was valuable because it enabled them to bridge black-white gulfs and tap into social and informational networks otherwise unavailable to them.[b] (Note that *Milliken I* generally precludes federal courts from requiring localities to engage in the kind of interdistrict programs that have been successful according to these studies.) Leonard Rubinowitz and James Rosenbaum's study of Chicago's interdistrict relocation program found that students of color who attended school in largely white suburbs were more likely to attend college and less likely to drop out of high school than students who remained in city schools; they were also much more likely to have jobs and higher pay than their counterparts.[c]

This is the rosy scenario. This is a contested scenario, however, and must be offset by plenty of dispiriting facts and claims.

Political scientist Gerald Rosenberg maintains that *Brown* itself did not "cause" the advances noted above, which were the result of national legislative

---

z. See *id.* at 538-39.

aa. See Amy Stuart Wells & Robert Crain, *Perpetuation Theory and the Long-Term Effects of School Desegregation*, 64 Rev. Educ. Res. 531-55 (1994); Marvin Dawkins & Jomills Henry Braddock II, *The Continuing Significance of Desegregation: School Racial Composition and African American Inclusion in American Society*, 63 J. Negro Educ. 394 (1994).

a. See Amy Stuart Wells & Robert Crain, *Stepping Over the Color Line: African-American Students in White Suburban Schools* (1997).

b. See Susan Eaton, *The Other Boston Busing Story: What's Won and Lost Across the Boundary Line* (2001); see id. at 117-55 (network benefits; 92% of the participants in the program went to college).

c. See Leonard Rubinowtiz & James Rosenbaum, *Crossing the Class and Color Lines: From Public Housing to White Suburbia* (2000). The success of the Chicago *Gatreaux* program inspired the federal government to implement a similar program (Moving to Opportunity) in Baltimore, Boston, Los Angeles, and New York in 1994.

and executive pressures; that *Brown* instead contributed to white backlash against black progress; and that *Brown* did little good even in the school districts under direct judicial supervision.[d] The first claim is particularly controversial; by other accounts, *Brown* figured prominently in the evolution of the civil rights movement, which was responsible for the civil rights statutes of the 1960s.[e] Also contested is David Armour's claim that the narrowing of the black-white achievement gap owes nothing to *Brown* and everything to the improving socio-economic situation of African-American families.[f] (Recall the evidence that *Brown* and school desegregation have contributed to the improving socio-economic situation.)

What is not contested is that American public schools have partially resegregated. The nation's schools, including those in the South, steadily desegregated between 1964 and 1978. (Progress was highly uneven. Public schools in the District of Columbia and Wilmington, desegregated as a matter of law by *Bolling* and *Brown*, resegregated as a matter of fact, as the percentage of black students in the two districts went from 60.8% and 27.1% in 1954 to 95.3% and 84.7% in 1975.[g]) This process stagnated in the 1980s and reversed course by the end of the decade. Between 1986 and 1991, the proportion of black school children attending schools with a majority of minority students returned to pre-*Swann* levels.[h] By 1998, most of the progress made in integrating the South after 1970 had been lost, although the level of integration remained higher than it had been before 1964.[i] Latinos, currently the largest minority group in the country, are even more segregated than African-Americans, and their isolation has been increasing.[j]

Desegregation decrees have been undermined by "white flight" — the migration of white families away from school systems having a large percentage of African-American students. The exact "causes" of white flight are hard to figure. As Lewis Powell first argued in his *Swann amicus* brief, some scholars believe that desegregation plans themselves cause (or significantly exacerbate)

---

d. See Gerald Rosenberg, *The Hollow Hope: Can Courts Bring About Social Change?* (1991, 2d ed. 2008).

e. See David Garrow, *Hopelessly Hollow History: Revisionist Devaluing of* Brown v. Board of Education, 80 Va. L. Rev. 151 (1994) (leading historian of the civil rights movement arguing that *Brown* directly contributed to its success); Michael Klarman, *How* Brown *Changed Race Relations: The Backlash Thesis*, 81 J. Am. Hist. 81 (1994) (*Brown* indirectly contributed to success of civil rights movement by fueling southern violence that elevated race discrimination and white racism to a major place on the national political agenda).

f. See David Armour, *Forced Justice: School Desegregation and the Law* (1995), and *The End of School Desegregation and the Achievement Gap*, 28 Hastings Cont'l L.Q. 629 (2001).

g. See Raymond Wolters, *The Burden of* Brown: *Thirty Years of School Desegregation* 16, 182 (1984).

h. See Gary Orfield & Susan Eaton, *Dismantling Desegregation: The Quiet Reversal of* Brown v. Board of Education 54 (1996).

i. On this point and many others, consult Gary Orfield, *Schools More Separate: Consequences of a Decade of Resegregation* 29-31 (Civil Rights Project, Harvard Univ., July 2001).

j. See id. at 32-33, 43.

white flight, with mandatory ones triggering the most flight.[k] Others argue that "flight" would have occurred in any event because of low white birth rates and high levels of immigration; these scholars also believe that metropolitan-wide (interdistrict) desegregation plans can do much to mitigate the trend.[l] Also, white flight began before *Brown* remedies in most cities (such as Wilmington and the District of Columbia) and occurred in some cities with no desegregation plans.

Because of white flight, residential housing patterns, and the Supreme Court's limitations on courts' remedial powers, most school children in America today attend substantially segregated schools. Additionally, even when children attend schools that are technically "integrated," they are often "resegregated" within the school. Administrators sometimes assign students to essentially segregated classrooms, or assign minority school children in disproportionate numbers to lower "tracks" within the school system.[m]

Trends in achievement scores have followed the same pattern as desegregation. After almost 20 years of narrowing, the black-white achievement gap in test scores began to widen again in the late 1980s and early 1990s — just as resegregation was occurring.[n] Positive changes in black family characteristics, such as increased education and higher wages, may explain some of black gains, but not all of them.[o] Some students of color suffer even in integrated schools; several studies have suggested that some black students may lose confidence and perform more poorly in integrated schools than in all-black schools, because of discriminatory tracking programs and resegregation, poor teacher attitudes, lack of role models, and biases in the curriculum and its administration.[p] This argument turns the rationale of *Brown* on its head: While segregation marginalized and stigmatized blacks by excluding them from white school systems, integration can and sometimes does marginalize and stigmatize blacks

---

k. See Armour, *Forced Justice* 174-80; Christine Rossell, *An Analysis of the Court Decisions in* Sheff v. O'Neill *and Possible Remedies for Racial Isolation*, 29 Conn. L. Rev. 1187, 1214-15 (1997).

l. See Orfield & Eaton, *Dismantling Desegregation* 61-64.

m. See U.S. Commission on Civil Rights, *Fulfilling the Letter and Spirit of the Law: Desegregation of the Nation's Public Schools* 233-40 (1976). See also Roy Brooks, *Rethinking the American Race Problem* 77-78 (1990).

n. See J.R. Campbell et al., *1999 NAEP Trends in Academic Progress: Three Decades of Student Performance* 32-33, 38-39 (Nat'l Center for Educ. Statistics, U.S. Dep't of Educ. 2000).

o. Armour, *Forced Justice* 91-98, argues that the gap is explainable by socioeconomic factors alone and suggests that changes in socioeconomic factors can explain changes in the achievement gap. Stephan and Abigail Thernstrom, *America in Black and White* 357-59, disagree with Armour's conclusion because the achievement gap widened in the 1990s even though the black middle class was not shrinking. They believe that increased violence and disorder in public schools have contributed to the widening gap. Id. at 359, 376-81.

p. Jacqueline Jordan Irvine, *Black Students and School Failure: Policies, Practices, and Prescriptions* 9-12 (1990); Sonia Jarvis, Brown *and the Afrocentric Curriculum*, 101 Yale L.J. 1285 (1992).

by including them within white school systems that are unreceptive to their needs, interests, and concerns.

———

PARENTS INVOLVED IN COMMUNITY SCHOOLS v. SEATTLE SCHOOL DISTRICT No. 1
___ U.S. ___, 127 S.Ct. 2738, 168 L.Ed.2d 508 (2007)

[As elaborated in the previous Note, many school districts have sought further de facto integration through voluntary plans. In *Parents Involved*, the Supreme Court invalidated plans adopted in Seattle and Louisville, based upon the Court's recent affirmative action jurisprudence, which is excerpted and discussed in detail in Chapter 3, § 3A-C of this casebook. *Parents Involved* is excerpted and discussed in § 3D, but you may want to read the case here.]

———

A NOTE ON CONSTITUTIONAL LAW AND LEGAL EDUCATION

The study of *Brown* suggests that constitutional law is not just a system of immutable rules that can be objectively discovered once one learns the tricks of the lawyering trade. Indeed, the NAACP's efforts to overturn *Plessy* indicate that not just constitutional law, but the role of the attorney herself, is creative, interactive, and nonmechanical. Consider the suggestions made in Richard Posner, *The Problems of Jurisprudence* 100 (1990)[q]:

> The most important thing that law school imparts to its students is a feel for the outer bounds of permissible legal argumentation at the time when the education is being imparted. (Later those bounds will change, of course.) What "thinking like a lawyer" means is not the use of special analytic powers but an awareness of approximately how plastic law is at the frontiers — neither infinitely plastic, * * * nor rigid and predetermined, as many laypersons think — and of the permissible "moves" in arguing for, or against, a change in the law. It is neither method nor doctrine, but a repertoire of acceptable arguments and a feel for the degree and character of doctrinal stability, or, more generally, for the contours of a professional culture — a professional culture lovable to some, hateful to others.

This kind of realism about law can be depressing. Why can't law be more predictable, determinate, even objective? There is, in fact, a predictable component to constitutional law, but it cannot be grasped by merely searching for the apparent holdings of decided cases and compiling them into an outline of rules. We believe it is best to confront the fuzzy edges of constitutional law at the outset of this course, before you seek to master particular doctrinal areas.

Accordingly, our next section takes up the central question of constitutional law introduced by *Brown*: By what method(s) should the Supreme Court give meaning to the Constitution? To use Judge Posner's terms, in "thinking like a lawyer" about "how plastic [constitutional] law is at the frontiers," a central task is to identify and evaluate a variety of potential theories by which the Supreme Court can ascertain constitutional meaning. Unsurprisingly, each potential

———

q. Reprinted by permission of the publisher from THE PROBLEMS OF JURISPRUDENCE by Richard A. Posner, p. 100, Cambridge, Mass.: Harvard University Press, Copyright © 1990 by the President and Fellows of Harvard College.

technique of constitutional interpretation is controversial. The goal is not to indoctrinate you with any given approach to solving the fundamental problems of constitutional law but rather, as Posner puts it, to provide you with the skills to begin thinking like a lawyer about them. Whatever your views, we invite you to bring vigor, even passion, to the enterprise.

SECTION 3. *BROWN* AND THEORIES OF CONSTITUTIONAL DECISIONMAKING

Marbury held that the Constitution is the supreme law of the land and, as interpreted in *Cooper*, that the Supreme Court's constructions of the Constitution are binding on the other branches of the national as well as state governments. *Brown* is a vivid example of the exercise of this power of judicial review — the power to invalidate the acts of a democratically elected legislature as inconsistent with the Constitution. In a democracy, however, it is troubling that nine unelected judges with life tenure have this authority. In *The Least Dangerous Branch: The Supreme Court at the Bar of Politics* (1962), Alexander Bickel expressed this problem as the "countermajoritarian difficulty": The power of judicial review is in tension with our commitment to representative democracy.[a] *Marbury* and *Cooper*, if correctly decided, answer Bickel's question as to the Court's authority to displace majoritarian law. But those precedents do not answer other important questions: By what criteria does the Court evaluate the constitutionality of laws? What limits are there on judicial decisionmaking, lest we substitute judicial tyranny for legislative tyranny?

These are questions that arose in our discussion of *Plessy* and *Brown*. An early academic theory of judicial review, by James Bradley Thayer, maintained that courts should invalidate statutes only when there is no reasonable doubt as to their constitutionality. This theory lends some support to *Plessy* and problematizes *Brown*, either as to its precise result (which is now virtually beyond question in American constitutional law) or as to the possibility of generalizing from it (about which there is no consensus). "*Brown* represented one of the most agonizing movements in American jurisprudence. In some sense, all of American constitutional law * * * has revolved around trying to justify the judicial role in *Brown* while trying simultaneously to show that such a course will not lead to another *Lochner* era,"[b] where activist judicial review of labor legislation and ultimately the New Deal did the country no good and got the Supreme Court into political trouble (Chapter 1, §§ 4-5).

---

a. As Barry Friedman has shown, the countermajoritarian difficulty was not a primary concern with judicial review before the New Deal era, but has become an obsession with critics of the Court in the last third of the twentieth century. Friedman, *The History of the Countermajoritarian Difficulty, Part One: The Road to Judicial Supremacy*, 73 NYU L. Rev. 333 (1998); see also Friedman, *Dialogue and Judicial Review*, 91 Mich. L. Rev. 577 (1993) (post-Bickel constitutional scholarly focus on countermajoritarian difficulty).

b. Morton Horwitz, *The Jurisprudence of* Brown *and the Dilemmas of Liberalism*, 14 Harv. C.R.-C.L. L. Rev. 599, 602 (1979).

The remainder of this chapter introduces you to the leading theories justifying, guiding, and constraining judicial review. Originalist theories (Part A) posit that the Court's authority rests upon the consent of "We the People" who entered into the Constitution, our social contract. Current majorities can only be overruled, under the Constitution, if they thwart the will of the founding super-majority, as expressed in the Constitution and its amendments. The lodestar for originalist theories is the "original meaning" of constitutional provisions. Legal process theories (Part B) maintain that the Supreme Court must consider its institutional advantages and limitations when exercising its power of judicial review. One prominent theory, for example, infers from the structure and principles of the Constitution as well as the capacities of judges that judicial review is appropriate when the political process has been dysfunctional or procedurally flawed. Theories of popular constitutionalism (Part C) maintain that the Constitution must be read dynamically and should reflect new norms (such as the notion that the state cannot discriminate against citizens because of their race) as which our constitutional culture accepts as fundamental. Although there are many such academic theories, we focus on those grounded in the republican tradition, newer critical theory, and common law reasoning — and we explore each in the context of *Brown*. If you reject *Brown* as a litmus test and choose to treat it as simply exceptional, the following materials still provide a coherent overview of current constitutional theory.

A.   ORIGINAL MEANING THEORIES OF JUDICIAL REVIEW

Historically, judicial review has been justified on the ground that it enforces the original social contract, created in a moment of supermajoritarian popular consent. As the Supremacy Clause suggests and *Marbury* held, the Constitution is a supervening authority, trumping federal and state laws inconsistent with it. If a law can be shown to be inconsistent with the Constitution, then it is invalid, and a federal court will require parties in a case or controversy to disregard that law (*Cooper*). Under this analysis, a court is only enforcing the "original deal," for which there is ongoing consent, and its action is neither countermajoritarian nor violative of the consent of the governed.

Originalists seek to construct a foundation for judicial review that is consistent with the consent of the people, that is intersubjective (does not depend upon the judge's own values), and that can be applied in a predictable manner. What this entails, and how the theory is expressed, have evolved in the last generation.[c] In the 1970s, scholars such as Raoul Berger and Robert Bork challenged Warren Court precedents as inconsistent with the *original intent* of the Framers. H. Jefferson Powell, *The Original Understanding of Original Intent*, 98 Harv. L. Rev. 885 (1985), however, demonstrated that the "Framers" did not "intend" that their "intent" would be binding on future generations. Powell's article did not slow down the advance of originalist thinking but did impel a shift in vocabulary, toward the notion of *original understanding* — the understanding of the Constitution that would have been shared by those who

---

c.   See Vasan Kesavan & Michael Stokes Paulsen, *The Interpretive Force of the Constitution's Secret Drafting History*, 91 Geo. L.J. 1113 (2003).

ratified what the Framers drafted.[d]   In the wake of Jack Rakove, *Original Meanings: Politics and Ideas in the Making of the Constitution* (1996), another linguistic shift occurred, away from original understanding toward *original meaning*.[e] In the new millennium, original (public) meaning is the dominant concept: What meaning did constitutional language have for We the People — the public, as well as the ratifiers and the Framers? See Henry Monaghan, *Stare Decisis and Constitutional Adjudication*, 88 Colum. L. Rev. 723 (1988).

In figuring out "original meaning," an interpreter might consider (1) the text of the Constitution, including its structure and other provisions bearing on the issue; (2) the context within which that text was drafted, debated, and ratified, including legal background and traditions; and (3) the original goals and norms that were accepted by those ratifying (and perhaps those framing) the constitutional provision(s) in question. We shall devote a subpart to each of these sources of original meaning.

As you read these materials, keep in mind some general difficulties with originalist, consent-based theories of judicial review: (a) *The dead-hand of the past problem*: Is it appropriate to assume that there is an ongoing implicit consent to the original Constitution, which was negotiated and ratified by only a tiny minority of the population who could not possibly have envisioned much of what our world would be like?[f] (b) *The indeterminacy problem*: How can one ever know what more than a handful of founding era people thought about an issue? Can it be seriously maintained that there is a knowable "original meaning" as to issues that the framing generation could not have anticipated?[g] (c) *The cognitive dissonance problem*: For normatively charged issues of constitutional law, can any judge remain genuinely objective? Or will judges

---

d. Compare John Yoo, *The Continuation of Politics by Other Means: The Original Understanding of War Powers*, 84 Cal. L. Rev. 167 (1996), with William Michael Treanor, *Fame, the Founding, and the Power to Declare War*, 82 Cornell L. Rev. 695 (1997).

e. For examples of original meaning methodology in action, compare Saikrishna Prakash & Michael Ramsey, *The Executive Power over Foreign Affairs*, 111 Yale L.J. 231 (2001), with Curtis Bradley & Martin Flaherty, *Executive Power Essentialism and Foreign Affairs*, 102 Mich. L. Rev. 545 (2004). And compare Saikrishna Prakash, *Unleashing the Dogs of War: What the Constitution Means by "Declare War,"* 93 Cornell L. Rev. 45 (2007), with Robert Delahunty & John Yoo, *Making War*, 93 Cornell L. Rev. 123 (2007), and Michael Ramsey, *The President's Power to Respond to Attacks*, 93 Cornell L. Rev. 169 (2007).

f. See Dorothy Roberts, *The Meaning of Blacks' Fidelity to the Constitution*, 65 Fordham L. Rev. 1761 (1997). More specifically, the great majority of us today would not have had any political standing when the Constitution was ratified. Most African Americans in 1789 were enslaved (a condition sanctioned in the Constitution), and most women were nonparticipants in political life, as were most people without property. Among those who did have standing in 1789, the vote was close.

g. Paul Brest, *The Misconceived Quest for the Original Understanding*, 60 B.U. L. Rev. 204 (1980); Mark Tushnet, *Following the Rules Laid Down: A Critique of Interpretivism and Neutral Principles*, 96 Harv. L. Rev. 781 (1983); Michael Dorf & Laurence Tribe, *Levels of Generality in the Definition of Rights*, 57 U. Chi. L. Rev. 1057 (1990); Martin Flaherty, *History "Lite" in Modern American Constitutionalism*, 95 Colum. L. Rev. 523 (1995).

sift through evidence of original meaning, cherry-picking sources that support their own perspective and ignoring the rest?[h]

1. *Constitutional Text*

Text is the most relevant evidence when interpreting any legal document. It is the starting point and usually the ending point for interpreting contracts, wills, and statutes. Unfortunately, the Constitution is a relatively short document, filled with open-textured terms (like "equal protection" and "due process"), that was for the most part drafted more than 200 years ago. How can such a document address any of the important modern problems of governance? There are a number of judges and theorists who have propounded useful textualist approaches to constitutional decisionmaking.[i] Consider some techniques of textual exegesis:

(a) *Clause-Bound Textualism: What is the "plain meaning" of the constitutional language? How would a reasonable person in the Framers' era have understood the language?* The most obvious textual approach would ask how a normal reader of the English language would construe the provision in question, bringing to bear the conventional tools of grammar and word meaning into play.[j] This was the approach Chief Justice Marshall followed to construe Article III, § 2, clause 2 in *Marbury*. Sentence 1 gave the Supreme Court original jurisdiction but did not include the mandamus action Marbury was pressing; therefore, as a matter of ordinary inference, the Constitution did not authorize Congress to give the Court original jurisdiction in mandamus cases. Recall, however, that the meaning of Article III is not as "plain" as Marshall claimed. Thus, clause 2 could be limited to the proposition that Congress cannot restrict the Court's original jurisdiction in the enumerated categories but otherwise has a great deal of freedom to create "Regulations" and "Exceptions" for the Court's jurisdiction. *Marbury* thus exemplifies the key problem with textualism as a constitutional methodology: The text may not be clear. *Marbury* itself is unusual, insofar as it involves a constitutional provision that is relatively directive, specific, and focused. The constitutional provisions providing details for the structure of government are generally much easier to apply than the broader, "open-textured" provisions such as the Equal Protection Clause interpreted in *Brown*.

Marbury's textual reasoning involved more than grammar and word meaning. Marshall's interpretation rested upon a conversational *convention*: If

---

h. For evidence that original meaning jurisprudence, in action, is like looking out over the crowd and picking out your friends, see, e.g., Peter Smith, *Sources of Federalism: An Empirical Analysis of the Court's Quest for Original Meaning*, 52 UCLA L. Rev. 217 (2004).

i. See generally Charles Black, *Structure and Relationship in Constitutional Law* (1969); Antonin Scalia, *A Matter of Interpretation: Federal Courts and the Law* (1997); Akhil Reed Amar, *America's Constitution, A Biography* (2005), and *The Supreme Court, 1999 Term — Foreword: The Document and the Doctrine*, 114 Harv. L. Rev. 26 (2000).

j. Oliver Wendell Holmes, Jr., *The Theory of Legal Interpretation*, 12 Harv. L. Rev. 417 (1899) ("normal speaker of English" is the standard for legal interpretation), embraced and elaborated in Scalia, *Matter of Interpretation*.

I authorize you to do "x", I am implicitly not authorizing you to do "y" as well. The maxim *inclusio unius est exclusio alterius* (inclusion of one thing implies exclusion of all others) is a widely accepted common law presumption for construing legal instruments. Other textualist conventions include the notions that

- the meaning of words not defined in the statute can be ascertained by consulting authoritative dictionaries, and the "preferred" dictionary meaning is presumptively the right one (depending on context, of course);

- items in a series are presumed to be of the same kind (*noscitur a sociis*);

- one part of a sentence should not be construed in such a way that it renders another part unnecessary (the rule against surplusage); and so forth.[k]

These conventions are controversial in some circles. If Mother tells Sally, "Don't hit or kick your sister Anne," is Sally authorized to pinch little sister? Or hit sister Martha? (Hint: no!) At most, these conventions are presumptions; some academics would abolish them altogether.

Should a textualist limit her inquiry to meanings (and conventions) as they would have been understood at the time of the framing of the original Constitution or of a relevant amendment? The answer to that question sometimes makes a difference. The term "commerce" used in Article I, § 8 probably had a narrower meaning in 1787-89, when the Constitution was ratified, than it has today. See *United States v. Lopez*, 514 U.S. 549, 585-87 (1995) (Thomas, J., concurring) (surveying dictionaries of the time as well as ratification debates to show that "commerce" only included trade or barter and did not involve agriculture or manufacturing). Most judicial textualists prefer "original meanings" to current ones, but they are open to reasonable updating. The Framers of the Second Amendment's right "to keep and bear arms" could not have imagined modern firearms, but the Supreme Court has held that the right is not limited to weapons existing in 1791. *District of Columbia v. Heller*, 128 S.Ct. 2783, 2791-92 (2008).

In the same vein, an original meaning person would construe terms in accord with settled legal or constitutional meanings they had when added to the Constitution. The Fourteenth Amendment terms *privileges and immunities* and *due process* had established constitutional meanings in 1868; those should presumptively be followed. Note that this suggests that *The Slaughter House Cases* were wrongly decided, insofar as they gave the Privilege and Immunities Clause of the Fourteenth Amendment a different and narrower reading (inapplicable to state restrictions of occupation) than the then-established reading of a similar clause in Article IV. This suggests a dilemma for the modern textualist: Under what circumstances, if any, should the Court overrule

---

k. For an introduction to these and other traditional "canons of construction," see William Eskridge, Jr., Philip Frickey & Elizabeth Garrett, *Cases and Materials on Legislation: Statutes and the Creation of Public Policy* ch. 8, § 1 (4th ed. 2007).

important precedents because they are inconsistent with (original) constitutional plain meaning?

(b) *Holistic Interpretation: Read the provision in light of the whole document.* The Constitution can be read "holistically," as a coherent document, where all parts are presumed to fit together in a consistent whole.[l] Like the Bible, the Constitution should be read, where possible (or not absurd), as if it had a single author. Akhil Amar provides a justification: "The American People ratified the Philadelphia Convention not clause by clause, but as a single document. Later generations of Americans have added amendments one by one, but no amendment stands alone as a discrete legal regime. Each amendment aims to fit with, and be read as part of, the larger document."[m]

Holistic interpretation can be a means of fixing plain meaning. Consider the issue debated in Washington's Cabinet in 1790 and resolved in *M'Culloch v. Maryland*, 17 U.S. (4 Wheat.) 316 (1819) (Chapter 7, § 1): Is Congress authorized to charter a national bank? Secretary of Treasury Hamilton and, later, Chief Justice Marshall opined that Congress had such authority under the Article I, § 8 powers of Congress to lay and collect taxes, to borrow money etc., and to make all laws "necessary and proper" for carrying out those activities. A plain meaning problem with the Hamilton-Marshall view is that a national bank does not seem "essential" — the primary meaning of "necessary" then and now — to the enumerated Article I, § 8 activities.

Hamilton and Marshall responded with the Constitution's deployment of the term "necessary" elsewhere. Where the Constitution meant to limit governments strictly, as in Article I, § 10, it limited their actions to that which "may be *absolutely* necessary" to achieve stated goals. In contrast, Article II, § 3 authorizes the President to propose legislation to Congress "as he shall judge necessary and expedient." There, it is clear that "necessary" means something like "useful to attaining a goal" (the secondary definition) rather than "essential." See also U.S. Const. art. IV, § 3, cl. 2 ("needful"); id. art. V ("necessary"). Given the holistic presumption that a document uses the same term consistently throughout, a textualist might conclude that the Necessary and Proper Clause

---

l. The best introduction and defense can be found in Akhil Reed Amar, *Intratextualism*, 112 Harv. L. Rev. 747 (1999), and *The Bill of Rights: Creation and Reconstruction* (1998). Professor Amar's intratextual approach is criticized as too narrow by Mark Tushnet, *The Possibilities of Comparative Constitutional Law*, 108 Yale L.J. 1225 (1999); William Michael Treanor, *Taking Text Too Seriously: Modern Textualism, Original Meaning, and the Case of Amar's* Bill of Rights, 106 Mich. L. Rev. 487 (2007); Adrian Vermeule & Ernest Young, *Hercules, Herbert, and Amar: The Trouble with Intratextualism*, 113 Harv. L. Rev. 730 (2000).

m. Akhil Reed Amar, *The Supreme Court, 1999 Term: Foreword — The Document and the Doctrine*, 114 Harv. L. Rev. 26, 29-30 (2000). But see Treanor, *Taking Text Too Seriously*, 106 Mich. L. Rev. at 507-43, who argues that such an approach is not consistent with original "public" meaning and is prone to the idiosyncracies of particular drafters, namely, Gouverneur Morris (Constitution of 1789) and James Madison (Bill of Rights).

authorizes statutes useful, rather than absolutely essential, to the many activities specifically enumerated for Congress.[n]

The holistic presumption that a term means the same thing everywhere it appears in the Constitution is at odds with *Bolling v. Sharpe*, interpreting the Fifth Amendment's Due Process Clause to have an equal protection component. Why does the Fourteenth Amendment have an Equal Protection as well as Due Process Clause, if unequal treatment is actionable under the latter? This is an intratextual conundrum, and violates the rule against surplusage to boot: What does the Equal Protection Clause "add" to the Fourteenth Amendment if a Due Process Clause means what *Bolling* says?

Another holistic precept is that a judge should not construe one constitutional provision in a way plainly inconsistent with another current provision or its underlying assumptions. The Supreme Court in *The Insular Cases* (1901) rejected arguments that the Constitution prohibits Congress from acquiring and governing territories (The Philippines, Guam, and Puerto Rico) that it does not intend to assimilate into the United States as new states over time. The Court rejected a simple dichotomy between "domestic" (part of the United States) and "foreign" territories, in part because such a dichotomy is inconsistent with the text-based assumptions of the Thirteenth Amendment's prohibition of involuntary servitude "within the United States, or in any place subject to their jurisdiction." *Downes v. Bidwell*, 182 U.S. 244, 251 (1901).

For a current example, Justice Scalia rejects constitutional attacks on capital punishment, because he reads the Fifth Amendment's Grand Jury and Due Process Clauses as contemplating the existence of the death penalty. Cf. U.S. Const. art. III, § 3 (Treason Clauses; normal punishment for treason in the eighteenth century was death). If one part of the Constitution contemplates capital punishment, another part, the Eighth Amendment, surely cannot prohibit it, argues Justice Scalia. Query: Because the Eighth Amendment was added *later*, might it not change the original constitutional assumptions?

Another example is the Second Amendment's guarantee that "the *people*'s right to keep and bear Arms, shall not be infringed." Arguing from the Second Amendment's prefatory clause ("A well-regulated Militia, being necessary to the security of a free State"), some have claimed that the right to bear arms is only a collective right held by We the People as a group, and not an enforceable individual right. The Supreme Court unanimously rejected this intratextual argument based upon a holistic analysis. Justice Scalia's opinion for the Court in *Heller* argued that because rights recognized for "the people" in the First, Fourth, and Ninth Amendments are enforceable individual rights, the Second

---

n. There are also intratextual arguments against the Hamilton-Marshall interpretation. The Tenth Amendment's command that "powers not delegated to the United States by the Constitution, nor prohibited by it to the States, are reserved to the States respectively, or to the people" can be read as a constitutional principle of interpretation: construe Congress's enumerated powers narrowly rather than broadly — a rule that is violated by Hamilton and Marshall's elastic construction of the Necessary and Proper Clause.

Amendment ought to be read the same way. *Heller*, 128 S.Ct. at 2790; *id.* at 2822 (Stevens, J., dissenting, but agreeing on this point).

(c) *Structuralism: Read the text in light of overall constitutional principles.* A textualist who follows the aforementioned precepts might well dissent in *Bolling*, but it is unclear how she should vote in *Brown*. Yet über-textualist Justice Scalia is sure that *Brown* was correctly decided, on the ground that the Reconstruction Amendments reflect a legal commitment to complete formal equality for the freed slaves. *Rutan v. Republican Party of Illinois*, 497 U.S. 62, 96 n.1 (1990) (Scalia, J., dissenting). This might not resolve the interpretive dilemma, as *Plessy* presented its separate-but-equal formula as satisfying the requirements of formal equality. To attack *Plessy*, the textualist might need to ratchet up his theory one generality notch: Rather than looking just at the plain meaning of the Constitution (read as a whole document), the interpreter should also consider how competing constructions fit with the *principles* instinct in the Constitution.[o] Those principles include democratic representation and accountability of representatives to their constituents, as well as the text-based notion that accidents of birth ought not make a difference in state policy.[p]

Once the textualist attends to these constitutional principles, she has available to her some new defenses of *Brown*, for an understanding of equality that rejects state-supported racial segregation comports well with most theories of democracy and is strongly supported by the "accidents of birth" principle. But the southern opponents of *Brown* also had a structural argument based upon federalism and a holistic argument based on the Fourteenth Amendment's vesting (primary?) enforcement authority with Congress. This reflects a problem with structural or principle-based textualism: principles instinct in the Constitution often cut in different directions in a given case, and they are set at such a high level of generality that even the same principle is often susceptible of application either way regarding contested issues.

If *Brown* is correct, moreover, Justice Scalia might have a principled basis for joining *Bolling*. Chief Justice Warren's opinion in that case centrally relied on notions of coherence: It would be "unthinkable that the same Constitution would impose a lesser duty on the Federal Government" in a matter of such importance as apartheid. As Vicki Jackson and Akhil Amar have suggested, the constitutional commitment to national citizenship and equal protection represented by the Fourteenth Amendment might, under a structural understanding of the Constitution, be "read into" the Fifth Amendment.[q] See also *Adarand*

---

o. See Black, *Structure and Relationship*; Akhil Reed Amar, *America's Constitution, a Biography* (2005); Vicki Jackson, *Holistic Interpretation:* Fitzpatrick v. Bitzer *and Our Bifurcated Constitution*, 53 Stan. L. Rev. 1259 (2001).

p. See Amar, *America's Constitution*, 124-27, 380-85; *Adarand Constructors, Inc. v. Pena*, 515 U.S. 200, 239 (1995) (Scalia, J., concurring), both recognizing a general principle, reflected in the Constitution's bars to "Title[s] of Nobility" (Art. I, § 9, Cl. 8), and to "Corruption of Blood" (Art. III, § 3, Cl. 2), that strongly counsels against any race-based discrimination in American law.

q. Jackson, *Holistic Interpretation*, 53 Stan. L. Rev. at 1279-81 & n.91; Amar, *Intratextualism*, 112 Harv. L. Rev. at 766-73; see also Akhil Reed Amar, *The Bill of Rights and the Fourteenth Amendment*, 101 Yale L.J. 1193, 1277-82 (1992) (Fourteenth Amendment had a "feedback effect"

Constructors, Inc. v. Pena, 515 U.S. 200 (1995) (Chapter 3, § 3) (applying the principle of "congruence" to interpret equal protection guarantees of the Fifth and Fourteenth Amendments in a similar fashion).

The broader point is that the original meanings of the Constitution of 1787 and the Bill of Rights must, as a matter of formal law, be updated by reference to the transformations of the Reconstruction Amendments. For example, in *Fitzpatrick v. Bitzer*, 427 U.S. 445 (1976), the Court read the Fourteenth Amendment to modify the original meaning of the Eleventh: When acting under its authority to enforce the Fourteenth Amendment, Congress may abrogate state immunity which it cannot do under its Article I powers (Chapter 7, § 3D). See also *Adkins v. Children's Hospital*, 261 U.S. 525, 552-53 (1923) (updating Court's interpretation of Due Process Clause to allow labor legislation protecting women, in light of Nineteenth Amendment, giving women the right to vote and suggesting women are not a class needing special protections).

2. *Original Context for Constitutional Text*

Purely textual analysis of the Constitution will only get the interpreter so far, and Dean William Treanor has cautioned that examining only the text will often lead to *misreading* original meaning.[r] He says the originalist must also consider context. But what counts as valid context? For example, we have extensive notes of the Framers' debates at Philadelphia and public reports of debates at the state conventions ratifying the original Constitution, including the celebrated *Federalist Papers*. There is a vigorous debate among scholars and judges as to whether the secret deliberations at Philadelphia or public congressional deliberations as to constitutional amendments ought to be consulted in determining original meaning.[s] Those materials probably ought to be consulted, but the ratifying materials are more important for a practical reason. Ratification of the Constitution of 1789 and some of the amendments involved a process

---

on First Amendment, not only pressing it against the states, but also transforming its application to the federal government).

r. William Michael Treanor, *Taking Text Too Seriously: Modern Textualism, Original Meaning, and the Case of Amar's* Bill of Rights, 106 Mich. L. Rev. 487 (2007).

s. Compare Ronald Rotunda, *Original Intent, the View of the Framers, and the Role of the Ratifiers*, 41 Vand. L. Rev. 507 (1988) (arguing against consideration of the Philadelphia Convention's secret drafting history), with Vasan Kesavan & Michael Stokes Paulsen, *The Interpretive Force of the Constitution's Secret Drafting History*, 91 Geo. L.J. 1113 (2003) (arguing for such consideration). See also *District of Columbia v. Heller*, 128 S.Ct. 2783 (2008), where dissenting Justice Stevens relies on Congress's drafting history of the Second Amendment, which is belittled by Justice Scalia, writing for the Court; *City of Boerne v. Flores*, 521 U.S. 507 (1997), where Justice Kennedy's opinion for the Court relies on Congress's drafting history for the Fourteenth Amendment, over objection from Justice Scalia.

of give and take where the public understanding of the provisions "evolved" (or was "clarified") during the course of the debate.[t]

For complex issues or those whose contours have changed over time, an approach true to original understanding might be "imaginative reconstruction": How would the Framers have answered this question if it had been posed to them? Leading legal historians, such as Martin Flaherty, William Treanor, and Saikrishna Prakash, have suggested the proper historicist methodology for reconstructing original meaning: The interpreter must consider not just the drafting deliberations and the state ratification debates, but also the background legal context and the conceptual framework of the Framers.[u] Consider the excerpt that follows, which is also a leading attack on non-originalist judicial review of the sort Chief Justice Warren followed in *Brown*.

Robert H. Bork
The Tempting of America: The Political Seduction of the Law
75, 76-77, 143-45, 154-55 (1990)[v]

Brown was a great and correct decision, but it must be said in all candor that the decision was supported by a very weak opinion. Those two facts, taken together, have caused an enormous amount of trouble in the law. [The opinion was weak, indeed disingenuous, in several ways. It failed to deal with the fact that the drafters and ratifiers of the Fourteenth Amendment did not think it outlawed state-required segregation in any aspect of society, especially in education. The Court refused to admit, forthrightly, that much of the originalist evidence cut against its holding. The opinion's reliance on social science evidence about the alleged impact of segregation on black children's self-esteem was nonsense. No one believed it critical for the decision, and the Court immediately proved the cynics correct by summarily invalidating state-required segregation in public accommodations and parks, upon the authority of *Brown*. Clearly, the decision rested upon a broader, more principled foundation than doll studies.]

But the combined disingenuousness of the *Brown* opinion and the obvious moral rightness of its result had, I believe, a calamitous effect upon the law. This was massively ironic, because the result in *Brown* is consistent with, indeed is compelled by, the original understanding of the fourteenth amendment's equal

---

t.   E.g., John Yoo, *The Powers of War and Peace: The Constitution and Foreign Affairs After 9/11* (2005) (evolving Federalist position on war powers); William Eskridge, Jr., *All About Words: Early Understandings of the "Judicial Power" in Statutory Interpretation, 1776–1806*, 101 Colum. L. Rev. 990 (2001) (evolving Federalist position on Article III judicial power).

u.   Compare, e.g., John Yoo, *Globalism and the Constitution: Treaties, Non-Self-Execution, and the Original Understanding*, 99 Colum. L. Rev. 1955 (1999), with Martin Flaherty, *History Right? Historical Scholarship, Original Understanding, and Treaties as "Supreme Law of the Land,"* 99 Colum. L. Rev. 2095 (1999).

v.   Reprinted and edited with the permission of The Free Press, a Division of Simon & Schuster Inc., from THE TEMPTING OF AMERICA: The Political Seduction of the Law by Robert H. Bork. Copyright © 1990 by Robert H. Bork. All rights reserved.

protection clause. The disastrous fact was that the Supreme Court did not think so. The Court, judging by its opinion, thought that it had departed from the original understanding in order to do the socially desirable thing. What is more, the Court triumphed over intense political opposition despite that fact.

[Worse, the Court's reputation not only survived its lawless opinion and the controversy it aroused, but was enhanced for a generation of citizens, including future constitutional theorists, who found the Court's moral triumph over narrow "law" inspiring. Worst, when those budding constitutionalists started writing about constitutional theory they marched lock-step away from original understanding: Because *Brown* was the high ground, no constitutional theory that did not explain *Brown* could be legitimate. Because original understanding so dramatically flunked the *Brown* test, it could not be an acceptable constitutional theory. But, argues Bork, *Brown* is defensible under a proper application of original understanding, and even if *Brown* were not consistent with original understanding, its inconsistency could not negate that as the only acceptable philosophy, which follows.]

When we speak of "law," we ordinarily refer to a rule that we have no right to change except through prescribed procedures. That statement assumes that the rule has a meaning independent of our own desires. Otherwise there would be no need to agree on procedures for changing the rule. Statutes, we agree, may be changed by amendment or repeal. The Constitution may be changed by amendment pursuant to the procedures set out in article V. It is a necessary implication of the prescribed procedures that neither statute nor Constitution should be changed by judges. Though that has been done often enough, it is in no sense proper.

What is the meaning of a rule that judges should not change? It is the meaning understood at the time of the law's enactment. Though I have written of the understanding of the ratifiers of the Constitution, since they enacted it and made it law, that is actually a shorthand formulation, because what the ratifiers understood themselves to be enacting must be taken to be what the public of that time would have understood the words to mean. It is important to be clear about this. The search is not for a subjective intention. If someone found a letter from George Washington to Martha telling her that what he meant by the power to lay taxes was not what other people meant, that would not change our reading of the Constitution in the slightest. * * * Law is a public act. Secret reservations or intentions count for nothing. All that counts is how the words used in the Constitution would have been understood at the time. The original understanding is thus manifested in the words used and in secondary materials, such as debates at conventions, public discussion, newspaper articles, dictionaries in use at the time, and the like. * * *

[Original meaning is the methodology for constitutional interpretation that best assures *neutrality* in the deriving, defining, and applying of constitutional principle. Without neutrality in constitutional decisionmaking, the Court becomes nothing but a naked power organ, Bork argues. The Court becomes an arbiter of political rather than legal rights and duties.]

The structure of government the Founders of this nation intended most certainly did not give courts a political role. The debates surrounding the Constitution focused much more upon theories of representation than upon the judiciary, which was thought to be a comparatively insignificant branch. There were, however, repeated attempts at the Constitutional Convention in Philadelphia to give judges a policymaking role. The plan of the Virginia delegation, which, amended and expanded, ultimately became the Constitution of the United States, included a proposal that the new national legislature be controlled by placing a veto power in a Council of Revision consisting of the executive and "a convenient number of the National Judiciary." That proposal was raised four times and defeated each time. Among the reasons, as reported in James Madison's notes, was the objection raised by Elbridge Gerry of Massachusetts that it "was quite foreign from the nature of ye. office to make them judges of policy of public measures." Rufus King, also of Massachusetts, added that judges should "expound the law as it should come before them, free from the bias of having participated in its formulation." Judges who create new constitutional rights are judges of the policy of public measures and are biased by having participated in the policy's formulation. * * *

Even if evidence of what the Founders thought about the judicial role were unavailable, we would have to adopt the rule that judges must stick to the original meaning of the Constitution's words. If that method of interpretation were not common in the law, if James Madison and Justice Joseph Story had never endorsed it, if Chief Justice John Marshall had rejected it, we would have to invent the approach of original understanding in order to save the constitutional design. No other method of constitutional adjudication can confine courts to a defined sphere of authority and thus prevent them from assuming powers whose exercise alters, perhaps radically, the design of the American Republic. The philosophy of original understanding is thus a necessary inference from the structure of government apparent on the face of the Constitution.

PROBLEM 2-1
IS *BROWN* CONSISTENT WITH THE ORIGINAL
MEANING OF THE FOURTEENTH AMENDMENT?

Whichever side you represented in *Brown*, you would have been required to take original meaning seriously for purposes of the reargument in the case, because the original "intent" of the drafters of the Fourteenth Amendment was the stated agenda of the reargument. This problem presents the evidence pro and con, then concludes with some methodological questions.

Originalist evidence that Brown *was wrong.*[w]

---

w. See Raoul Berger, *Government by Judiciary: The Transformation of the Fourteenth Amendment* 22-27, 117-27 (1977); Andrew Kull, *The Color-Blind Constitution* (1992); Earl Maltz, *Civil Rights, the Constitution, and Congress, 1863-1869* (1990); Alfred Avins, *De Facto and De Jure School Segregation: Some Reflected Light On the Fourteenth Amendment From the Civil Rights Act of 1875*, 38 Miss. L.J. 179 (1967); Alfred Kelly, *The Congressional Controversy Over*

(i) *Segregationist attitudes and laws in or around 1868.* Segregation was the norm in 1868 [Kelly, 539]: An overwhelming majority of the black children in the North attended segregated schools or attended no public school at all; although several states formally desegregated their schools after the Civil War, most did not, and eight states (California, Kansas, Kentucky, Indiana, Maryland, Missouri, Nevada, West Virginia) enacted laws creating or recognizing segregated schools after the Fourteenth Amendment took effect; the rebel states of the South reentered the union with constitutions having no such provision, but they all quickly adopted laws or policies of school segregation soon after 1868. In 1862, Congress had established racially segregated schools in Washington, D.C., over which Congress has plenary jurisdiction. 12 Stat. 407. A month after Congress passed the Fourteenth Amendment, it provided that an 1864 statute should be construed to require the cities of Washington and Georgetown to pay over certain funds for the support of separate schools. 14 Stat. 216 (also *id.* at 343). The Senate galleries were racially segregated in 1866, when Congress was drafting and debating the Fourteenth Amendment.

There was an underlying intellectual structure behind the country's willingness to assure African Americans "equality" and its disinclination to require "integration."[x] Most Americans, including many of the supporters of radical Reconstruction, believed that "mixing the races" was not desirable, based upon stereotypes about African Americans and fears that racial mixing would lead to racial dilution. Many supporters of the Fourteenth Amendment also seem to have had a different conception of equality than the one many of us share today: Civil equality only assured rights of formal access to courts, contracting, and property ownership, not any kind of social equality. *Plessy,* therefore, may have been an accurate reflection of one strand of the Framers' notions about equality.

(ii) *Drafting history and debates.* The supporters of the Fourteenth Amendment said little about exactly what § 1 would prohibit, but they did emphasize its similarities to the Civil Rights Act of 1866. Representative George Latham said that "the 'civil rights bill' which is now a law * * * covers exactly the same ground as the [proposed] amendment," and many others agreed. What did the 1866 statute have to say about school segregation? Indeed, opponents of the proposed statute attacked it for opening up segregated schools to federal question. Supporters of the proposed statute, first, denied it would have any such effect[y] and, then, narrowed the proposal to drop language

---

School Segregation, 1867–1875, 64 Am. Hist. Rev. 537 (1959). Support for this account can also be drawn from two excellent accounts that find evidence on both sides of the issue: William Nelson, *The Fourteenth Amendment: From Political Principle to Judicial Doctrine* (1988), and Alexander Bickel, *The Original Understanding and the Segregation Decision,* 69 Harv. L. Rev. 1 (1955).

x. See Herbert Hovenkamp, *Social Service and Segregation Before* Brown, 1985 Duke L.J. 624, 637-51.

y. Representative Wilson, the House manager for the bill, explicitly said that the "civil rights" protected by the bill "do not mean that all citizens shall sit on juries, or that their children shall attend the same schools." Cong. Globe, 39th Cong., 1st Sess. 1117 (Mar. 1, 1866). This reflected the well-known distinction among *civil rights* (to sue, to contract) protected by the bill, and *political*

prohibiting "discrimination" against civil rights and immunities. Historians have read this as a deliberate choice to put the school segregation issue entirely to rest. [Bickel, 56-57; Berger 119.] That it was not revisited, even by opponents, during debate on the proposed constitutional amendment, may confirm that it was thought to be politically settled once and for all.

(iii) *Post-amendment practice and construction.* Between 1868 and 1883, nine northern state high courts addressed the validity of school segregation. Five courts upheld segregation against state and federal constitutional attack;[z] four courts invalidated segregation under state law;[a] no appeals court held that public school segregation violated the Fourteenth Amendment.[b] In the southern and border states, there were neither federal nor state court lawsuits challenging the de facto, and then de jure, school segregation practiced after 1868. Justice Thomas Cooley of the Michigan Supreme Court, an opponent of school segregation, wrote in his influential *General Principles of Constitutional Law* 230-31 (1880), that it was "admissible" under the Fourteenth Amendment "to require colored persons to attend separate schools, provided the schools are equal in advantages."

Congressional practice was to the same effect. In 1871, the District of Columbia Committee of the United States Senate reported a bill to abolish racial segregation in the District's schools. Cong. Globe, 41st Cong., 3d Sess. 1054 (1871). Anti-apartheid Senator Charles Sumner insisted that this was required by the equality principle in the Fourteenth Amendment. *Id.* at 1055, 1056, 1058. None of the bill's opponents disputed this, but the bill never proceeded to a vote in the Senate; a parallel bill was voted down, 71-88, in the House. *Id.* at 1367. Sumner introduced similar bills later in 1871 and in 1873. His 1873 bill passed the Senate but not the House. Congress continued, without interruption, to fund the D.C. school system, which had been formally and continuously segregated by race since 1862.

Enacting the Civil Rights Act of 1875, Congress rejected the provision in Sumner's original bill that would have required "equal and impartial enjoyment" of facilities furnished by "common schools and other public institutions of learning." Cong. Globe, 42d Cong., 2d Sess. 244 (Dec. 20, 1871). Proponents of the bill emphasized that legalized segregation was tantamount to creating a "caste" system, where African Americans were treated as degraded second-class citizens, or legal "lepers," as Representative Rainey put it. *Id.* app. 16 (Feb. 3,

---

rights (to vote) and *social rights* (to associate) not protected.

z. See *State ex rel. Garnes v. McCann*, 21 Ohio St. 198 (1871); *State ex rel. Stoutmeyer v. Duffy*, 7 Nev. 342 (1872); *Ward v. Flood*, 48 Cal. 36 (1874); *Cory v. Carter*, 48 Ind. 327 (1874); *People ex rel. King v. Gallagher*, 93 N.Y. 438 (1883).

a. See *Clark v. Board of Directors*, 24 Iowa 266 (1868); *People v. Board of Educ.*, 18 Mich. 400 (1869); *Chase v. Stephenson*, 71 Ill. 383 (1874); *Board of Educ. v. Tinnon*, 26 Kan. 1 (1881).

b. J. Morgan Kousser, *Dead End: The Development of Nineteenth-Century Litigation on Racial Discrimination in Schools* 22 (1986) reports an 1881 lower court decision in Pennsylvania ruling that education is a privilege or immunity protected under § 1 of the Fourteenth Amendment and that segregation was therefore invalid.

1872). Opponents of the Sumner bill, led by Senator Lyman Trumbull, the author of the 1866 Civil Rights Act, argued that "the right to go to school is not a civil right," of the sort the 1866 statute and the Fourteenth Amendment were aimed at protecting. *Id.* at 3189-90 (May 8, 1872). Schooling was a matter of local discretion, not federal rights. After Sumner's death, the Senate deleted the schools provision from the bill. Before it was invalidated in *The Civil Rights Cases* in 1883, the 1875 Act's requirement of "equal access" to public accommodations was immediately and pervasively interpreted *not* to mean integrated access.[c] According to those federal judges, even if the schools provision had remained in the bill and the statute had not been invalidated, *Plessy* would just have arrived twenty years earlier as an interpretation of the statute itself.

Originalist evidence that Brown *was right.*[d]

(i) *State recognition that segregated schools violated the Fourteenth Amendment.* Before they could rejoin the union, the rebel states of the South had to submit state constitutions conforming to the U.S. Constitution, including the Fourteenth Amendment. Almost all the southerners who spoke to the issue said that a state constitution separating the races in public education would flunk the Fourteenth Amendment; no state constitution had such a provision, and those of Louisiana and South Carolina explicitly barred school segregation. [Frank & Munro 459.] Ambiguous but apparently prohibitory provisions were in the constitutions of Florida and Alabama, and three other states (Mississippi, Texas, Virginia) were readmitted upon a federal statutory stipulation that their constitutions could never be amended to deprive any class of citizens of "school rights and privileges." [McConnell 963-65.] That these southern states failed to implement such assurances is less important than the consensus that the Fourteenth Amendment did not permit them to segregate schools openly under color of law.

The northern states came to recognize the inconsistency of school segregation and racial equality. After 1855, when Massachusetts repealed its segregation law, none of the New England states had such a law. Although some states enacted school segregation statutes after 1868, most went in the other direction: New Jersey, Michigan, and Illinois desegregated right after ratifying the Fourteenth Amendment; New York, Pennsylvania, Ohio, California, and other

---

c. See *Charge to Grand Jury — The Civil Rights Act*, 30 Fed. Cas. 999, 1000 (C.C. W.D.N.C. 1875) (No. T8,258); Stephen Riegel, *The Persistent Career of Jim Crow: Lower Federal Courts and the "Separate But Equal" Doctrine, 1865-1896*, 28 Am. J. Legal Hist. 17 (1984).

d. See John Frank & Robert Munro, *The Original Understanding of "Equal Protection of the Laws,"* 1972 Wash. U.L.Q. 421; Michael McConnell, *Originalism and the Desegregation Decisions*, 81 Va. L. Rev. 947 (1995); Note, *Is Racial Segregation Consistent with Equal Protection of the Laws? Plessy v. Ferguson Reexamined*, 49 Colum. L. Rev. 629 (1949). For responses to McConnell's case for *Brown*, see Earl Maltz (a leading originalist), *Originalism and the Desegregation Decisions — A Response to Professor McConnell*, 13 Const. Comm. 223 (1996), and Michael Klarman (not an originalist), *Brown, Originalism, and Constitutional Theory: A Response to Professor McConnell*, 81 Va. L. Rev. 1881 (1995).

states followed in the 1870s and 1880s, in some instances overriding court decisions allowing segregation. [McConnell, 968-75.]

(ii) *Congressional recognition that school segregation violated the Fourteenth Amendment.* While Congress funded segregated schools in the District, the decision to segregate was made in 1862-64, several Congresses before the Reconstruction Congress, whose main sin was one of omission, failing to take a direct vote on Sumner's proposal to desegregate. The post-1868 debate treated the issue as one of policy, and none focused on the Fourteenth Amendment, which, of course, does not apply to the District. [McConnell, 977-80.] After 1870, Sumner focused attention on his more ambitious national bill.

The 1870 Sumner bill banning segregation in schools, common carriers, and public accommodations was inspired by constitutional values: Sumner and his supporters — the same people who had pushed for the Fourteenth Amendment — maintained that the bill was an effort to enforce the guarantees of § 1 of the Fourteenth Amendment under Congress' § 5 powers.[e] Thus, the proponents believed that school segregation was already illegal; their proposal would simply provide a federal court remedy for rights unenforced by state courts, especially in the South. [McConnell, 990-1005.] The Democrats and some Republicans opposed the bill, and their arguments anticipated those accepted in *Plessy*: segregation is not racial "inequality," as each race is equally affected, and education is a social right rather than a civil right. [McConnell, 1005-29.] The Senate decisively and repeatedly rejected these arguments and passed the bill in 1874, soon after Sumner's death, but the bill died in the House. When Congress reconvened for its lame-duck session in 1875, after the Democrats had won the 1874 election, the House and Senate passed the Sumner bill, but without the controversial education provision. The wind then went out of the sails of Reconstruction, and Jim Crow came to power in the South.

(iii) *The clear error of* Plessy. Whatever might be the case with segregated schools (the *Brown* issue), segregated transportation (the *Plessy* issue) was clearly outlawed by the Fourteenth Amendment. Interstate travel was a civil right and not just a social right as understood by the Framers; Congress and even the states repeatedly legislated against racial segregation in transportation, with the 1875 Act confirming that principle. [McConnell, 1029-36.] If *Plessy* was wrong, then arguably everything building upon *Plessy* (including the school cases, *Cumming* and *Gong Lum*) was wrong as well.

Methodological problems with original meaning scholarship.

For originalism to subserve its core goals — respecting the terms of the social contract and constraining the discretion of judges — its methodology must generate predictable results in the hands of a broad array of jurists. Critics claim that changed circumstances render the original deal either an incoherent aspiration or impossible to discover in a neutral way; hence, original meaning

---

e. Sumner and his supporters generally believed that § 5 did not permit legislation that went beyond § 1, a theory ratified by the Court in *City of Boerne v. Flores* (Chapter 7, § 3C).

jurisprudence is indeterminate and does not constrain interpreters. Some key points made by the critics:

(i) *The problem of the counterfactual.* Because the Constitution and most of its amendments are old, their Framers failed to discuss or anticipate a lot of the issues in which we are interested today. For example, the debates about the Fourteenth Amendment focused on the now-forgotten §§ 2 and 3, which were of immediate concern in the context of Reconstruction but had no lasting importance. Section 1 of the amendment, which today looms larger in judicial application than any other provision of the Constitution, received only the most cursory attention. Because neither the Congress that proposed the amendment nor the states that ratified it focused on the issue of school segregation, originalists like McConnell and Maltz — the main adversaries on the *Brown* issue — must argue from other contemporary sources, which are as plentiful as they are indirect.

Most issues of constitutional interpretation are even more speculative than that in *Brown*. They are speculative because of changed circumstances. Who can tell how the Framers would have expected the Fourth Amendment to apply to wiretapping, the First Amendment to apply to television and radio, and so forth? Public education in 1868 was not as widely available as it is today, and providing even segregated education for blacks in the South was a major breakthrough. Shouldn't that affect the way we answer the *Brown* question? Unanticipated constitutional circumstances more dramatically illustrate the counterfactual nature of the originalist inquiry. The Reconstruction Congress was surprised when the Supreme Court gave a narrow construction to the Privileges and Immunities Clause in *The Slaughter House Cases* (1872), an event that made the Equal Protection Clause critical overnight. The *Brown* question then becomes: How would Framers who thought of education as a possible privilege of national citizenship conceptualize education in equal protection terms?

(ii) *Aggregation problems.* How can individual views, even if on point, be aggregated to establish "public meaning" in 1868? Note how the *Brown* debaters make all kinds of speculative leaps — from the intent of senators in 1874 to those in 1866 and from Congress in 1866 to ratifying states in 1868 (Michael McConnell), from the intent of Congress as to D.C. schools in 1862-66 to the intent of Congress on segregation in southern states in 1866 (Raoul Berger), and from the intent of Congress in passing the 1866 Civil Rights Act to the intent of Congress in proposing the Fourteenth Amendment (Alexander Bickel). No one can actually demonstrate that *two-thirds of each chamber in Congress* and *three-quarters of the states* even thought about the application of the Fourteenth Amendment to the issue of public school segregation, much less agreed that the amendment prohibited — or allowed — separate but equal segregation. Nor can anyone say with assurance what We the People thought about these topics.

These problems are just as acute, if not more so, for the original Constitution. For instance, it cannot be demonstrated that the views of the Philadelphia Convention delegates were known to the public or the state ratifying conventions, or were even accurately recorded by James Madison. The oft-cited

Federalist Papers are even worse in this regard: They represented the views of Madison and Hamilton, and were read by the New York ratifiers, but they have little determinate value for figuring out what most of the Philadelphia delegates thought about issues, what other ratifying states thought, what the New York delegates thought, or perhaps even what Madison and Hamilton thought (the two main authors had different views as to some issues; the papers were written with strategic purposes in mind).

(iii) *Level of generality problems.* A lot turns on how the level of generality at which the interpretive question is posed to the "Framers" or the "Public" as a group. Rather than asking, "How would the Framers or The Public have addressed this precise issue?" (a specific question), the interpreter might ask, "What goals were We the People pursuing in this provision, and which interpretation best meets the goals in the context of this case?" (a more general question), or even, "How did We the People expect interpreters to go about applying this provision?" (a meta-question).

Judge Bork faults *Brown* for ignoring original meaning, but recall that the Court sought and received extensive briefing on the original meaning of the Fourteenth Amendment. Having read our summary of the evidence, is Chief Justice Warren so far off base when he announced that the originalist evidence was not decisive, at least as to the specific question? One way to read *Brown* is that the Court moved to a higher level of generality and decided the case based upon the general purpose of the Equal Protection Clause. If it was unclear at the time of *Plessy* whether a separate-but-equal regime was a kind of "caste" legislation, it was pellucidly clear by 1954. And that spelled the doom for apartheid. Is this not an original meaning approach? See the next subpart.

Consider a meta-critique of original meaning as a methodology, a critique resting upon a deep tension between disciplines.[f] Professional historians, the "experts" in a true original meaning enterprise, tend to understand past events as complicated, evolving, and multifaceted. Lawyers and judges wielding original meaning tend to view the same past events as simple, perseverant, and single-focused. The former accuse the latter of engaging in "law office history," while the latter grumble that the former threaten to render our rich history a dead and unuseful exercise.

NOTE ON PRAGMATIC ARGUMENTS FOR ORIGINAL MEANING

Professor Randy Barnett is a libertarian and has long been a nonoriginalist. But he announced his conversion in *An Originalism for Nonoriginalists*, 45 Loy. L. Rev. 611 (1999). He observes that many today start with, and often end with, originalist arguments. In the Clinton impeachment proceedings of 1998, the battle for Florida's electoral votes in the 2000 election, and debates in 2002 over presidential power to invade Iraq without congressional authorization, law

---

f. William Eskridge, Jr., *Sodomy and Guns: "Tradition" in Constitutional Interpretation*, Harv. J.L. & Pol'y (2008); Martin Flaherty, *"History Lite" in Modern American Constitutionalism*, 95 Colum. L. Rev. 523 (1995); Mark Tushnet, *Interdisciplinary Legal Scholarship: The Case of History-in-Law*, 71 Chi.-Kent L. Rev. 909, 917-18 (1996).

professors, lawyers, and pundits emphasized the consistency of their views with those of the Framers. After years touting "noninterpretivism," many legal theorists have re-embraced originalist methodologies, to some extent. The pragmatic lesson of recent experience: When you want to *persuade* those who may not share your politics, argue originalism!

Barnett offers two pragmatic reasons for adopting an "original meaning" approach to constitutional interpretation. The first emphasizes that the Constitution is *written*. Though lacking the unanimous consent that contracts require, a constitution, like a contract, is put into writing to "lock in" a particular arrangement. A contracts teacher and scholar, Barnett recalls that contracts are put in writing and interpreted according to their meaning *at the time of formation* to gain certain practical advantages — reliable evidence as to terms, channeling of those who wish to modify the terms to preexisting procedures for change, and incentives for drafters to work out the details of their relationship before signing off on the document. These pragmatic virtues apply to written constitutions as well. Indeed, in *Constitutional Legitimacy*, 103 Colum. L. Rev. 111 (2003), Barnett posits the legitimacy of the Constitution along pragmatic rather than social contract lines: a constitution is legitimate, even in the absence of consent, if it provides procedural assurances that the commands it imposes on the people are likely to be both necessary and proper.

In *Restoring the Lost Constitution: The Presumption of Liberty* (2004), Barnett provides another pragmatic argument for originalism. If a constitution is supposed to be the law governing law makers, then it cannot be remade by the very parties — legislatures, courts, or executive branch officials — upon whom it is imposed. The practical benefits and protections of placing legal constraints on the government could not be obtained if those who are subject to the Constitution's restrictions, such as legislators and judges, could escape these bonds and alter its meaning on their own. For this reason, *the meaning of the Constitution must remain the same until it is properly changed* and some "outside" procedure for change must exist, such as the procedures specified in Article V.

3. *Original Purpose*

Robert H. Bork, *The Tempting of America: The Political Seduction of the Law* 81-82 (1990).[g] Following Alexander Bickel, *The Original Understanding of the Segregation Decision*, 69 Harv. L. Rev. 1 (1955), Judge Bork concedes that the Framers of the Fourteenth Amendment did not intend to invalidate state-enforced racial segregation immediately. Like Bickel, though, Bork advances an originalist theory in support of the *Brown* result:

"Let us suppose that *Plessy v. Ferguson* correctly represented the original understanding of the fourteenth amendment, that those who ratified it intended black equality, which they demonstrated by adopting the equal protection clause. But they also assumed that equality and state-compelled separation of the races were consistent, an assumption which they demonstrated by leaving in place various state laws segregating the races. Let us also suppose, along with the Court in *Plessy*, as I think we must, that the ratifiers had no objection to the psychological harm segregation inflicted. If those things are true, then it is impossible to square the *opinion* in *Brown* with the original understanding. It is, however, entirely possible to square the *result* in *Brown* with that understanding. * * *

"By 1954, when *Brown* came up for decision, it had been apparent for some time that segregation rarely if ever produced equality. Quite aside from any question of psychology, the physical facilities provided for blacks were not as good as those provided for whites. That had been demonstrated in a long series of cases. The Supreme Court was faced with a situation in which the courts would have to go on forever entertaining litigation about primary schools, secondary schools, colleges, washrooms, golf courses, swimming pools, drinking fountains, and the endless variety of facilities that were segregated, or else the separate-but-equal doctrine would have to be abandoned. Endless litigation, aside from the burden on the courts, also would never produce the equality the Constitution promised. The Court's realistic choice, therefore, was either to abandon the quest for equality by allowing segregation or to forbid segregation in order to achieve equality. There was no third choice. Either choice would violate one aspect of the original understanding, but there was no possibility of avoiding that. Since equality and segregation were mutually inconsistent, though the ratifiers did not understand that, both could not be honored. When that is seen, it is obvious that the Court must choose equality and prohibit state-imposed segregation. The purpose that brought the fourteenth amendment into being was equality before the law, and equality, not separation, was written into the text.

"Had the *Brown* opinion been written that way, its result would have clearly been rooted in the original understanding, and its legitimacy would have been enhanced for those troubled by the way in which the Court arrived at a moral result without demonstrating its mooring in the historic Constitution. There might have been an even more important benefit. The Court might not have been encouraged to embark on more adventures in policymaking, which is what it thought it had done in *Brown*, and academic constitutional lawyers might not have gone on to construct the apparently endless set of theories that not only attempt to justify *Brown* on grounds other than the original understanding but, in order to do so, advance arguments that necessarily justify departure from the historic Constitution in general. Perhaps constitutional theory would be in a far happier state today if *Brown* had been written, as it could have been, in terms of the original understanding." [Although *Brown* could have come out the same way under an originalist approach, *Bolling v. Sharpe* could not, according to Judge Bork.]

NOTE ON ORIGINAL PURPOSE AND TRANSLATING GOALS FROM ONE ERA TO THE NEXT

Bork believes that the Framers of the Fourteenth Amendment accepted state-enforced segregation generally, and school segregation specifically. Yet he ultimately argues that *Brown* was correctly decided, essentially based upon carrying out the original goal once circumstances have changed. Is this really "original meaning"? Recall that, except for the Radicals, the Framers of the Fourteenth Amendment were not committed to racial equality across the board; most of them favored equality only as to "civil rights," which they understood as not including public schooling. One problem with Bork's "originalist" argument is that he seems to abandon the Framers' understanding of equality for one based on contemporary moral criteria.

Paul Brest, *The Fundamental Rights Controversy: The Essential Contradictions of Normative Constitutional Scholarship*, 90 Yale L.J. 1063 (1981), argues that the original principle implicated in the Equal Protection Clause can be stated at several levels of generality: equality for the freed slaves; equality for African Americans generally; equality for people of all races; equality simpliciter. There is no neutral way to choose which level of generality for one's constitutional inquiry. It is also a matter of judgment and not routine for a judge to figure out how the chosen principle applies in the context of the case. Bork responds that "a judge should state the principle at the level of generality that the text and the historical evidence warrant." *Tempting of America* 149. But Bork himself seems to violate that precept, as the original evidence does not support the high level of generality Bork has chosen. How can the judge be justified in disregarding that original understanding simply because circumstances have changed? Aren't changed circumstances supposed to be handled, as Bork argues elsewhere in the book, by constitutional amendments under Article V?

Consider similarities between Bork's argument and Mark Tushnet's idea that *Brown* can be defended as the Court's *translation* of the nineteenth century's understanding of civil rights into the modern regulatory state era, when civil rights most naturally mean equal treatment in important state programs, the most important of which is public education.[h] If the Framers of the Fourteenth Amendment intended to ensure equality for all "civil rights," their idea applied in 1868 might be different from application in 1954 because cultural or political facts have changed. As a descriptive matter, public education was not routinely provided by governments in 1868 — but it was by 1954. As a normative matter,

---

h. Mark Tushnet, *Following the Rules Laid Down: A Critique of Interpretivism and Neutral Principles*, 96 Harv. L. Rev. 781, 800-01 (1983). For other deployments of the translation idea in constitutional law, see Paul Brest, *The Misconceived Quest for the Original Understanding*, 60 B.U.L. Rev. 204 (1980); Lawrence Lessig, *Fidelity in Translation*, 71 Tex. L. Rev. 1165, 1171-72 n.32 (1993) (listing scholars who deploy the translation metaphor); *id.* at 1242-47 (applying translation theory to *Brown*). Although translation has an originalist component, most originalists consider translation too dynamic to qualify as a good theory of original meaning. E.g., Steven Calabresi, *The Tradition of the Written Constitution: A Comment on Professor Lessig's Theory of Translation*, 65 Fordham L. Rev. 1435 (1997).

public education was not considered central to citizenship in 1868 — but it was by 1954. Can an originalist theory swallow Tushnet's translation idea without creating a "Living Constitution"?[i] If not, should an honest originalist reject Judge Bork's own dynamic interpretation defending the result in *Brown?*

B. LEGAL PROCESS THEORIES OF JUDICIAL REVIEW

"Legal process" theory views the rule of law from an *institutionalist* and *procedural* perspective.[j] That is, the rule of law is not just a law of rules, but is rather an institutional and procedural structure by which recognizable legal rules are made and changed in an orderly way, with each institution contributing to the project in ways that reflect its comparative competence. Under our Constitution, the overall structure is easy to understand in principle, but complicated in operation. Law's legitimacy owes as much to the process by which it is enacted as its formal pedigree. Hence, statutes are legitimate not only because they have formally met the Article I, § 7 requirements, but also because they have been adopted in an open and deliberative way by representatives elected by the people and accountable to them. The legitimacy of judicial decisions overturning such laws is trickier and must be considered in light of the proper institutional role that courts play in our constitutional system. That proper role depends, in turn, on (1) judges' special *institutional competence*, the things that the judiciary as an institution does really well; (2) the institutional limitations that justified Hamilton's referring to the judiciary as the "least dangerous branch"; and (3) the judiciary's *comparative* competence and limitation — the same issues viewed against the strengths and limitations of the legislative and executive branches. Consider some legal process theories of judicial review.

1. *Neutral Principles and Representation-Reinforcement Theory*

Legal process thinkers like Felix Frankfurter, Henry Hart, Albert Sacks, and Lon Fuller understood adjudication as the "reasoned elaboration" of principles and policies as applied to particular cases. Seizing upon this idea, Herbert Wechsler, *Toward Neutral Principles of Constitutional Law*, 73 Harv. L. Rev. 1 (1959), maintained that, in constitutional adjudication, the Court has a responsibility to issue decisions that are "genuinely principled, resting with respect to every step that is involved in reaching judgment on analysis and reasons quite transcending the immediate result that is achieved. * * * A principled decision * * * is one that rests on reasons with respect to all the

---

i. Charles Reich, *Mr. Justice Black and the Living Constitution*, 76 Harv. L. Rev. 673, 733 (1963), describes Justice Black's philosophy: "He asks what a given provision of the Bill of Rights was designed to accomplish — what evils it was intended to prevent. Then he seeks to give the provision a meaning which will, in a contemporary setting, accomplish the same general purposes and prevent the same kinds of evils." This is much like Judge Bork's justification for *Brown*.

j. For an introduction to this school of thought, see William Eskridge, Jr. & Philip Frickey, *An Historical and Critical Introduction to* The Legal Process, in Henry Hart, Jr. & Albert Sacks, *The Legal Process: Basic Problems in the Making and Application of Law* li–cxxxix (Eskridge & Frickey eds. 1994) (1958 tent. ed.).

issues in the case, reasons that in their generality and their neutrality transcend any immediate result that is involved."

Wechsler criticized *Brown* as unprincipled. "[*Brown*] must have rested on the view that racial segregation is, in principle, a denial of equality to the minority against whom it is directed * * * . In the context of a charge that segregation *with equal facilities* is a denial of equality, is there not a point in *Plessy* in the statement that if 'enforced separation stamps the colored race with a badge of inferiority' it is solely because its members choose 'to put that construction upon it?' Does enforced separation of the sexes discriminate against females merely because it may be the females who resent it and it is imposed by judgments predominantly male? Is a prohibition of miscegenation a discrimination against the [minority] member of the couple who would like to marry?

"For me, assuming equal facilities, the question posed by state-enforced segregation is not one of discrimination at all. Its human and its constitutional dimensions lie entirely elsewhere, in the denial by the state of freedom to associate, a denial that impinges in the same way on any groups or races that may be involved. * * * But if freedom of association is denied by segregation, integration forces an association upon those for whom it is unpleasant or repugnant. * * * Given a situation where the state must practically choose between denying the association to those individuals who wish it or imposing it on those who would avoid it, is there any basis in neutral principles for holding that the Constitution demands that the claims for association should prevail? I should like to think there is, but I confess that I have not yet written the opinion. To write it is for me the challenge of the school-segregation cases."

Wechsler's article triggered sharp attacks because of his perceived insensitivity to the appeal of *Brown* and to the injustice of segregation,[k] but his article was also a challenge to legal scholars to justify *Brown* along lines of traditional, consent-based theories of democracy: Even if *Brown* could not be defended by reference to the Framers' original intent, the Court could still be loyal to consent-based theory by grounding its result upon constitutional principles. Scholars struggled to come up with a principled defense of *Brown*. Arguably, the most successful effort was the "representation reinforcing" approach to judicial review developed by Professor John Hart Ely. He argued that certain provisions of the Constitution, including the Equal Protection Clause, are too elastic to constrain the Supreme Court — indeed, are so "open-textured" as to invite dynamic interpretation over time. To provide meaning to these clauses, Ely argued that judges should supply answers "derived from the general themes of the entire constitutional document and not from some source entirely beyond its four corners." In Ely's view, those themes are best captured by footnote four of *Carolene Products* (quoted in Chapter 1, § 6).

---

k. See Charles Black, *The Lawfulness of the Segregation Decisions*, 69 Yale L.J. 421 (1960); Louis Pollak, *Racial Discrimination and Judicial Integrity: A Reply to Professor Wechsler*, 108 U. Pa. L. Rev. 1 (1959). See generally Gary Peller, *Neutral Principles in the 1950's*, 21 U. Mich. J.L. Reform 561 (1989).

John Hart Ely
Democracy and Distrust: A Theory of Judicial Review
88-103 (1980)[1]

[Ely starts with the observation that the complaints giving rise to the American Revolution emphasized "participational themes * * * that (1) their input into the process by which they were governed was insufficient, and that (partly as a consequence) (2) they were being denied what others were receiving." Continuing those same themes, the original Constitution] is devoted almost entirely to structure, explaining who among the various actors — federal government, state government, Congress, executive, judiciary — has authority to do what, and going on to fill in a good bit of detail about how these persons are to be selected and to conduct their business. Even provisions that at first glance might seem primarily designed to assure or preclude certain substantive results seem on reflection to be principally concerned with process. Thus, for example, the provision that treason "shall consist only in levying War against [the United States], or in adhering to their Enemies, giving them Aid and Comfort," appears at least in substantial measure to have been a precursor of the First Amendment, reacting to the recognition that persons in power can disable their detractors by charging disagreement as treason. The prohibitions against granting titles of nobility seem rather plainly to have been designed to buttress the democratic ideal that all are equals in government. The Ex Post Facto and Bill of Attainder Clauses prove on analysis to be separation of powers provisions, enjoining the legislature to act prospectively and by general rule (just as the judiciary is implicitly enjoined by Article III to act retrospectively and by specific decree). And * * * the Privileges and Immunities Clause of Article IV, and at least in one aspect — the other being a grant of congressional power — the Commerce Clause as well, function as equality provisions, guaranteeing virtual representation to the politically powerless. * * *

* * * [M]y claim is only that the original Constitution was principally, indeed I would say overwhelmingly, dedicated to concerns of process and structure and not to the identification and preservation of specific substantive values. Any claim that it was exclusively so conceived would be ridiculous (as would any comparable claim about any comparably complicated human undertaking). And indeed there are other provisions in the original document that seem almost entirely value-oriented, though my point, of course, is that they are few and far between. Thus "corruption of blood" is forbidden as a punishment for treason. Punishing people for their parents' transgressions is outlawed as a substantively unfair outcome: it just can't be done, irrespective of procedures and also irrespective of whether it is done to the children of all offenders. The federal government, along with the states, is precluded from taxing articles exported from any state. Here too an outcome is simply precluded; what might be styled a value, the economic value of free trade among the states, is protected. This short list, however, covers just about all the values protected in the original Constitution — save one. And a big one it was. Although an understandable

---

squeamishness kept the word out of the document, *slavery* must be counted a substantive value to which the original Constitution meant to extend unusual protection from the ordinary legislative process, at least temporarily. Prior to 1808, Congress was forbidden to prohibit the slave trade into any state that wanted it, and the states were obliged to return escaping slaves to their "homes."

The idea of a bill of rights was not even brought up until close to the end of the Constitutional Convention, at which time it was rejected. The reason is not that the framers were unconcerned with liberty, but rather that by their lights a bill of rights did not belong in a constitution, at least not in the one they had drafted. As Hamilton explained in *Federalist* 84, * * * "The additional securities to republican government, to liberty, and to property, to be derived from the adoption of the plan under consideration, consist chiefly in the restraints which the preservation of the Union will impose on local factions . . . in the express guarantee of a republican form of government to each [state]; in the absolute and universal exclusion of titles of nobility . . ."

Of course a number of the state ratifying conventions remained apprehensive, and a bill of rights did emerge. Here too, however, the data are unruly. The expression-related provisions of the First Amendment * * * were centrally intended to help make our governmental processes work, to ensure the open and informed discussion of political issues, and to check our government when it gets out of bounds. We can attribute other functions to freedom of expression, and some of them must have played a role, but the exercise has the smell of the lamp about it: the view that free expression per se, without regard to what it means to the process of government, is our pre-eminent right has a highly elitist cast. [Moreover,] the linking of the politically oriented protections of speech, press, assembly, and petition is highly informative.

The First Amendment's religious clauses — "Congress shall make no law respecting an establishment of religion, or prohibiting the free exercise thereof" — are a different matter. Obviously part of the point of combining these cross-cutting commands was to make sure the church and the government gave each other breathing space: the provision thus performs a structural or separation of powers function. But we must not infer that because one account fits the data it must be the only appropriate account, and here the obvious cannot be blinked: part of the explanation of the Free Exercise Clause has to be that for the framers religion was an important substantive value they wanted to put significantly beyond the reach of at least the federal legislature.

[The Second Amendment (right to bear arms) and the Third Amendment (no quartering of troops) may sound like substantive amendments in part, but have been construed very narrowly. The Fifth through Eighth Amendments tend to be most relevant during lawsuits, and so we think of them as procedural, for the most part. For each amendment, Ely notes an arguable substantive feature, such as the Fifth Amendment's anti-self-incrimination privilege and the Fourth Amendment's privacy protection, but maintains that the primary role of each amendment is procedural, to assure fair trials.]

With one important exception, the Reconstruction Amendments do not designate substantive values for protection from the political process. The

Fourteenth Amendment's Due Process Clause, we have seen, is concerned with process writ small, the processes by which regulations are enforced against individuals. Its Privileges or Immunities Clause is quite inscrutable, indicating only that there should exist some set of constitutional entitlements not explicitly enumerated in the document: it is one of the provisions for which we are seeking guides to construction. The Equal Protection Clause is also unforthcoming with details, though it at least gives us a clue: by its explicit concern with equality among the persons within a state's jurisdiction it constitutes the document's clearest, though not sole, recognition that technical access to the process may not always be sufficient to guarantee good-faith representation of all those putatively represented. The Fifteenth Amendment, forbidding abridgment of the right to vote on account of race, opens the process to persons who had previously been excluded and thus by another strategy seeks to enforce the representative's duty of equal concern and respect. The exception, of course, involves a value I have mentioned before, slavery. The Thirteenth Amendment can be forced into a "process" mold — slaves don't participate effectively in the political process — and it surely significantly reflects a concern with equality as well. Just as surely, however, it embodies a substantive judgment that human slavery is simply not morally tolerable. Thus at no point has the Constitution been neutral on this subject. Slavery was one of the few values the original document singled out for protection from the political branches; *non*slavery is one of the few values it singles out for protection now.

What has happened to the Constitution in the second century of our nationhood, though ground less frequently plowed, is most instructive on the subject of what jobs we have learned our basic document is suited to. There were no amendments between 1870 and 1913, but there have been eleven since. Five of them have extended the franchise: the Seventeenth extends to all of us the right to vote for our Senators directly, the Twenty-Fourth abolishes the poll tax as a condition of voting in federal elections, the Nineteenth extends the vote to women, the Twenty-Third to residents of the District of Columbia, and the Twenty-Sixth to eighteen-year-olds. Extension of the franchise to groups previously excluded has therefore been the dominant theme of our constitutional development since the Fourteenth Amendment, and it pursues both of the broad constitutional themes we have observed from the beginning: the achievement of a political process open to all on an equal basis and a consequent enforcement of the representative's duty of equal concern and respect to minorities and majorities alike. Three other amendments — the Twentieth, Twenty-Second, and Twenty-Fifth — involve Presidential eligibility and succession. The Sixteenth, permitting a federal income tax, adds another power to the list of those that had previously been assigned to the central government. That's it, save two, and indeed one of those two did place a substantive value beyond the reach of the political process. The amendment was the Eighteenth, and the value shielded was temperance. It was, of course, repealed fourteen years later by the Twenty-First Amendment, precisely, I suggest, because such attempts to freeze substantive values do not belong in a constitution. In 1919 temperance obviously seemed like a fundamental value; in 1933 it obviously did not.

What has happened to the Constitution's other value-enshrining provisions is similar, and similarly instructive. Some surely have survived, but typically because they are so obscure that they don't become issues (corruption of blood, quartering of troops) or so interlaced with procedural concerns they seem appropriate in a constitution (self-incrimination, double jeopardy). Those sufficiently conspicuous and precise to be controvertible have not survived. The most dramatic examples, of course, were slavery and prohibition. Both were removed by repeal, in one case a repeal requiring unprecedented carnage. Two other substantive values that at least arguably were placed beyond the reach of the political process by the Constitution have been "repealed" by judicial construction — the right of individuals to bear arms, and freedom to set contract terms without significant state regulation. Maybe in fact our forebears did not intend very seriously to protect those values, but the fact that the Court, in the face of what must be counted at least plausible contrary arguments, so readily read these values out of the Constitution is itself instructive of American expectations of a constitution. Finally, there is the value of religion, still protected by the Free Exercise Clause. Something different has happened here. In recent years that clause has functioned primarily to protect what must be counted as discrete and insular minorities, such as the Amish, Seventh Day Adventists, and Jehovah's Witnesses. Whatever the original conception of the Free Exercise Clause, its function during essentially all of its effective life has been one akin to the Equal Protection Clause and thus entirely appropriate to a constitution.

Don't get me wrong: our Constitution has always been substantially concerned with preserving liberty. If it weren't, it would hardly be worth fighting for. The question that is relevant to our inquiry here, however, is how that concern has been pursued. The principal answers to that, we have seen, are by a quite extensive set of procedural protections, and by a still more elaborate scheme designed to ensure that in the making of substantive choices the decision process will be open to all on something approaching an equal basis, with the decision-makers held to a duty to take into account the interests of all those their decisions affect. (Most often the document has proceeded on the assumption that assuring access is the best way of assuring that someone's interests will be considered, and so in fact it usually is. Other provisions, however — centrally but not exclusively the Equal Protection Clause — reflect a realization that access will not always be sufficient.) The general strategy has therefore not been to root in the document a set of substantive rights entitled to permanent protection. The Constitution has instead proceeded from the quite sensible assumption that an effective majority will not inordinately threaten its own rights, and has sought to assure that such a majority not systematically treat others less well than it treats itself — by structuring decision processes at all levels to try to ensure, first, that everyone's interests will be actually or virtually represented (usually both) at the point of substantive decision, and second, that the processes of individual application will not be manipulated so as to reintroduce in practice the sort of discrimination that is impermissible in theory. We have noted a few provisions that do not comfortably conform to this pattern. But they're an odd assortment, the understandable products of particular historical circumstances — guns, religion, contract, and so on — and in any event they are few and far between. To represent them as a dominant theme of our constitutional document one would have to concentrate quite single-mindedly on hopping from stone to stone and averting one's eyes from the mainstream.

The American Constitution has thus by and large remained a constitution properly so called, concerned with constitutive questions. What has distinguished it, and indeed the United States itself, has been a process of government, not a governing ideology. Justice Linde has written: "As a charter of government a constitution must prescribe legitimate processes, not legitimate outcomes, if like ours (and unlike more ideological documents elsewhere) it is to serve many generations through changing times."

As I have tried to be scrupulous about indicating, the argument from the general contours of the Constitution is necessarily a qualified one. In fact the documentary dictation of particular substantive outcomes has been rare (and generally unsuccessful), but our Constitution is too complex a document to lie still for *any* pat characterization. Beyond that, the premise of the argument, that aids to construing the more open-ended provisions are appropriately found in the nature of the surrounding document, though it is a premise that seems to find acceptance on all sides, is not one with which it is impossible to disagree. Thus the two arguments that follow, each overtly normative, are if anything more important than the one I have just reviewed. The first is entirely obvious by now, that unlike an approach geared to the judicial imposition of "fundamental values," the representation-reinforcing orientation whose contours I have sketched and will develop further is not inconsistent with, but on the contrary is entirely supportive of, the American system of representative democracy. It recognizes the unacceptability of the claim that appointed and life-tenured judges are better reflectors of conventional values than elected representatives, devoting itself instead to policing the mechanism by which the system seeks to ensure that our elected representatives will actually represent. There may be an illusion of circularity here: my approach is more consistent with representative democracy because that's the way it was planned. But of course it isn't any more circular than setting out to build an airplane and ending up with something that flies.

The final point worth serious mention is that (again unlike a fundamental-values approach) a representation-reinforcing approach assigns judges a role they are conspicuously well situated to fill. My reference here is not principally to expertise. Lawyers *are* experts on process writ small, the processes by which facts are found and contending parties are allowed to present their claims. And to a degree they are experts on process writ larger, the processes by which issues of public policy are fairly determined: lawyers do seem genuinely to have a feel, indeed it is hard to see what other special value they have, for ways of insuring that everyone gets his or her fair say. But too much shouldn't be made of this. Others, particularly the fulltime participants, can also claim expertise on how the political process allocates voice and power. And of course many legislators are lawyers themselves. So the point isn't so much one of expertise as it is one of perspective.

The approach to constitutional adjudication recommended here is akin to what might be called an "antitrust" as opposed to a "regulatory" orientation to economic affairs — rather than dictate substantive results it intervenes only when the "market," in our case the political market, is systemically malfunctioning. (A referee analogy is also not far off: the referee is to intervene only when one team is gaining unfair advantage, not because the "wrong" team has scored.) Our government cannot fairly be said to be "malfunctioning" simply because it sometimes generates outcomes with which we disagree, however strongly (and claims that it is reaching results with which "the people" really disagree — or would "if they understood" — are likely to be little more than self-deluding projections). In a representative democracy value determinations are to be made by our elected representatives, and if in fact most of us disapprove we can vote them out of office. Malfunction occurs when the process is undeserving of trust, when (1) the ins are choking off the channels of political change to ensure that they will stay in and the outs will stay out, or (2) though no one is actually denied a voice or a vote, representatives beholden to an effective majority are systematically disadvantaging some minority out of simple hostility or a prejudiced refusal to recognize commonalities of interest, and thereby denying that minority the protection afforded other groups by a representative system.

Obviously our elected representatives are the last persons we should trust with identification of either of these situations. Appointed judges, however, are comparative outsiders in our governmental system, and need worry about continuance in office only very obliquely. This does not give them some special pipeline to the genuine values of the American people: in fact it goes far to ensure that they won't have one. It does, however, put them in a position objectively to assess claims — though no one could suppose the evaluation won't be full of judgment calls — that either by clogging the channels of change or by acting as accessories to majority tyranny, our elected representatives in fact are not representing the interests of those whom the system presupposes they are.

NOTES ON REPRESENTATION REINFORCEMENT
AND PUBLIC CHOICE THEORY

Ely's theory, if robust, solves the *Brown* problem: Apartheid is questionable because it flunks both of Ely's representation-reinforcing concerns — the "ins" were disadvantaging a discrete and insular minority out of prejudice and were blocking channels of change or liberation. Moreover, Ely solves the *Brown* puzzle in a way that is faithful to the principles of the Constitution and that limits the amount of spillover judicial activism (it would not lead to another *Lochner* era), Wechsler's two concerns. Or does it?[m]

1. *The Substance-Procedure Problem.* Is Ely right in characterizing the Constitution as essentially a proceduralist document? Many of the provisions

---

m. Critiques of Ely's theory include Laurence Tribe, *The Puzzling Persistence of Process-Based Constitutional Theories,* 89 Yale L.J. 1063 (1980); Mark Tushnet, *Darkness on the Edge of the Town: The Contributions of John Hart Ely to Constitutional Theory,* 89 Yale L.J. 1037 (1980); Archibald Cox, Book Review, 94 Harv. L. Rev. 700 (1981).

that might be viewed that way can also be viewed as protecting important substantive rights. For example, the First Amendment's protection of free speech does contribute to lively public debate and criticism, but it also protects personal rights of individuals. Is it not odd to think that we fought a bloody Revolution and a bloody Civil War to obtain nothing but procedure? Are there no rights so fundamental that courts should not protect them? How about a right to personal privacy, which seems implicated in the First, Fourth, and Fifth Amendments? If a majority of blacks voted for educational segregation, would that be constitutional under Ely's analysis?

Even if the Constitution is largely procedural, applying it Ely's way might involve more substantive judgment than Ely suggests. Key to his theory is the *Carolene* judicial role of protecting "discrete and insular minorities" against the operation of "prejudice" in the political system. In 1954, southerners and many northerners believed that segregation rested on practical grounds, and not "prejudice." Today, Americans are evenly divided on whether lesbians and gay men should be treated equally. "Prejudice"? Or "Traditional Family Values"?[n]

2. *The Indeterminacy Problem. Brown* is not as easy a case for representation-reinforcement review as might first appear. While blacks were formally excluded from the political process in the South, they were not in Kansas, where *Brown* arose. Indeed, Topeka itself was abandoning de jure segregation through the democratic process in 1954-55. How, then, does Ely's theory support *Brown*? The easiest way would be to show that even though blacks were not formally excluded from the political process in Topeka, they were marginalized politically and were the objects of stereotype and prejudice. Indeed, there was substantial evidence at trial that segregation itself contributed to this marginalization and reified it in the hearts of its intended victims. The difficulty with this type of argument is that once Ely's thesis encompasses functional problems with our democracy, judicial review becomes potentially broad. Poor people are systematically marginalized from local political systems today just as blacks were in Topeka in 1951. Should judicial review tackle the many economic decisions made by the government that hurt the poor, or fail to help them?

While the genius of Ely's theory is that it appears to tie much of the Warren Court's constitutional activism to a primary constitutional policy, it may tend toward judicial activism once one starts evaluating the system of representation functionally. If one abandons functional analysis and only looks at the formal system of representation, then Ely's theory tends toward little judicial review at all, enhancing the danger of legislative tyranny.

3. *The Public Choice Problem.* An appeal of Ely's theory is its focus on protecting discrete and insular minorities, because they will find it hard to protect themselves in the political process. This thesis may be undermined by "public choice theory," the application of economic insights to political

---

n. Daniel Ortiz, *Pursuing a Perfect Politics: The Allure and Failure of Process Theory*, 77 Va. L. Rev. 721 (1991).

behavior.[o] According to public choice, legislation is the result of a political market, with demand and supply features. Interest groups demand legislation, and legislators supply it. Hence, the ability of an identifiable group to secure advantages in the political process depends upon the group's ability to mobilize, to organize its members into an interest group that becomes a political player (lobbying, campaign contributions, political action committees). This, in turn, depends upon the ability of the group to overcome the "free rider problem." Political advantages available to a group are usually available to every member of the group, whether or not she contributed to its procurement (it is a "public good"). As a result, individual members of the group have incentives not to contribute to the formation of the public good, and instead to "free ride" on the efforts of others. The problem is that if everyone, or most people, take this attitude, not much of the public good will be provided.

Given the plethora of interest groups in our society, the free rider problem can often be overcome. Some groups, such as farmers and labor unions, have pre-existing economic organizations that can be turned to political purposes, with a coercive mechanism for getting contributions from its members (e.g., union dues). Absent such historical or organizational features, however, it is hard for large, diffuse groups of people to overcome the free rider problem, because it is impossible to monitor free riders. The smaller the group (e.g., three big auto manufacturers rather than 40 million car buyers) the more likely it is to organize effectively, because the small group can monitor free riders (often by excluding them from the public good) and form a consensus without undue transactions costs. The more a group feels a unique sense of identity (its members see themselves primarily as members of that one group and less as members of other groups and society), the more likely it is to organize, because the impulse to free ride is overridden by the community feeling.

The paradox suggested by public choice theory is that "discrete and insular minorities" are precisely those groups that ought to organize and protect themselves in the political process. [Ackerman 722-31]. While some discrete and insular minorities may be the objects of special prejudice, once the formal barriers to their political participation are removed, they tend systematically to become active in the political process. Having been the object of prejudice actually helps break down the free rider problem, and often they will bloc vote to maximize their power. If public choice theory is right about this, then Ely's theory is less progressive than it might otherwise seem. *Brown* is right, insofar as it broke down formal barriers to political participation, but perhaps there is not much of a "representation-reinforcement" reason to remain concerned about

---

o. See Bruce Ackerman, *Beyond* Carolene Products, 98 Harv. L. Rev. 713 (1985). See generally William Eskridge, Jr., Philip Frickey & Elizabeth Garrett, *Cases and Materials on Legislation: Statutes and the Creation of Public Policy* 47-73 (3d ed. 2001); Daniel Farber & Philip Frickey, *Law and Public Choice: A Critical Introduction* (1991); Einer Elhauge, *Does Interest Group Theory Justify More Intrusive Judicial Review?*, 101 Yale L.J. 31 (1991).

such issues in the new millennium.[p] If things such as a resurgence of prejudice and the continuing effects of slavery and apartheid trouble you, representation-reinforcement theory may not help you attack them.

On the other hand, Ely's theory could be more radical than he suspected. Among groups excluded from the political process are those that tend to be "discrete and anonymous," such as gay men and lesbians; "diffuse and noninsular," such as women; and "diffuse and anonymous," such as the poor. It is harder for these groups to organize politically. Large diffuse groups (such as women and the poor) are particularly subject to the free rider problem, especially to the extent that they do not have monetary resources. Anonymous groups (such as gay people) are also subject to the free rider problem because many people are physically and professionally afraid to "come out," and societal prejudice against such groups may undermine their effectiveness even when they are organized. If we take seriously Ely's point that judicial review might correct for inequities in the political system, we should protect the interests of those against whom the political process reflects systematic "prejudice," emphasized in *Carolene*. [Ackerman 731-40.] Yet one person's "prejudice" against gay people is another person's moral "principle." Ultimately, therefore, a representation-reinforcing theory might have to make substantive determinations of value that Ely says are not properly part of the Constitution.

PROBLEM 2-2
REPRESENTATION-REINFORCING JUDICIAL REVIEW

How would Professor Ely's theory suggest that the Supreme Court resolve the following constitutional challenges?

(A) Remedial Race-Based Criteria. Jefferson County, Kentucky maintained a de jure segregated public school system which was adjudged unconstitutional in 1973. Although the federal court gave up *Swann* remedial jurisdiction in 2000, the School Board in 2001 adopted a voluntary program seeking to maintain racial balance in as many schools as possible; both black and white representatives supported the plan. Decisions to assign students to schools are based on available space within the schools and the racial guidelines in the District's current student assignment plan. If a school has reached the "extremes of the racial guidelines" (15% minimum black enrollment, 50% maximum), a student whose race would contribute to the school's racial imbalance will not be assigned there. After assignment, students at all grade levels are permitted to apply to transfer between non-magnet schools in the district. Constitutional? See *Parents Involved v. Seattle School District No. 1*, 127 S.Ct. 2738 (2007) (excerpted and discussed in Chapter 3, § 3D).

(B) Challenging the Bilingual Juror. Prosecutors in criminal cases can strike jurors from the venire without providing reasons, but if it appears that

---

p. For an argument that the predictions of public choice do not accurately reflect African-American political power, see Daniel Farber & Philip Frickey, *Is* Carolene Products *Dead? Reflections on Affirmative Action and the Dynamics of Civil Rights Legislation*, 79 Cal. L. Rev. 685 (1991).

prosecutorial strikes are race-based, the prosecutor must provide a race-neutral explanation. If the judge finds the explanation unpersuasive, the entire jury selection process must start over; an appellate court will overturn the conviction of a defendant whose jury is tainted with race discrimination in this way. See *Batson v. Kentucky*, 476 U.S. 79 (1986); *Snyder v. Louisiana*, 128 S.Ct. 1203 (2008). Dionisio Hernandez challenges his conviction of attempted murder and possession of a weapon along precisely these lines. The prosecutor in his case struck several Latino jurors; upon defense objection, the prosecutor explained that it was because much testimony in the trial would be in Spanish, with an official translator for the jury. "I felt there was a great deal of uncertainty as to whether they could accept the interpreter as the final arbiter of what was said by each of the witnesses." The judge allowed the strikes on the ground that the explanation was race-neutral. Should the *Batson* doctrine be applied to invalidate this conviction? See *Hernandez v. New York*, 500 U.S. 352 (1991) (Chapter 4, § 3B); Juan Perea, *Buscando América: Why Integration and Equal Protection Fail to Protect Latinos*, 117 Harv. L. Rev. 1420 (2004).

(C) Cost-Exporting Laws. A New Jersey law prohibits the importation of most "solid or liquid waste which originated or was collected outside the territorial limits of the State." The Legislature found that the state was becoming a "dumping ground" for New York and Philadelphia waste, an intolerable situation. Environmentalists urged that caps be placed on in-state waste as well, but state Senator Frankly Unctuous responded: "We want to protect the environment—but not at the expense of our own citizens!" The bill passed unanimously in both chambers of the Legislature. Assume that the Commerce Clause (art. I, § 8, cl. 3) has a negative feature, barring state "interference" with interstate commerce in some circumstances. Is this a good case for application of a Negative Commerce Clause, from an Elysian perspective? See *City of Philadelphia v. New Jersey,* 437 U.S. 617 (1978) (Chapter 7, § 6B1); Mark Tushnet, *Rethinking the Dormant Commerce Clause*, 1979 Wis. L. Rev. 125.

2. *Institutional Competence and Theories of Judicial Restraint*

Some kinds of actions should be taken only by entities with special democratic legitimacy, and courts might police the "structures through which policies are both formed and applied."[q] The idea is that major policy decisions in a representative democracy should be made by elected officials and not by administrators or perhaps even more local representatives. For example, the Court has invalidated agency decisions that reflect major policy choices more legitimately made by the President or Congress, *Hampton v. Mow Sun Wong,* 426 U.S. 88 (1976) (invalidating Civil Service bar to federal employment by noncitizens but inviting President or Congress to act); presidential or executive department decisions raising constitutional problems that should be addressed by Congress, e.g., *Kent v. Dulles*, 357 U.S. 116 (1958) (Secretary of State cannot deny passport because of political beliefs without more specific congressional authorization); or local decisions that are better made at the state or national

---

q. Laurence Tribe, *Structural Due Process*, 10 Harv. C.R.-C.L. L. Rev. 269 (1975).

level, e.g., *Regents of the Univ. of Calif. v. Bakke*, 438 U.S. 265 (1978) (opinion of Powell, J.) (Board of Regents is not best institution to adopt racial quotas for university; statewide elected officials would be more legitimate decisionmakers).

Under most legal process theories of judicial review, a key role for the Court is to enforce constitutional rules of jurisdiction. Former Oregon Supreme Court Justice Hans Linde argues that "the central function of judicial review" is "to guarantee the democratic legitimacy of political decisions by establishing essential rules of the political process."[r] This has been a neglected source of review at the federal level until recently, as the Rehnquist Court has revived interest in enforcing the rules of federalism (Chapter 7). The most sweeping judicial activism of the last generation may have been the Court's decision invalidating hundreds of legislative vetoes, as inconsistent with the bicameralism and presentment requirements of Article I, § 7, *Immigration & Naturalization Service v. Chadha*, 462 U.S. 919 (1982) (Chapter 8, § 2A). State constitutions tend to have more procedural requirements for lawmaking than the U.S. Constitution does, and some state supreme courts vigorously enforce those requirements. See, e.g., *Department of Educ. v. Lewis*, 416 So. 2d 455 (Fla. 1982) (enforcing state single-subject rule to invalidate substantive rider in appropriations bill).

Finally, and most generally, the Court might encourage the deliberative, republican government instinct in the Constitution and expressly contemplated by some of its Framers, see *Federalist* No. 10 (App. 2). Thus, the Court might follow Thayer's "give the legislature the benefit of the doubt" approach to statutes that reflect a reasoned, factually based, openly debated policy choice, and a more scrutinizing approach to undeliberated choices. Compare *Romer v. Evans*, 517 U.S. 620 (1996) (Chapter 4, § 3D) (invalidating state initiative targeting gay people based upon open appeal to prejudice), with *Bowers v. Hardwick*, 478 U.S. 186 (1986) (Chapter 5, § 4C) (upholding state sodomy law reflecting longstanding, deliberate state policy).

Alexander Bickel, *The Least Dangerous Branch: The Supreme Court at the Bar of Politics* (1962). Like Ely's theory, the foregoing discussion has suggested process-based justifications for active judicial review, situations where the Supreme Court should intervene in the political process and reverse the burden of inertia (i.e., require a political response, considering the judicial input). A different kind of legal process theory is that developed by Professor Bickel's book, which famously discussed the Court's "passive virtues," its "techniques of 'not doing,' devices for disposing of a case while avoiding judgment on the constitutional issue it raises." In some cases, the Supreme Court has a constitutional obligation to avoid decision. The Case or Controversy requirement of Article III disables the Court from adjudicating cases where the plaintiff lacks standing to sue, the case is moot, or the issue is not ripe or is reserved for the political processes by the Constitution (Chapter 9, § 2).

---

r. Hans Linde, *Due Process of Lawmaking*, 55 Neb. L. Rev. 197, 251 (1976).

Bickel maintained that there are instances where the Court is authorized to adjudicate a constitutional question, but should choose not to decide it. The Court has many procedural devices at its disposal that allow it to avoid exercising its *Marbury* power: (1) declining to hear a case altogether, by denying review or certiorari and leaving the lower court decision in place; (2) dismissing an appeal or petition on grounds of "prudential" ripeness, standing, mootness, or political question even though the dispute satisfies the Case or Controversy requirements of Article III; or (3) deciding the case on narrow grounds, usually as a matter of statutory interpretation that avoids the constitutional question. Declining to decide a constitutional issue properly presented to the Court is a "passive virtue," deployed as a matter of wise judging or even constitutional politics, rather than as a matter of constitutional principle. The passive virtues are most needed in cases where the Court is not prepared to invalidate legislation, but the effect of upholding the legislation would be to legitimate it in ways that would be lamentable. Instead, the Court stays its hand, allowing the political process to continue to work on the problem, and perhaps develop the factual contours of it.

The *Brown* line of cases illustrates Bickel's theory. Before 1954, the Supreme Court repeatedly ducked the question whether it should overrule *Plessy*, as the Justices invalidated segregated education under the criteria of the earlier decision, while accumulating evidence that separate was never equal. In the course of the *Brown* litigation, the Court asked for further briefing (on an issue that ultimately made no difference to any Justice) because the Justices needed more time to resolve their personal and collective uncertainties. Bickel also defended the Court's judgment in *Naim v. Naim*, 350 U.S. 985 (1956), where it dismissed an appeal from the Virginia Supreme Court, which had upheld the state's law criminalizing different-race marriages. The state law was explicitly premised upon the policy of "White Supremacy" and was probably inconsistent with whatever principle animated *Brown*. Yet the Court ducked the issue on a trumped-up technicality, because it feared, with justification, that invalidating different-race marriage bans would embroil the Court in too much controversy and would undermine the needed political support for *Brown* (Bickel, *Least Dangerous Branch* 174). The Court invalidated the law in *Loving v. Virginia*, 388 U.S. 1 (1967), after the political climate lent more support to its action, and after almost all states outside the South had repealed their miscegenation statutes.

NOTE ON THE PASSIVE VIRTUES AND OTHER THEORIES OF JUDICIAL RESTRAINT

Gerald Gunther, *The Subtle Vices of the "Passive Virtues" — A Comment on Principle and Expediency in Judicial Review*, 64 Colum. L. Rev. 1 (1964), objected that Bickel's theory was neither passive nor virtuous. It was not passive, as it required judges actively to manipulate existing procedural doctrines, often in pursuit of a long-term goal of invalidating laws enjoying popular support. It was not virtuous, as it required judges to lie. Bickel might have responded that some strategic behavior is needed to assure the efficacy of our constitutional rule of law: Constitutional rules will not "stick" if the political culture revolts against them;[s] applying bad constitutional rules to avoid the backlash is even worse; the "least bad" option is to follow one of the avoidance strategies. Although he died a generation ago, Professor Bickel's theory of cautious constitutionalism has inspired a new generation of legal academics.

In the spirit of Bickel, we have suggested that the Court will be passive in enforcing constitutional values when there is a political consensus to the contrary, will be cautious and incremental once political consensus dissolves or is in flux, and will be bold only when it can implement its constitutional understanding with the support of the political culture. See William Eskridge, Jr. & Philip Frickey, *The Supreme Court, 1993 Term — Foreword: Law as Equilibrium*, 108 Harv. L. Rev. 26 (1994). Thus, the post-Reconstruction Court abdicated any responsibility for enforcing the Equal Protection Clause against apartheid (*Plessy*), but once African Americans and their allies made the national political culture nervous about apartheid the Court had room to enforce equality guarantees at important margins (*Buchanan, Herndon, Gaines*). When the Truman and Eisenhower Administrations signaled their strong support for overruling *Plessy*, the Court was emboldened to act decisively to denounce apartheid (*Brown I*) — but not to demand immediate desegregation (*Brown II*, following the remedial moderation suggested in the Eisenhower Administration's *amicus* brief). It was not until the 1960s, when Congress as well as the President moved decisively toward actual integration (the Civil Rights Act of 1964 and other initiatives) that the Supreme Court demanded immediate implementation of unitary school systems (*Green*). Our largely descriptive theory does make a normative claim: A Supreme Court that moved too far "ahead" of the political culture would not only have a hard time implementing its decrees, but would lose much of its overall political capital or legitimacy.

Also elaborating on Bickelian themes, Cass Sunstein, *The Supreme Court, 1995 Term — Foreword: One Case at a Time*, 110 Harv. L. Rev. 4 (1996), argues for a *minimalist* approach to judicial review most of the time. "Minimalism is best understood as an effort to leave things open by limiting the width and depth of judicial judgments. Minimalist judges try to keep their judgments as narrowly and as incompletely theorized as possible, consistent with the obligation to offer reasons. They are enthusiastic about avoiding constitutional questions; they like to use doctrines of justiciability, and their authority over their docket, to limit the occasions for judicial intervention into politically contentious areas; the ban on advisory opinions guides much of their work. They try * * * to minimize the risks of error introduced by broad rules and abstract theories, and to maximize the space for democratic deliberation about basic political and moral issues. Minimalist courts also respond to the sheer practical problem of obtaining consensus amidst pluralism."

"Whether minimalism makes sense cannot be decided in the abstract. The answer has a great deal to do with costs of decisions and costs of error. The

---

s. For a formal demonstration that appellate courts must consider the possibility that their directives will not be respected or enforced, see Dan Kahan, *Gentle Nudges vs. Hard Shoves: Solving the Sticky Norms Problem*, 67 U. Chi. L. Rev. 607 (2000).

case for minimalism is strongest when courts lack information that would justify confidence in a comprehensive ruling; when the need for planning is not especially insistent; when the decision costs of an incremental approach do not seem high; and when minimalist judgments not do create a serious risk of unequal treatment. Thus minimalism is usually the appropriate course when circumstances are changing rapidly or when the Court cannot be confident that a broad rule would make sense in future cases." Was *Brown II* a minimalist decision that complemented *Brown I*'s maximalist symbolism? How would a neo-Bickelian respond to the charge that *Brown II*'s minimalism was both a retreat from a great principle and a practical failure?

3. Common Law Constitutionalism

Because it involves the interpretation of written texts, constitutional law is usually considered more analogous to statutory interpretation than to common law decisionmaking. That analogy may be misleading. See Henry Monaghan, *Stare Decisis and Constitutional Adjudication*, 88 Colum. L. Rev. 723 (1988); David Strauss, *Common Law Constitutional Interpretation*, 63 U. Chi. L. Rev. 877 (1996). Many constitutional decisions, including *Brown*, have a casual relationship to the text of the Constitution — and some of them, including *Bolling* and *Marbury*, seem contrary to the text. Much constitutional doctrine, including liberty of contract (Chapter 5, § 2) and the right to privacy (id. § 4), has no text-based anchor at all, while some texts (such as the First Amendment) have assumed a primacy not apparent from their place in the Constitution or from the ratification debates. Like the common law, modern constitutional law is less concerned with divining the expectations of the Framers than with applying precedent in new factual settings.[t]

Descriptively, there seems to be little doubt that a great deal of constitutional law is common law with bite. Is this normatively defensible? Justice Scalia denounces such an approach as undemocratic, and his followers claim that judges are institutionally incompetent to carry out common law reasoning where the stakes are so high.[u] On the other hand, there are normative virtues of a common law approach, as Professor Ernest Young argues below.

Ernest Young, *Rediscovering Conservatism: Burkean Political Theory and Constitutional Interpretation*, 72 N.C. L. Rev. 619, 689-90, 691-93, 701-03 (1994).[v] The political thought of Edmund Burke valorized a polity's traditions as a source of norms superior to the contingent rationalizations of human

---

t. And the list of precedents that are hard to defend based solely on constitutional text and original meaning is a long one — the affirmative action and the racial gerrymandering cases (Chapter 3, § 3); the sex discrimination cases (Chapter 4, § 2); the selective incorporation cases (Chapter 5, § 1); the contraception and abortion cases (Chapter 5, § 4); the flagburning cases (Chapter 6, § 1); the freedom of association cases (Chapter 6, § 6); the "dormant" Commerce Clause cases (Chapter 7, § 6B) and perhaps some of the regular Commerce Clause cases (Chapter 7, § 2); and the voting rights cases (Chapter 5, § 3A and Chapter 9, § 1).

u. Antonin Scalia, *A Matter of Interpretation: Federal Courts and the Law* (1997); Adrian Vermeule, *Judging Under Uncertainty: An Institutional Theory of Legal Interpretation* (2006).

v. Reprinted by permission of the North Carolina Law Review.

decisionmakers. A Burkean constitutionalism would interpret foundational texts in an incremental common law manner, respecting without fetishizing original meaning, majority decisionmaking, and bright-line rules. "[A] common-law model fairly describes much of what courts actually do when interpreting the Constitution, and * * * such interpretation would generally be more successful if the common-law model were more candidly acknowledged and more broadly employed.

"By common-law model, I mean a process that attempts to emulate Burke's rejection of abstract theory and his corresponding emphasis on tradition and incremental change. * * * [N]one of the generally accepted modes of constitutional argument are ruled out; arguments from the constitutional text, the intent of the framers, judicial precedent, the broader philosophical purposes of the constitution, moral philosophy, and social policy may all be relevant in any given case. Given a Burkean set of assumptions, however, some of these arguments are more persuasive than others. For example, even the most fervent nonoriginalists tend to concede that originalist history is an important factor for judges to consider. For the Burkean, that history is primarily valuable as an aid in ascertaining the tradition as a whole as it has evolved from the original period to the present. Similarly, a Burkean judge will tend to reject arguments based on abstract moral theory except insofar as that theory can be shown to reflect and clarify the moral intuitions of society at large. * * *

"In a jurisprudence of doctrine, the primary tool of constitutional interpretation will be judicial precedent rather than originalist history or abstract moral theory. This approach mirrors the reality of constitutional advocacy; although lawyers may make arguments about original understanding or moral philosophy to courts, they generally emphasize the requirements of doctrine as articulated in prior decisions. [Eds.: Recall the NAACP Inc. Fund's argumentation in *Brown*.] Many precedents, of course, will themselves rely in whole or in part upon arguments about the original understanding. By incorporating originalism in this indirect way, however, adherence to precedent also takes account of a constitutional provision's line of growth from the original period down to the present. * * * Use of precedent in this way allows the judge to tap into a cumulative wisdom that transcends his own rationality. As Dean Brest observes, a doctrine that survives over a period of time has the approval of a court composed, in effect, of all the judges who have ever had occasion to consider and apply it. [*The Misconceived Quest for the Original Understanding*, 60 B.U. L. Rev. 204, 228 (1980).] * * *

"When specific precedents cannot directly determine a result, judges pursuing the common-law model are nonetheless constrained to some extent by the conventions of legal argument and reasoning. These considerations confine the range of arguments presented to courts by advocates. * * * An important part of this shared vision of what it means to argue like a lawyer is a commitment to the method of analogical reasoning, which Professor Sunstein describes as our legal culture's most characteristic way of proceeding. [*On Analogical Reasoning*, 106 Harv. L. Rev. 741 (1993).] According to Sunstein, the doctrine of stare decisis means that a certain number of outcomes must be respected as starting points for further reasoning; as a result, within the legal culture, analogical reasoning imposes a certain discipline that can help courts to reach determinate results even in the absence of widespread moral or political consensus. [Judges are also constrained by norms and procedures of adjudication, including a focus on the facts of particular cases and the need to justify decisions by reasons that could persuade a neutral observer, including judges at the top of the hierarchy or in the future.]

[Tradition is critical to a common-law constitutionalism — but what of "bad traditions"?] "It is true that, in 1954, it was possible to make traditionalist arguments for segregation. Nonetheless, * * * it was possible to make better traditionalist arguments against it.

"The first step in such an argument is based on the observation that abstract principles can serve as a source of progressive pressure. These principles are not the product of metaphysical theory; rather, they are simply the traditions of a society taken at a higher level of generality. * * * Any institution of even moderate complexity will also have an aspirational component — it will reflect certain ideals and be oriented toward the attainment of certain values that are never fully realized in practice. The existence of this aspirational component means that one can always argue that the currently prevailing interpretation of an institution's ideals is faulty or incomplete, and attempt to show that from the standpoint of a more adequate interpretation, certain of the institution's existing features must be judged wanting and in need of reform. * * *

"This fact is nowhere more evident than in the struggle against slavery and racism * * *. Although some elements of the civil rights movement rejected American liberalism in favor of more radical ideologies, the more successful groups — both within and without the African-American community — grounded their arguments in an appeal to the classical liberal ideals of freedom and equality. * * * Dr. Martin Luther King, Jr. was able to strengthen his moral appeal by drawing on the democratic elements of the American political tradition. * * *

"The philosophy of the struggle against racism in America is, of course, more complicated than this thumbnail sketch can convey. It is striking, however, that the opponents of segregation were able to tap into the traditions of the establishment they were fighting. What is equally striking, moreover, is that the defenders of segregation were cut off from those democratic traditions, and forced to fall back on the naked fact of segregation's existence without any way of justifying the institution itself in terms of shared American values. * * * [T]he history of resistance to racism in this country shows the liberating potential of tradition at work, constantly undermining the claims of unjust institutions and providing a consensual basis for arguments in favor of reform."

Query: Professor Young left out traditions that powerfully supported the South in its intense campaign to preserve apartheid — federalism's commitment to local decisionmaking (*Brown I*) and the separation of powers aversion to judicial policymaking (*Brown II*). How does the common law judge arbitrate these different traditions? Consider the next Note.

NOTE ON PRAGMATISM AS ANOTHER RESOURCE FOR COMMON LAW CONSTITUTIONALISM

Pragmatism follows Burke in rejecting the dogmatic assertions of "foundationalist" theories that posit a single template (original intent, representation-reinforcement) and deduce "right" answers to all cases from it. Unlike Burke, these commentators do not give priority to tradition. Following William James, pragmatic legal thought is interested in the consequences of different interpretations. Pragmatic legal scholars attempt to define a mediating path between foundational theory (thinking too big) and deciding each case on its facts without concern about the overall development of the law (thinking too small). Like Ernie Young, legal pragmatists find the common law method to be the appropriate approach for "construct[ing] midlevel theories drawing out the patterns governing large areas of decisions" in constitutional law.[w]

In place of searches for *the* right answer, the pragmatist proposes eclectic — but by no means unfamiliar — methodologies to construct the best answer available. A supportable answer may sometimes descend from deductive analysis alone. More often, such an answer will ascend from a combination of arguments, none of which standing alone would constitute a sufficient justification. Such "supporting arguments" operate more like the legs of a chair than the links of a chain. The leading pragmatic, or eclectic, theories of constitutional law posit that the following considerations are relevant: (1) the constitutional text, especially if focused and not open-textured; (2) original intent, to the extent determinable; (3) precedent and historical practice; (4) the original or evolved purpose of the provision; (5) practicality and potential resistance; and (6) ethical and political (*e.g.*, representation-reinforcement)

---

w. The account in text is taken from Daniel Farber & Philip Frickey, *Practical Reason and the First Amendment*, 34 UCLA L. Rev. 1615, 1645-56 (1987). On pragmatism, see *Pragmatism in Law and Society* (Michael Brint and William Weaver eds. 1991). On the common law as a pragmatic, workable method, consider this:

> It is the merit of the common law that it decides the case first and determines the principle afterwards. Looking at the forms of logic it might be inferred that when you have a minor premise and a conclusion, there must be a major, which you are also prepared then and there to assert. But in fact lawyers * * * frequently see well enough how they ought to decide on a given state of facts without being very clear as to the *ratio decidendi*. In cases of first impression Lord Mansfield's often-quoted advice to the business man who was suddenly appointed judge, that he should state his conclusions and not give his reasons, as his judgment would probably be right and the reasons certainly wrong, is not without its application to more educated courts. It is only after a series of determinations on the same subject-matter, that it becomes necessary to "reconcile the cases," as it is called, that is, by a true induction to state the principle which has until then been obscurely felt. And this statement is often modified more than once by new decisions before the abstracted general rule takes its final shape. A well settled legal doctrine embodies the work of many minds, and has been tested in form as well as substance by trained critics whose practical interest it is to resist it at every step. These are advantages the want of which cannot be supplied by any faculty of generalization, however brilliant * * * .

Oliver Wendell Holmes, Jr., *Codes, and the Arrangement of the Law*, 44 Harv. L. Rev. 725, 725 (1931) (reprinting Holmes, *Codes, and the Arrangement of the Law*, 5 Am. L. Rev. 1 (1870)).

norms.[x] As we and others have argued, the listing is also a hierarchy: The first items are more authoritative than the last. For example, a strong textual argument will trump an equally strong original intent or purpose argument.

Although the above factors are taken from legal *practice* and therefore lack the sharp normative edge of critical or republican theory, they may offer greater normative bite or constraint than foundationalist theories. Practical reason's freedom from the necessity of foundationalist justifications makes many cases easy to decide. Even in close cases, moreover, some objective standards of evaluation are available. In this view, then, "the tyranny of the judiciary" is neither inherent in all exercises of judicial review nor beyond evaluation in individual cases. The reasoned exercise of limited judicial discretion may not satisfy the purist, but it can hardly be considered a form of tyranny.

Richard Posner, *The Problems of Jurisprudence* 302-09 (1990).[y] Judge Posner says that because the language of the Equal Protection Clause "is not obviously incompatible with a system of segregated schools" and because the Framers of the Fourteenth Amendment perhaps did not intend "to bring about true equality between whites and blacks, * * * the ultimate justification for the *Brown* decision must be sought not in technical legal materials but in such political and ethical desiderata as improving the position of blacks; adopting a principle of racial (and implicitly also religious and ethnic) equality to vindicate the ideals for which World War II had recently been fought; raising public consciousness about racial injustice; promoting social peace through racial harmony; eradicating an institution that was an embarrassment to America's foreign policy; reducing the social and political autonomy of the South ('completing the work of the Civil War'); finding a new institutional role for the Supreme Court to replace the discredited one of protecting economic liberty; breathing new life into the Equal Protection Clause. * * *

"* * * In addition to (but related to) the natural law justification offered earlier (*Brown* as vindication of a moral norm that was influential then and that now commands a consensus), consider what we would think of a decision by the Supreme Court overruling *Brown* tomorrow on the ground that the decision was an incorrect interpretation of the Fourteenth Amendment. We would pronounce such a decision wrong even if we agreed that it rested on a defensible theory of constitutional interpretation. The decision would be an enormous provocation, stirring racial fears and hostilities in a nation more rather than less racially heterogeneous than when *Brown* was decided; it would be promptly overruled by Congress in the exercise of its powers under section 5 [of the Fourteenth Amendment] or the commerce clause; it would unsettle all of constitutional law,

---

x. This list is taken from William Eskridge, Jr. & Philip Frickey, *Statutory Interpretation as Practical Reasoning*, 42 Stan. L. Rev. 321 (1990), and is generally similar to the constitutional theories in Philip Bobbitt, *Constitutional Interpretation* (1991), and Richard Fallon, *A Constructivist Coherence Theory of Constitutional Interpretation*, 100 Harv. L. Rev. 1189 (1987). Elaboration of this kind of thinking can be found in Dennis Patterson, *Law and Truth* (1996).

y. Reprinted by permission of the publisher from THE PROBLEMS OF JURISPRUDENCE by Richard A. Posner, pp. 303, 304, 308, 309, Cambridge, Mass.: Harvard University Press, Copyright © 1990 by the President and Fellows of Harvard College.

most of which rests on interpretive grounds no more powerful (and often much less so) than those of *Brown*; and whatever its actual motivations it would be thought to bespeak the politicization of the Court. It would in short be socially, politically, and legally destabilizing.

"The example suggests that our legal certitudes are pragmatically rather than analytically grounded. The strongest defense of *Brown* is that the consequences of overruling it would be untoward. To borrow William James's formula, we believe that *Brown* is correct because that is a good, a useful, thing to believe. This may be true of most judicial decisions whose authority we are not disposed to question, whether they are ostensibly interpretive decisions or are leading cases in common law fields."

In response to the criticism that *Brown* rested on faulty social psychological research, Posner maintains that "there are firmer grounds" for *Brown*, but they "are matters of facts and consequence too, not matters of legal theory or distinctive legal materials. They are not grounds that hit one between the eyes after a careful reading of the equal protection clause and the debates that preceded its enactment and ratification. They are grounds based on political history, common sense and common knowledge, and ethical insight."

C. CIVIC REPUBLICANISM AND THE CONSTITUTION OUTSIDE THE COURTS

Both original meaning and legal process theories of constitutional law assume that the Constitution embodies a "liberal" understanding of government, as a social contract among self-interested individuals willing to give up their liberties only through the established organs of majority rule, namely, legislation by elected representatives. Alongside the liberal tradition, however, a "republican" tradition has animated American constitutionalism from Madison through Lincoln through *Brown*.[a] Unlike the liberal conception of government, republicanism does not start with atomistic individuals bargaining to form the state, but instead starts with a conception of civic virtue, in which citizens would work for the common good of the republic, from which they would derive a form of "public happiness" (philosopher Hannah Arendt's term) or civic virtue.

For republicans, the role of government is not to cut deals among interest groups, but rather to deliberate for the common good. Liberals, of course, also seek the common good, often defined in terms of overall social utility (typically defined in a materialistic way). The republican has a different focus: citizens are enriched through their participation in politics and self-governance, whose goal is to create *security* for all citizens, so that they and their families can

---

a. See Michael Sandel, *Democracy's Discontent: America in Search of a Public Philosophy* (1996); *Debating* Democracy's Discontent: *Essays on American Politics, Law, and Public Philosophy* (Anita Allen & Milton Regan, Jr. eds., 1998). See also William Eskridge, Jr. & John Ferejohn, *A Republic of Statutes* ch. 2 (forthcoming 2009); Bruce Ackerman, *The Storrs Lectures: Discovering the Constitution*, 93 Yale L.J. 1013 (1984); Tracy Higgins, *Democracy and Feminism*, 110 Harv. L. Rev. 1657 (1997); Frank Michelman, *The Supreme Court, 1985 Term — Foreword: Traces of Self-Government*, 100 Harv. L. Rev. 4 (1986); Cass Sunstein, *Interest Groups in American Public Law*, 38 Stan. L. Rev. 29 (1985).

pursue flourishing lives. Liberals usually consider people's preferences to be *exogenous* (outside) the political process; republicans consider them *endogenous*, that is, shaped and transformed by the political process.

Dialogue and discussion among the citizenry are the means by which people go beyond their narrow interests and perspectives and seek to solve social problems and advance the general interest of the republic as a whole. Debate in which all views are considered is likely to result in a better solution than closed discussion, and republicans have great faith in the ability of education to bring about agreement. Decisionmaking by consensus is preferred over coercive majority-vote wins. See *Federalist* 10 (App. 2 to this casebook).

A republican reading of *Federalist* 78 would be different from a liberal understanding of judicial review such as that in *Marbury* (and may explain why Marshall did not refer to *Federalist* 78 in his opinion). A republican reading would emphasize that the Constitution's system of checks and balances sought to yield a system of deliberative democracy in which a number of different institutional filters would weed out measures that did not pursue the common good — filters that include not just bicameralism, the presidential veto, and possible state resistance, but also judicial review. Correlatively, the Constitution provides We the People with different institutional forms of access to political participation, not just through elected legislators, but also through the nationally elected President and the unelected judiciary. While Hamilton cautioned that judges should exercise "judgment" and not "will" in striking down laws, he left it to the Court to devise standards of review that would discourage — ex ante (before the fact, as an incentive) as well as ex post (after the fact) — legislative action that was unjust or oppressive.

Republicanism also values perspective. Unlike many liberal theories which insist that the Constitution has an acontextual meaning stable over time, modern republican theorists insist that meaning is influenced by perspective, and that a variety of perspectives must be considered. Feminists and race theorists maintain that constitutional law cannot be "neutral" so long as the constitutional text and history are viewed only from insider perspectives.[b] Although people of color were not generally treated as full citizens before the Reconstruction Amendments nor were women before the Nineteenth Amendment, the Constitution should be construed in ways that reflect their full citizenship today. Judges and other public servants should emulate Justice Harlan, who viewed Jim Crow laws from the standpoint of Homer Plessy and through his eyes was able to see how deeply apartheid undermined the norms of Reconstruction.[c]

---

b. See Derrick Bell, *And We Are Not Saved* (1987); Catharine MacKinnon, *Toward a Feminist Theory of the State* (1989); Katharine Bartlett, *Feminist Legal Methods*, 103 Harv. L. Rev. 829 (1990); Mary Coombs, *Outsider Scholarship: The Law Review Stories*, 63 U. Colo. L. Rev. 683 (1992); Richard Delgado, *Storytelling for Oppositionists and Others: A Plea for Narrative*, 87 Mich. L. Rev. 2411 (1989); Mari Matsuda, *When the First Quail Calls: Multiple Consciousness as Jurisprudential Method*, 11 Women's Rts. L. Rep. 7 (1989); Suzanna Sherry, *Civic Virtue and the Feminine Voice in Constitutional Adjudication*, 72 Va. L. Rev. 543 (1986).

c. See Martha Minow, *The Supreme Court, 1986 Term — Foreword: Justice Engendered*, 101 Harv. L. Rev. 10, 59-60 (1987).

1. *Social Movements as Engines for Civic Republican Engagement*

A civic republican understanding of constitutionalism immediately stimulates the rejoinder that, however energized they were in 1776, Americans today are not civically engaged. They are consumers and observers of politics, not agents of political change and fervor. Indeed, most public choice theorists (discussed in the notes following the Ely excerpt) presume that Americans' preferences are exogenously determined, usually by material self-interest, the antithesis of the republican vision. There is much force to these observations, but such a starkly liberal view of politics is punctuated by a great deal of civic republican engagement— starting with the ferocious debates between the Jeffersonians and the Federalists in the 1790s and early 1800s, continuing with the Jacksonian assault on the U.S. Bank and the abolitionists' assault on slavery, reaching a tremendous apex during and after the Civil War, continuing during the Progressive Era, the New Deal, the Great Society, and the post-9/11 era.

Throughout American history, civic engagement has dramatically occurred through *social movements* (mass mobilizations of citizens supporting a norm change), which drive most evolution in constitutional law, in our view. (Social movements do not drive all evolution, as wars, external threats, and technological change trigger and motivate significant constitutional change as well.) The American Revolution itself was a social movement, the brash revolt of a younger generation of colonists unwilling to be treated by Parliament and King George III like pampered children rather than as full and equal citizens. Other social movements important to constitutional change are the abolitionist (Reconstruction Amendments), temperance (XVIII Amendment), women's rights (XIX Amendment; Chapters 4 & 5), civil rights for African and Latino Americans (Chapters 2-4 & 6), lesbian and gay rights (Chapter 4, § 3D), pro-choice and right-to-life (Chapter 5, §§ 3 & 4) movements. Consider some of the ways that social movements influence formal constitutional law as well as informal constitutional culture.

William Eskridge, Jr., *Some Effects of Identity-Based Social Movements on Constitutional Law in the Twentieth Century,*[d] 100 Mich. L. Rev. 2062, 2064-68 (2002). "What motivated big changes in constitutional law doctrine during the twentieth century? Rarely did important constitutional doctrine or theory change because of formal amendments to the document's text, and rarer still because scholars or judges 'discovered' new information about the Constitution's original meaning. Precedent and common law reasoning were the mechanisms by which changes occurred rather than their driving force. My thesis is that most twentieth century changes in the constitutional protection of individual rights were driven by or in response to the great identity-based social movements (IBSMs) of the twentieth century.

"Race, sex, and sexual orientation were markers of social inferiority and legal exclusion throughout the twentieth century. People of color, women, and gay people all came to resist their social and legal disabilities in the civil rights movement seeking to end apartheid; various feminist movements seeking

---

d. Reprinted with permission of the author.

women's control over their own bodies and equal rights with men; and the gay rights movement, seeking equal rights for [lesbian, gay,] and transgendered people. * * * [T]hese IBSMs became involved in constitutional litigation as part of three different kinds of politics in which they were engaged: their own *politics of protection* against state-sponsored threats to the life, liberty, and property of its members; their *politics of recognition*, seeking to end legal discriminations and exclusions of group members and to establish legal protections against private discrimination; and a *politics of remediation*, to rectify material as well as stigmatic legacies of previous state discrimination. At every stage, but particularly the last, these IBSMs were confronted with a *politics of preservation*, whereby countermovements sought to limit or roll back legal protections won or sought by the social movement. Each kind of politics offered opportunities for different kinds of constitutional arguments. The politics of protection most successfully invoked the First Amendment and the Due Process Clauses of the U.S. Constitution; the politics of recognition was most closely associated with the Equal Protection Clause; and the politics of preservation invoked arguments based upon constitutional federalism, separation of powers, and various libertarian doctrines.

"* * * IBSMs and their countermovements brought constitutional litigation that required the Court to apply old constitutional texts and precedents to new circumstances, not just in a single case, but in a string of cases that ran like a chain novel whose audience shifted in the course of narration. Moreover, IBSMs transformed the normative context in which these cases were decided, either by linking the new cases with established norms or by persuading society and its judges to change the normative context in which social traits were evaluated. As to the latter, IBSMs have moved public norms away from understanding race, sex, and (to a lesser extent) sexual orientation as *malign variations* toward understanding them as *tolerable* and (for race and sex) *benign variations*. Finally, as these social movements and countermovements have become institutionalized players in American constitutional litigation and politics, they have become ongoing constituencies for particular ways of thinking about certain provisions of the Constitution. Thus, the oxymoronic notion of 'substantive' due process has become an established part of constitutional jurisprudence because of the importance of the privacy right to women and sexual minorities; waves of minority groups' politics of recognition have transformed the Equal Protection Clause from the last resort to the cutting edge of individual rights claims; and the First Amendment's imperialism in constitutional law owes much to its ability to protect speech and expressive activities most dear to traditionalists as well as gay people; pro-life protesters as well as pro-choice advocates; and racial segregationists as well as people of color. IBSMs and their allies did not single-handedly work these transformations, but they have provided impetus and then support for judges when they have moved in the direction of those stances."

IBSM counsel originated and persuaded the Court to adopt particular doctrines as well, including the strict scrutiny standard in equal protection cases (Chapters 3-4) as well as the alternative sliding scale approach (Chapter 5, § 3); the incorporation of most of the Bill of Rights guarantees against the states through the Fourteenth Amendment (Chapter 5, § 1); the fundamental rights to vote, travel, and privacy (Chapter 5, §§ 2-4); an Imperial First Amendment (Chapter 6); the expansion of congressional authority to enforce the Reconstruction Amendments (Chapter 7, § 3); and the enforcement of human rights limits against the President's conduct of war (Chapter 8, § 3). Although not covered in this casebook, the Eighth Amendment's death penalty jurisprudence is substantially a creation of the civil rights movement.

"Judges adopting these constitutional transformations have usually not accepted the IBSM perspective uncritically or without amendment, however. Judges have rejected the most radical proposals, such as a bar to the death penalty, and have diluted other proposals, such as a robust de novo review of state criminal convictions by federal judges, an anti-subordination reading of the Equal Protection Clause, and strong First Amendment protection for sexual speech. Even when judges have accepted IBSM constitutional visions and doctrines, the constitutional transformations movement lawyers argued for have had limited utility for actual minority group members. Some IBSM-inspired doctrines have been turned to the advantage of countermovements. Examples include heightened scrutiny for suspect classifications, which has discouraged open affirmative action measures [Chapter 5, § 3], and the First Amendment rights of expressive conduct and association, which now protect enclaves of exclusion against state anti-discrimination laws [Chapter 6].

"The fate of particular proposals and doctrines has depended on context, but one rule stands out: judges are rarely willing to insist on massive transfers of social or economic entitlements in American society, and when they have — as with school desegregation and abortion — they have been incompletely successful. This rule owes much to the institutional limits of the federal judiciary. Judges do not have the resources to undertake initiatives requiring administrative capacity, nor do they have the political legitimacy to engage in much actual activism not otherwise acceptable to the political system. * * *

"In addition, IBSMs were the key impulse supporting a global shift in the way the Supreme Court applied the Constitution in the twentieth century. The shift was away from the *structural* Constitution of the founding generation and the *vested property/contract rights* Constitution of the *Lochner* era and toward the *Carolene* Constitution, which justified judicial activism along legal process lines. Under the *Carolene* Constitution, the role of the Court is to protect the integrity of the pluralist political process, and especially to check the political process' tendency toward self-perpetuation and persecution or suppression of minorities. This entails protecting despised minority groups against state *Kulturkampfs*, assuring groups that are able to organize themselves into mass movements that they will be integrated into the political process, and protecting traditionalists from excessive state burdens once a formerly subordinated minority has become part of the political mainstream."

Finally, the author explores the inevitable disappointments of IBSMs in constitutional litigation, which has fueled a vigorous *constitutional skepticism*. Theoretically, the origins of skepticism can be expressed in this way: social movement progressives are thoroughgoing civic republicans who aim to revolutionize social as well as political preferences, but constitutional litigation not only limits their agenda to whatever rights against the state that liberal judges are willing to grant, but also tends to channel the social movement's energies in a liberal, universalizing direction. Moreover, because successful countermovements (such as pro-life and traditional values movements) also influence the evolution of constitutional law, the resulting rules are not only incomplete from the progressive point of view, but are often counterproductive. This has given rise to *constitutional law drop-out* as well as *popular constitutionalism* approaches.

Robin West, *Constitutional Skepticism*, 72 B.U.L. Rev. 765-66, 774-78 (1992).[e] "[T]he prominence of the debate over the Constitution's *meaning*, whether it can be said to have one, and the implications for the coherence of liberalism that these questions of interpretation seem to raise, has pushed to the background an older and possibly more important debate about the Constitution's *value*. By asking relentlessly whether the Constitution's meaning can be made sufficiently determinate to serve the Rule of Law — by focusing almost exclusively on whether constitutionalism is *possible* within liberal theory and whether liberalism is possible, given an indeterminate Constitution — we have neglected to ask whether our Constitution is *desirable*. Does it further the 'good life' for the individuals, communities, and subcommunities it governs?"

In answering the question of the Constitution's value, Professor West contrasts a "progressive" constitutional vision from a traditional "liberal" one: Both seek personal flourishing and interconnection. "What *distinguishes* progressives from liberals is that while liberals tend to view the dangers of an over-oppressive state as the most serious obstacle to the attainment of such a world, progressives * * * argue that *for the most part* the most serious impediments emanate from unjust concentrations of *private* power — the social power of whites over blacks, the intimate power of men over women, the economic power of the materially privileged over the materially deprived. * * * [I]t is those concentrations of private power that must be targeted, challenged, and reformed by progressive political action. That action, in turn, will often involve state intervention into the private spheres within which hierarchies of private power are allowed to thrive, and that simple fact will commonly pit the progressive strategy of ending private domination against the liberal goal of minimizing the danger of an oppressive state.

"This difference between progressives and liberals largely accounts for the degree of conflict between their respective analyses and goals. For example, liberals and progressives generally agree, and lament, that the freedom of gays and lesbians to form and maintain nurturing intimate relationships is threatened by discriminatory state action. At the same time, progressives, far more than liberals, are sensitive to the degree to which that freedom is threatened by the continuing and seemingly unshakable hegemonic rage of an intolerant, abusive, and often violent minority of heterosexual private citizens. That hegemonic rage, not just state action, must somehow be challenged and transformed if gays and lesbians are to thrive." West makes the same point for women and people

---

e. Reprinted with permission of the Boston University Law Review.

of color: Private sexism and racism rather than public discrimination is an ongoing problem that is severely disabling and dangerous for women and people of color. * * *

"If [the] progressive insight is basically correct, then at least two problems exist with the scheme of individual rights and liberties protected by the Constitution. First, the Constitution does not prohibit the abuse of private power that interferes with the equality or freedom of subordinated peoples. The Constitution simply does not reach private power, and therefore cannot possibly prohibit its abuse. Even the most far reaching liberal interpretations of the Reconstruction Amendments — the only amendments that *seemingly* reach private power — refuse or fail to find either a constitutional prohibition of private societal racism, intimate sexual violence, or economic coercion or a constitutional imperative that the states take affirmative action to eradicate it. Justice Harlan's famous liberal dissent in *Plessy v. Ferguson*, for example, made painfully clear that, even on his reading of the amendment (which, of course, would have outlawed Jim Crow laws), the Fourteenth Amendment does not challenge the sensed or actual cultural and social superiority of the white race. * * *

"The incompatibility, however, of progressivism and the Constitution goes deeper. Not only does the Constitution fail to prohibit subordinating abuses of private power, but, at least a good deal of the time, in the name of guaranteeing constitutional protection of individual freedom, it also aggressively *protects* the very hierarchies of wealth, status, race, sexual preference, and gender that facilitate those practices of subordination." West notes the Constitution's protection of hate speech, pornography, misogynistic religion, patriarchal family structures, and class- and race-constructed notions of meritocracy.

Professor West maintains that "this incompatibility of the Constitution with progressive ideals is neither momentary nor contingent." First, it rests upon the Constitution's negative vision of liberty (freedom from state interference), which not only fails to protect positive liberty (empowerment) but also stands in the way of the positive liberty of women, gays, the poor, and people of color. "Second, the Fourteenth Amendment's mandate of equality, rather than being a limit to the Constitution's celebration of liberty, is also a bar to progressive progress, the heroic efforts of progressive litigators, judges, and commentators to prove the contrary notwithstanding. The 'equal protection of the laws' guaranteed by the Fourteenth Amendment essentially guarantees that one's membership in a racially or sexually defined group will not adversely affect one's treatment by the state. As such, the mandate powerfully reinforces the liberal understanding that the only attributes that matter to the state are those shared universally by all members of the community: the possession of equal dignity, the power to form one's own plan of life, and the universal aspirations to autonomy and so forth. Precisely this understanding of equality, grounded in the liberal claim and promise of universality and equal treatment, however, renders the Equal Protection Clause an obstacle to progressive progress. The need to acknowledge and compensate for the individual's membership in profoundly non-universal subordinate groups — whether racially, sexually, or economically defined — is what distinguishes the progressive political impulse from the liberal. It is precisely that membership in non-universal groups, and the centrality of the non-universal attributes that distinguish them, that both liberalism and the liberally defined constitutional mandate of equality are poised not simply to ignore, but also to oppose. It is, then, both unsurprising and inevitable that the Fourteenth Amendment's Equal Protection Clause is understood as not requiring, and indeed forbidding, the state and public interventions into private, intimate, and economic spheres of life needed to interrupt the patterns of domination, subordination, and inequality that continue to define the lives of those within these protected private realms."

NOTE ON PROGRESSIVE CONSTITUTIONALISM

Notwithstanding the critical account in the foregoing excerpt, Robin West believes that progressives should not submit to disabling *constitutional skepticism* and should remain actively engaged among the *constitutional faithful*. Drawing from radical feminist and critical race theories, as well as Professor West's own work, consider these important features of progressive constitutionalism.

1. *An Anti-Subordination Understanding of the Constitution.* An important critical theme is that the Fourteenth Amendment embodies an *anti-subordination* norm, and that this norm must inform the entire constitutional enterprise. The anti-subordination norm posits that the central goal of the Reconstruction Amendments was to overturn laws and practices that unfairly subordinated social groups and to assure all persons the same protection of law that white males have traditionally enjoyed. Although the Supreme Court has occasionally paid lip-service to this goal, its analytical approach, especially after 1968, has been dominated by a *rationality* goal that the Justices have attributed to the Reconstruction Amendments.

Catharine MacKinnon, *Reflections on Sex Equality under the Law*, 100 Yale L.J. 1281 (1991), suggests how the judiciary's rationality model has operated doctrinally: "[C]ourts in racial equality cases have largely confined themselves to the Aristotelian framework [where equality means treating like things alike]: qualification for admission into liberal humanity implicitly meant being like the white man. In *Plessy v. Ferguson*, for example, where segregation with equal facilities was held to be equality, the reason given was that Blacks were different from whites, so could be treated differently. When *Brown v. Board of Education* repudiated *Plessy* and held that educational segregation with equal facilities was inherently unequal, what changed was that *Brown* implicitly considered Blacks to be the same as whites. At least, Black school children were potentially so. This was a substantive shift in the political and ideological ground beneath the case law, not a pure doctrinal development. What was different was now the same. Difference could still justify differentiation, presumably including exclusion and subordination as well as segregation (maybe even affirmative action). Being the same as the dominant group remained the equality test."

Several consequences of this doctrinal structure have been of specific concern to critical theorists. This kind of thinking allows — and perhaps invites

— the modernization of anti-minority norms.[f] Thus, the Court's *Brown* jurisprudence disallows arguments that people of color should be excluded because of white prejudice and stereotypes about racial minorities, but it allows continued exclusion based on modern standards of performance and cultural familiarity that many minorities do not meet, in part because of the effects of prior discrimination. This analytic not only permits continued subordination of minorities, but also cloaks it in an aura of enhanced legitimacy. This kind of thinking also has an assimilative effect. To win an equal protection case, minorities and women must show (a la Aristotle) that they are similar to the unspoken white male norm. This means that women and minorities who are already most like the norm will have the greatest success in equal protection cases; their success in court may translate into status within their cohort, a phenomenon which might press toward indirect suppression of distinctive minority cultures.

2. *Affirmative, Not Just Negative, State Responsibilities.* The Supreme Court's articulation of constitutional values sometimes imposes *limitations* on state action, but almost never on private action; the Court rarely imposes *duties* on the state to provide affirmative protections for citizens. Even the desegregation cases have this feature, especially after *Milliken*, when the Court has diluted state responsibility for the ongoing consequences of slavery and apartheid to the libertarian presumption that white people ought to be able to avoid "too much integration" by moving away from people of color. Critics have also objected to the Court's failure to sustain the *Green-Swann* idea that the state has an affirmative obligation to reconstitute once-unconstitutional systems "root and branch" and to work toward a functionally and not just formally fair and equal system. Chapter 3 will show how the Court has not only refused to hold the state responsible for deeper remedial obligations, but has invalidated some of the remedial responses that state and local governments have made.

Judges would say they are just applying the libertarian Constitution as it is written — but the Constitution is filled with admonitions that demand *affirmative* assistance and not just noninterference from government.[g] Reading the Equal Protection Clause both literally and in light of its abolitionist roots, Robin West maintains that it requires the state to *protect* women and minorities to the same effect that it protects white men. West, *Progressive Constitutionalism* (1994). For feminist theorists, it is important that most violence against women occurs within the home or the family and is committed by men whom they know — an arena the law has not policed with the vigor it has exercised in protecting property and assaults by strangers. Both critical race and feminist

---

f. Kimberlé Crenshaw, *Race, Reform, and Retrenchment: Transformation and Legitimation in Antidiscrimination Law*, 101 Harv. L. Rev. 1331 (1988); see also Charles Lawrence, III, *The Id, the Ego, and Equal Protection: Reckoning with Unconscious Racism*, 39 Stan. L. Rev. 317 (1987); Reva Siegel, *"The Rule of Love": Wife Beating as Prerogative and Privacy*, 105 Yale L.J. 2117 (1996).

g. E.g., U.S. Const., preamble (We the People form the Constitution in order to advance "the general Welfare"); *id.*, art. IV (Congress has a responsibility to preserve and protect national property and to assure each state a "Republican form of government").

theorists have similarly urged the state to regulate hate speech and other forms of oppressive conduct that the Supreme Court has traditionally protected from regulation under a libertarian reading of the First Amendment.[h]

The Equal Protection Clause is not the only part of the Constitution that, on its face, imposes affirmative obligations on government. Among them are the General Welfare Clause of the Preamble, the Commander-in-Chief Clause of Article II, the Vesting Clause of Article III, the Property Protection and Guarantee Clauses of Article IV, and the Debt Assumption and Oath of Office Clauses of Article VI. From a progressive, civic republican point of view, the Constitution is a libertarian document *not* because it is written that way, or because such was the original goal of the Framers (quite the opposite), but because *judges* have read the Constitution that way. The primary explanation for such a slanted reading is the institutional limitations of the "least dangerous branch" (*Federalist* No. 78).

3. *Rejection of Dichotomies Between Liberty and Equality, Public and Private.* The Supreme Court has resisted — sometimes passively (*Plessy*), sometimes aggressively (*The Civil Rights Cases*) — progressive arguments that longstanding status alignments should be changed significantly. Primary doctrinal mechanisms for the resistance have been the public-private distinction and a preference for liberty over equality. The former prevents courts from applying constitutional norms to social practices (Chapter 3, § 2), and the second prevents courts from imposing equality norms on state actors and invalidates state equalization measures (e.g., Chapter 6, § 5). Both moves, of course, are contrary to the anti-subordination norm that critical theorists find in the Reconstruction Amendments.

Critical theorists also find fault in the Court's reliance on and manipulation of such categories. The distinction between state action and private choice, they argue, cannot be neutrally drawn. As the NAACP and its Inc. Fund have maintained, "white flight" cannot be understood as simply a matter of private choice, for white people's housing choices are framed by governmental decisions leaving identifiably white and black schools in place and facilitating gated communities by protective zoning and other property regulations. Even white prejudice against some people of color cannot be understood without reference to centuries of state support for the institutions of slavery and apartheid. And white efforts to avoid integration typically depend on state property and contract law to give effect to their preferences.[i]

Likewise, the liberty-equality distinction is overdrawn, according to the critics. As Mari Matsuda has argued to justify regulation of hate speech, the

---

h. Mari Matsuda, *Public Response to Racist Speech: Considering the Victim's Story*, 87 Mich. L. Rev. 2320 (1989); see Charles Lawrence, III, *If He Hollers Let Him Go: Regulating Racist Speech on Campus*, 1990 Duke L.J. 431.

i. There is no logical reason why the availability of state remedies cannot be considered sufficient to meet the state action requirement. See *Shelley v. Kraemer*, 334 U.S. 1 (1948) (Chapter 3, § 2) (state court enforcement of a racially restrictive covenant is state action); Mark Tushnet, *Shelley v. Kraemer* and Theories of Equality, 33 N.Y.L. Sch. L. Rev. 383 (1988).

First Amendment has egalitarian as well as libertarian features: Not only does the First Amendment flatly reject content-based discriminations, but it has sometimes been deployed to allow state regulations that enhance the ability of marginalized people to feel empowered to speak (Matsuda, *Racist Speech*). Although mainstream scholars may question *Bolling's* holding that the Fifth Amendment's Due Process Clause has an equal protection component, an outsider perspective suggests its cogency: Due process has always included a nonarbitrariness feature — What could be more arbitrary than blanket denial of state benefits or even respect simply because of one's minority trait?[j]

2. Polycentric Constitutionalism

The primary civic republican response to Professor West's dilemma is *politics*. The guarded success story surrounding *Brown* — widespread rejection of state-imposed racial segregation and general support for the value of racial diversity — is as much a product of the civil rights movement's successes in Congress during the 1960s. The Civil Rights Act of 1964 elevated the anti-discrimination norm to widely accepted national policy, and the Elementary and Secondary Education Act of 1965 provided federal funds to school districts, with the stipulation (from the 1964 Act) that segregated districts could not receive such needed monies.[k]

The general point suggested by this experience is that the Constitution (or simply our small "c" political constitution) should be viewed as an authorization and encouragement for the political process, after deliberation where everyone is represented, to create rules and structures that provide security and guarantee civic engagement for all citizens. Examples of republican constitutionalism along these lines include the Sherman Act of 1890 and the Clayton Act of 1914; the Social Security act of 1935 and the Medicare Act of 1965; the Voting Rights Act of 1965 (as expanded in its reauthorizations in 1970, 1975, 1982, and 2006); the Clean Air Act Amendments of 1970 and the Clean Water Act of 1970, as well as other environmental-protective laws; and so forth.[l]

Bruce Ackerman has expanded upon this idea and has sought to give it a formal grounding as Large "C" Constitutional Law.[m] He argues that there have been three big "Constitutional Moments": the Founding, Reconstruction, and the New Deal. Although the third did not produce Constitutional text, the texts

---

j. See Kenneth Karst, *The Supreme Court, 1976 Term — Foreword: Equal Citizenship Under the Fourteenth Amendment*, 91 Harv. L. Rev. 1 (1977) (both due process and equal protection must be understood as guarantees of national citizenship); William Eskridge, Jr., *Destabilizing Due Process and Evolutive Equal Protection*, 47 UCLA L. Rev. 1183 (2000).

k. Gerald Rosenberg, *Hollow Hope: Can Courts Bring About Social Change?* (1991, 2d ed. 2008); James Dunn, *Title VI, the Guidelines and School Desegregation in the South*, 53 Va. L. Rev. 42 (1967).

l. See William Eskridge, Jr. & John Ferejohn, *A Republic of Statutes* (forthcoming, 2009).

m. Bruce Ackerman, *We The People: Foundations* (1991).

produced by the first two were of questionable pedigree,[n] and the New Deal's regulatory statism was ratified by a similar process as the other two moments: a political crisis, followed by an intense period of high-politics debate, followed by a popular electoral ratification of a new order of governance (the ratifying conventions of 1787-89, the election of 1866, the election of 1936). Note how this theory sidesteps Article V, which most Constitutionalists consider the only formal mechanism by which the Constitution can be amended.

Once Constitutional law is viewed as having three rather than two Constitutional Moments, *Brown* and *Bolling* become an exercise, not just in translating the precepts of the Founding in light of Reconstruction, but also in translating precepts of Reconstruction in light of the New Deal. Ackerman terms this a process of *synthesis*, whereby the meaning of the Constitution and the Bill of Rights must be accommodated to reflect the normative changes wrought by the Reconstruction Amendments *and* by the New Deal. (Note the similarity of constitutional synthesis with structural interpretation.)

Bruce Ackerman, *Constitutional Politics/Constitutional Law*, 99 Yale L.J. 453, 531-36 (1989)[o]. Justice Brown gave two reasons for rejecting Plessy's attack on Jim Crow laws. The first reason was that "in the nature of things" the Fourteenth Amendment "could not have been intended * * * to enforce social, as distinguished from political equality." This was the thinking in the 1890s, but "the great constitutional debate of the 1930s was defined precisely by the Old Court's effort to insist that twentieth-century Americans could not legitimately use state power to pursue 'social, as distinguished from political equality' by requiring the payment of a minimum wage, or the recognition of a labor union, or the guarantee of a retirement pension. Given the New Deal's embrace of activist government in the late 1930s, the Warren Court could hardly respond to the petitioner's complaint about school segregation in *Brown* by reaffirming Justice Brown's assertion that 'the nature of things' precluded a reading of 'equal protection' that demanded something more than a thin political equality."

Justice Brown's second reason was that any "badge of inferiority" Homer Plessy drew from forced segregation "is not by reason of anything found in the act, but solely because the colored race chooses to put that construction upon it." This reason was more metaphysical: government in nineteenth century thinking could not be held responsible for "choices" like that which Plessy made. As Ackerman put it: "Rather than participating actively in the construction of public understandings, the state stands to one side and allows social groups to give any meaning they 'choose' to the state's treatment of them. * * *

"Once again, whatever the legal plausibility of this claim in 1896, such a view was judicially untenable after the New Deal. It is precisely the Old Court's

---

n. The original Constitution provided that it would take effect when nine states ratified it, contrary to the Articles of Confederation, which required unanimity to amend or supersede. The Fourteenth Amendment's ratification was owing to Congress' refusal to readmit rebel southern states unless they ratified the amendment and to recognize the effort by two states to rescind their ratifications.

o. Reprinted with permission of the Yale Law Journal..

insistence that the state must not intervene to alter the result of private 'choices' in the economy that precipitated the constitutional struggle of the 1930s that decisively legitimated activist government. In repudiating *Lochner*, the modern Court recognized that the government was an important actor in the process by which groups made their 'choices' in American society." Exemplary of the modern rejection of *Lochner* was compulsory public education (a notion in its infancy in 1896), positing that parents as well as children could be required to submit to a community process of education and inculcation. Echoing Tushnet, Ackerman concludes: "Public schools exemplified the newly-legitimated claims of the activist state to shape the conditions under which individual citizens ultimately come to make their mature choices. * * *

"Within this activist setting, it was absurd to accept Justice Brown's assurance that the meaning of segregated schools was up to the 'choices' of 'the colored race.' Was not the state in the business of public education precisely because children were in no position to make an informed 'choice' about the meaning of social reality? Rather than standing passively to one side, the activist state was now intimately involved in the way children — both black and white — would interpret the fact that they were being bussed to different schools on the basis of race."

NOTE ON THE CIVIL RIGHTS REVOLUTION AS A CONSTITUTIONAL MOMENT

The process of what Ackerman calls *higher lawmaking* (his term for widespread civic republican engagement by We the People) is what connects both Reconstruction and the New Deal as Constitutionally transformative. The formal Ackermanian model is this: Interbranch Impasse → Decisive Election → Reformist Challenge to Conservative Branch → Switch in Time.[p] In recent work, Ackerman argues that the civil rights laws of the 1960s constituted another Constitutional Moment: Congress at an impasse in the 1950s, unable to adopt needed civil rights laws →1960 Election and the Kennedy Assassination (1963) generate civil rights momentum →civil rights leaders gain important allies (President Johnson) to challenge South-dominated Senate →Senate backs down and goes along with landmark legislation (1964-68).[q] Indeed, Ackerman's 2006 Holmes Lectures identify *eight* periods of Constitutional

---

p. Ackerman, *We the People*, 49-50. The precise parallels: President Johnson vetoed the Civil Rights Act of 1866, the Old Court voided early New Deal legislation; the Radical Republicans triumphed over Johnson in the realigning 1866 election, the New Deal triumphed over the Old Court in the realigning 1936 election; the Republicans tried to impeach Johnson, Roosevelt tried to pack the Court; Johnson backed down, the Old Court backed down. In each case the country moved on, but was permanently transformed in its foundational assumptions about the structure of official power. For a much more complicated model, see Bruce Ackerman, *We the People 2: Transformations* 359-60 (1998).

q. Bruce Ackerman, *The Living Constitution*, 120 Harv. L. Rev. 1737 (2007) (delivered as the Oliver Wendell Holmes, Jr. Lectures); Bruce Ackerman & Jennifer Nou, *Canonizing the Civil Rights Revolution: The People and the Poll Tax*, 103 Nw. U.L. Rev. (forthcoming 2009).

transformation in American history — the original three plus the civil rights era plus four more.

Critics have pointed to several dangers. There is an increasing fuzziness as to exactly what makes a Constitutional Moment. Conservative critics suspect that Ackerman is at bottom just trying to transform the good old Constitution into liberalism's last stand.[r] For example, Ackerman scoffs at the notion that the Reagan Revolution of the 1980s was a Constitutional Moment, even though his model seems to invite that thesis.[s] Critics of all sorts worry that making so many things constitutional moments risks entrenching too many contingent commitments or diluting what it means to be "constitutional," or both.[t]

Reva Siegel, *She the People: The Nineteenth Amendment, Sex Equality, Federalism, and the Family*, 115 Harv. L. Rev. 947 (2002), extends the Constitutional Moment theory to sex discrimination. She argues that the great national debate that gave women the right to vote in the Nineteenth Amendment (1920) was a referendum on whether women's place should be rooted in the domestic sphere. Professor Siegel views the defeat of traditionalists on the franchise issue as a larger affirmation that women ought to be considered full and equal citizens in the public sphere. Although the Nineteenth Amendment does not fit the Ackerman model, because it was a formal addition to the Constitution, Siegel reads the amendment using the Ackermanian *synthesis* idea: the Fourteenth Amendment needs to be reinterpreted in light of the Nineteenth Amendment's rejection of women's confinement to domestic roles. Hence, the Equal Protection Clause should, since 1920, be understood to bar traditional sex discriminations on the part of the state. The problem with this view is that immediately after the Nineteenth Amendment was adopted, feminists started pressing for an Equal Rights Amendment (ERA) that specifically addressed that issue — and the ERA languished for decades before Congress in 1972 sent it to the states for ratification, and then an insufficient number of states ratified (Chapter 4, § 2B1). Hence, the Nineteenth Amendment does not seem to be the most successful way of thinking about the constitutional case for sex equality. A more successful effort follows.

---

r. Richard Posner, *Overcoming Law* (1995); Michael Gerhardt, *Ackermania: The Quest for a Common Law of Higher Lawmaking*, 40 Wm. & Mary L. Rev. 1731 (1999); Suzanna Sherry, *The Ghost of Liberalism Past*, 105 Harv. L. Rev. 918 (1992).

s. Like Roosevelt, Reagan won a landslide election on a platform that promised bold new policies and implemented many of them in the first term of his presidency. Just as Roosevelt faced down the Old Republican Court with labor and security laws, Reagan faced down the Old Democrat House with laws returning power to the states and private individuals. Roosevelt won the 1934 off-year election and a smashing reelection in 1936, in partial contrast to Reagan's near-draw in the 1982 off-year election and decisive reelection in 1984. Both Presidents were succeeded by like-minded but one-term Vice-Presidents (Truman and Bush 41). Even when the opposing party recaptured the presidency (in 1952 and 1992, respectively), it did so with me-too candidates (Eisenhower and Clinton) who on the whole declined to challenge the New Deal and the Reagan Revolution. And the me-too Presidents were in turn succeeded by administrations (Kennedy-Johnson and Bush 43) that pressed the New Deal and the Reagan Revolution even further.

t. Eskridge & Ferejohn, *Republic of Statutes*, ch. 1.

Robert Post & Reva Siegel, *Legislative Constitutionalism and Section Five Power: Policentric Interpretation of the Family and Medical Leave Act,* 112 Yale L.J. 1943, 1946-47, 1951, 2022-23 (2003). The Family and Medical Leave Act of 1993 (FMLA) is the kind of constitutionalism that Robin West and other progressives warmly support, for it pro-actively responds to the sexist stereotyping in American workplaces and imposes affirmative duties on public and private employers to accommodate family responsibilities for both male and female employees. But precisely as West argues, this progressive measure came under fire from liberal constitutionalism, because its application to public employers went well beyond what the Supreme Court had been willing to do under § 1 of the Fourteenth Amendment. In a move that surprised many constitutionalists, the Supreme Court upheld Congress's § 5 power to "enforce" the Fourteenth Amendment in *Nevada Department of Human Resources v. Hibbs,* 538 U.S. 721 (2003) (Chapter 7, § 3F). This is another example of Professor Eskridge's point that IBSMs have exercised strong influence on the Court's jurisprudence, but Professors Siegel and Post explore another dimension of this case.

"Our Constitution contains a variety of structures and arrangements that facilitate [the] necessary connections between constitutional law and constitutional culture. These mechanisms range from the amendment procedures of Article V to the political appointment of Article III judges. Section 5 is best conceived as another such mechanism." These also illustrate the general theory of what Post and Siegel call *policentric constitutional interpretation,* whereby "the Constitution should be regarded as having multiple interpreters, both political and legal." Recall Attorney General Meese's analysis of *Cooper v. Aaron* and his departmentalist notion that each branch should decide for itself how the Constitution should be interpreted.

As our notes following *Brown* suggest, the dismantling of apartheid was polycentric (our preferred spelling): the Supreme Court announced a new constitutional regime in *Brown,* but it was not until Congress and the President implemented the regime with monetary inducements as well as legal penalties that desegregation actually occurred and the Supreme Court itself actually announced a more positive norm of integration. Siegel and Post flip the account for the dismantling of state sex discrimination. The Supreme Court left state discriminations alone until Congress enacted a series of anti-sex-discrimination measures between 1963 and 1972, culminating in its passage of the ERA. Indeed, the Court *relied* on Congress's constitutional activism in *Frontiero v. Richardson,* 411 U.S. 677 (1973) (plurality opinion) (Chapter 4, § 2B1). "It was only after Congress used its lawmaking powers to validate the [women's] movement's understanding of equality that the Court proved willing to modify its own Section 1 doctrine to protect citizens against state action that discriminates on the basis of sex. The Court altered its jurisprudence to reflect the evolving constitutional culture of the country, as that culture was evidenced by congressional lawmaking."

Professors Post and Siegel call this model "policentric," referring to "the distribution of constitutional interpretation in our legal system across multiple institutions, many of which are political in character. A central premise of the policentric model is that both Congress and the Court should be regarded as having independent authority to ascertain constitutional meaning for purposes of delineating the parameters of Section 5 power. The policentric model holds that Congress can exercise Section 5 power to enact legislation establishing statutory rights (Rs), even when Congress is acting to enforce an understanding of constitutional rights (Rc) that differs from judicial interpretations of constitutional rights (Rj). The policentric model holds that courts can also act upon their own constitutional understandings (Rj) to subject Section 5 legislation to judicial review. Courts can invalidate Section 5 legislation that violates judicially enforceable rights or that impermissibly impairs other constitutional values such as federalism. The policentric model insists, however, that congressional enforcement of Rc is not itself a sufficient reason to render Section 5 legislation unconstitutional as a violation of separation of powers."

Query. Under what circumstances should the Supreme Court's "legal" understanding of § 5 (or any other constitutional provision) be influenced by legislative interpretations? For an argument that the Court should be *delibe-ration-respecting* and therefore careful *not* to override federal super-statutes or state statutory convergences, see William Eskridge, Jr. & John Ferejohn, *A Republic of Statutes* (forthcoming 2009).

3. Taking the Constitutional Away from the Courts

The constitutional skepticism Professor West attributes to many progressives has blossomed into an academic mini-movement to eliminate judicial review altogether. What a reversal of *Brown*! The antecedents to such an impulse lie in the nineteenth century, as revealed by the following excerpt.

James Bradley Thayer, *John Marshall* **(1901),** pp. 103-04, 106, 107. In an 1893 law review article, Thayer had propounded a "rule of administration" limiting judicial review to statutes that no reasonable person could consider consistent with the Constitution. Although the Supreme Court had followed his rule in *Plessy*, the Court violated it in other cases, impelling Thayer to offer this further argument in favor of judicial leniency when reviewing legislative decisions: "The legislatures are growing accustomed to this distrust [stimulated by activist judicial review] and more and more readily incline to justify it, and to shed the consideration of constitutional restraints, — certainly as concerning the exact extent of these restrictions, — turning that subject over to the courts; and, what is worse, they insensibly fall into a habit of assuming that whatever they can constitutionally do they may do, — as if honor and fair dealing and common honesty were not relevant to their inquiries.

"The people, all this while, become careless as to whom they send to the legislature; too often they cheerfully vote for men whom they would not trust with an important private affair, and when these unfit persons are found to pass foolish and bad laws, and the courts step in and disregard them, the people are glad that these few wiser gentlemen on the bench are so ready to protect them against their more immediate representatives. * * *

"* * * [I]t should be remembered that the exercise of [judicial review], even when unavoidable, is always attended with a serious evil, namely, that the correction of legislative mistakes comes from the outside, and the people thus lose the political experience, and the moral education and stimulus that come from fighting the question out in the ordinary way, and correcting their own errors. * * *

"The tendency of a common and easy resort to this great function, now lamentably too common, is to dwarf the political capacity of the people, and to deaden its sense of moral responsibility. It is no light thing to do that."

Mark Tushnet, *Taking the Constitution Away from the Courts* 11-12, 182-83 (1999). Professor Tushnet starts with a distinction between the *Thin* Constitution and the full Constitution of 1789, as amended and interpreted. "Political scientist Gary Jacobsohn has helpfully retrieved an obscure note written by Abraham Lincoln, describing '[t]he Union and the Constitution' as 'the picture of silver,' the 'frame[],' around the 'apple of gold,' the principles of the Declaration of Independence: 'The picture was made for the apple — not the apple for the picture.' The project the Constitution established for the people of the United States, Lincoln believed, was the vindication of the Declaration's principles: the principle that all people were created equal, the principle that all had inalienable rights. This is the Thin Constitution. * * *

Populist constitutional law vindicates the thin Constitution. [As] Lincoln knew, ordinary people could be committed to the thin Constitution in ways they could never be committed to the thick Constitution. And the thin Constitution is indeed admirable in ways the thick Constitution is not. The thin Constitution protects rights that it has taken centuries of struggle for people to appreciate as truly fundamental. Perhaps more important, the nation's commitment to the thin Constitution constitutes us as the people of the United States, and constituting a people is a morally worthy project."

So long as the Supreme Court is the primary (or exclusive) authority on what the Constitution means, the thin Constitution will always be subordinated to the thick (legalized) Constitution. Hence, Tushnet argues that progressives ought to support the return of constitutional discourse to "We the People" rather than "We the Court." Tushnet joins former Attorney General Meese in rejecting the doctrine of judicial supremacy suggested by dicta in *Cooper v. Aaron*; urges legislators and citizens to form their own constitutional conclusions independent of what the Supreme Court has said; recommends that the Constitution be amended to abrogate the Court's *Marbury* power of judicial review; and urges that constitutional law be reconceived as *populist*. Populist constitutionalism "treats constitutional law not as something in the hands of lawyers and judges but in the hands of the people themselves."

"Constitutional law creates the people of the United States *as a people* by providing a narrative that connects us to everyone who preceded us." Its project would take the Declaration of Independence, the Preamble to the Constitution, and the great constitutional principles such as equality and free speech (the thin Constitution) and elaborate upon them by application to the problems facing the modern regulatory state. These days, such problems include the validity of the federal government's indefinite detention of suspected terrorists, the legitimacy of race- or sex-based affirmative action, and the proper scope of state regulation of a woman's pregnancy. "One advantage of the thin Constitution is that it leaves a wide range [of fundamental issues] open for resolution through principled political discussions — principled because they are oriented toward the Declaration's principles. In this way the thin Constitution may constitute us as a people."

NOTE ON TAKING THE CONSTITUTION AWAY FROM THE COURTS

Professor Tushnet's idea has had a receptive audience among law professors — and, ironically, almost no interest among We the People![u] What should the student make of this? Consider a few points.

First, isn't this a project already afoot? Political scientists have found that Supreme Court dispositions in important constitutional decisions typically track public opinion. There is no perfect convergence of course. Sometimes, as with the famous *Miranda* warning, the Court is "ahead" of and shapes public opinion; sometimes, as in the "homosexual sodomy" cases, the Court lags somewhat behind public opinion; in a majority of constitutional cases, especially those involving technical issues such as full faith and credit for interstate judgments, there is no strong public opinion. But there is usually rough parallelism: Constitutional law, as announced by the Supreme Court, almost never trumps entrenched constitutional arrangements, rarely ventures beyond public consensus, and seldom corrects "injustices" that the political system wants to preserve.[v]

If the Supreme Court is already tracking public opinion, is there such a need for Tushnet's proposal? On the other hand, is it really the case that the Court's activism is usually "wrong" from a progressive point of view? In *Brown*, the Court not only contributed mightily to public deliberations about the injustice of racial segregation, but also had an important political effect: by *reversing the burden of inertia*, the Court forced the political system to deal with an issue it had been avoiding for decades.[w] Another civic republican virtue of judicial review, even by conservative judges, is that it provides a portal into the governance structure for groups excluded from local politics (as African Americans were in the South) and unable to get the attention of Congress.

Imagine what American government, politics, and constitutional law would be like without the Supreme Court as the arbiter. You need to perform this

---

u. E.g., Larry Kramer, *The People Themselves: Popular Constitutionalism and Judicial Review* (2004) (urging drastic curtailment of judicial review); Jeremy Waldron, *Law and Disagreement* (1999) (abolition); Adrian Vermeule, *Judging Under Uncertainty: An Institutional Theory of Legal Interpretation* (2006) (drastic curtailment).

v. Nathan Persily, Jack Citrin & Patrick Egan, *Public Opinion and Constitutional Controversy* (2008); William Mishler & Reginald S. Sheehan, *The Supreme Court as a Countermajoritarian Institution? The Impact of Public Opinion on Supreme Court Opinions*, 87 Am. Pol. Sci. Rev. 87 (1993).

w. On the important role of courts in "reversing the burden of inertia," see Eskridge & Ferejohn, *Republic of Statutes*, ch. 8 & postscript.

thought experiment *now*, because after a few chapters of study from this book, you will find it harder to imagine the Constitution *without* the Court.

PROBLEM 2-3
THE CONSTITUTIONALITY OF GUN CONTROL LAWS:
AN EXERCISE IN CONSTITUTIONAL METHODOLOGY

In 2008, the District of Columbia had the strictest gun control law in the country. The District required a license for anyone to own a handgun, and other District regulations made it virtually impossible to procure a license for most ordinary residents and homeowners. Moreover, the lawful owner of a firearm was required to keep his weapon "unloaded and disassembled or bound by a trigger lock or similar device" unless it was kept at his place of business or being used for lawful recreational purposes. See D.C. Code § 7-2507.02. Thus, even if registered, a handgun stored at home could not be operational.

Police officer Dick Heller felt insecure in his own home because he could not have and use his (police-issued) weapon there. Heller sued the District to overturn D.C.'s regulation as a violation of his Second Amendment right as a law-abiding citizen to possess a firearm in his own home for self-defense. A majority of the Supreme Court, in an opinion by Justice Scalia, agreed with this argument. *District of Columbia v. Heller*, 128 S.Ct. 2783 (2008). Justice Stevens, joined by Justices Souter, Ginsburg, and Breyer, did not; he argued that the Second Amendment's protection is limited to Heller's participation in a citizen militia and does not extend to his home use of a firearm.

Try to set aside your own political views and analyze this constitutional issue in light of the following evidence. Is all of this evidence relevant? (If not, what would you delete?) What relevant evidence ought to be most weighty? And how does the evidence cut? How would you vote?

(A) *Constitutional Text and Structure.* The Second Amendment says: "A well regulated Militia, being necessary to the security of a free State, *the right of the people to keep and bear Arms, shall not be infringed.*" The italicized portion is the operative clause; the other portion is the prefatory clause. No other rights-conferring provision of the Constitution has this structure. Justice Scalia read the operative clause to be broader than the prefatory clause and read it liberally. Justice Stevens read the operative clause to be limited to the concerns of the prefatory clause. Which is more linguistically sound? Which is better linked to the meaning of the terms the framers used?

The 1773 edition of Samuel Johnson's *Dictionary of the English Language* (4th ed.) defined *arms* as "weapons of offence, or armour of defence." Timothy Cunningham's *New and Complete Dictionary* (1771) defined arms as "any thing that a man wears for his defence, or takes into his hands, or useth in wrath to cast at or strike another." Accord, Noah Webster, *American Dictionary of the English Language* (1828). "By *arms*, we understand those instruments of offence generally made use of in war; such as firearms, swords, & c. By *weapons*, we more particularly mean instruments of other kinds (exclusive of fire-arms), made use of as offensive, on special occasions." 1 J. Trusler, *The*

Distinction Between Words Esteemed Synonymous in the English Language 37 (1794).

The same dictionaries defined *keep* as "hav[ing] in custody"and *bear* as "to carry." *Bear arms* comes from the Latin *arma ferre*, which means "to bear [*ferre*] war equipment [*arma*]." Brief for Professors of Linguistics and English as *Amici Curiae*, at 19, *Heller.* Virginia's military law directed that "every one of the said officers, non-commissioned officers, and privates, shall constantly *keep* the aforesaid arms, accoutrements, and ammunition, ready to be produced whenever called for by his commanding officer." Act for Regulating and Disciplining the Militia, 1785 Va. Acts ch. 1, § 3.

As for the prefatory clause, *militia* in the eighteenth century meant both the state-organized militia, but also "all males physically capable of acting in concert for the common defense." *United States v. Miller*, 307 U.S. 174, 179 (1939). The "security of a Free state" referred to the notion that a citizen "militia," i.e., an armed populace, "is the natural defence of a free country." Joseph Story, *Commentaries on the Constitution of the United States* § 189 (4th ed. 1873).

Justice Scalia said that the ordinary linguistic meaning of the Second Amendment's operative clause is the regular law-abiding citizen's right to possess and deploy weapons (especially firearms). Justice Stevens said the ordinary meaning is the right of the citizen to maintain and bear weapons in the context of his service to the militia.

(B) *Background, Drafting, Ratification History, and Original Purpose.* Between the Restoration (1661) and the Glorious Revolution (1688), the Stuart Kings suppressed dissent, in part by disarming opponents of their regime and by deploying militias loyal to them. See Joyce Lee Malcolm, *To Keep and Bear Arms: The Origins of an American Right* 103-06 (1994). After secret-Catholic King James II was deposed, the Parliament secured an assurance from the new Protestant monarchs, William of Orange and Mary Stuart, in the Declaration of Right (codified as the English Bill of Rights): "That the subjects which are Protestants may have arms for their defense suitable to their conditions and as allowed by law." 1 W. & M., c. 2, § 7, in 3 Eng. Stat. at Large 441 (1689). Blackstone considered "the right of having and using arms for self-preservation and defence" in the Bill of Rights to be one of the fundamental rights of Englishmen. *Commentaries on the Laws of England* vol. 1, at 139-40 (1765); see also Thomas Hobbes, *Leviathan* (1651), who argued for a retained right of self-defense as instinct in the social contract.

One of the American grievances against George III was his effort to disarm the colonists. "It is a natural right which the people have reserved to themselves, confirmed by the Bill of Rights, to keep arms for their own defence." *N.Y. Journal*, Supp. 1, Apr. 13, 1769. It is not clear how widely held a view this was, but in the wake of the Revolution several early state constitutions had constitutional protections for citizens to keep and bear arms. Pennsylvania's Declaration of Rights (1776) said, in § XIII: "That the people have a right to bear arms for the defence of themselves and the state." And North Carolina's Declaration of Rights (1776), § XVII, stated: "That the people have a right to bear arms, for the defence of the State." Also, the Massachusetts Constitution (1780), First Part, Art. XVII, said: "The people have a right to keep and to bear arms for the common defence."

The Constitution presented for ratification gave Congress and the President authority over the national armed forces and the authority to call forth the militia in Article I, § 8, clause 16; the same clause vested the training of the militia with the states. During ratification, most states expressed concern about the strong national authority over armed citizens, and several states proposed (nonbinding) amendments to the document they ratified. George Mason expressed this objection: "The militia may be here destroyed by that method which has been practiced in other parts of the world before; that is, by rendering them useless — by disarming them. Under various pretences, Congress may neglect to provide for arming and disciplining the militia; and the state governments cannot do it, for Congress has the exclusive right to arm them." Virginia ratified over his objection but included the following proposals for amending the Constitution (*Elliott's Debates* 659):

> 17th, That the people have a right to keep and bear arms; that a well regulated Militia composed of the body of the people trained to arms is the proper, natural and safe defence of a free State. That standing armies are dangerous to liberty, and therefore ought to be avoided, as far as the circumstances and protection of the Community will admit; and that in all cases the military should be under strict subordination to and be governed by the civil power.

> 19th. That any person religiously scrupulous of bearing arms ought to be exempted, upon payment of an equivalent to employ another to bear arms in his stead.

North Carolina adopted exactly the same language, and New York similar language ("keep and bear arms") in proposing amendments after ratifying. Similar concerns were expressed in amendments proposed by New Hampshire and Massachusetts; Maryland rejected similar amendments, as did Pennsylvania, whose rejection was taken up by opponents as a critique of the Constitution.

The drafter of the Bill of Rights, Madison was aware of these amendments and was intimately familiar with the Virginia debates and the amendment proposed there. His initial draft of what became the Second Amendment was as follows: "The right of the people to keep and bear arms shall not be infringed; a well armed, and well regulated militia being the best security of a free country; but no person religiously scrupulous of bearing arms, shall be compelled to render military service in person." *The Complete Bill of Rights: The Drafts, Debates, Sources, and Origins* 183 (Neil H. Cogan ed. 1997). Madison later dropped the last clause and simplified the language into the Second Amendment now in the Constitution.

Is the drafting history relevant to determining original meaning? Does it make a difference that we do not know why Madison rewrote the amendment the way he did? Are the Virginia and other proposed amendments relevant? If so, how do they cut? Based on the foregoing materials, how would you view the purpose of the amendment? How broad?

(C) *Contemporaneous Construction.* There is much debate in *Heller* regarding the understanding of contemporaries. Should this be relevant? Here are some of the materials bruited about by the Justices.

St. George Tucker's American edition of Blackstone's *Commentaries* (1803) included as Note "D" Tucker's "View of the Constitution of the United States." As to the Second Amendment, Tucker (a prominent Anti-Federalist and law professor) said: "This may be considered as the true palladium of liberty . . . . The right to self-defence is the first law of nature: in most governments it has been the study of rulers to confine the right within the narrowest limits possible. Wherever standing armies are kept up, and the right of the people to keep and bear arms is, under any colour or pretext whatsoever, prohibited, liberty, if not already annihilated, is on the brink of destruction." Vol. 1, App. 300. Tucker believed that the English game laws had abridged the right by prohibiting "keeping a gun or other engine for the destruction of game." *Id..* He grouped the Second Amendment right with some of the individual rights included in the First Amendment and enforceable through judicial review. *Id.,* App. 357.

Originally published in 1833, Justice Joseph Story's *Commentaries* include discussion of the Second Amendment. In § 189, Story equated the Second Amendment with the arms provision in the English Declaration (Bill) of Rights. The most relevant portion is worth extensive quotation:

> The importance of [the Second Amendment] will scarcely be doubted by any persons who have duly reflected upon the subject. The militia is the natural defence of a free country against sudden foreign invasions, domestic insurrections, and domestic usurpations of power by rulers. It is against sound policy for a free people to keep up large military establishments and standing armies in time of peace, both from the enormous expenses with which they are attended and the facile means which they afford to ambitious and unprincipled rulers to subvert the government, or trample upon the rights of the people. The right of the citizens to keep and bear arms has justly been considered as the palladium of the liberties of a republic, since it offers a strong moral check against the usurpation and arbitrary power of rulers, and will generally, even if these are successful in the first instance, enable the people to resist and triumph over them. And yet, though this truth would seem so clear, and the importance of a well-regulated militia would seem so undeniable, it cannot be disguised that, among the American people, there is a growing indifference to any system of militia discipline, and a strong disposition, from a sense of its burdens, to be rid of all regulations. How it is practicable to keep the people duly armed without some organization, it is difficult to see. There is certainly no small danger that indifference may lead to disgust, and disgust to contempt; and thus gradually undermine all the protection intended by the clause of our national bill of rights.

It is not entirely clear that Story's is "contemporaneous," in which case his account might be shifted to the next section.

Consider a different view: "The provision of the constitution, declaring the right of the people to keep and bear arms, &c. was probably intended to apply to the right of the people to bear arms for such [militia-related] purposes only, and not to prevent congress or the legislatures of the different states from enacting laws to prevent the citizens from always going armed. A different construction however has been given to it." Benjamin L. Oliver, *The Rights of an American Citizen* 177 (1832).

(D) *Post-Enactment Understanding and History.* Recall that the challengers in *Brown,* and ultimately the Court itself, argued that whatever ambiguities there might have been at the time of the Fourteenth Amendment's framing, they had disappeared by 1954. One might argue that ambiguities as to the ambit of the

Second Amendment might be clarified by practice after 1791 (when the amendment was adopted). Under almost all theories of constitutional interpretation, this kind of evidence is much weaker than constitutional text, original (and contemporaneous) understanding and purpose, and judicial precedent. Some theories would discount the following information entirely.

Between 1789 and 1820, nine States adopted Second Amendment analogues. Four (Kentucky, Ohio, Indiana, and Missouri) recognized the right of the people to "bear arms in defence of themselves and the State." Another three (Mississippi, Connecticut, and Alabama) found that each citizen has the "right to bear arms in defence of himself and the State." Two (Tennessee and Maine) followed the "common defence" language of the 1780 Massachusetts Constitution.

A number of state courts gave federal or state constitutional protections for the right to bear arms a broad reading in the nineteenth century. In *Nunn v. State*, 1 Ga. 243, 251 (1846), the Georgia Supreme Court invalidated a state ban on open carrying of pistols based upon the defendant's Second Amendment "*natural* right of self-defence." Consider the court's broad rhetoric:

> The right of the whole people, old and young, men, women and boys, and not militia only, to keep and bear *arms* of every description, and not *such* merely as are used by the *militia*, shall not be *infringed*, curtailed, or broken in upon, in the smallest degree; and all this for the important end to be attained: the rearing up and qualifying a well-regulated militia, so vitally necessary to the security of a free State. Our opinion is, that any law, State or Federal, is repugnant to the Constitution, and void, which contravenes this *right*, originally belonging to our forefathers, trampled under foot by Charles I. and his two wicked sons and successors, re-established by the revolution of 1688, conveyed to this land of liberty by the colonists, and finally incorporated conspicuously in our own Magna Charta!

Accord, *State v. Chandler*, 5 La. Ann. 489, 490 (La. 1850) (right of citizens to carry arms openly). On the other hand, the Tennessee Supreme Court in *Aymette v. State*, 21 Tenn. 154 (1840), held that the state constitutional guarantee of the right to "bear" arms did not prohibit the banning of concealed weapons. The court read that right to refer only to "protect[ion of] the public liberty" and "keep[ing] in awe those in power."

After the Civil War, advocates for rights of the freed slaves assumed broad readings of the Second Amendment when they cited state restrictions on gun use by people of color as an example of southern deprivation of constitutional liberties. See generally Stephen Halbrook, *Freedman, the Fourteenth Amendment, and the Right to Bear Arms, 1866-1876* (1998). Section 14 of the Freedmen's Bureau Act on July 16, 1866, 14 Stat. at 176-77, said this:

> [T]he right . . . to have full and equal benefit of all laws and proceedings concerning personal liberty, personal security, and the acquisition, enjoyment, and disposition of estate, real and personal, including the constitutional right to bear arms, shall be secured to and enjoyed by all the citizens . . . without respect to race or color, or previous condition of slavery . . . .

It was assumed during congressional debate that the founding generation "were for every man bearing his arms about him and keeping them in his house, his castle, for his own defense." Cong. Globe, 39th Cong., 1st Sess., 362, 371 (1866) (Sen. Davis, an opponent of the 1866 Act). Similar legislator statements were made during the congressional debates regarding the Fourteenth Amendment and the Civil Rights Act of 1871.

Thomas Cooley, *General Principles of Constitutional Law* 271 (1880) (leading constitutional law treatise), described the Second Amendment:

> The meaning of the provision undoubtedly is, that the people, from whom the militia must be taken, shall have the right to keep and bear arms; and they need no permission or regulation of law for the purpose. But this enables government to have a well-regulated militia; for to bear arms implies something more than the mere keeping; it implies the learning to handle and use them in a way that makes those who keep them ready for their efficient use; in other words, it implies the right to meet for voluntary discipline in arms, observing in doing so the laws of public order.

Other nineteenth century commentators generally followed Cooley, but by the twentieth century the Second Amendment (like the state militias) seemed to recede in debates about public policy and constitutional law.

The first two federal laws directly restricting civilian use and possession of firearms — the 1927 Act prohibiting mail delivery of "pistols, revolvers, and other firearms capable of being concealed on the person," Ch. 75, 44 Stat. 1059, and the 1934 Act prohibiting the possession of sawed-off shotguns and machine guns — were enacted over minor Second Amendment objections dismissed by legislators who participated in the debates. After the New Deal, Congress, state legislatures, and city councils have adopted hundreds of gun control laws. In adopting gun control laws, however, Congress has *always* steered clear of or exempted homeowners' use of guns for self-defense. See 27 Stat. 116 (1892) (crime to carry concealed pistol in the District except in one's place of business or "dwelling house"); Pub. L. No. 275, § 4, 47 Stat. 650, 651 (1932) (same); Pub. L. No. 274, 55 Stat. 742 (1941) (eve-of-war property requisition law, with prominent exception disallowing requisitioning of guns held for one's "personal use or sport"); Pub. L. No. 90-618, § 101, 82 Stat. 1213 (1968) (similar exclusion from the leading gun control statute); Pub. L. No. 99-308, 100 Stat. 449 (1986) (amending 1968 law to further protect people's Second Amendment rights).[x]

(E) *Precedent and Stare Decisis.* In terms of authority, Supreme Court precedent is second only to constitutional text (and original meaning) as a matter of legal authority. We treat this evidence here because that's how it best fits chronologically. The leading precedent does not come until 1939, but a few earlier ones reflect the Supreme Court's ungenerous approach to the Second Amendment before *Heller*.

In *United States v. Cruikshank*, 92 U. S. 542 (1876), the Court sustained a challenge to convictions under the Enforcement Act of 1870 for conspiring to deprive any individual of "any right or privilege granted or secured to him by the constitution or laws of the United States." Counts 2 and 10 of the indictment

---

x. Stephen Halbrook, *Congress Interprets the Second Amendment,* 62 Tenn. L. Rev. 597 (1995); Brief for Amici Curiae 55 Members of the U.S. Senate, the President of the U.S. Senate, and 250 Members of the U.S. House of Representatives in Support of Respondent, *District of Columbia v. Heller* (Supreme Court, Docket No. 07-290), authored by Halbrook.

related to defendants' alleged efforts to restrict the lawful use of weapons by other citizens; the Court declined to view this activity by the defendants as raising a constitutional concern:

> The right there specified [in the indictment] is that of "bearing arms for a lawful purpose." This is not a right granted by the Constitution. Neither is it in any manner dependent on that instrument for its existence. The second amendment declares that it shall not be infringed; but this, as has been seen, means no more than that it shall not be infringed by Congress. This is one of the amendments that has no other effect than to restrict the powers of the national government.

Other nineteenth century Supreme Court cases took a narrow view of the Second Amendment, but none was primarily concerned with that amendment. See also *Presser v. Illinois,* 116 U.S. 252 (1886), where the Court held that the right to keep and bear arms was not violated by a law that forbade "bodies of men to associate together as military organizations, or to drill or parade with arms in cities and towns unless authorized by law."

The leading Supreme Court case was *United States v. Miller,* 307 U.S. 174 (1939), where the Court upheld a conviction for transporting a double-barreled shotgun in violation of the National Firearms Act of 1934. Rejecting the defendant's Second Amendment argument, Justice McReynolds' opinion for a unanimous Court ruled that the amendment's operative clause had to be construed in light of the prefatory clause; this was fatal for the defendant's individual rights claim:

> In the absence of any evidence tending to show that possession or use of a 'shotgun having a barrel of less than eighteen inches in length' at this time has some reasonable relationship to the preservation or efficiency of a well regulated militia, we cannot say that the Second Amendment guarantees the right to keep and bear such an instrument. Certainly it is not within judicial notice that this weapon is any part of the ordinary military equipment or that its use could contribute to the common defense. (307 U.S. at 178.)

Miller was the last Supreme Court decision directly addressing individual rights claims under the Second Amendment, and that precedent has been treated as binding interpretation. E.g., *Lewis v. United States,* 445 U.S. 55, 65-66 n. 8 (1980) (following *Miller* for the proposition that the Second Amendment guarantees no right to keep and bear a firearm that does not have "some reasonable relationship to the preservation or efficiency of a well regulated militia").

Based on the foregoing materials, should *Miller* be overruled? (Recall that *Brown* substantially overruled *Plessy,* illustrating how the Supreme Court is more willing to overrule constitutional precedents than common law or statutory precedents.) Or is there another way to handle *Miller* if you agree with Justice Scalia?

(F) *Norms.* Norms come into play at two points: Is there a constitutional interest in possessing handguns in your home, or elsewhere? If so, what state interests justify regulation of guns, and what kinds of regulations are constitutionally permissible?

As to the first issue, there has been a normative shift in the United States as the result of a social movement very different from the civil rights movement that brought *Brown* and other race discrimination cases to the Supreme Court. Represented most effectively in the National Rifle Association (NRA), the right to own and use guns has gained significant traction in the United States in the last generation — at the same time women's, gay rights, and disability rights movements have also been successful in changing public opinion as to a broad range of issues. In the middle of the New Deal, when gun control was widely accepted, a Second Amendment right outside the militia context was largely unthinkable to conservative as well as progressive judges — while at the dawn of the New Millennium all nine Justices agreed that there is an individual right to gun ownership, and the main debate among the Justices were how broadly to define that right. Justice Scalia did not believe the right extended to "dangerous and unusual weapons" or to weapons used for illegal or harmful purposes.

All nine Justices also accepted the New Deal norm that the public interest can justify extensive state regulation of handguns. Justice Scalia explicitly said that he would not question the constitutionality of "longstanding prohibitions on the possession of firearms by felons and the mentally ill, or laws forbidding the carrying of firearms in sensitive places such as schools and government buildings, or laws imposing conditions and qualifications on the commercial sale of arms." He did not take a clear position on what level of scrutiny he would apply to laws regulating handguns used outside the home or other than for self-defense. Cf. Adam Winkler, *Scrutinizing the Second Amendment,* 105 Mich. L. Rev. 683, 687, 716-718 (2007) (describing hundreds of gun-law decisions issued in the last half-century by Supreme Courts in 42 States, which courts with "surprisingly little variation" have adopted a standard more deferential than strict scrutiny).

Justice Breyer (in a separate dissent) would have gone considerably further, based in part on founding era precedent. A 1783 Massachusetts law forbade the residents of Boston to "take into" or "receive into" "any Dwelling House, Stable, Barn, Out-house, Ware-house, Store, Shop or other Building" loaded firearms, and permitted the seizure of any loaded firearms that "shall be found" there. Act of Mar. 1, 1783, ch. 13, 1783 Mass. Acts p. 218. Notwithstanding that state's constitutional protection for firearm possession, this statute was similar to the District of Columbia law banning loaded firearms in one's home.

Justice Breyer had a broader concern. The D.C. Council found in 1976 that the proliferation of guns in the District contributed directly to increased levels of violence and death and further concluded that a ban on private possession of firearms was the best way of dealing with this problem of social and personal security. Post-1976 evidence suggests uncertainty whether a firearm ban serves this purpose (especially because Virginia and Maryland, bordering the District, allow gun ownership). Some studies suggest the ban has had no effect, others say that it has had some retarding effect. Why not allow legislatures to experiment in this way, and see over the longer term what works? Is it not irresponsible "judicial activism" to overturn the District's relatively far-reaching law, based upon speculative original meaning evidence?

Theoretical Queries. (1) *Original Meaning.* Judge Bork asks you to draft a memorandum as to which interpretation best reflects "original constitutional meaning," as applied to the District's ban of handguns in the home for self-defense. How would you come down? Jot down your thoughts now, and then consult the Justices' debate over original meaning in *District of Columbia v. Heller*, 128 S.Ct.2783 (2008). Do the original materials prevent the Justices from reading their own values into the Constitution? Or is using original materials more like looking out over the crowd and picking out your friends?

(2) *Common Law, Burkean Constitutionalism*. Professor Ernest Young decides to write a law review article explaining how the Supreme Court should resolve the constitutional issue in *Heller* — and how the majority should explain their reasons. Provide a roadmap for him to follow, given his Burkean pragmatism. Does the case-by-case approach of the common law provide a useful way of approaching an emotional issue (gun control) such as this one?

(3) *Popular Constitutionalism*. It is clear that this issue would never have reached the Supreme Court absent the gun rights social movement, spearheaded by the National Rifle Association (NRA). Social movements can expand or narrow the issues that are worth discussing in our legal-political system. Writing for the majority in *Heller,* Justice Scalia's opinion struck down the District's bar to handguns in the home for self-defense but did not mention the NRA, or even the various congressional carve-outs cited above. How would Professor Eskridge analyze this? See William Eskridge, Jr., *Sodomy and Guns: "Tradition" in Constitutional Interpretation*, Harv. J.L. & Pol'y (forthcoming). Professors Siegel and Post? See Reva Siegel, *Dead or Alive: Originalism as Popular Constitutionalism in* Heller, 122 Harv. L. Rev. 191 (2008). Would Professor Ackerman find this to be a constitutional moment?

Chapter 3

THE CONSTITUTION AND
RACIAL DISCRIMINATION

Since *Brown*, the Court has developed an elaborate approach to resolving racial discrimination cases. Section 1 of this chapter considers judicial review of statutes that disproportionally disadvantage racial minorities. Section 1 first analyzes current doctrine concerning such statutes that on their face take race into account, and then turns to the different approach taken to facially neutral statutes. Section 2 considers the important limitation upon federal power to outlaw racial discrimination imposed by the state action doctrine, which restricts the coverage of the Equal Protection Clause to governmental conduct rather than private behavior. In Section 3, we turn to how "affirmative action" — the use of a racial classification to advantage historically disadvantaged minorities — is scrutinized. By way of introduction, consider three sets of issues.

1. *Race and the Equal Protection Clause.* The Equal Protection Clause does not mention racial discrimination. Its context and history, however, establish that it was intended to target discrimination against African Americans. For example, the Court in *Strauder v. West Virginia*, 100 U.S. 303 (1879), held that the state's exclusion of African-American men from juries violated the equal protection of the laws (see Chapter 2, § 1A). One way to understand the result in *Brown* is that the states' segregation had to overcome a strong presumption against distinctions grounded upon race, and the states never overcame that presumption. (This may seem more persuasive than Chief Justice Warren's reliance on social science studies.)

Given the origins of the Equal Protection Clause, should it only be concerned with racial discrimination against African Americans? In *The Slaughter House Cases*, 83 U.S. (16 Wall.) 36 (1872), the Court said that it "doubt[ed] very much whether any action of a state not directed by way of discrimination against the negroes as a class, or on account of their race, will ever be held to come within the purview of this provision." Yet in 1886, in *Yick Wo v. Hopkins* (§ 1B of this chapter), the Supreme Court forcefully applied the Equal Protection Clause to strike down municipal practices discriminating against citizens of China living in the United States.

Indeed, current doctrine concerning discrimination against African Americans is derived in part from two cases involving Asian Americans.

During World War II, the federal government forcibly evacuated from the West Coast residents of Japanese ancestry, including those who were American citizens. (Earl Warren, later the Chief Justice, was then Governor of California and enthusiastically helped implement this program.) *Hirabayashi v. United States*, 320 U.S. 81 (1943), unanimously upheld the criminal conviction of an American citizen for refusing to obey a curfew order requiring all persons of Japanese ancestry to remain in their homes from 8:00 p.m. to 6:00 a.m. daily. *Korematsu v. United States*, 323 U.S. 214 (1944), by a 6-3 vote, upheld the criminal conviction of an American citizen who refused to leave the West Coast and be relocated. The subjects of intense criticism to this day, *Hirabayashi* and *Korematsu* seem impossible to defend from the current perspective, for the government programs appear to have been based on racist notions about the lack of loyalty of citizens of Japanese extraction. (German-Americans and Italian-Americans were not subjected to such severe wartime treatment.)[a]

As the Court often does in uncomfortable cases, the opinions in *Hirabayashi* and *Korematsu* tried to put a good face on a bad situation. These cases articulated what has become known as the "strict scrutiny" approach to racial discrimination claims. *Hirabayashi* stated that "[d]istinctions between citizens solely because of their ancestry are by their very nature odious to a free people whose institutions are founded upon the doctrine of equality. * * * [R]acial discriminations are in most circumstances irrelevant and therefore prohibited[.]" *Korematsu* elaborated on this theme:

> [A]ll legal restrictions which curtail the civil rights of a single racial group are immediately suspect. That is not to say that all such restrictions are unconstitutional. It is to say that courts must subject them to the most rigid scrutiny. Pressing public necessity may sometimes justify the existence of such restrictions; racial antagonism never can.

Although *Brown* did not cite *Hirabayashi* or *Korematsu*, the strict scrutiny approach growing out of those cases has become the test for judging (and invalidating) statutes that disadvantage racial minorities through the overt use of racial criteria, as § 1A of this chapter explains. *Korematsu* is the last case in which the Court has upheld intentional governmental discrimination against a racial or national-origin minority.

2. *Why Race? What Is Race?* Perhaps the most curious thing about equal protection law is that it proceeds without any reflection on why it is focusing on certain categories, such as race. The biologists tell us that there is a human "race" and that otherwise the term is pretty much a social construction: Human genetic variability among the populations of Europe, Africa, and Asia is not significantly different from the ethnic variations within the so-called racial

---

a. Indeed, in 1988 Congress enacted legislation apologizing for the relocation and internment program and awarding $20,000 to each surviving internee. See Civil Liberties Act of 1988, 50 U.S.C. app. § 1989b-4(a)(1) (1988). In 1987 a federal appeals court vacated Hirabayashi's conviction because of a showing that the federal government had concealed evidence supporting his claim that the prosecution was rooted in racial prejudice rather than military necessity. See *Hirabayashi v. United States*, 828 F.2d 591 (9th Cir. 1987). A few years earlier a district court had vacated Korematsu's conviction for the same reason. See *Korematsu v. United States*, 584 F. Supp. 1406 (N.D. Cal. 1984).

groups associated with each continent. See Anthony Appiah, *The Uncompleted Argument: DuBois and the Illusion of Race*, 12 Crit. Inquiry, Aut. 1985, at 21. Yet the history of the United States is a history of race obsession — as revealed not only in the institution of slavery and its repercussions, but also our country's treatment of Indians, the servitude of Asians in the West, and the reaction to a growing Latino population.

Perhaps the treatment of race in American law can be understood (descriptively, not normatively) as the reaction of the long-predominant Anglo-Saxon culture to different racial and ethnic groups. From the earliest colonial times, the Anglo-Saxon culture strongly differentiated itself from the Indians (with whom they were in conflict to obtain land) and Africans (the slaves), and the law reflected that differentiation with severe restrictions on interactions with the subordinated groups. This social differentiation has never fully dissipated, and being African American or Native American continues to have significant consequences today. The differentiation has dissipated more for other groups — such as Irish, Jewish, and Italian immigrants — who shared much of the same European background as the dominant culture and were more easily "assimilated" into it. Other differentiations have occurred for other immigrant groups, especially Asians and Latinos. Classifications also may generate a sense of cultural self-identification among members of the group, with various cross-cutting consequences.[b]

The obsession with race has also generated peculiar constructions of racial and ethnic categories. People like Homer Plessy, who had but one African ancestor, were classified as "black" in American culture (and still are to some extent), even when they were genetically much more ethnically white. The dominant culture tends to classify anyone with a Spanish-sounding last name or with a Cuban, Mexican, Central American, Puerto Rican, or South American parent as "Hispanic," even though such a classification cuts across various ethnic and racial categories internalized by people in the various groups. One consequence of this complexity is that virtually any legal discussion about race and ethnicity will be oversimplified. We apologize in advance for our own sacrifices of precision to space considerations.

3. *The Legacy of* Brown. This chapter considers the struggle over the meaning of *Brown v. Board of Education*, for African Americans in particular, but also for other racial and ethnic groups. As we discovered in Chapter 2, *Brown* is vulnerable to criticism, which has become more intense as *Brown* was implemented (Chapter 2, § 2) and applied to other problems implicating race and ethnicity (this chapter). The struggle for constructing what *Brown* means has focused on what the antidiscrimination principle means.

---

b. Theoretical analysis of the ways in which a dominant group uses labeling to create patterns of domination and marginalization can be found in Mary McIntosh, *The Homosexual Role*, 16 Social Problems 182-93 (1968), reprinted in *The Forms of Desire: Sexual Orientation and the Social Constructionist Controversy* ch. 3 (Edward Stein ed. 1990), and Michel Foucault, *The Subject and Power*, in *Michel Foucault: Beyond Structuralism and Hermeneutics* 208 (Hebert Dreyfuss & Paul Rabinow eds. 1982).

Civil rights movement lawyers and their allies focused on the *anti-subordination* feature of equality and the *affirmative responsibilities* of the state.[c] For Thurgood Marshall and his colleagues at the Inc. Fund, the process initiated by *Brown* was a "Second Reconstruction," whereby the state would not only recognize the full citizenship of a class of Americans who had been treated as second-class citizens by the state and stigmatized by racism, but would also attack the vestiges and effects of apartheid through an affirmative remedial program. The first, a politics of recognition, yielded *Brown I* and entailed a campaign against state policies having racially discriminatory effects, including many criminal laws, the operation of the death penalty, some employment testing and other requirements. The second, a politics of remediation, yielded *Brown II* and then *Green* (p.106, *supra*) — cases requiring the state to dismantle segregated schools and affirmatively integrate them. It entailed a campaign in favor of state policies restructuring race-tainted institutions, barring private parties from discriminating, and redistributing state resources toward people of color. Some of these policies, such as the remedial decree in *Swann* (p. 106, *supra*) and affirmative action programs, were themselves race-based.

Libertarians, including many who had opposed apartheid as well as (former) supporters of racial segregation, focused on the *rationality* feature of equality and the *negative responsibilities* of the state.[d] The author of an important memorandum to Justice Frankfurter supporting the Inc. Fund in *Brown*, Alexander Bickel (whose later scholarly work is discussed throughout Chapter 2), personally agreed that race-based statutory classifications were suspect, mainly because they were not relevant to rational state policies; once the state purged itself of the irrational classifications, the equality principle was satisfied. The state had the freedom but not the responsibility to enact laws prohibiting discrimination by private persons and firms. But most libertarians were not willing to go along with eliminating rational state policies because of their race-based effects, and most were skeptical of new race-based policies seeking to remediate the legacy of apartheid. Indeed, Bickel believed that race-based affirmative action deepened the evil legacy of apartheid by reinforcing negative stereotypes about black people and fanning racist prejudices.[e]

Consider these competing visions of equality and state responsibility as you read the materials in this chapter. Consider also how the original meaning of

---

c. See, e.g., Derrick Bell, Jr., *Race, Racism, and American Law* (6th ed. 2008); Kimberlé Crenshaw, *Race, Reform, and Retrenchment: Transformation and Legitimation in Antidiscrimination Law*, 101 Harv. L. Rev. 1331 (1988); Ruth Colker, *Anti-Subordination Above All: Sex, Race, and Equal Protection*, 61 NYU L. Rev. 1003 (1986); Neil Gotanda, *A Critique of "Our Constitution Is Color-Blind*," 44 Stan. L. Rev. 1 (1991).

d. See, e.g., Thomas Sowell, *Civil Rights: Rhetoric or Reality?* (1984) (excerpted in § 3A of this chapter); Walter Williams, *The State Against Blacks* (1982); Jim Chen, *Diversity and Damnation*, 43 UCLA L. Rev. 1839 (1996); Charles Fried, Metro Broadcasting v. FCC: *Two Concepts of Equality*, 104 Harv. L. Rev. 107 (1990).

e. See Brief of the Anti-Defamation League of B'nai B'rith *Amicus Curiae, DeFunis v. Odegaard* (U.S. Supreme Court, No. 73-235) (*amicus* brief filed by Bickel and Philip Kurland in Supreme Court's first constitutional affirmative action case).

the Fourteenth Amendment, the institutional limits of the judiciary (including Bickel's passive virtues), and precedents as well as common law values should influence the way these different visions were received by Supreme Court Justices who were neither strongly egalitarian nor absolutely libertarian in their approach to these issues.

SECTION 1. RACIAL CLASSIFICATIONS AFTER *BROWN*

A.   FACIAL RACIAL CLASSIFICATIONS THAT DISADVANTAGE MINORITIES OR EVIDENCE RACIAL HOSTILITY

All statutes overtly classify people on the basis of one or more criteria. For example, driver's license regulations classify people on the basis of eyesight, written test results, and so on. In considering modern equal protection doctrine concerning racial discrimination, it is first necessary to distinguish statutes that *on their face* classify on the basis of race or national origin ("it shall be unlawful for any person of Japanese ancestry to fail to . . .") and those that are facially neutral concerning race or national origin ("it shall be unlawful for any person to assist a country at war with the United States by . . ."). The governmental orders attacked in *Korematsu* and *Hirabayashi* contained facial national-origin classifications; the school segregation statutes in *Brown* contained facial racial classifications.

The facial classifications in *Korematsu* and *Hirabayashi* disadvantaged a national-origin minority. *Brown*, too, fits this pattern of facial classification and selective disadvantage once the Court accepted the proposition that segregated public schools are inherently unequal and therefore selectively harmful to African Americans. Following *Brown*, the Court, through *per curiam* summary orders without accompanying opinions, applied the antidiscrimination principle to outlaw segregation in other public facilities.[a]

In the 1960s, the Court began facing a somewhat different problem with statutes containing facial racial classifications. Consider *Anderson v. Martin*, 375 U.S. 399 (1964), in which the Court struck down a Louisiana statute that required that election ballots indicate the race of the candidates. The statute applied equally to all candidates, white and non-white alike, and thus was not like the Japanese relocation and curfew orders. Nonetheless, are there arguments flowing from *Brown* that could justify invalidating the law? Similarly, in *McLaughlin v. Florida*, 379 U.S. 184 (1964), the Court struck down a statute prohibiting an unmarried interracial couple from "habitually liv[ing] in and occupy[ing] in the nighttime the same room." The Court noted

---

a. See *Schiro v. Bynum*, 375 U.S. 395 (1964) (municipal auditorium); *New Orleans City Park Improvement Ass'n v. Detiege*, 358 U.S. 54 (1958) (municipal golf course and parks); *Gayle v. Browder*, 352 U.S. 903 (1956) (city buses); *Holmes v. Atlanta*, 350 U.S. 879 (1955) (municipal golf course); *Mayor & City Council of Baltimore City v. Dawson*, 350 U.S. 877 (1955) (public bathhouses and beaches).

that this behavior was not a crime if engaged in by a man and woman of the same race. Finally, consider *Loving v. Virginia* in this light.

LOVING v. VIRGINIA
388 U.S. 1, 87 S.Ct. 1817, 18 L.Ed.2d 1010 (1967)

CHIEF JUSTICE WARREN delivered the opinion of the Court.

[In 1958, an African-American woman and a white man, both residents of Virginia, got married in the District of Columbia. Upon returning to Virginia and making their home there, they were prosecuted for violating the state anti-miscegenation law. After they pleaded guilty in 1959, the Virginia trial judge imposed a one-year jail sentence, but suspended it for 25 years on condition that the Lovings leave Virginia and not return together for 25 years. The state courts later denied the Lovings' motion to vacate the conviction and sentence on the ground that the antimiscegenation law was unconstitutional.]

Virginia is now one of 16 States which prohibit and punish marriages on the basis of racial classifications.[5] Penalties for miscegenation arose as an incident to slavery and have been common in Virginia since the colonial period. The present statutory scheme dates from the adoption of the Racial Integrity Act of 1924, passed during the period of extreme nativism which followed the end of the First World War. * * *

I. In upholding the constitutionality of these provisions in the decision below, the Supreme Court of Appeals of Virginia referred to its 1955 decision in *Naim v. Naim*, 197 Va. 80, 87 S.E.2d 749. * * * In *Naim*, the state court concluded that the State's legitimate purposes were "to preserve the racial integrity of its citizens," and to prevent "the corruption of blood," "a mongrel breed of citizens," and "the obliteration of racial pride," obviously an endorsement of the doctrine of White Supremacy. * * *

* * * [T]he State argues that the meaning of the Equal Protection Clause, as illuminated by the statements of the Framers, is only that state penal laws containing an interracial element as part of the definition of the offense must apply equally to whites and Negroes in the sense that members of each race are punished to the same degree. Thus, the State contends that, because its miscegenation statutes punish equally both the white and the Negro participants in an interracial marriage, these statutes, despite their reliance on racial classifications do not constitute an invidious discrimination based upon race. The second argument advanced by the State assumes the validity of its equal application theory. The argument is that, if the Equal Protection Clause does not outlaw miscegenation statutes because of their reliance on racial classifications, the question of constitutionality would thus become whether there was any rational basis for a State to treat interracial marriages differently from other marriages. On this question, the State argues, the scientific evidence is substantially in doubt and, consequently, this Court should defer to the wisdom

---

5. * * * Over the past 15 years, 14 states have repealed laws outlawing interracial marriages. * * *

of the state legislature in adopting its policy of discouraging interracial marriages.

Because we reject the notion that the mere "equal application" of a statute containing racial classifications is enough to remove the classifications from the Fourteenth Amendment's proscription of all invidious racial discriminations, we do not accept the State's contention that these statutes should be upheld if there is any possible basis for concluding that they serve a rational purpose. The mere fact of equal application does not mean that our analysis of these statutes should follow the approach we have taken in cases involving no racial discrimination where the Equal Protection Clause has been arrayed against a statute discriminating between the kinds of advertising which may be displayed on trucks in New York City, *Railway Express Agency, Inc. v. New York* [Chapter 4, § 1], or an exemption in Ohio's ad valorem tax for merchandise owned by a non-resident in a storage warehouse, *Allied Stores of Ohio, Inc. v. Bowers*, 358 U.S. 522 (1959). In these cases, involving distinctions not drawn according to race, the Court has merely asked whether there is any rational foundation for the discriminations, and has deferred to the wisdom of the state legislatures. In the case at bar, however, we deal with statutes containing racial classifications, and the fact of equal application does not immunize the statute from the very heavy burden of justification which the Fourteenth Amendment has traditionally required of state statutes drawn according to race.

The State argues that statements in the Thirty-ninth Congress about the time of the passage of the Fourteenth Amendment indicate that the Framers did not intend the Amendment to make unconstitutional state miscegenation laws. Many of the statements alluded to by the State concern the debates over the Freedmen's Bureau Bill, which President Johnson vetoed, and the Civil Rights Act of 1866, 14 Stat. 27, enacted over his veto. While these statements have some relevance to the intention of Congress in submitting the Fourteenth Amendment, it must be understood that they pertained to the passage of specific statutes and not to the broader, organic purpose of a constitutional amendment. As for the various statements directly concerning the Fourteenth Amendment, we have said in connection with a related problem, that although these historical sources "cast some light" they are not sufficient to resolve the problem; "[a]t best, they are inconclusive. The most avid proponents of the post-War Amendments undoubtedly intended them to remove all legal distinctions among 'all persons born or naturalized in the United States.' Their opponents, just as certainly, were antagonistic to both the letter and the spirit of the Amendments and wished them to have the most limited effect." *Brown*. We have rejected the proposition that the debates in the Thirty-ninth Congress or in the state legislatures which ratified the Fourteenth Amendment supported the theory advanced by the State, that the requirement of equal protection of the laws is satisfied by penal laws defining offenses based on racial classifications so long as white and Negro participants in the offense were similarly punished. *McLaughlin*.

The State finds support for its "equal application" theory in the decision of the Court in *Pace v. Alabama*, 106 U.S. 583 (1883). In that case, the Court upheld a conviction under an Alabama statute forbidding adultery or fornication between a white person and a Negro which imposed a greater penalty than that of a statute proscribing similar conduct by members of the same race. The Court reasoned that the statute could not be said to discriminate against Negroes because the punishment for each participant in the offense was the same. However, as recently as the 1964 Term, in rejecting the reasoning of that case, we stated "*Pace* represents a limited view of the Equal Protection Clause which has not withstood analysis in the subsequent decisions of this Court." *McLaughlin.* As we there demonstrated, the Equal Protection Clause requires the consideration of whether the classifications drawn by any statute constitute an arbitrary and invidious discrimination. The clear and central purpose of the Fourteenth Amendment was to eliminate all official state sources of invidious racial discrimination in the States.

There can be no question but that Virginia's miscegenation statutes rest solely upon distinctions drawn according to race. The statutes proscribe generally accepted conduct if engaged in by members of different races. Over the years, this Court has consistently repudiated "[d]istinctions between citizens solely because of their ancestry" as being "odious to a free people whose institutions are founded upon the doctrine of equality." *Hirabayashi.* At the very least, the Equal Protection Clause demands that racial classifications, especially suspect in criminal statutes, be subjected to the "most rigid scrutiny," *Korematsu*, and, if they are ever to be upheld, they must be shown to be necessary to the accomplishment of some permissible state objective, independent of the racial discrimination which it was the object of the Fourteenth Amendment to eliminate. * * *

There is patently no legitimate overriding purpose independent of invidious racial discrimination which justifies this classification. The fact that Virginia prohibits only interracial marriages involving white persons demonstrates that the racial classifications must stand on their own justification, as measures designed to maintain White Supremacy.[11] We have consistently denied the constitutionality of measures which restrict the rights of citizens on account of race. There can be no doubt that restricting the freedom to marry solely because

---

11.   Appellants point out that the State's concern in these statutes, as expressed in the words of the 1924 Act's title, "An Act to Preserve Racial Integrity," extends only to the integrity of the white race. While Virginia prohibits whites from marrying any nonwhite (subject to the exception for the descendants of Pocahontas), Negroes, Orientals, and any other racial class may intermarry without statutory interference.   Appellants contend that this distinction renders Virginia's miscegenation statutes arbitrary and unreasonable even assuming the constitutional validity of an official purpose to preserve "racial integrity." We need not reach this contention because we find the racial classifications in these statutes repugnant to the Fourteenth Amendment, even assuming an even-handed state purpose to protect the "integrity" of all races. [*Editors' note*: The Virginia statutes stated that "the term 'white person' shall apply only to such person as has no trace whatever of any blood other than Caucasian; but persons who have one-sixteenth or less of the blood of the American Indian and have no other non-Caucasic blood shall be deemed to be white persons." In an earlier footnote, Chief Justice Warren explained this exception by quoting a 1925 publication by a state official, who wrote that it reflected " 'the desire of all to recognize as an integral and honored part of the white race the descendants of John Rolfe and Pocahontas.' "]

of racial classifications violates the central meaning of the Equal Protection Clause.

II. These statutes also deprive the Lovings of liberty without due process of law in violation of the Due Process Clause of the Fourteenth Amendment. The freedom to marry has long been recognized as one of the vital personal rights essential to the orderly pursuit of happiness by free men. Marriage is one of the "basic civil rights of man," fundamental to our very existence and survival. *Skinner v. State of Oklahoma* [Chapter 5, § 1]. To deny this fundamental freedom on so unsupportable a basis as the racial classifications embodied in these statutes, classifications so directly subversive of the principle of equality at the heart of the Fourteenth Amendment, is surely to deprive all the State's citizens of liberty without due process of law. * * * [Reversed.]

[The concurring opinion of **JUSTICE STEWART** is omitted.]

NOTES ON *LOVING* AND GOVERNMENT ACTIONS CLASSIFYING BY RACE

1. *Different Avenues to Attack the Virginia Statutes.* The state faced at least three hurdles in defending the laws involved in *Loving*: (1) If the statutes embodied racial discrimination, *Brown* would subject them to close judicial examination under the Equal Protection Clause. (2) Even if the statutes were not racially discriminatory, the state acknowledged that they violated equal protection if no rational basis could be discerned for the distinctions among persons found in them. (3) By burdening the liberty to marry, the statutes potentially violated the Due Process Clause. Each theory is discussed below.

2. *Defining and Invalidating Racial Discrimination.* Virginia contended that its statutes were not subject to close constitutional examination because persons of all races were equally disadvantaged. This argument attempts to distinguish statutes that *classify* on the basis of race from statutes that *discriminate* on the basis of race. As footnote 11 suggests, the "equal application" argument would have been sounder factually if all miscegenation had been outlawed. *Loving* makes clear, though, that even such an across-the-board approach would run afoul of the "central meaning" of the Equal Protection Clause. Why? Because it is inconsistent with the text of the Fourteenth Amendment or the intentions of its Framers? (See note 8 below.) Because, under appropriate theories of justice, race, an immutable characteristic, should be always irrelevant in appropriate governmental decisionmaking? Another avenue of analysis would harken back to footnote 4 of *Carolene Products* (Chapter 1, § 6), which suggested a special role for the Supreme Court in protecting "discrete and insular minorities" against prejudice, and the representation-reinforcement theory of Professor Ely (Chapter 2, § 3B). Under this approach, should the statutes be struck down because they were adopted during a period in which African Americans were politically powerless in Virginia? Because the statutes were adopted out of hostility toward African Americans or stigmatized them as inferior? Because race is an immutable characteristic? Do any (or all) of these theories necessarily follow from *Brown*?

3. *Colorblindness versus Prejudice.* Consider *Palmore v. Sidoti*, 466 U.S. 429 (1984). Upon the divorce of a white couple, the state judge awarded the mother custody of their daughter under the usual "best interests of the child" standard applicable to child custody. Later, when the mother married a black man, the state court reconsidered the best interests of the girl and concluded that her father should have custody. The state judge said that, despite improvement in race relations, it was inevitable that the girl would suffer social stigmatization if she lived in the home of a racially mixed marriage. A unanimous Supreme Court held that the judge's order violated equal protection. The Court acknowledged that the child "may be subject to a variety of pressures and stresses not present if the child were living with parents of the same racial or ethnic origin," but concluded that these were not permissible considerations for the state judge: Such private "biases may be outside the reach of the law, but the law cannot, directly or indirectly, give them effect." Was the problem with the judge's actions that they took race into account — that the judge was not colorblind — or that they deferred to private biases against racial minorities?

4. *Racial Classification and Harmed Groups.* The distinction between an equal protection theory based on colorblindness and one based on prejudice is often drawn by examining the groups benefitted or harmed by a racial classification. All criteria used to classify people create two or more affected groups — for example:

Government Regulation	Criterion	Ideology/ Purpose	Harmed Group
Antimiscegenation laws (*Loving*)	race	white supremacy	stigmatizing people of color
affirmative action by state university (*Bakke*, this chapter, § 3A)	race	remediation of social disadvantages	white people
exclusion of women from state military college (VMI case, chapter 4, § 2B1)	sex	separate spheres	women
vision test for driver's license	visual acuity	traffic safety	poorly sighted

The *Loving* opinion emphasized the suspect *classification*, which had the effect of harming a subordinated *class* by reinforcing the *ideology* of white supremacy. The rationality (use of race not rationally related to legitimate government interest) and anti-subordination (use of race to subordinate or stigmatize people of color) features of the Equal Protection Clause pressed in the same directions here — as they later would in the VMI case, which struck down a sex-based classification excluding women from a state military college on the basis of a separate-spheres ideology (men = warriors protecting women, who tend the home fires). An easy case in the opposite direction is the vision test for driver's licenses: the criterion of good vision is a rational one in this context, and the purpose of preventing traffic accidents is a splendid basis for state policy. Unlike the other items in the chart, affirmative action disaggregates the rationality (focus on the fishy classification) and anti-subordination (focus on the harmed class) features of the Equal Protection Clause. Consider also Problem 3-1, which follows these notes.

5. *Current Formulation of the "Strict Scrutiny" Standard: A Means/Ends Inquiry*. Although the Court does not always use precisely the same words in formulating the strict scrutiny standard derived from *Korematsu*, it has indicated that the variations are not legally significant. See, e.g., *In re Griffiths*, 413 U.S. 717, 721-22 & n.9 (1973). An illustrative formulation, taken from *Palmore*, *supra*, says that racial classifications "are subject to the most exacting scrutiny; to pass constitutional muster, they must be justified by a compelling governmental interest and must be 'necessary * * * to the accomplishment' of their legitimate purpose."

Note that this approach first says that the goal, or end, of the legislation must be "compelling," which presumably means something more than "permissible" or even "important." Recall *Korematsu*'s use of the phrase "[p]ressing public necessity." *Palmore*, for example, specifically held that satisfying widely held popular prejudices (against interracial households, in that case and in *Loving*) does not qualify as a compelling government interest. The approach then requires that the means chosen be "necessary" to effectuate the goal. Thus, merely a rational relationship between ends and means will not do, and presumably even a "significant" relationship is not good enough. The "means" scrutiny is designed to strike down statutes that create a greater burden than is necessary to achieve admittedly important goals. Note how this formulation would work in *Loving*: The statutes in question would be unconstitutional because the goal of racial integrity is not a compelling governmental interest; even if it were, as footnote 11 of the opinion indicates, the means chosen were hardly necessary to effectuate the goal.

6. *Rational Basis Review*. As noted above, the attorneys representing Virginia conceded that the Equal Protection Clause provided some limitation even on state legislation that did not constitute racial discrimination. This "rational basis" inquiry is discussed in Chapter 4, § 1. For present purposes, note the distinction in *Loving* between invidious racial discrimination (however that is defined), which is subject to heightened equal protection scrutiny, and discrimination in economic regulation, which *Loving* indicates is subject to deferential review inquiring only whether there is a rational connection between the goal of the statute and the means chosen to effectuate that goal.

7. *Judicial Restraint and the Right to Marry*. In only one paragraph, the Court struck down the Virginia statutes as violating the right to marry provided by the Due Process Clause of the Fourteenth Amendment. We will discuss such fundamental rights in Chapter 5. For present purposes, ask yourself: Why did the Chief Justice include Part II of the opinion, when he had already struck down the statutes in Part I? Should the Court ever decide more questions than are necessary to dispose of a case? Is there something about a *constitutional* question that especially suggests that the Court should decide it only if necessary? If the Court should engage in this kind of judicial restraint, how

should it pick which dispositive ground — in *Loving*, equal protection or fundamental right/due process — to invoke? A similar point can be made about the equal protection issue in *Loving*: As footnote 11 demonstrates, the Court could have avoided deciding whether the "equal application" argument could save the statutes by holding that the statutes really did not equally apply to persons of all races. Should the Court have done this?

8. *The Complexities of History.* As he had done in *Brown*, Chief Justice Warren concluded that the intentions of the Framers of the Fourteenth Amendment were sufficiently unclear so that they could be set aside in *Loving*. This may be problematic. Herbert Hovenkamp, *Social Science and Segregation Before* Brown, 1985 Duke L.J. 624, argues that before the mid-twentieth century, the prevailing culture in the United States believed in strict separation of the races. In the nineteenth century, even "progressives," such as the Radical Republicans who pushed through the Fourteenth Amendment, often believed that the white race was different and superior to the black race and that "mixing of the races" was a bad idea mainly because it would lead to interracial marriages, which were widely considered to produce defective children and even to "dilute" the white race. Under this view of nineteenth century ideology, any doubts about educational integration would have been pale in comparison with marital integration.[b] If this historical analysis is correct, should that change the result in *Loving*? If not, when should such evidence of original intent ever be relevant? See generally Problem 2-1, *Is* Brown *Consistent with the Original Intent of the Fourteenth Amendment?*, Chapter 2, § 3A.

9. *Implementing* Brown: *Federal Antidiscrimination Legislation.* The antidiscrimination principle of *Brown* and its progeny has been implemented most broadly not by judges under the Constitution, but by Congress under its authority to pass civil rights legislation. (The sources of, and limitations on, this congressional power are examined in Chapter 7.) One of the most important statutes implementing *Brown* is the Civil Rights Act of 1964. For instance, Title VI of this statute provides that "No person in the United States shall, on the ground of race, color, or national origin, be excluded from participation in, be denied the benefits of, or be subjected to discrimination under any program or activity receiving Federal financial assistance." Title VII forbids certain employers from engaging in employment discrimination on account of race and other specified criteria, such as gender.

---

b. In 1956, the Supreme Court dismissed on seemingly unsupportable jurisdictional grounds the appeal in *Naim v. Naim*, 350 U.S. 985 (1956), discussed in *Loving*. Alexander Bickel conceded that affirmance of *Naim* would have been "unthinkable" after *Brown*, but justified what the Court did on practical grounds: "[W]ould it have been wise, at a time when the Court had just pronounced its new integration principle, when it was subject to scurrilous attack by men who predicted that integration of the schools would lead to 'mongrelization of the race' and that this was the result the Court had really willed, * * * to declare that the states may not prohibit racial intermarriage?" Alexander Bickel, *The Least Dangerous Branch* 174 (1962). *Naim* suggests the power, as late as the 1950s, of fears of interracial marriage.

PROBLEMS INVOLVING RACIAL CLASSIFICATIONS
IN LAW ENFORCEMENT AND ADOPTION

Problem 3-1. *Prudential uses of race in the criminal justice system?* (1) May a state law enforcement agency take race into account in determining what officers to assign to work undercover as purported members of a gang defined by race (e.g., to infiltrate the Klu Klux Klan)? (2) Assume that a large city has a substantial community of persons of color, and that there have been serious racial tensions between members of that community and the police force. May the police chief order the reassignment of officers so that more officers who are persons of color are responsible for patrolling areas with high minority population? (3) Same city: May the police chief adjust the department's hiring criteria, if need be, to ensure that a higher percentage of new officers will be persons of color? (4) May prison officials, immediately following a prison riot triggered by racial tension among inmates, racially segregate the inmates for a cooling-off period? (5) Same prison system: If after months of problems the officials decide that the best way to protect inmates from violence is to segregate all inmates by race for the indefinite future, is that constitutional? Cf. *Johnson v. California*, 543 U.S. 499 (2005) (placing new inmates in cells with persons of same race during initial evaluation period is subject to strict scrutiny); *Lee v. Washington*, 390 U.S. 333 (1968) (striking down state statutes requiring ongoing racial segregation of prisons and jails). (6) What if law enforcement officials believe there is a correlation between race and likelihood to commit certain kinds of crimes in certain places? May race be part of a "profile" used to identify suspects? See, e.g., David Harris, *The Stories, the Statistics, and the Law: Why "Driving While Black" Matters*, 84 Minn. L. Rev. 265 (1999).[c]

Problem 3-2. *Race-matching in adoption?* Under *Loving* and *Palmore*, is it constitutional for a state-run adoption agency to follow a policy of "race matching," whereby the agency prefers to place children in homes of racially similar parents — children of color with parents of color, biracial children with different-race parents, white children in white homes? See, e.g., Elizabeth Bartholet, *Where Do Black Children Belong? The Politics of Race Matching in Adoption*, 139 U. Pa. L. Rev. 1163 (1991).[d]

---

c. In *United States v. Brignoni-Ponce*, 422 U.S. 873 (1975), the Court stated that "the characteristic appearance of persons who live in Mexico [such as] the mode of dress and haircut" could be a factor, but not the only factor, used by the Border Patrol in stopping and questioning possible illegal immigrants near the Mexican border. No Justice disagreed with this conclusion, which was based on an analysis of the factors that can provide "reasonable suspicion" justifying an investigative "stop" for Fourth Amendment purposes. Would, or should, the analysis be any different if the issue were viewed as one of equal protection?

d. Cf. the Indian Child Welfare Act, 25 U.S.C. § 1901 et seq., which in some circumstances mandates tribal-court rather than state-court jurisdiction over the placement of Indian children and otherwise strongly prefers that such children be in Indian homes. The statute defines "Indian child" as someone (1) who is a member of a federally recognized Indian tribe or (2) who is eligible for membership in such a tribe and is the biological child of a member of such a tribe. Are classifications based on membership in a federally recognized Indian tribe "racial" classifications? See *Morton v. Mancari*, 417 U.S. 535 (1974) (such classifications are "political," not racial). Many tribes define their membership at least in part by blood quantum (e.g., a tribe might require that , to

Problem 3-3. *Colorblindness in adoption?* Assume that it would be unconstitutional for adoption agencies to follow a policy of race matching. Would it also be constitutionally required for the state agency not to reveal the racial background of children to prospective parents? It is apparently true that a large majority of prospective parents, knowing the racial background of the children, will choose a child whose background is the same as theirs. It is also true that such discrimination has a disproportionate impact on children of color: There are many more children of color (especially African-American children) available for adoption than there are interested parents of color. Compare R. Richard Banks, *The Color of Desire: Fulfilling Adoptive Parents' Racial Preferences Through Discriminatory State Action*, 107 Yale L.J. 875 (1998), with Elizabeth Bartholet, Correspondence, *Private Race Preferences in Family Formation*, 107 Yale L.J. 2351 (1998).

B.   FACIALLY NEUTRAL CLASSIFICATIONS (DISCRIMINATORY INTENT AND EFFECT)

In *Brown* and *Loving*, the racial nature of the statute was plainly evident on the face of the statute. Could a statute or practice that is facially neutral concerning race nonetheless violate the Equal Protection Clause? Consider the following case.

YICK WO v. HOPKINS
118 U.S. 356, 6 S.Ct. 1064, 30 L.Ed. 220 (1886)

JUSTICE MATTHEWS delivered the opinion of the Court.

[In 1880, the San Francisco Board of Supervisors adopted a series of ordinances providing that a laundry located in a building constructed of material other than brick or stone could be operated only by obtaining the consent of the Board. Yick Wo, a citizen of China, was imprisoned for operating a laundry in a wood building without the Board's consent, and he brought this action for habeas corpus relief. He demonstrated that he had operated his laundry in the same location for 22 years and had been licensed to do so by the board of fire wardens. It was conceded that in 1880 "there were about 320 laundries in [San Francisco], of which about 240 were owned and conducted by subjects of China, and of the [320], about 310 were constructed of wood, the same material that constitutes nine-tenths of the houses in [San Francisco]." Moreover, all the applications of the approximately 200 Chinese who had applied for permits had been denied; with only one exception, all the 80 or so applications of non-Chinese had been granted. The California state courts denied the application for habeas corpus.]

The Fourteenth Amendment to the Constitution is not confined to the protection of citizens. It says: "Nor shall any State deprive any person of life, liberty, or property without due process of law; nor deny to any person within

---

be eligible to enroll as a member, the person must be the child of a tribal member and have at least a certain percentage of her lineage traceable to this tribe). Should that make any difference in the analysis?

its jurisdiction the equal protection of the laws." These provisions are universal in their application, to all persons within the territorial jurisdiction, without regard to any differences of race, of color, or of nationality; and the equal protection of the laws is a pledge of the protection of equal laws. * * *

It is contended on the part of the petitioners that the ordinances for violations of which they are severally sentenced to imprisonment are void on their face, as being within the prohibitions of the Fourteenth Amendment; and, in the alternative, if not so, that they are void by reason of their administration, operating unequally, so as to punish in the present petitioners what is permitted to others as lawful, without any distinction of circumstances — an unjust and illegal discrimination, it is claimed, which, though not made expressly by the ordinances is made possible by them.

* * * In the present cases we are not obliged to reason from the probable to the actual, and pass upon the validity of the ordinances complained of, as tried merely by the opportunities which their terms afford, of unequal and unjust discrimination in their administration. For the cases present the ordinances in actual operation, and the facts shown establish an administration directed so exclusively against a particular class of persons as to warrant and require the conclusion that, whatever may have been the intent of the ordinances as adopted, they are applied by the public authorities charged with their administration, and thus representing the State itself, with a mind so unequal and oppressive as to amount to a practical denial by the State of that equal protection of the laws which is secured to the petitioners, as to all other persons, by the broad and benign provisions of the Fourteenth Amendment to the Constitution of the United States. Though the law itself be fair on its face and impartial in appearance, yet, if it is applied and administered by public authority with an evil eye and an unequal hand, so as practically to make unjust and illegal discriminations between persons in similar circumstances, material to their rights, the denial of equal justice is still within the prohibition of the Constitution. * * *

The present cases, as shown by the facts disclosed in the record, are within this class. It appears that both petitioners have complied with every requisite, deemed by the law or by the public officers charged with its administration, necessary for the protection of neighboring property from fire, or as a precaution against injury to the public health. No reason whatever, except the will of the supervisors, is assigned why they should not be permitted to carry on, in the accustomed manner, their harmless and useful occupation, on which they depend for a livelihood. And while this consent of the supervisors is withheld from them and from 200 others who have also petitioned, all of whom happen to be Chinese subjects, 80 others, not Chinese subjects, are permitted to carry on the same business under similar conditions. The fact of this discrimination is admitted. No reason for it is shown, and the conclusion cannot be resisted, that no reason for it exists except hostility to the race and nationality to which the petitioners belong, and which in the eye of the law is not justified. The discrimination is, therefore, illegal, and the public administration which enforces it is a denial of the equal protection of the laws and a violation of the Fourteenth Amendment of the Constitution. The imprisonment of the petitioners is, therefore, illegal, and they must be discharged.

NOTES ON *YICK WO* AND DISCRIMINATORY INTENT

1. *The Relevance of Discriminatory Purposes for Enactment.* In *Yick Wo*, the Court did not need to address what motivated the passage of the law in question because it was clear that the law had been implemented discriminatorily.[e] But suppose Yick Wo had contacted an attorney the day after the law had been enacted, suspecting that the Board of Supervisors had adopted it for the purpose of driving Chinese laundries out of business. How could you prove the Board's evil intent? And even if you could prove that discriminatory reasons motivated the passage of the ordinances, should evil intent, standing alone, justify striking down these facially neutral laws? There has been a longstanding debate throughout American constitutional history about whether enactment of legislation for bad reasons, standing alone, could justify judicial invalidation.

Consider Chief Justice Marshall's discussion in *Fletcher v. Peck*, 10 U.S. (6 Cranch.) 87 (1810), a case in which a Georgia statute that had provided for the sale of public land was said to be the result of fraud and undue influence on the state legislature. Chief Justice Marshall cautioned against consideration of legislative motives:

> [That] impure motives should contribute to the passage of a law [is] most deeply to be deplored. * * * [Nonetheless, it] may well be doubted how far the validity of a law depends upon the motives of its framers * * *. If the principle be conceded, that an act of the supreme sovereign power may be declared null by a court, in consequence of the means which procured it, still would there be much difficulty in saying to what extent those means must be applied to produce this effect. * * * Must the vitiating cause operate on a majority, or on what number of the members? Would the act be null, whatever might be the wish of the nation, or would its * * * nullity depend upon the public sentiment?

> If the majority of the legislature be corrupted, it may well be doubted, whether it be within the province of the judiciary to control their conduct, and, if less than a majority act from impure motives, the principle by which judicial interference would be regulated, is not clearly discerned.

Many years later, in *Gomillion v. Lightfoot*, 364 U.S. 339 (1960), the Court considered an Alabama statute that altered the boundaries of the City of Tuskegee from the shape of a square to an irregular 28-sided figure. Justice Frankfurter's unanimous opinion for the Court noted that "the essential inevitable effect of this [statute] is to remove from the city all save only four or five of its 400 Negro voters while not removing a single white voter or resident." Consistent with the concerns mentioned in *Fletcher v. Peck*, may the Constitution be invoked to attack this racial gerrymander? Without citing *Fletcher*, *Gomillion* held that such a gerrymander was unconstitutional:

> The result of the Act is to deprive the Negro petitioners discriminatorily of the benefits of residence in Tuskegee, including, *inter alia*, the right to vote in municipal elections.

---

e. This is the usual understanding of the case. But see Gabriel Chin, *Unexplainable on Grounds of Race: Doubts about* Yick Wo (unpublished paper, Dec. 2007) (properly understood historically, case actually turned on property right to operate laundry, not race discrimination).

These allegations, if proven, would abundantly establish that Act 140 was not an ordinary geographic redistricting measure even within familiar abuses of gerrymandering. If these allegations upon a trial remained uncontradicted or unqualified, the conclusion would be irresistible, tantamount for all practical purposes to a mathematical demonstration, that the legislation is solely concerned with segregating * * * voters by fencing Negro citizens out of town so as to deprive them of their pre-existing municipal vote.

It is difficult to appreciate what stands in the way of adjudging a statute having this inevitable effect invalid in light of the principles by which this Court must judge, and uniformly has judged, statutes that, howsoever speciously defined, obviously [racially] discriminate[.]   "The [Fifteenth] Amendment nullifies sophisticated as well as simple-minded modes of discrimination." *Lane v. Wilson*, 307 U.S. 268, 275. * * *

* * * According to the allegations here made, the Alabama Legislature has not merely redrawn the Tuskegee city limits with incidental inconvenience to the petitioners; it is more accurate to say that it has deprived the petitioners of the municipal franchise and consequent rights and to that end it has incidentally changed the city's boundaries. While in form this is merely an act redefining metes and bounds, if the allegations are established, the inescapable human effect of this essay in geometry and geography is to despoil [blacks, and only blacks], of their theretofore enjoyed voting rights. * * *

What is the basis for the holding in *Gomillion* — discriminatory intent, discriminatory effect, or some combination of the two?

In *Palmer v. Thompson*, 403 U.S. 217 (1971), the Court returned to the issue of discriminatory motives for legislation. In 1962, Jackson, Mississippi operated five public segregated swimming pools: four for whites, one for blacks. Following a lawsuit in which this segregation was declared illegal, the city council simply closed down all the pools. Writing for a five-member majority in *Palmer*, Justice Black stated that "no case in this Court has held that a legislative act may violate equal protection solely because of the motivations of the men who voted for it." Alluding to Chief Justice Marshall's admonitions in *Fletcher v. Peck*, Justice Black assayed the "hazards of declaring a law unconstitutional because of the motivations of its sponsors":

* * * [P]etitioners have argued that the Jackson pools were closed because of ideological opposition to racial integration in swimming pools. Some evidence in the record appears to support this argument. On the other hand the courts below found that the pools were closed because the city felt they could not be operated safely and economically on an integrated basis. There is substantial evidence in the record to support this conclusion. It is difficult or impossible for any court to determine the "sole" or "dominant" motivation behind the choices of a group of legislators. Furthermore, there is an element of futility in a judicial attempt to invalidate a law because of the bad motives of its supporters. If the law is struck down for this reason, rather than because of its facial content or effect, it would presumably be valid as soon as the legislature or relevant governing body repassed it for different reasons.

It is true there is language in some of our cases interpreting the Fourteenth and Fifteenth Amendments which may suggest that the motive or purpose behind a law is relevant to its constitutionality. *Griffin v. County School Board*, [377 U.S. 218 (1964)]; *Gomillion*. But the focus in those cases was on the actual effect of the enactments, not upon the motivation which led the States to behave as they did. In *Griffin*[,] the State was in fact perpetuating a segregated public school system by financing segregated "private" academies. And in *Gomillion* the Alabama Legislature's gerrymander of the boundaries of Tuskegee excluded virtually all

Negroes from voting in town elections. Here the record indicates only that Jackson once ran segregated public swimming pools and that no public pools are now maintained by the city. Moreover, there is no evidence in this record to show that the city is now covertly aiding the maintenance and operation of pools which are private in name only. It shows no state action affecting blacks differently than whites.

Is this consistent with *Gomillion*? *Loving*?

2. *Discriminatory Intent or Effect?* *Hawkins v. Town of Shaw*, 437 F.2d 1286 (5th Cir. 1971), *aff'd en banc*, 461 F.2d 1171 (5th Cir. 1972), illustrates one way in which judges could react to *Palmer*. Consider the facts:

> The town of Shaw, Mississippi, was incorporated in 1886 and is located in the Mississippi Delta. Its population * * * consists of about 2,500 people — 1,500 black and 1,000 white residents. Residential racial segregation is almost total. There are 451 dwelling units occupied by blacks in town, and, of these, 97% (439) are located in neighborhoods in which no whites reside. That the town's policies in administering various municipal services have led to substantially less attention being paid to the black portion of town is clear.

> Nearly 98% of all homes that front on unpaved streets in Shaw are occupied by blacks. Ninety-seven percent of the homes not served by sanitary sewers are in black neighborhoods. Further, while the town has acquired a significant number of medium and high intensity mercury vapor street lighting fixtures, every one of them has been installed in white neighborhoods. The record further discloses [similar] statistical evidence of grave disparities in both the level and kinds of services offered regarding surface water drainage, water mains, fire hydrants, and traffic control apparatus * * *.

After *Palmer*, should these facts constitute an equal protection violation? Judge Tuttle's panel opinion, written just prior to *Palmer*, concluded that the facts amounted to "a prima facie case of racial discrimination," that the only remaining question was whether "these disparities can possibly be justified by any compelling state interests," and that no such compelling state interests were revealed by the record. Judge Tuttle continued:

> Yet, despite the fact that we conclude that no compelling state interests can justify the disparities * * *, it may be argued that this result was not intended. That is to say, the record contains no direct evidence aimed at establishing bad faith, ill will or an evil motive on the part of the Town of Shaw and its public officials. We feel, however, that the law on this point is clear. In a civil rights suit alleging racial discrimination in contravention of the Fourteenth Amendment, actual intent or motive need not be directly proved, for:

>> "equal protection of the laws" means more than merely the absence of governmental action designed to discriminate; . . . we now firmly recognize that the arbitrary quality of thoughtlessness can be as disastrous and unfair to private rights and the public interest as the perversity of a willful scheme. [Citing other lower court cases.]

Fletcher, *Gomillion*, *Palmer*, and *Hawkins* suggest a dilemma about using the Equal Protection Clause to attack facially neutral statutes that have a disproportionate racial impact. *Fletcher* and *Palmer* suggest at least three reasons why courts should not inquire whether the adoption of such statutes was discriminatorily motivated: (1) *deference to legislatures*: labeling a co-equal branch (Congress) or a state or local legislature "wicked" raises serious separation of powers problems; (2) *evidentiary problems*: what kind of proof should be admissible, and how much proof is enough; (3) *remedial problems and judicial futility*: the same statute if reenacted with pure motives would be valid.   But doesn't common sense suggest that the core purpose of the Reconstruction Amendments was to forbid intentional discrimination against racial minorities? Moreover, there seems to be only one obvious alternative to a discriminatory-intent approach if the courts are to nullify "sophisticated as well as simple-minded modes of discrimination" — a discriminatory-effects approach, as in *Hawkins*, where courts balance the degree of discriminatory effects against any plausible public policies that might support retaining the statute in question. But that kind of balancing will strike many as a quintessential legislative, not judicial, function.

3. *Three Models of Discriminatory Intent and Effect.*   Consider three possibilities of the interplay between discriminatory purpose and discriminatory effect in the context of facially neutral statutes:

• Model 1: *Results are what matter.*   A showing of disproportionate racial effect, by itself, should trigger strict scrutiny. Because so many government actions have such effects, however, this approach would have to be limited to narrow circumstances in which the discriminatory effect is very substantial (perhaps rising to the level of "statistical significance"), lest it call into question more governmental decisions than courts could possibly review.[f] This approach would fit comfortably with the results (if not the precise reasoning) in *Yick Wo* and *Gomillion* and would view *Hawkins* as a paradigmatic application. It would embrace the concern in *Fletcher* and *Palmer* about the conundrums that arise from investigating the intentions of lawmakers. It would, in effect, adopt a negligence or recklessness model instead of an intentional-tort model: the government would be required to avoid at least some foreseeable racially disproportionate effects of its policies, regardless of whether the policies were improperly motivated. Under this approach, the primary harm the Equal Protection Clause is designed to prevent is a *practical* one, in which carelessness, thoughtlessness, indifference, or other qualities lead the government to adopt policies that severely disproportionally harm minorities who already tend to be at the bottom rungs of socio-economic status. "Institutional racism" is a label sometimes applied to such an approach, because it indicts the outcomes of government processes that reinforce pre-existing inequality, regardless of the reasons that motivated the government to undertake the policy. Thus, this approach is consistent with the *anti-subordination* rationale for equal protection review.

---

f.   For example, under Title VII of the 1964 Civil Rights Act, as interpreted, facially neutral job requirements that have a statistically significant exclusionary effect upon a protected class (e.g., people of color, women) can constitute prima facie violations of the statute. When that occurs, the burden of proof shifts to the employer to justify the exclusionary policy by showing that it is "job related." For example, if a municipal fire department requires all firefighters to be at least five feet ten inches tall and weigh 160 pounds, that excludes women from the fire department in a statistically significant way. Thus, even if these requirements were adopted for reasons other than a desire to exclude women, they are illegal unless the department can show that they are job-related. See generally *Griggs v. Duke Power Co.*, 401 U.S. 424 (1971). Model 1 in the text would embrace this approach for purposes of equal protection analysis.

- Model 2: *The indignity and irrationality of intentional racism.* A showing of discriminatory purpose, by itself, should trigger strict scrutiny, at least so long as the action in question also results in some tangible harm to the minority community. To reach this conclusion, the concerns about investigating discriminatory intent raised in *Palmer* would have to be deemed insubstantial. Under this approach, *Palmer* seems wrong: the city apparently closed the pools at least in large measure for racist reasons, and the minority community in town was worse off (now no place to swim), albeit perhaps no worse off than the rest of the residents (who supposedly also had no place to swim). This approach assumes that the primary harm that the Equal Protection Clause is designed to prevent is a *dignitary or psychological* one: knowing that the government did something because of negative views about your race. Racism here is equated with an "irrational" mindset of the decisionmaker in question — the assumption is that race is not relevant to rational governmental policies, and prejudice is a particularly pernicious form of irrationality. Thus, this model is consistent with the rationality rather than the anti-subordination theory of equal protection review. (Note that Model 2 and Model 1 could both be embraced by courts: bad intent alone can trigger strict scrutiny, some bad effects alone do so as well. This seems similar to tort law, where intentional torts, recklessness, and negligence are all viable causes of action. Note also that, although the government action in *Palmer* might survive scrutiny under Model 1 (because perhaps there was no disproportionate racial impact), it would flunk Model 2 (because it was improperly motivated).)

- Model 3: *Disproportionate harm resulting from improper motives.* A showing of both discriminatory purpose and discriminatory effect should be necessary to trigger strict scrutiny. The outcomes in most of the cases, if not their reasoning, can be made consistent with this approach: for *Yick Wo* and *Gomillion*, the application of the statute had such a strong (statistical) discriminatory effect that discriminatory intent in the way the statute was administered (*Yick Wo*) or enacted (*Gomillion*) could be inferred; *Palmer* was correct because, although there was likely discriminatory intent present, there was no disproportionate racial impact; but *Hawkins* was wrong to conclude that discriminatory impact by itself can trigger strict scrutiny (of course, the impact there seems strong enough to allow an inference of discriminatory intent). Under this narrower approach, actionable racism is limited to situations in which the government disproportionally harms people of color because of racial animus, consistent with the rationality theory of equal protection review.

Consider the facts of the next case, and then apply each of these three models to those facts. Which of the models does the Court embrace in this case? Why does it do so? Should it have accepted a different model?

WASHINGTON v. DAVIS
426 U.S. 229, 96 S.Ct. 2040, 48 L.Ed.2d 597 (1976)

JUSTICE WHITE delivered the opinion of the Court.

[Plaintiffs, African Americans whose applications for the District of Columbia police department were rejected, alleged that the department's hiring practices were racially discriminatory because they included a written personnel test, "Test 21," that operated to exclude a disproportionate number of African-American applicants. Plaintiffs based their claim on federal civil service laws and on the equal protection component of the Due Process Clause of the Fifth Amendment (recall *Bolling v. Sharpe*, Chapter 2, § 1C), since at the time of their lawsuit Title VII of the 1964 Civil Rights Act, which prohibits employment discrimination on account of race, did not apply to the federal government. The court of appeals looked to the primary case interpreting Title VII, *Griggs v. Duke Power Co.*, 401 U.S. 424 (1971), and held that the *Griggs* standard for proving employment discrimination under Title VII should also be the constitutional standard. The court of appeals held that Test 21 violated the Fifth Amendment because a far greater proportion of African Americans than whites failed the test and defendants had not shown that the test was an adequate measure of job performance.]

As the Court of Appeals understood Title VII, employees or applicants proceeding under it need not concern themselves with the employer's possibly discriminatory purpose but instead may focus solely on the racially differential impact of the challenged hiring or promotion practices. This is not the constitutional rule. * * *

The central purpose of the Equal Protection Clause * * * is the prevention of official conduct discriminating on the basis of race. * * * [O]ur cases have not embraced the proposition that a law or other official act, without regard to whether it reflects a racially discriminatory purpose, is unconstitutional *solely* because it has a racially disproportionate impact. * * *

The school desegregation cases * * * adhered to the basic equal protection principle that the invidious quality of a law claimed to be racially discriminatory must ultimately be traced to a racially discriminatory purpose. That there are both predominantly black and predominantly white schools in a community is not alone violative of the Equal Protection Clause. The essential element of *de jure* segregation is "a current condition of segregation resulting from intentional state action." *Keyes v. School District No. 1*, 413 U.S. 189 (1973). "The differentiating factor between *de jure* segregation and so-called *de facto* segregation . . . is *purpose* or *intent* to segregate." The Court has also recently rejected allegations of racial discrimination based solely on the statistically disproportionate racial impact of various provisions of the Social Security Act because "[t]he acceptance of appellants' constitutional theory would render suspect each difference in treatment among the grant classes, however lacking in racial motivation and however otherwise rational the treatment might be." *Jefferson v. Hackney*, 406 U.S. 535 (1972). * * *

This is not to say that the necessary discriminatory racial purpose must be express or appear on the face of the statute, or that a law's disproportionate impact is irrelevant in cases involving Constitution-based claims of racial discrimination. A statute, otherwise neutral on its face, must not be applied so as invidiously to discriminate on the basis of race. *Yick Wo.* * * *

Necessarily, an invidious discriminatory purpose may often be inferred from the totality of the relevant facts, including the fact, if it is true, that the law bears more heavily on one race than another. It is also not infrequently true that the discriminatory impact — in the jury cases for example, the total or seriously disproportionate exclusion of Negroes from jury venires — may for all practical purposes demonstrate unconstitutionality because in various circumstances the discrimination is very difficult to explain on nonracial grounds. Nevertheless, we have not held that a law, neutral on its face and serving ends otherwise within the power of government to pursue, is invalid under the Equal Protection Clause simply because it may affect a greater proportion of one race than of another. Disproportionate impact is not irrelevant, but it is not the sole touchstone of an invidious racial discrimination forbidden by the Constitution. Standing alone, it does not trigger the rule that racial classifications are to be subjected to the strictest scrutiny and are justifiable only by the weightiest of considerations.

There are some indications to the contrary in our cases. In *Palmer v. Thompson*, the city of Jackson, Miss., following a court decree to this effect, desegregated all of its public facilities save five swimming pools which had been operated by the city and which, following the decree, were closed by ordinance pursuant to a determination by the city council that closure was necessary to preserve peace and order and that integrated pools could not be economically operated. Accepting the finding that the pools were closed to avoid violence and economic loss, this Court rejected the argument that the abandonment of this service was inconsistent with the outstanding desegregation decree and that the otherwise seemingly permissible ends served by the ordinance could be impeached by demonstrating that racially invidious motivations had prompted the city council's action. The holding was that the city was not overtly or covertly operating segregated pools and was extending identical treatment to both whites and Negroes. The opinion warned against grounding decision on legislative purpose or motivation, thereby lending support for the proposition that the operative effect of the law rather than its purpose is the paramount factor. But the holding of the case was that the legitimate purposes of the ordinance to preserve peace and avoid deficits were not open to impeachment by evidence that the councilmen were actually motivated by racial considerations. Whatever dicta the opinion may contain, the decision did not involve, much less invalidate, a statute or ordinance having neutral purposes but disproportionate racial consequences. * * *

That [*Palmer* was not] understood to have changed the prevailing rule is apparent from *Keyes*, where the principal issue in litigation was whether and to what extent there had been purposeful discrimination resulting in a partially or wholly segregated school system. * * *

* * * [V]arious Courts of Appeals have held in several contexts, including public employment, that the substantially disproportionate racial impact of a statute or official practice standing alone and without regard to discriminatory

purpose, suffices to prove racial discrimination violating the Equal Protection Clause absent some justification going substantially beyond what would be necessary to validate most other legislative classifications.[12] The cases impressively demonstrate that there is another side to the issue; but * * * we are in disagreement.

As an initial matter, we have difficulty understanding how a law establishing a racially neutral qualification for employment is nevertheless racially discriminatory and denies "any person . . . equal protection of the laws" simply because a greater proportion of Negroes fail to qualify than members of other racial or ethnic groups. Had respondents, along with all others who had failed Test 21, whether white or black, brought an action claiming that the test denied each of them equal protection of the laws as compared with those who had passed with high enough scores to qualify them as police recruits, it is most unlikely that their challenge would have been sustained. Test 21, which is administered generally to prospective Government employees, concededly seeks to ascertain whether those who take it have acquired a particular level of verbal skill; and it is untenable that the Constitution prevents the Government from seeking modestly to upgrade the communicative abilities of its employees rather than to be satisfied with some lower level of competence, particularly where the job requires special ability to communicate orally and in writing. Respondents, as Negroes, could no more successfully claim that the test denied them equal protection than could white applicants who also failed. The conclusion would not be different in the face of proof that more Negroes than whites had been disqualified by Test 21. That other Negroes also failed to score well would, alone, not demonstrate that respondents individually were being denied equal protection of the laws by the application of an otherwise valid qualifying test being administered to prospective police recruits.

Nor on the facts of the case before us would the disproportionate impact of Test 21 warrant the conclusion that it is a purposeful device to discriminate against Negroes and hence an infringement of the constitutional rights of respondents as well as other black applicants. As we have said, the test is neutral on its face and rationally may be said to serve a purpose the Government is constitutionally empowered to pursue. Even agreeing with the District Court that the differential racial effect of Test 21 called for further inquiry, we think the District Court correctly held that the affirmative efforts of the Metropolitan Police Department to recruit black officers, the changing racial composition of the recruit classes and of the force in general, and the relationship of the test to the training program negated any inference that the Department discriminated on the basis of race[.] * * *

Under Title VII, Congress provided that when hiring and promotion practices disqualifying substantially disproportionate numbers of blacks are challenged, discriminatory purpose need not be proved, and that it is an insufficient response to demonstrate some rational basis for the challenged practices. It is necessary, in addition, that they be "validated" in terms of job performance in any one of

---

12. [Justice White cited a number of decisions, including *Hawkins v. Town of Shaw.*]

several ways, perhaps by ascertaining the minimum skill, ability, or potential necessary for the position at issue and determining whether the qualifying tests are appropriate for the selection of qualified applicants for the job in question. However this process proceeds, it involves a more probing judicial review of, and less deference to, the seemingly reasonable acts of administrators and executives than is appropriate under the Constitution where special racial impact, without discriminatory purpose, is claimed. We are not disposed to adopt this more rigorous standard for the purposes of applying the Fifth and the Fourteenth Amendments * * * .

A rule that a statute designed to serve neutral ends is nevertheless invalid, absent compelling justification, if in practice it benefits or burdens one race more than another would be far reaching and would raise serious questions about, and perhaps invalidate, a whole range of tax, welfare, public service, regulatory, and licensing statutes that may be more burdensome to the poor and to the average black than to the more affluent white.[14]

Given that rule, such consequences would perhaps be likely to follow. However, in our view, extension of the rule beyond those areas where it is already applicable by reason of statute, such as in the field of public employment, should await legislative prescription. [The Court also held that, assuming that the applicable federal civil service statutes incorporated Title VII prohibitions against employment discrimination, plaintiffs had not satisfied Title VII standards for invalidating Test 21.]

JUSTICE STEVENS, concurring.

[Frequently] the most probative evidence of intent will be objective evidence of what actually happened rather than evidence describing the subjective state of mind of the actor. For normally the actor is presumed to have intended the natural consequences of his deeds. This is particularly true in the case of governmental action which is frequently the product of compromise, of collective decisionmaking, and of mixed motivation. It is unrealistic, on the one hand, to require the victim of alleged discrimination to uncover the actual subjective intent of the decisionmaker or, conversely, to invalidate otherwise legitimate action simply because an improper motive affected the deliberation of a participant in the decisional process. A law conscripting clerics should not be invalidated because an atheist voted for it.

My point [is] that the line between discriminatory purpose and discriminatory impact is not nearly as bright, and perhaps not quite as critical, as the reader of the Court's opinion might assume. I agree, of course, that a constitutional issue does not arise every time some disproportionate impact is shown. On the other hand, when the disproportion is as dramatic as in *Gomillion* or *Yick Wo* it

---

14.   * * * [D]isproportionate-impact analysis might invalidate "tests and qualifications for voting, draft deferment, public employment, jury service, and other government-conferred benefits and opportunities . . .; [s]ales taxes, bail schedules, utility rates, bridge tolls, license fees, and other state-imposed charges." It has also been argued that minimum wage and usury laws as well as professional licensing requirements would require major modifications in light of the unequal-impact rule. * * *

really does not matter whether the standard is phrased in terms of purpose or effect. Therefore, although I accept the statement of the general rule in the Court's opinion, I am not yet prepared to indicate how that standard should be applied in the many cases which have formulated the governing standard in different language. * * *

[**JUSTICE BRENNAN**, joined by **JUSTICE MARSHALL**, dissented on the statutory issue, but did not address the Court's constitutional holding.]

NOTES ON *DAVIS* AND PROVING DISCRIMINATORY INTENT

1. *Constitutional Theory and* Washington v. Davis. *Washington v. Davis* did not turn on the text and ratification debates surrounding the Equal Protection Clause. Consider other factors: (a) *Precedent.* Neither *Brown* nor *Loving* answers the question as to which theory of equality — the rationality feature or the anti-subordination feature — should prevail when a seemingly rational classification has the effect of disadvantaging a historically subordinated class of citizens. *Palmer v. Thompson,* and the century of case law it reflects, certainly cut against the Court's approach. On the other hand, the Court in the public school cases of the early 1970s distinguished sharply between intentional discrimination remediable under the Equal Protection Clause and unintended but discriminatory effects, which were not. See *San Antonio Indep. Sch. Dist. v. Rodriguez* (Chapter 5, § 3B), where the Court implicitly rejected a claim that Texas's school funding scheme violated the Equal Protection Clause because it had discriminatory effects against Mexican- as well as African-American school children. *Jefferson v. Hackney*, cited in the Court's opinion, involved a dramatic showing that Texas's welfare policies systematically benefitted white over black and Latino recipients; that the Court was unwilling to find an equal protection claim under those circumstances was a precedent-based reason not to do so in *Davis.* But did these recent precedents justify departing from the older ones like *Fletcher v. Peck?*

(b) *Institutional Competence and Capacity.* As Justice White's reference to *Keyes* (a school desegregation case) suggests, the Justices were worried that the federal judiciary was already overextended with the *Brown II* cases and were unprepared to open up another arena of equal protection litigation requiring courts to monitor local policies. (According to Justice Brennan's notes, this was the stated reason Justices Blackmun and Powell were opposed to recognizing the equality claims in *Rodriguez.*) Should Professor Bickel's passive virtues approach to cautious judicial review (Chapter 3, § 3) extend this far — denying relief in a whole class of cases, rather than temporarily as to one issue, where equality might be served?

(c) *Constitutional Principles: Federalism and Separation of Powers.* Although *Davis* involved a Fifth Amendment claim against the federal government (which controls the District of Columbia), the Court was concerned about the federalism implications of any holding that racially discriminatory effects would be subject to strict scrutiny. A huge number of state and local policies would be litigable under such a constitutional regime, which would place a large burden on state and local governments and intrude federal judges into their decisionmaking — at a point in time when a majority of the Court may have felt that judges had already gone too far. An oddity of the case was that the Court in 1971 had interpreted Title VII to render employers liable for policies having a racially discriminatory effect (unless the employer could show the policy served a valid business purpose) and Congress in 1972 had extended Title VII to cover federal, state, and local governments.[g] Because the Court had to address the Title VII question (and did so, resolving it against the challengers), it was unnecessary to have ruled that the Equal Protection Clause and Title VII rules were different — unless the Court majority was trying to make an important constitutional point. It is possible that the broad coverage of Title VII gave the Court cover for its narrow ruling: The unelected Court would not subject state and local governments to broad liability, but this might be accomplished in certain areas by Congress, where state governments were well-represented by senators, the party system, and powerful lobbyists.

2. *Proving Discriminatory Intent and Effect.* Later cases have understood *Washington v. Davis* as requiring a showing of both discriminatory purpose and discriminatory effect. See, e.g, *United States v. Armstrong*, 517 U.S. 456 (1996). The "effects" prong seems clear enough — it compels proof of disproportionate impact. The "intent" prong is murkier. In *Village of Arlington Heights v. Metropolitan Housing Development Corp.*, 429 U.S. 252 (1977), explained the evidentiary burdens concerning intent that are imposed by *Davis*:

> *Davis* made it clear that official action will not be held unconstitutional solely because it results in a racially disproportionate impact. * * * *Davis* does not require a plaintiff to prove that the challenged action rested solely on racially discriminatory purposes. Rarely can it be said that a legislature or administrative body operating under a broad mandate made a decision motivated solely by a single concern, or even that a particular purpose was the "dominant" or "primary" one. In fact, it is because legislators and administrators are properly concerned with balancing numerous competing considerations that courts refrain from reviewing the merits of their decisions, absent a showing of arbitrariness or irrationality. But racial discrimination is not just another competing consideration. When there is proof that a discriminatory purpose has been a motivating factor in the decision, this judicial deference is no longer justified.

> Determining whether invidious discriminatory purpose was a motivating factor demands a sensitive inquiry into such circumstantial and direct evidence of intent as may be available. The impact of the official action — whether it "bears more heavily on one race than another," *Davis* — may provide an important starting point. Sometimes a clear pattern, unexplainable on grounds other than race, emerges from the effect of the state action even when the governing legislation appears neutral on its face. *Yick Wo.* The evidentiary inquiry is then relatively easy. But such cases are rare. Absent a pattern as stark as that in *Yick Wo*, impact alone is not determinative, and the Court must look to other evidence.

> The historical background of the decision is one evidentiary source, particularly if it reveals a series of official actions taken for invidious purposes. The specific sequence of events leading up to the challenged decision also may shed some light

---

g. The lower court had granted the challengers relief only on Title VII grounds, and the petitioners relied only on Title VII. At oral argument, Justices Rehnquist and Powell fed the counsel their winning equal protection argument — and the attorneys rejected it, reaffirming their position that Title VII and the Equal Protection Clause provided the same assurances against policies having race-based effects but arguing that the local employment policy was justified for good business reasons.

on the decisionmaker's purposes. * * * Departures from the normal procedural sequence also might afford evidence that improper purposes are playing a role. Substantive departures too may be relevant, particularly if the factors usually considered important by the decisionmaker strongly favor a decision contrary to the one reached.

The legislative or administrative history may be highly relevant, especially where there are contemporary statements by members of the decisionmaking body, minutes of its meetings, or reports. In some extraordinary instances the members might be called to the stand at trial to testify concerning the purpose of the official action, although even then such testimony frequently will be barred by privilege.

At the end of this discussion, the Court said, in a footnote:

This Court has recognized, ever since *Fletcher v. Peck*, that judicial inquiries into legislative or executive motivation represent a substantial intrusion into the workings of other branches of government. Placing a decisionmaker on the stand is therefore "usually to be avoided."

Two years later, in a gender discrimination case, *Personnel Administrator v. Feeney*, 442 U.S. 256 (1979), the Court further elaborated:

The appellee's ultimate argument rests upon the presumption, common to the criminal and civil law, that a person intends the natural and foreseeable consequences of his voluntary actions. * * * "Discriminatory purpose," however, implies more than intent as volition or intent as awareness of consequences. It implies that the decisionmaker * * * selected or reaffirmed a particular course of action at least in part "because of," not merely "in spite of," its adverse effects upon an identifiable group.

In a footnote, the Court continued:

This is not to say that the inevitability or foreseeability of consequences of a neutral rule has no bearing upon the existence of discriminatory intent. Certainly, when the adverse consequences of a law upon an identifiable group are [plainly] inevitable * * *, a strong inference that the adverse effects were desired can reasonably be drawn. But in this inquiry * * * an inference is a working tool, not a synonym for proof. When * * * the impact is essentially an unavoidable consequence of legislative policy that has in itself always been deemed to be legitimate, and when * * * the statutory history and all of the available evidence effectively demonstrate the opposite, the inference simply fails to ripen into proof.

Do these cases require a showing of outright racial animus? Reconsider *Palmer*. Assume that the Jackson city council was ideologically opposed to integration. Would proof along those lines satisfy the *Feeney* standard? What if the Jackson city council was ideologically neutral about integration, but decided to close the swimming pools because of a justifiable fear that violence would result from integrated swimming? Dicta in *Davis*, discussing *Palmer*, suggests that this purpose might survive equal protection review. But wouldn't this theory allow the city council to maintain segregated swimming pools in the first place, if the council could demonstrate that was the only way to allow safe public swimming? And isn't that inconsistent with *Cooper v. Aaron* (Chapter 2, § 2B), which refused to allow local officials to postpone compliance with a *Brown II* order based on a fear of backlash? Compare *Palmore v. Sidoti* (note 3 following *Loving* in § 1A of this chapter), where the Court invalidated a state judge's order revoking a divorced white mother's custody of her white child when she married a black man because the judge feared that the child would suffer because of societal prejudice. Can the *Davis* dicta concerning *Palmer* be squared with *Palmore*?

Consider a different problem. Assume that a city council decides to build an interstate highway bypass through an African-American neighborhood, knowing that the project will dislocate hundreds of families. When asked why, council members point out that this was the least expensive place to route the bypass. Is there any way, under *Davis* and its progeny, to attack that decision? In answering this question, consider Paul Brest, *In Defense of the Antidiscrimination Principle*, 90 Harv. L. Rev. 1, 6 (1976):

> * * * [T]he antidiscrimination principle disfavors race-dependent decisions and conduct — at least when they selectively disadvantage the members of a minority group. By race-dependent, I mean decisions and conduct * * * that would have been different but for the race of those benefited or disadvantaged by them.

Under *Davis* and the later cases, is it relevant to inquire, as Brest suggested, whether the city council would have put the bypass through a white neighborhood, had that been the cheapest route? *Should* this inquiry be relevant to any meaningful approach based on discriminatory intent? Consider Brest's concept of "racially selective sympathy and indifference" — "the unconscious failure to extend to a minority the same recognition of humanity, and hence the same sympathy and care, given as a matter of course to one's own group." Does *Feeney* make it impossible to attack decisions rooted in racial indifference rather than racial hostility? Consider this additional language from *Feeney*: "When there is no 'reason to infer antipathy' * * * it is presumed that 'even improvident decisions will eventually be rectified by the democratic process.' "

3. *More Problems of Proof: Failure to Act and Partial Motivation.* If an official fails to act because of discriminatory reasons, can this inaction violate the Fourteenth Amendment? In *Rogers v. Lodge*, 458 U.S. 613 (1982), the Court accepted the lower courts' finding that an at-large voting scheme in a Georgia county had been *maintained* for discriminatory reasons and then invalidated the scheme even though it assumed that at-large elections had been adopted for valid reasons. Conversely, may a legislature refuse to repeal a statute that was adopted for discriminatory reasons and that continues to have a discriminatory effect if the refusal to repeal is motivated by nondiscriminatory factors? Consider *Hunter v. Underwood*, 471 U.S. 222 (1985), which invalidated a provision in the Alabama Constitution of 1901 that disenfranchised a person convicted of any crime "involving moral turpitude," which had been interpreted broadly to include minor offenses like presenting a bad check. The Court concluded that "the delegates to the all-white [constitutional] convention were not secretive about their purpose" for this provision, which was largely to disenfranchise African Americans, and that at present the statute continued to disenfranchise them disproportionately. Does *Hunter* suggest an affirmative duty to repeal legislation that was enacted for discriminatory reasons and that has a discriminatory effect, even if today's legislators think the statute serves legitimate contemporary purposes? How can this be, if the state legislature could constitutionally respond to *Hunter* by enacting a law containing the same substance so long as its motive is simply to limit voting to persons of high moral

character? Note that state statutes disenfranchising persons convicted of certain kinds of crimes are common throughout the United States.[h]

In footnote 21 in *Arlington Heights*, the Court stated that proof of improper motivation shifts to the defendant decisionmaker "the burden of establishing that the same decision would have resulted even had the impermissible purpose not been considered. If this were established, the complaining party * * * no longer fairly could attribute the injury complained of to improper consideration of a discriminatory purpose." In *Hunter*, the Court stated that even if the "real purpose" of the constitutional provision was to disenfranchise poor whites as well as blacks, the provision was nonetheless unconstitutional because discriminatory animus against blacks was a but-for motivation for the enactment of the provision.

The proof problems explored in these notes and a feeling that *Davis* represents a retreat from *Brown* have left numerous commentators highly critical of the Court's intent approach.[i]

C.   CONCLUDING THOUGHTS ABOUT STATUTES THAT HAVE DISCRIMINATORY EFFECTS

The cases we have examined seem to divide the world of statutes into two categories. Statutes that on their face take race into account are subject to strict scrutiny, even if they equally disadvantage whites and blacks, at least so long as the use of race can be traced to hostility toward a racial minority or the view that the minority is inferior. *Loving*. Facially neutral statutes that have a disparate

---

h. See *Richardson v. Ramirez*, 418 U.S. 24, 54 (1974) (upholding ban of voting by convicted felons on the ground that "the exclusion of felons from the vote has an affirmative sanction in § 2 of the Fourteenth Amendment"). Challenges to felon disenfranchisement under the Voting Rights Act have generally failed as well, but in recent years several states have softened their disenfranchisement statutes. See, e.g., *Developments in the Law — One Person, No Vote: The Laws of Felon Disenfranchisement*, 115 Harv. L. Rev. 1939 (2002).

i. See, e.g., Derrick Bell, *Foreword: Equal Employment Law and the Continuing Need for Self-Help*, 8 Loy. U. Chi. L.J. 681 (1977); Michael Selmi, *Proving Intentional Discrimination: The Reality of Supreme Court Rhetoric*, 86 Geo. L.J. 279 (1997); David Strauss, *Discriminatory Intent and the Taming of Brown*, 56 U. Chi. L. Rev. 935 (1989). See generally *Colloquium on Legislative and Administrative Motivation in Constitutional Law*, 15 San Diego L. Rev. 925 (1978). See also *Mobile v. Bolden*, 446 U.S. 55 (1980) (Marshall, J., dissenting), arguing that the *Davis* approach should not apply to voting discrimination claims under the Fifteenth Amendment. Justice Marshall understood *Davis* as premised on doubts about judicial competence to second-guess governmental-benefit distribution schemes and on a strong presumption that officials involved with a racially disparate scheme "either had made an honest error or had foreseen that the [scheme] would have a discriminatory impact and had found persuasive, legitimate reasons for imposing it nonetheless. These assumptions about the good faith of officials allowed the Court to conclude that, standing alone, a showing that a governmental policy had a racially discriminatory impact did not indicate that the affected minority had suffered the stigma, frustration, and unjust treatment prohibited under * * * equal protection jurisprudence." He argued that, although this deference might make sense for limiting the reach of the general prohibition found in the Equal Protection Clause, it was inappropriate in the context of the narrow prohibition concerning the right to vote found in the Fifteenth Amendment. Nonetheless, the Court has applied the *Davis* approach to the Fifteenth Amendment as well. See *Rogers v. Lodge*, 458 U.S. 613 (1982).

impact upon persons of color are subject to strict scrutiny only if *Davis* discriminatory intent can be shown; without that showing, as explained in Chapter 4, § 1, such statutes are subject only to rational-basis review, the most minimal form of equal protection scrutiny.

To prove a *Davis* claim, *Feeney* requires a showing that the decisionmaker acted at least in part because of a desire to harm a protected minority; foreseeable harmful effects upon a protected minority are not unconstitutional so long as the decision was made in spite of, not because of, them. So understood, these cases seem to view the Equal Protection Clause as designed primarily to root out the evil decisionmaker and to protect individuals against the stigma of disadvantage flowing from hostility or visions of inferiority based on race, and not against disadvantage flowing from more general social conditions.

Similarly, *Davis* and its progeny may be seen as designed to perfect the political process. Footnote 4 of *Carolene Products* (Chapter 1, § 6) spoke of how prejudice against discrete and insular minorities distorts the political process. Racially discriminatory motives result in harms to individuals that would not occur if the political process were cleansed of those motives. As *Feeney* said, if there is no reason to infer antipathy, the Court will presume that even improvident decisions will be rectified by the political process. Outright racial animus is a political distortion that the Equal Protection Clause invalidates; other distortions of the political process do not count.[j]

One problem with this approach is that it cannot attack the perpetuation of past discrimination. Choosing public employees based on civil service examinations will have a discriminatory impact because of the nation's history of inferior and segregated public educational opportunities for racial minorities. Although by using standardized tests the government is not using race impermissibly in a *Brown* sense (it is not overtly segregating) or a *Davis* sense (it did not choose the test because it wished to exclude racial minorities), real harm with a disproportionate racial impact results nonetheless. Not having the job, or not getting into a professional school, may strike many as a much more concrete form of disadvantage than the psychological harm of stigma and the

---

j. In a few contexts, the Court has been more willing to infer discriminatory purpose from a showing of discriminatory effects. See *Dayton Board of Educ. v. Brinkman*, 443 U.S. 526 (1979) (school desegregation); *Columbus Board of Educ. v. Penick*, 443 U.S. 449 (1979) (same); *Castaneda v. Partida*, 430 U.S. 482 (1977) (jury selection); *Rogers v. Lodge, supra* (racial vote dilution). Professor Daniel Ortiz argues in *The Myth of Intent in Equal Protection*, 41 Stan. L. Rev. 1105, 1137 (1989), that in all the cases since *Washington v. Davis* "[i]ntent takes into account not only the invidiousness of the government's classification but also the importance of the individual interest at stake." Thus, the important thing about *Davis*, *Arlington Heights*, and *Feeney* is that the individual interest at stake in them (employment, housing) is of less constitutional significance than jury composition for a criminal defendant (*Castaneda*), voting (*Rogers*), and public education (the school desegregation cases cited above). Ortiz acknowledges that this hierarchy of values is controversial and explains it by suggesting that the Court has essentially embraced a free-market allocational system and its associated disparities in wealth except where our society has not relegated an area to market control — thus, a distinction between "ordinary" social and economic goods (jobs and housing) and political, criminal, and educational "rights."

barriers to political influence that *Davis* considers important.[k] In short, *Davis* looks for evil decisionmakers who have harmed identifiable people because of their race, rather than government decisions that disadvantage historically subordinated racial groups. See Alan Freeman, *Legitimating Racial Discrimination Through Antidiscrimination Law: A Critical Review of Supreme Court Doctrine*, 62 Minn. L. Rev. 1049 (1978).

A contrary vision might try to avoid this all-or-nothing approach to laws that have discriminatory effects. Consider the following argument.

Charles Lawrence, III
The Id, the Ego, and Equal Protection:
Reckoning with Unconscious Racism
39 Stan. L. Rev. 317, 319-24, 366-67 (1987)[l]

* * * [The critics of *Washington v. Davis*] advance two principal arguments. The first is that a motive-centered doctrine of racial discrimination places a very heavy, and often impossible, burden of persuasion on the wrong side of the dispute. Improper motives are easy to hide. And because behavior results from the interaction of a multitude of motives, government officials will always be able to argue that racially neutral considerations prompted their actions. Moreover, where several decisionmakers are involved, proof of racially discriminatory motivation is even more difficult.

The second objection to the *Davis* doctrine is more fundamental. It argues that the injury of racial inequality exists irrespective of the decisionmakers' motives. Does the black child in a segregated school experience less stigma and humiliation because the local school board did not consciously set out to harm her? * * *

---

k. Consider this criticism:

[W]hite people tend to view intent as an essential element of racial harm; nonwhites do not. The white perspective can be, and frequently is, expressed succinctly and without any apparent perceived need for justification: "[W]ithout concern about past and present intent, racially discriminatory effects of legislation would be quite innocent." For black people, however, the fact of racial oppression exists largely independent of the motives or intentions of its perpetrators. Second, both in principle and in application the *Davis* rule presupposes the existence of race-neutral decisionmaking. Whites' level of confidence in race neutrality is much greater than nonwhites'; a skeptic (nonwhite, more likely than not) would not adopt a rule that presumes the neutrality of criteria of decision absent the specific intent to do racial harm. Finally, retaining the intent requirement in the face of its demonstrated failure to effectuate substantive racial justice is indicative of a complacency concerning, or even a commitment to, the racial status quo that can only be enjoyed by those who are its beneficiaries — by white people.

Barbara Flagg, *"Was Blind, But Now I See": White Race Consciousness and the Requirement of Discriminatory Intent*, 91 Mich. L. Rev. 953, 968-69 (1993).

l. Copyright © 1987 by the Board of Trustees of the Leland Stanford Junior University. For an interesting retrospective of this article, see Charles Lawrence III, *Unconscious Racism Revisited: Reflections on the Impact and Origins of "the Id, the Ego, and Equal Protection,"* 40 Conn. L. Rev. 931 (2008).

Supporters of the intent requirement * * * echo the four main arguments that the Court itself set forth in *Davis*: (1) A standard that would subject all governmental action with a racially disproportionate impact to strict scrutiny would cost too much * * *; (2) a disproportionate impact standard would make innocent people bear the costs of remedying a harm in which they played no part; (3) an impact test would be inconsistent with equal protection values, because the judicial decisionmaker would have to explicitly consider race; and (4) it would be inappropriate for the judiciary to choose to remedy the racially disproportionate impact of otherwise neutral governmental actions at the expense of other legitimate social interests.

My own sympathies lie with the critics * * * [b]ut I do not intend to simply add another chapter to the intent/impact debate. Rather, I wish to suggest another way to think about racial discrimination, a way that more accurately describes both its origins and the nature of the injury it inflicts. * * *

Scholarly and judicial efforts to explain the constitutional significance of disproportionate impact and government motive in cases alleging racial discrimination treat these two categories as mutually exclusive. * * * [T]he Court thinks of facially neutral actions as either [1] intentionally and unconstitutionally or [2] unintentionally and constitutionally discriminatory.

I argue this is a false dichotomy. Traditional notions of intent do not reflect the fact that decisions about racial matters are influenced in large part by factors that can be characterized as neither intentional — in the sense that certain outcomes are self-consciously sought — nor unintentional — in the sense that the outcomes are random, fortuitous, and uninfluenced by the decisionmaker's beliefs, desires, and wishes.

Americans share a common historical and cultural heritage in which racism has played and still plays a dominant role. Because of this shared experience, we also inevitably share many ideas, attitudes, and beliefs that attach significance to an individual's race and induce negative feelings and opinions about nonwhites. To the extent that this cultural belief system has influenced all of us, we are all racists. At the same time, most of us are unaware of our racism. We do not recognize the ways in which our cultural experience has influenced our beliefs about race or the occasions on which those beliefs affect our actions. In other words, a large part of the behavior that produces racial discrimination is influenced by unconscious racial motivation.

There are two explanations for the unconscious nature of our racially discriminatory beliefs and ideas. First, Freudian theory states that the human mind defends itself against the discomfort of guilt by denying or refusing to recognize those ideas, wishes, and beliefs that conflict with what the individual has learned is good or right. While our historical experience has made racism an integral part of our culture, our society has more recently embraced an ideal that rejects racism as immoral. When an individual experiences conflict between racist ideas and the societal ethic that condemns those ideas, the mind excludes his racism from consciousness.

Second, the theory of cognitive psychology states that the culture — including, for example, the media and an individual's parents, peers, and authority figures — transmits certain beliefs and preferences. Because these beliefs are so much a part of the culture, they are not experienced as explicit lessons. Instead, they seem part of the individual's rational ordering of her perceptions of the world. The individual is unaware, for example, that the ubiquitous presence of a cultural stereotype has influenced her perception that blacks are lazy or unintelligent. Because racism is so deeply ingrained in our culture, it is likely to be transmitted by tacit understandings: Even if a child is not told that blacks are inferior, he learns that lesson by observing the behavior of others. These tacit understandings, because they have never been articulated, are less likely to be experienced at a conscious level.

In short, requiring proof of conscious or intentional motivation as a prerequisite to constitutional recognition that a decision is race-dependent ignores much of what we understand about how the human mind works. It also disregards both the irrationality of racism and the profound effect that the history of American race relations has had on the individual and collective unconscious. * * * The equal protection clause requires the elimination of governmental decisions that take race into account without good and important reasons. Therefore, equal protection doctrine must find a way to come to grips with unconscious racism.

In pursuit of that goal, this article proposes a new test to trigger judicial recognition of race-based behavior. It posits a connection between unconscious racism and the existence of cultural symbols that have racial meaning. It suggests that the "cultural meaning" of an allegedly racially discriminatory act is the best available analogue for, and evidence of, a collective unconscious that we cannot observe directly. This test would thus evaluate governmental conduct to determine whether it conveys a symbolic message to which the culture attaches racial significance. A finding that the culture thinks of an allegedly discriminatory governmental action in racial terms would also constitute a finding regarding the beliefs and motivations of the governmental actors: The actors are themselves part of the culture and presumably could not have acted without being influenced by racial considerations, even if they were unaware of their racist beliefs. Therefore, the court would apply strict scrutiny.

[Professor Lawrence applies his test to some easy cases, like *Brown*, where there is a direct historical link between slavery, the black codes, and Jim Crow laws, including educational segregation; forcing black and white children into different schools had a cultural significance — subordination of blacks — that was inescapable. Also an easy case for Professor Lawrence would be a city's increase in a railway fare; even if blacks were relatively less able to absorb the increased cost, this would not be suspicious unless there were a history of using fares as a way to harm African Americans.

[He also applies his approach to *Memphis v. Greene*, 451 U.S. 100 (1981). Upon the request of residents in an all-white area, the City of Memphis closed a road passing through the area that was largely used by blacks. The street closing effectively created a barrier between the all-white area and the black portion of town. The Court upheld the action under *Washington v. Davis*. Justice Marshall in dissent pointed to testimony in the record that the street closing operated as both a physical and psychological barrier between the white and black communities, and that such a barrier reinforced feelings of racial hostility and favoritism. In light of our history of segregation based upon supposed racial inferiority, Professor Lawrence argues that the cultural meaning of Memphis' action is racist regardless of what consciously went through the minds of officials making the decision.]

[Consider, finally, how Professor Lawrence applies his test to *Arlington Heights*, note 1 following *Davis* earlier in this chapter, where the zoning board denied a developer's request to build an integrated townhouse project in an all-white neighborhood:]

Several kinds of evidence would be available to demonstrate that denying the zoning variance in these circumstances has a cultural meaning that demeans blacks. Initially, plaintiffs could present evidence of the historical and contemporaneous meaning of residential segregation in the culture as a whole. This would include the history of statutorily mandated housing segregation as well as the use of restrictive covenants among private parties that aim to prevent blacks from purchasing property in white neighborhoods. Studies of racially segregated housing patterns throughout the United States and in the areas surrounding Arlington Heights as well as data and attitudinal surveys on residential segregation and "white flight" would also be relevant. Such studies * * * agree substantially on the prominence of race in the minds of both those who flee and those who stay. They also note whites' continuing aversion to housing integration.

The body of evidence that documents our culture's frequent attachment of racial meaning to the very existence of segregated housing is extensive and should be more than sufficient to establish the cultural meaning of the Arlington Heights city officials' action. We have rarely come to live in racially segregated enclaves as the result of happenstance or out of mutual choice. We live in segregated neighborhoods because whites have believed that living with or close to blacks lowers their own status. Where one lives is an important index of one's status in our culture, and to live in proximity to those who are looked down upon is to be looked down upon oneself.[m]

---

m. In addition, see Linda Hamilton Krieger, *The Content of Our Categories: A Cognitive Bias Approach to Discrimination and Equal Employment Opportunity*, 47 Stan. L. Rev. 1161, 1199, 1216-17 (1995), a thorough study of scholarship in cognitive psychology that suggests that the intentional discrimination model is too narrow to capture the true nature of much biased decisionmaking, which is often the result not of outright racial animus at the precise moment the decision in made, but by distorted perceptions arising out of stereotypes:

* * * Stereotypes are viewed as social schemas or person prototypes. They operate as implicit expectancies that influence how incoming information is interpreted, the causes to which events are attributed, and how events are encoded into, retained in, and retrieved from memory. In other words, stereotypes cause discrimination by biasing how we process information about other people. * * *

A substantial body of empirical and theoretical work supports the proposition that cognitive biases in social judgment operate automatically and must be controlled, if at all, through subsequent "mental correction." Intergroup discrimination, or at least that variant which results from cognitive sources of bias, is automatic. It does not result from a motive or intent to discriminate; it is an unwelcome byproduct of otherwise adaptive cognitive processes. But, like

PROBLEMS CONCERNING DISCRIMINATORY INTENT

Problem 3-4: *Unequal Application of Death Penalty.* Under Georgia law, a jury may impose the death penalty for murder only if the crime involved certain aggravating circumstances (*e.g.*, prior conviction for a capital felony; murder occurred in the commission of certain specified crimes; defendant greatly risked death of more than one person by means of weapon; murder for hire; murder of judicial official or member of her family; murder was "outrageously or wantonly vile, horrible, or inhuman in that it involved torture, depravity of mind, or an aggravated battery"). An African-American criminal defendant alleged that the death penalty assessed to him by a jury for the murder of a white victim violated the Equal Protection Clause. The argument was based on statistical evidence. An empirical study examined over 2,000 murder cases arising in Georgia in the 1970s. The death penalty was imposed "in 22% of the cases involving black defendants and white victims; 8% of the cases involving white defendants and white victims; 1% of the cases involving black defendants and black victims; and 3% of the cases involving white defendants and black victims. * * * [P]rosecutors sought the death penalty in 70% of the cases involving black defendants and white victims; 32% of the cases involving white defendants and white victims; 15% of the cases involving black defendants and black victims; and 19% of the cases involving white defendants and black victims." After statistical analysis of variables that could explain these disparities on nonracial grounds, the study suggested that "defendants charged with killing white victims were 4.3 times as likely to receive a death sentence as defendants charged with killing blacks. [B]lack defendants were 1.1 times as likely to receive a death sentence as other defendants. Thus, [the study] indicates that black defendants, like [petitioner], who kill white victims have the greatest likelihood of receiving the death penalty." The author of the study

---

many unwanted byproducts, it can be controlled, sometimes even eliminated, through careful process re-engineering. Cognitive biases in intergroup perception and judgment, though unintentional and largely unconscious, can be recognized and prevented by a decisionmaker who is motivated not to discriminate and who is provided with the tools required to translate that motivation into action. Seen in this way, disparate treatment does not necessarily manifest discriminatory motive or intent, but a motive or intent not to discriminate must be present to prevent it.

Given this psychologically more accurate view of discrimination, what would a reformulated definition of nondiscrimination look like? To say that a decisionmaker lacks discriminatory motivation is not to say that his perceptions and judgments are unaffected by cognitive sources of intergroup bias. Indeed, we should expect that a self-professed "colorblind" decisionmaker will fall prey to the various sources of cognitive bias we have examined. For even if this decisionmaker's conscious inferential process is colorblind, the categorical structures through which he collects, sorts, and recalls information are not. In a culture in which race, gender, and ethnicity are salient, even the well-intentioned will inexorably categorize along racial, gender, and ethnic lines. And once these categorical structures are in place, they can be expected to distort social perception and judgment. Our decisionmaker is not colorblind; he is simply "color-clueless," likely unaware that his perceptions, judgments, and decisions are being distorted by cognitive sources of intergroup bias.

For more on implicit bias and antidiscrimination law, see, e.g., Linda Hamilton Krieger & Susan Fiske, *Behavioral Realism in Employment Discrimination Law: Implicit Bias and Disparate Impact*, 94 Cal. L. Rev. 997 (2006).

testified: "[W]hen the cases become tremendously aggravated so that everybody would agree that if we're going to have a death sentence, these are the cases that should get it, the race effects go away. It's only in the mid-range of cases where the decision makers have a real choice as to what to do. If there's room for the exercise of discretion, then the [racial] factors begin to play a role."

Assuming that petitioner's case falls in this "mid-range" of aggravating factors, should the Court find an equal protection violation and invalidate his death sentence? Should the Court consider other factors bearing on motivation, such as the racial composition of his jury? Or should the Court take more clear-cut action — either invalidating the capital punishment statutes themselves because of their disparate impact, or holding the statistical evidence irrelevant? See *McCleskey v. Kemp*, 481 U.S. 279 (1987). How should the case come out under Professor Lawrence's approach? See generally David Baldus, George Woodworth & Charles Pulaski, Jr., *Equal Justice and the Death Penalty: A Legal and Empirical Study* (1990); Randall Kennedy, *Race, Crime, and the Law* 328-50 (1997).

Problem 3-5: *Prosecutorial Discretion and Punishment for Crack Cocaine Offenses versus Powder Cocaine Offenses.* Suppose that, under state law, possession of three grams of "crack cocaine" (a crystalline form of the substance) carries a penalty of up to 20 years in prison, while possession of a similar amount of powder cocaine carries only a sentence of up to 5 years. If defendants, who are African American, show that 96.6% of all defendants in the state charged with crack cocaine possession are African American, while only 20.4% of all state defendants charged with powder cocaine are African American, have they demonstrated a violation of the federal Equal Protection Clause? If not, should a state supreme court invoke the state constitution's equality clause to strike down the disparity? See *State v. Russell*, 477 N.W.2d 866 (Minn. 1991).

Would it change your analysis if an African-American crack-cocaine defendant charged by the United States in the Central District of California demonstrated that federal penalties for crack-cocaine possession were more severe than state penalties, that all 24 crack-cocaine cases brought by the United States Attorney for the Central District of California in the last year were against African Americans, and that criminal defense attorneys were willing to testify as expert witnesses that non-African Americans involved in alleged cocaine offenses were being prosecuted in state rather than federal court? Would you at least allow the defendant to obtain discovery on recent cocaine cases in the District, including the race of the defendants, and to require the United States Attorney to explain her criteria for deciding whom to prosecute? See *United States v. Armstrong*, 517 U.S. 456 (1996). How would these cases come out under Professor Lawrence's theory of "unconscious racism"? See generally Randall Kennedy, *supra*, at 357-59, 364-86; David Sklansky, *Cocaine, Race, and Equal Protection*, 47 Stan. L. Rev. 1283 (1995).

SECTION 2. THE STATE ACTION DOCTRINE AS A LIMIT ON THE JUDICIAL POWER TO ADDRESS RACIAL DISCRIMINATION

Washington v. Davis holds that racially discriminatory effects are subject to heightened scrutiny only if they result from intentional discrimination by the state. The materials that we just examined suggest why the Court required a showing of *discriminatory intent*. In this section, we address why it is only discrimination *by the state*, and not by private persons, that implicates the Equal Protection Clause.

A.   INTRODUCTION

At first glance, the question concerning whether the Equal Protection Clause reaches private conduct seems easily answered by its text.   After all, the provision says that "no state," rather than "no person," shall deny anyone the equal protection of the laws. Compare the language of the Thirteenth Amendment, which by providing that "[n]either slavery nor involuntary servitude . . . shall exist within the United States" directly prohibits a certain kind of private conduct.[a]

In addition to this textualist point, there are other strong arguments against applying the Fourteenth Amendment to private persons. The regulation of private conduct has always been the domain of the common law, supplemented by statutes, and it would seem surprising if the framers of the Fourteenth Amendment would have intended to alter this fundamental aspect of our legal regime. Moreover, applying constitutional prohibitions to private parties would drastically increase the degree to which the government would be regulating private life. It would also greatly shift the responsibility of determining the appropriateness of private conduct from state judges (applying the common law and interpreting state statutes) and state legislators (considering whether to adopt new statutory provisions) to federal judges (interpreting the Constitution) and to Congress (considering whether to exercise its legislative power, under Section 5 of the Fourteenth Amendment, to enforce the amendment by appropriate legislation).

To take an obvious example: If, as in *Yick Wo*, government officials close down the businesses of a certain ethnic group out of animus toward such persons, that seems an obvious violation of the government's responsibility of providing equal protection of the laws. In contrast, the common law has always assumed that a private person has the freedom to contract with whomever she wishes, and if she decides not to take her clothes to a laundry because she is biased against its owners, that is within her freedom of choice. If she does more than that — for example, burning down the business out of spite — the common law and state criminal statutes provide remedies.

---

a. See *United States v. Reynolds*, 235 U.S. 133 (1914) (Thirteenth Amendment forbids compelling someone to work for another to pay off a debt); *The Civil Rights Cases*, 109 U.S. 3 (1883) (Thirteenth Amendment "by its own unaided force and effect . . . abolished slavery").

It is thus unsurprising that the Supreme Court has always understood the Fourteenth Amendment as targeting state governmental conduct, not private activity. In *The Civil Rights Cases*, 109 U.S. 3 (1883), the Court held that the Fourteenth Amendment only regulated "State action of a particular character."[b] Justice Bradley explained:

> [C]ivil rights, such as are guaranteed by the Constitution against State aggression, cannot be impaired by the wrongful acts of individuals, unsupported by State authority in the shape of laws, customs, or judicial or executive proceedings. The wrongful act of an individual, unsupported by any such authority, is simply a private wrong, or a crime of that individual; an invasion of the rights of the injured party, it is true * * * but if not sanctioned in some way by the State, or not done under State authority, his rights remain in full force, and may presumably be vindicated by resort to the laws of the State for redress. * * *

Civil rights lawyers and some Justices have sometimes urged that this precedent should have suffered the same fate as *Plessy*, because a rigid state action doctrine would prevent the Court from protecting racial minorities from the systemwide discriminatory effects of racism. But the Supreme Court has never overruled or even limited this holding of the case — for some of the same libertarian, federalism, and institutional reasons that animated the Court's decision in *Washington v. Davis* in the previous section.

But neither has the Court been capable of applying the doctrine with any degree of consistency. The essential problem is conceptual in nature. The state action principle is designed to limit the reach of the Constitution, but it is an analytically limitless concept. In every instance, the state, through its common law and statutes, is prohibiting conduct, requiring conduct, or permitting persons to choose whether to engage in conduct. There is no such thing as a pre-political "state of nature" existing prior to the application of a state regulatory regime.

For example, if a homeowner orders a visitor to leave because of the visitor's race and gets police assistance to expel her if she refuses to leave, the home-owner is discriminating with the assistance of state (police) action. Even if the visitor goes quietly without police intervention, that action operates against a backdrop of the state's legal rule that property owners may exclude anyone they wish and obtain state assistance in doing so. In this sense, even the most seemingly private of personal choices is infused with state authority.

Because just about anything can be attributed in part to state action, yet applying the Constitution to all private conduct seems inconsistent with constitutional text, the value of personal autonomy, and the primary state legislative and judicial responsibility to regulate private conduct, courts have an analytically challenging task when they try to make sense of the state action doctrine. The general approach is clear enough: The Fourteenth Amendment

---

b. We excerpt more of *The Civil Rights Cases* in Chapter 7, § 3A. Note that for purposes of this requirement the state includes all of its formal governmental subdivisions. Thus, the actions of a city, a county, a public school board, and so on — whether by formal lawmaking, such as the adoption of an ordinance, or by the actions of their employees — are subject to the Fourteenth Amendment.

is usually triggered only by the actions of government officials. Yet in some cases, to which we now turn, the Supreme Court has applied the Fourteenth Amendment to the conduct of private parties — those who seem to be exercising de facto governmental power, or to be intertwined with the government, to such an extent that it is deemed important to impose constitutional limitations upon their activities. The cases are "a conceptual disaster area,"[c] so do not expect bright-line distinctions and logical consistency. Instead, attempt to identify the values that are being balanced and to appreciate the difficulty of this enterprise.

B.   THE PUBLIC/PRIVATE DISTINCTION TODAY

1. *Private Actors and Public Functions*

The doctrinal developments involving *private actors performing public functions* and thereby being subjected to constitutional constraint began in response to the racism of the Texas Democratic Party in the early twentieth century, when Texas was effectively a one-party, Democratic state. In *Nixon v. Herndon*, 273 U.S. 536 (1927), the Court struck down Texas statutes that excluded blacks from voting in Democratic Party primary elections. The state action requirement was easily satisfied by the presence of state statutes compelling discrimination by a private organization (a political party is in form a private association, not a branch of the state government). Texas then responded by granting the executive committee of the party the authority to decide who could vote in the primary. Discriminatory Democratic Party rules adopted pursuant to this authority were struck down in *Nixon v. Condon*, 286 U.S. 73 (1932). The Court in *Condon* concluded that the inherent authority to regulate membership lies with a state political party's convention, not the executive committee, and therefore when the executive committee acted to adopt the rules in question it was acting as the agent of the state, not of the convention.

Ever determined to discriminate, the Texas Democratic Party convention then adopted racially exclusionary rules. The Court first held that the party convention's conduct was not state action, *Grovey v. Townsend*, 295 U.S. 45 (1935), but nine years later overruled *Grovey* in *Smith v. Allwright*, 321 U.S. 649 (1944). *Smith* stated:

> [S]tate delegation to a party of the power to fix the qualifications of primary elections is delegation of a state function that may make the party's action the action of the state. * * * If the State requires a certain electoral procedure, prescribes a general election ballot made up of party nominees so chosen and limits the choice of the electorate in general elections for state offices, practically speaking, to those whose names appear on such a ballot, it endorses, adopts and enforces the discrimination against Negroes, practiced by a party entrusted by Texas law with the determination of the qualifications of participants in the primary. This is state action within the meaning of the Fifteenth Amendment.

---

c. Charles Black, *The Supreme Court, 1966 Term — Foreword, "State Action," Equal Protection, and California's Proposition 14*, 81 Harv. L. Rev. 69, 95 (1967).

The shift from *Grovey* to *Smith* reflected both a change in Court personnel and in social context. Between 1935 and 1943, President Roosevelt remade the Court, and the New Deal Justices were open to the kind of anti-apartheid activism suggested in *Carolene Products* (Chapter 1, § 6). Similarly, the values associated with apartheid were under fire, as the civil rights movement was gaining steam and an increasing number of thoughtful people (including the Justices) were embarrassed by the similarities between American apartheid and Nazi racism.

Undaunted, Texas Democrats then turned to yet another technique, relying on private groups formally independent of the Democratic Party that effectively controlled the slating of candidates for the Democratic primary. As explained in *Terry v. Adams*, 345 U.S. 461 (1953):

> * * * This case raises questions concerning the constitutional power of a Texas county political organization called the Jaybird Democratic Association or Jaybird Party to exclude Negroes from its primaries on racial grounds. The Jaybirds deny that their racial exclusions violate the Fifteenth Amendment. They contend that the Amendment applies only to elections or primaries held under state regulation, that their association is not regulated by the state at all, and that it is not a political party but a self-governing voluntary club. * * *

> * * * The Jaybird Association or Party was organized in 1889. Its membership was then and always has been limited to white people; they are automatically members if their names appear on the official list of county voters. It has been run like other political parties with an executive committee named from the county's voting precincts. Expenses of the party are paid by the assessment of candidates for office in its primaries. Candidates for county offices submit their names to the Jaybird Committee in accordance with the normal practice followed by regular political parties all over the country. Advertisements and posters proclaim that these candidates are running subject to the action of the Jaybird primary. While there is no legal compulsion on successful Jaybird candidates to enter Democratic primaries, they have nearly always done so and with few exceptions since 1889 have run and won without opposition in the Democratic primaries and the general elections that followed. Thus the party has been the dominant political group in the county since organization, having endorsed every county-wide official elected since 1889.

It may seem difficult to distinguish the Jaybird Association from other local political groups, such as a business owners' association, that slate candidates. Nonetheless, although the Court could not muster a majority opinion, it did hold that the conduct of the Jaybird Association was state action. Speaking for himself and Justices Douglas and Burton, Justice Black said:

> For a state to permit such a duplication of its election processes is to permit a flagrant abuse of those processes to defeat the purposes of the Fifteenth Amendment. * * * It violates the Fifteenth Amendment for a state, by such circumvention, to permit within its borders the use of any device that produces an equivalent of the prohibited election.

Justice Frankfurter, writing for himself only, found the "vital component" of "State responsibility" in the "practical politics" of the situation, including participation by state officials in the Jaybird primary. Four other Justices said that the Jaybird Association operated "as an auxiliary of the local Democratic Party organization."

With no majority opinion and no clear consensus in the separate opinions about the nature of the crucial factors in the case, *Terry v. Adams* may have little precedential force outside its facts. It is an important case, nonetheless, because (if we may be a bit irreverent) the Court essentially adopted what might be called the "duck" test: If it walks like a duck, quacks like a duck, etc., it will be treated as a duck. It's sometimes a hard test to apply, but, as *Terry* suggests, without it the protections of the Reconstruction Amendments could be seriously eroded through subterfuge. *Terry* is a rare case in which the Court seemingly suggested that "private" power, if great enough, can erode constitutional values so much that, as a practical matter, the Constitution must be brought to bear on it. Moreover, *Terry* must be understood as the culmination of a series of cases about political racism in Texas, not as an isolated case announcing an analytically pure principle of state action.

These "white primary" cases exemplify our first category of state action cases, those involving *public functions* (like elections) that will be subject to the Constitution even if carried out by putatively private entities. Probably the broadest application of this approach is *Marsh v. Alabama*, 326 U.S. 501 (1946), involving a "company town." Chicasaw, a suburb of Mobile, Alabama, was owned by Gulf Shipbuilding Corp. It looked and functioned pretty much like any other town; it had a main street with merchants, residential streets, and so on. A Mobile County deputy sheriff, paid by the company, provided police protection. Marsh, a Jehovah's Witness, attempted to distribute religious material on the sidewalk near the post office. After she declined the request that she leave town, she was arrested and convicted of trespassing. Justice Black's majority opinion held that her conviction violated her First Amendment rights, made applicable to this "state action" by virtue of the Due Process Clause of the Fourteenth Amendment:

> The more an owner, for his advantage, opens up his property for use by the public in general, the more do his rights become circumscribed by the statutory and constitutional rights of those who use it. Thus, the owners of privately held bridges, ferries, turnpikes, and railroads may not operate them as freely as a farmer does his farm. Since these facilities are built and operated primarily to benefit the public and since their operation is essentially a public function, it is subject to state regulation. * * *

> We do not think it makes any significant constitutional difference as to the relationship between the rights of the owner and those of the public that here the State, instead of permitting the corporation to operate a highway, permitted it to use its property as a town. * * * Whether a corporation or a municipality owns or possesses the town the public in either case has an identical interest in the functioning of the community in such manner that the channels of communication remain free.

In *Marsh*, Justice Black acknowledged that he was "balanc[ing] the Constitutional rights of owners of property against those of the people to enjoy freedom of press and religion." He justified the result by noting that the many persons living in company towns were, like everyone else, "free citizens of their State and country" who "must make decisions which affect the welfare of community and nation." "To act as good citizens they must be informed. In order to enable them to be properly informed their information must be uncensored. There is no more reason for depriving these people of the liberties guaranteed by the First and Fourteenth Amendments than there is for curtailing these freedoms with respect to any other citizen."

This kind of balancing approach, where the interest in individual autonomy protected by the state action doctrine is weighed against the societal interest in avoiding erosion of constitutional rights by private actors performing public functions, has not overtly been a factor in most recent cases. In fact, after the liberal Warren Court, the Supreme Court has declined to apply the public function exception broadly. It is no coincidence that most of the refusals have *not* involved racial equal protection claims. For example, *Hudgens v. National Labor Relations Board*, 424 U.S. 507 (1976), overruled a 1968 decision holding that, by analogy to *Marsh*, a private shopping center was subject to the Constitution.[d] In *Jackson v. Metropolitan Edison Co.*, 419 U.S. 345 (1974), the Court held that an privately owned utility with a state-granted monopoly on providing electricity to a locale was not a "state actor" and therefore could terminate services without providing a hearing or otherwise concerning itself with due process requirements. The Court distinguished *Terry* and *Marsh* as cases that "found state action present in the exercise by a private entity of powers traditionally exclusively reserved to the State"; providing electricity, the Court said, was an essential public service, but "is not traditionally the exclusive prerogative of the State."

A similar case is *Flagg Brothers v. Brooks*, 436 U.S. 149 (1978), which involved a provision of the Uniform Commercial Code adopted in many states that provides that a warehouse company may sell goods in its possession to satisfy unpaid storage charges. The Court held that such conduct of the warehouse company was not state action, and thus not subject to any procedural limitations that might otherwise have been required by the Due Process Clause of the Fourteenth Amendment. The Court said that it "has never held that a State's mere acquiescence in a private action converts that action into that of the State," and that it makes no difference if the State "has embodied its decision not to act in statutory form." It made no difference that the state statute seemingly delegated much of the authority to resolve a private dispute to one of the private parties involved, for the majority referred to *Terry* and *Marsh* as involving functions "exclusively reserved to the State" and explained that commercial disputes between private persons are subject to resolution in a variety of private ways. Thus, *Flagg Brothers* and *Metropolitan Edison* indicate that it is not the functional importance of the interest sought to be protected, but the presence of some exclusive state attribute, that today will render putatively private conduct to be state action under the "public function" theory. Cf. *Lugar v. Edmondson Oil Co.*, 457 U.S. 922 (1982) (state action present when creditor

---

d. *PruneYard Shopping Center v. Robins*, 447 U.S. 74 (1980), is the flip side of *Hudgens*. The California Supreme Court held that, under the state constitution, peaceful picketers could not be excluded from a private shopping center. The U.S. Supreme Court found no federal constitutional infirmity with the state constitution as interpreted. The general point is that a state constitution may provide persons in the state more rights than granted by the federal Constitution so long as the state-created rights do not violate any federal constitutional protection (for example, the shopping center owner in *PruneYard* argued that the California Constitution as interpreted violated its federal constitutional free speech and property rights).

obtained a prejudgment writ of attachment from state court clerk and county sheriff executed the writ and seized debtor's property).[e]

2. *State Encouragement of or Entanglement with Private Actors*

Two other categories of state action cases are worth exploring. Sometimes, state action has been found when the state encouraged or reinforced private conduct that would violate the Constitution if done by the state directly. *Shelley v. Kraemer* is the principal case, and, as the trite adage goes, it raises many more questions than it answers. The other category involves situations in which the state has intertwined itself with a private entity. *Moose Lodge No. 107 v. Irvis* illustrates this problem.

SHELLEY v. KRAEMER
334 U.S. 1, 68 S.Ct. 836, 92 L.Ed. 1161 (1948)

CHIEF JUSTICE VINSON delivered the opinion of the Court.

[In 1911, thirty property owners on an avenue in St. Louis entered into a "racially restrictive covenant": an agreement binding them and their successors to restrict the occupancy of their property for the next fifty years to white persons. In 1945 the Shelleys, a black couple, bought one of the parcels of land covered by this agreement. Shortly thereafter, several neighboring landowners filed suit, alleging that the Shelleys' purchase was void because it violated the covenant. The Supreme Court of Missouri granted the relief sought, rejecting the Shelleys' argument that judicial enforcement of the restrictive covenant constituted state action violating the Equal Protection Clause. Chief Justice Vinson's opinion disposed of *Shelley* as well as a similar case from Michigan.]

---

e. As the Note on State Action Under State Constitutions at the end of this section suggests, the *Marsh* kind of balancing has been more popular in cases adjudicated under some state constitutions. In addition to *PruneYard Shopping Center, supra*, where the California Supreme Court held that state constitutional guarantees of free expression applied to a shopping mall, that court also applied state constitutional guarantees to a sidewalk owned by a grocery store, *In re Lane*, 71 Cal. 2d 872, 457 P.2d 561, 79 Cal. Rptr. 729 (1969), and to a train station, *In re Hoffman*, 67 Cal. 2d 845, 434 P.2d 353, 64 Cal. Rptr. 97 (1967), in both cases protecting people's right to leaflet in "public spaces" owned by private parties. In *Sharrock v. Dell Buick-Cadillac, Inc.*, 45 N.Y.2d 152, 379 N.E.2d 1169, 408 N.Y.S.2d 39 (1978), the New York Court of Appeals invalidated on due process grounds the private sale of a person's car pursuant to New York's lien law (which did not require prior notice to the owner). The court recognized that *Flagg Brothers* probably precluded its reaching the merits of the plaintiff's federal law claim, but held that New York constitutional law offered broader protection, in part because its state due process clause did not have a state action requirement on its face. Because state law authorized otherwise illegal conduct (selling someone's car without her consent), state involvement was present. The court further emphasized (in contrast to *Flagg Brothers*) that the lienor in that situation is performing functions traditionally performed by a sheriff, and therefore traditional limitations on the state, such as the due process requirement of prior notice, were appropriate.

In recent years, governments have hired private contractors to carry out many governmental functions. On the problematic reach of the Constitution in such instances, see Gillian Metzger, *Privatization as Delegation*, 103 Colum. L. Rev. 1367 (2003).

I. * * * Here the particular patterns of discrimination and the areas in which the restrictions are to operate, are determined, in the first instance, by the terms of agreements among private individuals. Participation of the State consists in the enforcement of the restrictions so defined. The crucial issue * * * is whether this distinction removes these cases from the operation of the * * * Fourteenth Amendment.

Since [*The Civil Rights Cases*, 109 U.S. 3 (1883)] the principle has become firmly embedded in our constitutional law that the action inhibited by the first section of the Fourteenth Amendment is only such action as may fairly be said to be that of the States. That Amendment erects no shield against merely private conduct, however discriminatory or wrongful.

We conclude, therefore, that the restrictive agreements standing alone cannot be regarded as violative of any rights guaranteed to petitioners by the Fourteenth Amendment. So long as the purposes of those agreements are effectuated by voluntary adherence to their terms, it would appear clear that there has been no action by the State * * * .

But here there was more. These are cases in which the purposes of the agreements were secured only by judicial enforcement by state courts of the restrictive terms of the agreements. The respondents urge that judicial enforcement of private agreements does not amount to state action; or, in any event, the participation of the State is so attenuated in character as not to amount to state action within the meaning of the Fourteenth Amendment. Finally, it is suggested, even if the States in these cases may be deemed to have acted in the constitutional sense, their action did not deprive petitioners of rights guaranteed by the Fourteenth Amendment. We move to a consideration of these matters.

II. * * * [T]he examples of state judicial action which have been held by this Court to violate the Amendment's commands are not restricted to situations in which the judicial proceedings were found in some manner to be procedurally unfair. It has been recognized that the action of state courts in enforcing a substantive common-law rule formulated by those courts, may result in the denial of rights guaranteed by the Fourteenth Amendment, even though the judicial proceedings in such cases may have been in complete accord with the most rigorous conceptions of procedural due process. * * *

The short of the matter is that from the time of the adoption of the Fourteenth Amendment until the present, it has been the consistent ruling of this Court that the action of the States to which the Amendment has reference, includes action of state courts and state judicial officials. * * * [I]t has never been suggested that state court action is immunized from the operation of those provisions simply because the act is that of the judicial branch of the state government.

III. Against this background of judicial construction, extending over a period of some three-quarters of a century, we are called upon to consider whether enforcement by state courts of the restrictive agreements in these cases may be deemed to be the acts of those States; and, if so, whether that action has denied these petitioners the equal protection of the laws which the Fourteenth Amendment was intended to insure.

We have no doubt that there has been state action in these cases in the full and complete sense of the phrase. The undisputed facts disclose that petitioners were willing purchasers of properties upon which they desired to establish homes. The owners of the properties were willing sellers; and contracts of sale were accordingly consummated. It is clear that but for the active intervention of the state courts, supported by the full panoply of state power, petitioners would have been free to occupy the properties in question without restraint.

These are not cases, as has been suggested, in which the States have merely abstained from action, leaving private individuals free to impose such discriminations as they see fit. Rather, these are cases in which the States have made available to such individuals the full coercive power of government to deny to petitioners, on the grounds of race or color, the enjoyment of property rights in premises which petitioners are willing and financially able to acquire and which the grantors are willing to sell. The difference between judicial enforcement and nonenforcement of the restrictive covenants is the difference to petitioners between being denied rights of property available to other members of the community and being accorded full enjoyment of those rights on an equal footing.

The enforcement of the restrictive agreements by the state courts in these cases was directed pursuant to the common-law policy of the States as formulated by those courts in earlier decisions. In the Missouri case, enforcement of the covenant was directed in the first instance by the highest court of the State after the trial court had determined the agreement to be invalid for want of the requisite number of signatures. In the Michigan case, the order of enforcement by the trial court was affirmed by the highest state court. The judicial action in each case bears the clear and unmistakable imprimatur of the State. We have noted that previous decisions of this Court have established the proposition that judicial action is not immunized from the operation of the Fourteenth Amendment simply because it is taken pursuant to the state's common-law policy. Nor is the Amendment ineffective simply because the particular pattern of discrimination, which the State has enforced, was defined initially by the terms of a private agreement. * * *

Respondents urge, however, that since the state courts stand ready to enforce restrictive covenants excluding white persons from the ownership or occupancy of property covered by such agreements, enforcement of covenants excluding colored persons may not be deemed a denial of equal protection of the laws to the colored persons who are thereby affected. This contention does not bear scrutiny. The parties have directed our attention to no case in which a court, state or federal, has been called upon to enforce a covenant excluding members of the white majority from ownership or occupancy of real property on grounds of race or color. But there are more fundamental considerations. The rights created by the first section of the Fourteenth Amendment are, by its terms, guaranteed to the individual. The rights established are personal rights. It is, therefore, no answer to these petitioners to say that the courts may also be induced to deny white persons rights of ownership and occupancy on grounds of race or color. Equal protection of the laws is not achieved through indiscriminate imposition of inequalities.

Nor do we find merit in the suggestion that property owners who are parties to these agreements are denied equal protection of the laws if denied access to the courts to enforce the terms of restrictive covenants and to assert property rights which the state courts have held to be created by such agreements. The Constitution confers upon no individual the right to demand action by the State which results in the denial of equal protection of the laws to other individuals. And it would appear beyond question that the power of the State to create and enforce property interests must be exercised within the boundaries defined by the Fourteenth Amendment. Cf. *Marsh*. * * * [Reversed.]

[**JUSTICES REED**, **JACKSON**, and **RUTLEDGE** took no part in the consideration or decision of these cases.]

NOTES ON *SHELLEY*

1. *State Support/Encouragement/Ratification of Private Discrimination.* On the surface, *Shelley* may appear to be an easy case for finding state action, as it involves an act of a state judge. But consider some questions suggested earlier. To return to an earlier example, is there state action if a landowner orders someone off her property solely because she does not like the person's race? What if, when the trespasser refuses, (a) the police arrive at the behest of the landowner and arrest the person, or (b) the landowner obtains an injunction ordering the person to leave? It is unlikely that today's Court would find state action in either instance.[f] Why should it make a difference that in *Shelley* third parties are interfering with a willing buyer and seller, where in the questions asked above the unwilling property owner is allowed to discriminate? The problem may boil down to this inquiry: Consistent with both the goals of the Equal Protection Clause and the purpose of the state action doctrine (which is designed to preserve a distinction between the public and private spheres of life), where should the power to assert individual autonomy lie? Should the personal autonomy of Shelley and the seller be preferred to that of the complaining neighbors? Should the personal autonomy of the landowner be preferred to that of the trespasser?

In all these examples, there is obvious action by the state (the judge or police intervening in the private dispute; the baseline of state common law empowering a property owner to eject an unwanted intruder); the hard question is whether this should constitute "state action" for Fourteenth Amendment purposes. In this sense, "the state action doctrine" is a very misleading term, for, as was stressed earlier, in every circumstance the state either forbids

---

f. In the sit-in cases of the early 1960s, the Supreme Court found state action when lunch counter owners were following state or local laws prohibiting nondiscriminatory service, e.g., *Petersen v. City of Greenville*, 373 U.S. 244 (1963), and in one case where there was no such ordinance the Court found official encouragement. *Lombard v. Louisiana*, 373 U.S. 267 (1963). The Court has read these precedents narrowly. See *Adickes v. S.H. Kress Co.*, 398 U.S. 144 (1970). See also *Bell v. Maryland*, 378 U.S. 226 (1964), in which three Justices stated that the Equal Protection Clause should apply where a business owner refuses to serve blacks because of local custom. These Justices said that they would not take the same position with respect to discrimination by a homeowner; they saw the business as a quasi-public entity.

conduct, requires conduct, or allows the person to decide whether to engage in conduct, and state officers stand ready to enforce these rules. In the first and second instances, where the state compulsion is obvious, state action seems obvious. The problem of "state action" generally arises in the third category, when a private person is allowed by law to exercise freedom of choice and undertakes a course of conduct that would be forbidden by the Constitution if done by the government. Maybe the doctrine should be renamed "the state responsibility doctrine" and focus on the unusual situations in which the state is deemed to bear sufficient responsibility associated with the exercise of private choice that constitutional limitations should be imposed. Consider the next note.

2. *Explaining* Shelley *and Narrowing Its Implications.* One way to justify the outcome in *Shelley* without expanding the state action concept is to note that the common law disfavored restraints on alienation like the covenant involved in *Shelley,* but had an exception allowing racial covenants. This exception giving preferred status to racial covenants seems impossible to defend in the twentieth century and appears to be state encouragement or ratification of private discrimination.

Another rather narrow way to view *Shelley* is to note that the racially restrictive covenant involved quite a large area of land. When the covenant was enforced by the Missouri courts, it operated much like a zoning ordinance — and there is no doubt that a zoning ordinance forbidding the sale of certain property to blacks violates equal protection.

A third narrowing understanding of *Shelley* would posit that the state actor in the case, the judge, should be "colorblind." A "colorblind" judge could convict the trespasser in the hypothetical above because her race would be legally irrelevant, but could not enforce the covenant because the judge would need to know the race of the buyer.

All of these rationales for *Shelley* would still allow a private homeowner to distinguish among guests on the basis of race and allow the homeowner to get state actors (police, a judge) to assist in excluding someone on the basis of race. Perhaps the essential difference is one of "baselines." The common law has always considered it the right of a landowner to exclude persons for almost any reason. The idea of a common law baseline against which to measure state action is incoherent to some extent, since (as we have continually stressed) the common law is judge-created and therefore reliance on common law rights by private persons could always be seen as state action. But if we move away from technicalities and ask "in this situation, is the state doing anything *extraordinary* to encourage, or even ratify, racial discrimination," we may be asking the relevant practical question. State encouragement might be seen if the state uses its coercive power to allow persons tangential to a transaction (the complaining neighbors in *Shelley*) for facially racially discriminatory reasons to prevent a transaction between a willing, nondiscriminatory buyer and seller. State encouragement might be even more apparent if the judge-made common law disfavors certain agreements but allows them if they are for racist purposes.

3. Shelley *as a Balancing Test.* The inquiry suggested in the previous note is essentially a balancing test focusing on the impact and appearance of holding one way or the other on the state action question. Perhaps what the Equal Protection Clause requires is that the state avoid the appearance as well as the reality of state-endorsed racial superiority. The Jaybird Case (*Terry v. Adams*) is a hard case theoretically, but as a practical matter a result contrary to the one reached there would have solidified the politics of racial superiority in Texas. In effect, Texas had an affirmative duty (a "responsibility") not to allow white primaries, and the Court had the authority to strike them down under the Equal Protection Clause or the Fifteenth Amendment. A contrary result in *Shelley* would have allowed bigots to take advantage of a racist exception in the common law to carve out huge residential areas for whites only and would have required judges to order facially racist results.

In contrast, if the police remove a trespasser from land because the owner dislikes the trespasser's race, the state could be seen as simply vindicating the individual autonomy of the owner (however misguided) and preserving a realm of private conduct within which the individual may be accorded freedom of association (cf. note *f* above). This result places no affirmative obligation on the state to attack "private" discrimination in this context. The state legislature would, however, have authority under its police power to enact legislation forbidding many kinds of private discrimination.[g] Essentially, the inquiry we are suggesting focuses on whether on the facts the antidiscrimination principle is so threatened that direct judicial intervention is necessary, or whether it is enough to allow the state or federal legislature discretion about whether to outlaw the "private" discrimination in question.

The line we are suggesting is drawn more on the basis of pragmatics than of theory. It assumes that the essential task is promoting the antidiscrimination principle without destroying individual autonomy. Under this view, state action questions in race cases should be resolved by overall considerations of equal protection, rather than by some unified theory of state action that applies to all cases, including those outside the equal protection arena. See generally Robert Glennon & John Nowak, *A Functional Analysis of the Fourteenth Amendment "State Action" Requirement*, 1976 Sup. Ct. Rev. 221.

Recall, however, that recent cases have not been willing overtly to engage in a balancing inquiry like the one suggested above. See Mark Tushnet, Shelley v. Kraemer *and Theories of Equality*, 33 N.Y. L. Sch. L. Rev. 383 (1988). Nonetheless, their outcomes might be supportable by a balancing approach. For example, *Metropolitan Edison* and *Flagg Brothers* presented the issue whether

---

g. Although we know of no state laws forbidding discrimination by the owner of one private home, many states and cities have open-housing laws that require those renting or selling multiple units to avoid racial discrimination. The federal Fair Housing Act of 1968 also forbids private racial discrimination in housing in some contexts, and a Reconstruction-era federal statute, 42 U.S.C. § 1982, has been interpreted as outlawing a racially discriminatory refusal to sell a home, see *Jones v. Alfred H. Mayer Co.* (Chapter 7, § 3A). If a state statute attempted to prohibit the owner of a family home from racially discriminating in the choice of guests, the owner could argue that the state law violated the owner's federal constitutional property rights and privacy rights.

the actions of private entities should be regulated by due process requirements, which often mandate notice and a hearing before someone may be deprived of "property" or "liberty." Absent legislative guidance, the judiciary might reasonably be hesitant to apply procedural due process guarantees to wide sections of the private sector, for fear that the economy could be ground to a halt. Had Metropolitan Edison responded to an energy shortage by shutting off power only to black customers, could the Court have possibly reached the same result about state action? Of course, this hypothetical is unlikely to arise, even if the utility were operated by racists, considering the heavy regulation to which public utilities are now subjected by state law.

On the whole, do the state action cases suggest that the Court was willing to engage in balancing in racial discrimination cases where allowing the "private" conduct would seriously threaten implementation of the antidiscrimination principle, whereas in more recent cases arising outside the Equal Protection Clause the Court has more rigidly attempted to preserve a wide sphere of private autonomy? Would it be unacceptable if state action means different things in different contexts?[h]

MOOSE LODGE NO. 107 v. IRVIS
407 U.S. 163, 92 S.Ct. 1965, 32 L.Ed.2d 627 (1972)

JUSTICE REHNQUIST delivered the opinion of the Court.

[A member of Moose Lodge No. 107 in Harrisburg, Pennsylvania, invited Irvis, an African American, to dine there. The club refused to serve him, consistent with rules of its national organization that limited membership to white males and allowed members to have only white guests.]

Moose Lodge is a private club in the ordinary meaning of that term. It is a local chapter of a national fraternal organization having well-defined requirements for membership. It conducts all of its activities in a building that is owned by it. It is not publicly funded. * * *

Appellee [Irvis], while conceding the right of private clubs to choose members upon a discriminatory basis, asserts that the licensing of Moose Lodge to serve liquor by the Pennsylvania Liquor Control Board amounts to such state involvement with the club's activities as to make its discriminatory practices forbidden by the Equal Protection Clause of the Fourteenth Amendment. The relief sought and obtained by appellee in the District Court was an injunction forbidding the licensing by the liquor authority of Moose Lodge until it ceased its discriminatory practices. * * *

Our cases make clear that the impetus for the forbidden discrimination need not originate with the State if it is state action that enforces privately originated discrimination. *Shelley.* The Court held in [*Burton v. Wilmington Parking*

---

h. For a thorough examination of the attempts to rationalize the *Shelley* result and a suggested reformulation under which *Shelley* could be understood as arising in a setting implicating the Thirteenth Amendment's prohibition on the badges and incidents of slavery even when private action is involved, see Mark Rosen, *Was* Shelly v. Kramer *Incorrectly Decided? Some New Answers*, 95 Cal. L. Rev. 451 (2007).

Authority, 365 U.S. 715 (1961)] that a private restaurant owner who refused service because of a customer's race violated the Fourteenth Amendment, where the restaurant was located in a building owned by a state-created parking authority and leased from the authority. The Court * * * concluded that the [parking authority] had "so far insinuated itself into a position of interdependence with Eagle [the restaurant operator] that it must be recognized as a joint participant in the challenged activity, which, on that account, cannot be considered to have been so 'purely private' as to fall without the scope of the Fourteenth Amendment."

The Court has never held, of course, that discrimination by an otherwise private entity would be violative of the Equal Protection Clause if the private entity receives any sort of benefit or service at all from the State, or if it is subject to state regulation in any degree whatever. Since state-furnished services include such necessities of life as electricity, water, and police and fire protection, such a holding would utterly emasculate the distinction between private as distinguished from state conduct * * * . Our holdings indicate that where the impetus for the discrimination is private, the State must have "significantly involved itself with invidious discriminations," *Reitman v. Mulkey*, 387 U.S. 369 (1967), in order for the discriminatory action to fall within the ambit of the constitutional prohibition.

Our prior decisions dealing with discriminatory refusal of service in public eating places are significantly different factually from the case now before us. *Peterson v. City of Greenville*, 373 U.S. 244 (1963), dealt with the trespass prosecution of persons who "sat in" at a restaurant to protest its refusal of service to Negroes. There the Court held that although the ostensible initiative for the trespass prosecution came from the proprietor, the existence of a local ordinance requiring segregation of races in such places was tantamount to the State having "commanded a particular result." With one exception, which is discussed *infra*, there is no suggestion in this record that the Pennsylvania statutes and regulations governing the sale of liquor are intended either overtly or covertly to encourage discrimination.

In *Burton*, the Court's full discussion of the facts in its opinion indicates the significant differences between that case and this: "The land and building were publicly owned. As an entity, the building was dedicated to 'public uses' in performance of the Authority's 'essential governmental functions.' The costs of land acquisition, construction, and maintenance are defrayed entirely from donations by the City of Wilmington, from loans and revenue bonds and from the proceeds of rentals and parking services out of which the loans and bonds were payable. Assuming that the distinction would be significant, the commercially leased areas were not surplus state property, but constituted a physically and financially integral and, indeed, indispensable part of the State's plan to operate its project as a self-sustaining unit. Upkeep and maintenance of the building, including necessary repairs, were responsibilities of the Authority and were payable out of public funds. It cannot be doubted that the peculiar relationship of the restaurant to the parking facility in which it is located confers on each an incidental variety of mutual benefits. Guests of the restaurant are afforded a convenient place to park their automobiles, even if they cannot enter the restaurant directly from the parking area. Similarly, its convenience for diners may well provide additional demand for the Authority's parking facilities. Should any improvements effected in the leasehold by Eagle become part of the realty, there is no possibility of increased taxes being passed on to it since the fee is held by a tax-exempt government agency. Neither can it be ignored, especially in view of Eagle's affirmative allegation that for it to serve Negroes would injure its business, that profits earned by discrimination not only contribute to, but also are indispensable elements in, the financial success of a governmental agency."

Here there is nothing approaching the symbiotic relationship between lessor and lessee that was present in *Burton*, where the private lessee obtained the benefit of locating in a building owned by the state-created parking authority, and the parking authority was enabled to carry out its primary public purpose of furnishing parking space by advantageously leasing portions of the building constructed for that purpose to commercial lessees such as the owner of the Eagle Restaurant. Unlike *Burton*, the Moose Lodge building is located on land owned by it, not by any public authority. Far from apparently holding itself out as a place of public accommodation, Moose Lodge quite ostentatiously proclaims the fact that it is not open to the public at large. Nor is it located and operated in such surroundings that although private in name, it discharges a function or performs a service that would otherwise in all likelihood be performed by the State. In short, while Eagle was a public restaurant in a public building, Moose Lodge is a private social club in a private building.

With the exception hereafter noted, the Pennsylvania Liquor Control Board plays absolutely no part in establishing or enforcing the membership or guest policies of the club that it licenses to serve liquor. There is no suggestion in this record that Pennsylvania law, either as written or as applied, discriminates against minority groups either in their right to apply for club licenses themselves or in their right to purchase and be served liquor in places of public accommodation. The only effect that the state licensing of Moose Lodge to serve liquor can be said to have on the right of any other Pennsylvanian to buy or be served liquor on premises other than those of Moose Lodge is that for some purposes club licenses are counted in the maximum number of licenses that may be issued in a given municipality.

Basically each municipality has a quota of one retail license for each 1,500 inhabitants. Licenses issued to hotels, municipal golf courses, and airport restaurants are not counted in this quota, nor are club licenses until the maximum number of retail licenses is reached. Beyond that point, neither additional retail licenses nor additional club licenses may be issued so long as the number of issued and outstanding retail licenses remains at or above the statutory maximum.

The District Court was at pains to point out in its opinion what it considered to be the "pervasive" nature of the regulation of private clubs by the Pennsylvania Liquor Control Board. As that court noted, an applicant for a club license must make such physical alterations in its premises as the board may require, must file a list of the names and addresses of its members and employees, and must keep extensive financial records. The board is granted the right to inspect the licensed premises at any time when patrons, guests, or members are present.

However detailed this type of regulation may be in some particulars, it cannot be said to in any way foster or encourage racial discrimination. Nor can it be said to make the State in any realistic sense a partner or even a joint venturer in the club's enterprise. The limited effect of the prohibition against obtaining additional club licenses when the maximum number of retail licenses allotted to a municipality has been issued, when considered together with the availability of liquor from hotel, restaurant, and retail licensees, falls far short of conferring upon club licensees a monopoly in the dispensing of liquor in any given municipality or in the State as a whole. We therefore hold that, with the exception hereafter noted, the operation of the regulatory scheme enforced by the Pennsylvania Liquor Control Board does not sufficiently implicate the State in the discriminatory guest policies of Moose Lodge to make the latter "state action" within the ambit of the Equal Protection Clause of the Fourteenth Amendment.

The District Court found that the regulations of the Liquor Control Board adopted pursuant to statute affirmatively require that "[e]very club licensee shall adhere to all of the provisions of its Constitution and By-Laws." Appellant argues that the purpose of this provision "is purely and simply and plainly the prevention of subterfuge," pointing out that the bona fides of a private club, as opposed to a place of public accommodation masquerading as a private club, is a matter with which the State Liquor Control Board may legitimately concern itself. * * * [T]he label "private club" can be and has been used to evade both regulations of state and local liquor authorities, and statutes requiring places of public accommodation to serve all persons without regard to race, color, religion, or national origin. * * *

Even though the Liquor Control Board regulation in question is neutral in its terms, the result of its application in a case where the constitution and bylaws of a club required racial discrimination would be to invoke the sanctions of the State to enforce a concededly discriminatory private rule. * * * *Shelley* makes it clear that the application of state sanctions to enforce such a rule would violate the Fourteenth Amendment. * * *

Appellee was entitled to a decree enjoining the enforcement of § 113.09 of the regulations promulgated by the Pennsylvania Liquor Control Board insofar as that regulation requires compliance by Moose Lodge with provisions of its constitution and bylaws containing racially discriminatory provisions. He was entitled to no more.

[Reversed and remanded.]

JUSTICE DOUGLAS, with whom JUSTICE MARSHALL joins, dissenting.

* * * Liquor licenses in Pennsylvania, unlike driver's licenses, or marriage licenses, are not freely available to those who meet racially neutral qualifications. There is a complex quota system * * * [, and] the quota for Harrisburg, where Moose Lodge No. 107 is located, has been full for many years. No more club licenses may be issued in that city.

This state-enforced scarcity of licenses restricts the ability of blacks to obtain liquor, for liquor is commercially available *only* at private clubs for a significant portion of each week. Access by blacks to places that serve liquor is further limited by the fact that the state quota is filled. A group desiring to form a nondiscriminatory club which would serve blacks must purchase a license held by an existing club, which can exact a monopoly price for the transfer. The availability of such a license is speculative at best, however, for, as Moose Lodge itself concedes, without a liquor license a fraternal organization would be hard pressed to survive. Thus, the State of Pennsylvania is putting the weight of its liquor license, concededly a valued and important adjunct to a private club, behind racial discrimination. * * *

[The dissent of **JUSTICE BRENNAN**, joined by **JUSTICE MARSHALL**, is omitted.]

NOTES ON *MOOSE LODGE*

1. *State Action in* Moose Lodge. Was the Court correct in deciding to prefer individual autonomy to the antidiscrimination principle in *Moose Lodge*? Is *Burton* legitimately distinguishable? Note the two arguments for finding state action in *Moose Lodge*: (1) The quota on liquor licenses means that the discrimination of Moose Lodge, although done in a narrowly defined private context, has potentially broad external racially discriminatory effects. (2) Under the Twenty-First Amendment, the states have nearly plenary authority to regulate liquor. According to the district court in *Moose Lodge*, the Pennsylvania Liquor Control Board pervasively regulated liquor licensees. For example, the Board could order physical alterations to the premises and could inspect the premises at any time during business hours. The licensee was required to file a list of its employees, to conform its financial arrangements to statutory requirements, to keep extensive records, not to permit persons of "ill repute" to frequent the club or allow any "lewd, immoral or improper entertainment." The court concluded that "[i]t would be difficult to find a more pervasive interaction of state authority with personal conduct." Yet the state failed to forbid racial discrimination by licensees. As an advocate, how would you articulate and use these two theories to support state action here, and how should your opposing counsel respond?

2. *Unified Versus Contextual Concepts of State Action.* If state action means the same thing in all constitutional contexts — that is, if procedural due process cases, free speech cases, and equal protection cases all must approach state action the same way — then maybe *Moose Lodge* is correctly decided.[i] It might

---

i.   In cases that do not involve equal protection, the trend since *Moose Lodge* has been to find no state action. See *National Collegiate Athletic Association v. Tarkanian*, 488 U.S. 179 (1988) (procedural due process claim against private athletic association that strongly encouraged state university to discipline coach); *Blum v. Yaretsky*, 457 U.S. 991 (1982) (procedural due process claim against privately owned nursing homes extensively regulated and subsidized by the state); *Rendell-Baker v. Kohn*, 457 U.S. 830 (1982) (free speech and procedural due process objections to termination of employees by heavily regulated and subsidized private school). *Cf. DeShaney v. Winnebago County Social Services Department*, 489 U.S. 189 (1989) (denying due process claim

seem silly to say that an employee dismissed by the lodge could argue that she was entitled to "due process" — notice and the opportunity to be heard — prior to the dismissal as a matter of federal constitutional law, or that her firing violated the First Amendment because it was in retaliation for her criticisms of the lodge or for her religion. These problems are perhaps best handled by sources of law other than the Constitution — *i.e.*, by whatever federal and state statutes, supplemented by state common law, have to say about the matter. Only by approaching state action as a question of judicial authority under specific constitutional provisions, rather than as a unitary concept limiting all constitutional provisions uniformly, could *Moose Lodge* be decided differently in the equal protection context and the due process or free speech context. For example, consider whether the state's failure to prevent racial discrimination by liquor licensees is any greater a federal concern than its failure to provide procedural protections to employees of licensees when they are discharged.

David Strauss, in *State Action After the Civil Rights Era*, 10 Const. Comm. 409 (1993), elaborated upon this point as an historical perspective on the state action cases. *Shelley*, the white primary cases, and *Burton* involved someone directly discriminating on the basis of race in a context in which no statute prohibited the act. Congress and the state legislatures not only had failed to outlaw racial discrimination, some state legislatures had actually engaged in it systematically with Jim Crow laws. Waiting for legislative reform seemed futile: Neither Congress nor many state legislatures were capable of addressing the issue for political reasons (*e.g.*, avoiding a "hot potato," structural problems that lead to legislative deadlock such as filibusters and malapportionment). If a law were to attack this racial discrimination, it would have to be the Equal Protection Clause, and thus the requirement of state action became "the enemy" of racial progress, a picky formalism that stood in the way of federal judges performing an important social role. Moreover, in many contexts, especially in the South — the white primary cases are perhaps the most obvious example — there was a substantial blurring of the "public" and the "private," situations in which the same elite whites ruled both the government and the social and business realms and drew little practical distinction among them, imposing government regulation or private pressure or social custom based simply on which seemed the most expedient. In such a context, it might well make sense to avoid formalistic applications of the state action doctrine. In contrast, one might suggest that today, in changed circumstances — Congress and the state legislatures are more able to respond to such social problems, and many current legal issues lack the clear moral imperative of those found in the earlier civil rights era — invoking the state action doctrine to limit the reach of the Constitution may often be more justified; it allows Congress and the state legislatures greater capacity to experiment and find different local solutions to problems, and it allows the private marketplace to have a role as well.

3. *Routine Versus Extraordinary Intertwining with the State. Burton*, discussed in *Moose Lodge*, seemingly held that a private actor can be subjected to the Constitution if it is symbiotically intertwined with the state. But *Moose*

---

against county for failure of social workers to protect child against abusive parent).

Lodge and *Metropolitan Edison* indicate that state licensing and regulation are not enough to render the private entity a state actor. Moreover, *Moose Lodge* states that private entities are entitled to receive the general benefits of all citizens or taxpayers (police and fire protection, for example) without thereby subjecting themselves to the Constitution.

Norwood v. Harrison, 413 U.S. 455 (1973), involved a Mississippi program, in effect since 1940, under which the state provided free textbooks to all students in the state. The Court held that the state could not constitutionally lend textbooks to students attending racially discriminatory private schools:

> Textbooks are a basic educational tool [and] are to be distinguished from generalized services government might provide to schools in common with others. Moreover, the textbooks * * * are a form of assistance readily available from sources entirely independent of the State — unlike, for example, "such necessities of life as electricity, water, and police and fire protection." * * * [T]he Constitution does not permit the State to aid discrimination even when there is no precise causal relationship between state financial aid to a private school and the continued well-being of that school. A State may not grant the type of tangible financial aid here involved if that aid has a significant tendency to facilitate, reinforce, and support private discrimination.

How can *Norwood* be distinguished from *Moose Lodge*, where in the circumstances the state's granting of a liquor license can be considered a subsidy? Given the *Norwood* Court's focus on effects rather than purpose, is *Norwood* good law after *Washington v. Davis*? Could it be defended on the ground that Mississippi had earlier engaged in de jure school segregation?

4. *An Analogy to the Establishment of Religion*? The First Amendment forbids government from establishing a state religion (Chapter 6, § 7). In many ways, Establishment Clause questions (for example, whether a state may provide free textbooks to religious private schools, whether a state may display a creche at Christmas) are similar to state action questions, in that both ask the Court to draw a line between the public and private sectors. Justice O'Connor has proposed an "endorsement" test in religion cases that asks, essentially, whether the government policy has the purpose or effect of conveying a message "that religion or a particular religious belief is favored or preferred." See *Wallace v. Jaffree*, 472 U.S. 38, 70 (1985) (O'Connor, J., concurring in the judgment). How many of the principal state action cases we have examined — the white primary cases, *Marsh, Hudgens, Metropolitan Edison, Flagg Brothers, Shelley, Moose Lodge, Burton*, and *Norwood* — could be explained by an endorsement test?

5. *Contrasting State Court Approaches.* Even when state courts purport to follow federal state action doctrines, they often apply them differently. Consider *Gay Law Students Association v. Pacific Telegraph & Telephone*, 24 Cal. 3d 458, 595 P.2d 592, 156 Cal. Rptr. 14 (1979), in which gay men and lesbians challenged the utility's policy excluding them from employment. The California Supreme Court held that its state equal protection provision (Article I, § 7(a)) applied to state-licensed utilities and that their discrimination on grounds of sexual orientation was actionable. The court held that the California equal protection guarantee does not always require the presence of a state actor to be applicable and, further, that under traditional public function analysis

(*Metropolitan Edison*) the utility was a public actor because of the monopoly power granted it by the state. The court distinguished its result from that in *Metropolitan Edison* on the ground that a utility's decision to cut off a customer's electricity was an ad hoc decision that did not implicate the utility's monopoly power so much as a blanket policy of discriminating against gays and lesbians. Is this persuasive, or is the court implicitly suggesting that it would have decided *Metropolitan Edison* differently under the state constitution?

6. *A Substantive Theory of State Action.* Consider this theory of state action: Every private dispute involves state action, because the parties rely upon state-created interests — *e.g.*, a property right, a tort duty, predictable rules on how a contract will be read. Where one party is claiming a violation of equal protection, she can always articulate her claim as in *Shelley*: The state's protection of the other private party through a common law or regulatory rule undermines constitutional values. Where racial distinctions are not being made (as in *Flagg Brothers*), the state regulation is subject to a very low level of scrutiny and will usually be upheld; the state action doctrine is a convenient (if confusing) surrogate for review on the merits that such statutes almost always pass. Where racial distinctions are made by state law (either explicitly as in *Brown* or by obvious implication as in *Shelley* and the white primary cases), the state action requirement falls away. Where race distinctions are not obvious and are only indirectly the result of state law (as in *Moose Lodge*), the state action requirement reemerges as a convenience. As Mark Tushnet has argued, the state action requirement in this third set of cases allows the Supreme Court to avoid the appearance that it is endorsing discrimination against African Americans. See Mark Tushnet, Shelley v. Kraemer *and Theories of Equality*, 33 N.Y.L. Sch. L. Rev. 383 (1988).

Recall the state cases we have discussed in this chapter, especially the California cases such as *PruneYard* and *Gay Law Students Association.* This theory would suggest that the California court's expansive treatment of state action in those cases merely reflects a more expansive vision of free expression and equal protection than that held by the U.S. Supreme Court. Or would it be more plausible to attribute the federal Court's more restrictive view to federalism concerns (preserving the authority of the state itself to address these issues), which do not enter the state courts' analysis? Might some combination of these factors be at work?

3. *The Special Context of the Courtroom*

In *Batson v. Kentucky,* the Court held that a prosecutor may not use peremptory challenges in a criminal case for the purpose of excluding racial minorities from the jury. This seems to be a straightforward application of *Washington v. Davis*: a state actor intentionally used race in a way that disadvantages persons of color (even if the defendant is not a person of color, excluding people of color from the jury is a cognizable racial harm). Notice how this fits the *Davis* intentional discrimination model: even though the prosecutor has discretion to use her peremptory challenges to exclude anyone from a jury without having to show cause why the person should be excluded, she may not use this authority granted by the courts for racially discriminatory reasons.

A much more difficult conceptual setting arose in *Edmonson v. Leesville Concrete Co.*, 500 U.S. 614 (1991). In this civil case, defense counsel used two of its three peremptory challenges to remove African-American persons from the prospective jury. Of course, defense counsel in a civil case is not a government officer, so state action is not so clear in this context. Nonetheless, the majority of the Court, per Justice Kennedy, concluded that state action was present. First, the Court emphasized that the power of defense counsel to exercise the peremptory challenge flowed from state authority: "Peremptory challenges are permitted only when the government, by statute or decisional law, deems it appropriate to allow parties to exclude a given number of persons who otherwise would satisfy the requirements for service on the petit jury." Second, the Court concluded that is was appropriate to consider the private actor (defense counsel) should be deemed a government actor. In evaluating this issue, the Court seemingly breathed life into precedents that many had considered dormant:

> Our precedents establish that, in determining whether a particular action or course of conduct is governmental in character, it is relevant to examine the following: the extent to which the actor relies on governmental assistance and benefits, see *Tulsa Professional Collection Services, Inc. v. Pope*, 485 U.S. 478 (1988); *Burton v. Wilmington Parking Authority*; whether the actor is performing a traditional governmental function, see *Terry v. Adams*; *Marsh v. Alabama*; and whether the injury caused is aggravated in a unique way by the incidents of governmental authority, see *Shelley v. Kraemer*.

As for the first factor, the Court stressed that, "without the overt, significant participation of the government, the peremptory challenge system, as well as the jury trial system of which it is a part, simply could not exist." It also emphasized the appearance to potential jurors of extensive state involvement in jury selection: the role of the court clerk in summoning them and requiring them to complete jury questionnaires, the use of the open courtroom for voir dire, the presence and activity of the judge, who (rather than counsel) dismisses jurors challenged peremptorily, and so on.

As for the second factor, the Court concluded that the jury is a "quintessential governmental body," so that the process of comprising it should be viewed as a traditional governmental function. "If a government confers on a private body the power to choose the government's employees or officials, the private body will be bound by the constitutional mandate of race-neutrality. At least a plurality of the Court recognized this principle in *Terry v. Adams*."

Concerning the third factor, the Court stated:

> Finally, we note that the injury caused by the discrimination is made more severe because the government permits it to occur within the courthouse itself. Few places are a more real expression of the constitutional authority of the government than a courtroom, where the law itself unfolds. Within the courtroom, the government invokes its laws to determine the rights of those who stand before it. In full view of the public, litigants press their cases, witnesses give testimony, juries render verdicts, and judges act with the utmost care to ensure that justice is done.

Race discrimination within the courtroom raises serious questions as to the fairness of the proceedings conducted there. Racial bias mars the integrity of the judicial system and prevents the idea of democratic government from becoming a reality. In the many times we have addressed the problem of racial bias in our system of justice, we have not "questioned the premise that racial discrimination in the qualification or selection of jurors offends the dignity of persons and the integrity of the courts." To permit racial exclusion in this official forum compounds the racial insult inherent in judging a citizen by the color of his or her skin.

Justice O'Connor, joined by Chief Justice Rehnquist and Justice Scalia, dissented, contending that the peremptory challenge was "an enclave of private action in a government-managed proceeding" and that "[t]he entirety of the Government's actual participation in the peremptory process boils down to a single fact: 'When a lawyer exercises a peremptory challenge, the judge advises the juror he or she has been excused.' " This, she said, is a far cry from active governmental participation in, much less encouragement of, discrimination. She distinguished *Shelley* as a case where judicial power was exercised to enforce a facially discriminatory contract so as to compel discrimination on the part of those who did not wish to discriminate. Here, in contrast, no one was compelled to discriminate, and the peremptory challenge is merely an unexplained (not facially objectionable) request to excuse a juror. Did Justice O'Connor persuasively distinguish *Shelley*? How did the Court — and how can a court generally — measure how much governmental participation is "significant"? Isn't this lack of a precise or easily applied standard present in all of the state action cases you have read?

Justice O'Connor also argued that the exercise of a peremptory challenge is not a traditional governmental function because "[w]hatever reason a private litigant may have for using a peremptory challenge, it is not the government's reason. The government otherwise establishes its requirements for jury service, leaving to the private litigant the unfettered discretion to use the strike for any reason. This is not part of the government's function in establishing the requirements for jury service." While the majority seemed to focus on resolution of disputes by jury trial as a traditional governmental function, Justice O'Connor viewed the function in question here much more narrowly (the exercise of peremptory challenges). She stressed that "[t]he peremptory challenge forms no part of the *government's* responsibility in selecting a jury." Moreover, pointing out that the "peremptory challenge is a practice of ancient origin, part of our common law heritage in criminal trials," and harkening back to the "exclusivity" requirement of *Metropolitan Edison*, she contended that

> [i]n order to constitute state action under [the traditional governmental function doctrine,] private conduct must not only comprise something that the government traditionally does, but something that *only* the government traditionally does. Even if one could fairly characterize the use of a peremptory strike as the performance of the traditional government function of jury selection, it has never been exclusively the function of the government to select juries; peremptory strikes are older than the Republic.

How could the majority respond?[j]

PROBLEM ON STATE ACTION: ENTWINEMENT REVISITED

Problem 3-6.   The Tennessee Secondary School Athletic Association (TSSAA), formed in 1925, is a not-for-profit membership corporation that regulates interscholastic sport among the private and public high schools that belong to it. The great majority of public schools in the state are members; 55 private schools also belong. According to its rules, absent a waiver, a member school's team may play or scrimmage only against the team of another member. The Tennessee State Board of Education at one time officially designated TSSAA as the organization to supervise public school athletics, but in recent years the State Board dropped the official designation and merely acknowledged TSSAA's role "in coordinating interscholastic athletic competition" and "authorized" public schools to join TSSAA. TSSAA staff members are not paid by the state, but are eligible to join the state's public employee retirement system. TSSAA's revenue comes from dues from member schools and gate receipts at athletic tournaments. TSSAA found that Brentwood Academy, a private parochial school and member, had violated association rules against exercising "undue influence" in recruiting athletes when the Academy wrote to incoming students and their parents about spring football practice. TSSAA imposed sanctions upon Brentwood's athletic program (e.g., barring teams from participating in state playoffs for two years). When these penalties were imposed, all the members of TSSAA's governing bodies were public school administrators. Should the penalties be subject to constitutional review? See *Brentwood Academy v. TSSAA*, 531 U.S. 288 (2001).

C. STATE ACTION UNDER STATE CONSTITUTIONS

The state action doctrine has been followed in many state courts when interpreting their state constitutions. As alluded to earlier, however, in several states–especially California, New Jersey, New York, Pennsylvania, Washington–state constitutional protections have been held applicable to what the U.S. Supreme Court would consider private controversies. See Note, *State Court Approaches to the State Action Requirement: Private Rights, Public Values & Constitutional Choices*, 39 Kan. L .Rev. 495 (1991).

Sometimes state constitutions seem directly applicable to private action (like the federal Thirteenth Amendment). Article I, § 2(a) of the California Constitution provides: "Every person may freely speak, write and publish his or her sentiments on all subjects, being responsible for the abuse of this right. A law may not restrain or abridge liberty of speech or press." The California Supreme Court has interpreted this guarantee to apply against at least some private parties, most notably shopping mall owners, and the U.S. Supreme Court found no federal constitutional objection to this ruling. See *Robins v. PruneYard Shopping Center*, 23 Cal. 3d 899, 592 P.2d 341, 153 Cal. Rptr. 854

---

j.   See also *Georgia v. McCollum*, 505 U.S. 42 (1992) (*Batson* applies to peremptory challenges by counsel for a criminal defendant). For a recent case finding a violation of the *Batson* standard, see *Snyder v. Louisiana*, 128 S.Ct. 1203 (2008).

(1979), *aff'd*, 447 U.S. 74 (1980). See also *Fashion Valley Mall, LLC v. NLRB*, 42 Cal. 4th 850, 172 P.3d 742, 69 Cal. Rptr. 3d 288 (2007) (4-3 decision declining to overrule *Pruneyard*). Compare *State v. Wicklund*, 589 N.W.2d 793 (1999) (Minnesota Constitution does not require the Mall of America, the largest shopping mall in the United States, to allow protestors to display signs and distribute leaflets on topic of public concern).

Some state courts have applied a functional approach, balancing one party's interest in a constitutional activity against the other party's interest in noninterference. In *State v. Schmid*, 84 N.J. 535, 423 A.2d 615 (1980), *appeal dismissed*, 455 U.S. 100 (1982), for example, the New Jersey Supreme Court upheld a candidate's state constitutional right to distribute campaign materials on the campus of Princeton University (a private college). The court held that people have state free speech rights against the state government, against persons exercising government power, and against people who have implicitly "assumed a constitutional obligation not to abridge the individual exercise of such freedoms because of the public use of their property." The court found Schmid's interest in distribution considerable, in light of the broad public interest in free debate and political activity, and found Princeton's interest in excluding him less weighty because his actions did not intrude upon, and indeed were consonant with, the institution's educational purposes. See also *Commonwealth v. Tate*, 495 Pa. 158, 432 A.2d 1382 (1981).

Perhaps the more functional approach followed in some states represents a rejection of the ideology suggested by *Washington v. Davis*, in which the state's only obligation is to act neutrally. Under an alternative conception, the state cannot be neutral when private discriminatory arrangements rely upon the state's coercive power. For example, in *Schmid*, the state was implicated in Princeton's exclusionary conduct, because the University was ultimately relying upon the state-created doctrine of private property and trespass to exclude protesters. If the state stands ready to support Princeton, can it be said to be participating in the discriminatory conduct? Or would that go too far?

SECTION 3. THE AFFIRMATIVE ACTION CONTROVERSY: BENIGN RACIAL CLASSIFICATIONS OR REVERSE DISCRIMINATION?

A. AN INTRODUCTION TO THE DEBATE

Following *Brown*, a state university law school that limited the number of racial minorities it admitted would surely violate the Equal Protection Clause. To return to an earlier theme (see notes 3 and 4 following *Loving*), that practice would be unconstitutional regardless of whether heightened scrutiny is triggered merely by the use of a racial classification, or alternatively by only those racial classifications that disadvantage a racial minority. The first approach turns on a strong presumption that race is never relevant to government decisionmaking (a "race neutrality" approach). Under the second approach, the government might sometimes have legitimate reasons to consider race, but not when the group disadvantaged by the classification is a racial minority — a comparatively powerless group that has suffered a history of prejudice and thus cannot be expected to defend itself adequately in the political process. This approach might be called the "discrete and insular minority" approach, based on its linkage to *Carolene Products* footnote 4 (Chapter 1, § 6) and the representation-reinforcement theory of Professor Ely (Chapter 2, § 3B). In addition, the second approach might be defended not on the basis of political power, but on the ground that the government has, at least in theory, an affirmative obligation to attack racial subordination. Even if courts will not enforce this obligation by compelling the government to act, courts should not interfere when the government does in fact act consistent with the obligation.

Sometimes, as in the law-school example above, it makes no difference which theory is chosen. But if a state law school set aside a minimum, rather than maximum, number of places for racial minorities, the constitutional treatment of the admissions plan would vary greatly depending upon which of these two approaches was invoked. In cases where it makes a difference, which approach should be used?

Some of the cases we have examined, such as *Washington v. Davis*, seem premised on the second approach — that heightened scrutiny is reserved to protect those most likely to be disadvantaged because of prejudice. Other cases, such as *Loving*, contain language supporting a colorblind or race-neutrality approach. But in none of these cases was it necessary to choose between the two approaches because they all involved discrimination against a racial minority. Beginning in the 1970s, the Court faced a series of cases in which affirmative action — the overt use of racial criteria to benefit racial minorities — was challenged, and accordingly the Court had to choose between the two approaches.

We use the famous *Bakke* case, from 1978, to introduce this debate,[a] then consider the issue in a larger theoretical framework, and finally examine the most recent decisions. As you read these materials, consider whether the Court's vision of what racial discrimination means has changed since *Brown*, or whether these cases follow from a proper understanding of *Brown*.

Regents of the University of California v. Bakke, 438 U.S. 265 (1978). The University of California at Davis medical school reserved sixteen of the 100 places in its class for minority group members (defined as "Blacks, Chicanos, Asians, and American Indians"). Alan Bakke, a rejected white applicant with

---

a. Two earlier cases raised affirmative-action issues. In *DeFunis v. Odegaard*, 416 U.S. 312 (1974), a rejected white applicant to a state law school whose "paper credentials" were stronger than some minority students who had been admitted brought suit, and a lower court had ordered the school to admit him. The Supreme Court eventually dismissed the case as moot because he was about to graduate. The only Justice to address the merits, Justice Douglas, proposed that strict scrutiny be applied even to this "benign" use of race. In *Morton v. Mancari*, 417 U.S. 535 (1974), the Court upheld a preference for hiring and promotions for Indians in the Bureau of Indian Affairs, the federal agency primarily concerned with administering federal programs for Indians. The Court justified the decision on narrow, *sui generis* grounds. According to the Court, the preference was a political, rather than a racial, one because it benefitted only members of federally recognized Indian tribes, not all persons of Native American ancestry. Indian tribes are sovereigns under American law and have a government-to-government relationship with the federal government.

arguably better "paper credentials" than some minority students who had been admitted, brought suit. Four Justices (**Burger**, **Stewart**, **Rehnquist**, and **Stevens**) concluded that the admissions program violated Title VI of the Civil Rights Act of 1964 because it constituted racial discrimination by a recipient of federal financial assistance, and accordingly these Justices did not reach the constitutional issue. The other five Justices concluded that Title VI forbids only those racial classifications that would violate the Equal Protection Clause, and accordingly they considered the meaning of equal protection in this context. In a joint opinion, four Justices (**Brennan**, **White**, **Marshall**, and **Blackmun**) would have upheld the program; **Justice Powell** concluded that the program violated equal protection. Thus, a majority of five Justices (Justice Powell and the four who rested their decision on Title VI) held the program illegal, but no rationale had the support of a majority of the Court. The debate between Justice Powell and the "Brennan four" on the constitutional issue illustrates many central issues concerning affirmative action.

1. *Nature of Discrimination and Level of Scrutiny.* Justice Powell stressed the universal language of the Equal Protection Clause and concluded that it protects all individuals equally, not some groups more than others. Strict scrutiny should apply regardless of whether whites are a "discrete and insular minority" under *Carolene Products* footnote 4:

> The concepts of "majority" and "minority" necessarily reflect temporary arrangements and political judgments. * * * [T]he white "majority" itself is composed of various minority groups, most of which can lay claim to a history of prior discrimination at the hands of the State and private individuals. Not all of these groups can receive preferential treatment and corresponding judicial tolerance of distinctions drawn in terms of race and nationality, for then the only "majority" left would be a new minority of white Anglo-Saxon Protestants. There is no principled basis for deciding which groups would merit "heightened judicial solicitude" and which would not. Courts would be asked to evaluate the extent of the prejudice and consequent harm suffered by various minority groups. Those whose societal injury is thought to exceed some arbitrary level of tolerability then would be entitled to preferential classifications at the expense of individuals belonging to other groups. * * * As these preferences began to have their desired effect, and the consequences of past discrimination were undone, new judicial rankings would be necessary. The kind of variable sociological and political analysis necessary to produce such rankings simply does not lie within the judicial competence — even if they otherwise were politically feasible and socially desirable.

He suggested that even seemingly "benign" preferences might simply be a product of racial politics, that such preferences might reinforce "common stereotypes holding that certain groups are unable to achieve success without special protection based on a factor having no relationship to individual worth," and that "innocent" persons like Bakke should not bear the burdens of redressing wrongs not of their making. Ultimately, he took it as axiomatic that strict scrutiny (which he phrased as requiring (a) a "constitutionally permissible and substantial" purpose and (b) the use of a racial classification as "necessary to the accomplishment" of the purpose) should apply in these circumstances, quoting *Hirabayashi* for the proposition that "[d]istinctions between citizens solely because of their ancestry are by their very nature odious to a free people whose institutions are founded upon the doctrine of equality."

According to the "Brennan four," strict scrutiny was inappropriate for "benign" racial classifications, which they defined as those that do not stigmatize those disadvantaged by the classification. The Davis plan was not based on the assumption that those disadvantaged by it were inferior, much less on racial hatred or separatism. Ultimately, they opted for "intermediate scrutiny":

> [B]ecause of the significant risk that racial classifications established for ostensibly benign purposes can be misused, causing effects not unlike those created by invidious classifications, it is inappropriate to inquire only whether there is any conceivable basis that might sustain such a classification. Instead, to justify such a classification an important and articulated purpose for its use must be shown. In addition, any statute must be stricken that stigmatizes any group or that singles out those least well represented in the political process to bear the brunt of a benign purpose.

2. *Applying Strict Scrutiny: Justice Powell.* Justice Powell concluded that remedying societal discrimination was too amorphous a "concept of injury that may be ageless in its reach into the past." Nor was the Davis program justified by the goal of improving the delivery of health care to underserved communities, since there was no evidence that the program was "either needed or geared to promote that goal."

Justice Powell did conclude that ameliorating the effects of identified past discrimination would be a constitutionally permissible purpose for affirmative action. But even if the Davis program were designed to achieve this purpose, it could not pass constitutional muster under the "means" portion of strict scrutiny analysis. Justice Powell stated that the Court had never "approved a classification that aids persons perceived as members of relatively victimized groups at the expense of other innocent individuals in the absence of judicial, legislative, or administrative findings of constitutional or statutory violations." The Davis plan had been created and adopted by the medical faculty of the university, whose "broad mission is education, not the formulation of any legislative policy or the adjudication of particular claims of illegality. [I]solated segments of our vast governmental structures are not competent to make those decisions, at least in the absence of legislative mandates and legislatively determined criteria."[b]

Justice Powell accepted, as a constitutionally sufficient purpose, "the attainment of a diverse student body," which he saw as linked to creating the best academic environment for the school. Again, however, the Davis plan failed to be a constitutionally acceptable means of promoting this purpose: "The diversity that furthers a compelling state interest encompasses a far broader array of qualifications and characteristics of which racial or ethnic origin is but a single though important element." Powell favorably compared the admissions program at Harvard College, where race may be deemed a "plus" but "does not insulate the individual from comparison with all other candidates for the

---

b. The Brennan four responded that it is California's business how it allocates lawmaking power, and that under the state constitution the authority over the university is lodged in the board of regents, which had delegated admissions decisions to the medical school faculty.

available seats. * * * This kind of program treats each applicant as an individual in the admissions process."

3. *Applying "Intermediate Scrutiny": The Brennan Four.* The Brennan four concluded that Davis's "purpose of remedying the effects of past societal discrimination" is "sufficiently important to justify the use of race-conscious admissions programs where there is a sound basis for concluding that minority underrepresentation is substantial and chronic, and that the handicap of prior discrimination is impeding access of minorities to the Medical School." They found sufficient evidence of the factual premises of these conclusions. Unlike Justice Powell, they found nothing superior about the Harvard admissions plan:

> The "Harvard" program, as those employing it readily concede, openly and successfully employs a racial criterion for the purpose of ensuring that some of the scarce places in institutions of higher education are allocated to disadvantaged minority students. That the Harvard approach does not also make public the extent of the preference and the precise workings of the system while the Davis program employs a specific, openly stated number, does not condemn the latter plan for purposes of Fourteenth Amendment adjudication. It may be that the Harvard plan is more acceptable to the public than is the Davis "quota." If it is, any State * * * is free to adopt it * * *. But there is no basis for preferring a particular preference program simply because in achieving the same goals that the Davis Medical School is pursuing, it proceeds in a manner that is not immediately apparent to the public.

JUSTICE MARSHALL wrote separately to emphasize the deep and pervasive historical discrimination against African Americans in this country. **JUSTICE BLACKMUN**'s separate opinion suggested that "to get beyond racism, we must first take account of race. There is no other way."

————

NOTES ON AFFIRMATIVE ACTION IN A BROADER THEORETICAL CONTEXT

How would the following theories suggest that *Bakke* be decided?

1. *Original Intent Theories.* Return to our brief history of the Fourteenth Amendment in Chapter 2, §§ 1A, 3A. Would the original drafters of the Fourteenth Amendment have disapproved of state or municipal preferences benefitting only African Americans or other racial minorities? Recall that the Reconstruction Congress passed the Fourteenth Amendment in part to protect the constitutionality of the Civil Rights Act of 1866, which was viewed by its critics as partial to the freed slaves. Also, between 1866 and 1871, Congress adopted eight reconstructive measures that established programs benefitting primarily African Americans; the Freedman's Bureau Act of 1866, 14 Stat. 173, was the most important of these.[c]

2. *Representation-Reinforcing Theories.* Recall Professor Ely's representation-reinforcing theory of judicial review (Chapter 2, § 3B). How would he analyze *Bakke*? See John Hart Ely, *The Constitutionality of Reverse Racial Discrimination*, 41 U. Chi. L. Rev. 723 (1974).

---

c. Contrasting views of original intent on this issue are offered by Robert Bork, *The Tempting of America: The Political Seduction of the Law* 101-10 (1989), and Eric Schnapper, *Affirmative Action and the Legislative History of the Fourteenth Amendment*, 71 Va. L. Rev. 753 (1985).

3. *Justice-Oriented Theories.* We also describe "progressive" approaches to constitutional discourse in Chapter 2, § 3C. Many such theories are driven by an assessment of the ultimate justice, in the current context, that can be achieved through constitutional interpretation. Consider two competing views about the appropriateness of adopting racial preferences benefitting traditional minority groups.

Thomas Sowell
Civil Rights: Rhetoric or Reality?
37, 42, 50-53, 118-19 (1984)[d]

The very meaning of the phrase "civil rights" has changed greatly since the *Brown* decision in 1954. * * * Initially, civil rights meant, quite simply, that all individuals should be treated the same under the law, regardless of their race, religion, sex or other such social categories. For blacks, especially, this would have represented a dramatic improvement in those states where law and public policy mandated racially separate institutions and highly discriminatory treatment.

Many Americans who supported the initial thrust of civil rights * * * later felt betrayed as the original concept of equal individual *opportunity* evolved toward the concept of equal group *results*. * * *

Those who carry the civil rights vision to its ultimate conclusion see no great difference between promoting equality of opportunity and equality of results. If there are not equal results among groups presumed to have equal genetic potential, then some inequality of opportunity must have intervened somewhere, and the question of precisely where is less important than the remedy of restoring the less fortunate to their just position. The fatal flaw in this kind of thinking is that there are many reasons, besides genes and discrimination, why groups differ in their economic performances and rewards. Groups differ by large amounts demographically, culturally, and geographically — and all of these differences have profound effects on incomes and occupations.

[Sowell argues that many of the apparent statistical disparities between the economic success of different racial and ethnic groups (especially blacks and whites) are the result of differing age and geographic distributions of the people in the different groups, the culture and goals that have been inculcated into people, and the choices they tend to have made. He argues, therefore, that it is indeterminate exactly how much of blacks' economic disadvantage *vis-a-vis* whites is due to discrimination of any sort. He further argues that the gap between earnings of blacks and whites narrowed before blacks gained efficacious remedies for discrimination in the Civil Rights Act of 1964.]

* * * Those blacks with less education and less job experience — the truly disadvantaged — have been falling farther and farther behind their white counterparts under affirmative action, during the very same years when blacks with more education and job experience have been advancing economically, both absolutely and relative to their white counterparts. First, the disadvan-

---

taged: Black male high school dropouts with less than six years of work experience earned 79% of the income of white male high school dropouts with less than six years of work experience in 1967 (before affirmative action quotas) and this *fell* to 69% by 1978 (after affirmative action quotas). Over these very same years, the income of black males who had completed college and had more than six years of work experience *rose* from 75% of the income of their white counterparts to 98%.

* * * The pattern of diametrically opposite trends in economic well-being among advantaged and disadvantaged blacks is also shown by the general internal distribution of income among blacks. The top fifth of blacks have absorbed a growing proportion of all income received by blacks, while each of the bottom three-fifths has received declining shares. * * *

Affirmative action hiring pressures make it costly to have no minority employees, but continuing affirmative action pressures at the promotion and discharge phases also make it costly to have minority employees who do not work out well. The net effect is to increase the demand for highly qualified minority employees while decreasing the demand for less qualified minority employees or for those without a sufficient track record to reassure employers. * * *

* * * Among the [dangers of affirmative action] are the undermining of minority * * * self-confidence by incessant reiteration of the themes of pervasive discrimination, hypocritical standards, and shadowy but malign enemies relentlessly opposing their progress. * * * [I]t also obscures the urgency of acquiring economically meaningful skills or developing the attitudes to apply them with the best results. Pride of achievement is also undermined by the civil rights vision that assumes credit for minority * * * advancement. This makes minority * * * achievement suspect in their own eyes and in the eyes of the larger society.

The more acute dangers are longer run. The spread of hate organizations may be a symptom of much more unorganized sentiment among people * * * . The dangers of continually adding to those resentments are all the greater the more heedlessly preferential doctrines are pushed in the courts, in the federal bureaucracy and by activists.

Patricia Williams
Metro Broadcasting, Inc. v. FCC: *Regrouping*
in Singular Times
104 Harv. L. Rev. 525, 541-44 (1990)[e]

* * * [A] student recently demanded of me, "Don't you think affirmative action is what creates a David Duke?" (David Duke is the former Ku Klux Klan leader who recently lost a race for U.S. Senator from Louisiana — but only narrowly, with sixty percent of the white vote and, according to one estimate, seventy percent of the white male vote.) Blacks are positioned in this query as responsible for the bitterest backlash against them, an eerie repeat of the

---

e. Copyright © 1990 by the Harvard Law Review Association.

responses (one being the founding of the Ku Klux Klan) to black gains * * * during Reconstruction.

In fact, affirmative action and minority set-aside programs are vastly more complicated than this "you're in, I'm out" conception suggests. Nothing in this rigid win-loss dichotomy permits the notion that everyone could end up a beneficiary, that expansion rather than substitution might be possible, and that the favoring of multiple cultures is enhancement of the total rather than a sweepingly reflexive act of favoritism for anything other than the monolithic purity of an all-white nation.

This particular evocation, of a corrupt system of favoritism seesawing between "the deserving" and "the preferred," caters to an assumption that those who are included by the grace of affirmative action systems are therefore *un*deserving. I want to underscore that I do mean that it "*caters to*," rather than *creates*, an assumption of inferiority, for the assumption of inferiority has a life that precedes and, unfortunately, will probably outlive affirmative action programs. The subtlety of this distinction has terrified even some few blacks into distorting historic assumptions of blacks as inferior into their weird acceptance of their exclusion as its cure. Sitting on university admissions committees, for example, I have seen black candidates who write on their applications comments such as, "Don't admit me if you have to lower your standards." I have never seen the same acutely self-conscious disavowals from students who are admitted because they meet some geographic criterion * * * or who are older re-entry students, or football heroes, or alumni children. I think this is so because these latter inclusionary categories are thought to indicate group life experiences * * * that "enrich" rather than "lower."

The question, then, becomes not how to undo the inclusionary affirmative action programs, but how to undo the stigma of inferiority that resides not merely in the label or designation of race, but that, according to our national symbology, is actually *embodied* in black presence. * * *

The tenacity of this devalued condition is perhaps captured by something I saw not long ago in a five-and-dime store: a huge bin of identically molded plastic sets of mother and father dolls. Some dolls in the bin were priced at $3.99 a set. Others had been originally priced at $2.99, now marked down to the "Must Sacrifice!" price of $1.99 a set. As a neutral market phenomenon, this obviously makes little sense, and one would assume that a rational vendor would quickly adjust one way or another for the discrepancy. As a less-than-neutral observer, however, I should add that although all the dolls were obviously cast from the same mold, they had not been privileged to share the same dye lot. The higher-priced dolls were white; the dolls priced for sacrificial sale were black. I was struck by how central the information about color was to my analysis of this situation: in a color-blind frame, the pricing was so irrational that I might comfortably assume a laissez-faire approach, confident that market pressures would assure a rapid adjustment. Knowing the dolls' color, however, exposed a more grim social reality: the irrationality of racism not only perpetuated, but also made "rational" by market forces. The absolute necessity of a corrective response to the silent tenacity of this status quo is the heart of what affirmative action is all about. * * *

* * * [T]he idea that an egalitarian society can be achieved or maintained through the mechanism of blind neutrality is fallacious. Racial discrimination is powerful precisely because of its frequent invisibility, its felt neutrality. * * * Racism inscribes culture with generalized preferences and routinized notions of propriety. It is aspiration as much as condemnation; it is an aesthetic. It empowers the mere familiarity and comfort of the status quo by labeling that status quo as "natural." If we are to reach the deep roots of this legacy, antidiscrimination must be a commitment not merely to undo the words of this forced division, but also to undo the consequences of oppressive acts. As in the old saw about the two horses given "equal" opportunity to run a race, but one of whom has a stone in his shoe, the failure to take into account history and context can radically alter whether mere neutrality can be deemed just.

NOTES ON SPECIFIC ARGUMENTS IN
THE AFFIRMATIVE ACTION DEBATE

These excerpts only scratch the surface of the affirmative action debate, and we can hardly hope to do more than highlight some of the lines of argument as well as some useful sources. The following notes attempt to cram a great deal of information and several different perspectives into a short space. You should regard the notes primarily as material to be mined for your own thinking, rather than as teachings to be mastered.[f]

1. *Formal versus Functional Equality.* As noted at the beginning of this chapter, scholars such as Dr. Sowell, who emphasize colorblindness, work within a very different ideological framework than those such as Professor Williams, who emphasize historical subordination. The former speak in terms of formal equality and emphasize the importance of equal process; the latter speak in terms of functional equality and emphasize equal results.

At one level, the formal versus functional equality debate is, therefore, an ideological one. Your agreement with Dr. Sowell or with Professor Williams might be connected with your views about the history of African Americans in our society, your interpretation of *Brown* (and exactly what it was rejecting in *Plessy*), your receptiveness to *Washington v. Davis* and the Court's state action doctrine, and your overall views about whether African Americans have been treated differently than other ethnic or racial groups. Obviously, one's views are not necessarily connected to one's own race or ethnicity. For example, Dr. Sowell and Professor Williams are both African American, and each claims adherents within that community.

----

f. For much deeper discussions, see, e.g., William Bowen & Derek Bok, *The Shape of the River: Long-Term Consequences of Considering Race in College and University Admissions* (1998), and Orlando Patterson, *The Ordeal of Integration: Progress and Resentment in America's "Racial" Crisis* (1997) (both contending that affirmative action should be continued); Peter Schuck, *Affirmative Action: Past, Present, and Future*, 20 Yale L. & Pol. Rev. 1 (2002) (affirmative action should be abandoned).

At another level, the debate is about experience and data: Is affirmative action either necessary or useful in narrowing the economic gaps between white people and black people? James Smith & Finis Welch, *Black Economic Progress After Myrdal*, 27 J. Econ. Lit. 519 (1989), report that between 1940 and 1980 wage differentials between white and black workers diminished greatly (Tables 1-8). Black income as a percentage of white income steadily progressed from 43.3% in 1940 to 72.6% in 1980 (Table 2). Based upon a multiple regression analysis, Smith and Welch concluded that better education for black workers explained most of the progress that was made, though in 1980 African Americans with the same educational attainment only made 80-87% of the income of similarly situated whites (Table 11). They also found that migration of African Americans from rural areas to urban areas contributed to erosion of wage differentials (Table 20); that rising black unemployment in the 1970s did not appreciably affect African Americans' progress in the 1970s but may have in the 1980s; and that affirmative action had the following apparent effects: (a) It did increase employment opportunities for African Americans, especially for firms with federal business (Table 26), but (b) was not a statistically significant determinant for the declining black-white wage differential (Table 27), though (c) it did contribute significantly to the big jump in income for young African Americans in 1967-72 (Table 28) and weakly to the general income improvement for African Americans with college degrees (Table 28).

James Heckman & Brook Payner, *Determining the Impact of Federal Antidiscrimination Policy in the Status of Blacks: A Study of South Carolina*, 79 Am. Econ. Rev. 138 (1989), present similar findings from their study of the South Carolina textile industry. Richard Epstein, *Forbidden Grounds: The Case Against Employment Discrimination Laws* 245-62 (1992), argues that the improvement of black economic opportunities in the South came as a result of the federal government's crushing of Jim Crow laws that impeded minority entry into the marketplace.[g]

In a major survey of the existing literature, Harry Holzer & David Neumark, *Assessing Affirmative Action*, 38 J. Econ. Lit. 483 (2000)[h], conclude that, although the "theoretical literature from labor economics generates ambiguous results on whether affirmative action programs result in efficiency gains or losses," the "empirical literature — both in economics and other disciplines — on the presence of discrimination and the effects of affirmative action is much more extensive." According to them, "the following inferences . . . seem justified:"

- "Significant labor market discrimination against minorities and women persists . . . ."

---

g. John Donohue III & James Heckman, *Re-Evaluating Federal Civil Rights Policy*, 79 Geo. L.J. 1713 (1991), respond to this point and others raised by skeptics of the contributions of federal civil rights policy and also provide a survey of the economic literature.

h. Reprinted with permission.

- "Affirmative action programs redistribute employment, university admissions, and government business from white males to minorities and women, though the extent of the redistribution may not be large."

- "There is virtually no evidence of weaker educational qualifications or job performance among females who benefit from affirmative action relative to males, especially within occupational grade."

- "The educational performance and labor market credentials of minority beneficiaries are weaker than those of their white counterparts. But evidence of weaker performance in the labor market among these groups is much less frequently observed or is less credible. Evidence on the performance of the minority businesses who benefit from special procurement programs is also mixed."

- "The potential effects of affirmative action on performance, at least in the labor market, appear to depend on how it is implemented. Employers that practice affirmative action can (and often do) mitigate its potentially negative effects on performance by extensive recruitment and screening before workers are hired, as well as special training and evaluation efforts afterwards."

- "Although minority students admitted to colleges and universities perform less well, on average, than nonminority students, this evidence is generally no stronger at the most selective schools that have been the focus of the affirmative action debate. Both black and white students benefit from attending selective colleges and universities."

- "There is some evidence consistent with positive externalities from affirmative action, but not for each type of externality that has been posited by its advocates. For example, minority doctors are more likely to treat minority and/or low-income patients than are other physicians. Evidence on role-model/mentoring effects in universities is weaker and more mixed, especially with respect to coeducational institutions. There is no evidence of positive (or negative) effects of a diverse student body on educational quality."

- "There is mixed evidence regarding whether affirmative action in contracting and procurement props up weak companies. In some studies, firms that initially benefit from these programs but then move into an environment without set-asides do not appear to fail at higher rates than comparable firms. On the other hand, there is some evidence that minority business enterprises deriving a large percentage of their revenue from local government are relatively more likely to go out of business. Some evidence suggests, however, that this phenomenon is attributable to the fraudulent formation of front companies for the sole purpose of qualifying for these programs. Local government programs with genuine assistance to small enterprises, and penalties for fraudulent behavior, appear able to promote success of minority business enterprises."

Obviously, these conclusions are not only provisional, but controversial. For example, Walter Williams, *The State Against Blacks* (1982), argues that federal intervention in the economy has held African Americans back. Historically, groups "at the bottom" start with low-paying jobs, with the second generation doing better and climbing the economic ladder. Federal minimum wage laws have impeded this sequence for African Americans, he argues, by discouraging employers from offering market rates, which affects African Americans disproportionately. The welfare system has also broken the cycle of progress for African Americans by making it tempting to get by without the work ethic. Even federal affirmative action policies have hurt African Americans, by discouraging employers from locating in majority-black areas and thereby being subjected to higher quotas.[i] David Strauss, *The Law and Economics of Racial Discrimination in Employment: The Case for Numerical Standards*, 79 Geo. L.J. 1619 (1991), argues exactly the opposite — that African-American under-employment and wage differentials are caused by patterns of secret or unconscious racism that can only be remedied through disparate impact numerical standards, and through remedial employment quotas. More recently, Stephan Thernstrom & Abigail Thernstrom, *America in Black and White* 449-51 (1997), consider the effect of affirmative action exceedingly hard to assess because African American progress would have occurred at some pace anyway even without affirmative action, the few studies on the subject have reached mixed results, and entrepreneurial politicians who have created affirmative action programs naturally claim credit for improving minority economic status through their efforts even though there are often few good reasons to be confident about cause and effect.[j]

2. *Positive Values of Affirmative Action.* Generally, the Supreme Court's willingness sometimes to allow affirmative action by state actors has been premised upon a backward-looking approach, justifying affirmative action as a remedy for past discrimination against African Americans; the Court has treated past discrimination very narrowly and refuses to see continuing victimization of African Americans by conscious and unconscious racism today. See Patricia Williams, *The Alchemy of Race and Rights* (1991) (especially the tale of the author's encounter with a bored Bennetton sales clerk). Kathleen Sullivan, *Sins of Discrimination: Last Term's Affirmative Action Cases*, 100 Harv. L. Rev. 78

---

i.   See also Richard Posner, *The Efficiency and Efficacy of Title VII*, 136 U. Pa. L. Rev. 513, 519 (1987). But see John Donohue III, *Is Title VII Efficient?*, 134 U. Pa. L. Rev. 1411 (1986).

j.   See also Christopher Edley, Jr., *Not All Black and White: Affirmative Action, Race, and American Values* (1996) (by former special counsel to President Clinton on affirmative action issues).

Recently, an extensive debate has occurred about the effects of preferential admission to law schools. Compare Richard Sander, *A Systemic Analysis of Affirmative Action in American Law Schools*, 57 Stan L Rev 367 (2004) (affirmative action strongly affects which schools African American students attend but only slightly affects whether they attend law school at all, and if such persons attended law schools where the median student was closer to their "predictors" their success rates (law school grades, graduation rates, bar passage rates, and postgraduation employment) would be better) with, e.g., Jesse Rothstein & Albert Yoon, *Affirmative Action in Law School Admissions: What Do Racial Preferences Do?*, 75 U. Chi. L. Rev. 649 (2008) (one of many critical responses to Sander, which purports to demonstrate, among other things, that without racial preferences many African Americans would not attend law school, especially at the elite schools).

(1986), argues that such a backward-looking approach also has the effect of presenting affirmative action as a "penalty" against specified "sinners." This is unrealistic, presenting excessively hard burdens of proof for employers wanting to engage in affirmative action, and divisive, inviting claims by "nonsinners" that they should not have to share the costs of prior sins.

Randall Kennedy, *Persuasion and Distrust: A Comment on the Affirmative Action Debate*, 99 Harv. L. Rev. 1327 (1986), argues that affirmative action can offer many "positive externalities" for employers, and Professor Sullivan urges such a forward-looking approach to affirmative action. "[E]mployers might advance [a number of] forward-looking reasons for affirmative action: improving their services to black constituencies, averting racial tension over the allocation of jobs in a community, or increasing the diversity of a work force, to name but a few examples. Or they might adopt affirmative action simply to eliminate from their operations all *de facto* embodiment of a system of racial caste." The Kennedy-Sullivan point might be developed in the school desegregation cases, interpreting *Brown* as offering positive benefits for white as well as black students. Contrast Richard Epstein, *Forbidden Grounds*, *supra* at 59-78, who argues that diversity in an employer's workforce will tend to create greater transactions costs. "Any social policy that requires that membership in a private association should be randomly drawn from a subset of the larger whole is an invitation to trouble," *id.* at 64, because diversity of tastes tends to create friction and disagreement over routine matters. "To the extent, therefore, that individual tastes are grouped by race, by sex, by age, by national origin — and to some extent they are — then there is a necessary conflict between the commands of any antidiscrimination law and the smooth operation of the firm. Firms whose members have diverse and clashing views may well find it more difficult to make collective decisions than firms with a closer agreement over tastes." *Id.* at 66. Epstein would leave it open to private employers to decide whether to discriminate either in favor of or against minority groups, based on the employer's view of its own business interests. How would Professor Patricia Williams or Professor Charles Lawrence, author of the article on unconscious racism excerpted in § 1C of this chapter, respond to this argument?

One value of the affirmative action debate may be to impel our culture to think more deeply about issues of "merit" and "entitlement."[k] The simplest example is the preference in our system for seniority — the idea behind last hired/first fired, tenure and lockstep promotions, union hierarchies, and so forth. It remains to be shown that seniority, especially strictly applied, is economically efficient, but it is quite clear that seniority systems greatly slowed the integration of African Americans into the workforce: If there were prior discrimination in, say, union membership, a sudden adoption of nondiscriminatory admission policies would still leave black workers at the bottom of the seniority ladder for years, so that when layoffs came (as they did throughout the 1970s and 1980s) African Americans would be the first to go. (See *Wygant*.) This critique

---

k. See generally Duncan Kennedy, *A Cultural Pluralist Case for Affirmative Action in Legal Academia*, 1990 Duke L.J. 705.

applies, of course, not just to the unionized work force, where seniority holds in place traditional patterns of access to employment, but also to universities, where tenure has a similar impact on the composition of faculties.[1]

3. *Affirmative Action, Allocational Politics, and the "New Ethnicity."* Relevant to the affirmative-action debate is what the sociologists call the "new ethnicity."[m] Traditional ethnicity tended to be expressive, backward-looking, and integrative toward the larger culture, but the new ethnicity tends to be instrumental and forward-looking (get more of the pie for us) and inward-turning and resistant to assimilation into the larger culture. Affirmative action might be viewed as an expression of this new ethnicity. Of course, this suggests that affirmative action has relevance far beyond the African-American population that we have been examining in this chapter.

Many affirmative action programs, both state and private, provide preferences not only to African Americans, but also to Latinos (usually quite vaguely defined), Asians, and Native Americans; many programs also include or focus on women, discussed in Chapter 4. One is immediately struck by the disparity of the various groups. African Americans generally share the common heritage of slavery and apartheid, and most affirmative action discourse (such as that above) focuses on their experience. Are the experiences of other groups similar enough to justify similar treatment? That of Native Americans, as documented by Rennard Strickland, *Genocide-at-Law: An Historic and Contemporary View of the Native American Experience*, 34 Kan. L. Rev. 713 (1986), might even be considered worse.

At the risk of saying something to offend everyone, one might venture some further speculations. For example, the situation of Asians may be significantly better than that of African Americans, since most Asians came to this country at least with consent — though one might divide Asians into groups, such as many Chinese, who came as indentured workers, as opposed to others, such as Vietnamese, who came here as refugees. Yet Japanese Americans were subjected to outrageous treatment during World War II (in contrast to Italian and German Americans, who were largely left alone by the government). Asian Americans are often penalized by racial prejudice, yet as a group they have done quite well economically.

The situation of Hispanics is perhaps the most complex of all, and one might well be skeptical of the Anglo term "Hispanic" itself. Latino groups are at least as diverse as Asian groups. Cuban Americans, for example, tend to be refugees or children of refugees from Castro's Cuba and to be economically advantaged, as opposed to Puerto Ricans or Mexican Americans, who have suffered the more

---

l. To take another example even closer to home, the increasing (albeit slow) diversification of law school faculties has had a dramatic impact on legal scholarship. Much of the scholarship excerpted or discussed in this chapter and in Chapter 2 is the work of African Americans or other scholars of color. Critical Race Theory is the most vivid, but by no means the only, contribution resulting from this diversification.

m. See *Ethnicity: Theory and Experience* (Nathan Glazer & Daniel Moynihan eds. 1975), especially Daniel Bell's essay on "Ethnicity and Social Change."

traditional problems (poverty and open discrimination) of marginalized groups. Should Cubans benefit from affirmative action programs?

What binds all these groups together, thereby justifying affirmative action? It's not clear. If it's traditions of poverty, does that set them apart from Appalachians, who are also victims of "accent discrimination"?[n] If it's the existence of traditions of vicious discrimination against them, does that set them apart from Jews, for example? Or gay men and lesbians? Steven Epstein, *Gay Politics, Ethnic Identity: The Limits of Social Constructionism*, 93/94 Socialist Rev. 9-54 (May/Aug. 1987), argues that gay men and lesbians are an "ethnic group" for purposes of the new ethnicity scholarship. Should gays and lesbians be included in affirmative action programs?

Richard Fallon, Jr. & Paul Weiler, Firefighters v. Stotts: *Conflicting Models of Racial Justice*, 1984 Sup. Ct. Rev. 1, 46-50 (1984), argue that a group should be entitled to preferential treatment if "(i) there has been an historic pattern of legally sanctioned, group-based discrimination; (ii) the legacy of historical discrimination includes a current condition of group disadvantage, resulting in social problems at least partly remediable through affirmative discrimination; and (iii) social and psychological factors give current meaning to the group as more than an arbitrary collection of individuals." They claim that only Native Americans have as powerful a claim to affirmative relief as African Americans. Why not Latinos? The poor? The disabled? Michael Gottesman, *Twelve Topics to Consider Before Opting for Racial Quotas*, 79 Geo. L.J. 1737, 1761-67 (1991) wonders why the criteria don't apply to women. None of these authors discusses whether the criteria apply to gay men and lesbians.

B. THE EVOLUTION OF THE MODERN CASE LAW, 1980-1995

As was the case in *Bakke*, in the 1980s the Supreme Court remained deeply divided over the question of affirmative action and was unable to produce any majority opinions that significantly clarified the issue. Adding to the disarray in the Court was whether affirmative action adopted by Congress should be treated differently from affirmative action at the state or local level. By 1995, however, after the Court had changed composition, clearer constitutional approaches had emerged. Nonetheless, the Court has continued to struggle with affirmative action in the new millenium.

Fullilove v. Klutznick, 448 U.S. 448 (1980). Six Justices voted to uphold against against a facial challenge a 1977 federal statute providing federal funds to state and local government building projects that required that, absent an administrative waiver, at least 10% of the money had to be spent procuring goods or services from minority business enterprises ("MBEs"), which were defined as businesses owned or controlled by "citizens of the United States who are Negroes, Spanish-speaking, Orientals, Indians, Eskimos, and Aleuts." **Justice Marshall**, joined by **Justices Brennan** and **Blackmun**, concluded that

---

n. Cf. Mari Matsuda, *Voices of America: Accent, Antidiscrimination Law, and a Jurisprudence for the Last Reconstruction*, 100 Yale L.J. 1329 (1991).

the statute survived the "intermediate scrutiny" approach they adopted in *Bakke*. **Chief Justice Burger**, joined by **Justices White** and **Powell**, also voted to uphold the statute, but did not adopt either approach suggested in *Bakke* — he simply stated that the use "of racial or ethnic criteria, even in a remedial context, calls for close examination." Burger stressed that "in no organ of government, state or federal, does there repose a more comprehensive remedial power than in Congress, expressly charged by the Constitution with competence and authority to enforce equal protection guarantees." He concluded that the objective of the statute — which he defined as attacking the perpetuation of the effects of past intentional discrimination — was constitutionally permissible. He acknowledged that Congress had made no "preambulary 'findings' on the subject," but concluded that Congress had a sufficient factual basis (largely because of prior congressional and executive branch reports and studies) to conclude that "minority businesses have been denied effective participation in public contracting opportunities by procurement practices that perpetuated the effects of prior discrimination." "Congress, of course, may legislate without compiling the kind of 'record' appropriate with respect to judicial or administrative proceedings." He also concluded that the means chosen to effectuate this purpose were unobjectionable, stressing the statute's limited nature (it allocated money on a one-shot basis) and its administrative waiver provisions for instances in which compliance with the MBE requirement was too difficult.

Justice Powell, writing separately, explained that the statute survived his approach in *Bakke* because it "serves the compelling government interest in eradicating the continuing effects of past discrimination identified by Congress." He reasoned that, "[b]ecause the distinction between permissible remedial action and impermissible racial preference rests on the existence of a constitutional or statutory violation, the legitimate interest in creating a race-conscious remedy is not compelling unless an appropriate governmental authority has found that such a violation has occurred." Unlike the college regents or faculty in *Bakke*, Congress was authorized, by its enforcement powers under the Civil War Amendments, to address and remedy problems of discrimination. As did Burger, Powell looked to the broad evidence before Congress in the era surrounding the passage of the statute to conclude that Congress had a reasonable basis for the use of racial criteria in the statute.

Justices Stewart and **Rehnquist** dissented, contending that the Constitution requires governmental colorblindness. **Justice Stevens** also dissented; he argued that, even if it is assumed that Congress has the authority to use racial criteria for remedial purposes, the legislative history and other evidence provided no sure basis for concluding that Congress carefully considered what it was doing in adopting the MBE provision.

———

Wygant v. Jackson Board of Education, 476 U.S. 267 (1986). Again with no majority opinion, the Court struck down a collective bargaining agreement between a public school board and a teacher's union that provided that layoffs be made on a seniority basis (last hired, first laid off) "except that at no time will there be a greater percentage of minority personnel laid off than the current percentage of minority personnel employed at the time of the layoff." Minority personnel were defined as employees who were "Black, American Indian, Oriental, or of Spanish descendancy." **Justice Powell**, in a plurality opinion joined in part by **Chief Justice Burger** and **Justices Rehnquist** and **O'Connor**, rejected the school district's major defense — that the protections ensured minority students with role models — as having "no logical stopping point" and having no necessary connection to any harm caused by prior discriminatory hiring practices. The district, which had never been found to have discriminated in hiring, tried for the first time before the Supreme Court to justify the agreement as a remedy for its past hiring practices, but Justice Powell refused to consider the argument without a district court finding "that the employer had a strong basis in evidence for its conclusion that remedial action was necessary." He also rejected the contention that the school district was authorized to remedy "societal discrimination," as opposed to its own illegal practices. Finally, he concluded that the means chosen — layoff protection — was less justifiable than affirmative action in hiring because, "[w]hile hiring goals impose a diffuse burden, often foreclosing only one of several opportunities, layoffs impose the entire burden of achieving racial equality on particular individuals, often resulting in serious disruption of their lives."

CITY OF RICHMOND v. J.A. CROSON CO.
488 U.S. 469, 109 S.Ct. 706, 102 L.Ed.2d 854 (1989)

JUSTICE O'CONNOR announced the judgment of the Court and delivered the opinion of the Court with respect to Parts I, III-B, and IV, an opinion with respect to Part II, in which **THE CHIEF JUSTICE [REHNQUIST]** and **JUSTICE WHITE** join, and an opinion with respect to Part III-A * * *, in which **THE CHIEF JUSTICE, JUSTICE WHITE,** and **JUSTICE KENNEDY** join.

[In 1983, the Richmond, Virginia City Council adopted the Minority Business Utilization Plan, requiring non-minority prime contractors receiving city construction contracts "to subcontract at least 30% of the dollar amount of the contract to one or more Minority Business Enterprises (MBEs)." "MBE was defined as '[a] business at least fifty-one (51) percent of which is owned and controlled . . . by minority group members' " (defined as "[c]itizens of the United States who are Blacks, Spanish-speaking, Orientals, Indians, Eskimos, or Aleuts"). "There was no geographic limit to the Plan; an otherwise qualified MBE from anywhere in the United States could avail itself of the 30% set-aside. The Plan declared that it was 'remedial' in nature, and enacted 'for the purpose of promoting wider participation by minority business enterprises in the construction of public projects.' " Supporters relied on the following information: "while the general population of Richmond was 50% black, only .67% of the city's prime construction contracts had been awarded to minority businesses in the 5-year period from 1978 to 1983"; virtually no minority businesses belonged to local contractors' associations; the city's attorney thought the ordinance was constitutional under *Fullilove*; Councilmember Marsh, a supporter of the ordinance and an attorney, stated that he was familiar with widespread racial discrimination in the construction industry, both locally and nationally. "There was no direct evidence of race discrimination on the part of the city in letting contracts or any evidence that the city's prime contractors had discriminated against minority-owned subcontractors," and opponents expressed concern that there were too few MBEs in the Richmond area to satisfy the 30% requirement. J.A. Croson Co., a non-minority contractor, ultimately brought this suit challenging the plan.]

II. * * * Appellant and its supporting amici rely heavily on *Fullilove* for the proposition that a city council, like Congress, need not make specific findings of discrimination to engage in race-conscious relief. * * *

That Congress may identify and redress the effects of society-wide discrimination does not mean that, *a fortiori*, the States and their political subdivisions are free to decide that such remedies are appropriate. Section 1 of the Fourteenth Amendment is an explicit constraint on state power, and the States must undertake any remedial efforts in accordance with that provision. * * *

[A] state or local subdivision (if delegated the authority from the State) has the authority to eradicate the effects of private discrimination within its own legislative jurisdiction. This authority must, of course, be exercised within the constraints of § 1 of the Fourteenth Amendment. * * * Richmond has legislative authority over its procurement policies, and can use its spending powers to remedy private discrimination, if it identifies that discrimination with the particularity required by the Fourteenth Amendment. * * *

Thus, if the city could show that it had essentially become a "passive participant" in a system of racial exclusion practiced by elements of the local construction industry, we think it clear that the city could take affirmative steps to dismantle such a system. It is beyond dispute that any public entity, state or federal, has a compelling interest in assuring that public dollars, drawn from the tax contributions of all citizens, do not serve to finance the evil of private prejudice.

IIIA. The Equal Protection Clause of the Fourteenth Amendment provides that "[N]o State shall . . . deny to *any person* within its jurisdiction the equal protection of the laws" (emphasis added). * * * The Richmond Plan denies certain citizens the opportunity to compete for a fixed percentage of public contracts based solely upon their race. To whatever racial group these citizens belong, their "personal rights" to be treated with equal dignity and respect are implicated by a rigid rule erecting race as the sole criterion in an aspect of public decisionmaking.

Absent searching judicial inquiry into the justification for such race-based measures, there is simply no way of determining what classifications are "benign" or "remedial" and what classifications are in fact motivated by illegitimate notions of racial inferiority or simple racial politics. Indeed, the purpose of strict scrutiny is to "smoke out" illegitimate uses of race by assuring that the legislative body is pursuing a goal important enough to warrant use of a highly suspect tool. The test also ensures that the means chosen "fit" this compelling goal so closely that there is little or no possibility that the motive for the classification was illegitimate racial prejudice or stereotype.

Classifications based on race carry a danger of stigmatic harm. Unless they are strictly reserved for remedial settings, they may in fact promote notions of racial inferiority and lead to a politics of racial hostility. *See Bakke* (opinion of Powell, J). We thus reaffirm the view expressed by the plurality in *Wygant* that the standard of review under the Equal Protection Clause is not dependent on the race of those burdened or benefitted by a particular classification. * * *

Even were we to accept a reading of the guarantee of equal protection under which the level of scrutiny varies according to the ability of different groups to defend their interests in the representative process, heightened scrutiny would still be appropriate in the circumstances of this case. One of the central arguments for applying a less exacting standard to "benign" racial classifications is that such measures essentially involve a choice made by dominant racial groups to disadvantage themselves. If one aspect of the judiciary's role under the Equal Protection Clause is to protect "discrete and insular minorities" from majoritarian prejudice or indifference, see *Carolene Products* n.4, some maintain that these concerns are not implicated when the "white majority" places burdens upon itself. *See* J. Ely, Democracy and Distrust 170 (1980).

In this case, blacks comprise approximately 50% of the population of the city of Richmond. Five of the nine seats on the City Council are held by blacks. The concern that a political majority will more easily act to the disadvantage of a minority based on unwarranted assumptions or incomplete facts would seem to militate for, not against, the application of heightened judicial scrutiny in this case. * * *

In *Wygant*, four Members of the Court applied heightened scrutiny to a race-based system of employee layoffs. * * * The challenged classification in that case tied the layoff of minority teachers to the percentage of minority students enrolled in the school district. The lower courts had upheld the scheme, based on the theory that minority students were in need of "role models" to alleviate the effects of prior discrimination in society. This Court reversed, with a plurality of four Justices reiterating the view expressed by Justice Powell in *Bakke* that "[s]ocietal discrimination, without more, is too amorphous a basis for imposing a racially classified remedy."

The role model theory employed by the lower courts failed for two reasons. First, the statistical disparity between students and teachers had no probative value in demonstrating the kind of prior discrimination in hiring or promotion that would justify race-based relief. Second, because the role model theory had no relation to some basis for believing a constitutional or statutory violation had occurred, it could be used to "justify" race-based decisionmaking essentially limitless in scope and duration.

B. * * * Like the "role model" theory employed in *Wygant*, a generalized assertion that there has been past discrimination in an entire industry provides no guidance for a legislative body to determine the precise scope of the injury it seeks to remedy. * * * "Relief" for such an ill-defined wrong could extend until the percentage of public contracts awarded to MBEs in Richmond mirrored the percentage of minorities in the population as a whole.

Appellant argues that it is attempting to remedy various forms of past discrimination that are alleged to be responsible for the small number of minority businesses in the local contracting industry. Among these the city cites the exclusion of blacks from skilled construction trade unions and training programs. This past discrimination has prevented them "from following the traditional path from laborer to entrepreneur." The city also lists a host of nonracial factors which would seem to face a member of any racial group attempting to establish a new business enterprise, such as deficiencies in working capital, inability to meet bonding requirements, unfamiliarity with bidding procedures, and disability caused by an inadequate track record.

While there is no doubt that the sorry history of both private and public discrimination in this country has contributed to a lack of opportunities for black entrepreneurs, this observation, standing alone, cannot justify a rigid racial quota in the awarding of public contracts in Richmond, Virginia. Like the claim that discrimination in primary and secondary schooling justifies a rigid racial preference in medical school admissions, an amorphous claim that there has been past discrimination in a particular industry cannot justify the use of an unyielding racial quota.

It is sheer speculation how many minority firms there would be in Richmond absent past societal discrimination, just as it was sheer speculation how many minority medical students would have been admitted to the medical school at Davis absent past discrimination in educational opportunities. Defining these sorts of injuries as "identified discrimination" would give local governments license to create a patchwork of racial preferences based on statistical generalizations about any particular field of endeavor. * * *

None of [the district court's findings], singly or together, provide the city of Richmond with a "strong basis in evidence for its conclusion that remedial action was necessary." *Wygant*. There is nothing approaching a prima facie case of a constitutional or statutory violation by *anyone* in the Richmond construction industry. [The plan was based on undocumented assertions of racial discrimination around the country and in Richmond that were undocumented.]

Reliance on the disparity between the number of prime contracts awarded to minority firms and the minority population of the city of Richmond is similarly misplaced. There is no doubt that "[w]here gross statistical disparities can be shown, they alone in a proper case may constitute prima facie proof of a pattern or practice of discrimination" under Title VII. But it is equally clear that "[w]hen special qualifications are required to fill particular jobs, comparisons to the general population (rather than to the smaller group of individuals who possess the necessary qualifications) may have little probative value."

[Justice O'Connor concluded that the city had too little evidence to support the set-aside. The city did not know how many qualified MBEs were in the market or the percentage of total city construction dollars that went to MBEs as subcontractors on city contracts. The dearth of minority participation in local contractors' associations "is not probative of any discrimination in the local construction industry" without a showing of great statistical disparity between eligible MBEs and MBE membership in the association.]

Finally, the city and the District Court relied on Congress' finding in connection with the set-aside approved in *Fullilove* that there had been nationwide discrimination in the construction industry. The probative value of these findings for demonstrating the existence of discrimination in Richmond is extremely limited. By its inclusion of a waiver procedure in the national program addressed in *Fullilove*, Congress explicitly recognized that the scope of the problem would vary from market area to market area.

Moreover, as noted above, Congress was exercising its powers under § 5 of the Fourteenth Amendment in making a finding that past discrimination would cause federal funds to be distributed in a manner which reinforced prior patterns of discrimination. While the States and their subdivisions may take remedial action when they possess evidence that their own spending practices are exacerbating a pattern of prior discrimination, they must identify that discrimination, public or private, with some specificity before they may use race-conscious relief. Congress has made national findings that there has been societal discrimination in a host of fields. If all a state or local government need do is find a congressional report on the subject to enact a set-aside program, the constraints of the Equal Protection Clause will, in effect, have been rendered a nullity. * * *

The foregoing analysis applies only to the inclusion of blacks within the Richmond set-aside program. There is *absolutely no evidence* of past discrimination against Spanish-speaking, Oriental, Indian, Eskimo, or Aleut persons in any aspect of the Richmond construction industry. * * * The random inclusion of racial groups that, as a practical matter, may never have suffered from discrimination in the construction industry in Richmond, suggests that perhaps the city's purpose was not in fact to remedy past discrimination. If a 30% set-aside was "narrowly tailored" to compensate black contractors for past discrimination, one may legitimately ask why they are forced to share this "remedial relief" with an Aleut citizen who moves to Richmond tomorrow? The gross overinclusiveness of Richmond's racial preference strongly impugns the city's claim of remedial motivation.

IV. * * * [I]t is almost impossible to assess whether the Richmond Plan is narrowly tailored to remedy prior discrimination since it is not linked to identified discrimination in any way. We limit ourselves to two observations in this regard.

First, there does not appear to have been any consideration of the use of race-neutral means to increase minority business participation in city contracting. * * * If MBEs disproportionately lack capital or cannot meet bonding requirements, a race-neutral program of city financing for small firms would, *a fortiori*, lead to greater minority participation. The principal opinion in *Fullilove* found that Congress had carefully examined and rejected race-neutral alternatives before enacting the MBE set-aside. There is no evidence in this record that the Richmond City Council has considered any alternatives to a race-based quota.

Second, the 30% quota cannot be said to be narrowly tailored to any goal, except perhaps outright racial balancing. It rests upon the "completely unrealistic" assumption that minorities will choose a particular trade in lockstep proportion to their representation in the local population.

Since the city must already consider bids and waivers on a case-by-case basis, it is difficult to see the need for a rigid numerical quota. * * * [T]he congressional scheme upheld in *Fullilove* allowed for a waiver of the set-aside provision where an MBE's higher price was not attributable to the effects of past discrimination. Based upon proper findings, such programs are less problematic from an equal protection standpoint because they treat all candidates individually, rather than making the color of an applicant's skin the sole relevant consideration. Unlike the program upheld in *Fullilove*, the Richmond Plan's waiver system focuses solely on the availability of MBEs; there is no inquiry into whether or not the particular MBE seeking a racial preference has suffered from the effects of past discrimination by the city or prime contractors.

Given the existence of an individualized procedure, the city's only interest in maintaining a quota system rather than investigating the need for remedial action in particular cases would seem to be simple administrative convenience. But the interest in avoiding the bureaucratic effort necessary to tailor remedial relief to those who truly have suffered the effects of prior discrimination cannot justify a rigid line drawn on the basis of a suspect classification. Under Richmond's scheme, a successful black, Hispanic, or Oriental entrepreneur from anywhere in the country enjoys an absolute preference over other citizens based solely on their race. We think it obvious that such a program is not narrowly tailored to remedy the effects of prior discrimination.

JUSTICE STEVENS, concurring in part and concurring in the judgment.

* * * I believe the Constitution requires us to evaluate our policy decisions — including those that govern the relationships among different racial and ethnic groups — primarily by studying their probable impact on the future. I therefore do not agree with the premise that seems to underlie today's decision, as well as [*Wygant*], that a governmental decision that rests on a racial classification is never permissible except as a remedy for a past wrong. I do, however, agree with the Court's explanation of why the Richmond ordinance cannot be justified as a remedy for past discrimination. [Justice Stevens stressed that the benefits of the ordinance were not limited to victims of past discrimination, nor were its burdens limited to white contractors who had some demonstrable relationship to actual discrimination.]

JUSTICE KENNEDY, concurring in part and concurring in the judgment.

Part II examines our caselaw upholding Congressional power to grant preferences based on overt and explicit classification by race. *See Fullilove.* With the acknowledgment that the summary in Part II is both precise and fair, I must decline to join it. The process by which a law that is an equal protection violation when enacted by a State becomes transformed to an equal protection guarantee when enacted by Congress poses a difficult proposition for me; but as it is not before us, any reconsideration of that issue must await some further case. * * *

[**JUSTICE MARSHALL**, joined by **JUSTICES BRENNAN** and **BLACKMUN**, dissented. Justice Marshall argued that the Richmond plan passed the "intermediate scrutiny" he would apply to affirmative action measures. The city had two important governmental interests — eradicating the present effects of past racial discrimination and ensuring that the city's money did not perpetuate those effects — that, he contended, were adequately supported by the record. He stressed that minority-owned businesses received only "one-seventy-fifth the public contracting funds that other businesses receive." The means chosen were reasonable because they were similar to those approved in *Fullilove*. He contended that, since the Civil War Amendments were adopted because of fears that states would inadequately respond to "racial violence or discrimination against newly freed slaves," "[t]o interpret any aspect of these Amendments as proscribing state remedial measures * * * turns the Amendments on their heads." He also objected to Justice O'Connor's characterization of "racial politics" in Richmond, stressing that white and black councilmembers had increasingly cooperated on controversial matters.]

[The opinion of **JUSTICE SCALIA** concurring the judgment and the dissenting opinion of **JUSTICE BLACKMUN** are omitted.]

Metro Broadcasting, Inc. v. Federal Communications Commission, 497 U.S. 547 (1990). This case concerned federal race-based preferences for increasing minority ownership of television and radio stations. In 1986, only 2.1% of such stations were minority owned. Over several decades, a federal policy had evolved through congressional initiatives and FCC policies whereby minority applicants for new broadcast licenses would receive a preference, and where a limited number of existing stations could be transferred only to minority-controlled firms. The FCC had defined "minority" to include "those of Black, Hispanic Surnamed, American Eskimo, Aleut, American Indian and Asiatic American extraction." The Court upheld these measures by a 5-4 vote. **Justice Brennan**'s majority opinion, joined by **Justices White**, **Marshall**, **Blackmun**, and **Stevens**, concluded that *Fullilove* had not imposed strict scrutiny upon the federal program challenged there, and then adopted "intermediate scrutiny" — a standard asking whether the classification in question "serve[s] important governmental objectives and [is] substantially related to the achievement of those objectives" — as the appropriate standard for assessing federal "benign" racial classifications. The majority stressed that intermediate scrutiny was appropriate regardless of whether the federal classification was "remedial" (designed to compensate victims of past governmental or societal discrimination) or was instead a "forward-looking" effort to diversify society, *cf.* Justice Stevens' separate opinion in *Croson*. The majority concluded that the interest in enhancing broadcast diversity was an important governmental objective because "the diversity of views and information on the airwaves serves important First Amendment values." The means chosen were substantially related to the achievement of broadcast diversity because there is a sufficient connection between expanded minority ownership and greater broadcast diversity.

Justice O'Connor, joined by **Chief Justice Rehnquist** and **Justices Scalia** and **Kennedy**, issued a long dissenting opinion. Relying upon *Croson*, she asserted that strict scrutiny applied to the FCC policies. She distinguished *Fullilove* on the basis that there Congress (1) was exercising its powers under § 5 of the Fourteenth Amendment, which provides Congress power to enforce equal protection guarantees *against the states*, and (2) was attempting to remedy identified discrimination. Turning first to the government interest at stake, Justice O'Connor concluded that in the circumstances the only interest that could be considered "compelling" is remedying the effects of identified racial discrimination, an interest that the FCC had conceded could not be shown. "Like the vague assertion of societal discrimination, a claim of insufficiently diverse broadcasting viewpoints might be used to justify [unconstrained] racial preferences, linked to nothing other than proportional representation of various races." She found the means chosen to effectuate the government's interest equally infirm because they impermissibly equated race with belief and behavior; the means were overinclusive (benefitting minority group members who had no interest in advancing the viewpoints the FCC believed were under-represented) and underinclusive (failing to benefit nonminorities who were well situated to advance underrepresented viewpoints). She disputed how thoroughly the FCC had attempted to use race-neutral approaches to encourage broadcast-ing diversity, and she concluded that the policies unduly burdened nonminorities seeking licenses. **Justice Kennedy**, joined by **Justice Scalia**, also issued a dissenting opinion urging strict scrutiny, if not absolute colorblindness, as the appropriate standard.

ADARAND CONSTRUCTORS, INC. v. PENA
515 U.S. 200, 115 S.Ct. 2097, 132 L.Ed.2d 158 (1995)

JUSTICE O'CONNOR announced the judgment of the Court and delivered an opinion with respect to Parts I, II, III–A, III–B, III–D, and IV, which is for the Court except insofar as it might be inconsistent with the views expressed in **JUSTICE SCALIA**'s concurrence, and an opinion with respect to Part III–C in which **JUSTICE KENNEDY** joins.

[The federal government awarded the prime contract for a highway construction project to Mountain Gravel & Construction Co. Mountain Gravel solicited bids from subcontractors for a portion of the work. Adarand Constructors submitted the low bid. Mountain Gravel chose Gonzales Construction Co., however, because Mountain Gravel would receive additional compensation from the federal government for hiring subcontractors, such as Gonzales Construction, certified as small businesses controlled by "socially and economically disadvantaged persons." "Social disadvantage" referred to those "subjected to racial or ethnic prejudice or cultural bias because of their identity as a member of a group without regard to their individual qualities"; "economic disadvantage" referred to "those socially disadvantaged individuals whose ability to compete in the free enterprise system has been impaired due to diminished capital and credit opportunities as compared to others in the same business area who are not socially disadvantaged." Women and racial minorities were presumed to be socially and economically disadvantaged, but this presumption was subject to rebuttal by a third party. A subcontractor who was not a woman or a racial minority could nonetheless qualify by proving social disadvantage "on the basis of clear and convincing evidence" and then by proving economic disadvantage as well. Adarand challenged this scheme as unconstitutional.]

IIIA. * * * Through the 1940s, this Court had routinely taken the view in non-race-related cases that, "[u]nlike the Fourteenth Amendment, the Fifth contains no equal protection clause and it provides no guaranty against discriminatory legislation by Congress." *Detroit Bank v. United States*, 317 U.S. 329, 337 (1943)[.] When the Court first faced a Fifth Amendment equal protection challenge to a federal racial classification, it adopted a similar approach, with most unfortunate results. *Hirabayashi* [p. 38, *supra*] considered a curfew applicable only to persons of Japanese ancestry. The Court observed — correctly — that "[d]istinctions between citizens solely because of their ancestry are by their very nature odious to a free people whose institutions are founded upon the doctrine of equality," and that "racial discriminations are in most circumstances irrelevant and therefore prohibited." But it also cited *Detroit Bank* for the proposition that the Fifth Amendment "restrains only such discriminatory legislation by Congress as amounts to a denial of due process," and upheld the curfew because "circumstances within the knowledge of those charged with the responsibility for maintaining the national defense afforded a rational basis for the decision which they made."

Eighteen months later, the Court again approved wartime measures directed at persons of Japanese ancestry. *Korematsu* [p. 38, *supra*] concerned an order that completely excluded such persons from particular areas. The Court did not address the view, expressed in cases like *Hirabayashi* and *Detroit Bank*, that the Federal Government's obligation to provide equal protection differs significantly from that of the States. Instead, it began by noting that "all legal restrictions which curtail the civil rights of a single racial group are immediately suspect . . . [and] courts must subject them to the most rigid scrutiny." That promising dictum might be read to undermine the view that the Federal Government is under a lesser obligation to avoid injurious racial classifications than are the States. But in spite of the "most rigid scrutiny" standard it had just set forth, the Court then inexplicably relied on "the principles we announced in the *Hirabayashi* case" to conclude that, although "exclusion from the area in which one's home is located is a far greater deprivation than constant confinement to the home from 8 p.m. to 6 a.m.," the racially discriminatory order was nonetheless within the Federal Government's power.

In *Bolling v. Sharpe* [Chapter 2, § 1C], the Court for the first time explicitly questioned the existence of any difference between the obligations of the Federal Government and the States to avoid racial classifications. *Bolling* did note that "[t]he 'equal protection of the laws' is a more explicit safeguard of prohibited unfairness than 'due process of law.' " But *Bolling* then concluded that, "[i]n view of [the] decision that the Constitution prohibits the states from maintaining racially segregated public schools, it would be unthinkable that the same Constitution would impose a lesser duty on the Federal Government."

Bolling's facts concerned school desegregation, but its reasoning was not so limited. The Court's observations that "[d]istinctions between citizens solely because of their ancestry are by their very nature odious," *Hirabayashi*, and that "all legal restrictions which curtail the civil rights of a single racial group are immediately suspect," *Korematsu*, carry no less force in the context of federal action than in the context of action by the States — indeed, they first appeared in cases concerning action by the Federal Government. *Bolling* relied on those observations and reiterated " 'that the Constitution of the United States, in its present form, forbids, so far as civil and political rights are concerned, discrimination *by the General Government, or by the States,* against any citizen because of his race.' " The Court's application of that general principle to the case before it, and the resulting imposition on the Federal Government of an obligation equivalent to that of the States, followed as a matter of course. * * *

* * * *Loving* * * * cited *Korematsu* for the proposition that "the Equal Protection Clause demands that racial classifications . . . be subjected to the 'most rigid scrutiny.' " * * * [I]n 1975, the Court stated explicitly that "[t]his Court's approach to Fifth Amendment equal protection claims has always been precisely the same as to equal protection claims under the Fourteenth Amendment." *Weinberger v. Wiesenfeld* [Chapter 4, § 2B1]. * * * We do not understand a few contrary suggestions appearing in cases in which we found special deference to the political branches of the Federal Government to be appropriate, *e.g., Hampton v. Mow Sun Wong,* 426 U.S. 88 (1976) (federal power over immigration), to detract from this general rule.

B. [Justice O'Connor reviewed *Bakke, Fullilove,* and *Wygant.*] The Court resolved the confusion, at least in part, in 1989. * * * A majority of the Court in *Croson* held that "the standard of review under the Equal Protection Clause is not dependent on the race of those burdened or benefitted by a particular classification," and that the single standard of review for racial classifications should be "strict scrutiny." As to the classification before the Court, the plurality agreed that "a state or local subdivision . . . has the authority to eradicate the effects of private discrimination within its own legislative jurisdiction," but the Court thought that the city had not acted with "a 'strong basis in evidence for its conclusion that remedial action was necessary.' " The Court also thought it "obvious that [the] program is not narrowly tailored to remedy the effects of prior discrimination."

With *Croson,* the Court finally agreed that the Fourteenth Amendment requires strict scrutiny of all race-based action by state and local governments. But *Croson* of course had no occasion to declare what standard of review the Fifth Amendment requires for such action taken by the Federal Government. * * * Thus, some uncertainty persisted with respect to the standard of review for federal racial classifications.

Despite lingering uncertainty in the details, however, the Court's cases through *Croson* had established three general propositions with respect to governmental racial classifications. First, skepticism: " '[a]ny preference based on racial or ethnic criteria must necessarily receive a most searching examination.' " *Wygant* (plurality opinion of Powell, J.); *Fullilove* (opinion of Burger, C.J.); *McLaughlin; Hirabayashi.* Second, consistency: "the standard of review under the Equal Protection Clause is not dependent on the race of those burdened or benefitted by a particular classification," *Croson* (plurality opinion); *id.* (Scalia, J., concurring in judgment); see also *Bakke* (opinion of Powell, J.), *i.e.,* all racial classifications reviewable under the Equal Protection Clause must be strictly scrutinized. And third, congruence: "[e]qual protection analysis in the Fifth Amendment area is the same as that under the Fourteenth

Amendment[.]" Taken together, these three propositions lead to the conclusion that any person, of whatever race, has the right to demand that any governmental actor subject to the Constitution justify any racial classification subjecting that person to unequal treatment under the strictest judicial scrutiny. * * *

A year later, however, the Court took a surprising turn. [*Metro Broadcasting* held] that "benign" federal racial classifications need only satisfy intermediate scrutiny[.]   * * *   The Court did not explain how to tell whether a racial classification should be deemed "benign," other than to express "confiden[ce] that an 'examination of the legislative scheme and its history' will separate benign measures from other types of racial classifications." * * *

By adopting intermediate scrutiny as the standard of review for congressionally mandated "benign" racial classifications, *Metro Broadcasting* departed from prior cases in two significant respects. First, it turned its back on *Croson*'s explanation of why strict scrutiny of all governmental racial classifications is essential:

> Absent searching judicial inquiry into the justification for such race-based measures, there is simply no way of determining what classifications are "benign" or "remedial" and what classifications are in fact motivated by illegitimate notions of racial inferiority or simple racial politics. Indeed, the purpose of strict scrutiny is to "smoke out" illegitimate uses of race by assuring that the legislative body is pursuing a goal important enough to warrant use of a highly suspect tool. The test also ensures that the means chosen "fit" this compelling goal so closely that there is little or no possibility that the motive for the classification was illegitimate racial prejudice or stereotype. *Croson* [plurality opinion].

We adhere to that view today * * * .

Second, *Metro Broadcasting* squarely rejected one of the three propositions established by the Court's earlier equal protection cases, namely, congruence between the standards applicable to federal and state racial classifications, and in so doing also undermined the other two — skepticism of all racial classifications, and consistency of treatment irrespective of the race of the burdened or benefitted group. * * *

The three propositions undermined by *Metro Broadcasting* all derive from the basic principle that the Fifth and Fourteenth Amendments to the Constitution protect *persons*, not *groups*. It follows from that principle that all governmental action based on race — a *group* classification long recognized as "in most circumstances irrelevant and therefore prohibited," *Hirabayashi* — should be subjected to detailed judicial inquiry to ensure that the *personal* right to equal protection of the laws has not been infringed. * * * Accordingly, we hold today that all racial classifications, imposed by whatever federal, state, or local governmental actor, must be analyzed by a reviewing court under strict scrutiny. In other words, such classifications are constitutional only if they are narrowly tailored measures that further compelling governmental interests. To the extent that *Metro Broadcasting* is inconsistent with that holding, it is overruled. * * *

Justice Stevens chides us for our "supposed inability to differentiate between 'invidious' and 'benign' discrimination," because it is in his view sufficient that "people understand the difference between good intentions and bad." But, as we have just explained, the point of strict scrutiny is to "differentiate between" permissible and impermissible governmental use of race. And Justice Stevens himself has already explained in his dissent in *Fullilove* why "good intentions" alone are not enough to sustain a supposedly "benign" racial classification: "[E]ven though it is not the actual predicate for this legislation, a statute of this kind inevitably is perceived by many as resting on an assumption that those who are granted this special preference are less qualified in some respect that is identified purely by their race. Because that perception — *especially when fostered by the Congress of the United States* — can only exacerbate rather than reduce racial prejudice, it will delay the time when race will become a truly irrelevant, or at least insignificant, factor. *Unless Congress clearly articulates the need and basis* for a racial classification, *and also tailors the classification to its justification,* the Court should not uphold this kind of statute." [Emphasis added] * * * [This passage makes] a persuasive case for requiring strict scrutiny of congressional racial classifications.

Perhaps it is not the standard of strict scrutiny itself, but our use of the concepts of "consistency" and "congruence" in conjunction with it, that leads Justice Stevens to dissent. According to Justice Stevens, our view of consistency "equate[s] remedial preferences with invidious discrimination" and ignores the difference between "an engine of oppression" and an effort "to foster equality in society," or, more colorfully, "between a 'No Trespassing' sign and a welcome mat." It does nothing of the kind. The principle of consistency simply means that whenever the government treats any person unequally because of his or her race, that person has suffered an injury that falls squarely within the language and spirit of the Constitution's guarantee of equal protection. It says nothing about the ultimate validity of any particular law; that determination is the job of the court applying strict scrutiny. The principle of consistency explains the circumstances in which the injury requiring strict scrutiny occurs. The application of strict scrutiny, in turn, determines whether a compelling governmental interest justifies the infliction of that injury. * * *

Justice Stevens also claims that we have ignored any difference between federal and state legislatures. But requiring that Congress, like the States, enact racial classifications only when doing so is necessary to further a "compelling interest" does not contravene any principle of appropriate respect for a co-equal Branch of the Government. * * *

C. [In this Part, in which only Justice Kennedy joined, Justice O'Connor attempted to reconcile the treatment of *stare decisis* in this case and in the abortion case, *Planned Parenthood v. Casey* (Chapter 5, § 4B). The votes of Justices O'Connor and Kennedy in *Casey* had been essential to avoid the overruling of *Roe v. Wade* (Chapter 5, § 4B).]

D. * * * We think that requiring strict scrutiny is the best way to ensure that courts will consistently give racial classifications that kind of detailed examination, both as to ends and as to means. *Korematsu* demonstrates vividly that even "the most rigid scrutiny" can sometimes fail to detect an illegitimate racial classification, compare *Korematsu* ("To cast this case into outlines of racial prejudice, without reference to the real military dangers which were presented, merely confuses the issue. Korematsu was not excluded from the Military Area because of hostility to him or his race"), with Pub. L. 100–383,

§ 2(a), 102 Stat. 903–904 ("[T]hese actions [of relocating and interning civilians of Japanese ancestry] were carried out without adequate security reasons . . . and were motivated largely by racial prejudice, wartime hysteria, and a failure of political leadership"). Any retreat from the most searching judicial inquiry can only increase the risk of another such error occurring in the future.

Finally, we wish to dispel the notion that strict scrutiny is "strict in theory, but fatal in fact." The unhappy persistence of both the practice and the lingering effects of racial discrimination against minority groups in this country is an unfortunate reality, and government is not disqualified from acting in response to it. * * * When race-based action is necessary to further a compelling interest, such action is within constitutional constraints if it satisfies the "narrow tailoring" test this Court has set out in previous cases. [The Court remanded the case for application of the strict-scrutiny standard.]

JUSTICE SCALIA, concurring in part and concurring in the judgment.

I join the opinion of the Court, except Part III–C, and except insofar as it may be inconsistent with the following: In my view, government can never have a "compelling interest" in discriminating on the basis of race in order to "make up" for past racial discrimination in the opposite direction. Individuals who have been wronged by unlawful racial discrimination should be made whole; but under our Constitution there can be no such thing as either a creditor or a debtor race. That concept is alien to the Constitution's focus upon the individual, see Amdt. 14, § 1 ("[N]or shall any State . . . deny *to any person*" the equal protection of the laws) (emphasis added), and its rejection of dispositions based on race, see Amdt. 15, § 1 (prohibiting abridgment of the right to vote "on account of race") or based on blood, see Art. III, § 3 ("[N]o Attainder of Treason shall work Corruption of Blood"); Art. I, § 9 ("No Title of Nobility shall be granted by the United States"). To pursue the concept of racial entitlement — even for the most admirable and benign of purposes — is to reinforce and preserve for future mischief the way of thinking that produced race slavery, race privilege and race hatred. In the eyes of government, we are just one race here. It is American. * * *

JUSTICE THOMAS, concurring in part and concurring in the judgment.

* * * I [disagree] with the premise underlying [the dissents]: that there is a racial paternalism exception to the principle of equal protection. I believe that there is a "moral [and] constitutional equivalence," *post* (Stevens, J., dissenting), between laws designed to subjugate a race and those that distribute benefits on the basis of race in order to foster some current notion of equality. Government cannot make us equal; it can only recognize, respect, and protect us as equal before the law. * * *

These programs * * * undermine the moral basis of the equal protection principle. Purchased at the price of immeasurable human suffering, the equal protection principle reflects our Nation's understanding that such classifications ultimately have a destructive impact on the individual and our society. * * * [T]here can be no doubt that racial paternalism and its unintended consequences can be as poisonous and pernicious as any other form of discrimination. So-called "benign" discrimination teaches many that because of chronic and apparently immutable handicaps, minorities cannot compete with them without their patronizing indulgence. Inevitably, such programs engender attitudes of superiority or, alternatively, provoke resentment among those who believe that they have been wronged by the government's use of race. These programs stamp minorities with a badge of inferiority and may cause them to develop dependencies or to adopt an attitude that they are "entitled" to preferences. * * *

JUSTICE STEVENS, with whom **JUSTICE GINSBURG** joins, dissenting.

The Court's concept of "consistency" assumes that there is no significant difference between a decision by the majority to impose a special burden on the members of a minority race and a decision by the majority to provide a benefit to certain members of that minority notwithstanding its incidental burden on some members of the majority. * * * [But] [t]here is no moral or constitutional equivalence between a policy that is designed to perpetuate a caste system and one that seeks to eradicate racial subordination. Invidious discrimination is an engine of oppression, subjugating a disfavored group to enhance or maintain the power of the majority. Remedial race-based preferences reflect the opposite impulse: a desire to foster equality in society. No sensible conception of the Government's constitutional obligation to "govern impartially" should ignore this distinction.

To illustrate the point, consider * * * *Hirabayashi* and *Korematsu*. The discrimination at issue in those cases was invidious because the Government imposed special burdens — a curfew and exclusion from certain areas on the West Coast — on the members of a minority class defined by racial and ethnic characteristics. Members of the same racially defined class exhibited exceptional heroism in the service of our country during that War. Now suppose Congress decided to reward that service with a federal program that gave all Japanese-American veterans an extraordinary preference in Government employment. If Congress had done so, the same racial characteristics that motivated the discriminatory burdens in *Hirabayashi* and *Korematsu* would have defined the preferred class of veterans. Nevertheless, "consistency" surely would not require us to describe the incidental burden on everyone else in the country as "odious" or "invidious" as those terms were used in those cases. We should reject a concept of "consistency" that would view the special preferences that the National Government has provided to Native Americans since 1834 as comparable to the official discrimination against African Americans that was prevalent for much of our history.

The consistency that the Court espouses would disregard the difference between a "No Trespassing" sign and a welcome mat. It would treat a Dixiecrat Senator's decision to vote against Thurgood Marshall's confirmation in order to keep African Americans off the Supreme Court as on a par with President Johnson's evaluation of his nominee's race as a positive factor. It would equate a law that made black citizens ineligible for military service with a program aimed at recruiting black soldiers. An attempt by the majority to exclude members of a minority race from a regulated market is fundamentally different from a subsidy that enables a relatively small group of newcomers to enter that market. An interest in "consistency" does not justify treating differences as though they were similarities.

The Court's explanation for treating dissimilar race-based decisions as though they were equally objectionable is a supposed inability to differentiate between "invidious" and "benign" discrimination. But the term "affirmative action" is common and well understood. Its presence in everyday parlance shows that people understand the difference between good intentions and bad. * * * [O]ur equal protection jurisprudence has identified a critical difference between state action that imposes burdens on a disfavored few and state action that benefits the few "in spite of" its adverse effects on the many. * * *

[T]he Court may find that its new "consistency" approach to race-based classifications is difficult to square with its insistence upon rigidly separate categories for discrimination against different classes of individuals.* * * [A]s the law currently stands, the Court will apply "intermediate scrutiny" to cases of invidious gender discrimination and "strict scrutiny" to cases of invidious race discrimination, while applying the same standard for benign classifications as for invidious ones. If this remains the law, then today's lecture about "consistency" will produce the anomalous result that the Government can more easily enact affirmative-action programs to remedy discrimination against women than it can enact affirmative-action programs to remedy discrimination against African Americans — even though the primary purpose of the Equal Protection Clause was to end discrimination against the former slaves. * * *

As a matter of constitutional and democratic principle, a decision by representatives of the majority to discriminate against the members of a minority race is fundamentally different from those same representatives' decision to impose incidental costs on the majority of their constituents in order to provide a benefit to a disadvantaged minority.[5] * * * [T]he former is virtually always repugnant to the principles of a free and democratic society, whereas the latter is, in some circumstances, entirely consistent with the ideal of equality. By insisting on a doctrinaire notion of "consistency" in the standard applicable to all race-based governmental actions, the Court obscures this essential dichotomy.

The Court's concept of "congruence" assumes that there is no significant difference between a decision by the Congress of the United States to adopt an affirmative-action program and such a decision by a State or a municipality. In my opinion that assumption is untenable. It ignores important practical and

---

5. * * * It is one thing to question the wisdom of affirmative-action programs: there are many responsible arguments against them, including the one based upon stigma [argued by Justice Thomas in this case], that Congress might find persuasive when it decides whether to enact or retain race-based preferences. It is another thing altogether to equate the many well-meaning and intelligent lawmakers and their constituents — whether members of majority or minority races — who have supported affirmative action over the years, to segregationists and bigots.

Finally, although Justice Thomas is more concerned about the potential effects of these programs than the intent of those who enacted them (a proposition at odds with this Court's jurisprudence, see *Washington v. Davis*, but not without a strong element of common sense, see *id.* (Stevens, J., concurring)), I am not persuaded that the psychological damage brought on by affirmative action is as severe as that engendered by racial subordination. That, in any event, is a judgment the political branches can be trusted to make. * * *

legal differences between federal and state or local decisionmakers. [Both *Fullilove* and *Metro Broadcasting* had stressed the importance of deference to Congress, even in the area of affirmative action, because of Congress' unique powers under the Fourteenth Amendment. Because oppression by faction is less likely to occur at the national level, see *Federalist* 10 (Madison) (App. 2), Congress could be trusted more than the legislatures of the states and localities. Moreover, the Congress is elected by all Americans, "whereas a state or local program may have an impact on nonresident entities who played no part in the decision to enact it. Thus, in the state or local context, individuals who were unable to vote for the local representatives who enacted a race-conscious program may nonetheless feel the effects of that program."] * * *

* * * *Metro Broadcasting*'s holding rested on more than its application of "intermediate scrutiny." Indeed, I have always believed that, labels notwithstanding, the FCC program we upheld in that case would have satisfied any of our various standards in affirmative-action cases — including the one the majority fashions today. What truly distinguishes *Metro Broadcasting* from our other affirmative-action precedents is the distinctive goal of the federal program in that case. Instead of merely seeking to remedy past discrimination, the FCC program was intended to achieve future benefits in the form of broadcast diversity. * * *

* * * [P]rior to *Metro Broadcasting*, the interest in diversity had been mentioned in a few opinions, but it is perfectly clear that the Court had not yet decided whether that interest had sufficient magnitude to justify a racial classification. *Metro Broadcasting*, of course, answered that question in the affirmative. The majority today overrules *Metro Broadcasting* only insofar as it is "inconsistent with [the] holding" that strict scrutiny applies to "benign" racial classifications promulgated by the Federal Government. The proposition that fostering diversity may provide a sufficient interest to justify such a program is *not* inconsistent with the Court's holding today — indeed, the question is not remotely presented in this case — and I do not take the Court's opinion to diminish that aspect of our decision in *Metro Broadcasting*. * * *

[The dissent of **JUSTICE SOUTER**, joined by **JUSTICES GINSBURG** and **BREYER**, and the dissent of **JUSTICE GINSBURG**, joined by **JUSTICE BREYER**, are omitted.]

NOTES ON *CROSON* AND *ADARAND*

1. Croson *and Strict Scrutiny.* *Croson* provides that all state and local racial classifications are subject to strict scrutiny. Thus, on the issue of the standard of equal protection scrutiny to be applied, it seems irrelevant whether such measures are designed as affirmative action steps or are rooted in a desire to disadvantage a racial minority. Yet Justice O'Connor in *Croson* went out of her way to indicate that affirmative action classifications are not *per se* unconstitutional. How could the *application* of strict scrutiny differ for affirmative action measures? After *Croson*, what compelling government interest(s) might benign classifications serve? For example, does Justice Powell's view in *Bakke* that diversity may be a compelling state interest survive *Croson*? How may a state or locality satisfy the "narrow tailoring" requirement? Consider the woeful

statistics in Richmond about business for minority contractors. What additional facts would be necessary to support a benign set-aside?

2. Adarand: *Formalism and Precedent.* The Constitution contains no Equal Protection Clause applicable to the federal government, and thus there is no obvious textual support for Justice O'Connor's "congruence" argument. Moreover, following the Civil War, in the Freedman's Bureau Acts, Congress engaged in race-based affirmative action by providing land, education, medical care, and other benefits to the newly freed former slaves. This historical record calls into question any argument that the Framers of the Fourteenth Amendment thought that their handiwork expressly or impliedly forbade *federal* usage of benign racial classifications. Moreover, to reach its result in *Adarand* the majority had to overcome the traditional presumption of *stare decisis* and overrule *Fullilove* and *Metro Broadcasting.* With all these formalist (textualist, originalist, precedential) arguments cutting against the result in *Adarand*, it seems odd to see that the Justices most inclined toward formalist arguments are in the majority. What arguments support the majority in *Adarand*?

To understand *Adarand*, consider the legacy of *Bolling, Korematsu,* and *Hirabayashi. Bolling,* which considered school segregation in the District of Columbia, stated: "In view of our decision that the Constitution prohibits the states from maintaining racially segregated schools, it would be unthinkable that the same Constitution would impose a lesser duty on the Federal Government." Is it equally "unthinkable" that the city council of Richmond, Virginia, and the Congress of the United States should be subjected to differing constitutional standards concerning the "benign" usage of race? Maybe it is "unthinkable" only when these two governments are operating similarly — *i.e.,* governing a city (Richmond; Washington, D.C.), and not when the Congress legislates on a nationwide basis. But would that mean that *Korematsu* and *Hirabayashi* were correctly decided? On *Bolling* and its progeny, see, e.g., Richard Primus, Bolling *Alone,* 104 Colum. L. Rev. 975 (2004); Peter Rubin, *Taking its Proper Place in the Constitutional Canon:* Bolling v. Sharpe, Korematsu, *and the Equal Protection Component of Fifth Amendment Due Process,* 92 Va. L. Rev. 1879 (2006).

3. *The* Adarand/Croson *Variety of Strict Scrutiny and Forward-Looking Affirmative Action. Adarand* and *Croson* involved remedial, backward-looking affirmative action (purporting to remedy past discrimination). Justice Stevens, in his *Adarand* dissent, contended that they do not foreclose forward-looking affirmative action (designed to promote policies improving society in the present and future, such as more diversity in broadcast programming, cf. *Metro Broadcasting*). Consider the next cases.

C. REVISITING THE DIVERSITY RATIONALE AND ADMISSION TO STATE UNIVERSITY PROFESSIONAL SCHOOLS

GRUTTER v. BOLLINGER
539 U.S. 306, 123 S.Ct. 2325, 156 L.Ed.2d 304 (2003)

JUSTICE O'CONNOR delivered the opinion of the Court.

[The University of Michigan Law School] ranks among the Nation's top law schools. It receives more than 3,500 applications each year for a class of around 350 students. Seeking to "admit a group of students who individually and collectively are among the most capable," the Law School looks for individuals with "substantial promise for success in law school" and "a strong likelihood of succeeding in the practice of law and contributing in diverse ways to the well-being of others." More broadly, the Law School seeks "a mix of students with varying backgrounds and experiences who will respect and learn from each other." * * *

The hallmark of [the law school's admissions policy, adopted in 1992,] is its focus on academic ability coupled with a flexible assessment of applicants' talents, experiences, and potential "to contribute to the learning of those around them." The policy requires admissions officials to evaluate each applicant based on all the information available in the file, including a personal statement, letters of recommendation, and an essay describing the ways in which the applicant will contribute to the life and diversity of the Law School. In reviewing an applicant's file, admissions officials must consider the applicant's undergraduate grade point average (GPA) and Law School Admissions Test (LSAT) score because they are important (if imperfect) predictors of academic success in law school. The policy stresses that "no applicant should be admitted unless we expect that applicant to do well enough to graduate with no serious academic problems."

The policy makes clear, however, that even the highest possible score does not guarantee admission to the Law School. Nor does a low score automatically disqualify an applicant. Rather, the policy requires admissions officials to look beyond grades and test scores to other criteria that are important to the Law School's educational objectives. So-called " 'soft' variables" such as "the enthusiasm of recommenders, the quality of the undergraduate institution, the quality of the applicant's essay, and the areas and difficulty of undergraduate course selection" are all brought to bear in assessing an "applicant's likely contributions to the intellectual and social life of the institution."

The policy aspires to "achieve that diversity which has the potential to enrich everyone's education and thus make a law school class stronger than the sum of its parts." The policy does not restrict the types of diversity contributions eligible for "substantial weight" in the admissions process, but instead recognizes "many possible bases for diversity admissions." The policy does, however, reaffirm the Law School's longstanding commitment to "one particular type of diversity," that is, "racial and ethnic diversity with special reference to the inclusion of students from groups which have been historically discriminated against, like African-Americans, Hispanics and Native Americans, who without this commitment might not be represented in our student body in meaningful numbers." By enrolling a " 'critical mass' of [underrepresented] minority students," the Law School seeks to "ensur[e] their ability to make unique contributions to the character of the Law School."

The policy does not define diversity "solely in terms of racial and ethnic status." Nor is the policy "insensitive to the competition among all students for admission to the [L]aw [S]chool." Rather, the policy seeks to guide admissions officers in "producing classes both diverse and academically outstanding, classes made up of students who promise to continue the tradition of outstanding contribution by Michigan Graduates to the legal profession."

Petitioner Barbara Grutter is a white Michigan resident who applied to the Law School in 1996 with a 3.8 grade point average and 161 LSAT score[, who was rejected for admission. She brought suit challenging the constitutionality of the admissions policy.]

[At trial,] the parties introduced extensive evidence concerning the Law School's use of race in the admissions process. Dennis Shields, Director of Admissions when petitioner applied to the Law School, testified that he did not direct his staff to admit a particular percentage or number of minority students, but rather to consider an applicant's race along with all other factors. Shields testified that at the height of the admissions season, he would frequently consult the so-called "daily reports" that kept track of the racial and ethnic composition of the class (along with other information such as residency status and gender). This was done, Shields testified, to ensure that a critical mass of underrepresented minority students would be reached so as to realize the educational benefits of a diverse student body. Shields stressed, however, that he did not seek to admit any particular number or percentage of underrepresented minority students.

Erica Munzel, who succeeded Shields as Director of Admissions, testified that " 'critical mass' " means " 'meaningful numbers' " or " 'meaningful representation,' " which she understood to mean a number that encourages underrepresented minority students to participate in the classroom and not feel isolated. Munzel stated there is no number, percentage, or range of numbers or percentages that constitute critical mass. Munzel also asserted that she must consider the race of applicants because a critical mass of underrepresented minority students could not be enrolled if admissions decisions were based primarily on undergraduate GPAs and LSAT scores.

The current Dean of the Law School, Jeffrey Lehman, also testified. Like the other Law School witnesses, Lehman did not quantify critical mass in terms of numbers or percentages. He indicated that critical mass means numbers such that underrepresented minority students do not feel isolated or like spokespersons for their race. When asked about the extent to which race is considered in admissions, Lehman testified that it varies from one applicant to another. In some cases, according to Lehman's testimony, an applicant's race may play no role, while in others it may be a " 'determinative' " factor.

The District Court heard extensive testimony from Professor Richard Lempert, who chaired the faculty committee that drafted the 1992 policy. Lempert emphasized that the Law School seeks students with diverse interests and backgrounds to enhance classroom discussion and the educational experience both inside and outside the classroom. When asked about the policy's " 'commitment to racial and ethnic diversity with special reference to the inclusion of students from groups which have been historically discriminated against,' " Lempert explained that this language did not purport to remedy past discrimination, but rather to include students who may bring to the Law School a perspective different from that of members of groups which have not been the victims of such discrimination. Lempert acknowledged that other groups, such as Asians and Jews, have experienced discrimination, but explained they were not mentioned in the policy because individuals who are members of those groups were already being admitted to the Law School in significant numbers.

Kent Syverud was the final witness to testify about the Law School's use of race in admissions decisions. Syverud was a professor at the Law School when the 1992 admissions policy was adopted and is now Dean of Vanderbilt Law School. In addition to his testimony at trial, Syverud submitted several expert reports on the educational benefits of diversity. Syverud's testimony indicated that when a critical mass of underrepresented minority students is present, racial stereotypes lose their force because nonminority students learn there is no " 'minority viewpoint' " but rather a variety of viewpoints among minority students.

In an attempt to quantify the extent to which the Law School actually considers race in making admissions decisions, the parties introduced voluminous evidence at trial. Relying on data obtained from the Law School, petitioner's expert, Dr. Kinley Larntz, generated and analyzed "admissions grids" for the years in question (1995-2000). These grids show the number of applicants and the number of admittees for all combinations of GPAs and LSAT scores. Dr. Larntz made " 'cell-by-cell' " comparisons between applicants of different races to determine whether a statistically significant relationship existed between race and admission rates. He concluded that membership in certain minority groups " 'is an extremely strong factor in the decision for acceptance,' " and that applicants from these minority groups " 'are given an extremely large allowance for admission' " as compared to applicants who are members of nonfavored groups. Dr. Larntz conceded, however, that race is not the predominant factor in the Law School's admissions calculus.

Dr. Stephen Raudenbush, the Law School's expert, focused on the predicted effect of eliminating race as a factor in the Law School's admission process. In Dr. Raudenbush's view, a race-blind admissions system would have a " 'very dramatic,' " negative effect on underrepresented minority admissions. He testified that in 2000, 35 percent of underrepresented minority applicants were admitted. Dr. Raudenbush predicted that if race were not considered, only 10 percent of those applicants would have been admitted. Under this scenario, underrepresented minority students would have comprised 4 percent of the entering class in 2000 instead of the actual figure of 14.5 percent.

[The district court found the admissions program unconstitutional, but a sharply divided en banc court of appeals reversed.]

Since this Court's splintered decision in *Bakke*, Justice Powell's opinion announcing the judgment of the Court has served as the touchstone for constitutional analysis of race-conscious admissions policies. Public and private universities across the Nation have modeled their own admissions programs on Justice Powell's views on permissible race-conscious policies. * * * [T]oday we endorse Justice Powell's view that student body diversity is a compelling state interest that can justify the use of race in university admissions. * * *

[Justice O'Connor noted that under *Adarand* all racial classifications receive strict scrutiny review, but that strict scrutiny is not "strict in theory, but fatal in fact."] Not every decision influenced by race is equally objectionable and strict scrutiny is designed to provide a framework for carefully examining the importance and the sincerity of the reasons advanced by the governmental decisionmaker for the use of race in that particular context.

With these principles in mind, we turn to the question whether the Law School's use of race is justified by a compelling state interest. * * * [T]he Law School asks us to recognize, in the context of higher education, a compelling state interest in student body diversity.

We first wish to dispel the notion that the Law School's argument has been foreclosed, either expressly or implicitly, by our affirmative-action cases decided since *Bakke*. It is true that some language in those opinions might be read to suggest that remedying past discrimination is the only permissible justification for race-based governmental action. See, e.g., *Croson* (plurality opinion) (stating that unless classifications based on race are "strictly reserved for remedial settings, they may in fact promote notions of racial inferiority and lead to a politics of racial hostility"). But we have never held that the only governmental use of race that can survive strict scrutiny is remedying past discrimination. Nor, since *Bakke*, have we directly addressed the use of race in the context of public higher education. Today, we hold that the Law School has a compelling interest in attaining a diverse student body.

The Law School's educational judgment that such diversity is essential to its educational mission is one to which we defer. The Law School's assessment that diversity will, in fact, yield educational benefits is substantiated by respondents and their *amici*. Our scrutiny of the interest asserted by the Law School is no less strict for taking into account complex educational judgments in an area that lies primarily within the expertise of the university. * * *

We have long recognized that, given the important purpose of public education and the expansive freedoms of speech and thought associated with the university environment, universities occupy a special niche in our constitutional tradition. See, e.g., *Wieman v. Updegraff*, 344 U.S. 183, 195 (1952) (Frankfurter, J., concurring); *Sweezy v. New Hampshire,* 354 U.S. 234, 250 (1957); *Shelton v. Tucker*, 364 U.S. 479, 487 (1960); *Keyishian v. Board of Regents of Univ. of State of N. Y.,* 385 U.S. at 603. In announcing the principle of student body diversity as a compelling state interest, Justice Powell invoked our cases recognizing a constitutional dimension, grounded in the First Amendment, of educational autonomy: "The freedom of a university to make its own judgments as to education includes the selection of its student body." From this premise,

Justice Powell reasoned that by claiming "the right to select those students who will contribute the most to the 'robust exchange of ideas,'" a university "seek[s] to achieve a goal that is of paramount importance in the fulfillment of its mission." Our conclusion that the Law School has a compelling interest in a diverse student body is informed by our view that attaining a diverse student body is at the heart of the Law School's proper institutional mission, and that "good faith" on the part of a university is "presumed" absent "a showing to the contrary."

As part of its goal of "assembling a class that is both exceptionally academically qualified and broadly diverse," the Law School seeks to "enroll a 'critical mass' of minority students." [Quoting law school's brief.] The Law School's interest is not simply "to assure within its student body some specified percentage of a particular group merely because of its race or ethnic origin." *Bakke* (opinion of Powell, J.). That would amount to outright racial balancing, which is patently unconstitutional. Rather, the Law School's concept of critical mass is defined by reference to the educational benefits that diversity is designed to produce.

These benefits are substantial. As the District Court emphasized, the Law School's admissions policy promotes "cross-racial understanding," helps to break down racial stereotypes, and "enables [students] to better understand persons of different races." These benefits are "important and laudable," because "classroom discussion is livelier, more spirited, and simply more enlightening and interesting" when the students have "the greatest possible variety of backgrounds." [Quoting district court opinion.]

The Law School's claim of a compelling interest is further bolstered by its *amici*, who point to the educational benefits that flow from student body diversity. In addition to the expert studies and reports entered into evidence at trial, numerous studies show that student body diversity promotes learning outcomes, and "better prepares students for an increasingly diverse workforce and society, and better prepares them as professionals." Brief for American Educational Research Association et al. as *Amici Curiae* 3; see, e.g., W. Bowen & D. Bok, The Shape of the River (1998); Diversity Challenged: Evidence on the Impact of Affirmative Action (G. Orfield & M. Kurlaender eds. 2001); Compelling Interest: Examining the Evidence on Racial Dynamics in Colleges and Universities (M. Chang, D. Witt, J. Jones, & K. Hakuta eds. 2003).

These benefits are not theoretical but real, as major American businesses have made clear that the skills needed in today's increasingly global marketplace can only be developed through exposure to widely diverse people, cultures, ideas, and viewpoints. Brief for 3M et al. as *Amici Curiae* 5; Brief for General Motors Corp. as *Amicus Curiae* 3-4. What is more, high-ranking retired officers and civilian leaders of the United States military assert that, "[b]ased on [their] decades of experience," a "highly qualified, racially diverse officer corps . . . is essential to the military's ability to fulfill its principle mission to provide national security." Brief for Julius W. Becton, Jr. et al. as *Amici Curiae* 27. The primary sources for the Nation's officer corps are the service academies and the Reserve Officers Training Corps (ROTC), the latter comprising students already admitted to participating colleges and universities. At present, "the military cannot achieve an officer corps that is *both* highly qualified *and* racially diverse unless the service academies and the ROTC used limited race-conscious recruiting and admissions policies." *Ibid.* (emphasis in original). To fulfill its mission, the military "must be selective in admissions for training and education for the officer corps, *and* it must train and educate a highly qualified, racially diverse officer corps in a racially diverse setting." *Id.*, at 29 (emphasis in original). We agree that "[i]t requires only a small step from this analysis to conclude that our country's other most selective institutions must remain both diverse and selective." *Ibid.*

We have repeatedly acknowledged the overriding importance of preparing students for work and citizenship, describing education as pivotal to "sustaining our political and cultural heritage" with a fundamental role in maintaining the fabric of society. *Plyler v. Doe* [p. 534, *infra*]. This Court has long recognized that "education ... is the very foundation of good citizenship." *Brown v. Board of Education.* For this reason, the diffusion of knowledge and opportunity through public institutions of higher education must be accessible to all individuals regardless of race or ethnicity. The United States, as *amicus curiae*, affirms that "[e]nsuring that public institutions are open and available to all segments of American society, including people of all races and ethnicities, represents a paramount government objective." And, "[n]owhere is the importance of such openness more acute than in the context of higher educa-tion." *Ibid.* Effective participation by members of all racial and ethnic groups in the civic life of our Nation is essential if the dream of one Nation, indivisible, is to be realized.

Moreover, universities, and in particular, law schools, represent the training ground for a large number of our Nation's leaders. Individuals with law degrees occupy roughly half the state governorships, more than half the seats in the United States Senate, and more than a third of the seats in the United States House of Representatives. The pattern is even more striking when it comes to highly selective law schools. A handful of these schools accounts for 25 of the 100 United States Senators, 74 United States Courts of Appeals judges, and nearly 200 of the more than 600 United States District Court judges.

In order to cultivate a set of leaders with legitimacy in the eyes of the citizenry, it is necessary that the path to leadership be visibly open to talented and qualified individuals of every race and ethnicity. All members of our heterogeneous society must have confidence in the openness and integrity of the educational institutions that provide this training. As we have recognized, law schools "cannot be effective in isolation from the individuals and institutions with which the law interacts." See *Sweatt v. Painter* [see p. 78, *supra*]. Access to legal education (and thus the legal profession) must be inclusive of talented and qualified individuals of every race and ethnicity, so that all members of our heterogeneous society may participate in the educational institutions that provide the training and education necessary to succeed in America.

The Law School does not premise its need for critical mass on "any belief that minority students always (or even consistently) express some characteristic minority viewpoint on any issue." To the contrary, diminishing the force of such stereotypes is both a crucial part of the Law School's mission, and one that it cannot accomplish with only token numbers of minority students. Just as growing up in a particular region or having particular professional experiences is likely to affect an individual's views, so too is one's own, unique experience of being a racial minority in a society, like our own, in which race unfortunately still matters. The Law School has determined, based on its experience and expertise, that a "critical mass" of underrepresented minorities is necessary to further its compelling interest in securing the educational benefits of a diverse student body.

[Justice O'Connor then turned to the second element of strict scrutiny: the narrow tailoring requirement.] The purpose of the narrow tailoring requirement is to ensure that "the means chosen 'fit' . . . th[e] compelling goal so closely that there is little or no possibility that the motive for the classification was illegitimate racial prejudice or stereotype." *Croson.* * * *

To be narrowly tailored, a race-conscious admissions program cannot use a quota system — it cannot "insulat[e] each category of applicants with certain desired qualifications from competition with all other applicants." *Bakke* (opinion of Powell, J.). Instead, a university may consider race or ethnicity only as a " 'plus' in a particular applicant's file," without "insulat[ing] the individual from comparison with all other candidates for the available seats." *Id.* In other words, an admissions program must be "flexible enough to consider all pertinent elements of diversity in light of the particular qualifications of each applicant, and to place them on the same footing for consideration, although not necessarily according them the same weight." *Ibid.*

We find that the Law School's admissions program bears the hallmarks of a narrowly tailored plan. * * * We are satisfied that the Law School's admissions program, like the Harvard plan described by Justice Powell, does not operate as a quota. Properly understood, a "quota" is a program in which a certain fixed number or proportion of opportunities are "reserved exclusively for certain minority groups." *Croson.* * * * In contrast, "a permissible goal . . . require[s] only a good-faith effort . . . to come within a range demarcated by the goal itself," and permits consideration of race as a "plus" factor in any given case while still ensuring that each candidate "compete[s] with all other qualified applicants."

Justice Powell's distinction between the medical school's rigid 16-seat quota and Harvard's flexible use of race as a "plus" factor is instructive. Harvard certainly had minimum *goals* for minority enrollment, even if it had no specific number firmly in mind. See *Bakke* (opinion of Powell, J.) ("10 or 20 black students could not begin to bring to their classmates and to each other the variety of points of view, backgrounds and experiences of blacks in the United States"). What is more, Justice Powell flatly rejected the argument that Harvard's program was "the functional equivalent of a quota" merely because it had some " 'plus' " for race, or gave greater "weight" to race than to some other factors, in order to achieve student body diversity.

The Law School's goal of attaining a critical mass of underrepresented minority students does not transform its program into a quota. As the Harvard plan described by Justice Powell recognized, there is of course "some relationship between numbers and achieving the benefits to be derived from a diverse student body, and between numbers and providing a reasonable environment for those students admitted." "[S]ome attention to numbers," without more, does not transform a flexible admissions system into a rigid quota. *Ibid.* Nor, as JUSTICE KENNEDY posits, does the Law School's consultation of the "daily reports," which keep track of the racial and ethnic composition of the class (as well as of residency and gender), "suggest [ ] there was no further attempt at individual review save for race itself" during the final stages of the admissions process. See *post* (dissenting opinion). To the contrary, the Law School's admissions officers testified without contradiction that they never gave race any more or less weight based on the information contained in these reports. Moreover, * * * between 1993 and 2000, the number of African-American, Latino, and Native-American students in each class at the Law School varied from 13.5 to 20.1 percent, a range inconsistent with a quota.

THE CHIEF JUSTICE believes that the Law School's policy conceals an attempt to achieve racial balancing, and cites admissions data to contend that the Law School discriminates among different groups within the critical mass. *Post* (dissenting opinion). But * * * the number of underrepresented minority students who ultimately enroll in the Law School differs substantially from their representation in the applicant pool and varies considerably for each group from year to year.

That a race-conscious admissions program does not operate as a quota does not, by itself, satisfy the requirement of individualized consideration. When using race as a "plus" factor in university admissions, a university's admissions program must remain flexible enough to ensure that each applicant is evaluated as an individual and not in a way that makes an applicant's race or ethnicity the defining feature of his or her application. The importance of this individualized consideration in the context of a race-conscious admissions program is paramount. See *Bakke* (opinion of Powell, J.) (identifying the "denial . . . of th[e] right to individualized consideration" as the "principal evil" of the medical school's admissions program).

Here, the Law School engages in a highly individualized, holistic review of each applicant's file, giving serious consideration to all the ways an applicant might contribute to a diverse educational environment. The Law School affords this individualized consideration to applicants of all races. There is no policy, either *de jure* or *de facto*, of automatic acceptance or rejection based on any single "soft" variable. Unlike the program at issue in *Gratz v. Bollinger*, the Law School awards no mechanical, predetermined diversity "bonuses" based on race or ethnicity. Like the Harvard plan, the Law School's admissions policy "is flexible enough to consider all pertinent elements of diversity in light of the particular qualifications of each applicant, and to place them on the same footing for consideration, although not necessarily according them the same weight." *Bakke* (opinion of Powell, J.).

We also find that, like the Harvard plan Justice Powell referenced in *Bakke*, the Law School's race-conscious admissions program adequately ensures that all factors that may contribute to student body diversity are meaningfully considered alongside race in admissions decisions. With respect to the use of race itself, all underrepresented minority students admitted by the Law School have been deemed qualified. By virtue of our Nation's struggle with racial inequality, such students are both likely to have experiences of particular importance to the Law School's mission, and less likely to be admitted in meaningful numbers on criteria that ignore those experiences.

The Law School does not, however, limit in any way the broad range of qualities and experiences that may be considered valuable contributions to student body diversity. To the contrary, the 1992 policy makes clear "[t]here are many possible bases for diversity admissions," and provides examples of admittees who have lived or traveled widely abroad, are fluent in several languages, have overcome personal adversity and family hardship, have exceptional records of extensive community service, and have had successful careers in other fields. The Law School seriously considers each "applicant's promise of making a notable contribution to the class by way of a particular strength, attainment, or characteristic — e.g., an unusual intellectual achievement, employment experience, nonacademic performance, or personal background." All applicants have the opportunity to highlight their own potential diversity contributions through the submission of a personal statement, letters of recommendation, and an essay describing the ways in which the applicant will contribute to the life and diversity of the Law School.

What is more, the Law School actually gives substantial weight to diversity factors besides race. The Law School frequently accepts nonminority applicants with grades and test scores lower than underrepresented minority applicants (and other nonminority applicants) who are rejected. This shows that the Law School seriously weighs many other diversity factors besides race that can make a real and dispositive difference for nonminority applicants as well. By this flexible approach, the Law School sufficiently takes into account, in practice as well as in theory, a wide variety of characteristics besides race and ethnicity that contribute to a diverse student body. JUSTICE KENNEDY speculates that "race is likely outcome determinative for many members of minority groups" who do not fall within the upper range of LSAT scores and grades. *Post* (dissenting opinion). But the same could be said of the Harvard plan discussed approvingly by Justice Powell in *Bakke*, and indeed of any plan that uses race as one of many factors. See *Bakke* (" 'When the Committee on Admissions reviews the large middle group of applicants who are "admissible" and deemed capable of doing good work in their courses, the race of an applicant may tip the balance in his favor' ").

Petitioner and the United States argue that the Law School's plan is not narrowly tailored because race-neutral means exist to obtain the educational benefits of student body diversity that the Law School seeks. We disagree. Narrow tailoring does not require exhaustion of every conceivable race-neutral alternative. Nor does it require a university to choose between maintaining a reputation for excellence or fulfilling a commitment to provide educational opportunities to members of all racial groups. Narrow tailoring does, however, require serious, good faith consideration of workable race-neutral alternatives that will achieve the diversity the university seeks.

* * * The District Court took the Law School to task for failing to consider race-neutral alternatives such as "using a lottery system" or "decreasing the emphasis for all applicants on undergraduate GPA and LSAT scores." But these alternatives would require a dramatic sacrifice of diversity, the academic quality of all admitted students, or both.

The Law School's current admissions program considers race as one factor among many, in an effort to assemble a student body that is diverse in ways broader than race. Because a lottery would make that kind of nuanced judgment impossible, it would effectively sacrifice all other educational values, not to mention every other kind of diversity. So too with the suggestion that the Law School simply lower admissions standards for all students, a drastic remedy that would require the Law School to become a much different institution and sacrifice a vital component of its educational mission. The United States advocates "percentage plans," recently adopted by public undergraduate institutions in Texas, Florida, and California to guarantee admission to all students above a certain class-rank threshold in every high school in the State. The United States does not, however, explain how such plans could work for graduate and professional schools. Moreover, even assuming such plans are race-neutral, they may preclude the university from conducting the individualized assessments necessary to assemble a student body that is not just racially diverse, but diverse along all the qualities valued by the university. We are satisfied that the Law School adequately considered race-neutral alternatives currently capable of producing a critical mass without forcing the Law School to abandon the academic selectivity that is the cornerstone of its educational mission.

We acknowledge that "there are serious problems of justice connected with the idea of preference itself." *Bakke* (opinion of Powell, J.). Narrow tailoring, therefore, requires that a race-conscious admissions program not unduly harm members of any racial group. Even remedial race-based governmental action generally "remains subject to continuing oversight to assure that it will work the least harm possible to other innocent persons competing for the benefit." To be narrowly tailored, a race-conscious admissions program must not "unduly burden individuals who are not members of the favored racial and ethnic groups."

We are satisfied that the Law School's admissions program does not. Because the Law School considers "all pertinent elements of diversity," it can (and does) select nonminority applicants who have greater potential to enhance student body diversity over underrepresented minority applicants. See *Bakke* (opinion of Powell, J.). As Justice Powell recognized in *Bakke*, so long as a race-conscious admissions program uses race as a "plus" factor in the context of individualized consideration, a rejected applicant

> will not have been foreclosed from all consideration for that seat simply because he was not the right color or had the wrong surname. . . . His qualifications would have been weighed fairly and competitively, and he would have no basis to complain of unequal treatment under the Fourteenth Amendment.

* * * We are mindful, however, that "[a] core purpose of the Fourteenth Amendment was to do away with all governmentally imposed discrimination

based on race." *Palmore v. Sidoti* [p. 202, *supra*]. Accordingly, race-conscious admissions policies must be limited in time. This requirement reflects that racial classifications, however compelling their goals, are potentially so dangerous that they may be employed no more broadly than the interest demands. Enshrining a permanent justification for racial preferences would offend this fundamental equal protection principle. We see no reason to exempt race-conscious admissions programs from the requirement that all governmental use of race must have a logical end point. The Law School, too, concedes that all "race-conscious programs must have reasonable durational limits." Brief at 32.

In the context of higher education, the durational requirement can be met by sunset provisions in race-conscious admissions policies and periodic reviews to determine whether racial preferences are still necessary to achieve student body diversity. Universities in California, Florida, and Washington State, where racial preferences in admissions are prohibited by state law, are currently engaged in experimenting with a wide variety of alternative approaches. Universities in other States can and should draw on the most promising aspects of these race-neutral alternatives as they develop.

The requirement that all race-conscious admissions programs have a termination point "assure[s] all citizens that the deviation from the norm of equal treatment of all racial and ethnic groups is a temporary matter, a measure taken in the service of the goal of equality itself." *Croson* (plurality opinion). * * *

We take the Law School at its word that it would "like nothing better than to find a race-neutral admissions formula" and will terminate its race-conscious admissions program as soon as practicable. See Brief for law school; *Bakke* (opinion of Powell, J.) (presuming good faith of university officials in the absence of a showing to the contrary). It has been 25 years since Justice Powell first approved the use of race to further an interest in student body diversity in the context of public higher education. Since that time, the number of minority applicants with high grades and test scores has indeed increased. We expect that 25 years from now, the use of racial preferences will no longer be necessary to further the interest approved today. [Affirmed.]

[**JUSTICE GINSBURG**, with whom **JUSTICE BREYER** joined, concurred, agreeing that affirmative action must have a logical stopping point but expressing concern that, in light of ongoing discrimination and social inequality, the Court's suggestion of a 25-year sunset on affirmative action might be optimistic.]

CHIEF JUSTICE REHNQUIST, with whom **JUSTICE SCALIA**, **JUSTICE KENNEDY**, and **JUSTICE THOMAS** join, dissenting.

* * * From 1995 through 2000, the Law School admitted between 1,130 and 1,310 students. Of those, between 13 and 19 were Native American, between 91 and 108 were African-Americans, and between 47 and 56 were Hispanic. If the Law School is admitting between 91 and 108 African-Americans in order to achieve "critical mass," thereby preventing African-American students from feeling "isolated or like spokespersons for their race," one would think that a

number of the same order of magnitude would be necessary to accomplish the same purpose for Hispanics and Native Americans. Similarly, even if all of the Native American applicants admitted in a given year matriculate, which the record demonstrates is not at all the case, how can this possibly constitute a "critical mass" of Native Americans in a class of over 350 students? In order for this pattern of admission to be consistent with the Law School's explanation of "critical mass," one would have to believe that the objectives of "critical mass" offered by respondents are achieved with only half the number of Hispanics and one-sixth the number of Native Americans as compared to African-Americans. But respondents offer no race-specific reasons for such disparities. Instead, they simply emphasize the importance of achieving "critical mass," without any explanation of why that concept is applied differently among the three underrepresented minority groups.

These different numbers, moreover, come only as a result of substantially different treatment among the three underrepresented minority groups, as is apparent in an example offered by the Law School and highlighted by the Court: The school asserts that it "frequently accepts nonminority applicants with grades and test scores lower than underrepresented minority applicants (and other nonminority applicants) who are rejected." Specifically, the Law School states that "[s]ixty-nine minority applicants were rejected between 1995 and 2000 with at least a 3.5 [Grade Point Average (GPA)] and a [score of] 159 or higher on the [Law School Admissions Test (LSAT)]" while a number of Caucasian and Asian-American applicants with similar or lower scores were admitted.

Review of the record reveals only 67 such individuals. Of these 67 individuals, *56* were Hispanic, while only 6 were African-American, and only 5 were Native American. This discrepancy reflects a consistent practice. For example, in 2000, 12 Hispanics who scored between a 159-160 on the LSAT and earned a GPA of 3.00 or higher applied for admission and only 2 were admitted. Meanwhile, 12 African-Americans in the same range of qualifications applied for admission and all 12 were admitted. Likewise, that same year, 16 Hispanics who scored between a 151-153 on the LSAT and earned a 3.00 or higher applied for admission and only 1 of those applicants was admitted. Twenty-three similarly qualified African-Americans applied for admission and 14 were admitted.

These statistics have a significant bearing on petitioner's case. Respondents have *never* offered any race-specific arguments explaining why significantly more individuals from one underrepresented minority group are needed in order to achieve "critical mass" or further student body diversity. They certainly have not explained why Hispanics, who they have said are among "the groups most isolated by racial barriers in our country," should have their admission capped out in this manner. True, petitioner is neither Hispanic nor Native American. But the Law School's disparate admissions practices with respect to these minority groups demonstrate that its alleged goal of "critical mass" is simply a sham. Petitioner may use these statistics to expose this sham, which is the basis for the Law School's admission of less qualified underrepresented minorities in preference to her. Surely strict scrutiny cannot permit these sort of disparities without at least some explanation.

Only when the "critical mass" label is discarded does a likely explanation for these numbers emerge. The Court states that the Law School's goal of attaining a "critical mass" of underrepresented minority students is not an interest in merely " 'assur[ing] within its student body some specified percentage of a particular group merely because of its race or ethnic origin.' " *Ante* (quoting *Bakke* (opinion of Powell, J.)). The Court recognizes that such an interest "would amount to outright racial balancing, which is patently unconstitutional." The Court concludes, however, that the Law School's use of race in admissions, consistent with Justice Powell's opinion in *Bakke*, only pays " '[s]ome attention to numbers.' "

But the correlation between the percentage of the Law School's pool of applicants who are members of the three minority groups and the percentage of the admitted applicants who are members of these same groups is far too precise to be dismissed as merely the result of the school paying "some attention to [the] numbers." * * * [F]rom 1995 through 2000 the percentage of admitted applicants who were members of these minority groups closely tracked the percentage of individuals in the school's applicant pool who were from the same groups. * * *

For example, in 1995, when 9.7% of the applicant pool was African-American, 9.4% of the admitted class was African-American. By 2000, only 7.5% of the applicant pool was African-American, and 7.3% of the admitted class was African-American. This correlation is striking. Respondents themselves emphasize that the number of underrepresented minority students admitted to the Law School would be significantly smaller if the race of each applicant were not considered. But, as the examples above illustrate, the measure of the decrease would differ dramatically among the groups. The tight correlation between the percentage of applicants and admittees of a given race, therefore, must result from careful race based planning by the Law School. It suggests a formula for admission based on the aspirational assumption that all applicants are equally qualified academically, and therefore that the proportion of each group admitted should be the same as the proportion of that group in the applicant pool. * * *

I do not believe that the Constitution gives the Law School such free rein in the use of race. The Law School has offered no explanation for its actual admissions practices and, unexplained, we are bound to conclude that the Law School has managed its admissions program, not to achieve a "critical mass," but to extend offers of admission to members of selected minority groups in proportion to their statistical representation in the applicant pool. But this is precisely the type of racial balancing that the Court itself calls "patently unconstitutional."

Finally, I believe that the Law School's program fails strict scrutiny because it is devoid of any reasonably precise time limit on the Law School's use of race in admissions. * * *

[**JUSTICE KENNEDY**, dissenting, endorsed Justice Powell's approach in *Bakke* but believed that the majority was not true to it, engaging in "nothing short of perfunctory" review that was too accepting of the Law School's assurances that its admissions process satisfied constitutional requirements, when in fact "the Law School's pursuit of critical mass mutated into the equivalent of a quota."]

[JUSTICE SCALIA filed a short dissenting statement contending, among other things, that the majority's work will lead to further confusion and litigation about the constitutionality of affirmative action.]

[JUSTICE THOMAS, joined by JUSTICE SCALIA, lampooned Michigan's supposed compelling state interest as simply one seeking to maintain a prestigious law school that uses admissions criteria that disproportionally disadvantage racial minorities. He suggested that the law school could achieve its goal of a more racially diverse student body by using nonracial means: for example, it could expand the class size or simply drop some of its elite admissions criteria (e.g., stop using LSAT scores, which are generally lower for minority applicants). Even if diversity is a compelling government interest, he argued that narrow tailoring would require the use of such neutral criteria before considering engaging in race-based means of achieving diversity.]

———

Gratz v. Bollinger, 539 U.S. 244 (2003). In a companion case to *Grutter*, disappointed white applicants challenged the affirmative action policy used for admission to the undergraduate college of liberal arts and sciences of the University of Michigan. Out of a scheme with 150 total points and in which 100 points guaranteed admission, the program automatically awarded 20 points to any underrepresented minority applicant. **Chief Justice Rehnquist**, joined by **Justices O'Connor**, **Scalia**, **Kennedy**, and **Thomas**, struck down the program as failing to provide the individualized evaluation of each applicant required by *Grutter* and the Powell opinion in *Bakke*. The approach amounted to a practical quota because, as the majority understood the facts, it resulted in the admission of virtually any minimally qualified minority applicant. Thus, even though under *Grutter* educational diversity is a compelling government interest, the undergraduate admissions plan flunked the narrow-tailoring requirement. The majority was unmoved by the university's argument that it could not easily provide individualized consideration to the large number of applications it received. **Justice O'Connor** concurred, stressing the differences between the mechanical, nonindividualized process for undergraduate admissions and the individualized approach her majority opinion approved in the law-school case. **Justice Breyer** concurred in the judgment and expressed agreement with Justice O'Connor's views. Among the dissenting opinions, the most relevant for current concerns were filed by **Justice Souter** and by **Justice Ginsburg**. Justice Souter stressed that, even under the automatic process of awarding 20 points to minority applicants, all applicants contended for all seats in the class, and nonminority applicants could easily obtain admission over minority applicants by gaining more points based on other criteria (grades, test scores, strength of high school, quality of course of study, residence, alumni relationships, leadership, personal character, socioeconomic disadvantage, athletic ability, and quality of a personal essay). Thus, in his view the program operated more like a plus-factor scheme than a quota. Justice Ginsburg suggested that, in light of ongoing racial inequality and the distinction between benign and pernicious racial preferences, colleges and universities should continue to have ways to attempt to ameliorate racial differences in admissions. In her view, it is better to do this forthrightly, as Michigan had done, than to encourage applicants and admissions officers to do it by "resort to camouflage": "Seeking to improve their chances for admission, applicants may highlight the minority group associations to which they belong, or the Hispanic surnames of their mothers or grandparents. In turn, teachers' recommendations may emphasize who a student is as much as what he or she has accomplished. * * * If honesty is the best policy, surely Michigan's accurately described, fully disclosed College affirmative action program is preferable to achieving similar numbers through winks, nods, and disguises."

NOTES ON THE MICHIGAN CASES

1. *Why Revive Justice Powell's Approach Concerning the "Compelling" Nature of the Diversity Rationale?* The majority of the deeply divided Court settles on embracing Justice Powell's approach in *Bakke* but then divides on what that approach entails — for example, the narrow-tailoring point at which a plus factor becomes a quota. Strictly speaking, *stare decisis* in no way compels this outcome, as Justice Powell was writing only for himself, and in any event the current Court certainly has the authority to overrule the holding or implications of an earlier decision. What factors seem to have led Justice O'Connor to endorse the Powell approach, noting along the way that the *Croson* plurality opinion (written by her) had suggested that only remedial purposes could serve as compelling government interests in the affirmative action context?

In prior cases, one government interest found by a majority of the Court to be "compelling" was remedying past illegal discrimination (*Swann* and the de jure segregation cases involving busing as a remedy, see p. 106, *supra*; cf. dictum in the *Croson* and *Adarand* cases regarding the capacity of government to consider taking race into account to remedy past illegal discrimination in the contracting industry). There is no suggestion in the Michigan cases that the University engaged in past illegal discrimination against persons of color in admissions. The other governmental interest found by a majority of the Court to be compelling is national security (*Korematsu*; *Hirabayashi*). This might have suggested that, outside the context of past illegality, a "compelling" government interest justifying the use of a racial classification must amount to something analogous to self-defense or the necessity defense in tort law and criminal law — a compulsion to act to save life or limb that authorizes the use of conduct (even deadly force in tort and criminal law) that society almost always otherwise forbids. (An arguable context would be separation of the races in a prison following a race riot.) In the Michigan cases, there is no contention that colorblind law school admissions will cause the University to unravel or result in lethal results to the citizenry. So what is "compelling" about the diversity rationale, in the context of law school admissions?

Despite *Croson*'s and *Adarand*'s insistence that strict scrutiny does not vary regardless of whether the use of race is hostile toward a racial minority or "benign," can the Michigan cases be explained in any way other than that a majority of the Court (embodied in the swing vote of Justice O'Connor) truly became comfortable that race was used here in a "benign" way in which the public interest in a future society that is both more racially integrated and racially compatible greatly outweighs the harm caused to non-minority law school applicants? Has strict scrutiny turned into a balancing test, not very different from the intermediate scrutiny approach (important government interest achieved by reasonable means) promoted by the Brennan Four in *Bakke* and Justice Brennan's majority opinion in *Metro Broadcasting* (a case overruled at least in part in *Adarand*)?

What exactly is/are the compelling interest(s)? Diversity of viewpoints and experiences in the educational milieu? Diversifying the legal profession? Diversifying the elite segment of the legal profession? Diversifying the professions, generally? As for that, consider all the professionals trained by state universities — how might *Grutter* affect the constitutionality of admissions to state university programs that train, e.g., accountants, architects, doctors, engineers, military officers, morticians, pharmacists, psychologists (those who provide mental health counseling), optometrists, nurses, and social workers? To what extent, if any, does the socioeconomic status the person might attain or the power the person might wield in society, regardless of whether she is in a profession, make a difference (note that Justice O'Connor cited the amicus brief filed by big business (3M et al.) supporting the diversity rationale)? To what extent does the racial composition of the profession or industry play a role (note that she cited the amicus brief by retired high-ranking military officers, which argued that diversifying the officer corps was essential to the effective functioning of the military)? Does any of this have anything to do with undergraduate admissions?

2. *Narrow Tailoring?* Is there any important difference between the law school's "holistic" review of applications and the undergraduate college's review of all applications with some applicants getting an automatic 20 points and others not? Focusing on the law school, is there any good response to the Chief Justice's contention that "critical mass" is a hollow concept that is a cover for loose proportional representation? Or to Justice Thomas's argument that race-neutral means (e.g., a lottery) should have been used before race-conscious means were considered?

3. *Nature of the Harm and Causation.* No Justice quarreled with the assumption that Ms. Grutter had suffered an injury that entitled her to have standing to object to the consideration of race in the law school admissions policy. But note that there is a serious question of causation: had the law school used a colorblind policy, there is no way to know whether she would have been admitted. Thus, the harm that she suffered is not that she was wrongfully denied admission (though had she prevailed, she could have attempted to prove that on remand); the harm must be that she was denied some sort of "equal treatment" in the admissions process. This is a kind of "expressive harm" or "dignitary harm," somewhat similar to that suffered by non-minority voters who end up in electoral districts that are carved out to create a majority-minority district, see *Shaw v. Reno* (in the next Part of this Chapter). Could these questions about causation, standing, and nature of harm have softened the way strict scrutiny

was applied? Compare the Seattle and Louisville cases, which immediately follow.

D. STUDENT ASSIGNMENT IN K-12 PUBLIC EDUCATION

Chief Justice Rehnquist died and Justice O'Connor retired between the Michigan cases and the Seattle and Louisville cases. They were replaced by Chief Justice Roberts and Justice Alito.

PARENTS INVOLVED IN COMMUNITY SCHOOLS v. SEATTLE SCHOOL DISTRICT No. 1
___ U.S. ___, 127 S.Ct. 2738, 168 L.Ed.2d 508 (2007)

CHIEF JUSTICE ROBERTS announced the judgment of the Court, and delivered the opinion of the Court with respect to Parts I, II, III-A, and III-C, and an opinion with respect to Parts III-B and IV, in which **JUSTICES SCALIA, THOMAS,** and **ALITO** join.

The school districts in these cases voluntarily adopted student assignment plans that rely upon race to determine which public schools certain children may attend. The Seattle[, Washington] school district classifies children as white or nonwhite; the Jefferson County [Kentucky] school district as black or "other." In Seattle, this racial classification is used to allocate slots in oversubscribed high schools. In Jefferson County, it is used to make certain elementary school assignments and to rule on transfer requests. In each case, the school district relies upon an individual student's race in assigning that student to a particular school, so that the racial balance at the school falls within a predetermined range based on the racial composition of the school district as a whole. Parents of students denied assignment to particular schools under these plans solely because of their race brought suit, contending that allocating children to different public schools on the basis of race violated the Fourteenth Amendment guarantee of equal protection. The Courts of Appeals below upheld the plans. We granted certiorari, and now reverse.

[I] Both cases present the same underlying legal question — whether a public school that had not operated legally segregated schools or has been found to be unitary may choose to classify students by race and rely upon that classification in making school assignments. Although we examine the plans under the same legal framework, the specifics of the two plans, and the circumstances surrounding their adoption, are in some respects quite different.

[The Chief Justice described the two plans and their backgrounds. Seattle's school district had never been segregated by law, but concern with racial imbalances led the district in 1998 to adopt the following plan (in effect 1999-2002). Students would submit a list of high schools they preferred to attend. If too many students choose the same high schools, as is typically the case, the district adopted several tiebreaker rules: (1) the applicant has a sibling enrolled in that school; (2) for schools that are more than 10% off the city's overall racial balance (41% "white" and 59% "nonwhite") the applicant gets in if he or she helps bring the school into racial balance; and (3) geographic proximity.

[Jefferson County (where Louisville is located) had maintained a de jure segregated public school system which was adjudged unconstitutional in 1973. The schools operated under this decree until 2000, when the District Court dissolved the decree after finding that the district had achieved unitary status by eliminating "[t]o the greatest extent practicable" the vestiges of its prior policy of segregation. In 2001, the County adopted a voluntary program seeking to maintain racial balance (overall, about 66% of the district's schoolchildren are white, 34% nonwhite). Parents of kindergartners, first-graders, and students new to the district may submit an application indicating a first and second choice among the schools within their cluster; students who do not submit such an application are assigned within the cluster by the district. Decisions to assign students to schools within each cluster are based on available space within the schools and the racial guidelines in the District's current student assignment plan. If a school has reached the "extremes of the racial guidelines" (15% minimum black enrollment, 50% maximum), a student whose race would contribute to the school's racial imbalance will not be assigned there. After assignment, students at all grade levels are permitted to apply to transfer between nonmagnet schools in the district. A similar system works for middle and high schools.

[In Part II of his opinion, the Chief Justice rejected Seattle's objections that Parents Involved lacks standing to litigate their equal protection claims.]

[III.A] It is well established that when the government distributes burdens or benefits on the basis of individual racial classifications, that action is reviewed under strict scrutiny. *Grutter.* As the Court recently reaffirmed, " 'racial classifications are simply too pernicious to permit any but the most exact connection between justification and classification.' " *Gratz.* In order to satisfy this searching standard of review, the school districts must demonstrate that the use of individual racial classifications in the assignment plans here under review is "narrowly tailored" to achieve a "compelling" government interest. *Adarand.*

Without attempting in these cases to set forth all the interests a school district might assert, it suffices to note that our prior cases, in evaluating the use of racial classifications in the school context, have recognized two interests that qualify as compelling. The first is the compelling interest of remedying the effects of past intentional discrimination. See *Freeman v. Pitts* [p. 113, *supra*]. Yet the Seattle public schools have not shown that they were ever segregated by law, and were not subject to court-ordered desegregation decrees. The Jefferson County public schools were previously segregated by law and were subject to a desegregation decree entered in 1975. In 2000, the District Court that entered that decree dissolved it, finding that Jefferson County had "eliminated the vestiges associated with the former policy of segregation and its pernicious effects," and thus had achieved "unitary" status. Jefferson County accordingly does not rely upon an interest in remedying the effects of past intentional discrimination in defending its present use of race in assigning students.

Nor could it. We have emphasized that the harm being remedied by mandatory desegregation plans is the harm that is traceable to segregation, and that "the Constitution is not violated by racial imbalance in the schools, without more." *Milliken* [p. 111, *supra*]. Once Jefferson County achieved unitary status, it had remedied the constitutional wrong that allowed race-based assignments. Any continued use of race must be justified on some other basis.[10]

The second government interest we have recognized as compelling for purposes of strict scrutiny is the interest in diversity in higher education upheld in *Grutter*. The specific interest found compelling in *Grutter* was student body diversity "in the context of higher education." The diversity interest was not focused on race alone but encompassed "all factors that may contribute to student body diversity." We described the various types of diversity that the law school sought:

> [The law school's] policy makes clear there are many possible bases for diversity admissions, and provides examples of admittees who have lived or traveled widely abroad, are fluent in several languages, have overcome personal adversity and family hardship, have exceptional records of extensive community service, and have had successful careers in other fields.

The Court quoted the articulation of diversity from Justice Powell's opinion in *Bakke*, noting that "it is not an interest in simple ethnic diversity, in which a specified percentage of the student body is in effect guaranteed to be members of selected ethnic groups, that can justify the use of race." Instead, what was upheld in *Grutter* was consideration of "a far broader array of qualifications and characteristics of which racial or ethnic origin is but a single though important element."

The entire gist of the analysis in *Grutter* was that the admissions program at issue there focused on each applicant as an individual, and not simply as a member of a particular racial group. The classification of applicants by race upheld in *Grutter* was only as part of a "highly individualized, holistic review." As the Court explained, "[t]he importance of this individualized consideration in the context of a race-conscious admissions program is paramount." The point of the narrow tailoring analysis in which the *Grutter* Court engaged was to ensure that the use of racial classifications was indeed part of a broader assessment of diversity, and not simply an effort to achieve racial balance, which the Court explained would be "patently unconstitutional."

In the present cases, by contrast, race is not considered as part of a broader effort to achieve "exposure to widely diverse people, cultures, ideas, and viewpoints"; race, for some students, is determinative standing alone. The districts argue that other factors, such as student preferences, affect assignment decisions under their plans, but under each plan when race comes into play, it is decisive by itself. It is not simply one factor weighed with others in reaching

---

10. The districts point to dicta in a prior opinion in which the Court suggested that, while not constitutionally mandated, it would be constitutionally permissible for a school district to seek racially balanced schools as a matter of "educational policy." See *Swann* [p. 106, *supra*]. * * * [But] *Swann*, evaluating a school district engaged in court-ordered desegregation, had no occasion to consider whether a district's voluntary adoption of race-based assignments in the absence of a finding of prior *de jure* segregation was constitutionally permissible, an issue that was again expressly reserved in *Washington v. Seattle School Dist. No. 1,* 458 U.S. 457, 472, n. 15 (1982). * * *

a decision, as in *Grutter*; it is *the* factor. Like the University of Michigan undergraduate plan struck down in *Gratz*, the plans here "do not provide for a meaningful individualized review of applicants" but instead rely on racial classifications in a "nonindividualized, mechanical" way. *Id.* (O'Connor, J., concurring).

Even when it comes to race, the plans here employ only a limited notion of diversity, viewing race exclusively in white/nonwhite terms in Seattle and black/"other" terms in Jefferson County. The Seattle "Board Statement Reaffirming Diversity Rationale" speaks of the "inherent educational value" in "[p]roviding students the opportunity to attend schools with diverse student enrollment." But under the Seattle plan, a school with 50 percent Asian-American students and 50 percent white students but no African-American, Native-American, or Latino students would qualify as balanced, while a school with 30 percent Asian-American, 25 percent African-American, 25 percent Latino, and 20 percent white students would not. It is hard to understand how a plan that could allow these results can be viewed as being concerned with achieving enrollment that is " 'broadly diverse,' " *Grutter.* * * *

In upholding the admissions plan in *Grutter*, * * * this Court relied upon considerations unique to institutions of higher education, noting that in light of "the expansive freedoms of speech and thought associated with the university environment, universities occupy a special niche in our constitutional tradition." See also *Bakke* (opinion of Powell, J.). The Court explained that "[c]ontext matters" in applying strict scrutiny, and repeatedly noted that it was addressing the use of race "in the context of higher education." *Grutter.* The Court in *Grutter* expressly articulated key limitations on its holding — defining a specific type of broad-based diversity and noting the unique context of higher education — but these limitations were largely disregarded by the lower courts in extending *Grutter* to uphold race-based assignments in elementary and secondary schools. The present cases are not governed by *Grutter*.

[III.B] Perhaps recognizing that reliance on *Grutter* cannot sustain their plans, both school districts assert additional interests, distinct from the interest upheld in *Grutter,* to justify their race-based assignments. In briefing and argument before this Court, Seattle contends that its use of race helps to reduce racial concentration in schools and to ensure that racially concentrated housing patterns do not prevent nonwhite students from having access to the most desirable schools. Jefferson County has articulated a similar goal, phrasing its interest in terms of educating its students "in a racially integrated environment." Each school district argues that educational and broader socialization benefits flow from a racially diverse learning environment, and each contends that because the diversity they seek is racial diversity — not the broader diversity at issue in *Grutter* — it makes sense to promote that interest directly by relying on race alone.

The parties and their *amici* dispute whether racial diversity in schools in fact has a marked impact on test scores and other objective yardsticks or achieves intangible socialization benefits. The debate is not one we need to resolve, however, because it is clear that the racial classifications employed by the districts are not narrowly tailored to the goal of achieving the educational and social benefits asserted to flow from racial diversity. In design and operation, the plans are directed only to racial balance, pure and simple, an objective this Court has repeatedly condemned as illegitimate.

The plans are tied to each district's specific racial demographics, rather than to any pedagogic concept of the level of diversity needed to obtain the asserted educational benefits. In Seattle, the district seeks white enrollment of between 31 and 51 percent (within 10 percent of "the district white average" of 41 percent), and nonwhite enrollment of between 49 and 69 percent (within 10 percent of "the district minority average" of 59 percent). In Jefferson County, by contrast, the district seeks black enrollment of no less than 15 or more than 50 percent, a range designed to be "equally above and below Black student enrollment systemwide," based on the objective of achieving at "all schools . . . an African-American enrollment equivalent to the average district-wide African-American enrollment" of 34 percent. In Seattle, then, the benefits of racial diversity require enrollment of at least 31 percent white students; in Jefferson County, at least 50 percent. There must be at least 15 percent nonwhite students under Jefferson County's plan; in Seattle, more than three times that figure. This comparison makes clear that the racial demographics in each district — whatever they happen to be — drive the required "diversity" numbers. The plans here are not tailored to achieving a degree of diversity necessary to realize the asserted educational benefits; instead the plans are tailored, in the words of Seattle's Manager of Enrollment Planning, Technical Support, and Demographics, to "the goal established by the school board of attaining a level of diversity within the schools that approximates the district's overall demographics."

The districts offer no evidence that the level of racial diversity necessary to achieve the asserted educational benefits happens to coincide with the racial demographics of the respective school districts — or rather the white/nonwhite or black/"other" balance of the districts, since that is the only diversity addressed by the plans. Indeed, in its brief Seattle simply assumes that the educational benefits track the racial breakdown of the district. When asked for "a range of percentage that would be diverse," however, Seattle's expert said it was important to have "sufficient numbers so as to avoid students feeling any kind of specter of exceptionality." The district did not attempt to defend the proposition that anything outside its range posed the "specter of exceptionality." Nor did it demonstrate in any way how the educational and social benefits of racial diversity or avoidance of racial isolation are more likely to be achieved at a school that is 50 percent white and 50 percent Asian-American, which would qualify as diverse under Seattle's plan, than at a school that is 30 percent Asian-American, 25 percent African-American, 25 percent Latino, and 20 percent white, which under Seattle's definition would be racially concentrated. [The same was true of Jefferson County.]

In *Grutter,* the number of minority students the school sought to admit was an undefined "meaningful number" necessary to achieve a genuinely diverse student body. Although the matter was the subject of disagreement on the Court, the majority concluded that the law school did not count back from its applicant pool to arrive at the "meaningful number" it regarded as necessary to diversify its student body. Here the racial balance the districts seek is a defined range set solely by reference to the demographics of the respective school districts.

This working backward to achieve a particular type of racial balance, rather than working forward from some demonstration of the level of diversity that provides the purported benefits, is a fatal flaw under our existing precedent. We have many times over reaffirmed that "[r]acial balance is not to be achieved for its own sake." *Freeman.* See also *Croson*; *Bakke* (opinion of Powell, J.) ("If petitioner's purpose is to assure within its student body some specified percentage of a particular group merely because of its race or ethnic origin, such a preferential purpose must be rejected . . . as facially invalid"). *Grutter* itself reiterated that "outright racial balancing" is "patently unconstitutional."

Accepting racial balancing as a compelling state interest would justify the imposition of racial proportionality throughout American society, contrary to our repeated recognition that "[a]t the heart of the Constitution's guarantee of equal protection lies the simple command that the Government must treat citizens as individuals, not as simply components of a racial, religious, sexual or national class." *Miller v. Johnson*, 515 U.S. 900, 911 (1995) (quoting *Metro Broadcasting* (O'Connor, J., dissenting)).[14] Allowing racial balancing as a compelling end in itself would "effectively assur[e] that race will always be relevant in American life, and that the 'ultimate goal' of 'eliminating entirely from governmental decisionmaking such irrelevant factors as a human being's race' will never be achieved." *Croson* (plurality opinion of O'Connor, J.). An interest "linked to nothing other than proportional representation of various races . . . would support indefinite use of racial classifications, employed first to obtain the appropriate mixture of racial views and then to ensure that the [program] continues to reflect that mixture." *Metro Broadcasting* (O'Connor, J., dissenting).

The validity of our concern that racial balancing has "no logical stopping point," *Croson*; see also *Grutter*, is demonstrated here by the degree to which the districts tie their racial guidelines to their demographics. As the districts' demographics shift, so too will their definition of racial diversity. See App. in No. 05-908, at 103a (describing application of racial tiebreaker based on "*current* white percentage" of 41 percent and "*current* minority percentage" of 59 percent (emphasis added)).* * *

The principle that racial balancing is not permitted is one of substance, not semantics. Racial balancing is not transformed from "patently unconstitutional" to a compelling state interest simply by relabeling it "racial diversity." While

---

14.   In contrast, Seattle's website formerly described "emphasizing individualism as opposed to a more collective ideology" as a form of "cultural racism," and currently states that the district has no intention "to hold onto unsuccessful concepts such as [a] . . . colorblind mentality." Harrell, School Web Site Removed: Examples of Racism Sparked Controversy, Seattle Post-Intelligencer, June 2, 2006, pp. B1, B5. Compare *Plessy v. Ferguson* (Harlan, J., dissenting) ("Our Constitution is color-blind, and neither knows nor tolerates classes among citizens. In respect of civil rights, all citizens are equal before the law").

the school districts use various verbal formulations to describe the interest they seek to promote — racial diversity, avoidance of racial isolation, racial integration — they offer no definition of the interest that suggests it differs from racial balance. See, *e.g.,* App. in No. 05-908, at 257a ("Q. What's your understanding of when a school suffers from racial isolation? A. I don't have a definition for that"); *id.,* at 228a-229a ("I don't think we've ever sat down and said, 'Define racially concentrated school exactly on point in quantitative terms.' I don't think we've ever had that conversation"); Tr. in *McFarland I,* at 190 (Dec. 8, 2003) ("Q. How does the Jefferson County School Board define diversity . . . ?" "A. Well, we want to have the schools that make up the percentage of students of the population"). * * *

The en banc Ninth Circuit declared that "when a racially diverse school system is the goal (or racial concentration or isolation is the problem), there is no more effective means than a consideration of race to achieve the solution." For the foregoing reasons, this conclusory argument cannot sustain the plans. However closely related race-based assignments may be to achieving racial balance, that itself cannot be the goal, whether labeled "racial diversity" or anything else. To the extent the objective is sufficient diversity so that students see fellow students as individuals rather than solely as members of a racial group, using means that treat students solely as members of a racial group is fundamentally at cross-purposes with that end.

[III.C] The districts assert, as they must, that the way in which they have employed individual racial classifications is necessary to achieve their stated ends. The minimal effect these classifications have on student assignments, however, suggests that other means would be effective. Seattle's racial tiebreaker results, in the end, only in shifting a small number of students between schools. Approximately 307 student assignments were affected by the racial tiebreaker in 2000-2001; the district was able to track the enrollment status of 293 of these students. Of these, 209 were assigned to a school that was one of their choices, 87 of whom were assigned to the same school to which they would have been assigned without the racial tiebreaker. Eighty-four students were assigned to schools that they did not list as a choice, but 29 of those students would have been assigned to their respective school without the racial tiebreaker, and 3 were able to attend one of the oversubscribed schools due to waitlist and capacity adjustments. In over one-third of the assignments affected by the racial tiebreaker, then, the use of race in the end made no difference, and the district could identify only 52 students who were ultimately affected adversely by the racial tiebreaker in that it resulted in assignment to a school they had not listed as a preference and to which they would not otherwise have been assigned. [A similarly miminal effect came from Jefferson County's use of racial classifications.]

While we do not suggest that *greater* use of race would be preferable, the minimal impact of the districts' racial classifications on school enrollment casts doubt on the necessity of using racial classifications. * * *

The districts have also failed to show that they considered methods other than explicit racial classifications to achieve their stated goals. Narrow tailoring requires "serious, good faith consideration of workable race-neutral alternatives," *Grutter*, and yet in Seattle several alternative assignment plans — many of which would not have used express racial classifications — were rejected with little or no consideration. Jefferson County has failed to present any evidence that it considered alternatives, even though the district already claims that its goals are achieved primarily through means other than the racial classifications. Compare *Croson* (Kennedy, J., concurring in part and concurring in judgment) (racial classifications permitted only "as a last resort").

[In Part IV, Chief Justice Roberts responds to Justice Breyer's dissent. The Chief Justice contends that Justice Breyer errs in relying upon precedents recognizing the compelling interest in remedying past intentional discrimination, because in these cases the Seattle school district never engaged in such discrimination, and the Louisville district remedied its past discrimination and achieved unitary status before adopting the plan in question. The Chief Justice also responds that Justice Breyer unduly relies upon mere dicta from *Swann*. Furthermore, "[w]e simply do not understand how Justice Breyer can maintain that classifying every schoolchild as black or white, and using that classification as a determinative factor in assigning children to achieve pure racial balance, can be regarded as 'less burdensome, and hence more narrowly tailored' than the consideration of race in *Grutter,* when the Court in *Grutter* stated that '[t]he importance of . . . individualized consideration' in the program was 'paramount,' and consideration of race was one factor in a 'highly individualized, holistic review.' " The Chief Justice contends that Justice Breyer is simply resisting the Court's precedents in *Adarand* and other cases that hold that all racial classifications, including "benign" ones, must be subjected to strict scrutiny. He quotes Justice O'Connor's dissent in *Metro Broadcasting* (" '[B]enign' carries with it no independent meaning, but reflects only acceptance of the current generation's conclusion that a politically acceptable burden, imposed on particular citizens on the basis of race, is reasonable."). "Accepting Justice Breyer's approach would do no more than move us from 'separate but equal' to 'unequal but benign.' *Metro Broadcasting* (Kennedy, J., dissenting)." Furthermore, Chief Justice Roberts states, Justice Breyer, in speaking of bringing the races together, ignores that the Equal Protection Clause " 'protects *persons*, not *groups*,' " quoting *Adarand* (emphasis in original) and referring to similar language in *Brown II*.]

JUSTICE BREYER's position comes down to a familiar claim: The end justifies the means. He admits that "there is a cost in applying 'a state-mandated racial label,' " but he is confident that the cost is worth paying. Our established strict scrutiny test for racial classifications, however, insists on "detailed examination, both as to ends *and* as to means." *Adarand* (emphasis added). Simply because the school districts may seek a worthy goal does not mean they are free to discriminate on the basis of race to achieve it, or that their racial classifications should be subject to less exacting scrutiny. * * *

If the need for the racial classifications embraced by the school districts is unclear, even on the districts' own terms, the costs are undeniable. "[D]istinctions between citizens solely because of their ancestry are by their very nature odious to a free people whose institutions are founded upon the doctrine of equality." *Adarand*. Government action dividing us by race is inherently suspect because such classifications promote "notions of racial inferiority and lead to a politics of racial hostility," *Croson,* "reinforce the belief, held by too many for too much of our history, that individuals should be judged by the color of their skin," *Shaw v. Reno* [p. 325, *infra*?], and "endorse race-based reasoning and the conception of a Nation divided into racial blocs, thus contributing to an escalation of racial hostility and conflict." *Metro Broadcasting* (O'Connor, J., dissenting). As the Court explained in *Rice v. Cayetano,* 528 U.S. 495, 517 (2000), "[o]ne of the principal reasons race is treated as a forbidden classification is that it demeans the dignity and worth of a person to be judged by ancestry instead of by his or her own merit and essential qualities."

All this is true enough in the contexts in which these statements were made — government contracting, voting districts, allocation of broadcast licenses, and electing state officers — but when it comes to using race to assign children to schools, history will be heard. In *Brown I,* we held that segregation deprived black children of equal educational opportunities regardless of whether school facilities and other tangible factors were equal, because government classification and separation on grounds of race themselves denoted inferiority. It was not the inequality of the facilities but the fact of legally separating children on the basis of race on which the Court relied to find a constitutional violation in 1954. The next Term, we accordingly stated that "full compliance" with *Brown I* required school districts "to achieve a system of determining admission to the public schools *on a nonracial basis.*" *Brown II* (emphasis added).

The parties and their *amici* debate which side is more faithful to the heritage of *Brown,* but the position of the plaintiffs in *Brown* was spelled out in their brief and could not have been clearer: "[T]he Fourteenth Amendment prevents states from according differential treatment to American children on the basis of their color or race." Brief for Appellants in Nos. 1, 2, and 4 and for Respondents in No. 10 on Reargument in *Brown I,* O.T.1953, p. 15 (Summary of Argument). What do the racial classifications at issue here do, if not accord differential treatment on the basis of race? As counsel who appeared before this Court for the plaintiffs in *Brown* put it: "We have one fundamental contention which we will seek to develop in the course of this argument, and that contention is that no State has any authority under the equal-protection clause of the Fourteenth Amendment to use race as a factor in affording educational opportunities among its citizens." Tr. of Oral Arg. in *Brown I,* p. 7 (Robert L. Carter, Dec. 9, 1952). There is no ambiguity in that statement. And it was that position that prevailed in this Court, which emphasized in its remedial opinion that what was "[a]t stake is the personal interest of the plaintiffs in admission to public schools as soon as practicable *on a nondiscriminatory basis,*" and what was required was "determining admission to the public schools *on a nonracial basis.*" *Brown II* (emphasis added). What do the racial classifications do in these cases, if not determine admission to a public school on a racial basis?

Before *Brown,* schoolchildren were told where they could and could not go to school based on the color of their skin. The school districts in these cases have not carried the heavy burden of demonstrating that we should allow this once again — even for very different reasons. For schools that never segregated on the basis of race, such as Seattle, or that have removed the vestiges of past segregation, such as Jefferson County, the way "to achieve a system of determining admission to the public schools on a nonracial basis," *Brown II*, is to stop assigning students on a racial basis. The way to stop discrimination on the basis of race is to stop discriminating on the basis of race.

JUSTICE KENNEDY, concurring in part and concurring in the judgment.

[Justice Kennedy faulted the Jefferson County assignment plan as internally contradictory and confusing, qualities immediately fatal under the strict scrutiny required by *Adarand* and the Court's other precedents. Seattle did a better job of explaining its plan.] The district, nevertheless, has failed to make an adequate showing in at least one respect. It has failed to explain why, in a district composed of a diversity of races, with fewer than half of the students classified as "white," it has employed the crude racial categories of "white" and "non-white" as the basis for its assignment decisions.

The district has identified its purposes as follows: "(1) to promote the educational benefits of diverse school enrollments; (2) to reduce the potentially harmful effects of racial isolation by allowing students the opportunity to opt out of racially isolated schools; and (3) to make sure that racially segregated housing patterns did not prevent non-white students from having equitable access to the most popular over-subscribed schools." Yet the school district does not explain how, in the context of its diverse student population, a blunt distinction between "white" and "non-white" furthers these goals. As the Court explains, "a school with 50 percent Asian-American students and 50 percent white students but no African-American, Native-American, or Latino students would qualify as balanced, while a school with 30 percent Asian-American, 25 percent African-American, 25 percent Latino, and 20 percent white students would not." Far from being narrowly tailored to its purposes, this system threatens to defeat its own ends, and the school district has provided no convincing explanation for its design. * * * As the district fails to account for the classification system it has chosen, despite what appears to be its ill fit, Seattle has not shown its plan to be narrowly tailored to achieve its own ends; and thus it fails to pass strict scrutiny.

* * * [P]arts of the opinion by The Chief Justice imply an all-too-unyielding insistence that race cannot be a factor in instances when, in my view, it may be taken into account. The plurality opinion is too dismissive of the legitimate interest government has in ensuring all people have equal opportunity regardless of their race. The plurality's postulate that "[t]he way to stop discrimination on the basis of race is to stop discriminating on the basis of race" is not sufficient to decide these cases. Fifty years of experience since *Brown I* should teach us that the problem before us defies so easy a solution. School districts can seek to reach *Brown*'s objective of equal educational opportunity. The plurality opinion is at least open to the interpretation that the Constitution requires school districts to ignore the problem of *de facto* resegregation in schooling. I cannot endorse that conclusion. To the extent the plurality opinion suggests the Constitution mandates that state and local school authorities must accept the status quo of racial isolation in schools, it is, in my view, profoundly mistaken.

The statement by Justice Harlan that "[o]ur Constitution is color-blind" was most certainly justified in the context of his dissent in *Plessy v. Ferguson* [Chapter 2, § 1A]. The Court's decision in that case was a grievous error it took far too long to overrule. *Plessy,* of course, concerned official classification by race applicable to all persons who sought to use railway carriages. And, as an aspiration, Justice Harlan's axiom must command our assent. In the real world, it is regrettable to say, it cannot be a universal constitutional principle.

In the administration of public schools by the state and local authorities it is permissible to consider the racial makeup of schools and to adopt general policies to encourage a diverse student body, one aspect of which is its racial composition. If school authorities are concerned that the student-body compositions of certain schools interfere with the objective of offering an equal educational opportunity to all of their students, they are free to devise race-conscious measures to address the problem in a general way and without treating each student in different fashion solely on the basis of a systematic, individual typing by race.

School boards may pursue the goal of bringing together students of diverse backgrounds and races through other means, including strategic site selection of new schools; drawing attendance zones with general recognition of the demographics of neighborhoods; allocating resources for special programs; recruiting students and faculty in a targeted fashion; and tracking enrollments, performance, and other statistics by race. These mechanisms are race conscious but do not lead to different treatment based on a classification that tells each student he or she is to be defined by race, so it is unlikely any of them would demand strict scrutiny to be found permissible. Executive and legislative branches, which for generations now have considered these types of policies and procedures, should be permitted to employ them with candor and with confidence that a constitutional violation does not occur whenever a decision-maker considers the impact a given approach might have on students of different races. Assigning to each student a personal designation according to a crude system of individual racial classifications is quite a different matter; and the legal analysis changes accordingly.

Each respondent has asserted that its assignment of individual students by race is permissible because there is no other way to avoid racial isolation in the school districts. Yet, as explained, each has failed to provide the support necessary for that proposition. [I]ndividual racial classifications employed in this manner may be considered legitimate only if they are a last resort to achieve a compelling interest.

In the cases before us it is noteworthy that the number of students whose assignment depends on express racial classifications is limited. I join Part III-C of the Court's opinion because I agree that in the context of these plans, the small number of assignments affected suggests that the schools could have achieved their stated ends through different means. These include the facially race-neutral means set forth above or, if necessary, a more nuanced, individual evaluation of school needs and student characteristics that might include race as a component. The latter approach would be informed by *Grutter,* though of course the criteria relevant to student placement would differ based on the age of the students, the needs of the parents, and the role of the schools.

[Justice Kennedy suggested that the state may have compelling interests that go beyond remedying past discrimination (*Swann*) or creating educational diversity (*Grutter*).] This Nation has a moral and ethical obligation to fulfill its historic commitment to creating an integrated society that ensures equal opportunity for all of its children. A compelling interest exists in avoiding racial isolation, an interest that a school district, in its discretion and expertise, may choose to pursue. Likewise, a district may consider it a compelling interest to achieve a diverse student population. Race may be one component of that diversity, but other demographic factors, plus special talents and needs, should also be considered. What the government is not permitted to do, absent a showing of necessity not made here, is to classify every student on the basis of race and to assign each of them to schools based on that classification. Crude measures of this sort threaten to reduce children to racial chits valued and traded according to one school's supply and another's demand.

That statement, to be sure, invites this response: A sense of stigma may already become the fate of those separated out by circumstances beyond their immediate control. But to this the replication must be: Even so, measures other than differential treatment based on racial typing of individuals first must be exhausted.

The decision today should not prevent school districts from continuing the important work of bringing together students of different racial, ethnic, and economic backgrounds. Due to a variety of factors — some influenced by government, some not — neighborhoods in our communities do not reflect the diversity of our Nation as a whole. Those entrusted with directing our public schools can bring to bear the creativity of experts, parents, administrators, and other concerned citizens to find a way to achieve the compelling interests they face without resorting to widespread governmental allocation of benefits and burdens on the basis of racial classifications.

[The concurring opinion of **JUSTICE THOMAS** and the dissenting opinion of **JUSTICE STEVENS** are omitted. Both Justices' views are discussed in the Notes following the case. The dissenting opinion of **JUSTICE BREYER**, joined by **JUSTICE STEVENS, JUSTICE SOUTER,** and **JUSTICE GINSBURG**, is summarized in the Notes as well.]

NOTES ON THE SEATTLE AND LOUISVILLE SCHOOL CASES

1. *Justice Stevens' Dissent.* Justice Stevens called it a "cruel irony" to invoke *Brown* as mandating color-blindness when in the case it was only African American children who suffered segregation by race. The Court of the 1960's and 1970's was truer to the real meaning of *Brown* than the current Court, he argued. He concluded: "It is my firm conviction that no Member of the Court that I joined in 1975 would have agreed with today's decision."

2. *Justice Breyer's Dissent.* The dissent runs 77 pages and cannot be easily digested or summarized. Students especially interested in any of the following points should consult the opinion directly.

(a) *Precedent and Practice.* In *Swann*, decided in 1971, the opinion for the Court by Chief Justice Burger stated in dictum:

> School authorities are traditionally charged with broad power to formulate and implement educational policy and might well conclude, for example, that in order to prepare students to live in a pluralistic society each school should have a prescribed ratio of Negro to white students reflecting the proportion for the district as a whole. *To do this as an educational policy is within the broad discretionary powers of school authorities.* (Emphasis added).

Justice Breyer stressed that this language provided a basis for much innovation over three decades, both by judges and by school boards, to tackle the difficult problem of racial isolation in public schools, whether easily traceable to *de jure* segregation or not. Congress, too, has enacted numerous race-conscious statutes in the context of schools. See, *e.g.,* 20 U.S.C. § 6311(b)(2)(C)(v) (No Child Left Behind Act); § 1067 *et seq.* (authorizing aid to minority institutions).

(b) *The Reality of Racial Isolation in Public Schools.* "Between 1968 and 1980, the number of black children attending a school where minority children constituted more than half of the school fell from 77% to 63% in the Nation (from 81% to 57% in the South) but then reversed direction by the year 2000, rising from 63% to 72% in the Nation (from 57% to 69% in the South). Similarly, between 1968 and 1980, the number of black children attending schools that were more than 90% minority fell from 64% to 33% in the Nation (from 78% to 23% in the South), but that too reversed direction, rising by the year 2000 from 33% to 37% in the Nation (from 23% to 31% in the South). As of 2002, almost 2.4 million students, or over 5% of all public school enrollment, attended schools with a white population of less than 1%. Of these, 2.3 million were black and Latino students, and only 72,000 were white. Today, more than one in six black children attend a school that is 99-100% minority. In light of the evident risk of a return to school systems that are in fact (though not in law) resegregated, many school districts have felt a need to maintain or to extend their integration efforts."

(c) *The Murkiness of the De Jure/De Facto Distinction.* No law ever required segregation of the Seattle schools, but they were highly segregated in fact and in practice (white students were routinely allowed to transfer out of majority-black schools). Ultimately the NAACP brought suit, contending that the government building and teacher-assignment policies perpetuated the segregation. The parties settled after the school district pledged to undertake a desegregation plan. The district then implemented a plan requiring race-based transfers and busing. In response to concerns from the Department of Education, the district agreed to remedy racially imbalanced schools through mandatory busing, starting in 1978. The Supreme Court protected the busing plan against a state constitutional amendment in *Washington v. Seattle School Dist. No. 1,* 458 U.S. 457, 461-466 (1982). Subsequently, in an effort to achieve school integration without busing, the district adopted race-based student assignment plans, culminating in the 1998 plan challenged in this litigation Justice Breyer queries, was Seattle's school system *de jure* or *de facto*? Why should it matter whether a federal district court had adjudicated the matter? "Are courts really to treat as merely *de facto* segregated those school districts that avoided a federal order by voluntarily complying with *Brown*'s requirements?"

(d) *The Complexity of Reducing Racial Isolation.* "[School] boards work in communities where demographic patterns change, where they must meet traditional learning goals, where they must attract and retain effective teachers, where they should (and will) take account of parents' views and maintain *their* commitment to public school education, where they must adapt to court intervention, where they must encourage voluntary student and parent action — where they will find that their own good faith, their knowledge, and their understanding of local circumstances are always necessary but often insufficient to solve the problems at hand.

"These facts and circumstances help explain why in this context, as to means, the law often leaves legislatures, city councils, school boards, and voters with a broad range of choice, thereby giving 'different communities' the opportunity to 'try different solutions . . . .' "

(e) *The Nature of the Compelling Government Interest*:

Justice Breyer identified the government interest as "the school districts' interest in eliminating school-by-school racial isolation and increasing the degree to which racial mixture characterizes each of the district's schools and each individual student's public school experience." He posited three elements to this interest:

(1) remediating prior conditions of segregation, including "an interest in continuing to combat the remnants of segregation caused in whole or in part by [school-related] policies, which have often affected not only schools, but also housing patterns, employment practices, economic conditions, and social attitudes. It is an interest in maintaining hard-won gains. And it has its roots in preventing what gradually may become the *de facto* resegregation of America's public schools."

(2) "an interest in overcoming the adverse educational effects produced by and associated with highly segregated schools. Studies suggest that children taken from those schools and placed in integrated settings often show positive academic gains."

(3) "a democratic element: an interest in producing an educational environment that reflects the 'pluralistic society' in which our children will live. *Swann.* It is an interest in helping our children learn to work and play together with children of different racial backgrounds. It is an interest in teaching children to engage in the kind of cooperation among Americans of all races that is necessary to make a land of three hundred million people one Nation.

"* * * [T]his Court from *Swann* to *Grutter* has treated these civic effects as an important virtue of racially diverse education. In *Grutter,* in the context of law school admissions, we found that these types of interests were, constitutionally speaking, 'compelling.' See *Grutter* (recognizing that Michigan Law School's race-conscious admissions policy 'promotes cross-racial understanding, helps to break down racial stereotypes, and enables [students] to better understand persons of different races,' and pointing out that 'the skills needed in today's increasingly global marketplace can only be developed through exposure to widely diverse people, cultures, ideas, and viewpoints').

"In light of this Court's conclusions in *Grutter,* the 'compelling' nature of these interests in the context of primary and secondary public education follows here *a fortiori.* Primary and secondary schools are where the education of this Nation's children begins, where each of us begins to absorb those values we carry with us to the end of our days. * * *

"The compelling interest at issue here, then, includes an effort to eradicate the remnants, not of general 'societal discrimination,' but of primary and secondary school segregation; it includes an effort to create school environments that provide better educational opportunities for all children; it includes an effort to help create citizens better prepared to know, to understand, and to work with people of all races and backgrounds, thereby furthering the kind of democratic government our Constitution foresees. If an educational interest that combines these three elements is not 'compelling,' what is?"

(f) *The Question of Narrow Tailoring*:

"[First,] the defining feature of both plans is greater emphasis upon student choice. In Seattle, for example, in more than 80% of all cases, that choice alone determines which high schools Seattle's ninth graders will attend. After ninth grade, students can decide voluntarily to transfer to a preferred district high school (without any consideration of race-conscious criteria). *Choice,* therefore, is the 'predominant factor' in these plans. *Race* is not.

"Indeed, the race-conscious ranges at issue in these cases often have no effect, either because the particular school is not oversubscribed in the year in question, or because the racial makeup of the school falls within the broad range, or because the student is a transfer applicant or has a sibling at the school. * * *

"Second, broad-range limits on voluntary school choice plans are less burdensome, and hence more narrowly tailored, see *Grutter*, than other race-conscious restrictions this Court has previously approved. See, *e.g., Swann.* Indeed, the plans before us are *more narrowly tailored* than the race-conscious admission plans that this Court approved in *Grutter.* Here, race becomes a factor only in a fraction of students' non-merit-based assignments — not in large numbers of students' merit-based applications. Moreover, the effect of applying race-conscious criteria here affects potentially disadvantaged students *less severely,* not more severely, than the criteria at issue in *Grutter.* Disappointed students are not rejected from a State's flagship graduate program; they simply attend a different one of the district's many public schools, which in aspiration and in fact are substantially equal. And, in Seattle, the disadvantaged student loses at most one year at the high school of his choice. One will search *Grutter* in vain for similarly persuasive evidence of narrow tailoring as the school districts have presented here.

"Third, the manner in which the school boards developed these plans itself reflects 'narrow tailoring.' Each plan was devised to overcome a history of segregated public schools. Each plan embodies the results of local experience and community consultation. Each plan is the product of a process that has sought to enhance student choice, while diminishing the need for mandatory busing. And each plan's use of race-conscious elements is *diminished* compared to the use of race in preceding integration plans. * * *

"Experience in Seattle and Louisville is consistent with experience elsewhere. In 1987, the U.S. Commission on Civil Rights studied 125 large school districts seeking integration. It reported that most districts — 92 of them, in fact — adopted desegregation policies that combined two or more highly race-conscious strategies, for example, rezoning or pairing.

"Having looked at dozens of *amicus* briefs, public reports, news stories, and the records in many of this Court's prior cases, which together span 50 years of desegregation history in school districts across the Nation, I have discovered many examples of districts that sought integration through explicitly race-conscious methods, including mandatory busing. Yet, I have found *no* example or model that would permit this Court to say to Seattle and to Louisville: 'Here is an instance of a desegregation plan that is likely to achieve your objectives and also makes less use of race-conscious criteria than your plans.' And, if the plurality cannot suggest such a model — and it cannot — then it seeks * * * to impose a 'narrow tailoring' requirement that in practice would never be met.

"* * * Why does Seattle's plan group Asian-Americans, Hispanic-Americans, Native-Americans, and African-Americans together, treating all as similar minorities? The majority suggests that Seattle's classification system could permit a school to be labeled 'diverse' with a 50% Asian-American and 50% white student body, and no African-American students, Hispanic students, or students of other ethnicity.

"The 50/50 hypothetical has no support in the record here; it is conjured from the imagination. In fact, Seattle apparently began to treat these different minority groups alike in response to the federal Emergency School Aid Act's requirement that it do so. Moreover, maintaining this federally mandated system of classification makes sense insofar as Seattle's experience indicates that the relevant circumstances in respect to each of these different minority groups are roughly similar, *e.g.,* in terms of residential patterns, and call for roughly similar responses. This is confirmed by the fact that Seattle has been able to achieve a desirable degree of diversity without the *greater* emphasis on race that drawing fine lines among minority groups would require. Does the plurality's view of the Equal Protection Clause mean that courts must give no weight to such a board determination? Does it insist upon especially strong evidence supporting inclusion of multiple minority groups in an otherwise lawful government minority-assistance program? If so, its interpretation threatens to produce divisiveness among minority groups that is incompatible with the basic objectives of the Fourteenth Amendment. Regardless, the plurality cannot object that the constitutional defect is the individualized use of race and simultaneously object that not enough account of individuals' race has been taken."

3. *What is the Holding of the Seattle and Louisville Cases?* Because Justice Kennedy's vote is needed to create a majority *judgment* for the Court and because his opinion would allow greater use of race-based criteria, the *holding* of these cases would appear no broader than would be allowed by his opinion. Under this criterion, strict scrutiny applies to all race-based classifications. What state interests are "compelling," aside from remediation and (possibly) diversity? What kind of evidence must the district produce to show narrow tailoring?

4. *Theories of Judicial Review.* Can the striking down of the chosen policies of democratically elected school boards here be justified by any theory of judicial review? Consider factors discussed in Chapter 2, *supra*:

(a) *Original Meaning.* In passages we have omitted, the Chief Justice makes some appeal to the Constitution's original meaning, but Justice Breyer responds that the Reconstruction Congress itself engaged in race-conscious programs to assist people of color after the Civil War. Justice Thomas, in the concurring opinion we have omitted, responds:

> What the dissent fails to understand, however, is that the color-blind Constitution does not bar the government from taking measures to remedy past state-sponsored discrimination — indeed, it requires that such measures be taken in certain circumstances. Race-based government measures during the 1860's and 1870's to remedy *state-enforced slavery* were therefore not inconsistent with the color-blind Constitution.

Note, however, that the Reconstruction statutes were usually not narrowly tailored, that is, limited to former slaves alone; any person of color could take advantage of their largesse.

Is there a better way to make an original meaning argument for the Court's result? The plurality Justices, especially Justices Thomas (who writes a strong colorblindness concurring opinion) and Scalia (who in *Adarand* made a similar point), believe that the Constitution as a coherent document lends support to Justice Harlan's famous *Plessy* dissent, which is a leading cite for color-blindness. See if you can construct such an argument from the Constitution, as it was changed by the Reconstruction (and perhaps other amendments).

(b) *Representation-Reinforcement.* Representation-reinforcement theories have generally supported the Breyer position in cases such as this one. Professor Ely was openly critical of judicial invalidation when the state was deploying race for remedial or other problem-solving "benign" reasons. Justice Stevens made this kind of argument in his *Adarand* dissent as well.

One possible argument for the Court along these lines is the pluralism argument originally suggested by Professors Bickel and Kurland in the *DeFunis* case (p. 253, *supra*). Bickel and Kurland argued that "benign" affirmative action would stigmatize racial minorities and create animosities against them — contributing to social anxieties and political polarization. Justices Scalia and Thomas seemed persuaded by this kind of point in earlier cases, such as *Adarand*. Indeed, left academics are now making a similar point. Arguing from the social constructionist philosophy of Michel Foucault, Professor Richard Ford argues that when the state creates race-based categories, it is perpetuating and intensifying a discourse of racial line-drawing that has the effect of socially hard-wiring race into American culture, often to the disadvantage of "racial" minorities. *See* Ford, *Racial Culture: A Critique* (2005). Although Ford supports affirmative action and is probably sympathetic to Breyer's arguments in the Seattle and Louisville School Cases, his theory provides a postmodern edge to the Bickel and Kurland argument.

(c) *Pragmatism*. Justice Breyer does not have a monopoly on pragmatic arguments. Although Justice Thomas's position is based upon the color-blindness principle of *Plessy*'s dissent and original meaning (as he understands it), he responded at some length to Justice Breyer's pragmatic points in the Seattle and Louisville School Cases.

According to Justice Thomas, there is no hard, rigorous empirical evidence that racial integration in schools *causes* populations to achieve greater understanding or attain better educations. Thus, even according to one of Breyer's main sources, "the main reason white and minority students perform better academically in majority white schools is likely that these schools provide greater opportunities to learn. In other words, it is not desegregation per se that improves achievement, but rather the learning advantages some desegregated schools provide." Hallinan, *Diversity Effects on Student Outcomes: Social Science Evidence*, 59 Ohio St. L.J. 733, 744 (1998). Conversely, students of color often achieve *better* educations in segregated environments. Indeed, Seattle maintains a school aimed at black students (99% of the student body, by design), for that very reason.

Justice Thomas sharply disputes Justice Breyer's argument that integrated education will contribute to greater racial harmony in society and politics. First, he points out that there is little evidence of a causal link between school integration and harmony. Although many social scientists believe there is a link, others do not:

> Some studies have even found that a deterioration in racial attitudes seems to result from racial mixing in schools. See N. St. John, School Desegregation Outcomes for Children 67-68 (1975) ("A glance at [the data] shows that for either race positive findings are less common than negative findings"); Stephan, The Effects of School Desegregation: An Evaluation 30 Years After Brown, in Advances in Applied Social Psychology 183-186 (M. Saks & L. Saxe eds.1986).

Third, Thomas points out that even when students of different races attend the same schools, they are often educationally and socially resegregated within the schools.

5. *The Legacy of* Brown: *Chief Justice Roberts and Justice Breyer*. As our excerpt indicates, Chief Justice Roberts claimed that his opinion was true to the legacy of *Brown*, but so did Justice Breyer in dissent. For Breyer, *Brown* was "this Court's finest hour," which "held out a promise . . . of true racial equality — not as a matter of fine words on paper, but as a matter of everyday life in the Nation's cities and schools." He applauded the racial progress in the 50 years since *Brown* and deplored the majority's holding taking from school districts "the instruments they have used to rid their schools of racial segregation,

instruments that they believe are needed to overcome the problems of cities divided by race and poverty."[n]

Without unduly stressing the point, it could be suggested that these widely different invocations of *Brown* are evidence that people tend to rewrite history to suit their own fundamental commitments, that such rewriting is especially keen to appropriate and reinterpret canonical texts (*Brown* as much as the Constitution) to celebrate and cement one's own vision for America, and that those canonical texts are susceptible to such interpretive appropriations and revisions. Indeed, one of the features, shared by *Brown* and the Constitution, that enables a text to *become* canonical is its articulation of a simple but powerful principle at a level of generality that defies easy cabining.

6. *The Legacy of Brown: Justice Thomas.* In this process of claiming the legacy of *Brown*, Justice Thomas's concurring opinion makes a distinctive contribution. Part III of his opinion lays out the ways in which the arguments made by the Seattle and Jefferson County school districts and Justice Breyer may echo the arguments made by the *de jure* segregated school districts in South Carolina and Virginia more than 50 years ago in *Brown*:[o]

- Justice Breyer says that "[e]ach plan embodies the results of local experience and community consultation," the same appeal to local practice and mores made by the segregationists;

- "weight [must be given] to a local school board's knowledge, expertise, and concerns," the same appeal that the segregationists made for deference to the expertise of elected school boards;

- the Court's decision "threatens to substitute for present calm a disruptive round of race-related litigation" and "risks serious harm to the law and for the Nation," echoes of the segregationists' claims that desegregation would generate violence and turmoil in the South;

- Justice Breyer wraps his dissent in many older precedents and complains that the majority has abandoned them for newer ones, the same charge made by the segregationists in 1952-55;

- states using race-based criteria for good goals and with benign motives should not be judged harshly, the same attitude taken by the segregationists, who saw themselves as benignly inspired and even protective of minority interests; and

---

n. For discussion of such diverse, competing, and common invocations of *Brown* as involving either a principle of racial antisubordination (Justice Breyer's position) or a principle forbidding racial classification (Chief Justice Roberts' position), see, e.g., Goodwin Liu, *"History Will Be Heard": An Appraisal of the* Seattle/Louisville *Decision*, 2 Harv. Law & Policy Rev. ___ (2008) (forthcoming); Reva Siegel, *Equality Talk: Antisubordination and Anticlassification Values in Constitutional Struggles over* Brown, 117 Harv. L. Rev. 1470 (2004).

o. All of the quotations are from Justice Breyer's dissent, until the last one, which is from Justice Thomas's opinion. Each parallel for the segregationists' arguments in 1952-55 is massively supported by references to the *Brown I* and *Brown II* briefs and arguments.

- "just as the dissent argues that the need for these programs will lessen over time, the segregationists claimed that reliance on segregation was lessening and might eventually end."

"What was wrong in 1954 cannot be right today," concluded Justice Thomas. Is there a good answer to him?[p]

PROBLEMS ON REDUCING RACIAL ISOLATION IN PUBLIC SCHOOLS

Apply the Seattle and Louisville cases to the following circumstances:

Problem 3-7. School district is completely segregated by race (all "non-white" schools have 0% whites, all "white" schools have 0% nonwhites) and adopts a plan allowing "integrative" transfers, i.e., only those breaking down segregated patterns. (This example is similar to the plan Seattle adopted in 1963, in response to complaints from the NAACP.)

Problem 3-8. School district faces substantial racial segregation (most children are in 80% segregated schools) and adopts a plan that places children in schools based upon a balance for each child, including where she lives, where her sibling(s) are in school, specialized educational opportunities available at magnet schools, and the pupil's own race (race being a plus when diluting segregated patterns). (The example is similar to the plan Seattle adopted in 1998, but adapted to be more like the balance-of-factors approach the Court approved in *Grutter*.)

Problem 3-9. School district faces substantial racial segregation (most children are in 80% segregated schools) and adopts a plan that creates new schools and populates those schools by a selective admissions process that considers students' race and aims at a balance in the new schools reflecting the racial population of the city. (The example bears some similarities to the plan Seattle adopted in the 1970s, in response to the NAACP's lawsuit against the school district.)

Would it make a difference if the district has been legally segregated before 1954, and that experts believe the current segregation can be traced to housing patterns, etc., created by that earlier regime? Note that the plurality Justices, and apparently also Justice Kennedy, are strongly resistant to Justice Breyer's criticism of the *de jure/de facto* distinction; rooted in the state action doctrine, the distinction strikes Breyer as fuzzy and indeterminate as applied to Seattle.

E. FACIALLY NEUTRAL CLASSIFICATIONS DESIGNED TO BENEFIT RACIAL MINORITIES

1. *Introduction*

---

p. For commentary on the Seattle and Louisville decisions, see, e.g., Heather Gerken, *Justice Kennedy and the Domains of Equal Protection*, 121 Harv. L. Rev. 104 (2007); James Ryan, *The Supreme Court and Voluntary Integration*, 121 Harv. L. Rev. 131 (2007); J. Harvie Wilkinson III, *The Seattle and Louisville School Cases: There Is No Other Way*, 121 Harv. L. Rev. 158 (2007).

In the affirmative action cases, the Supreme Court considered the governmental use of race to be highly suspicious. In this context of a *facial racial classification*, the Court rejected the idea that a desire to help minorities is legally distinct from a desire to harm whites.

Would the Court be equally suspicious of all *facially neutral* classifications attributable at least in part to racial considerations? *Washington v. Davis*, combined with *Adarand*'s "consistency" axiom, may suggest that all such facially neutral classifications trigger strict scrutiny because they are racial classifications in disguise. The question may be a good deal more complicated than that, however.

In *Davis* and similar cases, the statutory scheme had a disparate impact on minorities. Because the statute was facially neutral, *Brown* and its progeny did not require applying strict scrutiny. *Davis* held that this discriminatory impact creates no serious constitutional problem unless the government adopted the law at least in part out of a desire to achieve those effects; "selective racial indifference" is not enough to state a claim. Thus, the practical harm caused by the statute (in *Davis*, failure to get a government job) must be linked to another kind of injury to be actionable. Why such racial motivation is the right kind of extra harm is left unclear in *Davis*.

One explanation is that *Davis* adopts an intentional-tort model: Injury is not actionable unless the actor intended it to occur. Thus, the government's negligence or selective racial indifference — *i.e.*, failure to focus upon and avoid foreseeable racially discriminatory effects through reasonable steps — provides no basis for relief. This *mens rea* requirement may be supportable in many ways, but we will identify two that seem particularly relevant here.

First, perhaps the injury should not legally "count" as racial unless there is a realization that the government intended it to happen. This explanation links *Davis* to the *Brown* tradition through the requirement of "stigma." *Brown* suggested that the problem with "separate but equal" school segregation was stigma — the "brand of inferiority" that it placed upon even those African-American children receiving an otherwise allegedly equal education. School segregation sent a message of the inferiority of African-American children, even of the antipathy of white society toward them. The presence of *Davis* intent surrounding the adoption of a government employment test signals similar antipathy or stereotypes of inferiority, causing stigma to the excluded individual and assaulting her dignity. When no *Davis* intent is shown, the injury hurts less and is just one of those disappointments that must be borne in a complex society.

This conclusion about the "individuation" of the cause of action in *Davis*, whereby group effects are beside the point (except where they are so dramatic as to suggest wrongful intent) and individual disappointment must be linked with individual psychological harm, is suggested by a passage in *Davis* (reprinted earlier in this chapter). After noting that no one has a constitutional claim just because she fails the employment test, the Court continued:

> The conclusion would not be different in the face of proof that more Negroes than whites had been disqualified by Test 21. That other Negroes also failed to score

well would, alone, not demonstrate that respondents individually were being denied equal protection of the laws by the application of an otherwise valid qualifying test being administered to prospective police recruits.

Although this passage leaves obscure exactly why illicit intent would demonstrate an equal protection violation, it does suggest that there must be some harm to the individual beyond the loss of the job. One understanding of that additional injury is a requirement of dignitary harm.

Second, from the perspective of the government, the *Davis* approach avoids imposing limitations upon governmental decisionmaking that may be unrealistic. The government often finds itself in "zero sum" situations where helping one group disadvantages another. Scarce resources prevent the government from addressing all social problems. Moreover, the government has an interest in expeditious decisionmaking. Holding the government responsible for "negligent failure to take reasonable steps to avoid racially discriminatory effects" could seriously intrude upon these interests, perhaps to the point of suggesting separation of powers concerns about courts invading the legislative domain. Moreover, the "negligent failure" theory would place in constitutional jeopardy all sorts of government actions. This political-process and "slippery slope" defense of *Davis* also resonates well with footnote 14 in the case and the paragraph to which it is attached.

This reading of *Davis* is in tension with *Croson* (and with its federal offspring, *Adarand*). The Court in *Croson* did not inquire whether the minority set-aside program caused dignitary harm to the white contractors. Moreover, the Court seemed troubled by the appearance of "selective racial indifference" on the part of the Richmond city council.

One could maintain both *Davis* and *Croson* by drawing a bright line between them. When a facial racial classification is used, a "red flag" goes up, concerns about stigma vanish, and strict scrutiny is invoked. In contrast, when the classification is facially neutral, the plaintiff must show both practical injury (failure to get a government job) and dignitary harm. Would it make sense to draw this bright line? Consider an example.

Assume that a city council is considering two bills appropriating funds for a job-training program. One would define the qualifications for spots in the program to assist the retraining of skilled workers who have lost their jobs. The majority of skilled workers are unionized, and thus labor unions are promoting the bill. The majority of skilled workers are also white, but many minorities would benefit from it as well. The second bill would use economic status to define the qualifications for getting into the program; only the very poor would qualify. This bill is being promoted by a variety of community groups, including the African-American Alliance, which is concerned about the disproportionate poverty and unemployment of African Americans.

If the city council adopts the first bill and an African American who cannot qualify for its benefits brings suit, a straightforward application of *Davis* would result in the denial of relief. The plaintiff could not show that the city council adopted the bill at least in part because of a desire disproportionately to exclude African Americans from its coverage. The city council will defend itself by noting that the ordinance is facially neutral and was adopted for bona fide reasons. All African Americans who are skilled workers may enjoy the benefits of the bill, and the thought never entered anyone's mind that it was a way to engage in hateful racial exclusion. "We weren't trying to hurt anyone, just trying to help skilled, unemployed people."

If the city council adopts the second bill and an unemployed, skilled worker who is white and above the poverty line (because of spousal income, for example) brings suit, a similarly straightforward application of *Davis* should result in the denial of relief as well. Again, the classification is facially neutral (all people defined as "poor" qualify, which includes many whites), and the city council did not adopt this ordinance because of antipathy toward whites or stereotypes about their inferiority.

These are hardly controversial examples. But the reasons that real-world analogues to them are not controversial may be subtle. We will suggest two. First, even a facially neutral classification that disproportionately benefits racial minorities usually benefits a greater absolute number of whites. When Congress adopts a statute benefitting the poor, the statute may well disproportionately benefit racial minorities (because they are disproportionately poor), but in absolute terms a greater number of whites than minorities are benefitted (because there are also lots of poor whites, and so many more whites than minorities generally). Thus, upon cursory examination, the statute does not resemble a racial preference at all.

Second, and relatedly, when legislators adopt such a statute, it is easy to view them as being motivated by a desire to help a class of people not defined by race (the poor), and not being motivated by a desire to harm anyone. True, the money allocated to this project is unavailable for competing proposals to help the non-poor; true, the bill disproportionately helps racial minorities, who may have lobbied for it on that basis. The legislature's action, however, seems benevolent — "benign" toward all and rooted in antipathy or visions of inferiority toward none, including those who are not benefitted by the statute and perhaps even lobbied against it in favor of proposals that would have helped them.

Both of these reasons why a facially neutral statute infrequently generates hostility from the general community are easy to destroy, however. In some situations, at least, it is possible to craft the legislation in a way that helps a larger aggregate number of minorities than whites. Imagine a state law school establishing a minimum quota (subject to some grade point average and LSAT requirements) for graduates of "inner city public high schools," defined as those located in the fifteen or twenty largest cities in the United States. If a law school did that, would its intent still be viewed as "benign," desiring only to help a certain class not defined by race? (Note that many whites would benefit from this classification as well.) If your intuitions about constitutionality change when the comparative number of beneficiaries according to racial makeup is flipped, why?

All of this becomes more complicated when it is recognized that, at least sometimes, government cannot avoid considering racial impact. When the city council in the hypothetical above chooses between the union-promoted bill and the bill designed to help the poor, its members not only know the racially differential effects of the choice, that racial impact has been thrust upon them by lobbyists as well. "Help our people," say the lobbyists for the African-American community. Is that somehow an illicit lobbying campaign? (If you think so, you might want to peek ahead to Chapter 6, on the First Amendment.) If a councilmember votes that way, does the councilmember have the kind of illicit motivation condemned by *Davis*? Or may she say, "I was simply trying to help one part of the community, and the bill helps lots of other kinds of people as well"? Should it matter whether the councilmember votes that way for political reasons (to pick up minority votes for reelection) or for high-minded reasons of promoting social progress?

2. *The Context of Electoral Redistricting*

Probably the starkest context in which elected officials simply cannot avoid racial considerations is electoral redistricting. As explained in Chapter 5, § 3A, the Constitution requires state legislatures and the federal House of Representatives to be reapportioned on a "one person, one vote" basis following each decennial census. The state legislature reapportions itself as well as the state's federal congressional districts. Reapportionment is an intensely political affair in which the majority party tries to maximize its influence, the minority party fights back, and incumbents of both parties hope for district configurations favorable for reelection.

In America, of course, the racial composition of an area affects its politics. Thus, a reapportionment involves racial considerations. Moreover, racial minorities may argue that some "majority-minority" districts (*e.g.*, ones with a majority of African Americans) be created, because otherwise in the presence of racial bloc voting by both whites and African Americans the latter can neither elect a candidate of their choice nor hope for much responsiveness from the white candidate who is elected.

In areas covered by the Voting Rights Act, legislative consideration of race in the reapportionment context becomes even more inevitable. The original Act covers jurisdictions that had low voter turnout and a "test or device" as a prerequisite to voting. (See Chapter 7, § 3B.) Large portions of the South remain covered by the Act. In such a jurisdiction, any change in voting structure, like a reapportionment, may not take effect without federal "preclearance" under § 5 of the Act — that is, the approval of either the federal Justice Department or the federal District Court for the District of Columbia based on a finding that the change has neither the purpose nor the effect of diminishing minority voting strength. Since 1982, § 2 of the Act has provided an independent, nationwide prohibition on electoral structures that "result" in the dilution of the minority vote. Thus, a jurisdiction covered by the Act must reapportion in a way that does not diminish minority political power from the pre-existing baseline (§ 5) and does not result in minority political power being manifestly lower than it could be under other districting (§ 2). Even if inevitable, however, this consideration of race is not necessarily immune from constitutional scrutiny. Complicating the doctrinal question is the fact that a reapportionment is facially neutral: The statute drawing district lines says nothing about race on its face.

It is in the context of electoral redistricting, and only in that context, that the Court has addressed (and sometimes invalidated) a facially neutral scheme adopted for the purpose of benefitting racial minorities. The principal case follows.

Shaw v. Reno, 509 U.S. 630 (1993). The North Carolina General Assembly's reapportionment of the state's twelve seats in the federal House of Representatives based on the 1990 census included one majority-black congressional district. After the federal Attorney General objected to the plan pursuant to § 5 of the Voting Rights Act, the General Assembly revised the plan and created a second majority-black district. "The first of the two majority-black districts contained in the revised plan, District 1, is somewhat hook shaped. Centered in the northeast portion of the State, it moves southward until it tapers to a narrow band; then, with finger-like extensions, it reaches far into the southern-most part of the State near the South Carolina border. District 1 has been compared to a 'Rorschach ink-blot test' and a 'bug splattered on a windshield.'

"The second majority-black district, District 12, is even more unusually shaped. It is approximately 160 miles long and, for much of its length, no wider than the I-85 corridor. It winds in snake-like fashion through tobacco country, financial centers, and manufacturing areas 'until it gobbles in enough enclaves of black neighborhoods.' *** Northbound and southbound drivers on I-85 sometimes find themselves in separate districts in one county, only to 'trade' districts when they enter the next county. Of the 10 counties through which District 12 passes, five are cut into three different districts; even towns are divided. At one point the district remains contiguous only because it intersects at a single point with two other districts before crossing over them."

The majority opinion of **Justice O'Connor** held that strict scrutiny applied to this redistricting. She upheld as constitutionally cognizable the plaintiffs' complaint "that the deliberate segregation of voters into separate districts on the basis of race violated their constitutional right to participate in a 'color-blind' electoral process. * * * What appellants object to is redistricting legislation that is so extremely irregular on its face that it rationally can be viewed only as an effort to segregate the races for purposes of voting, without regard for traditional districting principles and without sufficiently compelling justification. * * *

"[W]e believe that reapportionment is one area in which appearances do matter. A reapportionment plan that includes in one district individuals who belong to the same race, but who are otherwise widely separated by geographical and political boundaries, and who may have little in common with one another but the color of their skin, bears an uncomfortable resemblance to political apartheid. It reinforces the perception that members of the same racial group — regardless of their age, education, economic status, or the community in which they live — think alike, share the same political interests, and will prefer the same candidates at the polls. We have rejected such perceptions elsewhere as impermissible racial stereotypes. By perpetuating such notions, a racial gerrymander may exacerbate the very patterns of racial bloc voting that majority-minority districting is sometimes said to counteract.

"The message that such districting sends to elected representatives is equally pernicious. When a district obviously is created solely to effectuate the perceived common interests of one racial group, elected officials are more likely to believe that their primary obligation is to represent only the members of that group, rather than their constituency as a whole. This is altogether antithetical to our system of representative democracy. * * *

"The state appellees suggest that a covered jurisdiction may have a compelling interest in creating majority-minority districts in order to comply with the Voting Rights Act." Justice O'Connor acknowledged that § 5 of the Voting Rights Act forbade preclearance of a reapportionment "if it will lead to 'a retrogression in the position of racial minorities with respect to their effective exercise of the electoral franchise.' " She cautioned, however, against reading the Court's "§ 5 cases to give covered jurisdictions *carte blanche* to engage in racial gerrymandering in the name of nonretrogression. A reapportionment plan would not be narrowly tailored to the goal of avoiding retrogression if the State went beyond what was reasonably necessary to avoid retrogression." She noted that on remand the state could attempt to prove that the plan was necessary to "avoid dilution of black voting strength in violation of § 2."

"The state appellees alternatively argue that the General Assembly's plan advanced a [different] compelling interest. * * * We previously have recognized a significant state interest in eradicating the effects of past racial discrimination. But the State must have a 'strong basis in evidence for [concluding] that remedial action [is] necessary.' *Croson.*" The Court remanded for consideration of the state's defenses.

Justices White, **Blackmun**, **Stevens**, and **Souter** dissented. For them, it blinked reality to think that a redistricting could be done without race being considered. Redistricting is inherently partisan, with politically salient factors such as race inevitably taken into account. In addition, the plaintiffs had not demonstrated any cognizable harm from the redistricting (everyone in the district had the same right to vote, for example). Moreover, Justice White explained, "[w]hites constitute roughly 76 percent of the total population and 79 percent of the voting age population in North Carolina. Yet, under the State's plan, they still constitute a voting majority in 10 (or 83 percent) of the 12 congressional districts. Though they might be dissatisfied at the prospect of casting a vote for a losing candidate — a lot shared by many, including a disproportionate number of minority voters — surely they cannot complain of discriminatory treatment."

Justice Souter maintained that, "[u]nlike other contexts in which we have addressed the State's conscious use of race, see, *e.g.*, *Croson* (city contracting); *Wygant* (teacher layoffs), electoral districting calls for decisions that nearly always require some consideration of race for legitimate reasons where there is a racially mixed population. As long as members of racial groups have the commonality of interest implicit in our ability to talk about concepts like "minority voting strength" and "dilution of minority votes," and as long as racial bloc voting takes place, legislators will have to take race into account in order to avoid dilution of minority voting strength in the districting plans they adopt. One need look no further than the Voting Rights Act to understand that this may be required * * * .

"A second distinction between districting and most other governmental decisions in which race has figured is that those other decisions using racial criteria characteristically occur in circumstances in which the use of race to the advantage of one person is necessarily at the obvious expense of a member of a different race. Thus, for example, awarding government contracts on a racial basis excludes certain firms from competition on racial grounds. See *Croson.* * * *

"In districting, by contrast, the mere placement of an individual in one district instead of another denies no one a right or benefit provided to others. All citizens may register, vote, and be represented. In whatever district, the individual voter has a right to vote in each election, and the election will result in the voter's representation. As we have held, one's constitutional rights are not violated merely because the candidate one supports loses the election or because a group (including a racial group) to which one belongs winds up with a representative from outside that group. It is true, of course, that one's vote may be more or less effective depending on the interests of the other individuals who are in one's district, and our cases recognize the reality that members of the same race often have shared interests. 'Dilution' thus refers to the effects of districting decisions not on an individual's political power viewed in isolation, but on the political power of a group. * * *

"Our different approaches to equal protection in electoral districting and nondistricting cases reflect these differences. There is a characteristic coincidence of disadvantageous effect and illegitimate purpose associated with the State's use of race in those situations in which it has immediately triggered at least heightened scrutiny (which every Member of the Court to address the issue has agreed must be applied even to race-based classifications designed to serve some permissible state interest). Presumably because the legitimate consideration of race in a districting decision is usually inevitable under the Voting Rights Act when communities are racially mixed, however, and because, without more, it does not result in diminished political effectiveness for anyone, we have not taken the approach of applying the usual standard of such heightened 'scrutiny' to race-based districting decisions."

––––––––––

Limitations of length preclude our full exploration of the cases following *Shaw v. Reno.*[q] For present purposes, it should suffice to note the following:

––

q. *Shaw* has generated an enormous scholarly literature. For a sample, see Alexander Aleinikoff & Samuel Isaacharoff, *Race and Redistricting: Drawing Constitutional Lines After* Shaw v. Reno, 92 Mich. L. Rev. 588 (1993); Heather Gerken, *Understanding The Right to an Undiluted Vote*, 114 Harv. L. Rev. 1663 (2001); Pamela Karlan, *Easing the Spring: Strict Scrutiny and Affirmative Action After the Redistricting Cases*, 43 Wm. & Mary L. Rev. 1569 (2002); Richard Pildes & Richard Niemi, *Expressive Harms, "Bizarre Districts," and Voting Rights: Evaluating Election-*

- *The nature of the harm.* Justice O'Connor, in her plurality opinion in *Bush v. Vera*, 517 U.S. 952 (1996), wrote that some majority-minority districts "cause constitutional harm insofar as they convey the message that political identity is, or should be, predominantly racial." She labeled this an "expressive harm," which Justice Souter, in dissent, defined as "one that 'results from the idea or attitudes expressed through a governmental action, rather than from the more tangible or material consequences the action brings about' " (quoting Pildes & Niemi, *supra* note *b*). Why is expressive harm, rather than more concrete harm, sufficient in this context to constitute a constitutional claim? Compare Professor Lawrence's argument (§ 1C of this chapter) for modifying the *Washington v. Davis* approach to bring within constitutional cognizance those governmental acts that send a racist message. If expressive harm counts in *Shaw*, should it count in the contexts identified by Professor Lawrence as well?

- *Bizarre shape?* In *Miller v. Johnson*, 515 U.S. 900 (1995), the majority held that "[s]hape is relevant not because bizarreness is a necessary element of the constitutional wrong or a threshold requirement of proof, but because it may be persuasive circumstantial evidence that race for its own sake, and not other districting principles, was the legislature's dominant and controlling rationale in drawing its district lines. The logical implication * * * is that parties may rely on evidence other than bizarreness to establish race-based districting."

- *Predominant motive.* Recall that under *Washington v. Davis*, racially discriminatory intent need not be the predominant motive; it is actionable if it is a substantial factor. But when it is recognized that racial considerations will play a role in any redistricting, the majority of Justices who support *Shaw v. Reno* limited its cause of action to situations of predominant motive. In *Miller*, the Court stated: "The plaintiff's burden is to show, either through circumstantial evidence of a district's shape and demographics or more direct evidence going to legislative purpose, that race was the predominant factor motivating the legislature's decision to place a significant number of voters within or without a particular district. To make this showing, a plaintiff must prove that the legislature subordinated traditional race-neutral districting principles, including but not limited to compactness, contiguity, respect for political subdivisions or communities defined by actual shared interests, to racial considerations. Where these or other race-neutral considerations are the basis for redistricting legislation, and are not subordinated to race, a state can 'defeat a claim that a district has been gerrymandered on racial lines.' " As one might imagine, the requirement of

---

District Appearances After Shaw v. Reno, 92 Mich. L. Rev. 483 (1993); Peter Rubin, *Reconnecting Doctrine and Purpose: A Comprehensive Approach to Strict Scrutiny After* Adarand *and* Shaw, 149 U. Pa. L. Rev. 1 (2000).

"predominant motive" has proved bedeviling in practice because of the close correlation of racial and political considerations in redistricting.[r]

PROBLEM: CUMULATIVE VOTING AS AN ALTERNATIVE

Problem 3-10. Any time single-member districts are used, some interests are advantaged and others harmed.[s] One way around this problem, for example, would be to elect all twelve North Carolina Congressmembers at large (*i.e.*, statewide) rather than from single-member districts. Article I of the Constitution would allow this, and there would be no "one person, one vote" problem. But in the context of racial bloc voting, this approach would ensure the election of twelve whites. Thus, any switch to this system would be disapproved by the Justice Department under § 5 of the Voting Rights Act. Minority voters in North Carolina would also have a cause of action against this switch under the Act.

If North Carolina wanted to adopt at-large elections, therefore, it would have to find some way to neutralize the racial impact. One way would be to use cumulative voting, in which each voter receives a number of votes equivalent to the number of seats being filled and may cast more than one vote for a particular candidate. Under this scheme, for example, a North Carolina voter might cast all twelve of her votes for one candidate, or six votes each for two candidates. Strategic use of cumulative voting by minority voters would ensure the election of at least one or two minority-preferred candidates. If, for the above reasons, North Carolina adopted at-large elections with cumulative voting, would there be a constitutional problem? What if it were clear that

---

r. Consider a later development in the North Carolina litigation. On later remand from *Shaw v. Reno*, the three-judge district court, with one dissent, struck down the districting on the ground that the motivation for it was primarily racial rather than political. Again the Supreme Court granted review. In *Easley v. Cromartie*, 532 U.S. 234 (2001), Justice O'Connor broke ranks with the four Justices routinely objecting to North Carolina's practices. This time, she joined the majority opinion of Justice Breyer, which set aside the district court's conclusion as clearly erroneous. The five-member majority concluded that plaintiffs had not carried their burden of showing that the North Carolina legislature had drawn the district primarily to promote racial balancing rather than primarily to serve the interests of the Democratic Party. Because African Americans in North Carolina who are registered Democrats are much less likely to cross over and vote for Republicans than other North Carolinians who are registered Democrats, the legislature's tendency to create Democratic districts by locating African Americans in them was not necessarily a decision that was motivated predominantly by race rather than by politics. The majority summarized its holding this way: "In a case such as this one where majority-minority districts (or the approximate equivalent) are at issue and where racial identification correlates highly with political affiliation, the party attacking the legislatively drawn boundaries must show at the least that the legislature could have achieved its legitimate political objectives in alternative ways that are comparably consistent with traditional districting principles. That party must also show that those districting alternatives would have brought about significantly greater racial balance. Appellees failed to make any such showing here." Justice Thomas, joined by Chief Justice Rehnquist, Justice Scalia, and Justice Kennedy, dissented, on the ground that the district court's findings of fact were not clearly erroneous.

s. See, e.g., Lani Guinier, *The Tyranny of the Majority: Fundamental Fairness in Representative Democracy* (1994).

cumulative voting had been adopted to ensure African-American representation in the state's congressional delegation?

3. *Extending Strict Scrutiny for Facially Neutral Classifications Designed to Benefit Racial Minorities Beyond the Redistricting Setting?*

As noted, *Shaw* has been applied only in the redistricting setting. Consider how the decision might be deployed to attack the following hypothetical state programs, which involve facially neutral classifications adopted at least in part to open doors to historically disadvantaged persons of color. How should the state defend the programs?

PROBLEMS ON FACIALLY NEUTRAL UNIVERSITY ADMISSIONS PROGRAMS DESIGNED TO BENEFIT RACIAL MINORITIES

Problem 3-11. *The "10% Solution."* May a state university, fearful that diversity admissions in which race is taken into account as a plus factor may be unconstitutional, adopt a program under which undergraduate admission is guaranteed to any student in the state who graduates in the top 10% of her high school class? Should it matter if the reason why this method was chosen is that it will make admission possible for more students of color? See, e.g., Michelle Adams, *Isn't It Ironic? The Central Paradox at the Heart of "Percentage Plans,"* 62 Ohio St. L.J. 1729 (2001); Brian Fitzpatrick, *Strict Scrutiny of Facially Race-Neutral State Action and the Texas Ten Percent Plan*, 53 Baylor L. Rev. 289 (2001).

Problem 3-12. *Affirmative Action Based on Low Socioeconomic Status.* Suppose in the aftermath of *Gratz* that the University of Michigan gave an automatic 20 points in the admission calculus not to persons on the basis of race, but on the basis of very low socioeconomic status. Assuming this was motivated at least in large part to increase the enrollment of persons of color, should the approach be subject to strict scrutiny? See, e.g., Richard Fallon, *Affirmative Action Based on Economic Disadvantage*, 43 UCLA L. Rev. 1913 (1996); Kim Forde-Mazrui, *The Constitutional Implications of Race-Neutral Affirmative Action*, 88 Geo. L.J. 2331 (2000).

F. A CONCLUDING THOUGHT: GROUP RIGHTS, APOLOGY, AND REPARATIONS

In the material on affirmative action and majority-minority districting, it is clear that the Supreme Court has understood the Equal Protection Clause as creating individual rather than group rights. This doctrinal understanding has obviously undercut efforts to promote justice for racial groups:

> Strong biases exist in American law against concepts of group rights. Rights are seen as belonging to individuals, not groups or communities. This individualistic approach cannot be lightly set aside without doing violence to much of American constitutional doctrine, doctrine that has been painfully achieved over the course of two centuries. And yet, a too rigid adherence to this individualistic model will leave American government and society with

little ability to deal with the cultural devastation that has occurred in America's inner cities. Courts presented with this question seem to have the Hobson's choice of either permitting what appears to be an assault on the concept of individual rights or precluding measures that can break down long-term cycles of exclusion.[t]

Nonetheless, in a few instances Congress has recognized past injustice, formally or informally apologized for it, and sometimes provided reparations. As mentioned at the beginning of this chapter, in 1988 Congress apologized for the relocation and internment program of Japanese Americans during World War II and awarding $20,000 to each surviving internee. Earlier, in 1946, Congress adopted the Indian Claims Commission Act, ch. 959, 60 Stat. 1049, which waived the sovereign immunity of the United States and provided that historical wrongs against Indian tribes could be brought before a claims commission, which had jurisdiction to award damages. In 1993, Congress adopted a Joint Resolution apologizing for the actions of American citizens and government officials that resulted in the takeover of Hawaii by American interests a century before. See 107 Stat. 1510.

In recent years, a lively debate has ensued concerning apology and reparations for slavery and its aftermath. For an introduction to the subject that cites much of the relevant literature, see Note, *Bridging the Color Line: The Power of African-American Reparations To Redirect America's Future*, 115 Harv. L. Rev. 1689 (2002). Consider some of the many questions that arise from this inquiry. How should the class of beneficiaries be defined? What benefits should be provided? How would federal legislation of this sort mesh with the affirmative action and majority-minority districting cases? Cf. *Jacobs v. Barr*, 959 F.2d 313 (D.C. Cir.), *cert. denied*, 506 U.S. 831 (1992) (rejecting equal protection attack to Japanese American reparations plan brought by German American who had been detained during World War II). With continuing efforts to find ways to implement affirmative action despite these decisions?

---

t. Robert Cottrol, *A Tale of Two Cultures: Or Making the Proper Connections Between Law, Social History and the Political Economy of Despair*, 25 San Diego L. Rev. 989, 1021 (1988).

Chapter 4

SEX AND GENDER DISCRIMINATION AND OTHER EQUAL PROTECTION CONCERNS

In *The Slaughter-House Cases*, 83 U.S. (16 Wall.) 36 (1872), the first Supreme Court case to interpret the Fourteenth Amendment, the Court said that it "doubt[ed] very much whether any action of a state not directed by way of discrimination against the negroes as a class, or on account of their race, will ever be held to come within the purview of this provision." This prediction proved to be inaccurate, as the Court held discrimination against Chinese Americans to violate the Equal Protection Clause in *Yick Wo v. Hopkins*, 118 U.S. 356 (1886) (Chapter 3, § 1B), and suggested in *Strauder v. West Virginia*, 100 U.S. 303 (1879) (Chapter 2, § 1A) that national origin discrimination (against, for example, "Celtic Irishmen") would violate the clause. By the turn of the century, the Equal Protection Clause had been construed as a general protection against arbitrary classifications, requiring "some reasonable ground — some difference which bears a just and proper relation to the attempted classification." *Gulf, C. & S.F. Ry. v. Ellis*, 165 U.S. 150 (1897). Today, the clause is read in accord with its broad plain meaning — to apply to any state classification. As § 1 of this chapter indicates, however, the requirement of a "rational basis" for the state's line-drawing is an easy test for a statute to pass.

Race-based classifications, of course, trigger strict scrutiny (recall Chapter 3). An important question is when, if ever, something more stringent than rational-basis review should be applied to classifications other than race or national origin. A note at the end of § 1 of this chapter traces the Supreme Court's consideration of this issue for statutory discrimination along lines of alienage, illegitimacy, age, and wealth. The most important line of cases deals with discrimination based upon sex or gender (§ 2 of this chapter).[a] Recall that

---

a. In this chapter, two terms, "sex" and "gender," are used to describe discrimination between men and women. "Sex" refers to biological classifications as *man* and *woman*, and "gender" refers to characteristics associated with being a man (*masculine*) and a woman (*feminine*). For discussion and critique, see Mary Anne Case, *Disaggregating Gender from Sex and Sexual Orientation: The Effeminate Man in the Law and Feminist Jurisprudence*, 105 Yale L.J. 1 (1995); Richard Epstein, *Gender Is for Nouns*, 41 DePaul L. Rev. 981 (1992); Katherine Franke, *The Central Mistake of Sex Discrimination Law: The Disaggregation of Sex from Gender*, 144 U. Pa. L. Rev. 1 (1995).

African Americans earlier engaged in a constitutionalized politics of recognition that transformed the Equal Protection Clause by creating a higher standard for race as a "suspect classification" (Chapter 3, § 1A). The women's movement engaged in a similar constitutional campaign in the 1970s, seeking recognition of sex as another suspect classification.[b] Because the Framers of the Fourteenth Amendment did not intend to protect against sex classifications as they did for at least some racial classifications, one needs a different theory of equal protection to justify its expansion. Is there a special justification for subjecting sex or gender classifications to stricter scrutiny than the rational-basis test? If so, should such classifications be scrutinized as severely as classifications based upon race?

Other identity-based social movements, most notably the disability rights and gay liberation movements, sought similar equal protection scrutiny to sweep away hundreds of statutory discriminations. Section 3 of this chapter traces the Court's ambiguous response to these movements. Without subjecting either classification to strict scrutiny (like race) or intermediate scrutiny (like sex), the Supreme Court has on a few occasions invalidated disability and sexual orientation classifications under rational-basis review. This not only creates potential problems for the many disability and sexual orientation discriminations in American law, but raises the question whether the so-called "double standard" (rational basis = easy to pass; strict scrutiny = bound to fail) still holds in equal protection cases or is being (and should be) replaced by a sliding-scale approach such as that proposed by Thurgood Marshall, the greatest social movement lawyer of the last century.[c]

SECTION 1. MINIMAL EQUAL PROTECTION SCRUTINY (THE RATIONAL-BASIS TEST)

The Equal Protection Clause speaks in general language, protecting "any person" against the denial of "the equal protection of the laws." Just as equal protection has not been limited to race claims, so also it cannot practically require the state to treat all persons the same. People differ in many ways relevant to public policy. A sensible way to begin thinking about equal protection as a generalized requirement is to consider whether, as a federal constitutional matter, a state must treat *all similarly situated people similarly*.[d] For purposes of driving an automobile, the blind and the sighted are not similarly situated; people with blue eyes and people with brown eyes are.

---

b. The historical parallels are explored in Serena Mayeri, *Constitutional Choices: Legal Feminism and the Historical Dynamics of Change,* 92 Calif. L. Rev. 755 (2004).

c. Justice Marshall's most elaborate statement of this approach was in his dissent in *San Antonio Ind. School Dist. v. Rodriguez* (Chapter 5, § 3B), discussed in William Eskridge, Jr., *Some Effects of Identity-Based Social Movements on Constitutional Law in the Twentieth Century,* 100 Mich. L. Rev. 2062, 2269-79 (2002).

d. This understanding of the Equal Protection Clause (and the over- and underinclusion analysis in the next paragraph) was classically articulated in Joseph Tussman & Jacobus tenBroek, *The Equal Protection of the Laws,* 37 Calif. L. Rev. 341 (1949).

A state that wishes to prevent dangerous drivers from operating motor vehicles might start by requiring that all drivers have a certain level of visual acuity. Standing alone, this requirement is *underinclusive*: It would eliminate only one of a variety of kinds of dangerous drivers. At first glance, the problem of underinclusion may not seem important, for the person complaining about underinclusion has been properly identified as contributing to the problem the state is attempting to remedy. States ought to be able to pursue partial remedies rather than be compelled to take an all-or-nothing approach; reform may be taken "one step at a time." But if equal protection requires even a minimal degree of fairness in regulation, underinclusion can be troubling. Imagine that California must reduce auto emissions by 40%, and the state responds by revoking the licenses of all persons who make less than $15,000 a year. These persons were contributing to the air pollution problem — perhaps even disproportionally, if they tend to have older autos with less effective emissions controls — but picking out these people and forcing them to bear the full brunt of a general societal problem seems grossly unfair. These persons also are probably less politically powerful than the class of drivers left untouched by the remedy, which may heighten our concerns.

Overinclusion is the flip side of the equal protection coin. A statute that forbids a driver's license to someone with poor eyesight will probably keep off the road some drivers who can operate a vehicle safely despite their poor visual acuity, and if so the statute is overinclusive. If these persons could demand a driving test, they might well pass it. In some ways, we may be more sympathetic with the victims of overinclusive statutes than with the victims of underinclusive statutes, for the former are not even contributing to the problem the state is attempting to remedy. The state, however, has a legitimate interest in adopting regulatory approaches that are administratively convenient and cost effective; allowing anyone to demand a driver's test before a license could be denied would be inefficient and costly (and sometimes even dangerous).

Many of the cases involving arguments about underinclusion and overinclusion concern economic regulation. From the beginning of this century until the late 1930s, the Supreme Court took an activist posture in protecting economic interests from "unfair" regulation, pursuant to the Due Process Clause (the *Lochner* case, discussed in Chapter 1, § 4, and Chapter 5, § 2B). The Court treated the Due Process Clause's protection against a deprivation of (economic) "liberty" without due process of law as forbidding the government from regulating where the goal of the regulation was either deemed illegitimate or too minor compared to the importance of the liberty to the person being regulated. The person being regulated could and often did also make an equal protection challenge to the regulation based on underinclusion or overinclusion. For example, if the government decided to promote workplace health by forbidding bakers from working more than sixty hours each week, a bakery or its employees could argue that due process was violated because the goal (promoting employee health) was insufficient when weighed against the employer's and employee's interests in being free to choose how long the work week should be. Alternatively, they could argue that equal protection was violated because the statute was *underinclusive* (it did not limit the work week in other occupations such as mining or cotton-mill work, where long hours pose a greater threat to worker health than in the bakery trade) and *overinclusive* (most bakery workers could work more than sixty hours per week and suffer no discernible deterioration in health).

By the late 1930s, the Court had abandoned rigorous review of economic regulation under either the Due Process or Equal Protection Clauses. Indeed, one of the principal cases announcing the Court's new refusal to review such statutes vigorously was *Carolene Products*, in which Justice Stone inserted his famous footnote 4 containing dictum about a potential new judicial role: protecting "discrete and insular minorities" (Chapter 1, § 6; Chapter 2, § 3B). The next case demonstrates the general approach the Court has taken to equal protection review of economic regulation since the late 1930s.

RAILWAY EXPRESS AGENCY, INC. v. NEW YORK
336 U.S. 106, 69 S.Ct. 463, 93 L.Ed. 533 (1949)

JUSTICE DOUGLAS delivered the opinion of the Court.

Section 124 of the Traffic Regulations of the City of New York promulgated by the Police Commissioner provides: "No person shall operate, or cause to be operated, in or upon any street an advertising vehicle; provided that nothing herein contained shall prevent the putting of business notices upon business delivery vehicles, so long as such vehicles are engaged in the usual business or regular work of the owner and not used merely or mainly for advertising."

Appellant is engaged in a nation-wide express business. It operates about 1,900 trucks in New York City and sells the space on the exterior sides of these trucks for advertising. That advertising is for the most part unconnected with its own business. It was convicted in the magistrate's court and fined. The judgment of conviction was sustained in the Court of Special Sessions. The Court of Appeals affirmed without opinion by a divided vote. The case is here on appeal. * * *

The Court of Special Sessions concluded that advertising on vehicles using the streets of New York City constitutes a distraction to vehicle drivers and to pedestrians alike and therefore affects the safety of the public in the use of the streets. We do not sit to weigh evidence on the due process issue in order to determine whether the regulation is sound or appropriate; nor is it our function to pass judgment on its wisdom. We would be trespassing on one of the most intensely local and specialized of all municipal problems if we held that this regulation had no relation to the traffic problem of New York City. It is the judgment of the local authorities that it does have such a relation. And nothing has been advanced which shows that to be palpably false.

The question of equal protection of the laws is pressed more strenuously on us. It is pointed out that the regulation draws the line between advertisements of products sold by the owner of the truck and general advertisements. It is argued that unequal treatment on the basis of such a distinction is not justified by the aim and purpose of the regulation. It is said, for example, that one of appellant's trucks carrying the advertisement of a commercial house would not cause any greater distraction of pedestrians and vehicle drivers than if the commercial house carried the same advertisement on its own truck. Yet the regulation allows the latter to do what the former is forbidden from doing. It is therefore contended that the classification which the regulation makes has no relation to the traffic problem since a violation turns not on what kind of advertisements are carried on trucks but on whose trucks they are carried.

That, however, is a superficial way of analyzing the problem, even if we assume that it is premised on the correct construction of the regulation. The local authorities may well have concluded that those who advertised their own wares on their trucks do not present the same traffic problem in view of the nature or extent of the advertising which they use. It would take a degree of omniscience which we lack to say that such is not the case. If that judgment is correct, the advertising displays that are exempt have less incidence on traffic than those of appellants.

We cannot say that that judgment is not an allowable one. Yet if it is, the classification has relation to the purpose for which it is made and does not contain the kind of discrimination against which the Equal Protection Clause affords protection. It is by such practical considerations based on experience rather than by theoretical inconsistencies that the question of equal protection is to be answered. And the fact that New York City sees fit to eliminate from traffic this kind of distraction but does not touch what may be even greater ones in a different category, such as the vivid displays on Times Square, is immaterial. It is no requirement of equal protection that all evils of the same genus be eradicated or none at all.

JUSTICE RUTLEDGE acquiesces in the Court's opinion and judgment, *dubitante* on the question of equal protection of the laws.

JUSTICE JACKSON, concurring.

The burden should rest heavily upon one who would persuade us to use the due process clause to strike down a substantive law or ordinance. Even its provident use against municipal regulations frequently disables all government — state, municipal and federal — from dealing with the conduct in question because the requirement of due process is also applicable to State and Federal Governments. Invalidation of a statute or an ordinance on due process grounds leaves ungoverned and ungovernable conduct which many people find objectionable.

Invocation of the equal protection clause, on the other hand, does not disable any governmental body from dealing with the subject at hand. It merely means that the prohibition or regulation must have a broader impact. I regard it as a salutary doctrine that cities, states and the Federal Government must exercise their powers so as not to discriminate between their inhabitants except upon some reasonable differentiation fairly related to the object of regulation. This equality is not merely abstract justice. The framers of the Constitution knew, and we should not forget today, that there is no more effective practical guaranty against arbitrary and unreasonable government than to require that the principles of law which officials would impose upon a minority must be imposed generally. Conversely, nothing opens the door to arbitrary action so effectively as to allow those officials to pick and choose only a few to whom they will apply legislation and thus to escape the political retribution that might be visited upon them if larger numbers were affected. Courts can take no better measure to assure that laws will be just than to require that laws be equal in operation.

This case affords an illustration. Even casual observations from the sidewalks of New York will show that an ordinance which would forbid all advertising on vehicles would run into conflict with many interests, including some, if not all, of the great metropolitan newspapers, which use that advertising extensively. Their blandishment of the latest sensations is not less a cause of diverted attention and traffic hazard than the commonplace cigarette advertisement which this truck-owner is forbidden to display. But any regulation applicable to all such advertising would require much clearer justification in local conditions to enable its enactment than does some regulation applicable to a few. I do not mention this to criticize the motives of those who enacted this ordinance, but it dramatizes the point that we are much more likely to find arbitrariness in the regulation of the few than of the many. Hence, for my part, I am more receptive to attack on local ordinances for denial of equal protection than for denial of due process, while the Court has more often used the latter clause.

In this case, if the City of New York should assume that display of any advertising on vehicles tends and intends to distract the attention of persons using the highways and to increase the dangers of its traffic, I should think it fully within its constitutional powers to forbid it all. The same would be true if the City should undertake to eliminate or minimize the hazard by any generally applicable restraint, such as limiting the size, color, shape or perhaps to some extent the contents of vehicular advertising. Instead of such general regulation of advertising, however, the City seeks to reduce the hazard only by saying that while some may, others may not exhibit such appeals. The same display, for example, advertising cigarettes, which this appellant is forbidden to carry on its trucks, may be carried on the trucks of a cigarette dealer and might on the trucks of this appellant if it dealt in cigarettes. And almost an identical advertisement, certainly one of equal size, shape, color and appearance, may be carried by this appellant if it proclaims its own offer to transport cigarettes. But it may not be carried so long as the message is not its own but a cigarette dealer's offer to sell the same cigarettes. * * *

The question in my mind comes to this. Where individuals contribute to an evil or danger in the same way and to the same degree, may those who do so for hire be prohibited, while those who do so for their own commercial ends but not for hire be allowed to continue? I think the answer has to be that the hireling may be put in a class by himself and may be dealt with differently than those who act on their own. But this is not merely because such a discrimination will enable the lawmaker to diminish the evil. That might be done by many classifications, which I should think wholly unsustainable. It is rather because there is a real difference between doing in self-interest and doing for hire, so that it is one thing to tolerate action from those who act on their own and it is another thing to permit the same action to be promoted for a price.

NOTES ON *RAILWAY EXPRESS*
AND THE RATIONAL-BASIS STANDARD

1. *Some Rational Basics.* Any equal protection standard evaluating whether there is a rational basis for a classification must somehow identify a goal for the statute and decide whether the means chosen in the statute to effectuate that goal are rational. This is simply a much weaker form of means/ends scrutiny than the strict scrutiny applied to racial discrimination (which we analyzed in means/ends terms in the notes following *Loving* in Chapter 3). The Court has phrased the standard for minimal equal protection scrutiny in a variety of ways. A weak formulation is found in *Lindsley v. Natural Carbonic Gas Co.*, 220 U.S. 61 (1911):

> 1. The equal protection clause * * * does not take from the State the power to classify in the adoption of police laws, but admits the exercise of a wide scope of discretion in that regard, and avoids what is done only when it is without any reasonable basis and therefore is purely arbitrary. 2. A classification having some rational basis does not offend against that clause merely because it is not made with mathematical nicety or because in practice it results in some inequality. 3. When the classification in such a law is called in question, if any state of facts reasonably can be conceived that would sustain it, the existence of that state of facts at the time the law was enacted must be assumed. 4. One who assails the classification in such a law must carry the burden of showing that it does not rest upon any reasonable basis, but is essentially arbitrary.

A stronger standard is set forth in *Royster Guano Co. v. Virginia*, 253 U.S. 412 (1920):

> The classification must be reasonable, not arbitrary and must rest upon some ground of difference having a fair and substantial relation to the object of the legislation, so that all persons similarly circumstanced shall be treated alike.

Note some of the important differences in these formulations, as well as some broader possibilities. *Goals*: Should any goal or end for the statute suffice, even one dreamed up by counsel, after the fact, to put a good face on the statute? Or should the Court consider only the goal the legislature actually had in mind? How can the Court determine the actual goal? Should the Court require the legislature to say what the goal is? *Means*: May counsel, after the fact, justify the means chosen by pointing to evidence not before the legislature? Is it enough to find some minimal rational connection between goals and means, or must the rationality of the statute be substantial?

2. *Theories of Economic Legislation and Judicial Review.* *Railway Express* is a lenient (minimalist) application of the rational-basis test, upholding an ordinance that was highly underinclusive and entailed lines drawn to avoid hurting powerful interests. Whether such a lenient approach is defensible depends upon theories of legislation as well as judicial review. Consider some possibilities:

(A) *Public-Spirited Legislatures and Cautious Courts.* Most of the *Railway Express* Justices seemed to be optimistic that legislatures would deliberate in the public interest most of the time and skeptical that courts were institutionally competent to second-guess most policy judgments made by legislatures. This is the legal process vision that prevailed during the New Deal and is still influential today.[e]

(B) *Unprincipled Legislatures and Cautious Courts.* Justice Jackson took a more beady-eyed view of the legislature in this case, viewing the ordinance as a political compromise, whereby lines were drawn to exempt powerful interests from regulation. A cautious court would still uphold such a regulation, as Jackson did, because there are no principles by which the court can draw better lines, and dealmaking among interest groups is part of the normal political process. Pure policy decisions and line-drawing — including special interest deals and compromises — should be left to the legislature.[f]

(C) *Rent-Seeking Legislatures and Representation-Reinforcing Courts.* According to public choice theory (Chapter 2, § 3B), many laws are not just deals, but are "rent-seeking" distributions of public funds or authority to special interest groups without a public-regarding justification. The New York law might have drawn its regulatory lines to provide a competitive advantage for local companies over interstate ones, for example. A court following Ely's representation-reinforcing theory (Chapter 2, § 3B) might consider rent-seeking laws to be political dysfunctions which independent courts could correct.[g]

3. *Equal Protection Scrutiny: An Underenforced Constitutional Norm?* In economic regulation cases, the Court usually finds a way to uphold the regulation in question.[h] The Court has upheld some apparent special-interest laws by deploying the rational basis test in a highly lenient manner: (a) accepting counsel's post-hoc justifications or supplying the Court's own "plausible reasons" for the legislature's line-drawing, *e.g., United States Railroad Retirement Bd. v. Fritz*, 449 U.S. 166 (1980); *Williamson v. Lee Optical*, 348 U.S. 483 (1955); (b) deferring to legislative assertion of an "at least debatable" connection between a legitimate end and the means chosen by the legislature, *e.g., Minnesota v. Clover Leaf Creamery Co.*, 449 U.S. 456 (1981); and (c) accepting "administrative convenience" or general "public sentiment" as a rational state goal.

Although the many decisions are not easy to aggregate into any simple test, perhaps at a minimum they stand for the proposition that equal protection in the

---

e. See Henry Hart, Jr. & Albert Sacks, *The Legal Process: Materials on the Making and Application of Law* (William Eskridge, Jr. & Philip Frickey eds. 1994) (1958 tent. ed.).

f. See Alexander Bickel, *The Least Dangerous Branch: The Supreme Court at the Bar of Politics* (1962).

g. Other approaches along these lines are animated by republican theory. See, e.g., Bruce Ackerman, *Beyond* Carolene Products, 98 Harv. L. Rev. 713 (1985); Cass Sunstein, *Interest Groups in American Law*, 38 Stan. L. Rev. 29 (1985).

h. For the occasional modern exception, see *Metropolitan Life Ins. Co. v. Ward*, 470 U.S. 869 (1985) (impermissible for state to encourage growth of in-state insurance industry by taxing in-state companies at much lower rate than out-of-state companies doing business in state); *Logan v. Zimmerman Brush Co.*, 455 U.S. 422 (1982) (irrational for statute to bar employment discrimination complaint simply because state agency with which complaint was filed did not schedule hearing before statutory time period for relief expired).

economic arena is an "underenforced constitutional norm."[i] Under this view, state officials, who are duty-bound to follow the federal Constitution, are required by the Equal Protection Clause to treat similarly situated people similarly with respect to all manner of regulation, including economic. Federal judges should not, however, second-guess state officials concerning economic regulation, both for normative reasons (the latter, but not the former, are elected) and for practical reasons (the difficulty of developing workable standards for evaluating and enforcing equal protection in the sphere of economic regulation). Under this construct, one might say that the New York officials might have acted unconstitutionally in imposing the regulation in *Railway Express*, but the Supreme Court properly refused to invalidate it.

One reason for underenforcing the rationality norm is federalism: National courts should defer to local regulations not having interstate ramifications. In that event, state courts might — and in fact often do — apply rational-basis review with greater bite to state legislation under state, rather than federal, constitutional law.[j] Thus, the New York courts could apply the state constitutional protections against arbitrary legislative line-drawing with more bite than the U.S. Supreme Court did in *Railway Express*.

Another reason for underenforcing the rationality norm is that it might often duplicate routine review of administrative decisions. For example, when a zoning variance is denied, the property owner may be able to identify seemingly similar properties that were allowed a similar variance. Is it possible to distinguish honest but inept or arbitrary state or local administrative decisions, for which the remedy perhaps should simply be found under state law, from violations of the constitutional rationality requirement? In *Village of Willowbrook v. Olech*, 528 U.S. 562 (2000) (*per curiam*), which involved local zoning, the Court concluded that its decisions "have recognized successful equal protection claims brought by a 'class of one,' where the plaintiff alleges that she has been intentionally treated differently from others similarly situated and that there is no rational basis for the difference in treatment. In so doing, we have explained that 'the purpose of the equal protection clause * * * is to secure every person within the State's jurisdiction against intentional and arbitrary discrimination, whether occasioned by express terms of a statute or by its improper execution through duly constituted agents.' " The Court did not address an alternative theory advanced by the Court of Appeals, which relied upon plaintiff's allegation that the local officials had been motivated solely by a spiteful effort to "get" her. Justice Breyer, concurring in the judgment, stressed that this additional factor of illegitimate animus was "sufficient to

---

i. See Lawrence Sager, *Fair Measure: The Legal Status of Underenforced Constitutional Norms*, 91 Harv. L. Rev. 1212 (1978); Stephen Ross, *Legislative Enforcement of Equal Protection*, 72 Minn. L. Rev. 311 (1987). Much the same point could be made about the discriminatory-intent requirement of *Washington v. Davis*, 426 U.S. 229 (1976) (Chapter 3, § 1B).

j. See William Brennan, *State Constitutions and the Protection of Individual Rights*, 90 Harv. L. Rev. 489 (1977); *Developments in the Law — The Interpretation of State Constitutional Rights*, 95 Harv. L. Rev. 1324, 1463-93 (1982).

minimize any concern about transforming run-of-the-mill zoning cases into cases of constitutional right."

Federal Communications Commission v. Beach Communications, Inc., 508 U.S. 307 (1993). The Court upheld a federal statute requiring cable television systems to be franchised by local governmental authorities, but exempting facilities serving "only subscribers in one or more multiple unit dwellings under common ownership, control, or management." As construed by the FCC, this provision applied not just to traditional cable systems (which send signals through cables laid under city streets or along utility lines), but also to satellite master antenna television (SMATV) systems (a satellite dish on a rooftop receives signals from a satellite and retransmits the signal by wire to units in a building or complex of buildings). Thus, whether a SMATV system that links multiple buildings must be franchised by the local government depended upon whether the buildings were separately or commonly owned or managed. The Court found no constitutional infirmity in this distinction between common and separate ownership or management, in part because in the common-ownership setting the cost of regulation might outweigh the benefits to consumers (because the system was more likely to be small, or because consumers could more easily negotiate with the single property owner or manager).

"Whether embodied in the Fourteenth Amendment or inferred from the Fifth, equal protection is not a license for courts to judge the wisdom, fairness, or logic of legislative choices. In areas of social and economic policy, a statutory classification that neither proceeds along suspect lines nor infringes fundamental constitutional rights must be upheld against equal protection challenge if there is any reasonably conceivable state of facts that could provide a rational basis for the classification. Where there are 'plausible reasons' for Congress' action, 'our inquiry is at an end.' This standard of review is a paradigm of judicial restraint. 'The Constitution presumes that, absent some reason to infer antipathy, even improvident decisions will eventually be rectified by the democratic process and that judicial intervention is generally unwarranted no matter how unwisely we may think a political branch has acted.'

"On rational-basis review, a classification in a statute such as the Cable Act comes to us bearing a strong presumption of validity, and those attacking the rationality of the legislative classification have the burden 'to negative every conceivable basis which might support it.' Moreover, because we never require a legislature to articulate its reasons for enacting a statute, it is entirely irrelevant for constitutional purposes whether the conceived reason for the challenged distinction actually motivated the legislature. Thus, the absence of ' "legislative facts" ' explaining the distinction '[o]n the record' has no significance in rational-basis analysis. In other words, a legislative choice is not subject to courtroom fact-finding and may be based on rational speculation unsupported by evidence or empirical data. ' "Only by faithful adherence to this guiding principle of judicial review of legislation is it possible to preserve to the legislative branch its rightful independence and its ability to function." '

"These restraints on judicial review have added force 'where the legislature must necessarily engage in a process of line-drawing.' Defining the class of persons subject to a regulatory requirement — much like classifying governmental beneficiaries — 'inevitably requires that some persons who have an almost equally strong claim to favored treatment be placed on different sides of the line, and the fact [that] the line might have been drawn differently at some points is a matter for legislative, rather than judicial, consideration.' The distinction at issue here represents such a line: By excluding from the definition of 'cable system' those facilities that serve commonly owned or managed buildings without using public rights-of-way, § 602(7)(B) delineates the bounds of the regulatory field. Such scope-of-coverage provisions are unavoidable components of most economic or social legislation. In establishing the franchise requirement, Congress had to draw the line somewhere; it had to choose which facilities to franchise. This necessity renders the precise coordinates of the resulting legislative judgment virtually unreviewable, since the legislature must be allowed leeway to approach a perceived problem incrementally."

PROBLEM 4-1
APPLYING RATIONAL-BASIS SCRUTINY TO
DRIVER'S LICENSING

Under the cases you have read (*Beach Communications, Railway Express,* and the race cases in Chapters 2 and 3), is it a denial of the equal protection of the laws if the state forbids issuance of a driver's license to:

(a) any person on public welfare or with an income at a defined poverty level, based upon a statistical showing that such persons have been engaged in a disproportionate number of auto accidents;

(b) men under the age of 18 and women under the age of 16, with the sex differential based upon insurance studies showing that young men aged 16-18 are two times more likely than young women aged 16-18 to have a serious auto accident;

(c) any person who is not an American citizen, based upon a legislative finding that such people are not as likely to understand English (needed to read road signs, etc.);

(d) gay men and lesbians, based upon the announced legislative policy to discourage and not to "promote the homosexual lifestyle" in the state;

(e) any person who has ever had a diagnosed instance of epilepsy or "any mental disease or emotional disturbance," based upon a legislative finding that such people are more likely to cause accidents;

(f) any person who was "born out of wedlock," based upon a legislative policy to encourage people to procreate within the institution of marriage.

Work through each of these exclusions, with an eye toward whether each policy meets the rational basis test of *Railway Express/Beach Communications,* whether some of the criteria above should be subjected to a stricter examination, and how the array of results you reach fits together. The remainder of this chapter describes some of the lines the Supreme Court has drawn.

NOTE ON THE COURT'S APPLICATION OF HEIGHTENED SCRUTINY TO NON-RACE CLASSIFICATIONS: A "DOUBLE STANDARD"?

Gerald Gunther wrote in 1972 that the Supreme Court had developed a "double standard" in equal protection cases: easy-to-pass rational-basis review for economic and most other classifications, contrasted with automatically lethal strict scrutiny for race, ethnicity, and a few other classifications.[k] Under such an approach, the key was whether a classification triggered strict rather than rational basis scrutiny. Accordingly, lawyers petitioned the Court to recognize other classifications as similarly "suspect." Consider the Court's analysis of the following classifications, and see if criteria emerge that justify elevating a classification to strict scrutiny (also, revisit your answers to Problem 4-1).

1. *Alienage.* Under longstanding precedent, the federal authority over foreign relations and immigration has included nearly plenary power over "aliens." Thus, federal regulation of noncitizens is ordinarily subject at most to the most lenient rationality review when challenged on equal protection grounds.[1] For the same federal plenary authority reasons, however, the states have less justification for treating noncitizens differently from citizens, and the Supreme Court has reviewed their discriminations more strictly.[m] In *Graham v. Richardson*, 403 U.S. 365 (1971), the Court held that states could not, without substantial justification, deny welfare benefits to noncitizens lawfully present in the country. "[C]lassifications based on alienage, like those based on nationality or race, are inherently suspect and subject to close judicial scrutiny. Aliens as a class are a prime example of a 'discrete and insular' minority (see *Carolene Products* n.4) for whom such heightened judicial solicitude is appropriate."[n]

---

k. Gerald Gunther, *The Supreme Court, 1971 Term — Foreword: In Search of Evolving Doctrine on a Changing Court: A Model for a Newer Equal Protection*, 86 Harv. L. Rev. 1 (1972).

l. See, e.g., *Mathews v. Diaz*, 426 U.S. 67 (1976). Cf. *Hampton v. Mow Sun Wong*, 426 U.S. 88 (1976) (invalidating Civil Service Commission bar to federal employment of noncitizens on ground that only President or Congress is institutionally competent to make such policy judgments; after the Court's decision, President issued a similar bar, which was upheld by the lower courts).

m. In *Oyama v. California*, 332 U.S. 633 (1948), and *Takahashi v. Fish & Game Comm'n*, 334 U.S. 410, 420 (1948), the Court struck down California statutes discriminating against aliens and their children. For theoretical support of the Court's higher standard for reviewing state alienage classifications, see Gerald Neuman, *Aliens as Outlaws: Government Services, Proposition 187, and the Structure of Equal Protection Doctrine*, 42 UCLA L. Rev. 1425 (1995); Michael Wishnie, *Laboratories of Bigotry? Devolution of the Immigration Power, Equal Protection and Federalism*, 76 NYU L. Rev. 493 (2001); Note, *The Equal Treatment of Aliens: Preemption or Equal Protection?*, 31 Stan. L. Rev. 1069 (1979).

n. Louis Lusky, the law clerk who drafted the celebrated footnote four in *Carolene Products*, believed that noncitizens are not discrete and insular minorities because "many of them, who are anglophones, pass unnoticed, and many if not most others fit into the social scene with little difficulty." Lusky, *Footnote Redux: A* Carolene Products *Reminiscence*, 82 Colum. L. Rev. 1093,

After *Graham*, the Court struck down across-the-board rules excluding all noncitizens from employment in the state civil service, *Sugarman v. Dougall*, 413 U.S. 634 (1973), and from admission to the state bar, *In re Griffiths*, 413 U.S. 717 (1973). The Court has backed away from strict-meaning-fatal scrutiny in this context, however. States are allowed to bar noncitizens from certain state positions that are involved in the governance or functioning of the state as a political entity. In *Foley v. Connelie*, 435 U.S. 291 (1978), for example, the Court upheld a state law excluding noncitizens from the state police force.[o] Although the noncitizen cases are not easy to aggregate into any simple formula, it appears that the Court has attempted to apply a pragmatic distinction between state statutes that are economically protectionist — that reserve economic benefits for citizens (*Graham*) — and ones that are deemed to be rationally related to reserving sovereign functions for citizens (*Foley*).

2. *Illegitimacy.* Historically, many state laws have treated children born outside of marriage less favorably than marital children, particularly in such areas as inheritance rights. Beginning in 1968, when the Court struck down two Louisiana statutes, *Levy v. Louisiana*, 391 U.S. 68 (1968) (equal protection violated when state allowed marital, but not nonmarital, child to sue for damages for wrongful death of mother); *Glona v. American Guarantee & Liability Ins. Co.*, 391 U.S. 73 (1968) (equal protection violated when state allowed parent to sue for wrongful death of marital, but not nonmarital, child), something more than *Railway Express* rationality review has been applied to classifications based upon parental status. The Court has rejected the argument that statutes penalizing a child for the status of her parents are a justified means of encouraging marriage. "[N]o child is responsible for his birth and penalizing the illegitimate child is an ineffective — as well as an unjust — way of deterring the parent." *Weber v. Aetna Casualty & Surety Co.*, 406 U.S. 164 (1972). In essence, the decisions are based on the premises that persons born outside of marriage have suffered from irrational societal prejudice that imposes burdens upon them bearing no relation to their own responsibility or wrongdoing.

The more recent precedents apply an "intermediate" level of scrutiny, *e.g., Clark v. Jeter*, 486 U.S. 456 (1988). The Court's path has been anything but straightforward, and it has upheld some distinctions between children of marital and nonmarital birth. A common problem has concerned the situation where a man dies intestate (without a will) and someone comes forward and claims to be his child for purposes of inheriting his property. The Court has held that a state may not categorically deny intestate inheritance to children born out of marriage, *Trimble v. Gordon*, 430 U.S. 762 (1977), but may limit intestate inheritance to persons who, during the life of the deceased, were adjudged by a state court to be his children, *Lalli v. Lalli*, 439 U.S. 259 (1978).

1105 n.72 (1982).

o. Other such decisions upholding exclusionary state laws include *Cabell v. Chavez-Salido*, 454 U.S. 432 (1982) (probation officers); *Ambach v. Norwick*, 441 U.S. 68 (1979) (public school teachers). Compare *Bernal v. Fainter*, 467 U.S. 216 (1984) (striking down requirement that notary public be citizen because official functions are clerical and do not go "to the heart of representative government").

Another common problem has involved child support obligations for nonmarital children. Not only is a state prohibited from restricting such obligations to marital children, *Gomez v. Perez*, 409 U.S. 535 (1973), but the state must provide nonmarital children a meaningful opportunity to establish paternity, upon which the support obligation is based. A final matter of dispute has concerned whether states may distinguish between mothers and fathers in obtaining consent for adoption of nonmarital children, a question the Court has treated as involving a gender rather than an illegitimacy classification. *Lehr v. Robertson*, 463 U.S. 248 (1983), and *Caban v. Mohammed*, 441 U.S. 380 (1979), when read together, seem to indicate that a state may provide that only the mother must consent to the adoption when the putative father has not formally claimed paternity or developed any substantial relationship with the child.

3. *Age.* Age is different in nature from other potentially sensitive equal protection classifications: Everybody is young once, and — notwithstanding 1960s rock music dictum to the contrary — few hope to die before they get old. But the very young are formally politically powerless (they have no vote), and there is a history of discrimination against older workers, who have suffered the loss of employment to make way for younger, more modestly paid substitutes. On the other hand, some elderly persons — such as many federal judges and members of Congress — wield considerable power, and in recent years groups such as the American Association of Retired Persons have lobbied effectively in Congress and the state legislatures.

The Court has been unwilling to apply any form of heightened scrutiny to age classifications. It has upheld mandatory retirement laws for state and federal employees. See *Massachusetts Board of Retirement v. Murgia*, 427 U.S. 307 (1976) (upholding 50-year-old retirement age for state police); *Vance v. Bradley*, 440 U.S. 93 (1979) (upholding 60-year-old retirement age for federal foreign service personnel).[p] More recently, the Court found no equal protection violation in a municipal ordinance that allowed only persons between the ages of fourteen and eighteen to be admitted to certain dance halls. *Dallas v. Stanglin*, 490 U.S. 19 (1989). See also *Kimel v. Florida Board of Regents*, 528 U.S. 62 (2000) (applying the *Murgia* principle to limit Congress's Fourteenth Amendment authority to "enforce" norms against age discrimination).

---

p. In *Murgia*, the Court explained that "unlike, say, those who have been discriminated against on the basis of race or national origin," the aged "have not experienced a 'history of purposeful unequal treatment' or been subjected to unique disabilities on the basis of stereotyped characteristics not truly indicative of their abilities." Moreover, "old age does not define a 'discrete and insular' group, *Carolene Products* n.4, in need of 'extraordinary protection from the majoritarian political process.' Instead, it marks a stage that each of us will reach if we live out our normal span." The federal Age Discrimination in Employment Act of 1967, as amended, 29 U.S.C. § 621 et seq., provides statutory protection against age discrimination in the workplace. In some senses, *Murgia* is like *Washington v. Davis* (Chapter 3, § 1B), in that both cases refused to adopt stringent constitutional approaches to employment discrimination when Congress had already statutorily addressed the problem to some extent.

United States Department of Agriculture v. Moreno, 413 U.S. 528 (1973). The Food Stamp Act of 1964, as amended in 1971, 84 Stat. 2048, was a program of subsidized food for the poor. Excluded from participation was any household containing an individual unrelated to any other member of the household. Ermina Sanchez and her three children were threatened with termination of the food stamps they needed, because they shared their home with Jacinta Moreno, a 56-year-old diabetic whom Sanchez cared for. The Court, in an opinion by **Justice Brennan**, held that the "statutory classification (households of related persons versus households containing one or more unrelated persons) is clearly irrelevant to the stated purposes of the Act," which were to assure minimal nutrition and alleviate hunger, as well as distribution of agricultural surpluses. 7 U.S.C. § 2011.

The legislative history suggested that the 1971 amendment was meant to prevent "hippie communes" from taking advantage of the food stamp program, but Justice Brennan ruled that this was an impermissible purpose. "For if the constitutional conception of 'equal protection of the laws' means anything, it must at the very least mean that a bare congressional desire to harm a politically unpopular group cannot constitute a *legitimate* government interest." Justice Brennan rejected government arguments that the classification was an effort to regulate morality, for that would raise serious constitutional problems under the right to privacy (Chapter 5, § 4), or to prevent fraud, for the classification would have been very under- as well as overinclusive for such a purpose.

Justice Rehnquist, joined by **Chief Justice Burger**, dissented. They found the classification not quite so irrational as the Court did and pointed to *Dandridge v. Williams*, 397 U.S. 471 (1970), where the Court upheld a state limit on the amount of welfare a single family could receive. The limit upheld in *Dandridge* burdened large families in a similar way that the limit struck down in *Moreno* disadvantaged unrelated families, and for a similar rational basis: conservation of scarce state monies allocated for helping poor people. How can *Moreno* and *Dandridge* be reconciled?[q] Note that these cases illustrate a broader equal protection puzzle: What *conditions* can *constitutionally* be imposed upon the receipt of government benefits?

SECTION 2. SEX- AND GENDER-BASED DISCRIMINATION

Law has long treated women differently from men. For most of our history this has not been considered constitutionally problematic, based upon a traditional "jurisprudence of difference," which considered differences between men and women rooted in biology and social roles a sufficient justification for statutes making sex-based distinctions. This traditional jurisprudence was the basis for the Court's early application of the Fourteenth Amendment to sex discriminations and exclusions (Part A).

---

q. For one effort at reconciliation, see Lynn Baker, *The Prices of Rights: Toward a Positive Theory of Unconstitutional Conditions*, 75 Cornell L. Rev. 1185 (1990).

In the last hundred years many women's rights advocates have argued for a "jurisprudence of equal treatment," which posits that men and women, as equal citizens of this country, are entitled to be treated by precisely the same legal rules. Part B traces the impact of this line of thought upon equal protection doctrine, which in the 1970s began to scrutinize gender-based discrimination more strictly and to invalidate such statutes. Many of the Supreme Court cases invalidated statutes that seemingly gave women advantages over men.

Throughout the last century, some women's rights advocates have questioned the jurisprudence of sameness, on the ground that by seeking to treat women the "same" as men, the jurisprudence accepts "men" as the norm and perpetuates structural inequality between women and men in American society. Recent theorists have worked toward a new "jurisprudence of difference," which rejects the fundamental structure of equal protection law ("similarly situated" women must be treated the same as men) and argues for a new constitutional baseline where women actually enjoy the equal *protection* of the laws. Part C summarizes this line of theory and contrasts it with the jurisprudence of formal equality.

A. WOMEN OUTSIDE THE CONSTITUTION: THE TRADITIONAL JURISPRUDENCE OF DIFFERENCE[a]

The role of women in colonial society was not an elevated one. They had no right to vote, did not serve on juries, had few economic rights if they were married, and were assigned economic and family roles that were rarely better than drudgery. From the birth of our nation, some women have had a vision of a different society. In 1776, for example, Abigail Adams urged her husband John to "Remember the Ladies, and be more generous and favourable to them than your ancestors," in crafting laws for the emerging republic. "Do not put such unlimited power into the hands of the Husbands. Remember all Men would be tyrants if they could. If particular care and attention is not paid to the Ladies we are determined to foment a Rebellion, and will not hold ourselves bound by any laws in which we have no voice, or Representation."[b] Within

---

a. This account is drawn from Barbara Allen Babcock, Ann Freedman, Susan Deller Ross, Wendy Webster Williams, Rhonda Copelon, Deborah Rhode & Nadine Taub, *Sex Discrimination and the Law: History, Practice, and Theory* ch. 1 (1996); Deborah Rhode, *Justice and Gender: Sex Discrimination and the Law* chs. 1-3 (1989).

b. Letter from Abigail Adams to John Adams (March 31, 1776), in 1 *Adams Family Correspondence* 369-71 (L. Butterfield ed. 1963). John treated it as a lark: "As to your extraordinary Code of Laws, I cannot but laugh. We have been told that our Struggle has loosened the bands of Government every where. That Children and Apprentices were disobedient — that schools and Colleges were grown turbulent — that Indians slighted their Guardians and Negroes grew insolent to their Masters. But your Letter was the first Intimation that another Tribe more numerous and powerful than all the rest were grown discontented. — This is rather too coarse a Compliment but you are so saucy, I wont blot it out." Letter from John Adams to Abigail Adams (Apr. 14, 1776), in *id.* at 381. Abigail replied: "[W]hilst you are proclaiming peace and good will to Men, Emancipating all Nations, you insist upon retaining an absolute power over Wives. But you must remember that Arbitrary power is like most other things which are very hard, very liable to be broken * * *." Letter from Abigail Adams to John Adams (May 7, 1776), in *id.* at 401.

months of this letter, the Continental Congress adopted the Declaration of Independence and its precept that "all men are created equal." The "Ladies" were not "Remembered."

The Constitution and the Bill of Rights were little more sensitive to the political rights of women, though they were written in a gender-neutral fashion that assured some formal rights to women as well as men. For example, women as well as men were assured freedom of religion by the First Amendment. On the other hand, the background assumption, completely unchanged by the Constitution, was that women were not part of the public citizenry. They were considered submerged in the family unit headed by the husband.[c] Like slaves and poor men, women were not entitled to vote.

Notwithstanding their subordination in both the family and the polity, women in the early United States (especially those in the upper classes) asserted their personal and political rights against the traditional claims of their "inferiority."[d] Women gained important political experience as leaders in the abolitionist and temperance movements of the early and mid-nineteenth century. Leaders included Lucretia Mott, Elizabeth Cady Stanton, and Harriet Tubman in the abolitionist movement and Susan B. Anthony in the temperance movement. Led by Mott and Stanton, an assembly of women and men at Seneca Falls, New York (Stanton's home) issued a "Declaration of Sentiments" on July 19, 1848, which asserted the formal human equality of men and women (tracking the language of the Declaration of Independence but expanding it to include women) and protested the "entire disenfranchisement of one-half the people of this country."

Although women were among the leading abolitionists, and many abolitionist leaders such as Stanton and Frederick Douglass called for suffrage for women as well as the former slaves, the male chiefs of the movement abandoned female suffrage after the Civil War and focused their attention on the former *male* slaves. Thus the Fifteenth Amendment to the Constitution said nothing about women's right to vote, and § 2 of the Fourteenth Amendment explicitly wrote "male" into the Constitution. Bitterly disappointed by the betrayal of their supposed male abolitionist and Republican allies, Anthony and Stanton emerged as voices urging women to take direct action against oppression. "Reconstruction politics shattered feminists' dependence on abolitionism and opened the way for woman suffrage to develop into an organized movement of women, ultimately one of mass proportions."[e] It took a half century for that movement to find its way into the Constitution (the Nineteenth Amendment (1920)) and a century to be reflected in Supreme Court

---

c. See Sir William Blackstone, *Commentaries on the Laws of England* book I, ch. XV (1765) (no separate legal existence of wife apart from her husband). On the confining features of early marriage law, see Nancy Cott, *Public Vows: A History of Marriage and the Nation* 9-55 (2000).

d. See, e.g., Mary Wollstonecraft, *Vindication of the Rights of Women* (1792); Sarah Grimke, *Letters on the Equality of the Sexes* (1838).

e. Ellen DuBois, *Feminism and Suffrage: The Emergence of an Independent Women's Movement in America 1848-1869*, at 201 (1978).

opinions concerning the Fourteenth Amendment (*Reed v. Reed* (1971)). Consider the inauspicious beginnings.

———

Bradwell v. Illinois, 83 U.S. (16 Wall.) 130 (1873). Myra Bradwell's application for a license to practice law had been denied by the Illinois Supreme Court solely because she was a married woman. The U.S. Supreme Court affirmed this judgment with only one dissent.[f] **Justice Miller**'s opinion addressed Bradwell's argument that she was denied a constitutional "privilege or immunity": Because Bradwell was a citizen of Illinois, the Privileges and Immunities Clause of Article IV was inapplicable to her claim; because admission to the bar of a state is not one of the privileges and immunities of United States citizenship, the Fourteenth Amendment (as interpreted in *The Slaughter House Cases* (Chapter 5, § 1), decided the day before) did not secure the asserted right either.

Justice Bradley, who dissented in *The Slaughter House Cases*, concurred in the judgment on broader grounds, reflecting a theory of gender: "[T]he civil law, as well as nature herself, has always recognized a wide difference in the respective spheres and destinies of man and woman. Man is, or should be, woman's protector and defender. The natural and proper timidity and delicacy which belongs to the female sex evidently unfits it for many of the occupations of civil life. The constitution of the family organization, which is founded in the divine ordinance, as well as in the nature of things, indicates the domestic sphere as that which properly belongs to the domain and functions of womanhood. The harmony, not to say identity, of interests and views which belong, or should belong, to the family institution is repugnant to the idea of a woman adopting a distinct and independent career from that of her husband. So firmly fixed was this sentiment in the founders of the common law that it became a maxim of that system of jurisprudence that a woman had no legal existence separate from her husband. * * *

"It is true that many women are unmarried and not affected by any of the duties, complications, and incapacities arising out of the married state, but these are exceptions to the general rule. The paramount destiny and mission of woman are to fulfil the noble and benign offices of wife and mother. This is the law of the Creator. And the rules of civil society must be adapted to the general constitution of things, and cannot be based upon exceptional cases.

"The humane movements of modern society, which have for their object the multiplication of avenues for woman's advancement, and of occupations adapted to her condition and sex, have my heartiest concurrence. But I am not prepared to say that it is one of her fundamental rights and privileges to be admitted into every office and position, including those which require highly special qualifications and demanding special responsibilities. In the nature of things it is not every citizen of every age, sex, and condition that is qualified for every calling and position. It is the prerogative of the legislator to prescribe regulations founded on nature, reason, and experience for the due admission of

---

f.   Bradwell was subsequently admitted to the Illinois bar anyway, by additional legislation.

qualified persons to professions and callings demanding special skill and confidence. This fairly belongs to the police power of the State; and, in my opinion, in view of the peculiar characteristics, destiny, and mission of woman, it is within the province of the legislature to ordain what offices, positions, and callings shall be filled and discharged by men, and shall receive the benefit of those energies and responsibilities, and that decision and firmness which are presumed to predominate in the sterner sex."

In *Minor v. Happersett*, 88 U.S. (21 Wall.) 162 (1874), the Supreme Court ruled that the right to vote was not among the "privileges and immunities of United States citizenship." Consequently, the states were not inhibited by the Constitution from committing "that important trust to men alone." But the Court also said that women are "persons" and may be "citizens" within the meaning of the Fourteenth Amendment. In 1878, the National Women's Suffrage Association voted to fight for a constitutional amendment assuring women the right to vote. For the next two generations, feminists campaigned for such an amendment, arguing that women ought to be considered autonomous and equal citizens — a norm requiring that they be given the right to vote.[g] Opponents argued that (1) women were not in fact autonomous and ought to be happy ruling over their natural province, the domestic sphere (the Bradley stance in *Bradwell*); (2) recognition of women's citizenship by assuring women the right to vote would undermine the family and introduce discord into husband-wife relations; and (3) the normative arguments were best resolved on a state-by-state basis rather than by a blanket national constitutional rule. After decades of debate, Congress propounded the Nineteenth Amendment, and three-quarters of the states ratified it in 1920.

At the same time women were seeking the right to vote, they were petitioning the Supreme Court for interpretations of the Due Process and Equal Protection Clauses protecting against sex-exclusionary legislation. In this campaign, feminists came up empty-handed; whatever the basis of constitutional challenges, the Court followed the prevailing jurisprudence of difference accepted by the American legal establishment.

Due Process. Most of the due process cases involved industry attacks on legislation providing workplace protections for women. Early in the women's rights movement, Stanton and Anthony had advocated equal pay for equal work, eight-hour days, and better workplace conditions for women, but most legislation "protecting" women in the workplace was adopted for other reasons.[h]

---

g. See Aileen Kraditor, *The Ideas of the Woman Suffrage Movement, 1890-1920* (1965); Ellen Carol DuBois, *Outgrowing the Compact of the Fathers: Equal Rights, Woman Suffrage, and the United States Constitution, 1820-1878*, 74 J. Am. Hist. 836 (1987); Reva Siegel, *She the People: The Nineteenth Amendment, Sex Equality, and the Family*, 115 Harv. L. Rev. 947 (2002).

h. On women in the workplace, male resistance, and gendered labor laws, see Alice Kessler-Harris, *Out to Work: A History of Wage-Earning Women in the United States* 201-02 (1982); Philip Foner, *Women and the American Labor Movement* (1979); Julie Matthei, *An Economic History of Women in America* (1982); Elizabeth Brandeis, *Labor Legislation*, in 3 *History of Labor in the United States* 462 (John Commons et al. eds. 1935).

Unions sought maximum hour laws for women and children, arguably as a way to prevent women from competing on equal terms with men in the workplace. As a result of this and many other factors, women — who constituted about one-fifth of the workforce at the turn of the century — tended to be segregated into "women's work," jobs reflecting home-based values (teaching and helping, subordinate as well as nurturing).

When Oregon's law setting maximum hours for women was challenged by employers in *Muller v. Oregon*, 208 U.S. 412 (1908), the Supreme Court unanimously upheld the law, based upon the state's important interest in protecting women:

> That woman's physical structure and the performance of maternal functions place her at a disadvantage in the struggle for subsistence is obvious. * * * [B]y abundant testimony of the medical fraternity continuance for a long time on her feet at work, repeating this from day to day, tends to injurious effects upon the body, and as healthy mothers are essential to vigorous offspring, the physical well-being of woman becomes an object of public interest and care in order to preserve the strength and vigor of the race.

> Still again, history discloses the fact that woman has always been dependent upon man. * * * As minors * * * she has been looked upon in the courts as needing especial care that her rights may be preserved. * * * Differentiated by these matters from the other sex, she is properly placed in a class by herself, and legislation designed for her protection may be sustained even when like legislation is not necessary for men and could not be sustained. It is impossible to close one's eyes to the fact that she still looks to her brother and depends upon him. * * *

Most middle-class progressive groups applauded the decision in *Muller*, and the National Consumers' League's brief, filed by Louis Brandeis, containing detailed empirical policy arguments became a new standard for influencing the Court (the so-called "Brandeis brief"). Progressives were more ambivalent about decisions upholding other "protective" legislation that effectively closed off employment options for women. See *Radice v. New York*, 264 U.S. 292 (1924) (upholding law forbidding nightwork for waitresses but exempting female entertainers and ladies' room attendants); *Bosley v. McLaughlin*, 236 U.S. 385 (1915) (rejecting challenge by female pharmacist to 8-hour law preventing her employment with hospital).

In the wake of cases like *Radice*, many women came to oppose "protective" legislation, arguing that "unequal wages and bad factory conditions, and not special laws for adult women workers, are the things in which we should all interest ourselves. * * * When we limit women's opportunities to work, we simply create more poverty, and we postpone the day when equal pay for equal work will be universal."[i] They invoked the Nineteenth Amendment's implicit recognition of women's equal citizenship as a basis for criticizing protective legislation. Accepting a Nineteenth Amendment argument made by employers, the Supreme Court in *Adkins v. Children's Hospital*, 261 U.S. 525 (1923), struck down a federal statute fixing minimum wages for women and children in the District of Columbia. Although *Adkins* was primarily a *Lochner*-style liberty of contract decision, it also reflected society's and the Court's tentative movement

---

i. Views of Rheta Childe Dorr, *Good Housekeeping*, Sept. 1925, at 156 ff.

away from complete acceptance of the separate spheres philosophy and the jurisprudence of natural difference.

Equal Protection. The early equal protection cases generally involved efforts by men to overturn laws that discriminated in favor of women — without success, because of the jurisprudence of difference embedded in *Muller*. For example, in *Quong Wing v. Kirkendall*, 223 U.S. 59 (1912), the Court upheld against equal protection attack a statute that imposed a $10 licensing charge for laundries but exempted any laundry operation of two or fewer women. Justice Holmes wrote for the Court, finding the legislature's "ground of distinction in sex * * * not without precedent," citing *Muller*. "If Montana deems it advisable to put a lighter burden upon women than upon men with regard to an employment that our people commonly regard as more appropriate for the former, the Fourteenth Amendment does not interfere by creating a fictitious equality where there is a real difference." See also *Breedlove v. Suttles*, 302 U.S. 277 (1937) (upholding Georgia statute exempting nonvoting women from state poll tax "[i]n view of burdens necessarily borne by them for the preservation of the race").

Later cases were brought by women seeking to overturn statutes segregating them from job opportunities. There was particular enthusiasm for these efforts after World War II, during which many women moved into the workplace, doing traditionally "men's work" as well as serving in the armed forces. The second wave of feminism began after the war, but the Supreme Court remained deaf to women's voices. For example, in *Goesaert v. Cleary*, 335 U.S. 464 (1948), the Court upheld a statute allowing a woman to work as a bartender only if she was the wife or daughter of the bar owner. *Goesaert* approached the problem as simply a matter of *Railway Express* rationality review: "The fact that women may now have achieved the virtues that men have long claimed as their prerogatives and now indulge in vices that men have long practiced, does not preclude the State from drawing a sharp line between the sexes," certainly in such matters as the regulation of the liquor traffic.[j] The Constitution does not require legislatures to reflect sociological insight, or shifting social standards, any more than it requires them to keep abreast of the latest scientific standards." The Court rejected the sex discrimination claim on the basis of deference (*Railway Express*) rather than the old separate spheres idea (*Muller*).

Also reflecting the erosion of the public separate spheres ideology was erosion in traditional state exclusions of women from jury service. Before World War I, all states excluded women, but as the nation entered World War II, only 13 states required the same jury service of women that they required of men; 15 states allowed women to opt out of compulsory jury service; 20 states disqualified women as a class. After the war, the situation shifted rapidly, and the Supreme Court gave it a push in 1946. Relying on a statute regulating federal jury service, the Court overturned the conviction of defendants, because the federal judge excluded women from the jury venire in *Ballard v. United*

---

j. Note the possible influence of the Twenty-First Amendment, which was later construed as granting the states extraordinary authority, for example, to censor expressive conduct that would otherwise be protected by the First Amendment. See *California v. LaRue*, 409 U.S. 109 (1972).

States, 329 U.S. 187 (1946). In response to the government's argument that the discrimination was not prejudicial to defendants's jury trial rights, Justice Douglas responded that women and men are "not fungible; a community made up exclusively of one is different from a community composed of both." He then posed the question: "[I]f the shoe were on the other foot, who would claim that a jury was truly representative of the community if all men were intentionally and systematically excluded from the panel?" A Court majority declined to constitutionalize that principle in *Fay v. New York*, 332 U.S. 261 (1947), but four dissenters maintained that a "blue ribbon" jury substantially excluding women and working class people violated the Equal Protection Clause.

B. THE JURISPRUDENCE OF EQUAL TREATMENT AND HEIGHTENED SCRUTINY OF SEX-BASED DISTINCTIONS

The erosion of separate spheres was not immediately accompanied by a single positive feminist vision of equal protection. Between 1920 and 1960, the women's rights movement was deeply divided between feminists like Eleanor Roosevelt who accepted natural differences between men and women and supported female-protective legislation, and those who rejected that jurisprudence and insisted on the autonomy of women and their complete equality with men.[k] Feminists and their allies in the latter camp pressed for the adoption of an Equal Rights Amendment, which was first introduced in Congress in 1923 but which made little progress because of the opposition of women and their allies in the former group.

After World War II, political and constitutional activism among women moved slowly toward the full equality stance. Exemplifying this shift was the ACLU's alliance with ERA feminists in the jury cases. By 1961, only three states retained complete exclusions of women from juries, and three others permitted women to serve only if they opted in. Gwendolyn Hoyt killed her husband in Florida, one of the states in the latter group. A jury of 12 men found her guilty of murder, and she appealed on the ground that the Equal Protection Clause prohibited the exclusion of women from the jury that convicted her. Dorothy Kenyon's *amicus* brief for the ACLU (its first in a sex discrimination case) argued that representation on juries is an important civil right, as illustrated by the experience of blacks, who did not achieve genuine citizenship until the Court required that they be invited to its burdens such as jury service. The same was true of women. They continued to be excluded, either by law or in practice, because "the thinking of older times, when women were no part of the body politic" persisted and suggested that jury service would detract from women's "primary duties" of housekeeping and childrearing within the home. This rationale was anachronistic, as "a revolution has taken place in the lives and status of women." Not only was the discrimination against all women

---

k. See Cynthia Harrison, *On Account of Sex: The Politics of Women's Issues, 1945-1968* (1988); Ruth Rosen, *The World Split Wide Open: How the Modern Women's Movement Changed America* 27, 66 (2000); Verta Taylor, *Social Movement Continuity: The Women's Movement in Abeyance*, 54 Am. Soc. Rev. 761 (1989).

therefore unreasonable, but it was a discrimination that the "fully emancipated, fully enfranchised woman citizen" would no longer tolerate.

The Supreme Court unanimously rejected these arguments, holding in *Hoyt v. Florida*, 368 U.S. 57 (1961), that an opt-in system did not clearly discriminate against women's service on juries in the way that the Court had criticized in *Ballard* (a statutory case). *Hoyt* cast into bold relief the fact that the Supreme Court had never struck down a sex discrimination as unconstitutional. Ironically, the decision came just as the women's movement was taking flight again. Responding to feminist demands, President Kennedy established the President's Commission on the Status of Women (PCSW), which served as a consciousness-raising and idea-sharing forum for feminist lawyers and thinkers from all around the country. In an important memorandum to the PCSW, civil rights activist Pauli Murray argued that the Equal Protection Clause could be interpreted to question sex-based discriminations for the same reasons the Court had deployed it against race-based discriminations: Sex discriminations (like race discriminations) rested upon a natural law understanding of "inherent differences" that had been deployed to support disadvantages and social inferiority of women; the naturalized view of sex differences rested upon unproven stereotypes or myths about women that were usually an irrational basis for subordinating them; like blacks, women needed to mobilize against pervasive state discrimination through the formation of an organization like the NAACP.[1]

Murray's arguments persuaded the Commission to proclaim that "equality of rights under the law for all persons, male or female, is so basic to democracy and its commitment to the ultimate value of the individual that it must be reflected in the fundamental law of the land." Moreover, Murray's memorandum helped bridge the concerns of various civil rights activists: Her Fourteenth Amendment strategy sought equality for women (desired by liberal ERA feminists), but without sacrificing laws genuinely remedying women's disadvantages in the workplace (desired by labor feminists and ERA opponents). Murray, an African American active in the civil rights movement, also sought to unite blacks and women in a common campaign against prejudice and discrimination.

Murray's arguments found their way into the congressional debates over the addition of "sex discrimination" to the jobs title of the Kennedy Administration's civil rights bill. Although the amendment was propounded by anti-civil rights (but pro-ERA) Representative Howard Smith of Virginia, Murray and other feminists supported it and ensured that it was preserved in the final statute. The EEOC, however, refused to make sex discrimination a priority in its enforcement of the new law, a stance that drew strong protests. When officials ignored their complaints at a 1966 conference on women's status, Murray, Betty Friedan, and other feminists stormed out in protest and founded the National Organization for Women (NOW). The feminist political energy harnessed by

---

1. Pauli Murray, A Proposal to Reexamine the Applicability of the Fourteenth Amendment to State Laws and Practices Which Discriminate on the Basis of Sex Per Se (Dec. 1962), discussed in Harrison, *On Account of Sex* 126-34.

NOW sought a relatively unified political agenda: serious enforcement of the Equal Pay Act and Title VII by the EEOC, to assure equality in the workplace; liberalization or repeal of restrictive abortion laws; adoption of legislation barring sex discrimination in education, accomplished with the enactment of Title IX in 1972; and adoption of the ERA, which would assure constitutional equality.[m]

The last point underscores a conscious decision made by these groups, based upon their experience and upon feminist theory: The jurisprudence of difference embedded in *Bradwell* and *Muller* should be repudiated, because it subordinated women as humans and citizens. Even when gender differences "protected" or "benefitted" women, special treatment of women only perpetuated gender stereotypes of women as the "weaker sex" who need protection at the grace of men. Aside from this critique of the jurisprudence of difference, women's rights groups developed an affirmative vision of equal protection, a "jurisprudence of equal treatment." A good statement of this jurisprudence from one of the main women's rights lawyers of the 1970s is Wendy Webster Williams' article (excerpted immediately below). In the remainder of this part, following the Williams excerpt, we shall trace the Supreme Court's reaction to the various strands of the equal-treatment argument.

Wendy Webster Williams
Equality's Riddle: Pregnancy and the Equal
Treatment/Special Treatment Debate
13 N.Y.U. Rev. L. & Soc. Change 325, 329-31 (1984-85)[n]

The first proposition essential to this analysis is that sex-based generalizations are generally impermissible whether derived from physical differences such as size and strength, from cultural role assignments such as breadwinner or homemaker, or from some combination of innate and ascribed characteristics, such as the greater longevity of the average woman compared to the average man. Instead of classifying on the basis of sex, lawmakers and employers must classify on the basis of the trait or function or behavior for which sex was used as a proxy. Strength, not maleness, would be the criterion for certain jobs; economic dependency, not femaleness, the criterion for alimony upon divorce. The basis for this proposition is a belief that a dual system of rights inevitably produces gender hierarchy and, more fundamentally, treats women and men as statistical abstractions rather than as persons with individual capacities, inclinations and aspirations — at enormous cost to women and not insubstantial cost to men.

The second essential proposition is that laws and rules which do not overtly classify on the basis of sex, but which have a disproportionately negative effect upon one sex, warrant, under appropriate circumstances, placing a burden of justification upon the party defending the law or rule in court. In the view of its proponents, the proposition is an essential companion to the first proposition and

---

m. See generally Serena Mayeri, *Constitutional Choices: Legal Feminism and the Historical Dynamics of Change*, 92 Calif. L. Rev. 755, 761-801 (2004).

n. Reprinted by permission from vol. 13 (1984), N.Y.U. Rev. L. & Soc. Change.

is necessary for the ultimate equality of the sexes. Society has been tailored to predefined sex roles not only through overt gender classifications, but also through laws and rules neutral on their face but inspired by the same assumptions, stereotypes and ideologies as sex-based classifications.

The goal of the feminist legal movement that began in the early seventies is not and never was the integration of women into a male world any more than it has been to build a separate but better place for women. Rather, the goal has been to break down the legal barriers that restricted each sex to its predefined role and created a hierarchy based on gender. The ability to challenge covert as well as overt gender sorting laws is essential both for challenging in court a male defined set of structures and institutions and for requiring their reconstitution to reflect the full range of our human concerns. The first proposition (sex classifications are generally impermissible) facilitates the elimination of legislation that overtly classifies by sex. The second proposition (perpetrators of rules with a disparate effect must justify them) provides a doctrinal tool with which to begin to squeeze the male tilt out of a purportedly neutral legal structure and thus substitute genuine for merely formal gender neutrality.

1. *From Rational Basis to Intermediate Scrutiny (and Beyond?) in Gender Cases*

Like the NAACP before it, NOW established a Legal Defense and Education Fund to litigate issues of women's equality. Also, the ACLU in 1971 established its Women's Rights Project, headed by Ruth Bader Ginsburg. Representing a new generation of litigators, Ginsburg followed Kenyon and Murray in pressing the Court to rule that women should have all the same legal rights and duties as men. These lawyers had filed constitutional challenges to statutory sex discriminations, and state and federal judges found many of the challenged policies unconstitutional — notwithstanding *Hoyt*. E.g., *White v. Crook*, 251 F. Supp. 401 (M.D. Ala. 1966) (three-judge court) (state exclusion of women from juries violates the Equal Protection Clause) (not appealed); *Sail'er Inn, Inc. v. Kirby*, 485 P.2d 529 (Cal. 1971) (applying heightened equal protection scrutiny to exclusion of women from employment as bartenders).

In *Reed v. Reed*, the ACLU attorneys — Kenyon, Murray, and Ginsburg — urged the Court to renounce the constitutional philosophy of *Muller*, *Goesaert*, and *Hoyt*. In their brief, counsel announced that "a new appreciation of women's place has been generated in the United States." Feminists "of both sexes" were pressing for women's "full membership" in the benefits and duties of constitutional citizenship. "But the distance to equal opportunity for women — in the face of the pervasive social, cultural, and legal roots of sex-based discrimination — remains considerable. In the absence of a firm constitutional foundation for equal treatment of men and women by the law, women seeking to be judged on their individual merits will continue to encounter law-sanctioned obstacles." Accordingly, the ACLU lawyers maintained that sex was a suspect classification for the same reasons race was: Both were natural traits that the dominant culture has treated as a badge of inferiority and stigmatized legally, based upon inaccurate stereotypes about the group defined by the trait. Consider the Court's response in *Reed* and in the next case, *Frontiero v.*

Richardson, where the ACLU reiterated its arguments for strict scrutiny in an *amicus* brief.

Reed v. Reed, 404 U.S. 71 (1971). Idaho statutes provided a "tie-breaker" preference for males over females of equal degrees of relationship to be appointed to administer an estate. (Thus, a son would be preferred over a daughter to administer a deceased parent's estate.) A unanimous Supreme Court, per **Chief Justice Burger**, struck down the statute under the rational basis standard. The Court relied upon the *Royster Guano* formulation (note 1 following *Railway Express*), under which the classification "must be reasonable, not arbitrary, and must rest upon some ground of difference having a fair and substantial relation to the object of the legislation, so that all persons similarly circumstanced shall be treated alike." The state relied upon the justification of administrative convenience: In general, men are more likely than women to have the sophistication in business affairs needed to administer an estate, and by eliminating one area of controversy where two or more persons seek to be appointed administrator, probate courts avoid time-consuming issues. Rejecting this argument, the Court stated: "To give a mandatory preference to members of either sex over members of the other, merely to accomplish the elimination of hearings on the merits, is to make the very kind of arbitrary legislative choice forbidden by the Equal Protection Clause." *Query*: Is this really an example of *Railway Express* rational-basis scrutiny? Even *Moreno* scrutiny?

FRONTIERO v. RICHARDSON
411 U.S. 677, 93 S.Ct. 1764, 36 L.Ed.2d 583 (1973)

JUSTICE BRENNAN announced the judgment of the Court in an opinion in which **JUSTICE DOUGLAS, JUSTICE WHITE**, and **JUSTICE MARSHALL** join.

[Pursuant to 37 U.S.C. §§ 401, 403, and 10 U.S.C. §§ 1072, 1076, a serviceman could claim his wife as a "dependent" without regard to whether she was in fact dependent upon him for any part of her support. A servicewoman, on the other hand, could not claim her husband as a "dependent" under these programs unless he was in fact dependent upon her for over one-half of his support. Rejecting the Frontieros' equal protection attack, the lower court held that Congress might reasonably have concluded that, since the husband in our society is generally the "breadwinner" in the family — and the wife typically the "dependent" partner — "it would be more economical to require married female members claiming husbands to prove actual dependency than to extend the presumption of dependency to such members." The Supreme Court reversed.]

At the outset, appellants contend that classifications based upon sex, like classifications based upon race, alienage, and national origin, are inherently suspect and must therefore be subjected to close judicial scrutiny. We agree and, indeed, find at least implicit support for such an approach in our unanimous decision only last Term in *Reed v. Reed*. [In *Reed*], the Court implicitly rejected appellee's apparently rational explanation of the statutory scheme, and concluded that, by ignoring the individual qualifications of particular applicants, the challenged statute provided "dissimilar treatment for men and women who are . . . similarly situated." The Court therefore held that, even though the State's interest in achieving administrative efficiency "is not without some legitimacy," "[t]o give a mandatory preference to members of either sex over members of the other, merely to accomplish the elimination of hearings on the merits, is to make the very kind of arbitrary legislative choice forbidden by the [Constitution.]" This departure from "traditional" rational-basis analysis with respect to sex-based classifications is clearly justified.

There can be no doubt that our Nation has had a long and unfortunate history of sex discrimination. Traditionally, such discrimination was rationalized by an attitude of "romantic paternalism" which, in practical effect, put women, not on a pedestal, but in a cage. [As an example of such a "paternalistic attitude," Justice Brennan quoted from Justice Bradley's concurring opinion in *Bradwell*, *supra*.]

As a result of notions such as these, our statute books gradually became laden with gross, stereotyped distinctions between the sexes and, indeed, throughout much of the 19th century the position of women in our society was, in many respects, comparable to that of blacks under the pre-Civil War slave codes. Neither slaves nor women could hold office, serve on juries, or bring suit in their own names, and married women traditionally were denied the legal capacity to hold or convey property or to serve as legal guardians of their own children. And although blacks were guaranteed the right to vote in 1870, women were denied even that right * * * until adoption of the Nineteenth Amendment half a century later.

It is true, of course, that the position of women in America has improved markedly in recent decades. Nevertheless, it can hardly be doubted that, in part because of the high visibility of the sex characteristic, women still face pervasive, although at times more subtle, discrimination in our educational institutions, in the job market and, perhaps most conspicuously, in the political arena.[17]

Moreover, since sex, like race and national origin, is an immutable characteristic determined solely by the accident of birth, the imposition of special disabilities upon the members of a particular sex because of their sex would seem to violate "the basic concept of our system that legal burdens should bear some relationship to individual responsibility . . . ." And what differentiates sex from such non-suspect statuses as intelligence or physical disability, and aligns it with the recognized suspect criteria, is that the sex characteristic frequently bears no relation to ability to perform or contribute to society. As a result, statutory distinctions between the sexes often have the effect of

---

17. It is true, of course, that when viewed in the abstract, women do not constitute a small and powerless minority. Nevertheless, in part because of past discrimination, women are vastly underrepresented in this Nation's decisionmaking councils. There has never been a female President, nor a female member of this Court. Not a single woman presently sits in the United States Senate, and only 14 women hold seats in the House of Representatives. And, as appellants point out, this underrepresentation is present throughout all levels of our State and Federal Government.

invidiously relegating the entire class of females to inferior legal status without regard to the actual capabilities of its individual members.

We might also note that, over the past decade, Congress has itself manifested an increasing sensitivity to sex-based classifications. In Tit. VII of the Civil Rights Act of 1964, for example, Congress expressly declared that no employer, labor union, or other organization subject to the provisions of the Act shall discriminate against any individual on the basis of "race, color, religion, *sex*, or national origin." Similarly, the Equal Pay Act of 1963 provides that no employer covered by the Act "shall discriminate . . . between employees on the basis of *sex*." And § 1 of the Equal Rights Amendment, passed by Congress on March 22, 1972, and submitted to the legislatures of the States for ratification, declares that "[e]quality of rights under the law shall not be denied or abridged by the United States or by any State on account of sex." Thus, Congress itself has concluded that classifications based upon sex are inherently invidious, and this conclusion of a coequal branch of Government is not without significance to the question presently under consideration. *Cf. Oregon v. Mitchell* (opinion of Brennan, White, and Marshall, JJ.); *Katzenbach v. Morgan* [both cases in Chapter 7, § 3B].

With these considerations in mind, we can only conclude that classifications based upon sex, like classifications based upon race, alienage, or national origin, are inherently suspect, and must therefore be subjected to strict judicial scrutiny. Applying the analysis mandated by that stricter standard of review, it is clear that the statutory scheme now before us is constitutionally invalid.

[On their face, the statutes commanded "dissimilar treatment for men and women who are . . . similarly situated," *Reed*, and the government conceded that the differential treatment accorded men and women under these statutes serves no purpose other than mere "administrative convenience." But the government offered no evidence that the differential treatment actually saved it money. "In order to satisfy the demands of strict judicial scrutiny, the Government must demonstrate, for example, that it is actually cheaper to grant increased benefits with respect to *all* male members, than it is to determine which male members are in fact entitled to such benefits and to grant increased benefits only to those members whose wives actually meet the dependency requirement. Here, however, there is substantial evidence that, if put to the test, many of the wives of male members would fail to qualify for benefits." Moreover, administrative convenience, even if established, cannot support a statutory classification under strict scrutiny. "On the contrary, any statutory scheme which draws a sharp line between the sexes, *solely* for the purpose of achieving administrative convenience, necessarily commands 'dissimilar treatment for men and women who are . . . similarly situated,' and therefore involves the 'very kind of arbitrary legislative choice forbidden by the [Constitution] . . . .' *Reed*." Justice Brennan found the statutory policy violative of the equal protection component of the Fifth Amendment.]

JUSTICE STEWART concurs in the judgment, agreeing that the statutes before us work an invidious discrimination in violation of the Constitution. *Reed*.

JUSTICE REHNQUIST dissents for the reasons stated by Judge Rives in his opinion for the District Court[.]

JUSTICE POWELL, with whom THE CHIEF JUSTICE [BURGER] and JUSTICE BLACKMUN join, concurring in the judgment.

I agree that the challenged statutes constitute an unconstitutional discrimination against servicewomen in violation of the Due Process Clause of the Fifth Amendment, but I cannot join the opinion of Justice Brennan, which would hold that all classifications based upon sex, "like classifications based upon race, alienage, and national origin," are "inherently suspect and must therefore be subjected to close judicial scrutiny." It is unnecessary for the Court in this case to characterize sex as a suspect classification, with all of the far-reaching implications of such a holding. *Reed*, which abundantly supports our decision today, did not add sex to the narrowly limited group of classifications which are inherently suspect. In my view, we can and should decide this case on the authority of *Reed* and reserve for the future any expansion of its rationale.

There is another, and I find compelling, reason for deferring a general categorizing of sex classifications as invoking the strictest test of judicial scrutiny. The equal rights amendment, which if adopted will resolve the substance of this precise question, has been approved by the Congress and submitted for ratification by the States. If this Amendment is duly adopted, it will represent the will of the people accomplished in the manner prescribed by the Constitution. By acting prematurely and unnecessarily, as I view it, the Court has assumed a decisional responsibility at the very time when state legislatures, functioning within the traditional democratic process, are debating the proposed Amendment. It seems to me that this reaching out to pre-empt by judicial action a major political decision which is currently in process of resolution does not reflect appropriate respect for duly prescribed legislative processes.

NOTES ON THE RACE ANALOGY AND WHETHER SEX-BASED CLASSIFICATIONS SHOULD BE SUBJECT TO STRICT SCRUTINY

1. *Objections to the Race-Sex Analogy—and the Odd Insistence on Immutability.* Justice Brennan's plurality opinion maintained, as the ACLU had argued, that sex-based classifications are enough "like" race-based classifications to require strict scrutiny; the opinion points to pervasive past and continuing discrimination against women, the immutability of sex, and its typical irrelevance to legitimate state goals. Note, initially, that some feminists believe the ACLU's race-analogy was the wrong strategy for arguing women's equality.[o] To begin with, the strategy accepted the traditional equal protection trope that "similarly situated people should be treated similarly." In a society where "man is the measure of all things," this approach unfairly required women

---

o. For an excellent analysis of the pitfalls of the race analogy for women's rights, see Serena Mayeri, Note, *"A Common Fate of Discrimination": Race-Gender Analogies in Legal and Historical Perspective*, 110 Yale L.J. 1045 (2001).

to demonstrate that they are "similarly situated" to men and failed to meet women's particular needs. Moreover, women's rights counsel were analogizing sex to race at precisely the point in time when the Court was reinterpreting the race cases to foreclose most constitutional claims based upon the disparate impact of state policies on racial minorities (Chapter 3, § 1B). As Wendy Williams' article emphasized, women's equality required heightened scrutiny of policies not deploying sex-based classifications but still directly affecting women — most notably policies discriminating on the basis of pregnancy. The race analogy undermined women's arguments in the pregnancy cases, as Williams immediately learned in *Geduldig v. Aiello* (§ 2B3 below).

Finally, and perhaps most interestingly, the ACLU and the plurality both emphasized the immutability of sex as a key factor motivating heightened scrutiny. Is immutability a necessary *or* sufficient condition to trigger strict scrutiny? Alienage is not immutable (many aliens can become citizens), yet it had just been recognized as a suspect classification, at least for state laws. Neither the civil rights movement nor the Warren Court gave any emphasis to immutability as a reason to treat race as a suspect classification, and with good reason: Race is not as immutable as some people assume, because one's race depends upon context and the person's presentation. Homer Plessy thought himself "white," but the state deemed him "colored." Nor is immutability a sufficient criterion for strict scrutiny. If it could be shown that most shoplifters act out of an "immutable" compulsion (kleptomania), could they challenge discrimination against them in those criminal laws?

Note how the immutability criterion in *Frontiero* disaggregates *sex* and *gender*. Sex is viewed as natural, prepolitical, *immutable*, while gender is treated as socially created, political, *mutable*. This is a feminist "advance" over the traditional jurisprudence of difference, which viewed both sex and gender as natural and immutable — but why treat sex as immutable?[p] Transsexuals, for example, feel that their gender identity but not their sex is fixed; many transsexuals have surgery to change their sex. The disaggregation of sex and gender links up with the analytical structure of the Court's subsequent cases: A law classifying on the basis of *sex* will be most questionable when it subserves traditional *gender* "stereotypes." How would the Court analyze the issue if it considered both sex and gender social constructs?

2. *Original Intent and the De Facto ERA.* The Framers of the Fourteenth Amendment were particularly solicitous of protecting the rights of the former slaves; thus, heightened scrutiny could be limited to classifications based upon race and ethnicity, as the majority suggested in *The Slaughter House Cases.* These Framers turned their backs on their former allies in the women's movement and rejected proposals for "equal treatment" for women. As a matter of original intent, one might argue that the Court should not read extra protections into the Constitution that the Framers considered but left out, nor

---

p. See Katherine Franke, *The Central Mistake of Sex Discrimination Law: The Disaggregation of Sex from Gender*, 144 U. Pa. L. Rev. 1 (1995) (detailed critique of this disaggregation).

should the Court overrule precedents without better originalist evidence.[q] Ruth Bader Ginsburg later conceded that "[b]oldly dynamic interpretation, departing radically from the original understanding, is required to tie to the fourteenth amendment's equal protection clause a command that government treat men and women as individuals equal in rights, responsibilities and opportunities."[r] She invoked *Loving v. Virginia* (Chapter 3, § 1A) and *Brown v. Board of Education* (Chapter 2, § 1), to argue that the Equal Protection Clause *should* be dynamically interpreted. Again, note the race-sex analogy and the implicit argument that the Court should update the Constitution to recognize women's full equal citizenship for the same reasons that motivated the Court to recognize the full equal citizenship for people of color. But because the core goal of the Fourteenth Amendment was to assure black people full citizenship, the originalist case for sex discrimination dynamism is much weaker than that for race discrimination dynamism.

Moreover, the 1789 Framers intended that the mechanism for "updating" the Constitution be the amendment process outlined in Article V, a procedure under way when Ginsburg sought a judicial updating. In 1972, Congress submitted the Equal Rights Amendment (ERA) to the states. Section 1 said: "Equality of rights under the law shall not be denied or abridged by the United States or by any State on account of sex." Within months of its submission, the ERA was ratified by half of the 38 states needed for amendment of the Constitution, but then it became stalled by opposition. In 1978, Congress extended the deadline for ratification until 1982, by which point the ERA still only had 35 of the 38 states needed, and the amendment died. Is it appropriate for the Court to "amend" the Constitution on its own, or anticipate an amendment's passage, while the amendment is pending under the procedures sanctioned by Article V? The four concurring Justices in *Frontiero* thought not; some scholars have concluded that the *Frontiero* plurality's willingness to adopt a "de facto ERA" through interpretation is inconsistent with Article V and the rule of law.[s]

Other scholars have been friendly to the Court's creation of a de facto ERA.[t] One of us suggests this caveat: there was normative significance to the *reasons* Americans agreed with Phyllis Schlafly and STOP-ERA. Schlafly charged that

---

q. See Earl Maltz, *Gender Discrimination and the Original Understanding*, 18 Harv. J.L. & Pub. Pol'y 415 (1995).

r. Ruth Bader Ginsburg, *Sexual Equality under the Fourteenth and Equal Rights Amendments*, 1979 Wash. U.L.Q. 161, 161.

s. E.g., Henry Monaghan, *We the People[s], Original Understanding, and Constitutional Amendment*, 96 Colum. L. Rev. 121 (1996); David Dow, *When Words Mean What We Believe They Say: The Case of Article V*, 76 Iowa L. Rev. 1 (1990). See also Akhil Reed Amar, *The Consent of the Governed: Constitutional Amendment Outside Article V*, 94 Colum. L. Rev. 457 (1994) (Constitution can also be amended by a national referendum).

t. Michael Dorf, *Equal Protection Incorporation*, 88 Va. L. Rev. 951 (2002); William Eskridge, Jr., *Some Effects of Identity-Based Social Movements on Constitutional Law in the twentieth Century*, 100 Mich. L. Rev. 2062, 2130-38 (2002); Reva Siegel, *Constitutional Culture, Social Movement Conflict and Constitutional Change*, 94 Calif. L. Rev. 1323 (2006); David Strauss, *The Irrelevance of Constitutional Amendments*, 114 Harv. L. Rev. 1457, 1476-78 (2001).

the ERA would (1) sweep away legislation *protecting* women, including statutory rape laws, labor and tax benefits for working wives and mothers, and exemption from military service; (2) destroy traditional family values by "liberating" husbands from alimony obligations and pregnant women from restrictions on abortion; and (3) impose homosexual marriage and the rest of the "homosexual agenda" on the nation. Most Americans, including most women, did *not* want all the logical consequences of a totally sex-blind jurisprudence, and even ERA supporters denied the ERA would have these effects. Our suggestion is that these counter-arguments molded the Supreme Court's sex discrimination jurisprudence from the very beginning: unlike in the race cases, where the Court has pressed a colorblind perspective, the Court in the sex cases has allowed a lot of sex-based distinctions, precisely along the lines advocated by Schlafly.[u]   Does this hypothesis render the de facto ERA more legitimate?

3. *Was There a Political Need for the Court to Intervene? Women as a Discrete and Dispersed Majority.* Recall the *Carolene Products* idea that special constitutional protection might be extended to "discrete and insular minorities" (like blacks) whose problems will not be fairly addressed by a biased political process (Chapter 1, § 6). Women, however, are discrete but not insular (wherever you find men in our society, you also find women) and are certainly not a minority, as they constitute a majority of our population. After the Nineteenth Amendment, women have potentially great political power. Not only does the race-sex analogy break down, but a representation-reinforcing Supreme Court has much less incentive to protect women against discriminations; such problems ought to be remedied in the political process, yes?

John Hart Ely, *Democracy and Distrust: A Theory of Judicial Review* 164-70 (1980), makes these points but notes that women might be appropriate beneficiaries of his representation-reinforcement interpretation of the Constitution (Chapter 2, § 3B). Women have long been victims of laws that reflect invidious stereotypes, many of which were enacted in periods when women had no political representation (before 1920), and even after women could vote their political participation was hampered by the continuing effects of their traditional subordination. Sex discrimination is based upon a "highly visible" trait that "lends itself to a system of thought dominated by stereotype, which automatically consigns an individual to a general category (such as race or gender), often implying the inferiority of the person so categorized."[v]

Conceding all this, Ely argues that women are more than capable of being heard politically, and that if the political process fails to correct such outdated statutes it is more because women as a group are ambivalent about some of them or don't organize against them. Also, the success of the ERA, the adoption of equal rights amendments in sixteen state constitutions, and the enactment of

---

    u. Eskridge, *Identity-Based Social Movements*, 100 Mich. L. Rev. at 2138-56. On the reasons for the ERA's defeat, see Jane Mansbridge, *Why We Lost the ERA* (1986); Donald Mathews & Jane Sherron De Hart, *Sex, Gender, and the Politics of the ERA: A State and the Nation* (1990).

    v. Kenneth Karst, *The Supreme Court, 1976 Term — Foreword: Equal Citizenship under the Fourteenth Amendment*, 91 Harv. L. Rev. 1, 23 (1977).

Title VII of the Civil Rights Act and other laws assuring women's rights all suggest that women in the 1960s and 1970s were a political force who overcame the stigmatization of gender stereotypes by their own efforts. Ely's theory suggests that, although "older" statutes (especially those enacted before women had the right to vote) might be strictly scrutinized, newer statutes (such as the one in *Frontiero*, which was adopted in 1967) might be left alone.

NOTE ON THE COURT'S SEX-DISCRIMINATION CASES, 1973-76

For several years after *Frontiero*, the Court managed to avoid deciding the level of scrutiny it would apply in sex discrimination cases. An ancillary theme in the cases was the relationship of sex (one's biology) to gender (one's social role). Generally, the Court struck down *sex-based classifications* which reflected what the Court considered *gender stereotypes*. Thus, in *Stanton v. Stanton*, 421 U.S. 7 (1975), a father relied upon a state statute under which females reached majority at 18 and males at 21 to justify stopping child support payments to his 18-year-old daughter. The state court had upheld the statute, concluding that it was based on the notion that, because males are the primary breadwinners, they need the opportunity to obtain an education. The Supreme Court reversed, on the ground that education was equally important to both sexes and that the statute's distinction was based upon outmoded stereotypes about women's roles.

In *Schlesinger v. Ballard*, 419 U.S. 498 (1975), a male Navy officer challenged a statute providing that male officers had a shorter period in which to attain promotion or be discharged than female officers. Upholding the statute, the Court concluded that the sex classification was not based on "archaic or overbroad generalizations," like those in *Frontiero*, but rather reflected the real differences between male and female Navy officers in terms of promotions; because women were prohibited from serving in combat and many forms of sea duty, they could not be expected to compile a record for promotion as quickly as men. The Court was willing to allow a sex-based remedial law which arguably helped women overcome structural disadvantages and pursue nonstereotypical careers.

Similarly, the Court in *Kahn v. Shevin*, 416 U.S. 351 (1974), upheld a state statute allowing widows, but not widowers, a small property tax exemption on the ground that, "[w]hether from overt discrimination or from the socialization process," such women faced more difficult barriers in the job market than widowers. Contrast *Weinberger v. Wiesenfeld*, 420 U.S. 636 (1975), which struck down a Social Security provision under which a surviving widow and minor children received benefits based on the earnings of the deceased husband and father, but under which only minor children received benefits if the mother died. The Court conceptualized the statute as discrimination against women — their survivors received less protection than men — and concluded that it was based on archaic and overbroad generalizations that assume that the earnings of male, but not female, workers are vital to supporting their families.

Without addressing the strict scrutiny question, the Court was usually following the ACLU's view that "persons similarly situated, whether male or female, must be accorded even-handed treatment by the law." Legislative classifications "may not be premised on sex-role stereotypes or unalterable sex characteristics that bear no necessary relationship to an individual's need, ability, or life situation." Brief for Appellants, at 11, *Kahn* (No. 73-78). In *Taylor v. Louisiana*, 419 U.S. 522 (1975), the Court interpreted the Sixth Amendment to overrule *Hoyt*'s ruling that the state can have a separate opt-in system for jury service by women. In the next major case, involving the sale of liquor, the ACLU urged the Court to overrule *Goesaert*.

CRAIG v. BOREN
429 U.S. 190, 97 S.Ct. 451, 50 L.Ed.2d 397 (1976)

JUSTICE BRENNAN delivered the opinion of the Court.

[An Oklahoma statute prohibited the sale of 3.2% beer to males under the age of 21 and to females under the age of 18; it did not prohibit the possession or consumption of such beer by males aged 18-20. A male in the 18-20 age group and a bar owner filed suit for declaratory and injunctive relief, alleging that the law was unconstitutional. The three-judge district court upheld the statute.]

Analysis may appropriately begin with the reminder that *Reed* emphasized that statutory classifications that distinguish between males and females are "subject to scrutiny under the Equal Protection Clause." To withstand constitutional challenge, previous cases establish that classifications by gender must serve important governmental objectives and must be substantially related to achievement of those objectives. Thus, in *Reed*, the objectives of "reducing the workload on probate courts" and "avoiding intrafamily controversy" were deemed of insufficient importance to sustain use of an overt gender criterion in the appointment of administrators of intestate decedents' estates. Decisions following *Reed* similarly have rejected administrative ease and convenience as sufficiently important objectives to justify gender-based classifications. *See, e.g., Stanley v. Illinois*, 405 U.S. 645 (1972); *Frontiero*; *cf. Schlesinger v. Ballard*. And only two Terms ago, *Stanton v. Stanton*, expressly stating that *Reed v. Reed* was "controlling," held that *Reed* required invalidation of a Utah differential age-of-majority statute, notwithstanding the statute's coincidence with and furtherance of the State's purpose of fostering "old notions" of role typing and preparing boys for their expected performance in the economic and political worlds.[6]

Reed v. Reed has also provided the underpinning for decisions that have invalidated statutes employing gender as an inaccurate proxy for other, more germane bases of classification. Hence, "archaic and overbroad" generalizations, *Ballard*, concerning the financial position of servicewomen, *Frontiero*, and

---

6. *Kahn v. Shevin* and *Schlesinger v. Ballard*, upholding the use of gender-based classifications, rested upon the Court's perception of the laudatory purposes of those laws as remedying disadvantageous conditions suffered by women in economic and military life. Needless to say, in this case Oklahoma does not suggest that the age-sex differential was enacted to ensure the availability of 3.2% beer for women as compensation for previous deprivations.

working women, *Weinberger v. Wiesenfeld*, could not justify use of a gender line in determining eligibility for certain governmental entitlements. Similarly, increasingly outdated misconceptions concerning the role of females in the home rather than in the "marketplace and world of ideas" were rejected as loose-fitting characterizations incapable of supporting state statutory schemes that were premised upon their accuracy. *Stanton.* In light of the weak congruence between gender and the characteristic or trait that gender purported to represent, it was necessary that the legislatures choose either to realign their substantive laws in a gender-neutral fashion, or to adopt procedures for identifying those instances where the sex-centered generalization actually comported with fact. * * *

We accept for purposes of discussion the District Court's identification of the objective underlying [the statute] as the enhancement of traffic safety. Clearly, the protection of public health and safety represents an important function of state and local governments. However, appellees' statistics in our view cannot support the conclusion that the gender-based distinction closely serves to achieve that objective and therefore the distinction cannot under *Reed* withstand equal protection challenge.

The appellees introduced a variety of statistical surveys. First, an analysis of arrest statistics for 1973 demonstrated that 18 - 20-year-old male arrests for "driving under the influence" and "drunkenness" substantially exceeded female arrests for that same age period. Similarly, youths aged 17-21 were found to be overrepresented among those killed or injured in traffic accidents, with males again numerically exceeding females in this regard. Third, a random roadside survey in Oklahoma City revealed that young males were more inclined to drive and drink beer than were their female counterparts. Fourth, Federal Bureau of Investigation nationwide statistics exhibited a notable increase in arrests for "driving under the influence." Finally, statistical evidence gathered in other jurisdictions, particularly Minnesota and Michigan, was offered to corroborate Oklahoma's experience by indicating the pervasiveness of youthful participation in motor vehicle accidents following the imbibing of alcohol. Conceding that "the case is not free from doubt," the District Court nonetheless concluded that this statistical showing substantiated "a rational basis for the legislative judgment underlying the challenged classification."

Even were this statistical evidence accepted as accurate, it nevertheless offers only a weak answer to the equal protection question presented here. The most focused and relevant of the statistical surveys, arrests of 18-20 year-olds for alcohol-related driving offenses, exemplifies the ultimate unpersuasiveness of this evidentiary record. Viewed in terms of the correlation between sex and the actual activity that Oklahoma seeks to regulate — driving while under the influence of alcohol — the statistics broadly establish that .18% of females and 2% of males in that age group were arrested for that offense. While such a disparity is not trivial in a statistical sense, it hardly can form the basis for employment of a gender line as a classifying device. Certainly if maleness is to serve as a proxy for drinking and driving, a correlation of 2% must be considered an unduly tenuous "fit." Indeed, prior cases have consistently rejected the use of sex as a decisionmaking factor even though the statutes in question certainly rested on far more predictive empirical relationships than this.[13]

Moreover, the statistics exhibit a variety of other shortcomings that seriously impugn their value to equal protection analysis. Setting aside the obvious methodological problems, the surveys do not adequately justify the salient features of Oklahoma's gender-based traffic-safety law. None purports to measure the use and dangerousness of 3.2% beer as opposed to alcohol generally, a detail that is of particular importance since, in light of its low alcohol level, Oklahoma apparently considers the 3.2% beverage to be "nonintoxicating." Okla. Stat., Tit. 37, § 163.1 (1958). Moreover, many of the studies, while graphically documenting the unfortunate increase in driving while under the influence of alcohol, make no effort to relate their findings to age-sex differentials as involved here. Indeed, the only survey that explicitly centered its attention upon young drivers and their use of beer — albeit apparently not of the diluted 3.2% variety — reached results that hardly can be viewed as impressive in justifying either a gender or age classification.

There is no reason to belabor this line of analysis. It is unrealistic to expect either members of the judiciary or state officials to be well versed in the rigors of experimental or statistical technique. But this merely illustrates that proving broad sociological propositions by statistics is a dubious business, and one that inevitably is in tension with the normative philosophy that underlies the Equal Protection Clause. Suffice to say that the showing offered by the appellees does not satisfy us that sex represents a legitimate, accurate proxy for the regulation of drinking and driving. In fact, when it is further recognized that Oklahoma's statute prohibits only the selling of 3.2% beer to young males and not their drinking the beverage once acquired (even after purchase by their 18 - 20-year-old female companions), the relationship between gender and traffic safety becomes far too tenuous to satisfy *Reed*'s requirement that the gender-based difference be substantially related to achievement of the statutory objective. * * *

JUSTICE STEVENS, concurring.

There is only one Equal Protection Clause. It requires every State to govern impartially. It does not direct the courts to apply one standard of review in some cases and a different standard in other cases. Whatever criticism may be leveled at a judicial opinion implying that there are at least three such standards applies with the same force to a double standard.

I am inclined to believe that what has become known as the two-tiered analysis of equal protection claims does not describe a completely logical method of deciding cases, but rather is a method the Court has employed to

---

13.   For example, we can conjecture that in *Reed*, Idaho's apparent premise that women lacked experience in formal business matters (particularly compared to men) would have proved to be accurate in substantially more than 2% of all cases. And in both *Frontiero* and *Wiesenfeld*, we expressly found appellees' empirical defense of mandatory dependency tests for men but not women to be unsatisfactory, even though we recognized that husbands are still far less likely to be dependent on their wives than vice versa.

explain decisions that actually apply a single standard in a reasonably consistent fashion. I also suspect that a careful explanation of the reasons motivating particular decisions may contribute more to an identification of that standard than an attempt to articulate it in all-encompassing terms. It may therefore be appropriate for me to state the principal reasons which persuaded me to join the Court's opinion.

In this case, the classification is not as obnoxious as some the Court has condemned,[1] nor as inoffensive as some the Court has accepted. It is objectionable because it is based on an accident of birth, because it is a mere remnant of the now almost universally rejected tradition of discriminating against males in this age bracket, and because, to the extent it reflects any physical difference between males and females, it is actually perverse.[4] The question then is whether the traffic safety justification put forward by the State is sufficient to make an otherwise offensive classification acceptable.

The classification is not totally irrational. For the evidence does indicate that there are more males than females in this age bracket who drive and also more who drink. Nevertheless, there are several reasons why I regard the justification as unacceptable. It is difficult to believe that the statute was actually intended to cope with the problem of traffic safety, since it has only a minimal effect on access to a not very intoxicating beverage and does not prohibit its consumption. Moreover, the empirical data submitted by the State accentuate the unfairness of treating all 18 - 21-year-old males as inferior to their female counterparts. The legislation imposes a restraint on 100% of the males in the class allegedly because about 2% of them have probably violated one or more laws relating to the consumption of alcoholic beverages. It is unlikely that this law will have a significant deterrent effect either on that 2% or on the law-abiding 98%. But even assuming some such slight benefit, it does not seem to me that an insult to all of the young men of the State can be justified by visiting the sins of the 2% on the 98%.

[We have omitted the opinions of **JUSTICE POWELL**, concurring; of **JUSTICE BLACKMUN**, concurring in part; of **JUSTICE STEWART**, concurring in the judgment; and of **CHIEF JUSTICE BURGER**, dissenting.]

JUSTICE REHNQUIST, dissenting.

Most obviously unavailable to support any kind of special scrutiny in this case, is a history or pattern of past discrimination, such as was relied on by the plurality in *Frontiero* to support its invocation of strict scrutiny. There is no suggestion in the Court's opinion that males in this age group are in any way peculiarly disadvantaged, subject to systematic discriminatory treatment, or otherwise in need of special solicitude from the courts. * * *

---

1. Men as a general class have not been the victims of the kind of historic, pervasive discrimination that has disadvantaged other groups.

4. Because males are generally heavier than females, they have a greater capacity to consume alcohol without impairing their driving ability than do females.

The Court's conclusion that a law which treats males less favorably than females "must serve important governmental objectives and must be substantially related to achievement of those objectives" apparently comes out of thin air. The Equal Protection Clause contains no such language, and none of our previous cases adopt that standard. I would think we have had enough difficulty with the two standards of review which our cases have recognized — the norm of "rational basis," and the "compelling state interest" required where a "suspect classification" is involved — so as to counsel weightily against the insertion of still another "standard" between those two. How is this Court to divine what objectives are important? How is it to determine whether a particular law is "substantially" related to the achievement of such objective, rather than related in some other way to its achievement? Both of the phrases used are so diaphanous and elastic as to invite subjective judicial preferences or prejudices relating to particular types of legislation, masquerading as judgments whether such legislation is directed at "important" objectives or whether the relationship to those objectives is "substantial" enough.

I would have thought that if this Court were to leave anything to decision by the popularly elected branches of the Government, where no constitutional claim other than that of equal protection is invoked, it would be the decision as to what governmental objectives to be achieved by law are "important," and which are not. As for the second part of the Court's new test, the Judicial Branch is probably in no worse position than the Legislative or Executive Branches to determine if there is *any* rational relationship between a classification and the purpose which it might be thought to serve. But the introduction of the adverb "substantially" requires courts to make subjective judgments as to operational effects, for which neither their expertise nor their access to data fits them. And even if we manage to avoid both confusion and the mirroring of our own preferences in the development of this new doctrine, the thousands of judges in other courts who must interpret the Equal Protection Clause may not be so fortunate.

NOTE ON THE COURT'S "MIDDLE TIER" SCRUTINY

Do we now have three tiers of equal protection scrutiny, with *Craig* establishing "intermediate scrutiny" for a "semi-suspect classification," or is Justice Stevens correct in his concurring opinion in *Craig*, that the same standard explains the outcomes in all equal protection cases? What justifications — based upon original intent, representation reinforcement, or justice-based theories — might there be for the majority's approach? What difference does the level of scrutiny make? The Oklahoma statute would have passed the rational basis test, because there was an empirical connection between a legitimate state goal (safety) and the classification chosen by the state (young men statistically threatened the goal more than young women). How is Justice Brennan's application of intermediate scrutiny materially different from strict scrutiny? Consider this angle: Although the federal ERA died in 1982, at least sixteen state constitutions have ERAs protecting against discrimination because of sex.[w] Assuming that an ERA would require strict rather than intermediate scrutiny, in what sort of case would strict scrutiny invalidate, but *Craig*'s intermediate scrutiny would affirm, a statute containing a sex-based classification?

In a series of cases after *Craig*, the Court made short shrift of sex-based classifications which rested upon traditional gender roles for men and women: *Califano v. Goldfarb*, 430 U.S. 199 (1977), invalidating a federal law paying survivors' benefits to widows routinely but to a widower only if he was receiving at least one-half of his support from his deceased wife, followed in *Califano v. Westcott*, 443 U.S. 76 (1979) and *Wengler v. Druggists Mut. Ins. Co.*, 446 U.S. 142 (1980); *Orr v. Orr*, 440 U.S. 268 (1979), invalidating an Alabama law exempting wives from payment of alimony upon the dissolution of a marriage; *Kirchberg v. Feenstra*, 450 U.S. 455 (1981), invalidating a Louisiana law giving the husband, as "head and master" of the household, the right to dispose of property jointly owned by his wife without her consent. Justice Marshall's opinion for the Court in *Kirchberg* said that when the state deploys a sex-based classification, it has a burden of demonstrating an "exceedingly persuasive justification for the classification."

Richard Epstein, *The Rule of Sex-Blind Jurisprudence Isn't Always Fair*, Wall Street Journal, July 21, 1993, at A15.[x] In connection with Ruth Bader Ginsburg's nomination to the Court, Professor Epstein evaluated several cases where she had won Supreme Court rulings to invalidate sex discriminations. Epstein felt that *Reed v. Reed* was defensible, because the state made no showing that decedents generally preferred men to women as executors. He cautioned, however, that the sex discrimination would have been rational if the state had made such a showing, because the state ought to have the authority to set up "a default rule that best mirrors the preferences of ordinary citizens who have the right to choose executors of their choice."

Epstein questioned the results in *Frontiero* and *Goldfarb*, where the statutory schemes "made a good deal more sense than the one in *Reed*. In justifying sex-based classifications, why must the law treat unlike cases alike? If 90% of women were in fact dependent on husbands and only 3% of men on wives — roughly the numbers in *Goldfarb* — then it is good economics, not insidious stereotypes, to treat the two situations differently.

---

w. See Alaska Const. art. I, § 3; Colorado Const. art. II, § 29; Connecticut Const. art. I, § 20; Hawaii Const. art. I, § 3; Illinois Const. art. I, § 18; Louisiana Const. art. I, § 3; Maryland Const., Declaration of Rights, art. 46; Massachusetts Const. pt 1, art. I; Montana Const. art. II, § 4; New Mexico Const. art. II, § 18; Pennsylvania Const. art. I, § 28; Texas Const. art. I, § 3a; Utah Const. art. IV, § 1; Virginia Const. art. I, § 11; Washington Const. art. XXXI, § 1; Wyoming Const. art. I, § 3. Half of these provisions were modeled on the proposed federal Equal Rights Amendment. Other states as well as the District of Columbia have statutes protecting against discrimination because of sex in employment and other arenas.

x. Materials reprinted with permission of Professor Richard Epstein.

"To require proof of dependency for wives creates an unnecessary administrative headache since an automatic rule already reaches the right result 90% of the time. Better to spare the paperwork and use the savings to increase the overall benefit levels. To pay benefits to male spouses without scrutiny leads to massive overpayments requiring either additional budget appropriations or benefit reductions. The sex classifications in *Frontiero* and *Goldfarb* are perfectly sensible and should have been sustained unless and until the underlying behavioral patterns shift."

As for *Craig v. Boren*, Epstein argued: "The social gain of denying alcohol to males at 18 is far greater than the gain from denying it to females at 18. A rule that keeps women from drinking until 21 imposes unnecessary deprivation; a rule that allows men to drink at 18 creates unnecessary risk. Clearly the law is not designed to oppress or stigmatize men, and nothing in the Constitution forbids this sensible accommodation."

From the foregoing analysis, Epstein concluded that a "rigid" sex-equality jurisprudence saddled the country with "inferior social outcomes for the small benefit of striking down sex-based statutes that are likely to fall anyhow of their own political weight." Does his analysis undervalue the goals of the Court's sex discrimination jurisprudence? Is his analysis persuasive as a matter of neutral cost-benefit economics? Compare Mary Anne Case, *Of Richard Epstein and Other Radical Feminists*, 18 Harv. J.L. & Pub. Pol'y 369, 382-85 (1995). How would Epstein's treat-like-cases-alike analysis resolve the next case, where the sex discrimination served a remedial goal?

————

Califano v. Webster, 430 U.S. 313 (1977). Until it was amended in 1972, the Social Security Act provided for old-age benefits to be calculated on the basis of the wage earner's "average monthly wage" (AMW) for a specified number of years (to be chosen by the employee, hence, her or his highest earning years). The AMW for male and female wage earners was calculated differently, such that female earners could exclude more low-earning years from the formula than male earners could. Will Webster claimed this formula discriminated against him under the *Craig* test and was inconsistent with *Wiesenfeld* and *Goldfarb*.

The Court, in a *per curiam* opinion, disagreed. It read *Ballard* and *Kahn* for the proposition that "[r]eduction of the disparity in economic condition between men and women caused by the long history of discrimination against women [is] an important governmental objective" under *Craig*. But " 'the mere recitation of a benign, compensatory purpose is not an automatic shield which protects against any inquiry into the actual purposes underlying a statutory scheme,' " as *Wiesenfeld* held. The Court found the provision more analogous to *Ballard* and *Kahn* than *Wiesenfeld* and *Goldfarb*. "The more favorable treatment of the female wage earner enacted here was not a result of 'archaic and overbroad generalizations' about women, *Ballard*, or of 'the role-typing society has long imposed' upon women, *Stanton*, such as casual assumptions that women are 'the weaker sex' or are more likely to be child-rearers or dependents. Rather 'the only discernible purpose of [this statute's more favorable treatment is] the permissible one of redressing our society's longstanding disparate treatment of women.' *Goldfarb*."

The Court found in the legislative history of the 1956 statute evidence that Congress was responding to the well-documented fact that women's wages and economic opportunities were wrongfully depressed by traditionalist attitudes; the differential of the statute was defended and tailored to rectify some of this past discrimination. (Significantly, *Wiesenfeld* and *Goldfarb* struck down provisions that disadvantaged female wage earners, though they advantaged female survivors, while the *Webster* provision advantaged female wage earners as well as their spouses.) Congress repealed the favorable treatment in 1972 prospectively, because statutes prohibiting sex discrimination in the workplace made remediation less necessary.

Chief Justice Burger, joined by **Justices Stewart, Blackmun**, and **Rehnquist**, concurred in the judgment, but believed the result inconsistent with *Goldfarb*, from which he had dissented. "I question whether certainty in the law is promoted by hinging the validity of important statutory schemes on whether five Justices view them to be more akin to the 'offensive' provisions struck down in *Wiesenfeld* and *Frontiero*, or more like the 'benign' provisions upheld in *Ballard* and *Kahn*." Compare these Justices' tolerance for remedial sex-based classifications in *Webster* with their objection (except for Blackmun) to remedial race-based classifications in *Bakke* (Chapter 3, § 3A), decided the next Term of the Court.

————

J.E.B. v. Alabama ex rel. T.B., 511 U.S. 127 (1994). In a state action to establish J.E.B.'s paternity, the state exercised nine of its ten peremptory challenges to strike male jurors; although J.E.B. used all but one of his challenges to strike female jurors, the jury ended up all-female. The Supreme Court declared the process inconsistent with the Equal Protection Clause and extended *Batson*, prohibiting discriminatory use of race-based peremptory challenges, to prohibit sex-based peremptory challenges. **Justice Blackmun**'s opinion for the Court noted that sex-discriminating peremptory challenges were only recently the subject of challenge, because women were long excluded from jury service, even longer than African Americans (see *Hoyt*). Indeed, the stereotypes invoked to exclude women from juries were similar to those invoked by the state to strike male jurors: Women will empathize with the jilted complainant, while men will be skeptical of her charges. Blackmun cited empirical studies casting doubt on generalizations that women will vote differently on juries than men and, more pointedly, maintained that sex or gender stereotypes are no more defensible than race stereotypes.

"Discrimination in jury selection, whether based on race or on gender, causes harm to the litigants, the community, and the individual jurors who are wrongfully excluded from participation in the judicial process. The litigants are harmed by the risk that the prejudices which motivated the discriminatory selection of the jury will infect the entire proceedings. The community is harmed by the State's participation in the perpetuation of invidious group stereotypes and the inevitable loss of confidence in our judicial system that state-sanctioned discrimination in the courtroom engenders." The Court insisted on the same protections as in *Batson* for race-based challenges: The party alleging gender discrimination must make a prima facie showing of intentional discrimination, and the party challenged must then explain the basis for the strike; the explanation need not rise to the level of for-cause challenges but must persuade the judge that the strike was motivated by non-gender reasons.

Justice Scalia, writing for himself and **Chief Justice Rehnquist** and **Justice Thomas**, dissented. His initial point was that the discrimination in question was *sex discrimination* (men were excluded), not *gender discrimination* (masculine people were not at issue). His second point was that he didn't understand how it is sex discrimination when each side is free to exercise offsetting peremptory challenges: J.E.B. struck women, the state struck men. Why isn't the system as a whole satisfactory under ideas of functional as well as formal equality? His third point was that group-based characteristics are the whole point of peremptory challenges, and extending *Batson* to sex-based challenges further undermines their role in an adversarial system. Is there any principled reason why *J.E.B.* should not be extended to religion-based challenges? Ethnicity or alienage-based? Non-speakers of the English language? Sexual orientation? See *People v. Garcia,* 92 Cal. Rptr. 2d 339 (App. 2000) (extending state constitutional rule to monitor peremptory exclusion of lesbians, gay men, and bisexuals from juries).

––––––

Mississippi University for Women v. Hogan, 458 U.S. 718 (1982). The Mississippi University for Women (MUW) was created in 1884 to provide higher education for white women, who before 1882 were excluded from the state university (which did not encourage women to attend until 1920) and all other state colleges. MUW remained all-female until Joe Hogan applied to its School of Nursing. The Supreme Court ruled that the exclusion of men violated the Equal Protection Clause. **Justice O'Connor**'s opinion for the Court summarized the precedents as establishing that "the party seeking to uphold a statute that classifies individuals on the basis of their gender must carry the burden of showing an 'exceedingly persuasive justification for the classification.' *Kirchberg*. The burden is met only by showing at least that the classification serves 'important governmental objectives and that the discriminatory means employed' are 'substantially related to the achievement of those objectives.' *Wengler*."

Justice O'Connor found the state justification, compensation for workplace discrimination against women, unsupported. "In limited circumstances, a gender-based classification favoring one sex can be justified if it intentionally and directly assists members of the sex that is disproportionately burdened," as in *Webster* and *Ballard*. But where the "benign, compensatory purpose" is no more than a shield for archaic gender norms, it cannot save the statute, as in *Wiesenfeld*. The Court found that women in Mississippi lacked no opportunities to become nurses; at all points in the last generation, more than 90% of the nurses in the state have been female. "Rather than compensate for discriminatory barriers faced by women, MUW's policy of excluding males from admission to the School of Nursing tends to perpetuate the stereotyped view of nursing as an exclusively woman's job. By assuring that Mississippi allots more openings in its state-supported nursing schools to women than it does to men, MUW's admissions policy lends credibility to the old view that women, not men, should become nurses, and makes the assumption that nursing is a field for women a self-fulfilling prophecy."

Four dissenting Justices (**Chief Justice Burger** and **Justices Blackmun, Powell, Rehnquist**) lamented the possibility that the Court was threatening educational diversity. Specifically, the dissenters eulogized all-female schools, which experts had found useful in creating a preferable learning environment for women who found coeducational schools unfriendly to women and dominated by men. (See Note: Is Sex Segregation in Schools Ever Constitutional?, p. 402, *infra*, for references.) Are the dissenters' fears magnified by the next case, *United States v. Virginia*?

NOTE ON THEORIES OF CULTURAL FEMINISM AND SOCIOBIOLOGY

Carol Gilligan, *In a Different Voice: Psychological Theory and Women's Development* (1982), argued that female and male children develop differently in our society. Her prototypical children, Jake and Amy, approached problem-solving differently. In response to the dilemma of a man whose wife was dying and the medicine needed to treat her was beyond his ability to pay, Jake reasoned deductively that the man should steal the needed drugs, because the wife's death was more lamentable than the theft. Amy, in contrast, resisted the question and wondered whether there were ways of accommodating the two values (life and property); perhaps the man could work out a deal with a druggist whereby he could obtain the needed medicine in return for working extra hours for the druggist. Gilligan maintained that girls approach a wide range of issues looking for connection, empathy, and accommodation, while boys are more likely to view issues and problems in the abstract and as yes/no propositions. Girls tend to embrace an "ethic of care," boys an "ethic of rights."

Cultural feminism has been controversial within feminist thought, with some feminists urging the ethic of care as a different and more productive way of analyzing legal problems generally,[y] and other feminists worrying that Gilligan's dichotomy replicates traditional stereotypes about women.[z] Gilligan responded to her critics in *Making Connections: The Relational Worlds of Adolescent Girls at Emma Willard School* (1990). She denied taking the position that the Jake/Amy dichotomy is hard-wired into male and female children, but insisted that, under the particular circumstances of our culture today, boys and girls tend

---

y. See Katharine Bartlett, *Feminist Legal Methods*, 103 Harv. L. Rev. 829 (1990); Carrie Menkel-Meadow, *Portia in a Different Voice: Speculations on a Woman's Lawyering Process*, 1 Berkeley Women's L.J. 39 (1985); Suzanna Sherry, *Civic Virtue and the Feminine Voice in Constitutional Adjudication*, 72 Va. L. Rev. 543 (1986); Robin West, *Jurisprudence and Gender*, 55 U. Chi. L. Rev. 1 (1988). See also Martha Minow, *The Supreme Court, 1986 Term — Foreword: Justice Engendered*, 101 Harv. L. Rev. 10 (1987).

z. See, e.g., Catharine MacKinnon, *Feminism Unmodified: Discourses on Life and Law* (1987); Christine Littleton, *Reconstructing Sexual Equality*, 75 Calif. L. Rev. 1279 (1987); Joan Williams, *Deconstructing Gender*, 87 Mich. L. Rev. 797 (1989).

to reason differently and that Amy's ethic of care should be more widely appreciated.

Scientific theories of evolutionary psychology or "sociobiology" likewise point to differences between men and women.[a] According to such theories, gender differences are the result of evolutionary adaptation: Sexual differentiation results from, or is strongly influenced by, the different reproductive roles of men and women. Men have the ability to engage in rivalrous, aggressive, and promiscuous behavior and have not as much incentive to stick around for the rearing of offspring as women, whose pregnancies incapacitate them as well as connect them with their offspring. Natural selection would be expected to favor females whose character is nurturant and loyal, and males whose character is bold and aggressive (Posner, *Sex and Reason*, 93).

These descriptive features of evolutionary psychology are subject to argument and dispute, and even more controversial are the normative conclusions sometimes drawn from them by legal scholars. Richard Epstein, for example, cautions that "men and women are more comfortable in playing the roles that are congenial to their biological roles, and will find themselves uneasy with powerful social [or legal] conventions that dictate a parity in social roles in courtship, marriage, and parenting" (Epstein, *Two Challenges,* 336). Although such scholars concede that nature is not a sure guide to regulation, the general thrust of their prescriptive arguments is that legal regulations cutting against the grain of evolutive imperative are doomed to expensive failure, just as are legal regulations cutting against the grain of free markets.

Notwithstanding their profound intellectual differences, both cultural feminists and sociobiologists would seem presumptively open to the idea of same-sex schooling, an issue unresolved in *Hogan*. Their different-yet-similar takes on gender were on vivid display in the litigation surrounding the sex integration of two all-male public paramilitary colleges, The Citadel in South Carolina and Virginia Military Institute in Virginia. The latter generated the following Supreme Court decision. How does Justice Ginsburg respond to the general points raised by cultural feminism and evolutionary psychology?

---

a. Sociobiology classics include Edward Wilson, *Sociobiology: The New Synthesis* (1976); Richard Dawkins, *The Selfish Gene* (1976); Jerome Barkow, Leda Cosmides & John Tooby, *The Adapted Mind: Evolutionary Psychology and the Generation of Culture* (1992). An excellent journalistic account is Robert Wright, *The Moral Animal — Why We Are the Way We Are: The New Science of Evolutionary Psychology* (1994). Leading applications of sociobiology to legal regulatory issues include Richard Posner, *Sex and Reason* 88-98 (1992), reviewed by Gillian Hadfield, *Flirting with Science: Richard Posner on the Bioeconomics of Sexual Man*, 106 Harv. L. Rev. (1992), and by Jane Larson, *The New Home Economics*, 10 Const. Comm. 443 (1993); Richard Epstein, *Two Challenges for Feminist Thought*, 18 Harv. J.L. & Pub. Pol'y 321 (1995), with a response in Mary Anne Case, *Of Richard Epstein and Other Radical Feminists, id.* at 369.

UNITED STATES v. VIRGINIA
518 U.S. 515, 116 S.Ct. 2264, 135 L.Ed. 2d 735 (1996)

JUSTICE GINSBURG delivered the opinion of the Court.

[Virginia Military Institute (VMI) was the sole single-sex school among Virginia's public institutions of higher learning. VMI's distinctive mission was to produce "citizen-soldiers," men prepared for leadership in civilian life and in military service. Using an "adversative," or constantly challenging and doubting, method of training not available elsewhere in Virginia,[b] VMI endeavored to instill physical and mental discipline in its cadets. The United States sued Virginia and VMI, alleging that VMI's exclusively male admission policy violated the Equal Protection Clause, as construed in *Hogan*. The Fourth Circuit agreed and ordered Virginia to remedy the constitutional violation. In response, Virginia proposed a parallel program for women: Virginia Women's Institute for Leadership (VWIL), located at Mary Baldwin College, a private liberal arts school for women. In lieu of VMI's adversative method, the VWIL Task Force favored "a cooperative method which reinforces self-esteem." In addition to the standard bachelor of arts program offered at Mary Baldwin, VWIL students would take courses in leadership, complete an off-campus leadership externship, participate in community service projects, and assist in arranging a speaker series. The lower courts found this parallel program provided "substantively comparable" benefits and held it met equal protection requirements. The Supreme Court reversed.]

* * * To summarize the Court's current directions for cases of official classification based on gender: Focusing on the differential treatment or denial of opportunity for which relief is sought, the reviewing court must determine whether the proffered justification is "exceedingly persuasive." The burden of justification is demanding and it rests entirely on the State. See *Hogan*. The State must show "at least that the [challenged] classification serves 'important governmental objectives and that the discriminatory means employed' are 'substantially related to the achievement of those objectives.' " *Id*. The justification must be genuine, not hypothesized or invented *post hoc* in response to litigation. And it must not rely on overbroad generalizations about the different talents, capacities, or preferences of males and females.

[Sex is not a proscribed classification, however.] "Inherent differences" between men and women, we have come to appreciate, remain cause for celebration, but not for denigration of the members of either sex or for artificial constraints on an individual's opportunity. Sex classifications may be used to compensate women "for particular economic disabilities [they have] suffered," *Webster*, to "promot[e] equal employment opportunity," see *Guerra*, to advance

---

b. *Editors' note*: According to the record in the case, the adversative model of education features "[p]hysical rigor, mental stress, absolute equality of treatment, absence of privacy, minute regulation of behavior, and indoctrination in desirable values." The cadets live in spartan barracks where surveillance is constant and privacy nonexistent; they wear uniforms, eat together in the mess hall, and regularly participate in drills. Freshmen students are exposed to the rat line, comparable in intensity to Marine Corps boot camp.

full development of the talent and capacities of our Nation's people.[7] But such classifications may not be used, as they once were, to create or perpetuate the legal, social, and economic inferiority of women. * * *

[Virginia asserted two justifications in defense of VMI's exclusion of women. The Court agreed that the first justification, diversity of educational benefits, is a benign goal (*Webster*), but not one of the "actual state purposes" that motivated the policy. Justice Ginsburg's review of the record of single-sex education in Virginia revealed that it originated in the state's belief that only men would benefit from higher education. Virginia persisted in that belief much longer than other states; its public university, the University of Virginia, did not admit female students until 1970. The state only came to its diversity purpose for VMI after the Supreme Court called such policies into question in *Hogan*; that was too late to save the state justification, however.

[Justice Ginsburg then addressed the state's second justification: preserving the adversative method of education. The District Court forecast from expert witness testimony that coeducation would materially affect physical training, the absence of privacy, and the adversative approach. The lower court found, as matters of fact, that women developed differently from men, that men "tend to need an atmosphere of adversativeness," while women "tend to thrive in a cooperative atmosphere," but also that some women desired VMI's adversative method and would benefit from it.] The notion that admission of women would downgrade VMI's stature, destroy the adversative system and, with it, even the school, is a judgment hardly proved, a prediction hardly different from other "self-fulfilling prophec[ies]," see *Hogan*, once routinely used to deny rights or opportunities. When women first sought admission to the bar and access to legal education, concerns of the same order were expressed. For example, in 1876, the Court of Common Pleas of Hennepin County, Minnesota, explained why women were thought ineligible for the practice of law. Women train and educate the young, the court said, which

> forbids that they shall bestow that time (early and late) and labor, so essential in attaining to the eminence to which the true lawyer should ever aspire. It cannot therefore be said that the opposition of courts to the admission of females to practice . . . is to any extent the outgrowth of . . . "old fogyism[.]" . . . [I]t arises rather from a comprehension of the magnitude of the responsibilities connected with the successful practice of law, and a desire to *grade up* the profession (emphasis added).

[Similar fears were voiced by law schools refusing to admit women in the early twentieth century. The medical profession and the military academies made the same kinds of arguments. None of the fears about debasing the legal, medical,

---

7. Several *amici* have urged that diversity in educational opportunities is an altogether appropriate governmental pursuit and that single-sex schools can contribute importantly to such diversity. Indeed, it is the mission of some single-sex schools "to dissipate, rather than perpetuate, traditional gender classifications." See Brief for Twenty-Six Private Women's Colleges as *Amici Curiae* 5. We do not question the State's prerogative evenhandedly to support diverse educational opportunities. * * * Cf. *Hogan* [Mississippi had no other single-sex college except the nursing school].

or military professions came to pass after women were admitted to those careers.]

The State's misunderstanding and, in turn, the District Court's, is apparent from VMI's mission: to produce "citizen-soldiers," individuals

> imbued with love of learning, confident in the functions and attitudes of leadership, possessing a high sense of public service, advocates of the American democracy and free enterprise system, and ready . . . to defend their country in time of national peril. [Quoting Mission Study Committee of the VMI Board of Visitors, Report, May 16, 1986.]

Surely that goal is great enough to accommodate women, who today count as citizens in our American democracy equal in stature to men. Just as surely, the State's great goal is not substantially advanced by women's categorical exclusion, in total disregard of their individual merit, from the State's premier "citizen-soldier" corps. Virginia, in sum, "has fallen far short of establishing the 'exceedingly persuasive justification,' " *Hogan*, that must be the solid base for any gender-defined classification.

[Justice Ginsburg then turned to the remedial plan, whose constitutionality had been upheld in the lower courts. The Supreme Court's race discrimination precedents establish that the remedial decree must closely fit the constitutional violation; it must be shaped to place persons unconstitutionally denied an opportunity or advantage in "the position they would have occupied in the absence of [discrimination]." See *Milliken v. Bradley*, 433 U.S. 267, 280 (1977). Justice Ginsburg found that the establishment of the VWIL did not practically remedy the discrimination, in large part because the women's program was qualitatively different and quantitatively inferior to that retained for males at VMI. Tangible differences included fewer courses for VWIL students, less qualified faculty members, lower admissions standards for students, no comparable athletic facilities, a much smaller educational endowment, and incomplete access to VMI's impressive alumni network. Intangible differences included loss of the adversative method and the bonding it seems to achieve. Virginia defended its solution based upon "real differences" in the preference most women have for a more cooperative, and less competitive, learning environment.]

[G]eneralizations about "the way women are," estimates of what is appropriate for *most women*, no longer justify denying opportunity to women whose talent and capacity place them outside the average description. Notably, Virginia never asserted that VMI's method of education suits *most men*. * * *

Virginia's VWIL solution is reminiscent of the remedy Texas proposed 50 years ago, in response to a state trial court's 1946 ruling that, given the equal protection guarantee, African Americans could not be denied a legal education at a state facility. See *Sweatt v. Painter*, 339 U.S. 629 (1950) [Chapter 2, § 1B]. Reluctant to admit African Americans to its flagship University of Texas Law School, the State set up a separate school for Heman Sweatt and other black law students. As originally opened, the new school had no independent faculty or library, and it lacked accreditation.

[Although the lower courts found the parallel law school "substantially equivalent" to the whites' law school, the Supreme Court struck down the remedy on the ground that the tangible facilities and faculty of the new law school were distinctly inferior and that there was an even greater disparity for intangible elements such as reputation.] In line with *Sweatt*, we rule here that Virginia has not shown substantial equality in the separate educational opportunities the State supports at VWIL and VMI. * * *

A prime part of the history of our Constitution * * * is the story of the extension of constitutional rights and protections to people once ignored or excluded. VMI's story continued as our comprehension of "We the People" expanded. There is no reason to believe that the admission of women capable of all the activities required of VMI cadets would destroy the Institute rather than enhance its capacity to serve the "more perfect Union." * * *

[**JUSTICE THOMAS** took no part in the consideration of this case. Although objecting to the Court's apparently "strict" scrutiny, **CHIEF JUSTICE REHNQUIST** concurred in the judgment.]

JUSTICE SCALIA, dissenting. * * *

Much of the Court's opinion is devoted to deprecating the closed-mindedness of our forebears with regard to women's education, and even with regard to the treatment of women in areas that have nothing to do with education. Closed-minded they were — as every age is, including our own, with regard to matters it cannot guess, because it simply does not consider them debatable. The virtue of a democratic system with a First Amendment is that it readily enables the people, over time, to be persuaded that what they took for granted is not so, and to change their laws accordingly. That system is destroyed if the smug assurances of each age are removed from the democratic process and written into the Constitution. So to counterbalance the Court's criticism of our ancestors, let me say a word in their praise: they left us free to change. The same cannot be said of this most illiberal Court, which has embarked on a course of inscribing one after another of the current preferences of the society (and in some cases only the counter-majoritarian preferences of the society's law-trained elite) into our Basic Law. Today it enshrines the notion that no substantial educational value is to be served by an all-men's military academy — so that the decision by the people of Virginia to maintain such an institution denies equal protection to women who cannot attend that institution but can attend others. Since it is entirely clear that the Constitution of the United States — the old one — takes no sides in this educational debate, I dissent.

* * * [I]n my view the function of this Court is to *preserve* our society's values regarding (among other things) equal protection, not to *revise* them; to prevent backsliding from the degree of restriction the Constitution imposed upon democratic government, not to prescribe, on our own authority, progressively higher degrees. For that reason it is my view that, whatever abstract tests we may choose to devise, they cannot supersede — and indeed ought to be crafted *so as to reflect* — those constant and unbroken national traditions that embody the people's understanding of ambiguous constitutional texts. More specifically, it is my view that "when a practice not expressly prohibited by the text of the

Bill of Rights bears the endorsement of a long tradition of open, widespread, and unchallenged use that dates back to the beginning of the Republic, we have no proper basis for striking it down." *Rutan v. Republican Party of Ill.*, 497 U.S. 62, 95 (1990) (Scalia, J., dissenting). The same applies, *mutatis mutandis*, to a practice asserted to be in violation of the post-Civil War Fourteenth Amendment. * * *

[Justice Scalia then made the following arguments: The Court was silently replacing the intermediate scrutiny standard traditionally applied in sex-discrimination cases with a strict scrutiny standard akin to that in race-discrimination cases; the Court's requirement that VMI must open its adversative method to women so long as there are any women who would benefit from it imported a least-restrictive-means requirement characteristic only of strict scrutiny and not of intermediate scrutiny as articulated in precedents such as *Hogan*; and the Court's approach destabilized equal protection law without any firm theoretical basis. With respect to his last charge, Justice Scalia adverted to *Carolene Products'* justification for judicial review when "prejudice against discrete and insular minorities may be a special condition, which tends seriously to curtail the operation of those political processes ordinarily to be relied upon to protect minorities, and which may call for a correspondingly more searching judicial inquiry."]

* * * It is hard to consider women a "discrete and insular minorit[y]" unable to employ the "political processes ordinarily to be relied upon," when they constitute a majority of the electorate. And the suggestion that they are incapable of exerting that political power smacks of the same paternalism that the Court so roundly condemns. Moreover, a long list of legislation proves the proposition false. See, *e.g.*, Equal Pay Act of 1963, 29 U.S.C. § 206(d); Title VII of the Civil Rights Act of 1964, 42 U.S.C. § 2000e-2; Title IX of the Education Amendments of 1972, 20 U.S.C. § 1681; Women's Business Ownership Act of 1988, Pub. L. 100-533, 102 Stat. 2689; Violence Against Women Act of 1994, Pub. L. 103-322, Title IV, 108 Stat. 1902.

[Justice Scalia also criticized the Court for ignoring the lower court findings of fact that women and men do, on the whole, have different educational needs that are adequately reflected in the different designs of VMI and VWIL. He lamented the sacrifice of educational diversity that the Court's opinion required and concluded with quotations from the *Code of a Gentleman* the Court, in his view, was destroying.]

NOTE ON THE CURRENT STATE OF THE COURT'S
SEX DISCRIMINATION JURISPRUDENCE

Two Justices in the VMI case (Rehnquist and Scalia) felt the Court's analysis departed from *Craig*'s intermediate scrutiny. The suggestion is that the *Frontiero* plurality opinion, which adopted attorney Ruth Bader Ginsburg's effort to read the ERA into the Equal Protection Clause, had been furtively adopted by now-Justice Ginsburg's opinion for the Court. On the one hand, Justice Ginsburg framed her test almost exclusively from Justice O'Connor's opinion in *Hogan*, which struck down a sex segregation that disadvantaged men. Indeed, it is Justice Scalia's approach that seems inconsistent with the Court's precedents, for it was specifically rejected by Court majorities in *Hogan* and *J.E.B.* On the other hand, note how tightly Justice Ginsburg's opinion held the state to the policies that had actually motivated its exclusion of women, which focused the debate on stereotype-ridden reasons that dominated Virginian education a hundred years ago and deflected the diversity justification offered by *amici* (note 7 of the Court's opinion). Note also how Ginsburg's opinion closely associated the Court's sex and race discrimination jurisprudence on the matter of remedy (*Sweatt*).

The VMI case also illustrates this pattern in the Court's jurisprudence: However the Justices verbally articulate the test for review of laws deploying a sex-based classification, they generally strike down laws that deny women opportunities that men have (*Reed*; *Stanton*; *Kirchberg*; VMI) or that deny men opportunities that women have when the state was motivated by archaic stereotypes (*Craig*; *Hogan*), but uphold laws benefitting women when the Court believes the state was motivated by remedial justifications rather than archaic stereotypes (*Ballard*; *Kahn*; *Webster*). Unfortunately, this neat categorization does not capture three other kinds of cases, where a sex-based law (1) is plausibly tied to the "inherent differences" between men and women that even Ginsburg "celebrat[ed]" in her VMI opinion; (2) has been adopted under circumstances where the Court for institutional reasons "defers" to other branches of government; or (3) advantages neither women nor men systematically. Examples of all three phenomena appear in the next subpart; most of these cases reflect the normative compromises entailed in a de facto ERA adopted without strong public consensus favoring a purely sex-blind jurisprudence (see note "u" *supra*).

2. *Deference to Traditional Gender Classifications Based Upon "Real Differences"*

The Supreme Court has accepted most of the jurisprudence of equal treatment, as outlined by Justice Ginsburg and Professor Williams. But others, such as Justice Scalia and Professor Epstein, believe that the Court has not sufficiently defended its new level of equal protection scrutiny to justify using it as a sharp tool against controversial targets. Indeed, two lines of thought have existed side by side: the principle of equal treatment, and the exception for "real differences," a phrase used in *Ballard* and echoed in *United States v. Virginia*.

The intellectual debate about real differences between men and women assumes, as all the opinions in *Frontiero* did, that sex is biologically fixed, perhaps even immutable. As you read the following cases, note these further inquiries: (1) The biggest "real difference" is assumed to be women's ability to be pregnant and bear children. Is this a general difference, or is it one affecting only some women? (2) For each case, separate the examination of whether there is a real difference between men and women from the examination of the regulatory strategy the state has adopted. Is the strategy a rational and gender-neutral response to sex differences, or is it gendered in ways that reinforce unproductive stereotypes? (3) Baselines make a big difference. Someone who follows sociobiology or natural law and thinks sex differences are relatively hard-wired may be much more open to sex-based regulations than someone who follows most strands of feminist theory and thinks that many supposed sex differences are just gender stereotypes.

———

Michael M. v. Superior Court of Sonoma County, 450 U.S. 464 (1981). Section 261.5 of California's Penal Code included as unlawful sexual intercourse "an act of sexual intercourse accomplished with a female not the wife of the perpetrator, where the female is under the age of 18 years." The statute made men alone criminally liable for the act of statutory rape. Michael M., a 17½-year-old male charged with statutory rape of Sharon, a 16½-year-old female, moved to have § 261.5 invalidated as unlawful sex discrimination, an effort rebuffed by the California courts. Following cases where it had upheld laws "where the gender classification is not invidious, but rather realistically reflects the fact that the sexes are not similarly situated in certain circumstances," the Supreme Court affirmed.

Justice Rehnquist's plurality opinion, joined by three other Justices, reasoned that the statutory sex discrimination was substantially related to the goal of preventing illegitimate pregnancy, an important state interest. "We need not be medical doctors to discern that young men and young women are not similarly situated with respect to the problems and the risks of sexual intercourse. Only women may become pregnant, and they suffer disproportionately the profound physical, emotional, and psychological consequences of sexual activity. The statute at issue here protects women from sexual intercourse at an age when those consequences are particularly severe. * * *

"Because virtually all of the significant harmful and inescapably identifiable consequences of teenage pregnancy fall on the young female, a legislature acts well within its authority when it elects to punish only the participant who, by nature, suffers few of the consequences of his conduct. It is hardly unreasonable for a legislature acting to protect minor females to exclude them from punishment. Moreover, the risk of pregnancy itself constitutes a substantial deterrence to young females. No similar natural sanctions deter males. A criminal sanction imposed solely on males thus serves to roughly 'equalize' the deterrents on the sexes. * * *

"In any event, we cannot say that a gender-neutral statute would be as effective as the statute California has chosen to enact. The State persuasively contends that a gender-neutral statute would frustrate its interest in effective enforcement. Its view is that a female is surely less likely to report violations of the statute if she herself would be subject to criminal prosecution. In an area already fraught with prosecutorial difficulties, we decline to hold that the Equal Protection Clause requires a legislature to enact a statute so broad that it may well be incapable of enforcement."

Justice Blackmun concurred only in the judgment. He pointed out that Sharon "appears not to have been an unwilling participant in at least the initial stages of the intimacies that took place the night of June 3, 1978." As evidence, Justice Blackmun pointed to Sharon's testimony at the preliminary hearing:

> "Yeah. We was laying there and we were kissing each other, and then he asked me if I wanted to walk him over to the park; so we walked over to the park and we sat down on a bench and then he started kissing me again and we were laying on the bench. And he told me to take my pants off.

> "I said, 'No,' and I was trying to get up and he hit me back down on the bench and then I just said to myself, 'Forget it,' and I let him do what he wanted to do * * *."

Michael's and Sharon's "nonacquaintance with each other before the incident; their drinking; their withdrawal from the others of the group; their foreplay, in which she willingly participated and seems to have encouraged; and the closeness of their ages (a difference of only one year and 18 days) are factors that should make this case an unattractive one to prosecute at all, and especially to prosecute as a felony, rather than as a misdemeanor chargeable under § 261.5."

Justice Brennan, in dissent, argued that California had presented no evidence that a gender-neutral statutory rape law (such as the laws adopted by 37 other states) would be less enforceable or less effective in deterring minor females from having intercourse than its males-only statute. "Until very recently, no California court or commentator had suggested that the purpose of California's statutory rape law was to protect young women from the risk of pregnancy. Indeed, the historical development of § 261.5 demonstrates that the law was initially enacted on the premise that young women, in contrast to young men, were to be deemed legally incapable of consenting to an act of sexual intercourse. Because their chastity was considered particularly precious, those young women were felt to be uniquely in need of the State's protection. In contrast, young men were assumed to be capable of making such decisions for themselves; the law therefore did not offer them any special protection."

NOTE ON THE GENDERED TREATMENT OF RAPE

After the Court's decision, California amended its statutory rape law to be gender-neutral, and as of June 2008 all states except Idaho follow a gender-neutral policy for statutory rape. Has *Michael M.* been effectively overruled by the VMI case, where the Court insisted upon considering only the *actual, historical purposes* of the exclusion of women, not (as the Court did in *Michael M.*) current justifications? Most feminists criticized *Michael M.* for upholding a law that rested upon gender stereotypes like those in *Bradwell* and *Craig.*[c] Has their point of view been accepted by the VMI Court?

Another criticism is that statutory rape laws may undercut the public perception of rape as a violent attack, by reducing a "real" rape that is a savage assault to a "statutory" rape that is only unlawful because of the "accident" of

---

c. See Frances Olsen, *Statutory Rape: A Feminist Critique of Rights Analysis*, 63 Tex. L. Rev. 387 (1984); Wendy Webster Williams, *The Equality Crisis: Reflections on Culture, Courts and Feminism*, 7 Women's Rts. L. Rep. 175, 181-82 (Spring 1982).

age.[d] On the other hand, prosecutors may use statutory rape prosecutions in cases where they are doubtful that they can win on a rape charge, so making statutory rape a crime may counter some of the other flaws of rape law.[e] Note how Justice Blackmun's concurring opinion can be read to support both the feminist criticism and the prosecutorial defense.

———

Parham v. Hughes, 441 U.S. 347 (1979). A Georgia law allowed the mother but not the father of a child born outside of marriage to bring suit for the child's wrongful death. Although the father acknowledged his paternity and had established a relationship with the child, the Court upheld the statute against a charge of sex discrimination. **Justice Stewart**'s plurality opinion for four Justices contrasted cases, such as *Frontiero*, where statutory classifications rested upon gender stereotypes, with "cases where men and women are not similarly situated * * * and a statutory classification is realistically based upon the differences in their situations, [where] this Court has upheld its validity," citing *Ballard* as an example. "[M]others and fathers of illegitimate children are not similarly situated. Under Georgia law, only a father can by voluntary unilateral action make an illegitimate child legitimate," by filing a motion with the court declaring his paternity. "Since fathers who do legitimate their children can sue for wrongful death in precisely the same circumstances as married fathers whose children were legitimate *ab initio*, the statutory classification does not discriminate against fathers as a class but instead distinguishes between fathers who have legitimated their children and those who have not." Justice Stewart concluded, therefore, that the state discrimination only required a rational basis, which his plurality opinion found in preventing fraud by requiring fathers to claim paternity through regularized procedures.

Writing for four dissenters, **Justice White** argued that it was still *sex discrimination* to treat fathers differently in any way than mothers; the plurality approach was circular, confusing the issue of sex discrimination with the issue of state justification. Indeed, on the same day it handed down *Parham*, the Court (the *Parham* dissenters plus Justice Powell) in *Caban v. Mohammed*, 441 U.S. 380 (1979), struck down a New York law requiring the consent of the mother, but not the father, for the adoption of their nonmarital child. The Court treated the statutory classification as a routine discrimination on the basis of sex and rejected the "real differences" argument (mothers are more bonded to their children than fathers) on the ground that, even if generally true, it was not true in *Caban*, where the father had bonded with the child. New York responded to *Caban* with a statute requiring the mother of a child born outside of marriage to be notified of any proposed adoption and allowing her to veto the adoption, but not according either notice or veto power to the biological father unless he had

———

d. See Kristin Bumiller, *Rape as a Legal Symbol: An Essay on Sexual Violence and Racism*, 42 U. Miami L. Rev. 75, 88 (1987).

e. Cf. Heidi Kitrosser, *Meaningful Consent: Toward a New Generation of Statutory Rape Laws*, 4 Va. J. Soc. Pol'y & L. 287 (1997); Jane Larson, *"Even a Worm Will Turn at Last": Rape Reform in Late Nineteenth-Century America*, 9 Yale J. L. & Human. 1 (1997); Michelle Oberman, *Turning Girls into Women: Re-Evaluating Modern Statutory Rape Law*, 85 J. Crim. L. & Crimin. 15 (1994).

claimed paternity by registering with the state or had established a substantial relationship with the child. The Court upheld this law in *Lehr v. Robertson*, 463 U.S. 248 (1983), again over a dissenting opinion by Justice White.

Concurring only in the *Parham* judgment (and writing the opinion for the Court in *Caban*), **Justice Powell** agreed with the dissenters that the state was discriminating against fathers, but agreed with the plurality's result, on the ground that the sex discrimination narrowly served an important state goal — encouraging fathers to acknowledge paternity and form relationships with their nonmarital children. Compose arguments from feminist and sociobiological premises that would support Justice Powell's position.

Rostker v. Goldberg, 453 U.S. 57 (1981). Section 3 of the Military Selective Service Act [MSSA] empowered the President, by proclamation, to require the registration of "every male citizen" and male resident aliens between the ages of 18 and 26. The purpose of this registration was to facilitate any eventual conscription; those persons required to register were liable for training and service in the Armed Forces. The MSSA was challenged on equal protection grounds for its exclusion of women. **Justice Rehnquist**'s opinion for the Court upheld the sex discrimination.

"The Solicitor General argues, largely on the basis of * * * cases emphasizing the deference due Congress in the area of military affairs and national security, that this Court should scrutinize the MSSA only to determine if the distinction drawn between men and women bears a rational relation to some legitimate government purpose, and should not examine the Act under the heightened scrutiny with which we have approached gender-based discrimination [citing *Michael M.*, *Craig*, and *Reed*]. We do not think that the substantive guarantee of due process or certainty in the law will be advanced by any further 'refinement' in the applicable tests as suggested by the Government. * * *

"No one could deny that under the test of *Craig v. Boren*, the Government's interest in raising and supporting armies is an 'important governmental interest.' Congress and its Committees carefully considered and debated two alternative means of furthering that interest: the first was to register only males for potential conscription, and the other was to register both sexes. Congress chose the former alternative." It saw registration under the MSSA as prefatory to a subsequent draft of those registered, to serve as combat troops in an emergency situation. "Women as a group, however, unlike men as a group, are not eligible for combat. The restrictions on the participation of women in combat in the Navy and Air Force are statutory. Under 10 U.S.C. § 6015 (1976 ed., Supp. III), 'women may not be assigned to duty on vessels or in aircraft that are engaged in combat missions,' and under 10 U.S.C. § 8549 female members of the Air Force 'may not be assigned to duty in aircraft engaged in combat missions.' The Army and Marine Corps preclude the use of women in combat as a matter of established policy. Congress specifically recognized and endorsed the exclusion of women from combat in exempting women from registration. [Quoting several statements from the Senate Report supporting this statement.] Men and women, because of the combat restrictions on women, are simply not similarly situated for purposes of a draft or registration for a draft." Hence, the decision of

Congress and the President to exclude women from registration was a sex-based classification "closely related to Congress' [important] purpose in authorizing registration."

Justice Marshall's dissenting opinion (joined by **Justice Brennan**) noted that "[t]he Government does not defend the exclusion of women from registration on the ground that preventing women from serving in the military is substantially related to the effectiveness of the Armed Forces." Indeed, the top brass repeatedly told Congress that "the participation of women in the All-Volunteer Armed Forces has contributed substantially to military effectiveness. * * * Congress has repeatedly praised the performance of female members of the Armed Forces, and has approved efforts by the Armed Services to expand their role." The Court's reasoning — that the MSSA's exclusion of women from registration is permissible because registration seeks only persons who would be drafted for possible combat duty, from which women have traditionally been excluded — focuses on the wrong question.

"The relevant inquiry under the *Craig v. Boren* test is not whether a *gender-neutral* classification would substantially advance important governmental interests. Rather, the question is whether the gender-based classification is itself substantially related to the achievement of the asserted governmental interest. Thus, the Government's task in this case is to demonstrate that excluding women from registration substantially furthers the goal of preparing for a draft of combat troops. Or to put it another way, the Government must show that registering women would substantially impede its efforts to prepare for such a draft. Under our precedents, the Government cannot meet this burden without showing that a gender-neutral statute would be a less effective means of attaining this end. * * * In this case, the Government makes no claim that preparing for a draft of combat troops cannot be accomplished just as effectively by *registering* both men and women but *drafting* only men if only men turn out to be needed. Nor can the Government argue that this alternative entails the additional cost and administrative inconvenience of registering women. This Court has repeatedly stated that the administrative convenience of employing a gender classification is not an adequate constitutional justification under the *Craig v. Boren* test."

Justice Marshall also maintained that the Court's opinion rested upon its own rationale, not the one considered by Congress. The Defense Department and Congress believed that only about two-thirds of those registered would be needed for combat; the other one-third would be needed to staff non-combat positions of the sort that women could fill. All four Service Chiefs agreed that there were no military reasons for refusing to register women, and uniformly advocated requiring registration of women. (**Justice White** dissented in a separate opinion.)

———

Nguyen v. INS, 533 U.S. 53 (2001). The Supreme Court rejected a challenge to a federal statute, 8 U.S.C. § 1409(a)(4), that accorded American citizenship automatically, upon birth, to a child born out of wedlock in a foreign country to an American mother, but denied citizenship to such a child whose only American parent was her father, unless the child were legally legitimated or paternity were established in a court of law or by paternal oath before the child's eighteenth birthday. In *Miller v. Albright*, 523 U.S. 420 (1998), a divided Court had failed to resolve the constitutionality of § 1409(a)(4), essentially because two Justices believed that the child plaintiff seeking a declaration of citizenship did not have standing to raise her father's sex discrimination claim. In *Nguyen*, both the child and the father were plaintiffs, so there was no problem of standing.

Justice Kennedy's opinion for the Court found the sex discrimination justified by two governmental interests. "The first governmental interest to be served is the importance of assuring that a biological parent-child relationship exists. In the case of the mother, the relation is verifiable from the birth itself. The mother's status is documented in most instances by the birth certificate or hospital records and the witnesses who attest to her having given birth.

"In the case of the father, the uncontestable fact is that he need not be present at the birth. If he is present, furthermore, that circumstance is not incontrovertible proof of fatherhood. See *Lehr v. Robertson*. Fathers and mothers are not similarly situated with regard to the proof of biological parenthood. The imposition of a different set of rules for making that legal determination with respect to fathers and mothers is neither surprising nor troublesome from a constitutional perspective. Section 1409(a)(4)'s provision of three options for a father seeking to establish paternity — legitimation, paternity oath, and court order of paternity — is designed to ensure an acceptable documentation of paternity. * * *

"[T]o require Congress to speak without reference to the gender of the parent with regard to its objective of ensuring a blood tie between parent and child would be to insist on a hollow neutrality. * * * Congress could have required both mothers and fathers to prove parenthood within 30 days or, for that matter, 18 years, of the child's birth. Given that the mother is always present at birth, but that the father need not be, the facially neutral rule would sometimes require fathers to take additional affirmative steps which would not be required of mothers, whose names will appear on the birth certificate as a result of their presence at the birth, and who will have the benefit of witnesses to the birth to call upon. The issue is not the use of gender specific terms instead of neutral ones. Just as neutral terms can mask discrimination that is unlawful, gender specific terms can mark a permissible distinction. The equal protection question is whether the distinction is lawful. Here, the use of gender specific terms takes into account a biological difference between the parents. The differential treatment is inherent in a sensible statutory scheme, given the unique relationship of the mother to the event of birth.

"The second important governmental interest furthered in a substantial manner by § 1409(a)(4) is the determination to ensure that the child and the citizen parent have some demonstrated opportunity or potential to develop not just a relationship that is recognized, as a formal matter, by the law, but one that consists of the real, everyday ties that provide a connection between child and citizen parent and, in turn, the United States. In the case of a citizen mother and a child born overseas, the opportunity for a meaningful relationship between citizen parent and child inheres in the very event of birth, an event so often critical to our constitutional and statutory understandings of citizenship. The mother knows that the child is in being and is hers and has an initial point of contact with him. There is at least an opportunity for mother and child to develop a real, meaningful relationship.

"The same opportunity does not result from the event of birth, as a matter of biological inevitability, in the case of the unwed father. Given the 9-month interval between conception and birth, it is not always certain that a father will know that a child was conceived, nor is it always clear that even the mother will be sure of the father's identity. This fact takes on particular significance in the case of a child born overseas and out of wedlock. One concern in this context has always been with young people, men for the most part, who are on duty with the Armed Forces in foreign countries." Justice Kennedy finally concluded that the statutory differentiation was narrowly enough tailored to fit this asserted interest, as well as the first.

Justice Scalia, joined by **Justice Thomas**, concurred in the Court's opinion but reiterated their view, stated in *Miller*, that Congress has plenary and unreviewable power in the arena of immigration and naturalization.

Justice O'Connor, joined by **Justices Souter**, **Ginsburg**, and **Breyer**, dissented. Justice O'Connor maintained that the Court's approach deviated from the heightened scrutiny its precedents bound it to apply in sex discrimination cases, such as the VMI case. Specifically, she criticized the Court's first justification (proof of parental relationship) as insufficient because (1) there was scant evidence that this was the actual reason for the sex-based classification; (2) the requirements of § 1409(a)(4) add nothing to what § 1409(a)(1) already requires, namely, a blood test showing a parental relationship between the American father and the child claiming citizenship; and (3) sex-neutral criteria, such as the blood-test requirement of § 1409(a)(1) for the child-claimant whatever the sex of its American parent, would fully serve the asserted governmental interest. Justice O'Connor suggested that the Court's willingness to attribute a rational goal to Congress and to allow much leeway in the fit between the statutory criterion and the valid state interest was more characteristic of rational basis review than heightened scrutiny as required by the VMI Case and other precedents.

Justice O'Connor made two of the same criticisms of the Court's second justification (opportunity of the American parent and foreign-born child to develop a relationship): It was hypothetical and could be met by a more direct — and ungendered — statutory criterion (*e.g.*, the child and the parent, whatever the gender, have enjoyed a relationship). By stressing an "opportunity" for a relationship, the Court was more successful in creating a closer fit between the end and the means — but at the expense of creating an end that is not sufficiently important to justify a statutory sex discrimination.

"The claim that § 1409(a)(4) substantially relates to the achievement of the goal of a 'real, practical relationship' thus finds support not in biological differences but instead in a stereotype — *i.e.*, 'the generalization that mothers are significantly more likely than fathers . . . to develop caring relationships with their children.' *Miller* (Breyer, J., dissenting). Such a claim relies on 'the very stereotype the law condemns,' *J.E.B.*, 'lends credibility' to the generalization, *Hogan*, and helps to convert that 'assumption' into 'a self-fulfilling prophecy,' *ibid.* Indeed, contrary to this stereotype, Boulais [the father] has reared Nguyen, while Nguyen apparently has lacked a relationship with his mother. * * *

"In denying petitioner's claim that § 1409(a)(4) rests on stereotypes, the majority articulates a misshapen notion of 'stereotype' and its significance in our equal protection jurisprudence. The majority asserts that a 'stereotype' is 'defined as a frame of mind resulting from irrational or uncritical analysis.' This Court has long recognized, however, that an impermissible stereotype may enjoy empirical support and thus be in a sense 'rational.' See, e.g., *J.E.B.* ('We have made abundantly clear in past cases that gender classifications that rest on impermissible stereotypes violate the Equal Protection Clause, even when some statistical support can be conjured up for the generalization'); *Craig* (invalidating a sex-based classification even though the evidence supporting the distinction was 'not trivial in a statistical sense'). Indeed, the stereotypes that underlie a sex-based classification 'may hold true for many, even most, individuals.' *Miller* (Ginsburg, J., dissenting). But in numerous cases where a measure of truth has inhered in the generalization, 'the Court has rejected official actions that classify unnecessarily and overbroadly by gender when more accurate and impartial functional lines can be drawn.' *Ibid.*"

NOTE ON *ROSTKER*, *NGUYEN*, AND JUDICIAL DEFERENCE TO CERTAIN NATIONAL LEGISLATIVE AND EXECUTIVE POLICIES

The Court's decisions in *Rostker* and *Nguyen* are hard to square with the *Craig* test, as applied in the VMI case: Although the Court invoked important state goals, the connection between those goals and the sex-based classification was weak in both cases. In *Rostker*, it was not clear why women had to be excluded for registration to meet the needs of military preparedness. Wouldn't we be *better prepared* if the Armed Forces had more able personnel whom it could call into duty? In *Nguyen*, it was not clear why Congress should not have imposed a real relationship test on all children with one American parent, whatever the parent's sex. Wouldn't the connection between biological parentage and American values (etc.) be *firmer* without the sex-based classification? In both cases, the sex-based scheme also tracked traditional stereotypes (male warriors protecting womenfolk; nurturing mother, wandering father). According to its legislative history, the statutory sex discrimination in *Nguyen* was motivated by the sexist common law presumption that the mother of a nonmarital child is its guardian and that the father has no legal rights. Finally, the most plausible current justification for both statutory policies was that a simple sex-based scheme was easier or cheaper to administer — but *Craig* and other precedents have specifically rejected ease-of-administration as a justification for sex-based classifications. (Recall Professor Epstein's critique of *Craig*.)

Were these cases wrongly decided? It is plausible to say that *Rostker* was just a mistake, superseded by the Court's tougher post-1981 sex discrimination jurisprudence. But the same cannot be said of *Nguyen*, a post-VMI precedent.

Consider this theory: Although the Court cited the *Parham* line of cases only to support the state interest in assuring good proof of biological parenthood, *Nguyen* is like *Parham* in that the government is imposing extra proof requirements for fatherhood claims than for motherhood ones.[f] And so *Nguyen* might be justified as resting on the "real differences" rationale accepted in *Parham* and *Lehr*. But is *Parham* consistent with the VMI case? The approach of the *Nguyen* dissenters, tightly patterned on the VMI case, would suggest that it is not — yet five Justices (including two who joined Justice Ginsburg's VMI opinion) thought otherwise.

Consider both *Rostker* and *Nguyen* from the perspective of comparative institutional competence. As the Court emphasized in *Rostker*, the federal judiciary defers to Congress and the President with regard to matters of military policy and war. As Justice Scalia noted in *Nguyen*, the judiciary also defers to Congress in matters of immigration and naturalization. See *Fiallo v. Bell*, 430 U.S. 787 (1977). *Deference* to another institution's line-drawing means that the Court will give the institution some latitude to make decisions the Court would not have made — or would not allow other institutions to make. (The Court does not *defer* to another institution's policy if the Justices *agree* with the policy or its constitutionality.) The Court might defer to the other institution by accepting its normative understanding of its proper or acceptable *ends*, by giving it leeway in the choice of *means* through which it pursues its ends, or by giving it the benefit of the doubt as to factual assertions needed to connect proper ends with sex-based means.

This was Justice Powell's approach to affirmative action. He disliked the policy but was willing to allow institutions to adopt it if they believed race-based preferences suited one of several acceptable needs. In *Bakke*, Powell further opined that a state legislature or even chief executive had more leeway to adopt an affirmative action policy than the unelected Board of Regents. Although he disapproved a racial quota program in *Bakke*, Powell in *Fullilove* voted to uphold a racial quota program adopted by Congress (Chapter 3, § 3B). Likewise, the Court might give Congress more leeway in adopting sex-based classifications for immigration and military policy than it would tolerate by state legislatures — or than it would give Congress in regulating interstate commerce. Recall *Korematsu* and *Hirabayashi* (Chapter 1, § 6), where the Court gave Congress and the President (too much) leeway to adopt race-based national security policies and credited questionable military assertions about the presumptive disloyalty of Japanese Americans.

Deference can be justified on grounds of the other institution's (1) greater competence in drawing lines in a particular policy arena, (2) greater democratic legitimacy, or (3) constitutional authorization to make such decisions (see the

---

f. Also, the sex-based classification relates to the parents, who are not directly injured, and not to the child. Tuan Anh Nguyen was treated differently from other offspring in part because he was a nonmarital child (the *Levy* line of cases) and in part because his American parent was his father—but not because of his sex. Is this a legitimate distinction in light of *Loving v. Virginia* (Chapter 3, § 1A), which subjected race-based classifications to strict scrutiny even when they affected each race the same as a formal matter?

political question doctrine materials in Chapter 9, § 1). All three justifications might apply to a President-Congress military or immigration policy: (1) Federal judges concede that they have little competence in military policy, which often rests upon secret and fast-changing intelligence as well as important judgments about how to manage the armed forces most effectively. Judicial competence to handle immigration matters is surely greater because of less need for secrecy but still inferior to that of the political branches. (2) The President and Congress are elected by and accountable to the people; their decisions in dealing with military and foreign affairs are intensely scrutinized by the media and within the political process, and the effects of their decisions are often easy to trace back to the decisionmakers. (3) The Constitution vests those institutions with unique authority to create and command the armed forces and to regulate immigration and naturalization, with little or no textual role for the Court. The issue of deference will recur in this casebook, especially in Chapters 6, 8, and 9. The Court also defers to other institutional decisions in such contexts as prisons, internal state employment policies, primary and secondary schools, and state funding decisions.

Note that the degree of deference accorded Congress in *Rostker* could well have saved the federal armed forces statute struck down in *Frontiero*. How can the two decisions be reconciled? *Query* also: Before 1948, the Defense Department followed a policy of race-based segregation in our armed forces; the main justification was that integration would undermine unit cohesion and morale, because white soldiers were uncomfortable with, and often hostile to, black soldiers.[g] President Truman ended this policy by executive order in 1948. If he had not acted, would the Supreme Court have invalidated the de jure segregation in the armed forces after *Brown* and *Bolling*? Or would the Court have deferred?

NOTE ON THE MILITARY'S EXCLUSION OF WOMEN FROM COMBAT ROLES

Consider, generally, the debate over whether women can be excluded from combat.[h] See *Owens v. Brown*, 455 F. Supp. 291 (D.D.C. 1978) (pre-*Rostker* decision disapproving statutory naval combat exclusion). The effects of excluding women from combat positions include their exclusion from some leadership positions, lower salaries and fewer opportunities, and a general need for fewer women in the armed forces. This is a major arena of sex discrimination that arguably harms women's interests a lot more than the discriminatory

---

g. For histories of the white resistance to ending armed forces segregation, and the changed attitudes of white soldiers when desegregation occurred in 1948-54, see Richard Dalfiume, *Desegregation of the U.S. Armed Forces* (1969); Morris MacGregor, Jr., *Integration of the Armed Forces, 1940-1965* (1981); Bernard Nalty, *Strength for the Fight: A History of Black Americans in the Military* (1986).

h. See generally *Female Soldiers — Combatants or Noncombatants?: Historical and Contemporary Perspectives* (Nancy Loring Goldman ed. 1982); *Loaded Question: Women in the Military* (Wendy Chapkis ed. 1981), as well as Kenneth Karst, *The Pursuit of Manhood and the Desegregation of the Armed Forces*, 38 UCLA L. Rev. 499 (1991); Lori Kornblum, *Women Warriors in a Men's World: The Combat Exclusion*, 2 L. & Inequality 351 (1984).

laws struck down in *Frontiero*, *Craig*, and *Wiesenfeld*. Apart from the extraordinary deference suggested in *Rostker*, can the discrimination be justified? Some scholars contend that, because "combat is a synonym for power," the reason women are excluded is to preserve male power, and even to preserve fragile conceptions of "manhood" itself, as uniquely involving fighting and protecting home and family from invaders[i] — a justification that would seem unacceptable under the VMI case, perhaps even after considering the deference arguments in the previous Note. In short, the armed forces do have to justify this exclusion even under a deferential regime. The armed forces have traditionally maintained that men are better suited for combat roles (*i.e.,* they are stronger) than women.[j] This kind of argument seems increasingly inconsistent with the realities of modern warfare, which relies less and less on muscle power and more and more on firepower and technology. Moreover, the VMI decision suggests that the military's need for strong soldiers is not a valid reason for having a sex-based exclusion, because the military could (and does) exclude people who do not meet minimal strength requirements.

Today, the main argument for the combat exclusion is that women in the foxholes would be a sexual force disrupting morale and unit cohesion.[k] Soldiers are asked to risk their lives for their comrades and for the overall plan of battle; this level of altruistic behavior, military experts believe, can only be achieved through the bonding experience that goes on within a unit. Not only do men not bond with women in the same way they do with other men (most men will tend to be protective of women, for example), but the introduction of women into combat situations will generate sexual rivalries that risk setting comrade against comrade. Also, combat conditions tend to be rough and crude, with little privacy, embarrassing to women as well as men. These are conditions conducive to sexual harassment, diminished bonding, and general trouble. Note that this kind of argument is most likely to trigger a judicial response of deference, not only because it has been endorsed by the executive branch, but also because it relies on hard-to-refute experience of military commanders (who generally support some version of the foregoing argument).

Notwithstanding these arguments, Congress repealed the statutory exclusion and vested the Defense Department with discretion to assign women to any military assignment in P.L. 103-160, §§ 541-542, 107 Stat. 1659 (1993). In January 1994, the Secretary of Defense lifted the "risk rule" that had blocked women from serving in units which had a high probability of engaging in combat. This change opened more than 250,000 positions to women; now over 80% of the total jobs in the armed services are open to women, compared with 33% before the new rule. An independent study of the new rule's implementa-

---

i. See Helen Rogan, *Mixed Company: Women in the Modern Army* 296 (1981); Karst, *Pursuit of Manhood*; Kornblum, *Women Warriors*.

j. See Brian Mitchell, *Weak Link: Feminization of the American Military* (1989). Contrast *Female Soldiers*; Jill Laurie Goodman, *Women, War, and Equality: An Examination of Sex Discrimination in the Military*, 5 Women's Rts. L. Rptr. 243 (1979).

k. See Mady Wechsler Segal, *The Argument for Female Combatants*, in *Female Soldiers* 267, 278-81; William Eskridge, Jr. & Nan Hunter, *Sexuality, Gender, and the Law* 357-65 (1997).

tion found that "when compared with the effects of training, operational tempo, leadership, and materiel, gender is not perceived as affecting readiness." The majority of officers and experienced enlisted personnel surveyed asserted that women perform about as well as men do. Women's integration also appears not to have eroded cohesion. "Any divisions caused by gender were minimal or invisible in units with high cohesion. Gender was reported as a secondary issue in units that had conflicting groups, and then it took a back seat to divisions along work group or rank lines." Integration also had some positive effects on cohesion: "The presence of women was also cited as raising the level of professional standards." The report concluded with several concerns. First, men resented what they perceived as double standards in service, such as different physical standards for women or an inclination on the part of leaders not to demand as much of women. Second, morale problems sometimes were created by dating and sexual relationships among soldiers. Third and most important, sexual harassment of female soldiers by their male comrades was pervasive and created serious morale problems.[1]

Although the Department does not (as of 2008) authorize women to serve in combat units, they have served with distinction in combat situations. In the recent wars in Afghanistan and Iraq, women participated in bombing campaigns, have commanded ships, and have served in on-the-ground combat. According to recent polls, most Americans believe that women should be eligible to serve in combat. Given these developments, would an equal protection challenge to the combat exclusion succeed today? What arguments could the Department of Defense make in support of the remaining exclusion?

3.   *Classifications That Have a Disparate Impact Upon Women*

Liberal feminists have been just as opposed to policies that have a discriminatory impact upon women as to those that discriminate on their face. Both before and after *Craig*, however, such policies proved impervious to constitutional attack, even though they had pervasive discriminatory effects on women's opportunities in the workplace. Note the parallel to *Washington v. Davis* (Chapter 3, § 1B) in the race discrimination context. Is there a persuasive reason not to follow the *Davis* approach in either of the following cases?

Geduldig v. Aiello, 417 U.S. 484 (1974). California's disability insurance program paid benefits to persons temporarily disabled from work, but excluded pregnancy-related disabilities from coverage. Challenging the pregnancy-based discrimination, Wendy Williams maintained that "the individual who receives a benefit or suffers a detriment because of a physical characteristic unique to one sex benefits or suffers because he or she belongs to one or the other sex" — which was sex discrimination, because men were treated differently (Brief for Appellees, at 31, *Geduldig* (No. 73-640)). Moreover, men were treated more favorably than women, and for exactly the reasons rejected in *Reed* and *Frontiero* (and later in *Craig*): men were privileged and women were denigrated

---

1.   The quotations in text are all taken from Margaret Harrell & Laura Miller, *New Opportunities for Military Women: Effects Upon Readiness, Cohesion, and Morale* (Rand 1997).

in the public and workplace sphere because of women's unique ability to bear children and the concomitant special responsibility for rearing them in the domestic sphere. "Those who would make these unique physical differences a touchstone for unscrutinized differential treatment offer nothing other than the modern version of the historical rationales which were for so long the source of women's second class citizenship under the law." (Id. at 36.) Indeed, "[t]his last prejudice — that women are not serious and permanent members of the workforce and that lurking somewhere in each woman's life is a man fully able to support her — underlies and reinforces discrimination against women in all realms of their lives." (Id. at 39-40.)

But the nine men on the Court were not persuaded that this was the right focus. According to Justice Douglas's conference notes, most of the Justices agreed with Chief Justice Burger's complaint that the pregnancy exclusion involves "a different kind of risk than illness covered by [the] Act. [P]rostate problem is covered — as is hysterectomy — different from pregnancy." **Justice Stewart**'s opinion for the Court ruled that the pregnancy exclusion was rationally related to the insurance program's self-supporting goals; benefits are covered by premiums, and some lines have to be drawn. Three dissenting Justices argued that such lenient rational basis review was inappropriate under either *Reed* or the just-decided *Frontiero*, which required more exacting scrutiny for sex-based classifications. Justice Stewart responded that the exclusion was not "gender discrimination as such": It does not divide the world into men and women, but merely classifies the world into men-plus-nonpregnant-women and pregnant women. Indeed, there was not necessarily a sex-discriminatory impact on men, as the annual claim rate and cost were higher for women than men in California.

———

Personnel Administrator of Massachusetts v. Feeney, 442 U.S. 256 (1979). Massachusetts General Laws, ch. 31, § 23 (originally enacted 1884), provided that all veterans who qualified for state civil service positions be given a preference over nonveterans. During her 12-year tenure as a public employee, Helen Feeney took and passed several competitive civil service exams. In 1971, she received the second highest score on an exam for a job with the Board of Dental Examiners, but she was ranked sixth behind five male veterans on the Dental Examiner list because of the veterans' preference; a lower-scoring veteran got the job. In 1973, she received the third highest score on an exam for an administrative assistant position with a mental health center but was placed twelfth on the hiring list, behind eleven male veterans with lower scores. This pattern of getting high scores but losing the job to lower-scoring male veterans recurred. Feeney challenged the veterans' preference as a violation of equal protection.

In the 1970s, over 98% of the veterans in Massachusetts were male; only 1.8% were female. Between 1963 and 1973, when Feeney was competing for state merit jobs, 47,005 new permanent appointments were made, 43% women and 57% men. Of the women appointed, 1.8% were veterans, while 54% of the men had veteran status. A large unspecified percentage of the female appointees were serving in lower paying positions for which males traditionally had not applied. On each of 50 sample eligible lists that are part of the record in this case, one or more women who would have been certified as eligible for appointment on the basis of test results were displaced by veterans whose test scores were lower.

The Court, in another opinion by **Justice Stewart**, upheld the statutory classification. It relied on *Washington v. Davis* and *Arlington Heights* (Chapter 3, § 1B) for the proposition that "even if a neutral law has a disproportionately adverse effect upon a racial minority [or, in Feeney's case, women], it is unconstitutional under the Equal Protection Clause only if that impact can be traced to a discriminatory purpose."

The trial court found, as a matter of fact, that the veterans' preference "was not established for the purpose of discriminating against women." The key issue was whether Feeney had shown "that a gender-based discriminatory purpose has, at least in some measure, shaped the Massachusetts veterans' preference legislation." Feeney first argued that the preference was inherently sex-biased because it favored a status reserved under federal military policy primarily to men. The Court rejected this argument as inconsistent with Feeney's concession that some kind of veterans' preference would be allowable: If a more limited "sex-biased" preference were okay, why not a broad one? Feeney also argued that the state had to have realized that an extensive invocation of a veterans' preference would naturally exclude women from the better state jobs; indeed, the statute until 1971 exempted from operation of the preference jobs "especially calling for women," namely secretarial and other "women's work." The Court found this to be the most weighty argument but was unpersuaded.

" 'Discriminatory purpose,' however, implies more than intent as volition or intent as awareness of consequences. It implies that the decisionmaker, in this case a state legislature, selected or reaffirmed a particular course of action at least in part 'because of,' not merely 'in spite of,' its adverse effects upon an identifiable group. Yet nothing in the record demonstrates that this preference for veterans was originally devised or subsequently re-enacted because it would accomplish the collateral goal of keeping women in a stereotypic and predefined place in the Massachusetts Civil Service.

"To the contrary, the statutory history shows that the benefit of the preference was consistently offered to 'any person' who was a veteran. That benefit has been extended to women under a very broad statutory definition of the term veteran. The preference formula itself, which is the focal point of this challenge, was first adopted — so it appears from this record — out of a perceived need to help a small group of older Civil War veterans. It has since been reaffirmed and extended only to cover new veterans. When the totality of legislative actions establishing and extending the Massachusetts veterans' preference are considered, the law remains what it purports to be: a preference for veterans of either sex over nonveterans of either sex, not for men over women."

Justice Marshall, joined by **Justice Brennan**, dissented. Under *Arlington Heights* (Chapter 3, § 1B), a discriminatory purpose can be inferred by looking at the "degree, inevitability, and foreseeability of any disproportionate impact as well as the alternatives reasonably available." The district court's finding that the veterans' preference essentially supplanted test results as the determinant of upper-level civil service appointments underscored the overwhelming impact of the preference upon women. Given the armed forces' longstanding exclusion of women from service (until World War I) and from combat and other positions, such an overwhelming impact was inevitable and foreseeable. "Although neutral in form, the statute is anything but neutral in application. It inescapably reserves a major sector of public employment to 'an already established class which, as a matter of historical fact, is 98% male.' Where the foreseeable impact of a facially neutral policy is so disproportionate, the burden should rest on the State to establish that sex-based considerations played no part in the choice of the particular legislative scheme." Indeed, the statute's exclusion of traditional women's work from the veterans' preference revealed that it embodied the same "archaic assumptions about women's roles" the Court invoked to invalidate statutes in *Craig* and *Wiesenfeld*.

NOTES ON *FEENEY* AND DISCRIMINATORY IMPACT ON WOMEN

1. *Application of the Discriminatory Intent Test to Issues of Jobs and Abortion.* Recall the argument that the *Washington v. Davis/Arlington Heights* discriminatory-intent test should be softened, so that it may be satisfied by a showing of "selective racial indifference." See Chapter 3, § 1B. Could Massachusetts have been any more indifferent to the interests of women seeking civil service employment and promotion? Also consider whether Professor Lawrence's arguments about "unconscious racism" (Chapter 3, § 1C) can be applied to issues of "unconscious sexism" in cases like *Feeney*.

Consider also state regulation of abortion. The issue has traditionally been analyzed under fundamental rights theories (see Chapter 5, § 4B), but can also be viewed as a violation of a woman's right to be treated equally.[m] Note that if *Geduldig* and *Feeney* had invalidated their respective state classifications (pregnancy and nonveteran status) because of their disparate impact upon women, the same kind of equal protection argument could easily have been raised against all abortion restrictions. Would such restrictions survive middle-tier scrutiny, as applied in the VMI case?

2. Geduldig, Feeney, *and the Court's Theory of Equal Protection.* These cases reflect several features of the Court's philosophy for interpreting the Equal Protection Clause. Most important, the Court has privileged the clause's rationality goal and suppressed its anti-subordination goal, perhaps even more

---

m. See, e.g., Ruth Bader Ginsburg, *Some Thoughts on Autonomy and Equality in Relation to Roe v. Wade*, 63 N.C. L. Rev. 375 (1985); Kenneth Karst, *Women's Constitution*, 1984 Duke L.J. 447; Sylvia Law, *Rethinking Sex and the Constitution*, 132 U. Pa. L. Rev. 955 (1984); Catharine MacKinnon, *Reflections on Sex Equality Under Law*, 100 Yale L.J. 1281 (1991); Frances Olsen, *Unraveling Compromise*, 103 Harv. L. Rev. 105 (1989); Reva Siegel, *Reasoning from the Body: A Historical Perspective on Abortion Regulation and Questions of Equal Protection*, 44 Stan. L. Rev. 261 (1992).

in the sex cases than in the race cases. See generally Ruth Colker, *Anti-Subordination Above All: Sex, Race, and Equal Protection*, 61 NYU L. Rev. 1003 (1986). Compare *Craig* with *Feeney*. In the former case, where the sex-based discrimination inconvenienced young men, the Court struck it down because it appeared on the face of the statute. In the latter case, where the sex-based discrimination severely disadvantaged women, the Court upheld it because the sex differential was not "intended" and the veteran-based classification was rational. (Yet one reason the sex discrimination was an inevitable consequence is the traditional discrimination against women by the military, which has been embodied in facial classifications. See notes following *Rostker*.)

Also, Court majorities have been reluctant, for institutional reasons, to require states to rearrange their workplace policies, absent invidious motivation. The Court's baseline is that state governments should be given leeway to make the complicated allocative judgments required for disability plans such as the one in *Geduldig* and personnel policies such as that in *Feeney*. While open and invidious sex- or race-based criteria trump such a baseline, it snaps back into place when challengers are "merely" asserting disparate impact. Finally, as Justice Stewart said in *Feeney*, "when there is no 'reason to infer antipathy,' it is presumed that 'even improvident decisions will eventually be rectified by the democratic process.' " Recall that women are a majority of the voting public. Public choice theory, however, would suggest that a statute benefitting veterans, a tightly (male-) bonded and well organized group, would be hard to change in the democratic process; even though they might be outnumbered by the Helen Feeneys, as well as the male victims, of the veterans preference, they have legislative inertia on their side.[n]

3. Disparate Impact on Women under State Constitutional Law. Recall that many states have state constitutional equal rights amendments. One is Massachusetts: "Equality under the law shall not be denied *or abridged* because of sex, race, color, creed or national origin" (emphasis added).[o] Feeney challenged the veterans preference only under the U.S. Constitution in federal court. Would she have been more successful bringing her lawsuit in state court and invoking the state constitution as well?

NOTE ON STATUTORY RIGHTS AGAINST SEX AND PREGNANCY DISCRIMINATION IN PRIVATE AND PUBLIC EMPLOYMENT

SHOULD *GEDULDIG* BE OVERRULED?

Congress in Title VII of the Civil Rights Act of 1964 prohibited private job discrimination or adverse job classification "because of" an employee's "race,

---

n. For other ironies of the case, see Michael Seidman, *Public Principle and Private Choice: The Uneasy Case for a Boundary Maintenance Theory of Constitutional Law*, 96 Yale L.J. 1006 (1987).

o. The ERAs in Maryland, Pennsylvania, Washington say that "equality of rights shall not be abridged or denied because of sex," and there is similar language in the ERAs of three other states (Colorado, Hawaii, Texas).

color, religion, sex, or national origin." 42 U.S.C. § 2000e-2(a)(1)-(2). The sex discrimination component was neither thoroughly considered by Congress nor vigorously enforced at the outset, but it was an unmistakable command that Congress extended to state and local employers in the statute's 1972 amendments. Moreover, the Supreme Court construed the statute to prohibit employment policies having an unjustified "disparate impact" on employees because of their race, sex, etc., *Griggs v. Duke Power Co.*, 401 U.S. 424 (1971) — precisely the kind of claim that the Court refused to constitutionalize five years later in *Washington v. Davis*. Note that Title VII as amended would seemingly require a different result in *Feeney* — were it not for the fact that § 712 preserves federal, state, and local veterans' preferences. 42 U.S.C. § 2000e-11. Recall the public choice point in the previous Note.

Griggs would also suggest that Title VII as amended would require a different result in *Geduldig*, at least as applied to insurance programs tied to state employment, but the Court followed *Geduldig* rather than *Griggs* in *General Electric v. Gilbert*, 429 U.S. 125 (1976), upholding an employer disability plan which excluded disability arising from pregnancy. The Court found that the exclusion of pregnancy was not a statutory discrimination "because of * * * sex" (it's because of pregnancy!) and that the whole package of disability benefits was not worth more to men than to women. The attorneys in *Gilbert*, Professors Wendy Webster Williams and Susan Deller Ross, lobbied Congress to override the Court, on the ground that pregnancy-based discriminations have traditionally been a barrier to women's obtaining certain jobs and advancing up employment ladders. Congress agreed and overrode the Court with the Pregnancy Discrimination Act of 1978 (PDA), which defined "sex" in Title VII to include "pregnancy, childbirth, or related medical conditions"; the PDA further provided that "women affected by pregnancy, childbirth, or related medical conditions shall be treated the same for all employment-related purposes, including receipt of benefits under fringe benefit programs, as other persons not so affected but similar in their ability or inability to work." 42 U.S.C. § 2000e(k). The Supreme Court has applied the PDA to invalidate on statutory grounds employer policies disqualifying pregnant women from certain jobs the employer considered potentially harmful to the fetus. See *United Auto Workers v. Johnson Controls*, 499 U.S. 187 (1991).

In *Price Waterhouse v. Hopkins*, 490 U.S. 228 (1989), the Court held that it is sex discrimination if an employer disadvantages an employee because she violates traditional gender roles. The plaintiff, Ann Hopkins, had allegedly been denied partnership at Price Waterhouse on the ground that some partners felt she was "macho" and uncharming; even her supporters urged her to "walk more femininely, talk more femininely," etc. Again, Congress picked up on this idea when it enacted the Family and Medical Leave Act of 1993 (FMLA). One purpose of the FMLA was to require employers to provide such leaves to *both* male and female employees, for it was often assumed that only female employees wanted such leaves, a classic gender stereotype that Congress believed held women back in the workplace.

In *Nevada Department of Human Resources v. Hibbs*, 538 U.S. 721 (2003) (reproduced in Chapter 7, § 3F), the Supreme Court ruled that Congress in the

FMLA was attacking sex discrimination along the following lines: "Historically, denial or curtailment of women's employment opportunities has been traceable directly to the pervasive presumption that women are mothers first, and workers second. This prevailing ideology about women's roles has in turn justified discrimination against women when they are mothers or mothers-to-be." (Quoting the FMLA's legislative history.) The Court held that it was a violation of the Equal Protection Clause for state employers to provide family leave only to female employees or to administer such leaves in a discriminatory manner. The Court also said that this was the problem Congress was trying to address, with incomplete success, in the PDA. The Court further said that it was a violation of equal protection for states to offer no family leave at all, as "such a policy would exclude far more women than men from the workplace." This was precisely the argument that the Court rejected in *Geduldig*. Should *Geduldig* be overruled?

PROBLEM 4-2
FRONTIER ISSUES IN STATUTORY AND CONSTITUTIONAL DISCRIMINATION ON THE BASIS OF SEX OR GENDER

For a state employer covered by both Title VII and the Equal Protection Clause, which, if any, of the following employment exclusions is illegal discrimination because of sex:[p]

(a) firing a female physical education teacher because she is considered too "macho" and "unladylike";

(b) firing a male kindergarten teacher because he is considered too "effeminate";

(c) firing a female secretary because she wears "men's" suits rather than traditional female attire (dresses);

(d) firing a male secretary because he wears an earring (or dresses?);

(e) firing a female high school guidance counselor because she is openly lesbian;

(f) firing a female high school guidance counselor because she is a male-to-female transsexual.

C. CRITIQUES OF ABSTRACT EQUALITY AND THE EMERGENCE OF A JURISPRUDENCE OF DIFFERENCE

For a number of feminist legal scholars, the litigation strategy adopted by women's groups in the 1970s, and reflected in many of the Court's decisions, erroneously glorified abstract principle over concrete result. "Formal equality * * * can effect only limited change. It cannot, for example, ensure that jobs are

---

p. See generally Eskridge & Hunter, *Sexuality, Gender, and the Law* 913-37, 1102-09, 1140-44 (discussing and excerpting the cases); Mary Anne Case, *Disaggregating Gender from Sex and Sexual Orientation: The Effeminate Man in the Law and Feminist Jurisprudence*, 105 Yale L.J. 1 (1995).

structured so that female workers and male workers are equally able to combine wage work and parenthood. Nor can it ensure that social security, unemployment compensation, and other safety nets are structured so as to provide for women's financial security as well as they provide for men's. Moreover, women, especially ordinary mothers and wives, have been harmed by the changes effected to date by the movement towards formal equality." Mary Becker, *Prince Charming: Abstract Equality*, 1987 Sup. Ct. Rev. 201, 247.[q] Because some of the most harmful discriminations against women were sex-neutral, such as those in *Geduldig* and *Feeney*, formal equality failed to address the big issues. Because men were often the plaintiffs, some of the feminist "victories" took away preferences women enjoyed in law. Consider three areas of concern:

1. *Alimony and Child Support.* The Court in *Orr v. Orr*, 440 U.S. 268 (1979), invalidated state laws imposing alimony (or, by implication, child support) payments on husbands but not wives. The Court found the sex-based classification grounded in gender stereotypes (the woman is always the dependent) and rejected Alabama's claim that it was remedial (the only women helped by the classification were well-to-do). Although defensible under *Craig*, *Orr* came at a time when many wives were being paupered by the no-fault divorce revolution, which allowed wandering males to abandon their supportive spouses more readily and, often, without easily enforceable alimony and child support obligations.[r]

2. *Benefit and Tax Statutes.* Women's groups persuaded the Court to strike down (or Congress to change) most of the sex-based distinctions in federal statutes setting Social Security and other work-related benefits. Yet the beneficiaries of these victories are usually men (the widowers in *Wiesenfeld* and *Goldfarb*), who continue to earn a lot more on average than female wage earners. More important, sex-based classifications on the face of the statute are not the problem for most women. "[T]he major problem with social security was *and is* its treatment of ordinary women, women who are primarily responsible for domestic production and reproduction and who often participate, on a limited basis, in wage employment. The social security system is structured to afford greater financial security in old age to breadwinners than to full or part-time homemakers. Thus, the major problem from the perspective of women's inequality is not, as the cases suggest, that the social security system has treated

---

q. For other critiques of equality feminism, see Ann Freedman, *Sex Equality, Sex Differences, and the Supreme Court*, 92 Yale L.J. 913 (1983); Christine Littleton, *Reconstructing Sexual Equality*, 75 Calif. L. Rev. 1279 (1987). An effort at synthesis is Elizabeth Schneider, *The Dialectic of Rights and Politics: Perspectives from the Women's Movement*, 61 N.Y.U. L. Rev. 589 (1986). A scholarly review of the equality problems still facing women in the workplace, the home, and elsewhere can be found in Deborah Rhode, *Justice and Gender: Sex Discrimination and the Law* chs. 6-11 (1989), with a concluding essay on the sameness/difference debates within feminism.

r. See generally *Symposium: Divorce and Feminist Legal Theory*, 82 Geo. L.J. 2119-2569 (1994).

the atypical woman differently from a similar man, but rather that it gives less effective old-age financial security to typical women than to typical men."[s]

3. *Preferences for Women.* Equality theory has arguably put women in the same bind the NAACP's victories put blacks in: By problematizing sex-based classifications at the very point when women were gaining real political clout, equal protection theory became a sharp tool to criticize, and perhaps overturn, statutes seeking to remedy the functional barriers to women's equal participation in society and the economy and to address women's unique experiences and problems. That is why some feminist legal scholars argue for a jurisprudence of difference: "[P]regnancy, abortion, reproduction, and creation of another human being *are* special — very special. Women have these experiences. Men do not. An equality doctrine that ignores the unique quality of these experiences implicitly says that women can claim equality only insofar as they are like men. Such doctrine demands that women deny an important aspect of who they are." Sylvia Law, *Rethinking Sex and the Constitution*, 132 U. Pa. L. Rev. 955, 1007 (1984).

The debate over formal equality shows up most sharply in cases where a recently enacted statute draws sex-based distinctions that benefit women, but usually in response to a traditional inequity. E.g., *California Fed. Savs. & Loan Ass'n v. Guerra*, 479 U.S. 272 (1987) (ruling that Title VII did not preempt a state law ensuring family leave time for female but not male employees).

NOTE ON AFFIRMATIVE ACTION
FOR WOMEN IN THE WORKPLACE

Because women have been excluded or discouraged from a wide array of jobs, and because the continued absence of women from those jobs may be evidence of continuing sex discrimination, some employers have adopted "affirmative action plans" which give female applicants a preference. Has such an employer "discriminated" on the basis of sex? Such claims against public employers can be raised under either the Equal Protection Clause or Title VII. Review the race-based affirmative action cases in Chapter 3, § 3, especially *Wygant v. Jackson Board of Educ.*, 476 U.S. 267 (1987).

The leading case on sex-based affirmative action is *Johnson v. Transportation Agency*, 480 U.S. 616 (1987). Pursuant to an affirmative action plan, the Agency chose Diane Joyce over Paul Johnson for the position of road dispatcher, even though Johnson had a slightly higher score from the interviewing process. What gave Joyce an edge was that she was a female applicant for a position (skilled craft worker) with no female employees and a long tradition of no representation of women. Justice Brennan, writing for five Justices, upheld the Agency's decision based upon a flexible interpretation of Title VII to permit affirmative action when there is a "manifest imbalance" in the relevant workforce. The Court did not consider the equal protection standard because it had been abandoned by the plaintiff.

---

s. Mary Becker, *Obscuring the Struggle: Sex Discrimination, Social Security, and Stone, Seidman, Sunstein & Tushnet's* Constitutional Law, 89 Colum. L. Rev. 264, 276 (1989).

Justice O'Connor, concurring in the judgment, argued that the Title VII and equal protection standards are the same (*Wygant*). That is, "the employer must have had a firm basis for believing that remedial action was required. An employer would have such a firm basis if it can point to a statistical disparity sufficient to support a prima facie claim under Title VII by the employee beneficiaries of the affirmative action plan of a pattern or practice claim of discrimination." She found that standard met in the *Johnson* case, where there had never been a female among the 238 skilled craft workers. While agreeing with the dissenting Justices that "an affirmative action program that automatically and blindly promotes those marginally qualified candidates falling within a preferred race or gender category, or that can be equated with a permanent plan of 'proportionate representation by race and sex,' would violate Title VII" and the Equal Protection Clause, Justice O'Connor believed this was not such a case, for Diane Joyce's sex was merely a "plus" factor and not the only factor that got her the job.

Justice Scalia, joined by Chief Justice Rehnquist and for the most part by Justice White, sharply dissented. He argued that no affirmative action is allowed under Title VII, a view consistent with his interpretation of the Equal Protection Clause in *Croson* (Chapter 3, § 3B). Relying on the district court's findings of fact, Justice Scalia also argued that sex was the only reason Joyce was promoted ahead of Johnson, which would be inadmissible even under Justice O'Connor's approach. Justice Thomas, not on the Court in 1987, has taken a similar stance in race-based affirmative action cases (see *Adarand*, Chapter 3, § 3B).

Evaluate the clashing views on the Court. Doctrinally, shouldn't affirmative action for women (receiving intermediate scrutiny) pass constitutional muster more easily than affirmative action for racial minorities (receiving strict scrutiny)? Can *Webster* and *Ballard* be cited for the proposition that state efforts to remedy prior sex discrimination through affirmative action should be reviewed more leniently than efforts to remedy prior race discrimination (*Croson*)? Should conservatives find sex-based affirmative action less, or more, troubling than race-based programs?

PROBLEM 4-3
IS SEX SEGREGATION IN SCHOOLS EVER CONSTITUTIONAL?

(A) *All-Girls' Elementary School.* In a series of publications informed by expert surveys, the American Association of University Women (AAUW) concluded that girls as early as third grade are disadvantaged by being educated with boys. See AAUW, *How Schools Shortchange Girls* (1992), and *Achieving Gender Equity in the Classroom and on the Campus: The Next Steps* (1995). Reasons may include greater teacher (including female teacher) attention to the boys, an overwhelming male focus in the teaching materials, and the channeling of the girls' social attention toward the boys. Some studies have found that girls in single-sex schools score a half-grade above their coeducational counterparts on four academic ability tests, and a full grade higher on science tests.[t] Following school boards in New York, California, Virginia, and other states, a local school board finds these theories to have merit and wants to apply them in a single school, open to female but not male applicants from the county school system. Is this constitutional after the VMI case? Compare *Garrett v. Board of Educ.*, 775 F. Supp. 1004 (E.D. Mich. 1991) (all-male academies in inner city are unconstitutional).

(B) *All-Girls' Schools Revisited?* Would your answer to the previous inquiry change in light of the AAUW's more recent study, *Separated by Sex: A Critical Look at Single-Sex Education for Girls* (1998), which concluded that "there is no evidence in general that single-sex education works or is better for girls than coeducation." The new AAUW study specifically found: (1) "girls and boys succeed" wherever and whenever elements of a good education are present, like small classes and schools, equitable teaching practices, and focused academic curriculum; (2) while "some kinds of single-sex programs produce positive results" for some girls, including a preference for math and science, increased risk-taking, and increased confidence, it was unclear whether these benefits "derive from factors unique to single-sex programs or factors that promote good education such as small classes," etc.; (3) there is no escape from sexism, even in single-sex schools and classes, which have drawbacks of their own, such as depriving girls of the social benefits of coeducation. On the other hand, the Department of Education has come down the other way, concluding that single-sex education is better for many girls and proposing that federal law explicitly acknowledge that (controversial) conclusion. 67 Fed. Reg. 31,098 (May 8, 2002).

(C) *Sex-Segregated Sports.* Almost all public schools maintain athletic programs that are sex-segregated. Swanson Junior High School has a boys' but not a girls' football team. Jane Doe is an athletic girl who wants to play football; sports medical experts tell the school that she is as qualified as the boys to play several positions, and she has in fact played in recreational leagues. The school refuses to allow her to compete for a position on the boys' team. Constitutional? Compare *O'Connor v. Board of Educ.*, 449 U.S. 1301 (1980) (Stevens, J., as circuit Justice, denying a petition against sex-segregated sports); 45 C.F.R. § 86.41(b) (Title IX regulations to same effect: schools are obligated to provide parity for female and male athletic programs, but parity does not require sex-integration of particular sports). Should Justice Stevens' disposition be revisited after the VMI case? Suppose a school has football for boys and soccer for girls. Should a boy be allowed to compete for a spot on the soccer team?

––––––––

---

t. See Note, *Inner-City Single-Sex Schools: Educational Reform or Invidious Discrimination?*, 105 Harv. L. Rev. 1741, 1757 (1992).

Catharine A. MacKinnon
Toward a Feminist Theory of the State
220-22, 225-27, 232, 244-45 (1991)[u]

The philosophy underlying the sameness/difference approach applies liberalism to women. Sex is a natural difference, a division, a distinction, beneath which lies a stratum of human commonality, sameness. The moral thrust of the sameness branch of the doctrine conforms normative rules to empirical reality by granting women access to what men have: to the extent women are no different from men, women deserve what men have. The differences branch, which is generally regarded as patronizing and unprincipled but necessary to avoid absurdity, exists to value or compensate women for what they are or have become distinctively as women — by which is meant, unlike men, or to leave women as "different" as equality law finds them.

Most scholarship on sex discrimination law concerns which of these paths to sex equality is preferable in the long run * * * as if they were all there is. As a prior matter, however, treating issues of sex equality as issues of sameness and difference is to take a particular approach. This approach is here termed the sameness/difference approach because it is obsessed with the sex difference. Its main theme is: "we're the same, we're the same, we're the same." Its counterpoint theme (in a higher register) goes: "but we're different, but we're different, but we're different." * * *

Concealed is the substantive way in which man has become the measure of all things. Under the sameness rubric, women are measured according to correspondence with man, their equality judged by proximity to his measure. Under the difference rubric, women are measured according to their lack of correspondence from man, their womanhood judged by their distance from his measure. Gender neutrality is the male standard. The special protection rule is the female standard. Masculinity or maleness is the referent for both. * * *

The sameness standard has mostly gotten men the benefit of those few things women have historically had — for all the good they did. Under gender neutrality, the law of custody and divorce has shifted once again, giving men what is termed an equal chance at custody of children and at alimony. Men often look like better parents under gender-neutral rules like level of income and presence of nuclear family, because men make more money and * * * initiate the building of family units. They also have greater credibility and authority in court. Under gender neutrality, men are in effect granted a preference as parents because society advantages them before they get to court. * * *

Missing in sex equality law is what Aristotle missed in his empiricist notion that equality means treating likes alike and unlikes unlike. * * * Why should one have to be the same as a man to get what a man gets simply because he is one? Why does maleness provide an original entitlement * * * ?

The women that gender neutrality benefits, and there are some, expose this method in highest relief. They are mostly women who have achieved a

---

u. Reprinted with permission of Professor Catharine MacKinnon, the copyright holder.

biography that somewhat approximates the male norm, at least on paper. They are the qualified, the least of sex discrimination's victims. When they are denied a man's chance, it looks the most like sex bias. [*E.g., Hopkins.*] * * *

The special benefits side of the sameness/difference approach has not compensated women for being second class. Its double standard does not give women the dignity of the single standard, nor does it suppress the gender of its referent: female. The special benefits rule is the only place in mainstream sex equality doctrine where one can identify as a woman and not have that mean giving up all claim to equal treatment. But it comes close. Originally, women were permitted to be protected in the workforce, with dubious benefit. Then, under its double standard, women who stood to inherit something when their husbands died were allowed to exclude a small percentage of inheritance tax, Justice Douglas waxing eloquent about the difficulties of all women's economic situation. [*Kahn.*] If women are going to be stigmatized as different, the compensation should at least fit the disparity. Women have also gotten three more years than men get before being advanced or kicked out of the military hierarchy. [*Ballard.*] This is to compensate them for being precluded from combat, the usual way to advance. [*Rostker.*] Making exceptions for women, as if they are a special case, often seems preferable to correcting the rule itself, even when women's "specialness" is dubious or shared or statutorily created. * * *

The result of gender neutrality is that at the same time that very few women gain access to the preconditions effectively to assert equality on male terms, women created in society's traditional mold lose the guarantees of those roles to men asserting sex equality. Women asking courts to enforce the guarantees that have been part of the bargain of women's roles receive less and less, while also not receiving the benefits of the social changes that would qualify them for rights on the same terms as men. This is not a transitional problem. Abstract equality necessarily reinforces the inequalities of the status quo to the extent that it evenly reflects an unequal social arrangement. The law of sex discrimination has largely refused to recognize that it is women who are unequal to men, and has called this refusal the equality principle. * * *

* * * [This analysis] does challenge the view that neutrality, specifically gender neutrality as an expression of objectivity, is adequate to the nonneutral objectified social reality women experience. If differentiation were the problem, gender neutrality would make sense as an approach to it. Since hierarchy is the problem, it is not only inadequate, it is perverse. * * * [C]urrent law to rectify sex inequality is premised upon, and promotes, its continued existence.

The analytical point of departure and return of sex discrimination law is thus the liberal one of gender differences, understood rationally or irrationally to create gender inequalities. The feminist issue, by contrast, is gender hierarchy, which not only produces inequalities but shapes the social meaning, hence legal relevance, of the sex difference. * * *

* * * Can women, demanding actual equality through law, be part of changing the state's relation to women and women's relation to men?

The first step [toward an adequate sex equality argument] is to claim women's concrete reality. Women's inequality occurs in a context of unequal pay, allocation to disrespected work, demeaned physical characteristics, targeting for rape, domestic battery, sexual abuse as children, and systematic sexual harassment. Women are daily dehumanized, used in denigrating entertainment, denied reproductive control, and forced by the conditions of their lives into prostitution. These abuses occur in a legal context historically characterized by disenfranchisement, preclusion from property ownership, exclusion from public life, and lack of recognition of sex-specific injuries. Sex inequality is thus a social and political institution.

The next step is to recognize that male forms of power over women are affirmatively embodied as individual rights in law. When men lose power, they feel they lose rights. Often they are not wrong. Examples include the defense of mistaken belief in consent in the rape law, which legally determines whether or not a rape occurred from the rapists' perspective; freedom of speech, which gives pimps rights to torture, exploit, use, and sell women to men through pictures and words, and gives consumers rights to buy them; the law of privacy, which defines home and sex as presumptively consensual and protects the use of pornography in the home; the law of child custody, which purports gender neutrality while applying a standard of adequacy of parenting based on male-controlled resources and male-defined norms, sometimes taking children away from women but more generally controlling women through the threat and fear of loss of their children. Real sex equality under law would qualify or eliminate these powers of men, hence men's current "rights" to use, access, possess, and traffic women and children.

NOTES ON RADICAL AND CRITICAL FEMINIST THEORIES

As the MacKinnon excerpt suggests, it can be argued that, notwithstanding judicial decisions striking down "archaic" sex-based classifications and purporting to deliver formal equality, women are not equal citizens in the United States. Women make less money than similarly qualified males, are sexually harassed on the job and in the classroom, and are subject to rape by dates and spouses as well as by strangers.[v] Arguably, the statutory or constitutional reforms only nibble at the margins — treating women like men for purposes of drinking (*Craig*), alimony (*Orr*), property (*Reed*), survivors' benefits (*Wiesenfeld*), education (the VMI case), and leaving a few minor compensatory measures in place (*Ballard, Webster, Guerra*). By lining up marginal victories that mean little, perhaps legal feminism has deflected attention from the real problems that remain. See also Robin West, *Progressive Constitutionalism: Restructuring the Fourteenth Amendment* (1994), which makes similar constitutional arguments for the affirmative responsibilities of the state to address private violence and

---

v. See generally Justice Souter's dissent in *United States v. Morrison*, Chapter 7, § 3E (summarizing extensive congressional findings regarding the high level of violence against women in the United States); Susan Estrich, *Sex at Work*, 43 Stan. L. Rev. 813 (1991) (pervasive sexual harassment of women in the workplace); Vicki Schultz, *Life's Work*, 100 Colum. L. Rev. 1881 (2000) (continuing sex segregation and employment discrimination against women).

discrimination against women. How would liberal feminists respond to such critique? Scholars influenced by sociobiology? Consider also some larger questions of constitutional theory raised by MacKinnon and West:

1. *Transforming Law.* If law is thoroughly gendered, law needs to be rethought from the ground up, not just at the margins (the mistake of equality feminism) or with special remedial exceptions (the mistake of difference feminism). Radical feminism insists that a state founded on male baselines is not constitutionally legitimate for the non-male majority. To sustain its legitimacy in a polity where women are full and equal citizens, law needs to be reconceived from women's point of view.

Consider a radical approach to the VMI case. The Court interrogated the historical arguments for sex-segregated colleges and thereby exposed their sexist philosophy — but then failed to interrogate the linkages between VMI's pedagogy and its all-male culture. Such an interrogation might have exposed a sexist philosophy underlying the adversative method and the ritual (fraternity-like) hazing entailed in that culture. In that event, the remedy sought by the Department of Justice and accepted by the Court might be shallow, for it might leave VMI as an institution profoundly hostile to women and it might have female taxpayers fund an institution that almost none of them would want to attend. Under a radical critique, the VMI Court's analogy to *Sweatt* was telling, for that was a race case where the Court simply ordered a person of color admitted to an extremely inhospitable white institution, with no protection for the minority nor any requirement that the institution protect the student from inevitable harassment. Just as tellingly, the VMI Court did not invoke *Green* or *Swann*, desegregation cases where the Department of Justice requested and the Court required long-segregated state institutions to take affirmative steps to restructure themselves.

Recall the liberal feminist critique of *Michael M.*, reflected in Justice Brennan's dissent: The gendered rape law was invalid because it rested on traditional notions of female virginity as valuable and the older male as the only responsible actor. MacKinnon has criticized the dissent for being more concerned "with avoiding the stereotyping attendant to the ideological message the law communicated than with changing the facts that make the stereotype largely true. In the interest of opposing facial distinctions and debunking the supposed myth of male sexual aggression, the fact that it is overwhelmingly girls who are sexually victimized by older males for reasons wholly unrelated to their capacity to become pregnant was completely obscured. * * * Underage girls form a credible disadvantaged group for equal protection purposes when the social facts of sexual assault are faced, facts which prominently feature one-sided sexual aggression by older males." Catharine MacKinnon, *Reflections on Sex Equality Under Law*, 100 Yale L.J. 1281, 1305 (1991). If you agree with MacKinnon's critique, how would you vote to uphold the sex-based law in *Michael M*? Does MacKinnon's critique run the risk of perpetuating a view of adolescent girls as fragile creatures in need of protection from predatory boys? Consider the next Note.

2. *Equality and Liberty.* Radical feminists argue that the Supreme Court overemphasizes the libertarian features of the original Constitution, which they

maintain has been modified or even trumped by the egalitarian features of the Reconstructed Constitution and the Nineteenth Amendment. These are *not* just another set of amendments — they rescued the original Constitution from illegitimacy in a polity where people of color and, later, women are citizens whose interests must be respected. For women, equality values are particularly important, and traditional liberty values must give way through the kind of constitutional holism or synthesis described in Chapter 2, § 3C.

Accordingly, Professor MacKinnon, *Francis Biddle's Sister: Pornography, Civil Rights, and Speech*, in *Feminism Unmodified* 163 (1987), argues that the state must suppress misogynistic pornography, because it perpetuates a culture where women are sexualized and therefore objectified. This is not a culture where women *can* be equal citizens. MacKinnon recognizes the obvious response, that such suppression would infringe on men's First Amendment liberties. She replies that this kind of liberty for men cannot justify more serious deprivations of liberty for women (whom she claims suffer sexual assaults as a result of pornography). When two kinds of liberty are at stake, a "neutral" Court cannot cogently prefer the liberty of those who are inclined to *commit* the violence over the liberty of those who will *suffer* it. If women's equal citizenship is to mean anything, it has got to mean that the state can suppress violence-inducing "speech."

MacKinnon's critique of pornography has called forth vigorous feminist responses. By defining women too much by male sexual oppression against them, pro-sex feminists such as Carole Vance argue that MacKinnon's brand of feminism denies women's personal and sexual agency.[w] MacKinnon's dominance thesis, they maintain, oversimplifies women's experience and denies women a resource needed for self-understanding and even resistance. Robin West, *The Difference in Women's Hedonic Lives: A Phenomenological Critique of Feminist Legal Theory*, 3 Wis. Women's L.J. 81 (1987), criticizes MacKinnon for not attending to women's own accounts of pleasure and fulfillment. Just as some women apparently want to attend VMI and participate in its culture of ritualized hazing, so some women enjoy dominance forms of sexual intercourse popularized in soft-core pornography. It is a departure from feminist method, West argues, to elevate abstract conceptions of women's equality above concrete experiences women consider valuable as a matter of their own sexual liberty.

West's article also criticizes liberal constitutionalism for its assumption that citizens are autonomous, utility-maximizing agents. Liberal constitutionalism seeks to prevent the state from unduly restricting people's range of choices and from coercing choices. Drawing from cultural feminist thought, West argues that this rests upon male-centered and thereby biased assumptions. Women are more relational than men; they often "choose" options because of the benefits that flow to people with whom they feel connected (children, spouses, friends). So to give them more choices (the goal of liberalism) will not necessarily benefit women, and the fact that they have the same formal choices as men does not

---

w. See *Pleasure and Danger: Exploring Female Sexuality* (Carole Vance ed., 2d ed. 1992); *Powers of Desire: The Politics of Sexuality* (Anne Snitow et al. eds. 1983); Kathryn Abrams, *Sex Wars Redux: Agency and Coercion in Feminist Legal Theory*, 95 Colum. L. Rev. 304 (1995).

mean that women are being treated equally by the state. The *circumstances* of choice are more important than the *possibility* of choice. If the circumstances offer women few realistic choices, because of continuing sexist structures and ideology, women will lose rather than exercise liberty through choice, which is perverse. From these Westian ideas, formulate a possible defense for the constitutionality of the sex-based law in *Michael M*. Is *Nguyen* defensible under her theory?

   3. *Feminist Critique of the Public-Private Distinction and the State Action Doctrine*. For libertarian and institutionalist reasons, the state action requirement plays a central role in the Supreme Court's narrow enforcement of the Equal Protection Clause (Chapter 3, § 2). The Court's constitutionalism reaches the conduct of "public" but not "private" actors. An expansive state action doctrine is objectionable from a feminist perspective. Most violence and discrimination against women are carried out by private actors; such violence and discrimination harm women and deny them both genuine liberty and full equality. The Constitution ought to be concerned about this — but the traditional state action doctrine has been the doctrinal basis for judicial abnegation. The state action doctrine, and not the Constitution, ought to give way.[x]

   One feminist approach would be to view the idea of state action expansively, as the NAACP's Inc. Fund and its allies did in the lunch counter sit-in cases. See *Lombard v. Louisiana*, 373 U.S. 267 (1963) (refusal of lunch place to serve people of color can be attributed to the state because of the state's long support of racist attitudes through apartheid). State entanglement theories could justify attributing some private action to the state. Another approach would be to take an expansive view of state responsibility for failing to act. Robin West, *Equality Theory, Marital Rape, and the Promise of the Fourteenth Amendment*, 42 Fla. L. Rev. 45 (1990), makes this kind of argument: State laws long exempted domestic rape and violence against women from sexual assault statutes and still exempt marital rape under some circumstances; state police and prosecutors do not vigorously enforce the laws that do exist; these policies of state neglect as well as action give rise to state responsibility for domestic violence against women. To be sure, American courts generally do not take the state to task for its inaction — but this is another legacy of the Constitution's original sexism. As before, the baseline should be the Reconstructed Constitution: Just as the state in *Green* and *Swann* had an obligation to restructure a status quo founded on racist policies, so the state now has an obligation to restructure a status quo founded on sexist policies.

   Some feminists deny the constitutional imperative of the state action doctrine through an expansive reading of the Thirteenth Amendment. Thus, one might argue that private as well as public obstacles to women's exercising their right to choose abortions constitute efforts to impose "involuntary servitude" on women that is directly actionable under the Thirteenth Amendment. Other feminists undercut the state action requirement through a literal reading of the

---

x. See Ruth Gavison, *Feminism and the Public/Private Distinction*, 45 Stan. L. Rev. 1 (1992); Frances Olsen, *Statutory Rape: A Feminist Critique of Rights Analysis*, 63 Tex. L. Rev. 387 (1984).

Fourteenth Amendment that dovetails with its anti-subordination purpose. Kenneth Karst, *The Supreme Court, 1976 Term — Foreword: Equal Citizenship Under the Fourteenth Amendment*, 91 Harv. L. Rev. 1 (1977), maintains that the Fourteenth Amendment must be read in light of its first sentence, the National Citizenship Clause, which does not have a state action requirement. Robin West argues in *Progressive Constitutionalism* (1994) that the state's obligation, in the second sentence, to assure "equal protection of the laws" *literally* requires the state to protect women where they are most vulnerable (within the family) at least as strongly as the state protects men in the public sphere (streets, business).

Under Karst's or West's theory, the state has an obligation to adopt statutory rape laws to protect girls against sexual assault. Justice Rehnquist's *Michael M.* arguments are enriched by this line of thought: If the state has reason to believe (as Rehnquist claimed) that a sex-neutral statutory rape law would discourage female minors from reporting assaults by male minors, the efficacy of the law would be undermined; under those circumstances, the state has a strong equal *protection* interest in defining the crime in gendered terms. If the factual predicate of this argument is correct, is this argument a cogent defense of *Michael M.*? Was the case rightly decided?

Consider the following case, which raises all the issues discussed in this Note, in the context of Operation Rescue's campaign to prevent women from exercising their rights to choose abortions.

———

Bray v. Alexandria Women's Health Clinic, 506 U.S. 263 (1993). Section 1985(3) of 42 U.S.C. (Civil Rights Act of 1871) gives a cause of action against two or more persons who deprive "any person or class of persons of the equal protection of the laws, or of equal privileges and immunities under the laws." Generally, the Supreme Court has read this law to provide a claim only against state actors or those conspiring with state actors. But the Court in *Griffin v. Breckenridge*, 403 U.S. 88 (1971), interpreted § 1985(3) to provide relief against private conspirators who are motivated by animus that is "racial, or perhaps otherwise class-based, invidiously discriminatory," and who also interfere with rights protected against private as well as official encroachment, in that case the right to interstate travel (see Chapter 5, § 3C). Under *Griffin*, the lower courts upheld lawsuits by abortion clinics against participants in Operation Rescue, who allegedly conspired to deprive women of the right to travel interstate to use abortion clinics in the District of Columbia metropolitan area.

The Supreme Court, in an opinion by **Justice Scalia**, reversed, holding that "women seeking abortion" did not qualify as a class for purposes of the statute. Justice Scalia left open the possibility that women could be a class protected by § 1985(3), because the record did not support the charge that Operation Rescue was motivated by animus against women generally; *Geduldig* had rejected the proposition that discrimination based upon pregnancy is ipso facto sex discrimination. The Court also ruled that the clinics had presented no right that is constitutionally protected against private as well as public action. The right to interstate travel is protected against private action but was not the target of Operation Rescue; the right to an abortion was the target of Operation Rescue but is not assured against private action.

Justice Souter concurred in this analysis of the *deprivation clause* of § 1985(3), construed in *Griffin*, but argued that the plaintiffs had a claim under the *hindrance clause* of the statute, giving a claim for relief against conspiracies "for the purpose of preventing or hindering the constituted authorities of any State or Territory from giving or securing to all persons within such State or Territory the equal protection of the laws." Because plaintiffs alleged that the defendants' conspiracy was to deprive women of their right to abortions, they were alleging facts entitling them to relief under the plain meaning of the hindrance clause, and Justice Souter saw no reason to import extratextual criteria into that clause, as *Griffin* had done for the deprivation clause.

Justice Stevens, joined by **Justice Blackmun**, disagreed with the Court as to both the deprivation and hindrance clauses. As to the deprivation clause, Justice Stevens maintained that actions targeting abortion are not sex neutral, because they are penalizing a physical characteristic present only in women; he felt that a broad reading of *Geduldig* is simply too false to be valid law, and the Court in that case relied mainly on the evidence in the record that the benefits offered by the disability program were in fact as generous for women as they were for men. Moreover, in protecting the equal protection of the laws, he assumed Congress is not limited by the state action doctrine limiting judicial enforcement of the Fourteenth Amendment.

Justice O'Connor, also joined by Justice Blackmun, dissented from the Court's construction of the hindrance clause, which struck her as squarely applicable to the allegations against Operation Rescue. "Like the Klan conspiracies Congress tried to reach in enacting § 1985(3), '[p]etitioners intended to hinder a particular group in the exercise of their legal rights because of their membership in a specific class.' [*Griffin*.] The controversy associated with the exercise of those rights, although legitimate, makes the clinics and the women they serve especially vulnerable to the threat of mob violence." Justice O'Connor disputed the central premise of the Court's opinion: The goal of the statute was not simply to implement the negative features of the Fourteenth Amendment, which prohibits states from discriminating, but was to invoke the affirmative features of the amendment, to reach private discrimination as well.

Postscript. In *United States v. Morrison*, 529 U.S. 598 (2000) (Chapter 7, § 3E), the Court invalidated that part of the Violence Against Women Act that imposed liability on persons who commit gender-motivated offences, such as the rape complained of in *Morrison*. The Court concluded that Congress had no Fourteenth Amendment § 5 (enforcement) authority; gender-motivated violence could not be the basis for Fourteenth Amendment liability against private parties, even when the plaintiff maintained that they were benefitting from lax local enforcement of rape laws. You might want to read *Morrison* at this point, as it provides support for the *Bray* majority and undercuts assumptions made in the Stevens and O'Connor dissents; ironically, O'Connor was the critical fifth vote for the majority in *Morrison*.

Note also that the *Bray* majority relied on *Geduldig*, while the dissenters were critical of that decision. Recall from our employment discrimination note that *Nevada Department of Human Resources v. Hibbs*, 538 U.S. 721 (2003) (Chapter 7, § 3F) contains reasoning that calls *Geduldig* into question. If

Geduldig were no longer good law, how might a § 1985(3) claim be crafted for abortion clinics subject to violence from Operation Rescue?

SECTION 3. WHAT LEVEL OF SCRUTINY FOR OTHER "SUSPICIOUS" CLASSIFICATIONS?

A central lesson of the race discrimination cases, amplified in the sex discrimination cases, was that a group could sweep away almost all formal state discriminations stigmatizing its members if social movement lawyers could persuade the Supreme Court to recognize the trait marking the group's members as a "suspect" or "quasi-suspect" classification. For reasons of federalism, institutional legitimacy, and the capacity of the judiciary to handle large numbers of claims, the Court after 1976 was leery of creating more such classifications. In this section, we examine the claims of several social movements and the Court's response. Consider, also, the Court's uncertainty as to what criteria should determine which classifications should be subjected to strict scrutiny. Finally, reflect on the thesis, first advanced by Justice Thurgood Marshall, that the "double standard" of strict and usually fatal scrutiny for a few classifications and rational basis and easy to pass scrutiny for all others, has never adequately explained the Court's actual decisionmaking and that the Court does and should follow a context-specific approach where it considers the reliability of the classification, the importance of the state benefit discriminatorily apportioned, and the cogency of the state justification for the particular discrimination. *San Antonio Indep. Sch. Dist. v. Rodriguez* (Marshall, J., dissenting) (Chapter 5, § 3B).[a]

A. WEALTH

Early American history was filled with statutes discriminating on the basis of wealth; property ownership, for example, was often a requirement for the exercise of the franchise. Since the Civil War, most laws formally excluding or discriminating against people on the basis of wealth have disappeared. But countless statutes have the effect of excluding or discriminating against people without much money. A law requiring a couple to pay a state fee to obtain a marriage license may not formally bar poor people from getting married, but it would have the effect of discouraging some poor people from being able to take advantage of the institution of civil marriage. From the perspective of the person without much money, the statutes are equivalent. In the world of *Washington v. Davis* (Chapter 3, § 1B), their constitutional status might be different.

---

a. Academics have been especially receptive to Justice Marshall's functional (anti-tiers) approach. See Suzanne Goldberg, *Equality Without Tiers,* 77 S. Cal. L. Rev. 481 (2004); Toni Massaro, *Gay Rights, Thick and Thin,* 49 Stan. L. Rev. 45 (1996), as well as Leslie Friedman Goldstein, *Between the Tiers: The New(est) Equal Protection and* Bush v. Gore, 4 U. Pa. J. Const. L. 372 (2002); Peter Smith, Note, *The Demise of Three-Tier Review: Has the United States Supreme Court Adopted a "Sliding Scale" Approach Toward Equal Protection Jurisprudence?,* J Contemp. L. 475 (1997).

For a time, the Court seemed to apply heightened scrutiny to statutes disadvantaging the poor by imposing a charge for governmental services or, even more broadly, failing to provide support for the necessary expenditures of life. For example, the Court held that in most circumstances a poor person charged with a crime has a right to free counsel at trial and on appeal, *Gideon v. Wainwright*, 372 U.S. 335 (1963) (right to counsel in felony cases); *Argersinger v. Hamlin*, 407 U.S. 25 (1972) (right to counsel in misdemeanor cases if a prison term is imposed), and that the state may not impose appellate filing fees or a charge for a transcript on appeal if that would preclude access to the appellate process. *Griffin v. Illinois*, 351 U.S. 12 (1956) (felony cases); *Mayer v. Chicago*, 404 U.S. 189 (1971) (misdemeanor cases). Another case outlawed imposing a filing fee on a poor person seeking to file a divorce action. *Boddie v. Connecticut*, 401 U.S. 371 (1971). In the course of invalidating a poll tax — a tax on the privilege of voting — the Court said that "[l]ines drawn on the basis of wealth or property, like those of race, are traditionally disfavored." *Harper v. Virginia Board of Elections*, 383 U.S. 663 (1966). These cases helped fuel a welfare rights movement that sought protections for affirmative state benefits for poor people. See *Goldberg v. Kelly*, 397 U.S. 254 (1970) (requiring the state to afford a due process hearing before depriving recipients of welfare benefits, which the Court treated as an "entitlement" rather than a "privilege").[b]

In the early 1970s, however, the Court rejected the proposition that wealth-based classifications and access fees are suspect. In *San Antonio Independent School District v. Rodriguez*, 411 U.S. 1 (1973) (Chapter 5, § 3B), the Court rejected a challenge to Texas' funding of public education on the ground that it distinguished between rich and poor neighborhoods and areas. Anticipating *Washington v. Davis*, Justice Powell's opinion for the Court noted that wealth-based equal protection claimants like those in *Rodriguez* typically challenge policies that only have discriminatory effects on the poor and do not formally exclude them from state services. Without evidence of invidious intent, such claims cannot succeed, Powell concluded. He also ruled that wealth as a classification had "none of the indicia of suspectness: the class is not saddled with such disabilities, or subjected to a history of purposeful unequal treatment, or relegated to such a position of political powerlessness as to command extraordinary protection from the majoritarian political process." Justice Marshall's dissenting opinion witheringly criticized this reasoning. See also *Dandridge v. Williams*, 397 U.S. 471 (1970). It is very doubtful that *Rodriguez* provides any support for the proposition that the state can provide important services like education only to people who own property or have a certain income, but it probably allows states to provide a better quality education for students who live in high-income districts than to those in low-income ones.

In *United States v. Kras*, 409 U.S. 434 (1973), the Court held that you can be too poor to go bankrupt. Justice Blackmun's opinion upheld an across-the-board filing fee for bankruptcy proceedings and admonished the petitioner that

---

b. On the background for *Goldberg*, and a wonderful introduction to much of the welfare rights social movement, see Martha Davis, *Brutal Need: Lawyers and the Welfare Rights Movement, 1960-1973* (1993).

the modest cost (as prorated over several months, the cost of a movie each week) was something he ought to be able to pay. The Court in *Ortwein v. Schwab*, 410 U.S. 656 (1973) (per curiam), held that *Griffin*'s waiver of criminal appeal filing fees for the indigent did not extend to civil cases generally: There was no due process right to appeal, nor was there an equal protection violation for state charges that discriminated against the indigent. On the other hand, where the state imposes special, and costly, procedural requirements on only one class of litigants, the Court has scrutinized more vigorously. See *Lindsey v. Normet*, 405 U.S. 56 (1972), invalidating a double-bond requirement imposed only on tenants appealing their evictions.

Just as the Court seemed to be confining *Griffin* to criminal cases, another arena for challenge opened up in litigation involving parental rights. Thus, in *Lassiter v. Department of Soc. Servs.*, 452 U.S. 18 (1981), the Court ruled that parents were sometimes entitled to attorneys paid for by the state, and in *Little v. Streater*, 452 U.S. 1 (1981), the Court required the state to pay for blood tests to enable an indigent defendant to contest a paternity claim.

––––––

M.L.B. v. S.L.J., 519 U.S. 102 (1996). The Mississippi chancery court terminated the parental rights of M.L.B., who was unable to appeal because she could not afford the $ 2,352.36 in fees required by the state to prepare a record for appeal. The U.S. Supreme Court, in an opinion by **Justice Ginsburg**, ruled that the state could not constitutionally apply the fee requirement to M.L.B. Justice Ginsburg recognized that the precedents involved both equal protection and due process concerns. "The equal protection concern relates to the legitimacy of fencing out would-be appellants based solely on their inability to pay core costs. *Griffin* (Frankfurter, J., concurring in the judgment). The due process concern homes in on the essential fairness of the state-ordered proceedings anterior to adverse state action." Because due process does not require the state to provide an appeal (*Ortwein*), Ginsburg focused on the equal protection feature of M.L.B.'s claim. In line with the precedents, she considered "the character and intensity of the individual interest at stake, on the one hand, and the State's justification for its exaction, on the other." Even more than in *Mayer*, where the stakes of a lost appeal for the misdemeanor offender (in his case, loss of professional opportunities but not of liberty) outweighed the state's mere pecuniary costs, M.L.B.'s stakes (the loss of her children) were most severe and greatly outweighed the state pecuniary interest (further diluted by the state interest in correcting lower court errors).

Justice Kennedy concurred only in the judgment; he believed the fee invalid as an undue burden on the fairest possible process when family relations are under state control. **Justice Thomas**, joined by **Chief Justice Rehnquist** and **Justice Scalia**, dissented. Those Justices would have overruled *Griffin* and its line of cases in light of *Washington v. Davis* and *Feeney*. The Equal Protection Clause, warned Justice Thomas, "is not a panacea for perceived social or economic inequity; it seeks to 'guarante[e] equal laws, not equal results.' *Feeney*."

B. LANGUAGE AND ETHNICITY

It is typically forgotten that southern apartheid extended to Mexican as well as African Americans in states like Texas. Outside the South, state discrimination against Mexican Americans was pervasive in California, Arizona, and New Mexico; New York discriminated in some respects against Puerto Ricans.[c] Recall that *Yick Wo v. Hopkins* (Chapter 3, § 1) had held that state discrimination on grounds of (Chinese) ethnicity could violate the Equal Protection Clause.

As we noted in Chapter 2, the first successful court challenge to apartheid came in a challenge by Mexican-American families. *Méndez v. Westminster School District*, 64 F.Supp. 544 (C.D. Cal. 1946), aff'd, 161 F.2d 774 (9ᵗʰ Cir. 1947). On the eve of *Brown,* the Supreme Court ruled that states could not exclude Mexican-Americans from juries in *Hernandez v. Texas*, 347 U.S. 475 (1954). Ironically, both the defendant (represented by the League of United Latin American Citizens, LULAC) and the state treated Mexican Americans as "white" in the jury case. Hence, the Court treated the exclusion as nonracial and invalidated it on the basis of analogy to race. "Community prejudices are not static," wrote Chief Justice Warren (who as Governor or California had presided over legal desegregation of the public schools for Latinos). Warren catalogued the José Crow regime that Texas had constructed for Mexican Americans and concluded that "persons of Mexican descent constitute a separate class * * * distinct from 'whites.'"[d]

Pure and open ethnicity-based discriminations have gradually melted away, yet Latinos still face what many thoughtful observers consider pervasive discrimination. Today, Latino Americans are more de facto segregated in schools, housing, and jobs than any other big ethnic or racial group, outside Native Americans. Why is that? Is constitutional equality at stake?

Juan Perea, *Buscando América: Why Integration and Equal Protection Fail to Protect Latinos,* 117 Harv. L. Rev. 1420, 1425, 1432-34 (2004)[e]. Professor Perea's argument is that de jure as well as de facto language discrimination is at the heart of the ongoing discrimination against Latinos. According to the 2000 Census, 17.9% of American residents speak a language other than English at home; 10.7% speak Spanish at home. "I argue that the Equal Protection Clause, as currently implemented through assimilation and integration, actually denies equality to Latinos, many of whom are native or bilingual Spanish speakers."

---

c. E.g., Thomas Carter, *Mexican Americans in School: A History of Educational Neglect* (1970); Gilbert González, *Segregation and the Education of Mexican Children, 1900-1940*, in José Moreno, ed., *The Elusive Quest for Equality: 150 Years of Chicano-Chicana Education* 53 (1999).

d. See Ian Haney-López, *Race and Colorblindness After* Hernandez *and* Brown, 25 Chicao-Latino L. Rev. 61 (2005). Unlike California, Texas continued de jure discrimination long after *Brown.* As late as 1970s, Latino's were challenging de jure school discrimination on the basis of Mexican ethnicity. E.g., *Alvarado v. El Paso Independent School District*, 326 F.Supp. 674 (S.D. Tex. 1971), rev'd, 445 F.2d 1011 (5th Cir. 1971).

e. Reprinted with permission of the Harvard Law Review.

"Negative social valuations are attributed to native speakers of Spanish and certain other non-English languages. Historically, native speakers of languages other than English have been viewed as threatening to the safety of the state." Slaves were forced to give up their African languages, German and other immigrants were derided by the Framers, and nineteenth century nativist movements are all examples.

"Bilinguals deviate from the norm of English monolingualism and are often 'raced' because of it. Majoritarian fears of disloyalty, loss of control, and exclusion are directed at bilinguals who speak their native, non-English languages in the presence of English monolinguals. * * * Many teachers further devalue these students and their language abilities by presuming that they are of low intelligence and that their knowledge of Spanish constitutes no knowledge at all, and by adopting educational goals that include the elimination of the native Spanish."

"Language difference itself, independent of skin color and other physical features that we usually equate with race, often triggers racism and discrimination." Perea invokes the standard notion that race is a social rather than biological construction, "a concept which signifies and symbolizes social conflicts and interests by referring to different types of human bodies." Michael Omi & Howard Winant, *Racial Formation in the United States* 55 (2d ed. 1994). "Because language differences are used to subordinate members of Latino and other language minority communities—in employment, in education, and more generally in the assignment of low prestige and dignity—language should be understood as part of a dynamic understanding of race itself.

"A secondary argument is that language discrimination is analogous to the more commonly understood notion of race discrimination. The Equal Protection Clause forbids intentional discrimination based on race. Since intentional discrimination based on language or accent often functions like race discrimination, it should be redressable in the same way. Language discrimination functions like race discrimination when employees are fired or disciplined for speaking Spanish in the workplace, when language qualifications are imposed that bear no relation to legitimate government or employment requirements, and when language regulations are used to deny equal education to, or disparage the native cultures of, language minority students. This argument from analogy, however, is weaker than the more direct argument outlined above because, given a general lack of understanding of bilingualism and language discrimination, judges often miss or reject the analogy."

HERNANDEZ v. NEW YORK
500 U.S. 352, 111 S.Ct. 1859, 114 L.Ed.2d 395 (1991)

JUSTICE KENNEDY announced the judgment of the Court and delivered an opinion in which **THE CHIEF JUSTICE [REHNQUIST], JUSTICE WHITE** and **JUSTICE SOUTER** join.

[Dionisio Hernandez was convicted of attempted murder and possession of a weapon. After nine jurors had been impaneled, defense counsel objected to the prosecutor's striking several Latino jurors. In response, the prosecutor volunteered his reasons for striking the jurors in question:

> * * * I felt there was a great deal of uncertainty as to whether they could accept the interpreter as the final arbiter of what was said by each of the witnesses, especially where there were going to be Spanish-speaking witnesses, and I didn't feel, when I asked them whether or not they could accept the interpreter's translation of it, I didn't feel that they could. They each looked away from me and said with some hesitancy that they would try, not that they could, but that they would try to follow the interpreter, and I feel that in a case where the interpreter will be for the main witnesses, they would have an undue impact upon the jury.

The issue was whether the prosecutor's explanation provided a race-neutral explanation for his peremptory strikes or constituted discriminatory challenges in violation of the Equal Protection Clause as interpreted in *Batson v. Kentucky*, 476 U.S. 79 (1986).]

The prosecutor here offered a race-neutral basis for these peremptory strikes. As explained by the prosecutor, the challenges rested neither on the intention to exclude Latino or bilingual jurors, nor on stereotypical assumptions about Latinos or bilinguals. The prosecutor's articulated basis for these challenges divided potential jurors into two classes: those whose conduct during *voir dire* would persuade him they might have difficulty in accepting the translator's rendition of Spanish-language testimony and those potential jurors who gave no such reason for doubt. Each category would include both Latinos and non-Latinos. While the prosecutor's criterion might well result in the disproportionate removal of prospective Latino jurors, that disproportionate impact does not turn the prosecutor's actions into a *per se* violation of the Equal Protection Clause. * * *

Once the prosecutor offers a race-neutral basis for his exercise of peremptory challenges, "[t]he trial court then [has] the duty to determine if the defendant has established purposeful discrimination." *Batson*. While the disproportionate impact on Latinos resulting from the prosecutor's criterion for excluding these jurors does not answer the race-neutrality inquiry, it does have relevance to the trial court's decision on this question. "[A]n invidious discriminatory purpose may often be inferred from the totality of the relevant facts, including the fact, if it is true, that the [classification] bears more heavily on one race than another." *Washington v. Davis*. If a prosecutor articulates a basis for a peremptory challenge that results in the disproportionate exclusion of members of a certain race, the trial judge may consider that fact as evidence that the prosecutor's stated reason constitutes a pretext for racial discrimination.

In the context of this trial, the prosecutor's frank admission that his ground for excusing these jurors related to their ability to speak and understand Spanish raised a plausible, though not a necessary, inference that language might be a pretext for what in fact were race-based peremptory challenges. This was not a case where by some rare coincidence a juror happened to speak the same language as a key witness, in a community where few others spoke that tongue. If it were, the explanation that the juror could have undue influence on jury deliberations might be accepted without concern that a racial generalization had come into play. But this trial took place in a community with a substantial Latino population, and petitioner and other interested parties were members of that ethnic group. It would be common knowledge in the locality that a significant percentage of the Latino population speaks fluent Spanish, and that many consider it their preferred language, the one chosen for personal communication, the one selected for speaking with the most precision and power, the one used to define the self.

The trial judge can consider these and other factors when deciding whether a prosecutor intended to discriminate. For example, though petitioner did not suggest the alternative to the trial court here, Spanish-speaking jurors could be permitted to advise the judge in a discreet way of any concerns with the translation during the course of trial. A prosecutor's persistence in the desire to exclude Spanish-speaking jurors despite this measure could be taken into account in determining whether to accept a race-neutral explanation for the challenge. [But the trial judge believed the prosecutor's race-neutral explanation for striking the two jurors in question, and the Court held that appeals courts must defer to trial court findings under *Batson*. The Court found such deference particularly appropriate because *Batson* cases will turn on the credibility of prosecutors and their explanations.]

Language permits an individual to express both a personal identity and membership in a community, and those who share a common language may interact in ways more intimate than those without this bond. Bilinguals, in a sense, inhabit two communities, and serve to bring them closer. Indeed, some scholarly comment suggests that people proficient in two languages may not at times think in one language to the exclusion of the other. The analogy is that of a high-hurdler, who combines the ability to sprint and to jump to accomplish a third feat with characteristics of its own, rather than two separate functions. This is not to say that the cognitive processes and reactions of those who speak two languages are susceptible of easy generalization, for even the term "bilingual" does not describe a uniform category. It is a simple word for a more complex phenomenon with many distinct categories and subdivisions. Sanchez, Our Linguistic and Social Context, in Spanish in the United States 9, 12 (J. Amastae & Elias-Olivares 1982); Dodson, Second Language Acquisition and Bilingual Development: A Theoretical Framework, 6 J. Multilingual & Multicultural Development 325, 326-327 (1985).

Our decision today does not imply that exclusion of bilinguals from jury service is wise, or even that it is constitutional in all cases. It is a harsh paradox that one may become proficient enough in English to participate in trial, see, e.g., 28 U.S.C. §§ 1865(b)(2), (3) (English-language ability required for federal jury service), only to encounter disqualification because he knows a second language as well. As the Court observed in a somewhat related context: "Mere knowledge of [a foreign] language cannot reasonably be regarded as harmful. Heretofore it has been commonly looked upon as helpful and desirable." *Meyer v. Nebraska*, 262 U.S. 390 (1923).

Just as shared language can serve to foster community, language differences can be a source of division. Language elicits a response from others, ranging from admiration and respect, to distance and alienation, to ridicule and scorn. Reactions of the latter type all too often result from or initiate racial hostility. In holding that a race-neutral reason for a peremptory challenge means a reason other than race, we do not resolve the more difficult question of the breadth with which the concept of race should be defined for equal protection purposes. We would face a quite different case if the prosecutor had justified his peremptory challenges with the explanation that he did not want Spanish-speaking jurors. It may well be, for certain ethnic groups and in some communities, that proficiency in a particular language, like skin color, should be treated as a surrogate for race under an equal protection analysis. Cf. *Yu Cong Eng v. Trinidad*, 271 U.S. 500 (1926) (law prohibiting keeping business records in other than specified languages violated equal protection rights of Chinese businessmen); *Meyer v. Nebraska* (striking down law prohibiting grade schools from teaching languages other than English). And, as we make clear, a policy of striking all who speak a given language, without regard to the particular circumstances of the trial or the individual responses of the jurors, may be found by the trial judge to be a pretext for racial discrimination. But that case is not before us.

[**JUSTICE O'CONNOR**, with whom **JUSTICE SCALIA** joined, concurred in the judgment. Her view was that the plurality opinion contained dicta unnecessary to the decision which invited language-based challenges to jury venires.]

JUSTICE STEVENS, with whom **JUSTICE MARSHALL** joins, dissenting. [**JUSTICE BLACKMUN** dissented, "essentially" for the reasons in Part II of this dissent.]

[I.] An avowed justification that has a significant disproportionate impact will rarely qualify as a legitimate, race-neutral reason sufficient to rebut the prima facie case because disparate impact is itself evidence of discriminatory purpose. *Arlington Heights*; *Washington v. Davis*. An explanation based on a concern that can easily be accommodated by means less drastic than excluding the challenged venireperson from the petit jury will also generally not qualify as a legitimate reason because it is not in fact "related to the particular case to be tried." *Batson*. And, as in any other equal protection challenge to a government classification, a justification that is frivolous or illegitimate should not suffice to rebut the prima facie case.

If any explanation, no matter how insubstantial and no matter how great its disparate impact, could rebut a prima facie inference of discrimination provided only that the explanation itself was not facially discriminatory, "the Equal Protection Clause 'would be but a vain and illusory requirement.' " *Batson*. The Court mistakenly believes that it is compelled to reach this result because an equal protection violation requires discriminatory purpose. The Court overlooks, however, the fact that the "discriminatory purpose" which characterizes violations of the Equal Protection Clause can sometimes be established by objective evidence that is consistent with a decisionmaker's honest belief that his motive was entirely benign. "Frequently the most probative evidence of intent will be objective evidence of what actually happened," *Washington v. Davis* (Stevens, J., concurring), including evidence of disparate impact. See, e.g., *Yick Wo v. Hopkins*; *Gomillion v. Lightfoot*. The line between discriminatory purpose and discriminatory impact is neither as bright nor as critical as the Court appears to believe.

The Court therefore errs in focusing the entire inquiry on the subjective state of mind of the prosecutor. In jury selection challenges, the requisite invidious intent is established once the defendant makes out a prima facie case. No additional evidence of this intent is necessary unless the explanation provided by the prosecutor is sufficiently powerful to rebut the prima facie proof of discriminatory purpose. By requiring that the prosecutor's explanation itself provide additional, direct evidence of discriminatory motive, the Court has imposed on the defendant the added requirement that he generate evidence of the prosecutor's actual subjective intent to discriminate. Neither *Batson* nor our other equal protection holdings demand such a heightened quantum of proof.

[II.] The prosecutor's explanation was insufficient for three reasons. First, the justification would inevitably result in a disproportionate disqualification of Spanish-speaking venirepersons. An explanation that is "race-neutral" on its face is nonetheless unacceptable if it is merely a proxy for a discriminatory practice. Second, the prosecutor's concern could easily have been accommodated by less drastic means. As is the practice in many jurisdictions, the jury could have been instructed that the official translation alone is evidence; bilingual jurors could have been instructed to bring to the attention of the judge any disagreements they might have with the translation so that any disputes could be resolved by the court. Third, if the prosecutor's concern was valid and substantiated by the record, it would have supported a challenge for cause. The fact that the prosecutor did not make any such challenge should disqualify him from advancing the concern as a justification for a peremptory challenge.

NOTES ON LANGUAGE & ETHNICITY-BASED DISCRIMINATION

1. *Juror Selection.* Professor Perea objects to the Court's approach in *Hernandez.* Because "[b]ilinguals understand and think in two languages similtaneously and interdependently," the prosecutor "was asking the impossible." And he was making a demand of potential Latino jurors — to ignore their own judgment of the truth — that no one was making of Anglo jurors. The only jurors excused for bilingual ability, here and in other cases, are Latinos. There was nothing race-neutral about the prosecutor's actions. Perea, *Buscando América*, 117 Harv. L. Rev. at 1436.

Might Justice Kennedy have decided/voted differently if the record reflected that the prosecutor *only* asked Latinos whether they were bilingual and (then) whether they could accept the official translation? Many non-Latino Americans are bilingual; many speak Spanish. If these questions were never asked of non-Latino jurors, would that be sufficient evidence of *race* discrimination to satisfy *Batson*? Ought it be sufficient?

2. *Workplace.* Most workplace discrimination based on language has been analyzed under Title VII, which makes discrimination on the basis of "national origin" actionable. Courts have been reluctant to view language-based discrimination as actionable, e.g., *Garcia v. Gloor*, 618 F.2d 264 (5th Cir.1980). Responding to *Garcia,* the EEOC developed guidelines presuming that English-only workplace rules are national origin discrimination; employers can rebut the presumption if they can show a business necessity for the English-only policy.

See 29 C.F.R. § 1606.7 (2007). Such complaints comprise a rapidly increasing part of the EEOC's workload, though few lawsuits have been successful. See Cristina Rodriguez, *Language Diversity in the Workplace*, 100 Nw. U.L. Rev. 1689 (2006). For public employers (covered by Title VII), is the EEOC's guideline a fair statement of the equal protection requirement, or does the Constitution demand less than Title VII?

3. *Voting.* Again, this is an arena regulated by statute. The Voting Rights Act Amendments of 1975, Pub. L. No. 94-73, title III, 89 Stat. 402 (1975), codified as amended at 42 U.S.C. § 1973aa-1a, protect language-minority voters against discrimination and assure most such voters access to voting materials in their language.[f] Congress was acting under its authority to "enforce" the Fifteenth Amendment. As you will see in Chapter 7, § 3, Congress can only adopt laws that redress problems the Supreme Court would consider constitutional violations; if Congress and the Court are on the same page as to a constitutional violation, Congress has significant discretion in crafting a remedial statute addressing the problem. So is there a constitutional problem when language-minority citizens with limited command of English (thus, *not* bilinguals like the jurors in *Hernandez*) cannot understand the ballot and the state provides them with no assistance?[g]

PROBLEM 4-4
CONSTITUTIONALITY OF ENGLISH-ONLY LAWS?

(A) *English-Only Laws.* About half the states have enacted some type of English-only law. Most laws just declare English as the "official" language of the state, but without imposing specific legal rules to implement this symbolism. Would Professor Perea have a constitutional problem with such laws? See Juan Perea, *Demography and Distrust: An Essay on American Languages, Cultural Pluralism, and Official English,* 77 Minn. L. Rev. 269 (1992). How should a state attorney general respond to equal protection questions about such a law? See Cristina Rodriguez, *Language and Participation,* 94 Calif. L. Rev. 687, 751-54 (2006).

(B) *English-Only Law with Bite.* Arizona's English-only law struck more deeply: "As the official language of this State, the English language is the language of the ballot, the public schools and all government functions and actions." Assume that this law is invoked to discharge Juana Richardson, a bilingual teacher who occasionally spoke Spanish in the government class she taught to public high school students. Richardson brings suit for a declaratory judgment that the statute is unconstitutional as applied to her. You are the lawyer for the state attorney general defending the statute. What are its prospects? For First Amendment problems with such laws, see *Yñiguez v.*

---

f. The Voting Rights Act of 1965, § 4(e), imposed language assistance for Puerto Rican voters under certain circumstances and was the basis for a federalism challenge in *Katzenbach v. Morgan* (excerpted and discussed in Chapter 7, § 3B).

g. We use the present tense, because the Voting Rights Act was renewed in 2006, with the language-assistance provision intact (after strong opposition).

Arizonans for Official English, 69 F.3d 920 (9th Cir. 1995) (en banc), vacated on other grounds, 520 U.S. 43 (1997); *Ruiz v. Hall,* 191 Ariz. 441 (1998). See also *In re Initiative Petition No. 366*, 46 P.3d 123 (Okla. 2002).

(C) *No Bilingual Education.* The Equal Educational Opportunity Act imposes upon states an affirmative duty to help schoolchildren "overcome language barriers that impede equal participation by its students in its instructional programs" but do not direct the states toward one particular method. Like California and Massachusetts, Arizona also has a statute, adopted by popular initiative, that requires "all children in Arizona public schools shall be taught English by being taught in English." Ariz. Rev. Stat. § 15-752. On its face this law requires that English be taught through the immersion method, through constant exposure to English; conversely, the law precludes the use of bilingual education, where the children's native language is used to help teach English.

Most educators believe that bilingual education is a better way to teach English, and most Latino intellectuals believe that it is preferable because it gives the children more of a choice to retain their parent tongue. See Cristina Rodriguez, *Accommodating Linguistic Difference: Toward a Comprehensive Theory of Language Rights in the United States*, 36 Harv. C.R.-C.L. L. Rev. 133 (2001). Does the Arizona law constitute an equal protection violation? Does the fact that it was adopted by popular initiative make a difference? Cf. *Romer v. Evans*, below in Part D1.

C. PHYSICAL OR MENTAL DISABILITY

Disability-based discrimination is deeply rooted in American history. Individuals with mental and physical disabilities have been routinely denied marriage licenses, excluded from classrooms and workplaces by law or official practice, institutionalized for indefinite periods of time, and even sterilized. In *Buck v. Bell*, 274 U.S. 200 (1927) (Chapter 5, § 1), Justice Holmes, in a flippant opinion, dismissed an equal protection challenge to a sterilization law. For decades after *Buck v. Bell*, no one raised constitutional arguments against disability-based classifications. Although there were a number of organizations dedicated to protective legislation, it was not until the 1970s that people with disabilities and their allies were energized into a mass social movement demanding dignified treatment for disabled citizens.[h] The Rehabilitation Act of 1973, which formally banned discrimination by reason of one's handicap, was left unimplemented until disability rights activists engaged in civil disobedience and political protest and established a lobbying organization in Washington, D.C. The Carter Administration finally issued strong implementing regulations in 1977.

The new grass roots movement was normative as well as political. Disability has traditionally been viewed as malignant — unnatural, medically degenerate,

---

h. For the history of this social movement, see Doris Zames Fleischer & Freda Zames, *The Disability Rights Movement: From Charity to Confrontation* (2001); Richard Scotch, *From Good Will to Civil Rights: Transforming Federal Disability Policy* (2d ed. 2001); Joseph Shapiro, *No Pity: People with Disabilities Forging a New Civil Rights Movement* (1993).

socially disruptive, at best pitiable. The movement not only rejected those characterizations, but maintained that the governmental and societal discrimination they engendered were more disabling than the physical or mental variations themselves. By working against those barriers, the disability rights movement has sought to advance the self-determination, independence, and equal citizenship of its members. Like the other identity-based social movements, the disability rights movement created litigating institutions that have sought constitutional protections. Specifically, those organizations sought judicial recognition that disability is a suspect or quasi-suspect classification like race or sex — a recognition that would have called into question hundreds of state and local laws formally discriminating against people with disabilities.

CITY OF CLEBURNE v. CLEBURNE LIVING CENTER

473 U.S. 432, 105 S.Ct. 3249, 87 L.Ed.2d 313 (1985)

JUSTICE WHITE delivered the opinion of the Court.

[Cleburne Living Center attempted to establish a group home for the developmentally disabled in Cleburne, Texas. Under that city's zoning regulations applicable to the proposed site of the home, a special use permit was required for the construction of "[h]ospitals for the insane or feeble-minded, or alcoholic [sic] or drug addicts, or penal or correctional institutions." The city classified the proposed home as one for the "feeble-minded," and after a hearing the city council voted to deny a special use permit. The federal court of appeals overturned the city's action, concluding that the developmentally disabled are a "quasi-suspect class" and that, under intermediate scrutiny, the city's zoning regulation was invalid both on its face and as applied. Justice White's opinion began by surveying the cases applying minimal scrutiny to economic regulation; strict scrutiny to classifications based on race, alienage, or national origin; intermediate scrutiny for classifications based on gender or illegitimacy; and the Court's refusal in *Murgia* (see p. 345, *supra*) "to extend heightened scrutiny to differential treatment based on age."]

The lesson of *Murgia* is that where individuals in the group affected by a law have distinguishing characteristics relevant to interests the State has the authority to implement, the courts have been very reluctant, as they should be in our federal system and with our respect for the separation of powers, to closely scrutinize legislative choices as to whether, how, and to what extent those interests should be pursued. In such cases, the Equal Protection Clause requires only a rational means to serve a legitimate end.

Against this background, we conclude for several reasons that the Court of Appeals erred in holding mental retardation a quasi-suspect classification calling for a more exacting standard of judicial review than is normally accorded economic and social legislation. First, * * * those who are mentally retarded have a reduced ability to cope with and function in the everyday world. * * * [T]hey range from those whose disability is not immediately evident to those who must be constantly cared for. They are thus different, immutably so, in relevant respects, and the States' interest in dealing with and providing for them is plainly a legitimate one. How this large and diversified group is to be treated under the law is a difficult and often a technical matter, very much a task for legislators guided by qualified professionals and not by the perhaps ill-informed opinions of the judiciary. Heightened scrutiny inevitably involves substantive judgments about legislative decisions, and we doubt that the predicate for such judicial oversight is present where the classification deals with mental retardation.

Second, the distinctive legislative response, both national and state, to the plight of those who are mentally retarded demonstrates not only that they have unique problems, but also that the lawmakers have been addressing their difficulties in a manner that belies a continuing antipathy or prejudice and a corresponding need for more intrusive oversight by the judiciary. Thus, the Federal Government has not only outlawed discrimination against the mentally retarded in federally funded programs, see § 504 of the Rehabilitation Act of 1973, but it has also provided the retarded with the right to receive "appropriate treatment, services, and habilitation" in a setting that is "least restrictive of [their] personal liberty." [Developmental Disabilities Assistance and Bill of Rights Act.]

[Justice White discussed other federal and Texas legislation designed to help the developmentally disabled. These affirmative rights would come into question if the Court made disability a suspect classification.] Even assuming that many of these laws could be shown to be substantially related to an important governmental purpose, merely requiring the legislature to justify its efforts in these terms may lead it to refrain from acting at all. Much recent legislation intended to benefit the retarded also assumes the need for measures that might be perceived to disadvantage them. The Education of the Handicapped Act, for example, requires an "appropriate" education, not one that is equal in all respects to the education of nonretarded children. * * * Especially given the wide variation in the abilities and needs of the retarded themselves, governmental bodies must have a certain amount of flexibility and freedom from judicial oversight in shaping and limiting their remedial efforts.

Third, the legislative response, which could hardly have occurred and survived without public support, negates any claim that the mentally retarded are politically powerless in the sense that they have no ability to attract the attention of the lawmakers. Any minority can be said to be powerless to assert direct control over the legislature, but if that were a criterion for higher level scrutiny by the courts, much economic and social legislation would now be suspect.

Fourth, if the large and amorphous class of the mentally retarded were deemed quasi-suspect * * *, it would be difficult to find a principled way to distinguish a variety of other groups who have perhaps immutable disabilities setting them off from others, who cannot themselves mandate the desired legislative responses, and who can claim some degree of prejudice from at least part of the public at large. One need mention in this respect only the aging, the disabled, the mentally ill, and the infirm. We are reluctant to set out on that course, and we decline to do so.

Doubtless, there have been and there will continue to be instances of discrimination against the retarded that are in fact invidious, and that are properly subject to judicial correction under constitutional norms. But the appropriate method of reaching such instances is not to create a new quasi-suspect classification and subject all governmental action based on that classification to more searching evaluation. Rather, we should look to the likelihood that governmental action premised on a particular classification is valid as a general matter, not merely to the specifics of the case before us. Because mental retardation is a characteristic that the government may legitimately take into account in a wide range of decisions, and because both State and Federal Governments have recently committed themselves to assisting the retarded, we will not presume that any given legislative action, even one that disadvantages retarded individuals, is rooted in considerations that the Constitution will not tolerate.

Our refusal to recognize the retarded as a quasi-suspect class does not leave them entirely unprotected from invidious discrimination. To withstand equal protection review, legislation that distinguishes between the mentally retarded and others must be rationally related to a legitimate governmental purpose. This standard, we believe, affords government the latitude necessary both to pursue policies designed to assist the retarded in realizing their full potential, and to freely and efficiently engage in activities that burden the retarded in what is essentially an incidental manner. The State may not rely on a classification whose relationship to an asserted goal is so attenuated as to render the distinction arbitrary or irrational. See *Zobel v. Williams*, 457 U.S. 55 (1982); *Moreno*. Furthermore, some objectives — such as "a bare . . . desire to harm a politically unpopular group," *Moreno* — are not legitimate state interests. * * *

[Rather than first entertain a *facial* challenge to the requirement of a special-use permit for homes for the developmentally disabled, the Court chose first to consider whether requiring a special-use permit for this home was, on the facts of the case, an "as applied" violation of equal protection.] The City does not require a special use permit in an R-3 zone for apartment houses, multiple dwellings, boarding and lodging houses, fraternity or sorority houses, dormitories, apartment hotels, hospitals, sanitariums, nursing homes for convalescents or the aged (other than for the insane or feeble-minded or alcoholics or drug addicts), private clubs or fraternal orders, and other specified uses. * * * May the city require the permit for this facility when other care and multiple dwelling facilities are freely permitted?

It is true, as already pointed out, that the mentally retarded as a group are indeed different from others not sharing their misfortune, and in this respect they may be different from those who would occupy other facilities that would be permitted in an R-3 zone without a special permit. But this difference is largely irrelevant unless the Featherston home and those who would occupy it would threaten legitimate interests of the city in a way that other permitted uses such as boarding houses and hospitals would not. Because in our view the record does not reveal any rational basis for believing that the Featherston home would pose any special threat to the city's legitimate interests, we affirm the judgment below insofar as it holds the ordinance invalid as applied in this case.

The District Court found that the City Council's insistence on the permit rested on several factors. First, the Council was concerned with the negative attitude of the majority of property owners located within 200 feet of the

Featherston facility, as well as with the fears of elderly residents of the neighborhood. But mere negative attitudes, or fear, unsubstantiated by factors which are properly cognizable in a zoning proceeding, are not permissible bases for treating a home for the mentally retarded differently from apartment houses, multiple dwellings, and the like. * * * "Private biases may be outside the reach of the law, but the law cannot, directly or indirectly, give them effect." *Palmore v. Sidoti* [Chapter 3, § 1 of this casebook].

Second, the Council had two objections to the location of the facility. It was concerned that the facility was across the street from a junior high school, and it feared that the students might harass the occupants of the Featherston home. But the school itself is attended by about 30 mentally retarded students, and denying a permit based on such vague, undifferentiated fears is again permitting some portion of the community to validate what would otherwise be an equal protection violation. The other objection to the home's location was that it was located on "a five hundred year flood plain." This concern with the possibility of a flood, however, can hardly be based on a distinction between the Featherston home and, for example, nursing homes, homes for convalescents or the aged, or sanitariums or hospitals, any of which could be located on the Featherston site without obtaining a special use permit. The same may be said of another concern of the Council — doubts about the legal responsibility for actions which the mentally retarded might take. If there is no concern about legal responsibility with respect to other uses that would be permitted in the area, such as boarding and fraternity houses, it is difficult to believe that the groups of mildly or moderately mentally retarded individuals who would live at 201 Featherston would present any different or special hazard.

Fourth, the Council was concerned with the size of the home and the number of people that would occupy it. The District Court found, and the Court of Appeals repeated, that "[i]f the potential residents of the Featherston Street home were not mentally retarded, but the home was the same in all other respects, its use would be permitted under the city's zoning ordinance." Given this finding, there would be no restrictions on the number of people who could occupy this home as a boarding house, nursing home, family dwelling, fraternity house, or dormitory. The question is whether it is rational to treat the mentally retarded differently. It is true that they suffer disability not shared by others; but why this difference warrants a density regulation that others need not observe is not at all apparent. At least this record does not clarify how, in this connection, the characteristics of the intended occupants of the Featherston home rationally justify denying to those occupants what would be permitted to groups occupying the same site for different purposes. * * * In the words of the Court of Appeals, "[T]he City never justifies its apparent view that other people can live under such 'crowded' conditions when mentally retarded persons cannot." * * *

The short of it is that requiring the permit in this case appears to us to rest on an irrational prejudice against the mentally retarded. * * *

JUSTICE STEVENS, with whom **THE CHIEF JUSTICE [BURGER]** joins, concurring. [Justice Stevens reiterated his view, first expressed in *Craig*, that equal protection review involves a "continuum" of responses rather than "tiers" of review. "Rationality" always insists that the sovereign's line-drawing be defensible by reference to criteria that are "neutral" and "legitimate."]

In every equal protection case, we have to ask certain basic questions. What class is harmed by the legislation, and has it been subjected to a "tradition of disfavor" by our laws? What is the public purpose that is being served by the law? What is the characteristic of the disadvantaged class that justifies the disparate treatment? In most cases the answer to these questions will tell us whether the statute has a "rational basis." The answers will result in the virtually automatic invalidation of racial classifications and in the validation of most economic classifications, but they will provide differing results in cases involving classifications based on alienage, gender, or illegitimacy. But that is not because we apply an "intermediate standard of review" in these cases; rather it is because the characteristics of these groups are sometimes relevant and sometimes irrelevant to a valid public purpose, or, more specifically, to the purpose that the challenged laws purportedly intended to serve.

Every law that places the mentally retarded in a special class is not presumptively irrational. The differences between mentally retarded persons and those with greater mental capacity are obviously relevant to certain legislative decisions. An impartial lawmaker — indeed, even a member of a class of persons defined as mentally retarded — could rationally vote in favor of a law providing funds for special education and special treatment for the mentally retarded. A mentally retarded person could also recognize that he is a member of a class that might need special supervision in some situations, both to protect himself and to protect others. * * *

Even so, the Court of Appeals correctly observed that through ignorance and prejudice the mentally retarded "have been subjected to a history of unfair and often grotesque mistreatment." The discrimination against the mentally retarded that is at issue in this case is the city's decision to require an annual special use permit before property in an apartment house district may be used as a group home for persons who are mildly retarded. The record convinces me that this permit was required because of the irrational fears of neighboring property owners, rather than for the protection of the mentally retarded persons who would reside in respondent's home.

[**JUSTICE MARSHALL**, joined by **JUSTICES BRENNAN** and **BLACKMUN**, concurred in the judgment in part and dissented in part. Justice Marshall applied the "sliding scale" approach to equal protection developed in his dissent in *San Antonio Independent School District v. Rodriguez* (Chapter 5, § 3B), under which the "substantiality of the state interests to be served" and "the reasonableness of the means by which the State has sought to advance it interests" are crucial factors. "Differences in the application of this test [are] a function of the constitutional importance of the interests at stake and the invidiousness of the particular classification." Applying this approach in *Cleburne*, Justice Marshall maintained that developmentally disabled people, like blacks and women in the past, are subject to laws that discriminate on their face against them, based upon irrational prejudices. Justice Marshall invoked the *Carolene Products* idea that citizens have no firm equality baseline as regards economic legislation but are assured substantial equality in other arenas by the Fourteenth Amendment.

[Where legislatures have systematically ignored those baselines in the past, the Court has been justified in conducting a "more searching judicial inquiry" of such frequently invoked, but typically irrational, classifications.] Heightened scrutiny does not allow courts to second-guess reasoned legislative or professional judgments tailored to the unique needs of a group like the retarded, but it does seek to assure that the hostility or thoughtlessness with which there is reason to be concerned has not carried the day. By invoking heightened scrutiny, the Court recognizes, and compels lower courts to recognize, that a group may well be the target of the sort of prejudiced, thoughtless, or stereotyped action that offends principles of equality found in the Fourteenth Amendment. Where classifications based on a particular characteristic have done so in the past, and the threat that they may do so remains, heightened scrutiny is appropriate.[9]

In light of the scrutiny that should be applied here, Cleburne's ordinance sweeps too broadly to dispel the suspicion that it rests on a bare desire to treat the retarded as outsiders, pariahs who do not belong in the community. The Court, while disclaiming that special scrutiny is necessary or warranted, reaches the same conclusion. Rather than striking the ordinance down, however, the Court invalidates it merely as applied to respondents. I must dissent from the novel proposition that "the preferred course of adjudication" is to leave standing a legislative act resting on "irrational prejudice," thereby forcing individuals in the group discriminated against to continue to run the act's gauntlet.

---

9. No single talisman can define those groups likely to be the target of classifications offensive to the Fourteenth Amendment and therefore warranting heightened or strict scrutiny; experience, not abstract logic, must be the primary guide. The "political powerlessness" of a group may be relevant, but that factor is neither necessary, as the gender cases demonstrate, nor sufficient, as the example of minors illustrates. Minors cannot vote and thus might be considered politically powerless to an extreme degree. Nonetheless, we see few statutes reflecting prejudice or indifference to minors, and I am not aware of any suggestion that legislation affecting them be viewed with the suspicion of heightened scrutiny. Similarly, immutability of the trait at issue may be relevant, but many immutable characteristics, such as height or blindness, are valid bases of governmental action and classifications under a variety of circumstances. The political powerlessness of a group and the immutability of its defining trait are relevant insofar as they point to a social and cultural isolation that gives the majority little reason to respect or be concerned with that group's interests and needs. Statutes discriminating against the young have not been common nor need be feared because those who do vote and legislate were once themselves young, typically have children of their own, and certainly interact regularly with minors. Their social integration means that minors, unlike discrete and insular minorities, tend to be treated in legislative arenas with full concern and respect, despite their formal and complete exclusion from the electoral process.

The discreteness and insularity warranting a "more searching judicial inquiry," *Carolene Products* n.4., must therefore be viewed from a social and cultural perspective as well as a political one. To this task judges are well suited, for the lessons of history and experience are surely the best guide as to when, and with respect to what interests, society is likely to stigmatize individuals as members of an inferior caste or view them as not belonging to the community. Because prejudice spawns prejudice, and stereotypes produce limitations that confirm the stereotype on which they are based, a history of unequal treatment requires sensitivity to the prospect that its vestiges endure. In separating those groups that are discrete and insular from those that are not, as in many important legal distinctions, "a page of history is worth a volume of logic." *New York Trust Co. v. Eisner*, 256 U.S. 345 (1921) (Holmes, J.).

The Court appears to act out of a belief that the ordinance might be "rational" as applied to some subgroup of the retarded under some circumstances, such as those utterly without the capacity to live in a community, and that the ordinance should not be invalidated *in toto* if it is capable of ever being validly applied. But the issue is not "whether the city may never insist on a special use permit for the mentally retarded in an R-3 zone." The issue is whether the city may require a permit pursuant to a blunderbuss ordinance drafted many years ago to exclude all the "feebleminded," or whether the city must enact a new ordinance carefully tailored to the exclusion of some well defined subgroup of retarded people in circumstances in which exclusion might reasonably further legitimate city purposes. * * *

To my knowledge, the Court has never before treated an equal protection challenge to a statute on an as-applied basis. When statutes rest on impermissibly overbroad generalizations, our cases have invalidated the presumption on its face. We do not instead leave to the courts the task of redrafting the statute through an ongoing and cumbersome process of "as applied" constitutional rulings. * * *

NOTE ON *CLEBURNE* AND EQUAL PROTECTION TIERS

1. *Is There a New Level of Scrutiny (Rational Basis with Bite) for Disability-Based Classifications?* In *Cleburne*, the six Justices who joined the opinion for the Court seem to have accepted *four* tiers of scrutiny: (1) "anything goes" rational basis (*Railway Express*); (2) rational basis "with teeth" (*Cleburne*); (3) intermediate scrutiny (*Craig*); (4) strict scrutiny (the race cases). One reason *Cleburne* seems not to be an example of ordinary rational basis review is that Justice White was unwilling to attribute legitimate goals to the governmental decision, such as protection of property values or even safety concerns, because they were not documented in the public record.

It is hard to tell how broadly to read *Cleburne*. According to Justice Brennan's notes of the first *Cleburne* conference, the Justices were evenly split on whether to uphold the ordinance, with four Justices voting to strike under heightened scrutiny and four voting to uphold under rational basis. On reargument, Justice Powell broke the tie: No heightened scrutiny, but the ordinance as applied fell on rational basis grounds. But what, exactly, was irrational about the decision? The Court in *Board of Trustees v. Garrett*, 531 U.S. 356 (2001) (Chapter 7, § 3D3), interpreted *Cleburne* as *not* resting on improper (prejudice- or stereotype-based) motives alone; the negative attitudes must be accompanied by a showing that the local decision did not rest on other, legitimate bases, the Court said in *Garrett*. It is possible that *Cleburne* could be limited to cases where the legislative record contains evidence of improper bias and no evidence of legitimate considerations. In that event, would it be too easy for prejudice-based laws to withstand scrutiny? Would judicial review then have any value for people with disabilities?

One way of articulating a new (*Cleburne*) tier of scrutiny is this: Heightened scrutiny in the race and sex discrimination cases starts with a presumption of unconstitutionality, shifts the burden of justification to the government, and limits the kinds of arguments the government can make. Ordinary rational basis review starts with a presumption of constitutionality, which the challenger can rebut only by demonstrating that there is no reasonable connection with any plausible state goal. *Cleburne*-style rational basis review also starts with a presumption of validity, but might be understood to allow the challenger to create a prima facie case of invalidity by showing no rational fit with the asserted purpose or by demonstrating antipathy. Such a prima facie case would shift the burden to the state to demonstrate a rational and neutral justification for its discrimination.

2. *Should the Court Abandon the Tiers Approach and Follow a Single Unified Standard in Equal Protection Cases?* Five *Cleburne* Justices (the three dissenters and the two concurring Justices) seemingly endorsed a balancing approach rather than the tiers approach. Elaborating on his earlier *Rodriguez* dissent, Justice Marshall argued for a sliding scale. Elaborating on his concurring opinion in *Craig*, Justice Stevens argued for a single standard asking mostly the same questions Marshall had laid out in *Rodriguez*. How would this work? In the spirit of Dan Ortiz's recharacterization of the role of intent in equal protection law, one of us has structured the Marshall-Stevens balancing approach in the following way.[h]

Almost all laws have arguable purposes that can be expressed in terms of the public interest, but the statutory criteria are usually both overinclusive (regulating activities not needed to meet the statute's rational goals) and underinclusive (failing to regulate some activities inconsistent with the goals). Where the state is regulating the market and the classification is a purely economic one, courts will not be interested in the actual, typically messy, motivations of the legislature and will be willing to attribute plausible public interests to such laws; additionally, they will tolerate a great deal of over- and underinclusion in the choice of statutory criteria. Where important rights are involved and the classification one that has been found consistently invidious, courts will attribute irrational motives (prejudice and stereotypes) to the legislature and may strike down the law on that ground alone, as the Court did in *Loving*. The hardest cases are those where important rights are involved and the classification somewhat fishy but not meeting all the criteria for suspectness the Court laid out in *Frontiero* and *Cleburne*. In those cases, the Court will follow a presumption of validity that can be trumped by evidence of prejudice- or stereotype-based motivation. Such evidence makes the Court reluctant to attribute legitimate governmental goals not found in the record and unwilling to tolerate much over- or underinclusion. Does this standard make sense? Note its similarity with some of the analysis in the previous Note: Does that suggest the substantial irrelevance of the verbal formulation of the equal protection test?

3. *The Disability Rights Movement and the Goals of the Equal Protection Clause.* Like earlier identity movements, the disability rights movement has challenged disability-based discriminations and exclusions. In contrast to the

---

h. William Eskridge, Jr., *Some Effects of Identity-Based Social Movements on Constitutional Law in the Twentieth Century*, 100 Mich. L. Rev. 2062 (2002), drawing from Daniel Ortiz, *The Myth of Intent in Equal Protection*, 41 Stan. L. Rev. 1105 (1989).

initial focus of those earlier movements, the disability rights movement from the beginning has viewed benign neglect as just as big a problem for its members as formal discrimination and has demanded not just formal equality but functional equality as well: The state must not only admit disabled people into its programs, but must also take reasonable measures to accommodate the needs of the disabled.[i] The *Cleburne* Justices probably did not perceive this, but they would surely have rejected it, for the same institutional and ideological reasons they were unwilling to press hard for *Brown II* remedies or accept the remedial ideas of radical feminists. Like *Freeman v. Pitts* (Chapter 2, § 2C2) and *Bray v. Alexandria Health Clinic* (above), *Cleburne* assumes the primacy of the rationality goal of the Fourteenth Amendment and slights its anti-subordination goal. Given the disability rights constitutional vision, therefore, *Cleburne* was a significant defeat — notwithstanding the fact that the challengers won a remand. Consider the next case.

———

Heller v. Doe, 509 U.S. 312 (1993). Under Kentucky law, both mentally ill and mentally retarded persons could be involuntarily committed only upon a showing that they were dangerous to themselves or others, that they could reasonably benefit from treatment, and that no less restrictive alternative existed. For the mentally ill, the burden of proof for these factors was "beyond a reasonable doubt"; for the mentally retarded, however, the burden was only "clear and convincing evidence." Thus, it was easier for the state to institutionalize a retarded person. **Justice Kennedy**'s opinion for the Court accepted the apparent legislative assumptions that mental retardation is easier to diagnose than mental illness, and predictions of future dangerousness are also more reliable for the former group. These differences justified different standards of proof because of the plausibly different " 'risk of error' faced by the subject of the proceedings." Justice Kennedy also relied on the gravity of erroneous institutionalization: Because treatment methods for the retarded are "much less invasive" than those for the mentally ill, it was rational for the state to believe that the liberty deprivation would be much more grievous for the wrongfully institutionalized mentally ill person than the wrongfully institutionalized mentally retarded person.

Justice Souter, joined by **Justices Blackmun** and **Stevens**, dissented on *Cleburne* grounds. "While the Court cites *Cleburne* once, and does not purport to overrule it, neither does the Court apply it, and at the end of the day *Cleburne*'s status is left uncertain. I would follow *Cleburne* here. * * * Without plausible justification, Kentucky is being allowed to draw a distinction that is difficult to see as resting on anything other than the stereotypical assumption that the retarded are 'perpetual children,' an assumption that has historically been taken to justify the disrespect and 'grotesque mistreatment' to which the retarded have been subjected." Justice Blackmun also dissented on the ground that the statutory distinction could not survive heightened scrutiny.

---

    i. See Arlene Mayerson & Sylvia Yee, *The ADA and Models of Equality*, 62 Ohio St. L.J. 535 (2001).

D. SEXUAL ORIENTATION

Unlike race, sex, wealth, and disability classifications, sexual orientation classifications are relatively new to American statutory history; the concept of "homosexuality" was not developed until around 1890.[j] In the early twentieth century, cities and states adopted rules to suppress and exclude "degenerates" and "sexual inverts." After World War II, anti-homosexual laws, rules, and state practices exploded in a Kulturkampf seeking to purge public life of "homosexuals and sex perverts," as a Senate investigating subcommittee deemed these people in 1950. They were barred from the state and federal civil service and from the armed forces, hunted and exposed by the FBI and several state investigatory commissions, rounded up and deported by the INS, expelled from state colleges and universities, denied or stripped of professional licenses and certifications, prohibited from congregating together or from being served in bars, harassed and arrested by the police in large numbers for cross-dressing and alleged sexual solicitations, beaten and raped by police officers, incarcerated in state prisons and mental hospitals, and made the objects of state-sponsored medical experiments, castrations, sterilizations, and electrical shock treatments — all because of their (perceived) sexual orientation or their (supposed) private consensual activities.[k]

Like other stigmatized minorities, some lesbians, gay men, and bisexuals — terms they prefer to the old medical term "homosexuals" — came to resist state persecution and asserted, initially, that homosexuality is a tolerable variation from the norm and, later, that it is a benign variation ("Gay is Good"). The June 1969 riots outside New York City's Stonewall Inn, when gay and transgendered people fought back against police violence, galvanized thousands of gays to "come out" of their "closets" and organize themselves politically and legally. Several decades of political activism and court challenges have eliminated most antigay laws and policies in states of the Northeast and Pacific Coast. Success in those jurisdictions has not been matched elsewhere, however; a normative traditional family values countermovement has not only sought to preserve prior antigay laws, but has introduced new ones.

Accordingly, laws or judicial decisions formally discriminating on the basis of sexual orientation are not only widespread, but are more numerous than ever before.[l] They include (a) the federal exclusion of openly gay people from the armed forces, (b) exclusions of gay people from teaching or police jobs at the local and state level, (c) state laws prohibiting educators from teaching anything that would place "homosexuality" in a favorable light, (d) federal laws

---

j. See Jonathan Ned Katz, *Gay American History* (1976), as well as Lillian Faderman, *Surpassing the Love of Men: Romantic Friendship and Love Between Women, from the Renaissance to the Present* (1981).

k. On the anti-homosexual Kulturkampf of 1946-61, see William Eskridge, Jr., *Dishonorable Passions: Sodomy Laws in America, 1861-2003*, at 73-108 (2008); David Johnson, *The Lavender Scare: The Cold War Persecution of Gays and Lesbians in the Federal Government* (2004).

l. See William Eskridge, Jr., *Gaylaw: Challenging the Apartheid of the Closet* 139-41, 362-71 (1999) (app. B3).

conditioning spending programs on their not "promoting" homosexuality, (e) ordinances singling out "homosexual" but not "heterosexual" solicitation for criminalization, and (f) state presumptions or rules against child custody or adoption by lesbians or gay men. Other state policies discriminate on the basis of sex but have their primary effect on lesbians, bisexuals, gay men, and transgendered people, that is, state bars to same-sex marriage and laws refusing to recognize valid same-sex marriages entered into in another state and the federal law refusing to recognize such marriages in federal statutes invoking marriage or spousehood. Yet other policies discriminate on the basis of gender presentation, namely, excluding transsexuals or transvestites from state employment and family recognition. Are any of these policies invalid as a matter of equal protection?

PROBLEM 4-5
THE CONSTITUTIONALITY OF AN ANTIGAY INITIATIVE

Aspen, Boulder, and Denver, Colorado adopted ordinances prohibiting private as well as public workplace, housing, and public accommodations discrimination on the basis of sexual orientation. In 1992, Colorado for Family Values (CFV) proposed Amendment 2 to the state constitution:

> Neither the State of Colorado, through any of its branches or departments, nor any of its agencies, political subdivisions, municipalities or school districts, shall enact, adopt or enforce any statute, regulation, ordinance or policy whereby homosexual, lesbian or bisexual orientation, conduct, practices or relationships shall constitute or otherwise be the basis of or entitle any person or class of persons to have or claim any minority status, quota preferences, protected status or claim of discrimination.

In Colorado, as in most states, the voters can amend the state constitution through a majority vote for "initiatives" like Amendment 2. Gay groups and their allies opposed the initiative on the ground that it would preempt needed local protections and subject gay people to affirmative and unfair state discrimination.

Typical of the initiative process, CFV prepared a ballot pamphlet setting forth its case for Amendment 2, "equal rights — not special rights."[m] The pamphlet made the following arguments: (1) "Homosexuals" are not a "disadvantaged minority" meriting anti-discrimination protections, as they are much wealthier than average citizens, have never been subject to legal segregation, and are marked by immoral behavior rather than immutable traits such as race, sex, and disability. Instead, "special class status for gays threaten[s] the hard-won gains of disadvantaged minorities." (2) "Target: Children." Pedophilia, said CFV, "is actually an accepted part of the homosexual community!" "Homosexuals" account for more than one-third of all child molestations. And "Homosexual indoctrination in the schools? It's Happening in Colorado," through educational materials that "try and convince children — maybe even your own — that they should consider homosexuality!" (3) "Homosexuals" are sexually promiscuous. " 'Monogamy' is virtually unknown

---

m. The ballot materials are reproduced as an appendix to Robert Nagel, *Playing Defense*, 6 Wm. & Mary Bill of Rights L.J. 167 (1997).

in the homosexual lifestyle." Gay men tend to be afflicted with AIDS: "Gays have been unwilling (or unable) to curb their voracious, unsafe sex practices in the face of AIDS." Even those not afflicted with AIDS die young; according to CFV, the average reported age of death for gay men is 42 years old, lesbians 45 years old. (4) "To this angry, alienated minority, the family is the symbol of everything they attack." "Militant" gay rights people want to destroy the family and the state's churches. (5) "Homosexuality" is a choice and not an innate trait. (6) " 'Gay-rights' destroys basic freedoms." The freedom of "your child" at the University of Colorado not to have a gay roommate has been taken away by Boulder's anti-discrimination law. Gay rights will suppress free speech and deny straight people jobs they ought to have. A cartoon depicted a day care center telling a rejected applicant that he cannot be hired because "we haven't filled our quota of homosexuals."

These arguments are representative of those made by Amendment 2 supporters in other forums; gay rights advocates claimed that most of these factual assertions are false, and none could be empirically supported. Colorado voters approved the initiative 54%-46%, but it was challenged as a violation of the Equal Protection Clause before it could go into effect. You are the trial judge ruling on the constitutionality of Amendment 2. What level of equal protection scrutiny should you impose on this state constitutional rule? Would it pass rational basis review? Rational basis review with (*Cleburne*) bite? What justifications should the state press in defense of Amendment 2? Would they pass muster under any of the tiers of equal protection scrutiny? Jot down your analysis before reading further.

ROMER v. EVANS
517 U.S. 620, 116 S.Ct. 1620, 134 L.Ed. 2d 855 (1996)

JUSTICE KENNEDY delivered the opinion of the Court.

One century ago, the first Justice Harlan admonished this Court that the Constitution "neither knows nor tolerates classes among citizens." *Plessy v. Ferguson*, 163 U.S. 537, 559 (1896) (dissenting opinion). Unheeded then, those words now are understood to state a commitment to the law's neutrality where the rights of persons are at stake. The Equal Protection Clause enforces this principle and today requires us to hold invalid a provision of Colorado's Constitution [Amendment 2, quoted in Problem 4-5]. * * *

The State's principal argument in defense of Amendment 2 is that it puts gays and lesbians in the same position as all other persons. So, the State says, the measure does no more than deny homosexuals special rights. This reading of the amendment's language is implausible. [The Colorado Supreme Court interpreted the amendment as repealing local protections for gay people and preventing further protections from being adopted unless the state constitution were first amended.]

Sweeping and comprehensive is the change in legal status effected by this law. So much is evident from the ordinances that the Colorado Supreme Court declared would be void by operation of Amendment 2. Homosexuals, by state decree, are put in a solitary class with respect to transactions and relations in both the private and governmental spheres. The amendment withdraws from homosexuals, but no others, specific legal protection from the injuries caused by discrimination, and it forbids reinstatement of these laws and policies.

The change that Amendment 2 works in the legal status of gays and lesbians in the private sphere is far-reaching, both on its own terms and when considered in light of the structure and operation of modern anti-discrimination laws. [Justice Kennedy explained that the common law afforded no protection against discrimination by public accommodations because of race, sex, etc. The common law also placed few, if any, restrictions on employment discrimination. The Aspen, Boulder, and Denver ordinances are typical of antidiscrimination regulations adopted in hundreds of jurisdictions filling this gap in the common law. Additionally, those regulations, like others, prohibit discrimination on the basis of criteria that have not triggered constitutional strict scrutiny, including age, military status, marital status, pregnancy, parenthood, custody of a minor child, political affiliation, physical or mental disability of an individual or of his or her associates, and sexual orientation. The effect of Amendment 2 was to deprive gay people of those protections in public accommodations, housing, sale of real estate, insurance, health and welfare services, private education, and employment.]

Amendment 2's reach may not be limited to specific laws passed for the benefit of gays and lesbians. It is a fair, if not necessary, inference from the broad language of the amendment that it deprives gays and lesbians even of the protection of general laws and policies that prohibit arbitrary discrimination in governmental and private settings. See, *e.g.*, Colo. Rev. Stat. § 24-4-106(7) (1988) (agency action subject to judicial review under arbitrary and capricious standard); § 18-8-405 (making it a criminal offense for a public servant knowingly, arbitrarily or capriciously to refrain from performing a duty imposed on him by law); * * * 4 Colo. Code of Regulations 801-1, Policy 11-1 (1983) (prohibiting discrimination in state employment on grounds of specified traits or "other non-merit factor"). At some point in the systematic administration of these laws, an official must determine whether homosexuality is an arbitrary and thus forbidden basis for decision. Yet a decision to that effect would itself amount to a policy prohibiting discrimination on the basis of homosexuality, and so would appear to be no more valid under Amendment 2 than the specific prohibitions against discrimination the state court held invalid.

If this consequence follows from Amendment 2, as its broad language suggests, it would compound the constitutional difficulties the law creates. [The Colorado Supreme Court made the limited observation that the amendment is not intended to affect many anti-discrimination laws protecting non-suspect classes, but the state court's construction left open the possibility of broader application. Justice Kennedy specifically rejected the view that Amendment 2's prohibition on specific legal protections does no more than deprive homosexuals of special rights.] We find nothing special in the protections Amendment 2 withholds. These are protections taken for granted by most people either because they already have them or do not need them; these are protections against exclusion from an almost limitless number of transactions and endeavors that constitute ordinary civic life in a free society. * * *

Amendment 2 fails, indeed defies, [rational basis] inquiry. First, the amendment has the peculiar property of imposing a broad and undifferentiated disability on a single named group, an exceptional and, as we shall explain, invalid form of legislation. Second, its sheer breadth is so discontinuous with the reasons offered for it that the amendment seems inexplicable by anything but animus toward the class that it affects; it lacks a rational relationship to legitimate state interests.

Taking the first point, even in the ordinary equal protection case calling for the most deferential of standards, we insist on knowing the relation between the classification adopted and the object to be attained. The search for the link between classification and objective gives substance to the Equal Protection Clause; it provides guidance and discipline for the legislature, which is entitled to know what sorts of laws it can pass; and it marks the limits of our own authority. In the ordinary case, a law will be sustained if it can be said to advance a legitimate government interest, even if the law seems unwise or works to the disadvantage of a particular group, or if the rationale for it seems tenuous. [Citing, *inter alia*, *Railway Express*.] By requiring that the classification bear a rational relationship to an independent and legitimate legislative end, we ensure that classifications are not drawn for the purpose of disadvantaging the group burdened by the law.

Amendment 2 confounds this normal process of judicial review. It is at once too narrow and too broad. It identifies persons by a single trait and then denies them protection across the board. The resulting disqualification of a class of persons from the right to seek specific protection from the law is unprecedented in our jurisprudence. The absence of precedent for Amendment 2 is itself instructive; "[d]iscriminations of an unusual character especially suggest careful consideration to determine whether they are obnoxious to the constitutional provision."

It is not within our constitutional tradition to enact laws of this sort. Central both to the idea of the rule of law and to our own Constitution's guarantee of equal protection is the principle that government and each of its parts remain open on impartial terms to all who seek its assistance. " 'Equal protection of the laws is not achieved through indiscriminate imposition of inequalities.' " *Sweatt v. Painter*, 339 U.S. 629, 635 (1950) (quoting *Shelley v. Kraemer*, 334 U.S. 1, 22 (1948)). Respect for this principle explains why laws singling out a certain class of citizens for disfavored legal status or general hardships are rare. A law declaring that in general it shall be more difficult for one group of citizens than for all others to seek aid from the government is itself a denial of equal protection of the laws in the most literal sense. * * *

A second and related point is that laws of the kind now before us raise the inevitable inference that the disadvantage imposed is born of animosity toward the class of persons affected. "[I]f the constitutional conception of 'equal protection of the laws' means anything, it must at the very least mean that a bare . . . desire to harm a politically unpopular group cannot constitute a *legitimate* governmental interest." *Moreno*. Even laws enacted for broad and ambitious purposes often can be explained by reference to legitimate public policies which justify the incidental disadvantages they impose on certain persons. Amendment

2, however, in making a general announcement that gays and lesbians shall not have any particular protections from the law, inflicts on them immediate, continuing, and real injuries that outrun and belie any legitimate justifications that may be claimed for it. We conclude that, in addition to the far-reaching deficiencies of Amendment 2 that we have noted, the principles it offends, in another sense, are conventional and venerable; a law must bear a rational relationship to a legitimate governmental purpose, and Amendment 2 does not.

The primary rationale the State offers for Amendment 2 is respect for other citizens' freedom of association, and in particular the liberties of landlords or employers who have personal or religious objections to homosexuality. Colorado also cites its interest in conserving resources to fight discrimination against other groups. The breadth of the Amendment is so far removed from these particular justifications that we find it impossible to credit them. We cannot say that Amendment 2 is directed to any identifiable legitimate purpose or discrete objective. It is a status-based enactment divorced from any factual context from which we could discern a relationship to legitimate state interests; it is a classification of persons undertaken for its own sake, something the Equal Protection Clause does not permit. "[C]lass legislation . . . [is] obnoxious to the prohibitions of the Fourteenth Amendment . . . . " *Civil Rights Cases.* * * *

JUSTICE SCALIA, with whom **THE CHIEF JUSTICE [REHNQUIST]** and **JUSTICE THOMAS** join, dissenting.

The Court has mistaken a Kulturkampf for a fit of spite. The constitutional amendment before us here is not the manifestation of a " 'bare . . . desire to harm' " homosexuals, but is rather a modest attempt by seemingly tolerant Coloradans to preserve traditional sexual mores against the efforts of a politically powerful minority to revise those mores through use of the laws. That objective, and the means chosen to achieve it, are not only unimpeachable under any constitutional doctrine hitherto pronounced (hence the opinion's heavy reliance upon principles of righteousness rather than judicial holdings); they have been specifically approved by the Congress of the United States and by this Court. * * *

[Justice Scalia criticized the Court for suggesting that Amendment 2 had a potentially broad impact upon gay people, for the Colorado Supreme Court authoritatively construed Amendment 2 "only to prevent the adoption of antidiscrimination laws intended to protect gays, lesbians, and bisexuals."] The amendment prohibits *special treatment* of homosexuals, and nothing more. It would not affect, for example, a requirement of state law that pensions be paid to all retiring state employees with a certain length of service; homosexual employees, as well as others, would be entitled to that benefit. But it would prevent the State or any municipality from making death-benefit payments to the "life partner" of a homosexual when it does not make such payments to the long-time roommate of a nonhomosexual employee. Or again, it does not affect the requirement of the State's general insurance laws that customers be afforded coverage without discrimination unrelated to anticipated risk. Thus, homosexuals could not be denied coverage, or charged a greater premium, with respect to auto collision insurance; but neither the State nor any municipality could require that distinctive health insurance risks associated with homosexuality (if there are any) be ignored.

Despite all of its hand-wringing about the potential effect of Amendment 2 on general antidiscrimination laws, the Court's opinion ultimately does not dispute all this, but assumes it to be true. The only denial of equal treatment it contends homosexuals have suffered is this: They may not obtain *preferential* treatment without amending the state constitution. That is to say, the principle underlying the Court's opinion is that one who is accorded equal treatment under the laws, but cannot as readily as others obtain *preferential* treatment under the laws, has been denied equal protection of the laws. If merely stating this alleged "equal protection" violation does not suffice to refute it, our constitutional jurisprudence has achieved terminal silliness. * * *

I turn next to whether there was a legitimate rational basis for the substance of the constitutional amendment — for the prohibition of special protection for homosexuals. It is unsurprising that the Court avoids discussion of this question, since the answer is so obviously yes. The case most relevant to the issue before us today is not even mentioned in the Court's opinion: In *Bowers v. Hardwick* [Chapter 5, § 4C], we held that the Constitution does not prohibit what virtually all States had done from the founding of the Republic until very recent years — making homosexual conduct a crime. That holding is unassailable, except by those who think that the Constitution changes to suit current fashions. But in any event it is a given in the present case: Respondents' briefs did not urge overruling *Bowers*, and at oral argument respondents' counsel expressly disavowed any intent to seek such overruling. If it is constitutionally permissible for a State to make homosexual conduct criminal, surely it is constitutionally permissible for a State to enact other laws merely *disfavoring* homosexual conduct. * * * And *a fortiori* it is constitutionally permissible for a State to adopt a provision *not even* disfavoring homosexual conduct, but merely prohibiting all levels of state government from bestowing *special protections* upon homosexual conduct. Respondents (who, unlike the Court, cannot afford the luxury of ignoring inconvenient precedent) counter *Bowers* with the argument that a greater-includes-the-lesser rationale cannot justify Amendment 2's application to individuals who do not engage in homosexual acts, but are merely of homosexual "orientation." * * *

But assuming that, in Amendment 2, a person of homosexual "orientation" is someone who does not engage in homosexual conduct but merely has a tendency or desire to do so, *Bowers* still suffices to establish a rational basis for the provision. If it is rational to criminalize the conduct, surely it is rational to deny special favor and protection to those with a self-avowed tendency or desire to engage in the conduct. Indeed, where criminal sanctions are not involved, homosexual "orientation" is an acceptable stand-in for homosexual conduct. * *.* Just as a policy barring the hiring of methadone users as transit employees does not violate equal protection simply because *some* methadone users pose no threat to passenger safety, see *New York City Transit Authority v. Beazer*, 440 U.S. 568 (1979), and just as a mandatory retirement age of 50 for police officers does not violate equal protection even though it prematurely ends the careers of many policemen over 50 who still have the capacity to do the job, see *Murgia*,

Amendment 2 is not constitutionally invalid simply because it could have been drawn more precisely so as to withdraw special antidiscrimination protections only from those of homosexual "orientation" who actually engage in homosexual conduct. * * *

* * * The Court's opinion contains grim, disapproving hints that Coloradans have been guilty of "animus" or "animosity" toward homosexuality, as though that has been established as Unamerican. Of course it is our moral heritage that one should not hate any human being or class of human beings. But I had thought that one could consider certain conduct reprehensible — murder, for example, or polygamy, or cruelty to animals — and could exhibit even "animus" toward such conduct. Surely that is the only sort of "animus" at issue here: moral disapproval of homosexual conduct, the same sort of moral disapproval that produced the centuries-old criminal laws that we held constitutional in *Bowers*. The Colorado amendment does not, to speak entirely precisely, prohibit giving favored status to people who are *homosexuals*; they can be favored for many reasons — for example, because they are senior citizens or members of racial minorities. But it prohibits giving them favored status *because of their homosexual conduct* — that is, it prohibits favored status *for homosexuality*.

[Justice Scalia maintained that Colorado had, in fact, engaged in a measured response to homosexuality. The state in 1971 repealed its law making consensual sodomy a crime, but that repeal was not intended to connote an approval of homosexuality.] The problem (a problem, that is, for those who wish to retain social disapprobation of homosexuality) is that, because those who engage in homosexual conduct tend to reside in disproportionate numbers in certain communities, see Record, Exh. MMM, have high disposable income, see *ibid*.; App. 254 (affidavit of Prof. James Hunter), and of course care about homosexual-rights issues much more ardently than the public at large, they possess political power much greater than their numbers, both locally and statewide. Quite understandably, they devote this political power to achieving not merely a grudging social toleration, but full social acceptance, of homosexuality. * * *

That is where Amendment 2 came in. It sought to counter both the geographic concentration and the disproportionate political power of homosexuals by (1) resolving the controversy at the statewide level, and (2) making the election a single-issue contest for both sides. It put directly, to all the citizens of the State, the question: Should homosexuality be given special protection? They answered no. The Court today asserts that this most democratic of procedures is unconstitutional. Lacking any cases to establish that facially absurd proposition, it simply asserts that it *must* be unconstitutional, because it has never happened before. [This is completely false, says Justice Scalia. In the late nineteenth century, the federal government enacted a series of statutes singling out polygamists for special criminal, civil, and juridical treatment; the Court upheld all the legal disabilities, including one that disenfranchised not only polygamists, but also people who taught or counseled polygamy. *Davis v. Beason*, 133 U.S. 333 (1890). Although abstract advocacy cannot today be punished, *Beason* remains good for the proposition that disapproved status can be the basis for civil penalty.] Has the Court concluded that the perceived social harm of polygamy is a "legitimate concern of government," and the perceived social harm of homosexuality is not? [Justice Scalia concluded his opinion:]

When the Court takes sides in the culture wars, it tends to be with the knights rather than the villeins — and more specifically with the Templars, reflecting the views and values of the lawyer class from which the Court's Members are drawn. How that class feels about homosexuality will be evident to anyone who wishes to interview job applicants at virtually any of the Nation's law schools. The interviewer may refuse to offer a job because the applicant is a Republican; because he is an adulterer; because he went to the wrong prep school or belongs to the wrong country club; because he eats snails; because he is a womanizer; because she wears real-animal fur; or even because he hates the Chicago Cubs. But if the interviewer should wish not to be an associate or partner of an applicant because he disapproves of the applicant's homosexuality, *then* he will have violated the pledge which the Association of American Law Schools requires all its member-schools to exact from job interviewers: "assurance of the employer's willingness" to hire homosexuals. This law-school view of what "prejudices" must be stamped out may be contrasted with the more plebeian attitudes that apparently still prevail in the United States Congress, which has been unresponsive to repeated attempts to extend to homosexuals the protections of federal civil rights laws, see, *e.g.*, Employment Non-Discrimination Act of 1994, S. 2238, 103d Cong., 2d Sess. (1994); Civil Rights Amendments of 1975, H.R. 5452, 94th Cong., 1st Sess. (1975), and which took the pains to exclude them specifically from the Americans With Disabilities Act of 1990, see 42 U.S.C. § 12211(a) (1988 ed., Supp. V). * * *

NOTES ON *ROMER* AND ITS IMPLICATIONS FOR JUDICIAL REVIEW OF ANTIGAY STATE POLICIES

1. *What Is the Holding of* Romer? What exactly was wrong with Amendment 2? Some possibilities:

(a) it deprived gay people of the right to participate equally in the political process;[n]

(b) the law was a denial of the "equal protection of the laws" in the most literal sense, as it closed off state process to one vulnerable group;[o]

---

n. This was the theory followed by the Colorado Supreme Court, *Evans v. Romer*, 854 P.2d 1270 (1993), and has been viewed by some commentators as essentially the Court's theory. See Pamela Karlan, *Just Politics? Five Not So Easy Pieces of the 1995 Term*, 34 Houston L. Rev. 289, 296 (1997); Nicholas Zeppos, *The Dynamics of Democracy: Travel, Premature Predation, and the Components of Political Identity*, 50 Vand. L. Rev. 445 (1997).

o. Brief by Laurence Tribe et al., in *Evans*, the so-called "Scholars' Brief" filed in the case.

(c) the law may not draw moral distinctions based upon sexual practices between consenting adults (therefore overruling *Hardwick*);[p]

(d) the state cannot, without justification, single out one social group for "pariah" status by creating a constitutional right to discriminate against that group,[q] or the state has an obligation to remedy pervasive discrimination against a vulnerable group similar to those the state does protect;[r]

(e) the law's goal — state action reflecting widespread animus against gay people — was impermissible;[s]

(f) the measure, unprecedented in its sweep, was way overbroad.[t]

Which basis is the *best* (most persuasive) basis for *Romer*? Does the best reading of the case meet Justice Scalia's criticisms that the result is inconsistent with *Hardwick* and with the general precepts underlying rational basis review?

2. *The War of Analogies; Classification versus Class.* Justice Scalia argued that a state that can discourage polygamy by penalizing "polygamosexuals" is a state that can discourage sodomy by penalizing "homosexuals." Would equal protection law allow the state to deny fundamental rights to people who identified themselves as polygamosexuals? Justice Kennedy invoked a counter-analogy, *Plessy*. Is it fair to analogize racial apartheid, a pervasive and violent state regime, with the regime of Amendment 2? Note the potential power of race-based analogies in equal protection law — but it is a power that can backfire if the analogy is incorrect or even insulting as Justice Scalia argued in dissent. Like Colorado for Family Values, Scalia depicted gays as a group earning high incomes and wielding political power much greater than their numbers would suggest. The result is "special rights" legislation such as the ordinances prohibiting sexual orientation discrimination. Justice Kennedy rejected this rhetoric and treated gays and lesbians as a group beset by "animus" which threatened to close them out of the Colorado political process. Which view is more accurate?[u]

---

p. Robert Bork, *Slouching Towards Gomorrah* 112-14 (1996) (disapproving); Ronald Dworkin, *Sex, Death, and the Courts*, N.Y. Rev. Books, Aug. 8, 1996, at 49 (approving); Cass Sunstein, *The Supreme Court, 1995 Term — Foreword: Leaving Things Undecided*, 110 Harv. L. Rev. 4, 62 (1996) (approving).

q. Daniel Farber & Suzanna Sherry, *The Pariah Principle*, 13 Const. Comm. 257 (1996), as well as Akhil Amar, *Attainder and Amendment 2:* Romer's *Rightness*, 95 Mich. L. Rev. 203 (1996).

r. Louis Michael Seidman, Romer's *Radicalism: The Unexpected Revival of Warren Court Activism*, 1996 Sup. Ct. Rev. 67.

s. Eskridge, *Gaylaw* 205-18; Andrew Koppelman, Romer v. Evans *and Invidious Intent*, 6 Wm. & Mary Bill of Rights J. (1997).

t. Richard Duncan, *The Narrow and Shallow Bite of* Romer *and the Eminent Rationality of Dual-Gender Marriage: A (Partial) Response to Professor Koppelman*, 6 Wm. & Mary Bill of Rights J. (1997).

u. M.V. Lee Badgett, *The Wage Effects of Sexual Orientation Discrimination*, 48 Indus. & Labor Rel. Rev. 726 (1995), analyzed pooled data from a national random sample, and found that bisexual and gay male workers earned 11-27% less money than heterosexual workers with the same

Justice Kennedy's focus on the "classification" (sexual orientation) contrasts with Justice Scalia's focus on the "class" ("homosexuals"). Recall *Loving v. Virginia* (Chapter 3). Although *Carolene Products* and Ely's "representation-reinforcing" theory (Chapter 2, § 3B) make the discriminated-against class the focus, like Justice Scalia did, others believe that Justice Kennedy's is the better approach in the general run of cases. An advantage of this approach would be to escape the implicit issue of whether a particular group is sufficiently "victimized" to merit heightened scrutiny of an invidious classification. Can such an inquiry really be avoided, though? Which is more consistent with the sex discrimination cases such as VMI? Which focus (if either) makes the best sense for the body politic as a whole?

3. *Equal Protection Review After* Romer: *Channeling Antigay Discourse.* *Romer* can be read narrowly, e.g., *Shahar v. Bowers*, 114 F.3d 1097 (11th Cir. 1997) (en banc), *cert. denied*, 522 U.S. 1049 (1998) (prosecutor can refuse to hire lesbian who planned to marry another woman, because her sexuality could undermine public confidence in the office), or can be read broadly, e.g., *Stemler v. City of Florence*, 126 F.3d 856 (6th Cir. 1997), *cert. denied*, 523 U.S. 1118 (1998) (ruled that a lesbian arrested by the police because of her orientation had a valid equal protection claim for selective prosecution). One effect of *Romer*'s focus on "animus" has been to transform public discourse about homosexuality. Proponents of laws and initiatives that discriminate against gay people have focused on neutral policies; to minimize the chance of a successful equal protection challenge, they have abstained from arguments which demonize gay people or which make wild claims about them. *Romer* and equal protection law *channel* antigay discourse into more tolerant tropes.[v] Antigay policies are now justified as preventing harm to third parties or as signaling that the state should *tolerate* "homosexuals" but should *not promote* "homosexuality."

Consider the judicial presumption against child custody by lesbian or gay parents. Consistent with a broad reading of *Romer*, most states have abandoned this presumption on the ground that it rests upon unproven stereotypes about lesbian and gay parents. E.g., *Boswell v. Boswell*, 721 A.2d 662 (Md. 1998). Consistent with a narrow reading of *Romer*, southern states retaining the presumption justify it by reference to harmful effects encountered by children being raised by openly lesbian or gay parents. E.g., *Weigand v. Houghton*, 730 So.2d 581 (Miss. 1999); see Lynn Wardle, *The Potential Impact of Homosexual Parenting on Children*, 1997 U. Ill. L. Rev. 833. Gay parents object that the supposed harms to children are fictitious (according to social science surveys). See Carlos Ball & Janice Pea, *Warring with Wardle: Morality, Social Science, and Gay and Lesbian Parents*, 1998 U. Ill. L. Rev. 233. If the parents are right about the social science data, can the state nonetheless justify a presumption against custody by lesbian and gay parents upon the no promo homo rationale

---

experience, education, occupation, etc. Badgett found that lesbians and bisexual women earned less than heterosexual women, but the difference was not statistically significant.

v. See William Eskridge, Jr., *No Promo Homo: The Sedimentation of Antigay Discourse and the Channeling Effect of Judicial Review*, 75 NYU L. Rev. 1327 (2000).

that the state should signal that it is on the whole "better" for children to be raised in mom-dad households? How should *Romer* be applied to this issue?

NOTE ON JUDICIAL REVIEW
OF POPULAR INITIATIVES AND REFERENDA

State constitutions are routinely subject to amendment by ballot proposal, and in about half the states citizens may adopt ordinary legislation by initiative as well. The Supreme Court has rarely reviewed the constitutionality of such direct lawmaking, and until *Romer* its review had largely focused on initiatives having a race-based impact.[w] With few dissenting voices, scholars have urged the Court to scrutinize popular initiatives for equal protection violations more vigorously than the Court reviews ordinary statutes adopted by legislatures.[x] *Evans* might be an example of that realist argument. If so, it and the other cases are vulnerable to the argument from democracy: Perhaps courts should be more rather than less reluctant to overturn legislation when it is clearly responsive to majority preferences.

The main argument for heightened review is that the Constitution adopts a "republican" structure rather than direct democracy (see *Federalist* 10 [App. 2]) for the national government and expresses a preference for the same at the state level (see U.S. Const., Art. IV, § 4, requiring Congress to "guarantee to every State [a] Republican Form of Government"). The reason for the Constitution's policy is the greater preference for the status quo and for deliberation assured by republican governance. Before a bill becomes law, it must pass through two legislative chambers and a possible executive veto. This assures more opportunities for affected minorities to block or ameliorate the harm to them from representative than popular legislation. Possibilities for distortion and emotional appeals are more likely in direct democracy, where voters are often confused by the phrasing of initiatives and subject to demagogy by professional politicians or grass-roots organizers. Also, because voting is open and public in the representative but not initiative process, critics of direct democracy fear that prejudice will be more readily expressed in the latter than the former.

---

w. See *Reitman v. Mulkey*, 387 U.S. 369 (1967); *Hunter v. Erickson*, 393 U.S. 385 (1969); *James v. Valtierra*, 402 U.S. 137 (1971); *Washington v. Seattle Sch. Dist. No. 1*, 458 U.S. 457 (1982); *Crawford v. Board of Educ.*, 458 U.S. 527 (1982). In all but *James* and *Crawford*, the Court invalidated the initiative because it impaired racial minority equality.

x. Among the scholars urging such heightened scrutiny are Derrick Bell, Jr., *The Referendum: Democracy's Barrier to Racial Equality*, 54 Wash. L. Rev. 1 (1978); Julian Eule, *Judicial Review of Direct Democracy*, 99 Yale L.J. 1503 (1990); Daniel Lowenstein, *California Initiatives and the Single-Subject Rule*, 30 UCLA L. Rev. 936 (1983) (state constitutional review); Lawrence Sager, *Insular Majorities Unabated:* Warth v. Seldin *and* City of Eastlake v. Forest City Enterprises, Inc., 91 Harv. L. Rev. 1373 (1978). Along the same lines, see Philip P. Frickey, *Interpretation on the Borderline: Constitution, Canons, Direct Democracy*, 1996 Ann. Surv. Am. L. 477 (urging narrow interpretation of ballot measures).

Other scholars reject or caution against this academic conventional wisdom.[y] Initiatives are an intrinsically fair way for the voting population to focus on an issue that concerns them — and are often a better path to active citizen engagement in substantive issues. Public choice theory, for example, suggests that legislators have incentives not to confront or resolve conflictual issues, and this may have been the reason the Colorado legislature ducked the issue of sexual orientation protections at the local level. Moreover, the same kinds of questions raised against direct democracy — the inability of minorities to win, the lack of genuine deliberation, private interests winning over the common good — have been posed by public choice theorists criticizing representative democracy. Lynn Baker criticizes opponents of direct democracy for employing "an interest group or pluralist model of lawmaking by ordinary citizens, but a republican or public-interest model of lawmaking by legislatures" [Baker 751].

How does the Colorado experience bear on these arguments? Judge Hans Linde contends that the history of antigay initiatives supports the conventional academic wisdom and heightened judicial review under Article IV.[z] One argument is that, as soon as states and municipalities stopped discriminating against lesbian and gay employees and couples and started granting these citizens equal rights, antigay initiatives sought to overturn positive laws, in part by appeals to arguments that gay people are child molesters (the main argument in the 1970s) or that the community should not "promote the homosexual lifestyle" by providing "special rights" (the main argument in the 1990s). In considering this contention, note that antigay initiatives have had a remarkably high success rate.[a]

PROBLEM 4-6
DON'T ASK, DON'T TELL

President Clinton in 1993 proposed to end the military's exclusion of homosexuals but backed away quickly in the face of opposition. Clinton, key senators, and the Joint Chiefs of Staff agreed on a policy of "don't ask, don't tell," codified in 10 U.S.C. § 654(b), which requires separation of a member of the armed forces if the military finds:

---

y. See Lynn Baker, *Direct Democracy and Discrimination: A Public Choice Perspective*, 67 Chi-Kent L. Rev. 707 (1991); Richard Briffault, *Distrust of Democracy*, 63 Tex. L. Rev. 1347 (1985) (book review); Clayton Gillette, *Plebiscites, Participation, and Collective Action in Local Government Law*, 86 Mich. L. Rev. 930 (1988).

z. See Hans Linde, *When Is Initiative Lawmaking Not "Republican Government"?*, 17 Hast. Const. L.Q. 159 (1989). On the intellectual history of antigay initiatives, see William Eskridge, Jr., *Challenging the Apartheid of the Closet*, 25 Hofstra L. Rev. 817, 928-30 (1997); Jane Schacter, *The Gay Civil Rights Debate in the States: Decoding the Discourse of Equivalents*, 29 Harv. C.R.-C.L. L. Rev. 283 (1994).

a. One scholar found that, although only about one-third of all ballot measures pass, voters approved thirty of the thirty-eight state or local ballot measures seeking to restrict gay rights that she identified between 1959 and 1993, a 79% success rate. See Barbara Gamble, *Putting Civil Rights to a Popular Vote*, 41 Am. J. Pol. Sci. 245 (1997).

(1) That the member has engaged in, attempted to engage in, or solicited another to engage in a homosexual act or acts unless there are further findings, made and approved in accordance with procedures set forth in such regulations, that the member has demonstrated that —

(A) such conduct is a departure from the member's usual and customary behavior;

(B) such conduct, under all the circumstances, is unlikely to recur;

(C) such conduct was not accomplished by use of force, coercion, or intimidation;

(D) under the particular circumstances of the case, the member's continued presence in the armed forces is consistent with the interests of the armed forces in proper discipline, good order, and morale; and

(E) the member does not have a propensity or intent to engage in homosexual acts.

(2) That the member has stated that he or she is a homosexual or bisexual, or words to that effect, unless there is a further finding, made and approved in accordance with procedures set forth in the regulations, that the member has demonstrated that he or she is not a person who engages in, attempts to engage in, has a propensity to engage in, or intends to engage in homosexual acts.

(3) That the member has married or attempted to marry a person known to be of the same biological sex.

The primary justification for this statute is the one developed by General Colin Powell, then-Chair of the Joint Chiefs of Staff: Many straight soldiers are uncomfortable serving with openly gay soldiers,[b] and military commanders from all the branches agreed (and testified before Congress) that allowing openly gay personnel would undermine morale and unit cohesion.[c] Several military leaders testified that allowing anyone who commits sodomy to serve would be similarly objectionable.

Under this statute, is the Army obligated to discharge someone who tells her commanding officer that she is a lesbian in orientation but makes no admission that she has ever had sex with another woman? Would the application of the statute to a "celibate homosexual" be constitutional? In answering this question, consider how you would frame the level of judicial scrutiny, whether *Romer* is relevant, and how much to defer to the collective judgment of Congress, the President, and the Joint Chiefs of Staff (recall *Rostker*). Relevant lower court opinions include *Thomasson v. Perry*, 80 F.3d 915 (4th Cir. 1996) (en banc); *Able v. United States*, 88 F.3d 1280 (2d Cir. 1996), *on remand*, 968 F. Supp. 850 (E.D.N.Y. 1997), *rev'd*, 155 F.3d 628 (2d Cir. 1998); *Richenberg v. Perry*, 97 F.3d 256 (8th Cir. 1996); *Holmes v. California Army Nat'l Guard*, 124 F.3d 1126 (9th Cir. 1997).

———

b. See General Powell's testimony in *Fiscal Year 1993 Defense Budget: Hearings Before the House Comm. on the Budget*, 102d Cong., 2d Sess. 45 (1992).

c. Relevant testimony is reproduced in William Eskridge, Jr. & Nan Hunter, *Sexuality, Gender, and the Law* ch. 4, § 3C (2d ed. 2003). Historical background for the exclusion can be found in Allan Bérubé, *Coming Out Under Fire: The History of Gay Men and Women in World War Two* (1990); Randy Shilts, *Conduct Unbecoming: Lesbians and Gays in the U.S. Military — Vietnam to the Persian Gulf* (1993).

Watkins v. United States Army, 847 F.2d 1329, vacated en banc, 872 F.2d 699 (9th Cir. 1989). Writing for a panel of the Ninth Circuit, **Judge Norris** ruled that the Army's pre-1993 policy of excluding bisexuals, gay men, and lesbians violated equal protection strict scrutiny. Judge Norris' argument for strict scrutiny tracked the factors he found in the Supreme Court cases:

(A) Whether the group at issue has suffered a history of purposeful discrimination. The Army conceded that "homosexuals have historically been the object of pernicious and sustained hostility."

(B) Whether the discrimination embodies a gross unfairness that is sufficiently inconsistent with the ideals of equal protection to term it invidious. "Considering this additional factor makes sense. After all, discrimination exists against some groups because the animus is warranted — no one could seriously argue that burglars form a suspect class. In giving content to this concept of gross unfairness, the Court has considered (1) whether the disadvantaged class is defined by a trait that 'frequently bears no relation to ability to perform or contribute to society'; (2) whether the class has been saddled with unique disabilities because of prejudice or inaccurate stereotypes; and (3) whether the trait defining the class is immutable." Judge Norris found that (1) sexual orientation does not impair a person's ability to perform well in the military (the Army did not seriously dispute that point); (2) classifications based on sexual orientation reflect prejudice and inaccurate stereotypes; and (3) sexual orientation, whether immutable or not, rests outside the conscious control or choice of the individual.

The Army argued, and dissenting **Judge Reinhardt** agreed, that its regulations reflected the fact that most homosexuals are "sodomists" and that sodomy is a major military crime, constitutional under *Hardwick*. "In essence, the Army argues that homosexuals, like burglars, cannot form a suspect class because they are criminals." Judge Norris responded: "First, the class burdened by the regulations is defined by the sexual *orientation* of its members, not by their sexual conduct. To our knowledge, homosexual orientation itself has never been criminalized in this country. * * * Second, little of the homosexual *conduct* covered by the regulations is criminal. The regulations reach many forms of homosexual conduct other than sodomy such as kissing, handholding, caressing, and hand-genital contact. Yet, sodomy is the only consensual adult sexual conduct that Congress has criminalized."

(C) Whether the penalized group lacks effective political representation needed to protect itself from social and state prejudice. Judge Norris argued that gay people are a minority that the majority has a hard time understanding or empathizing with. Most gay people are in the "closet," undermining the group's ability to organize politically, and even when political organization occurs it is frequently met with public prejudice and unusual hostility. The courts are needed to correct for this defect in the political process.

Postscript. The en banc Ninth Circuit vacated Judge Norris' opinion but ordered Sergeant Watkins reinstated on estoppel grounds: The Army had several times reenlisted Watkins notwithstanding his known orientation, and it was too late to make a point of it near the end of his distinguished career.

NOTES ON STRICT SCRUTINY FOR SEXUAL ORIENTATION

1. *Strict Scrutiny in the United States.* Academics have been persuaded by Judge Norris's reasons for treating sexual orientation classifications as suspect,[d] but judges have been a much harder audience. As of 2008, no federal appellate court has followed Judge Norris to find that sexual orientation discrimination requires strict scrutiny—even after *Romer* and *Lawrence v. Texas* (Chapter 5, § 4C), which invalidated Texas's Homosexual Conduct Law on constitutional privacy grounds.

Several state appellate courts followed Judge Norris and interpreted their *state* constitutions to treat sexual orientation as a suspect classification. See *The Marriage Cases*, 183 P.3d 384 (Cal. 2008) (excerpted below); *Baehr v. Miike*, 994 P.2d 566 (Haw. 1999) (summary disposition); *Commonwealth v. Wasson*, 842 S.W.2d 487 (Ky. 1992); *Tanner v. Oregon Health Servs.*, 971 P.2d 435 (Or. App. 1998). Some state appellate courts have provided strong constitutional protection for gay people without addressing the level-of-scrutiny question. See *Baker v. State*, 744 A.2d 864 (Vt. 1999) (striking down the state exclusion of lesbian and gay couples from all of the benefits and duties of marriage, but leaving the remedy to the legislature). As this short list suggests, the large majority of state appellate courts have *not* embraced Judge Norris's reasoning; in most states it is not even worth litigating.

2. *International Strict Scrutiny.* The Canadian Supreme Court unanimously ruled in *Egan v. The Queen*, [1995] 2 S.C.R. 513 (Sup. Ct. Can.), that sexual orientation is an "analogous ground" to those the Canadian Charter bars as the basis for state discrimination. The Court expanded upon this holding with decisions striking down important state discriminations in *Vriend v. Alberta*, [1998] 1 S.C.R. 493 (Sup. Ct. Can.) (provincial anti-discrimination law must protect against sexual orientation discrimination), and *Attorney General v. M. and H.*, 171 D.L.R. (4th) 577 (Sup. Ct. Can. 1999) (provinces cannot bar lesbian and gay couples from all the state benefits associated with marriage). In *M. and H.*, Justice Cory articulated the factors the Court would consider in evaluating a law discriminating against gay people: (1) "the existence of pre-existing disadvantage, stereotyping, prejudice, or vulnerability experienced by the individual or group at issue," and the statute's contribution to that problem; (2) the human needs of the claimant and the fit between her needs and the statutory distinction; and (3) "the nature of the interest affected by the impugned legislation," including "whether the distinction in question restricts access to a fundamental social institution, or affects a basic aspect of full membership in Canadian society."

Constitutional decisions in Europe, Columbia, Israel, and South Africa have also moved toward treating sexual orientation as a disapproved classification.[e]

---

d. E.g., Eskridge, *Gaylaw*, 217-18; Nan Hunter, *Life After* Hardwick, 27 Harv. C.R.-C.L. L. Rev. 531 (1992).

e. The best country-by-country survey is Robert Wintemute & Mads Andenaes, eds., *Legal Recognition of Same-Sex Partnerships: A Study of National, European, and International Law* (2001).

On the other hand, judicial decisions have not been notably gay-protective in the United Kingdom, India, China, Japan, and most of South America. In most countries of the world, there has not even been gay rights litigation.

3. *Strict Scrutiny and Social Movement Theory.* One of us has theorized the constitutional movement from the discriminatory regime of the Cold War to the regime envisioned by Judge Norris, and has linked it with similar movements relating to race and sex discrimination.[f] Traditionally, Americans have understood variation in race, sex, or (last in time) sexual orientation as *malign* and therefore naturally subject to stigma; at best, racial minorities, women, and sodomites were second-class citizens, at worst slaves or criminals. So long as this was the consensus, constitutional rights were unthinkable. In each case, minorities demanded *tolerance* and begrudgingly received it, but under conditions of inequality. Slaves were freed into apartheid; wives escaped coverture but remained subject to many legal restrictions; homosexuals were liberated from sodomy laws but remained under the disability of "no promo homo" measures. This regime of tolerable sexual variation has given way to one of *benign* variation for women and racial minorities: there is no longer a sex or race norm, and different variations are all equal as a formal matter. In the United States, gay people aspire to this regime but have not achieved it nationally. Canada, California, and New England have taken this final step toward benign sexual variation as a matter of their constitutional norms.

Why do some jurisdictions move more quickly from malign to tolerable to benign variation? The main variables determining the level of judicial scrutiny of state antigay discriminations have been the importance of fundamentalist religions in the jurisdiction's politics and the level of cohabitation (rather than marriage) among straight citizens.[g] Thus, there have been no protections for gay people in the fundamentalist Islamic countries of the Arab world, but there have been protections for gay people in Israel, with much higher cohabitation rates and somewhat lower fundamentalist religiosity. In the United States, none of the gay-protective decisions has come in states of the South or the West, where traditionalist religious groups are politically active and engaged; the most gay-protective states are those of the university-saturated Northeast and the post-industrial Pacific Rim, none of which has a politics much influenced by religions and all of which have relatively high nonmarital cohabitation rates.[h] See how this theory plays out in the same-sex marriage debate, where the emotions have been intense and the arguments all over the map (literally).

––––––––

–––––––––––––––––––––––––––––

f. Eskridge, *Gaylaw*, 205-18; William Eskridge, Jr., *Some Effects of Identity-Based Social Movements on Constitutional Law in the Twentieth Century,* 100 Mich. L. Rev. 2062, 2069-94 (2002).

g. See M. Lee Badgett, *Something Old, Something New: Will Gay People Change Marriage?* (draft 2008).

h. For a map of the United States as regards public rights for gay people, see William Eskridge, Jr. & Darren Spedale, *Gay Marriage: For Better or For Worse?* 234-49 (2006).

Goodridge v. Department of Public Health, 798 N.E.2d 941 (Mass. 2003). Seven lesbian and gay couples sued the state to invalidate its exclusion of same-sex couples from marriage. **Chief Justice Margaret Marshall** delivered the opinion of a closely (4-3) divided Court striking down the discrimination under the Massachusetts Constitution. "Whether and whom to marry, how to express sexual intimacy, and whether and how to establish a family — these are among the most basic of every individual's liberty and due process rights. And central to personal freedom and security is the assurance that the laws will apply equally to persons in similar situations. The liberty interest in choosing whether and whom to marry would be hollow if the Commonwealth could, without sufficient justification, foreclose an individual from freely choosing the person with whom to share an exclusive commitment in the unique institution of civil marriage." Notwithstanding this language, Chief Justice Marshall concluded that the Court need not reach the issue whether to apply heightened scrutiny, for the discrimination had no rational basis.

"The department posits three legislative rationales for prohibiting same-sex couples from marrying: (1) providing a 'favorable setting for procreation'; (2) ensuring the optimal setting for child rearing, which the department defines as 'a two-parent family with one parent of each sex'; and (3) preserving scarce State and private financial resources."

The Chief Justice found the first reason a justifiable state interest, but not one advanced by excluding lesbian and gay couples from marriage. "General Laws c. 207 contains no requirement that the applicants for a marriage license attest to their ability or intention to conceive children by coitus. Fertility is not a condition of marriage, nor is it grounds for divorce. People who have never consummated their marriage, and never plan to, may be and stay married. People who cannot stir from their deathbed may marry. While it is certainly true that many, perhaps most, married couples have children together (assisted or unassisted), it is the exclusive and permanent commitment of the marriage partners to one another, not the begetting of children, that is the *sine qua non* of civil marriage. * * *

"The 'marriage is procreation' argument singles out the one unbridgeable difference between same-sex and opposite-sex couples, and transforms that difference into the essence of legal marriage. Like Amendment 2 to the Constitution of Colorado, which effectively denied homosexual persons equality under the law and full access to the political process, the marriage restriction impermissibly 'identifies persons by a single trait and then denies them protection across the board.' *Romer v. Evans.* In so doing, the State's action confers an official stamp of approval on the destructive stereotype that same-sex relationships are inherently unstable and inferior to opposite-sex relationships and are not worthy of respect.

"The department's first stated rationale, equating marriage with unassisted heterosexual procreation, shades imperceptibly into its second: that confining marriage to opposite-sex couples ensures that children are raised in the 'optimal' setting. Protecting the welfare of children is a paramount State policy. Restricting marriage to opposite-sex couples, however, cannot plausibly further this policy. * * * Moreover, we have repudiated the common-law power of the

State to provide varying levels of protection to children based on the circumstances of birth. The 'best interests of the child' standard does not turn on a parent's sexual orientation or marital status.

"The department has offered no evidence that forbidding marriage to people of the same sex will increase the number of couples choosing to enter into opposite-sex marriages in order to have and raise children. There is thus no rational relationship between the marriage statute and the Commonwealth's proffered goal of protecting the 'optimal' child rearing unit. Moreover, the department readily concedes that people in same-sex couples may be 'excellent' parents. These couples (including four of the plaintiff couples) have children for the reasons others do — to love them, to care for them, to nurture them. But the task of child rearing for same-sex couples is made infinitely harder by their status as outliers to the marriage laws. * * *

"The third rationale advanced by the department is that limiting marriage to opposite-sex couples furthers the Legislature's interest in conserving scarce State and private financial resources. The marriage restriction is rational, it argues, because the General Court logically could assume that same-sex couples are more financially independent than married couples and thus less needy of public marital benefits, such as tax advantages, or private marital benefits, such as employer-financed health plans that include spouses in their coverage.

"An absolute statutory ban on same-sex marriage bears no rational relationship to the goal of economy. First, the department's conclusory generalization — that same-sex couples are less financially dependent on each other than opposite-sex couples — ignores that many same-sex couples, such as many of the plaintiffs in this case, have children and other dependents (here, aged parents) in their care. The department does not contend, nor could it, that these dependents are less needy or deserving than the dependents of married couples. Second, Massachusetts marriage laws do not condition receipt of public and private financial benefits to married individuals on a demonstration of financial dependence on each other; the benefits are available to married couples regardless of whether they mingle their finances or actually depend on each other for support.

"The department suggests additional rationales for prohibiting same-sex couples from marrying, which are developed by some *amici*. It argues that broadening civil marriage to include same-sex couples will trivialize or destroy the institution of marriage as it has historically been fashioned. Certainly our decision today marks a significant change in the definition of marriage as it has been inherited from the common law, and understood by many societies for centuries. But it does not disturb the fundamental value of marriage in our society.

"Here, the plaintiffs seek only to be married, not to undermine the institution of civil marriage. They do not want marriage abolished. They do not attack the binary nature of marriage, the consanguinity provisions, or any of the other gate-keeping provisions of the marriage licensing law. Recognizing the right of an individual to marry a person of the same sex will not diminish the validity or dignity of opposite-sex marriage, any more than recognizing the right of an individual to marry a person of a different race devalues the marriage of a person who marries someone of her own race. If anything, extending civil marriage to same-sex couples reinforces the importance of marriage to individuals and communities. That same-sex couples are willing to embrace marriage's solemn obligations of exclusivity, mutual support, and commitment to one another is a testament to the enduring place of marriage in our laws and in the human spirit.

"* * * Alarms about the imminent erosion of the 'natural' order of marriage were sounded over the demise of antimiscegenation laws, the expansion of the rights of married women, and the introduction of 'no-fault' divorce. Marriage has survived all of these transformations, and we have no doubt that marriage will continue to be a vibrant and revered institution."

In a concurring opinion, **Justice Greaney** concluded that the case should be decided on an equal protection basis; specifically, on the ground that the marriage law discriminated on the basis of sex. In dissent, **Justice Spina** argued that the court should not have resolved the validity of the marriage statute, but left it for the legislature "to effectuate social change without interference from the courts." The second dissent, by **Justice Sosman**, found that the primary basis for the majority's opinion was that the benefits of civil marriage could not be withheld from same-sex couples raising children; she argued that the legislature had a rational basis for limiting those benefits to marital households because marriages were the only environment proven to support healthy child-rearing.

Justice Cordy's dissenting opinion made the marriage-is-for-procreation argument. "As long as marriage is limited to opposite-sex couples who can at least theoretically procreate, society is able to communicate a consistent message to its citizens that marriage is a (normatively) necessary part of their procreative endeavor; that if they are to procreate, then society has endorsed the institution of marriage as the environment for it and for the subsequent rearing of their children; and that benefits are available explicitly to create a supportive and conducive atmosphere for those purposes. If society proceeds similarly to recognize marriages between same-sex couples who cannot procreate, it could be perceived as an abandonment of this claim, and might result in the mistaken view that civil marriage has little to do with procreation: just as the potential of procreation would not be necessary for a marriage to be valid, marriage would not be necessary for optimal procreation and child rearing to occur. In essence, the Legislature could conclude that the consequence of such a policy shift would be a diminution in society's ability to steer the acts of procreation and child rearing into their most optimal setting."

NOTES ON THE MASSACHUSETTS SAME-SEX MARRIAGE CASE

1. *Was There No Rational Basis for the Statutory Discrimination?* By applying rational basis review, the Court avoided thorny questions as to whether sexual orientation is a suspect classification. But that meant that the Court had to find no "rational basis" for the discrimination. All three of the state's arguments rested upon legitimate state goals, but the Court found the classifica-

tion did not closely fit the goal. Consider each reason in light of *Railway Express*, the leading case for rationality review.

(a) The favorable-setting-for-procreation argument was inconsistent with the marriage statutes, which have never made procreation a condition of marriage. But under *Railway Express*, the legislature does not have to tackle the entire problem all at once; it can tackle problems piecemeal, excluding only a portion of couples who do not meet the procreation aspiration.[i]

(b) The optimal-setting-for-childraising argument was not supported by evidence showing that the exclusion of same-sex couples induces more people to enter into and raise children within heterosexual marriages. The Court here is passing over another form of this argument: traditionalists believe that children do not do as well in lesbian or gay households and that the nuclear family of dad-mom-kids is the only one the state should sanction. Could reasonable legislators believe that? The Eleventh Circuit found evidence to that effect when it upheld Florida's exclusion of lesbian, gay, and bisexual adults from adoption in *Lofton v. Secretary of the Dep't of Children & Family Servs.*, 358 F.3d 804 (11th Cir. 2004) (en bac review denied). In any event, *Railway Express* does not require a legislature to prove facts; that "reasonable" legislators could accept facts supporting either form of the argument could suffice. Is this argument unreasonable in that sense?

(c) The economy argument was found to be both over-inclusive (many straight couples do not need the state's support) and under-inclusive (many lesbian and gay couples do need such support). But *Railway Express* upheld an advertising statute that was way under-inclusive (it allowed a lot of diverting ads) and over-inclusive (it banned many ads that would not have been safety hazards).

Obviously, *Goodridge* is not an example of *Railway Express* review. It looks more like *Craig v. Boren* than like *Railway Express* in the kind of scrutiny given to the statute. Like the drinking law in *Craig*, the marriage law in *Goodridge* was defended by reference to valid state goals, but fell because the supporting evidence was weak and the classification seemed driven by stereotypes rather than good policy. So is this really "heightened scrutiny" in disguise? Think about this question, and return to it when you read *Rodriguez*, where Justice Thurgood Marshall suggests a sliding scale approach.

2. *Animus? Or Morality? Goodridge* could be analogized to both *Cleburne* and *Romer*, where so-called "rational basis" review was fatal to statutes with plausible justifications (protecting property values in *Cleburne* and conserving scarce prosecutorial resources in *Romer*). The big difference, however, is that the Court in both *Cleburne* and *Romer* found that the discrimination rested upon "prejudice" against the disabled and anti-gay "animus," respectively. Both cases involved recent regulatory policies that were, the Court found, motivated by exclusion. This explains the bite rational basis review had in those cases.

---

i. For a more sympathetic account of the argument, see Douglas Kmiec, *The Procreative Argument for Proscribing Same-Sex Marriage*, 32 Hastings Const. L.Q. 653 (2004-05).

In contrast, the discrimination in *Goodridge* was longstanding and existed long before society even had a name for "homosexuals." So the case is different. The Chief Justice suggests that the state's second defense rested upon anti-gay stereotypes, but that was not true of the other two. Perhaps she was suggesting that, whatever the original motivations for the different-sex requirement for marriage, it was resistant to change "because of" anti-gay stereotypes and, perhaps, prejudice. Such a move might be defensible, but wouldn't it require a much more elaborate discussion? And is it not credible that many Massachusetts citizens opposed same-sex marriage for genuine religious reasons?

Finally, and most important, the *traditional* reason marriage is limited to different-sex couples is the *noninstrumental* natural law argument: procreative sex between a husband and a wife within marriage is intrinsically good and is the only nondegraded forum for human sexual expression.[j] Because the state did not advance this argument, *amici* did, and it is probably the strongest justification for the marriage exclusion—and a justification that does not sound like prejudice. Should pure moral signaling be sufficient to justify the discrimination under rational basis review?

3. *Amending Constitutions.* On May 17, 2004, as the *Goodridge* mandate required, Massachusetts started issuing marriage licenses to same-sex couples, but a process was already afoot to override the decision by amending the state constitution. Unlike Article V of the U.S. Constitution, the Massachusetts Constitution can be amended by simple majorities — but only through a deliberative process extending over several years. Two successive Legislatures must approve the same new constitutional language, which must then be ratified by a majority of the voters at the next general election. The Legislature deliberated two different amendments between 2004 and 2007 but could not agree on one; the Legislature killed the second amendment, when it failed to achieve support from even one-quarter of the Legislature (50 members).

As this constitutional moment was playing out in Massachusetts, a parallel one was going on in Congress, starting with the Federal Marriage Amendment (FMA) to the U.S. Constitution. The original version of the FMA was introduced in 2003. An amended version (2004) read as follows:

> Marriage in the United States shall consist only of the union of a man and a woman. Neither this Constitution, nor the constitution of any State, shall be construed to require that marriage or the legal incidents thereof be conferred upon any union other than the union of a man and a woman.

The FMA's rationale was to head off "activist judges" from interpreting state constitutions to require same-sex marriage, as was done in Massachusetts. Might it have swept more broadly, for example to preempt "domestic partnership" health and life insurance benefits for lesbian and gay municipal and state employees that were the same as those provided for married straight employees? The FMA and a similar Marriage Protection Amendment both failed to achieve even simple majorities in the Senate in 2004 and 2006.

---

j. E.g., Robert George, *In Defense of Natural Law* (1999); Robert George & Gerard Bradley, *Marriage and the Liberal Imagination*, 84 Geo. L.J. 301 (1995).

Consider the "optimal" process for amending constitutions. Consider the advantages and disadvantages of the Massachusetts amendment process, compared with that in Article V. Note that Canada and most European countries have constitutional amendment processes that are more like those in Massachusetts than Article V. See Donald Lutz, *Toward a Theory of Constitutional Amendment*, in *Responding to Imperfection: The Theory and Practice of Constitutional Amendment* 248-49, 254-67 (Sanford Levinson ed., 1995). Professor Lutz asserts that the Article V process is much too demanding. Are there values that such a demanding process serves? Are they counterbalanced by the greater freedom Article V gives the Supreme Court to create new constitutional rights? (Revisit the cases discussed in Chapters 2 and 3, where there is tremendous constitutional activism by both "conservative" and "liberal" judges.)

NOTE ON RECOGNITION OF LESBIAN AND GAY FAMILIES AFTER THE MASSACHUSETTS MARRIAGE CASE, 2003-2008

Six months after the decision in *Goodridge*, Massachusetts started issuing marriage licenses to same-sex couples, mostly from inside the state. Governor Romney, President Bush, and many religious leaders felt that the beach head for "gay marriage" in Massachusetts would be a national calamity — and many feared that judges from other jurisdictions would deliver gay marriage, against the wishes of state populations that overwhelmingly favored traditional family values. Gay marriage was an issue in the 2004 presidential campaign, and anti-marriage ballot initiatives to amend state constitutions passed in several states. As of June 2008, twenty-six states have amended their state constitutions to bar gay marriages or their recognition (or, in the case of Hawaii, to authorize the legislature to do so). Another fifteen have statutes barring judges from recognizing out-of-state same-sex marriages such as those recognized in Massachusetts. Typically, the campaigns supporting such marriage bars have avoided the excesses of the Colorado Amendment 2 campaign that yielded the family values fiasco in *Romer v. Evans*.[k]

In many of the states without constitutional nonrecognition provisions, lesbian and gay couples brought *Goodridge* lawsuits asserting state constitutional equality and fundamental right to marry claims. Between 2003 and 2007, every state appeals court to address such claims rejected them and upheld same-sex marriage bars.[l] On the one hand, therefore, *Goodridge* seemed to be a dead end. On the other hand, state legislatures were not idle, especially in the Northeast and Pacific Rim regions. Following Vermont's lead, Connecticut, New Jersey, and New Hampshire adopted *civil union* statutes granting all the state benefits and duties of marriage to same-sex couples. In 1999, California's legislature had adopted a *domestic partnership* law conferring some marriage rights to registered

---

k. An up-to-date survey of each state's marriage recognition law can be found on www.lamdbalegal.org.

l. See *Standhardt v. Superior Court*, 77 P.3d 451 (Ariz. App. 2003); *Morrison v. Sadler*, 821 N.E.2d 15 (Ind. App. 2005); *Hernandez v. Robles*, 855 N.E. 2d 1 (N.Y. 2006); *Andersen v. King County*, 138 P.3d 963 (Wash. 2006); *Lewis v. Harris*, 908 A.2d 196 (N.J. 2006) (accepting equality claim but not requiring same-sex marriage); *Conaway v. Deane*, 932 A.2d 571 (Md. 2007).

lesbian and gay couples. In 2003, the legislature expanded the law to cover almost all the rights, benefits, and duties associated with marriage, making the California Domestic Partnership Act essentially the same as the East Coast civil union laws. See also 2006 D.C. Law 16-79 (Act 16-265) (expanding that jurisdiction's domestic partnership law to include almost all the rights and duties of marriage). Oregon followed this approach with its own comprehensive domestic partnership law, 2007 Ore. Laws ch. 99. Maine (2004, 2007) and Washington (2007) adopted statewide *domestic partnership* laws granting only some of the rights and benefits of marriage to registered same-sex partners.

Just as the litigation phase of the marriage equality movement seemed to be winding down, the California Supreme Court decided six same-sex marriage cases on May 18, 2008. That opinion follows. California had a domestic partnership law that gave almost all the rights, benefits, and duties of marriage to registered same-sex couples — but of course not the name. Should this make a constitutional difference? Recall *Loving v. Virginia* (Chapter 3, § 1), as you contemplate the debate in these cases, and note that it is point of great pride for the California Supreme Court that it anticipated *Loving* in its landmark decision in *Perez v. Sharp*, 198 P.2d 17 (1948) (reported as *Perez v. Lippold* in the West reporters; the California judges prefer *Perez v. Sharp*, however).

IN RE MARRIAGE CASES
43 Cal.4th 757, 183 P.3d 384, 76 Cal.Rptr.3d 683 (California Supreme Court, 2008)

[These appeals consolidated six cases where lesbian and gay couples sought recognition of their committed relationships as *marriages*. Since statehood in 1850, California's family law had implicitly limited civil marriage to different-sex relationships. A 1977 statute limited marriage to unions between one man and one woman, and a 2000 initiative reaffirmed the limitation of marriage to different-sex couples and provided that the state would not recognize out-of-state same-sex marriages. Plaintiffs argued that the discrimination against their relationships violated the equality guarantee of the California Constitution. They argued that the discrimination was subject to strict scrutiny for three independent reasons: the exclusion of same-sex couples from state marriage law rested upon two "suspect" classifications, namely, (1) sex and (2) sexual orientation and, moreover, (3) denied those couples a "fundamental" interest in marriage. The excerpt here treats the first two arguments; in an excerpt in Chapter 5, § 4, we treat the fundamental interest argument and its relationship to *Lawrence v. Texas*.]

CHIEF JUSTICE GEORGE delivered the opinion for the Court.

[V. Sex-based classifications have long been subject to strict scrutiny under the California Constitution, see *Sail'er Inn, Inc. v. Kirby,* 5 Cal.3d 1 (1971). The California Supreme Court had not decided what level of scrutiny to apply to sexual orientation classifications.]

[A. The Sex Discrimination Argument.] * * * In drawing a distinction between opposite-sex couples and same-sex couples, the challenged marriage statutes do not treat men and women differently. Persons of either gender are treated equally and are permitted to marry only a person of the opposite gender. In light of the equality of treatment between genders, the distinction prescribed by the relevant statutes plainly does not constitute discrimination on the basis of sex as that concept is commonly understood.

Plaintiffs contend, however, that the statutory distinction nonetheless should be viewed as sex or gender discrimination because the statutory limitation upon marriage in a particular case is dependent upon an individual person's sex or gender. Plaintiffs argue that because a woman who wishes to marry another woman would be permitted to do so if she were a man rather than a woman, and a man who wishes to marry another man would be permitted to do so if he were a woman rather than a man, the statutes must be seen as embodying discrimination on the basis of sex. Plaintiffs rely on the decisions in [*Perez v. Sharp*, 32 Cal.2d 711 (1948)], and *Loving v. Virginia*, in which this court and subsequently the United States Supreme Court found that the antimiscegenation statutes at issue in those cases discriminated on the basis of race, even though the statutes prohibited White persons from marrying Black persons and Black persons from marrying White persons.

The decisions in *Perez* and *Loving v. Virginia*, however, are clearly distinguishable from this case, because the antimiscegenation statutes at issue in those cases plainly treated members of minority races differently from White persons, prohibiting only intermarriage that involved White persons in order to prevent (in the undisguised words of the defenders of the statute in *Perez*) "the Caucasian race from being contaminated by races whose members are by nature physically and mentally inferior to Caucasians." (*Perez*; see also *Loving*.) Under these circumstances, there can be no doubt that the reference to race in the statutes at issue in *Perez* and *Loving* unquestionably reflected the kind of racial discrimination that always has been recognized as calling for strict scrutiny under equal protection analysis.

In *Perez, Loving*, and a number of other decisions (see, e.g., *McLaughlin v. Florida* (1964) 379 U.S. 184, 192), courts have recognized that a statute that treats a couple differently based upon whether the couple consists of persons of the same race or of different races generally reflects a policy disapproving of the integration or close relationship of individuals of different races in the setting in question, and as such properly is viewed as embodying an instance of *racial discrimination* with respect to the interracial couple and both of its members. By contrast, past judicial decisions, in California and elsewhere, virtually uniformly hold that a statute or policy that treats men and women equally but that accords differential treatment either to a couple based upon whether it consists of persons of the same sex rather than opposite sexes, or to an individual based upon whether he or she generally is sexually attracted to persons of the same gender rather than the opposite gender, is more accurately characterized as involving differential treatment on the basis of *sexual orientation* rather than an instance of *sex discrimination*, and properly should be analyzed on the *former* ground. These cases recognize that, in realistic terms, a statute or policy that treats same-sex couples differently from opposite-sex couples, or that treats individuals who are sexually attracted to persons of the same gender differently from individuals who are sexually attracted to persons of the opposite gender, does not treat an individual man or an individual woman differently *because of* his or her *gender* but rather accords differential treatment *because of* the individual's *sexual orientation.* * * *

Although plaintiffs further contend that the difference in treatment prescribed by the relevant statutes should be treated as sex discrimination for equal protection purposes because the differential treatment reflects illegitimate gender-related stereotyping based on the view that men are attracted to women and women are attracted to men, this argument again improperly conflates two concepts — discrimination on the basis of sex, and discrimination on the basis of sexual orientation — that traditionally have been viewed as distinct phenomena. Under plaintiffs' argument, discrimination on the basis of sexual orientation always would constitute a subset of discrimination on the basis of sex. * * *

Accordingly, we conclude that in the context of California's equal protection clause, the differential treatment prescribed by the relevant statutes cannot properly be found to constitute discrimination on the basis of sex, and thus that the statutory classification embodied in the marriage statutes is not subject to strict scrutiny on that ground.

[B. Sexual Orientation Discrimination.] In arguing that the marriage statutes do not discriminate on the basis of sexual orientation, defendants rely upon the circumstance that these statutes, on their face, do not refer explicitly to sexual orientation and do not prohibit gay individuals from marrying a person of the opposite sex. Defendants contend that under these circumstances, the marriage statutes should not be viewed as directly classifying or discriminating on the basis of sexual orientation but at most should be viewed as having a "disparate impact" on gay persons.

In our view, the statutory provisions restricting marriage to a man and a woman cannot be understood as having merely a disparate impact on gay persons, but instead properly must be viewed as directly classifying and prescribing distinct treatment on the basis of sexual orientation. By limiting marriage to opposite-sex couples, the marriage statutes, realistically viewed, operate clearly and directly to impose different treatment on gay individuals because of their sexual orientation. By definition, gay individuals are persons who are sexually attracted to persons of the same sex and thus, if inclined to enter into a marriage relationship, would choose to marry a person of their own sex or gender.[59] A statute that limits marriage to a union of persons of opposite sexes,

---

59.   As explained in the amicus curiae brief filed by a number of leading mental health organizations, including the American Psychological Association and the American Psychiatric Association: "Sexual orientation is commonly discussed as a characteristic of the *individual*, like biological sex, gender identity, or age. This perspective is incomplete because sexual orientation is always defined in relational terms and necessarily involves relationships with other individuals. Sexual acts and romantic attractions are categorized as homosexual or heterosexual according to the biological sex of the individuals involved in them, relative to each other. Indeed, it is by acting — or desiring to act — with another person that individuals express their heterosexuality, homosexuality, or bisexuality. . . . Thus, sexual orientation is integrally linked to the intimate personal relationships that human beings form with others to meet their deeply felt needs for love, attachment, and intimacy. In addition to sexual behavior, these bonds encompass nonsexual physical affection between partners, shared goals and values, mutual support, and ongoing commitment. [¶]

thereby placing marriage outside the reach of couples of the same sex, unquestionably imposes different treatment on the basis of sexual orientation. In our view, it is sophistic to suggest that this conclusion is avoidable by reason of the circumstance that the marriage statutes permit a gay man or a lesbian to marry someone of the opposite sex, because making such a choice would require the negation of the person's sexual orientation. * * *

Having concluded that the California marriage statutes treat persons differently on the basis of sexual orientation, we must determine whether sexual orientation should be considered a "suspect classification" under the California equal protection clause, so that statutes drawing a distinction on this basis are subject to strict scrutiny. * * *

In addressing this issue, the majority in the Court of Appeal stated: "For a statutory classification to be considered 'suspect' for equal protection purposes, generally three requirements must be met. The defining characteristic must (1) be based upon an 'immutable trait'; (2) 'bear[] no relation to [a person's] ability to perform or contribute to society'; and (3) be associated with a 'stigma of inferiority and second class citizenship,' manifested by the group's history of legal and social disabilities. (*Sail'er Inn*.) While the latter two requirements would seem to be readily satisfied in the case of gays and lesbians, the first is more controversial." Concluding that "whether sexual orientation is immutable presents a factual question" as to which an adequate record had not been presented in the trial court, the Court of Appeal ultimately held that "[l]acking guidance from our Supreme Court or decisions from our sister Courts of Appeal," the court would review the marriage statutes under the rational basis, rather than the strict scrutiny, standard.

Past California cases fully support the Court of Appeal's conclusion that sexual orientation is a characteristic (1) that bears no relation to a person's ability to perform or contribute to society, and (2) that is associated with a stigma of inferiority and second-class citizenship, manifested by the group's history of legal and social disabilities. [See *People v. Garcia* (2000) 77 Cal.App.4th 1269, treating lesbians and gay men as a social group like blacks and women that prosecutors could not exclude from juries through peremptory challenges.]

We disagree, however, with the Court of Appeal's conclusion that it is appropriate to reject sexual orientation as a suspect classification, in applying the California Constitution's equal protection clause, on the ground that there is a question as to whether this characteristic is or is not "immutable." Although we noted in *Sail'er Inn* that generally a person's gender is viewed as an immutable trait, immutability is not invariably required in order for a characteristic to be considered a suspect classification for equal protection purposes. California cases establish that a person's religion is a suspect classification for equal protection purposes, and one's religion, of course, is not immutable but is a

---

Consequently, sexual orientation is not merely a personal characteristic that can be defined in isolation. Rather, one's sexual orientation defines the universe of persons with whom one is likely to find the satisfying and fulfilling relationships that, for many individuals, comprise an essential component of personal identity."

matter over which an individual has control. (See also *Raffaelli v. Committee of Bar Examiners* (1972) 7 Cal.3d 288, 292 [alienage treated as a suspect classification notwithstanding circumstance that alien can become a citizen].) Because a person's sexual orientation is so integral an aspect of one's identity, it is not appropriate to require a person to repudiate or change his or her sexual orientation in order to avoid discriminatory treatment.

In his briefing before this court, the Attorney General does not maintain that sexual orientation fails to satisfy the three requirements for a suspect classification discussed by the Court of Appeal, but instead argues that a *fourth* requirement should be imposed before a characteristic is considered a constitutionally suspect basis for classification for equal protection purposes — namely, that "a 'suspect' classification is appropriately recognized only for minorities who are unable to use the political process to address their needs." The Attorney General's brief asserts that "[s]ince the gay and lesbian community in California is obviously able to wield political power in defense of its interests, this Court should not hold that sexual orientation constitutes a suspect classification."

Although some California decisions in discussing suspect classifications have referred to a group's "political powerlessness" (see, e.g., *Raffaelli*), our cases have not identified a group's *current* political powerlessness as a necessary *prerequisite* for treatment as a suspect class. Indeed, if a group's *current* political powerlessness were a prerequisite to a characteristic's being considered a constitutionally suspect basis for differential treatment, it would be impossible to justify the numerous decisions that continue to treat sex, race, and religion as suspect classifications. Instead, our decisions make clear that the most important factors in deciding whether a characteristic should be considered a constitutionally suspect basis for classification are whether the class of persons who exhibit a certain characteristic historically has been subjected to invidious and prejudicial treatment, and whether society now recognizes that the characteristic in question generally bears no relationship to the individual's ability to perform or contribute to society. Thus, "courts must look closely at classifications based on that characteristic lest *outdated* social stereotypes result in invidious laws or practices." (*Sail'er Inn.*) This rationale clearly applies to statutory classifications that mandate differential treatment on the basis of sexual orientation. In sum, we conclude that statutes imposing differential treatment on the basis of sexual orientation should be viewed as constitutionally suspect under the California Constitution's equal protection clause. * * *

There is no persuasive basis for applying to statutes that classify persons on the basis of the suspect classification of sexual orientation a standard less rigorous than that applied to statutes that classify on the basis of the suspect classifications of gender, race, or religion. Because sexual orientation, like gender, race, or religion, is a characteristic that frequently has been the basis for biased and improperly stereotypical treatment and that generally bears no relation to an individual's ability to perform or contribute to society, it is appropriate for courts to evaluate with great care and with considerable skepticism any statute that embodies such a classification. The strict scrutiny standard therefore is applicable to statutes that impose differential treatment on the basis of sexual orientation. * * *

[D.] [I]n circumstances, as here, in which the strict scrutiny standard of review applies, the state bears a heavy burden of justification. In order to satisfy that standard, the state must demonstrate not simply that there is a rational, constitutionally legitimate interest that supports the differential treatment at issue, but instead that the state interest is a *constitutionally compelling* one that justifies the disparate treatment prescribed by the statute in question. Furthermore, unlike instances in which the rational basis test applies, the state does not meet its burden of justification under the strict scrutiny standard merely by showing that the classification established by the statute is rationally or reasonably related to such a compelling state interest. Instead, the state must demonstrate that the distinctions drawn by the statute (or statutory scheme) are *necessary* to further that interest.

[The Chief Justice summarily rejected the argument made by the Proposition 22 Legal Defense Fund that the California Constitution required the Legislature to follow the traditional definition of "marriage" as one man, one woman, as well as the Attorney General's argument that constitutional separation of powers precluded the judiciary from second-guessing legislative policy judgments. The Court gave greater attention to the argument that it ought to defer to the popular judgment, reflected in the Knight Initiative approved by a large majority in 2000, that the state ought to preserve the traditional definition of marriage.]

Although defendants maintain that this court has an obligation to defer to the statutory definition of marriage contained in section 308.5 because that statute — having been adopted through the initiative process — represents the expression of the "people's will," this argument fails to take into account the very basic point that the provisions of the California Constitution itself constitute the ultimate expression of the people's will, and that the fundamental rights embodied within that Constitution for the protection of all persons represent restraints that the people themselves have imposed upon the statutory enactments that may be adopted either by their elected representatives or by the voters through the initiative process. As the United States Supreme Court explained in *West Virginia State Board of Education v. Barnette* (1943) 319 U.S. 624, 638: "The very purpose of a Bill of Rights was to withdraw certain subjects from the vicissitudes of political controversy, to place them beyond the reach of majorities and officials and to establish them as legal principles to be applied by the courts. One's right to life, liberty, and property, to free speech, a free press, freedom of worship and assembly, and other fundamental rights may not be submitted to vote; they depend on the outcome of no elections."

[The Chief Justice then treated the Attorney General's argument that the state had a compelling interest in following the definition of marriage followed almost everywhere else in the United States, and indeed in the world.] Although the understanding of marriage as limited to a union of a man and a woman is undeniably the predominant one, if we have learned anything from the significant evolution in the prevailing societal views and official policies toward members of minority races and toward women over the past half-century, it is that even the most familiar and generally accepted of social practices and traditions often mask an unfairness and inequality that frequently is not recognized or appreciated by those not directly harmed by those practices or traditions. It is instructive to recall in this regard that the traditional, well-established legal rules and practices of our not-so-distant past (1) barred interracial marriage, (2) upheld the routine exclusion of women from many occupations and official duties, and (3) considered the relegation of racial minorities to separate and assertedly equivalent public facilities and institutions as constitutionally equal treatment. As the United States Supreme Court observed in its decision in *Lawrence v. Texas* [Chapter 5, § 4C], the expansive and protective provisions of our constitutions, such as the due process clause, were drafted with the knowledge that "times can blind us to certain truths and later generations can see that laws once thought necessary and proper in fact serve only to oppress." For this reason, the interest in retaining a tradition that excludes an historically disfavored minority group from a status that is extended to all others — even when the tradition is long-standing and widely shared — does not necessarily represent a compelling state interest for purposes of equal protection analysis.

After carefully evaluating the pertinent considerations in the present case, we conclude that the state interest in limiting the designation of marriage exclusively to opposite-sex couples, and in excluding same-sex couples from access to that designation, cannot properly be considered a compelling state interest for equal protection purposes. To begin with, the limitation clearly is not necessary to preserve the rights and benefits of marriage currently enjoyed by opposite-sex couples. Extending access to the designation of marriage to same-sex couples will not deprive any opposite-sex couple or their children of any of the rights and benefits conferred by the marriage statutes, but simply will make the benefit of the marriage designation available to same-sex couples and their children. As Chief Judge Kaye of the New York Court of Appeals succinctly observed in her dissenting opinion in *Hernandez v. Robles*: "There are enough marriage licenses to go around for everyone." Further, permitting same-sex couples access to the designation of marriage will not alter the substantive nature of the legal institution of marriage; same-sex couples who choose to enter into the relationship with that designation will be subject to the same duties and obligations to each other, to their children, and to third parties that the law currently imposes upon opposite-sex couples who marry. Finally, affording same-sex couples the opportunity to obtain the designation of marriage will not impinge upon the religious freedom of any religious organization, official, or any other person; no religion will be required to change its religious policies or practices with regard to same-sex couples, and no religious officiant will be required to solemnize a marriage in contravention of his or her religious beliefs.

While retention of the limitation of marriage to opposite-sex couples is not needed to preserve the rights and benefits of opposite-sex couples, the exclusion of same-sex couples from the designation of marriage works a real and appreciable harm upon same-sex couples and their children. As discussed above, because of the long and celebrated history of the term "marriage" and the widespread understanding that this word describes a family relationship unreservedly sanctioned by the community, the statutory provisions that continue to limit access to this designation exclusively to opposite-sex couples — while providing only a novel, alternative institution for same-sex couples — likely will be viewed as an official statement that the family relationship of same-sex couples is not of comparable stature or equal dignity to the family relationship of opposite-sex couples. Furthermore, because of the historic disparagement of gay persons, the retention of a distinction in nomenclature by which the term "marriage" is withheld only from the family relationship of same-sex couples is all the more likely to cause the new parallel institution that has been established for same-sex couples to be considered a mark of second-class citizenship. Finally, in addition to the potential harm flowing from the lesser stature that is likely to be afforded to the family relationships of same-sex couples by designating them domestic partnerships, there exists a substantial risk that a judicial decision upholding the differential treatment of opposite-sex and same-sex couples would be understood as *validating* a more general proposition that our state by now has repudiated: that it is permissible, under the law, for society to treat gay individuals and same-sex couples differently from, and less favorably than, heterosexual individuals and opposite-sex couples. * * *

[Another portion of **CHIEF JUSTICE GEORGE**'s opinion, discussing the fundamental right to marry, is excepted in Chapter 5, § 4D. We omit the concurring opinion of **JUSTICE KENNARD** as well as the concurring and dissenting opinions of **JUSTICE BAXTER** and **JUSTICE CORRIGAN**. Four Justices joined the opinion for the Court; three dissented.]

NOTES ON THE CALIFORNIA SAME-SEX MARRIAGE CASES

1. *Strict Scrutiny for Sexual Orientation Classifications and Theories of Constitutional Interpretation.* Announcing that sexual orientation classifications ought to be subjected to strict scrutiny, the California Supreme was following the analysis laid out in *Watkins*. What is the precise constitutional theory for these holdings?

(A) *Text and Original Meaning?* Article I, § 7(a) of the California Constitution tracks the Fourteenth Amendment: "A person may not be deprived of life, liberty, or property without due process of law or denied equal protection of the laws * * *." When that Constitution was adopted, California had not only made sodomy a crime, but had also created a separate crime for "oral copulation" between consenting adults and a series of laws targeting "sex perverts" and "degenerates," synonyms in that era for "homosexuals." When California amended its state constitution to render "sex" a suspect classification, in 1972, consensual sodomy and oral copulation were still felonies.

The Chief Justice's rejection of the sex discrimination argument for gay marriage can most easily be justified under an original meaning approach to the California Constitution, because in 1972 supporters of both federal and state ERAs repeatedly rejected claims by ERA opponents that such an amendment would constitutionalize same-sex marriage. See *Singer v. Hara*, 522 P.2d 1187 (Wash. App. 1974) (appeal denied) (thorough examination of rejection of gay marriage arguments by ERA supporters). But original meaning also cuts against expanding the state equal protection clause to make sexual orientation a suspect classification like race (the core equal protection category) and sex (added by a constitutional amendment). Is there any kind of original meaning or textual argument to support the Chief Justice's result?

(B) *Representation-Reinforcement Theory?* Consider Ely's representation-reinforcement theory (Chapter 2, § 3B). The Attorney General made a representation-reinforcement argument *against* strict scrutiny. Conceding that gay people were subject to unfair treatment in the past, the Attorney General argued that they were no longer politically powerless — and so the judiciary ought to leave matters to the political process, the baseline for most constitutional review. The Chief Justice responded that the Attorney General's theory would negate the suspectness of "race, sex, and religion." Not so clear. When the California Supreme Court overruled the state different-race marriage bar in 1948, racial minorities were politically powerless in the state. Sex was rendered suspect by a constitutional amendment, albeit one codifying the state supreme court's holding in *Sail'er Inn*. While mainstream religion is hardly powerless, a representation-reinforcing reason religion is a suspect classification is that *minority religions* like the Jehovah's Witnesses have been and probably remain politically marginalized. Is there a good Elysian argument against the Attorney General's caution in these cases?[m]

(C) *Pragmatic or Common Law Constitutionalism.* Perhaps the Chief Justice's best response rests upon the common law method, whereby law evolves through reasoning by analogy (Chapter 2, § 3B). Sexual orientation is "like" race and sex and religion, the core suspect classifications, and so ought to be suspect as well. On the one hand, though, sexual orientation is *not* like race and sex and religion in all respects. Sexual orientation is more closely tied to particular *conduct* (indeed, conduct that had traditionally been a felony in California) than the other three traits. Moreover, sexual orientation is quite different from race and sex in that it is rarely apparent from outward appearances; "passing" as straight is pretty easy for most gay people. While religion, like sexual orientation, is also not typically apparent to the naked eye, religious identity is closely associated with public conduct (religious worship, holidays, etc.), while sexual identity is closely associated with private conduct. Are these distinctions persuasive? What responses would the Chief Justice have to them?

On the other hand, reasoning by analogy might have slippery slope problems. If sexual orientation is "like" race and religion because it is fundamental to one's identity, as the Chief Justice reasons, then why should other "orientations" not be suspect for similar reasons? How about an exhibitionist orientation as a basis for striking down laws that discriminate against nudity? Weight orientation as a suspect classification for re-examining restrictions for service as a police officer or firefighter? What if one's sexual orientation is toward group sex? Is this also suspect? Would it support a challenge to anti-polygamy laws?

2. *Popular Constitutionalism.* Justice Baxter's dissenting opinion objected that the Court's result not only ran against the state's traditional understanding of the definition of marriage and repeated affirmations of that traditional

---

m. Ely himself believed that *Romer v. Evans* was rightly decided, but not for strict scrutiny reasons: he signed an *amicus* brief arguing that Amendment 2 was a core violation of the Equal Protection Clause because its plain meaning swept away all claims of discrimination and arbitrary treatment by sexual minorities.

understanding in legislative enactments, but also against the will of the people. In 2000, voters by a wide margin passed the Knight Initiative, which added this language to the California Family Code: "Only marriage between a man and a woman is valid or recognized in California." Under the California Constitution, the Legislature could not retract any part of this Knight Initiative without putting the matter to another vote of the people. Justice Baxter suggested that this deepens the countermajoritarian difficulty with the majority's activism. The Chief Justice responded that the Constitution itself is a supermajoritarian expression of the people's will and trumps the Knight Initiative as well as legislated portions of the Family Code.

An *amicus* brief one of us filed in the *Marriage Cases* suggested another response to the countermajoritarian difficulty. The brief recounted the history of state regulation of sexual and gender minorities in California, demonstrating that the Legislature was responsible for decades of oppressive anti-gay measures that reinforced social beliefs that gay people were predatory and anti-family. The only relief came from California court decisions overturning or narrowly construing measures criminalizing homosexual solicitation, cross-dressing, etc. and excluding gay people from teaching positions, as well as decisions affirmatively prohibiting anti-gay discrimination:

> The California Legislature would not have enacted laws accomplishing what this Court * * * did in that period. By protecting sexual minorities, this Court * * * *reversed the burden of inertia*: Did the Legislature or the People really believe gay people were such immediate threats that majorities in both chambers were willing to override the Court? Reversing the burden of inertia also created *conditions for disproving stereotypes.* Popular fears, long fanned by the State, that homosexuals prey on schoolchildren proved unfounded in the wake of [court decisions protecting gay schoolteachers]; myths that homosexuals disrupted workplaces, accepted by the federal as well as state governments, also failed to materialize after [court decisions and an executive order protecting them from job discrimination]. By creating a tolerant space for gay people within the State itself, this Court and the Governor gave gay people opportunities to contribute to public projects, sometimes as openly gay people. That was educational for all concerned.[n]

Less than six months after *The Marriage Cases* were decided, California voters had an opportunity to amend the state constitution to override the Court through a constitutional initiative, Proposition 8, on the November 2008 ballot. Prop 8 stated: "Only marriage between a man and a woman is valid or recognized in California." Unlike the Knight Initiative, however, voters were be able to consider the 2008 initiative in light of some experience with same-sex marriage in their state. On June 17, the state issued the first official marriage licenses to lesbian and gay couples, and no catastrophe has occurred. How could Justice Baxter respond to this argument, that popular opinion is shaped by the state, and the Court was right to give gay marriage a chance? In any event, to the surprise of many observers, the California voters passed Prop 8 by a 52.3-47.7% margin.

---

n. Brief of Professor William N. Eskridge, Jr., as *Amicus Curiae*, at *The Marriage Cases* (California Supreme Court, Case No. S147999).

3. *Social Movements Theory, Incrementalism, and Gay Rights.* The California Court of Appeal, which had denied the marriage claims, worried that the judiciary's legitimacy would be imperiled if courts were too far ahead of public opinion. Inspired by *Perez,* which helped change social norms regarding different-race marriage, the Chief Justice was not as worried, perhaps for the reason suggested by the previous note. In fact, public opinion on the gay marriage issue has been changing in California in the last decade: public disapproval fell from wide to narrow margins, and some polls (June 2008) had suggested that most Californians are not troubled by same-sex marriage, a stunning reversal.

The marriage experience suggests an incrementalist model for social movement influence on public law.[o] An incrementalist model assumes that traditional attitudes or prejudices do not change easily, or perhaps at all, except generationally. This step-by-step process has three features. First, start with the easiest issue, in this instance sodomy reform; some conservative libertarians as well as liberal humanitarians can go along with this reform, and there are strong constitutional arguments for it (even if they did not prevail in *Bowers,* they were more persuasive to a wide array of state judges). Be opportunistic: if judges are unreceptive, turn to legislators or prosecutors for relief. Once sodomy reform is procured, move on to the harder issues, those requiring affirmative government effort or rules, and not just hands-off policies. Even if one victory is preceded by ten defeats, a victory that sticks advances the cause. Success creates both momentum and a feeling of political efficacy, and wins over new political allies.

Second, success also brings more people out of their closets, either as openly gay people or as straight allies. Sodomy reform might embolden more gays to come out of the closet, because they have fewer fears of being arrested; more come out of the closet once anti-discrimination laws protect them against job discrimination. Once more people are openly lesbian or gay, stereotypes can be undermined; officials are more reluctant to demonize gays if they work with openly gay people, or even count them as friends, neighbors, or relatives. State recognition of relationships and child-rearing is most important, for that helps gays come out as families.

Third, each success can discredit opposition, which tends to rely on the same, now-falsifiable stereotyping to oppose each pro-gay move. So a gay-fearful parent who opposes sodomy reform because he or she believes that it will "promote homosexuality" and child abuse may be surprised when there appear to be no malignant effects of sodomy reform. When similar end-of-morality arguments are raised against anti-discrimination laws, some previous skeptics are more persuadable — and even more join them if anti-discrimination laws, too, fail to have the bad effects traditionalists predict. President Clinton's "Defense of Marriage Act" rested upon the silly, and now falsified, assertion that gay marriage was a "threat" to his and other different-sex marriages.

---

o. The account in text is taken from William N. Eskridge, Jr., *Equality Practice: Civil Unions and the Future of Gay Rights* (2002); Kees Waaldijk, *Small Change: How the Road to Same-Sex Marriage Got Paved in The Netherlands,* in *Legal Recognition of Same-Sex Partnerships: A Study of National, European and International Law* (Robert Wintemute & Mads Andenaes eds. 2001).

This "equality practice" model explains why it was safer for judges to require gay marriage in Canada, Massachusetts, and California than in Florida, Ohio, or even New York. Reflect on how a similar equality practice model helps explain the Supreme Court's slow movement from *Brown II*, which allowed school boards broad leeway in moving away from de jure segregation, to *Green*, which required actual and immediate dismantling of dual (race-divided) school systems. How might the equality practice model explain advances in women's rights? People with disabilities?[p]

Equality practice also suggests that reforms such as same-sex marriage ought to be debated at the state level before the U.S. Supreme Court takes a firm position. Indeed, the Supreme Court's decision in *Loving v. Virginia* (1967) was preceded by widespread state abandonment of anti-miscegenation laws. Between *Brown*, when 30 states had such laws, and *Loving,* when only 16 did, equality practice paved the way for the Court to invalidate the remaining southern laws, without significant backlash.[q]

NOTE ON THE SEX DISCRIMINATION ARGUMENT FOR GAY RIGHTS

The "miscegenation analogy" was first offered by Professor Paul Freund as a reason to oppose the ERA: If sex discrimination were forbidden, he told Congress, then states would have to permit same-sex marriage. The reason was that *Loving v. Virginia* held that denying a black/white couple a marriage license is race discrimination because the only variable — the classification — is the race of one partner (the black/black couple got a license). This parallels the state's denial of a marriage license to a woman/woman couple: It is sex discrimination because the only variable — the classification — is the sex of one partner (the woman/man couple get a license). In the late 1980s, Sylvia Law and Andy Koppelman revived this argument in support of gay marriage.[r] It received a big shot in the arm when the Hawaii Supreme Court accepted it as a reason to provide strict scrutiny for the same-sex marriage exclusion in *Baehr v. Lewin*, 852 P.2d 44 (1993).

In response to this argument, the California Supreme Court observed that there is a disconnect among the *classification*, the disadvantaged *class*, and the

---

p. On the greater difficulty of political incrementalism for people with disabilities, see Michael Selmi, *Interpreting the Americans with Disabilities Act: Why the Supreme Court Rewrote the Statute, and Why Congress Did Not Care*, 76 Geo. Wash. L. Rev. 522 (2008).

q. On the interconnections between *Loving* and gay marriage, see Randall Kennedy, *Marriage and the Struggle for Gay, Lesbian, and Black Liberation*, 2005 Utah L. Rev. 781.

r. Sylvia Law, *Homosexuality and the Social Meaning of Gender*, 1988 Wis. L. Rev. 187; Andrew Koppelman, *Why Discrimination Against Lesbians and Gay Men Is Sex Discrimination*, 69 N.Y.U. L. Rev. 197 (1994). For excellent responses, see David Orgon Coolidge, *Playing the* Loving *Card: Same-Sex Marriage and the Politics of Analogy*, 12 BYU L. Rev. 201 (1998); John Gardner, *On the Ground of Her Sex(uality)*, 18 Oxford J. Legal Stud. 167 (1998); Edward Stein, *Evaluating the Sex Discrimination Argument for Lesbian and Gay Rights*, 49 UCLA L. Rev. 471 (2001). Koppelman responds to the critics in *Defending the Sex Discrimination Argument for Lesbian and Gay Rights: A Reply to Edward Stein*, 49 UCLA L. Rev. 519 (2001).

ideology in the same-sex marriage case that does not exist in the different-race marriage case. The difference can be outlined in this way:

	Classification	Disadvantaged Class	Ideology
Loving	race	racial minorities	racism
ERA	sex	women	sexism
Baehr	sex	sexual orientation minorities	compulsory hetero- sexuality

Thus, *Baehr* has a transvestic quality, dressing up gay rights in feminist garb (and, indirectly, in racial garb), and the miscegenation analogy fails. Do Koppelman and Law have a response to this line of thought? Consider the argument that compulsory heterosexuality is one way that culture preserves the rigid gender roles disapproved in the Court's sex discrimination jurisprudence.

NOTE ON INTERSTATE RECOGNITION OF CALIFORNIA AND MASSACHUSETTS MARRIAGES

States routinely recognize marriages celebrated in other states as a matter of state choice of law rules. Since 1993, more than two-thirds of the states have enacted statutes directing their courts not to recognize same-sex marriages from other jurisdictions. E.g., Miss. Code § 93-1-1 (1997): "Any marriage between persons of the same gender is prohibited and null and void from the beginning. Any marriage between persons of the same gender that is valid in another jurisdiction does not constitute a legal or valid marriage in Mississippi." Is this law "sex discrimination" that must be justified by something more than a rational basis? What is its rational basis, under *Romer*?

There may be another basis for challenging these nonrecognition laws. Article IV, § 1 requires each state to give "Full Faith and Credit" to the "public Acts, Records and judicial Proceedings of every other State." Divorces, which are judgments, are accorded full faith and credit, see *Williams v. North Carolina*, 317 U.S. 287 (1942), but marriages are at best only public acts or records, whose full faith and credit status is more ambiguous. What is the purpose of the Full Faith & Credit Clause? Would its purpose be undermined by Mississippi's nonrecognition statute? For an excellent account, see Andrew Koppelman, *Same Sex, Different States: When Same-Sex Marriages Cross State Lines* (2006).

Also in response to the possibility of same-sex marriage, President Clinton and Congress adopted the Defense of Marriage Act ("DOMA"), Pub. L. No. 104-199, 110 Stat. 2419 (1996). DOMA § 2 authorized the states to refuse to recognize marriages "between persons of the same sex" for purposes of the Full Faith and Credit Clause. (Can Congress repeal the Full Faith and Credit Clause? Consult Art. IV, § 1 (second sentence), and compare Am. XIV, § 5, as construed in the cases excerpted in Chapter 7, § 3.) DOMA § 3 said: "In determining the meaning of any Act of Congress * * * the word 'marriage' means only a legal union between one man and one woman as husband and wife, and the word 'spouse' refers only to a person of the opposite sex who is a husband or a wife." For questions about DOMA's constitutionality under *Romer* as well as the Court's sex discrimination jurisprudence, see Andrew Koppelman, *The Gay Rights Question in Contemporary American Law* (2002).

CONCLUDING NOTE ON EQUAL PROTECTION

Having traveled from equal protection review of one tier (rational basis), to two tiers (adding strict scrutiny), to three tiers (adding intermediate scrutiny, most prominently for gender classifications), to four tiers (adding *Cleburne*'s "rational basis with attitude") and possibly beyond (*Evans*), evaluate the utility of "tiered analysis" in this area. What factors explain why judges seem to want tiers of scrutiny? Among other things, presumably the impetus here is to provide predictability and certainty in law, both for the benefit of the citizenry and the lower courts. Are those goals satisfied by the materials you have read? Are there other reasons for the creation and maintenance of the tiered approach? What factors seem to inhibit the success of the approach?

Have we progressed much beyond the obvious: Although equal protection requires the government to treat "similarly situated" people "similarly," the definition and application of the two quoted terms in this phrase are exceedingly difficult and normatively charged? Does this suggest that a return to originalism would be in order, to promote greater predictability and certainty? This chapter demonstrates that originalism has had little impact in the contemporary interpretation of the Equal Protection Clause. Should it?

Finally, consider *Carolene Products* footnote 4 and the "discrete and insular minority" theory. To what extent does this theory explain the presence of the tiers or the outcomes when that approach is applied? Does there remain any necessary relationship between political powerlessness and heightened judicial scrutiny of classifications disadvantaging the group in question? Hasn't increased judicial solicitude actually paralleled the *increase* in political power of the affected group (*Frontiero* and the women's movement, *Evans* and the gay rights movement, and so on)?

Indeed, does the story of this chapter boil down to the lesson that judges will sometimes attempt to promote progress, as viewed by the elite segment of society in which they reside? Recall Justice Scalia's dissenting arguments in the VMI and Colorado initiative cases about the differences in attitude between the "law-trained elite" and the society at large. It's easy, in the abstract, to attack judges as both unauthorized and poorly equipped to be vanguards of social change. Do Chapters 2-4 validate this criticism as a practical matter, or have the judges done pretty well at it, all things considered? Or does this social/political perspective miss important other factors? The next chapter continues the consideration of this problem, but in the context of the identification and enforcement of constitutional rights not easily linked to constitutional text — the most prominent example being *Roe v. Wade*, the landmark abortion decision.

Chapter 5

PROTECTING FUNDAMENTAL RIGHTS

From the right to free speech to the right to bear arms to the right against self-incrimination, the Constitution directly provides a rich mix of rights against governmental intrusion. Other rights are indirectly protected in terms of equal treatment. The Constitution provides no absolute right to vote, for example. But when voting is the method selected for choosing a public official, the vote must be *equally* open to racial minorities as well as whites (the Fifteenth Amendment), to women as well as men (the Nineteenth Amendment), and to those aged eighteen years as well as those who are older (the Twenty-Sixth Amendment).

Yet, there are important interests the Framers did not specifically protect. Nowhere is there any express right to subsistence or education, to engage in intimate personal relationships, or to run for office. Is the Supreme Court precluded from declaring that any such interests have constitutional status? Are other forms of liberty protected by the Constitution? And if so, how? Those questions are the subject of this chapter.

SECTION 1. SHOULD COURTS EVER ENFORCE UNENUMERATED RIGHTS?

Before considering whether specific rights are "fundamental," it behooves us to consider whether courts should ever enforce rights that are not specifically designated in the Constitution. The issue is obviously controversial, and you will have to form your own conclusion. We begin by considering the historical origins of today's "fundamental rights" jurisprudence.

NOTE ON THE HISTORICAL ROOTS OF UNENUMERATED RIGHTS

American thought in the revolutionary period was permeated with natural-rights concepts.[a] The most notable embodiment of this view is the Declaration of Independence itself, which speaks of a right "to life, liberty, and happiness" not because the government granted it, but because all people naturally have it

---

a. For discussion of this history, see Thomas Grey, *Origins of the Unwritten Constitution: Fundamental Law in American Revolutionary Thought*, 30 Stan. L. Rev. 843 (1978).

simply because they are people. Another example is James Otis's argument against the power of Parliament to authorize unreasonable searches:

> As to Acts of Parliament, an Act against the Constitution is void; an Act against natural Equity is void; and if an Act of Parliament should be made, in the very Words of this Petition, it would be void. The Executive Courts must pass such Acts into disuse.

Similarly, in protesting the Stamp Act, the Whigs turned to the courts for support, contending that the act was unconstitutional and therefore void.

Some scholars suggest that this belief in natural law as a judicially enforceable restriction on legislatures persisted into the early nineteenth century.[b] On this view, enforcement of natural rights by courts would not even require a textual basis. Alternatively, the Ninth Amendment might provide such a textual basis for fundamental rights.

There is also some historical evidence that the natural-law tradition influenced the drafters of the Fourteenth Amendment. The idea of "higher law" was deeply embedded in the jurisprudence of the time, particularly in what was then called the "law of nations," a term that included a variety of subjects such as public international law, conflict of laws, and even parts of commercial law.[c] Anti-slavery Republicans, including Abraham Lincoln, placed a great deal of emphasis on the Declaration of Independence, with its natural-law philosophy. Although the legislative history of the Fourteenth Amendment is sparse, there was extensive debate on the closely related Civil Rights Act of 1866, in which fundamental rights figured prominently.[d] For example, Senator Trumbull, in a major speech defending the bill after President Johnson's veto, asserted that

> [t]o be a citizen of the United States carries with it some rights; * * * They are those inherent, fundamental rights which belong to free citizens or free men in all countries, such as the rights enumerated in this bill, and they belong to them in all the States of the Union. The right of American citizenship means something. [Cong. Globe, 39th Cong., 1st Sess. 1757 (1866).]

The fundamental rights idea has also been a recurring theme in Supreme Court decisions. Early nineteenth century decisions by Chief Justice Marshall and others had a strong natural-law tinge. Later in the nineteenth century (and consistently through the present day), the Court has viewed the Due Process Clause as embodying those rights fundamental to citizens in a free country. This formulation received its most notable modern phrasing in Justice Cardozo's opinion in *Palko v. Connecticut*, 302 U.S. 319 (1937) (reprinted in this chapter), which held that the test for incorporation under the Fourteenth Amendment is whether a right found in the Bill of Rights is "implicit in the concept of ordered liberty." As we shall see, this test became the basis for the selective incorporation doctrine, under which most provisions of the Bill of Rights were read into

---

b. See Suzanna Sherry, *The Founders' Unwritten Constitution*, 54 U. Chi. L. Rev. 1127 (1987).

c. See Daniel Farber & Suzanna Sherry, *A History of the Constitution* ch. 9 (1990).

d. Remnants of this statute survive as 42 U.S.C. §§ 1981 and 1982. See *Jones v. Alfred H. Mayer Co.* and accompanying text (Chapter 7, § 3A).

the Due Process Clause of the Fourteenth Amendment and thereby made applicable to state as well as federal action.

It may seem odd that a provision regarding "process" has come to protect "substance." Nevertheless, history seems to have settled that issue. The provisions of the Bill of Rights have been applied to the states by way of the Due Process Clause for many years. The Privileges or Immunities Clause of the Fourteenth Amendment might have provided a more appropriate textual anchor for substantive rights, but the following case seems to have foreclosed that possibility.

———

The Slaughter House Cases, 83 U.S. 36 (1873). A Louisiana law banned slaughter houses within the New Orleans city limits but made an exception for the Crescent City Company, which was thereby essentially given a monopoly. In an opinion by **Justice Miller**, the Supreme Court rejected a broad-gauged attack on the statute brought by New Orleans butchers. One of the butchers' arguments was based on the Privileges or Immunities Clause of the Fourteenth Amendment, which they asserted protected their fundamental right to work at their trade. The Court held, however, that this clause protected only a limited set of national privileges, such as the right of access to federal agencies and the right to use navigable waters.

In limiting the Fourteenth Amendment "P or I Clause" to protecting a limited set of national rights, the Court stressed that the language of the Fourteenth Amendment says that no state shall abridge "the privileges or immunities *of citizens of the United States*." Justice Miller contrasted this language to that found in the Privileges and Immunities Clause of Article IV, which refers to the privileges and immunities of citizens of a state. The Article IV clause had been held to protect nonresidents from discrimination affecting a broad range of significant interests, such as the right to own property or the right to protection by the government. The right to pursue a trade was probably within the range of interests protected by the Article IV clause, but that clause applied only to discrimination against nonresidents. If the same interests were protected by the Fourteenth Amendment against state abridgement, then the effect would be a massive transfer of power to the federal government:

> For not only are these rights subject to the control of Congress whenever in its discretion any of them are supposed to be abridged by State legislation, but that body may also pass laws in advance, limiting and restricting the exercise of legislative power by the States, in their most ordinary and usual functions, as in its judgment it may think proper on all such subjects. And still further, such a construction followed by the reversal of the judgments of the Supreme Court of Louisiana in these cases, would constitute this court a perpetual censor upon all legislation of the States, on the civil rights of their own citizens, with authority to nullify such as it did not approve as consistent with those rights, as they existed at the time of the adoption of this amendment. * * * We are convinced that no such results were intended by the Congress which proposed these amendments, nor by the legislatures of the States which ratified them.

Justice Field, joined by **Chief Justice Chase** and **Justices Swayne** and **Bradley**, argued in dissent for a broad reading of the P or I Clause. What the Article IV clause did to protect citizens against discrimination by other states, "the fourteenth amendment does for the protection of every citizen of the United

States against hostile and discriminating legislation against him in favor of others, whether they reside in the same or in different States." In particular, Field said, "all pursuits, all professions, all avocations are open" to American citizens equally. "The State may prescribe such regulations for every pursuit and calling of life as will promote the public health, secure the good order and advance the general prosperity of society, but when once prescribed, the pursuit or calling must be free to be followed by every citizen who is within the conditions designated, and will conform to the regulations."

NOTES ON THE AFTERMATH OF THE
SLAUGHTER HOUSE CASES

1. *Incorporation and the P or I Clause.* Interestingly, Justice Miller listed among the national privileges and immunities the rights to "peaceably assemble and petition for redress of grievances." Thus, his interpretation left open the possibility that the Bill of Rights might be incorporated into the P or I Clause. There is also some support for this view in the debates on the Fourteenth Amendment — and also support for the view, so emphatically rejected by Justice Miller, that the Fourteenth Amendment clause was meant to protect the same rights as the Article IV clause.[e] For example, in introducing the amendment in the Senate, Senator Howard explained the P or I Clause by reading at length from an opinion broadly construing the Article IV Clause. He then went on to say:

> Such is the character of the privileges and immunities spoken of in the second section of the fourth article of the Constitution. To these privileges and immunities, whatever they may be — for they are not and cannot be fully defined in their entire extent and precise nature — to those should be added the personal rights guaranteed and secured by the first eight amendments of the Constitution [which he then proceeded to list].

2. *The Due Process Clause and the* Slaughter House Cases. After the *Slaughter House Cases*, the P or I Clause became essentially defunct. The decision was less successful, however, in disposing of the Due Process Clause. According to Justice Miller, due process provides only procedural protections — not an unreasonable reading, given the language of the clause. (At least one prominent pre-Fourteenth Amendment case had viewed a state due process clause as providing substantive protection for property, however, so it is conceivable that the Framers of the Fourteenth Amendment did have more than procedural protections in mind.[f]) By the time it decided *Mugler v. Kansas*, 123 U.S. 623 (1887), however, the Court had concluded that due process protects more than procedure — that someone is deprived of their property without due process of *law* if the deprivation is based on an arbitrary legislative fiat.

---

e. See Bryan Wildenthal, *The Lost Compromise: Reassessing the Early Understanding in Court and Congress on Incorporation of the Bill of Rights in the Fourteenth Amendment*, 61 Ohio St. L.J. 1053 (2000); Daniel Farber & Suzanna Sherry, *A History of the American Constitution* ch. 11 (1990); John Harrison, *Reconstructing the Privileges or Immunities Clause*, 101 Yale L.J. 1385 (1992).

f. The state cases are reviewed in Edward Corwin, *The Doctrine of Due Process of Law Before the Civil War*, 24 Harv. L. Rev. 460 (1911).

Some cases raised issues of both substance and procedure. In *Twining v. New Jersey*, 211 U.S. 78 (1908), the Court rejected defendant's claim that the Fifth Amendment's privilege against self-incrimination applies in state criminal proceedings as a matter of due process. The Court's methodology was historicist: Because such rights were not widely recognized at the time of the Fourteenth Amendment, they would not be read into its Due Process Clause.

3. *The Civil Rights Campaign to Save the Lives of Black Defendants.* The NAACP and other civil rights groups deliberately sought to loosen up the *Twining* approach, by showing the Justices that southern trials of black men were mockeries of due process and needed to be monitored. The civil rights strategy was to invoke federal standards as the basis for rights that the Due Process Clause ought to protect in state courts. They were remarkably successful, persuading Justices of all ideologies to recognize due process rights to counsel in capital cases, *Powell v. Alabama*, 287 U.S. 45 (1932); against the use of coerced or involuntary confessions in their trials, *Brown v. Mississippi*, 297 U.S. 278 (1936); and to juries drawn from a cross-section of the community, *Smith v. Texas*, 311 U.S. 128 (1940). These cases, and the dozens of follow-up appeals, left several Supreme Court Justices receptive to the long-rejected idea that the Due Process Clause "incorporates" all or most of the specific guarantees of the Bill of Rights. The Justices debated that issue in the next two cases, the latter of which was another black defendant case.

PALKO v. CONNECTICUT
302 U.S. 319, 58 S.Ct. 149, 82 L.Ed. 288 (1937)

JUSTICE CARDOZO delivered the opinion of the Court.

[Palko had been indicted for first-degree murder. The jury found him guilty of second-degree murder, and he received a life sentence. The state appealed, as allowed by a Connecticut statute, contending that the trial judge had erred in excluding certain evidence and had wrongly instructed the jury on the difference between first-degree and second-degree murder. The Connecticut Supreme Court of Errors agreed with the state and ordered a new trial. Palko objected that a new trial would place him twice in jeopardy for the same offense, which he claimed would violate the Fourteenth Amendment. The state trial court overruled the objection, this time the jury convicted him of first-degree murder, and he was sentenced to death.

[Justice Cardozo assumed that, in a federal prosecution, allowing the appeal and retrial in these circumstances would violate the privilege against double jeopardy found in the Fifth Amendment. The case turned on whether, as Palko claimed, "the Fourteenth Amendment is to be taken as embodying the prohibitions of the Fifth," and more generally whether "[w]hatever would be a violation of the original bill of rights (Amendments I to VIII) if done by the federal government is now equally unlawful by force of the Fourteenth Amendment if done by a state." The Court held that "[t]here is no such general rule," and then continued in the following passages, from which citations to precedent have been removed:]

The Fifth Amendment provides, among other things, that no person shall be held to answer for a capital or otherwise infamous crime unless on presentment or indictment of a grand jury. This court has held that, in prosecutions by a state, presentment or indictment by a grand jury may give way to informations at the instance of a public officer. The Fifth Amendment provides also that no person shall be compelled in any criminal case to be a witness against himself. This court has said that, in prosecutions by a state, the exemption will fail if the state elects to end it. The Sixth Amendment calls for a jury trial in criminal cases and the Seventh for a jury trial in civil cases at common law where the value in controversy shall exceed $20. This court has ruled that consistently with those amendments trial by jury may be modified by a state or abolished altogether. * * *

On the other hand, the due process clause of the Fourteenth Amendment may make it unlawful for a state to abridge by its statutes the freedom of speech which the First Amendment safeguards against encroachment by the Congress or the like freedom of the press, or the free exercise of religion, or the right of peaceable assembly, without which speech would be unduly trammeled, or the right of one accused of crime to the benefit of counsel. In these and other situations immunities that are valid as against the federal government by force of the specific pledges of particular amendments have been found to be implicit in the concept of ordered liberty, and thus, through the Fourteenth Amendment, become valid as against the states.

The line of division may seem to be wavering and broken if there is a hasty catalogue of the cases on the one side and the other. Reflection and analysis will induce a different view. There emerges the perception of a rationalizing principle which gives to discrete instances a proper order and coherence. The right to trial by jury and the immunity from prosecution except as the result of an indictment may have value and importance. Even so, they are not of the very essence of a scheme of ordered liberty. To abolish them is not to violate a "principle of justice so rooted in the traditions and conscience of our people as to be ranked as fundamental." Few would be so narrow or provincial as to maintain that a fair and enlightened system of justice would be impossible without them. What is true of jury trials and indictments is true also, as the cases show, of the immunity from compulsory self-incrimination. This too might be lost, and justice still be done. Indeed, today as in the past there are students of our penal system who look upon the immunity as a mischief rather than a benefit, and who would limit its scope, or destroy it altogether.[g] No doubt there would remain the need to give protection against torture, physical or mental. Justice, however, would not perish if the accused were subject to a duty to respond to orderly inquiry. The exclusion of these immunities and privileges from the privileges and immunities protected against the action of the States has not been arbitrary or casual. It has been dictated by a study and appreciation of the meaning, the essential implications, of liberty itself.

We reach a different plane of social and moral values when we pass to the privileges and immunities that have been taken over from the earlier articles of the Federal Bill of Rights and brought within the Fourteenth Amendment by a

---

g. See, e.g., Bentham, *Rationale of Judicial Evidence*, Book IX, Pt. 4, c.III[.] Compulsory self-incrimination is part of the established procedure in the law of Continental Europe.

process of absorption. These in their origin were effective against the federal government alone. If the Fourteenth Amendment has absorbed them, the process of absorption has had its source in the belief that neither liberty nor justice would exist if they were sacrificed. This is true, for illustration, of freedom of thought and speech. Of that freedom one may say that it is the matrix, the indispensable condition, of nearly every other form of freedom. With rare aberrations a pervasive recognition of that truth can be traced in our history, political and legal. So it has come about that the domain of liberty, withdrawn by the Fourteenth Amendment from encroachment by the states, has been enlarged by latter-day judgments to include liberty of the mind as well as liberty of action. The extension became, indeed, a logical imperative when once it was recognized, as long ago it was, that liberty is something more than exemption from physical restraint, and that even in the field of substantive rights and duties the legislative judgment, if oppressive and arbitrary, may be overridden by the courts. Fundamental too in the concept of due process, and so in that of liberty, is the thought that condemnation shall be rendered only after trial. The hearing, moreover, must be a real one, not a sham or a pretense. For that reason, ignorant defendants in a capital case were held to have been condemned unlawfully when in truth, though not in form, they were refused the aid of counsel. The decision did not turn upon the fact that the benefit of counsel would have been guaranteed to the defendants by the provisions of the Sixth Amendment if they had been prosecuted in a federal court. The decision turned upon the fact that in the particular situation laid before us in the evidence the benefit of counsel was essential to the substance of a hearing.

[The Court concluded that allowing the state to appeal, when a defendant had been acquitted due to a legal error at trial, did not violate any fundamental principle of justice.].

ADAMSON v. CALIFORNIA
332 U.S. 46, 67 S.Ct. 1672, 91 L.Ed. 1903 (1947)

JUSTICE REED delivered the opinion of the Court. [Adamson was convicted of murder in a California court. He challenged the constitutionality of California provisions that allowed the judge and the prosecutor to point out to the jury that he did not testify and thus made no effort to explain or to deny the evidence against him. Justice Reed first assumed that such practices would violate the Fifth Amendment's privilege against self-incrimination if done in federal court.]

* * * Such an assumption does not determine appellant's rights under the Fourteenth Amendment. It is settled law that the clause of the Fifth Amendment, protecting a person against being compelled to be a witness against himself, is not made effective by the Fourteenth Amendment as a protection against state action on the ground that freedom from testimonial compulsion is a right of national citizenship, or because it is a personal privilege or immunity secured by the Federal Constitution as one of the rights of man that are listed in the Bill of Rights. * * *

Appellant secondly contends that if the privilege against self-incrimination is not a right protected by the privileges and immunities clause of the Fourteenth

Amendment against state action, this privilege, to its full scope under the Fifth Amendment, inheres in the right to a fair trial. A right to a fair trial is a right admittedly protected by the due process clause of the Fourteenth Amendment. Therefore, appellant argues, the due process clause of the Fourteenth Amendment protects his privilege against self-incrimination. The due process clause of the Fourteenth Amendment, however, does not draw all the rights of the federal Bill of Rights under its protection. That contention was made and rejected in *Palko*. * * * Nothing has been called to our attention that either the framers of the Fourteenth Amendment or the states that adopted intended its due process clause to draw within its scope the earlier amendments to the Constitution. *Palko* held that such provisions of the Bill of Rights as were "implicit in the concept of ordered liberty" became secure from state interference by the clause. But it held nothing more.

[The Court concluded that, although the Due Process Clause of the Fourteenth Amendment forbade compulsion to testify through torture or other coercion, the California procedure at issue here did not violate "the concept of ordered liberty." The Court was impressed that the California procedure did not compel the jury to find guilt or even create a rebuttable presumption of guilt, but merely "was a method for advising the jury in the search for truth."]

JUSTICE FRANKFURTER, concurring.

Between the incorporation of the Fourteenth Amendment into the Constitution and the beginning of the present membership of the Court — a period of 70 years — the scope of that Amendment was passed upon by 43 judges. Of all these judges, only one, who may respectfully be called an eccentric exception, ever indicated the belief that the Fourteenth Amendment was a shorthand summary of the first eight Amendments theretofore limiting only the Federal Government, and that due process incorporated those eight Amendments as restrictions upon the powers of the States. Among these judges were not only those who would have to be included among the greatest in the history of the Court, but — it is especially relevant to note — they included those whose services in the cause of human rights and the spirit of freedom are the most conspicuous in our history. It is not invidious to single out Miller, Davis, Bradley, Waite, Matthews, Gray, Fuller, Holmes, Brandeis, Stone and Cardozo (to speak only of the dead) as judges who were alert in safeguarding and promoting the interests of liberty and human dignity through law. But they were also judges mindful of the relation of our federal system to a progressively democratic society and therefore duly regardful of the scope of authority that was left to the States even after the Civil War. And so they did not find that the Fourteenth Amendment, concerned as it was with matters fundamental to the pursuit of justice, fastened upon the States procedural arrangements which, in the language of Mr. Justice Cardozo, only those who are "narrow or provincial" would deem essential to "a fair and enlightened system of justice." *Palko*. To suggest that it is inconsistent with a truly free society to begin prosecutions without an indictment, to try petty civil cases without the paraphernalia of a common law jury, to take into consideration that one who has full opportunity to make a defense remains silent is, in de Tocqueville's phrase, to confound the familiar with the necessary. * * *

A construction which gives to due process no independent function but turns it into a summary of the specific provisions of the Bill of Rights would, as has been noted, tear up by the roots much of the fabric of law in the several States, and would deprive the States of opportunity for reforms in legal process designed for extending the area of freedom. It would assume that no other abuses would reveal themselves in the course of time than those which had become manifest in 1791. Such a view not only disregards the historic meaning of "due process." It leads inevitably to a warped construction of specific provisions of the Bill of Rights to bring within their scope conduct clearly condemned by due process but not easily fitting into the pigeon-holes of the specific provisions. It seems pretty late in the day to suggest that a phrase so laden with historic meaning should be given an improvised content consisting of some but not all of the provisions of the first eight Amendments, selected on an undefined basis, with improvisation of content for the provisions so selected.

And so, when, as in a case like the present, a conviction in a State court is here for review under a claim that a right protected by the Due Process Clause of the Fourteenth Amendment has been denied, the issue is not whether an infraction of one of the specific provisions of the first eight Amendments is disclosed by the record. The relevant question is whether the criminal proceedings which resulted in conviction deprived the accused of the due process of law to which the United States Constitution entitled him. Judicial review of that guaranty of the Fourteenth Amendment inescapably imposes upon this Court an exercise of judgment upon the whole course of the proceedings in order to ascertain whether they offend those canons of decency and fairness which express the notions of justice of English-speaking peoples even toward those charged with the most heinous offenses. These standards of justice are not authoritatively formulated anywhere as though they were prescriptions in a pharmacopoeia. But neither does the application of the Due Process Clause imply that judges are wholly at large. The judicial judgment in applying the Due Process Clause must move within the limits of accepted notions of justice and is not to be based upon the idiosyncrasies of a merely personal judgment. The fact that judges among themselves may differ whether in a particular case a trial offends accepted notions of justice is not disproof that general rather than idiosyncratic standards are applied. An important safeguard against such merely individual judgment is an alert deference to the judgment of the State court under review.

JUSTICE BLACK, dissenting.

* * * I am attaching to this dissent, an appendix which contains a resume, by no means complete, of the Amendment's history. In my judgment that history conclusively demonstrates that the language of the first section of the Fourteenth Amendment, taken as a whole, was thought by those responsible for its submission to the people, and by those who opposed its submission, sufficiently explicit to guarantee that thereafter no state could deprive its citizens of the privileges and protections of the Bill of Rights. Whether this Court ever will, or whether it now should, in the light of past decisions, give full effect to what the Amendment was intended to accomplish is not necessarily essential to a decision here. However that may be, [prior decisions] do not prevent our

carrying out that purpose, at least to the extent of making applicable to the states, not a mere part, as the Court has, but the full protection of the Fifth Amendment's provision against compelling evidence from an accused to convict him of crime. And I further contend that the "natural law" formula which the Court uses to reach its conclusion in this case should be abandoned as an incongruous excrescence on our Constitution. I believe that formula to be itself a violation of our Constitution, in that it subtly conveys to courts, at the expense of legislatures, ultimate power over public policies in fields where no specific provision of the Constitution limits legislative power. * * *

[Justice Black here contended that the Court had subverted the Fourteenth Amendment in two ways. First, in decisions such as *Lochner v. New York* (§ 2B of this chapter)], it held that "the Fourteenth Amendment guarantees the liberty of all persons under 'natural law' to engage in their chosen business or vocation." Justice Black considered this an unjustified expansion of the Fourteenth Amendment, which he believed was not designed to interfere with state regulation of property rights or business practices. Second, the Court imported this natural law/balancing approach to decide cases involving alleged state infringement of "individual liberties enumerated in the Bill of Rights," such as in *Twining* and the present case. This, Justice Black contended, was an unjustified contraction of the Fourteenth Amendment that made cases turn on "this Court's notions of 'civilized standards,' 'canons of decency,' and 'fundamental justice[.]' " (Quoting precedents). Justice Black also noted that, despite the language of precedent suggesting that reliance upon the Bill of Rights was precluded in deciding what "due process" meant in the Fourteenth Amendment, in a series of cases the Court had already held that the following rights were "fundamental" and therefore applicable to the states through the Fourteenth Amendment: right to counsel in some criminal cases; freedom of assembly; the rights to be free from certain kinds of cruel and unusual punishment and from double jeopardy; the right of a criminal defendant to be informed of the charge against him; the right to just compensation when private property is taken for public use; and First Amendment guarantees generally.]

I cannot consider the Bill of Rights to be an outworn 18th Century "strait jacket" * * *. Its provisions may be thought outdated abstractions by some. And it is true that they were designed to meet ancient evils. But they are the same kind of human evils that have emerged from century to century wherever excessive power is sought by the few at the expense of the many. In my judgment the people of no nation can lose their liberty so long as a Bill of Rights like ours survives and its basic purposes are conscientiously interpreted, enforced and respected so as to afford continuous protection against old, as well as new, devices and practices which might thwart those purposes. I fear to see the consequences of the Court's practice of substituting its own concepts of decency and fundamental justice for the language of the Bill of Rights as its point of departure in interpreting and enforcing that Bill of Rights. * * * I would follow what I believe was the original purpose of the Fourteenth Amendment — to extend to all the people of the nation the complete protection of the Bill of Rights. To hold that this Court can determine what, if any, provisions of the Bill of Rights will be enforced, and if so to what degree, is to frustrate the great design of a written Constitution.

JUSTICE DOUGLAS joins in this opinion.

[The appendix to Justice Black's dissent, in which he made his historical argument about the original meaning of the Fourteenth Amendment, is not excerpted, but is discussed in the notes following this case.]

JUSTICE MURPHY, with whom **JUSTICE RUTLEDGE** concurs, dissenting.

While in substantial agreement with the views of Justice Black, I have one reservation and one addition to make.

I agree that the specific guarantees of the Bill of Rights should be carried over intact into the first section of the Fourteenth Amendment. But I am not prepared to say that the latter is entirely and necessarily limited by the Bill of Rights. Occasions may arise where a proceeding falls so far short of conforming to fundamental standards of procedure as to warrant constitutional condemnation in terms of a lack of due process despite the absence of a specific provision in the Bill of Rights.

That point, however, need not be pursued here inasmuch as the Fifth Amendment is explicit in its provision that no person shall be compelled in any criminal case to be a witness against himself. That provision, as Justice Black demonstrates, is a constituent part of the Fourteenth Amendment. * * *

NOTES ON THE INCORPORATION DEBATE

1. *Justice Black's Historical Argument.* Justice Black's dissent touched off a substantial scholarly dispute about whether he accurately described the intentions of the Framers of the Fourteenth Amendment.[h] Suffice it to say that the scholars are still divided and that the Supreme Court never accepted Justice Black's theory as a matter of constitutional interpretation.

Consider Justice Black's best evidence, contained in a speech by Senator Howard presenting to the Senate the joint resolution proposing the Fourteenth Amendment. Senator Howard said that, under the proposed amendment, "privileges and immunities" included whatever rights were secured by the Privileges and Immunities Clause of Article IV of the original Constitution. He then continued:

> * * * [T]o these should be added the personal rights guaranteed and secured by the first eight amendments of the Constitution; such as the freedom of speech and of the press; the right of the people peaceably to assemble and petition the Government for a redress of grievances, a right appertaining to each and all the people; the right to keep and to bear arms; the right to be exempted from the quartering of soldiers in a house without the consent of the owner; the right to be exempt from unreasonable searches and seizures, and from any search or seizure except by virtue of a warrant

---

h. See Charles Fairman, *Does the Fourteenth Amendment Incorporate the Bill of Rights? The Original Understanding,* 2 Stan. L. Rev. 5 (1949), for arguments by a leading historian that the Due Process Clause does not incorporate the Bill of Rights. For a critique of Fairman's analysis, see Richard Aynes, *On Misreading John Bingham and the Fourteenth Amendment,* 103 Yale L.J. 57, 61 (1993) (arguing that Fairman "misread critical sources, relied on information taken out of context, ignored important contemporary materials, and buttressed his argument with a flawed legal theory").

issued upon a formal oath or affidavit; the right of an accused person to be informed of the nature of the accusation against him, and his right to be tried by an impartial jury of the vicinage; and also the right to be secure against excessive bail and against cruel and unusual punishments.

How much weight should be given to Howard's statement? Black's critics suggest that (a) Senator Howard was not a key player in formulating the Fourteenth Amendment (he presented the proposal because the Senate chairman of the joint committee was ill); (b) such a major proposal as full incorporation would have been discussed and debated frequently and thoroughly (which it wasn't); and (c) subsequent congressional practice was inconsistent with incorporation (Congress admitted some states whose constitutions did not embody all Bill of Rights protections, and Congress considered some federal constitutional amendments that would have been superfluous had full incorporation been encompassed within the Fourteenth Amendment).

2. *The Judicial Reception of Incorporation.* As *Adamson* indicates, *The Slaughter House Cases* are usually read as rejecting the argument that the P or I Clause of the Fourteenth Amendment incorporates Bill of Rights guarantees. Even though the Supreme Court never accepted Justice Black's argument, it has accomplished much the same thing by essentially incorporating the important protections of the Bill of Rights on a case-by-case basis. This so-called "selective incorporation" technique, which Justice Black disparaged in *Adamson*, asked the Court to consider whether the Bill of Rights guarantee in question was "fundamental." In the 1960s especially, the Supreme Court incorporated into the Due Process Clause virtually all of the provisions of the Bill of Rights.[i] Along the way the Court modified its incorporation inquiry from whether the right was "implicit in the concept of ordered liberty" (*Palko*) to whether it was "fundamental to the American scheme of justice" (*Duncan v. Louisiana*, 391 U.S. 145 (1968)) — a change that shifted the focus from whether the right was necessary in any system of democratic government to whether it was important in American society. See Jerold Israel, *Selective Incorporation Revisited*, 71 Geo. L.J. 253 (1982). See also William Eskridge, Jr., *Some Effects of Identity-Based Social Movements on Constitutional Law in the Twentieth Century*, 100 Mich. L. Rev. 2062 (2002) (continuing role of the race cases in

---

i. In particular: the Fourth Amendment right to be free from unreasonable searches and seizures, *Mapp v. Ohio*, 367 U.S. 643 (1961); the Fifth Amendment right against self-incrimination, *Griffin v. California*, 380 U.S. 609 (1965), and *Malloy v. Hogan*, 378 U.S. 1 (1964) (overruling *Adamson*), and its prohibition against double jeopardy, *Benton v. Maryland*, 395 U.S. 784 (1969) (overruling *Palko*); the Sixth Amendment rights to counsel, *Gideon v. Wainwright*, 372 U.S. 335 (1963), to a speedy and public trial, *Klopfer v. North Carolina*, 386 U.S. 213 (1967), to confrontation of opposing witnesses, *Pointer v. Texas*, 380 U.S. 400 (1965), to compulsory process for obtaining witnesses, *Washington v. Texas*, 388 U.S. 14 (1967), and to a jury trial in criminal cases, *Duncan v. Louisiana*, 391 U.S. 145 (1968); and the Eighth Amendment prohibitions against cruel and unusual punishment, *Robinson v. California*, 370 U.S. 660 (1962), and excessive bail, *Schilb v. Kuebel*, 404 U.S. 357 (1971). (Well before *Adamson*, the First Amendment rights of free speech, press, and religion and the Fifth Amendment right to just compensation had been applied to the states through the Due Process Clause.) Today, the few Bill of Rights guarantees that have not been applied to the states include the Second Amendment guarantee of a right to bear arms, the Fifth Amendment requirement of grand-jury indictment for major crimes, and the Seventh Amendment right to jury trial in civil cases.

creating a national code of criminal procedure). Under this test, is the Second Amendment incorporated?

3. *"Incorporation Plus."* Justice Murphy in *Adamson* believed that the Due Process Clause of the Fourteenth Amendment could be *broader* than the original Bill of Rights. Later in this chapter, we will trace developments along these lines that, ironically, flowed in part from the *Palko* formulation about values "implicit in the concept of ordered liberty." As originally conceived, this standard was a way to avoid applying to the states certain rights that the Bill of Rights provided against federal action. But because of the way it was phrased, this standard is not necessarily linked to the Bill of Rights — anything sufficiently important, whether recognized as such by the Bill of Rights, would seem to qualify.

SKINNER v. OKLAHOMA ex rel. WILLIAMSON
316 U.S. 535, 62 S.Ct. 1110, 86 L.Ed. 1655 (1942)

JUSTICE DOUGLAS delivered the opinion of the Court.

This case touches a sensitive and important area of human rights. Oklahoma deprives certain individuals of a right which is basic to the perpetuation of a race — the right to have offspring. * * *

[Oklahoma's Habitual Criminal Sterilization Act] defines an "habitual criminal" as a person who, having been convicted two or more times for crimes "amounting to felonies involving moral turpitude," either in an Oklahoma court or in a court of any other State, is thereafter convicted of such a felony in Oklahoma and is sentenced to a term of imprisonment in an Oklahoma penal institution. Machinery is provided for the institution by the Attorney General of a proceeding against such a person in the Oklahoma courts for a judgment that such person shall be rendered sexually sterile. Notice, an opportunity to be heard, and the right to a jury trial are provided. The issues triable in such a proceeding are narrow and confined. If the court or jury finds that the defendant is an "habitual criminal" and that he "may be rendered sexually sterile without detriment to his or her general health," then the court "shall render judgment to the effect that said defendant be rendered sexually sterile" by the operation of vasectomy in case of a male, and of salpingectomy in case of a female. [The Act] provides that "offenses arising out of the violation of the prohibitory laws, revenue acts, embezzlement, or political offenses, shall not come or be considered within the terms of this Act."

[Between 1926-34, Skinner had been convicted twice for robbery with firearms and once for stealing chickens.] In 1936 the Attorney General instituted proceedings against him. Petitioner in his answer challenged the Act as unconstitutional by reason of the Fourteenth Amendment. A jury trial was had. The court instructed the jury that the crimes of which petitioner had been convicted were felonies involving moral turpitude, and that the only question for the jury was whether the operation of vasectomy could be performed on petitioner without detriment to his general health. The jury found that it could be. A judgment directing that the operation of vasectomy be performed on petitioner was affirmed by the Supreme Court of Oklahoma by a five to four decision.

Several objections to the constitutionality of the Act have been pressed upon us. It is urged that the Act cannot be sustained as an exercise of the police power, in view of the state of scientific authorities respecting inheritability of criminal traits. It is argued that due process is lacking because, under this Act, unlike the Act upheld in *Buck v. Bell*, 274 U.S. 200 [1927], the defendant is given no opportunity to be heard on the issue as to whether he is the probable potential parent of socially undesirable offspring. It is also suggested that the Act is penal in character and that the sterilization provided for is cruel and unusual punishment and violative of the Fourteenth Amendment. We pass those points without intimating an opinion on them, for there is a feature of the Act which clearly condemns it. That is, its failure to meet the requirements of the equal protection clause of the Fourteenth Amendment.

We do not stop to point out all of the inequalities in this Act. A few examples will suffice. In Oklahoma, grand larceny is a felony. Larceny is grand larceny when the property taken exceeds $20 in value. Embezzlement is punishable "in the manner prescribed for feloniously stealing property of the value of that embezzled." Hence, he who embezzles property worth more than $20 is guilty of a felony. A clerk who appropriates over $20 from his employer's till and a stranger who steals the same amount are thus both guilty of felonies. If the latter repeats his act and is convicted three times, he may be sterilized. But the clerk is not subject to the pains and penalties of the Act no matter how large his embezzlements nor how frequent his convictions. * * * [T]he nature of the two crimes is intrinsically the same and they are punishable in the same manner. Furthermore, the line between them follows close distinctions. * * *[j]

It was stated in *Buck v. Bell, supra*, that the claim that state legislation violates the equal protection clause of the Fourteenth Amendment is "the usual last resort of constitutional arguments." Under our constitutional system the States in determining the reach and scope of particular legislation need not provide "abstract symmetry." * * * Thus, if we had here only a question as to a State's classification of crimes, such as embezzlement or larceny, no substantial federal question would be raised. * * *

But * * * [w]e are dealing here with legislation which involves one of the basic civil rights of man. Marriage and procreation are fundamental to the very existence and survival of the race. The power to sterilize, if exercised, may have subtle, far-reaching and devastating effects. In evil or reckless hands it can cause races or types which are inimical to the dominant group to wither and disappear. There is no redemption for the individual whom the law touches. Any experiment which the State conducts is to his irreparable injury. He is forever deprived of a basic liberty. We mention these matters not to reexamine

---

j. *Editors' note*: One "close distinction" noted by Justice Douglas was that under Oklahoma law an employee who receives personal property intended for his employer but converts the property for his own use commits larceny by fraud if at the time of receipt he intended to convert the property, but is guilty of embezzlement if his intent to convert arises later. "Whether a particular act is larceny by fraud or embezzlement thus turns not on the intrinsic quality of the act but on when the felonious intent arose[.]"

the scope of the police power of the States. We advert to them merely in emphasis of our view that strict scrutiny of the classification which a State makes in a sterilization law is essential, lest unwittingly, or otherwise, invidious discriminations are made against groups or types of individuals in violation of the constitutional guaranty of just and equal laws. The guaranty of "equal protection of the laws is a pledge of the protection of equal laws." *Yick Wo v. Hopkins* [Chapter 3, § 1B]. When the law lays an unequal hand on those who have committed intrinsically the same quality of offense and sterilizes one and not the other, it has made as invidious a discrimination as if it had selected a particular race or nationality for oppressive treatment. Sterilization of those who have thrice committed grand larceny, with immunity for those who are embezzlers, is a clear, pointed, unmistakable discrimination. Oklahoma makes no attempt to say that he who commits larceny by trespass or trick or fraud has biologically inheritable traits which he who commits embezzlement lacks. Oklahoma's line between larceny by fraud and embezzlement is determined "with reference to the time when the fraudulent intent to convert the property to the taker's own use" arises. We have not the slightest basis for inferring that that line has any significance in eugenics, nor that the inheritability of criminal traits follows the neat legal distinctions which the law has marked between those two offenses. In terms of fines and imprisonment, the crimes of larceny and embezzlement rate the same under the Oklahoma code. Only when it comes to sterilization are the pains and penalties of the law different. The equal protection clause would indeed be a formula of empty words if such conspicuously artificial lines could be drawn. * * *

[The concurring opinions of **CHIEF JUSTICE STONE** and **JUSTICE JACKSON** are omitted.]

NOTES ON *SKINNER* AND PROTECTING IMPLIED FUNDAMENTAL RIGHTS

1. *Equal Protection.* Is *Skinner*'s approach at all similar to any you have seen in earlier equal protection cases? This doesn't seem to be the normal rational basis test, or even the *Cleburne* version of that test (Chapter 4, § 3C). Regarding issues of empirical uncertainty, such as whether certain behavioral traits are inherited, it matters a good deal whether the Court adopts a rational-basis test (under which the factual basis for the regulation is presumed, with plaintiff bearing the burden of demonstrating the contrary) or some form of higher scrutiny (which has the effect of shifting the burden of justification to the state). Since proof either way is probably not available, the standard of review essentially dictates the outcome.

2. *Examining the Potential Theories in* Skinner. In this chapter, we will discuss some cases after *Skinner* involving voting and education, in which the Court has based its recognition of an implied fundamental right upon the Equal Protection Clause. This chapter also considers the alternative theory of substantive due process and concludes with some consideration of procedural due process. As in *Skinner*, in the other cases in this chapter there might be an explicit constitutional right — like the right to be free from "cruel and unusual punishment" — that could be invoked. In each instance, sort out how the

potential theories might apply. For example, had *Skinner* been decided on cruel and unusual punishment grounds, could it have any bearing on whether a state might sterilize mentally retarded adults who reside in state institutions? Does the actual holding in *Skinner* prevent a state from sterilizing such persons? How would you make a "substantive due process" or "procedural due process" argument against such a state practice concerning such developmentally disabled adults?

A WORLD WITHOUT IMPLIED FUNDAMENTAL RIGHTS: A NOTE ON THE SOCIAL CONTEXT OF *BUCK v. BELL* AND *SKINNER*

It is easy to indict *Skinner* and other fundamental rights cases as exercises in improper judicial activism. Consider the facts of *Skinner*. Can the result be justified under any approach we have mentioned to the problem of judicial review? Reconsider your answer after considering the following.

In the early part of the twentieth century, state legislatures embraced the notion that compulsory sterilization was an appropriate strategy to rid our society of "defective people." Although today the idea seems repulsive, for many people prior to World War II it seemed like a progressive reform.[k] *Buck v. Bell*, 274 U.S. 200 (1927), cited in *Skinner*, lent legitimacy to the practice. Justice Holmes' opinion for the Court upheld a Virginia statute that established a process for the sterilization of mentally retarded persons in state institutions. The statute was based on the assumptions that developmental disability is inheritable; that reproduction by such adults is against society's interests; and that if sterilized some of these persons could be discharged from state institutions and, free from state supervision, could become self-supporting contributors to society. The state invoked the statute against Carrie Buck, an institutionalized woman. According to findings made by the state trial court, Ms. Buck was retarded, and both her mother and her illegitimate child were likewise retarded. Because the Virginia practice allowed some procedural protections before

---

k. See generally Daniel Kevles, *In the Name of Eugenics: Genetics and the Uses of Human Heredity* (1985). Consider Stephen Jay Gould, *Carrie Buck's Daughter*, 2 Const. Comm. 331, 332 (1985):

The movement for compulsory sterilization began in earnest during the 1890s, abetted by two major factors — the rise of eugenics as an influential political movement and the perfection of safe and effective operations * * * to replace castration and other obvious mutilation. Indiana passed the first sterilization act based on eugenic principles in 1907. * * * Like so many others to follow, it provided for sterilization of afflicted people residing in the state's "care," either as inmates of mental hospitals and homes for the feebleminded or as inhabitants of prisons. Sterilization could be imposed upon those judged insane, idiotic, imbecilic, or moronic, and upon convicted rapists or criminals when recommended by a board of experts.

By the 1930s, more than thirty states had passed similar laws, often with an expanded list of so-called hereditary defects, including alcoholism and drug addiction in some states, and even blindness and deafness in others. It must be said that these laws were continually challenged and rarely enforced in most states; only California and Virginia applied them zealously. By January 1935, some 20,000 forced "eugenic" sterilizations had been performed in the United States, nearly half in California.

sterilization could be performed, Buck argued that the statute was unconstitutional only because it intruded into her bodily integrity in violation of substantive due process and, in applying only to institutionalized persons, the statute was so underinclusive as to violate equal protection.

Justice Holmes dismissed both arguments in his characteristically pithy way. Finding a sufficient state interest in promoting the public welfare to justify the statute against substantive due process attack, Justice Holmes relied upon *Jacobson v. Massachusetts*, 197 U.S. 11 (1905), which upheld a state law requiring people to submit to vaccination against infectious disease. Justice Holmes said:

> It is better for all the world, if instead of waiting to execute degenerate offspring for crime, or to let them starve for their imbecility, society can prevent those who are manifestly unfit from continuing their kind. The principle that sustains compulsory vaccination is broad enough to cover cutting the Fallopian tubes. *Jacobson*. Three generations of imbeciles are enough.

Turning to Buck's second contention, Justice Holmes labeled the Equal Protection Clause "the usual last resort of constitutional arguments" and said that "the answer is that the law does all that is needed when it does all that it can, indicates a policy, applies it to all within the lines, and seeks to bring within the lines all similarly situated so far and so fast as its means allow."

As Chapters 2-4 indicate, the Equal Protection Clause has become far more than the constitutional doormat it was in Justice Holmes' day. But note that Holmes may have been right in *Buck v. Bell* if, as many commentators believe, the Court should never create a right that cannot be directly supported by constitutional language and history. These sources of constitutional meaning might well provide the Due Process Clause no role beyond guaranteeing notice and the opportunity to be heard before liberty or property can be deprived by a state, and the Virginia statute did include such procedural protections. If the Constitution allows a state to sterilize persons who have undesirable inheritable traits, then the Equal Protection Clause, under rational basis review, provides no barrier when the state implements the policy on those most easily accessible — those within state institutions. Moreover, as Holmes pointed out, these sterilized persons can then be released into society, increasing their liberty and making room in the institutions for others.[1] A rational basis for the Virginia statute is thus easily invoked, and there is no obvious way to obtain heightened equal protection scrutiny — the statute was not aimed at racial minorities (Carrie Buck was white, for example) or women (lots of men were sterilized as well). Recall that even today *Cleburne* (Chapter 4, § 3C) stands for the proposition that statutes disadvantaging people with mental disabilities are subject only to rational basis review.

---

1. Influenced no doubt by the social Darwinism of his time, Holmes said this in contemporary correspondence: "I wrote and delivered a decision [*Buck v. Bell*] upholding the constitutionality of a state law for sterilizing imbeciles the other day — and felt that I was getting near to the first principle of real reform." Letter to Harold Laski of May 12, 1927, in 2 *Holmes-Laski Letters* 942 (Mark DeWolfe Howe ed. 1953).

Buried beneath the constitutional theory operating in *Buck v. Bell* are tragic facts that remained hidden for a half-century [see Gould, *supra*]. In 1980, a Virginia official found Carrie Buck still alive, living near Charlottesville with her sister Doris, who had also been sterilized (she had been told that the operation was for appendicitis). Carrie Buck was found to be a woman of normal intelligence. She had been shunted off to the state institution by her foster parents when she became pregnant (apparently the result of rape by a relative of her foster parents). The only evidence presented at her commitment hearing came from her foster parents. Later, she and her mother were administered an IQ test, which purported to show that both were "retarded." During the trial on whether Carrie Buck could be sterilized, the only evidence put forward concerning the supposed retardation of her daughter — who at that time was *seven months old* — came from a social worker who said that "there is a look about [the baby] that is not quite normal, but just what it is, I can't tell." The daughter later received adequate grades in elementary school before dying at the age of eight from an illness.

The compulsory sterilization movement, as exposed by the real facts of *Buck v. Bell*, was concerned essentially with eliminating the genes of "the most worthless one-tenth of our present population," to use the language of the movement's leader, Harry Laughlin. Indeed, Laughlin's report on the Buck family, used in the litigation, began: "These people belong to the shiftless, ignorant, and worthless class of anti-social whites of the South." According to Stephen Jay Gould, the case really stands for the proposition that "[t]wo generations of bastards are enough." [Gould 336-37.]

For lawyers, the problem is that our constitutional document says nothing that clearly protects the Carrie Bucks of the world on these facts. Her sterilization was not in punishment for crime, and thus could not be considered an Eighth Amendment problem. The Virginia statute did provide her some procedural protections, but people like her are unlikely to be able to afford an attorney, and even if an attorney is provided he or she might have been unable to find enough scientific evidence to counter the prevailing wisdom of the day. A flat prohibition on sterilization for eugenic purposes — or at least a strong presumption against it, with the state bearing a high burden of justification — may be the only practical way to protect society against such fundamental abuses. And yet the judge who entertains creating such a fundamental constitutional right will surely be criticized for usurping the legislative function, and those criticisms have considerable theoretical force.

A final lesson of *Buck v. Bell* is that the Constitution, as construed by the Court, rarely provides more than marginal protection for the victims of such policy fads as the eugenics movement — until public norms change. The case of J.L. Skinner illustrates this idea. He was convicted and sentenced to sterilization in 1930s Oklahoma, when legislators, prosecutors, and ordinary people were anxious about the perpetuation of so-called "degenerates." But as the case made its way up the appellate system, the eugenics policy encountered increased skepticism. Scientists in the 1930s cast doubt on these theories, and national policymakers by the end of the decade were acutely aware of the philosophical similarities between American and Nazi eugenics. Once the case reached the Supreme Court, scientific experts, elite lawyers, and national policymakers had set their minds against sterilization and other eugenics policies.

Review Justice Douglas's opinion and see if you can detect Nazi Germany in the background. The concern is more explicit in Justice Jackson's concurring opinion in *Skinner*, which we have omitted. Jackson stated in part: "There are limits to the extent to which a legislatively represented majority may conduct biological experiments at the expense of the dignity and personality and natural powers of a minority — even those who have been guilty of what the majority define as crimes. But this Act falls down before reaching this problem, which I mention only to avoid the implication that such a question may not exist because not discussed." Note the tension between this language and Jackson's concurring opinion in *Railway Express*, decided seven years later, in which he scorned substantive due process review in favor of somewhat searching equal protection analysis. Also note that Justice Black, who condemned judicial creation of rights beyond the constitutional text in *Adamson*, silently joined the majority opinion in *Skinner*, presumably because the clever equal-protection rationale avoided the need to address whether compulsory sterilization violated substantive due process.

SECTION 2. PROTECTING ECONOMIC LIBERTY AND PROPERTY

A.   HISTORICAL INTRODUCTION

The state of New York enacts a law restricting the hours that bakers can work and another law restricting the owners' use of designated historic buildings. Such statutes regulate important economic interests. What federal constitutional restrictions apply? This is an unexpectedly complicated question.

If the first law were applied to rewrite existing labor-management contracts, it might fall athwart the Contracts Clause of Article I, § 10, which says that "[n]o State shall * * * pass any * * * Law impairing the Obligation of Contracts." The Contracts Clause was originally aimed at debtor-relief legislation by the states and was liberally applied in the early nineteenth century. Thus, in *Fletcher v. Peck*, 10 U.S. (6 Cranch) 87 (1810), the Marshall Court refused to allow Georgia to rescind land grants that had been obtained by bribing the state legislature, because rescission would impair vested rights that the ultimate purchasers had acquired by contract. In the *Dartmouth College Case*, 17 U.S. (4 Wheat.) 518 (1819), the Court struck down a New Hampshire law changing the provisions of the college's state charter, which the Court viewed as a contract. The same principle was applied by the Marshall Court to limit state regulation of business corporations.

The Taney Court (1836-64) retreated from the Marshall Court's broad use of the Contracts Clause, however. In *Charles River Bridge v. Warren Bridge*, 36 U.S. (11 Pet.) 420 (1837), the Court upheld the right of Massachusetts to adopt new policies in derogation of a public charter granted to a ferry company. Justice Story (a Marshall Court holdover) adamantly objected that the Court was sanctioning a violation of the Contracts Clause and undermining vested rights. But Chief Justice Taney's opinion for the Court insisted that "contract" rights should not be needlessly constructed when they would derogate from the public interest. This was obviously a different attitude toward state regulation of private property than that followed by the Marshall Court. A broadly utilitarian justification for state regulation of private property is set forth in Chief Judge Lemuel Shaw's opinion in *Commonwealth v. Alger*, 61 Mass. 53 (1851).[a]

What Chief Justice Taney did to the Contracts Clause in *Charles River* Justice Miller did to the Privileges or Immunities Clause in *The Slaughter House Cases* (described above) — substantially removing both as federal constitutional protections against state regulation of "vested" private rights, whether expressed in contract or in property. Justice Miller's decision also dismissed due process objections to state regulation, indicating that the Fourteenth Amendment's Due Process Clause spoke only to procedural requirements of state actions. But before the ink was dry on *The Slaughter House Cases*, the state courts were interpreting the Due Process Clause to protect liberty of private contracting and the sanctity of private property.[b]

Some of the state court judges who saw the Due Process Clause in economic terms — Judges David Brewer of the Kansas Supreme Court (1871-84) and Rufus Peckham of the New York Court of Appeals (1886-95) — were later appointed to the U.S. Supreme Court. In the 1890s they transformed American constitutional law, under cover of the Due Process Clause. The primary innovation of the state cases in the 1880s, e.g., *In re Jacobs*, 98 N.Y. 98 (1885) (a leading case), and of the Supreme Court cases in the 1890s was its recognition of a "liberty of contract" right in the Due Process Clause. "So long as any single man, the humblest and the weakest in the land, may not enter into business or engage in labor such as his means will permit and his inclination determine, just so long is personal liberty an unaccomplished fact." Justice Brewer, *The Liberty of Each Individual* (address, July 4, 1893). This line of cases is explored in Part B.

A second innovation adopted by the Supreme Court during this period was an embryonic version of the incorporation doctrine. *Chicago, Burlington & Quincy Railroad v. Chicago*, 166 U.S. 226 (1897), which held the Fifth Amendment's Takings Clause applicable to the states through the Fourteenth Amendment's Due Process Clause, was the Court's first incorporation of a Bill

---

a. On the ideological features of judicial approaches to economic regulation in this period, see Morton Horwitz, *The Transformation of American Law, 1780-1860* (1977).

b. In *Bertholf v. O'Reilly*, 74 N.Y. 509, 511 (1878), the New York Court of Appeals recognized that due process "right to liberty [includes] the right to exercise his faculties and to follow a lawful avocation for the support of life; the right to property [includes] the right to acquire possession and enjoy it in any way consistent with the equal rights of others." For other authorities to the same effect, see *Hanson v. Vernon*, 27 Iowa 28, 73 (1869); *Carew v. Rutherford*, 106 Mass. 1, 10-15 (1870); *People v. Salem*, 20 Mich. 452, 484-85 (1870); Thomas Cooley, *A Treatise on the Constitutional Limitations Which Rest Upon Legislative Power of the States of the American Union* (1868).

of Rights guarantee to the states. The line of cases created by this particular incorporation is explored in Part C.

B. THE RISE AND DECLINE OF LIBERTY OF CONTRACT AND SUBSTANTIVE DUE PROCESS REVIEW

In *Allgeyer v. Louisiana*, 165 U.S. 578 (1897), the Court struck down a Louisiana law requiring all insurance on Louisiana property to be issued by insurers registered to do business in the state. The Court characterized the law as an infringement on the right of out-of-state brokers to pursue their livelihoods and subjected the law to strict scrutiny, which it flunked. In contrast, in *Holden v. Hardy*, 169 U.S. 366 (1898), the Court, over the dissent of Justices Brewer and Peckham, upheld against due process attack a Utah statute which limited mining and smelting workers to eight-hour days. Although the Court recognized that the statute limited employers' and employees' freedom of contract, it found the regulation justified in order to protect the health and safety of those working in such hazardous jobs.

Between 1898 and 1905, the U.S. Supreme Court upheld a series of state laws limiting freedom of contract, sometimes relying upon an idea suggested in *Holden* that placing an employer and employee on a more equal footing was itself a sufficient state interest to justify labor regulation. E.g., *Knoxville Iron Co. v. Harbison*, 183 U.S. 13 (1901). The state courts grew more moderate in their application of substantive due process review after the late 1890s, as illustrated by the New York Court of Appeals' decision in *State v. Lochner*, 177 N.Y. 145 (1904). Justice Peckham's former court had been at the forefront in strictly scrutinizing economic regulations, but under the leadership of Chief Judge Alton Parker the court upheld the New York "bakers' law," which prohibited employers from requiring bakers to work more than 60 hours in one week. Chief Judge Parker relied on *Holden*. The U.S. Supreme Court disagreed and reversed, in a landmark decision.

LOCHNER v. NEW YORK
198 U.S. 45, 25 S.Ct. 539, 49 L.Ed. 937 (1905)

JUSTICE PECKHAM delivered the opinion of the Court.

[Lochner was charged with violating a New York statute that prohibited employers from requiring bakers to work over sixty hours in a week.] The statute necessarily interferes with the right of contract between the employer and employees, concerning the number of hours in which the latter may labor in the bakery of the employer. The general right to make a contract in relation to his business is part of the liberty of the individual protected by the Fourteenth Amendment of the Federal Constitution. *Allgeyer*. Under that provision no State can deprive any person of life, liberty or property without due process of law. The right to purchase or to sell labor is part of the liberty protected by this amendment, unless there are circumstances which exclude the right. There are, however, certain powers, existing in the sovereignty of each State in the Union, somewhat vaguely termed police powers, the exact description and limitation of which have not been attempted by the courts. Those powers, broadly stated and without, at present, any attempt at a more specific limitation, relate to the safety, health, morals and general welfare of the public. Both property and liberty are held on such reasonable conditions as may be imposed by the governing power of the State in the exercise of those powers, and with such conditions the Fourteenth Amendment was not designed to interfere. * * *

It must, of course, be conceded that there is a limit to the valid exercise of the police power by the State. There is no dispute concerning this general proposition. Otherwise the Fourteenth Amendment would have no efficacy and the legislatures of the States would have unbounded power, and it would be enough to say that any piece of legislation was enacted to conserve the morals, the health or the safety of the people; such legislation would be valid, no matter how absolutely without foundation the claim might be. The claim of the police power would be a mere pretext — become another and delusive name for the supreme sovereignty of the State to be exercised free from constitutional restraint. This is not contended for. In every case that comes before this court, therefore, where legislation of this character is concerned and where the protection of the Federal Constitution is sought, the question necessarily arises: Is this a fair, reasonable and appropriate exercise of the police power of the State, or is it an unreasonable, unnecessary and arbitrary interference with the right of the individual to his personal liberty or to enter into those contracts in relation to labor which may seem to him appropriate or necessary for the support of himself and his family? Of course the liberty of contract relating to labor includes both parties to it. The one has as much right to purchase as the other to sell labor.

This is not a question of substituting the judgment of the court for that of the legislature. If the act be within the power of the State it is valid, although the judgment of the court might be totally opposed to the enactment of such a law. But the question would still remain: Is it within the police power of the State? and that question must be answered by the court.

The question whether this act is valid as a labor law, pure and simple, may be dismissed in a few words. There is no reasonable ground for interfering with the liberty of person or the right of free contract, by determining the hours of labor, in the occupation of a baker. There is no contention that bakers as a class are not equal in intelligence and capacity to men in other trades or manual occupations, or that they are not able to assert their rights and care for themselves without the protecting arm of the State, interfering with their independence of judgment and of action. They are in no sense wards of the State. Viewed in the light of a purely labor law, with no reference whatever to the question of health, we think that a law like the one before us involves neither the safety, the morals nor the welfare of the public, and that the interest of the public is not in the slightest degree affected by such an act. The law must be upheld, if at all, as a law pertaining to the health of the individual engaged in the occupation of a baker. * * *

We think the limit of the police power has been reached and passed in this case. There is, in our judgment, no reasonable foundation for holding this to be necessary or appropriate as a health law to safeguard the public health or the health of the individuals who are following the trade of a baker. If this statute be valid, and if, therefore, a proper case is made out in which to deny the right of an individual, sui juris, as employer or employee, to make contracts for the labor of the latter under the protection of the provisions of the Federal Constitution, there would seem to be no length to which legislation of this nature might not go.

* * * We think that there can be no fair doubt that the trade of a baker, in and of itself, is not an unhealthy one to that degree which would authorize the legislature to interfere with the right to labor, and with the right of free contract on the part of the individual, either as employer or employee. In looking through statistics regarding all trades and occupations, it may be true that the trade of a baker does not appear to be as healthy as some other trades, and is also vastly more healthy than still others. To the common understanding the trade of a baker has never been regarded as an unhealthy one. * * * It is unfortunately true that labor, even in any department, may possibly carry with it the seeds of unhealthiness. But are we all, on that account, at the mercy of legislative majorities? A printer, a tinsmith, a locksmith, a carpenter, a cabinetmaker, a dry goods clerk, a bank's, a lawyer's or a physician's clerk, or a clerk in almost any kind of business, would all come under the power of the legislature, on this assumption. No trade, no occupation, no mode of earning one's living, could escape this all-pervading power, and the acts of the legislature in limiting the hours of labor in all employments would be valid, although such limitation might seriously cripple the ability of the laborer to support himself and his family. * * *

It is manifest to us that the limitation of the hours of labor as provided for in this section of the statute under which the indictment was found, and the plaintiff in error convicted, has no such direct relation to and no such substantial effect upon the health of the employee, as to justify us in regarding the section as really a health law. It seems to us that the real object and purpose were simply to regulate the hours of labor between the master and his employees (all being men, sui juris), in a private business, not dangerous in any degree to morals or in any real and substantial degree, to the health of the employees. Under such circumstances the freedom of master and employee to contract with each other in relation to their employment, and in defining the same, cannot be prohibited or interfered with, without violating the Federal Constitution.

JUSTICE HOLMES, dissenting.

This case is decided upon an economic theory which a large part of the country does not entertain. If it were a question whether I agreed with that theory, I should desire to study it further and long before making up my mind. But I do not conceive that to be my duty, because I strongly believe that my agreement or disagreement has nothing to do with the right of a majority to embody their opinions in law. It is settled by various decisions of this court that state constitutions and state laws may regulate life in many ways which we as legislators might think as injudicious or if you like as tyrannical as this, and which equally with this interfere with the liberty to contract. Sunday laws and usury laws are ancient examples. A more modern one is the prohibition of lotteries. The liberty of the citizen to do as he likes so long as he does not interfere with the liberty of others to do the same, which has been a shibboleth for some well-known writers, is interfered with by school laws, by the Post Office, by every state or municipal institution which takes his money for purposes thought desirable, whether he likes it or not. The Fourteenth Amendment does not enact Mr. Herbert Spencer's Social Statics. The other day we sustained the Massachusetts vaccination law. United States and state statutes and decisions cutting down the liberty to contract by way of combination are familiar to this court. Two years ago we upheld the prohibition of sales of stock on margins or for future delivery in the constitution of California. The decision sustaining an eight hour law for miners is still recent. Some of these laws embody convictions or prejudices which judges are likely to share. Some may not. But a constitution is not intended to embody a particular economic theory, whether of paternalism and the organic relation of the citizen to the State or of Laissez faire. It is made for people of fundamentally differing views, and the accident of our finding certain opinions natural and familiar or novel and even shocking ought not to conclude our judgment upon the question whether statutes embodying them conflict with the Constitution of the United States.

General propositions do not decide concrete cases. The decision will depend on a judgment or intuition more subtle than any articulate major premise. But I think that the proposition just stated, if it is accepted, will carry us far toward the end. Every opinion tends to become a law. I think that the word "liberty" in the Fourteenth Amendment is perverted when it is held to prevent the natural outcome of a dominant opinion, unless it can be said that a rational and fair man necessarily would admit that the statute proposed would infringe fundamental principles as they have been understood by the traditions of our people and our law. It does not need research to show that no such sweeping condemnation can be passed upon the statute before us. A reasonable man might think it a proper measure on the score of health. Men whom I certainly could not pronounce unreasonable would uphold it as a first installment of a general regulation of the hours of work. Whether in the latter aspect it would be open to the charge of inequality I think it unnecessary to discuss.

JUSTICE HARLAN, with whom **JUSTICE WHITE** and **JUSTICE DAY** concurred, dissenting.

It is plain that this statute was enacted in order to protect the physical well-being of those who work in bakery and confectionery establishments. It may be that the statute had its origin, in part, in the belief that employers and employees in such establishments were not upon an equal footing, and that the necessities of the latter often compelled them to submit to such exactions as unduly taxed their strength. Be this as it may, the statute must be taken as expressing the belief of the people of New York that, as a general rule, and in the case of the average man, labor in excess of sixty hours during a week in such establishments may endanger the health of those who thus labor. Whether or not this be wise legislation it is not the province of the court to inquire. * * *

Professor Hirt in his treatise on the "Diseases of the Workers" has said: "The labor of the bakers is among the hardest and most laborious imaginable, because it has to be performed under conditions injurious to the health of those engaged in it. It is hard, very hard work, not only because it requires a great deal of physical exertion in an overheated workshop and during unreasonably long hours, but more so because of the erratic demands of the public, compelling the baker to perform the greater part of his work at night thus depriving him of an opportunity to enjoy the necessary rest and sleep, a fact which is highly injurious to his health." Another writer says: "The constant inhaling of flour dust causes inflammation of the lungs and of the bronchial tubes. The eyes also suffer through this dust, which is responsible for the many cases of running eyes among the bakers. The long hours of toil to which all bakers are subjected produce rheumatism, cramps and swollen legs. The intense heat in the workshops induces the workers to resort to cooling drinks, which together with their habit of exposing the greater part of their bodies to the change in the atmosphere, is another source of a number of diseases of various organs. Nearly all bakers are pale-faced and of more delicate health than the workers of other crafts, which is chiefly due to their hard work and their irregular and unnatural mode of living, whereby the power of resistance against disease is greatly diminished. The average age of a baker is below that of other workmen; they seldom live over their fiftieth year, most of them dying between the ages of forty and fifty. During periods of epidemic diseases the bakers are generally the first to succumb to the disease[.]" * * *

I do not stop to consider whether any particular view of this economic question presents the sounder theory. What the precise facts are it may be difficult to say. It is enough for the determination of this case, and it is enough for this court to know, that the question is one about which there is room for debate and for an honest difference of opinion. There are many reasons of a weighty, substantial character, based upon the experience of mankind, in support of the theory that, all things considered, more than ten hours' steady work each day, from week to week, in a bakery or confectionery establishment, may endanger the health, and shorten the lives of the workmen, thereby diminishing their physical and mental capacity to serve the State, and to provide for those dependent upon them.

If such reasons exist that ought to be the end of this case, for the State is not amenable to the judiciary, in respect of its legislative enactments, unless such enactments are plainly, palpably, beyond all question, inconsistent with the Constitution of the United States. We are not to presume that the State of New York has acted in bad faith. Nor can we assume that its legislature acted without due deliberation, or that it did not determine this question upon the fullest attainable information, and for the common good. We cannot say that the State has acted without reason nor ought we to proceed upon the theory that its action is a mere sham. * * *

NOTES ON *LOCHNER* AND THE HEYDAY OF SUBSTANTIVE DUE PROCESS

1. *What's Wrong with* Lochner? Justice Peckham's decision came as something of a surprise to the legal world, and in fact depended upon an unexplained shift in position by Justice Brown, the author of *Holden v. Hardy*. The decision was criticized when it was handed down (though not so much as other anti-labor decisions of the Fuller Court, 1888-1910), and the level of

criticism has only grown over time. Consider these ways to disagree with the Court.

(a) Justice Holmes' dissent might be read for the proposition that the Court should afford only minimal scrutiny to socio-economic regulations adopted by the legislature. Recall Thayer, *The Origin and Scope of the American Doctrine of Constitutional Law*, 7 Harv. L. Rev. 129 (1883) (Chapter 2 § 1). Justice Holmes challenged the Court to justify its adoption of a particular theory of economics (laissez faire) when it recognized invasions of "liberty of contract" as a basis for strict scrutiny of labor legislation.

(b) Justice Harlan's dissent might be read for the proposition that the Court overlooked legitimate state justifications for its intrusion into the parties' liberty of contract — either the health and safety of bakers (more thoroughly documented in the encyclopedic opinion by Chief Judge Parker of the New York Court of Appeals) or the disparity in bargaining power between workers and employers (*Holden*).

(c) A more recent attack on *Lochner* focuses on its assumption that there is a "private" sphere of worker-management "liberty" into which the state should presumptively not intrude. But the state is already there, for the possibility of worker-management contracting is premised upon the state's standing ready to enforce the terms of that contract — as it frequently did in the 1890s when employers would call upon the police and the courts to enjoin "unlawful" strikes. Hence, the private sphere is already infected with public participation, and there is no neutral reason for the Court to presume against state regulation of contracting activity.[c]

2. *Defense of* Lochner. Arguably the New York bakers' statute was not really enacted as a health measure, nor did it reflect inequality of bargaining position; instead, it was possibly rent-seeking by unions and employers.[d] The bakers' unions in the 1890s obtained maximum hour rules from the major employers, but small-time bakeries that were not unionized then had a competitive advantage over the big bakeries that were, because the former had lower labor costs per hour. The *Lochner* statute was a measure by which the unions and the big bakeries could raise the labor costs — and incidentally the prices charged to consumers — of the small bakeries, so that they would not outsell the big bakeries. Some theories of economics suggest that this might be economically inefficient, and some theories of public choice suggest that the state is often the cover for precisely this sort of rent-seeking.[e]

3. Lochner*'s Aftermath.* The Court's decision in *Lochner* signaled a reinvigorated judicial hostility (at both the state and federal level) to legislation enacted at the behest of labor unions. Most prominently, *Lochner* was the basis

---

c. See Gary Peller, *The Metaphysics of American Law*, 73 Cal. L. Rev. 1151 (1985) (retrieving this insight from the work of the legal realists); Cass Sunstein, Lochner*'s Legacy*, 87 Colum. L. Rev. 873 (1987) (reinterpreting *Lochner* in light of this insight).

d. See Sidney Tarrow, Lochner v. New York: *A Political Analysis*, 5 Labor History 277 (1964).

e. See generally Bernard Siegan, *Economic Liberties and the Constitution* (1980); Richard Epstein, *Toward a Revitalization of the Contract Clause*, 51 U. Chi. L. Rev. 703 (1984).

for subsequent invalidation of state laws making "yellow dog contracts" (whereby the employer would require a promise by employees that they not join a union) unlawful. See *Coppage v. Kansas*, 236 U.S. 1 (1915); *People v. Marcus*, 185 N.Y. 257 (1906); see also *Adair v. United States*, 208 U.S. 161 (1908) (invalidating federal law as beyond Congress' Commerce Clause power). On the other hand, the Supreme Court refused to apply *Lochner* to strike down a law regulating the hours women could work, see *Muller v. Oregon*, 208 U.S. 412 (1908) (Chapter 4, § 2A), and in *Bunting v. Oregon*, 243 U.S. 426 (1917), refused to follow *Lochner* in upholding a state law generally restricting work days to ten hours. Any implication that *Bunting* overruled the *Lochner* approach was dispelled, however, in *Adkins v. Children's Hospital of the District of Columbia*, 261 U.S. 525 (1923), which struck down a minimum wage law for female employees.

Lochner, as well as other cases that limited the authority of Congress and the state legislatures, caused a constitutional crisis in the 1930s, when the Great Depression led to tremendous political pressure for more national and state economic regulation (Chapter 1, §§ 4-5). See *Home Building & Loan Ass'n v. Blaisdell*, 290 U.S. 398 (1934) (upholding a temporary moratorium on mortgage foreclosures). President Franklin Roosevelt's Court-packing plan may have had something to do with the "switch in time that saved nine." In any event, changes in composition of the Court coupled with the crushing economic realities of the time led a majority of the Justices to abandon *Lochner*. *Nebbia v. New York*, 291 U.S. 502 (1934), a 5-4 decision that upheld a New York law allowing a state board to fix minimum and maximum retail prices for milk, was the first major signal of a retreat from economic substantive due process. See Daniel Farber, *Who Killed* Lochner?, 90 Geo. L.J. 985 (2002). The doctrine was firmly interred in the next two cases. The first case decisively rejects the constitutional baseline at the heart of *Lochner*; the second goes quite far in deferring to potentially protectionist economic regulation.

West Coast Hotel v. Parrish, 300 U.S. 379 (1937). In a 5-4 decision, **Chief Justice Hughes** upheld a state law establishing a minimum wage for women, overruling the *Lochner*-like *Adkins v. Children's Hospital, supra*. The opinion stated that "[t]he Constitution does not speak of freedom of contract. It speaks of liberty and prohibits the deprivation of liberty without due process of law. [Regulation] which is reasonable in relation to its subject and is adopted in the interests of the community is due process." The opinion stressed that the legislature "was clearly entitled to consider the situation of women in employment, the fact that they are in the class receiving the least pay, that their bargaining power is relatively weak, and that they are the ready victims of those who would take advantage of their necessitous circumstances. The legislature was entitled to adopt measures to reduce the evils of the 'sweating system,' the exploiting of workers at wages so low as to be insufficient to meet the bare cost of living, thus making their very helplessness the occasion of a most injurious competition. * * * The adoption of similar requirements by many States evidences a deep-seated conviction both as to the presence of the evil and as to the means adopted to check it. Legislative response to that conviction cannot be regarded as arbitrary or capricious, and that is all we have to decide. Even if the wisdom of the policy be regarded as debatable and its effects uncertain, still the legislature is entitled to its judgment." The opinion then seemingly junked the baseline of *Lochner*: "There is an additional and compelling consideration which recent economic experience has brought into a strong light. The exploitation of a class of workers who are in an unequal bargaining position with respect to bargaining power and are thus relatively defenseless against the denial of a living wage is not only detrimental to their health and well being but casts a direct burden for their support upon the community. What these workers lose in wages the taxpayers are called upon to pay. The bare cost of living must be met. We may take judicial notice of the unparalleled demands for relief which arose during the recent period of depression. * * * The community is not bound to provide what is in effect a subsidy for unconscionable employers. The community may direct its law-making power to correct the abuse which springs from their selfish disregard of the public interest."

Williamson v. Lee Optical, 348 U.S. 483 (1955). An Oklahoma statute prohibited opticians from duplicating or replacing lenses without a written prescription from an ophthalmologist or optometrist, even though opticians have the expertise and equipment to take a whole (or, frequently, even broken) lens and determine the prescription for it. The Court, per **Justice Douglas**, conceded that the statute was perhaps "a needless, wasteful requirement in many cases" and that the law was "not in every respect logically consistent with its aims." Nevertheless, the statute did not violate due process: "[I]t is for the legislature, not the courts, to balance the advantages and disadvantages. * * * The legislature might have concluded that the frequency of occasions when a prescription is necessary was sufficient to justify this regulation, [or] the legislature may have concluded that eye examinations were so critical, not only for correction of vision but also for detection of latent ailments or diseases, that every change in frames and every duplication of a lens should be accompanied by a prescription from a medical expert. * * * It is enough that there is an evil at hand for correction, and that it might be thought that the particular legislative measure was a rational way to correct it. The day is gone when this Court uses the Due Process Clause * * * to strike down state laws, regulatory of business and industrial conditions, because they may be unwise, improvident, or out of harmony with a particular school of thought. * * * 'For protection against abuses by legislatures the people must resort to the polls, not to the courts.' " The Court also rejected an equal protection challenge, for reasons similar to those accepted in the majority opinion in *Railway Express* (Chapter 4).

NOTE ON STATE SUBSTANTIVE DUE PROCESS

Since the New Deal, the U.S. Supreme Court has almost completely abandoned the *Lochner* strict scrutiny approach to social and economic legislation. As *Lee Optical* illustrates, the Court not only defers to legislative goals but is willing to uphold social and economic regulations based upon any conceivable basis the Court itself can imagine to support the statute. But economic substantive due process lives on at the state level.[f] Is it more appropriate for state supreme courts to engage in *Lochner*-style judicial review of state statutes then for the U.S. Supreme Court to do the same? Consider the advantages state courts have in spotting state legislative rent-seeking.

For a frequently litigated example, consider state laws requiring "full crews" on all runs of intrastate railroads. There is some suspicion that such laws amount to little more than legislated featherbedding — full employment laws for railroad workers (who have politically powerful unions) — and this has stimulated challenges to such laws under state Due Process Clauses. The New York Court of Appeals upheld its law in *New York Central Railroad Co. v. Lefkowitz*, 23 N.Y.2d 1 (1968), appeal dismissed, 393 U.S. 536 (1969), but only over a spirited dissent by Judge Breitel, and the full court agreed that a pure featherbedding law would be unconstitutional because not supported by a truly public justification. The Wisconsin Supreme Court struck down part of its law in *Chicago & North Western Railway v. La Follette*, 169 N.W.2d 441 (1969), on the ground that the costs it imposed on railroads were "grossly disproportionate" to the public justification.

The U.S. Supreme Court's opinion in *Lee Optical* would be vulnerable under some of these state precedents, because the law smacks of rent-seeking legislation by ophthalmologists and optometrists at the expense of consumers (who pay higher prices) and opticians (not as wealthy a group as the doctors). Compare also *United States v. Carolene Products Co.*, 304 U.S. 144 (1938) (upholding prohibition of interstate transportation of cheaper "filled milk," notwithstanding charges that the statute only served the interests of local "whole milk" producers), with *Gillette Dairy, Inc. v. Nebraska Dairy Products Board*, 219 N.W.2d 214 (Neb. 1974) (striking down state law requiring agency to set minimum prices for milk because law did not really meet stated goal of freeing dairy industry from anti-competitive influences), and *Defiance Milk Products Co. v. Du Mond*, 309 N.Y. 537 (1956) (striking down a law requiring condensed skim milk to be sold only in packages of ten pounds or more).

C.   THE TAKINGS CLAUSE

KELO v. CITY OF NEW LONDON
545 U.S. 469, 125 S.Ct. 2655, 162 L.Ed.2d 439 (2005)

JUSTICE STEVENS delivered the opinion of the Court.

In 2000, the city of New London approved a development plan that, in the words of the Supreme Court of Connecticut, was "projected to create in excess of 1,000 jobs, to increase tax and other revenues, and to revitalize an economically distressed city, including its downtown and waterfront areas." In assembling the land needed for this project, the city's development agent has purchased property from willing sellers and proposes to use the power of eminent domain to acquire the remainder of the property from unwilling owners

---

f. See, e.g., John Hetherington, *State Economic Regulation and Substantive Due Process of Law*, 53 Nw. U.L. Rev. 13, 226 (1958) (parts 1 and 2); Jeff Strnad, Note, *State Economic Substantive Due Process: A Proposed Approach*, 88 Yale L.J. 1487 (1979).

in exchange for just compensation. The question presented is whether the city's proposed disposition of this property qualifies as a "public use" within the meaning of the Takings Clause of the Fifth Amendment to the Constitution. * * *

Two polar propositions are perfectly clear. On the one hand, it has long been accepted that the sovereign may not take the property of *A* for the sole purpose of transferring it to another private party *B,* even though *A* is paid just compensation. On the other hand, it is equally clear that a State may transfer property from one private party to another if future "use by the public" is the purpose of the taking; the condemnation of land for a railroad with common-carrier duties is a familiar example. Neither of these propositions, however, determines the disposition of this case.

As for the first proposition, the City would no doubt be forbidden from taking petitioners' land for the purpose of conferring a private benefit on a particular private party. Nor would the City be allowed to take property under the mere pretext of a public purpose, when its actual purpose was to bestow a private benefit. The takings before us, however, would be executed pursuant to a "carefully considered" development plan. The trial judge and all the members of the Supreme Court of Connecticut agreed that there was no evidence of an illegitimate purpose in this case.

On the other hand, this is not a case in which the City is planning to open the condemned land — at least not in its entirety — to use by the general public. Nor will the private lessees of the land in any sense be required to operate like common carriers, making their services available to all comers. But although such a projected use would be sufficient to satisfy the public use requirement, this "Court long ago rejected any literal requirement that condemned property be put into use for the general public." Indeed, while many state courts in the mid-19th century endorsed "use by the public" as the proper definition of public use, that narrow view steadily eroded over time. Not only was the "use by the public" test difficult to administer (*e.g.,* what proportion of the public need have access to the property? at what price?), but it proved to be impractical given the diverse and always evolving needs of society. Accordingly, when this Court began applying the Fifth Amendment to the States at the close of the 19th century, it embraced the broader and more natural interpretation of public use as "public purpose." Thus, in a case upholding a mining company's use of an aerial bucket line to transport ore over property it did not own, Justice Holmes' opinion for the Court stressed "the inadequacy of use by the general public as a universal test." We have repeatedly and consistently rejected that narrow test ever since.

The disposition of this case therefore turns on the question whether the City's development plan serves a "public purpose." Without exception, our cases have defined that concept broadly, reflecting our longstanding policy of deference to legislative judgments in this field.

In *Berman v. Parker,* 348 U.S. 26 (1954), this Court upheld a redevelopment plan targeting a blighted area of Washington, D.C., in which most of the housing for the area's 5,000 inhabitants was beyond repair. Under the plan, the area would be condemned and part of it utilized for the construction of streets, schools, and other public facilities. The remainder of the land would be leased or sold to private parties for the purpose of redevelopment, including the construction of low-cost housing.

The owner of a department store located in the area challenged the condemnation, pointing out that his store was not itself blighted and arguing that the creation of a "better balanced, more attractive community" was not a valid public use. Writing for a unanimous Court, Justice Douglas refused to evaluate this claim in isolation, deferring instead to the legislative and agency judgment that the area "must be planned as a whole" for the plan to be successful. The Court explained that "community redevelopment programs need not, by force of the Constitution, be on a piecemeal basis — lot by lot, building by building." The public use underlying the taking was unequivocally affirmed:

> We do not sit to determine whether a particular housing project is or is not desirable. The concept of the public welfare is broad and inclusive . . . . The values it represents are spiritual as well as physical, aesthetic as well as monetary. It is within the power of the legislature to determine that the community should be beautiful as well as healthy, spacious as well as clean, well-balanced as well as carefully patrolled. In the present case, the Congress and its authorized agencies have made determinations that take into account a wide variety of values. It is not for us to reappraise them. If those who govern the District of Columbia decide that the Nation's Capital should be beautiful as well as sanitary, there is nothing in the Fifth Amendment that stands in the way.

In *Hawaii Housing Authority v. Midkiff*, 467 U.S. 229 (1984), the Court considered a Hawaii statute whereby fee title was taken from lessors and transferred to lessees (for just compensation) in order to reduce the concentration of land ownership. We unanimously upheld the statute and rejected the Ninth Circuit's view that it was "a naked attempt on the part of the state of Hawaii to take the property of A and transfer it to B solely for B's private use and benefit." Reaffirming *Berman*'s deferential approach to legislative judgments in this field, we concluded that the State's purpose of eliminating the "social and economic evils of a land oligopoly" qualified as a valid public use. Our opinion also rejected the contention that the mere fact that the State immediately transferred the properties to private individuals upon condemnation somehow diminished the public character of the taking. "[I]t is only the taking's purpose, and not its mechanics," we explained, that matters in determining public use. * * *

Viewed as a whole, our jurisprudence has recognized that the needs of society have varied between different parts of the Nation, just as they have evolved over time in response to changed circumstances. Our earliest cases in particular embodied a strong theme of federalism, emphasizing the "great respect" that we owe to state legislatures and state courts in discerning local public needs. For more than a century, our public use jurisprudence has wisely eschewed rigid formulas and intrusive scrutiny in favor of affording legislatures broad latitude in determining what public needs justify the use of the takings power.

Those who govern the City were not confronted with the need to remove blight in the Fort Trumbull area, but their determination that the area was sufficiently distressed to justify a program of economic rejuvenation is entitled to our deference. The City has carefully formulated an economic development plan that it believes will provide appreciable benefits to the community, including — but by no means limited to — new jobs and increased tax revenue. As with other exercises in urban planning and development, the City is endeavoring to coordinate a variety of commercial, residential, and recreational uses of land, with the hope that they will form a whole greater than the sum of its parts. To effectuate this plan, the City has invoked a state statute that specifically authorizes the use of eminent domain to promote economic development. Given the comprehensive character of the plan, the thorough deliberation that preceded its adoption, and the limited scope of our review, it is appropriate for us, as it was in *Berman,* to resolve the challenges of the individual owners, not on a piecemeal basis, but rather in light of the entire plan. Because that plan unquestionably serves a public purpose, the takings challenged here satisfy the public use requirement of the Fifth Amendment.

To avoid this result, petitioners urge us to adopt a new bright-line rule that economic development does not qualify as a public use. Putting aside the unpersuasive suggestion that the City's plan will provide only purely economic benefits, neither precedent nor logic supports petitioners' proposal. Promoting economic development is a traditional and long accepted function of government. There is, moreover, no principled way of distinguishing economic development from the other public purposes that we have recognized. * * * It would be incongruous to hold that the City's interest in the economic benefits to be derived from the development of the Fort Trumbull area has less of a public character than any of those other interests. Clearly, there is no basis for exempting economic development from our traditionally broad understanding of public purpose.

It is further argued that without a bright-line rule nothing would stop a city from transferring citizen A's property to citizen B for the sole reason that citizen B will put the property to a more productive use and thus pay more taxes. Such a one-to-one transfer of property, executed outside the confines of an integrated development plan, is not presented in this case. While such an unusual exercise of government power would certainly raise a suspicion that a private purpose was afoot, the hypothetical cases posited by petitioners can be confronted if and when they arise. They do not warrant the crafting of an artificial restriction on the concept of public use.

Alternatively, petitioners maintain that for takings of this kind we should require a "reasonable certainty" that the expected public benefits will actually accrue. Such a rule, however, would represent an even greater departure from our precedent. "When the legislature's purpose is legitimate and its means are not irrational, our cases make clear that empirical debates over the wisdom of takings — no less than debates over the wisdom of other kinds of socioeconomic legislation — are not to be carried out in the federal courts." *Midkiff.* * * * The disadvantages of a heightened form of review are especially pronounced in this type of case. Orderly implementation of a comprehensive redevelopment plan obviously requires that the legal rights of all interested parties be established before new construction can be commenced. A constitutional rule that required postponement of the judicial approval of every condemnation until the likelihood of success of the plan had been assured would unquestionably impose a significant impediment to the successful consummation of many such plans.

JUSTICE KENNEDY, concurring.

A court applying rational-basis review under the Public Use Clause should strike down a taking that, by a clear showing, is intended to favor a particular private party, with only incidental or pretextual public benefits, just as a court applying rational-basis review under the Equal Protection Clause must strike down a government classification that is clearly intended to injure a particular class of private parties, with only incidental or pretextual public justifications. See *Cleburne* [p. 423].

A court confronted with a plausible accusation of impermissible favoritism to private parties should treat the objection as a serious one and review the record to see if it has merit, though with the presumption that the government's actions were reasonable and intended to serve a public purpose. Here, the trial court conducted a careful and extensive inquiry into "whether, in fact, the development plan is of primary benefit to . . . the developer [*i.e.,* Corcoran Jennison], and private businesses which may eventually locate in the plan area [*e.g.,* Pfizer], and in that regard, only of incidental benefit to the city." * * * Even the dissenting justices on the Connecticut Supreme Court agreed that respondents' development plan was intended to revitalize the local economy, not to serve the interests of Pfizer, Corcoran Jennison, or any other private party. This case, then, survives the meaningful rational basis review that in my view is required under the Public Use Clause.

Petitioners and their *amici* argue that any taking justified by the promotion of economic development must be treated by the courts as *per se* invalid, or at least presumptively invalid. Petitioners overstate the need for such a rule, however, by making the incorrect assumption that review under *Berman* and *Midkiff* imposes no meaningful judicial limits on the government's power to condemn any property it likes. A broad *per se* rule or a strong presumption of invalidity, furthermore, would prohibit a large number of government takings that have the purpose and expected effect of conferring substantial benefits on the public at large and so do not offend the Public Use Clause.

My agreement with the Court that a presumption of invalidity is not warranted for economic development takings in general, or for the particular takings at issue in this case, does not foreclose the possibility that a more stringent standard of review than that announced in *Berman* and *Midkiff* might be appropriate for a more narrowly drawn category of takings. There may be private transfers in which the risk of undetected impermissible favoritism of private parties is so acute that a presumption (rebuttable or otherwise) of invalidity is warranted under the Public Use Clause. This demanding level of scrutiny, however, is not required simply because the purpose of the taking is economic development.

This is not the occasion for conjecture as to what sort of cases might justify a more demanding standard, but it is appropriate to underscore aspects of the instant case that convince me no departure from *Berman* and *Midkiff* is appropriate here. This taking occurred in the context of a comprehensive development plan meant to address a serious city-wide depression, and the projected economic benefits of the project cannot be characterized as *de minimus*. The identity of most of the private beneficiaries were unknown at the time the city formulated its plans. The city complied with elaborate procedural requirements that facilitate review of the record and inquiry into the city's purposes. In sum, while there may be categories of cases in which the transfers are so suspicious, or the procedures employed so prone to abuse, or the purported benefits are so trivial or implausible, that courts should presume an impermissible private purpose, no such circumstances are present in this case.

JUSTICE O'CONNOR, with whom CHIEF JUSTICE REHNQUIST, JUSTICE SCALIA, and JUSTICE THOMAS join, dissenting.

This case returns us for the first time in over 20 years to the hard question of when a purportedly "public purpose" taking meets the public use requirement. It presents an issue of first impression: Are economic development takings constitutional? I would hold that they are not. We are guided by two precedents about the taking of real property by eminent domain. * * *

The Court's holdings in *Berman* and *Midkiff* were true to the principle underlying the Public Use Clause. In both those cases, the extraordinary, precondemnation use of the targeted property inflicted affirmative harm on society — in *Berman* through blight resulting from extreme poverty and in *Midkiff* through oligopoly resulting from extreme wealth. And in both cases, the relevant legislative body had found that eliminating the existing property use was necessary to remedy the harm. Thus a public purpose was realized when the harmful use was eliminated. Because each taking *directly* achieved a public benefit, it did not matter that the property was turned over to private use. Here, in contrast, New London does not claim that Susette Kelo's and Wilhelmina Dery's well-maintained homes are the source of any social harm. Indeed, it could not so claim without adopting the absurd argument that any single-family home that might be razed to make way for an apartment building, or any church that might be replaced with a retail store, or any small business that might be more lucrative if it were instead part of a national franchise, is inherently harmful to society and thus within the government's power to condemn.

In moving away from our decisions sanctioning the condemnation of harmful property use, the Court today significantly expands the meaning of public use. It holds that the sovereign may take private property currently put to ordinary private use, and give it over for new, ordinary private use, so long as the new use is predicted to generate some secondary benefit for the public — such as increased tax revenue, more jobs, maybe even aesthetic pleasure. But nearly any lawful use of real private property can be said to generate some incidental benefit to the public. Thus, if predicted (or even guaranteed) positive side-effects are enough to render transfer from one private party to another constitutional, then the words "for public use" do not realistically exclude *any* takings, and thus do not exert any constraint on the eminent domain power. * * *

Any property may now be taken for the benefit of another private party, but the fallout from this decision will not be random. The beneficiaries are likely to be those citizens with disproportionate influence and power in the political process, including large corporations and development firms. As for the victims, the government now has license to transfer property from those with fewer resources to those with more. The Founders cannot have intended this perverse result. "[T]hat alone is a *just* government," wrote James Madison, "which *impartially* secures to every man, whatever is his *own*."

JUSTICE THOMAS, dissenting.

The most natural reading of the [Takings] Clause is that it allows the government to take property only if the government owns, or the public has a legal right to use, the property, as opposed to taking it for any public purpose or necessity whatsoever. At the time of the founding, dictionaries primarily defined the noun "use" as "[t]he act of employing any thing to any purpose." 2 S. Johnson, A Dictionary of the English Language 2194 (4th ed. 1773) (hereinafter Johnson). The term "use," moreover, "is from the Latin *utor,* which means "to use, make use of, avail one's self of, employ, apply, enjoy, etc." J. Lewis, Law of Eminent Domain § 165, p. 224, n. 4 (1888) (hereinafter Lewis). When the government takes property and gives it to a private individual, and the public has no right to use the property, it strains language to say that the public is "employing" the property, regardless of the incidental benefits that might accrue to the public from the private use. The term "public use," then, means that either the government or its citizens as a whole must actually "employ" the taken property. * * *

The Court relies almost exclusively on this Court's prior cases to derive today's far-reaching, and dangerous, result. * * * When faced with a clash of constitutional principle and a line of unreasoned cases wholly divorced from the text, history, and structure of our founding document, we should not hesitate to resolve the tension in favor of the Constitution's original meaning.

NOTES ON *KELO* AND THE PUBLIC USE REQUIREMENT

1. *Disparate Impact.* Justice Thomas noted in his dissent that "[o]ver 97 percent of the individuals forcibly removed from their homes by the "slum-clearance" project upheld by this Court in *Berman* were black." Of course, if economic development programs are successful, the beneficiaries from increased employment and better funded government services are also disproportionately poor and minority. How, if at all, should the Court take into account potential racial and class dimensions of the problem?

2. *Stare Decisis.* Are you persuaded by Justice O'Connor's effort to distinguish prior cases (including the Hawaiian decision, which she wrote)? Is Justice Thomas right that the Court "should not hesitate" to discard a century of precedent?

3. *The Limits of "Public Use."* Under the majority opinion, are there any limits to the doctrine of public use? Under Justice Kennedy's concurrence? How much independent weight should Justice Kennedy's opinion carry? On the

one hand, he was the swing vote; on the other hand, he did join the majority opinion without qualification.

4. *What is a "Taking"?* Acquisition of property is an obvious form of "taking." But the takings clause has also been expanded to other government actions. The critical case was an opinion by Justice Holmes, *Pennsylvania Coal v. Mahon*, 260 U.S. 393 (1922). In *Mahon*, the Court held that a taking could exist if the government "went too far" in regulating the uses of private property, even though the government did not physically invade or take title to the property. In *Mahon*, a Pennsylvania statute required mining companies to maintain adequate support for surface lands. Under Pennsylvania law, the right to adequate support was a separate property right, which did not necessarily accompany ownership of the surface. In *Mahon*, the effect of the property was to make coal mining completely uneconomic, rendering the company's mining rights worthless and therefore constituting a taking. (Compare *Keystone Bituminous Coal Ass'n v. DeBenedictis*, 480 U.S. 470 (1987), upholding a nearly identical statute where there were no findings that the statute deprived the owners of all reasonable use of their coal holdings.)

PENN CENTRAL TRANSPORTATION CO.
v. CITY OF NEW YORK
438 U.S. 104, 98 S.Ct. 2646, 57 L.Ed.2d 631 (1978)

JUSTICE BRENNAN delivered the opinion of the Court.

[Following refusal of the New York City Landmarks Preservation Commission to approve plans for construction of 50-story office building over Grand Central Terminal, which had been designated a "landmark," the terminal owner filed a taking challenge to the landmarks preservation law.]

Before considering appellants' specific contentions, it will be useful to review the factors that have shaped the jurisprudence of the Fifth Amendment injunction "nor shall private property be taken for public use, without just compensation." The question of what constitutes a "taking" for purposes of the Fifth Amendment has proved to be a problem of considerable difficulty. While this Court has recognized that the "Fifth Amendment's guarantee . . . [is] designed to bar Government from forcing some people alone to bear public burdens which, in all fairness and justice, should be borne by the public as a whole," this Court, quite simply, has been unable to develop any "set formula" for determining when "justice and fairness" require that economic injuries caused by public action be compensated by the government, rather than remain disproportionately concentrated on a few persons. Indeed, we have frequently observed that whether a particular restriction will be rendered invalid by the government's failure to pay for any losses proximately caused by it depends largely "upon the particular circumstances [in that] case."

In engaging in these essentially ad hoc, factual inquiries, the Court's decisions have identified several factors that have particular significance. The economic impact of the regulation on the claimant and, particularly, the extent to which the regulation has interfered with distinct investment-backed expectations are, of course, relevant considerations. So, too, is the character of the governmental action. A "taking" may more readily be found when the interference with property can be characterized as a physical invasion by government, than when interference arises from some public program adjusting the benefits and burdens of economic life to promote the common good.

"Government hardly could go on if to some extent values incident to property could not be diminished without paying for every such change in the general law," and this Court has accordingly recognized, in a wide variety of contexts, that government may execute laws or programs that adversely affect recognized economic values. Exercises of the taxing power are one obvious example. A second are the decisions in which this Court has dismissed "taking" challenges on the ground that, while the challenged government action caused economic harm, it did not interfere with interests that were sufficiently bound up with the reasonable expectations of the claimant to constitute "property" for Fifth Amendment purposes.

* * *

Stated baldly, appellants' position appears to be that the only means of ensuring that selected owners are not singled out to endure financial hardship for no reason is to hold that any restriction imposed on individual landmarks pursuant to the New York City scheme is a "taking" requiring the payment of "just compensation." Agreement with this argument would, of course, invalidate not just New York City's law, but all comparable landmark legislation in the Nation. We find no merit in it. * * *

Rejection of appellants' broad arguments is not, however, the end of our inquiry, for all we thus far have established is that the New York City law is not rendered invalid by its failure to provide "just compensation" whenever a landmark owner is restricted in the exploitation of property interests, such as air rights, to a greater extent than provided for under applicable zoning laws. We now must consider whether the interference with appellants' property is of such a magnitude that "there must be an exercise of eminent domain and compensation to sustain [it]." That inquiry may be narrowed to the question of the severity of the impact of the law on appellants' parcel, and its resolution in turn requires a careful assessment of the impact of the regulation on the Terminal site.

[T]he New York City law does not interfere in any way with the present uses of the Terminal. Its designation as a landmark not only permits but contemplates that appellants may continue to use the property precisely as it has been used for the past 65 years: as a railroad terminal containing office space and concessions. So the law does not interfere with what must be regarded as Penn Central's primary expectation concerning the use of the parcel. More importantly, on this record, we must regard the New York City law as permitting Penn Central not only to profit from the Terminal but also to obtain a "reasonable return" on its investment.

JUSTICE REHNQUIST, with whom **THE CHIEF JUSTICE [BURGER]** and **JUSTICE STEVENS** join, dissenting.

Even where the government prohibits a noninjurious use, the Court has ruled that a taking does not take place if the prohibition applies over a broad cross section of land and thereby "secure[s] an average reciprocity of advantage." [Citing *Pennsylvania Coal Co. v. Mahon.*] It is for this reason that zoning does not constitute a "taking." While zoning at times reduces *individual* property values, the burden is shared relatively evenly and it is reasonable to conclude that on the whole an individual who is harmed by one aspect of the zoning will be benefitted by another.

Here, however, a multimillion dollar loss has been imposed on appellants; it is uniquely felt and is not offset by any benefits flowing from the preservation of some 400 other "landmarks" in New York City. Appellees have imposed a substantial cost on less than one one-tenth of one percent of the buildings in New York City for the general benefit of all its people. It is exactly this imposition of general costs on a few individuals at which the "taking" protection is directed.

NOTES ON *PENN CENTRAL* AND THE TAKINGS CLAUSE

1. *The Takings Clause, Public Benefits, and Baselines.* Justice Rehnquist argues that the owner of a landmark is being required to provide a benefit to the public, and that the cost of providing this benefit should be paid by the public. On the other hand, if they were harming the public, their activity would constitute a nuisance, and no compensation would be required. The central concept is that individuals may be prohibited from doing harm, but not required to bestow benefits. How clear is this distinction?

Consider *Miller v. Schoene*, 276 U.S. 272 (1928), which upheld a Virginia statute requiring owners of blighted cedar trees to cut down their trees to protect apple trees that might be infected by the blight. Justice Stone's opinion held there was no compensable taking, only a regulation. His reason could have been that the rule was efficient (see the previous note), because the apple industry was much more important to Virginia than the cedar industry, meaning that the apple owners would in the absence of statute and transactions costs have been able to buy out the cedar owners. But Justice Stone disclaimed reliance on that argument, and on the alternative argument that the blighted cedars could have been considered a common law nuisance.

Instead, Justice Stone reasoned that the state was faced with a choice of competing interests (cedar and apple). The state could vest a "property" right in the apple owners, thereby creating a tort "duty" on the part of the cedar owners to cut down their trees. Or the state could vest the "property" right in the cedar owners, thereby creating a tort "duty" on the part of the apple owners not to trespass on the cedar property. In short, whatever decision the state made would be constructive of "property" rights and "tort" duties — and that such rights and duties did not preexist the problem but were an outgrowth of "considerations of social policy which are not unreasonable." In the following case, however, the Court took a different approach, relying on the common law to set the baseline.

LUCAS v. SOUTH CAROLINA COASTAL COUNCIL
505 U.S. 1003, 112 S.Ct. 2886, 120 L.Ed.2d 798 (1992)

JUSTICE SCALIA delivered the opinion of the Court.

In 1986, petitioner David H. Lucas paid $975,000 for two residential lots on the Isle of Palms in Charleston County, South Carolina, on which he intended to build single family homes. In 1988, however, the South Carolina Legislature enacted the Beachfront Management Act, which had the direct effect of barring petitioner from erecting any permanent habitable structures on his two parcels. A state trial court found that this prohibition rendered Lucas's parcels "valueless." This case requires us to decide whether the Act's dramatic effect on the economic value of Lucas's lots accomplished a taking of private property under the Fifth and Fourteenth Amendments requiring the payment of "just compensation." * * *

Prior to Justice Holmes' exposition in *Mahon*, it was generally thought that the Takings Clause reached only a "direct appropriation" of property, or the functional equivalent of a "practical ouster of [the owner's] possession." Justice Holmes recognized in *Mahon*, however, that if the protection against physical appropriations of private property was to be meaningfully enforced, the government's power to redefine the range of interests included in the ownership of property was necessarily constrained by constitutional limits. * * *

Nevertheless, our decision in *Mahon* offered little insight into when, and under what circumstances, a given regulation would be seen as going "too far" for purposes of the Fifth Amendment. In 70-odd years of succeeding "regulatory takings" jurisprudence, we have generally eschewed any " 'set formula' " for determining how far is too far, preferring to "engag[e] in . . . essentially ad hoc, factual inquiries," [quoting *Penn Central*]. We have, however, described at least two discrete categories of regulatory action as compensable without case-specific inquiry into the public interest advanced in support of the restraint. The first encompasses regulations that compel the property owner to suffer a physical "invasion" of his property. * * *

The second situation in which we have found categorical treatment appropriate is where regulation denies all economically beneficial or productive use of land. As we have said on numerous occasions, the Fifth Amendment is violated when land-use regulation "does not substantially advance legitimate state interests *or denies an owner economically viable use of his land.*"

We have never set forth the justification for this rule. Perhaps it is simply, as Justice Brennan suggested [in *Penn Central*], that total deprivation of beneficial use is, from the landowner's point of view, the equivalent of a physical appropriation. * * *

Where the State seeks to sustain regulation that deprives land of all economically beneficial use, we think it may resist compensation only if the logically antecedent inquiry into the nature of the owner's estate shows that the proscribed use interests were not part of his title to begin with.[g] This accords, we think, with our "takings" jurisprudence, which has traditionally been guided by the understandings of our citizens regarding the content of, and the State's power over, the "bundle of rights" that they acquire when they obtain title to property. * * *

It seems unlikely that common-law principles would have prevented the erection of any habitable or productive improvements on petitioner's land; they rarely support prohibition of the "essential use" of land. The question, however, is one of state law to be dealt with on remand. We emphasize that to win its case South Carolina must do more than proffer the legislature's declaration that the uses Lucas desires are inconsistent with the public interest, or the conclusory assertion that they violate a common-law maxim such as *sic utere tuo ut alienum non laedas*. As we have said, a "State, by *ipse dixit*, may not transform private property into public property without compensation. . . ." Instead, as it would be required to do if it sought to restrain Lucas in a common-law action for public nuisance, South Carolina must identify background principles of nuisance and property law that prohibit the uses he now intends in the circumstances in which the property is presently found. Only on this showing can the State fairly claim that, in proscribing all such beneficial uses, the Beachfront Management Act is taking nothing.[h]

JUSTICE KENNEDY, concurring in the judgment.

In my view, reasonable expectations must be understood in light of the whole of our legal tradition. The common law of nuisance is too narrow a confine for the exercise of regulatory power in a complex and interdependent society. The State should not be prevented from enacting new regulatory initiatives in response to changing conditions, and courts must consider all reasonable expectations whatever their source. The Takings Clause does not require a static body of state property law; it protects private expectations to ensure private investment. I agree with the Court that nuisance prevention accords with the most common expectations of property owners who face regulation, but I do not believe this can be the sole source of state authority to impose severe

---

g. Drawing on our First Amendment jurisprudence, see, *e.g.*, *Employment Division v. Smith*, [Chapter 6, § 7A], Justice Stevens would "loo[k] to the *generality* of a regulation of property" to determine whether compensation is owing. The Beachfront Management Act is general, in his view, because it "regulates the use of the coastline of the entire state." There may be some validity to the principle Justice Stevens proposes, but it does not properly apply to the present case. The equivalent of a law of general application that inhibits the practice of religion without being aimed at religion, see *Smith*, *supra*, is a law that destroys the value of land without being aimed at land. Perhaps such a law — the generally applicable criminal prohibition on the manufacturing of alcoholic beverages challenged in *Mugler v. Kansas*, 123 U.S. 623 (1887), comes to mind — cannot constitute a compensable taking. But a regulation *specifically directed to land use* no more acquires immunity by plundering landowners generally than does a law specifically directed at religious practice acquire immunity by prohibiting all religions. Justice Stevens' approach renders the Takings Clause little more than a particularized restatement of the Equal Protection Clause.

h. * * * We stress that an affirmative decree eliminating all economically beneficial uses may be defended only if an *objectively reasonable application* of relevant precedents would exclude those beneficial uses in the circumstances in which the land is presently found.

restrictions. Coastal property may present such unique concerns for a fragile land system that the State can go further in regulating its development and use than the common law of nuisance might otherwise permit.

[Justice Kennedy concluded, however, that some of the state's goals, such as promotion of tourism, "ought not to suffice to deprive specific property of all value without a corresponding duty to compensate." Also, he observed, "the State did not act until after the property had been zoned for individual lot development and most other parcels had been improved, throwing the whole burden of the regulation on the remaining lots."]

JUSTICE BLACKMUN, dissenting.

[T]he Court justifies its new rule that the legislature may not deprive a property owner of the only economically valuable use of his land, even if the legislature finds it to be a harmful use, because such action is not part of the "long recognized" "understandings of our citizens." These "understandings" permit such regulation only if the use is a nuisance under the common law. Any other course is "inconsistent with the historical compact recorded in the Takings Clause." It is not clear from the Court's opinion where our "historical compact" or "citizens' understanding" comes from, but it does not appear to be history.

The principle that the State should compensate individuals for property taken for public use was not widely established in America at the time of the Revolution. * * *

Even into the 19th century, state governments often felt free to take property for roads and other public projects without paying compensation to the owners. As one court declared in 1802, citizens "were bound to contribute as much of [land], as by the laws of the country, were deemed necessary for the public convenience." * * *

In short, I find no clear and accepted "historical compact" or "understanding of our citizens" justifying the Court's new taking doctrine. Instead, the Court seems to treat history as a grab-bag of principles, to be adopted where they support the Court's theory, and ignored where they do not. If the Court decided that the early common law provides the background principles for interpreting the Taking Clause, then regulation, as opposed to physical confiscation, would not be compensable. If the Court decided that the law of a later period provides the background principles, then regulation might be compensable, but the Court would have to confront the fact that legislatures regularly determined which uses were prohibited, independent of the common law, and independent of whether the uses were lawful when the owner purchased. What makes the Court's analysis unworkable is its attempt to package the law of two incompatible eras and peddle it as historical fact.

JUSTICE STEVENS, dissenting.

The Just Compensation Clause "was designed to bar Government from forcing some people alone to bear public burdens which, in all fairness and justice, should be borne by the public as a whole." Accordingly, one of the central concerns of our takings jurisprudence is "prevent[ing] the public from loading upon one individual more than his just share of the burdens of government." We have, therefore, in our takings law frequently looked to the *generality* of a regulation of property. [The Beachfront Management Act regulated the coastline of the entire state, did not single out owners of undeveloped land, and did impose some special burdens on owners of developed land (*e.g.*, prohibiting them from rebuilding if their structures were destroyed). Thus, it was not the kind of regulation properly triggering the concerns underlying the Takings Clause.]

[JUSTICE SOUTER filed a separate opinion arguing that certiorari should have been dismissed as improvidently granted, because the finding regarding total loss of market value was not before the Court.]

TAHOE-SIERRA PRESERVATION COUNCIL, INC. v. TAHOE REGIONAL PLANNING AGENCY
535 U.S. 302, 122 S.Ct. 1465, 152 L.Ed.2d 517 (2002)

JUSTICE STEVENS delivered the opinion of the Court.

[Lake Tahoe was described by the Court (quoting President Clinton) as a "national treasure that must be protected and preserved." The Court also quoted Mark Twain's description of the clarity of its waters as "not *merely* transparent, but dazzlingly, brilliantly so." But the clarity of the lake is threatened by algae, which in turn are fed by runoff. Development, particularly on steep ground, increases runoff because of the heavy water flow from paved areas. The Tahoe Regional Planning Agency (TRPA) was established by an interstate compact with the goal of preserving the lake. Because of the complexity of the planning process, a moratorium was imposed for 32 months on all development in the area. TRPA's proposed new plan was challenged in court by the state of California, and development was prohibited for roughly three additional years under an injunction. The dissenters viewed the entire construction freeze to be relevant. However, the majority considered only the initial moratorium. The plaintiff claimed that the moratorium was a taking. The district court agreed, applying the *Lucas* theory, but the court of appeals held that the *Penn Central* test applied instead.]

Certainly, our holding that the permanent "obliteration of the value" of a fee simple estate constitutes a categorical taking does not answer the question whether a regulation prohibiting any economic use of land for a 32-month period has the same legal effect. Petitioners seek to bring this case under the rule announced in *Lucas* by arguing that we can effectively sever a 32-month segment from the remainder of each landowner's fee simple estate, and then ask whether that segment has been taken in its entirety by the moratoria. Of course, defining the property interest taken in terms of the very regulation being challenged is circular. With property so divided, every delay would become a total ban; the moratorium and the normal permit process alike would constitute categorical takings. Petitioners' "conceptual severance" argument is unavailing because it ignores *Penn Central's* admonition that in regulatory takings cases we must focus on "the parcel as a whole." We have consistently rejected such an approach to the "denominator" question. Thus, the District Court erred when it disaggregated petitioners' property into temporal segments corresponding to the regulations at issue and then analyzed whether petitioners were deprived of all economically viable use during each period. The starting point for the court's analysis should have been to ask whether there was a total taking of the entire parcel; if not, then *Penn Central* was the proper framework.

An interest in real property is defined by the metes and bounds that describe its geographic dimensions and the term of years that describes the temporal aspect of the owner's interest. Both dimensions must be considered if the interest is to be viewed in its entirety. Hence, a permanent deprivation of the owner's use of the entire area is a taking of "the parcel as a whole," whereas a temporary restriction that merely causes a diminution in value is not. Logically, a fee simple estate cannot be rendered valueless by a temporary prohibition on economic use, because the property will recover value as soon as the prohibition is lifted.

Neither *Lucas* * * * nor any of our other regulatory takings cases compels us to accept petitioners' categorical submission. In fact, these cases make clear that the categorical rule in *Lucas* was carved out for the "extraordinary case" in which a regulation permanently deprives property of all value; the default rule remains that, in the regulatory taking context, we require a more fact specific inquiry. Nevertheless, we will consider whether the interest in protecting individual property owners from bearing public burdens "which, in all fairness and justice, should be borne by the public as a whole," justifies creating a new rule for these circumstances. * * *

[T]he ultimate constitutional question is whether the concepts of "fairness and justice" that underlie the Takings Clause will be better served [here] by . . . categorical rules or by a *Penn Central* inquiry into all of the relevant circumstances in particular cases. From that perspective, the extreme categorical rule that any deprivation of all economic use, no matter how brief, constitutes a compensable taking surely cannot be sustained. * * *

It may well be true that any moratorium that lasts for more than one year should be viewed with special skepticism. But given the fact that the District Court found that the 32 months required by TRPA to formulate the 1984 Regional Plan was not unreasonable, we could not possibly conclude that every delay of over one year is constitutionally unacceptable. * * * We conclude, therefore, that the interest in "fairness and justice" will be best served by relying on the familiar *Penn Central* approach when deciding cases like this, rather than by attempting to craft a new categorical rule.

CHIEF JUSTICE REHNQUIST, with whom **JUSTICE SCALIA** and **JUSTICE THOMAS** join, dissenting.

For over half a decade petitioners were prohibited from building homes, or any other structures, on their land. Because the Takings Clause requires the government to pay compensation when it deprives owners of all economically viable use of their land, and because a ban on all development lasting almost six years does not resemble any traditional land-use planning device, I dissent.

NOTES ON *LAKE TAHOE*
AND THE CURRENT STATE OF TAKINGS LAW

1. *The Denominator Problem. Lucas* applies only when virtually all of the utility of property has been destroyed. This makes it critical to define the "denominator" — the total property interest considered relevant to the claim. For example, a set-back requirement could be considered a complete taking of the strip where construction is forbidden, or it could be considered a restriction on only a minor percentage of the full parcel. Similarly, a five-day freeze on development could be considered a total taking of a five-day interest in the property, or an negligible intrusion on the fee simple as a whole. In *Lake Tahoe*, the Court defines the denominator (the total property interest) quite broadly, rather than separating the various "sticks" in the bundle of property rights.

In a brief separate dissent, Justice Thomas (joined by Justice Scalia) called into question the Court's focus on the "parcel as a whole." Justice Thomas observed that if the agency had enacted a permanent ban on development, there would have been a taking under *Lucas* even if the ban had been repealed 32 months later. The repeal would only be relevant to the amount of compensation. Is Justice Thomas right that the two situations are indistinguishable? If this is true, does it mean that the exercise of determining the denominator is arbitrary?

2. *Is the Takings Revival Over?* After *Tahoe-Sierra*, the takings revival seems to have lost momentum. The Court gives no sign of repudiating its holdings in *Lucas* or similar cases, but seems disinclined to vigorously police regulations of property. Current indications that expansion of current takings doctrine, if it takes place at all, will probably be cautious.

In the 2004 Term, the Court decided a cluster of three takings cases. None of them was a victory for property rights advocates. We have already seen that in *Kelo* a majority declined an invitation to vigorously police the "public use" requirement. In a second 2005 case, the Court increased the procedural barriers for bringing a regulatory takings case in federal court (though four Justices agreed with the outcome in the case but wanted to lower the ripeness barrier for takings cases.) See *San Remo Hotel v. City and County of San Francisco*, 545 U.S. 323 (2005). Consider a third case, in which the Court rejected the opportunity to scrutinize the efficacy of land use regulations.

Lingle v. Chevron U.S.A., Inc., 544 U.S. 528 (2005), repudiated dicta in previous cases that required government land use regulations to "substantially advance legitimate state interests." This requirement had appeared in a half dozen early opinions, beginning with *Agins v. City of Tiburon*, 447 U.S. 255 (1980). Based on this dictum, the Ninth Circuit struck down a Hawaii statute that limits the rent oil companies may charge service-station operators, on the ground that the statute did not serve its purported purpose of helping to control retail gas prices. In a unanimous opinion by **Justice O'Connor**, the Court rejected this dicta. The Court emphasized that the governing standard for takings is provided by *Penn Central*, outside of the "relatively narrow categories" of permanent physical invasions and total takings, and the "special context of land-use exactions." The Court characterized all of the takings tests as seeking "to identify regulatory actions that are functionally equivalent to the classic taking in which government directly appropriates private property or ousts the owner from his domain." Hence, the tests focus on the burden to owner, not the strength of the government's interest. The touchstone is whether the government has "singled out" a property owner to bear a burden that should be more widely borne by the government.

SECTION 3. EQUAL PROTECTION AND "FUNDAMENTAL INTERESTS"

In Chapters 3 and 4, we considered equal protection as concerned with the fair allocation of governmental benefits or detriments, not with the underlying question of whether the government has the authority to regulate the benefit or detriment in the first place. Moreover, the allocation of benefits or detriments generally need only be minimally rational to pass equal protection scrutiny. From the cases we have seen, heightened scrutiny under the Equal Protection Clause is warranted only if the government action overtly classifies people on the basis of a sensitive criterion (e.g., race) or, although facially neutral, is rooted in intentional discrimination against such a group.

For a simple illustration, consider three state statutes: one outlaws the ownership of guns by anyone; the second outlaws the ownership of guns by convicted felons; the third outlaws the ownership of guns by women. The first statute probably does not even raise any conventional equal protection problems. (It has no underinclusion or overinclusion at all unless the goal is not just to regulate guns but to regulate dangerous objects generally, and even then it easily survives equal protection review.) The second statute is clearly overinclusive (some convicted felons won't harm people if they own guns). It is also underinclusive — it does nothing about convicted felons who possess but don't own guns, and in any event lots of nonfelons are bad bets to own guns, from society's standpoint. Nonetheless, the second statute survives equal protection review because under the Court's decisions only rational-basis scrutiny is available, and the statute clearly passes muster under that standard. The third statute violates equal protection, because the Court's precedents prescribe higher scrutiny for statutes that overtly disadvantage women. Under conventional theory, each of these equal protection inquiries is *egalitarian* in nature, focusing on the extent of overinclusion and underinclusion and the degree to which our norms of equal treatment are offended by the nature of the group disadvantaged (e.g., felons, women) or by the criterion used to classify (e.g., felony convictions, sex).

Of course, even if the statute in question survives conventional equal protection review, it might be unconstitutional nonetheless for some other reason. For example, the Constitution might protect the liberty to own guns explicitly (cf. the Second Amendment) or implicitly (e.g., as an aspect of the "liberty" protected against deprivation without "due process of law" by the Fourteenth Amendment). In contrast to the egalitarian inquiry of classic equal protection, the Second Amendment or due process argument here is *libertarian* and "rights oriented" in nature: It contends that people have a "right" to be free from government regulation of gun ownership even if the government regulation in question is fairly drawn from an egalitarian standpoint. Again, note that the libertarian argument, which focuses on the personal interest being deprived or regulated (e.g., gun ownership), is not a part of the classic equal protection approach.

Now consider a statute that gives veterans of the armed services special preferences. If the preference the state has granted violates an independent constitutional right — such as giving only veterans the right to speak on foreign policy issues — then of course the statute is unconstitutional under the libertarian, rights-oriented approach to which we will soon turn our attention. If, however, no independent constitutional right is involved, our materials so far suggest that the usual challenge will be based on the Equal Protection Clause. But note that our hypothetical statute does not use race, sex, or other established "sensitive factors" to classify people. Also, let us assume that the legislature had no covert intent to discriminate against such a class. It might seem that the only thing left to do under the Equal Protection Clause is apply minimal scrutiny for underinclusion and overinclusion, which the statute will almost surely survive.

Under this analysis, if only "constitutional gratuities" are involved — things to which no one has a constitutional right — the nature of the particular privilege or detriment is irrelevant, and the only questions from the equal protection standpoint are whether the statute (1) flunks higher scrutiny because it overtly or covertly embodies discrimination on the basis of race, gender, and so on; or (2) is so irrationally overinclusive or underinclusive as to flunk minimal scrutiny. This is the conventional approach to equal protection, based on Justice Jackson's concurring opinion in *Railway Express* and on the tiers of higher scrutiny for race, gender, and so on that have arisen since the Jackson opinion.

What the conventional approach ignores, however, is that our fundamental norms about equality are sometimes hard to divorce from a consideration of the particular interests being regulated. For example, our basic sense of equal treatment may not be violated by a law that gives veterans a special preference in getting state jobs. (Even that, of course, is controversial, given the impact of this preference on women, as discussed in *Feeney* (Chapter 4, § 2B).) But surely we would have graver doubts about a law that gives a veteran more than one vote in state judicial elections or that gives only the children of veterans the right to a free public education. Even though such laws might serve the rational purpose of encouraging and rewarding military service, we might well demand a stronger justification for a state decision touching on such important interests.

If we wish to subject these hypothetical veterans preferences to heightened scrutiny, there are three reasons why we might want to look to equal protection rather than due process or some other libertarian constitutional provision as a basis. First, to some extent, our objection to these laws is based on equality — that in giving veterans extra votes or the exclusive right to educate their children free of charge, the government is essentially treating the rest of the populace as second-class citizens. Giving one group certain crucial benefits while depriving others creates a hierarchy that may offend our notion of equality.

Second, a libertarian approach may not work as a source of protection here. How can the Constitution be said to guarantee the right to vote in state judicial elections, given the undisputed power of the government to abolish judicial elections entirely in favor of appointment by the governor? Similarly, it is far from clear that the Constitution requires the state to establish public schools at all. Hence, if state power is limited, it must be on the basis of some kind of equal-treatment principle, rather than by a substantive individual right.

Third, equal protection is a lesser intrusion on legislative autonomy. It leaves to the state, for example, the question of whether to appoint or elect judges, merely requiring that if the electoral route is taken the state must give everyone an equal vote. Similarly, the decision to establish public education may be left to the states even though the courts might police arbitrary exclusions from the public schools.

Despite these potential attractions, equal protection has only sporadically served as a basis for protecting "fundamental interests" that are not independent constitutional rights. One of the relatively few cases is *Skinner* (this Chapter, § 1). Another is *Harper v. Virginia Board of Elections*, 383 U.S. 663 (1966). *Harper* struck down, as violating equal protection, a Virginia statute that imposed a poll tax not exceeding $1.50 upon each voter. The opinion was wonderfully ambiguous, both casually referring to voting as a fundamental right and stating that "[l]ines drawn on the basis of wealth or property, like those of race are traditionally disfavored." Nowhere does the Constitution expressly provide an individual right to vote, however, and probably the Framers of both the original Constitution and the Reconstruction Amendments considered it the prerogative of the states to set the basic requirements for voting. Nor, despite language in *Harper*, has the Court ever held that the poor are a suspect class for equal protection purposes. Since the poll tax statute had a rational basis — more than just raising revenue, the statute could be said to encourage voting only by those persons who consider voting important enough to pay a little something for the privilege — *Harper* is difficult to square with the classical approach to equal protection. Contrast *Lassiter v. Northampton County Board of Elections*, 360 U.S. 45 (1959), where the Court upheld a statute requiring literacy as a precondition to voting.

In this section, we will trace the current developments in voting and wealth discrimination cases. Be careful to examine precisely how the Court defines what is protected in each case, and then consider whether the Equal Protection Clause is the appropriate locus in the Constitution for the protection involved.

A. VOTING

Throughout much of the twentieth century, many state legislatures failed to reapportion their seats in light of shifting population. Because this was a period of urbanization, legislative districts in urban areas tended to have increasingly more voters in them than did rural districts. Could an urban voter challenge the failure to reapportion as unconstitutionally diluting her voting power in the state legislature? One obvious problem with this type of challenge is finding some constitutional provision to serve as its basis. To be sure, as with any governmental allocation of benefits, the Equal Protection Clause can be invoked to challenge this distribution of legislative seats. Unless something more than rational-basis review can be invoked, however, the failure to reapportion would survive traditional equal protection review, since it is probably "rational" for a legislature to accord increased political power to rural residents (for example, to offset the inherent power of urban economic centers). Another textual basis for the challenge might be the Guarantee Clause, Art. IV, § 4, which provides that "[t]he United States shall guarantee to every State in this Union a Republican Form of Government." A severely malapportioned legislature might not seem "republican." A problem with this theory is, however, that under longstanding precedent the Court has held that issues under the Guarantee Clause are nonjusticiable "political questions." See *Luther v. Borden*, 48 U.S. (7 How.) 1 (1849) (Chapter 9, § 1).[a] Indeed, no matter what the constitutional theory, the Court had traditionally seemed very reluctant to address malapportionment claims, considering them "political thickets" that were not amenable to judicial remedy.

All this changed with the cases brought by the NAACP Inc. Fund challenging voting practices in the South that excluded or diluted the votes of African Americans. Building on their earlier Supreme Court decisions which intruded deeply into southern voting rules, the Inc. Fund and the ACLU persuaded the Supreme Court in *Gomillion v. Lightfoot*, 364 U.S. 339 (1960), to adjudicate and invalidate a gerrymander that effectively diluted the votes of blacks in Tuskegee. Once the Court had crossed the political Rubicon in *Gomillion*, it was easier to decide *Baker v. Carr*, 369 U.S. 186 (1962) (Chapter 9, § 1), which held that allegations that a state legislature was malapportioned were justiciable and were properly conceptualized as equal protection claims. In *Gray v. Sanders*, 372 U.S. 368 (1963), the Court invoked the Equal Protection Clause to invalidate the Georgia "county unit system" used in state primary elections for statewide offices, under which a candidate who received the highest number of votes in a county received two votes for each representative the county had in the lower state legislative chamber. The winner of the primary was the candidate who received the most county unit votes. Because counties were represented in the lower state house on a basis other than population, counties with only about a third of the state's population could control the primary election outcome. *Wesberry v. Sanders*, 376 U.S. 1 (1964), struck down a Georgia statute allocating that state's districts in the federal House of Representatives under which some districts had more than twice the population of others. *Wesberry* was based upon Article I, § 2, not the Equal Protection Clause. Then came the following case.

---

a. In *Luther v. Borden*, the Court refused to decide which of two competing groups constituted the lawful government of Rhode Island, which was in a state of some insurrection. The Court thought that the Guarantee Clause contained no judicially manageable standards for determining whether a government was republican and suggested that the clause was enforceable only by the Congress or the President.

REYNOLDS v. SIMS
377 U.S. 533, 84 S.Ct. 1362, 12 L.Ed.2d 506 (1964)

CHIEF JUSTICE WARREN delivered the opinion of the Court.

[Notwithstanding provisions in the Alabama Constitution requiring the state legislature to reapportion its seats in response to the federal census taken every ten years, the last reapportionment of the legislature apparently was based on the 1900 census. Since 1900, the population of Alabama had grown substantially in urban, but not rural, areas, resulting in many more persons in urban than in rural legislative districts. "Under the existing provisions, applying 1960 census figures, only 25.1% of the State's total population resided in districts represented by a majority of the members of the Senate, and only 25.7% lived in counties which could elect a majority of the members of the House of Representatives. Population-variance ratios of up to about 41-to-1 existed in the Senate, and up to about 16-to-1 in the House. Bullock County, with a population of only 13,462, and Henry County, with a population of only 15,286, each were allocated two seats in the Alabama House, whereas Mobile County, with a population of 314,301, was given only three seats, and Jefferson County, with 634,864 people, had only seven representatives. With respect to senatorial apportionment, because the pertinent Alabama constitutional provisions had been consistently construed as prohibiting the giving of more than one Senate seat to any one county, Jefferson County, with over 600,000 people, was given only one senator, as was Lowndes County, with a 1960 population of only 15,417, and Wilcox County, with only 18,739 people."

[In a suit by residents of a large Alabama county against state officials and political party officers, the federal district court concluded that the population inequality among districts violated the Equal Protection Clause, rejected as inadequate two reapportionment plans proposed by the legislature, and developed its own reapportionment plan for the 1962 elections.]

Undeniably the Constitution of the United States protects the right of all qualified citizens to vote, in state as well as in federal elections. A consistent line of decisions by this Court in cases involving attempts to deny or restrict the right of suffrage has made this indelibly clear. [Here Chief Justice Warren cited Fifteenth Amendment cases involving racial gerrymandering or other racially exclusionary tactics and cases involving prosecutions under federal criminal statutes designed to protect the right to vote for federal elected officials or to protect against racial discrimination in voting.] And history has seen a continuing expansion of the scope of the right of suffrage in this country.[b] The right to vote freely for the candidate of one's choice is of the essence of a democratic society, and any restrictions on that right strike at the heart of representative government. And the right of suffrage can be denied by a debasement or dilution of the weight of a citizen's vote just as effectively as by wholly prohibiting the free exercise of the franchise. * * *

---

b. The Fifteenth, Seventeenth, Nineteenth, Twenty-third and Twenty-fourth Amendments to the Federal Constitution all involve expansions of the right of suffrage. Also relevant, in this regard, is the [voting] rights legislation enacted by Congress in 1957 and 1960.

Legislators represent people, not trees or acres. Legislators are elected by voters, not farms or cities or economic interests. As long as ours is a representative form of government, and our legislatures are those instruments of government elected directly by and directly representative of the people, the right to elect legislators in a free and unimpaired fashion is a bedrock of our political system. It could hardly be gainsaid that a constitutional claim had been asserted by an allegation that certain otherwise qualified voters had been entirely prohibited from voting for members of their state legislature. And, if a State should provide that the votes of citizens in one part of the State should be given two times, or five times, or 10 times the weight of votes of citizens in another part of the State, it could hardly be contended that the right to vote of those residing in the disfavored areas had not been effectively diluted. * * * Of course, the effect of state legislative districting schemes which give the same number of representatives to unequal numbers of constituents is identical. * * *

* * * [R]epresentative government is in essence self-government through the medium of elected representatives of the people, and each and every citizen has an inalienable right to full and effective participation in the political processes of his State's legislative bodies. Most citizens can achieve this participation only as qualified voters through the election of legislators to represent them. Full and effective participation by all citizens in state government requires, therefore, that each citizen have an equally effective voice in the election of members of his state legislature. * * *

We are told that the matter of apportioning representation in a state legislature is a complex and many-faceted one. We are advised that States can rationally consider factors other than population in apportioning legislative representation. We are admonished not to restrict the power of the States to impose differing views as to political philosophy on their citizens. We are cautioned about the dangers of entering into political thickets and mathematical quagmires. Our answer is this: a denial of constitutionally protected rights demands judicial protection; our oath and our office require no less of us. * * * Population is, of necessity, the starting point for consideration and the controlling criterion for judgment in legislative apportionment controversies. A citizen, a qualified voter, is no more nor no less so because he lives in the city or on the farm. * * * The Equal Protection Clause demands no less than substantially equal state legislative representation for all citizens, of all places as well as of all races. * * *

Since neither of the houses of the Alabama Legislature, under any of the three plans considered by the District Court, was apportioned on a population basis, we would be justified in proceeding no further. However, one of the proposed plans * * * at least superficially resembles the scheme of legislative representation followed in the Federal Congress [because each county got one representative in the state senate, while the house was apportioned on the basis of population]. * * *

* * * [We] find the federal analogy inapposite and irrelevant to state legislative districting schemes. * * * The original constitutions of 36 of our States provided that representation in both houses of the state legislatures would be based completely, or predominantly, on population. And the Founding

Fathers clearly had no intention of establishing a pattern or model for the apportionment of seats in state legislatures when the system of representation in the Federal Congress was adopted. Demonstrative of this is the fact that the Northwest Ordinance, adopted in the same year, 1787, as the Federal Constitution, provided for the apportionment of seats in territorial legislatures solely on the basis of population.

The system of representation in the two Houses of the Federal Congress is one ingrained in our Constitution, as part of the law of the land. It is one conceived out of compromise and concession indispensable to the establishment of our federal republic. Arising from unique historical circumstances, it is based on the consideration that in establishing our type of federalism a group of formerly independent States bound themselves together under one national government. * * *

* * * [N]either history alone, nor economic or other sorts of group interests, are permissible factors in attempting to justify disparities from population-based representation. Citizens, not history or economic interests, cast votes. Considerations of area alone provide an insufficient justification for deviations from the equal-population principle. Again, people, not land or trees or pastures, vote. * * *

A consideration that appears to be of more substance in justifying some deviations from population-based representation in state legislatures is that of insuring some voice to political subdivisions, as political subdivisions. * * * Local governmental entities are frequently charged with various responsibilities incident to the operation of state government. In many States much of the legislature's activity involves the enactment of so-called local legislation, directed only to the concerns of particular political subdivisions. And a State may legitimately desire to construct districts along political subdivision lines to deter the possibilities of gerrymandering. However, permitting deviations from population-based representation does not mean that each local governmental unit or political subdivision can be given separate representation, regardless of population. Carried too far, a scheme of giving at least one seat in one house to each political subdivision (for example, to each county) could easily result, in many States, in a total subversion of the equal-population principle in that legislative body. * * *

We do not consider here the difficult question of the proper remedial devices which federal courts should utilize in state legislative apportionment cases. Remedial techniques in this new and developing area of the law will probably often differ with the circumstances of the challenged apportionment and a variety of local conditions. It is enough to say now that, once a State's legislative apportionment scheme has been found to be unconstitutional, it would be the unusual case in which a court would be justified in not taking appropriate action to insure that no further elections are conducted under the invalid plan. However, under certain circumstances, such as where an impending election is imminent and a State's election machinery is already in progress, equitable considerations might justify a court in withholding the granting of immediately effective relief in a legislative apportionment case, even though the existing apportionment scheme was found invalid. * * *

[The opinion of **JUSTICE CLARK**, concurring in the affirmance, the separate opinion of **JUSTICE STEWART**, and the dissenting opinion of **JUSTICE HARLAN** are omitted.]

NOTES ON *REYNOLDS*
AND THE "FUNDAMENTAL RIGHT" TO VOTE

1. *Defining the Right.* How does *Reynolds* define the protection the Equal Protection Clause accords voting? Why not adopt a weaker standard, such as the one proposed in a separate opinion by Justice Stewart, who suggested that the Equal Protection Clause be read as outlawing only differences in voting strength that are not rationally defensible or that "permit the systematic frustration of the will of a majority of the electorate of the State"? After all, political influence can be asserted in many ways, not just through the ballot. Moreover, techniques such as providing that one state legislative chamber (like the federal Senate) be smaller than the other and apportioned on some basis other than population could be rational attempts to provide some insulation from the influence of faction (the dominant political currents that Madison feared might overwhelm minority rights).

Following *Wesberry*, the Court has applied the one person, one vote requirement very strictly in the context of apportionment of the House of Representatives, relying upon Article I, § 2, cl. 1. See *Karcher v. Daggett*, 462 U.S. 725 (1983) (invalidating apportionment that had a maximum population deviation of only .7%). The Court has been considerably more flexible under *Reynolds* in reviewing the apportionment of state and local legislative bodies, allowing political subdivision lines and other factors to influence apportionment to some extent. Although generalizations are not simple to construct, it appears that the Court will uphold state and local apportionment plans that contain less than 10% maximum population deviation among districts. For a particularly lenient decision, see *Brown v. Thomson*, 462 U.S. 835 (1983).

2. *History.* In *Reynolds*, Justice Harlan in dissent contended that the Framers of the Fourteenth Amendment did not intend the Equal Protection Clause to be applied to voting.[c] Indeed, the constitutional text itself raises some hard questions about *Reynolds*. Why would the Framers of the Fourteenth Amendment have included § 2 of the Fourteenth Amendment if, as *Reynolds* suggests, the Equal Protection Clause in § 1 outlaws discrimination in voting? Moreover, why adopt the Fifteenth Amendment shortly thereafter if the Equal Protection Clause applied to voting? The legislative history of the Fourteenth Amendment also provides support for Harlan's position. Representative Bingham, a primary congressional sponsor, stated that "[t]he amendment does not give, as the second section shows, the power to Congress of regulating suffrage in the several states." Representative Garfield expressed "profound regret" that the right to vote had not been included in the Amendment, but remarked that "I am willing * * * when I cannot get all I wish to take what I can get." In introducing the Amendment in the Senate, Howard said that § 1 "does not give to either of these

---

c. See also William Van Alstyne, *The Fourteenth Amendment, the "Right" to Vote, and the Understanding of the Thirty-ninth Congress*, 1965 Sup. Ct. Rev. 33.

classes the right of voting," because voting is not one of the "privileges or immunities" secured by the Constitution but is "merely the creature of law." The conclusion that discrimination in voting rights was not covered by the Amendment seems startling today, but was consistent with the distinction drawn at the time between "political" and "civil" rights.[d] If this is a correct rendition of the original understanding, should the Court overrule *Reynolds v. Sims* (not to mention *Shaw v. Reno*, Chapter 3, § 3E, and its successors)?

3. *Denial of the Vote.* In a variety of circumstances, the Supreme Court has held that the Equal Protection Clause forbids a state from denying the vote to otherwise qualified citizens. The principal cases include *Kramer v. Union Free School District*, 395 U.S. 621 (1969) (state may not limit vote in school district election only to those who own or lease taxable real property in the district or who have children enrolled in the school), and *Carrington v. Rash*, 380 U.S. 89 (1965) (state may not bar members of military service from voting in state elections). Recall also *Harper v. Virginia Board of Elections*, the poll tax case mentioned earlier in this Section.

PROBLEM 5-1
POLITICAL GERRYMANDERING

In *Karcher v. Daggett*, 462 U.S. 725 (1983), the plaintiffs seeking a declaratory judgment that the New Jersey congressional districting was unconstitutional included all the Republican members of the federal House of Representatives from New Jersey. Among other arguments, they contended that "the bizarre configuration of New Jersey's Congressional districts is sufficient to demonstrate that the plan was not adopted in 'good faith.' This argument [is] a claim that the district boundaries are unconstitutional because they are the product of political gerrymandering." *Id.* (Stevens, J., concurring). Invoking the Equal Protection Clause, Justice Stevens, in a concurring opinion in *Karcher*, was willing to strike down the redistricting based solely upon the taking of partisan advantage and to consider the noncompact shape of district configurations and "extensive deviation from established political boundaries" as evidence of illicit political gerrymandering. (Justice Powell voiced similar concerns in a separate opinion in *Karcher*.) Justice Stevens also stated:

> A procedural standard * * * may also be enlightening. If the process for formulating and adopting a plan excluded divergent viewpoints, openly reflected the use of partisan criteria, and provided no explanation of the reasons for selecting one plan over another, it would seem appropriate to conclude that an adversely affected plaintiff group is entitled to have the majority explain its action. On the other hand, if neutral decisionmakers developed the plan on the basis of neutral criteria, if there was an adequate opportunity for the presentation and consideration of differing points of view, and if the guidelines used in selecting a plan were explained, a strong presumption of validity should attach to whatever plan such a process produced. * * *

> A glance at the [districting] map * * * shows district configurations well deserving the kind of descriptive adjectives — "uncouth" and "bizarre" — that have traditionally been used to describe acknowledged gerrymanders. * * * In addition

---

d. See Daniel Farber & Suzanna Sherry, *A History of the American Constitution* 310-11, 314, 365 (1990).

[to] disregarding geographical compactness, the redistricting scheme wantonly disregards county boundaries. For example, in the words of a commentator: "In a flight of cartographic fancy, the Legislature packed New Jersey Republicans into a new district many call 'the Swan.' Its long neck and twisted body stretch from the New York suburbs to the rural upper reaches of the Delaware River." That district, the Fifth, contains segments of at least seven counties. The same commentator described the Seventh District, comprised of parts of five counties, as tracing "a curving partisan path through industrial Elizabeth, liberal, academic Princeton and largely Jewish Marlboro in Monmouth County. The resulting monstrosity was called 'the Fishhook' by detractors." 40 Cong.Q. 1193-1195 (1982).

Such a map prompts an inquiry into the process that led to its adoption. The plan was sponsored by the leadership in the Democratic Party, which controlled both houses of the state legislature as well as the Governor's office, and was signed into law the day before the inauguration of a Republican Governor. The legislators never formally explained the guidelines used in formulating their plan or in selecting it over other available plans. Several [other plans] contained districts that were more nearly equal in population, more compact, and more consistent with subdivision boundaries. * * * [T]he record indicates that the decisionmaking process leading to adoption of the challenged plan was far from neutral. It was designed to increase the number of Democrats, and to decrease the number of Republicans, that New Jersey's voters would send to Congress in future years.

Should this amount to a violation of Article I, § 2 or the Equal Protection Clause? Cf. *Davis v. Bandemer*, 478 U.S. 109 (1986); Samuel Issacharoff, *Judging Politics: The Elusive Quest for Judicial Review of Political Fairness*, 71 Tex. L. Rev. 1643 (1993).

The Court returned to the topic of political gerrymandering in *Vieth v. Jubelirer*, 541 U.S. 267 (2004), but was unable to produce a majority opinion. Compare the opinion of Justice Scalia, joined by Chief Rehnquist and Justices O'Connor & Thomas (political gerrymandering claims should be nonjusticiable) with opinion of Justice Kennedy, concurring in the judgment (agreeing with dismissal of this case but unwilling to decide that such claims are always nonjusticiable) and with dissenting opinions of Justice Stevens, Justice Souter (joined by Justice Ginsburg), and Justice Breyer (such claims should be justiciable). In addition, see *League of United Latin American Citizens v. Perry*, 548 U.S. 399 (2006) (again leaving the justiciability question unresolved).

BUSH v. GORE
531 U.S. 98, 121 S.Ct. 525, 148 L.E.2d 388 (2000)

PER CURIAM.

[This case arose out of the hotly contested election of 2000. Al Gore emerged with a slight lead in the national popular vote, but the electoral college vote depended on Florida, where George W. Bush had a razor-thin margin on the initial count (about 1,700 votes out of roughly six million cast). Because Bush's margin was less than .5%, an automatic machine recount was conducted, which showed Bush still winning but by a smaller margin. Pursuant to Florida law, Gore then demanded manual recounts in four counties. A dispute arose about the deadline for local canvassing boards to submit their returns to the Secretary of State. The Florida Supreme Court overturned the Secretary's refusal to extend the deadline, but the U.S. Supreme Court remanded that decision for further consideration. Since Article II, § 1, cl. 2 requires presidential electors to be selected in "such Manner as the [state legislature] may direct," the Court sought further clarification on whether the Florida court's decision was based on ordinary principles of construing state statutes adopted by the legislature or, instead, was based on the state constitution's guarantee of the right to vote. In the meantime, the Florida court's new deadline had expired, and the state electoral commission had declared Bush the victor. Gore then filed a state court complaint, pursuant to a state statute providing that "[r]eceipt of a number of illegal votes or rejection of a number of legal votes sufficient to change or place in doubt the result of the election" is grounds for contesting the result. In response, the Florida Supreme Court ordered a statewide manual recount under the supervision of a single trial judge. To complicate matters further, a federal statute purported to give a presumption of validity to the state's electors if the state finally determined the validity of its returns by December 12. The Supreme Court stayed the Florida decision on December 9 by a 5-4 vote.]

___The individual citizen has no federal constitutional right to vote for electors for the President of the United States unless and until the state legislature chooses a statewide election as the means to implement its power to appoint members of the electoral college. U.S. Const., Art. II, § 1. This is the source for the statement in *McPherson v. Blacker*, 146 U.S. 1 (1892), that the State legislature's power to select the manner for appointing electors is plenary; it may, if it so chooses, select the electors itself, which indeed was the manner used by state legislatures in several States for many years after the framing of our Constitution. History has now favored the voter, and in each of the several States the citizens themselves vote for Presidential electors. When the state legislature vests the right to vote for President in its people, the right to vote as the legislature has prescribed is fundamental; and one source of its fundamental nature lies in the equal weight accorded to each vote and the equal dignity owed to each voter. The State, of course, after granting the franchise in the special context of Article II, can take back the power to appoint electors. See *id.* ("[T]here is no doubt of the right of the legislature to resume the power at any time, for it can neither be taken away nor abdicated").

The right to vote is protected in more than the initial allocation of the franchise. Equal protection applies as well to the manner of its exercise. Having once granted the right to vote on equal terms, the State may not, by later arbitrary and disparate treatment, value one person's vote over that of another. It must be remembered that "the right of suffrage can be denied by a debasement or dilution of the weight of a citizen's vote just as effectively as by wholly prohibiting the free exercise of the franchise." *Reynolds v. Sims.*

There is no difference between the two sides of the present controversy on these basic propositions. Respondents say that the very purpose of vindicating the right to vote justifies the recount procedures now at issue. The question before us, however, is whether the recount procedures the Florida Supreme Court has adopted are consistent with its obligation to avoid arbitrary and disparate treatment of the members of its electorate.

Much of the controversy seems to revolve around ballot cards designed to be perforated by a stylus but which, either through error or deliberate omission, have not been perforated with sufficient precision for a machine to register the perforations. In some cases a piece of the card — a chad — is hanging, say, by two corners. In other cases there is no separation at all, just an indentation.

The Florida Supreme Court has ordered that the intent of the voter be discerned from such ballots. For purposes of resolving the equal protection challenge, it is not necessary to decide whether the Florida Supreme Court had the authority under the legislative scheme for resolving election disputes to define what a legal vote is and to mandate a manual recount implementing that definition. The recount mechanisms implemented in response to the decisions of the Florida Supreme Court do not satisfy the minimum requirement for nonarbitrary treatment of voters necessary to secure the fundamental right. Florida's basic command for the count of legally cast votes is to consider the "intent of the voter." This is unobjectionable as an abstract proposition and a starting principle. The problem inheres in the absence of specific standards to ensure its equal application. The formulation of uniform rules to determine intent based on these recurring circumstances is practicable and, we conclude, necessary.

The law does not refrain from searching for the intent of the actor in a multitude of circumstances; and in some cases the general command to ascertain intent is not susceptible to much further refinement. In this instance, however, the question is not whether to believe a witness but how to interpret the marks or holes or scratches on an inanimate object, a piece of cardboard or paper which, it is said, might not have registered as a vote during the machine count. The factfinder confronts a thing, not a person. The search for intent can be confined by specific rules designed to ensure uniform treatment.

The want of those rules here has led to unequal evaluation of ballots in various respects. As seems to have been acknowledged at oral argument, the standards for accepting or rejecting contested ballots might vary not only from county to county but indeed within a single county from one recount team to another. * * *

The recount process, in its features here described, is inconsistent with the minimum procedures necessary to protect the fundamental right of each voter in the special instance of a statewide recount under the authority of a single state judicial officer. Our consideration is limited to the present circumstances, for the problem of equal protection in election processes generally presents many complexities.

The question before the Court is not whether local entities, in the exercise of their expertise, may develop different systems for implementing elections. Instead, we are presented with a situation where a state court with the power to assure uniformity has ordered a statewide recount with minimal procedural safeguards. When a court orders a statewide remedy, there must be at least some assurance that the rudimentary requirements of equal treatment and fundamental fairness are satisfied. * * *

The Supreme Court of Florida has said that the legislature intended the State's electors to "participat[e] fully in the federal electoral process," as provided in 3 U.S.C. § 5. That statute, in turn, requires that any controversy or contest that is designed to lead to a conclusive selection of electors be completed by December 12. That date is upon us, and there is no recount procedure in place under the State Supreme Court's order that comports with minimal constitutional standards. Because it is evident that any recount seeking to meet the December 12 date will be unconstitutional for the reasons we have discussed, we reverse the judgment of the Supreme Court of Florida ordering a recount to proceed.

Seven Justices of the Court agree that there are constitutional problems with the recount ordered by the Florida Supreme Court that demand a remedy [citing the dissents by Justices Souter and Breyer, agreeing that the Florida procedure raised equal protection concerns.] The only disagreement is as to the remedy. Because the Florida Supreme Court has said that the Florida Legislature intended to obtain the safe-harbor benefits of 3 U.S.C. § 5, Justice Breyer's proposed remedy — remanding to the Florida Supreme Court for its ordering of a constitutionally proper contest until December 18 — contemplates action in violation of the Florida Election Code, and hence could not be part of an "appropriate" order authorized by Fla. Stat. § 102.168(8) (2000). [The majority concluded that remand would not be appropriate.]

None are more conscious of the vital limits on judicial authority than are the Members of this Court, and none stand more in admiration of the Constitution's design to leave the selection of the President to the people, through their legislatures, and to the political sphere. When contending parties invoke the process of the courts, however, it becomes our unsought responsibility to resolve the federal and constitutional issues the judicial system has been forced to confront.

[**CHIEF JUSTICE REHNQUIST**, joined by **JUSTICES SCALIA** and **THOMAS**, concurred on the ground that the Florida Supreme Court had so blatantly misapplied Florida election law as to violate the mandate of Article II that the election be conducted in the manner dictated by the state legislature.]

JUSTICE STEVENS, with whom **JUSTICE GINSBURG** and **JUSTICE BREYER** join, dissenting.

The Constitution assigns to the States the primary responsibility for determining the manner of selecting the Presidential electors. See Art. II, § 1, cl. 2. When questions arise about the meaning of state laws, including election laws, it is our settled practice to accept the opinions of the highest courts of the States as providing the final answers. On rare occasions, however, either federal statutes or the Federal Constitution may require federal judicial intervention in state elections. This is not such an occasion. * * *

Nor are petitioners correct in asserting that the failure of the Florida Supreme Court to specify in detail the precise manner in which the "intent of the voter" is to be determined rises to the level of a constitutional violation. We found such a violation when individual votes within the same State were weighted unequally, but we have never before called into question the substantive standard by which a State determines that a vote has been legally cast. And there is no reason to think that the guidance provided to the factfinders, specifically the various canvassing boards, by the "intent of the voter" standard is any less sufficient — or will lead to results any less uniform — than, for example, the "beyond a reasonable doubt" standard employed every day by ordinary citizens in courtrooms across this country.

Admittedly, the use of differing substandards for determining voter intent in different counties employing similar voting systems may raise serious concerns. Those concerns are alleviated — if not eliminated — by the fact that a single impartial magistrate will ultimately adjudicate all objections arising from the recount process. Of course, as a general matter, "[t]he interpretation of constitutional principles must not be too literal. We must remember that the machinery of government would not work if it were not allowed a little play in its joints." If it were otherwise, Florida's decision to leave to each county the determination of what balloting system to employ — despite enormous differences in accuracy — might run afoul of equal protection. So, too, might the similar decisions of the vast majority of state legislatures to delegate to local authorities certain decisions with respect to voting systems and ballot design.

Even assuming that aspects of the remedial scheme might ultimately be found to violate the Equal Protection Clause, I could not subscribe to the majority's disposition of the case. As the majority explicitly holds, once a state legislature determines to select electors through a popular vote, the right to have one's vote counted is of constitutional stature. As the majority further acknowledges, Florida law holds that all ballots that reveal the intent of the voter constitute valid votes. Recognizing these principles, the majority nonetheless orders the termination of the contest proceeding before all such votes have been tabulated. Under their own reasoning, the appropriate course of action would be to remand to allow more specific procedures for implementing the legislature's uniform general standard to be established. * * *

What must underlie petitioners' entire federal assault on the Florida election procedures is an unstated lack of confidence in the impartiality and capacity of the state judges who would make the critical decisions if the vote count were to proceed. Otherwise, their position is wholly without merit. The endorsement of that position by the majority of this Court can only lend credence to the most cynical appraisal of the work of judges throughout the land. It is confidence in the men and women who administer the judicial system that is the true backbone of the rule of law. Time will one day heal the wound to that confidence that will be inflicted by today's decision. One thing, however, is certain. Although we may never know with complete certainty the identity of the winner of this year's Presidential election, the identity of the loser is perfectly clear. It is the Nation's confidence in the judge as an impartial guardian of the rule of law.

[Dissenting opinions by **JUSTICES GINSBURG**, **SOUTER**, and **BREYER** are omitted.]

NOTES ON *BUSH v. GORE*

1. *The Equality/Substantive Right Distinction. Bush* dramatically illustrates the difference between a substantive claim and an equality claim. Because the right to vote for President is fundamental only for equality purposes, completely abolishing the right — either for all voters, or merely for those whose ballots were poorly marked — would seem to raise no federal constitutional problem.

(Recall that the President is formally elected by the Electoral College, and electors are chosen in such manner as the state legislatures provide.) But using different methods in different counties to decipher poorly marked ballots raises an equality issue. Thus, it would seem, by mandating that none of the votes be counted unless all can be counted alike, the Court vindicates the fundamental right to vote. That, at least, is the theory of the opinion.

2. *Precedential Implications.* The dissenters suggest that the majority opinion raises grave doubts about the use of voting methods in different districts having different levels of reliability. (For example, optical scanners used in some other places are much more reliable than the card punch method used in the disputed Florida counties). Do you agree? Similarly, in Florida, different counties used different standards for accepting absentee ballots. Is this permissible? Ultimately, in order to avoid the risk of having elections halted or set aside by the federal courts, will states be required to adopt uniform statewide election methods and procedures?

3. *Political and Jurisprudential Implications. Bush v. Gore* produced the strongest popular and scholarly reaction to a Supreme Court decision in recent years. For a sampling of academic views, see Bush v. Gore: *The Question of Legitimacy* (Bruce Ackerman ed. 2002); *A Badly Flawed Election: Debating* Bush v. Gore, *the Supreme Court, and American Democracy* (Ronald Dworkin ed. 2002); Richard Posner, *Breaking the Deadlock: The 2000 Election, the Constitution, and the Courts* (2001); *The Vote: Bush, Gore, and the Supreme Court* (Cass Sunstein & Richard Epstein eds. 2001); Jack Balkin, Bush v. Gore *and the Boundary Between Law and Politics,* 110 Yale L.J. 1407 (2001); Jesse Choper, *Why the Supreme Court Should Not Have Decided the Presidential Election of 2000,* 18 Const. Comm. 335 (2002); Symposium, *The Law of Presidential Elections: Issues in the Wake of Florida 2000,* 29 Fla. State U. L. Rev. (2001). (Comprehensive background on the case can be found in Samuel Issacharoff, Pamela Karlan & Richard Pildes, *When Elections Go Bad: The Law of Democracy and the Presidential Election of 2000* (2001).) Defenders of the Court tend to proclaim that the Florida vote-counting process had become unconscionably arbitrary or biased and that the Court properly stepped in to end what was becoming a national political catastrophe. Opponents argue, among other things, that the Court should have remanded the case so that the Florida trial court could have attempted to achieve compliance with the new requirements. More broadly, opponents tend to condemn the Court for taking the issue away from the political process (a contested election would have been resolved in the U.S. House of Representatives) on flimsy doctrinal grounds and writing an opinion seemingly designed to apply to no other situation. Opponents also note the irony that the five Justices in the majority that deprived the Florida courts of authority are the five Justices who routinely vote to limit federal intrusions into state affairs (see Chapter 7). One response to such complaints might be to say that *Bush v. Gore* is simply the same sort of activism as *Roe v. Wade*, just to different political and social ends.

Whatever might be said about the decision jurisprudentially, the American people (other than Democratic Party loyalists) have apparently supported it. If anything, the decision has increased the Court's legitimacy with the citizenry.

This development may turn the notion of and justifications for judicial restraint on their head.

Crawford v. Marion County Election Bd., 128 S.Ct. 1610 (2008). A coalition of plaintiffs challenged an Indiana law, which had passed on a party-line vote in the state legislature, that required persons seeking to vote to present a government-issued photo identification. **Justice Stevens**, joined by **Chief Justice Roberts** and **Justice Kennedy**, concluded that the law was not susceptible to a facial challenge. Stevens applied a balancing test and concluded that the statute was facially justified by the state's interest in preventing voter fraud and instilling confidence in the electoral process. The Stevens opinion left open the possibility that a narrower attack on the statute's application to specific groups might be sustainable on a different factual record.

Justice Scalia, joined by **Justices Thomas** and **Alito**, maintained that "weighing the burden of a nondiscriminatory voting law upon each voter and concomitantly requiring exceptions for vulnerable voters would effectively turn back decades of equal-protection jurisprudence. A voter complaining about such a law's effect on him has no valid equal-protection claim because, without proof of discriminatory intent, a generally applicable law with disparate impact is not unconstitutional." Justice Scalia continued:

> * * * This is an area where the dos and don'ts need to be known in advance of the election, and voter-by-voter examination of the burdens of voting regulations would prove especially disruptive. A case-by-case approach naturally encourages constant litigation. Very few new election regulations improve everyone's lot, so the potential allegations of severe burden are endless. * * *
>
> That sort of detailed judicial supervision of the election process would flout the Constitution's express commitment of the task to the States. See Art. I, § 4. It is for state legislatures to weigh the costs and benefits of possible changes to their election codes, and their judgment must prevail unless it imposes a severe and unjustified overall burden upon the right to vote, or is intended to disadvantage a particular class. Judicial review of their handiwork must apply an objective, uniform standard that will enable them to determine, *ex ante*, whether the burden they impose is too severe.

Justice Souter, joined by **Justice Ginsburg**, dissented. Justice Souter maintained that the statute failed the balancing test because it "threatens to impose nontrivial burdens on the voting right of tens of thousands of the State's citizens, and a significant percentage of those individuals are likely to be deterred from voting." **Justice Breyer** also dissented. Curiously, none of the opinions in the case cited *Bush v. Gore*, which seems to have had little or no precedential impact.

B.   BASIC RIGHTS FOR THE LEAST ADVANTAGED

Once the NAACP's Inc. Fund had substantially won its campaign against apartheid, its focus shifted from policies discriminating on the basis of race to those having racially disproportionate effects. A big variable correlating with race was poverty; state policies shortchanging the poor typically harmed Latinos and African Americans the most. Progressive attorneys in the Inc. Fund, ACLU, and other public interest groups brought lawsuits to recognize rights of poor people — including "welfare rights," a minimal standard of living for all Americans.[e] In 1970, the welfare rights movement won a surprising victory in *Goldberg v. Kelly* (§ 6A of this chapter), which held that welfare recipients have a constitutional entitlement that cannot be taken away without notice and a right to be heard. *Goldberg*, however, was the movement's high-water point. Once all four Nixon Justices were in place, the Court trimmed back welfare rights, rejecting claims that state welfare programs discriminated against certain kinds of poor families. See *Dandridge v. Williams*, 397 U.S. 471 (1970) (rejecting challenge to Maryland's policy of capping family grants regardless of family size); *Jefferson v. Hackney*, 406 U.S. 535 (1972) (rejecting challenge to Texas's policy of underfunding family grants, which had a hugely disproportionate effect on Latino and African American welfare recipients). Confirming that the Court was closing the doors to at least most challenges to state policies hurting the poor, the Burger Court applied those precedents to the field of education in the following case. Was there a limit to what states could do?

SAN ANTONIO INDEPENDENT SCHOOL DISTRICT v. RODRIGUEZ
411 U.S. 1, 93 S.Ct. 1278, 36 L.Ed.2d 16 (1973)

JUSTICE POWELL delivered the opinion of the Court.

[In this suit attacking the Texas system of financing public education, Mexican-American parents whose children attended schools in the Edgewood Independent School District in San Antonio brought a class action on behalf of schoolchildren throughout the State who are members of minority groups or who are poor and live in school districts having a low property tax base.]

* * * [Edgewood District] has been compared throughout this litigation with the Alamo Heights Independent School District[, a] comparison between the least and most affluent districts in the San Antonio area [that] serves to illustrate the manner in which the dual system of finance operates and to indicate the extent to which substantial disparities exist despite the State's impressive progress in recent years. Edgewood is one of seven public school districts in the metropolitan area. Approximately 22,000 students are enrolled in its 25 elementary and secondary schools. The district is situated in the core-city sector of San Antonio in a residential neighborhood that has little commercial or industrial property. The residents are predominantly of Mexican-American descent: approximately 90% of the student population is Mexican-American and over 6% is Negro. The average assessed property value per pupil is $5,960 — the lowest in the metropolitan area — and the median family income ($4,686) is also the lowest. At an equalized tax rate of $1.05 per $100 of assessed property — the highest in the metropolitan area — the district contributed $26 to the education of each child for the 1967-1968 school year

---

e. See generally Martha Davis, *Brutal Need: Lawyers and the Welfare Rights Movement, 1960-1973* (1994); Elizabeth Bussiere, *(Dis)Entitling the Poor: The Warren Court, Welfare Rights, and the American Political Tradition* (1997); Shep Melnick, *Between the Lines: Interpreting Welfare Rights* (1994).

above its Local Fund Assignment for the [Texas State] Minimum Foundation Program. The Foundation Program contributed $222 per pupil for a state-local total of $248. Federal funds added another $108 for a total of $356 per pupil.

Alamo Heights is the most affluent school district in San Antonio. Its six schools, housing approximately 5,000 students, are situated in a residential community quite unlike the Edgewood District. The school population is predominantly "Anglo," having only 18% Mexican-Americans and less than 1% Negroes. The assessed property value per pupil exceeds $49,000, and the median family income is $8,001. In 1967-1968 the local tax rate of $.85 per $100 of valuation yielded $333 per pupil over and above its contribution to the Foundation Program. Coupled with the $225 provided from that Program, the district was able to supply $558 per student. Supplemented by a $36 per-pupil grant from federal sources, Alamo Heights spent $594 per pupil. * * *

* * * [Substantial interdistrict] disparities, largely attributable to differences in the amounts of money collected through local property taxation, * * * led the District Court to conclude that Texas' dual system of public school financing violated the Equal Protection Clause. * * * Finding that wealth is a "suspect" classification and that education is a "fundamental" interest, the District Court held that the Texas system could be sustained only if the State could show that it was premised upon some compelling state interest. On this issue the court concluded that "[n]ot only are defendants unable to demonstrate compelling state interests * * * they fail even to establish a reasonable basis for these classifications."

[The Court rejected the wealth-discrimination argument for two reasons: "First, in support of their charge that the system discriminates against the 'poor,' appellees have made no effort to demonstrate that it operates to the peculiar disadvantage of any class fairly definable as indigent, or as composed of persons whose incomes are beneath any designated poverty level. Indeed, there is reason to believe that the poorest families are not necessarily clustered in the poorest property districts." And second: "The argument here is not that the children in districts having relatively low assessable property values are receiving no public education; rather, it is that they are receiving a poorer quality education than that available to children in districts having more assessable wealth. Apart from the unsettled and disputed question whether the quality of education may be determined by the amount of money expended for it, a sufficient answer to appellees' argument is that, at least where wealth is involved, the Equal Protection Clause does not require absolute equality or precisely equal advantages."]

In *Brown v. Board of Education*, a unanimous Court recognized that "education is perhaps the most important function of state and local governments." * * *

Nothing this Court holds today in any way detracts from our historic dedication to public education. We are in complete agreement with the conclusion of the three-judge panel below that "the grave significance of education both to the individual and to our society" cannot be doubted. But the importance of a service performed by the State does not determine whether it must be regarded as fundamental for purposes of examination under the Equal Protection Clause. Mr. Justice Harlan, dissenting from the Court's application of strict scrutiny to a law impinging upon the right of interstate travel, admonished that "[v]irtually every state statute affects important rights." *Shapiro v. Thompson*[, 394 U.S. 618 (1969)] (Harlan, J., dissenting). In his view, if the degree of judicial scrutiny of state legislation fluctuated, depending on a majority's view of the importance of the interest affected, we would have gone "far toward making this Court a " 'super-legislature.' " We would, indeed, then be assuming a legislative role and one for which the Court lacks both authority and competence. * * *

The lesson of these cases in addressing the question now before the Court is plain. It is not the province of this Court to create substantive constitutional rights in the name of guaranteeing equal protection of the laws. Thus, the key to discovering whether education is "fundamental" is not to be found in comparisons of the relative societal significance of education as opposed to subsistence or housing. Nor is it to be found by weighing whether education is as important as the right to travel. Rather, the answer lies in assessing whether there is a right to education explicitly or implicitly guaranteed by the Constitution. * * * *Dunn v. Blumstein*, 405 U.S. 330 (1972);[f] * * * *Skinner v. Oklahoma*.[g]

Education, of course, is not among the rights afforded explicit protection under our Federal Constitution. Nor do we find any basis for saying it is implicitly so protected. * * * It is appellees' contention, however, that education is distinguishable from other services and benefits provided by the State because it bears a peculiarly close relationship to other rights and liberties accorded protection under the Constitution. Specifically, they insist that education is itself a fundamental personal right because it is essential to the effective exercise of First Amendment freedoms and to intelligent utilization of the right to vote. In asserting a nexus between speech and education, appellees urge that the right to speak is meaningless unless the speaker is capable of articulating his thoughts intelligently and persuasively. The "marketplace of ideas" is an empty forum for those lacking basic communicative tools. Likewise, they argue that the corollary right to receive information becomes little more than a hollow privilege when the recipient has not been taught to read, assimilate, and utilize available knowledge.

A similar line of reasoning is pursued with respect to the right to vote. Exercise of the franchise, it is contended, cannot be divorced from the educational foundation of the voter. The electoral process, if reality is to conform to the democratic ideal, depends on an informed electorate * * * .

---

f. *Dunn* fully canvasses this Court's voting rights cases and explains that "this Court has made clear that a citizen has a *constitutionally protected right* to participate in elections on an equal basis with other citizens in the jurisdiction." (Emphasis supplied.)

g. *Skinner* applied the standard of close scrutiny to a state law permitting forced sterilization of "habitual criminals." Implicit in the Court's opinion is the recognition that the right of procreation is among the rights of personal privacy protected under the Constitution. See *Roe v. Wade*, 410 U.S. 113 (1973).

* * * [W]e have never presumed to possess either the ability or the authority to guarantee to the citizenry the most *effective* speech or the most *informed* electoral choice. That these may be desirable goals of a system of freedom of expression and of a representative form of government is not to be doubted. * * * But they are not values to be implemented by judicial intrusion into otherwise legitimate state activities.

Even if it were conceded that some identifiable quantum of education is a constitutionally protected prerequisite to the meaningful exercise of either right, we have no indication that the present levels of educational expenditures in Texas provide an education that falls short. * * * Whatever merit appellees' argument might have if a State's financing system occasioned an absolute denial of educational opportunities to any of its children, that argument provides no basis for finding an interference with fundamental rights where only relative differences in spending levels are involved and where — as is true in the present case — no charge fairly could be made that the system fails to provide each child with an opportunity to acquire the basic minimal skills necessary for the enjoyment of the rights of speech and of full participation in the political process.

[The concurring opinion of **JUSTICE STEWART**, the dissenting opinion of **JUSTICE BRENNAN**, and the dissenting opinion of **JUSTICE WHITE**, joined by **JUSTICES DOUGLAS** and **BRENNAN**, are omitted.]

JUSTICE MARSHALL, joined by **JUSTICE DOUGLAS**, dissenting.

* * * The Court apparently seeks to establish today that equal protection cases fall into one of two neat categories which dictate the appropriate standard of review — strict scrutiny or mere rationality. But this Court's decisions in the field of equal protection defy such easy categorization. A principled reading of what this Court has done reveals that it has applied a spectrum of standards in reviewing discrimination allegedly violative of the Equal Protection Clause. This spectrum clearly comprehends variations in the degree of care with which the Court will scrutinize particular classifications, depending, I believe, on the constitutional and societal importance of the interest adversely affected and the recognized invidiousness of the basis upon which the particular classification is drawn. I find in fact that many of the Court's recent decisions embody the very sort of reasoned approach to equal protection analysis for which I previously argued — that is, an approach in which "concentration [is] placed upon the character of the classification in question, the relative importance to individuals in the class discriminated against of the governmental benefits that they do not receive, and the asserted state interests in support of the classification." *Dandridge* ([Marshall's] dissenting opinion).

I therefore cannot accept the majority's labored efforts to demonstrate that fundamental interests, which call for strict scrutiny of the challenged classification, encompass only established rights which we are somehow bound to recognize from the text of the Constitution itself. To be sure, some interests which the Court has deemed to be fundamental for purposes of equal protection analysis are themselves constitutionally protected rights. Thus, discrimination against the guaranteed right of freedom of speech has called for strict judicial scrutiny. See *Police Dept. Of Chicago v. Mosley*, 408 U.S. 92 (1972). Further, every citizen's right to travel interstate, although nowhere expressly mentioned in the Constitution, has long been recognized as implicit in the premises underlying that document: the right "was conceived from the beginning to be a necessary concomitant of the stronger Union the Constitution created." *United States v. Guest*, 383 U.S. 745, 758 (1966). * * * But it will not do to suggest that the "answer" to whether an interest is fundamental for purposes of equal protection analysis is always determined by whether that interest "is a right . . . explicitly or implicitly guaranteed by the Constitution."

I would like to know where the Constitution guarantees the right to procreate, *Skinner*, or the right to vote in state elections, e. g., *Reynolds*, or the right to an appeal from a criminal conviction, e. g., *Griffin v. Illinois*, 351 U.S. 12 (1956). These are instances in which, due to the importance of the interests at stake, the Court has displayed a strong concern with the existence of discriminatory state treatment. But the Court has never said or indicated that these are interests which independently enjoy full-blown constitutional protection. * * *

[T]he right to vote in state elections has been recognized as a "fundamental political right," because the Court concluded very early that it is "preservative of all rights." *Yick Wo*; see also *Reynolds*. * * *

The majority is, of course, correct when it suggests that the process of determining which interests are fundamental is a difficult one. But I do not think the problem is insurmountable. And I certainly do not accept the view that the process need necessarily degenerate into an unprincipled, subjective "picking-and-choosing" between various interests or that it must involve this Court in creating "substantive constitutional rights in the name of guaranteeing equal protection of the laws." Although not all fundamental interests are constitutionally guaranteed, the determination of which interests are fundamental should be firmly rooted in the text of the Constitution. The task in every case should be to determine the extent to which constitutionally guaranteed rights are dependent on interests not mentioned in the Constitution. As the nexus between the specific constitutional guarantee and the nonconstitutional interest draws closer, the nonconstitutional interest becomes more fundamental and the degree of judicial scrutiny applied when the interest is infringed on a discriminatory basis must be adjusted accordingly. Thus, it cannot be denied that interests such as procreation, the exercise of the state franchise, and access to criminal appellate processes are not fully guaranteed to the citizen by our Constitution. But these interests have nonetheless been afforded special judicial consideration in the face of discrimination because they are, to some extent, interrelated with constitutional guarantees. Procreation is now understood to be important because of its interaction with the established constitutional right of privacy. The exercise of the state franchise is closely tied to basic civil and political rights inherent in the First Amendment. And access to criminal appellate processes enhances the integrity of the range of rights implicit in the Fourteenth Amendment guarantee of due process of law. Only if we closely protect the related interests from state discrimination do we ultimately ensure the integrity of the constitutional guarantee itself. This is the real lesson that must be taken from our previous decisions involving interests deemed to be fundamental. [Justice Marshall compared this process of analogy to the process the Court has used to determine which classifications should trigger heightened equal protection scrutiny.]

In summary, it seems to me inescapably clear that this Court has consistently adjusted the care with which it will review state discrimination in light of the constitutional significance of the interests affected and the invidiousness of the particular classification. In the context of economic interests, we find that discriminatory state action is almost always sustained, for such interests are generally far removed from constitutional guarantees. * * * But the situation differs markedly when discrimination against important individual interests with constitutional implications and against particularly disadvantaged or powerless classes is involved. The majority suggests, however, that a variable standard of review would give this Court the appearance of a "superlegislature." I cannot agree. Such an approach seems to me a part of the guarantees of our Constitution and of the historic experiences with oppression of and discrimination against discrete, powerless minorities which underlie that document. * * *

———

Plyler v. Doe, 457 U.S. 202 (1982). By a 1975 amendment to state education statutes, the Texas legislature refused to provide state funds to local school districts for the education of children not "legally admitted" into the United States, and school districts were authorized to deny enrollment to such children. In several class actions brought by school-age children of Mexican descent living in Texas who could not document legal immigration status, the lower courts concluded that this statute violated the Equal Protection Clause. In an opinion by **Justice Brennan**, a sharply divided Court affirmed. Justice Brennan began with the premise that the "Equal Protection Clause was intended to work nothing less than the abolition of all caste-based and invidious class-based legislation." The Court rejected the claim that "illegal aliens" are a "suspect class" for two reasons: Illegal entry is a voluntary action, and it is not in general a "constitutional irrelevancy" (given the government's power to control access to the United States). "At the least, those who elect to enter our territory by stealth and in violation of our law should be prepared to bear the consequences, including, but not limited to, deportation." But their children are not "comparably situated," having no control over the situation; thus, the legislation violated the fundamental premise that " 'no child is responsible for his birth and penalizing the * * * child is an ineffectual — as well as unjust — way of deterring the parent' " (quoting a case involving discrimination against illegitimate children). Moreover, although public education is not a fundamental right, "neither is it merely some governmental 'benefit' indistinguishable from other forms of social welfare legislation." The statute "imposes a lifetime hardship on a discrete class of children not accountable for their disabling status," because the "stigma of illiteracy will mark them for the rest of their lives." Thus, the discrimination "can hardly be considered rational unless it furthers some substantial goal of the State." Justice Brennan found no legitimate state interest.

Two members of the *Rodriguez* majority wrote concurring opinions in *Plyler*. **Justice Blackmun** argued that classifications "involving the complete denial of education are in a sense unique, for they strike at the heart of equal protection values by involving the State in the creation of permanent class distinctions," thereby being analogous to a deprivation of the vote. **Justice Powell** agreed that a "legislative classification that threatens the creation of an underclass of future citizens and residents cannot be reconciled with one of the fundamental purposes of the Fourteenth Amendment." He found *Rodriguez* distinguishable: "in *Rodriguez* no group of children was singled out by the State and then penalized because of their parents' status," "[n]or * * * was any group of children totally deprived of all education as in these cases."

The four dissenters, led by **Chief Justice Burger**, applied a simple syllogism: "Once it is conceded — as the Court does — that illegal aliens are not a suspect class, and that education is not a fundamental right," the only issue logically was whether "the legislative classification at issue bears a rational relationship to a legitimate state purpose." Without "laboring what will undoubtedly seem obvious to many, it simply is not 'irrational' for a state to conclude that it does not have the same responsibility to provide benefits for persons whose very presence in the state and this country is illegal as it does to provide for persons lawfully present." That the majority's motives "are noble and compassionate does not alter the fact that the Court distorts our constitutional function to make amends for the defaults of others."

NOTES ON *RODRIGUEZ* AND *PLYLER*

1. *Quo Vadis Fundamental Interests?* Jot down a list of "fundamental" interests that the *Rodriguez* majority would accept as justifying heightened equal protection scrutiny. Do the same for the dissenters. What interests are on both lists? What are only on the dissent's list?

After *Rodriguez*, one would expect the Court not to recognize more fundamental interests as a mechanism for equal protection heightened scrutiny. So, for example, even though, as we shall see, the Court recognized the right to choose an abortion as a fundamental due process right, it did not subject state medical and hospital plans to heightened scrutiny when they refused to cover abortion. See *Maher v. Roe*, 432 U.S. 464 (1977) (medicaid programs can refuse to fund abortions); *Poelker v. Doe*, 432 U.S. 519 (1977) (per curiam) (municipal hospital could refuse to provide abortion services). On the other hand, the Court in *Zablocki v. Redhail*, 434 U.S. 374 (1978), recognized the right to marry as a fundamental right and struck down a state law barring remarriages by people with outstanding family support obligations (the proverbial deadbeat dads). Marshall wrote the opinion; Powell concurred. Is the "right to marry" any more "in" the Constitution than the right to an education? Is it more "preservative" of other rights?

2. *Rights and Remedies.* Keep in mind that the Court deciding *Rodriguez* was a Court struggling with the difficulty of judicial remediation of school segregation. Justice Blackmun spoke for all four Nixon Justices when he reportedly said in conference on *Rodriguez*, "if we affirm, federal courts will destroy the state systems; we cannot legislate equality in education." Justice

Powell had been chair of the Richmond School Board and was a powerful voice in conference for minimal judicial "interference" with local school systems. Any Justice who felt that the federal judiciary was overextended in the school desegregation cases would have been aghast at the prospect of parallel litigation over school financing. Note that Justices Blackmun and Powell were both in the *Plyler* majority, in part because remediation was much easier: the Texas law was struck down, and the children of aliens could attend school. That there was little need for ongoing judicial supervision made it easier for those Justices to join Justice Brennan's opinion.

Even more difficult was the question of what the constitutional standard would be for determining whether a school system violated the rights articulated in the *Rodriguez* dissent. In the voting cases, one problem with a less expansive right — such as the one Justice Stewart suggested in his separate opinion in *Reynolds*, which would protect against only irrational allocations of political power that absolutely frustrate the preferences of a majority of citizens — is that figuring out whether it had been violated would require much more difficult judicial judgment calls than the simple standard of *Reynolds* (which in light of later cases amounts to something like "one person, one vote, plus or minus 10%"). Note, too, that Justice Stewart's approach in *Reynolds* and the approach to education rejected in *Rodriguez* would create difficult problems of implementation and remedy, while *Reynolds* and *Plyer* were remedially simple.

3. *How to Explain* Plyler? Given the powerful forces generating the result in *Rodriguez*, how does one explain *Plyler*, an activist result by a much more conservative Court? Probably the best explanation is that Texas's law looked punitive and short-sighted to the Court. According to Brennan's conference notes, the Justices were deeply troubled that Texas was engaging in renegade immigration politics which penalized "helpless" children (Powell's phrase, echoing Marshall's arguments at conference) and risked creating a "permanent underclass" (Blackmun and Stevens). Burger and O'Connor expressed dismay at the law and opined that the political process was unresponsive to this unfairness. The strongest statement at conference in favor of the law was Rehnquist's: Illegal immigration was "an intractable problem in the southwest." Whatever doctrinal difficulties Justice Brennan had on cobbling together an opinion,[h] he had at least five Justices who wanted to join it.

A complementary explanation for *Plyler* is that it illustrates the "sliding scale" that Marshall articulated in his *Rodriguez* dissent (and that we saw in his and Stevens' opinions in *Cleburne*, Chapter 4, § 3C). Marshall anticipated *Plyler* when he maintained that the Court should be particularly militant against laws discriminating "against important individual interests with constitutional implications and against particularly disadvantaged or powerless classes." Marshall's might be a more accurate descriptive theory of the Court's case law in this area, for it also helps us understand cases like *Cleburne* and *Romer v. Evans* (Chapter 4, § 3C & D). But the spirit in which this kind of equal protection review has been carried out has unquestionably been that of Justice

---

h. Cf. Mark Tushnet, *The Optimist's Tale*, 132 U. Pa. L. Rev. 1257 (1989) (Brennan's opinion cobbled together different theories appealing to different Justices in order to get five votes).

Powell's philosophy — cautious in its definition of "rights" and deferential to well-motivated state policies and even experiments, pragmatic and attentive to institutional concerns before engaging the Court in activist review, but open to selective interventions when apparently ill-motivated policies hurt people who are not well represented in the political process.

EDGEWOOD INDEPENDENT SCHOOL DISTRICT v. KIRBY
777 S.W.2d 391 (Supreme Court of Texas, 1989)

MAUZY, Justice.

At issue is the constitutionality of the Texas system for financing the education of public school children. * * *

There are approximately three million public school children in Texas. The legislature finances the education of these children through a combination of revenues supplied by the state itself and revenues supplied by local school districts which are governmental subdivisions of the state. Of total education costs, the state provides about forty-two percent, school districts provide about fifty percent, and the remainder comes from various other sources including federal funds. School districts derive revenues from local ad valorem property taxes, and the state raises funds from a variety of sources including the sales tax and various severance and excise taxes. * * *

Because of the disparities in district property wealth, spending per student varies widely, ranging from $2,112 to $19,333. Under the existing system, an average of $2,000 more per year is spent on each of the 150,000 students in the wealthiest districts than is spent on the 150,000 students in the poorest districts.

The lower expenditures in the property-poor districts are not the result of lack of tax effort. Generally, the property-rich districts can tax low and spend high while the property-poor districts must tax high merely to spend low. In 1985-86, local tax rates ranged from $.09 to $1.55 per $100 valuation. The 100 poorest districts had an average tax rate of 74.5 cents and spent an average of $2,978 per student. The 100 wealthiest districts had an average tax rate of 47 cents and spent an average of $7,233 per student. * * *

The amount of money spent on a student's education has a real and meaningful impact on the educational opportunity offered that student. High-wealth districts are able to provide for their students broader educational experiences including more extensive curricula, more up-to-date technological equipment, better libraries and library personnel, teacher aides, counseling services, lower student-teacher ratios, better facilities, parental involvement programs, and drop-out prevention programs. They are also better able to attract and retain experienced teachers and administrators. * * *

Article VII, section 1 of the Texas Constitution provides:

A general diffusion of knowledge being essential to the preservation of the liberties and rights of the people, it shall be the duty of the Legislature of the State to establish and make suitable provision for the support and maintenance of an efficient system of public free schools.

* * * [T]he language of article VII, section 1 imposes on the legislature an affirmative duty to establish and provide for the public free schools. This duty

is not committed unconditionally to the legislature's discretion, but instead is accompanied by standards. By express constitutional mandate, the legislature must make "suitable" provision for an "efficient" system for the "essential" purpose of a "general diffusion of knowledge." While these are admittedly not precise terms, they do provide a standard by which this court must, when called upon to do so, measure the constitutionality of the legislature's actions. We do not undertake this responsibility lightly and we begin with a presumption of constitutionality. * * *

The Texas Constitution derives its force from the people of Texas. This is the fundamental law under which the people of this state have consented to be governed. In construing the language of article VII, section 1, we consider "the intent of the people who adopted it." In determining that intent, "the history of the times out of which it grew and to which it may be rationally supposed to have direct relationship, the evils intended to be remedied and the good to be accomplished, are proper subjects of inquiry." However, because of the difficulties inherent in determining the intent of voters over a century ago, we rely heavily on the literal text. We seek its meaning with the understanding that the Constitution was ratified to function as an organic document to govern society and institutions as they evolve through time. * * *

Considering "the general spirit of the times and the prevailing sentiments of the people," it is apparent from the historical record that those who drafted and ratified article VII, section 1 never contemplated the possibility that such gross inequalities could exist within an "efficient" system. At the Constitutional Convention of 1875, delegates spoke at length on the importance of education for *all* the people of this state, rich and poor alike. The chair of the education committee, speaking on behalf of the majority of the committee, declared:

> [Education] must be classed among the abstract rights, based on apparent natural justice, which we individually concede to the State, for the general welfare, when we enter into a great compact as a commonwealth. I boldly assert that it is for the general welfare of all, rich and poor, male and female, that the means of a common school education should, if possible, be placed within the reach of every child in the State.

Other delegates recognized the importance of a diffusion of knowledge among the masses not only for the preservation of democracy, but for the prevention of crime and for the growth of the economy. * * *

* * * The economic development of the state has not been uniform. Some cities have grown dramatically, while their sister communities have remained static or have shrunk. Formulas that once fit have been knocked askew. Although local conditions vary, the constitutionally imposed state responsibility for an efficient education system is the same for all citizens regardless of where they live.

We conclude that, in mandating "efficiency," the constitutional framers and ratifiers did not intend a system with such vast disparities as now exist. Instead, they stated clearly that the purpose of an efficient system was to provide for a "*general* diffusion of knowledge." (Emphasis added.) The present system, by contrast, provides not for a diffusion that is general, but for one that is limited and unbalanced. The resultant inequalities are thus directly contrary to the constitutional vision of efficiency. * * *

Some have argued that reform in school finance will eliminate local control, but this argument has no merit. An efficient system does not preclude the ability of communities to exercise local control over the education of their children. It requires only that the funds available for education be distributed equitably and evenly. An efficient system will actually allow for more local control, not less. It will provide property-poor districts with economic alternatives that are not now available to them. Only if alternatives are indeed available can a community exercise the control of making choices.

Our decision today is not without precedent. Courts in nine other states with similar school financing systems have ruled those systems to be unconstitutional for varying reasons. * * *

Although we have ruled the school financing system to be unconstitutional, we do not now instruct the legislature as to the specifics of the legislation it should enact; nor do we order it to raise taxes. The legislature has primary responsibility to decide how best to achieve an efficient system. We decide only the nature of the constitutional mandate and whether that mandate has been met. Because we hold that the mandate of efficiency has not been met, we reverse the judgment of the court of appeals. The legislature is duty-bound to provide for an efficient system of education, and only if the legislature fulfills that duty can we launch this great state into a strong economic future with educational opportunity for all.

NOTES ON *EDGEWOOD*, STATE CONSTITUTIONAL PROTECTIONS, AND CONSTITUTIONAL BALANCING

1. *State Constitutional Rights in a Federal System.* A decision of a state supreme court on state law is definitive, except in exceptional circumstances where a blatant misinterpretation of state law might undermine the enforcement of a federal constitutional right. Thus, the Supreme Court of the United States may not review whether the Supreme Court of Texas properly interpreted the Texas Constitution in *Edgewood*. Indeed, since no federal issue is found in *Edgewood*, the Supreme Court of the United States may not review the case at all. See U.S. Const., art. III, § 2. Because state constitutions can expand (but not contract) the rights of state citizens beyond those they hold as a matter of federal law, students in Texas public schools have a broader right to equality in school finance than do students in states where the state constitution provides no more protection than the federal Constitution, as interpreted in *Rodriguez*. Indeed, it is precisely this facet of state constitutional law that once led Justice Brennan to suggest that attorneys consider whether litigation attempting to establish new individual rights might have a better chance of success if based on a state constitutional claim rather than a federal one. See William Brennan, *State Constitutions and the Protection of Individual Rights*, 90 Harv. L. Rev. 489 (1977).

A considerable number of state judiciaries have addressed the *Rodriguez* issue, with about half granting some kind of relief. For a survey and critical analysis, see James Ryan, *Schools, Race, and Money*, 109 Yale L.J. 249 (1999). The state courts are divided on whether the goal should be to equalize funding or assure every child access to a minimally adequate education.

2. *The Openly Utilitarian Reasoning in* Edgewood: *Arguments for Balancing.* Recall the theories of judicial review discussed at the end of Chapter 2: textualism, originalism, process theory (exemplified by representation reinforcement), progressivism, practical reason. Do any of them resemble the approach taken to the Texas Constitution in *Edgewood*? The text of the Texas Constitution provides a source of argument in the case, but does it compel the outcome?

One way to view *Edgewood* is the following: Utilitarianism views with suspicion policies that distribute a lot more resources to the rich than to the poor (classification based upon wealth) or that deprive poor people of an important public good (education, a fundamental public right). Why? Because in such circumstances moving one dollar from a rich district to a poor district would presumably have a higher marginal payoff, and the total social utility would be higher. If the state is making such an obvious sacrifice of aggregate social utility, it is not adequately doing its job of serving the "general welfare," and the court might usefully step in.

The judicial process arguably might have three types of institutional advantages in making utility-maximizing social and economic policy.[i] Consider the strengths and weaknesses of the following arguments:

(a) *The problem of inertia.* Much social policy is the result of legislative and executive inertia and inactivity rather than continuing choice. Because they often do not get sufficient credit for addressing vexing social problems and, indeed, often must make unpleasant allocational choices, legislators often have incentives to avoid tinkering with outdated policies. And because the legislature is not required to act on proposed measures (which can be bottled up indefinitely in committee), obsolescent policies can linger unchanged for long periods of time. Unlike the legislature, a court cannot control its agenda: It must decide the case before it, and must justify its decision by reasons (also in some contrast to legislative failures to act). Hence, courts will be willing to correct inefficient policies in a number of cases where the legislature is content to be inactive, and judicial review can serve "action-forcing" functions even when the legislature must ultimately make the utilitarian judgments. State funding of school districts is a conflictual issue that the Texas legislature perhaps wanted to avoid, and *Edgewood* was a good way to put the issue on the political agenda.

(b) *The problem of rent-seeking.* When they do focus on social problems, the legislature and agencies often seem to favor the interests of well-organized groups, arguably at the expense of the general welfare. Economists call this "rent-seeking" (a group or individual extracts money or a privilege from the state, which is not justified on utilitarian/efficiency grounds for the polity as a whole). Legislative earmarks, bloated defense contracts, monopolistic licensing arrangements, tobacco subsidies (paying farmers to grow stuff that kills us) are

---

i. The following discussion is drawn from Guido Calabresi, *A Common Law for the Age of Statutes* (1982); Daniel Farber & Philip Frickey, *Law and Public Choice: A Critical Introduction* (1991); William Eskridge, Jr., *Politics Without Romance: Implications of Public Choice Theory for Statutory Interpretation*, 74 Va. L. Rev. 274 (1988).

all examples of rent-seeking legislative policy. Precisely because judges either have life tenure (in the federal system) or serve long, relatively insulated terms (the norm in state systems), they are somewhat free from interest group pressures and bring to bear a more scrutinizing perspective upon these issues. Even if Texas' legislature had seriously considered the school funding issue, well-heeled parent groups would have been powerful impediments to major reform. The same socio-economic inequities that yielded different expenditures in Edgewood and Alamo Heights also would yield different political clout in Austin.

(c) *The problem of prejudice.* An underlying issue in both the *Edgewood* and *Serrano* litigations, politely submerged by the courts in each state, is race and ethnicity. Alamo Heights is overwhelmingly white as well as affluent. Many of the poor school districts in Texas are predominantly African American or Latino. The failure of the Texas legislature to provide more funding for the poor districts might have been in part due to their racial and ethnic composition. "Have not" groups tend to lose in our political system, and when they are of a different skin color they tend to lose more often. One lesson of *Brown* is that courts can be a means of forcing the legislature to treat "discrete and insular" minority groups more fairly. But do courts in the broad range of cases protect groups that are truly politically powerless? One might suggest that courts are more likely to become involved when the group in question begins to have enhanced political power and a capacity to place issues on the public agenda. Consider, for example, when the Court intervened in the school segregation controversy in *Brown*, when it began providing more meaningful scrutiny of sex classifications in *Reed* and *Frontiero* (Chapter 4, § 2B), and when it struck down a measure disadvantaging lesbians and gay males in *Romer v. Evans* (Chapter 4, § 3D).

3. *Problems with Judicial Balancing.* Some of the problems with "balancing" as a technique of judicial review are suggested in T. Alexander Aleinikoff, *Constitutional Law in the Age of Balancing*, 96 Yale L.J. 943 (1987). The problem that looms largest is the indeterminacy problem: it is not clear that utilitarian analysis — balancing — can be anything but indeterminate. Consider some of the questions unaddressed in *Edgewood* and *Serrano*.

(a) *What interests should be considered?* The *Edgewood* majority mainly considers the interest in equality of resources, but without much consideration of the traditional interest in local control and fiscal management of school districts. Once those interests are considered, the balance becomes less clear.

(b) *How can the various interests be measured and compared? Serrano* makes a case for valuing educational equality quite highly, which *Edgewood* seems to accept, and both cases assume a low valuation for local control (though there is little justification in the opinions). But the Alamo Hills people might value their local control quite highly, and indeed also derive a lot of satisfaction out of spending a lot more money than Edgewood does. For all the Court tells us, their total satisfaction might indeed be higher than the aggregate dissatisfaction of the Edgewood people with their system of local control but fewer resources.

(c) *What would be the effect of the court's decision upon the interests it is balancing?* The court's result has an intuitive appeal — splitting up a limited pie more evenly might yield overall greater utility because of the greater marginal utility of each dollar for the poor as opposed to the rich districts. But that assumes a static analysis. What if the court's result has consequences for the size of the pie? One benefit of local control might be an incentive for school districts to engage in a competition with one another to put more resources into education, to make their local communities relatively attractive. If the funding of education becomes a completely statewide decision, then the local efforts may diminish, and with it the overall quality of education in the state — defeating the goal of greatest happiness for the greatest number.

If you believe that the balancing inquiry is essentially indeterminate, you might be more likely to defer to the legislative judgment; at least its balancing (which may be equally indeterminate) is done by elected representatives, and therefore is subject to some external check. If the elected representatives compromise overall social utility, they might be voted out of office.

Finally, Aleinikoff suggests that balancing is "transforming constitutional discourse into a general discussion of the reasonableness of governmental conduct." He finds this troubling:

> Balancing opinions give one the eerie sense that constitutional law as a distinct form of discourse is slipping away. The balancing drum beats the rhythm of reasonableness, and we march to it because the cadence seems so familiar, so sensible. But our eyes are no longer focused on the Constitution. If each constitutional provision, every constitutional value, is understood simply as an invitation for a discussion of good social policy, it means little to talk of constitutional "theory."[j]

PROBLEM 5-2
RACIAL DISPARITIES AND STATE CONSTITUTIONAL LAW

The State of Westland's constitution provides for an "adequate and efficient educational system." Under state law, school districts are funded exclusively by the state government, and every district gets the same funding per pupil. The major city in Westland is Metropolis. Students in Metropolis have much lower test scores and higher drop-out rates than those elsewhere in the state. They are also disproportionately people of color. Suburban schools with higher performance indicators do not accept transfers from outside their own districts. Moreover, school segregation has increased because the local public housing district has constructed all of its public housing within the Metropolis city limits rather than the suburbs. A civil rights group files suit in state court based on these allegations (but not alleging any racial animus). The group seeks (a) an order directing the state legislature to devote additional resources to Metropolis schools in light of the more difficult problems of those schools, (b) an order requiring suburban schools to accept inner-city transfer students, and (c) an order that the public housing authority build new projects outside of the city

---

j. For a more recent analysis and partial defense of balancing approaches, see Richard Fallon, *The Supreme Court, 1996 Term — Foreword: Implementing the Constitution*, 111 Harv. L. Rev. 54, 77-83 (1997).

limits. Should the court find any violation of the state constitution? If so, what would be the appropriate remedial order?

C. THE RIGHT TO TRAVEL

Shapiro v. Thompson, 394 U.S. 618 (1969). The Court struck down rules in several states and the District of Columbia that denied welfare assistance to residents who had not resided in the jurisdiction for at least one year. The decision said it was based on the Equal Protection Clause, and thus it fueled the debate (prior to *Dandridge* and *Rodriguez*) whether the poor could be a suspect class, wealth could be a suspect classification, or welfare could be a fundamental right. The opinion in *Shapiro* also alluded to a right of interstate travel, however:

> This Court long ago recognized that the nature of our Federal Union and our constitutional concepts of personal liberty unite to require that all citizens be free to travel throughout the length and breadth of our land uninhibited by statutes, rules, or regulations which unreasonably burden or restrict this movement.

The Court noted that its precedents have not "ascribed the source of this right to * * * a particular constitutional provision," and in a footnote stated that some cases linked the right to the Privileges and Immunities Clause of Article IV, § 2, other cases tied it to the Privileges or Immunities Clause of the Fourteenth Amendment, and yet other cases saw it connected to the Commerce Clause. See the debate within the Court in *Edwards v. California*, 314 U.S. 160 (1941), as well as *Crandall v. Nevada*, 73 U.S. (6 Wall.) 35 (1868).

Having recognized a right to travel, the Court demanded a compelling state interest to justify its residence requirement. **Justice Brennan's** opinion held that the apparent purpose of deterring in-migration of poor people "cannot serve as justification * * * since that purpose is constitutionally impermissible" as a penalty chilling people's exercise of their constitutional rights. His opinion recognized that planning the state budget, having an objective test for apportioning welfare benefits, and minimizing fraud were permissible state purposes, but held that these interests were not constitutionally compelling.

It was not clear whether *Shapiro* is a fundamental rights/equal protection case or (as *Rodriguez* interpreted it) a penalty-on-interstate-travel case. No matter how it is characterized, *Shapiro* has had a robust legacy in several lines of cases. To begin, the right to travel has been the basis for invalidating state benefit schemes that discriminate based upon residence in the state. In *Zobel v. Williams*, 457 U.S. 55 (1982), the Court struck down Alaska's statute distributing its oil and gas windfalls to its citizens, with the rebate dependent upon length of residency in Alaska. The Court relied on the Equal Protection Clause and invoked *Shapiro* to dismiss the state's rationale that the statute rewarded citizens for their "past contributions." Justice Brennan, the author of *Shapiro*, wrote a concurring opinion arguing that "it is difficult to escape from the recognition that underlying any scheme of classification on the basis of duration of residence, we shall almost invariably find the unstated premise that 'some citizens are more equal than others,' " a premise starkly inconsistent with the Equal Protection Clause. The Court followed *Zobel* to invalidate benefit statutes based upon residency criteria in *Attorney General of New York v. Soto-*

Lopez, 476 U.S. 898 (1986), and *Hooper v. Bernalillo County Assessor*, 472 U.S. 612 (1985).

The right to travel has been the main basis for striking down one-year residence requirements for voting, see *Dunn v. Blumstein*, 405 U.S. 330 (1972), but not a 50-day period, see *Marston v. Lewis*, 410 U.S. 679 (1973) (*per curiam*). The right has also been invoked to strike down a one-year residence requirement for receiving nonemergency medical care at public expense, see *Memorial Hospital v. Maricopa County*, 415 U.S. 250 (1974), but was not sufficient to invalidate a one-year residence requirement for bringing a divorce action against a nonresident, see *Sosna v. Iowa*, 419 U.S. 393 (1975). See if you can figure out a rationale to reconcile *Sosna* with the other cases.

Additionally, consider whether some of these cases should not have been decided on grounds of the Privileges and Immunities Clause of Article IV, which Justice O'Connor believed was the soundest basis for *Zobel* (she concurred in the Court's result but did not join its right-to-travel discussion). See also *Supreme Court of New Hampshire v. Piper*, 470 U.S. 274 (1985) (relying on Article IV to strike down state residence requirement for admission to the bar).

SAENZ v. ROE
526 U.S. 489, 119 S.Ct. 1518, 143 L.Ed.2d 689 (1999)

JUSTICE STEVENS delivered the opinion of the Court.

In 1992, California enacted a statute [§ 11450.03] limiting the maximum welfare benefits available to newly arrived residents. The scheme limits the amount payable to a family that has resided in the State for less than 12 months to the amount payable by the State of the family's prior residence. The questions presented by this case are whether the 1992 statute was constitutional when it was enacted and, if not, whether an amendment to the Social Security Act enacted by Congress in 1996 affects that determination. * * *

The "right to travel" discussed in our cases embraces at least three different components. It protects the right of a citizen of one State to enter and to leave another State, the right to be treated as a welcome visitor rather than an unfriendly alien when temporarily present in the second State, and, for those travelers who elect to become permanent residents, the right to be treated like other citizens of that State.

* * * Given that § 11450.03 imposed no obstacle to respondents' entry into California, we think the State is correct when it argues that the statute does not directly impair the exercise of the right to free interstate movement. For the purposes of this case, therefore, we need not identify the source of that particular right in the text of the Constitution. The right of "free ingress and regress to and from" neighboring States, which was expressly mentioned in the text of the Articles of Confederation, may simply have been "conceived from the beginning to be a necessary concomitant of the stronger Union the Constitution created."

The second component of the right to travel is, however, expressly protected by the text of the Constitution. The first sentence of Article IV, § 2, provides:

> The Citizens of each State shall be entitled to all Privileges and Immunities of Citizens in the several States.

Thus, by virtue of a person's state citizenship, a citizen of one State who travels in other States, intending to return home at the end of his journey, is entitled to enjoy the "Privileges and Immunities of Citizens in the several States" that he visits. * * *

What is at issue in this case [is the] third aspect of the right to travel — the right of the newly arrived citizen to the same privileges and immunities enjoyed by other citizens of the same State. That right is protected not only by the new arrival's status as a state citizen, but also by her status as a citizen of the United States. That additional source of protection is plainly identified in the opening words of the Fourteenth Amendment:

> All persons born or naturalized in the United States, and subject to the jurisdiction thereof, are citizens of the United States and of the State wherein they reside. No State shall make or enforce any law which shall abridge the privileges or immunities of citizens of the United States; . . . .

Despite fundamentally differing views concerning the coverage of the Privileges or Immunities Clause of the Fourteenth Amendment, most notably expressed in the majority and dissenting opinions in the *Slaughter-House Cases* (§ 1 of this chapter), it has always been common ground that this Clause protects the third component of the right to travel. * * *

It is undisputed that respondents and the members of the class that they represent are citizens of California and that their need for welfare benefits is unrelated to the length of time that they have resided in California. We thus have no occasion to consider what weight might be given to a citizen's length of residence if the bona fides of her claim to state citizenship were questioned. Moreover, because whatever benefits they receive will be consumed while they remain in California, there is no danger that recognition of their claim will encourage citizens of other States to establish residency for just long enough to acquire some readily portable benefit, such as a divorce or a college education, that will be enjoyed after they return to their original domicile. * * *

Disavowing any desire to fence out the indigent, California has instead advanced an entirely fiscal justification for its multitiered scheme. The enforcement of § 11450.03 will save the State approximately $10.9 million a year. The question is not whether such saving is a legitimate purpose but whether the State may accomplish that end by the discriminatory means it has chosen. An evenhanded, across-the-board reduction of about 72 cents per month for every beneficiary would produce the same result. But our negative answer to the question does not rest on the weakness of the State's purported fiscal justification. It rests on the fact that the Citizenship Clause of the Fourteenth Amendment expressly equates citizenship with residence: "That Clause does not provide for, and does not allow for, degrees of citizenship based on length of residence." It is equally clear that the Clause does not tolerate a hierarchy of 45 subclasses of similarly situated citizens based on the location of their prior residence.[20] Thus § 11450.03 is doubly vulnerable: Neither the duration of respondents' California residence, nor the identity of their prior States of residence, has any relevance to their need for benefits. Nor do those factors bear any relationship to the State's interest in making an equitable allocation of the funds to be distributed among its needy citizens. * * * In short, the State's legitimate interest in saving money provides no justification for its decision to discriminate among equally eligible citizens.

The question that remains is whether congressional approval of durational residency requirements in the 1996 amendment to the Social Security Act somehow resuscitates the constitutionality of § 11450.03. That question is readily answered, for we have consistently held that Congress may not authorize the States to violate the Fourteenth Amendment. Moreover, the protection afforded to the citizen by the Citizenship Clause of that Amendment is a limitation on the powers of the National Government as well as the States.

CHIEF JUSTICE REHNQUIST, with whom JUSTICE THOMAS joins, dissenting.

* * * I agree with the proposition that a "citizen of the United States can, of his own volition, become a citizen of any State of the Union by a *bona fide* residence therein, with the same rights as other citizens of that State." [*Slaughter-House Cases.*]

But I cannot see how the right to become a citizen of another State is a necessary "component" of the right to travel, or why the Court tries to marry these separate and distinct rights. A person is no longer "traveling" in any sense of the word when he finishes his journey to a State which he plans to make his home. Indeed, under the Court's logic, the protections of the Privileges or Immunities Clause recognized in this case come into play only when an individual *stops* traveling with the intent to remain and become a citizen of a new State. * * *

The Court today recognizes that States retain the ability to determine the bona fides of an individual's claim to residence, but then tries to avoid the issue. It asserts that because respondents' need for welfare benefits is unrelated to the length of time they have resided in California, it has "no occasion to consider what weight might be given to a citizen's length of residence if the bona fides of her claim to state citizenship were questioned." But I do not understand how the absence of a link between need and length of residency bears on the State's ability to objectively test respondents' resolve to stay in California. There is no link between the need for an education or for a divorce and the length of residence, and yet States may use length of residence as an objective yardstick to channel their benefits to those whose intent to stay is legitimate.

---

20. See Cohen, Discrimination Against New State Citizens: An Update, 11 *Const. Comm.* 73, 79 (1994) ("[J]ust as it would violate the Constitution to deny these new arrivals state citizenship, it would violate the Constitution to concede their citizenship in name only while treating them as if they were still citizens of other states").

JUSTICE THOMAS, with whom **THE CHIEF JUSTICE [REHNQUIST]** joins, dissenting.

The colonists' repeated assertions that they maintained the rights, privileges, and immunities of persons "born within the realm of England" and "natural born" persons suggests that, at the time of the founding, the terms "privileges" and "immunities" (and their counterparts) were understood to refer to those fundamental rights and liberties specifically enjoyed by English citizens and, more broadly, by all persons. Presumably members of the Second Continental Congress so understood these terms when they employed them in the Articles of Confederation, which guaranteed that "the free inhabitants of each of these States, paupers, vagabonds and fugitives from justice excepted, shall be entitled to all privileges and immunities of free citizens in the several States." Art. IV. The Constitution, which superseded the Articles of Confederation, similarly guarantees that "[t]he Citizens of each State shall be entitled to all Privileges and Immunities of Citizens in the several States." Art. IV, § 2, cl. 1.

Justice Bushrod Washington's landmark opinion in *Corfield v. Coryell*, 6 F. Cas. 546 (No. 3, 230) (CCED Pa. 1825), reflects this historical understanding. In *Corfield*, a citizen of Pennsylvania challenged a New Jersey law that prohibited any person who was not an "actual inhabitant and resident" of New Jersey from harvesting oysters from New Jersey waters. Justice Washington, sitting as Circuit Justice, rejected the argument that the New Jersey law violated Article IV's Privileges and Immunities Clause. He reasoned, "we cannot accede to the proposition . . . that, under this provision of the constitution, the citizens of the several states are permitted to participate in all the rights which belong exclusively to the citizens of any other particular state, merely upon the ground that they are enjoyed by those citizens." * * * Washington rejected the proposition that the Privileges and Immunities Clause guaranteed equal access to all public benefits (such as the right to harvest oysters in public waters) that a State chooses to make available. Instead, he endorsed the colonial-era conception of the terms "privileges" and "immunities," concluding that Article IV encompassed only *fundamental* rights that belong to all citizens of the United States.

Justice Washington's opinion in *Corfield* indisputably influenced the Members of Congress who enacted the Fourteenth Amendment. When Congress gathered to debate the Fourteenth Amendment, Members frequently, if not as a matter of course, appealed to *Corfield*, arguing that the Amendment was necessary to guarantee the fundamental rights that Justice Washington identified in his opinion. For just one example, in a speech introducing the Amendment to the Senate, Senator Howard explained the Privileges or Immunities Clause by quoting at length from *Corfield*. Furthermore, it appears that no Member of Congress refuted the notion that Washington's analysis in *Corfield* undergirded the meaning of the Privileges or Immunities Clause.

That Members of the 39th Congress appear to have endorsed the wisdom of Justice Washington's opinion does not, standing alone, provide dispositive insight into their understanding of the Fourteenth Amendment's Privileges or Immunities Clause. Nevertheless, their repeated references to the *Corfield* decision, combined with what appears to be the historical understanding of the

Clause's operative terms, supports the inference that, at the time the Fourteenth Amendment was adopted, people understood that "privileges or immunities of citizens" were fundamental rights, rather than every public benefit established by positive law. Accordingly, the majority's conclusion — that a State violates the Privileges or Immunities Clause when it "discriminates" against citizens who have been domiciled in the State for less than a year in the distribution of welfare benefits — appears contrary to the original understanding and is dubious at best.

NOTES ON *SAENZ*

1. *Alignment of the Justices.* The alignment of the Justices in *Saenz* is of some interest. On the one hand, Justice Scalia joined the majority, apparently untroubled by Justice Thomas's appeal to the original understanding. On the other hand, Chief Justice Rehnquist joined Thomas's call for a possibly fundamental rethinking of the Fourteenth Amendment, giving central place to the "P or I" clause.

2. *Has the P or I Clause Been Resurrected?* Obviously, the majority's interpretation of the clause is not fully fleshed out. *Saenz* has been hailed for resurrecting the P or I clause as a formidable constitutional provision. See Akhil Amar, "Lost Clause," *New Republic*, June 14, 1999, at 14. Clearly, Justice Thomas would like to do so. It is unclear, however, whether the majority views its holding as at all related to the broader issues about the clause discussed by Justice Thomas. Thomas focuses on the "nationally protected rights" covered by the clause. At one point, the majority speaks of two separate prongs, the right to equal treatment for new state residents, and the "nationally protected" rights covered by the clause. Perhaps the implication is that the second, potentially much more expansive prong (the part discussed by Justice Thomas), remains dormant; only the first prong is resurrected by *Saenz*. On the other hand, the P or I clause itself draws no such distinction, and speaks only of certain national rights ("the privileges or immunities of citizens of the United States"). A more natural reading of the clause might be that the right to equal treatment as a new resident is simply one of the nationally protected "privileges or immunities."

Perhaps the Court meant to base its ruling on the residence-based definition of state citizenship in the first sentence of the Fourteenth Amendment, which it also quotes, rather than simply the P or I clause. It would not be too much of a stretch to read the grant of state citizenship to mean a grant of *equal* state citizenship, regardless of duration; otherwise, the southern states could have discriminated against African Americans by creating disabilities of individuals who had only recently acquired state citizenship. The Court's opinion at least hints at this, and it provides a limiting principle that may have made Justice Scalia more comfortable about joining. In any event, the status of the "nationally protected rights" under the clause seems unclear after *Saenz*, as opposed to the previous situation in which the clause seemed simply defunct. In reading the cases in Section 4, consider whether reliance on the P or I clause would have changed the result or strengthened the analysis.

SECTION 4. FUNDAMENTAL PRIVACY RIGHTS

In the first three sections of this chapter we saw how the Constitution might protect rights necessary to "ordered liberty," rights of private property and economic freedom, and equal rights to vote, to receive a public education, and to travel. In this section we explore rights of privacy. The earliest cases involving this right were decided during the *Lochner* era. Note how the Court's approach to substantive due process with respect to economic regulation might have influenced its analysis of privacy.

MEYER v. NEBRASKA
262 U.S. 390, 43 S.Ct. 625, 67 L.Ed. 1042 (1923)

[A Nebraska law prohibited teaching young children in any public or private school in any language other than English. Writing for the Court, JUSTICE MCREYNOLDS ruled this law inconsistent with the Due Process Clause.]

While this court has not attempted to define with exactness the liberty thus guaranteed [by the Due Process Clause], the term has received much consideration and some of the included things have been definitely stated. Without doubt, it denotes not merely freedom from bodily restraint but also the right of the individual to contract, to engage in any of the common occupations of life, to acquire useful knowledge, to marry, establish a home and bring up children, to worship God according to the dictates of his own conscience, and generally to enjoy those privileges long recognized at common law as essential to the orderly pursuit of happiness by free men. [Citing many cases, including *Lochner* and *Adkins v. Children's Hospital*.] The established doctrine is that this liberty may not be interfered with, under the guise of protecting the public interest, by legislative action which is arbitrary or without reasonable relation to some purpose within the competency of the state to effect. Determination by the Legislature of what constitutes proper exercise of police power is not final or conclusive but is subject to supervision by the courts.

The American people have always regarded education and acquisition of knowledge as matters of supreme importance which should be diligently promoted. * * *

Practically, education of the young is only possible in schools conducted by especially qualified persons who devote themselves thereto. The calling always has been regarded as useful and honorable, essential, indeed, to the public welfare. Mere knowledge of the German language cannot reasonably be regarded as harmful. Heretofore it has been commonly looked upon as helpful and desirable. Plaintiff in error taught this language in school as part of his occupation. His right thus to teach and the right of parents to engage him so to instruct their children, we think, are within the liberty of the amendment.

The challenged statute forbids the teaching in school of any subject except in English; also the teaching of any other language until the pupil has attained and successfully passed the eighth grade, which is not usually accomplished before the age of twelve. The Supreme Court of the state has held that "the so-called ancient or dead languages" are not "within the spirit or the purpose of the act." Latin, Greek, Hebrew are not proscribed; but German, French, Spanish,

Italian, and every other alien speech are within the ban. Evidently the Legislature has attempted materially to interfere with the calling of modern language teachers, with the opportunities of pupils to acquire knowledge, and with the power of parents to control the education of their own.

It is said the purpose of the legislation was to promote civic development by inhibiting training and education of the immature in foreign tongues and ideals before they could learn English and acquire American ideals, and "that the English language should be and become the mother tongue of all children reared in this state." It is also affirmed that the foreign born population is very large, that certain communities commonly use foreign words, follow foreign leaders, move in a foreign atmosphere, and that the children are thereby hindered from becoming citizens of the most useful type and the public safety is imperiled.

That the state may do much, go very far, indeed, in order to improve the quality of its citizens, physically, mentally and morally, is clear; but the individual has certain fundamental rights which must be respected. The protection of the Constitution extends to all, to those who speak other languages as well as to those born with English on the tongue. Perhaps it would be highly advantageous if all had ready understanding of our ordinary speech, but this cannot be coerced by methods which conflict with the Constitution — a desirable end cannot be promoted by prohibited means. * * *

The desire of the Legislature to foster a homogeneous people with American ideals prepared readily to understand current discussions of civic matters is easy to appreciate. Unfortunate experiences during the late war and aversion toward every character of truculent adversaries were certainly enough to quicken that aspiration. But the means adopted, we think, exceed the limitations upon the power of the state and conflict with rights assured to plaintiff in error. The interference is plain enough and no adequate reason therefor in time of peace and domestic tranquility has been shown.

The power of the state to compel attendance at some school and to make reasonable regulations for all schools, including a requirement that they shall give instructions in English, is not questioned. Nor has challenge been made of the state's power to prescribe a curriculum for institutions which it supports. Those matters are not within the present controversy. Our concern is with the prohibition approved by the Supreme Court. * * * We are constrained to conclude that the statute as applied is arbitrary and without reasonable relation to any end within the competency of the state.

As the statute undertakes to interfere only with teaching which involves a modern language, leaving complete freedom as to other matters, there seems no adequate foundation for the suggestion that the purpose was to protect the child's health by limiting his mental activities. It is well known that proficiency in a foreign language seldom comes to one not instructed at an early age, and experience shows that this is not injurious to the health, morals or understanding of the ordinary child.

MR. JUSTICE HOLMES and **MR. JUSTICE SUTHERLAND** dissent.

NOTE: WHAT KINDS OF "LIBERTY" ARE SUBSTANTIVELY PROTECTED BY THE DUE PROCESS CLAUSE?

Following *Meyer*, the Court in *Pierce v. Society of Sisters*, 268 U.S. 510 (1925), ruled that the state could not require all children to attend public schools. The Due Process Clause barred the state from using compulsory education laws to suppress private, especially religious, schools. Today, *Pierce* and *Meyer* could be defended on First Amendment grounds, but as written they stand for the proposition that the Constitution protects certain zones of "privacy" from state control.[a] There were in the 1920s a number of different ways one could understand these zones of privacy:[b] (1) *Privacy as Family Governance.* Presumptively, the state cannot interfere in the individual's choices as to marriage and the married couple's choices as to how to raise its family. *Meyer* and *Pierce* might also be read to support the notion of parental rights to govern their children, without "excessive" state "protection" of the children. Cf. *Hammer v. Dagenhart* (Chapter 7, § 2) (striking down federal law aimed at stopping child labor). (2) *Privacy as Life Choices. Meyer*'s list of common law privileges "essential to the orderly pursuit of happiness by free men" boil down to certain kinds of life choices with which the state cannot readily interfere. Indeed, the facts of *Meyer* — the state during World War I was disrespecting German-American communities — suggest that activities and knowledge that help bind together minority groups are entitled to some protection against state suppression. (3) *Privacy as Inaccessibility. Meyer* starts with the proposition that liberty naturally includes "freedom from bodily restraint." The Court in *Union Pacific Railroad v. Botsford*, 141 U.S. 250 (1891) (essentially overruled by *Sibbach v. Wilson & Co.*, 312 U.S. 1 (1941)), held that the state could not require a personal injury plaintiff to submit to a medical examination. *Skinner* is an application of this privacy right. Presumptively, one's body is inaccessible to the state — as is one's home. See *Boyd v. United States*, 116 U.S. 616, 630 (1886) (Fourth Amendment protects the "sanctities of a man's home and the privacies of his life"); see also Anita Allen, *Uneasy Access: Privacy for Women in a Free Society* (1988).

The cases in this section will explore the Court's application of the nascent privacy right. As you read the cases, consider (1) the legitimacy of the Court's jurisprudence, (2) exactly what the Court considers to be "privacy," and (3) how issues of sex and gender discrimination relate to the privacy reasoning.

A.   CONTRACEPTION, MARRIAGE, AND FAMILY

By World War I, most states and the federal government made it a crime to distribute articles of contraception, and almost half the states criminalized a

---

a. These cases did not explicitly rely on the right to be let alone articulated in Louis Brandeis & Samuel Warren, *The Right to Privacy,* 4 Harv. L. Rev. 193 (1890), which was mainly about what we would call "informational privacy," the tort right to avoid publicity. On the early cases and their ambiguous relationship to the right to be let alone, see Ken Gormley, *One Hundred Years of Privacy,* 1992 Wis. L. Rev. 1335.

b. See William Eskridge, Jr., *Some Effects of Identity-Based Social Movements on Constitutional Law in the Twentieth Century,* 100 Mich. L. Rev. 2062 (2002), for the analysis that follows.

doctor's providing contraceptive information to patients.[c] These laws bore harshly on women, and feminists such as Emma Goldman and Margaret Sanger objected that these laws not only threatened women's health, but also deprived them of life choices. The state went after both women, deporting Goldman and arresting Sanger, her sister, and even her husband. New York closed her birth control clinic in 1916, and Sanger appealed the conviction to the U.S. Supreme Court. Her argument was that the state's suppression of birth control information and devices was a severe and unacceptable intrusion into a woman's due process liberties, specifically, her right to protect her own health and her right to make important life choices without state interference. By thwarting reproductive choice, the state was essentially controlling the entire lives of women. *"The State has no more right to compel 'motherhood' than the individual has to compel [sexual] relations."* Brief on Behalf of the Plaintiff in Error, at 31, *Sanger v. People* (1919 Term, No. 75) (emphasis in original). Although Sanger made her argument in the substantive due process argot the Court would accept in *Meyer*, the Court dismissed her appeal on the ground that it raised no substantial federal question. *Sanger v. People*, 251 U.S. 537 (1919) (per curiam). Notwithstanding the Court's deaf ear, Sanger and Planned Parenthood (which she founded) engaged in a relentless and ultimately successful campaign to nullify state and federal anti-contraception laws, usually through legislative amendment or repeal and administrative construction, but sometimes through judicial review.[d]

The Connecticut statute criminalizing birth control was before the Supreme Court as early as 1943. In the 1943 case, a physician argued that the statute prevented him from providing birth-control advice to patients whose health would be threatened by pregnancy and birth. The Court refused to address whether the statute violated the Fourteenth Amendment. The Court avoided the issue because, it said unanimously, the doctor did not have "standing" in this situation: He had alleged no injury to himself caused by the statute, and he could not get into court merely by asserting the standing of other persons, such as his patients. *Tileston v. Ullman*, 318 U.S. 44 (1943) (*per curiam*).

POE v. ULLMAN
367 U.S. 497, 81 S.Ct. 1752, 6 L.Ed.2d 989 (1961)

[Not quite two decades after *Tileston* a new lawsuit was brought that avoided the standing problem. The plaintiffs included married women who allegedly had a medical need for, but could not receive, birth-control advice because of the statute. The Court again ducked the issue, this time concluding that the lawsuit was not "ripe." Essentially, a bare majority (five Justices) thought there was no practical dispute. Apparently only one prosecution for violation of the

---

    c. See generally Janet Farrell Brodie, *Contraception and Abortion in Nineteenth-Century America* (1994); Thomas Dienes, *Law, Politics, and Birth Control* (1974).

    d. See Ellen Chesler, *Woman of Valor: Margaret Sanger and the Birth Control Movement in America* (1992); Carole McCann, *Birth Control Politics in the United States* 1916-1945 (1994); see also David Garrow, *Liberty and Sexuality: The Right of Privacy and the Making of* Roe v. Wade (1994) (useful combination of social movement and legal history).

statute had been brought since its adoption in 1879, and in that case the prosecutor eventually refused to proceed. Contraceptives were readily available in Connecticut drug stores, notwithstanding the statute. As Justice Frankfurter explained for four Justices, "[t]he undeviating policy of nullification by Connecticut of its anti-contraceptive laws throughout all the long years that they have been on the statute books bespeaks more than prosecutorial paralysis." Justice Brennan, who provided the crucial fifth vote not to hear the case, stated that he was not convinced that plaintiffs "as individuals are truly caught in an inescapable dilemma." Justice Harlan's dissent provided an important opening chapter to the privacy debate.]

JUSTICE HARLAN, dissenting.

[P]recisely because it is the Constitution alone which warrants judicial interference in sovereign operations of the State, the basis of judgment as to the Constitutionality of state action must be a rational one, approaching the [constitutional] text which is the only commission for our power not in a literalistic way, as if we had a tax statute before us, but as the basic charter of our society, setting out in spare but meaningful terms the principles of government. *McCulloch v. Maryland* [Chapter 7, § 1]. But as inescapable as is the rational process in Constitutional adjudication in general, nowhere is it more so than in giving meaning to the prohibitions of the Fourteenth Amendment and, where the Federal Government is involved, the Fifth Amendment, against the deprivation of life, liberty or property without due process of law.

It is but a truism to say that this provision of both Amendments is not self-explanatory. As to the Fourteenth, which is involved here, the history of the Amendment also sheds little light on the meaning of the provision. It is important to note, however, that two views of the Amendment have not been accepted by this Court as delineating its scope. * * *

Were due process merely a procedural safeguard it would fail to reach those situations where the deprivation of life, liberty or property was accomplished by legislation which by operating in the future could, given even the fairest possible procedure in application to individuals, nevertheless destroy the enjoyment of all three. [Citing, *inter alia, Korematsu v. United States*, 323 U.S. 214 (1944).] Thus the guaranties of due process, though having their roots in Magna Carta's "*per legem terrae*" and considered as procedural safeguards "against executive usurpation and tyranny," have in this country "become bulwarks also against arbitrary legislation."

However it is not the particular enumeration of rights in the first eight Amendments which spells out the reach of Fourteenth Amendment due process, but rather, as was suggested in another context long before the adoption of that Amendment, those concepts which are considered to embrace those rights "which are . . . *fundamental*; which belong . . . to the citizens of all free governments," *Corfield v. Coryell*, Fed.Cas.No.3,230, 4 Wash.C.C. 371, 380, for "the purposes [of securing] which men enter into society," *Calder v. Bull*, 3 Dall. 386, 388, 1 L.Ed. 648. Again and again this Court has resisted the notion that the Fourteenth Amendment is no more than a shorthand reference to what is explicitly set out elsewhere in the Bill of Rights. [Citing, *inter alia,*

Slaughter-House Cases and *Palko*.] Indeed the fact that an identical provision limiting federal action is found among the first eight Amendments, applying to the Federal Government, suggests that due process is a discrete concept which subsists as an independent guaranty of liberty and procedural fairness, more general and inclusive than the specific prohibitions. [Citing, *inter alia, Bolling v. Sharpe* (Chapter 2, § 1C).]

Due process has not been reduced to any formula; its content cannot be determined by reference to any code. The best that can be said is that through the course of this Court's decisions it has represented the balance which our Nation, built upon postulates of respect for the liberty of the individual, has struck between that liberty and the demands of organized society. If the supplying of content to this Constitutional concept has of necessity been a rational process, it certainly has not been one where judges have felt free to roam where unguided speculation might take them. The balance of which I speak is the balance struck by this country, having regard to what history teaches are the traditions from which it developed as well as the traditions from which it broke. That tradition is a living thing. A decision of this Court which radically departs from it could not long survive, while a decision which builds on what has survived is likely to be sound. No formula could serve as a substitute, in this area, for judgment and restraint.

It is this outlook which has led the Court continuingly to perceive distinctions in the imperative character of Constitutional provisions, since that character must be discerned from a particular provision's larger context. And inasmuch as this context is one not of words, but of history and purposes, the full scope of the liberty guaranteed by the Due Process Clause cannot be found in or limited by the precise terms of the specific guarantees elsewhere provided in the Constitution. This "liberty" is not a series of isolated points pricked out in terms of the taking of property; the freedom of speech, press, and religion; the right to keep and bear arms; the freedom from unreasonable searches and seizures; and so on. It is a rational continuum which, broadly speaking, includes a freedom from all substantial arbitrary impositions and purposeless restraints, and which also recognizes, what a reasonable and sensitive judgment must, that certain interests require particularly careful scrutiny of the state needs asserted to justify their abridgment. Cf. *Skinner*; *Bolling v. Sharpe*.

[Justice Harlan endorsed *Meyer* and *Pierce*.] I do not think it was wrong to put those decisions on "the right of the individual to . . . establish a home and bring up children," *Meyer*, or on the basis that "The fundamental theory of liberty upon which all governments in this Union repose excludes any general power of the State to standardize its children by forcing them to accept instruction from public teachers only," *Pierce*. I consider this so, even though today those decisions would probably have gone by reference to the concepts of freedom of expression and conscience assured against state action by the Fourteenth Amendment, concepts that are derived from the explicit guarantees of the First Amendment against federal encroachment upon freedom of speech and belief. For it is the purposes of those guarantees and not their text, the reasons for their statement by the Framers and not the statement itself, see

Palko, which have led to their present status in the compendious notion of "liberty" embraced in the Fourteenth Amendment.

Each new claim to Constitutional protection must be considered against a background of Constitutional purposes, as they have been rationally perceived and historically developed. Though we exercise limited and sharply restrained judgment, yet there is no "mechanical yard-stick," no "mechanical answer." The decision of an apparently novel claim must depend on grounds which follow closely on well-accepted principles and criteria. The new decision must take "its place in relation to what went before and further [cut] a channel for what is to come." The matter was well put in *Rochin v. California*, 342 U.S. 165, 170-171:

> The vague contours of the Due Process Clause do not leave judges at large. We may not draw on our merely personal and private notions and disregard the limits that bind judges in their judicial function. Even though the concept of due process of law is not final and fixed, these limits are derived from considerations that are fused in the whole nature of our judicial process. . . . These are considerations deeply rooted in reason and in the compelling traditions of the legal profession.

[For Justice Harlan, the intrusion into the privacy of the "most intimate details of the marital relation with the full force of the criminal law" was of constitutional significance because marital privacy is an aspect of the privacy of the home, expressly protected against certain governmental intrusions by the Third and Fourth Amendments and more generally protected, under a series of precedents, by the "principle of liberty" found in the Due Process Clause "against all unreasonable intrusion of whatever character." He conceded that the state may regulate to promote public morality, and even that perhaps a state might reasonably view the use of contraceptives as immoral. But he concluded:]

Adultery, homosexuality and the like are sexual intimacies which the State forbids altogether, but the intimacy of husband and wife is necessarily an essential and accepted feature of the institution of marriage, an institution which the State not only must allow, but which always and in every age it has fostered and protected. It is one thing when the State exerts its power either to forbid extra-marital sexuality altogether, or to say who may marry, but it is quite another when, having acknowledged a marriage and the intimacies inherent in it, it undertakes to regulate by means of the criminal law the details of that intimacy.

In sum, even though the State has determined that the use of contraceptives is as iniquitous as any act of extra-marital sexual immorality, the intrusion of the whole machinery of the criminal law into the very heart of marital privacy, requiring husband and wife to render account before a criminal tribunal of their uses of that intimacy, is surely a very different thing indeed from punishing those who establish intimacies which the law has always forbidden and which can have no claim of social protection.

[Justice Harlan therefore concluded that "a closer scrutiny and stronger justification" for the statute was required than merely a rational relationship to a proper state purpose; that even the state itself apparently conceded that the moral judgment underlying the statute was not an important one, or the means chosen to effectuate that judgment appropriate, because it was not enforcing the statute against individual marital users; and that the infirmity of the statute was confirmed by the fact that no other state or the federal government has ever made use of contraceptives a crime.]

GRISWOLD v. CONNECTICUT
381 U.S. 479, 85 S.Ct. 1678, 14 L.Ed.2d 510 (1965)

JUSTICE DOUGLAS delivered the opinion of the Court.

[Estelle Griswold was Executive Director of the Planned Parenthood League of Connecticut. Another appellant, Lee Buxton, was a professor at the Yale Medical School who served as Medical Director for Planned Parenthood at its Center in New Haven. They gave information, instruction, and medical advice to married couples about birth control. They examined the wife and prescribed the best contraceptive device or material for her use. Fees were usually charged, although some couples were serviced free. No statute prohibited the sale of birth control devices. But it was a crime to use "any drug, medicinal article or instrument for the purpose of preventing conception," and they were charged as accessories to that offense.]

Coming to the merits, we are met with a wide range of questions that implicate the Due Process Clause of the Fourteenth Amendment. Overtones of some arguments suggest that *Lochner* should be our guide. But we decline that invitation . * * * We do not sit as a super-legislature to determine the wisdom, need, and propriety of laws that touch economic problems, business affairs, or social conditions. This law, however, operates directly on an intimate relation of husband and wife and their physician's role in one aspect of that relation.

The association of people is not mentioned in the Constitution nor in the Bill of Rights. The right to educate a child in a school of the parents' choice — whether public or private or parochial — is also not mentioned. Nor is the right to study any particular subject or any foreign language. Yet the First Amendment has been construed to include certain of those rights. [The Court then reviewed *Meyer* and *Pierce*, as well as First Amendment cases dealing with freedom of association.]

The foregoing cases suggest that specific guarantees in the Bill of Rights have penumbras, formed by emanations from those guarantees that help give them life and substance. *See Poe v. Ullman* (dissenting opinion). Various guarantees create zones of privacy. The right of association contained in the penumbra of the First Amendment is one, as we have seen. The Third Amendment in its prohibition against the quartering of soldiers "in any house" in time of peace without the consent of the owner is another facet of that privacy. The Fourth Amendment explicitly affirms the "right of the people to be secure in their persons, houses, papers, and effects, against unreasonable searches and seizures." The Fifth Amendment in its Self-Incrimination Clause enables the citizen to create a zone of privacy which government may not force him to surrender to his detriment. The Ninth Amendment provides: "The enumeration in the Constitution, of certain rights, shall not be construed to deny or disparage others retained by the people."

The Fourth and Fifth Amendments were described in *Boyd v. United States*, 116 U.S. 616, 630, as protection against all governmental invasions "of the sanctity of a man's home and the privacies of life." We recently referred in *Mapp v. Ohio*, 367 U.S. 643, 656, to the Fourth Amendment as creating a "right to privacy, no less important than any other right carefully and particularly reserved to the people." * * *

The present case, then, concerns a relationship lying within the zone of privacy created by several fundamental constitutional guarantees. And it concerns a law which, in forbidding the use of contraceptives rather than regulating their manufacture or sale, seeks to achieve its goals by means having a maximum destructive impact upon that relationship. Such a law cannot stand in light of the familiar principle, so often applied by this Court, that a "governmental purpose to control or prevent activities constitutionally subject to state regulation may not be achieved by means which sweep unnecessarily broadly and thereby invade the area of protected freedoms." *NAACP v. Alabama*, 377 U.S. 288, 307. Would we allow the police to search the sacred precincts of marital bedrooms for telltale signs of the use of contraceptives? The very idea is repulsive to the notions of privacy surrounding the marriage relationship.

We deal with a right of privacy older than the Bill of Rights — older than our political parties, older than our school system. Marriage is a coming together for better or for worse, hopefully enduring, and intimate to the degree of being sacred. It is an association that promotes a way of life, not causes; a harmony in living, not political faiths; a bilateral loyalty, not commercial or social projects. Yet it is an association for as noble a purpose as any involved in our prior decisions.

JUSTICE GOLDBERG, whom **THE CHIEF JUSTICE [WARREN]** and **JUSTICE BRENNAN** join, concurring.

This Court, in a series of decisions, has held that the Fourteenth Amendment absorbs and applies to the States those specifics of the first eight amendments which express fundamental personal rights. The language and history of the Ninth Amendment reveal that the Framers of the Constitution believed that there are additional fundamental rights, protected from governmental infringement, which exist alongside those fundamental rights specifically mentioned in the first eight constitutional amendments.

The Ninth Amendment reads, "The enumeration in the Constitution, of certain rights, shall not be construed to deny or disparage others retained by the people." The Amendment is almost entirely the work of James Madison. It was introduced in Congress by him and passed the House and Senate with little or no debate and virtually no change in language. It was proffered to quiet expressed fears that a bill of specifically enumerated rights could not be sufficiently broad to cover all essential rights and that the specific mention of certain rights would be interpreted as a denial that others were protected.

In presenting the proposed Amendment, Madison said:

It has been objected also against a bill of rights, that, by enumerating particular exceptions to the grant of power, it would disparage those rights which were not placed in that enumeration; and it might follow by implication, that those rights which were not singled out, were intended to be assigned into the hands of the General Government, and were consequently insecure. This is one of the most plausible arguments I have ever heard urged against the admission of a bill of rights into this system; but, I conceive, that it may be guarded against. I have attempted it, as gentlemen may see by turning to the last clause of the fourth resolution [the Ninth Amendment]. * * *

[This statement by Madison makes] clear that the Framers did not intend that the first eight amendments be construed to exhaust the basic and fundamental rights which the Constitution guaranteed to the people. * * *

While this Court has had little occasion to interpret the Ninth Amendment, "[i]t cannot be presumed that any clause in the constitution is intended to be without effect." *Marbury v. Madison.* In interpreting the Constitution, "real effect should be given to all the words it uses." The Ninth Amendment to the Constitution may be regarded by some as a recent discovery and may be forgotten by others, but since 1791 it has been a basic part of the Constitution which we are sworn to uphold. To hold that a right so basic and fundamental and so deep-rooted in our society as the right of privacy in marriage may be infringed because that right is not guaranteed in so many words by the first eight amendments to the Constitution is to ignore the Ninth Amendment and to give it no effect whatsoever. Moreover, a judicial construction that this fundamental right is not protected by the Constitution because it is not mentioned in explicit terms by one of the first eight amendments or elsewhere in the Constitution would violate the Ninth Amendment, which specifically states that "[the] enumeration in the Constitution, of certain rights, shall not be *construed* to deny or disparage others retained by the people." (Emphasis added.)

* * * I do not mean to imply that the Ninth Amendment is applied against the States by the Fourteenth. Nor do I mean to state that the Ninth Amendment constitutes an independent source of rights protected from infringement by either the States or the Federal Government. Rather, the Ninth Amendment shows a belief of the Constitution's authors that fundamental rights exist that are not expressly enumerated in the first eight amendments and an intent that the list of rights included there not be deemed exhaustive. * * * [Justice Goldberg endorsed the view that fundamental rights are those rooted in the traditions of our people.] "Liberty" also "gains content from the emanations of . . . specific [constitutional] guarantees" and "from experience with the requirements of a free society." *Poe v. Ullman* (dissenting opinion of Justice Douglas). * * *

Although the Constitution does not speak in so many words of the right of privacy in marriage, I cannot believe that it offers these fundamental rights no protection. The fact that no particular provision of the Constitution explicitly forbids the State from disrupting the traditional relation of the family — a relation as old and as fundamental as our entire civilization — surely does not show that the Government was meant to have the power to do so. Rather, as the Ninth Amendment expressly recognizes, there are fundamental personal rights such as this one, which are protected from abridgment by the Government though not specifically mentioned in the Constitution. * * *

The logic of the dissents would sanction federal or state legislation that seems to me even more plainly unconstitutional than the statute before us. Surely the Government, absent a showing of a compelling subordinating state interest, could not decree that all husbands and wives must be sterilized after two children have been born to them. Yet by their reasoning such an invasion of marital privacy would not be subject to constitutional challenge because, while it might be "silly," no provision of the Constitution specifically prevents the Government from curtailing the marital right to bear children and raise a family. While it may shock some of my Brethren that the Court today holds that the Constitution protects the right of marital privacy, in my view it is far more shocking to believe that the personal liberty guaranteed by the Constitution does not include protection against such totalitarian limitation of family size, which is at complete variance with our constitutional concepts. Yet, if upon a showing of a slender basis of rationality, a law outlawing voluntary birth control by married persons is valid, then, by the same reasoning, a law requiring compulsory birth control also would seem to be valid. In my view, however, both types of law would unjustifiably intrude upon rights of marital privacy which are constitutionally protected. * * *

Finally, it should be said of the Court's holding today that it in no way interferes with a State's proper regulation of sexual promiscuity or misconduct. As my Brother Harlan so well stated in his dissenting opinion in *Poe v. Ullman*[:]

> Adultery, homosexuality and the like are sexual intimacies which the State forbids . . . but the intimacy of husband and wife is necessarily an essential and accepted feature of the institution of marriage, an institution which the State not only must allow, but which always and in every age it has fostered and protected. It is one thing when the State exerts its power either to forbid extra-marital sexuality . . . or to say who may marry, but it is quite another when, having acknowledged a marriage and the intimacies inherent in it, it undertakes to regulate by means of the criminal law the details of that intimacy.

In sum, I believe that the right of privacy in the marital relation is fundamental and basic — a personal right "retained by the people" within the meaning of the Ninth Amendment. Connecticut cannot constitutionally abridge this fundamental right, which is protected by the Fourteenth Amendment from infringement by the States. I agree with the Court that petitioners' convictions must therefore be reversed.

JUSTICE HARLAN, concurring in the judgment.

[Justice Harlan followed his *Poe* dissent to find that the statute violated the Due Process Clause. He then responded to Justice Black's contention that his approach lacked judicial restraint and that judicial restraint requires limiting the reach of the Fourteenth Amendment's Due Process Clause to those rights expressly found in the Bill of Rights.]

While I could not more heartily agree that judicial "self restraint" is an indispensable ingredient of sound constitutional adjudication, I do submit that the formula suggested for achieving it is more hollow than real. "Specific" provisions of the Constitution, no less than "due process," lend themselves as readily to "personal" interpretations by judges whose constitutional outlook is simply to keep the Constitution in supposed "tune with the times." * * *

Judicial self-restraint will not, I suggest, be brought about in the "due process" area by the historically unfounded incorporation formula long advanced by my Brother Black, and now in part espoused by my Brother Stewart. It will be achieved in this area, as in other constitutional areas, only by continual insistence upon respect for the teachings of history, solid recognition of the basic values that underlie our society, and wise appreciation of the great roles that the doctrines of federalism and separation of powers have played in establishing and preserving American freedoms. See *Adamson v. California* (Justice Frankfurter, concurring). Adherence to these principles will not, of course, obviate all constitutional differences of opinion among judges, nor should it. Their continued recognition will, however, go farther toward keeping most judges from roaming at large in the constitutional field than will the interpolation into the Constitution of an artificial and largely illusory restriction on the content of the Due Process Clause.

JUSTICE WHITE, concurring in the judgment.

In my view this Connecticut law as applied to married couples deprives them of "liberty" without due process of law, as that concept is used in the Fourteenth Amendment. I therefore concur in the judgment of the Court reversing these convictions under Connecticut's aiding and abetting statute. * * *

As I read the opinions of the Connecticut courts and the argument of Connecticut in this Court, the State claims but one justification for its anti-use statute. There is no serious contention that Connecticut thinks the use of artificial or external methods of contraception immoral or unwise in itself, or that the anti-use statute is founded upon any policy of promoting population expansion. Rather, the statute is said to serve the State's policy against all forms of promiscuous or illicit sexual relationships, be they premarital or extramarital, concededly a permissible and legitimate legislative goal.

Without taking issue with the premise that the fear of conception operates as a deterrent to such relationships in addition to the criminal proscriptions Connecticut has against such conduct, I wholly fail to see how the ban on the use of contraceptives by married couples in any way reinforces the State's ban on illicit sexual relationships. Connecticut does not bar the importation or possession of contraceptive devices; they are not considered contraband material under state law, and their availability in that State is not seriously disputed. The only way Connecticut seeks to limit or control the availability of such devices is through its general aiding and abetting statute whose operation in this context has been quite obviously ineffective and whose most serious use has been against birth-control clinics rendering advice to married, rather than unmarried, persons. Cf. *Yick Wo v. Hopkins*. Indeed, after over 80 years of the State's proscription of use, the legality of the sale of such devices to prevent disease has never been expressly passed upon, although it appears that sales have long occurred and have only infrequently been challenged. This "undeviating policy . . . throughout all the long years . . . bespeaks more than prosecutorial paralysis." *Poe v. Ullman.* Moreover, it would appear that the sale of contraceptives to prevent disease is plainly legal under Connecticut law.

JUSTICE BLACK, with whom **JUSTICE STEWART** joins, dissenting.

The Court talks about a constitutional "right of privacy" as though there is some constitutional provision or provisions forbidding any law ever to be passed which might abridge the "privacy" of individuals. But there is not. There are, of course, guarantees in certain specific constitutional provisions which are designed in part to protect privacy at certain times and places with respect to certain activities. Such, for example, is the Fourth Amendment's guarantee against "unreasonable searches and seizures." * * *

The due process argument which my Brothers Harlan and White adopt here is based, as their opinions indicate, on the premise that this Court is vested with power to invalidate all state laws that it considers to be arbitrary, capricious, unreasonable, or oppressive, or on this Court's belief that a particular state law under scrutiny has no "rational or justifying" purpose, or is offensive to a "sense of fairness and justice." If these formulas based on "natural justice," or others which mean the same thing, are to prevail, they require judges to determine what is or is not constitutional on the basis of their own appraisal of what laws are unwise or unnecessary. The power to make such decisions is of course that of a legislative body. * * *

* * * [The Ninth] Amendment was passed, not to broaden the powers of this Court or any other department of "the General Government," but, as every student of history knows, to assure the people that the Constitution in all its provisions was intended to limit the Federal Government to the powers granted expressly or by necessary implication. If any broad, unlimited power to hold laws unconstitutional because they offend what this Court conceives to be the "[collective] conscience of our people" is vested in this Court by the Ninth Amendment, the Fourteenth Amendment, or any other provision of the Constitution, it was not given by the Framers, but rather has been bestowed on the Court by the Court. This fact is perhaps responsible for the peculiar phenomenon that for a period of a century and a half no serious suggestion was ever made that the Ninth Amendment, enacted to protect state powers against federal invasion, could be used as a weapon of federal power to prevent state legislatures from passing laws they consider appropriate to govern local affairs. Use of any such broad, unbounded judicial authority would make of this Court's members a day-to-day constitutional convention. * * *

The late Judge Learned Hand, after emphasizing his view that judges should not use the due process formula suggested in the concurring opinions today or any other formula like it to invalidate legislation offensive to their "personal preferences," made the statement, with which I fully agree, that:

> For myself it would be most irksome to be ruled by a bevy of Platonic Guardians, even if I knew how to choose them, which I assuredly do not.

So far as I am concerned, Connecticut's law as applied here is not forbidden by any provision of the Federal Constitution as that Constitution was written, and I would therefore affirm.

JUSTICE STEWART, whom JUSTICE BLACK joins, dissenting.

Since 1879 Connecticut has had on its books a law which forbids the use of contraceptives by anyone. I think this is an uncommonly silly law. As a practical matter, the law is obviously unenforceable, except in the oblique context of the present case. As a philosophical matter, I believe the use of contraceptives in the relationship of marriage should be left to personal and private choice, based upon each individual's moral, ethical, and religious beliefs. As a matter of social policy, I think professional counsel about methods of birth control should be available to all, so that each individual's choice can be meaningfully made. But we are not asked in this case to say whether we think this law is unwise, or even asinine. We are asked to hold that it violates the United States Constitution. And that I cannot do.

NOTES ON *GRISWOLD* AND THE RIGHT OF PRIVACY

1. *Alternative Methods in* Griswold. What is a "penumbra" and how does it generate rights? (No fair to answer, "Only the Shadow knows!") See generally Paul Kauper, *Penumbras, Peripheries, Emanations, Things Fundamental and Things Forgotten: The* Griswold *Case*, 64 Mich. L. Rev. 235 (1965). Of the Justices writing in support of the majority decision, who has the strongest arguments? What sources do they suggest that the Court should examine to determine whether a given right is fundamental? For a skeptical survey, see John Hart Ely, *The Supreme Court, 1977 Term — Foreword: On Discovering Fundamental Values*, 92 Harv. L. Rev. 5 (1978).

2. *Linking* Griswold, *the Incorporation Doctrine, and the "Reverse Incorporation" Problem.* Justice Harlan again invoked *Palko* to define what substantive due process rights are provided by the Due Process Clause of the Fourteenth Amendment. Justice Goldberg, in a footnote we have not reproduced, asserted that the Court "has never held that the Bill of Rights or the Fourteenth Amendment protects only those rights that the Constitution specifically mentions by name." As you would expect, he cited *Meyer* and *Pierce*; in addition, he cited *Bolling v. Sharpe*, the companion case to *Brown* in which the Court held that school segregation in the District of Columbia violated the Due Process Clause of the Fifth Amendment. Does the "reverse incorporation" holding in *Bolling* lend any support to *Griswold*? Note how Justice Harlan deployed *Palko* and *Bolling v. Sharpe* in his *Poe* dissent.

3. *Equal Protection as an Alternative?* It is clear that in Connecticut the women who had the most difficulty receiving birth-control information and supplies were poor women, who had to rely upon birth-control clinics. Should the Court have based its result on these facts, invoking the Equal Protection Clause? The statute's harm to the poor was perpetuated in Connecticut because of continued support for the statute by the Roman Catholic Church — suggesting the statute served a "sectarian" religious purpose and not even a minimal secular one. Might this explain Justice White's position in *Griswold*?

Because women obviously bear disproportionate burdens from unwanted pregnancies, the Connecticut law had a strikingly disparate impact on women.

Recall *Yick Wo v. Hopkins* (Chapter 3, § 1B). Should this have influenced the outcome in *Griswold*?

4. *Unmarried People and the Expanding Ambit of the Right of Privacy.* *Griswold* involved only the rights of married couples to use birth control. In *Eisenstadt v. Baird*, 405 U.S. 438 (1972), the Court struck down a law prohibiting the sale of contraceptives to unmarried individuals. The majority decision, by Justice Brennan, purported to apply "rational basis" equal protection analysis. According to Justice Brennan, the state surely could not have meant to make the threat of unwanted pregnancy a punishment for non-marital sex (which is almost surely what the state in fact did mean to do). (Might Justice Brennan have implicitly rejected this purpose as embodying sex discrimination, since the effect of the "punishment" would fall primarily on women?) Having refused to consider the statute's most probable purpose, the Court then examined a variety of trumped-up justifications, not surprisingly finding all of them to be unconvincing.

Eisenstadt said: "If the right of privacy means anything, it is the right of the *individual*, married or single, to be free from unwarranted governmental intrusion into matters so fundamentally affecting a person as the decision whether to bear or beget a child." Although *Griswold* articulated the privacy right in *family governance* terms, *Eisenstadt* rearticulated it in terms of the individual's *life choices*. This libertarian rearticulation was important in the next cases, involving abortions and regulation of contraceptives by minors, as both decisions certainly viewed privacy in *inaccessibility* terms.

5. *Minors.* In a later contraception case, *Carey v. Population Services International*, 431 U.S. 678 (1977), the Court considered the sale of contraceptives to minors. Justice Brennan's plurality opinion concluded that restrictions on such sales infringed minors' right to privacy. Three concurring Justices made it clear that they did not believe that minors had a constitutional right to be sexually active, but instead that denying them access to birth control was an inappropriate means of deterring sexual activity. Concurring, Justice Stevens remarked that "[i]t is as though a State decided to dramatize its disapproval of motorcycles by forbidding the use of safety helmets." Dissenting alone, Justice Rehnquist observed that if the men who struggled to establish the Constitution or the Reconstruction Amendments "could have lived to know that their efforts had enshrined in the Constitution the right of commercial vendors of contraceptives to peddle them to unmarried minors, [it] is not difficult to imagine their reaction."

6. *A Right of "Sexual" Privacy?* Echoing Margaret Sanger's 1919 appeal, Professor Fowler Harper's brief for Planned Parenthood in *Poe* argued that "sexual pleasure" is an important end in human life, and that frustration of one's preferred sexual outlet, by the state or otherwise, is psychologically harmful to the individual as well as the entire family. This was an open appeal for the Court to recognize the important role of sexuality in people's lives — but the Justices ducked *Poe* and dodged the issue in subsequent cases. Justice Brennan's opinion in *Eisenstadt* pretended that the state was not trying to regulate nonmarital sexuality, and his opinion in *Carey* conceded that the Court had never ruled that a particular sexual act is constitutionally protected. Richard

Posner, *Sex and Reason* 331 (1992), reads *Eisenstadt* for the proposition that "unmarried persons have a constitutional right to engage in sexual intercourse." Would the Supreme Court agree? If it did, could the state continue to criminalize adultery, namely, sexual intercourse between a man and a woman, at least one of whom is married to someone else? Incest, or intercourse between two closely related persons? Sex between first cousins, which many states consider incest? Sex with animals? Where does precedent draw the line? Where would you draw the line if you were a legislator? Are the two lines notably different?

Robert H. Bork
Neutral Principles and Some First Amendment Problems
47 Ind. L.J. 1, 8-9 (1971)[e]

[In *Griswold,* Justice Douglas] performed a miracle of transubstantiation. He called the first amendment's penumbra a protection of "privacy" and then asserted that other amendments create "zones of privacy." He had no better reason to use the word "privacy" than that the individual is free within these zones, free to act in public as well as in private. None of these penumbral zones — from the first, third, fourth or fifth amendments, all of which he cited, along with the ninth — covered the case before him. One more leap was required. Justice Douglas asserted that these various "zones of privacy" created an independent right of privacy, a right not lying within the penumbra of any specific amendment. He did not disclose, however, how a series of specified rights combined to create a new and unspecified right.

The *Griswold* opinion fails every test of neutrality. The derivation of the principle was utterly specious, and so was its definition. In fact, we are left with no idea of what the principle really forbids. Derivation and definition are interrelated here. Justice Douglas called the amendments and their penumbras "zones of privacy," though of course they are not that at all. They protect both private and public behavior and so would more properly be labelled "zones of freedom." If we follow Justice Douglas in his next step, these zones would then add up to an independent right of freedom, which is to say, a general constitutional right to be free of legal coercion, a manifest impossibility in any imaginable society.

Griswold, then, is an unprincipled decision, both in the way in which it derives a new constitutional right and in the way it defines that right, or rather fails to define it. We are left with no idea of the sweep of the right of privacy and hence no notion of the cases to which it may or may not be applied in the future. The truth is that the Court could not reach its result in *Griswold* through principle. The reason is obvious. Every clash between a minority claiming freedom and a majority claiming power to regulate involves a choice between the gratifications of the two groups. When the Constitution has not spoken, the Court will be able to find no scale, other than its own value preferences, upon which to weigh the respective claims to pleasure. Compare the facts in *Griswold* with a hypothetical suit by an electric utility company and one of its

---

customers to void a smoke pollution ordinance as unconstitutional. The cases are identical.

In *Griswold* a husband and wife assert that they wish to have sexual relations without fear of unwanted children. The law impairs their sexual gratifications. The State can assert, and at one stage in that litigation did assert, that the majority finds the use of contraceptives immoral. Knowledge that it takes place and that the State makes no effort to inhibit it causes the majority anguish, impairs their gratifications.

The electrical company asserts that it wishes to produce electricity at low cost in order to reach a wide market and make profits. Its customer asserts that he wants a lower cost so that prices can be held low. The smoke pollution regulation impairs his and the company's stockholders' economic gratifications. The State can assert not only that the majority prefer clean air to lower prices, but also that the absence of the regulation impairs the majority's physical and aesthetic gratifications.

Neither case is covered specifically or by obvious implication in the Constitution. Unless we can distinguish forms of gratification, the only course for a principled Court is to let the majority have its way in both cases. It is clear that the Court cannot make the necessary distinction. There is no principled way to decide that one man's gratifications are more deserving of respect than another's or that one form of gratification is more worthy than another. Why is sexual gratification more worthy than moral gratification? Why is sexual gratification nobler than economic gratification? There is no way of deciding these matters other than by reference to some system of moral or ethical values that has no objective or intrinsic validity of its own and about which men can and do differ. Where the Constitution does not embody the moral or ethical choice, the judge has no basis other than his own values upon which to set aside the community judgment embodied in the statute. That, by definition, is an inadequate basis for judicial supremacy. The issue of the community's moral and ethical values, the issue of the degree of pain an activity causes, are matters concluded by the passage and enforcement of the laws in question. The judiciary has no role to play other than that of applying the statutes in a fair and impartial manner.

One of my colleagues refers to this conclusion, not without sarcasm, as the "Equal Gratification Clause." The phrase is apt, and I accept it, though not the sarcasm. Equality of human gratifications, where the document does not impose a hierarchy, is an essential part of constitutional doctrine because of the necessity that judges be principled. To be perfectly clear on the subject, I repeat that the principle is not applicable to legislatures. Legislation requires value choice and cannot be principled in the sense under discussion. Courts must accept any value choice the legislature makes unless it clearly runs contrary to a choice made in the framing of the Constitution.

It follows, of course, that broad areas of constitutional law ought to be reformulated. Most obviously, it follows that substantive due process, revived by the *Griswold* case, is and always has been an improper doctrine. Substantive due process requires the Court to say, without guidance from the Constitution, which liberties or gratifications may be infringed by majorities and which may not. This means that *Griswold's* antecedents were also wrongly decided, *e.g., Meyer v. Nebraska*, which struck down a statute forbidding the teaching of subjects in any language other than English; *Pierce v. Society of Sisters*, which set aside a statute compelling all Oregon school children to attend public schools; *Adkins v. Children's Hospital*, which invalidated a statute of Congress authorizing a board to fix minimum wages for women and children in the District of Columbia; and *Lochner v. New York*, which voided a statute fixing maximum hours of work for bakers. With some of these cases I am in political agreement, and perhaps *Pierce*'s result could be reached on acceptable grounds, but there is no justification for the Court's methods. In *Lochner*, Justice Peckham, defending liberty from what he conceived as a mere meddlesome interference, asked, "[A]re we all . . . at the mercy of legislative majorities?" The correct answer, where the Constitution does not speak, must be "yes."

———

Professor Bork's suggestion that *Griswold* was not good law generated controversy when President Reagan nominated then-Judge Bork to be a Justice on the Supreme Court. When Bork refused to back away from his principled opposition to a general constitutional right of privacy, large majorities of Americans viewed his nomination in a negative light, and the Senate rejected it on a bipartisan 58-42 vote.[f] Bork's obedience to principle is admirable, but is it fair to say that the Constitution's text says *nothing* relevant to the issue? Consider the following Note.

NOTE ON THE NINTH AMENDMENT

1. *The Text.* There is a maxim of interpretation that the expression of certain things implies the exclusion of all other things (in lawyer's Latin, *expressio unius est exclusio alterius*). To take a simple example, when a parent sends a child to the corner store with a grocery list, the listing of certain items implies that the child is not to buy anything else. Read the Ninth Amendment carefully, for it seems to embody an instruction that at least some parts of the Constitution are *not* to be interpreted according to this maxim.

Justice Goldberg in *Griswold* argued that the amendment commands that *expressio unius* is not an appropriate method of interpreting the Bill of Rights. To be specific, his argument is that, according to the Ninth Amendment, the existence of a list of express rights (Amendments 1-8) is not to be taken as creating a negative implication about the existence of other, unexpressed rights. On this reading, the Ninth Amendment does not itself protect any unenumerated rights; it simply assumes that such rights exist and are to be protected by courts in the same way as listed rights. There is some historical evidence that the authors of the Ninth Amendment intended to refer to unwritten "natural rights."

---

f. See generally Ethan Bronner, *Battle for Justice: How the Bork Nomination Shook America* (1989). Bork's unapologetic response is *The Tempting of America: The Political Seduction of the Law* (1990), excerpted in Chapter 2, § 3A.

See Daniel Farber, Retained by the People (2008); Suzanna Sherry, *The Founders' Unwritten Constitution*, 54 U. Chi. L. Rev. 1127 (1987).

Even on Goldberg's reading, does the use of the word "retained" in the Ninth Amendment restrict the meaning of it to those freedoms that have always been fundamental in our traditions, or at least were fundamental in 1791, thus making the extension of *Griswold* to unmarried persons and minors quite problematic? More dramatically, could "rights retained by the people" simply mean that those rights already provided under state law (state constitutional law, statutory law, or common law) continue after the adoption of the Bill of Rights unless and until they are modified or abolished by the state, by an act of Congress constitutionally preempting the state law, or by a judicial declaration that the state law is unconstitutional? This reading of the Ninth Amendment would completely undercut Justice Goldberg's approach. But this reading seems merely to duplicate the Tenth Amendment, which appears to make clear that states remain free to define individual rights not otherwise guaranteed by the federal Constitution.

Contrast Justice Black's approach in *Griswold*. He contended that the Ninth Amendment is designed to refute any implication that the expression of certain rights against federal action (Amendments 1-8) indicates that the federal government, which is limited to exercising the powers delegated to it under the original Constitution (see Article I), had been transformed by the existence of the Bill of Rights into a government that can do anything not expressly prohibited in the Bill of Rights. Is Black's reading of the Amendment as compatible with its words as Goldberg's reading? Does Black's reading of the Ninth Amendment just duplicate the Tenth Amendment?

Consider Bork's attack on *Griswold*. Does he violate his own interpretive model by, in effect, reading the word "not" out of the Ninth Amendment?[g]

2. *The Historical Context.* Justices Goldberg and Black reformulated their textual disagreement into a disagreement about original intentions as well. Consider their disagreement, as well as the third approach identified above, in terms of constitutional originalism:

(1) *The Goldberg view.* Goldberg argued that the Framers of the Bill of Rights intended to rebut the *expressio unius* negative implication about the existence of unenumerated *rights*.

---

g. In his Senate confirmation hearings concerning his nomination to the Supreme Court, Judge Bork was asked about the Ninth Amendment. He responded:

I do not think that you can use the ninth amendment unless you know something of what it means. For example, if you had an amendment that says "Congress shall make no" and then there is an ink blot and you cannot read the rest of it and that is the only copy you have, I do not think the court can make up what might be under the ink blot.

Nomination of Robert H. Bork to be Associate Justice of the Supreme Court of the United States: Hearings Before the Senate Comm. on the Judiciary, 100th Cong., 1st Sess. 249 (1987).

(2) *The Black view.* Black contended that, to the contrary, the Framers intended to rebut the *expressio unius* negative implication about the existence of unenumerated federal *powers*.

(3) *The state-law view.* The third argument noted above — that the Ninth Amendment was designed simply to preserve rights recognized under state law — is also subscribed to by some scholars.[h]

During the period in which the Constitution was ratified, it and its Framers were attacked for failing to include a Bill of Rights against federal action. Supporters of the Constitution argued in defense that, under the document they drafted, a Bill of Rights was unnecessary: The federal government was already quite limited, as its authority was confined to those powers delegated to it.[i] The defenders also contended that including a Bill of Rights could work mischief. James Iredell, a supporter of the Constitution, argued in the North Carolina ratifying convention:

> [I]t would be not only useless, but dangerous, to enumerate a number of rights which are not intended to be given up; because it would be implying, in the strongest manner, that every right not included in the exception might be impaired by the government without usurpation; and it would be impossible to enumerate every one. Let any one make what collection or enumeration of rights he pleases, I will immediately mention twenty or thirty more rights not contained in it.[j]

Iredell's speech typified the sentiments of supporters of the Constitution. One way to read Iredell's argument is Justice Black's: Adding a Bill of Rights might create ambiguity about whether the federal government remained one solely of enumerated, delegated powers. Another way to read the argument is compatible with Justice Goldberg's views: Adding a Bill of Rights would endanger the unwritten individual rights already "retained" by the people. Which is the more plausible understanding? Whichever reading you accept explains what the Ninth Amendment was supposed to guard against.

In part, the historical record is somewhat ambiguous because of a lack of clarity about what "rights" meant in this context. One could say, with Justice Goldberg, that the Framers understood "rights retained by the people" as those individual rights found in natural law. There was a strong tradition of natural law in colonial America, which is reflected in the Declaration of Independence

---

h. See, e.g., Russell Caplan, *The History and Meaning of the Ninth Amendment*, 69 Va. L. Rev. 223 (1983). For a discussion of the overall problem, see generally Thomas McAffee, *The Original Meaning of the Ninth Amendment*, 90 Colum. L. Rev. 1215 (1990).

i. An illustration of this argument is provided in McAffee, *supra*, at 1227:

 * * * The objection that the Constitution should include a bill of rights was first raised near the end of the Convention, in August and September of 1787. Even after the Convention had rejected the call to form a committee to draft a bill of rights, on September 14, just three days before the Convention adjourned, Charles Pinckney and Elbridge Gerry moved to insert a provision for freedom of the press. But Roger Sherman * * * argued that the proposal was "unnecessary" because "[t]he power of Congress does not extend to the Press."

j. North Carolina Ratifying Convention, (July 29, 1788), in 4 Jonathan Elliot, *Debates in the Several State Conventions on the Adoption of the Federal Constitution* 167 (1891). See Daniel Farber & Suzanna Sherry, *A History of the American Constitution* 224-25, 230 (1990).

("all men have certain inalienable rights, including life, liberty, and the pursuit of happiness") and in the early state constitutions. Whether this tradition of natural law continued unabated into the framing of the Constitution is more debatable, however. In any event, even if many of the Framers believed in natural law, in our contemporary, skeptical world many intellectuals reject the idea — they would contend that natural law is just some sort of quasi-religious superstition, or that we cannot hope to ascertain what list of rights the Framers thought were contained in natural law and that the contents of it are too debatable and subjective to be left to the Supreme Court. Thus, even if Goldberg was right about the historical context, some would argue that our contemporary context is so different that we ought to ignore the Ninth Amendment.

An alternative reading of the historical context fits Justice Black's understanding. For the drafters of the Constitution, one can argue, "the scheme of limited government embodied in the system of enumerated powers was a means of reserving rights to the people." [McAffee 1219]. Here "right" is not being used in the contemporary sense of a specific limitation on otherwise lawful governmental power — as we would say today, for example, that Congress has the power to regulate interstate commerce, but cannot exercise that power in a way that violates the First Amendment. Rather, on this reading "right" means the absence of governmental authority to operate in the first place — the unenumerated rights are those "retained" by the simple device of enumerating a list of limited powers. This, of course, raises again the question whether this reading of the Ninth Amendment simply duplicates the Tenth Amendment — why would the Framers have inserted one amendment dealing with "rights" and one with "powers" if the two terms had the same effect?

We cannot hope to give you any way to resolve the historical dispute. We can give you one potential source of historical understanding, however. Appendix 3 reproduces an edited version of James Madison's speech to the House of Representatives presenting his draft of the Bill of Rights (including the Ninth Amendment). Read it and see what you think.

3. *Alternatives.* Consider Randy Barnett, *Reconceiving the Ninth Amendment*, 74 Cornell L. Rev. 1, 37 (1988):

> As a practical matter, we must choose between two fundamentally different constructions of the Constitution, each resting on a different presumption. We either accept the presumption that in pursuing happiness persons may do whatever is not justly prohibited or we are left with a presumption that the government may do whatever is not expressly prohibited. The presence of the Ninth Amendment in the Constitution strongly supports the first of these two presumptions. According to this interpretation of the Ninth Amendment, the Constitution established what Steven Macedo has called islands of governmental powers "surrounded by a sea of individual rights." It did not establish "islands [of rights] surrounded by a sea of governmental powers."

On this reading, is there any way to distinguish between unenumerated economic rights and unenumerated personal rights? Should there be? How might Bork respond?

PROBLEM 5-3
STATE REGULATION OF SEXUALITY

In light of the cases you have read thus far in this chapter (and earlier in the book), which of the following state laws are unconstitutional as applied in the prescribed circumstances:

(a)   A law prohibiting oral sex between consenting adults in private places, as applied to (i) a husband and wife, (ii) an unmarried man and woman, (iii) a woman and woman. See *People v. Onofre*, 415 N.E.2d 936 (N.Y. 1980).

(b)   An obscenity law applied to a man who views obscene movies in his own home but says he has not shared the movies with others. See *Stanley v. Georgia*, 394 U.S. 557 (1969).

(c)   A child custody law, applied to take award custody to the child's biological grandmother on the ground that her daughter (the child's biological mother) is a lesbian and the child is being raised in a "lesbian household" with the mother's female partner. See *Bottoms v. Bottoms*, 457 S.E.2d 102 (Va. 1995).

B.   ABORTION

ROE v. WADE
410 U.S. 113, 93 S. Ct. 705, 35 L.Ed.2d 147 (1973)

JUSTICE BLACKMUN delivered the opinion of the Court.

[Jane Roe, an unmarried pregnant woman, brought a class action challenging the constitutionality of the Texas criminal abortion laws. Texas prohibited all abortions except for the purpose of saving the pregnant woman's life. The Court undertook a detailed examination of the history of abortion law, beginning with the ancient Greeks. The Court observed that "the restrictive criminal abortion laws in effect in a majority of States today are of relatively recent vintage," generally dating from the second half of the nineteenth century. In contrast, the common law did not prohibit abortion before "quickening" — the first noticeable movement of the fetus, usually around the seventeenth week of pregnancy:

> It is thus apparent that at common law, at the time of the adoption of our Constitution, and throughout the major portion of the 19th century, abortion was viewed with less disfavor than under most American statutes currently in effect. Phrasing it another way, a woman enjoyed a substantially broader right to terminate a pregnancy than she does in most States today. At least with respect to the early stage of pregnancy, and very possibly without such a limitation, the opportunity to make this choice was present in this country well into the 19th century. Even later, the law continued for some time to treat less punitively an abortion procured in early pregnancy.

The Court noted that the move toward more severe abortion laws seems to have been caused by medical concerns about the risks to women posed by abortions under the medical technology of the time. After a lengthy discussion of this background, the Court turned to the constitutional issues.]

The Constitution does not explicitly mention any right of privacy. In a line of decisions, however, going back perhaps as far as *Union Pacific R. Co. v.*

Botsford, 141 U.S. 250, 251 (1891), the Court has recognized that a right of personal privacy, or a guarantee of certain areas or zones of privacy, does exist under the Constitution. In varying contexts, the Court or individual Justices have, indeed, found at least the roots of that right in the First Amendment, in the Fourth and Fifth Amendments, in the penumbras of the Bill of Rights [citing *Griswold*], in the Ninth Amendment, or in the concept of liberty guaranteed by the first section of the Fourteenth Amendment. These decisions make it clear that only personal rights that can be deemed "fundamental" or "implicit in the concept of ordered liberty," *Palko*, are included in this guarantee of personal privacy. They also make it clear that the right has some extension to activities relating to marriage, procreation, contraception, family relationships, and child rearing and education.

This right of privacy, whether it be founded in the Fourteenth Amendment's concept of personal liberty and restrictions upon state action, as we feel it is, or, as the District Court determined, in the Ninth Amendment's reservation of rights to the people, is broad enough to encompass a woman's decision whether or not to terminate her pregnancy. The detriment that the State would impose upon the pregnant woman by denying this choice altogether is apparent. Specific and direct harm medically diagnosable even in early pregnancy may be involved. Maternity, or additional offspring, may force upon the woman a distressful life and future. Psychological harm may be imminent. Mental and physical health may be taxed by child care. There is also the distress, for all concerned, associated with the unwanted child, and there is the problem of bringing a child into a family already unable, psychologically and otherwise, to care for it. In other cases, as in this one, the additional difficulties and continuing stigma of unwed motherhood may be involved. All these are factors the woman and her responsible physician necessarily will consider in consultation.

On the basis of elements such as these, appellant and some *amici* argue that the woman's right is absolute and that she is entitled to terminate her pregnancy at whatever time, in whatever way, and for whatever reason she alone chooses. With this we do not agree. Appellant's arguments that Texas either has no valid interest at all in regulating the abortion decision, or no interest strong enough to support any limitation upon the woman's sole determination, are unpersuasive. The Court's decisions recognizing a right of privacy also acknowledge that some state regulation in areas protected by that right is appropriate. [A] State may properly assert important interests in safeguarding health, in maintaining medical standards, and in protecting potential life. At some point in pregnancy, these respective interests become sufficiently compelling to sustain regulation of the factors that govern the abortion decision. The privacy right involved, therefore, cannot be said to be absolute. In fact, it is not clear to us that the claim asserted by some *amici* that one has an unlimited right to do with one's body as one pleases bears a close relationship to the right of privacy previously articulated in the Court's decisions. The Court has refused to recognize an unlimited right of this kind in the past. *Jacobson v. Massachusetts*, 197 U.S. 11 (1905) (vaccination); *Buck v. Bell* (sterilization).

We, therefore, conclude that the right of personal privacy includes the abortion decision, but that this right is not unqualified and must be considered against important state interests in regulation. [Justice Blackmun found this approach consistent with the trend in the lower courts and concluded that, where " 'fundamental rights' are involved, * * * regulation limiting these rights may be justified only by a 'compelling state interest,' and that legislative enactments must be narrowly drawn to express only the legitimate state interests at stake," citing *Griswold*.]

The appellee and certain *amici* argue that the fetus is a "person" within the language and meaning of the Fourteenth Amendment. In support of this, they outline at length and in detail the well-known facts of fetal development. If this suggestion of personhood is established, the appellant's case, of course, collapses, for the fetus' right to life is then guaranteed specifically by the Amendment. The appellant conceded as much on reargument. On the other hand, the appellee conceded on reargument that no case could be cited that holds that a fetus is a person within the meaning of the [Amendment].

The Constitution does not define "person" in so many words. Section 1 of the Fourteenth Amendment contains three references to "person." The first, in defining "citizens," speaks of "persons born or naturalized in the United States." The word also appears both in the Due Process Clause and in the Equal Protection Clause. "Person" is used in other places in the Constitution. But in nearly all these instances, the use of the word is such that it has application only postnatally. None indicates, with any assurance, that it has any possible pre-natal application.

All this, together with our observation that throughout the major portion of the 19th century prevailing legal abortion practices were far freer than they are today, persuades us that the word "person," as used in the Fourteenth Amendment, does not include the unborn. This is in accord with the results reached in those few cases where the issue has been squarely presented. * * *

This conclusion, however, does not of itself fully answer the contentions raised by Texas, and we pass on to other considerations.

The pregnant woman cannot be isolated in her privacy. She carries an embryo and, later, a fetus, if one accepts the medical definitions of the developing young in the human uterus. The situation therefore is inherently different from marital intimacy, or bedroom possession of obscene material, or marriage, or procreation, or education, with which [prior cases] were respectively concerned. As we have intimated above, it is reasonable and appropriate for a State to decide that at some point in time another interest, that of health of the mother or that of potential human life, becomes significantly involved. The woman's privacy is no longer sole and any right of privacy she possesses must be measured accordingly.

Texas urges that, apart from the Fourteenth Amendment, life begins at conception and is present throughout pregnancy, and that, therefore, the State has a compelling interest in protecting that life from and after conception. We need not resolve the difficult question of when life begins. When those trained in the respective disciplines of medicine, philosophy, and theology are unable to arrive at any consensus, the judiciary, at this point in the development of man's knowledge, is not in a position to speculate as to the answer. * * *

In view of all this, we do not agree that, by adopting one theory of life, Texas may override the rights of the pregnant woman that are at stake. We repeat, however, that the State does have an important and legitimate interest in preserving and protecting the health of the pregnant woman, whether she be a resident of the State or a nonresident who seeks medical consultation and treatment there, and that it has still *another* important and legitimate interest in protecting the potentiality of human life. These interests are separate and distinct. Each grows in substantiality as the woman approaches term and, at a point during pregnancy, each becomes "compelling."

With respect to the State's important and legitimate interest in the health of the mother, the "compelling" point, in the light of present medical knowledge, is at approximately the end of the first trimester. This is so because of the now-established medical fact * * * that until the end of the first trimester mortality in abortion may be less than mortality in normal childbirth. It follows that, from and after this point, a State may regulate the abortion procedure to the extent that the regulation reasonably relates to the preservation and protection of maternal health. Examples of permissible state regulation in this area are requirements as to the qualifications of the person who is to perform the abortion; as to the licensure of that person; as to the facility in which the procedure is to be performed, that is, whether it must be a hospital or may be a clinic or some other place of less-than-hospital status; as to the licensing of the facility; and the like.

This means, on the other hand, that, for the period of pregnancy prior to this "compelling" point, the attending physician, in consultation with his patient, is free to determine, without regulation by the State, that, in his medical judgment, the patient's pregnancy should be terminated. If that decision is reached, the judgment may be effectuated by an abortion free of interference by the State.

With respect to the State's important and legitimate interest in potential life, the "compelling" point is at viability. This is so because the fetus then presumably has the capability of meaningful life outside the mother's womb. State regulation protective of fetal life after viability thus has both logical and biological justifications. If the State is interested in protecting fetal life after viability, it may go so far as to proscribe abortion during that period, except when it is necessary to preserve the life or health of the mother. * * *

This holding, we feel, is consistent with the relative weights of the respective interests involved, with the lessons and examples of medical and legal history, with the lenity of the common law, and with the demands of the profound problems of the present day. The decision leaves the State free to place increasing restrictions on abortion as the period of pregnancy lengthens, so long as those restrictions are tailored to the recognized state interests. The decision vindicates the right of the physician to administer medical treatment according to his professional judgment up to the points where important state interests provide compelling justifications for intervention. Up to those points, the abortion decision in all its aspects is inherently, and primarily, a medical decision, and basic responsibility for it must rest with the physician. If an individual practitioner abuses the privilege of exercising proper medical judgment, the usual remedies, judicial and intra-professional, are available.

[Concurring opinions by **CHIEF JUSTICE BURGER**, **JUSTICE DOUGLAS**, and **JUSTICE STEWART** are omitted, as is the dissenting opinion of **JUSTICE WHITE**.]

JUSTICE REHNQUIST, dissenting.

The Court's opinion brings to the decision of this troubling question both extensive historical fact and a wealth of legal scholarship. While the opinion thus commands my respect, I find myself nonetheless in fundamental disagreement with those parts of it that invalidate the Texas statute in question, and therefore dissent. * * *

* * * I have difficulty in concluding, as the Court does, that the right of "privacy" is involved in this case. Texas, by the statute here challenged, bars the performance of a medical abortion by a licensed physician on a plaintiff such as Roe. A transaction resulting in an operation such as this is not "private" in the ordinary usage of that word. Nor is the "privacy" that the Court finds here even a distant relative of the freedom from searches and seizures protected by the Fourth Amendment to the Constitution, which the Court has referred to as embodying a right to privacy.

* * * The test traditionally applied in the area of social and economic legislation is whether or not a law such as that challenged has a rational relation to a valid state objective. *Williamson v. Lee Optical Co.* The Due Process Clause of the Fourteenth Amendment undoubtedly does place a limit, albeit a broad one, on legislative power to enact laws such as this. If the Texas statute were to prohibit an abortion even where the mother's life is in jeopardy, I have little doubt that such a statute would lack a rational relation to a valid state objective under the test stated in *Williamson.* But the Court's sweeping invalidation of any restrictions on abortion during the first trimester is impossible to justify under that standard, and the conscious weighing of competing factors that the Court's opinion apparently substitutes for the established test is far more appropriate to a legislative judgment than to a judicial one. * * *

To reach its result, the Court necessarily has had to find within the scope of the Fourteenth Amendment a right that was apparently completely unknown to the drafters of the Amendment. As early as 1821, the first state law dealing directly with abortion was enacted by the Connecticut Legislature. By the time of the adoption of the Fourteenth Amendment in 1868, there were at least 36 laws enacted by state or territorial legislatures limiting abortion. While many States have amended or updated their laws, 21 of the laws on the books in 1868 remain in effect today. Indeed, the Texas statute struck down today was, as the majority notes, first enacted in 1857 and "has remained substantially unchanged to the present time."

There apparently was no question concerning the validity of this provision or of any of the other state statutes when the Fourteenth Amendment was adopted. The only conclusion possible from this history is that the drafters did not intend to have the Fourteenth Amendment withdraw from the States the power to legislate with respect to this matter.

NOTES ON *ROE* AND THE ABORTION CONTROVERSY

1. *Should the Statute's Age Make a Difference?* In a companion case, *Doe v. Bolton*, 410 U.S. 179 (1973), the Court invalidated a more modern abortion statute that required abortions to be performed in hospitals and set up special procedures for hospital approval of abortions, on the ground that such procedures unduly restricted the exercise of the *Roe* right. Should the more modern statute, adopted after women obtained the right to vote, have been treated differently than the nineteenth century Texas law in *Roe*?

2. *Did the Court Act Too Soon? Was the Political Process Working?* Consider whether the Court would have done better to follow its own example in the contraception cases and try to establish a dialogue with the legislatures before attempting a definitive statement about abortion rights. Such a dialogue might well have been productive. In 1962, the influential American Law Institute, in its Model Penal Code, proposed liberalizing criminal abortion statutes. Beginning in 1968, thirteen states had softened their abortion statutes to allow abortions not only if the woman's life was threatened, but also if the pregnancy seriously endangered her physical or mental health, if the child would have major physical or mental abnormalities, or if the pregnancy resulted from rape. Four states essentially allowed abortion on demand if performed early in the pregnancy. Both the American Bar Association and the American Medical Association had gone on record favoring a liberalization of access to abortion. Although in the early 1970s many states continued to have restrictive approaches to abortion, the trend in the states, if left unimpeded, might well have led to a national consensus or at least to much wider availability of abortion through state legislation. Indeed, in 1973 immediately following *Roe*, 52% of those polled in a national survey said that they approved of *Roe*'s holding, which was described to them as "making abortions up to three months of pregnancy legal."[k]

3. *Aggressive Rational Basis Review as an Alternative.* As with the birth-control statute in *Griswold*, many of the abortion statutes on the books in the early 1970s were a century old, adopted in a different time and climate, both moral and political. The primary purpose for the statutes apparently was to protect the life and health of the mother from the comparative dangers of abortion instead of childbirth. By 1973, the medical basis for the criminal statutes had evaporated: abortion in the early stages of pregnancy had become safer than carrying the fetus to term. These facts led one thoughtful lower-court judge to contend that the old abortion statutes should be invalidated because there was no longer any logical connection between the nineteenth century legislature's purpose and the means chosen to effectuate that purpose. See *Abele v. Markle*, 342 F. Supp. 800, 809 (D. Conn. 1972) (three-judge court) (Newman, J., concurring in the result). Should the Court have taken this more limited tack in *Roe*? Or would it have been ducking its constitutional responsibilities if it had done so? How would this analysis be affected by considering

---

k. See Eric Uslander & Ronald Weber, *Public Support for Pro-Choice Abortion Policies in the Nation and States: Changes and Stability After the* Roe *and* Doe *Decisions*, 77 Mich. L. Rev. 1772, 1775 (1979). See also Garrow, *Liberty and Sexuality, supra.*

the law's disproportionate affect on women? (Note that Justice White, who concurred in *Griswold* on rational basis grounds, dissented in *Roe*.)

4. *Revisiting* Lochner. Is *Roe* just *Lochner* in feminist garb, or is there a principled reason for viewing abortion as a fundamental right? Consider how *Roe* would be decided by a judge applying originalism, representation reinforcement,[l] or normative interpretation.[m] Does it matter whether we phrase the question in terms of "abortion" or "control over reproduction"?

5. *The Role of the Physician.* In his concurring opinion, Chief Justice Burger stressed that the Court was not simply endorsing abortion on demand, because the physician's independent medical judgment remained a crucial element in the abortion decision. Would an independent medical judgment be desirable, or would it in fact give undue control of women's lives to their (at the time, at least) predominantly male doctors? In any event, the creation of abortion clinics seems to have undercut whatever expectation of direct patient-physician dialogue the *Roe* majority may have expected as a barrier to on-demand abortions.

6. *Comparative Law Perspective.* Mary Ann Glendon, *Abortion and Divorce in Western Law* (1987), found only five major western countries besides the United States in which the law allows abortion essentially on demand (Austria, Denmark, Greece, Norway, and Sweden).

Reva Siegel
Reasoning from the Body: A Historical Perspective on Abortion Regulation and Questions of Equal Protection
44 Stan. L. Rev. 261, 276-77, 350-51 (1992)[n]

[*Roe*] holds that the state has an interest in potential life which becomes compelling at the point of viability. It defines this regulatory interest in potential life physiologically, without reference to the sorts of constitutional considerations that normally attend the use of state power against a citizen. In the Court's reasoning, facts concerning the physiological development of the unborn provide "logical and biological justifications" both limiting and legitimating state action directed against the pregnant woman. Because *Roe* analyzes an exercise of state power from a medical, rather than a social, point of view, it authorizes state action against the pregnant woman on the basis of physiological criteria, requiring no inquiry into the state's reasons for acting against the

---

l. See John Hart Ely, *The Wages of Crying Wolf: A Comment on* Roe v. Wade, 82 Yale L.J. 920 (1973).

m. See Sylvia Law, *Rethinking Sex and the Constitution*, 132 U. Pa. L. Rev. 955 (1984); Michael Perry, *Abortion, the Public Morals, and the Police Power: The Ethical Function of Substantive Due Process*, 23 UCLA L. Rev. 689 (1976). Compare Michael Perry, *The Constitution, the Courts, and Human Rights* 94 (1982) (author changes his mind about normative consensus).

n. Copyright © 1991 by the Board of Trustees of the Leland Stanford, Jr. University. Reprinted by permission.

pregnant woman, or the impact of its actions on her. Indeed, *Roe* analyzes the state's interest in potential life as a benign exercise of state power for the protection of the unborn, and not as a coercive exercise of state power against pregnant women, often reasoning as if the state's interest in protecting potential life scarcely pertained to the pregnant woman herself. Thus, in the course of justifying its decision to protect the abortion decision as a right of privacy, the Court recognized an antagonistic state interest in restricting women's access to abortion on which it imposed temporal, but few principled, restraints.

To the extent that *Roe* relied upon physiological reasoning to define the state's interest in potential life, it unleashed a legal discourse of indeterminate content and scope — one legitimating boundless regulation of women's reproductive lives should the Court abandon the trimester framework that presently constrains it. In recognizing the state's interest in potential life, the Court ignored a simple social fact that should be of critical constitutional significance: When a state invokes an interest in potential life to justify fetal-protective regulation, the proposed use of public power concerns not merely the unborn, but women as well. Abortion-restrictive regulation is sex-based regulation, the use of public power to force women to bear children. Yet, the Court has never described the state's interest in protecting potential life as an interest in forcing women to bear children. *Roe*'s physiological reasoning obscures that simple social fact. "[I]f one accepts the medical definitions of the developing young in the human uterus" as a sufficient, objective, and authoritative framework for evaluating the state's regulatory interest in abortion — as *Roe* did — state action compelling women to perform the work of motherhood can be justified without ever acknowledging that the state is enforcing a gender status role. In part, this is because analyzing abortion-restrictive regulation within physiological paradigms obscures its social logic, but also, and as importantly, it is because physiological reasons for regulating women's conduct are already laden with socio-political import: Facts about women's bodies have long served to justify regulation enforcing judgments about women's roles.

Abortion-restrictive regulation is state action compelling pregnancy and motherhood, and this simple fact cannot be evaded by invoking nature or a woman's choices to explain the situation in which the pregnant woman subject to abortion restrictions finds herself. A pregnant woman seeking an abortion has the practical capacity to terminate a pregnancy, which she would exercise but for the community's decision to prevent or deter her. If the community successfully effectuates its will, it is the state, and not nature, which is responsible for causing her to continue the pregnancy. * * *

When abortion-restrictive regulation is analyzed as state action compelling motherhood, it presents equal protection concerns that *Roe*'s physiological reasoning obscures[.]

NOTE ON ABORTION REGULATION AS
SEX DISCRIMINATION

Was the Due Process Clause the best place to ground an argument against abortion statutes? Would the Equal Protection Clause have been preferable? What doctrinal obstacles were there? (See Chapter 4, § 2.)[o]

Ruth Bader Ginsburg, *Some Thoughts on Autonomy and Equality in Relation to* Roe v. Wade, 63 N.C. L. Rev. 375, 382-83 (1985)[p], suggests that *Roe* might have been more firmly grounded "had the Court placed the woman alone, rather than the woman tied to her physician, at the center of its attention":

> It is not a sufficient answer to charge it all to women's anatomy — a natural, not man-made, phenomenon. Society, not anatomy, "places a greater stigma on unmarried women who become pregnant than on the men who father their children." Society expects, but nature does not command, that "woman take the major responsibility * * * for child care" and that they will stay with their children, bearing nurture and support burdens alone, when fathers deny paternity or otherwise refuse to provide care or financial support for unwanted offspring.

> I do not pretend that, if the Court had added a distinct sex discrimination theme to its medically oriented opinion, the storm *Roe* generated would have been less furious. I appreciate the intense divisions of opinion on the moral question and recognize that abortion today cannot fairly be described as nothing more than birth control delayed. The conflict, however, is not simply one between a fetus' interests and a woman's interests, narrowly conceived, nor is the overriding issue state versus private control of a woman's body for a span of nine months. Also in the balance is a woman's autonomous charge of her full life's course — as Professor Karst put it, her ability to stand in relation to man, society, and the state as an independent, self-sustaining, equal citizen.

The conceptualization of abortion as forcing a burden on women is expressed in a well-known philosophical article, Judith Jarvis Thompson, *A Defense of Abortion*, 1 Phil. & Pub. Aff. 47 (1971). Professor Thompson asks the reader to consider the possibility of being kidnapped and hooked up to a blood circulation machine in order to save the life of a famous violinist. After nine months, the violinist will be well enough to be unplugged. This would plainly be an invasion of your moral rights, and Thompson argues by analogy that (even if the fetus is a person) coercing a woman's participation in the pregnancy is no different than the violinist hypothetical. See also Judith Jarvis Thompson, *The Realm of Rights* 289-93 (1990) (what claims does a "fertilized egg" have against a woman?). Is this argument persuasive, or is the violinist analogy contrived?

Some of these arguments illustrate the importance of baselines. Is the pregnant woman being required to confer a benefit to the fetus, or is she being prevented from harming it? This depends on whether the baseline is a world in which women control their pregnancies, or one where pregnancies proceed to term. (Compare the problem of picking baselines in an economic substantive

---

o. Is it relevant to this argument that public opinion polls show that women favor restricting abortion slightly more than men? See Daniel Farber, *Legal Pragmatism and the Constitution*, 72 Minn. L. Rev. 1331, 1369 n.186 (1988).

p. Reprinted with permission.

due process case (§ 2B of this chapter) and in a Takings Clause case (§ 2C).) Which is the proper baseline?

NOTE: THE ABORTION RIGHT FROM *ROE* TO *CASEY*

Just as the Equal Rights Amendment was to generate an anti-ERA politics seeking to preserve traditional gender roles against state liberalization, so the pro-choice movement triggered a "pro-life" countermovement seeking to preserve traditional ideas about family and the origins of human life.[q] *Roe v. Wade* energized the countermovement, which persuaded state legislatures to adopt numerous measures to make abortions more difficult for women, including (1) rules against abortions for minors without parental consent or (2) for wives without their husbands' consent; (3) requirements that women be given state-specified information (meant to discourage this choice) and (4) be required to wait for a period of time before they could have abortions; (5) refusal to fund abortions in state medicaid and employee health insurance programs; and (6) closure of municipal hospitals to abortions. Reread *Roe*. Which of these new state policies would you expect the Court to invalidate as inconsistent with *Roe*? Jot down your answer and then read the following account.

In the wake of *Roe*, the Court invalidated most of the new restrictions. In *Planned Parenthood v. Danforth*, 428 U.S. 52 (1976), the Court invalidated requirements of parental consent for minors and spousal consent for wives. Reaffirming the individualist, rather than family, nature of the privacy right declared in *Eisenstadt* and *Roe*, Justice Blackmun's opinion for the Court ruled that parents and husbands cannot have vetoes over a right personal to the pregnant woman. The pregnancy of minors troubled most of the Justices, however. Although invalidating a less restrictive parental consent law as an "undue burden" on the minor's right to choose in *Bellotti v. Baird*, 443 U.S. 622 (1979), Justice Powell's plurality opinion recognized "the peculiar vulnerability of children; their inability to make critical decisions in an informed, mature manner; and the importance of the parental role in child rearing." In dictum, Powell opined that states could require parents to consent so long as there were a judicial procedure available for the minor to petition in lieu of a parental dialogue. Thus, it was no great surprise when the Court in *Planned Parenthood v. Ashcroft*, 462 U.S. 476 (1983), upheld a state law requiring a minor to obtain either parental consent or judicial approval of her choice to abort. See also *H.L. v. Matheson*, 450 U.S. 398 (1981) (approving law requiring that parents be notified whenever possible).

In *Akron v. Akron Center for Reproductive Health*, 462 U.S. 416 (1983), the Court struck down a requirement that dilatation-and-evacuation abortions be performed in hospitals, because the ban imposed a heavy and unnecessary burden on women's access to a relatively inexpensive, otherwise accessible, and safe abortion procedure in clinics. The Court also invalidated the government's blanket determination that *all* minors under the age of 15 are too immature to make an abortion decision or that an abortion never may be in the minor's best

---

q. See generally Dallas Blanchard, *The Anti-Abortion Movement and the Rise of the Religious Right: From Polite to Firey Protest* (1994) (institutional history and ideology of pro-life movement).

interests without parental approval. The statute did not provide any opportunity for case-by-case evaluations of the maturity of pregnant minors. The Court was similarly unsympathetic with an "informed consent" requirement. By requiring the attending physician to give the woman a lengthy and inflexible list of information, and by imposing a twenty-four-hour waiting period, the state had placed a burden on abortions that was not reasonably related to health or safety. See also *Thornburgh v. American College of Obstetricians and Gynecologists*, 476 U.S. 747 (1986) (striking down a similar informed-consent law). Perhaps the post-*Roe* case going the furthest in protecting abortion rights was *Colautti v. Franklin*, 439 U.S. 379 (1979), which involved a Pennsylvania statute requiring doctors to determine viability before performing abortions. The Court held the statute to be unconstitutionally vague, largely because it was unclear how much evidence of viability was required.

For poor women, the rights granted in theory by *Roe* were not necessarily available in practice. In *Maher v. Roe*, 432 U.S. 464 (1977), and *Harris v. McRae*, 448 U.S. 297 (1980), the Court held that the government has no affirmative obligation to pay for abortions, even if it does pay for childbirth. *Maher* found no violation of substantive due process because the government was imposing no "unduly burdensome interference" with the freedom to decide whether to terminate the pregnancy. On the equal protection front, the Court applied only a rational basis test, because wealth is not a suspect class and because the Court had already determined that no fundamental right was infringed. A sufficient rational basis was present because of the government's legitimate (though not always, according to *Roe*, compelling) interest in protecting the potential life of the fetus.

The Reagan Administration mounted a constitutional attack on *Roe*. In *Akron* and *Thornburgh*, the Solicitor General urged the Court to abandon *Roe*'s "rigid" trimester framework and adopt *Maher*'s "undue burden" approach. Three Justices — including newly appointed Justice O'Connor — dissented from the invalidation of an informed consent law in *Akron*, and they were joined by Chief Justice Burger in *Thornburgh*. The retirement of Justice Powell in 1987 cost the Court a fairly loyal adherent to *Roe*. Although Reagan's nomination of anti-privacy Judge Robert Bork was defeated, his substitute, Judge Anthony Kennedy, a devout Roman Catholic, was not considered a friend of *Roe*. In the next case, digested below, Missouri asked the Court to overrule *Roe* — a petition joined by dozens of *amici* and by the Solicitor General. The Reagan Administration maintained to the Court that *Roe* created a fundamental right that was not supported by constitutional text, intent, or traditions; denigrated the state's interest in potential human life without any legal or moral basis; and engaged in judicial activism in the teeth of popular demands for regulation of this controversial activity.

———

Webster v. Reproductive Health Services, 492 U.S. 490 (1989). A Missouri law required doctors to determine viability before performing an abortion after the twentieth week of pregnancy. The plurality opinion, written by **Chief Justice Rehnquist**, declined to revisit *Roe*'s holding that abortion has some constitutional protection, but did concede that it involved a "liberty interest protected by the Due Process Clause." It then contended that the trimester system should be rejected. Applying an unspecified level of review, it concluded: "The Missouri testing requirement here is reasonably designed to ensure that abortions are not performed where the fetus is viable — an end which all concede is legitimate — and that is sufficient to sustain its constitutionality." Interestingly, in light of later developments, **Justice Kennedy** joined Rehnquist's opinion. **Justice O'Connor** concurred on the basis that Missouri law did not impose an "undue burden" and in any event was consistent with the Court's previous decisions. Her support for *Roe* remained unclear, however. In an angry concurrence, **Justice Scalia** berated the majority for refusing to overrule *Roe* outright:

> The outcome of today's case will doubtless be heralded as a triumph of judicial statesmanship. It is not that, unless it is statesmanlike needlessly to prolong this Court's self-awarded sovereignty over a field where it has little proper business since the answer to most of the cruel questions posed are political and not juridical — a sovereignty which therefore quite properly, but to the great damage of the Court, makes it the object of the sort of organized public pressure that political institutions in a democracy ought to receive.

Justices Blackmun, **Brennan**, **Marshall,** and **Stevens** dissented on the ground that the Court's ruling was inconsistent with *Roe*.

Hodgson v. Minnesota, 497 U.S. 417 (1990). Based upon *Ashcroft* and subsequent cases, 38 states enacted laws requiring notification or consent of one or both parents before a minor could obtain an abortion. Arguably the most restrictive law was that of Minnesota, which required notification of both parents (one of eight states to do so) and had virtually no loopholes except for an alternate procedure for judicial bypass, as required by *Danforth*. The trial judge made these findings of fact: (1) the requirement that the father be notified was a significant burden on a minor's right to obtain abortion, and was a prohibitive barrier for many minors because they legitimately feared violence from their fathers, and the same minors were too intimidated by the judicial bypass to use it; (2) the legislature intended the two-parent notification procedure to deter abortions by minors and to "save lives" of fetuses; and (3) both bypass judges and public defenders who had worked on such cases believed the notification and bypass procedures did not serve any goal of informed consent or dialogue with mature decisionmakers, and merely deterred young women from making their own decisions about abortion. The judge invalidated the two-parent notification law, even with the judicial bypass.

The Supreme Court reversed. **Justice Kennedy**'s controlling opinion simply applied *Ashcroft* and the other precedents upholding parental notification and consent requirements that had opportunities for judicial bypass. He did not disagree with the lower court's findings of fact but considered them, essentially, irrelevant. Concurring, **Justice O'Connor** maintained that the two-parent notification requirement was in fact an *undue burden* on a minor woman's right to abortion but agreed with the Court that the availability of a judicial bypass saved the statute.

When Justices Brennan and Marshall were replaced by Justices Souter and Thomas, the future of *Roe* looked even dimmer. When *Casey*, excerpted below, was argued, the Solicitor General for the George W. Bush Administration and the State of Pennsylvania both asked the Court to overrule *Roe*. Planned Parenthood, which challenged the state restrictions on abortion, asked the Court to overrule *Roe* if it was not willing to give the right of privacy real bite. Consider the Court's response.

PLANNED PARENTHOOD OF SOUTHEASTERN PENNSYLVANIA v. CASEY
505 U.S. 833, 112 S.Ct. 2791, 120 L.Ed.2d 674 (1992)

JUSTICE O'CONNOR, JUSTICE KENNEDY, and **JUSTICE SOUTER** announced the judgment of the Court and delivered the opinion of the Court with respect to Parts I, II, and III. [This is referred to by the other Justices and in our Notes as the "Joint Opinion."]

[Pennsylvania required a woman seeking an abortion to wait 24 hours (except in a medical emergency), so that she could consider information regarding the nature and risks of the procedure and the probable gestational age of the fetus, which the law required the physician to provide. The law required minors to obtain the consent of one parent, with a judicial-bypass option. Married women were required to notify their spouses.]

I. Liberty finds no refuge in a jurisprudence of doubt. Yet 19 years after our holding that the Constitution protects a woman's right to terminate her pregnancy in its early stages, *Roe v. Wade*, that definition of liberty is still questioned. Joining the respondents as *amicus curiae*, the United States, as it has done in five other cases in the last decade, again asks us to overrule *Roe*. * * *

After considering the fundamental constitutional questions resolved by *Roe*, principles of institutional integrity, and the rule of *stare decisis*, we are led to conclude this: the essential holding of *Roe v. Wade* should be retained and once again reaffirmed.

It must be stated at the outset and with clarity that *Roe*'s essential holding, the holding we reaffirm, has three parts. First is a recognition of the right of the woman to choose to have an abortion before viability and to obtain it without undue interference from the State. Before viability, the State's interests are not strong enough to support a prohibition of abortion or the imposition of a substantial obstacle to the woman's effective right to elect the procedure. Second is a confirmation of the State's power to restrict abortions after fetal viability, if the law contains exceptions for pregnancies which endanger a woman's life or health. And third is the principle that the State has legitimate interests from the outset of the pregnancy in protecting the health of the woman and the life of the fetus that may become a child. These principles do not contradict one another; and we adhere to each.

II. Constitutional protection of the woman's decision to terminate her pregnancy derives from the Due Process Clause of the Fourteenth Amendment. It declares that no State shall "deprive any person of life, liberty, or property, without due process of law." The controlling word in the case before us is "liberty." Although a literal reading of the Clause might suggest that it governs only the procedures by which a State may deprive persons of liberty, for at least 105 years * * * the Clause has been understood to contain a substantive component as well, one "barring certain government actions regardless of the fairness of the procedures used to implement them." * * * "[T]he guaranties of due process, though having their roots in Magna Carta's *per legem terrae*' and considered as procedural safeguards 'against executive usurpation and tyranny,' have in this country 'become bulwarks also against arbitrary legislation.' " *Poe v. Ullman* (Harlan, J., dissenting from dismissal on jurisdictional grounds).

The most familiar of the substantive liberties protected by the Fourteenth Amendment are those recognized by the Bill of Rights. We have held that the Due Process Clause of the Fourteenth Amendment incorporates most of the Bill of Rights against the States. It is tempting, as a means of curbing the discretion of federal judges, to suppose that liberty encompasses no more than those rights already guaranteed to the individual against federal interference by the express provisions of the first eight amendments to the Constitution. See *Adamson* (Black, J., dissenting). But of course this Court has never accepted that view.

It is also tempting, for the same reason, to suppose that the Due Process Clause protects only those practices, defined at the most specific level, that were protected against government interference by other rules of law when the Fourteenth Amendment was ratified. See *Michael H. v. Gerald D.*, 491 U.S. 110, 127-128, n.6 (1989) (opinion of Scalia, J.).[r] But such a view would be inconsistent with our law. It is a premise of the Constitution that there is a realm of personal liberty which the government may not enter. We have vindicated this principle before. Marriage is mentioned nowhere in the Bill of Rights and interracial marriage was illegal in most States in the 19th century, but the Court was no doubt correct in finding it to be an aspect of liberty protected against state interference by the substantive component of the Due Process Clause in *Loving.* * * *

Neither the Bill of Rights nor the specific practices of States at the time of the adoption of the Fourteenth Amendment marks the outer limits of the substantive sphere of liberty which the Fourteenth Amendment protects. See U.S. Const., Amend. 9. As the second Justice Harlan recognized in [*Poe v. Ullman*]:

> [T]he full scope of the liberty guaranteed by the Due Process Clause cannot be found in or limited by the precise terms of the specific guarantees elsewhere provided in the Constitution. This "liberty" is not a series of isolated points pricked out in terms of the taking of property; the freedom of speech, press, and religion; the right to keep and bear arms; the freedom from unreasonable searches and seizures; and so on. It is a rational continuum which, broadly speaking, includes a freedom from all substantial arbitrary impositions and purposeless restraints, . . . and which also recognizes, what a reasonable and sensitive judgment must, that certain interests require particularly careful scrutiny of the state needs asserted to justify their abridgment.

---

r. *Editors' note:* The issue in *Michael H.* was whether a biological father could claim paternal rights to a child whose mother was married to someone else.

Justice Harlan wrote these words in addressing an issue the full Court did not reach in *Poe v. Ullman*, but the Court adopted his position four Terms later in *Griswold v. Connecticut.* * * * It is settled now, as it was when the Court heard arguments in *Roe v. Wade*, that the Constitution places limits on a State's right to interfere with a person's most basic decisions about family and parenthood, as well as bodily integrity.

The inescapable fact is that adjudication of substantive due process claims may call upon the Court in interpreting the Constitution to exercise that same capacity which by tradition courts always have exercised: reasoned judgment. Its boundaries are not susceptible of expression as a simple rule. That does not mean we are free to invalidate state policy choices with which we disagree; yet neither does it permit us to shrink from the duties of our office. [The Joint Opinion again quoted Justice Harlan's *Poe* dissent.]

Men and women of good conscience can disagree, and we suppose some always shall disagree, about the profound moral and spiritual implications of terminating a pregnancy, even in its earliest stage. Some of us as individuals find abortion offensive to our most basic principles of morality, but that cannot control our decision. Our obligation is to define the liberty of all, not to mandate our own moral code. The underlying constitutional issue is whether the State can resolve these philosophic questions in such a definitive way that a woman lacks all choice in the matter, except perhaps in those rare circumstances in which the pregnancy is itself a danger to her own life or health, or is the result of rape or incest.

It is conventional constitutional doctrine that where reasonable people disagree the government can adopt one position or the other. That theorem, however, assumes a state of affairs in which the choice does not intrude upon a protected liberty. Thus, while some people might disagree about whether or not the flag should be saluted, or disagree about the proposition that it may not be defiled, we have ruled that a State may not compel or enforce one view or the other.

Our law affords constitutional protection to personal decisions relating to marriage, procreation, contraception, family relationships, child rearing, and education. Our cases recognize "the right of the *individual*, married or single, to be free from unwarranted governmental intrusion into matters so fundamentally affecting a person as the decision whether to bear or beget a child." *Eisenstadt v. Baird* (emphasis in original). Our precedents "have respected the private realm of family life which the state cannot enter." These matters, involving the most intimate and personal choices a person may make in a lifetime, choices central to personal dignity and autonomy, are central to the liberty protected by the Fourteenth Amendment. At the heart of liberty is the right to define one's own concept of existence, of meaning, of the universe, and of the mystery of human life. Beliefs about these matters could not define the attributes of personhood were they formed under compulsion of the State.

These considerations begin our analysis of the woman's interest in terminating her pregnancy but cannot end it, for this reason: though the abortion decision may originate within the zone of conscience and belief, it is more than a philosophic exercise. Abortion is a unique act. It is an act fraught with consequences for others: for the woman who must live with the implications of her decision; for the persons who perform and assist in the procedure; for the spouse, family, and society which must confront the knowledge that these procedures exist, procedures some deem nothing short of an act of violence against innocent human life; and, depending on one's beliefs, for the life or potential life that is aborted. Though abortion is conduct, it does not follow that the State is entitled to proscribe it in all instances. That is because the liberty of the woman is at stake in a sense unique to the human condition and so unique to the law. The mother who carries a child to full term is subject to anxieties, to physical constraints, to pain that only she must bear. That these sacrifices have from the beginning of the human race been endured by woman with a pride that ennobles her in the eyes of others and gives to the infant a bond of love cannot alone be grounds for the State to insist she make the sacrifice. Her suffering is too intimate and personal for the State to insist, without more, upon its own vision of the woman's role, however dominant that vision has been in the course of our history and our culture. The destiny of the woman must be shaped to a large extent on her own conception of her spiritual imperatives and her place in society.

It should be recognized, moreover, that in some critical respects the abortion decision is of the same character as the decision to use contraception, to which *Griswold v. Connecticut, Eisenstadt v. Baird,* and *Carey v. Population Services International* afford constitutional protection. We have no doubt as to the correctness of those decisions. They support the reasoning in *Roe* relating to the woman's liberty because they involve personal decisions concerning not only the meaning of procreation but also human responsibility and respect for it. As with abortion, reasonable people will have differences of opinion about these matters. One view is based on such reverence for the wonder of creation that any pregnancy ought to be welcomed and carried to full term no matter how difficult it will be to provide for the child and ensure its well-being. Another is that the inability to provide for the nurture and care of the infant is a cruelty to the child and an anguish to the parent. These are intimate views with infinite variations, and their deep, personal character underlay our decisions in *Griswold, Eisenstadt,* and *Carey.* The same concerns are present when the woman confronts the reality that, perhaps despite her attempts to avoid it, she has become pregnant.

It was this dimension of personal liberty that *Roe* sought to protect, and its holding invoked the reasoning and the tradition of the precedents we have discussed, granting protection to substantive liberties of the person. *Roe* was, of course, an extension of those cases and, as the decision itself indicated, the separate States could act in some degree to further their own legitimate interests in protecting pre-natal life. The extent to which the legislatures of the States might act to outweigh the interests of the woman in choosing to terminate her pregnancy was a subject of debate both in *Roe* itself and in decisions following it.

While we appreciate the weight of the arguments made on behalf of the State in the case before us, arguments which in their ultimate formulation conclude that *Roe* should be overruled, the reservations any of us may have in reaffirming the central holding of *Roe* are outweighed by the explication of individual liberty we have given combined with the force of *stare decisis*. We turn now to that doctrine.

III. The obligation to follow precedent begins with necessity, and a contrary necessity marks its outer limit. With Cardozo, we recognize that no judicial system could do society's work if it eyed each issue afresh in every case that raised it. Indeed, the very concept of the rule of law underlying our own Constitution requires such continuity over time that a respect for precedent is, by definition, indispensable. At the other extreme, a different necessity would make itself felt if a prior judicial ruling should come to be seen so clearly as error that its enforcement was for that very reason doomed. * * *

So in this case we may inquire whether *Roe*'s central rule has been found unworkable; whether the rule's limitation on state power could be removed without serious inequity to those who have relied upon it or significant damage to the stability of the society governed by the rule in question; whether the law's growth in the intervening years has left *Roe*'s central rule a doctrinal anachronism discounted by society; and whether *Roe*'s premises of fact have so far changed in the ensuing two decades as to render its central holding somehow irrelevant or unjustifiable in dealing with the issue it addressed. [Addressing each of these factors, the Court concluded that *Roe* remains "viable."]

The sum of the precedential inquiry to this point shows *Roe*'s underpinnings unweakened in any way affecting its central holding. While it has engendered disapproval, it has not been unworkable. An entire generation has come of age free to assume *Roe*'s concept of liberty in defining the capacity of women to act in society, and to make reproductive decisions; no erosion of principle going to liberty or personal autonomy has left *Roe*'s central holding a doctrinal remnant; *Roe* portends no developments at odds with other precedent for the analysis of personal liberty; and no changes of fact have rendered viability more or less appropriate as the point at which the balance of interests tips. Within the bounds of normal *stare decisis* analysis, then, and subject to the considerations on which it customarily turns, the stronger argument is for affirming *Roe*'s central holding, with whatever degree of personal reluctance any of us may have, not for overruling it. * * *

* * * Where, in the performance of its judicial duties, the Court decides a case in such a way as to resolve the sort of intensely divisive controversy reflected in *Roe* and those rare, comparable cases, its decision has a dimension that the resolution of the normal case does not carry. It is the dimension present whenever the Court's interpretation of the Constitution calls the contending sides of a national controversy to end their national division by accepting a common mandate rooted in the Constitution.

The Court is not asked to do this very often, having thus addressed the Nation only twice in our lifetime, in the decisions of *Brown* and *Roe*. But when the Court does act in this way, its decision requires an equally rare precedential force to counter the inevitable efforts to overturn it and to thwart its implementation. Some of those efforts may be mere unprincipled emotional reactions;

others may proceed from principles worthy of profound respect. But whatever the premises of opposition may be, only the most convincing justification under accepted standards of precedent could suffice to demonstrate that a later decision overruling the first was anything but a surrender to political pressure, and an unjustified repudiation of the principle on which the Court staked its authority in the first instance. So to overrule under fire in the absence of the most compelling reason to reexamine a watershed decision would subvert the Court's legitimacy beyond any serious question. Cf. *Brown II* ("[I]t should go without saying that the vitality of th[e] constitutional principles [announced in *Brown I*] cannot be allowed to yield simply because of disagreement with them"). * * *

The Court's duty in the present case is clear. In 1973, it confronted the already-divisive issue of governmental power to limit personal choice to undergo abortion, for which it provided a new resolution based on the due process guaranteed by the Fourteenth Amendment. Whether or not a new social consensus is developing on that issue, its divisiveness is no less today than in 1973, and pressure to overrule the decision, like pressure to retain it, has grown only more intense. A decision to overrule *Roe*'s essential holding under the existing circumstances would address error, if error there was, at the cost of both profound and unnecessary damage to the Court's legitimacy, and to the Nation's commitment to the rule of law. It is therefore imperative to adhere to the essence of *Roe*'s original decision, and we do so today.

IV. From what we have said so far it follows that it is a constitutional liberty of the woman to have some freedom to terminate her pregnancy. We conclude that the basic decision in *Roe* was based on a constitutional analysis which we cannot now repudiate. The woman's liberty is not so unlimited, however, that from the outset the State cannot show its concern for the life of the unborn, and at a later point in fetal development the State's interest in life has sufficient force so that the right of the woman to terminate the pregnancy can be restricted.

That brings us, of course, to the point where much criticism has been directed at *Roe*, a criticism that always inheres when the Court draws a specific rule from what in the Constitution is but a general standard. We conclude, however, that the urgent claims of the woman to retain the ultimate control over her destiny and her body, claims implicit in the meaning of liberty, require us to perform that function. Liberty must not be extinguished for want of a line that is clear. And it falls to us to give some real substance to the woman's liberty to determine whether to carry her pregnancy to full term.

We conclude the line should be drawn at viability, so that before that time the woman has a right to choose to terminate her pregnancy. We adhere to this principle for two reasons. First * * * is the doctrine of *stare decisis*. Any judicial act of line-drawing may seem somewhat arbitrary, but *Roe* was a reasoned statement, elaborated with great care. We have twice reaffirmed it in the face of great opposition. *Thornburgh*; *Akron*.

The second reason is that the concept of viability, as we noted in *Roe*, is the time at which there is a realistic possibility of maintaining and nourishing a life outside the womb, so that the independent existence of the second life can in reason and all fairness be the object of state protection that now overrides the rights of the woman. Consistent with other constitutional norms, legislatures may draw lines which appear arbitrary without the necessity of offering a justification. But courts may not. We must justify the lines we draw. And there is no line other than viability which is more workable. To be sure, * * * there may be some medical developments that affect the precise point of viability, but this is an imprecision within tolerable limits given that the medical community and all those who must apply its discoveries will continue to explore the matter. The viability line also has, as a practical matter, an element of fairness. In some broad sense it might be said that a woman who fails to act before viability has consented to the State's intervention on behalf of the developing child.

The woman's right to terminate her pregnancy before viability is the most central principle of *Roe v. Wade.* It is a rule of law and a component of liberty we cannot renounce.

On the other side of the equation is the interest of the State in the protection of potential life. The *Roe* Court recognized the State's "important and legitimate interest in protecting the potentiality of human life." The weight to be given this state interest, not the strength of the woman's interest, was the difficult question faced in *Roe.* We do not need to say whether each of us, had we been Members of the Court when the valuation of the State interest came before it as an original matter, would have concluded, as the *Roe* Court did, that its weight is insufficient to justify a ban on abortions prior to viability even when it is subject to certain exceptions. The matter is not before us in the first instance, and coming as it does after nearly 20 years of litigation in *Roe*'s wake we are satisfied that the immediate question is not the soundness of *Roe*'s resolution of the issue, but the precedential force that must be accorded to its holding. And we have concluded that the essential holding of *Roe* should be reaffirmed.

Yet it must be remembered that *Roe v. Wade* speaks with clarity in establishing not only the woman's liberty but also the State's "important and legitimate interest in potential life." That portion of the decision in *Roe* has been given too little acknowledgment and implementation by the Court in its subsequent cases. Those cases decided that any regulation touching upon the abortion decision must survive strict scrutiny, to be sustained only if drawn in narrow terms to further a compelling state interest. Not all of the cases decided under that formulation can be reconciled with the holding in *Roe* itself that the State has legitimate interests in the health of the woman and in protecting the potential life within her. In resolving this tension, we choose to rely upon *Roe,* as against the later cases.

Roe established a trimester framework to govern abortion regulations. Under this elaborate but rigid construct, almost no regulation at all is permitted during the first trimester of pregnancy; regulations designed to protect the woman's health, but not to further the State's interest in potential life, are permitted during the second trimester; and during the third trimester, when the fetus is viable, prohibitions are permitted provided the life or health of the mother is not at stake. Most of our cases since *Roe* have involved the application of rules derived from the trimester framework. * * *

We reject the trimester framework, which we do not consider to be part of the essential holding of *Roe*. See *Webster*. Measures aimed at ensuring that a woman's choice contemplates the consequences for the fetus do not necessarily interfere with the right recognized in *Roe*, although those measures have been found to be inconsistent with the rigid trimester framework announced in that case. A logical reading of the central holding in *Roe* itself, and a necessary reconciliation of the liberty of the woman and the interest of the State in promoting prenatal life, require, in our view, that we abandon the trimester framework as a rigid prohibition on all previability regulation aimed at the protection of fetal life. The trimester framework suffers from these basic flaws: in its formulation it misconceives the nature of the pregnant woman's interest; and in practice it undervalues the State's interest in potential life, as recognized in *Roe*.

As our jurisprudence relating to all liberties save perhaps abortion has recognized, not every law which makes a right more difficult to exercise is, *ipso facto*, an infringement of that right. An example clarifies the point. We have held that not every ballot access limitation amounts to an infringement of the right to vote. Rather, the States are granted substantial flexibility in establishing the framework within which voters choose the candidates for whom they wish to vote.

The abortion right is similar. Numerous forms of state regulation might have the incidental effect of increasing the cost or decreasing the availability of medical care, whether for abortion or any other medical procedure. The fact that a law which serves a valid purpose, one not designed to strike at the right itself, has the incidental effect of making it more difficult or more expensive to procure an abortion cannot be enough to invalidate it. Only where state regulation imposes an undue burden on a woman's ability to make this decision does the power of the State reach into the heart of the liberty protected by the Due Process Clause. * * *

A finding of an undue burden is a shorthand for the conclusion that a state regulation has the purpose or effect of placing a substantial obstacle in the path of a woman seeking an abortion of a nonviable fetus. A statute with this purpose is invalid because the means chosen by the State to further the interest in potential life must be calculated to inform the woman's free choice, not hinder it. And a statute which, while furthering the interest in potential life or some other valid state interest, has the effect of placing a substantial obstacle in the path of a woman's choice cannot be considered a permissible means of serving its legitimate ends. To the extent that the opinions of the Court or of individual Justices use the undue burden standard in a manner that is inconsistent with this analysis, we set out what in our view should be the controlling standard. In our considered judgment, an undue burden is an unconstitutional burden. Understood another way, we answer the question, left open in previous opinions discussing the undue burden formulation, whether a law designed to further the State's interest in fetal life which imposes an undue burden on the woman's decision before fetal viability could be constitutional. The answer is no.

Some guiding principles should emerge. What is at stake is the woman's right to make the ultimate decision, not a right to be insulated from all others in doing so. Regulations which do no more than create a structural mechanism by which the State, or the parent or guardian of a minor, may express profound respect for the life of the unborn are permitted, if they are not a substantial obstacle to the woman's exercise of the right to choose. Unless it has that effect on her right of choice, a state measure designed to persuade her to choose childbirth over abortion will be upheld if reasonably related to that goal. Regulations designed to foster the health of a woman seeking an abortion are valid if they do not constitute an undue burden. * * *

[V. The Joint Opinion upheld the informed consent, 24-hour waiting period, and one-parent consent provisions of the Pennsylvania law (see notes 1 and 2 following the case). In holding that the state can require the physician to provide the woman seeking abortion with truthful information about the procedure, the health risks, and the probable gestational age of the fetus, the Joint Opinion overruled *Akron* and *Thornburgh* to the extent they held to the contrary. Chief Justice Rehnquist and Justices White, Scalia, and Thomas concurred with the Joint Opinion on these points. The Joint Opinion ruled that the spousal notification provision was an undue, and therefore unconstitutional, burden on the right to abortion. Justices Blackmun and Stevens concurred with the Joint Opinion on this point.]

VI. Our Constitution is a covenant running from the first generation of Americans to us and then to future generations. It is a coherent succession. Each generation must learn anew that the Constitution's written terms embody ideas and aspirations that must survive more ages than one. We accept our responsibility not to retreat from interpreting the full meaning of the covenant in light of all of our precedents. We invoke it once again to define the freedom guaranteed by the Constitution's own promise, the promise of liberty.

[**JUSTICES BLACKMUN** and **STEVENS** filed concurring opinions, applauding Parts I through III of the Joint Opinion, but arguing that the *Roe* trimester system should be retained.]

[**CHIEF JUSTICE REHNQUIST**, joined by **JUSTICES WHITE**, **SCALIA**, and **THOMAS**, concurred in the portions of the judgment upholding most of Pennsylvania's law, but dissented from the reaffirmance of *Roe*. The Chief Justice argued that the right to abortion fails the "implicit in the concept of ordered liberty" test of *Palko*: Abortion is *sui generis* — and therefore different from parenting (*Meyer* and *Pierce*), contraception (*Griswold*), and marriage (*Loving*) — because it involves the "purposeful termination of potential life. * * * Nor do the historical traditions of the American people support the view that the right to terminate one's pregnancy is 'fundamental.' The common law which we inherited from England made abortion after 'quickening' an offense. At the time of the adoption of the Fourteenth Amendment, statutory prohibitions or restrictions on abortion were commonplace; in 1868, at least 28 of the then-37 States and 8 Territories had statutes banning or limiting abortion. By the turn of the century virtually every State had a law prohibiting or restricting abortion on its books. By the middle of the present century, a liberalization trend had set in. But 21 of the restrictive abortion laws in effect in 1868 were still in effect in 1973 when *Roe* was decided, and an overwhelming majority of the States prohibited abortion unless necessary to preserve the life or health of the mother. On this record, it can scarcely be said that any deeply rooted tradition of relatively unrestricted abortion in our history supported the classification of the right to abortion as 'fundamental' " for due process purposes.]

JUSTICE SCALIA, with whom THE CHIEF JUSTICE, JUSTICE WHITE, and JUSTICE THOMAS join, concurring in the judgment in part and dissenting in part.

* * * Laws against bigamy, for example — which entire societies of reasonable people disagree with — intrude upon men and women's liberty to marry and live with one another. But bigamy happens not to be a liberty specially "protected" by the Constitution.

That is, quite simply, the issue in this case: not whether the power of a woman to abort her unborn child is a "liberty" in the absolute sense; or even whether it is a liberty of great importance to many women. Of course it is both. The issue is whether it is a liberty protected by the Constitution of the United States. I am sure it is not. I reach that conclusion not because of anything so exalted as my views concerning the "concept of existence, of meaning, of the universe, and of the mystery of human life." [Quoting Joint Opinion.] Rather, I reach it for the same reason I reach the conclusion that bigamy is not constitutionally protected — because of two simple facts: (1) the Constitution says absolutely nothing about it, and (2) the longstanding traditions of American society have permitted it to be legally proscribed.[s]

The Court destroys the proposition, evidently meant to represent my position, that "liberty" includes "only those practices, defined at the most specific level, that were protected against government interference by other rules of law when the Fourteenth Amendment was ratified," [citing *Michael H.*]. That is not, however, what *Michael H.* says; it merely observes that, in defining "liberty," we may not disregard a specific, "relevant tradition protecting, or denying protection to, the asserted right." But the Court does not wish to be fettered by any such limitations on its preferences. The Court's statement that it is "tempting" to acknowledge the authoritativeness of tradition in order to "cur[b] the discretion of federal judges" is of course rhetoric rather than reality; no

---

s. The Court's suggestion that adherence to tradition would require us to uphold laws against interracial marriage is entirely wrong. Any tradition in [*Loving*] was contradicted *by a text* — an Equal Protection Clause that explicitly establishes racial equality as a constitutional value. See *Loving v. Virginia* ("In the case at bar, ... we deal with statutes containing racial classifications, and the fact of equal application does not immunize the statute from the very heavy burden of justification which the Fourteenth Amendment has traditionally required of state statutes drawn according to race"). The enterprise launched in *Roe*, by contrast, sought to *establish* — in the teeth of a clear, contrary tradition — a value found nowhere in the constitutional text.

There is, of course, no comparable tradition barring recognition of a "liberty interest" in carrying one's child to term free from state efforts to kill it. For that reason, it does not follow that the Constitution does not protect childbirth simply because it does not protect abortion. The Court's contention that the only way to protect childbirth is to protect abortion shows the utter bankruptcy of constitutional analysis deprived of tradition as a validating factor. It drives one to say that the only way to protect the right to eat is to acknowledge the constitutional right to starve oneself to death.

government official is "tempted" to place restraints upon his own freedom of action, which is why Lord Acton did not say "Power tends to purify." The Court's temptation is in the quite opposite and more natural direction — towards systematically eliminating checks upon its own power; and it succumbs. * * *

Assuming that the question before us is to be resolved at such a level of philosophical abstraction, in such isolation from the traditions of American society, as by simply applying "reasoned judgment," I do not see how that could possibly have produced the answer the Court arrived at in *Roe v. Wade*. Today's opinion describes the methodology of *Roe*, quite accurately, as weighing against the woman's interest the State's " 'important and legitimate interest in protecting the potentiality of human life.' " But "reasoned judgment" does not begin by begging the question, as *Roe* and subsequent cases unquestionably did by assuming that what the State is protecting is the mere "potentiality of human life." The whole argument of abortion opponents is that what the Court calls the fetus and what others call the unborn child *is a human life*. Thus, whatever answer *Roe* came up with after conducting its "balancing" is bound to be wrong, unless it is correct that the human fetus is in some critical sense merely potentially human. There is of course no way to determine that as a legal matter; it is in fact a value judgment. Some societies have considered newborn children not yet human, or the incompetent elderly no longer so.

The authors of the joint opinion, of course, do not squarely contend that *Roe v. Wade* was a *correct* application of "reasoned judgment"; merely that it must be followed, because of *stare decisis*. But in their exhaustive discussion of all the factors that go into the determination of when *stare decisis* should be observed and when disregarded, they never mention "how wrong was the decision on its face?" Surely, if "[t]he Court's power lies . . . in its legitimacy, a product of substance and perception," [quoting Joint Opinion], the "substance" part of the equation demands that plain error be acknowledged and eliminated. *Roe* was plainly wrong — even on the Court's methodology of "reasoned judgment," and even more so (of course) if the proper criteria of text and tradition are applied.

The emptiness of the "reasoned judgment" that produced *Roe* is displayed in plain view by the fact that, after more than 19 years of effort by some of the brightest (and most determined) legal minds in the country, after more than 10 cases upholding abortion rights in this Court, and after dozens upon dozens of *amicus* briefs submitted in this and other cases, the best the Court can do to explain how it is that the word "liberty" *must* be thought to include the right to destroy human fetuses is to rattle off a collection of adjectives that simply decorate a value judgment and conceal a political choice. The right to abort, we are told, inheres in "liberty" because it is among "a person's most basic decisions," it involves a "most intimate and personal choic[e]," it is "central to personal dignity and autonomy," it "originate[s] within the zone of conscience and belief," it is "too intimate and personal" for state interference, it reflects "intimate views" of a "deep, personal character," it involves "intimate relationships," and notions of "personal autonomy and bodily integrity," and it concerns a particularly " 'important decisio[n].' " But it is obvious to anyone applying "reasoned judgment" that the same adjectives can be applied to many forms of conduct that this Court (including one of the Justices in today's majority, see *Bowers v. Hardwick*) has held are *not* entitled to constitutional protection — because, like abortion, they are forms of conduct that have long been criminalized in American society. Those adjectives might be applied, for example, to homosexual sodomy, polygamy, adult incest, and suicide, all of which are equally "intimate" and "deep[ly] personal" decisions involving "personal autonomy and bodily integrity," and all of which can constitutionally be proscribed because it is our unquestionable constitutional tradition that they are proscribable. It is not reasoned judgment that supports the Court's decision; only personal predilection. * * *

[W]hether it would "subvert the Court's legitimacy" or not, the notion that we would decide a case differently from the way we otherwise would have in order to show that we can stand firm against public disapproval is frightening. It is a bad enough idea, even in the head of someone like me, who believes that the text of the Constitution, and our traditions, say what they say and there is no fiddling with them. But when it is in the mind of a Court that believes the Constitution has an evolving meaning; that the Ninth Amendment's reference to "othe[r]" rights is not a disclaimer, but a charter for action; and that the function of this Court is to "speak before all others for [the people's] constitutional ideals" unrestrained by meaningful text or tradition — then the notion that the Court must adhere to a decision for as long as the decision faces "great opposition" and the Court is "under fire" acquires a character of almost czarist arrogance. We are offended by these marchers who descend upon us, every year on the anniversary of *Roe*, to protest our saying that the Constitution requires what our society has never thought the Constitution requires. These people who refuse to be "tested by following" must be taught a lesson. We have no Cossacks, but at least we can stubbornly refuse to abandon an erroneous opinion that we might otherwise change — to show how little they intimidate us. * * *

We should get out of this area, where we have no right to be, and where we do neither ourselves nor the country any good by remaining.

NOTES ON *CASEY* AND
THE FUNDAMENTAL RIGHT TO ABORTION

1. *Spousal Notification.* The Pennsylvania statute required, with certain exceptions, that a married woman sign a statement indicating that she had notified her husband of the abortion decision. Regarding the spousal notice provision, the majority had this to say:

> There was a time, not so long ago, when a different understanding of the family and of the Constitution prevailed. In *Bradwell v. Illinois*, 16 Wall. 130 (1873), three Members of this Court reaffirmed the common-law principle that "a woman had no legal existence separate from her husband, who was regarded as her head and representative in the social state; and, notwithstanding some recent modifications of this civil status, many of the special rules of law flowing from and dependent upon this cardinal principle still exist in full force in most States." Only one generation has passed since this Court observed that "woman is still regarded as the center of home and family life," with attendant "special responsibilities" that precluded full and independent legal status under the Constitution. *Hoyt v. Florida*, 368 U.S. 57,

62 (1961). These views, of course, are no longer consistent with our understanding of the family, the individual, or the Constitution.

In keeping with our rejection of the common-law understanding of a woman's role within the family, the Court held in *Danforth* that the Constitution does not permit a State to require a married woman to obtain her husband's consent before undergoing an abortion. The principles that guided the Court in *Danforth* should be our guides today. For the great many women who are victims of abuse inflicted by their husbands, or whose children are the victims of such abuse, a spousal notice requirement enables the husband to wield an effective veto over his wife's decision. Whether the prospect of notification itself deters such women from seeking abortions, or whether the husband, through physical force or psychological pressure or economic coercion, prevents his wife from obtaining an abortion until it is too late, the notice requirement will often be tantamount to the veto found unconstitutional in *Danforth*. The women most affected by this law — those who most reasonably fear the consequences of notifying their husbands that they are pregnant — are in the gravest danger.

The husband's interest in the life of the child his wife is carrying does not permit the State to empower him with this troubling degree of authority over his wife. The contrary view leads to consequences reminiscent of the common law. A husband has no enforceable right to require a wife to advise him before she exercises her personal choices. If a husband's interest in the potential life of the child outweighs a wife's liberty, the State could require a married woman to notify her husband before she uses a postfertilization contraceptive. Perhaps next in line would be a statute requiring pregnant married women to notify their husbands before engaging in conduct causing risks to the fetus. After all, if the husband's interest in the fetus' safety is a sufficient predicate for state regulation, the State could reasonably conclude that pregnant wives should notify their husbands before drinking alcohol or smoking. Perhaps married women should notify their husbands before using contraceptives or before undergoing any type of surgery that may have complications affecting the husband's interest in his wife's reproductive organs. And if a husband's interest justifies notice in any of these cases, one might reasonably argue that it justifies exactly what the *Danforth* Court held it did not justify — a requirement of the husband's consent as well. A State may not give to a man the kind of dominion over his wife that parents exercise over their children.

Section 3209 embodies a view of marriage consonant with the common-law status of married women but repugnant to our present understanding of marriage and of the nature of the rights secured by the Constitution. Women do not lose their constitutionally protected liberty when they marry. * * *

Is this a fair characterization of the Pennsylvania statute? If marriage is a "bilateral loyalty," as *Griswold* said, why doesn't the husband have a colorable interest in notification?

Chief Justice Rehnquist's dissenting opinion argued that this provision should be upheld:

The question before us is therefore whether the spousal notification requirement rationally furthers any legitimate state interests. We conclude that it does. First, a husband's interests in procreation within marriage and in the potential life of his unborn child are certainly substantial ones. The State itself has legitimate interests both in protecting these interests of the father and in protecting the potential life of the fetus, and the spousal notification requirement is reasonably related to advancing those state interests. By providing that a husband will usually know of his spouse's intent to have an abortion, the provision makes it more likely that the husband will participate in deciding the fate of his unborn child, a possibility that might otherwise have been denied him. This participation might in some cases result in a decision to proceed with the pregnancy. As Judge Alito observed in his dissent below, "[t]he Pennsylvania legislature could have rationally believed that some married women are initially inclined to obtain an abortion without their husbands' knowledge because of perceived problems — such as economic constraints, future plans, or the husbands' previously expressed opposition — that may be obviated by discussion prior to the abortion."

Is the Chief Justice's position sufficiently attentive to the concern that the husband may attempt to coerce the wife, through violence or threats, to forego her right to abortion?[s]

2. *Waiting Periods.* The Pennsylvania statute required a twenty-four hour waiting period after a doctor provided specified information about abortion. Parallel requirements had been invalidated in *Akron*. Nevertheless, the Joint Opinion concluded that these provisions were valid. Requiring information about the fetus was acceptable as part of informed consent:

> We also see no reason why the State may not require doctors to inform a woman seeking an abortion of the availability of materials relating to the consequences to the fetus, even when those consequences have no direct relation to her health. An example illustrates the point. We would think it constitutional for the State to require that in order for there to be informed consent to a kidney transplant operation the recipient must be supplied with information about risks to the donor as well as risks to himself or herself.

Can this overruling of *Akron* be squared with the Joint Opinion's ode to stare decisis? Was there something about *Akron* that made it less important than *Roe* for purposes of stare decisis? Justices Blackmun and Stevens argued that the waiting period was a gratuitous burden on the woman's choice and reflected a disturbing distrust of the ability of women to make considered decisions on their own.

3. *Parental Consent (with Judicial Bypass).* On the authority of *Hodgson* and *Akron*, the Joint Opinion held that the state may require a minor seeking abortion to obtain the consent of a parent, so long as there was the opportunity for a judicial bypass (where the minor could explain to a judge her reasons for not notifying her parents). Yet there was strong evidence in *Hodgson* and *Casey* (and findings of fact by the trial judge in *Hodgson*) that (1) many adolescent girls legitimately fear violence or coercion from their fathers[t] and (2) therefore fear notifying them or their mothers, and often (3) are too intimidated and humiliated to tell their fears and reasons to a judicial stranger. The Joint Opinion found spousal *notification* an "undue burden." Why was parental *consent* not also an "undue burden," given documented dangers of coercion?

4. *The Fetus as a Person.* Most laypeoples' evaluation of *Roe* probably turns on their view of the status of the fetus: If they believe that the fetus is a person, they oppose *Roe*; otherwise, they probably favor some degree of free choice regarding abortion. A more sophisticated critique of *Roe* does not depend on the

---

s. Cf. American Medical Association Council on Scientific Affairs, *Violence Against Women* 7 (1991): "Researchers on family violence agree that the true incidence of partner violence is probably * * * four million severely assaulted women per year. Studies suggest that from one-fifth to one-third of all women will be physically assaulted by a partner or ex-partner during their lifetime."

t. See also the sources collected in William Eskridge, Jr. & Nan Hunter, *Sexuality, Gender, and the Law* 190-202 (1997).

status of the fetus, but rather on the absence of a sufficient foundation for rejecting the state's judgment about the undesirability of abortion. In *Roe* itself, Justice Blackmun avoided the issue, concluding that the fetus is not a "person" protected by the Fourteenth Amendment, and that when life begins is a philosophical question beyond judicial resolution.

Interestingly, in *Casey* this issue seems to have reemerged as a focal point of debate. Arguing that abortion is not a protected right, Chief Justice Rehnquist contended that abortion is *sui generis* because of the effect on potential human life, quoting a statement from an earlier case that to look "at the act which is assertedly the subject of a liberty interest in isolation from its effect upon other people [is] like inquiring whether there is a liberty interest in firing a gun where the case at hand happens to involve its discharge into another person's body." This analogy rather loses its force without the comparison between the fetus and "another person's body." Even more pointedly, Justice Scalia says:

> The whole argument of abortion opponents is that what the Court calls the fetus and what others call the unborn child *is a human life*. Thus, whatever answer *Roe* came up with after conducting its "balancing" is bound to be wrong, unless it is correct that the human fetus is in some critical sense merely potentially human. There is of course no way to determine that as a legal matter; it is in fact a value judgment. Some societies have considered newborn children not yet human, or the incompetent elderly no longer so.

In response to Justice Scalia, Justice Stevens pointed to the *Roe* Court's holding that unborn children are not "persons" within the meaning of the Fourteenth Amendment:

> From this holding, there was no dissent; indeed, no member of the Court has ever questioned this fundamental proposition. Thus, as a matter of federal constitutional law, a developing organism that is not yet a "person" does not have what is sometimes described as a "right to life." This has been and, by the Court's holding today, remains a fundamental premise of our constitutional law governing reproductive autonomy.

5. *Conservation and Tradition*. Given the general trend toward conservative dominance of the Court in recent years, the schism between the authors of the Joint Opinion and the four dissenters may turn out to have permanent importance. One particularly interesting point is the differing views of tradition expressed by the Joint Opinion and Justice Scalia's dissent. Justice Scalia views tradition as consisting of a number of discrete, static practices and beliefs. These traditions play something of the role of "trade usages" in construing contracts. Under Scalia's view, just as we know that the word "dozen" in a contract between bakers does not mandate twelve donuts because of a consistent history of past performances, so we know that the word "liberty" does not include abortion because of a consistent history of past legislation. Similarly, Justice Scalia views the tradition of public nonsectarian prayer as putting a gloss on the phrase "establishment of religion" found in the First Amendment (see his dissent in *Lee v. Weisman*, Chapter 6, § 7B).

In stark contrast, the Joint Opinion, like Justice Frankfurter (in *Adamson*) and Justice Harlan (in *Poe* and *Griswold*), portrays tradition as subject to growth and reconsideration. (Cf. Ernest Young's Burkean defense of evolutive judicial review in Chapter 2, § 3B3.) This view of tradition parallels the Joint Opinion's concern about stare decisis. The common law, with its deep respect for precedent but also its historic ability to evolve, provides a model that connects both living tradition and stare decisis. In this light, the Joint Opinion seems to be a quintessential act of common law judging. Moreover, to determine the scope of "liberty," the Joint Opinion relies on common law techniques like analogy with other precedents, rather than on the kind of clear deductive logic that Justice Scalia demands in his dissent. Thus, the two conservative camps seem to be separated by a deep jurisprudential gulf.

To an extraordinary degree, the jurisprudential debate in *Casey* is reminiscent of the debate between Justices Black and Frankfurter in *Adamson*. Like Frankfurter, the authors of the Joint Opinion rely on the common law tradition to define the scope of protected liberty under the Fourteenth Amendment. Like Scalia, Black was intensely skeptical of what he saw to be the subjectivity of this enterprise. Also like Scalia, Black relied on text and history to construct clear legal rules as barriers to subjectivity. Both feared an "imperial judiciary."

6. *The Central but Ambiguous Role of Justice Harlan.* Notice that the Joint Opinion in *Casey* not only follows Justice Harlan's *Poe* dissent in locating the right to privacy in the due process approach of *Palko*, but quotes extensively from his justification for substantive due process review. But recall that Justice Harlan carefully distanced his protection of marital intimacy from activity he considered beyond the pale, such as "adultery and homosexuality." Is there any reason to think that Justice Harlan would have expanded a right of joint marital contraceptive privacy to allow a *married* woman to abort a fetus without even providing notice to her husband? To allow an *unmarried* woman any privacy rights at all? Does the Joint Opinion in *Casey* embrace the abstract approach of Justice Harlan while deviating rather substantially from the ways in which he probably would have applied his methodology in concrete circumstances? If so, is that of any significance?

Stenberg v. Carhart, 530 U.S. 914 (2000). At issue was Nebraska's ban on "partial birth abortion," defined as a procedure in which the doctor "partially delivers vaginally a living unborn child before killing the unborn child." The statute defined this phrase to mean "intentionally delivering into the vagina a living unborn child, or a substantial portion thereof, for the purpose of performing a procedure that the [abortionist] knows will kill the unborn child and does kill the unborn child." Thus, the statute prohibited an abortion procedure, not abortion per se, and banned that procedure both pre- and postviability. The statute was aimed at a procedure called "dilation and extraction" (D&X), where during the later stages of pregnancy the fetus is withdrawn intact.

In a majority opinion by **Justice Breyer**, joined by **Justices Stevens, O'Connor**, **Souter**, and **Ginsburg**, the Court struck down the statute. (All except Justice Souter also wrote concurring opinions.) First, the majority concluded that the statute could not constitutionally be applied even postviability. In the language of *Casey*, any regulation of abortion, whether pre- or postviability, must allow abortions "necessary, in appropriate medical judgment, for the preservation of the life or health of the mother," and the statutory ban contained no such exception. Relying upon the district court's findings, based on a contested record at trial, that in some circumstances the D&X is the safest procedure, the Court rejected the state's argument that no exception was required because other safe abortion procedures were available. The Court emphasized the judicial need to tolerate reasonable differences in medical opinion.

Second, the Court held that the statute imposed an undue burden on a woman's ability to choose an abortion because the wording of the ban reached beyond the D&X to illegalize the most common procedure for previability second trimester abortions, the "dilation and evacuation" (D&E), in which at least some fetal tissue is removed by surgical instruments. In the later stages of pregnancy, the D&E sometimes involves dismemberment and removal of significant portions of the fetus, which for the majority ran afoul of the statute's prohibition of "delivering into the vagina a living unborn child, or a substantial portion thereof."

In a lengthy and emotional dissent, **Justice Kennedy**, joined by **Chief Justice Rehnquist**, argued that the state intended only to prohibit the D&X and should be allowed to make the moral decision that killing the fetus outside the womb (D&X) is more gruesome or horrifying — more like infanticide — than killing it in the womb (D&E). The dissent further contended that the D&X is highly controversial even within the medical community, and restricting pregnant women to the D&E would deprive none of them of a safe abortion. The state, they concluded, should be able to take sides on a disputed medical question.

Justice Thomas, joined by **Chief Justice Rehnquist** and **Justice Scalia**, also dissented, contending that the statutory text only reached the D&X and should be so interpreted to avoid deciding the second constitutional question reached by the majority. As for the need for an exception to protect the health of the mother, Justice Thomas argued that the court should distinguish between the situation in which a woman seeks an abortion because her pregnancy risks her health and that in which she elects abortion for whatever reason and simply prefers one procedure over another. The "health exception" of *Casey* should apply only to the former situation, he contended.

Justice Scalia also dissented, lumping the case together with *Roe* and *Casey* as "policy-judgment[s]-couched as law" and expressed hope that someday the invalidation of this "humane law" barring "[t]he method of killing a human child . . . so horrible that the most clinical description of it evokes a shudder of revulsion" will be "assigned its rightful place in the history of this court's jurisprudence beside *Korematsu* and *Dred Scott*."

GONZALES v. CARHART
___ U.S. ___, 127 S.Ct. 1610, 167 L.Ed.2d 480 (2007)

JUSTICE KENNEDY delivered the opinion of the Court.

[In the usual second-trimester abortion procedure, "dilation and evacuation" (D&E), the doctor dilates the cervix and then inserts surgical instruments into the uterus in order to separate portions of the fetus and remove them one by one.

A variation of the standard D&E, usually termed an "intact D&E," and sometimes called "dilation and extraction" (D&X), requires a doctor to extract the fetus intact or largely intact with only a few passes, pulling out its entire body instead of ripping it apart. In order to allow the head to pass through the cervix, the doctor typically pierces or crushes the skull. In 2000, the Supreme Court in *Stenberg v. Carhart* (casebook, pp. 570-71), overturned a Nebraska "partial-birth abortion" law that banned intact D&E procedures and, possibly, some regular D&E procedures as well. The Court found two constitutional problems: first, the law was vague as to what procedures it actually criminalized, and second, there was no exception to protect the health of the mother.

[After *Stenberg,* Congress passed a national Partial-Birth Abortion Ban Act of 2003. The federal statute prohibits "knowingly perform[ing] a partial-birth abortion . . . that is [not] necessary to save the life of a mother." There is no exclusion for the mother's health. The statute defines a partial birth abortion as a procedure in which the doctor: "(A) deliberately and intentionally vaginally delivers a living fetus until, in the case of a head-first presentation, the entire fetal head is outside the [mother's] body . . ., or, in the case of breech presentation, any part of the fetal trunk past the navel is outside the [mother's] body . . ., for the purpose of performing an overt act that the person knows will kill the partially delivered living fetus"; and "(B) performs the overt act, other than completion of delivery, that kills the fetus."]

[I. As he and Justice Thomas had done in their *Stenberg* dissenting opinions, Justice Kennedy began his *Carhart* majority opinion with a detailed description of the D&E and intact D&E (or D&X) procedures. Justice Kennedy started with an "abortion doctor's clinical description," followed by "another description from a nurse who witnessed the same method performed on a 26½-week fetus and who testified before the Senate Judiciary Committee:

> Dr. Haskell went in with forceps and grabbed the baby's legs and pulled them down into the birth canal. Then he delivered the baby's body and the arms — everything but the head. The doctor kept the head right inside the uterus. . . .
>
> The baby's little fingers were clasping and unclasping, and his little feet were kicking. Then the doctor stuck the scissors in the back of his head, and the baby's arms jerked out, like a startle reaction, like a flinch, like a baby does when he thinks he is going to fall.
>
> The doctor opened up the scissors, stuck a high-powered suction tube into the opening, and sucked the baby's brains out. Now the baby went completely limp. .
> . . .
>
> He cut the umbilical cord and delivered the placenta. He threw the baby in a pan, along with the placenta and the instruments he had just used."

Based upon testimony such as this, Congress found that "[a] moral, medical, and ethical consensus exists that the practice of performing a partial-birth abortion . . . is a gruesome and inhumane procedure that is never medically necessary and should be prohibited." Congressional Findings, 117 Stat. 1202, notes following 18 U.S.C. § 1531.]

II. The principles set forth in the joint opinion in *Casey* did not find support from all those who join the instant opinion. Whatever one's views concerning the *Casey* joint opinion, it is evident a premise central to its conclusion — that the government has a legitimate and substantial interest in preserving and promoting fetal life — would be repudiated were the Court now to affirm the judgments of the Courts of Appeals. * * *

We assume the following principles for the purposes of this opinion. Before viability, a State "may not prohibit any woman from making the ultimate decision to terminate her pregnancy." *Casey* (plurality opinion). It also may not impose upon this right an undue burden, which exists if a regulation's "purpose or effect is to place a substantial obstacle in the path of a woman seeking an abortion before the fetus obtains viability." On the other hand, "[r]egulations which do no more than create a structural mechanism by which the State, or the parent or the guardian of a minor, may express profound respect for the life of the unborn are permitted, if they are not a substantial obstacle to the woman's exercise of the right to choose." *Casey*, in short, struck a balance. The balance was central to its holding. We now apply its standard to the cases at bar.

[III.B] Respondents contend * * * the Act is unconstitutionally vague on its face. "As generally stated, the void-for-vagueness doctrine requires that a penal statute define the criminal offense with sufficient definiteness that ordinary people can understand what conduct is prohibited and in a manner that does not encourage arbitrary and discriminatory enforcement." *Kolender v. Lawson,* 461 U.S. 352, 357 (1983). The Act satisfies both requirements.

The Act provides doctors "of ordinary intelligence a reasonable opportunity to know what is prohibited." *Grayned v. City of Rockford,* 408 U.S. 104, 108 (1972). Indeed, it sets forth "relatively clear guidelines as to prohibited conduct" and provides "objective criteria" to evaluate whether a doctor has performed a prohibited procedure. *Posters 'N' Things v. United States,* 511 U.S. 513, 525-26 (1994). Unlike the statutory language in *Stenberg* that prohibited the delivery of a " 'substantial portion' " of the fetus — where a doctor might question how much of the fetus is a substantial portion — the Act defines the line between potentially criminal conduct on the one hand and lawful abortion on the other. Doctors performing D&E will know that if they do not deliver a living fetus to an anatomical landmark they will not face criminal liability.

This conclusion is buttressed by the intent that must be proved to impose liability. The Court has made clear that scienter requirements alleviate vagueness concerns. * * * Because a doctor performing a D&E will not face criminal liability if he or she delivers a fetus beyond the prohibited point by mistake, the Act cannot be described as "a trap for those who act in good faith."

Respondents likewise have failed to show that the Act should be invalidated on its face because it encourages arbitrary or discriminatory enforcement. Just as the Act's anatomical landmarks provide doctors with objective standards, they also "establish minimal guidelines to govern law enforcement." * * * The Act is not vague.

C. We next determine whether the Act imposes an undue burden, as a facial matter, because its restrictions on second-trimester abortions are too broad. A review of the statutory text discloses the limits of its reach. The Act prohibits intact D&E; and, notwithstanding respondents' arguments, it does not prohibit the D&E procedure in which the fetus is removed in parts. * * *

The Act excludes most D&Es in which the fetus is removed in pieces, not intact. If the doctor intends to remove the fetus in parts from the outset, the doctor will not have the requisite intent to incur criminal liability. A doctor performing a standard D&E procedure can often "tak[e] about 10-15 'passes' through the uterus to remove the entire fetus." Removing the fetus in this manner does not violate the Act because the doctor will not have delivered the living fetus to one of the anatomical landmarks or committed an additional overt act that kills the fetus after partial delivery. § 1531(b)(1).

A comparison of the Act with the Nebraska statute struck down in *Stenberg* confirms this point. The statute in *Stenberg* prohibited " 'deliberately and intentionally delivering into the vagina a living unborn child, or a substantial portion thereof, for the purpose of performing a procedure that the person performing such procedure knows will kill the unborn child and does kill the unborn child.' " The Court concluded that this statute encompassed D&E because "D&E will often involve a physician pulling a 'substantial portion' of a still living fetus, say, an arm or leg, into the vagina prior to the death of the fetus." The Court also rejected the limiting interpretation urged by Nebraska's Attorney General that the statute's reference to a "procedure" that " 'kill[s] the unborn child' " was to a distinct procedure, not to the abortion procedure as a whole. [Justice Kennedy concluded that the language of the new statute avoided these concerns.]

[IV. Finally, Justice Kennedy considered the *Casey*-based argument that the Act imposed a substantial obstacle to late-term but pre-viability abortions.]

A. The Act's purposes are set forth in recitals preceding its operative provisions. A description of the prohibited abortion procedure demonstrates the rationale for the congressional enactment. The Act proscribes a method of abortion in which a fetus is killed just inches before completion of the birth process. Congress stated as follows: "Implicitly approving such a brutal and inhumane procedure by choosing not to prohibit it will further coarsen society to the humanity of not only newborns, but all vulnerable and innocent human life, making it increasingly difficult to protect such life." Congressional Findings. The Act expresses respect for the dignity of human life. * * *

Respect for human life finds an ultimate expression in the bond of love the mother has for her child. The Act recognizes this reality as well. Whether to have an abortion requires a difficult and painful moral decision. *Casey.* While we find no reliable data to measure the phenomenon, it seems unexceptionable to conclude some women come to regret their choice to abort the infant life they once created and sustained. See Brief for Sandra Cano et al. As *Amici Curiae.* Severe depression and loss of esteem can follow. See *ibid.*

In a decision so fraught with emotional consequence some doctors may prefer not to disclose precise details of the means that will be used, confining themselves to the required statement of risks the procedure entails. From one standpoint this ought not to be surprising. Any number of patients facing imminent surgical procedures would prefer not to hear all details, lest the usual anxiety preceding invasive medical procedures become the more intense. This is likely the case with the abortion procedures here in issue.

It is, however, precisely this lack of information concerning the way in which the fetus will be killed that is of legitimate concern to the State. *Casey* (plurality opinion). The State has an interest in ensuring so grave a choice is well informed. It is self-evident that a mother who comes to regret her choice to abort must struggle with grief more anguished and sorrow more profound when she learns, only after the event, what she once did not know: that she allowed a doctor to pierce the skull and vacuum the fast-developing brain of her unborn child, a child assuming the human form.

It is a reasonable inference that a necessary effect of the regulation and the knowledge it conveys will be to encourage some women to carry the infant to full term, thus reducing the absolute number of late-term abortions. The medical profession, furthermore, may find different and less shocking methods to abort the fetus in the second trimester, thereby accommodating legislative demand. The State's interest in respect for life is advanced by the dialogue that better informs the political and legal systems, the medical profession, expectant mothers, and society as a whole of the consequences that follow from a decision to elect a late-term abortion.

It is objected that the standard D&E is in some respects as brutal, if not more, than the intact D&E, so that the legislation accomplishes little. What we have already said, however, shows ample justification for the regulation. Partial-birth abortion, as defined by the Act, differs from a standard D&E because the former occurs when the fetus is partially outside the mother to the point of one of the Act's anatomical landmarks. It was reasonable for Congress to think that partial-birth abortion, more than standard D&E, "undermines the public's perception of the appropriate role of a physician during the delivery process, and perverts a process during which life is brought into the world." Congressional Findings   There would be a flaw in this Court's logic, and an irony in its jurisprudence, were we first to conclude a ban on both D&E and intact D&E was overbroad and then to say it is irrational to ban only intact D&E because that does not proscribe both procedures. In sum, we reject the contention that the congressional purpose of the Act was "to place a substantial obstacle in the path of a woman seeking an abortion." *Casey* (plurality opinion).

B. The Act's furtherance of legitimate government interests bears upon, but does not resolve, the next question: whether the Act has the effect of imposing an unconstitutional burden on the abortion right because it does not allow use of the barred procedure where " 'necessary, in appropriate medical judgment, for [the] preservation of the . . . health of the mother.' " [W]hether the Act creates significant health risks for women has been a contested factual question. The evidence presented in the trial courts and before Congress demonstrates both sides have medical support for their position.

[For example, "abortion doctors" testified that intact D&E is safer for the pregnant woman, because it poses less risk of cervical laceration or uterine perforation and of leaving fetal material in the uterus. On the other hand, Justice Kennedy pointed to trial and congressional testimony "by other doctors" that

D&E is "always" a safe alternative to intact D&E. "There is documented medical disagreement whether the Act's prohibition would ever impose significant health risks on women."]

The question becomes whether the Act can stand when this medical uncertainty persists. The Court's precedents instruct that the Act can survive this facial attack. The Court has given state and federal legislatures wide discretion to pass legislation in areas where there is medical and scientific uncertainty.

This traditional rule is consistent with *Casey*, which confirms the State's interest in promoting respect for human life at all stages in the pregnancy. Physicians are not entitled to ignore regulations that direct them to use reasonable alternative procedures. The law need not give abortion doctors unfettered choice in the course of their medical practice, nor should it elevate their status above other physicians in the medical community. * * *

Medical uncertainty does not foreclose the exercise of legislative power in the abortion context any more than it does in other contexts. The medical uncertainty over whether the Act's prohibition creates significant health risks provides a sufficient basis to conclude in this facial attack that the Act does not impose an undue burden.

The conclusion that the Act does not impose an undue burden is supported by other considerations. Alternatives are available to the prohibited procedure. As we have noted, the Act does not proscribe D&E. One District Court found D&E to have extremely low rates of medical complications. In addition the Act's prohibition only applies to the delivery of "a living fetus." 18 U.S.C. § 1531(b)(1)(A). If the intact D&E procedure is truly necessary in some circumstances, it appears likely an injection that kills the fetus is an alternative under the Act that allows the doctor to perform the procedure.

      * * *

In reaching the conclusion the Act does not require a health exception we reject certain arguments made by the parties on both sides of these cases. On the one hand, the Attorney General urges us to uphold the Act on the basis of the congressional findings alone. Although we review congressional factfinding under a deferential standard, we do not in the circumstances here place dispositive weight on Congress' findings. The Court retains an independent constitutional duty to review factual findings where constitutional rights are at stake.

As respondents have noted, and the District Courts recognized, some recitations in the Act are factually incorrect. Whether or not accurate at the time, some of the important findings have been superseded. Two examples suffice. Congress determined no medical schools provide instruction on the prohibited procedure. The testimony in the District Courts, however, demonstrated intact D&E is taught at medical schools. Congress also found there existed a medical consensus that the prohibited procedure is never medically necessary. The evidence presented in the District Courts contradicts that conclusion. Uncritical deference to Congress' factual findings in these cases is inappropriate.

On the other hand, relying on the Court's opinion in *Stenberg*, respondents contend that an abortion regulation must contain a health exception "if 'substantial medical authority supports the proposition that banning a particular procedure could endanger women's health.' " As illustrated by respondents' arguments and the decisions of the Courts of Appeals, *Stenberg* has been interpreted to leave no margin of error for legislatures to act in the face of medical uncertainty.

A zero tolerance policy would strike down legitimate abortion regulations, like the present one, if some part of the medical community were disinclined to follow the proscription. This is too exacting a standard to impose on the legislative power, exercised in this instance under the Commerce Clause, to regulate the medical profession. Considerations of marginal safety, including the balance of risks, are within the legislative competence when the regulation is rational and in pursuit of legitimate ends. When standard medical options are available, mere convenience does not suffice to displace them; and if some procedures have different risks than others, it does not follow that the State is altogether barred from imposing reasonable regulations. The Act is not invalid on its face where there is uncertainty over whether the barred procedure is ever necessary to preserve a woman's health, given the availability of other abortion procedures that are considered to be safe alternatives.

V. The considerations we have discussed support our further determination that these facial attacks should not have been entertained in the first instance. In these circumstances the proper means to consider exceptions is by as-applied challenge. The Government has acknowledged that pre-enforcement, as-applied challenges to the Act can be maintained. This is the proper manner to protect the health of the woman if it can be shown that in discrete and well-defined instances a particular condition has or is likely to occur in which the procedure prohibited by the Act must be used. In an as-applied challenge the nature of the medical risk can be better quantified and balanced than in a facial attack.

* * *

Respondents have not demonstrated that the Act, as a facial matter, is void for vagueness, or that it imposes an undue burden on a woman's right to abortion based on its overbreadth or lack of a health exception. For these reasons the judgments of the Courts of Appeals for the Eighth and Ninth Circuits are reversed.

[JUSTICE THOMAS, joined by JUSTICE SCALIA, concurred. They reiterated their view that "the Court's abortion jurisprudence, including *Casey* and *Roe v. Wade*, has no basis in the Constitution." Justice Thomas also noted that the parties had not raised the question of whether the statute exceeded Congress's Article I powers and, therefore, that the validity of Congress's exercising authority over this issue was not before the Court.]

JUSTICE GINSBURG, with whom JUSTICE STEVENS, JUSTICE SOUTER, and JUSTICE BREYER join, dissenting. * * *

Today's decision is alarming. It refuses to take *Casey* and *Stenberg* seriously. It tolerates, indeed applauds, federal intervention to ban nationwide a procedure found necessary and proper in certain cases by the American College of Obstetricians and Gynecologists (ACOG). It blurs the line, firmly drawn in *Casey*, between previability and postviability abortions. And, for the first time since *Roe*, the Court blesses a prohibition with no exception safeguarding a woman's health.

I dissent from the Court's disposition. Retreating from prior rulings that abortion restrictions cannot be imposed absent an exception safeguarding a woman's health, the Court upholds an Act that surely would not survive under the close scrutiny that previously attended state-decreed limitations on a woman's reproductive choices.

I. As *Casey* comprehended, at stake in cases challenging abortion restrictions is a woman's "control over her own destiny." * * * [L]egal challenges to undue restrictions on abortion procedures do not seek to vindicate some generalized notion of privacy; rather, they center on a woman's autonomy to determine her life's course, and thus to enjoy equal citizenship stature. See, e.g., Siegel, Reasoning from the Body: A Historical Perspective on Abortion Regulation and Questions of Equal Protection, 44 Stan. L. Rev. 261 (1992); Law, Rethinking Sex and the Constitution, 132 U. Pa. L. Rev. 955, 1002-28 (1984).

In keeping with this comprehension of the right to reproductive choice, the Court has consistently required that laws regulating abortion, at any stage of pregnancy and in all cases, safeguard a woman's health. *Stenberg.*

[Justice Ginsburg noted that the federal statute had no health exception, based upon incorrect assumptions, such as the congressional finding that "[t]here is no credible medical evidence that partial-birth abortions are safe or are safer than other abortion procedures." Yet ACOG and other medical associations attested to Congress and the trial courts that "intact D&E carries meaningful safety advantages over other methods." Intact D&E minimizes the number of times a physician must insert instruments through the cervix and into the uterus, a minimization that helps the woman avoid risks of tearing and infection. Intact D&E reduces the risk that fetal material will be left in the uterus, which can cause infection, hemorrhage, and infertility. Intact D&E diminishes the chances of exposing the woman's tissues to sharp bony fragments sometimes resulting from dismemberment of the fetus. Intact D&E takes less operating time, thereby reducing risks of complications relating to anesthesia. Justice Ginsburg maintained that there was no reasonable basis to believe otherwise, as reflected in the trial records.]

II. The Court offers flimsy and transparent justifications for upholding a nationwide ban on intact D&E *sans* any exception to safeguard a women's health. Today's ruling, the Court declares, advances "a premise central to [*Casey*'s] conclusion" — *i.e.,* the Government's "legitimate and substantial interest in preserving and promoting fetal life." But the Act scarcely furthers that interest: The law saves not a single fetus from destruction, for it targets only a *method* of performing abortion. And surely the statute was not designed to protect the lives or health of pregnant women. In short, the Court upholds a law that, while doing nothing to "preserv[e] . . . fetal life," bars a woman from choosing intact D&E although her doctor "reasonably believes [that procedure] will best protect [her]."

* * * Ultimately, the Court admits that "moral concerns" are at work, concerns that could yield prohibitions on any abortion. Notably, the concerns expressed are untethered to any ground genuinely serving the Government's interest in preserving life. By allowing such concerns to carry the day and case, overriding fundamental rights, the Court dishonors our precedent.

Revealing in this regard, the Court invokes an antiabortion shibboleth for which it concededly has no reliable evidence: Women who have abortions come to regret their choices, and consequently suffer from "[s]evere depression and loss of esteem." Because of women's fragile emotional state and because of the "bond of love the mother has for her child," the Court worries, doctors may withhold information about the nature of the intact D&E procedure. The solution the Court approves, then, is *not* to require doctors to inform women, accurately and adequately, of the different procedures and their attendant risks. Instead, the Court deprives women of the right to make an autonomous choice, even at the expense of their safety.

This way of thinking reflects ancient notions about women's place in the family and under the Constitution — ideas that have long since been discredited.

Though today's majority may regard women's feelings on the matter as "self-evident," this Court has repeatedly confirmed that "[t]he destiny of the woman must be shaped . . . on her own conception of her spiritual imperatives and her place in society." *Casey.* * * *

III. If there is anything at all redemptive to be said of today's opinion, it is that the Court is not willing to foreclose entirely a constitutional challenge to the Act. "The Act is open," the Court states, "to a proper as-applied challenge in a discrete case." But the Court offers no clue on what a "proper" lawsuit might look like. Nor does the Court explain why the injunctions ordered by the District Courts should not remain in place, trimmed only to exclude instances in which another procedure would safeguard a woman's health at least equally well. Surely the Court cannot mean that no suit may be brought until a woman's health is immediately jeopardized by the ban on intact D&E. A woman "suffer[ing] from medical complications" needs access to the medical procedure at once and cannot wait for the judicial process to unfold. The Court appears, then, to contemplate another lawsuit by the initiators of the instant actions. In such a second round, the Court suggests, the challengers could succeed upon demonstrating that "in discrete and well-defined instances a particular condition has or is likely to occur in which the procedure prohibited by the Act must be used." One may anticipate that such a preenforcement challenge will be mounted swiftly, to ward off serious, sometimes irremediable harm, to women whose health would be endangered by the intact D&E prohibition. * * *

[IV] As the Court wrote in *Casey*, "overruling *Roe*'s central holding would not only reach an unjustifiable result under principles of *stare decisis*, but would seriously weaken the Court's capacity to exercise the judicial power and to function as the Supreme Court of a Nation dedicated to the rule of law." * * *

Though today's opinion does not go so far as to discard *Roe* or *Casey*, the Court, differently constituted than it was when we last considered a restrictive abortion regulation, is hardly faithful to our earlier invocations of the "rule of law" and the "principles of *stare decisis.*" * * *

* * * In candor, the Act, and the Court's defense of it, cannot be understood as anything other than an effort to chip away at a right declared again and again by this Court — and with increasing comprehension of its centrality to women's lives. * * *

NOTE ON *GONZALES v. CARHART*

Justice Ginsburg's dissenting opinion essentially accuses the majority of writing their morality into the Constitution. She suggests that a Court that once included two women would not have ruled this way. Justice O'Connor was in the *Stenberg* majority, while her replacement, Justice Alito, was in the *Carhart* majority.

Women may still have a "liberty" to choose abortions, but not after viability and, now, not the safest procedure for late-term (previability) abortions. The Court responds that *Casey* set a "balance," and the woman's liberty is just one prong of that balance. But if women's possible regret and state concern for the sanctity of life can trump women's liberty to choose intact D&E, why can these concerns also not trump women's ability to choose D&E itself, which destroys the fetus (or baby) in gruesome ways and therefore also triggers regrets?

PROBLEM 5-4
PROHIBITION ON SEX-SPECIFIC ABORTIONS

In some cultures, it is common for couples to abort female fetuses in order to increase their chances of male offspring. This phenomenon may occur in some subcultures of our own society. In addition, couples whose children are all of one gender might abort a fetus of that gender in the hope that a new pregnancy will give them a more diverse brood. There are no available statistics about sex-specific abortions in America. Having heard testimony about such incidents, however, the Eastland legislature passes a law making it unlawful for a physician to perform any abortion if he knows that the abortion is motivated by the sex of the fetus. It is a misdemeanor to perform such an abortion before viability but a felony if the physician knows that the fetus is viable. The legislation does not impose any duty on the physician to inquire into the parents' motivation, but he is required to inform any pregnant woman seeking an abortion that under state law, she is not supposed to consider the gender of the fetus in making a decision about abortion. Furthermore, a state court may not issue a by-pass order for a minor whose parents have not consented to the abortion, if the court finds that the abortion is sex-motivated. How should a court rule on the provisions of this statute under current law? Would a court rule differently under an equal protection approach to abortion?

C.   CONSENSUAL SEXUAL ACTIVITY

In 1961 (*Poe*) and 1965 (*Griswold*), almost all gay men, lesbians, and bisexuals were deeply closeted, and their venues for socialization (bars, restaurants) regularly harassed by police and state regulators.   After the celebrated Stonewall riots of June 1969, many gay people "came out" of their closets and challenged state and federal laws criminalizing their consensual conduct and discriminating against them in government employment, immigration, state licensing and censorship, police surveillance, child custody proceedings, recognition of families, educational programs, and so forth.[u]   Central to the "gay rights" efforts was the repeal or nullification of state laws prohibiting consensual "sodomy."   By 1986, the laws of twenty-five states had been repealed or judicially nullified under *Griswold* and its progeny.   Does the *Griswold* line of cases *require* the state to allow private same-sex intimacy?

Bowers v. Hardwick, 478 U.S. 186 (1986).   Hardwick challenged the Georgia statute criminalizing sodomy[v] by committing that act with another adult male in the bedroom of respondent's home.   **Justice White** delivered the opinion of the Court.   The Court rejected Hardwick's substantive due process claim on the following grounds:

> Sodomy was a criminal offense at common law and was forbidden by the laws of the original 13 States when they ratified the Bill of Rights.   In 1868, when the Fourteenth Amendment was ratified, all but 5 of the 37 States in the Union had criminal sodomy laws.   In fact, until 1961, all 50 States outlawed sodomy, and today, 24 States and the District of Columbia continue to provide criminal penalties for sodomy performed in private and between consenting adults.   Against this background, to claim that a right to engage in such conduct is "deeply rooted in this Nation's history and tradition" or "implicit in the concept of ordered liberty" is, at best, facetious.

Justice Powell concurred but suggested that the statute's twenty-year sentence might violate the Eighth Amendment.   In dissent, **Justice Blackmun** maintain:

> Only the most willful blindness could obscure the fact that sexual intimacy is "a sensitive, key relationship of human existence, central to family life, community welfare, and the development of human personality," *Paris Adult Theatre I v. Slaton*, 413 U.S. 49, 63 (1973).   The fact that individuals define themselves in a significant way through their intimate sexual relationships with others suggests, in a Nation as diverse as ours, that there may be many "right" ways of conducting those relationships, and that much of the richness of a relationship will come from the

---

u. See William Eskridge, Jr., *Challenging the Apartheid of the Closet: Establishing Conditions for Lesbian and Gay Intimacy, Nomos, and Citizenship*, 25 Hofstra L. Rev. 817 (1997).

v. Georgia Code Ann. § 16-6-2 (1984) provides, in pertinent part, as follows:

"(a) A person commits the offense of sodomy when he performs or submits to any sexual act involving the sex organs of one person and the mouth or anus of another. . . .

"(b) A person convicted of the offense of sodomy shall be punished by imprisonment for not less than one nor more than 20 years. . . ."

freedom an individual has to *choose* the form and nature of these intensely personal bonds. * * *

Justice Stevens also dissented on the ground that the statute banned certain sexual acts regardless of gender, and the state had failed to justify a policy of applying the statute only to same-sex acts.

———

Commonwealth of Kentucky v. Wasson, 842 S.W.2d 487 (Ky. 1992). Jeffrey Wasson was charged with violating § 510.100 of the Kentucky Statutes, which criminalizes "deviate sexual intercourse with another person of the same sex" and specifies that "consent of the other person shall not be a defense." Writing for a four-Justice majority, **Justice Leibson**'s opinion invalidated the statute as a violation of state right to privacy and equal protection guarantees. Justice Leibson found the reasoning of *Bowers* inapposite for the following reasons:

(1) *Textual differences*. The bill of rights in Kentucky's 1891 Constitution is more supportive of a right of privacy than the one cobbled together from the federal bill of rights. Consider the following:

§ 1. All men are, by nature, free and equal, and have certain inherent and inalienable rights, among which may be reckoned:

First: The right of enjoying and defending their lives and liberties. * * *

Third: The right of seeking and pursuing their safety and happiness.

§ 2. Absolute and arbitrary power over the lives, liberty and property of freemen exists nowhere in a republic, not even in the largest majority.

(2) *Kentucky precedent. Commonwealth v. Campbell*, 133 Ky. 50, 117 S.W. 383, 385 (1909), early on recognized that "it is not within the competency of government to invade the privacy of a citizen's life and to regulate his conduct in matters in which he alone is concerned, or to prohibit him any liberty the exercise of which will not directly injure society." Quoting and essentially codifying John Stuart Mill's *On Liberty* (1857), this precedent establishes as Kentucky law the obligation of the Commonwealth not to adopt statutes that reflect the "nosy preferences" of citizens.

(3) *Flaws in* Bowers. The Court found *Bowers* "misdirected" in its "application of the theory of original intent" and factually ignorant (as in its belief that laws prohibiting oral sex have "ancient roots," when sodomy laws until the late nineteenth century only targeted anal sex).

———

Postscript: With *Wasson*, Kentucky became the first state to repeal or nullify its consensual sodomy law after *Bowers*. Since 1992, three states (Arizona, Nevada, Rhode Island) have repealed their consensual sodomy laws, the highest courts in four states (Arkansas, Georgia (the *Bowers* state), Massachusetts, Montana) have nullified their laws through narrow interpretation or invalidation under state constitutions, and four states (Maryland, Minnesota, Missouri, Tennessee) have essentially nullified their laws through lower court opinions that state attorneys general have not appealed or that the state's highest court has apparently ratified by denying review (Tennessee). In a few states

(Kansas, Louisiana, Texas), state constitutional challenges have failed. One such failed challenge, *Lawrence v. State*, 41 S.W.3d 349 (Tex. App. 2001), then reached the U.S. Supreme Court.

LAWRENCE v. TEXAS
539 U.S. 558, 123 S.Ct. 2472, 156 L.Ed.2d 508 (2003)

JUSTICE KENNEDY delivered the opinion of the Court.

Liberty protects the person from unwarranted government intrusions into a dwelling or other private places. In our tradition the State is not omnipresent in the home. And there are other spheres of our lives and existence, outside the home, where the State should not be a dominant presence. Freedom extends beyond spatial bounds. Liberty presumes an autonomy of self that includes freedom of thought, belief, expression, and certain intimate conduct. The instant case involves liberty of the person both in its spatial and more transcendent dimensions.

[Acting on a reported weapons disturbance, the Harris County Police entered the apartment of John Lawrence and found him engaging in anal sex with another adult man, Tyron Garner. The police arrested and detained the men overnight for violating Texas's "Homosexual Conduct Law." Tex. Penal Code § 21.06(a) (2003). The law provides: "A person commits an offense if he engages in deviate sexual intercourse with another individual of the same sex." The statute defines deviate sexual intercourse to include oral and anal sex. The defendants pleaded *nolo contendere*, were fined $200 apiece (plus court costs of $141.25), and appealed their convictions, on the ground that the Homosexual Conduct Law was unconstitutional. The Texas courts rejected their federal constitutional claims, largely on the authority of *Bowers v. Hardwick*. The Supreme Court reversed.]

[II.] The Court began its substantive discussion in *Bowers* as follows: "The issue presented is whether the Federal Constitution confers a fundamental right upon homosexuals to engage in sodomy and hence invalidates the laws of the many States that still make such conduct illegal and have done so for a very long time." That statement, we now conclude, discloses the Court's own failure to appreciate the extent of the liberty at stake. To say that the issue in *Bowers* was simply the right to engage in certain sexual conduct demeans the claim the individual put forward, just as it would demean a married couple were it to be said marriage is simply about the right to have sexual intercourse. The laws involved in *Bowers* and here are, to be sure, statutes that purport to do no more than prohibit a particular sexual act. Their penalties and purposes, though, have more far-reaching consequences, touching upon the most private human conduct, sexual behavior, and in the most private of places, the home. The statutes do seek to control a personal relationship that, whether or not entitled to formal recognition in the law, is within the liberty of persons to choose without being punished as criminals.

This, as a general rule, should counsel against attempts by the State, or a court, to define the meaning of the relationship or to set its boundaries absent injury to a person or abuse of an institution the law protects. It suffices for us to acknowledge that adults may choose to enter upon this relationship in the confines of their homes and their own private lives and still retain their dignity as free persons. When sexuality finds overt expression in intimate conduct with another person, the conduct can be but one element in a personal bond that is more enduring. The liberty protected by the Constitution allows homosexual persons the right to make this choice.

Having misapprehended the claim of liberty there presented to it, and thus stating the claim to be whether there is a fundamental right to engage in consensual sodomy, the *Bowers* Court said: "Proscriptions against that conduct have ancient roots." In academic writings, and in many of the scholarly *amicus* briefs filed to assist the Court in this case, there are fundamental criticisms of the historical premises relied upon by the majority and concurring opinions in *Bowers*. Brief for Cato Institute as *Amicus Curiae* 16-17; Brief for American Civil Liberties Union et al. as *Amici Curiae* 15-21; Brief for Professors of History et al. as *Amici Curiae* 3-10. We need not enter this debate in the attempt to reach a definitive historical judgment, but the following considerations counsel against adopting the definitive conclusions upon which *Bowers* placed such reliance.

At the outset it should be noted that there is no longstanding history in this country of laws directed at homosexual conduct as a distinct matter. [Both English and early American "crime against nature" laws regulated relations between men and women as well as between men and men.] The absence of legal prohibitions focusing on homosexual conduct may be explained in part by noting that according to some scholars the concept of the homosexual as a distinct category of person did not emerge until the late 19th century. * * *

It was not until the 1970's that any State singled out same-sex relations for criminal prosecution, and only nine States have done so. [Citing Arkansas, Kansas, Kentucky, Missouri, Montana, Nevada, Tennessee, and Texas statutes]; see also *Post v. State*, 715 P. 2d 1105 (Okla. Crim. App. 1986) (sodomy law invalidated as applied to different-sex couples). Post-*Bowers* even some of these States did not adhere to the policy of suppressing homosexual conduct. Over the course of the last decades, States with same-sex prohibitions have moved toward abolishing them.

In summary, the historical grounds relied upon in *Bowers* are more complex than the majority opinion and the concurring opinion by Chief Justice Burger indicate. Their historical premises are not without doubt and, at the very least, are overstated.

It must be acknowledged, of course, that the Court in *Bowers* was making the broader point that for centuries there have been powerful voices to condemn homosexual conduct as immoral. The condemnation has been shaped by religious beliefs, conceptions of right and acceptable behavior, and respect for the traditional family. For many persons these are not trivial concerns but profound and deep convictions accepted as ethical and moral principles to which they aspire and which thus determine the course of their lives. These considerations do not answer the question before us, however. The issue is whether the majority may use the power of the State to enforce these views on the whole society through operation of the criminal law. "Our obligation is to define the liberty of all, not to mandate our own moral code." *Casey.*

* * *

The sweeping references by Chief Justice Burger to the history of Western civilization and to Judeo-Christian moral and ethical standards did not take account of other authorities pointing in an opposite direction. A committee advising the British Parliament recommended in 1957 repeal of laws punishing homosexual conduct. The Wolfenden Report: Report of the Committee on Homosexual Offenses and Prostitution (1963). Parliament enacted the substance of those recommendations 10 years later. Sexual Offences Act 1967, § 1.

Of even more importance, almost five years before *Bowers* was decided the European Court of Human Rights considered a case with parallels to *Bowers* and to today's case. An adult male resident in Northern Ireland alleged he was a practicing homosexual who desired to engage in consensual homosexual conduct. The laws of Northern Ireland forbade him that right. He alleged that he had been questioned, his home had been searched, and he feared criminal prosecution. The court held that the laws proscribing the conduct were invalid under the European Convention on Human Rights. *Dudgeon v. United Kingdom*, 45 Eur. Ct. H. R. (1981) ¶ 52. Authoritative in all countries that are members of the Council of Europe (21 nations then, 45 nations now), the decision is at odds with the premise in *Bowers* that the claim put forward was insubstantial in our Western civilization.

In our own constitutional system the deficiencies in *Bowers* became even more apparent in the years following its announcement. The 25 States with laws prohibiting the relevant conduct referenced in the *Bowers* decision are reduced now to 13, of which 4 enforce their laws only against homosexual conduct. In those States where sodomy is still proscribed, whether for same-sex or heterosexual conduct, there is a pattern of nonenforcement with respect to consenting adults acting in private. The State of Texas admitted in 1994 that as of that date it had not prosecuted anyone under those circumstances. *State v. Morales*, 869 S. W. 2d 941, 943.

Two principal cases decided after *Bowers* cast its holding into even more doubt. In *Casey*, the Court reaffirmed the substantive force of the liberty protected by the Due Process Clause. The *Casey* decision again confirmed that our laws and tradition afford constitutional protection to personal decisions relating to marriage, procreation, contraception, family relationships, child rearing, and education. In explaining the respect the Constitution demands for the autonomy of the person in making these choices, we stated as follows:

> These matters, involving the most intimate and personal choices a person may make in a lifetime, choices central to personal dignity and autonomy, are central to the liberty protected by the Fourteenth Amendment. At the heart of liberty is the right to define one's own concept of existence, of meaning, of the universe, and of the mystery of human life. Beliefs about these matters could not define the attributes of personhood were they formed under compulsion of the State.

Persons in a homosexual relationship may seek autonomy for these purposes, just as heterosexual persons do. The decision in *Bowers* would deny them this right.

The second post-*Bowers* case of principal relevance is *Romer v. Evans*, Chapter 4, § 3D. There the Court struck down class-based legislation directed at homosexuals as a violation of the Equal Protection Clause. *Romer* invalidated an amendment to Colorado's constitution which named as a solitary class persons who were homosexuals, lesbians, or bisexual either by "orientation, conduct, practices or relationships," and deprived them of protection under state antidiscrimination laws. We concluded that the provision was "born of animosity toward the class of persons affected" and further that it had no rational relation to a legitimate governmental purpose.

* * *

To the extent *Bowers* relied on values we share with a wider civilization, it should be noted that the reasoning and holding in *Bowers* have been rejected elsewhere. The European Court of Human Rights has followed not *Bowers* but its own decision in *Dudgeon v. United Kingdom*. See *P.G. & J.H. v. United Kingdom*, App. No. 00044787/98, ¶ ;56 (Eur. Ct. H. R., Sept. 25, 2001); *Modinos v. Cyprus*, 259 Eur. Ct. H. R. (1993); *Norris v. Ireland*, 142 Eur. Ct. H. R. (1988). Other nations, too, have taken action consistent with an affirmation of the protected right of homosexual adults to engage in intimate, consensual conduct. See Brief for Mary Robinson et al. as *Amici Curiae* 11-12. The right the petitioners seek in this case has been accepted as an integral part of human freedom in many other countries. There has been no showing that in this country the governmental interest in circumscribing personal choice is somehow more legitimate or urgent.

The doctrine of *stare decisis* is essential to the respect accorded to the judgments of the Court and to the stability of the law. It is not, however, an inexorable command. In *Casey* we noted that when a Court is asked to overrule a precedent recognizing a constitutional liberty interest, individual or societal reliance on the existence of that liberty cautions with particular strength against reversing course. The holding in *Bowers*, however, has not induced detrimental reliance comparable to some instances where recognized individual rights are involved. Indeed, there has been no individual or societal reliance on *Bowers* of the sort that could counsel against overturning its holding once there are compelling reasons to do so. *Bowers* itself causes uncertainty, for the precedents before and after its issuance contradict its central holding.

The rationale of *Bowers* does not withstand careful analysis. In his dissenting opinion in *Bowers* JUSTICE STEVENS came to these conclusions:

> Our prior cases make two propositions abundantly clear. First, the fact that the governing majority in a State has traditionally viewed a particular practice as immoral is not a sufficient reason for upholding a law prohibiting the practice; neither history nor tradition could save a law prohibiting miscegenation from constitutional attack. Second, individual decisions by married persons, concerning the intimacies of their physical relationship, even when not intended to produce offspring, are a form of "liberty" protected by the Due Process Clause of the Fourteenth Amendment.

Moreover, this protection extends to intimate choices by unmarried as well as married persons.

JUSTICE STEVENS' analysis, in our view, should have been controlling in *Bowers* and should control here.

Bowers was not correct when it was decided, and it is not correct today. It ought not to remain binding precedent. *Bowers v. Hardwick* should be and now is overruled.

The present case does not involve minors. It does not involve persons who might be injured or coerced or who are situated in relationships where consent might not easily be refused. It does not involve public conduct or prostitution. It does not involve whether the government must give formal recognition to any relationship that homosexual persons seek to enter. The case does involve two adults who, with full and mutual consent from each other, engaged in sexual practices common to a homosexual lifestyle. The petitioners are entitled to respect for their private lives. The State cannot demean their existence or control their destiny by making their private sexual conduct a crime. Their right to liberty under the Due Process Clause gives them the full right to engage in their conduct without intervention of the government. "It is a promise of the Constitution that there is a realm of personal liberty which the government may not enter." *Casey.* The Texas statute furthers no legitimate state interest which can justify its intrusion into the personal and private life of the individual.

Had those who drew and ratified the Due Process Clauses of the Fifth Amendment or the Fourteenth Amendment known the components of liberty in its manifold possibilities, they might have been more specific. They did not presume to have this insight. They knew times can blind us to certain truths and later generations can see that laws once thought necessary and proper in fact serve only to oppress. As the Constitution endures, persons in every generation can invoke its principles in their own search for greater freedom.

[**JUSTICE O'CONNOR** concurred in the judgment. She had joined the Court's opinion in *Bowers*, was not willing to join the Court's opinion overruling that precedent. But, she concluded, the Texas Homosexual Conduct Law did violate the Equal Protection Clause because it branded all homosexuals as criminals.]

JUSTICE SCALIA, with whom **THE CHIEF JUSTICE [REHNQUIST]** and **JUSTICE THOMAS** join, dissenting.

"Liberty finds no refuge in a jurisprudence of doubt." *Casey.* That was the Court's sententious response, barely more than a decade ago, to those seeking to overrule *Roe v. Wade.* The Court's response today, to those who have engaged in a 17-year crusade to overrule *Bowers v. Hardwick*, is very different. The need for stability and certainty presents no barrier.

Most of the rest of today's opinion has no relevance to its actual holding — that the Texas statute "furthers no legitimate state interest which can justify" its application to petitioners under rational-basis review. Though there is discussion of "fundamental proposition[s]" and "fundamental decisions," nowhere does the Court's opinion declare that homosexual sodomy is a "fundamental right" under the Due Process Clause; nor does it subject the Texas law to the standard of review that would be appropriate (strict scrutiny) if homosexual sodomy *were* a "fundamental right." Thus, while overruling the *outcome* of *Bowers*, the Court leaves strangely untouched its central legal conclusion: "[R]espondent would have us announce ... a fundamental right to engage in homosexual sodomy. This we are quite unwilling to do." Instead the Court simply describes petitioners' conduct as "an exercise of their liberty" — which it undoubtedly is — and proceeds to apply an unheard-of form of rational-basis review that will have far-reaching implications beyond this case.

* * *

Today's opinion is the product of a Court, which is the product of a law-profession culture, that has largely signed on to the so-called homosexual agenda, by which I mean the agenda promoted by some homosexual activists directed at eliminating the moral opprobrium that has traditionally attached to homosexual conduct. I noted in an earlier opinion the fact that the American Association of Law Schools (to which any reputable law school *must* seek to belong) excludes from membership any school that refuses to ban from its job-interview facilities a law firm (no matter how small) that does not wish to hire as a prospective partner a person who openly engages in homosexual conduct. See *Romer* [dissenting opinion].

* * *

The matters appropriate for this Court's resolution are only three: Texas's prohibition of sodomy neither infringes a "fundamental right" (which the Court does not dispute), nor is unsupported by a rational relation to what the Constitution considers a legitimate state interest, nor denies the equal protection of the laws. I dissent.

JUSTICE THOMAS, dissenting.

* * * I write separately to note that the law before the Court today "is . . . uncommonly silly." *Griswold v. Connecticut* (Stewart, J., dissenting). If I were a member of the Texas Legislature, I would vote to repeal it. Punishing someone for expressing his sexual preference through noncommercial consensual conduct with another adult does not appear to be a worthy way to expend valuable law enforcement resources.

Notwithstanding this, I recognize that as a member of this Court I am not empowered to help petitioners and others similarly situated. My duty, rather, is to "decide cases 'agreeably to the Constitution and laws of the United States.' " [*Id.*] And, just like Justice Stewart, I "can find [neither in the Bill of Rights nor any other part of the Constitution a] general right of privacy," [*id.*], or as the Court terms it today, the "liberty of the person both in its spatial and more transcendent dimensions."

NOTES ON *LAWRENCE*
AND THE FUTURE OF THE RIGHT OF PRIVACY

1. Stare Decisis *in Constitutional Cases.* Two authors of the joint opinion in *Casey* (Justices Kennedy and Souter) voted to overrule *Bowers*. As he candidly signaled in his *Casey* and *Carhart* dissents, Justice Scalia considers *stare decisis*

no big obstacle to overruling wrongly decided constitutional precedents — but in *Lawrence* he chided the majority Justices for giving nothing more than lip service to the principle that, they said, saved the abortion right from being overruled in *Casey*. (Scalia's criticism does not apply to Justice O'Connor, who took stare decisis just as seriously in *Lawrence* as she did in *Casey*.) The majority didn't say much in response, but consider some possible defenses:

(a) *The Libertarian Presumption.* The Constitution is a highly libertarian document, and its structural protection of people's freedom to act in their own interests without state interference was buttressed in the Bill of Rights and then in the Fourteenth Amendment. *Roe v. Wade*, a precedent protecting a liberty interest, gets more *stare decisis* support than *Bowers v. Hardwick*, a precedent declining to protect a liberty interest. Moreover, it cannot be ignored that the invasions of liberty were in criminal statutes, which have long been subjected to different, and more stringent, liberty-protective limitations than civil statutes.

(b) Stare Decisis *Cuts Both Ways.* *Bowers'* holding that anti-homosexual sentiment is a rational basis for a law criminalizing "homosexual sodomy" is inconsistent with *Romer's* holding that antigay "animus" is not a rational basis for a potentially sweeping anti-civil rights measure. Unless the rational basis test applies differently for the Due Process and Equal Protection Clauses — a proposition Justice O'Connor seems to accept — these two holdings cannot logically coexist. The Court chose *Romer* over *Bowers*, which is not only defensible but also supported by the litigation posture in the case: Harris County did not ask the Court to reconsider *Romer*, while Lawrence and dozens of *amici* asked the Court to reconsider and overrule *Bowers*.

(c) *Social Movements and Emerging National Consensus.* By 1992, the pro-choice movement had been successful in persuading substantial majorities of Americans that women have a right to abortion — but not an unlimited right. This was a script *Casey* followed carefully: the *Roe* right was reaffirmed, but state regulatory authority was expanded (and several recent decisions were overruled to do so). By 2003, the gay rights movement had been successful in persuading substantial majorities of Americans that lesbians, gay men, and bisexuals were an acceptable minority whose so-called "lifestyles" should be "tolerated" by the state — and that it was ridiculous for the state to criminalize their private intimate activities. This was a script *Lawrence* followed carefully: criminal sodomy laws were invalidated, but the majority disclaimed any endorsement of same-sex marriage or gays in the military, for example.

Do any of these theories (or a combination) justify the different deployment of *stare decisis* in the two cases?

2. *History and Political Theory: The Constitution as a Mechanism for Moderating Culture Wars.* Recall that Justice Scalia demands a long and unbroken history of affirmative protection before he will acknowledge some kind of fundamental right protection — but that view of the relationship between history and substantive due process was rejected in *Griswold, Roe* and *Casey*, and *Loving v. Virginia.* Justice Kennedy demonstrates that there can be relatively objective benchmarks for evolving tradition — the ALI's Model Penal Code, the adoption of its deregulatory principle in the next generation of state legislative

and judicial deliberation, the experience of other Western countries. All point in the same direction: consensual sodomy laws unnecessarily intrude into people's private lives.

Underlying Kennedy's and O'Connor's approach is *not* the idea that the Court decides great moral issues, but that the Court and its constitutional discourse contribute to a well-managed pluralism. America is a nation of social groups, and they constantly come into conflict. The political process is the arena where their conflicts are worked out, most of the time. But constitutionalism can serve a useful purpose of managing and channeling intergroup conflict. On the one hand, constitutionalism can prevent the state from being deployed as a means whereby a minority is turned into an outlaw group. That is not only an unfair deployment of the state, but creates resentments and the risk that the outlaws (and the inlaws) will go outside normal politics to fight. On the other hand, constitutionalism can protect groups against excessive state intrusion into their own bonding needs. Freedom of religion, of association (*Dale*, which Kennedy and O'Connor joined), the sanctity of the home, and the right of privacy are examples.

3. *Can State Morals Laws Survive* Lawrence? Justice Scalia also predicted in his dissent that *Lawrence* is the end of state morals regulation. This is an echo of Lord Patrick Devlin's famous attack on the Wolfenden Report urging the United Kingdom to decriminalize consensual sodomy; like Scalia, Devlin defended state morals regulation as an expression of popular norms. Scalia's list of morals laws that would fall if "homosexual sodomy" were deregulated is even an adaptation of Devlin's list in *On the Enforcement of Morals* (1959). H.L.A. Hart famously responded to Devlin in *Law, Liberty, and Morality* (1963). His argument was that however repugnant "homosexual sodomy" was, the state should not regulate private activities not harming third parties, the principle best articulated in John Stuart Mill, *On Liberty* ch. 4 (1857).

Lawrence does not purport to decide the constitutionality of other laws regulating morals, but lower courts will now have to adjudicate such challenges, if only because the dissenting opinion will inspire lawyers to bring them. The most obvious criterion for evaluating the laws is the Mill-Hart inquiry: Does this private conduct harm third parties? Consider the following array of morals legislation, loosely based on Justice Scalia's list. Which of these laws must fall after *Lawrence*? Which are easily defensible?

(1) Use of sex toys on oneself or on another person (yes, several states do outlaw the sale of such devices);

(2) Fornication: sexual intercourse between two people who are not married;

(3) Adult incest between first cousins (could it be made illegal if the incest were between adult siblings?; would it matter whether such incest increases the risk of birth defects to offspring?);

(4) Prostitution;

(5) Bestiality;

(6) Adultery: sex between two adults, at least one of whom is married to someone else.

NOTE ON THE RELATIONSHIP OF *CARHART* TO *LAWRENCE*

There are some similarities between *Carhart* and *Lawrence,* now the two most-discussed constitutional privacy decisions in the new millennium. Justice Kennedy, the author of five-Justice majority opinions in both cases, overrules (*Lawrence*) or narrowly construes *(Carhart)* recent precedents; abandons the "fundamental rights" rhetoric and treats privacy as simply a due process "liberty" that can be regulated in a number of ways, but not "too much"; and follows the moral consensus reached by large majorities of the states, which had repealed their sodomy laws (*Lawrence*) and adopted partial-birth abortion statutes (*Carhart*).

The differences between the two opinions are more notable, however. Paradoxically, the differences might help us understand the limits of *Lawrence* as well as the normative problems with *Carhart.*

First, equal citizenship plays a key role in *Lawrence,* as a reason to give the privacy right bite, while it seems ignored, perhaps even rhetorically inverted, in *Carhart.* Justice Ginsburg's dissent not only emphasizes the relationship of abortion choice to women's equal citizenship, but also charges that the Court's rhetoric reveals a contrary perspective.

This does not mean that *Carhart* returns women to a period where their "natural" role as domestics prevented or impeded their participation in public life — any more than *Lawrence* means that the state can never discriminate against lesbians, gay men, bisexuals, and transgendered people. Both *Carhart* and *Lawrence* are about how much majoritarian social attitudes must yield to personal liberty decisions that group members feel they need to carry out their life projects. Because it is overruling a decision that denied gay people any equal treatment (*Bowers*), *Lawrence* can honestly present itself as egalitarian, but that does not mean that the Court would go "all the way" to marriage for gay rights. Likewise, *Roe* can be imagined as an egalitarian decision (as the Court did in *Casey*), but *Carhart* indicates the Court will not go "all the way" in this regard, either.

Second, morality plays a strikingly different role in the two cases. *Lawrence* announces that sectarian morality cannot justify invading gay people's privacy — but *Carhart* says that the morality can require women seeking late-term abortions to fall back on potentially riskier procedures. Justice Kennedy does not see these different roles of morality to be inconsistent. Recall that he co-authored the Joint Opinion in *Casey,* so he has put himself on record that women's abortion choices cannot be completely foreclosed by moral views. From his point of view, *Lawrence* is analogous to *Casey. Carhart,* then, might be analogous to a decision upholding choices that Justice Kennedy believes are not central to the lives of homosexuals. In other words, *Carhart* makes it clear that, for the current Court, public morality remains relevant as a limitation on the privacy right.

Third, disgust seems to play important but contrasting roles in the two cases. In *Lawrence,* Justice Kennedy says nothing about what actually goes on in the homosexual bedroom, while his *Carhart* opinion lays out the process of partial-birth abortion from the perspective of a nurse who views it as killing a helpless baby. Most readers will be disgusted by what they read in Part I of *Carhart*, only the most dedicated homophobe would be disgusted by the sanitized presentation of gay relationships in *Lawrence*. It is apparent that the *Bowers* majority found homosexual relations disgusting and were unable to see any human connection there — and that directly generated the result in *Bowers*. See William Eskridge, Jr., *Dishonorable Passions: Sodomy Law in America, 1861-2003* (forthcoming 2008) (detailed account of *Bowers*). It appears that the majority of Justices (and at least one dissenter, Justice Thomas) found nothing particularly disgusting about homosexual relations in *Lawrence*. But these Justices are horrified by what they consider infanticide in *Carhart*.

All three points are related. Social scientists have found that people's moral opinions are shaped by what disgusts them, and public morality is shaped by creating disgusting images and associating them with certain people (homosexuals) or practices (sodomy) or both (the homosexual is always a disgusting sodomite). Reflecting modern social attitudes, *Lawrence* disrupts that process for homosexuals and sodomy, but *Carhart* initiates a new process that partially reverses what *Roe v. Wade* and *Casey* were trying to do, namely, disaggregate women's life choices from images of abortion as infanticide.

D. THE RIGHT TO MARRY

Griswold spoke of marriage as "an association for as noble a purpose as any involved in our prior decisions." An alternative ground for the Court's decision to strike down laws prohibiting different-race marriage in *Loving* (Chapter 3, § 1A) was a right to marry found in the Due Process Clause.

In *Zablocki v. Redhail*, 434 U.S. 374 (1978), the Court invalidated Wisconsin's law precluding the issuance of marriage licenses to people with outstanding support obligations to children from a previous marriage. Justice Thurgood Marshall's opinion for the Court started with the proposition that the "right to marry" is a fundamental right. "It is not surprising that the decision to marry has been placed on the same level of importance as decisions relating to procreation, childbirth, child rearing, and familial relationships. As the facts of these cases illustrate, it would make little sense to recognize a right to privacy with respect to other matters of family life and not with respect to the decision to enter into a relationship that is the foundation of the family in our society." Justice Marshall then reasoned that any state discrimination in allocating the right to marry must be scrutinized strictly under the Equal Protection Clause. "When a statutory classification significantly interferes with the exercise of a fundamental right, it cannot be upheld unless it is supported by sufficiently important state interests and is closely tailored to effectuate only those interests." The Wisconsin statute flunked this stringent test. Although ensuring collection of support obligations owed one's children is an important state interest, the state has other, less constitutionally intrusive, ways of effectuating that interest.

In *Turner v. Safley*, 482 U.S. 78 (1987), a unanimous Court, per Justice O'Connor, struck down a state regulation barring the ability of prisoners to marry. The Court held that the right to marry was implicated even in prison settings, where sex with outsiders is normally prohibited:

> First, inmate marriages, like others, are expressions of emotional support and public commitment. These elements are an important and significant aspect of the marital relationship. In addition, many religions recognize marriage as having spiritual significance; for some inmates and their spouses, therefore, the commitment of marriage may be an exercise of religious faith as well as an expression of personal dedication. Third, most inmates eventually will be released by parole or commutation, and therefore most inmate marriages are formed in the expectation that they will be fully consummated. Finally, marital status often is a precondition to the receipt of government benefits (e.g., Social Security benefits), property rights (e.g., tenancy by the entirety, inheritance rights), and other, less tangible benefits (e.g., legitimation of children born out of wedlock). These incidents of marriage, like the religious and personal aspects of the marriage commitment, are unaffected by the fact of confinement or the pursuit of legitimate corrections goals.

Because of the prison setting, Justice O'Connor applied the Court's precedents requiring a "reasonable relationship" between a prison regulation and legitimate penological objectives. Another part of her opinion (joined only by five Justices) upheld prison surveillance of inmate mail, usually protected under the First Amendment. Unlike opening inmate mail, preventing inmate marriages did not narrowly serve legitimate penological purposes, Justice O'Connor reasoned.

In re Marriage Cases, 43 Cal.4th 757, 183 P.3d 384, 76 Cal.Rptr.3d 683 (California Supreme Court, 2008). These appeals consolidated six cases where lesbian and gay couples sought recognition of their committed relationships as marriages; much of the Court's opinion is excerpted in Chapter 4. One of the plaintiffs' claims was grounded in the "fundamental right to marry." Although one of us had argued for such a fundamental right in 1996,[w] no appellate court had accepted this argument under either the U.S. Constitution or a state constitution. State courts recognizing equality rights for lesbian and gay couples did so under either a rational basis approach, or heightened scrutiny because of a suspect classification. **Chief Justice George**'s opinion for the California Supreme Court was the first appellate decision in the United States to recognize a "fundamental right to marry" for lesbian and gay couples.

Part IV of the Chief Justice's opinion held that the plaintiff lesbian and gay couples have a "fundamental right to marry." Unlike the U.S. Constitution, the California Constitution mentions privacy rights, in Article I, section 1, which provides: "All people are by nature free and independent and have inalienable rights. Among these are enjoying and defending life and *liberty*, acquiring, possessing, and protecting property, and pursuing and obtaining safety, happiness, and *privacy*." (Added 1972, emphasis added.) Like the U.S. Constitution, however, the California Constitution does not explicitly protect a fundamental right to marry, but the state supreme court has inferred such a right from the 1972 amendment, which was meant to codify *Griswold v. Connecticut* in the state constitution.

---

w. William N. Eskridge, Jr., *The Case for Same-Sex Marriage* 123-52 (1996), arguing that the *Loving-Zablocki-Turner* line of cases supported a constitutional right for lesbian and gay couples to marry.

The lower court had rejected plaintiffs' claim on the ground that lesbian and gay couples enjoyed no "fundamental right to marriage," because marriage had traditionally not included them. Although all other state appeals courts had accepted or acquiesced in a similar argument, Chief Justice George rejected it as circular. "In *Perez v. Sharp*, this court's 1948 decision holding that the California statutory provisions prohibiting interracial marriage were unconstitutional — the court did not characterize the constitutional right that the plaintiffs in that case sought to obtain as 'a right to interracial marriage' and did not dismiss the plaintiffs' constitutional challenge on the ground that such marriages never had been permitted in California. Instead, the *Perez* decision focused on the *substance* of the constitutional right at issue — that is, the importance to an individual of the freedom 'to join in marriage *with the person of one's choice*' — in determining whether the statute impinged upon the plaintiffs' fundamental constitutional right. * * * And, in addressing a somewhat analogous point, the United States Supreme Court in *Lawrence v. Texas,* concluded that its prior decision in *Bowers v. Hardwick* had erred in narrowly characterizing the constitutional right sought to be invoked in that case as the right to engage in intimate *homosexual* conduct, determining instead that the constitutional right there at issue properly should be understood in a broader and more neutral fashion so as to focus upon the substance of the interests that the constitutional right is intended to protect."

When understood at the proper level of generality, the question becomes, what is the point of the important constitutional interest in marriage? *Perez* and other cases established a "linkage between marriage, establishing a home, and raising children in identifying civil marriage as the means available to an individual to establish, with a loved one of his or her choice, an officially recognized family relationship. In *De Burgh v. De Burgh* (1952) 39 Cal.2d 858, for example, in explaining 'the public interest in the institution of marriage,' this court stated: 'The family is the basic unit of our society, the center of the personal affections that ennoble and enrich human life. It channels biological drives that might otherwise become socially destructive; it ensures the care and education of children in a stable environment; it establishes continuity from one generation to another; it nurtures and develops the individual initiative that distinguishes a free people. Since the family is the core of our society, the law seeks to foster and preserve marriage.' "

The Chief Justice emphasized the social utility of marriage as a broadly available institution. *De Burgh* and other cases described marriage as the "building block" of society, by providing a good structure for rearing children as well as channeling adult behaviors in productive ways. And of course many cases recognized marriage as the most important individual right, for marriage is typically "the most socially productive and individually fulfilling relationship that one can enjoy in the course of a lifetime." These values of marriage, and its critical role as an enforceable individual right, are recognized in Article 16 of the U.N. Universal Declaration of Human Rights; Article 23 of the International Covenant of Civil and Political Rights; Article 12 of the European Convention for the Protection of Human Rights and Fundamental Freedoms; Article 17 of the American Convention on Human Rights; and the constitutions of many other countries. See Lynn Wardle, *Federal Constitutional Protection for Marriage: Why and How*, 20 BYU J. Pub. L. 439, 453-61 (2006).

In response to the argument that marriage had traditionally been reserved for different-sex couples only, the Chief Justice noted that precisely that argument had been rejected in *Perez*. The point of constitutional review is to subject tradition to normative scrutiny. "There can be no question but that, in recent decades, there has been a fundamental and dramatic transformation in this state's understanding and legal treatment of gay individuals and gay couples. California has repudiated past practices and policies that were based on a once common viewpoint that denigrated the general character and morals of gay individuals, and at one time even characterized homosexuality as a mental illness rather than as simply one of the numerous variables of our common and diverse humanity. This state's current policies and conduct regarding homosexuality recognize that gay individuals are entitled to the same legal rights and the same respect and dignity afforded all other individuals and are protected from discrimination on the basis of their sexual orientation, and, more specifically, recognize that gay individuals are fully capable of entering into the kind of loving and enduring committed relationships that may serve as the foundation of a family and of responsibly caring for and raising children."

Amici argued that the main point of marriage is procreation, and that the valid state interest in channeling reproductive activity into marriage justified the omission of same-sex couples, who could not produce children through their sexual activities. The Chief Justice was unpersuaded, in part because as many as 70,000 children were being raised in California by same-sex couples (citing study that found that 28.4 percent of California lesbian and gay couples were raising children). Some of these children were adopted, others came through surrogates and artificial insemination, but the fact remained, for the Court, that even this traditional value of marriage was not served by excluding so many families from the state marriage law.

"Furthermore, although promoting and facilitating a stable environment for the procreation and raising of children is unquestionably one of the vitally important purposes underlying the institution of marriage and the constitutional right to marry, past cases make clear that this right is not confined to, or restrictively defined by, that purpose alone. As noted above, our past cases have recognized that the right to marry is the right to enter into a relationship that is 'the center of the personal affections that ennoble and enrich human life' (*De Burgh*) — a relationship that is 'at once the most socially productive and individually fulfilling relationship that one can enjoy in the course of a lifetime.' (*Marvin v. Marvin*.) The personal enrichment afforded by the right to marry may be obtained by a couple whether or not they choose to have children, and the right to marry never has been limited to those who plan or desire to have children. Indeed, in *Griswold v. Connecticut* — one of the seminal federal cases striking down a state law as violative of the federal constitutional right of privacy — the high court upheld a married couple's right to use contraception *to prevent procreation*, demonstrating quite clearly that the promotion of procreation is not the sole or defining purpose of marriage. Similarly, in *Turner v. Safley*, the court held that the constitutional right to marry extends to an individual confined in state prison — even a prisoner who has no right to conjugal visits with his would-be spouse — emphasizing that '[m]any important attributes of marriage remain . . . after taking into account the limitations imposed by prison life . . . [including the] expressions of emotional support and public commitment [that] are an important and significant aspect of the marital relationship.' Although *Griswold* and *Turner* relate to the right to marry under the federal Constitution, they accurately reflect the scope of the state constitutional right to marry as well. Accordingly, this right cannot properly be defined by or limited to the state's interest in fostering a favorable environment for the procreation and raising of children.

"The Proposition 22 Legal Defense Fund and the Campaign also rely upon several academic commentators who maintain that the constitutional right to marry should be viewed as inapplicable to same-sex couples because a contrary interpretation assertedly would sever the link that marriage provides between procreation and child rearing and would 'send a message' to the public that it is immaterial to the state whether children are raised by their biological mother and father. (See, e.g., Blankenhorn, The Future of Marriage (2007); Wardle, *"Multiply and Replenish": Considering Same-Sex Marriage in Light of State Interests in Marital Procreation* (2001) 24 Harv. J.L. & Pub. Pol'y 771, 797-799; Gallagher, *What Is Marriage For? The Public Purposes of Marriage Law* (2002) 62 La. L.Rev. 773, 779-780, 790-791.) Although we appreciate the genuine concern for the well-being of children underlying that position, we conclude this claim lacks merit. Our recognition that the core substantive rights encompassed by the constitutional right to marry apply to same-sex as well as opposite-sex couples does not imply in any way that it is unimportant or immaterial to the state whether a child is raised by his or her biological mother and father. By recognizing this circumstance we do not alter or diminish either the legal responsibilities that biological parents owe to their children or the substantial incentives that the state provides to a child's biological parents to enter into and raise their child in a stable, long-term committed relationship. Instead, such an interpretation of the constitutional right to marry simply confirms that a stable two-parent family relationship, supported by the state's official recognition and protection, is equally as important for the numerous children in California who are being raised by same-sex couples as for those children being raised by opposite-sex couples (whether they are biological parents or adoptive parents). This interpretation also guarantees individuals who are in a same-sex relationship, and who are raising children, the opportunity to obtain from the state the official recognition and support accorded a family by agreeing to take on the substantial and long-term mutual obligations and responsibilities that are an essential and inseparable part of a family relationship."

Finally, the Chief Justice rejected the Attorney General's argument that the Domestic Partnership Act, as amended to provide virtually all the legal benefits and duties of marriage for same-sex couples, satisfied the constitutional marriage right. "Whether or not the name 'marriage,' in the abstract, is considered a core element of the state constitutional right to marry, one of the core elements of this fundamental right is the right of same-sex couples to have their official family relationship accorded the same dignity, respect, and stature as that accorded to all other officially recognized family relationships. The current statutes — by drawing a distinction between the name assigned to the family relationship available to opposite-sex couples and the name assigned to the family relationship available to same-sex couples, and by reserving the historic and highly respected designation of marriage exclusively to opposite-sex couples while offering same-sex couples only the new and unfamiliar designation of domestic partnership — pose a serious risk of denying the official family relationship of same-sex couples the equal dignity and respect that is a core element of the constitutional right to marry. As observed by the City [and County of San Francisco] at oral argument, this court's conclusion in *Perez* that the statutory provision barring interracial marriage was unconstitutional, undoubtedly would have been the same even if alternative nomenclature, such as 'transracial union,' had been made available to interracial couples."

In sum, the Court ruled that the state's exclusion of lesbian and gay couples from civil marriage violated both the state constitution's privacy right and was an additional reason why the exclusion was subject to strict scrutiny under the state equal protection right. (See the excerpts from the *Marriage Cases* in Chapter 4, § __ for the Court's holding that the exclusion of same-sex couples violated constitutional equal protection because it relied on a suspect classification (sexual orientation) without a compelling public reason to do so.) Three other Justices joined the Chief Justice's opinion. **Justices Baxter, Corrigan**, and **Chin** dissented from the Court's opinion and judgment.

NOTE ON THE CONSTITUTIONAL RIGHT TO MARRY

The level-of-generality debate between the majority and the dissenters tracked the debate between *Lawrence* and *Bowers*. Thus, the *Bowers* majority and the *Marriage Cases* dissenters asked whether there was a tradition specifically protecting "homosexual sodomy" (*Bowers*) or assuring "gay marriage" (*Marriage Cases*) and, of course, found no such tradition. Those jurists defined the constitutionally protected right at a low level of generality — in contrast to the higher level at which the *Lawrence* and *Marriage Cases* majorities defined the fundamental right.

The *Marriage Cases* do go beyond *Lawrence* in this respect, however. Justice Kennedy in *Lawrence* argued that there was, actually, a great deal of historical support for the proposition that sodomy laws should not apply to consensual private behavior, while Chief Justice George announced no historical tradition in favor of same-sex marriage. (In fact, there is a literature demonstrating that many cultures, including Native American ones in the United States, have openly recognized same-sex unions and marriages. See Eskridge, *Case for Same-Sex Marriage*, 15-50.) So the contrast is quite striking. Even *Loving v. Virginia* and *Perez v. Sharp* could point to the fact that recognition of different-race marriages was the traditional norm in Asia, Africa, Europe and much of the Americas, a norm from which the South was an outlier.

Moreover, *amici* supporting the state argued that the California Constitution itself hard-wired the different-sex requirement for marriage. Tracking similar language in the California Constitution of 1849, Article XX, section 8 of the California Constitution of 1879 provided: "All property, real and personal, owned by either husband or wife before marriage, and that acquired by either of them afterwards by gift, devise, or descent, shall be their separate property." Although the current language is gender neutral, *amici* argued that this was a constitutional recognition of the historic requirement that civil marriage *always* entails one man (the husband) and one woman (the wife). There was no similar constitution hard-wiring as to different-race marriage, a key difference between *Perez* and the gay marriage cases.

In short, the disconnection between history and the fundamental right is especially striking in the *California Marriage Cases*. Is there a theoretical basis for pressing this case closer to *Loving/Perez*? Review the theories laid out in Chapter 2.

Related to the history point is the famous slippery slope argument, made in the *Marriage Cases* by Justice Baxter's dissenting opinion:

> The bans on incestuous and polygamous marriages are ancient and deep-rooted . . . . Yet here, the majority overturns, in abrupt fashion, an initiative statute confirming the equally deep-rooted assumption that marriage is a union of partners of the opposite sex. The majority does so by relying on its own assessment of contemporary community values . . . . Who can say that, in ten, fifteen, or twenty years, an activist court might not rely on the majority's analysis to conclude, on the basis of a perceived evolution in community values, that the laws prohibiting polygamous and incestuous marriages were no longer constitutionally justified?

The slippery slope point is probably one major reason why no previous appellate court had ever applied the fundamental right to marry jurisprudence to gay marriage. To say there is a general right to marry seems to invite Justice Baxter's point. How should the majority have responded to this argument?

Note, moreover, that the slippery slope argument has lost most of its cultural resonance: ordinary Americans just don't seem to care much about it anymore, in part because more of them support same-sex marriage and in part because the "prediction" has, thus far, not been borne out. Experience with same-sex marriage in The Netherlands (2001), Canada (2003), Massachusetts (2004), etc., as well as with civil unions in Denmark (1989), Norway (1993), Sweden (1994), Vermont (2000), etc. has been that state recognition of lesbian and gay unions has engendered zero public demand or movement toward legitimating incest, polygamy, etc. For an excellent analysis of the slippery slope argument from a social movement perspective, see Brett McDonnell, *Is Incest Next?*, 10 Cardozo Women's L.J. 337 (2004).

PROBLEM 5-5
SEXUAL CONDUCT LAWS AFTER *LAWRENCE*?

The dissenters in both *Lawrence v. Texas* and the *California Marriage Cases* say that those constitutional decisions mark the end of morals regulation. The student should take these dissenting views with a grain of salt, and the majority opinions in those cases cannot reasonably be read so broadly. But consider the following hypothetical morals laws. If you were the state attorney general, what is the best defense of each law? Is a federal court likely to accept your defense under *Lawrence*? Would a California state judge decide the case differently under its state constitutional precedents?

(A) Plural Marriage. Like every other state, California will not give marriage licenses to someone who is already married, and marriage with someone who is already married is void under California Family Code § 2201. A fundamentalist Mormon family (a husband and two wives raising children in a loving relationship) sues the state to recognize that family's plural marriage under both federal and state constitutions. Frame their claim and the state's response. Is there a principled reason not to recognize their "fundamental right to marry"?

(B) Seventeen-Year-Old Spouse. John is seventeen and Sally is eighteen. They want to marry, but California requires parental consent (or a court order) if one partner is under age eighteen. Cal. Family Code §§ 302, 353. Most states would allow such marriages, but California does not. Does this couple have a right to marry claim under either the U.S. or the California Constitution?

(C) First Cousin Marriage. California allows first cousins to marry, but most states do not. Assume that Ben and Juana are first cousins who marry one another in California and then relocate in a jurisdiction that does not grant marriage licenses to first-cousin couples. Most such jurisdictions will still "recognize" out-of-state first-cousin marriages if valid in the state of celebration (California), but assume the courts in State X do not recognize such marriages. The Supreme Court has not interpreted the Full Faith & Credit Clause of Article IV to require states to recognize sibling state marriages that are contrary to their public policy, so Ben and Juana's only federal constitutional claim is one resting on the fundamental right to marry. Would the U.S. Supreme Court recognize such a right for them? If California did not recognize first-cousin marriages, would Ben and Juana have a state constitutional claim under the *Marriage Cases*?

SECTION 5. THE "RIGHT TO DIE"

WASHINGTON v. GLUCKSBERG
521 U.S. 702, 117 S.Ct. 2258, 138 L.Ed.2d 772 (1997)

CHIEF JUSTICE REHNQUIST delivered the opinion of the Court.

[This case involved Washington State's prohibition against causing or aiding a suicide. Such prohibitions are long-standing and practically universal. Also, a recent federal statute bans use of federal funds to finance physician-assisted suicide. The suit was brought by several doctors who treat terminally ill patients in extreme pain, as well as three terminally ill patients who died while the case was on appeal, and by Compassion in Dying, an organization that counsels people considering physician assisted suicide. In an en banc opinion, the federal court of appeals held the Washington ban on assisted suicide unconstitutional as applied to terminally ill, mentally competent patients. The Supreme Court reversed.[a]]

---

a. *Editors' note:* In a companion case, *Vacco v. Quill*, 521 U.S. 793 (1997), the Court reviewed an equal protection challenge to a similar New York law. The federal court of appeals had found it irrational for the state to distinguish between active physician assistance to terminate a patient's

The Due Process Clause guarantees more than fair process, and the "liberty" it protects includes more than the absence of physical restraint. The Clause also provides heightened protection against government interference with certain fundamental rights and liberty interests. In a long line of cases, we have held that, in addition to the specific freedoms protected by the Bill of Rights, the "liberty" specially protected by the Due Process Clause includes the rights to marry, *Loving*; to have children, *Skinner*; to direct the education and upbringing of one's children, *Meyer*; *Pierce*; to marital privacy, *Griswold*; to use contraception, ibid; *Eisenstadt*; to bodily integrity, *Rochin v. California*, 342 U.S. 165 (1952), and to abortion, *Casey*. We have also assumed, and strongly suggested, that the Due Process Clause protects the traditional right to refuse unwanted lifesaving medical treatment. *Cruzan* [*v. Director, Missouri Dept. of Health*, 497 U.S. 261 (1990)].

But we "ha[ve] always been reluctant to expand the concept of substantive due process because guideposts for responsible decisionmaking in this unchartered area are scarce and open-ended." By extending constitutional protection to an asserted right or liberty interest, we, to a great extent, place the matter outside the arena of public debate and legislative action. We must therefore "exercise the utmost care whenever we are asked to break new ground in this field," lest the liberty protected by the Due Process Clause be subtly transformed into the policy preferences of the members of this Court.

Our established method of substantive-due-process analysis has two primary features: First, we have regularly observed that the Due Process Clause specially protects those fundamental rights and liberties which are, objectively, "deeply rooted in this Nation's history and tradition," and "implicit in the concept of ordered liberty," such that "neither liberty nor justice would exist if they were sacrificed." Second, we have required in substantive-due-process cases a "careful description" of the asserted fundamental liberty interest. Our Nation's history, legal traditions, and practices thus provide the crucial "guideposts for responsible decisionmaking" that direct and restrain our exposition of the Due Process Clause. As we stated recently[,] the Fourteenth Amendment "forbids the government to infringe ... 'fundamental' liberty interests *at all*, no matter what process is provided, unless the infringement is narrowly tailored to serve a compelling state interest."

Justice Souter, relying on Justice Harlan's dissenting opinion in *Poe v. Ullman*, would largely abandon this restrained methodology, and instead ask "whether [Washington's] statute sets up one of those 'arbitrary impositions' or 'purposeless restraints' at odds with the Due Process Clause of the Fourteenth

---

life and removing life support with the same purpose and effect. After concluding, in reliance on *Glucksberg*, that the case did not involve a fundamental right, the *Quill* Court concluded that the New York statute easily survived rational basis review. The Court relied on the overwhelming number of state statutes and judicial decisions making this distinction and found ample justification for the statute, "including prohibiting intentional killing and preserving life; preventing suicide; maintaining physicians' role as their patients' healers; protecting vulnerable people from indifference, prejudice, and psychological and financial pressure to end their lives and avoiding a possible slide toward euthanasia."

Amendment." In our view, however, the development of this Court's substantive-due-process jurisprudence * * * has been a process whereby the outlines of the "liberty" specially protected by the Fourteenth Amendment — never fully clarified, to be sure, and perhaps not capable of being fully clarified — have at least been carefully refined by concrete examples involving fundamental rights found to be deeply rooted in our legal tradition. This approach tends to rein in the subjective elements that are necessarily present in due-process judicial review. In addition, by establishing a threshold requirement — that a challenged state action implicate a fundamental right — before requiring more than a reasonable relation to a legitimate state interest to justify the action, it avoids the need for complex balancing of competing interests in every case.

Turning to the claim at issue here, the Court of Appeals stated that "[p]roperly analyzed, the first issue to be resolved is whether there is a liberty interest in determining the time and manner of one's death," or, in other words, "[i]s there a right to die?" Similarly, respondents assert a "liberty to choose how to die" and a right to "control of one's final days," and describe the asserted liberty as "the right to choose a humane, dignified death," and "the liberty to shape death." * * *.

We now inquire whether this asserted right has any place in our Nation's traditions. Here * * * we are confronted with a consistent and almost universal tradition that has long rejected the asserted right, and continues explicitly to reject it today, even for terminally ill, mentally competent adults. To hold for respondents, we would have to reverse centuries of legal doctrine and practice, and strike down the considered policy choice of almost every State.

Respondents contend, however, that the liberty interest they assert *is* consistent with this Court's substantive-due-process line of cases, if not with this Nation's history and practice. Pointing to *Casey* and *Cruzan*, respondents read our jurisprudence in this area as reflecting a general tradition of "self-sovereignty," and as teaching that the "liberty" protected by the Due Process Clause includes "basic and intimate exercises of personal autonomy." According to respondents, our liberty jurisprudence, and the broad, individualistic principles it reflects, protects the "liberty of competent, terminally ill adults to make end-of-life decisions free of undue government interference." The question presented in this case, however, is whether the protections of the Due Process Clause include a right to commit suicide with another's assistance. With this "careful description" of respondents' claim in mind, we turn to *Casey* and *Cruzan*.

In *Cruzan*, we considered whether Nancy Beth Cruzan, who had been severely injured in an automobile accident and was in a persistive vegetative state, "ha[d] a right under the United States Constitution which would require the hospital to withdraw life-sustaining treatment" at her parents' request. We began with the observation that "[a]t common law, even the touching of one person by another without consent and without legal justification was a battery." We then discussed the related rule that "informed consent is generally required for medical treatment." After reviewing a long line of relevant state cases, we concluded that "the common-law doctrine of informed consent is viewed as generally encompassing the right of a competent individual to refuse medical treatment." Next, we reviewed our own cases on the subject, and stated that "[t]he principle that a competent person has a constitutionally protected liberty interest in refusing unwanted medical treatment may be inferred from our prior decisions." Therefore, "for purposes of [that] case, we assume[d] that the United States Constitution would grant a competent person a constitutionally protected right to refuse lifesaving hydration and nutrition." We concluded that, notwithstanding this right, the Constitution permitted Missouri to require clear and convincing evidence of an incompetent patient's wishes concerning the withdrawal of life-sustaining treatment.

* * * The right assumed in *Cruzan*, however, was not simply deduced from abstract concepts of personal autonomy. Given the common-law rule that forced medication was a battery, and the long legal tradition protecting the decision to refuse unwanted medical treatment, our assumption was entirely consistent with this Nation's history and constitutional traditions. The decision to commit suicide with the assistance of another may be just as personal and profound as the decision to refuse unwanted medical treatment, but it has never enjoyed similar legal protection. Indeed, the two acts are widely and reasonably regarded as quite distinct. In *Cruzan* itself, we recognized that most States outlawed assisted suicide — and even more do today — and we certainly gave no intimation that the right to refuse unwanted medical treatment could be somehow transmuted into a right to assistance in committing suicide. * * *

The Court of Appeals, like the District Court, found *Casey* " 'highly instructive' " and " 'almost prescriptive' " for determining " 'what liberty interest may inhere in a terminally ill person's choice to commit suicide' ":

> Like the decision of whether or not to have an abortion, the decision how and when to die is one of "the most intimate and personal choices a person may make in a lifetime," a choice "central to personal dignity and autonomy."

Similarly, respondents emphasize the statement in *Casey* that:

> At the heart of liberty is the right to define one's own concept of existence, of meaning, of the universe, and of the mystery of human life. Beliefs about these matters could not define the attributes of personhood were they formed under compulsion of the State.

By choosing this language, the Court's opinion in *Casey* described, in a general way and in light of our prior cases, those personal activities and decisions that this Court has identified as so deeply rooted in our history and traditions, or so fundamental to our concept of constitutionally ordered liberty, that they are protected by the Fourteenth Amendment. The opinion moved from the recognition that liberty necessarily includes freedom of conscience and belief about ultimate considerations to the observation that "though the abortion decision may originate within the zone of conscience and belief, it is *more than a philosophic exercise*." [emphasis added] That many of the rights and liberties protected by the Due Process Clause sound in personal autonomy does not warrant the sweeping conclusion that any and all important, intimate, and personal decisions are so protected, *Rodriguez* [this chapter, § 3B], and *Casey* did not suggest otherwise.

The history of the law's treatment of assisted suicide in this country has been and continues to be one of the rejection of nearly all efforts to permit it. That being the case, our decisions lead us to conclude that the asserted "right" to assistance in committing suicide is not a fundamental liberty interest protected by the Due Process Clause. The Constitution also requires, however, that Washington's assisted-suicide ban be rationally related to legitimate government interests. This requirement is unquestionably met here. As the court below recognized,[b] Washington's assisted-suicide ban implicates a number of state interests.

[The lower court struck down Washington's assisted-suicide ban only "as applied to competent, terminally ill adults who wish to hasten their deaths by obtaining medication prescribed by their doctors." The Supreme Court was concerned, however, that any such limitations on the right to die might be eroded.]

This concern is further supported by evidence about the practice of euthanasia in the Netherlands. The Dutch government's own study revealed that in 1990, there were 2,300 cases of voluntary euthanasia (defined as "the deliberate termination of another's life at his request"), 400 cases of assisted suicide, and more than 1,000 cases of euthanasia without an explicit request. In addition to these latter 1,000 cases, the study found an additional 4,941 cases where physicians administered lethal morphine overdoses without the patients' explicit consent. This study suggests that, despite the existence of various reporting procedures, euthanasia in the Netherlands has not been limited to competent, terminally ill adults who are enduring physical suffering, and that regulation of the practice may not have prevented abuses in cases involving vulnerable persons, including severely disabled neonates and elderly persons suffering from dementia. * * * Washington, like most other States, reasonably ensures against this risk by banning, rather than regulating, assisting suicide.

We need not weigh exactingly the relative strengths of these various interests. They are unquestionably important and legitimate, and Washington's ban on assisted suicide is at least reasonably related to their promotion and protection. We therefore hold that [Washington law] does not violate the Fourteenth Amendment, either on its face or "as applied to competent, terminally ill adults who wish to hasten their deaths by obtaining medication prescribed by their doctors."[c]

---

b. The court identified and discussed six state interests: (1) preserving life; (2) preventing suicide; (3) avoiding the involvement of third parties and use of arbitrary, unfair, or undue influence; (4) protecting family members and loved ones; (5) protecting the integrity of the medical profession; and (6) avoiding future movement toward euthanasia and other abuses.

c. Justice Stevens states that "the Court does conceive of respondents' claim as a facial challenge — addressing not the application of the statute to a particular set of plaintiffs before it, but the constitutionality of the statute's categorical prohibition. . . ." We emphasize that we today reject the Court of Appeals' specific holding that the statute is unconstitutional "as applied" to a particular class. Justice Stevens agrees with this holding, but would not "foreclose the possibility that an individual plaintiff seeking to hasten her death, or a doctor whose assistance was sought, could prevail in a more particularized challenge." Our opinion does not absolutely foreclose such a claim. However, given our holding that the Due Process Clause of the Fourteenth Amendment does not provide heightened protection to the asserted liberty interest in ending one's life with a physician's assistance, such a claim would have to be quite different from the ones advanced by

Throughout the Nation, Americans are engaged in an earnest and profound debate about the morality, legality, and practicality of physician-assisted suicide. Our holding permits this debate to continue, as it should in a democratic society. The decision of the en banc Court of Appeals is reversed, and the case is remanded for further proceedings consistent with this opinion.

JUSTICE O'CONNOR, concurring.[d]

Death will be different for each of us. For many, the last days will be spent in physical pain and perhaps the despair that accompanies physical deterioration and a loss of control of basic bodily and mental functions. Some will seek medication to alleviate that pain and other symptoms.

The Court frames the issue in this case as whether the Due Process Clause of the Constitution protects a "right to commit suicide which itself includes a right to assistance in doing so," and concludes that our Nation's history, legal traditions, and practices do not support the existence of such a right. I join the Court's opinions because I agree that there is no generalized right to "commit suicide." But respondents urge us to address the narrower question whether a mentally competent person who is experiencing great suffering has a constitutionally cognizable interest in controlling the circumstances of his or her imminent death. I see no need to reach that question in the context of the facial challenges to the New York and Washington laws at issue here. The parties and *amici* agree that in these States a patient who is suffering from a terminal illness and who is experiencing great pain has no legal barriers to obtaining medication, from qualified physicians, to alleviate that suffering, even to the point of causing unconsciousness and hastening death. In this light, even assuming that we would recognize such an interest, I agree that the State's interests in protecting those who are not truly competent or facing imminent death, or those whose decisions to hasten death would not truly be voluntary, are sufficiently weighty to justify a prohibition against physician-assisted suicide.

JUSTICE STEVENS, concurring in the judgments.

There may be little distinction between the intent of a terminally-ill patient who decides to remove her life-support and one who seeks the assistance of a doctor in ending her life; in both situations, the patient is seeking to hasten a certain, impending death. The doctor's intent might also be the same in prescribing lethal medication as it is in terminating life support. A doctor who fails to administer medical treatment to one who is dying from a disease could be doing so with an intent to harm or kill that patient. Conversely, a doctor who prescribes lethal medication does not necessarily intend the patient's death — rather that doctor may seek simply to ease the patient's suffering and to comply with her wishes. The illusory character of any differences in intent or causation is confirmed by the fact that the American Medical Association unequivocally endorses the practice of terminal sedation — the administration of sufficient

---

respondents here.

    d. **JUSTICE GINSBURG** concurs in the Court's judgments substantially for the reasons stated in this opinion. **JUSTICE BREYER** joins this opinion except insofar as it joins the opinion of the Court.

dosages of pain-killing medication to terminally ill patients to protect them from excruciating pain even when it is clear that the time of death will be advanced. The purpose of terminal sedation is to ease the suffering of the patient and comply with her wishes, and the actual cause of death is the administration of heavy doses of lethal sedatives. This same intent and causation may exist when a doctor complies with a patient's request for lethal medication to hasten her death.

Thus, although the differences the majority notes in causation and intent between terminating life-support and assisting in suicide support the Court's rejection of the respondents' facial challenge, these distinctions may be inapplicable to particular terminally ill patients and their doctors. Our holding today in *Vacco v. Quill* that the Equal Protection Clause is not violated by New York's classification, just like our holding in *Washington v. Glucksberg* that the Washington statute is not invalid on its face, does not foreclose the possibility that some applications of the New York statute may impose an intolerable intrusion on the patient's freedom.

JUSTICE SOUTER, concurring in the judgment.

In my judgment, the importance of the individual interest here, as within that class of "certain interests" demanding careful scrutiny of the State's contrary claim, cannot be gainsaid. Whether that interest might in some circumstances, or at some time, be seen as "fundamental" to the degree entitled to prevail is not, however, a conclusion that I need draw here, for I am satisfied that the State's interests described in the following section are sufficiently serious to defeat the present claim that its law is arbitrary or purposeless.

The State has put forward several interests to justify the Washington law as applied to physicians treating terminally ill patients, even those competent to make responsible choices: protecting life generally, discouraging suicide even if knowing and voluntary, and protecting terminally ill patients from involuntary suicide and euthanasia, both voluntary and nonvoluntary.

It is not necessary to discuss the exact strengths of the first two claims of justification in the present circumstances, for the third is dispositive for me. That third justification is different from the first two, for it addresses specific features of respondents' claim, and it opposes that claim not with a moral judgment contrary to respondents', but with a recognized state interest in the protection of nonresponsible individuals and those who do not stand in relation either to death or to their physicians as do the patients whom respondents describe. * * * The State thus argues, essentially, that respondents' claim is not as narrow as it sounds, simply because no recognition of the interest they assert could be limited to vindicating those interests and affecting no others. The State says that the claim, in practical effect, would entail consequences that the State could, without doubt, legitimately act to prevent. * * *

Respondents propose an answer to all this, the answer of state regulation with teeth. Legislation proposed in several States, for example, would authorize physician-assisted suicide but require two qualified physicians to confirm the patient's diagnosis, prognosis, and competence; and would mandate that the patient make repeated requests witnessed by at least two others over a specified time span; and would impose reporting requirements and criminal penalties for various acts of coercion.

But at least at this moment there are reasons for caution in predicting the effectiveness of the teeth proposed. Respondents' proposals, as it turns out, sound much like the guidelines now in place in the Netherlands, the only place where experience with physician-assisted suicide and euthanasia has yielded empirical evidence about how such regulations might affect actual practice. Dutch physicians must engage in consultation before proceeding, and must decide whether the patient's decision is voluntary, well considered, and stable, whether the request to die is enduring and made more than once, and whether the patient's future will involve unacceptable suffering. There is, however, a substantial dispute today about what the Dutch experience shows. Some commentators marshal evidence that the Dutch guidelines have in practice failed to protect patients from involuntary euthanasia and have been violated with impunity. The day may come when we can say with some assurance which side is right, but for now it is the substantiality of the factual disagreement, and the alternatives for resolving it, that matter. They are, for me, dispositive of the due process claim at this time.

JUSTICE BREYER, concurring in the judgments.

I believe that Justice O'Connor's views, which I share, have greater legal significance than the Court's opinion suggests. I join her separate opinion, except insofar as it joins the majority. And I concur in the judgments. I shall briefly explain how I differ from the Court. * * *

Justice Harlan concluded that marital privacy was such a "special interest." He found in the Constitution a right of "privacy of the home" — with the home, the bedroom, and "intimate details of the marital relation" at its heart — by examining the protection that the law had earlier provided for related, but not identical, interests described by such words as "privacy," "home," and "family." The respondents here essentially ask us to do the same. They argue that one can find a "right to die with dignity" by examining the protection the law has provided for related, but not identical, interests relating to personal dignity, medical treatment, and freedom from state-inflicted pain.

I do not believe, however, that this Court need or now should decide whether or not such a right is "fundamental." That is because, in my view, the avoidance of severe physical pain (connected with death) would have to comprise an essential part of any successful claim and because, as Justice O'Connor points out, the laws before us do not force a dying person to undergo that kind of pain. Rather, the laws of New York and of Washington do not prohibit doctors from providing patients with drugs sufficient to control pain despite the risk that those drugs themselves will kill. And under these circumstances the laws of New York and Washington would overcome any remaining significant interests and would be justified, regardless.

Medical technology, we are repeatedly told, makes the administration of pain-relieving drugs sufficient, except for a very few individuals for whom the ineffectiveness of pain control medicines can mean, not pain, but the need for sedation which can end in a coma. We are also told that there are many instances in which patients do not receive the palliative care that, in principle, is available, but that is so for institutional reasons or inadequacies or obstacles, which would seem possible to overcome, and which do *not* include *a prohibitive set of laws.*

This legal circumstance means that the state laws before us do not infringe directly upon the (assumed) central interest (what I have called the core of the interest in dying with dignity) as, by way of contrast, the state anticontraceptive laws at issue in *Poe* did interfere with the central interest there at stake — by bringing the State's police powers to bear upon the marital bedroom.

Were the legal circumstances different — for example, were state law to prevent the provision of palliative care, including the administration of drugs as needed to avoid pain at the end of life — then the law's impact upon serious and otherwise unavoidable physical pain (accompanying death) would be more directly at issue. And as Justice O'Connor suggests, the Court might have to revisit its conclusions in these cases.

NOTES ON THE "RIGHT TO DIE" CASE

1. *The Holding and the Role of Precedent.* What exactly is the holding of this case? Note the seeming presence of two majorities: Five Justices (Rehnquist, O'Connor, Scalia, Kennedy, Thomas) join the opinion of the Court broadly dismissing right-to-die arguments, but five Justices (O'Connor, Stevens, Souter, Ginsburg, Breyer) write separately to reserve a number of issues. Under what circumstances, if any, has the Court left room for a potential constitutional claim? Would it matter if the risk of abuse was particularly small in a particular case? Would it matter if the individual's pain was not capable of being controlled by medication? One medical observer suggests that, in effect, by endorsing potentially lethal sedation of terminal patients (which is normally accompanied by withholding of hydration and nutrition), the Court has rejected assisted suicide only to embrace euthanasia. See David Orentlicher, *The Supreme Court and Physician-Assisted Suicide*, 337 New England J. of Med. 1236 (1997).

One intriguing aspect of this case is the handling of precedent. Chief Justice Rehnquist sidesteps any criticism of *Roe* or *Casey* (perhaps to retain the votes of Justices Kennedy and O'Connor). He also conspicuously avoids any reliance on *Bowers*, and the concurring Justices seem to feel no need to deal with that precedent, either. At this point, is the case law on substantive due process internally consistent, or has the Court been weaving from one side to the other?

2. *Approaches to Substantive Due Process.* The dispute between the majority and Justice Souter over methodology deserves careful attention. In effect, Justice Souter defends the approach taken in the Joint Opinion in *Casey*, which is evolutive in a common-law-like way and looks at general principles of history; the Chief Justice defends the approach the Court took in *Bowers* (without citing that case, by the way), which is more static and looks at specific historical practices. Which most adequately channels judicial discretion? Most effectively protects individual liberty? To what extent is the quality of public deliberation on the issue relevant to the constitutional question? Consider the observation that the "earnestness, profundity, and widespread nature of the

debate [over assisted suicide] reduced and perhaps eliminated the Court's relative advantage over legislatures in formulating relevant principles and bringing these principles to bear on contested general issues." Richard Fallon, *The Supreme Court, 1996 Term — Foreword: Implementing the Constitution*, 111 Harv. L. Rev. 54, 145 (1997).

3. *Substantive Due Process and Executive Action.* The issue in *County of Sacramento v. Lewis*, 523 U.S. 833 (1998), was whether a police officer violated substantive due process by causing death through "deliberate indifference to life" in the course of a high-speed chase. The Court held that "only a purpose to cause harm unrelated to the legitimate object of arrest will satisfy the element of arbitrary conduct shocking to the conscience, necessary for a due process violation." The Court called for a flexible, contextual approach to due process: "Rules of due process are not, however, subject to mechanical application. Deliberate indifference that shocks in one environment may not be so patently egregious in another, and our concern with preserving the constitutional proportions of substantive due process demands an exact analysis of circumstances before any abuse of power is condemned as conscience shocking." Justice Scalia, joined by Justice Thomas, concurred only in the judgment. He lambasted the Court for abandoning *Glucksberg*'s focus on whether the specific conduct in question violated an entrenched tradition.

Query: Under what circumstances, if any, might the application to a suspected terrorist of "harsh interrogation techniques" such as sleep deprivation or water-boarding violate due process?

PROBLEM 5-6
HUMAN CLONING

In response to the success of scientists in cloning a sheep, a special commission recommended a federal ban on cloning humans. At this writing, Congress is actively considering legislation on the subject. Critics of the proposal argue that cloning would have some clinical uses:

> [Consider] a couple each carrying a recessive gene for a serious disorder. Cloning would allow them to avoid conceiving an embryo with the disorder and facing selective abortion. In another case, a woman might carry a dominant gene for a disorder. Cloning would permit her to avoid genetic contribution from an egg donor and thus would keep the genetic parenting between the woman and her partner, something of value to many couples. Other cases would include a couple entirely lacking gametes.

Susan Wolf, *Ban Cloning? Why NAC Is Wrong*, 27 Hastings Center Report, Sept.-Oct. 1997, at 12, 13. Under the various opinions in *Glucksberg*, how would you analyze whether a complete ban on cloning would violate substantive due process?

SECTION 6. PROCEDURAL DUE PROCESS

A. INTRODUCTORY NOTES ON PROCEDURAL DUE PROCESS

1. *Procedural versus Substantive Due Process.* Whatever force there might be to the criticism that "substantive due process" is logically an oxymoron and without support in the Constitution's text and history, the Due Process Clauses of the Fifth and Fourteenth Amendments clearly have *some* content. Both amendments state that a person is entitled to "due process of law" before she is deprived of certain important interests by the government. Even if this language is given a purely procedural definition, it could still be a source of great protection against governmental abuse.

Suppose, for example, that the government establishes a rule that a supervisor can fire any employee he believes guilty of using illegal drugs. Neither public employment nor drug use is a fundamental right, nor are public employees a "suspect class." The basic policy of the statute seems immune to constitutional attack; presumably, it would not be hard to imagine a rational purpose. Thus, the state seems to be free to establish non-use of drugs as a criterion for public employment. But the application of this criterion seems to be left to the unchecked discretion of the supervisor, with no guarantee that the employee will have a right to be heard. The absence of a hearing process may violate procedural due process, even though no substantive constitutional right is involved.

2. *Due Process Values.* One important aspect of due process is a guarantee of procedural fairness in adjudication, whether in the courts or in trial-like hearings before administrative agencies. In *Marshall v. Jerrico, Inc.*, 446 U.S. 238 (1980), the Supreme Court explained some of the significant values underlying procedural due process:

> The Due Process Clause entitles a person to an impartial and disinterested tribunal in both civil and criminal cases. This requirement of neutrality in adjudicative proceedings safeguards the two central concerns of procedural due process, the prevention of unjustified or mistaken deprivations and the promotion of participation and dialogue by affected individuals in the decisionmaking process. The neutrality requirement helps to guarantee that life, liberty, or property will not be taken on the basis of an erroneous or distorted conception of the facts or the law. At the same time, it preserves both the appearance and reality of fairness, "generating the feeling, so important to a popular government, that justice has been done," by ensuring that no person will be deprived of his interests in the absence of a proceeding in which he may present his case with assurance that the arbiter is not predisposed to find against him.

Consider the "two central concerns of procedural due process" identified in *Jerrico.* The first is utilitarian — the government should not deprive a person of an important interest unless the correct understanding of the facts and the law allows it to do so. The second is normative and is often called the "dignitary" or "intrinsic" value to due process — even if the government may lawfully deprive someone of an important interest, respect for that individual demands that she have the opportunity to be heard by a neutral decisionmaker under fair proceedings before the deprivation occurs. In other words, one concern relates to the actuality of justice, and the other involves the appearance of justice.

3. *Rules versus Adjudications*. Note that these two concerns of procedural due process make the most sense in contexts in which a judge or administrative official is enforcing a governmental directive in a way that deprives an individual of life, liberty, or property. The utilitarian concern suggests that the individual should be allowed to show that the deprivation is not justified under the governmental directive or that the directive itself is unenforceable. The normative concern highlights the individual's dignitary interest in observing and participating in a procedure that has singled her out for a potentially grievous loss. In contrast, the Supreme Court has held that due process does not require a legislature or other governmental lawmaking body adopting a statute or rule that applies across a class of persons to provide any special procedural protections. The notion is that the lawmaking process provides all the process that is due. See *Bi-Metallic Investment Co. v. State Board of Equalization*, 239 U.S. 441 (1915) (state agency may increase the valuation of all taxable property in a jurisdiction without providing hearing). In such situations, providing procedural protections becomes much more impracticable — how can the legislature identify all the persons who might be affected and provide them prior notice and the opportunity to be heard? Perhaps special procedural protections are also less important: the democratic process allows citizens to participate and generally provides legitimacy for the statute or rule, and no individual has been singled out for disparate treatment. Moreover, trial-type hearings with individual witnesses may generate information too geared to their own variable circumstances and insufficiently attuned to the broader issues of policy that are before the legislature or agency.

This distinction may be clarified by an example. Suppose the legislature imposes a tax on anyone who owns more than two cars. In passing the statute, the legislature is under no duty to conduct hearings of any kind. But imposing the tax is a different story. A taxpayer must be given some opportunity to establish that she does not in fact own more than two cars. In short, legislative policy decisions (should car owners be taxed?) are not generally subject to procedural due process. (The idea of legislative due process (Chapter 2, § 3B), is an unconventional effort to impose some process restrictions on legislation, but even so, nothing like a conventional trial-type hearing is contemplated.) On the other hand, individualized fact-determinations (how many cars does Jane Doe own?) are usually subject to some due process requirements.

4. *Critical Definitional Issues*. The Due Process Clause leaves all of its terms undefined. Consider another simple example. Assume that someone receiving public assistance from the state gets a letter informing him that his benefits will be cut off at the end of the month. This is the first time he learns that any questions had been raised about his eligibility. Upon phoning the welfare office, he is informed that the only avenue of relief available to him is to write a letter of protest, which will be reviewed administratively at some point (perhaps months) in the future.

How do the words of the Due Process Clause apply to this situation? The man is certainly a person, and the state is taking away from (and therefore arguably "depriving") him of a benefit he has been enjoying. Beyond that, many questions arise. It is hard to consider his deprivation one of "life" — but what if he starves as a result of the loss of welfare? Should "liberty" include the ability to continue to rely upon governmental benefits? Could the benefits be considered "property"? To make the example even harder, consider a second person who has not been receiving welfare, considers herself eligible for it despite the government's rejection of her application, and is given no avenue to challenge the rejection of her application. In this situation, is the state even "depriving" her of anything? Could "liberty" or "property" be defined in a way to reach her situation? Note that we are again back in the quagmire of defining "baselines."

Assuming that either or both persons have suffered a deprivation of life, liberty, or property, the inquiry then turns to what "process" is "due." Here the questions relate to the formality and complexity of the required procedures. Must the state engage in trial-like proceedings before cutting off his benefits? Before denying benefits to her in the first place? If trial-like proceedings are unnecessary, what kind of process short of them will suffice? Once the basic format of the proceedings is ascertained, other important procedural questions remain: (1) Who bears the burden of proving the welfare recipient or applicant eligible or ineligible? (2) What is the burden of proof (beyond a reasonable doubt, or by a clear and convincing evidence, or by a preponderance of the evidence)? (3) May the recipient or applicant be represented by an attorney? (4) If the recipient cannot afford counsel, must the state provide some form of assistance? (5) Is there a right to confront and cross-examine adverse witnesses? (6) Must an administrative appeal and/or the chance to challenge the administrative decision in court be made available? And so on.

Note that in considering what process is due, the two values identified in *Jerrico* can point in different directions. The utilitarian concern might suggest that the determination of what process is due should be done by cost/benefit analysis (balancing the cost of additional procedures against their utilitarian value — i.e., the product of the likelihood that they would prevent erroneous deprivations and the magnitude of those deprivations). The dignitary or intrinsic value to due process might suggest that better procedures are required as long as they do not unduly burden the government and tend to foster the appearance of justice and to reduce psychological harm.[e]

---

e. For example, suppose that you believe that you did far better on a law school examination than the grade awarded for your performance. Assuming that some process should be available to you in these circumstances (maybe your "contract" with the law school constitutes a "property" interest and contains an implied term of fair grading), is it enough for the school to require the professor to provide you a short written, truthful response, such as "I graded the exam according to my usual grading processes, which include anonymous grading, and thus you were treated just like everyone else"? Or should the professor be required to discuss the exam with you, or even regrade it? The written response might satisfy the utilitarian value of due process, since requiring any additional procedure is very unlikely to result in a change of grade and would involve some burden to the professor. The dignitary or intrinsic value of due process is premised on the notion that you'll justifiably feel better if, at a minimum, the professor stares you in the eye and tells you personally, even if your grade remains the same.

5. *The Interplay Between Federal and State Law.* Before we turn to a consideration of current doctrine, we should alert you to an issue that many students find confusing: the interplay between federal and state law in procedural due process cases. When a state program does not involve any substantive constitutional right, the state has a virtually free hand over eligibility standards. Thus, for example, it is up to the state to decide the requirements for revoking a driver's license. Consequently, we have to look to *state law* to answer the following question: "What factual findings are necessary to determine continued eligibility for this benefit?" The character of the inquiry changes, however, when we switch from the question of standards for driver's licenses to that of procedure, where we must decide whether denial of a driver's license triggers procedural due process at all and if so, whether the state's procedures are sufficient. At this point, *federal law* takes over with the following two questions: First, given the way the state has structured the benefit, does the benefit amount to the kind of "liberty" or "property" protected by the Due Process Clause? Second, if the Due Process Clause does apply, do the state-established procedures for awarding the benefit provide "enough of a hearing"? Thus, the state has great leeway in determining eligibility standards, but it is up to federal law whether to apply the liberty or property labels and to determine if procedures are adequate.

6. *Introduction to the Doctrinal Debate.* Prior to the 1960s, the Supreme Court tended to look to the common law for guidance in defining what constituted a "liberty" or "property" interest. If one of these interests was present, the Court ordinarily assumed that the "process" that was "due" included notice and an opportunity to be heard before the deprivation occurred.

The common law considered government benefits (public employment, welfare, and so on) mere privileges rather than rights. Thus, due process was not triggered when a public employee lost her job or a recipient of governmental benefits like welfare or social security was cut off from those funds. In essence, this approach allowed the government to grant the "privilege" subject to whatever conditions the government chose to impose, including revocation without any accompanying procedural protections. The absence of procedural protections in these circumstances may seem harsh, however, in light of the post-New Deal expansion in the role of government as employer, regulator, and provider of "social security" in the broad sense.

Professor Charles Reich argued in *The New Property*, 73 Yale L.J. 733 (1964), that the promised receipt of state benefits constituted an "entitlement" that is the "new property" characteristic of life in the modern regulatory state. The nascent welfare rights movement seized upon this idea as the basis for arguing that the state could not arbitrarily cut off welfare benefits. Their efforts bore almost immediate doctrinal fruit.

———

Goldberg v. Kelly, 397 U.S. 254 (1970). Welfare recipients challenged the termination of their benefits without a prior evidentiary hearing. Citing Reich's article, **Justice Brennan**'s opinion for the Court ruled that the continued receipt of welfare benefits is *property* whose deprivation triggers the protections of the Due Process Clause. "Such benefits are a matter of statutory entitlement for persons qualified to receive them. Their termination involves state action that adjudicates important rights."

As to the *process* that is *due*, Brennan suggested: "The extent to which procedural due process must be afforded the recipient is influenced by the extent to which he may be 'condemned to suffer grievous loss,' *Joint Anti-Fascist Refugee Committee v. McGrath*, 341 U.S. 123, 168 (1951) (Frankfurter, J., concurring), and depends upon whether the recipient's interest in avoiding that loss outweighs the governmental interest in summary adjudication." "Welfare provides the means to obtain essential food, clothing, housing, and medical care. Thus the crucial factor in this context * * * is that termination of aid pending resolution of a controversy over eligibility may deprive an eligible recipient of the very means by which to live while he waits." Moreover, "important governmental interests are promoted by affording recipients a pre-termination evidentiary hearing. From its founding the Nation's basic commitment has been to foster the dignity and well-being of all persons within its borders. We have come to recognize that forces not within the control of the poor contribute to their poverty. This perception, against the background of our traditions, has significantly influenced the development of the contemporary public assistance system. Welfare, by meeting the basic demands of subsistence, can help bring within the reach of the poor the same opportunities that are available to others to participate meaningfully in the life of the community. At the same time, welfare guards against the societal malaise that may flow from a widespread sense of unjustified frustration and insecurity. Public assistance, then, is not mere charity, but a means to 'promote the general Welfare, and secure the Blessings of Liberty to ourselves and our Posterity.' The same governmental interests that counsel the provision of welfare, counsel as well its uninterrupted provision to those eligible to receive it; pre-termination evidentiary hearings are indispensable to that end." The state's justification, resting on the conservation of "fiscal and administrative resources," could not offset these interests.

Chief Justice Burger and **Justices Black** and **Stewart** dissented. Justice Black objected to the essentially legislative nature of the Court's balancing. "I would have little, if any, objection to the majority's decision in this case if it were written as the report of the House Committee on Education and Labor, but as an opinion ostensibly resting on the language of the Constitution I find it woefully deficient. * * * Although the majority attempts to bolster its decision with limited quotations from prior cases, it is obvious that today's result does not depend on the language of the Constitution itself or the principles of other decisions, but solely on the collective judgment of the majority as to what would be a fair and humane procedure in this case." Invoking his famous debate with Justice Frankfurter in *Adamson* (§ 1 of this chapter), Justice Black charged that "fairness" approaches to the Due Process Clause, unmoored to the constitutional text or original intent, were invitations to jurocracy. "In fact, if that view of due process is correct, the Due Process Clause could easily swallow up all other parts of the Constitution. And truly the Constitution would always be 'what the judges say it is' at a given moment, not what the Founders wrote into the document. A written constitution, designed to guarantee protection against governmental abuses, including those of judges, must have written standards that mean something definite and have an explicit content."

Goldberg was, as Justice Black feared, a potentially revolutionary opinion. But once the four Nixon Justices were in place, the *Goldberg* revolution was tamed at both ends of its analysis — what government benefits were entitlements triggering due process protection (Part B of this section) and what protection would be triggered (Part C). As you read the following materials, consider whether they meet Justice Black's demand that the Due Process Clause be construed by reference to standards that "mean something definite and have an explicit content."

B.   DEFINING "LIBERTY" AND "PROPERTY"

Almost all law schools have parking problems. Suppose an employee of a state law school arrives at work one morning and discovers that his parking permit has been canceled. Presumably, the right to a workplace parking space is not "fundamental to ordered liberty," even under the most generous conception of that concept. But is the employee at least entitled to an explanation of the decision or a chance to contest it? It would seem in the abstract that the answer might be influenced by either an evaluation of the importance of the employee's interest and the utility of providing some procedures, or whether the law school's rules limit the administrator's discretion in lifting the permit, so the employee might be able to force a favorable decision at the hearing. It might also be relevant if the school gave a damaging explanation for the decision — for instance, perhaps the employee should get some kind of hearing before the school issued an interoffice memo announcing that the permit was lifted because the employee was a drunken driver. Consider, in light of the following materials, whether the Court has picked the right factors for determining whether the right to due process exists in a given situation.

BOARD OF REGENTS v. ROTH
408 U.S. 564, 92 S.Ct. 2701, 33 L.Ed.2d 548 (1972)

JUSTICE STEWART delivered the opinion of the Court.

[Roth was hired to teach at a state university for one year, and he lacked "tenure" under state law. The university president informed him that he would not be rehired, giving no reason for the decision and providing Roth no opportunity to challenge it. The president's action complied with state law and university rules. Roth contended that the failure to provide him a statement of reasons and a hearing violated due process. The Supreme Court ruled against Roth's claim.]

The requirements of procedural due process apply only to the deprivation of interests encompassed by the Fourteenth Amendment's protection of liberty and property. When protected interests are implicated, the right to some kind of prior hearing is paramount.[f] But the range of interests protected by procedural due process is not infinite.

The District Court decided that procedural due process guarantees apply in this case by assessing and balancing the weights of the particular interests involved. It concluded that the respondent's interest in re-employment at [the University] outweighed the University's interest in denying him re-employment summarily. Undeniably, the respondent's re-employment prospects were of major concern to him — concern that we surely cannot say was insignificant. And a weighing process has long been a part of any determination of the *form* of hearing required in particular situations by procedural due process. But, to determine whether due process requirements apply in the first place, we must look not to the "weight" but to the *nature* of the interest at stake. We must look to see if the interest is within the Fourteenth Amendment's protection of liberty and property.

* * * [T]he Court has fully and finally rejected the wooden distinction between "rights" and "privileges" that once seemed to govern the applicability of procedural due process rights. The Court has also made clear that the property interests protected by procedural due process extend well beyond actual ownership of real estate, chattels, or money. By the same token, the Court has required due process protection for deprivations of liberty beyond the sort of formal constraints imposed by the criminal process.

Yet, while the Court has eschewed rigid or formalistic limitations on the protection of procedural due process, it has at the same time observed certain boundaries. For the words "liberty" and "property" in the Due Process Clause of the Fourteenth Amendment must be given some meaning.

"While this Court has not attempted to define with exactness the liberty . . . guaranteed [by the Fourteenth Amendment], . . . [w]ithout doubt, it denotes not merely freedom from bodily restraint but also the right of the individual to contract, to engage in any of the common occupations of life, to acquire useful knowledge, to marry, establish a home and bring up children, to worship God according to the dictates of his own conscience, and generally to enjoy those privileges long recognized . . . as essential to the orderly pursuit of happiness by free men." *Meyer*.

There might be cases in which a State refused to reemploy a person under such circumstances that interests in liberty would be implicated. But this is not such a case. [Justice Stewart stressed that it would be "a different case" if the State had made "any charge against him that might seriously damage his standing and associations in his community," because " '[w]here a person's good name, reputation, honor, or integrity is at stake because of what the government is doing to him, notice and an opportunity to be heard are essential.' *Wisconsin v. Constantineau*, 400 U.S. 433, 437 (1971)." There was also "no

---

f. Before a person is deprived of a protected interest, he must be afforded opportunity for some kind of a hearing, "except for extraordinary situations where some valid governmental interest is at stake that justifies postponing the hearing until after the event." *Boddie v. Connecticut*, 401 U.S. 371, 379 [1971]. * * *

suggestion that the State, in declining to re-employ the respondent, imposed on him a stigma or other disability that foreclosed his freedom to take advantage of other employment opportunities."]

The Fourteenth Amendment's procedural protection of property is a safeguard of the security of interests that a person has already acquired in specific benefits. These interests — property interests — may take many forms.

Thus, the Court has held that a person receiving welfare benefits under statutory and administrative standards defining eligibility for them has an interest in continued receipt of those benefits that is safeguarded by procedural due process. *Goldberg v. Kelly.* Similarly, in the area of public employment, the Court has held that a public college professor dismissed from an office held under tenure provisions, and college professors and staff members dismissed during the terms of their contracts have interests in continued employment that are safeguarded by due process. The Court [has also] held that this principle "proscribing summary dismissal from public employment without hearing or inquiry required by due process" also applied to a teacher recently hired without tenure or a formal contract, but nonetheless with a clearly implied promise of continued employment.

* * * To have a property interest in a benefit, a person clearly must have more than an abstract need or desire for it. He must have more than a unilateral expectation of it. He must, instead, have a legitimate claim of entitlement to it. It is a purpose of the ancient institution of property to protect those claims upon which people rely in their daily lives, reliance that must not be arbitrarily undermined. It is a purpose of the constitutional right to a hearing to provide an opportunity for a person to vindicate those claims.

Property interests, of course, are not created by the Constitution. Rather, they are created and their dimensions are defined by existing rules or understandings that stem from an independent source such as state law — rules or understandings that secure certain benefits and that support claims of entitlement to those benefits. Thus, the welfare recipients in *Goldberg* had a claim of entitlement to welfare payments that was grounded in the statute defining eligibility for them. The recipients had not yet shown that they were, in fact, within the statutory terms of eligibility. But we held that they had a right to a hearing at which they might attempt to do so.

Just as the welfare recipients' "property" interest in welfare payments was created and defined by statutory terms, so the respondent's "property" interest in employment at [the University] was created and defined by the terms of his appointment. Those terms secured his interest in employment up to June 30, 1969. But the important fact in this case is that they specifically provided that the respondent's employment was to terminate on June 30. They did not provide for contract renewal absent "sufficient cause." Indeed, they made no provision for renewal whatsoever.

Thus, the terms of the respondent's appointment secured absolutely no interest in re-employment for the next year. They supported absolutely no possible claim of entitlement to re-employment. Nor, significantly, was there any state statute or University rule or policy that secured his interest in re-employment or that created any legitimate claim to it. In these circumstances, the respondent surely had an abstract concern in being rehired, but he did not have a *property* interest sufficient to require the University authorities to give him a hearing when they declined to renew his contract of employment.

[JUSTICE POWELL took no part in the decision. The concurring opinion of CHIEF JUSTICE BURGER and the dissenting opinions of JUSTICES DOUGLAS, BRENNAN, and MARSHALL are omitted.]

NOTES ON DEFINING "PROPERTY" AND "LIBERTY"

1. *Defining "Property": Entitlements.* *Roth* rejected one plausible interpretation of *Goldberg* (which was followed by the lower court in *Roth*): that "property" in the administrative state might include all of the many important economic interests flowing from the government. *Roth* did not go all the way back to the old common law right/privilege distinction, however. At common law a public employee had no right to employment, and his or her working terms were purely a matter of contract. *Roth* recognizes that a bona fide expectation of continuing employment arising from state law is "property" for due process purposes.[g] After *Roth*, does an applicant for welfare who is not currently receiving benefits qualify for due process protection? (Hint: Note how *Roth* conceptualizes the interests safeguarded by "[t]he Fourteenth Amendment's procedural protection of property," just before it discusses *Goldberg*. This is just dictum, however, and the Court has never definitively resolved the issue.) Determining whether state law creates an "entitlement" is no easy task. Compare, e.g., *Bishop v. Wood*, 426 U.S. 341 (1976) (police officer held job at will of city despite being classified as "permanent employee") with *Goss v. Lopez*, 419 U.S. 565 (1975) (school children were deprived of a property interest by their temporary suspension from school because state law stated that students could be suspended only for "misconduct").

2. *The Purposes of a Hearing.* In the introduction to this section, we remarked that policy decisions normally do not require due process, but individualized fact-finding does. *Roth* can be seen as resting on a similar concept. If a person is an "employee at will," the decision of whether to retain him or her is essentially an open-ended policy decision, in which individual traits, financial considerations, and institutional priorities may all factor in. Indeed, at common law, an employee at will could be discharged for any reason or no reason at all ("I felt like it" is an adequate legal justification for the employer). On the other hand, a tenured employee can only be discharged on specific grounds, and thus the discharge will involve narrowly focused factual inquiries. Or, to put it another way, the tenured employee can prevail by proving certain facts at the hearing, while the untenured employee can be fired no matter what facts she can prove at the hearing. So the hearing serves a clear instrumental purpose for the tenured employee, but not for the employee at will.

---

g. In a companion case, *Perry v. Sindermann*, 408 U.S. 593 (1972), the Court held that a professor had a property interest in continued employment, even if his college had no formal contractual tenure system, so long as the college and he had a mutual expectation that his employment would be renewed each year.

Of course, even the employee at will might gain some benefit from the opportunity to have a dialogue with the employer, not to mention whatever intangible elements of personal respect accompany the right to a hearing. *Roth* and other cases, however, take a more hardboiled approach — a hearing is only required if the individual can legally *force* the government to make a favorable decision by proving certain facts.

3. *The Consequences of Finding "Property": A Rejection of "the Bitter with the Sweet" Argument.* If the entitlement under state law is shown, then "property" is present and procedural due process applies notwithstanding any procedural conditions found in the employee's contract. *Cleveland Board of Education v. Loudermill*, 470 U.S. 532 (1985), demonstrates how this approach works. An employee fired by the school board contended that he should have been granted a pretermination hearing. The Supreme Court first asked whether he had a "property" interest for procedural due process purposes. It concluded that he did because Ohio statutes provided that "classified civil service employees" like him were entitled to retain their positions "during good behavior and efficient service" and could not be dismissed except for "misfeasance, malfeasance, or nonfeasance in office." Next, the Court asked whether the procedures accorded him complied with procedural due process, and it concluded that they did not. But the same Ohio statutes that created an entitlement to future employment also purported to specify the procedures for termination. Should this matter — should the claimant have to accept the "bitter" (procedural limitations) with the "sweet" (the entitlement)? Rejecting the plurality opinion in *Arnett v. Kennedy*, 416 U.S. 134 (1974), the Court considered it irrelevant that the school board had followed the statutory procedures:

> [T]he "bitter with the sweet" approach misconceives the constitutional guarantee. * * * [T]he Due Process Clause provides that certain substantive rights — life, liberty, and property — cannot be deprived except pursuant to constitutionally adequate procedures. The categories of substance and procedure are distinct. Were the rule otherwise, the Clause would be reduced to a mere tautology. "Property" cannot be defined by the procedures provided for its deprivation any more than can life or liberty. The right to due process "is conferred, not by legislative grace, but by constitutional guarantee. While the legislature may elect not to confer a property interest in [public] employment, it may not constitutionally authorize the deprivation of such an interest, once conferred, without appropriate procedural safeguards."

4. *Liberty Interests.* Many government actions do not directly deprive an individual of property, even in the broad form of government assistance, and yet cause substantial hardship. Some of these government actions invade "liberty interests," as defined for procedural due process purposes. Prior to *Roth* the courts relied upon common law conceptions (e.g., false imprisonment, battery) for guidance in defining "liberty." Hence, the government may accomplish physical restraint (e.g., imprisonment) or physical intrusion only if appropriate procedures are followed.[h] Speaking more broadly, in general an individual has been deprived of a "liberty interest" for procedural due process purposes if she

---

h. A post-*Roth* example is *Ingraham v. Wright*, 430 U.S. 651 (1977) (paddling of public-school children implicates liberty interest).

is the subject of a coercive government order prohibiting her from engaging in previously lawful activity. (In *Roth*, the Court found no such liberty interest when a person "simply is not rehired in one job but remains free as before to seek another." Contrast this with an order disbarring an attorney, who is then unable to seek a job in the field in which she is trained.) In some situations, a liberty interest might encompass a status, such as marriage or parental custody. Such a status will be considered a liberty interest if it has constitutional protection as a fundamental right. (Note the quotation from *Meyer* in *Roth*.)[i]

For example, suppose the state allows the mother of an illegitimate child to be deprived of parental rights whenever that decision is in "the best interests of the child," as determined by a judge after an *ex parte* hearing. She could make a substantive claim that the "best interests" standard is unconstitutional (because of her fundamental right relating to parenting, see again the excerpt from *Meyer* in *Roth*) and that the state must instead prove her unfitness to be a parent. She can also make a procedural claim that, whatever the substantive standard, an *ex parte* hearing violates her right to be heard before being deprived of such an important liberty interest. In practice, of course, she would usually want to make both claims: The only permissible substantive standard is unfitness, and the only permissible procedure is an adversary hearing.

5. *Liberty and Imprisonment.* Prisoners' cases have been a particularly troublesome area for defining liberty interests. If there is "a valid conviction, the criminal defendant has been constitutionally deprived of his liberty, to the extent that the State may confine him and subject him to the rules of its prison system so long as the conditions of confinement do not otherwise violate the Constitution." *Meachum v. Fano*, 427 U.S. 215 (1976) (holding that transfer from medium-security to maximum-security prison involved no liberty interest). But prisoners may sometimes still be able to claim a residual liberty interest. For example, the particular confinement at issue might not seem subsumed within the deprivation of liberty authorized by a criminal conviction. See *Vitek v. Jones*, 445 U.S. 480 (1980) (transfer from prison to state mental hospital for treatment involves a liberty interest because of resulting stigma and increased restrictions on action). Moreover, a protectable interest could be found if it is linked to a statutory entitlement. See *Board of Pardons v. Allen*, 482 U.S. 369 (1987) (parole statute created an expectancy of release).

6. *Procedural Due Process, Incorporation, and National Rules of Procedure.* As Justice Black's dissent in *Goldberg* explicitly argued, there is a connection between *Goldberg/Roth* and the "incorporation cases" of § 1 of this chapter. Most of these cases involved defendants' *procedural* rights in state criminal trials: rights against unreasonable searches and seizures (Fourth

---

i. *Roth*'s discussion of *Wisconsin v. Constantineau* might suggest that personal reputation is also a liberty interest. In *Paul v. Davis*, 424 U.S. 693 (1976), however, the Court held that due process was not triggered when police circulated a flyer to merchants that labeled a person a shoplifter. *Paul* concluded that injury to reputation, without some other injury, did not qualify as a deprivation of a liberty interest. (*Constantineau* thus could be conceptualized as involving an injury to reputation plus a ban on the purchase of liquor.) *Paul* is perhaps explicable as an attempt to avoid equating common law torts (e.g., libel) with due process liberty interests.

Amendment); against self-incrimination (Fifth Amendment); to a speedy trial by jury and to confront opposing witnesses (Sixth Amendment); and to reasonable punishments (Eighth Amendment). Justice Black would have incorporated all of them pursuant to the Due Process Clause, and the Court ultimately incorporated almost all of them — its announced approach of "selective incorporation" was less selective and more incorporation. The effect of this process was to create *national rights of criminal procedure*, applicable in state as well as federal courts. Note that many of the national rules — such as the right to counsel in criminal cases resulting in defendant's incarceration — are not drawn from the text or original intent of the Bill of Rights, but were Supreme Court glosses on the Constitution. And the Court used some of the state cases, like *Miranda v. Arizona*, to create new constitutional rights applicable to federal law enforcement as well. See *Dickerson v. United States*, 530 U.S. 428 (2000).

Although *Goldberg* was not the start of a revolution in welfare law, it stimulated poverty law cases that revolutionized state civil procedure. In *Fuentes v. Shevin*, 407 U.S. 67 (1972), for example, the Court ruled that the state could not enforce prejudgment attachments against consumers without a prior hearing. The Court has refined the *Fuentes* approach in such a way that it tracks the procedural protections the Court provides in Rule 65 of the Federal Rules of Civil Procedure for issuing temporary restraining orders: Judicial process usually cannot be used to attach or garnish a debtor's property until the debtor has had an opportunity to be heard (*Fuentes*); in the exceptional case where such opportunity would pose a genuine threat to the creditor's interest in the litigated property, the state can remove it into neutral hands only upon proof of such compelling need reviewed by a neutral officer of the court, the posting of a bond to protect the debtor's interest, and the availability of an immediate post-deprivation hearing. See *Connecticut v. Doehr*, 501 U.S. 1 (1991); *North Georgia Finishing Co. v. Di-Chem, Inc.*, 419 U.S. 601 (1975). These cases have contributed to the Court's longstanding (and pre-*Goldberg*) practice of creating national rules (or minimum standards) for state as well as federal civil practice under the aegis of a highly dynamic Due Process Clause. The Supreme Court's nationalizing tendency in civil procedure has also extended to rules of notice, see *Mullane v. Central Hanover Bank & Trust Co.*, 339 U.S. 306 (1950); personal jurisdiction, see *World-Wide Volkswagen Corp. v. Woodson*, 444 U.S. 286 (1980); waiver of procedural rights to notice and a chance to be heard, see *D.H. Overmyer v. Frick Co.*, 405 U.S. 174 (1972); pretrial discovery, see *Société Internationale v. Rogers*, 357 U.S. 197 (1958); joinder and class action practice, see *Amchem Products, Inc. v. Windsor*, 521 U.S. 591 (1997); and res judicata, see *Hansberry v. Lee*, 311 U.S. 32 (1940) — all decided under the Due Process Clause.

C. DEFINING "WHAT PROCESS IS DUE"

It is all very well to have the right to "due process" in a given situation, but this begs the question of what process is actually required. In various circumstances, the state might argue that anything from an informal phone call to a full-blown trial constituted the appropriate process. The following case is the leading authority on how to determine which procedures are required by due process. (Don't forget, however, that you must always consider the antecedent question raised above — whether *any* procedures *at all* are required by due process in a given situation.)

MATHEWS v. ELDRIDGE
424 U.S. 319, 96 S.Ct. 893, 47 L.Ed.2d 18 (1976)

JUSTICE POWELL delivered the opinion of the Court.

[The Social Security Act provides benefits to workers while they are disabled. When the state agency responsible for investigating ongoing eligibility believes that a recipient is no longer "disabled," it informs him or her that benefits may be terminated and that he or she may respond in writing and may furnish new evidence. If the agency decides to terminate benefits, a federal official must approve it before it takes effect. If benefits are terminated, there is a statutory right to an evidentiary hearing, and if the termination is shown to be erroneous the worker may receive benefits retroactively. Subsequent judicial review is also available. In this case, a worker whose benefits were terminated contended that the absence of a pretermination evidentiary hearing violated due process. The government conceded that these benefits were "property" for procedural due process purposes, but argued that the procedures in place provided all the process that was constitutionally due.]

This Court consistently has held that some form of hearing is required before an individual is finally deprived of a property interest. * * * The fundamental requirement of due process is the opportunity to be heard "at a meaningful time and in a meaningful manner." * * * [This] dispute centers upon what process is due prior to the initial termination of benefits, pending review. * * *

* * * "[D]ue process is flexible and calls for such procedural protections as the particular situation demands." Accordingly, resolution of the issue whether the administrative procedures provided here are constitutionally sufficient requires analysis of the governmental and private interests that are affected. More precisely, our prior decisions indicate that identification of the specific dictates of due process generally requires consideration of three distinct factors: First, the private interest that will be affected by the official action; second, the risk of an erroneous deprivation of such interest through the procedures used, and the probable value, if any, of additional or substitute procedural safeguards; and finally, the Government's interest, including the function involved and the fiscal and administrative burdens that the additional or substitute procedural requirement would entail. See, e.g., *Goldberg.* * * *

Since a recipient whose benefits are terminated is awarded full retroactive relief if he ultimately prevails, his sole interest is in the uninterrupted receipt of this source of income pending final administrative decision on his claim. * * *

[*Goldberg* is the only case in which] the Court [has] held that due process requires an evidentiary hearing prior to a temporary deprivation. It was emphasized there that welfare assistance is given to persons on the very margin of subsistence. * * * Eligibility for disability benefits, in contrast, is not based upon financial need [but rather upon the worker's average monthly earnings during the period prior to disability, his age, and other factors not directly related to financial need that are specified by statute].

As *Goldberg* illustrates, the degree of potential deprivation that may be created by a particular decision is a factor to be considered in assessing the validity of any administrative decisionmaking process. The potential deprivation here is generally likely to be less than in *Goldberg*, although the degree of difference can be overstated. * * * [T]o remain eligible for benefits a recipient must be "unable to engage in substantial gainful activity." 42 U.S.C. § 423. Thus, * * * there is little possibility that the terminated recipient will be able to find even temporary employment to ameliorate the interim loss.

* * * "[T]he possible length of wrongful deprivation of * * * benefits [also] is an important factor in assessing the impact of official action on the private interests." The Secretary concedes that the delay between a request for a hearing before an administrative law judge and a decision on the claim is currently between 10 and 11 months. Since a terminated recipient must first obtain a reconsideration decision as a prerequisite to invoking his right to an evidentiary hearing, the delay between the actual cutoff of benefits and final decision after a hearing exceeds one year.

In view of the torpidity of this administrative review process and the typically modest resources of the family unit of the physically disabled worker, the hardship imposed upon the erroneously terminated disability recipient may be significant. Still, the disabled worker's need is likely to be less than that of a welfare recipient. In addition to the possibility of access to private resources, other forms of government assistance will become available where the termination of disability benefits places a worker or his family below the subsistence level. In view of these potential sources of temporary income, there is less reason here than in *Goldberg* to depart from the ordinary principle, established by our decisions, that something less than an evidentiary hearing is sufficient prior to adverse administrative action.

An additional factor to be considered here is the fairness and reliability of the existing pretermination procedures, and the probable value, if any, of additional procedural safeguards. Central to the evaluation of any administrative process is the nature of the relevant inquiry. In order to remain eligible for benefits the disabled worker must demonstrate by means of "medically acceptable clinical and laboratory diagnostic techniques" that he is unable "to engage in any substantial gainful activity by reason of any *medically determinable* physical or mental impairment . . . ." In short, a medical assessment of the worker's physical or mental condition is required. This is a more sharply focused and easily documented decision than the typical determination of welfare entitlement. * * *

[T]he decision whether to discontinue disability benefits will turn, in most cases, upon "routine, standard, and unbiased medical reports by physician specialists" concerning a subject whom they have personally examined. * * * To be sure, credibility and veracity may be a factor in the ultimate disability assessment in some cases. But procedural due process rules are shaped by the risk of error inherent in the truthfinding process as applied to the generality of cases, not the rare exceptions. The potential value of an evidentiary hearing, or even oral presentation to the decisionmaker, is substantially less in this context than in *Goldberg*. * * *

[A]mici point to the significant reversal rate for appealed cases as clear evidence that the current process is inadequate. Depending upon the base selected and the line of analysis followed, the relevant reversal rates urged by the contending parties vary from a high of 58.6% for appealed reconsideration decisions to an overall reversal rate of only 3.3%. Bare statistics rarely provide a satisfactory measure of the fairness of a decision-making process. Their adequacy is especially suspect here since the administrative review system is operated on an open file basis. A recipient may always submit new evidence, and such submissions may result in additional medical examinations. Such fresh examinations were held in approximately 30% to 40% of the appealed cases in fiscal 1973, either at the reconsideration or evidentiary hearing stage of the administrative process. In this context, the value of reversal rate statistics as one means of evaluating the adequacy of the pretermination process is diminished. * * *

In striking the appropriate due process balance the final factor to be assessed is the public interest. This includes the administrative burden and other societal costs that would be associated with requiring, as a matter of constitutional right, an evidentiary hearing upon demand in all cases prior to the termination of disability benefits. The most visible burden would be the incremental cost resulting from the increased number of hearings and the expense of providing benefits to ineligible recipients pending decision. No one can predict the extent of the increase, but the fact that full benefits would continue until after such hearings would assure the exhaustion in most cases of this attractive option. Nor would the theoretical right of the Secretary to recover undeserved benefits result, as a practical matter, in any substantial offset to the added outlay of public funds. The parties submit widely varying estimates of the probable additional financial cost. We only need say that experience with the constitutionalizing of government procedures suggests that the ultimate additional cost in terms of money and administrative burden would not be insubstantial.

Financial cost alone is not a controlling weight in determining whether due process requires a particular procedural safeguard prior to some administrative decision. But the Government's interest, and hence that of the public, in conserving scarce fiscal and administrative resources is a factor that must be weighed. At some point the benefit of an additional safeguard to the individual affected by the administrative action and to society in terms of increased assurance that the action is just, may be outweighed by the cost. Significantly, the cost of protecting those whom the preliminary administrative process has identified as likely to be found undeserving may in the end come out of the pockets of the deserving since resources available for any particular program of social welfare are not unlimited.

But more is implicated in cases of this type than ad hoc weighing of fiscal and administrative burdens against the interests of a particular category of claimants. The ultimate balance involves a determination as to when, under our constitutional system, judicial-type procedures must be imposed upon administrative action to assure fairness. We reiterate the wise admonishment of Mr. Justice Frankfurter that differences in the origin and function of administrative agencies "preclude wholesale transplantation of the rules of procedure, trial, and review which have evolved from the history and experience of courts." The judicial model of an evidentiary hearing is neither a required, nor even the most effective, method of decisionmaking in all circumstances. The essence of due process is the requirement that "a person in jeopardy of serious loss [be given] notice of the case against him and opportunity to meet it." All that is necessary is that the procedures be tailored, in light of the decision to be made, to "the capacities and circumstances of those who are to be heard," *Goldberg*, to insure that they are given a meaningful opportunity to present their case. In assessing what process is due in this case, substantial weight must be given to the good-faith judgments of the individuals charged by Congress with the administration of social welfare programs that the procedures they have provided assure fair consideration of the entitlement claims of individuals. This is especially so where, as here, the prescribed procedures not only provide the claimant with an effective process for asserting his claim prior to any administrative action, but also assure a right to an evidentiary hearing, as well as to subsequent judicial review, before the denial of his claim becomes final.

[**JUSTICE STEVENS** took no part in the consideration or decision of this case. The dissenting opinion of **JUSTICE BRENNAN**, joined by **JUSTICE MARSHALL**, is omitted.]

NOTES ON DEFINING "WHAT PROCESS IS DUE"

1. *Utilitarianism and Due Process.* Does *Eldridge* slight the dignitary or intrinsic value of due process?[j] Note that the loss of disability benefits can be devastating. (Justice Brennan's dissent noted that because of the loss of benefits "there was a foreclosure upon the Eldridge home and the family's furniture was repossessed, forcing Eldridge, his wife, and their children to sleep in one bed.") Wouldn't the termination of benefits have far more legitimacy, at least in the eyes of the Eldridge family, if they had been heard in person before the cutoff occurred? From the standpoint of legal process values (e.g., creating judicially manageable standards, discouraging continuous litigation on an issue), would a more categorical approach be preferable to case-by-case application of the *Eldridge* balancing approach? (On balancing, see pp. 541-42, *supra*.) In considering questions of efficiency, fairness, and individual dignity, one should not ignore the possibility that the greater the procedural rights accorded, the greater will be the state's expenses in administering a program, which may reduce the amount of benefits available for bona fide claimants.

---

j. See Jerry Mashaw, *The Supreme Court's Due Process Calculus for Administrative Adjudication in* Mathews v. Eldridge*: Three Factors in Search of a Theory of Value*, 44 U. Chi. L. Rev. 28 (1976).

2. *Determining "What Process Is Due."* In considering "what process is due," several central questions arise. One is the question of *timing*: may a prompt post-deprivation hearing suffice, or must there be a hearing prior to the deprivation? Another is the question of *formality*: the possibilities for a hearing extend from an oral, evidentiary trial before a neutral tribunal to a decision by a government official involved in the dispute based on a written or brief oral record, with none of the rights described above. As one would predict in light of *Eldridge*, the Court has answered the question of "what process is due" on a case-by-case basis, and it seems impossible to generalize about the issue in the space available to us. At one extreme remains *Goldberg v. Kelly*, which requires that a welfare recipient be allowed to retain an attorney (at his or her own expense) and receive "timely and adequate notice detailing the reasons for a proposed termination, and an effective opportunity to defend by confronting any adverse witnesses and by presenting his own arguments and evidence orally."

At the other end of the continuum are cases in which the Court found a liberty or property interest but nonetheless almost entirely deferred to the existing state scheme. For example, in *Ingraham v. Wright*, 430 U.S. 651 (1977), the Court concluded that the "paddling" of students in public schools involved a liberty interest, but said that the availability of a later tort action under state law to obtain damages provided "what process is due" in these circumstances. Another illustration is *Goss v. Lopez*, 419 U.S. 565 (1975). In *Goss*, the Court held that suspension of students from public schools for disciplinary reasons involved both a property interest (because state law said that students could be suspended only for "misconduct") and a liberty interest. Yet the process "due" in these circumstances was only a conversation before the suspension in which the school official told the student of the charge against her, informed her of the evidence supporting the charge, and provided her an opportunity to give her side of the events.

3. *Due Process and Especially Sensitive Areas of Liberty.* Although most of the "action" in recent years has involved accommodating procedural due process to the modern administrative state, other decisions have considered what process is due outside the administrative context. For example, in addition to retaining the longstanding "beyond a reasonable doubt" approach to the burden of proof in criminal cases, the Court has held that "clear and convincing evidence" rather than a mere preponderance of the evidence is the required burden of proof in other sensitive areas of loss of liberty. See *Santosky v. Kramer*, 455 U.S. 745 (1982) (termination of parental rights with respect to child requires clear and convincing evidence of statutory criteria); *Addington v. Texas*, 441 U.S. 418 (1979) (involuntary commitment of adult to mental hospital requires clear and convincing evidence that person is dangerous to him/herself or to others).

In *Little v. Streater*, 452 U.S. 1 (1981), the Supreme Court ruled that due process required the state to provide indigent male defendants in paternity suits with free paternity testing. But the same day, the Court ruled that the Due Process Clause does not assure an indigent mother free counsel in an adversary proceeding initiated by the state to terminate her parental rights. Justice

Stewart's opinion for the Court in *Lassiter v. Department of Social Servs.*, 452 U.S. 18 (1981), noted that a man accused of a misdemeanor cannot constitutionally be sentenced to one day in jail without representation by appointed counsel. But this reflects a presumption that an indigent litigant has a right to appointed counsel only when, if he loses, he may be deprived of his physical liberty. The indigent mother, the Court concluded, was entitled to counsel only if the *Eldridge* factors — the private interest at stake, the government's interest, and the risk that the procedures used will lead to erroneous decisions — were satisfied. Because the parent's interest in the accuracy and justice of the decision to terminate parental status is a "commanding" one, the state shares with the parent an interest in a correct decision and has a relatively weak pecuniary interest in avoiding the expense of appointed counsel and the cost of the lengthened proceedings his presence may cause, and judges as well as litigants believe that appointed counsel would both facilitate parental termination hearings and prevent arbitrary terminations, the Court ruled that *in some cases* the *Eldridge* factors would be able to overcome the presumption against counsel. But the Court found the added value of counsel insufficient to overcome the presumption in Lassiter's case.

PROBLEM 5-7
ISSUES OF PROCEDURAL DUE PROCESS

(a) Under state law, it is illegal in some circumstances to discharge an employee because of a physical disability. Logan filed a claim with the state agency, which triggered the agency's obligation to begin a proceeding within 120 days. The agency scheduled the proceeding five days after that period, and the state courts held that the failure to start the procedure in timely fashion deprived the agency of jurisdiction. Assess whatever constitutional claims Logan might have. See *Logan v. Zimmerman Brush Co.*, 455 U.S. 422 (1982).

(b) A school board requires pregnant schoolteachers to take an unpaid maternity leave, commencing five months before the expected birth. A school teacher objects that the board's "irrebuttable presumption" of incapacity to teach violates her due process rights. The board responds that the rule is substantive (*Lochner*-like) and not procedural (*Goldberg*-ish). Who wins? See *Cleveland Board of Education v. LaFleur*, 414 U.S. 632 (1974).

(c) A more dramatic due process question: In 2002, an American citizen was arrested as he entered the country. He was allegedly connected with a terrorist organization and was seeking to assemble a "dirty bomb" (one that would spread radioactive contaminants). Suppose that the government seeks to detain him indefinitely, both to allow questioning and to keep him from carrying through on the plan. Assume for present purposes that such a detention is not per se unconstitutional. Under the due process clause, does he have the right to some kind of a hearing regarding the allegations? If so, what procedures are required? [See *Hamdan v. Rumsfeld*, Chapter 8.]

Chapter 6

CIVIL SOCIETY, POLITICAL ACTION, AND THE FIRST AMENDMENT

One of our themes has been the role of social and political movements in helping to shape constitutional law. But constitutional law also helps create the context in which these movements function. It plays the same role with respect to religious groups, voluntary associations, media, and political groups. The First Amendment sets limits on government intrusions into these important aspects of civil society. It also limits government intrusion into public debate, thereby safeguarding the political process. In the course of providing this protection, however, it may leave some groups vulnerable to forms of discourse that help other, more entrench dominant groups.

In this regard, consider some key aspects of First Amendment law that bear on democracy and the political process:

- Dissident political groups can vehemently attack the government and other groups, so long as a communication does not pose an imminent risk of violence or constitute a true threat.

- The media, as well as other groups, can criticize public officials and public figures without restraint, so long as they do not make knowingly false statements of fact.

- Some forms of economic influence on the political process are subject to significant government regulations (such as direct candidate contributions), whereas others (such as independent expenditures to support a candidate) are constitutionally protected from regulation.

The First Amendment also sets rules governing regulation of inter-group relations. It limits the ability of government to smooth group relations by regulating speech that offends the members of particular groups. It sharply limits the ability of the government to prohibit verbal attacks on groups, speech that group members find demeaning, or speech that might encourage discrimination. In the cultural realm, groups are left free to act toward each other as they will, without any requirement of civility. And where religious groups are concerned, the First Amendment provides some protection of group practices (but not much), while limiting the ability of government to channel assistance to religious education or other church activities. Thus, the First Amendment plays an important role in deregulating some aspects of group relations, while imposing special regulations on how religious groups and government can interact.

Notably, although the First Amendment does a lot to set the ground rules for collective activities, the Court is much more prone to discuss the First Amendment in terms of *individual* rights. As you read this chapter, consider whether this emphasis is helpful or whether it obscures the First Amendment's role in setting ground rules for civil society.

SECTION 1. FREE SPEECH AND COMPETING VALUES

The Supreme Court has decided well over three hundred First Amendment cases, the majority of them since 1970. They deal with a wide range of factual and legal issues, from copyright law to nude dancing. It would be impossible to examine fully this enormous, complex body of case law, and we make no pretense of doing so. Instead, this chapter covers key aspects of First Amendment doctrine, while emphasizing applications that connect with our major theme.

Because the doctrine is so intricate, it is easy to become lost in the details. A brief overview may be helpful before we begin. Historically, the central struggle in free speech doctrine has involved subversive speech. It was only in the 1960s that the Supreme Court finally resolved that issue. At around the same time, the Court began giving serious attention to other categories of speech. Previously, obscenity, commercial advertising, and defamation had all been relegated to outlaw status, completely lacking in First Amendment protection. Today, the government still has authority to regulate speech falling into these categories, but that authority is subject to substantial restrictions. With regard to speech falling outside of these historic categories, the Court is extremely suspicious of government efforts to ban harmful messages. This rule against "content regulation" has become the centerpiece of current doctrine. This system of categories, combined with the rule against regulating other forms of content, is now fairly well settled. But the Court is much more forgiving of laws which ignore content completely and regulate only the time, place, or manner of speech.

The Court has also confronted a number of problems that do not fit neatly within this framework. First, there are several settings where the government seems to have a legitimate interest in controlling the content of speech. The Court has developed special doctrines to deal with many of these settings, involving speech by public employees, students, recipients of government grants, broadcasters, and others. These doctrines give the government more control over the content of speech than it is allowed to exercise over the general public. Second, the Court has developed another set of doctrines dealing with the form (rather than the substance) of government regulations. These doctrines require an unusual degree of precision in laws regulating speech. They also favor after-the-fact sanctions over before-the-fact restrictions on speech. Third, the Court has recognized a right of freedom of association, connected with (but distinct from) the right to free expression.

NOTE ON THE ORIGINAL UNDERSTANDING
OF FREEDOM OF SPEECH

As we saw in Chapter 2, there is considerable dispute about just how important original intent should be in constitutional interpretation, but almost no one denies its relevance. We begin our study of the First Amendment, then, with a quick look at its historical context.[a]

When the printing press was invented, governments were quick to respond. The new ability to circulate thousands of copies of a work threatened social stability and government authority. The response was a system of licensing for authors and printers. The poet John Milton was a prominent early critic of the sweeping censorship of the period. See Vincent Blasi, *Milton's Areopagitica and the Modern First Amendment*, 13 Communications Lawyer 1 (1996). By the mid-eighteenth century, however, the English were proud of themselves for having abolished this system. Indeed, for at least some, the absence of licensing was pretty much the definition of free speech. As Blackstone said, "the liberty of the press" consists of "laying no previous restraints upon publication," rather than "freedom from censure for criminal matter when published." Licensing makes a single censor the absolute authority over what is said. But punishing "any dangerous writings, which, when published, shall on a fair and impartial trial be adjudged of a pernicious tendency, is necessary for the preservation of peace and good order, of government and religion, the only solid foundations of civil liberty."

Even in England, Blackstone's definition of free speech was not universally accepted. Opposition writers (so-called because they opposed the group in power) emphasized that freedom of speech was a check on the power of tyrants. The opposition writers found a ready audience, where their theories helped provide the intellectual framework for the American Revolution. In the colonies, efforts to repress dissent were less frequent than in England. Probably the most notable was the Zenger trial. The governor of New York, whom Zenger had criticized, charged him with seditious libel. Contrary to existing English practice, his lawyers argued that he had a right to have the jury determine the truth of his remarks. One of his lawyers proclaimed the right "publicly to remonstrate the abuse of power in the strongest terms, to put their neighbors upon their guard against the craft of open violence of men in authority." The jury disobeyed its instructions from the judge and acquitted Zenger, to the accompaniment of loud cheers from the audience.

Unfortunately, the incomplete materials concerning the legislative history of the amendment shed little light about just what was meant by freedom of speech and of the press. The upshot is that the modern Supreme Court's interpretations of the First Amendment have drawn from this history, but the Court has rarely found decisive historical evidence on the issues before it. Instead, it has been

---

a. For background on this history, see Leonard Levy's books, *Legacy of Suppression: Freedom of Speech and Press in Early American History* (1960) and *Emergence of a Free Press* (1985), along with William Van Alstyne's review of the latter in 99 Harv. L. Rev. 1089 (1986).

guided largely by its interpretation of the First Amendment's purposes, with some deference to historical practices such as long-established regulations of obscenity and slander.

Before we begin any serious doctrinal exploration, it is important to consider the fundamental issues of why speech receives special constitutional protection and to what degree other values should be sacrificed in the name of free speech. The following two cases raise those issues.

TEXAS v. JOHNSON
491 U.S. 397, 109 S.Ct. 2533, 105 L.Ed.2d 342 (1989)

JUSTICE BRENNAN delivered the opinion of the Court.

After publicly burning an American flag [near the Republican National Convention] as a means of political protest, Gregory Lee Johnson was convicted of desecrating a flag in violation of Texas law.[b] This case presents the question whether his conviction is consistent with the First Amendment. We hold that it is not. * * *

Texas claims that its interest in preventing breaches of the peace justifies Johnson's conviction for flag desecration. However, no disturbance of the peace actually occurred or threatened to occur because of Johnson's burning of the flag. * * * The only evidence offered by the State at trial to show the reaction to Johnson's actions was the testimony of several persons who had been seriously offended by the flag-burning.

The State's position, therefore, amounts to a claim that an audience that takes serious offense at particular expression is necessarily likely to disturb the peace and that the expression may be prohibited on this basis. Our precedents do not countenance such a presumption. On the contrary, they recognize that a principal "function of free speech under our system of government is to invite dispute. It may indeed best serve its high purpose when it induces a condition of unrest, creates dissatisfaction with conditions as they are, or even stirs people to anger." It would be odd indeed to conclude *both* that "if it is the speaker's opinion that gives offense, that consequence is a reason for according it constitutional protection," *and* that the Government may ban the expression of certain disagreeable ideas on the unsupported presumption that their very disagreeableness will provoke violence. * * *

It remains to consider whether the State's interest in preserving the flag as a symbol of nationhood and national unity justifies Johnson's conviction.* * *

---

b. *Editors' note*: The Texas statute, entitled "Desecration of Venerated Object," provided:

(a) A person commits an offense if he intentionally or knowingly desecrates:
* * *
   (3) a state or national flag.

(b) For purposes of this section, "desecrate" means deface, damage, or otherwise physically mistreat in a way that the actor knows will seriously offend one or more persons likely to observe or discover his action.

(c) An offense under this section is a Class A misdemeanor.

If there is a bedrock principle underlying the First Amendment, it is that the Government may not prohibit the expression of an idea simply because society finds the idea itself offensive or disagreeable. * * *

Texas' focus on the precise nature of Johnson's expression, moreover, misses the point of our prior decisions: their enduring lesson, that the Government may not prohibit expression simply because it disagrees with its message, is not dependent on the particular mode in which one chooses to express an idea. If we were to hold that a State may forbid flag-burning wherever it is likely to endanger the flag's symbolic role, but allow it wherever burning a flag promotes that role — as where, for example, a person ceremoniously burns a dirty flag — we would be saying that when it comes to impairing the flag's physical integrity, the flag itself may be used as a symbol — as a substitute for the written or spoken word or a "short cut from mind to mind" — only in one direction. We would be permitting a State to "prescribe what shall be orthodox" by saying that one may burn the flag to convey one's attitude toward it and its referents only if one does not endanger the flag's representation of nationhood and national unity.

[The concurring opinion of **JUSTICE KENNEDY** is omitted.]

CHIEF JUSTICE REHNQUIST, with whom **JUSTICE WHITE** and **JUSTICE O'CONNOR** join, dissenting.

* * * The Court decides that the American flag is just another symbol, about which not only most opinions pro and con be tolerated, but for which the most minimal public respect may not be enjoined. The government may conscript men into the Armed Forces where they must fight and perhaps die for the flag, but the government may not prohibit the public burning of the banner under which they fight. I would uphold the Texas statute as applied in this case.

[**JUSTICE STEVENS'** dissenting opinion is omitted.]

R.A.V. v. CITY OF ST. PAUL
505 U.S. 377, 112 S.Ct. 2538, 120 L.Ed.2d 305 (1992)

JUSTICE SCALIA delivered the opinion of the Court.

In the predawn hours of June 21, 1990, petitioner and several other teenagers allegedly assembled a crudely-made cross by taping together broken chair legs. They then allegedly burned the cross inside the fenced yard of a black family that lived across the street from the house where petitioner was staying. Although this conduct could have been punished under any of a number of laws, one of the two provisions under which respondent city of St. Paul chose to charge petitioner (then a juvenile) was the St. Paul Bias-Motivated Crime Ordinance, which provides:

> Whoever places on public or private property a symbol, object, appellation, characterization or graffiti, including, but not limited to, a burning cross or Nazi swastika, which one knows or has reasonable grounds to know arouses anger, alarm or resentment in others on the basis of race, color, creed, religion or gender commits disorderly conduct and shall be guilty of a misdemeanor.

* * *

The First Amendment generally prevents government from proscribing speech, or even expressive conduct because of disapproval of the ideas expressed. Content-based regulations are presumptively invalid. From 1791 to the present, however, our society, like other free but civilized societies, has permitted restrictions upon the content of speech in a few limited areas, which are "of such slight social value as a step to truth that any benefit that may be derived from them is clearly outweighed by the social interest in order and morality." We have recognized that "the freedom of speech" referred to by the First Amendment does not include a freedom to disregard these traditional limitations. [Editors note: These exceptions include defamation, obscenity, and fighting words. According to the "fighting words" doctrine of *Chaplinsky v. New Hampshire*, 315 U.S. 568 (1942), the First Amendment does not protect personal insults against the audience that are likely to cause retaliation.] * * *

       * * *

In other words, the exclusion of "fighting words" from the scope of the First Amendment simply means that, for purposes of that Amendment, the unprotected features of the words are, despite their verbal character, essentially a "nonspeech" element of communication. Fighting words are thus analogous to a noisy sound truck: Each is, as Justice Frankfurter recognized, a "mode of speech," both can be used to convey an idea; but neither has, in and of itself, a claim upon the First Amendment. As with the sound truck, however, so also with fighting words: The government may not regulate use based on hostility — or favoritism — towards the underlying message expressed. * * *

Even the prohibition against content discrimination that we assert the First Amendment requires is not absolute. It applies differently in the context of proscribable speech than in the area of fully protected speech. * * *

When the basis for the content discrimination consists entirely of the very reason the entire class of speech at issue is proscribable, no significant danger of idea or viewpoint discrimination exists. Such a reason, having been adjudged neutral enough to support exclusion of the entire class of speech from First Amendment protection, is also neutral enough to form the basis of distinction within the class. To illustrate: A State might choose to prohibit only that obscenity which is the most patently offensive *in its prurience* — *i.e.*, that which involves the most lascivious displays of sexual activity. But it may not prohibit, for example, only that obscenity which includes offensive *political* messages. * * *

Another valid basis for according differential treatment to even a content-defined subclass of proscribable speech is that the subclass happens to be associated with particular "secondary effects" of the speech, so that the regulation is "*justified* without reference to the content of the . . . speech," *Renton v. Playtime Theatres, Inc.* [this chapter, § 3A]. A State could, for example, permit all obscene live performances except those involving minors. * * * Thus, for example, sexually derogatory "fighting words," among other words, may produce a violation of Title VII's general prohibition against sexual discrimination in employment practices. Where the government does not target conduct on the basis of its expressive content, acts are not shielded from regulation merely because they express a discriminatory idea or philosophy.

These bases for distinction refute the proposition that the selectivity of the restriction is "even arguably 'conditioned upon the sovereign's agreement with what a speaker may intend to say.'" There may be other such bases as well. Indeed, to validate such selectivity (where totally proscribable speech is at issue) it may not even be necessary to identify any particular "neutral" basis, so long as the nature of the content discrimination is such that there is no realistic possibility that official suppression of ideas is afoot. (We cannot think of any First Amendment interest that would stand in the way of a State's prohibiting only those obscene motion pictures with blue-eyed actresses.) Save for that limitation, the regulation of "fighting words," like the regulation of noisy speech, may address some offensive instances and leave other, equally offensive, instances alone.

Applying these principles to the St. Paul ordinance, we conclude that, even as narrowly construed by the Minnesota Supreme Court, the ordinance is facially unconstitutional. Although the phrase in the ordinance, "arouses anger, alarm or resentment in others," has been limited by the Minnesota Supreme Court's construction to reach only those symbols or displays that amount to "fighting words," the remaining, unmodified terms make clear that the ordinance applies only to "fighting words" that insult, or provoke violence, "on the basis of race, color, creed, religion or gender." Displays containing abusive invective, no matter how vicious or severe, are permissible unless they are addressed to one of the specified disfavored topics. Those who wish to use "fighting words" in connection with other ideas — to express hostility, for example, on the basis of political affiliation, union membership, or homosexuality — are not covered. The First Amendment does not permit St. Paul to impose special prohibitions on those speakers who express views on disfavored subjects.

In its practical operation, moreover, the ordinance goes even beyond mere content discrimination, to actual viewpoint discrimination. Displays containing some words — odious racial epithets, for example — would be prohibited to proponents of all views. But "fighting words" that do not themselves invoke race, color, creed, religion, or gender — aspersions upon a person's mother, for example — would seemingly be usable *ad libitum* in the placards of those arguing *in favor* of racial, color, etc. tolerance and equality, but could not be used by that speaker's opponents. One could hold up a sign saying, for example, that all "anti-Catholic bigots" are misbegotten; but not that all "papists" are, for that would insult and provoke violence "on the basis of religion." St. Paul has no such authority to license one side of a debate to fight freestyle, while requiring the other to follow Marquis of Queensbury Rules.
* * *

Let there be no mistake about our belief that burning a cross in someone's front yard is reprehensible. But St. Paul has sufficient means at its disposal to prevent such behavior without adding the First Amendment to the fire.

JUSTICE WHITE, with whom **JUSTICE BLACKMUN** and **JUSTICE O'CONNOR** join, and with whom **JUSTICE STEVENS** joins [in part], concurring in the judgment.

The majority's observation that fighting words are "quite expressive indeed" is no answer. Fighting words are not a means of exchanging views, rallying supporters, or registering a protest; they are directed against individuals to provoke violence or to inflict injury. Therefore, a ban on all fighting words or on a subset of the fighting words category would restrict only the social evil of hate speech, without creating the danger of driving viewpoints from the marketplace.

[Justice White disagreed with the Court's reasoning but agreed that the ordinance was invalid because it was "overbroad."]

[**JUSTICE BLACKMUN**'s opinion concurring in the judgment is omitted.]

JUSTICE STEVENS, with whom **JUSTICE WHITE** and **JUSTICE BLACKMUN** join as to Part I, concurring in the judgment.

* * * Just as Congress may determine that threats against the President entail more severe consequences than other threats, so St. Paul's City Council may determine that threats based on the target's race, religion, or gender cause more severe harm to both the target and to society than other threats. This latter judgment — that harms caused by racial, religious, and gender-based invective are qualitatively different from that caused by other fighting words — seems to me eminently reasonable and realistic.

NOTES ON *JOHNSON* AND *R.A.V.*

1. *Dissenting speech.* Flag burning, almost by definition, is not a form of mainstream expression. It derives its emotional punch from the very fact that the larger culture invests meaning in the flag. For some groups, such as veterans, this use of a venerated symbol may seem assaultive. Why is the Court unwilling to allow Congress to regulate this means of expression? Should it matter if this kind of expression is used by dissident groups to assault majority values rather than being used by dominant groups against marginalized ones?

2. *The Content Distinction.* Both the *Johnson* and *R.A.V.* stress that particular types of communication have been singled out for regulation because of their content. Suppose the defendants in these two cases had been prosecuted for starting a fire without a permit. Should enforcement of such laws against speakers be subject to anything more than the rationality test?

3. *Why do we protect speech?* Would society be the poorer if it were illegal to burn flags or crosses? Why do we bother protecting speech that offends what many consider to be basic national values?

NOTES ON FIRST AMENDMENT VALUES

1. *First Amendment Values.* There is an unusually large academic literature on the overall values served by the First Amendment. The following values are most frequently invoked. How well do they hold up? Do the flag-burning and cross-burning cases subserve the values that hold up?

(a) *The "marketplace of ideas" and the search for truth.* Truth cannot be decided by the fiat of a government authority, but only by a free and open debate. From the competition of ideas, truth will emerge. This is the teaching of John Stuart Mill, *On Liberty* (1859), and is important to both the decisions we have reproduced. But how does burning a cross on someone's lawn contribute to free and open debate, or to search for truth?

(b) *Systemic political values.* If people are to govern, they must first be informed. Hence, the channels of communication about political and social issues must be unimpaired. This is the teaching of Alexander Meiklejohn, *Free Speech and Its Relation to Self-Government* (1948), who analogizes the First Amendment's protection of informative public speech to the free flow of debate in a town meeting. (Is this a realistic vision?) Other systemic political values have been argued as a basis for privileging the First Amendment. For example, human beings have a tendency to be intolerant of people who are different from themselves or who espouse unfamiliar ideas. By carving out arenas where society restrains itself from suppressing not only disagreement but offensive behavior, the First Amendment encourages our polity to consider tolerance as a norm that might be fruitful elsewhere.[c]

(c) *Individualism and autonomy values.* Speech is a primary method for people to express their individuality and personhood. A libertarian would argue that the state must leave the individual alone when she is engaged in speech, unless there is compelling evidence of harm to the autonomy of others.[d] A communitarian would argue that the state should be encouraging individualism, anti-authoritarianism, and nonconformity.[e] Does either variation support the right of R.A.V. to burn a cross in the middle of the night? What about Johnson's right to burn a stolen flag?

2. *"Slippery Slopes," Absolutism, and Balancing.* While "slippery slope" arguments are found in other areas of the law, they are particularly prevalent in First Amendment cases, as *Johnson* illustrates. Part of the debate in *Johnson* involves the feasibility of treating flag burning differently from other forms of conduct. Justice Brennan argues that allowing a ban on flag burning will open the door to other forms of repression; Chief Justice Rehnquist believes that flag burning can be properly singled out for special treatment. (Note that Justice Scalia sided with Justice Brennan in *Johnson*, perhaps because he is a strong believer in "bright line" rules.) A generation ago, the major debate was between First Amendment "absolutists" and "balancers." Although the rhetoric was somewhat different, the methodological issue was similar: To what extent

---

c. This is the teaching of Lee Bollinger, *The Tolerant Society: Freedom of Speech and Extremist Speech in America* (1986), criticized in David Strauss, *Why Be Tolerant?*, 53 U. Chi. L. Rev. 1485 (1986).

d. See Edwin Baker, *Scope of the First Amendment Freedom of Speech*, 25 UCLA L. Rev. 964 (1978); Martin Redish, *The Value of Free Speech*, 130 U. Pa. L. Rev. 591 (1982).

e. See Steven Shiffrin, *The First Amendment, Democracy, and Romance* (1990). More recently, Shiffrin has stressed dissent as the core concern of the First Amendment. See Steven Shiffrin, *Dissent, Injustice, and the Meanings of America* (1999).

should speech be protected by broad categorical rules as opposed to more finely tuned, fact-sensitive standards?

The argument for broad categorical rules is based on the dynamics of censorship. Once allowed to operate at all, censorship gains acceptability and will tend to expand. Because the application of fact-sensitive doctrines is unpredictable, self-censorship will silence even those who might ultimately win if their cases were litigated. Moreover, the First Amendment is most needed in times of public hysteria, when careful weighing of the facts is most difficult, and when judges will be under the most pressure to bend to popular fears. Even in normal times, First Amendment cases often will involve the most despised members of society, and judges will often be tempted to give way to their own prejudices. Only categorical rules can protect against the ultimate erosion of First Amendment protection.

The counter-argument is that no set of rules can be effective if we do not trust the judges who administer them. If we trust the judges, we ought to allow them the leeway to consider the full range of facts relevant to a particular case, rather than limiting them with oversimplistic rules. First Amendment cases often involve conflicts between important social values, to which categorical rules simply cannot do justice.[f]

As applied to *Johnson*, which set of arguments is more convincing? Is it possible to give both viewpoints some credence, by using categorical rules in some areas and fact-sensitive balancing in others? In the *R.A.V.* situation, can we draw a workable line between cross burning and other forms of "speech"?[g]

In connection with the Equal Protection Clause, we considered a number of justifications for heightened judicial scrutiny. Do any of those justifications apply to *Johnson* or *R.A.V.*?

United States v. O'Brien, 391 U.S. 367 (1968). One of the major issues in *Johnson* is the extent to which the Constitution protects "symbolic speech" — that is, the use of nonverbal methods of expression. *O'Brien*, which involved draft-card burning, is the leading case on this issue. In an opinion by **Chief Justice Warren**, the Court upheld O'Brien's conviction for burning his draft card at an anti-war rally, on the ground that the government had valid reasons for protecting draft cards that had nothing to do with O'Brien's message. (It was clear from the legislative history, however, that the legislative motive was to target dissenters; nevertheless, in this pre-*Washington v. Davis* decision, the Court said that legislative motivation was irrelevant.) In the course of the opinion, the Court laid down the following four-part test to be applied when

---

f. For discussions of these issues, see Frederick Schauer, *The Second-Best First Amendment*, 31 Wm. & Mary L. Rev. 1 (1989); Kathleen Sullivan, *Post-Liberal Judging: The Roles of Categorization and Balancing*, 63 U. Colo. L. Rev. 293 (1992).

g. For a discussion of *R.A.V.* and the current evolution of the categorical approach, see Keith Werhan, *The Liberalization of Freedom of Speech on a Conservative Court*, 80 Iowa L. Rev. 51 (1994).

" 'speech' and 'non-speech' elements are combined in the same course of conduct":

> [A] government regulation is sufficiently justified if it is within the constitutional power of the Government; if it furthers an important or substantial governmental interest; if the governmental interest is unrelated to the suppression of free expression; and if the incidental restriction on alleged First Amendment freedoms is no greater than is essential to the furtherance of that interest.

At the time, *O'Brien* was mostly considered to be a "symbolic speech" case, although its test has now been applied in many other contexts. *O'Brien* and subsequent cases distinguish sharply between content-based restrictions and content-neutral regulations.[h]

SECTION 2. REGULATION OF POLITICAL EXPRESSION

It is commonly agreed that political speech is at the "core" of the First Amendment. Indeed, some theorists would provide protection only to political speech. In this section, we consider the circumstances under which such speech is protected and those in which, despite its core status, it can nevertheless be regulated. We begin by reviewing some history, including some classical opinions that are universally classed as part of the First Amendment canon.

A. ILLEGAL ADVOCACY

Historically, the most stringent controls on speech have been imposed during periods of national emergency to prevent subversion. For an early example, the Sedition Act of 1798, 1 Stat. 596, criminalized "false, scandalous, and malicious writing or writings against the government of the United States," as well as Congress and the President, "with intent to defame [them]; or to bring them [into] contempt or disrepute." Although the Supreme Court never adjudicated the constitutionality of the Act, several Justices applied it sitting on circuit, and there is some reason to believe that it would have been upheld.[a]

Between the Sedition Act of 1798 and the Espionage Act of 1917, the federal and state governments continued to repress speech, especially in periods of emergency. For example, southern states suppressed abolitionist literature and speech before the Civil War, both North and South stifled dissent during the Civil War, the Reconstruction as well as the Jim Crow South suppressed opposition political activity, and courts as well as executive officers brutally suppressed workers and labor leaders seeking to better their lot. The nineteenth century was in fact filled with repression of speech, and much of it was litigated

---

h. For efforts to justify the distinction, see Elena Kagan, *Private Speech, Public Purpose: The Role of Governmental Motive in First Amendment Doctrine*, 63 U. Chi. L. Rev. 413 (1996); Geoffrey Stone, *Content Regulation and the First Amendment*, 25 Wm. & Mary L. Rev. 189 (1983). For the contrary view, see Martin Redish, *The Content Distinction in First Amendment Analysis*, 34 Stan. L. Rev. 113 (1981).

a. See generally Leonard Levy, *Legacy of Suppression* (1960); Walter Berns, *Freedom of the Press and the Alien and Sedition Laws: A Reappraisal*, 1970 Sup. Ct. Rev. 109; Philip Hamburger, *The Development of the Law of Seditious Libel and the Control of the Press*, 37 Stan. L. Rev. 661 (1985).

and written about. See David Rabban, *The First Amendment in Its Forgotten Years* (1997). Nonetheless, the First Amendment did not "come into its own" until World War I.

———

Masses Publishing Co. v. Patten, 244 Fed. 535 (S.D.N.Y. 1917), *rev'd*, 246 Fed. 24 (2d Cir. 1917). The case arose when the post office refused to mail a magazine called "The Masses" on the ground that its contents would hamper the war effort. The Espionage Act of 1917 barred publications from the mail if they made false statements with the intent of hindering the war effort, willfully caused military insubordination, or obstructed military recruiting. **Judge Learned Hand** construed the statute narrowly to criminalize only speech or writings that on their face constituted a "direct incitement to violent resistance" to the law. For example, he had the following to say about the provision regarding causing insubordination:

> [The government's position] is that to arouse discontent and disaffection among the people with the prosecution of the war and with the draft tends to promote a mutinous and insubordinate temper among the troops. This, too, is true; men who become satisfied that they are engaged in an enterprise dictated by the unconscionable selfishness of the rich, and effectuated by a tyrannous disregard for the will of those who must suffer and die, will be more prone to insubordination than those who have faith in the cause and acquiesce in the means. Yet to interpret the word "cause" so broadly would * * * involve necessarily as a consequence the suppression of all hostile criticism, and of all opinion except what encouraged and supported the existing policies, or which fell within the range of temperate argument. It would contradict the normal assumption of democratic government that the suppression of hostile criticism does not turn upon the justice of its substance or the decency and propriety of its temper. Assuming that the power to repress such opinion may rest in Congress in the throes of a struggle for the very existence of the state, its exercise is so contrary to the use and wont of our people that only the clearest expression of such a power justified the conclusion that it was intended.

Similarly, with regard to the draft-resistance provision, Hand distinguished between language that might "arouse a seditious disposition," which was not forbidden, and "language that directly advocated resistance to the draft," which was illegal. Hand's statutory analysis was not adopted by the Supreme Court, though it did ultimately influence later opinions such as *Brandenburg v. Ohio* (this chapter, *infra*).[b]

———

Schenck v. United States, 249 U.S. 47 (1919). Schenck had mailed a leaflet to draft-age men arguing that the draft violated the Thirteenth Amendment. **Justice Holmes**, for the Court, first concluded that the leaflet Schenck distributed "would not have been sent unless it had been intended to have some effect, and we do not see what effect it could be expected to have upon persons subject to the draft except to influence them to obstruct the carrying of it out." Then Holmes announced the "clear and present danger test" and found it satisfied on the facts:

———

b. See Gerald Gunther, *Learned Hand and the Origins of Modern First Amendment Doctrine: Some Fragments of History*, 27 Stan. L. Rev. 719 (1975).

We admit that in many places and in ordinary times the defendants in saying all that was said in the circular would have been within their constitutional rights. But the character of every act depends upon the circumstances in which it is done. The most stringent protection of free speech would not protect a man in falsely shouting fire in a theatre and causing a panic. * * * The question in every case is whether the words used are used in such circumstances and are of such a nature as to create a clear and present danger that they will bring about the substantive evils that Congress has a right to prevent. It is a question of proximity and degree. When a nation is at war many things that might be said in time of peace are such a hindrance to its effort that their utterance will not be endured so long as men fight, and that no Court could regard them as protected by any constitutional right. It seems to be admitted that if an actual obstruction of the recruiting service were proved, liability for words that produced that effect might be enforced. [The Espionage Act] punishes conspiracies to obstruct as well as actual obstruction. If the act (speaking, or circulating a paper), its tendency and the intent with which it is done are the same, we perceive no ground for saying that success alone warrants making the act a [crime].

Our next case, also decided in 1919, marked a turning point in First Amendment law. While the majority continued to brush aside First Amendment concerns, Justice Holmes' dissent announced a bold new perspective on freedom of speech.

ABRAMS v. UNITED STATES
250 U.S. 616, 40 S.Ct. 17, 63 L.Ed. 1173 (1919)

JUSTICE CLARKE delivered the opinion of the Court.

[The defendants were charged with violating the 1917 Espionage Act in a four-count indictment by using language that was "disloyal, scurrilous and abusive . . . about the form of Government of the United States," "intended to bring the form of Government of the United States into contempt, scorn, contumely and disrepute"; and "intended to incite, provoke and encourage resistance to the United States in said war."   The two leaflets in question attacked the Allied invasion of Russia, which was intended to quash the Bolsheviks and bring Russia back into World War I on the Allies' side. One leaflet accused President Wilson of "cowardly silence" about the intervention in Russia. The other pamphlet warned workers that munitions might be used not to fight the Germans but to fight the Bolsheviks. Neither pamphlet supported the Germans, and the first one said "[w]e hate and despise German militarism . . . ."]

On the record thus described it is argued, somewhat faintly, that the acts charged against the defendants were not unlawful because within the protection of that freedom of speech and of the press which is guaranteed by the First Amendment to the Constitution of the United States, and that the entire Espionage Act is unconstitutional because in conflict with that Amendment.

This contention is sufficiently discussed and is definitely negatived in *Schenck v. United States* and *Baer v. United States*, 249 U.S. 47 [1919]; and in *Frohwerk v. United States*, 249 U.S. 204 [1919].[c]

* * *

It will not do to say, as is now argued, that the only intent of these defendants was to prevent injury to the Russian cause. Men must be held to have intended, and to be accountable for, the effects which their acts were likely to produce. Even if their primary purpose and intent was to aid the cause of the Russian Revolution, the plan of action which they adopted necessarily involved, before it could be realized, defeat of the war program of the United States, for the obvious effect of this appeal, if it should become effective, as they hoped it might, would be to persuade persons of character such as those whom they regarded themselves as addressing, not to aid government loans and not to work in ammunition factories, where their work would produce "bullets, bayonets, cannon" and other munitions of war, the use of which would cause the "murder" of Germans and Russians. * * *

JUSTICE HOLMES, dissenting.

I never have seen any reason to doubt that the questions of law that alone were before this Court in the cases of *Schenck, Frohwerk* and *Debs*, 249 U.S. 47, 204, 211, were rightly decided. I do not doubt for a moment that by the same reasoning that would justify punishing persuasion to murder, the United States constitutionally may punish speech that produces or is intended to produce a clear and imminent danger that it will bring about forthwith certain substantive evils that the United States constitutionally may seek to prevent. The power undoubtedly is greater in time of war than in time of peace because war opens dangers that do not exist at other times.

But as against dangers peculiar to war, as against others, the principle of the right to free speech is always the same. It is only the present danger of immediate evil or an intent to bring it about that warrants Congress in setting a limit to the expression of opinion where private rights are not concerned. Congress certainly cannot forbid all effort to change the mind of the country. Now nobody can suppose that the surreptitious publishing of a silly leaflet by an unknown man, without more, would present any immediate danger that its opinions would hinder the success of the government arms or have any appreciable tendency to do so. Publishing those opinions for the very purpose of obstructing however, might indicate a greater danger and at any rate would have the quality of an attempt. So I assume that the second leaflet if published for the purposes alleged in the fourth count might be punishable. But it seems pretty clear to me that nothing less than that would bring these papers within the scope of this law. An actual intent in the sense that I have explained is

---

c. *Editors' note*: Justice Holmes wrote for the Court in *Frohwerk*, upholding the conviction of publishers of a German-language newspaper for criticizing the sending of troops to France and deploring the pathetic condition of the drafted American soldier. See also *Debs v. United States*, 249 U.S. 211 (1919) (upholding Debs' conviction for obstructing the recruitment of American soldiers).

necessary to constitute an attempt, where a further act of the same individual is required to complete the substantive crime * * * . It is necessary where the success of the attempt depends upon others because if that intent is not present the actor's aim may be accomplished without bringing about the evils sought to be checked. An intent to prevent interference with the revolution in Russia might have been satisfied without any hindrance to carrying on the war in which we were engaged.

* * *

Persecution for the expression of opinions seems to me perfectly logical. If you have no doubt of your premises or your power and want a certain result with all your heart you naturally express your wishes in law and sweep away all opposition. To allow opposition by speech seems to indicate that you think the speech impotent, as when a man says that he has squared the circle, or that you do not care whole-heartedly for the result, or that you doubt either your power or your premises. But when men have realized that time has upset many fighting faiths, they may come to believe even more than they believe the very foundations of their own conduct that the ultimate good desired is better reached by free trade in ideas — that the best test of truth is the power of the thought to get itself accepted in the competition of the market, and that truth is the only ground upon which their wishes safely can be carried out. That at any rate is the theory of our Constitution. It is an experiment, as all life is an experiment. Every year if not every day we have to wager our salvation upon some prophecy based upon imperfect knowledge. While that experiment is part of our system I think that we should be eternally vigilant against attempts to check the expression of opinions that we loathe and believe to be fraught with death, unless they so imminently threaten immediate interference with the lawful and pressing purposes of the law that an immediate check is required to save the country. I wholly disagree with the argument of the Government that the First Amendment left the common law as to seditious libel in force. History seems to me against the notion. I had conceived that the United States through many years had shown its repentance for the Sedition Act of 1798, by repaying fines that it imposed. Only the emergency that makes it immediately dangerous to leave the correction of evil counsels to time warrants making any exception to the sweeping command, "Congress shall make no law ... abridging the freedom of speech." Of course I am speaking only of expressions of opinion and exhortations, which were all that were uttered here, but I regret that I cannot put into more impressive words my belief that in their conviction upon this indictment the defendants were deprived of their rights under the Constitution of the United States.

JUSTICE BRANDEIS concurs with the foregoing opinion.

A NOTE ON SUBVERSIVE SPEECH FROM 1920-1960

Note the transformation of Justice Holmes' views from *Schenck, Frohwerk,* and *Debs,* where he wrote opinions for the Court upholding convictions that don't seem much different from the one in *Abrams,* where he dissented. Essentially, Holmes moved toward the libertarian approach urged by Professor Zechariah Chafee, who believed it important to carve out an arena of protected speech.[d] Holmes' clear and present danger approach in *Abrams* is different from the incitement approach taken by Hand in *Masses*, even though both judges were influenced by Chafee. Hand was critical of the Holmes approach, because its contextual determination was too subjective to constrain lemming-like judges in times of national crisis. See Gunther, *supra* note *b*, 27 Stan. L. Rev. at 749 (Hand's criticism of Holmes' dissent). Consider the irony of the next case.

Gitlow v. New York, 268 U.S. 652 (1925). The Court upheld the conviction of Benjamin Gitlow for violating New York's law prohibiting the advocacy of criminal anarchy. His offense was helping to publish a "Left Wing Manifesto," which advocated worldwide class struggle, mass industrial revolts and strikes, and the establishment of a "revolutionary dictatorship of the proletariat." This is the first opinion where the Court held (really assumed) that the guarantees of the First Amendment were applicable to the states as protections assured by the Due Process Clause of the Fourteenth Amendment. The Court held that "utterances inciting to the overthrow of organized government by unlawful means present a sufficient danger of substantive evil" to justify legislative prohibition. "A single revolutionary spark may kindle a fire that, smoldering for a time, may burst into a sweeping and destructive conflagration."

Justice Holmes, joined by **Justice Brandeis**, dissented. Holmes responded to the majority's "incitement" rationale: "Every idea is an incitement. It offers itself for belief, and, if believed, it is acted on unless some other belief outweighs it, or some failure of energy stifles the movement at its birth. * * * If, in the long run, the beliefs expressed in proletarian dictatorship are destined to be accepted by the dominant forces of the community, the only meaning of free speech is that they should be given their chance and have their way."

Whitney v. California, 274 U.S. 357 (1927), upheld the conviction for "criminal syndicalism" of a member of the Communist Labor Party, whose only individual activities had been attending meetings. **Justice Brandeis'** opinion was technically a concurrence but rejected the majority's reasoning entirely. One of the most famous passages in First Amendment law comes from that Brandeis opinion:

> This Court has not yet fixed the standard by which to determine when a danger shall be deemed clear; how remote the danger may be and yet be deemed present; and what degree of evil shall be deemed sufficiently substantial to justify resort to abridgement of free speech and assembly as the means of protection. To reach sound conclusions on these matters, we must bear in mind why a State is, ordinarily, denied the power to prohibit dissemination of social, economic and political doctrine which a vast majority of its citizens believes to be false and fraught with evil consequence.

---

d. The story of the change in Holmes' thinking is told in David Bogen, *The Free Speech Metamorphosis of Mr. Justice Holmes*, 11 Hofstra L. Rev. 97 (1982), and in David Rabban, *The Emergence of Modern First Amendment Doctrine*, 50 U. Chi. L. Rev. 1205 (1983). See also Fred Ragan, *Justice Oliver Wendell Holmes, Jr., Zechariah Chafee, Jr., and the Clear and Present Danger Test for Free Speech: The First Year, 1919*, 58 J. Am. Hist. 24 (1971).

Those who won our independence believed that the final end of the State was to make men free to develop their faculties; and that in its government the deliberative forces should prevail over the arbitrary. They valued liberty both as an end and as a means. They believed liberty to be the secret of happiness and courage to be the secret of liberty. They believed that freedom to think as you will and to speak as you think are means indispensable to the discovery and spread of political truth; that without free speech and assembly discussion would be futile; that with them, discussion affords ordinarily adequate protection against the dissemination of noxious doctrine; that the greatest menace to freedom is an inert people; that public discussion is a political duty; and that this should be a fundamental principle of the American government.[e] They recognized the risks to which all human institutions are subject. But they knew that order cannot be secured merely through fear of punishment for its infraction; that it is hazardous to discourage thought, hope and imagination; that fear breeds repression; that repression breeds hate; that hate menaces stable government; that the path of safety lies in the opportunity to discuss freely supposed grievances and proposed remedies; and that the fitting remedy for evil counsels is good ones. Believing in the power of reason as applied through public discussion, they eschewed silence coerced by law — the argument of force in its worst form. Recognizing the occasional tyrannies of governing majorities, they amended the Constitution so that free speech and assembly should be guaranteed.

Fear of serious injury cannot alone justify suppression of free speech and assembly. Men feared witches and burnt women. It is the function of speech to free men from the bondage of irrational fears. To justify suppression of free speech there must be reasonable ground to fear that serious evil will result if free speech is practiced. There must be reasonable ground to believe that the danger apprehended is imminent. * * *

Those who won our independence by revolution were not cowards. They did not fear political change. They did not exalt order at the cost of liberty. To courageous, self-reliant men, with confidence in the power of free and fearless reasoning applied through the processes of popular government, no danger flowing from speech can be deemed clear and present, unless the incidence of the evil apprehended is so imminent that it may befall before there is opportunity for full discussion. If there be time to expose through discussion the falsehood and fallacies, to avert the evil by the processes of education, the remedy to be applied is more speech, not enforced silence. Only an emergency can justify repression. Such must be the rule if authority is to be reconciled with freedom. Such, in my opinion, is the command of the Constitution. It is therefore always open to Americans to challenge a law abridging free speech and assembly by showing that there was no emergency justifying it.

———

This may be a somewhat idealized portrait of the Framers, but it is one that has helped inspire modern First Amendment jurisprudence.

During the post-war "red scare," the Court continued to uphold state repression. By the 1930s, however, a majority of the Court had been converted

———

e. In a footnote at this point, Justice Brandeis added the following historical reference: "Compare Thomas Jefferson: 'We have nothing to fear from the demoralizing reasonings of some, if others are left free to demonstrate their errors and especially when the law stands ready to punish the first criminal act produced by the false reasonings; these are safer corrections than the conscience of the judge.' Quoted by Charles A. Beard, The Nation, July 7, 1926, vol. 123, p. 8. Also in first Inaugural Address: 'If there be any among us who would wish to dissolve this union or change its republican form, let them stand undisturbed as monuments of the safety with which error of opinion may be tolerated where reason is left free to combat it.' "

to the more libertarian position espoused by Brandeis and Holmes and used their approach to invalidate convictions under state "syndicalism" laws. See *De Jonge v. Oregon*, 299 U.S. 353 (1937); *Herndon v. Lowry*, 301 U.S. 242 (1937). The Court then adopted the "clear and present danger" test as a general standard for First Amendment cases. The test requires a particularized showing of an immediate threat of serious harm.

Dennis v. United States, 341 U.S. 494 (1951). After World War II, the country again was faced with a period of serious repression. In what is now called the McCarthy era (but which actually began before Senator Joseph McCarthy attained national prominence), a variety of actions were taken to suppress "Communist influences." The Court gave its backing to these efforts by upholding the convictions of leading Communist Party figures for violating the Smith Act, which made it unlawful for any person "to knowingly or willfully advocate, abet, advise, or teach the duty, necessity, or propriety of overthrowing or destroying any government in the United States by force or violence." Following the lead of Chief Judge Learned Hand's opinion for the Second Circuit (affirming the convictions), the Court in an opinion by **Chief Justice Vinson** watered down the clear and present danger test, saying that the immediacy and probability of the harm were only factors to be offset against its gravity. Apparently, since an eventual Communist revolution would be such a disaster, not much was required in the way of present risk to justify suppression of the party.[f] **Justices Black** and **Douglas** wrote stinging dissents in this and other McCarthy-era cases.

Yates v. United States, 354 U.S. 298 (1957). *Yates* was the Court's first attempt to clarify *Dennis*. Writing for the Court, **Justice Harlan** rejected the government's position that *Dennis* allowed abstract discussion about overthrowing the government but not "advocacy" of conduct. Instead, Justice Harlan narrowly defined the class of speech punishable under the Smith Act. Mere doctrinal justification of forcible overthrow, "even though uttered with the hope that it may ultimately lead to violent revolution, is too remote from concrete action to be regarded as the kind of indoctrination preparatory to action which was condemned in *Dennis*." Instead, "those to whom the advocacy is addressed must be urged to *do* something, rather than merely to *believe* in something" (emphasis in original). He then proceeded to examine the record, ordering retrials for defendants connected with Communist Party classes on sabotage and street fighting. For the other defendants, there was not enough evidence even to justify a retrial. Similarly, in *Scales v. United States*, 367 U.S. 203 (1961), Justice Harlan narrowly construed the provision of the Smith Act that made it a felony to be a knowing member of any group advocating forceful overthrow of the government. Under the *Scales* doctrine, party members could only be convicted upon proof that they specifically intended to incite the overthrow of

---

f. But see Richard Posner, *Free Speech in an Economic Perspective*, 20 Suffolk U. L. Rev. 1, 34-35 (1986) (Court should have discounted to present value the cost of a future revolution).

the government. As a result of this judicial reworking of the statute, Smith Act prosecutions ground to a halt.[g]

The Court's application of the clear and present danger test in *Dennis* raised considerable doubt about whether that test offered sufficient protection to subversive speech. After the McCarthy era, though, the test was applied with greater bite. See *Watts v. United States*, 394 U.S. 705 (1969); *Bond v. Floyd*, 385 U.S. 116 (1966). At the end of the Warren Court era, in the following case, the Court revamped the test, creating the standard which currently applies to advocacy of illegal action.

BRANDENBURG v. OHIO
395 U.S. 444, 89 S.Ct. 1827, 23 L.Ed.2d 430 (1969)

PER CURIAM.

The appellant, a leader of a Ku Klux Klan group, was convicted under the Ohio Criminal Syndicalism statute for "advocat[ing] . . . the duty, necessity, or propriety of crime, sabotage, violence, or unlawful methods of terrorism as a means of accomplishing industrial or political reform" and for "voluntarily assembl[ing] with any society, group, or assemblage of persons formed to teach or advocate the doctrines of criminal syndicalism." He was fined $1,000 and sentenced to one to 10 years' imprisonment. [Brandenburg was convicted on the basis of Klan events filmed by a television reporter.]

One film showed 12 hooded figures, some of whom carried firearms. They were gathered around a large wooden cross, which they burned. No one was present other than the participants and the newsmen who made the film. Most of the words uttered during the scene were incomprehensible when the film was projected, but scattered phrases could be understood that were derogatory of Negroes and, in one instance, of Jews.[1]

Another scene on the same film showed the appellant, in Klan regalia, making a speech. The speech, in full, was as follows:

> This is an organizers' meeting. We have had quite a few members here today which are — we have hundreds, hundreds of members throughout the State of Ohio. I can quote from a newspaper clipping from the Columbus, Ohio Dispatch, five weeks ago Sunday morning. The Klan has more members in the State of Ohio than does any other organization. We're not a revengent organization, but if our President, our Congress, our Supreme Court, continues to suppress the white, Caucasian race, it's possible that there might have to be some revengeance taken.

---

g. See Daniel Farber & John Nowak, *Justice Harlan and the First Amendment*, 2 Const. Comm. 425 (1985); Norman Dorsen, *John Marshall Harlan, Civil Liberties, and the Warren Court*, 36 N.Y.L. Sch. L. Rev. 81 (1991).

1. The significant portions that could be understood were: "How far is the nigger going to - yeah." "This is what we are going to do to the niggers." "A dirty nigger." "Send the Jews back to Israel." "Let's give them back to the dark garden." "Save America." "Let's go back to constitutional betterment." "Bury the niggers." "We intend to do our part." "Give us our state rights." "Freedom for the whites." "Nigger will have to fight for every inch he gets from now on."

We are marching on Congress July the Fourth, four hundred thousand strong. From there we are dividing into two groups, one group to march on St. Augustine, Florida, the other group to march into Mississippi. Thank you.

* * * The Ohio Criminal Syndicalism Statute was enacted in 1919. From 1917 to 1920, identical or quite similar laws were adopted by 20 States and two territories. In 1927, this Court sustained the constitutionality of California's Criminal Syndicalism Act, the text of which is quite similar to that of the laws of Ohio. *Whitney v. California.* The Court upheld the statute on the ground that, without more, "advocating" violent means to effect political and economic change involves such danger to the security of the State that the State may outlaw it. But *Whitney* has been thoroughly discredited by later decisions. *See Dennis v. United States.* These later decisions have fashioned the principle that the constitutional guarantees of free speech and free press do not permit a State to forbid or proscribe advocacy of the use of force or of law violation except where such advocacy is directed to inciting or producing imminent lawless action and is likely to incite or produce such action.[2] As we said in *Noto v. United States*, 367 U.S. 290, 297-298 (1961), "the mere abstract teaching . . . of the moral propriety or even moral necessity for a resort to force and violence, is not the same as preparing a group for violent action and steeling it to such action." A statute which fails to draw this distinction impermissibly intrudes upon the freedoms guaranteed by the First and Fourteenth Amendments. It sweeps within its condemnation speech which our Constitution has immunized from governmental control.

Measured by this test, Ohio's Criminal Syndicalism Act cannot be sustained. The Act punishes persons who "advocate or teach the duty, necessity, or propriety" of violence "as a means of accomplishing industrial or political reform"; or who publish or circulate or display any book or paper containing such advocacy; or who "justify" the commission of violent acts "with intent to exemplify, spread or advocate the propriety of the doctrines of criminal syndicalism"; or who "voluntarily assemble" with a group formed "to teach or advocate the doctrines of criminal syndicalism." Neither the indictment nor the trial judge's instructions to the jury in any way refined the statute's bald definition of the crime in terms of mere advocacy not distinguished from incitement to imminent lawless action.

Accordingly, we are here confronted with a statute which, by its own words and as applied, purports to punish mere advocacy and to forbid, on pain of criminal punishment, assembly with others merely to advocate the described type of action. Such a statute falls within the condemnation of the First and Fourteenth Amendments. The contrary teaching of *Whitney v. California* cannot be supported, and that decision is therefore overruled.

---

2. It was on the theory that the Smith Act embodied such a principle and that it had been applied only in conformity with it that this Court sustained the Act's constitutionality. *Dennis.* That this was the basis for *Dennis* was emphasized in *Yates v. United States*, 354 U.S. 298, 320-324 (1957), in which the Court overturned convictions for advocacy of the forcible overthrow of the Government under the Smith Act, because the trial judge's instructions had allowed conviction for mere advocacy, unrelated to its tendency to produce forcible action.

[The concurring opinions of **JUSTICE BLACK** and **JUSTICE DOUGLAS** are omitted.]

NOTES ON *BRANDENBURG*

1. *"Clear and Present Danger."* How does *Brandenburg* modify the clear and present danger test? Is the modification justified? Note how the first element of the *Brandenburg* test ("advocacy is directed to inciting") follows Hand's *Masses* opinion (discussed above) in distinguishing direct incitement from mere advocacy. Does *Brandenburg* essentially overrule *Abrams, Gitlow*, and *Dennis*, as well as *Whitney*?[j]

Even as liberally applied in *Brandenburg*, the clear and present danger test allows radical political expression to be suppressed as soon as it shows signs of becoming effective.[k] Justice Douglas' concurring opinion argued that the test should be whether the inciting speech is accompanied by "overt acts" violating the law. For example, yelling "fire" in a theatre is "speech brigaded with action" and can be regulated under his approach.

Note that in *Brandenburg*, the speech in question involved threats against minority groups, as opposed to earlier cases in which the threats had been directed against the government. The Court seems to assume that the same test should apply to both kinds of speech. Do you agree? Or should the government have greater power to protect minority groups from threatening speech? Recall the *R.A.V.* case.

2. *The Flag Salute Case.* What about affirmative efforts to instill loyalty, such as requiring children to salute the flag? During World War II, the Court overruled a case decided just three years earlier and held that compulsory flag salutes violated the First Amendment. *West Virginia State Bd. of Education v. Barnette*, 319 U.S. 624 (1943). Justice Jackson's opinion for the Court contained some eloquent passages reminiscent of Brandeis in *Whitney*:

> The case is made difficult not because the principles of its decision are obscure but because the flag involved is our own. * * * [F]reedom to differ is not limited to things that do not matter much. That would be a mere shadow of freedom. The test of its substance is the right to differ as to things that touch the heart of the existing order.

> If there is any fixed star in our constitutional constellation, it is that no official, high or petty, can prescribe what shall be orthodox in politics, nationalism, religion, or other matters of opinion or force citizens to confess by word or act their faith therein. If there are any circumstances which permit an exception, they do not now occur to us.

VIRGINIA v. BLACK
538 U.S. 343, 123 S.Ct. 1536, 155 L.Ed.2d 535 (2003)

JUSTICE O'CONNOR announced the judgment of the Court and delivered the opinion of the Court with respect to Parts I, II, and III, and an opinion with

---

j. See Hans Linde, *"Clear and Present Danger" Reexamined: Dissonance in the* Brandenburg *Concerto*, 22 Stan. L. Rev. 1163 (1970).

k. See Thomas Emerson, *First Amendment Doctrine and the Burger Court*, 68 Cal. L. Rev. 422 (1980).

respect to Parts IV and V, in which **CHIEF JUSTICE REHNQUIST**, **JUSTICE STEVENS**, and **JUSTICE BREYER** join.

I. Respondents Barry Black, Richard Elliott, and Jonathan O'Mara were convicted separately of violating Virginia's cross-burning statute, [which] provides:

> It shall be unlawful for any person or persons, with the intent of intimidating any person or group of persons, to burn, or cause to be burned, a cross on the property of another, a highway or other public place. Any person who shall violate any provision of this section shall be guilty of a Class 6 felony.

> Any such burning of a cross shall be prima facie evidence of an intent to intimidate a person or group of persons.

[Black led a Ku Klux Klan rally attended by around thirty people. The rally was located on private party in an open field near a state highway. At the conclusion of the rally, the crowd circled around a 25- to 30-foot cross. The cross was between 300 and 350 yards away from the road. According to the sheriff, the cross "then all of a sudden . . . went up in a flame. In a separate case, two other defendants attempted to burn a cross on the yard of an African-American, was Elliott's next-door neighbor. The two defendants drove a truck onto the neighbor's property, planted a cross, and set it on fire. Their apparent motive was to "get back" at the neighbor for complaining about shooting in their backyard.]

[Part II of the opinion is devoted to a review of the history of cross-burning. It concludes: "In sum, while a burning cross does not inevitably convey a message of intimidation, often the cross burner intends that the recipients of the message fear for their lives. And when a cross burning is used to intimidate, few if any messages are more powerful."]

[III.] "True threats" encompass those statements where the speaker means to communicate a serious expression of an intent to commit an act of unlawful violence to a particular individual or group of individuals. The speaker need not actually intend to carry out the threat. Rather, a prohibition on true threats "protect[s] individuals from the fear of violence" and "from the disruption that fear engenders," in addition to protecting people "from the possibility that the threatened violence will occur." Intimidation in the constitutionally proscribable sense of the word is a type of true threat, where a speaker directs a threat to a person or group of persons with the intent of placing the victim in fear of bodily harm or death. Respondents do not contest that some cross burnings fit within this meaning of intimidating speech, and rightly so. As noted in Part II, the history of cross burning in this country shows that cross burning is often intimidating, intended to create a pervasive fear in victims that they are a target of violence.

* * *

[Moreover,] Virginia's statute does not run afoul of the First Amendment insofar as it bans cross burning with intent to intimidate. Unlike the statute at issue in *R.A.V.*, the Virginia statute does not single out for opprobrium only that speech directed toward "one of the specified disfavored topics." It does not matter whether an individual burns a cross with intent to intimidate because of the victim's race, gender, or religion, or because of the victim's "political affiliation, union membership, or homosexuality." Moreover, as a factual matter it is not true that cross burners direct their intimidating conduct solely to racial or religious minorities. Indeed, in the case of Elliott and O'Mara, it is at least unclear whether the respondents burned a cross due to racial animus.

The First Amendment permits Virginia to outlaw cross burnings done with the intent to intimidate because burning a cross is a particularly virulent form of intimidation. Instead of prohibiting all intimidating messages, Virginia may choose to regulate this subset of intimidating messages in light of cross burning's long and pernicious history as a signal of impending violence. Thus, just as a State may regulate only that obscenity which is the most obscene due to its prurient content, so too may a State choose to prohibit only those forms of intimidation that are most likely to inspire fear of bodily harm. A ban on cross burning carried out with the intent to intimidate is fully consistent with our holding in *R.A.V.* and is proscribable under the First Amendment.

[In Parts IV and V of her plurality opinion, Justice O'Connor concluded that the state's prima facie evidence provision was facially unconstitutional because of its indiscriminate coverage. Since the instruction was given in Black's case, the plurality voted to reverse his conviction, but it remanded the convictions of Elliott and O'Mara to determine whether the prima facie evidence provision was severable or whether it was subject to a narrowing construction. In a partial concurrence, Justice Scalia (joined by Justice Thomas) argued that the provision had such a modest potential impact on prosecutions that it should not be subject to a facial attack].

[The concurring opinion of **JUSTICE STEVENS**, as well as the opinion of **JUSTICE SCALIA**, joined in part by **JUSTICE THOMAS**, concurring in part and dissenting in part, are omitted.]

JUSTICE SOUTER, with whom **JUSTICE KENNEDY** and **JUSTICE GINSBURG** join, concurring in the judgment in part and dissenting in part.

The majority's approach could be taken as recognizing an exception to *R.A.V.* when circumstances show that the statute's ostensibly valid reason for punishing particularly serious proscribable expression probably is not a ruse for message suppression, even though the statute may have a greater (but not exclusive) impact on adherents of one ideology than on others.

My concern here, in any event, is not with the merit of a pragmatic doctrinal move. For whether or not the Court should conceive of exceptions to *R.A.V.*'s general rule in a more practical way, no content-based statute should survive even under a pragmatic recasting of *R.A.V.* without a high probability that no "official suppression of ideas is afoot." I believe the prima facie evidence provision stands in the way of any finding of such a high probability here. * * *

JUSTICE THOMAS, dissenting.

That in the early 1950s the people of Virginia viewed cross burning as creating an intolerable atmosphere of terror is not surprising: Although the cross took on some religious significance in the 1920's when the Klan became connected with certain southern white clergy, by the postwar period it had reverted to its original function "as an instrument of intimidation." * * *

It strains credulity to suggest that a state legislature that adopted a litany of segregationist laws self-contradictorily intended to squelch the segregationist message. Even for segregationists, violent and terroristic conduct, the Siamese twin of cross burning, was intolerable. The ban on cross burning with intent to intimidate demonstrates that even segregationists understood the difference between intimidating and terroristic conduct and racist expression. It is simply beyond belief that, in passing the statute now under review, the Virginia legislature was concerned with anything but penalizing conduct it must have viewed as particularly vicious.

Accordingly, this statute prohibits only conduct, not expression. And, just as one cannot burn down someone's house to make a political point and then seek refuge in the First Amendment, those who hate cannot terrorize and intimidate to make their point. In light of my conclusion that the statute here addresses only conduct, there is no need to analyze it under any of our First Amendment tests. * * *

NOTES ON *VIRGINIA v. BLACK*

1. *Distinguishing* R.A.V. While cross-burning may be among the most virulent forms of threats, are there any other threats that are equally virulent? If so, does the state's decision to punish one subcategory of the super-virulent threats but not the others fit within the *R.A.V.* exception? Under the *Black* analysis, could a state punish only pornography containing homosexual acts on the theory that those were more offensive to community standards than heterosexual acts? What about punishing only incitements to violence directed against minority groups, based on the history of the Klan and of lynch mobs in the South? Can "virulence" really be defined in a way that eliminates the threat of viewpoint-based animus? For that matter, what was wrong with the City of St. Paul's view, endorsed by the four concurring Justices in *R.A.V.*, that racial epithets are a particularly virulent form of fighting words?

2. *Distinguishing* Brandenburg. Recall that the cross-burning in *Brandenburg* was filmed for TV, so presumably the defendant knew it would be communicated to a broader audience. Suppose that the cross-burning and accompanying speeches were meant to communicate a threat of violence to local minority group members. Could Brandenburg have been prosecuted under an anti-crossburning statute with an appropriate intent requirement? If so, the only distinction between an incitement and a threat seems to be that the audience for the threat includes the victims, whereas the incitement includes only potential participants. But this makes it puzzling why the definitions are so different — in particular, why incitement requires a dangerous probability of success while threats apparently do not.

3. *Law and Social Meaning. Virginia v. Black* stresses the historical context of cross-burning and the ways in which this symbol is understood by observers. We will see this concern with social meaning again at the end of the chapter, when we discuss the Court's jurisprudence regarding public religious symbols. Are the Court's perceptions of social meaning a valuable assist to

decisionmaking or an unreliable guide? For reflections on how the Court should think about these issues, see Kenneth L. Karst, *Threats and Meanings: How the Facts Govern First Amendment Doctrine*, 58 Stan. L. Rev. 1337 (2006); Frederick Schauer, *Intentions, Conventions, and the First Amendment*, 2003 Sup. Ct. Rev. 197 (2004).

B.   DEFAMATION, PRIVACY, AND POLITICAL SPEECH

Political speech is not always accurate, deliberately or otherwise, and it can involve discussion of otherwise private aspects of a person's life. This section considers the use of tort law to discipline such speech, and the role of the First Amendment in constraining tort law.

NEW YORK TIMES CO. v. SULLIVAN
376 U.S. 254, 84 S.Ct. 710, 11 L.Ed.2d 686 (1964)

JUSTICE BRENNAN delivered the opinion of the Court.

We are required in this case to determine for the first time the extent to which the constitutional protections for speech and press limit a State's power to award damages in a libel action brought by a public official against critics of his official conduct.

Respondent L. B. Sullivan is one of the three elected Commissioners of the City of Montgomery, Alabama. He testified that he was "Commissioner of Public Affairs and the duties are supervision of the Police Department, Fire Department, Department of Cemetery and Department of Scales." He brought this civil libel action against the four individual petitioners, who are Negroes and Alabama clergymen, and against petitioner the New York Times Company, a New York corporation which publishes the New York Times, a daily newspaper. A jury in the Circuit Court of Montgomery County awarded him damages of $500,000, the full amount claimed, against all the petitioners, and the Supreme Court of Alabama affirmed.

Respondent's complaint alleged that he had been libeled by statements in a full-page advertisement that was carried in the New York Times on March 29, 1960. Entitled "Heed Their Rising Voices," the advertisement began by stating that "As the whole world knows by now, thousands of Southern Negro students are engaged in widespread non-violent demonstrations in positive affirmation of the right to live in human dignity as guaranteed by the U.S. Constitution and the Bill of Rights." It went on to charge that "in their efforts to uphold these guarantees, they are being met by an unprecedented wave of terror by those who would deny and negate that document which the whole world looks upon as setting the pattern for modern freedom. . . ." Succeeding paragraphs purported to illustrate the "wave of terror" by describing certain alleged events. The text concluded with an appeal for funds for three purposes: support of the student movement, "the struggle for the right-to-vote," and the legal defense of Dr. Martin Luther King, Jr., leader of the movement, against a perjury indictment then pending in Montgomery.

[The text contained several references to police brutality in Montgomery. Although Sullivan wasn't named, the state courts said these were sufficient as a reference to him as police commissioner. Also, the text contained some minor and largely irrelevant inaccuracies.]

[W]e consider this case against the background of a profound national commitment to the principle that debate on public issues should be uninhibited, robust, and wide-open, and that it may well include vehement, caustic, and sometimes unpleasantly sharp attacks on government and public officials. The present advertisement, as an expression of grievance and protest on one of the major public issues of our time, would seem clearly to qualify for the constitutional protection. The question is whether it forfeits that protection by the falsity of some of its factual statements and by its alleged defamation of respondent.

Authoritative interpretations of the First Amendment guarantees have consistently refused to recognize an exception for any test of truth — whether administered by judges, juries, or administrative officials — and especially one that puts the burden of proving truth on the speaker. The constitutional protection does not turn upon "the truth, popularity, or social utility of the ideas and beliefs which are offered." *N.A.A.C.P. v. Button*, 371 U.S. 415, 445. As Madison said, "Some degree of abuse is inseparable from the proper use of every thing; and in no instance is this more true than in that of the press." In *Cantwell v. Connecticut*, 310 U.S. 296, 310, the Court declared:

> In the realm of religious faith, and in that of political belief, sharp differences arise. In both fields the tenets of one man may seem the rankest error to his neighbor. To persuade others to his own point of view, the pleader, as we know, at times, resorts to exaggeration, to vilification of men who have been, or are, prominent in church or state, and even to false statement. But the people of this nation have ordained in the light of history, that, in spite of the probability of excesses and abuses, these liberties are, in the long view, essential to enlightened opinion and right conduct on the part of the citizens of a democracy.

That erroneous statement is inevitable in free debate, and that it must be protected if the freedoms of expression are to have the "breathing space" that they "need . . . to survive," *N.A.A.C.P. v. Button*, was also recognized by the Court of Appeals for the District of Columbia Circuit in *Sweeney v. Patterson*, 76 U.S. App. D.C. 23, 24, 128 F. 2d 457, 458 (1942), *cert. denied*, 317 U.S. 678. Judge Edgerton spoke for a unanimous court which affirmed the dismissal of a Congressman's libel suit based upon a newspaper article charging him with anti-Semitism in opposing a judicial appointment. He said:

> Cases which impose liability for erroneous reports of the political conduct of officials reflect the obsolete doctrine that the governed must not criticize their governors. . . . The interest of the public here outweighs the interest of appellant or any other individual. The protection of the public requires not merely discussion, but information. Political conduct and views which some respectable people approve, and others condemn, are constantly imputed to Congressmen. Errors of fact, particularly in regard to a man's mental states and processes, are inevitable. . . . Whatever is added to the field of libel is taken from the field of free debate.

Injury to official reputation affords no more warrant for repressing speech that would otherwise be free than does factual error. Where judicial officers are involved, this Court has held that concern for the dignity and reputation of the courts does not justify the punishment as criminal contempt of criticism of the judge or his decision. This is true even though the utterance contains "half-truths" and "misinformation." Such repression can be justified, if at all, only by a clear and present danger of the obstruction of justice. If judges are to be treated as "men of fortitude, able to thrive in a hardy climate," surely the same must be true of other government officials, such as elected city commission-ers.[14] Criticism of their official conduct does not lose its constitutional protection merely because it is effective criticism and hence diminishes their official reputations.

If neither factual error nor defamatory content suffices to remove the constitutional shield from criticism of official conduct, the combination of the two elements is no less inadequate. This is the lesson to be drawn from the great controversy over the Sedition Act of 1798, which first crystallized a national awareness of the central meaning of the First Amendment. * * * The Act allowed the defendant the defense of truth, and provided that the jury were to be judges both of the law and the facts. Despite these qualifications, the Act was vigorously condemned as unconstitutional in an attack joined in by Jefferson and Madison. In the famous Virginia Resolutions of 1798, the General Assembly of Virginia resolved that it

> doth particularly protest against the palpable and alarming infractions of the Constitution, in the two late cases of the "Alien and Sedition Acts," passed at the last session of Congress . . . [The Sedition Act] exercises . . . a power not delegated by the Constitution, but, on the contrary, expressly and positively forbidden by one of the amendments thereto — a power which, more than any other, ought to produce universal alarm, because it is levelled against the right of freely examining public characters and measures, and of free communication among the people thereon, which has ever been justly deemed the only effectual guardian of every other right.

Madison prepared the Report in support of the protest. His premise was that the Constitution created a form of government under which "The people, not the government, possess the absolute sovereignty." The structure of the government dispersed power in reflection of the people's distrust of concentrated power, and of power itself at all levels. This form of government was "altogether different" from the British form, under which the Crown was sovereign and the people were subjects. "Is it not natural and necessary, under such different circum-stances," he asked, "that a different degree of freedom in the use of the press should be contemplated?" Earlier, in a debate in the House of Representatives, Madison had said: "If we advert to the nature of Republican Government, we shall find that the censorial power is in the people over the Government, and not in the Government over the people." Of the exercise of that power by the press, his Report said: "In every state, probably, in the Union, the press has exerted a freedom in canvassing the merits and measures of public men, of every description, which has not been confined to the strict limits of the common law. On this footing the freedom of the press has stood; on this foundation it yet

---

14. The climate in which public officials operate, especially during a political campaign, has been described by one commentator in the following terms: "Charges of gross incompetence, disregard of the public interest, communist sympathies, and the like usually have filled the air; and hints of bribery, embezzlement, and other criminal conduct are not infrequent." Noel, *Defamation of Public Officers and Candidates*, 49 Col. L. Rev. 875 (1949). * * *

stands . . . ." The right of free public discussion of the stewardship of public officials was thus, in Madison's view, a fundamental principle of the American form of government.[15]

Although the Sedition Act was never tested in this Court, the attack upon its validity has carried the day in the court of history. Fines levied in its prosecution were repaid by Act of Congress on the ground that it was unconstitutional. Calhoun, reporting to the Senate on February 4, 1836, assumed that its invalidity was a matter "which no one now doubts." Jefferson, as President, pardoned those who had been convicted and sentenced under the Act and remitted their fines, stating: "I discharged every person under punishment or prosecution under the sedition law, because I considered, and now consider, that law to be a nullity, as absolute and as palpable as if Congress had ordered us to fall down and worship a golden image." The invalidity of the Act has also been assumed by Justices of this Court. These views reflect a broad consensus that the Act, because of the restraint it imposed upon criticism of government and public officials, was inconsistent with the First Amendment. * * *

The constitutional guarantees require, we think, a federal rule that prohibits a public official from recovering damages for a defamatory falsehood relating to his official conduct unless he proves that the statement was made with "actual malice" — that is, with knowledge that it was false or with reckless disregard of whether it was false or not. * * *

We hold today that the Constitution delimits a State's power to award damages for libel in actions brought by public officials against critics of their official conduct. Since this is such an action, the rule requiring proof of actual malice is applicable. [The Court concluded that the record would not support a finding of malice or a finding that the police commissioner was personally defamed.]

[The concurring opinion of **JUSTICE BLACK**, joined by **JUSTICE DOUGLAS**, is omitted.]

15.　　The Report on the Virginia Resolutions further stated:

[It] is manifestly impossible to punish the intent to bring those who administer the government into disrepute or contempt, without striking at the right of freely discussing public characters and measures; . . . which, again, is equivalent to a protection of those who administer the government, if they should at any time deserve the contempt or hatred of the people, against being exposed to it, by free animadversions on their characters and conduct. Nor can there be a doubt . . . that a government thus intrenched in penal statutes against the just and natural effects of a culpable administration, will easily evade the responsibility which is essential to a faithful discharge of its duty.

Let it be recollected, lastly, that the right of electing the members of the government constitutes more particularly the essence of a free and responsible government. The value and efficacy of this right depends on the knowledge of the comparative merits and demerits of the candidates for public trust, and on the equal freedom, consequently, of examining and discussing these merits and demerits of the candidates respectively.

Gertz v. Robert Welch, Inc., 418 U.S. 323 (1974). This case involved an article accusing the plaintiff of organizing a "communist frameup" of a policeman. The police officer was convicted of killing a youth, and the plaintiff, an attorney, had represented the family in a damage suit. The Court, per **Justice Powell**, held that the *New York Times v. Sullivan* rule did not apply because the plaintiff was neither a public official nor a public figure. The Court laid down two rules governing liability in such cases:

"[S]o long as they do not impose liability without fault, the States may define for themselves the appropriate standard of liability for a publisher or broadcaster of defamatory falsehood injurious to a private individual." Thus, the plaintiff need only prove negligence.

"It is necessary to restrict defamation plaintiffs who do not prove knowledge of falsity or reckless disregard for the truth to compensation for actual injury." Thus, to recover "presumed" or punitive damages, the plaintiff must satisfy the *New York Times* test even if he is a private figure.

Hustler Magazine v. Falwell, 485 U.S. 46 (1988). In a heavy-handed parody, *Hustler* portrayed Jerry Falwell, a well-known minister and commentator on public affairs, as having committed incest with his mother in an outhouse. Falwell sued for libel and intentional infliction of emotional distress. The jury found that the parody could not be reasonably understood as purporting to communicate facts and so did not constitute libel, but did find *Hustler* liable for intentional infliction of emotional distress. In an opinion by **Chief Justice Rehnquist**, the Court held that a public figure cannot recover damages for emotional distress without satisfying *New York Times*, and that the plaintiff had failed to prove that the parody constituted a false "statement of fact." The Court rejected the argument that a malicious motive should be a basis for liability: "Were we to hold otherwise, there can be little doubt that political cartoonists and satirists would be subject to damage awards. * * * The appeal of the political cartoon or caricature is often based on exploration of unfortunate physical traits or politically embarrassing events — an exploration often calculated to injure the feelings of the subject of the portrayal." The Court also rejected "outrageousness" as a standard for liability:

> Respondent contends, however, that the caricature in question here was so "outrageous" as to distinguish it from more traditional political cartoons. * * * If it were possible by laying down a principled standard to separate the one from the other, public discourse would probably suffer little or no harm. But we doubt that there is any such standard, and we are quite sure that the pejorative description "outrageous" does not supply one. "Outrageousness" in the area of political and social discourse has an inherent subjectiveness about it which would allow a jury to impose liability on the basis of the jurors' tastes or views, or perhaps on the basis of their dislike of a particular expression. An "outrageousness" standard thus runs afoul of our longstanding refusal to allow damages to be awarded because the speech in question may have an adverse emotional impact on the audience.

NOTES ON POST-*NEW YORK TIMES* DEVELOPMENTS IN DEFAMATION LAW

The Supreme Court has been faced with a plethora of cases requiring it to apply the *New York Times* rule in various factual settings. For this reason, a rich body of constitutional doctrine has evolved that defines the limits of the rule. Consider several critical issues.

Who Is a Public Figure? A few years after *New York Times*, the Court was faced with the question whether it applied to other prominent individuals who were not on the state payroll. In two tandem cases, the Court ruled that at least some such individuals were covered by the rule.[16] One of the cases involved allegations of misconduct by the athletic director at a state university, who was technically an employee of a privately incorporated athletic association. The other involved a retired general who had become active in national politics, and was accused of haranguing a mob to resist a desegregation order. As "public figures," these plaintiffs were covered by the same rule as public officials.

Later cases make it clear that the category of public figures is limited. For example, involvement in well-publicized litigation is not enough to make a person a public figure.[17] Nor does a lawyer become a public figure by representing a client in civil rights litigation.[18] Similarly, a government researcher was not considered a public figure when a U.S. Senator attacked his work as a waste of public funds, since he had not assumed any role of public prominence in debate over government research expenditures and had not otherwise invited a high level of public attention.[19]

What Is Defamatory? In *Milkovich v. Lorain Journal Co.*, 497 U.S. 1 (1990), the plaintiff was a high school wrestling coach whose team was placed on probation for misconduct. The local courts overturned the ruling against the team. The coach sued because of press coverage implying that he had lied at the hearing. The Court rejected the argument that this was merely a matter of opinion and therefore not defamatory under the *New York Times* rule. Rather than using the "opinion" label, the Court preferred to ask whether a statement has provably false factual implications, and whether it used language in a loose, figurative, or hyperbolic sense which might dispel the factual implications. Although *Milkovich* rejects the idea of a separate privilege for "opinion," it provides the functional equivalent of such a privilege by careful tailoring of the plaintiff's duty to prove falsity.

What Is Malice? In common usage, malice means personal animosity. This is clearly not the meaning of the term under *New York Times v. Sullivan*. Rather, the plaintiff must prove by clear and convincing evidence that the

---

16. See *Curtis Publishing Co. v. Butts*, 388 U.S. 130 (1967) (also presenting the opinion in the companion case of *Associated Press v. Walker*).

17. See *Wolston v. Reader's Digest Ass'n*, 443 U.S. 157 (1979); *Time, Inc. v. Firestone*, 424 U.S. 448 (1976).

18. See *Gertz v. Robert Welch, Inc.*, 418 U.S. 323 (1974).

19. See *Hutchinson v. Proxmire*, 443 U.S. 111 (1979).

defendant knew the statement was false or acted with reckless disregard of the truth. And "recklessness" here means something more than a high degree of negligence, as the cases also indicate.[20]

Private Libels. As we saw in *Gertz*, the *New York Times* rule does not apply to claims of defamation brought by private citizens (as opposed to public figures). *Gertz* and other libel cases have emphasized the identity of the plaintiff rather than other potentially relevant factors. Some of these other factors have, however, occasionally been pivotal.[21]   Thus, although the *New York Times* rule seems to be well settled, the situation for private libel is less clear. There seems to be a broad consensus that at least some private defamation cases should be subject to constitutional restraints. What is unclear is whether there are some examples of defamation that are so truly private, and so far removed from public discourse, that they should be exempted from these restraints.

---

20.   In *Harte-Hanks Communications v. Connaughton*, 491 U.S. 657 (1989), the plaintiff was a county judge who was under investigation by a grand jury. The defendant ran a front-page story alleging that the judge had used "dirty tricks" to influence a witness and had offered her and her sister a trip to Florida in appreciation of their help during the investigation. The Court held that a showing of "highly unreasonable conduct constituting an extreme departure from the standards of investigation and reporting ordinarily adhered to by responsible publishers" is not enough to show malice. Thus, as the Court indicated in another case, the crucial point is whether in fact the publisher had serious doubts about the accuracy of the statement, not whether a prudent publisher would have had such doubts. See *St. Amant v. Thompson*, 390 U.S. 727 (1968). To show malice, it is not enough to show that the journalist knew that a story was not literally accurate in all regards. In *Masson v. New Yorker Magazine*, 501 U.S. 496 (1991), a published interview contained lengthy passages in quotations that did not in fact reflect verbatim transcripts of the subject's statements. The question, according to the Court, was whether the jury could find that the quotations had substantially the same meaning as the plaintiff's actual statements, or whether they had been changed in ways that rendered them defamatory.

21.   The concept of "public concern" surfaced in *Dun & Bradstreet, Inc. v. Greenmoss Builders, Inc.*, 472 U.S. 749 (1985), in which a credit reporting agency had erroneously informed some of its clients that the plaintiff corporation was bankrupt. A plurality opinion by Justice Powell refused to apply *Gertz*, even though the jury had apparently awarded punitive damages without finding *New York Times* malice. Finding the kind of speech involved in the case to be peripheral to the First Amendment, like commercial speech, Justice Powell could find "no credible argument that this type of credit reporting requires special protection to ensure that 'debate on public issues [will] be uninhibited, robust, and wide-open.' " Chief Justice Burger and Justice White concurred on the ground that *Gertz* was wrongly decided anyway.

One point that had clear majority support in *Dun & Bradstreet* is that the media enjoy no special privileges under libel law. But this point too has been called into question. In *Philadelphia Newspapers, Inc. v. Hepps*, 475 U.S. 767 (1986), the Court considered whether in a private libel case, the state may apply the common law rule that puts the burden of proof on the defendant to establish truth as a defense. Rejecting the common law rule, the Court said that to "ensure that true speech on matters of public concern is not deterred, we hold that the common-law presumption that defamatory speech is false cannot stand when a plaintiff seeks damages against a media defendant for speech of public concern."

As the following case shows, tort-related concepts also intersect the First Amendment outside of defamation law. The Court has repeatedly encountered the question whether the First Amendment protects certain invasions of privacy.

Bartnicki v. Vopper, 532 U.S. 514 (2001). Bartnicki was the chief negotiator for a local teacher's union. She used the cell phone in her car to call Kane, the union's president. In the process of discussing the negotiations, the president said, "If they're not gonna move for three percent, we're gonna have to go to their, their homes . . . . To blow off their front porches, we'll have to do some work on some of those guys." The school district later accepted a proposal favorable to the teachers. In connection with news reports about the settlement, Vopper played a tape of the intercepted conversation on his radio talk show. Bartnicki sued under a federal anti-wiretapping law. Section 2511(1)(a) of the statute prohibits interception of certain communications, including cell phone calls. Section 2511(1)(c) prohibits disclosure of the contents of any illegally intercepted material. The statute provides a private cause of action. In its presentation of the facts, the Court stressed three aspects of the facts: Vopper had nothing to do with the interception and did not even know the name of the person responsible; the tapes were obtained legally by the radio station; and the tapes involved a matter of public concern. In an opinion by **JUSTICE STEVENS**, the Court held that the First Amendment shielded the radio station from liability. Justice Stevens concluded that "the enforcement of that provision in these cases, however, implicates the core purposes of the First Amendment because it imposes sanctions on the publication of truthful information of public concern." The court did not find a sufficiently weighty public interest on the facts of the case to justify imposing liability. **JUSTICE BREYER**, joined by **JUSTICE O'CONNOR**, filed a concurring opinion, stressing that the Court's holding was limited to "the special circumstances present here: (1) the radio broadcasters acted lawfully (up to the time of final public disclosure); and (2) the information publicized involved a matter of unusual public concern, namely a threat of potential physical harm to others."

C.   CAMPAIGN EXPENDITURES

INTRODUCTORY NOTE ON CAMPAIGN FINANCE

Campaign finance reform became a major issue as a result of scandals during the Nixon Administration. In 1974, Congress passed its first major campaign finance legislation, the Federal Election Campaign Act (FEC). The FEC was immediately challenged on First Amendment grounds. Like its successors, the FEC contained special fast-track provisions, intended to move the constitutional issues up to the Supreme Court as quickly as possible. The fast-track provision, plus the need to make decisions without disrupting the election cycle, have placed the Court under great time pressure.

The Court's ensuing landmark decision in *Buckley v. Valeo*, 424 U.S. 1 (1976), has determined the shape of current campaign finance law. One of the most important holdings was the validity of public funding for campaigns, even when subject to some conditions on candidates who chose to accept the funds. The Court's response to direct restrictions on campaign spending, however, was much more mixed.

The *Buckley* Court distinguished sharply between limits on expenditures and limits on contributions. The Court found the interests invoked by the government to be insufficient to justify the spending restrictions. The majority scorned the argument that the expenditure limits were necessary to neutralize the effects of wealth on political campaigns. According to the Court, "the concept that government may restrict the speech of some elements of our society in order to enhance the relative voice of others is wholly foreign to the First Amendment," which was intended "to secure 'the widest possible dissemination of information from diverse and antagonistic sources' and 'to assure unfettered interchange of ideas for the bringing about of political and social changes desired by the people.'"

The Court was less hostile to the contribution restrictions. Unlike restrictions on a person's expenditures, a contribution limitation places "little direct restraint on his political communication, for it permits the symbolic expression of support evidenced by a contribution but does not in any way infringe the contributor's freedom to discuss candidates and issues." In short, the Court seemed to consider contribution restrictions as mostly involving associational rather than speech rights, and as burdening those rights only marginally. The Court found ample justification for the restriction:

> To the extent that large contributions are given to secure a political *quid pro quo* from current and potential office holders, the integrity of our system of representative democracy is undermined. Although the scope of such pernicious practices can never be reliably ascertained, the deeply disturbing examples surfacing after the 1972 election demonstrate that the problem is not an illusory one.

"Of almost equal concern," the Court added, was the "appearance of corruption" due to public awareness of the potential for abuse created by large contributions.

Buckley's distinction between expenditures and contributions was followed in later cases, despite considerable criticism from some Justices and scholars. *Nixon v. Shrink Missouri Government PAC,* 528 U.S. 377 (2000), was a replay of the contribution prong of *Buckley*. A Missouri statute imposed strict contribution limits for candidates for state office. Reaffirming *Buckley*, Justice Souter's opinion for the Court upheld these contribution limits, finding them to be "closely drawn" to match a "sufficiently important interest." He found a legitimate interest not only in preventing actual corruption but in avoiding "the broader threat from politicians too compliant with the wishes of large contributors." "Leave the perception of impropriety unanswered, and the cynical assumption that large donors call the tune could jeopardize the willingness of voters to take part in democratic governance."

Some commentators on campaign finance speak of the hydraulic effect, where blocking campaign spending in one area just causes it to pop up somewhere else. There is some historical support for the hydraulic view. One effect of *Buckley* was to increase the importance of campaign spending by organizations such as political action committees (PACs), corporations, and other groups. PACs are organizations that are designed to receive contributions from some group of people for election purposes. They therefore provide an alternative pathway for individuals to aggregate their election spending, outside of political parties or direct contributions to candidates. The upshot of the cases is that PACs can spend unlimited amounts of money, so long as no individual contributor gave more than $5,000. See *California Medical Ass'n v. Federal Election Comm'n*, 453 U.S. 182 (1981); *Federal Election Comm'n v. National Conservative PAC*, 470 U.S. 480 (1985).

In the 1990s, the flood of campaign funding jumped into a different channel called "soft money." To an increasing extent, contributions from corporations, unions, and other large donors were funneled through political parties, which then used the money to support the election of their party candidates. Typically, the money was used to increase voter registration and election turnout by party members or people thought to be sympathetic to the party. The Court held that the First Amendment shielded "independent" expenditures by political parties, just as it would shield independent expenditures by individuals, but that soft money can be treated a candidate contributions when the party pays for certain campaign ads over which the candidate has some degree of control. *Colorado Republican Fed. Campaign Comm. v. Federal Election Comm'n*, 518 U.S. 604 (1996) (*Colorado Republicans I*); *Federal Election Comm'n v. Colorado Republican Fed. Campaign Comm.*, 533 U.S. 431 (2001)(*Colorado Republicans II*).

The only (partial) deviation from the pattern of upholding contribution limits and invalidating expenditure limits was in the area of corporate speech, where the Court's approach wobbled. In *First National Bank v. Bellotti*, 435 U.S. 765 (1978), the Court struck down a statute prohibiting corporations from spending money to influence referendums on subjects unrelated to their business. Federal law has long prohibited corporations from making campaign contributions to candidates, however, and the Court has found sufficient potential for corruption to justify such restrictions. See *FEC v. National Right to Work Comm.*, 459 U.S. 197 (1982). These cases do fit the *Buckley* pattern, but the next decision took a different turn.

In *Austin v. Michigan Chamber of Commerce*, 494 U.S. 652 (1990), the Court upheld a state prohibition on corporate expenditures in political campaigns except through special political action funds. The Court found that the statute burdened the corporation's First Amendment rights. Nevertheless, the Court upheld the statute because it was supported by the compelling state interest in preventing corporations from channeling funds obtained from consumers and investors into political campaigns. Rather than being aimed at corruption, the ban on partisan corporate expenditures was designed to end "the corrosive and distorting effects of immense aggregations of wealth that are accumulated with the help of the corporate form and that have little or no correlation to the public's support for the corporation's political ideas." Instead of attempting to equalize the relative influence of speakers — a purpose found to be illegitimate in *Buckley* — the corporate expenditure ban "ensures that expenditures reflect actual public support for the political ideas espoused by corporations" by forcing the corporation to raise money for political expenditures separately.

This brings us to 2002, when Congress passed its most important campaign finance legislation in three decades, the Bipartisan Campaign Reform Act (BCRA). BCRA is a massive, complex piece of legislation (leading to an equally massive, complex set of opinions by the Justices). Our focus will be on two of the main provisions. Section 323 attempts to eliminate "soft money" donations. It prohibits national political parties from soliciting, receiving or spending any money except in compliance with federal funding limits — in effect, forcing them to rely entirely on "hard money" that is subject to federal regulation. Section 203 attempted to deal with a problem created by *Buckley* concerning corporate speech. Congress had attempted to ban all use of corporate and union funds (except through PACs) for campaign ads. But the *Buckley* Court, in order to avoid overbreadth concerns, had construed the statute narrowly to apply only to ads containing "express advocacy" of a candidate. Section 203 expanded the ban to include all "electioneering communications," whether or not they explicitly told the audience to vote for or against a candidate.

Like the original 1974 statute, the 2002 version was immediately challenged on First Amendment grounds. Many observers expected the Court to strike down substantial portions of BCRA, if not the entire statute. Some even anticipated a decision overruling *Buckley* and striking down all limits on contributions. The ensuing decision is widely considered the Court's most important statement on campaign finance since Gerald Ford's administration.

McCONNELL v. FEDERAL ELECTION COMMISSION
540 U.S. 93, 124 S.Ct. 619, 157 L.Ed.2d 491 (2003)

JUSTICE STEVENS and **JUSTICE O'CONNOR** delivered the opinion of the Court.[22]

* * *The Government defends § 323(a)'s ban on national parties' involvement with soft money as necessary to prevent the actual and apparent corruption of federal candidates and officeholders. Our cases have made clear that the prevention of corruption or its appearance constitutes a sufficiently important interest to justify political contribution limits. We have not limited that interest to the elimination of cash-for-votes exchanges. * * *

Of "almost equal" importance has been the Government's interest in combating the appearance or perception of corruption engendered by large campaign contributions. Take away Congress' authority to regulate the appearance of undue influence and "the cynical assumption that large donors call the tune could jeopardize the willingness of voters to take part in democratic governance." And because the First Amendment does not require Congress to ignore the fact that "candidates, donors, and parties test the limits of the current law," *Colorado II*, these interests have been sufficient to justify not only contribution limits themselves, but laws preventing the circumvention of such limits.

---

22. Due to the complexity of the case, there were actually multiple "opinions of the Court," authored by different Justices. We will focus only on the lead opinion, which dealt with the soft money and electioneering issues. (Challenges to others aspects of the statute were covered in opinions for the Court written by Chief Justice Rehnquist and Justice Breyer.) Unusually, the lead opinion is co-authored, probably in order to expedite the process so that the case could be handed down before the 2004 campaign began in earnest. There were also multiple dissenting and concurring opinions, some of which will be partially excerpted.

"The quantum of empirical evidence needed to satisfy heightened judicial scrutiny of legislative judgments will vary up or down with the novelty or the plausibility of the justification raised." The idea that large contributions to a national party can corrupt or, at the very least, create the appearance of corruption of federal candidates and officeholders is neither novel nor implausible. For nearly 30 years, FECA has placed strict dollar limits and source restrictions on contributions that individuals and other entities can give to national, state, and local party committees for the purpose of influencing a federal election. The premise behind these restrictions has been, and continues to be, that contributions to a federal candidate's party in aid of that candidate's campaign threaten to create — no less than would a direct contribution to the candidate — a sense of obligation. This is particularly true of contributions to national parties, with which federal candidates and officeholders enjoy a special relationship and unity of interest. This close affiliation has placed national parties in a unique position, "whether they like it or not," to serve as "agents for spending on behalf of those who seek to produce obligated officeholders." As discussed below, rather than resist that role, the national parties have actively embraced it.

The question for present purposes is whether large *soft-money* contributions to national party committees have a corrupting influence or give rise to the appearance of corruption. Both common sense and the ample record in these cases confirm Congress' belief that they do. [T]he FEC's allocation regime has invited widespread circumvention of FECA's limits on contributions to parties for the purpose of influencing federal elections. Under this system, corporate, union, and wealthy individual donors have been free to contribute substantial sums of soft money to the national parties, which the parties can spend for the specific purpose of influencing a particular candidate's federal election. It is not only plausible, but likely, that candidates would feel grateful for such donations and that donors would seek to exploit that gratitude.

The evidence in the record shows that candidates and donors alike have in fact exploited the soft-money loophole, the former to increase their prospects of election and the latter to create debt on the part of officeholders, with the national parties serving as willing intermediaries. Thus, despite FECA's hard-money limits on direct contributions to candidates, federal officeholders have commonly asked donors to make soft-money donations to national and state committees "solely in order to assist federal campaigns," including the office-holder's own. Parties kept tallies of the amounts of soft money raised by each officeholder, and "the amount of money a Member of Congress raise[d] for the national political committees often affect[ed] the amount the committees g[a]ve to assist the Member's campaign." Donors often asked that their contributions be credited to particular candidates, and the parties obliged, irrespective of whether the funds were hard or soft. National party committees often teamed with individual candidates' campaign committees to create joint fundraising committees, which enabled the candidates to take advantage of the party's higher contribution limits while still allowing donors to give to their preferred candidate. Even when not participating directly in the fundraising, federal officeholders were well aware of the identities of the donors: National party committees would distribute lists of potential or actual donors, or donors themselves would report their generosity to officeholders.

* * *

The evidence from the federal officeholders' perspective is similar. For example, one former Senator described the influence purchased by nonfederal donations as follows:

> Too often, Members' first thought is not what is right or what they believe, but how it will affect fundraising. Who, after all, can seriously contend that a $100,000 donation does not alter the way one thinks about — and quite possibly votes on — an issue? . . . When you don't pay the piper that finances your campaigns, you will never get any more money from that piper. Since money is the mother's milk of politics, you never want to be in that situation.

* * * By bringing soft-money donors and federal candidates and officeholders together, "[p]arties are thus necessarily the instruments of some contributors whose object is not to support the party's message or to elect party candidates across the board, but rather to support a specific candidate for the sake of a position on one narrow issue, or even to support any candidate who will be obliged to the contributors." *Colorado II.*

Plaintiffs argue that without concrete evidence of an instance in which a federal officeholder has actually switched a vote (or, presumably, evidence of a specific instance where the public believes a vote was switched), Congress has not shown that there exists real or apparent corruption. But the record is to the contrary. The evidence connects soft money to manipulations of the legislative calendar, leading to Congress' failure to enact, among other things, generic drug legislation, tort reform, and tobacco legislation. To claim that such actions do not change legislative outcomes surely misunderstands the legislative process.

More importantly, plaintiffs conceive of corruption too narrowly. Our cases have firmly established that Congress' legitimate interest extends beyond preventing simple cash-for-votes corruption to curbing "undue influence on an officeholder's judgment, and the appearance of such influence." Many of the "deeply disturbing examples" of corruption cited by this Court in *Buckley* to justify FECA's contribution limits were not episodes of vote buying, but evidence that various corporate interests had given substantial donations to gain access to high-level government officials. Even if that access did not secure actual influence, it certainly gave the "appearance of such influence."

The record in the present case is replete with similar examples of national party committees peddling access to federal candidates and officeholders in exchange for large soft-money donations. * * * So pervasive is this practice that the six national party committees actually furnish their own menus of opportunities for access to would-be soft-money donors, with increased prices reflecting an increased level of access. * * *

In sum, there is substantial evidence to support Congress' determination that large soft-money contributions to national political parties give rise to corruption and the appearance of corruption. * * *

BCRA § 203's Prohibition of Corporate and Labor Disbursements for Electioneering Communications

Since our decision in *Buckley,* Congress' power to prohibit corporations and unions from using funds in their treasuries to finance advertisements expressly advocating the election or defeat of candidates in federal elections has been firmly embedded in our law. The ability to form and administer separate segregated funds [PACs] has provided corporations and unions with a constitutionally sufficient opportunity to engage in express advocacy. That has been this Court's unanimous view, and it is not challenged in this litigation.

Section 203 of BCRA [extends] this rule, which previously applied only to express advocacy, to all "electioneering communications" covered by the definition of that term in amended FECA § 304(f)(3). [That subsection defines electioneering communications as any broadcast, cable, or satellite communication that clearly identifies a candidate, airs within sixty days of a general election or thirty days of a primary, and is targeted at the relevant electorate.] Thus, under BCRA, corporations and unions may not use their general treasury funds to finance electioneering communications, but they remain free to organize and administer segregated funds, or PACs, for that purpose. Because corporations can still fund electioneering communications with PAC money, it is "simply wrong" to view the provision as a "complete ban" on expression rather than a regulation. * * *

Rather than arguing that the prohibition on the use of general treasury funds is a complete ban that operates as a prior restraint, plaintiffs instead challenge the expanded regulation on the grounds that it is both overbroad and underinclusive. * * *

In light of our precedents, plaintiffs do not contest that the Government has a compelling interest in regulating advertisements that expressly advocate the election or defeat of a candidate for federal office. Nor do they contend that the speech involved in so-called issue advocacy is any more core political speech than are words of express advocacy. * * * Rather, plaintiffs argue that the justifications that adequately support the regulation of express advocacy do not apply to significant quantities of speech encompassed by the definition of electioneering communications.

This argument fails to the extent that the issue ads broadcast during the 30- and 60-day periods preceding federal primary and general elections are the functional equivalent of express advocacy. The justifications for the regulation of express advocacy apply equally to ads aired during those periods if the ads are intended to influence the voters' decisions and have that effect. The precise percentage of issue ads that clearly identified a candidate and were aired during those relatively brief preelection time spans but had no electioneering purpose is a matter of dispute between the parties and among the judges on the District Court. * * * Moreover, whatever the precise percentage may have been in the past, in the future corporations and unions may finance genuine issue ads during those time frames by simply avoiding any specific reference to federal candidates, or in doubtful cases by paying for the ad from a segregated fund. * * *

JUSTICE KENNEDY, concurring in the judgment in part and dissenting in part with respect to BCRA Titles I and II.

The First Amendment guarantees our citizens the right to judge for themselves the most effective means for the expression of political views and to decide for themselves which entities to trust as reliable speakers. Significant portions of Titles I and II of the Bipartisan Campaign Reform Act of 2002 (BCRA or Act) constrain that freedom. These new laws force speakers to abandon their own preference for speaking through parties and organizations. And they provide safe harbor to the mainstream press, suggesting that the corporate media alone suffice to alleviate the burdens the Act places on the rights and freedoms of ordinary citizens.

* * *

Though the majority cites common sense as the foundation for its definition of corruption, in the context of the real world only a single definition of corruption has been found to identify political corruption successfully and to distinguish good political responsiveness from bad — that is *quid pro quo*. Favoritism and influence are not, as the Government's theory suggests, avoidable in representative politics. It is in the nature of an elected representative to favor certain policies, and, by necessary corollary, to favor the voters and contributors who support those policies. It is well understood that a substantial and legitimate reason, if not the only reason, to cast a vote for, or to make a contribution to, one candidate over another is that the candidate will respond by producing those political outcomes the supporter favors. Democracy is premised on responsiveness. *Quid pro quo* corruption has been, until now, the only agreed upon conduct that represents the bad form of responsiveness and presents a justiciable standard with a relatively clear limiting principle: Bad responsiveness may be demonstrated by pointing to a relationship between an official and a *quid*. * * *

The hostility toward corporations and unions that infuses the majority opinion is inconsistent with the viewpoint neutrality the First Amendment demands of all Government actors, including the members of this Court. Corporations, after all, are the engines of our modern economy. They facilitate complex operations on which the Nation's prosperity depends. To say these entities cannot alert the public to pending political issues that may threaten the country's economic interests is unprecedented. Unions are also an established part of the national economic system. They, too, have their own unique insights to contribute to the political debate, but the law's impact on them is just as severe. The costs of the majority's misplaced concerns about the "corrosive and distorting effects of immense aggregations of wealth," moreover, will weigh most heavily on budget-strapped nonprofit entities upon which many of our citizens rely for political commentary and advocacy. These groups must now choose between staying on the sidelines in the next election or establishing a PAC against their institutional identities. PACs are a legal construct sanctioned by Congress. They are not necessarily the means of communication chosen and preferred by the citizenry. * * *

The First Amendment commands that Congress "shall make no law . . . abridging the freedom of speech." The command cannot be read to allow

Congress to provide for the imprisonment of those who attempt to establish new political parties and alter the civic discourse. Our pluralistic society is filled with voices expressing new and different viewpoints, speaking through modes and mechanisms that must be allowed to change in response to the demands of an interested public. As communities have grown and technology has evolved, concerted speech not only has become more effective than a single voice but also has become the natural preference and efficacious choice for many Americans. The Court, upholding multiple laws that suppress both spontaneous and concerted speech, leaves us less free than before. Today's decision breaks faith with our tradition of robust and unfettered debate.

NOTES ON *McCONNELL*

1. *Organizational Speech.* One of the fracture lines within the Court concerns the status of speech by corporations and unions. Are there legitimate reasons for allowing greater regulation of speech by these entities? The majority, following the earlier decision in *Austin*, obviously thinks so; the dissenters disagree. If there is to be greater regulation, is that because organizational speech has lower First Amendment value, or because the government's regulatory interests are higher? Has the Court underestimated the "need for vibrant election-related participation by a large group of non-governmental actors"? See Richard L. Hasen, *Buckley is Dead, Long Live Buckley: the New Campaign Finance Incoherence of McConnell v. Federal Election Commission*, 153 U. Pa. L. Rev. 31 (2004).

2. *The Meaning of Corruption.* Another fracture line involves the definition of corruption. The majority believes that gaining access to a candidate is a form of corruption. The dissenters would limit corruption to payments that actually change an elected official's votes, perhaps limited to payments made directly to a candidate. Loosely, the majority thinks corruption includes "influence peddling," while the dissent defines it as bribery. Is the grant of access as a reward for political contributions and expenditures something that we should be worried about? Or is it an inevitable component of democracy?

3. *Later developments.* Cases since *McConnell* have been less receptive to campaign finance regulation. First, in *Randall v. Sorrell*, 548 U.S. 230 (2006), the Court struck down a 1997 Vermont law that imposed especially stringent limits on contributions and campaign expenditures. Perhaps the most interesting aspect of the decision was Chief Justice Roberts' view about *Buckley*. He joined a portion of Justice Breyer's decision that refused to overrule *Buckley*'s limits on expenditures, but that spoke more broadly about adherence to *Buckley*:

Second, in *Federal Election Comm'n v. Wisconsin Right to Life*, 127 S.Ct. 2652 (2007), a closely divided Court sharply contracted the prohibition on union and corporate advertising during the so-called blackout period before elections. Hearing an as-applied challenge to the prohibition, Chief Justice Roberts' controlling opinion held that "a court should find that an ad is the functional equivalent of express advocacy only if the ad is susceptible of no reasonable interpretation other than as an appeal to vote for or against a specific candidate." He was joined by Justice Alito. Justice Scalia, joined by Justices Kennedy and Thomas, argued that *McConnell* should be overruled on this point. The dissenters protested that the Chief Justice's opinion had in effect eviscerated *McConnell*. Were they right? See Richard L. Hasen, *Beyond Incoherence: The Roberts Court's Deregulatory Turn in FEC v. Wisconsin Right to Life*, 92 Minn. L. Rev. 1064 (2008).

Third, in *Davis v. Federal Election Commission*, 128 S.Ct. 2759 (2008), the Court struck down the so-called "Millionaire's Amendment." This amendment modifies the usual restrictions on expenditures by candidates receiving public financing when the opposing candidate finances his or her campaign out of personal wealth. Justice Alito's opinion for the Court rejected as illegitimate any government interest in providing a level playing field between wealthy and less affluent candidates.   In contrast, Justice Stevens' dissent for four Justices said that it "cannot be gainsaid that the twin rationales at the heart of the Millionaire's Amendment — reducing the importance of wealth as a criterion for public office and countering the perception that seats in the United States Congress are available for purchase by the wealthiest bidder — are important Government interests. It is also evident that Congress, in enacting the provision, crafted a solution that was carefully tailored to those concerns."

SECTION 3. GOVERNMENT POLICING OF CULTURAL DISCOURSE AND INTERGROUP RELATIONS

People can come to identify themselves as part of groups in various ways, including the way that the culture identifies and characterizes individuals and their behaviors. Challenging, transgressing, or defending these characterizations is an important aspect of public discourse, and the contestants often call upon government assistance. For instance, sex-related expression can help define how people think about men, women, and sexuality. In response, religious groups call for regulation of obscenity in order to defend traditional understandings of sex roles, while some feminists call for regulation of pornography in order to change attitudes and behavior toward women. Similar disputes arise with respect to ethnic, language, and racial minorities. Overlayed on these debates is the question of how to structure the public sphere, so that on the one hand all groups are free to use it for self-expression but on the other hand all groups can navigate it freely.

A.   SEXUALITY AND GENDER

When the First Amendment was ratified, all fourteen states made either blasphemy or profanity a statutory crime, and some of the states made it a crime to promulgate "any filthy, obscene, or profane song, pamphlet, libel or mock sermon," *Mass. Bay Colony Charters and Laws* 399 (1814). In the first half of the nineteenth century, most states and many municipalities adopted laws criminalizing the promulgation of obscene printed materials — but never defining what was meant by *obscenity*. Materials advertising contraceptives, describing the biology of human reproduction, treating homosexuality as a tolerable condition, or recounting episodes of fornication or sodomy were seized as obscene, without any noticeable judicial cavil until the 1930s.

After Judge Augustus Hand overturned the Customs Service seizure of James Joyce's *Ulysses* on the ground that the First Amendment protected serious literature, see *United States v. One Book Entitled Ulysses,* 72 F.2d 705 (2d Cir. 1934), federal and state judges began scrutinizing sexual censorship more carefully. Although the Supreme Court in *Roth v. United States,* 354 U.S. 476 (1957), held for the first time that obscenity was not protected by the First Amendment, the Court rejected the "tends to deprave vulnerable minds" test followed since the 1880s and redefined obscenity as material which, if considered as a whole, predominantly appeals to "prurient interest, i.e., a shameful or morbid interest in nudity, sex, or excretion." During the 1960s, the Court expanded and sought to refine the *Roth* definition, but could never obtain the agreement of five Justices for any precise formulation. Then, in 1973, the Court handed down two decisions that commanded five-Justice majority opinions.

Miller v. California, 413 U.S. 15 (1973). The Court held in an opinion by **Chief Justice Burger** that "the basic guidelines for the trier of fact must be: (a) whether "the average person, applying contemporary community standards" would find that the work, taken as a whole, appeals to the prurient interest; (b) whether the work depicts or describes, in a patently offensive way, sexual conduct specifically defined by the applicable state law; and (c) whether the work, taken as a whole, lacks serious literary, artistic, political, or scientific value." As the Court explained:

Sex and nudity may not be exploited without limit by films or pictures exhibited or sold in places of public accommodation any more than live sex and nudity can be exhibited or sold without limit in such public places. At a minimum, prurient, patently offensive depiction or description of sexual conduct must have serious literary, artistic, political, or scientific value to merit First Amendment protection. For example, medical books for the education of physicians and related personnel necessarily use graphic illustrations and descriptions of human anatomy. In resolving the inevitably sensitive questions of fact and law, we must continue to rely on the jury system, accompanied by the safeguards that judges, rules of evidence, presumption of innocence, and other protective features provide, as we do with rape, murder, and a host of other offenses against society and its individual members. * * *

Paris Adult Theatre I v. Slaton, 413 U.S. 49 (1973). In another opinion by **Chief Justice Burger**, the Court rejected the argument that the First Amendment protects the right of consenting adults to purchase obscene materials. The Court held that the government had valid regulatory interests, including "the interest of the public in the quality of life and the total community environment, the tone of commerce in the great city centers, and, possibly, the public safety itself." The Court also noted that "there is at least an arguable correlation between obscene material and crime." Although (then as now) the empirical evidence was at least subject to dispute, the Court concluded that the legislature was entitled to assume that obscene materials were harmful:

If we accept the unprovable assumption that a complete education requires the reading of certain books, and the well nigh universal belief that good books, plays, and art lift the spirit, improve the mind, enrich the human personality, and develop character, can we then say that a state legislature may not act on the corollary assumption that commerce in obscene books, or public exhibitions focused on obscene conduct, have a tendency to exert a corrupting and debasing impact leading to antisocial behavior? * * * The sum of experience, including that of the past two decades, affords an ample basis for legislatures to conclude that a sensitive, key relationship of human existence, central to family life, community welfare, and the development of human personality, can be debased and distorted by crass commercial exploitation of sex. Nothing in the Constitution prohibits a State from reaching such a conclusion and acting on it legislatively simply because there is no conclusive evidence or empirical data.

Are such assumptions a sufficient basis for preventing adults from reading whatever books they want to?

NOTES ON REGULATING SEXUALLY EXPLICIT MATERIALS

1. *Privacy.* In connection with *Paris Adult Theatre*, consider *Stanley v. Georgia*, 394 U.S. 557 (1969), in which the Court reversed a conviction for possession of obscene films. The police had discovered the films during a search of the defendant's home for evidence of illegal gambling. Justice Marshall's opinion for the Court held that the regulations for regulating obscenity do not reach into the privacy of the home: "If the First Amendment means anything, it means that a State has no business telling a man, sitting alone in his own house, what books he may read or what films he may watch." Apparently, under *Stanley*, the government cannot arrest a person for possessing a videotape of an obscene movie, but under *Paris Adult Theatre*, it can prosecute the store that sold the tape.

2. *Local Communities and the Internet.* In *Ashcroft v. ACLU*, 535 U.S. 564 (2002), the Court grappled with the question of how to apply the "community standard" portion of *Miller* to the Internet. In response to *Reno v. ACLU*, 521 U.S. 844 (1997), which struck down Congress' first effort to shield children from pornographic material on the Internet, Congress passed the Child Online Protection Act, which restricts only commercial material on the World Wide Web that is "harmful to minors." The statute incorporates the *Miller* test. The lower court held that using contemporary community standards made the statute unconstitutional on its face, since it would in effect limit the entire country to whatever material was acceptable to the most restrictive local community. The case produced such a badly fractured Court that we are reluctant to attempt a summary. The only thing that almost everyone on the Court did agree about was that the lower court's first effort was unsatisfactory.

3. *Child Pornography.* The Court has made only one significant departure from the *Miller* obscenity test. In *New York v. Ferber*, 458 U.S. 747 (1982), the Court upheld a statute banning "child pornography," which was defined as sexual material involving children as models or actors. The Court found that the state's interest in protecting children from participating in the production of these materials was strong enough to justify banning the materials themselves, so as to dry up the market.

Ashcroft v. The Free Speech Coalition, 535 U.S. 234 (2002). The issue in this case was whether to expand *Ferber* to encompass "virtual child pornography" — pornography in which adult actors portray juveniles or in which computer images appearing like real children are used. **Justice Kennedy's** opinion for the Court stressed that no children were actually used in making such pornography. He emphasized that *"Ferber's* judgment about child pornography was based upon how it was made, not on what it communicated." To the government's argument that virtual pornography encourages pedophiles, the Court responded:

> The mere tendency of speech to encourage unlawful acts is not a sufficient reason for banning it. The government "cannot constitutionally premise legislation on the desirability of controlling a person's private thoughts." First Amendment freedoms are most in danger when the government seeks to control thought or to justify its laws for that impermissible end. The right to think is the beginning of freedom, and speech must be protected from the government because speech is the beginning of thought.

The government also argued that makers of real child pornography would evade conviction if they were allowed to offer a "virtual pornography" defense. But the Court said that banning protected speech in order to expedite the prosecution of unprotected speech "turns the First Amendment on its head."

Regina v. Butler, 134 National Reporter 81 (Canadian Sup. Ct. 1992), is the Canadian counterpart of *Miller*. The defendants ran an "adults only" video store in Winnipeg. They were charged with violating the Canadian obscenity statute. (The same statute, by the way, bans obscene materials, "crime comics," any instrument for causing an abortion, and advertisements for cures for venereal diseases.) The statute bans "the undue exploitation of sex or of sex and * * * crime, horror, cruelty and violence." The Court construed this provision to ban "degrading or dehumanizing material" that violates community standards. In particular, the opinion by **Justice Sopinka** explained:

> Among other things, degrading or dehumanizing materials place women (and sometimes men) in positions of subordination, servile submission or humiliation. They run against the principles of equality and dignity of all human beings. * * * Consent cannot save materials that otherwise contain degrading or dehumanizing scenes.

As to what materials are forbidden, the Court said that the portrayal of "sex coupled with violence" is "almost always" the undue exploitation of sex; explicit sex "which is degrading or dehumanizing" may be undue if "the risk of harm" is substantial; but apart from child pornography, explicit sex that is neither violent nor dehumanizing is permitted. Finally, "[a]rtistic expression rests at the heart of freedom of expression values and any doubt in this regard must be resolved in favour of freedom of expression." As in *Miller*, the court held that community standards would be applied. Also, the Court had previously held that the statute did "not extend to the private use or viewing of obscene materials."

Turning to the issue of whether the statute violated the Canadian Charter, the Court concluded that pornography does involve "expression" and therefore is entitled to prima facie protection under the Charter. The statute, however, served "pressing and substantial objectives which justify overriding the freedom to distribute obscene materials." There is "a growing concern that the exploitation of women and children, depicted in publications and films can, in certain circumstances, lead to 'abject and servile victimization.' " If "true equality between male and female persons is to be achieved, we cannot ignore the threat to equality resulting from exposure to audiences of certain types of violent and degrading material."

A NOTE ON FEMINIST ANTI-PORNOGRAPHY THEORIES

It seems somewhat odd to say that obscenity is not "speech" because it is not communication (wrong: it is like other pictures and writings) or because it serves none of the First Amendment values that speech can serve (wrong: personal autonomy, perhaps also informational values). Perhaps the Court has concluded that the social detriment of obscene materials so much outweighs their possible First Amendment value that such materials should be excluded under a per se rule. But what is the social detriment? Is it the nosy preferences of sexual prudes, their disgust that people might be reading this stuff? Isn't the point of the First Amendment to carve out protections for expression that riles some people? In light of the recent decisions protecting flag-burning and cross-burning, can the obscenity cases stand?

Professor Catharine A. MacKinnon, *Francis Biddle's Sister: Pornography, Civil Rights, and Speech*, in *Feminism Unmodified* 163 (1987), sets forth another line of defense for anti-pornography statutes — their third-party effects. Based upon empirical studies, published stories, and testimony at hearings on her proposed anti-pornography ordinance in Minneapolis, MacKinnon argues for several different third-party effects.

"The first victims of pornography are the ones in it." *Id.* at 179. Linda Marchiano, also known as "Linda Lovelace" (star of *Deep Throat*), described the degradation she suffered in a book, *Ordeal*. Her story is one of brutal coercion: she was beaten, imprisoned, threatened, intimidated, humiliated, and tortured by people involved in making the movies. Other stars, even in "soft porn" films, report systematic coercion and pain as a regular part of the moviemaking process. Children as well as women are coerced into performing in pornographic films, sometimes physically and sometimes psychologically, as through blackmail.

Second, pornography directly and specifically causes sexual abuse, particularly against women, argues MacKinnon. "Some rapes are performed by men with paperback books in their pockets." Experimental studies, MacKinnon writes, show that exposure to pornography as defined in the proposed ordinance "cause[s] measurable harm to women through increasing men's attitudes and behaviors of discrimination in both violent and nonviolent forms. Exposure to some of the pornography in our definition increases the immediately subsequent willingness of normal men to aggress against women under laboratory conditions. * * * Exposure to pornography also significantly increases attitudinal measures known to correlate with rape and self-reports of aggressive acts, measures such as hostility toward women, propensity to rape, condoning rape, and predicting that one would rape or force sex on a woman if one knew one would not get caught." *Id.* at 187.[23]

Third, MacKinnon argues that pornography contributes generally to women's inequality. It does this by contributing to violence against women (as described above), but also by reinforcing subordinating attitudes toward women. Generally, pornography eroticizes male domination of women, and its various corollaries — women are objects, masculinity is domination, and hierarchy is sexy. Pornography "makes dominance and submission into sex. * * * Inequality is its central dynamic; the illusion of freedom coming together with the reality of force is central to this working. * * * Pornography in this view is a * * * practice of sexual politics, an institution of gender inequality." *Id.* at 172.

Does MacKinnon's theory, as echoed in *Butler*, provide a sounder basis for regulation than the *Miller* approach?

PROBLEM 6-1
FEMINIST ANTI-PORNOGRAPHY ORDINANCES

In 1983, an ordinance was introduced in the Minneapolis city council that provided various civil sanctions (such as injunctions) against the sale of pornography. The purpose section of the ordinance stated that:

> The council finds that pornography is central in creating and maintaining the civil inequality of the sexes. Pornography is a systematic practice of exploitation and subordination based on sex which differentially harms women. The bigotry and contempt it promotes, with the acts of aggression it fosters, harm women's opportunities for equality of rights in employment, education, property rights, public accommodations and public services; create public harassment and private denigration; promote injury and degradation such as rape, battery and prostitution and inhibit just enforcement of laws against these acts; contribute significantly to restricting women from full exercise of citizenship and participation in public life, including in neighborhoods; damage relations between the sexes; and undermine women's equal exercise of rights to speech and action guaranteed to all citizens under the Constitutions and laws of the United States and the State of Minnesota.

Based on these findings, the city's civil rights ordinance was to be amended to make the sale of pornography a violation of the civil rights of women. Pornography was defined as follows:

> Pornography is the sexually explicit subordination of women, graphically depicted, whether in pictures or in words, that also includes one or more of the following:
>
> (i) women are presented dehumanized as sexual objects, things or commodities; or
>
> (ii) women are presented as sexual objects who enjoy pain or humiliation; or

---

23. Other examinations of research on possible linkages between pornography and violence or oppression against women include James Weinstein, *Hate Speech, Pornography, and the Radical Attack on Free Speech Doctrine* 191-217 (1999); Richard Posner, *Sex and Reason* 366-73 (1992); Frederick Schauer, *Causation Theory and the Causes of Sexual Violence*, 1987 Am. Bar Found. Res. J. 737 (analyzing the results of the Report of the Attorney General's Commission on Pornography, on which Schauer served); Cass Sunstein, *Pornography and the First Amendment*, 1986 Duke L.J. 589.

(iii) women are presented as sexual objects who experience sexual pleasure in being raped; or

(iv) women are presented as sexual objects tied up or cut up or mutilated or bruised or physically hurt; or

(v) women are presented in postures of sexual submission; or

(vi) women's body parts — including but not limited to vaginas, breasts, and buttocks — are exhibited, such that women are reduced to those parts; or

(vii) women are presented as whores by nature; or

(viii) women are presented being penetrated by objects or animals; or

(ix) women are presented in scenarios of degradation, injury, abasement, torture, shown as filthy or inferior, bleeding, bruised, or hurt in a context that makes these conditions sexual.[24]

A modified form of the ordinance was later passed in Indianapolis.

Would this ordinance be constitutional under current judicial standards? See *American Booksellers Ass'n v. Hudnut*, 771 F.2d 323 (7th Cir. 1985) (Easterbrook, J.), *aff'd mem.*, 475 U.S. 1001 (1986) (reviewing a similar ordinance). Should material of the kind described in the ordinance be protected by the First Amendment?[25] If the ordinance were limited to material that both "subordinates women" *and* is classified as obscene under *Miller*, would it be constitutional? In this connection, reread *R.A.V.*

Although the courts have refused to embrace the feminist position, pornography and other sexual suppression seems to be subject to an unusual amount of regulation in the Court's eyes, as illustrated by the following decisions. In considering these cases, ask whether the Courts would have upheld similar restraints on political expression.

City of Renton v. Playtime Theatres, Inc. 475 U.S. 41, 106 S.Ct. 925, 89 L.Ed.2d 29 (1986). A city ordinance in Renton, Washington, prohibited adult movie theaters within 1,000 feet of any residence, church, park, or school. The plaintiffs had purchased two theatres with the intention of exhibiting adult films. In an opinion by **Chief Justice Rehnquist**, the Court upheld the ordinance, reasoning that "at least with respect to businesses that purvey sexually explicit materials, zoning ordinances designed to combat the undesirable secondary effects of such businesses are to be reviewed under the standards applicable to "content-neutral" time, place, and manner regulations." The ordinance satisfied this standard, in the Court's view. The Court was unimpressed by the facts that Renton had relied entirely on the experience of other cities to show that adult businesses would cause harm rather than presenting evidence relating

---

24. For the full text of the Minneapolis proposal, see 2 Const. Comm. 181-89 (1985). The background of the ordinance is recounted in David Bryden, *Between Two Constitutions: Feminism and Pornography,* 2 Const. Comm. 147 (1985).

25. Compare MacKinnon's arguments, above, with Nadine Strossen, *The Convergence of Feminist and Civil Liberties Principles in the Pornography Debate* (Book Review), 62 N.Y.U. L. Rev. 201 (1987) (rejecting MacKinnon's views).

specifically to its own situation, and that the ordinance left open very few sites that were actually commercially available.[26]

Barnes v. Glen Theatre, Inc., 501 U.S. 560 (1991). This case involved the application of Indiana's ban on public nudity to barroom dancing. **Chief Justice Rehnquist**'s plurality opinion accepted the premise that nude dancing was sufficiently expressive to receive some First Amendment protection. He considered the state's interest in preventing public nudity to be content neutral, and upheld the ordinance under the *O'Brien* test. **Justice Scalia**, concurring in the judgment, argued that a general law regulating conduct (and not targeted at expressive conduct) should not be subject to First Amendment scrutiny at all. ("Were it the case that Indiana *in practice* targeted only expressive nudity, while turning a blind eye to nude beaches and unclothed purveyors of hot dogs and machine tools, it might be said that what posed as a regulation of conduct in general was in reality a regulation of only communicative conduct.") **Justice Souter** also concurred in the judgment, on the basis that the state had a "substantial interest in combating the secondary effects of adult entertainment establishments" such as prostitution and sexual assaults. **Justice White**, joined by **Justices Marshall**, **Blackmun**, and **Stevens**, dissented, arguing that the statute was aimed at the "communicative aspect of the erotic dance" and therefore was not content-neutral.

City of Erie v. Pap's A.M., 529 U.S. 277 (2000), presented the Court with the opportunity to clarify its holding in *Barnes*, but the Justices once again proved unable to agree on a rationale. The plaintiff operated an adult entertainment establishment featuring nude dancing. Erie passed an ordinance against nude dancing, with language tracking the ordinance upheld in *Barnes*, thus requiring that the dancers wear pasties and G-strings. The introduction to the ordinance recited the city's concern about the secondary effects of nude dancing establishments like the plaintiff's. Once again, the Court upheld the ban on nude dancing, but with no consensus on the reasoning. According to the plurality opinion by **Justice O'Connor**, the propensity of adult entertainment establishments to attract crime and prostitution is a content-neutral secondary effect that the city could validly seek to suppress. Consequently, she found that the *O'Brien* test was applicable and was satisfied by the ordinance. **Justices Scalia** and **Thomas** once again concluded that a general ban on public nudity

---

26.   *Renton* purports to leave open the opportunity to operate an adult bookstore or movie theater, though subjecting these activities to special land-use restrictions. In practice, however, administrators might either delay issuing permits or arbitrarily deny them, in effect turning what is supposed to be a system of zoning into a flat prohibition. *City of Littleton v. Z.J. Gifts D-4, L.L.C.*, 541 U.S. 774 (2004), considers what procedural safeguards are required to prevent this abuse. *City of Littleton* held that the state's "ordinary judicial review procedures suffice as long as the courts remain sensitive to the need to prevent First Amendment harms and administer those procedures accordingly. And whether the courts do so is a matter normally fit for case-by-case determination rather than a facial challenge."

regulates conduct rather than speech, and is therefore immune from First Amendment scrutiny. In dissent, **Justice Souter** found an inadequate factual record to support the city's concerns. In another dissent, **Justice Stevens**, joined by **Justice Ginsburg**, argued that the ban was content-based since it was aimed entirely at erotic dancing rather than other nude dancing — the city having conceded that it had not applied the ordinance to serious theatrical productions such as the play "Equus."

———

What exactly is the state's interest in banning public nudity, where only consenting adults are involved? How is it different from the state's interest in banning photographs of nude individuals, which clearly would not be subject to the *O'Brien* test?

The state courts had indicated that the ban did not apply to theatrical performances. Is there any constitutional obstacle to applying the ban in that context? If not, why should the state have the power to ban a live performance of a play involving nudity, but not the power to ban a movie showing exactly the same thing?

B. FIGHTING WORDS, CAPTIVE AUDIENCES, AND HATE SPEECH

COHEN v. CALIFORNIA
403 U.S. 15, 91 S.Ct. 1780, 29 L.Ed.2d 284 (1971)

JUSTICE HARLAN delivered the opinion of the Court.

This case may seem at first blush too inconsequential to find its way into our books, but the issue it presents is of no small constitutional significance.

Appellant Paul Robert Cohen was convicted [of] "maliciously and willfully disturb[ing] the peace or quiet of any neighborhood or person . . . by . . . offensive conduct . . ." He was given 30 days' imprisonment. The facts upon which his conviction rests are detailed in the opinion of the Court of Appeal of California, Second Appellate District, as follows:

> On April 26, 1968, the defendant was observed in the Los Angeles County Courthouse in the corridor outside of division 20 of the municipal court wearing a jacket bearing the words "Fuck the Draft" which were plainly visible. There were women and children present in the corridor. The defendant was arrested. The defendant testified that he wore the jacket knowing that the words were on the jacket as a means of informing the public of the depth of his feelings against the Vietnam War and the draft.

> The defendant did not engage in, nor threaten to engage in, nor did anyone as the result of his conduct in fact commit or threaten to commit any act of violence. The defendant did not make any loud or unusual noise, nor was there any evidence that he uttered any sound prior to his arrest.

* * *

In order to lay hands on the precise issue which this case involves, it is useful first to canvass various matters which this record does *not* present. * * *

In the first place, Cohen was tried under a statute applicable throughout the entire State. Any attempt to support this conviction on the ground that the statute seeks to preserve an appropriately decorous atmosphere in the courthouse where Cohen was arrested must fail in the absence of any language in the statute that would have put appellant on notice that certain kinds of otherwise permissible speech or conduct would nevertheless, under California law, not be tolerated in certain places. No fair reading of the phrase "offensive conduct" can be said sufficiently to inform the ordinary person that distinctions between certain locations are thereby created.[3]

In the second place, as it comes to us, this case cannot be said to fall within those relatively few categories of instances where prior decisions have established the power of government to deal more comprehensively with certain forms of individual expression simply upon a showing that such a form was employed. This is not, for example, an obscenity case. Whatever else may be necessary to give rise to the States' broader power to prohibit obscene expression, such expression must be, in some significant way, erotic. It cannot plausibly be maintained that this vulgar allusion to the Selective Service System would conjure up such psychic stimulation in anyone likely to be confronted with Cohen's crudely defaced jacket.

This Court has also held that the States are free to ban the simple use, without a demonstration of additional justifying circumstances, of so-called "fighting words," those personally abusive epithets which, when addressed to the ordinary citizen, are, as a matter of common knowledge, inherently likely to provoke violent reaction. *Chaplinsky.* While the four-letter word displayed by Cohen in relation to the draft is not uncommonly employed in a personally provocative fashion, in this instance it was clearly not "directed to the person of the hearer." No individual actually or likely to be present could reasonably have regarded the words on appellant's jacket as a direct personal insult. Nor do we have here an instance of the exercise of the State's police power to prevent a speaker from intentionally provoking a given group to hostile reaction. *Cf. Feiner v. New York [supra].* There is, as noted above, no showing that anyone who saw Cohen was in fact violently aroused or that appellant intended such a result.

Finally, in arguments before this Court much has been made of the claim that Cohen's distasteful mode of expression was thrust upon unwilling or unsuspecting viewers, and that the State might therefore legitimately act as it did in order to protect the sensitive from otherwise unavoidable exposure to appellant's crude form of protest. Of course, the mere presumed presence of unwitting listeners or viewers does not serve automatically to justify curtailing all speech capable of giving offense. While this Court has recognized that government may properly act in many situations to prohibit intrusion into the privacy of the home of unwelcome views and ideas which cannot be totally banned from the

---

3. It is illuminating to note what transpired when Cohen entered a courtroom in the building. He removed his jacket and stood with it folded over his arm. Meanwhile, a policeman sent the presiding judge a note suggesting that Cohen be held in contempt of court. The judge declined to do so and Cohen was arrested by the officer only after he emerged from the courtroom.

public dialogue, we have at the same time consistently stressed that "we are often 'captives' outside the sanctuary of the home and subject to objectionable speech." The ability of government, consonant with the Constitution, to shut off discourse solely to protect others from hearing it is, in other words, dependent upon a showing that substantial privacy interests are being invaded in an essentially intolerable manner. Any broader view of this authority would effectively empower a majority to silence dissidents simply as a matter of personal predilections.

In this regard, persons confronted with Cohen's jacket were in a quite different posture than, say, those subjected to the raucous emissions of sound trucks blaring outside their residences. Those in the Los Angeles courthouse could effectively avoid further bombardment of their sensibilities simply by averting their eyes. And, while it may be that one has a more substantial claim to a recognizable privacy interest when walking through a courthouse corridor than, for example, strolling through Central Park, surely it is nothing like the interest in being free from unwanted expression in the confines of one's own home. Given the subtlety and complexity of the factors involved, if Cohen's "speech" was otherwise entitled to constitutional protection, we do not think the fact that some unwilling "listeners" in a public building may have been briefly exposed to it can serve to justify this breach of the peace conviction where, as here, there was no evidence that persons powerless to avoid appellant's conduct did in fact object to it, and where that portion of the statute upon which Cohen's conviction rests evinces no concern, either on its face or as construed by the California courts, with the special plight of the captive auditor, but, instead, indiscriminately sweeps within its prohibitions all "offensive conduct" that disturbs "any neighborhood or person." * * *

Against this background, the issue flushed by this case stands out in bold relief. It is whether California can excise, as "offensive conduct," one particular scurrilous epithet from the public discourse, either upon the theory of the court below that its use is inherently likely to cause violent reaction or upon a more general assertion that the States, acting as guardians of public morality, may properly remove this offensive word from the public vocabulary.

The rationale of the California court is plainly untenable. At most it reflects an "undifferentiated fear or apprehension of disturbance [which] is not enough to overcome the right to freedom of expression." We have been shown no evidence that substantial numbers of citizens are standing ready to strike out physically at whoever may assault their sensibilities with execrations like that uttered by Cohen. There may be some persons about with such lawless and violent proclivities, but that is an insufficient base upon which to erect, consistently with constitutional values, a governmental power to force persons who wish to ventilate their dissident views into avoiding particular forms of expression. The argument amounts to little more than the self-defeating proposition that to avoid physical censorship of one who has not sought to provoke such a response by a hypothetical coterie of the violent and lawless, the States may more appropriately effectuate that censorship themselves.

Admittedly, it is not so obvious that the First and Fourteenth Amendments must be taken to disable the States from punishing public utterance of this unseemly expletive in order to maintain what they regard as a suitable level of discourse within the body politic. We think, however, that examination and reflection will reveal the shortcomings of a contrary viewpoint.

At the outset, we cannot overemphasize that, in our judgment, most situations where the State has a justifiable interest in regulating speech will fall within one or more of the various established exceptions, discussed above but not applicable here, to the usual rule that governmental bodies may not prescribe the form or content of individual expression. Equally important to our conclusion is the constitutional backdrop against which our decision must be made. The constitutional right of free expression is powerful medicine in a society as diverse and populous as ours. It is designed and intended to remove governmental restraints from the arena of public discussion, putting the decision as to what views shall be voiced largely into the hands of each of us, in the hope that use of such freedom will ultimately produce a more capable citizenry and more perfect polity and in the belief that no other approach would comport with the premise of individual dignity and choice upon which our political system rests. *See Whitney v. California* (Brandeis, J., concurring).

To many, the immediate consequence of this freedom may often appear to be only verbal tumult, discord, and even offensive utterance. These are, however, within established limits, in truth necessary side effects of the broader enduring values which the process of open debate permits us to achieve. That the air may at times seem filled with verbal cacophony is, in this sense not a sign of weakness but of strength. We cannot lose sight of the fact that, in what otherwise might seem a trifling and annoying instance of individual distasteful abuse of a privilege, these fundamental societal values are truly implicated. That is why "[w]holly neutral futilities . . . come under the protection of free speech as fully as do Keats' poems or Donne's sermons," and why "so long as the means are peaceful, the communication need not meet standards of acceptability."

Against this perception of the constitutional policies involved, we discern certain more particularized considerations that peculiarly call for reversal of this conviction. First, the principle contended for by the State seems inherently boundless. How is one to distinguish this from any other offensive word? Surely the State has no right to cleanse public debate to the point where it is grammatically palatable to the most squeamish among us. Yet no readily ascertainable general principle exists for stopping short of that result were we to affirm the judgment below. For, while the particular four-letter word being litigated here is perhaps more distasteful than most others of its genre, it is nevertheless often true that one man's vulgarity is another's lyric. Indeed, we think it is largely because governmental officials cannot make principled distinctions in this area that the Constitution leaves matters of taste and style so largely to the individual.

[**JUSTICE WHITE**'s dissenting opinion is omitted.]

JUSTICE BLACKMUN, with whom **THE CHIEF JUSTICE [BURGER]** and **JUSTICE BLACK** join, dissenting.

Cohen's absurd and immature antic, in my view, was mainly conduct and little speech. The California Court of Appeal appears so to have described it, and I cannot characterize it otherwise. Further, the case appears to me to be well within the sphere of *Chaplinsky v. New Hampshire*, where Justice Murphy, a known champion of First Amendment freedoms, wrote for a unanimous bench. As a consequence, this Court's agonizing over First Amendment values seems misplaced and unnecessary.

NOTES ON *COHEN* AND OFFENSIVE SPEECH

1. *The Distinction Between Profanity and Fighting Words.* Justice Harlan's decision suggests that even if fighting words can be regulated, ordinarily profanity cannot. Should there be such a wide distinction drawn between these two categories of expression? Presumably *Cohen* would have greatly surprised the Framers, who operated against the backdrop of state laws criminalizing blasphemy and other forms of profanity. Should state actions clearly allowable at the time of the Framers be restricted? Are the purposes or values of the First Amendment more implicated in profanity cases than in fighting-words cases?

The regulation of both fighting words and profanity relates to the maintenance of public civility.[e] By protecting profanity and narrowly construing the fighting-words doctrine, *Cohen* reduces the state's ability to maintain such civility. If that is a good idea, why not overrule *Chaplinsky*?

Could the Court be wrong in suggesting that profanity has fewer third-party effects than fighting words? In cases where profanity is not also fighting words, the listeners might often be vulnerable people (e.g., children, the elderly) unable to escape the onslaught. Is Justice Harlan undervaluing parents' interest in protecting children from foul language? On the other hand, if you can burn a flag or a cross with the intent of upsetting targeted persons, perhaps the display of language in *Cohen* is tame by comparison.

2. *The Special Cases of the Captive Audience and Government Property.* Justice Harlan also distinguished *Cohen* from the speech-on-government-property cases (§ 3A of this chapter) and the captive-audience cases. As to the latter, the Court held in *Public Utilities Comm'n v. Pollak*, 343 U.S. 451 (1952), that citizens in public places have no right to be protected from unwelcome noises and utterances. Later, however, the Court held that noisy sound trucks could be regulated in residential settings, lest a captive audience in their homes be incommoded by unwanted expression. See *Kovacs v. Cooper*, 336 U.S. 77 (1949). Cf. *Frisby v. Schultz*, 487 U.S. 474 (1988) (allowing ban on targeted

---

e. For explorations of this question, see Walter Berns, *The First Amendment and the Future of American Democracy* (1976); Daniel Farber, *Civilizing Public Discourse: An Essay on Professor Bickel, Justice Harlan, and the Enduring Significance of* Cohen v. California, 1980 Duke L.J. 283; Robert Post, *The Constitutional Concept of Public Discourse: Outrageous Opinion, Democratic Deliberation, and* Hustler Magazine v. Falwell, 103 Harv. L. Rev. 601 (1990). See also William Cohen, *A Look Back at* Cohen v. California, 34 UCLA L. Rev. 1595 (1987).

residential picketing on the theory that the homeowner is a captive audience in her own home).[f]

3. *May the State Regulate Harassing Expression?* In *Plummer v. City of Columbus*, 414 U.S. 2 (1973), the Court struck down an ordinance prohibiting "menacing, insulting, slanderous, or profane language." The defendant was a taxicab driver who addressed a female passenger with a series of "vulgar, suggestive, and abhorrent, sexually-oriented statements." In *State v. Harrington*, 67 Or. App. 608, 680 P.2d 666 (1984), the Oregon Supreme Court interpreted its state constitution to overturn a conviction for uttering racial epithets in violation of a harassment law. The court ruled that "abusive language spoken with intent to annoy or alarm" could not constitutionally be regulated. Should the U.S. Supreme Court carry *Cohen* that far?

1. *An Exception for Hate Speech?*

The results in *Plummer* and *Harrington* noted above can be criticized — and distinguished from *Cohen* — by invoking an antisubordination principle suggested by the equal protection cases (Chapters 2-4) and by critical theory of the sort outlined by Professor Robin West (Chapter 2, § 3C2). Mari Matsuda, *Public Response to Racist Speech: Considering the Victim's Story*, 87 Mich. L. Rev. 2320 (1989), argues for a reading of the First Amendment that accounts for such an antisubordination principle. She defines hate speech to include only that which contains a message of racial inferiority, directed against a historically oppressed group and is persecutory and hateful in its message. Is her reconciliation of free speech and equal protection precepts a persuasive one? Is it constitutional, in light of *Plummer*, *R.A.V.*, and the following decisions?

Beauharnais v. Illinois, 343 U.S. 250 (1952). Defendant Beauharnais was the president of the White Circle League. He was prosecuted for distributing a leaflet calling for white citizens of Chicago "to halt the further encroachment, harassment and invasion of white people, their property, neighborhoods and person by the Negro" and to unite "to prevent the white race from becoming mongrelized by the negro." The legal basis for the prosecution was an Illinois law making it a crime to distribute a publication that "portrays depravity, criminality, unchastity, or lack of virtue of a class of citizens, of any race, color, creed or religion" or which "exposes the citizens of any race, color, creed or religion to contempt, derision, or obloquy or which is productive of breach of the peace or riots." The trial judge did not allow Beauharnais to put on evidence of the truth of the statements.

A divided (5-4) Supreme Court affirmed the conviction. **Justice Frankfurter**'s opinion for the Court ruled that (1) libel is not speech protected by the First Amendment, (2) "collectivities" as well as individuals can be libeled, and (3) it was within the realm of reasonable legislative choice to create such a law

---

f. See also *Federal Communications Commission v. Pacifica Foundation*, § 3B2 *infra*, upholding FCC sanctions against a radio station that played George Carlin's monologue concerning "seven dirty words" that cannot be said on the broadcast media.

to ease racial tensions in the state. "[T]he Illinois Legislature may warrantably believe that a man's job and his educational opportunities and the dignity accorded him may depend as much on the reputation of the racial and religious group to which he willy-nilly belongs, as on his own merits. This being so, we are precluded from saying that speech concededly punishable when immediately directed at individuals cannot be outlawed if directed at groups with whose position and esteem in society the affiliated individual may be inextricably involved."

___

Some lower courts have suggested that Justice Frankfurter's disposition does not survive *New York Times v. Sullivan* (§ 2B, *supra*). See, e.g., *Collin v. Smith*, 578 F.2d 1197 (7th Cir. 1978) (Illinois town of Skokie could not constitutionally prevent white supremacist, antisemitic Nazi Party march; *Beauharnais* no longer good law). *R.A.V.* seems even more contrary to *Beauharnais*. Does *R.A.V.* draw into question any law making only some group libels illegal? Any rule — such as Matsuda's — protecting against race-based animus? Consider the next case.

___

Wisconsin v. Mitchell, 508 U.S. 476 (1993), explored the implications of the Court's holding in *R.A.V., supra*. After seeing a movie in which a white man had beaten a young black, the defendant, who was black, asked his friends, "Do you all feel hyped up to move on some white people?" Soon afterward, at the defendant's direction, the group beat up a young white. The defendant was convicted of aggravated battery, but his sentence was increased under a statute providing extra punishment for "hate crimes" (that is, crimes in which the victim was selected on the basis of a prohibited criterion, such as race). The Court affirmed the enhanced sentence in an opinion by **Chief Justice Rehnquist**. He distinguished *R.A.V.* as follows:

"[Defendant] argues that the Wisconsin penalty-enhancement statute is invalid because it punishes the defendant's discriminatory motive, or reason, for acting. But motive plays the same role under the Wisconsin statute as it does under federal and state antidiscrimination laws, which we have previously upheld against constitutional challenge. * * * [I]n *R.A.V.*, we cited Title VII (as well as [other federal antidiscrimination statutes]) as an example of a permissible content-neutral regulation of conduct.

"Nothing in our decision last Term in *R.A.V.* compels a different result here. * * * Because the ordinance only proscribed a class of 'fighting words' deemed particularly offensive by the city — *i.e.*, those 'that contain . . . messages of "bias-motivated" hatred' — we held that it violated the rule against content-based discrimination. But whereas the ordinance struck down in *R.A.V.* was explicitly directed at expression (*i.e.*, 'speech' or 'messages'), the statute in this case is aimed at conduct unprotected by the First Amendment.

"Moreover, the Wisconsin statute singles out for enhancement bias-inspired conduct because this conduct is thought to inflict greater individual and societal harm. For example, according to the State and its *amici*, bias-motivated crimes are more likely to provoke retaliatory crimes, inflict distinct emotional harms on their victims, and incite community unrest. The State's desire to redress these perceived harms provides an adequate explanation for its penalty-enhancement provision over and above mere disagreement with offenders' beliefs or biases. * * * "

What are the implications of *Mitchell*? Suppose that the sentence enhancement was applied in a case where the crime was "making terroristic threats"? Valid under *Mitchell*? Under *R.A.V.* itself?

NOTE ON THE HATE SPEECH DEBATE

Hate speech in general and proposals to regulate it in particular have received a great deal of attention from commentators. A complete discussion of the scholarship on the subject is precluded by space limitations. Our goal here is simply to give you a flavor of the contending positions.

Richard Delgado, *Campus Antiracism Rules: Constitutional Narratives in Collision*, 85 Nw. U.L. Rev. 343 (1991)[g], argues that hate speech does little to promote First Amendment values:

> Uttering racial slurs may afford the racially troubled speaker some immediate relief, but hardly seems essential to self-fulfillment in any ideal sense. Indeed, social science writers hold that making racist remarks impairs, rather than promotes, the growth of the person who makes them, by encouraging rigid, dichotomous thinking and impeding moral development. * * *

> Additionally, slurs contribute little to the discovery of truth. Classroom discussion of racial matters and even the speech of a bigot aimed at proving the superiority of the white race might move us closer to the truth. But one-on-one insults do not. They neither state nor attack a proposition; they are like a slap in the face. * * * "More speech" is rarely a solution. Epithets often strike suddenly, immobilizing their victim and rendering her speechless. Often they are delivered in cowardly, anonymous fashion — for example, in the form of a defaced poster or leaflet slipped under a student's door, or hurled by a group against a single victim, rendering response foolhardy.

Turning to an equality perspective, Delgado observes that regulation of hate speech "may be necessary for full effectuation of the values of equal personhood we hold equally dear."[h]

Charles Lawrence III, *Acknowledging the Victim's Cry*, Academe 10 (November-December 1990), draws an intriguing analogy between hate speech regulation and the *Brown* decision:

> [*Brown*] speaks directly to the psychic injury inflicted by racist speech by noting that the symbolic message of segregation affected "the hearts and minds" of African-American children "in a way unlikely ever to be undone." Racial epithets

---

g. Reprinted by special permission of Northwestern University School of Law, *Northwestern University Law Review*.

h. For a summary of Delgado's views, see Richard Delgado, *Toward a Legal Realist View of the First Amendment*, 113 Harv. L. Rev. 778 (2000) (book review). For a critique of this line of argument, see Gary Goodpaster, *Equality and Free Speech: The Case Against Substantive Equality*, 82 Iowa L. Rev. 645 (1997).

and harassment often cause deep emotional scarring and feelings of anxiety and fear that pervade every aspect of a victim's life.

Brown also recognized that African-American children did not have an equal opportunity to learn and participate in the school's community when they bore the additional burden of being subject to the humiliation and psychic assault contained in the message of segregation. * * *

African-Americans and other people of color are skeptical about the argument that even the most injurious speech must remain unregulated because, in an unregulated marketplace of ideas, the best ones will rise to the top and gain acceptance. Experience tells quite the opposite. People of color have seen too many demagogues elected by appealing to America's racism. * * *

Whenever we decide that racist speech must be tolerated because of the importance of maintaining societal tolerance for all unpopular speech, we are asking African-Americans and other subordinated groups to bear the burden of the good of all. We must be careful that the ease with which we strike the balance against the regulation of racist speech is in no way influenced by the fact that the cost will be borne by others. We must be certain that those who will pay that price are fairly represented in our deliberations and that they are heard.[i]

In a response to Professor Lawrence, Gerald Gunther, *Freedom for the Thought We Hate*, Academe 10 (November-December 1990), argued:

Lest it be thought that I am insensitive to the pain imposed by expressions of racial or religious hatred, let me say that I have suffered that pain and empathize with others under similar verbal assault. My deep belief in the principles of the First Amendment arises in part from my own experiences. I received my elementary education in a public school in a very small town in Nazi Germany. There I was subject to vehement anti-Semitic remarks from my teacher, classmates, and others — Judensau (Jew pig) was far from the harshest. I can assure you that they hurt.

More generally, I lived in a country where ideological orthodoxy reigned and where the opportunity for dissent was severely limited.

The lesson I have drawn from my childhood in Nazi Germany and my happier adult life in this country is the need to walk the sometimes difficult path of denouncing the bigots' hateful ideas with all my power, yet at the same time challenging any community's attempt to suppress hateful ideas by force of law. * * *

[S]peech should not and cannot be banned simply because it is "offensive" to substantial parts or a majority of the community. The refusal to suppress offensive speech is one of the most difficult obligations the free speech principle imposes upon all of us; yet it is also one of the First Amendment's greatest glories — indeed, it is a central test of a community's commitment to free speech.[j]

Like Professor Gunther, Nadine Strossen, *Regulating Racist Speech on Campus: A Modest Proposal?*,[k] 1990 Duke L.J. 484, argues that hate speech cannot be banned consistent with existing First Amendment analysis. She also argues that hate speech regulation has a tendency to backfire, harming minority groups:

---

i. See also Charles Lawrence, III, *If He Hollers Let Him Go: Regulating Racist Speech on Campus*, 1990 Duke L.J. 431.

j. Other notable responses to Professors Delgado, Lawrence, and Matsuda include James Weinstein, *Hate Speech, Pornography, and the Radical Attack on Free Speech Doctrine* (1999), and Robert Post, *Racist Speech, Democracy, and the First Amendment*, 32 Wm. & Mary L. Rev. 267 (1991).

k. Reprinted with permission.

The first reason that laws censoring racist speech may undermine the goal of combating racism flows from the discretion such laws inevitably vest in prosecutors, judges, and the other individuals who implement them. One ironic, even tragic, result of this discretion is that members of minority groups themselves — the very people whom the law is intended to protect — are likely targets of punishment. For example, among the first individuals prosecuted under the British Race Relations Act of 1965 were black power leaders. Their overtly racist messages undoubtedly expressed legitimate anger at real discrimination, yet the statute drew no such fine lines, nor could any similar statute possibly do so.* * *

The British experience * * * parallels the experience in the United States under the one [hate speech] rule that has led to a judicial decision. During the approximately one year that [the rule] was in effect, there were more than twenty cases of whites charging blacks with racist speech. More importantly, the only two instances in which the rule was invoked to sanction racist speech (as opposed to sexist and other forms of hate speech) involved the punishment of speech by or on behalf of black students. Additionally, the only student who was subject to a full-fledged disciplinary hearing * * * was a black student accused of homophobic and sexist expression. * * * Likewise, the student who recently brought a lawsuit challenging the University of Connecticut's hate speech policy, under which she had been penalized for an allegedly homophobic remark, was Asian-American.[1]

PROBLEM 6-2
UNIVERSITY REGULATION OF HATE SPEECH

In 1988, the University of Michigan adopted a policy on discriminatory harassment. One set of provisions applied to "educational and academic centers, such as classroom buildings, libraries, research laboratories, recreation and study centers." In those locations, students were forbidden to engage in "[a]ny behavior, verbal or physical, that stigmatizes or victimizes an individual on the basis of race, ethnicity, religion, sex, sexual orientation, creed, national origin, ancestry, age, marital status, handicap or Vietnam-era veteran status," and that

(a) Involves an express or implied threat to an individual's academic efforts, employment, participation in University sponsored extra-curricular activities or personal safety; or

(b) Has the purpose or reasonably foreseeable effect of interfering with an individual's academic efforts, employment, participation in University sponsored extra-curricular activities or personal safety; or

(c) Creates an intimidating, hostile, or demeaning environment for educational pursuits, employment, or participation in University sponsored extracurricular activities.

Possible sanctions, depending on the severity of the offense, ranged from a formal reprimand or required performance of community services, through removal from University housing, to suspension or expulsion.

---

1. For responses to Strossen and other critics of hate speech regulation, see W. Bradley Wendel, *"Certain Fundamental Truths": A Dialectic on Negative and Positive Liberty in Hate-Speech Cases*, 65 Law & Contemp. Probs. 33 (2002) (presenting a thoughtful dialogue on the issue); Jean Stefancic & Richard Delgado, *A Shifting Balance: Freedom of Expression and Hate-Speech Restriction*, 78 Iowa L. Rev. 737 (1993).

The rationale for such regulation was explained in Professor Matsuda's article:

> Universities are special places, charged with pedagogy, and duty-bound to a constituency with special vulnerabilities. Many of the new adults who come to live and study at the major universities are away from home for the first time, and at a vulnerable stage of psychological development. Students are particularly dependent on the university for community, for intellectual development, and for self-definition. Official tolerance of racist speech in this setting is more harmful than generalized tolerance in the community-at-large. It is harmful to student perpetrators in that it is a lesson in getting-away-with-it that will have lifelong repercussions. It is harmful to targets, who perceive the university as taking sides through inaction, and who are left to their own resources in coping with the damage wrought. Finally, it is a harm to the goals of inclusion, education, development of knowledge, and ethics that universities exist and stand for. Lessons of cynicisms and hate replace lessons in critical thought and inquiry.

Mari Matsuda, *Public Response to Racist Speech: Considering the Victim's Story*, 87 Mich. L. Rev. 2310, 2370-71 (1989).

A different perspective, more skeptical of such rules, is presented by Peter Byrne, *Racial Insults and Free Speech Within the University*, 79 Geo. L.J. 399 (1991). Professor Byrne suggests several nonhypothetical cases that arose or were specifically prohibited by the Michigan regulations:

"A" says in class: "Women just aren't as good in this field as men."

"B" says in class: "Homosexuality is a treatable disease."

"A" and "B" make their statements in a lunchroom conversation.

If the University subjected "A" or "B" to discipline for these comments, would it be acting constitutionally under *Cohen* and *R.A.V.*?

Could you suggest drafting changes or alternative types of regulation that might make the regulation less vulnerable to challenge? Should First Amendment doctrine be realigned, as Professor Matsuda suggests, to eliminate constitutional protection for hate speech — defined as messages of racial inferiority, directed against a historically oppressed group, and characterized as persecutorial, hateful, and degrading?

For purposes of this problem, assume that the state does not have any special power to regulate speech merely because it owns and operates the University. We will reconsider that assumption later.

2. *Offensive Speech in the Electronic Media*

The precepts of *Cohen* and *R.A.V.* apply with full force to print media such as newspapers, but not necessarily to electronic media, such as television or radio. *Red Lion Broadcasting Co. v. Federal Communications Commission*, 395 U.S. 367 (1969), upheld the FCC's fairness doctrine, which required radio and television to provide equal time to opposing viewpoints on important political issues. Such a holding, unthinkable for newspaper regulation, was justified for television regulation by the scarcity of possible channels. Cf. *Turner Broadcasting Sys. v. FCC*, 512 U.S. 622 (1994) (conceding that this rationale has been overtaken by changed circumstances). Consider the different rationale for allowing regulation of dirty words on the airwaves.

Federal Communications Commission v. Pacifica Foundation, 438 U.S. 726 (1978). George Carlin recorded a monologue which featured "seven dirty words" that you couldn't say on the airwaves; the comic point of the monologue was Carlin's mocking and defying the ban by iterating the seven dirty words in a variety of contexts. Pacifica's New York radio station played the monologue. In response to complaints from a father whose son was exposed to it, the FCC ruled it "patently offensive" but not obscene and banned it pursuant to 18 U.S.C. § 1464, which forbids the use of "any obscene, indecent, or profane language by means of radio communication." A fractured Supreme Court upheld the FCC action.

Justice Stevens wrote a plurality opinion emphasizing the special nature of radio transmissions. "Patently offensive, indecent material presented over the airwaves confronts the citizen, not only in public, but also in the privacy of the home, where the individual's right to be left alone plainly outweighs the First Amendment rights of an intruder." Additionally, "broadcasting is uniquely accessible to children, even those too young to read. Although Cohen's written message might have been incomprehensible to a first grader, Pacifica's broadcast could have enlarged a child's vocabulary in an instant. Other forms of offensive expression may be withheld from the young without restricting the expression at its source. Bookstores and motion picture theaters, for example, may be prohibited from making indecent material available to children."[m]

Justice Powell, joined by **Justice Blackmun**, concurred in that portion of Justice Stevens' opinion. They emphasized the Commission's factual findings, the intrusion into the home, and the exposure of children to the monologue. But they stated that state censorship would not necessarily be permissible against radio broadcasts late at night, when children were not likely to be listening, or against sale of the monologue in record form.

Four Justices dissented. **Justice Brennan**'s dissenting opinion, joined by **Justice Marshall**, argued that the Court's result was inconsistent with *Cohen*'s rule that the state cannot silence speech to protect others from hearing it, unless substantial privacy interests are being invaded in an intolerable manner. "[A]n individual's actions in switching on and listening to communications transmitted over the public airways and directed to the public at large do not implicate fundamental privacy interests, even when engaged in within the home. * * * [U]nlike other intrusive modes of communication, such as sound trucks, '[t]he radio can be turned off.' " More pointedly, Justice Brennan argued that the majority displayed a "depressing inability to appreciate that in our land of cultural pluralism, there are many who think, act, and talk differently from the Members of this Court, and who do not share their fragile sensibilities. It is

---

m. In a portion of his opinion (Part IVB) joined only by Chief Justice Burger and Justice Rehnquist, Justice Stevens invoked the sliding-scale approach he had crafted in *American Mini Theatres*: Like obscenity, indecent speech is low-value expression, more easily regulable than political expression, a core concern of the First Amendment (see note 1 following *Renton*). The other six Justices explicitly rejected such an approach.

only an acute ethnocentric myopia that enables the Court to approve the censorship of communications solely because of the words they contain."

NOTE ON REGULATION OF INDECENT SPEECH IN THE ELECTRONIC MEDIA: *SABLE, DENVER AREA, RENO v. ACLU*

Notwithstanding *Pacifica*, a unanimous Court in *Sable Communications, Inc. v. Federal Communications Commission*, 492 U.S. 115 (1989), invalidated a 1988 federal law that criminally prohibited "sexually oriented pre-recorded [dial-a-porn] telephone messages" that were either indecent or obscene. Justice White's opinion for the Court held that indecent but nonobscene speech is protected by the First Amendment and presumptively cannot be banned. He distinguished *Pacifica* as involving only a partial ban on programming that intruded into the home without prior warning as to indecent content. Placing a telephone call requires affirmative choice by the listener as to precisely what she or he wants to hear. The danger that children would be exposed to indecent material did not justify a total ban, because less restrictive means — special access codes, blocking porn numbers at parents' request — could achieve substantially the same end.

After *Sable*, it was accepted that Congress could not completely ban indecency on cable television. A plurality opinion in *Denver Area Educational Telecommunications Consortium v. Federal Communications Commission*, 518 U.S. 727 (1996), adopted a balancing approach to legislation authorizing the FCC and cable operators to censor indecent material. The law allowed cable operators to bar "sexually explicit" as well as obscene material on leased access and public access channels, for which such operators normally have no editorial discretion.

The next year, the application of the First Amendment to the Internet came before the Supreme Court. In *Reno v. American Civil Liberties Union*, 521 U.S. 844 (1997), the Supreme Court invalidated provisions of the Communications Decency Act (CDA) of 1996 prohibiting transmission of indecent communications to persons under age eighteen on the Internet. Justice Stevens' opinion for the Court ruled that cyberspace is subject to normal First Amendment precepts, which were automatically fatal to the Act's content-based regulation of indecency. The Internet is not as invasive as radio or television, nor can a user come upon sexually explicit materials by accident and without prior warning. Hence, the Court said, the statutory regulation was much more like that in *Sable* than in *Pacifica*. The Act was overbroad, for it suppressed speech adults are entitled to send and receive, and the statutory goal of protecting minors could be achieved through less restrictive means, as in *Denver Area*.

The Court revisited the issue of indecent speech in the electronic media in *United States v. Playboy Entertainment Group*, 529 U.S. 803 (2000). The Telecommunications Act required cable operators either to scramble sexually explicit channels in full or to limit programming on those channels to certain hours, because of the possibility that "signal bleed" from incomplete scrambling would allow children to see portions of the programming. Justice Kennedy's opinion for the Court held the provision to be content-based and struck it down. He emphasized that the statute was concerned with the "direct impact that speech has on its listeners" rather than on secondary effects. The plaintiff had offered a "plausible, less restrictive alternative": requiring cable operators to block undesired channels at the request of individual households, combined with advertising and other efforts to notify households of this option. The government failed to show that this alternative would be ineffective at protecting children. Justice Kennedy emphasized that current technology "expands the capacity to choose; and it denies the potential of this revolution if we assume the Government is best positioned to make these choices for us."

After remand, the Court upheld a ruling by the district court that the plaintiffs were likely to prevail on the merits of their claim. *Ashcroft v. ACLU*, 542 U.S. 656 (2004). Justice Kennedy's opinion for the Court stressed that upon remand for trial the government would have a full opportunity to demonstrate that the district court's initial conclusions about less restrictive alternatives were incorrect. He also emphasized that five years had passed since the district court's decision, suggesting that a new examination was in order in light of the rapidly evolving nature of Internet technology. Finally, he concluded that leaving the preliminary injunction in place guarded against chilling effect and self-censorship threatened by the statute pending final resolution of the case.

NOTES ON COMMERCIAL SPEECH

1. *Constitutional protection for commercial speech.* Commercial advertising was long considered to be outside the scope of First Amendment protection. That rule changed in *Virginia State Board of Pharmacy v. Virginia Citizens Consumer Council*, 425 U.S. 748, 96 S.Ct. 1817, 48 L.Ed.2d 346 (1976). In striking down a state ban on price advertising by pharmacists, Justice Blackmun's opinion for the Court rejected the traditional doctrine for several reasons:

> Focusing first on the individual parties to the transaction that is proposed in the commercial advertisement, we may assume that the advertiser's interest is a purely economic one. That hardly disqualifies him from protection under the First Amendment. The interests of the contestants in a labor dispute are primarily economic, but it has long been settled that both the employee and the employer are protected by the First Amendment when they express themselves on the merits of the dispute in order to influence its outcome. * * *

> As to the particular consumer's interest in the free flow of commercial information, that interest may be as keen, if not keener by far, than his interest in the day's most urgent political debate. * * * When drug prices vary as strikingly as they do, information as to who is charging what becomes more than a convenience. It could mean the alleviation of physical pain or the enjoyment of basic necessities.

>   * * *

> Moreover, there is another consideration that suggests that no line between publicly "interesting" or "important" commercial advertising and the opposite kind could ever be drawn. Advertising, however tasteless and excessive it sometimes may seem, is nonetheless dissemination of information as to who is producing and selling what product, for what reason, and at what price. So long as we preserve a

predominantly free enterprise economy, the allocation of our resources in large measure will be made through numerous private economic decisions. It is a matter of public interest that those decisions, in the aggregate, be intelligent and well informed. To this end, the free flow of commercial information is indispensable. And if it is indispensable to the proper allocation of resources in a free enterprise system, it is also indispensable to the formation of intelligent opinions as to how that system ought to be regulated or altered. Therefore, even if the First Amendment were thought to be primarily an instrument to enlighten public decisionmaking in a democracy, we could not say that the free flow of information does not serve that goal. * * *

The rationale for the state regulation was the price regulation would lead to a race to the bottom – cheaper prices but a loss of professionalism. Justice Blackmun found this rationale to be unacceptable:

It appears to be feared that if the pharmacist who wishes to provide low cost, and assertedly low quality, services is permitted to advertise, he will be taken up on his offer by too many unwitting customers. They will choose the low-cost, low-quality service and drive the "professional" pharmacist out of business. They will respond only to costly and excessive advertising, and end up paying the price. They will go from one pharmacist to another, following the discount, and destroy the pharmacist-customer relationship. They will lose respect for the profession because it advertises. All this is not in their best interests, and all this can be avoided if they are not permitted to know who is charging what.

There is, of course, an alternative to this highly paternalistic approach. That alternative is to assume that this information is not in itself harmful, that people will perceive their own best interests if only they are well enough informed, and that the best means to that end is to open the channels of communication rather than to close them. If they are truly open, nothing prevents the "professional" pharmacist from marketing his own assertedly superior product, and contrasting it with that of the low-cost, high-volume prescription drug retailer. But the choice among these alternative approaches is not ours to make or the Virginia General Assembly's. It is precisely this kind of choice, between the dangers of suppressing information, and the dangers of its misuse if it is freely available, that the First Amendment makes for us. * * *

Nevertheless, Justice Blackmun said, commercial speech remained subject to greater regulation than other forms of protected speech. In the concluding part of the opinion, the Court stressed that it was not precluding time, place, and manner regulations; restrictions on false or misleading advertising; or bans on advertising for illegal products or services.

2. *The Current Test. Central Hudson Gas & Electric Corp. v. Public Service Comm'n*, 447 U.S. 557 (1980), involved a state regulation that banned public utility ads promoting the use of electricity. The Court struck down the ban, despite the state's attempt to rely on energy conservation as a justification. In the course of the decision, the Court set forth a four-part test for regulations of commercial speech:

At the outset we must determine whether the expression is protected by the First Amendment. For commercial speech to come within that provision, it at least must concern lawful activity and not be misleading. Next we ask whether the asserted governmental interest is substantial. If both inquiries yield positive answers, we must determine whether the regulation directly advances the governmental interest asserted, and whether it is not more extensive than is necessary to serve that interest.[n]

Presumably this test would yield the same result the Court reached in *Virginia Board*. Reconsider *Railway Express* (Chapter 4, § 1) in light of this approach. Would New York City's restriction of advertising on vehicles pass muster?

3. *Advertising by Lawyers*. Lawyers have been traditionally prohibited from soliciting business by advertising or otherwise. "Ambulance chasing" is a long-standing basis for disbarment. Soon after *Virginia Board*, however, the Court made it clear that the First Amendment also covered advertising by lawyers. *Bates v. State Bar*, 433 U.S. 350 (1977). Since then, the state bars have attempted to continue as much regulation of legal advertising as possible, resulting in a spate of later Supreme Court opinions.

__4. *Regulation of Truthful Information*. In *44 Liquormart, Inc. v. Rhode Island*, 517 U.S. 484 (1996), two liquor stores filed suit to challenge a Rhode Island statute banning price advertising for alcoholic beverages except at the place of sale. The Justices were unanimous in agreeing to strike down the law, but badly divided in terms of the rationale. The lead opinion was by Justice Stevens. He read *Central Hudson* as requiring "special care" in reviewing a "blanket ban" on truthful, nonmisleading speech about a lawful product for reasons unrelated to consumer protection. In a portion of his opinion joined by Justices Kennedy, Souter, and Ginsburg, he concluded that the Rhode Island statute failed even the usual *Central Hudson* test without the need for such a particularly careful review. Justice Thomas did not join this portion of the opinion, but instead argued that regulations designed to keep consumers ignorant are per se invalid. In another portion of his opinion, Stevens was joined by Justices Kennedy, Thomas, and Ginsburg (but not by Souter) in disavowing *Posadas*: "The reasoning in *Posadas* does support the State's argument, but, on reflection, we are now persuaded that *Posadas* erroneously performed the First Amendment analysis. The casino advertising ban was designed to keep truthful, nonmisleading speech from members of the public for fear that they would be more likely to gamble if they received it. As a result, the advertising ban served to shield the State's antigambling policy from the public scrutiny that more direct, nonspeech regulation would draw.

"Given our longstanding hostility to commercial speech regulation of this type, *Posadas* clearly erred in concluding that it was 'up to the legislature' to choose suppression over a less speech-restrictive policy. The *Posadas* majority's conclusion on that point cannot be reconciled with the unbroken line of prior cases striking down similarly broad regulations on truthful, nonmisleading advertising when non-speech-related alternatives were available.

---

n. The final factor has been interpreted as a "reasonableness" or "narrow tailoring" test, rather than as a more stringent test requiring the least restrictive alternative. See *Board of Trustees v. Fox*, 492 U.S. 469 (1989).

"Because the 5-to-4 decision in *Posadas* marked such a sharp break from our prior precedent, and because it concerned a constitutional question about which this Court is the final arbiter, we decline to give force to its highly deferential approach."

Justice O'Connor, joined by Chief Justice Rehnquist and Justices Souter and Breyer, applied *Central Hudson* and concluded that the statute was unconstitutional. This group of four Justices also agreed that *Posadas* had been too hasty in accepting Puerto Rico's justifications without giving them "[t]he closer look that we have required since *Posadas*." This group of four Justices saw no reason, however, to revisit *Central Hudson*. Finally, Justice Scalia indicated an inclination to revisit the entire area of commercial speech in some later case: "I will take my guidance as to what the Constitution forbids, with regard to a text as indeterminate as the First Amendment's preservation of 'the freedom of speech,' and where the core offense of suppressing particular political ideas is not at issue, from the long accepted practices of the American people." Because this historical evidence was not before the Court, Justice Scalia concurred in the judgment on the basis of existing doctrine.

Thus, four Justices in *44 Liquormart* were prepared not only to overrule *Posadas* but to go beyond *Central Hudson* in prohibiting regulation of commercial speech for purposes unrelated to consumer protection; four Justices retreated less sharply from *Posadas* and declined to reexamine *Central Hudson*; and one Justice was apparently willing to put almost all of current First Amendment doctrine up for grabs. Although the Court has decided several commercial speech cases since *44 Liquormart*, in each case it invalidated the government regulation under the *Central Hudson* test, without revisiting the question of the test's validity.

SECTION 4. SPEECH WITH A GOVERNMENT NEXUS

The government may relate to civil society in a variety of ways. In the previous sections, we have considered situations in which the government's role was purely regulatory. Often, however, non-governmental actors want more from government than being free from regulation. They may want to use government-owned streets and parks for demonstrations, parades, or leafletting. They may want government funding for some of their activities. Or they may want to mobilize public employees, students, or other participants in government institutions. In this section, we consider the extent to which the government may foreclose the use of these avenues for expression or condition their use on restrictions on speech.

A. PUBLIC FORUM DOCTRINE

The government may have additional powers to regulate speech when it is not only acting as a regulator but also as an employer, property owner, or source of funding. Indeed, at one time, it was thought that the government's proprietary activities were simply outside the scope of the First Amendment, just like the activities of firms in the private sector. See *Commonwealth v. Davis*, 162 Mass. 510, 39 N.E. 113 (1895) (Holmes, J.), *aff'd*, 167 U.S. 43 (1897). The unarticulated premise may have been that constitutional restrictions should apply only when the government is using its unique power of legal coercion, rather than when it is engaging in the same kinds of conduct also found in the private sector. Today, that position has clearly been rejected, but First Amendment protection is sometimes weaker when speech has a government nexus.

A classic example involves speech on government property. *Hague v. Committee for Industrial Organization*, 307 U.S. 496 (1939), suggested an approach for reviewing government regulation of expressive activities in streets and parks:

> [T]hey have immemorially * * * been used for purposes of assembly, communicating thoughts between citizens, and discussing public questions. * * * The privilege of a citizen of the United States to use the streets and parks for communication of views on national questions may be regulated in the interest of all; it is not absolute, but relative, and must be exercised in subordination to the general comfort and convenience, and in consonance with peace and good order; but it must not, in the guise of regulation, be abridged or denied.

See also *Schneider v. State*, 308 U.S. 147 (1939).

Hague contained the outlines of the *public forum doctrine*: State property traditionally open for expressive purposes may not be closed off or abridged for reasons relating to the content of the proposed expression, but the state may impose reasonable "time, place, and manner" restrictions on the use of public property. See *Cox v. New Hampshire*, 312 U.S. 569 (1941).

UNITED STATES v. GRACE
461 U.S. 171, 103 S.Ct. 1702, 75 L.Ed.2d 736 (1983)

JUSTICE WHITE delivered the opinion of the Court.

In this case we must determine whether 40 U.S.C. § 13k, which prohibits, among other things, the "display [of] any flag, banner, or device designed or adapted to bringing into public notice any party, organization, or movement" in the United States Supreme Court building and on its grounds, violates the First Amendment. [The Court construed the "bring into public notice" clause to apply to "almost any sign or leaflet carrying a communication."]

Around noon on March 17, 1980, appellee Mary Grace entered upon the sidewalk in front of the Court and began to display a four foot by two and a half foot sign on which was inscribed the verbatim text of the First Amendment. A Court police officer approached Grace and informed her that she would have to go across the street if she wished to display the sign. Grace was informed that Title 40 of the United States Code prohibited her conduct and that if she did not cease she would be arrested. Grace left the grounds. [The other appellee had passed out leaflets on the sidewalk. They filed suit for an injunction against continued enforcement of the statute. The Court first determined that the statute did apply to their activities, and then turned to the constitutional issue.]

* * * The sidewalks comprising the outer boundaries of the Court grounds are indistinguishable from any other sidewalks in Washington, D.C., and we can discern no reason why they should be treated any differently. Sidewalks, of course, are among those areas of public property that traditionally have been held open to the public for expressive activities and are clearly within those

areas of public property that may be considered, generally without further inquiry, to be public forum property. The inclusion of the public sidewalks within the scope of § 13k's prohibition, however, results in the destruction of public forum status that is at least presumptively impermissible. Traditional public forum property occupies a special position in terms of First Amendment protection and will not lose its historically recognized character for the reason that it abuts government property that has been dedicated to a use other than as a forum for public expression. Nor may the government transform the character of the property by the expedient of including it within the statutory definition of what might be considered a nonpublic forum parcel of property. The public sidewalks forming the perimeter of the Supreme Court grounds, in our view, are public forums and should be treated as such for First Amendment purposes.
* * *

Based on its provisions and legislative history, it is fair to say that the purpose of the Act was to provide for the protection of the building and grounds and of the persons and property therein, as well as the maintenance of proper order and decorum. [Section 13k] was one of the provisions apparently designed for these purposes. At least, no special reason was stated for its enactment.

We do not denigrate the necessity to protect persons and property or to maintain proper order and decorum within the Supreme Court grounds, but we do question whether a total ban on carrying a flag, banner, or device on the public sidewalks substantially serves these purposes. There is no suggestion, for example, that appellees' activities in any way obstructed the sidewalks or access to the building, threatened injury to any person or property, or in any way interfered with the orderly administration of the building or other parts of the grounds. As we have said, the building's perimeter sidewalks are indistinguishable from other public sidewalks in the city that are normally open to the conduct that is at issue here and that § 13k forbids. A total ban on that conduct is no more necessary for the maintenance of peace and tranquility on the public sidewalks surrounding the building than on any other sidewalks in the city. Accordingly, § 13k cannot be justified on this basis.

The United States offers another justification for § 13k that deserves our attention. It is said that the federal courts represent an independent branch of the Government and that their decisionmaking processes are different from those of the other branches. Court decisions are made on the record before them and in accordance with the applicable law. The views of the parties and of others are to be presented by briefs and oral argument. Courts are not subject to lobbying, judges do not entertain visitors in their chambers for the purpose of urging that cases be resolved one way or another, and they do not and should not respond to parades, picketing, or pressure groups. Neither, the Government urges, should it appear to the public that the Supreme Court is subject to outside influence or that picketing or marching, singly or in groups, is an acceptable or proper way of appealing to or influencing the Supreme Court. Hence, we are asked to hold that Congress was quite justified in preventing the conduct in dispute here from occurring on the sidewalks at the edge of the Court grounds.

As was the case with the maintenance of law and order on the Court grounds, we do not discount the importance of this proffered purpose for § 13k. But, again, we are unconvinced that the prohibitions of § 13k that are at issue here sufficiently serve that purpose to sustain its validity insofar as the public sidewalks on the perimeter of the grounds are concerned. Those sidewalks are used by the public like other public sidewalks. There is nothing to indicate to the public that these sidewalks are part of the Supreme Court grounds or are in any way different from other public sidewalks in the city. We seriously doubt that the public would draw a different inference from a lone picketer carrying a sign on the sidewalks around the building than it would from a similar picket on the sidewalks across the street.

We thus perceive insufficient justification for § 13k's prohibition of carrying signs, banners, or devices on the public sidewalks surrounding the building. We hold that under the First Amendment the section is unconstitutional as applied to those sidewalks. Of course, this is not to say that those sidewalks, like other sidewalks, are not subject to reasonable time, place, and manner restrictions[.]

_____

Hill v. Colorado, 530 U.S. 703 (2000), illustrates the difficulty the Court has sometimes encountered in applying the principle of content neutrality. A Colorado statute made it unlawful for anyone within 100 feet of a healthcare facility to "knowingly approach" within eight feet of another person, without that person's consent, in order to pass out leaflets, display a sign, or engage in "oral protest, education, or counseling." The statute was prompted by anti-abortion activities at clinics offering abortions.

In an opinion by **Justice Stevens**, the Court upheld the statute as a valid time, place or manner regulation. As to why the statute should be considered content-neutral, the Court stressed that it applied on its face to all viewpoints and subjects. The fact that the statute did not cover routine social interactions (such as asking the time) was not enough to make it suspect, nor was the fact that the impetus for the statute came from demonstrations supporting a particular viewpoint. Having found the statute content-neutral, the Court upheld it because it left open many methods of communicating with pedestrians near clinics, and because it was narrowly tailored to the permissible statutory purpose of protecting unwilling listeners from unwanted communications.

Justice Souter, in a concurring opinion, stressed that the statute had no effect on stationary speakers, making it implausible that it was motivated by disfavor toward the content of the speech, as opposed to "protecting people already tense or distressed in anticipation of medical attention (whether an abortion or some other procedure) from the unwanted intrusion of close personal importunity by strangers." He was joined by **Justices O'Connor**, **Ginsburg**, and **Breyer**.

Accusing the majority of favoritism toward abortion, **Justice Scalia**, joined by **Justice Thomas**, argued that it was obvious that the statute was targeted at anti-abortion demonstrators and that it distinguished on the basis of content by singling out protest, education, and counseling. He also denied that the state had a legitimate interest in protecting individuals from unwanted speech in a public forum. **Justice Kennedy** also considered the statute unconstitutional, though he did not join the Scalia dissent. In a passionate dissent of his own, he asserted that the majority had denied "these protesters, in the face of what they consider to be one of life's gravest moral crises, even the opportunity to try to offer a fellow citizen a little pamphlet, a handheld paper seeking to reach a higher law."

NOTES ON *GRACE, HILL,* AND THE TRADITIONAL PUBLIC FORUM

Consistent with the famous statement in *Hague,* the *Grace* opinion stresses the special constitutional status of sidewalks as a traditional "public forum." But *why* do these places have special status?[a] Is it because history has given the public a sort of constitutional easement? Or because these places are especially well suited for these purposes? Or simply because there has to be *someplace* where people can exercise their First Amendment rights?

What kind of limitations can the state place on our use of a public forum? Contrast *Grace* with *Cox v. Louisiana,* 379 U.S. 559 (1965), which upheld a Louisiana statute prohibiting picketing "near" a courthouse with the intent to influence the administration of justice.[b] The Louisiana statute had been modeled on a federal statute, which was passed in 1950 as a response to picketing of federal courthouses to protest the trials of Communist Party leaders. Does *Grace* overrule *Cox* sub silentio? If not, does *Grace* mean that people have the constitutional right to picket on the sidewalk in front of the Court only if their message doesn't relate to the Court's business?

WARD v. ROCK AGAINST RACISM
491 U.S. 781, 109 S.Ct. 2746, 105 L.Ed.2d 661 (1989)

JUSTICE KENNEDY delivered the opinion of the Court.

In the southeast portion of New York City's Central Park, about 10 blocks upward from the park's beginning point at 59th Street, there is an amphitheater and stage structure known as the Naumberg Acoustic Bandshell. The bandshell faces west across the remaining width of the park. In close proximity to the bandshell, and lying within the directional path of its sound, is a grassy open area called the Sheep Meadow. The city has designated the Sheep Meadow as a quiet area for passive recreations like reclining, walking, and reading. Just beyond the park, and also within the potential sound range of the bandshell, are the apartments and residences of Central Park West.

---

a. See generally Ronald Cass, *First Amendment Access to Government Facilities,* 65 Va. L. Rev. 1287 (1979); Robert Post, *Between Governance and Management: The History and Theory of the Public Forum,* 34 UCLA L. Rev. 1713 (1987); Geoffrey Stone, *Fora Americana: Speech in Public Places,* 1974 Sup. Ct. Rev. 233.

b. See Harry Kalven, *The Concept of the Public Forum:* Cox v. Louisiana, 1965 Sup. Ct. Rev. 1.

This case arises from the city's attempt to regulate the volume of amplified music at the bandshell so the performances are satisfactory to the audience without intruding upon those who use the Sheep Meadow or live on Central Park West and in its vicinity.

The city's regulation requires bandshell performers to use sound-amplification equipment and a sound technician provided by the city. [The sound technician controls both the volume and the mix of sound — that is, the way the sound from various microphones and instruments is combined. The city adopted this regulation after considering various alternatives, and also after prolonged difficulties with concerts by Rock Against Racism, at one of which the police ultimately "pulled the plug" after issuing noise citations.] The challenge to this volume control technique comes from the sponsor of a rock concert. * * *

Music is one of the oldest forms of human expression. From Plato's discourse in the Republic to the totalitarian state in our own times, rulers have known its capacity to appeal to the intellect and to the emotions, and have censored musical compositions to serve the needs of the state. The Constitution prohibits any like attempts in our own legal order. Music, as a form of expression and communication, is protected under the First Amendment. In the case before us the performances apparently consisted of remarks by speakers, as well as rock music, but the case has been presented as one in which the constitutional challenge is to the city's regulation of the musical aspects of the concert; and, based on the principle we have stated, the city's guidelines must meet the demands of the First Amendment. The parties do not appear to dispute that proposition.

We need not here discuss whether a municipality which owns a band stand or stage facility may exercise, in some circumstances, a proprietary right to select performances and control their quality. Though it did demonstrate its own interest in the effort to insure high quality performance by providing the equipment in question, the city justifies its guideline as a regulatory measure to limit and control noise. Here the bandshell was open, apparently, to all performers; and we decide the case as one in which the bandshell is a public forum for performances in which the government's right to regulate expression is subject to the protections of the First Amendment. Our cases make clear, however, that even in a public forum the government may impose reasonable restrictions on the time, place, or manner of protected speech, provided the restrictions "are justified without reference to the content of the regulated speech, that they are narrowly tailored to serve a significant governmental interest, and that they leave open ample alternative channels for communication of the information." *Clark v. Community for Creative Non-Violence*, 468 U.S. 288, 293 (1984). We consider these requirements in turn.

It is undeniable that the city's substantial interest in limiting sound volume is served in a direct and effective way by the requirement that the city's sound technician control the mixing board during performances. Absent this requirement, the city's interests would have been served less well, as is evidenced by the complaints about excessive volume generated by respondent's past concerts. The alternative regulatory methods hypothesized by the Court of

Appeals reflect nothing more than a disagreement with the city over how much control of volume is appropriate or how that level of control is to be achieved. The Court of Appeals erred in failing to defer to the city's reasonable determination that its interest in controlling volume would be best served by requiring bandshell performers to utilize the city's sound technician.

[The Court also upheld the city's second justification, to ensure "that the sound amplification [is] sufficient to reach all listeners within the defined concert ground." In response to Rock Against Racism's argument that the guideline was overbroad (requiring a city technician when the sponsor had equally expert personnel), the Court relied on the lower court's finding that the city's technician was able to accommodate all sponsor needs. Finally, the Court found that the guidelines left ample alternative means of communication, since it did not restrict access to the bandshell but merely reduced volume.]

NOTES ON *ROCK AGAINST RACISM* AND TIME, PLACE AND MANNER REGULATION

1. *Content Neutrality*. *Rock Against Racism* highlights the importance of the content distinction in First Amendment analysis. Content-neutral regulations receive lower scrutiny. See *O'Brien*. But is there ever such a thing as a *truly* content-neutral regulation? Even in *Rock Again Racism*, is the noise level completely unrelated to the "message" of the music? Is punk rock played at a whisper still the real thing? (Like the members of the Court, the authors of this book are probably disqualified by age from answering this question!)

2. *Completely Foreclosing a Mode of Communication*. Normally, content-neutral regulations survive review with little difficulty, given the leniency of the test. The primary exception seems to be for regulations that shut off a traditional mode of communication. In *City of Ladue v. Gilleo*, 512 U.S. 43 (1994), the Court struck down a local ordinance banning lawn signs, as applied to a woman who wanted to post a sign protesting the Persian Gulf War on her front lawn. The Court was unpersuaded that "adequate substitutes exist for the important medium of speech" that the city had closed: "especially for persons of modest means or limited mobility, a yard or window sign may have no practical substitute."

3. *Other Government Property*. We have already considered the government's (quite limited) ability to restrict speech on some government-owned property. Government ownership of streets, parks, and sidewalks seems to add only marginally to its regulatory power. But the Court has also had occasion to consider speech activities involving other types of government property. In *Widmar v. Vincent*, 454 U.S. 263 (1981), for example, the Court held that the government could not exclude religious groups from using university classrooms for after-hours meetings, since other student groups were allowed to use the rooms. On the other hand, in *United States Postal Service v. Greenburgh Civic Ass'ns*, 453 U.S. 114 (1981), the Court held that the government could ban civic groups from putting leaflets in home mailboxes without paying for postage, and in *City Council v. Taxpayers for Vincent*, 466 U.S. 789 (1984), the Court upheld a municipal ban against posting signs on public property.

Perry Educ. Ass'n v. Perry Local Educators' Ass'n, 460 U.S. 37 (1983). The issue before the Court in *Perry* was whether an insurgent faculty union could have access to school mailboxes. The Court held that the faculty mailboxes were a nonpublic forum and that restricting access to the recognized union was reasonable. The Court attempted to provide a framework for analyzing speech restrictions on government property. *Perry* created a tripartite framework for evaluating regulations of speech on government property. The degree of scrutiny depends on whether the property in question is (1) a traditional public forum such as a park, (2) a "limited" forum that the government has expressly dedicated to speech purposes, or (3) other government property ("nonpublic forum"). In a traditional forum, time, place, and manner regulations are allowed, but the government cannot close the forum to expressive activities, and it has no more power to regulate on the basis of content than it has on private property. The rules for a "limited" forum are the same, except that the government can close the forum to expressive activity altogether if it chooses. In a nonpublic forum, the government can impose any reasonable regulation so long as it avoids discriminating on the basis of viewpoint.

Applying the *Perry* test to public spaces is not always easy. The difficulties are compounded, however, when the test is applied to metaphorical forums: opportunities for speech that are not defined by location. *Arkansas Educational Television Comm'n v. Forbes*, 523 U.S. 666 (1998), is illustrative. A public television decided that Forbes was not a serious candidate and excluded him from a televised debate. The Court decided that candidate debates should be treated as nonpublic forums, allowing reasonable, nonviewpoint restrictions on access. The Court concluded, however, that the decision to exclude Forbes had been made on neutral grounds. How useful is forum analysis here? Would it have been better for the Court to simply analyze candidate debates as sui generis rather than applying *Perry*?

B. GOVERNMENT-SUPPORTED SPEECH

A pervasive issue in constitutional law is the extent to which the government can use its financial resources to obtain results that it could not obtain through direct regulation. For instance, although *Roe* and *Casey* restrict governmental regulation of abortion, whether the government has to fund abortions may be a different matter. The issue of "unconstitutional conditions" has been particularly significant in the area of free speech. We begin with the relatively straightforward situation in which the financial leverage takes the form of a government paycheck, and then consider the more general problems of restrictions on government funding.

NOTE ON PUBLIC EMPLOYEE SPEECH

The speech in *Perry* was doubly subject to regulation: not only were the mailboxes government property but the speakers were employees and their would-be union representatives. The government has a greater interest in limiting the speech of its employees than that of the general public. The government has no legitimate interest in restricting the street-corner speaker who says the governor is an idiot; it does have an interest in eliminating members of his own staff who are openly insulting at the office.

In *Pickering v. Board of Education,* 391 U.S. 563 (1968), a teacher had been fired for writing a newspaper letter criticizing the school board's fiscal policies. The Court saw its task as finding "a balance between the interests of the teacher, as a citizen, in commenting upon matters of public concern and the interest of the State, as an employer, in promoting the efficiency of the public services it performs through its employees." The teacher's statements obviously related to matters of public concern. Because the letter was not shown to undermine the performance of his teaching duties or otherwise interfere with the operation of the schools, the school had no more interest in restricting this speech than that of any citizen. Although the letter did contain some factual misstatements, they did not rise to the level of unprotected defamation under the *New York Times* test. Hence, the letter was protected speech.

One issue left open by *Pickering* is the role of subject matter in the analysis. Although the Court characterized the speech as relating to matters of public concern, it was not clear whether this was essential to the holding. Also, it was not clear how broadly this term swept — recall that in defamation law only a narrow category of speech has been excluded from the "public concern" category. In *Connick v. Myers,* 461 U.S. 138 (1983), the Court made it clear that *Pickering* only applies to matters of public concern, and that the term is defined somewhat narrowly.

Connick involved a disgruntled assistant district attorney who circulated a questionnaire to fellow workers. The questions covered office transfer policy (her particular gripe), office morale, the need for a grievance committee, confidence in supervisors, and whether employees felt pressured to work in political campaigns. She was fired for insubordination. The Court attempted to draw a line between matters of public concern and "matters of only personal interest" such as "employee grievances." With the possible exception of the "most unusual circumstances," the Court said, "a federal court is not the appropriate forum in which to review the wisdom of a personnel decision" relating to employee grievances that lack public concern.

In *Garcetti v. Ceballos,* 547 U.S. 410 (2006), the Court further limited *Pickering* by holding that "when public employees make statements pursuant to their official duties, the employees are not speaking as citizens for First Amendment purposes, and the Constitution does not insulate their communications from employer discipline."

———

As the foregoing materials show, the First Amendment establishes limits on how the government treats its employees. (See also the procedural due process rights of state employees, Chapter 5, § 6B.) May the government employee *waive* these rights? Although most personal constitutional rights — such as the right not to incriminate oneself, the right to counsel, and the right to a jury trial in civil or criminal cases — may be waived by the recipient, the weight of scholarly opinion is to the effect that the public employee cannot waive all or most of her First Amendment rights.[c] The best reasons against allowing total waivers is the social benefit of protecting these rights of public employees — such as the assurance of meritocracy and robust public discussion, not to mention the possibility of whistleblowing.

Now, expand the inquiry: If the government may not ordinarily condition public employment upon the waiver of First Amendment rights, may it condition the payment of other benefits upon the recipient's waiver of her First Amendment rights? Is there a class of cases where the government cannot control speech *directly*, through criminal bars or license requirements or injunctions, but can control speech *indirectly*, through subsidies and grants conditioned upon nonspeech? Consider also the restrictions the First Amendment places on the government's ability to condition the use of government property upon the user's conformity to state guidelines.

RUST v. SULLIVAN
500 U.S. 173, 111 S.Ct. 1759, 114 L.Ed.2d 233 (1991)

CHIEF JUSTICE REHNQUIST delivered the opinion of the Court.

[Title X of the Public Health Services Act established funding for family-planning services. Section 1008 of the Act provided that none of the funds "shall be used in programs where abortion is a method of family planning." In 1989, the Department of Health and Human Services (HHS) issued new regulations implementing the statute. Under the 1989 regulations, Title X projects must refer every pregnant client "for appropriate prenatal and/or social services by furnishing a list of available providers that promote the welfare of the mother and the unborn child." The list may not be used indirectly to encourage or promote abortion, "such as by weighing the list of referrals in favor of health care providers which perform abortions, by including on the list of referral providers health care providers whose principal business is the provision of abortions, by excluding available providers who do not provide abortions, or by 'steering' clients to providers who offer abortion as a method of family planning." The Title X project is expressly prohibited from referring a pregnant woman to an abortion provider, even upon specific request. One permissible response to such an inquiry is that "the project does not consider abortion an appropriate method of family planning and therefore does not counsel or refer for abortion."]

The challenged regulations implement the statutory prohibition by prohibiting counseling, referral, and the provision of information regarding

---

c. See Daniel Farber, *Free Speech Without Romance: Public Choice and the First Amendment*, 105 Harv. L. Rev. 554 (1991). On the tougher question of whether a public employee may be held to contracts promising confidentiality, compare Frank Easterbrook, *Insider Trading, Secret Agents, Evidentiary Privileges, and the Production of Information*, 1981 Sup. Ct. Rev. 309, with Cass Sunstein, *Government Control of Information*, 74 Cal. L. Rev. 889 (1986).

abortion as a method of family planning. They are designed to ensure that the limits of the federal program are observed. The Title X program is designed not for prenatal care, but to encourage family planning. A doctor who wished to offer prenatal care to a project patient who became pregnant could properly be prohibited from doing so because such service is outside the scope of the federally funded program. The regulations prohibiting abortion counseling and referral are of the same ilk; "no funds appropriated for the project may be used in programs where abortion is a method of family planning," and a doctor employed by the project may be prohibited in the course of his project duties from counseling abortion or referring for abortion. This is not a case of the Government "suppressing a dangerous idea," but of a prohibition on a project grantee or its employees from engaging in activities outside of its scope.

To hold that the Government unconstitutionally discriminates on the basis of viewpoint when it chooses to fund a program dedicated to advance certain permissible goals, because the program in advancing those goals necessarily discourages alternate goals, would render numerous government programs constitutionally suspect. When Congress established a National Endowment for Democracy to encourage other countries to adopt democratic principles, 22 U.S.C. § 4411(b), it was not constitutionally required to fund a program to encourage competing lines of political philosophy such as Communism and · Fascism. Petitioners' assertions ultimately boil down to the position that if the government chooses to subsidize one protected right, it must subsidize analogous counterpart rights. But the Court has soundly rejected that proposition. Within far broader limits than petitioners are willing to concede, when the government appropriates public funds to establish a program it is entitled to define the limits of that program. * * *

[H]ere the government is not denying a benefit to anyone, but is instead simply insisting that public funds be spent for the purposes for which they were authorized. The Secretary's regulations do not force the Title X grantee to give up abortion-related speech; they merely require that the grantee keep such activities separate and distinct from Title X activities. Title X expressly distinguishes between a Title X *grantee* and a Title X *project.* The grantee, which normally is a health care organization, may receive funds from a variety of sources for a variety of purposes. The grantee receives Title X funds, however, for the specific and limited purpose of establishing and operating a Title X project. The regulations govern the scope of the Title X *project*'s activities, and leave the grantee unfettered in its other activities. The Title X *grantee* can continue to perform abortions, provide abortion-related services, and engage in abortion advocacy; it simply is required to conduct those activities through programs that are separate and independent from the project that receives Title X funds.

In contrast, our "unconstitutional conditions" cases involve situations in which the government has placed a condition on the *recipient* of the subsidy rather than on a particular program or service, thus effectively prohibiting the recipient from engaging in the protected conduct outside the scope of the federally funded program. * * *

This is not to suggest that funding by the Government, even when coupled with the freedom of the fund recipients to speak outside the scope of the Government-funded project, is invariably sufficient to justify government control over the content of expression. For example, this Court has recognized that the existence of a Government "subsidy," in the form of Government-owned property, does not justify the restriction of speech in areas that have "been traditionally open to the public for expressive activity," or have been "expressly dedicated to speech activity." Similarly, we have recognized that the university is a traditional sphere of free expression so fundamental to the functioning of our society that the Government's ability to control speech within that sphere by means of conditions attached to the expenditure of Government funds is restricted by the vagueness and overbreadth doctrines of the First Amendment. It could be argued by analogy that traditional relationships such as that between doctor and patient should enjoy protection under the First Amendment from government regulation, even when subsidized by the Government. We need not resolve that question here, however, because the Title X program regulations do not significantly impinge upon the doctor-patient relationship. Nothing in them requires a doctor to represent as his own any opinion that he does not in fact hold. Nor is the doctor-patient relationship established by the Title X program sufficiently all-encompassing so as to justify an expectation on the part of the patient of comprehensive medical advice. The program does not provide post-conception medical care, and therefore a doctor's silence with regard to abortion cannot reasonably be thought to mislead a client into thinking that the doctor does not consider abortion an appropriate option for her. The doctor is always free to make clear that advice regarding abortion is simply beyond the scope of the program. In these circumstances, the general rule that the Government may choose not to subsidize speech applies with full force.

JUSTICE BLACKMUN, with whom JUSTICE MARSHALL joins, and with whom JUSTICE STEVENS joins [as to the portions excerpted here], dissenting.

Until today, the Court never has upheld viewpoint-based suppression of speech simply because that suppression was a condition upon the acceptance of public funds. Whatever may be the Government's power to condition the receipt of its largess upon the relinquishment of constitutional rights, it surely does not extend to a condition that suppresses the recipient's cherished freedom of speech based solely upon the content or viewpoint of that speech. * * *

Remarkably, the majority concludes that "the Government has not discriminated on the basis of viewpoint; it has merely chosen to fund one activity to the exclusion of another." But the majority's claim that the Regulations merely limit a Title X project's speech to preventive or precon-ceptional services rings hollow in light of the broad range of non-preventive services that the Regulations authorize Title X projects to provide. By refusing to fund those family-planning projects that advocate abortion *because* they advocate abortion, the Government plainly has targeted a particular viewpoint. The majority's reliance on the fact that the Regulations pertain solely to funding decisions simply begs the question. Clearly, there are some bases upon which government may not rest its decision to fund or not to fund. For example, the

Members of the majority surely would agree that government may not base its decision to support an activity upon considerations of race. As demonstrated above, our cases make clear that ideological viewpoint is a similarly repugnant ground upon which to base funding decisions. * * *

[The dissents of JUSTICES STEVENS and O'CONNOR are omitted.]

Rosenberger v. Rector and Visitors of the University of Virginia, 515 U.S. 819 (1995). The University of Virginia has a fund, supported by student fees, which is used, among other things, to cover printing costs for various student groups. The University refused to provide such payment, however, for a group called Wide Awake Productions, because its student newspaper ("Wide Awake: A Christian Perspective at the University of Virginia") primarily promotes religion. On behalf of the group, Rosenberger mounted a free speech challenge to the restriction. The court of appeals upheld the funding refusal on the basis that it was required in order to comply with the Establishment Clause. (The funding question is discussed more fully later in this chapter.) Before reaching the Establishment Clause issue, the Court began with an analysis of the free speech issue. The case gave rise to an interesting debate about free speech issues in government funding cases. In his opinion for the Court, **Justice Kennedy** concluded that the University had engaged in viewpoint-based regulation. By the terms of the religious-funding prohibition, "the University does not exclude religion as a subject matter but selects for disfavored treatment those student journalistic efforts with religious editorial viewpoints." In striking down the funding ban, Justice Kennedy concluded that fundamental First Amendment principles were at stake:

> The first danger to liberty lies in granting the State the power to examine publications to determine whether or not they are based on some ultimate idea and if so for the State to classify them. The second, and corollary, danger to speech is from the chilling of individual thought and expression. That danger is especially real in the University setting, where the State acts against a background and tradition of thought and experiment that is at the center of our intellectual and philosophic tradition. * * * For the University, by regulation, to cast disapproval on particular viewpoints of its students risks the suppression of free speech and creative inquiry in one of the vital centers for the nation's intellectual life, its college and university campuses.

Rust v. Sullivan was distinguishable, he said, because in that program the government was hiring private speakers to convey the government's own messages, rather than expending funds "to encourage a diversity of views from private speakers."

In dissent, **Justice Souter**, joined by **Justices Stevens, Ginsburg**, and **Breyer**, argued that the funding ban was not based on viewpoint. The dissenters defined "viewpoint discrimination" as being present "when government allows one message while prohibiting the messages of those who can reasonably be expected to respond." Here, that was not true, because the University refused to fund advocacy by other religious groups and even by agnostics and atheists. Hence, the University did not "skew debate by funding one position but not its competitors." In response, Justice Kennedy said: "It is as objectionable to exclude both a theistic and an atheistic perspective on the debate as it is to exclude one, the other, or yet another political, economic, or social viewpoint. The dissent's declaration that debate is not skewed so long as multiple voices are silenced is simply wrong; the debate is skewed in multiple ways."[d]

LEGAL SERVICES CORP. v. VELAZQUEZ
531 U.S. 533, 121 S.Ct. 1043, 149 L.Ed.2d 63 (2001)

JUSTICE KENNEDY delivered the opinion of the Court.

[The Legal Services Corporation (LSC) was established as a nonprofit corporation to distribute federal funds to local legal aid organizations for the poor. This case involves a condition on the use of LSC funds added by § 504(a)(16) of a 1996 appropriations act. This condition prohibits grant recipients from engaging in efforts to amend or otherwise challenge existing welfare law. As interpreted by the government, the statute bars a lawyer from arguing to a court that a state law conflicts with federal law or that either a state or federal statute is unconstitutional. However, grantees can argue that an agency made an erroneous factual determination or misread or misapplied a term contained in an existing welfare statute. When a constitutional or statutory issue becomes apparent after a case is underway, LSC requires that its attorneys withdraw. The restriction applies to all of the grantee's activities, including those funded from other sources. LSC argued that these restrictions were permissible under *Rust v. Sullivan*.]

The Court in *Rust* did not place explicit reliance on the rationale that the counseling activities of the doctors under Title X amounted to governmental speech; when interpreting the holding in later cases, however, we have explained *Rust* on this understanding. * * * As we said in *Rosenberger*, "[w]hen the government disburses public funds to private entities to convey a governmental message, it may take legitimate and appropriate steps to ensure that its message is neither garbled nor distorted by the grantee." * * *

Neither the latitude for government speech nor its rationale applies to subsidies for private speech in every instance, however. As we have pointed out, "[i]t does not follow . . . that viewpoint-based restrictions are proper when the [government] does not itself speak or subsidize transmittal of a message it favors but instead expends funds to encourage a diversity of views from private speakers." *Rosenberger*.

Although the LSC program differs from the program at issue in *Rosenberger* in that its purpose is not to "encourage a diversity of views," the salient point is that, like the program in *Rosenberger,* the LSC program was designed to facilitate private speech, not to promote a governmental message. Congress funded LSC grantees to provide attorneys to represent the interests of indigent clients. In the specific context of § 504(a)(16) suits for benefits, an LSC-funded attorney speaks on the behalf of the client in a claim against the government for welfare benefits. The lawyer is not the government's speaker. The attorney defending the decision to deny benefits will deliver the government's message

---

d. On the general significance of viewpoint neutrality in funding decisions, see Martin Redish & Daryl Kessler, *Government Subsidies and Free Expression*, 80 Minn. L. Rev. 543 (1996).

in the litigation. The LSC lawyer, however, speaks on the behalf of his or her private, indigent client. Cf. *Polk County v. Dodson,* 454 U.S. 312 (1981) (holding that a public defender does not act "under color of state law" because he "works under canons of professional responsibility that mandate his exercise of independent judgment on behalf of the client" and because there is an "assumption that counsel will be free of state control").

The Government has designed this program to use the legal profession and the established Judiciary of the States and the Federal Government to accomplish its end of assisting welfare claimants in determination or receipt of their benefits. The advice from the attorney to the client and the advocacy by the attorney to the courts cannot be classified as governmental speech even under a generous understanding of the concept. In this vital respect this suit is distinguishable from *Rust.*

* * *

When the government creates a limited forum for speech, certain restrictions may be necessary to define the limits and purposes of the program. The same is true when the government establishes a subsidy for specified ends. As this suit involves a subsidy, limited forum cases * * * may not be controlling in a strict sense, yet they do provide some instruction. Here the program presumes that private, nongovernmental speech is necessary, and a substantial restriction is placed upon that speech. At oral argument and in its briefs the LSC advised us that lawyers funded in the Government program may not undertake representation in suits for benefits if they must advise clients respecting the questionable validity of a statute which defines benefit eligibility and the payment structure. The limitation forecloses advice or legal assistance to question the validity of statutes under the Constitution of the United States. It extends further, it must be noted, so that state statutes inconsistent with federal law under the Supremacy Clause may be neither challenged nor questioned.

By providing subsidies to LSC, the Government seeks to facilitate suits for benefits by using the State and Federal courts and the independent bar on which those courts depend for the proper performance of their duties and responsibilities. Restricting LSC attorneys in advising their clients and in presenting arguments and analyses to the courts distorts the legal system by altering the traditional role of the attorneys in much the same way broadcast systems or student publication networks were changed in the limited forum cases we have cited. Just as government in those cases could not elect to use a broadcasting network or a college publication structure in a regime which prohibits speech necessary to the proper functioning of those systems, see *Arkansas Ed. Television Comm'n* and *Rosenberger*, it may not design a subsidy to effect this serious and fundamental restriction on advocacy of attorneys and the functioning of the judiciary.

LSC has advised us, furthermore, that upon determining a question of statutory validity is present in any anticipated or pending case or controversy, the LSC-funded attorney must cease the representation at once. This is true whether the validity issue becomes apparent during initial attorney-client consultations or in the midst of litigation proceedings. A disturbing example of the restriction was discussed during oral argument before the Court. It is well understood that when there are two reasonable constructions for a statute, yet one raises a constitutional question, the Court should prefer the interpretation which avoids the constitutional issue. Yet, as the LSC advised the Court, if, during litigation, a judge were to ask an LSC attorney whether there was a constitutional concern, the LSC attorney simply could not answer.

Interpretation of the law and the Constitution is the primary mission of the judiciary when it acts within the sphere of its authority to resolve a case or controversy. An informed, independent judiciary presumes an informed, independent bar. Under § 504(a)(16), however, cases would be presented by LSC attorneys who could not advise the courts of serious questions of statutory validity. It is fundamental that the First Amendment "was fashioned to assure unfettered interchange of ideas for the bringing about of political and social changes desired by the people." *New York Times Co. v. Sullivan.* There can be little doubt that the LSC Act funds constitutionally protected expression; and in the context of this statute there is no programmatic message of the kind recognized in *Rust* and which sufficed there to allow the Government to specify the advice deemed necessary for its legitimate objectives. This serves to distinguish § 504(a)(16) from any of the Title X program restrictions upheld in *Rust,* and to place it beyond any congressional funding condition approved in the past by this Court. * * *

JUSTICE SCALIA, with whom **THE CHIEF JUSTICE**, **JUSTICE O'CONNOR**, and **JUSTICE THOMAS** join, dissenting.

* * * The Court contends that *Rust* is different because the program at issue subsidized government speech, while the LSC funds private speech. This is so unpersuasive it hardly needs response. If the private doctors' confidential advice to their patients at issue in *Rust* constituted "government speech," it is hard to imagine what subsidized speech would *not* be government speech. Moreover, the majority's contention that the subsidized speech in these cases is not government speech because the lawyers have a professional obligation to represent the interests of their clients founders on the reality that the doctors in *Rust* had a professional obligation to serve the interests of their patients. * * *

The Court further asserts that these cases are different from *Rust* because the welfare funding restriction "seeks to use an existing medium of expression and to control it . . . in ways which distort its usual functioning." This is wrong on both the facts and the law. It is wrong on the law because there is utterly no precedent for the novel and facially implausible proposition that the First Amendment has anything to do with government funding that — though it does not actually abridge anyone's speech — "distorts an existing medium of expression." * * *

NOTE ON STUDENT SPEECH

"All men are created equal," according to the Declaration of Independence, but some are more equal than others, according to George Orwell's *Animal Farm*. With respect to the First Amendment, soldiers, prisoners, and high school students are not quite as equal as the rest of us. Unlike the public forum cases, decisions dealing with members of these groups rely less on the idea that the government has special powers to manage certain *places*, and more on the idea of special power to control certain *people*. Prison authorities have broad (but not unlimited) powers to regulate prisoners' correspondence, including their reading materials, subject only to a deferential reasonableness standard. See *Thornburgh v. Abbott*, 490 U.S. 401 (1989). Because of the Court's willingness to defer to the demands of military discipline, military personnel also have diminished First Amendment rights.

High schools have also given rise to a substantial body of First Amendment litigation. In *Tinker v. Des Moines School District*, 393 U.S. 503 (1969), the Court held over Justice Black's vehement dissent that students could not be expelled for wearing black armbands to protest the Vietnam War. In *Bethel School District No. 403 v. Fraser*, 478 U.S. 675 (1986), however, the Court stressed the school's role in inculcating moral values and upheld the suspension of a student for using sexual innuendos in a speech at a school assembly.

In *Hazelwood School District v. Kuhlmeier*, 484 U.S. 260 (1988), the Court upheld a principal's censorship of two articles in a high school newspaper. One article described some students' experiences with pregnancy, and the other discussed the impact of divorce on students at the school. Because the newspaper was written and edited by a journalism class, the Court held that "educators do not offend the First Amendment by exercising editorial control over the style and content of student speech in school-sponsored expressive activities so long as their actions are reasonably related to legitimate pedagogical concerns."

Finally, in *Morse v. Frederick*, __U.S. ___, 127 S.Ct. 2618, 168 L.Ed.2d 290 (2007), the Court further contracted protection for student speech. Students at an Alaska high school were released from classes so that they could view the Olympic Torch Relay in 2002. One student waived a huge banner reading "BONG HiTS 4 JESUS." The student was disciplined by the principal, who considered the banner to be advocating drug use. Chief Justice Roberts' opinion for the Court held that it was reasonable for the principal to "conclude that the banner promoted illegal drug use — in violation of established school policy — and that failing to act would send a powerful message to the students in her charge, including Frederick, about how serious the school was about the dangers of illegal drug use. The First Amendment does not require schools to tolerate at school events student expression that contributes to those dangers." A concurring opinion by Justice Alito agreed that " illegal drug use presents a grave and in many ways unique threat to the physical safety of students. I therefore conclude that the public schools may ban speech advocating illegal drug use. But I regard such regulation as standing at the far reaches of what the First Amendment permits. I join the opinion of the Court with the understanding that the opinion does not endorse any further extension." Justice Stevens' dissent protested that "this case began with a silly, nonsensical banner, it ends with the Court inventing out of whole cloth a special First Amendment rule permitting the censorship of any student speech that mentions drugs, at least so long as someone could perceive that speech to contain a latent pro-drug message."

SECTION 5. PROCESS-BASED PROTECTIONS FOR SPEECH

To get a complete view of First Amendment doctrine, it is necessary to understand not only the substantive restrictions on speech regulation, but also the special process-based protections that apply to speech. Even if a speech restriction would otherwise be permissible, it may be struck down because it takes the form of a prior restraint or because it is badly drafted. In this section, we briefly touch upon these process-based protections.

A. PRIOR RESTRAINTS AND PERMIT SYSTEMS

As noted at the beginning of this chapter, Blackstone identified the "liberty of the press" with the absence of prior restrictions on publication such as licensing. So long as the press was able to publish what it wanted, the government could impose a suitable punishment after the fact for abuses. An early opinion by Justice Holmes suggested a Blackstonian interpretation of the First Amendment. The defendant had been held in contempt of court for publishing an editorial and cartoon questioning the motives of the Colorado Supreme Court. Holmes said that the main purpose of the First Amendment was to "prevent all such *previous restraints* upon publication as had been practiced by other governments," not the "subsequent punishment of such as may be deemed contrary to the public welfare." *Patterson v. People of State of Colorado ex rel. Attorney General*, 205 U.S. 454 (1907). By the end of World War I, however, Holmes had clearly changed his mind about this point, and today's Court endorses his later view. Later decisions, for example, limit the use of contempt citations to actual violations of court orders or out-of-court conduct that presents a "clear and present danger" to the integrity of pending judicial proceedings. See *Wood v. Georgia*, 370 U.S. 375 (1962); *Bridges v. California*, 314 U.S. 252 (1941). Thus, the First Amendment is clearly not limited to prior restraints. Nevertheless, it does apply to them with particular vigor.[a]

Near v. Minnesota, 283 U.S. 697 (1931), is the leading case on prior restraints. A newspaper had charged that certain public officials had been protecting local gangsters and called for a special grand jury. Acting under a state statute, the government obtained an injunction forbidding the defendants from circulating "any publication whatsoever which is a malicious, scandalous or defamatory newspaper." **Chief Justice Hughes** wrote the opinion for the Court. He emphasized that "unless the owner or publisher is able and disposed to bring competent evidence to satisfy the judge that the charges are true and are published with good motives and for justifiable ends, his newspaper or

---

a. For commentary, see Stephen Barnett, *The Puzzle of Prior Restraint*, 29 Stan. L. Rev. 539 (1977); Thomas Emerson, *The Doctrine of Prior Restraint*, 20 Law & Contemp. Probs. 648 (1955); Paul Freund, *The Supreme Court and Civil Liberties*, 4 Vand. L. Rev. 533 (1951); William Mayton, *Toward a Theory of First Amendment Process: Injunctions of Speech, Subsequent Punishment, and the Costs of the Prior Restraint Doctrine*, 67 Cornell L. Rev. 245 (1982); Marin Scordato, *Distinction Without a Difference: A Reappraisal of the Doctrine of Prior Restraint*, 68 N.C. L. Rev. 1 (1989).

periodical is suppressed and further publication is made punishable as a contempt." Thus, the state had instituted the equivalent of a licensing system, covering only the defendants. "This," said Hughes, "is of the essence of censorship." He stressed the powerful objections to prior restraints voiced by Blackstone, as well as later history: "The fact that for approximately one hundred and fifty years there has been almost an entire absence of attempts to impose previous restraints upon publications relating to the malfeasance of public officers is significant of the deep-seated convictions that such restraints would violate constitutional right." Hughes did admit that the rule against prior restraints was not absolute, but the rule applied except in a few special cases: "[N]o one would question but that a government might prevent actual obstruction to its recruiting service or the publication of the sailing dates of transports or the number or location of troops. On similar grounds, the primary requirements of decency may be enforced against obscene publications. The security of the community life may be protected against incitements to acts of violence."

Shuttlesworth v. City of Birmingham, 394 U.S. 147 (1969), illustrates how the prior restraint concept can be used to challenge permit systems as well as injunctions. Civil rights marchers were convicted under an ordinance that gave complete discretion to city officials over parade permits. In an opinion by **Justice Stewart**, the Court reversed the convictions for violating the ordinance: "This ordinance as it was written, therefore, fell squarely within the ambit of the many decisions of this Court over the last 30 years, holding that a law subjecting the exercise of First Amendment freedoms to the prior restraint of a license, without narrow, objective, and definite standards to guide the licensing authority, is unconstitutional. * * * And our decisions have made clear that a person faced with such an unconstitutional licensing law may ignore it and engage in impunity in the exercise of the right of free expression * * * ." The state unsuccessfully argued that the ordinance had been cured by a later interpretation of the state supreme court, limiting the discretion of the municipal officials.

New York Times Co. v. United States, 403 U.S. 713 (1971). This case arose out of the Vietnam War. To make a long story short, the *New York Times* and *Washington Post* had obtained copies of a classified study entitled *History of U.S. Decision-Making Process on Viet Nam Policy* (also known as "the Pentagon Papers"). The study indicated that the government had concealed important facts or actively misled the public with respect to decisions to escalate the war. The government sought an injunction against publication of the study. In a short *per curiam*, accompanied by lengthy concurring opinions, the Court rejected the government's arguments. The *per curiam* contains one paragraph explaining the Court's rationale, which (apart from citations) reads as follows: " 'Any system of prior restraints of expression comes to this Court bearing a heavy presumption against its constitutional validity.' The Government 'thus carries a heavy burden of showing justification for the imposition of such a restraint.' The District Court for the Southern District of New York in the *New*

York Times case and the Court of Appeals for the District of Columbia Circuit in the *Washington Post* case held that the government had not yet met that burden. We agree." In addition to the *per curiam*, every Justice wrote a separate opinion, six concurring in the judgment and three dissenting.

Justices Black, Douglas, Brennan, and **Marshall** would have summarily reversed all the lower court orders staying the newspapers' publication. Justice Black (joined by Douglas) stated that "every moment's continuance of the injunctions against these newspapers amounts to a flagrant, indefensible, and continuing violation of the First Amendment." He sternly scolded the Executive Branch for having "forgotten the essential purpose and history of the First Amendment," which gave special protection to the press "so that it could bare the secrets of government and inform the people. Only a free and unrestrained press can effectively expose deception in government. And paramount among the responsibilities of a free press is the duty to prevent any part of the government from deceiving the people and sending them off to distant lands to die of foreign fevers and foreign shot and shell." Justice Brennan wrote that "the First Amendment tolerates absolutely no judicial restraints of the press predicated upon surmise or conjecture that untoward consequences may result."

Justices Stewart and **White** were more cautious. "In the absence of the governmental checks and balances present in other areas of our national life, the only effective restraint upon executive policy and power in the areas of national defense and international affairs may lie in an enlightened citizenry * * *. For this reason, it is perhaps here that a press that is alert, aware, and free most vitally serves the basic purpose of the First Amendment. For without an informed and free press there cannot be an enlightened citizenry," wrote Justice Stewart. "Yet it is elementary that the successful conduct of international diplomacy and the maintenance of an effective national defense require both confidentiality and secrecy." Justice Stewart ruled against the government because he could not say that disclosure of any of the "Pentagon Papers" would "surely result in direct, immediate, and irreparable damage to our Nation or its people." Justice White joined Stewart's opinion, but also wrote a concurrence of his own (which was joined by Stewart). Justice White emphasized that there were a number of criminal statutes that were "potentially relevant to these cases."

Chief Justice Burger, Justice Harlan, and **Justice Blackmun** dissented on the ground that the Court should not have heard and decided the case so hastily. (Oral argument took place only three days after the lower courts entered their orders. The Court's decision was handed down another four days later.) Justice Blackmun also expressed fear that the release of the papers might cause serious repercussions: "If, however, damage has been done, and if, with the Court's action today, these newspapers proceed to publish the critical documents and there results therefrom 'the death of soldiers, the destruction of alliances, the greatly increased difficulty of negotiation with our enemies, the inability of our diplomats to negotiate,' to which list I might add the factors of prolongation of the war and of further delay in the freeing of United States prisoners, then the Nation's people will know where the responsibility for these sad consequences rests."

Madsen v. Women's Health Center, Inc., 512 U.S. 753 (1994). Anti-abortion picketers had demonstrated outside a Florida abortion clinic. A state court permanently enjoined them from blocking access or physically abusing people entering or leaving the clinic. Despite the initial injunction, the trial court found, protesters continued to impede access to the clinic, creating a high level of noise with loudspeakers and bullhorns, and they also picketed the homes of clinic workers. Concluding that the initial injunction had been ineffective, the state court issued a new, more detailed injunction. Among other provisions, the injunction created a 36-foot buffer zone around the clinic in which picketing was banned, limiting the noise level, and prohibiting any uninvited approach to clinic patients within 300 feet of the clinic. In an opinion by **Chief Justice Rehnquist**, the Court held that this injunction should be scrutinized under a standard somewhere between strict scrutiny and content neutrality: "We must ask instead whether the challenged provisions of the injunction burden no more speech than necessary to serve a significant government interest." Applying this standard, the Court upheld the 36-foot buffer zone in front of the clinic and the noise restrictions as burdening "no more speech than necessary to accomplish the governmental interest at stake." But several portions of the injunction were invalidated: the restriction on approaching patients within 300 feet of the clinic, a prohibition on using images "visible within the clinic," and the 300-foot buffer zone around the residences of clinic workers. **Justice Scalia** protested in dissent that the "entire injunction in this case departs so far from the established course of our jurisprudence that in any other context it would have been regarded as a candidate for summary reversal." He attributed the result to the Court's favoritism toward abortion.

B. (DUE PROCESS) VAGUENESS AND THE FIRST AMENDMENT

The Supreme Court has frequently invalidated broadly written statutes on the ground that they are "void for vagueness." Traditionally, the Court has understood the void-for-vagueness doctrine in due process terms: criminal laws must "give a person of ordinary intelligence fair notice that his contemplated conduct is forbidden by statute." *United States v. Harriss*, 347 U.S. 612, 617 (1954); accord, *Lanzetta v. New Jersey*, 306 U.S. 451 (1939); *Stromberg v. California*, 283 U.S. 359 (1931). The doctrine is also an example of a structural approach to due process: the important moral judgments made in the criminal law must be made by the legislature, directly accountable to the people, and not by the police, prosecutors, or even judges. See *Grayned v. Rockford*, 408 U.S. 104 (1972); Chapter 8, § 2A (the nondelegation doctrine). Most of the Justices in *Roe v. Wade* (chapter 5, § 4B) thought the nineteenth century Texas abortion law was void-for-vagueness, and Justice Blackmun's original draft opinion invalidated the law only on those grounds. Consider the advantages of an opinion in that case which left the states free to adopt more precise abortion laws, which could then have been reviewed on privacy grounds with a more complete record of the evidence and public opinion.

In response to the civil rights cases of the 1960s, the Court rethought the doctrine along equal protection lines: another vice of vague statutes is that they give enforcement authorities (e.g., southern police) too much discretion to apply criminal sanctions arbitrarily.[b] Thus, obstruction of sidewalk laws were enforced against civil rights protesters and not white citizens, see *Cox v. Louisiana*, 379 U.S. 536, 551-52 (1965); *id.* at 579 (Black, J.); disturbing the peace laws tended to spring into action only when racial minorities were engaged in peaceful protests, see *Shuttlesworth v. Birmingham*, 382 U.S. 87, 90-92 (1968); "crime against nature" laws were used only against gay or bisexual men (even though straight men and women engaged in equally unconventional acts), see *Wainwright v. Stone*, 414 U.S. 21 (1973); "lewd vagrancy" and cross-dressing laws were deployed only against lesbians, gay men, and transgendered people, see *Pryor v. Municipal Court*, 599 P.2d 636 (Cal. 1979); *City of Columbus v. Rogers*, 324 N.E.2d 563 (Ohio 1975); and "psychopathic personality" bars were applied only to gay and bisexual people. See *Boutilier v. INS*, 387 U.S. 118 (1967).

The leading case for this newer problem with vague statutes was *Papachristou v. Jacksonville*, 405 U.S. 156 (1972). Jacksonville made it a crime to be "vagabonds," "lewd, wanton and lascivious persons," "habitual loafers," and so forth. The lead defendants were two white women and two black men who were doing nothing more sinister than riding around together in an automobile. On appeal of their conviction to the Supreme Court, they argued that the state and local "vagrancy laws are archaic vestiges of long-past economic conditions and social philosophies" which posed risks of arbitrary enforcement. According to Justice Douglas's conference notes, the Justices were less concerned about notice than about the discretion these laws gave "police or judges . . . to go after anyone they do not like." A secondary theme of the conference was the obsolescence of these laws. Justice Douglas's opinion for a unanimous Court ruled that the "archaic" law was unconstitutionally vague, because it "makes criminal actions which by modern standards are normally innocent," and which are indeed fundamental freedoms traditionally enjoyed by Americans; was "not intelligible to the poor among us, the minorities, the average householder"; and seemed to be enforced mainly against "nonconformists" and "suspicious persons."

Papachristou confirmed the conventional wisdom that two bases for the void-for-vagueness doctrine were fair notice and preventing arbitrary enforcement, but expanded the lesson of the protest cases of the 1960s: the Court will be particularly vigilant when broad, ill-defined statutes touch upon any fundamental rights. This concern has been particularly strong when broadly written laws can be applied to activities protected under the First Amendment. In *NAACP v. Button*, 371 U.S. 415 (1963), the Court struck down a Virginia law

---

b. This idea was advanced by Anthony Amsterdam, *The Void-for-Vagueness Doctrine in the Supreme Court*, 109 U. Pa. L. Rev. 67 (1960) (student note), and its influence on the civil rights cases is developed in William Eskridge, Jr., *Some Effects of Identity-Based Social Movements on Constitutional Law in the Twentieth Century*, 100 Mich. L. Rev. 501 (2002) (Part II.A.3 of the article).

barring organizations from retaining counsel to represent persons in litigation as to which the organizations had no direct interest. On its face, the law seemed justified on grounds of legal ethics (as Justice Harlan maintained in his dissent), but a Court suspicious of the legislature's (anti-NAACP) motives struck it down because of concern that it could be deployed to penalize protected speech and association. Justice Brennan's opinion urged courts to err against censorship, lest citizens and their associations not have the "breathing space" they need to exercise their First Amendment rights. This was the origin of the famous "chilling effect" argument: Because citizens do not know exactly where the statutory line is drawn between permitted and prohibited expression, they will typically err on the side of caution and refrain from exercising their expressive rights.

C. (EQUAL PROTECTION) OVERBREADTH AND THE FIRST AMENDMENT

The introduction to Chapter 4 discussed the idea of overinclusiveness or *overbreadth*, which occurs when a statute's prohibition sweeps beyond its stated purpose. In ordinary equal protection cases, some overbreadth is not fatal to the statute's constitutionality; one hallmark of strict scrutiny, where the statutory classification is suspect (like race) or impinges a fundamental interest (like voting), is that it does not tolerate much overbreadth. Similarly, statutes impinging fundamental First Amendment interests are not allowed much overbreadth. The rationales for the overbreadth doctrine are similar to those of the vagueness doctrine just examined: (a) minimizing official discretion in the enforcement of statutes that might curtail speech, (b) expanding the range of people who can bring constitutional challenges, and (c) minimizing the chilling effect of rules on people's willingness to engage in expression.[c]

On the other hand, not all statutes which might seem chilling have been invalidated by the Supreme Court. In *Broadrick v. Oklahoma*, 413 U.S. 601 (1973), a closely divided Court upheld a state law restricting political activities by public employees. Although the law seemed to reach core First Amendment activities that posed no danger to state policies (e.g., display of campaign buttons or bumper stickers), the Court declined to strike down the law. Justice White's opinion required that overbreadth "must not only be real, but substantial as well," to justify invalidation. *Broadrick* suggests that there may also be costs to the overbreadth doctrine, such as dangers that (a) it becomes too easy for courts to invalidate statutes, (b) it can invalidate statutes whose harms may be more hypothetical than real, and (c) it slights legitimate state policies.

---

c. See Richard Fallon, Jr., *Making Sense of Overbreadth*, 100 Yale L.J. 853 (1991); Kenneth Karst, *Equality as a Central Principle in the First Amendment*, 43 U. Chi. L. Rev. 20 (1975); Note, *The First Amendment Overbreadth Doctrine*, 83 Harv. L. Rev. 844 (1970).

BOARD OF AIRPORT COMMISSIONERS
v. JEWS FOR JESUS, INC.
482 U.S. 569, 107 S.Ct. 2568, 96 L.Ed.2d 500 (1987)

JUSTICE O'CONNOR delivered the opinion of the Court.

[The Board of Airport Commissioners of Los Angeles adopted a resolution banning all "First Amendment activities" within the "Central Terminal Area" at Los Angeles International Airport (LAX). After an airport officer told a minister affiliated with Jews for Jesus that he must stop distributing religious literature in the Central Terminal Area, the plaintiff commenced this action, contending that the resolution was unconstitutional on its face.]

Under the First Amendment overbreadth doctrine, an individual whose own speech or conduct may be prohibited is permitted to challenge a statute on its face "because it also threatens others not before the court — those who desire to engage in legally protected expression but who may refrain from doing so rather than risk prosecution or undertake to have the law declared partially invalid." *Brockett v. Spokane Arcades, Inc.*, 472 U.S. 491, 503 (1985). A statute may be invalidated on its face, however, only if the overbreadth is "substantial." *Broadrick v. Oklahoma*, 413 U.S. 601, 615 (1973). The requirement that the overbreadth be substantial arose from our recognition that application of the overbreadth doctrine is, "manifestly, strong medicine," *Broadrick*, and that "there must be a realistic danger that the statute itself will significantly compromise recognized First Amendment protections of parties not before the Court for it to be facially challenged on overbreadth grounds."

On its face, the resolution at issue in this case reaches the universe of expressive activity, and, by prohibiting all protected expression, purports to create a virtual "First Amendment Free Zone" at LAX. The resolution does not merely regulate expressive activity in the Central Terminal Area that might create problems such as congestion or the disruption of the activities of those who use LAX. Instead, the resolution expansively states that LAX "is not open for First Amendment activities by any individual and/or entity," and that "any individual and/or entity [who] seeks to engage in First Amendment activities within the Central Terminal Area . . . shall be deemed to be acting in contravention of the stated policy of the Board of Airport Commissioners." The resolution therefore does not merely reach the activity of respondents at LAX; it prohibits even talking and reading, or the wearing of campaign buttons or symbolic clothing. Under such a sweeping ban, virtually every individual who enters LAX may be found to violate the resolution by engaging in some "First Amendment activit[y]." We think it obvious that such a ban cannot be justified even if LAX were a nonpublic forum because no conceivable governmental interest would justify such an absolute prohibition of speech.

Additionally, we find no apparent saving construction of the resolution. The resolution expressly applies to all "First Amendment activities," and the words of the resolution simply leave no room for a narrowing construction. In the past the Court sometimes has used either abstention or certification when, as here, the state courts have not had the opportunity to give the statute under challenge a definite construction. Neither option, however, is appropriate in this case because California has no certification procedure, and the resolution is not "fairly subject to an interpretation which will render unnecessary or substantially modify the federal constitutional question." The difficulties in adopting a limiting construction of the resolution are not unlike those found in *Baggett v. Bullitt*, 377 U.S. 360 (1964). At issue in *Baggett* was the constitutionality of several statutes requiring loyalty oaths. The *Baggett* Court concluded that abstention would serve no purpose given the lack of any limiting construction, and held the statutes unconstitutional on their face under the First Amendment overbreadth doctrine. We observed that the challenged loyalty oath was not "open to one or a few interpretations, but to an indefinite number," and concluded that "[i]t is fictional to believe that anything less than extensive adjudications, under the impact of a variety of factual situations, would bring the oath within the bounds of permissible constitutional certainty." Here too, it is difficult to imagine that the resolution could be limited by anything less than a series of adjudications, and the chilling effect of the resolution on protected speech in the meantime would make such a case-by-case adjudication intolerable.

The petitioners suggest that the resolution is not substantially overbroad because it is intended to reach only expressive activity unrelated to airport-related purposes. Such a limiting construction, however, is of little assistance in substantially reducing the overbreadth of the resolution. Much nondisruptive speech — such as the wearing of a T-Shirt or button that contains a political message — may not be "airport related," but is still protected speech even in a nonpublic forum. *See Cohen.* Moreover, the vagueness of this suggested construction itself presents serious constitutional difficulty. The line between airport-related speech and nonairport-related speech is, at best, murky. The petitioners, for example, suggest that an individual who reads a newspaper or converses with a neighbor at LAX is engaged in permitted "airport-related" activity because reading or conversing permits the traveling public to "pass the time." We presume, however, that petitioners would not so categorize the activities of a member of a religious or political organization who decides to "pass the time" by distributing leaflets to fellow travelers. In essence, the result of this vague limiting construction would be to give LAX officials alone the power to decide in the first instance whether a given activity is airport related. Such a law that "confers on police a virtually unrestrained power to arrest and charge persons with a violation" of the resolution is unconstitutional because "[t]he opportunity for abuse, especially where a statute has received a virtually open-ended interpretation, is self-evident."

We conclude that the resolution is substantially overbroad, and is not fairly subject to a limiting construction. Accordingly, we hold that the resolution violates the First Amendment. * * *

JUSTICE WHITE, with whom **THE CHIEF JUSTICE [REHNQUIST]** joins, concurring.

I join the Court's opinion but suggest that it should not be taken as indicating that a majority of the Court considers the Los Angeles International Airport to be a traditional public forum. That issue was one of the questions on which we granted certiorari, and we should not have postponed it for another day.

NOTES ON *JEWS FOR JESUS* AND OVERBREADTH

1. *What's Wrong with the Ordinance*? Is the L.A. ordinance in *Jews for Jesus* overbroad, or is it vague? If read literally, it's certainly overbroad, since it forbids people from reading books in the terminal. But obviously no one would really apply the ordinance that way, so just what kind of activities are actually covered by the ordinance? And who would decide that issue: the airport police or management, the county prosecutor, the jury, or a state judge? As a practical matter, doesn't the ordinance really mean that activities will be allowed in the terminal at the discretion of various state officials? On this reading, doesn't it fall afoul of *Shuttlesworth*?

2. *The Standing Issue.* If a defendant's own conduct is constitutionally protected, she doesn't need the overbreadth doctrine (or a vagueness challenge, for that matter). On the other hand, if her conduct isn't protected, why should she escape prosecution because the statute is overbroad and infringes other people's rights? Normally, standing rules only allow people to litigate their own rights, not someone else's (see Chapter 9, § 1). So what *is* the basis of overbreadth analysis? See Henry Monaghan, *Third Party Standing*, 84 Colum. L. Rev. 277 (1984).

The Court has typically been unwilling to apply overbreadth or vagueness analysis to regulations that apply purely to commercial speech. Is this just another reflection of the "second class" status of commercial speech, or is there some principled justification? Recall the earlier discussion of commercial speech as being less of a public good economically, and therefore less at risk of overdeterrence.

The Court distinguished between standing and overbreadth analysis in *Virginia v. Hicks*, 539 U.S. 113 (2003). The case involved regulations by the Richmond housing authority, which allowed the police to service notice on any person lacking "a legitimate business or social purpose" for being on the premises and to arrest for trespassing any person who remains or returns after having been given this notice. Allegedly, an unwritten rule required advance permission from the management for leafleting and demonstrations. Hicks was given written notice barring him from the residence. When he was arrested after his return to the premises, he challenged the regulation as facially overbroad, although he himself had not engaged in any speech-related activities. The state supreme court ruled in his favor. The Court held that it had jurisdiction because the state had standing to appeal the ruling against it, regardless of whether Hicks would have had standing to bring a challenge in federal court. (That seems a little weird, doesn't it?) On the merits, it rejected the overbreadth argument on the ground that any invalid application to speech activities was not substantial compared with the breadth of the rule's legitimate applications to nonspeech activities (such as Hicks').

3. *Reconsidering the Pornography Ordinance.* Review the pornography ordinance discussed in Problem 6-1. Assume that the basic theory of the

ordinance is sound (that pornography is central to the subordination of women in our society and that this is a compelling basis for government regulation). Is the ordinance vulnerable to overbreadth or vagueness attacks?

SECTION 6. FREEDOM OF ASSOCIATION

Most of the Court's decisions regarding freedom of association have involved politically oriented organizations. Freedom of association first received explicit constitutional protection in cases involving the efforts of southern states to harass the NAACP. The leading case was *NAACP v. Alabama ex rel. Patterson*, 357 U.S. 449 (1958), in which Justice Harlan wrote for a unanimous Court in holding that the NAACP couldn't be required to turn over its membership list to the state. See also *NAACP v. Button*, 371 U.S. 415 (1963) (striking down Virginia law prohibiting organizations like the NAACP from retaining lawyers in connection with litigation to which it was not a party). On the other hand, in *Federal Trade Commission v. Superior Court Trial Lawyers Ass'n*, 493 U.S. 411 (1990), the Court upheld the application of the antitrust laws to another boycott. That boycott was organized by lawyers in private practice who acted as court-appointed counsel for indigents in criminal cases in the District of Columbia. They were protesting the low fees for criminal representation.

Besides the freedom to associate, there is also the freedom not to associate. In *Abood v. Detroit Bd. Of Ed.*, 431 U.S. 209 (1977), the Court held that school teachers could not be forced to join a union as a condition of employment. Although the teachers could be required to pay dues to support the union's collective bargaining activities, from which they benefitted, they could not be required to pay for the union's social or political programs.

————

NAACP v. Claiborne Hardware Co., 458 U.S. 886 (1982). This case arose from a boycott of white stores by African Americans in Claiborne County, Mississippi. The boycott was intended to force business and civic leaders to agree to a series of civil rights demands. Although the boycott was largely peaceful, there were some violent episodes. In a state antitrust action, some of the merchants recovered over $1 million in damages against the boycott organizers. Applying the principles of *Scales* (p. 671, *supra*), **Justice Stevens** concluded on behalf of a unanimous Court that liability cannot be imposed simply because an individual belonged to a group that also contained some violent members; instead, "it is necessary to establish that the group itself possessed unlawful goals and that the individual held a specific intent to further those illegal aims." The opinion closed with some general observations about "guilt by association": "In litigation of this kind the stakes are high. Concerted action is a powerful weapon. History teaches that special dangers are associated with conspiratorial activity. And yet one of the foundations of our society is the right of individuals to combine with other persons in pursuit of a common goal by lawful means. * * *

"The taint of violence colored the conduct of some of the petitioners. They, of course, may be held liable for the consequences of their violent deeds. The burden of demonstrating that it colored the entire collective effort, however, is not satisfied by evidence that violence occurred or even that violence contributed to the success of the boycott. A massive and prolonged effort to change the social, political, and economic structure of a local environment cannot be characterized as a violent conspiracy simply by reference to the ephemeral consequences of relatively few violent acts. * * * A court must be wary of a claim that the true color of forest is better revealed by reptiles hidden in the weeds than by the foliage of countless freestanding trees."

BOARD OF DIRECTORS OF ROTARY INTERNATIONAL v. ROTARY CLUB OF DUARTE
481 U.S. 537, 107 S.Ct. 1940, 95 L.Ed.2d 474 (1987)

JUSTICE POWELL delivered the opinion of the Court.

[The international Rotary organization revoked the charter of a local rotary club because it had admitted women. The local club and two of its women members filed suit in state court challenging the action as a violation of California's Unruh Civil Rights Act (so called by reference to the name of its legislative sponsor).]

In *Roberts v. United States Jaycees*, 468 U.S. 609 (1984), we upheld against First Amendment challenge a Minnesota statute that required the Jaycees to admit women as full voting members. *Roberts* provides the framework for analyzing appellants' constitutional claims. As we observed in *Roberts*, our cases have afforded constitutional protection to freedom of association in two distinct senses. First, the Court has held that the Constitution protects against unjustified government interference with an individual's choice to enter into and maintain certain intimate or private relationships. Second, the Court has upheld the freedom of individuals to associate for the purpose of engaging in protected speech or religious activities. In many cases, government interference with one form of protected association will also burden the other form of association. In *Roberts* we determined the nature and degree of constitutional protection by considering separately the effect of the challenged state action on individuals' freedom of private association and their freedom of expressive association. We follow the same course in this case.

The Court has recognized that the freedom to enter into and carry on certain intimate or private relationships is a fundamental element of liberty protected by the Bill of Rights. Such relationships may take various forms, including the most intimate. We have not attempted to mark the precise boundaries of this type of constitutional protection. The intimate relationships to which we have accorded constitutional protection include marriage; the begetting and bearing of children; child rearing and education; and cohabitation with relatives. Of course, we have not held that constitutional protection is restricted to relationships among family members. We have emphasized that the First Amendment protects those relationships, including family relationships, that presuppose "deep attachments and commitments to the necessarily few other individuals with whom one shares not only a special community of thoughts, experiences, and beliefs but also distinctively personal aspects of one's life." *Roberts*. But in *Roberts* we observed that "[d]etermining the limits of state authority over an individual's freedom to enter into a particular association . . . unavoidably entails a careful assessment of where that relationship's objective characteristics locate it on a spectrum from the most intimate to the most attenuated of personal attachments." In determining whether a particular association is sufficiently personal or private to warrant constitutional protection, we consider factors such as size, purpose, selectivity, and whether others are excluded from critical aspects of the relationship.

The evidence in this case indicates that the relationship among Rotary Club members is not the kind of intimate or private relation that warrants constitutional protection. The size of local Rotary Clubs ranges from fewer than 20 to more than 900. There is no upper limit on the membership of any local Rotary Club. About ten percent of the membership of a typical club moves away or drops out during a typical year. The clubs therefore are instructed to "keep a flow of prospects coming" to make up for the attrition and gradually to enlarge the membership. The purpose of Rotary "is to produce an inclusive, not exclusive, membership, making possible the recognition of all useful local occupations, and enabling the club to be a true cross section of the business and professional life of the community." The membership undertakes a variety of service projects designed to aid the community, to raise the standards of the members' businesses and professions, and to improve international relations. Such an inclusive "fellowship for service based on diversity of interest," however beneficial to the members and to those they serve, does not suggest the kind of private or personal relationship to which we have accorded protection under the First Amendment. To be sure, membership in Rotary Clubs is not open to the general public. But each club is instructed to include in its membership "all fully qualified prospective members located within its territory," to avoid "arbitrary limits on the number of members in the club," and to "establish and maintain a membership growth pattern."

Many of the Rotary Clubs' central activities are carried on in the presence of strangers. Rotary Clubs are required to admit any member of any other Rotary Club to their meetings. Members are encouraged to invite business associates and competitors to meetings. At some Rotary Clubs, the visitors number "in the tens and twenties each week." Joint meetings with the members of other organizations, and other joint activities, are permitted. The clubs are encouraged to seek coverage of their meetings and activities in local newspapers. In sum, Rotary Clubs, rather than carrying on their activities in an atmosphere of privacy, seek to keep their "windows and doors open to the whole world." We therefore conclude that application of the Unruh Act to local Rotary Clubs does not interfere unduly with the members' freedom of private association.

The Court also has recognized that the right to engage in activities protected by the First Amendment implies "a corresponding right to associate with others in pursuit of a wide variety of political, social, economic, educational, religious, and cultural ends." *Roberts*. For this reason, "[i]mpediments to the exercise of one's right to choose one's associates can violate the right of association protected by the First Amendment . . . ." In this case, however, the evidence fails to demonstrate that admitting women to Rotary Clubs will affect in any significant way the existing members' ability to carry out their various purposes.

As a matter of policy, Rotary Clubs do not take positions on "public questions," including political or international issues. To be sure, Rotary Clubs engage in a variety of commendable service activities that are protected by the First Amendment. But the Unruh Act does not require the clubs to abandon or alter any of these activities. It does not require them to abandon their basic goals of humanitarian service, high ethical standards in all vocations, goodwill, and peace. Nor does it require them to abandon their classification system or admit members who do not reflect a cross-section of the community. Indeed, by opening membership to leading business and professional women in the community, Rotary Clubs are likely to obtain a more representative cross-section of community leaders with a broadened capacity for service.

Even if the Unruh Act does work some slight infringement on Rotary members' right of expressive association, that infringement is justified because it serves the State's compelling interest in eliminating discrimination against women. On its face the Unruh Act, like the Minnesota public accommodations law we considered in *Roberts*, makes no distinctions on the basis of the organization's viewpoint. Moreover, public accommodations laws "plainly serv[e] compelling state interests of the highest order." In *Roberts* we recognized that the State's compelling interest in assuring equal access to women extends to the acquisition of leadership skills and business contacts as well as tangible goods and services. The Unruh Act plainly serves this interest. We therefore hold that application of the Unruh Act to California Rotary Clubs does not violate the right of expressive association afforded by the First Amendment.

Boy Scouts of America v. Dale, 530 U.S. 640 (2000). The Boy Scouts of America (BSA) is a private, not-for-profit organization engaged in instilling its system of values in boys. James Dale, a former Eagle Scout, was an Assistant Scoutmaster as an adult until the BSA expelled him on the ground that he was an "avowed homosexual and gay rights activist." Dale sued BSA for violating a New Jersey statute that prohibits discrimination by public accommodations on the basis of sexual orientation. The New Jersey state appellate courts ruled that BSA was a public accommodation covered by the law and that application of the statute did not unconstitutionally infringe BSA's First Amendment rights of free speech and expressive association. In a majority opinion by **Chief Justice Rehnquist**, the U.S. Supreme Court reversed, holding that the state violated BSA's right of expressive association. "In *Roberts v. United States Jaycees*, we observed that 'implicit in the right to engage in activities protected by the First Amendment' is 'a corresponding right to associate with others in pursuit of a wide variety of political, social, economic, educational, religious, and cultural ends.' This right is crucial in preventing the majority from imposing its views on groups that would rather express other, perhaps unpopular, ideas. Government actions that may unconstitutionally burden this freedom may take many forms, one of which is 'intrusion into the internal structure or affairs of an association' like a 'regulation that forces the group to accept members it does not desire.' Forcing a group to accept certain members may impair the ability of the group to express those views, and only those views, that it intends to express. Thus, '[f]reedom of association . . . plainly presupposes a freedom not to associate.' "

The Chief Justice found that the BSA was an intensely expressive association, seeking to inculcate Scout values in boys, and that exclusion of gay people from BSA leadership positions was consistent with their expressive purpose. "The Scout Oath and Law includes a vow '[t]o keep myself physically strong, mentally awake, and morally straight.' Although this oath does not explicitly speak to issues of sexuality, '[t]he Boy Scouts asserts that it "teach[es] that homosexual conduct is not morally straight," ' Brief for Petitioners 39, and that it does 'not want to promote homosexual conduct as a legitimate form of behavior,' Reply Brief for Petitioners 5. We accept the Boy Scouts' assertion. We need not inquire further to determine the nature of the Boy Scouts' expression with respect to homosexuality. But because the record before us contains written evidence of the Boy Scouts' viewpoint, we look to it as instructive, if only on the question of the sincerity of the professed beliefs." The Chief Justice pointed to an internal 1978 position statement, written by the BSA president to the BSA executive committee; a public 1991 position statement issued in connection with litigation under California's antidiscrimination law; and a 1993 public position statement — all affirming that BSA 'has always reflected the expectations that Scouting families have had for the organization. We do not believe that homosexuals provide a role model consistent with these expectations. Accordingly, we do not allow for the registration of avowed homosexuals as members or as leaders of the BSA.' [1993 statement.] * * *

"We must * * * determine whether Dale's presence as an assistant scoutmaster would significantly burden the Boy Scouts' desire to not 'promote homosexual conduct as a legitimate form of behavior.' Reply Brief for Petitioners 5. As we give deference to an association's assertions regarding the nature of its expression, we must also give deference to an association's view of what would impair its expression. That is not to say that an expressive association can erect a shield against antidiscrimination laws simply by asserting that mere acceptance of a member from a particular group would impair its message. But here Dale, by his own admission, is one of a group of gay Scouts who have 'become leaders in their community and are open and honest about their sexual orientation.' Dale was the copresident of a gay and lesbian organization at college and remains a gay rights activist. Dale's presence in the Boy Scouts would, at the very least, force the organization to send a message, both to the youth members and the world, that the Boy Scouts accepts homosexual conduct as a legitimate form of behavior."

The Court relied on *Hurley v. Irish-American Gay, Lesbian and Bisexual Group of Boston*, 515 U.S. 557 (1995), as support for its holding: "There we considered whether the application of Massachusetts' public accommodations law to require the organizers of a private St. Patrick's Day parade to include among the marchers an Irish-American gay, lesbian, and bisexual group, GLIB, violated the parade organizers' First Amendment rights. We noted that the parade organizers did not wish to exclude the GLIB members because of their sexual orientations, but because they wanted to march behind a GLIB banner. . . . Here, we have found that the Boy Scouts believes that homosexual conduct is inconsistent with the values it seeks to instill in its youth members; it will not 'promote homosexual conduct as a legitimate form of behavior.' Reply Brief for Petitioners 5. As the presence of GLIB in Boston's St. Patrick's Day parade would have interfered with the parade organizers' choice not to propound a particular point of view, the presence of Dale as an assistant scoutmaster would just as surely interfere with the Boy Scout's choice not to propound a point of view contrary to its beliefs. * * *

"Dale makes much of the claim that the Boy Scouts does not revoke the membership of heterosexual Scout leaders that openly disagree with the Boy Scouts' policy on sexual orientation. But if this is true, it is irrelevant. The presence of an avowed homosexual and gay rights activist in an assistant scoutmaster's uniform sends a distinctly different message from the presence of a heterosexual assistant scoutmaster who is on record as disagreeing with Boy Scouts policy. The Boy Scouts has a First Amendment right to choose to send one message but not the other. The fact that the organization does not trumpet its views from the housetops, or that it tolerates dissent within its ranks, does not mean that its views receive no First Amendment protection."

The Chief Justice distinguished cases such as *Rotary Club*, where the Court allowed states to apply their public accommodations laws to commercial organizations for the compelling interest of eliminating discrimination against women. "But in each of these cases we went on to conclude that the enforcement of these statutes would not materially interfere with the ideas that the organization sought to express." As in *Hurley*, the state regulation directly interfered with the organization's ideas. As to the state's justification for burdening BSA's expressive rights, the Chief Justice simply said: "The state interests embodied in New Jersey's public accommodations law do not justify such a severe intrusion on the Boy Scouts' rights to freedom of expressive association. That being the case, we hold that the First Amendment prohibits the State from imposing such a requirement through the application of its public accommodations law."

Four Justices joined a dissenting opinion authored by **Justice Stevens**. Three of those Justices (all but Stevens) also joined a dissent by **Justice Souter** (who had authored the unanimous opinion for the Court in *Hurley*).

NOTE: CAN *ROTARY/ROBERTS* AND *DALE/HURLEY* BE RECONCILED?

Hurley (an expressive conduct case) and *Dale* (expressive association) seem to support the proposition that an expressive association has a First Amendment right to exclude people who would dilute or undermine its message. But the Jaycees (in *Roberts*) and Rotary Clubs made similar arguments supporting their exclusion of women, to no avail. Why the different results? Some possibilities: (1) The Court viewed the Boston Parade and the Boy Scouts as truly "expressive" associations, and the Jaycees and Rotary as social clubs. As Justice

Stevens's dissent argued, however, the Boy Scouts were "expressive" only in the same apple-pie sense that the Jaycees and Rotary Clubs were. And in one sense, the latter were more expressive, for their exclusionary policies were articulated in their foundational documents, while the Boy Scouts' exclusion of gay people was ad hoc and its justifications substantially coined by their Supreme Court counsel. (2) The Court viewed the state interest in combatting sex discrimination as compelling in *Roberts* and *Rotary*, in contrast to the state interest in opposing discrimination against gay people in *Hurley* and *Dale*. Recall that the Court views sex-based classifications as quasi-suspect; while the Court has not formally ruled on the level of scrutiny for sexual orientation classifications, it has regularly upheld every antigay discrimination that has ever come before it, until *Romer v. Evans* (Chapter 4, § 3D). (3) As a political matter, the Court's baseline in *Roberts* and *Rotary* is that sex is a benign trait as regards public policy; women should be included in any and all institutions of public life. In *Hurley* and *Dale*, the baseline for most of the Justices is that sexual orientation is a trait that is relevant to many "reasonable" people, perhaps in part because of its links with conduct which many Americans find unmentionable or disgusting. (This theory explains why the Massachusetts and New Jersey Supreme Courts would have come out the other way: in those urbanized states, sexual orientation is more generally considered a benign trait, irrelevant to public policy.) Is any of these a persuasive justification for deciding *Roberts/Rotary* differently from *Hurley/Dale*? Can you think of other justifications?[d]

RUMSFELD v. FORUM FOR ACADEMIC AND INSTITUTIONAL RIGHTS (FAIR)
547 U.S. 47, 126 S.Ct. 1297, 164 L.Ed.2d 156 (2006)

[FAIR was an association of law schools and law faculties. Its members opposed discrimination based on sexual orientation. The law schools had rules that prohibited use of their recruiting facilities by employers who engaged in such discrimination. Under these rules, the military's anti-gay policies would disqualify it from recruiting on campus. A federal statute, the Solomon Amendment, cuts off federal funding to universities that deny military recruiters access equal to that provided other recruiters. The court of appeals had declared the Solomon Amendment unconstitutional.]

CHIEF JUSTICE ROBERTS delivered the opinion of the Court [joined by all members of the Court, except for Justice Alito, who did not participate].

The Solomon Amendment neither limits what law schools may say nor requires them to say anything. Law schools remain free under the statute to

---

d. *Dale* has already given rise to considerable controversy. For discussion of the decision and its implications for freedom of association, see Evelyn Broady, *Entrance, Voice, and Exit: The Constitutional Bounds of the Right of Association*, 35 U.C. Davis L. Rev. 821 (2002); Dale Carpenter, *Expressive Association and Anti-Discrimination Law After* Dale: *A Tripartite Approach*, 85 Minn. L. Rev. 1515 (2001); Daniel Farber, *Speaking in the First Person Plural: Expressive Associations and the First Amendment*, 85 Minn. L. Rev. 1483 (2001); David McGowan, *Making Sense of* Dale, 18 Const. Comm. 121 (2001).

express whatever views they may have on the military's congressionally mandated employment policy, all the while retaining eligibility for federal funds. See Tr. of Oral Arg. 25 (Solicitor General acknowledging that law schools "could put signs on the bulletin board next to the door, they could engage in speech, they could help organize student protests"). As a general matter, the Solomon Amendment regulates conduct, not speech. It affects what law schools must *do* — afford equal access to military recruiters — not what they may or may not *say*.

Nevertheless, the Third Circuit concluded that the Solomon Amendment violates law schools' freedom of speech in a number of ways. First, in assisting military recruiters, law schools provide some services, such as sending e-mails and distributing flyers, that clearly involve speech. The Court of Appeals held that in supplying these services law schools are unconstitutionally compelled to speak the Government's message. Second, military recruiters are, to some extent, speaking while they are on campus. The Court of Appeals held that, by forcing law schools to permit the military on campus to express its message, the Solomon Amendment unconstitutionally requires law schools to host or accommodate the military's speech. Third, although the Court of Appeals thought that the Solomon Amendment regulated speech, it held in the alternative that, if the statute regulates conduct, this conduct is expressive and regulating it unconstitutionally infringes law schools' right to engage in expressive conduct. We consider each issue in turn.

* * *

The compelled speech to which the law schools point is plainly incidental to the Solomon Amendment's regulation of conduct, and "it has never been deemed an abridgment of freedom of speech or press to make a course of conduct illegal merely because the conduct was in part initiated, evidenced, or carried out by means of language, either spoken, written, or printed." Congress, for example, can prohibit employers from discriminating in hiring on the basis of race. The fact that this will require an employer to take down a sign reading "White Applicants Only" hardly means that the law should be analyzed as one regulating the employer's speech rather than conduct. See *R.A.V. v. St. Paul* [casebook, pp. 619-23] ("[W]ords can in some circumstances violate laws directed not against speech but against conduct"). Compelling a law school that sends scheduling e-mails for other recruiters to send one for a military recruiter is simply not the same as forcing a student to pledge allegiance, or forcing a Jehovah's Witness to display the motto "Live Free or Die" * * *.

Our compelled-speech cases are not limited to the situation in which an individual must personally speak the government's message. We have also in a number of instances limited the government's ability to force one speaker to host or accommodate another speaker's message. Relying on these precedents, the Third Circuit concluded that the Solomon Amendment unconstitutionally compels law schools to accommodate the military's message "[b]y requiring schools to include military recruiters in the interviews and recruiting receptions the schools arrange."

The compelled-speech violation in each of our prior cases, however, resulted from the fact that the complaining speaker's own message was affected by the speech it was forced to accommodate. * * *

In this case, accommodating the military's message does not affect the law schools' speech, because the schools are not speaking when they host interviews and recruiting receptions. Unlike a parade organizer's choice of parade contingents, a law school's decision to allow recruiters on campus is not inherently expressive. Law schools facilitate recruiting to assist their students in obtaining jobs. A law school's recruiting services lack the expressive quality of a parade, a newsletter, or the editorial page of a newspaper; its accommodation of a military recruiter's message is not compelled speech because the accommodation does not sufficiently interfere with any message of the school. * * *

Having rejected the view that the Solomon Amendment impermissibly regulates *speech,* we must still consider whether the expressive nature of the *conduct* regulated by the statute brings that conduct within the First Amendment's protection. In *O'Brien* [casebook, pp. 628-29], we recognized that some forms of " 'symbolic speech' " were deserving of First Amendment protection. But we rejected the view that "conduct can be labeled 'speech' whenever the person engaging in the conduct intends thereby to express an idea." Instead, we have extended First Amendment protection only to conduct that is inherently expressive. In *Texas v. Johnson* [casebook, pp. 617-19], for example, we applied *O'Brien* and held that burning the American flag was sufficiently expressive to warrant First Amendment protection.

Unlike flag burning, the conduct regulated by the Solomon Amendment is not inherently expressive. Prior to the adoption of the Solomon Amendment's equal-access requirement, law schools "expressed" their disagreement with the military by treating military recruiters differently from other recruiters. But these actions were expressive only because the law schools accompanied their conduct with speech explaining it. For example, the point of requiring military interviews to be conducted on the undergraduate campus is not "overwhelmingly apparent." An observer who sees military recruiters interviewing away from the law school has no way of knowing whether the law school is expressing its disapproval of the military, all the law school's interview rooms are full, or the military recruiters decided for reasons of their own that they would rather interview someplace else.

The expressive component of a law school's actions is not created by the conduct itself but by the speech that accompanies it. The fact that such explanatory speech is necessary is strong evidence that the conduct at issue here is not so inherently expressive that it warrants protection under *O'Brien.* If combining speech and conduct were enough to create expressive conduct, a regulated party could always transform conduct into "speech" simply by talking about it. For instance, if an individual announces that he intends to express his disapproval of the Internal Revenue Service by refusing to pay his income taxes, we would have to apply *O'Brien* to determine whether the Tax Code violates the First Amendment. Neither *O'Brien* nor its progeny supports such a result.

* * *

The Solomon Amendment does not violate law schools' freedom of speech, but the First Amendment's protection extends beyond the right to speak. We have recognized a First Amendment right to associate for the purpose of speaking, which we have termed a "right of expressive association." [citing *Dale*.] The reason we have extended First Amendment protection in this way is clear: The right to speak is often exercised most effectively by combining one's voice with the voices of others. If the government were free to restrict individuals' ability to join together and speak, it could essentially silence views that the First Amendment is intended to protect.

FAIR argues that the Solomon Amendment violates law schools' freedom of expressive association. According to FAIR, law schools' ability to express their message that discrimination on the basis of sexual orientation is wrong is significantly affected by the presence of military recruiters on campus and the schools' obligation to assist them. Relying heavily on our decision in *Dale,* the Court of Appeals agreed.

In *Dale,* we held that the Boy Scouts' freedom of expressive association was violated by New Jersey's public accommodations law, which required the organization to accept a homosexual as a scoutmaster. After determining that the Boy Scouts was an expressive association, that "the forced inclusion of Dale would significantly affect its expression," and that the State's interests did not justify this intrusion, we concluded that the Boy Scout's First Amendment rights were violated.

The Solomon Amendment, however, does not similarly affect a law school's associational rights. To comply with the statute, law schools must allow military recruiters on campus and assist them in whatever way the school chooses to assist other employers. Law schools therefore "associate" with military recruiters in the sense that they interact with them. But recruiters are not part of the law school. Recruiters are, by definition, outsiders who come onto campus for the limited purpose of trying to hire students — not to become members of the school's expressive association. This distinction is critical. Unlike the public accommodations law in *Dale,* the Solomon Amendment does not force a law school " 'to accept members it does not desire.' " The law schools *say* that allowing military recruiters equal access impairs their own expression by requiring them to associate with the recruiters, but just as saying conduct is undertaken for expressive purposes cannot make it symbolic speech, so too a speaker cannot "erect a shield" against laws requiring access "simply by asserting" that mere association "would impair its message."

FAIR correctly notes that the freedom of expressive association protects more than just a group's membership decisions. For example, we have held laws unconstitutional that require disclosure of membership lists for groups seeking anonymity, or impose penalties or withhold benefits based on membership in a disfavored group. Although these laws did not directly interfere with an organization's composition, they made group membership less attractive, raising the same First Amendment concerns about affecting the group's ability to express its message.

The Solomon Amendment has no similar effect on a law school's associational rights. Students and faculty are free to associate to voice their disapproval of the military's message; nothing about the statute affects the composition of the group by making group membership less desirable. The Solomon Amendment therefore does not violate a law school's First Amendment rights. A military recruiter's mere presence on campus does not violate a law school's right to associate, regardless of how repugnant the law school considers the recruiter's message.

NOTE ON *FAIR*

To what extent does *FAIR* limit the implications of *Dale*? Suppose Congress banned discrimination against members of the military in law school admissions or against the hiring of reservists as faculty members. Are students or faculty "members" as in *Dale* or are they more like the recruiters in *FAIR*? Would your answer be the same if Congress banned discrimination against gays in hiring or admissions?

The Court says that an organization cannot satisfy *Dale* by simply saying that association would impair its message. What made the Boy Scouts' claim that Dale's presence as a Scoutmaster would impair its message more credible than the law schools' claim in *FAIR*?

SECTION 7. THE RELIGION CLAUSES

Religion is an important component of civil society. In this section, we will consider the government's relationship with religious groups. Although the trend in recent years has been to loosen the restrictions, significant constitutional restrictions still apply to laws that hinder religious practices, provide financial assistance to the activities of religious groups, or endorse religious symbols.

The Framers of the Bill of Rights held a variety of views about the relation of religion and the state, according to Arlin Adams & Charles Emmerich, *A Nation Dedicated to Religious Liberty: The Constitutional Heritage of the Religion Clauses* (1990).[a] Pietistic separatists (e.g., John Witherspoon) followed the traditions of the Pennsylvania Quakers and Rhode Island's Roger Williams, who believed in the "wall of separation between the garden of the Church and the wilderness of the world," *id.* at 6 (quoting Williams), and in a confessional pluralism that left every person free to pursue his or her own faith. Enlightenment separatists (e.g., Tom Paine, Thomas Jefferson) were not especially religious and saw religious liberty as an individual right; in the Lockean tradition, they taught liberty of conscience and plurality of religions.

---

a. Helpfully reviewed by John Witte, Jr., *The Integration of Religious Liberty*, 90 Mich. L. Rev. 1363 (1992). See also William Miller, *The First Liberty: Religion and the American Republic* (1986); Laurence Tribe, *American Constitutional Law* 1158-60 (2d ed. 1988); Michael McConnell, *The Origins and Historical Understanding of the Free Exercise of Religion*, 103 Harv. L. Rev. 1410 (1990). See generally *Church and State in America: A Bibliographical Guide* (John Wilson ed. 1986).

Political centrists (e.g., George Washington, John Adams) favored state nonintrusion, mainly because they "believed that religion was an essential cornerstone for morality, civic virtue and democratic government." *Id.* at 26. Hence, this group favored government fostering of a religious attitude (e.g., Thanksgiving Day prayers), but not state intrusion.

Adams and Emmerich do not believe that any one of these schools dominated in the framing of the Religion Clauses of the First Amendment but instead believe the clauses a result of a dialogue among all three views. All the views believed strongly in religious liberty but sought to protect that liberty in different ways — precluding the establishment of a state church (as in England), refraining from regulations that unnecessarily burden people's exercise of their faiths, requiring state neutrality, and avoiding favoritism for or discrimination against different religions. At least some of the Framers believed that these protections not only assured people their freedom of faith, but also served as a more general protection of liberty for all, because flourishing churches and religious groups could serve as buffers between the individual and the state and contributors to the marketplace of ideas.

The lesson Adams and Emmerich draw from history is that the different goals of the Religion Clauses must be integrated with one another and not viewed in isolation. For example, they argue that Justices who emphasize religious liberty as a "wall of separation" (see Part B) marginalize the Free Exercise Clause, while those who emphasize religious liberty as state accommodation to religious practices (see Part A) marginalize the Establishment Clause. This is easier said than done. Read the following materials and see if you can do the job better than the Court has done. Then consider the material at the end of this section, which presents a modern theory of religious pluralism and its implications for liberty/equality clashes, such as those raised in *Rotary* and *Hurley, supra*.

A. FREE EXERCISE

STANSBURY v. MARKS
2 Dall. 213 (Pa. 1793)

In this case (which was tried on Saturday, the 5th of April), the defendant offered Jonas Phillips, a Jew, as a witness; but he refused to be sworn, because it was his Sabbath. The court, therefore, fined him 10£; but the defendant, afterwards, waived the benefit of his testimony, and he was discharged from the fine.

NOTES ON *STANSBURY*

1. *State Constitutional Rights.* The foregoing is the complete report of the case — probably the shortest opinion you will ever read. In evaluating the opinion, consider the language of the Pennsylvania Constitution of 1790, Art. IX, § 3, which was in effect at the time of the decision:

That all men have a natural and indefeasible right to worship Almighty God according to the dictates of their own consciences; that no man can of right be compelled to attend, erect, or support any place of worship, or maintain any ministry, against his consent; that no human authority can, in any case whatever, control or interfere with their rights of conscience; and that no preference shall ever be given, by law, to any religious establishment or modes of worship.

Compare this provision with the language of the First Amendment. Which is more protective of religious freedom?

2. *Values in the Free Exercise of Religion.* In light of this introductory history and modern constitutional theory, what values does the Free Exercise Clause protect? There are a number of possibilities:[b] (a) *Autonomy.* An important element of our personal autonomy is our faith (or lack thereof), and the state shouldn't be able to coerce (or penalize?) us for our faith. (b) *Pluralism and Representation-Reinforcement.* Communities of faith contribute to the pluralist richness of the United States, but there may also be a tendency of the majority to "pick on" minority faiths (this has been the experience of Jews, Mormons, Amish, and Jehovah's Witnesses at various points in our history). The Free Exercise Clause provides a bulwark for such "discrete and insular" minority communities against majoritarian oppression. (c) *Tolerant Society.* The Free Exercise Clause enforces norms of tolerance in a diverse society, which can carry over into other areas of society as well. *Query*: In light of these values, how much does or should a (state or federal constitutional) Free Exercise Clause add to a Speech Clause, which provides an independent (but perhaps not very strong) justification for not requiring Jonas Phillips to testify?

3. *Protecting Free Exercise Values: Neutrality versus Accommodation.* Assuming that the Free Exercise Clause embodies important constitutional values, how strongly should they be enforced? Consider some analogies. Paralleling the Court's interpretation of the Equal Protection Clause to prohibit only intentional state discrimination (and not state action having discriminatory effects), see *Washington v. Davis* (Chapter 3, § 1B), the Free Exercise Clause might be applied only against state policies intentionally harming one group's free exercise of religion, but not against state laws whose infringement on religion is only incidental and unintended. (Recall the language of the clause: "Congress shall make no law . . . *prohibiting* the free exercise" of religion.)

Under this view, the requirement in *Stansbury* might seem permissible, so long as the Saturday trial day was not intended to harass Jonas Phillips. But the representation-reinforcement rationale for the Free Exercise Clause suggests that the majority's insensitivity to the genuine needs of religious minorities may result in major deprivations that would be imperfectly policed by an intent approach. The better analogy might be to the Speech Clause of the First Amendment. (But note the different text: "Congress shall make no law . . . *abridging* the freedom of speech . . . .") A rule such as the mandatory equipment-and-technician rule in *Rock Against Racism* (§ 4A of this chapter) might not be intended to chill speech, but the speaker can still challenge it if it

---

b. See Lee Bollinger, *The Tolerant Society* (1986); Frederick Gedicks & Roger Hendrix, *Democracy, Autonomy, and Values: Some Thoughts on Religion and Law in Modern America,* 60 S. Cal. L. Rev. 1579 (1987); Robert Rodes, *Sub Deo et Lege: A Study of Free Exercise,* 4 Relig. & Pub. Order 3 (1968); Michael Sandel, *Religious Liberty — Freedom of Conscience or Freedom of Choice?,* 1989 Utah L. Rev. 597 (1989).

has the effect of burdening speech and is not supported by a legitimate state interest that is also "neutral" toward religion.

Was the law requiring the attendance of witnesses "neutral" in its effect on religion? True, the law does not distinguish on its face between religious beliefs, but of course trials were never held on Sunday, so that compulsory attendance would never burden those whose Sabbath was on Sunday. Then perhaps Jonas Phillips could not constitutionally be required to testify on his Sabbath. But consider *McGowan v. Maryland*, 366 U.S. 420 (1961), in which the Court rejected attacks on Sunday closing laws. Chief Justice Warren's opinion for the Court held that the laws originally had a religious purpose, but now have the secular purpose of providing a "uniform day of rest for all citizens." In *Braunfeld v. Brown*, 366 U.S. 599 (1961), the Court rejected a challenge to a Sunday closing law by Orthodox Jews, who argued that the law placed them at a competitive disadvantage because their religion required them to close on Saturday as well. The Court concluded that there was no less burdensome alternative, since allowing exemptions for Saturday Sabbatarians would cause enforcement problems and undermine the purpose of providing a noncommercial day of rest for the population. Doesn't this statute favor one religion over another? See also *Goldman v. Weinberger*, 475 U.S. 503 (1986) (divided Court permitted Air Force to prohibit the wearing of a Jewish yarmulke by military officer who was an orthodox Jew and ordained rabbi). Can these cases be distinguished from *Stansbury*?

————

Wisconsin v. Yoder, 406 U.S. 205 (1972). Defendants, who were members of the Old Order Amish religion, were convicted for refusing to send their children to school after eighth grade, violating the state-law requirement that children attend school until age 16. The evidence showed that Amish children received vocational training at home and that the defendants believed that attending high school would destroy the Amish way of life. The defendants offered expert testimony in support of their view that a high school education was unnecessary for their agrarian way of life and that the public schools transmitted values such as competitiveness and independence that were inconsistent with their culture. In an opinion by **Chief Justice Burger**, the Court upheld their free exercise claim. He found that conclusion "inescapable that secondary schooling, by exposing Amish children to worldly influences in terms of attitudes, goals, and values contrary to beliefs, and by substantially interfering with the way of life of the Amish faith community at the crucial adolescent stage of development, contravenes the basic religious tenets and practice of the Amish faith, both as to the parent and the child." Under the circumstances of the case, he did not find any compelling interest in requiring continued school attendance, finding that an eighth-grade education was ample to prepare Amish children for life in their community, and that the history of the Amish showed the viability of their way of life. He also rejected the state's asserted interest in protecting the interests of Amish children who might ultimately decide to leave the community: "when the interests of parenthood are combined with a free exercise claim of the nature revealed by this record," a particularly strong showing on the part of the state was required.

NOTES ON *YODER* AND RELIGIOUS EXEMPTIONS

1. *A Special Rule for the Amish?* Consider how the holding of *Yoder* would apply in the following two situations:

(a) A commune pursuing an agrarian way of life like that of the Amish, but based on the reading of secular writers.

(b) A small religious community established in 1985 by a group professing allegiance to a belief in a new sect, Baptist Buddhism, embracing a way of life similar to that of the Amish but without the history of Amish culture.

Would *Yoder* protect either of these groups? If not, has the Court violated the Establishment Clause by giving the Amish special status?

2. *Unemployment Compensation. Yoder* has its strongest doctrinal support in *Sherbert v. Verner*, 374 U.S. 398 (1963), the first case in which the Supreme Court held that the Free Exercise Clause was a limitation on state regulation independent of the other provisions of the First Amendment. *Sherbert* involved the denial of unemployment benefits to a Sabbatarian who refused to work on Saturdays. The Court held that the denial of benefits "force[d] her to choose between following the precepts of her religion and forfeiting benefits, on the one hand, and abandoning of the precepts of her religion in order to accept work, on the other hand. Governmental imposition of such a choice puts the same kind of burden upon the free exercise of religion as would a fine." Hence, the *Sherbert* Court applied a compelling interest test. Is *Sherbert* consistent with *Rust v. Sullivan* in its treatment of funding denials? See Richard Epstein, *The Supreme Court, 1987 Term — Foreword: Unconstitutional Conditions, State Power, and the Limits of Consent*, 102 Harv. L. Rev. 4, 83-85 (1988) (defending *Sherbert*). If the state gives unemployment compensation to a woman who refuses to take a job for religious reasons, but denies compensation to one who refuses a job for equally firm secular reasons, isn't the state subsidizing religion?

3. *Applications of* Yoder *and* Sherbert. Consider the following possible applications of the Court's precedents:

(a) The local high school teaches biology from a purely Darwinian (evolutionist) perspective. Baptist parents are opposed to exposing their children to what they consider an atheistic approach inconsistent with the teachings of their Church and their own religious belief in creationism. These parents petition the school to excuse their children from the mandatory biology requirement. Does the school have to accommodate their request? See Wendell Bird, *Freedom of Religion and Science Instruction in Public Schools*, 87 Yale L.J. 515 (1978) (student note).

(b) Lee is an Old Order Amish self-employed farmer who employed other Amish on his farm. He did not pay social security taxes for his employees, because Amish faith considers the social security system unnecessary for their people, who take seriously their moral responsibility to care for the elderly. Assume that this factual claim is true. Can the government nevertheless require Lee to pay the taxes? See *United States v. Lee*, 455 U.S. 252 (1982).

(c) The Forest Service proposed to permit timber harvesting and road building in a portion of the National Forest System that is considered sacred by Native American tribes, and where they have held religious rituals. Can the tribes prevent this intrusion? See *Lyng v. Northwest Indian Cemetery Protective Association*, 485 U.S. 439 (1988).

Assume that the Court denies relief in all three of these cases. What is left of *Sherbert* and *Yoder* in that event? Consider the next case.

EMPLOYMENT DIVISION, DEPARTMENT OF HUMAN RESOURCES v. SMITH
494 U.S. 872, 110 S.Ct. 1595, 108 L.Ed.2d 876 (1990)

JUSTICE SCALIA delivered the opinion of the Court.

[Smith and Black were fired by a private drug rehabilitation organization because they used peyote, a hallucinogen, at a ceremony of the Native American Church. Their applications for unemployment compensation were denied under a state law disqualifying employees discharged for work-related "misconduct." When the case was first brought before the Supreme Court, the Court remanded for a determination of whether sacramental peyote use violates Oregon's criminal law. On remand, the Oregon court held that the criminal statute did apply to their conduct.]

* * * It is no more necessary to regard the collection of a general tax, for example, as "prohibiting the free exercise [of religion]" by those citizens who believe support of organized government to be sinful, than it is to regard the same tax as "abridging the freedom . . . of the press" of those publishing companies that must pay the tax as a condition of staying in business. It is a permissible reading of the text, in the one case as in the other, to say that if prohibiting the exercise of religion (or burdening the activity of printing) is not the object of the tax but merely the incidental effect of a generally applicable and otherwise valid provision, the First Amendment has not been offended.

Our decisions reveal that the latter reading is the correct one. We have never held that an individual's religious beliefs excuse him from compliance with an otherwise valid law prohibiting conduct that the State is free to regulate. On the contrary, the record of more than a century of our free exercise jurisprudence contradicts that proposition. * * *

The only decisions in which we have held that the First Amendment bars application of a neutral, generally applicable law to religiously motivated action have involved not the Free Exercise Clause alone, but the Free Exercise Clause in conjunction with other constitutional protections, such as freedom of speech and of the press, see *Cantwell v. Connecticut*, 310 U.S. 296 (1940) (invalidating a licensing system for religious and charitable solicitations under which the administrator had discretion to deny a license to any cause he deemed nonreligious); *Murdock v. Pennsylvania*, 319 U.S. 105 (1943) (invalidating a flat tax on solicitation as applied to the dissemination of religious ideas); *Follett v. McCormick*, 321 U.S. 573 (1944) (same), or the right of parents, acknowledged in *Pierce v. Society of Sisters*, 268 U.S. 510 (1925), to direct the education of their children, see *Wisconsin v. Yoder* (invalidating compulsory school-attendance laws as applied to Amish parents who refused on religious grounds to send their children to school).   Some of our cases prohibiting compelled expression, decided exclusively upon free speech grounds, have also involved freedom of religion.   And it is easy to envision a case in which a challenge on freedom of association grounds would likewise be reinforced by Free Exercise Clause concerns. * * *

The present case does not present such a hybrid situation, but a free exercise claim unconnected with any communicative activity or parental right. Respondents urge us to hold, quite simply, that when otherwise prohibitable conduct is accompanied by religious convictions, not only the convictions but the conduct itself must be free from governmental regulation.   We have never held that, and decline to do so now. * * *

Respondents argue that even though exemption from generally applicable criminal laws need not automatically be extended to religiously motivated actors, at least the claim for a religious exemption must be evaluated under the balancing test set forth in *Sherbert v. Verner*, 374 U.S. 398 (1963).   Under the *Sherbert* test, governmental actions that substantially burden a religious practice must be justified by a compelling governmental interest.   Applying that test we have, on three occasions, invalidated state unemployment compensation rules that conditioned the availability of benefits upon an applicant's willingness to work under conditions forbidden by his religion.   We have never invalidated any governmental action on the basis of the *Sherbert* test except the denial of unemployment compensation.   Although we have sometimes purported to apply the *Sherbert* test in contexts other than that, we have always found the test satisfied.   In recent years we have abstained from applying the *Sherbert* test (outside the unemployment compensation field) at all. * * *

Even if we were inclined to breathe into *Sherbert* some life beyond the unemployment compensation field, we would not apply it to require exemptions from a generally applicable criminal law.   The *Sherbert* test, it must be recalled, was developed in a context that lent itself to individualized governmental assessment of the reasons for the relevant conduct.   [A] distinctive feature of unemployment compensation programs is that their eligibility criteria invite consideration of the particular circumstances behind an applicant's unemployment: "The statutory conditions [in *Sherbert*] provided that a person was not eligible for unemployment compensation benefits if, 'without good cause,' he had quit work or refused available work.   The 'good cause' standard created a mechanism for individualized exemptions."   [O]ur decisions in the unemployment cases stand for the proposition that where the State has in place a system of individual exemptions, it may not refuse to extend that system to cases of "religious hardship" without compelling reason.

Whether or not the decisions are that limited, they at least have nothing to do with an across-the-board criminal prohibition on a particular form of conduct.   Although, as noted earlier, we have sometimes used the *Sherbert* test to analyze free exercise challenges to such laws, we have never applied the test to invalidate one.   We conclude today that the sounder approach, and the approach in accord with the vast majority of our precedents, is to hold the test inapplicable to such challenges. * * * To make an individual's obligation to obey such a law contingent upon the law's coincidence with his religious beliefs, except where the State's interest is "compelling" — permitting him, by virtue of his beliefs, "to become a law unto himself" — contradicts both constitutional tradition and common sense.

Nor is it possible to limit the impact of respondents' proposal by requiring a "compelling state interest" only when the conduct prohibited is "central" to the individual's religion. It is no more appropriate for judges to determine the "centrality" of religious beliefs before applying a "compelling interest" test in the free exercise field, than it would be for them to determine the "importance" of ideas before applying the "compelling interest" test in the free speech field. * * *

If the "compelling interest" test is to be applied at all, then, it must be applied across the board, to all actions thought to be religiously commanded. Moreover, if "compelling interest" really means what it says (and watering it down here would subvert its rigor in the other fields where it is applied), many laws will not meet the test. Any society adopting such a system would be courting anarchy, but that danger increases in direct proportion to the society's diversity of religious beliefs, and its determination to coerce or suppress none of them. * * * The rule respondents favor would open the prospect of constitutionally required religious exemptions from civic obligations of almost every conceivable kind — ranging from compulsory military service, to the payment of taxes, to health and safety regulation such as manslaughter and child neglect laws, compulsory vaccination laws, drug laws, and traffic laws * * *. The First Amendment's protection of religious liberty does not require this.

Values that are protected against government interference through enshrine-ment in the Bill of Rights are not thereby banished from the political process. Just as a society that believes in the negative protection accorded to the press by the First Amendment is likely to enact laws that affirmatively foster the dissemination of the printed word, so also a society that believes in the negative protection accorded to religious belief can be expected to be solicitous of that value in its legislation as well. It is therefore not surprising that a number of States have made an exception to their drug laws for sacramental peyote use. But to say that a nondiscriminatory religious-practice exemption is permitted, or even that it is desirable, is not to say that it is constitutionally required, and that the appropriate occasions for its creation can be discerned by the courts. It may fairly be said that leaving accommodation to the political process will place at a relative disadvantage those religious practices that are not widely engaged in; but that unavoidable consequence of democratic government must be preferred to a system in which each conscience is a law unto itself or in which judges weight the social importance of all laws against the centrality of all religious beliefs.

JUSTICE O'CONNOR, concurring in the judgment. [Although JUSTICE BRENNAN, JUSTICE MARSHALL, and JUSTICE BLACKMUN joined parts of this opinion, they did not concur in the judgment.]

The Court today gives no convincing reason to depart from settled First Amendment jurisprudence. There is nothing talismanic about neutral laws of general applicability or general criminal prohibitions, for laws neutral toward religion can coerce a person to violate his religious conscience or intrude upon his religious duties just as effectively as laws aimed at religion. Although the Court suggests that the compelling interest test, as applied to generally applicable laws, would result in a "constitutional anomaly," the First Amendment unequivocally makes freedom of religion, like freedom from race discrimination and freedom of speech, a "constitutional nor[m]," not an "anomaly." Nor would application of our established free exercise doctrine to this case necessarily be incompatible with our equal protection cases. We have in any event recognized that the Free Exercise Clause protects values distinct from those protected by the Equal Protection Clause. As the language of the Clause itself makes clear, an individual's free exercise of religion is a preferred constitutional activity. A law that makes criminal such an activity therefore triggers constitutional concern — and heightened judicial scrutiny — even if it does not target the particular religious conduct at issue. Our free speech cases similarly recognize that neutral regulations that affect free speech values are subject to a balancing, rather than categorical, approach. *See, e.g., United States v. O'Brien; City of Renton v. Playtime Theatres, Inc.* The Court's parade of horribles not only fails as a reason for discarding the compelling interest test, it instead demonstrates just the opposite: that courts have been quite capable of applying our free exercise jurisprudence to strike sensible balances between religious liberty and competing state interests.

Finally, the Court today suggests that the disfavoring of minority religions is an "unavoidable consequence" under our system of government and that accommodation of such religions must be left to the political process. In my view, however, the First Amendment was enacted precisely to protect the rights of those whose religious practices are not shared by the majority and may be viewed with hostility. The history of our free exercise doctrine amply demonstrates the harsh impact majoritarian rule has had on unpopular or emerging religious groups such as the Jehovah's Witnesses and the Amish. Indeed, the words of Justice Jackson in *West Virginia Board of Education v. Barnette* are apt:

> The very purpose of a Bill of Rights was to withdraw certain subjects from the vicissitudes of political controversy, to place them beyond the reach of majorities and officials and to establish them as legal principles to be applied by the courts. One's right to life, liberty, and property, to free speech, a free press, freedom of worship and assembly, and other fundamental rights may not be submitted to vote; they depend on the outcome of no elections.

[Justice O'Connor argued, however, that the government had a compelling health interest in forbidding peyote use. **JUSTICE BLACKMUN**, joined by **JUSTICES BRENNAN** and **MARSHALL**, dissented; in their view, the fact that almost half the states exempted ceremonial use of peyote established that there was no compelling interest.]

Michael McConnell
Free Exercise Revisionism and the Smith *Decision*
57 U. Chi. L. Rev. 1109, 1133-35, 1148 (1990)[c]

Throughout the *Smith* opinion, generally applicable laws are treated as presumptively neutral, with religious accommodations a form of special preference, akin to affirmative action. The opinion describes religious accommodations as laws that "affirmatively foster" the "value" of "religious belief." In *Sherbert v. Verner*, by contrast, Justice Brennan's majority opinion characterized a religious exemption as "reflect[ing] nothing more than the governmental obligation of neutrality in the face of religious differences." In a sense, then, both *Smith* and *Sherbert* are about neutrality toward religion. But which has the correct understanding of neutrality?

To examine this question I will use the facts of *Stansbury v. Marks* [*supra*], the first recorded case raising free exercise issues after adoption of the First Amendment. * * * We can assume that, in those days of the six-day work week, the courts of Pennsylvania were routinely open for business on Saturday. The decision to operate on Saturday, we may assume, was not aimed at members of the Jewish faith, but was simply a matter of convenience. Nor was the law allowing parties to civil suits to compel witnesses to attend court proceedings, on pain of paying a fine, instituted for the purpose of restricting religious exercise. This is an example of a generally applicable, otherwise valid, law. Is it neutral toward religion?

No, it is not. The courts were closed on Sundays, the day on which the Christian majority of Pennsylvania observed the sabbath. The effect of the six-day calendar was to impose a burden on Saturday sabbath observers (mostly Jews) that is not imposed on others (mostly Christians). It is anything *but* neutral — not because the burden happened to fall disproportionately on Jews, but because the burden was attached to a practice that, among others, defines what it means to be a faithful Jew.

What would neutrality require? Surely it is not necessary to conduct court business on Sunday. Since the vast majority of Pennsylvanians were Christians and observed Sunday as the day of sabbath, that would create conflict and administrative costs. * * * The best, least costly, and most neutral solution is to exempt Saturday sabbath observers from the obligation of testifying on Saturday. Thus, an exemption is not "affirmative fostering" of religion; it is more like *Sherbert*'s neutrality in the face of differences.

It may be objected that this example is loaded because the selection of days of rest is fraught with religious significance. The selection of Sunday as the day on which the courts would not operate was itself a religious choice, almost an establishment of religion. It might be said that an exemption is required in that case only to equalize a situation in which Christians had already been granted a benefit on account of religious practice.

---

c. Reprinted with permission.

But this objection presupposes that there are decisions that are *not* fraught with religious significance. And perhaps there are — but those decisions will not give rise to free exercise claims. All free exercise claims involve government decisions that are fraught with religious significance, at least from the point of view of the religious minority. In this respect, *Stansbury v. Marks* cannot be distinguished from *Smith*. In *Smith*, the generally applicable law was the prohibition on the use of hallucinogenic drugs. The Native American Church uses peyote as its sacrament. Application of the anti-drug laws to the sacramental use of peyote effectively destroys the practice of the Native American Church. Is this neutral?

No, it is not. Christians and Jews use wine as part of their sacrament, and wine is not illegal. Even when wine was illegal during Prohibition, Congress exempted the sacramental use of wine from the proscription. The effect of laws prohibiting hallucinogenic drugs but not alcohol, or of allowing exemptions from one law but not the other, is to impose a burden on the practice of the Native American Church that is not imposed on Christians or Jews. It is no more neutral than operating courts on Saturday and not on Sunday.

* * * Evidence in the *Smith* case showed that ingestion of peyote by members of the Native American Church is *not* dangerous and does not lead to drug problems or substance abuse. Indeed, it is statistically and culturally associated with resistance to substance abuse. The federal government and twenty-three of the states have approved the use of peyote in Native American church ceremonies for this reason, and the federal government even licenses a facility for the production of peyote.

If this evidence is valid, then the decision to ban the sacramental use of peyote but not the sacramental use of wine is not based on any objective differences between the effects of the two substances. Rather, it is based on the fact that most ordinary Americans are familiar with the use of wine and consider Christian and Jewish sacramental use harmless and perhaps even a good thing; but the same ordinary Americans consider peyote a bizarre and threatening substance and have no respect or solicitude for the Native American Church. In short, the difference is attributable to prejudice. * * *

[A] court faced with a free exercise claim is not required to determine, in the abstract, how important a governmental purpose is or how central a religious practice is. The court instead must engage in the hypothetical exercise of comparing burdens. The degree of protection for religious minorities should be no less than that which our society would provide for the majority. This should be enough to decide many cases quite easily. Who can doubt that unobtrusive exceptions to military uniform regulations would be made if Christians, like Orthodox Jews, had to wear yarmulkes at all times? Who can doubt that there would be exceptions to social security (or, more likely, no social security at all) if mainstream Christians were forbidden by their religion to participate? Who can doubt that the United States Forest Service would find a way to avoid despoiling Christian worship sites when building logging roads?

Other cases would come out the other way. A country could probably not survive if it allowed selective conscientious objection to war. Nor would it allow trespass or interference with the private rights of others. A government interest is sufficient if it is so important that it is not conceivable that the government would waive it even if the religious needs of the majority so required.

NOTES ON *SMITH* AND FREE EXERCISE

1. *Is Religious Freedom Disfavored?* Does *Smith* give religious practices the same degree of protection given free speech? (Note that in *Barnes*, the nude dancing case in § 3A, *supra*, Justice Scalia was alone in his view that *Smith* should extend to free speech claims.) How does the protection given religious minorities under the First Amendment compare with that given racial minorities under the Equal Protection Clause? If some relatively minor legal prohibition makes the practice of a religion into a crime, without serving any important government purpose, why shouldn't the courts require an exemption? How much bite is left in the Free Exercise Clause after *Smith*? See Douglas Laycock, *The Remnants of Free Exercise*, 1990 Sup. Ct. Rev. 1.

2. *Where's the Baseline?* As McConnell argues, distinguishing penalties from affirmative accommodations requires defining a baseline. His baseline for neutrality is the (sometimes hypothetical) accommodation that would be made to a majority religion. The government would nearly always accommodate a majority of its citizens, at least if a practice was mandatory under the majority religion. Even the exceptions that McConnell gives seem dubious; for example, he suggests that the government would not allow trespass by members of the majority religion, but of course, the laws of property would probably not define actions required by the majority religion as trespasses. At the very least, under McConnell's baseline, the baseline will almost always be set from the perspective of the religious minority seeking the exemption.

In McConnell's analysis of *Stansbury*, note how he builds his way toward a religious exemption. He argues that a Sunday closing is warranted in order to avoid "needless conflict and administrative costs." Then he argues that in the interests of neutrality, an exemption from court attendance should be extended to other Sabbatarians. Note, however, that the justification for the Saturday exemption (neutrality) has now shifted away from the justification for the Sunday closing (conflict and administrative costs). Consider the following government response: "We don't care about anyone's religion, one way or another, but if enough people have a problem with court attendance on a given day, whether for religious reasons or some other reason, we have to make accommodations. On the other hand, we just can't accommodate every small group that comes along, whether religious or not." Given the practicalities of governance, why isn't sheer size a neutral basis for distinguishing among groups? (Recall that in *McGowan v. Maryland*, *supra*, the Supreme Court upheld Sunday closing laws on a somewhat similar theory.)

Consider how McConnell's test would apply to *Yoder*. If the majority religion favored pastoral life by uneducated farmers, presumably a democratic government would find compulsory education laws unmanageable. On the other hand, in the long run, this situation seems about as compatible with national security as selective conscientious objection laws, which McConnell finds unjustifiable. For a critique of McConnell's approach to the religion clauses, see Kathleen Sullivan, *Religion and Liberal Democracy*, 59 U. Chi. L. Rev. 195 (1992). See also William Marshall, *In Defense of* Smith *and Free Exercise Revisionism*, 58 U. Chi. L. Rev. 308 (1990).

3. *Airport Terminals Revisited.* Krishna Consciousness is a religion, and adherents are required to solicit funds for it publicly. If such persons seek to solicit funds at public airports, would McConnell require that this be allowed? (If Krishna Consciousness were the majority religion, wouldn't airports have been designed with plenty of room for this practice? Note that the airport does have a chapel for those with more conventional religions.) What is the result under *Smith*? Could this be considered a "hybrid" claim based on both free exercise and free speech rights?

4. Smith *v.* Sherbert. The majority in *Smith* distinguishes unemployment compensation (in *Sherbert*) as a unique setting, but don't forget that *Smith* itself involves unemployment compensation. What difference does it make that Oregon also has a criminal penalty for religious use of peyote? Why couldn't another state say that it won't ban religious use but that it won't encourage such use by giving users state benefits when they lose their jobs? This isn't a rhetorical question: we're puzzled about it ourselves. Should *Sherbert* be overruled? Consider the next note.

5. *An Economic Theory for* Smith. Granting a free exercise claim entails two different costs for state policy — the cost of exempting sincere religious observants from the policy *and* the costs of policing the exemption to ensure that it goes only to the sincere (to avoid the costs of insincere "strategic" observants taking advantage of the exemption). *Yoder* and *Goldman* (the yarmulke case) involve only the first cost, because there were few incentives for non-Amish to take their children out of public schools or for non-Jews to wear yarmulkes. See Mayer Freed & Daniel Polsby, *Race, Religion, and Public Policy*, 1983 Sup. Ct. Rev. 1. Because nonobservants might want to use peyote, *Smith* presents both types of costs. But we think the second type of costs would be small in that case. They were much greater in *Sherbert*. Shouldn't the Court overrule it?

6. *Voluntary Exemptions.* The *Smith* majority says that the states are free to provide religious exemptions. But if such special exemptions for religion aren't required for the free exercise of religion, why isn't this preferred treatment a violation of the Establishment Clause? For example, suppose that a state college allows Sabbatarians to reschedule Saturday exams, but not individuals with pressing personal commitments (e.g., a doctor's appointment for a sick child). Does this violate the Establishment Clause? Consider this issue again when you read § 6B of this chapter.

———

Church of the Lukumi Babalu Aye, Inc. v. Hialeah, 508 U.S. 520 (1993). Hialeah, Florida, passed a series of ordinances that, though facially neutral, were targeted against the church's use of animal sacrifice, a religious ritual central to the church's religious practice. All nine Justices concluded that the ordinances were unconstitutional. The majority opinion of **Justice Kennedy** applied the *Smith* standard, found that the ordinances were not "neutral and of general applicability" but rather were enacted with the intention and had the effect of suppressing a religion, and accordingly applied strict scrutiny. The ordinances flunked rigid review because they were underinclusive with respect to the two interests advanced in support of them — protecting public health and preventing cruelty to animals. Few killings of animals were regulated at all unless the death was through religious ritual. **Justice Scalia**, joined by **Chief Justice Rehnquist**, filed a separate statement agreeing with much of the majority opinion, but objecting to the inquiry concerning the subjective motivations of the city council.

Justice Blackmun, joined by **Justice O'Connor**, concurred in the judgment, writing separately to continue to express his disagreement with the *Smith* test. **Justice Souter** also wrote separately and voiced his disapproval of *Smith* (which was decided before he came to the Court). Perhaps because of his strong endorsement of *stare decisis* in the *Casey* abortion decision (Chapter 5, § 4B), Justice Souter wrote at length concerning why he believed *Smith* could be reconsidered.

––––––––

In response to *Smith*, Congress adopted the Religious Freedom Restoration Act of 1993 (RFRA), 42 U.S.C. §§ 2000bb-2000bb-4, which sought to "restore" federal law to the strict-scrutiny approach found in pre-*Smith* precedents to judge the legality of incidental burdens on religious freedom.

City of Boerne v. Flores (Chapter 7, § 3C). In *Boerne*, the Supreme Court in 1997 invalidated those portions of RFRA applying to state and local governments, concluding that Congress lacked the authority to adopt these provisions under § 5 of the Fourteenth Amendment. *Boerne* also provided the occasion for an important debate over the original understanding of the Free Exercise Clause. In her dissent in *Boerne*, **Justice O'Connor** mustered much of the historical evidence against *Smith*, drawing on the work of legal scholars.[d] For instance, several state constitutions protected religious exercise except when it harmed specific state interests. In New York, the exception was for "acts of licentiousness" and "practices inconsistent with the peace or safety of this State." In Maryland, it was any disturbance of "the good order, peace or safety of the State," infringement of "the laws of morality," or injury to "others, in their natural, civil, or religious rights." The Northwest Ordinance provided that no person "demeaning himself in a peaceable and orderly manner" shall be "molested on account of his mode of worship or religious sentiments."

Justice O'Connor devoted particular attention to James Madison's views, appropriately enough given his central role in the adoption of the First Amendment. In the debates over the Virginia Declaration of Rights, Madison's proposed language would have safeguarded the "full and free exercise" of

––

d. See Adams & Emmerich, *A Nation Dedicated to Religious Liberty*, *supra*; Leonard Levy, *Judgments: Essays on American Constitutional History* (1972); McConnell, *The Origins and Original Understanding of the Free Exercise of Religion*, *supra*.

religion, "unless under color of religion the preservation of equal liberty, and the existence of the State be manifestly endangered." Later, in supporting a Bill for Establishing Religious Freedom drafted by Jefferson, Madison drafted his famous "Memorial and Remonstrance Against Religious Assessments." In the "Memorial and Remonstrance," Madison argued that free exercise entails a "duty toward the Creator":

> This duty is precedent both in order of time and degree of obligation to the claims of Civil Society . . .[E]very man who becomes a member of any Civil Society, [must] do it with a saving of his allegiance to the Universal Sovereign. We maintain therefore that in matters of Religion, no man's right is abridged by the institution of Civil Society, and that Religion is wholly exempt from its cognizance.

Similarly, Jefferson held that the federal government was constitutionally forbidden "from intermeddling with religious institutions, their doctrines, discipline, or exercises."

Justice O'Connor also observed that the "practice of the colonies and early States bears out the conclusion that, at the time the Bill of Rights was ratified, it was accepted that government should, when possible, accommodate religious practice." For examples, Quakers were often exempted from the duty to swear an oath of allegiance, and most legislators exempted conscientious objectors from conscription. In addition, she noted, "North Carolina and Maryland excused Quakers from the requirement of removing their hats in courts; Rhode Island exempted Jews from the requirements of the state marriage laws; and Georgia allowed groups of European immigrants to organize whole towns according to their own faith."

Justice Scalia responded to Justice O'Connor in his *Boerne* concurrence, making the following points:[e] The early state constitutions typically applied only to state actions taken "for," "in respect of," or "on account of" religion, a description that Scalia said did not apply to neutral laws of general application. Moreover, the provisos about "good order" and so forth could be read broadly, since "peace" and "order" were often taken to encompass the obligations to obey general laws in eighteenth century usage. Nor are the religious exemptions granted by legislatures decisive, since they do not show that the legislators felt constitutionally obligated to provide the exemptions. Thus, the debate on the original understanding continues.

B. THE ESTABLISHMENT CLAUSE

1. *Basic Premises*

EVERSON v. BOARD OF EDUCATION
330 U.S. 1, 67 S.Ct. 504, 91 L.Ed. 711 (1947)

JUSTICE BLACK delivered the opinion of the Court.

[A New Jersey statute authorized local school districts to pay for transportation of children to and from school (both public and private). The issue in the

---

e. Accord, Philip Hamburger, *A Constitutional Right of Religious Exemption: An Historical Perspective*, 60 Geo. Wash. L. Rev. 915 (1992).

case was whether a local school district violated the Establishment Clause by reimbursing parents for transportation of their children to Catholic parochial schools.]

Whether this New Jersey law is one respecting the "establishment of religion" requires an understanding of the meaning of that language, particularly with respect to the imposition of taxes. Once again, therefore, it is not inappropriate briefly to review the background and environment of the period in which that constitutional language was fashioned and adopted.

A large proportion of the early settlers of this country came here from Europe to escape the bondage of laws which compelled them to support and attend government favored churches. The centuries immediately before and contemporaneous with the colonization of America had been filled with turmoil, civil strife, and persecutions, generated in large part by established sects determined to maintain their absolute political and religious supremacy. With the power of government supporting them, at various times and places, Catholics had persecuted Protestants, Protestants had persecuted Catholics, Protestant sects had persecuted other Protestant sects, Catholics of one shade of belief had persecuted Catholics of another shade of belief, and all of these had from time to time persecuted Jews. In efforts to force loyalty to whatever religious group happened to be on top and in league with the government of a particular time and place, men and women had been fined, cast in jail, cruelly tortured, and killed. Among the offenses for which these punishments had been inflicted were such things as speaking disrespectfully of the views of ministers of government-established churches, non-attendance at those churches, expressions of non-belief in their doctrines, and failure to pay taxes and tithes to support them.

These practices of the old world were transplanted to and began to thrive in the soil of the new America. The very charters granted by the English Crown to the individuals and companies designated to make the laws which would control the destinies of the colonials authorized these individuals and companies to erect religious establishments which all, whether believers or non-believers, would be required to support and attend. An exercise of this authority was accompanied by a repetition of many of the old-world practices and persecutions. Catholics found themselves hounded and proscribed because of their faith; Quakers who followed their conscience went to jail; Baptists were peculiarly obnoxious to certain dominant Protestant sects; men and women of varied faiths who happened to be in a minority in a particular locality were persecuted because they steadfastly persisted in worshipping God only as their own consciences dictated. And all of these dissenters were compelled to pay tithes and taxes to support government-sponsored churches whose ministers preached inflammatory sermons designed to strengthen and consolidate the established faith by generating a burning hatred against dissenters.

These practices became so commonplace as to shock the freedom-loving colonials into a feeling of abhorrence. The imposition of taxes to pay ministers' salaries and to build and maintain churches and church property aroused their indignation. It was these feelings which found expression in the First Amendment. No one locality and no one group throughout the Colonies can rightly be given entire credit for having aroused the sentiment that culminated in adoption of the Bill of Rights' provisions embracing religious liberty. But Virginia, where the established church had achieved a dominant influence in political affairs and where many excesses attracted wide public attention, provided a great stimulus and able leadership for the movement. The people there, as elsewhere, reached the conviction that individual religious liberty could be achieved best under a government which was stripped of all power to tax, to support, or otherwise to assist any or all religions, or to interfere with the beliefs of any religious individual or group.

The movement toward this end reached its dramatic climax in Virginia in 1785-86 when the Virginia legislative body was about to renew Virginia's tax levy for the support of the established church. Thomas Jefferson and James Madison led the fight against this tax. Madison wrote his great Memorial and Remonstrance against the law. In it, he eloquently argued that a true religion did not need the support of law; that no person, either believer or non-believer, should be taxed to support a religious institution of any kind; that the best interest of a society required that the minds of men always be wholly free; and that cruel persecutions were the inevitable result of government-established religions. Madison's Remonstrance received strong support throughout Virginia, and the Assembly postponed consideration of the proposed tax measure until its next session. When the proposal came up for consideration at that session, it not only died in committee, but the Assembly enacted the famous "Virginia Bill for Religious Liberty" originally written by Thomas Jefferson. The preamble to that Bill stated among other things that

> Almighty God hath created the mind free; that all attempts to influence it by temporal punishments, or burdens, or by civil incapacitations, tend only to beget habits of hypocrisy and meanness, and are a departure from the plan of the Holy author of our religion, who being Lord both of body and mind, yet chose not to propagate it by coercions on either . . .; that to compel a man to furnish contributions of money for the propagation of opinions which he disbelieves, is sinful and tyrannical; that even the forcing him to support this or that teacher of his own religious persuasion, is depriving him of the comfortable liberty of giving his contributions to the particular pastor, whose morals he would make his pattern. * * *

And the statute itself enacted

> That no man shall be compelled to frequent or support any religious worship, place, or ministry whatsoever, nor shall be enforced, restrained, molested, or burthened in his body or goods, nor shall otherwise suffer on account of his religious opinions or belief. . . .

This Court has previously recognized that the provisions of the First Amendment, in the drafting and adoption of which Madison and Jefferson played such leading roles, had the same objective and were intended to provide the same protection against governmental intrusion on religious liberty as the Virginia statute. Prior to the adoption of the Fourteenth Amendment, the First Amendment did not apply as a restraint against the states. Most of them did soon provide similar constitutional protections for religious liberty. But some states persisted for about half a century in imposing restraints upon the free exercise of religion and in discriminating against particular religious groups. In recent years, so far as the provision against the establishment of a religion is concerned, the question has most frequently arisen in connection with proposed state aid to church schools and efforts to carry on religious teachings in the public schools in accordance with the tenets of a particular sect. Some churches have either sought or accepted state financial support for their schools. Here again the efforts to obtain state aid or acceptance of it have not been limited to any one particular faith. The state courts, in the main, have remained faithful to the language of their own constitutional provisions designed to protect religious freedom and to separate religions and governments. Their decisions, however, show the difficulty in drawing the line between tax legislation which provides funds for the welfare of the general public and that which is designed to support institutions which teach religion. * * *

The "establishment of religion" clause of the First Amendment means at least this: Neither a state nor the Federal Government can set up a church. Neither can pass laws which aid one religion, aid all religions, or prefer one religion over another. Neither can force nor influence a person to go to or to remain away from church against his will or force him to profess a belief or disbelief in any religion. No person can be punished for entertaining or professing religious beliefs or disbeliefs, for church attendance or non-attendance. No tax in any amount, large or small, can be levied to support any religious activities or institutions, whatever they may be called, or whatever form they may adopt to teach or practice religion. Neither a state nor the Federal Government can, openly or secretly, participate in the affairs of any religious organizations or groups and *vice versa*. In the words of Jefferson, the clause against establishment of religion by law was intended to erect "a wall of separation between Church and State." * * *

Measured by these standards, we cannot say that the First Amendment prohibits New Jersey from spending tax-raised funds to pay the bus fares of parochial school pupils as a part of a general program under which it pays the fares of pupils attending public and other schools. It is undoubtedly true that children are helped to get to church schools. There is even a possibility that some of the children might not be sent to the church schools if the parents were compelled to pay their children's bus fares out of their own pockets when transportation to a public school would have been paid for by the State. The same possibility exists where the state requires a local transit company to provide reduced fares to school children including those attending parochial schools, or where a municipally owned transportation system undertakes to carry all school children free of charge. Moreover, state-paid policemen, detailed to protect children going to and from church schools from the very real hazards of traffic, would serve much the same purpose and accomplish much the same result as state provisions intended to guarantee free transportation of a kind which the state deems to be best for the school children's welfare. And parents might refuse to risk their children to the serious danger of traffic accidents going to and from parochial schools, the approaches to which were not protected by policemen. Similarly, parents might be reluctant to permit their children to attend schools which the state had cut off from such general government services as ordinary police and fire protection, connections for sewage disposal, public highways and sidewalks. Of course, cutting off church schools from these services, so separate and so indisputably marked off from the religious function, would make it far more difficult for the schools to operate. But such is obviously not the purpose of the First Amendment. That Amendment requires the state to be a neutral in its relations with groups of religious believers and non-believers; it does not require the state to be their adversary.

State power is no more to be used so as to handicap religions, than it is to favor them. * * *

The First Amendment has erected a wall between church and state. That wall must be kept high and impregnable. We could not approve the slightest breach. New Jersey has not breached it here.

[The dissenting opinion of **JUSTICE JACKSON**, joined by **JUSTICE FRANKFURTER**, and the dissenting opinion of **JUSTICE RUTLEDGE**, joined by **JUSTICES FRANKFURTER**, **JACKSON**, and **BURTON** are omitted.]

Wallace v. Jaffree, 472 U.S. 38 (1985). This case involved a state law mandating a moment of silence "for meditation or voluntary prayer" in public classrooms. In an opinion by **Justice Stevens**, the Court held the statute unconstitutional because its purpose was to foster school prayer, rejecting the argument that the Establishment Clause prohibits only government discrimination between various sects: "Just as the right to speak and the right to refrain from speaking are complementary components of a broader concept of individual freedom of mind, so also the individual's freedom to choose his own creed is the counterpart of his right to refrain from accepting the creed established by the majority. At one time it was thought that this right merely proscribed the preference of one Christian sect over another, but would not require equal respect for the conscience of the infidel, the atheist, or the adherent of a non-Christian faith such as Islam or Judaism. But when the underlying principle has been examined in the crucible of litigation, the Court has unambiguously concluded that the individual freedom of conscience protected by the First Amendment embraces the right to select any religious faith or none at all. This conclusion derives support not only from the interest in respecting the individual's freedom of conscience, but also from the conviction that religious beliefs worthy of respect are the product of free and voluntary choice by the faithful, and from recognition of the fact that the political interest in forestalling intolerance extends beyond intolerance among Christian sects — or even intolerance among 'religions' — to encompass intolerance of the disbeliever and the uncertain."

In dissent, **Justice Rehnquist** argued that the Court's Establishment Clause jurisprudence has been warped by Jefferson's misleading "wall of separation" metaphor: "James Madison was undoubtedly the most important architect among the Members of the House of the Amendments which became the Bill of Rights, but it was James Madison speaking as an advocate of sensible legislative compromise, not as an advocate of incorporating the Virginia Statute of Religious Liberty into the United States Constitution. * * * His original language 'nor shall any national religion be established' obviously does not conform to the 'wall of separation' between church and State idea which latter-day commentators have ascribed to him. His explanation on the floor of the meaning of his language — 'that Congress should not establish a religion, and enforce the legal observation of it by law' is of the same ilk. When he replied to Huntington in the debate over the proposal which came from the Select Committee of the House, he urged that the language 'no religion shall be established by law' should be amended by inserting the word 'national' in front of the word 'religion.' "

NOTES ON *EVERSON, JAFFREE,* AND ESTABLISHMENT CLAUSE ANALYSIS

1. *The Debate Over Justice Black's History of the Religion Clauses.* Adams & Emmerich, *A Nation Dedicated to Religious Liberty, supra,* object to historical theories, like Justice Black's, that emphasize only one historical value (wall of separation) to the exclusion of others (equal treatment). Of course, the actual holding in *Everson* permitted the New Jersey bus fare program. Other historians fault Justice Black for an ahistorical reading of what early Americans meant by "wall of separation." Anticipating the views of the pietistic separatists, Roger Williams himself (who coined the phrase) believed that the wall was one-way: It prevented the state from interfering with religion but not from fostering religion generally. Jefferson and the other Enlightenment separatists wanted a wall that worked both ways — protecting church from state and state from church. See Laurence Tribe, *American Constitutional Law* 1158-60 (2d ed. 1988). But both pietistic groups and Enlightenment thinkers may have shared an avowal of the critical value of liberty of conscience and its incompatibility with religious establishment. See Noah Feldman, *The Intellectual Origins of the Establishment Clause,* 77 NYU L. Rev. 346 (2002).

Robert Cord, *Separation of Church and State* (1982), takes on some of Justice Black's specific evidence to argue that few of the Framers absolutely opposed state aid to religion, and most believed that nondiscriminatory state aid was fine. For example, he argues that Madison's Memorial and Remonstrance objected that the statute was discriminatory, by privileging one religion, Christianity, and that Madison did not object to general state fostering of religious attitudes. Additionally, the United States during Madison's and Jefferson's presidential terms (1801-17) entered into treaties agreeing to subsidize schools for Native Americans run by several different Christian groups — without recorded objection from either Jefferson or Madison, and without recorded court challenges.

2. *Applying General Lessons of History to Specific Problems.* The dissenters in *Everson* protested that upholding the school busing statute was inconsistent with Justice Black's general theory of the Establishment Clause. The Court's decisions about aid to parochial schools have continued to produce some very odd line-drawing. For example, while *Everson* allows the state to bus students to parochial schools, the state may not supply them with transportation for field trips; it can give them textbooks but cannot provide classroom maps or charts. See *Wolman v. Walter,* 433 U.S. 229 (1977). If this makes any sense to you, you're ahead of most of the scholars in the field.

Based on his *Jaffree* dissent, would Chief Justice Rehnquist allow the state to subsidize purely religious events (e.g., Sunday school classes), so long as the subsidy was open to members of all religions? (What counts as a religion, by the way — could the "United Church of Atheism" qualify?)

3. *Does History Solve Cases Like* Everson *and* Jaffree? In connection with the dispute over the original understanding of the religion clauses, consider *Marsh v. Chambers*, 463 U.S. 783 (1983), a challenge to the practice of opening state legislative sessions each day with a prayer by a state-paid chaplain. Chief Justice Burger's opinion for the Court upheld the practice based on its unique historical roots, because legislators since the time of the first Congress had followed the practice without challenge. Note, here, the dispute over the level of generality at which original intent is to be determined, which parallels that in the racial discrimination area:

Generality Level	Race Discrimination	Establishment
high	colorblindness	wall of separation
medium	ending discrimination against minorities	equality among religions
low	specific intent about school segregation	specific intent about legislative chaplains

Within an originalist approach, is there any systematic way of deciding these issues? (Note, by the way, how liberals and conservatives are both inconsistent: The conservative position is to take a highly general view of intent in race cases, but a medium or low generality view of the Establishment Clause, while with liberals the positions are reversed.)

———

Lemon v. Kurtzman, 403 U.S. 602 (1971). A Rhode Island statute provided for a salary supplement for teachers at private schools to equalize spending on secular education with that in public schools. Teachers were eligible if they taught *only* courses offered in public schools using the public schools' texts. The Court struck down the statute because it required too much government supervision of the teaching in parochial schools, thereby "entangling" religious and governmental institutions. **Chief Justice Burger** announced a three-prong test for Establishment Clause claims. To survive, a "statute must have a secular legislative purpose; second, its principal or primary effect must be one that neither advances nor inhibits religions; finally, the statute must not foster 'an excessive government entanglement with religion.' "

The *Lemon* test became controversial within the Court in the 1980s, though it remained the controlling standard for determining Establishment Clause cases. See *Lynch v. Donnelly*, 465 U.S. 668 (1984), in which Chief Justice Burger applied *Lemon* to uphold Pawtucket, Rhode Island's display of a crèche (the Nativity scene, with the baby Jesus, flanked by Mary and Joseph, and surrounded by congeries of adoring wisemen, angels, shepherds, sheep, and assorted barn animals), over doubts about the test in **Justice O'Connor's** concurring opinion and doubts about its application in **Justice Brennan's** dissent. Chief Justice Burger's opinion stressed that more secular holiday symbols were also on display. We explore this issue in the next subsection.

2. *Government Endorsement of Religion*

County of Allegheny v. American Civil Liberties Union, 492 U.S. 573 (1989). This case involved two religious displays: a crèche on the staircase of a county courthouse and a menorah outside a government building next to a Christmas tree. **Justice Blackmun** wrote the lead opinion, parts of which were joined by a majority, and other parts of which were joined by no one else. **Justices Blackmun** and **O'Connor** were the swing voters. They joined with **Justices Kennedy**, **Rehnquist**, **White**, and **Scalia** to uphold the menorah, while joining **Justices Brennan, Marshall,** and **Stevens** to reject the crèche.

Three portions of Justice Blackmun's opinion commanded a majority. In Part IIIA of the opinion, he articulated a standard for Establishment Clause cases forbidding government "endorsements" of religion. In Part IV, he concluded that the crèche did convey a message of religious endorsement in context. In *Lynch*, the Court had found no message of endorsement because the crèche had been combined with various secularized Christmas displays such as Santa Claus. But in *Allegheny*, these secularized materials were absent, and instead an angel in the crèche announced "Glory to God in the Highest!" The majority found this to be an unmistakable endorsement of religion. In Part V of Justice Blackmun's opinion, a majority again coalesced to reject the arguments made in Justice Kennedy's dissent.

Justice Kennedy (joined by Rehnquist, White, and Scalia) advocated a broader role for government promotion of religion. "Non-coercive government action within the realm of flexible accommodation or passive acknowledgment of existing symbols does not violate the Establishment Clause unless it benefits religion in a way more direct and more substantial than practices that are accepted in our national heritage." Thus, he would use a three-part test: (a) non-coerciveness, (b) accommodation or passive acknowledgment, (c) similarity to accepted historical practices. On this basis, he found both the crèche and the menorah unobjectionable. He rejected the majority's "endorsement" test because it would invalidate some long-standing government practices, such as the use of the slogan "In God we trust," which he said obviously endorsed religion. On the other hand, he said, the government may not "proselytize on behalf of a particular religion."

The majority rejected Justice Kennedy's effort to distinguish between government support for a particular religion and government endorsement of religion in general. The Court's language about the dissent was strong:

> Although Justice Kennedy repeatedly accuses the Court of harboring a "latent hostility" or "callous indifference" toward religion, nothing could be further from the truth, and the accusations could be said to be as offensive as they are abused. Justice Kennedy apparently has misperceived a respect for religious pluralism, a respect commanded by the Constitution, as hostility or indifference to religion. No misperception could be more antithetical to the values embodied in the Establishment Clause.

Because the crèche display "demonstrated the county's endorsement of Christianity," the Court said, an injunction against the display "does not represent a hostility or indifference to religion, but, instead, the respect for religious diversity that the Constitution requires."

The menorah display received different treatment. For the four Justices joining the Kennedy dissent the issue was easy: The menorah was merely a noncoercive display of a conventional religious symbol. On the other hand, Justices Brennan, Marshall, and Stevens were equally sure that the menorah display was unconstitutional, based on a "strong presumption against the display of religious symbols on public property."

For Justices Blackmun and O'Connor, who cast the decisive votes, the issue was more difficult. Justice Blackmun believed that the menorah's message is not exclusively religious because Chanukah, like Christmas, has both religious and secular dimensions. Moreover, the presence of a Christmas tree and a sign saluting religious liberty helped communicate "a secular celebration of Christmas coupled with an acknowledgment of Chanukah as a contemporaneous alternative tradition." Justice O'Connor agreed that the Christmas tree is primarily a secular symbol. The menorah, however, is "the central religious symbol and ritual object" of a religious holiday. By displaying both the menorah and the Christmas tree, in Justice O'Connor's view, the city had not secularized the menorah; the total holiday display did convey an overall message of pluralism rather than endorsement of religion.

———

Capitol Square Review and Advisory Board v. Pinette, 515 U.S. 753 (1995). Capitol Square, the Statehouse plaza in Columbus, Ohio, is defined as a public forum by state law. The Ku Klux Klan applied to place an unattended cross on the square during the 1993 Christmas season, a request that was denied on Establishment Clause grounds. The Court voted 7-2 in favor of the Klan, but was split as to the rationale. **Justice Scalia**, writing for himself, **Chief Justice Rehnquist**, and **Justices Kennedy** and **Thomas**, argued that the endorsement test does not apply at all to private religious expression in a public forum. Erroneous impressions of state sponsorship should not change the reality that the government has not endorsed the speech in any way. "Private religious speech cannot be subject to veto by those who see favoritism where there is none." **Justices O'Connor, Souter**, and **Breyer** concurred in the judgment. They believed that the endorsement test applied on these facts, but that a reasonable observer would not have believed that the government was endorsing the Klan's message, given the fact that the square is a public forum. **Justice Stevens** argued in dissent that the "very fact that a sign is installed on public property implies official recognition and reinforcement of its message." **Justice Ginsburg** also dissented, referring to the principle that the "negative bar against establishment of religion implies affirmative establishment of secular public order."

McCREARY COUNTY v. ACLU
545 U.S. 844, 125 S.Ct. 2722, 162 L.Ed.2d 729 (2005)

JUSTICE SOUTER delivered the opinion of the Court.

Executives of two counties posted a version of the Ten Commandments on the walls of their courthouses. After suits were filed charging violations of the Establishment Clause, the legislative body of each county adopted a resolution calling for a more extensive exhibit meant to show that the Commandments are

Kentucky's "precedent legal code." The result in each instance was a modified display of the Commandments surrounded by texts containing religious references as their sole common element. After changing counsel, the counties revised the exhibits again by eliminating some documents, expanding the text set out in another, and adding some new ones.

The issues are whether a determination of the counties' purpose is a sound basis for ruling on the Establishment Clause complaints, and whether evaluation of the counties' claim of secular purpose for the ultimate displays may take their evolution into account. We hold that the counties' manifest objective may be dispositive of the constitutional enquiry, and that the development of the presentation should be considered when determining its purpose. * * *

Ever since *Lemon v. Kurtzman* summarized the three familiar considerations for evaluating Establishment Clause claims, looking to whether government action has "a secular legislative purpose" has been a common, albeit seldom dispositive, element of our cases. Though we have found government action motivated by an illegitimate purpose only four times since *Lemon,* and "the secular purpose requirement alone may rarely be determinative . . . , it nevertheless serves an important function."

The touchstone for our analysis is the principle that the "First Amendment mandates governmental neutrality between religion and religion, and between religion and nonreligion." When the government acts with the ostensible and predominant purpose of advancing religion, it violates that central Establishment Clause value of official religious neutrality, there being no neutrality when the government's ostensible object is to take sides. Manifesting a purpose to favor one faith over another, or adherence to religion generally, clashes with the "understanding, reached . . . after decades of religious war, that liberty and social stability demand a religious tolerance that respects the religious views of all citizens . . . ." By showing a purpose to favor religion, the government "sends the . . . message to . . . nonadherents 'that they are outsiders, not full members of the political community, and an accompanying message to adherents that they are insiders, favored members . . . .' " * * *

Despite the intuitive importance of official purpose to the realization of Establishment Clause values, the Counties ask us to abandon *Lemon*'s purpose test, or at least to truncate any enquiry into purpose here. Their first argument is that the very consideration of purpose is deceptive: according to them, true "purpose" is unknowable, and its search merely an excuse for courts to act selectively and unpredictably in picking out evidence of subjective intent. The assertions are as seismic as they are unconvincing.

Examination of purpose is a staple of statutory interpretation that makes up the daily fare of every appellate court in the country, and governmental purpose is a key element of a good deal of constitutional doctrine, *e.g., Washington v. Davis* [Chapter 3, § 1B] (discriminatory purpose required for Equal Protection violation); *Hunt v. Washington State Apple Advertising Comm'n* [Chapter 7, § 6B] (discriminatory purpose relevant to dormant Commerce Clause claim); *Church of Lukumi Babalu Aye, Inc. v. Hialeah* [Chapter 6 § 7A] (discriminatory purpose raises level of scrutiny required by free exercise claim). With enquiries into purpose this common, if they were nothing but hunts for mares' nests deflecting attention from bare judicial will, the whole notion of purpose in law would have dropped into disrepute long ago.

But scrutinizing purpose does make practical sense, as in Establishment Clause analysis, where an understanding of official objective emerges from readily discoverable fact, without any judicial psychoanalysis of a drafter's heart of hearts. The eyes that look to purpose belong to an " 'objective observer,' " one who takes account of the traditional external signs that show up in the " 'text, legislative history, and implementation of the statute,' " or comparable official act. There is, then, nothing hinting at an unpredictable or disingenuous exercise when a court enquires into purpose after a claim is raised under the Establishment Clause. * * *

Even the Counties' own cited authority confirms that we have not made the purpose test a pushover for any secular claim. [T]he Court often does accept governmental statements of purpose, in keeping with the respect owed in the first instance to such official claims. But in those unusual cases where the claim was an apparent sham, or the secular purpose secondary, the unsurprising results have been findings of no adequate secular object, as against a predominantly religious one.

The Counties' second proffered limitation can be dispatched quickly. They argue that purpose in a case like this one should be inferred, if at all, only from the latest news about the last in a series of governmental actions, however close they may all be in time and subject. But the world is not made brand new every morning, and the Counties are simply asking us to ignore perfectly probative evidence; they want an absentminded objective observer, not one presumed to be familiar with the history of the government's actions and competent to learn what history has to show. The Counties' position just bucks common sense: reasonable observers have reasonable memories, and our precedents sensibly forbid an observer "to turn a blind eye to the context in which [the] policy arose."

This case comes to us on appeal from a preliminary injunction. We accordingly review the District Court's legal rulings *de novo,* and its ultimate conclusion for abuse of discretion.

[The Commandments] proclaim the existence of a monotheistic god (no other gods). They regulate details of religious obligation (no graven images, no sabbath breaking, no vain oath swearing). And they unmistakably rest even the universally accepted prohibitions (as against murder, theft, and the like) on the sanction of the divinity proclaimed at the beginning of the text. Displaying that text is thus different from a symbolic depiction, like tablets with 10 roman numerals, which could be seen as alluding to a general notion of law, not a sectarian conception of faith. Where the text is set out, the insistence of the religious message is hard to avoid in the absence of a context plausibly suggesting a message going beyond an excuse to promote the religious point of view. The display in *Stone* [*v. Graham,* 449 U.S. 39 (1980)] had no context that might have indicated an object beyond the religious character of the text, and the Counties' solo exhibit here did nothing more to counter the sectarian implication than the postings at issue in *Stone*. Actually, the posting by the Counties lacked even the *Stone* display's implausible disclaimer that the Commandments were set out to show their effect on the civil law. What is more, at the ceremony for posting the framed Commandments in Pulaski County, the county executive was accompanied by his pastor, who testified to the certainty of the existence of God. The reasonable observer could only think that the Counties meant to emphasize and celebrate the Commandments' religious message. * * *

Once the Counties were sued, they modified the exhibits and invited additional insight into their purpose in a display that hung for about six months. This new one was the product of forthright and nearly identical Pulaski and McCreary County resolutions listing a series of American historical documents with theistic and Christian references, which were to be posted in order to furnish a setting for displaying the Ten Commandments and any "other Kentucky and American historical documen[t]" without raising concern about "any Christian or religious references" in them. As mentioned, the resolutions expressed support for an Alabama judge who posted the Commandments in his courtroom, and cited the fact the Kentucky Legislature once adjourned a session in honor of "Jesus Christ, Prince of Ethics."

In this second display, unlike the first, the Commandments were not hung in isolation, merely leaving the Counties' purpose to emerge from the pervasively religious text of the Commandments themselves. Instead, the second version was required to include the statement of the government's purpose expressly set out in the county resolutions, and underscored it by juxtaposing the Commandments to other documents with highlighted references to God as their sole common element. The display's unstinting focus was on religious passages, showing that the Counties were posting the Commandments precisely because of their sectarian content. That demonstration of the government's objective was enhanced by serial religious references and the accompanying resolution's claim about the embodiment of ethics in Christ. Together, the display and resolution presented an indisputable, and undisputed, showing of an impermissible purpose.

Today, the Counties make no attempt to defend their undeniable objective, but instead hopefully describe version two as "dead and buried." Their refusal to defend the second display is understandable, but the reasonable observer could not forget it. * * *

After the Counties changed lawyers, they mounted a third display, without a new resolution or repeal of the old one. The result was the "Foundations of American Law and Government" exhibit, which placed the Commandments in the company of other documents the Counties thought especially significant in the historical foundation of American government. In trying to persuade the District Court to lift the preliminary injunction, the Counties cited several new purposes for the third version, including a desire "to educate the citizens of the county regarding some of the documents that played a significant role in the foundation of our system of law and government." The Counties' claims did not, however, persuade the court, intimately familiar with the details of this litigation, or the Court of Appeals, neither of which found a legitimizing secular purpose in this third version of the display. " 'When both courts [that have already passed on the case] are unable to discern an arguably valid secular purpose, this Court normally should hesitate to find one.' " The conclusions of the two courts preceding us in this case are well warranted. * * *

In holding the preliminary injunction adequately supported by evidence that the Counties' purpose had not changed at the third stage, we do not decide that the Counties' past actions forever taint any effort on their part to deal with the subject matter. We hold only that purpose needs to be taken seriously under the Establishment Clause and needs to be understood in light of context; an implausible claim that governmental purpose has changed should not carry the day in a court of law any more than in a head with common sense. It is enough to say here that district courts are fully capable of adjusting preliminary relief to take account of genuine changes in constitutionally significant conditions.

Nor do we have occasion here to hold that a sacred text can never be integrated constitutionally into a governmental display on the subject of law, or American history. We do not forget, and in this litigation have frequently been reminded, that our own courtroom frieze was deliberately designed in the exercise of governmental authority so as to include the figure of Moses holding tablets exhibiting a portion of the Hebrew text of the later, secularly phrased Commandments; in the company of 17 other lawgivers, most of them secular figures, there is no risk that Moses would strike an observer as evidence that the National Government was violating neutrality in religion.

The importance of neutrality as an interpretive guide is no less true now than it was when the Court broached the principle in *Everson* [Chapter 6, § 7B], and a word needs to be said about the different view taken in today's dissent. We all agree, of course, on the need for some interpretative help. The First Amendment contains no textual definition of "establishment," and the term is certainly not self-defining. No one contends that the prohibition of establishment stops at a designation of a national (or with Fourteenth Amendment incorporation, a state) church, but nothing in the text says just how much more it covers. There is no simple answer, for more than one reason.

The prohibition on establishment covers a variety of issues from prayer in widely varying government settings, to financial aid for religious individuals and institutions, to comment on religious questions. In these varied settings, issues of about interpreting inexact Establishment Clause language, like difficult interpretative issues generally, arise from the tension of competing values, each constitutionally respectable, but none open to realization to the logical limit.

The First Amendment has not one but two clauses tied to "religion," the second forbidding any prohibition on the "the free exercise thereof," and sometimes, the two clauses compete: spending government money on the clergy looks like establishing religion, but if the government cannot pay for military chaplains a good many soldiers and sailors would be kept from the opportunity to exercise their chosen religions. At other times, limits on governmental action that might make sense as a way to avoid establishment could arguably limit freedom of speech when the speaking is done under government auspices.

[T]radeoffs are inevitable, and an elegant interpretative rule to draw the line in all the multifarious situations is not to be had.

Given the variety of interpretative problems, the principle of neutrality has provided a good sense of direction: the government may not favor one religion over another, or religion over irreligion, religious choice being the prerogative of individuals under the Free Exercise Clause. The principle has been helpful simply because it responds to one of the major concerns that prompted adoption of the Religion Clauses. The Framers and the citizens of their time intended not only to protect the integrity of individual conscience in religious matters, but to guard against the civic divisiveness that follows when the Government weighs in on one side of religious debate; nothing does a better job of roiling society, a point that needed no explanation to the descendants of English Puritans and Cavaliers (or Massachusetts Puritans and Baptists). A sense of the past thus points to governmental neutrality as an objective of the Establishment Clause, and a sensible standard for applying it. To be sure, given its generality as a principle, an appeal to neutrality alone cannot possibly lay every issue to rest, or tell us what issues on the margins are substantial enough for constitutional significance, a point that has been clear from the Founding era to modern times. But invoking neutrality is a prudent way of keeping sight of something the Framers of the First Amendment thought important.

The dissent, however, puts forward a limitation on the application of the neutrality principle, with citations to historical evidence said to show that the Framers understood the ban on establishment of religion as sufficiently narrow to allow the government to espouse submission to the divine will. The dissent identifies God as the God of monotheism, all of whose three principal strains (Jewish, Christian, and Muslim) acknowledge the religious importance of the Ten Commandments. On the dissent's view, it apparently follows that even rigorous espousal of a common element of this common monotheism is consistent with the establishment ban.

But the dissent's argument for the original understanding is flawed from the outset by its failure to consider the full range of evidence showing what the Framers believed. * * * But the fact is that we do have more to go on, for there is also evidence supporting the proposition that the Framers intended the Establishment Clause to require governmental neutrality in matters of religion, including neutrality in statements acknowledging religion. The very language of the Establishment Clause represented a significant departure from early drafts that merely prohibited a single national religion, and the final language instead "extended [the] prohibition to state support for 'religion' in general."

The historical record, moreover, is complicated beyond the dissent's account by the writings and practices of figures no less influential than Thomas Jefferson and James Madison. Jefferson, for example, refused to issue Thanksgiving Proclamations because he believed that they violated the Constitution.

Historical evidence thus supports no solid argument for changing course (whatever force the argument might have when directed at the existing precedent), whereas public discourse at the present time certainly raises no doubt about the value of the interpretative approach invoked for 60 years now.

We are centuries away from the St. Bartholomew's Day massacre and the treatment of heretics in early Massachusetts, but the divisiveness of religion in current public life is inescapable. This is no time to deny the prudence of understanding the Establishment Clause to require the Government to stay neutral on religious belief, which is reserved for the conscience of the individual.

JUSTICE O'CONNOR, concurring.

I join in the Court's opinion. The First Amendment expresses our Nation's fundamental commitment to religious liberty by means of two provisions — one protecting the free exercise of religion, the other barring establishment of religion. They were written by the descendants of people who had come to this land precisely so that they could practice their religion freely. Together with the other First Amendment guarantees — of free speech, a free press, and the rights to assemble and petition — the Religion Clauses were designed to safeguard the freedom of conscience and belief that those immigrants had sought. They embody an idea that was once considered radical: Free people are entitled to free and diverse thoughts, which government ought neither to constrain nor to direct.

Reasonable minds can disagree about how to apply the Religion Clauses in a given case. But the goal of the Clauses is clear: to carry out the Founders' plan of preserving religious liberty to the fullest extent possible in a pluralistic society. By enforcing the Clauses, we have kept religion a matter for the individual conscience, not for the prosecutor or bureaucrat. At a time when we see around the world the violent consequences of the assumption of religious authority by government, Americans may count themselves fortunate: Our regard for constitutional boundaries has protected us from similar travails, while allowing private religious exercise to flourish. * * * Those who would renegotiate the boundaries between church and state must therefore answer a difficult question: Why would we trade a system that has served us so well for one that has served others so poorly?

Our guiding principle has been James Madison's — that "[t]he Religion . . . of every man must be left to the conviction and conscience of every man." To that end, we have held that the guarantees of religious freedom protect citizens from religious incursions by the States as well as by the Federal Government. Government may not coerce a person into worshiping against her will, nor prohibit her from worshiping according to it. It may not prefer one religion over another or promote religion over nonbelief. And government may not, by "endorsing religion or a religious practice," "mak[e] adherence to religion relevant to a person's standing in the political community."

When we enforce these restrictions, we do so for the same reason that guided the Framers — respect for religion's special role in society. Our Founders conceived of a Republic receptive to voluntary religious expression, and provided for the possibility of judicial intervention when government action threatens or impedes such expression. Voluntary religious belief and expression may be as threatened when government takes the mantle of religion upon itself as when government directly interferes with private religious practices. When the government associates one set of religious beliefs with the state and identifies nonadherents as outsiders, it encroaches upon the individual's decision about whether and how to worship. In the marketplace of ideas, the government has vast resources and special status. Government religious expression therefore risks crowding out private observance and distorting the natural interplay between competing beliefs. Allowing government to be a potential mouthpiece for competing religious ideas risks the sort of division that might easily spill over into suppression of rival beliefs. Tying secular and religious authority together poses risks to both.

Given the history of this particular display of the Ten Commandments, the Court correctly finds an Establishment Clause violation. The purpose behind the counties' display is relevant because it conveys an unmistakable message of endorsement to the reasonable observer.

It is true that many Americans find the Commandments in accord with their personal beliefs. But we do not count heads before enforcing the First Amendment. Nor can we accept the theory that Americans who do not accept the Commandments' validity are outside the First Amendment's protections. There is no list of approved and disapproved beliefs appended to the First Amendment — and the Amendment's broad terms ("free exercise," "establishment," "religion") do not admit of such a cramped reading. It is true that the Framers lived at a time when our national religious diversity was neither as robust nor as well recognized as it is now. They may not have foreseen the variety of religions for which this Nation would eventually provide a home. They surely could not have predicted new religions, some of them born in this country. But they did know that line-drawing between religions is an enterprise that, once begun, has no logical stopping point. They worried that "the same authority which can establish Christianity, in exclusion of all other Religions, may establish with the same ease any particular sect of Christians, in exclusion of all other Sects." The Religion Clauses, as a result, protect adherents of all religions, as well as those who believe in no religion at all. * * *

We owe our First Amendment to a generation with a profound commitment to religion and a profound commitment to religious liberty — visionaries who held their faith "with enough confidence to believe that what should be rendered to God does not need to be decided and collected by Caesar." * * *

JUSTICE SCALIA, with whom the **CHIEF JUSTICE** and **JUSTICE THOMAS** join, and with whom **JUSTICE KENNEDY** joins as to Parts II and III, dissenting. [Only excerpts from Part I of Justice Scalia's dissent are included here. Part II of the dissent argues that the *Lemon* test has been applied in a manipulative way, and Part III argues that the counties had not been shown to have any impermissible intent under *Lemon*.]

The same week that Congress submitted the Establishment Clause as part of the Bill of Rights for ratification by the States, it enacted legislation providing for paid chaplains in the House and Senate. The day after the First Amendment was proposed, the same Congress that had proposed it requested the President to proclaim "a day of public thanksgiving and prayer, to be observed, by acknowledging, with grateful hearts, the many and signal favours of Almighty

God."   President Washington offered the first Thanksgiving Proclamation shortly thereafter, devoting November 26, 1789 on behalf of the American people " 'to the service of that great and glorious Being who is the beneficent author of all the good that is, that was, or that will be,' " thus beginning a tradition of offering gratitude to God that continues today. The same Congress also reenacted the Northwest Territory Ordinance of 1787: "Religion, morality, and knowledge, being necessary to good government and the happiness of mankind, schools and the means of education shall forever be encouraged." And of course the First Amendment itself accords religion (and no other manner of belief) special constitutional protection.

With all of this reality (and much more) staring it in the face, how can the Court *possibly* assert that " 'the First Amendment mandates governmental neutrality between . . . religion and nonreligion,' " and that "[m]anifesting a purpose to favor . . . adherence to religion generally" is unconstitutional? Who says so? Surely not the words of the Constitution. Surely not the history and traditions that reflect our society's constant understanding of those words. Surely not even the current sense of our society, recently reflected in an Act of Congress adopted *unanimously* by the Senate and with only 5 nays in the House of Representatives, criticizing a Court of Appeals opinion that had held "under God" in the Pledge of Allegiance unconstitutional. Nothing stands behind the Court's assertion that governmental affirmation of the society's belief in God is unconstitutional except the Court's own say-so, citing as support only the unsubstantiated say-so of earlier Courts going back no farther than the mid-20th century. And it is, moreover, a thoroughly discredited say-so. It is discredited, to begin with, because a majority of the Justices on the current Court (including at least one Member of today's majority) have, in separate opinions, repudiated the brain-spun "*Lemon* test" that embodies the supposed principle of neutrality between religion and irreligion. And it is discredited because the Court has not had the courage (or the foolhardiness) to apply the neutrality principle consistently. * * *

Besides appealing to the demonstrably false principle that the government cannot favor religion over irreligion, today's opinion suggests that the posting of the Ten Commandments violates the principle that the government cannot favor one religion over another. That is indeed a valid principle where public aid or assistance to religion is concerned, or where the free exercise of religion is at issue, but it necessarily applies in a more limited sense to public acknowledgment of the Creator. If religion in the public forum had to be entirely nondenominational, there could be no religion in the public forum at all. One cannot say the word "God," or "the Almighty," one cannot offer public supplication or thanksgiving, without contradicting the beliefs of some people that there are many gods, or that God or the gods pay no attention to human affairs. With respect to public acknowledgment of religious belief, it is entirely clear from our Nation's historical practices that the Establishment Clause permits this disregard of polytheists and believers in unconcerned deities, just as it permits the disregard of devout atheists. The Thanksgiving Proclamation issued by George Washington at the instance of the First Congress was scrupulously nondenominational — but it was monotheistic. * * *

Historical practices thus demonstrate that there is a distance between the acknowledgment of a single Creator and the establishment of a religion.* * * The three most popular religions in the United States, Christianity, Judaism, and Islam — which combined account for 97.7% of all believers — are monotheistic. Publicly honoring the Ten Commandments is thus indistinguishable, insofar as discriminating against other religions is concerned, from publicly honoring God. Both practices are recognized across such a broad and diverse range of the population — from Christians to Muslims — that they cannot be reasonably understood as a government endorsement of a particular religious viewpoint.[d]

NOTES ON THE TEN COMMANDMENTS CONTROVERSY

1. *Distinguishing the Indistinguishable?* On the same day as *McCreary*, the Court also decided *Van Orden v. Perry*, 545 U.S. 677 (2005), which also involved the Ten Commandments. In *Van Orden*, the Ten Commandments had been displayed on a six-foot monolith in front of the Texas State Capitol. The monument had been given to the state by a private fraternal order (thus involving no expenditure of state money.) Not surprisingly, the four dissenters in *McCreary* all voted to uphold the monument against Establishment Clause challenge. Somewhat more surprisingly, this outcome also received the support of Justice Breyer. Concurring only in the judgment, Breyer maintained that:

> The case before us is a borderline case. It concerns a large granite monument bearing the text of the Ten Commandments located on the grounds of the Texas State Capitol. On the one hand, the Commandments' text undeniably has a religious message, invoking, indeed emphasizing, the Deity. On the other hand, focusing on the text of the Commandments alone cannot conclusively resolve this case. Rather, to determine the message that the text here conveys, we must examine how the text is *used*. And that inquiry requires us to consider the context of the display.

He stressed that the group that donated the memorial did so to "highlight the Commandments' role in shaping civic morality," that it "sits in a large park containing 17 monuments and 21 historical markers, all designed to illustrate the 'ideals' of those who settled in Texas and of those who have lived there since that time," and that the monument went unchallenged for forty years. The remaining members of the *McCreary* majority dissented.

2. *The Meaning of Neutrality.* Justices Scalia and Souter seem to agree that the government must be neutral regarding theological issues, but they seem to differ about the scope of the neutrality in cases involving "endorsement" of religion. According to Souter, the government must be neutral regarding all issues related to religion, including the existence or nonexistence of God; according to Scalia, the government need only remain neutral regarding disputes among monotheists. (Of course, even Scalia's characterization would not be

---

d. This is not to say that a display of the Ten Commandments could never constitute an impermissible endorsement of a particular religious view. The Establishment Clause would prohibit, for example, governmental endorsement of a particular version of the Decalogue as authoritative. Here the display of the Ten Commandments alongside eight secular documents, and the plaque's explanation for their inclusion, make clear that they were not posted to take sides in a theological dispute.

accepted universally — some Muslims and Jews consider Christianity to be imperfectly monotheistic because of the doctrine of the trinity, a characterization most Christians would reject.) Which of these positions makes the most sense historically or analytically? As part of its endorsement of monotheism, could a state explicitly condemn Hinduism, or would that be going to far?

3. *Rewind and Erase?* Justice Thomas, concurring in the judgment in *Van Orden*, argued that the Court should abandon its precedents and "return to the original meaning" of the Establishment Clause. He argued first, that the Establishment Clause should not be applied to the states, and that in any event, the Court should return to the original meaning of the word "establishment" as involving "actual legal coercion." Would it be unobjectionable under his view for a state to pass a law endorsing a specific Christian denomination as the official religion of that state, assuming no coercion was involved? Or is that hypothetical too far-fetched to be worth considering?

NOTE ON *ALLEGHENY COUNTY* AND THE *LEMON* DEBATE

In her *Lynch* concurrence, Justice O'Connor queried whether the *Lemon* test really serves any of the values enshrined in the Establishment Clause. On the one hand, one might argue that *Lemon* is a justifiable retreat from Justice Black's strict wall-of-separation approach in *Everson*, which arguably sacrifices the pro-religion attitude of some Framers. On the other hand, one might argue that the latter goal was never agreed to by all the Framers and is increasingly out of date in our modern secular society. Cf. *United States v. Seeger*, 380 U.S. 163 (1965) (interpreting federal draft exemption for "religious" conscientious objection to include someone who was agnostic as to whether there is a "Supreme Being" but believed in "goodness and virtue" and the ethical life).

On yet a third hand (!), the *Lemon* test might be impossible to apply to tough problems, such as that in *Allegheny County*. Note how fractured the Court was. Would it have been more fractured if the menorah had been displayed inside a public building (like a school gym)? Would Justice Blackmun be satisfied that this was merely the presentation of the secular aspects of two winter holidays?

Justice Scalia delivered a blistering attack on *Lemon*'s motivation prong in *Edwards v. Aguillard*, 482 U.S. 578 (1987). That case involved an Establishment Clause challenge to Louisiana's law requiring the teaching of creationism whenever Darwinian evolutionist theory was taught (usually in high school biology classes). He argued that the examination of legislative motivations required by the *Lemon* test is an incoherent enterprise. How would Justice O'Connor or Justice Kennedy analyze such a statute?[e] How would you vote in

---

e. Compare Steven Goldberg, *The Constitutional Status of American Science*, 1979 U. Ill. L.F. 1, who believes that good science should prevail over religious zeal, with Wendell Bird, *Freedom of Religion and Science Instruction in Public Schools*, 87 Yale L.J. 515 (1978) (student note), who argues that creationism is better "science" than Darwinian evolution and must in any event be protected under the Free Exercise Clause, and Stephen Carter, *Evolutionism, Creationism, and Treating Religion as a Hobby*, 1987 Duke L.J. 977, who believes that creationism is bad science but that excluding it may threaten religious freedom.

this case? The Supreme Court struck down the statute. See also *Epperson v. Arkansas*, 393 U.S. 97 (1968).

NOTE ON THE SCHOOL PRAYER CASES

Among the Supreme Court's most controversial decisions were those relating to school prayer. In *Engel v. Vitale*, 370 U.S. 421 (1962), the Court struck down a New York law requiring students to recite a nonsectarian prayer ("Almighty God, we acknowledge our dependence upon Thee, and we beg Thy blessings upon us, our parents, our teachers and our Country.") Justice Black's opinion for the Court said that "it is no part of the business of government to compose official prayers for any group of the American people to recite as a part of a religious program carried on by government." Nor was the prayer saved because individual students were allowed to remain silent or be excused from the room. In *School District of Abington Township v. Schempp*, 374 U.S. 203 (1963), another opinion by Justice Black declared unconstitutional a Pennsylvania statute requiring every school day to begin with a recitation of the Lord's Prayer and a Bible reading. In dissent, Justice Stewart argued that the government's only duty "in connection with religious exercises in the public schools is that of refraining from so structuring the school environment as to put any kind of pressure on a child to participate in those exercises." These precedents have been among the most controversial the Court has ever handed down, and constitutional amendments regularly have been proposed to override them.

LEE v. WEISMAN
505 U.S. 577, 112 S.Ct. 2649, 120 L.Ed.2d 467 (1992)

JUSTICE KENNEDY delivered the opinion of the Court.

School principals in the public school system of the city of Providence, Rhode Island, are permitted to invite members of the clergy to offer invocation and benediction prayers as part of the formal graduation ceremonies for middle schools and for high schools. The question before us is whether including clerical members who offer prayers as part of the official school graduation ceremony is consistent with the Religion Clauses of the First Amendment, provisions the Fourteenth Amendment makes applicable with full force to the States and their school districts.

Deborah Weisman graduated from Nathan Bishop Middle School, a public school in Providence, at a formal ceremony in June 1989. She was about 14 years old. For many years it has been the policy of the Providence School Committee and the Superintendent of Schools to permit principals to invite members of the clergy to give invocations and benedictions at middle school and high school graduations. Many, but not all, of the principals elected to include prayers as part of the graduation ceremonies. Acting for himself and his daughter, Deborah's father, Daniel Weisman, objected to any prayers at Deborah's middle school graduation, but to no avail. The school principal, petitioner Robert E. Lee, invited a rabbi to deliver prayers at the graduation exercises for Deborah's class. Rabbi Leslie Gutterman, of the Temple Beth El in Providence, accepted.

It has been the custom of Providence school officials to provide invited clergy with a pamphlet entitled "Guidelines for Civic Occasions," prepared by the National Conference of Christians and Jews. The Guidelines recommend that public prayers at nonsectarian civic ceremonies be composed with "inclusiveness and sensitivity," though they acknowledge that "[p]rayer of any kind may be inappropriate on some civic occasions." The principal gave Rabbi Gutterman the pamphlet before the graduation and advised him the invocation and benediction should be nonsectarian. * * *

The principle that government may accommodate the free exercise of religion does not supersede the fundamental limitations imposed by the Establishment Clause. It is beyond dispute that, at a minimum, the Constitution guarantees that government may not coerce anyone to support or participate in religion or its exercise, or otherwise act in a way which "establishes a [state] religion or religious faith, or tends to do so." The State's involvement in the school prayers challenged today violates these central principles.

That involvement is as troubling as it is undenied. A school official, the principal, decided that an invocation and a benediction should be given; this is a choice attributable to the State, and from a constitutional perspective it is as if a state statute decreed that the prayers must occur. The principal chose the religious participant, here a rabbi, and that choice is also attributable to the State. The reason for the choice of a rabbi is not disclosed by the record, but the potential for divisiveness over the choice of a particular member of the clergy to conduct the ceremony is apparent. * * *

We are asked to recognize the existence of a practice of nonsectarian prayer, prayer within the embrace of what is known as the Judeo-Christian tradition, prayer which is more acceptable than one which, for example, makes explicit references to the God of Israel, or to Jesus Christ, or to a patron saint. There may be some support, as an empirical observation, to the statement of the Court of Appeals for the Sixth Circuit, picked up by Judge Campbell's dissent in the Court of Appeals in this case, that there has emerged in this country a civic religion, one which is tolerated when sectarian exercises are not. If common ground can be defined which permits once conflicting faiths to express the shared conviction that there is an ethic and a morality which transcend human invention, the sense of community and purpose sought by all decent societies might be advanced. But though the First Amendment does not allow the government to stifle prayers which aspire to these ends, neither does it permit the government to undertake that task for itself.

The First Amendment's Religion Clauses mean that religious beliefs and religious expression are too precious to be either proscribed or prescribed by the State. The design of the Constitution is that preservation and transmission of religious beliefs and worship is a responsibility and a choice committed to the private sphere, which itself is promised freedom to pursue that mission. It must not be forgotten then, that while concern must be given to define the protection granted to an objector or a dissenting nonbeliever, these same Clauses exist to protect religion from government interference. James Madison, the principal author of the Bill of Rights, did not rest his opposition to a religious establishment on the sole ground of its effect on the minority. A principal ground for his view was: "[E]xperience witnesseth that ecclesiastical establishments, instead of maintaining the purity and efficacy of Religion, have had a contrary operation." Memorial and Remonstrance Against Religious Assessments (1785).

These concerns have particular application in the case of school officials, whose effort to monitor prayer will be perceived by the students as inducing a participation they might otherwise reject. Though the efforts of the school officials in this case to find common ground appear to have been a good-faith attempt to recognize the common aspects of religions and not the divisive ones, our precedents do not permit school officials to assist in composing prayers as an incident to a formal exercise for their students. And these same precedents caution us to measure the idea of a civic religion against the central meaning of the Religion Clauses of the First Amendment, which is that all creeds must be tolerated and none favored. The suggestion that government may establish an official or civic religion as a means of avoiding the establishment of a religion with more specific creeds strikes us as a contradiction that cannot be accepted. * * *

As we have observed before, there are heightened concerns with protecting freedom of conscience from subtle coercive pressure in the elementary and secondary public schools. Our decisions in *Engel v. Vitale* and *Abington School District* recognize, among other things, that prayer exercises in public schools carry a particular risk of indirect coercion. The concern may not be limited to the context of schools, but it is most pronounced there. What to most believers may seem nothing more than a reasonable request that the nonbeliever respect their religious practices, in a school context may appear to the nonbeliever or dissenter to be an attempt to employ the machinery of the State to enforce a religious orthodoxy. * * *

There was a stipulation in the District Court that attendance at graduation and promotional ceremonies is voluntary. Petitioners and the United States, as amicus, made this a center point of the case, arguing that the option of not attending the graduation excuses any inducement or coercion in the ceremony itself. The argument lacks all persuasion. Law reaches past formalism. And to say a teenage student has a real choice not to attend her high school graduation is formalistic in the extreme. True, Deborah could elect not to attend commencement without renouncing her diploma; but we shall not allow the case to turn on this point. Everyone knows that in our society and in our culture high school graduation is one of life's most significant occasions. A school rule which excuses attendance is beside the point. Attendance may not be required by official decree, yet it is apparent that a student is not free to absent herself from the graduation exercise in any real sense of the term "voluntary," for absence would require forfeiture of those intangible benefits which have motivated the student through youth and all her high school years. Graduation is a time for family and those closest to the student to celebrate success and express mutual wishes of gratitude and respect, all to the end of impressing upon the young person the role that it is his or her right and duty to assume in the community and all of its diverse parts.

[The concurring opinion of JUSTICE BLACKMUN, which was joined by JUSTICES STEVENS and O'CONNOR, is omitted.]

JUSTICE SOUTER, with whom JUSTICE STEVENS and JUSTICE O'CONNOR join, concurring.

Some have challenged [current doctrine] by reading the Establishment Clause to permit "nonpreferential" state promotion of religion. The challengers argue that, as originally understood by the Framers, "[t]he Establishment Clause did not require government neutrality between religion and irreligion nor did it prohibit the Federal Government from providing nondiscriminatory aid to religion." While a case has been made for this position, it is not so convincing as to warrant reconsideration of our settled law; indeed, I find in the history of the Clause's textual development a more powerful argument supporting the Court's jurisprudence following *Everson*.

When James Madison arrived at the First Congress with a series of proposals to amend the National Constitution, one of the provisions read that "[t]he civil rights of none shall be abridged on account of religious belief or worship, nor shall any national religion be established, nor shall the full and equal rights of conscience be in any manner, or on any pretext, infringed." Madison's language did not last long. It was sent to a Select Committee of the House, which, without explanation, changed it to read that "no religion shall be established by law, nor shall the equal rights of conscience be infringed." Thence the proposal went to the Committee of the Whole, which was in turn dissatisfied with the Select Committee's language and adopted an alternative proposed by Samuel Livermore of New Hampshire: "Congress shall make no laws touching religion, or infringing the rights of conscience." Livermore's proposal would have forbidden laws having anything to do with religion and was thus not only far broader than Madison's version, but broader even than the scope of the Establishment Clause as we now understand it. The House rewrote the amendment once more before sending it to the Senate, this time adopting, without recorded debate, language derived from a proposal by Fisher Ames of Massachusetts: "Congress shall make no law establishing Religion, or prohibiting the free exercise thereof, nor shall the rights of conscience be infringed." Perhaps, on further reflection, the Representatives had thought Livermore's proposal too expansive, or perhaps, as one historian has suggested, they had simply worried that his language would not "satisfy the demands of those who wanted something said specifically against establishments of religion." L. Levy, The Establishment Clause 81 (1986). We do not know; what we do know is that the House rejected the Select Committee's version, which arguably ensured only that "no religion" enjoyed an official preference over others, and deliberately chose instead a prohibition extending to laws establishing "religion" in general.

The sequence of the Senate's treatment of this House proposal, and the House's response to the Senate, confirm that the Framers meant the Establishment Clause's prohibition to encompass nonpreferential aid to religion. In

September 1789, the Senate considered a number of provisions that would have permitted such aid, and ultimately it adopted one of them. First, it briefly entertained this language: "Congress shall make no law establishing One Religious Sect or Society in preference to others, nor shall the rights of conscience be infringed." After rejecting two minor amendments to that proposal, the Senate dropped it altogether and chose a provision identical to the House's proposal, but without the clause protecting the "rights of conscience." With no record of the Senate debates, we cannot know what prompted these changes, but the record does tell us that, six days later, the Senate went half circle and adopted its narrowest language yet: "Congress shall make no law establishing articles of faith or a mode of worship, or prohibiting the free exercise of religion." The Senate sent this proposal to the House along with its versions of the other constitutional amendments proposed.

Though it accepted much of the Senate's work on the Bill of Rights, the House rejected the Senate's version of the Establishment Clause and called for a joint conference committee, to which the Senate agreed. The House conferees ultimately won out, persuading the Senate to accept this as the final text of the Religion Clauses: "Congress shall make no law respecting an establishment of religion, or prohibiting the free exercise thereof." What is remarkable is that, unlike the earliest House drafts or the final Senate proposal, the prevailing language is not limited to laws respecting an establishment of "a religion," "a national religion," "one religious sect," or specific "articles of faith." The Framers repeatedly considered and deliberately rejected such narrow language and instead extended their prohibition to state support for "religion" in general. * * *

While these considerations are, for me, sufficient to reject the non-preferentialist position, one further concern animates my judgment. In many contexts, including this one, nonpreferentialism requires some distinction between "sectarian" religious practices and those that would be, by some measure, ecumenical enough to pass Establishment Clause muster. Simply by requiring the enquiry, nonpreferentialists invite the courts to engage in comparative theology. I can hardly imagine a subject less amenable to the competence of the federal judiciary, or more deliberately to be avoided where possible.

Petitioners rest most of their argument on a theory that, whether or not the Establishment Clause permits extensive nonsectarian support for religion, it does not forbid the state to sponsor affirmations of religious belief that coerce neither support for religion nor participation in religious observance. I appreciate the force of some of the arguments supporting a "coercion" analysis of the Clause. But we could not adopt that reading without abandoning our settled law, a course that, in my view, the text of the Clause would not readily permit. Nor does the extratextual evidence of original meaning stand so unequivocally at odds with the textual premise inherent in existing precedent that we should fundamentally reconsider our course. * * *

Petitioners contend that because the early Presidents included religious messages in their inaugural and Thanksgiving Day addresses, the Framers could not have meant the Establishment Clause to forbid noncoercive state endorsement of religion. The argument ignores the fact, however, that Americans today find such proclamations less controversial than did the founding generation, whose published thoughts on the matter belie petitioners' claim. President Jefferson, for example, steadfastly refused to issue Thanksgiving proclamations of any kind, in part because he thought they violated the Religion Clauses. * * *

During his first three years in office, James Madison also refused to call for days of thanksgiving and prayer, though later, amid the political turmoil of the War of 1812, he did so on four separate occasions. * * *

Madison's failure to keep pace with his principles in the face of congressional pressure cannot erase the principles. He admitted to backsliding, and explained that he had made the content of his wartime proclamations inconsequential enough to mitigate much of their impropriety. While his writings suggest mild variations in his interpretation of the Establishment Clause, Madison was no different in that respect from the rest of his political generation. That he expressed so much doubt about the constitutionality of religious proclamations, however, suggests a brand of separationism stronger even than that embodied in our traditional jurisprudence. So too does his characterization of public subsidies for legislative and military chaplains as unconstitutional "establishments," for the federal courts, however expansive their general view of the Establishment Clause, have upheld both practices.

To be sure, the leaders of the young Republic engaged in some of the practices that separationists like Jefferson and Madison criticized. * * * Yet in the face of the separationist dissent, those practices prove, at best, that the Framers simply did not share a common understanding of the Establishment Clause, and, at worst, that they, like other politicians, could raise constitutional ideals one day and turn their backs on them the next. * * *

JUSTICE SCALIA, with whom **THE CHIEF JUSTICE [REHNQUIST]**, **JUSTICE WHITE**, and **JUSTICE THOMAS** join, dissenting.

From our Nation's origin, prayer has been a prominent part of governmental ceremonies and proclamations. The Declaration of Independence, the document marking our birth as a separate people, "appeal[ed] to the Supreme Judge of the world for the rectitude of our intentions" and avowed "a firm reliance on the protection of divine Providence." In his first inaugural address, after swearing his oath of office on a Bible, George Washington deliberately made a prayer a part of his first official act as President:

> it would be peculiarly improper to omit in this first official act my fervent supplications to that Almighty Being who rules over the universe, who presides in the councils of nations, and whose providential aids can supply every human defect, that His benediction may consecrate to the liberties and happiness of the people of the United States a Government instituted by themselves for these essential purposes.

Such supplications have been a characteristic feature of inaugural addresses ever since. Thomas Jefferson, for example, prayed in his first inaugural address: "may that Infinite Power which rules the destinies of the universe lead our councils to what is best, and give them a favorable issue for your peace and prosperity." * * * Most recently, President Bush, continuing the tradition established by President Washington, asked those attending his inauguration to bow their heads, and made a prayer his first official act as President. * * *

The Court presumably would separate graduation invocations and benedictions from other instances of public "preservation and transmission of religious beliefs" on the ground that they involve "psychological coercion." I find it a sufficient embarrassment that our Establishment Clause jurisprudence regarding holiday displays, see *Allegheny County*, has come to "requir[e] scrutiny more commonly associated with interior decorators than with the judiciary." *American Jewish Congress v. Chicago*, 827 F.2d 120, 129 (7th Cir. 1987) (Easterbrook, J., dissenting). But interior decorating is a rock-hard science compared to psychology practiced by amateurs. A few citations of "[r]esearch in psychology" that have no particular bearing upon the precise issue here cannot disguise the fact that the Court has gone beyond the realm where judges know what they are doing. The Court's argument that state officials have "coerced" students to take part in the invocation and benediction at graduation ceremonies is, not to put too fine a point on it, incoherent.

[Justice Scalia then argued that a student who fails to participate in the prayer is not subject to meaningful coercion, and that the involvement of state officials in the drafting of the prayer was minimal.]

The deeper flaw in the Court's opinion does not lie in its wrong answer to the question whether there was state-induced "peer-pressure" coercion; it lies, rather, in the Court's making violation of the Establishment Clause hinge on such a precious question. The coercion that was a hallmark of historical establishments of religion was coercion of religious orthodoxy and of financial support *by force of law and threat of penalty*. Typically, attendance at the state church was required; only clergy of the official church could lawfully perform sacraments; and dissenters, if tolerated, faced an array of civil disabilities. L. Levy, The Establishment Clause 4 (1986). Thus, for example, in the colony of Virginia, where the Church of England had been established, ministers were required by law to conform to the doctrine and rites of the Church of England; and all persons were required to attend church and observe the Sabbath, were tithed for the public support of Anglican ministers, and were taxed for the costs of building and repairing churches.

The Establishment Clause was adopted to prohibit such an establishment of religion at the federal level (and to protect state establishments of religion from federal interference). I will further acknowledge for the sake of argument that, as some scholars have argued, by 1790 the term "establishment" had acquired an additional meaning — "financial support of religion generally, by public taxation" — that reflected the development of "general or multiple" establishments, not limited to a single church. But that would still be an establishment coerced *by force of law*. And I will further concede that our constitutional tradition, from the Declaration of Independence and the first inaugural address of Washington, quoted earlier, down to the present day, has, with a few aberrations, ruled out of order government-sponsored endorsement of religion — even when no legal coercion is present, and indeed even when no ersatz, "peer-pressure" psycho-coercion is present — where the endorsement is sectarian, in the sense of specifying details upon which men and women who believe in a benevolent, omnipotent Creator and Ruler of the world, are known to differ (for example, the divinity of Christ). But there is simply no support for the proposition that the officially sponsored nondenominational invocation and benediction read by Rabbi Gutterman — with no one legally coerced to recite them — violated the Constitution of the United States. To the contrary, they are so characteristically American they could have come from the pen of George Washington or Abraham Lincoln himself.

NOTES ON *WEISMAN* AND ESTABLISHMENT DOCTRINE

1. *Different Visions of Conservative Jurisprudence.* We have included unusually long excerpts from *Weisman* because the opinions so clearly set out the principal contending positions on the Court regarding the Establishment Clause. We leave it to you to weigh the opposing arguments of the Justices. Obviously, *Weisman* reflects a very real split among the views of conservatives. You might want to compare the line-up of the Justices in *Casey* (Chapter 5, § 4B), decided at almost the same time. Notice again how varying attitudes toward history and tradition are reflected in the division between the Scalia-Thomas camp and Justices Souter, Kennedy, and O'Connor. Interestingly enough, Professor McConnell, who takes issue with Justice Scalia's opinion in *Smith*, also differs from his view about graduation prayers:

> I would have thought that gathering a captive audience is a classic example of coercion; participation is hardly voluntary if the cost of avoiding the prayer is to miss one's graduation. Equally seriously, it appears that the content of the prayer was subject to indirect governmental control, which is a species of coercion. For the Court to embrace the coercion test in this form would be a small step back toward permitting the government to indoctrinate children in the favored civil religion of nondenominational theism.

Michael McConnell, *Religion Freedom at a Crossroads*, 59 U. Chi. L. Rev. 115, 158-59 (1992).

2. *Religion and American Traditions.* Justice Scalia's dissenting opinion is interesting for its views of both tradition and religion. Note his definition of sectarianism as "specifying details upon which men and women who believe in a benevolent, omnipotent Creator and Ruler of the world are known to differ (for example, the divinity of Christ)." Many Christians (and most non-Christians) might consider that particular religious doctrine to be something more than a "detail." In the same sentence of Scalia's opinion, he also seems to acknowledge that "tradition" can provide an affirmative basis for constitutional restrictions; in most previous opinions, he has referred to tradition only as a means of validating practices that might otherwise be constitutionally troublesome. He has not yet provided a theory, however, that explains the role of tradition in constitutional interpretation. (Justice Souter also seems to have a reverential attitude toward tradition, but his vision of American tradition regarding religion is quite different than Scalia's.)

While revering tradition, Scalia (unlike Souter) seems to have less respect for precedent. One commentator has suggested that these attitudes are only superficially contradictory:

> * * * Justice Scalia's traditionalism can be reconciled with his disdain for stare decisis if one recognizes that his traditionalism takes the form not of a cool counsel of restraint and humility but of an urgent sense that something has gone awry and that the world should be returned to its older, more solid, traditional foundations. Certain recent developments are, for Justice Scalia, what the French Revolution was for Burke: a source not of new traditions to be accepted, but of innovations to be overthrown, in the name of deeper traditions, as soon as possible.

David Strauss, *Tradition, Precedent, and Justice Scalia*, 12 Cardozo L. Rev. 1699, 1714 (1991).

3. *The Scope of Accommodation.* Justice Kennedy rejects the argument that the graduation prayer merely "accommodates" religion, on the ground that there is no significant burden to accommodate. In other settings, like *Sherbert* and *Smith*, the accommodation issue has often proved difficult: It often isn't easy to distinguish an accommodation from an affirmative benefit. Under *Smith*, the Court seems prepared to take a favorable view toward accommodations, but it remains to be seen whether these accommodations can be implemented without running afoul of establishment concerns. For a suggestion that accommodation presents an essentially irreconcilable conflict between free exercise and establishment values, see Suzanna Sherry, Lee v. Weisman: *Paradox Redux*, 1992 Sup. Ct. Rev. 123. Consider that suggestion in light of the following case.

Santa Fe Independent School Dist. v. Doe, 530 U.S. 290 (2000). Before 1995, a student elected as the high school "student council chaplain" delivered a prayer over the public address system before each home football game. After suit was filed challenging the constitutionality of this practice, the school district adopted a different policy: students would vote to decide whether to have an "invocation" delivered before each game, and if so, to elect a student to deliver it. The Court, per **Justice Stevens**, invalidated the policy on its face, viewing the outcome largely controlled by *Lee v. Weisman*. The Court rejected the argument that this was private, not public, speech, noting that the speech was over the school's public address system at a school-sponsored event by a speaker representing the student body pursuant to a school policy that, the Court concluded, explicitly and implicitly encouraged public prayer, involving both perceived and actual endorsement of religion. The Court considered attendance at football games to have a coercive aspect similar to the graduation ceremony in *Weisman*. For some students (football players, band members, cheerleaders), attendance was mandatory. As for others, "[t]o assert that high school students do not feel immense social pressure, or have a truly genuine desire, to be involved in the extracurricular event that is American high school football is 'formalistic in the extreme.' " (Quoting *Weisman*.) For at least some students, "the choice between whether to attend these games or to risk facing a personally offensive religious ritual is in no practical sense an easy one." In any event, even if every student's decision to attend were viewed as voluntary, " 'the government may no more use social pressure to enforce orthodoxy than it may use more direct means.' " (Again quoting *Weisman*.) "[N]othing in the Constitution * * * prohibits any public school student from voluntarily praying at any time before, during, or after the schoolday[,]" but "the religious liberty protected by the Constitution is abridged when the State affirmatively sponsors the particular religious practice of prayer." The Court invalidated the policy on its face even though it had never been put into practice, invoking the *Lemon* standard and concluding that, in light of the policy's history and context, it lacked a secular legislative purpose. "[T]he simple enactment of this policy, with the purpose and perception of school endorsement of student prayer, was a constitutional violation." **Chief Justice Rehnquist**, joined by **Justices Scalia** and **Thomas**, dissented, objecting to the invalidation of the policy on its face. Acknowledging that it might be applied unconstitutionally, the dissenters contended that the policy allowed students to choose to forgo any student speech before games or to elect a speaker who would not engage in religious speech. Moreover, they argued, the school district had articulated plausible secular purposes for the policy: to solemnize the event, promote good sportsmanship, and establish the appropriate environment for the competition.

————

Board of Education of Kiryas Joel Village School Dist. v. Grumet, 512 U.S. 687 (1994). This case illustrates the difficulty of identifying the limits of permissible accommodation. Most of the children in a community of ultra-Orthodox Jews, the Satmar Hasidim, went to private school, but children with disabilities were sent to public school to participate in special educational programs. They were the subject of harassment by other public school children. Under a then-current interpretation of the Establishment Clause, now overruled,[f] it was not possible to provide the public programs on the grounds of the private school. To accommodate their needs, the state government passed special legislation authorizing them to form their own public school district, so that their children would not have to attend county schools. **Justice Souter**, writing for the Court, held the special school district unconstitutional as a delegation of government power to a religious group. **Justice O'Connor** concurred because the accommodation was in effect limited to a particular religious group rather than being stated in general terms applicable to other groups. **Justice Kennedy** viewed the new school district as a form of religious gerrymandering. In dissent, **Justice Scalia**, joined by **Chief Justice Rehnquist** and **Justice Thomas**, ridiculed the idea that New York was "establishing" this obscure religious sect. Instead, he found the case to exemplify a "characteristically and admirably American accommodation of the religious practices (or more precisely, cultural peculiarities) of a tiny minority sect."

———————————————————————

f. See *Agostini v. Felton*, 521 U.S. 203 (1997).

3. *Financial Support of Religious Programs*

Most of the post-*Lemon* cases have (like *Lemon* and *Everson*) involved state aid to nonpublic schools.[g] Tribe, *American Constitutional Law*, *supra* at 1219-20, views the cases allowing public funding as falling into two basic categories: (a) funded equipment is supplied directly to parents and not through parochial schools, or (b) funded services at parochial schools are not subject to supervision or control of content by the parochial schools. He argues that the underlying principle enforced by the Court is to limit "symbolic links" between the state and church schools, but that otherwise most forms of nondiscriminatory state aid are permissible. Assuming this is the Court's evolving practice, is it justifiable under the values you believe are embodied in the Establishment Clause? Consider Professor Tribe's synthesis of the cases in light of more recent decisions.

In *Lamb's Chapel v. Center Moriches Union Free School District*, 508 U.S. 384 (1993), the Court, per Justice White, struck down a school district practice of routinely opening its facilities for after-hours use for essentially all but religious purposes, such that a film on family values and child rearing could be shown by a civic group, but not a religious group. In part, the school district defended its practice as a method of preventing an Establishment Clause violation. In rejecting this argument, the Court stated:

> * * * The showing of this film would not have been during school hours, would not have been sponsored by the school, and would have been open to the public, not just to church members. The District property had repeatedly been used by a wide variety of private organizations. Under these circumstances, * * * there would have been no realistic danger that the community would think that the District was endorsing religion or any particular creed, and any benefit to religion or to the Church would have been no more than incidental. * * * [P]ermitting District property to be used to exhibit the film involved in this case would not have been an establishment of religion under the three-part test articulated in *Lemon*: The challenged governmental action has a secular purpose, does not have the principal or primary effect of advancing or inhibiting religion, and does not foster an excessive entanglement with religion.

Justices Kennedy, Scalia, and Thomas, concurring in the judgment, complained that the citation to *Lemon*, a decision they viewed as moribund, was unnecessary.

Zobrest v. Catalina Foothills School District, 509 U.S. 1 (1993), involved the federal Individuals with Disabilities Education Act, which was assumed

---

g. Leading cases include *Aguilar v. Felton*, 473 U.S. 402 (1985) (prohibiting state teachers from going to parochial schools to teach remedial courses to their students); *Mueller v. Allen*, 463 U.S. 388 (1983) (permitting state tax deduction for tuition and expenses for children to attend private as well as public schools); *Committee for Public Education v. Nyquist*, 413 U.S. 756 (1973) (invalidating tuition tax credits to low-income parents having children in nonpublic schools and tax deductions to higher-income parents). *Aguilar* was overruled in *Agostini v. Felton*, 521 U.S. 203 (1997), which was in fact a successful effort to reopen the same litigation. To reach the merits in *Agostini*, the Court had to leap past some formidable procedural obstacles, as you might imagine, since it was necessary to reopen a final judgment which the Court itself had issued in the earlier decision.

generally to require a local school district to provide a sign-language interpreter to accompany a deaf student to classes. A school district, on Establishment Clause grounds, refused to provide such an interpreter to a student at a parochial high school, Salpointe. The Court, per Chief Justice Rehnquist, found no constitutional bar to public financial assistance in these circumstances. Justice Blackmun, joined by Justice Souter, dissented in *Zobrest*, complaining that in an educational environment in which the secular and the sectarian are "inextricably intertwined," "governmental assistance to the educational function of the school necessarily entails governmental participation in the school's inculcation of religion. A state-employed sign-language interpreter would be required to communicate the material covered in religion class, the nominally secular subjects that are taught from a religious perspective, and the daily Masses at which Salpointe encourages attendance for Catholic students."

In *Mitchell v. Helms*, 530 U.S. 793 (2000), a divided Court upheld a federal statute that provides aid to local schools, allocating funds to purchase certain supplies for parochial and other private schools on a per capita basis. Six Justices agreed that previous cases, which had limited provision of instructional materials such as maps to parochial schools, were inconsistent with recent doctrine and should be overruled. But these six Justices split in their analysis. The plurality opinion of Justice Thomas, joined by Chief Justice Rehnquist and Justices Scalia and Kennedy, placed heavy stress on the fact that the same aid was available to all schools on a nondiscriminatory basis. The district court's holding that the statute had a secular purpose was not challenged on appeal. Justice Thomas concluded that the statute also had a secular effect because the program did not define its recipients on the basis of religion, it allocated funds based on the independent private decisions of parents about where to send their children, and it provided no incentive to engage in religious indoctrination. The plurality put aside the possible special problems caused by government payments directly to parochial schools, as opposed to in-kind grants of nonreligious materials. Justice Thomas was unimpressed by the showing that some of the materials had been diverted to purely religious use. Justice O'Connor, joined by Justice Breyer, said that the plurality had put too much weight on the "neutrality" of the aid program, but concluded that the evidence of diversion to religious purposes was de minimis. The three dissenters, led by Justice Souter, argued that the program constituted impermissible direct aid to religious activities. Although Justice Souter isolated a list of relevant factors from previous decisions, he considered Establishment Clause cases ultimately to involve "a matter of judgment" based on "[p]articular factual circumstances."

ZELMAN v. SIMMONS-HARRIS
536 U.S. 639, 122 S.Ct. 2460, 153 L.Ed.2d 604 (2002)

CHIEF JUSTICE REHNQUIST delivered the opinion of the Court

[The Cleveland public schools were in disastrous condition. As part of a plan to improve educational opportunities in the city, Ohio's Pilot Project Scholarship Program provides (a) tuition aid for some Cleveland students to attend participating public or private schools of their parent's choosing and (b) tutorial aid for students who choose to remain enrolled in their usual public school. Both religious and nonreligious schools in the district may participate, as may public schools in suburbs. Tuition aid is distributed to parents according to financial need, and the parents decide which school to choose. The number of tutorial assistance grants provided to students remaining in public school must equal the number of tuition aid scholarships (but the tutoring grants are much smaller). In the 1999-2000 school year, 82% of the participating private schools were religious, none of the suburban public schools participated, and 96% of the students participating in the scholarship program were enrolled in religiously affiliated schools. Sixty percent of the students were from families at or below the poverty line. Besides the regular public schools, Cleveland children also have two other non-private options. They can attend community schools, which are funded under state law but run by their own school boards and receive twice the per-student funding as participating private schools. Or they can attend magnet schools, which are public schools emphasizing a particular subject area, teaching method, or service.]

The Establishment Clause of the First Amendment, applied to the States through the Fourteenth Amendment, prevents a State from enacting laws that have the "purpose" or "effect" of advancing or inhibiting religion. There is no dispute that the program challenged here was enacted for the valid secular purpose of providing educational assistance to poor children in a demonstrably failing public school system. Thus, the question presented is whether the Ohio program nonetheless has the forbidden "effect" of advancing or inhibiting religion.

To answer that question, our decisions have drawn a consistent distinction between government programs that provide aid directly to religious schools, and programs of true private choice, in which government aid reaches religious schools only as a result of the genuine and independent choices of private individuals, *Mueller v. Allen,* 463 U. S. 388 (1983); *Witters v. Washington Dept. of Servs. for Blind,* 474 U. S. 481 (1986); *Zobrest v. Catalina Foothills School Dist.,* 509 U. S. 1 (1993). While our jurisprudence with respect to the constitutionality of direct aid programs has "changed significantly" over the past two decades, our jurisprudence with respect to true private choice programs has remained consistent and unbroken. Three times we have confronted Establishment Clause challenges to neutral government programs that provide aid directly to a broad class of individuals, who, in turn, direct the aid to religious schools or institutions of their own choosing. Three times we have rejected such challenges. * * *

We believe that the program challenged here is a program of true private choice, consistent with *Mueller, Witters,* and *Zobrest,* and thus constitutional. As was true in those cases, the Ohio program is neutral in all respects toward religion. It is part of a general and multifaceted undertaking by the State of Ohio to provide educational opportunities to the children of a failed school district. It confers educational assistance directly to a broad class of individuals defined without reference to religion, *i.e.,* any parent of a school-age child who resides in the Cleveland City School District. The program permits the participation of *all* schools within the district, religious or nonreligious. Adjacent public schools also may participate and have a financial incentive to do so. Program benefits are available to participating families on neutral terms, with no reference to religion. The only preference stated anywhere in the program is a preference for low-income families, who receive greater assistance and are given priority for admission at participating schools.

There are no "financial incentive[s]" that "ske[w]" the program toward religious schools. Such incentives "[are] not present . . . where the aid is allocated on the basis of neutral, secular criteria that neither favor nor disfavor religion, and is made available to both religious and secular beneficiaries on a nondiscriminatory basis." The program here in fact creates financial *dis*incentives for religious schools, with private schools receiving only half the government assistance given to community schools and one-third the assistance given to magnet schools. Adjacent public schools, should any choose to accept program students, are also eligible to receive two to three times the state funding of a private religious school. Families too have a financial disincentive to choose a private religious school over other schools. Parents that choose to participate in the scholarship program and then to enroll their children in a private school (religious or nonreligious) must copay a portion of the school's tuition. Families that choose a community school, magnet school, or traditional public school pay nothing. Although such features of the program are not necessary to its constitutionality, they clearly dispel the claim that the program "creates . . . financial incentive[s] for parents to choose a sectarian school."

Respondents suggest that even without a financial incentive for parents to choose a religious school, the program creates a "public perception that the State is endorsing religious practices and beliefs." But we have repeatedly recognized that no reasonable observer would think a neutral program of private choice, where state aid reaches religious schools solely as a result of the numerous independent decisions of private individuals, carries with it the *imprimatur* of government endorsement. * * *

There also is no evidence that the program fails to provide genuine opportunities for Cleveland parents to select secular educational options for their school-age children. Cleveland schoolchildren enjoy a range of educational choices: They may remain in public school as before, remain in public school with publicly funded tutoring aid, obtain a scholarship and choose a religious school, obtain a scholarship and choose a nonreligious private school, enroll in a community school, or enroll in a magnet school. That 46 of the 56 private schools now participating in the program are religious schools does not condemn it as a violation of the Establishment Clause. The Establishment Clause question is whether Ohio is coercing parents into sending their children to religious schools, and that question must be answered by evaluating *all* options Ohio provides Cleveland schoolchildren, only one of which is to obtain a program scholarship and then choose a religious school. * * *

Respondents and Justice Souter claim that even if we do not focus on the number of participating schools that are religious schools, we should attach constitutional significance to the fact that 96% of scholarship recipients have enrolled in religious schools. They claim that this alone proves parents lack genuine choice, even if no parent has ever said so. We need not consider this argument in detail, since it was flatly rejected in *Mueller*, where we found it irrelevant that 96% of parents taking deductions for tuition expenses paid tuition at religious schools. Indeed, we have recently found it irrelevant even to the constitutionality of a direct aid program that a vast majority of program benefits went to religious schools. *Agostini v. Felton*, 521 U.S. 203 (1997). The constitutionality of a neutral educational aid program simply does not turn on whether and why, in a particular area, at a particular time, most private schools are run by religious organizations, or most recipients choose to use the aid at a religious school. As we said in *Mueller*, "[s]uch an approach would scarcely provide the certainty that this field stands in need of, nor can we perceive principled standards by which such statistical evidence might be evaluated." * * *

In sum, the Ohio program is entirely neutral with respect to religion. It provides benefits directly to a wide spectrum of individuals, defined only by financial need and residence in a particular school district. It permits such individuals to exercise genuine choice among options public and private, secular and religious. The program is therefore a program of true private choice. In keeping with an unbroken line of decisions rejecting challenges to similar programs, we hold that the program does not offend the Establishment Clause.

JUSTICE O'CONNOR, concurring.

There is little question in my mind that the Cleveland voucher program is neutral as between religious schools and nonreligious schools. Justice Souter rejects the Court's notion of neutrality, proposing that the neutrality of a program should be gauged not by the opportunities it presents but rather by its effects. * * *

I do not agree that the nonreligious schools have failed to provide Cleveland parents reasonable alternatives to religious schools in the voucher program. For nonreligious schools to qualify as genuine options for parents, they need not be superior to religious schools in every respect. They need only be adequate substitutes for religious schools in the eyes of parents. The District Court record demonstrates that nonreligious schools were able to compete effectively with Catholic and other religious schools in the Cleveland voucher program. The best evidence of this is that many parents with vouchers selected nonreligious private schools over religious alternatives and an even larger number of parents send their children to community and magnet schools rather than seeking vouchers at all. Moreover, there is no record evidence that any voucher-eligible student was turned away from a nonreligious private school in the voucher program, let alone a community or magnet school. * * *

I find the Court's answer to the question whether parents of students eligible for vouchers have a genuine choice between religious and nonreligious schools persuasive. In looking at the voucher program, all the choices available to potential beneficiaries of the government program should be considered. In these cases, parents who were eligible to apply for a voucher also had the option, at a minimum, to send their children to community schools. Yet the Court of Appeals chose not to look at community schools, let alone magnet schools, when evaluating the Cleveland voucher program. That decision was incorrect. Focusing in these cases only on the program challenged by respondents ignores how the educational system in Cleveland actually functions. The record indicates that, in 1999, two nonreligious private schools that had previously served 15 percent of the students in the voucher program were prompted to convert to community schools because parents were concerned about the litigation surrounding the program, and because a new community schools program provided more per-pupil financial aid. Many of the students that enrolled in the two schools under the voucher program transferred to the community schools program and continued to attend these schools. This incident provides strong evidence that both parents and nonreligious schools view the voucher program and the community schools program as reasonable alternatives.

[**JUSTICE THOMAS** also filed a concurring opinion. He questioned whether the Establishment Clause is incorporated by the Fourteenth Amendment. He suggested that "the States may pass laws that include or touch on religious matters so long as these laws do not impede free exercise rights or any other individual religious liberty interest." Justice Thomas also stressed the importance of the voucher program to improving educational opportunities for minority children.]

JUSTICE SOUTER, with whom **JUSTICE STEVENS**, **JUSTICE GINSBURG**, and **JUSTICE BREYER** join, dissenting.

The Court's majority holds that the Establishment Clause is no bar to Ohio's payment of tuition at private religious elementary and middle schools under a scheme that systematically provides tax money to support the schools' religious missions. The occasion for the legislation thus upheld is the condition of public education in the city of Cleveland. The record indicates that the schools are failing to serve their objective, and the vouchers in issue here are said to be needed to provide adequate alternatives to them. If there were an excuse for giving short shrift to the Establishment Clause, it would probably apply here. But there is no excuse. Constitutional limitations are placed on government to preserve constitutional values in hard cases, like these. * * * I therefore respectfully dissent.

The applicability of the Establishment Clause to public funding of benefits to religious schools was settled in *Everson v. Board of Ed.,* 330 U. S. 1 (1947), which inaugurated the modern era of establishment doctrine. The Court stated the principle in words from which there was no dissent:

> No tax in any amount, large or small, can be levied to support any religious activities or institutions, whatever they may be called, or whatever form they may adopt to teach or practice religion.

The Court has never in so many words repudiated this statement, let alone, in so many words, overruled *Everson*.

Today, however, the majority holds that the Establishment Clause is not offended by Ohio's Pilot Project Scholarship Program, under which students may be eligible to receive as much as $2,250 in the form of tuition vouchers transferable to religious schools. In the city of Cleveland the overwhelming proportion of large appropriations for voucher money must be spent on religious schools if it is to be spent at all, and will be spent in amounts that cover almost all of tuition. The money will thus pay for eligible students' instruction not only in secular subjects but in religion as well, in schools that can fairly be characterized as founded to teach religious doctrine and to imbue teaching in all subjects with a religious dimension. Public tax money will pay at a systemic level for teaching the covenant with Israel and Mosaic law in Jewish schools, the primacy of the Apostle Peter and the Papacy in Catholic schools, the truth of reformed Christianity in Protestant schools, and the revelation to the Prophet in Muslim schools, to speak only of major religious groupings in the Republic.

How can a Court consistently leave *Everson* on the books and approve the Ohio vouchers? The answer is that it cannot. It is only by ignoring *Everson* that the majority can claim to rest on traditional law in its invocation of neutral aid provisions and private choice to sanction the Ohio law. It is, moreover, only by ignoring the meaning of neutrality and private choice themselves that the majority can even pretend to rest today's decision on those criteria.

The majority's statements of Establishment Clause doctrine cannot be appreciated without some historical perspective on the Court's announced limitations on government aid to religious education, and its repeated repudiation of limits previously set. My object here is not to give any nuanced exposition of the cases, which I tried to classify in some detail in an earlier opinion, see *Mitchell v. Helms*, 530 U.S. 793, 873-899 (2000) (dissenting opinion), but to set out the broad doctrinal stages covered in the modern era, and to show that doctrinal bankruptcy has been reached today.

Viewed with the necessary generality, the cases can be categorized in three groups. In the period from 1947 to 1968, the basic principle of no aid to religion through school benefits was unquestioned. Thereafter for some 15 years, the Court termed its efforts as attempts to draw a line against aid that would be divertible to support the religious, as distinct from the secular, activity of an institutional beneficiary. Then, starting in 1983, concern with divertibility was gradually lost in favor of approving aid in amounts unlikely to afford substantial benefits to religious schools, when offered evenhandedly without regard to a recipient's religious character, and when channeled to a religious institution only by the genuinely free choice of some private individual. Now, the three stages are succeeded by a fourth, in which the substantial character of government aid is held to have no constitutional significance, and the espoused criteria of neutrality in offering aid, and private choice in directing it, are shown to be nothing but examples of verbal formalism. * * *

* * * *Everson*'s statement is still the touchstone of sound law, even though the reality is that in the matter of educational aid the Establishment Clause has largely been read away. True, the majority has not approved vouchers for religious schools alone, or aid earmarked for religious instruction. But no scheme so clumsy will ever get before us, and in the cases that we may see, like these, the Establishment Clause is largely silenced. I do not have the option to leave it silent, and I hope that a future Court will reconsider today's dramatic departure from basic Establishment Clause principle.

[The dissenting opinions of **JUSTICE STEVENS** and of **JUSTICE BREYER**, joined by **JUSTICES STEVENS** and **SOUTER**, are omitted.]

NOTES ON *ZELMAN*

1. *The Scope of* Zelman. Does *Zelman* provide blanket approval for all voucher programs? Consider the following hypothetical voucher programs:

a. Maxopolis has only regular public schools (not magnet or "community") and no nonreligious private schools. (Does it matter whether the effect of the vouchers is to allow additional children to attend religious schools or to reduce the financial burden on existing students?)

b. The State of Northland adopts a voucher system as the result of a vigorous lobbying effort by religious schools.

c. The State of Westland eliminates its public school system, privatizing existing schools by selling them to community groups. The state also converts its school financing entirely to a voucher system. Among the previously public schools, many favor school prayer and other religious activities.

Are these voucher programs constitutional under *Zelman*?

2. *The Problem of Entanglement.* Justice Breyer emphasized in his dissent that recipient schools in the Ohio program were required to meet certain criteria. They must accept students of all religions. They are also forbidden to "advocate or foster unlawful behavior or teach hatred of any person or group on the basis of race, ethnicity, national origin, or religion." State officials must exclude any noncomplying school from the program. Justice Breyer was concerned that determining whether a particular religion "teaches hatred" of other religious groups would be extremely divisive, not to mention requiring sensitive judgments about religious creeds. Does the inclusion of these provisions in the voucher program raise Establishment Clause concerns? You might also consider whether these provisions would be vulnerable to challenge as infringements on free speech or freedom of association. Is a voucher program a limited public forum?

3. *"Proximate Cause" in Constitutional Law.* The Establishment Clause is one of several areas of constitutional law in which the same question is critical: How far do we hold the government responsible for the unintended consequences of its actions? (As *Washington v. Davis* and the "secular purpose" test both show, we generally do hold the government responsible for the *intended* effects of its actions). This question arises in standing law (under the "fairly traceable" prong of the standing test). Obviously, it is central to the state action doctrine. The question also arises in other areas of law, most notably in the guise of "proximate cause" in tort law. Apparently, these issues of causal responsibility are very difficult: legal doctrine in every one of these areas is notoriously opaque and muddled.

In its Establishment Clause setting, the question is whether the government is responsible (in a constitutional sense) when its policies reduce the cost of engaging in religious activities. In *Zelman*, the effect of the voucher system is to make attendance at religious schools less expensive, and hence to increase demand. The *Zelman* Court suggests that the school choices of the parents break the chain of causal responsibility between the state subsidy and the religious exercises of the schools. In torts terms, the actions of the parents are an independent intervening cause. Is the torts analogy illuminating, or is this kind of reasoning leading the Court astray?

4. *Vouchers and Establishment Clause Values.* What is the constitutional worry about school vouchers for religious schools? Consider the following list of possibilities:

(a) This use of vouchers carries a message of endorsement of the religious mission of the schools.

(b) Administration of the voucher program will require excessive state involvement in the operations of religious schools.

(c) Religious groups will be involved in socially divisive political struggles over the funding and structure of the programs.

(d) Some of the funds will be used to subsidize purely religious activities.

(e) All of the funds will be used to subsidize religious teachings, because religion is an integral part of every class.

Which of these seem to you to be serious concerns? Are any of them serious enough that the voucher programs should be banned?

5. *Purely Secular Vouchers.* Would it be constitutional for a state to establish a voucher program that did *not* include religious schools? Reconsider your answer in light of the following two cases.

Rosenberger v. Rector and Visitors of the University of Virginia, 515 U.S. 819 (1995). The University of Virginia authorizes payments from its student activity fees to cover printing costs for various student groups. The University refused to provide such payment, however, for a group called Wide Awake Productions (WAP), because its student newspaper ("Wide Awake: A Christian Perspective at the University of Virginia") primarily promotes religion. On behalf of the group, Rosenberger mounted a free speech challenge to the restriction. (The free speech issue is discussed earlier in § 3B2 of this chapter.) The court of appeals upheld the funding ban on the basis that it was required in order to comply with the Establishment Clause. The Supreme Court sharply divided on this issue.

Justice Kennedy wrote the opinion of the Court. He stressed that the scheme for funding student publications was completely neutral in its application, did not involve the use of general tax revenues, and paid only for the discrete activity of printing for otherwise eligible groups. "We do not confront a case where, even under a neutral program that includes nonsectarian recipients, the government is making direct money payments to an institution or group that is engaged in religious activity. Neither the Court of Appeals nor the dissent, we believe, takes sufficient cognizance of the undisputed fact that no public funds flow directly to WAP's coffers."

Although she joined the majority opinion, **Justice O'Connor** viewed the case as more difficult. In her view, it represented the collision of two important principles: (1) the mandate of government neutrality toward religion, and (2) the ban on using public funds to finance religious messages. "When two bedrock principles so conflict, understandably neither can provide the definitive answer. Reliance on categorical platitudes is unavailing. Resolution instead depends on the hard task of judging — sifting through the details and determining whether the challenged program offends the Establishment Clause." In concluding that no Establishment Clause violation was present, she relied on the facts cited by the majority, as well as the strict independence of student groups from the University, the broad range of messages receiving assistance, and the possibility that students would have the right to withhold a pro-rata share of their activity fees if they disapproved of WAP's message.

Justice Souter dissented, joined by **Justices Stevens**, **Ginsburg**, and **Breyer**. He stressed the proselytizing nature of WAP's publications. "Using public funds for the direct subsidization of preaching the word is categorically forbidden under the Establishment Clause, and if the Clause was meant to accomplish nothing else, it was meant to bar this use of public money." He distinguished a number of prior cases as involving only "indirect aid" to religion. In response to the dissent, **Justice Thomas**'s concurring opinion argued that the Framers were only concerned about preferential funding for religion, and that the difference between "direct" and "indirect" aid lacks any economic substance. Thomas described himself as leaning toward the view that the Framers only meant to prohibit funding preferences for particular religions (as opposed to religion generally), but in any event, he found no basis for believing that the Framers meant to require the exclusion of religions from more generally available financial aid.

————

Good News Club v. Milford Central School, 533 U.S. 98 (2001). This case involved after-school use of an elementary school. Good News Club, a private Christian organization for elementary school children, submitted a request to use a room for singing, hearing Bible lessons, memorizing scripture, and prayer. The request was denied on the basis that the proposed use was "the equivalent of religious worship." It was stipulated that the after-school program was a limited public forum. **Justice Thomas**'s opinion for the Court ruled in favor of the religious group. He found it clear that "teaching morals and character development to children is a permissible purpose" under the school's policy, and that the "Club teaches morals and character development to children." Thus, exclusion of the Club from the limited forum was impermissible: "We disagree that something that is 'quintessentially religious' or 'decidedly religious in nature' cannot also be characterized properly as the teaching of morals and character development from a particular viewpoint. What matters for purposes of the Free Speech Clause is that we can see no logical difference in kind between the invocation of Christianity by the Club and the invocation of teamwork, loyalty, or patriotism by other associations to provide a foundation for their lessons." He reserved the question whether the state's interest in avoiding an Establishment Clause violation would justify viewpoint discrimination, but found no such violation because the meetings were held after school hours, not sponsored by the school, and open to any student who obtained parental consent, not just to club members. The school district faced an "uphill battle" in its Establishment Clause claim because "allowing the Club to speak on school grounds would ensure neutrality, not threaten it." Moreover, "to the extent we consider whether the community would feel coercive pressure to engage in the Club's activities," the requirement of parental consent prevented any confusion about whether the school was endorsing religion and made the impressionability of elementary school children irrelevant.

In dissent, **Justice Stevens** said that the school was entitled to distinguish between "meetings to discuss political issues from meetings whose principal purpose is to recruit new members to join a political organization," and similarly could distinguish between meeting to discuss religious issues and meetings to recruit members for the religion. Similarly, **Justice Souter**, joined by **Justice Ginsburg**, said "[i]t is beyond question that Good News intends to use the public school premises not for the mere discussion of a subject from a particular, Christian point of view, but for an evangelical service of worship calling children to commit themselves in an act of Christian conversion." Unless read narrowly, Souter said, "this case would stand for the remarkable proposition that any public school opened for civic meetings must be opened for use as a church, synagogue, or mosque." In response, **Justice Scalia**'s concurrence said that the Court had "previously rejected the attempt to distinguish worship from other religious speech," and that any such distinction "would be beyond the courts' competence to administer." The dissenters also chided the majority for ruling on the Establishment Clause argument, which had not been passed upon by the lower courts.

———

Does the majority opinion imply that the Free Speech Clause would require a state to include pervasively religious schools in a voucher program? Query whether depriving legislatures of any discretion in this regard will make it more difficult to enact voucher programs or other forms of school aid.

LOCKE v. DAVEY
540 U.S. 712, 124 S.Ct. 1307, 158 L.Ed.2d 1 (2004)

CHIEF JUSTICE REHNQUIST delivered the opinion of the Court.

The State of Washington established the Promise Scholarship Program to assist academically gifted students with postsecondary education expenses. In accordance with the State Constitution, students may not use the scholarship at an institution where they are pursuing a degree in devotional theology. We hold that such an exclusion from an otherwise inclusive aid program does not violate the Free Exercise Clause of the First Amendment. * * *

To be eligible for the scholarship, a student must meet academic, income, and enrollment requirements. A student must graduate from a Washington public or private high school and either graduate in the top 15% of his graduating class, or attain on the first attempt a cumulative score of 1,200 or better on the Scholastic Assessment Test I or a score of 27 or better on the American College Test. The student's family income must be less than 135% of the State's median. Finally, the student must enroll "at least half time in an eligible postsecondary institution in the state of Washington," and may not pursue a degree in theology at that institution while receiving the scholarship. Private institutions, including those religiously affiliated, qualify as "eligible postsecondary institution[s]" if they are accredited by a nationally recognized accrediting body. A "degree in theology" is not defined in the statute, but, as both parties concede, the statute simply codifies the State's constitutional prohibition on providing funds to students to pursue degrees that are "devotional in nature or designed to induce religious faith."

A student who applies for the scholarship and meets the academic and income requirements is notified that he is eligible for the scholarship if he meets the enrollment requirements. Once the student enrolls at an eligible institution, the institution must certify that the student is enrolled at least half time and that the student is not pursuing a degree in devotional theology. The institution, rather than the State, determines whether the student's major is devotional. If the student meets the enrollment requirements, the scholarship funds are sent to the institution for distribution to the student to pay for tuition or other educational expenses.

Respondent, Joshua Davey, was awarded a Promise Scholarship, and chose to attend Northwest College. Northwest is a private, Christian college affiliated with the Assemblies of God denomination, and is an eligible institution under the Promise Scholarship Program. Davey had "planned for many years to attend a Bible college and to prepare [himself] through that college training for a lifetime of ministry, specifically as a church pastor." To that end, when he enrolled in Northwest College, he decided to pursue a double major in pastoral ministries and business management/administration. There is no dispute that the pastoral ministries degree is devotional and therefore excluded under the Promise Scholarship Program. * * *

The Religion Clauses of the First Amendment provide: "Congress shall make no law respecting an establishment of religion, or prohibiting the free exercise thereof." These two Clauses, the Establishment Clause and the Free Exercise Clause, are frequently in tension. Yet we have long said that "there is room for play in the joints" between them. In other words, there are some state actions permitted by the Establishment Clause but not required by the Free Exercise Clause.

This case involves that "play in the joints" described above. Under our Establishment Clause precedent, the link between government funds and religious training is broken by the independent and private choice of recipients. As such, there is no doubt that the State could, consistent with the Federal Constitution, permit Promise Scholars to pursue a degree in devotional theology, and the State does not contend otherwise. The question before us, however, is whether Washington, pursuant to its own constitution, which has been authoritatively interpreted as prohibiting even indirectly funding religious instruction that will prepare students for the ministry, can deny them such funding without violating the Free Exercise Clause.

Davey urges us to answer that question in the negative. He contends that under the rule we enunciated in *Church of Lukumi Babalu Aye, Inc. v. Hialeah* [Chapter 6, § 7A], the program is presumptively unconstitutional because it is not facially neutral with respect to religion. We reject his claim of presumptive unconstitutionality, however; to do otherwise would extend the *Lukumi* line of cases well beyond not only their facts but their reasoning. In *Lukumi,* the city of Hialeah made it a crime to engage in certain kinds of animal slaughter. We found that the law sought to suppress ritualistic animal sacrifices of the Santeria religion. In the present case, the State's disfavor of religion (if it can be called that) is of a far milder kind. It imposes neither criminal nor civil sanctions on any type of religious service or rite. It does not deny to ministers the right to participate in the political affairs of the community. And it does not require students to choose between their religious beliefs and receiving a government benefit.[d] The State has merely chosen not to fund a distinct category of instruction.

Justice Scalia argues, however, that generally available benefits are part of the "baseline against which burdens on religion are measured." Because the Promise Scholarship Program funds training for all secular professions, Justice Scalia contends the State must also fund training for religious professions. But training for religious professions and training for secular professions are not fungible. Training someone to lead a congregation is an essentially religious endeavor. Indeed, majoring in devotional theology is akin to a religious calling as well as an academic pursuit. And the subject of religion is one in which both the United States and state constitutions embody distinct views — in favor of free exercise, but opposed to establishment — that find no counterpart with respect to other callings or professions. That a State would deal differently with religious education for the ministry than with education for other callings is a product of these views, not evidence of hostility toward religion.

Even though the differently worded Washington Constitution draws a more stringent line than that drawn by the United States Constitution, the interest it seeks to further is scarcely novel. In fact, we can think of few areas in which a State's antiestablishment interests come more into play. Since the founding of our country, there have been popular uprisings against procuring taxpayer funds to support church leaders, which was one of the hallmarks of an "established" religion.

Most States that sought to avoid an establishment of religion around the time of the founding placed in their constitutions formal prohibitions against using tax funds to support the ministry. The plain text of these constitutional provisions prohibited *any* tax dollars from supporting the clergy. We have found nothing to indicate, as Justice Scalia contends, that these provisions

---

d. Promise Scholars may still use their scholarship to pursue a secular degree at a different institution from where they are studying devotional theology.

would not have applied so long as the State equally supported other professions or if the amount at stake was *de minimis*. That early state constitutions saw no problem in explicitly excluding *only* the ministry from receiving state dollars reinforces our conclusion that religious instruction is of a different ilk.[g]

Far from evincing the hostility toward religion which was manifest in *Lukumi,* we believe that the entirety of the Promise Scholarship Program goes a long way toward including religion in its benefits. The program permits students to attend pervasively religious schools, so long as they are accredited. As Northwest advertises, its "concept of education is distinctly Christian in the evangelical sense." It prepares *all* of its students, "through instruction, through modeling, [and] through [its] classes, to use . . . the Bible as their guide, as the truth," no matter their chosen profession. And under the Promise Scholarship Program's current guidelines, students are still eligible to take devotional theology courses. Davey notes all students at Northwest are required to take at least four devotional courses, "Exploring the Bible," "Principles of Spiritual Development," "Evangelism in the Christian Life," and "Christian Doctrine," and some students may have additional religious requirements as part of their majors.

In short, we find neither in the history or text of Article I, § 11 of the Washington Constitution, nor in the operation of the Promise Scholarship Program, anything that suggests animus towards religion. Given the historic and substantial state interest at issue, we therefore cannot conclude that the denial of funding for vocational religious instruction alone is inherently constitutionally suspect.

Without a presumption of unconstitutionality, Davey's claim must fail. The State's interest in not funding the pursuit of devotional degrees is substantial and the exclusion of such funding places a relatively minor burden on Promise Scholars. If any room exists between the two Religion Clauses, it must be here. We need not venture further into this difficult area in order to uphold the Promise Scholarship Program as currently operated by the State of Washington.

JUSTICE SCALIA, with whom **JUSTICE THOMAS** joins, dissenting.

* * * When the State makes a public benefit generally available, that benefit becomes part of the baseline against which burdens on religion are measured; and when the State withholds that benefit from some individuals solely on the

---

g. The *amici* contend that Washington's Constitution was born of religious bigotry because it contains a so-called "Blaine Amendment," which has been linked with anti-Catholicism. As the State notes and Davey does not dispute, however, the provision in question is not a Blaine Amendment. The enabling Act of 1889, which authorized the drafting of the Washington Constitution, required the state constitution to include a provision "for the establishment and maintenance of systems of public schools, which shall be . . . free from sectarian control." This provision was included in Article IX, § 4, of the Washington Constitution ("All schools maintained and supported wholly or in part by the public funds shall be forever free from sectarian control or influence"), and is not at issue in this case. Neither Davey nor *amici* have established a credible connection between the Blaine Amendment and Article I, § 11, the relevant constitutional provision. Accordingly, the Blaine Amendment's history is simply not before us.

basis of religion, it violates the Free Exercise Clause no less than if it had imposed a special tax.

That is precisely what the State of Washington has done here. It has created a generally available public benefit, whose receipt is conditioned only on academic performance, income, and attendance at an accredited school. It has then carved out a solitary course of study for exclusion: theology. No field of study but religion is singled out for disfavor in this fashion. Davey is not asking for a special benefit to which others are not entitled. He seeks only *equal* treatment — the right to direct his scholarship to his chosen course of study, a right every other Promise Scholar enjoys.

The Court's reference to historical "popular uprisings against procuring taxpayer funds to support church leaders" is therefore quite misplaced. That history involved not the inclusion of religious ministers in public benefits programs like the one at issue here, but laws that singled them out for financial aid. For example, the Virginia bill at which Madison's Remonstrance was directed provided: "[F]or the support of Christian teachers . . . [a] sum payable for tax on the property within this Commonwealth, is hereby assessed . . . ." Laws supporting the clergy in other States operated in a similar fashion. One can concede the Framers' hostility to funding the clergy *specifically,* but that says nothing about whether the clergy had to be excluded from benefits the State made available to all. No one would seriously contend, for example, that the Framers would have barred ministers from using public roads on their way to church.

The Court does not dispute that the Free Exercise Clause places some constraints on public benefits programs, but finds none here, based on a principle of " 'play in the joints.' " I use the term "principle" loosely, for that is not so much a legal principle as a refusal to apply *any* principle when faced with competing constitutional directives. There is nothing anomalous about constitutional commands that abut. A municipality hiring public contractors may not discriminate *against* blacks or *in favor of* them; it cannot discriminate a little bit each way and then plead "play in the joints" when haled into court. If the Religion Clauses demand neutrality, we must enforce them, in hard cases as well as easy ones.

Even if "play in the joints" were a valid legal principle, surely it would apply only when it was a close call whether complying with one of the Religion Clauses would violate the other. But that is not the case here. It is not just that "the State could, consistent with the Federal Constitution, permit Promise Scholars to pursue a degree in devotional theology." The establishment question *would not even be close,* as is evident from the fact that this Court's decision in *Witters v. Washington Dept. of Servs. for Blind,* 474 U.S. 481 (1986), was unanimous. Perhaps some formally neutral public benefits programs are so gerrymandered and devoid of plausible secular purpose that they might raise specters of state aid to religion, but an evenhanded Promise Scholarship Program is not among them.

In any case, the State already has all the play in the joints it needs. There are any number of ways it could respect both its unusually sensitive concern for the conscience of its taxpayers *and* the Federal Free Exercise Clause. It could make the scholarships redeemable only at public universities (where it sets the curriculum), or only for select courses of study. Either option would replace a program that facially discriminates against religion with one that just happens not to subsidize it. The State could also simply abandon the scholarship program altogether. If that seems a dear price to pay for freedom of conscience, it is only because the State has defined that freedom so broadly that it would be offended by a program with such an incidental, indirect religious effect. * * *

It may be that Washington's original purpose in excluding the clergy from public benefits was benign, and the same might be true of its purpose in maintaining the exclusion today. But those singled out for disfavor can be forgiven for suspecting more invidious forces at work. Let there be no doubt: This case is about discrimination against a religious minority. Most citizens of this country identify themselves as professing some religious belief, but the State's policy poses no obstacle to practitioners of only a tepid, civic version of faith. Those the statutory exclusion actually affects — those whose belief in their religion is so strong that they dedicate their study and their lives to its ministry — are a far narrower set. One need not delve too far into modern popular culture to perceive a trendy disdain for deep religious conviction. In an era when the Court is so quick to come to the aid of other disfavored groups, see, e.g., *Romer v. Evans* [casebook, p. 402], its indifference in this case, which involves a form of discrimination to which the Constitution actually speaks, is exceptional.

Today's holding is limited to training the clergy, but its logic is readily extendible, and there are plenty of directions to go. What next? Will we deny priests and nuns their prescription-drug benefits on the ground that taxpayers' freedom of conscience forbids medicating the clergy at public expense? This may seem fanciful, but recall that France has proposed banning religious attire from schools, invoking interests in secularism no less benign than those the Court embraces today. When the public's freedom of conscience is invoked to justify denial of equal treatment, benevolent motives shade into indifference and ultimately into repression. Having accepted the justification in this case, the Court is less well equipped to fend it off in the future. I respectfully dissent.

JUSTICE THOMAS, dissenting.

[T]he parties agree that a "degree in theology" means a degree that is "devotional in nature or designed to induce religious faith." * * * With this understanding, I join Justice Scalia's dissenting opinion. I write separately to note that, in my view, the study of theology does not necessarily implicate religious devotion or faith. The contested statute denies Promise Scholarships to students who pursue "a degree in theology." But the statute itself does not define "theology." And the usual definition of the term "theology" is not limited to devotional studies. "Theology" is defined as "[t]he study of the nature of God and religious truth" and the "rational inquiry into religious questions." These definitions include the study of theology from a secular perspective as well as from a religious one.

Assuming that the State denies Promise Scholarships only to students who pursue a degree in devotional theology, I believe that Justice Scalia's application of our precedents is correct. Because neither party contests the validity of these precedents, I join Justice Scalia's dissent.

NOTES ON *LOCKE*

1. *Unconstitutional Conditions. Locke* also involved a free speech claim, which the Court brusquely dismissed in footnote three of its opinion:

> Davey, relying on *Rosenberger* [Chapter 6, § 4B], contends that the Promise Scholarship Program is an unconstitutional viewpoint restriction on speech. But the Promise Scholarship Program is not a forum for speech. The purpose of the Promise Scholarship Program is to assist students from low- and middle-income families with the cost of postsecondary education, not to " 'encourage a diversity of views from private speakers.' " Our cases dealing with speech forums are simply inapplicable.

> Davey also argues that the Equal Protection Clause protects against discrimination on the basis of religion. Because we hold that the program is not a violation of the Free Exercise Clause, however, we apply rational-basis scrutiny to his equal protection claims. For the reasons stated herein, the program passes such review.

Is this analysis consistent with *Rosenberger*? With *Velazquez*?

2. *Voucher Programs.* Based on *Locke*, is it clear that the state can exclude primarily sectarian schools from voucher programs? Is this the sort of decision that should be left to legislatures, or (as Justice Scalia suggests) should policing the boundaries of state funding for religion be a job for the courts?

3. *A Cryptic Dissent?* Justice Thomas joins Scalia's dissent only on the basis of an understanding that the statute includes only devotional theological studies. Does that mean that he would uphold a ban that covered all study, whether devotional or secular? Also note that he agrees with Scalia's interpretation of existing precedent, carefully adding that the parties have not challenged that precedent. Does that mean he would reject free exercise cases such as *Lukumi* if the issue were squarely before him?

Chapter 7

FEDERALISM: CONGRESSIONAL POWER AND STATE AUTHORITY

SECTION 1. ENUMERATED FEDERAL POWER, RESERVED STATE AUTHORITY: INTRODUCTION

Our constitutional system contemplates two levels of power, the national power and that of the individual states.[a] Three different types of constitutional issues derive from the federal structure of our government. First, under what circumstances can the national government act? The structure of the Constitution and the expectations of the Framers suggest that Congress could only act pursuant to one of the "enumerated powers," almost all of which are set forth in Article I. As a result, decisions about the reach of the national government's power involve a categorization game, in which proponents try to fit the exercise into one of the enumerated cubbyholes, and opponents argue that no cubbyhole will accommodate the exercise. We trace the history of the most extensive such "game," that involving the Commerce Clause and the regulation of economic activity, in Section 2. Section 3 considers the congressional authority to enact civil rights legislation, which requires an examination of the powers delegated to Congress under the Thirteenth, Fourteenth, and Fifteenth Amendments. Section 4 briefly examines several other potential sources of wideranging congressional authority.

Second, how does this federal power relate to state power? The Constitution makes plain that the states delegated only limited power to the federal government and retained (or "reserved," if you will) general regulatory power — sometimes called the "local police power" — over their geographic domains and the persons within them. It is inevitable under such a federal structure that conflicting claims of state and national power will arise. The Supremacy Clause of Article VI tells us that a constitutional exercise of congressional power is the supreme law of the land, displacing any state laws inconsistent with it. This "preemption" doctrine is discussed in Section 6, but has important implications throughout the chapter. For instance, many of the cases examined in Sections

---

a. A third layer of government exists in areas within the sovereignty of Indian tribes. The complex questions of federal Indian law are beyond the scope of this course, but we do introduce them briefly in the Note on Triadic Federalism: Indian Tribal Sovereignty, at the end of this chapter.

2, 3, and 4 consider claims that the supremacy of federal power must be carefully confined to its constitutionally defined spheres, lest Congress run roughshod over appropriate state authority to regulate the persons found within their borders. In addition, as Section 5 demonstrates, as a further protection of state autonomy from federal encroachment, the Supreme Court has found an implicit "intergovernmental immunity doctrine," which limits congressional power to regulate the states themselves (and not merely persons found within the states).

Third, in what ways does the Constitution limit the exercise of state power? Of course, Chapters 2-6 considered several important such limitations found in the First, Fourteenth, and Fifteenth Amendments. Section 6 of this chapter considers several more limitations upon state power that are more directly related to our federal structure of shared power between the national and state governments. In addition to the preemption doctrine briefly explained above, Section 6 traces approaches that sometimes prevent the states from taking advantage of our federal structure to benefit their citizens at the expense of citizens of other states. It considers an express constitutional limitation to this effect, the Privileges and Immunities Clause of Article IV, and an implicit limitation, the so-called "dormant commerce clause doctrine," which seeks to prevent states from regulating interstate commerce in ways that discriminate in favor of in-state economic interests.

All three of these issues are implicated in our opening case, *McCulloch v. Maryland*, which is viewed by some as "the greatest decision John Marshall ever handed down — the one most important to the future of America, most influential in the Court's own doctrinal history, and most revealing of Marshall's unique talent for stately argument."[b] We start with this case not only because it is a "great case" raising all these issues in a single opinion, but also because it illustrates important themes of constitutional decisionmaking — reasoning from the constitutional structure, the role of original intent in constitutional decisionmaking, and the representation-reinforcement theory of judicial review. Think more broadly. What are the origins of national sovereignty? What is the proper relationship between state and federal sovereignty? What is federalism good for?

McCULLOCH v. MARYLAND
17 U.S. (4 Wheat.) 316, 4 L.Ed. 579 (1819)

CHIEF JUSTICE MARSHALL delivered the opinion of the Court.

[Congress created the Second Bank of the United States in 1816 to provide loans to the national government and assist in the collection of taxes (see Note 1 following this case for background history). The Bank was blamed for the economic recession of 1818, and several states sought to tax it. One was Maryland, which sued James McCulloch, cashier of the Baltimore branch of the

---

b. Robert McCloskey, *The American Supreme Court* 66 (1960).

Bank,[c] when the Bank refused to pay. Maryland argued that the Bank's charter was itself invalid legislation and that, in any event, the states have authority to tax national instrumentalities such as the Bank.]

The first question made in the cause is, has Congress power to incorporate a bank?

It has been truly said, that this can scarcely be considered as an open question, entirely unprejudiced by the former proceedings of the nation respecting it. The principle now contested was introduced at a very early period of our history, has been recognized by many successive legislatures, and has been acted upon by the judicial department, in cases of peculiar delicacy, as a law of undoubted obligation.

It will not be denied, that a bold and daring usurpation might be resisted, after an acquiescence still longer and more complete than this. But it is conceived, that a doubtful question, one on which human reason may pause, and the human judgment be suspended, in the decision of which the great principles of liberty are not concerned, but the respective powers of those who are equally the representatives of the people, are to be adjusted; if not put at rest by the practice of the government, ought to receive a considerable impression from that practice. An exposition of the constitution, deliberately established by legislative acts, on the faith of which an immense property has been advanced, ought not to be lightly disregarded.

The power now contested was exercised by the first Congress elected under the present constitution. The bill for incorporating the [first] bank of the United States did not steal upon an unsuspecting legislature, and pass unobserved. Its principle was completely understood, and was opposed with equal zeal and ability. After being resisted, first in the fair and open field of debate, and afterwards in the executive cabinet, with as much persevering talent as any measure has ever experienced, and being supported by arguments which convinced minds as pure and as intelligent as this country can boast, it became a law. The original act was permitted to expire; but a short experience of the embarrassments to which the refusal to revive it exposed the government, convinced those who were most prejudiced against the measure of its necessity, and induced the passage of the present law. It would require no ordinary share of intrepidity to assert that a measure adopted under these circumstances was a bold and plain usurpation, to which the constitution gave no countenance. * * *

In discussing this question, the counsel for the State of Maryland have deemed it of some importance, in the construction of the constitution, to consider that instrument not as emanating from the people, but as the act of sovereign and independent States. The powers of the general government, it has been said, are delegated by the States, who alone are truly sovereign; and must

---

c. *Editors' note:* McCulloch was himself a controversial figure, hated in Maryland as an important lobbyist for the Bank in Washington and suspected of looting the Bank by making unsecured loans to cronies. He was removed from office shortly after his case was decided. Later he was unsuccessfully criminally prosecuted by Maryland.

be exercised in subordination to the States, who alone possess supreme dominion.

It would be difficult to sustain this proposition. The Convention which framed the constitution was indeed elected by the State legislatures. But the instrument, when it came from their hands, was a mere proposal, without obligations, or pretensions to it. * * * [This] instrument was submitted to the people. They acted upon it in the only manner in which they can act safely, effectively, and wisely, on such a subject, by assembling in Convention [, from which] the constitution derives its whole authority. The government proceeds directly from the people. * * *

The government of the Union, then, * * * is, emphatically, and truly, a government of the people. In form and in substance it emanates from them. Its powers are granted by them, and are to be exercised directly on them, and for their benefit.

This government is acknowledged by all to be one of enumerated powers. The principle, that it can exercise only the powers granted to it, * * * is now universally admitted. But the question respecting the extent of the powers actually granted, is perpetually arising, and will probably continue to arise, as long as our system shall exist. * * *

If any one proposition could command the universal assent of mankind, we might expect it would be this — that the government of the Union, though limited in its powers, is supreme within its sphere of action. This would seem to result necessarily from its nature. It is the government of all; its powers are delegated by all; it represents all, and acts for all. Though any one State may be willing to control its operations, no State is willing to allow others to control them. The nation, on those subjects on which it can act, must necessarily bind its component parts. But this question is not left to mere reason: the people have, in express terms, decided it, by saying, "this constitution, and the laws of the United States, which shall be made in pursuance thereof," "shall be the supreme law of the land," and by requiring that the members of the State legislatures, and the officers of the executive and judicial departments of the States, shall take the oath of fidelity to it.

Among the enumerated powers, we do not find that of establishing a bank or creating a corporation. But there is no phrase in the instrument which, like the articles of confederation, excludes incidental or implied powers; and which requires that everything granted shall be expressly and minutely described. Even the 10th amendment, which was framed for the purpose of quieting the excessive jealousies which had been excited, omits the word "expressly," and declares only that the powers "not delegated to the United States, nor prohibited to the States, are reserved to the States or to the people;" thus leaving the question, whether the particular power which may become the subject of contest has been delegated to the one government, or prohibited to the other, to depend on a fair construction of the whole instrument. The men who drew and adopted this amendment had experienced the embarrassments resulting from the insertion of this word in the articles of confederation, and probably omitted it to avoid those embarrassments. A constitution, to contain an accurate detail of all the subdivisions of which its great powers will admit, and of all the means by which they may be carried into execution, would partake of the prolixity of a legal code, and could scarcely be embraced by the human mind. It would probably never be understood by the public. Its nature, therefore, requires, that only its great outlines should be marked, its important objects designated, and the minor ingredients which compose those objects be deduced from the nature of the objects themselves. That this idea was entertained by the framers of the American constitution, is not only to be inferred from the nature of the instrument, but from the language. Why else were some of the limitations, found in the ninth section of the 1st article, introduced? It is also, in some degree, warranted by their having omitted to use any restrictive term which might prevent its receiving a fair and just interpretation. In considering this question, then, we must never forget, that it is a *constitution* we are expounding.

Although, among the enumerated powers of government, we do not find the word "bank" or "incorporation," we find the great powers to lay and collect taxes; to borrow money; to regulate commerce; to declare and conduct a war; and to raise and support armies and navies. The sword and the purse, all the external relations, and no inconsiderable portion of the industry of the nation, are entrusted to its government. It can never be pretended that these vast powers draw after them others of inferior importance, merely because they are inferior. Such an idea can never be advanced. But it may with great reason be contended, that a government, entrusted with such ample powers, on the due execution of which the happiness and prosperity of the nation so vitally depends, must also be entrusted with ample means for their execution. The power being given, it is the interest of the nation to facilitate its execution. It can never be their interest, and cannot be presumed to have been their intention, to clog and embarrass its execution by withholding the most appropriate means. Throughout this vast republic, from the St. Croix to the Gulf of Mexico, from the Atlantic to the Pacific, revenue is to be collected and expended, armies are to be marched and supported. The exigencies of the nation may require that the treasure raised in the north should be transported to the south, that raised in the east conveyed to the west, or that this order should be reversed. Is that construction of the constitution to be preferred which would render these operations difficult, hazardous, and expensive? Can we adopt that construction, (unless the words imperiously require it,) which would impute to the framers of that instrument, when granting these powers for the public good, the intention of impeding their exercise by withholding a choice of means? If, indeed, such be the mandate of the constitution, we have only to obey; but that instrument does not profess to enumerate the means by which the powers it confers may be executed; nor does it prohibit the creation of a corporation, if the existence of such a being be essential to the beneficial exercise of those powers. It is, then, the subject of fair inquiry, how far such means may be employed.

It is not denied, that the powers given to the government imply the ordinary means of execution. That, for example, of raising revenue, and applying it to national purposes, is admitted to imply the power of conveying money from place to place, as the exigencies of the nation require, and of employing the usual means of conveyance. * * *

But the constitution of the United States has not left the right of Congress to employ the necessary means, for the execution of the powers conferred on the government, to general reasoning. To its enumeration of powers is added that of making "all laws which shall be necessary and proper, for carrying into execution the foregoing powers, and all other powers vested by this constitution, in the government of the United States, or in any department thereof."

The counsel for the State of Maryland have urged various arguments, to prove that this clause, though in terms a grant of power, is not so in effect; but is really restrictive of the general right, which might otherwise be implied, of selecting means for executing the enumerated powers. * * *

[The] argument on which most reliance is placed, is drawn from the peculiar language of this clause. Congress is not empowered by it to make all laws, which may have relation to the powers conferred on the government, but such only as may be *"necessary and proper"* for carrying them into execution. The word *"necessary,"* is considered as controlling the whole sentence, and as limiting the right to pass laws for the execution of the granted powers, to such as are indispensable, and without which the power would be nugatory. That it excludes the choice of means, and leaves to Congress, in each case, that only which is most direct and simple.

Is it true, that this is the sense in which the word "necessary" is always used? Does it always import an absolute physical necessity, so strong, that one thing, to which another may be termed necessary, cannot exist without that other? * * * To employ the means necessary to an end, is generally understood as employing any means calculated to produce the end, and not as being confined to those single means, without which the end would be entirely unattainable. * * * The word "necessary" * * * has not a fixed character peculiar to itself. It admits of all degrees of comparison; and is often connected with other words, which increase or diminish the impression the mind receives of the urgency it imports. A thing may be necessary, very necessary, absolutely or indispensably necessary. To no mind would the same idea be conveyed, by these several phrases. This comment on the word is well illustrated, by the passage cited at the bar, from the 10th section of the 1st article of the constitution. It is, we think, impossible to compare the sentence which prohibits a State from laying "imposts, or duties on imports or exports, except what may be *absolutely* necessary for executing its inspection laws," with that which authorizes Congress "to make all laws which shall be necessary and proper for carrying into execution" the powers of the general government, without feeling a conviction that the convention understood itself to change materially the meaning of the word "necessary," by prefixing the word "absolutely." This word, then, like others, is used in various senses; and, in its construction, the subject, the context, the intention of the person using them, are all to be taken into view.

* * * It must have been the intention of those who gave these powers, to insure, as far as human prudence could insure, their beneficial execution. This could not be done by confiding the choice of means to such narrow limits as not to leave it in the power of Congress to adopt any which might be appropriate, and which were conducive to the end. This provision is made in a constitution

intended to endure for ages to come, and, consequently, to be adapted to the various *crises* of human affairs. To have prescribed the means by which government should, in all future time, execute its powers, would have been to change, entirely, the character of the instrument, and give it the properties of a legal code. It would have been an unwise attempt to provide, by immutable rules, for exigencies which, if foreseen at all, must have been seen dimly, and which can be best provided for as they occur. * * * If we apply this principle of construction to any of the powers of the government, we shall find it so pernicious in its operation that we shall be compelled to discard it. * * *

So, with respect to the whole penal code of the United States: whence arises the power to punish in cases not prescribed by the constitution? All admit that the government may, legitimately, punish any violation of its laws; and yet, this is not among the enumerated powers of Congress. The right to enforce the observance of law, by punishing its infraction, might be denied with the more plausibility, because it is expressly given in some cases. Congress is empowered "to provide for the punishment of counterfeiting the securities and current coin of the United States," and "to define and punish piracies and felonies committed on the high seas, and offences against the law of nations." The several powers of Congress may exist, in a very imperfect state to be sure, but they may exist and be carried into execution, although no punishment should be inflicted in cases where the right to punish is not expressly given.

Take, for example, the power "to establish post offices and post roads." This power is executed by the single act of making the establishment. But, from this has been inferred the power and duty of carrying the mail along the post road, from one post office to another. And, from this implied power, has again been inferred the right to punish those who steal letters from the post office, or rob the mail. It may be said, with some plausibility, that the right to carry the mail, and to punish those who rob it, is not indispensably necessary to the establishment of a post office and post road. This right is indeed essential to the beneficial exercise of power, but not indispensably necessary to its existence. * * *

In ascertaining the sense in which the word "necessary" is used in this clause of the constitution, we may derive some aid from that with which it is associated. Congress shall have power "to make all laws which shall be necessary and proper to carry into execution" the powers of the government. If the word "necessary" was used in that strict and rigorous sense for which the counsel for the State of Maryland contend, it would be an extraordinary departure from the usual course of the human mind, as exhibited in composition, to add a word, the only possible effect of which is to qualify that strict and rigorous meaning; to present to the mind the idea of some choice of means of legislation not straitened and compressed within the narrow limits for which gentlemen contend.

But the argument which most conclusively demonstrates the error of the construction contended for by the counsel for the State of Maryland, is founded on the intention of the Convention, as manifested in the whole clause. To waste time and argument in proving that, without it, Congress might carry its powers into execution, would be not much less idle than to hold a lighted taper to the sun. * * * We think so for the following reasons:

1st. The clause is placed among the powers of Congress, not among the limitations on those powers.

2nd. Its terms purport to enlarge, not to diminish the powers vested in the government. It purports to be an additional power, not a restriction on those already granted. No reason has been, or can be assigned for thus concealing an intention to narrow the discretion of the national legislature under words which purport to enlarge it. * * *

The result of the most careful and attentive consideration bestowed upon this clause is, that if it does not enlarge, it cannot be construed to restrain the powers of Congress, or to impair the right of the legislature to exercise its best judgment in the selection of measures to carry into execution the constitutional powers of the government. If no other motive for its insertion can be suggested, a sufficient one is found in the desire to remove all doubts respecting the right to legislate on that vast mass of incidental powers which must be involved in the constitution, if that instrument be not a splendid bauble.

We admit, as all must admit, that the powers of the government are limited, and that its limits are not to be transcended. But we think the sound construction of the constitution must allow to the national legislature that discretion, with respect to the means by which the powers it confers are to be carried into execution, which will enable that body to perform the high duties assigned to it, in the manner most beneficial to the people. Let the end be legitimate, let it be within the scope of the constitution, and all means which are appropriate, which are plainly adapted to that end, which are not prohibited, but consist with the letter and spirit of the constitution, are constitutional. * * *

If a corporation may be employed indiscriminately with other means to carry into execution the powers of the government, no particular reason can be assigned for excluding the use of a bank, if required for its fiscal operations. To use one, must be within the discretion of Congress, if it be an appropriate mode of executing the powers of government. That it is a convenient, a useful, and essential instrument in the prosecution of its fiscal operations, is not now a subject of controversy. * * *

But, were its necessity less apparent, none can deny its being an appropriate measure; and if it is, the degree of its necessity, as has been very justly observed, is to be discussed in another place. Should Congress, in the execution of its powers, adopt measures which are prohibited by the constitution; or should Congress, under the pretext of executing its powers, pass laws for the accomplishment of objects not entrusted to the government; it would become the painful duty of this tribunal, should a case requiring such a decision come before it, to say that such an act was not the law of the land. But where the law is not prohibited, and is really calculated to effect any of the objects entrusted to the government, to undertake here to inquire into the degree of its necessity, would be to pass the line which circumscribes the judicial department, and to tread on legislative ground. This court disclaims all pretensions to such a power. * * *

It being the opinion of the Court, that the act incorporating the bank is constitutional; and that the power of establishing a branch in the State of Maryland might be properly exercised by the bank itself, we proceed to inquire—

2. Whether the State of Maryland may, without violating the constitution, tax that branch?

That the power of taxation is one of vital importance; that it is retained by the States; that it is not abridged by the grant of a similar power to the government of the Union; that it is to be concurrently exercised by the two governments: are truths which have never been denied. But, such is the paramount character of the constitution that its capacity to withdraw any subject from the action of even this power, is admitted. The States are expressly forbidden to lay any duties on imports or exports, except what may be absolutely necessary for executing their inspection laws. If the obligation of this prohibition must be conceded — if it may restrain a State from the exercise of its taxing power on imports and exports — the same paramount character would seem to restrain, as it certainly may restrain, a State from such other exercise of this power, as is in its nature incompatible with, and repugnant to, the constitutional laws of the Union. A law, absolutely repugnant to another, as entirely repeals that other as if express terms of repeal were used.

On this ground the counsel for the bank place its claim to be exempted from the power of a State to tax its operations. There is no express provision for the case, but the claim has been sustained on a principle which so entirely pervades the constitution, is so intermixed with the materials which compose it, so interwoven with its web, so blended with its texture, as to be incapable of being separated from it without rending it into shreds.

This great principle is, that the constitution and the laws made in pursuance thereof are supreme; that they control the constitution and laws of the respective States, and cannot be controlled by them. * * *

That the power to tax involves the power to destroy; that the power to destroy may defeat and render useless the power to create; that there is a plain repugnance, in conferring on one government a power to control the constitutional measures of another, which other, with respect to those very measures, is declared to be supreme over that which exerts the control, are propositions not to be denied. But all inconsistencies are to be reconciled by the magic of the word *confidence.* Taxation, it is said, does not necessarily and unavoidably destroy. To carry it to the excess of destruction would be an abuse, to presume which, would banish that confidence which is essential to all government.

But is this a case of confidence? Would the people of any one State trust those of another with a power to control the most insignificant operations of their State government? We know they would not. Why then, should we suppose that the people of any one State should be willing to trust those of another with a power to control the operations of a government to which they have confided the most important and most valuable interests? In the legislature of the Union alone, are all represented. The legislature of the Union alone, therefore, can be trusted by the people with the power of controlling measures which concern all, in the confidence that it will not be abused. This, then, is not a case of confidence, and we must consider it as it really is. * * *

If the States may tax one instrument, employed by the government in the execution of its powers, they may tax any and every other instrument. They may tax the mail; they may tax the mint; they may tax patent-rights; they may tax the papers of the custom-house; they may tax judicial process, they may tax all the means employed by the government, to an excess which would defeat all the ends of government. This was not intended by the American people. They did not design to make their government dependent on the States. * * *

It has also been insisted, that, as the power of taxation in the general and State governments is acknowledged to be concurrent, every argument which would sustain the right of the general government to tax banks chartered by the States, will equally sustain the right of the States to tax banks chartered by the general government.

But the two cases are not on the same reason. The people of all the States have created the general government, and have conferred upon it the general power of taxation. The people of all the States, and the States themselves, are represented in Congress, and, by their representatives, exercise this power. When they tax the chartered institutions of the States, they tax their constituents; and these taxes must be uniform. But, when a State taxes the operations of the government of the United States, it acts upon institutions created, not by their own constituents, but by people over whom they claim no control. It acts upon the measures of a government created by others as well as themselves, for the benefit of others in common with themselves. The difference is that which always exists, and always must exist, between the action of the whole on a part, and the action of a part on the whole — between the laws of a government declared to be supreme, and those of a government which, when in opposition to those laws, is not supreme.

But if the full application of this argument could be admitted, it might bring into question the right of Congress to tax the State banks, and could not prove the right of the States to tax the Bank of the United States.

The court has bestowed on this subject its most deliberate consideration. The result is a conviction that the States have no power, by taxation or otherwise to retard, impede, burden, or in any manner control the operations of the constitutional laws enacted by Congress to carry into execution the powers vested in the general government. This is, we think, the unavoidable consequence of that supremacy which the constitution has declared.

We are unanimously of opinion that the law passed by the legislature of Maryland, imposing a tax on the Bank of the United States, is unconstitutional and void.

This opinion does not deprive the States of any resources which they originally possessed. It does not extend to a tax paid by the real property of the bank, in common with the other real property within the State, nor to a tax imposed on the interest which the citizens of Maryland may hold in this institution, in common with other property of the same description throughout the State. But this is a tax on the operations of the bank, and is, consequently, a tax on the operation of an instrument employed by the government of the Union to carry its powers into execution. Such a tax must be unconstitutional.

NOTES ON CONSTITUTIONAL REASONING IN *McCULLOCH*: ORIGINAL INTENT, CONSTITUTIONAL STRUCTURES AND REPRESENTATION REINFORCEMENT

1. *Original Intent: The Curious Role of History in the Bank Case.* During the Philadelphia Convention in 1787, Madison proposed that Congress in Article I, § 8, be empowered "to grant charters of incorporation," but the Convention rejected this suggestion. Chief Justice Marshall does not mention this argument, and slides by the question of original intent by invoking something like a constitutional rule of adverse possession: Because the political system has acquiesced in the Bank's constitutionality for so long, it would require extremely strong arguments to invalidate the Bank. Persuasive? Why isn't the rejection of the power to incorporate banks at the Philadelphia Convention precisely the sort of strong argument needed to rebut the long acquiescence? Consider the following history of the argument from the rejected proposal.[d]

Within three years of the Convention, legislation creating the Bank sailed through the Senate, about half of whose Members in 1790 had been at the Philadelphia Convention. The records reveal no objections in the Senate that were based upon the original expectations of the Framers. Madison, who had proposed a clause authorizing national banks at the Philadelphia Convention, raised a constitutional objection to the bank bill in the House, but virtually no one else expressed interest in the argument, and the House passed the bill overwhelmingly.

Before signing the bill, President Washington asked for the advice of his cabinet. Secretary of State Thomas Jefferson opposed the Bank, at least in part on constitutional grounds. He relied on the Tenth Amendment and the requirement in Article I, § 8 that "the Constitution allows only the means which are necessary, not merely 'convenient,' for effecting the enumerated powers. If such a latitude of construction be allowed to this phrase as to give any non-enumerated power [to Congress], it would swallow up all the delegated powers, and reduce the whole to one power." 19 *Papers of Thomas Jefferson* 275, 278 (1974) ("Opinion on the Constitutionality of the Bill for Establishing a National Bank"). Attorney General Edmund Randolph and Secretary of Treasury Alexander Hamilton rejected the relevance of arguments based upon original intent and argued that the text of the Constitution gave firm support to the validity of the Bank charter. Hamilton claimed that the Bank charter had "a relation more or less direct to the power of collecting taxes; to that of borrowing money; to that of regulating trade between the states; and to those of raising,

---

d. See Paul Finkelman, *The Constitution and the Intentions of the Framers: The Limits of Historical Analysis*, 50 U. Pitt. L. Rev. 349, 358-71 (1989); David McGowan, *Ethos in Law and History: Alexander Hamilton*, The Federalist, *and the Supreme Court*, 85 Minn. L. Rev. 794, 804-19 (2001).

supporting & maintaining fleets and armies." If more confirmation were needed, Hamilton argued, it came from the Necessary and Proper Clause. Against Jefferson, Hamilton argued that the term "necessary" means "no more than needful, requisite, incidental, useful, or conducive to." 8 *Papers of Alexander Hamilton* 97 (1965) ("Opinion on the Constitutionality of an Act to Establish a Bank"). The President signed the Bank bill into law.

Congress declined to recharter the bank in 1811, but the War of 1812 fueled a ruinous inflation that impelled Congress to pass a new charter in 1815. President Madison vetoed it — but not for constitutional reasons. The earlier objections were "precluded by repeated recognitions under varied circumstances of the validity of such an institution in acts of the legislative, executive, and judicial branches of the Government." Within a year, Congress passed a bill that President Madison could sign, and the second Bank was established in 1816. What conclusions might you draw about constitutional theory from the debates about the Bank's constitutionality in 1790, and the nondebate in 1815-16? About *McCulloch* generally?

2. *The Text: Structural Arguments.* Notice how deftly the Chief Justice leaps over the technical argument that there is no clause in Article I, § 8 listing the chartering of banks as an enumerated power of Congress. Separate out the many arguments Marshall uses to dance around this omission and consider whether those textual arguments escape the dilemma.

(a) *Nature of constitutions.* What does the Chief Justice mean when he says "that it is a *constitution* we are expounding"? Does he mean that, unlike a statute, a constitution should be interpreted flexibly over time to subserve its purposes of an organizationally flourishing government? (If so, why shouldn't statutes be interpreted the same way?) Or should only certain parts of a constitution be interpreted so liberally? Philip Kurland, *Curia Regis: Some Comments on the Divine Right of Kings and Courts "to Say What the Law Is,"* 23 Ariz L. Rev. 582, 591 (1981), argues that when modern judges cite to this precept from *McCulloch* "you can be sure that the court will be throwing the constitutional text, its history, and its structure to the winds in reaching its conclusion." Is this a fair statement of Chief Justice Marshall's methodology?

(b) *Textual context.* Note the Chief Justice's strategy in massaging the word "necessary." He argues that the word has several different dictionary meanings and that the precise meaning depends on context. Then he observes that in Article I, § 10, the Constitution prohibits state taxes on imports and exports, "except what may be *absolutely* necessary for executing its inspection laws." The Chief Justice infers also from the words associated with necessary, mainly "proper," and suggests that the associated words further clarify the meaning of necessary. Finally, he looks to the "whole clause" and its purpose and argues that Maryland's strict interpretation of "necessary" would "almost annihilate" the usefulness of the clause. This is confirmed by the placement of the Necessary and Proper Clause "among the powers of Congress." Since the clause is part of the empowering provisions, Chief Justice Marshall posits that it must be broadly construed.

Are these arguments persuasive, either individually or collectively? If they are persuasive, is the Chief Justice right in his final argument that the Bank passes the "convenience" test? Are there any limits to the Chief Justice's test: "Let the end be legitimate * * * and all means which are appropriate, which are plainly adapted to that end, which are not prohibited * * * are constitutional"?

(c) *Constitutional principles.* Note that the Chief Justice's textual arguments become even more abstract when he reaches the second part of his opinion, dealing with the federal immunity from state taxation. There is no precise clause to analyze here, but Marshall creates his own text by seizing upon "a principle which so entirely pervades the constitution" that it must be considered as important as the actual written text. The great principle is the supremacy of the national power from state interference. Where does the Chief Justice find that principle in the Constitution? How does it support his holding that Maryland cannot tax the operations of the Bank?

3. *Representation-Reinforcement Argument.* The most celebrated argument in *McCulloch* is the representation-reinforcement one at the end: The United States and its instrumentalities are vulnerable to attack by the state political processes, because they are not "represented" therein, and hence the Court has a special duty to protect the United States against potentially oppressive laws. The obverse, however, is not true: The United States can tax the states (so long as such taxation is "uniform"), which are well represented in the national legislature.

Is this distinction persuasive as a general proposition? Why should we care that the United States is not "well represented" in state legislatures, since Congress can simply expressly preempt state legislation that unduly penalizes it? Why isn't that a more than adequate political process check on the states? Moreover, as a policy matter, shouldn't the states be able to tax U.S. instrumentalities on a nondiscriminatory basis? *McCulloch* can be read to suggest that even non-discriminatory taxes are invalid, as the opinion emphasizes the destructive potential of taxation, but the representation-reinforcement rationale ought not apply when there is no indication that the state is treating the United States' instrumentality any differently from other corporations.

Consider, also, that the *McCulloch* formulation is asymmetrical, protecting the United States against state taxation but not necessarily vice versa. Are the states really protected against unfair treatment because they are "represented" in the national legislature? Does the Chief Justice's argument depend upon the fact that before the Seventeenth Amendment the state legislatures elected U.S. senators (Art. I, § 3, cl. 1)? If so, what about today, when senators are elected directly by the people?

———

U.S. Term Limits, Inc. v. Thornton, 514 U.S. 779 (1995). In 1992, Arkansas voters amended the state constitution to prevent certification as a candidate for the U.S. House from Arkansas any person already elected to three or more House terms, and as a candidate for the U.S. Senate from Arkansas any person already elected to two or more Senate terms. Read the Constitution. Is there an answer suggested by the text and structure? The Supreme Court was passionately divided on this issue, with five Justices voting to invalidate the amendment. Apart from a debate about the originalist sources, the case generated a debate over the nature of the federalist arrangement, because one's resolution of the interpretive issue depended in large part upon the normative baseline about federal/state sovereignty from which one started.

Proponents of state-imposed term limits on federal officials argued that because the Constitution does not expressly prohibit them, the states are authorized to impose them. The opinion for the Court by **Justice Stevens** followed Chief Justice Marshall's opinion in *Sturges v. Crowninshield*, 4 Wheat. 122, 193 (1819) (as well as *McCulloch*), and Hamilton's *Federalist* No. 32, to read the Constitution and the Tenth Amendment to stand for the proposition that the states retained all the rights of sovereignty they had before 1789, except those divested of the states by the Constitution. The national government, in turn, owed its sovereignty, not to the states, but directly to "We the People."

Under this view of federal/state sovereignty, Stevens rejected the proponents' argument on the grounds that the power to add qualifications was not within the original powers of the pre-Constitution states, and that the Framers intended that the Constitution be the exclusive source of qualifications for members of Congress. As to the first reason, Justice Stevens interpreted *McCulloch* to stand for the proposition that, before the federal government existed, the states had no original power to tax federal entities (*McCulloch*) or to regulate federal representatives (*U.S. Term Limits*). As to the second reason, the Constitution generally and the Qualifications Clauses in particular assured that for the "National Government, representatives owe primary allegiance not to the people of a State, but to the people of the Nation." See also Art. I, § 5, cl. 1; § 6. Compare Art. II, § 1, cl. 2; *Powell v. McCormack*, 395 U.S. 486 (1969) (surveying originalist evidence).

Justice Thomas, joined by **Chief Justice Rehnquist** and **Justices O'Connor** and **Scalia**, dissented. He started with a different baseline for thinking about federal sovereignty: "The ultimate source of the Constitution's authority is the consent of the people of each individual State, not the consent of the undifferentiated people of the Nation as a whole.

"The ratification procedure erected by Article VII makes this point clear. The Constitution took effect once it had been ratified by the people gathered in convention in nine different States. But the Constitution went into effect only 'between the States so ratifying the same,' Art. VII; it did not bind the people of North Carolina until they had accepted it. In Madison's words, the popular consent upon which the Constitution's authority rests was 'given by the people, not as individuals composing one entire nation, but as composing the distinct and independent States to which they respectively belong.' *The Federalist* No. 39."

Because the federal government is a creature of state agreement, its powers are narrowly limited to those enumerated in the Constitution; conversely, state powers remain plenary, unlimited except insofar as the Constitution limits them. "In each State, the remainder of the people's powers — '[t]he powers not delegated to the United States by the Constitution, nor prohibited by it to the

States,' Amdt. 10 — are either delegated to the state government or retained by the people. The Federal Constitution does not specify which of these two possibilities obtains; it is up to the various state constitutions to declare which powers the people of each State have delegated to their state government. As far as the Federal Constitution is concerned, then, the States can exercise all powers that the Constitution does not withhold from them. The Federal Government and the States thus face different default rules: where the Constitution is silent about the exercise of a particular power — that is, where the Constitution does not speak either expressly or by necessary implication — the Federal Government lacks that power and the States enjoy it."

Justice Kennedy concurred in the opinion for the Court and wrote a separate opinion responding to Justice Thomas' theory of federal/state sovereignty. "Federalism was our Nation's own discovery. The Framers split the atom of sovereignty. It was the genius of their idea that our citizens would have two political capacities, one state and one federal, each protected from incursion by the other. The resulting Constitution created a legal system unprecedented in form and design, establishing two orders of government, each with its own direct relationship, its own privity, its own set of mutual rights and obligations to the people who sustain it and are governed by it. *McCulloch*." Because the Arkansas amendment directly affected the unique federal right to vote, a right also implicating the First Amendment, Justice Kennedy believed it crossed the line. But his concurring opinion emphasized, contrary to *McCulloch*, that the states must be equally well-protected against federal incursions.

NOTE ON THEORIES OF FEDERAL/STATE SOVEREIGNTY AND ON THE ADVANTAGES OF A FEDERALIST ARRANGEMENT

Step back from the debate over the precise powers at issue in the National Bank and Term Limits Cases. In analyzing the issues throughout this chapter, the baseline matters. Who has it right: Marshall (*McCulloch*, followed in *U.S. Term Limits*) or Thomas (the dissent in *Term Limits*) or Kennedy (concurring in *Term Limits*)? In resolving this issue in your own mind, you might consider, first, the text and debates behind the Constitution of 1789. Most of the relevant sources are in appendices to this casebook: the Constitution, of course (App. 1); the letter from George Washington, president of the Convention, speaking for the Convention on these issues (App. 2); and *Federalist* No. 51 (App. 2). Which view of federal/state sovereignty do these sources support?[e]

A second source of materials would be the Reconstruction Amendments to the Constitution and their debating history, recounted in Chapter 2. Do the Civil War and the Reconstruction Amendments reflect a victory of Lincoln's view, which was even more nationalistic than Marshall's in *McCulloch*? Or do they leave in place the separate sovereign spheres that New Federalists say prevailed during the Constitution's Founding? If you accept Bruce Ackerman's thesis that

---

e. For speculations in different directions, compare Raoul Berger, *Federalism: The Founders' Design* (1987), with Daniel Farber, *The Constitution's Forgotten Cover Letter: An Essay on the New Federalism and the Original Understanding*, 94 Mich. L. Rev. 615 (1995), and Charles Fried, *Federalism — Why Should We Care?*, 6 Harv. J.L. & Pub. Pol'y 1 (1982).

the New Deal was a third great *constitutional moment*, you are more likely to reject the separate-sovereign-spheres argument entirely.[f]

A third possible source of insight involves an inquiry into the *values or goals* federalism is supposed to play or might productively play in our polity.[g] At least three goals can be identified:

(1) *Protecting Liberty*. Madison in *Federalist* 51 argued that the federal arrangement would assure a "double security" for citizen liberty, because the states would protect citizens against federal overregulation or tyranny. See also Clarence Thomas, *Why Federalism Matters*, 48 Drake L. Rev. 231 (2000). States can accomplish this because they have an independent lobbying voice in the nation's capital, are needed to administer most national programs, and are the building blocks of national political parties (Merritt, *State Autonomy*). If the states balk at bad national regulation, they can stop it or ameliorate its harms by bargaining or ongoing resistance. Nineteenth century abolitionists relied on northern state governments to resist slavery and to protect the liberty of escaped or freed slaves (Chapter 1, § 3). The federal arrangement also provides libertarian sanctuaries for people mistreated in their home states. Women needing birth control advice in the early nineteenth century or abortions before *Roe v. Wade* could move or travel to states whose regulatory regimes were relatively liberal. Racial and sexual minorities brutalized by the police in repressive states could and did move in large numbers to more tolerant states.

On the other hand, the federal arrangement protects both the policies and perhaps also the locked-in political structures of the so-called "repressive" states (Cashin, *Minority Poor*). Indeed, Madison in *Federalist* 10 warned that tyranny

---

f. For example, Robert Bork, *The Tempting of America: The Political Seduction of the Law* 52-58 (1990), argues that the New Deal was nothing of the kind; it was, rather, a constitutional betrayal of federalism.

g. *Gregory v. Ashcroft*, 501 U.S. 452 (1991); *FERC v. Mississippi*, 456 U.S. 742 (1982) (O'Connor, J., dissenting). For academic analyses of the values of a federalist arrangement generally, see Paul Peterson, *The Price of Federalism* (1995); Ann Althouse, *Variations on a Theory of Normative Federalism: A Supreme Court Dialogue*, 42 Duke L.J. 979 (1993); Akhil Amar, *Of Sovereignty and Federalism*, 96 Yale L.J. 1425 (1987); Jenna Bednar & William Eskridge, Jr., *Steadying the Court's "Unsteady Path": A Theory of Judicial Enforcement of Federalism*, 68 S. Cal. L. Rev. 1447 (1995); Michael McConnell, *Federalism: Evaluating the Founders' Design*, 54 U. Chi. L. Rev. 1484 (1987); Deborah Jones Merritt, *Three Faces of Federalism: Finding a Formula for the Future*, 47 Vand. L. Rev. 1563 (1994); Deborah Jones Merritt, *The Guarantee Clause and State Autonomy: Federalism for a Third Century*, 88 Colum. L. Rev. 1 (1988); Edward Purcell, Jr., *Evolving Understandings of American Federalism: Some Shifting Parameters*, 50 N.Y.L. Sch. L.Rev. 635 (2005-06); Gordon Tullock, *Federalism: Problems of Scale*, 6 Pub. Choice 19 (1969); John Yoo, *The Judicial Safeguards of Federalism*, 70 S. Cal. L. Rev. 1311 (1997); Ernest Young, *The Conservative Case for Federalism*, 74 Geo. Wash. L. Rev. 874 (2006). For trenchant critiques, see Sheryll Cashin, *Federalism, Welfare Reform, and the Minority Poor: Accounting for the Tyranny of State Majorities*, 99 Colum. L. Rev. 552 (1999); Frank Cross, *The Folly of Federalism*, 24 Cardozo L. Rev. 1 (2002); Edward Rubin & Malcolm Feeley, *Federalism: Some Notes on a National Neurosis*, 41 UCLA L. Rev. 903 (1994). Responding to Cross, Rubin, and Feeley is Roderick Hills, Jr., *Is Federalism Good for Localism? The Localist Case for Federal Regimes*, 21 J.L. & Pol. 187 (2005).

was more likely in a smaller republic and that this was a republican advantage of a strong national government. Are states likely to protect us against federal overregulation, with the federal government protecting us against state overregulation? Or is there an off-setting danger that a double layer of government (state/federal) will impose a double layer of regulation — a double risk of tyranny?

(2) *Republicanism.* Because citizens are more likely to be politically active at the local level, federalism "assures a decentralized government that will be more sensitive to the diverse needs of a heterogeneous society; it increases opportunity for citizen involvement in the political process; it allows for more innovation and experimentation in government" (*Gregory*, 501 U.S. at 458; see Amar, *Sovereignty and Federalism*; Merritt, *Three Faces*). Most political groups in American history — from Irish and Italian immigrants early in the century, to African Americans after World War II, to women and gay people today — started their political participation and gained a measure of political respectability at the state and local level before becoming nationally significant (Merritt, *State Autonomy*). On the other hand, is *federalism* necessary or even useful for fostering local autonomy in an era where major metropolitan areas cross state boundaries in some regions? (Rubin & Feeley, *National Neurosis* say no; Hills, *Local Case for Federalist Regimes* says yes.) Moreover, as *Federalist* 10 suggested, local governments might also be more prone to ossification and interest-group capture than the national government.

(3) *Efficiency and Diversity.* A third value is efficiency. A federal arrangement allows better satisfaction of peoples' preferences. Assume a unitary state with 100 people, 60 of whom prefer Policy *A* and 40 prefer Policy *B*. Under majority rule, the state will choose Policy *A*, leaving 40 citizens unhappy. If the state were a federation, more citizen preferences could usually be satisfied. Divide up the hypothetical polity in this way (Tullock, *Problems of Scale*):

	Prefer Policy A	Prefer Policy B
Province 1	50	10
Province 2	10	30

Under this scenario, the policies adopted by the different provinces (*A* in Prov. 1, *B* in Prov. 2) would satisfy the preferences of 80 citizens total, already a net gain in overall citizen happiness. If some citizens of each polity "voted with their feet" and moved to satisfy their preferences, even greater satisfaction could be achieved. Finally, the two provinces over time could gauge the relative effectiveness of their different policies, and one policy might prove superior and then be adopted by both.

This simple game dynamic suggests why local allocative and distributive policies (the traditional police powers) are best left to the control of local governments: such governments have an incentive to do the job well, lest they lose citizens to more efficient local governments (Peterson, *Price of Federal-*

ism).[h] This game dynamic also suggests that the federal arrangement can serve the equal citizenship and diversity goals advanced by identity-based social movements. For almost a generation, federalism had a bad odor because southern supporters of apartheid rallied under the constitutional banner of "states rights," but one reason for the success of the civil rights movement was that people of color were able to leave the South and resettle in northern cities, where they were able to exercise political power. Lesbians and gay men have suffered from one discriminatory national program after another, yet have flourished in states like California and Massachusetts, where the local political processes have affirmatively protected them against private discrimination and violence and have recognized their relationships as marriages.

This efficiency value is one that was developed during the twentieth century, and was not important during the framing era (Purcell, *Evolving Understandings of American Federalism*). Should that make a difference? As before, one might ask whether federalism is being confused with localism. Your municipal or county rather than state government picks up the trash and educates your children. Gay men and lesbians have found much more governmental hospitality in New York City than in Albany, the state capital. One response to this concern is the "commitment problem": without some kind of enforcement mechanism to guarantee localism, power will gravitate to the national level, and local governments will lose interest, possibly seeking to break away (Bednar & Eskridge, *Unsteady Path*). This has, in fact, been the fate of most federations, and it might be argued that ours has been unprecedentedly robust in large part because there has been enforcement of federalism outside the ordinary political process.

NOTE ON THE ORIGINAL MEANING

One central purpose of the Philadelphia Convention was to create a government that could act more decisively in the national interest than the Articles of Confederation government had been able to do.[i] Edmund Randolph of Virginia expressed his view of the defects of the Articles on May 29, 1787: (1) They offered little "security against foreign invasion," because the national government lacked the power to tax and raise armies and because the states were free to provoke foreign conflicts. (2) "That there were many advantages, which the U.S. might acquire, which were not attainable under the confederation — such as a productive impost — counteraction of the commercial regulations of other nations — pushing of commerce ad libitum — &c &c." (3)

---

h. Note here that in the nineteenth century, municipal governments were not only the primary regulatory authorities, but regulated pervasively. By the mid-nineteenth century, many local authorities had detailed rules relating to public health, environmental nuisances, criminal offenses, land use, the sale of liquor, the licensing of many businesses and occupations, etc. See William Novak, *The People's Welfare: Law and Regulation in Nineteenth-Century America* (1996).

i. On the discussions about federalism at the Convention and the ratifying debates, see generally Raoul Berger, *Federalism: The Founders' Design* (1987); Daniel Farber & Suzanna Sherry, *A History of the American Constitution* (1990); Daniel Farber, *The Constitution's Forgotten Cover Letter: An Essay on the New Federalism and the Original Understanding*, 94 Mich. L. Rev. 615 (1995). The original sources are generally cited in the text of our explication that follows.

The federal government could not resolve conflicts among the states, could not defend itself against state encroachment, and was not even supreme over state constitutions. II Max Farrand, *The Records of Federal Constitution of 1787*, at 19 (1911) [hereinafter "Farrand"].

There was agreement that the national government had to be more powerful, and much of the debate at the Convention dealt with how to define the national authority. Initially, the grant of power was highly generalized. On May 29, the Convention voted for the Sixth Resolution, which stated: "That the national legislature ought to be empowered to enjoy the legislative rights vested in Congress by the Confederation; and moreover To legislate in all cases to which the separate States are incompetent or in which the harmony of the United States may be interrupted by the exercise of individual legislation." I Farrand 47. Part of the debate is reported in Madison's notes:

> Mr. Pinckney [S. Car.] & Mr. Rutledge [S. Car.] objected to the vagueness of the term *incompetent*, and said they could not well decide how to vote until they should seen an exact enumeration of the powers comprehended by this definition.

> Mr. Butler [S. Car.] repeated his fear that we were running into an extreme in taking away the powers of the States, and called on Mr. Randolph for the extent of his meaning.

> Mr. Randolph [Va.] disclaimed any intention to give indefinite powers to the national Legislature, declaring that he was entirely opposed to such an inroad of the State jurisdictions, and that he did not think any considerations whatever could ever change his determination. His opinion was fixed on this point.

> Mr. Madison [Va.] said that he had brought with him into the Convention a strong bias in favor of an enumeration and definition of the powers necessary to be exercised by the national Legislature; but had also brought doubts concerning its practicability. His wishes remained unaltered; but his doubts had become stronger. What his opinion might ultimately be he could not yet tell. But he should shrink from nothing which should be found essential to such a form of Govt. as would provide for the safety, liberty and happiness of the Community. This being the end of all our deliberations, all the necessary means for attaining it must, however reluctantly be submitted to.

(The States then voted 9-0, with one divided state, in favor of the proposition.)

Later the Convention considered amending the second clause of the Sixth Resolution. One amendment, which read as follows, failed by a 2-8 vote:

> To make laws binding on the People of the United States in all cases which may concern the common interests of the Union; but not to interfere with the government of the individual States in any matters of internal policy, which respect the government of such States only, and wherein the general welfare of the United States is not concerned.

A second amendment to the same clause was adopted by an 8-2 vote:

> and moreover to legislate in all cases for the general interests of the Union, and also in those to which the States are separately incompetent, or in which the harmony of the United States may be interrupted by the exercise of individual legislation.

A third amendment to the same clause was then adopted: "(and moreover) to legislate in all cases for the general interests of the Union, and also in those to which the States are separately incompetent, (or in which the harmony of the U. States may be interrupted by the exercise of individual Legislation)."

On August 6, the Committee of Detail reported a draft Constitution based upon the Resolutions passed by the Convention. Section 1 of Article VII listed 18 enumerated powers of the "Legislature of the United States," very similar to the enumerated powers in the ultimately adopted Article I, § 8. On August 16, the Convention adopted the Committee's recommendation that the Legislature be permitted "To regulate commerce with foreign nations, and among the several States." Southern states subsequently objected that the clause would enable Northern states to obtain advantageous commercial laws, to the detriment of Southern states, and sought to amend the clause to require a two-thirds vote of Congress to enact commercial regulations. The motion was defeated on August 28. Some of the debate (II Farrand 449-53):

> Mr. Sherman [Conn.], alluding to Mr. Pinckney's enumeration of particular interests, as requiring a security agst. abuse of the power; observed that, the diversity was of itself a security, adding that to require more than a majority to decide a question was always embarrassing as had been experience in cases [under the Articles of Confederation] requiring the votes of nine States of Congress. * * *

> Mr. Madison [Va.] went into pretty full view of the subject. He observed that the disadvantage to the S. States from a navigation act, lay chiefly in a temporary rise of freight, attended however with an increase of Southn. as well as Northern Shipping — with the emigration of Northern seamen & merchants to the Southern States — & with a removal of the existing & injurious retaliations among States (on each other). The power of foreign nations to obstruct our retaliating measures on them by a corrupt influence would also be less if a majority shd. be made competent than if 2/3 of each House shd. be required to legislative acts in this case. An abuse of the power would be qualified with all these good effects. But he thought an abuse was rendered improbable by the provision of 2 branches — by the independence of the Senate, by the negative of the Executive, by the interest of Connecticut & New Jersey which were agricultural, not commercial States; by the interior interest which was also agricultural in the most commercial States — by the accession of Western States which wd. be altogether agricultural. He added that the Southern States would derive an essential advantage in the general security afforded by the increase of our maritime strength. He stated the vulnerable situation of them all, and of Virginia in particular. The increase of Coasting trade, and of seamen, would also be favorable to the S. States, by increasing, the consumption of their produce. If the Wealth of the Eastern should be in still greater proportion be augmented, that wealth wd. contribute the more to the public wants, and be otherwise a national benefit.

These excerpts, as well as Numbers 45-46 & 78 of *The Federalist*, give some flavor of the original discussions surrounding the nature and scope of the national legislative authority. On the surface, it seems clear that Congress was expected to exercise only those powers delegated to it, and the Tenth Amendment confirmed that all other powers were reserved to the states or to the people. It is less clear from these original sources how the Framers expected these structural limitations to operate. For example, some debate among the Framers indicated a desire to treat Congress' powers as rather open-ended. Moreover, attempts to modify the language of the Tenth Amendment more clearly to cabin congressional power, by stating that "the powers not *expressly* delegated" to the federal government belonged to the states or the people, failed (Farber & Sherry, *Constitution* 134-42, 241-42).

Our discussion of the powers of the federal Congress in this chapter will be selective, focusing on the Commerce Clause (Section 2) and Congress's authority to enact civil rights legislation (Section 3), which have shown the most interesting development. We shall next turn to the Taxing and Spending Clause and the problem of unconstitutional conditions, along with a brief look at the Treaty Power (Section 4). We shall not deal with other powers of Congress in this chapter, although several of them are involved in our discussion of *McCulloch*. (Chapter 8 will explore Congress' war and foreign affairs powers, especially as they have fallen into competition with those of the President.)

SECTION 2. CONGRESSIONAL POWER UNDER THE COMMERCE CLAUSE

The federal commerce power clearly provides a grant of legislative authority to Congress. It has also been judicially construed to create an implied limitation upon state legislative authority to burden interstate commerce. Congressional power is our primary topic in this section; we turn to implied limits on the states in Section 6A of this chapter.

PROBLEM 7-1
REGULATION OF PUBLIC ACCOMMODATIONS UNDER THE COMMERCE CLAUSE

Consider a federal statute that makes it unlawful for a public accommodation, such as a restaurant, to refuse to serve people on the basis of their race or ethnic background. Assuming that the statute was enacted under Congress' Commerce Clause powers, could it be constitutionally applied to (a) Trader Rick's, a restaurant in a northern Virginia suburb of Washington, D.C., that is located in a posh hotel and caters to customers from out-of-town, especially tourists; (b) The Greasy Spoon, a restaurant in Paw Paw, West Virginia, that is located off a state road and caters to distinctly local clientele, though occasionally an out-of-stater wanders in; (c) Leslie's Lemonade Stand, a neighborhood lemonade stand in Richmond, Virginia, operated two months during the summer by an eight-year-old entrepreneur and serving only a local clientele. Based upon the language of the clause and the Framers' discussions, could Congress regulate any of these businesses under the Commerce Clause? Reconsider your answer after you read each of the major cases reproduced below, namely, *Gibbons v. Ogden, Hammer v. Dagenhart, United States v. Darby, Katzenbach v. McClung,* and *United States v. Lopez.*

GIBBONS v. OGDEN
22 U.S. (9 Wheat.) 1, 6 L.Ed. 23 (1824)

CHIEF JUSTICE MARSHALL delivered the opinion of the Court.

[In 1803, the New York legislature granted Robert Livingston and Robert Fulton an exclusive license to operate steamships in New York waters. Livingston and Fulton assigned Aaron Ogden the right to operate a ferry between New York City and Elizabethtown Point, New Jersey. Thomas Gibbons, a competing ferry operator, technically violated the New York license, because it entered New York waters. But Gibbons' ferries were, however, licensed as "vessels [in] the coasting trade" pursuant to a 1793 federal statute. Ogden obtained an injunction in New York state courts, prohibiting Gibbons from operating his vessels in New York waters. Gibbons appealed, claiming the judgment was inconsistent with the Commerce Clause.]

The subject to be regulated is commerce; and our constitution being, as was aptly said at the bar, one of enumeration, and not of definition, to ascertain the extent of the power, it becomes necessary to settle the meaning of the word. The counsel for the appellee would limit it to traffic, to buying and selling, or the interchange of commodities, and do not admit that it comprehends navigation. This would restrict a general term, applicable to many objects, to one of its significations. Commerce, undoubtedly, is traffic, but it is something more; it is intercourse. It describes the commercial intercourse between nations, and parts of nations, in all its branches, and is regulated by prescribing rules for carrying on that intercourse. The mind can scarcely conceive a system for regulating commerce between nations, which shall exclude all laws concerning navigation, which shall be silent on the admission of the vessels of the one nation into the ports of the other, and be confined to prescribing rules for the conduct of individuals, in the actual employment of buying and selling, or of barter.

If commerce does not include navigation, the government of the Union has no direct power over that subject, and can make no law prescribing what shall constitute American vessels, or requiring that they shall be navigated by American seamen. Yet this power has been exercised from the commencement of the government, has been exercised with the consent of all, and has been understood by all to be a commercial regulation. All America understands, and has uniformly understood, the word "commerce" to comprehend navigation. It was so understood, and must have been so understood when the constitution was framed. The power over commerce, including navigation, was one of the primary objects for which the people of America adopted their government, and must have been contemplated in forming it. The convention must have used the word in that sense; because all have understood it in that sense, and the attempt to restrict it comes too late.

If the opinion that "commerce" as the word is used in the constitution, comprehends navigation also, requires any additional confirmation, that additional confirmation is, we think, furnished by the words of the instrument itself. * * * The 9th section of the 1st article declares, that "no preference shall be given, by any regulation of commerce or revenue, to the ports of one state over those of another." This clause cannot be understood as applicable to those laws only which are passed for the purposes of revenue, because it is expressly applied to commercial regulations; and the most obvious preference which can be given to one port over another, in regulating commerce, relates to navigation. But the subsequent part of the sentence is still more explicit. It is, "nor shall vessels bound to or from one state, be obliged to enter, clear, or pay duties, in another." These words have a direct reference to navigation.

The universally acknowledged power of the government to impose embargoes, must also be considered as showing that all America is united in that construction which comprehends navigation in the word commerce. * * *

The word used in the constitution, then, comprehends, and has been always understood to comprehend, navigation within its meaning; and a power to regulate navigation, is as expressly granted, as if that term had been added to the word "commerce."

To what commerce does this power extend? The constitution informs us, to commerce "with foreign nations, and among the several States, and with the Indian tribes."

It has, we believe, been universally admitted that these words comprehend every species of commercial intercourse between the United States and foreign nations. No sort of trade can be carried on between this country and any other, to which this power does not extend. It has been truly said, that commerce, as the word is used in the constitution, is a unit, every part of which is indicated by the term.

If this be the admitted meaning of the word, in its application to foreign nations, it must carry the same meaning throughout the sentence, and remain a unit, unless there be some plain intelligible cause which alters it.

The subject to which the power is next applied, is to commerce "among the several states." The word "among" means intermingled with. A thing which is among others, is intermingled with them. Commerce among the states cannot stop at the external boundary line of each state, but may be introduced into the interior. It is not intended to say that these words comprehend that commerce, which is completely internal, which is carried on between man and man in a State, or between different parts of the same State, and which does not extend to or affect other states. Such a power would be inconvenient, and is certainly unnecessary.

Comprehensive as the word "among" is, it may very properly be restricted to that commerce which concerns more States than one. The phrase is not one which would probably have been selected to indicate the completely interior traffic of a State, because it is not an apt phrase for that purpose; and the enumeration of the particular classes of commerce to which the power was to be extended, would not have been made had the intention been to extend the power to every description. The enumeration presupposes something not enumerated; and that something, if we regard the language or the subject of the sentence, must be the exclusively internal commerce of a state. The genius and character of the whole government seem to be, that its action is to be applied to all the external concerns of the nation, and to those internal concerns which affect the States generally; but not to those which are completely within a particular state, which do not affect other states, and with which it is not necessary to interfere, for the purpose of executing some of the general powers of the government. The completely internal commerce of a state, then, may be considered as reserved for the state itself.

But, in regarding commerce with foreign nations, the power of Congress does not stop at the jurisdictional lines of the several states. It would be a very useless power, if it could not pass those lines. The commerce of the United States with foreign nations, is that of the whole United States. Every district has a right to participate in it. The deep streams which penetrate our country in every direction, pass through the interior of almost every state in the Union, and furnish the means of exercising this right. If Congress has the power to regulate it, that power must be exercised whenever the subject exists. If it exists within the States, if a foreign voyage may commence or terminate at a port within a State, then the power of Congress may be exercised within a State. * * *

We are now arrived at the inquiry — What is this power?

It is the power to regulate; that is, to prescribe the rule by which commerce is to be governed. This power, like all others vested in Congress, is complete in itself, may be exercised to its utmost extent, and acknowledges no limitations, other than are prescribed in the constitution. These are expressed in plain terms, and do not affect the questions which arise in this case, or which have been discussed at the bar. If, as has always been understood, the sovereignty of Congress, though limited to specified objects, is plenary as to those objects, the power over commerce with foreign nations, and among the several States is vested in Congress, as absolutely as it would be in a single government, having in its constitution the same restrictions on the exercise of the power as are found in the constitution of the United States. The wisdom and the discretion of Congress, their identity with the people, and the influence which their constituents possess at election, are, in this, as in many other instances, as that, for example, of declaring war, the sole restraints on which they have relied, to secure them from its abuse. They are the restraints on which the people must often rely solely, in all representative governments.

The power of Congress, then, comprehends navigation, within the limits of every state in the Union; so far as that navigation may be, in any manner, connected with "commerce with foreign nations, or among the several States, or with the Indian tribes." It may, of consequence, pass the jurisdictional line of New York, and act upon the very waters to which the prohibition now under consideration applies.

[Thus, Chief Justice Marshall concluded that Congress' commerce power was expansive enough to enact the federal statute in question. In the remainder of the opinion, Chief Justice Marshall considered how to resolve the conflict between the federal statute and the state grant of monopoly, and also discussed whether the state monopoly would be lawful in the absence of any federal statute covering the same subject. This portion of the opinion is reproduced at the beginning of § 6 of this Chapter.]

NOTES ON *GIBBONS* AND THE COURT'S ARTICULATION OF COMMERCE CLAUSE LIMITS ON NATIONAL POWER

1. *Should the Supreme Court Enforce the Article I, § 8 Limits on National Power?* Note that a premise of Chief Justice Marshall's opinion is that Ogden wins the case if the federal statute is not within the powers enumerated in Article I, § 8. This assumes that the reach of the Commerce Clause (and probably also other enumerated powers) is a limitation on national power that should be enforced by the courts. Although this assumption pervades the cases in this part, it does not necessarily follow from the original expectations of the Framers.

In *Federalist* Nos. 45-46, Madison refuted the Anti-Federalists' charge that the stronger national government in the Constitution will swallow up the state governments. In a nutshell, Madison's argument was that the people's first loyalty will always be to the states (the governments closer to the people), that the Constitution is written to ensure the states' participation in the national government (as by election of senators and the President), and that the states would have a variety of means to resist unlawful or unjust encroachments against them by the national government. If Madison's arguments were correct, why shouldn't the Supreme Court in cases like *Gibbons* simply assume — either presumptively or irrebuttably — that Congress has acted properly in adopting statutes, and that the chief or only protection against congressional usurpation is objection and resistance by the states?

Updating Madison's arguments, several modern scholars have read the Constitution to suggest that the Article I limits on national power should be enforced only through the political process.[a] Such authors argue that the Supreme Court should not decide constitutional questions arising out of the national government's alleged usurpation of state authority, on the ground that the states are well represented in the national political process. (Recall Chief Justice Marshall's discussion in *McCulloch*. Why was a similar argument not made in *Gibbons*?) Note that a similar argument could be made as to the enforcement of some of the individual rights treated in earlier chapters. For example, because the press is extremely well-represented in the state as well as national political process, should the protections of *New York Times v. Sullivan* (Chapter 6, § 2B) be diluted or not enforced? Has the Supreme Court been justified in lenient review of state policies having racially significant effects (see *Washington v. Davis*, Chapter 3, § 1B), on the ground that racial minorities are well-represented in state and local political processes? Consider these arguments pro and con as you read the Court's historical efforts to set limits on the power of Congress to act.

2. *Theories for Limiting Congress' Commerce Clause Power.* On the issue of Congress' power under the Commerce Clause, *Gibbons* seems like an easy case, for interstate navigation was directly contemplated as the clause's object by the Framers. Yet Congress surely cannot do anything it wants under the aegis of the Commerce Clause; several possible limitations on that power were suggested in *Gibbons* and were then elaborated in subsequent Supreme Court cases. The different limiting strategies focus on different words in the Commerce Clause.

---

a. See Herbert Wechsler, *The Political Safeguards of Federalism*, in *Principles, Politics and Fundamental Law* 49-82 (1954); Jesse Choper, *Judicial Review and the National Political Process* 171-259 (1980). For commentary suggesting the many ways state governments can influence national political decisions, see Akhil Amar, *Of Sovereignty and Federalism*, 96 Yale L.J. 1425 (1987); Larry Kramer, *Understanding Federalism*, 45 Vand. L. Rev. 1485 (1994) (political parties as conduit of influence); Deborah Jones Merritt, *The Guarantee Clause and State Autonomy: Federalism for a Third Century*, 88 Colum. L. Rev. 1 (1988). A more thorough examination of the Wechsler thesis is in § 5B of this chapter.

(a) *"Commerce."* Navigation is clearly "commerce," and Marshall's opinion suggests that an activity not falling within a commonly accepted notion of commerce would not be within Congress' power. This became a popular strategy through which the Court could uphold state regulation, by finding that the regulated activity was not commerce. Later in the nineteenth century, the Court used the same strategy, in reverse, to strike down certain federal statutes. For example, in *Paul v. Virginia*, 75 U.S. (8 Wall.) 168 (1868), the Court held that federal law could not regulate insurance contracts. "Issuing a policy of insurance is not a transaction of commerce," because the policy is a contract, not something offered in barter and trade.

(b) *"Among the Several States."* Another implicit limitation on Congress' Commerce Clause power is that it can only be exercised for commercial transactions that operate across state lines, that are not local. *Gibbons* stated: "The completely internal commerce of a State, then, may be considered as reserved for the State itself." For example, the Court in *Federal Baseball Club v. National League*, 259 U.S. 200 (1922), held that the Sherman Act (prohibiting conspiracies to monopolize trade or commerce "among the several states") did not apply to organized baseball, whose "exhibitions" were held to be "purely state affairs." The Court rejected the argument that transportation of players across state lines rendered the sport interstate in nature, because "the transport is a mere incident, not the essential thing." (The Court also seemed to rely on the "commerce" requirement, for it suggested that the "personal effort" involved in baseball is not commerce.)

(c) *"Regulate."* Finally, Congress can only "regulate" interstate commerce. Several early Presidents believed that it prevented Congress from passing legislation that "facilitated" (rather than "regulated") interstate commerce. For example, President Madison in 1817 vetoed the Internal Improvement Bill because " '[t]he power to regulate commerce among the several States,' cannot include a power to construct roads and canals, and to improve the navigation of water courses, in order to facilitate, promote, and secure such a commerce, without a latitude of construction departing from the ordinary import of the terms, strengthened by the known inconveniences which doubtless led to the grant of this remedial power to Congress." II *Messages and Papers of the Presidents* 569, 570 (1897).

3. *Congress' Efforts to Regulate New Problems Under its Commerce Clause Power, 1887-1920.* The analytical structure in *Gibbons* was not often tested in the nineteenth century, because Congress did not engage in much economic regulation. Congress fought pirates, regulated rivers and harbors, established safety standards for steamboats, and engaged in other activities that did not raise serious Commerce Clause questions.[b] This changed after the Civil War and the industrialization of the United States. The advent of railroads, large-scale manufacturing, the telephone and telegraph, sweat shops, labor unions, and cartels introduced social and economic issues that could not be adequately dealt

---

b. See Jerry Mashaw, *Administration and "The Democracy": Administrative Law from Jackson to Lincoln, 1829-1861*, 117 Yale L.J. 1568 (2008), for an excellent discussion of the detailed federal regime for regulating steamboat safety and other matters.

with at the local or even state level. National legislation of three sorts was adopted pursuant to Congress' Commerce Clause power.

(a) *Impediments to an Efficient National Market.* Once business and transportation were no longer local, markets became national, and market abuses could no longer be effectively addressed by the states acting singly or even in concert.[c] The most significant federal statutes of the period dealt with this kind of problem. The Interstate Commerce Act of 1887 established a regulatory structure (the Interstate Commerce Commission) to respond to allegedly unfair railroad practices, such as price discrimination (preferred wealthy customers paid lower prices than farmers), rebates to certain customers, and artificially high prices. Theoretically, the act would ensure a smoothly functioning interstate transportation system. To the same end, Congress later adopted statutes seeking to ensure fair labor conditions on the railroads, including employer liability for accidents and a ban of anti-union contracts. The Sherman Anti-Trust Act of 1890 prohibited, in § 1, any contract, combination, or conspiracy "in restraint of trade or commerce among the several states" and, in § 2, any effort or conspiracy to "monopolize any part of the trade or commerce among the several states." The Sherman Act was amended and strengthened by the Clayton Act of 1914, which expanded upon the anti-monopoly prohibition and added new prohibitions against interlocking directorates of competing companies.

(b) *Interstate and International Contagion.* With increased mobility of people and goods came fears of migrating people and evils. National immigration regulations began in earnest in the 1880s, to keep out "undesirable" persons: persons of color (mainly from China), prostitutes and other "degenerates" (applied to include "sexual inverts"), paupers and people destined to be public charges, and so forth.[d] Other statutes tried to prevent the interstate transmission of vice. The Comstock Act of 1873 criminalized using the U.S. mails for sending "obscene" material, including contraception and abortion information. The Federal Lottery Act of 1895 prohibited the importing, mailing, or interstate transporting of lottery tickets (seeking to discourage gambling). An 1897 statute prohibited the "carrying of obscene literature and articles designed for indecent and immoral use from one state to another." The Mann Act of 1910 prohibited the transportation of women in interstate or foreign commerce for "immoral purposes." Yet other statutes were concerned with interstate disease and health menaces. The Pure Food & Drugs Act of

---

c. As Section 6 details, states were probably prohibited by the Commerce Clause itself from exercising much, if any, jurisdiction outside their individual borders, for the defensible reason that states would create a cacophony of regulations and might create self-seeking ones. One solution would have been for the states to form interstate agreements, allowed under Art. I, § 10, cl. 3 if consented to by Congress, but collective action problems would have made that difficult, if not impossible.

d. These statutes were enacted under Congress' "Naturalization" authority of Article I, § 8, cl. 4, which has been broadly construed to permit Congress virtually unlimited power to limit immigration.

1906 prohibited the interstate transportation of adulterated or unsafe foods and drugs and established the Food & Drug Administration to set standards.

(c) *National Standards of Safety and Fairness.* Although not so numerous in this period as the other two kinds of regulation, most notable for the future were congressional enactments setting national standards for safety and fairness. If the new national marketplace developed on its own, there were fears that the public interest could be sacrificed in ways the national government could prevent. For the easiest example, national standards could be useful *focal points* for private activity, channeling it in ways that could improve safety and even efficiency. Thus in 1893, Congress required all common carriers engaged in interstate commerce to have a power driving wheel brake system and to have couplers between the cars that worked automatically (so that workers need not risk injury by going between the cars). For a harder example, national standards could be useful to avoid local *races to the bottom,* by which individual states decline to adopt needed business regulations out of fear that businesses will "vote with their feet" by relocating in more lenient jurisdictions.[e] In an important application of this idea, the Child Labor Act of 1916 prohibited the transportation in interstate commerce of goods produced in factories employing children under the age of fourteen or employing children aged fourteen to sixteen for more than eight hours a day, for six days a week, or for nighttime work.

Many of these laws were questionable under the Court's traditional conception of the restrictions on congressional power. Not only did they have a less certain connection with *commerce* than the law upheld in *Gibbons*, but they regulated matters that seemed to be *intrastate* as well as *interstate*. This was a big problem for a Court committed to the conceptual framework of *dual federalism*. "There are certain matters over which the National Government has absolute control, and no action of the State can interfere therewith, and there are others in which the State is supreme, and in respect to them the National Government is powerless. To preserve the even balance between the two governments and hold each in its separate sphere is the peculiar duty of all courts." *South Carolina v. United States,* 199 U.S. 437, 448 (1905). Consider how the following decisions by the Court accommodate or sacrifice that principle. Are the decisions consistent with *Gibbons*? With one another?

――――

United States v. E.C. Knight, 156 U.S. 1 (1895): *Incidental effects on commerce.* The Court refused to apply the Sherman Act to break up the Sugar Trust (a monopoly of the production of sugar), on the ground that this was a

――

    e. A race to the bottom is a standard prisoners' dilemma game, whereby two players are collectively best off by cooperating but, acting not in concert, will tend to cheat on one another, yielding a result that is poorer for both. Thus, each of two states has strong incentives to pollute the atmosphere, even though it is in their joint interest to reduce overall pollution. See Richard Musgrave, *The Theory of Public Finance* 132-33 (1959); Wallace Oates, *An Economist's Perspective on Fiscal Federalism,* in *The Political Economy of Fiscal Federalism* 3 (Oates ed. 1977); Daniel Farber, *Environmental Federalism in a Global Economy,* 83 Va. L. Rev. 1283 (1997).

regulation of *manufacturing*, rather than *commerce*. **Chief Justice Fuller**'s opinion for the Court rejected the government's argument that production of a necessity of life, such as sugar, pervasively involved commerce. "Doubtless the power to control the manufacture of a given thing involves in a certain sense the control of its disposition, but this is a secondary and not the primary sense; and although the exercise of that power may result in bringing the operation of commerce into play, it does not control it, and affects it only incidentally and indirectly. Commerce succeeds to manufacture, and is not a part of it." Because American Sugar's manufacturing operations bore "no direct relation" to interstate commerce, the Sherman Act could not constitutionally be applied to them.

Although refined sugar was certainly shipped in interstate commerce, it was, again, just incidental to the manufacturing monopoly that the government alleged. It might be convenient to stretch the Commerce Clause in the instant case, the Chief Justice warned, but any such bow to convenience would breech the sharp wall erected by the Constitution between the police powers, to be exercised only by state and local governments, and the power over interstate commerce, exercised by Congress. **Justice Harlan** dissented. He considered the alleged monopoly to have a direct rather than incidental effect on interstate commerce.[f]

Champion v. Ames (The Lottery Case), 188 U.S. 321 (1903): *Outlaws of commerce*. The Court by a 5-4 vote, in an opinion by **Justice Harlan**, upheld the constitutionality of the federal Lottery Act, which outlawed carrying lottery tickets across state lines. **Chief Justice Fuller**'s dissenting opinion argued that Congress could not use its Commerce Clause powers to prohibit noncommercial activities, invoking *McCulloch*'s dictum: "Should Congress under the pretext of executing its powers, pass laws for the accomplishment of objects not entrusted to the Government; it would become the painful duty of this tribunal, should a case requiring such a decision come before it, to say that such an act was not the law of the land."

Justice Harlan agreed that the purpose of the statute was to suppress "the widespread pestilence of lotteries," a threat to public morals, but argued that the

---

f. *E.C. Knight* was an intensely controversial decision and a major theme of the election of 1896. The Court quickly retreated from such a broad position. In *Addyston Pipe & Steel Co. v. United States*, 175 U.S. 211 (1899), the Court upheld a Sherman Act suit against iron pipe companies conspiring to fix prices, which the Court characterized as not only a manufacturing restraint, but also a "direct restraint upon interstate commerce." The Court in the twentieth century routinely reviewed, and usually affirmed, Sherman Act prosecutions of anticompetitive behavior by manufacturers.

In contrast to the manufacturing case, the Supreme Court liberally applied the Sherman Act to a labor union boycott in *Loewe v. Lawlor*, 208 U.S. 274 (1908). In *Coronado Coal Co. v. United Mine Workers*, 268 U.S. 295 (1925), the Court affirmed a Sherman Act injunction against a local labor strike, on the ground that there was an intent "to restrain interstate commerce, and the means employed were calculated to carry that intent into effect." Note the relevance of this reasoning to the Court's decision upholding the National Labor Relations Act in *Jones & Laughlin, infra*.

structure of federalism supported the statute. State statutes prohibited lotteries within their borders but could not clearly reach the interstate market in lotteries. "[If] the carrying of lottery tickets from one State to another be interstate commerce, and if Congress is of opinion that an effective regulation for the suppression of lotteries, carried on through such commerce, is to make it a criminal offense to cause lottery tickets to be carried from one State to another, we know of no authority in the courts to hold that the means thus devised are not appropriate and necessary to protect the country at large against a species of interstate commerce which * * * has grown into disrepute and has become offensive to the entire people of the Nation."

Chief Justice Fuller objected to the implication that something could become an object of national regulation "the moment it is taken to be transported from place to place." "An invitation to dine, or to take a drive, or a note of introduction, all become articles of commerce under the ruling in this case, by being deposited with an express company for transportation. This in effect breaks down all the differences between that which is, and that which is not, an article of commerce . * * * It is a long step in the direction of wiping out all traces of state lines, and the creation of a centralized Government." Justice Harlan responded that this case hardly required the Court to explore the limits to which Congress could take the general rule in the case. He closed his opinion for the Court with an invocation of *Gibbons'* defense of leaving most issues to the political process. The same relaxed ends/means test of The Lottery Case was applied to uphold the Pure Food & Drugs Act in *Hipolite Egg Co. v. United States*, 220 U.S. 45 (1911), and the Mann Act (prohibiting the transportation of a woman across state lines for prostitution or "other immoral purposes") in *Hoke v. United States*, 227 U.S. 308 (1913).

Swift & Co. v. United States, 196 U.S. 375 (1905): *Current (stream) of commerce.* The Court, in an opinion by **Justice Holmes**, upheld a Sherman Act injunction against price-fixing by meat-packers. Against objection that this was federal regulation of intrastate commerce, Holmes responded: "When cattle are sent for sale from a place in one State, with the expectation that they will end their transit, after purchase in another, and when in effect they do so, with only the interruption necessary to find a purchaser at the stockyard, and when this is a typical, constantly recurring course, the current thus existing is a current of commerce among the States, and the purchase of the cattle is a part and incident of such commerce." *Swift* was followed in *Stafford v. Wallace*, 258 U.S. 495 (1922), which upheld regulation of animal stockyards because they were in a "stream of commerce" that Congress could surely regulate. According to Chief Justice Taft's opinion for the Court in *Stafford*, a reasonable fear by Congress that a course of conduct "usually lawful and affecting only intrastate commerce when considered alone, will probably and more or less constantly be used in conspiracies against interstate commerce or constitute a direct and undue burden on it," could serve "the same purpose as the intent charged in the Swift indictment to bring acts of a similar character into the current of interstate commerce for federal restraint." Taft also emphasized that the Court should defer to Congress's judgment as to the nature and extent of the connection between apparently local acts and interstate commerce. Yet the Court did not defer to Congress in *The First Employers' Liability Cases*, 207 U.S. 463 (1908) (invalidating a requirement that railroads insure employees against accidents), and *Adair v. United States*, 208 U.S. 161 (1908) (overturning a federal prohibition of yellow-dog contracts between railroads and their employees).

———

Houston, East & West Texas Railway v. United States (The Shreveport Rate Case), 234 U.S. 342 (1914): *Close and substantial relation.* The Interstate Commerce Commission directed the railway to equalize its rates between Dallas and Marshall, Texas and Marshall and Shreveport, Louisiana. The Supreme Court held that the ICC had jurisdiction over the intrastate (Dallas/Marshall) as well as interstate (Marshall/Shreveport) rates. **Justice Hughes**' opinion for the Court reasoned that congressional "authority, extending to these interstate carriers as instruments of interstate commerce, necessarily embraces the right to control their operations in all matters having such a close and substantial relation to interstate traffic that the control is essential or appropriate to the security of that traffic, to the efficiency of the interstate service, and to the maintenance of conditions under which interstate commerce may be conducted upon fair terms and without molestation or hindrance. As it is competent for Congress to legislate to these ends, unquestionably it may seek their attainment by requiring that the agencies of interstate commerce shall not be used in such manner as to cripple, retard or destroy it. * * * Wherever the interstate and intrastate transactions of carriers are so related that the government of the one involves the control of the other, it is Congress, and not the State, that is entitled to prescribe the final and dominant rule[.]" Two Justices dissented.

———

Hammer v. Dagenhart (The Child Labor Case), 247 U.S. 251 (1918): *Commerce versus manufacture.* The Court, in an opinion by **Justice Day**, held that Congress had no Commerce Clause power to prohibit interstate transportation of goods made by child labor. Congress relied on *Ames*, *Hipolite*, and *Hoke*, where the Court allowed Congress to prohibit disapproved items from entering interstate commerce. Justice Day distinguished these precedents: "In each of these instances the use of interstate transportation was necessary to the accomplishment of harmful results. In other words, although the power over interstate transportation was to regulate, that could only be accomplished by prohibiting the use of the facilities of interstate commerce to effect the evil intended. This element is wanting in the present case. The thing intended to be accomplished by this statute is the denial of the facilities of interstate commerce to those manufacturers in the States who employ children within the prohibited ages. The act in its effect does not regulate transportation among the States, but aims to standardize the ages at which children may be employed in mining and manufacturing within the States. The goods shipped are of themselves harmless."

Justice Day argued that this was essentially a case of federal regulation of manufacture, rather than commerce, and so *E.C. Knight* governed. "There is no power vested in Congress to require the States to exercise their police power so as to prevent possible unfair competition. Many causes may cooperate to give one State, by reason of local laws or conditions, an economic advantage over to others. The Commerce Clause was not intended to give to Congress a general authority to equalize such conditions. In some of the States laws have been passed fixing minimum wages for women, in others the local law regulates the hours of labor of women in various employments. Business done in such States may be at an economic disadvantage when compared with States which have no such regulations; surely, this fact does not give Congress the power to deny transportation in interstate commerce to those who carry on business where the hours of labor and the rate of compensation for women have not been fixed by a standard in use in other States and approved by Congress. * * *

"In our view the necessary effect of this act is, by means of a prohibition against the movement in interstate commerce of ordinary commercial commodities, to regulate the hours of labor of children in factories and mines within the States, a purely state authority. Thus the act in a two-fold sense is repugnant to the Constitution. It not only transcends the authority delegated to Congress over commerce but also exerts a power as to a purely local matter to which the federal authority does not extend. The far reaching result of upholding the act cannot be more plainly indicated than by pointing out that if Congress can thus regulate matters entrusted to local authority by prohibition of the movement of commodities in interstate commerce, all freedom of commerce will be at an end, and the power of the States over local matters may be eliminated, and thus our system of government be practically destroyed."

Writing for four Justices, **Justice Holmes** dissented. "The statute confines itself to prohibiting the carriage of certain goods in interstate or foreign commerce. Congress is given power to regulate such commerce in unqualified terms. It would not be argued today that the power to regulate does not include the power to prohibit. Regulation means the prohibition of something, and when interstate commerce is the matter to be regulated I cannot doubt that the regulation may prohibit any part of such commerce that Congress sees fit to forbid. At all events it is established by the *Lottery Case* and others that have followed it that a law is not beyond the regulative power of Congress merely because it prohibits certain transportation out and out. So I repeat that this statute in its immediate operation is clearly within the Congress's constitutional power.

"The question then is narrowed to whether the exercise of its otherwise constitutional power by Congress can be pronounced unconstitutional because of its possible reaction upon the conduct of the States in a matter upon which I have admitted that they are free from direct control. I should have thought that that matter had been disposed of so fully as to leave no room for doubt. I should have thought that the most conspicuous decisions of this Court had made it clear that the power to regulate commerce and other constitutional powers could not be cut down or qualified by the fact that it might interfere with the carrying out of the domestic policy of any State. * * * [N]otwithstanding *E.C. Knight Co.*, the Sherman Act has been made an instrument for the breaking up of combinations in restraint of trade and monopolies, using the power to regulate commerce as a foothold, but not proceeding because that commerce was the end actually in mind [see footnote *e* above]. The objection that the control of the States over production was interfered with was urged again and again but always in vain." Holmes also relied on *Hoke* for the proposition that "[i]t does not matter whether the supposed evil precedes or follows the transportation. It is enough that in the opinion of Congress the transportation encourages the evil."

"But I had thought that the propriety of the exercise of a power admitted to exist in some cases was for the consideration of Congress alone and that this Court always had disavowed the right to intrude its judgment upon questions of policy or morals. It is not for this Court to pronounce when prohibition is necessary to regulation if it ever may be necessary — to say that it is permissible as against strong drink but not as against the product of ruined lives."

NOTES ON THE CHILD LABOR CASE AND THE COURT'S NARROW VIEW OF THE COMMERCE CLAUSE

1. *The Manufacture/Commerce Distinction and The Demise of the Outlaws of Commerce Argument?* The Child Labor Case was a return to the core precept of *E.C. Knight*, that *manufacture* was local and left to state regulation, in contrast to *commerce*, which might be regulated by the national government. The case was also a departure from the lenient attitude the Court had shown in the outlaws-of-commerce precedents, as Holmes trenchantly demonstrated.[g] In *Hoke*, the unanimous Court said: "Let an article be debased by adulteration, let it be misrepresented by false branding, and Congress may exercise its prohibitive power. It may be that Congress could not prohibit the manufacture of the article in a state. It may be that Congress could not prohibit in all of its conditions its sale within a state. But Congress may prohibit its transportation between the states, and by that means defeat the motive and evils of its manufacture." Why isn't a product of child labor just as much an "outlaw of commerce" as adulterated food (*Hipolite Egg*) or lottery tickets (The Lottery Case)?

2. *Possible Escape Hatches: Current of Commerce and Affecting Commerce.* The Child Labor Case left relatively untouched the escape hatches of *Swift* (local activity in the current of commerce) and *Shreveport* (local activity affecting commerce), and the Court vigorously applied *Swift* in *Stafford v. Wallace*, which held that meat-packing practices in a "stream of commerce" could be regulated by the federal government. If you were a legislative drafter for a Congress that still wanted a child labor law, how might you draft a measure to pass constitutional scrutiny? Consider several options, and you are not limited to the Commerce Clause!

3. *Substantive Features of the Child Labor Case.* The decision may be viewed as substantive rather than purely jurisdictional: (a) *Anti-Redistribution.* The Court was worried that the child labor statute had the *Lochner* problem, being a naked redistribution from business to labor — like the statutes struck

---

g. None of the important contemporary commentators thought the Court had adequate answers to Holmes' dissent. See, e.g., Thurlow Gordon, *The Child Labor Law Case*, 32 Harv. L. Rev. 45 (1918); William Carey Jones, *The Child Labor Decision*, 6 Calif. L. Rev. 395 (1918); William Sutherland, *The Child Labor Cases & the Constitution*, 8 Cornell L.Q. 338 (1923).

down in *Adair* and *The First Employer Liability Cases*. Congress, of course, could regulate labor unions when they threatened to disrupt interstate commerce, as the Court held in *Loewe v. Lawlor*, 208 U.S. 274 (1908); *In re Debs*, 158 U.S. 564 (1895). Note that a race-to-the bottom argument was made in the Child Labor Case, but the Court could not distinguish it from a naked redistribution, or perhaps thought that the argument was too far-reaching. (b) *Disapproval of Federalizing Employment Law.* A more neutral distinction between the Child Labor Case and the transportation cases was the Court's concern with national regulation of the employment relationship. There was great anxiety, fueled by the expansion of the national government during World War I, that federal regulation was expanding into new areas and that such expansion carried with it tremendous bureaucratic costs. Judges believed that such costs were not nearly as justified for employment relations as they were for transportation and commercial activities, which contemporaries viewed as "affected with a public interest" (almost like common carrier activities). (c) *Family and Privacy.* At that time, three-quarters of the children working were engaged in agriculture, and most of those were employed by their own parents on family farms.[h] Although the statute covered only factory work, there may have been concerns that it interfered with decisions best left to families themselves and that it could be expanded in the future to reach farm work.

Barry Cushman suggests a synthesis of these early cases, based upon the Court's premise that matters Congress could regulate were usually barred or preempted from state regulation. *Formalism and Realism in Commerce Clause Jurisprudence*, 67 U. Chi. L. Rev. 1089 (2000). The Court in these cases wanted to give Congress breathing room to regulate matters where national uniformity was necessary, but without depriving the states of power over ordinary economic transactions and relations. The Great Depression and demands for more national regulation created a crisis for this jurisprudence, Cushman argues.

NOTE ON THE NEW DEAL'S EARLY DIFFICULTIES MEETING COMMERCE CLAUSE SCRUTINY, 1934-36

President Franklin Roosevelt's plan to bring the country out of the Great Depression of 1929 involved unprecedented national direction of the economy, through national standards for conditions of labor, fair business practices, unionizing, social welfare and insurance, and so forth. These new kinds of statutes were more creative invocations of the Commerce Clause than the Child Labor Act. Because the Court for the first four years of the New Deal (1933-37) was peopled entirely with pre-New Deal Justices committed to the line-drawing of cases like the *Child Labor Case* or the *Shreveport Rate Case*, there was bound to be trouble. And trouble there was.[i]

---

h. See Lawrence Berger & S. Rayan Johansson, *Child Health in the Workplace: The Supreme Court in* Hammer v. Dagenhart, 5 J. Health Politics, Policy & Law 81 (1980).

i. See Barry Cushman, *Rethinking the New Deal Court: The Structure of a Constitutional Revolution* (1998); Peter Irons, *The New Deal Lawyers* (1982); G. Edward White, *The Constitution and the New Deal* (2000); Robert Stern, *The Commerce Clause and the National Economy, 1933-*

The New Deal survived several early cases, but in *Railroad Retirement Board v. Alton Railroad*, 295 U.S. 330 (1935), the Court by a 5-4 vote struck down the Railroad Retirement Act of 1934. Although Congress had the power to regulate railroad transportation and safety under the Commerce Clause, that power did not extend to establishment of a mandatory retirement plan for railroad workers, which Justice Roberts' opinion for the Court characterized as "essentially related to the social welfare of the worker, and therefore remote from any regulation of commerce as such." This was an invalid Commerce Clause goal under the *Child Labor Case*.

Three weeks after *Alton Railroad*, the Court in *A.L.A. Schechter Poultry Corp. v. United States*, 295 U.S. 495 (1935), invalidated the National Industry Recovery Act's (NIRA) labor rules for the New York poultry market. NIRA authorized the President to establish codes of fair competition for various industries, to be written by experts within those industries, a move which the Court in *Panama Refining Co. v. Ryan*, 293 U.S. 388 (1935), invalidated as an excessive delegation of congressional power to the President (and in turn to private parties (see Chapter 8, § 2A)). In *Schechter*, the Court held that the Poultry Code — prohibiting child labor, setting a minimum wage and maximum hours, and assuring workers the right to unionize — was an excessive delegation *and* beyond Congress' Commerce Clause power, even though the Code only applied to "transaction[s] in or affecting interstate commerce." Schechter argued, however, that the Code was applied to his business, which only sold chickens in New York.

Because chickens generally were shipped across state lines, the government argued that the poultry industry was part of a current of commerce that could be regulated (*Swift*) and that defects in the industry "directly affected" commerce (the *Shreveport Rate Case*). In an opinion by Chief Justice Hughes, the Court rejected the current of commerce argument because the wage and work week limitations did not relate to commerce and only applied to slaughterhouse and sales work performed locally, after the chickens had arrived in New York. "The mere fact that there may be a constant flow of commodities into a State does not mean that the flow continues after the property has arrived and has become commingled with the mass of property within the State and is there held solely for local disposition and use. So far as the poultry here in question is concerned, the flow in interstate commerce had ceased." The Court rejected the affecting-commerce argument on the ground that the regulations' effect on commerce was "indirect" and not "direct." *Schechter* concluded with a classic statement of the formalist position (in response to the government's overall argument that the nation as a practical matter needed national wage and hour rules to climb out of the Depression): "It is not the province of this Court to consider the economic advantages or disadvantages of such a centralized system. It is sufficient to say that the Federal Constitution does not provide for it."

The New Deal's defeat in *Schechter* was particularly stinging because not a single Justice believed the NIRA constitutional. Justice Cardozo, a critic of the Court's activism in other Commerce Clause cases, wrote a concurring opinion rejecting the government's "affecting commerce" theory: If Schechter's local chicken processing implicated interstate commerce, there were no limits to federal government power. Stung but undaunted, the New Deal Congress continued to legislate, immediately adopting the National Labor Relations Act to assure workers' rights to organize and bargain and the Bituminous Coal Conservation Act, which established an NIRA-type Code for the coal industry.

In *Carter v. Carter Coal Co.*, 298 U.S. 238 (1936), the Court by a 6-3 vote struck down the Coal Conservation Act. The government again relied on the flow of coal in interstate commerce and the effects of the market collapse; the Court (per Sutherland, J.) again rebuffed the arguments, based on *Schechter*: "The only perceptible difference between that case and this is that in the *Schechter* case the federal power was asserted with respect to commodities which had come to rest after their interstate transportation; while here, the case deals with commodities at rest before interstate commerce has begun. That difference is without significance." Chief Justice Hughes concurred; Justices Cardozo, Stone, and Brandeis dissented on the ground that there was a sufficient connection between the Code's price controls and interstate commerce.[j]

The decisions in *Schechter* and *Carter Coal* precipitated a constitutional crisis (recall Chapter 1, § 5). Right after the 1936 election, in which he carried every state but Maine and Vermont, President Roosevelt proposed that he be authorized to appoint one additional Justice (up to six) for each Justice over the age of 70. Since six Justices were over 70 (including all the conservative Justices known as the "Four Horsemen"), Roosevelt could have appointed enough justices to turn the six-to-three loss in *Carter Coal* into an easy nine-to-six victory.

The 1937 Court-packing plan aroused significant opposition among both Democrats and Republicans. Opponents considered the proposal a usurpation of power by the President and an unconstitutional infringement upon the Article III independence of the Court. (Was the proposal unconstitutional?) In any event, the plan was derailed by action within the Court. First, Justice VanDevanter retired in 1937 (ultimately to be replaced by Justice Hugo Black, a New Deal Senator from Alabama). Second, in two important cases the Court indicated a more pragmatic approach to economic regulation. In *West Coast*

---

j. Nor was the Court willing to allow Congress to use its taxing and spending powers, rather than its commerce power, to regulate such matters as agricultural production. In *United States v. Butler*, 297 U.S. 1 (1936), the Court struck down a federal tax on processors of agricultural commodities that was designed to fund a program paying farmers to reduce their productive acreage. The Court concluded that the tax violated the Tenth Amendment by "invad[ing] the reserved rights of the states. It is a statutory plan to regulate and control agricultural production, a matter beyond the powers delegated to the federal government." This was so even though Article I, § 8, in defining Congress's taxing and spending powers, contains no limitation to interstate or national matters other than the "general welfare" (the power is "to lay and collect Taxes, Duties, Imposts and Excises, to pay the Debts and to provide for the common Defence and general Welfare of the United States"). Thus, *Butler* was based on the proposition that the Tenth Amendment, and more generally the structures of federalism built into the Constitution, operated as an independent barrier to congressional regulation. The current status of this congressional power is considered in § 4, *infra*.

Hotel Co. v. Parrish, 300 U.S. 379 (1937), the Court, by a five-to-four vote, upheld a state minimum wage statute. While the "Four Horsemen" (VanDevanter, McReynolds, Butler, Sutherland) — the Justices most committed to formalism under the Commerce Clause — dissented, Justices historically committed to flexibility under the Commerce Clause (Brandeis, Stone, and Cardozo) were joined by Chief Justice Hughes and Justice Owen Roberts.[k] After the "switch in time that saved nine," the Court-packing bill was reported with an unfavorable recommendation "as a needless, futile, and utterly dangerous abandonment of constitutional principle." S. Rep. No. 711, 75th Cong., 1st Sess. (1937). On July 22 the bill was killed by recommitment to the Senate Judiciary Committee.

National Labor Relations Board v. Jones & Laughlin Steel Corp., 301 U.S. 1 (1937). Speaking for five Justices, **Chief Justice Hughes** upheld the application of the NLRA's labor-management provisions to a national steel company. Relying on *E.C. Knight* and *Carter Coal*, Jones & Laughlin argued that Congress could not regulate manufacturing. The government responded, first, that because the steel company was a large, vertically integrated enterprise, disruption of manufacturing operations would disrupt the stream of interstate commerce (*Swift*) and, in the alternative, that disruption of intrastate manufacturing by labor strife would directly affect commerce and that Congress can act to prevent obstructions to the overall free flow of commerce (the *Shreveport Rate Case*).

Chief Justice Hughes proceeded carefully. Answering Jones & Laughlin's broad facial attack on the statute, he ruled that the law was written in a constitutional manner and could be limited to contexts "affecting commerce." "It is a familiar principle that acts which directly burden or obstruct interstate or foreign commerce, or its free flow, are within the reach of the congressional power. Acts having that effect are not rendered immune because they grow out of labor disputes. [It] is the effect upon commerce, not the source of the injury, which is the criterion." Applying that test, which Hughes himself had devised in the *Shreveport Rate Case*, the Chief Justice addressed the steel company's argument that the NLRA could not be applied to its local manufacturing workers.

Hughes avoided taking a position on the government's stream of commerce theory but accepted its affecting commerce theory. "The congressional authority to protect interstate commerce from burdens and obstructions is not

---

k. Justice Roberts' vote is the most interesting, for it has been called the "switch in time that saved nine." He had voted in *Morehead v. New York ex rel. Tipaldo*, 298 U.S. 587 (1936), to invalidate a state minimum wage law for women (another five-to-four decision), and then seemingly changed his mind one year later in *West Coast Hotel*. In his defense, it can be pointed out that he had voted in *West Coast Hotel* before Roosevelt submitted his Court-packing plan. Moreover, Roberts claimed in a subsequent memorandum that he had joined the majority in *Morehead* only because the dissenters had not forthrightly faced the fact that they had to overrule earlier precedents to sustain the minimum wage law (which Roberts claimed to be willing to do). See generally Richard Friedman, *Switching Time and Other Thought Experiments: The Hughes Court and Constitutional Transformation*, 142 U. Pa. L. Rev. 1891 (1994).

limited to transactions which can be deemed to be an essential part of a 'flow' of interstate or foreign commerce. * * * Although activities may be intrastate in character when separately considered, if they have such a close and substantial relation to interstate commerce that their control is essential or appropriate to protect that commerce from burdens and obstructions, Congress has the power to exercise that control." The Court cited *Schechter* for this last proposition! The Court also laid to rest the *E.C. Knight* idea that manufacturing could not be regulated under the Commerce Clause. "[T]hat the employees here concerned were engaged in production is not determinative. The question remains as to the effect upon interstate commerce of the labor practice involved."

The Court also stated: "Giving full weight to the [company's] contention with respect to a break in the complete continuity of the 'stream of commerce' by reason of [its] manufacturing operations, the fact remains that the stoppage of these operations by industrial strife would have a most serious effect upon interstate commerce. In view of [the company's] far-flung activities, it is idle to say that the effect would be indirect and remote. It is obvious that it would be immediate and might be catastrophic. * * * We have often said that interstate commerce itself is a practical conception. It is equally true that interferences with that commerce must be appraised by a judgment that does not ignore actual experience."

Writing for four Justices, **Justice McReynolds** objected to "this chain of indirect and progressively remote events" by which the government and the Court justified NLRA jurisdiction over a dispute in which but ten men were discharged, because the unfair labor practice affected interstate commerce. Justice MacReynolds' dissenting colleagues then left the Court seriatim: Justice VanDevanter in 1937 (replaced by New Deal Senator Hugo Black), Justice Sutherland in 1938 (replaced by New Deal Solicitor General Stanley Reed), and Justice Butler in 1939 (replaced by New Deal Michigan Governor Frank Murphy). MacReynolds himself retired in 1941, shortly before the next major Commerce Clause precedent was handed down — by a unanimous Court populated mostly by New Deal Justices.

UNITED STATES v. DARBY
312 U.S. 100, 61 S.Ct. 451, 85 L.Ed. 609 (1941)

JUSTICE STONE delivered the opinion of the Court.

[The Fair Labor Standards Act of 1938 regulated hours, wages, and other conditions of employment. Darby, who manufactured lumber in Georgia and shipped some of it to customers in other states, was indicted for violating the Act, but the district court quashed the indictment on the ground that the statute was unconstitutional under *Hammer v. Dagenhart*.]

The two principal questions raised by the record in this case are, *first*, whether Congress has constitutional power to prohibit the shipment in interstate commerce of lumber manufactured by employees whose wages are less than a prescribed minimum or whose weekly hours of labor at that wage are greater than a prescribed maximum, and, *second*, whether it has power to prohibit the employment of workmen in the production of goods "for interstate commerce" at other than prescribed wages and hours. * * *

The prohibition of shipment of the proscribed goods in interstate commerce. * * * While manufacture is not of itself interstate commerce, the shipment of manufactured goods interstate is such commerce and the prohibition of such shipment by Congress is indubitably a regulation of the commerce. The power to regulate commerce is the power "to prescribe the rule by which commerce is governed." *Gibbons.* It extends not only to those regulations which aid, foster and protect the commerce, but embraces those which prohibit it. It is conceded that the power of Congress to prohibit transportation in interstate commerce includes noxious articles, stolen articles, kidnapped persons, and articles such as intoxicating liquor or convict made goods, traffic in which is forbidden or restricted by the laws of the state of destination.

But it is said that the present prohibition falls within the scope of none of these categories; that while the prohibition is nominally a regulation of the commerce its motive or purpose is regulation of wages and hours of persons engaged in manufacture, the control of which has been reserved to the states and upon which Georgia and some of the states of destination have placed no restriction; that the effect of the present statute is not to exclude the proscribed articles from interstate commerce in aid of state regulation, but instead, under the guise of a regulation of interstate commerce, it undertakes to regulate wages and hours within the state contrary to the policy of the state which has elected to leave them unregulated. * * *

Such regulation is not a forbidden invasion of state power merely because either its motive or its consequence is to restrict the use of articles of commerce within the states of destination; and is not prohibited unless by other Constitutional provisions. It is no objection to the assertion of the power to regulate interstate commerce that its exercise is attended by the same incidents which attend the exercise of the police power of the states.

* * * The motive and purpose of a regulation of interstate commerce are matters for the legislative judgment upon the exercise of which the Constitution places no restriction and over which the courts are given no control. * * * Whatever their motive and purpose, regulations of commerce which do not infringe some constitutional prohibition are within the plenary power conferred on Congress by the Commerce Clause. Subject only to that limitation, presently to be considered, we conclude that the prohibition of the shipment interstate of goods produced under the forbidden substandard labor conditions is within the constitutional authority of Congress.

In the more than a century which has elapsed since the decision of *Gibbons v. Ogden*, these principles of constitutional interpretation have been so long and repeatedly recognized by this Court as applicable to the Commerce Clause, that there would be little occasion for repeating them now were it not for the decision of this Court twenty-two years ago in *Hammer v. Dagenhart*. In that case it was held by a bare majority of the Court over the powerful and now classic dissent of Mr. Justice Holmes setting forth the fundamental issues involved, that Congress was without power to exclude the products of child labor from interstate commerce. The reasoning and conclusion of the Court's opinion there cannot be reconciled with the conclusion which we have reached, that the power of Congress under the Commerce Clause is plenary to exclude any article from interstate commerce subject only to the specific prohibitions of the Constitution.

Hammer v. Dagenhart has not been followed. The distinction on which the decision was rested that Congressional power to prohibit interstate commerce is limited to articles which in themselves have some harmful or deleterious property — a distinction which was novel when made and unsupported by any provision of the Constitution — has long since been abandoned. The thesis of the opinion that the motive of the prohibition or its effect to control in some measure the use or production within the states of the article thus excluded from the commerce can operate to deprive the regulation of its constitutional authority has long since ceased to have force. *Lottery Case.* And finally we have declared "The authority of the federal government over interstate commerce does not differ in extent or character from that retained by the states over intrastate commerce."

The conclusion is inescapable that *Hammer v. Dagenhart* was a departure from the principles which have prevailed in the interpretation of the Commerce Clause both before and since the decision and that such vitality, as a precedent, as it then had has long since been exhausted. It should be and now is overruled.

Validity of the wage and hour requirements. * * * As the Government seeks to apply [§ 15(a)(2)] in the indictment, and as the court below construed the phrase "produced for interstate commerce," it embraces at least the case where an employer engaged, as is appellee, in the manufacture and shipment of goods in filling orders of extrastate customers, manufactures his product with the intent or expectation that according to the normal course of his business all or some part of it will be selected for shipment to those customers.

Without attempting to define the precise limits of the phrase, we think the acts alleged in the indictment are within the sweep of the statute. * * *

There remains the question whether such restriction on the production of goods for commerce is a permissible exercise of the commerce power. The power of Congress over interstate commerce is not confined to the regulation of commerce among the states. It extends to those activities intrastate which so affect interstate commerce or the exercise of the power of Congress over it as to make regulation of them appropriate means to the attainment of a legitimate end, the exercise of the granted power of Congress to regulate interstate commerce. See *McCulloch v. Maryland.* * * *

* * * [T]he power of Congress to regulate interstate commerce extends to the regulation through legislative action of activities intrastate which have a substantial effect on the commerce or the exercise of the Congressional power over it. * * *

Congress, having by the present Act adopted the policy of excluding from interstate commerce all goods produced for the commerce which do not conform to the specified labor standards, it may choose the means reasonably adapted to the attainment of the permitted end, even though they involve control of intrastate activities. [Thus] Congress may require inspection and preventive treatment of all cattle in a disease infected area in order to prevent shipment in interstate commerce of some of the cattle without the treatment. And we have recently held that Congress in the exercise of its power to require inspection and grading of tobacco shipped in interstate commerce may compel such inspection and grading of all tobacco sold at local auction rooms from which a substantial part but not all of the tobacco sold is shipped in interstate commerce. *Currin v. Wallace*, [306 U.S. 1]. * * *

The means adopted by § 15(a)(2) for the protection of interstate commerce by the suppression of the production of the condemned goods for interstate commerce is so related to the commerce and so affects it as to be within the reach of the commerce power. Congress, to attain its objective in the suppression of nationwide competition in interstate commerce by goods produced under substandard labor conditions, has made no distinction as to the volume or amount of shipments in the commerce or of production for commerce by any particular shipper or producer. It recognized that in present day industry, competition by a small part may affect the whole and that the total effect of the competition of many small producers may be great. The legislation aimed at a whole embraces all its parts.

So far as *Carter v. Carter Coal Co.* is inconsistent with this conclusion, its doctrine is limited in principle by the decisions under the Sherman Act and the National Labor Relations Act, which we have cited and which we follow.

Our conclusion is unaffected by the Tenth Amendment. * * * The amendment states but a truism that all is retained which has not been surrendered. There is nothing in the history of its adoption to suggest that it was more than declaratory of the relationship between the national and state governments as it had been established by the Constitution before the amendment or that its purpose was other than to allay fears that the new national government might seek to exercise powers not granted, and that the states might not be able to exercise fully their reserved powers.

Wickard v. Filburn, 317 U.S. 111 (1942). The Court applied the new learning on the Commerce Clause (*Darby*) to uphold the Agricultural Adjustment Act's quota on agricultural production. Under the Act, the Secretary of Agriculture imposed a quota on the production of wheat because, he concluded, the total supply of wheat would exceed domestic and export needs, driving down prices. Filburn had a dairy farm and grew small amounts of wheat to feed to his animals and for other purposes. He exceeded his quota and was fined. Even though the federal regulation of Filburn had nothing like a "direct" effect on interstate commerce, **Justice Jackson**'s opinion for a unanimous Court viewed the regulation as the federal government's effort to stabilize national wheat prices by limiting the supply. "That appellee's own contribution to the demand for wheat may be trivial by itself is not enough to remove him from the scope of federal regulation where, as here, his contribution, taken together with that of many others similarly situated, is far from trivial. *Darby*.

"It is well established by decisions of this Court that the power to regulate commerce includes the power to regulate the prices at which commodities in that commerce are dealt in and practices affecting such prices. One of the primary purposes of the Act in question was to increase the market price of wheat, and to that end to limit the volume thereof that could affect the market. It can hardly be denied that a factor of such volume and variability as home-consumed wheat would have a substantial influence on price and market conditions. This may arise because being in marketable condition such wheat overhangs the market and, if induced by rising prices, tends to flow into the market and check price increases. But if we assume that it is never marketed, it supplies a need of the man who grew it which would otherwise be reflected by purchases in the open market. Home-grown wheat in this sense competes with wheat in commerce. The stimulation of commerce is a use of the regulatory function quite as definitely as prohibitions or restrictions thereon. This record leaves us in no doubt that Congress may properly have considered that wheat consumed on the farm where grown, if wholly outside the scheme of regulation, would have a substantial effect in defeating and obstructing its purpose to stimulate trade therein at increased prices.

"It is said, however, that this Act, forcing some farmers into the market to buy what they could provide for themselves, is an unfair promotion of the markets and prices of specializing wheat growers. It is of the essence of regulation that it lays a restraining hand on the self-interest of the regulated and that advantages from the regulation commonly fall to others. The conflicts of economic interest between the regulated and those who advantage by it are wisely left under our system to resolution by the Congress under its more flexible and responsible legislative process. Such conflicts rarely lend themselves to judicial determination. And with the wisdom, workability, or fairness, of the plan of regulation we have nothing to do."

NOTE ON CIVIL RIGHTS AND FEDERALISM

After being associated with *Lochner*'s liberty of contract jurisprudence before 1937, federalism became even more closely associated with *Plessy*'s jurisprudence of apartheid after 1937. Representing Clarendon County, South Carolina in *Brown I*, John W. Davis's main argument was that racial segregation was a matter of local custom to which the Court should defer. In *Brown II*, southern states insisted, from federalist premises, that federal trial judges should defer to local political processes in determining the manner and speed of school desegregation. When the Supreme Court rejected their stance in *Brown I* and *II*, the South denounced the Court's actions as violating the federal arrangement.[1] States rights became the shibboleth for die-hard opposition to racial integration and for the constitutional right of localities to choose apartheid. In contrast, the civil rights movement was associated with national human rights trumping localism.

---

1. See Numan Bartley, *The Rise of Massive Resistance: Race and Politics in the South in the 1950's* (1969); Francis Wilhoit, *The Politics of Massive Resistance* (1973).

This was just as apparent in the political as in the constitutional arena. Rejecting states rights arguments, Congress adopted the Civil Rights Act of 1964 to make the anti-discrimination norm applicable on a national and uniform basis. Title II of the new law prohibited specified public accommodations (such as motels and restaurants) from discriminating on the basis of race. The law was immediately challenged. The jurisdictional statement of Moreston Rolleston, Jr., representing the Heart of Atlanta Motel, presented an odd amalgam of federalist and original meaning arguments. "George Washington," he argued, "did not intend that the new Constitution would provide any rights of personal freedom for his Negro slaves and certainly not the right to use the taverns and inns in which George Washington slept." Solicitor General Archibald Cox defended Title II as an exercise of Congress's Commerce Clause powers and rejected his advisers' plea to rely also on Congress's power under the Fourteenth Amendment (which is examined in § 3 of this chapter).[m]

HEART OF ATLANTA MOTEL v. UNITED STATES
379 U.S. 241, 85 S.Ct. 348, 13 L.Ed.2d 258 (1964)

JUSTICE CLARK delivered the opinion of the Court.

[Title II of the Civil Rights Act of 1964 assures that "[a]ll persons shall be entitled to the full and equal enjoyment of the goods, services, facilities, privileges, advantages, and accommodations of any place of public accommodation, as defined in this section, without discrimination or segregation on the ground of race, color, religion, or national origin" (§ 201(a)). Section 201(b) lists four classes of business establishments, each of which "serves the public" and "is a place of public accommodation" within the meaning of the title "if its operations affect commerce, or if discrimination or segregation by it is supported by State action." The covered establishments include "(1) any inn, hotel, motel, or other establishment which provides lodging to transient guests, other than an establishment located within a building which contains not more than five rooms for rent or hire and which is actually occupied by the proprietor of such establishment at his residence." Section 201(c) defines the phrase "affect commerce" as applied to the above establishments. It first declares that "any inn, hotel, motel, or other establishment which provides lodging to transient guests" affects commerce *per se*.

[The Heart of Atlanta was a 216-room motel located close to posh Peachtree Street in Atlanta, as well as major state and national highways. The motel refused to accommodate African Americans. Conceding that it fell within § 201, the motel sought an order invalidating Title II as applied to its business.]

The sole question posed is, therefore, the constitutionality of the Civil Rights Act of 1964 as applied to these facts. The legislative history of the Act indicates that Congress based the Act on § 5 and the Equal Protection Clause of the Fourteenth Amendment as well as its power to regulate interstate commerce. * * *

---

m. An excellent account of the litigation, the parties' strategies, and the Justices' deliberation is Richard Cortner, *Civil Rights and Public Accommodations: The* Heart of Atlanta Motel *and* McClung *Cases* (2001).

The Senate Commerce Committee made it quite clear that the fundamental object of Title II was to vindicate "the deprivation of personal dignity that surely accompanies denials of equal access to public establishments." At the same time, however, it noted that such an objective has been and could be readily achieved "by congressional action based on the commerce power of the Constitution." [S.Rep. No. 872, at 16-17.] Our study of the legislative record, made in the light of prior cases, has brought us to the conclusion that Congress possessed ample power in this regard, and we have therefore not considered the other grounds relied upon. * * *

While the Act as adopted carried no congressional findings the record of its passage through each house is replete with evidence of the burdens that discrimination by race or color places upon interstate commerce. * * * This testimony included the fact that our people have become increasingly mobile with millions of people of all races travelling from State to State; that Negroes in particular have been the subject of discrimination in transient accommodations, having to travel great distances to secure the same; that often they have been unable to obtain accommodations and have had to call upon friends to put them up overnight, * * * ; and that these conditions had become so acute as to require the listing of available lodging for Negroes in a special guidebook which was itself "dramatic testimony to the difficulties" Negroes encounter in travel. * * * We shall not burden this opinion with further details since the voluminous testimony presents overwhelming evidence that discrimination by hotels and motels impedes interstate travel. * * *

[T]he determinative test of the exercise of power by the Congress under the Commerce Clause is simply whether the activity sought to be regulated is "commerce which concerns more States than one" and has a real and substantial relation to the national interest. Let us now turn to this facet of the problem.

That the "intercourse" of which the Chief Justice [Marshall] spoke [in *Gibbons*] included the movement of persons through more States than one was settled as early as 1849. * * * Nor does it make any difference whether the transportation is commercial in character. * * *

The same interest in protecting interstate commerce which led Congress to deal with segregation in interstate carriers and the white-slave traffic has prompted it to extend the exercise of its power to gambling, *Lottery Case*, * * * and to racial discrimination by owners and managers of terminal restaurants, *Boynton v. Virginia*, 364 U.S. 454 (1960).

That Congress was legislating against moral wrongs in many of these areas rendered its enactments no less valid. In framing Title II of this Act Congress was also dealing with what it considered a moral problem. But that fact does not detract from the overwhelming evidence of the disruptive effect that racial discrimination has had on commercial intercourse. It was this burden which empowered Congress to enact appropriate legislation, and, given this basis for the exercise of its power, Congress was not restricted by the fact that the particular obstruction to interstate commerce with which it was dealing was also deemed a moral and social wrong.

It is said that the operation of the motel here is of a purely local character. But, assuming this to be true, "[i]f it is interstate commerce that feels the pinch, it does not matter how local the operation which applies the squeeze." *United States v. Women's Sportswear Mfrs. Assn.*, 336 U.S. 460, 464 (1949). * * *

We, therefore, conclude that the action of the Congress in the adoption of the Act as applied here to a motel which concededly serves interstate travelers is within the power granted it by the Commerce Clause of the Constitution, as interpreted by this Court for 140 years. * * *

[**JUSTICE DOUGLAS**' concurring opinion stated that he was reluctant to rest solely on the Commerce Clause because of his belief that the right of people to be free of state action that discriminates against them because of race "occupies a more protected position in our constitutional system than does the movement of cattle, fruit, steel and coal across state lines." He would also have relied upon § 5 of the Fourteenth Amendment. **JUSTICES BLACK** and **GOLDBERG** filed concurring opinions. All of these opinions also applied to the following case.]

Katzenbach v. McClung, 379 U.S. 294 (1964). Under Title II, any restaurant "principally engaged in selling food for consumption on the premises" was subject to the Act "if it serves or offers to serve interstate travelers or a substantial portion of the food which it serves * * * has moved in interstate commerce." This case involved Ollie's Barbecue, a Birmingham, Alabama, restaurant specializing in barbecued meats and homemade pies. Ollie's had a seating capacity of 220. It was located on a state highway, 11 blocks from an interstate. Although two-thirds of its employees were African American, Ollie's refused to serve African Americans. The district court found that, if forced to serve African Americans, the restaurant would lose a substantial amount of business.

A unanimous Court held that Title II constitutionally applied to Ollie's. **Justice Clark**'s opinion emphasized the "impressive array of testimony" during the 1963-64 congressional hearings "that discrimination in restaurants had a direct and highly restrictive effect upon interstate travel by Negroes. This resulted, it was said, because discriminatory practices prevent Negroes from buying prepared food served on the premises while on a trip * * *. This obviously discourages travel and obstructs interstate commerce for one can hardly travel without eating."

The Court also emphasized that "this testimony afforded ample basis for the conclusion that established restaurants in such areas sold less interstate goods because of the discrimination, * * * that business in general suffered and that many new businesses refrained from establishing there as a result of [the discrimination]." During the twelve months prior to the Civil Rights Act of 1964, Ollie's purchased about $150,000 worth of food, $69,683 of which was meat that had been shipped interstate. "It goes without saying that, viewed in isolation, the volume of food purchased by Ollie's Barbecue from sources supplied from out of state was insignificant when compared with the total foodstuffs moving in commerce. But, as our late Brother Jackson said for the

Court in *Wickard v. Filburn*: 'That appellee's own contribution to the demand for wheat may be trivial by itself is not enough to remove him from the scope of federal regulation where, as here, his contribution, taken together with that of many others similarly situated, is far from trivial.' "

The Court rejected the argument that Ollie's could not be "presumptively" swept into Title II based upon such a *Wickard*-like aggregation: "In *Darby*, this Court held constitutional the Fair Labor Standards Act. * * * Here, as there, Congress has determined for itself that refusals of service to Negroes have imposed burdens both upon the interstate flow of food and upon the movement of products generally. Of course, the mere fact that Congress has said when particular activity shall be deemed to affect commerce does not preclude further examination by this Court. But where we find that the legislators, in light of the facts and testimony before them, have a rational basis for finding a chosen regulatory scheme necessary to the protection of commerce, our investigation is at an end. The only remaining question — one answered in the affirmative by the court below — is whether the particular restaurant either serves or offers to serve interstate travelers or serves food a substantial portion of which has moved in interstate commerce."

Justice Black concurred, with some hesitation about the breadth of the Court's opinion. "I recognize too that some isolated and remote lunchroom which sells only to local people and buys almost all its supplies in the locality may possibly be beyond the reach of the power of Congress to regulate commerce, just as such an establishment is not covered by the present Act." **Justices Douglas** and **Goldberg** also concurred separately, arguing that Congress also had authority to enact Title II under § 5 of the Fourteenth Amendment.

NOTE ON THE COMMERCE CLAUSE AFTER THE NEW DEAL AND CIVIL RIGHTS ACT DECISIONS

The post-*Darby* precedents can be read to demolish many of the old Commerce Clause limitations:

- The Tenth Amendment has been reduced to a "truism" (*Darby*), the dual federalism idea underlying *E.C. Knight* has been abandoned, and formal distinctions as to subject matter marginalized (*Heart of Atlanta*).

- Congress can regulate anything once it actually enters commerce, under the outlaws-of-commerce theory (Lottery Case), and even beforehand under the current-of-commerce theory (*Swift*).

- Congress can regulate intrastate activities by showing a substantial effect on interstate commerce (*Darby*), and to show such effect Congress can aggregate lots of little transactions (*Wickard*) and even search through trash cans and food bins (*McClung*).

In *Perez v. United States*, 402 U.S. 146 (1971), the Court upheld a federal statute prohibiting "extortionate credit transactions" (*i.e.*, loan-sharking enforced by threats of violence). Perez was convicted without any showing that his loan-sharking affected interstate commerce in any way, but the Court upheld the law as applied to him, because he was "clearly a *member of the class* which engages in 'extortionate credit transactions' * * *. Where the *class of activities* is regulated and that *class* is within the reach of federal power, the courts have no power 'to excise, as trivial, individual instances' of the class." After *Perez*, is there any basis left for Commerce Clause review? Compare *Hodel v. Virginia Surface Mining & Reclamation Ass'n*, 452 U.S. 264 (1981) (deferring to congressional findings that linked the regulation to interstate commerce), with *United States v. Bass*, 404 U.S. 336 (1971) (interpreting a criminal statute to require a connection between the defendant's possession of a firearm was connected with interstate commerce).

UNITED STATES v. LOPEZ
514 U.S. 549, 115 S.Ct. 1624, 131 L.Ed.2d 626 (1995)

CHIEF JUSTICE REHNQUIST delivered the opinion of the Court.

[Alfonso Lopez, a twelfth-grade student, was arrested for carrying a concealed .38 caliber handgun and five bullets. He was originally charged under Texas law with firearm possession on school premises. The state charges were dismissed after federal agents charged Lopez with violating the federal Gun-Free School Zones Act of 1990, 18 U.S.C. § 922(q), which made it a federal offense "for any individual knowingly to possess a firearm at a place that the individual knows, or has reasonable cause to believe, is a school zone." The term "school zone" is defined as "in, or on the grounds of, a public, parochial or private school" or "within a distance of 1,000 feet from the grounds of a public, parochial or private school." At trial and on appeal, Lopez challenged the authority of Congress to legislate concerning local gun possession. The Court of Appeals held that Congress did not have this authority under the Commerce Clause.]

We start with first principles. The Constitution creates a Federal Government of enumerated powers. See U.S. Const., Art. I, § 8. As James Madison wrote, "[t]he powers delegated by the proposed Constitution to the federal government are few and defined. Those which are to remain in the State governments are numerous and indefinite." *The Federalist* No. 45, pp. 292-293 (C. Rossiter ed. 1961). This constitutionally mandated division of authority "was adopted by the Framers to ensure protection of our fundamental liberties." *Gregory v. Ashcroft*, 501 U.S. 452, 458 (1991) (internal quotation marks omitted). "Just as the separation and independence of the coordinate branches of the Federal Government serves to prevent the accumulation of excessive power in any one branch, a healthy balance of power between the States and the Federal Government will reduce the risk of tyranny and abuse from either front." *Ibid.*

[The Chief Justice then traced the history of the Court's analysis of Congress' power under the Commerce Clause: *Gibbons* as the foundational case; *E.C. Knight* and the other turn-of-the-century cases seeking principled limits, culminating with "the watershed case of *Jones & Laughlin*"; *Darby* and *Wickard*, "which ushered in an era of Commerce Clause jurisprudence that greatly expanded the previously defined authority of Congress."]

But even these modern-era precedents which have expanded congressional power under the Commerce Clause confirm that this power is subject to outer limits. In *Jones & Laughlin*, the Court warned that the scope of the interstate commerce power "must be considered in the light of our dual system of government and may not be extended so as to embrace effects upon interstate commerce so indirect and remote that to embrace them, in view of our complex society, would effectually obliterate the distinction between what is national and what is local and create a completely centralized government." Since that time, the Court has heeded that warning and undertaken to decide whether a rational basis existed for concluding that a regulated activity sufficiently affected interstate commerce. [Citing *Hodel, Perez, McClung, Heart of Atlanta Motel*.]
* * *

Consistent with this structure, we have identified three broad categories of activity that Congress may regulate under its commerce power. First, Congress may regulate the use of the channels of interstate commerce. See, *e.g.*, *Darby*; *Heart of Atlanta Motel*. Second, Congress is empowered to regulate and protect the instrumentalities of interstate commerce, or persons or things in interstate commerce, even though the threat may come only from intrastate activities. See, *e.g.*, *Shreveport Rate Case*. Finally, Congress' commerce authority includes the power to regulate those activities having a substantial relation to interstate commerce, *Jones & Laughlin*, *i.e.*, those activities that substantially affect interstate commerce. * * *

We now turn to consider the power of Congress, in the light of this framework, to enact § 922(q). The first two categories of authority may be quickly disposed of: § 922(q) is not a regulation of the use of the channels of interstate commerce, nor is it an attempt to prohibit the interstate transportation of a commodity through the channels of commerce; nor can § 922(q) be justified as a regulation by which Congress has sought to protect an instrumentality of interstate commerce or a thing in interstate commerce. Thus, if § 922(q) is to be sustained, it must be under the third category as a regulation of an activity that substantially affects interstate commerce. * * *

Even *Wickard*, which is perhaps the most far reaching example of Commerce Clause authority over intrastate activity, involved economic activity in a way that the possession of a gun in a school zone does not. Roscoe Filburn operated a small farm in Ohio, on which, in the year involved, he raised 23 acres of wheat. It was his practice to sow winter wheat in the fall, and after harvesting it in July to sell a portion of the crop, to feed part of it to poultry and livestock on the farm, to use some in making flour for home consumption, and to keep the remainder for seeding future crops. The Secretary of Agriculture assessed a penalty against him under the Agricultural Adjustment Act of 1938 because he harvested about 12 acres more wheat than his allotment under the Act permitted. The Act was designed to regulate the volume of wheat moving in interstate and foreign commerce in order to avoid surpluses and shortages, and concomitant fluctuation in wheat prices, which had previously obtained. [In sustaining the Act, the Court stressed that home-grown and -consumed wheat affected the interstate market price of wheat because its use obviated the need to buy that wheat on the market.]

Section 922(q) is a criminal statute that by its terms has nothing to do with "commerce" or any sort of economic enterprise, however broadly one might define those terms.[3] Section 922(q) is not an essential part of a larger regulation of economic activity, in which the regulatory scheme could be undercut unless the intrastate activity were regulated. It cannot, therefore, be sustained under our cases upholding regulations of activities that arise out of or are connected with a commercial transaction, which viewed in the aggregate, substantially affects interstate commerce.

Second, § 922(q) contains no jurisdictional element which would ensure, through case-by-case inquiry, that the firearm possession in question affects interstate commerce. For example, in *United States v. Bass*, 404 U.S. 336 (1971), the Court interpreted former 18 U.S.C. § 1202(a), which made it a crime for a felon to "receiv[e], posses[s], or transpor[t] in commerce or affecting commerce . . . any firearm." The Court interpreted the possession component of § 1202(a) to require an additional nexus to interstate commerce both because the statute was ambiguous and because "unless Congress conveys its purpose clearly, it will not be deemed to have significantly changed the federal-state balance." The *Bass* Court set aside the conviction because although the Government had demonstrated that Bass had possessed a firearm, it had failed "to show the requisite nexus with interstate commerce." The Court thus interpreted the statute to reserve the constitutional question whether Congress could regulate, without more, the "mere possession" of firearms. Unlike the statute in *Bass*, § 922(q) has no express jurisdictional element which might limit its reach to a discrete set of firearm possessions that additionally have an explicit connection with or effect on interstate commerce.

Although as part of our independent evaluation of constitutionality under the Commerce Clause we of course consider legislative findings, and indeed even congressional committee findings, regarding effect on interstate commerce, the Government concedes that "[n]either the statute nor its legislative history contain[s] express congressional findings regarding the effects upon interstate commerce of gun possession in a school zone." Brief for United States 5–6. We agree with the Government that Congress normally is not required to make formal findings as to the substantial burdens that an activity has on interstate commerce. But to the extent that congressional findings would enable us to evaluate the legislative judgment that the activity in question substantially

---

3. Under our federal system, the " 'States possess primary authority for defining and enforcing the criminal law.' " When Congress criminalizes conduct already denounced as criminal by the States, it effects a " 'change in the sensitive relation between federal and state criminal jurisdiction.' " The Government acknowledges that § 922(q) "displace[s] state policy choices in . . . that its prohibitions apply even in States that have chosen not to outlaw the conduct in question." Brief for United States 29, n.18; see also Statement of President George Bush on Signing the Crime Control Act of 1990, 26 Weekly Comp. of Pres. Doc. 1944, 1945 (Nov. 29, 1990) ("Most egregiously, section [922(q)] inappropriately overrides legitimate state firearms laws with a new and unnecessary Federal law. The policies reflected in these provisions could legitimately be adopted by the States, but they should not be imposed upon the States by Congress").

affected interstate commerce, even though no such substantial effect was visible to the naked eye, they are lacking here.[4] * * *

The Government's essential contention, *in fine*, is that we may determine here that § 922(q) is valid because possession of a firearm in a local school zone does indeed substantially affect interstate commerce. The Government argues that possession of a firearm in a school zone may result in violent crime and that violent crime can be expected to affect the functioning of the national economy in two ways. First, the costs of violent crime are substantial, and, through the mechanism of insurance, those costs are spread throughout the population. Second, violent crime reduces the willingness of individuals to travel to areas within the country that are perceived to be unsafe. Cf. *Heart of Atlanta Motel*. The Government also argues that the presence of guns in schools poses a substantial threat to the educational process by threatening the learning environment. A handicapped educational process, in turn, will result in a less productive citizenry. That, in turn, would have an adverse effect on the Nation's economic well-being. As a result, the Government argues that Congress could rationally have concluded that § 922(q) substantially affects interstate commerce.

We pause to consider the implications of the Government's arguments. The Government admits, under its "costs of crime" reasoning, that Congress could regulate not only all violent crime, but all activities that might lead to violent crime, regardless of how tenuously they relate to interstate commerce. Similarly, under the Government's "national productivity" reasoning, Congress could regulate any activity that it found was related to the economic productivity of individual citizens: family law (including marriage, divorce, and child custody), for example. Under the theories that the Government presents in support of § 922(q), it is difficult to perceive any limitation on federal power, even in areas such as criminal law enforcement or education where States historically have been sovereign. Thus, if we were to accept the Government's arguments, we are hard-pressed to posit any activity by an individual that Congress is without power to regulate. * * *

Admittedly, a determination whether an intrastate activity is commercial or noncommercial may in some cases result in legal uncertainty. But, so long as Congress' authority is limited to those powers enumerated in the Constitution, and so long as those enumerated powers are interpreted as having judicially enforceable outer limits, congressional legislation under the Commerce Clause always will engender "legal uncertainty." [The Chief Justice quoted *McCulloch*, *Gibbons*, and *Marbury*.]

---

4. We note that on September 13, 1994, President Clinton signed into law the Violent Crime Control and Law Enforcement Act of 1994, Pub.L. 103–322, 108 Stat. 1796. Section 320904 of that Act amends § 922(q) to include congressional findings regarding the effects of firearm possession in and around schools upon interstate and foreign commerce. The Government does not rely upon these subsequent findings as a substitute for the absence of findings in the first instance. Tr. of Oral Arg. 25 ("[W]e're not relying on them in the strict sense of the word, but we think that at a very minimum they indicate that reasons can be identified for why Congress wanted to regulate this particular activity").

* * * The possession of a gun in a local school zone is in no sense an economic activity that might, through repetition elsewhere, substantially affect any sort of interstate commerce. Respondent was a local student at a local school; there is no indication that he had recently moved in interstate commerce, and there is no requirement that his possession of the firearm have any concrete tie to interstate commerce.

To uphold the Government's contentions here, we would have to pile inference upon inference in a manner that would bid fair to convert congressional authority under the Commerce Clause to a general police power of the sort retained by the States. Admittedly, some of our prior cases have taken long steps down that road, giving great deference to congressional action. The broad language in these opinions has suggested the possibility of additional expansion, but we decline here to proceed any further. To do so would require us to conclude that the Constitution's enumeration of powers does not presuppose something not enumerated, and that there never will be a distinction between what is truly national and what is truly local. This we are unwilling to do.

JUSTICE KENNEDY, with whom JUSTICE O'CONNOR joins, concurring. * * *

The history of our Commerce Clause decisions contains at least two lessons of relevance to this case. The first * * * is the imprecision of content-based boundaries used without more to define the limits of the Commerce Clause. The second, related to the first but of even greater consequence, is that the Court as an institution and the legal system as a whole have an immense stake in the stability of our Commerce Clause jurisprudence as it has evolved to this point. *Stare decisis* operates with great force in counseling us not to call in question the essential principles now in place respecting the congressional power to regulate transactions of a commercial nature. That fundamental restraint on our power forecloses us from reverting to an understanding of commerce that would serve only an 18th-century economy, dependent then upon production and trading practices that had changed but little over the preceding centuries; it also mandates against returning to the time when congressional authority to regulate undoubted commercial activities was limited by a judicial determination that those matters had an insufficient connection to an interstate system. Congress can regulate in the commercial sphere on the assumption that we have a single market and a unified purpose to build a stable national economy.

[Justice Kennedy lamented that the Court has had such difficulty articulating standards for enforcing federalist restraints on the national government. This was, in fact, ironic, because of the four structural elements in the Constitution (separation of powers, checks and balances, judicial review, federalism), federalism was the unique contribution of the Framers to political science and political theory. Justice Kennedy emphasized Madison's "double security" argument in *Federalist* No. 51.]

The theory that two governments accord more liberty than one requires for its realization two distinct and discernable lines of political accountability: one between the citizens and the Federal Government; the second between the citizens and the States. If, as Madison expected, the federal and state governments are to control each other, see *The Federalist* No. 51, and hold each other in check by competing for the affections of the people, see *The Federalist* No. 46, those citizens must have some means of knowing which of the two governments to hold accountable for the failure to perform a given function. * * * Were the Federal Government to take over the regulation of entire areas of traditional state concern, areas having nothing to do with the regulation of commercial activities, the boundaries between the spheres of federal and state authority would blur and political responsibility would become illusory. The resultant inability to hold either branch of the government answerable to the citizens is more dangerous even than devolving too much authority to the remote central power.

To be sure, one conclusion that could be drawn from *The Federalist Papers* is that the balance between national and state power is entrusted in its entirety to the political process. Madison's observation that "the people ought not surely to be precluded from giving most of their confidence where they may discover it to be most due," *The Federalist* No. 46, p. 295 (C. Rossiter ed. 1961), can be interpreted to say that the essence of responsibility for a shift in power from the State to the Federal Government rests upon a political judgment, though he added assurance that "the State governments could have little to apprehend, because it is only within a certain sphere that the federal power can, in the nature of things, be advantageously administered," *ibid*. Whatever the judicial role, it is axiomatic that Congress does have substantial discretion and control over the federal balance. * * *

At the same time, the absence of structural mechanisms to require those officials to undertake this principled task, and the momentary political convenience often attendant upon their failure to do so, argue against a complete renunciation of the judicial role. Although it is the obligation of all officers of the Government to respect the constitutional design, the federal balance is too essential a part of our constitutional structure and plays too vital a role in securing freedom for us to admit inability to intervene when one or the other level of Government has tipped the scales too far. * * *

The statute before us upsets the federal balance to a degree that renders it an unconstitutional assertion of the commerce power, and our intervention is required. As the Chief Justice explains, unlike the earlier cases to come before the Court here neither the actors nor their conduct have a commercial character, and neither the purposes nor the design of the statute have an evident commercial nexus. The statute makes the simple possession of a gun within 1,000 feet of the grounds of the school a criminal offense. In a sense any conduct in this interdependent world of ours has an ultimate commercial origin or consequence, but we have not yet said the commerce power may reach so far. If Congress attempts that extension, then at the least we must inquire whether the exercise of national power seeks to intrude upon an area of traditional state concern.

An interference of these dimensions occurs here, for it is well established that education is a traditional concern of the States. The proximity to schools, including of course schools owned and operated by the States or their subdivisions, is the very premise for making the conduct criminal. In these circumstances, we have a particular duty to insure that the federal-state balance is not destroyed. [Justice Kennedy concluded that this is an area best left to state "experimentation," and he noted that over 40 states have adopted laws criminalizing possession of guns near a school.]

JUSTICE THOMAS, concurring. * * *

In an appropriate case, I believe that we must further reconsider our "substantial effects" test with an eye toward constructing a standard that reflects the text and history of the Commerce Clause without totally rejecting our more recent Commerce Clause jurisprudence. * * *

At the time the original Constitution was ratified, "commerce" consisted of selling, buying, and bartering, as well as transporting for these purposes. See 1 S. Johnson, *A Dictionary of the English Language* 361 (4th ed. 1773) (defining commerce as "Intercour[s]e; exchange of one thing for another; interchange of any thing; trade; traffick"); [further dictionaries of the period]. This understanding finds support in the etymology of the word, which literally means "with merchandise." See 3 *Oxford English Dictionary* 552 (2d ed. 1989) (com— "with"; merci— "merchandise"). In fact, when Federalists and Anti-Federalists discussed the Commerce Clause during the ratification period, they often used trade (in its selling/bartering sense) and commerce interchangeably.

[Justice Thomas also argued that the term "commerce" was used in contradistinction to productive activities such as manufacturing and agriculture. See *Federalist* Nos. 21, 36, 74 (all by Hamilton); state ratification conventions.] Moreover, interjecting a modern sense of commerce into the Constitution generates significant textual and structural problems. For example, one cannot replace "commerce" with a different type of enterprise, such as manufacturing. When a manufacturer produces a car, assembly cannot take place "with a foreign nation" or "with the Indian Tribes." Parts may come from different States or other nations and hence may have been in the flow of commerce at one time, but manufacturing takes place at a discrete site. Agriculture and manufacturing involve the production of goods; commerce encompasses traffic in such articles.

The Port Preference Clause also suggests that the term "commerce" denoted sale and/or transport rather than business generally. According to that Clause, "[n]o Preference shall be given by any Regulation of Commerce or Revenue to the Ports of one State over those of another." U.S. Const., Art. I, § 9, cl. 6. Although it is possible to conceive of regulations of manufacturing or farming that prefer one port over another, the more natural reading is that the Clause prohibits Congress from using its commerce power to channel commerce through certain favored ports.

The Constitution not only uses the word "commerce" in a narrower sense than our case law might suggest, it also does not support the proposition that Congress has authority over all activities that "substantially affect" interstate commerce. The Commerce Clause does not state that Congress may "regulate matters that substantially affect commerce with foreign Nations, and among the several States, and with the Indian Tribes." In contrast, the Constitution itself temporarily prohibited amendments that would "affect" Congress' lack of authority to prohibit or restrict the slave trade or to enact unproportioned direct taxation. U.S. Const., Art. V. Clearly, the Framers could have drafted a Constitution that contained a "substantially affects interstate commerce" clause had that been their objective. * * *

[Finally], much if not all of Art. I, § 8 (including portions of the Commerce Clause itself) would be surplusage if Congress had been given authority over matters that substantially affect interstate commerce. An interpretation of cl. 3 that makes the rest of § 8 superfluous simply cannot be correct. Yet this Court's Commerce Clause jurisprudence has endorsed just such an interpretation: the power we have accorded Congress has swallowed Art. I, § 8. * * *

Our construction of the scope of congressional authority has the additional problem of coming close to turning the Tenth Amendment on its head. Our case law could be read to reserve to the United States all powers not expressly prohibited by the Constitution. Taken together, these fundamental textual problems should, at the very least, convince us that the "substantial effects" test should be reexamined.

[Justice Thomas would read *Gibbons* in a more restricted way than the Court's post-New Deal precedents (especially *Wickard* and *Darby*) have done. Chief Justice Marshall explicitly rejected the idea of a completely elastic Commerce Clause, argued Justice Thomas. "I am aware of no cases prior to the New Deal that characterized the power flowing from the Commerce Clause as sweepingly as does our substantial effects test. My review of the case law indicates that the substantial effects test is but an innovation of the 20th century." It would have the effect of giving Congress a national "police power" inconsistent with the Framers' original design. Justice Thomas found the majority opinion in this case a useful corrective and left open the possibility of a modification of recent Commerce Clause jurisprudence in another case.]

[The dissenting opinion of **JUSTICE STEVENS** has been omitted.]

JUSTICE SOUTER, dissenting.

[Justice Souter defended a strongly deferential approach to Commerce Clause review, both because it "reflects our respect for the institutional competence of the Congress on a subject expressly assigned to it by the Constitution and our appreciation of the legitimacy that comes from Congress's political accountability in dealing with matters open to a wide range of possible choices," and because the Court's activist reading of Commerce Clause restrictions during the *Lochner* era (Chapter 1, § 3) was an experiment from which the Court wisely retreated.]

There is today, however, a backward glance at both the old pitfalls, as the Court treats deference under the rationality rule as subject to gradation according to the commercial or noncommercial nature of the immediate subject of the challenged regulation. The distinction between what is patently commercial and what is not looks much like the old distinction between what directly affects commerce and what touches it only indirectly. And the act of calibrating the level of deference by drawing a line between what is patently commercial and what is less purely so will probably resemble the process of deciding how much interference with contractual freedom was fatal. Thus, it seems fair to ask whether the step taken by the Court today does anything but portend a return to the untenable jurisprudence from which the Court extricated itself almost 60 years ago. The answer is not reassuring. To be sure, the occasion for today's decision reflects the century's end, not its beginning. But if it seems anomalous that the Congress of the United States has taken to regulating school yards, the act in question is still probably no more remarkable than state regulation of bake shops 90 years ago. In any event, there is no reason to hope that the Court's qualification of rational basis review will be any more successful than the efforts at substantive economic review made by our predecessors as the century began. Taking the Court's opinion on its own terms, Justice Breyer has explained both the hopeless porosity of "commercial" character as a ground of Commerce Clause distinction in America's highly connected economy, and the inconsistency of this categorization with our rational basis precedents from the last 50 years.

Further glosses on rationality review, moreover, may be in the offing. Although this case turns on commercial character, the Court gestures toward two other considerations that it might sometime entertain in applying rational basis scrutiny (apart from a statutory obligation to supply independent proof of a jurisdictional element): does the congressional statute deal with subjects of traditional state regulation, and does the statute contain explicit factual findings supporting the otherwise implicit determination that the regulated activity substantially affects interstate commerce? Once again, any appeal these considerations may have depends on ignoring the painful lesson learned in 1937, for neither of the Court's suggestions would square with rational basis scrutiny. * * *

JUSTICE BREYER, with whom **JUSTICE STEVENS**, **JUSTICE SOUTER**, and **JUSTICE GINSBURG** join, dissenting.

* * * I apply three basic principles of Commerce Clause interpretation. First, the power to "regulate Commerce . . . among the several States" encompasses the power to regulate local activities insofar as they significantly affect interstate commerce. See, *e.g.*, *Gibbons*; *Wickard*. As the majority points out, the Court, in describing how much of an effect the Clause requires, sometimes has used the word "substantial" and sometimes has not. Compare, *e.g.*, *Wickard* ("substantial economic effect") with *Hodel* ("affects interstate commerce"). * * * I use the word "significant" because the word "substantial" implies a somewhat narrower power than recent precedent suggests. See, *e.g.*, *Perez*.

Second, in determining whether a local activity will likely have a significant effect upon interstate commerce, a court must consider, not the effect of an individual act (a single instance of gun possession), but rather the cumulative effect of all similar instances (i.e., the effect of all guns possessed in or near schools). See, *e.g.*, *Wickard*. * * *

Third, the Constitution requires us to judge the connection between a regulated activity and interstate commerce, not directly, but at one remove. Courts must give Congress a degree of leeway in determining the existence of a significant factual connection between the regulated activity and interstate commerce — both because the Constitution delegates the commerce power directly to Congress and because the determination requires an empirical judgment of a kind that a legislature is more likely than a court to make with accuracy. The traditional words "rational basis" capture this leeway. Thus, the specific question before us, as the Court recognizes, is not whether the "regulated activity sufficiently affected interstate commerce," but, rather, whether Congress could have had *a rational basis* for so concluding. * * *

* * * Could Congress rationally have found that "violent crime in school zones," through its effect on the "quality of education," significantly (or substantially) affects "interstate" or "foreign commerce"? 18 U.S.C.A. - §§ 922(q)(1)(F), (G) (Nov.1994 Supp.). As long as one views the commerce connection, not as a "technical legal conception," but as "a practical one," *Swift & Co.*, the answer to this question must be yes. Numerous reports and studies — generated both inside and outside government — make clear that Congress could reasonably have found the empirical connection that its law, implicitly or explicitly, asserts.

[Justice Breyer compendiously documented the extent to which guns in and around schools have become widespread and have contributed to increased school violence, with a concomitant decline in the learning environment.] Having found that guns in schools significantly undermine the quality of education in our Nation's classrooms, Congress could also have found, given the effect of education upon interstate and foreign commerce, that gun-related violence in and around schools is a commercial, as well as a human, problem. Education, although far more than a matter of economics, has long been inextricably intertwined with the Nation's economy. * * * Scholars estimate that nearly a quarter of America's economic growth in the early years of this century is traceable directly to increased schooling; that investment in "human capital" (through spending on education) exceeded investment in "physical capital" by a ratio of almost two to one; and that the economic returns to this investment in education exceeded the returns to conventional capital investment. [The link between secondary education and business has become more important in recent decades, owing to increased emphasis on technology and service in the economy, global competition, and firm preferences for areas with good educational facilities.]

The economic links I have just sketched seem fairly obvious. Why then is it not equally obvious, in light of those links, that a widespread, serious, and substantial physical threat to teaching and learning *also* substantially threatens the commerce to which that teaching and learning is inextricably tied? That is to say, guns in the hands of six percent of inner-city high school students and gun-related violence throughout a city's schools must threaten the trade and commerce that those schools support. The only question, then, is whether the latter threat is (to use the majority's terminology) "substantial." And, the evidence of (1) the *extent* of the gun-related violence problem, (2) the *extent* of the resulting negative effect on classroom learning, and (3) the *extent* of the consequent negative commercial effects, when taken together, indicate a threat to trade and commerce that is "substantial." At the very least, Congress could rationally have concluded that the links are "substantial."

Specifically, Congress could have found that gun-related violence near the classroom poses a serious economic threat (1) to consequently inadequately educated workers who must endure low paying jobs, and (2) to communities and businesses that might (in today's "information society") otherwise gain, from a well-educated work force, an important commercial advantage of a kind that location near a railhead or harbor provided in the past. Congress might also have found these threats to be no different in kind from other threats that this Court has found within the commerce power, such as the threat that loan sharking poses to the "funds" of "numerous localities," *Perez*, and that unfair labor practices pose to instrumentalities of commerce. As I have pointed out, Congress has written that "the occurrence of violent crime in school zones" has brought about a "decline in the quality of education" that "has an adverse impact on interstate commerce and the foreign commerce of the United States." 18 U.S.C.A. §§ 922(q)(1)(F), (G) (Nov. 1994 Supp.). The violence-related facts, the educational facts, and the economic facts, taken together, make this conclusion rational. And, because under our case law the sufficiency of the constitutionally necessary Commerce Clause link between a crime of violence and interstate commerce turns simply upon size or degree, those same facts make the statute constitutional. * * *

The majority's holding — that § 922 falls outside the scope of the Commerce Clause — creates three serious legal problems. First, the majority's holding runs contrary to modern Supreme Court cases that have upheld congressional actions despite connections to interstate or foreign commerce that are less significant than the effect of school violence. [Specifically, *Perez*, where Congress found a link between local loansharking, violence, and commerce, and *McClung*, where Congress found a link between prejudicial discrimination, interstate travel, and economic integration.]

The second legal problem the Court creates comes from its apparent belief that it can reconcile its holding with earlier cases by making a critical distinction between "commercial" and noncommercial "transaction[s]." That is to say, the Court believes the Constitution would distinguish between two local activities, each of which has an identical effect upon interstate commerce, if one, but not the other, is "commercial" in nature. As a general matter, this approach fails to heed this Court's earlier warning not to turn "questions of the power of Congress" upon "formula[s]" that would give "controlling force to nomenclature such as 'production' and 'indirect' and foreclose consideration of the actual effects of the activity in question upon interstate commerce." *Wickard*. See also *Darby* (overturning the Court's distinction between "production" and "commerce" in the child labor case, *Hammer v. Dagenhart*). Moreover, the majority's test is not consistent with what the Court saw as the point of the cases that the majority now characterizes. Although the majority today attempts to categorize *Perez, McClung*, and *Wickard* as involving intrastate "economic activity," the Courts that decided each of those cases did *not* focus upon the economic nature of the activity regulated. Rather, they focused upon whether that activity *affected* interstate or foreign commerce. In fact, the *Wickard* Court expressly held that Wickard's consumption of home grown wheat, "though it may not be regarded as commerce," could nevertheless be regulated —

"whatever its nature" — so long as "it exerts a substantial economic effect on interstate commerce."

More importantly, if a distinction between commercial and noncommercial activities is to be made, this is not the case in which to make it. The majority clearly cannot intend such a distinction to focus narrowly on an act of gun possession standing by itself, for such a reading could not be reconciled with *McClung* or *Perez* — in each of those cases the specific transaction (the race-based exclusion, the use of force) was not itself "commercial." And, if the majority instead means to distinguish generally among broad categories of activities, differentiating what is educational from what is commercial, then, as a practical matter, the line becomes almost impossible to draw. Schools that teach reading, writing, mathematics, and related basic skills serve both social and commercial purposes, and one cannot easily separate the one from the other. American industry itself has been, and is again, involved in teaching. When, and to what extent, does its involvement make education commercial? Does the number of vocational classes that train students directly for jobs make a difference? Does it matter if the school is public or private, nonprofit or profit-seeking? Does it matter if a city or State adopts a voucher plan that pays private firms to run a school? Even if one were to ignore these practical questions, why should there be a theoretical distinction between education, when it significantly benefits commerce, and environmental pollution, when it causes economic harm? * * *

The third legal problem created by the Court's holding is that it threatens legal uncertainty in an area of law that, until this case, seemed reasonably well settled. Congress has enacted many statutes (more than 100 sections of the United States Code), including criminal statutes (at least 25 sections), that use the words "affecting commerce" to define their scope, and other statutes that contain no jurisdictional language at all, see, *e.g.*, 18 U.S.C. § 922(o)(1) (possession of machine guns). Do these, or similar, statutes regulate noncommercial activities? If so, would that alter the meaning of "affecting commerce" in a jurisdictional element? More importantly, in the absence of a jurisdictional element, are the courts nevertheless to take *Wickard* (and later similar cases) as inapplicable, and to judge the effect of a single noncommercial activity on interstate commerce without considering similar instances of the forbidden conduct? However these questions are eventually resolved, the legal uncertainty now created will restrict Congress' ability to enact criminal laws aimed at criminal behavior that, considered problem by problem rather than instance by instance, seriously threatens the economic, as well as social, well-being of Americans. * * *

NOTES ON *LOPEZ* AND THE
COMMERCE CLAUSE'S NEW TEETH

1. *Reconciling the Precedents?* How can *Lopez* be distinguished from *Perez*, *McClung*, and *Wickard*? The educational setting? That gun-toting is not as obviously "commercial" as loan-sharking, restaurants, and farming? The absence of congressional findings in the 1990 statute? The absence of a jurisdictional feature to the statute? Is there any answer to Justice Breyer's

charge that the gun-control statute can be factually connected with commerce at least as persuasively as the statutes upheld in the earlier cases? His argument that there is no reason to believe that the Court's new test will work any better than the failed tests of the past?

Justice Thomas's concurring opinion can be read as suggesting that *Perez* and the other precedents should be read narrowly (perhaps some overruled), because a broad reading would press the Court's Commerce Clause jurisprudence further from the original intent of the Framers. Should some of the twentieth-century precedents be overruled? In response to Justice Kennedy's and Justice Breyer's invocation of *stare decisis*, Justice Thomas invokes *Gibbons* — the leading precedent — as thoroughly at odds with the Court's twentieth-century jurisprudence. Do the other Justices have good responses to Justice Thomas's analysis of *Gibbons*?

2. *Institutional Concerns.* Institutional concerns can be raised for either side of the debate. Justice Souter worried that the new bout of line-drawing and litigation that *Lopez* will stimulate threatens a new *Lochner* era, in which the Court will trump democratic values without appropriate reference to a valid or even administrable constitutional principle. Justice Breyer argued that the commercial/noncommercial principle cannot be neutrally or predictably administered.[n]

The majority believed that if such a weak statute were upheld against Commerce Clause attack, Congress would view itself as essentially unlimited, thereby usurping more and more state terrain and wasting the potential benefits of federalism — double security for liberty, which depends upon clear lines of state/national authority; civic involvement, which is easier at the local level; and efficiency, which is sacrificed with increased centralization. Most important, an opinion affirming this much of a congressional reach would raise the *commitment problem*: Why should the states continue to have enthusiasm for the federal arrangement if they see the federal government as encroaching without limits? *Lopez* might then be considered a "constitutional wake-up call," in which the Court is reminding Congress that it must attend to jurisdictional limits when it adopts legislation.[o] Under this view, the Court could still be very lenient in reviewing congressional enactments but will not make up reasons for Congress, as Justice Breyer was willing to do.

3. *Justifying National Regulation Under the Commerce Clause.* Professor Donald Regan criticizes the Court's Commerce Clause decisions from the New Deal onward for failing to ask whether the regulation should or should not come

---

n. For an argument that the Court's line-drawing in Commerce Clause cases is no worse than its line-drawing in equal protection, free speech, and privacy cases, see Lynn Baker & Ernest Young, *Federalism and the Double Standard of Judicial Review*, 51 Duke L.J. 75, 94-100 (2001).

o. See Jenna Bednar & William Eskridge, Jr., *Steadying the Court's "Unsteady Path": A Theory of Judicial Enforcement of Federalism*, 68 S. Cal. L. Rev. 1447 (1995).

from the federal government.[p] Given the values of federalism and presumptive state regulation of allocative and developmental projects such as education, roadbuilding, police and fire protection, he argues that national regulation of such issues must be affirmatively, and deliberately in Congress, justified along the lines suggested above, especially facilitating an efficient national market, creating public goods, and avoiding races to the bottom. Could *Darby*, *Wickard*, *Heart of Atlanta Motel*, *McClung*, and *Perez* all be defended under this revised line of inquiry? How about federal environmental regulation? If Justice Breyer's opinion had been written into the statute and its legislative history, would it have passed this test?

PROBLEM 7-2
THE REACH OF COMMERCE CLAUSE POWER AFTER *LOPEZ*

(A) You are Counsel to the President, who wants to propose new federal laws regulating guns near schools, but in a form that will probably pass constitutional muster. What drafting strategies would you suggest to the President? What are the odds of constitutionality for each kind of strategy?

(B) Angel McClary Raich and Diane Monson, California residents suffering from serious medical conditions, grow and use marijuana for medical purposes pursuant to the terms of the state Compassionate Use Act. Federal agents seize and destroy all of Monson's cannabis plants because even their private production violated the federal Controlled Substances Act (CSA). Enacted in 1970, the CSA classifies marijuana as a Schedule I drug, because of its supposed high potential for abuse and lack of accepted medical use. (Nine states, including California, have found to the contrary, but of course their medical marijuana statutes would be preempted if the CSA is a proper use of Congress's Commerce Clause power.) Raich and Monson brought suit to enjoin enforcement of the CSA against their private cultivation and use of marijuana for medical purposes. After *Lopez*, does Congress have the authority to regulate private production of marijuana? For the Supreme Court's post-*Lopez* answer, see *Gonzales v. Raich*, 545 U.S. 1 (2005).

(C) Federal law makes it a crime for a person subject to a domestic violence protection order to possess any kind of firearm. 18 U.S.C. § 922(g)(8). Frankly Unctuous is under such an order for making obscene and abusive phone calls to his estranged wife; they both live in Midland, Texas. FBI agents arrest him for possession of a handgun in his home. Unctuous challenges his prosecution on the ground that Congress has no authority to regulate domestic disputes that have no possible connection to interstate commerce and that have been traditionally regulated only at the state level. He also invokes the Supreme Court's ruling in *District of Columbia v. Heller*, 128 S.Ct. 2783 (2008), that the

---

p. See Donald Regan, *How To Think About the Federal Commerce Power and Incidentally Rewrite* United States v. Lopez, 94 Mich. L. Rev. 554 (1995). For other scholarly discussions of *Lopez* and its implications, see, e.g., Steven Calabresi, *"A Government of Limited and Enumerated Powers": In Defense of* United States v. Lopez, 94 Mich. L. Rev. 752 (1995); Lawrence Lessig, *Translating Federalism:* United States v. Lopez, 1995 Sup. Ct. Rev. 125; Symposium, 46 Case Western Res. L. Rev. 633 (1996).

Second Amendment recognizes an individual right for law-abiding citizens to keep handguns in the home for self-defense and perhaps other purposes. *Heller* accepted all of the arguments made by Justice Scalia and described in our problem at the end of Chapter 2. Although Justice Scalia's opinion for the Court only extended the right to "law-abiding" citizens, Unctuous argues that he is law-abiding, and points out that the domestic enforcement order was generated by nonviolent phone calls alone. How should the government respond to these arguments? Is the Supreme Court likely to agree?

Jot down your answers to these questions. We will return to them later in the chapter, after *United States v. Morrison* in § 3E.

SECTION 3. CONGRESSIONAL AUTHORITY TO PROMOTE CIVIL RIGHTS

After *Lopez* — the first case in 60 years to strike down a federal statute as beyond the commerce power — Congress was on notice that the Commerce Clause no longer served as the source of a virtually limitless national police power for Congress. *Heart of Atlanta* and *McClung* are probably safe from post-*Lopez* reconsideration, as both deal with the refusal to enter into a commercial transaction (renting a hotel room, buying food in a restaurant). But other civil rights measures may lack this obvious economic connection, including the following: (1) The Voting Rights Act of 1965 forbids certain state and local electoral practices that diminish the voting strength of minority groups. (2) The Religious Freedom Restoration Act of 1993 forbade state and local governments from substantially burdening a person's free exercise of religion unless it did so for a compelling government interest achieved by the least restrictive means. (3) The Violence Against Women Act of 1991 provided the victim of a crime of violence motivated by gender with a cause of action in federal court against the perpetrator.

The constitutionality of provisions such as these are at the cutting edge of current constitutional law. The logical sources of congressional power for civil rights legislation of these types are the enforcement provisions of the Reconstruction Amendments (§ 2 of the Thirteenth and Fifteenth Amendments and § 5 of the Fourteenth Amendment). A potential limit upon congressional power is the Eleventh Amendment, which, as interpreted by the Court, sometimes forbids Congress from authorizing a suit by a private party against a state. This section turns to these provisions and evaluates the constitutionality of statutes in each of the six categories mentioned above. We take a largely chronological approach to the statutes and cases, evaluating the post-Civil War statutes first, then turning to the major cases that arose under the Voting Rights Act and later enactments. We end with the Court's consideration of the Violence Against Women Act, where Commerce Clause and civil-rights-enforcement rationales were both invoked in defense of the statute.

A. THE RECONSTRUCTION AMENDMENTS AND FEDERAL STATUTES ADOPTED UNDER THEM

Recall the discussion of the adoption of the Reconstruction Amendments following the Civil War in Chapter 1, § 4 and Chapter 2, § 1. Read § 2 of the Thirteenth and Fifteenth Amendments and § 5 of the Fourteenth Amendment carefully. What should it mean for Congress "to enforce" these provisions "by appropriate legislation"?

In 1866, when only the Thirteenth Amendment had been ratified, Congress enacted the Civil Rights Act of 1866. In addition to providing criminal penalties for the deprivation of federal rights under color of state law, the statute, as currently codified, contains two important protections. 42 U.S.C. § 1981(a) provides: "All persons within the jurisdiction of the United States shall have the same right in every State and Territory to make and enforce contracts, to sue, be parties, give evidence, and to the full and equal benefit of all laws and proceedings for the security of persons and property as is enjoyed by white citizens, and shall be subject to like punishment, pains, penalties, taxes, licenses, and exactions of every kind, and to no other." 42 U.S.C. § 1982 provides: "All citizens of the United States shall have the same right, in every State and Territory, as is enjoyed by white citizens thereof to inherit, purchase, lease, sell, hold, and convey real and personal property." Serious questions were raised concerning whether the 1866 statute was within Congress's enumerated legislative power under § 2 of the Thirteenth Amendment, and for that reason and others President Johnson vetoed the bill. Read § 1 of the Thirteenth Amendment: What was the constitutional problem? Congress overrode the presidential veto, but recognized that more needed to be done.

Much of the impetus for the Fourteenth Amendment was to make certain that the 1866 Act was constitutional — and even more so, to protect those rights by constitutional text so that they would not be subject to repeal by a later Congress. Read § 1 of the Fourteenth Amendment and compare it to the language of the 1866 Act. The Framers of the Fourteenth Amendment contemplated a large role for § 5 of the amendment as well, for it appears that they viewed Congress, through the enactment of legislation, and not the courts, through the interpretation of the Reconstruction Amendments, as the primary enforcers of the Amendments.[a] Indeed, Congress adopted new civil rights measures in 1870 and 1871. The latter provided, among other things, a federal cause of action for violations of federal rights by state officers. Now codified as 42 U.S.C. § 1983, this important provision states:

> Every person who, under color of any statute, ordinance, regulation, custom, or usage, of any State or Territory, subjects, or causes to be subjected, any citizen of the United States or other persons with the jurisdiction thereof to the deprivation of any rights, privileges or immunities secured by the Constitution and laws, shall be

---

a. See, e.g., Steven Engel, Note, *The* McCulloch *Theory of the Fourteenth Amendment:* City of Boerne v. Flores *and the Original Understanding of Section 5*, 109 Yale L.J. 115 (1999).

liable to the person injured in an action at law, suit in equity, or other proper proceeding for redress.[b]

The last federal civil rights statute adopted during Reconstruction, the Civil Rights Act of 1875, provided: "That all persons within the jurisdiction of the United States shall be entitled to the full and equal enjoyment of the accommodations, advantages, facilities, and privileges of inns, public conveyances of land or water, theatres, and other places of public amusement; subject only to the conditions and limitations established by law, and applicable alike to citizens of every race and color, regardless of any previous condition of servitude." Violation of the statute was a misdemeanor, and persons whose rights were violated could recover $500 for every offense. This statute provoked the most important constitutional challenge to any Reconstruction civil rights measure and resulted in the following decision.

THE CIVIL RIGHTS CASES
109 U.S. 3, 3 S.Ct. 18, 27 L.Ed. 835 (1883)

JUSTICE BRADLEY delivered the opinion of the Court.

[It was conceded that Congress lacked any such power under Article I. The Court first rejected an argument based on § 5 of the Fourteenth Amendment. The Court understood § 1 of the Amendment only to reach state action, not private action like that of the defendants in the case. (Recall the discussion of the state action doctrine in Chapter 3, § 2.) Accordingly, the Court reasoned, § 5's authorization of legislative power to enforce § 1 allows Congress] to adopt appropriate legislation for correcting the effects of such prohibited State law and State acts, and thus to render them effectually null, void, and innocuous. This is the legislative power conferred upon Congress, and this is the whole of it. It does not invest Congress with power to legislate upon subjects which are within the domain of State legislation; but to provide modes of relief against State legislation, or State action, of the kind referred to. It does not authorize Congress to create a code of municipal law for the regulation of private rights; but to provide modes of redress against the operation of State laws, and the action of State officers, executive or judicial, when these are subversive of the fundamental rights specified in the amendment. * * *

If this legislation is appropriate for enforcing the prohibitions of the amendment, it is difficult to see where it is to stop. Why may not Congress, with equal show of authority, enact a code of laws for the enforcement and vindication of all rights of life, liberty, and property? * * * The truth is, that the implication of a power to legislate in this manner is based upon the assumption that if the States are forbidden to legislate or act in a particular way on a particular subject, and power is conferred upon Congress to enforce the prohibition, this gives Congress power to legislate generally upon that subject, and not merely power to provide modes of redress against such State legislation or action. The assumption is certainly unsound. It is repugnant to the Tenth Amendment of the Constitution, which declares that powers not delegated to the

---

b. An important additional remedy available to prevailing plaintiffs in § 1983 cases is the award of reasonable attorneys' fees. See 42 U.S.C. § 1988.

United States by the Constitution, nor prohibited by it to the States, are reserved to the States respectively or to the people. * * *

In this connection it is proper to state that civil rights, such as are guarantied by the Constitution against State aggression, cannot be impaired by the wrongful acts of individuals, unsupported by State authority in the shape of laws, customs, or judicial or executive proceedings. The wrongful act of an individual, unsupported by any such authority, is simply a private wrong, or a crime of that individual; an invasion of the rights of the injured party, it is true, whether they affect his person, his property, or his reputation; but if not sanctioned in some way by the State, or not done under State authority, his rights remain in full force, and may presumably be vindicated by resort to the laws of the State for redress. An individual cannot deprive a man of his right to vote, to hold property, to buy and to sell, to sue in the courts, or to be a witness or a juror; he may, by force or fraud, interfere with the enjoyment of the right in a particular case; he may commit an assault against the person, or commit murder, or use ruffian violence at the polls, or slander the good name of a fellow-citizen; but, unless protected in these wrongful acts by some shield of State law or State authority, he cannot destroy or injure the right; he will only render himself amenable to satisfaction or punishment; and amenable therefor to the laws of the State where the wrongful acts are committed. Hence, in all those cases where the Constitution seeks to protect the rights of the citizen against discriminative and unjust laws of the State by prohibiting such laws, it is not individual offenses, but abrogation and denial of rights, which it denounces, and for which it clothes the Congress with power to provide a remedy. This abrogation and denial of rights, for which the States alone were or could be responsible, was the great seminal and fundamental wrong which was intended to be remedied. And the remedy to be provided must necessarily be predicated upon that wrong. It must assume that in the cases provided for, the evil or wrong actually committed rests upon some State law or State authority for its excuse and perpetration. * * *

By its own unaided force and effect [the Thirteenth Amendment] abolished slavery, and established universal freedom. Still, legislation may be necessary and proper to meet all the various cases and circumstances to be affected by it, and to prescribe proper modes of redress for its violation in letter or spirit. And such legislation may be primary and direct in its character; for the amendment is not a mere prohibition of State laws establishing or upholding slavery, but an absolute declaration that slavery or involuntary servitude shall not exist in any part of the United States.

It is true that slavery cannot exist without law, any more than property in lands and goods can exist without law; and, therefore, the Thirteenth Amendment may be regarded as nullifying all State laws which establish or uphold slavery. But it has a reflex character also, establishing and decreeing universal civil and political freedom throughout the United States; and it is assumed that the power vested in Congress to enforce the article by appropriate legislation, clothes Congress with power to pass all laws necessary and proper for abolishing all badges and incidents of slavery in the United States; and upon this assumption it is claimed that this is sufficient authority for declaring by law that all persons shall have equal accommodations and privileges in all inns, public conveyances, and places of amusement; the argument being, that the denial of such equal accommodations and privileges is, in itself, a subjection to a species of servitude within the meaning of the amendment. * * *

The only question * * *, therefore, is, whether the refusal to any persons of the accommodations of an inn, or a public conveyance, or a place of public amusement, by an individual, and without any sanction or support from any State law or regulation, does inflict upon such persons any manner of servitude, or form of slavery, as those terms are understood in this country? Many wrongs may be obnoxious to the prohibitions of the Fourteenth Amendment which are not, in any just sense, incidents or elements of slavery. Such, for example, would be the taking of private property without due process of law; or allowing persons who have committed certain crimes (horse-stealing, for example) to be seized and hung by the *posse comitatus* without regular trial; or denying to any person, or class of persons, the right to pursue any peaceful avocations allowed to others. * * *

Now, conceding, for the sake of the argument, that the admission to an inn, a public conveyance, or a place of public amusement, on equal terms with all other citizens, is the right of every man and all classes of men, is it any more than one of those rights which the States by the Fourteenth Amendment are forbidden to deny to any person? And is the Constitution violated until the denial of the right has some State sanction or authority? Can the act of a mere individual, the owner of the inn, the public conveyance or place of amusement, refusing the accommodation, be justly regarded as imposing any badge of slavery or servitude upon the applicant, or only as inflicting an ordinary civil injury, properly cognizable by the laws of the State, and presumably subject to redress by those laws until the contrary appears?

After giving to these questions all the consideration which their importance demands, we are forced to the conclusion that such an act of refusal has nothing to do with slavery or involuntary servitude, and that if it is violative of any right of the party, his redress is to be sought under the laws of the State; or if those laws are adverse to his rights and do not protect him, his remedy will be found in the corrective legislation which Congress has adopted, or may adopt, for counteracting the effect of State laws, or State action, prohibited by the Fourteenth Amendment. It would be running the slavery argument into the ground to make it apply to every act of discrimination which a person may see fit to make as to the guests he will entertain, or as to the people he will take into his coach or cab or car, or admit to his concert or theater, or deal with in other matters of intercourse or business. Innkeepers and public carriers, by the laws of all the States, so far as we are aware, are bound, to the extent of their facilities, to furnish proper accommodation to all unobjectionable persons who in good faith apply for them. If the laws themselves make any unjust discrimination, amenable to the prohibitions of the Fourteenth Amendment, Congress has full power to afford a remedy under that amendment and in accordance with it.

When a man has emerged from slavery, and by the aid of beneficent legislation has shaken off the inseparable concomitants of that state, there must be some stage in the progress of his elevation when he takes the rank of a mere citizen, and ceases to be the special favorite of the laws, and when his rights as a citizen, or a man, are to be protected in the ordinary modes by which other men's rights are protected. There were thousands of free colored people in this country before the abolition of slavery, enjoying all the essential rights of life, liberty, and property the same as white citizens; yet no one, at that time, thought that it was any invasion of their personal status as freemen because they were not admitted to all the privileges enjoyed by white citizens, or because they were subjected to discriminations in the enjoyment of accommodations in inns, public conveyances, and places of amusement. Mere discriminations on account of race or color were not regarded as badges of slavery. * * *

JUSTICE HARLAN, dissenting.

* * * I do not contend that the Thirteenth Amendment invests Congress with authority, by legislation, to define and regulate the entire body of the civil rights which citizens enjoy, or may enjoy, in the several States. But I hold that since slavery, as the court has repeatedly declared, was the moving or principal cause of the adoption of that amendment, and since that institution rested wholly upon the inferiority, as a race, of those held in bondage, their freedom necessarily involved immunity from, and protection against, all discrimination against them, because of their race, in respect of such civil rights as belong to freemen of other races. Congress, therefore, under its express power to enforce that amendment, by appropriate legislation, may enact laws to protect that people against the deprivation, *because of their race*, of any civil rights granted to other freemen in the same State; and such legislation may be of a direct and primary character, operating upon States, their officers and agents, and, also, upon, at least, such individuals and corporations as exercise public functions and wield power and authority under the State.

[Justice Harlan then discussed cases holding that common carriers, inns, and places of public amusement have been given special privileges by the law and, under well-established common law doctrine, owe special duties to the public beyond those owed by other privately owned establishments.]

* * * Congress has not, in [this statute], entered the domain of State control and supervision. It does not assume to prescribe the general conditions and limitations under which inns, public conveyances, and places of public amusement, shall be conducted or managed. It simply declares, in effect, that since the nation has established universal freedom in this country, for all time, there shall be no discrimination, based merely upon race or color, in respect of the accommodations and advantages of public conveyances, inns, and places of public amusement.

I am of the opinion that such discrimination practised by corporations and individuals in the exercise of their public or quasi-public functions is a badge of servitude the imposition of which Congress may prevent under its power, by appropriate legislation, to enforce the Thirteenth Amendment . * * *

The assumption that [the Fourteenth Amendment] consists wholly of prohibitions upon State laws and State proceedings in hostility to its provisions, is unauthorized by its language. The first clause of the first section — "All persons born or naturalized in the United States, and subject to the jurisdiction thereof, are citizens of the United States, and of the State wherein they reside" — is of a distinctly affirmative character. In its application to the colored race, previously liberated, it created and granted, as well as citizenship of the United States, citizenship of the State in which they respectively resided. * * *

The citizenship thus acquired, by that race, in virtue of an affirmative grant from the nation, may be protected, not alone by the judicial branch of the government, but by Congressional legislation of a primary direct character; this, because the power of Congress is not restricted to the enforcement of prohibitions upon State laws or State action. It is, in terms distinct and positive, to enforce "the *provisions* of *this article*" of amendment; not simply those of a prohibitive character, but the provisions — *all* of the provisions — affirmative and prohibitive, of the amendment. It is, therefore, a grave misconception to suppose that the fifth section of the amendment has reference exclusively to express prohibitions upon State laws or State action. * * *

But what was secured to colored citizens of the United States — as between them and their respective States — by the national grant to them of State citizenship? With what rights, privileges, or immunities did this grant invest them? There is one, if there be no others — exemption from race discrimination in respect of any civil right belonging to citizens of the white race in the same State. * * * [S]uch must be their constitutional right, in their own State, unless the recent amendments be "splendid baubles," thrown out to delude those who deserved fair and generous treatment at the hands of the nation. Citizenship in this country necessarily imports at least equality of civil rights among citizens of every race in the same State. It is fundamental in American citizenship that, in respect of such rights, there shall be no discrimination by the State, or its officers, or by individuals, or corporations exercising public functions or authority, against any citizen because of his race or previous condition of servitude. * * *

* * * I agree that government has nothing to do with social, as distinguished from technically legal, rights of individuals. * * * Whether one person will permit or maintain social relations with another is a matter with which government has no concern. * * * What I affirm is that no State, nor the officers of any State, nor any corporation or individual wielding power under State authority for the public benefit or the public convenience, can, consistently either with the freedom established by the fundamental law, or with that equality of civil rights which now belongs to every citizen, discriminate against freemen or citizens, in those rights, because of their race, or because they once labored under the disabilities of slavery imposed upon them as a race. * * *

My brethren say, that when a man has emerged from slavery, and by the aid of beneficent legislation has shaken off the inseparable concomitants of that State, there must be some stage in the progress of his elevation when he takes the rank of a mere citizen, and ceases to be the special favorite of the laws, and when his rights as a citizen, or a man, are to be protected in the ordinary modes by which other men's rights are protected. It is, I submit, scarcely just to say that the colored race has been the special favorite of the laws. * * * Today, it is the colored race which is denied, by corporations and individuals wielding public authority, rights fundamental in their freedom and citizenship. At some future time it may be that some other race will fall under the ban of racial discrimination. If the constitutional amendments be enforced, according to the intent with which, as I conceive, they were adopted, there cannot be, in this republic, any class of human beings in practical subjection to another class, with power in the latter to dole out to the former just such privileges as they may choose to grant. * * *

NOTES ON *THE CIVIL RIGHTS CASES*

1. *Relationship Between the Substantive and Enforcement Sections, Between Judicial and Congressional Power.* In *The Civil Rights Cases*, the majority narrowly construed § 1 of both the Thirteenth and Fourteenth Amendment (the former limited to the badges and incidents of slavery, the latter limited to state rather than private misconduct). Even if those are defensible interpretations, does it follow that the enforcement provisions of both amendments grant Congress no power to create statutory civil rights transcending those limitations? For example, is it unimaginable that *judicial* power to reach private conduct through constitutional interpretation should be so circumspect, but that *congressional* power could be more expansive?

Read the text of § 2 of the Thirteenth Amendment and of § 5 of the Fourteenth Amendment: Can the words be reasonably understood more broadly than the Court read them in *The Civil Rights Cases*? Where do you suppose Congress got those words? (Hint: recall that *McCulloch* formulates the test for congressional authority under the Necessary and Proper Clause this way: "Let the end be legitimate, let it be within the scope of the constitution, and all means which are appropriate, which are plainly adapted to that end, which are not prohibited, but consist with the letter and spirit of the constitution, are constitutional.")

Even under this unitary view of judicial and congressional authority — under which Congress seems to have legislative authority only "to enforce" whatever the judiciary says § 1 of the amendments mean — the constitutionality of 42 U.S.C. § 1983 (the basic civil rights enforcement provision quoted earlier) is not in doubt. This statute simply provides commonplace legal remedies (damages, injunctive relief) for conduct that the judiciary defines as violating § 1 of the amendments and thus easily fits under congressional power to "enforce" the (judicially defined) amendments. In addition, note that the "under color of state law" element of § 1983 accommodates the Court's requirement of state action to trigger the Fourteenth Amendment.

2. *Section 5 of the Fourteenth Amendment: From* The Civil Rights Cases *of 1883 to* United States v. Guest. Recall that *The Civil Rights Cases* were decided after Reconstruction had ended and after the Compromise of 1877, in which the Republicans effectively abandoned the interests of the freed slaves to accommodate the resurgent whites in the South. In such a climate, Justice Bradley's opinion was a precursor to *Plessy*. Although decided more than a decade later, *Plessy* bears many similarities to *The Civil Rights Cases*: Both decisions denied any state responsibility for redressing private discrimination against the freed slaves, and both found Justice Harlan in solo dissent, arguing that the remedial

agenda of Reconstruction was betrayed. The civil rights movement of the twentieth century challenged *Plessy* but neglected *The Civil Rights Cases*, largely because Congresses dominated by southern Democrats enacted no civil rights law between 1875 and 1957. Because *The Civil Rights Cases* had never been revisited, the Justice Department relied on Congress's spending and commerce powers to justify the 1964 Civil Rights Act, and the Solicitor General defended Title II in *Heart of Atlanta* and *McClung* only on Commerce Clause grounds. Within the Court, however, there were three Justices (Black, Douglas, Goldberg) prepared to overrule *The Civil Rights Cases*. (Ironically, the staunchest supporter of the precedent was Justice John Harlan, the grandson of the 1883 dissenter.) Was it appropriate, these Justices wondered, for the Court to uphold the nation's landmark civil rights legislation under Congress's Commerce Clause rather than Fourteenth Amendment authority?

In *United States v. Guest*, 383 U.S. 745 (1966), the Court ruled that § 5 authorized Congress to make it a crime for white supremacists to conspire to deprive African Americans of their civil rights. Justice Stewart's majority opinion rested upon the allegation that the defendants had acted in concert with state officials, thereby satisfying *The Civil Rights Cases* (liberally construed). But six Justices joined Justice Brennan's concurring statement that § 5 empowers Congress "to enact laws punishing *all* conspiracies to interfere with the exercise of Fourteenth Amendment rights, whether or not state officers or others acting under the color of state law are implicated in the conspiracy." Id. at 782 (Brennan, joined by Warren and Douglas); see id. at 762 (Clark, Black, and Fortas, joining the Brennan statement). Although *Guest* did not formally overrule *The Civil Rights Cases* as to Congress's § 5 powers, it did suggest the votes were there for such an overruling. We return to this issue in *United States v. Morrison*, § 3E, below.

3. *Section 2 of the Thirteenth Amendment: From* The Civil Rights Cases *to* Jones v. Alfred Mayer. Unlike the Fourteenth, the Thirteenth Amendment reaches private activities. Like *Plessy*, *The Civil Rights Cases* took a narrow view of the rights recognized by § 1 of the Thirteenth Amendment and Congress's authority under § 2. In the early twentieth century, the Supreme Court recognized that the Thirteenth Amendment justified judicial relief and congressional legislation against "peonage" practices in the South, whereby poor people (typically people of color) became indentured to plantation owners to pay off debts owed them. E.g., *Bailey v. Alabama*, 219 U.S. 219 (1911). The Justice Department in the late 1930s and early 1940s asserted a broader federal power to attack private violence against as well as economic control over poor blacks in the South, but those efforts were stymied by southern influence in the New Deal and (ironically) by the Justice Department's focus on the anti-apartheid campaign under the Fourteenth Amendment after World War II. The Thirteenth Amendment lay in desuetude until the 1960s, when civil rights lawyers and the Justice Department sought to enforce the Civil Rights Act of 1866 against private parties. Their campaign led to the decision that follows.

JONES v. ALFRED H. MAYER CO.
392 U.S. 409, 88 S.Ct. 2186, 20 L.Ed.2d 1189 (1968)

JUSTICE STEWART delivered the opinion of the Court.

[A part of the Civil Rights Act of 1866, now codified as 42 U.S.C. § 1982, provides: "All citizens of the United States shall have the same right, in every State and Territory, as is enjoyed by white citizens thereof to inherit, purchase, lease, sell, hold, and convey real and personal property." Plaintiffs, who were African American, contended that a real estate developer refused to sell them a home because of race. The Court first held that § 1982 bars all racial discrimination, including private discrimination, in the sale or rental of property.]

The remaining question is whether Congress has power under the Constitution to do what § 1982 purports to do: to prohibit all racial discrimination, private and public, in the sale and rental of property. Our starting point is the Thirteenth Amendment, for it was pursuant to that constitutional provision that Congress originally enacted what is now § 1982. * * *

As its text reveals, the Thirteenth Amendment "is not a mere prohibition of State laws establishing or upholding slavery, but an absolute declaration that slavery or involuntary servitude shall not exist in any part of the United States." *The Civil Rights Cases.* It has never been doubted, therefore, "that the power vested in Congress to enforce the article by appropriate legislation," *ibid.*, includes the power to enact laws "direct and primary, operating upon the acts of individuals, whether sanctioned by State legislation or not." *Id.* * * *

"By its own unaided force and effect," the Thirteenth Amendment "abolished slavery, and established universal freedom." *Id.* Whether or not the Amendment *itself* did any more than that — a question not involved in this case — it is at least clear that the Enabling Clause of that Amendment empowered Congress to do much more. For that clause clothed "Congress with power to pass *all laws necessary and proper for abolishing all badges and incidents of slavery in the United States." Ibid.* (Emphasis added.)

* * * [T]he majority leaders in Congress — who were, after all, the authors of the Thirteenth Amendment — had no doubt that its Enabling Clause contemplated the sort of positive legislation that was embodied in the 1866 Civil Rights Act. Their chief spokesman, Senator Trumbull of Illinois, the Chairman of the Judiciary Committee, had brought the Thirteenth Amendment to the floor of the Senate in 1864. In defending the constitutionality of the 1866 Act, he argued[:] * * *

> * * * I have no doubt that under this provision * * * we may destroy all these discriminations in civil rights against the black man; and if we cannot, our constitutional amendment amounts to nothing. It was for that purpose that the second clause of that amendment was adopted, which says that Congress shall have authority, by appropriate legislation, to carry into effect the article prohibiting slavery. Who is to decide what that appropriate legislation is to be? The Congress of the United States; and it is for Congress to adopt such appropriate legislation as it may think proper, so that it be a means to accomplish the end.

Surely Senator Trumbull was right. Surely Congress has the power under the Thirteenth Amendment rationally to determine what are the badges and the incidents of slavery, and the authority to translate that determination into effective legislation. Nor can we say that the determination Congress has made is an irrational one. For this Court recognized long ago that, whatever else they may have encompassed, the badges and incidents of slavery — its "burdens and disabilities" — included restraints upon "those fundamental rights which are the essence of civil freedom, namely, the same right . . . to inherit, purchase, lease, sell and convey property, as is enjoyed by white citizens." *The Civil Rights Cases.*[78] Just as the Black Codes, enacted after the Civil War to restrict the free exercise of those rights, were substitutes for the slave system, so the exclusion of Negroes from white communities became a substitute for the Black Codes. And when racial discrimination herds men into ghettos and makes their ability to buy property turn on the color of their skin, then it too is a relic of slavery.

Negro citizens, North and South, who saw in the Thirteenth Amendment a promise of freedom — freedom to "go and come at pleasure" and to "buy and sell when they please" — would be left with "a mere paper guarantee" if Congress were powerless to assure that a dollar in the hands of a Negro will purchase the same thing as a dollar in the hands of a white man. At the very least, the freedom that Congress is empowered to secure under the Thirteenth Amendment includes the freedom to buy whatever a white man can buy, the right to live wherever a white man can live. If Congress cannot say that being a free man means at least this much, then the Thirteenth Amendment made a promise the Nation cannot keep.

[**JUSTICE DOUGLAS**' concurring opinion and **JUSTICE HARLAN**'s dissenting opinion, joined by **JUSTICE WHITE**, are omitted.]

NOTES ON *JONES* AND THIRTEENTH AMENDMENT POWER

1. *Stare Decisis.* How faithful is *Jones* to the approach taken in *The Civil Rights Cases* concerning congressional power under § 2 of the Thirteenth Amendment? Note that, because of its date of adoption as well as its legislative history, Congress had to be attempting to exercise its Thirteenth Amendment enforcement authority with the 1866 Act; in contrast, the 1875 Act struck down

---

78. The Court did conclude in the *Civil Rights Cases* that "the act of . . . the owner of the inn, the public conveyance or place of amusement, refusing . . . accommodation" cannot be "justly regarded as imposing any badge of slavery or servitude upon the applicant." "It would be running the slavery argument into the ground," the Court thought, "to make it apply to every act of discrimination which a person may see fit to make as to the guests he will entertain, or as to the people he will take into his coach or cab or car, or admit to his concert or theatre, or deal with in other matters of intercourse or business." * * *

Whatever the present validity of the position taken by the majority on that issue — a question rendered largely academic by Title II of the Civil Rights Act of 1964, 78 Stat. 243 (see *Heart of Atlanta Motel v. United States*, 379 U.S. 241; *Katzenbach v. McClung*, 379 U.S. 294) — we note that the entire Court agreed upon at least one proposition: The Thirteenth Amendment authorizes Congress not only to outlaw all forms of slavery and involuntary servitude but also to eradicate the last vestiges and incidents of a society half slave and half free, by securing to all citizens, of every race and color, "the same right to make and enforce contracts, to sue, be parties, give evidence, and to inherit, purchase, lease, sell and convey property, as is enjoyed by white citizens." * * *

in *The Civil Rights Cases* was arguably justified by either the Thirteenth or Fourteenth Amendments.

Read the statute at issue in *Jones*. Do its words indicate that Congress intended it to reach private conduct? Both the language and the legislative history of the Act have suggested to many observers, contra Justice Stewart in *Jones*, that Congress was attempting only to outlaw state statutes or practices that interfered with the property rights of racial minorities. See, e.g., Barry Sullivan, *Historical Reconstruction: Reconstruction History and the Proper Scope of Section 1981*, 98 Yale L.J. 541, 546 n.36 (1989) (reviewing division among historians on this issue).

Nonetheless, the Court stuck with the *Jones* approach in *Runyon v. McCrary*, 427 U.S. 160 (1976), which interpreted 42 U.S.C. § 1981, another provision derived from the 1866 Civil Rights Act, as reaching private conduct.[c] More recently, the Court asked the parties whether *Runyon*'s interpretation of § 1981 as reaching private conduct should be overruled. Ultimately, because of *stare decisis* factors, the Court did not overrule *Runyon*, but did interpret § 1981 narrowly in the employment context, holding that the statute did not apply to racial harassment on the job. See *Patterson v. McLean Credit Union*, 491 U.S. 164 (1989). *Patterson* says that *stare decisis* should be stronger for precedents interpreting statutes than for precedents interpreting the Constitution. Can you discern a basis for this argument, and if so how strong is the argument?

2. *Title II Revisited.* *Jones* was decided in 1968, four years after *Heart of Atlanta* and *McClung*. Had the chronology been reversed, so *Jones* was a precedent Congress could have considered in enacting Title II of the 1964 Civil Rights Act, should Congress have relied upon § 2 of the Thirteenth Amendment rather than (or in addition to) the commerce power?

3. *Beyond Title II.* Using § 2 of the Thirteenth Amendment to justify congressional civil rights measures aimed against private actors is often difficult because of the amendment's limitation to issues related to slavery. For example, Title VII of the 1964 Civil Rights Act forbids private employment discrimination on such factors as race and gender — while the former might come within an expansive view of § 2 power, it is difficult to make the case for the latter.

---

c. Section 1981 states: "All persons within the jurisdiction of the United States shall have the same right in every State and Territory to make and enforce contracts, to sue, be parties, give evidence, and to the full and equal benefit of all laws and proceedings for the security of persons and property as is enjoyed by white citizens, and shall be subject to like punishment, pains, penalties, taxes, licenses, and exactions of every kind, and to no other." *Runyon* held that the right to make and enforce contracts provided in § 1981 outlawed the refusal of a private school to admit a student on the basis of race. Note that the private schools in question were described as "commercially operated" and had advertised and offered schooling to members of the general public, and thus *Runyon* does not necessarily extend § 1981 to forbid racial discrimination by all private clubs or organizations.

B. "THE SECOND RECONSTRUCTION" AND THE VOTING RIGHTS ACT

In 1875, Congress passed the most radical of its civil rights statutes, but within a brief time Reconstruction was over, in the aftermath of the contested presidential election of 1876 and the political compromises that followed it. Congress went over 80 years before passing another civil rights statute, and it was not until the Civil Rights Act of 1964 and the Voting Rights Act of 1965 that federal law provided stringent new protections for civil rights. As we have seen, the Court upheld Title II of the 1964 Civil Rights Act in *Heart of Atlanta* and *McClung* on commerce grounds. The Voting Rights Act contained no obvious commercial aspect, however, and Congress had justified it squarely on its authority under § 2 of the Fifteenth Amendment. An introduction to the statute and its background is necessary to understand the cases considering its constitutionality.

For a century, the promise of § 1 of the Fifteenth Amendment — that African Americans shall have access to voting without racial discrimination — remained largely unfulfilled. The Voting Rights Act of 1965 was adopted after Congress found "that racial discrimination in voting was an insidious and pervasive evil which had been perpetuated in certain parts of the country through unremitting and ingenious defiance of the Constitution." *South Carolina v. Katzenbach, infra.*

The 1965 statute was not the first exercise in the modern era of congressional power under § 2 of the Fifteenth Amendment. Legislation adopted in 1957, 1960, and 1964 had gradually expanded the authority of the Attorney General to seek injunctive relief against racial voting discrimination and of the federal courts to provide relief. Litigation under these statutes had, however, been largely ineffectual. In considering the 1965 statute, Congress concluded that case-by-case litigation had failed to enforce compliance with the Fifteenth Amendment because it had proved too slow, too expensive, and too cumbersome, and because a decree outlawing a discriminatory device could easily be circumvented simply by adopting a different method of discrimination. Consider, for example, the sequence of events alleged in *United States v. Mississippi*, 380 U.S. 128 (1965):

> 1. In 1890, a majority of qualified voters in Mississippi were blacks. A new state constitution adopted in that year required that persons otherwise qualified to vote be able to read any section of the Mississippi Constitution, *or* understand the same when read to them, *or* "give a reasonable interpretation thereof." This requirement, coupled with the fact that until 1952 blacks could not vote in the Democratic primary (victory in which was tantamount to election because the Republican Party was virtually nonexistent), decreased the percentage of registered voters who were black to 9% in 1899 and 5% in 1954.

> 2. By the 1950s the white primary was unlawful and black literacy had improved. In response, in 1954 the state constitution was amended to require a prospective voter to be able to read and copy in writing any section of the Mississippi Constitution, *and* give a reasonable interpretation of it, *and* demonstrate "a reasonable understanding of the duties and obligations of citizenship under a

constitutional form of government." These provisions lent themselves to even greater discriminatory application in the hands of voting registrants.[d]

3. In 1960 the state constitution was amended to add a new voting qualification of "good moral character." Moreover, in 1962 the state adopted laws requiring that application forms be filled out "properly and responsively" without any assistance. Both of these devices were obviously subject to discriminatory application.

Congress responded to this kind of evidence by adopting the Voting Rights Act of 1965, codified as amended at 42 U.S.C. § 1973 *et seq.* The Act had two essential strategies for jurisdictions having low minority voting rates: to remove barriers to registering and voting by racial minorities and then to protect them against future attempts to dilute their new voting power. Accordingly, the Act first outlawed or suspended "tests and devices" prerequisite to voting, such as literacy tests. Second, § 5 of the Act provided that no change in voting qualifications or procedures could be implemented without the prior determination of either the Attorney General or the United States District Court for the District of Columbia (*not* by the local district court that would ordinarily have jurisdiction over such matters) that the change did not have the purpose *and* would not have the effect of causing a retrogression in minority voting strength.

It is important to note that this statute was adopted eleven years before the Court decided *Washington v. Davis* (Chapter 3, § 1B), which held that, for equal protection purposes, facially neutral laws with disparate racial impact are unconstitutional only upon a showing that they are contaminated by discriminatory intent. By outlawing discriminatory effects even when discriminatory intent is not present, the Voting Rights Act might seem vulnerable to constitutional objection, as violating *The Civil Rights Cases* model by which congressional authority to adopt civil rights legislation pursuant to the enforcement clauses of the Reconstruction Amendments is limited by the judicial understanding of what the substantive provisions of those amendments outlaw. Watch for this problem as we proceed through these materials.

The provisions of the Voting Rights Act noted above did not apply nationwide. They reached only those jurisdictions that on November 1, 1964,

---

d. *Editors' note:* A vivid example of discriminatory application of a "read and understand" requirement is given in *United States v. Louisiana*, 225 F. Supp. 353, 384 (E.D. La. 1963) (3-judge court), *aff'd*, 380 U.S. 145 (1965):

Registrars were easily satisfied with answers from white voters. In one instance "FRDUM FOOF SPETGH" was an acceptable response to the request to interpret Article I, § 3 of the Louisiana Constitution.

On the other hand, the record shows that Negroes whose application forms and answers indicate that they are highly qualified by literacy standards and have a high degree of intelligence have been turned down although they have given a reasonable interpretation of fairly technical clauses of the Constitution. For example, the Louisiana Constitution, Article X, § 16 provides: "Rolling stock operated in this State, the owners of which have no domicile therein, shall be assessed by the Louisiana Tax Commission, and shall be taxed for State purposes only, at a rate not to exceed forty mills on the dollar assessed value." The rejected interpretation was: "My understanding is that it means if the owner of which does not have residence within the State, his rolling stock shall be taxed not to exceed forty mills on the dollar."

maintained any "test or device" and had less than 50% of the voting-age population registered to vote or in which less than 50% of such persons voted in the presidential election of 1964. Although the coverage formula was written in neutral terms, the Act was designed to have, and did have, the effect of bringing the Deep South within its coverage. The 1965 Act was drafted as a temporary remedy, having a five-year life span.

South Carolina v. Katzenbach, 383 U.S. 301 (1966). In upholding the constitutionality of the Voting Rights Act against a facial challenge, **Chief Justice Warren** relied upon the *McCulloch* test for congressional power (quoted in Note 1 following *The Civil Rights Cases*). The Court first concluded that the statute's remedies, which apply without the need for prior adjudication, were an appropriate response to the demonstrated ineffectiveness of case-by-case adjudication. Second, notwithstanding principles of federalism, the Act could constitutionally apply only to certain regions of the country in light of the "local evils" found there. Moving to the heart of the statute, the Court upheld the dual strategy of suspending "tests and devices" for five years and using federal preclearance to prevent erosion of the minority vote by new discriminatory techniques.

" * * * South Carolina assails the temporary suspension of existing voting qualifications, reciting the rule laid down by *Lassiter v. Northampton County Bd. of Elections*, 360 U.S. 45, that literacy tests and related devices are not in themselves contrary to the Fifteenth Amendment. In that very case, however, the Court went on to say, 'Of course a literacy test, fair on its face, may be employed to perpetuate that discrimination which the Fifteenth Amendment was designed to uproot.' * * *

"The Act suspends literacy tests and similar devices for a period of five years from the last occurrence of substantial voting discrimination. * * * Underlying [this approach] was the feeling that States and political subdivisions which had been allowing white illiterates to vote for years could not sincerely complain about 'dilution' of their electorates through the registration of Negro illiterates. Congress knew that continuance of the tests and devices in use at the present time, no matter how fairly administered in the future, would freeze the effect of past discrimination in favor of unqualified white registrants. Congress permissibly rejected the alternative of requiring a complete re-registration of all voters, believing that this would be too harsh on many whites who had enjoyed the franchise for their entire adult lives.

"The Act suspends new voting regulations pending scrutiny by federal authorities to determine whether their use would violate the Fifteenth Amendment. This may have been an uncommon exercise of congressional power, as South Carolina contends, but the Court has recognized that exceptional conditions can justify legislative measures not otherwise appropriate. Congress knew that some of the [covered States] had resorted to the extraordinary stratagem of contriving new rules of various kinds for the sole purpose of perpetuating voting discrimination in the face of adverse federal court decrees. Congress had reason to suppose that these States might try similar maneuvers in the future in order to evade the remedies for voting discrimination contained in the Act itself. Under the compulsion of these unique circumstances, Congress responded in a permissibly decisive manner."

Query: If a state that had been using a literacy test in discriminatory ways began applying it in a color-blind manner, would its current use of the test violate the Constitution? If not, how can the five-year suspension of those tests be within Congress' power under § 2 of the Fifteenth Amendment?

KATZENBACH v. MORGAN
384 U.S. 641, 86 S.Ct. 1717, 16 L.Ed.2d 828 (1966)

JUSTICE BRENNAN delivered the opinion of the Court.

[At issue was § 4(e) of the 1965 Act, which provided that no person who had completed the sixth grade in school in Puerto Rico in which the language of instruction was other than English could be denied the right to vote on account of inability to read or write English. This provision was aimed primarily at stopping New York City from using the New York state literacy test to prevent many of its citizens of Puerto Rican descent from voting.]

The Attorney General of the State of New York argues that * * * § 4(e) cannot be sustained as appropriate legislation to enforce the Equal Protection Clause unless the judiciary decides * * * that the application of the English literacy requirement prohibited by § 4(e) is forbidden by the Equal Protection Clause itself. We disagree.

* * * A construction of § 5 that would require a judicial determination that the enforcement of the state law precluded by Congress violated the Amendment, as a condition of sustaining the congressional enactment, would depreciate both congressional resourcefulness and congressional responsibility for implementing the Amendment. It would confine the legislative power in this context to the insignificant role of abrogating only those state laws that the judicial branch was prepared to adjudge unconstitutional, or of merely informing the judgment of the judiciary by particularizing the "majestic generalities" of § 1 of the Amendment.

Thus our task in this case is not to determine whether the New York English literacy requirement as applied to deny the right to vote to a person who successfully completed the sixth grade in a Puerto Rican school violates the Equal Protection Clause. Accordingly, our decision in *Lassiter* sustaining the North Carolina English literacy requirement as not in all circumstances prohibited by the first sections of the Fourteenth and Fifteenth Amendments, is inapposite. *Lassiter* did not present the question before us here: Without regard to whether the judiciary would find that the Equal Protection Clause itself nullifies New York's English literacy requirement as so applied, could Congress prohibit the enforcement of the state law by legislating under § 5 of the Fourteenth Amendment? In answering this question, our task is limited to determining whether such legislation is, as required by § 5, appropriate legislation to enforce the Equal Protection Clause.

By including § 5 the draftsmen sought to grant to Congress, by a specific provision applicable to the Fourteenth Amendment, the same broad powers expressed in the Necessary and Proper Clause, Art. I, § 8, cl. 18. * * * Thus the *McCulloch v. Maryland* standard is the measure of what constitutes "appropriate legislation" under § 5 of the Fourteenth Amendment. Correctly viewed, § 5 is a positive grant of legislative power authorizing Congress to exercise its discretion in determining whether and what legislation is needed to secure the guarantees of the Fourteenth Amendment. * * * [10]

There can be no doubt that § 4(e) may be regarded as an enactment to enforce the Equal Protection Clause. Congress explicitly declared that it enacted § 4(e) "to secure the rights under the fourteenth amendment of persons educated in American-flag schools in which the predominant classroom language was other than English." The persons referred to include those who have migrated from the Commonwealth of Puerto Rico to New York and who have been denied the right to vote because of their inability to read and write English, and the Fourteenth Amendment rights referred to include those emanating from the Equal Protection Clause. More specifically, § 4(e) may be viewed as a measure to secure for the Puerto Rican community residing in New York nondiscriminatory treatment by government — both in the imposition of voting qualifications and the provision or administration of governmental services, such as public schools, public housing and law enforcement.

Section 4(e) may be readily seen as "plainly adapted" to furthering these aims of the Equal Protection Clause. The practical effect of § 4(e) is to prohibit New York from denying the right to vote to large segments of its Puerto Rican community. Congress has thus prohibited the State from denying to that community the right that is "preservative of all rights." This enhanced political power will be helpful in gaining nondiscriminatory treatment in public services for the entire Puerto Rican community. * * * It was well within congressional authority to say that this need of the Puerto Rican minority for the vote warranted federal intrusion upon any state interests served by the English literacy requirement. It was for Congress, as the branch that made this judgment, to assess and weigh the various conflicting considerations — the risk or pervasiveness of the discrimination in governmental services, the effectiveness of eliminating the state restriction on the right to vote as a means of dealing with the evil, the adequacy or availability of alternative remedies, and the nature and significance of the state interests that would be affected by the nullification of the English literacy requirement as applied to residents who have successfully completed the sixth grade in a Puerto Rican school. It is not for us to review the congressional resolution of these factors. It is enough that we be able to perceive a basis upon which the Congress might resolve the conflict as it did. There plainly was such a basis to support § 4(e) in the application in question

---

10. Contrary to the suggestion of the dissent, § 5 does not grant Congress power to exercise discretion in the other direction and to enact "statutes so as in effect to dilute equal protection and due process decisions of this Court." We emphasize that Congress' power under § 5 is limited to adopting measures to enforce the guarantees of the Amendment; § 5 grants Congress no power to restrict, abrogate, or dilute these guarantees. Thus, for example, an enactment authorizing the States to establish racially segregated systems of education would not be — as required by § 5 — a measure "to enforce" the Equal Protection Clause since that clause of its own force prohibits such state laws.

in this case. Any contrary conclusion would require us to be blind to the realities familiar to the legislators.

The result is no different if we confine our inquiry to the question whether § 4(e) was merely legislation aimed at the elimination of an invidious discrimination in establishing voter qualifications. We are told that New York's English literacy requirement originated in the desire to provide an incentive for non-English speaking immigrants to learn the English language and in order to assure the intelligent exercise of the franchise. Yet Congress might well have questioned, in light of the many exemptions provided, and some evidence suggesting that prejudice played a prominent role in the enactment of the requirement, whether these were actually the interests being served. Congress might have also questioned whether denial of a right deemed so precious and fundamental in our society was a necessary or appropriate means of encouraging persons to learn English, or of furthering the goal of an intelligent exercise of the franchise. Finally, Congress might well have concluded that as a means of furthering the intelligent exercise of the franchise, an ability to read or understand Spanish is as effective as ability to read English for those to whom Spanish-language newspapers and Spanish-language radio and television programs are available to inform them of election issues and governmental affairs. Since Congress undertook to legislate so as to preclude the enforcement of the state law, and did so in the context of a general appraisal of literacy requirements for voting, to which it brought a specially informed legislative competence, it was Congress' prerogative to weigh these competing considerations. Here again, it is enough that we perceive a basis upon which Congress might predicate a judgment that the application of New York's English literacy requirement to deny the right to vote to a person with a sixth grade education in Puerto Rican schools in which the language of instruction was other than English constituted an invidious discrimination in violation of the Equal Protection Clause.

There remains the question whether the congressional remedies adopted in § 4(e) constitute means which are not prohibited by, but are consistent "with the letter and spirit of the constitution." The only respect in which appellees contend that § 4(e) fails in this regard is that the section itself works an invidious discrimination in violation of the Fifth Amendment by prohibiting the enforcement of the English literacy requirement only for those educated in American-flag schools (schools located within United States jurisdiction) in which the language of instruction was other than English, and not for those educated in schools beyond the territorial limits of the United States in which the language of instruction was also other than English. This is not a complaint that Congress, in enacting § 4(e), has unconstitutionally denied or diluted anyone's right to vote but rather that Congress violated the Constitution by not extending the relief effected in § 4(e) to those educated in non-American-flag schools. [The Court concluded that failing to extend relief to those educated in non-American-flag schools did not violate the equal protection component of the Fifth Amendment because reform measures such as § 4(e) may take a one-step-at-a-time approach.]

[The separate statement of **JUSTICE DOUGLAS** is omitted.]

JUSTICE HARLAN, with whom JUSTICE STEWART joins, dissenting.

When recognized state violations of federal constitutional standards have occurred, Congress is of course empowered by § 5 to take appropriate remedial measures to redress and prevent the wrongs. But it is a judicial question whether the condition with which Congress has thus sought to deal is in truth an infringement of the Constitution, something that is the necessary prerequisite to bringing the § 5 power into play at all. * * *

* * * The question here is not whether the statute is appropriate remedial legislation to cure an established violation of a constitutional command, but whether there has in fact been an infringement of that constitutional command. * * * That question is one for the judicial branch ultimately to determine. Were the rule otherwise, Congress would be able to qualify this Court's constitutional decisions under the Fourteenth and Fifteenth Amendments, let alone those under other provisions of the Constitution, by resorting to congressional power under the Necessary and Proper Clause. In view of this Court's holding in *Lassiter* that an English literacy test is a permissible exercise of state supervision over its franchise, I do not think it is open to Congress to limit the effect of that decision as it has undertaken to do by § 4(e). In effect the Court reads § 5 of the Fourteenth Amendment as giving Congress the power to define the *substantive* scope of the Amendment. If that indeed be the true reach of § 5, then I do not see why Congress should not be able as well to exercise its § 5 "discretion" by enacting statutes so as in effect to dilute equal protection and due process decisions of this Court. In all such cases there is room for reasonable men to differ as to whether or not a denial of equal protection or due process has occurred, and the final decision is one of judgment. Until today this judgment has always been one for the judiciary to resolve.

I do not mean to suggest in what has been said that a legislative judgment of the type incorporated in § 4(e) is without any force whatsoever. Decisions on questions of equal protection and due process are based not on abstract logic, but on empirical foundations. To the extent "legislative facts" are relevant to a judicial determination, Congress is well equipped to investigate them, and such determinations are of course entitled to due respect. In *South Carolina v. Katzenbach* such legislative findings were made to show that racial discrimination in voting was actually occurring. * * *

But no such factual data provide a legislative record supporting § 4(e)[9] by way of showing that Spanish-speaking citizens are fully as capable of making informed decisions in a New York election as are English-speaking citizens. * * *

Thus, we have here not a matter of giving deference to a congressional estimate, based on its determination of legislative facts, bearing upon the validity *vel non* of a statute, but rather what can at most be called a legislative

---

9. There were no committee hearings or reports referring to this section, which was introduced from the floor during debate on the full Voting Rights Act.

announcement that Congress believes a state law to entail an unconstitutional deprivation of equal protection. * * *

NOTE ON *MORGAN*

Under *Morgan*, what are the limits on Congress's § 5 power? Must there be a violation (conceivable violation?) of the Constitution, as judicially construed, for Congress to remedy? Or did the Court abandon the limitations of *The Civil Rights Cases* and hold that Congress may pass statutes that outlaw state action that does not violate constitutional rights as judicially defined? This distinction is between a *remedial* theory and a *substantive* theory of § 5 power. Under the former, the judiciary has a monopoly on the substantive meaning of § 1 of the amendment so that Congress may provide statutory remedies only for violations of § 1 as it is judicially understood. Under the latter, Congress and the Court have a shared interpretive power over the substantive meaning of § 1 such that, for example, Congress may enact legislation under § 5 providing remedies for what Congress believes are equal protection violations even if the Court would not read the Equal Protection Clause that way. Justice Harlan, in dissent, argued that the logic of the majority opinion would allow Congress to dilute rights as easily as expand them. The majority's response, in footnote 10, is that Congress may only expand, not contract, constitutional rights. The footnote is sometimes called the "one-way-rachet" theory of congressional power (§ 5 is a tool that allows Congress to "turn" § 1 meaning in only one direction). Does footnote 10 make sense? Can the substantive theory be defended under the theories of constitutional interpretation earlier examined: text and original intent (Chapter 2, § 3A); representation-reinforcement (Chapter 2, § 3B)?

Oregon v. Mitchell, 400 U.S. 112 (1970). A fractured Court, with no majority opinion, upheld one key provision and struck down another of the Voting Rights Act Amendments of 1970. First, the amendments expanded the suspension of literacy tests beyond the jurisdictions covered by the original Voting Rights Act to include all state and national elections throughout the United States. The Court unanimously held that the nationwide ban on such tests was constitutional, but no majority opinion was issued. **Justice Douglas** thought that the statute was constitutional under § 5 of the Fourteenth Amendment; the other eight Justices, in four separate opinions, concluded that it was appropriate legislation under § 2 of the Fifteenth Amendment. The Justices all stressed that Congress had evidence before it showing that literacy tests reduced voter participation in a discriminatory manner. For example, **Justice Harlan** said: "Despite the lack of evidence of specific instances of discriminatory application or effect, Congress could have determined that racial prejudice is prevalent throughout the Nation, and that literacy tests unduly lend themselves to discriminatory application, either conscious or unconscious. This danger of violation of § 1 of the Fifteenth Amendment was sufficient to authorize the exercise of congressional power under § 2." Harlan added: "[t]he legislative history of the Voting Rights Act Amendments contains sufficient evidence to this effect, if any be needed."

Section 302 of the amendments lowered the minimum age for voting in state and national elections from 21 to 18. **Justice Black** concluded that the statute was constitutional as applied to federal, but not state, elections. Although he wrote for himself, his conclusion controlled the outcome, because the other eight justices were evenly divided. Four Justices (**Burger**, **Harlan**, **Stewart**, **Blackmun**) would have struck down § 302 in its entirety. Justice Stewart, joined by Chief Justice Burger and Justice Blackmun, interpreted *Morgan* this way:

> [In *Morgan* the] Court upheld the statute on two grounds: that Congress could conclude that enhancing the political power of the Puerto Rican community by conferring the right to vote was an appropriate means of remedying discriminatory treatment in public services; and that Congress could conclude that the New York statute was tainted by the impermissible purpose of denying the right to vote to Puerto Ricans. * * *

> But it is necessary to go much further to sustain § 302. The state laws that it invalidates do not invidiously discriminate against any discrete and insular minority. Unlike the statute considered in *Morgan*, § 302 is valid only if Congress has the power not only to provide the means of eradicating situations that amount to a violation of the Equal Protection Clause, but also to determine as a matter of substantive constitutional law what situations fall within the ambit of the clause. * * * I cannot but conclude that § 302 was beyond the constitutional power of Congress to enact.

Justices Douglas, **Brennan**, **White**, and **Marshall** would have upheld § 302 in all respects. The joint opinion of the latter three argued:

> We believe there is a serious question whether a statute granting the franchise to citizens 21 and over while denying it to those between the ages of 18 and 21 could * * * withstand present scrutiny under the Equal Protection Clause. Regardless of the answer to this question, however, it is clear to us that proper regard for the special function of Congress in making determinations of legislative fact compels this Court to respect those determinations unless they are contradicted by evidence far stronger than anything that has been adduced in these cases. * * *

> * * * When a state legislative classification is subjected to judicial challenge as violating the Equal Protection Clause, it comes before the courts cloaked by the presumption that the legislature has, as it should, acted within constitutional limitations. Accordingly, "[a] statutory discrimination will not be set aside as the denial of equal protection of the laws if any state of facts reasonably may be conceived to justify it."

> But * * * this limitation on judicial review of state legislative classifications is a limitation stemming, not from the Fourteenth Amendment itself, but from the nature of judicial review. It is simply a "salutary principle of judicial decision," one of the "self-imposed restraints intended to protect [the Court] and the state against irresponsible exercise of [the Court's] unappealable power." The nature of the judicial process makes it an inappropriate forum for the determination of complex factual questions of the kind so often involved in constitutional adjudication. * * *

> Limitations stemming from the nature of the judicial process, however, have no application to Congress. * * * Should Congress, pursuant to [§ 5 of the Fourteenth Amendment], undertake an investigation in order to determine whether the factual basis necessary to support a state legislative discrimination actually exists, it need not stop once it determines that some reasonable men could believe the factual basis exists. Section 5 empowers Congress to make its own determination on the matter. See *Morgan*. It should hardly be necessary to add that if the asserted factual basis necessary to support a given state discrimination does not exist, § 5 of the Fourteenth

Amendment vests Congress with power to remove the discrimination by appropriate means.

The scope of our review in such matters has been established by a long line of consistent decisions. * * * "[W]here we find that the legislators, in light of the facts and testimony before them, have a rational basis for finding a chosen regulatory scheme necessary * * * our investigation is at an end."

* * * The core of the dispute * * * is a conflict between state and federal legislative determinations of the factual issues upon which depends decision of a federal constitutional question — the legitimacy, under the Equal Protection Clause, of state discrimination against persons between the ages of 18 and 21. Our cases have repeatedly emphasized that, when state and federal claims come into conflict, the primacy of federal power requires that the federal finding of fact control. The Supremacy Clause requires an identical result when the conflict is one of legislative, not judicial, findings.

NOTE ON *OREGON*

How did Justice Brennan's theory for upholding wide-ranging congressional enforcement power change from *Morgan* to *Oregon v. Mitchell*? Could his *Oregon v. Mitchell* approach allow Congress to dilute constitutional rights (the "rachet" problem mentioned in connection with *Morgan*)? Consider Justice Harlan's separate opinion in *Oregon v. Mitchell*.

* * * To allow a simple majority of Congress to have final say on matters of constitutional interpretation is * * * fundamentally out of keeping with the constitutional structure. * * *

Judicial deference is based, not on relative factfinding competence, but on due regard for the decision of the body constitutionally appointed to decide. Establishment of voting qualifications is a matter for state legislatures. Assuming any authority at all, only when the Court can say with some confidence that the legislature has demonstrably erred in adjusting the competing interests is it justified in striking down the legislative judgment. * * *

The same considerations apply, and with almost equal force, to Congress' displacement of state decisions with its own ideas of wise policy. The sole distinction between Congress and the Court in this regard is that Congress, being an elective body, presumptively has popular authority for the value judgment it makes. But since the state legislature has a like authority, this distinction between Congress and the judiciary falls short of justifying a congressional veto on the state judgment. The perspectives and values of national legislators on the issue of voting qualifications are likely to differ from those of state legislators, but I see no reason *a priori* to prefer those of the national figures, whose collective decision, applying nationwide, is necessarily less able to take account of peculiar local conditions. Whether one agrees with this judgment or not, it is the one expressed by the Framers in leaving voter qualifications to the States.

City of Rome v. United States, 446 U.S. 156 (1980). The Voting Rights Act requires covered jurisdictions to submit electoral changes made after November 1964 for preclearance either to the Department of Justice or to the federal District Court for the District of Columbia. Under the Act, preclearance is granted only if the jurisdiction proves the absence of both discriminatory intent and discriminatory effect. Rome, Georgia, persuaded the district court that a variety of electoral changes (described in note 1 following this case) had not been discriminatorily motivated. The court nonetheless denied preclearance because the changes would have a discriminatory impact.

On the same day it decided *Rome,* the Court ruled in *Mobile v. Bolden*, 446 U.S. 55 (1980), that the Fifteenth Amendment only reached intentional discrimination. In *Rome*, however, the Court ruled that Congress appropriately used its § 2 power to outlaw voting practices that are discriminatory in effect. **Justice Marshall**'s opinion for the Court relied on *South Carolina v. Katzenbach*. "The Court had earlier held in *Lassiter* that the use of a literacy test that was fair on its face and was not employed in a discriminatory fashion did not violate § 1 of the Fifteenth Amendment. In upholding the Act's *per se* ban on such tests in *South Carolina v. Katzenbach*, the Court found no reason to overrule *Lassiter*. Instead, the Court recognized that the prohibition was an appropriate method of enforcing the Fifteenth Amendment because for many years most of the covered jurisdictions had imposed such tests to effect voting discrimination and the continued use of even nondiscriminatory, fairly administered literacy tests would 'freeze the effect' of past discrimination by allowing white illiterates to remain on the voting rolls while excluding illiterate Negroes. This holding makes clear that Congress may, under the authority of § 2 of the Fifteenth Amendment, prohibit state action that, though in itself not violative of § 1, perpetuates the effects of past discrimination." Accord, *Katzenbach v. Morgan; Oregon v. Mitchell*, both of which upheld Voting Rights Act provisions regulating discriminatory effects.

"It is clear, then, that under § 2 of the Fifteenth Amendment Congress may prohibit practices that in and of themselves do not violate § 1 of the Amendment, so long as the prohibitions attacking racial discrimination in voting are 'appropriate[.]' In the present case, we hold that the Act's ban on electoral changes that are discriminatory in effect is an appropriate method of promoting the purposes of the Fifteenth Amendment, even if it is assumed that § 1 of the Amendment prohibits only intentional discrimination in voting. Congress could rationally have concluded that, because electoral changes by jurisdictions with a demonstrable history of intentional racial discrimination in voting create the risk of purposeful discrimination, it was proper to prohibit changes that have a discriminatory impact."

Justice Rehnquist dissented, on the ground that if Congress wanted to regulate hard-to-prove discriminatory intents, it may shift the burden of proof in such cases. But Rome had shown that it did not have a discriminatory intent, and so Congress had no authority to "enforce" the Fifteenth Amendment in that case. "Absent other circumstances, it would be a topsy-turvy judicial system which held that electoral changes which have been affirmatively proved to be permissible under the Constitution nonetheless violate the Constitution."

NOTES ON *ROME*

Justice Rehnquist has a good argument: If Rome *proved* that it had not violated the Fifteenth Amendment (by showing that the electoral changes were not discriminatorily motivated), what business does Congress have outlawing the changes under its power to "enforce" the Fifteenth Amendment? The majority responds that the changes can be outlawed because they create the risk of intentional discrimination. The obvious answer to this argument would seem to be that Rome had demonstrated the absence of that risk. Consider several responses to Justice Rehnquist's argument:

1. *Remedial theory: Congress may paint with a broad brush and adopt a prophylactic rule.* Where there's smoke there's fire, the adage goes. By analogy, where there are discriminatory effects, we might well worry whether there is also discriminatory intent, especially because such intent is hard to prove. In some situations, we might adopt a broad, prophylactic rule that forbids smoke-causing behavior that often (although not always) is related to the threat of fire. This seems to be a homespun way of explaining how the Court in *South Carolina v. Katzenbach* and *Oregon v. Mitchell* upheld a federal statutory ban on literacy tests even though, under *Lassiter*, literacy tests are not unconstitutional per se. As Justice Stewart said in *Oregon*, "[i]n the interests of uniformity, Congress may paint with a much broader brush than may this Court, which must confine itself to the judicial function of deciding individual cases and controversies upon individual records. Cf. *Lassiter*."

Consider a few of the many electoral changes made in Rome. Prior to the alterations in question, Rome had a nine-member city commission elected at-large (each voter could vote for all nine positions), but the city was carved into nine wards, and each commissioner had to reside in the ward from which he or she was elected. Commissioners were elected by plurality vote. The 1966 electoral changes, which were embodied in local legislation adopted by the Georgia legislature at the request of Rome officials, retained a nine-member city commission elected at-large. But under the new plan the nine commissioners came from only three wards, each ward producing three commissioners, and candidates were required to run for a numbered post in the ward (Post 1, Ward 1, for example). In addition, under the new approach each commissioner had to be elected by a majority vote (for example, if no candidate for Post 1, Ward 1 received a majority of the citywide vote, the two candidates who had received the most votes would be subjected to a runoff election). In the context of at-large elections, a majority-white population, and strong racial bloc voting, which the district court found to be present in Rome, these electoral changes dilute the voting power of the minority community.[d] Although, as Justice Rehnquist in *Rome* stressed, the district court found that these changes were not improperly motivated, the district court's opinion provides little certainty about this factual conclusion.[e]

---

d. Justice Marshall explained: "[U]nder the pre-existing plurality-win system, a Negro candidate would have a fair opportunity to be elected by a plurality of the vote if white candidates split their votes among several white candidates and Negroes engage in 'single-shot' voting in his favor [that is, vote for the black candidate and for no one else]. The 1966 change to the majority vote/runoff election scheme significantly decreased the opportunity for such a Negro candidate since, 'even if he gained a plurality of votes in the general election, [he] would still have to face the runner-up white candidate in a head-to-head runoff election in which, given bloc voting by race and a white majority, [he] would be at a severe disadvantage.'" (Quoting the district court.)

e. The district court said "the issue is a close one." On the one hand, it was suspicious that the new voting rules were adopted right after the VRA went into effect; were a well-known mechanism for diluting the black vote; and were supported by a false assertion about the requirements of Georgia voting law. On the other hand, the city persuaded the district court of its clean hands

Rome seems to hold that, considering the difficulty of proving discriminatory intent in this context and the pervasive history of intentional racial discrimination in voting in the jurisdictions covered by the Voting Rights Act, Congress should be allowed to outlaw changes in electoral practices that have discriminatory effects under its power to "enforce" the Fifteenth Amendment. The theory is not that Congress has legitimately redefined § 1 of the Fifteenth Amendment to prohibit discriminatory effects (which would be a *substantive* theory of congressional power). Instead, the prophylactic approach is an expansive *remedial* theory: It prevents state action that runs afoul of judicially defined rights (actions tainted by discriminatory intent) by outlawing a broader category of state action (actions producing discriminatory effects). The notion is that discriminatory intent almost always produces discriminatory effects, and the latter are much easier to identify and prohibit.

A potential problem is that discriminatory effects also commonly arise in the absence of discriminatory intent (especially when that intent is defined as narrowly as the judiciary does, see notes following *Washington v. Davis*, Chapter 3, § 1B). This problem of overbreadth is true of any prophylactic theory: every child should be vaccinated against measles, for example, even though without the vaccination only a few would ever get the disease; you should always wash your hands before handling food even though only rarely will disease result if you don't. Should Congress be authorized to interfere with the sovereignty of the states by prohibiting quite a bit of constitutional state action (action that produces discriminatory effects in voting but not for reasons of discriminatory intent) so that it can prevent a largely unmeasurable degree of unconstitutional state action (action that produces such effects because of such intent)? How can Congress, the Court, or anybody else determine the degree to which the prophylactic remedy is overbroad? In *Rome*, perhaps the Court has a persuasive answer to this problem, because in jurisdictions with a long history of documented voting discrimination there is special reason to be suspicious of electoral changes that have discriminatory effects — that in this context the prophylactic remedy is overinclusive, but does not seem unduly so.

2. *Substantive theory of* Katzenbach v. Morgan. *Morgan* suggested that Congress is authorized to expand upon the protections of the Civil War Amendments, a theory that would justify the Voting Rights Act despite Justice Rehnquist's concerns. Does the *Rome* approach have the same "rachet" problem as *Morgan* has — could the *Rome* approach be used to dilute rather than expand rights? Should the Court in *Rome* have simply relied upon the substantive theory of *Morgan* rather than the prophylactic remedial theory?

---

through "sworn statements of participants at every stage in this process — the City Attorney, five Commissioners, the City Manager, and the local representatives in the State legislature — to the effect that their actions were not motivated by any consideration of race or color." The district court was unwilling to question their credibility. "Thus, on the present record we accept the argument that the majority vote and associated runoff election and numbered posts provisions were enacted primarily because of the City Attorney's mistaken belief that such a system was required under state law. Staggered terms were most likely adopted because City officials felt they would contribute to continuity in the City Government. And the Board of Election residency requirement, we find, was enacted to ensure responsiveness by Board members to the particular concerns of their wards."

Consider the changes in composition of the Court between the time of the two opinions.

3. *Institutional Competence and Discriminatory Effects as an Underenforced Constitutional Norm.* Also potentially relevant to the *Rome* issue is the opinion in *Oregon v. Mitchell* that was joined by Justices Brennan, Marshall, and White. That opinion suggests that the anti-discrimination rule of the Fourteenth and Fifteenth Amendments is an "underenforced constitutional norm" — a norm that the judiciary will enforce only narrowly because of institutional limitations.[f] Like the Court in *Washington v. Davis* four years earlier in the context of the Fourteenth Amendment, the Court in *Mobile v. Bolden* in the context of the Fifteenth Amendment was reluctant to give full force to the anti-discrimination rule when plaintiffs could not show that the racially discriminatory effects were the intended result of state action: Because constitutionalizing a "discriminatory effects" approach would create a permanent right that not only burdened states but also could prove hard for courts to administer, the Court itself was reluctant to enforce the Fifteenth Amendment in that way. By engaging in its own factfinding and deliberation, which would consider the interests of the states as well as minority persons and could fine-tune the rights and remedies involved so that they would be easier for courts to administer, Congress can provide precisely the kind of legitimacy and certitude that the Court, as an institution, cannot. Does this process-based substantive theory adequately answer Justice Rehnquist's concerns?

If (as earlier cases held) Congress may ban literacy tests rather than merely provide states and localities an opportunity to demonstrate that their test was not adopted and will not be applied in discriminatory fashion, why can't Congress outlaw other electoral devices that have discriminatory effects, as the Court in *Rome* held? Justice Rehnquist in *Rome* responded that there was a vast history of the misuse of literacy tests, that literacy tests are easily used to discriminate, and that a ban on them was necessary to remedy a prior constitutional violation (any future nondiscriminatory use of such a test that did not require all voters to re-register would effectively freeze in place the prior discrimination, for illiterate whites who were already registered would continue to be eligible to vote, while illiterate racial minorities who sought to register for the first time would be disqualified by the test). Consider the electoral changes at issue in *Rome* (discussed in Note 1 above). Are they sufficiently distinguishable from literacy tests to make them beyond congressional authority to prohibit based on discriminatory effects alone?

PROBLEM 7-3
LEGISLATIVE FACTFINDING AND
FOURTEENTH AMENDMENT PERSONS

In *Roe v. Wade* (Chapter 5, § 4B), which struck down state laws outlawing abortion as violating the Due Process Clause of the Fourteenth Amendment, the

---

f.   See Lawrence Gene Sager, *Fair Measure: The Legal Status of Underenforced Constitutional Norms*, 91 Harv. L. Rev. 1212 (1978).

Court stated: "We need not resolve the difficult question of when life begins. When those trained in the respective disciplines of medicine, philosophy, and theology are unable to arrive at any consensus, the judiciary, at this point in the development of man's knowledge, is not in a position to speculate as to the answer." Suppose that Congress held extensive hearings and, in response, adopted the following statute:

> The Congress finds that present-day scientific evidence indicates a significant likelihood that actual human life exists from conception.

> The Congress further finds that the fourteenth amendment to the Constitution of the United States was intended to protect all human beings.

> Upon the basis of these findings, and in the exercise of the powers of the Congress, including its power under section 5 of the fourteenth amendment to the Constitution of the United States, the Congress hereby declares that for the purpose of enforcing the obligation of the States under the fourteenth amendment not to deprive persons of life without due process of law, human life shall be deemed to exist from conception, without regard to race, sex, age, health, defect, or condition of dependency; and for this purpose "person" shall include all human life as defined herein.

Is the statute constitutional? Can any remedial theory be invoked in its defense? Any substantive theory?

C. THE RELIGIOUS FREEDOM RESTORATION ACT

Problem 7-3 illustrates how controversies concerning congressional substantive and remedial authority under § 5 of the Fourteenth Amendment range beyond those involving racial discrimination. In the 1996 Term, the Court finally returned to these issues, but this time in the context of the Free Exercise Clause of the First Amendment.

A bit of background, especially for those who have not studied the Free Exercise Clause: In many ways, the Free Exercise Clause raises similar questions to those that arise under the Equal Protection Clause. As Chapter 6, § 7 indicates, the Free Exercise Clause creates constitutional doubts about governmental regulation that interferes with religious freedom, whether by statutes that discriminate on their face against religion or are rooted in discriminatory intent. In these respects, at a minimum the case law under the Free Exercise Clause parallels equal-protection precedents, see *Loving v. Virginia* (Chapter 3, § 1A) (facial racial classifications); *Washington v. Davis* (Chapter 3, § 1B) (facially neutral laws). Several Supreme Court precedents indicated, however, that the Free Exercise Clause was even more protective than the *Washington v. Davis* approach — subjecting to strict scrutiny even facially neutral regulations that inhibit religious freedom but cannot be shown to be contaminated by intentional discrimination against religion. In *Employment Division, Department of Human Resources v. Smith* (Chapter 6, § 7), however, a closely divided Supreme Court in 1990 held that, at least in the context of criminal statutes, a facially neutral regulation of conduct that incidentally inhibits a religious practice is not subject to any stringent constitutional standard.

Smith met with a firestorm of criticism from the religious community. Congress ultimately responded by passing the Religious Freedom Restoration

Act (RFRA) of 1993, 42 U.S.C. §§ 2000bb-2000bb-4. Under RFRA, facially neutral laws that "substantially burden a person's exercise of religion" are legal only if the Government demonstrates "that application of the burden to the person" is "in furtherance of a compelling governmental interest" and "is the least restrictive means of furthering that compelling governmental interest." Congress relied upon its legislative authority under § 5 of the Fourteenth Amendment to impose this approach upon state and local governments. The Free Exercise Clause applies to the states through the Due Process Clause of the Fourteenth Amendment (see Chapter 5, § 1), so Congress maintained that it was applying RFRA to state and local governments to enforce that Fourteenth Amendment provision. It is to the constitutionality of RFRA that we now turn.

CITY OF BOERNE v. FLORES
521 U.S. 507, 117 S.Ct. 2157, 138 L.Ed.2d 624 (1997)

JUSTICE KENNEDY delivered the opinion of the Court.[g]

[The Archbishop of San Antonio applied for a building permit to enlarge St. Peter Catholic Church in Boerne, Texas. City authorities denied the application because, under a local historic preservation ordinance, the church was within a historic district. The Archbishop then brought suit, arguing that the permit denial violated RFRA. The city responded that RFRA was unenforceable because it was unconstitutional.]

II. Congress enacted RFRA in direct response to the Court's decision in *Smith*. There we considered a Free Exercise Clause claim brought by members of the Native American Church who were denied unemployment benefits when they lost their jobs because they had used peyote. Their practice was to ingest peyote for sacramental purposes, and they challenged an Oregon statute of general applicability which made use of the drug criminal. In evaluating the claim, we declined to apply the balancing test set forth in *Sherbert v. Verner*, 374 U.S. 398 (1963), under which we would have asked whether Oregon's prohibition substantially burdened a religious practice and, if it did, whether the burden was justified by a compelling government interest. We stated:

> [G]overnment's ability to enforce generally applicable prohibitions of socially harmful conduct . . . cannot depend on measuring the effects of a governmental action on a religious objector's spiritual development. To make an individual's obligation to obey such a law contingent upon the law's coincidence with his religious beliefs, except where the State's interest is "compelling" . . . contradicts both constitutional tradition and common sense.

The application of the *Sherbert* test, the *Smith* decision explained, would have produced an anomaly in the law, a constitutional right to ignore neutral laws of general applicability. * * *

Four Members of the Court disagreed. They argued the law placed a substantial burden on the Native American Church members so that it could be upheld only if the law served a compelling state interest and was narrowly tailored to achieve that end. * * *

---

g. *Editors' note:* **JUSTICE SCALIA** joined all but Part III-A-1 of this opinion.

These points of constitutional interpretation were debated by Members of Congress in hearings and floor debates. Many criticized the Court's reasoning, and this disagreement resulted in the passage of RFRA. [In RFRA,] Congress announced:

(1) [T]he framers of the Constitution, recognizing free exercise of religion as an unalienable right, secured its protection in the First Amendment to the Constitution;

(2) laws "neutral" toward religion may burden religious exercise as surely as laws intended to interfere with religious exercise;

(3) governments should not substantially burden religious exercise without compelling justification;

(4) in [*Smith*] the Supreme Court virtually eliminated the requirement that the government justify burdens on religious exercise imposed by laws neutral toward religion; and

(5) the compelling interest test as set forth in prior Federal court rulings is a workable test for striking sensible balances between religious liberty and competing prior governmental interests.

The Act's stated purposes are:

(1) to restore the compelling interest test as set forth in [*Sherbert*] and *Wisconsin v. Yoder*, 406 U.S. 205 (1972) and to guarantee its application in all cases where free exercise of religion is substantially burdened; and

(2) to provide a claim or defense to persons whose religious exercise is substantially burdened by government.

RFRA prohibits "[g]overnment" from "substantially burden[ing]" a person's exercise of religion even if the burden results from a rule of general applicability unless the government can demonstrate the burden "(1) is in furtherance of a compelling governmental interest; and (2) is the least restrictive means of furthering that compelling governmental interest." The Act's mandate applies to [both the federal government and state and local governments]. * * *

IIIA. * * * Legislation which deters or remedies constitutional violations can fall within the sweep of Congress' enforcement power even if in the process it prohibits conduct which is not itself unconstitutional and intrudes into "legislative spheres of autonomy previously reserved to the States." For example, the Court upheld a suspension of literacy tests and similar voting requirements under Congress' parallel power to enforce the provisions of the Fifteenth Amendment, as a measure to combat racial discrimination in voting, *South Carolina v. Katzenbach*, despite the facial constitutionality of the tests under *Lassiter*. We have also concluded that other measures protecting voting rights are within Congress' power to enforce the Fourteenth and Fifteenth Amendments, despite the burdens those measures placed on the States. *South Carolina v. Katzenbach*; *Katzenbach v. Morgan*; *Oregon v. Mitchell*; *City of Rome v. United States*.

It is also true, however, that "[a]s broad as the congressional enforcement power is, it is not unlimited." *Oregon v. Mitchell* (opinion of Black, J.). In assessing the breadth of § 5's enforcement power, we begin with its text. Congress has been given the power "to enforce" the "provisions of this article." We agree with respondent, of course, that Congress can enact legislation under § 5 enforcing the constitutional right to the free exercise of religion. The "provisions of this article," to which § 5 refers, include the Due Process Clause of the Fourteenth Amendment. Congress' power to enforce the Free Exercise Clause follows from our holding in *Cantwell v. Connecticut*, 310 U.S. 296, 303 (1940), that the "fundamental concept of liberty embodied in [the Fourteenth Amendment's Due Process Clause] embraces the liberties guaranteed by the First Amendment."

Congress' power under § 5, however, extends only to "enforc[ing]" the provisions of the Fourteenth Amendment. The Court has described this power as "remedial," *South Carolina v. Katzenbach*. The design of the Amendment and the text of § 5 are inconsistent with the suggestion that Congress has the power to decree the substance of the Fourteenth Amendment's restrictions on the States. Legislation which alters the meaning of the Free Exercise Clause cannot be said to be enforcing the Clause. Congress does not enforce a constitutional right by changing what the right is. It has been given the power "to enforce," not the power to determine what constitutes a constitutional violation. Were it not so, what Congress would be enforcing would no longer be, in any meaningful sense, the "provisions of [the Fourteenth Amendment]."

While the line between measures that remedy or prevent unconstitutional actions and measures that make a substantive change in the governing law is not easy to discern, and Congress must have wide latitude in determining where it lies, the distinction exists and must be observed. There must be a congruence and proportionality between the injury to be prevented or remedied and the means adopted to that end. Lacking such a connection, legislation may become substantive in operation and effect. * * *

[In Part III-A-1, Justice Kennedy supported his conclusion by contending that "[t]he Fourteenth Amendment's history confirms the remedial, rather than substantive, nature of the Enforcement Clause." The first draft of the Fourteenth Amendment, reported by Rep. Bingham (R-OH), provided:

> The Congress shall have power to make all laws which shall be necessary and proper to secure to the citizens of each State all privileges and immunities of citizens in the several States, and to all persons in the several States equal protection in the rights of life, liberty, and property.

"Members of Congress from across the political spectrum criticized the Amendment, and the criticisms had a common theme: The proposed Amendment gave Congress too much legislative power at the expense of the existing constitutional structure." For example, "Senator William Stewart of Nevada [stated] the Amendment would permit 'Congress to legislate fully upon all subjects affecting life, liberty, and property,' such that 'there would not be much left for the State Legislatures,' and would thereby 'work an entire change in our form of government.' " In response, the draft was taken off the table and replaced by a new version, which was adopted as the Fourteenth Amendment. "Under the revised Amendment, Congress' power was no longer plenary but remedial. Congress was granted the power to make the substantive constitutional prohibitions against the States effective. Representative Bingham said the new draft would give Congress 'the power . . . to protect by national law the privileges and immunities of all the citizens of the Republic . . . whenever the same shall be abridged or denied by the unconstitutional acts of any State.'

Representative Stevens described the new draft Amendment as 'allow[ing] Congress to correct the unjust legislation of the States.' * * * See generally H. Brannon, The Rights and Privileges Guaranteed by the Fourteenth Amendment to the Constitution of the United States 387 (1901) (Congress' 'powers are only prohibitive, corrective, vetoing, aimed only at undue process of law')[.] * * * "]

The design of the Fourteenth Amendment has proved significant also in maintaining the traditional separation of powers between Congress and the Judiciary. The first eight Amendments to the Constitution set forth self-executing prohibitions on governmental action, and this Court has had primary authority to interpret those prohibitions. The Bingham draft, some thought, departed from that tradition by vesting in Congress primary power to interpret and elaborate on the meaning of the new Amendment through legislation. Under it, "Congress, and not the courts, was to judge whether or not any of the privileges or immunities were not secured to citizens in the several States." [H. Flack, The Adoption of the Fourteenth Amendment 64 (1908).] While this separation of powers aspect did not occasion the widespread resistance which was caused by the proposal's threat to the federal balance, it nonetheless attracted the attention of various Members. See Cong. Globe, 39th Cong., 1st Sess., at 1064 (statement of Rep. Hale) (noting that Bill of Rights, unlike the Bingham proposal, "provide safeguards to be enforced by the courts, and not to be exercised by the Legislature"); *id.*, at App. 133 (statement of Rep. Rogers) (prior to Bingham proposal it "was left entirely for the courts . . . to enforce the privileges and immunities of the citizens"). As enacted, the Fourteenth Amendment confers substantive rights against the States which, like the provisions of the Bill of Rights, are self-executing. The power to interpret the Constitution in a case or controversy remains in the Judiciary.

The remedial and preventive nature of Congress' enforcement power, and the limitation inherent in the power, were confirmed in our earliest cases on the Fourteenth Amendment [discussing *The Civil Rights Cases*]. * * * Recent cases have continued to revolve around the question of whether § 5 legislation can be considered remedial. In *South Carolina v. Katzenbach*, we emphasized that "[t]he constitutional propriety of [legislation adopted under the Enforcement Clause] must be judged with reference to the historical experience . . . it reflects." There we upheld various provisions of the Voting Rights Act of 1965, finding them to be "remedies aimed at areas where voting discrimination has been most flagrant" and necessary to "banish the blight of racial discrimination in voting, which has infected the electoral process in parts of our country for nearly a century." We noted evidence in the record reflecting the subsisting and pervasive discriminatory — and therefore unconstitutional — use of literacy tests. The Act's new remedies, which used the administrative resources of the Federal Government, included the suspension of both literacy tests and, pending federal review, all new voting regulations in covered jurisdictions, as well as the assignment of federal examiners to list qualified applicants enabling those listed to vote. The new, unprecedented remedies were deemed necessary given the ineffectiveness of the existing voting rights laws and the slow costly character of case-by-case litigation.

After *South Carolina v. Katzenbach*, the Court continued to acknowledge the necessity of using strong remedial and preventive measures to respond to the widespread and persisting deprivation of constitutional rights resulting from this country's history of racial discrimination. See *Oregon v. Mitchell*; *City of Rome*; *Morgan*.

Any suggestion that Congress has a substantive, non-remedial power under the Fourteenth Amendment is not supported by our case law. In *Oregon v. Mitchell*, a majority of the Court concluded Congress had exceeded its enforcement powers by enacting legislation lowering the minimum age of voters from 21 to 18 in state and local elections. The five [Justices] who reached this conclusion explained that the legislation intruded into an area reserved by the Constitution to the States. Four of these five were explicit in rejecting the position that § 5 endowed Congress with the power to establish the meaning of constitutional provisions. See *id.* (opinion of Harlan, J.); *id.* (opinion of Stewart, J.[, joined by Burger, C.J., and Blackmun, J.]). * * *

There is language in our opinion in *Katzenbach v. Morgan* which could be interpreted as acknowledging a power in Congress to enact legislation that expands the rights contained in § 1 of the Fourteenth Amendment. This is not a necessary interpretation, however, or even the best one. * * * The Court provided two related rationales for its conclusion that § 4(e) [of the Voting Rights Act] could "be viewed as a measure to secure for the Puerto Rican community residing in New York nondiscriminatory treatment by government." Under the first rationale, Congress could prohibit New York from denying the right to vote to large segments of its Puerto Rican community, in order to give Puerto Ricans "enhanced political power" that would be "helpful in gaining nondiscriminatory treatment in public services for the entire Puerto Rican community." Section 4(e) thus could be justified as a remedial measure to deal with "discrimination in governmental services." The second rationale, an alternative holding, did not address discrimination in the provision of public services but "discrimination in establishing voter qualifications." The Court perceived a factual basis on which Congress could have concluded that New York's literacy requirement "constituted an invidious discrimination in violation of the Equal Protection Clause." Both rationales for upholding § 4(e) rested on unconstitutional discrimination by New York and Congress' reasonable attempt to combat it. As Justice Stewart explained in *Oregon v. Mitchell*, interpreting *Morgan* to give Congress the power to interpret the Constitution "would require an enormous extension of that decision's rationale."

If Congress could define its own powers by altering the Fourteenth Amendment's meaning, no longer would the Constitution be "superior paramount law, unchangeable by ordinary means." It would be "on a level with ordinary legislative acts, and, like other acts, . . . alterable when the legislature shall please to alter it." *Marbury*. Under this approach, it is difficult to conceive of a principle that would limit congressional power. Shifting legislative majorities could change the Constitution and effectively circumvent the difficult and detailed amendment process contained in Article V. * * *

B. Respondent contends that RFRA is a proper exercise of Congress' remedial or preventive power. The Act, it is said, is a reasonable means of protecting the free exercise of religion as defined by *Smith*. It prevents and remedies laws which are enacted with the unconstitutional object of targeting religious beliefs and practices. See *Church of the Lukumi Babalu Aye, Inc. v. Hialeah* [Chapter 6, § 7] ("[A] law targeting religious beliefs as such is never permissible"). To avoid the difficulty of proving such violations, it is said, Congress can simply invalidate any law which imposes a substantial burden on a religious practice unless it is justified by a compelling interest and is the least restrictive means of accomplishing that interest. If Congress can prohibit laws with discriminatory effects in order to prevent racial discrimination in violation of the Equal Protection Clause, see *City of Rome*, then it can do the same, respondent argues, to promote religious liberty.

While preventive rules are sometimes appropriate remedial measures, there must be a congruence between the means used and the ends to be achieved. The appropriateness of remedial measures must be considered in light of the evil presented. Strong measures appropriate to address one harm may be an unwarranted response to another, lesser one.

A comparison between RFRA and the Voting Rights Act is instructive. In contrast to the record which confronted Congress and the judiciary in the voting rights cases, RFRA's legislative record lacks examples of modern instances of generally applicable laws passed because of religious bigotry. The history of persecution in this country detailed in the hearings mentions no episodes occurring in the past 40 years. [Citing various statements made in legislative history.] The absence of more recent episodes stems from the fact that, as one witness testified, "deliberate persecution is not the usual problem in this country." House Hearings [on RFRA] 334 (statement of Douglas Laycock). See also House [Committee] Report 2 ("[L]aws directly targeting religious practices have become increasingly rare"). Rather, the emphasis of the hearings was on laws of general applicability which place incidental burdens on religion. Much of the discussion centered upon anecdotal evidence of autopsies performed on Jewish individuals and Hmong immigrants in violation of their religious beliefs, and on zoning regulations and historic preservation laws (like the one at issue here), which as an incident of their normal operation, have adverse effects on churches and synagogues. It is difficult to maintain that they are examples of legislation enacted or enforced due to animus or hostility to the burdened religious practices or that they indicate some widespread pattern of religious discrimination in this country. Congress' concern was with the incidental burdens imposed, not the object or purpose of the legislation. This lack of support in the legislative record, however, is not RFRA's most serious shortcoming. Judicial deference, in most cases, is based not on the state of the legislative record Congress compiles but "on due regard for the decision of the body constitutionally appointed to decide." *Oregon v. Mitchell* (opinion of Harlan, J.). As a general matter, it is for Congress to determine the method by which it will reach a decision.

Regardless of the state of the legislative record, RFRA cannot be considered remedial, preventive legislation, if those terms are to have any meaning. RFRA is so out of proportion to a supposed remedial or preventive object that it cannot be understood as responsive to, or designed to prevent, unconstitutional behavior. It appears, instead, to attempt a substantive change in constitutional protections. Preventive measures prohibiting certain types of laws may be appropriate when there is reason to believe that many of the laws affected by the congressional enactment have a significant likelihood of being unconstitutional. See *City of Rome* (since "jurisdictions with a demonstrable history of intentional racial discrimination . . . create the risk of purposeful discrimination" Congress could "prohibit changes that have a discriminatory impact" in those jurisdictions). Remedial legislation under § 5 "should be adapted to the mischief and wrong which the [Fourteenth] [A]mendment was intended to provide against." *The Civil Rights Cases.*

RFRA is not so confined. Sweeping coverage ensures its intrusion at every level of government, displacing laws and prohibiting official actions of almost every description and regardless of subject matter. RFRA's restrictions apply to every agency and official of the Federal, State, and local Governments. 42 U.S.C. § 2000bb–2(1). RFRA applies to all federal and state law, statutory or otherwise, whether adopted before or after its enactment. § 2000bb–3(a). RFRA has no termination date or termination mechanism. Any law is subject to challenge at any time by any individual who alleges a substantial burden on his or her free exercise of religion.

The reach and scope of RFRA distinguish it from other measures passed under Congress' enforcement power, even in the area of voting rights. In *South Carolina v. Katzenbach*, the challenged provisions were confined to those regions of the country where voting discrimination had been most flagrant and affected a discrete class of state laws, *i.e.*, state voting laws. Furthermore, to ensure that the reach of the Voting Rights Act was limited to those cases in which constitutional violations were most likely (in order to reduce the possibility of overbreadth), the coverage under the Act would terminate "at the behest of States and political subdivisions in which the danger of substantial voting discrimination has not materialized during the preceding five years." *Id.* The provisions restricting and banning literacy tests, upheld in *Katzenbach v. Morgan* and *Oregon v. Mitchell*, attacked a particular type of voting qualification, one with a long history as a "notorious means to deny and abridge voting rights on racial grounds." In *City of Rome*, the Court rejected a challenge to the constitutionality of a Voting Rights Act provision which required certain jurisdictions to submit changes in electoral practices to the Department of Justice for preimplementation review. The requirement was placed only on jurisdictions with a history of intentional racial discrimination in voting. Like the provisions at issue in *South Carolina v. Katzenbach*, this provision permitted a covered jurisdiction to avoid preclearance requirements under certain conditions and, moreover, lapsed in seven years. This is not to say, of course, that § 5 legislation requires termination dates, geographic restrictions or egregious predicates. Where, however, a congressional enactment pervasively prohibits constitutional state action in an effort to remedy or to prevent unconstitutional state action, limitations of this kind tend to ensure Congress' means are proportionate to ends legitimate under § 5.

The stringent test RFRA demands of state laws reflects a lack of proportionality or congruence between the means adopted and the legitimate end to be achieved. If an objector can show a substantial burden on his free exercise, the State must demonstrate a compelling governmental interest and show that the law is the least restrictive means of furthering its interest. Claims that a law substantially burdens someone's exercise of religion will often be difficult to contest. Requiring a State to demonstrate a compelling interest and show that it has adopted the least restrictive means of achieving that interest is the most demanding test known to constitutional law. * * * Laws valid under *Smith* would fall under RFRA without regard to whether they had the object of stifling or punishing free exercise. * * * [RFRA] is a considerable congressional intrusion into the States' traditional prerogatives and general authority to regulate for the health and welfare of their citizens.

The substantial costs RFRA exacts, both in practical terms of imposing a heavy litigation burden on the States and in terms of curtailing their traditional general regulatory power, far exceed any pattern or practice of unconstitutional conduct under the Free Exercise Clause as interpreted in *Smith*. Simply put, RFRA is not designed to identify and counteract state laws likely to be unconstitutional because of their treatment of religion. In most cases, the state laws to which RFRA applies are not ones which will have been motivated by religious bigotry. If a state law disproportionately burdened a particular class of religious observers, this circumstance might be evidence of an impermissible legislative motive. Cf. *Washington v. Davis*. RFRA's substantial burden test, however, is not even a discriminatory effects or disparate impact test. It is a reality of the modern regulatory state that numerous state laws, such as the zoning regulations at issue here, impose a substantial burden on a large class of individuals. When the exercise of religion has been burdened in an incidental way by a law of general application, it does not follow that the persons affected have been burdened any more than other citizens, let alone burdened because of their religious beliefs. In addition, the Act imposes in every case a least restrictive means requirement — a requirement that was not used in the pre-*Smith* jurisprudence RFRA purported to codify — which also indicates that the legislation is broader than is appropriate if the goal is to prevent and remedy constitutional violations. * * *

Our national experience teaches that the Constitution is preserved best when each part of the government respects both the Constitution and the proper actions and determinations of the other branches. When the Court has interpreted the Constitution, it has acted within the province of the Judicial Branch, which embraces the duty to say what the law is. *Marbury*. When the political branches of the Government act against the background of a judicial interpretation of the Constitution already issued, it must be understood that in later cases and controversies the Court will treat its precedents with the respect due them under settled principles, including *stare decisis*, and contrary expectations must be disappointed. RFRA was designed to control cases and controversies, such as the one before us; but as the provisions of the federal statute here invoked are beyond congressional authority, it is this Court's precedent, not RFRA, which must control. * * *

[The concurring opinion of **JUSTICE STEVENS**; the opinion of **JUSTICE SCALIA**, joined by **JUSTICE STEVENS**, concurring in part; the dissenting opinion of **JUSTICE O'CONNOR**, joined in large part by **JUSTICE BREYER**; the dissenting opinion of **JUSTICE SOUTER**; and the dissenting opinion of **JUSTICE BREYER** are omitted.]

NOTES ON *BOERNE* AND CONGRESSIONAL ENFORCEMENT POWER

1. *Possible Objections to the Court's Rejection of Congressional Power To Protect the Free Exercise of Religion.* Although some academics had correctly predicted the demise of RFRA,[h] the Supreme Court's lopsided rejection of the statute came as something of a constitutional surprise.[i] Moreover, even the dissenters in *Boerne* pretty much conceded the Court's view that § 5 did not authorize Congress to override *Smith* and argued, instead, that *Smith* should be reconsidered. Are there good arguments for the proposition that § 5 of the Fourteenth Amendment gives Congress the authority to adopt RFRA?

Recall the argument in Note 3 following *Rome*, to the effect that there ought to be some room for Congress to take a broader view of the Constitution than the Supreme Court is willing to enforce. If the Court for institutional reasons "underenforces" individual rights, then Congress ought to have some latitude to enforce those underenforced constitutional norms. This provides one account of *South Carolina v. Katzenbach*. The Court had declined to invalidate literacy tests as a violation of the Fifteenth Amendment, but upheld Congress's power to suspend such tests under its § 5 powers. The Court's stance can be justified on the ground that Congress has more factfinding expertise to evaluate the effects of such tests, and its decision interfering with state electoral practices is more democratically legitimate than a similar intervention by the Court.

Even if the Court refused to recognize its own institutional caution as a reason to give Congress leeway, it might do so as part of an inter-branch dialogue about the meaning of the Free Exercise Clause. *Boerne* might be criticized for rejecting any substantive role for Congress in defining the rights protected by the Fourteenth Amendment.[j] Recall the critique developed in our notes after *Cooper v. Aaron* (Chapter 2, § 2B): Commentators from a variety of perspectives dispute the Supreme Court's insistence that it must always have the last word as to the meaning of the Constitution. Indeed, *Boerne* may be a more aggressive deployment of the judicial supremacy idea than *Cooper* was. *Smith* was a decision that not only divided the Court, but was immediately and overwhelmingly repudiated by Congress, while *Brown* was a unanimous decision of the Court that Congress did not try to override.

---

h. See, e.g., Christopher Eisgruber & Lawrence Gene Sager, *Why the Religious Freedom Restoration Act Is Unconstitutional*, 69 NYU L. Rev. 437 (1994); William Van Alstyne, *The Failure of the Religious Freedom Restoration Act Under Section 5 of the Fourteenth Amendment*, 46 Duke L.J. 291 (1996).

i. See, e.g., Robert Drinan, S.J., *Reflections on the Demise of the Religious Freedom Restoration Act*, 86 Geo. L.J. 101 (1997).

j. See David Cole, *The Value of Seeing Things Differently:* City of Boerne v. Flores *and Congressional Enforcement of the Bill of Rights*, 1997 S.Ct. Rev. 31.

2. *The Court, Congress, and Social Movements*. Admittedly, following the precedent on congressional authority to enforce the Reconstruction Amendments is a challenge. The path from *The Civil Rights Cases* to *Boerne* was anything but straightforward. Consider the discussion in Chapter 1 of the possible relationship between social movements and the evolution of constitutional doctrine. After Reconstruction ended, the Court narrowly interpreted congressional power to legislate under the Reconstruction Amendments (*The Civil Rights Cases*); during the "second Reconstruction" of the civil rights movement of the 1960s, the Court accorded Congress very expansive power in this area (*South Carolina v. Katzenbach* and, especially, *Katzenbach v. Morgan*). The cases in the next decade or so did not quarrel with this Court/Congress equilibrium, especially when Congress was legislating concerning a core, historical aspect of Reconstruction (race: *Rome*) rather than an issue of equality outside that core (age: *Oregon v. Mitchell*).

In the 1990s, however, a Court composed of a different set of Justices has shattered the earlier equilibrium of deference to congressional power.[k] *Lopez* is the paradigm-shifting Commerce Clause precedent, although it purports to overrule no precedent; *Boerne* takes a similar, but even bolder tack to congressional authority to enforce the Reconstruction Amendments, as it does expressly overrule a precedent (or, at least, repudiates the substantive theory of *Morgan*). What is driving the Court to undo what might have been thought to be the settled expectations concerning congressional power? Consider three possibilities, and then try to come up with some further suggestions on your own:

• *Federalism concerns*: The current majority of the Court considers federalism a core constitutional principle and does not trust Congress to respect it and stay within its constitutional boundaries. Nor have "the political safeguards of federalism" been sufficient to prevent congressional overreaching. For instance, how could states lobby against forbidding guns in schools, or the promotion of religious liberty? The Court sees itself as the lone institution in our country that can effectively protect the states against congressional encroachment. The earlier apparent equilibrium about congressional authority under the Commerce Clause and the Reconstruction Amendments gave Congress *carte blanche*, in effect a national police power contrary to constitutional text, to the historical expectations of the Framers, and to good policy (recall the values of federalism).

• *Separation of powers concerns*: Since *Marbury*, it has been clear that it is emphatically the province of the judiciary, not of Congress, to say what the law is. Questions such as whether a statute concerns something substantially related to interstate commerce or is designed to remedy constitutional violations are questions of law for courts, not questions of policy for Congress. The earlier equilibrium involved an improper shift of judicial power to the legislative branch. In this regard, note that the congressional

---

k. See, e.g., Robert Post & Reva Siegel, *Equal Protection by Law: Federal Antidiscrimination Legislation After* Morrison *and* Kimel, 110 Yale L.J. 441 (2000).

strategy with RFRA — lambasting the Court for misconstruing the Free Exercise Clause — and the very title to the statute, suggesting that religious liberty has been lost (through judicial foolishness) and must be "restored," are direct challenges to the Court. Note how this account is diametrically opposed to arguments contending that the Court should accord Congress some enforcement-power discretion based on Congress's better fact-finding capacity and on the notion that an inter-branch dialogue about constitutional meaning can be productive.

- *Easy cases and political appearances*: If the Court were ever to strike down anything as beyond the commerce power, *Lopez* is a great test case, for there was no obvious connection between the statute and interstate commerce, there was no obvious reason that federal regulation was necessary or state regulation was insufficient, and the Justices may have had the sense that Congress was engaged in symbolic legislation for political purposes. *Boerne* can be seen as similar: assuming there is no *Morgan*-like substantive power, the statute is very vulnerable to constitutional attack because, unlike with the Voting Rights Act, the legislative history of RFRA does not make any showing that the statute is appropriate to remedy constitutional violations as judicially defined (i.e., violations of the Free Exercise Clause as narrowly interpreted in *Smith*). The Court was dubious about the likelihood that states and local governments were routinely abusing free exercise rights (again, in contrast to the near-universal appreciation of the extent of voting discrimination on the basis of race before 1965 in the South). The Justices may have thought that Congress had responded to political pressure from a powerful political lobby, the religious community, rather than carefully evaluated the merits of the statute.

Were these changes potentially affected by a major shift in political equilibrium? Certainly federal policy from the Reagan Administration onward has been to devolve increasing authority to the states. In 1994, Republicans took control of the House of Representatives on a campaign platform called "The Contract with America," which included a promise to respect state prerogatives (e.g., to avoid unfunded federal mandates, which require states or local governments to do certain things but provide no federal funds to pay for these activities).

3. Boerne *as Precedent: The Congruence and Proportionality Test.* What does the Court mean by "congruence"? "Proportionality"? This test has been crucial in the post-*Boerne* cases, to which we now turn.

D. CONGRESSIONAL POWER AND THE ELEVENTH AMENDMENT

1. *An Overview of the Eleventh Amendment*

In addition to truncating the commerce power in *Lopez* and the civil rights enforcement power in *Boerne*, the Court in the 1990s took a third major step to cabin congressional authority in pursuit of federalism values: it interpreted the Eleventh Amendment as denying Congress the authority to subject unconsenting states to suit in federal court for violations of federal statutes adopted pursuant to Congress's Article I powers. The intricacies of the Eleventh Amendment are well beyond the scope of this book (we urge you to take the Federal Courts course at your law school, where you would study the subject in depth). For present purposes, a short overview should suffice.

As a matter of federal common law (with possible constitutional roots), the United States cannot be sued in the federal courts without its consent (a consent that has been given in a series of federal statutes partially waiving immunity). See *United States v. Nordic Village*, 503 U.S. 30 (1992). A similar immunity generally protects states from lawsuits in their own courts unless they have consented to suit. During the first decade of the Constitution, the question arose whether and under what circumstances the states might be sued in federal court.

In *Chisholm v. Georgia*, 2 U.S. (2 Dall.) 419 (1793), the Supreme Court took original jurisdiction in a lawsuit against the state of Georgia by a South Carolina creditor seeking payment for goods purchased by Georgia during the Revolution. Georgia argued that the Supreme Court did not have jurisdiction over the controversy. Four Justices read Article III's grant of jurisdiction over "Controversies * * * between a State and Citizens of another State" to embrace cases where the State is a defendant as well as those where it is a plaintiff. Only Justice Iredell dissented, primarily on statutory grounds.

Chisholm created a sensation, because several states were under pressure by creditors to pay their debts incurred during the Revolution, which the states were not in a position to do. Within a year, Congress proposed the Eleventh Amendment to the Constitution as a response to this problem, and the states ratified it.[1] The amendment provides: "The Judicial power of the United States shall not be construed to extend to any suit in law or equity, commenced or prosecuted against one of the United States by Citizens of another State, or by Citizens or Subjects of any Foreign State."

In *Hans v. Louisiana*, 134 U.S. 1 (1890), the Court gave this amendment a decidedly nonliteral interpretation by holding that it forbids a suit against an unconsenting state not only by a citizen of another state or foreign country, but also by one of its own citizens. In brief, the Court thought it would be "anomalous" if the state, without its consent, could be sued by one of its own citizens but not by others. In essence, the Court read the Eleventh Amendment as reflecting a broad principle, perhaps implicit in the original Constitution as well, that states generally have sovereign immunity when sued in federal court.

Hans seems at war with the text of the Constitution, for it reads the Eleventh Amendment to afford state immunity in cases not covered by its precise terms. Chief Justice Hughes rescued constitutional state immunity from this textualist embarrassment in *Monaco v. Mississippi*, 292 U.S. 313 (1934), which extended state immunity to cases brought by a foreign state. Hughes explained the state immunity not as an interpretation of the Eleventh Amendment, but instead as a construction of the "judicial Power" conferred by Article III. Given the sovereign immunity the common law invariably recognized as a defense from

---

1. Oddly enough, the purpose of the Eleventh Amendment seems to be to allow the states to engage in the very "impairments of contracts" supposedly forbidden by the Contract Clause (unless, of course, the Contract Clause applies only to private contracts).

lawsuits, the Framers surely did not intend for Article III to confer jurisdiction against the states (or the United States) without their consent.

Taken at full value, *Hans* (perhaps supplemented by *Monaco*) had the potential to destroy the capacity of federal courts to hear claims, including constitutional claims, against state action. The Court has created several important exceptions to this understanding of the Eleventh Amendment, all of which are based on complicated theories beyond our present scope. First, a federal suit may proceed against a state officer in her official capacity implementing an unconstitutional state statute, on the ground that the state is not really the defendant. See *Ex parte Young*, 209 U.S. 123 (1908). Such suits may be for prospective injunctive relief, but not for retrospective money damages. See *Edelman v. Jordan*, 415 U.S. 651 (1974). Second, the Court has recognized that a state may waive the immunity and allow itself to be sued, although for the waiver to be effective the state statute or state constitutional provision must clearly specify the state's intention to allow suits against it in federal court (thus, a general waiver of immunity in its own state courts is insufficient). See, e.g., *id.* Third, the United States may sue a state in federal court notwithstanding the Eleventh Amendment. See, e.g., *United States v. Mississippi*, 380 U.S. 128 (1965). Note also that the Eleventh Amendment does not bar suits against municipalities, counties, or other subdivisions of a state. See, e.g., *Lincoln County v. Luning*, 133 U.S. 529 (1890).

2. *May Congress Abrogate States' Eleventh Amendment Immunity?*

The text of the Eleventh Amendment is all about the jurisdiction of federal courts and tells us nothing about Congress's power to enact legislation that would alter or remove the jurisdictional bar. In *Fitzpatrick v. Bitzer*, 427 U.S. 445 (1976), the Court held that § 5 of the Fourteenth Amendment authorizes Congress to abrogate state Eleventh Amendment immunity. *Bitzer* emphasized the transformation of American federalism accomplished by the Reconstruction Amendments and ruled that the Eleventh Amendment had to be read in light of the subsequent-in-time Fourteenth Amendment.[m] As with state waivers, the Court has required a crystal-clear statement of abrogation on the face of a statute before it will find that Congress has exercised its *Bitzer* authority. E.g., *Quern v. Jordan*, 440 U.S. 332 (1979).

Bitzer did not address the question whether Congress could abrogate the states' immunity pursuant to its antecedent-in-time Article I powers. One argument in favor of such power is the following: Sovereign immunity is a common law doctrine that can be overridden by statute; therefore, the Supremacy Clause authorizes Congress to abrogate state sovereign immunity by a law adopted under any of its authorized powers, including those in Article I. Consistent with this common law notion of state immunity, in *Pennsylvania v. Union Gas Co.*, 491 U.S. 1 (1989), the Court ruled that Congress's legislative powers under Article I, such as the commerce power, also include the authority to subject states to suit in federal court. But *Union Gas* was a 5-4 decision with

---

m. See Vicki Jackson, *Holistic Interpretation:* Fitzpatrick v. Bitzer *and Our Bifurcated Constitution*, 53 Stan. L. Rev. 1259 (2001); Chapter 2, § 3A1.

no majority opinion, the basis for the critical fifth vote (Justice White) was inscrutable from his separate opinion, and the four dissenters (Justice Scalia writing for Chief Justice Rehnquist and Justices O'Connor and Kennedy) strongly contended that the result was forbidden by *Hans*. The Court turned around on this issue seven years later.

Seminole Tribe of Florida v. Florida, 517 U.S. 44 (1996). The Court invalidated the provision of the Indian Gaming Regulatory Act that allowed Indian tribes to sue states in federal court to enforce the statutory duty to negotiate in good faith to create Indian gaming enclaves. The Court, per **Chief Justice Rehnquist**, ruled that the "Indian Commerce Clause" does not authorize Congress to abrogate state Eleventh Amendment immunity. To reach that result, the Court overruled *Union Gas*.

To support its departure from stare decisis, the Court noted that there was no majority opinion in *Union Gas*; the fifth Justice (White) concurred only in the result and rejected the plurality opinion's rationale. This disarray within the Court majority created confusion among lower courts, which had difficulty applying the decision. More important, the Chief Justice criticized the plurality opinion in *Union Gas* because it "departed sharply from our established federalism jurisprudence and essentially eviscerated our decision in *Hans*," which had been followed for one hundred years until *Union Gas*. The Chief Justice maintained that the Court has always held that "the Eleventh Amendment stood for the constitutional principle that state sovereign immunity limited the federal courts' jurisdiction in Art. III. * * * And our decisions since *Hans* had been equally clear that the Eleventh Amendment reflects 'the fundamental principle of sovereign immunity [that] limits the grant of judicial authority under Article III.' *Pennhurst State Sch. & Hosp. v. Halderman*, 465 U.S. 89, 97-98 (1984). As the dissent in *Union Gas* recognized, the plurality's conclusion — that Congress could under Article I expand the scope of the federal courts' jurisdiction under Article III — 'contradict[ed] our unvarying approach to Article III as setting forth the *exclusive* catalog of permissible federal court jurisdiction.' " Hence, stare decisis cut both ways in *Seminole Tribe*.

Finally, and most important, the Court rejected the notion that state immunity from suit was nothing more than a common law doctrine. Entering the union as independent sovereigns, the states retained their immunity as part of the Constitution's plan. Thus, it was a fundamental constitutional " 'postulate that States of the Union, still possessing attributes of sovereignty, shall be immune from suits, without their consent, save where there has been a "surrender of this immunity in the plan of the [C]onvention." ' " *Monaco*. The Chief Justice distinguished *Bitzer* on the ground that "the Fourteenth Amendment, by expanding federal power at the expense of state autonomy, had fundamentally altered the balance of state and federal power struck by the Constitution." Thus, although Congress could not abrogate the states' Eleventh Amendment immunity under Article I (part of the original constitutional plan), Congress could do so under its legislative power under § 5 of the later-in-time Fourteenth Amendment.

Four Justices — **Stevens**, **Souter**, **Ginsburg**, and **Breyer** — dissented. In an opinion by Souter, the latter three argued that *Hans*, rather than *Union Gas*, should be narrowed if not overruled. Souter maintained that, as a matter of the Framers' original expectations, state sovereign immunity in 1789 was entirely unclear, and whatever immunity the states had was terminated by the Constitution, as *Chisholm* held for diversity cases and everyone assumed for federal question cases (such as *Seminole Tribe*). The plain language of the Eleventh Amendment reflected its purpose: to divest federal courts of diversity jurisdiction when an out-of-stater sues a state. Conversely, the amendment left federal question jurisdiction alone, and *Hans* was wrong to hold otherwise. "In sum, reading the Eleventh Amendment solely as a limit on citizen-state diversity jurisdiction has the virtue of coherence with this Court's practice, with the views of John Marshall, with the history of the Amendment's drafting, and with its allusive language," concluded Justice Souter. In light of this evidence, and *Hans'* own misreading of the common law and the Framers' expectations, Justice Souter objected to any extension of *Hans*. (The Chief Justice vigorously disagreed: no precedent of the Court has questioned *Hans*, which has been the foundational precedent; the majority opinion characterized the dissenters' approach as "highly speculative.")

Last of all, Justice Souter explored the relationship between immunity and sovereignty. The Founding rejected the idea of *indivisible sovereignty*, for the Constitution created an arrangement where both state and national governments were sovereign, within their respective spheres. (To the extent sovereignty remained indivisible, it rested with We the People.) Following Akhil Amar, *Of Federalism and Sovereignty*, 96 Yale L.J. 1425 (1987), Justice Souter argued that the logical implication of divided sovereignty was that each government would retain immunity only within their respective spheres, and be subject to suit where acting outside their constitutional authority. "When individuals sued States to enforce federal rights, the Government that corresponded to the 'sovereign' in the traditional common-law sense was not the State but the National Government, and any state immunity from the jurisdiction of the Nation's courts would have required a grant from the true sovereign, the people, in their Constitution, or from the Congress that the Constitution had empowered."

Alden v. Maine, 527 U.S. 706 (1999). In 1992 state probation officers and juvenile caseworkers in Maine sued the state to enforce the overtime-pay requirements of the Fair Labor Standards Act. *Seminole Tribe* required dismissal of their federal court lawsuit, but the state workers refiled in state court, upon the theory that the Eleventh Amendment only regulates *federal* jurisdiction (Article III) and does not affect the Supremacy Clause obligation of state courts to enforce federal law. Affirming the Maine Supreme Court, the U.S. Supreme Court ruled that, although the Eleventh Amendment was not technically applicable (because the suit was in state court), the principle underlying *Hans* and *Seminole Tribe* barred the state lawsuit as well as the federal one. **Justice Kennedy**'s opinion for the Court (the same five Justices who formed the majority in *Seminole Tribe*) relied on the common law notion, universally accepted at the Founding, that sovereigns are immune from lawsuits to which they have not expressly consented:

Although the Constitution grants broad powers to Congress, our federalism requires that Congress treat the states in a manner consistent with their status as residuary sovereigns and joint participants in the governance of the nation. The founding generation thought it "neither becoming nor convenient that the several States of the Union, invested with that large residuum of sovereignty which had not been delegated to the United States, should be summoned as defendants to answer the complaints of private persons." The principle of sovereign immunity preserved by constitutional design "thus accords the States the respect owed them as members of the federation."

The immunity principle undergirds *Hans'* reading of the Eleventh Amendment and *Monaco's* reading of Article III, but those precedents do not exhaust the constitutional importance of the sovereign immunity baseline. That principle would be defeated if state immunity were lost for lawsuits filed in state courts:

> In some ways, of course, a congressional power to authorize private suits against nonconsenting States in their own courts would be even more offensive to state sovereignty than a power to authorize the suits in a federal forum. Although the immunity of one sovereign in the courts of another has often depended in part on comity or agreement, the immunity of a sovereign in its own courts has always been understood to be within the sole control of the sovereign itself. A power to press a State's own courts into federal service to coerce the other branches of the State, furthermore, is the power first to turn the State against itself and ultimately to commandeer the entire political machinery of the State against its will and at the behest of individuals. Such plenary federal control of state governmental processes denigrates the separate sovereignty of the States.

"It is unquestioned that the Federal Government retains its own immunity from suit not only in state tribunals but also in its own courts. In light of our constitutional system recognizing the essential sovereignty of the States, we are reluctant to conclude that the States are not entitled to a reciprocal privilege." This reluctance was reinforced, Justice Kennedy reasoned, by functional considerations, particularly the "political accountability so essential to our liberty and republican form of government" which would be compromised by allowing the federal government to commandeer the states' courts against the states: "This case at one level concerns the formal structure of federalism, but in a Constitution as resilient as ours form mirrors substance. Congress has vast power but not all power. When Congress legislates in matters affecting the States, it may not treat these sovereign entities as mere prefectures or corporations."

Speaking for the same four Justices who dissented in *Seminole Tribe*, **Justice Souter** wrote a dissenting opinion in this case, objecting to the Court's hardwiring the eighteenth century concept of sovereign immunity into the Constitution. Not only is the concept unmentioned in the Constitution's text, but the Framers themselves were silent about its role in the new government, and none of the opinions in *Chisholm* mentioned it. Nor did Justice Souter find any tangible basis for the principle in the "structure" of the Constitution. Several different conceptions of sovereign immunity would be perfectly consistent with the Constitution and the Bill of Rights. Finally: "[T]here is much irony in the Court's profession that it grounds its opinion on a deeply rooted historical tradition of sovereign immunity, when the Court abandons a principle nearly as inveterate, and much closer to the hearts of the Framers: that where there is a right there must be a remedy." See *Marbury v. Madison*.

NOTES ON THE EXPANDING STATE IMMUNITY FROM SUIT

1. *Constitutional Theory.* The most remarkable thing about these decisions is how much they have rendered the actual text of the Eleventh Amendment irrelevant to the constitutional immunity. *Hans* commenced that process, by extending Eleventh Amendment immunity beyond the diversity cases targeted by the amendment; subsequent Supreme Court decisions extended the immunity to admiralty cases, see *Ex parte New York*, 256 U.S. 490 (1921), and cases where foreign states sued the states. *Monaco* (interpreting Article III). In effect, those cases lopped off "by Citizens of another State, or by Citizens or Subjects of any Foreign State" from the end of the Eleventh Amendment. *Alden* extended the constitutional immunity to suits to enforce federal statutes against the states in their own state courts. *Alden* is based on supposedly fundamental (unwritten) constitutional principles of dual federalism rather than on the Eleventh Amendment per se, but in practical effect it lopped off "of the United States" from the amendment. Following *Alden*, the Court in *Federal Maritime Comm'n v. South Carolina State Ports Auth.*, 122 S.Ct. 1864 (2002), held that dual federalism protects the states against being hailed before federal agencies performing adjudicative functions. Again, although the Eleventh Amendment was not the basis for this decision, it in effect rewrote "The Judicial Power" in the amendment to mean "Any Adjudicatory Power."

The current Court relies on the original intent of the Framers of the original Constitution as the basis for broadly construing state sovereign immunity. The main argument seems to be that because the common law recognized immunity of governments to lawsuits as to which they have not consented, that principle was assumed in the Constitution (*Monaco*; *Seminole*; *Alden*). Hamilton in *Federalist* No. 81 explicitly promised the states that they would retain their full immunity (*FMC*), and Madison and Marshall similarly defended the Constitution against attacks that it would deprive states of their immunity from private lawsuits (*Alden*). Do the representations of Hamilton, Madison, and Marshall, made after eight states had ratified the Constitution, bind the Framers? Justice Souter argued in his *Seminole* and *Alden* dissents that sovereign immunity was a highly unsettled concept among the colonists, and some states explicitly recognized lawsuits against their governments. Also, Framers such as Edmund Randolph and James Wilson assumed that the states would be giving up any immunity not retained when they ratified the Constitution. See also *Thornton, supra* (the term limits case). Finally, when they ratified, several states proposed that the Constitution be clarified or amended to protect states against suit — hardly the appropriate stance if immunity was already written into the Constitution.

The *Chisholm* Court — filled with important Framers (the lead opinion was written by James Wilson, who had delivered the leading address that kicked off the Federalists' campaign, but the dissenting opinion was by James Iredell, another prominent Framer) — believed that the states had surrendered most of their immunities. The constitutional override of *Chisholm* by the adoption of the Eleventh Amendment was limited to diversity cases in federal court and was so read by the Founding Generation, represented by Chief Justice Marshall. In *FMC*, Justice Stevens' dissent added this historical argument: *Chisholm* held that states were not immune from service of process in a federal lawsuit *and* that federal courts had subject matter jurisdiction over lawsuits between a state and citizens of another state. The first bill responding to *Chisholm*, introduced the day after the decision was handed down, would have overridden both holdings; the amendment Congress ultimately submitted to the states overrode only the subject matter jurisdiction holding.

The Court's ultimate theory for this line of cases is that they are consistent with the federalist structure adopted in the Constitution.[n] But the same Constitution that adopts a federalist structure also created a powerful national government whose statutes are the supreme law of the land, to be faithfully applied by state as well as federal judges. U.S. Const. art. VI. *Alden*'s invigoration of state governments comes at the price of Maine's obligation to obey the directives of the Fair Labor Standards Act. *FMC*'s extension of *Alden* comes at the price of South Carolina's obligation to obey the Shipping Act. Is there a neutral way to justify this trade-off from the structure of the Constitution?

The four Justices who dissented in *Seminole* and *Alden* and its companion cases charged the five-Justice majority with judicial activism akin to that of the Warren Court era. Justice Stevens' dissent in *Florida Prepaid Postsecondary Education Expense Fund v. College Savings Bank*, 527 U.S. 627 (1999), a companion case to *Alden*, said that the Court created a version of sovereign immunity "defined only by the present majority's perception of constitutional penumbras rather than constitutional text." Recall *Griswold v. Connecticut* (Chapter 5, § 4A). Stevens' charge, of course, can be turned around: If federalism and privacy are both robust ideas for a healthy polity, why not create constitutional space out of penumbras and background principles for both, just as the Rehnquist Court has done? A Court deciding both *Casey* (Chapter 5, § 4B) and *Alden* is surely not a passive Court, but that alone may not make it a bad Court.

2. *The Court's Theory of Strict Accountability.* There is a political theory afoot in *Seminole*, *Alden* (where it is most explicit), and *FMC*, a theory that is probably animating *Lopez* and *Boerne* as well. (It first appears in this book in *Freeman v. Pitts*, a fairly recent *Brown II* case (Chapter 2, § 2C2).) It is a theory of accountability and goes something like this: The allocation of scarce resources among competing needs is fundamental to the political process. State officials must make hard choices as to priorities — and they are accountable to the voters for unsatisfactory choices at election time. This political accountability is sacrificed whenever the federal government asserts authority over the state's political processes or highjacks part of the state budget for its own goals.

---

n. The *Seminole/Alden/FMC* line of cases might be defended by reference to precedent going back as far as *Hans*. But as Vicki Jackson, *The Supreme Court, the Eleventh Amendment, and State Sovereign Immunity*, 98 Yale L.J. 1 (1988), demonstrated, precedent cuts both ways. Since *Cohens v. Virginia*, 19 U.S. 264 (1821), the Supreme Court has reviewed state court judgments in actions against the states under its federal question authority, without any mention of the Eleventh Amendment. That should have been a strong precedent-based argument against the result in *Alden*, yet the Court did not even mention *Cohens*.

The underlying and broad purpose of the Eleventh Amendment was to prevent the distortions of state politics that would occur were the states suable for nonpayment of their debts. This accountability rationale applies regardless of whether the lawsuit is in state rather than federal court (*Alden*) or an administrative adjudication rather than a court case (*FMC*). Is this a cogent theory of politics and governance in a federal system? Is it cogent enough to trump the Supremacy Clause goals in these circumstances? (Again, under what meta-principle do you choose between the two great constitutional goals?) Indeed, would this rationale not supplant the Supremacy Clause altogether, if taken to its logical conclusion?

3. *Circumstances When States Can Be Sued, Notwithstanding the Eleventh Amendment.* Recall that, notwithstanding the Eleventh Amendment, the states can be sued if they waive their immunity, when the plaintiff is the United States, or if Congress has abrogated their immunity pursuant to its Fourteenth Amendment authority (*Bitzer*). Although *Seminole Tribe* explicitly reaffirms it, might *Bitzer* be revisited after *Alden*? Given its longstanding status as an unquestioned precedent of the Court, *Bitzer* seems to be in no immediate danger. Consider the next case.

Central Virginia Community College v. Katz, 546 U.S. 356 (2006). The Bankruptcy Clause of Article I provides Congress the authority to establish "uniform Laws on the subject of Bankruptcies throughout the United States." Dictum in *Seminole Tribe* assumed that its holding applied to limit congressional authority under the Bankruptcy Clause just as it does to other provisions in Article I. In *Katz*, however, the Court, in an opinion by **Justice Stevens**, held that bankruptcy is different: the Framers designed the Bankruptcy Clause to allow Congress to create a uniform, integrated national bankruptcy system to replace the inconsistent state approaches to the discharge of debts and the refusal of states to respect one another's discharge orders. Inherent in the constitutional plan was congressional authority to treat states as other creditors are treated. In dissent, **Justice Thomas**, joined by **Chief Justice Roberts**, **Justice Scalia**, and **Justice Kennedy**, argued that this holding was inconsistent with *Seminole Tribe* and earlier Eleventh Amendment decisions.

3. *Congress's Fourteenth Amendment Authority to Abrogate State Eleventh Amendment Immunity After* Boerne

Now let us apply these principles to a concrete situation. Title VII of the 1964 Civil Rights Act (as amended), the Age Discrimination in Employment Act (as amended), and the Americans with Disabilities Act all forbid states from discriminating against their employees on certain grounds (e.g., race, gender, age, disability) and provide that prevailing plaintiffs may recover damages. Even after *Lopez*, it would seem clear that these statutes are generally within Congress' commerce power, as they regulate an economic relationship (that of employer and employee). But under *Seminole Tribe*, Congress has no authority under the commerce power (which is in Article I) to abrogate the states' immunity to suit. Plaintiffs are therefore driven to argue that these statutes, and others like them, are justified by Congress' authority to enforce the Reconstruction Amendments. This argument has not fared well in the post-*Boerne* era.

Thus, in *Kimel v. Florida Board of Regents*, 528 U.S. 62 (2000), the five Federalism Justices held that the Age Discrimination in Employment Act (ADEA) could not be applied to state employers under Congress's authority to enforce the Fourteenth Amendment and, therefore, that Congress could not abrogate the states' immunity from suit. Justice O'Connor's opinion for the Court started with the proposition that the Fourteenth Amendment imposes only a minimal rationality requirement on state rules discriminating on the basis of age. See *Massachusetts Bd. of Retirement v. Murgia* (Chapter 4, § 1). "Judged against the backdrop of our equal protection jurisprudence, it is clear that the ADEA is 'so out of proportion to a supposed remedial or preventive object that it cannot be understood as responsive to, or designed to prevent, unconstitutional behavior.' *Boerne*. The Act, through its broad restriction on the use of age as a discriminating factor, prohibits substantially more state employment decisions and practices than would likely be held unconstitutional under the applicable equal protection, rational basis standard."

Justice O'Connor examined the ADEA's legislative record and found the extension of the statute to the states was "an unwarranted response to a perhaps inconsequential problem. Congress never identified any pattern of age discrimination by the States, much less any discrimination whatsoever that rose to the level of constitutional violation. The evidence compiled by petitioners to demonstrate such attention by Congress to age discrimination by the States falls well short of the mark. That evidence consists almost entirely of isolated sentences clipped from floor debates and legislative reports." Given the indiscriminate scope of the ADEA's substantive requirements, the dearth of evidence for widespread and unconstitutional age discrimination by the states brought the case within *Boerne*'s rule of invalidity. See also *Florida Prepaid Postsecondary Education Expense Board v. College Sav. Bank*, 527 U.S. 627 (1999) (ruling that a federal patent remedy statute could not be applied against state patent violators, because there was no pattern of unconstitutional behavior by the states to establish this as a "proportional and congruent" congressional enforcement response).

Board of Trustees v. Garrett, 531 U.S. 356 (2001). The Court, by the same 5-4 vote as in *Seminole* and *Kimel*, held that Congress had exceeded its § 5 power when it enacted the provisions of the Americans with Disabilities Act (ADA) forbidding states from engaging in employment discrimination against the disabled, which included a requirement that states take affirmative steps to accommodate disabled employees. In some senses, the case resembled *Kimel*, in that discrimination on the basis of disability, like age discrimination, draws only rational-basis review under the Equal Protection Clause. *Garrett* presented two factors not present in *Kimel*, however. First, unlike with age discrimination, the Court has found a violation of the Equal Protection Clause in the context of disability discrimination, concluding that a city's refusal to allow the construction of a group home for the developmentally disabled was motivated by irrational animus. See *Cleburne v. Cleburne Living Center* (Chapter 4, § 3C).

Thus, rational-basis review in this context seems to be a more aggressive judicial scrutiny than the "anything goes" review accorded to age classifications. Second, the text of the ADA and its legislative history contained elaborate findings and information seemingly documenting widespread disability discrimination.

Chief Justice Rehnquist's opinion for the usual majority first rejected the contention that *Cleburne* established a special kind of rationality review for disability claims. He then concluded that Congress had failed to document "a pattern of irrational state discrimination in employment against the disabled." Because the Eleventh Amendment shields only states, and not local governments or private parties, from suit in federal court, the majority considered irrelevant all information in the legislative history concerning supposed discrimination by any entity other than states.

"Congress made a general finding in the ADA that 'historically, society has tended to isolate and segregate individuals with disabilities, and, despite some improvements, such forms of discrimination against individuals with disabilities continue to be a serious and pervasive social problem.' 42 U.S.C. § 12101(a)(2). The record assembled by Congress includes many instances to support such a finding. But the great majority of these incidents do not deal with the activities of States.

"Respondents in their brief cite half a dozen examples from the record that did involve States. A department head at the University of North Carolina refused to hire an applicant for the position of health administrator because he was blind; similarly, a student at a state university in South Dakota was denied an opportunity to practice teach because the dean at that time was convinced that blind people could not teach in public schools. A microfilmer at the Kansas Department of Transportation was fired because he had epilepsy; deaf workers at the University of Oklahoma were paid a lower salary than those who could hear. The Indiana State Personnel Office informed a woman with a concealed disability that she should not disclose it if she wished to obtain employment.

"Several of these incidents undoubtedly evidence an unwillingness on the part of state officials to make the sort of accommodations for the disabled required by the ADA. Whether they were irrational under our decision in *Cleburne* is more debatable, particularly when the incident is described out of context. But even if it were to be determined that each incident upon fuller examination showed unconstitutional action on the part of the State, these incidents taken together fall far short of even suggesting the pattern of unconstitutional discrimination on which § 5 legislation must be based. Congress, in enacting the ADA, found that 'some 43,000,000 Americans have one or more physical or mental disabilities.' 42 U.S.C. § 12101(a)(1). In 1990, the States alone employed more than 4.5 million people. U.S. Dept. of Commerce, Bureau of Census, Statistical Abstract of the United States 338 (119th ed. 1999) (Table 534). It is telling, we think, that given these large numbers, Congress assembled only such minimal evidence of unconstitutional state discrimination in employment against the disabled.

"Justice Breyer maintains that Congress applied Title I of the ADA to the States in response to a host of incidents representing unconstitutional state discrimination in employment against persons with disabilities. A close review of the relevant materials, however, undercuts that conclusion. Justice Breyer's Appendix C consists not of legislative findings, but of unexamined, anecdotal accounts of 'adverse, disparate treatment by state officials.' Of course, as we have already explained, 'adverse, disparate treatment' often does not amount to a constitutional violation where rational-basis scrutiny applies. These accounts, moreover, were submitted not directly to Congress but to the Task Force on the Rights and Empowerment of Americans with Disabilities, which made no findings on the subject of state discrimination in employment.[7] And, had Congress truly understood this information as reflecting a pattern of unconstitutional behavior by the States, one would expect some mention of that conclusion in the Act's legislative findings. There is none. Although Justice Breyer would infer from Congress' general conclusions regarding societal discrimination against the disabled that the States had likewise participated in such action, the House and Senate committee reports on the ADA flatly contradict this assertion. After describing the evidence presented to the Senate Committee on Labor and Human Resources and its subcommittee (including the Task Force Report upon which the dissent relies), the Committee's report reached, among others, the following conclusion: 'Discrimination still persists in such critical areas as *employment in the private sector,* public accommodations, public services, transportation, and telecommunications.' S.Rep. No. 101-116, p. 6 (1989) (emphasis added). The House Committee on Education and Labor, addressing the ADA's employment provisions, reached the same conclusion: '[A]fter extensive review and analysis over a number of Congressional sessions, . . . there exists a compelling need to establish a clear and comprehensive Federal prohibition of discrimination on the basis of disability in the areas of *employment in the private sector,* public accommodations, public services, transportation, and telecommunications.' H.R.Rep. No. 101-485, pt. 2 p. 28 (1990) (emphasis added). Thus, not only is the inference Justice Breyer draws unwarranted, but there is also strong evidence that Congress' failure to mention States in its legislative findings addressing discrimination in employment reflects that body's judgment that no pattern of unconstitutional state action had been documented.

"Even were it possible to squeeze out of these examples a pattern of unconstitutional discrimination by the States, the rights and remedies created by the ADA against the States would raise the same sort of concerns as to congruence and proportionality as were found in *Boerne.* For example, whereas it would be entirely rational (and therefore constitutional) for a state employer to conserve scarce financial resources by hiring employees who are able to use

---

7. "Only a small fraction of the anecdotes Justice Breyer identifies * * * relate to state discrimination against the disabled in employment. At most, somewhere around 50 of these allegations describe conduct that could conceivably amount to constitutional violations by the States, and most of them are so general and brief that no firm conclusion can be drawn. The overwhelming majority of these accounts pertain to alleged discrimination by the States in the provision of public services and public accommodations, which areas are addressed in Titles II and III of the ADA."

existing facilities, the ADA requires employers to 'mak[e] existing facilities used by employees readily accessible to and usable by individuals with disabilities.' 42 U.S.C. §§ 12112(5)(B), 12111(9). The ADA does except employers from the 'reasonable accommodatio[n]' requirement where the employer 'can demonstrate that the accommodation would impose an undue hardship on the operation of the business of such covered entity.' § 12112(b)(5)(A). However, even with this exception, the accommodation duty far exceeds what is constitutionally required in that it makes unlawful a range of alternate responses that would be reasonable but would fall short of imposing an 'undue burden' upon the employer. The Act also makes it the employer's duty to prove that it would suffer such a burden, instead of requiring (as the Constitution does) that the complaining party negate reasonable bases for the employer's decision.

"The ADA also forbids 'utilizing standards, criteria, or methods of administration' that disparately impact the disabled, without regard to whether such conduct has a rational basis. § 12112(b)(3)(A). Although disparate impact may be relevant evidence of racial discrimination, such evidence alone is insufficient even where the Fourteenth Amendment subjects state action to strict scrutiny. *Washington v. Davis.*

Chief Justice Rehnquist contrasted the ADA with the VRA, where "Congress documented a marked pattern of unconstitutional action by the States. State officials, Congress found, routinely applied voting tests in order to exclude African-American citizens from registering to vote. Congress also determined that litigation had proved ineffective and that there persisted an otherwise inexplicable 50- percentage-point gap in the registration of white and African-American voters in some States." Under the *Cleburne* standard, the ADA record had established no such "pattern of discrimination by the States which violates the Fourteenth Amendment" that would justify the congressional remedy as "congruent and proportional to the targeted violation."

In a lengthy dissent seeking to document that Congress compiled a vast amount of evidence from which it "reasonably could have concluded that the remedy before us constitutes an 'appropriate' way to enforce" equal protection, **Justice Breyer** complained that the majority was "reviewing the congressional record as if it were an administrative agency record."

NOTES ON THE POST-*BOERNE* ELEVENTH AMENDMENT CASES

1. *Congressional Enforcement Power Revisited.* Perhaps *Boerne* was a fairly easy case, once the Court assumed that Congress had only remedial, and no substantive, power under the Reconstruction Amendments, because the legislative record was virtually devoid of evidence that in RFRA Congress was remedying or preventing widespread constitutional violations as judicially defined. As with the gun law in *Lopez*, one might have been concerned that, on this record, RFRA could be justified only if Congress has some sort of national police power contrary to constitutional text and history. But what of *Garrett*? Is disability discrimination not a "real" civil rights problem? Do these cases

suggest that congressional authority under the Reconstruction Amendments is largely limited to promoting the civil rights of groups that the Court considers worthy of the protections of heightened scrutiny under the Equal Protection Clause? Does that make any sense?

2. *What Is Congress To Do?* Consider the recent federalism cases from the perspective of Congress. In *Lopez*, the Court stressed that the gun statute lacked formal congressional findings of effect upon interstate commerce. In *Boerne*, the Court similarly stressed that Congress had not built a substantial record connecting RFRA to remedying or preventing constitutional violations as judicially defined. Then *Garrett* found the much more carefully assembled legislative history of the ADA insufficient. Both *Boerne* and *Garrett* refer to the legislative history of the Voting Rights Act as the model for Congress to follow — yet that history was developed in a far different time, when evidence of intentional discrimination was patent, really undeniable. Has the Court suggested that Congress can attack only those forms of discrimination that everybody knows exists even independent of the legislative record? Is the basic problem in *Garrett* that Congress did not gather enough information? The immediate scholarly reaction to *Garrett* has been overwhelmingly negative, in part on the ground that the Court may have imposed upon Congress a requirement of factual documentation that Congress cannot possibly satisfy.[o] But perhaps *Garrett* goes even further, imposing an additional requirement that Congress duly deliberate and conscientiously determine that the facts justify invoking its § 5 power. Thus, even if Congress could gather sufficient information — which interest groups supporting legislation invoking the § 5 power now have every incentive to give to Congress — the five Justices that decided *Garrett* might not be satisfied unless the congressional record revealed a kind of deliberative, objective quality similar to the way a federal district judge is supposed to apply the assembled facts to the legal standards developed by the Supreme Court.[p]

---

o. See, e.g., William Buzbee & Robert Schapiro, *Legislative Record Review*, 54 Stan. L. Rev. 87 (2001); Ruth Colker & James Brudney, *Dissing Congress*, 100 Mich. L. Rev. 80 (2001).

p. For the argument that any requirement of due deliberation fundamentally misconceives how Congress (or any other legislature) operates, see Philip Frickey & Steven S. Smith, *Judicial Review, The Congressional Process, and the Federalism Cases: An Interdisciplinary Critique*, 111 Yale L.J. 1707, 1744-45 (2002), reprinted with permission of the Yale Law Journal:

Students of deliberation have observed that successful deliberation is contingent on a commonality of interests or values to be pursued in public policy. If a commonality of interests or values does not exist, discussion will take the form of debate, decisions will be made by vote rather than by consensus, and the process will take the form of building majority coalitions through a variety of means rather than persuasion on the merits. The process of building majorities or supermajorities under conditions of a conflict of interests generates competition. Competition, in turn, produces strategies that undermine the purposes of deliberation. Legislators may reveal incomplete or misleading information about their own goals, objective conditions, or causal reasoning. Strategic disclosure muddies the legislative record and greatly complicates the task of applying a legal standard that asks judges to evaluate the quality of that record. * * *

The Court expects Congress to legislate differently when its exercise of Commerce Clause

3. *Why Should Congress Have To Do That? Or, the Court and Social Movements Revisited.*   Some scholars read *Lopez, Boerne, Seminole,* and *Garrett* as a repudiation of the cooperative relationship forged by the Court with Congress to implement the equality values of *Brown v. Board of Education.*[q] But note how carefully the majorities have distinguished the civil rights cases. Consider the following hypothesis: Because southern apartheid was entrenched and fundamentally inconsistent with core constitutional values (democracy as well as equality), and because drastic measures were called for, the civil rights precedents were exceptional. But legislators, judges, and commentators have taken the civil rights cases at face value and then expanded upon them to justify more aggressive congressional legislation for the benefit of other social groups — religious minorities (*Boerne*), the aged (*Kimel*), and the disabled (*Garrett*). The injustices faced by these minorities do not present the enormous constitutional problems apartheid did, and the current Court believes that the normal political process is sufficient to protect these minorities (*Smith; Murgia; Cleburne*). Hence, the need for congressional action was not as great as it was for people of color in the 1960s, and if the Court went along with these new congressional exercises of power there would be no limit to that power. Federalism is a core constitutional value, and it has been of enormous utility as well.   Hence, the time has come for the Court to reassert limitations on Congress's authority, under the Fourteenth Amendment as well as Article I. Persuasive? Consider this debate as you examine the next case.

E. THE VIOLENCE AGAINST WOMEN ACT

UNITED STATES v. MORRISON
529 U.S. 598, 120 S.Ct. 1740, 146 L.Ed.2d 658 (2000)

CHIEF JUSTICE REHNQUIST delivered the opinion of the Court.

[Petitioner Christy Brzonkala, a student at Virginia Polytechnic Institute (Virginia Tech), complained that respondents Antonio Morrison and James Crawford, football-playing students at Virginia Tech, assaulted and repeatedly raped her. After the rape, Morrison allegedly announced that he "like[d] to get girls drunk" and have his way with them sexually. He boasted of his sexual conquests of women. Brzonkala filed a complaint against respondents under Virginia Tech's Sexual Assault Policy. During the school-conducted hearing

---

and Section 5 authority threatens states' rights. When there is little conflict of interests within Congress, it is easy to see how congressional action, even with bicameralism and a process that builds majority decisions, might be improved to meet the Court's expectations. However, when conflict of interests is present and when policy is therefore constructed through a competitive process of coalition building, bargaining, and voting, the Court is asking too much. It is demanding more than a statute, which is a legislative *outcome*, that meets constitutional standards. It is requiring that a bargaining *process* have the major features of a hypothetical rational policymaking process. It is demanding that the legislative process become something it is not and cannot be in a system of competitive parties operating through several institutions with shared policymaking responsibilities.

q. See, e.g., Brudney & Colker, *supra*; Robert Post & Reva Siegel, *Equal Protection by Law: Federal Antidiscrimination Legislation After* Morrison *and* Kimel, 110 Yale L.J. 441 (2000).

on her complaint, Morrison admitted having sexual contact with her despite the fact that she had twice told him "no." After the hearing, Virginia Tech's Judicial Committee found insufficient evidence to punish Crawford, but found Morrison guilty of sexual assault and sentenced him to immediate suspension for two semesters. Virginia Tech's vice president later set this aside as excessive punishment. Brzonkala thereupon dropped out of the university and sued it and the male students under the Violence Against Women Act, 42 U.S.C. § 13981, which provides a federal cause of action for the victim of a "crime of violence motivated by gender" against the perpetrator. The Court considered whether either the Commerce Clause or § 5 of the Fourteenth Amendment authorized Congress to create this new cause of action.]

As we observed in *Lopez*, modern Commerce Clause jurisprudence has "identified three broad categories of activity that Congress may regulate under its commerce power." "First, Congress may regulate the use of the channels of interstate commerce." *Lopez* (citing *Heart of Atlanta Motel; Darby*). "Second, Congress is empowered to regulate and protect the instrumentalities of interstate commerce, or persons or things in interstate commerce, even though the threat may come only from intrastate activities." *Id.* (citing *Shreveport Rate Cases*). "Finally, Congress' commerce authority includes the power to regulate those activities having a substantial relation to interstate commerce, . . . *i.e.*, those activities that substantially affect interstate commerce." *Id.* (citing *Jones & Laughlin*).

[Petitioners United States and Brzonkala argued that § 13981 fell under the third category, which was also the focus of *Lopez*.] [A] fair reading of *Lopez* shows that the noneconomic, criminal nature of the conduct at issue was central to our decision in that case. *Lopez*'s review of Commerce Clause case law demonstrates that in those cases where we have sustained federal regulation of intrastate activity based upon the activity's substantial effects on interstate commerce, the activity in question has been some sort of economic endeavor. [*Lopez* also emphasized that the gun-free school zone law lacked a jurisdictional element tying the offense to interstate commerce and congressional findings regarding the effects of gun possession in a school zone on interstate commerce. Overall, the Court was worried that if the attenuated connection between guns in school zones and interstate commerce were accepted, Congress "could regulate any activity that it found was related to the economic productivity of individual citizens: family law (including marriage, divorce, and child custody), for example."]

With these principles underlying our Commerce Clause jurisprudence as reference points, the proper resolution of the present cases is clear. Gender-motivated crimes of violence are not, in any sense of the phrase, economic activity. While we need not adopt a categorical rule against aggregating the effects of any noneconomic activity in order to decide these cases, thus far in our Nation's history our cases have upheld Commerce Clause regulation of intrastate activity only where that activity is economic in nature.

Like the Gun-Free School Zones Act at issue in *Lopez*, § 13981 contains no jurisdictional element establishing that the federal cause of action is in pursuance of Congress' power to regulate interstate commerce. Although

Lopez makes clear that such a jurisdictional element would lend support to the argument that § 13981 is sufficiently tied to interstate commerce, Congress elected to cast § 13981's remedy over a wider, and more purely intrastate, body of violent crime.

In contrast with the lack of congressional findings that we faced in *Lopez*, § 13981 *is* supported by numerous findings regarding the serious impact that gender-motivated violence has on victims and their families. But the existence of congressional findings is not sufficient, by itself, to sustain the constitutionality of Commerce Clause legislation. As we stated in *Lopez*, " '[S]imply because Congress may conclude that a particular activity substantially affects interstate commerce does not necessarily make it so.' " Rather, " '[w]hether particular operations affect interstate commerce sufficiently to come under the constitutional power of Congress to regulate them is ultimately a judicial rather than a legislative question, and can be settled finally only by this Court.' " *Lopez* n.2 (quoting *Heart of Atlanta Motel* (Black, J., concurring)).

In these cases, Congress' findings are substantially weakened by the fact that they rely so heavily on a method of reasoning that we have already rejected as unworkable if we are to maintain the Constitution's enumeration of powers. Congress found that gender-motivated violence affects interstate commerce

> "by deterring potential victims from traveling interstate, from engaging in employment in interstate business, and from transacting with business, and in places involved in interstate commerce; . . . by diminishing national productivity, increasing medical and other costs, and decreasing the supply of and the demand for interstate products." H. R. Conf. Rep. No. 103-711, at 385.

Given these findings and petitioners' arguments, the concern that we expressed in *Lopez* that Congress might use the Commerce Clause to completely obliterate the Constitution's distinction between national and local authority seems well founded. The reasoning that petitioners advance seeks to follow the but-for causal chain from the initial occurrence of violent crime (the suppression of which has always been the prime object of the States' police power) to every attenuated effect upon interstate commerce. If accepted, petitioners' reasoning would allow Congress to regulate any crime as long as the nationwide, aggregated impact of that crime has substantial effects on employment, production, transit, or consumption. Indeed, if Congress may regulate gender-motivated violence, it would be able to regulate murder or any other type of violence since gender-motivated violence, as a subset of all violent crime, is certain to have lesser economic impacts than the larger class of which it is a part.

Petitioners' reasoning, moreover, will not limit Congress to regulating violence but may, as we suggested in *Lopez*, be applied equally as well to family law and other areas of traditional state regulation since the aggregate effect of marriage, divorce, and childrearing on the national economy is undoubtedly significant. Congress may have recognized this specter when it expressly precluded § 13981 from being used in the family law context. See 42 U.S.C. § 13981(e)(4). Under our written Constitution, however, the limitation of congressional authority is not solely a matter of legislative grace. See *Lopez* (Kennedy, J., concurring); *Marbury*.

We accordingly reject the argument that Congress may regulate noneconomic, violent criminal conduct based solely on that conduct's aggregate effect on interstate commerce. The Constitution requires a distinction between what is truly national and what is truly local. In recognizing this fact we preserve one of the few principles that has been consistent since the Clause was adopted. The regulation and punishment of intrastate violence that is not directed at the instrumentalities, channels, or goods involved in interstate commerce has always been the province of the States. See, *e.g., Cohens v. Virginia*, 6 Wheat. 264, 426, 428 (1821) (Marshall, C.J.) (stating that Congress "has no general right to punish murder committed within any of the States," and that it is "clear . . . that congress cannot punish felonies generally"). Indeed, we can think of no better example of the police power, which the Founders denied the National Government and reposed in the States, than the suppression of violent crime and vindication of its victims.

* * * Petitioners' § 5 argument is founded on an assertion that there is pervasive bias in various state justice systems against victims of gender-motivated violence. This assertion is supported by a voluminous congressional record. Specifically, Congress received evidence that many participants in state justice systems are perpetuating an array of erroneous stereotypes and assumptions. Congress concluded that these discriminatory stereotypes often result in insufficient investigation and prosecution of gender-motivated crime, inappropriate focus on the behavior and credibility of the victims of that crime, and unacceptably lenient punishments for those who are actually convicted of gender-motivated violence. Petitioners contend that this bias denies victims of gender-motivated violence the equal protection of the laws and that Congress therefore acted appropriately in enacting a private civil remedy against the perpetrators of gender-motivated violence to both remedy the States' bias and deter future instances of discrimination in the state courts.

* * * [T]he language and purpose of the Fourteenth Amendment place certain limitations on the manner in which Congress may attack discriminatory conduct. These limitations are necessary to prevent the Fourteenth Amendment from obliterating the Framers' carefully crafted balance of power between the States and the National Government. Foremost among these limitations is the time-honored principle that the Fourteenth Amendment, by its very terms, prohibits only state action. [Citing, e.g., *The Civil Rights Cases*. Petitioners argued that *United States v. Guest*, 383 U.S. 745 (1966) implicitly overruled the *Civil Rights Cases*. Although six concurring Justices expressed such a view in two separate statements, the opinion for the Court did not. It would require more than magic mathematics to dislodge the established rule of the *Civil Rights Cases*.]

Petitioners alternatively argue that, unlike the situation in the *Civil Rights Cases*, here there has been gender-based disparate treatment by state authorities, whereas in those cases there was no indication of such state action. There is abundant evidence, however, to show that the Congresses that enacted the Civil Rights Acts of 1871 and 1875 had a purpose similar to that of Congress in enacting § 13981: There were state laws on the books bespeaking equality of treatment, but in the administration of these laws there was discrimination against newly freed slaves. * * *

But even if that distinction were valid, we do not believe it would save § 13981's civil remedy. For the remedy is simply not "corrective in its character, adapted to counteract and redress the operation of such prohibited [s]tate laws or proceedings of [s]tate officers." *Civil Rights Cases.* Or, as we have phrased it in more recent cases, prophylactic legislation under § 5 must have a " 'congruence and proportionality between the injury to be prevented or remedied and the means adopted to that end.' " *Florida Prepaid*, quoting *Boerne*. Section 13981 is not aimed at proscribing discrimination by officials which the Fourteenth Amendment might not itself proscribe; it is directed not at any State or state actor, but at individuals who have committed criminal acts motivated by gender bias.

In the present cases, for example, § 13981 visits no consequence whatever on any Virginia public official involved in investigating or prosecuting Brzonkala's assault. The section is, therefore, unlike any of the § 5 remedies that we have previously upheld. For example, in *Katzenbach v. Morgan*, Congress prohibited New York from imposing literacy tests as a prerequisite for voting because it found that such a requirement disenfranchised thousands of Puerto Rican immigrants who had been educated in the Spanish language of their home territory. That law, which we upheld, was directed at New York officials who administered the State's election law and prohibited them from using a provision of that law. In *South Carolina v. Katzenbach*, Congress imposed voting rights requirements on States that, Congress found, had a history of discriminating against blacks in voting. The remedy was also directed at state officials in those States. * * *

Section 13981 is also different from these previously upheld remedies in that it applies uniformly throughout the Nation. Congress' findings indicate that the problem of discrimination against the victims of gender-motivated crimes does not exist in all States, or even most States. By contrast, the § 5 remedy upheld in *Katzenbach v. Morgan* was directed only to the State where the evil found by Congress existed, and in *South Carolina v. Katzenbach*, the remedy was directed only to those States in which Congress found that there had been discrimination. * * *

JUSTICE THOMAS, concurring.

The majority opinion correctly applies our decision in *United States v. Lopez*, and I join it in full. I write separately only to express my view that the very notion of a "substantial effects" test under the Commerce Clause is inconsistent with the original understanding of Congress' powers and with this Court's early Commerce Clause cases. By continuing to apply this rootless and malleable standard, however circumscribed, the Court has encouraged the Federal Government to persist in its view that the Commerce Clause has virtually no limits. Until this Court replaces its existing Commerce Clause jurisprudence with a standard more consistent with the original understanding, we will continue to see Congress appropriating state police powers under the guise of regulating commerce.

JUSTICE SOUTER, with whom **JUSTICE STEVENS**, **JUSTICE GINSBURG**, and **JUSTICE BREYER** join, dissenting. * * *

I. Our cases, which remain at least nominally undisturbed, stand for the following propositions. Congress has the power to legislate with regard to activity that, in the aggregate, has a substantial effect on interstate commerce. See *Wickard v. Filburn*. The fact of such a substantial effect is not an issue for the courts in the first instance, but for the Congress, whose institutional capacity for gathering evidence and taking testimony far exceeds ours. By passing legislation, Congress indicates its conclusion, whether explicitly or not, that facts support its exercise of the commerce power. The business of the courts is to review the congressional assessment, not for soundness but simply for the rationality of concluding that a jurisdictional basis exists in fact. Any explicit findings that Congress chooses to make, though not dispositive of the question of rationality, may advance judicial review by identifying factual authority on which Congress relied. Applying those propositions in these cases can lead to only one conclusion.

One obvious difference from *Lopez* is the mountain of data assembled by Congress, here showing the effects of violence against women on interstate commerce. Passage of the Act in 1994 was preceded by four years of hearings, which included testimony from physicians and law professors; from survivors of rape and domestic violence; and from representatives of state law enforcement and private business. The record includes reports on gender bias from task forces in 21 States, and we have the benefit of specific factual findings in the eight separate Reports issued by Congress and its committees over the long course leading to enactment. Compare *Hodel* (noting "extended hearings," "vast amounts of testimony and documentary evidence," and "years of the most thorough legislative consideration").

With respect to domestic violence, Congress received evidence for the following findings:

"Three out of four American women will be victims of violent crimes sometime during their life." H.R. Rep. No. 103-395 p. 25 (1993).

"Violence is the leading cause of injuries to women ages 15 to 44 . . . ." S. Rep. No. 103-138, p. 38 (1993). * * *

"Between 2,000 and 4,000 women die every year from [domestic] abuse." S. Rep. No. 101-545, at 36.

"[A]rrest rates may be as low as 1 for every 100 domestic assaults." S. Rep. No. 101-545, at 38.

"Partial estimates show that violent crime against women costs this country at least 3 billion — not million, but billion — dollars a year." S. Rep. No. 101-545, at 33. * * *

" '[A]n individual who commits rape has only about 4 chances in 100 of being arrested, prosecuted, and found guilty of any offense.' " S. Rep. No. 101-545, at 33, n. 30. * * *

Based on the data thus partially summarized, Congress found that

"crimes of violence motivated by gender have a substantial adverse effect on interstate commerce, by deterring potential victims from traveling interstate, from engaging in employment in interstate business, and from transacting with business, and in places involved, in interstate commerce . . . [,] by diminishing national productivity, increasing medical and other costs, and decreasing the supply of and the demand for interstate products . . . ." H. R. Conf. Rep. No. 103-711, p. 385 (1994).

Congress thereby explicitly stated the predicate for the exercise of its Commerce Clause power. Is its conclusion irrational in view of the data amassed? True, the methodology of particular studies may be challenged, and some of the figures arrived at may be disputed. But the sufficiency of the evidence before Congress to provide a rational basis for the finding cannot seriously be questioned.

Indeed, the legislative record here is far more voluminous than the record compiled by Congress and found sufficient in two prior cases upholding Title II of the Civil Rights Act of 1964 against Commerce Clause challenges. In *Heart of Atlanta Motel* and *McClung*, the Court referred to evidence showing the consequences of racial discrimination by motels and restaurants on interstate commerce. Congress had relied on compelling anecdotal reports that individual instances of segregation cost thousands to millions of dollars. Congress also had evidence that the average black family spent substantially less than the average white family in the same income range on public accommodations, and that discrimination accounted for much of the difference.

While Congress did not, to my knowledge, calculate aggregate dollar values for the nationwide effects of racial discrimination in 1964, in 1994 it did rely on evidence of the harms caused by domestic violence and sexual assault, citing annual costs of $3 billion in 1990 and $5 to $10 billion in 1993. Equally important, though, gender-based violence in the 1990's was shown to operate in a manner similar to racial discrimination in the 1960's in reducing the mobility of employees and their production and consumption of goods shipped in interstate commerce. Like racial discrimination, "[g]ender-based violence bars its most likely targets — women — from full partic[ipation] in the national economy." * * *

II. The Act would have passed muster at any time between *Wickard* in 1942 and *Lopez* in 1995, a period in which the law enjoyed a stable understanding that congressional power under the Commerce Clause, complemented by the authority of the Necessary and Proper Clause, Art. I. § 8 cl. 18, extended to all activity that, when aggregated, has a substantial effect on interstate commerce. * * *

The fact that the Act does not pass muster before the Court today is therefore proof, to a degree that *Lopez* was not, that the Court's nominal adherence to the substantial effects test is merely that. Although a new jurisprudence has not emerged with any distinctness, it is clear that some congressional conclusions about obviously substantial, cumulative effects on commerce are being assigned lesser values than the once-stable doctrine would assign them. These devaluations are accomplished not by any express repudiation of the substantial effects test or its application through the aggregation of individual conduct, but by supplanting rational basis scrutiny with a new criterion of review.

Thus the elusive heart of the majority's analysis in these cases is its statement that Congress's findings of fact are "weakened" by the presence of a disfavored "method of reasoning." This seems to suggest that the "substantial effects" analysis is not a factual enquiry, for Congress in the first instance with subsequent judicial review looking only to the rationality of the congressional conclusion, but one of a rather different sort, dependent upon a uniquely judicial competence.

This new characterization of substantial effects has no support in our cases (the self-fulfilling prophecies of *Lopez* aside), least of all those the majority cites. Perhaps this explains why the majority is not content to rest on its cited precedent but claims a textual justification for moving toward its new system of congressional deference subject to selective discounts. Thus it purports to rely on the sensible and traditional understanding that the listing in the Constitution of some powers implies the exclusion of others unmentioned. The majority stresses that Art. I, § 8 enumerates the powers of Congress, including the commerce power, an enumeration implying the exclusion of powers not enumerated. It follows, for the majority, not only that there must be some limits to "commerce," but that some particular subjects arguably within the commerce power can be identified in advance as excluded, on the basis of characteristics other than their commercial effects. Such exclusions come into sight when the activity regulated is not itself commercial or when the States have traditionally addressed it in the exercise of the general police power, conferred under the state constitutions but never extended to Congress under the Constitution of the Nation.

The premise that the enumeration of powers implies that other powers are withheld is sound; the conclusion that some particular categories of subject matter are therefore presumptively beyond the reach of the commerce power is, however, a non sequitur. From the fact that Art. I, § 8, cl. 3 grants an authority limited to regulating commerce, it follows only that Congress may claim no authority under that section to address any subject that does not affect commerce. It does not at all follow that an activity affecting commerce nonetheless falls outside the commerce power, depending on the specific character of the activity, or the authority of a State to regulate it along with Congress. My disagreement with the majority is not, however, confined to logic, for history has shown that categorical exclusions have proven as unworkable in practice as they are unsupportable in theory.

Obviously, it would not be inconsistent with the text of the Commerce Clause itself to declare "noncommercial" primary activity beyond or presumptively beyond the scope of the commerce power. That variant of categorical approach is not, however, the sole textually permissible way of defining the scope of the Commerce Clause, and any such neat limitation would at least be suspect in the light of the final sentence of Article I, § 8, authorizing Congress to make "all Laws . . . necessary and proper" to give effect to its enumerated powers such as commerce. Accordingly, for significant periods of our history, the Court has defined the commerce power as plenary, unsusceptible to categorical exclusions, and this was the view expressed throughout the latter part of the 20th century in the substantial effects test. These two conceptions of the commerce power, plenary and categorically limited, are in fact old rivals, and today's revival of their competition summons up familiar history * * * .

[Justice Souter surveyed the Court's vacillating approach, starting with *Gibbons*, which he interpreted as encompassing a broad understanding of Congress' power and anticipating the approach followed after the New Deal. The New Deal Court rejected earlier cases which had experimented, unsuccessfully, with various limiting principles.]

Since adherence to these formalistically contrived confines of commerce power in large measure provoked the judicial crisis of 1937, one might reasonably have doubted that Members of this Court would ever again toy with a return to the days before *NLRB v. Jones & Laughlin Steel Corp.*, which brought the earlier and nearly disastrous experiment to an end. And yet today's decision can only be seen as a step toward recapturing the prior mistakes. Its revival of a distinction between commercial and noncommercial conduct is at odds with *Wickard*, which repudiated that analysis, and the enquiry into commercial purpose, first intimated by the *Lopez* concurrence, see *Lopez* (opinion of *Kennedy*, J.), is cousin to the intent-based analysis employed in *Hammer*, but rejected for Commerce Clause purposes in *Heart of Atlanta* and *Darby*.

Why is the majority tempted to reject the lesson so painfully learned in 1937? An answer emerges from contrasting *Wickard* with one of the predecessor cases it superseded. It was obvious in *Wickard* that growing wheat for consumption right on the farm was not "commerce" in the common vocabulary, but that did not matter constitutionally so long as the aggregated activity of domestic wheat growing affected commerce substantially. Just a few years before *Wickard*, however, it had certainly been no less obvious that "mining" practices could substantially affect commerce, even though *Carter Coal Co.* had held mining regulation beyond the national commerce power. When we try to fathom the difference between the two cases, it is clear that they did not go in different directions because the *Carter Coal* Court could not understand a causal connection that the *Wickard* Court could grasp; the difference, rather, turned on the fact that the Court in *Carter Coal* had a reason for trying to maintain its categorical, formalistic distinction, while that reason had been abandoned by the time *Wickard* was decided. The reason was laissez-faire economics, the point of which was to keep government interference to a minimum. The Court in *Carter Coal* was still trying to create a laissez-faire world out of the 20th-century economy, and formalistic commercial distinctions were thought to be useful instruments in achieving that object. The Court in *Wickard* knew it could not do any such thing and in the aftermath of the New Deal had long since stopped attempting the impossible. Without the animating economic theory, there was no point in contriving formalisms in a war with Chief Justice Marshall's conception of the commerce power.

If we now ask why the formalistic economic/noneconomic distinction might matter today, after its rejection in *Wickard*, the answer is not that the majority fails to see causal connections in an integrated economic world. The answer is that in the minds of the majority there is a new animating theory that makes categorical formalism seem useful again. Just as the old formalism had value in the service of an economic conception, the new one is useful in serving a conception of federalism. It is the instrument by which assertions of national power are to be limited in favor of preserving a supposedly discernible, proper sphere of state autonomy to legislate or refrain from legislating as the individual States see fit. The legitimacy of the Court's current emphasis on the noncommercial nature of regulated activity, then, does not turn on any logic serving the text of the Commerce Clause or on the realism of the majority's view of the national economy. The essential issue is rather the strength of the majority's claim to have a constitutional warrant for its current conception of a federal relationship enforceable by this Court through limits on otherwise plenary commerce power. This conception is the subject of the majority's second categorical discount applied today to the facts bearing on the substantial effects test.

[Justice Souter also maintained that the Framers expected the relations between state and national authority to be regulated more by political than judicial checks. See *The Federalist* No. 46 (Madison); *Gibbons*; *Garcia* (§ 5B of this Chapter). He also found it ironic that, in the name of federalism, the Court was striking down a statute supported by attorneys general representing 38 states, who admitted that local remedies for violence against women were insufficient and insisted upon the need for a national regulatory response. Thirty-six states joined an amicus brief supporting the statute in this case; only one state has argued the unconstitutionality of the law.] It is, then, not the least irony of these cases that the States will be forced to enjoy the new federalism whether they want it or not. For with the Court's decision today, Antonio Morrison, like *Carter Coal*'s James Carter before him, has "won the states' rights plea against the states themselves." R. Jackson, The Struggle for Judicial Supremacy 160 (1941). * * *

JUSTICE BREYER, joined by **JUSTICE STEVENS**, dissenting. [We have omitted that portion of the dissent joined also by Justices Souter and Ginsburg.]

[Justice Breyer believed that Congress's authority under the Commerce Clause was sufficient for this statute.] Given my conclusion on the Commerce Clause question, I need not consider Congress' authority under § 5 of the Fourteenth Amendment. Nonetheless, I doubt the Court's reasoning rejecting that source of authority. The Court points out that * * * § 5 does not authorize Congress to use the Fourteenth Amendment as a source of power to remedy the conduct of *private persons*. That is certainly so. The Federal Government's argument, however, is that Congress used § 5 to remedy the actions of *state actors*, namely, those States which, through discriminatory design or the discriminatory conduct of their officials, failed to provide adequate (or any) state remedies for women injured by gender-motivated violence — a failure that the States, and Congress, documented in depth. * * *

But why can Congress not provide a remedy against private actors? Those private actors, of course, did not themselves violate the Constitution. But this Court has held that Congress at least sometimes can enact remedial "[l]egislation . . . [that] prohibits conduct which is not itself unconstitutional." *Boerne*; see also *Katzenbach v. Morgan*; *South Carolina v. Katzenbach*. The statutory remedy does not in any sense purport to "determine what constitutes a constitutional violation." *Boerne*. It intrudes little upon either States or private parties. It may lead state actors to improve their own remedial systems, primarily through example. It restricts private actors only by imposing liability for private conduct that is, in the main, already forbidden by state law. Why is the remedy "disproportionate"? And given the relation between remedy and violation — the creation of a federal remedy to substitute for constitutionally inadequate state remedies — where is the lack of "congruence"? * * *

NOTES ON *MORRISON* AND THE VALUES OF FEDERALISM

1. *The Need for a Limiting Principle?* As Justice Souter's dissent argues (without significant cavil from the majority), the Court could have read *Heart of Atlanta* and *McClung* broadly and approved VAWA as a Commerce Clause regulation, given the enormous record of economic effects resulting from gender-based violence. The Court, however, chose to draw the economic-noneconomic activity line. Justice Souter asks: Why do we need a line? Why not draw a line that allows Congress greater latitude in facilitating the operation of a national market?

One reason for drawing a line would be that the Supreme Court needs to enforce the limits implicit in Article I, § 8's delegation of authority for Congress to regulate interstate commerce; Justice Thomas believes that the Court has wandered far afield from the Framers' original expectations in this area (recall his concurring opinion in *Lopez*). But recall from our notes to *Gibbons* that commentators and perhaps Chief Justice Marshall drew from the Framers' discussions the conclusion that Article I limitations on Congress' authority were supposed to be enforced through the political rather than the judicial process. Is there a good reason to think that political checks on Congress' authority would be workable? To the extent there is slippage, and shirking, what are the possible costs? Keep these questions in mind when you read the federal-regulation-of-states cases, especially *Garcia* (in § 5B of this chapter).

If a limiting principle, enforceable by the judiciary, is desirable, is the Chief Justice's economic-noneconomic activity principle a good one? Is it workable? Why not go all the way, as Justice Thomas suggested in *Lopez*, and limit Congress to regulating activities that are mainly "commercial," rather than more broadly economic? Justice Thomas's approach has a closer relationship to the constitutional text and may be easier to administer than the Chief Justice's approach. Conversely, why not follow Justice Breyer's suggestion (in that portion of his dissent that we omitted) that judicial review of congressional decisions under Article I should be process-oriented: So long as Congress has openly deliberated and made appropriate findings relating to interstate commerce, the Court should defer to its judgment. Is this essentially no more than the leave-it-to-the-political-process approach?

As for a limiting principle for Congress' § 5 authority, the majority sticks with the state-action principle and finds evidence of state bias insufficient to support a remedy against a private actor under the *Boerne* congruence and proportionality test. What do you think of the majority's treatment of the *Guest* case? Is that further evidence supporting the view of Post & Siegel, *supra* note *q*, that the Court is reneging on the Court/Congress partnership to promote equality values forged in the post-*Brown* era? Or would it have been irresponsible for the current Court to defer to the principle apparently accepted by six Justices in *Guest*?

2. Morrison *and the Purposes of Federalism.* Consider the VAWA Case and its limiting principle in light of the purposes of federalism. As to the particular statute, the libertarian benefits of federalism are purchased at a high libertarian price. That is, the Court protects accused rapists like Antonio Morrison from "excessive" regulation: he and his friend were subject to three levels of regulation (the school's administrative proceeding, possible state prosecution or a tort suit in state court, the federal VAWA lawsuit), one of which the Supreme Court stripped away. From Morrison's point of view, he was being *over-regulated.* But from Christy Brzonkala's point of view, Morrison and those like him — whom the local and state authorities are unlikely to punish — are *under-regulated* without the VAWA remedy, and it is her liberty and the liberty of women like her that are sacrificed in the name of "libertarian" federalism. How should the libertarian risks of over- and under-regulation be balanced in this circumstance?

Consider a different perspective. VAWA is premised in part on the notion that local politics — in *Morrison,* the university officials and the county prosecutors — is unresponsive to the plight of rape victims and that the only way to break through these local lock-ins is through federal litigation such as that provided by VAWA. A response to this argument, based on notions of efficiency, is that potential rape victims and their friends should vote with their feet: if the university tolerates rapists, students should go elsewhere; if the county won't prosecute rapists, families should relocate to venues that do so. This, however, seems like a really odd and question-begging argument in the context of VAWA. Congress found — and the Court did not deny — that local political lock-ins prevented effective enforcement of sexual assault laws and that those lock-ins were resistant to change through voting-with-their-feet and other mechanisms. This was a rotten federalism. Under these circumstances, why shouldn't Congress have authority to regulate? In any event, relegating victims of local oppression to the vote-with-your-feet remedy seems hopelessly inconsistent with the Court's race cases. After all, for example, Mildred and Richard Loving (*Loving v. Virginia,* Chapter 3, § 1A), moved to the District of Columbia at the behest of Virginia. Their return to Virginia was motivated in large part by their desire to challenge its miscegenation statute.

3. Morrison *and the Costs of Federalism. Morrison* is a costly decision, both in terms of risking that rapists will escape punishment and that a new generation of women (and men) will be subjected to gender-motivated sexual assault without effective remedies. This would seem to be a terrible "cost" of federalism, but from the Supreme Court's point of view it is a cost of the rule of law as well as of federalism. The majority Justices understand federalism limitations on Congress's authority to be a matter of constitutional imperative. Failure to enforce those rules would be a default in the rule of law itself.

From this point of view, *Morrison* may be a *constitutional tragedy* — the application of the rule of law yields not only undesirable consequences but horrible and tragic ones. But the judge charged with applying the rule of law has no choice, and she imposes its iron rule regardless of consequences. Robert

Bolt's *A Man for All Seasons* (1962) portrays Sir Thomas More as such a tragic figure. He refused to bend the law to forward favored policies or persons or to punish persons he and his friends thought were "bad." When questioned whether he would apply the law to protect The Devil, he replied that he would. If the law were bent to get Satan, then the law can be similarly bent to get you and me. More died in support of his unbending view of the rule of law. See Lawrence Alexander, *Constitutional Tragedies and Giving Refuge to the Devil*, in *Constitutional Stupidities/Constitutional Tragedies* (William Eskridge, Jr. & Sanford Levinson eds. 1997).

From the dissenters' point of view, however, *Morrison* is a *constitutional stupidity* — a terrible result unjustified by the rule of law, especially the post-New Deal precedents concerning the extent of congressional power. In the post-legal realist world of law, there is always play in the hard cases. From this fact, Justice Souter argues that the majority Justices must defend their choice to strike down a much-needed federal statute. They cannot. Federalism gave way during the New Deal. And it gave way some more during the Civil Rights Revolution of the 1960s. Why should it not accommodate the Women's Rights Revolution in law of the last generation?

From yet another point of view, *Morrison* may be neither tragedy nor stupidity. One might speculate that the majority of the Court simply did not buy the factual premise of VAWA (that local jurisdictions throughout the country routinely neglect or refuse to provide women victims with equal protection of the law) or the logic of its remedy (that a tort action in federal court that duplicates, substantively, the tort action such victims would have in state court would somehow be effective in deterring or remedying such violations of equal protection). Under this view, *Morrison* is similar to *Lopez*: both involve symbolic legislation eagerly passed for political reasons by Members of Congress that merely duplicates the local police power. (On this view, the support for VAWA from many state attorneys' general was simply a political act by officials more interested in reelection than in whether the statute invaded states' rights.) There are insufficient political safeguards for federalism, and the Court is left as the only institution that can provide meaningful review. Is this kind of thinking uncomfortably close to *Lochner*, where a business-protecting Court questioned the pro-labor redistributive motives of the New York legislature?

F. THERMIDOR AFTER THE COURT'S FEDERALISM REVOLU-TION?

NEVADA DEPARTMENT OF HUMAN RESOURCES v. HIBBS
538 U.S. 721, 123 S.Ct. 1972, 155 L.Ed.2d 953 (2003)

CHIEF JUSTICE REHNQUIST delivered the opinion of the Court.

[The Family and Medical Leave Act of 1993, 29 U.S.C. § 2612(a)(1)(C), provides employees with the right to take up to twelve weeks of unpaid leave from work annually to care for a newborn child or for a spouse, child, or parent with a serious health condition. The statute applies to the states as employers and provides a cause of action for equitable relief and damages. In this case, a former employee sought damages from the state for the alleged violation of the statute.]

The FMLA aims to protect the right to be free from gender-based discrimination in the workplace.[2] * * * We now inquire whether Congress had evidence of a pattern of constitutional violations on the part of the States in this area.

The history of the many state laws limiting women's employment opportunities is chronicled in — and, until relatively recently, was sanctioned by — this Court's own opinions. For example, in *Bradwell v. State* (Illinois), and *Goesaert v. Cleary,* (Michigan), the Court upheld state laws prohibiting women from practicing law and tending bar, respectively. State laws frequently subjected women to distinctive restrictions, terms, conditions, and benefits for those jobs they could take. In *Muller v. Oregon*, for example, this Court approved a state law limiting the hours that women could work for wages, and observed that 19 States had such laws at the time. Such laws were based on the related beliefs that (1) woman is, and should remain, "the center of home and family life," and (2) "a proper discharge of [a woman's] maternal functions — having in view not merely her own health, but the well-being of the race — justif[ies] legislation to protect her from the greed as well as the passion of man." Until our decision in *Reed v. Reed*, "it remained the prevailing doctrine that government, both federal and state, could withhold from women opportunities accorded men so long as any 'basis in reason' " — such as the above beliefs — "could be conceived for the discrimination." *United States v. Virginia* (quoting *Goesaert*). [All of these precedents are excerpted in Chapter 4, § 2B of this casebook.]

Congress responded to this history of discrimination by abrogating States' sovereign immunity in Title VII of the Civil Rights Act of 1964, and we sustained this abrogation in *Fitzpatrick*. But state gender discrimination did not cease. "[I]t can hardly be doubted that . . . women still face pervasive, although at times more subtle, discrimination . . . in the job market." *Frontiero v. Richardson*. According to evidence that was before Congress when it enacted the FMLA, States continue to rely on invalid gender stereotypes in the employment context, specifically in the administration of leave benefits. Reliance on such stereotypes cannot justify the States' gender discrimination in this area. *Virginia*. The long and extensive history of sex discrimination prompted us to hold that measures that differentiate on the basis of gender warrant heightened scrutiny; here, as in *Fitzpatrick,* the persistence of such unconstitutional discrimination by the States justifies Congress' passage of prophylactic § 5 legislation.

---

2. The text of the Act makes this clear. Congress found that, "due to the nature of the roles of men and women in our society, the primary responsibility for family caretaking often falls on women, and such responsibility affects the working lives of women more than it affects the working lives of men." 29 U.S.C. § 2601(a)(5). In response to this finding, Congress sought "to accomplish the [Act's other] purposes . . . in a manner that . . . minimizes the potential for employment discrimination *on the basis of sex* by ensuring generally that leave is available . . . *on a gender-neutral basis*[,] and to promote the goal of equal employment opportunity *for women and men* . . . ." §§ 2601(b)(4) and (5) (emphasis added).

As the FMLA's legislative record reflects, a 1990 Bureau of Labor Statistics (BLS) survey stated that 37 percent of surveyed private-sector employees were covered by maternity leave policies, while only 18 percent were covered by paternity leave policies. S. Rep. No. 103-3, pp. 14-15 (1993). The corresponding numbers from a similar BLS survey the previous year were 33 percent and 16 percent, respectively. While these data show an increase in the percentage of employees eligible for such leave, they also show a widening of the gender gap during the same period. Thus, stereotype-based beliefs about the allocation of family duties remained firmly rooted, and employers' reliance on them in establishing discriminatory leave policies remained widespread.[3]

Congress also heard testimony that "[p]arental leave for fathers . . . is rare. Even . . . [w]here child-care leave policies do exist, men, *both in the public and private sectors,* receive notoriously discriminatory treatment in their requests for such leave." Many States offered women extended "maternity" leave that far exceeded the typical 4- to 8-week period of physical disability due to pregnancy and childbirth, but very few States granted men a parallel benefit: Fifteen States provided women up to one year of extended maternity leave, while only four provided men with the same. This and other differential leave policies were not attributable to any differential physical needs of men and women, but rather to the pervasive sex-role stereotype that caring for family members is women's work.

Finally, Congress had evidence that, even where state laws and policies were not facially discriminatory, they were applied in discriminatory ways. It was aware of the "serious problems with the discretionary nature of family leave," because when "the authority to grant leave and to arrange the length of that leave rests with individual supervisors," it leaves "employees open to discretionary and possibly unequal treatment." H.R. Rep. No. 103-8, pt. 2, pp. 10-11 (1993). Testimony supported that conclusion, explaining that "[t]he lack of uniform parental and medical leave policies in the work place has created an environment where [sex] discrimination is rampant."

In spite of all of the above evidence, JUSTICE KENNEDY argues in dissent that Congress' passage of the FMLA was unnecessary because "the States appear to have been ahead of Congress in providing gender-neutral family leave benefits" and points to Nevada's leave policies in particular. However, it was only "[s]ince Federal family leave legislation was first introduced" that the States had even "begun to consider similar family leave initiatives." [Quoting legislative history.]

---

3. While this and other material described leave policies in the private sector, a 50-state survey also before Congress demonstrated that "[t]he proportion and construction of leave policies available to public sector employees differs little from those offered private sector employees." The Parental and Medical Leave Act of 1986: Joint Hearing before the Subcommittee on Labor-Management Relations and the Subcommittee on Labor Standards of the House Committee on Education and Labor, 99th Cong., 2d Sess., 33 (1986) (hereinafter Joint Hearing) (statement of Meryl Frank, Director of the Yale Bush Center Infant Care Leave Project).

Furthermore, the dissent's statement that some States "had adopted some form of family-care leave" before the FMLA's enactment glosses over important shortcomings of some state policies. First, seven States had childcare leave provisions that applied to women only. * * * These laws reinforced the very stereotypes that Congress sought to remedy through the FMLA. Second, 12 States provided their employees no family leave, beyond an initial childbirth or adoption, to care for a seriously ill child or family member. Third, many States provided no statutorily guaranteed right to family leave, offering instead only voluntary or discretionary leave programs. Three States left the amount of leave time primarily in employers' hands. Congress could reasonably conclude that such discretionary family-leave programs would do little to combat the stereotypes about the roles of male and female employees that Congress sought to eliminate. Finally, four States provided leave only through administrative regulations or personnel policies, which Congress could reasonably conclude offered significantly less firm protection than a federal law. Against the above backdrop of limited state leave policies, no matter how generous petitioner's own may have been, Congress was justified in enacting the FMLA as remedial legislation.

In sum, the States' record of unconstitutional participation in, and fostering of, gender-based discrimination in the administration of leave benefits is weighty enough to justify the enactment of prophylactic § 5 legislation.

We reached the opposite conclusion in *Garrett* and *Kimel*. In those cases, the § 5 legislation under review responded to a purported tendency of state officials to make age- or disability-based distinctions. Under our equal protection case law, discrimination on the basis of such characteristics is not judged under a heightened review standard, and passes muster if there is "a rational basis for doing so at a class-based level, even if it 'is probably not true' that those reasons are valid in the majority of cases." *Kimel*; see also *Garrett*. Thus, in order to impugn the constitutionality of state discrimination against the disabled or the elderly, Congress must identify, not just the existence of age- or disability-based state decisions, but a "widespread pattern" of irrational reliance on such criteria. *Kimel*. We found no such showing with respect to the ADEA and Title I of the Americans with Disabilities Act of 1990 (ADA).

Here, however, Congress directed its attention to state gender discrimination, which triggers a heightened level of scrutiny. Because the standard for demonstrating the constitutionality of a gender-based classification is more difficult to meet than our rational-basis test — it must "serv[e] important governmental objectives" and be "substantially related to the achievement of those objectives," *Virginia* — it was easier for Congress to show a pattern of state constitutional violations. Congress was similarly successful in *South Carolina v. Katzenbach*, where we upheld the Voting Rights Act of 1965: Because racial classifications are presumptively invalid, most of the States' acts of race discrimination violated the Fourteenth Amendment.

The impact of the discrimination targeted by the FMLA is significant. Congress determined:

Historically, denial or curtailment of women's employment opportunities has been traceable directly to the pervasive presumption that women are mothers first, and workers second. This prevailing ideology about women's roles has in turn justified discrimination against women when they are mothers or mothers-to-be. [Quoting legislative history.]

Stereotypes about women's domestic roles are reinforced by parallel stereotypes presuming a lack of domestic responsibilities for men. Because employers continued to regard the family as the woman's domain, they often denied men similar accommodations or discouraged them from taking leave. These mutually reinforcing stereotypes created a self-fulfilling cycle of discrimination that forced women to continue to assume the role of primary family caregiver, and fostered employers' stereotypical views about women's commitment to work and their value as employees. Those perceptions, in turn, Congress reasoned, lead to subtle discrimination that may be difficult to detect on a case-by-case basis.

We believe that Congress' chosen remedy, the family-care leave provision of the FMLA, is "congruent and proportional to the targeted violation." Congress had already tried unsuccessfully to address this problem through Title VII and the amendment of Title VII by the Pregnancy Discrimination Act, 42 U.S.C. §2000e(k) [see p. 398]. Here, as in *South Carolina v. Katzenbach,* Congress again confronted a "difficult and intractable proble[m]," *Kimel,* where previous legislative attempts had failed. Such problems may justify added prophylactic measures in response.

By creating an across-the-board, routine employment benefit for all eligible employees, Congress sought to ensure that family-care leave would no longer be stigmatized as an inordinate drain on the workplace caused by female employees, and that employers could not evade leave obligations simply by hiring men. By setting a minimum standard of family leave for *all* eligible employees, irrespective of gender, the FMLA attacks the formerly state-sanctioned stereotype that only women are responsible for family caregiving, thereby reducing employers' incentives to engage in discrimination by basing hiring and promotion decisions on stereotypes.

The dissent characterizes the FMLA as a "substantive entitlement program" rather than a remedial statute because it establishes a floor of 12 weeks' leave. In the dissent's view, in the face of evidence of gender-based discrimination by the States in the provision of leave benefits, Congress could do no more in exercising its § 5 power than simply proscribe such discrimination. But this position cannot be squared with our recognition that Congress "is not confined to the enactment of legislation that merely parrots the precise wording of the Fourteenth Amendment," but may prohibit "a somewhat broader swath of conduct, including that which is not itself forbidden by the Amendment's text." *Kimel.* For example, this Court has upheld certain prophylactic provisions of the Voting Rights Act as valid exercises of Congress' § 5 power, including the literacy test ban and preclearance requirements for changes in States' voting procedures. See *Katzenbach v. Morgan*; *Oregon v. Mitchell*; *South Carolina v. Katzenbach.*

Indeed, in light of the evidence before Congress, a statute mirroring Title VII, that simply mandated gender equality in the administration of leave benefits, would not have achieved Congress' remedial object. Such a law would allow

States to provide for no family leave at all. Where "[t]wo-thirds of the nonprofessional caregivers for older, chronically ill, or disabled persons are working women," [quoting House and Senate committee reports], and state practices continue to reinforce the stereotype of women as caregivers, such a policy would exclude far more women than men from the workplace.

Unlike the statutes at issue in *City of Boerne, Kimel*, and *Garrett,* which applied broadly to every aspect of state employers' operations, the FMLA is narrowly targeted at the fault line between work and family — precisely where sex-based overgeneralization has been and remains strongest — and affects only one aspect of the employment relationship.

We also find significant the many other limitations that Congress placed on the scope of this measure. See *Florida Prepaid* ("[W]here 'a congressional enactment pervasively prohibits constitutional state action in an effort to remedy or to prevent unconstitutional state action, limitations of this kind tend to ensure Congress' means are proportionate to ends legitimate under § 5' " (quoting *City of Boerne*)). The FMLA requires only unpaid leave and applies only to employees who have worked for the employer for at least one year and provided 1,250 hours of service within the last 12 months. Employees in high-ranking or sensitive positions are simply ineligible for FMLA leave; of particular importance to the States, the FMLA expressly excludes from coverage state elected officials, their staffs, and appointed policymakers. Employees must give advance notice of foreseeable leave, and employers may require certification by a health care provider of the need for leave. In choosing 12 weeks as the appropriate leave floor, Congress chose "a middle ground, a period long enough to serve 'the needs of families' but not so long that it would upset 'the legitimate interests of employers.' " Moreover, the cause of action under the FMLA is a restricted one: The damages recoverable are strictly defined and measured by actual monetary losses, and the accrual period for backpay is limited by the Act's 2-year statute of limitations (extended to three years only for willful violations). [*Affirmed.*]

[The concurring opinion of **JUSTICE SOUTER**, joined by **JUSTICES GINSBURG** and **BREYER**; the opinion of **JUSTICE STEVENS** concurring in the judgment; and the dissenting opinion of **JUSTICE SCALIA** are omitted. The dissenting opinion of **JUSTICE KENNEDY**, joined by **JUSTICES SCALIA** and **THOMAS**, is discussed in the Notes after *Lane.*]

Tennessee v. Lane, 541 U.S. 509 (2004). Title II of the Americans with Disabilities Act provides that "no qualified individual with a disability shall, by reason of such disability, be excluded from participation in or be denied the benefits of the services, programs or activities of a public entity." Two physically handicapped persons who use wheelchairs for mobility brought suit for damages and equitable relief against the state and several of its counties on the ground that, because of physical barriers, they were denied access to state courts. To answer criminal charges against him, at his first appearance George Lane crawled up two flights of stairs to get to the courtroom; he refused to do so for a second hearing and also refused to be carried by officers and then was arrested and jailed for failure to appear. Beverly Jones, a certified court reporter, alleged that she could not get to several courtrooms and thereby was denied employment opportunities as well as the right to access to judicial proceedings. Lane and Jones claimed that the state was in violation of the ADA; the state responded that it was immune under the Eleventh Amendment and that Congress had not lawfully abrogated that immunity because Congress had no Fourteenth Amendment authority to enact Title II, like Title I evaluated in *Garrett*.

Justice Stevens' opinion for the Court noted that *Garrett* had emphasized that much of the evidence of discrimination in the legislative history of the ADA concerned the provision of public services and public accommodations, areas addressed by Titles II and III, rather than employment discrimination, addressed by Title I, and that *Garrett* had left open the question whether Title II was a valid exercise of § 5 power. Justice Stevens distinguished Title II from Title I in two important ways. First, Title I is an antidiscrimination provision seeking to enforce equal protection guarantees. Title II as well seeks to outlaw irrational disability discrimination, but it also seeks to enforce "a variety of other basic constitutional guarantees, infringements of which are subject to more searching judicial review." In Lane's factual context, the opinion noted the confrontation clause of the Sixth Amendment protecting the right of a criminal defendant to be present at all important stages of proceedings. More generally, Justice Stevens referred to the right of civil litigants to notice and the opportunity to be heard in court and to the First Amendment right of the public to access to judicial proceedings.

Moreover, the legislative record was stronger for Title II. "With respect to the particular services at issue in this case, Congress learned that many individuals, in many States across the country, were being excluded from courthouses and court proceedings by reason of their disabilities. A report before Congress showed that some 76% of public services and programs housed in state-owned buildings were inaccessible to and unusable by persons with disabilities, even taking into account the possibility that the services and programs might be restructured or relocated to other parts of the buildings. Congress itself heard testimony from persons with disabilities who described the physical inaccessibility of local courthouses. And its appointed task force heard numerous examples of the exclusion of persons with disabilities from state judicial services and programs, including exclusion of persons with visual impairments and hearing impairments from jury service, failure of state and local governments to provide interpretive services for the hearing impaired, failure to permit the testimony of adults with developmental disabilities in abuse cases, and failure to make courtrooms accessible to witnesses with physical disabilities."

Overall, Justice Stevens concluded that the record of state constitutional violations was stronger in this case than it had been in *Hibbs*. "Title II is aimed at the enforcement of a variety of basic rights, including the right of access to the courts at issue in this case, that call for a standard of judicial review at least as searching, and in some cases more searching, than the standard that applies to sex-based classifications." Supporting the conclusion that Title II was a "congruent and proportional" response to constitutional violations is the fact that Title II's remedy is a "reasonable accommodation" by public accommodations for people with disabilities. This gives states and their organs flexible options for providing access.

"This duty to accommodate is perfectly consistent with the well-established due process principle that, 'within the limits of practicability, a State must afford to all individuals a meaningful opportunity to be heard' in its courts. Our cases have recognized a number of affirmative obligations that flow from this principle: the duty to waive filing fees in certain family-law and criminal cases, the duty to provide transcripts to criminal defendants seeking review of their convictions, and the duty to provide counsel to certain criminal defendants. Each of these cases makes clear that ordinary considerations of cost and convenience alone cannot justify a State's failure to provide individuals with a meaningful right of access to the courts. Judged against this backdrop, Title II's affirmative obligation to accommodate persons with disabilities in the administration of justice cannot be said to be "so out of proportion to a supposed remedial or preventive object that it cannot be understood as responsive to, or designed to prevent, unconstitutional behavior." *Boerne*. It is, rather, a reasonable prophylactic measure, reasonably targeted to a legitimate end." In a footnote, Justice Stevens stated: "Because this case implicates the right of access to the courts, we need not consider whether Title II's duty to accommodate exceeds what the Constitution requires in the class of cases that implicate only *Cleburne*'s prohibition on irrational discrimination. See *Garrett*."

Dissenting and arguing that Title II was not a valid exercise of Congress's Fourteenth Amendment authority, **Chief Justice Rehnquist** (joined by **Justices Kennedy** and **Thomas**) distinguished *Hibbs* because it involved sex discrimination, where the standard of scrutiny is higher.

Justice Scalia dissented in a separate opinion. He had reluctantly joined the majority in *Boerne* and repudiated his acceptance of the congruence and proportionality test, which has been too "malleable" and subject to "individual judges' policy preferences," and makes the Court too much "Congress's taskmaster" in second-guessing legislative handiwork. Returning to the narrowness of *The Civil Rights Cases*, Justice Scalia would limit § 5 to simply "enforc[ing]" § 1 of the Fourteenth Amendment. Congress could, for example, provide a cause of action against a violation of § 1, make such violations federal crimes, and impose reporting obligations on the states to facilitate the enforcement of the Fourteenth Amendment, but Congress would have no prophylactic authority. Acknowledging that "[t]he major impediment" to this approach is stare decisis, he would accord a somewhat broader authority to congressional power to attack racial discrimination — what he saw as at the core of § 1 and which was the subject matter of the expansive § 5 precedents (*South Carolina, Morgan, Rome, Alfred H. Mayer Co.*).

NOTE ON *HIBBS* AND *LANE*

1. *Liberal Readings of the Record.* The most striking difference in these recent cases is that the Court majority reads the record of constitutional violations more sympathetically than it did in the earlier cases *and* views the record more the way Congress did (i.e., is more deferential). This is particularly notable in *Hibbs*, where Justice Kennedy's dissenting opinion picked apart the

record to demonstrate that there were few hard constitutional violations found by Congress. His charges: (a) The Court's focus was too broad. Properly understood, FMLA was not a response to general sex discrimination in the workplace, but to alleged discrimination in the granting of family and medical leaves. (b) The only evidence that state as well as private sector employers discriminated came in conclusory form from two witnesses to the 1986 precursor bill, which was very different from the FMLA. There was no empirical basis for Congress's conclusion. (c) Indeed, the states led the way. Thirty states had parental and medical leave statutes before Congress enacted the FMLA in 1993. At most, three states had "discriminatory" policies, because they had programs women but not men could take advantage of. These are excellent criticisms. Why were they not persuasive to the Chief Justice?[r]

2. *Pregnancy-Based Discrimination.* In his short list of state leave policies that arguably discriminated on the basis of sex, Justice Kennedy excluded state programs limited to pregnancy. The Supreme Court had ruled in *Geduldig v. Aiello* (Chapter 4, § 2) that pregnancy-based discrimination is *not* sex discrimination. The government conceded at oral argument that *Geduldig* was binding precedent, and the Chief Justice's opinion for the Court did not question it. But Congress in the Pregnancy Discrimination Act of 1978 found that pregnancy-based discrimination *was* sex discrimination, because it reflected sex stereotyping that held female employees back in the workplace, precisely the same kind of reasoning the Chief Justice invoked to uphold the FMLA. Should *Geduldig* be revisited?

3. *The Future of Congruence and Proportionality?* Unclear. In *Lane,* Justice Scalia jettisoned the *Boerne* approach, and other Justices might follow him. In *Hibbs,* Justice Stevens declined to join the Chief Justice's opinion for the Court, because he believed the *Boerne* approach was too confining. Three Justices seem comfortable with a deferential application of *Boerne*'s congruence and proportionality test but might also jettison it if given an opportunity. Swing Justice O'Connor—in the majority of every federalism case in this section—has left the Court, as has Chief Justice Rehnquist, so it is far from clear that the Court would follow the *Hibbs-Lane* deferential attitude in other cases. One hallmark of the Roberts Court, however, is that it is not keen on openly overruling earlier decisions, so the FMLA is safe. As applied to other kinds of public accommodations, Title II is ripe for further challenge. Assuming that Justice Kennedy (the author of *Boerne*) is the median Justice, would the Court uphold application of the ADA to a state public assistance office, where a plaintiff was unable to show up for his appointment to receive disability assistance because he could not get up stairs that did not comply with the ADA?

---

r. For a cogent account, see Reva Siegel, *You've Come a Long Way, Baby: Rehnquist's New Approach to Pregnancy Discrimination in* Hibbs, 58 Stan. L. Rev. 1871 (2006).

SECTION 4. BEYOND THE COMMERCE POWER AND THE CIVIL RIGHTS ENFORCEMENT POWER

In this section, we examine three other sources of congressional authority that might provide Congress a way around the limitations on the commerce power and the civil rights enforcement power that are found in the recent cases we just examined.

A. TAXING POWER

Recall the Child Labor Case (*Hammer v. Dagenhart*), where the Court said Congress could not prevent manufacturers from using child labor, at least under its Commerce Clause power. After the Court's decision, Congress enacted the Child Labor Tax Law, which imposed tax assessments on companies employing child labor. If the employer used child labor (defined in detail by the Act), it was required to pay the government 10% of its entire net business income. There was no plan to apportion the tax according to the extent of the employer's violation of the no-child-labor requirement, although the tax was not levied if the employer was actually unaware it was using child labor. Congress asserted authority for the law under the Tax and Spend Clause (Article I, § 8, cl. 1): "The Congress shall have Power To lay and collect Taxes, Duties, Imposts, and Excises, to pay the Debts and provide for the common Defence and general Welfare of the United States."

Although a transparent effort around the Child Labor Case, Congress had substantial authority for accomplishing its goal by the less controversial taxing authority. In *McCray v. United States*, 195 U.S. 27 (1904), the Court upheld a blatantly discriminatory tax of ten cents on yellow (looks like butter) oleomargarine and one one-quarter of a cent on white (doesn't look like butter). The Court refused to examine the possibly illicit motives of Congress in that case, and in *United States v. Doremus*, 249 U.S. 86 (1919), which upheld not only a special tax on opium, but set up a special inspection apparatus. Notwithstanding these precedents, the Supreme Court in *Bailey v. Drexel Furniture Co.* (The Child Labor Tax Case), 259 U.S. 20 (1922), invalidated the tax scheme, upon the ground that it was a "penalty" and not a "tax." "Where the sovereign enacting the law has power to impose both tax and penalty the difference between revenue production and mere regulation may be immaterial, but not so when one sovereign can impose a tax only, and the power of regulation rests in another. * * * [T]here comes a time in the extension of the penalizing features of the so-called tax when it loses its character as such and becomes a mere penalty with the characteristics of regulation and punishment." Interestingly, Justice Holmes and Brandeis (dissenters in the Child Labor Case) joined Chief Justice Taft's opinion.[a]

---

[a]. Cf. Alexander Bickel, *The Unpublished Opinions of Mr. Justice Brandeis* 3-4, 18-19 (1957) (Justice Brandeis sometimes failed to file dissents for strategic reasons, perhaps here to avoid offending the new Chief Justice).

As in the Commerce Clause cases, the New Deal Court was prepared to give Congress wider discretion under the Tax Clause. In *United States v. Kahriger*, the Court upheld the provisions of the Internal Revenue Act of 1951 that levied a special tax on persons involved in the business of accepting wagers ("bookies"). The taxpayer argued that this was beyond the federal taxing power, as interpreted in the Child Labor Tax Case. The Court disagreed: "As with [other] excise taxes which we have held to be valid, the instant tax has a regulatory effect. But regardless of its regulatory effect, the wagering tax produces revenue." Does this mean that the Child Labor Tax Case is overruled? It is not clear, for the *Kahriger* Court cited the case for the following proposition: "Penalty provisions in tax statutes added for breach of a regulation concerning activities in themselves subject only to state regulation have caused this Court to declare the enactments invalid. Unless there are provisions extraneous to any tax need, courts are without authority to limit the exercise of the taxing power." Although *Steward Machine,* 301 U.S. 548 (1937), distinguished *Butler*, 297 U.S. 1 (1936) and did not overrule that decision, and *Kahriger* even cited the Child Labor Tax Case, the pre-1937 precedents seemed drained of viability in the post-New Deal era.

B. SPENDING POWER

The Child Labor Tax Act (struck down in *Bailey v. Drexel Furniture*) relied on the coercive portion of Article I, § 8, cl. 1, namely, its taxing power. What if Congress had relied on the inducement portion, its spending power? For example, Congress could have voted a substantial subsidy to all American businesses, to enable them to pay for adult labor. The subsidy would of course not be paid to businesses employing child labor. Would this have passed constitutional muster during the *Lochner* era (i.e., before the "switch in time")? Probably not.

In *United States v. Butler*, 297 U.S. 1 (1936), the Court invalidated the Agricultural Adjustment Act of 1933, which was designed to encourage farmers to reduce their production so as to raise market prices. The Act conditioned farm subsidies upon farmers' agreements to curtail production in line with federal guidelines. In turn, the subsidies were paid from a fund financed by a "processing tax" on farm products. Thus, farmers were indirectly taxed to pay for subsidies to reduce their production. The Court held that Congress' taxing and spending power was an independent enumerated power, limited only by the requirement that the tax and expenditure be "in the General welfare." Thus, the Court rejected the view, held by Madison among others, that the taxing and spending powers could only be invoked in support of other enumerated powers of Congress. Nevertheless, the Court reasoned that the statute "invades the reserved rights of the states" and treated matters "beyond the powers delegated to the federal government. The tax, the appropriation of the funds raised, and the direction for their disbursement, are but parts of the plan. They are but means to an unconstitutional end. * * * If the taxing power may not be used as the instrument to enforce a regulation of matters of state concern with respect to which Congress has no authority to interfere [e.g., the Child Labor Tax Case], may it, as in the present case, be employed to raise the money necessary to purchase a compliance which the Congress is powerless to command?" The

Court said "no," while dissenting Justices Stone, Brandeis, and Cardozo said "yes."

As it has in the Commerce Clause and Tax Clause cases, the post-New Deal Court has been substantially more lenient in upholding Congress' authority to condition its grants upon the recipient's compliance with detailed substantive regulations. In *Steward Machine Company v. Davis*, 301 U.S. 548 (1937), the Court upheld the unemployment compensation provisions of the Social Security Act of 1935. Those provisions established a federal taxing and conditional spending program to encourage the states to adopt federal unemployment compensation standards. The Act imposed a federal payroll tax on employers, but the employer received a tax credit for any contributions made to a qualifying state plan. Among other requirements, a state plan had to place its contributions in a federal trust fund. Justice Cardozo's opinion for the Court in *Steward* found no invasion of the states' Tenth Amendment rights, because there was no "coercion," only "inducement" for the states to adopt progressive laws. His opinion openly praised the object of the Social Security Act: to encourage states to make their unemployment compensation plans more responsive to the suffering during the Great Depression.

As we saw in Chapter 6, § 4B, in connection with *Rust v. Sullivan*, the Court's interest in individual rights during and after the 1960s stimulated renewed interest in "unconstitutional conditions" as a limitation on the federal spending power.[b] To what extent may Congress use federal money to entice persons or entities (like the states) to forego their constitutional protections? Consider the following case in light of the unconstitutional conditions doctrine — and in light of the Court's new (post-*Lopez*) federalism jurisprudence.

SOUTH DAKOTA v. DOLE
483 U.S. 203, 107 S.Ct. 2793, 97 L.Ed.2d 171 (1987)

CHIEF JUSTICE REHNQUIST delivered the opinion of the Court.

[In 1984, Congress enacted 23 U.S.C. § 158, which directs the Secretary of Transportation to withhold 5% of the federal highway funds otherwise payable to states from any state which permits purchase or public possession of any alcoholic beverage by a person less than 21 years old. South Dakota, which permitted persons 19 years of age or older to purchase 3.2% beer, sought a declaratory judgment that § 158 violates constitutional limits on the congressional spending power and also violates the Twenty-first Amendment. The lower federal courts rejected these claims.]

* * * [W]e need not decide in this case whether [the Twenty-first Amendment] would prohibit an attempt by Congress to legislate directly a national minimum drinking age. Here, Congress has acted indirectly under its spending

---

b. See, e.g., Mitchell Berman, *Coercion Without Baselines: Unconstitutional Conditions in Three Dimensions*, 90 Geo. L.J. 1 (2001); Thomas McCoy & Barry Friedman, *Conditional Spending: Federalism's Trojan Horse*, 1988 Sup. Ct. Rev. 85; Kathleen Sullivan, *Unconstitutional Conditions*, 102 Harv. L. Rev. 1413 (1989).

power to encourage uniformity in the States' drinking ages. * * * [W]e find this legislative effort within constitutional bounds even if Congress may not regulate drinking ages directly.

* * * Incident to [the spending] power, Congress may attach conditions on the receipt of federal funds, and has repeatedly employed the power "to further broad policy objectives by conditioning receipt of federal moneys upon compliance by the recipient with federal . . . directives." The breadth of this power was made clear in *Butler.* * * * Thus, objectives not thought to be within Article I's "enumerated legislative fields" may nevertheless be attained through the use of the spending power and the conditional grant of federal funds.

The spending power is of course not unlimited, but is instead subject to several general restrictions articulated in our cases. The first of these limitations is derived from the language of the Constitution itself: the exercise of the spending power must be in pursuit of "the general welfare." In considering whether a particular expenditure is intended to serve general public purposes, courts should defer substantially to the judgment of Congress. Second, we have required that if Congress desires to condition the States' receipt of federal funds, it "must do so unambiguously . . ., enabl[ing] the States to exercise their choice knowingly, cognizant of the consequences of their participation." Third, our cases have suggested (without significant elaboration) that conditions on federal grants might be illegitimate if they are unrelated "to the federal interest in particular national projects or programs." Finally, we have noted that other constitutional provisions may provide an independent bar to the conditional grant of federal funds.

South Dakota does not seriously claim that § 158 is inconsistent with any of the first three restrictions mentioned above. * * * [T]he State itself, rather than challenging the germaneness of the condition to federal purposes, admits that it "has never contended that the congressional action was . . . unrelated to a national concern in the absence of the Twenty-first Amendment." Indeed, the condition imposed by Congress is directly related to one of the main purposes for which highway funds are expended — safe interstate travel. This goal of the interstate highway system had been frustrated by varying drinking ages among the States. A Presidential commission appointed to study alcohol-related accidents and fatalities on the Nation's highways concluded that the lack of uniformity in the States' drinking ages created "an incentive to drink and drive" because "young persons commut[e] to border States where the drinking age is lower." By enacting § 158, Congress conditioned the receipt of federal funds in a way reasonably calculated to address this particular impediment to a purpose for which the funds are expended.

The remaining question about the validity of § 158 — and the basic point of disagreement between the parties — is whether the Twenty-first Amendment constitutes an "independent constitutional bar" to the conditional grant of federal funds. Petitioner, relying on its view that the Twenty-first Amendment prohibits *direct* regulation of drinking ages by Congress, asserts that "Congress may not use the spending power to regulate that which it is prohibited from regulating directly under the Twenty-first Amendment." But our cases show that this "independent constitutional bar" limitation on the spending power is not of the kind petitioner suggests. *Butler*, for example, established that the constitutional limitations on Congress when exercising its spending power are less exacting than those on its authority to regulate directly.

We have also held that a perceived Tenth Amendment limitation on congressional regulation of state affairs did not concomitantly limit the range of conditions legitimately placed on federal grants. In *Oklahoma v. Civil Service Comm'n*, 330 U.S. 127 (1947), the Court considered the validity of the Hatch Act insofar as it was applied to political activities of state officials whose employment was financed in whole or in part with federal funds. The State contended that an order under this provision to withhold certain federal funds unless a state official was removed invaded its sovereignty in violation of the Tenth Amendment. Though finding that "the United States is not concerned with, and has no power to regulate, local political activities as such of state officials," the Court nevertheless held that the Federal Government "does have power to fix the terms upon which its money allotments to states shall be disbursed." The Court found no violation of the State's sovereignty because the State could, and did, adopt "the 'simple expedient' of not yielding to what she urges is federal coercion. The offer of benefits to a state by the United States dependent upon cooperation by the state with federal plans, assumedly for the general welfare, is not unusual."

These cases establish that the "independent constitutional bar" limitation on the spending power is not, as petitioner suggests, a prohibition on the indirect achievement of objectives which Congress is not empowered to achieve directly. Instead, we think that the language in our earlier opinions stands for the unexceptionable proposition that the power may not be used to induce the States to engage in activities that would themselves be unconstitutional. Thus, for example, a grant of federal funds conditioned on invidiously discriminatory state action or the infliction of cruel and unusual punishment would be an illegitimate exercise of the Congress'. broad spending power. But no such claim can be or is made here . * * *

Our decisions have recognized that in some circumstances the financial inducement offered by Congress might be so coercive as to pass the point at which "pressure turns into compulsion." [*Steward Machine.*] Here, however, Congress has directed only that a State desiring to establish a minimum drinking age lower than 21 lose a relatively small percentage of certain federal highway funds. Petitioner contends that the coercive nature of this program is evident from the degree of success it has achieved. We cannot conclude, however, that a conditional grant of federal money of this sort is unconstitutional simply by reason of its success in achieving the congressional objective.

When we consider, for a moment, that all South Dakota would lose if she adheres to her chosen course as to a suitable minimum drinking age is 5% of the funds otherwise obtainable under specified highway grant programs, the argument as to coercion is shown to be more rhetoric than fact . * * *

Here Congress has offered relatively mild encouragement to the States to enact higher minimum drinking ages than they would otherwise choose. But the enactment of such laws remains the prerogative of the States not merely in theory but in fact. Even if Congress might lack the power to impose a national minimum drinking age directly, we conclude that encouragement to state action found in § 158 is a valid use of the spending power.

[The dissenting opinion of **JUSTICE BRENNAN** is omitted.]

JUSTICE O'CONNOR, dissenting.

* * * [Section 158] is not a condition on spending reasonably related to the expenditure of federal funds and cannot be justified on that ground. Rather, it is an attempt to regulate the sale of liquor, an attempt that lies outside Congress' power to regulate commerce because it falls within the ambit of § 2 of the Twenty-first Amendment.

My disagreement with the Court is relatively narrow on the spending power issue: it is a disagreement about the application of a principle rather than a disagreement on the principle itself * * * .

* * * [T]he Court's application of the requirement that the condition imposed be reasonably related to the purpose for which the funds are expended is cursory and unconvincing. We have repeatedly said that Congress may condition grants under the spending power only in ways reasonably related to the purpose of the federal program. In my view, establishment of a minimum drinking age of 21 is not sufficiently related to interstate highway construction to justify so conditioning funds appropriated for that purpose. * * *

* * * [T]he Court asserts the reasonableness of the relationship between the supposed purpose of the expenditure — "safe interstate travel" — and the drinking age condition. The Court reasons that Congress wishes that the roads it builds may be used safely, that drunken drivers threaten highway safety, and that young people are more likely to drive while under the influence of alcohol under existing law than would be the case if there were a uniform national drinking age of 21. It hardly needs saying, however, that if the purpose of § 158 is to deter drunken driving, it is far too over- and under-inclusive. It is over-inclusive because it stops teenagers from drinking even when they are not about to drive on interstate highways. It is under-inclusive because teenagers pose only a small part of the drunken driving problem in this Nation.

When Congress appropriates money to build a highway, it is entitled to insist that the highway be a safe one. But it is not entitled to insist as a condition of the use of highway funds that the State impose or change regulations in other areas of the State's social and economic life because of an attenuated or tangential relationship to highway use or safety. Indeed, if the rules were otherwise, the Congress could effectively regulate almost any area of a State's social, political, or economic life on the theory that use of the interstate transportation system is somehow enhanced. If, for example, the United States were to condition highway moneys upon moving the state capital, I suppose it might argue that interstate transportation is facilitated by locating local governments in places easily accessible to interstate highways — or, conversely, that highways might become overburdened if they had to carry traffic to and from the state capital. In my mind, such a relationship is hardly more attenuated than the one which the Court finds supports § 158.

There is a clear place at which the Court can draw the line between permissible and impermissible conditions on federal grants. It is the line identified in the Brief for the National Conference of State legislatures et al. as *Amici Curiae*:

> Congress has the power to *spend* for the general welfare, it has the power to *legislate* only for delegated purposes. * * *
>
> The appropriate inquiry, then, is whether the spending requirement or prohibition is a condition on a grant or whether it is regulation. The difference turns on whether the requirement specifies in some way how the money should be spent, so that Congress' intent in making the grant will be effectuated. Congress has no power under the Spending Clause to impose requirements on a grant that go beyond specifying how the money should be spent. A requirement that is not such a specification is not a condition, but a regulation, which is valid only if it falls within one of Congress' delegated regulatory powers.

This approach harks back to *United States v. Butler*. The *Butler* Court saw the Agricultural Adjustment Act for what it was — an exercise of regulatory, not spending, power. The error in *Butler* was not the Court's conclusion that the Act was essentially regulatory, but rather its crabbed view of the extent of Congress' regulatory power under the Commerce Clause. The Agricultural Adjustment Act was regulatory but it was regulation that today would likely be considered within Congress' commerce power.

While *Butler*'s authority is questionable insofar as it assumes that Congress has no regulatory power over farm production, its discussion of the spending power and its description of both the power's breadth and its limitations remain sound. The Court's decision in *Butler* also properly recognizes the gravity of the task of appropriately limiting the spending power. If the spending power is to be limited only by Congress' notion of the general welfare, the reality, given the vast financial resources of the Federal Government, is that the Spending Clause gives "power to the Congress to tear down the barriers, to invade the states' jurisdiction, and to become a parliament of the whole people, subject to no restrictions save such as are self-imposed." *Butler*. This, of course, as *Butler* held, was not the Framers' plan and it is not the meaning of the Spending Clause.

Our later cases are consistent with the notion that, under the spending power, the Congress may only condition grants in ways that can fairly be said to be related to the expenditure of federal funds. * * * [Some] conditions that have been upheld by the Court may be viewed as independently justified under some regulatory power of the Congress.

This case, however, falls into neither class. As discussed above, a condition that a State will raise its drinking age to 21 cannot fairly be said to be reasonably related to the expenditure of funds for highway construction. The only possible connection, highway safety, has nothing to do with how the funds Congress has appropriated are expended. Rather than a condition determining how federal highway money shall be expended, it is a regulation determining who shall be able to drink liquor. As such it is not justified by the spending power.

Of the other possible sources of congressional authority for regulating the sale of liquor only the commerce power comes to mind. But in my view, the regulation of the age of the purchasers of liquor, just as the regulation of the price at which liquor may be sold, falls squarely within the scope of those powers reserved to the States by the Twenty-first Amendment. * * * Accordingly, Congress simply lacks power under the Commerce Clause to displace state regulation of this kind.

The immense size and power of the Government of the United States ought not obscure its fundamental character. It remains a Government of enumerated powers. *McCulloch.* Because § 158 cannot be justified as an exercise of any power delegated to the Congress, it is not authorized by the Constitution. The Court errs in holding it to be the law of the land, and I respectfully dissent.

NOTES ON *DOLE* AND CONDITIONAL FEDERAL SPENDING

1. *Another Relic of a Bygone Era?* There are at least three reasons to question whether *South Dakota v. Dole* will remain a viable precedent. First, *Dole* bespeaks an extreme deference to congressional intermeddling in states' affairs that is consistent with its pre-1990 origin, but incongruent with the Court's more recent scrutinizing review in *Lopez, Boerne,* and *Morrison.* "[I]f the Spending Clause is simultaneously interpreted to permit Congress to seek otherwise forbidden regulatory aims indirectly through a conditional offer of federal funds to the states, the notion of a 'federal government of enumerated powers' will have no meaning,"[c] precisely the argument that motivated the Court's aggressive review in *Morrison.* Could Congress condition receipt of federal monies for state programs upon the states' agreement to abide by federal anti-discrimination rules of the sort that were struck down in *Kimel* and *Garrett?* To enact laws similar to the VAWA? (Would it make a constitutional difference, for Justice O'Connor, that such a requirement were linked to the monies Congress is already providing the states under other portions of the VAWA?)

Second, some legal scholars who have examined the historical record believe the Framers intended that Congress is authorized to spend only for the "general Welfare" and that this limitation is one the Framers expected to be enforced through judicial review.[d] If Justice Thomas is right that the Court must give more attention to the original constitutional limits, see his concurring opinions in *Lopez* and *Morrison,* then this evidence also points to a revival of that limit and a narrowing of *Dole.* Third, Congress's conditional deployment of its Spending Clause power may be its greatest threat to state autonomy and the values of federalism. Almost 30% of state budgets now come from federal

---

c. Lynn Baker, *Conditional Federal Spending After* Lopez, 95 Colum. L. Rev. 1911, 1920 (1995).

d. See John Eastman, *Restoring the "General" to the General Welfare Clause*, 4 Chapman L. Rev. 63 (2001); David Engdahl, *The Basis of the Spending Power*, 18 Seattle U.L. Rev. 215 (1995).

monies, and this gives the federal government potentially enormous leverage to nationalize policies that might be better handled locally.[e]

If *Dole* were overruled or narrowed, what approach should the Court adopt for reviewing congressional conditions? To begin with, the Court already construes statutory conditions narrowly, see *Pennhurst State School & Hosp. v. Halderman*, 451 U.S. 1 (1981), and the rule of narrow construction might be applied with even greater rigor in cases where Congress is essentially trying to regulate local affairs.[f] As Justice O'Connor argued in her dissent, the Court might also apply *Dole*'s germaneness requirement more strictly, perhaps in the way the Court is now reviewing statutes enacted under Congress's Fourteenth Amendment authority. Rather than the lenient (rational basis) scrutiny of *Katzenbach v. Morgan* and *Dole*, the Court could carefully examine the connection between the condition on the states and the purpose of the federal spending and demand a tight fit, as the Court required in *Kimel* and *Garrett*. In addition, *Dole*'s suggestion that some federal offers are so "coercive" that they would violate the Spending Clause might be explored, as Justice Scalia suggested in *College Savs. Bank v. Florida Prepaid Postsecondary Educ. Expense Bd.*, 527 U.S. 666, 692 (1999). Lynn Baker has urged the Court to abandon the *Dole* framework altogether and adopt a new test, under which courts would presume invalid conditional offers of federal funds to the states that would regulate them in ways Congress could not directly mandate.[g]

2. *Or, Congress's Last Best Chance?* On the other hand, *Dole* could well survive.[h] First, there is the force of *stare decisis*. Are five Justices willing to overrule precedent in this area? Neither *Lopez* nor *Boerne* (or any cases following them) have purported to overrule any precedent; *Seminole Tribe* did jettison *Union Gas*, but it was a very vulnerable precedent (no majority opinion; crucial fifth vote provided in a separate opinion without much explanation). But couldn't the Court narrow *Dole* without overruling it? Second, the problem of unconstitutional conditions is a knotty one. Some of the pro-federalism Justices are inclined to say that the federal government gets to spend its money pretty much as it wants. E.g., *National Endowment for the Arts v. Finley*, 524 U.S. 569 (1998) (Scalia, J., joined by Thomas, J., concurring) ("I regard the distinction between 'abridging' speech and funding it as a fundamental divide, on this side of which the First Amendment is inapplicable."). Third, it is not clear what standard can be adopted that will sharply limit congressional intermeddling in state affairs through conditional spending and can be predictably applied by the lower courts. Surely lower courts could apply Professor Baker's even stricter rule (that the condition is presumptively

---

e. See Ilya Somin, *Closing the Pandora's Box of Federalism: The Case for Judicial Restriction of Federal Subsidies to State Governments*, 90 Geo. L.J. 461 (2002).

f. See William Eskridge, Jr. & Philip Frickey, *Quasi-Constitutional Law: Clear Statement Rules as Constitutional Lawmaking*, 45 Vand. L. Rev. 593 (1992) (examining this clear statement rule).

g. See Lynn Baker, *Conditional Federal Spending and States' Rights,* 574 Annals 104 (2001).

h. See, e.g., Richard Fallon, *The "Conservative" Paths of the Rehnquist Court's Federalism Decisions*, 69 U. Chi. L. Rev 429 (2002).

unconstitutional unless Congress has an independent ground for regulation) as well as they can apply *Lopez* and *Boerne* — but the Court might not be willing to go that far, especially if it means overruling *Dole*. Could *Dole*'s germaneness and no-coercion requirements, if beefed up along O'Connor lines, be predictably applied?

3. *Federalism, the Public/Private Distinction, and Conditional Spending.* Titles VI and IX of the Civil Rights Act require recipients of federal financial assistance (including private entities, like private colleges and universities) to avoid racial and gender discrimination. Thus, conditional federal spending not only provides Congress the opportunity to conflate the national and state governments (as in *Dole*), but to conflate the public and the private spheres as well. Is one conflation more of a threat to liberty than the other? What of the values of federalism, versus the values of private autonomy? Is it more appropriate to reach private entities through conditional funding than through direct regulation under the Commerce Clause?

PROBLEM 7-4
SPENDING CLAUSE AND THE SOLOMON AMENDMENT

As amended in 2004, the Solomon Amendment provides that if any part of an institution of higher education denies military recruiters access equal to that provided other recruiters, the entire institution would loses designated federal funds. 10 U.S.C. § 983. The purpose of the Amendment was to discipline universities whose law schools were refusing to allow Judge Advocate General recruiters to participate fully in their career services programs, because the armed forces by law cannot enlist openly lesbian, gay, or bisexual lawyers. Law schools challenged the Solomon Amendment as an "unconstitutional condition" in violation of the First Amendment, an argument unanimously rejected in *Rumsfeld v. Forum for Academic & Institutional Rights, Inc.,* 547 U.S. 47 (2006).

Consider a different kind of challenge. Polytechnical University is science-oriented and receives $100 million in science research funds from the federal government. Because Polytech's law school does not allow military recruiters to participate fully in its career services program, the federal government terminates all its research money. Not one penny of those funds came from the Department of Defense or any other military-related agency; all of the money was for medical research, and most of it came from the Department of Health & Human Services. Polytech argues that the Solomon Amendment violates the Spending Clause because there is no "nexus" between the medical research funds it receives and the military programs Congress is trying to protect. Is this a tenable argument under *Dole*? Under the O'Connor dissenting opinion? Should the plaintiffs in *FAIR* (above) have made this argument? Why do you suppose they did not?

C. POWERS GRANTED TO CONGRESS OUTSIDE OF ARTICLE I: A LOOK AT THE TREATY POWER

Not all of the federal government's enumerated powers are in Article I. Article III empowers Congress to establish federal courts, and the Sixteenth

Amendment empowers Congress to "lay and collect taxes on incomes." Several of the constitutional amendments empower Congress to enforce their mandates by appropriate legislation, as we saw in our detailed look at congressional authority to enforce the Reconstruction Amendments. Not the least of non-Article I powers is the authority in Article II, § 2, cl. 2, for the President and the Senate to make treaties.

Query: After being rebuffed in the Child Labor Case, and then again in the Child Labor Tax Case, the federal government (through the President and the Senate) enters into a treaty with foreign countries, wherein the signatories agree to abolish child labor in their respective jurisdictions. By now, you might consider this to be an easy case (the treaty is invalid, until *Hammer v. Dagenhart* is overruled), but consider the following case, which is still the leading case concerning the national treaty power.

MISSOURI v. HOLLAND
252 U.S. 416, 40 S.Ct. 382, 64 L.Ed. 641 (1920)

JUSTICE HOLMES delivered the opinion of the Court.

This is a bill in equity brought by the State of Missouri to prevent a game warden of the United States from attempting to enforce the Migratory Bird Treaty Act of July 3, 1918, and the regulations made by the Secretary of Agriculture in pursuance of the same. The ground of the bill is that the statute is an unconstitutional interference with the rights reserved to the States by the Tenth Amendment, and that the acts of the defendant done and threatened under that authority invade the sovereign right of the State and contravene its will manifested in statutes. The State also alleges a pecuniary interest, as owner of the wild birds within its border and otherwise, admitted by the Government to be sufficient, but it is enough that the bill is a reasonable and proper means to assert the alleged quasi sovereign rights of a State. A motion to dismiss was sustained by the District Court on the ground that the act of Congress is constitutional. The State appeals.

On December 8, 1916, a treaty between the United States and Great Britain was proclaimed by the President. It recited that many species of birds in their annual migrations traversed certain parts of the United States and of Canada, that they were of great value as a source of food and in destroying insects injurious to vegetation, but were in danger of extermination through lack of adequate protection. It therefore provided for specified close seasons and protection in other forms, and agreed that the two powers would take or propose to their law-making bodies the necessary measures for carrying the treaty out. The above mentioned Act of July 3, 1918, entitled an act to give effect to the convention, prohibited the killing, capturing or selling any of the migratory birds included in the terms of the treaty except as permitted by regulations compatible with those terms, to be made by the Secretary of Agriculture. Regulations were proclaimed on July 31, and October 25, 1918. It is unnecessary to go into any details, because as we have said, the question raised is the general one whether the treaty and statute are void as an interference with the rights reserved to the States.

To answer this question it is not enough to refer to the Tenth Amendment, reserving the powers not delegated to the United States, because by Article II, § 2, the power to make treaties is delegated expressly, and by Article VI treaties made under the authority of the United States, along with the Constitution and laws of the United States made in pursuance thereof, are declared the supreme law of the land. If the treaty is valid there can be no dispute about the validity of the statute under Article I, § 8, as a necessary and proper means to execute the powers of the Government. The language of the Constitution as to the supremacy of treaties being general, the question before us is narrowed to an inquiry into the ground upon which the present supposed exception is placed.

It is said that a treaty cannot be valid if it infringes the Constitution, that there are limits, therefore, to the treaty-making power, and that one such limit is that what an act of Congress could not do unaided, in derogation of the powers reserved to the States, a treaty cannot do. An earlier act of Congress that attempted by itself and not in pursuance of a treaty to regulate the killing of migratory birds within the States had been held bad in the District Court. *United States v. Shauver*, 214 Fed. Rep. 154[;] *United States v. McCullagh*, 221 Fed. Rep. 288. Those decisions were supported by arguments that migratory birds were owned by the States in their sovereign capacity for the benefit of their people, and that under cases like *Geer v. Connecticut*, 161 U.S. 519, this control was one that Congress had no power to displace. The same argument is supposed to apply now with equal force.

Whether the two cases cited were decided rightly or not they cannot be accepted as a test of the treaty power. Acts of Congress are the supreme law of the land only when made in pursuance of the Constitution, while treaties are declared to be so when made under the authority of the United States. It is open to question whether the authority of the United States means more than the formal acts prescribed to make the convention. We do not mean to imply that there are no qualifications to the treaty-making power; but they must be ascertained in a different way. It is obvious that there may be matters of the sharpest exigency for the national well being that an act of Congress could not deal with but that a treaty followed by such an act could, and it is not lightly to be assumed that, in matters requiring national action, "a power which must belong to and somewhere reside in every civilized government" is not to be found. * * * [W]hen we are dealing with words that also are a constituent act, like the Constitution of the United States, we must realize that they have called into life a being the development of which could not have been foreseen completely by the most gifted of its begetters. It was enough for them to realize or to hope that they had created an organism; it has taken a century and has cost their successors much sweat and blood to prove that they created a nation. The case before us must be considered in the light of our whole experience and not merely in that of what was said a hundred years ago. The treaty in question does not contravene any prohibitory words to be found in the Constitution. The only question is whether it is forbidden by some invisible radiation from the general terms of the Tenth Amendment. We must consider what this country has become in deciding what that Amendment has reserved.

The State as we have intimated founds its claim of exclusive authority upon an assertion of title to migratory birds, an assertion that is embodied in statute. No doubt it is true that as between a State and its inhabitants the State may regulate the killing and sale of such birds, but it does not follow that its authority is exclusive of paramount powers. To put the claim of the State upon title is to lean upon a slender reed. Wild birds are not in the possession of anyone; and possession is the beginning of ownership. The whole foundation of the State's rights is the presence within their jurisdiction of birds that yesterday had not arrived, tomorrow may be in another State and in a week a thousand miles away. If we are to be accurate we cannot put the case of the State upon higher ground than that the treaty deals with creatures that for the moment are within the state borders, that it must be carried out by officers of the United States within the same territory, and that but for the treaty the State would be free to regulate this subject itself.

As most of the laws of the United States are carried out within the States and as many of them deal with matters which in the silence of such laws the State might regulate, such general grounds are not enough to support Missouri's claim. Valid treaties of course "are as binding within the territorial limits of the States as they are elsewhere throughout the dominion of the United States." No doubt the great body of private relations usually fall within the control of the State, but a treaty may override its power. * * *

Here a national interest of very nearly the first magnitude is involved. It can be protected only by national action in concert with that of another power. The subject-matter is only transitorily within the State and has no permanent habitat therein. But for the treaty and the statute there soon might be no birds for any powers to deal with. We see nothing in the Constitution that compels the Government to sit by while a food supply is cut off and the protectors of our forests and our crops are destroyed. It is not sufficient to rely upon the States. The reliance is vain, and were it otherwise, the question is whether the United States is forbidden to act. We are of opinion that the treaty and statute must be upheld.

JUSTICE VANDEVANTER and **JUSTICE PITNEY** dissent.

NOTE ON THE TREATY POWER AND ORIGINAL MEANING

Missouri v. Holland is a "nationalist" reading of the Treaty Clause: Treaty obligations entered into by the President, with the advice and consent of the Senate, create domestic law under the Supremacy Clause (Art. VI, cl. 2) even if not supported by an independent Article I ground for federal authority.[i] Through most of our history, there has been a countervision of the Treaty Clause, a "states' rights" reading: Treaty obligations are not the law of the land

---

i. See David Golove, *Treaty-Making and the Nation: The Historic Foundations of the Nationalist Conception of the Treaty Power*, 98 Mich. L. Rev. 1075 (2000).

unless they fall under one of the powers delegated to the national government under Article I.[j] As a matter of law, which reading is correct?

Consider the Constitution's text. The Tenth Amendment "reserves" to the states those powers "not delegated to the United States" and reflects the fact that the federal government is one of limited powers. But Article II seems to create an explicit delegation of power that Article VI explicitly gives the same supremacy as it gives Article I statutes; unlike Article I, however, Article II does not set out limits as to what treaties may touch upon. If a treaty were self-executing, intended by the President and Senate to be operative law, it would presumably trump state law under Article VI. But most treaties (now) are *not* self-executing, and if they are to be the law of the land they must be implemented by legislation.[k] The migratory bird treaty apparently had this feature.

Can Congress enact such an implementing statute without an Article I foundation? Justice Holmes says yes, and he cites the Necessary and Proper Clause, which allows Congress "[t]o make all Laws which shall be necessary and proper for carrying into Execution the foregoing Powers [those in Article I], and all other Powers vested by this Constitution in the Government of the United States," including Article II's Treaty Clause. As Nick Rosenkranz has argued, if you put these clauses together, you have the following power of Congress: "To make all Laws which shall be necessary and proper for carrying into Execution * * * [the] Power * * * to make Treaties."[l] Rosenkranz argues that the plain meaning of the Constitution reveals that Justice Holmes was flat wrong: the migratory birds statute was *not* needed to carry into execution Congress's power to "make Treaties." Instead, it was a congressional implementation of a treaty already made, but without any basis (in 1921) in the Constitution's delegation of limited authority to Congress. Can the Holmes position be salvaged? David Golove and Louis Henkin, among others, believe that original meaning supports *Missouri v. Holland.* Curtis Bradley and Nick Rosenkranz do not. Consider the evidence.

1. *Pre-1787 Practice.* In eighteenth-century England, treaties were made by the King, and they were binding on the nation. The Articles of Confederation vested the exclusive right to enter into treaties with Congress, with the proviso that no commercial treaty could interfere with state legislative power to impose equal taxes on foreigners as they impose on their own citizens or from regulating trade in goods or commodities (Art. IX). The Articles also prohibited the states from imposing imposts or duties inconsistent with treaties proposed for France and Spain (Art. VI). These limitations, explicitly recognizing state power as a limit on the national treaty power, bedeviled American negotiators of the Treaty of Peace entered into with Great Britain in 1782. The nationalist-versus-states' rights debate over the treaty power began during this period.

---

j. See Curtis Bradley, *The Treaty Power and American Federalism*, 97 Mich. L. Rev. 391 (1998).

k. See *Medellín v. Texas*, 128 S.Ct. 1346 (2008), excerpted and discussed in Chapter 8, § 1B3.

l. Nicholas Rosenkranz, *Executing the Treaty Power*, 118 Harv. L. Rev. 1867, 1880-1903 (2005).

Most of the statesmen in the national government — most notably Jefferson and Madison — took the nationalist position, that Congress could accrue new commerce-regulatory powers through treaties than it was otherwise vested with by the Articles (Golove, *Treaty-Making*). Statesmen at the local level tended to disagree; Virginia, for example, insisted it was not bound to enforce the Treaty of Peace provision enforcing debt obligations to the British. But see *Ware v. Hylton*, 3 U.S. 199 (1796) (upholding Art. IV of the Peace Treaty, requiring restitution of confiscated debts to British citizens). Moreover, other countries doubted the United States had this power either, and refused to enter into commercial treaties with the new country for that reason.

2. *The Philadelphia Convention and the Ratifying Debates.* The frustrations of the Articles period created consensus at Philadelphia for the propositions that the national treaty power must be available to trump state law, but there was also a consensus that the national government would be one of limited authority, confined to those powers delegated to it by the Constitution. It is not apparent that anyone gave thought to the proposition that a treaty power in Article II could reach subjects about which Article I did not authorize Congress to legislate. Louis Henkin argues that an early draft of the Necessary and Proper Clause explicitly included the power to "enforce treaties," but that language was struck because it was "superfluous." Rosenkranz responds that the language struck was from the Militia Clause and that the Necessary and Proper Clause never had language relating to treaties.[m]

During the state ratifying debates, Anti-Federalists attacked the Constitution's treaty power on the ground that it was unbounded — and therefore represented an important threat to the viability of autonomous states (Golove, *Treaty-Making*). Of particular concern was the possibility that the President and Senate might cede territorial rights over individual state objections. In the Virginia ratifying debates, Madison confessed that the treaty power under both the Articles and the Constitution gave no power of "dismembering" the country, "or alienating any part of it," because that was not a treaty power recognized by the law of nations. The opponents, particularly Patrick Henry, also argued that the treaty power could override individual rights. The Federalists generally denied that this would be legal, but without detailed reasoning from their constitutional text — except for this defense by George Nicholas: The President and Senate can "make no treaty which shall be repugnant to the spirit of the Constitution, or inconsistent with the delegated powers." Scholars vigorously debate how Nicholas' statement should be interpreted and how broadly to attribute it to other Federalists.[n]

3. *Early Interpretation and Practice.* The notorious Jay Treaty with Great Britain ignited a great debate between the nationalist and states' rights visions of the treaty power. Article 9 of the treaty overrode state law to assure property

---

m. Compare Louis Henkin, *Foreign Affairs and the Constitution* 481 n.111 (2d ed. 1996), with Rosenkranz, *Executing the Treaty Power*, 118 Harv. L. Rev. at 1912-18.

n. Compare Bradley, *Treaty Power*, 97 Mich. L. Rev. at 413 with Golove, *Treaty-Making*, 98 Mich. L. Rev. at 1148.

rights of British subjects in the American states, and opponents argued that this was beyond the authority of the President and Senate to accomplish. These arguments were rejected by President Washington, who upon the advice of Hamilton signed and supported the treaty; by two-thirds of the Senate, which ratified the treaty; by a slender majority in the House, which voted to give the treaty effect (Golove, *Treaty-Making*, 98 Mich. L. Rev. at 1154-61); and by the U.S. Supreme Court in *Martin v. Hunter's Lessee*, 14 U.S. 304 (1816), which applied the treaty to override state law. On the other hand, some supporters of the Constitution opined that the treaty power did not authorize national action beyond the powers delegated by Article I. Jefferson opposed the treaty on this ground and wrote his view into the Senate's earliest manual of parliamentary practice, which said that the treaty power could not extend to objects not normally regulated by treaties, to matters where the Constitution vested the House with a role, or to matters "reserved to the States: for surely the President and Senate cannot do by treaty what the whole government is interdicted from doing in any way" (Bradley, *Treaty Power*, 97 Mich. L. Rev. at 415, quoting the manual). Note that Jefferson was not so particular about the treaty power when he used it to make the Louisiana Purchase (Golove, *Treaty-Making*, 98 Mich. L. Rev. at 1188-95).

Bottom line: Was *Missouri v. Holland* wrongly decided? Should it be overruled? Can stare decisis save *Holland*? See Rosenkranz, *Executing the Treaty Power*, 118 Harv. L. Rev. at 1935-37 (nope).

PROBLEM 7-5
SUMMARY PROBLEM ON NATIONAL POWERS

Recall *City of Boerne v. Flores* (§ 3C of this chapter), where the Supreme Court invalidated the Religious Freedom Restoration Act (RFRA) as exceeding Congress' Fourteenth Amendment authority to enforce individual rights. You are a member of Congress who would like to enact a statute that protects religious freedom from indirect abridgments, as RFRA tried to do, but in a manner that will pass constitutional scrutiny. Which, if any, strategy will be effective in this regard? See, e.g., Robert Drinan, S.J., *Reflections on the Demise of the Religious Freedom Restoration Act*, 86 Geo. L.J. 101 (1997).

(1) *Commerce Clause Authority.* Construct the best strategy you can to revise RFRA to meet Commerce Clause requirements. Is this strategy likely to prevail?

(2) *Spending Clause Authority.* Another idea is inspired by *South Dakota v. Dole*: require states to accommodate religious minorities as a condition for their accepting federal funds. What limits are there to this kind of strategy?

(3) *Treaty Power.* Another strategy could be fashioned around *Missouri v. Holland*. The United States has signed and ratified the International Convention on Civil and Political Rights. Article 18 of the Convention protects against state abridgment of religious liberty. It not only prohibits the state from interfering with the free exercise of religion, but also assures individual "freedom . . . to manifest his religion or belief in worship, observance, practice and teaching." This treaty is not self-enforcing, but Congress might enact legislation imple-

menting Article 18 along the lines suggested in RFRA. Would that treaty be a sufficient authority for congressional action? Or is this precisely the kind of case that would motivate the Roberts Court to narrow or overrule *Missouri v. Holland*?

SECTION 5. INTERGOVERNMENTAL IMMUNITIES AND CONGRESSIONAL POWER

A. INTRODUCTION

The existence of the federal and state levels of sovereignty in this country might impose additional limitations on the ability of each level to act, apart from the division of responsibilities entailed in the limited but supreme powers of the national government and the plenary but subordinate powers of state governments. *McCulloch* illustrates this phenomenon, whereby the Court inferred from the Constitution's structure a prohibition against state taxation of a national entity. *McCulloch* has been extended to prohibit other state regulations of or burdens on the national government.[a]

McCulloch suggests in dicta that national regulation of or burdens on state governments do not justify the same, or perhaps any, level of judicial enforcement. In addition to national *taxation* of the states, either directly imposed on the states or indirectly imposed, as by taxing the interest on state bonds, national intrusions might include:

- national *regulations* applicable to the states, either nondiscriminatory (regulations applicable to all, including the states) or discriminatory (Part B of this section);

- national *commandeering* of state legislatures or state officers to help administer national programs (Part C); or

- *jurisdiction* over the states in federal courts (see § 3D of this chapter).

We do not read *McCulloch* for the proposition that the values of federalism are not threatened by possible national impositions on state governments — for such impositions theoretically do pose threats to the federal arrangement.[b] And nothing in *McCulloch* denies that the national government has obvious

---

a. See generally Laurence Tribe, *American Constitutional Law* § 6-33 (3d ed. 2000).

b. To the contrary, such threats can be just as serious. Most federations (Yugoslavia, U.S.S.R.) have dissolved because of the commitment problem identified in Bednar & Eskridge, *Unsteady Path*, § 1 note *g*. That is, if the states are not assured that their ability to govern is protected against national burdens, the states might lose enthusiasm for the federal arrangement. In Canada, separatist movements apparently became serious only after the British House of Lords ceased reviewing federalism issues for that country. Once Canada's Supreme Court took up the task in the 1950s, almost all national assertions of jurisdiction were upheld, in contrast to frequent invalidations before 1949. At that point, provincial dissatisfaction became palpable, and separatist movements gained a credibility that today threatens the Canadian federation. See Katharine Swinton, *The Supreme Court and Canadian Federalism: The Laskin-Dickson Years* (1990); P.W. Hogg, *Is the Supreme Court of Canada Biased in Constitutional Cases?*, 57 Can. B. Rev. 721 (1979); K.M. Lysyk, *Reshaping Canadian Federalism*, 13 U. Brit. Colum. L. Rev. 1 (1979).

incentives to impose burdens on state governments, namely, to satisfy interest groups benefitting from federal legislation, to achieve national goals at a lower cost through reliance on state resources, and to assure state accountability for obeying national policies. Might these actions by the national government — direct taxation or regulation, commandeering, federal jurisdiction — be just as destructive of federalism as Congress' overreaching its Commerce Clause powers? Commandeering, in particular, might be especially destructive because it not only interferes with the operation of and imposes potentially large costs upon state governance, but blurs lines of accountability by allowing national officials to take credit for work done by the states.

The reasons for possible judicial passivity in the face of national encroachments, those suggested by Chief Justice Marshall, are what we today call legal process limits, similar to the representation-reinforcement theory of John Hart Ely (Chapter 2, § 3B), which *McCulloch* anticipates. But *McCulloch* poses the issue without definitively resolving it. Are the states well enough represented in the national political process to obviate the need for judicial protection? Is the Court institutionally capable of developing administrable limitations on national regulation? If so, what exactly are those standards?

B. STATE IMMUNITY FROM DIRECT NATIONAL REGULATION

National League of Cities v. Usery, 426 U.S. 833 (1976). The Fair Labor Standards Act (FLSA) upheld in *Darby* was amended in 1961 and 1966 to apply to certain classes of state employees who had since 1938 been excluded from the statute's minimum wage and other guarantees. The Supreme Court sustained this regulation of the terms and conditions of state employment in *Maryland v. Wirtz*, 392 U.S. 183 (1968). After Congress further expanded the statute's application to state employees in 1974, the Court not only invalidated the 1974 amendments, but overruled *Maryland v. Wirtz*. **Justice Rehnquist**'s opinion for the Court ruled that "there are limits upon the power of Congress to override state sovereignty, even when exercising its otherwise plenary powers to tax or to regulate commerce which are conferred by Art. I of the Constitution." He continued with this quotation from *Fry v. United States*, 421 U.S. 542 (1975):

> While the Tenth Amendment has been characterized as a "truism," stating merely that "all is retained which has not been surrendered," *Darby*, it is not without significance. The Amendment expressly declares the constitutional policy that Congress may not exercise power in a fashion that impairs the States' integrity or their ability to function effectively in a federal system.

See also *New York v. United States*, 326 U.S. 572 (1946); *Coyle v. Oklahoma*, 221 U.S. 559 (1911) (national government cannot, for example, tell state government where its seat of power shall be located).

"One undoubted attribute of state sovereignty is the States' power to determine the wages which shall be paid to those whom they employ in order to carry out their governmental functions, what hours those persons will work, and what compensation will be provided where these employees may be called upon to work overtime. The question we must resolve here, then, is whether these determinations are 'functions essential to separate and independent existence,' *Coyle*, so that Congress may not abrogate the States' otherwise plenary authority to make them." National League of Cities' complaint alleged "substantial costs which will be imposed upon them by the 1974 amendments," which revealed "a significant impact on the functioning of the governmental bodies involved.

"Quite apart from the substantial costs imposed upon the States and their political subdivisions, the Act displaces state policies regarding the manner in which they will structure delivery of those governmental services which their citizens require. The Act, speaking directly to the States *qua* States, requires that they shall pay all but an extremely limited minority of their employees the minimum wage rates currently chosen by Congress." This decision, Justice Rehnquist reasoned, "will impermissibly interfere with the integral governmental functions of these bodies" and will "significantly alter or displace the States' abilities to structure employer-employee relationships in such areas as fire prevention, police protection, sanitation, public health, and parks and recreation," core functions that state and local governments perform for citizens. "We hold that insofar as the challenged amendments operate to directly displace the States' freedom to structure integral operations in areas of traditional governmental functions, they are not within the authority granted Congress by Art. I, § 8, cl. 3."

Justice Blackmun joined the Court's opinion upon the understanding that it adopted a "balancing approach" that "does not outlaw federal power in areas such as environmental protection, where the federal interest is demonstrably greater and where state facility compliance with imposed federal standards would be essential." **Justices Brennan**, **White**, **Marshall**, and **Stevens** dissented.

NOTE ON THE CONSTITUTIONAL EXPERIMENT IN *NATIONAL LEAGUE OF CITIES*

Most constitutional commentators were surprised with the result and analysis in *National League of Cities*, not least because this was the first time since the 1930s that the Court had invalidated a federal statute as beyond Congress' enumerated powers.[c] Some believed that the decision rested upon a less than firm constitutional foundation, the Tenth Amendment, which had been consigned to "truism" status by *Darby*. Compounding these difficulties was the fuzziness of the actual limitation on federal authority, which the Court clarified in *Hodel v. Virginia Surface Mining & Reclamation Ass'n*, 452 U.S. 264, 287-88 (1981), announcing that to be unconstitutional under *National League of Cities*, a statute must meet all of the following requirements: "First, there must be a showing that the challenged statute regulates the 'States as States.' Second, the federal regulation must address matters that are indisputably 'attribute[s] of state sovereignty.' And third, it must be apparent that the States' compliance with the

---

c. See, e.g., Sotirios Barber, National League of Cities v. Usery: *New Meaning for the Tenth Amendment?*, 1976 Sup. Ct. Rev. 161. Some subsequent commentators were less critical of the decision. See Philip Bobbitt, *Constitutional Fate* 191-95 (1982); Robert Nagel, *Federalism as a Fundamental Value:* National League of Cities *in Perspective*, 1981 Sup. Ct. Rev. 81.

federal law would directly impair their ability 'to structure integral operations in areas of traditional governmental functions.' "

In no case did the Court invalidate a statute based upon the *Hodel* test. The regulation in *Hodel* itself was permissible because it only regulated private mining companies, and not the states as states (first prong). In *United Transportation Union v. Long Island Railroad*, 455 U.S. 678 (1982), the Court unanimously held that federal labor relations rules could be applied to state-owned railroads, because operating a railroad has traditionally been a function of private industry, not state action, and therefore not a "traditional" state function (third prong). Hence, federal regulation of state-owned railroads "does not impair a state's ability to function as a state."

A closely divided Court in *Equal Employment Opportunity Commission v. Wyoming*, 460 U.S. 226 (1983), upheld the application of federal prohibitions against compulsory retirement to state park employees. The Court recognized that management of parks is a traditional state function but held that the third prong of the *Hodel* test was not met, because it would only have a marginal effect on the state's ability to operate its parks efficiently.

GARCIA v. SAN ANTONIO METROPOLITAN TRANSIT AUTHORITY
469 U.S. 528, 105 S.Ct. 1005, 83 L.Ed.2d 1016 (1985)

JUSTICE BLACKMUN delivered the opinion of the Court.

[This case involved whether the San Antonio Metropolitan Transit Authority (SAMTA) was subject to the minimum-wage and overtime requirements of the FLSA. The district court ruled that SAMTA was immune from FLSA regulation under *National League of Cities* and *Long Island Railroad*. The Supreme Court reversed, and in the process overruled *National League of Cities*.]

The controversy in the present cases has focused on the third *Hodel* requirement — that the challenged federal statute trench on "traditional governmental functions." The District Court voiced a common concern: "Despite the abundance of adjectives, identifying which particular state functions are immune remains difficult." Just how troublesome the task has been is revealed by the results reached in other federal cases. Thus, [lower] courts have held that regulating ambulance services, licensing automobile drivers, operating a municipal airport, performing solid waste disposal, and operating a highway authority are functions *protected* under *National League of Cities*. At the same time, [lower] courts have held that issuance of industrial development bonds, regulation of intrastate natural gas sales, regulation of traffic on public roads, regulation of air transportation, operation of a telephone system, leasing and sale of natural gas, operation of a mental health facility, and provision of in-house domestic services for the aged and handicapped are *not* entitled to immunity. We find it difficult, if not impossible, to identify an organizing principle that places each of the cases in the first group on one side of a line and each of the cases in the second group on the other side. The constitutional distinction between licensing drivers and regulating traffic, for example, or between operating a highway authority and operating a mental health facility, is elusive at best.

Thus far, this Court itself has made little headway in defining the scope of the governmental functions deemed protected under *National League of Cities*. In that case the Court set forth examples of protected and unprotected functions, but provided no explanation of how those examples were identified. The only other case in which the Court has had occasion to address the problem is *Long Island*. * * * We relied in large part there on "the *historical reality* that the operation of railroads is not among the functions *traditionally* performed by state and local governments," but we simultaneously disavowed "a static historical view of state functions generally immune from federal regulation." (first emphasis added; second emphasis in original) We held that the inquiry into a particular function's "traditional" nature was merely a means of determining whether the federal statute at issue unduly handicaps "basic state prerogatives," but we did not offer an explanation of what makes one state function a "basic prerogative" and another function not basic. Finally, having disclaimed a rigid reliance on the historical pedigree of state involvement in a particular area, we nonetheless found it appropriate to emphasize the extended historical record of *federal* involvement in the field of rail transportation.

Many constitutional standards involve "undoubte[d] . . . gray areas," and, despite the difficulties that this Court and other courts have encountered so far, it normally might be fair to venture the assumption that case-by-case development would lead to a workable standard for determining whether a particular governmental function should be immune from federal regulation under the Commerce Clause. A further cautionary note is sounded, however, by the Court's experience in the related field of state immunity from federal taxation. [The Court had ruled the states immune from federal taxation in *Collector v. Day*, 78 U.S. (11 Wall.) 113 (1871). In *South Carolina v. United States*, 199 U.S. 437 (1905), the Court held that *Day*'s state tax immunity extended only to the "ordinary" and "strictly governmental" instrumentalities of state governments and not to instrumentalities "used by the State in the carrying on of an ordinary private business." The Court in *New York v. United States*, 326 U.S. 572 (1946), found that the distinction between "governmental" and "proprietary" functions was "untenable" and abandoned it.]

The distinction the Court discarded as unworkable in the field of tax immunity has proved no more fruitful in the field of regulatory immunity under the Commerce Clause. Neither do any of the alternative standards that might be employed to distinguish between protected and unprotected governmental functions appear manageable. We rejected the possibility of making immunity turn on a purely historical standard of "tradition" in *Long Island*, and properly so. The most obvious defect of a historical approach to state immunity is that it prevents a court from accommodating changes in the historical functions of States, changes that have resulted in a number of once-private functions like education being assumed by the States and their subdivisions. At the same time, the only apparent virtue of a rigorous historical standard, namely, its promise of a reasonably objective measure for state immunity, is illusory. Reliance on history as an organizing principle results in line-drawing of the most arbitrary sort; the genesis of state governmental functions stretches over a historical continuum from before the Revolution to the present, and courts would have to decide by fiat precisely how longstanding a pattern of state involvement had to be for federal regulatory authority to be defeated.

A nonhistorical standard for selecting immune governmental functions is likely to be just as unworkable as is a historical standard. The goal of identifying "uniquely" governmental functions, for example, has been rejected by the Court in the field of government tort liability in part because the notion of a "uniquely" governmental function is unmanageable. Another possibility would be to confine immunity to "necessary" governmental services, that is, services that would be provided inadequately or not at all unless the government provided them. The set of services that fits into this category, however, may well be negligible. The fact that an unregulated market produces less of some service than a State deems desirable does not mean that the State itself must provide the service; in most if not all cases, the State can "contract out" by hiring private firms to provide the service or simply by providing subsidies to existing suppliers. It also is open to question how well equipped courts are to make this kind of determination about the workings of economic markets.

We believe, however, that there is a more fundamental problem at work here, a problem that explains why the Court was never able to provide a basis for the governmental/proprietary distinction in the intergovernmental tax immunity cases and why an attempt to draw similar distinctions with respect to federal regulatory authority under *National League of Cities* is unlikely to succeed regardless of how the distinctions are phrased. The problem is that neither the governmental/proprietary distinction nor any other that purports to separate out important governmental functions can be faithful to the role of federalism in a democratic society. The essence of our federal system is that within the realm of authority left open to them under the Constitution, the States must be equally free to engage in any activity that their citizens choose for the common weal, no matter how unorthodox or unnecessary anyone else — including the judiciary — deems state involvement to be. Any rule of state immunity that looks to the "traditional," "integral," or "necessary" nature of governmental functions inevitably invites an unelected federal judiciary to make decisions about which state policies it favors and which ones it dislikes. * * * [T]he States cannot serve as laboratories for social and economic experiment, if they must pay an added price when they meet the changing needs of their citizenry by taking up functions that an earlier day and a different society left in private hands. * * *

We therefore now reject, as unsound in principle and unworkable in practice, a rule of state immunity from federal regulation that turns on a judicial appraisal of whether a particular governmental function is "integral" or "traditional." Any such rule leads to inconsistent results at the same time that it disserves principles of democratic self-governance, and it breeds inconsistency precisely because it is divorced from those principles. If there are to be limits on the Federal Government's power to interfere with state functions — as undoubtedly there are — we must look elsewhere to find them. We accordingly return to the underlying issue that confronted this Court in *National League of Cities* — the manner in which the Constitution insulates States from the reach of Congress' power under the Commerce Clause. * * *

The States unquestionably do "retai[n] a significant measure of sovereign authority." They do so, however, only to the extent that the Constitution has not divested them of their original powers and transferred those powers to the Federal Government. In the words of James Madison to the Members of the First Congress: "Interference with the power of the States was no constitutional criterion of the power of Congress. If the power was not given, Congress could not exercise it; if given, they might exercise it, although it should interfere with the laws, or even the Constitution of the States." * * *

* * * With rare exceptions, like the guarantee, in Article IV, § 3, of state territorial integrity, the Constitution does not carve out express elements of state sovereignty that Congress may not employ its delegated powers to displace. * * *

* * * Apart from the limitation on federal authority inherent in the delegated nature of Congress' Article I powers, the principal means chosen by the Framers to ensure the role of the States in the federal system lies in the structure of the Federal Government itself. It is no novelty to observe that the composition of the Federal Government was designed in large part to protect the States from overreaching by Congress. The Framers thus gave the States a role in the selection both of the Executive and the Legislative Branches of the Federal Government. The States were vested with indirect influence over the House of Representatives and the Presidency by their control of electoral qualifications and their role in presidential elections. U.S. Const., Art. I, § 2, and Art. II, § 1. They were given more direct influence in the Senate, where each State received equal representation and each Senator was to be selected by the legislature of his State. Art. I, § 3. The significance attached to the States' equal representation in the Senate is underscored by the prohibition of any constitutional amendment divesting a State of equal representation without the State's consent. Art. V. * * * The effectiveness of the federal political process in preserving the States' interests is apparent even today in the course of federal legislation. * * * [T]he States have been able to direct a substantial proportion of federal revenues into their own treasuries in the form of general and program-specific grants in aid.

* * * We realize that changes in the structure of the Federal Government have taken place since 1789, not the least of which has been the substitution of popular election of Senators by the adoption of the Seventeenth Amendment in 1913, and that these changes may work to alter the influence of the States in the federal political process. Nonetheless, against this background, we are convinced that the fundamental limitation that the constitutional scheme imposes on the Commerce Clause to protect the "States as States" is one of process rather than one of result. * * *

Insofar as the present cases are concerned, we need go no further than to state that we perceive nothing in the overtime and minimum-wage requirements of the FLSA, as applied to SAMTA, that is destructive of state sovereignty or violative of any constitutional provision. SAMTA faces nothing more than the same minimum-wage and overtime obligations that hundreds of thousands of other employers, public as well as private, have to meet. * * *

Of course, we continue to recognize that the States occupy a special and specific position in our constitutional system and that the scope of Congress' authority under the Commerce Clause must reflect that position. But the principal and basic limit on the federal commerce power is that inherent in all congressional action — the built-in restraints that our system provides through state participation in federal governmental action. The political process ensures that laws that unduly burden the States will not be promulgated. In the factual setting of these cases the internal safeguards of the political process have performed as intended. * * *

JUSTICE POWELL, with whom **THE CHIEF JUSTICE [BURGER]**, **JUSTICE REHNQUIST**, and **JUSTICE O'CONNOR** join, dissenting. * * *

More troubling than the logical infirmities in the Court's reasoning is the result of its holding, *i.e.*, that federal political officials, invoking the Commerce Clause, are the sole judges of the limits of their own power. This result is inconsistent with the fundamental principles of our constitutional system. At least since *Marbury v. Madison* it has been the settled province of the federal judiciary "to say what the law is" with respect to the constitutionality of acts of Congress. In rejecting the role of the judiciary in protecting the States from federal overreaching, the Court's opinion offers no explanation for ignoring the teaching of the most famous case in our history.

In our federal system, the States have a major role that cannot be preempted by the National Government. As contemporaneous writings and the debates at the ratifying conventions make clear, the States' ratification of the Constitution was predicated on this understanding of federalism. Indeed, the Tenth Amendment was adopted specifically to ensure that the important role promised the States by the proponents of the Constitution was realized.

[All eight States voting for the Constitution only after proposing amendments to be adopted after ratification included among their recommendations some version of what later became the Tenth Amendment. Justice Powell essentially charged the Court with acquiescing in a constitutional "bait and switch": a necessary inducement to states' ratification of the Constitution being taken away years after the fact by judicial fiat.]

[We omit the separate dissenting opinions of **JUSTICE O'CONNOR** and **JUSTICE REHNQUIST**. The latter conceded that there was no consensus as to exactly what the *National League of Cities* test should be but maintained that "under any one of these approaches the judgment in this case should be affirmed, and I do not think it incumbent on those of us in dissent to spell out further the fine points of a principle that will, I am confident, in time again command the support of a majority of this Court."]

NOTE ON *GARCIA*: SHOULD THE COURT ABSTAIN FROM ENFORCING FEDERALISM-BASED LIMITS ON CONGRESS?

Garcia followed Herbert Wechsler, *The Political Safeguards of Federalism*, in *Principles, Politics, and Fundamental Law* 49-82 (1961), in leaving enforcement of federalism-based limitations to the political process. See also *Federalist* Nos. 45-46; Jesse Choper, *Judicial Review and the National Political*

Process (1980). Like Chief Justice Marshall in *McCulloch*, Wechsler thought that intergovernmental immunities should be asymmetrical for political process reasons: The national government is vulnerable to state predation and so requires judicial protection, but states are well represented in the national process and thus can protect themselves against federal intrusion. Consider some criticisms of this approach:[d]

(1) *Original Meaning: The Bait and Switch Problem.* Would the states have ratified the Constitution if they had known that the Court would not enforce federalism limits on Congress *and* would not protect the states themselves against national intrusion? Is *Garcia* an example of constitutional "bait-and-switch"? In a twist on Wechsler, Larry Kramer argues not. By his account, the Constitution's drafters and the delegates at the ratifying conventions did not expect courts to enforce jurisdictional limits on Congress. "It was the legislature's delegated responsibility to decide whether a proposed law was constitutionally authorized, subject to oversight by the people. Courts simply had nothing to do with it, and they were acting as interlopers if they tried to second-guess the legislature's decision."[e] Others who have examined the original evidence disagree with Kramer. In addition to the support for judicial review found in *Federalist* No. 78 (which Kramer dismisses as a pamphlet almost no one read), other examinations of the historical evidence have concluded that the Framers expected courts to enforce the jurisdictional limits on Congress's power (e.g., Prakash & Yoo, *Puzzling Persistence*).

(2) *The Political Process Problem.* Does the political structure really protect the "states *qua* states," especially now that state legislatures no longer elect senators and the state-oriented electoral college is only a formality in electing the President? Consider the FLSA, which was amended in 1974 to include all state employees. Senators would have been under great pressure

---

d. For critiques of *Garcia* and Wechsler's "political safeguards" thesis, see Lynn Baker, *Putting the Safeguards Back into the Political Safeguards of Federalism*, 46 Vill. L. Rev. 951 (2001); Jenna Bednar & William Eskridge, Jr., *Steadying the Court's "Unsteady Path": A Theory of Judicial Enforcement of Federalism*, 68 S. Cal. L. Rev. 1447 (1995); Steven Calabresi, *"A Government of Limited and Enumerated Powers": In Defense of* United States v. Lopez, 94 Mich. L. Rev. 752, 790-99 (1995); John McGinnis & Ilya Somin, *Federalism v. States Rights: A Defense of Judicial Review in a Federal System,* 99 Nw. U.L. Rev. 89 (2004); Saikrishna Prakash & John Yoo, *The Puzzling Persistence of Process-Based Federalism Theories*, 79 Tex. L. Rev. 1459 (2001); Andrzej Rapaczynski, *From Sovereignty to Process: The Jurisprudence of Federalism After* Garcia, 1985 Sup. Ct. Rev. 341; Martin Redish & Karen Drizin, *Constitutional Federalism and Judicial Review: The Role of Textual Analysis*, 62 NYU L. Rev. 1 (1987); William Van Alstyne, *The Second Death of Federalism*, 83 Mich. L. Rev. 1709 (1985). Defenses of *Garcia* include Martha Field, Garcia v. San Antonio Metropolitan Transit Authority: *The Demise of a Misguided Doctrine*, 99 Harv. L. Rev. 84 (1985); Larry Kramer, *Putting the Politics Back into the Political Safeguards of Federalism*, 100 Colum. L. Rev. 215 (2000); Robert Mikos, *The Populist Safeguards of Federalism*, 68 Ohio St. L.J. 1669 (2007). See also Bradford Clark, *Separation of Powers as a Safeguard of Federalism*, 79 Tex. L. Rev. 1321 (2001).

e. Larry Kramer, *The Supreme Court, 2000 Term — Foreword: We the Court*, 115 Harv. L. Rev. 4, 49 (2001); see *id.* at 65-70 (surveying the original evidence); Kramer, *Political Safeguards of Federalism*.

from public employee unions, and indeed unions in general, to support such legislation, and those unions can turn out votes and contribute money and volunteers for (or against) the Senator at election time. Can her state do anything similar to affect her reelection chances? Nonetheless, states do seem to be an effective lobbying group in the nation's capital.[f] Within a year of *Garcia*, for example, Congress amended the FLSA to allow public employers some ability to substitute compensatory time off for costly overtime pay. The states *qua* states also have clout through the national political parties, which are organized at the state level, and through the national government's reliance on state cooperation to carry out most programs (Kramer, *Political Safeguards*).

Finally, note that the Court can tip the political process in favor of the states by the way it interprets potentially intrusive federal statutes. The Court took this step in *Gregory v. Ashcroft*, 501 U.S. 452 (1991), where it held that general federal legislation does not apply to core state governmental operations unless the statute contains a clear statement to that effect. Thus, because the Age Discrimination in Employment Act says nothing directly about whether it applies to appointed state judges, states may maintain their mandatory retirement rules for such judges even though mandatory retirement age is ordinarily considered a prima facie violation of the statute and the judges seemed to fall within the general coverage provisions of the Act. Is this revival of the Rehnquist approach in *National League of Cities* as a statutory-interpretation rather than constitutional approach a useful compromise in accommodating state sovereignty while maintaining congressional supremacy (because Congress can always amend the statute to make it clear that particular state operations are covered)?

(3) *The Rotten Federalism Argument.* Especially in times of governmental scarcity, the national government has every incentive to enact regulatory programs whose cost is borne mainly by private businesses and by the states. Private businesses can pass on many of these costs to consumers or resist their imposition through lobbying, but the states are less able to do so, because their taxpayers are increasingly resistant to tax increases. This is pretty rotten federalism: In the olden days (the sixties), the federal government followed a carrot approach — if the states took federal money (under the spending power), they had to abide by federal policy conditions. At least the states had a choice and got some assistance. Later, the federal government began to follow a stick approach — it just told the states they have to do federal bureaucratic chores or adopt within their governments preferred federal policies. (Following the election of 1994, however, in which Congress changed political composition, state protests over unfunded federal mandates have been much more effective.)

If *Garcia* fell by the constitutional wayside, what approach should the Court take? The Rehnquist approach in *National League of Cities*? A balancing approach? *Hodel*? Redish & Drizin, *Textual Analysis*, argue that both *National*

---

f. See William Eskridge, Jr., *Overriding Supreme Court Statutory Interpretation Decisions*, 101 Yale L.J. 331 (1991); Carol Lee, *The Political Safeguards of Federalism? Congressional Responses to Supreme Court Decisions on State and Local Liability*, 20 Urb. Law. 301 (1988).

League of Cities and *Garcia* are inconsistent with the text of the Constitution: The Tenth Amendment imposes no additional limits on Congress' power (contra *National League of Cities*) beyond the judicially enforceable limits mandated by the enumerated powers in Article I (contra *Garcia*). They argue that the best that can be done is to give some teeth to the Commerce Clause, by requiring a truly "rational basis" for Congress' exercise of powers thereunder (anticipating *Lopez*).

Field, *Misguided Doctrine*, cheered the overruling of *National League of Cities*, but also suggested a limiting principle: "A more satisfactory version of a 'core governmental functions' test would include traditional and nontraditional roles alike and would restrict immunity to essentially internal state activities. Such internal matters would include the organization of state and local governments, the treatment of the states' own employees, and other activities that fall under the rubric of housekeeping functions. Immunity would end where state actions impinge directly upon the outside world, however traditional the activity or slight the impact." Hence, she would immunize state employee rules and render FLSA essentially inapplicable to the states (thus the result in *National League of Cities* would survive).

NOTE ON INTERGOVERNMENTAL TAX IMMUNITIES

McCulloch's rule against state taxation of federal entities has never been questioned. Indeed, it was expanded by the Court to immunize indirect as well as direct state burdens on the federal government. Thus, the Court exempted from state taxation, interest from federal bonds, *Weston v. City Council of Charleston*, 2 Pet. 449 (1829); wages paid federal employees, *Dobbins v. Commissioners of Erie County*, 16 Pet. 435 (1842); and even income derived from a federal lease, *Gillespie v. Oklahoma*, 257 U.S. 501 (1922).

Although *McCulloch* suggested reasons why federal immunity from state taxation did not require state immunity from federal taxation, the Court later held not only that the federal government cannot tax the states directly, but cannot burden them indirectly, as by taxing the wages of state employees, *Collector v. Day*, 78 U.S. (11 Wall.) 113 (1871), or the income from the lease of lands to the state, *Burnet v. Coronado Oil Co.*, 285 U.S. 393 (1932). In *Pollock v. Farmers' Loan & Trust Co.*, 157 U.S. 429 (1895), the Court narrowly invalidated a federal tax on the interest earned on state bonds. (*Pollock* also invalidated the federal income tax, a holding that was overridden by the Seventeenth Amendment.)

The New Deal Court cut back on intergovernmental immunity restrictions. In *Graves v. New York ex rel. O'Keefe*, 306 U.S. 466 (1939), the Court repudiated the theory that a tax on income is constitutionally equivalent to a tax on its source (the state or federal government). Such taxes are incident to the normal operation of modern administrative governance, to be borne by both state and federal governments. Thus, the Court allowed federal taxation of state employee wages, *Helvering v. Gerhardt*, 304 U.S. 405 (1938), as well as state taxation of federal employee wages, *Graves*. All of the old indirect tax cases were overruled by *Graves* and its progeny, except *Pollock*.

The federal government itself remained immune from state taxation, but for a time state immunity from federal taxation was limited to state governmental, but not proprietary, activities. See *South Carolina v. United States*, 199 U.S. 437 (1905); *Helvering v. Powers*, 293 U.S. 214 (1934). This test was abandoned in *New York v. United States*, 326 U.S. 572 (1946), but the Court yielded no majority approach. Two Justices in that case believed that any nondiscriminatory tax on a state was constitutional, even if directly collected. A plurality of four Justices upheld the tax before them was constitutional even though it was directly levied against the state but left open the possibility that a tax "impair-[ing] the sovereign status" of a state might be vulnerable.

In *First Agricultural Bank v. State Tax Commission*, 392 U.S. 339 (1968), the Court reaffirmed the *McCulloch* holding that federal banks are immune from state taxation — over a dissent by Justice Marshall, who argued that intergovernmental tax immunities should not be read easily into federal statutes, because the doctrine itself has no textual support in the Constitution and is inconsistent with the premises of the modern regulatory state.

South Carolina v. Baker, 485 U.S. 505 (1988). In 1982, Congress removed the federal income tax exemption for interest on state and local bonds unless they are issued in registered form; this effectively eliminated bearer bonds, which the IRS found contributed to tax evasion. Although the statute did have a direct effect on state tax policy, the opinion for the Court by **Justice Brennan** ruled that there was no process defect in the statute, the only ground for Tenth Amendment challenge left by *Garcia*. "It suffices to observe that South Carolina has not even alleged that it was deprived of any right to participate in the national political process or that it was singled out in a way that left it politically isolated and powerless. Cf. *Carolene Products*, n.4. Rather, South Carolina argues that the political process failed here because [the provision] was 'imposed by the vote of an uninformed Congress relying upon incomplete information.' But nothing in *Garcia* or the Tenth Amendment authorizes courts to second-guess the substantive basis for congressional legislation."

The Court agreed with South Carolina that the effect of the law was to impose a tax upon interest earned on a state bond, which had been declared immune from national taxation in *Pollock*, discussed in the previous note. The *Pollock* rule was merely "one application of the more general rule that neither the federal nor the state governments could tax income an individual derived from *any* contact with another government," including income by state or federal employees (*Collector v. Day*). That rationale was repudiated by the New Deal Court, which considered such taxes constitutionally acceptable even if they had the indirect effect of increasing governmental costs. *E.g.*, *Graves*. "Subsequent cases have consistently reaffirmed the principle that a nondiscriminatory tax collected from private parties contracting with another government is constitutional even though part or all the financial burden falls on the other government." Justice Brennan applied this principle to overrule *Pollock*.

Only **Justice O'Connor** dissented from both parts of the Court's holding, viewing the 1982 statute as unacceptable congressional nibbling away at state sovereignty. **Chief Justice Rehnquist** and **Justice Scalia** concurred in the judgment but declined to join the Court's *Garcia* analysis.

C. STATE IMMUNITY FROM NATIONAL COMMANDEERING

The Supremacy Clause of Article VI contemplates that state judges can be commandeered to apply national law, see *Testa v. Katt*, 330 U.S. 386 (1947), but national commandeering of state legislatures or even executive officials was viewed as potentially threatening to state sovereignty during the *National League of Cities* era. In *FERC v. Mississippi*, 456 U.S. 742 (1982), the Court recognized this problem but upheld a federal law requiring state utility commissions to hold fact-finding hearings and carry out certain national energy policy tasks. In dissent, Justice O'Connor argued that this was commandeering contrary to the rule of *National League of Cities* and core values of federalism. "If Congress routinely required the state legislatures to debate bills drafted by congressional committees, it could hardly be questioned that the practice would affect an attribute of state sovereignty. [This statute], which sets the agendas of agencies exercising delegated legislative power in a specific field, has a similarly intrusive effect." Recall the "rotten federalism" point above. *Query*: After *Garcia* and *South Carolina v. Baker*, is a commandeering claim relegated to the political process, and the Court severely limited in its review?

NEW YORK v. UNITED STATES
505 U.S. 144, 112 S.Ct. 2408, 120 L.Ed.2d. 120 (1992)

JUSTICE O'CONNOR delivered the opinion of the Court.

[Low-level radioactive waste is commonplace, and when disposed it must be isolated from people for long periods of time. The dominant public sentiment on the issue is "NIMBY" — "Not In My Back Yard." Every state wants to engage in the activities producing this waste; no one wants it stored in their state. Since 1979, only three disposal sites had been in operation, and the nation's waste had been shipped to them. In 1980, Congress enacted legislation encouraging states to enter into regional compacts creating disposal sites. By 1985, only three compacts had been approved, and they were formed around the already-existing South Carolina, Nevada, and Washington sites; under the 1980 statute these three compacts were authorized to exclude waste from nonmembers starting in 1986. In response, Congress enacted the Low-Level Radioactive Waste Policy Amendments Act of 1985. The statute was designed to solve the NIMBY problem.

[Based largely upon a proposal of the National Governors' Association, the 1985 statute was a compromise between sited and unsited states (those containing or not containing disposal sites). The sited states agreed to accept waste for another seven years, and the unsited states agreed to handle their own waste by 1992. The statute provided three kinds of incentives to encourage states to tackle this problem, along with a series of deadlines that the states were expected to meet as they did so. *First*, the sited states were authorized to charge gradually increasing fees for waste from unsited states. One quarter of these surcharges went to the federal Department of Energy, which used these funds to make payments to states that met their deadlines. *Second*, states that failed to meet certain deadlines could be charged higher surcharges and, eventually, could be denied access to disposal facilities altogether. *Third*, the so-called "take title" provision told states that eventually they would literally own the problem themselves if they didn't cooperate. It provided:

> If a State (or, where applicable, a compact region) in which low-level radioactive waste is generated is unable to provide for the disposal of all such waste generated within such State or compact region by January 1, 1996, each State in which such waste is generated, upon the request of the generator or owner of the waste, shall take title to the waste, be obligated to take possession of the waste, and shall be liable for all damages directly or indirectly incurred by such generator or owner as a consequence of the failure of the State to take possession of the waste as soon after January 1, 1996, as the generator or owner notifies the State that the waste is available for shipment.

[New York joined no regional compact. It complied with the initial requirements of the statute by enacting legislation providing for the siting of a facility in the state. Residents of the two counties containing potential sites opposed the state's choice of location — a classic example of the NIMBY syndrome. Fearing that it could not comply with the statutory deadlines, New York and these two counties brought suit, contending that the statute was inconsistent with the Tenth Amendment and with the Guaranty Clause of Article IV.]

[Federalism] questions can be viewed in either of two ways. In some cases the Court has inquired whether an Act of Congress is authorized by one of the powers delegated to Congress in Article I of the Constitution. See, *e.g.*, *McCulloch*. In other cases the Court has sought to determine whether an Act of Congress invades the province of state sovereignty reserved by the Tenth Amendment. See, *e.g.*, *Garcia.* * * *

It is in this sense that the Tenth Amendment "states but a truism that all is retained which has not been surrendered." *Darby.* * * *

Congress exercises its conferred powers subject to the limitations contained in the Constitution. Thus, for example, under the Commerce Clause Congress may regulate publishers engaged in interstate commerce, but Congress is constrained in the exercise of that power by the First Amendment. The Tenth Amendment likewise restrains the power of Congress, but this limit is not derived from the text of the Tenth Amendment itself, which, as we have discussed, is essentially a tautology. Instead, the Tenth Amendment confirms that the power of the Federal Government is subject to limits that may, in a given instance, reserve power to the States. The Tenth Amendment thus directs us to determine, as in this case, whether an incident of state sovereignty is protected by a limitation on an Article I power. * * *

Petitioners do not contend that Congress lacks the power to regulate the disposal of low level radioactive waste. Space in radioactive waste disposal sites is frequently sold by residents of one State to residents of another. Regulation of the resulting interstate market in waste disposal is therefore well within Congress' authority under the Commerce Clause. Petitioners * * * do not dispute that under the Supremacy Clause Congress could, if it wished, pre-empt state radioactive waste regulation. Petitioners contend only that the Tenth

Amendment limits the power of Congress to regulate in the way it has chosen. Rather than addressing the problem of waste disposal by directly regulating the generators and disposers of waste, petitioners argue, Congress has impermissibly directed the States to regulate in this field.

Most of our recent cases interpreting the Tenth Amendment have concerned the authority of Congress to subject state governments to generally applicable laws. The Court's jurisprudence in this area has traveled an unsteady path. [Citing *Maryland v. Wirtz, National League of Cities, Garcia.*] This case presents no occasion to apply or revisit the holdings of any of these cases, as this is not a case in which Congress has subjected a State to the same legislation applicable to private parties.

This case instead concerns the circumstances under which Congress may use the States as implements of regulation; that is, whether Congress may direct or otherwise motivate the States to regulate in a particular field or a particular way. * * *

* * * While Congress has substantial powers to govern the Nation directly, including in areas of intimate concern to the States, the Constitution has never been understood to confer upon Congress the ability to require the States to govern according to Congress' instructions. The Court has been explicit about this distinction. "Both the States and the United States existed before the Constitution. The people, through that instrument, established a more perfect union by substituting a national government, acting, with ample power, *directly upon the citizens*, instead of the Confederate government, which acted with powers, greatly restricted, only upon the States." [*Lane County v. Oregon*, 7 Wall. 71, 76 (1869) (emphasis added).] The Court has made the same point with more rhetorical flourish, although perhaps with less precision, on a number of occasions. In Chief Justice Chase's much-quoted words, "the preservation of the States, and the maintenance of their governments, are as much within the design and care of the Constitution as the preservation of the Union and the maintenance of the National government. The Constitution, in all its provisions, looks to an indestructible Union, composed of indestructible States." *Texas v. White*, 7 Wall. 700, 725 (1869). * * *

In the end, the [Constitutional] Convention opted for a Constitution in which Congress would exercise its legislative authority directly over individuals rather than over States * * * . This choice was made clear to the subsequent state ratifying conventions. Oliver Ellsworth, a member of the Connecticut delegation in Philadelphia, explained the distinction to his State's convention: "This Constitution does not attempt to coerce sovereign bodies, states, in their political capacity. . . . But this legal coercion singles out the . . . individual." Charles Pinckney, another delegate at the Constitutional Convention, emphasized to the South Carolina House of Representatives that in Philadelphia "the necessity of having a government which should at once operate upon the people, and not upon the states, was conceived to be indispensable by every delegation present." Rufus King, one of Massachusetts' delegates, returned home to support ratification by recalling the Commonwealth's unhappy experience under the Articles of Confederation and arguing: "Laws, to be effective, therefore, must not be laid on states, but upon individuals." * * * At North Carolina's convention, Samuel Spencer recognized that "all the laws of the Confederation were binding on the states in their political capacities, . . . but now the thing is entirely different. The laws of Congress will be binding on individuals."

In providing for a stronger central government, therefore, the Framers explicitly chose a Constitution that confers upon Congress the power to regulate individuals, not States. As we have seen, the Court has consistently respected this choice. We have always understood that even where Congress has the authority under the Constitution to pass laws requiring or prohibiting certain acts, it lacks the power directly to compel the States to require or prohibit those acts. The allocation of power contained in the Commerce Clause, for example, authorizes Congress to regulate interstate commerce directly; it does not authorize Congress to regulate state governments' regulation of interstate commerce.

This is not to say that Congress lacks the ability to encourage a State to regulate in a particular way, or that Congress may not hold out incentives to the States as a method of influencing a State's policy choices. Our cases have identified a variety of methods, short of outright coercion, by which Congress may urge a State to adopt a legislative program consistent with federal interests. Two of these methods are of particular relevance here.

First, under Congress' spending power, "Congress may attach conditions on the receipt of federal funds." *South Dakota v. Dole*. Such conditions must (among other requirements) bear some relationship to the purpose of the federal spending; otherwise, of course, the spending power could render academic the Constitution's other grants and limits of federal authority. Where the recipient of federal funds is a State, as is not unusual today, the conditions attached to the funds by Congress may influence a State's legislative choices. *Dole* was one such case: The Court found no constitutional flaw in a federal statute directing the Secretary of Transportation to withhold federal highway funds from States failing to adopt Congress' choice of a minimum drinking age. Similar examples abound.

Second, where Congress has the authority to regulate private activity under the Commerce Clause, we have recognized Congress' power to offer States the choice of regulating that activity according to federal standards or having state law pre-empted by federal regulation. This arrangement, which has been termed "a program of cooperative federalism," is replicated in numerous federal statutory schemes. * * *

By either of these two methods, as by any other permissible method of encouraging a State to conform to federal policy choices, the residents of the State retain the ultimate decision as to whether or not the State will comply. If a State's citizens view federal policy as sufficiently contrary to local interests, they may elect to decline a federal grant. If state residents would prefer their government to devote its attention and resources to problems other than those deemed important by Congress, they may choose to have the Federal Government rather than the State bear the expense of a federally mandated regulatory program, and they may continue to supplement that program to the extent state law is not preempted. Where Congress encourages state regulation rather than compelling it, state governments remain responsive to the local electorate's preferences; state officials remain accountable to the people.

By contrast, where the Federal Government compels States to regulate, the accountability of both state and federal officials is diminished. If the citizens of New York, for example, do not consider that making provision for the disposal of radioactive waste is in their best interest, they may elect state officials who share their view. That view can always be preempted under the Supremacy Clause if it is contrary to the national view, but in such a case it is the Federal Government that makes the decision in full view of the public, and it will be federal officials that suffer the consequences if the decision turns out to be detrimental or unpopular. But where the Federal Government directs the States to regulate, it may be state officials who will bear the brunt of public disapproval, while the federal officials who devised the regulatory program may remain insulated from the electoral ramifications of their decision. Accountability is thus diminished when, due to federal coercion, elected state officials cannot regulate in accordance with the views of the local electorate in matters not pre-empted by federal regulation. * * *

[The Court upheld the Act's provision authorizing sited states to impose a surcharge on waste received from other states. As discussed above, these charges were intended to provide financial incentives for states to cooperate with the waste disposal scheme. The Court called this provision "an unexceptional exercise of Congress' power to authorize the states to burden interstate commerce." The Court also upheld the provision under which the federal government would collect a portion of this surcharge and place it into an escrow account, calling it "no more than a federal tax on interstate commerce." The Court also held valid the provision under which states achieving a series of milestones in combating radioactive waste receive portions of these federally collected funds, calling it a "conditional exercise of Congress' authority under the Spending Clause" consistent with *South Dakota v. Dole*.

[The Court also upheld the provision authorizing states and regional compacts with disposal sites to increase the costs of access to those sites, and deny access altogether, to waste generated in states that do not meet federal guidelines. This was viewed as a "conditional exercise of Congress' commerce power."] Where federal regulation of private activity is within the scope of the Commerce Clause, we have recognized the ability of Congress to offer states the choice of regulating that activity according to federal standards or having state law pre-empted by federal regulation. This is the choice presented to nonsited States by the Act's second set of incentives: States may either regulate the disposal of radioactive waste according to federal standards by attaining local or regional self-sufficiency, or their residents who produce radioactive waste will be subject to federal regulation authorizing sited States and regions to deny access to their disposal sites. The affected States are not compelled by Congress to regulate, because any burden caused by a State's refusal to regulate will fall on those who generate waste and find no outlet for its disposal, rather than on the State as a sovereign. A State whose citizens do not wish it to attain the Act's milestones may devote its attention and its resources to issues its citizens deem more worthy; the choice remains at all times with the residents of the State, not with Congress. The State need not expend any funds, or participate in any federal program, if local residents do not view such expenditures or participation as worthwhile. Nor must the State abandon the field if it does not accede to federal direction; the State may continue to regulate the generation and disposal of radioactive waste in any manner its citizens see fit.

The take title provision is of a different character. This * * * offers States, as an alternative to regulating pursuant to Congress' direction, the option of taking title to and possession of the low level radioactive waste generated within their borders and becoming liable for all damages waste generators suffer as a result of the States' failure to do so promptly. In this provision, Congress has crossed the line distinguishing encouragement from coercion. * * *

The take title provision offers state governments a "choice" of either accepting ownership of waste or regulating according to the instructions of Congress. Respondents do not claim that the Constitution would authorize Congress to impose either option as a freestanding requirement. On one hand, the Constitution would not permit Congress simply to transfer radioactive waste from generators to state governments. Such a forced transfer, standing alone, would in principle be no different than a congressionally compelled subsidy from state governments to radioactive waste producers. The same is true of the provision requiring the States to become liable for the generators' damages. Standing alone, this provision would be indistinguishable from an Act of Congress directing the States to assume the liabilities of certain state residents. Either type of federal action would "commandeer" state governments into the service of federal regulatory purposes, and would for this reason be inconsistent with the Constitution's division of authority between federal and state governments. On the other hand, the second alternative held out to state governments — regulating pursuant to Congress' direction — would, standing alone, present a simple command to state governments to implement legislation enacted by Congress. As we have seen, the Constitution does not empower Congress to subject state governments to this type of instruction. * * *

The take title provision appears to be unique. No other federal statute has been cited which offers a state government no option other than that of implementing legislation enacted by Congress. Whether one views the take title provision as lying outside Congress' enumerated powers, or as infringing upon the core of state sovereignty reserved by the Tenth Amendment, the provision is inconsistent with the federal structure of our Government established by the Constitution.

Respondents raise a number of objections to this understanding of the limits of Congress' power.

First, the United States argues that the Constitution's prohibition of congressional directives to state governments can be overcome where the federal interest is sufficiently important to justify state submission. This argument contains a kernel of truth: In determining whether the Tenth Amendment limits the ability of Congress to subject state governments to generally applicable laws, the Court *has* in some cases stated that it will evaluate the strength of federal interests in light of the degree to which such laws would prevent the State from functioning as a sovereign; that is, the extent to which such generally applicable laws would impede a state government's responsibility to represent and be accountable to the citizens of the State. See, *e.g.*, *National League of Cities*; *Garcia*. But whether or not a particularly strong federal interest enables Congress to bring state governments within the orbit of generally applicable *federal* regulation, no Member of the Court has ever suggested that such a federal interest would enable Congress to command a state government to enact *state* regulation. No matter how powerful the federal interest involved, the Constitution simply does not give Congress the authority to require the States to regulate. The Constitution instead gives Congress the authority to regulate matters directly and to pre-empt contrary state regulation. Where a federal interest is sufficiently strong to cause Congress to legislate, it must do so directly; it may not conscript state governments as its agents.

Second, the United States argues that the Constitution does, in some circumstances, permit federal directives to state governments. Various cases are cited for this proposition, but none support it. * * * Federal statutes enforceable in state courts do, in a sense, direct state judges to enforce them, but this sort of federal "direction" of state judges is mandated by the text of the Supremacy Clause. No comparable constitutional provision authorizes Congress to command state legislatures to legislate.

The sited State respondents focus their attention on the process by which the Act was formulated. They correctly observe that public officials representing the State of New York lent their support to the Act's enactment. A Deputy Commissioner of the State's Energy Office testified in favor of the Act. Senator Moynihan of New York spoke in support of the Act on the floor of the Senate. Respondents note that the Act embodies a bargain among the sited and unsited States, a compromise to which New York was a willing participant and from which New York has reaped much benefit. Respondents then pose what appears at first to be a troubling question: How can a federal statute be found an unconstitutional infringement of State sovereignty when state officials consented to the statute's enactment?

The answer follows from an understanding of the fundamental purpose served by our Government's federal structure. The Constitution does not protect the sovereignty of States for the benefit of the States or state governments as abstract political entities, or even for the benefit of the public officials governing the States. To the contrary, the Constitution divides authority between federal and state governments for the protection of individuals. State sovereignty is not just an end in itself: "Rather, federalism secures to citizens the liberties that derive from the diffusion of sovereign power." "Just as the separation and independence of the coordinate Branches of the Federal Government serve to prevent the accumulation of excessive power in any one Branch, a healthy balance of power between the States and the Federal Government will reduce the risk of tyranny and abuse from either front." *Gregory v. Ashcroft*. [Hence, the Court concluded, state officials "cannot consent to the enlargement of the powers of Congress beyond those enumerated in the Constitution."

[Finally, the Court turned to New York's argument that the Act violated the Guarantee Clause. The Court noted that disputes under the clause are ordinarily considered nonjusticiable, see generally Chapter 9, § 1, and concluded that even if the issue were justiciable, "neither the monetary incentives provided by the Act nor the possibility that a State's waste producers may find themselves excluded from the disposal sites of another State can reasonably be said to deny any State a republican form of government. As we have seen, these two incentives represent permissible conditional exercises of Congress' authority under the Spending and Commerce Clauses respectively, in forms that have now grown commonplace. Under each, Congress offers the States a legitimate choice rather than issuing an unavoidable command. The States thereby retain the ability to set their legislative agendas; state government officials remain accountable to the local electorate. The twin threats imposed by the first two challenged provisions of the Act — that New York may miss out on a share of federal spending or that those generating radioactive waste within New York may lose out-of-state disposal outlets — do not pose any realistic risk of altering the form or the method of functioning of New York's government."]

JUSTICE WHITE, with whom **JUSTICE BLACKMUN** and **JUSTICE STEVENS** join, concurring in part and dissenting in part.

Curiously absent from the Court's analysis is any effort to place the take title provision within the overall context of the legislation. * * * Congress could have pre-empted the field by directly regulating the disposal of this waste pursuant to its powers under the Commerce and Spending Clauses, but instead it *unanimously* assented to the States' request for congressional ratification of agreements to which they had acceded. * * * [T]he States wished to take the lead in achieving a solution to this problem and agreed among themselves to the various incentives and penalties implemented by Congress to insure adherence to the various deadlines and goals. The chief executives of the States proposed this approach, and I am unmoved by the Court's vehemence in taking away Congress' authority to sanction a recalcitrant unsited State now that New York has reaped the benefits of the sited States' concessions. * * *

The Court's distinction between a federal statute's regulation of States and private parties for general purposes, as opposed to a regulation solely on the activities of States, is unsupported by our recent Tenth Amendment cases. In no case has the Court rested its holding on such a distinction. Moreover, the Court makes no effort to explain why this purported distinction should affect the analysis of Congress' power under general principles of federalism and the Tenth Amendment. * * * An incursion on state sovereignty hardly seems more constitutionally acceptable if the federal statute that "commands" specific action also applies to private parties. * * *

Ultimately, I suppose, the entire structure of our federal constitutional government can be traced to an interest in establishing checks and balances to prevent the exercise of tyranny against individuals. But these fears seem extremely far distant to me in a situation such as this. We face a crisis of national proportions in the disposal of low-level radioactive waste, and Congress has acceded to the wishes of the States by permitting local decisionmaking rather than imposing a solution from Washington. New York itself participated and supported passage of this legislation at both the gubernatorial and federal representative levels, and then enacted state laws specifically to comply with the deadlines and timetables agreed upon by the States in the 1985 Act. For me, the Court's civics lecture has a decidedly hollow ring at a time when action, rather than rhetoric, is needed to solve a national problem. * * *

[The opinion of **JUSTICE STEVENS**, concurring in part and dissenting in part, is omitted.]

NOTES ON *NEW YORK* AND PROCESS FEDERALISM

1. *Federalism and Prisoners' Dilemmas.* In *New York*, as in many other federalism cases, the states were caught in a game of prisoners' dilemma. The states are all better off collectively if waste disposal sites are available, yet each individual state would prefer to opt out of the disposal process, dumping their waste on other states that have been responsible enough to develop their own waste disposal programs. Without some coordination scheme and some sanction for defectors, the rational strategy is for every state to produce waste and for no one to establish disposal sites. The Court's decision seems to undermine the availability of a national remedy for such dilemmas and, worse, to validate New York's predatory strategy toward states that attempted to implement the statute in good faith.

Justice O'Connor might respond that direct federal regulation can cure the coordination problem, but without interfering with state autonomy. To the extent that the effect of the decision is to require the federal government to displace more state regulation, however, it is unclear how state autonomy is served. In any event, is it likely that New York citizens were any more confused about responsibility for radioactive waste control than about the relative responsibility of the state, federal courts, and Congress regarding school desegregation, or about the responsibility of the state, the federal Environmental Protection Agency, and Congress regarding air pollution?

2. *State Autonomy, Republicanism, and Federalism.* Professor Deborah Merritt defends the anti-commandeering principle generally, and *New York* in particular, as required by the Guarantee Clause of Article IV, which assures the states a republican form of government and, therefore, governmental autonomy.[g] On this reading, state governments exist as organs representative of and accountable to local communities. For citizens of other states (via the national government) to seize control of a state's legislative process destroys the special relationship between the state government and its own citizens. This is important, not because it protects the individual rights of these citizens, but because it eliminates the nexus which gives their community a legal voice. A republican interpretation might provide a more powerful normative basis for O'Connor's opinion. One might wonder, however, whether this is an overly romanticized view of the nature of state governments. Compare Sheryll Cashin,

---

g. See Deborah Jones Merritt, *The Guarantee Clause and State Autonomy: Federalism for a Third Century*, 88 Colum. L. Rev. 1 (1988); Merritt, *Three Faces of Federalism: Finding a Formula for the Future*, 47 Vand. L. Rev. 1563 (1994). For a similar suggestion that Justice O'Connor's opinion in the *Croson* affirmative action case (Chapter 3, § 3B), is essentially republican, see Daniel Farber, Richmond *and Republicanism*, 41 U. Fla. L. Rev. 623 (1989).

Federalism, Welfare Reform, and the Minority Poor: Accounting for the Tyranny of State Majorities, 99 Colum. L. Rev. 552 (1999) (state and, especially, local governments are not responsive to racial minorities and, to the contrary, serve as mechanisms for resegregation).

3. *Structural Limits and Individual Rights.* First Amendment rights are subject to a compelling interest test (Chapter 6), as is the right to be free from racial discrimination (Chapter 3). Apparently, however, the right of state officials to be free from federally mandated enforcement is *absolute*, and would not be subject to modification even where national survival is at stake. The Court's rationale is that there will always be a temptation to bend structural limits in pursuit of whatever a given era regards as compelling national interests. Obviously, however, the same temptation also exists with respect to individual rights. Is the result to place structural limits on a higher plane than fundamental human rights? If, as Justice O'Connor suggests in *New York*, federalism is an indirect method of protecting human rights, why should this indirect mechanism be treated as more sacrosanct than the rights it is designed to protect? (Incidentally, it is far from clear that federalism was initially designed for this purpose, rather than for protecting provincial economic and social interests — most notably slavery — from potential federal interference.)

———

Saikrishna Prakash, *Field Office Federalism*, 79 Va. L. Rev. 1957 (1993). In our editing of *New York v. United States*, we omitted the historical debate between Justices O'Connor and Stevens over the original understanding the Framers had about commandeering. Professor Prakash's article presents a thoughtful review of that complicated topic. We summarize his conclusions, drawn from examination of the American experience during the Articles of Confederation, the drafting of the Constitution at Philadelphia, and the ratification debates:

The Framers were hostile to national commandeering of state legislatures. Unlike the Articles, the Constitution did not give Congress authority to "requisition" state legislatures, directing them to provide the national government with monies and men. A primary reason the Philadelphia Convention rejected the New Jersey Plan was its effort to continue the Articles' requisition system, and proponents of the Virginia Plan such as Edmond Randolph and James Madison made opposition to national requisitioning of state legislatures a central argument against the New Jersey Plan. Hamilton's *Federalist* No. 15 heartily criticized the Articles for their allowing coercion of state governments. Prakash concludes, after a balanced analysis of *The Federalist Papers*, that their authors advertised the Constitution as creating a federal government that acted directly upon individuals, and not states, and that this authority was a substitute for the old and unworkable requisitioning power.

The Framers were open to national commandeering of state magistracy (executive and judicial officers). The Continental Congress under the Articles assumed that it had authority to direct state executive officers, and none of the discussions at Philadelphia disputed this power, in contrast to the sharp dispute about the power to commandeer state legislatures. *The Federalist Papers*, by and large, continued that assumption. Madison, for example, responded to Anti-

Federalist fears of a dual (and doubly oppressive) set of tax collectors by observing that federal tax collection "will generally be made by the officers, and according to the rules, appointed by the several States." *Federalist* No. 45. Hamilton's *Federalist* No. 27 was the most extensive discussion, insisting that the Constitution "will enable the government to employ the ordinary magistracy of each [state], in the execution of its laws." Most speakers at the ratification debates (whose views were recorded) agreed with Madison and Hamilton.

Prakash argues that the distinction was grounded in *sovereignty*: The national government could not regulate the direct voices of state sovereignty (the legislatures), but could commandeer administrative individuals, including state judges as well as executives. Compare Evan Caminker, *State Sovereignty and Subordinacy: May Congress Commandeer State Officers to Implement Federal Law?*, 95 Colum. L. Rev. 1001 (1995) (arguing that Framers expected Congress to be able to commandeer both state legislatures and administrators). Consider how these arguments about the original understanding played out in the next case.

PRINTZ v. UNITED STATES
521 U.S. 898, 117 S.Ct. 2365, 138 L. Ed. 2d 914 (1997)

JUSTICE SCALIA delivered the opinion of the Court.

[The Gun Control Act of 1968 (GCA), 18 U.S.C. § 921 *et seq.*, prohibits firearms dealers from transferring handguns to any person under 21, to anyone not resident in the dealer's state, to convicted felons, and to certain others. In 1993, the Brady Act amended the GCA to require the Attorney General to establish a national instant background check system by November 30, 1998, Pub. L. 103-159, note following 18 U.S.C. § 922, and immediately put in place certain interim provisions until that system becomes operative. Under the interim provisions, a firearms dealer who proposes to transfer a handgun must (1) receive from the transferee a statement (the Brady Form), containing data on the proposed transferee, (2) verify the identity of the transferee, and (3) provide the "chief law enforcement officer" (CLEO) of the transferee's residence with the Brady Form. With some exceptions, the dealer must then wait five business days before consummating the sale, unless the CLEO earlier notifies the dealer that he has no reason to believe the transfer would be illegal. The Brady Act creates two significant alternatives to the foregoing scheme. A dealer may sell a handgun immediately if the purchaser possesses a state handgun permit issued after a background check or if state law provides for an instant background check. In states that have not rendered one of these alternatives applicable to all gun purchasers, CLEOs must "make a reasonable effort to ascertain within 5 business days whether receipt or possession would be in violation of the law." The Act does not require the CLEO to take any particular action if he determines that a pending transaction would be unlawful; he may notify the firearms dealer to that effect, but is not required to do so. If, however, the CLEO notifies a gun dealer that a prospective purchaser is ineligible to receive a handgun, he must, upon request, provide the would-be purchaser with a written statement of the reasons for that determination.]

[Three CLEOs challenged the statute, claiming that] congressional action compelling state officers to execute federal laws is unconstitutional. Because there is no constitutional text speaking to this precise question, the answer to the CLEOs' challenge must be sought in historical understanding and practice, in the structure of the Constitution, and in the jurisprudence of this Court. * * *

Petitioners contend that compelled enlistment of state executive officers for the administration of federal programs is, until very recent years at least, unprecedented. The Government contends, to the contrary, that "the earliest Congresses enacted statutes that required the participation of state officials in the implementation of federal laws." The Government's contention demands our careful consideration, since early congressional enactments "provid[e] 'contemporaneous and weighty evidence' of the Constitution's meaning." Indeed, such "contemporaneous legislative exposition of the Constitution . . ., acquiesced in for a long term of years, fixes the construction to be given its provisions." *Myers v. United States*, 272 U.S. 52, 175 (1926) (citing numerous cases). Conversely if, as petitioners contend, earlier Congresses avoided use of this highly attractive power, we would have reason to believe that the power was thought not to exist.

The Government observes that statutes enacted by the first Congresses required state courts to record applications for citizenship, to transmit abstracts of citizenship applications and other naturalization records to the Secretary of State, and to register aliens seeking naturalization and issue certificates of registry. * * * Other statutes of that era apparently or at least arguably required state courts to perform functions unrelated to naturalization, such as resolving controversies between a captain and the crew of his ship concerning the seaworthiness of the vessel, hearing the claims of slave owners who had apprehended fugitive slaves and issuing certificates authorizing the slave's forced removal to the State from which he had fled, taking proof of the claims of Canadian refugees who had assisted the United States during the Revolutionary War, and ordering the deportation of alien enemies in times of war.

These early laws establish, at most, that the Constitution was originally understood to permit imposition of an obligation on state *judges* to enforce federal prescriptions, insofar as those prescriptions related to matters appropriate for the judicial power. [But such laws are consistent with the Supremacy Clause, which explicitly requires state *judges* to give effect to federal law in their courts. Indeed, the existence of many statutes commandeering state judges contrasts with virtually no statute commandeering state administrators, suggesting an absence of congressional power to impose obligations on the latter.]

In addition to early legislation, the Government also appeals to other sources we have usually regarded as indicative of the original understanding of the Constitution. It points to portions of *The Federalist* which reply to criticisms that Congress's power to tax will produce two sets of revenue officers — for example, "Brutus's" assertion in his letter to the *New York Journal* of December 13, 1787, that the Constitution "opens a door to the appointment of a swarm of revenue and excise officers to prey upon the honest and industrious part of the community, eat up their substance, and riot on the spoils of the country."

"Publius" responded that Congress will probably "make use of the State officers and State regulations, for collecting" federal taxes, *The Federalist* No. 36 (Hamilton), and predicted that "the eventual collection [of internal revenue] under the immediate authority of the Union, will generally be made by the officers, and according to the rules, appointed by the several States," *id.*, No. 45 (J. Madison). The Government also invokes the *Federalist*'s more general observations that the Constitution would "enable the [national] government to employ the ordinary magistracy of each [State] in the execution of its laws," *id.*, No. 27, at 176 (A. Hamilton), and that it was "extremely probable that in other instances, particularly in the organization of the judicial power, the officers of the States will be clothed in the correspondent authority of the Union," *id.*, No. 45, at 292 (J. Madison). But none of these statements necessarily implies — what is the critical point here — that Congress could impose these responsibilities without the consent of the States. They appear to rest on the natural assumption that the States would consent to allowing their officials to assist the Federal Government, an assumption proved correct by the extensive mutual assistance the States and Federal Government voluntarily provided one another in the early days of the Republic, including voluntary federal implementation of state law, see, e.g., Act of Apr. 2, 1790, ch. 5, § 1, 1 Stat. 106 (directing federal tax collectors and customs officers to assist in enforcing state inspection laws).

Another passage of *The Federalist* reads as follows:

> It merits particular attention . . ., that the laws of the Confederacy as to the *enumerated* and *legitimate* objects of its jurisdiction will become the SUPREME LAW of the land; to the observance of which all officers, legislative, executive, and judicial in each State will be bound by the sanctity of an oath. Thus, the legislatures, courts, and magistrates, of the respective members will be incorporated into the operations of the national government as far as its just and constitutional authority extends; and will be rendered auxiliary to the enforcement of its laws.

The Federalist No. 27 (A. Hamilton) (emphasis in original). [Justice Scalia rejected any implication that this passage supports any federal commandeering of state executive officers, as Justice Souter maintained in his dissenting opinion.] First, the consequences in question ("incorporated into the operations of the national government" and "rendered auxiliary to the enforcement of its laws") are said in the quoted passage to flow automatically from the officers' oath to observe the "the laws of the Confederacy as to the enumerated and legitimate objects of its jurisdiction." Thus, if the passage means that state officers must take an active role in the implementation of federal law, it means that they must do so without the necessity for a congressional directive that they implement it. But no one has ever thought, and no one asserts in the present litigation, that that is the law. The second problem with Justice Souter's reading is that it makes state legislatures subject to federal direction. (The passage in question, after all, does not include legislatures merely incidentally, as by referring to "all state officers"; it refers to legislatures specifically and first of all.) We have held, however, that state legislatures are not subject to federal direction. *New York v. United States.*

These problems are avoided, of course, if the calculatedly vague consequences the passage recites — "incorporated into the operations of the national government" and "rendered auxiliary to the enforcement of its laws" — are taken to refer to nothing more (or less) than the duty owed to the National Government, on the part of all state officials, to enact, enforce, and interpret state law in such fashion as not to obstruct the operation of federal law, and the attendant reality that all state actions constituting such obstruction, even legislative acts, are ipso facto invalid. * * *

[Justice Scalia next examined the most relevant constitutional principle — the assurance that the states retained "a residuary and inviolable sovereignty," *The Federalist* No. 39 (J. Madison), a principle reflected in the Constitution's prohibition on any involuntary reduction or combination of a State's territory, Art. IV, § 3; the Judicial Power Clause, Art. III, § 2, and the Privileges and Immunities Clause, Art. IV, § 2, which speak of the "Citizens" of the States; Article V, which requires the votes of three-fourths of the States to amend the Constitution; the Guarantee Clause, Art. IV, § 4, which "presupposes the continued existence of the states and . . . those means and instrumentalities which are the creation of their sovereign and reserved rights," *Helvering v. Gerhardt*, 304 U.S. 405, 414-415 (1938); and of course the enumeration of congressional powers in Article I and reservation of other powers to the states in the Tenth Amendment. Justice Scalia quoted Justice Kennedy's concurring opinion in *U.S. Term Limits* for its claim that the Framers' great innovation was that "our citizens would have two political capacities, one state and one federal, each protected from incursion by the other" — "a legal system unprecedented in form and design, establishing two orders of government, each with its own direct relationship, its own privity, its own set of mutual rights and obligations to the people who sustain it and are governed by it." See also *The Federalist* No. 51, at 323. "The power of the Federal Government would be augmented immeasurably if it were able to impress into its service — and at no cost to itself — the police officers of the 50 States," reasoned Justice Scalia.]

The dissent of course resorts to the last, best hope of those who defend ultra vires congressional action, the Necessary and Proper Clause. * * * When a "La[w] . . . for carrying into Execution" the Commerce Clause violates the principle of state sovereignty reflected in the various constitutional provisions we mentioned earlier, it is not a "La[w] . . . proper for carrying into Execution the Commerce Clause," and is thus, in the words of *The Federalist*, "merely [an] ac[t] of usurpation" which "deserve[s] to be treated as such." *The Federalist* No. 33 (A. Hamilton). We in fact answered the dissent's Necessary and Proper Clause argument in *New York*: "[E]ven where Congress has the authority under the Constitution to pass laws requiring or prohibiting certain acts, it lacks the power directly to compel the States to require or prohibit those acts. . . . [T]he Commerce Clause, for example, authorizes Congress to regulate interstate commerce directly; it does not authorize Congress to regulate state governments' regulation of interstate commerce." * * *

The Government also maintains that requiring state officers to perform discrete, ministerial tasks specified by Congress does not violate the principle of *New York* because it does not diminish the accountability of state or federal officials. This argument fails even on its own terms. By forcing state governments to absorb the financial burden of implementing a federal regulatory program, Members of Congress can take credit for "solving" problems without having to ask their constituents to pay for the solutions with higher federal taxes. And even when the States are not forced to absorb the costs of implementing a federal program, they are still put in the position of taking the blame for its burdensomeness and for its defects. See Merritt, *Three Faces of Federalism: Finding a Formula for the Future*, 47 Vand. L. Rev. 1563, 1580, n.65 (1994). Under the present law, for example, it will be the CLEO and not some federal official who stands between the gun purchaser and immediate possession of his gun. And it will likely be the CLEO, not some federal official, who will be blamed for any error (even one in the designated federal database) that causes a purchaser to be mistakenly rejected. * * *

Finally, the Government puts forward a cluster of arguments that can be grouped under the heading: "The Brady Act serves very important purposes, is most efficiently administered by CLEOs during the interim period, and places a minimal and only temporary burden upon state officers." There is considerable disagreement over the extent of the burden, but we need not pause over that detail. Assuming all the mentioned factors were true, they might be relevant if we were evaluating whether the incidental application to the States of a federal law of general applicability excessively interfered with the functioning of state governments. See, e.g., *Usery* (overruled by *Garcia*) * * *. But where, as here, it is the whole object of the law to direct the functioning of the state executive, and hence to compromise the structural framework of dual sovereignty, such a "balancing" analysis is inappropriate. It is the very principle of separate state sovereignty that such a law offends, and no comparative assessment of the various interests can overcome that fundamental defect. * * *

We adhere to that principle today, and conclude categorically, as we concluded categorically in *New York*: "The Federal Government may not compel the States to enact or administer a federal regulatory program." The mandatory obligation imposed on CLEOs to perform background checks on prospective handgun purchasers plainly runs afoul of that rule. [Accordingly, the Court invalidated those parts of the Brady Act requiring CLEOs to make background checks and to accept notice of the contents of, and a copy of, the completed Brady Form, which the firearms dealer is required to provide to him. The other provisions of the Brady Act have no effect on the plaintiff CLEOs, and their constitutionality is not before the Court.]

[We omit the concurring opinions of **JUSTICES O'CONNOR** and **THOMAS** and the dissenting opinion of **JUSTICE BREYER**.]

JUSTICE STEVENS, joined by **JUSTICE SOUTER**, **JUSTICE GINSBURG**, and **JUSTICE BREYER**, dissenting. * * *

There is not a clause, sentence, or paragraph in the entire text of the Constitution of the United States that supports the proposition that a local police officer can ignore a command contained in a statute enacted by Congress pursuant to an express delegation of power enumerated in Article I. [This was no accident, Justice Stevens argued, because a key goal of the Constitution was to empower the national government.]

Indeed, the historical materials strongly suggest that the Founders intended to enhance the capacity of the federal government by empowering it — as a part of the new authority to make demands directly on individual citizens — to act through local officials. Hamilton made clear that the new Constitution, "by extending the authority of the federal head to the individual citizens of the several States, will enable the government to employ the ordinary magistracy of each, in the execution of its laws." *The Federalist* No. 27, at 180. * * *

More specifically, during the debates concerning the ratification of the Constitution, it was assumed that state agents would act as tax collectors for the federal government. Opponents of the Constitution had repeatedly expressed fears that the new federal government's ability to impose taxes directly on the citizenry would result in an overbearing presence of federal tax collectors in the States. Federalists rejoined that this problem would not arise because, as Hamilton explained, "the United States . . . will make use of the State officers and State regulations for collecting" certain taxes. [*The Federalist*] No. 36. Similarly, Madison made clear that the new central government's power to raise taxes directly from the citizenry would "not be resorted to, except for supplemental purposes of revenue . . . and that the eventual collection, under the immediate authority of the Union, will generally be made by the officers . . . appointed by the several States." *Id.*, No. 45. * * *

Bereft of support in the history of the founding, the Court rests its conclusion on the claim that there is little evidence the National Government actually exercised such a power in the early years of the Republic. This reasoning is misguided in principle and in fact. * * * [W]e have never suggested that the failure of the early Congresses to address the scope of federal power in a particular area or to exercise a particular authority was an argument against its existence. That position, if correct, would undermine most of our post-New Deal Commerce Clause jurisprudence. [More important, the early statutes delegating duties to state judges, such as immigration and naturalization duties, are on point, because in such statutes state judges were performing the same sort of reporting, checking, and housekeeping duties that the sheriffs must do under the Brady Act. E.g., Act of Mar. 26, 1790, ch. 3, § 1, 1 Stat. 103 (requiring state courts to consider immigration applications, specifying that the state courts "shall administer" an oath of loyalty to the United States, and that "the clerk of such court shall record such application"); Act of July 20, 1790, ch. 29, § 3, 1 Stat. 132-133 (requiring state courts to serve, functionally, like contemporary regulatory agencies in certifying the seaworthiness of vessels).]

* * * [T]he majority's opinion consists almost entirely of arguments against the substantial evidence weighing in opposition to its view; the Court's ruling is strikingly lacking in affirmative support. Absent even a modicum of textual foundation for its judicially crafted constitutional rule, there should be a presumption that if the Framers had actually intended such a rule, at least one of them would have mentioned it. * * *

Indeed, the presumption of validity that supports all congressional enactments has added force with respect to policy judgments concerning the impact of a federal statute upon the respective States. The majority points to nothing suggesting that the political safeguards of federalism identified in *Garcia* need be supplemented by a rule, grounded in neither constitutional history nor text, flatly prohibiting the National Government from enlisting state and local officials in the implementation of federal law. * * *

[JUSTICE SOUTER explained in his separate dissenting opinion that his vote was driven by his reading of *The Federalist*.]

Hamilton in No. 27 first notes that because the new Constitution would authorize the National Government to bind individuals directly through national law, it could "employ the ordinary magistracy of each [State] in the execution of its laws." *The Federalist* No. 27 (A. Hamilton). Were he to stop here, he would not necessarily be speaking of anything beyond the possibility of cooperative arrangements by agreement. But he then addresses the combined effect of the proposed Supremacy Clause, U.S. Const., Art. VI, cl. 2, and state officers' oath requirement, U.S. Const., Art. VI, cl. 3, and he states that "the Legislatures, Courts and Magistrates of the respective members will be incorporated into the operations of the national government, *as far as its just and constitutional authority extends*; and will be rendered auxiliary to the enforcement of its laws." *The Federalist* No. 27 (emphasis in original). The natural reading of this language is not merely that the officers of the various branches of state governments may be employed in the performance of national functions; Hamilton says that the state governmental machinery "will be incorporated" into the Nation's operation, and because the "auxiliary" status of the state officials will occur because they are "bound by the sanctity of an oath," *id.*, I take him to mean that their auxiliary functions will be the products of their obligations thus undertaken to support federal law, not of their own, or the States', unfettered choices. [In *Federalist* Nos. 36 and 45, Hamilton indicated that the national government can require state officials to assist in the collection of federal revenues. See also *Federalist* No. 44 (Madison).]

In the light of all these passages, I cannot persuade myself that the statements from No. 27 speak of anything less than the authority of the National Government, when exercising an otherwise legitimate power (the commerce power, say), to require state "auxiliaries" to take appropriate action. To be sure, it does not follow that any conceivable requirement may be imposed on any state official. I continue to agree, for example, that Congress may not require a state legislature to enact a regulatory scheme and that *New York v. United States* was rightly decided (even though I now believe its dicta went too far toward immunizing state administration as well as state enactment of such a scheme from congressional mandate); after all, the essence of legislative power, within the limits of legislative jurisdiction, is a discretion not subject to command. But insofar as national law would require nothing from a state officer inconsistent with the power proper to his branch of tripartite state government (say, by obligating a state judge to exercise law enforcement powers), I suppose that the reach of federal law as Hamilton described it would not be exceeded, cf. *Garcia* (without precisely delineating the outer limits of Congress's Commerce Clause power, finding that the statute at issue was not "destructive of state sovereignty"). * * *

NOTES ON *PRINTZ*, FEDERALISM, AND ORIGINAL MEANING

Printz illustrates the notion suggested by *U.S. Term Limits*: the importance of starting points. The dissenters presume that when Congress acts within its Commerce Clause power, it is presumptively lawful; the burden is on those challenging the congressional action. The majority presumes that when Congress regulates the states directly, there is cause for concern; the burden is on those defending the congressional action. How do you choose the baseline? The precedents (*FERC v. Mississippi* and *New York v. United States*) cut both ways and are not exactly on point. Some other possibilities:

1. *Constitutional Structure and the Values of Federalism.* Note Justice Scalia's core principle — the integrity of state governments — is nowhere set forth in the Constitution, but is teased out of various clauses in the document. Is it fair to compare that methodology with Justice Douglas' teasing a right of privacy out of the *penumbras* of the Bill of Rights (*Griswold*, Chapter 5, § 4A)? At the very least, however, the Constitution unmistakably creates a federal arrangement. Is it threatened by the kind of regulation invalidated in *Printz*?

Are the federalism values identified in our Note at the beginning of this chapter implicated in this kind of commandeering? How might liberty be threatened? Participatory democracy at the local level? Accountability? Efficiency? Justice Thomas's concurring opinion raised the link between the federalism and Second Amendment (right to keep and bear arms) issues in this case. In *District of Columbia v. Heller*, 128 S.Ct. 2783 (2008), the Court recognized an individual right of law-abiding citizens to gun ownership for self-defense. The majority in *Heller* was similar to the one in *Printz* (with Roberts and Alito replacing Rehnquist and O'Connor, respectively), and the four dissenters were the same. Does this right "bear" any relevance to the federalism problem?

Do the values of federalism support a bright-line rule such as that adopted by the Court: No commandeering of state officers, *period.* Or would these values support a balancing approach? Vicki Jackson, *Federalism and the Uses and Limits of Law:* Printz *and Principle*, 111 Harv. L. Rev. 2180, 2200-05 (1998), argues that the Constitution supports clear lines of accountability but sharply disputes, from the perspective of constitutional text and principles, the Court's nondeferential bright-line approach.

2. *Political Philosophy: The Nature of State Sovereignty.* The majority and dissenting Justices disagreed about the nature of federal and state sovereignty: Justice Scalia emphasized retained state sovereignty, Justice Stevens the supervening national sovereignty. Note that Justice Scalia did not follow Justice Thomas' theory in *U.S. Term Limits* and, instead, quoted Justice Kennedy (the only Justice in the majority for both cases). Kennedy's approach rejects the asymmetry suggested in *McCulloch* and supports an active role for the Court when either national or state sovereignties seek to encroach upon core features of the other. Does *Printz* represent a repudiation of the *McCulloch-U.S. Term Limits* idea that sovereignty resides wholly in We the People?

Note what is largely absent in the debate about state sovereignty: the *McCulloch-Garcia* argument that because the states are formally represented in the national government, the Court should leave the protection of their sovereignty to the political process. Justice Stevens makes this point in dissent, but the Court ignores it. Justice Breyer's dissent (which we omitted) makes the point that most federations in the world allow the national government to delegate duties to provincial governments, and some federations (the European Community, Switzerland) provide that the constituent states and not the national government will ordinarily implement national laws and regulations.

3. *Original Meaning.* Note also the methodological shift from the *Garcia-National League of Cities* debate to the debate among the Justices in *Printz* and *U.S. Term Limits.* The Justices in the latter cases de-emphasize or ignore the legal-process type arguments of institutional competence that were debated in the former cases. Original meaning arguments have replaced the legal process arguments. All nine Justices make such arguments in *Printz*; original meaning is the keystone of Justice Scalia's opinion for the Court and for Justice Stevens' lead dissent, and it is the only reason Justice Souter believed *New York v. United States* (which he joined) was not applicable. Note that Professor Prakash's leading article, *supra*, concludes that *New York* is correct, but *Printz* is wrong under the original meaning standard.

Does the debate in *Printz* surmount — or does it confirm — the theoretical difficulties with originalism raised in Chapter 2, § 3A2, namely: (1) for an old document like the Constitution, all the questions are counterfactual — *i.e.*, we attribute conclusions to long-dead people "as if" they had anticipated current states of affairs; (2) there is no reason to believe that the Framers "intended" us to be bound by their original intent or, even if so, by what level of intent (specific intent or general purpose); (3) even if we can "know" how Madison and Hamilton (authors of the always-quoted *Federalist Papers*) would have answered the interpretive puzzle, there is no reliable way to attribute the views of these authors (of blatant propaganda documents!) to other Framers or the state ratifying conventions?

———

Reno v. Condon, 528 U.S. 141 (2000). Congress enacted the Driver's Privacy Protection Act of 1994 (DPPA), 18 U.S.C. §§ 2721-2725 (as amended), to prevent state departments of motor vehicles from disclosing drivers' personal information to third parties, unless drivers have affirmatively consented to such disclosure. South Carolina, whose law allowed such personal information to be available to third parties, challenged the DPPA as violating constitutional principles of federalism. The Supreme Court, in an opinion by **Chief Justice Rehnquist**, unanimously rejected the challenge.

The Court first ruled that the law was within Congress' Commerce Clause powers, because the personal information the DPPA regulates is a "thing in interstate commerce," and therefore is a proper exercise of Congress' Commerce Clause powers under *Lopez.* See also The Lottery Case (§ 2 of this chapter). "The motor vehicle information which the States have historically sold is used by insurers, manufacturers, direct marketers, and others engaged in interstate commerce to contact drivers with customized solicitations. The information is also used in the stream of interstate commerce by various public and private entities for matters related to interstate motoring. Because drivers' information is, in this context, an article of commerce, its sale or release into the interstate stream of business is sufficient to support congressional regulation. We therefore need not address the Government's alternative argument that the States' individual, intrastate activities in gathering, maintaining, and distributing drivers' personal information has a sufficiently substantial impact on interstate commerce to create a constitutional base for federal legislation." (The Court did not consider it necessary to address the government's argument that the DPPA was also enacted pursuant to Congress' power to enforce the Fourteenth Amendment.)

A statute properly enacted under Congress' Commerce Clause power might still violate the Tenth Amendment, which was construed in *New York* and *Printz* to limit Congress' authority to direct state governmental activities. And the DPPA did impose new duties on state governments, with possible criminal penalties for violations. But the Court ruled that the law did not fall afoul the principles of *New York* or *Printz*. "We think, instead, that this case is governed by our decision in *South Carolina v. Baker*. In *Baker*, we upheld a statute that prohibited States from issuing unregistered bonds because the law 'regulate[d] state activities,' rather than 'seek[ing] to control or influence the manner in which States regulate private parties.' We further noted:

> The NGA [National Governor's Association] nonetheless contends that § 310 has commandeered the state legislative and administrative process because many state legislatures had to amend a substantial number of statutes in order to issue bonds in registered form and because state officials had to devote substantial effort to determine how best to implement a registered bond system. Such "commandeering" is, however, an inevitable consequence of regulating a state activity. Any federal regulation demands compliance. That a State wishing to engage in certain activity must take administrative and sometimes legislative action to comply with federal standards regulating that activity is a commonplace that presents no constitutional defect.

"Like the statute at issue in *Baker*, the DPPA does not require the States in their sovereign capacity to regulate their own citizens. The DPPA regulates the States as the owners of databases. It does not require the South Carolina Legislature to enact any laws or regulations, and it does not require state officials to assist in the enforcement of federal statutes regulating private individuals. We accordingly conclude that the DPPA is consistent with the constitutional principles enunciated in *New York* and *Printz*."

―――――

Jinks v. Richland County, 538 U.S. 456 (2003). Section 1367 of the U.S. Judicial Code provides that federal courts may under specified circumstances exercise supplemental jurisdiction over claims for which there is no independent basis for federal jurisdiction, so long as there is at least one claim that can be the basis for such jurisdiction. Section 1367(c) in most cases requires the federal court to dismiss supplemental claims if it dismisses all jurisdiction-conferring claims. Because Congress was mindful that the state statute of limitations might have expired by that point, § 1367(d) provides a tolling rule: "The period of limitations for any claim asserted under subsection (a), and for any other claim in the same action that is voluntarily dismissed at the same time as or after the dismissal of the claim under subsection (a), shall be tolled while the claim is pending and for a period of 30 days after it is dismissed unless State law provides for a longer tolling period."

Susan Jinks sued Richland County and officials of its detention center for wrongful death and civil rights violations grounded upon her husband's death in their custody. The defendants won summary judgment on the civil rights claim, the only one for which there was an independent ground for federal jurisdiction, and the federal court dismissed the state claims; they had been allowed pursuant to the court's supplemental jurisdiction, and § 1367(c) required that they be dismissed. Jinks refiled her wrongful death claims in state court and won a jury verdict. The South Carolina Supreme Court reversed, on the ground that the case was time-barred. The court ruled that § 1367(d) did not preempt the state statute of limitations, as it was an unconstitutional exercise of federal power. The Supreme Court unanimously reversed, in an opinion by **Justice Scalia**.

Justice Scalia rejected each of Richland County's three asserted reasons for invalidating § 1367(d). Richland first argued that § 1367(d) exceeded the enumerated powers of Congress. "We agree with petitioner and intervenor United States, however, that § 1367(d) is necessary and proper for carrying into execution Congress's power '[t]o constitute Tribunals inferior to the supreme Court,' U.S. Const., Art. I, § 8, cl. 9, and to assure that those tribunals may fairly and efficiently exercise '[t]he judicial Power of the United States,' Art. III, § 1. As to 'necessity': The federal courts can assuredly exist and function in the absence of § 1367(d), but we long ago rejected the view that the Necessary and Proper Clause demands that an Act of Congress be '*absolutely* necessary' to the exercise of an enumerated power. See *McCulloch*. Rather, it suffices that § 1367(d) is 'conducive to the due administration of justice' in federal court, and is 'plainly adapted' to that end. Section 1367(d) is conducive to the administration of justice because it provides an alternative to the unsatisfactory options that federal judges faced when they decided whether to retain jurisdiction over supplemental state-law claims that might be time barred in state court." Justice Scalia also found § 1367(d) conducive to the administration of justice for another reason — it eliminated an impediment to plaintiffs' access to federal courts in cases where there were closely related state and federal claims. Finally, there was "no suggestion by either of the parties that Congress enacted § 1367(d) as a 'pretext' for 'the accomplishment of objects not entrusted to the [federal] government,' *McCulloch*, nor is the connection between § 1367(d) and Congress's authority over the federal courts so attenuated as to undermine the enumeration of powers set forth in Article I, § 8, cf. *Lopez*; *Morrison*."

Invoking *Printz*, Richland County also maintained that § 1367(d) was not a proper exercise of Congress's Article I powers, because it intruded on state sovereignty. "Respondent views § 1367(d)'s tolling rule as a regulation of state-court 'procedure,' and contends that Congress may not, consistent with the Constitution, prescribe procedural rules for state courts' adjudication of purely state-law claims. See, e.g., Bellia, Federal Regulation of State Court Procedures, 110 Yale L. J. 947 (2001); *Congressional Authority to Require State Courts to Use Certain Procedures in Products Liability Cases*, 13 Op. Off. Legal Counsel 372, 373-374 (1989) (stating that 'potential constitutional questions' arise when Congress 'attempts to prescribe directly the state court procedures to be followed in products liability cases'). Assuming for the sake of argument that a principled dichotomy can be drawn, for purposes of determining whether an Act of Congress is 'proper,' between federal laws that regulate state-court 'procedure' and laws that change the 'substance' of state-law rights of action, we do not think that state-law limitations periods fall into the category of 'procedure' immune from congressional regulation." Justice Scalia noted that for *Erie* purposes, statutes of limitations are considered substantive. Without suggesting that Congress can set the rules of state court procedure, he found no Tenth Amendment violation.

Richland County also argued that the Eleventh Amendment barred application of § 1367(d) to lawsuits brought against a State's political subdivisions. This claim was squarely precluded by precedent, and the Court dismissed it summarily. "Although we have held that Congress lacks authority under Article I to override a *State*'s immunity from suit in its own courts, see *Alden v. Maine*, it may subject a *municipality* to suit in state court if that is done pursuant to a valid exercise of its enumerated powers [*Alden*]."

NOTE ON FEDERAL REGULATION OF STATE PROCESS

Applying much the same analysis as *Jinks*, the Court earlier ruled that Congress has the authority to impose an evidentiary privilege on state as well as federal courts if that privilege is "necessary and proper" to the operation of a federal statutory program seeking to identify and eliminate hazardous road conditions. *Pierce County v. Guillen*, 537 U.S. 129 (2003). But the Court interpreted the federal statute stingily, based upon a presumption that evidentiary privileges should be narrowly construed. As in *Jinks*, this might bespeak a constitutional concern that Congress does not have plenary authority to regulate state court procedures. Could Congress require state courts to follow the following rules as a matter of uniformity in national adjudicatory practice?

(A) A rule barring cross-examination of a rape victim based upon her or his previous sexual history. Assume Congress gathers extensive evidence showing that cross-examination of this sort has little bearing on the facts of rape, has a prejudicial effect on jury deliberations, and deters rape victims from complaining to authorities or supporting prosecution of their assailants.

(B) A rule requiring state courts to follow the liberal discovery rules adopted by the U.S. Supreme Court for federal civil practice, Fed. R. Civ. P. 26-37. Assume Congress gathers extensive evidence showing that the liberality of the Federal Rules produces greater fairness in civil litigation and facilitates settlement. There is some evidence that, when state courts allow much less discovery than the Federal Rules, plaintiffs will forum-shop their cases to other states that do have liberal discovery rules — thereby shifting litigation to fora less appropriate to their resolution.

(C) A rule requiring states to have jury trials in all cases arising under the common law or under statutes creating common law-type claims for relief (tort, contract, property, etc.). The Seventh Amendment does not apply to the states, and Congress finds that the legitimacy and efficiency added to civil adjudication justifies a statutory jury trial right.

PROBLEM 7-6
WHAT PRECEDENTS OUGHT TO BE OVERRULED NEXT?

Between *New York v. United States* and *Printz*, the Supreme Court has revived and apparently rethought federalism as a limit on congressional power. In light of this rethinking, which precedents should now be overruled? Make up a list — not based upon what you want, but upon a close reading of the new precedents. Some candidates for rethinking or overruling:

- *FERC v. Mississippi*, upholding a federal statute requiring — or commandeering — state regulatory agencies to initiate proceedings to develop energy conservation rules. Justice O'Connor dissented from the judgment in an opinion that reads like a roadmap for *Gregory*, *New York*, and *Printz*.

- *Garcia*. *Printz* and *New York* politely ignored *Garcia*, which is oftentimes a prelude to an overruling ("We have already retreated from the force of this precedent, and consistency with our recent decisions compels us, however reluctantly, to overrule * * * "). If *Garcia* falls, does *South Carolina v. Baker* fall too?

- *South Dakota v. Dole*. Does this broad authorization for congressional spending conditions undercut the other precedents — or is conditional spending different along some constitutional principle or policy?

- *Missouri v. Holland*. Justice Holmes's reasoning falls apart under the scrutiny of scholars like Nicholas Rosenkranz, and the holding seems strongly inconsistent with the New Federalism.

- *Darby et al*. The Tenth Amendment no longer seems like the "truism" *Darby* said it was. Should *Darby* or *Wickard* be revisited? *McClung*? *Perez*?

- *McCulloch v. Maryland*. It strikes us as doubtful that the Court would revisit the holdings of this constitutional chestnut, but its logic — or dicta — might be questioned, including Chief Justice Marshall's expansive view of the Necessary and Proper Clause,[h] or his suggestion that the national government can tax or regulate the states in ways the states cannot do to the national government (see *Garcia*). How about *U.S. Term Limits*? Has its baseline been rejected in *Printz*?

Would general principles of stare decisis save these decisions? Compare the stare decisis debate in *Planned Parenthood v. Casey* (Chapter 5, § 4B).

DOES ORIGINAL MEANING CONSTRAIN?
LESSONS FROM THE FEDERALISM CASES

Professor Peter Smith read all the Court's recent federalism decisions and coded for Justices' deployment of original meaning sources. *Sources of Federalism: An Empirical Analysis of the Court's Quest for Original Meaning*, 52 UCLA L. Rev. 217 (2004). He found that the Federalism Five (Rehnquist,

---

h. See John Yoo, McCulloch v. Maryland, in *Constitutional Stupidities/Constitutional Tragedies* (William Eskridge, Jr. & Sanford Levinson eds. 1998).

O'Connor, Scalia, Kennedy, Thomas) were much more likely to cite the Anti-Federalists for their affirmative statements than the Dissenting Four (Stevens, Souter, Ginsburg, Breyer). The Five positively cited defenders of the Constitution 81 times when they made pro-states rights statements and only 8 times when they made pro-national power statements. Conversely, the Four positively cited defenders of the Constitution 17 times when they made pro-states rights statements and 78 times when they made pro-national power statements. Is this evidence that the Justices are not using the historical materials in a dispassionate manner (Professor Smith's conclusion)? Or is there another reason for the disparity in treatment? Is using the sources of original meaning like looking out over the crowd and picking out your friends?

SECTION 6. NATIONALIST LIMITATIONS UPON STATE REGULATORY AUTHORITY

A. CONSTITUTIONAL PRINCIPLES, POLICIES, AND HISTORY

A central purpose of the Constitution was not just to authorize the federal government to deal with national problems, but also to disable the states from disrupting the plan of a national union. There are at least three policy concerns with state rulemaking embodied in the Constitution. First is the *uniformity policy*: Certain policies need to be uniform throughout the country, and allowing the states to adopt varying regulations would be counterproductive. One of the problems with the Articles of Confederation was that the country did not speak with one voice when it needed to do so. Second, the *free trade policy* seeks to integrate the states into one national marketplace, a "federal free trade unit." The Articles of Confederation allegedly contributed to economic "Balkanization," which is inefficient for the nation and "We the People." Third, and relatedly, is the *policy to avoid prisoners' dilemmas*. There was some fear that the individual states might discriminate against other states or their citizens in their laws and regulations. Once one state discriminated against another, the next state would retaliate, perhaps even raising the stakes into a full-blown trade war. This is the classic prisoners' dilemma, whereby the players left to their own devices will make a series of choices that leaves everyone worse off.

These policies suggested to the Framers the need to prevent the states from taking a variety of actions they otherwise might want to take. Apart from the Reconstruction Amendments, the constitutional text provides three types of explicit limits on the states.[a] First, the Constitution expressly prohibits the states from enacting certain types of legislation. Thus, Article I, § 10 prevents the states from entering into treaties, coining money, engaging in war, and many other activities. Another total prohibition is found in Article IV, § 2, which bars the states from depriving citizens of other states of their privileges and immunities.

---

a. See Martin Redish & Shane Nugent, *The Dormant Commerce Clause and the Constitutional Balance of Federalism*, 1987 Duke L.J. 569, 591-92.

Second, the Constitution contains certain waivable prohibitions on state action. Article I, § 10, cl. 2 provides that "[n]o State shall, without the consent of Congress, lay any Imposts or Duties on Imports or Exports, except what may be absolutely necessary for executing its inspection Laws." Clause 3 provides that "[n]o State shall, without the Consent of Congress, lay any Duty of Tonnage." For these potentially disruptive activities, the states may act only if authorized by Congress. Also under Clause 3, states may not enter into "Agreement[s] or Compact[s]" with one another without the consent of Congress.

Finally, the constitutional text forecloses state action where it clashes with national regulation. So long as Congress is acting under its enumerated powers, its statutes are superior to state law, according to the Supremacy Clause of Article VI. This is termed federal *preemption* of state law. State law is preempted if it is (1) contrary to the provisions of a federal statute, (2) inconsistent with federal policy, or (3) in an area wholly occupied by federal law.

Together, the Commerce Clause and the Supremacy Clause give Congress the power to override state barriers to interstate trade, as well as the ability to pursue other regulatory goals. But suppose a state attempts to exclude interstate commerce in the *absence* of federal legislation? In that situation, the Commerce Clause is "dormant" — Congress hasn't made active use of its power. But even in this dormant condition, according to longstanding doctrine, the Commerce Clause creates an implicit barrier to protectionist state laws. The origins of the "Dormant Commerce Clause" are something of a mystery. James Madison wrote in 1829 that he considered the Commerce Clause to be "a negative and preventive provision against injustice among the States themselves, rather than as a power to be used for the positive purpose of the General Government." Letter from Madison to J.C. Cabell (13 Feb. 1829), reproduced in III Farrand 478.[b] Consider an even earlier suggestion.

GIBBONS v. OGDEN
22 U.S. (9 Wheat.) 1, 6 L.Ed. 23 (1824)

[In a portion of **CHIEF JUSTICE MARSHALL**'s opinion for the Court that we omitted from § 2 of this chapter, the Chief Justice addressed the argument that] although the power of Congress to regulate commerce with foreign nations, and among the several states, be co-extensive with the subject itself, and have no other limits than are prescribed in the constitution, yet the states may severally exercise the same power, within their respective jurisdictions. In support of this argument, it is said that they possessed it as an inseparable attribute of sovereignty, before the formation of the constitution, and still retain it, except so far as they have surrendered it by that instrument; that this principle results from the nature of the government, and is secured by the tenth amendment; that an affirmative grant of power is not exclusive, unless in its own nature it be such that the continued exercise of it by the former possessor is inconsistent with the grant, and that this is not of that description.

---

b. Note that this letter was written a generation after the Founding, and that Madison does not say the *Court*, rather than *Congress*, should enforce this negative feature of the Commerce Clause.

The appellant, conceding these postulates, except the last, contends, that full power to regulate a particular subject, implies the whole power, and leaves no residuum; that a grant of the whole is incompatible with the existence of a right in another to any part of it. * * *

The grant of the power to lay and collect taxes is, like the power to regulate commerce, made in general terms, and has never been understood to interfere with the exercise of the same power by the states; and hence has been drawn an argument which has been applied to the question under consideration. But the two grants are not, it is conceived, similar in their terms or their nature. Although many of the powers formerly exercised by the states, are transferred to the government of the Union, yet the State governments remain, and constitute a most important part of our system. The power of taxation is indispensable to their existence, and is a power which, in its own nature, is capable of residing in, and being exercised by, different authorities at the same time. * * * In imposing taxes for State purposes, they are not doing what Congress is empowered to do. Congress is not empowered to tax for those purposes which are within the exclusive province of the states. When, then, each government exercises the power of taxation, neither is exercising the power of the other. But, when a State proceeds to regulate commerce with foreign nations, or among the several States, it is exercising the very power that is granted to Congress, and is doing the very thing which Congress is authorized to do. There is no analogy, then, between the power of taxation and the power of regulating commerce.

In discussing the question, whether this power is still in the States, in the case under consideration, we may dismiss from it the inquiry, whether it is surrendered by the mere grant to Congress, or is retained until Congress shall exercise the power. We may dismiss that inquiry, because it has been exercised, and the regulations which Congress deemed it proper to make, are now in full operation. The sole question is, can a State regulate commerce with foreign nations and among the states, while Congress is regulating it? * * *

It has been contended by the counsel for the appellant, that, as the word "to regulate" implies in its nature, full power over the thing to be regulated, it excludes, necessarily, the action of all others that would perform the same operation on the same thing. That regulation is designed for the entire result, applying to those parts which remain as they were, as well as to those which are altered. It produces a uniform whole, which is as much disturbed and deranged by changing what the regulating power designs to leave untouched, as that on which it has operated.

There is great force in this argument, and the court is not satisfied that it has been refuted.

Since, however, in exercising the power of regulating their own purely internal affairs, whether of trading or police, the states may sometimes enact laws, the validity of which depends on their interfering with, and being contrary to, an act of Congress passed in pursuance of the constitution, the court will enter upon the inquiry, whether the laws of New York, as expounded by the highest tribunal of that State, have, in their application to this case, come into collision with an act of Congress, and deprived a citizen of a right to which that act entitles him. Should this collision exist, it will be immaterial whether those laws were passed in virtue of a concurrent power "to regulate commerce with foreign nations and among the several States," or in virtue of a power to regulate their domestic trade and police. In one case and the other, the acts of New York must yield to the law of Congress; and the decision sustaining the privilege they confer, against a right given by a law of the Union, must be erroneous.

* * * In the exercise of this power [over commerce] Congress has passed "an act for enrolling or licensing ships or vessels to be employed in the coasting trade and fisheries, and for regulating the same." The counsel for the respondent contend that this act does not give the right to sail from port to port, but confines itself to regulating a preexisting right, so far only as to confer certain privileges on enrolled and licensed vessels in its exercise.

It will at once occur, that, when a legislature attaches certain privileges and exemptions to the exercise of a right over which its control is absolute, the law must imply a power to exercise the right. The privileges are gone, if the right itself be annihilated. It would be contrary to all reason, and to the course of human affairs, to say that a State is unable to strip a vessel of the particular privileges attendant on the exercise of a right, and yet may annul the right itself; that the State of New York cannot prevent an enrolled and licensed vessel, proceeding from Elizabethtown, in New Jersey, to New York, from enjoying, in her course, and on her entrance into port, all the privileges conferred by the act of Congress; but can shut her up in her own port, and prohibit altogether her entering the waters and ports of another State. To the court it seems very clear, that the whole act on the subject of the coasting trade, according to those principles which govern the construction of statutes, implies, unequivocally, an authority to license vessels to carry on the coasting trade. * * *

* * * A coasting vessel employed in the transportation of passengers, is as much a portion of the American marine as one employed in the transportation of a cargo; and no reason is perceived why such vessel should be withdrawn from the regulating power of that government, which has been thought best fitted for the purpose generally. The provisions of the law respecting native seamen, and respecting ownership, are as applicable to vessels carrying men as to vessels carrying manufacturers; and no reason is perceived why the power over the subject should not be placed in the same hands. * * *

[The Court then decreed that "so much of the several laws of the State of New York, as prohibits vessels, licensed according to the laws of the United States, from navigating the waters of the State of New York, by means of fire or steam, is repugnant to the" United States Constitution and void, because these state laws conflicted with the privileges granted by the federal licensing law.]

JUSTICE JOHNSON [concurring].

[The commerce] power must be exclusive; it can reside in but one potentate; and hence, the grant of this power [to Congress] carries with it the whole subject, leaving nothing for the State to act upon. * * * If there was any one object riding over every other in the adoption of the constitution, it was to keep the commercial intercourse among the States free from all invidious and partial restraints. And I cannot overcome the conviction, that if the licensing act was repealed tomorrow, the rights of the appellant to a reversal of the decision complained of, would be as strong as it is under this license. * * *

NOTE ON DUAL FEDERALISM AS A LIMIT ON STATE POWER

Analytically, the possibilities for federal/state regulation for interstate commerce are the following:

1. *Mutually exclusive regulation.* Whatever Congress can regulate as *interstate* under the Commerce Clause is closed to the states; whatever the states can regulate as *local* is closed to Congress under the Commerce Clause.

2. *Concurrent regulation.* Congressional and state jurisdiction overlap; each can regulate interstate commerce, but state regulation cannot violate other constitutionally prohibitions (*e.g.*, the Imposts Clause) or interfere with federal regulation (*preemption*).

3. *Authorized concurrent regulation.* The states can regulate interstate commerce in the absence of congressional negation *and* of any interference with the negative (i.e., anti-trade war) goals of the Commerce Clause.

Theory 1 is derived from the "dual federalism" idea, whereby state and federal sovereignty is plenary in the respective jurisdiction of each. This is the view defended by Justice Johnson, and it logically creates a negative or *dormant* feature of the Commerce Clause that should be enforced by the Court. Theory 2 does not logically or necessarily entail a dormant feature of the Commerce Clause, because the most obvious limitations on the states are those imposed by or implicit in federal statutes and those specifically enumerated in the Constitution. Theory 3 necessarily entails a dormant feature as a matter of constitutional policy but could logically be expressed without that feature.

Note that Chief Justice Marshall refrained from deciding which of the three options is embedded in the Constitution, although he did recognize "great force" in Theory 1. Instead, he decided the case as a *preemption* case. (Under all three theories, a congressional enactment properly adopted under the Commerce Clause trumps state policies because of the Supremacy Clause.) In *Willson v. Black-Bird Creek Marsh Co.*, 27 U.S. (2 Pet.) 245 (1829), Chief Justice Marshall continued to fudge the theoretical issue. There, a state law authorized a company to build a dam in a creek that fed into the Delaware River, a major interstate waterway. The dam excluded water from a marsh, thereby enhancing the value of the marshland and "probably improv[ing]" the health of nearby residents. But the dam also obstructed navigation of the creek by federally licensed ships. The Court upheld the state law, categorizing it as a local health measure.

Gibbons and *Black Bird Creek* left open the possibility that the federal commerce power was exclusive and, thus, that states could not regulate interstate commerce. Nonetheless, *Black Bird Creek* held that states could pursue other legitimate regulatory goals (like health) even if the regulation impinged to some extent upon interstate commerce. Until the middle of the nineteenth century, the decisions following these precedents engaged in labeling inquiries, invalidating state regulations that were deemed "regulations of interstate commerce" and upholding those "within the local police power."

Characteristic was *Mayor of New York v. Miln*, 36 U.S. (11 Pet.) 102 (1837), which upheld a state law requiring ship's masters to report the names and residences of passengers to local authorities. Again, the Court was able to avoid the theoretical question whether the power to regulate commerce is exclusively a federal power, by ruling that the law was "not a regulation of commerce, but of police." Echoing Justice Johnson's *Gibbons* separate opinion, Justice Story dissented on the ground that the law did regulate commerce and that such regulation is exclusive with the federal government. Contrast *The Passenger Cases*, 48 U.S. (7 How.) 283 (1849), where the Court struck down two state laws requiring ship's masters to pay a tax for each alien on the ship, to defray expenses incurred for the local examination of such aliens to assure that they would not become public charges if they were admitted to the state. (There was no opinion for the Court; five Justices justified the invalidation under five different rationales.) The theoretical confusion was ameliorated when the Court coalesced into a majority in the following case.

Cooley v. Board of Wardens of the Port of Philadelphia, 53 U.S. (12 How.) 299 (1851). The Court was faced with two statutes: an 1803 Pennsylvania statute regulating the pilots of ships entering and leaving the port of Philadelphia, and a 1789 federal statute providing that pilots should be regulated by state law. The opinion for the Court by **Justice Curtis** seemingly ended decades of indecision and adopted Theory 3. Justice Curtis first ruled that regulations of pilots "constitute regulation of navigation, and consequently of commerce, within the just meaning" of the Commerce Clause (*Gibbons*). Further, he declined to interpret the federal statute as an authorization of state law, in part on the notion that Congress could not authorize a violation of the Constitution. Thus the Court was squarely confronted with the question whether the Commerce Clause completely disabled the states from regulating in the area (Theory 1).

The Court rejected Theory 1 and seemed to adopt Theory 3: "Now the power to regulate commerce embraces a vast field, containing not only many, but exceedingly various subjects, quite unlike in their nature; some imperatively demanding a single uniform rule, operating equally on the commerce of the United States in every port; and some, like the subject now in question, as imperatively demanding that diversity, which alone can meet the local necessities of navigation." Under this standard, the Court upheld the state law, on the ground that the matter was intrinsically "local" in nature, and not an area needing national uniformity. "Whatever subjects of this [commerce] power are in their nature national, or admit only of one uniform system, or plan of regulation may justly be said to be of such a nature as to require exclusive legislation by Congress. That this cannot be affirmed of laws for the regulation of pilots and pilotage is plain," citing the 1789 statute, which thus played a role as a "signification" of the local nature of the regulation, and the value of diversity rather than uniformity in this area.

Although Justice Curtis confined the holding of the case to issues of navigation, his opinion was the first to commit a majority of the Court to one of the theories apportioning power over commerce as between the national and state governments. (Two Justices dissented, and one concurred in the result.)

NOTE ON THE EVOLUTION OF THE DORMANT
COMMERCE CLAUSE FROM *COOLEY* TO THE MODERN ERA

Cooley suggested that the Dormant Commerce Clause inquiry was no longer an exercise in labeling "interstate commerce," but rather turned on whether the subject matter of the regulation was so local in character as to justify differing treatment around the country, or so national in character as to suggest that a uniform rule is necessary. Unfortunately, drawing a line based on the subject matter of regulation proved difficult, and sometimes controversial. The Court's decision striking down state regulation of railroad rate discrimination in *Wabash, St. Louis & P. Ry. v. Illinois*, 118 U.S. 557 (1886), raised a firestorm of protests from farm states and was the direct impetus for Congress to adopt the Interstate Commerce Act in 1887. Indeed, after 1887, the Court frequently allowed state "safety" regulations for railroads, albeit based upon a theory that such regulations had only an "indirect" and not "direct effect" on interstate commerce. *E.g., Southern Ry. v. King*, 217 U.S. 524 (1910); *Smith v. Alabama*, 124 U.S. 465 (1888). *Cooley*'s national/local test was not considered the only approach to these issues, although its conceptual distinction between areas needing national uniformity and those permitting local diversity is an idea that has survived.

Less robust was *Cooley*'s suggestion that Congress cannot authorize states to regulate non-local commerce. In *Leisy v. Hardin*, 135 U.S. 100 (1890), the Court invalidated a state seizure of the interstate shipment of beer kegs on the ground that Congress' power to regulate interstate commerce is "plenary and exclusive." Congress thereupon passed a statute authorizing the states to regulate interstate-shipped liquor once it had arrived within their borders. The Court upheld that authorization. *In re Rahrer*, 140 U.S. 545 (1891). By the twentieth century, it became accepted doctrine that Congress could authorize state regulation of interstate commerce.[c] It is now universally recognized that there is an area of concurrent regulation by the states and Congress. As the Court has expanded Congress' Commerce Clause powers, this area of concurrent authority has become quite large.

The question arises, therefore, as to why the Court continues to enforce a Dormant Commerce Clause once the dual federalism idea (Theory 1) was rejected in *Cooley* and subsequent precedents. The doctrinal answer is that a dormant feature of the Commerce Clause is implicated in Theory 3, the theory tentatively accepted in *Cooley* and firmly entrenched in subsequent cases. But, unlike Theory 1, where a negative feature of the Commerce Clause is logically necessary, Theory 3 involves a negative feature only for functional — constitutional policy — reasons and, more important, says nothing about whether the

---

c. See *Prudential Ins. Co. v. Benjamin*, 328 U.S. 408 (1946) (reaffirming *Rahrer* and extending its rationale to allow state tax rule discriminating against interstate commerce because it was authorized by Congress); William Cohen, *Congressional Power to Validate Unconstitutional State Laws: A Forgotten Solution to an Old Enigma*, 35 Stan. L. Rev. 387 (1985). As it has done in other areas involving federalism values, the Rehnquist Court has imposed a clear statement requirement on the exercise of this power: "Congress must manifest its unambiguous intent before a federal statute will be read to permit or approve" what would otherwise be a Dormant Commerce Clause violation. *Wyoming v. Oklahoma*, 502 U.S. 437, 458 (1992).

Court rather than Congress should enforce the negative feature of the Commerce Clause.

NOTE ON THEORIES WHY THE COURT SHOULD ENFORCE THE "DORMANT" FEATURE OF THE COMMERCE CLAUSE

We believe the issue identified at the end of the previous Note has troubled the Court in recent decades. Hence, the Court and commentators have come up with theories for why the Dormant Commerce Clause is an important part of federalism and why the Court rather than just Congress should enforce the negative feature of the Commerce Clause.

1. *Economic Union as a Constitutional Value.* Justice Jackson laid out a compelling vision for Dormant Commerce Clause jurisprudence in his opinion for the Court in *H.P. Hood & Sons v. Du Mond*, 336 U.S. 525 (1949):

> [The] principle that our economic unit is the Nation, which alone has the gamut of powers necessary to control the economy, including the vital power of erecting customs barriers against foreign competition, has as its corollary that the states are not separable economic units. * * *

> Our system * * * is that every farmer and every craftsman shall be encouraged to produce by the certainty that he will have free access to every market in the Nation, that no home embargoes will withhold his exports, and no foreign state [within the Nation] will by customs duties or regulations exclude them.

This is a fine aspiration. But is it constitutional *law*, enforceable by the Court?

Donald Regan and Richard Collins, among others, maintain that the Dormant Commerce Clause is as lawlike as federalism and the right to privacy, for the *principle of economic union* is instinct in the structure of the Constitution.[d] That is, specific provisions in the constitutional text, supported by the overall goals the Framers had in mind when they adopted the Constitution to replace the "Balkanizing" Articles of Confederation, suggest the meta-concept that the Constitution creates a framework for an integrated economic union.[e] Inherent in any such union — even if not explicitly mentioned — is the compelling need to prevent economic Balkanization and protectionism among the states. Hence, as Madison suggested in 1829, the Dormant Commerce Clause is part of the structure of the Constitution. For the same reasons the Court enforces other structural protections, such as federalism, the Court should enforce the structural protections of the Dormant Commerce Clause.

The Dormant Commerce Clause jurisprudence is different from the federalism and privacy areas in that it does not create "nontrumpable" rights — that is, "rights" that cannot be overridden by the normal political process. While Congress could not have authorized Connecticut to regulate contraceptives (*Griswold*), nor could the states have authorized Congress's violation of the

---

d. See Donald Regan, *The Supreme Court and State Protectionism: Making Sense of the Dormant Commerce Clause*, 84 Mich. L. Rev. 1091 (1986); Richard Collins, *Economic Union as a Constitutional Value*, 63 N.Y.U.L. Rev. 43 (1988).

e. Compare *Printz v. United States* (§ 5C of this chapter) and *Griswold v. Connecticut* (Chapter 5, § 4A).

Commerce Clause or Fourteenth Amendment (*New York v. United States*; *Morrison*), Congress can authorize state laws that would otherwise violate the Dormant Commerce Clause. For this reason, Henry Monaghan, *The Supreme Court, 1974 Term — Foreword: Constitutional Common Law*, 89 Harv. L. Rev. 1 (1975), maintains that the Dormant Commerce Clause cases represent "constitutional common law" rather than normal constitutional law. Is such a body of law consistent with *Marbury*'s justifications for judicial review?

2. *Representation-Reinforcement Role of the Dormant Commerce Clause.* Another justification is suggested by *McCulloch*: State laws may be too protective of the interests of state political *insiders*, at the expense of *outsiders*, and the Supreme Court might be a useful check on such political dysfunction, because it is not only outside the political process, but it has a national rather than local perspective. This suggestion was fully developed as a justification for activist Dormant Commerce Clause review during the New Deal. The chief articulation was Justice Stone's opinion in *South Carolina State Highway Dep't v. Barnwell Bros.*, 303 U.S. 177 (1938):

> State regulations affecting interstate commerce, whose purpose or effect is to gain for those within the state an advantage at the expense of those without, or burden those out of the state without any corresponding advantage to those within, have been thought to impinge upon the constitutional prohibition even though Congress has not acted.
>
> Underlying the stated rule has been the thought, often expressed in judicial opinions, that when the regulation is of such a character that its burden falls principally upon those without the state, legislative action is not likely to be subjected to those political restraints which are normally exerted on legislation where it affects adversely some interests within the state.

Recall that later in 1938 Justice Stone also wrote the celebrated *Carolene Products* footnote four, which inspired Professor Ely's representation-reinforcement theory.[f]

Drawing from modern public choice (interest-group) theories of politics (Chapter 2, § 3B, Note), Professor Mark Tushnet has developed this idea most completely in a "cost-exporting" rationale for the Dormant Commerce Clause.[g] Tushnet argues that special interest groups will tend to organize and seek benefits from the political process. The ability of a group to extract *rents* (distributions to the group not justified by overall efficiency) depends in large part on the inability of cost-payers to mobilize against the group's lawmaking efforts. One

---

f. Representation-reinforcement theory posits that the role of the Court in constitutional law is to correct for serious defects in the political process (Chapter 2, § 3B). Much of this chapter can be viewed through the prism of representation-reinforcement theory, which was anticipated in some detail by Professor Wechsler's argument that the structures in the Constitution protect the states against federal encroachment and that judicial review is not needed (§ 5B). Cases like *Heart of Atlanta Motel* (§ 2) and *Garcia* (§ 5B) can be viewed as exemplars of Wechsler's insight and illustrations of Ely's theory applied to issues of federalism. Tushnet's theory, described in text, is an effort along similar lines.

g. See Mark Tushnet, *Rethinking the Dormant Commerce Clause*, 1979 Wis. L. Rev. 125. See also Daniel Farber, *State Regulation and the Dormant Commerce Clause*, 3 Const. Comm. 395 (1986).

way to assure this is for a group to pursue statutes that "export" the costs to outsiders unrepresented or less well-represented in the local political process. An important role of the Dormant Commerce Clause, therefore, is to prevent widespread rent-seeking by state "insiders" at the expense of state "outsiders" (and obviously also at the expense of the national free market). Put another way, Dormant Commerce Clause doctrine sets limits on state laws "exporting costs" of regulation to outsiders.

Another way the Court's enforcement of the Dormant Commerce Clause might be representation-reinforcing is that it corrects for congressional inertia. The Commerce and Supremacy Clauses give Congress authority to preempt state laws interfering with interstate commerce, but it is hard for Congress to monitor state violations: The violations are too numerous and too subtle to get on the crowded congressional agenda, and the Article I, § 7 requirements prevent Congress from rectifying most of the violations. The Court is better situated to monitor the violations: Case-by-case adjudication is ideal for sorting out the unjustified discriminations and burdens on commerce, and judicial invalidation of the most serious violations helps Congress conserve its resources while addressing the most thorny problem areas. This kind of representation-reinforcement argument not only justifies the Court's review of state laws burdening commerce, but also justifies the rule that Congress can override the Court and authorize state laws burdening interstate commerce.

3. *The Commitment Problem with Federalism.* Consider this further passage from Justice Jackson's opinion in *Hood*:

> The material success that has come to inhabitants of the states which make up this federal free trade unit has been the most impressive in the history of commerce, but the established interdependence of the states only emphasizes the necessity of protecting interstate movement of goods against local burdens and repressions. We need only consider the consequences if each of the few states that produce copper, lead, [etc.] should decree that industries located in that state shall have priority. What fantastic rivalries and dislocations and reprisals would ensue if such practices were begun!

The "dislocations and reprisals" problem is not just that the benefits of economic union will be lost and escalating rents will be extracted, but also goes to the political union itself.

Jenna Bednar and William Eskridge have identified the *commitment problem* as the chief reason for judicial enforcement of the Dormant Commerce Clause.[h] Under this theory, the temptation to cheat on the federal arrangement among the states not only threatens the free market, but undermines the federal arrangement itself. Unless there is a credible deterrent to such cheating, there is a risk that the states will turn on one another, putting pressure on the political stability of the federal arrangement. While there is little risk that the United States will degenerate the way Yugoslavia did, perhaps the risk is greater that the erosion seen in Canada would be replicated here if states could get away with cheating.

---

h. See Jenna Bednar & William Eskridge, Jr., *Steadying the Court's "Unsteady Path": A Theory of Judicial Enforcement of Federalism*, 68 S. Cal. L. Rev. 1447 (1995).

Bednar and Eskridge maintain, further, that Congress is not a sufficient check on state cheating. Congress' limited agenda and the many vetogates that legislation must pass through make it unlikely that Congress can easily address the many instances of state or local impositions on, or cost-exporting to, other states. Case-by-case adjudication by a relatively impartial judicial tribunal, on the other hand, seems well designed to regulate such cheating: the out-of-state (or even in-state) interests harmed by the rent-seeking have incentives to bring suit, courts cannot dodge the issue as Congress can and are well trained in gathering and evaluating the factual information needed to determine whether a state really is burdening interstate commerce unjustifiably, and federal judges as national officials would seem impartial enough to resolve matters credibly, such that states are assured that their own cheating and other states' cheating will be fairly handled.

B. MODERN DORMANT COMMERCE CLAUSE DOCTRINE

The Supreme Court now resolves Dormant Commerce Clause cases fairly often, and the doctrinal structure is pretty well set. The key doctrinal precepts are that *overt state discrimination* against interstate commerce is presumptively invalid and can only be sustained if needed to meet an important state interest (Subpart 1), and that *state policies burdening commerce* will be invalidated if the burden is clearly excessive compared with the legitimate local benefits (Subpart 2). The same rules apply to policies adopted at the municipal level, see *Dean Milk Co. v. Madison*, 340 U.S. 349 (1951), or county level, see *Fort Gratiot Sanitary Landfill, Inc. v. Michigan Dep't Nat. Resources*, 504 U.S. 353 (1992). The rules do not apply when the state is acting as a market participant rather than as a market regulator (Subpart 3).

1. *Discrimination Against Interstate Commerce*

As suggested by the goals of the Dormant Commerce Clause, the Court subjects overt state or local discrimination against interstate commerce to strict scrutiny. "When a state statute clearly discriminates against interstate commerce, it will be struck down unless the discrimination is demonstrably justified by a valid factor unrelated to economic protectionism. Indeed, when the state statute amounts to simple economic protectionism, a 'virtually per se rule of invalidity' has applied." *Wyoming v. Oklahoma*, 502 U.S. 437, 454-55 (1992). Laws discriminating on their face against interstate commerce on goods or services have included the following kinds:

(a) *Discrimination against outside competition.* The Court has traditionally applied strict scrutiny to laws that impose costs or restrictions on out-of-state (or out-of-area) goods or services. Few laws survive such scrutiny, because the Court usually finds that the local statute is designed to give local businesses artificial competitive advantages over out-of-state businesses, a per se invalid purpose under the Dormant Commerce Clause. In the leading case, *Welton v. Missouri*, 91 U.S. (1 Otto) 275 (1876), the Court struck down a Missouri law requiring that peddlers of goods "not the growth, produce, or manufacture of the State" obtain a license. The Court ruled that "the very object" of the Commerce Clause was to protect against "discriminating State legislation." See also

Crutcher v. Kentucky, 141 U.S. 47 (1891) (invalidating state statute requiring out-of-state express companies to obtain state license); *Buck v. Kuykendall*, 267 U.S. 307 (1925) (Brandeis, J.) (similar).

Many of the leading cases involve milk. In *Baldwin v. G.A.F. Seelig*, 294 U.S. 511 (1935), the Court invalidated a New York law that barred importation of out-of-state milk that did not adhere to local price minima. Justice Cardozo's opinion for the Court reasoned that the law "set a barrier to traffic between one state and another as effective as if customs duties, equal to the price differential, had been laid upon the milk," precisely the sort of barrier that triggers trade wars and other reprisals. In *Dean Milk Co. v. City of Madison*, 340 U.S. 349 (1951), the Court invalidated Madison, Wisconsin's ordinances making it unlawful to sell milk not pasteurized within five miles of the city and to sell, import, receive, or store milk unless from a source inspected by city officials (and within 25 miles of the city). The Court readily admitted the legitimacy of the state regulation and the dearth of federal statutes regulating the subject but invalidated the ordinances because their "practical effect" was to exclude milk produced and pasteurized out-of-state. "In thus erecting an economic barrier protecting a major local industry against competition from without the State, Madison plainly discriminates against interstate commerce. This it cannot do, even in the exercise of its unquestioned power to protect the health and safety of its people, if reasonable nondiscriminatory alternatives, adequate to serve legitimate local interest, are available." The Court found reasonable alternatives to be available. Compare *Minnesota v. Clover Leaf Creamery Co.*, 449 U.S. 456 (1981) (upholding state ban on selling milk in nonreturnable containers, because it did not on its face or in effect discriminate against interstate commerce).

(b) *Discrimination hoarding local resources or opportunities.* Statutes trying to prevent resources or businesses from going out-of-state are also immediately suspect under the Dormant Commerce Clause. In a leading case, *Pennsylvania v. West Virginia*, 262 U.S. 553 (1923), the Court invalidated a West Virginia statute requiring in-state pipeline companies to meet the domestic needs of West Virginia gas consumers before the companies could export West Virginia gas to out-of-state customers. The Court reasoned that the law on its face discriminated against interstate commerce and thus was invalid, notwithstanding the state's argument that it was merely preserving one of its natural advantages. See also *Hughes v. Oklahoma*, 441 U.S. 322 (1979), invalidating an Oklahoma statute seeking to conserve natural (non-hatchery) minnows by preventing their removal from the state; *New England Power Co. v. New Hampshire*, 455 U.S. 331 (1982), invalidating a New Hampshire statute requiring regulatory permission before hydroelectric power could be sold out of state; *Wyoming v. Oklahoma*, 502 U.S. 437 (1992), invalidating an Oklahoma statute requiring power plants to use at least 10% local coal.

Most of the hoarding cases have involved "local processing requirements," which channel business opportunities to in-state or in-area businesses. In a leading decision, *Foster-Fountain Packing Co. v. Haydel*, 278 U.S. 1 (1928), the Court invalidated a Louisiana law prohibiting the exportation of shrimp until the heads and hulls had been removed. The state justified the discrimination on the ground that shrimp hulls and heads were needed as fertilizer in the state, a goal the Court found not credible; the real purpose of the statute was to prevent Mississippi processing plants from competing with those in Louisiana. Other requirements held invalid have included local inspection of meat, *Minnesota v. Barber*, 136 U.S. 313 (1890); local packing of shrimp, *Toomer v. Witsell*, 334 U.S. 385 (1948); and local processing of timber, *South-Central Timber Dev., Inc. v. Wunnicke*, 467 U.S. 82 (1984).

(c) *Discrimination preventing outside burdens from flowing in-state.* This is the trickiest category. In the nineteenth century, the Court was tolerant of state efforts to prevent outside burdens from flowing into the state. For example, the law regulating the importation of potential public charges was sustained in *Milne.*[i] The Court also upheld quarantine laws honestly seeking to prevent the spread of contagious diseases. See *Bowman v. Chicago & Northwestern R.*, 125 U.S. 465 (1888) (leading case); *Kimmish v. Ball*, 129 U.S. 217 (1889); *Sligh v. Kirkwood*, 237 U.S. 52 (1915). Recall the "outlaws of commerce" theory of the Lottery Case and other Commerce Clause precedents in § 2. This kind of discrimination has faced tougher scrutiny in recent cases, starting with the leading decision, which follows.

CITY OF PHILADELPHIA v. NEW JERSEY
437 U.S. 617, 98 S.Ct. 2531, 57 L.Ed.2d 475 (1978)

JUSTICE STEWART delivered the opinion of the Court.

[A New Jersey law prohibited the importation of most "solid or liquid waste which originated or was collected outside the territorial limits of the State." Private landfill operators challenged the statute on preemption and Dormant Commerce Clause grounds. The state supreme court rejected both claims, finding that the statute "advanced vital health and environmental objectives with no economic discrimination against, and with little burden upon, interstate commerce." The Supreme Court reversed on the Dormant Commerce Clause claim.]

* * * All objects of interstate trade merit Commerce Clause protection; none is excluded by definition at the outset. * * * Hence, we reject the state court's suggestion that the banning of "valueless" out-of-state wastes by [the statute] implicates no constitutional protection. Just as Congress has power to regulate the interstate movement of these wastes, States are not free from constitutional scrutiny when they restrict that movement.

Although the Constitution gives Congress the power to regulate commerce among the States, many subjects of potential federal regulation under that power inevitably escape congressional attention "because of their local character and their number and diversity." In the absence of federal legislation, these subjects are open to control by the States so long as they act within the restraints imposed by the Commerce Clause itself. The bounds of these restraints appear nowhere

---

i. Such a law would not be sustained today. It would surely be found to interfere with national immigration policy if the outsiders were noncitizens from abroad, and would interfere with the right of interstate travel if the outsiders were citizens from other parts of this country (Chapter 5, § 3C). Also, after *City of Philadelphia*, such a law would seem to violate the Dormant Commerce Clause.

in the words of the Commerce Clause, but have emerged gradually in the decisions of this Court giving effect to its basic purpose. * * *

The opinions of the Court through the years have reflected an alertness to the evils of "economic isolation" and protectionism, while at the same time recognizing that incidental burdens on interstate commerce may be unavoidable when a State legislates to safeguard the health and safety of its people. Thus, where simple economic protectionism is effected by state legislation, a virtually per se rule of invalidity has been erected. The clearest example of such legislation is a law that overtly blocks the flow of interstate commerce at a State's borders. Cf. *Welton v. Missouri*. But where other legislative objectives are credibly advanced and there is no patent discrimination against interstate trade, the Court has adopted a much more flexible approach [described and illustrated in the Subpart 2, *infra*].

The crucial inquiry, therefore, must be directed to determining whether [the statute] is basically a protectionist measure, or whether it can fairly be viewed as a law directed to legitimate local concerns, with effects upon interstate commerce that are only incidental.

The purpose of [the statute] is set out in [it as] follows:

The Legislature finds and determines that . . . the volume of solid and liquid waste continues to rapidly increase, that the treatment and disposal of these wastes continues to pose an even greater threat to the quality of the environment of New Jersey, that the available and appropriate land fill sites within the State are being diminished, that the environment continues to be threatened by the treatment and disposal of waste which originated or was collected outside the State, and that the public health, safety and welfare require that the treatment and disposal within this State of all wastes generated outside of the State be prohibited.

The New Jersey Supreme Court accepted this statement of the state legislature's purpose. The state court additionally found that New Jersey's existing landfill sites will be exhausted within a few years; that to go on using these sites or to develop new ones will take a heavy environmental toll, both from pollution and from loss of scarce open lands; that new techniques to divert waste from landfills to other methods of disposal and resource recovery processes are under development, but that these changes will require time; and finally, that "the extension of the lifespan of existing landfills, resulting from the exclusion of out-of-state waste, may be of crucial importance in preventing further virgin wetlands or other undeveloped lands from being devoted to landfill purposes." Based on these findings, the court concluded that [the statute] was designed to protect, not the State's economy, but its environment, and that its substantial benefits outweigh its "slight" burden on interstate commerce.

[The parties disagreed over whether the statutory purpose was protectionist or remedial.] This dispute about ultimate legislative purpose need not be resolved, because its resolution would not be relevant to the constitutional issue to be decided in this case. Contrary to the evident assumption of the state court and the parties, the evil of protectionism can reside in legislative means as well as legislative ends. Thus, it does not matter whether the ultimate aim of [the statute] is to reduce the waste disposal costs of residents or to save remaining open lands from pollution, for we assume New Jersey has every right to protect its residents' pocketbooks as well as their environment. And it may be assumed as well that New Jersey may pursue those ends by slowing the flow of *all* waste into the State's remaining landfills, even though interstate commerce may incidentally be affected. But whatever New Jersey's ultimate purpose, it may not be accomplished by discriminating against articles of commerce from outside the State unless there is some reason, apart from their origin, to treat them differently. Both on its face and in its plain effect, [the statute] violates this principle of nondiscrimination.

The Court has consistently found parochial legislation of this kind to be constitutionally invalid, whether the ultimate aim of the legislation was to assure a steady supply of milk by erecting barriers to allegedly ruinous outside competition, *Baldwin v. G.A.F. Selig*; or to create jobs by keeping industry within the State, *Foster-Fountain Packing*; or to preserve the State's financial resources from depletion by fencing out indigent immigrants. *Edwards v. California* [Chapter 5, § 3C]. In each of these cases, a presumably legitimate goal was sought to be achieved by the illegitimate means of isolating the State from the national economy.

Also relevant here are the Court's decisions holding that a State may not accord its own inhabitants a preferred right of access over consumers in other States to natural resources located within its borders. *Pennsylvania v. West Virginia*. These cases stand for the basic principle that a "State is without power to prevent privately owned articles of trade from being shipped and sold in interstate commerce on the ground that they are required to satisfy local demands or because they are needed by the people of the State." *Foster-Fountain Packing Co.*

The New Jersey law at issue in this case falls squarely within the area that the Commerce Clause puts off limits to state regulation. On its face, it imposes on out-of-state commercial interests the full burden of conserving the state's remaining landfill space. It is true that in our previous cases the scarce natural resource was itself the article of commerce, whereas here the scarce resource and the article of commerce are distinct. But that difference is without consequence. In both instances, the State has overtly moved to slow or freeze the flow of commerce for protectionist reasons. It does not matter that the State has shut the article of commerce inside the State in one case and outside the State in the other. What is crucial is the attempt by one State to isolate itself from a problem common to many by erecting a barrier against the movement of interstate trade.

The appellees argue that not all laws which facially discriminate against out-of-state commerce are forbidden protectionist regulations. In particular, they point to quarantine laws, which this Court has repeatedly upheld even though they appear to single out interstate commerce for special treatment. In the appellees' view, [the statute] is analogous to such health-protective measures, since it reduces the exposure of New Jersey residents to the allegedly harmful effects of landfill sites.

It is true that certain quarantine laws have not been considered forbidden protectionist measures, even though they were directed against out-of-state commerce. But those quarantine laws banned the importation of articles such as diseased livestock that required destruction as soon as possible because their very movement risked contagion and other evils. Those laws thus did not discriminate against interstate commerce as such, but simply prevented traffic in noxious articles, whatever their origin.

The New Jersey statute is not such a quarantine law. There has been no claim here that the very movement of waste into or through New Jersey endangers health, or that waste must be disposed of as soon and as close to its point of generation as possible. The harms caused by waste are said to arise after its disposal in landfill sites, and at that point, as New Jersey concedes, there is no basis to distinguish out-of-state waste from domestic waste. If one is inherently harmful, so is the other. Yet New Jersey has banned the former while leaving its landfill sites open to the latter. The New Jersey law blocks the importation of waste in an obvious effort to saddle those outside the State with the entire burden of slowing the flow of refuse into New Jersey's remaining landfill sites. That legislative effort is clearly impermissible under the Commerce Clause of the Constitution.

Today, cities in Pennsylvania and New York find it expedient or necessary to send their waste into New Jersey for disposal, and New Jersey claims the right to close its borders to such traffic. Tomorrow, cities in New Jersey may find it expedient or necessary to send their waste into Pennsylvania or New York for disposal, and those States might then claim the right to close their borders. The Commerce Clause will protect New Jersey in the future, just as it protects her neighbors now, from efforts by one State to isolate itself in the stream of interstate commerce from a problem shared by all. The judgment is reversed.

JUSTICE REHNQUIST, with whom **THE CHIEF JUSTICE [BURGER]** joins, dissenting.

A growing problem in our Nation is the sanitary treatment and disposal of solid waste. For many years, solid waste was incinerated. Because of the significant environmental problems attendant on incineration, however, this method of solid waste disposal has declined in use in many localities, including New Jersey. "Sanitary" landfills have replaced incineration as the principal method of disposing of solid waste. * * * [But] landfills also present extremely serious health and safety problems. First, in New Jersey, "virtually all sanitary landfills can be expected to produce leachate, a noxious and highly polluted liquid which is seldom visible and frequently pollutes . . . ground and surface waters." The natural decomposition process which occurs in landfills also produces large quantities of methane and thereby presents a significant explosion hazard. Landfills can also generate "health hazards caused by rodents, fires and scavenger birds" and, "needless to say, do not help New Jersey's aesthetic appearance nor New Jersey's noise or water or air pollution problems."

The health and safety hazards associated with landfills present appellees with a currently unsolvable dilemma. Other, hopefully safer, methods of disposing of solid wastes are still in the development stage and cannot presently be used. But appellees obviously cannot completely stop the tide of solid waste that its citizens will produce in the interim. For the moment, therefore, appellees must continue to use sanitary landfills to dispose of New Jersey's own solid waste despite the critical environmental problems thereby created.

The question presented in this case is whether New Jersey must also continue to receive and dispose of solid waste from neighboring States, even though these will inexorably increase the health problems discussed above. The Court answers this question in the affirmative. New Jersey must either prohibit *all* landfill operations, leaving itself to cast about for a presently nonexistent solution to the serious problem of disposing of the waste generated within its own borders, or it must accept waste from every portion of the United States, thereby multiplying the health and safety problems which would result if it dealt only with such wastes generated within the State. Because past precedents establish that the Commerce Clause does not present appellees with such a Hobson's choice, I dissent. * * *

* * * I do not see why a State may ban the importation of items whose movement risks contagion, but cannot ban the importation of items which, although they may be transported into the State without undue hazard, will then simply pile up in an ever increasing danger to the public's health and safety. The Commerce Clause was not drawn with a view to having the validity of state laws turn on such pointless distinctions.

* * * [T]he Court implies that the challenged laws must be invalidated because New Jersey has left its landfills open to domestic waste. But, as the Court notes, this Court has repeatedly upheld quarantine laws "even though they appear to single out interstate commerce for special treatment." The fact that New Jersey has left its landfill sites open for domestic waste does not, of course, mean that solid waste is not innately harmful. Nor does it mean that New Jersey prohibits importation of solid waste for reasons other than the health and safety of its population. New Jersey must out of sheer necessity treat and dispose of its solid waste in some fashion, just as it must treat New Jersey cattle suffering from hoof-and-mouth disease. It does not follow that New Jersey must, under the Commerce Clause, accept solid waste or diseased cattle from outside its borders and thereby exacerbate its problems.

NOTES ON *CITY OF PHILADELPHIA* AND THE COURT'S ACTIVISM IN POLICING DISCRIMINATIONS AGAINST COMMERCE

Consider the similarities between *City of Philadelphia* and *Lochner*: A Court dedicated to free market principles in both cases struck down state laws based upon reasoning having only a broad, tenuous connection with the Constitution. If *Lochner* was a failed experiment, which at least could be linked to the Contract Clause, can one justify the *City of Philadelphia* line of cases, which are only inferentially (and some think unpersuasively) linked to the Commerce Clause, any better?[j] Return to the three justifications for Dormant Commerce Clause enforcement by the Supreme Court and see how they fit here:

1. *Economic Union and Efficiency.* Typically, as in *City of Philadelphia*, the Court simply applies heightened scrutiny to any overt discrimination against interstate commerce, without any analysis whether the particular discrimination might be efficient overall. A simple economic argument would support the efficiency of New Jersey's rule: Waste imposes *externalities* on the public, that is, costs (such as air pollution, stench, and visual blight) that are not internalized in the price charged. Hence, a state prohibition on such goods might be efficient overall, because the benefits (externalities avoided) outweigh the costs (opportunity costs lost by outsiders). Strict scrutiny short-circuits such analysis, because it requires super-efficiency: New Jersey's flat prohibition was invalid under strict scrutiny because it was overbroad; a tax on waste could have solved the externality problem without discriminating against interstate commerce. The super-efficiency required by strict scrutiny is not impossible to establish, see *Maine v. Taylor*, 477 U.S. 131 (1986) (allowing Maine to bar the importation of live baitfish, on the ground that there were proven dangers baitfish parasites would pose to indigenous wild fishes), but it disallows many state regulations that are efficient overall.

The Court ominously warns of a trade (or waste!) war, and theories of free trade emphasize that any barriers risk a series of reprisals and new barriers. But set against that possibility is the value of local autonomy — even more clearly embedded in the Constitution, according to the Court's recent federalism cases. Local autonomy is just as threatened by outside intrusions and options cut off from higher-level organs such as the Supreme Court, and the Court exposes citizens to what they view as increased risks and insecurities (Heinzerling, *Commercial Constitution,* 1995 Sup. Ct. Rev. at 237-39). How can the Court compare the risks New Jersey imposes on free trade in waste, with the risks Philadelphia imposes on local autonomy in New Jersey? Does the Constitution provide a basis to differentiate? Or is this just the same kind of unsupported value choice the Court made in *Lochner*?

2. *Political Process Defects?* Maybe there is a process defect that can serve as a surrogate for an efficiency defect. Consider the application of Professor Tushnet's insiders-exporting-costs-to-outsiders theory to this case. One might expect that the New Jersey law was sought by in-state industrial concerns, whose costs of waste-disposal would be increased by out-of-state competition for New Jersey landfill. The law burdens out-of-state industrial concerns, because it

---

j. For criticisms of *City of Philadelphia* for disabling states from engaging in productive activities such as containing externalities, see Stanley Cox, *Garbage In, Garbage Out: Court Confusion About the Dormant Commerce Clause,* 50 Okla. L. Rev. 155 (1997); Kirsten Engel, *Reconsidering the National Market in Solid Waste: Trade-Offs in Equity, Efficiency, Environmental Protection, and State Autonomy,* 73 N.C. L. Rev. 1481 (1995); Richard Epstein, *Waste and the Dormant Commerce Clause,* 3 Green Bag 29 (1999); Paul McGreal, *The Flawed Economics of the Dormant Commerce Clause,* 39 Wm. & Mary L. Rev. 1191 (1998). See also Lisa Heinzerling, *The Commercial Constitution,* 1995 Sup. Ct. Rev. 217 (making this criticism, but also arguing that the Dormant Commerce Clause jurisprudence is internally incoherent).

increases their costs of waste disposal, at least in the short term. Viewed this way, *City of Philadelphia* seems to fit within the theory, because in-state industrial concerns are exporting costs to their out-of-state competitors, who will have to pay more for waste disposal. The state's internal political process cannot be expected to prevent this sort of rent-seeking, so we need the Supreme Court to step in.

But this scenario neglects a number of problems. One is the externality problem developed above: New Jersey's policy is a response to outsiders' exporting their costs to New Jersey; the Court's approach prevents New Jersey from responding except by a highly calibrated and nondiscriminatory measure. (Note, also, that *New York v. United States* keeps Congress from stepping in and requiring Pennsylvania to find local sites for waste disposal.) In addition, as Tushnet himself points out, two other groups are involved in the state law — in-state landfill owners, who bear costs of the regulation, and out-of-state landfill owners, who benefit from the regulation. Hence, it is not true that the cost-bearers are entirely out-of-staters. While landfill owners are probably not a huge group within New Jersey, their very compactness and commonality of interest makes it quite likely that they will be well organized on any issue of landfill regulation and, hence, that their perspective will be heard during the legislative process.

Note further that if you want to play the cost-benefit game, you should consider long-run costs and benefits. Consider this argument: New Jersey is tired of being dumped on, and the cheapness of its landfill has discouraged industry in New York and Pennsylvania from developing technologies which dispose of wastes without damage to the environment and scenic beauty. In some ways, New Jersey's law may benefit everyone in the Northeast, as innovation-forcing regulation. To be sure, New Jersey's balance of policies may be self-interested, but in that event New York and Pennsylvania (with twice as many Senators and more than three times as many Representatives) can go to Congress to obtain a better allocation of costs and benefits. Indeed, why aren't these fatal problems with the representation-reinforcement justification for the Dormant Commerce Clause cases? Determining winners and losers, and costs and benefits, should be left to the political process, which has superior information-gathering capacity. It is no response to say that in many of these cases the losers are badly represented in the regulating state's political process, because they then have recourse to Congress.

3. *A Commitment Problem?* The Bednar and Eskridge theory relies on a domino effect, whereby any compromise of the free national marketplace will trigger state commitment problems and reprisals. But, as the next Note reveals, the Court's stringent approach in *City of Philadelphia* does not seem to have discouraged state and local governments from continuing to adopt environmental measures that burden or discriminate against interstate commerce. Does the popularity of environmental regulations suggest that states are willing to make the following counter-commitment: Each state is willing to tolerate some inconvenience because of neighbor state environmental regulations, so long as those regulations are reasonably related to environmental protection and are not

pretexts for economic advantage-seeking, and so long as the state can adopt its own reasonable environmental rules.

One can argue that Justice Rehnquist was right to dissent in *City of Philadelphia*: The pro-environmental regulations are more like quarantine laws than laws that hoard resources and business opportunities or that protect against interstate competition. By frustrating legitimate environmental protection efforts, is the Court undermining rather than protecting state enthusiasm for the federal arrangement?

NOTE ON THE POST-*PHILADELPHIA* WASTE CASES

Following *City of Philadelphia*'s stringent scrutiny, most state and local waste rules and taxes that discriminated on their face against interstate commerce have been declared unconstitutional by the Supreme Court. In *Chemical Waste Management, Inc. v. Hunt*, 504 U.S. 334 (1992), the Court struck down an Alabama law requiring commercial landfill owners to pay the state $25.60 per ton on all hazardous wastes disposed of, plus an additional $72.00 per ton for wastes generated outside Alabama. The Court applied *City of Philadelphia*'s strict scrutiny of a facial discrimination against interstate commerce. The additional fee was not justified by any evidence that out-of-state waste was more expensive to deal with, and other, nondiscriminatory methods were available for handling any problems that existed.

In *Oregon Waste Systems, Inc. v. Department of Environmental Quality*, 511 U.S. 93 (1994), the Court rejected a surcharge of $2.25 per ton for out-of-state waste, whose differential (three times the charge of $0.85 for in-state waste) the Court found unsupported by evidence of extra regulatory cost. The Court applied the same strict scrutiny to a state law forbidding private landfills from accepting solid waste generated outside its own county, not just outside the state, in *Fort Gratiot Sanitary Landfill, Inc. v. Michigan Dept. of Natural Resources*, 504 U.S. 353 (1992). The law failed strict scrutiny, because (again) there was no showing that out-of-state waste was more dangerous than in-state waste, and the purported state goal (accurate forecasting of the volume and composition of waste flows) could be better achieved by nondiscriminatory means such as caps on the total amount of waste that could be accepted.

In *C & A Carbone, Inc. v. Town of Clarkstown*, 511 U.S. 383 (1994), the Court struck down a municipal flow-control ordinance requiring all nonhazardous waste to be funneled through a privately operated waste treatment plant, even though it was sometimes cheaper to send it out-of-state. By limiting waste processing to a favored facility within its own jurisdiction, the town discriminated against interstate commerce and fell within the Court's local processing requirement precedents, which have almost always invalidated "laws hoard[ing] a local resource — be it meat, shrimp, or milk — for the benefit of local businesses that treat it. The flow control ordinance has the same design and effect. It hoards solid waste, and the demand to get rid of it, for the benefit of the preferred processing facility. The only conceivable distinction from the cases cited above is that the flow control ordinance favors a single local proprietor. But this difference just makes the protectionist effect of the ordinance more acute," because it "squelches competition in the waste-processing service altogether, leaving no room for investment from outside."

"Discrimination against interstate commerce in favor of local business or investment is per se invalid, save in a narrow class of cases in which the municipality can demonstrate, under rigorous scrutiny, that it has no other means to advance a legitimate local interest." *Amici* argued that the ordinance was needed to ensure safe handling of waste, given the shortage of landfill space and escalating environmental clean-up costs, but Justice Kennedy's opinion for the Court responded that the town could have achieved those safety goals through nondiscriminatory safety regulations. "State and local governments may not use their regulatory power to favor local enterprise by prohibiting patronage of out-of-state competitors or their facilities." Justice Souter's dissenting opinion viewed the regulation as a justified environmental regulation; it was anticompetitive but not protectionist. There was no exporting of costs to other jurisdictions.

UNITED HAULERS ASS'N, INC. v. ONEIDA-HERKIMER SOLID WASTE MANAGEMENT AUTHORITY
___ U.S. ___, 127 S.Ct. 1786, 167 L.Ed.2d 655 (2007)

CHIEF JUSTICE ROBERTS delivered the opinion of the Court.

[Oneida and Herkimer Counties adopted flow control ordinances requiring haulers to bring waste to facilities owned and operated by a state-created public benefit corporation.] We find this difference constitutionally significant. Disposing of trash has been a traditional government activity for years, and laws that favor the government in such areas — but treat every private business, whether in-state or out-of-state, exactly the same — do not discriminate against interstate commerce for purposes of the Commerce Clause. Applying the Commerce Clause test reserved for regulations that do not discriminate against interstate commerce, we uphold these ordinances because any incidental burden they may have on interstate commerce does not outweigh the benefits they confer on the citizens of Oneida and Herkimer Counties. [*Carbone* involved a similar flow-control ordinance, but the processing plant to which the flow was channeled was run by a *private* company, a point emphasized in the *Carbone* opinion.]

The flow control ordinances in this case benefit a clearly public facility, while treating all private companies exactly the same. Because the question is now squarely presented on the facts of the case before us, we decide that such flow control ordinances do not discriminate against interstate commerce for purposes of the dormant Commerce Clause.

Compelling reasons justify treating these laws differently from laws favoring particular private businesses over their competitors. "Conceptually, of course, any notion of discrimination assumes a comparison of substantially similar entities." But States and municipalities are not private businesses — far from it. Unlike private enterprise, government is vested with the responsibility of protecting the health, safety, and welfare of its citizens. * * *

Given these differences, it does not make sense to regard laws favoring local government and laws favoring private industry with equal skepticism. As our local processing cases demonstrate, when a law favors in-state business over out-of-state competition, rigorous scrutiny is appropriate because the law is often the product of "simple economic protectionism." Laws favoring local government, by contrast, may be directed toward any number of legitimate goals unrelated to protectionism. Here the flow control ordinances enable the Counties to pursue particular policies with respect to the handling and treatment of waste generated in the Counties, while allocating the costs of those policies on citizens and businesses according to the volume of waste they generate.

The contrary approach of treating public and private entities the same under the dormant Commerce Clause would lead to unprecedented and unbounded interference by the courts with state and local government. The dormant Commerce Clause is not a roving license for federal courts to decide what activities are appropriate for state and local government to undertake, and what activities must be the province of private market competition. In this case, the citizens of Oneida and Herkimer Counties have chosen the government to provide waste management services, with a limited role for the private sector in arranging for transport of waste from the curb to the public facilities. The citizens could have left the entire matter for the private sector, in which case any regulation they undertook could not discriminate against interstate commerce. But it was also open to them to vest responsibility for the matter with their government, and to adopt flow control ordinances to support the government effort. It is not the office of the Commerce Clause to control the decision of the voters on whether government or the private sector should provide waste management services. "The Commerce Clause significantly limits the ability of States and localities to regulate or otherwise burden the flow of interstate commerce, but it does not elevate free trade above all other values."

We should be particularly hesitant to interfere with the Counties' efforts under the guise of the Commerce Clause because "[w]aste disposal is both typically and traditionally a local government function." Congress itself has recognized local government's vital role in waste management, making clear that "collection and disposal of solid wastes should continue to be primarily the function of State, regional, and local agencies." Resource Conservation and Recovery Act of 1976, 42 U.S.C. § 6901(a)(4). The policy of the State of New York favors "displac[ing] competition with regulation or monopoly control" in this area. N.Y. Pub. Auth. Law Ann. § 2049-tt(3). We may or may not agree with that approach, but nothing in the Commerce Clause vests the responsibility for that policy judgment with the Federal Judiciary.

Finally, it bears mentioning that the most palpable harm imposed by the ordinances — more expensive trash removal — is likely to fall upon the very people who voted for the laws. Our dormant Commerce Clause cases often find discrimination when a State shifts the costs of regulation to other States, because when "the burden of state regulation falls on interests outside the state, it is unlikely to be alleviated by the operation of those political restraints normally exerted when interests within the state are affected." Here, the citizens and businesses of the Counties bear the costs of the ordinances. There is no reason to step in and hand local businesses a victory they could not obtain through the political process.

We hold that the Counties' flow control ordinances, which treat in-state private business interests exactly the same as out-of-state ones, do not "discriminate against interstate commerce" for purposes of the dormant Commerce Clause. * * *

[We omit the opinions of JUSTICE SCALIA, concurring in part, and of **JUSTICE THOMAS,** concurring in the judgment. The latter announced that he would jettison the Dormant Commerce Clause entirely; the former repeated that he would follow but not expand on binding precedents.]

JUSTICE ALITO, with whom **JUSTICE STEVENS** and **JUSTICE KENNEDY** join, dissenting. * * *

The fact that the flow control laws at issue discriminate in favor of a government-owned enterprise does not meaningfully distinguish this case from *Carbone*. The preferred facility in *Carbone* was, to be sure, nominally owned by a private contractor who had built the facility on the town's behalf, but it would be misleading to describe the facility as private. In exchange for the contractor's promise to build the facility for the town free of charge and then to sell it to the town five years later for $1, the town guaranteed that, during the first five years of the facility's existence, the contractor would receive "a minimum waste flow of 120,000 tons per year" and that the contractor could charge an above-market tipping fee. If the facility "received less than 120,000 tons in a year, the town [would] make up the tipping fee deficit." To prevent residents, businesses, and trash haulers from taking their waste elsewhere in pursuit of lower tipping fees (leaving the town responsible for covering any shortfall in the contractor's guaranteed revenue stream), the town enacted an ordinance "requir[ing] all nonhazardous solid waste within the town to be deposited at" the preferred facility. * * *

The only real difference between the facility at issue in *Carbone* and its counterpart in this case is that title to the former had not yet formally passed to the municipality. The Court exalts form over substance in adopting a test that turns on this technical distinction, particularly since, barring any obstacle presented by state law, the transaction in *Carbone* could have been restructured to provide for the passage of title at the beginning, rather than the end, of the 5-year period.* * *

In any event, we have never treated discriminatory legislation with greater deference simply because the entity favored by that legislation was a government-owned enterprise. * * *

The fallacy in the Court's approach can be illustrated by comparing a law that discriminates in favor of an in-state facility, owned by a corporation whose shares are publicly held, and a law discriminating in favor of an otherwise identical facility that is owned by the State or municipality. Those who are favored and disfavored by these two laws are essentially the same with one major exception: The law favoring the corporate facility presumably benefits the corporation's shareholders, most of whom are probably not local residents, whereas the law favoring the government-owned facility presumably benefits the people of the enacting State or municipality. I cannot understand why only the former law, and not the latter, should be regarded as a tool of economic protectionism. Nor do I think it is realistic or consistent with our precedents to condemn some discriminatory laws as protectionist while upholding other, equally discriminatory laws as lawful measures designed to serve legitimate local interests unrelated to protectionism. * * *

NOTES ON *UNITED HAULERS* AND THE KENTUCKY BONDS CASE

The debate among the Justices in *United Haulers* continued the next Term in *Department of Revenue of Kentucky v. Davis*, 128 S.Ct. 1801 (2008). The issue was whether Kentucky could exempt from state income taxation interest on its own bonds, but not interest on bonds issued by other states. Justice Souter's opinion for the Court upheld the discrimination against out-of-state bonds. The debate among the Justices illuminates some of the issues decided, or not, in *United Haulers*.

1. *Distinguishing* Carbone: *Does Government Ownership Make a Difference?* In *United Haulers,* the Chief Justice distinguished *Carbone* on the ground that the local government, rather than a private firm, owned and operated the waste treatment facility. In *Davis,* Justice Souter made a similar point, and Justice Stevens went along with allowing the discrimination in *Davis* that he disapproved in both *Carbone* and *United Haulers*.

If the goal of the Dormant Commerce Clause jurisprudence is protecting free markets and avoiding balkanization or "economic protectionism," why should government ownership make a difference? (Justice Alito raised this concern in his *United Haulers* dissent (joined by Justices Stevens and Kennedy), and Justice Kennedy raised it in his *Davis* dissent (joined by Justice Alito).) Does public operation provide evidence that the discrimination against interstate commerce is at least founded in a public-regarding purpose? The Chief Justice seemed to think so, a point that Justice Alito vigorously disputed, and for which the Chief presented no evidence. Relatedly, Justice Souter's *Davis* opinion applied the market participant exception to the Dormant Commerce Clause, but only Justices Stevens and Breyer joined that discussion.

2. *Balancing.* Although the Justices all claim to be applying per se rules and argue about how to categorize the schemes before them, we'd suggest that there is a fair amount of balancing afoot in these cases. When the Court applies the Dormant Commerce Clause to strike down state or local regulation, the Court is, to at least some extent, nationalizing that regulatory issue. In *United Haulers*, *amicus* briefs demonstrated that local waste processing was an issue of tremendous relevance to local governments. And Congress has repeatedly said that these issues are best handled at the local level. E.g., Resource Conservation and Recovery Act (RCRA) of 1976, Public Law No. 94-580, 90 Stat. 2795, codified at 42 U.S.C. § 6901(a)(4). Although the *United Haulers* dissenters responded that the Dormant Commerce Clause does not preempt all regulation, just discriminatory rules, the *amici* persuaded a plurality of Justices that monopolizing (i.e., discriminating against commerce) regulation was needed. Justice Souter made the same finding for the Kentucky exemption in *Davis*.

3. *Debate Over the Dormant Commerce Clause Generally.* The Dormant Commerce Clause represents an area of constitutional doctrine where the Court is even more internally divided than it is in the affirmative action, privacy, and federal power cases. There are three camps: (1) *The Zealous Enforcers.* Justices Stevens, Kennedy, and Alito zealously enforce the nationwide free market, anti-balkanization norm and are inclined to give the Dormant Commerce Clause precedents a normal or broad reading. (2) *The Anti-Enforcers.* Justices Scalia and Thomas object that the DCC jurisprudence is blatant judicial activism and ought not be extended one iota (Scalia) or ought to be abrogated (Thomas). (3) *The Pragmatists.* The remainder of the Justices are willing to apply the Dormant Commerce Clause precedents and the anti-balkanization norm, but with an eye to the value of local regulation and even discriminatory policies. They will also consider congressional signals (such as RCRA in *United Haulers*), how widespread a policy is and how long it has been in place, and perhaps also the apparent motivations for the policy.

If we are right about the current alignment of Justices, there is no stable majority position — or is there? Where would you take the Court's Dormant Commerce Clause jurisprudence? See generally Kenneth Karst, *From* Carbone *to* United Haulers: *The Advocates' Tales*, 2007 Sup. Ct. Rev. 237.

NOTE ON INTERSTATE TAXATION OF
INTERSTATE COMMERCE

What if Oneida County had financed its waste-treatment venture by a special tax applicable only on waste treated outside the town? A complex and perhaps not entirely coherent set of doctrines governs state taxation of interstate commerce. The prevailing approach to "discriminatory" state taxation is *Complete Auto Transit v. Brady*, 430 U.S. 274 (1977): To satisfy the Commerce Clause test, the tax must be "applied to an activity with substantial nexus with the taxing State, [must be] fairly apportioned, [must] not discriminate against interstate commerce, and [must be] fairly related to services provided by the State." Hence, a tax falling only on out-of-state haulers of waste would appear to be unconstitutional.

The Court's recent decisions suggest that the third and fourth prongs tend to collapse when the "discrimination" is in a statute's effect and not on its face: The brunt of a tax can be borne primarily by out-of-staters so long as there is some relationship between the tax and services or burdens on the state. E.g., *Commonwealth Edison v. Montana*, 453 U.S. 609 (1981) (upholding severance tax on coal, most of which is borne by out-of-state shippers and consumers). See also *Armco, Inc. v. Hardesty*, 467 U.S. 638 (1984); *Westinghouse Electric Corp. v. Tully*, 466 U.S. 388 (1984).

Commerce Clause restrictions on state taxation of multistate enterprises promise to remain an important area of constitutional law because of the increasingly multistate, and multinational, incidence of business operations.[k] See *General Motors Corp. v. Tracy*, 519 U.S. 278 (1997); *Barclays Bank PLC v. Franchise Tax Bd.*, 512 U.S. 298 (1994) (upholding state taxation of multinational companies, relying in part on congressional signals of approval).

NOTE ON STATE LAWS HAVING EXTRATERRITORIAL EFFECT

The Court identified state laws having extraterritorial effects as a Commerce Clause problem in *Brown-Forman Distillers Corp. v. New York State Liquor Auth.*, 476 U.S. 573 (1986). Under review was a New York law requiring liquor dealers selling wholesale in the state to file a price schedule every month and to sell in New York at the lowest price the distiller charged in any other state for that month. The Court struck it down under the *Baldwin* line of cases: "Economic protectionism is not limited to attempts to convey advantages to local merchants; it may include attempts to give local consumers an advantage over consumers in other States." New York could regulate the sale or even price of liquor within its borders, but the Commerce Clause sets limits on its ability to "project" its laws into other states by regulating the price to be paid in those states. In *Healy v. Beer Institute*, 491 U.S. 324 (1989), the Court invalidated a Connecticut law requiring beer companies to post prices every month and to certify that the posted prices were no higher than the prices they charged in three neighboring states. Because "the practical effect of the regulation is to control conduct beyond the boundaries of the State," the Court held the law subject to strict scrutiny. Because the "extraterritorial effect" of the law was to prevent "brewers from undertaking competitive pricing in Massachusetts based on prevailing market conditions," it was per se invalid.

It is not exactly clear how far the Court's rule against extraterritorial regulation reaches. Before these alcohol cases, the Due Process and Full Faith and Credit Clauses were the Constitution's mechanisms for reviewing extraterritorial application of state law. See *Allstate Ins. Co. v. Hague*, 449 U.S. 302 (1981). *Allstate* only bars extraterritorial application of state law when there are no meaningful contacts between the regulated activity and the regulating state. In contrast, *Brown-Forman* and *Healy* bar application of state law to extraterritorial economic activity even when it has substantial and harmful effects within the state. Note that *Allstate* construes a written constitutional provision, while *Healy* applies the nontextual Dormant Commerce Clause.[l]

2. *State Rules Burdening Interstate Commerce*

In a portion of *United Haulers* that we omitted, the Chief Justice considered a further argument, that the ordinance imposed an undue burden on interstate

---

k. See generally Jesse Choper & Tung Yin, *State Taxation and the Dormant Commerce Clause: The Object-Measure Approach*, 1998 Sup. Ct. Rev. 193; Howard Hunter, *Federalism and State Taxation of Multistate Enterprises*, 32 Emory L.J. 89 (1983); Daniel Shaviro, *A Political and Economic Look at Federalism in Taxation*, 90 Mich. L. Rev. 895 (1992).

l. For an argument that the Full Faith & Credit Clause should be more aggressively applied, see Kermit Roosevelt, III, *The Myth of Choice of Law: Rethinking Conflicts*, 97 Mich. L. Rev. 2448 (1999).

commerce and held that it did not. (Only three other Justices joined that part of Roberts's opinion.) He was invoking a line of cases evaluating state regulations having a *disruptive effect* on interstate commerce. Most of the cases involved transportation and inspection rules that on their face were neutral but in practice discriminated against interstate commerce. What to do with these cases has seriously divided the Supreme Court at least since the New Deal.

For example, in *South Carolina State Highway Dep't v. Barnwell Bros.*, 303 U.S. 177 (1938), the district court invalidated a South Carolina statute forbidding motor trucks whose width exceeded 90 inches and whose weight exceeded 20,000 pounds. The court found that the limitations imposed substantial burdens on interstate commerce, because 85% to 90% of the trucks in interstate commerce were 96 inches wide and weighed more than 20,000 pounds. Still, the Supreme Court reversed, because the state regulation was at least "fairly debatable."

In *Southern Pacific Co. v. Arizona*, 325 U.S. 761 (1945), however, the Court struck down an Arizona statute forbidding the operation of railroad trains of more than 14 passenger or 70 freight cars. The Court stated its now-classic rendition of the main dormant Commerce Clause inquiry: "Hence the matters for ultimate determination here are the nature and extent of the burden which the state regulation of interstate trains, adopted as a safety measure, imposes on interstate commerce, and whether the relative weights of the state and national interests involved are such as to make inapplicable the rule, generally observed, that the free flow of interstate commerce and its freedom from local restraints in matters requiring uniformity of regulation are interests safeguarded by the Commerce Clause from state interference." The Court concluded that the state went "too far," based upon factual findings that the rule greatly disrupted interstate train schedules and did not significantly enhance safety (because safety gains through shorter trains were more than offset by safety losses due to the larger number of trains). Why the different result from the *Barnwell Bros.* case (both opinions were by Justice Stone)? The Court emphasized the greater interest states have in highway safety versus the traditional federal interest in train regulation.

Since *Southern Pacific*, the Court has followed a fact-based balancing test (local benefits versus burden on interstate commerce), which has developed along the following lines: In determining the local benefits, the Court asks whether the state had a rational basis for enacting the law. Safety measures obviously qualify, and indeed carry a presumption of validity. See *Bibb v. Navajo Freight Lines, Inc.*, 359 U.S. 520 (1959). A finding of a legitimate localized purpose does not itself save the state law, however. The Court also evaluates the burden on interstate commerce and balances that against the local benefit. In balancing these interests, the Court considers the comparative impairment of the local and national interests (i.e., is the burden on commerce much more substantial than the benefit to safety, or vice versa?) and the even-handedness of the law (i.e., does it apply quite differently to intrastate transportation than to interstate transportation?). A leading statement of the test is in *Pike v. Bruce Church, Inc.*, 397 U.S. 137 (1970):

> Where the statute regulates evenhandedly to effectuate a legitimate local public interest, and its effects on interstate commerce are only incidental, it will be upheld unless the burden imposed on such commerce is clearly excessive in relation to the putative local benefits. If a legitimate local purpose is found, then the question becomes one of degree. And the extent of the burden that will be tolerated will of course depend on the nature of the local interest involved, and on whether it could be promoted as well with a lesser impact on interstate activities.

Consider the application of this test in the following celebrated case.

KASSEL v. CONSOLIDATED FREIGHTWAYS CORP.
450 U.S. 662, 101 S.Ct. 1309, 67 L.Ed.2d 580 (1981)

JUSTICE POWELL announced the judgment of the Court and delivered an opinion in which JUSTICE WHITE, JUSTICE BLACKMUN, and JUSTICE STEVENS joined.

[Consolidated Freightways Corporation of Delaware is one of the largest common carriers in the country. Consolidated carries commodities through Iowa on Interstate 80, the principal east-west route linking New York, Chicago, and the west coast, and on Interstate 35, a major north-south route. Consolidated mainly uses two kinds of trucks: a *semi*, a 55-foot long, three-axle tractor pulling a 40-foot two-axle trailer; and a *twin* or *double*, a 65-foot long, two-axle tractor pulling a single-axle trailer which, in turn, pulls a single-axle dolly and a second single-axle trailer. Consolidated would like to use 65-foot doubles on many of its trips through Iowa, but the state — alone in the Midwest or West — prohibits the use of 65-foot doubles within its borders.

[Under an Iowa statute, most truck combinations are restricted to 55 feet in length. Doubles, mobile homes, trucks carrying vehicles such as tractors and other farm equipment, and singles hauling livestock are permitted to be as long as 60 feet. Notwithstanding these restrictions, Iowa's statute permits cities abutting the state line by local ordinance to adopt the length limitations of the adjoining State. Where a city has exercised this option, otherwise oversized trucks are permitted within the city limits and in nearby commercial zones. Also, an Iowa truck manufacturer may obtain a permit to ship trucks that are as large as 70 feet, and permits are available to move oversized mobile homes, provided that the unit is to be moved from a point within Iowa or delivered for an Iowa resident.

[Consolidated challenged the statute as an unconstitutional burden on interstate commerce. Iowa defended the law as a reasonable safety measure. After a fourteen-day trial, the District Court ruled as a matter of fact that the double is as safe on the road as the semi and, more specifically, that the 65-foot double is as safe as, if not safer than, the 60-foot double and the 55-foot semi. "Twins and semis have different characteristics. Twins are more maneuverable, are less sensitive to wind, and create less splash and spray. However, they are more likely than semis to jackknife or upset. They can be backed only for a short distance. The negative characteristics are not such that they render the twin less safe than semis overall. Semis are more stable but are more likely to 'rear end' another vehicle." In light of these findings, the District Court applied the standard in *Raymond Motor Transportation, Inc. v. Rice*, 434 U.S. 429 (1978), and concluded that the state law impermissibly burdened interstate commerce. The Supreme Court affirmed.]

The Commerce Clause does not, of course, invalidate all state restrictions on commerce. * * * The extent of permissible state regulation is not always easy to measure. It may be said with confidence, however, that a State's power to regulate commerce is never greater than in matters traditionally of local concern. For example, regulations that touch upon safety — especially highway safety — are those that "the Court has been most reluctant to invalidate." *Raymond.* Indeed, "if safety justifications are not illusory, the court will not second-guess legislative judgment about their importance in comparison with related burdens on interstate commerce." *Raymond* (Blackmun, J., concurring). Those who would challenge such bona fide safety regulations must overcome a "strong presumption of validity." *Bibb.*

But the incantation of a purpose to promote the public health or safety does not insulate a state law from Commerce Clause attack. Regulations designed for that salutary purpose nevertheless may further the purpose so marginally, and interfere with commerce so substantially, as to be invalid under the Commerce Clause. In the Court's recent unanimous decision in *Raymond,* we declined to "accept the State's contention that the inquiry under the Commerce Clause is ended without a weighing of the asserted safety purpose against the degree of interference with interstate commerce." This "weighing" by a court requires — and indeed the constitutionality of the state regulation depends on — "a sensitive consideration of the weight and nature of the state regulatory concern in light of the extent of the burden imposed on the course of interstate commerce." * * *

In *Raymond,* the Court held that a Wisconsin statute that precluded the use of 65-foot doubles violated the Commerce Clause. This case is *Raymond* revisited. Here, as in *Raymond,* the State failed to present any persuasive evidence that 65-foot doubles are less safe than 55-foot singles. Moreover, Iowa's law is now out of step with the laws of all other Midwestern and Western States. Iowa thus substantially burdens the interstate flow of goods by truck. In the absence of congressional action to set uniform standards, some burdens associated with state safety regulations must be tolerated. But where, as here, the State's safety interest has been found to be illusory, and its regulations impair significantly the federal interest in efficient and safe interstate transportation, the state law cannot be harmonized with the Commerce Clause.

Iowa made a more serious effort to support the safety rationale of its law than did Wisconsin in *Raymond,* but its effort was no more persuasive. As noted above, the District Court found that the "evidence clearly establishes that the twin is as safe as the semi." The record supports this finding.

The trial focused on a comparison of the performance of the two kinds of trucks in various safety categories. The evidence showed, and the District Court found, that the 65-foot double was at least the equal of the 55-foot single in the ability to brake, turn, and maneuver. The double, because of its axle placement, produces less splash and spray in wet weather. And, because of its articulation in the middle, the double is less susceptible to dangerous "off-tracking," and to wind.

None of these findings is seriously disputed in Iowa. Indeed, the State points to only three ways in which the 55-foot single is even arguably superior: singles take less time to be passed and to clear intersections; they may back up for longer distances; and they are somewhat less likely to jackknife.

The first two of these characteristics are of limited relevance on modern interstate highways. As the District Court found, the negligible difference in the time required to pass, and to cross intersections, is insignificant on 4-lane divided highways because passing does not require crossing into oncoming traffic lanes, and interstates have few, if any, intersections. The concern over backing capability also is insignificant because it seldom is necessary to back up on an interstate. In any event, no evidence suggested any difference in backing capability between the 60-foot doubles that Iowa permits and the 65-foot doubles that it bans. Similarly, although doubles tend to jackknife somewhat more than singles, 65-foot doubles actually are less likely to jackknife than 60-foot doubles.

Statistical studies supported the view that 65-foot doubles are at least as safe overall as 55-foot singles and 60-foot doubles. One such study, which the District Court credited, reviewed Consolidated's comparative accident experience in 1978 with its own singles and doubles. Each kind of truck was driven 56 million miles on identical routes. The singles were involved in 100 accidents resulting in 27 injuries and one fatality. The 65-foot doubles were involved in 106 accidents resulting in 17 injuries and one fatality. Iowa's expert statistician admitted that this study provided "moderately strong evidence" that singles have a higher injury rate than doubles. Another study, prepared by the Iowa Department of Transportation at the request of the state legislature, concluded that "[s]ixty-five foot twin trailer combinations have *not* been shown by experiences in other states to be less safe than 60-foot twin trailer combinations *or* conventional tractor-semitrailers" (emphasis in original). Numerous insurance company executives, and transportation officials from the Federal Government and various States, testified that 65-foot doubles were at least as safe as 55-foot singles. Iowa concedes that it can produce no study that establishes a statistically significant difference in safety between the 65-foot double and the kinds of vehicles the State permits. Nor, as the District Court noted, did Iowa present a single witness who testified that 65-foot doubles were more dangerous overall than the vehicles permitted under Iowa law. In sum, although Iowa introduced more evidence on the question of safety than did Wisconsin in *Raymond*, the record as a whole was not more favorable to the State.

Consolidated, meanwhile, demonstrated that Iowa's law substantially burdens interstate commerce. Trucking companies that wish to continue to use 65-foot doubles must route them around Iowa or detach the trailers of the doubles and ship them through separately. Alternatively, trucking companies must use the smaller 55-foot singles or 60-foot doubles permitted under Iowa law. Each of these options engenders inefficiency and added expense. The record shows that Iowa's law added about $12.6 million each year to the costs of trucking companies. Consolidated alone incurred about $2 million per year in increased costs.

In addition to increasing the costs of the trucking companies (and, indirectly, of the service to consumers), Iowa's law may aggravate, rather than ameliorate, the problem of highway accidents. Fifty-five foot singles carry less freight than 65-foot doubles. Either more small trucks must be used to carry the same quantity of goods through Iowa, or the same number of large trucks must drive longer distances to bypass Iowa. In either case, as the District Court noted, the restriction requires more highway miles to be driven to transport the same quantity of goods. Other things being equal, accidents are proportional to distance traveled. Thus, if 65-foot doubles are as safe as 55-foot singles, Iowa's law tends to *increase* the number of accidents, and to shift the incidence of them from Iowa to other States.

Perhaps recognizing the weakness of the evidence supporting its safety argument, and the substantial burden on commerce that its regulations create, Iowa urges the Court simply to "defer" to the safety judgment of the State. It argues that the length of trucks is generally, although perhaps imprecisely, related to safety. The task of drawing a line is one that Iowa contends should be left to its legislature.

The Court normally does accord "special deference" to state highway safety regulations. *Raymond*. This traditional deference "derives in part from the assumption that where such regulations do not discriminate on their face against interstate commerce, their burden usually falls on local economic interests as well as other States' economic interests, thus insuring that a State's own political processes will serve as a check against unduly burdensome regulations." Less deference to the legislative judgment is due, however, where the local regulation bears disproportionately on out-of-state residents and businesses. Such a disproportionate burden is apparent here. Iowa's scheme, although generally banning large doubles from the State, nevertheless has several exemptions that secure to Iowans many of the benefits of large trucks while shunting to neighboring States many of the costs associated with their use.

At the time of trial there were two particularly significant exemptions. First, singles hauling livestock or farm vehicles were permitted to be as long as 60 feet. As the Court of Appeals noted, this provision undoubtedly was helpful to local interests. Cf. *Raymond* (exemption in Wisconsin for milk shippers). Second, cities abutting other States were permitted to enact local ordinances adopting the larger length limitation of the neighboring State. This exemption offered the benefits of longer trucks to individuals and businesses in important border cities without burdening Iowa's highways with interstate through traffic. Cf. *Raymond* (exemption in Wisconsin for shipments from local plants).

The origin of the "border cities exemption" also suggests that Iowa's statute may not have been designed to ban dangerous trucks, but rather to discourage interstate truck traffic. In 1974, the legislature passed a bill that would have permitted 65-foot doubles in the State. Governor Ray vetoed the bill. He said:

> I find sympathy with those who are doing business in our state and whose enterprises could gain from increased cargo carrying ability by trucks. However, with this bill, the Legislature has pursued a course that would benefit only a few Iowa-based companies while providing a great advantage for out-of-state trucking firms and competitors at the expense of our Iowa citizens.

After the veto, the "border cities exemption" was immediately enacted and signed by the Governor.

It is thus far from clear that Iowa was motivated primarily by a judgment that 65-foot doubles are less safe than 55-foot singles. Rather, Iowa seems to have hoped to limit the use of its highways by deflecting some through traffic. In the District Court and Court of Appeals, the State explicitly attempted to justify the law by its claimed interest in keeping trucks out of Iowa. The Court of Appeals correctly concluded that a State cannot constitutionally promote its own parochial interests by requiring safe vehicles to detour around it. * * *

JUSTICE BRENNAN, with whom JUSTICE MARSHALL joins, concurring in the judgment. * * *

For me, analysis of Commerce Clause challenges to state regulations must take into account three principles: (1) The courts are not empowered to second-guess the empirical judgments of lawmakers concerning the utility of legislation. (2) The burdens imposed on commerce must be balanced against the local benefits actually sought to be achieved by the State's lawmakers, and not against those suggested after the fact by counsel. (3) Protectionist legislation is unconstitutional under the Commerce Clause, even if the burdens and benefits are related to safety rather than economics.

Both the opinion of my Brother Powell and the opinion of my Brother Rehnquist are predicated upon the supposition that the constitutionality of a state regulation is determined by the factual record created by the State's lawyers in the trial court. But that supposition cannot be correct, for it would make the constitutionality of state laws and regulations depend on the vagaries of litigation rather than on the judgments made by the State's lawmakers.

In considering a Commerce Clause challenge to a state regulation, the judicial task is to balance the burden imposed on commerce against the local benefits sought to be achieved by the State's *lawmakers*. In determining those benefits, a court should focus ultimately on the regulatory purposes identified by the lawmakers and on the evidence before or available to them that might have supported their judgment. [The actual purpose of the Iowa lawmakers was to discourage interstate truck traffic on Iowa highways, not to improve traffic safety.]

[A 1974 statute] would have increased the maximum length of twin trailer trucks operable in Iowa from 60 to 65 feet. But Governor Ray * * * vetoed the legislation. The legislature did not override the veto, and the present regulation was thus maintained. In his veto, Governor Ray did not rest his decision on the conclusion that 55-foot singles and 60-foot doubles are any safer than 65-foot doubles, or on any other safety consideration inherent in the type or size of the trucks. Rather, his principal concern was that to allow 65-foot doubles would "basically ope[n] our state to literally thousands and thousands more trucks per year." This increase in interstate truck traffic would, in the Governor's estimation, greatly increase highway maintenance costs, which are borne by the citizens of the State, and increase the number of accidents and fatalities within the State. The legislative response was not to override the veto, but to accede to the Governor's action, and in accord with this basic premise, to enact a "border cities exemption." This permitted cities within border areas to allow 65-foot doubles while otherwise maintaining the 60-foot limit throughout the State to discourage interstate truck traffic. * * *

This Court's heightened deference to the judgments of state lawmakers in the field of safety is largely attributable to a judicial disinclination to weigh the interests of safety against other societal interests, such as the economic interest in the free flow of commerce. Thus, "if safety justifications are not illusory, the Court will not second-guess legislative judgment about their importance in *comparison with related burdens on interstate commerce.*" *Raymond* (Blackmun, J., concurring) (emphasis added). Here, the decision of Iowa's lawmakers to promote *Iowa's* safety and other interests at the direct expense of the safety and other interests of neighboring States merits no such deference. No special judicial acuity is demanded to perceive that this sort of parochial legislation violates the Commerce Clause. As Justice Cardozo has written, the Commerce Clause "was framed upon the theory that the peoples of the several states must sink or swim together, and that in the long run prosperity and salvation are in union and not division." *Baldwin v. G.A.F. Seelig, Inc.*

JUSTICE REHNQUIST, with whom **THE CHIEF JUSTICE [BURGER]** and **JUSTICE STEWART** join, dissenting.

The result in this case suggests, to paraphrase Justice Jackson, that the only state truck-length limit "that is valid is one which this court has not been able to get its hands on." * * *

It is necessary to elaborate somewhat on the facts as presented in the plurality opinion to appreciate fully what the Court does today. Iowa's action in limiting the length of trucks which may travel on its highways is in no sense unusual. Every State in the Union regulates the length of vehicles permitted to use the public roads. Nor is Iowa a renegade in having length limits which operate to exclude the 65-foot doubles favored by Consolidated. These trucks are prohibited in other areas of the country as well, some 17 States and the District of Columbia, including all of New England and most of the Southeast. While pointing out that Consolidated carries commodities through Iowa on Interstate 80, "the principal east-west route linking New York, Chicago, and the west coast," the plurality neglects to note that both Pennsylvania and New Jersey, through which Interstate 80 runs before reaching New York, also ban 65-foot doubles. In short, the persistent effort in the plurality opinion to paint Iowa as an oddity standing alone to block commerce carried in 65-foot doubles is simply not supported by the facts. * * *

The District Court approached the case as if the question were whether Consolidated's 65-foot trucks were as safe as others permitted on Iowa highways, and the Court of Appeals as if its task were to determine if the District Court's factual findings in this regard were "clearly erroneous." The question, however, is whether the Iowa Legislature has acted rationally in regulating vehicle lengths and whether the safety benefits from this regulation are more than slight or problematical. * * * "Since the adoption of one weight or width regulation, rather than another, is a legislative and not a judicial choice, its constitutionality is not to be determined by weighing in the judicial scales the merits of the legislative choice and rejecting it if the weight of evidence presented in court appears to favor a different standard." *Barnwell Brothers*. * * *

It must be emphasized that there is nothing in the laws of nature which make 65-foot doubles an obvious norm. Consolidated operates 65-foot doubles on many of its routes simply because that is the largest size permitted in many States through which Consolidated travels. Doubles can and do come in smaller sizes; indeed, when Iowa adopted the present 60-foot limit in 1963, it was in accord with [American Association of State Highway and Transportation Officials] recommendations. Striking down Iowa's law because Consolidated has made a voluntary business decision to employ 65-foot doubles, a decision based on the actions of other state legislatures, would essentially be compelling Iowa to yield to the policy choices of neighboring States. Under our constitutional scheme, however, there is only one legislative body which can pre-empt the rational policy determination of the Iowa Legislature and that is Congress. Forcing Iowa to yield to the policy choices of neighboring States perverts the primary purpose of the Commerce Clause, that of vesting power to regulate interstate commerce in Congress, where all the States are represented. * * *

Both the plurality and concurring opinions attach great significance to the Governor's veto of a bill passed by the Iowa Legislature permitting 65-foot doubles. Whatever views one may have about the significance of legislative motives, it must be emphasized that the law which the Court strikes down today was not passed to achieve the protectionist goals the plurality and the concurrence ascribe to the Governor. Iowa's 60-foot length limit was established in 1963, at a time when very few States permitted 65-foot doubles. Striking down legislation on the basis of asserted legislative motives is dubious enough, but the plurality and concurrence strike down the legislation involved in this case because of asserted impermissible motives for *not* enacting *other* legislation, motives which could not possibly have been present when the legislation under challenge here was considered and passed. Such action is, so far as I am aware, unprecedented in this Court's history.

NOTES ON *KASSEL* AND JUDICIAL BALANCING TO EVALUATE STATE LAWS BURDENING INTERSTATE COMMERCE

1. *The Ongoing Debate about the Legitimacy of Balancing.* The *Pike/Southern Pacific* balancing test recalls the Court's debate in the 1940s over whether or not the Court is institutionally competent to engage in serious utilitarian (cost-benefit) analysis. Compare the debate between Justices Frankfurter and Black in *Adamson v. California* (Chapter 5, § 1), over whether the Due Process Clause of the Fourteenth Amendment selectively "incorporates" only the most "fundamental" of the Bill of Rights protections and not all of them. Justice Black, who opposed "balancing" in *Adamson*, wrote a scathing dissent in *Southern Pacific*. He found the trial court proceeding in the case "extraordinary" in second-guessing the legislature's evaluation of the costs and benefits in a long-running battle between railroads and railroad workers at the state and national level. "[This] new pattern of trial procedure makes it necessary for a judge to hear all the evidence offered as to why a legislature passed a law and to make findings of fact as to the validity of those reasons. [In] this respect, [this] Court

today is acting as a 'super-legislature.' " What would Justice Black have said about the trial record in *Kassel*?

On the current Court, Justice Scalia has articulated a position similar to that of Justice Black:

> I do not know what qualifies us to make [the] ultimate (and most ineffable) judgment as to whether, given the importance-level x, and effectiveness-level y, the worth of the statute is "outweighed" by impact-on-commerce z. One commentator has suggested that * * * we do not in fact mean what we say when we declare that statutes that neither discriminate against commerce nor present a threat of multiple and inconsistent burdens might nonetheless be unconstitutional under a "balancing" test. If he is not correct, he ought to be. As long as a State's [law does] not discriminate against out-of-state interests [on its face], it should survive this Court's scrutiny. [Beyond] that, it is for Congress to prescribe its invalidity.

CTS Corporation v. Dynamics Corporation, 481 U.S. 69 (1987) (Scalia, J., concurring).[m] In *United Haulers*, Justice Scalia declined to join that part of the Chief Justice's opinion that applied the *Pike* balancing test. In *Department of Revenue of Kentucky v. Davis*, 128 S.Ct. 1801 (2008), the taxation of out-of-state municipal bonds case, Justice Souter's opinion for the Court declined to apply the *Pike* test on the ground that there were no comparable costs and benefits that could be weighed by judges.

Note also the obvious contrast between activist judicial review of facially neutral state laws having a *discriminatory effect on interstate commerce* (*Kassel*) and nonactivist judicial review of facially neutral state laws having a *discriminatory effect on racial minorities or women* (*Washington v. Davis* (Chapter 3, § 1B) and *Feeney* (Chapter 4, § 2B)). Can this contrast be defended?

Is *Kassel* a good example of academic and judicial criticisms of balancing? After you read the plurality and concurring opinions, is there any basis for deferring to the state judgment, as Justice Rehnquist argues? The evidence seemed overwhelming that there were no safety reasons supporting Iowa's policy — beyond the stated reason that, if Iowa could shift (export) interstate truck traffic to other states, *Iowa* drivers would be safer, even if at the expense of safety in *Minnesota* or *Missouri* (to which traffic would be diverted). This seems not only irrational, but politically perverse, and a much better example of the Stone/Tushnet representation-reinforcement analysis than the facial discrimination cases such as *City of Philadelphia* and *Carbone*. If you follow Justice Scalia and the commentators, are you not sacrificing the whole point of the Dormant Commerce Clause, namely, clearing the channels of interstate commerce?

2. *Congress as a Forum for Curing Discriminatory Effects on Interstate Commerce*. Maybe the point of the Commerce Clause is that it empowers

---

m. Scalia's reference in text was to Donald Regan, *The Supreme Court and State Protectionism: Making Sense of the Dormant Commerce Clause*, 84 Mich. L. Rev. 1091 (1986). Other commentators agree with Scalia and Regan that the Court is not the best decisionmaker in these kinds of cases. See Julian Eule, *Laying the Dormant Commerce Clause to Rest*, 91 Yale L.J. 425 (1982); Daniel Farber, *State Regulation and the Dormant Commerce Clause*, 3 Const. Comm. 395 (1986); Robert Sedler, *The Negative Commerce Clause as a Restriction on State Regulation and Taxation: An Analysis in Terms of Constitutional Structure*, 31 Wayne St. L. Rev. 885 (1985).

Congress (it's in Article I), not the Court. If the ills described in the *Kassel* opinions are genuine and interstate commerce really is being clogged, Congress and the President have incentives to intervene. Indeed, *Kassel* did trigger a response: In 1984, Congress amended the Surface Transportation Act to authorize state governors to petition the Secretary of Transportation to exclude doubles and other oversize vehicles from portions of the interstate highway system if the Secretary were persuaded by state showings of real safety problems.[n] Thus, state safety regulation is preempted, but safety issues are resolved at the national rather than state level and by a flexible fact-finding process that can respond to new evidence and political considerations. Is this not preferable to having the Court balance costs and benefits from case to case? Would the 1984 statute have been enacted without *Kassel*, though?

3. *The Anomaly of Creeping Unconstitutionality.* Iowa bought itself trouble by building exceptions into the state law that favored in-state interests. The Court has had few cases in which a truly nondiscriminatory state measure has been challenged because it unduly burdens interstate commerce. *Bibb* is perhaps the best example. In that case, Illinois required trucks operating in that state to have contour rear-fender mudguards; 45 states authorized the use of straight mudguards, and Arkansas actually required the straight ones and outlawed the contour ones. The Court concluded that the Illinois law was unconstitutional because it added little to highway safety and seriously disrupted interstate commerce (by requiring a carrier to shift cargo from one kind of carrier to another as state lines were crossed). Self-serving motives can be identified for the Illinois regulation, but the case stands for the proposition that even without them, and even without a clear showing that the regulation had effects favoring in-state interests, state regulation can nonetheless unduly burden the flow of interstate commerce.

Without the in-state exceptions, and Governor Ray's indiscreet veto statement, the Iowa situation was similar to that in *Bibb*: A regulation surely constitutional when it was adopted in 1963 became unconstitutional over time because it fell out of step with the allowances of other midwestern and western states, as Justice Rehnquist's dissent charged. Even Richard Collins, who endorses the Court's balancing approach, has expressed reservations about applying it to invalidate state statutes that burden commerce only because they have grown inconsistent with the laws of other states.[o] Why? Would his rationale apply to *Kassel*, where there was damning evidence concerning the reason Iowa declined to conform to the policy adopted by surrounding states?

Granholm v. Heald, 544 U.S. 460 (2005). Michigan and New York regulate the sale and importation of wine through three-tier systems requiring separate licenses for producers, wholesalers, and retailers. Their regulatory schemes allow in-state, but not out-of-state, wineries to make direct sales to

---

n. See Tandem Truck Safety Act of 1984, Pub. L. No. 98-554, §§ 102-03, 98 Stat. 2829-30.

o. See Richard Collins, *Justice Scalia and the Elusive Idea of Discrimination Against Interstate Commerce*, 20 N. Mex. L. Rev. 555 (1990).

consumers. Because this differential treatment explicitly discriminates against interstate commerce by limiting the emerging and significant direct-sale business, **Justice Kennedy**'s opinion for the Court found no difficulty holding it a violation of the Dormant Commerce Clause rule against "differential treatment of in-state and out-of-state economic interests that benefits the former and burdens the latter." Justice Kennedy waxed eloquent against the evils of a "low-level trade war" among the states created by such discriminatory rules, and invoked the virtual "per se rule of invalidity" recognized in *City of Philadelphia*.

No Justice disputed this much of Kennedy's analysis, but **Justice Thomas**'s dissenting opinion (joined by the **Chief Justice** and **Justices Stevens** and **O'Connor** — the three oldest Justices) argued that Congress authorized plenary state regulation of liquor in the Webb-Kenyon Act, which prohibits any "shipment or transportation" of alcoholic beverages "into any State" when those beverages are "intended, by any person interested therein, to be received, possessed, sold, or in any manner used . . . in violation of any law of such State." 27 U.S.C. § 122. The Court in *McCormick & Co. v. Brown*, 286 U.S. 131, 139-40 (1932), interpreted the Act to free the states of Dormant Commerce Clause claims, and Congress reenacted the statute in 1935 under this assumption about its meaning.

Justice Kennedy, in turn, did not dispute that Congress can authorize state laws that would otherwise violate the Dormant Commerce Clause but replied with a clear statement rule: the "Webb-Kenyon Act expresses no clear congressional intent to depart from the principle . . . that discrimination against out-of-state goods is disfavored." (*McCormick*, for example, upheld a state law that was nondiscriminatory.) Justice Thomas disagreed. He not only argued that the plain meaning of the statute was clear enough to demonstrate a congressional allowance of plenary state regulation of liquor, but also argued that the legislative history and background of the Act demonstrated a legislative intent to allow discriminatory state laws. The Court ruled in *Scott v. Donald*, 165 U.S. 58 (1897), that earlier congressional authorizing legislation did not allow the states to enact laws discriminating against out-of-state liquor by barring importation for personal use. Justice Thomas relied on legislative history to show that Congress meant to override *Scott* and reinstate the states' plenary authority when it enacted Webb-Kenyon. (Justice Kennedy maintained that the statute left *Scott*'s nondiscrimination holding intact.)

Justice Thomas also argued that the Michigan/New York schemes were saved by Section 2 of the Twenty-First Amendment: "The transportation or importation into any State, Territory, or possession of the United States for delivery or use therein of intoxicating liquors, in violation of the laws thereof, is hereby prohibited." The language is broader than that of Webb-Kenyon and broad enough to authorize discriminatory as well as nondiscriminatory state liquor statutes. Indeed, the Court so held in *State Bd. of Equalization of Cal. v. Young's Market Co.*, 299 U.S. 59 (1936). California law facially discriminated against beer importers and, by extension, out-of-state producers. The Court held that this explicit discrimination against out-of-state beer products came within the terms of the Twenty-first Amendment, and therefore did not run afoul of the Dormant Commerce Clause. The Court reasoned that the Twenty-first Amendment's words are "apt to confer upon the State the power to forbid all importations which do not comply with the conditions which it prescribes." The Court reaffirmed *Young's Market* in subsequent cases, and the states engaged in all manner of discriminatory liquor-regulatory schemes, similar to those in New York and Michigan, and without serious constitutional quarrel after the *Young's Market* cases. (In a separate dissent, **Justice Stevens** personally recalled the context of the Twenty-First Amendment to support Justice Thomas's analysis.)

Justice Kennedy responded that the Court's Twenty-First Amendment jurisprudence took the same turn its Commerce Clause jurisprudence did after the 1930s — toward greater limitations on state authority. In *Bacchus Imports, Ltd. v. Dias*, 468 U.S. 263 (1984), for example, the Court struck down a Hawaii statute exempting local products from the state's 20% excise tax on liquor. The Court held that the Twenty-First Amendment did not implicitly repeal or modify the Commerce Clause and therefore did not authorize state laws amounting to "mere economic protectionism." The Amendment's "central purpose ... was not to empower States to favor local liquor industries by erecting barriers to competition." Justice Thomas urged the Court to overrule or limit *Bacchus*, not cast aside a century of liquor jurisprudence and the plain meaning of the Twenty-First Amendment.

PROBLEM 7-7
DORMANT COMMERCE CLAUSE QUANDARIES

(a) *Apple Grading.* North Carolina has a small, struggling apple industry. It enacts a statute requiring all closed containers of apples sold or shipped into the state to bear "no grade other than the applicable U.S. grade or standard." The stated purpose of the statute was to prevent fraud in apple marketing. The state of Washington has the nation's largest apple industry, and boasts of the highest quality apples. Washington requires that its apples be graded on a scale superior to the standards used by the United States Department of Agriculture. To comply with the North Carolina law, Washington apple growers would have to use only the USDA labeling, and not their own higher-standard labeling. Washington apple growers challenge the North Carolina statute under the Dormant Commerce Clause. What evidence will the judges be interested in? Will the challengers likely prevail? Should they? See *Hunt v. Washington State Apple Advertising Commission*, 432 U.S. 333 (1977).

(b) *State Takeover Law.* Although federal law regulates corporate takeovers by imposing disclosure requirements, Illinois adopts a statute requiring registration with the state 20 days before a tender offer is made to take over companies incorporated in the state or doing business in the state. During the 20-day period, the offeror could not communicate with the shareholders of the targeted company, but that company's management could communicate with its shareholders. The state could refuse to allow the offer to proceed if the Illinois Secretary of State concluded that it did not fully disclose material information or was inequitable or fraudulent. Companies challenge the constitutionality of this law. What are their odds of prevailing under the *Pike/Kassel* balancing approach? *City of Philadelphia*? See *Edgar v. MITE Corp.*, 457 U.S. 624 (1982).[p]

(c) *State Regulation of the Internet.* New York adopts a law criminalizing intentional use of the Internet to "initiate or engage" in communications "harmful to minors," specifically, those depicting "actual or simulated nudity, sexual conduct, or sado-mascohistic abuse." Purveyors of such materials are protected against criminal liability if they (1) restrict minors' access by requiring credit card verification to enter their websites; (2) identify the not-for-minors content of their sites through means that facilitate parental blocking etc.; or (3) make other reasonable efforts to prevent minors from accessing the materials. A publishers' group brings suit for a declaratory judgment that this law unduly burdens commerce. What is the best argument for each side? How should the federal trial judge rule? See *American Libraries Ass'n v. Pataki*, 969 F. Supp. 160 (S.D.N.Y. 1997).[q]

3. *The Market Participant and Other Possible Exceptions*

The Court in *City of Philadelphia* noted a possible loophole in the Dormant Commerce Clause, for the Court expressed no opinion regarding a state's power to "restrict to state residents access to state-owned resources [or] to spend state funds solely on behalf of state residents and businesses" (footnote 6 of the Court's opinion). The latter exemption for discretionary state spending is related to the "market participant" exception to the Dormant Commerce Clause the Court recognized in *Hughes v. Alexandria Scrap Corp.*, 426 U.S. 794 (1976). Under this exception, when the state participates as an actor in the market, it can behave in discriminatory ways not permitted when it acts in its regulatory and taxing capacity. In *Alexandria Scrap*, Maryland offered a bounty for abandoned cars, in order to speed up their removal from public spaces, but conditioned the bounty in ways that favored in-state over out-of-state processing of the cars. The Court refused to apply the *Pike* balancing test, because it held that the Dormant Commerce Clause does not cover situations where "the entry by the State itself in the market as a purchaser, in effect, of a potential article of interstate commerce creates a burden upon that commerce if the State restricts its trade to its own citizens or businesses within the State." (Note that this exception might swallow up the rule of *City of Philadelphia*, as more than 80% of the nation's landfill is owned and operated by state and local governments.[r])

---

p. See Daniel Fischel, *From* MITE *to* CTS: *State Anti-Takeover Statutes, the Williams Act, the Commerce Clause, and Insider Trading*, 1987 Sup. Ct. Rev. 47.

q. Compare Dan Burk, *Federalism in Cyberspace*, 28 Conn. L. Rev. 1095 (1996) (urging strict judicial scrutiny of such laws), with Jack Goldsmith & Alan Sykes, *The Internet and the Dormant Commerce Clause*, 110 Yale L.J. 785 (2001) (supporting a wider berth for state regulation).

r. See David Pomper, Note, *Recycling* Philadelphia v. New Jersey: *The Dormant Commerce Clause, Postindustrial "Natural" Resources, and the Solid Waste Crisis*, 137 U. Pa. L. Rev. 1309 (1989).

Neither the reach nor the precise rationale for the market participant exception is clear.[s] *Alexandria Scrap*'s rationale was that the Dormant Commerce Clause only targets state regulation of a preexisting market, not state creation of a market on terms the state desires. There is no indication of a constitutional design to limit the ability of the states to spend their own money or to operate in the free market (see Madison's original statement of the dormant principle in the Commerce Clause, as well as the early cases, such as *Gibbons*). When states "act like" private proprietors, they are subject to more restrictions on their activities, and so ought to have at least some of the freedom of action that private proprietors have. But if the Dormant Commerce Clause has essentially been made up by the Court to prevent economic balkanization, why should the state's capacity as a proprietor versus a regulator, or as a spender rather than tax collector of money, make a constitutional difference? For example, if Clarkstown itself had owned the waste treatment plant, should its regulation have been acceptable in *Carbone*? Would it be constitutional for Clarkstown to tax all companies collecting waste, and then use those monies to subsidize the private waste treatment plant? To subsidize a waste treatment plant it owns?

Alternatively, the Court said in *Reeves, Inc. v. Stake*, 447 U.S. 429 (1980) (upholding South Dakota's policy of restricting the sale of cement from a state-owned plant to state residents), "the competing considerations in cases involving state proprietary action often will be subtle, complex, politically charged, and difficult to assess under traditional Commerce Clause analysis. Given these factors * * * as a rule, the adjustment of interests in this context is a task better suited for Congress than this Court." This seems at odds with *Kassel* and the activist philosophy of the Dormant Commerce Clause cases generally.

Professor Donald Regan argues that justification of the market participant exception rests upon the functional differences between discriminatory state spending, as opposed to discriminatory state taxes or regulations.[t] Spending discriminations are less likely to trigger the prisoners' dilemma of spiraling retaliations that open discriminations and even indirect regulations might trigger. In light of Regan's theory, is the following case wrongly decided, under either the market participant exception or general principles of the Dormant Commerce Clause?

---

s. *Alexandria Scrap* has been followed in *White v. Massachusetts Council of Constr. Employers, Inc.*, 460 U.S. 204 (1983), and *Reeves, Inc. v. Stake*, 447 U.S. 429 (1980). The Court in *South-Central Timber Dev. v. Wunnicke*, 467 U.S. 82 (1984), fractured badly on the application of the exception to Alaska's requirement tying the sale of timber owned by the state to processing the timber in Alaska, rather than out-of-state, by purchasers. The Court majority invalidated the state rule, but there was no rationale commanding a majority of the Justices. In *United Haulers*, the Chief Justice mentioned the market participant exception but did not rely on it.

t. See Donald Regan, *The Supreme Court and State Protectionism: Making Sense of the Dormant Commerce Clause*, 84 Mich. L. Rev. 1091, 1194 (1986); accord, Laurence Tribe, *Constitutional Choices* 145 (1985). For other thoughtful discussions, see Dan Coenen, *Untangling the Market-Participant Exemption to the Dormant Commerce Clause*, 88 Mich. L. Rev. 395 (1989); Mark Gergen, *The Selfish State and the Market*, 66 Tex. L. Rev. 1097 (1988); Jonathan Varat, *State "Citizenship" and Interstate Equality*, 48 U. Chi. L. Rev. 487 (1981).

West Lynn Creamery, Inc. v. Healy, 512 U.S. 186 (1994). Massachusetts imposed a nondiscriminatory tax on wholesale milk transactions and used the result to fund cash payments to the state's struggling dairy farmers. The Court, per **Justice Stevens**, held that this scheme, when viewed holistically, had the same economic effect as a tariff. "Its avowed purpose and its undisputed effect are to allow higher cost Massachusetts dairy farmers to compete with lower cost dairy farmers in other States. The 'premium payments' are effectively a tax which makes milk produced out of State more expensive. Although the tax also applies to milk produced in Massachusetts, its effect on Massachusetts producers is entirely (indeed more than) offset by the subsidy provided exclusively to Massachusetts dairy farmers. Like an ordinary tariff, the tax is thus effectively imposed on only out-of-state products. The pricing order thus allows Massachusetts dairy farmers who produce at a higher cost to sell at or below the price charged by lower cost out-of-state producers. This effect renders the program unconstitutional, because it, like a tariff, 'neutralize[s] advantages belonging to the place of origin.' "

The state defended with the argument that each of the components of its program — the nondiscriminatory tax and the discriminatory subsidy — was constitutional. Justice Stevens responded: "However, when a nondiscriminatory tax is coupled with a subsidy to one of the groups hurt by the tax, a state's political processes can no longer be relied upon to prevent legislative abuse, because one of the in-state interests which would otherwise lobby against the tax has been mollified by the subsidy." The state also claimed that the cost of the program was not exported in any sense, for it was borne entirely by in-state consumers (who therefore had political incentives to repeal the program if not in some longer-term public interest). Justice Stevens responded that much the same could be said of a tariff, the classic instance of a Dormant Commerce Clause violation. Moreover, this argument "ignores the fact that Massachusetts dairy farmers are part of an integrated interstate market. The purpose and effect of the pricing order are to divert market share to Massachusetts dairy farmers. This diversion necessarily injures the dairy farmers in neighboring States," making it oversimple to assume that only in-state consumers are harmed.

In a concurring opinion, **Justice Scalia**, joined by **Justice Thomas**, reiterated his view that Dormant Commerce Clause jurisprudence is illegitimate. Feeling obligated to follow existing precedent, however, he suggested this distinction: A subsidy for in-state businesses can be financed out of general revenue but not through an earmarked tax. "Perhaps, as some commentators contend, that line comports with an important economic reality: a State is less likely to maintain a subsidy when its citizens perceive that the money (in the general fund) is available for any number of competing, non-protectionist purposes."

Chief Justice Rehnquist dissented, in an opinion joined by **Justice Blackmun**. They objected to the Court's defense of the Dormant Commerce Clause based on supposed interest group alignment. The last time the Court had struck down a tax because of the use to which its revenues was put was in *United States v. Butler*, 297 U.S. 1 (1936), a *Lochner*-era precedent now viewed as discredited.

NOTE: SHOULD STATE SUBSIDIES BE EXEMPTED FROM DORMANT COMMERCE CLAUSE REGULATION?

A number of commentators agree with Justice Scalia that a subsidy supported by general tax revenues ought not be subjected to Dormant Commerce Clause scrutiny. They have argued that subsidies were not the original concerns of the Framers or the Justices developing the early history of this line of cases, see Dan Coenen, *Business Subsidies and the Dormant Commerce Clause*, 107 Yale L.J. 965 (1998); can be socially beneficial, especially when they confer positive externalities on the state and its economy, see Note, *Functional Analysis, Subsidies, and the Dormant Commerce Clause*, 110 Harv. L. Rev. 1537 (1997); and are less likely to have cost-exporting or protectionist effects. See Peter Enrich, *Saving the States from Themselves: Commerce Clause Constraints on State Tax Incentives for Business*, 110 Harv. L. Rev. 377 (1996). On the other hand, Edward Zelinsky, *Are Tax Benefits Constitutionally Equivalent to Direct Expenditures?*, 112 Harv. L. Rev. 379 (1998), argues that there is no functional difference between a state subsidy for in-state businesses, which Justice Scalia would immunize, and a state tax break for in-state businesses, which is invalid under the Court's interstate taxation cases. Enrich responds that tax incentives are more likely than subsidies to slide through the state appropriations process as special rent-seeking measures and therefore need greater judicial policing. Thus far, the lower courts have declined to apply *West Lynn Creamery* to state subsidy programs not connected to a specific tax. See, e.g., *Cumberland Farms, Inc. v. Mahany*, 943 F. Supp. 83 (D. Me. 1996).

C. SHOULD THE DORMANT COMMERCE CLAUSE BE LAID TO REST? ALTERNATIVE LIMITATIONS ON STATES

Several academic commentators, from a variety of perspectives, have called for laying the Dormant Commerce Clause to rest.[u] The defects of the doctrine are said to be manifold: It is not well grounded in either the text or original intent of the Constitution, asks the Court to make utilitarian (balancing) judgments it is not institutionally competent to perform, and substitutes the Court's market-based policy preferences, *Lochner*-style, for the regulatory preferences of elected state and local representatives. Perhaps in light of this sustained academic criticism, several of the Justices have become increasingly restive as well.

Camps Newfound/Owatonna, Inc. v. Town of Harrison, 520 U.S. 564 (1997). Maine provided a general exemption from real estate taxes for charitable institutions incorporated in the state. Because Camps Newfound/Owatonna was not a Maine company, it could not claim the exemption, and because most of its campers were also out-of-state, it was ineligible for a partial exemption as well. In an opinion by **Justice Stevens**, the Court held that (1) Camps' service was clearly in commerce and so triggered the Dormant Commerce Clause jurispru-

---

u. See, e.g., Julian Eule, *Laying the Dormant Commerce Clause to Rest*, 91 Yale L.J. 425 (1982); Lisa Heinzerling, *The Commercial Constitution*, 1995 Sup. Ct. Rev. 217; Martin Redish & Shane Nugent, *The Dormant Commerce Clause and the Constitutional Balance of Federalism*, 1987 Duke L.J. 569.

dence; (2) that jurisprudence is fully applicable to not-for-profit as well as profitmaking enterprises; and (3) the statute's facial discrimination against interstate commerce brought it within the rule of *New England Power Co. v. New Hampshire*, 455 U.S. 331, 338 (1982), that "the Commerce Clause * * * precludes a state from mandating that its residents be given a preferred right of access, over out-of-state consumers, to natural resources located within its borders or to the products derived therefrom." See also *City of Philadelphia*. This kind of regulation risked the sort of "economic Balkanization" and retaliatory spiral the Dormant Commerce Clause is supposed to prevent.

Although the ordinance discriminated on its face against interstate commerce, **Justice Scalia** wrote for himself and three other Justices (**Rehnquist, Thomas,** and **Ginsburg**) arguing for its validity under the Court's existing jurisprudence, basically because the state ought to be able to encourage charitable uses of state land. On the one hand, Justice Scalia argued that there was no *facial discrimination*, because land gratuitously devoted to relieving the state of its welfare obligations is not *similarly situated* to land not so devoted, and hence there is no discrimination to treat the two kinds of land differently. On the other hand, Justice Scalia argued that encouraging domestic charity ought to be the sort of state interest that would justify a facial discrimination against interstate commerce. If there is a market participant exception, why is there not a domestic charity exception to the Dormant Commerce Clause? Indeed, the Court in *Board of Educ. of Ky. Ann. Conf. of Methodist Episcopal Church v. Illinois*, 203 U.S. 553 (1906), upheld a state inheritance tax allowing exemption to in-state charities but denying a similar exemption to out-of-state charities.

Justice Thomas wrote a separate dissent, joined by Justice Scalia and Chief Justice Rehnquist. Drawing from the academic and judicial criticism of the "negative" Commerce Clause (his preferred terminology), Justice Thomas' dissent argued that its jurisprudence is both *overbroad*, because it brings state laws under judicial scrutiny without any basis in the Constitution and with insufficient regard for judicial policymaking limitations, and *unnecessary*, because the Constitution explicitly regulates state laws that discriminate against interstate commerce or travel. The problem, he said, is that the Constitution mandates a different regulatory regime than the one the Court has created on its own initiative. The remainder of this part discusses the textual limitations the Constitution places on state burdens against interstate commerce and travel.

1. *The Import-Export Clause*

In the portion of his *Camps* dissent joined only by Justice Scalia, Justice Thomas laid out the interpretive regime for evaluating discriminatory taxation under the Import-Export Clause, Article I, § 10, cl. 2: "No State shall, without the Consent of the Congress, lay any Imposts or Duties on Imports or Exports, except what may be absolutely necessary for executing its inspection Laws." Discriminatory state taxation can therefore be invalidated only if the challenger can show that (1) it is an "Impost" or a "Duty" (2) on "Imports or Exports," and (3) not "absolutely necessary for executing its inspection Laws." As with the Dormant Commerce Clause, Congress can authorize the discrimination otherwise prohibited.

The Import-Export Clause has been of little importance, because *Woodruff v. Parham*, 8 Wall. 123 (1868), held that the clause only applies to international trade. Justice Thomas' *Camps* dissent maintained, however, that contemporary usage of the terms Imports or Exports included trade between the states as well as trade between nations.[v] In an appropriate case, he would overrule *Woodruff* for that and other reasons. For Justice Thomas, the key inquiry would be whether a state tax is an Impost or Duty, as those terms were used in the eighteenth century.

An Impost was a tax levied on goods at the time of importation. A Duty included such taxes, but had a broader meaning, according to statements by James Wilson (who served on the Committee on Detail) at the Convention. "What seems likely from these descriptions is that a duty, though broader than an impost, was still a tax *on* particular *goods* or written instruments." What were excluded were so-called "direct taxes," such as taxes on real property. See *Federalist* No. 12 (Hamilton) (distinguishing direct taxes, such as property taxes, from indirect taxes, such as imposts, duties, and excises). Because discriminatory property taxes are neither "Imposts" nor "Duties," Justice Thomas concluded that the Maine tax scheme did not violate the Import-Export Clause.

2. *The Privileges and Immunities Clause*

Like Justice Thomas in *Camps*, Professor Julian Eule argued that the Dormant Commerce Clause should be laid to rest. He maintained that the Privileges and Immunities Clause, Article IV, § 2, cl. 1, ought to be the main protection against state burdens on interstate commerce.[w] The main issue under this provision is what are the "Privileges and Immunities" to which the "Citizens of each State" shall be entitled? The leading cases, excerpted below, start to answer that question. The Notes following the cases identify doctrinal details that have been resolved by the Supreme Court.

Corfield v. Coryell, 4 Wash. C.C. 371, Fed. Cas. No. 3,230 (1823). A New Jersey statute made it unlawful for any person who was not an inhabitant of the state to gather clams, oysters, or shells in the state's waters. The opinion, by **Justice Washington** sitting on federal circuit court, dismissed the Privileges and Immunities Clause claim on the ground that the complainant did not have a "privilege" or "immunity" to gather clams. Justice Washington admonished that

---

v. A comprehensive originalist examination of the terms is 1 William Crosskey, *Politics and the Constitution in the History of the United States* 295-323 (1953), which Justice Thomas' dissent endorses and supplements.

w. Article IV of the Articles of Confederation had provided that "the free inhabitants of each of these States * * * shall be entitled to all privileges and immunities of free citizens in the several States; and the people of each State shall have free ingress and egress to and from any other State, and shall enjoy therein all the privileges of trade and commerce, subject to the same duties, impositions and restrictions as the inhabitants thereof respectively . . . ." At the Philadelphia Convention, Charles Pinckney authored the Constitution's Privileges and Immunities Clause, which was accepted with virtually no debate. Pinckney wrote that Article IV of the Constitution was "formed exactly upon the principles of the 4th article of the present Confederation." III Farrand app. A, at 112.

"it would, in our opinion, be going quite too far to construe the grant of privileges and immunities of citizens, as amounting to a grant of co-tenancy in the common property of the State, to the citizens of all the other states." Hence, the privileges and immunities protected by the clause should be limited to those "which are, in their nature, *fundamental*" and "which belong, of right, to the citizens of all free governments." Among these rights are the "right of a citizen of one State to pass through, or to reside in any other state, for the purposes of trade, agriculture, professional pursuits, or otherwise"; the right "to take, hold, and dispose of property, either real or personal; and an exemption from higher taxes or impositions than are paid by the other citizens of the State."

UNITED BUILDING & CONSTRUCTION TRADES COUNCIL OF CAMDEN COUNTY v. MAYOR AND COUNCIL OF CAMDEN
465 U.S. 208, 104 S.Ct. 1020, 79 L.Ed.2d 249 (1984)

[A Camden, New Jersey, ordinance required that at least 40% of the employees of contractors and subcontractors working on city construction projects be Camden residents. The Supreme Court of New Jersey rejected the union's challenge to the ordinance, concluding that the Privileges and Immunities Clause was not violated because the ordinance discriminates on the basis of *municipal*, not state, residency. The Supreme Court reversed, per **JUSTICE REHNQUIST**, holding that the clause can apply to municipal decisions and then discussing the provision's precise ambit.]

* * * The New Jersey Supreme Court concluded that the Privileges and Immunities Clause does not apply to an ordinance that discriminates solely on the basis of *municipal* residency. The Clause is phrased in terms of *state* citizenship and was designed "to place the citizens of each State upon the same footing with citizens of other States, so far as the advantages resulting from citizenship in those States are concerned." *Paul v. Virginia*, 8 Wall. 168, 180 (1869). * * *

> The primary purpose of this clause, like the clauses between which it is located — those relating to full faith and credit and to interstate extradition of fugitives from justice — was to help fuse into one nation a collection of independent, sovereign States. It was designed to insure to a citizen of State A who ventures into State B the same privileges which the citizens of State B enjoy. For protection of such equality the citizen of State A was not to be restricted to the uncertain remedies afforded by diplomatic processes and official retaliation. *Toomer v. Witsell*, 334 U.S. 385, 395 (1948).

Municipal residency classifications, it is argued, simply do not give rise to the same concerns.

We cannot accept this argument. We have never read the Clause so literally as to apply it only to distinctions based on state citizenship. For example, in *Mullaney v. Anderson*, 342 U.S. 415, 419-420 (1952), the Court held that the Alaska Territory had no more freedom to discriminate against those not residing in the Territory than did any State to favor its own citizens. And despite some initial uncertainty, * * * it is now established that the terms "citizen" and "resident" are "essentially interchangeable" for purposes of analysis of most cases under the Privileges and Immunities Clause. A person who is not residing in a given State is *ipso facto* not residing in a city within that State. Thus, whether the exercise of a privilege is conditioned on state residency or on municipal residency he will just as surely be excluded.

Given the Camden ordinance, an out-of-state citizen who ventures into New Jersey will not enjoy the same privileges as the New Jersey citizen residing in Camden. It is true that New Jersey citizens not residing in Camden will be affected by the ordinance as well as out-of-state citizens. And it is true that the disadvantaged New Jersey residents have no claim under the Privileges and Immunities Clause. *The Slaughter-House Cases*, 16 Wall. 36, 77 (1873). But New Jersey residents at least have a chance to remedy at the polls any discrimination against them. Out-of-state citizens have no similar opportunity, and they must "not be restricted to the uncertain remedies afforded by diplomatic processes and official retaliation." We conclude that Camden's ordinance is not immune from constitutional review at the behest of out-of-state residents merely because some in-state residents are similarly disadvantaged.

Application of the Privileges and Immunities Clause to a particular instance of discrimination against out-of-state residents entails a two-step inquiry. As an initial matter, the court must decide whether the ordinance burdens one of those privileges and immunities protected by the Clause. *Baldwin v. Montana Fish and Game Comm'n*, 436 U.S. 371, 383 (1978). Not all forms of discrimination against citizens of other States are constitutionally suspect.

> Some distinctions between residents and nonresidents merely reflect the fact that this is a Nation composed of individual States, and are permitted; other distinctions are prohibited because they hinder the formation, the purpose, or the development of a single Union of those States. Only with respect to those "privileges" and "immunities" bearing upon the vitality of the Nation as a single entity must the state treat all citizens, resident and nonresident, equally.

As a threshold matter, then, we must determine whether an out-of-state resident's interest in employment on public works contracts in another State is sufficiently "fundamental" to the promotion of interstate harmony so as to "fall within the purview of the Privileges and Immunities Clause." * * *

Certainly, the pursuit of a common calling is one of the most fundamental of those privileges protected by the Clause. Many, if not most, of our cases expounding the Privileges and Immunities Clause have dealt with this basic and essential activity. Public employment, however, is qualitatively different from employment in the private sector; it is a subspecies of the broader opportunity to pursue a common calling. We have held that there is no fundamental right to government employment for purposes of the Equal Protection Clause. And in *White v. Massachusetts Council of Const. Employees*, 460 U.S. 204 (1983), we held that for purposes of the Commerce Clause everyone employed on a city public works project is, "in a substantial if informal sense, 'working for the city.'"

It can certainly be argued that for purposes of the Privileges and Immunities Clause everyone affected by the Camden ordinance is also "working for the city" and, therefore, has no grounds for complaint when the city favors its own residents. But we decline to transfer mechanically into this context an analysis fashioned to fit the Commerce Clause. Our decision in *White* turned on a distinction between the city acting as a market participant and the city acting as a market regulator. The question whether employees of contractors and subcontractors on public works projects were or were not, in some sense, working for the city was crucial to that analysis. The question had to be answered in order to chart the boundaries of the distinction. But the distinction between market participant and market regulator relied upon in *White* to dispose of the Commerce Clause challenge is not dispositive in this context. The two Clauses have different aims and set different standards for state conduct.

The Commerce Clause acts as an implied restraint upon state regulatory powers. Such powers must give way before the superior authority of Congress to legislate on (or leave unregulated) matters involving interstate commerce. When the State acts solely as a market participant, no conflict between state *regulation* and federal regulatory authority can arise. *White.* The Privileges and Immunities Clause, on the other hand, imposes a direct restraint on state action in the interests of interstate harmony. This concern with comity cuts across the market regulator-market participant distinction that is crucial under the Commerce Clause. It is discrimination against out-of-state residents on matters of fundamental concern which triggers the clause, not regulation affecting interstate commerce. Thus, the fact that Camden is merely setting conditions on its expenditures for goods and services in the marketplace does not preclude the possibility that those conditions violate the Privileges and Immunities Clause.

In *Hicklin v. Orbeck*, 437 U.S. 518 (1978), we struck down as a violation of the Privileges and Immunities Clause an "Alaska Hire" statute containing a resident hiring preference for all employment related to the development of the State's oil and gas resources. Alaska argued in that case "that because the oil and gas that are the subject of Alaska Hire are *owned* by the State, this ownership, of itself, is sufficient justification for the Act's discrimination against nonresidents, and takes the Act totally without the scope of the Privileges and Immunities Clause." We concluded, however, that the State's interest in controlling those things it claims to own is not absolute. "Rather than placing a statute completely beyond the Clause, a State's ownership of the property with which the statute is concerned is a factor — although often the crucial factor — to be considered in evaluating whether the statute's discrimination against noncitizens violates the Clause." * * * Much the same analysis, we think, is appropriate to a city's efforts to bias private employment decisions in favor of its residents on construction projects funded with public monies. The fact that Camden is expending its own funds or funds it administers in accordance with the terms of a grant is certainly a factor — perhaps the crucial factor — to be considered in evaluating whether the statute's discrimination violates the Privileges and Immunities Clause. But it does not remove the Camden ordinance completely from the purview of the Clause.

In sum, Camden may, without fear of violating the Commerce Clause, pressure private employers engaged in public works projects funded in whole or in part by the city to hire city residents. But that same exercise of power to bias the employment decisions of private contractors and subcontractors against out-of-state residents may be called to account under the Privileges and Immunities Clause. A determination of whether a privilege is "fundamental" for purposes of that Clause does not depend on whether the employees of private contractors and subcontractors engaged in public works projects can or cannot be said to be "working for the city." The opportunity to seek employment with such private employers is "sufficiently basic to the livelihood of the Nation," *Baldwin*, as to fall within the purview of the Privileges and Immunities Clause even though the contractors and subcontractors are themselves engaged in projects funded in whole or part by the city.

[Camden's infringement of the foregoing privilege or immunity of citizenship would be invalid under the clause unless the city could show a "substantial reason" for the difference in treatment. The city urged the policy as a way to arrest the middle class flight from the city and to tie work for the city to commitment in the city. Justice Rehnquist recognized that Camden's policy was not only a valid one, but its ordinance was more appropriately tailored to such a valid policy than, for example, the Alaska Hire statute at issue in *Hicklin*, which covered not only contractors and subcontractors dealing directly with the State's oil and gas, but also suppliers and other tangentially related concerns. Because there was no factual record, however, the case was remanded for further proceedings.]

JUSTICE BLACKMUN, dissenting.

Contrary to the Court's tacit assumption, discrimination on the basis of municipal residence is substantially different in this regard from discrimination on the basis of state citizenship. The distinction is simple but fundamental: discrimination on the basis of municipal residence penalizes persons within the State's political community as well as those without. The Court itself points out that while New Jersey citizens who reside outside Camden are not protected by the Privileges and Immunities Clause, they may resort to the State's political processes to protect themselves. What the Court fails to appreciate is that this avenue of relief for New Jersey residents works to protect residents of other States as well; disadvantaged state residents who turn to the State legislature to displace ordinances like Camden's further the interests of nonresidents as well as their own. Nor is this mechanism for relief merely a theoretical one; in the past decade several States, including California and Georgia, have repealed or forbidden protectionist ordinances like the one at issue here. In short, discrimination on the basis of municipal residence simply does not consign residents of other States to "the uncertain remedies afforded by diplomatic processes and official retaliation." The Court thus has applied the Privileges and Immunities Clause without regard for the political ills that it was designed to cure.

NOTES CONTRASTING THE DORMANT COMMERCE CLAUSE AND THE PRIVILEGES AND IMMUNITIES CLAUSE

Camden rendered the Privileges and Immunities Clause parallel to the Dormant Commerce Clause in one respect: Both apply to municipal and local discriminations as well as statewide ones. In most other respects, however, the two lines of cases follow different doctrinal rules and impose different limitations on states and municipalities. Among them are the following:

1. *Only Fundamental Rights.* *Corfield* held that the Privileges and Immunities Clause only protects fundamental privileges naturally belonging to the

citizens of any free government. Like *Camden*, most of the recent cases have dealt with state efforts to exclude nonresidents from professional opportunities. See, e.g., *Lunding v. New York Tax Appeals Tribunal*, 522 U.S. 287 (1998) ("right" secured by the P & I Clause is the right of a citizen of one state " 'to remove to and carry on business in another without being subjected in property or person to taxes more onerous than the citizens of the latter State are subjected to' "); *Supreme Court of Virginia v. Friedman*, 487 U.S. 59 (1988) (residency requirement to become member of Virginia bar violates P & I Clause); *Supreme Court of New Hampshire v. Piper*, 470 U.S. 274 (1985) (similar). Compare *Baldwin v. Montana Fish & Game Comm'n*, 436 U.S. 371 (1978) (rejecting challenge to elk-hunting license law imposing higher fees on nonresidents; elk-hunting is not a fundamental right). Can *Camden*'s protection of public employment be extended to qualify as a privilege the right to sell products across state boundaries (*Dean Milk Co.*)? The right to nondiscriminatory access to a state's resources (*City of Philadelphia*)? How about the right to drive your truck across the state of Iowa, as part of your business of trucking (*Kassel*)?

2. *Only "Citizens" (Not Corporations) Are Protected.* Although the clause itself only identifies "Citizens" as protected, *Camden* read the clause broadly to mean "nonresidents." Compare the Fourteenth Amendment, which makes us "citizens" of the states in which we "reside." A more thorny question is whether corporations are protected by the clause. The Supreme Court in *Bank of Augusta v. Earle*, 38 U.S. (13 Pet.) 519 (1839) (Taney, C.J.), held that corporations are not Citizens under the clause. See also *Paul v. Virginia*, 75 U.S. (8 Wall.) 168, 177 (1868). If corporations such as Consolidated Freightways are not Citizens, then surely government units, such as the City of Philadelphia, would not be either. Note that the Court has interpreted "person" in the Fourteenth Amendment to include corporations, e.g., *Railway Express Agency v. New York*, 336 U.S. 106 (1949), and *Camden* was willing to interpret "State" in the Privileges and Immunities Clause to mean "municipality." Should *Earle* be overruled?

3. *There Must Be Overt Discrimination — Discriminatory Effects Not Policed.* Unlike the Dormant Commerce Clause, the Privileges and Immunities Clause only applies when there is an overt discrimination. As the Court recognized in *Camden*, "[i]t is discrimination against out-of-state residents on matters of fundamental concern which triggers the Clause, not regulation affecting interstate commerce."[x] Hence, cases like *Pike* (Arizona required cantaloupe grower to pack produce in state) and *Kassel* (Iowa simply had a different truck-length rule from other states) would probably be decided differently under the Privileges and Immunities Clause, because they do not readily distinguish between state citizens and noncitizens. Indirect burdens on interstate commerce do not count for privileges and immunities purposes.

4. *No Market Participant Exception.* As the Court held in *Camden*, the Privileges and Immunities Clause has no market participant exception such as that created by *Alexandria Scrap* for the Dormant Commerce Clause. (Note,

---

x. See also Jonathan Varat, *State "Citizenship" and Interstate Equality*, 48 U. Chi. L. Rev. 487 (1981).

however, that the Court seemed willing to allow preferential economic concern for local residents as a valid legislative interest in *Camden*.)

5. *Standard of Review*. Compare the standard of review announced in *Toomer v. Witsell*, 334 U.S. 385 (1948) and applied in *Camden*: Discrimination against citizens of other states can be justified if there is "substantial reason" for the different treatment; the state or city must show that such reasons exist and that the particular discrimination bears a "close relation" to them. This seems like a more lenient standard than the Dormant Commerce Clause standard for overt discrimination against interstate commerce, but stiffer than the *Pike* test for evaluating discriminatory effects. Consider *Lunding, supra*, in which the Court struck down a New York law denying only nonresident taxpayers an income tax deduction for alimony. The Court reaffirmed that state legislatures have "considerable discretion" in drawing local taxing policy, but would be faulted if they violate the Court's rule of "substantial equality."

6. *No Congressional Validation*. The ruling in *Kassel* that Iowa's prohibition of doubles violated the Dormant Commerce Clause was properly overridden by congressionally authorized procedures. But if the Court held that the Iowa law discriminated against out-of-staters under the Privileges and Immunities Clause, presumably Congress could not validate the state law, although (of course) the state could simply reformulate the statute without the discrimination.

3. *The Supremacy Clause and Preemption*

Under the Supremacy Clause of Article VI, Congress can enact federal statutes that override, or "preempt," state law. The Court has held that duly authorized regulations promulgated by a federal agency may also have preemptive effect, see *Hillsborough County v. Automated Medical Laboratories*, 471 U.S. 707 (1985). Because today both sovereigns exercise so much regulatory authority over so many things, preemption issues are pervasive, yet they are so complicated by the diversity of their facts that no simple formula for federal preemption is evident. In any event, the Court has repeatedly stated that state regulation can be preempted in three different circumstances.[y]

First, Congress may expressly preempt state law by so stipulating in a federal statute. E.g., *Shaw v. Delta Air Lines*, 463 U.S. 85 (1983). This is but a simple application of the Supremacy Clause: if the federal statute is constitutional and says that state law is preempted, state law is preempted. Likewise, if Congress determines that state regulation should not be preempted by a federal statute, Congress may expressly say so in a "savings clause" in the statute. Not only will the savings clause prevent preemption, but, depending upon the wording of the clause, it may immunize the state regulation from Dormant Commerce Clause attack as well.

---

y. See *Ray v. Atlantic Richfield Co.*, 435 U.S. 151 (1978); see also *Crosby v. National Foreign Trade Council*, 530 U.S. 363 (2000); *Gade v. National Solid Wastes Management Ass'n*, 505 U.S. 88 (1992); *Pacific Gas & Elec. Co. v. State Energy Resources Conservation & Dev. Comm'n*, 461 U.S. 190 (1983).

Second, even without an explicit preemption provision, a federal statute will preempt state laws whose operation is inconsistent with that of the federal statute. Not surprisingly, a conflict will be found "where compliance with both federal and state regulations is a physical impossibility." *Florida Lime & Avocado Growers, Inc. v. Paul*, 373 U.S. 132, 142-43 (1963). A venerable example is *McDermott v. Wisconsin*, 228 U.S. 115 (1913), where compliance with federal food labeling requirements would have caused the food to have been mislabeled under state law. Much more difficult to apply is another strand of cases, under which the state law is preempted if it "stands as an obstacle to the accomplishment and execution of the full purposes and objectives of Congress." *Hines v. Davidowitz*, 312 U.S. 52, 67 (1941). Consider *Nash v. Florida Industrial Commission*, 389 U.S. 235 (1967), where the Court held that federal labor law preempted a provision of a state unemployment compensation scheme denying benefits to someone discharged from a job for filing an unfair labor practice charge with the federal National Labor Relations Board.

Third, federal statutes "occupying the field" comprehensively will preempt state law. "The scheme of federal regulations may be so pervasive as to make reasonable the inference that Congress left no room for the States to supplement it. Or the Act of Congress may touch a field in which the federal interest is so dominant that the federal system will be assumed to preclude enforcement of state laws of the same subject." *Rice v. Santa Fe Elevator Corp.*, 331 U.S. 218, 230 (1947). Note that this approach preempts state law even if it is not in actual conflict with the text or policies of federal law. This massive intrusion on federalism values is not easily assumed by the Court: There is a strong presumption against so-called "field preemption," and it will be found only if "the nature of the regulated subject matter permits no other conclusion, or [if] the Congress has unmistakably so ordained." *Florida Lime, supra*. Nonetheless, for example, the extensive federal regulation of aliens, coupled with the unique federal interest in foreign affairs, led the Court in *Hines, supra*, to hold that a federal statute governing the registration of aliens preempted a state alien registration statute.

NOTE ON PREEMPTION AND CONSTITUTIONAL NORMS

Preemption is a matter of both constitutional law (the Supremacy Clause) and statutory interpretation (congressional enactments are usually necessary to trigger a preemption inquiry). It might also be considered a matter of *quasi-constitutional law*, where constitutional norms inform statutory interpretation. Consider some of the ways this shows up:

1. *Interpretive Presumptions.* Inspired by the same federalism values that inspired the clear statement rule in *Gregory v. Ashcroft*, the Court "start[s] with the assumption that the historic police powers of the States [are] not to be superseded by . . . Federal Act unless that [is] the clear and manifest purpose of Congress." *Cipollone v. Liggett Group, Inc.*, 505 U.S. 504 (1992) (most state

tort remedies are unaffected by federal cigarette disclosure regulations).[z] See also *Silkwood v. Kerr-McGee Corp.*, 464 U.S. 238 (1984). Such a presumption does not apply, or might even be inverted, when the federal statute covers a policy area that is intrinsically and historically national in scope, such as foreign relations, immigration, and national defense. See *Toll v. Moreno*, 458 U.S. 1 (1982) (broad field preemption of state regulation of noncitizens and diplomats); *Banco Nacional de Cuba v. Sabbatino*, 376 U.S. 398 (1964) (broad preemption of state lawsuits to recover nationalized property traditionally left to presidential espousal and diplomatic channels). Note the similarity to *Cooley*, which distinguished between areas of intrinsic state and national regulation. (Some of the *Cooley*-era cases would come out differently today, because of the federalization of subject areas such as the immigration arena at issue in *Miln*.)

2. *Preemption and Dormant Commerce Clause Analysis.* Consider the argument made in Note, *Pre-emption as a Preferential Ground: A New Canon of Construction*, 12 Stan. L. Rev. 208, 220 (1959)[aa]:

> [T]he Court has adopted the same weighing of interests approach in pre-emption cases that it uses to determine whether a state law unjustifiably burdens interstate commerce. In a number of situations the Court has invalidated statutes on the pre-emption ground when it appeared that the state laws sought to favor local economic interests at the expense of the interstate market. On the other hand, when the Court has been satisfied that valid local interests, such as those in safety or in the reputable operation of local business, outweigh the restrictive effect on interstate commerce, the Court has rejected the pre-emption argument and allowed state regulation to stand.

As a general matter, this old assessment remains a valid generalization about both preemption cases and Dormant Commerce Clause cases. A qualification is that both kinds of cases seem rooted in ad hoc judicial balancing rather than in any more theoretical and predictable inquiry.

3. *Norms and Representation Reinforcement.* It strikes many observers as apparent that norms and fair deliberation make a difference in some preemption cases. Hypothesis: If a local law has substantial spillover effects in other states and seems to reflect parochial values, it should be preempted so that the issue will be pushed from the state to the federal agenda, where all of the interests are equally represented. If local law reflects more neutral, robust values — such as those of the common law — preemption ought not be preferred. *Cipollone* may be an example of this latter proposition; in light of the now-well-known hazards of cigarette smoking, the majority of the Justices were perhaps reluctant to read too much preemption into national disclosure rules.

---

z. Justice Stevens' opinion for the Court (on this issue) in *Cipollone* drew fire from both sides of the presumption. Justice Blackmun (joined by Justices Kennedy and Souter) objected that the presumption should have been stronger — "clear evidence" that Congress meant to displace state law. Justice Scalia (joined by Justice Thomas) objected that there should have been no presumption, and the Court in preemption cases should just apply the plain meaning of statutory texts. Contrast, however, Justice Scalia's invocation of an even stronger presumption against preemption in *BFP v. Resolution Trust Corp.*, 511 U.S. 531 (1994).

aa. Reprinted with permission.

REVISITING THE DORMANT COMMERCE CLAUSE CASES

Assume that the Supreme Court renounces the Dormant Commerce Clause precedents, and all the cases must be relitigated under the "proper" constitutional provisions. How would the Court decide the leading cases today: (a) *City of Philadelphia*, (b) *Kassel*, (c) *Southern Pacific*, (d) *Alexandria Scrap*, (e) *West Lynn Creamery*, and (f) *United Haulers*? After surveying the probable results, would you rethink your vote to renounce the Dormant Commerce Clause?

NOTE ON TRIADIC FEDERALISM:
INDIAN TRIBAL SOVEREIGNTY

"As every schoolchild learns," the Supreme Court said in *New York v. United States* (§ 5C above), "our Constitution establishes a dual sovereignty between the States and the Federal Government." That is not all the sovereignty exercised within the borders of this country, however. What is frequently ignored is that federalism was built on top of pre-existing Indian tribal governments without extinguishing all of their sovereignty. Indeed, Indian tribes today continue to possess important governmental authority over their lands and members. The rationale is that tribes were sovereign before European contact and have retained all pre-existing sovereignty that (1) remains consistent with the tribes' "dependent status,"[a] (2) has never been ceded away by them by treaty, and (3) has never been preempted by federal statute. Thus, when tribes exercise this retained sovereignty, the action is neither federal nor state action, and the Constitution's provisions usually considered so important in restraining governmental power within the borders of the United States (e.g., first amendment, due process, equal protection) do not apply. See *Talton v. Mayes*, 163 U.S. 376 (1896). Congress has, however, applied many of the Bill of Rights guarantees to the tribes by statute. See Indian Civil Rights Act of 1968, 25 U.S.C. §§ 1301-03.

Under the original conceptions of the Marshall Court, the federal-tribal relation was exclusive, such that the states had no role in Indian country. See

---

a. In *Cherokee Nation v. Georgia*, 30 U.S. (5 Pet.) 1 (1831), Chief Justice Marshall considered Indian tribes to be "domestic dependent sovereigns" having a relationship with the federal government resembling that of a ward to its guardian. The Marshall Court held that, because of their dependent status, tribes could engage in treaty relations and land transactions only with the European discovering sovereign or its successor (the United States). See *Johnson v. McIntosh*, 21 U.S. (8 Wheat.) 543 (1823). A century and a half later, the Supreme Court returned to this theory and held that a tribe had no criminal jurisdiction over a non-Indian present on the reservation even if the tribe had never ceded away such authority by treaty and Congress had never preempted that authority by federal statute. See *Oliphant v. Suquamish Indian Tribe*, 435 U.S. 191 (1978). Later cases have limited tribal civil regulatory power over non-Indians as well. See, e.g., *Montana v. United States*, 450 U.S. 544 (1981) (regulation of non-Indians on their own fee lands within reservations).

Worcester v. Georgia, 31 U.S. (6 Pet.) 515 (1832).[b] Later cases have weakened the *Worcester* rule into merely a presumption against state authority in Indian country.[c] The Court has held that Congress has "plenary power" over Indian affairs, see, e.g., *Lone Wolf v. Hitchcock*, 187 U.S. 553 (1903), although in recent years the Court has been willing to apply judicial review to federal statutes involving Indians. Today the field of federal Indian law is fascinating, complicated, and somewhat chaotic, with considerable controversy over the conflicting power of the federal government, the tribes, and the states. Indeed, over the past three decades the Supreme Court has had a steady diet of federal Indian law cases.

Not surprisingly, studying federal Indian law is great exercise for the mental faculties. For example, some decisions reach results that will strike students as at least initially surprising. See, e.g., *Morton v. Mancari*, 417 U.S. 535 (1974) (affirmative action program facially benefitting Indians for jobs in the Bureau of Indian Affairs received only rational-basis review because it was not a racial classification based on indigenous ethnicity, but a political one based on membership in tribes that had a government-to-government relationship with United States). More fundamentally, studying federal Indian law pushes one to consider what it means to live in a constitutional society that came about through colonialism. Consider the following response to the Supreme Court's comment about the education of schoolchildren concerning federalism, quoted above:

> The problem for schoolchildren as well as the rest of us is that the assumptions we make as proud Americans about our country and its Constitution run headlong into an alternative reality when our vision is expanded to include the historical facts and the ongoing nature of the colonization of this continent. The involuntary displacement of indigenous peoples from their lands and their political subjugation by a self-proclaimed superior sovereign is ironic, indeed, in a country that began by declaring itself independent of colonial status and that soon adopted a Constitution that has served as a model for restraining the abuse of public power. In both law and life, things are a good deal more complicated — both descriptively and normatively — than grade school history classes, high school civics classes, and law school constitutional law classes suggest.[d]

---

b. On the foundational opinions of the Marshall Court and their utility today, see Philip Frickey, *Marshalling Past and Present: Colonialism, Constitutionalism, and Interpretation in Federal Indian Law*, 107 Harv. L. Rev. 381 (1993).

c. Compare, e.g., *McClanahan v. Arizona State Tax Comm'n*, 411 U.S. 164 (1973) (state may not tax the income of tribal member earned on the reservation), with *Washington v. Confederated Tribes of the Colville Reservation*, 447 U.S. 134 (1980) (state may apply its cigarette tax to tribal sales of cigarettes to nonmembers).

d. Philip Frickey, *Domesticating Federal Indian Law*, 81 Minn. L. Rev. 31, 33 (1996).

Chapter 8

SEPARATION OF POWERS

The Constitution contemplates that the national government will have three branches: Congress, vested with "[a]ll legislative Powers" (Article I); the President, assisted by various Departments, who would carry out the "executive Power" (Article II); and the Supreme Court, and such "inferior courts" as Congress should establish, vested with the "judicial Power" (Article III). These three Articles describe the responsibilities of each branch of the national government, and Article I sets forth procedural and substantive limits on the authority of Congress to legislate. While it sounds simple enough, this scheme has given rise to vexing constitutional quandaries. Some of these quandaries have arisen in response to reformist demands of social movements in the twentieth century. For example, until the 1960s, Congress was completely unresponsive to the equality demands of the civil rights movement — and the policymaking void was filled by the Supreme Court and the President.[a] Hence, the Imperial Presidency (§ 1 of this chapter) and the Political Court (Chapter 9) were in no small part a product of identity politics. The most dramatic separation of powers controversies, however, have involved other activities of Congress and the President, most notably the War on Terrorism (§ 3). The great controversies of the last century have exposed a number of tensions in separation of powers jurisprudence.[b]

In examining these tensions, we start with the text and structure of the Constitution, particularly as explicated in *The Federalist Papers* and illuminated by commentators. Immediately following this conceptual overview is an excerpt from Professor Casper's presentation of the historical background

---

a. By executive orders in the 1940s, President Roosevelt desegregated the federal civil service and President Truman desegregated the armed forces. From the Roosevelt through the Carter Administrations, the Department of Justice engaged in law-inviting activism to support the civil rights movement's constitutional campaigns.

b. Our account draws from scholarship concerning the structure of the national government, especially *Symposium on The American Constitutional Tradition of Shared and Separated Powers*, 30 Wm. & Mary L. Rev. 209-432 (1989); Charles Black, *Structure and Relationship in Constitutional Law* (1969); Curtis Bradley & Martin Flaherty, *Executive Power Essentialism and Foreign Affairs*, 102 Mich. L. Rev. 545 (2004); Rebecca Brown, *Separated Powers and Ordered Liberty*, 139 U. Pa. L. Rev. 1513 (1991); Steven Calabresi & Saikrishna Prakash, *The President's Power To Execute the Laws*, 104 Yale L.J. 541 (1994); Victoria Nourse, *Toward a New Constitutional Anatomy*, 56 Stan. L. Rev. 835 (2004); Peter Strauss, *The Place of Agencies in Government: Separation of Powers and the Fourth Branch*, 84 Colum. L. Rev. 573 (1984).

against which the Framers drafted Articles I, II, and III. The rest of this chapter then explores these tensions in the Supreme Court's application of Articles I-III to cases where an imperial presidency, a grabby Congress, or even both Congress and the President acting in concert have arguably claimed powers they do not have or usurped the powers of another branch. Chapter 9 will explore these tensions in connection with the federal courts' assertion of authority.

1. *Separation of Powers versus Checks and Balances.* Read as a unit, the first three Articles of the Constitution have been interpreted to suggest two general organizing principles, which are in tension with one another. One is separation of powers, the notion that the three branches shall be separate from one another and shall concentrate on their respective functions (described in the "vesting clause" of each Article). A second is checks and balances, the notion that each of the three branches shall have some influence on how the other two branches perform their specialized roles. (A third principle, internal checks, is applicable only to Congress: According to Article I, § 7, Congress cannot accomplish its primary task, enacting statutes, unless both chambers agree to the same text and it is presented to the President.)

Although the Supreme Court and any duly established inferior courts alone exercise the "judicial Power of the United States" (Art. III, § 1), their authority depends upon the cooperation of the other branches. Congress has substantial power over the Court's appellate jurisdiction (Art. III, § 2, cl. 2) and has the power to create the inferior federal courts (Art. III, § 1). The President executes judgments entered by the courts (Art. II, § 1). Moreover, the political branches have a big say in who is a Justice of the Court. The President nominates Justices as well as judges on the "inferior" federal courts, who then must be approved by the Senate (Art. II, § 2, cl. 2). The House has the power to impeach federal judges and Justices (Art. I, § 2, cl. 5), who are removed from office if convicted by the Senate (Art. I, § 3, cl. 6).

Although Congress, and only Congress, exercises "[a]ll legislative Powers" (Art. I, § 1), before a bill becomes a law it must be presented to the President and (with specified exceptions) signed by the President (Art. I, § 7, cl. 2-3). Once a bill does become a law, it may be ineffective if the Supreme Court finds it unconstitutional (Art. VI, § 2, as interpreted in *Marbury* and later cases). The execution and interpretation of the laws are left to the executive and the judiciary. To take a specific example, Congress' power to declare war and regulate the armed forces (Art. I, § 8, cl. 11-14) depends very much on the cooperation of the President, who is the Commander-in-Chief of the armed forces (Art. II, § 2, cl. 1).

Although the President, and only the President, has the "executive Power" (Art. II, § 1), the Constitution makes clear that it is the "Laws" passed by Congress that must be executed (Art. II, § 3). The President, like Congress, is subject to judicial remedies (such as mandamus) for violating the laws and Constitution of the United States (Art. VI, § 2, as interpreted in *Marbury*). Additionally, the President's primary officers must meet with the approval of the Senate (Art. II, § 2, cl. 2). Like judges, the President and such officers can be impeached by the House (Art. I, § 2, cl. 5) and removed from office if convicted by the Senate (Art. I, § 3, cl. 6; Art. II, § 4).

The Framers and those defending the Constitution in the ratification debates were well aware of this tension between separation of powers and checks and balances. Rather than resolve the tension, however, they sought to justify it. Invoking Montesquieu's celebrated defense of separation of powers, the Anti-Federalists attacked the Constitution for permitting so much intermixing. Madison responded in *Federalist* No. 47 (App. 2) that neither Montesquieu nor the British system which inspired Montesquieu contemplated a complete separation. Madison read these sources to suggest that the optimal protection of citizens' liberty lay in a strategy combining separation of powers with checks and balances. A system in which each branch — especially the feared legislative power — needed some cooperation from another branch before setting policy would protect against arbitrary action better than a system in which the three branches acted entirely on their own and simply competed with one another.

2. *Ensuring Efficacy versus Preventing Tyranny.* The main policy emphasized in the ratification debates was the prevention of tyranny, and that policy was argued under both the separation of powers idea and the checks-and-balances idea. Following Montesquieu, *Federalist* No. 47 (App. 2) said: "The accumulation of all powers, legislative, executive, and judiciary, in the same hands, whether of one, a few, or many, and whether hereditary, self-appointed, or elective, may justly be pronounced the very definition of tyranny." The rationale was that the separation of rulemaking from the rule-executing and rule-adjudicating arms of government gives citizens some protection against being persecuted and treated unfairly — there is less danger of factional vendettas. Also important is that when legislators enact statutes, other branches will implement those statutes. The implementation by others, over whom the legislature has no absolute control, has two advantages. See *Federalist* No. 78 (App. 2). On the one hand, legislators will be more reluctant to pass unfair statutes, out of fear that tyrannical laws could be used against them and their supporters. On the other hand, if unfair laws were passed, they might be implemented in ways that avoid their most tyrannical features. Separation of powers strategies are a negative way of protecting against tyranny, by ensuring that circumstances do not unduly encourage it.[c]

Checks-and-balances strategies represent a more positive way of protecting against tyranny: By requiring the cooperation of more than a single branch to take action, it is more likely that the action will be reasonable and just. This idea is more subtle than the simple insight that "two heads are better than one." The ambitious legislator will be more reluctant to press for tyrannical laws favoring her faction, because her ambition is countered by that of the also ambitious executive, who can be expected to resist arbitrary legislative grabs for power — or who might even turn oppressive laws against their authors. Much of the Framers' attention seems to have been focused on heading off potential legislative tyranny. See *Federalist* Nos. 10, 48 and 51 (App. 2). For this reason, it is particularly hard for Congress to do anything.

---

c. See Paul Verkuil, *Separation of Powers, the Rule of Law, and the Idea of Independence*, 39 Wm. & Mary L. Rev. 301 (1989).

While protecting against tyranny was the Framers' most frequently discussed policy, in reaction to the colonists' objection to British rule, they also recognized a policy of ensuring efficacious national governance,[d] because the Framers also operated against their experience with the weak national government of the Articles of Confederation. (This was, after all, the reason for a new constitution.) Some of the Framers specifically criticized the Articles of Confederation for not providing a national executive and judiciary to implement national policy. James Wilson defended the Constitution's establishment of separate executive functions as needed to respond in "emergencies, in which the man [who] deliberates, is lost." *Federalist* No. 70 defended a strong executive as "essential to the protection of the community against foreign attacks," as well as "the steady administration of the laws; to the protection of property against those irregular and highhanded combinations which sometimes interrupt the ordinary course of justice; to the security of liberty against the enterprises and assaults of ambition, of faction, and of anarchy."

These two policies, against tyranny and in favor of efficacy, are sometimes in tension. Government may run roughshod over the interests of some to accomplish national goals expeditiously. Indeed, expeditious government action typically involves some sacrifice on the part of a minority of the citizenry, a phenomenon reflected in our nation's response to the events of September 11, 2001. Today, therefore, we worry about presidential tyranny more than we worry about legislative tyranny. The congeries of procedural roadblocks to efficacious legislative action have yielded legislative paralysis and encouraged the executive (and sometimes the courts) to take initiatives. The Constitution is quite vague about checks on the imperial presidency, or upon government by judiciary, which the Framers termed the "least dangerous branch." *Federalist* No. 78 (App. 2). Also, governance today is by independent agencies, which combine rulemaking (legislative), adjudication (judicial), and enforcement (executive) functions in one body. Government by agencies is justified on efficiency grounds, but might not the concentration of functions violate the central limiting precepts of separation of powers as well as checks and balances?

3. *Political versus Judicial Enforcement of Separation of Powers.* It is not clear that the Supreme Court should have much of a role in deciding separation of powers disputes. Recall Herbert Wechsler's "political safeguards" thesis (Chapter 7, §§ 1, 5B): Because political safeguards such as the state representation in the Senate provide sufficient protection for state autonomy, the Supreme Court's power of judicial review should not include the Constitution's federalism-based limits on congressional power. Jesse Choper makes the same kind of argument for separation of powers issues: Where the President is usurping power from Congress, the latter has plenty of political weapons with which to respond; the same is true when Congress seeks to usurp authority from

---

d. See Suzanna Sherry, *Separation of Powers: Asking a Different Question*, 30 Wm. & Mary L. Rev. 287 (1989).

the President. In those cases, and others, the Framers did not expect the Court to intervene, and its intervention is neither necessary nor productive.[e]

Commentators and judges remain deeply divided over the wisdom of judicial review for separation of powers issues. Recall that the first important case of judicial review (*Marbury*) involved a clash between a new President and the outgoing Congress — Jefferson and Secretary Madison were refusing to carry out mandatory duties established by the prior Congress. There was no hue and cry in 1803 that the Supreme Court had "betrayed" the original deal by announcing authority to review the Jefferson Administration's alleged failure to "take Care that the Laws be faithfully executed" (Art. II, § 3). Nor is it clear that the political safeguards will usually mobilize against usurpation. The gravest dangers to the separation of powers come in periods of emergency or alarm — precisely the time when the political organs are least likely to resist. As a relatively insulated branch, the Supreme Court might be most inclined to resist, but perhaps least able to stop, unwarranted assertions of authority.

An open question is the "productivity" of the Supreme Court's intervention in separation of powers disputes. As to that, the proof is in the pudding. We invite you to read the cases in this chapter — especially the cases involving the War on Terror (§ 3) — with these questions in mind: Has the Court developed a coherent body of law limiting the political branches along separation of powers lines? Do the cases sensibly mediate the tensions we find in the Constitution's framework for such issues? Do they reach a good balance, substantially protecting liberty without sacrificing efficacy?

4. *Formalist versus Functionalist Reasoning.* To the extent the Supreme Court does assume an active role in separation of powers conflicts (as it decidedly has), the challenge is how to draw the lines of national responsibilities "suitably." There are several different strategies the Court could take if it wants to police the Constitution's boundaries. For example, the Court could strictly enforce the lines apparently drawn in the Constitution.[f] The President is in charge of all executive functions, and if he tries to make rather than execute law he will be overruled; Congress does all the legislating, and if it tries to meddle in executive functions it will be overruled; the courts do all the adjudicating, and if they try to make policy they will be overruled. This approach has

---

e. Compare Jesse Choper, *Judicial Review and the National Political Process: A Functional Reconsideration of the Role of the Supreme Court* (1980) (separation of powers issues should be treated as nonjusticiable political questions), with Harold Koh, *The National Security Constitution: Sharing Power After the Iran-Contra Affair* (1990) (plenty of issues are appropriate for judicial resolution), and with John Choon Yoo,*The Powers of War and Peace: The Constitution and Foreign Affairs After 9/11* (2005) (urging a highly restrained judicial role in foreign affairs cases, leaving such issues to presidential and congressional accommodation), with Philip Bobbitt, *Terror and Consent: The Wars for the Twenty-First Century* (2008) (anti-terror measures must be grounded in the rule of law, including judicial review).

f. E.g., Stephen Calabresi & Kevin Rhodes, *The Structural Constitution: Unitary Executive, Plural Judiciary,*105 Harv. L. Rev. 1153 (1992) (sophisticated theoretical examination of the vesting clauses); John Manning, *Textualism as a Nondelegation Doctrine*, 97 Colum. L. Rev. 673 (1997) (similar, for bicameralism).

traditionally been considered an example of constitutional *formalism*. It has the advantage of providing rules for national decisionmaking that the Court might find easy to discern and implement: If a practice violates the Constitution's allocation, the Court strikes it down; if a practice does not fall athwart that allocation, the Court should permit it and leave the political branches to work out ultimate accommodations. A problem with the formalist approach is that it is not always clear what boundaries and rules for federal government decisionmaking are embodied in the Constitution. Even when the boundaries and rules are clear, they may not be responsive to the ultimate constitutional policies in light of modern conditions (the imperial presidency, independent agencies, and so forth).

In contrast, a *functionalist* approach would sacrifice or soften some of the sharp constitutional lines to permit "necessary" government action, unless such action generally threatens our freedoms.[g] A functionalist approach can be justified on the ground that it subserves the ultimate goal of the Constitution (the "general Welfare") and as such contributes to the overall legitimacy of government. A problem with a functionalist approach is that it is not always clear what situations justify a departure from the apparent commands of the Constitution. A particular case might seem to cry out for deviation, but the proper balance is not just whether a deviation is justified in this case (the costs of enforcing an apparent constitutional line are outweighed by the benefits of deviating this one time), but whether the deviation's long-term benefits outweigh its long-term costs, including the rule-of-law costs of occasional deviation from formal commands (a President who "gets away with" a usurpation of congressional power one time is more prone to make greater inroads into congressional authority in the future).

Finally, the Court can adopt an approach that is something of a hybrid of the formalist and functional approaches.[h] For example, the Court could decide, for functionalist reasons, that it will enforce some of the constitutional boundaries strictly (bicameralism and presentment) and, for equally functionalist reasons, that it will relax other boundaries to accommodate government in the modern regulatory state (such as allowing independent agencies that are part of neither Congress nor the presidency). Or, it could decide to enforce the textual boundaries and then add some functionalist restrictions of its own.

5. *Horizontal (Functional) versus Vertical (Political) Approaches.* As described above, both functional and formal perspectives approach separation of powers issues *horizontally*: Which branch is vested with the authority to do something (formalist) or is most capable of doing it (functionalist)? Does a

---

g. E.g., Abner Greene, *Checks and Balances in an Era of Presidential Lawmaking*, 61 U. Chi. L. Rev. 123 (1994) (on the fear of aggrandizement); Strauss, note *b, supra* (on the nature of the administrative state in light of separation of powers norms).

h. Many of the cases in this chapter will exemplify a dizzying array of both formalist and functionalist arguments. See William Eskridge, Jr., *Relationships Between Formalism and Functionalism in Separation of Powers Cases*, 22 Harv. J. L & Pub. Pol'y 21 (1998). For an example of functionalist argumentation for strictly formalist bright-line rules, see Adrian Vermeule, *Judging Under Uncertainty* (2006).

NUSL's Law Office Six cordially invites you to our presentation...
The Battlefield Back Home: Reducing Incarcerated Veterans' Financial Liabilities Through Jail-Based Legal Support
Tuesday, April 6, 2010 at 5:30pm
Northeastern University School of Law — Dockser Hall 250

novel arrangement cross institutional lines (formalist) or pose risks of usurpation by the empowered branch (functionalist)? Victoria Nourse argues that we should also consider the issues *vertically*:[i] What constituency does each branch represent, and what incentives does that create for decisionmakers in that branch? What new incentives does a shift in authority from one branch to another create? What new risks does the shift create for the ability of popular majorities to affect policy — or for minority groups or individuals who might be unduly harmed by majority-supported policies?[j] How does the shift affect the nation's overall posture as a representative democracy?

Say the President invaded another country without congressional authorization. As a formal matter, this would ask us to think about whether the President was acting (properly) as the Commander-in-Chief of the armed forces (Art. II, § 2, cl. 1) or was acting to declare war, a power vested in Congress (Art. I, § 8, cl. 11). As a functional matter, one might ask whether such action reflected a good balance between liberty and efficacy: The President would argue that his action was needed as a decisive measure to head off the escalating risk of devastating foreign attack. His critics would respond that such a drastic and aggressive step should only be taken after deliberation and vote in Congress (which as a practical matter has to fund the enterprise).

A vertical approach to the issue would look at constituencies and incentives. The President has a national constituency, with one person formally responsible for all actions taken under color of that office; Congress contains many members, all representing local (House) or state (Senate) constituencies, with no one person formally responsible for its deliberative actions. If the President acts against a foreign country, there is a risk that he is acting prematurely and without the support of all the constituencies needed for a unified national effort. A congressional declaration addresses those risks much better, but poses the risk of being too slow to respond and too fragmented to respond decisively. This balance of risks could support a rule that the Framers seem to have had in mind (see § 1B): The President may act to repel foreign attacks, but Congress must declare war when there is no immediate danger.

Nourse's theory is an example of a representation-reinforcing theory of separation of powers. (Recall *Carolene Products*, which set forth a representation-reinforcing theory of individual rights (Chapter 2, § 3B), and *Barnwell Brothers*, which set forth such a theory for the Dormant Commerce Clause (Chapter 7, § 6B).) If the Supreme Court is going to play a role in arbitrating separation of powers disputes, this might be an attractive basis for its decisions. Keep the vertical perspective in mind as you read the cases in this chapter.

---

i. See Victoria Nourse, *The Vertical Separation of Powers*, 49 Duke L.J. 749 (1999); Nourse, *Toward a "Due Foundation" for the Separation of Powers:* The Federalist Papers *as Political Narrative*, 74 Tex. L. Rev. 447 (1996); Nourse, *Toward a New Constitutional Anatomy Structure*, 56 Stan. L. Rev. 835 (2004).

j. The dual-risk analysis in Nourse's work is taken from Neil Komesar, *Imperfect Alternatives: Choosing Institutions in Law, Economics, and Public Policy* (1994).

6. *Fixed versus Evolving Rules.* Recall the debate in between originalist and evolutive theories of judicial review (Chapter 2, § 3). This debate plays out in distinctive ways for separation of powers issues. On the one hand, the Framers hardly anticipated the Civil War, the New Deal, or the War on Terror; indeed, they failed to anticipate challenges faced by the Washington Administration (1789-97). Not only have events blurred some of the lines suggested by the Constitution, but they have motivated what might be considered major changes in the constitutional balance. Because many separation of powers issues are not justiciable (Chapter 9), much of the evolution has occurred within the political process, with little or no input from the Supreme Court (recall tension #3). The cases in this chapter illustrate the allure of a constitutional rule of *adverse possession*: If Congress (to take the usual example) has acquiesced in a presidential usurpation of power over a period of years, that evidence significantly supports the constitutional acceptability of that practice once it reaches the Supreme Court.[k] Recall a similar point made by John Marshall in the opening portion of *McCulloch* (Chapter 7, § 1): Because the political process had come to embrace the legitimacy of the Bank of the United States, it came to the Court cloaked in a strong presumption of constitutionality.

On the other hand, the Framers' thinking about separation of powers issues retains a cogency it does not have as regards their ideas about free speech, due process, and equal protection. As with federalism cases, original meaning is taken seriously by lawyers and sometimes by politicians in separation of powers cases. So we start at the beginning — the drafting origins of the Constitution's separation of powers, introduced in the following essay. (You should also read *Federalist* Nos. 47 and 78, reproduced in Appendix 2 of this casebook.)

Gerhard Casper
An Essay in Separation of Powers:
Some Early Versions and Practices
30 Wm. & Mary L. Rev. 211, 212-22 (1989)[l]

* * * Article VI of the Maryland Declaration of Rights of 1776 provided "[t]hat the legislative, executive and judicial powers of government, ought to be forever separate and distinct from each other." Similar formulations appear elsewhere, for instance in the 1776 Virginia Bill of Rights. * * *

Invocation of the phrase "separation of powers" in bills of rights, such as those of Maryland, Massachusetts, New Hampshire, North Carolina, Virginia, and France * * * suggests a common linkage between the concept of liberty and the notion of separation of powers. * * * Montesquieu, perhaps the most frequently cited and most confused and confusing of the writers on separation of powers, provided the classical formulation concerning the linkage:

> When the legislative and executive powers are united in the same person, or in the same body of magistracy, there can be then no liberty; because apprehensions may

---

k. Adverse possession theories find support in the concurring and dissenting opinions in the *Steel Seizure Case*, excerpted in Section 1A below and is the explicit basis for much of the presidential authority asserted in Yoo, *Powers of War and Peace*, 9-10.

l. Copyright © 2000 by the *William and Mary Law Review.* Reprinted with permission.

arise, lest the same monarch or senate should enact tyrannical laws, to execute them in a tyrannical manner.

Again, there is no liberty, if the power of judging be not separated from the legislative and executive powers. Were it joined with the legislative, the life and liberty of the subject would be exposed to arbitrary control; for the judge would be then the legislator. Were it joined to the executive power, the judge might behave with all the violence of an oppressor.

As put forward by Montesquieu, separation of powers is a functional concept; separation is a necessary, if not a sufficient, condition of liberty. Its absence promotes tyranny. * * *

As one reviews the state constitutions adopted between 1776 and 1787 for the ways in which they implemented separation of powers notions, one is struck by the fact that the particulars display an exceedingly weak version of separation of powers. Most of the constitutions made a conceptual distinction, either explicitly or implicitly, between legislative, executive, and judicial functions, introduced more or less elaborate systems of interbranch ineligibilities, and gave some, although often a modest, measure of independence to the judiciary. The most distinct feature of the constitutions, however, was the dependence of the executive on the legislative branch on four counts. First, only New York, Massachusetts, and New Hampshire provided for the election of governors by voters. In the latter two states, the choice reverted to the legislature if no candidate received a majority of the votes. The other constitutions granted the legislature the power to elect the governor or president, typically on an annual basis. In Pennsylvania the legislature and the "supreme executive council," which was popularly elected, jointly chose the president. Second, only Massachusetts and New York recognized an overridable veto. In New York the veto power was lodged in a council of revision. Third, all states provided for some kind of executive or privy council, generally elected by the legislature. Fourth, states distributed the power of appointments in various ways, but legislative controls predominated.

[These state constitutional arrangements were criticized for intermingling executive, legislative, and judicial powers. The "Essex Result" of 1778, attacking the proposed Massachusetts Constitution, said:] "A little attention to the subject will convince us, that these three powers ought to be in different hands, and independent of one another, and so balanced, and each having that check upon the other, that their independence shall be preserved." * * *

The Bill of Rights of the 1784 New Hampshire Constitution expressed clearly that the doctrine of separation of powers, or for that matter the notion of checks and balances, could not supply neat formulas from which proper governmental organizational arrangements would follow automatically. Article XXXVII of the New Hampshire Bill of Rights displayed a deeper appreciation of the problem than the more barren assertions in all the other state constitutions:

In the government of this state, the three essential powers thereof, to wit, the legislative, executive and judicial, ought to be kept as separate from and independent of each other, as the nature of a free government will admit, or as is consistent with that chain of connection that binds the whole fabric of the constitution in one indissoluble bond of union and amity.

This provision, which is still in force, obviously views the separation of powers as essential to free government. However, it also reflects the concept of separate and independent powers as limited by the very notion of free government and by the necessity of maintaining "the whole fabric of the constitution." In short, New Hampshire emphasizes separation, coordination, and cooperation. Its dialectical view of the matter concisely summarizes the difficulties that awaited the federal constitutional convention as it faced the separation of powers "doctrine."

The Articles of Confederation had established a congress of state delegates as the central law-making and governing institution. Although its President, committees, and civil officers partook of an executive quality, and although after 1780 it established a court of appeals for cases of capture, the Confederation can hardly be seen as possessing the characteristics of a tripartite government. On the other hand, one should not overlook the fact that some institutional separation of administrative tasks had evolved, dictated, as it were, by the nature of things, and the need to free the Congress from concerning itself with too much administrative detail.

Although the absence of separation of powers was not generally viewed as the main weakness of the Confederation, Hamilton criticized the Articles as early as July 1783 for "confounding legislative and executive powers in a single body" and for lacking a federal judicature "having cognizance of all matters of general concern." In a draft resolution calling for a convention to amend the Articles, Hamilton wrote that the Confederation's structure was "contrary to the most approved and well founded maxims of free government which require that the legislative executive and judicial authorities should be deposited in distinct and separate hands." Hamilton had intended to submit the resolution to the Continental Congress, but abandoned the project for want of support.

When Randolph opened the substantive deliberations of the 1787 Convention with his enumeration of the defects of the Confederation, he apparently made no reference to separation of powers. The Virginia Plan, submitted the same day, however, implied separation of powers and called for a quadripartite governmental structure: a bicameral legislature, a national executive, and a national judiciary (to serve during good behavior), and a council of revision to be composed of the executive and members of the judiciary. The first house of the legislature was to elect the second from a pool of candidates to be nominated by the states, and the legislature was to elect the executive and judiciary. The executive was to enjoy "the Executive rights vested in Congress by the Confederation," but what these rights were was not adumbrated.

Other plans for a constitution all presupposed a three-branch structure of government. A resolution "that a national government ought to be established consisting of a supreme legislative, judiciary, and executive" was adopted overwhelmingly in the Committee of the Whole on May 30, the day following submission of the Virginia Plan. In a way, this event was the beginning and the end of the consideration of separation of powers *as such* in the Convention. To be sure, in the subsequent discussions of the structure and powers of the legislative, executive, and judicial branches as well as in the repeated debates concerning a council of revision, the delegates raised many points about the independence of the respective branches, the dangers of encroachments, and the need for checks and balances. What was strikingly absent, however, was anything that might be viewed as a coherent and generally shared view of separation of powers.

The constitutional text itself, although implying the notion of distinct branches, did not invoke the separation of powers as a principle. Some of the state ratifying conventions attempted to remedy this omission in their original proposals for bills of rights to be added to the Constitution. Madison also sought a remedy. * * *

Madison's 1789 proposal for a new Article VII to precede the existing one (which was to be renumbered) was ingenious in the manner in which it formulated a separation of powers doctrine that took account of the constitutional scheme of checks and balances:

> The powers delegated by this constitution, are appropriated to the departments to which they are respectively distributed: so that the legislative department shall never exercise the powers vested in the executive or judicial; nor the executive exercise the powers vested in the legislative or judicial; nor the judicial exercise the powers vested in the legislative or executive departments.

The separation of powers provision of Roger Sherman's draft bill of rights, also dating from the summer of 1789, captured even more clearly the point made by Madison's proposed Article VII:

> The legislative, executive and judiciary powers vested by the Constitution in the respective branches of the Government of the United States shall be exercised according to the distribution therein made, so that neither of said branches shall assume or exercise any of the powers peculiar to either of the other branches.

The House adopted Madison's amendment (with a minor change) despite objections that it was unnecessary and "subversive of the Constitution." Madison supposed "the people would be gratified with the amendment, as it was admitted that the powers ought to be separate and distinct; it might also tend to an explanation of some doubts that might arise respecting the construction of the Constitution." This was an intriguing suggestion: the amendment would provide a principle of interpretation for the Constitution — *in dubio, pro* separation of powers. In fact, Madison had taken this position earlier that year when discussing the removal power. Alas, the Senate rejected the amendment for reasons we shall never know. One can only surmise that the Senate was not eager to adopt separation of powers as an independent doctrine or even as a mere principle of construction for the many and subtle "mixing" decisions of the Framers, some of which benefited the Senate.

Addendum. In *Executive Power Essentialism and Foreign Affairs*, 102 Mich. L. Rev. 545, 571-85 (2002), Curtis Bradley and Martin Flaherty make the important point that the early state constitutions reflected important *shifts in political thinking*. The initial wave of state constitutions, adopted during the Revolution, were republican; there were ten such constitutions by 1777. They revealed strong distrust of executive power (associated with King George III) and hence concentrated power in legislatures. Some states had no chief executives; others created governors who shared power with privy councils drawn from or appointed by the legislature. In most states, the power to appoint judges and other officials was vested entirely in the legislature.

Founding Fathers such as James Madison and even Thomas Jefferson were disappointed by the performance of state legislatures under these arrangements, and state constitutions adopted in the 1780s vested less authority in legislatures and more in governors. The Massachusetts Constitution of 1780 made the governor popularly elected; although it defined his powers carefully, the governor had both appointment and veto authority (both missing from most of the other state constitutions in effect during the 1780s).

———

NOTE ON EARLY INTERACTIONS BETWEEN THE BRANCHES OF THE NATIONAL GOVERNMENT, 1790-1798

In addition to the intellectual and drafting origins of the constitutional separation of powers, early practice might be relevant to discerning the original understanding of Articles I-III.[m] While we reserve specific argumentation for later portions of this chapter, themes that emerge from the early years were an awareness by the leading players that early interactions were framed by separation of powers ideas, for they would set "precedents" for subsequent practice, but at the same time a frequent lack of consensus as to the precise contours or even root theory of separate powers.[n]

An example of both points involved the *Decision of 1789*.[o] In that first year of the Washington Administration, the House of Representatives' consideration of a bill to create a Department of Foreign Affairs turned to the question, Who would have the power to remove the Secretary of that Department? Some representatives thought that removal power must parallel appointment power — hence, the President could remove only with the consent of the Senate (accord, *Federalist* No. 77 (Hamilton)). Other representatives thought that the President, acting alone, should have the power to remove the Secretary — either because

---

m. For clashing historical treatments of early practice as shedding light on original understandings, compare Curtis Bradley & Martin Flaherty, *Executive Power Essentialism and Foreign Affairs,* 102 Mich. L. Rev. 545 (2002), with Saikrishna Prakash & Michael Ramsey, *The Executive Power over Foreign Affairs,* 111 Yale L.J. 231 (2001); and Steven Calabresi & Saikrishna Prakash, *The President's Power to Execute the Laws,* 104 Yale L.J. 541 (1994), with Martin Flaherty, *History "Lite" in Modern American Constitutionalism,* 95 Colum. L. Rev. 523 (1995); and William Michael Treanor, *Fame, the Founding and the Power to Declare War,* 82 Cornell L. Rev. 695 (1997), with John Yoo, *The Continuation of Politics by Other Means: The Original Understanding of War Powers,* 84 Cal. L. Rev. 167 (1996).

n. In 1790, John Jay observed that there was agreement that there should be three independent branches, but "how to constitute and ballance them in such a Manner as best to guard against Abuse and Fluctuation, & preserve the constitution from Encroachments, are Points on which there continues to be a great Diversity of opinions, and on which we have all as yet much to learn." [Maeva Marcus, *Separation of Powers in the Early National Period,* 30 Wm. & Mary L. Rev. 269, 270 (1989), quoting Jay's Charge to the Grand Jury of the Circuit Court for the District of New York, Apr. 12, 1790.]

o. Casper, *Some Early Versions and Practices,* 30 Wm. & Mary L. Rev. at 234-39; Curtis & Flaherty, *Executive Power Essentialism,* 102 Mich. L. Rev. at 656-64.

it was good policy that Congress in its discretion ought to choose (Representative Madison's original view) *or* because the Constitution required such power to rest with the President alone (Madison's view by the end of the debate). The House and Senate both ultimately voted for a law that indirectly left the removal power with the President alone, but with the basis for that power (the Constitution versus congressional choice) left dangling. On the other hand, the Decision of 1789 did set a precedent followed by subsequent Congresses.

Another precedent-setting episode arose out of a proposal in the House to request the President to initiate an investigation into the destruction of the army command under General St. Clair in Ohio.[p] Hostilities with the Indians had commenced in 1789, and the St. Clair disaster was an incident in that ongoing struggle. Representatives themselves objected that such a request was improper, because it amounted to an encroachment on executive powers, 3 Annals of Cong. 490-94 (1792). The proposal was defeated, and the House instead appointed its own committee of inquiry. President Washington and his cabinet were in agreement that the House acted properly and agreed to cooperate. The President insisted, however, that requests for executive department papers be made directly to the President, who would withhold any "the disclosure of which would injure the public." The House in turn followed the President's conditions when it formally requested papers.

During the course of the St. Clair investigation, the Secretary of War and another executive officer asked to present their views directly to the House, which instead asked them to present their views to the investigating committee. As this episode suggests, much thought was given to whether personal interactions among the branches were appropriate. The trend in the Washington Administration was away from face-to-face and informal dealings. Thus, President Washington himself refused a Senate request that he submit appointments in person to the senators, as inconsistent with his vision of the appointments process, and after one face-to-face encounter on a treaty with Native Americans both the President and Congress decided that complex treaty matters were best handled through formal communications.

Nonetheless, there was a great deal of interbranch communication. For example, the statute creating the Treasury Department directed the Secretary "to make report, and give information to either branch of the legislature, in person or in writing (as he may be required), respecting all matters referred to him by the Senate or House of Representatives," 1 Stat. 66. More important, the Washington Administration's foreign policy was conducted with constant coordination with Congress for practical reasons, as the Senate was needed to ratify treaties and the House as well as Senate were needed for appropriations.[q] Starting in 1790, the administration sought the return of American hostages taken by the Barbary Powers and an arrangement whereby the Powers would cease harassment of American shipping. At most points of his dealings with the Barbary Powers, the President sought to keep Congress apprized of the

---

p. Casper, *Some Early Versions and Practices*, 30 Wm. & Mary L. Rev. at 228-29.

q. Casper, *Some Early Versions and Practices*, 30 Wm. & Mary L. Rev. at 242-57.

diplomatic situation and the options being considered (including war), sought or received the advice of either chamber, and acted in conformity with legislative consensus. Over Senate objections, Washington even included the House of Representatives in his consultations about the possibility of a treaty, again for the practical reason that any treaty would involve monetary payments (ransom and tribute) requiring House initiation and approval. The President also demanded, and generally obtained, confidentiality for his messages to Congress and for most legislative deliberations. The careful coordination paid off: a treaty was ratified in 1796, and monies appropriated in 1797, although the House threw off the requirement of confidentiality that year.

The Adams Administration handled its big foreign crisis in a similarly cooperative way.[r] French raids on American commerce and a disrespectful demand of tribute from American envoys in 1797 generated outrage in the United States. The Adams Administration refused to pay a sixpence for tribute and commenced a Quasi-War with France in 1798. As had the Washington Administration in its dealings with the Barbary Powers, the Adams Administration needed and obtained Congress's cooperation to fund new ships and armed forces to confront the French. Although some hyperintensive Federalists wanted a formal declaration of war against France, Adams did not ask for, and Congress did not provide, such a declaration; naval hostilities lasted more than two years.

The federal judiciary was likewise attuned to its theoretical independence and the precedential nature of early arrangements. Hence, when in 1793 Secretary of State Jefferson asked the Supreme Court for its opinion on legal issues, the Court responded that it would not issue *advisory opinions.* "[T]he three departments of the government [being] in certain respects checks upon each other, and our being judges of a court of last resort, are considerations which accord strong arguments against the propriety of our extrajudicially deciding the questions alluded to, especially as the power given by the Constitution to the President, of calling the heads of departments for opinions, seems to have purposely as well as expressly united to the executive departments."[s] Also, federal judges refused to participate as judges deciding claims for pensions by veterans claiming to have been wounded, pursuant to the Invalid Pensions Act of 1792, 1 Stat. 243, because their findings were only recommendations to the Secretary of War.[t] Yet individual Justices gave their opinions to executive and legislative officials, and judges participated in the pension statute as extrajudicial *commissioners* rather than as judges.[u] Chief Justices John Jay and Oliver Ellsworth served as presidential envoys to negotiate treaties during

---

r. Yoo, *Continuation of Politics by Other Means,* 84 Cal. L. Rev. at 292-93.

s. Letter from John Jay, James Wilson, John Blair, James Iredell, and William Paterson to George Washington, Aug. 8, 1793, Record Group 59, National Archives, quoted and discussed in *Hart and Wechsler's The Federal Courts and the Federal System* 92-93 (4th ed. 1996); Maeva Marcus & Emily Van Tassel, *Judges and Legislators in the New Federal System 1789-1800,* in *Judges and Legislators: Toward Institutional Comity* 31, 42 (Robert Katzmann ed. 1988).

t. Marcus, *Early National Period,* 30 Wm. & Mary L. Rev. at 272-73.

u. Marcus, *Early National Period,* 30 Wm. & Mary L. Rev. at 173-75.

their tenures, over objections that were dismissed during the confirmation process.

SECTION 1. ISSUES OF EXECUTIVE AGGRANDIZEMENT (THE IMPERIAL PRESIDENCY)

Although President Washington initially walked on egg shells in his dealings with Congress, and tended to be solicitous of congressional opinions when he took either domestic or foreign affairs initiatives, as time went by he operated more independently, especially in matters of military or foreign policy. This was even more true of his successors. Illustrating aggressive executive department initiatives carried out without the close cooperation with Congress detailed in the previous Note were President Jefferson's doubling the size of the country through his agreement to purchase the Louisiana Territory from France; the "Monroe Doctrine," directing the European powers to leave Western Hemisphere matters to the United States; President Polk's leading us into the Mexican-American War; President Lincoln's leadership during the Civil War, including such bold strokes as the Emancipation Proclamation and such controversial practices as military trials of civilians and suspension of the writ of habeas corpus; President Andrew Johnson's defiance of the Reconstruction Congress and his insistence that the Tenure of Office Act, limiting his ability to discharge cabinet officers, was unconstitutional; President Teddy Roosevelt's deployment of "gunboat diplomacy" to protect American interests in other Western Hemisphere nations; and President Wilson's international role as a founder of the League of Nations (which the Congress then refused to permit our country to join). Political scientists have suggested a reason for these remarkable actions: the President has a huge "first mover" advantage, especially in crisis situations such as the Civil War, where the other branches face a double difficulty in opposing the President — they not only have to get their collective act together, but they would usually have to defy public opinion as well.[a]

Consistent with this political science wisdom, the growth of the national government witnessed an even bigger growth in presidential power, because there were more problems that activist Presidents could tackle, and We the People usually voted for aggressive rather than passive presidential candidates. The administrations of Presidents Teddy Roosevelt, Taft, and Wilson saw the President and his executive departments assume an increasingly activist role in domestic affairs, including labor-management relations, trust-busting, and business regulation. An "Imperial Presidency" was unmistakable during President Franklin Delano Roosevelt's New Deal, in which an exceptionally vigorous Chief Executive met the stupendous challenges of the Great Depression and World War II with an executive activism that threatened to eclipse the other branches of the national government, as well as the states.

---

a. See generally William Howell, *Power without Persuasion: The Politics of Direct Presidential Action* (2003); Terry Moe & William Howell, *The Presidential Power of Unilateral Action*, 15 J.L. Econ. & Org. 132 (1999).

This section examines three different contexts in which the Imperial Presidency has raised serious constitutional concerns: the President's alleged usurpation of legislative power in domestic (Part A) and foreign affairs (Part B), and the President's insistence that his office immunizes him from judicial process applicable to other citizens or even other federal officials (Part C). Interestingly, it was the administration of now-widely-admired President Harry Truman that most dramatically presented the first two issues: Truman committed the United States to the Korean War without a congressional declaration of war and, during the course of the war, seized the steel industry without congressional authorization. The last issue, of privilege and immunity, was pressed by President Richard Nixon's dramatic fall from power in 1974.

A. THE GENERAL POST-NEW DEAL FRAMEWORK

YOUNGSTOWN SHEET & TUBE CO. v. SAWYER (THE STEEL SEIZURE CASE)
343 U.S. 579, 72 S.Ct. 863, 96 L.Ed. 1153 (1952)

[The facts of the case were particularly complex.[b] Leading a United Nations-sanctioned peacekeeping force, the United States went to war with North Korea to repel its June 1950 attack on South Korea. Although Congress never declared war, it supported the war effort by authorizing a build-up of our armed forces to 3,500,000 people strong and appropriating unprecedented sums of money for national defense. In 1950, President Truman requested authority to requisition property and to allocate priorities for scarce goods. In Title IV of the Defense Production Act of 1950, Congress not only gave the President the powers requested, but also gave him authority to stabilize wages and prices and to provide for the settlement of labor disputes arising in the defense program. Congress extended the Act in 1951. A Senate committee expressed concern about inflation in some of the defense industries, because of the strain of producing for both military and domestic markets; the committee emphasized the steel industry as the exemplar of this problem. A three-way dispute broke out among the government, the steel companies, and the unions: the unions wanted a wage increase, which the companies wouldn't grant without a hefty price increase, which the government resisted.[c]

---

b. Our statement of facts is taken from Chief Justice Vinson's dissenting opinion, as well as Maeva Marcus, *Truman and the Steel Seizure Case: The Limits of Presidential Power* (1977); Alan Westin, *The Anatomy of a Constitutional Case* (1958); Henry Hart, Jr. & Albert Sacks, *The Legal Process* 1010-46 (William Eskridge, Jr. & Philip Frickey eds., 1994 [tent. ed. 1958]).

c. Pursuant to Title IV, President Truman established an Economic Stabilization Agency. On January 26, 1951, the Agency issued formal wage and price controls, to stem inflationary pressures in the steel industry, among others. On November 1, 1951, the United Steelworkers Union gave notice to the major steel companies that the Union intended to demand wage increases at the end of its contract. The companies resisted these demands. On December 22, President Truman referred the union-industry dispute to the Wage Stabilization Board (WSB) for recommendation of a fair solution, also as authorized by the 1950 Act. On March 22, 1952, the WSB issued its report, recommending a modest wage increase. The union embraced the recommendation, and the companies rejected it. Yet the companies pressed the Office of Price Stabilization (OPS) for a price increase, and it is probable that favorable action on prices would have made the companies

[On April 4, 1952, the union announced a nationwide strike to start on April 9. The President was in a bind. During World War II, the War Labor Disputes Act had authorized the President to seize industrial plants threatened with disruptive labor disputes. That authority ended in 1946. Congress replaced it with a more limited authority. The Taft-Hartley Act of 1947 provided: If in his opinion an actual or threatened strike imperiled the nation's health or safety, the President was authorized to appoint a special board to report the facts of the dispute and, if the report failed to induce resolution of the dispute, to seek a district court order enjoining the strike for 80 days, to facilitate efforts at settling the dispute (this is called a "cooling-off order"). President Truman was not willing to invoke the Taft-Hartley Act.[d] Nor was he willing to invoke the Selective Service Act of 1948. Whenever a producer failed to fill an order for goods required by the armed forces for defense purposes within a specified period of time, the Act authorized the President to take immediate possession of the producer's facilities and operate them for the production of the required goods (with "just compensation" to be paid to the producer). Nor was President Truman willing to invoke Title II of the Defense Production Act of 1950, which set up procedures for the President to "acquire by condemnation" facilities necessary for the national defense. A prerequisite to condemnation was an effort by the President to acquire the facilities by negotiation.

[Hours before the strike was to commence, the President issued Executive Order 10340, 17 Fed. Reg. 3139 (1952), which directed Secretary of Commerce Sawyer to take possession of the steel industry and to keep the mills operating, "in order to assure the continued availability of steel and steel products during the existing emergency." The order invoked "the authority vested in [the President] by the Constitution and laws of the United States, and as President of the United States and Commander in Chief of the armed forces of the United States."

[Executive Order 10340 had the advantage of maintaining production of an important war commodity without offending organized labor, which acquiesced in the order. It had the disadvantage of antagonizing the steel industry, which complied with the order but sued to have it overturned. On April 30, the steel companies obtained a preliminary injunction against the Secretary's action. The court of appeals stayed the effect of the injunction, pending review. In an extraordinary move, the Supreme Court took the case on certiorari on May 3; it was argued on May 12. The Court announced its decision affirming the injunction on June 2, 1952.]

JUSTICE BLACK delivered the opinion of the Court.

---

amenable to a wage increase. On March 28, the OPS suggested a modest price increase, which the companies rejected. On April 3, the companies offered the union a small wage increase, which the Union rejected.

d. It is not clear why. In his memoirs, the President claims that both he and Congress assumed that the WSB procedures were supposed to be substitutes for the Taft-Hartley procedures; since he had already exhausted the WSB procedures, Taft-Hartley was not available. See Harry S. Truman, *Memoirs — Years of Trial and Hope* 465-78 (1956) (vol. 2). Also note that the Taft-Hartley Act itself was bitterly opposed by organized labor and enacted over President Truman's veto.

We are asked to decide whether the President was acting within his constitutional power when he issued an order directing the Secretary of Commerce to take possession of and operate most of the Nation's steel mills. The mill owners argue that the President's order amounts to lawmaking, a legislative function which the Constitution has expressly confided to the Congress and not to the President. The Government's position is that the order was made on findings of the President that his action was necessary to avert a national catastrophe which would inevitably result from a stoppage of steel production, and that in meeting this grave emergency the President was acting within the aggregate of his constitutional powers as the Nation's Chief Executive and the Commander in Chief of the Armed Forces of the United States. * * *

The President's power, if any, to issue the order must stem either from an act of Congress or from the Constitution itself. There is no statute that expressly authorizes the President to take possession of property as he did here. Nor is there any act of Congress to which our attention has been directed from which such a power can fairly be implied. * * * There are two statutes which do authorize the President to take both personal and real property under certain conditions[, but] these conditions were not met and * * * the President's order was not rooted in either of the statutes. The Government refers to the seizure provisions of one of these statutes * * * as "much too cumbersome, involved, and time-consuming for the crisis which was at hand."

Moreover, the use of the seizure technique to solve labor disputes in order to prevent work stoppages was not only unauthorized by any congressional enactment; prior to this controversy, Congress had refused to adopt that method of settling labor disputes. When the Taft-Hartley Act was under consideration in 1947, Congress rejected an amendment which would have authorized such governmental seizures in cases of emergency. Apparently it was thought that the technique of seizure, like that of compulsory arbitration, would interfere with the process of collective bargaining. * * * Instead, the plan sought to bring about settlements by use of the customary devices of mediation, conciliation, investigation by boards of inquiry, and public reports. In some instances temporary injunctions were authorized to provide cooling-off periods. All this failing, unions were left free to strike. * * *

It is clear that if the President had authority to issue the order he did, it must be found in some provision of the Constitution. And it is not claimed that express constitutional language grants this power to the President. The contention is that presidential power should be implied from the aggregate of his powers under the Constitution. Particular reliance is placed on provisions in Article II which say that "The executive Power shall be vested in a President . . ."; that "he shall take Care that the Laws be faithfully executed"; and that he "shall be Commander in Chief of the Army and Navy of the United States."

The order cannot properly be sustained as an exercise of the President's military power as Commander in Chief of the Armed Forces. The Government attempts to do so by citing a number of cases upholding broad powers in military commanders engaged in day-to-day fighting in a theater of war. Such cases need not concern us here. Even though "theater of war" be an expanding concept, we cannot with faithfulness to our constitutional system hold that the Commander in Chief of the Armed Forces has the ultimate power as such to take possession of private property in order to keep labor disputes from stopping production. This is a job for the Nation's lawmakers, not for its military authorities.

Nor can the seizure order be sustained because of the several constitutional provisions that grant executive power to the President. In the framework of our Constitution, the President's power to see that the laws are faithfully executed refutes the idea that he is to be a lawmaker. The Constitution limits his functions in the lawmaking process to the recommending of laws he thinks wise and the vetoing of laws he thinks bad. And the Constitution is neither silent nor equivocal about who shall make laws which the President is to execute. The first section of the first Article says that "All legislative Powers herein granted shall be vested in a Congress of the United States . . . ." After granting many powers to the Congress, Article I goes on to provide that Congress may "make all Laws which shall be necessary and proper for carrying into Execution the foregoing Powers, and all other Powers vested by this Constitution in the Government of the United States, or in any Department or Officer thereof."

The President's order does not direct that a congressional policy be executed in a manner prescribed by Congress — it directs that a presidential policy be executed in a manner prescribed by the President. * * * The power of Congress to adopt such public policies as those proclaimed by the order is beyond question. It can authorize the taking of private property for public use. It can make laws regulating the relationships between employers and employees, prescribing rules designed to settle labor disputes, and fixing wages and working conditions in certain fields of our economy. The Constitution does not subject this lawmaking power of Congress to presidential or military supervision or control.

It is said that other Presidents without congressional authority have taken possession of private business enterprises in order to settle labor disputes. But even if this be true, Congress has not thereby lost its exclusive constitutional authority to make laws necessary and proper to carry out the powers vested by the Constitution "in the Government of the United States, or any Department or Officer thereof."

The Founders of this Nation entrusted the lawmaking power to the Congress alone in both good and bad times. It would do no good to recall the historical events, the fears of power and the hopes for freedom that lay behind their choice. Such a review would but confirm our holding that this seizure order cannot stand.

JUSTICE FRANKFURTER, concurring.

To be sure, the content of the three authorities of government is not to be derived from an abstract analysis. The areas are partly interacting, not wholly disjointed. The Constitution is a framework for government. Therefore the way the framework has consistently operated fairly establishes that it has operated according to its true nature. Deeply embedded traditional ways of conducting government cannot supplant the Constitution or legislation, but they give meaning to the words of a text or supply them. It is an inadmissibly narrow conception of American constitutional law to confine it to the words of the Constitution and to disregard the gloss which life has written upon them. In short, a systematic, unbroken, executive practice, long pursued to the knowledge of the Congress and never before questioned, engaged in by Presidents who have also sworn to uphold the Constitution, making as it were such exercise of power part of the structure of our government, may be treated as a gloss on "executive Power" vested in the President by § 1 of Art. II. * * *

Down to the World War II period * * * the record is barren of instances comparable to the one before us. Of twelve seizures by President Roosevelt prior to the enactment of the War Labor Disputes Act in June, 1943, three were sanctioned by existing law, and six others were effected after Congress, on December 8, 1941, had declared the existence of a state of war. In this case, reliance on the powers that flow from declared war has been commendably disclaimed by the Solicitor General. Thus the list of executive assertions of the power of seizure in circumstances comparable to the present reduces to three in the six-month period from June to December of 1941. We need not split hairs in comparing those actions to the one before us, though much might be said by way of differentiation. Without passing on their validity, as we are not called upon to do, it suffices to say that these three isolated instances do not add up, either in number, scope, duration or contemporaneous legal justification, to [a systematic and longstanding] executive construction of the Constitution. Nor do they come to us sanctioned by long-continued acquiescence of Congress giving decisive weight to a construction by the Executive of its powers.

A scheme of government like ours no doubt at times feels the lack of power to act with complete, all-embracing, swiftly moving authority. No doubt a government with distributed authority, subject to be challenged in the courts of law, at least long enough to consider and adjudicate the challenge, labors under restrictions from which other governments are free. It has not been our tradition to envy such governments. In any event our government was designed to have such restrictions. The price was deemed not too high in view of the safeguards which these restrictions afford. * * *

JUSTICE JACKSON, concurring in the judgment and opinion of the Court.

A judge, like an executive adviser, may be surprised at the poverty of really useful and unambiguous authority applicable to concrete problems of executive power as they actually present themselves. Just what our forefathers did envision, or would have envisioned had they foreseen modern conditions, must be divined from materials almost as enigmatic as the dreams Joseph was called upon to interpret for Pharaoh. A century and a half of partisan debate and scholarly speculation yields no net result but only supplies more or less apt quotations from respected sources on each side of any question. They largely cancel each other. And court decisions are indecisive because of the judicial practice of dealing with the largest questions in the most narrow way.

The actual art of governing under our Constitution does not and cannot conform to judicial definitions of the power of any of its branches based on isolated clauses or even single Articles torn from context. While the Constitution diffuses power the better to secure liberty, it also contemplates that practice will integrate the dispersed powers into a workable government. It enjoins upon its branches separateness but interdependence, autonomy but reciprocity. Presidential powers are not fixed but fluctuate, depending upon their disjunction or conjunction with those of Congress. We may well begin by a somewhat over-simplified grouping of practical situations in which a President may doubt, or others may challenge, his powers, and by distinguishing roughly the legal consequences of this factor of relativity.

1. When the President acts pursuant to an express or implied authorization of Congress, his authority is at its maximum, for it includes all that he possesses in his own right plus all that Congress can delegate. In these circumstances, and in these only, may he be said (for what it may be worth) to personify the federal sovereignty. If his act is held unconstitutional under these circumstances, it usually means that the Federal Government as an undivided whole lacks power. A seizure executed by the President pursuant to an Act of Congress would be supported by the strongest of presumptions and the widest latitude of judicial interpretation, and the burden of persuasion would rest heavily upon any who might attack it.

2. When the President acts in absence of either a congressional grant or denial of authority, he can only rely upon his own independent powers, but there is a zone of twilight in which he and Congress may have concurrent authority, or in which its distribution is uncertain. Therefore, congressional inertia, indifference or quiescence may sometimes, at least as a practical matter, enable, if not invite, measures on independent presidential responsibility. In this area, any actual test of power is likely to depend on the imperatives of events and contemporary imponderables rather than on abstract theories of law.

3. When the President takes measures incompatible with the expressed or implied will of Congress, his power is at its lowest ebb, for then he can rely only upon his own constitutional powers minus any constitutional powers of Congress over the matter. Courts can sustain exclusive presidential control in such a case only by disabling the Congress from acting upon the subject. Presidential claim to a power at once so conclusive and preclusive must be scrutinized with caution, for what is at stake is the equilibrium established by our constitutional system.

Into which of these classifications does this executive seizure of the steel industry fit? It is eliminated from the first by admission, for it is conceded that no congressional authorization exists for this seizure. * * *

Can it then be defended under flexible tests available to the second category? It seems clearly eliminated from that class because Congress has not left seizure of private property an open field but has covered it by three statutory policies inconsistent with this seizure. * * *

This leaves the current seizure to be justified only by the severe tests under the third grouping, where it can be supported only by any remainder of executive power after subtraction of such powers as Congress may have over the subject. In short, we can sustain the President only by holding that seizure of such strike-bound industries is within his domain and beyond control by Congress. * * *

The Solicitor General seeks the power of seizure in three clauses of the Executive Article, the first reading, "The executive Power shall be vested in a President of the United States of America." Lest I be thought to exaggerate, I quote the interpretation which his brief puts upon it: "In our view, this clause constitutes a grant of all the executive powers of which the Government is capable." If that be true, it is difficult to see why the forefathers bothered to add several specific items, including some trifling ones.

The example of such unlimited executive power that must have most impressed the forefathers was the prerogative exercised by George III, and the description of its evils in the Declaration of Independence leads me to doubt that they were creating their new Executive in his image. Continental European examples were no more appealing. And if we seek instruction from our own times, we can match it only from the executive powers in those governments we disparagingly describe as totalitarian. I cannot accept the view that this clause is a grant in bulk of all conceivable executive power but regard it as an allocation to the presidential office of the generic powers thereafter stated.

The clause on which the Government next relies is that "The President shall be Commander in Chief of the Army and Navy of the United States . . . ." [J]ust what authority goes with the [title] has plagued presidential advisers who would not waive or narrow it by nonassertion yet cannot say where it begins or ends. It undoubtedly puts the Nation's armed forces under presidential command. Hence, this loose appellation is sometimes advanced as support for any presidential action, internal or external, involving use of force, the idea being that it vests power to do anything, anywhere, that can be done with an army or navy. * * *

There are indications that the Constitution did not contemplate that the title Commander in Chief *of the Army and Navy* will constitute him also Commander in Chief of the country, its industries and its inhabitants. He has no monopoly of "war powers," whatever they are. * * *

The third clause in which the Solicitor General finds seizure powers is that "he shall take Care that the Laws be faithfully executed . . . ." That authority must be matched against words of the Fifth Amendment that "No person shall be . . . deprived of life, liberty or property, without due process of law . . . ." One gives a governmental authority that reaches so far as there is law, the other gives a private right that authority shall go no farther. These signify about all there is of the principle that ours is a government of laws, not of men, and that we submit ourselves to rulers only if under rules.

The Solicitor General lastly grounds support of the seizure upon nebulous, inherent powers never expressly granted but said to have accrued to the office from the customs and claims of preceding administrations. The plea is for a resulting power to deal with a crisis or an emergency according to the necessities of the case, the unarticulated assumption being that necessity knows no law. * * *

The appeal, however, that we declare the existence of inherent powers *ex necessitate* to meet an emergency asks us to do what many think would be wise, although it is something the forefathers omitted. They knew what emergencies were, knew the pressures they engender for authoritative action, knew, too, how they afford a ready pretext for usurpation. We may also suspect that they suspected that emergency powers would tend to kindle emergencies. Aside from suspension of the privilege of the writ of habeas corpus in time of rebellion or invasion, when the public safety may require it [U.S. Const., Art. I, § 9, cl. 2], they made no express provision for exercise of extraordinary authority because of a crisis. I do not think we rightfully may so amend their work. * * *

In view of the ease, expedition and safety with which Congress can grant and has granted large emergency powers, certainly ample to embrace this crisis, I am quite unimpressed with the argument that we should affirm possession of them without statute. Such power either has no beginning or it has no end. If it exists, it need submit to no legal restraint. I am not alarmed that it would plunge us straightway into dictatorship, but it is at least a step in that wrong direction.

As to whether there is imperative necessity for such powers, it is relevant to note the gap that exists between the President's paper powers and his real powers. The Constitution does not disclose the measure of the actual controls wielded by the modern presidential office. That instrument must be understood as an Eighteenth-Century sketch of a government hoped for, not as a blueprint of the Government that is. Vast accretions of federal power, eroded from that reserved by the States, have magnified the scope of presidential activity. Subtle shifts take place in the centers of real power that do not show on the face of the Constitution.

Executive power has the advantage of concentration in a single head in whose choice the whole Nation has a part, making him the focus of public hopes and expectations. In drama, magnitude and finality his decisions so far overshadow any others that almost alone he fills the public eye and ear. No other personality in public life can begin to compete with him in access to the public mind through modern methods of communications. By his prestige as head of state and his influence upon public opinion he exerts a leverage upon those who are supposed to check and balance his power which often cancels their effectiveness.

Moreover, rise of the party system has made a significant extraconstitutional supplement to real executive power. No appraisal of his necessities is realistic which overlooks that he heads a political system as well as a legal system. Party loyalties and interests, sometimes more binding than law, extend his effective control into branches of government other than his own and he often may win, as a political leader, what he cannot command under the Constitution. * * *

But I have no illusion that any decision by this Court can keep power in the hands of Congress if it is not wise and timely in meeting its problems. A crisis that challenges the President equally, or perhaps primarily, challenges Congress. If not good law, there was worldly wisdom in the maxim attributed to Napoleon that "The tools belong to the man who can use them." We may say that power to legislate for emergencies belongs in the hands of Congress, but only Congress itself can prevent power from slipping through its fingers.

[The concurring opinions of **JUSTICE DOUGLAS**, **JUSTICE CLARK** (concurring only in the judgment), and **JUSTICE BURTON** are omitted.]

CHIEF JUSTICE VINSON, with whom **JUSTICE REED** and **JUSTICE MINTON** join, dissenting.

A review of executive action demonstrates that our Presidents have on many occasions exhibited the leadership contemplated by the Framers when they made the President Commander in Chief, and imposed upon him the trust to "take Care that the Laws be faithfully executed." With or without explicit statutory authorization, Presidents have at such times dealt with national emergencies by acting promptly and resolutely to enforce legislative programs, at least to save those programs until Congress could act. Congress and the courts have responded to such executive initiative with consistent approval. * * *

Without declaration of war, President Lincoln took energetic action with the outbreak of the War Between the States. He summoned troops and paid them out of the Treasury without appropriation therefore. He proclaimed a naval blockade of the Confederacy and seized ships violating that blockade. Congress, far from denying the validity of these acts, gave them express approval. The most striking action of President Lincoln was the Emancipation Proclamation, issued in aid of the successful prosecution of the War Between the States, but wholly without statutory authority.

In an action furnishing a most apt precedent for this case, President Lincoln without statutory authority directed the seizure of rail and telegraph lines leading to Washington. Many months later, Congress recognized and confirmed the power of the President to seize railroads and telegraph lines and provided criminal penalties for interference with Government operation. * * *

President Hayes authorized the wide-spread use of federal troops during the Railroad Strike of 1877. President Cleveland also used the troops in the Pullman Strike of 1895 and his action is of special significance. No statute authorized this action. No call for help had issued from the Governor of Illinois; indeed Governor Altgeld disclaimed the need for supplemental forces. But the President's concern was that federal laws relating to the free flow of interstate commerce and the mails be continuously and faithfully executed without interruption. To further this aim his agent sought and obtained the injunction upheld by this Court in *In re Debs*, 158 U.S. 564 (1895). The Court scrutinized each of the steps taken by the President to insure execution of the "mass of legislation" dealing with commerce and the mails and gave his conduct full approval. Congress likewise took note of this use of Presidential power to forestall apparent obstacles to the faithful execution of the laws. By separate resolutions, both the Senate and the House commended the Executive's action.

President Theodore Roosevelt seriously contemplated seizure of Pennsylvania coal mines if a coal shortage necessitated such action. In his autobiography, President Roosevelt expounded the "Stewardship Theory" of Presidential power, stating that "the executive as subject only to the people, and, under the Constitution, bound to serve the people affirmatively in cases where the Constitution does not explicitly forbid him to render the service." * * *

Beginning with the Bank Holiday Proclamation and continuing through World War II, executive leadership and initiative were characteristic of President Franklin D. Roosevelt's administration. * * * [Before, as well as after, Pearl Harbor and the declaration of war] industrial concerns were seized to avert interruption of needed production. [After war was declared,] the President directed seizure of the Nation's coal mines to remove an obstruction to the effective prosecution of the war.

This is but a cursory summary of executive leadership. But it amply demonstrates that Presidents have taken prompt action to enforce the laws and protect the country whether or not Congress happened to provide in advance for the particular method of execution. * * * [T]he fact that Congress and the courts have consistently recognized and given their support to such executive action indicates that such a power of seizure has been accepted throughout our history.

NOTE ON FRAMEWORKS FOR THINKING ABOUT SEPARATION OF POWERS ISSUES

1. *Theoretical Approaches to Separation of Powers.* At least three different conceptual approaches can be gleaned from the opinions in the Steel Seizure Case. Drawing from the constitutional text, original understanding, historical practice, and political theory, consider the normative validity of each as a general theory of separation of powers.

(A) *Formalist categories (Black).* Justice Black's opinion for the Court, joined by four other Justices (Douglas, Jackson, Frankfurter, and Burton), sets forth a straightforward categorical approach. Its *ratio decidendi* seems to be that because the President's action falls under the legislative power defined in Article I and under none of the executive powers defined in Article II, the President was acting *ultra vires* (beyond his authority). This approach has the advantages of simplicity, compliance with a logical structure grounded in the constitutional text, and a clear message for future Presidents. It has the further advantage of taking the text of the Constitution seriously, consistent with the *textualist* and *holistic* theories of judicial review examined in Chapter 2, § 3A1. It has the disadvantages of seeming to render much of the President's historical activities unconstitutional and of tying the President's hands in times of emergency. Is this approach realistic? Is it defensible in light of the original expectations of the Framers, reflected in the Philadelphia Convention debates and *The Federalist Papers*? Early practice?[e]

(B) *Constrained functionalism (Jackson, Frankfurter).* A second approach is a process-based functional approach which seeks to draw constitutional lines flexibly so as to allow the President to take action in emergencies, but not so

---

e. Casper, *supra*, supports a functionalist approach. For a response to Casper and a defense of a categorical approach based on state practice in the 1770s, see Russell Osgood, *Early Versions and Practices of Separation of Powers: A Comment*, 30 Wm. & Mary L. Rev. 279 (1989).

flexibly as to ignore congressionally directed procedures for action. This approach is articulated in the concurring opinions of Justices Frankfurter and Jackson, as well as the opinion of Justice Clark (omitted in our excerpt). These Justices were leading *legal process* theorists of constitutional law, anticipating the work of Hart, Sacks, Bickel, and Ely (Chapter 2, § 3B). The advantage of this approach is that it allows constitutional authority to evolve as times change, while preserving the original objectives of checks and balances. A disadvantage is that its line-drawing might seem like judicial policymaking unsupported by the Constitution. How would Justice Jackson, for example, defend his scheme as a matter of constitutional policy?

(C) *Evolutive functionalism — constitutional adverse possession (Vinson).* A third approach is a lenient functional approach, which essentially defers to the political branch taking the challenged action, so long as it has some historical precedent. Note the possible conceptual basis for this approach in *pragmatic* or *common law* theories of judicial review (Chapter 2, § 3). Chief Justice Vinson and Justices Reed and Minton, the three dissenters, endorsed this approach. The dissenters thought that a long-established practice of executive power and congressional acquiescence provided concrete meaning to the vague constitutional clauses in question. This is a form of constitutional "adverse possession": If the President openly exercises power, with the knowledge and presumably the acquiescence of Congress, then after a certain period of time, the Constitution comes to consider this power as truly the President's. Can this be defended, in light of the background and history of separation of powers? Note that similar arguments prevailed in *McCulloch v. Maryland* (Chapter 7, § 1), but were rejected in *Brown v. Board of Education* (Chapter 2, § 1).

2. The Jackson Concurrence as the Now-Dominant Approach. Justice Jackson's concurring opinion has been the most influential of those penned in the Steel Seizure Case.[f] Jackson was one of the Justices President Truman might have expected to vote his way in the Steel Seizure Case. On June 9, 1941, President Roosevelt had ordered the U.S. Army to seize and occupy a bomber/airplane factory belonging to the North American Aviation Company, based upon threats of a wildcat, strike to close down the plant. The seizure was unprecedented in peacetime. Just days before his nomination to the Court, then-Attorney General Robert Jackson defended the seizure (89 Cong. Rec. 3992):

> [T]he Presidential proclamation [of seizure] rests upon the aggregate of the Presidential powers derived from the Constitution itself and from statutes enacted by the Congress.

> The Constitution lays upon the President the duty "to take care that the laws be faithfully executed." Among the laws which he is required to find means to execute are those which direct him to equip an enlarged army, [and] to provide for a strengthened navy [in preparation for anticipated U.S. entry into World War II]. * * *

---

f. E.g., *Medellín v. Texas,* 128 S.Ct. 1346 (2008) (excerpted *supra*); Erwin Chemerinsky, *Controlling Inherent Presidential Power: Providing a Framework for Judicial Review,* 56 S. Cal. L. Rev. 863 (1983); William Van Alstyne, *The Role of Congress in Determining Incidental Powers of the President and of the Federal Courts,* 40 Law & Contemp. Probs. 102 (Spring 1976).

The Government cited Jackson's defense of the 1941 seizure to defend the 1952 seizure of the steel mills. In his concurring opinion, Justice Jackson dismissed the Government's reliance upon earlier "partisan" statements.

Justice Jackson was probably inspired to resist the 1952 seizure because of his own experience as the Chief Prosecutor at the Nuremberg Trials of Nazi war criminals.[g] What he saw in his post-mortem of Nazi Germany was the ability of determined totalitarian groups to erode liberty by chipping away at the structural protections of citizens — namely, federalism, separation of powers, and the sanctity of private property. As Jackson put it in his oral biography:[h]

> In my view the freedom of the individual to engage in a business economically is a parallel to his freedom of speech and his freedom of action generally. I believe these are protected by a diffusion of power. If you concentrate the power over his living and ways of existence, I don't know whether it is possible to maintain other liberties.

An early draft of his Steel Seizure concurrence echoed a similar theme:[i]

> [I]f we are to preserve the art of government under a written Constitution that diffuses power to reduce the probability that liberty will ever be endangered by more than a fraction of the Government's total force at any one time, we must take a different approach to the questioned acts of the Executive, depending upon their classification.

This is a classic articulation of a functional approach to separation of powers, but it contains the seeds of something more.

Because it asks how shifting power from Congress to the President poses minoritarian risks to personal (and corporate) liberties, the draft as well as published opinion might be read as the germ of what Victoria Nourse calls the vertical approach. She would add that the President's decision also posed majoritarian risks, as it dislocated the national economy without sanction from the pluralistic process of congressional legislation (Jackson's category 3). Jackson's category 1, of course, is least problematic, because the constituencies of both President and Congress are mobilized, and the resulting policy most legitimate. For Nourse, as for Jackson, the hardest cases will often be those of category 2, where Congress has not asserted its authority. The President's assertion of authority may pose majoritarian or minoritarian risks, but their significance will depend on circumstances.

Unlike the Truman Administration in Steel Seizure, most administrations in subsequent cases have *not* conceded that their actions fell within category 3 and have, instead, affirmatively argued that their actions fell within statutory authorizations. (This is a constant theme in the recent War on Terror controversies.) Thus, many Steel Seizure cases end up being matters of statutory interpretation, where judges as well as politicians need to figure out

---

g. See Edward Reisman, "Justice Robert Jackson's Road to *Youngstown Sheet & Tube Co. v. Sawyer*: The Impact of Nuremberg" (Georgetown Univ. Law Center, Feb. 20, 1990).

h. "Justice Jackson's Story," Jackson Papers, Library of Congress (Madison Building), Container 190, folder 4, pp. 575-76, quoted in Reisman, *supra*, at 16.

i. Jackson Papers, Container 176 (draft 8 May 1952), quoted in Reisman, *supra*, at 16.

exactly what Congress has authorized, in order to decide which category the presidential action falls under. This is key. If authorized by statute (category 1), the presidential action is almost always going to prevail. If contrary to statutory authorization (category 3), the presidential action is almost always going to fail.

3. *Consequences of the Court's Decision.* When the Supreme Court granted quick certiorari in the Steel Seizure Case, the industry and union negotiators had just reached tentative agreement as to a settlement at the White House. Upon learning that the Court had granted review and stayed the effect of a takeover, the steel industry backed away from the agreement, according to legal historian Maeva Marcus.[j] After the Court handed the industry its victory on June 2, the union struck for 53 days; with further pressure from the President, the union and industry finally agreed upon a wage increase similar to that fixed by the Wage Stabilization Board months earlier. The strike was the longest and most costly ($400 million in lost wages, 21 million tons in lost steel output) in the country's history. Most current constitutional commentators follow Marcus in believing that the strike did not harm the war effort, but the Truman Administration believed otherwise. The President was wholly unswayed by the Court's justifications, and a leading historian of his administration concludes that the strike did impair the war effort.[k]

PROBLEM 8-1
DOES THE PRESIDENT HAVE THE AUTHORITY TO
"IMPOUND" FUNDS APPROPRIATED BY CONGRESS?

Deploying arguments made by his predecessors, President Richard Nixon asserted a presidential power not to spend all the money Congress allocated, as part of the President's Article II, § 3 "take Care" authority, to fight inflation in the 1970s.[l] The obvious problem was that the President failed to execute a fairly clear congressional directive, and thereby usurped the legislative power. See *Kendall v. United States*, 12 Pet. 524 (1838) (mandamus lay to compel the Postmaster General to pay to a contractor an award owing him under congressionally mandated procedures). Consider the following arguments the President might have to overcome this proposition:

1. *Emergency Powers.* President Nixon argued that impoundment was necessary to respond to an emergency in the 1970s, namely, inflation. Is the Steel Seizure Case fatal to the President's argument, for the Court required President Truman to follow congressional directives even during the Korean

---

j. Marcus, *Truman and the Steel Seizure Case,* 147-48.

k. 2 Harry Truman, *Memoirs* 478 (1956); David McCullough, *Truman* 901-02 (1992).

l. See generally Ralph Abascal & John Kramer, *Presidential Impoundment (Part I): Historical Genesis and Constitutional Framework,* 62 Geo. L.J. 1549 (1974); Abner Mikva & Michael Hertz, *Impoundment of Funds — the Courts, the Congress and the President: A Constitutional Triangle,* 69 Nw. U.L. Rev. 335 (1974). For an argument that the President enjoys an implicit Article II "completion power," see Jack Goldsmith & John Manning, *The President's Completion Power,* 115 Yale L.J. 2280 (2006).

War, which was a period of formally declared national emergency? Also, can it be said that inflation was an emergency similar to the Korean War?

2. *Enforcement Discretion.* It is a common practice for the President not to enforce all the laws that Congress enacts,[m] and this might rise to an historical practice entitled to the constitutional adverse possession rule pressed by Justice Frankfurter's concurrence in the Steel Seizure Case. Hence, the executive has virtually unlimited "prosecutorial discretion" in deciding how to enforce both criminal and civil statutory schemes. See *Heckler v. Chaney*, 470 U.S. 821 (1985). Moreover, the executive has substantial discretion in deciding exactly how to spend money Congress has allocated for certain programs. For example, if Congress allocates $100 million to build a dam on the New River in West Virginia, and the President can get the job done for $90 million, doesn't the Take Care Clause enable the President to save the country some money? If the President can do that in the New River case, why can't the President fight inflation by trimming several programs that Congress has "overfunded" (in the macroeconomic sense that spending all the money will fuel inflation)?

3. *Political Question.* The President also might argue that the correctness of these arguments cannot be tested in the courts, because the controversy must be left to the political process. Indeed, there was something of a political resolution in the Congressional Budget and Impoundment Control Act of 1974, 31 U.S.C. §§ 1400-1407, passed by Congress and signed by President Nixon. Under the statute, the President can "defer" an authorized expenditure for a year if the President notifies Congress. The deferral will take effect unless either House of Congress votes to disapprove it. The President can also "rescind" all or part of a budget authorization as unnecessary to effect congressional goals, again after notifying Congress, which has 45 days to veto it (this time by vote of both Houses). What constitutional problems might there be with this statute? What remedy if the President fails to notify Congress of a deferral or rescission?

B. FOREIGN RELATIONS AND WAR

Although the President's directive was aimed at domestic production, the Steel Seizure Case arose in the context of a foreign war. Among the most far-reaching assertions of presidential power are in the context of foreign relations, including presidential commitment of United States military forces abroad and entry into executive agreements with foreign countries. Even as its Justices were at loggerheads with President Franklin Roosevelt over the New Deal's domestic program (Chapter 1, § 6; Chapter 7, § 2), the Supreme Court endorsed a broad scope for presidential action in the foreign arena.

---

m. But consider the advice that then-Assistant Attorney General William Rehnquist wrote in an internal memorandum: "It may be argued that the spending of money is inherently an executive function, but the execution of any law is, by definition, an executive function and it seems an anomalous proposition that because the Executive Branch is bound to execute the laws, it is free to decline to execute them." Quoted in Arthur Miller, *The President and Faithful Execution of the Laws*, 40 Vand. L. Rev. 389, 397 (1987).

Several leading opinions were authored by Justice George Sutherland, who as a senator had set forth a constitutional theory sharply distinguishing between *internal* affairs, where the Constitution's allocation of authority between the states and the national government had to be rigidly enforced, and *external* affairs, where the national government exercised plenary authority (Chapter 7, § 4C). As to the latter, Sutherland suggested a "radically more liberal" rule of construction: The federal government, and its officers, were free to exercise any external powers normally exercised by sovereign states under international law, excepting only those explicitly forbidden by the Constitution, strongly contrary to fundamental constitutional principles, or not "essential" to governance. Sutherland, *Constitutional Power and World Affairs* 47 (1919).

———

United States v. Curtiss-Wright Export Corp., 299 U.S. 304 (1936). The Court upheld the President's action against Curtiss-Wright for selling guns to Bolivia. This case was different from the Steel Seizure Case, as Congress had by joint resolution authorized the President to place an embargo on arms sales to Bolivia and Paraguay, but **Justice Sutherland**'s opinion for the Court went beyond the facts. He stated not only that national power over external affairs is inherent and plenary, but also that the President plays a uniquely important role in foreign affairs. "In this vast external realm, with its important, complicated, delicate and manifold problems, the President alone has the power to speak or listen as a representative of the nation. He *makes* treaties with the advice and consent of the Senate; but he alone negotiates. * * *

"* * * It is quite apparent that if, in the maintenance of our international relations, embarrassment — perhaps serious embarrassment — is to be avoided and success for our aims achieved, congressional legislation which is to be made effective through negotiation and inquiry within the international field must often accord to the President a degree of discretion and freedom from statutory restriction which would not be admissible were domestic affairs alone involved." Buttressing this practical basis for presidential discretion was the "overwhelming support" for such broad delegation "which has prevailed almost from the inception of the national government to the present day. * * * Practically every volume of the United States Statutes contains one or more acts or joint resolutions of Congress authorizing action by the President in respect of subjects affecting foreign relations, which either leave the exercise of the power to his unrestricted judgment, or provide a standard far more general than that which has always been considered a requisite with regard to domestic affairs."

Commentators have been impressed by the breadth of Sutherland's reasoning and by his begging the central question in the case: Even if the national government has plenary authority to act in foreign affairs, hasn't the Constitution vested primary national authority in Congress, and not the President? Especially when the President's actions violate a company's liberty of contract, shouldn't it be the deliberative Congress, which is closer to the people, that should make the call?[a] Is the Court's subsequent disposition in the Steel Seizure Case inconsistent with *Curtiss-Wright*? If so, should *Curtiss-Wright* be narrowed — or is there a stronger constitutional basis for the sweeping dicta in this precedent? Consider the following Note.

NOTE ON THE VESTING CLAUSE THESIS FOR PRESIDENTIAL PRIMACY IN FOREIGN AFFAIRS

Reviving arguments first made by Thomas Jefferson, Saikrishna Prakash and Michael Ramsey, *The Executive Power over Foreign Affairs*, 111 Yale L.J. 231 (2001), argue that Article II's Vesting Clause delegates to the President primary authority to manage the nation's foreign relations. The authors make three kinds of arguments for this proposition, to which Curtis Bradley & Martin Flaherty, *Executive Power Essentialism and Foreign Affairs*, 102 Mich. L. Rev. 545 (2004), provide a detailed historiographical response. Prakash and Ramsey respond and defend their thesis in *Foreign Affairs and the Jeffersonian Executive: A Defense*, 89 Minn. L. Rev. 1591 (2005).

1. *Text: "Executive" authority means management of foreign relations, and all of that authority is vested in the President.* Contrast Article I, which vests Congress only with the "legislative Powers herein granted," with Article II, which vests the President with the "executive Power," simpliciter. Following Steven Calabresi, Prakash and Ramsey draw from this contrast the notion that the President has *all* powers that the framing era would have considered "executive," and not just the powers identified in Article II (such as receiving ambassadors). The leading political philosophers who influenced the Framers considered foreign affairs to be "essentially" executive tasks. For example, Montesquieu identified two kinds of executive power, the enforcement of laws and initiation of activities in the foreign affairs arena. Blackstone, the colonists' main source of knowledge about British law and constitutionalism, closely followed Montesquieu in considering the monarch's foreign affairs prerogatives to be "executive" in nature. Under Montesquieu's understanding, Article II's vesting all "executive power" with the President carried with it all foreign affairs power, as the typical American would have understood the matter in 1789.

Bradley and Flaherty respond, first, that the Foreign Affairs Vesting Thesis creates a mystery in the structure of Article II: If the Vesting Clause gives the President plenary authority in foreign affairs, why does Article II specifically vest the President with authority to receive ambassadors and to command American military forces in foreign campaigns? A second problem with the Prakash and Ramsey argument is that the Montesquieu-Blackstone model for executive control dominance in matters of foreign affairs was the monarchy —

---

a. See generally G. Edward White, *The Constitution and the New Deal* 69-77 (2000); Raoul Berger, *The Presidential Monopoly of Foreign Relations*, 71 Mich. L. Rev. 1, 45-48 (1972); David Levitan, *The Foreign Relations Power: An Analysis of Mr. Justice Sutherland's Theory*, 55 Yale L.J. 467 (1946). The contemporary response to Sutherland's opinion, however, was strongly supportive. E.g., James Garner, *Executive Discretion in the Conduct of Foreign Relations*, 31 Am. J. Int'l L. 289 (1937).

precisely what the Framers were *rejecting* as a model for their Article II President. More generally, historians of the founding era emphasize *discontinuities* between American and English practice (King George III aside) and offer strong doubt that there was a consensus, even in the United States, as to what duties were essentially executive and what were essentially legislative.

Finally, Bradley and Flaherty argue that state constitutions in effect in 1789 are strong evidence against the Foreign Affairs Vesting Thesis. No state constitution gave the governor *all* powers that could be understood as "executive," and *all* the constitutions followed the American approach of enumerating gubernatorial powers in the same way the U.S. Constitution would do in Articles I-III. Prakash and Ramsey respond with this mystery: states enjoyed foreign affairs power before 1789; who exercised that authority? Except for South Carolina, which vested treatymaking in both the governor and the legislature, the state constitutions do not tell us which organ exercised foreign affairs authority.

2. *Drafting and Ratifying the Constitution.* At the Convention, the Virginia Plan was the first comprehensive proposal for a constitution. Its Seventh Resolution, as presented by sponsor Edmund Randolph, called for the establishment of a national executive; "besides a general authority to execute the National laws, [this executive] ought to enjoy the Executive rights vested in Congress by the Confederation." Because the Confederation Congress (like the Continental Congress) exercised plenary authority over foreign affairs, Prakash and Ramsey argue that this broad understanding of "executive" power (consistent with their reading of Montesquieu-Blackstone) formed the unspoken baseline for subsequent deliberations.

Bradley and Flaherty counter that the Virginia Plan and this undefined resolution were not adopted by the Convention and that most speakers followed the state constitutional practice of focusing on specific grants of authority to the chief executive. In opposing a too-powerful executive, James Wilson said he "did not consider the Prerogatives of the British Monarch as a proper guide in defining the Executive powers. Some of these prerogatives were of a legislative nature. Among others that of war & peace &c. The only powers he conceived strictly Executive were those of executing the laws, and appointing officers." Madison agreed with Wilson that executive powers "do not include the Rights of war & peace &c" and that "the powers should be confined and defined" lest the country be afflicted with the "Evils of elective Monarchies." He moved that the executive be vested with three powers: "to carry into execution the national laws"; "to appoint to offices in cases not otherwise provided for"; and "to execute such powers, not legislative or judiciary in their nature, as may from time to time be delegated by the national legislature." The Committee of the Whole agreed to the motion, deleting the third power as included in the first. Bradley and Flaherty argue that Article II reflects this decision, with the addition of further specified powers. Prakash and Ramsey note that the Convention nonetheless vested the President with "executive Power," essentially the same term used in the Virginia Plan.

Bradley and Flaherty trade quotations from *The Federalist Papers* with Prakash and Ramsey, and we refer the student to those lengthy articles for the exact quotations and their warring constructions. It may be notable that only Bradley and Flaherty devote extensive attention to the debates within the state conventions, whose ratification in the name of We the People is the foundation of the Constitution's legitimacy. In Virginia, for example, the defenders of the Constitution said that the President's powers were very limited, the most important of which were to "see the laws executed" and to command the armed forces, while Congress would have the primary responsibility for national defense and foreign affairs. Prakash and Ramsey counter that no one at the Virginia or other state ratifying conventions denied that the Vesting Clause gave the President substantive powers, including residual authority (i.e., authority not delegated to Congress or the Senate) over foreign affairs.

3. *Early Practice: The Washington Administration.* Prakash and Ramsey's strongest evidence came from officials in the Washington Administration, which took many foreign affairs initiatives that were not clearly sanctioned by the enumerated powers in Article II. In 1790, Secretary of State Thomas Jefferson opined that the President (not Congress) could set diplomatic grades and destinations. His justification: "The Constitution . . . has declared that 'the Executive powers shall be vested in the President'. . . . The transaction of business with foreign nations is Executive altogether. It belongs then to the head of that department [Jefferson!], except as to such portion of it as are specially submitted to the Senate. Exceptions are to be construed strictly." In his diary, President Washington said that Representative Madison and Foreign Secretary John Jay concurred with Jefferson. Bradley and Flaherty say that Jefferson was right because of the Presidential Appointments Clause, Article II, § 2 (Jefferson himself disclaimed reliance on that clause, however).

In 1793, President Washington announced a Proclamation of Neutrality in the war then ensuing among Great Britain, France, and other European powers. The Proclamation forbade interference by American ships and citizens in these wars and of course came under attack by partisans of France, namely Jefferson and Madison (by then emerging as an oppositional force within the government). Defending the President, Secretary of Treasury Alexander Hamilton published a series of Letters from Pacificus, the first of which addressed the constitutionality of Washington's Proclamation.[b] Within the national government the executive branch is the "organ of intercourse between the [United States] and foreign Nations." As support for this proposition, Hamilton cited both the Vesting Clause and the Treaty Clause of Article II. Hamilton contrasted Article I's Vesting Clause with that of Article II, with the conclusion that Article II's clause had to be read broadly, and the Treaty Clause was merely an example of the larger power but did not exhaust it. Following Montesquieu, Hamilton read "executive" power to include all national foreign affairs powers.

As Bradley and Flaherty point out, Hamilton then argued from the Take Care Clause. Congress had the authority to declare war against England or France, but in the absence of such declaration, "the duty of the Executive is to preserve

---

b. Hamilton, Letters of Pacificus No. 1 (June 29, 1793), reprinted in 15 *The Papers of Alexander Hamilton* 33-42 (Harold Syrett & Jacob Cooke eds. 1969).

Peace till war is declared. * * * The President is charged with the execution of all laws, the laws of Nations as well as the Municipal law * * *. It is consequently bound, by faithfully executing the laws of neutrality, when that is the state of the Nation, to avoid giving a cause of war to foreign Powers." (Bradley himself does not agree with Hamilton's assumption that the Take Care Clause includes "the law of nations" with statutes and the Constitution as measures the President must enforce.)

Madison responded to Pacificus in a series of essays published under the name Helvidius. He argued, first, that the powers of declaring war and making peace were inherently "legislative" in nature and thus "can never fall within a proper definition of executive powers." Madison also argued that the Constitution does not allow concurrent exercise of powers that are purely "legislative" or "executive," and so the President was unconstitutionally invading Congress's power when he issued the Proclamation. (Bradley and Flaherty concede the "weakness" of Madison's argument but maintain that the main weakness, essentialist thinking about what is "executive," is a key weakness of the Foreign Affairs Vesting Thesis itself.)

Based on the foregoing evidence, do you consider the Foreign Affairs Vesting Thesis cogent? Or not? In part? Consider how this thesis or some variation plays out in the following areas of constitutional inquiry.

1. *Presidential Authority to Enter Binding Executive Agreements*

The President has Article II, § 2, cl. 2 power, "by and with the Advice and Consent of the Senate, to make Treaties." If two-thirds of the Senate concur, such a treaty becomes the "Law of the Land" under the Supremacy Clause of Article VI. Presidential practice, ratified by the Supreme Court, has both expanded and contracted this constitutional regime. On the one hand, executive agreements (entered without Senate ratification) may sometimes be the "Law of the Land." On the other than, most ratified treaties are *not* the "Law of the Land" without congressional enactment under Article I, § 7 (in addition to Senate ratification under Article II, § 2, cl. 2). This latter point will be developed in Part A.3, but for now consider the first point.

United States v. Belmont, 301 U.S. 324 (1937). The Court upheld and applied the "Litvinov Agreement" negotiated by President Franklin Roosevelt with the Soviet Union. That agreement assigned to the United States Russian claims against Americans who held funds of Russian companies seized after the Russian Revolution, and the Court held not only that it was enforceable but that it also preempted contrary state law. Responding to the argument that only *treaties* agreed to by the Senate pursuant to Article II are the law of the land preempting state law, **Justice Sutherland**'s opinion for the Court ruled that "an international compact, as this was, is not always a treaty which requires the participation of the Senate." But, like treaties, executive agreements trumped state law. "[W]hile this rule in respect of treaties is established by the express language of cl. 2, Art. VI of the Constitution, the same rule would result in the case of all international compacts and agreements, from the very fact that complete power over international affairs is in the national government and is not and cannot be subject to any curtailment or interference on the part of the several states. Compare *Curtiss-Wright*. * * * In respect of all international negotiations and compacts, and in respect of our foreign relations generally, state lines disappear."

Postscript. Unlike *Curtiss-Wright*, Justice Sutherland's broad reasoning in *Belmont* called forth much contemporary as well as modern criticism.[c] Even more than *Curtiss-Wright*, *Belmont* permitted matters of private property to be determined by the President and not by Congress. This was not only fishy in light of the Constitution's structure but was contrary to founding era precedent. See *Brown v. United States*, 12 U.S. 110 (1814), where the Marshall Court overruled the President's effort to condemn property owned in this country by citizens of Great Britain during the War of 1812; although the United States could seize such property consistent with international law, Chief Justice Marshall insisted that this authority rested with Congress, not the President.

On the other hand, the Foreign Affairs Vesting Thesis might justify the holding of *Belmont*, even though Justice Sutherland did not make that particular argument. The Court during World War II reaffirmed and expanded upon Sutherland's views in *United States v. Pink*, 315 U.S. 203 (1942). Is there any limit to the President's authority under this thesis? Note that the Supreme Court in the Steel Seizure Case did consider the Foreign Affairs Vesting Thesis and implicitly rejected it.

———

Dames & Moore v. Regan, 453 U.S. 654 (1981). On November 4, 1979, Iranian students seized 53 Americans as hostages after taking over the U.S. embassy in Tehran, Iran. In response, President Carter blocked the removal of all Iranian property and assets in the United States, pursuant to congressional authorization in the International Emergency Economic Powers Act (IEEPA). Both before and after the President's blocking of assets, private parties (including petitioner Dames & Moore) had filed lawsuits against Iran and Iranian entities in U.S. courts. On January 20, 1981, the United States and Iran entered into an international agreement, under which the hostages would be released; the U.S. would unblock Iranian assets by July 19, 1981 and allow most of them to return to Iran; and litigation against Iran in U.S. courts would be "terminated," and all cases referred to an Iran-United States Claims Tribunal, which would arbitrate any claims against Iran that were not settled within six months. Presidents Carter and Reagan issued a series of Executive Orders implementing the international agreement, including an order "suspending" the American lawsuits against Iran. But neither President submitted the agreement to the Senate for ratification as a "treaty," nor did they seek implementing legislation from Congress. Dames & Moore had a money judgment against Iran but was unable to enforce it because of the regulations; the district court

---

c. See Edwin Borchard, *Confiscations, Extraterritorial and Domestic*, 31 Am. J. Int'l L. 675 (1937); Stefan Riesenfeld, *The Power of Congress and the President in International Relations: Three Recent Supreme Court Decisions*, 25 Cal. L. Rev. 643 (1937). See generally White, *Constitution and the New Deal* 77-85.

suspended the lawsuit and referred Dames & Moore to the Iran-U.S. Tribunal. The Supreme Court granted expedited review of the order and affirmed.

Justice Rehnquist's opinion for the Court followed the framework suggested by Justice Jackson's opinion in the Steel Seizure Case. Under the Jackson framework, the President's nullification of attachments and direction that persons holding blocked Iranian assets transfer them to the United States were defensible under Category 1, because these actions were authorized by Congress: IEEPA § 203 on its face authorized the President pervasively to regulate foreign-owned property subject to the jurisdiction of the United States. Because IEEPA did not authorize suspension of the claims in United States courts, that action was more questionable. Still, under Category 2 of the Jackson framework, the President might have power to act, "where there is no contrary indication of legislative intent and when, as here, there is a history of congressional acquiescence in conduct of the sort engaged in by the President."

Justice Rehnquist pointed to a longstanding practice whereby the executive branch would "espouse" claims of U.S. nationals harmed by foreign state action and thereby negotiate agreements settling the claims of U.S. nationals. Under such agreements, the foreign state would provide a lump sum compensation package, in return for extinguishment of U.S. claims against the state. Typically these arrangements have been executive agreements and not treaties, and oftentimes the U.S. nationals have felt their interests slighted by a negotiation process emphasizing larger goals of national security and foreign policy.[d] Starting with the "Wilmington Packet" in 1799, no fewer than 80 executive agreements were entered into by the President to settle foreign claims. The International Claims Settlement Act of 1949 created a procedure whereby funds resulting from future settlements could be distributed. "By creating a procedure to implement future settlement agreements, Congress placed its stamp of approval on such agreements." Justice Rehnquist also relied on the legislative background of IEEPA, which suggested that "'[n]othing in this act is intended . . . to interfere with the authority of the President to [block assets], or to impede the settlement of claims of U.S. citizens against foreign countries.'"

Justice Powell dissented in part, because he thought there might be a taking of property under the Fifth Amendment (Chapter 5, § 2C).

NOTE ON EXECUTIVE AGREEMENTS AS "LAW OF THE LAND"

Justice Rehnquist's congressional acquiescence argument has some holes. None of the earlier claims settlements was quite like the one in the Iranian Hostages Case, where the President suspended ongoing litigation filed in U.S.

---

d. See generally *Restatement (Second) of Foreign Relations Law of the United States* § 213 (1965) (President "may waive or settle a claim against a foreign state . . . [even] without the consent of the [injured] national"); Louis Henkin, *Foreign Affairs and the Constitution* (1972).

courts.[e] After the earlier claims settlements, Congress asserted its authority in a statute setting forth the procedures to be followed when foreign states are sued, namely, the Foreign Sovereign Immunities Act (FSIA). Before 1976, when foreign states were sued in U.S. courts, the Department of State usually filed a statement seeking dismissal on immunity grounds, to which courts deferred. Setting forth legal criteria for federal jurisdiction and immunity, the FSIA was intended to take the Executive out of the business of interfering in such lawsuits. Congress rejected a proposal to make FSIA procedures "subject to * * * future international agreements" in order to "eliminate any possible question" that the FSIA permitted the President to interfere with the new rules.[f] Under this analysis, the President's suspension of lawsuits falls under Jackson's Category 3, where his authority it at its "lowest ebb."

The Court's decision is more defensible under *Curtiss-Wright* and *Belmont* than under the Steel Seizure Case. But those cases were different in material ways. In *Curtiss-Wright* the President was acting in concert with Congress (Jackson's Category 1), and in *Belmont* the President was acting independently to trump state law (Category 2). But as to the suspension of lawsuits issue in *Dames & Moore*, the President was acting on his own and was nullifying a congressional enactment, rather than just state law (Category 3). So *Dames & Moore* reaches well beyond any of the earlier precedents — and (like *Belmont*) is probably best-justified as an example of the Foreign Affairs Vesting Thesis. See Michael Ramsey, *Executive Agreements and the (Non)Treaty Power*, 77 N.C.L. Rev. 133, 207-16 (1998). Does that thesis justify overriding a federal statute (FSIA)? If the President wanted to nullify the FSIA, why shouldn't he have to seek legislation from Congress or a treaty from the Senate?[g] In the interim, the President could have sought stays from judges handling claims against Iran; most such cases were already on hold at the request of the Departments of Justice and State.

Justice Powell raised a "vertical" concern: By shifting power to settle foreign claims from Congress and the courts, *Dames & Moore* shifted governmental incentives away from majoritarian deliberation (Congress) and protection of individual rights (courts) toward decisive action during foreign

---

e. In the earlier settlements, the President had frozen foreign assets in this country and used them as a bargaining chip to obtain compensation for U.S. companies whose property in the foreign state had been nationalized; the companies in the earlier instances had not sued foreign states in U.S. courts, because foreign states enjoyed sovereign immunity from lawsuits arising out of their nationalization of assets within their borders. See Lee Marks & John Grabow, *The President's Foreign Economic Powers After* Dames & Moore v. Regan: *Legislation by Acquiescence*, 68 Cornell L. Rev. 68, 87-91 (1982).

f. Right after the FSIA was adopted, Beverly Carl, *Suing Foreign Governments in American Courts: The United States Foreign Sovereign Immunities Act in Practice*, 33 Sw. L.J. 1009, 1063 (1979), wrote: "Assume American hostages are being held by a foreign government. While negotiating for their release, the United States government wishes to offer as a quid pro quo the termination of pending litigation against that nation within this country. Under the FSIA, the executive would have no such authority * * *."

g. There was bipartisan support for the executive agreement, which was negotiated by Democrat Jimmy Carter and implemented by Republican Ronald Reagan.

crises (President). This shift threatens liberties as well as property rights. Is there any limit to the President's new power? For example, could the President have traded the Vice-President and his family for the 52 remaining hostages?

2. President's Commander-in-Chief Authority

Article II, § 2, cl. 1 says: "The President shall be Commander in Chief of the Army and Navy of the United States," etc. If Congress declares war, the President is in charge of the military operations, which Congress funds. This sounds simple enough, but there are dozens of issues that have arisen, many of which remain unresolved to this day. Consider whether the history recounted below sheds any light on the debate over the Foreign Affairs Vesting Thesis; even if not established as a matter of original meaning, the thesis might gain constitutional traction through congressional acquiescence (Steel Seizure; *Dames & Moore*).

The biggest issue is whether there is a core "commander-in-chief power" of the President that Congress cannot regulate. This issue was probably not one the Framers thought much about; some of the Framers would have found the notion of a standing army and navy alarming. Thus, when Congress wanted the country to prepare for possible war against France in 1898, it authorized President Adams to raise an army up to 10,000 men to serve for as many as three years. In other statutes, Congress authorized the President to seize French vessels and vessels heading to French ports under specified circumstances, thereby initiating a Quasi-War with France. Pursuant to an order from the Secretary of the Navy, Captain George Little seized a ship sailing *from* a French port. In *Little v. Barreme,* 6 U.S. 170 (1804), the Marshall Court ruled that the seizure was illegal because it did not fall within the terms of the statutory authorizations for the Quasi-War. Under *Little,* the President's commander-in-chief authority is subject to congressional direction.[h]

Early constitutional commentators considered the President's direction of wartime military activities to be either exclusive or nearly so; the country needed military campaigns to be run with a "single hand." 3 Joseph Story, *Commentaries on the Constitution of the United States* §§ 1163-1210, 1484-1486 (1833). But even Presidents themselves did not claim a commander-in-chief power that superseded congressional enactments. As Attorney General Jeremiah Black told President Buchanan, "the land and naval forces are under his orders as commander in chief. But his power is to be used only in the manner prescribed by the legislative department." *Power of the President in Executing the Laws,* 9 Op. Att'y Gen. 516, 518-19 (1860).

After South Carolina seceded in 1861, when Congress was not in session, President Lincoln took bold unilateral action, ordering a naval blockade of the South, calling up the militia, expanding the regular army, and essentially taking the nation to war. The President admitted that some of these actions "were

---

h. E.g., David Barron & Martin Lederman, *The Commander in Chief at the Lowest Ebb — A Constitutional History,* 121 Harv. L. Rev. 941, 944-50, 964-70 (2008); H. Jefferson Powell, *The Founders and the President's Authority over Foreign Affairs,* 40 Wm. & Mary L. Rev. 1471, 1511-28 (1999).

without the authority of law," but justified them as needed to ensure that the "Government was saved [from] overthrow." Cong. Glove, 37th Cong., 2d Sess. 2383 (1862) (message from President Lincoln). Within a month of Lincoln's justifications, Congress ratified Lincoln's actions by statute, except for his suspension of habeas corpus.[i]

Although Lincoln did not assert a preclusive power of the President to act contrary to congressional directives, some of his allies did. Concurring in *Ex parte Milligan*, 71 U.S. 2 (1866), Chief Justice Salmon Chase (Lincoln's Treasury Secretary and his replacement for Chief Justice Taney) rendered a broad construction of Congress's war powers — "except such as interferes with the command of the forces and the conduct of campaigns. That power and duty belong to the President as commander-in-chief." *Id.* at 141. Following this dictum (in a concurring opinion) was a broad statement of presidential power in John Norton Pomeroy, *An Introduction to the Constitutional Law of the United States* §§ 703-706 (1868), which opined that in his role as commander in chief the President cannot be bound by congressional statutes. Thus, "all direct management of warlike operations, all planning and organizing of campaigns, all establishment of blockages, all direction of marches, sieges, battles, and the like, are as much beyond the jurisdiction of the legislature, as they are beyond that of any assemblage of private citizens." *Id.*, § 455. Congress could make general rules, such as setting the size of the army or navy, but could not tell the President exactly how to deploy those troop levels.

The Chase-Pomeroy viewpoint was expressed more broadly in the twentieth century. Presidents such as Theodore Roosevelt, William Howard Taft, and Woodrow Wilson did not challenge the conventional wisdom that Congress could set limits on presidential military decisions.[j] After his presidency, and during his time as a professor at the Yale Law School, however, however, Taft opined that Congress could *not* prevent the President from deploying the armed forces to respond to an invasion, from deciding how to deploy the armed forces in time of war, or "order battles to be fought on a certain plan." William Howard Taft, *The Boundaries Between the Executive, the Legislative, and the Judicial Branches of the Government*, 25 Yale L.J. 599, 610 (1916).

World War II called forth some wildly dynamic statutory interpretations by the Franklin Roosevelt Administration. During the litigation surrounding the use of military tribunals to try war criminals in 1942, Attorney General Francis Biddle argued to a stunned Supreme Court that during time of war the President had extra-statutory authority to try war criminals: "the Commander-in-Chief, in

---

i. For detailed examination of Lincoln's actions, his justifications, and after-the-fact congressional ratifications, see Daniel Farber, *Lincoln's Constitution* (2003); Barron & Lederman, *Commander in Chief at the Lowest Ebb (History)*, 121 Harv. L. Rev. at 993-1025.

j. E.g., Attorney General George Wickersham, *Appropriations — Marine Corps — Service on Battle Ships, Etc.*, 27 Op. Att'y Gen. 259 (1909) (affirming congressional authority not only to establish a marine corps and set its numbers, but also to set directions that the corps "be employed in some designated way"); Attorney General James MacReynolds, *Detail of Staff Officers of Marine Corps to Duty Outside of Washington*, 30 Op. Att'y Gen. 234 (1913) (opining that navy regulation on deployment was invalid because inconsistent with implicit statutory directive).

time of war and to repel an invasion, is not bound by a statute." Transcript of Oral Argument, *Ex parte Quirin*, 317 U.S. 1 (1942). Following Biddle's main argument, the Court held that Congress had authorized the tribunals in that case. In a draft concurring opinion, Justice Jackson suggested that the Court's construction of the statute was required to avoid the serious constitutional question entailed by Congress's interfering with the commander-in-chief power. He questioned Congress's authority to limit the President's ability to deal with "those who come here as belligerents to destroy our institutions." Because no other Justice agreed with these views, Jackson joined the Chief Justice's opinion for the Court with no separate commentary.[k]

After World War II, Congress adopted a series of framework statutes and treaties to govern the nation's military affairs. These included the Geneva Conventions of 1949 (ratified in 1955), the Uniform Code of Military Justice of 1950, the National Security Act of 1947, and the Universal Military Training and Service Act of 1951. President Truman objected to none of this, and in the Steel Seizure Case his Department of Justice said that the President would follow any statute addressing the shortage of war materials. But in the course of the Korean War (1950 onwards), the President asserted a commander-in-chief authority to deploy troops without congressional limitation and to adjust military appropriations to meet changing battlefield needs.[l] Congress did not formally push back against these claims, but did do so in response to President Nixon's conduct of the undeclared War in Vietnam.

THE WAR POWERS RESOLUTION

Between 1954 and 1975, the United States was involved in the war between North and South Vietnam. There was never a congressionally declared "war," and our involvement came about through a series of presidential decisions, first to send advisers to help the Vietnamese fight "Communist aggression," then to commit U.S. soldiers to help fight the Communists, then to have U.S. soldiers take primary responsibility for the war, then to escalate the war through massive bombing and defoliation in both Vietnams, then to escalate the war into other countries (mainly Cambodia), and then to withdraw. Congress appropriated increasing amounts of money for the President's activities, and the Senate approved presidential authority to respond to events in Indochina through the Gulf of Tonkin Resolution in 1964.[m] During the Nixon Administration, Congress grew more restive with its marginal role and with the unproductive (but still expanding) war effort. One result was the enactment in 1973, over President Nixon's veto, of the War Powers Resolution,

---

k. Jackson's draft concurring opinion in *Quirin* and the Roosevelt Administration's dynamic statutory interpretations are discussed in Barron & Lederman, *Commander in Chief at the Lowest Ebb (History)*, 121 Harv. L. Rev. at 1041-54.

l. Barron & Lederman, *Commander in Chief at the Lowest Ebb (History)*, 121 Harv. L. Rev. at 1058-62.

m. On the chain or events drawing us into the Vietnam civil war, see Stanley Karnow, *Vietnam: A History* (1983), as well as John Hart Ely, *War and Responsibility: Constitutional Lessons of Vietnam and Its Aftermath* (1993).

Pub. L. No. 93-148, 87 Stat. 555 (1973), codified at 50 U.S.C. §§ 1541 et seq. The Resolution provides as follows:

§ 1541. Purpose and policy

(a) Congressional declaration. It is the purpose of this joint resolution to fulfill the intent of the framers of the Constitution of the United States and insure that the collective judgment of both the Congress and the President will apply to the introduction of United States Armed Forces into hostilities, or into situations where imminent involvement in hostilities is clearly indicated by the circumstances, and to the continued use of such forces in hostilities or in such situations.

(b) Congressional legislative power under necessary and proper clause. Under Article I, section 8, of the Constitution, it is specifically provided that the Congress shall have the power to make all laws necessary and proper for carrying into execution, not only its own powers but also all other powers vested by the Constitution in the Government of the United States, or in any department or officer thereof.

(c) Presidential executive power as Commander-in-Chief; limitation. The constitutional powers of the President as Commander-in-Chief to introduce United States Armed Forces into hostilities, or into situations where imminent involvement in hostilities is clearly indicated by the circumstances, are exercised only pursuant to (1) a declaration of war, (2) specific statutory authorization, or (3) a national emergency created by attack upon the United States, its territories or possessions, or its armed forces.

§ 1542. Consultation; initial and regular consultations

The President in every possible instance shall consult with Congress before introducing United States Armed Forces into hostilities or into situations where imminent involvement in hostilities is clearly indicated by the circumstances, and after every such introduction shall consult regularly with the Congress until United States Armed Forces are no longer engaged in hostilities or have been removed from such situations.

§ 1543. Reporting requirement

(a) Written report; time of submission; circumstances necessitating submission; information reported. In the absence of a declaration of war, in any case in which United States Armed Forces are introduced—

(1) into hostilities or into situations where imminent involvement in hostilities is clearly indicated by the circumstances;

(2) into the territory, airspace or waters of a foreign nation, while equipped for combat, except for deployments which relate solely to supply, replacement, repair, or training of such forces; or

(3) in numbers which substantially enlarge United States Armed Forces equipped for combat already located in a foreign nation;

the President shall submit within 48 hours to the Speaker of the House of Representatives and to the President pro tempore of the Senate a report, in writing, setting forth—

(A) the circumstances necessitating the introduction of United States Armed Forces;

(B) the constitutional and legislative authority under which such introduction took place; and

(C) the estimated scope and duration of the hostilities or involvement.

(b) Other information reported. The President shall provide such other information as the Congress may request in the fulfillment of its constitutional responsibilities with respect to committing the Nation to war and to the use of United States Armed Forces abroad.

(c) Periodic reports; semiannual requirement. Whenever United States Armed Forces are introduced into hostilities or into any situation described in subsection (a) of this section, the President shall, so long as such armed forces continue to be engaged in such hostilities or situation, report to the Congress periodically on the status of such hostilities or situation as well as on the scope and duration of such hostilities or situation, but in no event shall he report to the Congress less often than once every six months.

§ 1544. Congressional action * * *

(b) Termination of use of United States Armed Forces; exceptions; extension period. Within sixty calendar days after a report is submitted or is required to be submitted pursuant to section 4(a)(1) [50 U.S.C. § 1543(a)(1)], whichever is earlier, the President shall terminate any use of United States Armed Forces with respect to which such report was submitted (or required to be submitted), unless the Congress (1) has declared war or has enacted a specific authorization for such use of United States Armed Forces, (2) has extended by law such sixty-day period, or (3) is physically unable to meet as a result of an armed attack upon the United States. Such sixty-day period shall be extended for not more than an additional thirty days if the President determines and certifies to the Congress in writing that unavoidable military necessity respecting the safety of United States Armed Forces requires the continued use of such armed forces in the course of bringing about a prompt removal of such forces.

(c) Concurrent resolution for removal by President of United States Armed Forces. Notwithstanding subsection (b), at any time that United States Armed Forces are engaged in hostilities outside the territory of the United States, its possession and territories without a declaration of war or specific statutory authorization, such forces shall be removed by the President if the Congress so directs by concurrent resolution. * * *

§ 1547. Interpretation of joint resolution

(a) Inferences from any law or treaty. Authority to introduce United States Armed Forces into hostilities or into situations wherein involvement in hostilities is clearly indicated by the circumstances shall not be inferred—

(1) from any provision of law (whether or not in effect before the date of the enactment of this joint resolution), including any provision contained in any appropriation Act, unless such provision specifically authorizes the introduction of United States Armed Forces into hostilities or into such situations and states that it is intended to constitute specific statutory authorization within the meaning of this joint resolution; or

(2) from any treaty heretofore or hereafter ratified unless such treaty is implemented by legislation specifically authorizing the introduction of United States Armed Forces into hostilities or into such situations and stating that it is intended to constitute specific statutory authorization within the meaning of this joint resolution. * * *

(c) Introduction of United States Armed Forces. For purposes of this joint resolution, the term "introduction of United States Armed Forces" includes the assignment of members of such armed forces to command, coordinate, participate in the movement of, or accompany the regular or irregular military forces of any foreign country or government when such military forces are engaged, or there exists an imminent threat that such forces will become engaged, in hostilities.

(d) Constitutional authorities or existing treaties unaffected; construction against grant of Presidential authority respecting use of United States Armed Forces. Nothing in this joint resolution—

(1) is intended to alter the constitutional authority of the Congress or of the President, or the provisions of existing treaties; or

(2) shall be construed as granting any authority to the President with respect to the introduction of United States Armed Forces into hostilities or into situations wherein involvement in hostilities is clearly indicated by the circumstances which authority he would not have had in the absence of this joint resolution.

§ 1548. Separability of provisions

If any provision of this joint resolution or the application thereof to any person or circumstance is held invalid, the remainder of the joint resolution and the application of such provision to any other person or circumstance shall not be affected thereby.

NOTES ON THE WAR POWERS RESOLUTION: IS IT CONSTITUTIONAL?

President Ford notified Congress when he deployed armed force to rescue the merchant ship *Mayaguez* in May 1975. President Carter did not consult with Congress when he tried, unsuccessfully, to rescue the 52 hostages in Iran in April 1980, though he did notify Congress after the mission failed. President Reagan ignored the Resolution when he invaded Grenada in October 1983, to rescue American medical students. In September 1982, President Reagan committed U.S. armed forces to Lebanon but claimed that the Resolution did not apply because the troops were not involved in "hostilities." A year later, several hundred marines died in Beirut. In 1989, the first President Bush notified Congress of military action taken in Panama. The second President Bush in 2002 obtained congressional authorization for the use of force against Iraq. Although there has been a trend toward substantial compliance with the Resolution, no President has conceded its constitutionality.

Scholars are divided on whether the President has constitutional authority to defend the United States preemptively (i.e., by attacking opponents before they can attack us). For example, Dean Eugene Rostow, one of President Johnson's informal advisers during the Vietnam conflict, attacked the Resolution as contrary to traditional practice:[n]

> The pattern against which the [Resolution] protests is old, familiar, and rooted in the nature of things. There is nothing constitutionally illegitimate or even dubious about "undeclared" wars. We and other nations fought them frequently in the eighteenth and nineteenth centuries, as well as in the twentieth. [The Resolution] would turn the clock back to the Articles of Confederation, and destroy the Presidency which it was one of the chief aims of the men in Annapolis and Philadelphia to create.

Modern critics of the WPR, most prominently Professor John Yoo, have combined Dean Rostow's pragmatic arguments with the formalist and original meaning arguments supporting the Foreign Affairs Vesting Thesis or some variation.[o]

Among a host of constitutional scholars, Harold Koh and John Hart Ely defend the constitutionality of the Resolution, even while regretting its frequent inefficacy.[p] They maintain that the primacy of Congress in the making of war is one of the few arenas where the Framers of the Constitution operated under a clear consensus and that presidential appropriation of the power to make war is unconstitutional. They invoke both the Black and Jackson opinions in the Steel Seizure Case as precedential authority for their position. Scholars such as these criticize the Resolution as too narrow. Apparently, it does not apply to "covert wars," in which intelligence agents acting under civilian supervision

---

n. Rostow, *Great Cases Make Bad Law: The War Powers Act*, 50 Tex. L. Rev. 833, 855-56 (1972). Also arguing for broad presidential power are Eric A. Posner & Adrian Vermeule, *Terror in the Balance: Security, Liberty, and the Courts* (2007); H. Jefferson Powell, *The President's Authority Over Foreign Affairs: An Essay in Constitutional Interpretation* (2002); John Yoo, *The Powers of War and Peace: The Constitution and Foreign Affairs After 9/11* (2005); Leonard Ratner, *The Coordinated Warmaking Power — Legislative, Executive, and Judicial Roles*, 44 S. Cal. L. Rev. 461 (1971).

o. Yoo, *The Powers of War and Peace*; John Yoo, *The Continuation of Politics by Other Means: The Original Understanding of War Powers*, 84 Cal. L. Rev. 167 (1996). See also Phillip Trimble, *International Law: United States Foreign Relations Law* 10-46 (2002); Gary Lawson & Guy Seidman, *The Constitution of Empire: Territorial Expansion and American Legal History* (2004); Michael Stokes Paulsen, Youngstown *Goes to War*, 19 Const. Comm. 215, 237-38 (2002).

p. John Hart Ely, *War and Responsibility: Constitutional Lessons of Vietnam and Its Aftermath* (1993); Harold Koh, *The National Security Constitution: Sharing Power After the Iran-Contra Affair* (1990). Also arguing for a larger congressional role are Jacob Javits, *Who Makes War?: The President versus Congress* (1973); Louis Fisher, *Presidential War Power* (1995); Louis Henkin, *Constitutionalism, Democracy, and Foreign Affairs* (1990); Jane Stromseth, *Rethinking War Powers: Congress, the President, and the United Nations*, 81 Geo. L.J. 597 (1993); William Van Alstyne, *Congress, the President, and the Power to Declare War*, 121 U. Pa. L. Rev. 1 (1972).

conduct paramilitary activities against foreign governments and to "quick strikes" against foreign powers which can be completed well within the 60-day time span (e.g., President Reagan's strikes against Grenada in 1983, Libya in 1986, and Iran in 1987 and 1988).

In the historical material preceding our reprint of the WPR, we have seen how Presidents have fudged this issue for generations, but since Vietnam the matter has ripened into a genuine constitutional debate. Unfortunately, it is a debate where the President and Congress have taken opposing and self-interested positions and the Supreme Court (the only neutral institution on this issue) has not and probably will not resolve the impasse. Partly for this reason, each side resolutely appeals to constitutional text and original meaning.[q] How do these sources cut? Consider the evidence.

1. *Deliberations at the Philadelphia Convention.* Consider Madison's notes of the debate over the "Declare War" Clause, Art. I, § 8, cl. 11:

"To make war."

Mr. Pinkney [sic] opposed the [vest]ing this power in the Legislature. Its proceedings were too slow. It wd. meet but once a year. The Hs. of Reps. would be too numerous for such deliberations. The Senate would be the best depository, being more acquainted with foreign affairs, and most capable of proper resolutions. * * *

Mr. Butler. The Objections agst the Legislature lie in great degree agst the Senate. He was for vesting the power in the President, who will have all the requisite qualities, and will not make war but when the Nation will support in.

Mr. M[adison] and Mr. Gerry moved to insert "*declare*," striking out "*make*" war; leaving to the Executive the power to repel sudden attacks.

Mr. Sharman thought it stood very well. The Executive shd. be able to repel and not to commence war. "Make" better than "declare" the latter narrowing the power too much.

Mr. Gerry never expected to hear in a republic a motion to empower the Executive alone to declare war.

Mr. Mason was agst. giving the power of war to the Executive, because not (safely) to be trusted with it; or to the Senate, because not so constructed as to be entitled to it. He was for clogging rather than facilitating war; but for facilitating peace. He preferred "*declare*" to "*make*."

On the motion to insert *declare* — in place of *make*, (it was agreed to).

What conclusions would you draw from this discussion and the eventual decision made by the Framers?

---

q. Leading sources on the original meaning debate are Ely, *War and Responsibility* (arguing for broad congressional authority to regulate foreign military involvements); David J. Barron & Martin S. Lederman, *The Commander in Chief at the Lowest Ebb — Framing the Problem, Doctrine, and Original Understanding*, 121 Harv. L. Rev. 689, 772-800 (2008) (similar); William Michael Treanor, *Fame, the Founding, and the Power to Declare War*, 82 Cornell L. Rev. 695 (1997) (similar); Yoo, *Original Understanding of War Powers* (arguing for narrow congressional authority, with the funding power being the main way the Framers expected Congress to influence military policy). See also Jane Stromseth, *Understanding Constitutional War Powers Today: Why Methodology Matters*, 106 Yale L.J. 845, 860-61 (1996) (supporting congressional authority).

Notice that most of the delegates were thinking in functional, institutionalist terms. Thus, they emphasized the President's advantages of speedy response as a reason not to tie his hands when the nation was attacked by another country. There was support for a larger Senate role because it was thought that body would have more experience in foreign affairs. But there was also some voice for popular concerns, especially Butler's confidence that the President, who alone was elected by the entire nation, will be more responsive to national demands for war. Gerry's objection seems to be a popular response: But in a *republic*, it should be the deliberate judgment of localities and states assembled in Congress that must have the final word.

Consider John Yoo's argument that these debates must be read in light of eighteenth century understanding of what *declare war* meant. Blackstone and other eighteenth century legal synthesizers allowed that the monarch could initiate hostilities with other nations; a "declaration of war" was important in escalating *hostilities* to all-out *war*, with broader repercussions for relations between the nations and notice for their citizens that normal intercourse was disrupted. Parliament's increasingly important role focused on funding decisions, allowing elected representatives to veto royally initiated hostilities. The experience in the colonies was similar, with governors generally having control over militias, including the authority to initiate hostilities, but with legislatures exercising some negative authority through appropriations pressure.[r]

Jane Stromseth disputes this reading of pre-1789 practice and reads the originalist sources to support the proposition that "the Founders would have expected the President as Commander in Chief and Chief Executive to protect the United States in a dangerous and uncertain world by repelling actual or imminent attacks against the United States, its vessels, and its armed forces, but not, on his own, to go beyond this authority and effectively change the state of the nation from peace to war." (Stromseth, *Understanding Constitutional War Powers*, 106 Yale L.J. at 862.) Her reading receives support from the apparent purpose of the Framers' war clauses. As Madison put it, "[i]n no part of the constitution is more wisdom to be found, than in the clause which confides the question of war or peace to the legislature, and not to the executive department. * * * [T]he trust and the temptation would be too great for any one man. * * * War is in fact the true nurse of executive aggrandizement" (quoted in *id.* at 845).

2. *Ratification Debates.* James Wilson defended the Declare War Clause during the Pennsylvania ratifying convention with this argument:

> This system will not hurry us into war; it is calculated to guard against it. It will not be in the power of a single man, or a single body of men, to involve us in such distress; for the important power of declaring war is vested in the legislature at large: * * * nothing but our national interest can draw us into war. [Elliott, *Debates in the Several State Conventions* 528 (1836).]

This statement is cited by most of the scholars who favor congressional initiative to make war. At the Philadelphia Convention, however, Wilson had

---

r. See Yoo, *Original Understanding of War Powers*, 84 Calif. L. Rev. at 204-16, 218-35, 242-43.

been the author of the original Make War Clause, whose tilt toward congressional power had been reversed in some part by vote of the Convention.

John Yoo argues that the Federalist position matured after the Pennsylvania debates, and that by the time New York and Virginia ratified the defenders of the Constitution were taking a stronger pro-President position. At the critical Virginia convention, the Federalist response to charges of presidential aggrandizement rested largely upon the argument that Congress's power of the purse was the best practical limit on an imperial presidency.[s] Writing for the New York delegates, Hamilton in *Federalist* No. 25 deemphasized the significance of a declaration of war, saying it "has of late fallen into disuse."

Legal historians William Treanor, Curtis Bradley, and Martin Flaherty have disputed Yoo's account.[t] Hamilton's *Federalist* No. 69 responded to Anti-Federalist attacks on the strong presidency with the observation that the President's power as Commander-in-Chief was not as plenary as the authority of some governors to control their militias. Anti-Federalist charges that the President would be like the hated King of England were overstated. If the President were the Commander-in-Chief of the army and navy, Hamilton observed, he lacked the British King's power of "the *declaring* of war and the *raising* and *regulating* of fleets and armies; all which by the Constitution under consideration would appertain to the Legislature." Hamilton's concession was repeated by prominent Federalist James Iredell at the North Carolina convention.

3. *Practice and Precedent.* The Washington and Adams Administrations conducted hostilities in the 1790s without formal declarations of war, but they did seek congressional authorization for deploying the militia or raising a navy before they took action. The Supreme Court entertained several lawsuits in connection with the Quasi-War with France in 1798-1800, including *Little v. Barreme*, 6 U.S. 170 (1804), where Chief Justice Marshall enforced implicit congressional limits on presidential authority. For the first two generations under the Constitution, Presidents dependent upon congressional funds for ships and troops cooperated with Congress when hostilities were planned, but by the middle of the nineteenth century Presidents were more assertive. Also, Presidents throughout the nineteenth century engaged in small-scale military operations against pirates and bandits and to protect American interests abroad.

The Civil War commenced when southern states seceded from the Union and their forces fired on Fort Sumter. President Lincoln responded, inter alia, with a unilateral blockade of southern ports after the South's secession. Although his action was highly controversial, the Supreme Court upheld his action in *The Prize Cases*, 67 U.S. (2 Black) 635 (1863). Justice Grier's opinion for the Court interpreted the Constitution to give the President broad discretion when responding to national emergencies:

---

s. See Yoo, *Original Understanding of War Powers*, 84 Calif. L. Rev. at 281-86.

    t. Bradley & Flaherty, *Presidential Power Essentialism and Foreign Affairs*; Treanor, *Fame, the Founding and the Power to Declare War.*

By the Constitution, Congress alone has the power to declare a national or foreign war. It cannot declare war against a State, or any number of States, by virtue of any clause in the Constitution. The Constitution confers on the President the Whole Executive power. * * * He has no power to initiate or declare war either against a foreign nation or a domestic State. But by [Acts] of Congress, [he] is authorized to [call] out the militia and use the military and naval forces of the United States in case of invasion by foreign nations, and to suppress insurrection against the government of a State or of the United States.

If a war be made by invasion of a foreign nation, the President is not only authorized but bound to resist force by force. He does not initiate the war, but is bound to accept the challenge without waiting for any special legislative authority. * * *

Whether the President in fulfilling his duties, as Commander-in-Chief, in suppressing an insurrection, has met with such armed hostile resistance, and a civil war of such alarming proportions as will compel him to accord to them the character of belligerents, is a question to be decided *by him*, and this Court must be governed by the decisions and acts of the political department of the Government to which this power was entrusted.

Four Justices dissented from this opinion, arguing that only Congress could authorize the blockade. Do *The Prize Cases* provide some support for the President's executive agreement upheld in *Dames & Moore*?

Altogether, the United States has declared war five times in its history: the War of 1812, the Mexican-American War (1848), the Spanish-American War (1898), and World Wars I (1917) and II (1941). The United States has committed military forces somewhere between 125 and 215 times after the adoption of the Constitution, but many of those commitments were after consultation and some kind of authorization by Congress.

PROBLEM 8-2
THE WAR POWERS RESOLUTION, SEPARATION OF POWERS, AND HOSTILITIES AGAINST IRAQ

Consider, first, the abstract question, are any portions of the War Powers Resolution (WPR) unconstitutional in light of the materials in the previous Note? Next, consider the abstract problem in connection with the following sequence of events. Finally, consider what changes to the WPR might make it either constitutional or efficacious, depending on your point of view.[u]

In 1990, Iraq invaded Kuwait, an American ally and source of oil. The United Nations adopted a series of resolutions condemning the invasion of Kuwait and Iraq's alleged development of nuclear, chemical, and biological weapons. In House Resolution 77, 105 Stat. 3 (1991), Congress authorized the President "to use United States armed forces" to enforce the United Nations resolutions. On January 17, 1991, the United States went to war with Iraq. "Operation Desert Storm" was a quick success. Under a United Nations-sponsored cease-fire agreement, Iraq pledged to eliminate its nuclear and chemical and biological weapons programs and to end its support for interna-

---

u. John Hart Ely, *Suppose Congress Wanted a War Powers Act That Worked*, 88 Colum. L. Rev. 1379 (1988), suggests that Congress can strengthen the Resolution in ways that correct for repeated presidential refusal to follow it.

tional terrorism. United Nations inspectors were not given full access to Iraqi facilities and were withdrawn from Iraq in 1998. In Public Law 105-235 (1998), Congress concluded that Iraq's weapons program remained a national security threat to the United States and urged the President to "take appropriate action, in accordance with the Constitution and relevant laws of the United States, to bring Iraq into compliance with its international obligations." In the wake of the terrorist attacks of September 11, 2001, charges that Iraq provided support to al-Qaeda, the group responsible for the 9/11 attacks, were added to charges that Iraq was developing weapons of mass destruction that could be used against the United States as well as other countries.

In light of the foregoing legal regime, consider these constitutional and legal features relating to future military action against Iraq:

(A) The President deploys 100,000 American soldiers to U.S. military bases in the Near East. What obligations does the WPR impose on the President in this setting? Which ones are constitutional?

(B) Does the President have the authority to deploy these troops in an armed invasion of Iraq? What legal obligations would the WPR impose on the President at that point? Are they constitutional?

(C) In § 3(a) of the Authorization for Use of Military Force Against Iraq Resolution of 2002, Pub. Law No. 107-243 (2002), Congress provided: "The President is authorized to use the Armed Forces of the United States as he determines to be necessary and appropriate in order to (1) defend the national security of the United States against the continuing threat posed by Iraq; and (2) enforce all relevant United Nations Security Council resolutions concerning Iraq." (Sections 3(c) and 4 conform this authorization with the WPR in various respects.) Assume that the President deploys the armed forces to invade Iraq. Should there have been a formal declaration of war by Congress?

3. *Presidential Authority to Enforce or Terminate Treaties*

Although the Supremacy Clause of Article VI might be read, according to its plain meaning, to render all treaties the "Law of the Land," the Supreme Court has long held that some treaties are not "self-executing," that is, they are not binding law unless implemented through congressional legislation. Self-executing treaties are binding law. Is the President obliged to follow those directives? Without exception? Can the President *terminate* self-executing treaties on his own authority? The Foreign Affairs Vesting Thesis suggests that the President has that authority, which would parallel the President's authority to remove cabinet officers whose appointments were subject to the advice and consent of the Senate. See Prakash & Ramsey, *Executive Power over Foreign Affairs*, 111 Yale L.J. at 324-27. The Supreme Court has never resolved this issue, see *Goldwater v. Carter*, 444 U.S. 996 (1979) (no majority opinion, with the practical result being that President Carter was able to terminate our treaty with Taiwan), and most commentators treat the issue as unresolved.[v]

Consider the flip side: Does the President have any discretion to implement non-self-executing treaties as binding law on his own authority? Recall that *Belmont* allowed the President to override state law in a unilateral agreement. *Dames & Moore* treated the President's unilateral executive agreement as overriding a federal jurisdictional statute, the FSIA. The Foreign Affairs Vesting Thesis suggests that the President has some authority along these lines. Consider the Supreme Court's recent treatment of this issue.

    Medellín v. Texas, 128 S.Ct. 1346 (2008). In the Case Concerning Avena and Other Mexican Nationals (*Mex. v. U. S.*), 2004 I. C. J. 12, the International Court of Justice (ICJ) held that the United States had violated Article 36(1)(b) of the Vienna Convention on Consular Relations by failing to inform 51 Mexican nationals, including petitioner José Ernesto Medellín, of their Vienna Convention rights when they were prosecuted in state criminal proceedings. The ICJ found that those individuals were entitled to review and reconsideration of their U.S. state-court convictions and sentences regardless of their failure to comply with generally applicable state rules governing challenges to criminal convictions. In *Sanchez-Llamas v. Oregon*, 548 U. S. 331 (2006), the Supreme Court held, contrary to the ICJ's determination, that the Convention did not preclude the application of state default rules. President George W. Bush then issued a Memorandum to the Attorney General (Feb. 28, 2005), stating:

> I have determined, pursuant to the authority vested in me as President by the Constitution and the laws of the United States of America, that the United States will discharge its international obligations under the decision of the International Court of Justice in [*Avena*], by having State courts give effect to the decision in accordance with general principles of comity in cases filed by the 51 Mexican nationals addressed in that decision.

Relying on *Avena* and the President's Memorandum, Medellín filed a second Texas state-court habeas application challenging his state capital murder conviction and death sentence on the ground that he had not been informed of his Vienna Convention rights. The Texas Court of Criminal Appeals dismissed Medellín's application, ruling that neither *Avena* nor the President's Memorandum was binding federal law that could displace the state's limitations on filing successive habeas applications.

The U.S. Supreme Court affirmed. Writing for the majority, **Chief Justice Roberts** ruled that the *Avena* judgment was not binding "Law of the Land" pursuant to the Supremacy Clause, Article VI, § 2. To be sure, the judgment was binding on the United States pursuant to its international obligations under Article 94(1) of the United Nations Charter, which provides that "[e]ach Member of the United Nations *undertakes to comply* with the decision of the [ICJ] in any case to which it is a party." 59 Stat. 1051 (emphasis added). The

---

    v. *E.g.*, Oona Hathaway, *Treaties' End: The Past, Present, and Future of International Lawmaking in the United States*, 117 Yale L.J. 101, 192-96 (2008).

Solicitor General argued that the phrase "undertakes to comply" is not "an acknowledgment that an ICJ decision will have immediate legal effect in the courts of U.N. members," but rather "a *commitment* on the part of U.N. Members to take *future* action through their political branches to comply with an ICJ decision." Brief for United States as *Amicus Curiae.* The Court agreed with this interpretation, and said that the executive department's views were entitled to "great weight."

The President sought to carry out the nation's "commitment" to ICJ judgments through the foregoing Memorandum, which the Solicitor General urged upon the Court as a basis for overturning the Texas conviction. "In this case, the President seeks to vindicate United States interests in ensuring the reciprocal observance of the Vienna Convention, protecting relations with foreign governments, and demonstrating commitment to the role of international law. These interests are plainly compelling. Such considerations, however, do not allow us to set aside first principles. The President's authority to act, as with the exercise of any governmental power, 'must stem either from an act of Congress or from the Constitution itself.' *Youngstown; Dames & Moore.*"

The Chief Justice followed "Justice Jackson's familiar tripartite scheme," which "provides the accepted framework for evaluating executive action in this area." The Court ruled that the President has no authority to convert a non-self-executing treaty into a self-executing one, but took seriously the argument that the President's Memorandum fit within Jackson's Category 2, the "twilight zone" where longstanding presidential action, accompanied by congressional acquiescence, creates a field for future unilateral executive power. See *Dames & Moore; Belmont.* "The President's Memorandum is not supported by a 'particularly longstanding practice' of congressional acquiescence, but rather is what the United States itself has described as 'unprecedented action,' Brief for United States as *Amicus Curiae* in *Sanchez-Llamas,* O.T. 2005, Nos. 05-51 and 04-10566, pp. 29-30. Indeed, the Government has not identified a single instance in which the President has attempted (or Congress has acquiesced in) a Presidential directive issued to state courts, much less one that reaches deep into the heart of the State's police powers and compels state courts to reopen final criminal judgments and set aside neutrally applicable state laws."

Justice Stevens concurred in the Court's judgment affirming Medellín's conviction.

Justice Breyer, joined by **Justice Souter** and **Justice Ginsburg**, dissented, maintaining that Article 94(1) of the U.N. Convention was self-executing and therefore preempted state law and required Texas to follow *Avena.* On the separate issue of the status of the President's Memorandum, Justice Breyer seemed friendly to the Solicitor General's argument that the Memorandum fell close to or within Justice Jackson's "twilight zone" of concurrent authority. "It is difficult to believe that in the exercise of his Article II powers pursuant to a ratified treaty, the President can *never* take action that would result in setting aside state law. Suppose that the President believes it necessary that he implement a treaty provision requiring a prisoner exchange involving someone in state custody in order to avoid a proven military threat. Or suppose he believes it necessary to secure a foreign consul's treaty-based rights to move freely or to contact an arrested foreign national. Does the Constitution require the President in each and every such instance to obtain a special statute authorizing his action? On the other hand, the Constitution must impose significant restrictions upon the President's ability, by invoking Article II treaty-implementation authority, to circumvent ordinary legislative processes and to pre-empt state law as he does so.

"Previously this Court has said little about this question. It has held that the President has a fair amount of authority to make and to implement executive agreements, at least in respect to international claims settlement, and that this authority can require contrary state law to be set aside. See, *e.g., Pink*; *Belmont*. It has made clear that principles of foreign sovereign immunity trump state law and that the Executive, operating without explicit legislative authority, can assert those principles in state court. See *Ex parte Peru*, 318 U. S. 578, 588 (1943). It has also made clear that the Executive has inherent power to bring a lawsuit 'to carry out treaty obligations.' *Sanitary Dist. of Chicago v. United States*, 266 U. S. 405, 425, 426 (1925). But it has reserved judgment as to 'the scope of the President's power to preempt state law pursuant to authority delegated by . . . a ratified treaty' — a fact that helps to explain the majority's inability to find support in precedent for its own conclusions. *Barclays Bank PLC v. Franchise Tax Bd. of Cal.*, 512 U.S. 298, 329 (1994).

"Given the Court's comparative lack of expertise in foreign affairs; given the importance of the Nation's foreign relations; given the difficulty of finding the proper constitutional balance among state and federal, executive and legislative, powers in such matters; and given the likely future importance of this Court's efforts to do so, I would very much hesitate before concluding that the Constitution implicitly sets forth broad prohibitions (or permissions) in this area."

NOTE ON THE ICJ JUDGMENT CASE AND THE FOREIGN AFFAIRS VESTING THESIS

1. *Presumption Against Self-Executing Treaties.* The most important doctrinal point of *Medellín* is the Court's stinginess in declining to find that a treaty negotiated by the President and ratified by the Senate is the "Law of the Land," as the Supremacy Clause plainly says. Treaties will be considered self-executing "Law of the Land" only if there is clear evidence that the President and Congress expected them to be enforced through domestic legal mechanisms. But because treaties are typically international agreements that each country "undertakes" to comply, the *Medellín* approach seems to create a "presumption against self-executing treaties," as the dissenting opinion charged.[w] And if a

---

w. For an excellent debate over constitutional original meaning as regards self-executing treaties, compare Carlos Manuel Vásquez, *Laughing at Treaties*, 99 Colum. L. Rev. 2154 (1999) (arguing that the Constitution supports a presumption in favor of self-execution, anticipating and providing support for Justice Breyer's position), with John Choon Yoo, *Globalism and the Constitution: Treaties, Non-Self-Execution, and the Original Understanding*, 99 Colum. L. Rev. 1955 (1999) (arguing for a constitutional presumption against self-execution, anticipating and providing support for Chief Justice Roberts' position).

treaty is not self-executing, state law inconsistent with the treaty commitments is not preempted, either by force of the treaty or of presidential directives implementing the treaty.

Medellín may contribute to the end of treaties as a significant means by which the United States enters into international commitments. As Oona Hathaway, *Treaties' End: The Past, Present, and Future of International Lawmaking in the United States,* 117 Yale L.J. 101 (2008), documents, the last hundred years have seen congressional-executive agreements become the overwhelmingly dominant form of international commitment on the part of the United States. Treaties have not disappeared, but after *Medellín* any serious obligation will be through a congressional-executive agreement, which has "Law of the Land" status because it is statutory, while treaties will be even more marginalized, perhaps left to empty symbolic gestures. Ironically, this may mean "treaties' end," which Professor Hathaway lauds, but which other scholars lament as a violation of the text and original meaning of the Constitution.[x]

2. *The Triumph of the Jackson Framework and the Turn toward Statutory Interpretation.* Presidentialist scholars have sought to entrench the Foreign Affairs Vesting Thesis and to marginalize the Jackson framework as the baseline for separation of powers analysis touching on national security and foreign affairs. *Medellín* unanimously affirms the Jackson framework in a foreign relations context, and the majority explicitly rejects the Foreign Affairs Vesting Thesis as a basis for preempting state law, in seemingly absolute terms. What is the status of *Dames & Moore* (unilateral presidential override of a federal statute) and *Belmont* (override of state law) after *Medellín*? Neither decision has been overruled, but how can their reasoning stand after *Medellín*?

Medellín is a setback to the Foreign Affairs Vesting Thesis, but alternative defenses of broad presidential power have already come to the forefront. John Yoo, *The Powers of War and Peace: The Constitution and Foreign Affairs After 9/11* (2005), operates within the Jackson framework, arguing that the Constitution only establishes a general structure and leaves the details to be filled in by experience, practice, and acquiescence on the part of legislators and We the People. Thus, many foreign affairs issues fall within Jackson's "zone of twilight," where presidential initiatives + congressional acquiescence can expand presidential power over time. As *Medellín* suggests (confirming the lesson of Steel Seizure), twilight zone arguments will not be automatically accepted; the President has to show genuine similarity between powers his predecessors have exercised and those he now claims as his own, and perhaps also genuine congressional knowledge and acquiescence (which were not issues

---

x. Leading articles arguing the constitutional necessity of treaties as the primary engine for international agreement start with Edwin Borchard, *Shall the Executive Agreement Replace the Treaty?*, 53 Yale L.J. 664 (1944), continue with Laurence Tribe, *Taking Text Seriously: Reflections on Free-Form Method in Constitutional Interpretation,* 108 Harv. L. Rev. 1221 (1995), and are recently carried forward in innovative ways by Peter Spiro, *Treaties, Executive Agreements, and Constitutional Method,* 79 Tex. L. Rev. 961 (2001), and John Yoo, *Laws as Treaties?: The Constitutionality of Congressional-Executive Agreements*, 99 Mich. L. Rev. 757 (2001).

in *Medellín*). Scholarship by professional historians such as William Michael Treanor and Martin Flaherty is strongly dubious as to broad presidential claims.[y]

The triumph of the Jackson framework and the proliferation of national security statutes means that, increasingly, debates are going to be about how to interpret congressional enactments — for interpretation will reveal whether a case is Category 1, where the President wins, or the "lowest ebb" Category 3, where the President loses. As the stakes of statutory interpretation have gone up in separation of powers cases, there has been greater pressure to "constitutionalize" such interpretation through clear statement rules and other canons. Should there be a strong presumption in favor of the President's construction of statutes touching upon foreign and military affairs or national security, arenas where Article II vests the President with special authority?[z]

3. *Federalism.* Most of the *Medellín* majority Justices support strong presidential power vis-a-vis individual rights or congressional power — but here they take a very hard line against presidential authority. They key variable is federalism: the constitutional structure and original meaning preserve a key role for the states, whose autonomy is protected through constitutional law rules, as well as canons of statutory interpretation. Federalism also helps explain why the Roberts Court takes such a stingy view of the treaty self-execution doctrine: a major effect of self-executing treaties is that they preempt state law, and the presumption against self-execution is one way the Court makes sure that the Senate and the President explicitly take account of the federalism effects when they enter treaties. The Justices also may have worried that sometimes treaties are too easily entered into, and they want to assurance of the full Article I, Section 7 process before preempting state law.[aa]

---

y. E.g., Martin Flaherty, *More Real Than Apparent: Separation of Powers, the Rule of Law, and Comparative Executive "Creativity" in* Hamdan v. Rumsfeld, 2005-2006 Cato Sup. Ct. Rev. 51 (skeptical examination of presidential claims for preclusive authority to create military tribunals); William Michael Treanor, *Fame, the Founding, and the Power to Declare War*, 82 Cornell L. Rev. 695 (1997) (skeptical examination of presidential claims for preclusive warmaking authority); see also David Barron & Martin Lederman, *The Commander in Chief at the Lowest Ebb — A Constitutional History*, 121 Harv. L. Rev. 941 (2008) (skeptical examination of presidential claims for commander-in-chief authority).

z. *Department of Navy v. Egan*, 484 U.S. 518, 529 (1988) (suggesting such a deferential approach). Compare Curtis Bradley, *War on Terrorism: International Law, Clear Statement Requirements, and Constitutional Design*, 118 Harv. L. Rev. 2683 (2005), with William Eskridge, Jr. & Lauren Baer, *The Continuum of Deference: Supreme Court Treatment of Agency Statutory Interpretation from* Chevron *to* Hamdan, 96 Geo. L.J. 1083 (2008) (arguing that the Supreme Court is too deferential to executive department interpretations generally and that a "special" deference for national security and foreign affairs cases is uncalled for).

aa. Curtis Bradley, *Federalism and the Treaty Power*, 98 Am. J. Int'l L. 341 (2004), and Medellin v. Dretke: *Federalism and International Law*, 43 Colum. J. Transnat'l L. 667 (2005). On Article I, § 7 (and so implicitly Article II, § 2, the treaty power) as a safeguard of state autonomy, see Bradford R. Clark, *Separation of Powers as a Safegurard of Federalism*, 79 Tex. L. Rev. 1321 (2001).

C. EXECUTIVE PRIVILEGES AND IMMUNITIES

Since the Washington Administration, the President had maintained his privilege to withhold information from Congress or to divulge it under confidential circumstances, in order to protect the national interest. More ambiguous, because much less tested or discussed, was the President's amenability to or immunity from legal process. Executive privilege and presidential immunity for misdeeds are grounded in the notion that the needs of the job require compromise with the rule of law. Both issues came to the Supreme Court in cases arising out of alleged violations of law by President Nixon (1969-74). Both issues have recurred, as illustrated by the many legal problems faced by President Clinton (1993-2001).

UNITED STATES v. NIXON
418 U.S. 683, 94 S.Ct. 3090, 41 L.Ed.2d 1039 (1974)

CHIEF JUSTICE BURGER delivered the opinion of the Court.

[Agents of CREEP (Committee to Re-elect the President) broke into the Democratic National Headquarters at the Watergate Hotel on June 17, 1972 and were apprehended. They implicated officials in the campaign to reelect President Nixon, and in 1973-74 both Senate and House committees conducted hearings on the Watergate break-in and the apparent effort to cover it up. In May, the President named Archibald Cox as a special prosecutor to investigate any White House involvement in a cover-up. John Dean, former White House Counsel, implicated the President himself in June, and in February 1974 the House authorized the Judiciary Committee to commence impeachment proceedings against the President.

[On March 1, 1974, a grand jury returned indictments against seven defendants: former Attorney General John Mitchell, White House officials H.R. Haldeman and John Ehrlichman, and four others. Each was charged with conspiracy to defraud the United States and to obstruct justice in the Watergate affair. The President was named as an unindicted co-conspirator in *United States v. Mitchell*. On April 18, upon motion by the special prosecutor, a subpoena was issued by the district court, requiring the President to produce tapes, memoranda, and other writings relating to specified meetings with the President. The President released edited transcripts of some of the tapes in question and on May 1 moved to quash the subpoena on grounds of executive privilege. The district court denied the motion. As in the Steel Seizure Case and the Iranian Hostages Case, the Supreme Court took review before the case had been considered by the court of appeals. The Court affirmed and remanded the case to the district court for examination of the subpoenaed documents.]

* * * [W]e turn to the claim that the subpoena should be quashed because it demands "confidential conversations between a President and his close advisors that it would be inconsistent with the public interest to produce." The first contention is a broad claim that the separation of powers doctrine precludes judicial review of a President's claim of privilege. The second contention is that if he does not prevail on the claim of absolute privilege, the court should hold as a matter of constitutional law that the privilege prevails over the subpoena *duces tecum.* * * *

No holding of the Court has defined the scope of judicial power specifically relating to the enforcement of a subpoena for confidential Presidential communications for use in a criminal prosecution. * * * In a series of cases, the Court interpreted the explicit immunity conferred by express provisions of the Constitution on Members of the House and Senate by the Speech or Debate Clause, U.S. Const., Art. I, § 6. Since this Court has consistently exercised the power to construe and delineate claims arising under express powers, it must follow that the Court has authority to interpret claims with respect to powers alleged to derive from enumerated powers.

Our system of government "requires that federal courts on occasion interpret the Constitution in a manner at variance with the construction given the document by another branch." * * * Notwithstanding the deference each branch must accord the others, the "judicial Power of the United States" vested in the federal courts by Art. III, § 1, of the Constitution can no more be shared with the Executive Branch than the Chief Executive, for example, can share with the Judiciary the veto power, or the Congress share with the Judiciary the power to override a Presidential veto. Any other conclusion would be contrary to the basic concept of separation of powers and the checks and balances that flow from the scheme of a tripartite government. We therefore reaffirm that it is the province and duty of this Court "to say what the law is" with respect to the claim of privilege presented in this case. *Marbury v. Madison.*

In support of his claim of absolute privilege, the President's counsel urges two grounds, one of which is common to all governments and one of which is peculiar to our system of separation of powers. The first ground is the valid need for protection of communications between high Government officials and those who advise and assist them in the performance of their manifold duties; the importance of this confidentiality is too plain to require further discussion. Human experience teaches that those who expect public dissemination of their remarks may well temper candor with a concern for appearances and for their own interests to the detriment of the decisionmaking process. Whatever the nature of the privilege of confidentiality of Presidential communications in the exercise of Art. II powers, the privilege can be said to derive from the supremacy of each branch within its own assigned area of constitutional duties. Certain powers and privileges flow from the nature of enumerated powers; the protection of the confidentiality of Presidential communications has similar constitutional underpinnings.

The second ground asserted by the President's counsel in support of the claim of absolute privilege rests on the doctrine of separation of powers. Here it is argued that the independence of the Executive Branch within its own sphere, insulates a President from a judicial subpoena in an ongoing criminal prosecution, and thereby protects confidential Presidential communications.

However, neither the doctrine of separation of powers, nor the need for confidentiality of high-level communications, without more, can sustain an absolute, unqualified Presidential privilege of immunity from judicial process under all circumstances. The President's need for complete candor and objectivity from advisers calls for great deference from the courts. However, when the privilege depends solely on the broad, undifferentiated claim of public interest in the confidentiality of such conversations, a confrontation with other values arises. Absent a claim of need to protect military, diplomatic, or sensitive national security secrets, we find it difficult to accept the argument that even the very important interest in confidentiality of Presidential communications is significantly diminished by production of such material for *in camera* inspection with all the protection that a district court will be obliged to provide.

The impediment that an absolute, unqualified privilege would place in the way of the primary constitutional duty of the Judicial Branch to do justice in criminal prosecutions would plainly conflict with the function of the courts under Art. III. In designing the structure of our Government and dividing and allocating the sovereign power among three co-equal branches, the Framers of the Constitution sought to provide a comprehensive system, but the separate powers were not intended to operate with absolute independence. * * * To read the Art. II powers of the President as providing an absolute privilege as against a subpoena essential to enforcement of criminal statutes on no more than a generalized claim of the public interest in confidentiality of nonmilitary and nondiplomatic discussions would upset the constitutional balance of "a workable government" and gravely impair the role of the courts under Art. III. * * *

The expectation of a President to the confidentiality of his conversations and correspondence, like the claim of confidentiality of judicial deliberations, for example, has all the values to which we accord deference for the privacy of all citizens and, added to those values, is the necessity for protection of the public interest in candid, objective, and even blunt or harsh opinions in Presidential decisionmaking. * * * The privilege is fundamental to the operation of Government and inextricably rooted in the separation of powers under the Constitution. In *Nixon v. Sirica*, 159 U.S. App. D.C. 58, 487 F.2d 700 (1973), the Court of Appeals held that such Presidential communications are "presumptively privileged," and this position is accepted by both parties in the present litigation. * * *

But this presumptive privilege must be considered in light of our historic commitment to the rule of law. This is nowhere more profoundly manifest than in our view that "the twofold aim [of criminal justice] is that guilt shall not escape or innocence suffer." We have elected to employ an adversary system of criminal justice in which the parties contest all issues before a court of law. The need to develop all relevant facts in the adversary system is both fundamental and comprehensive. The ends of criminal justice would be defeated if judgments were to be founded on a partial or speculative presentation of the facts. The very integrity of the judicial system and public confidence in the system depend on full disclosure of all the facts, within the framework of the rules of evidence. To ensure that justice is done, it is imperative to the function of courts that compulsory process be available for the production of evidence needed either by the prosecution or by the defense.

Only recently the Court restated the ancient proposition of law, albeit in the context of a grand jury inquiry rather than a trial, "that 'the public . . . has a right to every man's evidence,' except for those persons protected by a constitutional, common-law, or statutory privilege." The privileges referred to by the Court are designed to protect weighty and legitimate competing interests. Thus, the Fifth Amendment to the Constitution provides that no man "shall be compelled in any criminal case to be a witness against himself." And, generally, an attorney or a priest may not be required to disclose what has been revealed in professional confidence. These and other interests are recognized in law by privileges against forced disclosure, established in the Constitution, by statute, or at common law. Whatever their origins, these exceptions to the demand for every man's evidence are not lightly created nor expansively construed, for they are in derogation of the search for truth.

In this case the President challenges a subpoena served on him as a third party requiring the production of materials for use in a criminal prosecution; he does so on the claim that he has a privilege against disclosure of confidential communications. He does not place his claim of privilege on the ground they are military or diplomatic secrets. As to these areas of Art. II duties the courts have traditionally shown the utmost deference to Presidential responsibilities. * * *

No case of the Court, however, has extended this high degree of deference to a President's generalized interest in confidentiality. Nowhere in the Constitution, as we have noted earlier, is there any explicit reference to a privilege of confidentiality, yet to the extent this interest relates to the effective discharge of a President's powers, it is constitutionally based.

The right to the production of all evidence at a criminal trial similarly has constitutional dimensions. The Sixth Amendment explicitly confers upon every defendant in a criminal trial the right "to be confronted with the witnesses against him" and "to have compulsory process for obtaining witnesses in his favor." Moreover, the Fifth Amendment also guarantees that no person shall be deprived of liberty without due process of law. It is the manifest duty of the courts to vindicate those guarantees, and to accomplish that it is essential that all relevant and admissible evidence be produced.

In this case we must weigh the importance of the general privilege of confidentiality of Presidential communications in performance of the President's responsibilities against the inroads of such a privilege on the fair administration of criminal justice. The interest in preserving confidentiality is weighty indeed and entitled to great respect. However, we cannot conclude that advisers will be moved to temper the candor of their remarks by the infrequent occasions of disclosure because of the possibility that such conversations will be called for in the context of a criminal prosecution.

On the other hand, the allowance of the privilege to withhold evidence that is demonstrably relevant in a criminal trial would cut deeply into the guarantee of due process of law and gravely impair the basic function of the courts. A President's acknowledged need for confidentiality in the communications of his office is general in nature, whereas the constitutional need for production of relevant evidence in a criminal proceeding is specific and central to the fair adjudication of a particular criminal case in the administration of justice. Without access to specific facts a criminal prosecution may be totally frustrated. The President's broad interest in confidentiality of communications will not be vitiated by disclosure of a limited number of conversations preliminarily shown to have some bearing on the pending criminal cases.

We conclude that when the ground for asserting privilege as to subpoenaed materials sought for use in a criminal trial is based only on the generalized interest in confidentiality, it cannot prevail over the fundamental demands of due process of law in the fair administration of criminal justice. The generalized assertion of privilege must yield to the demonstrated, specific need for evidence in a pending criminal trial.

[The Court further held that the district court did not err in authorizing the issuance of the subpoena: the court properly treated the material as presumptively privileged, proceeded to find that the Special Prosecutor had made a sufficient showing to rebut the presumption, and ordered an *in camera* examination of the subpoenaed material. In conducting the *in camera* inspection, the district court was instructed:] Statements that meet the test of admissibility and relevance must be isolated; all other material must be excised. At this stage the District Court is not limited to representations of the Special Prosecutor as to the evidence sought by the subpoena; the material will be available to the District Court. It is elementary that *in camera* inspection of evidence is always a procedure calling for scrupulous protection against any release or publication of material not found by the court, at that stage, probably admissible in evidence and relevant to the issues of the trial for which it is sought. That being true of an ordinary situation, it is obvious that the District Court has a very heavy responsibility to see to it that Presidential conversations, which are either not relevant or not admissible, are accorded that high degree of respect due the President of the United States. Mr. Chief Justice Marshall, sitting as a trial judge in the *Burr* case, was extraordinarily careful to point out that "[i]n no case of this kind would a court be required to proceed against a president as against an ordinary individual." Marshall's statement cannot be read to mean in any sense that a President is above the law, but relates to the singularly unique role under Art. II of a President's communications and activities, related to the performance of duties under that Article. Moreover, a President's communications and activities encompass a vastly wider range of sensitive material than would be true of any "ordinary individual." It is therefore necessary in the public interest to afford Presidential confidentiality the greatest protection consistent with the fair administration of justice. The need for confidentiality even as to idle conversations with associates in which casual reference might be made concerning political leaders within the country or foreign statesmen is too obvious to call for further treatment. We have no doubt that the District Judge will at all times accord to Presidential records [a] high degree of deference * * * and will discharge his responsibility to see to it that until released to the Special Prosecutor no *in camera* material is revealed to anyone. This burden applies with even greater force to excised material; once the decision is made to excise, the material is restored to its privileged status and should be returned under seal to its lawful custodian.

JUSTICE REHNQUIST took no part in the consideration or decision of these cases.

NOTES ON EXECUTIVE PRIVILEGES
AND THE NIXON TAPES CASE

1. *Why Should This Issue Be Resolved by the Court?* There may be something to President Nixon's argument that the Court should have stayed out of this controversy. Essentially, the case involved the creeping paralysis of Nixon's Administration. The Senate Select Committee that had publicized the Watergate affair, the House Judiciary Committee conducting the impeachment inquiry, and the Special Prosecutor all had access to the public documents and were interested in obtaining the subpoenaed transcripts. The President's refusal to release the tapes was of central concern in the impeachment proceedings, and the Nixon Tapes Case seems like a classic instance where the remedy for presidential recalcitrance is the political, and not judicial, process.

On July 27 (two days after the Supreme Court's decision), the House Judiciary Committee voted its first article of impeachment, charging the President with obstruction of justice. On July 29, it adopted a second article, charging the President with abuse of power. On July 30, it adopted a third article of impeachment, charging the President with willful disobedience of subpoenas issued by the Committee. The President released transcripts of the tapes to the public. The transcripts contained the smoking guns linking the President to the Watergate cover-up. President Nixon resigned on August 9. Was the Supreme Court's decision, in the midst of the impeachment process, appropriate?[a]

2. *Why Does the President Enjoy Any Executive Privilege?* One of the most striking things about the Chief Justice's opinion is its dismissive attitude toward the Special Prosecutor's argument that there is no constitutional basis for executive privilege. After all, the Speech or Debate Clause, Art. I, § 6, expressly protects Members of Congress against being "questioned" about their legislative activities. Why was there no similar privilege set out in Article II? The Court assumes that such a privilege is relevant and appropriate to the grants of power made to the President. How is that? Would the President not be able to execute the laws if the President had no privilege against testifying about such activities?[b]

Moreover, history and tradition weigh against the Court's casual treatment of the argument. In Aaron Burr's treason trial in 1807, Chief Justice Marshall (sitting as a circuit judge) ruled that President Jefferson was subject to a subpoena to testify and produce documents relating to presidential activities. In 1818, President Monroe was served with a subpoena to testify about his

---

a. See Gerald Gunther, *Judicial Hegemony and Legislative Autonomy: The* Nixon *Case and the Impeachment Process*, 22 UCLA L. Rev. 30 (1974) (not appropriate). Useful sources for the events leading up to President Nixon's resignation include Carl Bernstein & Robert Woodward, *All the President's Men* (1974); Ken Gormley, *Archibald Cox: Conscience of a Nation* (1997).

b. Compare Raoul Berger, *Executive Privilege: A Constitutional Myth* (1974), and Norman Dorsen & John Shattuck, *Executive Privilege, the Congress and the Courts*, 35 Ohio St. L.J. 1 (1974) (skeptical of the need for executive immunity), with Akhil Amar & Neal Katyal, *Executive Privileges and Immunities: The* Nixon *and* Clinton *Cases*, 108 Harv. L. Rev. 701 (1995) (big fans).

appointment of Dr. William Barton for a position at the Philadelphia naval hospital. Attorney General William Wirt advised the President that he could be subpoenaed, and the President offered to give his testimony by deposition or (as was ultimately done) by interrogatories. In light of this historical evidence, why should the President have a constitutional privilege against testifying?

3. *Why Is Executive Privilege Not Absolute?* If there is a constitutionally mandated executive privilege, why is it not absolute, at least as to presidential conversations pertinent to the President's executive duties? Compare other evidentiary privileges: The Fifth Amendment's privilege against self-incrimination is not subject to a balancing test to determine its applicability. If a statement might tend to incriminate you, you have an absolute right not to make it. The rationale is as follows: The purpose of evidentiary privileges is to assure complete and free conversations society wants to encourage (client to counsel, patient to doctor, the President to top advisers). To assure the interlocutors of completely candid discourse, society guarantees that the information will not turn up in trial and cannot be compelled by the government. Hence, the privilege must be absolute. Since the President's conversations with advisers are, according to the Court and received wisdom, so very important to the nation, doesn't this rationale apply with special force?

And what about the Court's "balancing" act? How can the Court balance executive privilege against other interests? Is executive privilege as weighty as the defendants' rights to fair trial? Why can't one's privilege against self-incrimination also be balanced away? The more one engages in this sort of balancing, the more the Court may begin to look like a legislature.[c]

PROBLEM 8-3
EXECUTIVE PRIVILEGE AND CONGRESSIONAL
INVESTIGATION OF U.S. ATTORNEY DISCHARGES

The Nixon Tapes Case involved a criminal trial proceeding, where the private interest in obtaining presidential materials was particularly strong. Presidents since Nixon have not often invoked executive privilege; most of the invocations have been to prevent congressional committees from examining presidential advisory documents.[d] The Supreme Court has affirmed that Congress has oversight authority "to enable it efficiently to exercise a legislative

---

c. See T. Alexander Aleinikoff, *Constitutional Law in the Age of Balancing*, 96 Yale L.J. 943 (1987).

d. Executive privilege was invoked by President Ford 1 time (against Congress), Carter 1 time (against Congress), President Reagan 3 times (all against Congress), first President Bush 1 time (against Congress), President Clinton 14 times (5 times against Congress), and the second President Bush 3 times (2 against Congress). See CRS Report for Congress: Morton Rosenberg, *Presidential Claims of Executive Privilege: History, Law, Practice and Recent Developments* appendix (Updated April 16, 2008), drawing from and supplementing Mark Rozelle, *Executive Privilege, Presidential Powers, Secrecy, and Accountability* (2d ed. 2002). For an excellent case study of a Reagan era investigation of the EPA, see Peter Shane, *Legal Disagreement and Negotiation in a Government of Laws: The Case of Executive Privilege Claims Against Congress*, 71 Minn. L. Rev. 461 (1987).

function belonging to it under the Constitution." *McGrain v. Daugherty*, 273 U.S. 135, 160 (1927); accord, *Watkins v. United States*, 354 U.S. 178 (1957).

The executive branch has developed a common law of privilege, partly codified in OLC opinion. See Rosenberg, *Presidential Claims of Executive Privilege*, 10-16. The President asserts executive privilege in three areas: (1) state secrets involving foreign and military affairs; (2) law enforcement investigations; and (3) confidential information that reveals the executive's "deliberative process." The Clinton Administration, the most aggressive in invoking executive privilege, claimed it for *any* communications within the White House or between the White House and agencies and departments. Generally, however, post-Nixon Presidents (including Clinton) have said they will not invoke privilege to block congressional inquiries into fraud, corruption, or other illegal or unethical conduct within the executive branch. *Id.*, 13-14. All post-Nixon Administrations have worked out most executive privilege disputes involving Congress informally. But sometimes negotiation does not work.

In 2007, a House committee investigated Attorney General Alberto Gonzalez's discharge of several U.S. Attorneys based upon allegations that the discharges were efforts to discipline U.S. Attorneys who did not follow a White House political agenda, including prosecuting Democrats and not Republicans. The committee issued subpoenas to several White House officials, including Chief of Staff Joshua Bolten and former White House Counsel Harriet Miers, to produce relevant documents, including communications (1) internal to the White House; (2) between White House officials and persons outside the executive branch; and (3) between White House and DOJ officials.

On June 27, 2007, the White House invoked executive privilege as to these documents, and Bolten/Miers subsequently declined to testify for these reasons. Upon the recommendation of the committee, the House voted to subpoena the witnesses and their documents. On March 10, 2008, the House Counsel filed an action for declaratory judgment and injunction for production of documents against Miers and Bolten. If you were a judge, how would you rule? Jot down your thoughts and then review the following document.

Letter from Acting Attorney General Paul Clement to The President, June 27, 2007. The letter lays out the objections to the Bolten/Miers documents. Our excerpts will focus on the internal White House communications, but the Clement analysis is similar for the other categories. "Among other things, these communications discuss the wisdom of such a proposal, specific U.S. Attorneys who could be removed, potential replacement candidates, and possible responses to congressional and media inquiries about the dismissals. These types of internal deliberations among White House officials fall squarely within the scope of executive privilege." Cites are to *Nixon*, D.C. Circuit authority, and previous presidential assertions of executive privilege.

"Under D.C. Circuit precedent, a congressional committee may not overcome an assertion of executive privilege unless it establishes that the documents and information are 'demonstrably critical to the responsible fulfillment of the Committee's functions.' *Senate Select Comm. on Presidential Campaign Activities v. Nixon*, 498 F.2d 725, 731 (D.C. Cir. 1974) (en banc).

And those functions must be in furtherance of Congress's legitimate legislative responsibilities. *McGrain.*

"As a threshold matter, it is not at all clear that internal White House communications about the possible dismissal and replacement of U.S. Attorneys fall within the scope of *McGrain* and its progeny. The Supreme Court has held that Congress's oversight powers do not reach 'matters which are within the exclusive province of one of the other branches of the Government." *Barenblatt v. United States,* 360 U.S. 109, 112 (1959). The Senate has the authority to approve or reject the appointment of officers whose appointment by law requires the advice and consent of the Senate (which has been the case for U.S. Attorneys since the founding of the Republic), but it is for the President to decide whom to nominate to such positions and whether to remove such officers once appointed. [*Public Citizen v. Department of Justice,* 491 U.S. 440, 483 (1989) (Kennedy, J., concurring in the judgment) (Congress cannot impose reporting requirements on the President's decision whom to nominate as judges).] Consequently, there is reason to question whether Congress has oversight authority to investigate deliberations by White House officials concerning proposals to dismiss and replace U.S. Attorneys, because such deliberations necessarily relate to the potential exercise by the President of an authority assigned to him alone."

The Acting Attorney General also opined that the committee had not shown a genuine need for the documents sufficient to override the executive privilege claim. Under *Senate Select Committee,* Congress must "point[] to . . .specific legislative decisions that cannot responsibly be made without access to [privileged] materials." DOJ had already turned over 8500 pages of documents relating to its own deliberations concerning the U.S. Attorney resignations.[e] Cf. *History of Refusals by Executive Branch Officials to Provide Information Demanded by Congress,* 6 Op. O.L.C. 751, 758-59, 767 (1982) (refusals by nineteenth-century Presidents to provide *any* information relating to decisions to remove executive branch officials, including a U.S. Attorney in one case).

"In a letter accompanying the subpoenas, the House Committee references the alleged 'written misstatements' and 'false statements' provided by the Department [of Justice] to the Committees about the U.S. Attorney dismissals. * * * This interest does not, however, justify the Committees' demand for White House documents and information about the U.S. Attorney resignations. Officials in the Department, not officials in the White House, presented the challenged statements, and as noted, the Department has provided unprecedented information to Congress concerning, *inter alia,* the process that led to the Department's statements. * * *"

---

e. *In re Sealed Case (Espy),* 121 F.3d 729 (D.C. Cir. 1997), ruled that departmental deliberations were protected only by a common law deliberative process privilege (not the constitutional privilege) that "disappears altogether when there is any reason to believe government misconduct has occurred." *Judicial Watch, Inc. v. Department of Justice,* 365 F.3d 1108 (D.C. 2004), extended that analysis to require disclosure of departmental documents to a congressional committee investigating presidential abuse of the pardon power. Only departmental documents "solicited and received" by the President are protected by constitutional executive privilege."

Nixon v. Administrator of General Services, 433 U.S. 425 (1977). The Presidential Recordings and Materials Preservation Act directed the Administrator of General Services (an executive official) to take possession of former President Nixon's presidential papers and tape recordings, screen them for personal and private materials (to be returned to the former President), and determine which of the retained materials should be made available to the public. The Court rejected the former President's executive privilege challenge to the law. **Justice Brennan**'s opinion for the Court invoked the "pragmatic, flexible approach" to separation of powers "expressly affirmed" in the Nixon Tapes Case, and which the Court characterized as "essentially embrac[ing] Mr. Justice Jackson's view" in the Steel Seizure Case. The Court agreed that the seizure of the presidential papers "would adversely affect the ability of future Presidents to obtain the candid advice necessary for effective decisionmaking" but ruled that the seizure would not be "unduly disruptive," that is, would not materially interfere with the President's ability to accomplish the "constitutionally assigned functions" of the office. Such a "limited intrusion into executive confidentiality" was justified by the "substantial public interest" in restoring "public confidence in our political processes by preserving the materials as a source for facilitating a full airing of the events leading to [President Nixon's] resignation."

Justice Rehnquist (who did not participate in the Nixon Tapes Case) dissented on the ground that the Act was a serious intrusion into the President's assurance of freely flowing information in executive decisionmaking and that separation of powers precludes balancing away such intrusions based upon the Court's "potpourri of reasons" why the Act represents good policy. Moreover, Rehnquist argued that the Court's willingness to balance away core powers was starkly inconsistent with the formalist approach in the Steel Seizure Case. "Surely if ever there were a case for 'balancing,' and giving weight to the asserted 'national interest' to sustain government action, it was in [the Steel Seizure Case]." **Chief Justice Burger** also dissented on separation of powers grounds: The statute was "an exercise of executive — not legislative — power by the Legislative Branch," inconsistent with the Steel Seizure majority, and it constituted a "sweeping modification of the constitutional privilege and historical practice of confidentiality of every Chief Executive since 1789," inconsistent with the Steel Seizure dissent as well as majority.

Nixon v. Fitzgerald, 457 U.S. 731 (1982). The Court, by a five-to-four vote, applied the Nixon Tapes Case balancing approach to hold former President Nixon absolutely immune from a civil damages lawsuit filed by a Defense Department whistleblower who was allegedly discharged by the President because of what Nixon considered his disloyalty. **Justice Powell**'s opinion for the Court interpreted Article II to assign to the President uniquely important discretionary decisionmaking that would be impaired by allowing his decisions to be second-guessed in damage lawsuits against him individually; decisions such as the Steel Seizure one could still, of course, be challenged in lawsuits for injunctive relief. Justice Powell also found support in the original understanding at the Philadelphia Convention: Senator Maclay recorded the views of John Adams and Oliver Ellsworth (key Framers) that "'the President, personally, was not subject to any process whatever,'" as such process "'would . . . put it in the power of a common justice to exercise any authority over him and stop the whole machine of Government.'" Likewise, Justice Joseph Story's constitutional commentary reasoned in 1833 that the President "'cannot be liable to arrest, imprisonment, or detention, while he is in the discharge of the duties of his office; and for this purpose his person must be deemed, in civil cases at least, to possess an official inviolability.'" Because civil lawsuits could "distract the President from his public duties, to the detriment of not only the President and his office but also the Nation that the Presidency was designed to serve," the Court found the individual interest in remedy insufficient to justify a civil lawsuit against the President for acts within his official responsibilities. Political remedies, including actual or threatened impeachment, were a sufficient deterrent for presidential misconduct.

The opinion of the Court was ambiguous as to whether the President's immunity was grounded in constitutional common law and, therefore, could be stripped by Congress. **Chief Justice Burger**'s concurring opinion argued that constitutional separation of powers requires the immunity, which, therefore, cannot be taken away.

Justice White wrote one of the most passionate dissents of his career, arguing that the Court's grant of absolute immunity to former President Nixon was inconsistent with the more limited immunity given Members of Congress only for their legislative acts in the Speech and Debate Clause, Art. I, § 6, e.g., *United States v. Brewster*, 408 U.S. 501 (1972) (Senator can be prosecuted for taking bribes); with the limited immunity accorded members of the President's Cabinet in *Butz v. Economou*, 438 U.S. 478 (1978); and with the rule of law articulated in *Marbury v. Madison* (Chapter 2, § 2A). Justice White subjected the historical materials to intense scrutiny and found no evidence sufficient to displace the normal presumption that every citizen is subject to the rule of law. As the President has been repeatedly held amenable to judicial process and even under the Court's analysis subject to criminal prosecution, Justice White found no justification, even under a balancing approach, for carving out damages cases for special immunity.

———

Clinton v. Jones, 520 U.S. 681 (1997). A unanimous Court rejected President Clinton's claim that a President could invoke *Fitzgerald* immunity to claims that arose before the President took office. Although she brought the lawsuit during Clinton's presidency, Paula Jones alleged that Clinton sexually harassed her when he was governor of Arkansas. The President maintained that the uniqueness of his office, recognized in *Fitzgerald*, demands that he be free of damage lawsuits during his term.

Justice Stevens' opinion for the Court accepted the premise of the President's argument but rejected its conclusion. The core concern of constitutional separation of powers is that one branch of government not usurp the powers or assume the responsibilities of another branch. "[I]n this case there is no suggestion that the Federal Judiciary is being asked to perform any function that might in some way be described as 'executive.' [Jones] is merely asking the courts to exercise their core Article III jurisdiction to decide cases and controversies. Whatever the outcome of this case, there is no possibility that the decision will curtail the scope of the official powers of the Executive Branch. The litigation of questions that relate entirely to the unofficial conduct of the individual who happens to be the President poses no perceptible risk of misallocation of either judicial power or executive power."

Justice Stevens recognized some force to the President's functional argument, that allowing the lawsuit to proceed would impair the President in the performance of his duties. Justice Stevens found little reason to believe that the lawsuit, and the prospect of similar ones in the future, would actually distract the President. (In American history, only three Presidents had been subject to such private actions.) In any event, the impairment claimed by the President was not constitutionally weighty enough to outweigh the judiciary's traditional Article III duties, for two related reasons.

"First, we have long held that when the President takes official action, the Court has the authority to determine whether he has acted within the law. Perhaps the most dramatic example of such a case is our holding that President Truman exceeded his constitutional authority when he issued an order directing the Secretary of Commerce to take possession of and operate most of the Nation's steel mills in order to avert a national catastrophe. *Youngstown.* Despite the serious impact of that decision on the ability of the Executive Branch to accomplish its assigned mission, and the substantial time that the President must necessarily have devoted to the matter as a result of judicial involvement, we exercised our Article III jurisdiction to decide whether his official conduct conformed to the law. * * *

"Second, it is also settled that the President is subject to judicial process in appropriate circumstances. Although Thomas Jefferson apparently thought otherwise, Chief Justice Marshall, when presiding in the treason trial of Aaron Burr, ruled that a subpoena *duces tecum* could be directed to the President. *United States v. Burr*, 25 F. Cas. 30 (No. 14,692d) (C.C.Va. 1807). We unequivocally and emphatically endorsed Marshall's position when we held that President Nixon was obligated to comply with a subpoena commanding him to produce certain tape recordings of his conversations with his aides. *United States v. Nixon.*" Justice Stevens noted several other instances where Presidents had responded to court orders requiring testimony, including two cases where President Clinton agreed to give video testimony.

"In sum, '[i]t is settled law that the separation-of-powers doctrine does not bar every exercise of jurisdiction over the President of the United States.' *Fitzgerald.* If the Judiciary may severely burden the Executive Branch by reviewing the legality of the President's official conduct, and if it may direct appropriate process to the President himself, it must follow that the federal courts have power to determine the legality of his unofficial conduct. The burden on the President's time and energy that is a mere by-product of such review surely cannot be considered as onerous as the direct burden imposed by judicial review and the occasional invalidation of his official actions. We therefore hold that the doctrine of separation of powers does not require federal courts to stay all private actions against the President until he leaves office."

The reasons for rejecting such a categorical rule also counseled against a constitutional requirement that the case be stayed during the President's term of office, but Justice Stevens allowed the trial judge substantial discretion. " '[E]specially in cases of extraordinary public moment, [a plaintiff] may be required to submit to delay not immoderate in extent and not oppressive in its consequences if the public welfare or convenience will thereby be promoted.' Although we have rejected the argument that the potential burdens on the President violate separation of powers principles, those burdens are appropriate matters for the District Court to evaluate in its management of the case. The high respect that is owed to the office of the Chief Executive, though not justifying a rule of categorical immunity, is a matter that should inform the conduct of the entire proceeding, including the timing and scope of discovery."

Although viewing the future burdens on the President as more substantial and constitutionally noteworthy, **Justice Breyer** concurred in the judgment.

NOTES ON THE PRESIDENTIAL IMMUNITY CASES

1. *Reconciling the Cases?* Justice Breyer's separate opinion in *Jones* argued that the Court's analysis was inconsistent with the reasoning of *Fitzgerald*. Justice Stevens responded that *Fitzgerald* was distinguishable, as it involved a President's official conduct during his presidency, not conduct before he attained that office. But *Fitzgerald*'s sweeping *claim immunity* deprived a plaintiff of his cause of action altogether, while *Jones' temporal immunity* would only have postponed a plaintiff's opportunity for her day in court.[f] Moreover, *Fitzgerald* involved a case that arose after the President left office, and therefore would not have distracted a sitting President, while *Jones* involved a President busily working away in the Oval Office, actually much more distracted from presidential duties by the lawsuit. Most important, by allowing a lawsuit against a sitting President for personal misdeeds to go forward, the Court was empowering the President's political opponents and perhaps needlessly injecting the federal courts into politics.[g] These ideas turn Stevens' distinction on its head: If either President should have gotten a break due to the nature of the office, it should have been sitting President Clinton, who would ultimately have faced his accuser under a temporal immunity, and not former President Nixon, who was freed completely by a claim immunity.

2. *The Ambiguous Role of Original Understanding.* Both Justice Breyer and the *Fitzgerald* majority invoked Justice Story's idea that the President "cannot be liable to arrest, imprisonment, or detention, while he is in the discharge of the duties of his office; and for this purpose his person must be deemed, in civil cases at least, to possess an official inviolability." 3 Joseph Story, *Commentaries on the Constitution of the United States* § 1563, at 418-19 (1833). Note that

---

f. See Akhil Amar & Neal Katyal, *Executive Privileges and Immunities: The* Nixon *and* Clinton *Cases*, 108 Harv. L. Rev. 701 (1995).

g. See Victoria Nourse, *The Vertical Separation of Powers*, 49 Duke L.J. 749, 768-72 (1999).

Story's words support only the temporal immunity involved in *Jones* (no lawsuits while the President is in office), but not the claim immunity involved in *Fitzgerald* (no claim, ever). Amar & Katyal, *Executive Privileges,* 108 Harv. L. Rev. at 715-18, argue that the same point can be made for the statements by Framers Oliver Ellsworth and John Adams, if you read them in context. Should both *Fitzgerald* and *Jones* be overruled?

Justice Stevens' most telling historical argument for rejecting a temporal immunity (made in a section of the opinion we omitted) was James Wilson's response at Pennsylvania's ratifying convention to charges that the President was a king-in-waiting. Wilson responded that the President is "placed high," but that "not a single privilege is annexed to his character; far from being above the laws, he is amenable to them in his private character as a citizen, and in his public character by impeachment." 2 Elliott, *Debates on the Federal Constitution* 480 (2d ed. 1863). If Wilson's statement is representative of the Framers' sentiments, does that confirm that *Fitzgerald* was wrongly decided? Should the Court revisit its dicta in *United States v. Nixon*, which found an executive privilege for communications within the Oval Office?

3. *Court-Created Immunities, Generally.* The only immunity from judicial process assured in the Constitution is that for Members of Congress in the Speech or Debate Clause, Art. I, § 6. All the other immunities have been created by the Supreme Court, essentially as constitutional common law — inspired by constitutional values but possibly subject to congressional override. In addition to the absolute immunity of the President and the qualified immunity of Cabinet members and other national executive officials created in *Butz v. Economou*, the Supreme Court has granted absolute immunity from private damage actions to federal judges, *Bradley v. Fisher*, 13 Wall. 335 (1872). All of these immunities, except for those in the Speech or Debate Clause, are creations of judicial policymaking. The maxim *inclusio unius est exclusio alterius* (including one thing in the text suggests the exclusion of all others) augurs against their being constitutional, and there is little if any support for them in the discussions surrounding the adoption of the Constitution. (Judicial immunity might be supported by reference to common law understandings in 1789. Compare the Court's elevation of the states' common law immunity to constitutional principle in Chapter 7, § 4). On the other hand, the functions of the various offices might be severely compromised without such immunities.

The Court's policymaking has been even more open in decisions construing 42 U.S.C. § 1983 (damages action against state officials for violating federal constitutional and statutory rights) to include various immunities for state legislators, *Tenney v. Brandlove*, 341 U.S. 367 (1951) (absolute); state judges, *Pierson v. Ray*, 386 U.S. 547 (1967) (absolute); state executive officials, *Scheuer v. Rhodes*, 416 U.S. 232 (1974) (qualified, for most); state prosecutors, *Imbler v. Pachtman*, 424 U.S. 409 (1976) (absolute for some functions, qualified for others).

NOTE ON CONGRESS'S IMPEACHMENT POWER: THE CASE OF WILLIAM JEFFERSON CLINTON

The President did indeed land in political hot water because the Court permitted *Jones v. Clinton* to proceed. During his deposition in the case, the President allegedly lied in response to a question whether he had "sex" with a subordinate federal government employee, Monica Lewinsky. Independent Counsel Kenneth Starr investigated this matter as part of his general inquiry of alleged improprieties on the part of that President and reported his evidence and findings to Congress. Under its authority vested by Article I, § 2, cl. 5, the House of Representatives initiated impeachment proceedings against the President and voted several articles of impeachment. There were constitutional issues involved in President Clinton's impeachment by the House and trial by the Senate. The most interesting issue was what kinds of misconduct would justify impeachment (by the House) and removal from office (by the Senate).

Article II, § 4 specifies that the President can be removed from office for "Treason, Bribery, or other high Crimes or Misdemeanors." Few seriously maintained that the President's adultery and oral sex (long a felonies in the District) constituted a "high Crime or Misdemeanor," but the House of Representatives determined that perjury (the original lie) and obstruction of justice (continuing to cover up the lie) did fall into those categories. Were they right? As a textual matter, one would expect an impeachable crime or misdemeanor to be something similarly serious as "Treason" or "Bribery." On the one hand, perjury and obstruction of justice are public crimes (like treason and bribery). On the other hand, they do not reflect betrayal of the President's core executive functions in the same way that treason and bribery do.

There was some deliberation as to this matter during the ratification debates.[h] In *Federalist* No. 70, Hamilton explained that the Convention rejected proposals for a committee-like chief executive; there should be one president, fully accountable to the people. He and the other Federalists understood that it was important to distance the President from Anti-Federalist charges of monarchy, and a chief distinction was that the President would be subject to impeachment.[i] In *Federalist* No. 65, he described the grounds for impeachment

---

h. See House Committee on the Judiciary, 93d Cong., 2d Sess., *Constitutional Grounds for Presidential Impeachment* (Report by the Staff of the Impeachment Inquiry [for President Nixon] Feb. 1974), confirmed and elaborated by House Committee on the Judiciary, 105th Cong., *Constitutional Grounds for Presidential Impeachment: Modern Precedents* (Report by the Staff of the Impeachment Inquiry [for President Clinton] Nov. 1998); Michael Gerhardt, *The Federal Impeachment Process: A Constitutional and Historical Analysis* (2d ed. 2000).

i. There was little dissent from this idea at the Convention. Early on, the delegates unanimously voted to make the executive removable for "malpractice or neglect of duty." In debate, Madison defended impeachment as "indispensable" to defend the community against "the incapacity, negligence or perfidy of the chief magistrate." The most serious argument against including the Impeachment Clause was Charles Pinckney's concern that the legislature would wield impeachment "as a rod over the Executive and by that means effectually destroy his independence." The Impeachment Clause was later rewritten to make the President removable for "treason and bribery." George Mason proposed adding "maladministration," but Madison objected that such a vague term would leave the President at the mercy of a politically hostile Senate. Mason withdrew that language

as "those offences which derive from the misconduct of public men, in other words, from the abuse or violation of some public trust. They are of a nature which may with peculiar propriety be denominated POLITICAL as they relate chiefly to injuries done immediately to the society itself." At the Virginia Convention, Edmond Randolph asserted that the President could not be impeached for mere errors of judgment. At the North Carolina Convention, James Iredell suggested that the President could be impeached not just for bribery, but also for inducing the Senate to go along with a foreign relations matter based upon presidential misrepresentations. (On the ratification discussions, see 1974 Judiciary Comm. Report 13-17.)

Also potentially relevant to this issue were the English parliamentary standards for impeachment, which were the linguistic and probable policy basis for "high Crimes and Misdemeanors" in the Impeachment Clause. The kinds of executive misconduct Parliament invoked included misappropriation of funds, abuse of official power, neglect of duty, encroachment on Parliament's prerogatives, and betrayal of public trust (1974 Judiciary Comm. Report 4-7). By the time President Clinton was impeached, the House had impeached one previous President, one cabinet officer, one Senator, and 13 federal judges (including Supreme Court Justice Chase). The conduct the House had charged fell into three broad categories: "(1) exceeding the constitutional bounds of the powers of the office in derogation of the powers of another branch of government; (2) behaving in a manner grossly incompatible with the proper function and purpose of the office; and (3) employing the power of the office for an improper purpose or for personal gain." (*Id.* at 18; see also 1998 Judiciary Comm. Report 4-14 (post-1974 impeachments of three federal judges included charges of perjury and making false statements in the course of a criminal investigation, filing false income tax returns, and bribery).)

Under these criteria, should President Clinton have been impeached if House members believed that he committed perjury during his deposition? Should the Senate have convicted?[j] In the end, the evenly balanced Senate vote came nowhere close to the two-thirds majority needed to remove the President from office. Did the impeachment exercise contribute to accountable governance? Did it make "good" constitutional law?

SECTION 2. ISSUES OF LEGISLATIVE OVERREACHING

The Framers of the Constitution and their opponents, the Anti-Federalists, felt that Congress, rather than the President, posed the greatest danger to liberty.

---

and substituted "high crimes and misdemeanors agst. the state," which was adopted, 8-3.

j. The Senate trial raised another interesting issue: What burden of proof did the House Managers carry in their prosecution of Clinton before the Senate? The managers claimed the Senate should have convicted if persuaded by a preponderance of the evidence, the standard in civil cases. The President's counsel claimed the burden was beyond a reasonable doubt, the standard for criminal cases. As to this issue, what valence would you give the requirement of Article I, § 3, cl. 6 that conviction should require the assent of two-thirds of the Senate?

Hence Congress alone among the three branches is fragmented into two equal bodies (Art. I, § 7), the better to prevent legislative usurpation by slowing down the Leviathan. Separation of powers jurisprudence, of the sort articulated in the Steel Seizure Case, is naturally concerned with direct congressional attacks on the President's exercise of his "executive Power" (Part B) and the Supreme Court's exercise of its "judicial Power" (Part C), but in the modern administrative state perhaps the biggest problem has been Congress' tendency to delegate broad lawmaking powers, often with strings attached (Part A). Although the Supreme Court says it has abandoned serious effort to enforce the *nondelegation doctrine* (Congress cannot delegate lawmaking power without clear standards as to the rules to be developed), the Court has indirectly discouraged such delegation by cutting some of the strings, including the legislative veto and the vesting of enforcement discretion in congressionally controlled agents.

A. "EXCESSIVE" CONGRESSIONAL DELEGATIONS AND THE ARTICLE I, SECTION 7 STRUCTURE FOR LAWMAKING

Operating within the framework of state common law, the Framers did not anticipate a great deal of legislating by Congress, but federal statutory law has become the norm, increasingly, since the Civil War. This has posed dilemmas for Members of Congress, dilemmas which can be and usually are resolved by delegation of some and often many conflictual issues to other government organs. The traditional explanation for delegation is legislative uncertainty and the availability of administrative expertise.[a] Congress often is called upon to solve problems for which there is no clear solution, or for which the details cannot be surmised. Delegation to a group of expert administrators allows Congress to address the problem, but to allow for the details of the solution to be worked out by people who know what they are doing and who can respond to new information about the problem.

Delegation can also be explained as a consequence of the rational operation of the legislative process.[b] Individual legislators risk fragile political support every time they take policy positions controversial within their districts. Presidents and governors often fall victim to this phenomenon of eroding support, which drives them from office with some regularity. Members of Congress have been better able to avoid such disastrous erosions of popularity, typically by focusing on issues about which their constituents agree and, for conflictual issues, by avoidance, compromise, and delegation of the controversial details to someone else, especially executive departments or independent agencies. The impulse to delegate is reinforced by the difficult processes of lawmaking, whereby numerous veto points (committees, negative chamber vote, filibuster, presidential veto) can kill a measure. These processes of lawmaking drive legislators not only toward compromise and moderate rather than radical

---

a. See, e.g., Henry Hart, Jr. & Albert Sacks, *The Legal Process: Basic Problems in the Making and Application of Law* (William Eskridge, Jr. & Philip Frickey eds. 1994 (tent. ed. 1958)).

b. See generally Daniel Farber & Philip Frickey, *Law and Public Choice: A Critical Introduction* (1991); William Eskridge, Jr., *Politics Without Romance: Implications of Public Choice Theory for Statutory Interpretation*, 74 Va. L. Rev. 275 (1988).

changes in the status quo, as the Framers expected, but also toward fudging divisive issues through delegation to other decisionmakers.[c]

The explosion in congressional delegation to agencies raises a host of constitutional problems, three of which we shall focus on here. First, is there any limit on Congress's authority to delegate *lawmaking* power to agencies? Second, Congress has been much more willing to delegate lawmaking power to agencies when it can attach strings to that delegation to allow future Congresses to have some kind of veto or control. Are there constitutional limits to this? Third, Congress has recently been willing to delegate to the President himself the ability to veto specific "lines" of tax and appropriations measures, without having to veto the entire bill. Is this constitutional? The primary constitutional provision relevant to all three of these issues is Article I, Section 7, which sets forth the structure by which Congress creates legislation.[d]

1. *The Decline and Potential Revival of the Nondelegation Doctrine*

A constitutional corollary to the precepts announced in Justice Black's opinion for the Court in the Steel Seizure Case is the *nondelegation doctrine*.[e] That doctrine posits that Congress cannot, consistent with Article I, delegate lawmaking powers to other groups (the executive, agencies, courts, private groups). Congress can delegate gap-filling authority to agencies and judges so long as Congress makes the important policy choices and lays down "an intelligible principle" to which the implementers must conform. *J.W. Hampton, Jr. & Co. v. United States*, 276 U.S. 394, 409 (1928).

In 1935, the Supreme Court used the nondelegation doctrine to invalidate federal legislation in *A.L.A. Schechter Poultry Corp. v. United States*, 295 U.S. 495 (1935). See also *Panama Refining v. Ryan*, 293 U.S. 388 (1935). President Franklin Roosevelt's National Industrial Recovery Act of 1933 authorized committees of management and labor in individual industries to draft codes of "fair competition," subject to Presidential approval, upon a finding that the codes contained no inequitable restrictions upon entry and no attempts to establish a monopoly or suppress small enterprises. The purpose of the statute, enacted during FDR's celebrated first "Hundred Days," was to stabilize wages and prices and restore stability and confidence in American businesses. The statute did so by prohibiting various practices deemed to be "unfair methods of competition."

---

c. Joseph A. Grundfest & A.C. Pritchard, *Statutes with Multiple Personality Disorders: The Value of Ambiguity in Statutory Design and Interpretation*, 54 Stan. L. Rev. 627 (2002) (describing and providing examples of Congress's use of ambiguous language as a means for enacting potentially controversial legislation); Lisa Schultz Bressman, *Chevron*'s Mistake (draft March 2008) (describing "deliberate ambiguities" as congressional delegations to agencies).

d. For constitutional-theoretic introductions, see Bradford Clark, *Separation of Powers as a Safeguard of Federalism*, 79 Tex. L. Rev. 1321 (2001); William Eskridge, Jr. & John Ferejohn, *The Article I, Section 7 Game*, 80 Geo. L.J. 523 (1992).

e. On the nondelegation doctrine as inherent in Article I's structure, see *Wayman v. Southard*, 23 U.S. 1 (1825) (Marshall, C.J.); David Schoenbrod, *Power Without Responsibility: How Congress Abuses the People Through Delegation* 181-89 (1993).

A unanimous Court in *Schechter* invalidated the "live poultry code." Starting with the axiom that "[t]he Congress is not permitted to abdicate or to transfer to others the essential legislative function with which it is thus vested," the Court found insufficient standards to guide the private groups and the President in implementing the statute. The Court was unpersuaded that the "fair competition" language imposed significant guidance and rejected Congress' justification that the delegation was justified by the knowledge and expertise of industry leaders. The Court emphasized the extraordinary nature of delegating regulatory authority to private groups.

Recall that in *Curtiss-Wright* the Supreme Court had no similar problem with broad congressional delegations to the President as to matters of foreign affairs. The New Deal majority that took control of the Court after 1937-38 relegated the nondelegation doctrine to the constitutional dustbin in domestic affairs cases as well. In *Yakus v. United States*, 321 U.S. 414 (1944), the Court upheld the delegation of price controls during wartime to the Price Administrator, with the only direction being that prices "in his judgment will be generally fair and equitable and will effectuate the purposes of this Act." How is this "fair and equitable" standard any more determinate than the "fair competition" standard of the NIRA? *Yakus* found that the statute "sufficiently marks the field within which the Administrator is to act so that it will be known whether he has kept within it in compliance with the legislative will."

The Economic Stabilization Act of 1970, 84 Stat. 799, did not even have this "fair and equitable" standard when it authorized the President "to issue such orders and regulations as he may deem appropriate to stabilize prices, rents, wages, and salaries at levels not less than those prevailing on May 25, 1970." Yet when President Nixon exercised that power to freeze wages and prices in 1971, a three-judge court rejected the nondelegation challenge. *Amalgamated Meat Cutters and Butcher Workmen of North American v. Connally*, 337 F. Supp. 737 (D.D.C. 1971). Judge Harold Leventhal constructed standards to guide presidential action from (1) the Act's legislative history, (2) prior price control statutes such as the one upheld in *Yakus*, and (3) principles implicit in the old "fair and equitable" standard used in prior statutes and mentioned in the legislative history.

The nondelegation doctrine continued to draw support from commentators, e.g., Theodore Lowi, *The End of Liberalism* 298 ff. (2d ed. 1979), long after the Supreme Court more or less abandoned it. Some state courts still enforce their version of the nondelegation doctrine. Hans Linde et al., *Legislative and Administrative Processes* 477-78 (2d ed. 1981), suggest several reasons for this: (1) the more slipshod work done by some state legislatures (with fewer staff), (2) the continuing appeal of substantive due process review at the state level, and (3) the dearth of legislative history in many states to guide administrators and judges to fill in details. A common test followed in the states is that of *Thygesen v. Callahan*, 74 Ill. 2d 404, 406-07, 385 N.E.2d 699, 700 (1979), which states that a legislative delegation is only valid if it sufficiently identifies:

(1) The *persons* and *activities* potentially subject to regulation;

(2) the *harm* sought to be prevented; and

(3) the general *means* intended to be available to the administrator to prevent the identified harm.

During the 1980s there was some support at the Supreme Court level for a revival of the nondelegation doctrine. *Industrial Union Department, AFL-CIO v. American Petroleum Institute*, 448 U.S. 607 (1980) (Rehnquist, J., dissenting); *American Textile Manufacturers Institute, Inc. v. Donovan*, 452 U.S. 490, 543 (1981) (Rehnquist, J., dissenting).

―――――

Mistretta v. United States, 488 U.S. 361 (1989). The Supreme Court unanimously rejected a nondelegation challenge to the Sentencing Reform Act of 1984, 18 U.S.C. § 3551 et seq., and 28 U.S.C. § 991-998, which charged the United States Sentencing Commission with developing Sentencing Guidelines to assure greater predictability and uniformity in the sentences received for violations of federal criminal law. The Sentencing Reform Act was a relatively easy case, because Congress had set forth its goals on the face of the statute and set limits on the Commission — it could not go beyond the sentencing maxima then provided in the criminal code and was directed to use current average sentences as a "starting point" for constructing the sentencing range, and specified seven factors in formulating categories of offenses and eleven factors in formulating categories of defendants that the Commission was to follow, as well as offender characteristics the Commission could not consider (e.g., race and sex) and aggravating (e.g., violence) and mitigating (e.g., cooperation with the government) circumstances the Commission should consider. As **Justice Blackmun**'s opinion for the Court put it, "although Congress granted the Commission substantial discretion in formulating guidelines, in actuality it legislated a full hierarchy of punishment — from near maximum imprisonment, to substantial imprisonment, to some imprisonment, to alternatives — and stipulated the most important offense and offender characteristics to place defendants within these categories."

That level of detail easily satisfied the *J.W. Hampton* test, but Justice Blackmun's opinion, joined by then-Chief Justice Rehnquist, closed its discussion with the extremely lenient approach in *Yakus*:

> It is no objection that the determination of facts and the inferences to be drawn from them in light of the statutory standards and declaration of policy call for the exercise of judgment, and for the formulation of subsidiary administrative policy within the prescribed statutory framework. * * * Only if we could say that there is an absence of standards for the guidance of the Administrator's action, so that it would be impossible in a proper proceeding to ascertain whether the will of Congress has been obeyed, would we be justified in overriding its choice of means for effecting its declared purpose. * * *

In a footnote, Justice Blackmun made clear that the earlier cases invoking the nondelegation doctrine would be narrowly read to apply only in cases where Congress made "crimes of acts never before criminalized [*Panama Refining*] or delegate[d] regulatory power to private individuals [*Schechter*]. In recent years, our application of the nondelegation doctrine principally has been limited to the interpretation of statutory texts, and, more particularly, to giving narrow constructions to statutory delegations that might otherwise be thought to be unconstitutional." **Justice Scalia**, who dissented on other grounds, agreed with the majority that the statute survived the nondelegation attack.

Whitman v. American Trucking Ass'ns, 531 U.S. 457 (2001). This case involved the Clean Air Act's requirement that the EPA promulgate air quality standards as are, in the Administrator's judgment, "requisite to protect the public health." 42 U.S.C. § 7409(b)(1). Notwithstanding *Mistretta,* the D.C. Circuit ruled that this statutory provision provided the EPA with no "intelligible principle" to guide its exercise of authority and therefore fell athwart the nondelegation doctrine. The Supreme Court reversed, finding the quoted language more than enough of a limiting principle to meet the *Hampton* standard for delegations. **Justice Scalia**'s opinion for the Court noted that, "even in sweeping regulatory schemes we have never demanded, as the Court of Appeals did here, that statutes provide a 'determinate criterion' for saying 'how much [of the regulated harm] is too much.'" The opinion reaffirmed *Mistretta*'s admonition that the Court has " 'almost never felt qualified to second-guess Congress regarding the permissible degree of policy judgment that can be left to those executing or applying the law.' "

Concurring opinions debated the theoretical viability of the nondelegation doctrine. **Justice Thomas** indicated that he would, in an appropriate case, consider judicial enforcement of the nondelegation doctrine. Accord, Gary Lawson, *Delegation and Original Meaning*, 88 Va. L. Rev. 327 (2002). In contrast, **Justice Stevens** argued that nothing in Article I limits Congress's authority to delegate lawmaking power to other officials. Accord, Thomas Merrill, *Rethinking Article I, Section 1: From Nondelegation to Exclusive Delegation*, 104 Colum. L. Rev. 2097 (2004).

Justice Scalia's opinion gave concrete meaning to the statutory principle, which the Court interpreted to require the EPA to set air quality standards "not lower or higher than is necessary * * * to protect the public health with an adequate margin of safety." This move suggests that the Court is no longer inclined to enforce the nondelegation doctrine by striking down broadly phrased statutory delegations but might be willing to deploy the nondelegation idea as a principle of statutory construction. Accord, Lisa Schultz Bressman, Schechter Poultry *at the Millennium: A Delegation Doctrine for the Administrative State*, 109 Yale L.J. 1399 (2000).

THE NONDELEGATION DOCTRINE AND CANONS OF STATUTORY INTERPRETATION

As applied by the Supreme Court, federalism and separation of powers are by most accounts "underenforced constitutional norms": the Court does not invoke them to invalidate congressional enactments nearly as often as it might. We have argued that another way to give effect to underenforced constitutional norms is through clear statement rules of statutory interpretation. William Eskridge, Jr. & Philip Frickey, *Quasi-Constitutional Law: Clear Statement Rules as Constitutional Lawmaking*, 45 Vand. L. Rev. 593 (1992). After *Mistretta* and *American Trucking*, the nondelegation doctrine is the most underenforced norm of all. What form might a clear statement approach to the nondelegation doctrine take? Consider some possibilities, and then apply what you know about constitutional law to the following Problem. Hint: Do *not* forget what you learned in previous chapters.

First, the Court might presume that broad and vague delegations contain within them a limiting principle that might be discerned from the legislative history and/or the statutory text. This is Judge Leventhal's idea in *Amalgamated Meat*, and Justice Scalia applied that idea in *American Trucking*. As agencies carry out their statutory duties under vague delegations, the Court will hold them accountable to Congress's purpose and will stop them when they go beyond or against that purpose. See Hart & Sacks, *The Legal Process* (William Eskridge, Jr. & Philip Frickey, eds., 1994) (1958 tent. ed.), which lays out a purpose-based theory of statutory interpretation.

Justice Scalia's opinion in *American Trucking* suggests a second nondelegation canon: the Supreme Court will presume that "Congress does not hide elephants in mouseholes." That is, broad and unspecified delegations of authority to an agency do not entitle it to make big public policy changes; agency "lawmaking" is interstitial, carrying out policies set by Congress rather than instituting new policies on its own. See also *FDA v. Brown & Williamson Corp.*, 529 U.S. 120 (2000) (interpreting food and drug law *not* to allow FDA unsettle a generation of tobacco regulatory policy); *MCI v. AT&T*, 512 U.S. 218 (1994) (presuming against major regulatory change when Congress gave the FCC authority to "modify" statutory requirements).

A third nondelegation-based clear statement rule might be the "avoidance canon": presume that Congress does not intend that agencies press broad delegations so far that they create "serious constitutional difficulties" or problems. See *NLRB v. Catholic Bishop of Chicago*, 440 U.S. 490 (1979) (interpreting NLRA narrowly and rejecting aggressive agency assertion of jurisdiction over religious schools, thereby avoiding delicate constitutional questions that should be decided by Congress). In *Hamdan v. Rumsfeld*, 548 U.S. 557 (2006), the Court interpreted a congressional authorization for the President to create military commissions by importing Geneva Convention protections that avoided possible due process problems with the summary process created by the President.

PROBLEM 8-4
THE ATTORNEY GENERAL'S AUTHORITY TO
PREEMPT STATE AID-IN-DYING LAWS

In 1994, Oregon became the first State to legalize assisted suicide when voters approved a ballot measure enacting the Oregon Death With Dignity Act (ODWDA). ODWDA, which survived a 1997 ballot measure seeking its repeal, exempts from civil or criminal liability state-licensed physicians who, in compliance with the specific safeguards in ODWDA, dispense or prescribe a lethal dose of drugs upon the request of a terminally ill patient.

The drugs Oregon physicians prescribe under ODWDA are regulated under a federal statute, the Controlled Substances Act (CSA). 84 Stat. 1242, as amended, 21 U.S.C. § 801 et seq. Congress classified a host of substances when it enacted the CSA, but the statute permits the Attorney General to add, remove, or reschedule substances, but only after making particular findings; on scientific and medical matters he is required to accept the findings of the Secretary of Health and Human Services (Secretary). These proceedings must be on the record after an opportunity for comment. See 21 U.S.C. A. § 811. The drugs used under the ODWDA are listed in Schedule II and can only be used pursuant to a prescription from a registered physician. 21 U.S.C. § 829(a).

To prevent diversion of controlled substances with medical uses, the CSA regulates the activity of physicians. To issue prescriptions of Schedule II drugs, physicians must "obtain from the Attorney General a registration issued in accordance with the rules and regulations promulgated by him." 21 U.S.C. § 822(a)(2). The Attorney General may deny, suspend, or revoke this registration if, as relevant here, the physician's registration would be "inconsistent with the public interest." § 824(a)(4); § 822(a)(2). When deciding whether a practitioner's registration is in the public interest, the Attorney General "shall" consider:

> "(1) The recommendation of the appropriate State licensing board or professional disciplinary authority.
>
> "(2) The applicant's experience in dispensing, or conducting research with respect to controlled substances.
>
> "(3) The applicant's conviction record under Federal or State laws relating to the manufacture, distribution, or dispensing of controlled substances.
>
> "(4) Compliance with applicable State, Federal, or local laws relating to controlled substances.
>
> "(5) Such other conduct which may threaten the public health and safety." § 823(f).

Also under the CSA: "The Attorney General is authorized to promulgate rules and regulations and to charge reasonable fees relating to the registration and control of the manufacture, distribution, and dispensing of controlled substances and to listed chemicals." 21 U.S.C. § 821. "The Attorney General may promulgate and enforce any rules, regulations, and procedures which he may deem necessary and appropriate for the efficient execution of his functions under this subchapter." 21 U.S.C. § 871(b).

On November 9, 2001, Attorney General John Ashcroft issued a Directive announcing that using controlled substances to assist suicide is not a legitimate medical practice and that dispensing or prescribing them for this purpose is unlawful under the CSA. The Directive was not issued through the notice-and-comment process used for legislative rulemaking, and the Attorney General did not seek input from other executive departments.

Oregon challenges the Attorney General's authority to issue this Directive; Ashcroft maintains that it has been validly issued pursuant to several explicit delegations of authority to him. What are some responses Oregon might make to the latter point? Would the Supreme Court agree? How would Justice Scalia, the Court's biggest critic of excessive delegation, vote in this case? For the debate among the Justices, see *Gonzalez v. Oregon*, 546 U.S. 243, 126 S.Ct. 904 (2006).

2. *The Legislative Veto*

Unchecked by the judiciary, broad congressional delegations to departments and agencies grew like weeds in a vacant lot during and after the New Deal. Yet Congress has been ambivalent about so much delegation and (especially after the 1960s, when divided government became a way of life) sought to exercise greater control over executive and agency enforcement of the broad statutory mandates. A great deal of control is exercised through legislative oversight and appropriations pressure,[f] but the frustrations of oversight during the Nixon Administration stimulated greater interest in the legislative veto. This is a statutory mechanism which renders the initial or continuing implementation of administrative decisions or actions subject to some further form of legislative review or control. Typically, a legislative veto provision of a statute provides that an agency or department must inform a congressional committee of specified actions, that those actions cannot have operative legal effect for a specified period of time, and that they can be nullified by vote of a committee, or of one chamber, or of both chambers of Congress.

The first federal legislative veto was adopted in 1932, over the objections of Attorney General William Mitchell that it was unconstitutional. Between 1932 and 1975, the Supreme Court calculated that 295 legislative vetoes were inserted into 196 different federal statutes (generally over the objections of Presidents or Attorneys General), including 24 statutes between 1932 and 1949, 34 statutes between 1950 and 1959, 49 statutes between 1960 and 1969, and 89 statutes between 1970 and 1975. The use of such vetoes was quickening even more after 1975. See Joseph Cooper, *The Legislative Veto in the 1980s*, in *Congress Reconsidered* 364, 367 (Lawrence Dodd & Bruce Oppenheimer eds. 3d ed. 1985) (counting 208 legislative vetoes between 1932 and 1978, and 78 between 1978 and 1982). Legislative veto provisions were attached to some of our nation's most important legislation after 1970, especially laws involving defense and foreign policy (e.g., the War Powers Resolution, reprinted in Section 1), energy and environmental policy (e.g., the Energy Policy and Conservation Act),

---

f. This sounds wonderful in theory, but at least some political scientists have found oversight disappointing in practice, in part because oversight committees can be captured by the same groups that capture the agencies themselves. E.g., Morris Ogul, *Congressional Oversight: Structures and Incentives*, in *Congress Reconsidered* 317 (Lawrence Dodd & Bruce Oppenheimer eds. 2d ed. 1981).

consumer welfare (e.g., Employee Retirement Income Security Act), and transportation policy (e.g., Regional Rail Reorganization Act of 1973).[g]

State legislatures in the 1970s adopted a similar array of legislative vetoes. The tendency at the state level was to create a committee to advise the legislature, and to suspend operation of agency rules until the legislature could study, and perhaps overturn, them. The states tended to be less ad hoc than Congress, with omnibus veto rules for all state agencies. Consider the following array in the early 1980s:

> No system of legislative supervision of agencies, relying on legislature to pass statutes if agency regulations are to be overturned (11 states).

> Advisory committee to legislature, reviewing agency regulations and making recommendations for legislative action (15 states).

> Advisory committee to legislature, reviewing agency regulations, with the committee's negative evaluation shifting the burden of the regulation's validity in the event of a legal challenge (3 states and model act).

> Legislative committee authorized to suspend the effectiveness of an agency rule pending legislative consideration of a statutory repeal (9 states).

> Two-house veto of agency rules (11 states).

> One-house veto of agency rules (1 state).

L. Harold Levinson, *Legislative and Executive Veto of Rules of Administrative Agencies: Models and Alternatives*, 24 Wm. & Mary L. Rev. 79, 81-83 (1982).

IMMIGRATION & NATURALIZATION SERVICE v. CHADHA
462 U.S. 919, 103 S.Ct. 2764, 77 L.Ed.2d 317 (1983)

CHIEF JUSTICE BURGER delivered the opinion of the Court.

[Jagdish Chadha, an East Indian born in Kenya who held a British passport, was lawfully admitted to the United States on a nonimmigrant student visa. After his visa expired and he was subject to deportation, an immigration judge, acting on behalf of the Attorney General, concluded that Chadha met the statutory grounds for a suspension of deportation: He had resided continuously in the United States for over seven years, was of good moral character, and would suffer "extreme hardship" if deported. Pursuant to the Immigration and Nationality Act, a report of this suspension of deportation was transmitted to Congress. Under § 244(c)(2) of the Act, one chamber of Congress had the authority to invalidate this decision by adopting a resolution to that effect either in the session of Congress in which the report was submitted or in the following session of Congress.]

On December 12, 1975, Representative Eilberg, Chairman of the Judiciary Subcommittee on Immigration, Citizenship, and International Law, introduced

---

g. See Jacob Javits & Joel Klein, *Congressional Oversight and the Legislative Veto: A Constitutional Analysis*, 52 N.Y.U. L. Rev. 455 (1977).

a resolution opposing "the granting of permanent residence in the United States to [six] aliens," including Chadha. The resolution was referred to the House Committee on the Judiciary. On December 16, 1975, the resolution was discharged from further consideration by the House Committee on the Judiciary and submitted to the House of Representatives for a vote. The resolution had not been printed and was not made available to other Members of the House prior to or at the time it was voted on. So far as the record before us shows, the House consideration of the resolution was based on Representative Eilberg's statement from the floor that "[i]t was the feeling of the committee, after reviewing 340 cases, that the aliens contained in the resolution [Chadha and five others] did not meet these statutory requirements, particularly as it relates to hardship; and it is the opinion of the committee that their deportation should not be suspended."   The resolution was passed without debate or recorded vote.[3] Since the House action was pursuant to § 244(c)(2), the resolution was not treated as an Art. I legislative act; it was not submitted to the Senate or presented to the President for his action. [Following the House action, the immigration judge ordered Chadha deported. By the time the controversy made its way to

---

3. It is not at all clear whether the House generally, or Subcommittee Chairman Eilberg in particular, correctly understood the relationship between H. Res. 926 and the Attorney General's decision to suspend Chadha's deportation. Exactly one year previous to the House veto of the Attorney General's decision in this case, Representative Eilberg introduced a similar resolution disapproving the Attorney General's suspension of deportation in the case of six other aliens. H. Res. 1518, 93d Cong., 2d Sess. (1974). The following colloquy occurred on the floor of the House:

"Mr. WYLIE. Mr. Speaker, further reserving the right to object, is this procedure to expedite the ongoing operations of the Department of Justice, as far as these people are concerned. Is it in any way contrary to whatever action the Attorney General has taken on the question of deportation; does the gentleman know?

"Mr. EILBERG. Mr. Speaker, the answer is no to the gentleman's final question. These aliens have been found to be deportable and the Special Inquiry Officer's decision denying suspension of deportation has been reversed by the Board of Immigration Appeals. We are complying with the law since all of these decisions have been referred to us for approval or disapproval, and there are hundreds of cases in this category. In these six cases however, we believe it would be grossly improper to allow these people to acquire the status of permanent resident aliens.

"Mr. WYLIE. In other words, the gentleman has been working with the Attorney General's office?

"Mr. EILBERG. Yes.

"Mr. WYLIE. This bill then is in fact a confirmation of what the Attorney General intends to do?

"Mr. EILBERG. The gentleman is correct insofar as it relates to the determination of deportability which has been made by the Department of Justice in each of these cases.

"Mr. WYLIE. Mr. Speaker, I withdraw my reservation of objection." 120 Cong. Rec. 41412 (1974).

Clearly, this was an obfuscation of the effect of a veto under § 244(c)(2). Such a veto in no way constitutes "a confirmation of what the Attorney General intends to do." To the contrary, such a resolution was meant to overrule and set aside, or "veto," the Attorney General's determination that, in a particular case, cancellation of deportation would be appropriate under the standards set forth in § 244(a)(1).

the Court of Appeals for the Ninth Circuit, the INS had agreed with Chadha and joined his arguments that the House action was unconstitutional. After entertaining briefs amici curiae from both the Senate and the House of Representatives, the Ninth Circuit held that the House action was unconstitutional. The Supreme Court affirmed.]

* * * [T]hat a given law or procedure is efficient, convenient or useful in facilitating functions of the government, standing alone, will not save it if it is contrary to the Constitution. Convenience and efficiency are not the primary objectives — or the hallmarks — of democratic government and our inquiry is sharpened rather than blunted by the fact that Congressional veto provisions are appearing with increasing frequency in statutes which delegate authority to executive and independent agencies * * * .

Explicit and unambiguous provisions of the Constitution prescribe and define the respective functions of the Congress and of the Executive in the legislative process. * * * Article I provides:

> All legislative Powers herein granted shall be vested in a Congress of the United States, which shall consist of a Senate *and* House of Representatives.

Art. I, § 1. (Emphasis added.)

> Every Bill which shall have passed the House of Representatives and the Senate, *shall*, before it becomes a law, be presented to the President of the United States . . .
>
> .

Art. I, § 7, cl. 2. (Emphasis added.)

> Every Order, Resolution, or Vote to which the Concurrence of the Senate and House of Representatives may be necessary (except on a question of Adjournment) *shall be* presented to the President of the United States; and before the Same shall take Effect, *shall be* approved by him, or being disapproved by him, *shall be* repassed by two thirds of the Senate and House of Representatives, according to the Rules and Limitations prescribed in the Case of a Bill.

Art. I, § 7, cl. 3. (Emphasis added.)

These provisions of Art. I are integral parts of the constitutional design for the separation of powers. * * *

The decision to provide the President with a limited and qualified power to nullify proposed legislation by veto was based on the profound conviction of the Framers that the powers conferred on Congress were the powers to be most carefully circumscribed. It is beyond doubt that lawmaking was a power to be shared by both Houses and the President. In *The Federalist* No. 73, Hamilton focused on the President's role in making laws:

> If even no propensity had ever discovered itself in the legislative body to invade the rights of the Executive, the rules of just reasoning and theoretic propriety would of themselves teach us that the one ought not to be left to the mercy of the other, but ought to possess a constitutional and effectual power of self-defense. * * *

The President's role in the lawmaking process also reflects the Framers' careful efforts to check whatever propensity a particular Congress might have to enact oppressive, improvident, or ill-considered measures. The President's veto role in the legislative process was described later during public debate on ratification:

It establishes a salutary check upon the legislative body, calculated to guard the community against the effects of faction, precipitancy, or of any impulse unfriendly to the public good, which may happen to influence a majority of that body. * * * The primary inducement to conferring the power in question upon the Executive is, to enable him to defend himself; the secondary one is to increase the chances in favor of the community against the passing of bad laws, through haste, inadvertence, or design.

The Federalist No. 73, *supra*, Appendix B (A. Hamilton). The Court also has observed that the Presentment Clauses serve the important purpose of assuring that a "national" perspective is grafted on the legislative process: "The President is a representative of the people just as the members of the Senate and of the House are, and it may be, at some times, on some subjects, that the President elected by all the people is rather more representative of them all than are the members of either body of the Legislature whose constituencies are local and not countrywide . . . ."

The bicameral requirement of Art. I, §§ 1, 7, was of scarcely less concern to the Framers than was the Presidential veto and indeed the two concepts are interdependent. By providing that no law could take effect without the concurrence of the prescribed majority of the Members of both Houses, the Framers reemphasized their belief, already remarked upon in connection with the Presentment Clauses, that legislation should not be enacted unless it has been carefully and fully considered by the Nation's elected officials. * * *

Hamilton argued that a Congress comprised of a single House was antithetical to the very purposes of the Constitution. Were the Nation to adopt a Constitution providing for only one legislative organ, he warned:

[W]e shall finally accumulate, in a single body, all the most important prerogatives of sovereignty, and thus entail upon our posterity one of the most execrable forms of government that human infatuation ever contrived. Thus we should create in reality that very tyranny which the adversaries of the new Constitution either are, or affect to be, solicitous to avert.

The Federalist No. 22.

This view was rooted in a general skepticism regarding the fallibility of human nature later commented on by Joseph Story:

Public bodies, like private persons, are occasionally under the dominion of strong passions and excitements; impatient, irritable, and impetuous. . . . If [a legislature] feels no check but its own will, it rarely has the firmness to insist upon holding a question long enough under its own view, to see and mark it in all its bearings and relations on society.

These observations are consistent with what many of the Framers expressed, none more cogently than Madison in pointing up the need to divide and disperse power in order to protect liberty:

In republican government, the legislative authority necessarily predominates. The remedy for this inconveniency is to divide the legislature into different branches; and to render them, by different modes of election and different principles of action, as little connected with each other as the nature of their common functions and their common dependence on the society will admit.

The Federalist No. 51 (sometimes attributed to "Hamilton or Madison" but now generally attributed to Madison).

However familiar, it is useful to recall that apart from their fear that special interests could be favored at the expense of public needs, the Framers were also concerned, although not of one mind, over the apprehensions of the smaller states. Those states feared a commonality of interest among the larger states would work to their disadvantage; representatives of the larger states, on the other hand, were skeptical of a legislature that could pass laws favoring a minority of the people. It need hardly be repeated here that the Great Compromise, under which one House was viewed as representing the people and the other the states, allayed the fears of both the large and small states.

We see therefore that the Framers were acutely conscious that the bicameral requirement and the Presentment Clauses would serve essential constitutional functions. The President's participation in the legislative process was to protect the Executive Branch from Congress and to protect the whole people from improvident laws. The division of the Congress into two distinctive bodies assures that the legislative power would be exercised only after opportunity for full study and debate in separate settings. The President's unilateral veto power, in turn, was limited by the power of two-thirds of both Houses of Congress to overrule a veto thereby precluding final arbitrary action of one person. It emerges clearly that the prescription for legislative action in Art. I, §§ 1, 7, represents the Framers' decision that the legislative power of the Federal Government be exercised in accord with a single, finely wrought and exhaustively considered, procedure.

The Constitution sought to divide the delegated powers of the new Federal Government into three defined categories, Legislative, Executive, and Judicial, to assure, as nearly as possible, that each branch of government would confine itself to its assigned responsibility. The hydraulic pressure inherent within each of the separate Branches to exceed the outer limits of its power, even to accomplish desirable objectives, must be resisted.

* * * When the Executive acts, he presumptively acts in an executive or administrative capacity as defined in Art. II. And when, as here, one House of Congress purports to act, it is presumptively acting within its assigned sphere.

Beginning with its presumption, we must nevertheless establish that the challenged action under § 244(c)(2) is of the kind to which the procedural requirements of Art. I, § 7, apply. Not every action taken by either House is subject to the bicameralism and presentment requirements of Art. I. Whether actions taken by either House are, in law and fact, an exercise of legislative power depends not on their form but upon "whether they contain matter which is properly to be regarded as legislative in its character and effect."

Examination of the action taken here by one House pursuant to § 244(c)(2) reveals that it was essentially legislative in purpose and effect. In purporting to exercise power defined in Art. I, § 8, cl. 4, to "establish an uniform Rule of Naturalization," the House took action that had the purpose and effect of altering the legal rights, duties, and relations of persons, including the Attorney General, Executive Branch officials and Chadha, all outside the Legislative Branch. * * * The one-House veto operated in these cases to overrule the Attorney General and mandate Chadha's deportation; absent the House action, Chadha would remain in the United States. Congress has *acted* and its action has altered Chadha's status.

The legislative character of the one-House veto in these cases is confirmed by the character of the congressional action it supplants. Neither the House of Representatives nor the Senate contends that, absent the veto provision in § 244(c)(2), either of them, or both of them acting together, could effectively require the Attorney General to deport an alien once the Attorney General, in the exercise of legislatively delegated authority,[16] had determined the alien should remain in the United States. Without the challenged provision in § 244(c)(2), this could have been achieved, if at all, only by legislation requiring deportation. * * *

The nature of the decision implemented by the one-House veto in these cases further manifests its legislative character. After long experience with the clumsy, time-consuming private bill procedure, Congress made a deliberate choice to delegate to the Executive Branch, and specifically to the Attorney General, the authority to allow deportable aliens to remain in this country in certain specified circumstances. It is not disputed that this choice to delegate authority is precisely the kind of decision that can be implemented only in accordance with the procedures set out in Art. I. Disagreement with the Attorney General's decision on Chadha's deportation — that is, Congress' decision to deport Chadha — no less than Congress' original choice to delegate to the Attorney General the authority to make that decision, involves determinations of policy that Congress can implement in only one way; bicameral passage followed by presentment to the President. Congress must abide by its delegation of authority until that delegation is legislatively altered or revoked.

---

16. Congress protests that affirming the Court of Appeals in these cases will sanction "lawmaking by the Attorney General." To be sure, some administrative agency action — rulemaking, for example — may resemble "lawmaking." This Court has referred to agency activity as being "quasi-legislative" in character. Clearly, however, "[i]n the framework of our Constitution, the President's power to see that the laws are faithfully executed refutes the idea that he is to be a lawmaker." *Youngstown.* When the Attorney General performs his duties pursuant to § 244, he does not exercise "legislative" power. The bicameral process is not necessary as a check on the Executive's administration of the laws because his administrative activity cannot reach beyond the limits of the statute that created it — a statute duly enacted pursuant to Art. I, §§ 1, 7. The constitutionality of the Attorney General's execution of the authority delegated to him by § 244 involves only a question of delegation doctrine. The courts, when a case or controversy arises, can always "ascertain whether the will of Congress has been obeyed," and can enforce adherence to statutory standards. It is clear, therefore, that the Attorney General acts in his presumptively Art. II capacity when he administers the Immigration and Nationality Act. Executive action under legislatively delegated authority that might resemble "legislative" action in some respects is not subject to the approval of both Houses of Congress and the President for the reason that the Constitution does not so require. That kind of Executive action is always subject to check by the terms of the legislation that authorized it; and if that authority is exceeded it is open to judicial review as well as the power of Congress to modify or revoke the authority entirely. A one-House veto is clearly legislative in both character and effect and is not so checked; the need for the check provided by Art. I, §§ 1, 7, is therefore clear. Congress' authority to delegate portions of its power to administrative agencies provides no support for the argument that Congress can constitutionally control administration of the laws by way of a congressional veto.

Finally, we see that when the Framers intended to authorize either House of Congress to act alone and outside of its prescribed bicameral legislative role, they narrowly and precisely defined the procedure for such action. There are four provisions in the Constitution, explicit and unambiguous, by which one House may act alone with the unreviewable force of law, not subject to the President's veto: [the House's power to initiate impeachments, Art. I, § 2, cl. 5; the Senate's power to conduct impeachment trials, Art. I, § 3, cl. 6; the Senate's power to confirm presidential appointments, Art. II, § 2, cl. 2; and the Senate's power to ratify treaties, Art, II, § 2, cl. 2. Chief Justice Burger concluded that these "narrow, explicit, and separately justified" exceptions to bicameralism and presentment "provide further support for the conclusion that congressional authority is not to be implied."]

The veto authorized by § 244(c)(2) doubtless has been in many respects a convenient shortcut; the "sharing" with the Executive by Congress of its authority over aliens in this manner is, on its face, an appealing compromise. In purely practical terms, it is obviously easier for action to be taken by one House without submission to the President; but it is crystal clear from the records of the Convention, contemporaneous writings and debates, that the Framers ranked other values higher than efficiency. The records of the Convention and debates in the States preceding ratification underscore the common desire to define and limit the exercise of the newly created federal powers affecting the states and the people. There is unmistakable expression of a determination that legislation by the national Congress be a step-by-step, deliberate and deliberative process.

The choices we discern as having been made in the Constitutional Convention impose burdens on governmental processes that often seem clumsy, inefficient, even unworkable, but those hard choices were consciously made by men who had lived under a form of government that permitted arbitrary governmental acts to go unchecked. There is no support in the Constitution or decisions of this Court for the proposition that the cumbersomeness and delays often encountered in complying with explicit constitutional standards may be avoided, either by the Congress or by the President. *See Youngstown.* With all the obvious flaws of delay, untidiness, and potential for abuse, we have not yet found a better way to preserve freedom than by making the exercise of power subject to the carefully crafted restraints spelled out in the Constitution.

[The opinion of **JUSTICE POWELL**, concurring in the judgment, is omitted. Rather than joining an opinion that "apparently will invalidate every use of the legislative veto," Justice Powell opted to decide the case on the ground that "[w]hen Congress finds that a particular person does not satisfy the statutory criteria for permanent residence in the country it has assumed a judicial function in violation of the principle of separation of powers." Justice Powell stressed the Framers' concern about the exercise of unchecked legislative power and noted that the congressional act here was surrounded by none of the traditional procedural protections that accompany adjudication.]

[The dissenting opinion of **JUSTICE REHNQUIST** is also omitted. Justice Rehnquist agreed that the legislative veto was unconstitutional but would not have severed it from the remainder of the law, thereby denying Chadha any relief.]

JUSTICE WHITE, dissenting.

[Justice White first stressed that the decision "sounds the death knell for nearly 200 other statutory provisions in which Congress has reserved a 'legislative veto.' " He then emphasized the utility of the legislative veto in allowing "the President and Congress to resolve major constitutional and policy differences, assur[ing] the accountability of independent regulatory agencies, and preserv[ing] Congress' control over lawmaking."]

The history of the legislative veto also makes clear that it has not been a sword with which Congress has struck out to aggrandize itself at the expense of the other branches — the concerns of Madison and Hamilton. Rather, the veto has been a means of defense, a reservation of ultimate authority necessary if Congress is to fulfill its designated role under Art. I as the Nation's lawmaker. While the President has often objected to particular legislative vetoes, generally those left in the hands of congressional committees, the Executive has more often agreed to legislative review as the price for a broad delegation of authority. To be sure, the President may have preferred unrestricted power, but that could be precisely why Congress thought it essential to retain a check on the exercise of delegated authority. * * *

* * * There is no question but that agency rulemaking is lawmaking in any functional or realistic sense of the term. The Administrative Procedure Act provides that a "rule" is an agency statement "designed to implement, interpret, or prescribe law or policy." When agencies are authorized to prescribe law through substantive rulemaking, the administrator's regulation is not only due deference, but is accorded "legislative effect." These regulations bind courts and officers of the Federal Government, may pre-empt state law, and grant rights to and impose obligations on the public. In sum, they have the force of law.

If Congress may delegate lawmaking power to independent and Executive agencies, it is most difficult to understand Art. I as prohibiting Congress from also reserving a check on legislative power for itself. Absent the veto, the agencies receiving delegations of legislative or quasi-legislative power may issue regulations having the force of law without bicameral approval and without the President's signature. It is thus not apparent why the reservation of a veto over the exercise of that legislative power must be subject to a more exacting test. In both cases, it is enough that the initial statutory authorizations comply with the Art. I requirements. * * *

The central concern of the presentment and bicameralism requirements of Art. I is that when a departure from the legal status quo is undertaken, it is done with the approval of the President and both Houses of Congress — or, in the event of a Presidential veto, a two-thirds majority in both Houses. This interest is fully satisfied by the operation of § 244(c)(2). The President's approval is found in the Attorney General's action in recommending to Congress that the deportation order for a given alien be suspended. The House and the Senate indicate their approval of the Executive's action by not passing a resolution of disapproval within the statutory period. Thus, a change in the legal status quo

— the deportability of the alien — is consummated only with the approval of each of the three relevant actors. The disagreement of any one of the three maintains the alien's pre-existing status: the Executive may choose not to recommend suspension; the House and Senate may each veto the recommendation. The effect on the rights and obligations of the affected individuals and upon the legislative system is precisely the same as if a private bill were introduced but failed to receive the necessary approval. "The President and the two Houses enjoy exactly the same say in what the law is to be as would have been true for each without the presence of the one-House veto, and nothing in the law is changed absent the concurrence of the President and a majority in each House." *Atkins v. United States*, 556 F.2d 1028, 1064 (1977), cert. denied, 434 U.S. 1009 (1978). * * *

NOTES ON *CHADHA* AND THE SUPREME COURT'S NEW DIRECTION IN SEPARATION OF POWERS CASES

1. *Different Visions of the Structure of the Constitution.* The opinions of Chief Justice Burger (for the Court), Justice Powell (concurring), and Justice White (dissenting) offer three different approaches to separation of powers. Justices White and Powell took a functionalist approach to separation of powers similar to that of Justice Jackson in the Steel Seizure Case. Their main concern was that Congress not take over duties given to the executive (Justice White) or the judiciary (Justice Powell). Chief Justice Burger's opinion, on the other hand, took a formalist, categorical approach similar to that of Justice Black in the Steel Seizure Case. Why did out-of-the-closet functionalists like Justices Brennan, Marshall, and Rehnquist join Chief Justice Burger's formalist opinion?

2. *Is* Chadha *Defensible Constitutional Law?* Most legal academics have been underwhelmed by the Chief Justice's reasoning.[h] Among the questions they have raised: Isn't the legislative veto formally consistent with Article I, § 7, insofar as it is just a condition subsequent of a statute validly adopted by both chambers of Congress, with presentment? The Chief Justice's broad definition of what's "legislative" (and his insistence that all of it be done by both chambers of Congress and presented to the President) seems to cover agency rulemaking itself, which if taken seriously would call into question the constitutionality of the administrative state. Congress delegates a lot of apparently "legislative" work to agencies, judges, and other actors, and has done so for decades without a whimper from the Court. Is it too late for the Court to start drawing lines? Once the Court abandoned serious enforcement of the nondelegation doctrine, is it fair to hold Congress to the bicameralism and presentment requirements so strictly?

Laurence Tribe, *The Legislative Veto Decision: A Law by Any Other Name?*, 21 Harv. J. Legis. 7 (1984), suggests that "the only imaginable justification" for

---

h. See Donald Elliott, INS v. Chadha: *The Administrative Constitution, the Constitution, and the Legislative Veto*, 1983 Sup. Ct. Rev. 125; William Eskridge, Jr. & John Ferejohn, *The Article I, Section 7 Game*, 80 Geo. L.J. 523 (1992); Girardeau Spann, *Deconstructing the Legislative Veto*, 68 Minn. L. Rev. 473 (1984); Peter Strauss, *Was There a Baby in the Bathwater?: A Comment on the Supreme Court's Legislative Veto Decision*, 1983 Duke L.J. 789.

the Court's apparent position is that "the legislature can delegate authority to others *but not to itself.*" Professor Tribe finds this position problematic, but there might be textual arguments for it drawn from the Appointments Clause, Art. II, § 2, cl. 2, or the Incompatibility Clause, Art. I, § 6, cl. 2.

3. *The Scope of the Court's Holding — and What Survives.* The Court could have written a narrow opinion in *Chadha*, striking down only legislative vetoes that interfered with adjudicatory proceedings (Justice Powell's position), or that permitted a veto upon the vote of only one house, or that permitted a veto of enforcement decisions made by an executive department and not by an agency. But, the Court's opinion seems applicable to virtually all of the legislative vetoes Congress has enacted. See *Process Gas Consumers Group v. Consumer Energy Council of America*, 463 U.S. 1216 (1983) (summarily affirming invalidation of legislative veto of agency rulemaking); *United States Senate v. FTC*, 463 U.S. 1216 (1983) (summarily affirming invalidation of two-house veto of agency rulemaking). On the other hand, lower courts have ruled that *Chadha* did not invalidate "report-and-wait" or "laying over" provisions, holding off the effective date of an agency action until Congress has an opportunity to review it. *Hechinger v. Metropolitan Washington Airports Auth.*, 36 F.3d 97 (D.C. Cir. 1994); *City of Alexandria v. United States*, 737 F.2d 1022 (Fed. Cir. 1984).

Also surviving *Chadha* are other mechanisms for legislative influence over agency actions: (a) hearings and informal pressure by congressional oversight committees, as well as publicity generated by legislator criticisms; (b) refusal by Congress to appropriate monies to wayward agencies, or to appropriate funds subject to substantive conditions (e.g., that the money will not be spent to carry out specified rules or policies); and (c) informal pressure by appropriations subcommittees and language in their committee reports earmarking funds for certain projects or policies and not for others. Jessica Korn, *The Power of Separation: American Constitutionalism and the Myth of the Legislative Veto* 36-37 (1996), reports that not only did all these practices survive intact, but that they had been more efficacious than the legislative veto all along. Louis Fisher says, in *Legislative Vetoes Enacted After* Chadha (1987), that the legislative veto itself has survived, insisted upon by congressional committees and acquiesced in by money-hungry agencies. So what's to like about a badly reasoned Supreme Court opinion that has not stuck with a body politic determined to perpetuate an unconstitutional practice?

4. *Functional (Public Choice) and Vertical (Popular) Problems with Legislative Vetoes.* While the veto has been defended as a way for Congress to monitor the enforcement of its statutes, it has also been subjected to serious functional criticism.[i] Madison argued in *Federalist* Nos. 10 and 51 (App. 2) that bicameralism and presentment were mechanisms whereby temporary, perhaps factional, majorities would be prevented from enacting unwise legislation.

---

i. See Stanley Brubaker, *Slouching Toward Constitutional Duty: The Legislative Veto & the Delegation of Authority*, 1 Const. Comm. 81 (1984); Eskridge & Ferejohn, *Article I, Section 7 Game, supra.*

Modern public choice theory provides rich support for Madison's insight.[j] The tendency of the legislature to distribute rents to special interest groups can be ameliorated if the groups must push their rents through two different chambers, which have different constituencies, and then must obtain the acquiescence of the President as well. As the costs and delays of obtaining legislation increase, this theory reasons, special interest groups will demand less of it. This phenomenon played itself out in several of the more notorious applications of legislative vetoes. When the FTC in the late 1970s adopted its "lemon rules," applicable to used car sales, used car dealers descended on Washington like locusts on the orchard, and within days procured a one-house veto of the proposed FTC rule. In other instances, of course, the mere threat of a legislative veto could be expected to skew agency policy to accommodate the interests of well-organized groups.[k]

Victoria Nourse, *Toward a New Anatomy of Constitutional Structure*, 56 Stan. L. Rev. 835 (2004), finds *Chadha* an easy case, because its veto represented an institutional power grab that posed threats both to popular majorities and to minorities. The one-chamber veto risked creating an "electoral aristocracy." A small group of people (Representative Eilberg and his subcommittee) basically made immigration policy for the entire country. Now there's always that risk in our complex government, but the bicameralism and presentment requirements are forms that minimize the risk — and the Burger opinion essentially rests upon this notion, not on its artificial idea of what's "legislative." Likewise, the Powell opinion rests upon the converse risk, that people like Chadha will be singled out by some faction in Congress and deprived of an important liberty for no publicly stated, judicially reviewable reason. The Constitution says that Congress cannot adopt bills of attainder (Art. I, § 9, cl. 3); what the House did to Chadha came too close to that, and Powell insisted on the Constitution's structural protection for that popular reason.

5. *Encouraging Too Much Delegation?* Perhaps another problem with the legislative veto was that it encouraged Congress to vote for broader and more abstract delegations to agencies and departments. Controversial delegations to a particular, often captured, agency might not have passed but for legislative veto provisions, which assured dubious legislators that if the agency went too far, a congressional subgroup could reverse unwanted individual decisions. This scheme allows a lot more legislation to be enacted, but greatly exacerbates the already-excessive tendency of Congress to delegate. In this way, *Chadha* may have been the Court's way of saying: We shall not revive the nondelegation doctrine, but we are not going to make it easy for Congress to delegate.

6. *Legislative Veto Challenges Under State Constitutions.* State courts have generally invalidated state legislative vetoes upon the same reasoning as that followed in *Chadha*, e.g., *State ex rel. Stephan v. Kansas House of Representatives*, 236 Kan. 45, 687 P.2d 622 (1984), and indeed some state supreme courts

---

j.　See James Buchanan & Gordon Tullock, *The Calculus of Consent* (1962).

k.　See Harold Bruff, *Legislative Formality, Administrative Rationality*, 63 Tex. L. Rev. 207, 222 (1984).

precisely anticipated *Chadha's* reasoning. See *State v. A.L.I.V.E. Voluntary*, 606 P.2d 769 (Alas. 1980); *General Assembly of New Jersey v. Byrne*, 90 N.J. 376, 448 A.2d 438 (1982); *State ex rel. Barker v. Manchin*, 279 S.E.2d 622 (W. Va. 1981).

The Idaho Supreme Court in *Mead v. Arnell*, 117 Idaho 660, 791 P.2d 410 (1990), upheld a statute allowing the legislature to override agency rules by a concurrent resolution passed by both chambers but not submitted to the governor for veto. The Court explicitly relied on the reasoning in Justice White's *Chadha* dissent. See also *Opinion of the Justices*, 121 N.H. 552, 431 A.2d 783 (1981) (dictum that laying-over requirement was constitutional).

NOTE ON SEVERABILITY

Because unconstitutional legislative vetoes were included in literally hundreds of federal statutes, *Chadha* also has occasioned a run of cases challenging the constitutionality of the entire statutes in which such vetoes were found. However, if an unconstitutional provision is "severable" from the remainder of the statute, the Court will not invalidate the statute — which was the approach taken by the Chief Justice in *Chadha* itself (with Justices Rehnquist and White in dissent). The Supreme Court's doctrine regarding severability has followed an unsteady path. Early in the twentieth century, the Court frequently refused to sever unconstitutional portions of regulatory legislation, thereby sweeping the whole statute away. E.g., *Carter v. Carter Coal Co.*, 298 U.S. 238 (1936) (Chapter 7, § 2). The New Deal Court abandoned that practice. Since 1938, the Court has followed a strong presumption of severability and rarely refused to sever unconstitutional provisions from statutes. E.g., See *Heckler v. Mathews*, 465 U.S. 728, 738 & n.5 (1984); *Regan v. Time*, 468 U.S. 641 (1984) (plurality opinion).

In the leading case of this new era, *Alaska Airlines v. Brock*, 480 U.S. 678 (1987), the Court held that an unconstitutional legislative veto provision found in the employee protections title of the Airline Deregulation Act of 1978, 92 Stat. 1705, was severable from the remainder of the title. The Court said:

> * * * In considering this question, in the context of a legislative veto, it is necessary to recognize that the absence of the veto necessarily alters the balance of powers between the Legislative and Executive Branches of the Federal Government. Thus, it is not only appropriate to evaluate the importance of the veto in the original legislative bargain, but also to consider the nature of the delegated authority that Congress made subject to a veto. Some delegations of power to the Executive or to an independent agency may have been so controversial or so broad that Congress would have been unwilling to make the delegation without a strong oversight mechanism. The final test, for legislative vetoes as well as for other provisions, is the traditional one: the unconstitutional provision must be severed unless the statute created in its absence is legislation Congress would not have enacted.

This seems like a sensible formulation, but its application strikes us as more than a little screwy. A unanimous Court in *Alaska Airlines* severed the legislative veto from the employee protections title, even though that title was the only one out of twenty-five in the statute to have a legislative veto attached to it; there was great concern about the title because it would be administered by the Secretary of Labor, not under the normal oversight responsibility of the transportation committees; a primary House sponsor specifically spoke to the importance of the legislative veto to the employee protection title and no one spoke against it. Contrary to the Court, it seems implausible that Congress would have adopted the title without the legislative veto.

The *Alaska Airlines* presumption of severability seems like a very strong one. Is it the best baseline under separation of powers precepts, however? See Michael Shumsky, *Severability, Inseverability, and the Rule of Law*, 41 Harv. J. Legis. 227 (2004) (no). One might argue that the presumption facilitates judicial activism. Because the Court shows its teeth in federalism and some free speech cases by striking down marginal provisions that the Court can then sever from the rest of the statute and diminish the dramatic consequences of its judgment, public outrage in cases of judicial usurpation is muted. Also, severability leaves in force a statute that Congress did not vote for. Does that fall athwart *Chadha*? Wouldn't presumptive nullification of the entire statute, or title, often be more appropriate, so that Congress itself could readjust the statutory scheme? See *Califano v. Westcott*, 443 U.S. 76, 93 (1979) (Powell, J., dissenting). Can the presumption of severability be defended as useful to protect private reliance interests that would be unsettled if entire statutes fell because of the invalidity of minor provisions? What burdens would a presumption of nonseverability impose on Congress?

Another angle deepens the mystery. The statute in *Alaska Airlines* had a severability clause, namely a provision directing that any portion found unconstitutional should be severed from the remainder of the law. There was some question whether the severability clause covered the title under consideration, but it is significant that the Supreme Court did not resolve that question first and announced its broad test without reference to a severability clause. Isn't it a violation of Article I, § 7 (as construed in *Chadha*) for the Court to ignore a controlling statutory provision? Why shouldn't the "presumption" of severability be conclusive when there is a statutory provision on point? Are there any circumstances under which a court might ignore a severability clause and strike down an entire statute? Cf. *Warren v. Mayor of Charlestown*, 68 Mass. (2 Gray) 84 (1854) (Shaw, C.J.) (refusing to sever when invalid and valid provisions were "so mutually connected with and dependent on each other, as conditions, considerations or compensations for each other" that it would be unreasonable to sever).

3. *The Line Item Veto*

Unlike Article I, § 7, the large majority of state constitutions allow their chief executives to veto particular lines or sections of tax and spending bills while signing the remainder into law. Budget-conscious politicians of both parties portrayed the line item veto as a panacea for the universally reviled "out of control federal spending." After *Chadha*, however, advocates of a federal line item veto realized that it was risky to follow the precise approach of the state constitutions. Instead, they took as their model presidential impoundment (Problem 8-1), allowing the President to "cancel" tax and spending provisions he disapproved. The GOP congressional leadership and a Democrat President bought this rationale. Should the Supreme Court? Jot down your thoughts and read on.

CLINTON v. CITY OF NEW YORK
524 U.S. 417, 118 S.Ct. 2091, 141 L.Ed.2d 393 (1998)

JUSTICE STEVENS delivered the opinion of the Court.

[The Line Item Veto Act, Pub. L. 104-130, 110 Stat. 1200, codified at 2 U.S.C. § 691 et seq., gave the President authority to *cancel* certain spending and tax benefit measures after he has signed them into law. Section 691(a) of the Act provides:

> [T]he President may, with respect to any bill or joint resolution that has been signed into law pursuant to Article I, section 7, of the Constitution of the United States, cancel in whole —
>
> (1) any dollar amount of discretionary budget authority;
>
> (2) any item of new direct spending; or
>
> (3) any limited tax benefit;
>
> if the President —
>
>   (A) determines that such cancellation will —
>
>   (i) reduce the Federal budget deficit;
>
>   (ii) not impair any essential Government functions; and
>
>   (iii) not harm the national interest; and
>
>   (B) notifies the Congress of such cancellation by transmitting a special message * * * within five calendar days (excluding Sundays) after the enactment of the law [to which the cancellation applies].

The President's *cancellation* under the Act would take effect when the special message notifying Congress of the cancellation was received in the House and Senate. With respect to dollar amounts of discretionary budget authority, a cancellation meant "to rescind." § 691e(4)(A). With respect to new direct spending items or limited tax benefits, a cancellation meant that the relevant legal provision, legal obligation, or budget authority is "prevent[ed] * * * from having legal force or effect." §§ 691e(4)(B), (C). The Act also established expedited procedures in both Houses for the consideration of disapproval bills, § 691d, bills or joint resolutions which, if enacted into law by the familiar procedures set out in Article I, § 7 of the Constitution, would render the President's cancellation null and void, § 691b(a).

[Appellees challenged two of the President's exercises of the cancellation power under the Line Item Veto Act. First, he canceled a provision in the Balanced Budget Act of 1997 that gave New York preferential treatment under the Medicaid law; no other state would have received such treatment. The federal government claimed that New York had inappropriately characterized taxes it had collected from Medicaid providers; unless granted a waiver, the state would owe the federal government as much as $2.6 billion. The canceled provision deemed the state's actions permissible and thereby waived the federal government's right to recoupment. New York City, a hospital and other related parties challenged the constitutionality of this cancellation. Second, President Clinton canceled a tax provision in the Taxpayer Relief Act of 1997 that allowed owners of certain food refiners and processors to defer paying tax on the gain from the sale of their stock if they sold to eligible farmers' cooperatives. Because very few taxpayers could take advantage of the tax expenditure, it was a limited tax benefit eligible for cancellation. An Idaho farmers' cooperative and an individual farmer challenged this second cancellation.]

[In the Court's first opportunity to consider the constitutionality of the line item veto, the Court had determined that the Members of Congress who brought that case lacked standing. See *Raines v. Byrd* (Chapter 9, § 2). In contrast, in this case the Court concluded that the appellees had standing because they each had a personal stake in having an actual injury redressed by the Court.]

The effect of a cancellation is plainly stated in § 691e, which defines the principal terms used in the Act. With respect to both an item of new direct spending and a limited tax benefit, the cancellation prevents the item "from having legal force or effect."[26] Thus, under the plain text of the statute, the two actions of the President that are challenged in these cases prevented one section of the Balanced Budget Act of 1997 and one section of the Taxpayer Relief Act of 1997 "from having legal force or effect." The remaining provisions of those statutes * * * continue to have the same force and effect as they had when signed into law.

In both legal and practical effect, the President has amended two Acts of Congress by repealing a portion of each. * * * There is no provision in the Constitution that authorizes the President to enact, to amend, or to repeal statutes. * * *

There are important differences between the President's "return" of a bill pursuant to Article I, § 7, and the exercise of the President's cancellation authority pursuant to the Line Item Veto Act. The constitutional return takes place *before* the bill becomes law; the statutory cancellation occurs *after* the bill becomes law. The constitutional return is of the entire bill; the statutory cancellation is of only a part. Although the Constitution expressly authorizes the President to play a role in the process of enacting statutes, it is silent on the subject of unilateral Presidential action that either repeals or amends parts of duly enacted statutes.

There are powerful reasons for construing constitutional silence on this profoundly important issue as equivalent to an express prohibition. The procedures governing the enactment of statutes set forth in the text of Article I were the product of the great debates and compromises that produced the Constitution itself. Familiar historical materials provide abundant support for the conclusion that the power to enact statutes may only "be exercised in accord with a single, finely wrought and exhaustively considered, procedure." *Chadha.* * * * What has emerged in these cases from the President's exercise of his statutory cancellation powers, however, are truncated versions of two bills that passed both Houses of Congress. They are not the product of the "finely wrought" procedure that the Framers designed. * * *

---

26.   The term "cancel," used in connection with any dollar amount of discretionary budget authority, means "to rescind." * * *

[The government's main defense of this unconventional arrangement was that the substance of the authority to cancel tax and spending items "is, in practical effect, no more and no less than the power to 'decline to spend' specified sums of money, or to 'decline to implement' specified tax measures." Recall our Note on Impoundment in § 1A of this chapter.] The Government has reviewed in some detail the series of statutes in which Congress has given the Executive broad discretion over the expenditure of appropriated funds. For example, the First Congress appropriated "sum[s] not exceeding" specified amounts to be spent on various Government operations. In those statutes, as in later years, the President was given wide discretion with respect to both the amounts to be spent and how the money would be allocated among different functions. It is argued that the Line Item Veto Act merely confers comparable discretionary authority over the expenditure of appropriated funds. The critical difference between this statute and all of its predecessors, however, is that unlike any of them, this Act gives the President the unilateral power to change the text of duly enacted statutes. None of the Act's predecessors could even arguably have been construed to authorize such a change. * * *

If there is to be a new procedure in which the President will play a different role in determining the final text of what may "become a law," such change must come not by legislation but through the amendment procedures set forth in Article V of the Constitution. *Cf. U.S. Term Limits, Inc. v. Thornton* (Chapter 7, § 1).

[**JUSTICE KENNEDY**'s concurring opinion is omitted.]

JUSTICE SCALIA, with whom **JUSTICE O'CONNOR** joins, and with whom **JUSTICE BREYER** joins as to Part III, concurring in part and dissenting in part.

* * * As much as the Court goes on about Art. I, § 7, therefore, that provision does not demand the result the Court reaches. It no more categorically prohibits the Executive *reduction* of congressional dispositions in the course of implementing statutes that authorize such reduction, than it categorically prohibits the Executive *augmentation* of congressional dispositions in the course of implementing statutes that authorize such augmentation — generally known as substantive rulemaking. There are, to be sure, limits upon the former just as there are limits upon the latter — and I am prepared to acknowledge that the limits upon the former may be much more severe. Those limits are established, however, not by some categorical prohibition of Art. I, § 7, which our cases conclusively disprove, but by what has come to be known as the doctrine of unconstitutional delegation of legislative authority: When authorized Executive reduction or augmentation is allowed to go too far, it usurps the nondelegable function of Congress and violates the separation of powers. * * *

Insofar as the degree of political, "law-making" power conferred upon the Executive is concerned, there is not a dime's worth of difference between Congress's authorizing the President to *cancel* a spending item, and Congress's authorizing money to be spent on a particular item at the President's discretion. And the latter has been done since the Founding of the Nation. * * *

Certain Presidents have claimed Executive authority to withhold appropriated funds even *absent* an express conferral of discretion to do so. [The action

of withholding appropriated funds is often termed "impoundment."] * * *
President Nixon, the Mahatma Gandhi of all impounders, asserted at a press
conference in 1973 that his "constitutional right" to impound appropriated funds
was "absolutely clear." Our decision two years later in *Train v. City of New
York*, 420 U.S. 35 (1975), proved him wrong, but it implicitly confirmed that
Congress may confer discretion upon the executive to withhold appropriated
funds, even funds appropriated for a specific purpose. The statute at issue in
Train authorized spending "not to exceed" specified sums for certain projects,
and directed that such "[s]ums authorized to be appropriated . . . shall be
allotted" by the Administrator of the Environmental Protection Agency. Upon
enactment of this statute, the President directed the Administrator to allot no
more than a certain part of the amount authorized. This Court held, as a matter
of statutory interpretation, that the statute *did not grant* the Executive discretion
to withhold the funds, but required allotment of the full amount authorized.

The short of the matter is this: Had the Line Item Veto Act authorized the
President to "decline to spend" any item of spending contained in the Balanced
Budget Act of 1997, there is not the slightest doubt that authorization would
have been constitutional. What the Line Item Veto Act does instead —
authorizing the President to "cancel" an item of spending — is technically
different. But the technical difference does *not* relate to the technicalities of the
Presentment Clause, which have been fully complied with; and the doctrine of
unconstitutional delegation, which *is* at issue here, is preeminently *not* a doctrine
of technicalities. The title of the Line Item Veto Act, which was perhaps
designed to simplify for public comprehension, or perhaps merely to comply
with the terms of a campaign pledge, has succeeded in faking out the Supreme
Court. The President's action it authorizes in fact is not a line-item veto and
thus does not offend Art. I, § 7; and insofar as the substance of that action is
concerned, it is no different from what Congress has permitted the President to
do since the formation of the Union. * * *

JUSTICE BREYER, with whom **JUSTICE O'CONNOR** and **JUSTICE SCALIA**
join as to Part III, dissenting. * * *

III. The Court believes that the Act violates the literal text of the Constitution. A simple syllogism captures its basic reasoning:

> Major Premise: The Constitution sets forth an exclusive method for enacting,
> repealing, or amending laws.

> Minor Premise: The Act authorizes the President to "repea[l] or amen[d]" laws
> in a different way, namely by announcing a cancellation of a portion of a previously
> enacted law.

> Conclusion: The Act is inconsistent with the Constitution.

I find this syllogism unconvincing, however, because its Minor Premise is faulty.
When the President "canceled" the two appropriation measures now before us,
he did not *repeal* any law nor did he *amend* any law. He simply *followed* the
law, leaving the statutes, as they are literally written, intact.

To understand why one cannot say, *literally speaking*, that the President has
repealed or amended any law, imagine how the provisions of law before us

might have been, but were not, written. Imagine that the canceled New York [Medicaid] provision at issue here had instead said the following:

> Section One. Taxes . . . that were collected by the State of New York from a health care provider before June 1, 1997 and for which a waiver of provisions [requiring payment] have been sought . . . are deemed to be permissible health care related taxes . . . *provided however that the President may prevent the just-mentioned provision from having legal force or effect if he determines x, y and z.* (Assume x, y and z to be the same determinations required by the Line Item Veto Act).

Whatever a person might say, or think, about the constitutionality of this imaginary law, there is one thing the English language would prevent one from saying. One could not say that a President who "prevent[s]" the deeming language from "having legal force or effect" has either *repealed* or *amended* this particular hypothetical statute. Rather, the President has *followed* that law to the letter. He has exercised the power it explicitly delegates to him. He has executed the law, not repealed it.

It could make no significant difference to this linguistic point were the italicized proviso to appear, not as part of what I have called Section One, but, instead, at the bottom of the statute page, say referenced by an asterisk, with a statement that it applies to every spending provision in the act next to which a similar asterisk appears. And that being so, it could make no difference if that proviso appeared, instead, in a different, earlier-enacted law, along with legal language that makes it applicable to every future spending provision picked out according to a specified formula.

But, of course, this last-mentioned possibility is this very case. The earlier law, namely, the Line Item Veto Act, says that "the President may . . . prevent such [future] budget authority from having legal force or effect." * * * For that reason, one cannot dispose of this case through a purely literal analysis as the majority does. Literally speaking, the President has not "repealed" or "amended" anything. He has simply *executed* a power conferred upon him by Congress, which power is contained in laws that were enacted in compliance with the exclusive method set forth in the Constitution. * * *

* * * This is not the first time that Congress has delegated to the President or to others this kind of power — a contingent power to deny effect to certain statutory language. See, *e.g.,* * * * 28 U.S.C. § 2072 (Supreme Court is authorized to promulgate rules of practice and procedure in federal courts, and "[a]ll laws in conflict with such rules *shall be of no further force and effect*") (emphasis added); Gramm-Rudman-Hollings Act, § 252(a)(4) (authorizing the President to issue a "final order" that has the effect of *"permanently cancell-[ing]"* sequestered amounts in spending statutes in order to achieve budget compliance) (emphasis added).

All of these examples, like the Act, delegate a power to take action that will render statutory provisions "without force or effect." Every one of these examples, like the present Act, delegates the power to choose between alternatives, each of which the statute spells out in some detail. None of these examples delegates a power to "repeal" or "amend" a statute, or to "make" a new law. Nor does the Act. Rather, the delegated power to nullify statutory language was *itself* created and defined by Congress, and included in the statute books on an equal footing with (indeed, as a component part of) the sections that are potentially subject to nullification. * * *

[In Part IV, Justice Breyer rejected arguments based upon separation of powers principles: (1) Has Congress given the President the wrong kind of power, *i.e.*, "non-executive" power? No. (2) Has Congress given the President the power to "encroach" upon Congress' own constitutionally reserved territory? No. (3) Has Congress given the President too much power, violating the nondelegation doctrine? No, because the law provides "intelligible" standards to guide the President.]

NOTES ON *CLINTON v. CITY OF NEW YORK*

1. *Should Spending and Taxing Cancellations Have Been Treated Differently? Is the President's Impoundment Authority Limited?* The cancellations before the Court concerned a tax provision and a spending provision. From a historical perspective, the taxing provision appears more questionable than the spending provision. As the dissents noted, Presidents have long used a power functionally indistinguishable from cancellation — the impoundment authority — to withhold funds that Congress had allocated to government programs in the annual appropriations process; in 1974 Congress okayed a regularized use of presidential impoundment (Problem 8-1). Is the cancellation power relating to discretionary spending, which consists of appropriated funds that have been the traditional target of presidential impoundments, unconstitutional after this case?[o]

As a formal matter, for the reasons developed in Problem 8-1, isn't the presidential impoundment authority more "executive" than an authority to rescind taxes, which looks more "legislative"? As a functional matter, is the problem of rent-seeking (Congress's dolloping out goodies to special interests) greater for tax statutes than for spending programs? As a matter of popular constitutionalism, does shifting power to the President pose unacceptable new risks to popular majorities or to minorities? As we read him, Justice Breyer would say that the functional and vertical inquiries suggest no big difference, and he would not rest upon the formality of the executive/legislative inquiry (contrary to the Burger approach in *Chadha*).

2. *The Congressional Reaction.* Congress could respond by a constitutional amendment giving the President the authority most state governors have to veto particular items in taxing and/or spending legislation. In the alternative, can you construct a statutory impoundment law that would meet the constitutional test.

---

o. Notice that the definition of *cancel* is different in the context of discretionary spending. Rather than rendering a provision of law without "legal force and effect," the President "rescinds" an item of discretionary spending when he cancels it. In budget parlance, a rescission is a congressionally authorized impoundment. Since 1974, federal law has allowed the President to propose to rescind federal spending, but his proposal would not go into effect unless approved by Congress within 45 days. One way to view the Line Item Veto Act's provisions affecting appropriated money is as merely a change in the way Congress authorizes rescissions. Rather than requiring ex post congressional approval, the Line Item Veto Act delegates a continuing power to rescind spending, as long as the President complies with the standards set forth in the Act.

What if "to cancel" was defined as "to decline to spend or enforce"? Or could Congress delegate to the President the power to "suspend" or federal spending programs if he finds his action would reduce the federal deficit, not impair any essential government functions, and not harm the national interest?

Another option is separate enrollment. Using this procedure, Congress would divide an omnibus spending bill, formally enrolling each provision allocating funds to particular programs as a separate bill. The group of bills would be passed by Congress (probably using a procedure that would require only one vote to enact the bundle of bills). The President would then have the ability to use his constitutional veto to cancel as many of the programs as he wishes; Congress would have the opportunity to override any veto with a supermajority vote. Are there reasons Congress might not want to follow this approach?

3. *How Significant Was the Cancellation Power?* President Clinton used this new power to cancel relatively small projects, cumulatively worth about $500 million. One explanation for the infrequent use of cancellation is that the effect of the new power occurred primarily during negotiations as Congress drafted and considered spending bills. Theoretically, the President's role in the content of legislation is determined in part by the possibility that he might veto bills containing provisions he dislikes; even when the veto threat is not carried out, it should influence the bargaining process that goes on in the legislative process. See William Eskridge, Jr. & John Ferejohn, *The Article I, Section 7 Game*, 80 Geo. L.J. 523 (1992). Thus, except for some symbolic uses of cancellation to score political points with voters, the President might never actually have to cancel or impound funds, having reached agreements with members of Congress before the bill reaches his desk.

A vertical perspective, therefore, would be concerned that the item veto reflects a big shift in lawmaking power — away from Congress's state and local constituencies and toward national ones (that elect the President). Evidence from studies of governors' use of their line-item veto power suggests it has little effect on the amount of state spending but allows the executives more influence over the shape of the budget. This latter outcome is more pronounced when the two branches are controlled by different parties. As a matter of the Constitution's balance of representation, therefore, the item veto law significantly altered the Article I, § 7 structure — and the Court was right to strike it down.

B. CONGRESSIONAL AND PRESIDENTIAL POWER TO CONTROL "EXECUTIVE" OFFICIALS

Another way Congress can delegate its cake and eat it too would be to grant authority to officials whom it controls to some extent through power over appointment, removal, or even threat of impeachment. Congress also might attempt to undercut presidential power by making officials removable only for "good cause." The validity of these kinds of arrangements might turn on how tightly the President must be viewed as controlling the *unitary executive* established in Article II, rather than on improper action by legislative subgroups under Article I, § 7. Thus, one might ask the formal question whether Article II assumes a unitary executive; the functional question whether congressional control over executive officials interferes with either the legislative duties of Congress or the executive duties of the President; and the vertical question whether congressional control (or presidential lack of control) over executive officials affects the President's constituency and his incentives to act. The theoretical possibilities are rich. The Supreme Court's precedents in this area are an unruly lot.

***

Myers v. United States, 272 U.S. 52 (1926). The Court invalidated an 1876 statute preventing the President from discharging postmasters without the consent of the Senate. **Chief Justice Taft**'s opinion for the Court rested in large part on the *Decision of 1789*, whereby a Congress filled with Framers expressed what the Chief Justice felt was a general understanding that the President must have the authority to remove executive department officers, without the need for Senate consent (Note on Early Interactions at the beginning of this chapter). The Chief Justice particularly relied on the position ultimately taken by Representative James Madison in the House, that "[i]f there is any point in which the separation of the Legislative and Executive powers ought to be maintained with great caution, it is that which relates to officers and offices." 1 Annals of Cong. 581 (1789). Drawing from the discussions at Philadelphia and the Framers' purpose to avoid the weaknesses of the Articles of Confederation, Chief Justice Taft (himself President from 1909 to 1913) viewed the executive as a unitary branch, hierarchically arrayed with the President in command of subordinate officers. The Vesting Clause of Article II was textual evidence of the proposition advanced by Madison and others in the Decision of 1789, that all executive powers were vested in the President and none in Congress. As the British system attested, the power of removal as well as the power of appointment were central features of the executive power.

The history of the Advise and Consent Clause for appointment proved that it was not intended by the Framers to spill over into removal. Typically, Madison said it best (1 Annals of Cong. 499):

> Vest this [removal] power in the Senate jointly with the President, and you abolish at once that great principle of unity and responsibility in the Executive department, which was intended for the security of liberty and the public good. If the President should possess alone the power of removal from office, those who are employed in the execution of the law will be in their proper situation, and the chain of dependence be preserved; the lowest officers, the middle grade, and the highest, will depend, as they ought, on the President, and the President on the community.

The Court considered the Decision of 1789 dispositive because it offered Madison a chance to speak so clearly, because his views were accepted by a Congress populated by Framers, and because even Hamilton (whose *Federalist* No. 77 supported the necessity of Senate consent for removal as well as appointment) acquiesced in the Madisonian consensus.

Justice Brandeis dissented, arguing that there was no consensus in 1789, but that by 1833, when Joseph Story penned his *Commentaries on the Constitution*, there was a consensus that Congress could require Senate consent for the removal of *inferior* executive officers. Brandeis also pointed out a logical problem in the Chief Justice's opinion: It conceded that Congress under the Appointments Clause (Art. II, § 2, cl. 2) could vest both appointment and removal of postmasters with the Postmaster General, and that Congress could condition removals upon Senate consent. See *United States v. Perkins*, 116 U.S. 483. If Congress could do this, consistent with Article II, why could it not impose the same condition on removals by the President? If Congress has the power to create the Post Office Department, why does it not have authority, under the Necessary and Proper Clause, to condition removals from office? Also dissenting, in separate opinions, were **Justices Holmes** and **MacReynolds**.

———

Humphrey's Executor v. United States, 295 U.S. 602 (1935). The Court upheld a provision in the Federal Trade Commission Act which permitted removal by the President, but only for "inefficiency, neglect of duty, or malfeasance in office." **Justice Sutherland**'s opinion for the Court reasoned that this limitation was needed to accomplish the goals of the statute. *Myers* was distinguishable, for it involved an "executive officer restricted to the performance of executive functions * * *. Putting aside *dicta*, which may be followed if sufficiently persuasive but which are not controlling, the necessary reach of the decision goes far enough to include all purely executive officers. It goes no farther; much less does it include an officer who occupies no place in the executive department and who exercises no part of the executive power vested by the Constitution in the President."

Justice Sutherland characterized the FTC as "an administrative body created by Congress to carry into effect legislative policies embodied in the statute in accordance with the legislative standard therein prescribed, and to perform other specified duties as a legislative or as a judicial aid. Such a body cannot in any proper sense be characterized as an arm or an eye of the executive." Because the FTC investigates, prosecutes, and adjudicates complaints of unfair trade practices, the Court characterized it as exercising "quasi-legislative or quasi-judicial powers, or as an agency of the legislative or judicial departments of the government." In creating such bodies, Congress can set the terms of the commissioners' office and limit the conditions of their removal, the latter to assure their independence of the President. The Supreme Court followed *Humphrey's Executor* in *Wiener v. United States*, 357 U.S. 349 (1958), to uphold congressional restrictions on the President's power to remove members of the War Claims Commission.

———

Buckley v. Valeo, 424 U.S. 1 (1976). The Federal Election Campaign Act of 1971, as amended in 1974, established the Federal Election Commission (FEC) and charged it with investigating, sanctioning, and rulemaking duties. The eight-member FEC included two members appointed by the President, two by the Speaker of the House, and two by the President *pro tempore* of the Senate. The Supreme Court, in a *per curiam* opinion, found that structure to violate the Appointments Clause (Art. II, § 2, cl. 2). Because the FEC members were "appointee[s] exercising significant authority pursuant to the laws of the United States," they were *Officers of the United States* and had to be appointed according to the terms of the Appointments Clause. The two members appointed by the President raised no difficulty, but the four appointed by Congress had no support in the clause.

The Court added that if the FEC were merely an investigative arm of Congress, the Appointments Clause would not apply. The Commission's enforcement and sanctioning power, however, rendered it something more. So, too, its rulemaking power: "These functions, exercised free from day-to-day supervision of either Congress or the Executive Branch, * * * are of kinds usually performed by independent regulatory agencies or by some department in the Executive Branch under the direction of an Act of Congress." Although under *Humphrey's Executor*, "the President may not insist that such functions be delegated to an appointee of his removable at will, none of them operates merely in aid of congressional authority to legislate or is sufficiently removed from the administration and enforcement of public law to allow it to be performed by the present Commission."

BOWSHER v. SYNAR
478 U.S. 714, 106 S.Ct. 3181, 92 L.Ed.2d 583 (1986)

CHIEF JUSTICE BURGER delivered the opinion of the Court.

[The "Gramm-Rudman-Hollings Act" sought to eliminate the federal budget deficit. To that end, the Act set a "maximum deficit amount" for federal spending for each of fiscal years 1986 through 1991 (when it would be zero). If in any fiscal year the federal budget deficit exceeded the maximum deficit amount by more than a specified sum, the Act required across-the-board cuts in federal spending to reach the targeted deficit level. Each year, the Directors of the Office of Management and Budget (OMB) and the Congressional Budget Office (CBO) would estimate the amount of the federal budget deficit for the upcoming fiscal year. If that deficit exceeded the maximum targeted deficit amount for that fiscal year by more than a specified amount, the Directors of OMB and CBO would independently calculate, on a program-by-program basis, the budget reductions necessary to ensure that the deficit does not exceed the maximum deficit amount. The Act then required the Directors to report jointly their deficit estimates and budget reduction calculations to the Comptroller General, who would then report his conclusions to the President. The President was required under the Act to issue a "sequestration" order mandating the spending reductions specified by the Comptroller General. After a certain period, the cuts required by the order would be implemented. Anticipating constitutional challenge to these procedures, the Act contained a "fallback" deficit reduction process to take effect in the event the foregoing procedures were invalidated.

[Twelve Members of Congress, the National Treasury Employees Union, and a union member brought suit challenging the Act on separation of powers grounds. A three-judge court invalidated the law, and the Supreme Court affirmed.]

The Constitution does not contemplate an active role for Congress in the supervision of officers charged with the execution of the laws it enacts. The President appoints "Officers of the United States" with the "Advice and Consent of the Senate . . . ." Art. II, § 2. Once the appointment has been made and confirmed, however, the Constitution explicitly provides for removal of Officers of the United States by Congress only upon impeachment by the House of

Representatives and conviction by the Senate. An impeachment by the House and trial by the Senate can rest only on "Treason, Bribery or other high Crimes and Misdemeanors." Art. II, § 4. A direct congressional role in the removal of officers charged with the execution of the laws beyond this limited one is inconsistent with separation of powers. * * *

[The Chief Justice reviewed the precedents — *Myers*, *Humphrey's Executor*, and *Wiener*.] In light of these precedents, we conclude that Congress cannot reserve for itself the power of removal of an officer charged with the execution of the laws except by impeachment. To permit the execution of the laws to be vested in an officer answerable only to Congress would, in practical terms, reserve in Congress control over the execution of the laws. As the District Court observed: "Once an officer is appointed, it is only the authority that can remove him, and not the authority that appointed him, that he must fear and, in the performance of his functions, obey." The structure of the Constitution does not permit Congress to execute the laws; it follows that Congress cannot grant to an officer under its control what it does not possess.

* * * To permit an officer controlled by Congress to execute the laws would be, in essence, to permit a congressional veto. Congress could simply remove, or threaten to remove, an officer for executing the laws in any fashion found to be unsatisfactory to Congress. This kind of congressional control over the execution of the laws, *Chadha* makes clear, is constitutionally impermissible. * * *

Appellants urge that the Comptroller General performs his duties independently and is not subservient to Congress. * * * [T]his contention does not bear close scrutiny.

The critical factor lies in the provisions of the statute defining the Comptroller General's office relating to removability. Although the Comptroller General is nominated by the President from a list of three individuals recommended by the Speaker of the House of Representatives and the President *pro tempore* of the Senate, and confirmed by the Senate, he is removable only at the initiative of Congress. He may be removed not only by impeachment but also by joint resolution of Congress "at any time" resting on any one of the following bases: [(i) permanent disability; (ii) inefficiency; (iii) neglect of duty; (iv) malfeasance; or (v) a felony or conduct involving moral turpitude.] 31 U.S.C. § 703(e)(1)(B). This provision was included, as one Congressman explained in urging passage of the Act, because Congress "felt that [the Comptroller General] should be brought under the sole control of Congress, so that Congress at any moment when it found he was inefficient and was not carrying on the duties of his office as he should and as the Congress expected, could remove him without the long, tedious process of a trial by impeachment." 61 Cong. Rec. 1081 (1921). * * *

* * * [T]he dissent is simply in error to suggest that the political realities reveal that the Comptroller General is free from influence by Congress. The Comptroller General heads the General Accounting Office (GAO), "an instrumentality of the United States Government independent of the executive departments," 31 U.S.C. § 702(a), which was created by Congress in 1921 as part of the Budget and Accounting Act of 1921. Congress created the office

because it believed that it "needed an officer, responsible to it alone, to check upon the application of public funds in accordance with appropriations." H. Mansfield, *The Comptroller General: A Study in the Law and Practice of Financial Administration* 65 (1939).

It is clear that Congress has consistently viewed the Comptroller General as an officer of the Legislative Branch. The Reorganization Acts of 1945 and 1949, for example, both stated that the Comptroller General and the GAO are "a part of the legislative branch of the Government." Similarly, in the Accounting and Auditing Act of 1950, Congress required the Comptroller General to conduct audits "as an agent of the Congress."

Over the years, the Comptrollers General have also viewed themselves as part of the Legislative Branch. [The Chief Justice quoted statements to that effect.]

Against this background, we see no escape from the conclusion that, because Congress has retained removal authority over the Comptroller General, he may not be entrusted with executive powers. The remaining question is whether the Comptroller General has been assigned such powers in the Balanced Budget and Emergency Deficit Control Act of 1985. * * *

Appellants suggest that the duties assigned to the Comptroller General in the Act are essentially ministerial and mechanical so that their performance does not constitute "execution of the law" in a meaningful sense. On the contrary, we view these functions as plainly entailing execution of the law in constitutional terms. Interpreting a law enacted by Congress to implement the legislative mandate is the very essence of "execution" of the law. Under § 251, the Comptroller General must exercise judgment concerning facts that affect the application of the Act. He must also interpret the provisions of the Act to determine precisely what budgetary calculations are required. Decisions of that kind are typically made by officers charged with executing a statute.

The executive nature of the Comptroller General's functions under the Act is revealed in § 252(a)(3) which gives the Comptroller General the ultimate authority to determine the budget cuts to be made. Indeed, the Comptroller General commands the President himself to carry out, without the slightest variation (with exceptions not relevant to the constitutional issues presented), the directive of the Comptroller General as to the budget reductions:

> The [Presidential] order *must provide* for reductions in the manner specified in section 251(a)(3), *must incorporate* the provisions of the [Comptroller General's] report submitted under section 251(b), and *must be consistent with such report in all respects.* The President *may not modify or recalculate any of the estimates, determinations, specifications, bases, amounts, or percentages* set forth in the report submitted under section 251(b) in determining the reductions to be specified in the order with respect to programs, projects, and activities, or with respect to budget activities, within an account . . . ." § 252(a)(3) (emphasis added).

Congress of course initially determined the content of the Balanced Budget and Emergency Deficit Control Act; and undoubtedly the content of the Act determines the nature of the executive duty. However, as *Chadha* makes clear, once Congress makes its choice in enacting legislation, its participation ends. Congress can thereafter control the execution of its enactment only indirectly —

by passing new legislation. By placing the responsibility for execution of the Balanced Budget and Emergency Deficit Control Act in the hands of an officer who is subject to removal only by itself, Congress in effect has retained control over the execution of the Act and has intruded into the executive function. The Constitution does not permit such intrusion. * * *

JUSTICE STEVENS, with whom **JUSTICE MARSHALL** joins, concurring in the judgment.

It is not the dormant, carefully circumscribed congressional removal power that represents the primary constitutional evil. Nor do I agree with the conclusion of both the majority and the dissent that the analysis depends on a labeling of the functions assigned to the Comptroller General as "executive powers." Rather, I am convinced that the Comptroller General must be characterized as an agent of Congress because of his longstanding statutory responsibilities; that the powers assigned to him under the Gramm-Rudman-Hollings Act require him to make policy that will bind the Nation; and that, when Congress, or a component or an agent of Congress, seeks to make policy that will bind the Nation, it must follow the procedures mandated by Article I of the Constitution — through passage by both Houses and presentment to the President. In short, Congress may not exercise its fundamental power to formulate national policy by delegating that power to one of its two Houses, to a legislative committee, or to an individual agent of the Congress such as the Speaker of the House of Representatives, the Sergeant at Arms of the Senate, or the Director of the Congressional Budget Office. *Chadha*. That principle, I believe, is applicable to the Comptroller General.

[Justice Stevens noted that the Court did not dispute that it would be constitutional for Congress to delegate to an executive official the authority provided to the Comptroller General in the Act. He saw the "central issue" in the case as follows: "If the delegation to a stranger is permissible, why may not Congress delegate the same responsibilities to one of its own agents?" His response was that intra-congressional delegations violate *Chadha*: "If Congress were free to delegate its policymaking authority to one of its components, or to one of its agents, it would be able to evade 'the carefully crafted restraints spelled out in the Constitution.' *Chadha*. That danger — congressional action that evades constitutional restraints — is not present when Congress delegates lawmaking power to the executive or to an independent agency."]

JUSTICE WHITE, dissenting.

[Justice White complained that the Court had struck down a novel legislative response to an economic crisis based on a removal power found in "a solitary provision of another statute that was passed sixty years ago and has lain dormant since that time." Justice White did not consider the Comptroller's authority under Gramm-Rudman to include substantial policymaking discretion and thought it sensible for Congress to entrust these duties to "an officer who is to the greatest degree possible nonpartisan and independent of the President and his political agenda and who therefore may be relied upon not to allow his calculations to be colored by political considerations." Moreover, he saw no intrusion into executive functions at work in the statute: The appropriation of funds is purely a congressional function, Congress has set a limit on the amount of appropriations, and Congress delegated the mechanics of enforcing the limitation to someone independent of the President.]

* * * [T]he Court baldly mischaracterizes the removal provision when it suggests that it allows Congress to remove the Comptroller for "executing the laws in any fashion found to be unsatisfactory"; in fact, Congress may remove the Comptroller only for one or more of five specified reasons * * *. Second, and more to the point, the Court overlooks or deliberately ignores the decisive difference between the congressional removal provision and the legislative veto struck down in *Chadha*: under the Budget and Accounting Act, Congress may remove the Comptroller only through a joint resolution, which by definition must be passed by both Houses and signed by the President. In other words, a removal of the Comptroller under the statute *satisfies the requirements of bicameralism and presentment laid down in Chadha.* * * *

The practical result of the removal provision is not to render the Comptroller unduly dependent upon or subservient to Congress, but to render him one of the most independent officers in the entire federal establishment. Those who have studied the office agree that the procedural and substantive limits on the power of Congress and the President to remove the Comptroller make dislodging him against his will practically impossible. * * *

* * * The wisdom of vesting "executive" powers in an officer removable by joint resolution may indeed be debatable — as may be the wisdom of the entire scheme of permitting an unelected official to revise the budget enacted by Congress — but such matters are for the most part to be worked out between the Congress and the President through the legislative process, which affords each branch ample opportunity to defend its interests. The Act vesting budget-cutting authority in the Comptroller General represents Congress' judgment that the delegation of such authority to counteract ever-mounting deficits is "necessary and proper" to the exercise of the powers granted the Federal Government by the Constitution; and the President's approval of the statute signifies his unwillingness to reject the choice made by Congress. Under such circumstances, the role of this Court should be limited to determining whether the Act so alters the balance of authority among the branches of government as to pose a genuine threat to the basic division between the lawmaking power and the power to execute the law. Because I see no such threat, I cannot join the Court in striking down the Act.

[**JUSTICE BLACKMUN** dissented separately. He would have invalidated the provisions of the 1921 statute allowing Congress to remove the Comptroller General, thereby saving the Gramm-Rudman-Hollings Act.]

NOTES ON *MYERS* THROUGH *BOWSHER*:
THE SUPREME COURT'S UNSTEADY PATH

1. *The Reasoning of* Bowsher. *Bowsher*'s categorization exercise is replete with logical holes and unanswered questions:[p]

(a) *Is the Comptroller an "Executive" Official?* An anomaly of the Court's opinion is its reliance on the simple idea that anyone who has a hand in enforcing the laws cannot be "controlled" by Congress. The Chief Justice views "control" functionally, but in that event congressional committees often exercise much more effective "control" over agencies than Congress does over the Comptroller, by means of oversight hearings, appropriations measures, and informal pressure. Also, there are plenty of congressional agents who execute the laws. The Capitol Hill Police who patrol the Capitol area, the Sergeant-at-Arms who manages the congressional payroll, and the Capitol Architect who maintains the grounds are all formally controlled by Congress. In a sense they all "execute" statutory directives. Does this violate separation of power precepts? Are these officials materially different from the Comptroller General in their "executive" duties?

(b) *Does Congress "Control" the Comptroller General?* Even if the Comptroller General were an executive official, she could act out her role in the statutory scheme if Congress didn't "control" her. The Court concedes that Congress has never "removed" a Comptroller General under the statute in question, and (as Justice White argued) any removal must be through a Joint Resolution meeting the bicameralism and presentment requirements. Is there any reason to believe that this official would kowtow to Congress under the Gramm-Rudman Act?[q] Aren't the Comptroller's duties under the Act substantially limited by the OMB and CBO projections?

Does *Bowsher* cast constitutional doubt on congressional efforts to control administrative policy except through substantive statutes (e.g., through oversight and appropriations)? For example, § 605 of Public Law No. 99-180, an appropriations measure, disapproved of Department of Justice efforts to liberalize antitrust rules concerning resale price maintenance. It provided that no funds appropriated to the Department of Justice "may be used for any activity to alter the per se prohibition on resale price maintenance in effect under Federal antitrust laws." Included was also a "sense of Congress" condemnation of the Department's "Guidelines" on vertical restraints, on grounds that they violated the Supreme Court's interpretation of the statute. Is § 605 constitutional?

(c) *What Happened to* Chadha? Having just read the Legislative and Line Item Veto Cases, you might think that the Gramm-Rudman Act had the same

---

p. Like most of the Court's separation of powers opinions, *Bowsher* has been the object of intense academic criticism of its strained exercise in categorization. E.g., Abner Greene, *Checks and Balances in an Era of Presidential Lawmaking*, 61 U. Chi. L. Rev. 123 (1994); Nourse, *Vertical Separation* 793-95; David Yassky, Note, *A Two-Tiered Theory of Consolidation and Separation of Powers*, 99 Yale L.J. 431 (1989).

q. Arguing not is Peter Strauss, *Formal and Functional Approaches to Separation of Powers Questions — A Foolish Inconsistency?*, 72 Cornell L. Rev. 488 (1987).

structural problem. It delegated important law-creating authority to an agent (like a subgroup) of the legislature, without requiring bicameral approval and presentment. Indeed, the Gramm-Rudman Case seems more constitutionally fishy than the Legislative Veto Case, since massive policy choices are potentially being made by a single unelected person. Moreover, if Chief Justice Burger is right that the Comptroller General is under Congress' thumb, there is even greater opportunity for rent-seeking behavior, as various lobbying groups and clusters of Members might pressure the Comptroller General's decisions.

But only Justices Marshall and Stevens believed that the Act was invalid because it delegated lawmaking power to a legislative agent. The Chief Justice, who authored the Legislative Veto decision, instead followed the concerns of Justice Powell's concurrence in that case: Separation of powers concerns are greatest when Congress invades judicial (*Chadha*) or executive (*Bowsher*) functions. Why this volte-face on the part of the Chief Justice? Does the Line Item Veto Case suggest that the *Chadha* approach has been abandoned?

2. *Theories for Reconciling the Cases.* In *Checks and Balances in an Era of Presidential Lawmaking*, 61 U. Chi. L. Rev. 123, 167 (1994), Abner Greene suggests that the laws in *Bowsher* and *Chadha* were both efforts at self-aggrandizement, and the Court was right to monitor that process defect. But under such a rationale, *Clinton v. New York* ought to come out differently, as Congress was giving away power, without strings attached, in the Line Item Veto Act. Is *Clinton v. New York* wrongly decided?

Victoria Nourse, in *The Vertical Separation of Powers*, 49 Duke L.J. 749, 793-95 (1999), argues that the cases can be reconciled through the vertical perspective. Forget the Court's categorization game, and do not end discussion with the aggrandizement problem. Instead, focus on how a shift in power is also a shift in political constituency and in popular accountability. Both *Chadha* and *Bowsher* shifted important federal decisionmaking away from the messy but deliberative *political* process and toward less accountable insiders (*Chadha*) and bureaucrats (*Bowsher*). Both cut the President, and his national constituency, out of important public decisions. *Clinton v. New York* is a harder case, because the line item veto does not take important decisions out of the political process, but does shift power in the other direction, to the President and away from Congress.

3. *Debate over Methodology: Triumph of Formalism?* After *Chadha* and *Bowsher*, one might tentatively conclude that the Supreme Court had opted for a formalist approach to separation of powers: each branch is limited to the particular power granted it in the Constitution, and is not to exercise other powers unless expressly authorized by the Constitution. (Although decided later, *Clinton v, New York* supports this conclusion.) Under such a formalist approach, does Justice Black's majority opinion in the Steel Seizure Case dominate Justice Jackson's concurring opinion, or can both be characterized as formalist along *Chadha* lines?

PROBLEM 8-5
HYBRID AIRPORT AGENCIES

Until 1987, the federal government owned and operated two airports near Washington, D.C. — National and Dulles Airports. With an eye toward making needed capital improvements, the Department of Transportation sought congressional authorization to transfer ownership and operation of the airports to a state-run regional authority. Congress passed such authorization for a Metropolitan Washington Airports Authority (MWAA) in 1986, but conditioned it upon the creation of a "review board" with veto power over major actions of MWAA's board of directors. The review board consisted of nine Members of Congress, but appointed in their capacities as users of D.C. airports and not as Members. The authorizing statute required major budgetary and regulatory decisions of MWAA to be approved by the review board. One unstated concern was that a state-dominated regional authority would shift air traffic from close-in National to far-out Dulles, making air travel more inconvenient for Members. The President had no problems with the review board idea. Frustrated that the review board would thwart efforts by the regional authority to shift air traffic from National to Dulles, citizens of northern Virginia brought suit to declare the statutory scheme unconstitutional. Is it? How do *Bowsher* and *Chadha* relate to this issue? See *Metropolitan Washington Airports Authority v. Citizens for the Abatement of Aircraft Noise, Inc.*, 501 U.S. 252 (1991).

NOTE ON THE CONSTITUTIONALITY OF
INDEPENDENT AGENCIES

The Chief Justice's opinion in the Gramm-Rudman Case was careful not to cast doubt on the constitutionality of independent agencies, whose officials are not removable by Congress.[r] But when the Court's precedents are read together, there might be substantial constitutional doubt about independent agencies, such as the FTC.[s] In short, should *Humphrey's Executor* be overruled?

Although *Bowsher* did not take that step, it gave new wind to such arguments by its respectful treatment of *Myers* and its broad understanding of executive functions. If, as *Myers* held, Article II vests the President with plenary authority to supervise the execution of the laws *and*, as *Bowsher* held, execution includes any step in the implementation of a law's policy, then follows that the FTC plays

---

r. In footnote 4, which we omitted, the Chief Justice rejected the appellants' slippery slope argument that the lower court opinion cast doubt on the constitutional status of independent agencies. "The statutes establishing independent agencies typically specify either that the agency members are removable by the President for specified causes * * * or else do not specify a removal procedure. This case involves nothing like these statutes, but rather a statute that provides for direct congressional involvement over the decision to remove the Comptroller General."

s. For different points of view, consult Address by Attorney General Edwin Meese, III, Federal Bar Ass'n, Detroit (13 Sept. 1985); Gary Lawson, *The Rise and Rise of the Administrative State*, 107 Harv. L. Rev. 1231 (1994); Geoffrey Miller, *Independent Agencies*, 1986 Sup. Ct. Rev. 41; Peter Strauss, *The Place of Agencies in Government: Separation of Powers and the Fourth Branch*, 84 Colum. L. Rev. 573 (1984); Michael Froomkin, Note, *In Defense of Agency Autonomy*, 96 Yale L.J. 787, 799 (1987).

an executive role that must be under the control of the President. Conversely, if the FTC is not part of the executive branch, where is it? The reasoning in *Humphrey's* treating the FTC as "quasi-legislative" might be questioned after *Bowsher*. In that event, the FTC becomes part of an unenumerated fourth branch of government — the legislative, executive, and judicial branches named in the Constitution are now joined by a "quasi" branch (to use the *Humphrey's* terminology) of independent agencies that are under the actual control of neither Congress nor the President. Forthright defenders of independent agencies such as Peter Strauss make this concession (see our excerpt from his article in Part C), but it seems like a riskier one after *Bowsher*.

Finally, as *Humphrey's* emphasized, many of the independent agencies make legislative rules based upon a broad statutory delegation, initiate enforcement actions, and adjudicate at least some of those actions. The FTC, for example, adjudicates unfair competition complaints brought by its own enforcement division and issues legislative rules. This combination of legislative, executive, and judicial functions in one institution might be said to violate the essential worry of the Framers (based upon Montesquieu) that these powers be separated lest they be (inevitably) abused.

Peter Strauss, *The Place of Agencies in Government: Separation of Powers and the Fourth Branch*, 84 Colum. L. Rev. 573, 578-80 (1984).[t] "[F]or any consideration of the structure given law-administration below the very apex of the governmental structure, the rigid separation of powers compartmentalization of governmental functions should be abandoned in favor of analysis in terms of separation of functions and checks and balances. Almost fifty years of experience has accustomed lawyers and judges to accepting the independent regulatory commissions, in the metaphor, as a 'headless "fourth branch" ' of government. Although the resulting theoretical confusion has certainly been noticed, we accept the idea of potent actors in government joining judicial, legislative, and executive functions, yet falling outside the constitutionally described schemata of three named branches embracing among them the entire allocated authority of government. * * * A shorthand way of putting the argument is that we should stop pretending that all our government (as distinct from its highest levels) can be allocated into three neat parts. * * *

"From the perspective suggested here, the important fact is that an agency is neither Congress nor President nor Court, but an inferior part of government. Each agency is subject to control relationships with some or all of the three constitutionally named branches, and those relationships give an assurance — functionally similar to that provided by the separation-of-powers notion for the constitutionally named bodies — that they will not pass out of control.[u]

---

t. This article originally appeared at 84 Colum. L. Rev. 573 (1984). Reprinted by permission.

u. For example, one may understand the delegation doctrine in this functional way, rather than as an indication "where" in government rulemaking occurs. That doctrine requires both statutory authorization (a relationship with Congress) and a capacity on the part of the courts to assure legality (a relationship with the courts). The availability of at least limited judicial review, indeed, appears to be identified with increasing frequency as an essential element of the grant of rulemaking authority.

Powerful and potentially arbitrary as they may be, the Secretary of Agriculture and the Chairman of the SEC for this reason do not present the threat that led the framers to insist on a splitting of the authority of government at its very top. What we have, then, are three named repositories of authorizing power and control, and an infinity of institutions to which parts of the authority of each may be lent. The three must share the reins of control; means must be found of assuring that no one of them becomes dominant. But it is not terribly important to number or allocate the horses that pull the carriage of government."

Strauss then lays out an analytical model along the following lines (pp. 596-97): (1) The formal *separation of powers* idea should govern relationships among the three named actors — Congress, the President, the Supreme Court — but not the inferior bodies and agencies. This formal approach is appropriate for evaluating the President's action in the Steel Seizure Case and presumably in the Line Item and Legislative Veto Cases, but not in *Myers*. (2) The guidepost for structuring agencies should be the fairness ideas derived from *separation of functions*, including clear policy statements to guide and limit agency rulemaking (*Hampton*), especially when citizen liberty is involved (*Mistretta*); relative independence for agencies performing adjudicative and prosecutorial functions (*Chadha* and *Buckley* (independence from Congress), *Humphrey's Executor* (from the President)); and avoidance of too many cooks spoiling the broth (*Bowsher*) and conflicts of interest (*Schechter* and *Metropolitan Washington Airports Authority*). (3) The relationship between the President and agencies should be guided by *checks and balances* precepts. "Whatever arrangements are made, one must remain able to characterize the President as the unitary, politically accountable head of all law-administration, sufficiently potent in his own relationships with those who actually perform it to serve as an effective counter to a feared Congress."

These theoretical precepts were soon enough put to a practical test in the following decision. Do they withstand the dissent's critique?

MORRISON v. OLSON
487 U.S. 654, 108 S.Ct. 2597, 101 L.Ed.2d 569 (1988)

CHIEF JUSTICE REHNQUIST delivered the opinion of the Court.

[In response to the Watergate scandal that drove President Nixon from office, Congress adopted the Ethics in Government Act of 1978. Title IV created the office of "Independent Counsel" to investigate and, if appropriate, prosecute certain high-ranking government officials for violations of federal criminal laws. After notification of a possible federal offense, the Attorney General must decide within 90 days whether there are "reasonable grounds to believe that further investigation is warranted." If such reasonable grounds exist, the Attorney General must apply to a Special Division of the U.S. Court of Appeals for the D.C. Circuit for appointment of a special prosecutor; the judicial panel appoints the prosecutor and defines her jurisdiction. The Independent Counsel proceeds until she reports that her job is "completed," *or* the Special Division finds her job completed, *or* the Attorney General removes her (but only for "good cause," as specified in the statute).

[Defendant Theodore Olson, then head of the Justice Department's Office of Legal Counsel, was accused of providing misleading testimony to a congressional subcommittee. Independent Counsel Alexia Morrison was appointed to investigate. Olson moved to quash her subpoenas on the ground that Title IV was unconstitutional. The court of appeals agreed, but the Supreme Court reversed.]

[In Part III of his opinion, the Chief Justice first held that Morrison's manner of appointment did not violate the Appointments Clause of Article II, which reads as follows:]

> [The President] shall nominate, and by and with the Advice and Consent of the Senate, shall appoint Ambassadors, other public Ministers and Consuls, Judges of the Supreme Court, and all other Officers of the United States, whose Appointments are not herein otherwise provided for, and which shall be established by Law: but the Congress may by Law vest the Appointment of such inferior Officers, as they think proper, in the President alone, in the Courts of Law, or in the Heads of Departments. U.S. Const., Art. II, § 2, cl. 2.

The initial question is * * * whether [Morrison] is an "inferior" or a "principal" officer. If she is the latter, * * * then the Act is in violation of the Appointments Clause.

The line between "inferior" and "principal" officers is one that is far from clear, and the Framers provided little guidance into where it should be drawn. We need not attempt here to decide exactly where the line falls between the two types of officers, because in our view [Morrison] clearly falls on the "inferior officer" side of that line [for the following reasons: She is subject to removal by the Attorney General for good cause, is empowered by the Act to perform only certain duties and is otherwise to comply with the policies of the Justice Department, and has a limited tenure in an office of strictly limited jurisdiction.]

This does not, however, end our inquiry under the Appointments Clause. [Olson et al.] argue that even if [Morrison] is an "inferior" officer, the Clause does not empower Congress to place the power to appoint such an officer outside the Executive Branch. * * * The relevant language of the Appointments Clause is worth repeating. It reads: ". . . but the Congress may by Law vest the Appointment of such inferior Officers, as they think proper, in the President alone, in the courts of Law, or in the Heads of Departments." On its face, the language of this "excepting clause" admits of no limitation on interbranch appointments. Indeed, the inclusion of "as they think proper" seems clearly to give Congress significant discretion to determine whether it is "proper" to vest the appointment of, for example, executive officials in the "courts of Law." * * *

We also note that the history of the clause provides no support for [Olson]'s position. * * * [T]here was little or no debate [at the Constitutional Convention] on the question of whether the Clause empowers Congress to provide for interbranch appointments, and there is nothing to suggest that the Framers intended to prevent Congress from having that power.

We do not mean to say that Congress' power to provide for interbranch appointments of "inferior officers" is unlimited. In addition to separation of powers concerns, which would arise if such provisions for appointment had the potential to impair the constitutional functions assigned to one of the branches,

[*Ex parte Siebold*, 100 U.S. 371 (1879)] suggested that Congress' decision to vest the appointment power in the courts would be improper if there was some "incongruity" between the functions normally performed by the courts and the performance of their duty to appoint. In this case, however, we do not think it impermissible for Congress to vest the power to appoint independent counsels in a specially created federal court. * * * We have recognized that courts may appoint private attorneys to act as prosecutor for judicial contempt judgments. * * * [W]e [have] approved court appointment of United States commissioners, who exercised certain limited prosecutorial powers. In *Siebold*, * * * we indicated that judicial appointment of federal marshals, who are "executive officer[s]," would not be inappropriate. * * *

Congress of course was concerned when it created the office of independent counsel with the conflicts of interest that could arise in situations when the Executive Branch is called upon to investigate its own high-ranking officers. If it were to remove the appointing authority from the Executive Branch, the most logical place to put it was in the Judicial Branch. In the light of the Act's provision making the judges of the Special Division ineligible to participate in any matters relating to an independent counsel they have appointed, we do not think that appointment of the independent counsels by the court runs afoul of the constitutional limitation on "incongruous" interbranch appointments.

[In Part IV of the opinion, Chief Justice Rehnquist rejected Olson's argument that the provisions giving judges the authority to appoint the special prosecutor violate Article III. "[O]nce it is accepted that the Appointments Clause gives Congress the power to vest the appointment of officials such as the independent counsel in the 'courts of Law,' there can be no Article III objection to the Special Division's exercise of that power, as the power itself derives from the Appointments Clause, a source of authority for judicial action that is independent of Article III."]

The Act also vests in the Special Division various powers and duties in relation to the independent counsel that, because they do not involve appointing the counsel or defining her jurisdiction, cannot be said to derive from the Division's Appointments Clause authority. These duties include granting extensions for the Attorney General's preliminary investigation; receiving the report of the Attorney General at the conclusion of his preliminary investigation; referring matters to the counsel upon request; receiving reports from the counsel regarding expenses incurred; receiving a report from the Attorney General following the removal of an independent counsel; granting attorney's fees upon request to individuals who were investigated but not indicted by an independent counsel; receiving a final report from the counsel; deciding whether to release the counsel's final report to Congress or the public and determining whether any protective orders should be issued; and terminating an independent counsel when his task is completed.

[The Chief Justice found most of the powers given the Special Division passive or ministerial, thereby posing no trespass on the executive branch.] We are more doubtful about the Special Division's power to terminate the office of the independent counsel. * * * As appellees suggest, the power to terminate, especially when exercised by the Division on its own motion, is "administrative" to the extent that it requires the Special Division to monitor the progress of proceedings of the independent counsel and come to a decision as to whether the counsel's job is "completed." It also is not a power that could be considered typically "judicial," as it has few analogues among the court's more traditional powers. Nonetheless, we do not * * * view this provision as a significant judicial encroachment upon executive power or upon the prosecutorial discretion of the independent counsel.

We think that the Court of Appeals overstated the matter when it described the power to terminate as a "broadsword and . . . rapier" that enables the court to "control the pace and depth of the independent counsel's activities." The provision has not been tested in practice, and we do not mean to say that an adventurous special court could not reasonably construe the provision as did the Court of Appeals; but it is the duty of federal courts to construe a statute in order to save it from constitutional infirmities, and to that end we think a narrow construction is appropriate here. The termination provisions of the Act do not give the Special Division anything approaching the power to *remove* the counsel while an investigation or court proceeding is still underway — this power is vested solely in the Attorney General. As we see it, "termination" may occur only when the duties of the counsel are truly "completed" or "so substantially completed" that there remains no need for any continuing action by the independent counsel. It is basically a device for removing from the public payroll an independent counsel who has served her purpose, but is unwilling to acknowledge the fact. So construed, the Special Division's power to terminate does not pose a sufficient threat of judicial intrusion into matters that are more properly within the Executive's authority to require that the Act be invalidated as inconsistent with Article III. * * *

[In Part V of the opinion, the Chief Justice turned to] whether the Act is invalid under the constitutional principle of separation of powers. Two related issues must be addressed: The first is whether the provision of the Act restricting the Attorney General's power to remove the independent counsel to only those instances in which he can show "good cause," taken by itself, impermissibly interferes with the President's exercise of his constitutionally appointed functions. The second is whether, taken as a whole, the Act violates the separation of powers by reducing the President's ability to control the prosecutorial powers wielded by the independent counsel. * * *

Unlike both *Bowsher* and *Myers*, this case does not involve an attempt by Congress itself to gain a role in the removal of executive officials other than its established powers of impeachment and conviction. The Act instead puts the removal power squarely in the hands of the Executive Branch; an independent counsel may be removed from office "only by the personal action of the Attorney General, and only for good cause." § 596(a)(1). There is no requirement of congressional approval of the Attorney General's removal decision, though the decision is subject to judicial review. In our view, the removal provisions of the Act make this case more analogous to *Humphrey's Executor* and *Weiner* than to *Myers* or *Bowsher*. * * *

[Olson et al.] contend that *Humphrey's Executor* and *Wiener* are distinguishable from this case because they did not involve officials who performed a "core executive function." They argue that our decision in *Humphrey's Executor* rests on a distinction between "purely executive" officials and officials who exercise "quasi-legislative" and "quasi-judicial" powers. In their view, when a "purely executive" official is involved, the governing precedent is *Myers*, not *Humphrey's Executor*. * * *

We undoubtedly did rely on the terms "quasi-legislative" and "quasi-judicial" to distinguish the officials involved in *Humphrey's Executor* and *Wiener* from those in *Myers*, but our present considered view is that the determination of whether the Constitution allows Congress to impose a "good cause"-type restriction on the President's power to remove an official cannot be made to turn on whether or not that official is classified as "purely executive." The analysis contained in our removal cases is designed not to define rigid categories of those officials who may or may not be removed at will by the President, but to ensure that Congress does not interfere with the President's exercise of the "executive Power" and his constitutionally appointed duty to "take Care that the laws be faithfully executed" under Article II. *Myers* was undoubtedly correct in its holding, and in its broader suggestion that there are some "purely executive" officials who must be removable by the President at will if he is to be able to accomplish his constitutional role. * * * At the other end of the spectrum from *Myers*, the characterization of the agencies in *Humphrey's Executor* and *Wiener* as "quasi-legislative" or "quasi-judicial" in large part reflected our judgment that it was not essential to the President's proper execution of his Article II powers that these agencies be headed up by individuals who were removable at will. We do not mean to suggest that an analysis of the functions served by the officials at issue is irrelevant. But the real question is whether the removal restrictions are of such a nature that they impede the President's ability to perform his constitutional duty, and the functions of the officials in question must be analyzed in that light.

Considering for the moment the "good cause" removal provision in isolation from the other parts of the Act at issue in this case, we cannot say that the imposition of a "good cause" standard for removal by itself unduly trammels on executive authority. There is no real dispute that the functions performed by the independent counsel are "executive" in the sense that they are law enforcement functions that typically have been undertaken by officials within the Executive Branch. As we noted above, however, the independent counsel is an inferior officer under the Appointments Clause, with limited jurisdiction and tenure and lacking policymaking or significant administrative authority. Although the counsel exercises no small amount of discretion and judgment in deciding how to carry out her duties under the Act, we simply do not see how the President's need to control the exercise of that discretion is so central to the functioning of the Executive Branch as to require as a matter of constitutional law that the counsel be terminable at will by the President.

Nor do we think that the "good cause" removal provision at issue here impermissibly burdens the President's power to control or supervise the independent counsel, as an executive official, in the execution of her duties under the Act. This is not a case in which the power to remove an executive official has been completely stripped from the President, thus providing no means for the President to ensure the "faithful execution" of the laws. Rather, because the independent counsel may be terminated for "good cause," the Executive, through the Attorney General, retains ample authority to assure that the counsel is competently performing her statutory responsibilities in a manner that comports with the provisions of the Act. Although we need not decide in this case exactly what is encompassed within the term "good cause" under the Act, the legislative history of the removal provision also makes clear that the Attorney General may remove an independent counsel for "misconduct." Here, as with the provision of the Act conferring the appointment authority of the independent counsel on the special court, the congressional determination to limit the removal power of the Attorney General was essential, in the view of Congress, to establish the necessary independence of the office. We do not think that this limitation as it presently stands sufficiently deprives the President of control over the independent counsel to interfere impermissibly with his constitutional obligation to ensure the faithful execution of the laws.

The final question to be addressed is whether the Act, taken as a whole, violates the principle of separation of powers by unduly interfering with the role of the Executive Branch. * * *

We observe first that this case does not involve an attempt by Congress to increase its own powers at the expense of the Executive Branch. Unlike some of our previous cases, most recently *Bowsher*, this case simply does not pose a "dange[r] of congressional usurpation of Executive Branch functions." [Also citing *Chadha*.] Indeed, with the exception of the power of impeachment — which applies to all officers of the United States — Congress retained for itself no powers of control or supervision over an independent counsel. The Act does empower certain members of Congress to request the Attorney General to apply for the appointment of an independent counsel, but the Attorney General has no duty to comply with the request, although he must respond within a certain time limit. Other than that, Congress' role under the Act is limited to receiving reports or other information and oversight of the independent counsel's activities, functions that we have recognized generally as being incidental to the legislative function of Congress.

Similarly, we do not think that the Act works any *judicial* usurpation of properly executive functions. As should be apparent from our discussion of the Appointments Clause above, the power to appoint inferior officers such as independent counsels is not in itself an "executive" function in the constitutional sense, at least when Congress has exercised its power to vest the appointment of an inferior office in the "courts of Law." We note nonetheless that under the Act the Special Division has no power to appoint an independent counsel *sua sponte*; it may only do so upon the specific request of the Attorney General, and the courts are specifically prevented from reviewing the Attorney General's decision not to seek appointment. In addition, once the court has appointed a counsel and defined her jurisdiction, it has no power to supervise or control the activities of the counsel. * * * The Act does give a federal court the power to review the Attorney General's decision to remove an independent counsel, but in our view this is a function that is well within the traditional power of the judiciary.

Finally, we do not think that the Act "impermissibly undermine[s]" the powers of the Executive Branch, or "disrupts the proper balance between the coordinate branches [by] prevent[ing] the Executive Branch from accomplishing its constitutionally assigned functions." It is undeniable that the Act reduces the amount of control or supervision that the Attorney General and, through him, the President exercises over the investigation and prosecution of a certain class of alleged criminal activity. The Attorney General is not allowed to appoint the individual of his choice; he does not determine the counsel's jurisdiction; and his power to remove a counsel is limited. Nonetheless, the Act does give the Attorney General several means of supervising or controlling the prosecutorial powers that may be wielded by an independent counsel. Most importantly, the Attorney General retains the power to remove the counsel for "good cause," a power that we have already concluded provides the Executive with substantial ability to ensure that the laws are "faithfully executed" by an independent counsel. No independent counsel may be appointed without a specific request by the Attorney General, and the Attorney General's decision not to request appointment if he finds "no reasonable grounds to believe that further investigation is warranted" is committed to his unreviewable discretion. The Act thus gives the Executive a degree of control over the power to initiate an investigation by the independent counsel. In addition, the jurisdiction of the independent counsel is defined with reference to the facts submitted by the Attorney General, and once a counsel is appointed, the Act requires that the counsel abide by Justice Department policy unless it is not "possible" to do so. Notwithstanding the fact that the counsel is to some degree "independent" and free from Executive supervision to a greater extent than other federal prosecutors, in our view these features of the Act give the Executive Branch sufficient control over the independent counsel to ensure that the President is able to perform his constitutionally assigned duties.

JUSTICE KENNEDY took no part in the consideration or decision of this case.

JUSTICE SCALIA, dissenting.

* * * That is what this suit is about. Power. The allocation of power among Congress, the President and the courts in such fashion as to preserve the equilibrium the Constitution sought to establish — so that "a gradual concentration of the several powers in the same department," *Federalist* No. 51, p. 321 (J. Madison), can effectively be resisted. Frequently an issue of this sort will come before the Court clad, so to speak, in sheep's clothing: the potential of the asserted principle to effect important change in the equilibrium of power is not immediately evident, and must be discerned by a careful and perceptive analysis. But this wolf comes as a wolf. * * *

[B]y the application of this statute in the present case, Congress has effectively compelled a criminal investigation of a high-level appointee of the President in connection with his action arising out of a bitter power dispute between the President and the Legislative Branch. Mr. Olson may or may not be guilty of a crime; we do not know. But we do know that the investigation of him has been commenced, not necessarily because the President or his authorized subordinates believe it is in the interest of the United States, in the sense that it warrants the diversion of resources from other efforts, and is worth the cost in money and in possible damage to other governmental interests; and not even, leaving aside those normally considered factors, because the President or his authorized subordinates necessarily believe that an investigation is likely to unearth a violation worth prosecuting; but only because the Attorney General cannot affirm, as Congress demands, that there are *no reasonable grounds to believe* that further investigation is warranted. The decision regarding the scope of that further investigation, its duration, and, finally, whether or not prosecution should ensue, are likewise beyond the control of the President and his subordinates. * * *

Art. II, § 1, cl. 1 of the Constitution provides: "The executive Power shall be vested in a President of the United States." * * * [T]his does not mean *some of* the executive power, but *all of* the executive power. It seems to me, therefore, that the decision of the Court of Appeals invalidating the present statute must be upheld on fundamental separation-of-powers principles if the following two questions are answered affirmatively: (1) Is the conduct of a criminal prosecution (and of an investigation to decide whether to prosecute) the exercise of purely executive power? (2) Does the statute deprive the President of the United States of exclusive control over the exercise of that power? Surprising to say, the Court appears to concede an affirmative answer to both questions, but seeks to avoid the inevitable conclusion that since the statute vests some purely executive power in a person who is not the President of the United States it is void. * * *

The utter incompatibility of the Court's approach with our constitutional traditions can be made more clear, perhaps, by applying it to the powers of the other two Branches. Is it conceivable that if Congress passed a statute depriving itself of less than full and entire control over some insignificant area of legislation, we would inquire whether the matter was "*so central* to the functioning of the Legislative Branch" as really to require complete control, or whether the statute gives Congress "*sufficient* control over the surrogate legislator to ensure that Congress is able to perform its constitutionally assigned duties"? Of course we would have none of that. Once we determined that a purely legislative power was at issue we would require it to be exercised, wholly and entirely, by Congress. * * *

Is it unthinkable that the President should have such exclusive power, even when alleged crimes by him or his close associates are at issue? No more so than that Congress should have the exclusive power of legislation, even when what is at issue is its own exemption from the burdens of certain laws. See Civil Rights Act of 1964, Title VII, 42 U.S.C. §§ 2000e *et seq.* (prohibiting "employers," not defined to include the United States, from discriminating on the basis of race, color, religion, sex or national origin). No more so than that this Court should have the exclusive power to pronounce the final decision on justiciable cases and controversies, even those pertaining to the constitutionality of a statute reducing the salaries of the Justices. A system of separate and coordinate powers necessarily involves an acceptance of exclusive power that can theoretically be abused. * * * The checks against any Branch's abuse of its exclusive powers are twofold: First, retaliation by one of the other Branch's use of *its* exclusive powers: Congress, for example, can impeach the Executive who willfully fails to enforce the laws; the Executive can decline to prosecute under unconstitutional statutes; and the courts can dismiss malicious prosecutions. Second, and ultimately, there is the political check that the people will replace those in the political branches (the branches more "dangerous to the political rights of the Constitution," *Federalist* No. 78) who are guilty of abuse. Political pressures produced special prosecutors — for Teapot Dome and for Watergate, for example — long before this statute created the independent counsel.

The Court has, nonetheless, replaced the clear constitutional prescription that the executive power belongs to the President with a "balancing test." What are the standards to determine how the balance is to be struck, that is, how much removal of presidential power is too much? * * * Once we depart from the text of the Constitution, just where short of that do we stop? The most amazing feature of the Court's opinion is that it does not even purport to give an answer. It simply *announces*, with no analysis, that the ability to control the decision whether to investigate and prosecute the President's closest advisors, and indeed the President himself, is not "so central to the functioning of the Executive Branch" as to be constitutionally required to be within the President's control. Apparently that is so because we say it is so. Having abandoned as the basis for our decision-making the text of Article II that "the executive Power" must be vested in the President, the Court does not even attempt to craft a *substitute* criterion — a "justiciable standard," however remote from the Constitution — that today governs, and in the future will govern, the decision of such questions. Evidently, the governing standard is to be what might be called the unfettered wisdom of a majority of this Court, revealed to an obedient people on a case-by-case basis. This is not only not the government of laws that the Constitution established; it is not a government of laws at all.

In my view, moreover, even as an ad hoc, standardless judgment the Court's conclusion must be wrong. Before this statute was passed, the President, in taking action disagreeable to the Congress, or an executive officer giving advice to the President or testifying before Congress concerning one of those many matters on which the two branches are from time to time at odds, could be assured that his acts and motives would be adjudged — insofar as the decision whether to conduct a criminal investigation and to prosecute is concerned — in the Executive Branch, that is, in a forum attuned to the interests and the policies of the Presidency. That was one of the natural advantages the Constitution gave to the Presidency, just as it gave Members of Congress (and their staffs) the advantage of not being prosecutable for anything said or done in their legislative capacities. See U.S. Const., Art. I, § 6, cl. 1. It is the very object of this legislation to eliminate that assurance of a sympathetic forum. * * *

[Justice Scalia contended that special prosecutors are in no sense "inferior" officers as they are in no sense subordinate to the President; hence, the statute violates the Appointments Clause even under the Court's functional reading. The Court's functionalism had the further disadvantage, Justice Scalia maintained, of departing from both *Myers* and *Humphrey's Executor* — the latter, by abandoning the "executive-versus-quasi-legislative-officer" distinction, and both precedents by explicitly announcing that some executive officers can be released from any presidential control.] There are now no lines. If the removal of a prosecutor, the virtual embodiment of the power to "take Care that the laws be faithfully executed," can be restricted, what officer's removal cannot? This is an open invitation for Congress to experiment. What about an Assistant Secretary of State, with responsibility for one very narrow area of foreign policy, who would not only have to be confirmed by the Senate but could also be removed only pursuant to certain carefully designed restrictions? * * * As far as I can discern from the Court's opinion, it is now open season upon the President's removal power for all executive offices, with not even the superficially principled restriction of *Humphrey's Executor* as cover. The Court essentially says to the President "Trust us. We will make sure that you are able to accomplish your constitutional role." I think the Constitution gives the President — and the people — more protection than that. * * *

NOTES ON THE INDEPENDENT COUNSEL CASE

1. *Formalist and Functionalist Theories for Reconciling the Precedents.* Is there any way to make *Morrison* consistent with *Bowsher*? With *Myers*? With *Buckley*? Note that in *Morrison* the Court approves a congressional plan that deprives the President of control over a "core" executive official. Doesn't that amount to a more drastic congressional intrusion upon the separation of powers than plans to deprive the President of control over a postmaster (*Myers*) or even over budget cuts (*Bowsher*) or federal campaign regulation (*Buckley*), for in this instance the uncontrollable officer is out to get one of the President's own officials — indeed, perhaps even the President himself! One way to reconcile *Morrison* with the earlier precedents is to read all the cases functionally, as Professor Strauss does in the preceding excerpt. Another way to reconcile them is suggested by Harold Krent, *Executive Control over Criminal Law Enforcement: Some Lessons from History*, 38 Am. U.L. Rev. 275 (1989), who contends that Justice Scalia misstated the historical record supporting the conclusion that criminal prosecutions are "core" executive functions.[v] Instead, Krent notes, the Attorney General did not preside over a core group of prosecutors until the late nineteenth century; in the early history under the Constitution, criminal prosecutions for violating federal laws were carried out by state prosecutors, private citizens, and district attorneys who reported to no one before 1820. Under Krent's reading, the independent counsel might be viewed as an officer not necessarily "executive" for *Myers* purposes.

Another way to read the cases would rely on the principle against self-aggrandizement. Under this principle, Congress itself cannot exercise direct control over officials "executing" the law (*Myers*, *Buckley*, and *Bowsher*), but it can authorize someone other than the President to control them (*Morrison*). Now consider this reading of *Humphrey's Executor*: Article II gives the President plenary authority over certain "purely executive" functions, but not

---

v. The pragmatic messiness of the historical record is also usefully explored by Susan Bloch, *The Early Role of the Attorney General in Our Constitutional Scheme: In the Beginning There Was Pragmatism*, 1989 Duke L.J. 561; Daniel Reisman, *Deconstructing Justice Scalia's Separation of Powers Jurisprudence: The Preeminent Executive*, 53 Alb. L. Rev. 49 (1988); Stephanie Dangel, Note, *Is Prosecution a Core Executive Function?* Morrison v. Olson *and the Framers' Intent*, 99 Yale L.J. 1069 (1990).

over all functions that might be classified as "executive." As to those functions, Congress under the Necessary and Proper Clause, Art. I, § 8, cl. 18, and under the Appointments Clause, Art. II, § 2, cl. 2, may exercise some influence, as a corollary of its own Article I authority as the nation's lawmaker. That influence cannot be through a congressional veto of executive action (*Chadha*) or through congressional control of an executive official (*Bowsher*), because of the self-aggrandizement involved. Similarly, that influence cannot be through congressional control over appointments to the commission (*Buckley*), but it can be through an appointments mechanism set up within the executive or judicial branches of government. Does this argument make sense of the cases? How should *Clinton v. New York* be decided under this theory? Were the *Clinton* dissenters right to object that the item veto, though novel, did not pose sufficient constitutional risks to be invalidated?

2. *The Vertical Perspective: Shifting Responsibility Away from Congress and Creating Terminator Risks.* Functionalism spawned the Independent Counsel idea. President Richard Nixon (1969-74) and his men violated the law at many levels but were protected from prosecution by a Justice Department headed by Nixon cronies who were themselves alleged to be part of the cover-up. Deeply underlying Chief Justice Rehnquist's opinion may be the Richard Nixon problem: If foxes are guarding the henhouse, who will guard the foxes? So Congress created a hound to monitor the foxes. Unfortunately, this functionalist experiment radically shifted responsibility in ways that pose both minoritarian and majoritarian risks.

The independence from political interference needed to solve the Richard Nixon Problem is also, unfortunately, independence from practical incentives that have traditionally supported the presumption of innocence accorded accused wrongdoers. A former student has analogized the independent counsel to *The Terminator*, a movie in which Arnold Schwarzenegger is a futuristic robot programmed to do nothing but hunt down a designated victim. Like the Terminator, the independent counsel is appointed for one purpose and one purpose only — to track down and get the goods on a designated federal official. She is given lots of money and the brightest assistants. Her decision whether to prosecute may be skewed by her own status (she goes out of business if she decides not to prosecute) and, more important, by her freedom from the many other factors prosecutors often have to consider (limited resources and executive enforcement priorities). Because the mere appointment of an independent counsel is a big media event, the suspect loses all presumption of innocence and is compelled to retain expensive counsel for long periods of time. The suspect stands a good chance of being wiped out financially even if never indicted. See Julie O'Sullivan, *The Independent Counsel Statute: Bad Law, Bad Policy*, 33 Am. Crim. L. Rev. 463 (1996).

More serious is the threat to majorities, because the law shifted responsibility for monitoring the President and his men and women from oversight and impeachment by Congress, with its political constituencies, to relentless investigation and exposure by the Independent Counsel, who has no constituency.[w] Contrast the public disgraces of Nixon and Clinton. Nixon's wrongdoing became public through a process by which his own Department of Justice and Congress slowly exposed links between criminal behavior and the White House. He resigned on the eve of impeachment votes that would surely have ended his presidency. Clinton's wrongdoing, in contrast, became public through a process by which a perceived political enemy (Republican IC Kenneth Starr) gathered evidence and turned it over to a hostile House of Representatives, which promptly impeached him (see the Note on Congress's Impeachment Power above). Whatever the merits of Starr's charges, the public was underwhelmed by them, and Clinton's impeachment and trial occupied the nation's political process for months — to the detriment of Congress's doing its Article I, § 7 job.

3. *Neo-Formalism in Separation of Powers Cases.* It is striking how functionalist the Chief Justice's opinion is in the Independent Counsel Case, and how little support Justice Scalia's powerful dissent garnered. Why is that? One reason may be that formalism does not automatically support the Scalia result, for the reasons raised in Note 1. Or it might be ambivalence about formalism's drawbacks. Its reliance on fitting novel arrangements into old categories has a Procrustean ring to it and, according to legal historiographers such as Martin Flaherty, typically relies on "originalist" analysis that is ahistorical or even amateurish.[x] Historians emphasize complexity and evolution; the legal archaeologist seeking categorical evidence tends to want, and therefore to find, simplicity and stability. The mechanical matchmaking (arrangement and category) of the legal archaeologist conveys a potentially misleading objectivity about constitutional law. Finally, one might find formalism simply inconvenient; a thoroughgoing formalism would make a mess of this century's modern regulatory state, says Strauss.

Nonetheless, formalism itself has a kind of Terminator quality to it: It is sort of indestructible — just when you think it has been crushed, it rises and renews pursuit. It seemed dead during the New Deal, but made a dramatic comeback in the Steel Seizure Case. When the judiciary embraced the functionalism of the Jackson concurrence (as in the Iranian Hostages Case), formalism came back even stronger in *Chadha* and *Bowsher*. Has *Morrison* been any more fatal? Hardly. If anything, *Morrison* reinvigorated formalism in the academy. Legal scholars, especially formalists and originalists, feasted on the Chief Justice's opinion like famished dieters.[y] Conservative contempt for *Morrison* created

---

w. Nourse, *Vertical Separation*, 49 Duke L.J. at 773-77; Julie O'Sullivan, *The Interaction Between Impeachment and the Independent Counsel Statute*, 86 Geo. L.J. 2193 (1998).

x. The point is made generally in Martin Flaherty, *History "Lite" in Modern American Constitutionalism*, 95 Colum. L. Rev. 523 (1995), and with specific reference to separation of powers debates in Flaherty, *The Most Dangerous Branch*, 105 Yale L.J. 1725 (1996).

y. See Martin Redish, *The Constitution as Political Structure* (1991); Steven Calabresi & Kevin Rhodes, *The Structural Constitution: Unitary Executive, Plural Judiciary*, 105 Harv. L. Rev. 1153 (1992); Stephen Carter, *From Sick Chicken to Synar: The Evolution and Subsequent De-Evolution of the Separation of Powers*, 1987 B.Y.U. L. Rev. 719; Lee Liberman, Morrison v. Olson: *A Formalistic Perspective on Why the Court Was Wrong*, 38 Am. U.L. Rev. 313 (1989); Thomas

sympathy for Gary Lawson's proposal that Supreme Court constitutional opinions should generally not count as binding precedent when they are inconsistent with original meaning.[a] (Justice Thomas, not on the Court for *Morrison*, is sympathetic to the Lawson thesis.) Correspondingly, the Scalia dissent energized a new generation of neo-formalist constitutional scholarship. Consider an exemplar of scholarship supporting Justice Scalia's approach.

Steven Calabresi & Saikrishna Prakash, *The President's Power To Execute the Laws*, 104 Yale L.J. 541, 663-64 (1994).[b] The conclusion to the authors' lengthy article sums up their claims: "First, our Constitution creates a trinity of types of governmental powers and personnel [Arts. I-III]. The constitutional text thus forecloses historical arguments for a headless fourth branch of government. Second, the Vesting Clauses of Article II (and Article III) are general grants of power that are explicated (to different degrees) by the subsequent Sections of those Articles. The Executive Power Clause [Art. II, § 1, cl. 1] in particular gives the President the authority to execute federal law.[c] Third, since the President's grant of 'the executive Power' is exclusive, Congress may not create other entities independent of the President and let them exercise his 'executive Power.' Fourth, the hierarchical structure of Article II is further confirmed by the language of the Take Care [Art. II, § 3], Opinions [Art. II, § 2, cl. 1], and Militia [*ibid.*] Clauses. Finally, the Necessary and Proper Clause does not give Congress any power to deviate from the basic constitutional structure. Congress can no more use that Clause to abolish the unitary Executive than it could use it to abolish the states. The pre-ratification history fully supports these understandings, and little in the post-ratification history calls any of this into question. Indeed, there is more post-ratification evidence to support our textual theories. We should not be surprised that the founding generation read the text according to its 'plain meaning.' * * *

"We can now appreciate our Constitution's elegant simplicity. Our grade school and high school civics teachers were right all along: The Constitution

---

Merrill, *The Constitutional Principle of Separation of Powers*, 1991 Sup. Ct. Rev. 225; Henry Monaghan, *The Protective Power of the Presidency*, 93 Colum. L. Rev. 1 (1993); Saikrishna Prakash, Note, *Hail to the Chief Administrator: The Framers and the President's Administrative Powers*, 102 Yale L.J. 991 (1992); Martin Redish & Elizabeth Cisar, *"If Angels Were to Govern": The Need for Pragmatic Formalism in Separation of Powers Theory*, 1992 Duke L.J. 449.

a. Gary Lawson, *The Constitutional Case Against Precedent,* 17 Harv. J.L. & Pub. Pol'y 23 (1994); accord, Randy Barnett, *Trumping Precedent with Original Meaning: Not As Radical As It Sounds*, 22 Const. Comm. 257 (2005); Michael Stokes Paulsen, *The Intrinsically Corrupting Influence of Precedent*, 22 Const. Comm. 289 (2005).

b. Reprinted by permission of The Yale Law Journal Company and Fred B. Rothman & Company from *The Yale Law Journal*, Vol. 104, pages 541-665.

c. *Editors' note*: Calabresi & Prakash contrast the Vesting Clause of Article II, which is a *general grant* of "executive Power" — presumably *all* of it, except as taken away elsewhere in the Constitution — with the Vesting Clause of Article I, which is a *limited grant* of "[a]ll legislative Powers *herein granted*." First articulated by Alexander Hamilton and a holding of *Myers*, this Vesting Clause Thesis is also the starting point for Prakash and Ramsey's Foreign Affairs Vesting Clause Thesis discussed in Section 1B.

separates our federal government into three branches, each exercising one of three types of powers. * * * The Framers and ratifiers consciously and deliberately chose to put one person in charge of executing *all* federal laws."

NOTE ON THE UNITARY EXECUTIVE THESIS

If accepted, the unitary executive thesis would require reconsidering a number of precedents, including *Humphrey's Executor, Clinton v. Jones,* other presidential immunity or privilege cases (surely *Nixon v. Administrator of General Services*), and perhaps even the Iranian Hostages Case — not to mention the Independent Counsel Case. A thesis that cuts against so much conventional wisdom has stimulated a host of responses over the last two decades.[d] Consider the following points:

1. *What Does "Executive Power" Include?* Peter Shane has suggested to us that most non-unitarists, from Peter Strauss onward, do not disagree that the President heads a unitary executive branch; instead, they contest the proposition that "executive Power" includes all of what we call "administration." There is some evidence that early nineteenth-century American political thought considered day-to-day administration different from higher-level executive decisionmaking. But the evidence is thin that this later thought influenced the Framers or accurately characterized the practice during the Washington Administration (Calabresi & Prakash, 104 Yale L.J. at 639-63). The stronger response to Calabresi and Prakash is that eighteenth-century political thought — either theoretical (Locke, Montesquieu) or practical (the experience before 1787) — did not organize government into the three neat categories modern formalists do (Flaherty, *Most Dangerous Branch*, 105 Yale L.J. at 1756-77). Recall Dean Casper's essay at the beginning of the chapter.

2. *Does the Necessary and Proper Clause Allow Congress a Role in Structuring Execution?* Over two decades ago, William Van Alstyne, *The Role of Congress in Determining Incidental Powers of the President and of the Federal Courts,* Law & Contemp. Probs. 102 (Spring 1976), argued that the Necessary and Proper Clause of Article I gives Congress a role in defining an administrative structure for execution of the laws. Calabresi & Prakash (104

---

d. The Strauss article excerpted above is a response to an earlier version of the unitary executive thesis and should be consulted in detail, as should Martin Flaherty, *The Most Dangerous Branch,* 105 Yale L.J. 1725 (1996). Other pragmatist — and non-unitarist — analysis of the issue include Michael Froomkin, *The Imperial Presidency's New Vestments,* 88 Nw. U.L. Rev. 1346 (1994); Abner Greene, *Checks and Balances in an Era of Presidential Lawmaking,* 61 U. Chi. L. Rev. 123 (1993); Larry Lessig & Cass Sunstein, *The President and Administration,* 94 Colum. L. Rev. 1 (1994); Geoffrey Miller, *The Unitary Executive in a Unified Theory of Constitutional Law: The Problem of Interpretation,* 15 Cardozo L. Rev. 201 (1993); Peter Shane, *Independent Policymaking and Presidential Power: A Constitutional Analysis,* 57 Geo. Wash. L. Rev. 596 (1989); Peter Strauss, *Formal and Functional Approaches to Separation-of-Powers Questions — A Foolish Inconsistency?,* 72 Cornell L. Rev. 488 (1987). For articles supporting the unitary executive thesis, see Steven Calabresi & Kevin Rhodes, *The Structural Constitution: Unitary Executive, Plural Judiciary,* 105 Harv. L. Rev. 1153 (1992); Gary Lawson & Guy Seidman, *The Jeffersonian Treaty Clause,* 2006 U. Ill. L. Rev. 1; Prakash & Ramsey, *Executive Power over Foreign Affairs,* 111 Yale L.J. 231.

Yale L.J. at 622-26) respond that such a broad reading of the clause was not contemplated by the Framers, who saw it only as giving Congress flexibility as to *means* and not adding to Congress' authorized powers (*ends*). Still, *McCulloch v. Maryland* (Chapter 7, § 1) read the clause more broadly, and the critics' deployment of the clause is not to allow Congress to regulate subjects otherwise forbidden by Article I, but only to give Congress some say in how administration is structured — Strauss' idea of pragmatic allocation below the top levels of the national government.

3. *Changed Circumstances.* The first two points rely on an originalist methodology. While Strauss and others make such arguments, their main arguments are nonoriginalist, based on constitutional precedent which reflects the needs of the modern administrative state, constitutional adverse possession (rationalizing longstanding practice), and translation or Ackermanian "constitutional moments" (Chapter 2, § 3C). Consider the last line of argument. Ackerman's New Deal constitutional moment involved a repudiation of the Old Court's substantive due process and Commerce Clause decisions, but note that the Old Court was rather *au current* in its toleration of presidential initiatives in foreign affairs (*Curtiss-Wright*), independent regulatory commissions (*Humphrey's Executor*), and agency adjudications (*Crowell v. Benson*, in § 2C of this chapter). Is it fair to say that the constitutional moment of the late 1930s formally transformed separation-of-powers issues in the way it assertedly transformed federalism and economic liberty issues?

———

Weiss v. United States, 510 U.S. 163 (1994). The Military Justice Act of 1968 established the position of "military judge," who presides over court-martial proceedings (ruling on legal issues and instructing court-martial board members regarding the law and procedures to be followed). Military trial and appellate judges must be commissioned officers of the armed forces and members of the bar. They are selected by the Judge Advocate General (JAG) of their respective branches of the armed forces; they do not serve for fixed terms and perform judicial duties only when assigned by the JAG; they perform nonjudicial functions simultaneous with their judicial performance. These judges are "Officers of the United States" subject to the Appointments Clause, Art. II, § 2, cl. 2. In an opinion by **Chief Justice Rehnquist**, the Court held that these officers meet the requirements of the clause because, as commissioned officers of the armed forces, all were already appointed by the President, with the advice and consent of the Senate. The Court held that no fresh appointment (to the position as military judge) was needed under the Appointments Clause.

Justice Souter, concurring, provided a more extensive analysis of the Appointments Clause issue. The Framers of the Constitution wanted to avoid *both* the executive's manipulation of official appointments *and* the legislature's factionalizing over appointments it controlled. *Freytag v. Commissioner*, 501 U.S. 868 (1991). The solution was the Appointments Clause, whose "grant to the President of the power to nominate principal officers would avert legislative despotism," just as "its requirement of Senate confirmation would serve as an 'excellent check' against Presidential missteps or wrongdoing." Quoting *The Federalist* No. 76. This ingenious solution did not apply, however, to "inferior

Officers," whose appointment could be structured by Congress (*Morrison v. Olson*). Justice Souter concluded that as far as principal Officers were concerned, the Court must protect against either branch's effort to aggrandize its own power and against either branch's abdication of its appointment responsibilities.

Justice Souter argued that if military judges were principal Officers, their method of appointment would amount to an abdication by both President and Congress of their nonwaivable responsibilities under the Appointments Clause. Because Article I Tax Court judges and Article III judges are principal Officers, the argument that military judges are as well "is far from frivolous." Under the *Morrison* factors, the military judge's tenure is not limited, nor is his or her jurisdiction; their powers over cases before them are similar to the powers of Article I and Article III judges; though they can be removed, that is true of most principal Officers. On the other hand, military judges can be removed for any reason, while Article I judges (for example) can only be removed for cause, and military judges have no fixed term and can be assigned and reassigned like functionaries. Given the tolerable arguments either way, Justice Souter deferred to Congress' (implicit) determination that military judges are inferior Officers.

For application of *Morrison* and *Weiss* to civilian judges on military courts, see *Ryder v. United States*, 515 U.S. 177 (1995), and *Edmond v. United States*, 520 U.S. 651 (1997).

C. CONGRESSIONAL STRUCTURING OF ADJUDICATION

Just as the modern regulatory state has pressed against the limits arguably imposed upon "legislative" and "executive" powers purportedly allocated in Articles I and II, so it has challenged limits arguably imposed on the "judicial Power" in Article III. The core feature of Article III is that the adjudications specified in § 2 be handled (or reviewed) by judges with assurances of independence — namely service for life "during good Behaviour" and with "Compensation, which shall not be diminished during their Continuance in Office" (§ 1).[a] Chapter 9 examines the self-imposed limits the Court has developed from Article III to restrain its own potentially self-aggrandizing exercise of power; the remainder of this chapter examines the limits Article III places on Congress: (1) May Congress assign Article III judges extrajudicial tasks? (2) May Congress assign adjudicative tasks to non-Article III judges? (3) What limits are there on Congress' ability to strip Article III courts of jurisdiction or to tinker with their judgments?

1. *Assigning Article III Judges Nonjudicial Duties*

Mistretta v. United States, 488 U.S. 361 (1989). In the Sentencing Reform Act of 1984, codified as 18 U.S.C. § 3551 *et seq.* and 28 U.S.C. §§ 991-998,

---

a. We do not treat the Good Behaviour and Compensation Clauses in this casebook. They are discussed in *Federalist* Nos. 78 and 79 (Hamilton). Leading cases on each are *United States ex rel. Toth v. Quarles*, 350 U.S. 11 (1955) (Good Behaviour); *United States v. Will*, 449 U.S. 200 (1980) (Compensation).

Congress created the United States Sentencing Guidelines Commission "as an independent commission in the judicial branch of the United States." 28 U.S.C. § 991(a). It has seven members appointed by the President and confirmed by the Senate. At least three members must be federal judges "selected after considering a list of six judges recommended to the President by the Judicial Conference of the United States." Members of the Commission are subject to removal by the President "only for neglect of duty or malfeasance in office or for other good cause shown."

After upholding the statute's delegation of authority to craft sentencing guidelines (§ 2A of this chapter), the Court rejected arguments that the Commission's composition and placement violated the separation of powers and Article III. **Justice Blackmun**'s opinion for the Court invoked the Nixon Cases and *Federalist* No. 47 (App. 2) for the proposition that "the Framers did not require — and indeed rejected — the notion that the three Branches must be entirely separate and distinct. * * * In a passage now commonplace in our cases, Justice Jackson summarized the pragmatic, flexible view of differentiated governmental power to which we are heir," when he said the Constitution " 'enjoins upon its branches separateness but interdependence, autonomy but reciprocity.' " Steel Seizure Case (Jackson, J., concurring).

"It is this concern of encroachment and aggrandizement that has animated our separation-of-powers jurisprudence and aroused our vigilance against the 'hydraulic pressure inherent within each of the separate Branches to exceed the outer limits of its power.' *Buckley v. Valeo.* Accordingly, we have not hesitated to strike down provisions of law that either accrete to a single Branch powers more appropriately diffused among separate Branches or that undermine the authority and independence of one or another coordinate Branch. * * * *Bowsher*; *Chadha.* By the same token, we have upheld statutory provisions that to some degree commingle the functions of the Branches, but that pose no danger of either aggrandizement or encroachment. *Morrison.*" Three issues were discussed: (1) the location of the Commission within the judicial branch, (2) the assignment of nonjudicial duties to Article III judges, and (3) excessive presidential control.

1. *The Location-of-the-Commission Issue.* To "ensure the independence of the Judicial Branch by precluding debilitating entanglements between the Judiciary and the two political Branches, and prevent the Judiciary from encroaching into areas reserved for the other Branches," the Court has refused to allow judges to issue advisory opinions or handle matters that are not justiciable (see Chapter 9, § 1). In *Morrison*, the Court repeated what it first said in *Buckley*, that " 'executive or administrative duties of a nonjudicial nature may not be imposed on judges holding office under Art. III.' "

But there is a "twilight area" in which the activities of the separate branches might properly overlap — including rulemaking authority for the Federal Rules governing Civil Procedure, Evidence, and so on ceded by Congress to the Supreme Court. *Sibbach v. Wilson & Co.*, 312 U.S. 1 (1941), construing the Rules Enabling Act, 28 U.S.C. § 2072. "[C]onsistent with the separation of powers, Congress may delegate to the Judicial Branch nonadjudicatory functions that do not trench upon the prerogatives of another Branch and are appropriate to the central mission of the Judiciary," pursuant to its powers under the Necessary and Proper Clause. See *Wayman v. Southard*, 23 U.S. (10 Wheat.) 1 (1825) (Marshall, C.J.). Justice Blackmun concluded that Congress had not vested in the judicial branch any powers more appropriately performed by other branches — sentencing is, after all, primarily a judicial function, despite the role of the executive branch in investigating the defendant and proposing sentences. Thus, the power to create rules for sentencing was found sufficiently similar to the longstanding power to create rules for practice and procedure to sustain Congress' discretion to place the Commission in the judicial branch of government.

Refusing to characterize the sentencing guidelines as *substantive* and in contrast to the *procedural* nature of prior judicial rulemaking, Justice Blackmun conceded that the power to craft sentencing guidelines involves more "political judgment about crime and criminality" and has "important effects on the substantive rights of litigants" that prior rulemaking was supposed to avoid. Nonetheless, locating the Commission in the judicial branch does not pose dangers of judicial aggrandizement, the Court held, because it leaves unaffected the ordinary work of Article III judges — applying law to facts — and is under the formal and functional control of Congress and the President.

"Although the Guidelines are intended to have substantive effects on public behavior (as do the rules of procedure), they do not bind or regulate the primary conduct of the public or vest in the Judicial Branch the legislative responsibility for establishing minimum and maximum penalties for every crime. They do no more than fetter the discretion of sentencing judges to do what they have done for generations — impose sentences within the broad limits established by Congress. Given their limited reach, the special role of the Judicial Branch in the field of sentencing, and the fact that the Guidelines are promulgated by an independent agency and not a court, it follows that as a matter of 'practical consequences' the location of the Sentencing Commission within the Judicial Branch simply leaves with the Judiciary what long has belonged to it."

2. *The Extralegal-Job-for-Judges Issue.* Although the Court found the requirement of judicial service on the Commission "somewhat troublesome," it found such participation did not interfere with the proper and independent functioning of the judiciary. In light of the Incompatibility Clause prohibiting certain kinds of extralegislative service by Members of Congress (Art. I, § 6, cl. 2), Justice Blackmun found it significant that the Constitution did not limit extrajudicial service by federal judges, a matter that was debated, inconclusively, at the Philadelphia Convention.

Remarkably, the first three Chief Justices also served in other capacities during their judicial terms: John Jay as Ambassador to England (where he negotiated the infamous Jay Treaty), Oliver Ellsworth as Minister to France, and John Marshall as Secretary of State (briefly overlapping with his initial service as Chief Justice) and member of the Sinking Fund Commission — all positions requiring Senate confirmation. Although some objected to Jay's double service, their objections were rebuffed in the Senate, as they had been at the Philadelphia Convention. Justice Blackmun conceded that "[i]t would be naive history * * * to suggest that the Framers, including the Justices who accepted extrajudicial service, were of one mind on the issue or believed that such service was in all cases appropriate and constitutional," but he concluded that, "at a minimum, both the Executive and Legislative Branches acquiesced in the assumption of extrajudicial duties by judges. * * * This contemporaneous practice by the Founders themselves is significant evidence that the constitutional principle of separation of powers does not absolutely prohibit extrajudicial service." Justice Blackmun then demonstrated that, after the Founding period, federal judges have frequently performed nonjudicial roles with the consent of the political branches. The particular composition of the Sentencing Commission was similar to prior service that had been ratified by history and political acquiescence and shown not to undermine the independence of the judiciary.

Because the "legitimacy of the Judicial Branch ultimately depends on its reputation for impartiality and nonpartisanship," the Court was "somewhat more troubled by [Mistretta's] argument that the Judiciary's entanglement in the political work of the Commission undermines public confidence in the disinterestedness of the Judicial Branch." Still, the Court rejected this challenge, too, because "the Sentencing Commission is devoted exclusively to the development of rules to rationalize a process that has been and will continue to be performed exclusively by the Judicial Branch. In our view, this is an essentially neutral endeavor and one in which judicial participation is peculiarly appropriate."

3. *The Presidential-Control-Power Issue.* The Court also concluded that the President's power to appoint and remove for cause did not threaten judicial independence. The appointment power might used as a carrot to get judges to do the President's bidding, but the President already has a better carrot in his ability to elevate lower federal judges to higher judicial positions, ultimately to the Supreme Court. The removal power, but only for cause, "poses a similarly negligible threat to judicial independence," because a judge removed from the Commission would retain her Article III job. *Bowsher* was a different case, as it involved self-aggrandizement: "Congress was accreting to itself," and not giving away, "the power to control the functions of another Branch."

Justice Scalia, in another solo dissent, objected that the problem with the statute was not a commingling of functions, but the creation of a whole new branch of government, "a sort of junior-varsity Congress."

"Precisely because the scope of delegation is largely uncontrollable by the courts, we must be particularly rigorous in preserving the Constitution's structural restrictions that deter excessive delegation. The major one, it seems to me, is that the power to make law cannot be exercised by anyone other than Congress, except in conjunction with the lawful exercise of executive or judicial power.

"The whole theory of *lawful* congressional 'delegation' is not that Congress is sometimes too busy or too divided and can therefore assign its responsibility of making law to someone else; but rather that a certain degree of discretion, and thus of lawmaking, *inheres* in most executive or judicial action, and it is up to Congress, by the relative specificity or generality of its statutory commands, to determine — up to a point — how small or how large that degree shall be.

Thus, the courts could be given the power to say precisely what constitutes a 'restraint of trade,' or to adopt rules of procedure, or to prescribe by rule the manner in which their officers shall execute their judgments, because that 'lawmaking' was ancillary to their exercise of judicial powers. * * * Or to take examples closer to the case before us: Trial judges could be given the power to determine what factors justify a greater or lesser sentence within the statutorily prescribed limits because that was ancillary to their exercise of the judicial power of pronouncing sentence upon individual defendants. * * *

"The lawmaking function of the Sentencing Commission is completely divorced from any responsibility for execution of the law or adjudication of private rights under the law. * * * The power to make law at issue here, in other words, is not ancillary but quite naked. The situation is no different in principle from what would exist if Congress gave the same power of writing sentencing laws to a congressional agency such as the General Accounting Office, or to members of its staff.

"The delegation of lawmaking authority to the Commission is, in short, unsupported by any legitimating theory to explain why it is not a delegation of legislative power. * * * The only governmental power the Commission possesses is the power to make law; and it is not the Congress." He found "no place within our constitutional system for an agency created by Congress to exercise no governmental power other than the making of laws."

"Today's decision follows the regrettable tendency of our recent separation-of-powers jurisprudence to treat the Constitution as though it were no more than a generalized prescription that the functions of the Branches should not be commingled too much — how much is too much to be determined, case-by-case, by this Court. * * * In designing [the constitutional] structure, the framers *themselves* considered how much commingling was, in the generality of things, acceptable, and set forth their conclusions in the document."

NOTE ON *MISTRETTA* AND JUNIOR VARSITY LAWMAKERS

The Sentencing Commission is the next step, after the Independent Counsel and the quasi-legislative FTC, in the sort of functional commingling tolerated by pragmatic theories of separation of powers, such as Peter Strauss's (§ 2B). This time, however, the independent agency is "placed" in the judicial branch, although it otherwise looks just like an executive branch agency. One early version of the proposed Commission, S. 1182, 98th Cong., 1st Sess. (1983), would have placed it within the Judicial Conference with its members appointed and removed by the judges of the Judicial Conference. But Congress ultimately chose to give the Commission a distinctly executive character: The Commissioners were appointed and could be removed by the President, the Attorney General and the Chair of the U.S. Parole Commission were ex officio members, and the guidelines had legal force much like those promulgated by executive and quasi-legislative agencies. The President's essential control over this matter was potentially troubling, because it vested the prosecutorial and sentencing functions in the same hands. How would a unitary executive theorist, such as Steven Calabresi or Saikrishna Prakash, evaluate this arrangement? Are there functional concerns sufficient to disturb a pragmatist like Strauss?

Victoria Nourse, *Vertical Separation*, 49 Duke L.J. at 790-91, suggests that *Mistretta* illustrates the limitations of both formalist and functionalist analyses. The formalist panic whenever Congress creates an unconventional arrangement like the Sentencing Commission deflects attention from genuine concerns about consequences — which are not completely captured by functionalist analyses. We read her vertical perspective as strongly concerned about the Commission. On the one hand, the law's effort to reduce or even eliminate judicial discretion in sentencing poses minoritarian risks of less individuated sentences and more power to prosecutors. On the other hand, the delegation of sentencing authority to a Commission generally without electoral constituency poses majoritarian risks that a critical policy has been taken out of the political process.

An originalist concern arises from the parallel between the Sentencing Commission and the proposed and rejected Council of Revision. At the Philadelphia Convention, a Council of Revision, consisting of members of the judicial and executive branches, was proposed as an organ to veto legislation passed by both chambers of Congress. The Council was rejected, as an "improper coalition between the Executive and the Judiciary." Is the Sentencing Commission a similarly "improper coalition" between the two branches? On the other hand, a proposal to prohibit Supreme Court Justices from holding other offices was made at the Philadelphia Convention but was never reported out of the Committee of Detail.[b]

2. *Assigning Adjudicative Tasks to Non-Article III Judges*

One problem addressed by the modern regulatory state has been the insufficiency of traditional adjudication as a way of resolving many cases and controversies. For example, the states in the early twentieth century shifted workplace injury cases from common law courts to state workers' compensation agencies, which were considered more reliable, efficient, and expert forums for handling these claims. The federal government in the first third of the century created federal agencies which conducted formal adjudications affecting the rights of private parties. For example, the Interstate Commerce Commission was transformed into an essentially adjudicatory body, where rates and service requirements were hashed out in a trial-like setting, but within an agency (not a court) and presided over by hearing examiners (not Article III judges).

In response, private interests argued that they had a constitutional right to have their claims adjudicated by the independent Article III judiciary, and not by civil servants without constitutional assurances of independence. The Supreme Court rejected these arguments in *Crowell v. Benson*, 285 U.S. 22 (1932), holding that agencies adjudicating regulatory claims were essentially handling matters of "public rights," and not simply "private rights." Hence, Congress ought to have flexibility to send these controversies to special Article I tribunals. Decided on the eve of the New Deal, *Crowell* was a magna carta for agency adjudications, which grew like weeds in a vacant lot. The Court

---

b. See Lewis Liman, Note, *The Constitutional Infirmities of the United States Sentencing Commission*, 96 Yale L.J. 1363, 1379 n.120 (1987) (arguing that the failure of the Committee to incorporate that proposal does not save the Sentencing Commission).

reaffirmed and expanded upon *Crowell* in *Glidden v. Zdanok*, 370 U.S. 530 (1962), which held that judges on the Court of Customs and Patent Appeals were essentially Article I creations and therefore did not have to have the life tenure and protection against wage cuts assured to Article III judges. Consider the recent cases in light of further congressional innovations and the separation of powers jurisprudence developed in this chapter.

———

Northern Pipeline Co. v. Marathon Pipe Line Co., 458 U.S. 50 (1982). The Bankruptcy Reform Act of 1978 established new Bankruptcy Courts in each federal judicial district. The Bankrutpcy Judges — appointed for 14-year terms, removable under specified conditions, and with no protection against salary diminution — were to have plenary jurisdiction over all civil proceedings arising under the Bankruptcy Act, which meant that Article I judges would be adjudicating not just federal regulatory claims, but also state law issues.[c] The Court invalidated the statute insofar as it empowered Article I judges to resolve contract disputes.

Justice Brennan delivered the judgment of the Court, but only three other Justices joined his plurality opinion. On its face, Article III, § 1, seems to prohibit the vesting of *any* judicial functions with officials who are not Article III judges having life tenure and salary protection. Following historical practice revealing negligible threats to separation of powers concerns, the Court has, however, recognized three narrow exceptions to the otherwise absolute mandate of Article III: territorial courts, e.g., *American Ins. Co. v. Canter*, 1 Pet. 511 (1828); courts-martial, e.g., *Dynes v. Hoover*, 20 How. 65 (1857); and courts that adjudicate certain disputes concerning "public rights," e.g., *Murray's Lessee v. Hoboken Land and Improvement Co.*, 18 How. 272 (1856); *Crowell v. Benson*. The public rights doctrine "extends only to matters arising 'between the Government and persons subject to its authority in connection with the performance of the constitutional functions of the executive or legislative departments,' *Crowell*, and only to matters that historically could have been determined exclusively by those departments. * * * In contrast, 'the liability of one individual to another under the law as defined,' *Crowell*, is a matter of private rights," that *must* be heard by Article III tribunals, for they "lie at the core of the historically recognized judicial power."

Defining "private rights" to include contract rights, grounded in state common law, independent of the federal regulatory statute, Justice Brennan concluded that the Bankrutpcy Judges were assigned adjudicatory tasks that could only be given to Article III judges and, therefore, were created in derogation of Article III. That the Bankruptcy Judges' factfinding was reviewable by an Article III judge did not save the statute. While Congress has discretion to assign factfinding functions to an administrative adjunct created to

———

c. The 1978 Act required the judges to interpret contracts involving the bankrupt under state law, and then to modify the rights of the parties along lines directed by the new federal law, as part of Congress' chosen method for restructuring debtor-creditor relations. On the 1978 Act and its constitutional problems, see Thomas Krattenmaker, *Article III and Judicial Independence: Why the New Bankruptcy Courts Are Unconstitutional*, 70 Geo. L.J. 297 (1981).

aid in the adjudication of congressionally created rights (*Crowell*), it has less discretion when the underlying rights are not created by Congress, including state common law as well as federal constitutional rights. See Steel Seizure Case (Frankfurter, J., concurring).

Because many federal regulatory statutes often displace analogous common law rights, the plurality's reasoning was potentially broad, and **Justices Rehnquist** and **O'Connor** concurred only in the Court's judgment. They believed that the lawsuit before them, essentially raising only state law claims, was one that non-Article III courts had never exercised jurisdiction over, and so that kind of lawsuit could not be heard by the new Bankruptcy Courts. Writing for three Justices, **Justice White** dissented.

Commodity Futures Trading Commission v. Schor, 478 U.S. 833 (1986). The Commodity Exchange Act (as interpreted by the Court) empowered the Commodity Futures Trading Commission (CFTC) to entertain state law counterclaims in adjudicatory proceedings in which disgruntled customers sought compensation from professional commodity brokers for the brokers' violation of the statute or CFTC regulations. **Justice O'Connor**'s opinion for the Court held that this delegation of adjudicatory authority over state law counterclaims does not violate the core purposes of Article III.

Justice O'Connor followed the pragmatic approach of the Court's decision in *Thomas v. Union Carbide Agricultural Products Co.*, 473 U.S. 568 (1985) (upholding a statutory requirement shifting private disputes from Article III courts to binding arbitration) and not the formalist approach of the *Northern Pipeline* plurality: " '[P]ractical attention to substance rather than doctrinaire reliance on formal categories should inform application of Article III,' " she ruled, quoting *Thomas*. Thus, the inquiry turned on the purposes of Article III.

"Article III, § 1, serves both to protect 'the role of the independent judiciary within the constitutional scheme of tripartite government,' *Thomas*, and to safeguard litigants' 'right to have claims decided before judges who are free from potential domination by other branches of government.' Although our cases have provided us with little occasion to discuss the nature or significance of this latter safeguard, our prior discussions of Article III, § 1's guarantee of an independent and impartial adjudication by the federal judiciary of matters within the judicial power of the United States intimated that this guarantee serves to protect primarily personal rather than structural interests. *Northern Pipeline* (Rehnquist, J., concurring in the judgment); *id.* (White, J., dissenting).

"Our precedents also demonstrate, however, that Article III does not confer on litigants an absolute right to the plenary consideration of every nature of claim by an Article III court. See, e.g., *Thomas*; *Crowell*. Moreover, as a personal right, Article III's guarantee of an impartial and independent federal adjudication is subject to waiver, just as are other personal constitutional rights that dictate the procedures by which civil and criminal matters must be tried." The Court held that Schor had waived his right to Article III adjudication of counterclaims against him by electing to proceed before the CFTC rather than suing the broker in federal district court, where he had a private right of action."

The structural interest served by Article III — assurance of the integrity of the Judicial Branch, *Northern Pipeline* (plurality) — could not be waived by the parties, of course. Again, Justice O'Connor insisted that the Court would not "adopt formalistic and unbending rules" that "might also unduly constrict Congress' ability to take needed and innovative action pursuant to its Article I powers. Thus, in reviewing Article III challenges, we have weighed a number of factors, [namely,] the extent to which the 'essential attributes of judicial power' are reserved to Article III courts, and, conversely, the extent to which the non-Article III forum exercises the range of jurisdiction and powers normally vested only in Article III courts, the origins and importance of the right to be adjudicated, and the concerns that drove Congress to depart from the requirements of Article III. See, e.g., *Thomas*; *Northern Pipeline*. * * *

"The CFTC, like the agency in *Crowell*, deals only with a 'particularized area of law,' whereas the jurisdiction of the bankruptcy courts found unconstitutional in *Northern Pipeline* extended broadly to 'all civil proceedings arising under title 11 or arising in or *related to* cases under title 11.' CFTC orders, like those of the agency in *Crowell*, but unlike those of the bankruptcy courts under the 1978 Act, are enforceable only by order of the district court. CFTC orders are also reviewed under the same 'weight of the evidence' standard sustained in *Crowell*, rather than the more deferential standard found lacking in *Northern Pipeline*. The legal rulings of the CFTC, like the legal determinations of the agency in *Crowell*, are subject to *de novo* review. Finally, the CFTC, unlike the bankruptcy courts under the 1978 Act, does not exercise 'all ordinary powers of district courts,' and thus may not, for instance, preside over jury trials or issue writs of habeas corpus."

Although the nature of the private right was owed some weight in the balance, it was negligible in this case, because of (1) the choice Schor had in going to the CFTC rather than federal court to press his statutory claims, per se evidence that Congress was not trying to displace Article III tribunals with administrative ones; (2) the obvious efficiency reasons for allowing the CFTC to adjudicate ancillary state claims, and the tight fit between this limited authority to hear counterclaims and the statutory purpose (the counterclaims must arise out of the same transaction or occurrence as the federal statutory claim); and (3) the dearth of evidence that Congress was trying either to aggrandize its own power or diminish the power of the independent judiciary.

Justice Brennan spoke for only two dissenters, defending the approach he developed in *Northern Pipeline*. Responding to the Court's balancing approach: "The Court requires that the legislative interest in convenience and efficiency be weighed against the competing interest in judicial independence. In doing so, the Court pits an interest the benefits of which are immediate, concrete, and easily understood against one, the benefits of which are almost entirely prophylactic, and thus often seem remote and not worth the cost in any single case. Thus, while this balancing creates the illusion of objectivity and ineluctability, in fact the result was foreordained, because the balance is weighted against judicial independence. The danger of the Court's balancing approach is, of course, that as individual cases accumulate in which the Court finds that the short-term benefits of efficiency outweigh the long-term benefits of judicial independence, the protections of Article III will be eviscerated."

NOTE ON *SCHOR*

Justice O'Connor emphasized that Schor was counterclaiming, and could have brought his claim in a regular judicial forum. Should the Court reach the same result if Schor could only have brought his claims in the CFTC and had no right to sue in federal court? See Paul Verkuil, *Separation of Powers, the Rule of Law, and the Idea of Independence*, 30 Wm. & Mary L. Rev. 301 (1989).

What if Congress finds that traditional state and federal adjudication of commodities fraud cases is too time-consuming and tends to produce bad results, because judges and juries tend to be biased in favor of sympathetic plaintiffs? Congress then sets up the CFTC as an exclusive forum where complaints will be handled more expeditiously, and where commodity brokers will get what Congress thinks will be a fairer hearing. In the name of efficiency, Congress makes the agency adjudication the exclusive forum for determining commodity broker fraud, preempts state fraud law but allows state law counterclaims and third party claims, and permits no appeal to an Article III court. The reason for the last requirement (no appeal) is Congress' finding that appeals would be inefficient, would place an excessive burden on broker defendants, and would subject defendants once again to the pro-plaintiff bias of federal judges. Constitutional? See Richard Fallon, *Of Legislative Courts, Administrative Agencies and Article III*, 101 Harv. L. Rev. 915 (1988).

Ex Parte Quirin, 317 U.S. 1 (1942). The defendants, one American citizen and several aliens, were convicted by Article II military tribunals of violating the law of war. The defendants, "being enemies of the United States and acting for * * * the German Reich, a belligerent enemy nation, secretly and covertly passed, in civilian dress, contrary to the law of war, through the military and naval lines and defenses of the United States * * * for the purpose of committing * * * hostile acts, and, in particular, to destroy certain war industries, war utilities and war materials within the United States." They brought a writ of habeas corpus objecting to the constitutionality of the tribunals and procedures under which they were convicted and sentenced to death. **Chief Justice Stone**'s opinion for the Court ruled that the writ was properly before the Court; military commission decisions could be set aside by courts on habeas petition when there is "clear conviction that they are in conflict with the Constitution or laws of Congress constitutionally enacted." Even during war, the courts have a duty "to preserve unimpaired the constitutional safeguards of civil liberty." On the merits, however, the Chief Justice ruled the convictions to have been validly obtained.

Articles of War adopted by statute authorized the President to establish "military commissions * * * appointed by military command as an appropriate tribunal for the trial and punishment of offenses against the law of war not ordinarily tried by court martial." [Article 16.] The President was also authorized to establish procedures for those commissions. "By universal agreement and practice, the law of war draws a distinction between the armed forces and the peaceful populations of belligerent nations and also between those who are lawful and unlawful combatants. Lawful combatants are subject to capture and detention as prisoners of war by opposing military forces. Unlawful combatants are likewise subject to capture and detention, but in addition they are subject to trial and punishment by military tribunals for acts which render their belligerency unlawful. The spy who secretly and without uniform passes the military lines of a belligerent in time of war, seeking to gather military information and communicate it to the enemy, or an enemy combatant who without uniform comes secretly through the lines for the purpose of waging war by destruction of life or property, are familiar examples of belligerents who are generally deemed not to be entitled to the status of prisoners of war, but to be offenders against the law of war subject to trial and punishment by military tribunals." This was the practice of the United States before the adoption of the Constitution, throughout the nineteenth century, and during World War I.

"By a long course of practical administrative construction by its military authorities, our Government has likewise recognized that those who during time of war pass surreptitiously from enemy territory into our own, discarding their uniforms upon entry, for the commission of hostile acts involving destruction of life or property, have the status of unlawful combatants punishable as such by military commission." The Court found that defendants' conduct fell within this violation of the law of war. That one of the defendants was an American citizen "does not relieve him from the consequences of a belligerency which is unlawful because in violation of the law of war. Citizens who associate themselves with the military arm of the enemy government, and with its aid, guidance and direction enter this country bent on hostile acts are enemy belligerents within the meaning of the Hague Convention and the law of war." The American defendant objected that his conviction was inconsistent with *Ex parte Milligan*, 71 U.S. (4 Wall.) 2 (1866), a Civil War case where the Court ruled that the law of war "can never be applied to citizens in states which have upheld the authority of the government, and where the courts are open and their process unobstructed." The Court distinguished *Milligan* as a case where the defendant had no association with the armed forces of a belligerent.

Defendants also contended that they had been convicted without grand jury indictment or a jury trial on the issues of fact, as required by the Fifth and Sixth Amendments. The Court ruled that these constitutional guarantees were "procedures unknown to military tribunals," at the time of the nation's founding. "Section 2 of the Act of Congress of April 10, 1806, 2 Stat. 371, derived from the Resolution of the Continental Congress of August 21, 1776, imposed the death penalty on alien spies 'according to the law and usage of nations, by sentence of a general court martial'. This enactment must be regarded as a contemporary construction of both Article III, and the Amendments as not foreclosing trial by military tribunals, without a jury, of offenses against the law of war committed by enemies not in or associated with our Armed Forces. It is a construction of the Constitution which has been followed since the founding of our government, and is now continued in the 82nd Article of War. Such a construction is entitled to the greatest respect."

Finally, the Court addressed the seeming inconsistency between the summary procedures of the commissions and several of the Articles of War enacted by Congress. "We need not inquire whether Congress may restrict the power of the Commander in Chief to deal with enemy belligerents. For the Court is unanimous in its conclusion that the Articles in question could not at any stage of the proceedings afford any basis for issuing the writ. But a majority of the full Court are not agreed on the appropriate grounds for decision. Some members of the Court are of opinion that Congress did not intend the Articles of War to govern a Presidential military commission convened for the determination of questions relating to admitted enemy invaders and that the context of the Articles makes clear that they should not be construed to apply in that class of cases. Others are of the view that — even though this trial is subject to whatever provisions of the Articles of War Congress has in terms made applicable to 'commissions' — the particular Articles in question, rightly construed, do not foreclose the procedure prescribed by the President or that shown to have been employed by the Commission in a trial of offenses against the law of war and the 81st and 82nd Articles of War, by a military commission appointed by the President."

Historical Note. The *Quirin* case was heard under an expedited schedule, and the Court delivered its judgment affirming the defendants' sentences immediately. The written opinion, excerpted above, was delivered several months after the saboteurs had been executed. Chief Justice Stone and his colleagues found the result somewhat harder to justify on paper than they had anticipated, and his opinion for the Court went through several drastic revisions. Some Justices were disturbed by the haste and post-hoc rationalization features of this case. For an excellent account, see David Danelski, *The Saboteurs' Case*, 1996 J. Sup. Ct. Hist. 61 (1996).

PROBLEM 8-6
POST-*QUIRIN* MILITARY COMMISSIONS

In 1950, Congress adopted the Uniform Code of Military Justice, to regularize processes in court-martials and other military proceedings. Closely following old Article 16 (construed in *Quirin*), new Article 21 states that the jurisdiction conferred on courts-martial "does not deprive military commissions ... of concurrent jurisdiction with respect to offenders or offenses that by statute or by the law of war may be tried by military commissions...." 10 U.S.C. § 821. New Article 36 authorizes the President to prescribe procedures for military commissions "consistent with" the UCMJ, and Article 36(b) says that there must be uniformity in procedural rules under the UCMJ (i.e., the rules for court-martials are the floor for all proceedings) unless the President finds that uniformity is "impracticable." 10 U.S.C. § 836(b).

The Senate in 1955 ratified the four Geneva Conventions that the United States had signed in 1949. The purpose of the Geneva Conventions was to modernize and update the international law of war. See Senate Comm. on Foreign Relations, Geneva Conventions for the Protection of War Victims, S. Exec. Rep. No. 84-9 at 1 (1955). Common Article 3 of the Conventions — that is, a provision applicable not just to prisoners of war (Third Convention), but also to noncombatants and others detained during military operations — provides that persons accused of violating the law of war and other wartime offenses are entitled to be tried by "a regularly constituted court" that affords "all the judicial guarantees which are recognized as indispensable by civilized people," including the rights to precise notice of charges and supporting evidence, to be present at trial and to be represented by counsel, and to confront adverse witnesses.[d]

During the War in Vietnam, roughly 1954 to 1975, the United States committed increasing numbers of "advisers" (initially) and then soldiers to a losing effort to preserve the pro-USA government in South Vietnam. The "Viet Cong" were guerillas in South Vietnam seeking to overthrow the regime and, ultimately, reunite North and South Vietnam under Communist leadership (exactly as occurred in 1975). The United States captured many Viet Cong guerillas. Could the President have created military commissions like those in *Quirin* to try these "enemy combatants" summarily (i.e., without rights of confrontation, jury trial, or appeal) and execute them for seeking to undermine what the United States believed was the lawful government in South Vietnam?

3. Congressional Attempts to Alter Federal Judicial Jurisdiction and Authority

Plaut v. Spendthrift Farm, Inc., 514 U.S. 211 (1996). Federal district court dismissed plaintiffs' securities fraud suit, with prejudice, following a Supreme Court decision setting a statute of limitations that plaintiffs' filing did not meet. After the judgment became final, Congress added a new § 27A to the Securities Act which provides for reinstatement of securities fraud lawsuits, on motion, which had been commenced before the Supreme Court decision but dismissed thereafter as time barred. The district court refused to reopen the judgment, on the ground that the new statute was unconstitutional. The Supreme Court, in an opinion by **Justice Scalia**, affirmed.

"Our decisions to date have identified two types of legislation that require federal courts to exercise the judicial power in a manner that Article III forbids. The first appears in *United States v. Klein*, 13 Wall. 128 (1872), where we refused to give effect to a statute that was said '[t]o prescribe rules of decision to the Judicial Department of the government in cases pending before it.' Whatever the precise scope of *Klein*, however, later decisions have made clear that its prohibition does not take hold when Congress 'amend[s] applicable law.' Section 27A(b) indisputably does set out substantive legal standards for the Judiciary to apply, and in that sense changes the law (even if solely retroactively). The second type of unconstitutional restriction upon the exercise of

---

d. This last point requires some elaboration. The specific access requirements in text might be deduced from the standard in Common Article 3 and represent the collective understanding of the treaty signatories. Moreover, Article 75 of Protocol 1 to the Geneva Conventions, adopted in 1977 specifically guarantees the right to be present for all stages of trial and the right to present and cross-examine witnesses. Article 75 at ¶ 4. The United States has not adopted the Protocols, but "regard[s] the provisions of Article 75 as an articulation of the safeguards to which all persons in the hands of an enemy are entitled." William H. Taft, IV, *The Law of Armed Conflict After 9/11*, 28 Yale J. Int'l L. 319, 322 (2003).

judicial power identified by past cases is exemplified by *Hayburn's Case*, 2 Dall. 409 (1792), which stands for the principle that Congress cannot vest review of the decisions of Article III courts in officials of the Executive Branch. Yet under any application of 27A(b) only courts are involved; no officials of other departments sit in direct review of their decisions. Section 27A(b) therefore offends neither of these previously established prohibitions.

"We think, however, that § 27A(b) offends a postulate of Article III just as deeply rooted in our law as those we have mentioned. Article III establishes a 'judicial department' with the 'province and duty . . . to say what the law is' in particular cases and controversies. *Marbury*. The record of history shows that the Framers crafted this charter of the judicial department with an expressed understanding that it gives the Federal Judiciary the power, not merely to rule on cases, but to decide them, subject to review only by superior courts in the Article III hierarchy — with an understanding, in short, that 'a judgment conclusively resolves the case' because 'a "judicial Power" is one to render dispositive judgments.' Easterbrook, *Presidential Review*, 40 Case W. Res. L. Rev. 905, 926 (1990). By retroactively commanding the federal courts to reopen final judgments, Congress has violated this fundamental principle.

[Justice Scalia reviewed the background of Article III. During the colonial and revolutionary period, legislatures regularly decided essentially private controversies and set aside court judgments. This practice became even more common in the 1780s, and fell under increasingly critical scrutiny.] "This sense of a sharp necessity to separate the legislative from the judicial power, prompted by the crescendo of legislative interference with private judgments of the courts, triumphed among the Framers of the new Federal Constitution. See Corwin, The Progress of Constitutional Theory Between the Declaration of Independence and the Meeting of the Philadelphia Convention, 30 Am. Hist. Rev. 511, 514-517 (1925). The Convention made the critical decision to establish a judicial department independent of the Legislative Branch by providing that 'the judicial Power of the United States shall be vested in one supreme Court, and in such inferior Courts as the Congress may from time to time ordain and establish.' Before and during the debates on ratification, Madison, Jefferson, and Hamilton each wrote of the factional disorders and disarray that the system of legislative equity had produced in the years before the framing; and each thought that the separation of the legislative from the judicial power in the new Constitution would cure them. [See *Federalist* No. 48 (Madison) (noting the phenomenon).]

"If the need for separation of legislative from judicial power was plain, the principal effect to be accomplished by that separation was even plainer. As Hamilton wrote in his exegesis of Article III, § 1, in *Federalist* No. 81:

> It is not true . . . that the parliament of Great Britain, or the legislatures of the particular states, can rectify the exceptionable decisions of their respective courts, in any other sense than might be done by a future legislature of the United States. The theory neither of the British, nor the state constitutions, authorises the revisal of a judicial sentence, by a legislative act. . . . A legislature without exceeding its province cannot reverse a determination once made, in a particular case; though it may prescribe a new rule for future cases.

The essential balance created by this allocation of authority was a simple one. The Legislature would be possessed of power to 'prescrib[e] the rules by which the duties and rights of every citizen are to be regulated,' but the power of '[t]he interpretation of the laws' would be 'the proper and peculiar province of the courts.' *The Federalist* No. 78. The Judiciary would be, 'from the nature of its functions, . . . the [department] least dangerous to the political rights of the constitution,' not because its acts were subject to legislative correction, but because the binding effect of its acts was limited to particular cases and controversies. Thus, 'though individual oppression may now and then proceed from the courts of justice, the general liberty of the people can never be endangered from that quarter: . . . so long as the judiciary remains truly distinct from both the legislative and executive.' [Id.]

"Judicial decisions in the period immediately after ratification of the Constitution confirm the understanding that it forbade interference with the final judgments of courts." Justice Scalia invoked dicta in *Calder v. Bull*, 3 Dall. 386 (1798), and a number of contemporaneous state cases for the proposition that the power to grant new trials was properly a judicial and not a legislative power. By the middle of the nineteenth century, this was conventional wisdom among American lawyers and judges. According to this understanding of the "judicial Power," only judges and not legislators could make the decision to reopen judgments, and § 27A was therefore a congressional encroachment upon the "judicial Power."

Justice Breyer concurred in the judgment, on the ground that "its exclusively retroactive effect, its application to a limited number of individuals, and its reopening of closed judgments" combined to yield an unconstitutional usurpation. **Justice Stevens**, joined by **Justice Ginsburg**, dissented. Justice Stevens argued that Congress unquestionably has the authority to override a Supreme Court decision interpreting a federal statute and to make the override rule applicable retroactively. E.g., *Sampeyreac v. United States*, 7 Pet. 222, 239 (1833) (very similar to present case). Under such a statute, courts would routinely reopen judgments. Why can Congress not make the process of reopening judgments more orderly and uniform? It had done so at least once, and the Court allowed it against constitutional attack. *United States v. Sioux Nation*, 448 U.S. 371 (1980).

"The Court has drawn the wrong lesson from the Framers' disapproval of colonial legislatures' appellate review of judicial decisions. The Framers rejected that practice, not out of a mechanistic solicitude for 'final judgments,' but because they believed the impartial application of rules of law, rather than the will of the majority, must govern the disposition of individual cases and controversies. Any legislative interference in the adjudication of the merits of a particular case carries the risk that political power will supplant evenhanded justice, whether the interference occurs before or after the entry of final judgment. Cf. *Klein*; *Hayburn's Case*. Section 27A(b) neither commands the reinstatement of any particular case nor directs any result on the merits. Congress recently granted a special benefit to a single litigant in a pending civil rights case, but the Court saw no need even to grant certiorari to review that disturbing legislative favor. In an ironic counterpoint, the Court today places a higher priority on protecting the Republic from the restoration to a large class of litigants of the opportunity to have Article III courts resolve the merits of their claims."

PROBLEM 8-7
CONGRESSIONAL EFFORTS TO STRIP FEDERAL COURTS OF AUTHORITY TO REQUIRE BUSING AS A REMEDY FOR *BROWN* VIOLATIONS

Recall *Swann* (Chapter 2, § 2C), in which the Supreme Court upheld an order requiring busing and other aggressive remedies for *Brown* violations. Federal court-required busing to achieve unitary school systems was extremely controversial, and proposals abounded in Congress to thwart it. In light of the Court's later decision in *Plaut*, it is notable that no one proposed that Congress vacate *Brown II* judgments and direct district judges to implement *Brown* without recourse to busing as a remedy.

Even in 1971, such legislation would have been problematic under *United States v. Klein*, 80 U.S. (13 Wall.) 128 (1872). The Court had previously held that a presidential pardon was admissible evidence for southerners seeking to regain confiscated property upon a showing they had not been disloyal during the Civil War. Congress responded with an 1870 statute making pardons inadmissable as proof of loyalty and, instead, conclusive evidence of disloyalty. The statute further provided that "in all cases where judgment shall have been heretofore rendered in the Court of Claims in favor of any claimant, on any other proof of loyalty then such as is above required and provided, * * * the Supreme Court shall, on appeal, have no further jurisdiction of the cause, and shall dismiss the same for want of jurisdiction." In such cases, the court of claims was required, on remand, to dismiss the claimant's petition for restitution of his or her property. In *Klein*, Chief Justice Chase refused to follow the 1870 statute, as it was an unconstitutional congressional usurpation of both the judicial power to adjudicate cases or controversies and of the executive power to grant pardons.

Three different kinds of proposals were floated in Congress to respond, politically, to *Swann*:

1. *Constitutional amendment.* On four occasions, the Constitution has been amended to override a Supreme Court interpretation of the Constitution.[e] Many other constitutional amendments have been proposed to override Supreme Court

---

e. The Eleventh Amendment (1798), insulating states from many federal court lawsuits, was a reaction to *Chisholm v. Georgia*, 2 U.S. (2 Dall.) 419 (1793), which had asserted federal jurisdiction against the state of Georgia for the payment of debt and past damages allegedly owed to out-of-staters. The Fourteenth Amendment (1868) specifically overrode *Dred Scott* (1857). The Sixteenth Amendment (1913) granting the federal government the authority to lay income taxes, overrode the Supreme Court's decision in *Pollock v. Farmers' Loan & Trust Co.*, 157 U.S. 429 (1895), which had invalidated the federal income tax. Finally, the Twenty-Sixth Amendment (1971) giving eighteen-year-olds the right to vote in state and national elections, overrode that part of *Oregon v. Mitchell*, 400 U.S. 112 (1970), which invalidated Congress' power to set voting-age rules for state elections.

decisions, but they have not been adopted.[f] A steady stream of political leaders called for amendments to overturn *Swann*, usually by restricting federal courts' remedial options in school desegregation cases. E.g., H.R.J. Res. 56, 97th Cong., 2d Sess. (1982). Because of the controversial nature of these proposals, none was ever recommended by the requisite two-thirds vote of each chamber of Congress.

2. *Legislation to curtail constitutional decisions.* Congress also may respond to Supreme Court decisions through normal legislation. Although Congress usually responds by elaborating or otherwise complying with the Court's decisions, as it did in the Civil Rights Act of 1964, Congress may have some room to resist Supreme Court decisions it dislikes. *Swann* stimulated some legislation of this sort. The Educational Amendments of 1972, 20 U.S.C. §§ 1651-1656, denied the use of federal money to bus students for racial balance. The Equal Education Opportunities Act of 1974 prohibited any "court, department, or agency of the United States [from ordering] transportation of any student to a school other than the school closest or next closest to his place of residence which provides the appropriate grade level, and type of education for such student." 20 U.S.C. § 1714. The EEOA seems at or beyond the constitutional boundary, but federal judges interpreted it to apply only to cases not raising constitutional violations. E.g., *Drummond v. Acree*, 409 U.S. 1228 (1972) (Powell, Circuit Justice). That is, of course, a problem with ordinary legislation: The Court can narrowly construe it or invalidate it.

3. *Limitations on jurisdiction.* Another strategy relies on Congress' authority under Article III to regulate federal jurisdiction.[g] While the Supreme Court has been loathe to interpret federal statutes to eliminate a federal forum for constitutional adjudication, e.g., *Webster v. Doe*, 486 U.S. 592 (1988) (judicial review available for Doe's allegations of CIA discrimination against him on grounds of sexual preference), Article III's plain meaning suggests that Congress might have a fair amount of power here.

Article III, § 1 states that the "[t]he judicial Power * * * shall be vested in one supreme Court, and in such inferior Courts as the Congress may from time to time ordain and establish." Article III, § 2, par. 2, provides that the Supreme Court "shall" have original jurisdiction over cases affecting ambassadors and other public ministers and cases in which a state is a party. "In all other Cases before mentioned [in paragraph 1], the supreme Court shall have appellate jurisdiction . . . with such Exceptions, and under such Regulations as the Congress shall make."

---

f. Amendments to overturn the Court's abortion, flagburning, and school prayer decisions have been stalled in Congress but continue to be proposed. Congress proposed an amendment to override *Hammer v. Dagenhart* (The Child Labor Case), 247 U.S. 251 (1918) (Chapter 7, § 2), but not enough states ratified the amendment.

g. See generally Richard Fallon et al., *Hart and Wechsler's The Federal Courts and the Federal System* (4th ed. 1996) (classic exploration of Congress' power to restrict federal jurisdiction); Michael Perry, *The Constitution, the Courts, and Human Rights* 128-37 (1982) (arguing that this is the ultimate and most workable political check on the Court's constitutional lawmaking authority).

The text of Article III suggests three ways Congress might try to curtail *Swann* — all of which have been proposed and deliberated in Congress: (1) Restrict or eliminate the Supreme Court's appellate jurisdiction in school desegregation cases. This approach receives some support (how much depends on how you read the opinion) from the leading Supreme Court case on this topic (excerpted below). (2) Restrict or eliminate the jurisdiction of lower federal courts in school desegregation cases. (3) Restrict or eliminate the jurisdiction of any federal court (lower federal courts' original jurisdiction as well as the Supreme Court's appellate jurisdiction) in school desegregation cases. This third approach has been the one most often proposed by legislative opponents of *Swann*. Some bills went even further and sought to restrict jurisdiction of any court in the United States (including state courts).

For each of these strategies — including the abrogation of jurisdiction in any court, state or federal — ask yourself the following questions: First, what is the argument for Congress' constitutional authority to enact each type of jurisdiction limitation? Second, what constitutional counterarguments might be constructed, and would they prevail? Third, even if Congress has the constitutional authority to adopt any or all of the different strategies, what policy problems accompany each strategy? You might want to reconsider your answers in light of the following material.

NOTE ON THE TEXTUAL ARGUMENTS FOR AND AGAINST CONGRESS' POWER TO RESTRICT FEDERAL JURISDICTION

Some scholars argue from the Vesting Clause's mandatory language — "The judicial Power * * * *shall be vested*" — that there is an irreducible minimum of jurisdiction Congress must vest in the Supreme Court and/or inferior federal courts.[h] Others emphasize that the Ordain and Establish Clause gives Congress seemingly total discretion whether even to create inferior federal courts and that the Exceptions Clause gives Congress arguably unlimited power to restrict the appellate jurisdiction of the Supreme Court.[i] The challenge for the former group of (mandatory jurisdiction) scholars is to explain how the Vesting Clause can avoid the cumulative trumping of the Ordain and Establish and the Exceptions Clauses. The challenge for the latter group of (discretionary jurisdiction) scholars is to explain how the judiciary can perform its core function if Congress can take away all its jurisdiction. Any ideas at this point? Read on.

---

h. See Akhil Amar, *A Neo-Federalist View of Article III: Separating the Two Tiers of Federal Jurisdiction*, 65 B.U.L. Rev. 205 (1985); Robert Clinton, *A Mandatory View of Federal Court Jurisdiction: A Guided Quest for the Original Understanding of Article III*, 132 U. Pa. L. Rev. 741 (1984); Lawrence Sager, *The Supreme Court, 1980 Term — Foreword: Constitutional Limitations on Congress' Authority To Regulate the Jurisdiction of the Federal Courts*, 95 Harv. L. Rev. 17 (1981).

i. See Paul Bator, *Congressional Power over the Jurisdiction of the Federal Courts*, 27 Vill. L. Rev. 1030 (1982); Gerald Gunther, *Congressional Power to Curtail Federal Court Jurisdiction: An Opinionated Guide to the Ongoing Debate*, 36 Stan. L. Rev. 895 (1984).

EX PARTE McCARDLE
74 U.S. (7 Wall.) 506, 19 L.Ed. 264 (1869)

CHIEF JUSTICE CHASE delivered the opinion of the Court.

[McCardle was a civilian being held for trial by military commission in Mississippi for allegedly publishing "incendiary and libellous" articles in his newspaper in violation of federal Reconstruction statutes. The federal circuit court denied his application for habeas corpus, and he appealed to the Supreme Court. McCardle relied on a February 5, 1867 federal statute providing the Supreme Court with appellate jurisdiction in habeas corpus cases. The case was argued in the Supreme Court in early March 1868. On March 27, 1868, Congress enacted a statute that provided "[t]hat so much of the act of February 5, 1867 * * * as authorized an appeal from the judgment of the Circuit Court to the Supreme Court of the United States, or the exercise of any such jurisdiction by said Supreme Court, on appeals which have been, or may hereafter be taken, be, and the same is hereby repealed."]

The first question necessarily is that of jurisdiction; for, if the act of March, 1868, takes away the jurisdiction defined by the act of February, 1867, it is useless, if not improper, to enter into any discussion of other questions.

It is quite true, as was argued by the counsel for the petitioner, that the appellate jurisdiction of this court is not derived from acts of Congress. It is, strictly speaking, conferred by the Constitution. But it is conferred "with such exceptions and under such regulations as Congress shall make."

It is unnecessary to consider whether, if Congress had made no exceptions and no regulations, this court might not have exercised general appellate jurisdiction under rules prescribed by itself. For among the earliest acts of the first Congress, at its first session, was the act of September 24th, 1789, to establish the judicial courts of the United States. That act provided for the organization of this court, and prescribed regulations for the exercise of its jurisdiction. * * *

The principle that the affirmation of appellate jurisdiction implies the negation of all such jurisdiction not affirmed having been thus established, it was an almost necessary consequence that acts of Congress, providing for the exercise of jurisdiction, should come to be spoken of as acts granting jurisdiction, and not as acts making exceptions to the constitutional grant of it.

The exception to appellate jurisdiction in the case before us, however, is not an inference from the affirmation of other appellate jurisdiction. It is made in terms. The provision of the act of 1867, affirming the appellate jurisdiction of this court in cases of *habeas corpus* is expressly repealed. It is hardly possible to imagine a plainer instance of positive exception.

We are not at liberty to inquire into the motives of the legislature. We can only examine into its power under the Constitution; and the power to make exceptions to the appellate jurisdiction of this court is given by express words.

What, then, is the effect of the repealing act upon the case before us? We cannot doubt as to this. Without jurisdiction the court cannot proceed at all in any cause. Jurisdiction is power to declare the law, and when it ceases to exist, the only function remaining to the court is that of announcing the fact and dismissing the cause. * * *

[T]he general rule, supported by the best elementary writers, is, that "when an act of the legislature is repealed, it must be considered, except as to transactions past and closed, as if it never existed." * * * [N]o judgment [can] be rendered in a suit after the repeal of the act under which it was brought and prosecuted.

It is quite clear, therefore, that this court cannot proceed to pronounce judgment in this case, for it has no longer jurisdiction of the appeal; and judicial duty is not less fitly performed by declining ungranted jurisdiction than in exercising firmly that which the Constitution and the laws confer.

Counsel seem to have supposed, if effect be given to the repealing act in question, that the whole appellate power of the court, in cases of *habeas corpus*, is denied. But this is an error. The act of 1868 does not except from that jurisdiction any cases but appeals from Circuit Courts under the act of 1867. It does not affect the jurisdiction which was previously exercised.

Felker v. Turpin, 518 U.S. 651 (1996), was a reprise of *McCardle*. The Antiterrorism and Effective Death Penalty Act of 1996 placed new limitations on petitions for habeas corpus. Especially in death penalty cases, it is common for prisoners to file successive habeas petitions, repeating earlier claims or attempting to raise new but untimely ones. The relevant provisions of the statute do not affect a prisoner's first habeas petition, but sharply limit subsequent petitions, which can only be heard if a special appellate panel grants a motion for leave to file the petition. The statute provides that the special panel's decision whether or not to grant leave is not appealable and not subject to a writ of certiorari to the Supreme Court. A prisoner on death row attempted to file a second petition for habeas relief, but the special court ruled that he had not met the statutory requirements. The issue before the Court was whether Congress had unconstitutionally eliminated the Supreme Court's jurisdiction. The Court unanimously held that it still had the power to hear the cases on an *original* writ of habeas corpus — that is, as a petition directly to the Court, rather than as a petition seeking review of a lower court order. (Recall that *Marbury v. Madison* was the flip side of this situation.) The Court also held that the limitations on second and later writs are not an unconstitutional "suspension of the writ."

NOTES ON *McCARDLE* AND CONGRESS' AUTHORITY TO RESTRICT THE SUPREME COURT'S JURISDICTION

McCardle can be read broadly, for the proposition that the Exceptions Clause empowers Congress to limit the Supreme Court's jurisdiction over cases of a certain type, even if they raise constitutional issues. But does *McCardle* have to be read to sanction an unlimited congressional power? Consider possible limitations:

1. *The Court's "Essential Role."* Henry Hart, *The Power of Congress to Limit the Jurisdiction of Federal Courts: An Exercise in Dialectic*, 66 Harv. L. Rev. 1362, 1365 (1953), argued for a narrow reading of *McCardle* and posited:

"The measure [of Congress' power under the Exceptions Clause] is simply that the exceptions must not be such as will destroy the essential role of the Supreme Court in the constitutional plan. *McCardle*, you will remember, meets that test. The circuit courts of the United States were still open in habeas corpus. And the Supreme Court itself could still entertain petitions for the writ which were filed with it in the first instance." What is the Court's "essential role in the constitutional plan"? Leonard Ratner argues that the Court's essential roles are "(1) to provide a tribunal for the ultimate resolution of inconsistent or conflicting interpretations of federal law by state or federal courts, and (2) to provide a tribunal for maintaining the supremacy of federal law when it conflicts with state law or is challenged by state authority."[j] Would a bill cutting off the Supreme Court's appellate jurisdiction in school desegregation cases violate these "essential roles"? Consider similar "essential roles" limitations suggested but not found to be violated by the Court's opinions in *Morrison v. Olson, Schor,* and *Mistretta,* albeit with little discussion of precisely what would violate the judiciary's core functions or its independent role (as dissenting Justices in each case duly noted).

2. *Bitter with the Sweet.* There is a political check on Congress' ability to restrict the Supreme Court's appellate jurisdiction: If the Court cannot review lower court decisions in school desegregation cases, for example, the results will be unpredictable — some state and federal courts might order massive busing, and then the Court is not available to check lower court excesses. (Even if Congress can strip lower federal courts as well as the Supreme Court of jurisdiction, the Supremacy Clause of Article VI seems to assure that state courts would remain as a forum for federal constitutional cases.)

Of course, then Congress might say the Court can review those cases, but it cannot order busing in any case. But this might fall afoul *United States v. Klein* (described in Problem 8-6). *Klein* might be read for the proposition that Congress must take the bitter with the sweet: If it allows the Supreme Court to take jurisdiction over a class of cases to assure uniformity (the sweet), it may not tell the Court how it has to decide the cases (the bitter).

3. *How Broadly Should* McCardle *Be Read?* Read broadly, *Klein* seems somewhat inconsistent with *McCardle*, even though both were written by Chief Justice Chase. If so, you might want to read *Klein* more narrowly — or reconsider the correctness of some of the language in *McCardle*, which may have read too much into the Exceptions Clause. For example, there is no indication in the original discussions that the Framers imagined, much less intended, that the Exceptions Clause would enable Congress to curtail the Court's appellate jurisdiction as a way to prevent decision on substantive grounds.[k] Moreover, a broad reading of *McCardle* raises questions of equal

---

j. Leonard Ratner, *Congressional Power over the Appellate Jurisdiction of the Supreme Court,* 109 U. Pa. L. Rev. 157, 160-61 (1960). Critical of the Hart argument and rejecting an "essential roles" limit is Martin Redish, *Federal Jurisdiction: Tensions in the Allocation of Judicial Power* 27-28 (2d ed. 1990).

k. See William Van Alstyne, *A Critical Guide to* Ex Parte McCardle, 15 Ariz. L. Rev. 229, 263-64 (1973).

protection, ex post facto penalization, and due process. Could *McCardle* be read more narrowly (particularly in light of the final paragraph of the opinion)?

NOTE ON CONGRESS' POWER TO RESTRICT THE JURISDICTION OF INFERIOR FEDERAL COURTS

If Congress has discretion not to create inferior federal courts at all under the Ordain and Establish Clause, does it not also have the authority to limit their jurisdiction in just about any way it desires? This is a familiar form of argument: The greater power includes the lesser power. Is there any way around it?

Justice Story said in *Martin v. Hunter's Lessee*, 14 U.S. (1 Wheat.) 304 (1816), that the language of Article III "is manifestly designed to be mandatory upon the legislature. Its obligatory force is so imperative, that congress could not, without a violation of its duty, have refused to carry it into operation. * * * If, then, it is a duty of congress to vest the judicial power of the United States, it is a duty to vest the whole judicial power." Justice Story argued that Congress was therefore required to establish the Supreme Court, and also at least some inferior federal courts. Since the Supreme Court only has original jurisdiction in two types of cases, its appellate jurisdiction is needed to exercise the other kinds of judicial power listed in Article III, § 2 (and, according to Justice Story, mandatory kinds of jurisdiction). Therefore:

> [I]f in any of the cases enumerated in [Art. III, § 2 of] the constitution, the state courts did not then possess jurisdiction, the appellate jurisdiction of the supreme court (admitting that it could act on state courts) could not reach those cases, and, consequently, the injunction of the constitution, that the judicial power "shall be vested," would be disobeyed. It would seem, therefore, to follow, that congress are bound to create some inferior courts, in which to vest all that jurisdiction which, under the constitution, is exclusively vested in the United States, and of which the supreme court cannot take original cognizance.

Justice Story's expansive dictum has been controversial. Many scholars argue that giving Congress discretion whether to create inferior federal courts at all was a deliberate compromise (some Framers favored mandatory inferior courts, some none at all).[1] And the Judiciary Act of 1789 vested the federal judiciary with much less than the jurisdiction authorized by Article III — it gave no general federal question jurisdiction, limited diversity jurisdiction to lawsuits involving more than $500, and did not authorize Supreme Court review of all federal questions.

Subsequent cases have not accepted the import of the *Martin v. Hunter's Lessee* dictum. In *Sheldon v. Sill*, 49 U.S. (8 How.) 441 (1850), for example, the Court held that a circuit court has no jurisdiction over a case meeting the constitutional but not the narrower statutory requirements. "[C]ongress may withhold from any court of its creation jurisdiction of any of the enumerated controversies. Courts created by statute can have no jurisdiction but such as the statute confers." If the *Sill* statement is credited, can Congress preclude federal

---

1. E.g., Henry Hart & Herbert Wechsler, *The Federal Courts and the Federal System* 11-12 (2d ed. 1973).

jurisdiction over just one kind of federal question case — school desegregation — or preclude jurisdiction to issue just one kind of remedy? Is the latter not tantamount to an unconstitutional congressional interference in civil rights? Or is it only Congress' exercise of its own Fourteenth Amendment, § 5 powers? Note here that any such statute would leave state courts with authority to enter busing orders.

Akhil Amar has suggested a synthesis of the Story and Hart arguments.[m] Hart was right that Congress cannot deprive the judiciary of its "essential role" in our constitutional system, but wrong to focus only on the Supreme Court. Story was right that Congress is obliged to vest some effective federal jurisdiction in the judiciary, but wrong to insist that Congress had to create inferior federal courts for such a purpose. In short, Amar argues that Congress cannot, consistent with the Vesting Clause and the central role of the Article III judiciary, give full effect to the Exceptions Clause and the Ordain and Establish Clause in the same constitutional subject matter. This thesis finds support in the Court's dicta in *Mistretta* and other cases, to the effect that Congress cannot deprive the Judicial Branch of its core functions, and with suggestions in prior cases that there must be some judicial forum to challenge unconstitutional actions. E.g., *Estep v. United States*, 327 U.S. 114 (1946). Responses? Does Amar's argument provide the solution to Problem 8-9?

Note the parallel between the broad Vesting Clauses in Articles II and III (executive and judicial power, apparently all of it, *shall be vested* in President and Supreme Court/inferior courts), especially in contrast to the more narrow one in Article I (only legislative powers *herein granted* shall be vested in Congress). Steven Calabresi and Kevin Rhodes, *The Structural Constitution: Unitary Executive, Plural Judiciary*, 105 Harv. L. Rev. 1153 (1992), note the parallel between Amar's argument against jurisdiction-stripping — the Exceptions and Ordain and Establish Clauses in Article III must be read narrowly in light of its broad and mandatory Vesting Clause — and Justice Scalia's argument in *Morrison* — the Appointments Clause in Article II must be read narrowly in light of its broad and mandatory Vesting Clause. But the Supreme Court in *Morrison* rejected the Scalia reading of Article II. Is there a better reason for the same Court to accept the Amar reading of Article II?

SECTION 3. SEPARATION OF POWERS, DUE PROCESS, AND THE WAR ON TERROR

Philip Bobbitt, *Terror and Consent: The Wars for the Twenty-First Century* (2008). An eminent constitutional theorist, Philip Bobbitt has also served as a foreign policy or national security capacity in the Administrations of Lyndon Johnson, Gerald Ford, Jimmy Carter, Ronald Reagan, George H.W. Bush, and William Clinton. *Terror and Consent* is an invaluable synthesis of constitutionalism, political history, and practical executive experience that, we

---

m. Starting with Amar, *Neo-Federalist View of Article III, supra*, and continuing with a bunch of follow-ups, e.g., Amar, *The Two-Tiered Structure of the Judiciary Act of 1789*, 138 U. Pa. L. Rev. 1499 (1990), and responses to attacks, e.g., Amar, *Reports of My Death Are Greatly Exaggerated: A Reply*, 138 U. Pa. L. Rev. 1651 (1990).

think, provides some valuable lessons for understanding the constitutional separation of powers showdowns between the George W. Bush Administration and civil libertarians that have followed the terrorist attacks on the World Trade Center and the Pentagon on 9/11/2001. (The cases and notes that follow will give the student a chronology of legal events that accompany the American response, loosely termed our "War Against Terrorism.") We recommend the book and draw the following general themes to the student's attention.

The New Face of War (Chapter 1 of *Terror and Consent*). Western civilization has always had "terrorism," or unconventional violent tactics for assaulting superior conventional forces. Different eras have known different kinds of terrorists, from the mercenaries of the Renaissance to the pirates of the early modern period to the national liberation movements of the twentieth century. In each era, terrorism represents a rejection and attempted disruption of the dominant form of constitutionalism, while at the same time mimicking its structure and characteristics. The current era, according to Bobbitt, is that of the *market state*. In contrast to the nation state, which advances the collective goals of a self-identified cohesive national community, the market state creates conditions conducive to individual self-fulfillment. The former is centralized, the latter decentralized, like a market.

The terrorism characteristic of our current age (al Qaeda is an exemplar) rejects the western consumerism and materialism of the market state, but its characteristic structure mimicks that state. "Market state terrorism will be just as global, networked, decentralized, and devolved and rely just as much on outsourcing and incentivizing as the market state. It does not depend on state sponsorship" (ch. 1, p. 45). Violence against civilians is the *goal* of this form of terrorism, not just a means to other goals: if terrorists can undermine civilians' sense of *security*, they have undermined the market state's source of legitimacy.

In this brave new world of stateless networked terrorism, it is hard to know who the "enemy" is — and this problem pervades America's confused response to al Qaeda. In nation state war, the typical prisoner was easy to identify as the enemy, and he was entitled to decent treatment under the Geneva Conventions of 1949, but few judicial protections under the Constitution; in the war on terror, the typical prisoner is someone the United States *suspects* is a collaborator with al Qaeda. The state would like to treat him worse that it treats POWs, in order to find out where his allegiance lies and to uncover other cells, but such a stance is morally vulnerable because of the risk that the detainee is actually an innocent bystander.

The Rule of Law as a Limitation and a Weapon in the War on Terror (Chapters 4 & 7). Bobbitt characterizes the United States and its allies as *states of consent*. Not only is the government accountable to We the People and so is vigorous in protecting our security, but the government is accountable to the rule of law and so is vigorous in setting forth bright-line rules that we all must obey, including government actors. Terrorism is the opposite: "*Terrorism is the pursuit of political goals through the use of violence against noncombatants in order to persuade them from doing what they have a lawful right to do.*" (Ch. 7, p. 352, emphasis in original.)

Bobbitt endorses "a counterterrorist strategy that scrupulously and transparently respects international standards . . . [and] a positive vision of societies built around democracy, human rights, and the rule of law — something that people can be *for* — to accompany the important but partial vision of being *against* terrorism." (P. 356, quoting Human Rights Watch's Kenneth Roth, "Counterterrorism and Human Rights: An Essential Alliance" (2004).) For Bobbitt, law provides several examples of what states of consent are and should be fighting *for*. One is inalienable rights, those that cannot be given or taken away. "Because consent is not merely a matter of saying Yes, but also of having the option of saying No, consent depends upon the availability of alternatives. Inalienability is one way — the law's way — of creating the necessity of citizens having to choose among alternatives." (Ch. 4, p. 183.) Another is the creation of governing rules through a process that is democratic, open, and deliberative. In discussing such a process, Bobbitt typically assumes but does not defend the proposition that Congress must ratify major changes in American anti-terrorist policy.

Bobbitt considers this an attractive political philosophy to offer world populations, and this is an advantage that states of consent have against terrorism. The goal of states of consent, therefore, is not just to protect their citizens against harm and violence, but also to do so within the parameters of the rule of law. Hence, Bobbitt is strongly opposed to separating law from (anti-terrorist) strategy (ch. 4, p. 237).

The Constitutional Relationship Between Rights and Powers (Chapters 5-8). From the ACLU to the Cato Institute, Americans of all political persuasions tend to understand state power and individual rights as a zero-sum game: when one gains traction, the other loses. Bobbitt revives the Hobbesian understanding of the state as *necessarily* limiting men's liberties "as they might not hurt, but assist one another, and join together against a common enemy." Hobbes, *Leviathan* ch. 26 (1651). Like Hamilton in *Federalist* No. 1, Bobbitt insists upon the *interdependence* rather than competition between the "vigor of government" and the "security of liberty" (Hamilton's words).

Bobbitt insists that this kind of synergy can only be effectuated if the war on terror is conducted with a proper appreciation for *strategy*: the rational connection between lawful ends and rational means. Thus, he forcefully denounces the unlawful torture of suspected terrorists: the end is at best ambiguous, as torture is in tension with the rule of law, and the means is lunatic, as torture rarely secures useful information. At the same time, Bobbitt savages old Cold War government approaches and structures because they do not match up against this new kind of non-state threat. He would expand government power to gather electronic information, insist upon a more cooperative structure for intelligence agencies, regularize procedures for detention and interrogation, and expand cooperative relationships with other governments and NGOs (ch. 6). Bobbitt endorses preemptive strikes: Are we better off after the preclusive strike against al Qaeda in Afghanistan after 9/11? Maybe not in absolute terms, but surely (Bobbitt argues) in relative terms: If we had not struck back, things would be a lot worse (ch. 4). Strategic thinking assumes a changing world and seeks to avoid future disasters through cost-effective prophylactics.

Normatively, Bobbitt insists upon the *duty of consequentialism* — "that is, any contemplated course of action must be measured in terms of the foreseeable costs and benefits that are its result and not against any absolute or categorical rule, including those regarding intentions" (ch. 7, p. 361). Thus, Bobbitt does not flinch from the "ticking bomb scenario": if Jack Bauer thinks that the malefactor he has captured can provide him with a valuable lead toward finding a ticking time bomb that will blow up Los Angeles, Jack must do what is required to extract that information, pronto. Including torture, presumably torture leading toward serious bodily injury or death. "It is an easy question" (p. 362). But this assumes Jack is sure the captive has relevant information.

At the same time, Bobbitt links this consequentialist philosophy to his rule of law institutionalism: "The states of consent must develop rules that define what terrorism is, who is a terrorist, and what states can lawfully do to fight terrorists and terrorism. * * * At the same time, we must * * * jettison nonconstitutional rules like those against information acquisition from the private sector of data voluntarily provided, and also many rules against data sharing among agencies. We must develop new practices like the requirement of national identity cards, including biometrics when these become reliable; increased CCTV surveillance of transportation, energy, and communication hubs; sophisticated data mining as well as standards for the detention of terrorist combatants on a noncriminal basis. We must do this because an open society depends upon a government strong enough and foresighted enough to protect individual rights." (Ch. 7, p. 394. Chapter 8 contains a more detailed set of proactive proposals for restructuring the government and improving our capacity for preventing and responding to terrorist attacks.)

HAMDI v. RUMSFELD

542 U.S. 507, 124 S.Ct. 2633, 159 L.Ed.2d 578 (2004)

[After the terrorist attacks of 9/11, Congress passed a resolution — the Authorization for Use of Military Force (AUMF) — authorizing the President to "use all necessary and appropriate force" against "nations, organizations, or persons" that he determines "planned, authorized, committed, or aided" in the attacks. As part of this response, President ordered an invasion of Afghanistan to attack al Qaeda and the Taliban regime that had harbored al Qaeda. Hamdi, an American citizen, was captured in Afghanistan and after some intermediate stops was detained at a naval brig in Charleston, S.C. No charges were filed against him. His father filed a habeas corpus petition on his behalf as next friend. Hamdi was not allowed any contact with outsiders, and hence was unable to file the petition himself or to communicate with his father. His father asserted that Hamdi went to Afghanistan to do "relief work" less than two months before September 11 and could not have received military training. In response to the petition, the government filed a declaration from Michael Mobbs (Mobbs Declaration), a Defense Department official. The Mobbs Declaration alleges various details regarding Hamdi's trip to Afghanistan, his affiliation there with a Taliban unit during a time when the Taliban was battling U.S. allies, and his subsequent surrender of an assault rifle.

[The Court was badly divided. Four Justices, led by Justice O'Connor, ruled that Hamdi was entitled to some form of due process hearing. You may want to reread *Mathews v. Eldridge* (Chapter 5, Section 6) in connection with the O'Connor opinion. Four other Justices, in two different opinions, would have held his detention squarely unlawful. Two of those Justices joined portions of O'Connor's opinion in order to provide a majority for some disposition of the case. The remaining member of the Court, Justice Thomas, agreed with the government's view that the Mobbs Declaration had provided a sufficient basis for Hamdi's indefinite detention.]

JUSTICE O'CONNOR announced the judgment of the Court and delivered an opinion, in which the **CHIEF JUSTICE**, **JUSTICE KENNEDY**, and **JUSTICE BREYER** join.

At this difficult time in our Nation's history, we are called upon to consider the legality of the Government's detention of a United States citizen on United States soil as an "enemy combatant" and to address the process that is constitutionally owed to one who seeks to challenge his classification as such. * * * We hold that although Congress authorized the detention of combatants in the narrow circumstances alleged here, due process demands that a citizen held in the United States as an enemy combatant be given a meaningful opportunity to contest the factual basis for that detention before a neutral decisionmaker. * * *

The threshold question before us is whether the Executive has the authority to detain citizens who qualify as "enemy combatants." There is some debate as to the proper scope of this term, and the Government has never provided any court with the full criteria that it uses in classifying individuals as such. It has made clear, however, that, for purposes of this case, the "enemy combatant" that it is seeking to detain is an individual who, it alleges, was " 'part of or supporting forces hostile to the United States or coalition partners' " in Afghanistan and who " 'engaged in an armed conflict against the United States' " there. We therefore answer only the narrow question before us: whether the detention of citizens falling within that definition is authorized.

The Government maintains that no explicit congressional authorization is required, because the Executive possesses plenary authority to detain pursuant to Article II of the Constitution. We do not reach the question whether Article II provides such authority, however, because we agree with the Government's alternative position, that Congress has in fact authorized Hamdi's detention, through the AUMF.

Our analysis on that point, set forth below, substantially overlaps with our analysis of Hamdi's principal argument for the illegality of his detention. He posits that his detention is forbidden by 18 U.S.C. § 4001(a). Section 4001(a) states that "[n]o citizen shall be imprisoned or otherwise detained by the United States except pursuant to an Act of Congress." Congress passed § 4001(a) in 1971 as part of a bill to repeal the Emergency Detention Act of 1950, which provided procedures for executive detention, during times of emergency, of individuals deemed likely to engage in espionage or sabotage. Congress was particularly concerned about the possibility that the Act could be used to reprise the Japanese internment camps of World War II. The Government again presses two alternative positions. First, it argues that § 4001(a), in light of its legislative history and its location in Title 18, applies only to "the control of civilian prisons and related detentions," not to military detentions. Second, it maintains that § 4001(a) is satisfied, because Hamdi is being detained "pursuant to an Act of Congress" — the AUMF. Again, because we conclude that the Government's second assertion is correct, we do not address the first. In other words, for the reasons that follow, we conclude that the AUMF is explicit congressional authorization for the detention of individuals in the narrow category we describe (assuming, without deciding, that such authorization is required), and that the AUMF satisfied § 4001(a)'s requirement that a detention be "pursuant to an Act of Congress" (assuming, without deciding, that § 4001(a) applies to military detentions). * * *

The capture and detention of lawful combatants and the capture, detention, and trial of unlawful combatants, by "universal agreement and practice," are "important incident[s] of war." *Ex parte Quirin.* The purpose of detention is to prevent captured individuals from returning to the field of battle and taking up arms once again.

There is no bar to this Nation's holding one of its own citizens as an enemy combatant. In *Quirin,* one of the detainees, Haupt, alleged that he was a naturalized United States citizen. We held that "[c]itizens who associate themselves with the military arm of the enemy government, and with its aid, guidance and direction enter this country bent on hostile acts, are enemy belligerents within the meaning of . . . the law of war." While Haupt was tried for violations of the law of war, nothing in *Quirin* suggests that his citizenship would have precluded his mere detention for the duration of the relevant hostilities. Nor can we see any reason for drawing such a line here. A citizen, no less than an alien, can be "part of or supporting forces hostile to the United States or coalition partners" and "engaged in an armed conflict against the United States"; such a citizen, if released, would pose the same threat of returning to the front during the ongoing conflict.

In light of these principles, it is of no moment that the AUMF does not use specific language of detention. Because detention to prevent a combatant's return to the battlefield is a fundamental incident of waging war, in permitting the use of "necessary and appropriate force," Congress has clearly and unmistakably authorized detention in the narrow circumstances considered here.

Hamdi objects, nevertheless, that Congress has not authorized the *indefinite* detention to which he is now subject. The Government responds that "the detention of enemy combatants during World War II was just as 'indefinite' while that war was being fought." We take Hamdi's objection to be not to the lack of certainty regarding the date on which the conflict will end, but to the substantial prospect of perpetual detention. We recognize that the national security underpinnings of the "war on terror," although crucially important, are broad and malleable. As the Government concedes, "given its unconventional nature, the current conflict is unlikely to end with a formal cease-fire agreement." The prospect Hamdi raises is therefore not far-fetched. If the Government does not consider this unconventional war won for two generations, and if it maintains during that time that Hamdi might, if released, rejoin forces fighting against the United States, then the position it has taken throughout the litigation of this case suggests that Hamdi's detention could last for the rest of his life.

It is a clearly established principle of the law of war that detention may last no longer than active hostilities. [Citing the Geneva Convention and other international materials.]

Hamdi contends that the AUMF does not authorize indefinite or perpetual detention. Certainly, we agree that indefinite detention for the purpose of interrogation is not authorized. Further, we understand Congress' grant of authority for the use of "necessary and appropriate force" to include the authority to detain for the duration of the relevant conflict, and our understanding is based on longstanding law-of-war principles. If the practical circumstances of a given conflict are entirely unlike those of the conflicts that informed the development of the law of war, that understanding may unravel. But that is not the situation we face as of this date. Active combat operations against Taliban fighters apparently are ongoing in Afghanistan. The United States may detain, for the duration of these hostilities, individuals legitimately determined to be Taliban combatants who "engaged in an armed conflict against the United States." If the record establishes that United States troops are still involved in active combat in Afghanistan, those detentions are part of the exercise of "necessary and appropriate force," and therefore are authorized by the AUMF.

Ex parte Milligan, 4 Wall. 2 (1866), does not undermine our holding about the Government's authority to seize enemy combatants, as we define that term today. In that case, the Court made repeated reference to the fact that its inquiry into whether the military tribunal had jurisdiction to try and punish Milligan turned in large part on the fact that Milligan was not a prisoner of war, but a resident of Indiana arrested while at home there. That fact was central to its conclusion. Had Milligan been captured while he was assisting Confederate soldiers by carrying a rifle against Union troops on a Confederate battlefield, the holding of the Court might well have been different. The Court's repeated explanations that Milligan was not a prisoner of war suggest that had these different circumstances been present he could have been detained under military authority for the duration of the conflict, whether or not he was a citizen.[14]

Moreover, as Justice Scalia acknowledges, the Court in *Ex parte Quirin*, dismissed the language of *Milligan* that the petitioners had suggested prevented them from being subject to military process. * * * Haupt * * * was accused of being a spy. The Court in *Quirin* found him "subject to trial and punishment by [a] military tribunal[ ]" for those acts, and held that his citizenship did not change this result.

Quirin was a unanimous opinion. It both postdates and clarifies *Milligan,* providing us with the most apposite precedent that we have on the question of whether citizens may be detained in such circumstances. Brushing aside such

---

14. Here the basis asserted for detention by the military is that Hamdi was carrying a weapon against American troops on a foreign battlefield; that is, that he was an enemy combatant. The legal category of enemy combatant has not been elaborated upon in great detail. The permissible bounds of the category will be defined by the lower courts as subsequent cases are presented to them.

precedent — particularly when doing so gives rise to a host of new questions never dealt with by this Court — is unjustified and unwise. * * *

Even in cases in which the detention of enemy combatants is legally authorized, there remains the question of what process is constitutionally due to a citizen who disputes his enemy-combatant status. Hamdi argues that he is owed a meaningful and timely hearing and that "extra-judicial detention [that] begins and ends with the submission of an affidavit based on third-hand hearsay" does not comport with the Fifth and Fourteenth Amendments. The Government counters that any more process than was provided below would be both unworkable and "constitutionally intolerable." Our resolution of this dispute requires a careful examination both of the writ of habeas corpus, which Hamdi now seeks to employ as a mechanism of judicial review, and of the Due Process Clause, which informs the procedural contours of that mechanism in this instance. * * *

[The government] asks us to hold that, given both the flexibility of the habeas mechanism and the circumstances presented in this case, the presentation of the Mobbs Declaration to the habeas court completed the required factual development. * * *

[To fit within the AUMF authorization, Hamdi would need to be "part of or supporting forces hostile to the United States or coalition partners" and "engaged in an armed conflict against the United States." The Government urged the Court to defer to the Mobbs Declaration on this point.] Under the Government's most extreme rendition of this argument, "[r]espect for separation of powers and the limited institutional capabilities of courts in matters of military decision-making in connection with an ongoing conflict" ought to eliminate entirely any individual process, restricting the courts to investigating only whether legal authorization exists for the broader detention scheme. At most, the Government argues, courts should review its determination that a citizen is an enemy combatant under a very deferential "some evidence" standard. Under this review, a court would assume the accuracy of the Government's articulated basis for Hamdi's detention, as set forth in the Mobbs Declaration, and assess only whether that articulated basis was a legitimate one.

In response, Hamdi emphasizes that this Court consistently has recognized that an individual challenging his detention may not be held at the will of the Executive without recourse to some proceeding before a neutral tribunal to determine whether the Executive's asserted justifications for that detention have basis in fact and warrant in law. * * * The District Court, agreeing with Hamdi, apparently believed that the appropriate process would approach the process that accompanies a criminal trial. It therefore disapproved of the hearsay nature of the Mobbs Declaration and anticipated quite extensive discovery of various military affairs. Anything less, it concluded, would not be "meaningful judicial review."

Both of these positions highlight legitimate concerns. And both emphasize the tension that often exists between the autonomy that the Government asserts is necessary in order to pursue effectively a particular goal and the process that a citizen contends he is due before he is deprived of a constitutional right. The ordinary mechanism that we use for balancing such serious competing interests, and for determining the procedures that are necessary to ensure that a citizen is not "deprived of life, liberty, or property, without due process of law," is the test that we articulated in *Mathews v. Eldridge* [Chapter 5, Section 6]. *Mathews* dictates that the process due in any given instance is determined by weighing "the private interest that will be affected by the official action" against the Government's asserted interest, "including the function involved" and the burdens the Government would face in providing greater process. The *Mathews* calculus then contemplates a judicious balancing of these concerns, through an analysis of "the risk of an erroneous deprivation" of the private interest if the process were reduced and the "probable value, if any, of additional or substitute safeguards." We take each of these steps in turn.

[The Court then emphasized the gravity of the government's interest in national security and the significance of the right to be free from arbitrary detention].

Striking the proper constitutional balance here is of great importance to the Nation during this period of ongoing combat. But it is equally vital that our calculus not give short shrift to the values that this country holds dear or to the privilege that is American citizenship. It is during our most challenging and uncertain moments that our Nation's commitment to due process is most severely tested; and it is in those times that we must preserve our commitment at home to the principles for which we fight abroad.

With due recognition of these competing concerns, we believe that neither the process proposed by the Government nor the process apparently envisioned by the District Court below strikes the proper constitutional balance when a United States citizen is detained in the United States as an enemy combatant. That is, "the risk of erroneous deprivation" of a detainee's liberty interest is unacceptably high under the Government's proposed rule, while some of the "additional or substitute procedural safeguards" suggested by the District Court are unwarranted in light of their limited "probable value" and the burdens they may impose on the military in such cases.

We therefore hold that a citizen-detainee seeking to challenge his classification as an enemy combatant must receive notice of the factual basis for his classification, and a fair opportunity to rebut the Government's factual assertions before a neutral decisionmaker. These essential constitutional promises may not be eroded.

At the same time, the exigencies of the circumstances may demand that, aside from these core elements, enemy combatant proceedings may be tailored to alleviate their uncommon potential to burden the Executive at a time of ongoing military conflict. Hearsay, for example, may need to be accepted as the most reliable available evidence from the Government in such a proceeding. Likewise, the Constitution would not be offended by a presumption in favor of the Government's evidence, so long as that presumption remained a rebuttable one and fair opportunity for rebuttal were provided. Thus, once the Government puts forth credible evidence that the habeas petitioner meets the enemy-combatant criteria, the onus could shift to the petitioner to rebut that evidence with more persuasive evidence that he falls outside the criteria. A burden-shifting scheme of this sort would meet the goal of ensuring that the errant tourist, embedded journalist, or local aid worker has a chance to prove military error while giving due regard to the Executive once it has put forth meaningful support for its conclusion that the detainee is in fact an enemy combatant. In the words of *Mathews,* process of this sort would sufficiently address the "risk of erroneous deprivation" of a detainee's liberty interest while eliminating certain procedures that have questionable additional value in light of the burden on the Government. * * *

In sum, while the full protections that accompany challenges to detentions in other settings may prove unworkable and inappropriate in the enemy-combatant setting, the threats to military operations posed by a basic system of independent review are not so weighty as to trump a citizen's core rights to challenge meaningfully the Government's case and to be heard by an impartial adjudicator.

In so holding, we necessarily reject the Government's assertion that separation of powers principles mandate a heavily circumscribed role for the courts in such circumstances. Indeed, the position that the courts must forgo any examination of the individual case and focus exclusively on the legality of the broader detention scheme cannot be mandated by any reasonable view of separation of powers, as this approach serves only to *condense* power into a single branch of government. We have long since made clear that a state of war is not a blank check for the President when it comes to the rights of the Nation's citizens. Whatever power the United States Constitution envisions for the Executive in its exchanges with other nations or with enemy organizations in times of conflict, it most assuredly envisions a role for all three branches when individual liberties are at stake. Likewise, we have made clear that, unless Congress acts to suspend it, the Great Writ of habeas corpus allows the Judicial Branch to play a necessary role in maintaining this delicate balance of governance, serving as an important judicial check on the Executive's discretion in the realm of detentions. Thus, while we do not question that our due process assessment must pay keen attention to the particular burdens faced by the Executive in the context of military action, it would turn our system of checks and balances on its head to suggest that a citizen could not make his way to court with a challenge to the factual basis for his detention by his government, simply because the Executive opposes making available such a challenge. Absent suspension of the writ by Congress, a citizen detained as an enemy combatant is entitled to this process.

Because we conclude that due process demands some system for a citizen detainee to refute his classification, the proposed "some evidence" standard is inadequate. Any process in which the Executive's factual assertions go wholly unchallenged or are simply presumed correct without any opportunity for the alleged combatant to demonstrate otherwise falls constitutionally short. As the Government itself has recognized, we have utilized the "some evidence" standard in the past as a standard of review, not as a standard of proof. That is, it primarily has been employed by courts in examining an administrative record developed after an adversarial proceeding — one with process at least of the sort that we today hold is constitutionally mandated in the citizen enemy-combatant setting. This standard therefore is ill suited to the situation in which a habeas petitioner has received no prior proceedings before any tribunal and had no prior opportunity to rebut the Executive's factual assertions before a neutral decisionmaker.

Today we are faced only with such a case. Aside from unspecified "screening" processes, and military interrogations in which the Government suggests Hamdi could have contested his classification, Hamdi has received no process. An interrogation by one's captor, however effective an intelligence-gathering tool, hardly constitutes a constitutionally adequate factfinding before a neutral decisionmaker. * * * Plainly, the "process" Hamdi has received is not that to which he is entitled under the Due Process Clause. * * *

JUSTICE SOUTER, joined by **JUSTICE GINSBURG**, concurring in part, dissenting in part, and concurring in the judgment.

[Justice Souter would follow the plain terms of the Non-Detention Act. The statute was passed in order to supersede a previous statute, the Emergency Detention Act of 1950, which had authorized the Attorney General to detain anyone reasonably thought likely to engage in espionage or sabotage during national emergencies. That statute was repealed in 1971 out of fear that it could authorize a repetition of the World War II internment of citizens of Japanese ancestry. "While Congress might simply have struck the 1950 statute, in considering the repealer the point was made that the existing statute provided some express procedural protection, without which the Executive would seem to be subject to no statutory limits protecting individual liberty. It was in these circumstances that a proposed limit on Executive action was expanded to the inclusive scope of § 4001(a) as enacted." Justice Souter rejected the government's arguments that § 4001(a) does not even apply to wartime military detentions or that the AUMF provided a blanket exemption for all terrorism-related detentions.]

Because the Force Resolution authorizes the use of military force in acts of war by the United States, the [Government's] argument goes, it is reasonably clear that the military and its Commander in Chief are authorized to deal with enemy belligerents according to the treaties and customs known collectively as the laws of war. Accordingly, the United States may detain captured enemies, and *Ex parte Quirin* may perhaps be claimed for the proposition that the American citizenship of such a captive does not as such limit the Government's power to deal with him under the usages of war. Thus, the Government here repeatedly argues that Hamdi's detention amounts to nothing more than customary detention of a captive taken on the field of battle: if the usages of war are fairly authorized by the Force Resolution, Hamdi's detention is authorized for purposes of § 4001(a). [Justice Souter responded that the government had failed to show that it was detaining Hamdi in accord with the laws of war. Its compliance with the Geneva Convention was questionable, because the Convention seems to give detainees in Hamdi's position the right to a hearing before a neutral tribunal, which the government had not provided.]

Since the Government has given no reason either to deflect the application of § 4001(a) or to hold it to be satisfied, I need to go no further; the Government hints of a constitutional challenge to the statute, but it presents none here. I will, however, stray across the line between statutory and constitutional territory just far enough to note the weakness of the Government's mixed claim of inherent, extrastatutory authority under a combination of Article II of the Constitution and the usages of war. It is in fact in this connection that the Government developed its argument that the exercise of war powers justifies the detention, and what I have just said about its inadequacy applies here as well. Beyond that, it is instructive to recall Justice Jackson's observation that the President is not Commander in Chief of the country, only of the military.

There may be room for one qualification to Justice Jackson's statement, however: in a moment of genuine emergency, when the Government must act with no time for deliberation, the Executive may be able to detain a citizen if there is reason to fear he is an imminent threat to the safety of the Nation and its people (though I doubt there is any want of statutory authority). This case, however, does not present that question, because an emergency power of necessity must at least be limited by the emergency; Hamdi has been locked up for over two years. Cf. *Ex parte Milligan* (martial law justified only by "actual and present" necessity as in a genuine invasion that closes civilian courts).

Whether insisting on the careful scrutiny of emergency claims or on a vigorous reading of § 4001(a), we are heirs to a tradition given voice 800 years ago by Magna Carta, which, on the barons' insistence, confined executive power by "the law of the land."

[In principle, Justice Souter said he would vote to hold the detention illegal. "Since this disposition does not command a majority of the Court, however, the need to give practical effect to the conclusions of eight members of the Court rejecting the Government's position calls for me to join with the plurality in ordering remand on terms closest to those I would impose." He added, however, that it "should go without saying that in joining with the plurality to produce a judgment, I do not adopt the plurality's resolution of constitutional issues that I would not reach."]

JUSTICE SCALIA, with whom **JUSTICE STEVENS** joins, dissenting.

* * * Where the Government accuses a citizen of waging war against it, our constitutional tradition has been to prosecute him in federal court for treason or some other crime. Where the exigencies of war prevent that, the Constitution's Suspension Clause, Art. I, § 9, cl. 2, allows Congress to relax the usual protections temporarily. Absent suspension, however, the Executive's assertion of military exigency has not been thought sufficient to permit detention without charge. No one contends that the congressional Authorization for Use of Military Force, on which the Government relies to justify its actions here, is an implementation of the Suspension Clause. Accordingly, I would reverse the decision below.

The very core of liberty secured by our Anglo-Saxon system of separated powers has been freedom from indefinite imprisonment at the will of the Executive. Blackstone stated this principle clearly:

> "Of great importance to the public is the preservation of this personal liberty: for if once it were left in the power of any, the highest, magistrate to imprison arbitrarily whomever he or his officers thought proper . . . there would soon be an end of all other rights and immunities. . . . To bereave a man of life, or by violence to confiscate his estate, without accusation or trial, would be so gross and notorious an act of despotism, as must at once convey the alarm of tyranny throughout the whole kingdom. But confinement of the person, by secretly hurrying him to gaol, where his sufferings are unknown or forgotten; is a less public, a less striking, and therefore a more dangerous engine of arbitrary government. * * * "

These words were well known to the Founders. Hamilton quoted from this very passage in The Federalist No. 84. The two ideas central to Blackstone's understanding — due process as the right secured, and habeas corpus as the instrument by which due process could be insisted upon by a citizen illegally imprisoned — found expression in the Constitution's Due Process and Suspension Clauses. See Amdt. 5; Art. I, § 9, cl. 2.

The gist of the Due Process Clause, as understood at the founding and since, was to force the Government to follow those common-law procedures traditionally deemed necessary before depriving a person of life, liberty, or property. When a citizen was deprived of liberty because of alleged criminal conduct, those procedures typically required committal by a magistrate followed by indictment and trial. * * *

Justice O'Connor, writing for a plurality of this Court, asserts that captured enemy combatants (other than those suspected of war crimes) have traditionally been detained until the cessation of hostilities and then released. That is probably an accurate description of wartime practice with respect to enemy *aliens.* The tradition with respect to American citizens, however, has been quite different. Citizens aiding the enemy have been treated as traitors subject to the criminal process. * * *

There are times when military exigency renders resort to the traditional criminal process impracticable. English law accommodated such exigencies by allowing legislative suspension of the writ of habeas corpus for brief periods. * * * Where the Executive has not pursued the usual course of charge, committal, and conviction, it has historically secured the Legislature's explicit approval of a suspension. * * *

Of course the extensive historical evidence of criminal convictions and habeas suspensions does not *necessarily* refute the Government's position in this case. When the writ is suspended, the Government is entirely free from judicial oversight. It does not claim such total liberation here, but argues that it need only produce what it calls "some evidence" to satisfy a habeas court that a detained individual is an enemy combatant. Even if suspension of the writ on the one hand, and committal for criminal charges on the other hand, have been the only *traditional* means of dealing with citizens who levied war against their own country, it is theoretically possible that the Constitution does not *require* a choice between these alternatives.

I believe, however, that substantial evidence does refute that possibility. First, the text of the 1679 Habeas Corpus Act makes clear that indefinite imprisonment on reasonable suspicion is not an available option of treatment for those accused of aiding the enemy, absent a suspension of the writ. In the United States, this Act was read as "enforc[ing] the common law," and shaped the early understanding of the scope of the writ. [Section] 7 of the Act specifically addressed those committed for high treason, and provided a remedy if they were not *indicted and tried* by the second succeeding court term. That remedy was *not* a bobtailed judicial inquiry into whether there were reasonable grounds to believe the prisoner had taken up arms against the King. Rather, if the prisoner was not indicted and tried within the prescribed time, "he shall be discharged from his Imprisonment." The Act does not contain any exception for wartime. That omission is conspicuous, since § 7 explicitly addresses the offense of "High Treason," which often involved offenses of a military nature. * * *

Further evidence comes from this Court's decision in *Ex parte Milligan*. There, the Court issued the writ to an American citizen who had been tried by military commission for offenses that included conspiring to overthrow the Government, seize munitions, and liberate prisoners of war. The Court rejected in no uncertain terms the Government's assertion that military jurisdiction was proper "under the 'laws and usages of war' ":

> "It can serve no useful purpose to inquire what those laws and usages are, whence they originated, where found, and on whom they operate; they can never be applied to citizens in states which have upheld the authority of the government, and where the courts are open and their process unobstructed."

Milligan is not exactly this case, of course, since the petitioner was threatened with death, not merely imprisonment. But the reasoning and conclusion of *Milligan* logically cover the present case. The Government justifies imprisonment of Hamdi on principles of the law of war and admits that, absent the war, it would have no such authority. But if the law of war cannot be applied to citizens where courts are open, then Hamdi's imprisonment without criminal trial is no less unlawful than Milligan's trial by military tribunal. * * *

The Government argues that our more recent jurisprudence ratifies its indefinite imprisonment of a citizen within the territorial jurisdiction of federal courts. It places primary reliance upon *Ex parte Quirin,* a World War II case upholding the trial by military commission of eight German saboteurs, one of whom, Hans Haupt, was a U.S. citizen. The case was not this Court's finest hour. The Court upheld the commission and denied relief in a brief *per curiam* issued the day after oral argument concluded; a week later the Government carried out the commission's death sentence upon six saboteurs, including Haupt. The Court eventually explained its reasoning in a written opinion issued several months later.

[Justice Scalia argued that *Quirin* misread *Milligan* and was wrong in principle.] But even if *Quirin* gave a correct description of *Milligan,* or made an irrevocable revision of it, *Quirin* would still not justify denial of the writ here. In *Quirin* it was uncontested that the petitioners were members of enemy forces. They were "*admitted* enemy invaders," and it was "undisputed" that they had landed in the United States in service of German forces. The specific holding of the Court was only that, "upon the *conceded* facts," the petitioners were "plainly within [the] boundaries" of military jurisdiction. But where those jurisdictional facts are *not* conceded — where the petitioner insists that he is *not* a belligerent — *Quirin* left the pre-existing law in place: Absent suspension of the writ, a citizen held where the courts are open is entitled either to criminal trial or to a judicial decree requiring his release. * * *

It follows from what I have said that Hamdi is entitled to a habeas decree requiring his release unless (1) criminal proceedings are promptly brought, or (2) Congress has suspended the writ of habeas corpus. A suspension of the writ could, of course, lay down conditions for continued detention, similar to those that today's opinion prescribes under the Due Process Clause. But there is a world of difference between the people's representatives' determining the need for that suspension (and prescribing the conditions for it), and this Court's doing so. * * *

There is a certain harmony of approach in the plurality's making up for Congress's failure to invoke the Suspension Clause and its making up for the Executive's failure to apply what it says are needed procedures — an approach that reflects what might be called a Mr. Fix-it Mentality. The plurality seems to view it as its mission to Make Everything Come Out Right, rather than merely to decree the consequences, as far as individual rights are concerned, of the other two branches' actions and omissions. Has the Legislature failed to suspend the writ in the current dire emergency? Well, we will remedy that failure by prescribing the reasonable conditions that a suspension should have included. And has the Executive failed to live up to those reasonable conditions? Well, we will ourselves make that failure good, so that this dangerous fellow (if he is dangerous) need not be set free. The problem with this approach is not only that it steps out of the courts' modest and limited role in a democratic society; but that by repeatedly doing what it thinks the political branches ought to do it encourages their lassitude and saps the vitality of government by the people.

Several limitations give my views in this matter a relatively narrow compass. They apply only to citizens, accused of being enemy combatants, who are detained within the territorial jurisdiction of a federal court. This is not likely to be a numerous group; currently we know of only two, Hamdi and Jose Padilla. Where the citizen is captured outside and held outside the United States, the constitutional requirements may be different. Moreover, even within the United States, the accused citizen-enemy combatant may lawfully be detained once prosecution is in progress or in contemplation. The Government has been notably successful in securing conviction, and hence long-term custody or execution, of those who have waged war against the state.

I frankly do not know whether these tools are sufficient to meet the Government's security needs, including the need to obtain intelligence through interrogation. It is far beyond my competence, or the Court's competence, to determine that. But it is not beyond Congress's. If the situation demands it, the Executive can ask Congress to authorize suspension of the writ — which can be made subject to whatever conditions Congress deems appropriate, including even the procedural novelties invented by the plurality today. To be sure, suspension is limited by the Constitution to cases of rebellion or invasion. But whether the attacks of September 11, 2001, constitute an "invasion," and whether those attacks still justify suspension several years later, are questions for Congress rather than this Court. If civil rights are to be curtailed during wartime, it must be done openly and democratically, as the Constitution requires, rather than by silent erosion through an opinion of this Court. * * *

Many think it not only inevitable but entirely proper that liberty give way to security in times of national crisis — that, at the extremes of military exigency, *inter arma silent leges.* Whatever the general merits of the view that war silences law or modulates its voice, that view has no place in the interpretation and application of a Constitution designed precisely to confront war and, in a manner that accords with democratic principles, to accommodate it. Because the Court has proceeded to meet the current emergency in a manner the Constitution does not envision, I respectfully dissent.

JUSTICE THOMAS, dissenting.

The Executive Branch, acting pursuant to the powers vested in the President by the Constitution and with explicit congressional approval, has determined that Yaser Hamdi is an enemy combatant and should be detained. This detention falls squarely within the Federal Government's war powers, and we lack the expertise and capacity to second-guess that decision. As such, petitioners' habeas challenge should fail, and there is no reason to remand the case. The plurality reaches a contrary conclusion by failing adequately to consider basic principles of the constitutional structure as it relates to national security and foreign affairs and by using the balancing scheme of *Mathews v. Eldridge.* I do not think that the Federal Government's war powers can be balanced away by this Court. Arguably, Congress could provide for additional procedural protections, but until it does, we have no right to insist upon them. But even if I were to agree with the general approach the plurality takes, I could not accept the particulars. The plurality utterly fails to account for the Government's compelling interests and for our own institutional inability to weigh competing concerns correctly. I respectfully dissent. * * *

Although the President very well may have inherent authority to detain those arrayed against our troops, I agree with the plurality that we need not decide that question because Congress has authorized the President to do so. [The AUMF] authorizes the President to "use all necessary and appropriate force against those nations, organizations, or persons he determines planned, authorized, committed, or aided the terrorist attacks" of September 11, 2001. Indeed, the Court has previously concluded that language materially identical to the AUMF authorizes the Executive to "make the ordinary use of the soldiers . . . ; that he may kill persons who resist and, of course, that he may use the milder measure of seizing [and detaining] the bodies of those whom he considers to stand in the way of restoring peace."

The plurality, however, qualifies its recognition of the President's authority to detain enemy combatants in the war on terrorism in ways that are at odds with our precedent. Thus, the plurality relies primarily on Article 118 of the Geneva Convention (III) for the proposition that "[i]t is a clearly established principle of the law of war that detention may last no longer than active hostilities." It then appears to limit the President's authority to detain by requiring that the record establish that United States troops are still involved in active combat in

Afghanistan because, in that case, detention would be "part of the exercise of 'necessary and appropriate force.' " But I do not believe that we may diminish the Federal Government's war powers by reference to a treaty and certainly not to a treaty that does not apply. Further, we are bound by the political branches' determination that the United States is at war. And, in any case, the power to detain does not end with the cessation of formal hostilities.

Accordingly, the President's action here is "supported by the strongest of presumptions and the widest latitude of judicial interpretation." [Citing *Dames & Moore*.] The question becomes whether the Federal Government (rather than the President acting alone) has power to detain Hamdi as an enemy combatant. More precisely, we must determine whether the Government may detain Hamdi given the procedures that were used.

I agree with the plurality that the Federal Government has power to detain those that the Executive Branch determines to be enemy combatants. But I do not think that the plurality has adequately explained the breadth of the President's authority to detain enemy combatants, an authority that includes making virtually conclusive factual findings. In my view, the structural considerations discussed above, as recognized in our precedent, demonstrate that we lack the capacity and responsibility to second-guess this determination. * * *

The Government's asserted authority to detain an individual that the President has determined to be an enemy combatant, at least while hostilities continue, comports with the Due Process Clause. As these cases also show, the Executive's decision that a detention is necessary to protect the public need not and should not be subjected to judicial second-guessing. Indeed, at least in the context of enemy-combatant determinations, this would defeat the unity, secrecy, and dispatch that the Founders believed to be so important to the warmaking function.

* * * Accordingly, I conclude that the Government's detention of Hamdi as an enemy combatant does not violate the Constitution. By detaining Hamdi, the President, in the prosecution of a war and authorized by Congress, has acted well within his authority. Hamdi thereby received all the process to which he was due under the circumstances. I therefore believe that this is no occasion to balance the competing interests, as the plurality unconvincingly attempts to do.

Companion Cases. On the same day the Court announced *Hamdi*, the Justices handed down two other opinions. In *Rumsfeld v. Padilla*, 542 U.S. 426 (2004), the Court ruled that an American citizen accused of being an enemy combatant had to bring his habeas suit in the jurisdiction (South Carolina) where he was incarcerated. Four Justices dissented, arguing that Padilla ought to be able to sue the Secretary of Defense in New York City. In *Rasul v. Rumsfeld*, 542 U.S. (2004), excerpted below, the Court ruled that accused enemy combatants detained in American facilities in Guantanamo Bay, Cuba, could bring habeas corpus lawsuits.

NOTES ON *HAMDI* AND THE WAR ON TERROR

1. *The Three Issues in* Hamdi. Because of the proliferation of opinions, the precise issues may not be clear to the student. As usefully framed by Jenny S.

Martinez, *Process and Substance in the "War on Terror,"* 108 Colum. L. Rev. 1013, 1045-48 (2008), there are, analytically, three issues for the Court to resolve.

First, does the federal government have the authority to detain American citizens indefinitely without a criminal charge or a congressional suspension of habeas? This is the issue addressed by Justices Scalia and Stevens (odd constitutional bedfellows indeed), and they correctly said that this issue should be answered by analysis of constitutional structure as well as history, which they provided. But they alone opined that the federal government did not have the power to detain without criminal process of habeas suspension. What could have persuaded the majority otherwise? Does Professor Bobbitt's book suggest a line of analysis for the majority?

Second, does the President have the authority to detain American citizens? On this issue, the Court was divided 5-4, with Justices Souter and Ginsburg joining Stevens and Scalia in saying no. The plurality Justices (Rehnquist, O'Connor, Kennedy, Breyer) asserted that Congress conferred authority on the President in the 2002 AUMF, and so the President was operating on the firm terrain of Jackson's Category 1. Souter and Ginsburg disagreed and believed the President was operating in Category 3 ("lowest ebb"), because contrary to statute (the anti-Detention Act). Justice Thomas agreed with the plurality and viewed this as a Category 1 case, but he also believed that the President has inherent Article II authority to detain citizens, and so would be prepared to treat this as a Category 2 case or perhaps even Category 3, where the President's commander-in-chief authority trumps the Anti-Detention Act or requires that the Act be construed narrowly.

Third, what process is constitutionally owed to detained citizens who dispute their enemy combatant status? On this issue Justices Souter and Ginsburg went along with Justice O'Connor's plurality opinion, not because they agreed with it, but apparently because they wanted an authoritative judgment for the Administration to obey. So this issue is decided 6-3. Justice Thomas disagreed; he asserted that once the political branches have determined the proper process for suspected enemies, the Court cannot second-guess it. Justices Scalia and Stevens complained about the plurality's Mr. Fix-It mentality and would not balance away citizens' rights.

2. *Should the Court be (very) reluctant to second-guess the President?* All the Justices except Thomas second-guessed the President's judgment on Hamdi's detention. There are three kinds of arguments in favor of some judicial monitoring of these detentions. First is the Bobbitt argument: the rule of law demands that even the President in a national emergency must respect citizens' presumptive liberty. It is decisions like *Hamdi* that distinguish our state of consent and the rule of law from the state of terror represented by al Qaeda. All eight second-guessing Justices believe that either statutory or constitutional rules prevent indefinite detention. The variety of viewpoints is striking, however: Was there a clear rule of law applicable here?

Second is a Steel Seizure argument: the Court should require the President to follow the processes established by Congress. This is consistent with both the

Constitution and democratic accountability. But only four Justices (Stevens, Scalia, Souter, Ginsburg) accepted this argument. The Non-Detention Act seems pretty sweeping and clear, while the AUMF says nothing about detention. Why does the plurality cut back on a clear congressional command — and then stick its neck out by imposing constitutionally required process on the Administration?

A third kind of argument might support the majority: representation-reinforcing judicial review of the sort laid out in Chapter 2, Section 3B. When the United States feels itself under attack or insecure, "the individuals whose rights are sacrificed are not those who make the laws, but minorities, dissidents, and noncitizens. In those circumstances, 'we' are making a decision to sacrifice 'their' rights — not a very prudent way to balance the competing interests." Geoffrey Stone, *Perilous Times* 531 (2004). Ethnic minorities such as Hamdi, accused of heinous associations in a time of fear and patriotic ferment, are in danger of being railroaded by the political process. Only independent judges can slow the juggernaut and seek more respectful and measured treatment. Perhaps more cynically, it is important in emotional times of crisis that the Supreme Court rhetorically reassure everyone (especially minorities) that there is one institution dedicated to ensuring people are treated fairly by the government. The Administration was holding Yaser Hamdi for years with no credible evidence that he was an "enemy" of any sort, and the government indeed released him soon after the Supreme Court's decision.

It is striking that conservative and liberal Justices alike joined in rebuking the Administration — especially in light of several serious arguments in favor of the Administration's (and Justice Thomas's) position that the Supreme Court should defer to the President's judgment here. To begin with, if you accept Prakash and Ramsey's Foreign Affairs Vesting Thesis, Article II vests the President with duties as the primary organ for the United States in matters of national security as well as foreign affairs. This thesis would be an argument for reading the AUMF broadly to create an exception to the Non-Detention Act, as the *Hamdi* majority does, but it is not as good an argument for a narrow reading of the Due Process Clause, which applies to the U.S. government generally. And if you are not persuaded by Prakash and Ramsey, then this argument gets you nowhere.

Second, and perhaps more important, the Foreign Affairs Vesting Clause argument can be buttressed in this case by the President's explicit commander-in-chief authority, surveyed in Section 1A2. Implicit in the commander-in-chief power is the authority to take needed action against the "enemy," without judicial second-guessing. Although Justice Scalia shrinks from this precedent, *Quirin* is a good citation for this idea. A la Bobbitt, the President might say that *Quirin* provides the rule of law cover for updating presidential power to deal with a new kind of enemy — not the treasonous citizen betraying his country, but the enemy within, the Trojan Horse technically living in our state of consent but whose loyalty is to a state or terror.

The Civil War cases are less supportive. President Lincoln issued an order authorizing his generals to detain citizens without conforming to normal process. Numerous individuals were held pursuant to this order, in one case in defiance of a habeas decree by Chief Justice Taney in *Ex parte Merryman*, 17 F. Cas. 144

(C.C.D. Md. 1861). Responding to Taney, Lincoln said he could not allow "all the laws but one" to remain unexecuted merely to uphold the habeas law. Lincoln also justified his action under the Suspension Clause: when Congress is not in session, the President himself has the authority to suspend habeas during national emergencies. In 1861, Congress declined to ratify this detention without habeas; when it did so in 1863, Congress required military commanders to discharge detainees, apart from prisoners of war, in states where courts were operating unimpaired and required officers to obey judicial orders in those states. The President accepted the 1863 statute but construed it narrowly. In *Ex parte Milligan,* 71 U.S. 2 (1866), the Supreme Court rejected the President's narrowing construction and directed that the detainee was entitled to habeas release.[a]

A third line of support for the President is pragmatic. Politically, the President's inherent first-mover advantage is most powerful in times of national emergency or threat (such as 9/11) and that the Supreme Court's institutional weakness is even more on display in such circumstances. Political scientists, for example, "find that judges are less likely to overturn presidents who appointed them to the bench, presidents who enjoy strong public approval ratings, and policies that involve foreign affairs." William Howell, *Power without Persuasion: The Politics of Direct Presidential Action* 151 (2003). Unfortunately for President Bush, no one on the *Hamdi* Court owed his or her seat to his appointment, the fact that a citizen was detained gave the case a domestic feature that worked against the President's position, and the Court was deliberating in the three companion cases just as news reports documented (with lurid photos) American abuse of Iraqi prisoners at Abu Ghraib prison. In light of the international black eye the United States acquired from Abu Ghraib, *Hamdi*'s mild affirmation of the rule of law was not likely to embroil the Court in controversy.

Some legal pragmatists worry that the Supreme Court has nothing to add when the country is making Bobbittian calculations about security and liberty. From an institutional cost-benefit point of view, the President is the best decisionmaker in times of emergency. Congressional framework statutes do not reliably anticipate the ever-changing technology of terrorist threats, and Congress moves too slowly to update such statutes in any event. Congress also lacks sufficient information to make reliable judgments. The President has access to information and experts on terrorism and can act quickly and in a tailored way to new threats. Judges have even less expertise than Congress and are, at best, second-guessers. They should defer to the President pretty much along the lines suggested by Justice Thomas.[b]

---

a. For detailed examinations of Lincoln's suspension of habeas, see Daniel Farber, *Lincoln's Constitution* (2003); David Barron & Martin Lederman, *The Commander in Chief at the Lowest Ebb — A Constitutional History,* 121 Harv. L. Rev. 941, 998-1000, 1004-08 (2008).

b. On institutional cost-benefit analysis and the weakness of the judiciary, see Neil Komesar, *Imperfect Alternatives: Choosing Institutions in Law, Economics, and Public Policy* (1994); Eric Posner & Adrian Vermeule, *Terror in the Balance: Security, Liberty, and the Courts* (2007); John Yoo, *Judicial Review and the War on Terrorism,* 72 Geo. Wash. L. Rev. 427 (2003).

3. *How Much Process Is Due?* Although there is a relationship between process and substance, notice how little discussion there is about liberty and structural constitutional limitations on the government's ability to detain citizens (the focus of the Scalia/Stevens dissent), and how much focus there is on process. Given the Court's institutional weakness, great uncertainty as to consequences of sharp constitutional lines (the Scalia/Stevens position) or of complete deference to the executive (the Thomas position), and the allure that process has for lawyers and judges, perhaps the focus on process is inevitable. See Martinez, *Process and Substance*, 108 Colum. L. Rev. at 1061-79. But what next? If you were advising the Bush Administration, how would you satisfy the Court's judgment in *Hamdi*, but without compromising the national security goals of the Administration?

PROBLEM 8-8
CRIMINAL RESPONSIBILITY FOR TORTURE
OF IRAQI PRISONERS?

At about the same time the Supreme Court was deliberating in *Hamdi,* there were reports of American misconduct regarding prisoners. In spring 2004, it was revealed that U.S. soldiers engaged in abusive practices against Iraqis in Abu Ghraib prison, including forced nudity, masturbation, and other forms of sexual humiliation; the piling up of naked bodies in pyramids; beatings; food and sleep deprivation; and other abuses. Assume that some of the above practices are "torture" in violation of the Convention Against Torture and the criminal statute implementing the Convention, 18 U.S.C. § 2340A.

Jack Bauer, a U.S. soldier who committed these offenses, is prosecuted in the United States. Bauer's attorney argues that his client was acting under Department of Defense imperatives to extract useful information from "suspected terrorists." Hence, Bauer was acting reasonably pursuant to policies that can be traced back to Secretary of Defense Rumsfeld and, through him, to the President. Assume that Bauer can make this connection. Does he have a valid constitutional argument that his prosecution for torture violates Article II and the constitutional separation of powers? In formulating your answer, consider (a) the Commander-in-Chief Clause (Notes in Section 1), as well as other relevant provisions of the Constitution; (b) presidential practice under the Commander-in-Chief Clause;[c] and (c) Supreme Court precedent such as *The Prize Cases*, 67 U.S. 635 (1862), discussed in the Note on the War Powers Resolution. Jot down your thoughts, and now read the following executive

---

c. George Washington was Commander in Chief both before and after there was a Constitution. According to B. Logan Beirne, "Battle Royale: George versus George versus George, Commander-in-Chief Power" (Yale Law School SAW, 2007), during the Revolution General Washington authorized torture of British agents and prisoners and considered such orders, however distasteful, part of his authority as the American Commander-in-Chief; Beirne also argues that the Continental Congress eventually found it necessary to vest General Washington with virtually plenary authority to conduct the war. Barron & Lederman, *The Commander in Chief at the Lowest Ebb*, 121 Harv. L. Rev. at 772-81, argue that General Washington was always faithful to specific directives of the Congress.

department memorandum. If you were a judge, would you accept or reject Jack Bauer's constitutional defense to the torture prosecution?

Memorandum from Jay S. Bybee, Assistant Attorney General, to Alberto R. Gonzales, Counsel to the President, *Re: Standards of Conduct for Interrogation under 18 U.S.C. §§ 2340-2340A* (Aug. 1, 2002). This memorandum advised the President as to the limitations possibly imposed on executive branch interrogation of prisoners taken in the "war on terrorism," by the Convention Against Torture and its implementing legislation (cited above). The memorandum advised the President that the anti-torture convention and legislation only "proscribe[] acts inflicting, and that are specifically intended to inflict, severe pain or suffering, whether mental or physical. Those acts must be of an extreme nature [to violate the Convention and statute]. We further conclude that certain acts may be cruel, inhuman, or degrading, but still not produce pain and suffering of the requisite intensity to fall within [the statutory] proscription against torture." (In a later section, the author also suggested that executive branch personnel engaged in torture out of "necessity" or in "self-defense" (of the country) would have defenses to prosecution for admitted torture of enemy combatants.) After its analysis of the statute's text and legislative background, the memorandum then concluded: "Even if an interrogation method arguably were to violate Section 2340A, the statute would be unconstitutional if it impermissibly encroached on the President's constitutional power to conduct a military campaign. As Commander-in-Chief, the President has the constitutional authority to order interrogations of enemy combatants to gain intelligence information concerning the military plans of the enemy. The demands of the Commander-in-Chief power are especially pronounced in the middle of a war in which the nation has already suffered a direct attack. In such a case, the information gained from interrogations may prevent future attacks by foreign enemies. Any effort to apply Section 2340A in a manner that interferes with the President's direction of such core war matters as the detention and interrogation of enemy combatants thus would be unconstitutional."

The memorandum describes "the War with Al Qaeda," as well as congressional authorizations for the President to use force to prevent and deter future attacks within and outside the United States, see S.J. Res. 23, Pub. Law No. 107-40, 115 Stat. 224 (2001), and to use expanded surveillance methods against terrorists, The USA Patriot Act, Pub. Law No. 107-56, 115 Stat. 272 (2001). Assistant Attorney General Bybee went beyond those resolutions to opine that "the President enjoys complete discretion in the exercise of his Commander-in-Chief authority and in conducting operations against hostile forces." Accordingly, he opined that the anti-torture statute and convention do not limit the President's authority in any way.

"* * * The President's constitutional power to protect the security of the United States and the lives and safety of its people must be understood in light of the Founders' intention to create a federal government 'cloathed with all the powers requisite to the complete execution of its trust.' *The Federalist* No. 23, at 147 (Alexander Hamilton) (Jacob E. Cooke ed. 1961). Foremost among the objectives committed to that trust by the Constitution is the security of the nation. As Hamilton explained in arguing for the Constitution's adoption, because 'the circumstances which may affect the public safety' are not 'reducible within certain determinate limits,'

> it must be admitted, as a necessary consequence, that there can be no limitation of that authority, which is to provide for the defence and protection of the community, in any matter essential to its efficacy.

Id. at 147-48. * * *

"The text, structure and history of the Constitution establish that the Founders entrusted the President with the primary responsibility, and therefore the power, to ensure the security of the United States in situations of grave and unforeseen emergencies. The decision to deploy military force in the defense of United States interests is expressly placed under Presidential authority by the Vesting Clause, U.S. Const. Art. I, § 1, cl. 1, and by the Commander-in-Chief Clause, *id.*, § 2, cl. 1. This Office [of Legal Counsel] has long understood the Commander-in-Chief Clause in particular as an affirmative grant of authority to the President. *See, e.g.,* Memorandum for Charles W. Colson, Special Counsel to the President, from William H. Rehnquist, Assistant Attorney General, Office of Legal Counsel, *Re: The President and the War Power: South Vietnam and the Cambodian Sanctuaries* (May 22, 1970) ("Rehnquist Memorandum"). The Framers understood the Clause as investing the President with the fullest range of power understood at the time of the ratification of the Constitution as belonging to the military commander. In addition, the structure of the Constitution demonstrates that any power traditionally understood as pertaining to the executive — which includes the conduct of warfare and the defense of the nation — unless expressly assigned in the Constitution to Congress, is vested in the President. Article II, Section 1 makes this clear by stating that the 'executive Power shall be vested in a President of the United States of America.' That sweeping grant vests in the President an unenumerated 'executive power' and contrasts with the specific enumeration of the powers — those 'herein' — granted to Congress in Article I. The implications of constitutional text and structure are confirmed by the practical consideration that national security decisions require the unity in purpose and energy in action that characterize the Presidency rather than Congress.

"As the Supreme Court has recognized, the Commander-in-Chief power and the President's obligation to protect the nation imply the ancillary powers necessary to their successful exercise. 'The first of the enumerated powers of the President is that he shall be Commander-in-Chief of the Army and Navy of the United States. And, of course, the grant of war power includes all that is necessary and proper for carrying those powers into execution.' *Johnson v. Eisentrager*, 339 U.S. 763, 788 (1950). In wartime, it is for the President alone to decide what methods to use to best prevail against the enemy. *See, e.g.,* Rehnquist Memorandum * * *. The President's complete discretion in exercising the Commander-in-Chief power has been recognized by the courts. In the *Prize Cases*, for example, the Court explained that whether the President 'in fulfilling his duties as Commander in Chief' had appropriately responded to the rebellion of the southern states was a question 'to be *decided by him*' and which the Court could not question, but must leave to 'the political department of the Government to which this power was entrusted.'

"One of the core functions of the Commander in Chief is that of capturing, detaining, and interrogating members of the enemy. [Six lines crossed out in the public version of this memorandum.] It is well settled that the President may seize and detain enemy combatants, at least for the duration of the conflict, and the laws of war make clear that prisoners may be interrogated for information concerning the enemy, its strength, and its plans. Numerous Presidents have ordered the capture, detention, and questioning of enemy combatants during virtually every major conflict in the Nation's history, including recent conflicts such as the Gulf, Vietnam, and Korean wars. Recognizing this authority, Congress has never attempted to restrict or interfere with the President's authority on this score.

"Any effort by Congress to regulate the interrogation of battlefield combatants would violate the Constitution's sole vesting of the Commander-in-Chief authority in the President. * * * It may be the case that only successful interrogations can provide the information necessary to prevent the success of covert terrorist attacks upon the United States and its citizens. Congress can no more interfere with the President's conduct of the interrogation of enemy combatants than it can dictate strategic or tactical decisions on the battlefield. Just as statutes that order the President to conduct warfare in a certain manner or for specific goals would be unconstitutional, so too are laws that seek to prevent the President from gaining the intelligence he believes necessary to prevent attacks upon the United States."

Postscript. The Office of Legal Counsel subsequently withdrew this Memorandum, in part because of its narrow interpretation of what is "torture" (not excerpted here), see Jack Goldsmith, *The Terror Presidency: Law and Judgment Inside the Bush Administration* 141-62 (2007), but has not backed away from the proposition that there is a core Commander-in-Chief power that Congress cannot regulate.

PROBLEM 8-9
PRESIDENTIAL SURVEILLANCE

Immediately after 9/11, President Bush secretly authorized the National Security Agency (NSA) to intercept international communications into and out of the United States of persons linked to al Qaeda or related terrorist organizations. After the NSA program came to light, the President explained that its purpose was to establish an "early warning system" to prevent another terrorist attack. "[A] two-minute phone conversation between somebody linked to al Qaeda here and an operative overseas could lead directly to the loss of thousands of lives." Presidential Press Conference, December 19, 2005. Because terrorists pose such a huge threat and move quickly from place to place, the President maintains that protocols Congress set in place in 1978 for long-term electronic communications monitoring are no longer appropriate and must be supplemented with emergency shorter-term measures. NSA activities are "carefully reviewed approximately every 45 days to ensure [they are] being used properly." Id. The Attorney General monitors for legality, and NSA officials themselves monitor to assure protection of civil liberties.

You are the General Counsel to the Senate Judiciary Committee, chaired by Senator Arlen Specter (R-Pa.). Senator Specter wonders whether the NSA program is legal. It might violate the Fourth Amendment, which the Supreme Court has construed to require warrants and probable cause for wiretaps, e.g., *Katz v. United States*, 389 U.S. 347 (1967), but the Court has never definitively ruled on the Fourth Amendment validity of surveillance to investigate foreign-sponsored terrorist activities. See *United States v. United States District Court*, 407 U.S. 297 (1972) (reserving this issue). Set the Fourth Amendment questions aside, as the Chair has assigned it to another staff member.

Instead, Senator Specter asks you to tell him whether the NSA program is a legitimate exercise of the President's authority, especially in light of prior legislation (described below) and general principles of separate powers at the national level. If the program is not constitutional, what should the Congress consider doing? The following materials might help you frame an answer for Senator Specter.[d]

January 9, 2006 Letter from Scholars and Former Government Officials [Curtis Bradley et al.] to Congressional Leadership in Response to Justice Department Letter of December 22, 2005.[e] "In 1978, after an extensive investigation of the privacy violations associated with foreign intelligence surveillance programs, Congress and the President enacted the Foreign Intelligence Surveillance Act (FISA). FISA comprehensively regulates electronic surveillance within the United States, striking a careful balance between protecting civil liberties and preserving the 'vitally important government purpose' of obtaining valuable intelligence in order to safeguard national security.

"With minor exceptions, FISA authorizes electronic surveillance only upon certain specified showings, and only if approved by a court. The statute specifically allows for warrantless *wartime* domestic electronic surveillance — but only for the first fifteen days of a war. 50 U.S.C. § 1811. It makes criminal any electronic surveillance not authorized by statute, id. § 1809; and it expressly establishes FISA and specified provisions of the federal criminal code (which govern wiretaps for criminal investigation) as the '*exclusive* means by which electronic surveillance . . . may be conducted.' 18 U.S.C. § 2511(2)(f) (emphasis added).

"The Department of Justice concedes that the NSA program [where the President's agents tapped thousands of electronic transmissions between people in the United States and those abroad, in order to monitor possible terrorist communications] was not authorized by the above provisions. * * * The DOJ nevertheless contends that the surveillance is authorized by the AUMF

---

d. These materials are taken from the appendices to David Cole & Martin Lederman, *The National Security Agency's Domestic Spying Program: Framing the Debate*, 81 Ind. L.J. 1363-1424 (2006).

e. This Letter, 81 *Ind. L.J.* at 1363-72, was a response to the December 22, 2005 Letter from Department of Justice to the Leadership of the Senate Select Committee on Intelligence and House Permanent Select Committee on Intelligence, id. at 1359-62.

[Authorization for the Use of Military Force], signed on September 18, 2001, which empowers the President to use 'all necessary and appropriate force against' al Qaeda. According to the DOJ, collecting 'signals intelligence' on the enemy, even if it involves tapping U.S. phones, without court approval or probable cause, is a 'fundamental incident of war' authorized by the AUMF.

[The scholars advanced several reasons the President was wrong about that: (1) The statute specifically addressing the matter of wiretaps (FISA) governs the more generally phrased law (AUMF), under accepted principles of statutory interpretation. Also, (2) repeals by implication, the effect of the DOJ's broad AUMF interpretation, are disfavored in the law. Finally, (3) the Attorney General admitted that he had consulted with Congress to determine whether FISA could be amended, and Members of Congress advised him that such legislation would be impossible to achieve. The scholars distinguished *Hamdi*, which involved presidential powers over combatants fighting against the United States in *Afghanistan*.] "It is one thing, however, to say that foreign battlefield capture of enemy combatants is an incident of waging war that Congress intended to authorize. It is another matter entirely to treat unchecked warrantless *domestic* spying as included in that authorization, especially where an existing statute specifies that other laws are the 'exclusive means' by which electronic surveillance may be conducted and provides that even a declaration of war authorizes such spying only for a fifteen-day emergency period.

"* * * [T]he [old] federal law involving wiretapping specifically provided that '[n]othing contained in this chapter or in section 605 of the Communications Act of 1934 shall limit the constitutional power of the President . . . to obtain foreign intelligence information deemed essential to the security of the United States." 18 U.S.C. § 2511(3) (1976).

"But FISA specifically repealed that provision, FISA § 201(c), and replaced it with language dictating that FISA and the criminal code are the 'exclusive means' of conducting electronic surveillance. In doing so, Congress did not deny that the President has constitutional power to conduct electronic surveillance for national security purposes; rather, Congress properly concluded that 'even if the President has the inherent authority in the absence of legislation to authorize warrantless electronic surveillance for foreign intelligence purposes, Congress has the power to regulate the conduct of such surveillance by legislating a reasonable procedure, which then becomes the exclusive means by which such surveillance can be conducted.' H.R. Rep. No. 95-1282 (1978). * * *

U.S. Department of Justice, "Legal Authorities Supporting the Activities of the National Security Agency Described by the President," January 19, 2006.[f] "As Congress expressly recognized in the AUMF, 'the President has authority under the Constitution to take action to deter and prevent acts of international terrorism against the United States,' AUMF pmbl., especially in the context of the current conflict. Article II of the Constitution vests in the

---

f. This Letter, 81 *Ind. L.J.* at 1373-1413, was a response to the Scholars' Letter of January 9 and a detailed elaboration of arguments suggested in the Department's Letter of December 22.

President all executive powers of the United States, including the power to act as Commander-in-Chief of the Armed Forces, and authority over the conduct of the Nation's foreign affairs. As the Supreme Court has explained, '[t]he President is the sole organ of the nation in its external relations, and its sole representative with foreign nations.' *Curtiss-Wright.* In this way, the Constitution gives the President inherent power to protect the Nation from foreign attack, *The Prize Cases*, and to protect national security information.

"To carry out these activities, the President must have authority to gather information necessary for the execution of his office. The Founders, after all, intended the federal Government to be clothed with all authority necessary to protect the Nation. Because of the structural advantages of the Executive Branch, the Founders also intended that the President would have the primary responsibility and necessary authority as Commander-in-Chief and Chief Executive to protect the Nation and to conduct the Nation's foreign affairs. See, e.g., *The Federalist* No.70, at 471-72 (Hamilton); see *Johnson v. Eisentrager*, 339 U.S. 763, 788 (1950) ('this [constitutional] grant of war power includes all that is necessary and proper for carrying these powers into execution'). Thus, it has long been recognized that the President has the authority to use secretive means to collect intelligence necessary for the conduct of foreign affairs and military campaigns. [*Curtiss-Wright* et al.]

"In reliance on these principles, a consistent understanding has developed that the President has inherent constitutional authority to conduct warrantless searches and surveillance within the United States for foreign intelligence purposes. Wiretaps for such purposes thus have been authorized by Presidents at least since the administration of Franklin Roosevelt in 1940. In a Memorandum to Attorney General Jackson, President Roosevelt wrote on May 21, 1940:

> You are, therefore, authorized and directed in such cases as you may approve, after investigation of the need in each case, to authorize the necessary investigation agents that they are at liberty to secure information by listening devices directed to the conversation or other communications of persons suspected of subversive activities against the Government of the United States, including suspected spies. You are requested furthermore to limit these investigations so conducted to a minimum and limit them insofar as possible to aliens.

President Truman approved a memorandum drafted by Attorney General Tom Clark in which the Attorney General advised that 'it is as necessary as it was in 1940 to take the investigative measures' authorized by President Roosevelt to conduct electronic surveillance 'in cases vitally affecting the domestic security.' Indeed, while the FISA was being debated during the Carter Administration, Attorney General Griffin Bell testified that 'the current bill recognizes no inherent power of the President to conduct electronic surveillance, and I want to interpolate here to say that *this does not take away the power [of] the President under the Constitution.*' Foreign Intelligence Electronic Surveillance Act of 1978: Hearings on H.R. 5764 [et al.] Before the Subcomm. on Legislation of the House Comm. on Intelligence, 95th Cong., 2d Sess. 15 (1978) (emphasis added)
* * *

"Among the President's most basic constitutional duties is the duty to protect the Nation from armed attack. The Constitution gives him all necessary authority to fulfill that responsibility. The courts have long acknowledged the President's inherent authority to take action to protect Americans abroad, see, e.g., *Durand v. Hollins*, 8 F. Cas. 111, 112 (C.C.S.D.N.Y. 1860) (No. 4186), and to protect the Nation from attack, see, e.g., *The Prize Cases*. See generally *Ex parte Quirin* (recognizing that the President has authority under the Constitution 'to direct the performance of those functions which may constitutionally be performed by the military arm of the nation in time of war,' including 'important incident[s] to the conduct of war,' such as 'the adoption of measures by the military command . . . to repel and defeat the enemy'). As the Supreme Court recognized in *The Prize Cases*, if the Nation is invaded, the President is 'bound to resist force by force'; '[h]e must determine the degree of force the crisis demands' and need not await congressional sanction to do so. * * *

"On September 14, 2001, in its first legislative response to the attacks of September 11th, Congress gave its express approval to the President's military campaign against al Qaeda and, in the process, confirmed the well-accepted understanding of the President's Article II powers. In the preamble to the AUMF, Congress stated that 'the President has authority under the Constitution to take action to deter and prevent acts of international terrorism against the United States,' AUMF pmbl., and thereby acknowledged the President's inherent constitutional authority to defend the United States. This clause 'constitutes an extraordinarily sweeping recognition of independent presidential *constitutional* power to employ the war power to combat terrorism.' Michael Stokes Paulsen, Youngstown *Goes to War*, 19 Constl. Comment. 215, 252 (2002). This striking recognition of presidential authority cannot be discounted as the product of excitement in the immediate aftermath of September 11th, for the same terms were repeated by Congress more than a year later in the AUMF Against Iraq Resolution of 2002. In the context of the conflict with al Qaeda and related terrorist organizations, therefore, Congress has acknowledged a broad executive authority to 'deter and prevent' further attacks against the United States.

"The AUMF passed by Congress on September 14, 2001, does not lend itself to a narrow reading. Its expansive language authorizes the President 'to use all *necessary and appropriate force* against those nations, organizations, or persons *he determines* planned, authorized, committed, or aided the terrorist attacks that occurred on September 11, 2001.' AUMF § 2(a) (emphasis added). In the field of foreign affairs, and particularly that of war powers and national security, congressional enactments are to be broadly construed where they indicate support for authority long asserted and exercised by the Executive Branch. [*Dames & Moore.*] This authorization transforms the struggle against al Qaeda and related terrorist organizations from what Justice Jackson called 'a zone of twilight,' in which the President and Congress have concurrent powers whose 'distribution is uncertain,' *Youngstown* (Jackson, J., concurring), into a situation in which the President's authority it at its maximum because 'it includes all that he possesses in his own right plus all that Congress can delegate,' id. With regard to these fundamental tools of warfare — and, as demonstrated below, warrantless electronic surveillance against the declared enemy is one such tool — the AUMF places the President's authority at its zenith under *Youngstown*. [The Letter also invokes *Hamdi*'s broad construction of the AUMF.]

"[Warrantless intelligence surveillance against the enemy is a "fundamental incident" of the use of military force authorized by the AUMF.] As one author has explained:

> It is *essential* in warfare for a belligerent to be as fully informed as possible about the enemy — his strength, his weakness, measures taken by him and measures contemplated by him. This applies not only to military matters, but . . . anything which bears on and is material to his ability to wage the war in which he is engaged. *The laws of war recognize and respect this aspect of warfare.*

Morris Greenspan, *The Modern Law of Land Warfare* 325 (1959) (emphasis added). Similarly, article 24 of the Hague Regulations of 1907 expressly states that 'the employment of measures necessary for obtaining information about the enemy [is] considered permissible.' [The Letter cites other international authorities, as well as court decisions and historical practice.]

"* * * Indeed, since its independence, the United States has intercepted communications for wartime intelligence purposes and, if necessary, has done so within its own borders. During the Revolutionary War, for example, George Washington received and used to his advantage reports from American intelligence agents on British military strength, British strategic intentions, and British estimates of American strength. In fact, Washington himself proposed that one of his Generals 'contrive a means of opening [British letters] without breaking the seals, take copies of the contents, and then let them go on.' [Similar examples during the Civil War, including "[t]elegraph wiretapping."]

"[During World War II, President Roosevelt authorized domestic wiretapping, as noted above.] The President's order gave the Government of the United States access to 'communications by mail, cable, radio, or other means of transmission passing between the United States and any foreign country.' See also Exec. Order No. 8985, § 1, 6 Fed. Reg. 6625, 6625 (Dec. 19, 1941). In addition, the United States systematically listened surreptitiously to electronic communications as part of the war effort. During World War II, signals intelligence assisted in, among other things, the destruction of the German U-boat fleet by the Allied naval forces, and the war against Japan. In general, signals intelligence 'helped to shorten the war by perhaps two years, reduce the loss of life, and make inevitable an Allied victory.' Carl Boyd, *American Command of the Sea Through Carriers, Codes, and the Silent Service: World War II and Beyond* 27 (1995). Significantly, not only was wiretapping in World War II used 'extensively by military intelligence and secret service personnel in combat areas abroad,' but also 'by the FBI and secret service in this country.' [Sam Dash et al., *The Eavesdroppers* 30 (1971).]

"In light of the long history of prior wartime practice, the NSA activities fit squarely within the sweeping terms of the AUMF. * * *

[The Letter then analyzed FISA, which requires the Attorney General to apply for an order from a special court when he wants to use "electronic surveillance" to obtain "foreign intelligence information." 50 U.S.C. §§ 1803-1804. The application must establish probable cause to believe that the target is a foreign power or agent of such power; must have a certification of a top specified executive official that the information cannot be obtained by normal investigative means; and must describe the measures it intends to take. The Letter described the FISA legislative history as expressing tentative congressional action, with signals that Congress did not intend to disturb the President's inherent powers. Section 109 of FISA prohibits any person from intentionally "engag[ing] . . . in electronic surveillance under color of law *except as authorized by statute.*" 50 U.S.C. § 1809(a)(1) (emphasis added).]

"The AUMF qualifies as a 'statute' authorizing electronic surveillance within the meaning of section 109 of FISA. [Analogy to *Hamdi*.] * * *

"[C]rucial to the Framers' decision to vest the President with primary constitutional authority to defend the Nation from foreign attack is the fact that the Executive can act quickly, decisively, and flexibly as needed. For Congress to have a role in that process, it must be able to act with similar speed * * *. Yet the need for prompt decisionmaking in the wake of a devastating attack on the United States is fundamentally inconsistent with the notion that to do so Congress must legislate at a level of detail more in keeping with a peacetime budget reconciliation bill. In emergency situations, Congress must be able to use broad language that effectively sanctions the President's use of the core incidents of military force. This is precisely what Congress did when it passed the AUMF on September 14, 2001 — just three days after the deadly attacks on America. * * * Under these circumstances, it would be unreasonable and wholly impractical to demand that Congress specifically amend FISA in order to assist the President in defending the Nation. Such specificity would also have been self-defeating because it would have apprised our adversaries of some of our most sensitive methods of intelligence gathering.

[Section 111 of FISA, 50 U.S.C. § 1811, which capped presidential surveillance even in time of war without court authorization at fifteen days,] "cannot reasonably be read as Congress's final word on electronic surveillance during wartime. * * * Rather, section 111 represents Congress's recognition that it would likely have to return to the subject and provide additional authorization to conduct warrantless electronic surveillance outside FISA during time of war.

[Even if § 111 and other provisions invoked by the Scholars were ambiguous,] "any doubt as to whether the AUMF and FISA should be understood to allow the President to make tactical military decisions to authorize surveillance outside the parameters of FISA must be resolved to avoid the serious constitutional questions that a contrary interpretation would raise."

"It is well established that the first task of any interpreter faced with a statute that may present an unconstitutional infringement on the powers of the President is to determine whether the statute may be construed to avoid the constitutional difficulty. Moreover, the canon of constitutional avoidance has particular importance in the realm of national security, where the President's constitutional authority is at its highest. See *Department of the Navy v. Egan*, 484 U.S. 518, 530 (1988); William N. Eskridge, Jr., *Dynamic Statutory Interpretation* 325 (1994) (describing "[s]uper-strong rule against congressional interference with the President's authority over foreign affairs and national security"). [The AUMF should be interpreted broadly, and FISA narrowly, to avoid constructions where FISA would unconstitutionally obstruct the President's Commander-in-Chief powers.]

"* * * The core of the Commander-in-Chief power is the authority to direct the Armed Forces in conducting a military campaign. Thus, the Supreme Court has made clear that the 'President alone' is 'constitutionally invested with the entire charge of hostile operations.' *Hamilton v. Dillin*, 88 U.S. 73, 87 (1874); *The Federalist* No. 74, at 500 (Hamilton). 'As Commander-in-chief, [the President] is authorized to direct the movements of the naval and military forces placed by law at his command, and to employ them in the manner he may deem most effectual to harass and conquer and subdue the enemy.' *Fleming v. Page*, 50 U.S. 603, 615 (1850). As Chief Justice Chase explained in 1866, although Congress has authority to legislate to support the prosecution of a war, Congress may not '*interfere[] with the command of the forces and the conduct of campaigns*. That power and duty belong to the President as commander-in-chief." *Ex parte Milligan*, 71 U.S. 2, 139 (1866) (Chase, C.J., concurring in judgment) (emphasis added).

"The Executive Branch uniformly has construed the Commander in Chief and foreign affairs powers to grant the President authority that is beyond the ability of Congress to regulate. In 1860, Attorney General Black concluded that an act of Congress, if intended to constrain the President's discretion in assigning duties to an officer in the army, would be unconstitutional:

> As commander-in-chief of the army it is your right to decide according to your own judgment what officer may perform any particular duty, and as the supreme executive magistrate you have the power of appointment. Congress could not, if it would, take away from the President, or in anywise diminish the authority conferred upon him by the Constitution.

Memorial of Captain Meigs, 9 Op. Att'y Gen. 462, 468 (1860). Attorney General Black went on to explain that, in his view, the statute involved there could probably be read as simply providing 'a recommendation' that the President could decline to follow at his discretion. Id. at 469-70.

[The concluding portion of the Letter argued that the NSA program did not violate the Fourth Amendment.]

February 2, 2006 Letter from Scholars and Former Government Officials to Congressional Leadership in Response to Justice Department Whitepaper of January 19, 2006. The Scholars continued to find no authorization for illegal wiretapping in the AUMF, especially in light of section 111, which also distinguishes this situation from that in *Hamdi*. The detention statute in *Hamdi* did not mention detention of citizens in wartime. "Had there been a statute on the books providing that when Congress declares war, the President may detain Americans as 'enemy combatants' *only* for the first fifteen days of the conflict, the Court could not reasonably have read the AUMF to authorize silently what Congress had specifically sought to limit. Yet that is what the DOJ's argument would require here." See also 18 U.S.C. § 2511(2)(f), which specifies that FISA and the criminal code are the "exclusive means" by which electronic surveillance can be conducted. DOJ concedes that its interpretation requires an implicit repeal of § 2511, which is strongly disfavored in the law.

"The argument that conduct undertaken by the Commander in Chief that has some relevance to 'engaging the enemy' is immune from congressional regulation finds no support in, and is directly contradicted by, both case law and historical precedent. *Every* time the Supreme Court has confronted a statute limiting the Commander-in-Chief's authority, it has upheld the statute. No precedent holds that the President, when acting as Commander in Chief, is free to disregard an Act of Congress, much less a *criminal statute* enacted by Congress, that was designed specifically to restrain the President as such." See, e.g., *Little v. Barreme*, 6 U.S. 170 (1804), holding unlawful a presidential seizure of a ship coming *from* France during the Quasi-War with France, when Congress authorized seizure only of ships going *to* France.

NOTES ON THE STEEL SEIZURE FORMULATION AND PRESIDENTIAL WIRETAPPING

The FISA controversy brings together many of the themes of this chapter, including the debate over the original meaning of Article II's Vesting Clause and its Commander-in-Chief Clause, and whether those powers trump Congress's Article I powers; the notion that presidential practice + congressional acquiescence = constitutional evolution; the role of important Supreme Court precedents such as the *Prize Cases*, the Steel Seizure Case, and *Hamdi*, with much debate as to how these precedents should be interpreted; *Whitman* concerns that the President's unilateral action represents an important shift in public policy that must involve Congress.

How would the Scholars respond to the following scenario? Agents of Badnikstan have obtained canisters of deadly nerve gas that they intend to set off in the center of Los Angeles, killing tens of thousands of innocent people. Federal agent Jack Bauer has 24 hours to find the bad guys. His only lead is the lover of one of the ring-leaders. The White House has been tapping the phone lines of the lover for three days (the FISA free period); in hour 73 (right after the FISA period lapses) Bauer learns through the phone tap that Chief Badnik Guy (CBG) will be at the lover's house at a certain time. Bauer and his associates ambush and capture the CBG. With only hours remaining before the canisters are expected to release the gas, Bauer asks the President for authorization to torture CBG. The President says yes, and Bauer extracts the information needed to save Los Angeles. CBG dies from the torture Bauer administered. Should Bauer or even the President be prosecuted for violating FISA and the new torture statute? Or do they have Bybee-like executive immunity?

How would DOJ deal with the following scenario? Same facts as in prior paragraph, except that Bauer has no leads on CBG, and the canister is set to go off within hours. Through scrambled phone lines, CBG tells Bauer that he will call off the attack and report the location of the canisters if the President will turn over the Vice-President and his family to Badnikstanian authorities (who plan to try the VP for war crimes). The VP stoically agrees to be turned over, but his wife and daughter refuse. Acting under direct orders from the President, Jack Bauer seizes them all and delivers them to the Badnikstanians, who reportedly torture the wife and daughter until the Vice President admits to all sorts of war crimes, for which he is executed.

———

Rasul v. Bush, 542 U.S. 466 (2004).　Several non-citizen detainees at Guantanamo Bay, Cuba brought habeas corpus actions seeking release from what they charged was illegal detention.　The government persuaded the lower court to dismiss these habeas petitions based upon *Johnson v. Eisentrager,* 339 U.S. 763 (1950).　In that case, the Supreme Court ruled that prisoners detained by the Americans in Landsberg Prison in post-WWII occupied Germany were beyond the habeas jurisdiction of the federal judiciary.　The Court said that the prisoners "at no relevant time were within any territory over which the United States is sovereign, and the scenes of their offense, their capture, their trial and their punishment were all beyond the territorial jurisdiction of any court of the United States."　But the Court also emphasized the difficulties of ordering the government to produce the prisoners in a habeas corpus proceeding in the United States, for that "would require allocation of shipping space, guarding personnel, billeting and rations" and would damage the prestige of military commanders at a sensitive time.

Justice Stevens' opinion for the *Rasul* Court rejected the government's argument and ruled that statutory habeas jurisdiction extends to territories (such as Guantanamo Bay) where the United States holds plenary and exclusive territorial jurisdiction, even if not ultimate sovereignty.　Cuba has never exercised practical control over Guantanamo Bay; from Cuban independence to the present, the United States has exercised practical control, but not sovereign control, pursuant to a long-term lease from Cuba.　Justice Stevens distinguished *Eisentrager* on three grounds: (1) its complainants had been adjudicated enemy combatants, while Rasul and his colleagues insisted that they were not; (2) Landsberg Prison was far away from this country, and it would have been highly inconvenient to bring them here for a habeas proceeding, while Guantanamo Bay is close at hand; and (3) Guantanamo Bay is territory over which the United States has exclusive and plenary control.　Justice Stevens's opinion also announced that *Eisentrager*'s interpretation of the habeas statute had been implicitly overruled by a subsequent Supreme Court decision.

Concurring only in the judgment, **Justice Kennedy** maintained that *Eisentrager* had not been overruled.　Moreover, *Eisentrager* stands for the correct proposition that there is a "realm of political authority over military affairs where the judiciary may not enter," and which must be left to the political branches.　But the Guantanamo Bay detentions, although implicitly authorized by Congress, see *Hamdi,* were not within that realm, and Justice Kennedy concluded that these detentions fell outside the *Eisentrager* realm, in part because the United States exercises plenary control over Guantanamo Bay and in part because there had not been an authoritative determination of Rasul's status as an enemy combatant.

Writing for three dissenters, **Justice Scalia** assailed the majority opinion as a "wrenching departure from precedent."　He relied on *Eisentrager* and claimed that it could not legitimately be distinguished from the Guantanamo Bay cases.　Additionally, Justice Scalia relied on the presumption that the Constitution does not apply extraterritorially, except under some circumstances to United States citizens (like Hamdi, but not Rasul).

NOTE ON THE NEW STATUTORY PROCESSES FOR GUANTANAMO DETAINEES AFTER *HAMDI* AND *RASUL*

1. *Post-*Hamdi *Process for Detainees Seeking Release.* To satisfy the Court's judgment in *Hamdi*, the Bush Administration established Combat Status Review Tribunals (CSRTs) to determine whether Hamdi and all other Guantanamo detainees should continue to be detained as suspected enemy combatants. Memorandum of the Secretary of the Navy, Implementation of Combatant Status Review Tribunal Procedures for Enemy Combatants Detained at Guantanamo Bay Naval Base (July 29, 2004). The tribunals followed the procedures of Army Regulation 190-8, *Enemy Prisoners of War, Retained Personnel, Civilian Internees and Other Detainees* (Dep't of Army, Nov. 11, 1997), which in turn follows the procedures outlined in the Geneva Convention. The process provided detainees with notice of the unclassified basis for his being considered an enemy combatant and opportunity to testify and present evidence to the CSRT, consisting of three military officers sworn to render an impartial decision and not involved in the detention or interrogation of the detainee. Each detainee was provided a "personal representative" who was charged with helping the detainee present his evidence. The decision of the tribunal is subject to mandatory review by the CSRT Legal Advisor and then the CSRT Director. As of November 2007, thirty-eight detainees were released pursuant to findings of their tribunals; another fifty-five (including Hamdi) were released after Department of Defense administrative review. Together, this was more than 25% of the detainees.

After *Rasul,* dozens Guantanamo Bay detainees filed habeas petitions. Section 1005(e) of the Detainee Treatment Act of 2005 (DTA) amended the habeas law, 28 U.S.C. § 2241, to provide that "no court, justice, or judge shall have jurisdiction to hear or consider . . . an application for a writ of habeas corpus filed by or on behalf of an alien detained by the Department of Defense at Guantanamo Bay, Cuba." 119 Stat. 2742. Section 1005(e) further provided that the Court of Appeals for the District of Columbia Circuit should have "exclusive" jurisdiction to review decisions of Department of Defense military commissions. The Supreme Court in *Hamdan v. Rumsfeld*, 548 U.S. 557 (2006), ruled that § 1005(e) did not apply to habeas petitions brought before the effective date of the statute.

2. *Military Commissions to Try Accused Enemy Combatants for Violations of the Law of War.* Soon after setting up the detention camp at Guantanamo Bay, the Administration established, by executive order, military commissions to try detainees for war crimes, similar to the tribunal in *Quirin*, and with possible death penalties (such as those meted out in *Quirin*). In *Hamdan*, the Supreme Court ruled that the President's military commissions were unlawful, because its procedures were legally insufficient because they were contrary to congressional enactments, primarily the Uniform Code of Military Justice (UCMJ). All eight participating *Hamdan* Justices followed and applied the Jackson framework from the *Steel Seizure Cases*. The Court (Stevens, Kennedy, Souter, Ginsburg, Breyer) ruled that the Administration's deployment of a military commission in Hamdan's case fell within Jackson's Category 3, namely, that this was "incompatible with the expressed or implied will of Congress." The dissenters (Scalia, Thomas, Alito), in contrast, found the matter to fall within Category 1,

where the President's "authority is at its maximum, for it includes all that he possesses in his own right plus all that Congress can delegate." (Chief Justice Roberts did not participate, because he had joined the lower court opinion the Court was reversing.)

The *Quirin* Court had ruled that Congress in the Articles of War had authorized the President to try the Nazi saboteurs by military commission. Even though UCMJ Article 21 was a reenactment of the Article upon which *Quirin* had relied (Congress was aware of that and approved of *Quirin*), the *Hamdan* Court ruled that the UCMJ, adopted in 1950, did not authorize the Bush Administration military commissions. Justice Stevens offered three reasons: (1) Article 21 authorizes military commissions to try "offenders or offenses" that "by statute or by the law of war may be tried by" such commissions. The government could point to no statute, and conspiracy to commit war crimes is not a recognized violation of the law of war. In contrast, the sabotage in *Quirin* was an accepted violation of the law of war. This reason commanded only a plurality of the eight-Justice Court (Stevens, Souter, Ginsburg, Breyer), but the other two commanded a majority. (2) The military commissions did not comport with UCMJ Article 36(b), which requires uniformity in procedural rules under the UCMJ unless "impracticable." The Court ruled that Article 36(b) creates a baseline whereby the court-martial procedures presumptively apply to military commissions; the Bush Administration's commission's relaxed evidentiary rules and its failure to give the defendant access to all the evidence against him were important departures from the court-martial rules that the Administration could not justify. (3) Until Hamdan is judged to be an enemy combatant, the 1949 Geneva Conventions require that he be subject to punishment only by a "regularly constituted court affording all the judicial guarantees which are recognized as indispensable by civilized peoples."

3. *Military Commissions Act of 2006 and a Tougher Statutory Restriction on Jurisdiction.* Four of the *Hamdan* majority Justices opined that Congress could speak more clearly if it chose, and Congress promptly did so, authorizing military commissions to try war crimes allegedly committed by the Guantanamo Bay detainees and setting forth detailed procedural rules for those commissions. Some of the rules were similar to those followed in courts martial, but with many notable exceptions, including the admissibility of hearsay and (under some tightly defined circumstances) evidence obtained by coercion, the composition of the jury and the appointment of a presiding officer, and so forth. Note that military commissions are different from CSRTs: the latter (responding to *Hamdi*) provide a process by which detained persons can challenge their continued detention and seek release; the former (responding to *Hamdan*) provide a process by which the government can seek penalties against detained persons for violating the law of war.

Section 7(a) of the Military Commissions Act of 2006 (MCA) further amended 28 U.S.C. § 2241(e) to read as follows:

> (1) No court, justice, or judge shall have jurisdiction to hear or consider an application for a writ of habeas corpus filed by or on behalf of an alien detained by the United States who has been determined by the United States to have been properly detained as an enemy combatant or is awaiting such determination.

(2) Except as provided in [DTA §§ 1005(e)(2) and (e)(3)] no court, justice, or judge shall have jurisdiction to hear or consider any other action against the United States or its agents relating to any aspect of the detention, transfer, treatment, trial, or conditions of confinement of an alien who is or was detained by the United States and has been determined by the United States to have been properly detained as an enemy combatant or is awaiting such determination.

Section 7(b) provided that the amended language added by § 7(a) "shall take effect on the date of the enactment of this Act, and shall apply to all cases, without exception, pending on or after the date of the enactment of this Act which relate to any aspect of the detention, transfer, treatment, trial, or conditions of detention of an alien detained by the United States since September 11, 2001."

The purpose of § 7 was to cut off habeas for all Guantanamo Bay detainees. Senator Arlen Specter, the Chair of the Judiciary Committee and a sponsor of the MCA, opposed the inclusion of § 7 and argued that it was an unconstitutional deprivation of habeas rights. Notwithstanding this argument, the Senate narrowly voted to add § 7.

BOUMEDIENE v. BUSH
___ U.S. ____, 128 S.Ct. 2229, ___ L.Ed.2d ____ (2008)

JUSTICE KENNEDY delivered the opinion of the Court.

[In consolidated appeals, Lakhdar Boumediene, Fawzi Khalid al Odah (through next friend Khalid al Odah), and other accused terrorists detained by the United States at Guantanamo argued that federal courts could continue to hear their habeas petitions, either because § 7 did not by its literal terms apply to them or because § 7 was unconstitutional as applied to their habeas appeals. In Part II of his opinion, Justice Kennedy relied on the litigation background and the legislative history of MCA to interpret § 7 as applicable to these appeals. The question then was whether the Suspension Clause guarantees a habeas forum to noncitizens held at Guantanamo Bay and adjudged by CSRTs to be enemy combatants.]

[III.A.] The Framers viewed freedom from unlawful restraint as a fundamental precept of liberty, and they understood the writ of habeas corpus as a vital instrument to secure that freedom. Experience taught, however, that the common-law writ all too often had been insufficient to guard against the abuse of monarchial power. That history counseled the necessity for specific language in the Constitution to secure the writ and ensure its place in our legal system.

[Justice Kennedy provided a brief history of the English writ, which enjoyed a roller-coaster deployment, as often suspended or laxly enforced as actually applied.] That the Framers considered the writ a vital instrument for the protection of individual liberty is evident from the care taken to specify the limited grounds for its suspension: "The Privilege of the Writ of Habeas Corpus shall not be suspended, unless when in Cases of Rebellion or Invasion the public Safety may require it." Art. I, § 9, cl. 2. The word "privilege" was used, perhaps, to avoid mentioning some rights to the exclusion of others. (Indeed, the only mention of the term "right" in the Constitution, as ratified, is in its clause giving Congress the power to protect the rights of authors and inventors. See Art. I, § 8, cl. 8.)

Surviving accounts of the ratification debates provide additional evidence that the Framers deemed the writ to be an essential mechanism in the separation-of-powers scheme. In a critical exchange with Patrick Henry at the Virginia ratifying convention Edmund Randolph referred to the Suspension Clause as an "exception" to the "power given to Congress to regulate courts." See 3 *Debates in the Several State Conventions on the Adoption of the Federal Constitution* 460-464 (J. Elliot 2d ed. 1876) (hereinafter *Elliot's Debates*). A resolution passed by the New York ratifying convention made clear its understanding that the Clause not only protects against arbitrary suspensions of the writ but also guarantees an affirmative right to judicial inquiry into the causes of detention. See Resolution of the New York Ratifying Convention (July 26, 1788), in 1 *Elliott's Debates* 328 (noting the convention's understanding "[t]hat every person restrained of his liberty is entitled to an inquiry into the lawfulness of such restraint, and to a removal thereof if unlawful; and that such inquiry or removal ought not to be denied or delayed, except when, on account of public danger, the Congress shall suspend the privilege of the writ of *habeas corpus*"). Alexander Hamilton likewise explained that by providing the detainee a judicial forum to challenge detention, the writ preserves limited government. As he explained in *The Federalist* No. 84:

> "[T]he practice of arbitrary imprisonments, have been, in all ages, the favorite and most formidable instruments of tyranny. The observations of the judicious Blackstone . . . are well worthy of recital: 'To bereave a man of life . . . or by violence to confiscate his estate, without accusation or trial, would be so gross and notorious an act of despotism as must at once convey the alarm of tyranny throughout the whole nation; but confinement of the person, by secretly hurrying him to jail, where his sufferings are unknown or forgotten, is a less public, a less striking, and therefore a *more dangerous engine* of arbitrary government.' And as a remedy for this fatal evil he is everywhere peculiarly emphatical in his encomiums on the *habeas corpus* act, which in one place he calls 'the *bulwark* of the British Constitution.' " (quoting Blackstone).

In our own system the Suspension Clause is designed to protect against these cyclical abuses. The Clause protects the rights of the detained by a means consistent with the essential design of the Constitution. It ensures that, except during periods of formal suspension, the Judiciary will have a time-tested device, the writ, to maintain the "delicate balance of governance" that is itself the surest safeguard of liberty. *Hamdi* (plurality opinion). The Clause protects the rights of the detained by affirming the duty and authority of the Judiciary to call the jailer to account. The separation-of-powers doctrine, and the history that influenced its design, therefore must inform the reach and purpose of the Suspension Clause.

[III.B. Justice Kennedy also examined founding-era materials to determine whether the writ could be denied because the prisoner was an alien or held outside the national boundaries.] In none of the cases cited do we find that a common-law court would or would not have granted, or refused to hear for lack of jurisdiction, a petition for a writ of habeas corpus brought by a prisoner deemed an enemy combatant, under a standard like the one the Department of Defense has used in these cases, and when held in a territory, like Guantanamo, over which the Government has total military and civil control.

We know that at common law a petitioner's status as an alien was not a categorical bar to habeas corpus relief. See, e.g., *Sommersett's Case*, 20 How. St. Tr. 1, 80-82 (1772) (ordering an African slave freed upon finding the custodian's return insufficient). We know as well that common-law courts entertained habeas petitions brought by enemy aliens detained in England — "entertained" at least in the sense that the courts held hearings to determine the threshold question of entitlement to the writ. [Unfortunately, Justice Kennedy believed there were no cases precisely paralleling the Guantanamo Bay cases. The detainees relied on English habeas decisions involving India and the Channel Islands, but those territories were under the direct control of the Crown, and therefore not similarly situated to Guantanamo Bay. Citing Lord Mansfield's decision in *King v. Cowle,* 2 Burr. 834, 854, 97 Eng. Rep. 587 (K.B.1759), the government relied on English decisions denying the writ to prisoners detained in Scotland and Hanover, territories subject to the Crown's control but not annexed to sovereign England. Justice Kennedy explained those decisions as probably involving "prudential" considerations: because Scotland and Hanover maintained their own separate court systems and codifications of law, the English courts were prudentially reluctant to process habeas petitions involving persons detained there. Confirming that intuition, the writ did run to persons detained in Ireland, which was not formally united to England but was subject to English law.]

* * * We decline, therefore, to infer too much, one way or the other, from the lack of historical evidence on point. Cf. *Brown v. Board of Education* (noting evidence concerning the circumstances surrounding the adoption of the Fourteenth Amendment, discussed in the parties' briefs and uncovered through the Court's own investigation, "convince us that, although these sources cast some light, it is not enough to resolve the problem with which we are faced. At best, they are inconclusive").

[IV.A. Justice Kennedy looked to the Court's precedents to see if the writ could only be issued to noncitizens held in territory subject to the de jure, and not just de facto, sovereignty of the United States. Between 1901 and 1904, the Court adjudicated a series of *Insular Cases* involving the application of American law to former Spanish colonies (Puerto Rico, Cuba, Philippines). He summarized the holdings of those cases: "the Constitution has independent force in these territories, a force not contingent upon acts of legislative grace," but dependent upon practical considerations varying from case to case. See generally Christina Burnett, Untied *States: American Expansion and Territorial Deannexation*, 72 U. Chi. L. Rev. 797 (2005). As the Court later made clear, "the real issue in the Insular Cases was not whether the Constitution extended to the Philippines or Porto Rico when we went there, but which of its provisions were applicable by way of limitation upon the exercise of executive and legislative power in dealing with new conditions and requirements." *Balzac v. Porto Rico*, 258 U.S. 298, 312 (1922). "[T]he Court took for granted that even in unincorporated Territories the Government of the United States was bound to provide to noncitizen inhabitants 'guaranties of certain fundamental personal rights declared in the Constitution.' "]

Practical considerations weighed heavily as well in *Johnson v. Eisentrager*, 339 U.S. 763 (1950), where the Court addressed whether habeas corpus jurisdiction extended to enemy aliens who had been convicted of violating the laws of war. The prisoners were detained at Landsberg Prison in Germany during the Allied Powers' postwar occupation. The Court stressed the difficulties of ordering the Government to produce the prisoners in a habeas corpus proceeding. It "would require allocation of shipping space, guarding personnel, billeting and rations" and would damage the prestige of military commanders at a sensitive time. In considering these factors the Court sought to balance the constraints of military occupation with constitutional necessities. See *Rasul* (discussing the factors relevant to *Eisentrager*'s constitutional holding).

True, the Court in *Eisentrager* denied access to the writ, and it noted the prisoners "at no relevant time were within any territory over which the United States is sovereign, and [that] the scenes of their offense, their capture, their trial and their punishment were all beyond the territorial jurisdiction of any court of the United States." The Government seizes upon this language as proof positive that the *Eisentrager* Court adopted a formalistic, sovereignty-based test for determining the reach of the Suspension Clause. We reject this reading for three reasons. [Namely, (1) other reasoning in *Eisentrager*, which emphasized practical concerns; (2) the fact that in *Eisentrager*, unlike this case, the United States lacked both de jure sovereignty *and* de facto authority over Landsberg Prison; and (3) respect for the holding of the Insular Cases and their functional approach.]

[IV.B.] The Government's formal sovereignty-based test raises troubling separation-of-powers concerns as well. [Guantanamo Bay illustrates this difficulty, where the President exercises complete de facto control, but without de jure sovereignty.] The necessary implication of the argument is that by surrendering formal sovereignty over any unincorporated territory to a third party, while at the same time entering into a lease that grants total control over the territory back to the United States, it would be possible for the political branches to govern without legal constraint.

Our basic charter cannot be contracted away like this. The Constitution grants Congress and the President the power to acquire, dispose of, and govern territory, not the power to decide when and where its terms apply. Even when the United States acts outside its borders, its powers are not "absolute and unlimited" but are subject "to such restrictions as are expressed in the Constitution." *Murphy v. Ramsey*, 114 U. S. 15, 44 (1885). Abstaining from questions involving formal sovereignty and territorial governance is one thing. To hold the political branches have the power to switch the Constitution on or off at will is quite another. The former position reflects this Court's recognition that certain matters requiring political judgments are best left to the political branches. The latter would permit a striking anomaly in our tripartite system of government, leading to a regime in which Congress and the President, not this Court, say "what the law is." *Marbury v. Madison*.

These concerns have particular bearing upon the Suspension Clause question in the cases now before us, for the writ of habeas corpus is itself an indispensable mechanism for monitoring the separation of powers. The test for determining the scope of this provision must not be subject to manipulation by those whose power it is designed to restrain.

[IV.C.] As we recognized in *Rasul*, the outlines of a framework for determining the reach of the Suspension Clause are suggested by the factors the Court relied upon in *Eisentrager*. In addition to the practical concerns discussed above, the *Eisentrager* Court found relevant that each petitioner:

> "(a) is an enemy alien; (b) has never been or resided in the United States; (c) was captured outside of our territory and there held in military custody as a prisoner of war; (d) was tried and convicted by a Military Commission sitting outside the United States; (e) for offenses against laws of war committed outside the United States; (f) and is at all times imprisoned outside the United States."

Based on this language from *Eisentrager*, and the reasoning in our other extraterritoriality opinions, we conclude that at least three factors are relevant in determining the reach of the Suspension Clause: (1) the citizenship and status of the detainee and the adequacy of the process through which that status determination was made; (2) the nature of the sites where apprehension and then detention took place; and (3) the practical obstacles inherent in resolving the prisoner's entitlement to the writ.

[Given these factors, the Guantanamo Bay detainees were not similarly situated to the Landsberg detainees of *Eisentrager*. First, although both were noncitizens, the Guantanamo Bay detainees had not been afforded the trial-type process of military commissions given the detainees in Landsberg.] In comparison the procedural protections afforded to the detainees in the CSRT hearings are far more limited, and, we conclude, fall well short of the procedures and adversarial mechanisms that would eliminate the need for habeas corpus review. Although the detainee is assigned a "Personal Representative" to assist him during CSRT proceedings, the Secretary of the Navy's memorandum makes clear that person is not the detainee's lawyer or even his "advocate." The Government's evidence is accorded a presumption of validity. The detainee is allowed to present "reasonably available" evidence, but his ability to rebut the Government's evidence against him is limited by the circumstances of his confinement and his lack of counsel at this stage. And although the detainee can seek review of his status determination in the Court of Appeals, that review process cannot cure all defects in the earlier proceedings.

[Second, although both were held outside the de jure sovereign territory of the United States, Guantanamo Bay is subject to American plenary and exclusive control as a practical matter.] The Court's holding in *Eisentrager* was thus consistent with the Insular Cases, where it had held there was no need to extend full constitutional protections to territories the United States did not intend to govern indefinitely. Guantanamo Bay, on the other hand, is no transient possession. In every practical sense Guantanamo is not abroad; it is within the constant jurisdiction of the United States. See *Rasul*.

[Third, the costs of habeas consideration for the Guantanamo Bay detainees would not be nearly so impressive as they would have been for the Landsberg ones, nor would there be friction with the host government or American allies.]

[V. Justice Kennedy considered the argument that the D.C. Circuit appeals process provided by § 1005(e) of the DTA was an adequate substitute for habeas and ruled that it was not. He started with the observation, drawn from the DTA's legislative history and a comparison of the DTA with previous habeas statutes, that Congress in the DTA and the MCA was seeking to curtail the procedural rights of the Guantanamo detainees.]

We do not endeavor to offer a comprehensive summary of the requisites for an adequate substitute for habeas corpus. We do consider it uncontroversial, however, that the privilege of habeas corpus entitles the prisoner to a meaningful opportunity to demonstrate that he is being held pursuant to "the erroneous application or interpretation" of relevant law. And the habeas court must have the power to order the conditional release of an individual unlawfully detained — though release need not be the exclusive remedy and is not the appropriate one in every case in which the writ is granted. See *Ex parte Bollman*, 4 Cranch 75, 136 (1807) (where imprisonment is unlawful, the court "can only direct [the prisoner] to be discharged"). These are the easily identified attributes of any constitutionally adequate habeas corpus proceeding. But, depending on the circumstances, more may be required. * * *

There is evidence from 19th-century American sources indicating that, even in States that accorded strong res judicata effect to prior adjudications, habeas courts in this country routinely allowed prisoners to introduce exculpatory evidence that was either unknown or previously unavailable to the prisoner. Justice McLean, on Circuit in 1855, expressed his view that a habeas court should consider a prior judgment conclusive "where there was clearly jurisdiction and a full and fair hearing; but that it might not be so considered when any of these requisites were wanting." *Ex parte Robinson*, 20 F. Cas. 969, 971, (No. 11,935) (CC Ohio 1855). To illustrate the circumstances in which the prior adjudication did not bind the habeas court, he gave the example of a case in which "[s]everal unimpeached witnesses" provided new evidence to exculpate the prisoner. *Ibid.* * * *

Accordingly, where relief is sought from a sentence that resulted from the judgment of a court of record, [the typical habeas case], considerable deference is owed to the court that ordered confinement. Likewise in those cases the prisoner should exhaust adequate alternative remedies before filing for the writ in federal court. Both aspects of federal habeas corpus review are justified because it can be assumed that, in the usual course, a court of record provides defendants with a fair, adversary proceeding. In cases involving state convictions this framework also respects federalism; and in federal cases it has added justification because the prisoner already has had a chance to seek review of his conviction in a federal forum through a direct appeal. The present cases fall outside these categories, however; for here the detention is by executive order.

Where a person is detained by executive order, rather than, say, after being tried and convicted in a court, the need for collateral review is most pressing. A criminal conviction in the usual course occurs after a judicial hearing before a tribunal disinterested in the outcome and committed to procedures designed to ensure its own independence. These dynamics are not inherent in executive detention orders or executive review procedures. In this context the need for habeas corpus is more urgent. The intended duration of the detention and the reasons for it bear upon the precise scope of the inquiry. Habeas corpus proceedings need not resemble a criminal trial, even when the detention is by executive order. But the writ must be effective. The habeas court must have sufficient authority to conduct a meaningful review of both the cause for detention and the Executive's power to detain.

[Justice Kennedy examined the process afforded by the CSRTs and found it insufficient.] Petitioners identify what they see as myriad deficiencies in the CSRTs. The most relevant for our purposes are the constraints upon the detainee's ability to rebut the factual basis for the Government's assertion that he is an enemy combatant. [A]t the CSRT stage the detainee has limited means to find or present evidence to challenge the Government's case against him. He does not have the assistance of counsel and may not be aware of the most critical allegations that the Government relied upon to order his detention. The detainee can confront witnesses that testify during the CSRT proceedings. But given that there are in effect no limits on the admission of hearsay evidence — the only requirement is that the tribunal deem the evidence "relevant and helpful" — the detainee's opportunity to question witnesses is likely to be more theoretical than real. * * *

[The government maintained that the CSRT process satisfied the *Hamdi* standards of due process, but Justice Kennedy responded that there was no opinion for the Court on the due process issue; in any event, habeas is *normally* available for state and federal trial proceedings that more than meet due process requirements.] Although we make no judgment as to whether the CSRTs, as currently constituted, satisfy due process standards, we agree with petitioners that, even when all the parties involved in this process act with diligence and in good faith, there is considerable risk of error in the tribunal's findings of fact. This is a risk inherent in any process that, in the words of the former Chief Judge of the Court of Appeals, is "closed and accusatorial." See [*Bismullah v. Gates*, 514 F.3d at 1296 (Ginsburg, C. J., concurring in denial of rehearing en banc)]. And given that the consequence of error may be detention of persons for the duration of hostilities that may last a generation or more, this is a risk too significant to ignore.

For the writ of habeas corpus, or its substitute, to function as an effective and proper remedy in this context, the court that conducts the habeas proceeding must have the means to correct errors that occurred during the CSRT proceedings. This includes some authority to assess the sufficiency of the Government's evidence against the detainee. It also must have the authority to admit and consider relevant exculpatory evidence that was not introduced during the earlier proceeding. Federal habeas petitioners long have had the means to supplement the record on review, even in the postconviction habeas setting. Here that opportunity is constitutionally required.

The DTA does not explicitly empower the Court of Appeals to order the applicant in a DTA review proceeding released should the court find that the standards and procedures used at his CSRT hearing were insufficient to justify detention. This is troubling. Yet, for present purposes, we can assume congressional silence permits a constitutionally required remedy. In that case it would be possible to hold that a remedy of release is impliedly provided for. The DTA might be read, furthermore, to allow the petitioners to assert most, if not all, of the legal claims they seek to advance, including their most basic claim: that the President has no authority under the AUMF to detain them indefinitely.

(Whether the President has such authority turns on whether the AUMF authorizes — and the Constitution permits — the indefinite detention of "enemy combatants" as the Department of Defense defines that term. Thus a challenge to the President's authority to detain is, in essence, a challenge to the Department's definition of enemy combatant, a "standard" used by the CSRTs in petitioners' cases.) At oral argument, the Solicitor General urged us to adopt both these constructions, if doing so would allow MCA § 7 to remain intact.

The absence of a release remedy and specific language allowing AUMF challenges are not the only constitutional infirmities from which the statute potentially suffers, however. The more difficult question is whether the DTA permits the Court of Appeals to make requisite findings of fact. The DTA enables petitioners to request "review" of their CSRT determination in the Court of Appeals, DTA § 1005(e)(2)(B)(i), 119 Stat. 2742; but the "Scope of Review" provision confines the Court of Appeals' role to reviewing whether the CSRT followed the "standards and procedures" issued by the Department of Defense and assessing whether those "standards and procedures" are lawful. § 1005(e)(C). Among these standards is "the requirement that the conclusion of the Tribunal be supported by a preponderance of the evidence . . . allowing a rebuttable presumption in favor of the Government's evidence." § 1005(e)(C)(I).

Assuming the DTA can be construed to allow the Court of Appeals to review or correct the CSRT's factual determinations, as opposed to merely certifying that the tribunal applied the correct standard of proof, we see no way to construe the statute to allow what is also constitutionally required in this context: an opportunity for the detainee to present relevant exculpatory evidence that was not made part of the record in the earlier proceedings.

On its face the statute allows the Court of Appeals to consider no evidence outside the CSRT record. In the parallel litigation, however, the Court of Appeals determined that the DTA allows it to order the production of all " 'reasonably available information in the possession of the U. S. Government bearing on the issue of whether the detainee meets the criteria to be designated as an enemy combatant,' " regardless of whether this evidence was put before the CSRT. See *Bismullah I*, 501 F.3d, at 180. The Government, with support from five members of the Court of Appeals, disagrees with this interpretation. For present purposes, however, we can assume that the Court of Appeals was correct that the DTA allows introduction and consideration of relevant exculpatory evidence that was "reasonably available" to the Government at the time of the CSRT but not made part of the record. Even so, the DTA review proceeding falls short of being a constitutionally adequate substitute, for the detainee still would have no opportunity to present evidence discovered after the CSRT proceedings concluded.

* * * One of the petitioners, Mohamed Nechla, requested at his CSRT hearing that the Government contact his employer. The petitioner claimed the employer would corroborate Nechla's contention he had no affiliation with al Qaeda. Although the CSRT determined this testimony would be relevant, it also found the witness was not reasonably available to testify at the time of the hearing. Petitioner's counsel, however, now represents the witness is available to be heard. If a detainee can present reasonably available evidence demonstrating

there is no basis for his continued detention, he must have the opportunity to present this evidence to a habeas corpus court. Even under the Court of Appeals' generous construction of the DTA, however, the evidence identified by Nechla would be inadmissible in a DTA review proceeding. The role of an Article III court in the exercise of its habeas corpus function cannot be circumscribed in this manner. * * *

[We omit **CHIEF JUSTICE ROBERTS'** dissenting opinion, joined by **JUSTICES SCALIA, THOMAS,** and **ALITO,** as well as the dissenting opinion of **JUSTICE SCALIA,** with whom **CHIEF JUSTICE ROBERTS, JUSTICE THOMAS,** and **JUSTICE ALITO** join. Their points are summarized in Notes in Chapter 9. We also omit the concurring opinion of **JUSTICE SOUTER,** who responded to some of the dissenters' concerns.]

NOTES ON *BOUMEDIENE* AND THE APPLICATION OF HABEAS TO NONCITIZEN DETAINEES

1. *Does Habeas Protect Noncitizens Held Outside American Sovereign Jurisdiction?* Justice Scalia presented three big arguments why habeas does not so extend.

(a) *Original Meaning.* When the Constitution of 1789 included the Suspension Clause, Justice Scalia assumed the framers would have assumed that the habeas remedy would have extended *no further* than it had already extended in 1789. Like the Court, Justice Scalia found no case where habeas had been extended to protect a noncitizen held by the Crown outside territories under the Crown's sovereign jurisdiction. The Court started from a different baseline, whereby habeas is available in all cases (and perhaps more) where it might have been available in 1789. Which is the more defensible baseline?

Even if you accept the Court's baseline, Justice Scalia made another historical argument. The common-law writ was codified by the Habeas Corpus Act of 1679, which was then adopted in several of the colonies. Section XI of the Act stated where the writ could run. It "may be directed and run into any county palatine, the cinque-ports, or other privileged places within the kingdom of England, dominion of Wales, or town of Berwick upon Tweed, and the islands of Jersey or Guernsey." 31 Car. 2, ch. 2. Justice Scalia then observed: "The cinque-ports and county palatine were so-called 'exempt jurisdictions' — franchises granted by the Crown in which local authorities would manage municipal affairs, including the court system, but over which the Crown maintained ultimate sovereignty. The other places listed — Wales, Berwick-upon-Tweed, Jersey, and Guernsey — were territories of the Crown even though not part England proper." Morever, "[t]he possibility of evading judicial review through such spiriting-away," the *Boumediene* majority's worry, "was eliminated, not by expanding the writ abroad, but by forbidding (in Article XII of the Act) the shipment of prisoners to places where the writ did not run or where its execution would be difficult. See 31 Car. 2, ch. 2." Is this not better evidence, for this codification of English habeas practice, known to the American colonists, affirmatively indicates that there were jurisdictional limits to the operation of the writ *and* suggests the means for controlling the Crown's temptation to evade the writ by shipping prisoners elsewhere (like Scotland~Guantanamo). If so, did

Justice Kennedy have a good reason for not following it, as a matter of original meaning?

(b) *Precedent.* Justice Scalia maintained that *Eisentrager* had settled the issue, because Justice Jackson's opinion for the Court had rested upon his conclusion that there was no historical precedent for extending the writ to a noncitizen held outside the United States. Justice Kennedy responded that Justice Jackson also gave functional reasons for not extending habeas to the Landsberg prisoners, to which Justice Scalia replied that, under a functional approach, the Guantanamo detainees ought to have been entitled to *less* process than the Landsberg ones, not more:

> The prisoners in *Eisentrager* were *prosecuted* for crimes after the cessation of hostilities; the prisoners here are enemy combatants *detained* during an ongoing conflict. The category of prisoner comparable to these detainees are not the *Eisentrager* criminal defendants, but the more than 400,000 prisoners of war detained in the United States alone during World War II. Not a single one was accorded the right to have his detention validated by a habeas corpus action in federal court — and that despite the fact that they were present on U.S. soil. The Court's analysis produces a crazy result: Whereas those convicted and sentenced to death for war crimes are without judicial remedy, all enemy combatants detained during a war, at least insofar as they are confined in an area away from the battlefield over which the United States exercises "absolute and indefinite" control, may seek a writ of habeas corpus in federal court. And, as an even more bizarre implication from the Court's reasoning, those prisoners whom the military plans to try by full-dress Commission at a future date may file habeas petitions and secure release before their trials take place.

Did Justice Kennedy have a persuasive response to this point? (Justice Souter's concurring opinion emphasized that the Court's interpretation of *Eisentrager* in *Rasul* was also entitled to stare decisis effect, and of course that interpretation supported Justice Kennedy.)

(c) *Constitutional Text.* Under Article I, § 9, cl. 1, habeas can be suspended only "in Cases of Rebellion or Invasion." Justice Scalia argued: "The latter case (invasion) is plainly limited to the territory of the United States; and while it is conceivable that a rebellion could be mounted by American citizens abroad, surely the overwhelming majority of its occurrences would be domestic. If the extraterritorial scope of habeas turned on flexible, 'functional' considerations, as the Court holds, why would the Constitution limit its suspension almost entirely to instances of domestic crisis? Surely there is an even greater justification for suspension in foreign lands where the United States might hold prisoners of war during an ongoing conflict. And correspondingly, there is less threat to liberty when the Government suspends the writ's (supposed) application in foreign lands, where even on the most extreme view prisoners are entitled to fewer constitutional rights. It makes no sense, therefore, for the Constitution generally to forbid suspension of the writ abroad if indeed the writ has application there." Is this a cogent argument? How could the Court have responded?

2. *Has Congress Provided an Adequate Substitute for Habeas?* Chief Justice Roberts's dissenting opinion argued that the process was more than adequate. He strenuously objected to the Court's characterization of the CSRT process as merely an executive determination and insisted that the CSRT was intended by the President and Congress to be treated as the first step in the process of

collateral review, namely, the kind of review that habeas corpus provides. Properly understood, the way the political process presented the matter, Congress was replacing the collateral review of a habeas trial court + federal appeals court review with the collateral review of a CSRT + federal appeals court review. What is wrong with that, given the traditional flexibility of habeas *and* the *Hamdi* Court's explication of due process for detainees? Chief Justice Roberts stated: "Today's Court opines that the Suspension Clause guarantees prisoners such as the detainees 'a meaningful opportunity to demonstrate that [they are] being held pursuant to the erroneous application or interpretation of relevant law.' Further, the Court holds that to be an adequate substitute, any tribunal reviewing the detainees' cases 'must have the power to order the conditional release of an individual unlawfully detained.' The DTA system — CSRT review of the Executive's determination followed by D.C. Circuit review for sufficiency of the evidence and the constitutionality of the CSRT process — meets these criteria," opined the Chief Justice. Under the DTA and the Department's post-*Hamdi* regulations, a detainee has the following rights (in the Chief Justice's language):

- "to present evidence that he has been wrongfully detained," including witnesses who are reasonably available, documentary evidence, the detainee's own testimony;

- access to a "personal representative" who may review "classified information" and explain its gist to the detainee, help the detainee arrange for witnesses, assist the detainee's preparation of his case, and even aid the detainee in presenting his evidence to the tribunal;

- appellate D.C. Circuit review of the sufficiency of the evidence justifying continued detention, as well as the constitutionality of the process the tribunal followed; the circuit court has the authority to direct the release of a detainee whose CSRT proceeding was unlawful.

"The DTA provides more opportunity and more process, in fact, than that afforded prisoners of war or any other alleged enemy combatants in history."

The Court's primary objection to this process was that the detainee cannot present newly discovered exculpatory evidence to the D.C. Circuit, evidence that well might be missed by the incarcerated detainee and his vaguely defined "personal representative." But the Chief Justice responded that (a) the D.C. Circuit has the authority to remand the case to the CSRT for further proceedings in light of newly discovered evidence; (b) the Department of Defense authority in charge of Guantanamo conducts her or his own reviews of detainee status (most of the detainees thus far released have been pursuant to such administrative review) and can consider such evidence; and (c) DOD regulations affirmatively entitle the detainee to a new CSRT if there is new evidence that is material to the legality of his detention.

The Chief Justice made a powerful analytical case here. As a matter of *law* — not your own potential disagreement with the Bush Administration's policies — is there a reasonable basis to object to the government's claim that it has provided detainees with an "adequate" substitute for habeas?

3. *Consequentialist Arguments: What Happens Next?* Interestingly, three leading conservative jurists traded consequentialist arguments that reveal, for each jurist, why he voted the way he did in this case.

Justice Kennedy concluded his opinion with some rhetoric we have omitted: "Security depends upon a sophisticated intelligence apparatus and the ability of our Armed Forces to act and to interdict. There are further considerations, however. Security subsists, too, in fidelity to freedom's first principles. Chief among these are freedom from arbitrary and unlawful restraint and the personal liberty that is secured by adherence to the separation of powers. It is from these principles that the judicial authority to consider petitions for habeas corpus relief derives. * * * Within the Constitution's separation-of-powers structure, few exercises of judicial power are as legitimate or as necessary as the responsibility to hear challenges to the authority of the Executive to imprison a person. Some of these petitioners have been in custody for six years with no definitive judicial determination as to the legality of their detention. Their access to the writ is a necessity to determine the lawfulness of their status, even if, in the end, they do not obtain the relief they seek."

Justice Scalia started his opinion with this: "America is at war with radical Islamists. * * * The game of bait-and-switch that today's opinion plays upon the Nation's Commander in Chief will make the war harder on us. It will almost certainly cause more Americans to be killed. * * * At least 30 of those prisoners hitherto released from Guantanamo Bay have returned to the battlefield. Some have been captured or killed. But others have succeeded in carrying on their atrocities against innocent civilians. In one case, a detainee released from Guantanamo Bay masterminded the kidnapping of two Chinese dam workers, one of whom was later shot to death when used as a human shield against Pakistani commandoes. Another former detainee promptly resumed his post as a senior Taliban commander and murdered a United Nations engineer and three Afghan soldiers. Still another murdered an Afghan judge. It was reported only last month that a released detainee carried out a suicide bombing against Iraqi soldiers in Mosul, Iraq."

Chief Justice Roberts ended his opinion thus: "So who has won? Not the detainees. The Court's analysis leaves them with only the prospect of further litigation to determine the content of their new habeas right, followed by further litigation to resolve their particular cases, followed by further litigation before the D. C. Circuit — where they could have started had they invoked the DTA procedure. Not Congress, whose attempt to 'determine — through democratic means — how best' to balance the security of the American people with the detainees' liberty interests, see *Hamdan* (Breyer, J., concurring), has been unceremoniously brushed aside. Not the Great Writ, whose majesty is hardly enhanced by its extension to a jurisdictionally quirky outpost, with no tangible benefit to anyone. Not the rule of law, unless by that is meant the rule of lawyers, who will now arguably have a greater role than military and intelligence officials in shaping policy for alien enemy combatants. And certainly not the American people, who today lose a bit more control over the conduct of this Nation's foreign policy to unelected, politically unaccountable judges."

Are *any* of these rhetorical flourishes fully justified? All three of these Justices rested their legal analysis largely upon formal criteria (original meaning, precedent, separation of powers principles). What role does such a functional flourish play in such analysis? We were especially surprised to see Justice Scalia *commence* his strongly formalist opinion with such dramatic consequentialist language. By the way, the deaths that Justice Scalia discusses were the result of Department of Defense decisions to release detainees. Recall that Scalia took the most absolute anti-Administration position in *Hamdi*, for he would have required the government either to charge the suspected terrorists or release them. Has he changed his mind about the proper framework for understanding suspected terrorists? What might this debate tell you about the relationship between *formalism* and *functionalism* in constitutional doctrine or judicial reasoning?

By the way, we believe that there is a more pragmatic, and less dramatic, way of thinking about the consequences of the *Boumediene* and *Hamdi* line of cases. This is the *proceduralization of enemy detention*. The old model of prisoners of war held without process (*Eisentrager*) is giving way to a new model of suspected terrorists who are entitled to some process (*Hamdi* and *Boumediene*). The big change is not that the latter are held at Guantanamo (*Boumediene*) or within the United States (*Rasul*), or that they are sometimes citizens (*Hamdi*). The big change is rampant ambiguity as to who is the "enemy." Now that the War on Terror has formally delinked "enemy" from "nation state," it is often hard to tell who is (potential) "ally" and who is (secret) "enemy." The Bush 43 Administration thinks that the President needs much leeway to hold suspected enemies with no judicial monitoring, see the Bybee Memorandum (2002), excerpted above in this Supplement, while the critics believe that judicial monitoring is needed to assure that the rule of law is followed. See Philip Bobbitt, *Terror and Consent: The Wars for the Twenty-First Century* (2008); Jenny S. Martinez, *Process and Substance in the "War on Terror,"* 108 Colum. L. Rev. 1013 (2008). Is this helpful? Or does it repackage the balance of uncertainty? Both?

Chapter 9

LIMITS ON THE JUDICIAL POWER

In the preceding two chapters, we explored the Supreme Court's role in policing the boundaries between Congress and the President within the federal government, and those between the federal and state governments. But the Court has also evolved an elaborate set of doctrines to police the boundaries between the federal judiciary itself and other organs of government. Besides being an important part of the constitutional structure, these doctrines are essential working tools of any lawyer who litigates in federal court. These doctrines are sufficiently complex and recondite that most law schools offer a separate course on federal jurisdiction. In this chapter, we will merely present the outlines of some of the major doctrines and consider how they relate to more general issues of constitutional interpretation.

Article III of the Constitution establishes and (rather vaguely) defines the authority of the federal judiciary. We will discuss in turn, three different kinds of limitations on federal courts' power to hear certain controversies, which have been teased out of Article III. First, the Supreme Court has held that the "judicial Power" granted in Article III does not permit courts to adjudicate lawsuits raising essentially "political questions" that are best left to resolution by the legislative (Article I) and executive (Article II) branches. Second, Article III, § 2's limitation of federal jurisdiction to "Cases" or "Controversies" has been read to establish other limits on the justiciability of certain types of lawsuits — primarily those where the plaintiff does not have a sufficient stake in the outcome. Third, the remedial power granted federal courts in Article III might authorize the provision of only those kinds of relief that parties have traditionally received in the Anglo-American system.

The civil rights cases of the second half of the twentieth century transformed the Court's justiciability doctrines. Matters that judges had traditionally left to state and local administrators — voting practices, public education, management of state institutions (e.g., prisons) — came under ever-closer scrutiny of federal judges. Specifically, federal courts came to adjudicate an increasing array of arguably "political" matters. They heard litigants whose cases were arguably premature or who sought remedies that would benefit other (future) beneficiaries. Most dramatically, they sometimes issued "structural injunctions" that went beyond relief ordinarily granted by courts of equity by forcing states and localities to restructure their governmental institutions and by retaining authority to oversee whether the restructuring was carried out and actually achieved its remedial purposes. See generally Owen Fiss, *The Civil Rights Injunction* (1978). The Warren and early Burger Courts encouraged such activism in support of the national campaign against southern apartheid. The apotheosis of the new model was *Swann* (Chapter 2, § 2C1), where the Court affirmed an ambitious injunction that restructured a city-county school system. Although the civil rights cases generally (and the *Brown II* cases in particular) inspired the era of relaxed limits on judicial authority, the relaxation extended beyond the race cases to litigation involving the antiwar movement, environmental challenges to state and private pollution, challenges to the rules and administration of public welfare programs, and vote dilution claims of all sorts.

Once the Supreme Court was reconstituted by President Nixon, however, the Justices reasserted some — but by no means all — traditional limits on the "judicial Power" granted them by Article III. Justices appointed by Presidents Reagan and Bush père in the 1980s have been more insistent on some justiciability limits. Unlike earlier Justices, those of the Reagan-Bush Court have relied on precepts of federalism and separation of powers to justify a more cautious approach to the "judicial Power" even in civil rights cases such as *Dowell* and *Freeman v. Pitts* (Chapter 2, § 2C). Justices O'Connor and Scalia were at the forefront of this reconceptualization. Other Justices, however, continue to be attracted to the more traditional strategy, often making the functionalist argument that the new approach slights the Court's proper role under *Marbury* in enforcing the Constitution.

SECTION 1. THE POLITICAL QUESTION DOCTRINE

The "political question doctrine" posits that some constitutional issues are not justiciable, because the issue is committed to the political branches of government (Congress and the President). Recall the suggestion in *Marbury* that, where the President or another executive branch official had "legal discretion," the judiciary would not grant relief. The modern way of putting this is to say that the issue is political and not legal, or that there are "no judicially cognizable standards" by which a court could resolve the dispute.

The constitutional basis for the political question doctrine is usually said to be separation of powers. One might say that its specific textual referent would be Article III's reservation of the "judicial Power" to the Supreme Court and inferior federal courts, because the "judicial Power" would not include the power to adjudicate political disputes. This rationale might strike you as curious, as it strikes us, because Chapter 8 is filled with cases — such as *Chadha*, which struck down the legislative veto; the Nixon Tapes Case, which rejected the President's claim of executive privilege to withhold evidence needed in a criminal trial; and *Morrison v. Olson*, which upheld the use of special prosecutors to investigate executive branch wrongdoing — that involved highly politicized conflicts between the executive and legislative branches.

The political question doctrine's link to separation of powers becomes even more curious in light of its history. The leading modern political question case, *Baker v. Carr*, excerpted below, presents a sharp debate between the majority and dissenting opinions over the source and ambit of the political question doctrine. Much of the debate in *Baker v. Carr* concerns the meaning of prior cases, especially decisions holding nonjusticiable questions arising under Article IV, § 4 (referred to as the "Guarantee Clause," the "Guaranty Clause," or the "Republican Form of Government Clause").

Luther v. Borden, 7 How. (48 U.S.) 1 (1849). Rhode Island was in a condition amounting to civil war: Some citizens who were disenfranchised under the original colonial charter went into rebellion, seeking a new and more democratic state constitution. The government organized under the colonial charter imposed martial law and gave its soldiers various police powers. The issue in the case was whether the soldiers had committed a trespass when breaking into a private home. The resolution of it turned in part on whether the original charter government was still in power, or whether the insurgents had successfully achieved the adoption of the new constitution and ousted the old government, thereby revoking any authority it had to impose martial law. The Court held that a federal court could not determine which of two competing state governments was authorized. The Court thought that a court was not well equipped to consider this problem, and it also took solace in the wording of the Guarantee Clause: It confirms that Congress has the authority to decide this question, and any congressional resolution of it should be not subject to second-guessing by any other branch. This holding turned out to be very important after the Civil War, when it gave the Reconstruction Congress the final authority to decide which southern states had reestablished lawful governments. Note that *Luther* does not necessarily hold that all Guarantee Clause claims are nonjusticiable; narrowly understood, the case merely stands for the proposition that some questions under the clause are beyond judicial resolution.[a]

Giles v. Harris, 189 U.S. 475 (1903). The case involved a claim that Montgomery County, Alabama unlawfully refused to register more than 5,000 qualified African-American voters. Although "traditional limits of proceedings in equity have not embraced a remedy for political wrongs," **Justice Holmes'** opinion for the Court assumed that the circuit court had jurisdiction, but ruled that the court properly declined to issue an injunction to remedy the wrongs. The main reasons were that popular opinion would defeat the injunction, rendering it pointless, and that only the national political process could truly

---

a. The Court did not read *Luther* narrowly in later cases, however. In *Pacific States Tel. & Tel. Co. v. Oregon*, 223 U.S. 118 (1912), Oregon's adoption of direct democracy, by which the voters could directly make law, allegedly violated the Guarantee Clause's requirement that states possess a "republican form of government." (Essentially, the argument would be that a "republican" government requires a representative legislative process, not direct democracy.) The Court held the issue nonjusticiable, concluding that the federal courts had no judicially manageable standards to determine when a state government loses the label of "republican."

In the heyday of the Progressive Era, in which direct democracy was a popular governmental reform, it is not surprising that the Court in this case was reluctant to adjudicate its compatibility with the Guarantee Clause. Whatever might be the practical utility of its outcome, however, *Pacific States Tel. & Tel.* broadly suggested that no claim that a state government failed to be "republican" could be adjudicated in federal court.

assure that voting rights could be enforced under these circumstances, making the injunction unnecessary. Justice Holmes suggested that the lower court had essentially no "practical power to deal with the people of the state in a body. The [complaint] imports that the great mass of the white population intends to keep the blacks from voting. To meet such an intent something more than ordering the plaintiff's name to be inscribed upon the lists of 1902 will be needed. * * * Unless we are prepared to supervise the voting in that state by officers of the court, it seems to us that all that the plaintiff could get from equity would be an empty form. Apart from damages to the individual, relief from a great political wrong, if done, as alleged, by the people of a state and the state itself, must be given by them or by the legislative and political department of the government of the United States."

———

To the extent that both *Luther* and *Giles* are considered political question cases, they suggest that the doctrine is an amalgam of several different concerns about the exercise of the "judicial Power": (1) *constitutional,* arising out of the Constitution's allocation of authority to other branches of government; (2) *pragmatic,* relating to the competence of the judiciary to develop and apply rules and principles of law to the matter; and (3) *administrability,* relating to the courts' supposed incapacity to administer a remedy.[b] All three policies came into play in the next big case.

———

Colegrove v. Green, 328 U.S. 549 (1946). Illinois had not redrawn its congressional districts for four decades despite major population shifts. Illinois voters living in districts with considerably more population than some other districts brought suit, objecting to the dilution of their vote on "one person, one vote" grounds. The state argued that *Giles* precluded equitable relief in this "political" matter. Writing for a plurality and invoking *Giles,* **Justice Frankfurter** reasoned from the constitutional structure and the greater institutional competence of the political branches that "courts ought not to enter this political thicket." Although not cited, *Giles* was even more central to **Justice Rutledge**'s concurring opinion, which argued that voting matters were not political questions in the constitutional sense, but posed "delicate" issues of remedy and enforcement such that judges should exercise their equitable discretion to refrain from issuing relief. Citing cases where the NAACP had successfully challenged exclusionary voting practices in damage actions (rather than *Giles* injunction suits), e.g., *Nixon v. Herndon,* 273 U.S. 536 (1927), three dissenting Justices (**Black**, **Douglas**, and **Murphy**) conceded that "voting is part

---

b. See William Eskridge, Jr., *Some Effects of Identity-Based Social Movements on Constitutional Law in the Twentieth Century,* 100 Mich. L. Rev. 2062 (2002). For a more elaborate typology, see Louis Henkin, *Is There a "Political Question" Doctrine?,* 85 Yale L.J. 597 (1976). For a simpler typology, see Rachel Barkow, *More Supreme Than Court? The Fall of the Political Question Doctrine and the Rise of Judicial Supremacy,* 102 Colum. L. Rev. 237 (2002) (emphasizing the "prudential" features of the political question doctrine). For an argument that the political question doctrine is merely an institutional safety valve, with no principled evolution, see Fritz Scharpf, *Judicial Review and the Political Question: A Functional Analysis,* 75 Yale L.J. 517 (1966).

of elections and that elections are 'political,' " but it does not follow that "courts are impotent in connection with evasions of all 'political' rights."

The Court's ultimate willingness to adjudicate these kinds of claims was influenced by its experience with the school desegregation cases, culminating in *Cooper v. Aaron* (Chapter 2, § 2B). Counsel for the Little Rock School Board extensively quoted *Giles* to support his assertion that desegregation orders could not be issued by federal judges when the people of the state were massively unwilling to go along. Given the Court's commitment to *Brown* and the district's underlying (but never directly asserted) challenge to its duty to follow that precedent, this was an argument that even Justice Frankfurter summarily dismissed. The Court did not even mention the *Giles* issue in its landmark opinion, which held that local opposition was no justification for a federal judge to delay entry of an injunction enforcing constitutional rights.

Gomillion v. Lightfoot, 364 U.S. 339 (1960). The NAACP challenged an Alabama statute altering the city limits of Tuskegee, to the effect that virtually all the black voters were moved outside the new limits. The challengers recognized that *Colegrove* was a problem for their lawsuit. The ACLU's brief distinguished between the constitutional dimension of the political question doctrine and the pragmatic-administrability dimension. The Court's prior cases, starting with *Herndon*, made clear that the first was no barrier. Nor was the second, because Congress in 1957 had explicitly authorized federal courts to exercise jurisdiction in voting rights cases. Unspoken but also relevant was the Solicitor General's participation in the case, suggesting that the Eisenhower Administration would back the Court up (as it had done in *Cooper*). Distinguishing *Colegrove* and ignoring *Giles*, Justice Frankfurter's opinion for a unanimous Court saw the challenged law as just the same as *Herndon*: a subterfuge to deny people of color their rights to vote and therefore no different from any other individual rights case. Notwithstanding Frankfurter's cautious opinion, *Gomillion* was a doctrinal fulcrum for the Court to reconsider *Colegrove*.

BAKER v. CARR
369 U.S. 186, 82 S.Ct. 691, 7 L.Ed.2d 663 (1962)

JUSTICE BRENNAN delivered the opinion of the Court.

[The Tennessee legislature had not been reapportioned since 1901. The state's demographics had changed dramatically since then. Plaintiffs, who lived in urban and suburban legislative districts that had many more voters than rural districts, claimed that their votes were diluted in violation of the Equal Protection Clause. They sought an injunction prohibiting elections under the current scheme and either a reapportionment of legislative seats in accordance with population or "at-large elections" for the legislature. The district court denied relief, holding the controversy a "political question" under *Colegrove*.]

Of course the mere fact that the suit seeks protection of a political right does not mean it presents a political question. Such an objection "is little more than a play upon words." *Herndon*. Rather, it is argued that apportionment cases, whatever the actual wording of the complaint, can involve no federal constitutional right except one resting on the guaranty of a republican form of government, and that complaints based on that clause have been held to present political questions which are nonjusticiable. * * *

We have said that "In determining whether a question falls within [the political question] category, the appropriateness under our system of government of attributing finality to the action of the political departments and also the lack of satisfactory criteria for a judicial determination are dominant considerations." The nonjusticiability of a political question is primarily a function of the separation of powers. Much confusion results from the capacity of the "political question" label to obscure the need for case-by-case inquiry. Deciding whether a matter has in any measure been committed by the Constitution to another branch of government, or whether the action of that branch exceeds whatever authority has been committed, is itself a delicate exercise in constitutional interpretation, and is a responsibility of this Court as ultimate interpreter of the Constitution. * * *

Foreign relations: There are sweeping statements to the effect that all questions touching foreign relations are political questions. Not only does resolution of such issues frequently turn on standards that defy judicial application, or involve the exercise of a discretion demonstrably committed to the executive or legislature; but many such questions uniquely demand single-voiced statement of the Government's views. Yet it is error to suppose that every case or controversy which touches foreign relations lies beyond judicial cognizance. Our cases in this field seem invariably to show a discriminating analysis of the particular question posed, in terms of the history of its management by the political branches, of its susceptibility to judicial handling in the light of its nature and posture in the specific case, and of the possible consequences of judicial action. [As an example, Justice Brennan noted that, although the Court would conclusively defer to a decision by the political branches to terminate a foreign treaty, "if there has been no conclusive 'governmental action' then a court can construe a treaty and may find it provides the answer."]

Dates of duration of hostilities: Though it has been stated broadly that "the power which declared the necessity is the power to declare its cessation, and what the cessation requires," here too analysis reveals isolable reasons for the presence of political questions, underlying this Court's refusal to review the political department's determination of when or whether a war has ended. Dominant is the need for finality in the political determination, for emergency's nature demands "A prompt and unhesitating obedience." * * * [But] clearly definable criteria for decision may be available. In such cases the political question barrier falls away. * * *

Validity of enactments: In *Coleman v. Miller*, [307 U.S. 433 (1939),] this Court held that the questions of how long a proposed amendment to the Federal Constitution remained open to ratification, and what effect a prior rejection had on a subsequent ratification, were committed to congressional resolution and involved criteria of decision that necessarily escaped the judicial grasp. Similar considerations apply to the enacting process: "The respect due to coequal and independent departments," and the need for finality and certainty about the status of a statute contribute to judicial reluctance to inquire whether, as passed, it complied with all requisite formalities. * * *

It is apparent that several formulations which vary slightly according to the settings in which the questions arise may describe a political question, although each has one or more elements which identify it as essentially a function of the separation of powers. Prominent on the surface of any case held to involve a political question is found a textually demonstrable constitutional commitment of the issue to a coordinate political department; or a lack of judicially discoverable and manageable standards for resolving it; or the impossibility of deciding without an initial policy determination of a kind clearly for nonjudicial discretion; or the impossibility of a court's undertaking independent resolution without expressing lack of the respect due coordinate branches of government; or an unusual need for unquestioning adherence to a political decision already made; or the potentiality of embarrassment from multifarious pronouncements by various departments on one question.

Unless one of these formulations is inextricable from the case at bar, there should be no dismissal for nonjusticiability on the ground of a political question's presence. The doctrine of which we treat is one of "political questions," not one of "political cases." * * *

But it is argued that this case shares the characteristics of decisions that constitute a category not yet considered, cases concerning the Constitution's guaranty of a republican form of government. * * * Guaranty Clause claims involve those elements which define a "political question," and for that reason and no other, they are nonjusticiable. In particular, * * * the nonjusticiability of such claims has nothing to do with their touching upon matters of state governmental organization.

* * * *Luther v. Borden*, though in form simply an action for damages for trespass was, as Daniel Webster said in opening the argument for the defense, "an unusual case." * * *

Chief Justice Taney's opinion for the Court reasoned as follows: (1) If a court were to hold the defendants' acts unjustified because the charter government had no legal existence during the period in question, it would follow that all of that government's actions — laws enacted, taxes collected, salaries paid, accounts settled, sentences passed — were of no effect; and that "the officers who carried their decisions into operation [were] answerable as trespassers, if not in some cases as criminals." * * * A decision for the plaintiff would inevitably have produced some significant measure of chaos. * * *

(2) No state court had recognized as a judicial responsibility settlement of the issue of the locus of state governmental authority. Indeed, the courts of Rhode Island had in several cases held that "it rested with the political power to decide whether the charter government had been displaced or not," and that that department had acknowledged no change.

(3) Since "[t]he question relates, altogether, to the constitution and laws of [the] . . . State," the courts of the United States had to follow the state courts' decisions unless there was a federal constitutional ground for overturning them.

(4) No provision of the Constitution could be or had been invoked for this purpose except Art. IV, § 4, the Guaranty Clause. Having already noted the absence of standards whereby the choice between governments could be made by a court acting independently, Chief Justice Taney now found further textual and practical reasons for concluding that, if any department of the United States was empowered by the Guaranty Clause to resolve the issue it was not the judiciary:

> Under this article of the Constitution it rests with Congress to decide what government is the established one in a State. * * *

> After the President has acted and called out the militia, is a Circuit Court of the United States authorized to inquire whether his decision was right? . . . If the judicial power extends so far, the guarantee contained in the Constitution of the United States is a guarantee of anarchy, and not of order. * * *

Clearly, several factors were thought by the Court in *Luther* to make the question there "political": the commitment to the other branches of the decision as to which is the lawful state government; the unambiguous action by the President, in recognizing the charter government as the lawful authority; the need for finality in the executive's decision; and the lack of criteria by which a court could determine which form of government was republican.

But the only significance that *Luther* could have for our immediate purposes is in its holding that the Guaranty Clause is not a repository of judicially manageable standards which a court could utilize independently in order to identify a State's lawful government. The Court has since refused to resort to the Guaranty Clause — which alone had been invoked for the purpose — as the source of a constitutional standard for invalidating state action. [Citing nine cases.]

Just as the Court has consistently held that a challenge to state action based on the Guaranty Clause presents no justiciable question so has it held, and for the same reasons, that challenges to congressional action on the ground of inconsistency with that clause present no justiciable question. * * *

We come, finally, to the ultimate inquiry whether our precedents as to what constitutes a nonjusticiable "political question" bring the case before us under the umbrella of that doctrine. A natural beginning is to note whether any of the common characteristics which we have been able to identify and label descriptively are present. We find none: The question here is the consistency of state action with the Federal Constitution. We have no question decided, or to be decided, by a political branch of government coequal with this Court. Nor do we risk embarrassment of our government abroad, or grave disturbance at home if we take issue with Tennessee as to the constitutionality of her action here challenged. Nor need the appellants, in order to succeed in this action, ask the Court to enter upon policy determinations for which judicially manageable standards are lacking. Judicial standards under the Equal Protection Clause are well developed and familiar, and it has been open to courts since the enactment of the Fourteenth Amendment to determine, if on the particular facts they must, that a discrimination reflects *no* policy, but simply arbitrary and capricious action.

This case does, in one sense, involve the allocation of political power within a State, and the appellants might conceivably have added a claim under the Guaranty Clause. Of course, as we have seen, any reliance on that clause would be futile. But because any reliance on the Guaranty Clause could not have succeeded it does not follow that appellants may not be heard on the equal protection claim which in fact they tender. True, it must be clear that the Fourteenth Amendment claim is not so enmeshed with those political question elements which render Guaranty Clause claims nonjusticiable as actually to present a political question itself. But we have found that not to be the case here.

JUSTICE FRANKFURTER, whom **JUSTICE HARLAN** joins, dissenting.

* * * From its earliest opinions this Court has consistently recognized a class of controversies which do not lend themselves to judicial standards and judicial remedies. * * *

1. The cases concerning war or foreign affairs, for example, are usually explained by the necessity of the country's speaking with one voice in such matters. While this concern alone undoubtedly accounts for many of the decisions, others do not fit the pattern. It would hardly embarrass the conduct of war were this Court to determine, in connection with private transactions between litigants, the date upon which war is to be deemed terminated. But the Court has refused to do so. * * * A controlling factor in such cases is that * * * there exists no standard ascertainable * * * by reference to which a political decision affecting the question at issue between the parties can be judged. * * *

2. The Court has been particularly unwilling to intervene in matters concerning the structure and organization of the political institutions of the States. The abstention from judicial entry into such areas has been greater even than that which marks the Court's ordinary approach to issues of state power challenged under broad federal guarantees. * * *

3. The cases involving Negro disfranchisement are no exception to the principle of avoiding federal judicial intervention into matters of state government in the absence of an explicit and clear constitutional imperative. For here the controlling command of Supreme Law is plain and unequivocal. An end of discrimination against the Negro was the compelling motive of the Civil War Amendments. * * *

4. The Court has refused to exercise its jurisdiction to pass on "abstract questions of political power, of sovereignty, of government." The "political question" doctrine, in this aspect, reflects the policies underlying the requirement of "standing": that the litigant who would challenge official action must claim infringement of an interest particular and personal to himself, as distinguished from a cause of dissatisfaction with the general frame and functioning of government — a complaint that the political institutions are awry. What renders cases of this kind non-justiciable is not necessarily the

nature of the parties to them, for the Court has resolved other issues between similar parties; nor is it the nature of the legal question involved, for the same type of question has been adjudicated when presented in other forms of controversy. The crux of the matter is that courts are not fit instruments of decision where what is essentially at stake is the composition of those large contests of policy traditionally fought out in non-judicial forums, by which governments and the actions of governments are made and unmade. * * *

5. The influence of these converging considerations — the caution not to undertake decision where standards meet for judicial judgment are lacking, the reluctance to interfere with matters of state government in the absence of an unquestionable and effectively enforceable mandate, the unwillingness to make courts arbiters of the broad issues of political organization historically committed to other institutions and for whose adjustment the judicial process is ill-adapted — has been decisive of the settled line of cases, reaching back more than a century, which holds that Art. IV, § 4 of the Constitution, guaranteeing to the States, "a Republican Form of Government," is not enforceable through the courts. * * *

The present case involves all of the elements that have made the Guarantee Clause cases non-justiciable. It is, in effect, a Guarantee Clause claim masquerading under a different label. But it cannot make the case more fit for judicial action that appellants invoke the Fourteenth Amendment rather than Art. IV, § 4, where, in fact, the gist of their complaint is the same — unless it can be found that the Fourteenth Amendment speaks with greater particularity to their situation. We have been admonished to avoid "the tyranny of labels." Art. IV, § 4, is not committed by express constitutional terms to Congress. It is the nature of the controversies arising under it, nothing else, which has made it judicially unenforceable. * * * But where judicial competence is wanting, it cannot be created by invoking one clause of the Constitution rather than another.

[Justice Frankfurter concluded that the plaintiffs' complaint "is simply that the representatives are not sufficiently numerous or powerful," and federal judicial consideration of it "will add a virulent source of friction and tension in federal-state relations."]

[Concurring opinions by **JUSTICES DOUGLAS, CLARK**, and **STEWART** are omitted. **JUSTICE CLARK** stressed that Tennessee's apportionment scheme was "a topsy turvical of gigantic proportions," for which there was no political remedy because the beneficiaries of the "crazy quilt" system had a vested interest in keeping their advantage — they controlled the Assembly and hence could block any legislative change, and Tennessee had no initiative or referendum by which the voters could change the apportionment directly. A dissenting opinion by **JUSTICE HARLAN**, arguing that no federal constitutional right was at stake, is also omitted. **JUSTICE WHITTAKER** did not participate in this case. The substantive rules governing reapportionment are discussed in Chapter 5, § 3A.]

NOTES ON THE POLITICAL QUESTION
DOCTRINE SINCE *BAKER*

Justice Brennan's *Baker* opinion was revolutionary. It not only overruled *Colegrove* and ushered in a generation of voting rights litigation, but its mode of analysis reconfigured the political question doctrine. Notice that Brennan's list of six factors the Court should consider in deciding whether an issue is a political question emphasized the pragmatic (factors 2-6) rather than constitutional (factor 1) dimensions of the doctrine and, within the pragmatic dimension, emphasized competence to discern rules of law rather than the administrability concerns. Indeed, *Baker* can be read as narrowing the kinds of administrability concerns courts ought to consider and as decisively rejecting *Giles*'s holding that problems with enforcement are a reason for refusing to exercise jurisdiction. Powerfully supporting this reading of *Baker* are the dozens of post-1962 voting and school desegregation cases, where the Court has affirmed or required federal court civil rights injunctions in the face of strong popular and official opposition. Even more dramatic have been the orders entered in other institutional reform litigation, especially in the many lawsuits seeking structural reform of state prison systems.[c] Consider other contexts in which federal courts have considered the applicability of the post-*Baker* political question doctrine:

1. *Exclusion of Members of Congress.* The House of Representatives in 1967 refused to seat Representative Adam Clayton Powell based upon a resolution asserting that he had "wrongfully diverted House funds for the use of others and himself" and had made "false reports on expenditures of foreign currency to the Committee on House Administration." Arguing that he met all the formal requirements of Article I, § 2, cl. 2, and had been overwhelmingly reelected by his constituents after full ventilation of these charges, Representative Powell sued to be seated. The House Speaker invoked Article I, § 5, cl. 1, that "each House shall be the Judge of the * * * Qualifications of its own Members." This is a textual commitment of the issue to another branch under *Baker v. Carr*, argued Speaker McCormack. He also asserted that judicial resolution of the claim would yield a "potentially embarrassing confrontation between coordinate branches."

Chief Justice Warren, writing for the Court in *Powell v. McCormack*, 395 U.S. 486 (1969), held the controversy justiciable:

> Our system of government requires that federal courts on occasion interpret the Constitution in a manner at variance with the construction given the document by another branch. The alleged conflict that such an adjudication may cause cannot justify the courts' avoiding their constitutional responsibility.

> Nor are any of the other formulations of a political question "inextricable from the case at bar." *Baker v. Carr*. Petitioners seek a determination that the House was without power to exclude Powell from the 90th Congress, which, we have seen, requires an interpretation of the Constitution — a determination for which clearly there are "judicially * * * manageable standards." Finally, a judicial resolution of

---

c. See Malcolm Feeley & Edward Rubin, *Judicial Policy Making and the Modern State: How the Courts Reformed America's Prisons* (1998) (institutional analysis of federal judicial decrees requiring detailed plans for reorganization of state prisons, often over intense local opposition).

petitioners' claim will not result in "multifarious pronouncements by various departments on one question." For [it] is the responsibility of this Court to act as the ultimate interpreter of the Constitution. *Marbury*.

2. *Adjudicating Expropriations by Foreign Countries.* Shortly after *Baker v. Carr*, the Supreme Court held in *Banco Nacional de Cuba v. Sabbatino*, 376 U.S. 398 (1964), that foreign expropriations of the property of U.S. citizens are nonjusticiable "acts of state." The Court gave two reasons for nonjusticiability: There was no accepted standard in international law for determining when nationalizations require just compensation for those who lose their property, and the usual remedy was for the executive branch to "espouse" its nationals' claims through diplomacy (as the United States was doing in response to Cuba's expropriations after Fidel Castro took power). Justice Harlan, a dissenter in *Baker v. Carr*, wrote the opinion for a unanimous Court. Is this consistent with *Baker*?

In response, Congress enacted the *Sabbatino* Amendment to the Foreign Assistance Act of 1964, Pub. L. No. 88-63, § 301(d)(4), 78 Stat. 1009, 1013, codified at 22 U.S.C. § 2370(e)(2), which directs courts to adjudicate claims that foreign state expropriations violate international law, unless the President states officially that such an adjudication in the particular case would inhibit the executive's conduct of foreign policy. Is this statute constitutional in requiring courts to adjudicate what they believe to be political questions? See *Banco Nacional de Cuba v. First National City Bank*, 431 F.2d 394 (2d Cir. 1970), *rev'd on other grounds*, 406 U.S. 759 (1972) (avoiding the constitutional question by construing statute narrowly).

The plurality opinion for four Justices in *Alfred Dunhill of London, Inc. v. Republic of Cuba*, 425 U.S. 682 (1976), sought to create a "commercial exception" for the act of state doctrine, rendering it inapplicable to "purely commercial operations" of a foreign state; four Justices dissented from the exception, and the fifth (Justice Stevens) expressed no view on it. Courts relied on *Dunhill* and other exceptions to adjudicate claims by American companies that the Islamic Republic of Iran owed them "just compensation" when it nationalized their Iranian subsidiaries and properties after the Shah was overthrown in 1979. Recall from *Dames & Moore* (Chapter 8, § 1B) that the President used the claims against Iran as a bargaining chip in his negotiations for the return of 52 hostages held in Tehran, and that the claims were referred to an international claims tribunal, one of the traditional means of resolving foreign nationalization claims. In light of this context, were American courts wise in distinguishing *Sabbatino*? See William Eskridge, Jr., *The Iranian Nationalization Cases*, 22 Harv. Int'l L.J. 525 (1981) (no).

3. *The Constitutionality of the Vietnam War.* During the 1950s and early 1960s, the executive branch eased the country into the Vietnam War, and after 1964 rather rapidly escalated our involvement to mammoth proportions. There was never a formal congressional declaration of war, though in August 1964 the Senate did pass the Gulf of Tonkin Resolution (with only two Senators dissenting), which broadly approved of the President's responding to Communist aggression in Vietnam. The ambiguous nature of this "war," the ultimately staggering commitment of people and resources to its conduct, and the

perception by the late 1960s that this was a losing effort all made the war legally as well as politically controversial.[d]

The Supreme Court ducked the legal issues, e.g., *Mora v. McNamara*, 389 U.S. 934 (1967) (denying certiorari on case raising issue of legality of the war, over dissents by Justices Douglas and Stewart), but they percolated quite actively in the courts of appeals. In *Orlando v. Laird*, 443 F.2d 1039 (2d Cir.), *cert. denied*, 404 U.S. 869 (1971), the Second Circuit held that the question whether or not Congress was required to take *some* action to authorize the Vietnam War was not a political question under *Baker v. Carr*, because it was possible to discern judicially manageable standards. The *Orlando* court found that Congress had authorized the President to commit military forces at various points, specifically in the Gulf of Tonkin Resolution and in continuing appropriations measures.

But in *DaCosta v. Laird*, 448 F.2d 1368 (2d Cir. 1971), *cert. denied*, 405 U.S. 979 (1972), the same court refused to adjudicate the claim that Congress' repeal of the Gulf of Tonkin Resolution removed the congressional authorization found sufficient (and justiciable) in *Orlando*. The Court relied on dicta in *Orlando* that the means by which Congress and the President cooperated in prosecuting the war was a political question. It extended that dicta to hold that "the method and means by which they mutually participate in winding down the conflict and in disengaging the nation from it, is also a political question." The Second Circuit later found to be political questions the President's unilateral decision to escalate the bombing of North Vietnam in 1973, see *DaCosta v. Laird*, 471 F.2d 1146 (1973), and the President's decision to continue military operations in Cambodia notwithstanding specific congressional directives to remove all U.S. forces from that country. See *Holtzman v. Schlesinger*, 484 F.2d 1307 (2d Cir. 1973), *cert. denied*, 416 U.S. 936 (1974). Are these decisions consistent with *Baker*?

4. *Treaty Termination.* By *per curiam* order without opinion, *Goldwater v. Carter*, 444 U.S. 996 (1979), reversed a lower court decision that the President had the authority to terminate a Senate-approved treaty with Taiwan without congressional approval. Justice Rehnquist (joined by Chief Justice Burger and Justices Stewart and Stevens) wrote a separate opinion arguing that the issue of treaty termination is a political question, on the ground that "while the Constitution is express as to the manner in which the Senate shall participate in the ratification of a treaty, it is silent as to that body's participation in the abrogation of a treaty, and the fact that different termination procedures may be appropriate for different treaties." Note the similarity to the Second Circuit's reasoning in *DaCosta*. Is this argument consistent with *Powell v. McCormack*? *Baker v. Carr*?

---

d. See John Hart Ely, *The American War in Indochina, Part I: The (Troubled) Constitutionality of the War They Told Us About*, 42 Stan. L. Rev. 877 (1990); John Hart Ely, *The American War In Indochina, Part II: The Unconstitutionality of the War They Didn't Tell Us About*, 42 Stan. L. Rev. 1093 (1990); Michael Tigar, *The "Political Question" Doctrine and Foreign Relations*, 17 UCLA L. Rev. 1135 (1970); Lawrence Velvel, *The War in Viet Nam: Unconstitutional, Justiciable, and Jurisdictionally Attackable*, 16 Kan. L. Rev. 449 (1968).

Justice Powell, concurring in the judgment on grounds that the dispute was not ripe for adjudication, rejected Justice Rehnquist's position, arguing that Article II, § 2 and Article VI provide plenty of constitutional text from which "judicially discoverable and manageable standards" can be discerned. "Interpretation of the Constitution does not imply lack of respect for a coordinate branch. If the President and Congress had reached irreconcilable positions, final disposition of the question presented by this case would eliminate, rather than create, multiple constitutional interpretations. The specter of the Federal Government brought to a halt because of the mutual intransigence of the President and the Congress would require this Court to provide a resolution pursuant to our duty 'to say what the law is.' "

Justice Brennan dissented from the *per curiam* opinion, finding no political question and arguing in favor of the President's power to terminate treaties. According to Brennan, the political question doctrine "does not pertain when a court is faced with an *antecedent* question whether a particular branch has been constitutionally designated as the repository of political decisionmaking power. The issue of decisionmaking authority must be resolved as a matter of constitutional law, not political discretion; accordingly, it falls within the competence of the courts."

5. *Reapportionment and Gerrymandering.* Every ten years the allocation of House of Representatives seats to the states is recalculated, and this triggers political battles over how many seats each state will get (the Census numbers not being beyond question) and how new districts will be drawn in each state (even states keeping the same number of seats have to reconfigure their districts so that they will be roughly equal). *Baker v. Carr* seems to have allowed these controversies to grow and flourish in the courts.

A unanimous Supreme Court in *United States Department of Commerce v. Montana*, 503 U.S. 442 (1992), held justiciable Montana's claim that the congressionally adopted method for computing House representation unfairly short-changed it under Article I, § 2, providing that Representatives shall be apportioned among the States "according to their respective Numbers." Relying on *Baker* and *Bandemer*, the Court simply said that "the interpretation of the apportionment provisions of the Constitution is well within the competence of the Judiciary," and then proceeded to a complex mathematical defense of Congress' chosen means of apportionment. Interestingly, the Court cited two leading sources advocating abolition of the political question doctrine, though it cited them for innocuous propositions. *Id.* at 1425 nn.36 & 37, citing Louis Henkin, *Is There a "Political Question" Doctrine?*, 85 Yale L.J. 597 (1976), and Martin Redish, *The Federal Courts in the Political Order* (1991).

NIXON v. UNITED STATES

506 U.S. 224, 113 S.Ct. 732, 122 L.Ed.2d 1 (1993)

CHIEF JUSTICE REHNQUIST delivered the opinion of the Court.

[The House of Representatives impeached Walter Nixon, a federal district judge, following his federal conviction and imprisonment for making false statements to a federal grand jury. Pursuant to Senate Rule XI, the Senate delegated much of its role in trying the impeachment to a committee of Senators. After receiving evidence and hearing testimony, the committee presented the full Senate with a transcript of the proceedings and a report specifying the uncontested facts and summarizing the evidence concerning the contested facts. Nixon and the House impeachment managers submitted briefs to the full Senate and were allowed to deliver arguments from the Senate floor. Nixon was also allowed to make a personal appeal to the Senate. Following his conviction by the Senate and his removal from office, Nixon brought this action, contending that his impeachment was unconstitutional because the full Senate did not take part in the evidentiary hearing. The lower courts dismissed the action on the ground that it was nonjusticiable.]

A controversy is nonjusticiable — *i.e.*, involves a political question — where there is "a textually demonstrable constitutional commitment of the issue to a coordinate political department; or a lack of judicially discoverable and manageable standards for resolving it. . . ." *Baker v. Carr*. But the courts must, in the first instance, interpret the text in question and determine whether and to what extent the issue is textually committed. As the discussion that follows makes clear, the concept of a textual commitment to a coordinate political department is not completely separate from the concept of a lack of judicially discoverable and manageable standards for resolving it; the lack of judicially manageable standards may strengthen the conclusion that there is a textually demonstrable commitment to a coordinate branch.

In this case, we must examine Art. I, § 3, cl. 6, to determine the scope of authority conferred upon the Senate by the Framers regarding impeachment. It provides:

> The Senate shall have the sole Power to try all Impeachments. When sitting for that Purpose, they shall be on Oath or Affirmation. When the President of the United States is tried, the Chief Justice shall preside: And no Person shall be convicted without the Concurrence of two thirds of the Members present.

The language and structure of this Clause are revealing. The first sentence is a grant of authority to the Senate, and the word "sole" indicates that this authority is reposed in the Senate and nowhere else. The next two sentences specify requirements to which the Senate proceedings shall conform: The Senate shall be on oath or affirmation, a two-thirds vote is required to convict, and when the President is tried the Chief Justice shall preside.

Petitioner argues that the word "try" in the first sentence imposes by implication an additional requirement on the Senate in that the proceedings must be in the nature of a judicial trial. From there petitioner goes on to argue that this limitation precludes the Senate from delegating to a select committee the task of hearing the testimony of witnesses[.] * * * Petitioner concludes from this that courts may review whether or not the Senate "tried" him before convicting him.

There are several difficulties with this position which lead us ultimately to reject it. The word "try," both in 1787 and later, has considerably broader meanings than those to which petitioner would limit it. Older dictionaries define try as "[t]o examine" or "[t]o examine as a judge." See 2 S. Johnson, A

Dictionary of the English Language (1785). In more modern usage the term has various meanings. For example, try can mean "to examine or investigate judicially," "to conduct the trial of," or "to put to the test by experiment, investigation, or trial." Webster's Third New International Dictionary 2457 (1971). Petitioner submits that "try," as contained in T. Sheridan, Dictionary of the English Language (1796), means "to examine as a judge; to bring before a judicial tribunal." Based on the variety of definitions, however, we cannot say that the Framers used the word "try" as an implied limitation on the method by which the Senate might proceed in trying impeachments. "As a rule the Constitution speaks in general terms, leaving Congress to deal with subsidiary matters of detail as the public interests and changing conditions may require[.]"

The conclusion that the use of the word "try" in the first sentence of the Impeachment Trial Clause lacks sufficient precision to afford any judicially manageable standard of review of the Senate's actions is fortified by the existence of the three very specific requirements that the Constitution does impose on the Senate when trying impeachments: The Members must be under oath, a two-thirds vote is required to convict, and the Chief Justice presides when the President is tried. These limitations are quite precise, and their nature suggests that the Framers did not intend to impose additional limitations on the form of the Senate proceedings by the use of the word "try" in the first sentence.

Petitioner devotes only two pages in his brief to negating the significance of the word "sole" in the first sentence of Clause 6. As noted above, that sentence provides that "[t]he Senate shall have the sole Power to try all Impeachments." We think that the word "sole" is of considerable significance. Indeed, the word "sole" appears only one other time in the Constitution — with respect to the House of Representatives' "*sole* Power of Impeachment." Art. I, § 2, cl. 5 (emphasis added). The commonsense meaning of the word "sole" is that the Senate alone shall have authority to determine whether an individual should be acquitted or convicted. The dictionary definition bears this out. "Sole" is defined as "having no companion," "solitary," "being the only one," and "functioning . . . independently and without assistance or interference." Webster's Third New International Dictionary 2168 (1971). If the courts may review the actions of the Senate in order to determine whether that body "tried" an impeached official, it is difficult to see how the Senate would be "functioning . . . independently and without assistance or interference." * * *

The history and contemporary understanding of the impeachment provisions support our reading of the constitutional language. The parties do not offer evidence of a single word in the history of the Constitutional Convention or in contemporary commentary that even alludes to the possibility of judicial review in the context of the impeachment powers. This silence is quite meaningful in light of the several explicit references to the availability of judicial review as a check on the Legislature's power with respect to bills of attainder, *ex post facto* laws, and statutes. See The Federalist No. 78 ("Limitations . . . can be preserved in practice no other way than through the medium of the courts of justice").

The Framers labored over the question of where the impeachment power should lie. Significantly, in at least two considered scenarios the power was placed with the Federal Judiciary. Indeed, Madison and the Committee of

Detail proposed that the Supreme Court should have the power to determine impeachments. Despite these proposals, the Convention ultimately decided that the Senate would have "the sole Power to try all Impeachments." Art. I, § 3, cl. 6. According to Alexander Hamilton, the Senate was the "most fit depositary of this important trust" because its Members are representatives of the people. See The Federalist No. 65. The Supreme Court was not the proper body because the Framers "doubted whether the members of that tribunal would, at all times, be endowed with so eminent a portion of fortitude as would be called for in the execution of so difficult a task" or whether the Court "would possess the degree of credit and authority" to carry out its judgment if it conflicted with the accusation brought by the Legislature — the people's representative. See *id.* In addition, the Framers believed the Court was too small in number: "The awful discretion, which a court of impeachments must necessarily have, to doom to honor or to infamy the most confidential and the most distinguished characters of the community, forbids the commitment of the trust to a small number of persons." *Id.*

There are two additional reasons why the Judiciary, and the Supreme Court in particular, were not chosen to have any role in impeachments. First, the Framers recognized that most likely there would be two sets of proceedings for individuals who commit impeachable offenses — the impeachment trial and a separate criminal trial. In fact, the Constitution explicitly provides for two separate proceedings. See Art. I, § 3, cl. 7. The Framers deliberately separated the two forums to avoid raising the specter of bias and to ensure independent judgments[.] * * * Certainly judicial review of the Senate's "trial" would introduce the same risk of bias as would participation in the trial itself.

Second, judicial review would be inconsistent with the Framers' insistence that our system be one of checks and balances. In our constitutional system, impeachment was designed to be the *only* check on the Judicial Branch by the Legislature. On the topic of judicial accountability, Hamilton wrote:

> The precautions for their responsibility are comprised in the article respecting impeachments. They are liable to be impeached for mal-conduct by the house of representatives, and tried by the senate, and if convicted, may be dismissed from office and disqualified for holding any other. *This is the only provision on the point, which is consistent with the necessary independence of the judicial character, and is the only one which we find in our own constitution in respect to our own judges.* [*The Federalist* No. 79 (emphasis added).]

Judicial involvement in impeachment proceedings, even if only for purposes of judicial review, is counterintuitive because it would eviscerate the "important constitutional check" placed on the Judiciary by the Framers. See *id.*, No. 81. Nixon's argument would place final reviewing authority with respect to impeachments in the hands of the same body that the impeachment process is meant to regulate.

Nevertheless, Nixon argues that judicial review is necessary in order to place a check on the Legislature. Nixon fears that if the Senate is given unreviewable authority to interpret the Impeachment Trial Clause, there is a grave risk that the Senate will usurp judicial power. The Framers anticipated this objection and created two constitutional safeguards to keep the Senate in check. The first safeguard is that the whole of the impeachment power is divided between the two legislative bodies, with the House given the right to accuse and the Senate given the right to judge. * * * The second safeguard is the two-thirds super-majority vote requirement. * * *

In addition to the textual commitment argument, we are persuaded that the lack of finality and the difficulty of fashioning relief counsel against justici-ability. We agree with the Court of Appeals that opening the door of judicial review to the procedures used by the Senate in trying impeachments would "expose the political life of the country to months, or perhaps years, of chaos." This lack of finality would manifest itself most dramatically if the President were impeached. The legitimacy of any successor, and hence his effectiveness, would be impaired severely, not merely while the judicial process was running its course, but during any retrial that a differently constituted Senate might conduct if its first judgment of conviction were invalidated. Equally uncertain is the question of what relief a court may give other than simply setting aside the judgment of conviction. Could it order the reinstatement of a convicted federal judge, or order Congress to create an additional judgeship if the seat had been filled in the interim?

Petitioner finally contends that a holding of nonjusticiability cannot be reconciled with our opinion in *Powell v. McCormack*, 395 U.S. 486 (1969). The relevant issue in *Powell* was whether courts could review the House of Representatives' conclusion that Powell was "unqualified" to sit as a Member because he had been accused of misappropriating public funds and abusing the process of the New York courts. We stated that the question of justiciability turned on whether the Constitution committed authority to the House to judge its Members' qualifications, and if so, the extent of that commitment. Article I, § 5 provides that "Each House shall be the Judge of the Elections, Returns and Qualifications of its own Members." In turn, Art. I, § 2 specifies three require-ments for membership in the House: The candidate must be at least 25 years of age, a citizen of the United States for no less than seven years, and an inhabitant of the State he is chosen to represent. We held that, in light of the three requirements specified in the Constitution, the word "qualifications" — of which the House was to be the Judge — was of a precise, limited nature.

Our conclusion in *Powell* was based on the fixed meaning of "[q]ualifi-cations" set forth in Art. I, § 2. The claim by the House that its power to "be the Judge of the Elections, Returns and Qualifications of its own Members" was a textual commitment of unreviewable authority was defeated by the existence of this separate provision specifying the only qualifications which might be imposed for House membership. The decision as to whether a Member satisfied these qualifications *was* placed with the House, but the decision as to what these qualifications consisted of was not.

In the case before us, there is no separate provision of the Constitution which could be defeated by allowing the Senate final authority to determine the meaning of the word "try" in the Impeachment Trial Clause. We agree with Nixon that courts possess power to review either legislative or executive action that transgresses identifiable textual limits. As we have made clear, "whether the action of [either the Legislative or Executive Branch] exceeds whatever authority has been committed, is itself a delicate exercise in constitutional interpretation, and is a responsibility of this Court as ultimate interpreter of the Constitution." *Baker v. Carr.* But we conclude, after exercising that delicate responsibility, that the word "try" in the Impeachment Clause does not provide an identifiable textual limit on the authority which is committed to the Senate.

[The concurring opinion of **JUSTICE STEVENS** is omitted.]

JUSTICE WHITE, with whom **JUSTICE BLACKMUN** joins, concurring in the judgment.

* * * [T]he Court's willingness to abandon its obligation to review the constitutionality of legislative acts merely on the strength of the word "sole" is perplexing. Consider, by comparison, the treatment of Art. I, § 1, which grants "All legislative powers" to the House and Senate. As used in that context "all" is nearly synonymous with "sole" — both connote entire and exclusive authority. Yet the Court has never thought it would unduly interfere with the operation of the Legislative Branch to entertain difficult and important questions as to the extent of the legislative power. * * *

The majority's review of the historical record * * * explains why the power to try impeachments properly resides with the Senate. It does not explain, however, the sweeping statement that the Judiciary was "not chosen to have any role in impeachments." Not a single word in the historical materials cited by the majority addresses judicial review of the Impeachment Trial Clause. And a glance at the arguments surrounding the Impeachment Clauses negates the majority's attempt to infer nonjusticiability from the Framers' arguments in support of the Senate's power to try impeachments.

What the relevant history mainly reveals is deep ambivalence among many of the Framers over the very institution of impeachment, which, by its nature, is not easily reconciled with our system of checks and balances. As they clearly recognized, the branch of the Federal Government which is possessed of the authority to try impeachments, by having final say over the membership of each branch, holds a potentially unanswerable power over the others. In addition, that branch, insofar as it is called upon to try not only members of other branches, but also its own, will have the advantage of being the judge of its own members' causes.

It is no surprise, then, that the question of impeachment greatly vexed the Framers. The pages of the Convention debates reveal diverse plans for resolving this exceedingly difficult issue. Both before and during the convention, Madison maintained that the judiciary ought to try impeachments. Shortly thereafter, however, he devised a quite complicated scheme that involved the participation of each branch. Jefferson likewise had attempted to develop an interbranch system for impeachment trials in Virginia. Even Hamilton's eloquent defense of the scheme adopted by the Constitution was based on a pragmatic decision to further the cause of ratification rather than a strong belief in the superiority of a scheme vesting the Senate with the sole power to try impeachments. While at the Convention, Hamilton advocated that impeachment trials be conducted by a court made up of state-court judges. Four months after publishing The Federalist Nos. 65 and 66, however, he urged the New York Ratifying Convention to amend the Clause he had so ably defended to have the Senate, the Supreme Court, and judges from each State jointly try impeachments.

The historical evidence reveals above all else that the Framers were deeply concerned about placing in any branch the "awful discretion, which a court of impeachments must necessarily have." The Federalist No. 65. Viewed against this history, the discord between the majority's position and the basic principles of checks and balances underlying the Constitution's separation of powers is clear. In essence, the majority suggests that the Framers conferred upon Congress a potential tool of legislative dominance yet at the same time rendered Congress' exercise of that power one of the very few areas of legislative authority immune from any judicial review. While the majority rejects petitioner's justiciability argument as espousing a view "inconsistent with the Framers' insistence that our system be one of checks and balances," it is the Court's finding of nonjusticiability that truly upsets the Framers' careful design. In a truly balanced system, impeachments tried by the Senate would serve as a means of controlling the largely unaccountable Judiciary, even as judicial review would ensure that the Senate adhered to a minimal set of procedural standards in conducting impeachment trials.

[Justice White then responded to the majority's conclusion that the term "try" did not present a judicially manageable standard. He asserted that "try" was obviously used in its legal sense, as shown "by the use of 'tried' in the third sentence of the Impeachment Trial Clause ('[w]hen the President of the United States is tried . . .'), and by Art. III, § 2, cl. 3 ('[t]he Trial of all Crimes, except in Cases of Impeachment . . .')." In its legal sense, Justice White argued, the term has a judicially manageable meaning. "Were the Senate, for example, to adopt the practice of automatically entering a judgment of conviction whenever articles of impeachment were delivered from the House, it is quite clear that the Senate will have failed to 'try' impeachments. Indeed in this respect, 'try' presents no greater, and perhaps fewer, interpretive difficulties than some other constitutional standards that have been found amenable to familiar techniques of judicial construction, including, for example, 'Commerce . . . among the several States' and 'due process of law.'"

[Accordingly, Justice White reached the merits. Based on a review of historical materials, he concluded that the Framers did not intend impeachment trials to be governed by the strict rules of procedure used in courts. He also found historical precedent in the House of Lords and in state legislatures for the use of fact-finding committees for impeachment. Accordingly, he found no constitutional infirmity in Nixon's impeachment and removal from office.]

[**JUSTICE SOUTER**, concurring in the judgment, argued that the political-question doctrine is "deriv[ed] in large part from prudential concerns about the respect we owe the political departments." Although agreeing with the majority that the issue in this case was a political question, Justice Souter opined that "[i]f the Senate were to act in a manner seriously threatening the integrity of its results, convicting, say, upon a coin toss, * * * judicial interference might well be appropriate. In such circumstances, the Senate's action might be so far beyond the scope of its constitutional authority, and the consequent impact on the Republic so great, as to merit a judicial response despite the prudential concerns that would ordinarily counsel silence."]

PROBLEMS ON POLITICAL QUESTIONS

Problem 9-1: *The Case of the Gulf War.* On August 2, 1990, Iraqi troops invaded Kuwait. Within ten days, the United States responded with an embargo and military blockade against all shipments into Iraq or Kuwait. On November 8, President George H.W. Bush announced a significant increase in U.S. troops in the Gulf, which he accomplished under his Article II powers as Commander in Chief, but over objections in Congress that he should have followed the procedures of the War Powers Resolution (Chapter 8, § 1B). On November 29, the United Nations passed a Resolution sanctioning the use of "all necessary means" to force Iraq out of Kuwait if there were not a voluntary withdrawal by January 15, 1991. Immediately after that, two lawsuits (one by U.S. soldiers and one by 54 Members of Congress) were filed to enjoin the President from committing troops to a war against Iraq without first obtaining a congressional declaration of war or, at least, without formally reporting to the Congress pursuant to the War Powers Resolution. Was this lawsuit a nonjusticiable political question? Compare *Ange v. Bush*, 752 F. Supp. 509 (D.D.C. 1990) (yes), with *Dellums v. Bush*, 752 F. Supp. 1141 (D.D.C. 1990) (no).

Problem 9-2: *The Case of the Senate-Originated Revenue Bill.* The Victims of Crime Act of 1984 established a Crime Victims Fund, 98 Stat. 2170, 42 U.S.C. § 10601(a), as a federal source of funds for programs to compensate crime victims. One source of money for the Fund is a provision requiring "special assessments" to be made against criminals, with the money going into the Fund, up to $100 million, with any amount beyond that going into the general federal Treasury. 42 U.S.C. § 10601. The statute also amended the federal criminal code to require, *inter alia*, courts to impose a special assessment on any person convicted of a federal misdemeanor. 18 U.S.C. § 3013. Defendant, convicted of a misdemeanor and assessed $50 under the statute, challenges its constitutionality. His argument is that the bill that was to become the 1985 statute originated in the Senate, in violation of the Origination Clause of the Constitution, Article I, § 7, cl. 1, which says: "All Bills for raising Revenue shall originate in the House of Representatives." Is this claim a nonjusticiable political question? See *United States v. Munoz-Flores*, 495 U.S. 385 (1990); *Millard v. Roberts*, 202 U.S. 429, 436-37 (1906).

Problem 9-3: *The Case of the Disputed Electors.* Recall the *Bush v. Gore* litigation (Chapter 5, § 3). Article II of the U.S. Constitution and 3 U.S.C. § 5 vest the state "Legislature" with the authority to determine the procedures by which the state chooses its electors for President. Applying state election laws that had been adopted by the Florida Legislature, the Florida Supreme Court on December 8, 2000, ordered Miami-Dade and other counties to conduct manual recounts of "undervotes" — those ballots the voting machines did not count but where the intent of the voter might be discerned through examination of "chads" created by a partial punch-through in the ballot and even of "dimples," or indentations not amounting to punch-throughs. The court ruled that the "intent of the voter" was the standard each county must follow. The recounts were to be completed by December 12, the federal safe-harbor date, assuring any state that its certified electors would not be challenged. (A second date, December 18, was important, because that's when the electors would cast their votes for President.) The recounts began but were stayed by the U.S. Supreme Court on December 9. Three days later, the Supreme Court reversed the second Florida Supreme Court decision on the ground that the state recount procedures violated the Equal Protection Clause. Florida certified its Bush electors, and the next day candidate Gore conceded the election to George W. Bush. Should the U.S. Supreme Court have treated this litigation as a political question? If not, should the Court have exercised one of the other "passive virtues" and declined to intervene in the matter?

A NOTE ON POLITICAL QUESTIONS
AND THE GUARANTEE CLAUSE

Since *Luther v. Borden*, the Court has refused to recognize claims that the Guarantee Clause provides individual rights enforceable in court. When individual rights are recognized that have "republican form of government" overtones, the Court transforms the claim so that it is based upon some other constitutional provision, like the Equal Protection Clause in *Baker v. Carr*.

Even if the Guarantee Clause provides no justiciable individual rights, however, it could conceivably be the source of structural protections. If Congress enacts a statute extensively regulating core state functions or coercing states into service to promote federal ends, it could conceivably be said to have violated its "guarantee" that state government be republican in form. (Note that by this standard, the residents of the District of Columbia are being denied a "republican form of government," but the clause only appears to cover the states.) *Baker* seems to cut both ways here. On the one hand, it contains extensive language suggesting that only one constitutional structural feature — separation of powers, not federalism — can produce political questions. On the other hand, it says that Guarantee Clause issues are nonjusticiable. Recall, too, *Garcia v. San Antonio Metropolitan Transportation Authority* (Chapter 7, § 5B), which held that, at least in all but the most unusual circumstances, states must rely upon the congressional process and not constitutional adjudication for protection against federal regulation.

Baker and other cases are often understood to preclude justiciability of all claims, whether individual or structural, raised under the Guarantee Clause. Somewhat recently, however, the Supreme Court suggested that it might entertain a reconsideration of this issue for structural federalism issues. In *New York v. United States* (Chapter 7, § 5C), the Court rejected federalism-based challenges to certain provisions of a federal statute regulating the disposal of low-level radioactive waste. In addition to the typical arguments (that the statute exceeded Congress' Article I powers or violated the Tenth Amendment), New York contended that the statute violated the Guarantee Clause. Justice O'Connor's majority opinion acknowledged that at least one post-*Baker* case, as well as several commentators, have suggested that not all Guarantee Clause questions should be nonjusticiable. She continued:

We need not resolve this difficult question [of justiciability] today. * * * The twin threats imposed by the first two challenged provisions of the Act — that New York may miss out on a share of federal spending or that those generating radioactive waste within New York may lose out-of-state disposal outlets — do not pose any realistic risk of altering the form or the method of functioning of New York's government. Thus even indulging the assumption that the Guarantee Clause provides a basis upon which a State or its subdivisions may sue to enjoin the enforcement of a federal statute, petitioners have not made out such a claim in this case.

One way to understand *New York v. United States* is to suggest that the policies of the Guarantee Clause provide the underlying rationale for the Court's Article I/Tenth Amendment rule in *New York v. United States*. On this reading, issues directly arising under the Guarantee Clause can remain nonjusticiable, while the policies of this clause provide a theory to assist the Court in its difficult line-drawing exercises under Article I and the Tenth Amendment.

A NOTE ON POLITICAL QUESTIONS
AND BELATED AMENDMENTS

A largely forgotten fact is that the Bill of Rights proposed by Congress in 1789 contained twelve, not ten, amendments. The first proposed amendment would have ensured that, as the country grew, there would be at least one member of the House of Representatives for every fifty thousand persons. The refusal of a sufficient number of states to ratify this amendment seems wise in retrospect: consider a current House of Representatives with about 5,000 members.

The second proposed amendment, preventing members of Congress from raising their own pay during the current congressional session,[e] was also rejected in 1790-91. When we speak of the Second Amendment today, we refer to the right to bear arms, not limitations on congressional pay raises. And yet the original second amendment, long supposed dead, was resurrected by state legislatures beginning in 1978, in part to protest the federal budget deficit. In 1992, the requisite thirty-eighth state ratified it, and so it is now the Twenty-Seventh Amendment – or is it?[f]

Venerable Supreme Court precedent suggests that, under Article V, the amendment process of proposal and ratification is one process and must be accomplished more or less contemporaneously, to ensure that the same societal consensus exists for both proposal and ratification. *Dillon v. Gloss*, 256 U.S. 368 (1921). A later case, however, seemingly treats the issue as a political question. See *Coleman v. Miller*, 307 U.S. 433 (1939). Note that the two cases

---

e. It provided: "No law varying the compensation for the services of the Senators and Representatives shall take effect, until an election of Representatives shall have intervened." Note that this provision also bans pay cuts until the required time has passed.

f. See generally William Van Alstyne, *What Do You Think About the Twenty-Seventh Amendment?*, 10 Const. Comm. 9 (1993).

can be made consistent: under *Dillon*, there is a "reasonable time" limitation upon ratification; under *Coleman*, only Congress can enforce it.[g]

Consider the political context in which the 1992 Congress received the question whether to declare the original second, and now new Twenty-Seventh, Amendment, a valid part of the Constitution. In that context (an election year; huge federal deficit; respect for Congress at a record low, in part due to congressional pay raises), few members of Congress had the temerity to suggest that perhaps an amendment proposed over two hundred years before was no longer ripe for ratification. On May 21, 1992, both houses of Congress adopted a concurrent resolution (Senate vote: 99-0; House vote: 414-3) declaring this amendment "valid * * * as part of the Constitution of the United States."

Is that the end of the matter — is the original second amendment now a valid Twenty-Seventh Amendment? Should anybody else get to consider this question now that Congress has accepted it? Does this story give you pause about absolute judicial deference to Congress in this instance? More broadly, does it undermine the whole notion of political questions — that judicial review is sometimes dispensable when a coordinate branch stands ready to make a conclusive judgment on a sensitive constitutional issue? Or is the problem not with the political question doctrine, but with the current sad lack of capacity of Congress to treat constitutional questions differently from political questions — a state for which the Court may be partly responsible?

One concluding note: In proposing an amendment, Congress does have the authority to fix a reasonable time for ratification. See *Dillon v. Gloss*, *supra*. Not a bad idea.

SECTION 2. "CASES" OR "CONTROVERSIES"

One can imagine a legal system in which any citizen who cares enough to litigate could obtain a hearing about whether government officials have violated the law. That has never been our system. Instead, courts are limited to hearing cases in which the plaintiff has some more definite personal connection with an alleged violation of law. The easiest cases are those in which the government action directly deprives the plaintiff of some specific legal right. In *Marbury*, for example, the plaintiff claimed to have the right to a specific government job which was being illegally withheld by the defendant. *Marbury* indicates the traditional willingness of courts to intervene in such situations. But today, government actions often affect the interests of millions of people with varying degrees of directness and tangibility, and courts have struggled to draw a line between political or ideological disputes and concrete legal controversies.

---

g. For a debate about the appropriateness of *Coleman*, compare Walter Dellinger, *The Legitimacy of Constitutional Change: Rethinking the Amendment Process*, 97 Harv. L. Rev. 386 (1983) (*Coleman* wrong, and judicial supervision of amendment process warranted) with Laurence Tribe, *A Constitution We Are Amending: In Defense of a Restrained Judicial Role*, 97 Harv. L. Rev. 433 (1983) (judicial supervision inappropriate, particularly for amendments that overturn Supreme Court decisions).

Ultimately, the effort to draw this line is rooted in the language of Article III itself. The "judicial Power" in Article III extends only to "Cases" or "Controversies" enumerated in § 2. These are abstract terms, and the judicial opinions defining them often serve to obscure rather than elucidate their meaning. But the basics are easy to understand.

The power of the federal courts is "judicial" — it is not "legislative," as is Congress' (Article I, § 1), nor is it "executive," as is the President's (Article II, § 1). If courts go beyond the "judicial" function, they invade the provinces of Congress and the President. But what is the judicial function? Article III defines it in terms of hearing "Cases" or "Controversies." These terms — which are essentially synonymous except that perhaps the latter refers only to civil cases — seem to encompass only adversarial lawsuits, not merely questions that somebody might have about what the law is.

Thus, limiting the power of federal judges to hear only adversarial lawsuits has at least two complementary justifications. As a functional matter, judges have experience and training in handling a live controversy between adverse parties adjudicated by our adversary system, but have no special expertise in considering abstract policy questions. Moreover, an adversarial dispute ensures that the courts will have a full basis for making a decision. As a formal matter, when judges reach beyond the adversarial situation and consider abstract policy questions, they arguably violate the separation of powers — they invade the legislative or executive domains.

The historical background provides further evidence that understanding Article III requires understanding the separation of powers and the nature of the judicial function. The Framers considered, but rejected, allowing "Each branch of the Legislature, as well as the supreme Executive [the] authority to require the opinions of the supreme Judicial Court upon important questions of law, and upon solemn occasions."[a] Consistent with this, in a 1793 exchange of letters, the Supreme Court refused to provide President Washington advice on a legal question he had posed. The Justices concluded that, under the separation of powers, in a merely advisory situation any declaration of law the Court uttered would exceed the powers of the judiciary and invade the province of other branches.[b] A year before, in refusing to provide legal advice to Congress and

---

a. See, e.g., Daniel Farber & Suzanna Sherry, *A History of the American Constitution* 60-61 (1990).

b. Chief Justice Jay wrote:

[T]he lines of separation [are] drawn by the Constitution between the three departments of the government. These being in certain respects checks upon each other, and our being judges in a court in the last resort, are considerations which afford strong arguments against the propriety of our extra-judicially deciding the questions [previously asked], especially as the power given by the Constitution to the President, of calling on the heads of departments for opinions [see Article II, § 2], seems to have been *purposely* as well as expressly united to the *executive* departments.

3 Henry Johnston, *Correspondence and Public Papers of John Jay* 486-89 (1891) (emphasis in original), quoted in John Nowak & Ronald Rotunda, *Constitutional Law* 66 (7th ed. 2004).

the Secretary of War, the Justices quoted language from a letter that a circuit court had written to the President referring to limitations based in part on the judicial function: " '[N]either the Legislative nor the Executive branches can constitutionally assign to the judicial any duties, but such as are properly judicial, and to be performed in a judicial manner.' "[c] Since these early precedents, the federal courts have refused to issue advisory opinions, requiring instead an actual case or controversy between adversary parties before invoking their Article III powers.

In this part, we will examine the most important doctrines limiting federal judicial power under Article III: standing, ripeness, and mootness. Each of these doctrines is quite murky at the margin, but each at its core is easy to understand. To use a homely example, suppose that law students think that Mr. Bill, their admittedly eccentric professor in the required first-year constitutional law course, graded their exams arbitrarily. They are considering filing complaints with the law school grievance committee. Consider the differing arguments that one of the students could make, and the responses available.

Standing. Michael, who received an A+, may think that Mr. Bill was wacko in giving him that grade (he claims to have learned "less than zero" in the course), but he has no "standing" to file a grievance — he suffered no harm from Mr. Bill's supposed wackiness. When the grievance committee throws out his grievance, it could couch its decision in the separation of powers — Mr. Bill's supposedly arbitrary award of an A+ to Michael may be something implicating the executive powers of the school (the Dean should investigate) or its legislative assembly (the faculty should investigate), but it is not appropriate for the grievance committee to take up the abstract issue of Mr. Bill's eccentricities. More likely, however, the grievance committee will justify denying his grievance on functional grounds: Michael has no concrete injury to grieve, and considering his complaints will waste the committee's time and force it to consider abstract possibilities. In other words, the committee could rule "no harm, no foul," or "if you want to grouse, go on a talk show" (or see the Dean, which has certain similarities).

Ripeness. Michael responds that he'll forego any direct complaint about his grade in constitutional law. But he thinks that he would like to take the law school's elective on international trade law, which unfortunately is taught only by Mr. Bill, and he fears that he'll get nailed this time when Mr. Bill grades that exam. This grievance would also almost certainly be denied. The most obvious reason is that the complaint comes far too early — it is not "ripe" for consideration — and therefore is far too abstract. Mr. Bill may never offer the course while Michael is a student (Michael might graduate before the course is offered again, Mr. Bill might get hit by a truck in the interim). If Mr. Bill does offer it, Michael might decide not to take it (it could be offered at the same time as a course offered by Ms. Suzanna, Michael's favorite teacher, for which Michael would opt). If Michael does take Mr. Bill's course, he might get another A+, or Mr. Bill might not be wacky, or . . . well, you get the idea. Again, if the

---

c. *Hayburn's Case*, 2 U.S. 408 (1792).

grievance committee heard this complaint, it would be stepping into a domain more appropriate for other institutional actors (the Dean, the faculty assembly), and it would be undertaking review of a complaint that it has no functional capacity to adjudicate.

Mootness. Michael restrains his litigious self and files no grievance based on his experience in constitutional law with Mr. Bill. Later, he takes international trade law from Mr. Bill, who in the interim has completely fallen off the deep end. Mr. Bill gives a mid-term exam (itself a sign of lunacy) and then admits to the class that he graded it by throwing the bluebooks down the stairs, awarding proportionally higher grades the farther down a bluebook ended up. Michael's bluebook landed on the second step and he receives a D- for the midterm exam. Michael files a grievance. He certainly has standing, his complaint seems ripe — but then Mr. Bill announces in class that he has had a change of heart (after a stern talk from the Dean) and will grade the exams carefully. He does so, and Michael gets another A+. His complaint has been "mooted" by Mr. Bill's subsequent action — it has been rendered no longer timely, and again too abstract.[d]

These examples are designed to suggest that there is a common-sense basis for notions of standing, ripeness, and mootness related to formal institutional responsibilities (which in constitutional law travel under the label of separation of powers) and to functional capacities. Now let us turn to a more legalistic assessment situating case or controversy requirements in our adversary system and translating the common-sense concerns noted above into their constitutional analogues.

The various case or controversy requirements reflect three different types of concerns. First, these requirements make for more reliable adjudicative decisions. If the plaintiff truly suffers an injury and the injury continues to hurt her, she will most likely press her case vigorously, and the defendant will respond in kind. This assures the sort of adversarial clash that the Anglo-American system of litigation traditionally assumed produces well-informed

---

d. Ripeness and mootness are usually both problems of timing — the complaint comes too early (not ripe) or too late (now moot). Assume that Susan, whose application to the law school has not yet been granted or denied, wants to complain that the school does not offer a course in international trade law. Her complaint is obviously not ripe — she may never be admitted, even if admitted might decide to go to another law school, and so on. Assume that she is admitted and forgets about this matter until she has graduated, and then files a grievance complaining about the failure to offer the course. Her complaint obviously comes too late — it is moot.

Note how at least simple examples of justiciability doctrine, like this one and the one involving Michael in the text, suggest that one virtue of the doctrine is that people who complain in the abstract — regardless of whether they are mere whiners or virtuous do-gooders — are forced to complain to institutions that are designed to consider abstract complaints (executive and legislative bodies), but also usually have the capacity to respond by ignoring them. In contrast, at least in theory, if federal courts have jurisdiction, they generally have the duty to render a decision rather than ignore or avoid the case. See generally, e.g., David Shapiro, *Jurisdiction and Discretion*, 60 N.Y.U. L. Rev. 543 (1985). This is another, quite important, aspect of the "judicial function" under Article III that may support limiting access to the federal courts.

results (perhaps even "truth"). By forcing the focus onto concrete, individual grievances rather than generalized political disputes, these requirements afford the Court a richer factual context for its deliberation and the possibility of writing a narrowly tailored decision. This means constitutional law develops incrementally, without sweeping pronouncements that might go too far and erode the Court's legitimacy.

Second, these requirements reflect the Court's understanding of its role within the Constitution's scheme of separation of powers. This strand of case or controversy policy is intimately related to the political question doctrine discussed in the previous part.[e] Under this policy, the "judicial Power" is not a roving authority to do good and *make* law. While courts do make law "interstitially" (filling the gaps left by the legislature), they should only do so as needed to resolve a concrete problem affecting individuals. What the "judicial Power" is *not*, but what *is* included in the "legislative Powers" of Article I, is the power to rearrange the rights and duties of groups of people; to create legal rules and standards without reference to an established authority or tradition; or to deal with problems which a mere judicial order cannot resolve or which are committed to the political branches of government. See generally *Valley Forge Christian College v. Americans United*, 454 U.S. 464 (1982), for a more complete statement of this philosophy.

Third, these requirements allow the Court to avoid confronting issues it is not ready to decide. The Court might choose not to speak for purely political reasons. Recall from Chapter 2 that at Justice Frankfurter's urging in the early 1950s, the Court put off the segregation issue (over the objections of Justices Black and Douglas) until it could reach a consensus and perhaps devise the most politically acceptable way of framing a decree. This philosophy inspired Professor Alexander Bickel, Justice Frankfurter's law clerk during the 1952 Term, to develop his theory extolling the Court's "passive virtues" — its willingness to defer resolution of hotly disputed constitutional issues — discussed above in connection with the political question doctrine.

Set against these values are the values enshrined in *Marbury*, namely, the obligation of the Court to say what the law is and to refuse to give effect to laws inconsistent with the Constitution. See also *The Federalist* No. 78 (Alexander Hamilton) (App. 2). Professor Martin Redish assails the passive virtues, and especially standing restrictions, in *The Federal Courts in the Political Order: Judicial Jurisdiction and American Political Theory* (1991), arguing that these restrictions are not apparent from the text and structure of Article III, needlessly displace constitutional debate from substance to procedure, and keep important issues of constitutional interpretation from the courts. He also argues that the private law model of adjudication (an adversarial clash between a person directly harmed and a person directly causing harm) is not appropriate for the

---

e. Note in this regard that, until *Nixon*, the last time the Supreme Court had dismissed a case as a nonjusticiable political question was *Gilligan v. Morgan*, 413 U.S. 1, 10-12 (1973). With the virtual abandonment of the political question doctrine at the Supreme Court level after the 1970s, some of the separation-of-powers concerns reflected in the political question doctrine have floated over into other doctrines, especially standing.

sort of public controversies involved in constitutional cases. This latter point was forcefully argued in Owen Fiss, *The Civil Rights Injunction* (1978), and Abram Chayes, *The Supreme Court, 1981 Term — Foreword: Public Law Litigation and the Burger Court*, 96 Harv. L. Rev. 4 (1982).

Consider the values and the costs of the passive virtues as we survey the doctrinal lay of the land for the three main passive virtues that have been teased out of the case or controversy requirement of Article III.

1. *Mootness.* Under traditional doctrine, " 'federal courts are without power to decide questions that cannot affect the rights of litigants in the case before them.' The inability of the federal judiciary 'to review moot cases derives from the requirement of Article III of the constitution under which the exercise of judicial power depends upon the existence of a case or controversy.' " *DeFunis v. Odegaard*, 416 U.S. 312 (1974) (*per curiam*). Any number of things might moot a case: Plaintiff no longer objects to defendant's conduct, defendant agrees to conform with plaintiff's demands, or the passage of time renders the court unable to grant plaintiff the remedy she seeks. In *DeFunis*, the Court found plaintiff's claim that he had been unconstitutionally denied admission to the University of Washington Law School (on the ground that the state law school's affirmative preferences for minority applicants gave his place to someone less well "qualified") moot because the school later admitted plaintiff and he was about to graduate when the matter reached the Court. Nothing the Court might rule would affect DeFunis' rights: If the Supreme Court agreed with the district court, which had ordered DeFunis admitted, obviously DeFunis would get his degree. But everyone in the case also agreed that he would get his degree even if the Supreme Court held that the law school had acted lawfully. Over the objections of four Justices, the Court held that the case did not present a justiciable case or controversy.

The standards enunciated in *DeFunis* often do not apply in the context of public law litigation, such as the desegregation cases. As a technical matter, parties usually litigate most such cases as class actions (*DeFunis* was not a class action, a point emphasized by the Court). This often seems to insulate a lawsuit against mootness problems. Even though the class representative's claim may become moot, other class members' claims usually remain alive. See *United States Parole Commission v. Geraghty*, 445 U.S. 388 (1980). As a class representative's claim expires, a fresh class representative may replace her.

The class action strategy might not work where the challenged public policy, like a state residency requirement for voting, has a short time fuse requiring constant rollover of the entire class. Thus, just because a class action can continue even though the case becomes moot as to a single class representative, *Sosna v. Iowa*, 419 U.S. 393 (1975), a mootness objection is not saved simply because the plaintiffs denominate their case a class action, *Hall v. Beals*, 396 U.S. 45 (1969). In response to this seemingly inequitable dilemma which favors defendants with the resources to stall litigation until the plaintiff's claim expires, the Court will sometimes hear a case notwithstanding its mootness where an issue is "capable of repetition yet evading review," because the lawsuit's duration systematically tends to moot individual grievances. *Southern Pacific Terminal Co. v. ICC*, 219 U.S. 498, 515 (1911).

The landmark abortion rights case, *Roe v. Wade* (Chapter 5, § 4B), provides a useful example of this phenomenon. There the Court decided the case even though Ms. Roe had already borne her child, holding that so long as some member of the class remained capable of raising a claim against the Texas law (e.g., some member of the class could seek to have or aid in an abortion), the case remained justiciable. Realistically, it is unlikely that an abortion case could reach the Supreme Court in time to be heard; the gestation period for litigation is much longer than nine months! Later, the Court further broadened this exception to its strict construction in *DeFunis*, even in suits not filed as class actions, where an otherwise moot issue is capable of repetition among the same litigants. *First National Bank v. Bellotti*, 435 U.S. 765 (1978).

2. *Ripeness.* In an effort to keep the judiciary from overstepping its Article III jurisdiction over cases and controversies, ripeness doctrine seeks to avoid "premature adjudication." *Pacific Gas & Electric Co. v. State Energy Resources Conservation & Development Commission*, 461 U.S. 190 (1983). Under traditional doctrine, "[d]etermination of the scope and constitutionality of legislation in advance of its immediate adverse effect in the context of a concrete case involves too remote and abstract an inquiry for the proper exercise of the judicial function." *International Longshoremen's & Warehousemen's Union, Local 37 v. Boyd*, 347 U.S. 222 (1954). In the leading case of *United Public Workers v. Mitchell*, 330 U.S. 75 (1947), government workers brought suit challenging provisions of the Hatch Act prohibiting their participation in political campaigns. While the Court found that one employee who had violated the Act had a ripe claim, those who merely wished to undertake political activities, but had not yet done so, were barred from adjudication. The Court said that the power of judicial review "arises only when the interests of litigants require the use of this judicial authority for their protection against actual interference. A hypothetical threat is not enough." Justice Douglas dissented on this issue, reasoning that it was unfair to government employees to require them to risk incurring the statute's penalties in order to challenge it.

In a host of cases, however, the Supreme Court has adjudicated important constitutional issues without demanding actual prosecutions. For example, in *Adler v. Board of Education*, 342 U.S. 485 (1952), the Court upheld New York's Feinberg Law, excluding "subversive persons" from employment in the public school system, without demanding that any of the plaintiffs had been prosecuted for violating the statute. The majority opinion did not even mention ripeness, even though Justice Frankfurter hotly dissented on ripeness grounds, citing *Mitchell*. In other cases, the Court has considered "hardship to the parties" and "fitness of the issues" in adjudicating controversies where there had been no actual prosecution. E.g., *Abbott Laboratories v. Gardner*, 387 U.S. 136 (1967).

As with mootness, plaintiffs alleging ongoing patterns of constitutional violations have sometimes been able to sue without proving that particular plaintiffs have been subject to the practices in question. In *Lankford v. Gelston*, 364 F.2d 197 (4th Cir. 1966), Judge Sobeloff held that African-American families in Baltimore were entitled to injunctive relief against the police department to prevent future violations of the families' privacy rights. The district court had refused relief, because it was satisfied that new police procedures were a good-faith effort to deal with the pattern of unjustified searches of blacks' homes. Judge Soboleff disagreed, based upon the "vast demonstration of disregard of private rights" and the persistence of "[a] sense of impending crisis in police-community relations."

The Supreme Court, however, did not follow this reasoning in refusing to hear (on ripeness grounds) challenges of ongoing discriminatory law enforcement in *O'Shea v. Littleton*, 414 U.S. 488 (1974). The Court refused to "conclude that the case or controversy requirement is satisfied by general assertions or inferences that in the course of their activities [plaintiffs] will be prosecuted for violating valid criminal laws." Sharply dissenting, Justice Douglas (joined by Justices Brennan and Marshall) said that the complaint alleged "a more pervasive scheme for suppression of Blacks and their civil rights than I have ever seen," in which a judge and magistrate were alleged to have consistently denied African Americans fair bonds, jury fees, and sentences. See also *Los Angeles v. Lyons*, 461 U.S. 95 (1983) (refusing to adjudicate the discriminatory use of chokeholds by Los Angeles police, based upon plaintiff's lack of standing to obtain an injunction against the practice, even though it had been applied to his own neck); *Rizzo v. Goode*, 423 U.S. 362 (1976) (refusing to adjudicate discriminatory police practices in Philadelphia for similar reasons). On the other hand, in *Duke Power Co. v. Carolina Environmental Study Group, Inc.*, 438 U.S. 59 (1978), the Court heard a case challenging the constitutionality of a federally mandated ceiling on liability for nuclear disasters, notwithstanding the absence of such a disaster and its future unlikelihood.

The right-to-privacy cases in Chapter 5, § 4, have had a particularly roller-coaster history with ripeness doctrine. In *Poe v. Ullman*, Justice Frankfurter's opinion for the Court dismissed challenges to Connecticut's prohibition against the use of contraceptives because none of the plaintiffs had been prosecuted and, given the state's general lack of interest in enforcing the statute, seemed unlikely to be prosecuted. In *Griswold v. Connecticut*, plaintiffs (according to Tom Emerson, who argued the case) orchestrated a cooked-up arrest and were able to escape ripeness problems. In *Bowers v. Hardwick*, the Court upheld Georgia's sodomy law even though charges against plaintiff had been dropped, and there was little if any indication that he would even be prosecuted in the future.

3. *Standing.* According to the doctrines associated with standing, a plaintiff must have "a personal stake in the outcome of a controversy as to assure that concrete adverseness which sharpens the presentation of issues upon which the court so largely depends for illumination of difficult constitutional questions." *Baker v. Carr*. In a sense, this is the most basic requirement: Roughly speaking, a case isn't ripe if the plaintiff does not yet have a sufficiently clear personal stake, and it's moot if the plaintiff no longer has a personal stake.

The traditional law of standing required the plaintiff to show that she had suffered a legal injury, typically to a right protected under common law. More recently, the Supreme Court has defined the law of standing more realistically to require that the plaintiff in a case or controversy be someone who has suffered only an "injury in fact," an actual injury to her interests, *and* who is within the "zone of interests" meant to be protected by constitutional or statutory provisions. *Association of Data Processing Service Organizations v. Camp*, 397 U.S. 150 (1970). The Supreme Court considers the injury in fact component of standing a constitutional requirement of Article III, but the zone of interests component only a prudential concern inspired by Article III. *Valley Forge Christian College, supra.* Therefore, the key concept is what constitutes an injury in fact.

The Supreme Court has broken injury in fact into three inquiries: (1) whether plaintiff has suffered an actual injury, (2) whether plaintiff's injury is the result of defendant's conduct, and (3) whether plaintiff's injury can be redressed by the judicial relief she requests. *Los Angeles v. Lyons*, 461 U.S. 95 (1983). If a showing of any of these three elements is lacking, the court will dismiss the suit for lack of constitutional standing.

The requirement of actual injury to plaintiff is often pretty easy to satisfy, since the Court will recognize not only economic injury, but also aesthetic, environmental, and certain emotional injuries as well. For example, in *Duke Power, supra*, the Court found standing for an environmental group challenging the liability limits for a local nuclear reactor. The Court found the possibility of environmental and thermal pollution to be an actual injury, as well as plaintiffs' "generalized concern about exposure to radiation and the apprehension flowing from the uncertainty about the health and genetic consequences of even small emissions like those concededly emitted by nuclear power plants." See also *United States v. SCRAP*, 412 U.S. 669 (1973).

Once a plaintiff has satisfactorily demonstrated that she suffered an injury in fact, she must prove a causal link between her injury and the defendant's conduct. In constitutional cases, the plaintiff must show that her injury is "fairly traceable" to a specific government action. In *Warth v. Seldin*, 422 U.S. 490 (1975), the Court denied standing to low-income and minority individuals who claimed to have been denied housing opportunities because of a town's exclusionary zoning ordinance. The Court held that the plaintiffs had not properly asserted that "absent [the town's] restrictive zone practices, there [was] a substantial probability that they would have been able to purchase and lease in Penfield," since they were unable to show that any developer who would build housing suitable to their needs and resources was being excluded by the zoning law. But a black plaintiff, who wished to purchase specific housing that a developer wished to build but could not under existing zoning laws, was held to have standing to challenge the law as racially discriminatory. *Village of Arlington Heights v. Metropolitan Housing Development*, 429 U.S. 252 (1977).

The third element required to demonstrate a personal stake in litigation is the ability of the court to correct the perceived wrong. To have standing, litigants must demonstrate that there is a "substantial likelihood" that they will benefit from the requested relief. In *Warth*, the Court questioned whether judicial redress was possible, holding that the plaintiffs had failed to show that "if the court affords the relief requested, the asserted liability of petitioners will be removed." Similarly, in *Simon v. Eastern Kentucky Welfare Rights Organization*, 426 U.S. 26 (1976), the Court denied standing to indigents and allied organizations challenging an IRS policy giving tax exemptions to nonprofit hospitals which limited access of poor people to their emergency room services. The Court found no standing because it would only be "speculative" whether the desired relief would actually change the hospitals' emergency room services to the poor.

Consider the following cases applying these justiciability doctrines, and how the doctrines work differently in (1) structural constitutional cases raising separation-of-powers issues (*Raines v. Byrd*), (2) *Brown*-type cases seeking to enforce civil rights guarantees (*Allen v. Wright*), and (3) private enforcement of statutory obligations (*Lujan v. Defenders of Wildlife*). Consider also whether Congress can overcome case or controversy requirements by authorizing lawsuits that otherwise would be nonjusticiable.

––––––

Raines v. Byrd, 521 U.S. 811 (1997), involved a challenge to federal legislation authorizing a "line item veto." Rather than having to veto an entire appropriations or tax bill, the President was authorized to "cancel" certain provisions within the bill. The President could do so by sending a "special message" to Congress, which could override his action only by passing a new "disapproval bill" through the normal Article I procedures. The suit was brought by legislators who had voted against the bill and argued that it violated the Presentment Clause of Article I, § 7. The Supreme Court ordered the complaint dismissed for lack of standing.

The majority opinion was by **Chief Justice Rehnquist.** He began by stressing that the existence of a case or controversy is a "bedrock requirement," one element of which is standing. The Court has "always insisted on strict compliance with this jurisdictional standing requirement," and the "standing inquiry has been especially rigorous when reaching the merits of the dispute would force us to decide whether an action taken by one of the other two branches of the Federal Government was unconstitutional." Stressing the "overriding and time-honored concern about keeping the Judiciary's power within its proper constitutional sphere," he called for a careful inquiry to determine whether the plaintiffs' claimed injury is "personal, particularized, concrete, and otherwise judicially cognizable."

The Chief Justice distinguished *Coleman v. Miller*, 307 U.S. 433 (1939), in which a narrow majority had granted state legislators standing. In *Coleman*, half of the members of the Kansas Senate had voted not to ratify the proposed Child Labor Amendment, but the lieutenant governor cast the deciding vote in favor of the amendment. Thus, Rehnquist said, *Coleman* "stands (at most) for the proposition that legislators whose votes would have been sufficient to defeat (or enact) a specific legislative act have standing to sue if that legislative action goes into effect (or does not go into effect), on the ground that their votes have been completely nullified." Hence, to "uphold standing here would require a drastic extension of *Coleman*. We are unwilling to take that step." In closing, the Court noted that the plaintiffs alleged no injury to themselves as individuals and "the institutional injury they allege is wholly abstract and widely dispersed." The Court "attach[ed] some importance to the fact" that the plaintiffs did not have formal authority to represent either branch of Congress. It also noted, without specifying whether these facts were decisive, that "our conclusion neither deprives Members of Congress of an adequate remedy (since they may repeal the Act or exempt appropriations bills from its reach), nor forecloses the Act from constitutional challenge (by someone who suffers judicially cognizable injury as a result of the Act)."

Concurring, **Justice Souter** (joined by **Justice Ginsburg**) found the standing issue "fairly debatable" in its own right. Hence, "it behooves us to resolve the question under more general separation-of-powers principles underlying our standing requirements." Souter remarked that a dispute "involving only officials, and the official interests of those, who serve in the branches of the National Government" is far removed "from the model of the traditional common-law cause of action at the conceptual core of the case-or-controversy requirement." In essence, the case presented "an interbranch controversy about calibrating the legislative and executive powers, as well as an intrabranch dispute between segments of Congress itself." "Intervention in such a controversy" would embroil "the federal courts in a power contest nearly at the height of its political tension."

Justices Stevens and **Breyer** dissented. Justice Breyer argued that the statute deprived legislators of the right to vote "for or against the truncated measure that survives the exercise of the President's cancellation authority." Because the right to cast such a vote is guaranteed by Article I, legislators should have standing to protest the violation of that right. Justice Breyer phrased the issue as whether the case "is so different in form from those 'matters that were the traditional concern of the courts at Westminster' that it falls outside the scope of Article III's judicial power." However, he said, he did not find *Coleman* distinguishable.

NOTES ON *RAINES v. BYRD*

1. *The Scope of the Holding.* Does *Raines* completely eliminate legislative standing? Consider the following scenarios:

(a) A state legislator claims that his state has cast the decisive vote necessary to require Congress to call a constitutional convention. He sues for an order requiring Congress to call such a convention.

(b) The President unilaterally sends troops into combat in Albania. A member of Congress (or the Congress as an institution) files suit, claiming that the President has infringed its exclusive power to declare war.

(c) The House of Representatives adopts a rule requiring a supermajority for tax increases. A proposed increase receives a majority, but not the required supermajority, and a proponent seeks a judicial declaration that the bill has passed the House.

2. *The Purposes of Standing Doctrine.* Note that the constitutionality of the line-item veto remains a justiciable controversy, and the majority specifically notes that a private party affected by the resulting loss in funds has standing. After *Raines*, the President exercised his authority under the statute frequently, creating considerable uncertainty as to the legal status of the affected appropria-

tion and tax provisions. The Court finally did hold the line-item veto unconstitutional in *Clinton v. City of New York* (Chapter 8, § 2A). Was anything gained by the delay? (Note that in some legal systems, constitutional issues can be decided only at the behest of legislators or other officials, rather than in suits by private parties.)

3. *Are Inter-Governmental Disputes Different?* Consider an analogous situation in the private sector. Suppose that a federal statute requires that bank documents involving large amounts of money be countersigned by the president of the bank. (Compare this with the constitutional requirements requiring certain other documents to be signed or vetoed by the President of the United States). Consider three possible litigation scenarios:

(a) The Board of Directors of the First Bank of Frostbite Falls passes a resolution authorizing these documents to be signed by a vice-president instead. May the president of the bank bring suit in federal court to enjoin enforcement of the resolution?

(b) Suppose instead that a bank board claims that the statute is unconstitutional, and brings a class action to enjoin its enforcement. Is there standing?

(c) Suppose that a shareholder in the bank brings suit against the Secretary of the Treasury, claiming that the Secretary is failing to enforce the statute, that violations are widespread, and that the result is to increase the risk of bank funds being misapplied.

Do any of these scenarios satisfy the *Raines* Court's call for a "personal, particularized, concrete, and otherwise judicially cognizable" injury? Which scenario is most analogous to *Raines*?

ALLEN v. WRIGHT
468 U.S. 737, 104 S.Ct. 3315, 82 L.Ed.2d 556 (1984)

JUSTICE O'CONNOR delivered the opinion of the Court.

[The federal Internal Revenue Code provides that certain "charitable institutions" are tax-exempt, and that contributions to those institutions are tax-deductible. In *Bob Jones University v. United States*, 461 U.S. 574 (1983), the Court held that racially discriminatory private schools do not qualify for such "charitable" status. In this action, a class of African-American parents alleged that the Internal Revenue Service was not complying with its obligations to investigate potentially discriminatory private schools and to deny tax-exempt status to those found to discriminate. The parents did not allege that their children had applied and been denied admission to the schools. Rather, they contended that the IRS had effectively encouraged segregation — not only in private schools, but also in public ones (because the existence of the private schools, fostered by tax-exempt status, drained off white students who would otherwise be available to effect desegregation of the public schools). The court of appeals agreed and ordered the IRS to make a better enforcement effort.]

[T]he "case or controversy" requirement defines with respect to the Judicial Branch the idea of separation of powers on which the Federal government is founded. The several doctrines that have grown up to elaborate that requirement are "founded in concern about the proper — and properly limited — role of the courts in a democratic society." *Warth*.

> All of the doctrines that cluster about Article III — not only standing but mootness, ripeness, political question, and the like — relate in part, and in different though overlapping ways, to an idea, which is more than an intuition but less than a rigorous and explicit theory, about the constitutional and prudential limits to the powers of an unelected, unrepresentative judiciary in our kind of government. *Vander Jagt v. O'Neill*, 699 F.2d 1166, 1178-1179 (CADC 1983) (Bork, J., concurring).

The case-or-controversy doctrines state fundamental limits on federal judicial power in our system of government.

The Article III doctrine that requires a litigant to have "standing" to invoke the power of a federal court is perhaps the most important of these doctrines. "In essence the question of standing is whether the litigant is entitled to have the court decide the merits of the dispute or of particular issues." Standing doctrine embraces several judicially self-imposed limits on the exercise of federal jurisdiction, such as the general prohibition on a litigant's raising another person's legal rights, the rule barring adjudication of generalized grievances more appropriately addressed in the representative branches, and the requirement that a plaintiff's complaint fall within the zone of interests protected by the law invoked. The requirement of standing, however, has a core component derived directly from the Constitution. A plaintiff must allege personal injury fairly traceable to the defendant's allegedly unlawful conduct and likely to be redressed by the requested relief.

Like the prudential component, the constitutional component of standing doctrine incorporates concepts concededly not susceptible of precise definition. The injury alleged must be, for example, "distinct and palpable," and not "abstract" or "conjectural" or "hypothetical." The injury must be "fairly" traceable to the challenged action, and relief from the injury must be "likely" to follow from a favorable decision. These terms cannot be defined so as to make application of the constitutional standing requirement a mechanical exercise. * * *

Respondents allege two injuries in their complaint to support their standing to bring this lawsuit. First, they say that they are harmed directly by the mere fact of Government financial aid to discriminatory private schools. Second, they say that the federal tax exemptions to racially discriminatory private schools in their communities impair their ability to have their public schools desegregated. * * *

Respondents' first claim of injury can be interpreted in two ways. It might be a claim simply to have the Government avoid the violation of law alleged in respondents' complaint. Alternatively, it might be a claim of stigmatic injury, or denigration, suffered by all members of a racial group when the Government discriminates on the basis of race. Under neither interpretation is this claim of injury judicially cognizable.

This Court has repeatedly held that an asserted right to have the Government act in accordance with law is not sufficient, standing alone, to confer jurisdiction on a federal court. In *Schlesinger v. Reservists Committee to Stop the War*,

418 U.S. 208 (1974), for example, the Court rejected a claim of citizen standing to challenge Armed Forces Reserve commissions held by Members of Congress as violating the Incompatibility Clause of Article I, § 6, of the Constitution. As citizens, the Court held, plaintiffs alleged nothing but "the abstract injury in nonobservance of the Constitution . . . ." More recently, in *Valley Forge*, we rejected a claim of standing to challenge a Government conveyance of property to a religious institution. Insofar as the plaintiffs relied simply on "their shared individuated right" to a government that made no law respecting an establishment of religion, we held that plaintiffs had not alleged a judicially cognizable injury. "[A]ssertion of a right to a particular kind of Government conduct, which the Government has violated by acting differently, cannot alone satisfy the requirements of Art. III without draining those requirements of meaning." Respondents here have no standing to complain simply that their Government is violating the law.

Neither do they have standing to litigate their claim based on the stigmatizing injury often caused by racial discrimination. There can be no doubt that this sort of noneconomic injury is one of the most serious consequences of discriminatory government action and is sufficient in some circumstances to support standing. Our cases make clear, however, that such injury accords a basis for standing only to "those persons who are personally denied equal treatment" by the challenged discriminatory conduct. * * *

The consequences of recognizing respondents' standing on the basis of their first claim of injury illustrate why our cases plainly hold that such injury is not judicially cognizable. If the abstract stigmatic injury were cognizable, standing would extend nationwide to all members of the particular racial groups against which the Government was alleged to be discriminating by its grant of a tax exemption to a racially discriminatory school, regardless of the location of that school. All such persons could claim the same sort of abstract stigmatic injury respondents assert in their first claim of injury. A black person in Hawaii could challenge the grant of a tax exemption to a racially discriminatory school in Maine. Recognition of standing in such circumstances would transform the federal courts into "no more than a vehicle for the vindication of the value interests of concerned bystanders." Constitutional limits on the role of the federal courts preclude such a transformation.

It is in their complaint's second claim of injury that respondents allege harm to a concrete, personal interest that can support standing in some circumstances. The injury they identify — their children's diminished ability to receive an education in a racially integrated school — is, beyond any doubt, not only judicially cognizable but * * * one of the most serious injuries recognized in our legal system. Despite the constitutional importance of curing the injury alleged by respondents, however, the federal judiciary may not redress it unless standing requirements are met. In this case, respondents' second claim of injury cannot support standing because the injury alleged is not fairly traceable to the Government conduct respondents challenge as unlawful.

The illegal conduct challenged by respondents is the IRS's grant of tax exemptions to some racially discriminatory schools. The line of causation between that conduct and desegregation of respondents' schools is attenuated at best. From the perspective of the IRS, the injury to respondents is highly indirect and "results from the independent action of some third party not before the court." "[T]he indirectness of the injury . . . may make it substantially more difficult to meet the minimum requirement of Art. III . . . ."

The diminished ability of respondents' children to receive a desegregated education would be fairly traceable to unlawful IRS grants of tax exemptions only if there were enough racially discriminatory private schools receiving tax exemptions in respondents' communities for withdrawal of those exemptions to make an appreciable difference in public school integration. Respondents have made no such allegation. It is, first, uncertain how many racially discriminatory private schools are in fact receiving tax exemptions. Moreover, it is entirely speculative * * * whether withdrawal of a tax exemption from any particular school would lead the school to change its policies. It is just as speculative whether any given parent of a child attending such a private school would decide to transfer the child to public school as a result of any changes in educational or financial policy made by the private school once it was threatened with loss of tax-exempt status. It is also pure speculation whether, in a particular community, a large enough number of the numerous relevant school officials and parents would reach decisions that collectively would have a significant impact on the racial composition of the public schools. * * *

The idea of separation of powers that underlies standing doctrine explains why our cases preclude the conclusion that respondents' alleged injury "fairly can be traced to the challenged action" of the IRS. That conclusion would pave the way generally for suits challenging, not specifically identifiable Government violations of the law, but the particular programs agencies establish to carry out their legal obligations. Such suits, even when premised on allegations of several instances of violations of law, are rarely if ever appropriate for federal-court adjudication.

> Carried to its logical end, [respondents'] approach would have the federal courts as virtually continuing monitors of the wisdom and soundness of Executive action; such a role is appropriate for the Congress acting through its committees and the "power of the purse"; it is not the role of the judiciary, absent actual present or immediately threatened injury resulting from unlawful governmental action.

The same concern for the proper role of the federal courts is reflected in cases [where] plaintiffs sought injunctive relief directed at certain systemwide law enforcement practices. The Court held in each case that, absent an allegation of a specific threat of being subject to the challenged practices, plaintiffs had no standing to ask for an injunction. Animating this Court's holdings was the principle that "[a] federal court . . . is not the proper forum to press" general complaints about the way in which government goes about its business.

Case-or-controversy considerations, the Court observed in *O'Shea v. Littleton*, 414 U.S. 488, 499 (1974), "obviously shade into those determining whether the complaint states a sound basis for equitable relief." The latter set of considerations should therefore inform our judgment about whether respondents have standing. Most relevant to this case is the principle articulated in *Rizzo v. Goode*, 423 U.S. 362, 378-379 (1976):

> When a plaintiff seeks to enjoin the activity of a government agency, even within a unitary court system, his case must contend with "the well-established rule that the Government has traditionally been granted the widest latitude in the 'dispatch of its own internal affairs.' "

When transported into the Art. III context, that principle, grounded as it is in the idea of separation of powers, counsels against recognizing standing in a case brought, not to enforce specific legal obligations whose violation works a direct harm, but to seek a restructuring of the apparatus established by the Executive Branch to fulfill its legal duties. The Constitution, after all, assigns to the Executive Branch, and not to the Judicial Branch, the duty to "take Care that the Laws be faithfully executed." We could not recognize respondents' standing in this case without running afoul of that structural principle.

JUSTICE MARSHALL took no part in the decisions of these cases.

JUSTICE BRENNAN, dissenting.

In these cases, the respondents have alleged at least one type of injury that satisfies the constitutional requirement of "distinct and palpable injury." In particular, they claim that the IRS's grant of tax-exempt status to racially discriminatory private schools directly injures their children's opportunity and ability to receive a desegregated education. * * *

Fully explicating the injury alleged helps to explain why it is fairly traceable to the governmental conduct challenged by the respondents. As the respondents specifically allege in their complaint:

> Defendants have fostered and encouraged the development, operation and expansion of many of these racially segregated private schools by recognizing them as "charitable" organizations and exempt from federal income taxation * * *. Once the schools are classified as tax-exempt . . ., contributions made to them are deductible from gross income on individual and corporate income tax returns. . . . Moreover, [the] organizations . . . are also exempt from federal social security taxes . . . and from federal unemployment taxes . . . . The resulting exemptions and deductions provide tangible financial aid and other benefits which support the operation of racially segregated private schools. In particular, the resulting deductions facilitate the raising of funds to organize new schools and expand existing schools in order to accommodate white students avoiding attendance in desegregating public school districts. Additionally, the existence of a federal tax exemption amounts to a federal stamp of approval which facilitates fund raising on behalf of racially segregated private schools. Finally, by supporting the development, operation and expansion of institutions providing racially segregated educational opportunities for white children avoiding attendance in desegregating public schools, defendants are thereby interfering with the efforts of courts, HEW and local school authorities to desegregate public school districts which have been operating racially dual school systems.

Viewed in light of the injuries they claim, the respondents have alleged a direct causal relationship between the Government action they challenge and the injury they suffer: their inability to receive an education in a racially integrated school is directly and adversely affected by the tax-exempt status granted by the IRS to racially discriminatory schools in their respective school districts. Common sense alone would recognize that the elimination of tax-exempt status for racially discriminatory private schools would serve to lessen the impact that those institutions have in defeating efforts to desegregate the public schools. * * *

More than one commentator has noted that the causation component of the court's standing inquiry is no more than a poor disguise for the Court's view of the merits of the underlying claim. The Court today does nothing to avoid that criticism. * * *

JUSTICE STEVENS, with whom JUSTICE BLACKMUN joins, dissenting.

We have held that when a subsidy makes a given activity more or less expensive, injury can be fairly traced to the subsidy for purposes of standing analysis because of the resulting increase or decrease in the ability to engage in the activity. Indeed, we have employed exactly this causation analysis in the same context at issue here — subsidies given private schools that practice racial discrimination. Thus, in *Gilmore v. City of Montgomery*, 417 U.S. 556 (1974), we easily recognized the causal connection between official policies that enhanced the attractiveness of segregated schools and the failure to bring about or maintain a desegregated public school system. Similarly, in *Norwood v. Harrison*, 413 U.S. 455 (1973), we concluded that the provision of textbooks to discriminatory private schools "has a significant tendency to facilitate, reinforce, and support private discrimination." * * *

This causation analysis is nothing more than a restatement of elementary economics: when something becomes more expensive, less of it will be purchased. Sections [of the Internal Revenue Code defining "charitable status"] are premised on that recognition. If racially discriminatory private schools lose the "cash grants" that flow from the operation of the statutes, the education they provide will become more expensive and hence less of their services will be purchased. Conversely, maintenance of these tax benefits makes an education in segregated private schools relatively more attractive, by decreasing its cost. Accordingly, without tax-exempt status, private schools will either not be competitive in terms of cost, or have to change their admissions policies, hence reducing their competitiveness for parents seeking "a racially segregated alternative" to public schools, which is what respondents have alleged many white parents in desegregating school districts seek. In either event the process of desegregation will be advanced in the same way that it was advanced in *Gilmore* and *Norwood* — the withdrawal of the subsidy for segregated schools means the incentive structure facing white parents who seek such schools for their children will be altered. Thus, the laws of economics, not to mention the laws of Congress embodied in [the Internal Revenue Code], compel the conclusion that the injury respondents have alleged — the increased segregation of their children's schools because of the ready availability of private schools that admit whites only — will be redressed if these schools' operations are inhibited through the denial of preferential tax treatment.

———

Northeastern Florida Chapter of the Associated General Contractors of America v. Jacksonville, 508 U.S. 656 (1993). In 1984, Jacksonville, Florida, "enacted an ordinance entitled 'Minority Business Enterprise Participation,' which required that 10% of the amount spent on city contracts be set aside each fiscal year for so-called 'Minority Business Enterprises' (MBE's). An MBE was defined as a business whose ownership was at least 51% 'minority' or female, and a 'minority' was in turn defined as a person who is or considers himself to be black, Spanish-speaking, Oriental, Indian, Eskimo, Aleut, or handicapped. Once projects were earmarked for MBE bidding by the city's chief purchasing officer, they were 'deemed reserved for minority business enterprises only.' "

The ordinance was challenged by an association of individuals and firms in the construction industry who did business in Jacksonville and did not qualify as MBE's under the city's ordinance. The Eleventh Circuit held that the association lacked standing, because it "has not demonstrated that, but for the program, any [association] member would have bid successfully for any of these contracts." The Supreme Court reversed. **Justice Thomas**'s opinion for the Court stated that the Court had frequently allowed standing for persons challenging discrimination, as in *Bakke* (Chapter 3, § 3A), where a twice-rejected white male applicant claimed that a medical school's admissions program, which reserved 16 of the 100 places in the entering class for minority applicants, was inconsistent with equal protection guarantees. See also *Turner v. Fouche*, 396 U.S. 346 (1970) (plaintiff had standing to challenge a Georgia law limiting school-board membership to property owners even though there was no allegation that plaintiff would have been appointed "but for" the property requirement); *Clements v. Fashing*, 457 U.S. 957 (1982) (allowing lawsuit against "automatic resignation" provision of the Texas Constitution, which requires the immediate resignation of some state officeholders upon their announcement of a candidacy for another office, and finding standing because plaintiffs had alleged that they would have announced their candidacy were it not for the consequences of doing so).

"Singly and collectively, these cases stand for the following proposition: When the government erects a barrier that makes it more difficult for members of one group to obtain a benefit than it is for members of another group, a member of the former group seeking to challenge the barrier need not allege that he would have obtained the benefit but for the barrier in order to establish standing. The 'injury in fact' in an equal protection case of this variety is the denial of equal treatment resulting from the imposition of the barrier, not the ultimate inability to obtain the benefit. And in the context of a challenge to a set-aside program, the 'injury in fact' is the inability to compete on an equal footing in the bidding process, not the loss of a contract."

Justice O'Connor, joined by **Justice Blackmun**, dissented on the ground that the case had been rendered moot when Jacksonville repealed its MBE ordinance and replaced it with a more narrowly tailored one, protecting only women and African Americans, establishing only "goals" and not requiring "quotas," and providing other methods to meet such goals. Justice O'Connor found the new ordinance tailored to meet the constitutional requirements of *Croson* (Chapter 3, § 3B), which she authored. *Query*: Why wasn't the case moot? Compare *City of Mesquite v. Aladdin's Castle*, 455 U.S. 283 (1982) (repeal of challenged statute does not deprive court of jurisdiction, especially if court suspects that was the goal), with *Diffenderfer v. Central Baptist Church* *of Miami*, 404 U.S. 412 (1972) (repeal of statute and replacement with statute responding to constitutional difficulties renders case moot).

NOTES ON *ALLEN* AND *NORTHEASTERN FLORIDA CHAPTER*

1. *Standing and Separation of Powers.* The traditional policy underlying standing doctrine is the desire to assure the Court a lively adversarial controversy. The controversy in *Allen* seems to be as lively and adversarial as they come, so why should the Court deny the parents standing? Of course, Justice O'Connor's opinion emphasizes that the "single basic idea" behind constitutional standing is separation of powers.[f] But if there is a separation-of-powers problem, such as judicial intrusion into executive discretionary programs, aren't there enough other protections? The Court can declare a controversy a "nonjusticiable" political question in such cases. Or it may take the case and decline to enter relief that would be an excessive intrusion.

Even if separation of powers is the central idea in standing cases, why shouldn't *Allen* be appropriate for federal adjudication? Justice O'Connor says that the Court will not hear these sorts of cases, where the alleged injury cannot fairly be traced to defendant's activity, lest the courts become "continuing monitors of the wisdom and soundness of Executive action." Does it follow that allowing plaintiffs to sue here will open the floodgates so that courts will monitor executive actions? In any event, why shouldn't they? If, as the parents alleged, the IRS was violating its statutory mandate to deny tax exemptions to segregating institutions, perhaps the courts should be monitoring the Executive, just as they had been doing to local school boards. Why should the Executive be "above the law"? Was the likelihood that the plaintiffs suffered a tangible injury greater in *Northeastern Florida Chapter* than in *Allen*?

2. *A Contrasting State Court Approach to Standing.* Contrast the following two standing cases. In *Gilmore v. Utah*, 429 U.S. 1012 (1976) (*per curiam*), the Supreme Court rejected the petition of Bessie Gilmore to challenge the legality of the upcoming execution of her son, Gary. Chief Justice Burger, concurring, admonished her for not being the proper plaintiff to challenge the death penalty; Gary Gilmore, the person sentenced to die under the questionable Utah death penalty statute, had waived his rights to object and, indeed, rebuffed efforts by his mother and others to delay his execution. After an evidentiary hearing, the Utah courts had concluded that Gilmore was legally competent to make this decision. The Court's action is troubling. If her son were killed, would she not be injured? How can the Court deny that? Compare *Singleton v. Wulff*, 428 U.S. 106 (1976). Arguably, even third parties, such as citizens of Utah, should be able to sue to invalidate an unconstitutional death statute. Are they not demeaned if their government executes someone unlawfully?

A different approach was taken by the Pennsylvania Supreme Court in *Commonwealth v. McKenna*, 476 Pa. 428, 383 A.2d 174 (1978). McKenna,

---

f. If you read the Court's precedents in this area, this announcement might come as quite a surprise. See Gene Nichol, *Abusing Standing: A Comment on* Allen v. Wright, 133 U. Pa. L. Rev. 635, 648 (1984).

sentenced to death, had raised various procedural challenges to his conviction but had not objected to his death sentence (assuming the conviction stood). *Amici* civil libertarians argued that the state's death penalty statute was unconstitutional under the U.S. Supreme Court's precedents. The Pennsylvania Court heard the third-party challenges, based upon its policy to "consider the interests of society as a whole in seeing to it that justice is done, regardless of what might otherwise be normal procedure." Does the U.S. Constitution permit Pennsylvania to do this? Does the Pennsylvania decision mean that in Pennsylvania any member of the public can appeal any criminal conviction on constitutional grounds, if the defendant fails to do so?

3. *Congressional Power.* Could Congress grant taxpayers standing to sue? Or consider two other arenas for congressional action. First, Congress might allow individuals to file a complaint with the IRS to protest giving tax exempt status to a segregated private school. If such a law was passed, would an IRS denial of such a claim constitute violation of a procedural right under *Northeastern Florida Contractors*? Second, suppose Congress made findings that improper tax exemptions for segregated private schools actually do harm minority students in public schools and that the same law created a private cause of action for these minority students. Would courts have Article III jurisdiction over such litigation? Consider your answers again after you have completed the standing materials.

NOTE ON TAXPAYER STANDING

The plaintiffs in *Allen* did not sue as taxpayers seeking full enforcement of federal tax law, or objecting to the way their tax dollars are being used. The problem with asserting federal taxpayer standing is the difficulty in proving a causal relationship between general governmental tax policies and specific injuries to individuals. Once collected, revenues become aggregated, losing their individual identity and connection to specific taxpayers. In *Frothingham v. Mellon*, 262 U.S. 447 (1923), the Court declined to hear a challenge to the Federal Maternity Act, which conditioned appropriations to states on compliance with provisions of the Act aimed at reducing maternal and infant mortality. The Court denied standing, stating: "The party who invokes the [judicial] power must be able to show that he has sustained or is immediately in danger of sustaining some direct injury as a result of the statute's enforcement, and not merely that he suffers in some indefinite way in common with people generally."

In *Flast v. Cohen*, 392 U.S. 83 (1968), on the other hand, the Court held that federal taxpayer standing could be recognized in those limited circumstances where litigants (1) challenge a specific exercise of the government's taxing or spending power, which (2) they contend is a violation of the constitutional limitations on the taxing or spending power. It is not enough to challenge appropriations incidental to federal regulations. *Flast* stands as an exception to the general rule which disfavors taxpayer standing, and it probably applies only to Establishment Clause violations (*Flast* dealt with a challenge to aid to religious schools).

The *Flast* decision was severely limited in *Valley Forge Christian College v. Americans United*, 454 U.S. 464 (1982). There, taxpayers challenged an HEW grant of surplus funds and a land transfer to a parochial college as violating the Establishment Clause. The Court refused standing, holding that the challenge was to an administrative agency's actions, not congressional legislation as in *Flast*. The Court denied standing to challenge the land transfer since it was made pursuant to the Property Clause of Article IV, not under the Article I spending power.

Hein v. Freedom From Religion Foundation, 127 S.Ct. 2553 (2007), furthered limited the scope of *Flast*. An organization that was opposed to government endorsement of religion, and three of its members, brought an Establishment Clause challenge against a federal agency's use of federal money to fund conferences to promote President George W. Bush's "faith-based initiatives." A plurality of the Court (Justice Alito, joined by Chief Justice Roberts and Justice Kennedy) concluded that *Flast* was inapplicable because the plaintiffs did not challenge any specific congressional action or appropriation. Thus, standing did not exist because the expenditures at issue were not made pursuant to any Act of Congress, but under general appropriations to the Executive Branch to fund day-to-day activities. Justice Scalia, joined by Justice Thomas, concurred in the judgment on the ground that *Flast* should be overruled. Justice Souter's dissent stressed that *Flast* had "deep historical roots going back to the ideal of religious liberty in James Madison's Memorial and Remonstrance Against Religious Assessments, that the government in a free society may not 'force a citizen to contribute three pence only of his property for the support of any one establishment' of religion."

Arguing in the alternative, the plaintiffs in *Valley Forge* claimed that even if they lacked taxpayer standing, they had standing as citizens of the United States to challenge the constitutionality of HEW policies. The Court has traditionally taken a dim view of citizen standing, and continued its trend in denying citizen standing in *Valley Forge*. A citizen *qua* citizen is held to have only a generalized grievance which cannot be differentiated from that of other citizens.

In *United States v. Richardson*, 418 U.S. 166 (1974), the Court held citizens could not challenge a statute keeping CIA expenditures secret from the public. The plaintiffs' contention that citizens need such information to enable them to make informed decisions as voters was held to be merely a "generalized grievance" common to all members of the public, not a particularized injury; such grievances were better handled through the political process. Concurring, Justice Powell expressed an "antipathy to efforts to convert the Judiciary into an open forum for the resolution of political or ideological disputes about the performance of government." He argued that the public's esteem for the countermajoritarian power of judicial review recognized in *Marbury* would be impaired if the Court used it too often as a roving tribunal of good government. Justice Powell's comments suggested that the Court's reluctance to grant citizen standing is more a prudential concern than one mandated by Article III.

NOTE ON THIRD-PARTY STANDING

Sometimes one party asserts standing on the basis of another party's legal injury. This is known as third-party standing or *jus tertii*. Generally, no one has the right to press another's claim. For example, in *Tileston v. Ullman*, 318 U.S. 44 (1943) (per curiam), the Court ruled that a doctor had no standing to press the liberty and privacy claims of his patients, who wished to have access to contraceptives that were illegal in Connecticut.

But exceptions have been recognized over the years. For instance, where it is difficult for the rightful plaintiff to assert her legal right, another plaintiff *with standing to sue in his own right* may also press her claim. Thus, the doctrine of *jus tertii* is not a rule of constitutional law required by Article III (because plaintiff has standing on her own), but is a judicially created prudential limitation — "a salutary 'rule of self-restraint' designed to minimize unwarranted intervention into controversies where the applicable constitutional questions are ill-defined and speculative." *Craig v. Boren* (Chapter 4, § 2B1). *Craig*, the case holding that equal protection was violated by a state law forbidding the sale of 3.2% beer to males under twenty-one years of age, but allowing its sale to females aged eighteen and older, is a good example. *Craig* allowed a beer seller to challenge the law: (1) the seller had standing in her own right because she suffered injury in fact flowing from the statute (her choice was either to obey the statute and forego beer sales to young males or to sell to them and risk sanctions and the loss of her beer license); and (2) the seller was ideally situated to assert the rights of the young males, for she had strong reasons to oppose the law, and compliance with the law would operate to violate the rights of third parties. In addition, see, e.g., *Singleton v. Wulff*, 428 U.S. 106 (1976) (physician may raise privacy rights of patients in challenging restrictive abortion law).

A striking issue of third-party standing was posed by *Bush v. Gore* (Chapter 5, § 3A), where a presidential candidate was allowed to litigate the equal protection rights of voters with "spoiled" ballots. The court did not even mention the standing issue. Did Bush have standing under *Craig v. Boren*? How is Bush's case different from *Tileston*?

Certain organizations may also press the claims of their members. Third-party standing has been granted in such cases where the organization's members have suffered an injury in fact sufficient to give them standing, but where the litigation is relevant to the entire organization. See, e.g., *Hunt v. Washington State Apple Advertising Commission*, 432 U.S. 333 (1977); *NAACP v. Alabama*, 357 U.S. 449 (1958).

Given the incoherence of standing doctrine and the anomalous policy consequences of it, some scholars have advocated its abolition or amelioration. E.g., Mark Tushnet, *The New Law of Standing: A Plea for Abandonment*, 62 Cornell L. Rev. 663 (1977). If not abandoned, could the law of standing be more narrowly formulated, as *McKenna* might suggest? Or perhaps politely ignored or excepted from, as the mootness and ripeness cases might suggest?

6. *The Issue of Congressional Authority over Standing.* Suppose Congress attempts to grant standing in a case that the Court would otherwise dismiss. Is such a statutory grant of authority ever relevant? Clearly, legislation may be a crucial part of the underlying claim that creates standing. For instance, if Congress had never created a local court system for the District of Columbia, Marbury would not have been able to claim any injury from the failure to issue him a commission for a nonexistent position. Thus, by creating new programs, Congress may in effect also extend the boundaries of standing by granting new legal rights. The more difficult problem is presented where the congressional action does not purport to create new private rights, but instead merely confers a "naked" grant of standing to a private party to challenge some public act. Presumably, Congress could not merely give the courts the authority to issue advisory opinions. But if the case arises in the context of a specific controversy, and if the plaintiffs have a sufficient connection with the controversy to provide an adversary presentation of the legal and factual issues, why shouldn't the Court be able to hear the case? If the concern is about the non-democratic nature of federal courts, that concern is addressed by the legislative authorization. But are there other constitutional policies at stake? Consider Justice Scalia's separation of powers analysis in the following case.

LUJAN v. DEFENDERS OF WILDLIFE
504 U.S. 555, 112 S.Ct. 2130, 119 L.Ed.2d 351 (1992)

JUSTICE SCALIA delivered the opinion of the Court with respect to Parts I, II, III-A, and IV, and an opinion with respect to Part III-B in which **THE CHIEF JUSTICE, JUSTICE WHITE,** and **JUSTICE THOMAS** join.

[The Endangered Species Act of 1973 (ESA) seeks to protect species of animals against threats to their continuing existence caused by humans. Endangered or threatened species are identified by a periodic list compiled by the Secretary of the Interior. Section 7(a)(2) of the Act then provides that each federal agency must ensure that "any action authorized, funded, or carried out by that agency * * * is not likely to jeopardize the continued existence of any endangered species or any threatened species or result in the destruction or adverse modification of the habitat of such species." The Secretary by regulation determined that § 7 is only applicable to species and habitats within the territorial borders of the United States or on the High Seas. Plaintiffs, organizations dedicated to wildlife conservation and other environmental causes, obtained an injunction requiring the Secretary to promulgate a revised regulation applying § 7 extraterritorially.]

II. While the Constitution of the United States divides all power conferred upon the Federal Government into "legislative Powers," Art. I, § 1, "[t]he executive Power," Art. II, § 1, and "[t]he judicial Power," Art. III, § 1, it does not attempt to define those terms. To be sure, it limits the jurisdiction of federal courts to "Cases" and "Controversies," but an executive inquiry can bear the name "case" (the Hoffa case) and a legislative dispute can bear the name "controversy" (the Smoot-Hawley controversy). Obviously, then, the Constitution's central mechanism of separation of powers depends largely upon common understanding of what activities are appropriate to legislatures, to executives, and to courts. In The Federalist No. 48, Madison expressed the view that "[i]t is not infrequently a question of real nicety in legislative bodies whether the operation of a particular measure will, or will not, extend beyond the legislative sphere," whereas "the executive power [is] restrained within a narrower compass and . . . more simple in its nature," and "the judiciary [is] described by landmarks still less uncertain." One of those landmarks, setting apart the "Cases" and "Controversies" that are of the justiciable sort referred to in Article III — "serv[ing] to identify those disputes which are appropriately resolved through the judicial process" — is the doctrine of standing. Though some of its elements express merely prudential considerations that are part of judicial self-government, the core component of standing is an essential and unchanging part of the case-or-controversy requirement of Article III.

Over the years, our cases have established that the irreducible constitutional minimum of standing contains three elements: First, the plaintiff must have suffered an "injury in fact" — an invasion of a legally-protected interest which is (a) concrete and particularized, and (b) "actual or imminent, not 'conjectural' or 'hypothetical.' " Second, there must be a causal connection between the injury and the conduct complained of — the injury has to be "fairly . . . trace[able] to the challenged action of the defendant, and not . . . th[e] result [of] the independent action of some third party not before the court." Third, it must be "likely," as opposed to merely "speculative," that the injury will be "redressed by a favorable decision." * * *

III. We think the Court of Appeals failed to apply the foregoing principles in denying the Secretary's motion for summary judgment. Respondents had not made the requisite demonstration of (at least) injury and redressability.

A. Respondents' claim to injury is that the lack of consultation with respect to certain funded activities abroad "increase[s] the rate of extinction of endangered and threatened species." * * * To survive the Secretary's summary judgment motion, respondents had to submit affidavits or other evidence showing, through specific facts, not only that listed species were in fact being threatened by funded activities abroad, but also that one or more of respondents' members would thereby be "directly" affected apart from their " 'special interest' in th[e] subject."

[The affidavits alleged that two members, Kelly and Skilbred, had visited two project areas in the past and intended to return in the future to observe endangered species.]

[The affidavits] plainly contain no facts * * * showing how damage to the species will produce "imminent" injury to Mss. Kelly and Skilbred. That the women "had visited" the areas of the projects before the projects commenced proves nothing. As we have said in a related context, " '[p]ast exposure to illegal conduct does not in itself show a present case or controversy regarding injunctive relief . . . if unaccompanied by any continuing, present adverse effects.' " And the affiants' profession of an "inten[t]" to return to the places they had visited before — where they will presumably, this time, be deprived of the opportunity to observe animals of the endangered species — is simply not enough. * * *

[Justice Scalia's opinion then identifies and rejects plaintiffs' "novel standing theories." Their "ecosystem nexus" theory proposed that any person who uses *any* part of a "contiguous ecosystem" adversely affected by a funded activity has standing even if the activity is located a great distance away. The Court rejected this theory as inconsistent with precedent holding that a plaintiff claiming injury from environmental damage must use the area affected by the challenged activity and not an area roughly "in the vicinity" of it. Plaintiffs' "animal nexus" theory asserted that anyone who has an interest in studying or seeing the endangered animals anywhere on the globe has standing; similar was their "vocational nexus" theory, under which anyone with a professional interest in such animals can sue.] This is beyond all reason. * * * It goes beyond the limit * * * and into pure speculation and fantasy, to say that anyone who observes or works with an endangered species, anywhere in the world, is appreciably harmed by a single project affecting some portion of that species with which he has no more specific connection.

B. The most obvious problem in the present case is redressability. Since the agencies funding the projects were not parties to the case, the District Court could accord relief only against the Secretary: He could be ordered to revise his regulation to require consultation for foreign projects. But this would not remedy respondents' alleged injury unless the funding agencies were bound by the Secretary's regulation, which is very much an open question. [Although the Secretary of Interior thought his regulation binding upon other federal agencies, the Solicitor General opined that it was not, and the other agencies agreed with the latter. Since these other agencies were not parties to the lawsuit, no relief could be entered against them.]

IV. The Court of Appeals found that respondents had standing for an additional reason: because they had suffered a "procedural injury." The so-called "citizen-suit" provision of the ESA provides, in pertinent part, that "any person may commence a civil suit on his own behalf (A) to enjoin any person, including the United States and any other governmental instrumentality or agency . . . who is alleged to be in violation of any provision of this chapter." The court held that, because § 7(a)(2) requires interagency consultation, the citizen-suit provision creates a "procedural righ[t]" to consultation in all "persons" — so that *anyone* can file suit in federal court to challenge the Secretary's (or presumably any other official's) failure to follow the assertedly correct consultative procedure, notwithstanding their inability to allege any discrete injury flowing from that failure. To understand the remarkable nature of this holding one must be clear about what it does *not* rest upon: This is not a case where plaintiffs are seeking to enforce a procedural requirement the disregard of which could impair a separate concrete interest of theirs (*e.g.*, the procedural requirement for a hearing prior to denial of their license application, or the procedural requirement for an environmental impact statement before a federal facility is constructed next door to them). Nor is it simply a case where concrete injury has been suffered by many persons, as in mass fraud or mass tort situations. Nor, finally, is it the unusual case in which Congress has created a concrete private interest in the outcome of a suit against a private party for the government's benefit, by providing a cash bounty for the victorious plaintiff. Rather, the court held that the injury-in-fact requirement had been satisfied by congressional conferral upon *all* persons of an abstract, self-contained, noninstrumental "right" to have the Executive observe the procedures required by law. We reject this view. * * *

* * * "The province of the court," as Chief Justice Marshall said in *Marbury v. Madison*, "is, solely, to decide on the rights of individuals." Vindicating the *public* interest (including the public interest in government observance of the Constitution and laws) is the function of Congress and the Chief Executive. The question presented here is whether the public interest in proper administration of the laws (specifically, in agencies' observance of a particular, statutorily prescribed procedure) can be converted into an individual right by a statute that denominates it as such, and that permits all citizens (or, for that matter, a subclass of citizens who suffer no distinctive concrete harm) to sue. If the concrete injury requirement has the separation-of-powers significance we have always said, the answer must be obvious: To permit Congress to convert the undifferentiated public interest in executive officers' compliance with the law into an "individual right" vindicable in the courts is to permit Congress to transfer from the President to the courts the Chief Executive's most important constitutional duty, to "take Care that the Laws be faithfully executed," Art. II, § 3. It would enable the courts, with the permission of Congress, "to assume a position of authority over the governmental acts of another and co-equal department," and to become " 'virtually continuing monitors of the wisdom and soundness of Executive action.' " We have always rejected that vision of our role * * * .

JUSTICE KENNEDY, with whom **JUSTICE SOUTER** joins, concurring in part and concurring in the judgment.

[I] join Part IV of the Court's opinion with the following observations. As government programs and policies become more complex and far-reaching, we must be sensitive to the articulation of new rights of action that do not have clear analogs in our common-law tradition. Modern litigation has progressed far from the paradigm of Marbury suing Madison to get his commission, or Ogden seeking an injunction to halt Gibbons' steamboat operations. *Gibbons v. Ogden*, 9 Wheat. 1 (1824). In my view, Congress has the power to define injuries and articulate chains of causation that will give rise to a case or controversy where none existed before, and I do not read the Court's opinion to suggest a contrary view. In exercising this power, however, Congress must at the very least identify the injury it seeks to vindicate and relate the injury to the class of persons entitled to bring suit. The citizen-suit provision of the Endangered Species Act does not meet these minimal requirements, because while the statute purports to confer a right on "any person . . . to enjoin . . . the United States and any other governmental instrumentality or agency . . . who is alleged to be in violation of any provision of this chapter," it does not of its own force establish that there is an injury in "any person" by virtue of any "violation." 16 U.S.C. § 1540(g)(1)(A).

[**JUSTICE STEVENS** concurred in the judgment; he rejected the plurality opinion's analysis of standing but found the Secretary's regulation a correct interpretation of the statute and so concurred in the reversal of the lower courts' orders. **JUSTICE BLACKMUN**, joined by **JUSTICE O'CONNOR**, dissented from the Court's holding that there was no standing.]

NOTES ON *DEFENDERS OF WILDLIFE* AND STANDING TO ENFORCE STATUTES

1. *The Court's Environmental Standing Precedents.* The leading case is *Sierra Club v. Morton*, 405 U.S. 727 (1972), in which the environmental group sued to overturn the Forest Service's approval of a private resort, which would allegedly have despoiled natural wooded areas. Over Justice Douglas' celebrated dissent arguing that "trees have standing," the Court held that the organization or its members would have to show a particularized injury to them (including aesthetic injury to members who had been to the forest and wanted to go back).

The Court indicated that *Sierra Club* might be an easy test to satisfy in *United States v. SCRAP*, 412 U.S. 669 (1973), where the Court held that environmental groups (in that case, a bunch of students) could challenge Interstate Commerce Commission rate policies. The injury in fact claimed was this: Higher rates proposed by the ICC would allegedly increase the use of non-recyclable goods, which would lead to the use of more resources to produce the goods, which in turn would further deplete forests that the plaintiffs enjoyed. Does this characterization of the plaintiffs' injury in fact seem too attenuated?

In *Duke Power Company v. Carolina Environmental Study Group, Inc.*, discussed above, the Court found that an environmental group had standing to challenge the constitutionality of federal limits on tort liability of nuclear power plants for meltdowns and other disasters. Relying on *SCRAP*, the Court held that plaintiffs had the requisite "personal stake" in the controversy because of their "direct and present injury" by reason of the alleged aesthetic and thermal pollution of their neighborhood by the nuclear plant. The Court did not reach the issue of whether their "fear and apprehension" of a nuclear disaster would, alone, justify their standing to sue.

The Supreme Court signaled a more conservative application of *Sierra Club* in *Lujan v. National Wildlife Federation*, 497 U.S. 871 (1990), which prevented the Federation from challenging the Bureau of Land Management's failure to follow congressionally mandated procedures. Those procedures were required for reviewing executive orders withdrawing public lands from resource development. Justice Scalia's opinion for the Court faulted the Federation for not providing *Sierra Club*-type affidavits alleging that its members used the very lands in question, not just those in the vicinity, and also for challenging the entire BLM program and not just its review of the lands directly affecting Federation members.

2. *Procedural Injuries, Citizen Suits, and Original Intent.* The Court in *Defenders of Wildlife* brushes aside the claim of procedural standing, calling it nothing more than "an abstract, self-contained, noninstrumental 'right' to have the Executive observe the procedures required by law." Are such "noninstrumental rights" ever a basis for standing? What about the right to a decision-making process free of racial motivation, which the Court found a sufficient

basis for standing in *Northeastern Florida Contractors* and in *Shaw v. Reno* (Chapter 3, § 3E)?

Cass Sunstein, *What's Standing After* Lujan? *Of Citizen Suits, "Injuries," and Article III*, 91 Mich. L. Rev. 163 (1992), argues that *Defenders of Wildlife* seems to expand Article III standing limits well beyond the boundaries assumed by the Framers of the Constitution. According to Sunstein, the strict injury-in-fact requirement of standing is of relatively recent origin, and giving it such bite against Congress' efforts to recognize regulatory interests subserved by citizen suits is inconsistent with the Framers' understanding that Congress would have such authority. Practice at the time of the Constitution's framing was tolerant of congressional authorization for citizens to seek mandamus against officials violating the law and to seek *qui tam* relief for private violations — actions that would not be allowed under a strict reading of *Defenders of Wildlife*. How might Justice Scalia respond? Cf. Harold Krent & Ethan Shenkman, *Of Citizen Suits and Citizen Sunstein*, 91 Mich. L. Rev. 1793 (1993) (arguing that allowing citizen suits would interfere with the ability of the President to "take Care" that the laws be faithfully and soberly executed).

3. *Separation of Powers Concerns with the New Standing.* Justice Blackmun's dissenting opinion in *Defenders of Wildlife* expressed concern that the new rigidity in applying standing precepts to environmental statutes would shift power away from Congress to the President. It seems obvious that Congress sets policy both by the substantive rules and by the procedures through which policy is implemented. Hence, when Congress delegates rulemaking power to agencies it does not control (and which are often now controlled by a President of a different political party), it typically "hard wires" into the statute procedures that will press the agency toward the policy equilibrium desired by Congress.[g] The use of process to direct agencies toward substantive results has been particularly popular in environmental statutes, such as the National Environmental Policy Act, which requires agencies to consider the environmental impact of their activities.

Procedural obligations can be as important as substantive obligations in the modern regulatory state, and judicial review to enforce both types of obligations is necessary if one accepts the premise of legislative supremacy, as Article I implicitly does.[h] The problem, highlighted in *Defenders of Wildlife*, is that if you take a narrow, private-law view of standing it is harder to find plaintiffs who can enforce procedural obligations. They run into problems of particularity and redressability — it's hard for plaintiffs to show that they are affected by every single procedural violation they challenge, and it's also hard for such plaintiffs to show that following the right procedures will help them.

---

g. Matthew McCubbins, Roger Noll & Barry Weingast, *Administrative Procedures as Instruments of Control*, 3 J.L. Econ. & Org. 243 (1987); see also Jonathan Macey, *Separated Powers and Positive Political Theory: The Tug of War Over Administrative Agencies*, 80 Geo. L.J. 671 (1992).

h. See Daniel Farber, *Politics and Procedure in Environmental Law*, 8 J. L. Econ. & Org. 59, 76-78 (1992).

Justice Blackmun concluded: "It is to be hoped that over time the Court will acknowledge that some classes of procedural duties are so enmeshed with the prevention of substantive, concrete harm that an individual plaintiff may be able to demonstrate a sufficient likelihood of injury just through the breach of that procedural duty."

———

Federal Election Commission v. Akins, 524 U.S. 11 (1998). Plaintiffs challenged the Commission's determination that the American Israel Public Affairs Committee (AIPAC) was not a "political committee" under the federal election laws and therefore was not covered by various disclosure requirements. In an opinion by **Justice Breyer**, the Court held that the plaintiffs had standing. Their injury in fact consisted of "their inability to obtain information" such as lists of donors that, on their view of the law, "the statute requires that AIPAC make public." The Court "found no reason to doubt their claim that the information would help them (and others to whom they would communicate it) to evaluate candidates for public office, especially candidates who received assistance from AIPAC, and to evaluate the role that AIPAC's financial assistance might play in a specific election." This "injury consequently seems concrete and particular." The government argued, however, that this was an undifferentiated injury shared by the voters generally, and hence not a basis for standing. The Court found it irrelevant, however, that the injury was shared generally: "Often the fact that an interest is abstract and the fact that it is widely shared go hand in hand. But their association is not invariable, and where a harm is concrete, though widely shared, the Court has found 'injury in fact.' " Thus, "the informational injury at issue here, directly related to voting, the most basic of political rights, is sufficiently concrete and specific such that the fact that it is widely shared does not deprive Congress of constitutional power to authorize its vindication in the federal courts."

Justice Scalia dissented, joined by **Justices O'Connor** and **Thomas** (but not, notably, by the Chief Justice). He viewed the Court's rejection of the "widely shared" test with alarm:

> The provision of law at issue in this case is an extraordinary one, conferring upon a private person the ability to bring an Executive agency into court to compel its enforcement of the law against a third party. * * * If provisions such as the present one were commonplace, the role of the Executive Branch in our system of separated and equilibrated powers would be greatly reduced, and that of the Judiciary greatly expanded.

> Because this provision is so extraordinary, we should be particularly careful not to expand it beyond its fair meaning. In my view the Court's opinion does that. Indeed, it expands the meaning beyond what the Constitution permits.

He stressed that a "system in which the citizenry at large could sue to compel Executive compliance with the law would be a system in which the courts, rather than the President, are given the primary responsibility to 'take Care that the Laws be faithfully executed,' Art. II, § 3." The barrier to this system of judicial control has been that "the common understanding of the interest necessary to sustain suit has included the requirement * * * that the complained-of injury be particularized and differentiated, rather than common to all the electorate." Besides criticizing the majority for being inconsistent with *Defenders of Wildlife*, Justice Scalia predicted sweeping consequences:

> If today's decision is correct, it is within the power of Congress to authorize any interested person to manage (through the courts) the Executive's enforcement of any law that includes a requirement for the filing and public availability of a piece of paper. This is not the system we have had, and is not the system we should desire.

In short, Justice Scalia concluded, the statute as construed by the majority "unconstitutionally transfers from the Executive to the courts the responsibility to 'take Care that the Laws be faithfully executed.' "

Was Justice Scalia correct in his implication that *Akins* overruled the Article II, separation of powers theory of *Defenders of Wildlife*? Putting aside the question whether this is "the system we have had," was he correct that this "is not the system we should desire"?

2. *Civil Penalties and Article II.* A concurrence by Justice Kennedy noted that the legitimacy of the civil penalty provision under Article II was not before the Court, a point also made in Justice Scalia's concurrence. Does allowing a private party to sue to collect a penalty payable to the government infringe on the President's "take care" power? Is it relevant that, at the time the Constitution was enacted, private individuals were sometimes allowed to bring criminal prosecutions? Would the Article II issue be any different if, like punitive damages in tort cases, the civil penalties were payable to the plaintiff rather than to the government?

NOTE ON REDRESS FOR PAST HARMS

In *Steel Co. v. Citizens for a Better Environment*, 523 U.S. 83 (1998), discussed in *Laidlaw*, the Court held that a civil penalty for a completely past violation could not be considered redress of that violation. Hence, Article III standing was lacking. The connection between redress and the "case or controversy" requirement has some intuitive appeal — what difference does it make if the plaintiff suffered an injury, if the Court is merely being asked to give a legal opinion about past events rather than remedy the harm? For instance, at different stages of the litigation, different parties might be seeking redress from a federal court, which raises the question of whose injury the remedy must "redress." Suppose a state statute allowed citizen suits to collect civil penalties for wholly past violations of some state law, and also suppose that the defendant argues that the statute violates the federal Constitution in some respect. According to *Steel Co.*, such a citizen suit does not present a "case or controversy" at the time it is brought, because the civil penalties do not "redress" the plaintiff's injury. If something is not a case or controversy — and therefore not within the federal judicial power — then presumably it remains that way regardless of which party prevails. Yet, the Supreme Court would have jurisdiction to hear the defendant's appeal under *ASARCO, Inc. v. Kadish*, 490 U.S. 605, 618 (1989). Does this make any sense? Can a genuine adversary lawsuit exist when one side but not the other has a "concrete stake" in the outcome?

The Court further complicated the issue of redress with its decision in *Friends of the Earth, Inc. v. Laidlaw Environmental Services, Inc.*, 528 U.S. 167 (2000). Friends of the Earth had filed a citizen suit against Laidlaw under the Clean Water Act, charging Laidlaw with numerous violations of the mercury limits in its water permit. The Court found standing on the basis of the local residents reluctance to use the water for boating and fishing because of the pollution, notwithstanding the trial court's finding that there was actually no threat to health. By the time the district court decided the case, the violations had ceased. The Court held that this was insufficient to constitute mootness, however, because it was less than completely certain at that point that the violations would not recur. The Court also said that the plaintiffs had standing to sue for civil penalties because, unlike *Steel Co.*, the plaintiffs alleged an on-going violation at the time the case was filed. The penalties for past violations would be effective, in the Court's view, in deterring future violations. The Court did, however, remand for further consideration of the fact that the plant closed permanently while the case was pending on appeal.

Friends of the Earth seemed to reflect a loosening of standing requirements in general and the redressability requirement in particular. That trend continued with the following case.

MASSACHUSETTS v. EPA
549 U.S. 497, 127 S.Ct. 1438, 167 L.Ed.2d 248 (2007)

JUSTICE STEVENS delivered the opinion of the Court.

[States, local governments, and environmental organizations petitioned for review of an order of the Environmental Protection Agency (EPA) denying a petition for rulemaking to regulate greenhouse gas emissions from motor vehicles under the Clean Air Act. A divided panel of the D.C. Circuit ruled in favor of the EPA, in part on the basis of questions about the petitioners' standing.]

A well-documented rise in global temperatures has coincided with a significant increase in the concentration of carbon dioxide in the atmosphere. Respected scientists believe the two trends are related. For when carbon dioxide is released into the atmosphere, it acts like the ceiling of a greenhouse, trapping solar energy and retarding the escape of reflected heat. It is therefore a species — the most important species — of a "greenhouse gas."

Calling global warming "the most pressing environmental challenge of our time," a group of States, local governments, and private organizations, alleged in a petition for certiorari that the Environmental Protection Agency (EPA) has abdicated its responsibility under the Clean Air Act to regulate the emissions of four greenhouse gases, including carbon dioxide. Specifically, petitioners asked us to answer two questions concerning the meaning of § 202(a)(1) of the Act: whether EPA has the statutory authority to regulate greenhouse gas emissions from new motor vehicles; and if so, whether its stated reasons for refusing to do so are consistent with the statute.

* * *

Article III of the Constitution limits federal-court jurisdiction to "Cases" and "Controversies." Those two words confine "the business of federal courts to questions presented in an adversary context and in a form historically viewed as capable of resolution through the judicial process." It is therefore familiar learning that no justiciable "controversy" exists when parties seek adjudication of a political question, when they ask for an advisory opinion, or when the question sought to be adjudicated has been mooted by subsequent developments. This case suffers from none of these defects.

The parties' dispute turns on the proper construction of a congressional statute, a question eminently suitable to resolution in federal court. Congress has moreover authorized this type of challenge to EPA action. See 42 U.S.C. § 7607(b)(1). That authorization is of critical importance to the standing inquiry: "Congress has the power to define injuries and articulate chains of causation that will give rise to a case or controversy where none existed before." "In exercising this power, however, Congress must at the very least identify the injury it seeks to vindicate and relate the injury to the class of persons entitled to bring suit." We will not, therefore, "entertain citizen suits to vindicate the public's nonconcrete interest in the proper administration of the laws." [The three preceding sentences are quotations from Justice Kennedy's *Lujan* concurrence.]

EPA maintains that because greenhouse gas emissions inflict widespread harm, the doctrine of standing presents an insuperable jurisdictional obstacle. We do not agree. At bottom, "the gist of the question of standing" is whether petitioners have "such a personal stake in the outcome of the controversy as to assure that concrete adverseness which sharpens the presentation of issues upon which the court so largely depends for illumination." *Baker v. Carr.* As JUSTICE KENNEDY explained in his *Lujan* concurrence:

> While it does not matter how many persons have been injured by the challenged action, the party bringing suit must show that the action injures him in a concrete and personal way. This requirement is not just an empty formality. It preserves the vitality of the adversarial process by assuring both that the parties before the court have an actual, as opposed to professed, stake in the outcome, and that the legal questions presented . . . will be resolved, not in the rarified atmosphere of a debating society, but in a concrete factual context conducive to a realistic appreciation of the consequences of judicial action.

To ensure the proper adversarial presentation, *Lujan* holds that a litigant must demonstrate that it has suffered a concrete and particularized injury that is either actual or imminent, that the injury is fairly traceable to the defendant, and that it is likely that a favorable decision will redress that injury. See *id.* However, a litigant to whom Congress has "accorded a procedural right to protect his concrete interests" — here, the right to challenge agency action unlawfully withheld — "can assert that right without meeting all the normal standards for redressability and immediacy." *Ibid.* When a litigant is vested with a procedural right, that litigant has standing if there is some possibility that the requested relief will prompt the injury-causing party to reconsider the decision that allegedly harmed the litigant. *Ibid.*

Only one of the petitioners needs to have standing to permit us to consider the petition for review. We stress here, as did Judge Tatel below, the special position and interest of Massachusetts. It is of considerable relevance that the party seeking review here is a sovereign State and not, as it was in *Lujan,* a private individual.

* * *

When a State enters the Union, it surrenders certain sovereign prerogatives. Massachusetts cannot invade Rhode Island to force reductions in greenhouse gas emissions, it cannot negotiate an emissions treaty with China or India, and in some circumstances the exercise of its police powers to reduce in-state motor-vehicle emissions might well be pre-empted.

These sovereign prerogatives are now lodged in the Federal Government, and Congress has ordered EPA to protect Massachusetts (among others) by prescribing standards applicable to the "emission of any air pollutant from any class or classes of new motor vehicle engines, which in [the Administrator's] judgment cause, or contribute to, air pollution which may reasonably be anticipated to endanger public health or welfare." 42 U.S.C. § 7521(a)(1). Congress has moreover recognized a concomitant procedural right to challenge the rejection of its rulemaking petition as arbitrary and capricious. 42 U.S.C. § 7607(b)(1). Given that procedural right and Massachusetts' stake in protecting its quasi-sovereign interests, the Commonwealth is entitled to special solicitude in our standing analysis.

With that in mind, it is clear that petitioners' submissions as they pertain to Massachusetts have satisfied the most demanding standards of the adversarial process. EPA's steadfast refusal to regulate greenhouse gas emissions presents a risk of harm to Massachusetts that is both "actual" and "imminent." There is, moreover, a "substantial likelihood that the judicial relief requested" will prompt EPA to take steps to reduce that risk.

The Injury

The harms associated with climate change are serious and well recognized. Indeed, the NRC Report itself — which EPA regards as an "objective and independent assessment of the relevant science" — identifies a number of environmental changes that have already inflicted significant harms, including "the global retreat of mountain glaciers, reduction in snow-cover extent, the earlier spring melting of rivers and lakes, [and] the accelerated rate of rise of sea levels during the 20th century relative to the past few thousand years . . . ." ["NRC" refers to the National Research Council of the National Academy of Sciences.]

* * *

That these climate-change risks are "widely shared" does not minimize Massachusetts' interest in the outcome of this litigation. According to petitioners' unchallenged affidavits, global sea levels rose somewhere between 10 and 20 centimeters over the 20th century as a result of global warming. These rising seas have already begun to swallow Massachusetts' coastal land. Because the Commonwealth "owns a substantial portion of the state's coastal property," it has alleged a particularized injury in its capacity as a landowner. The severity of that injury will only increase over the course of the next century: If sea levels continue to rise as predicted, one Massachusetts official believes that a significant fraction of coastal property will be "either permanently lost through inundation or temporarily lost through periodic storm surge and flooding events." Remediation costs alone, petitioners allege, could run well into the hundreds of millions of dollars.

Causation

EPA does not dispute the existence of a causal connection between man-made greenhouse gas emissions and global warming. At a minimum, therefore, EPA's refusal to regulate such emissions "contributes" to Massachusetts' injuries.

EPA nevertheless maintains that its decision not to regulate greenhouse gas emissions from new motor vehicles contributes so insignificantly to petitioners' injuries that the agency cannot be haled into federal court to answer for them. For the same reason, EPA does not believe that any realistic possibility exists that the relief petitioners seek would mitigate global climate change and remedy their injuries. That is especially so because predicted increases in greenhouse gas emissions from developing nations, particularly China and India, are likely to offset any marginal domestic decrease.

But EPA overstates its case. Its argument rests on the erroneous assumption that a small incremental step, because it is incremental, can never be attacked in a federal judicial forum. Yet accepting that premise would doom most challenges to regulatory action. Agencies, like legislatures, do not generally resolve massive problems in one fell regulatory swoop. They instead whittle away at them over time, refining their preferred approach as circumstances change and as they develop a more-nuanced understanding of how best to proceed. That a first step might be tentative does not by itself support the notion that federal courts lack jurisdiction to determine whether that step conforms to law.

And reducing domestic automobile emissions is hardly a tentative step. Even leaving aside the other greenhouse gases, the United States transportation sector emits an enormous quantity of carbon dioxide into the atmosphere — according to the MacCracken affidavit, more than 1.7 billion metric tons in 1999 alone. That accounts for more than 6% of worldwide carbon dioxide emissions. * * *

The Remedy

While it may be true that regulating motor-vehicle emissions will not by itself *reverse* global warming, it by no means follows that we lack jurisdiction to decide whether EPA has a duty to take steps to *slow* or *reduce* it. Because of the enormity of the potential consequences associated with man-made climate change, the fact that the effectiveness of a remedy might be delayed during the (relatively short) time it takes for a new motor-vehicle fleet to replace an older one is essentially irrelevant. Nor is it dispositive that developing countries such as China and India are poised to increase greenhouse gas emissions substantially over the next century: A reduction in domestic emissions would slow the pace of global emissions increases, no matter what happens elsewhere.

We moreover attach considerable significance to EPA's "agree[ment] with the President that 'we must address the issue of global climate change,'" and to EPA's ardent support for various voluntary emission-reduction programs. As Judge Tatel observed in dissent below, "EPA would presumably not bother with such efforts if it thought emissions reductions would have no discernable impact on future global warming."

In sum — at least according to petitioners' uncontested affidavits — the rise in sea levels associated with global warming has already harmed and will continue to harm Massachusetts. The risk of catastrophic harm, though remote, is nevertheless real. That risk would be reduced to some extent if petitioners received the relief they seek. We therefore hold that petitioners have standing to challenge the EPA's denial of their rulemaking petition.

[On the merits, the Court held that EPA did have authority to regulate greenhouse gases from vehicles and that EPA had relied on impermissible factors in deciding against regulation. The Court remanded for further consideration by the agency under the correct statutory standards.]

CHIEF JUSTICE ROBERTS, with whom JUSTICE SCALIA, JUSTICE THOMAS, and JUSTICE ALITO join, dissenting.

Global warming may be a "crisis," even "the most pressing environmental problem of our time." Pet. for Cert. 26, 22. Indeed, it may ultimately affect nearly everyone on the planet in some potentially adverse way, and it may be that governments have done too little to address it. It is not a problem, however, that has escaped the attention of policymakers in the Executive and Legislative Branches of our Government, who continue to consider regulatory, legislative, and treaty-based means of addressing global climate change.

Apparently dissatisfied with the pace of progress on this issue in the elected branches, petitioners have come to the courts claiming broad-ranging injury, and attempting to tie that injury to the Government's alleged failure to comply with a rather narrow statutory provision. I would reject these challenges as nonjusticiable. Such a conclusion involves no judgment on whether global warming exists, what causes it, or the extent of the problem. Nor does it render petitioners without recourse. This Court's standing jurisprudence simply recognizes that redress of grievances of the sort at issue here "is the function of Congress and the Chief Executive," not the federal courts. *Lujan.* I would vacate the judgment below and remand for dismissal of the petitions for review.

* * *

It is not at all clear how the Court's "special solicitude" for Massachusetts plays out in the standing analysis, except as an implicit concession that petitioners cannot establish standing on traditional terms. But the status of Massachusetts as a State cannot compensate for petitioners' failure to demonstrate injury in fact, causation, and redressability.

When the Court actually applies the three-part test, it focuses, as did the dissent below, on the State's asserted loss of coastal land as the injury in fact. If petitioners rely on loss of land as the Article III injury, however, they must ground the rest of the standing analysis in that specific injury. * * * Without "particularized injury, there can be no confidence of 'a real need to exercise the power of judicial review' or that relief can be framed 'no broader than required by the precise facts to which the court's ruling would be applied.'"

The very concept of global warming seems inconsistent with this particularization requirement. Global warming is a phenomenon "harmful to humanity at large," and the redress petitioners seek is focused no more on them than on the public generally — it is literally to change the atmosphere around the world.

If petitioners' particularized injury is loss of coastal land, it is also that injury that must be "actual or imminent, not conjectural or hypothetical," "real and immediate," and "certainly impending."

* * *

The Court's sleight-of-hand is in failing to link up the different elements of the three-part standing test. What must be *likely* to be redressed is the particular injury in fact. The injury the Court looks to is the asserted loss of land. The Court contends that regulating domestic motor vehicle emissions will reduce carbon dioxide in the atmosphere, *and therefore* redress Massachusetts's injury. But even if regulation *does* reduce emissions — to some indeterminate degree, given events elsewhere in the world — the Court never explains why that makes it *likely* that the injury in fact — the loss of land — will be redressed. Schoolchildren know that a kingdom might be lost "all for the want of a horseshoe nail," but "likely" redressability is a different matter. The realities make it pure conjecture to suppose that EPA regulation of new automobile emissions will *likely* prevent the loss of Massachusetts coastal land.

* * *

When dealing with legal doctrine phrased in terms of what is "fairly" traceable or "likely" to be redressed, it is perhaps not surprising that the matter is subject to some debate. But in considering how loosely or rigorously to define those adverbs, it is vital to keep in mind the purpose of the inquiry. The limitation of the judicial power to cases and controversies "is crucial in maintaining the tripartite allocation of power set forth in the Constitution." In my view, the Court today — addressing Article III's "core component of standing" — fails to take this limitation seriously.

NOTES ON *MASSACHUSETTS v. EPA*

1. *Is* Lujan *Still Standing?* The *EPA v. Mass.* majority purports to distinguish *Lujan*, but the Court clearly bases its ruling much more on the Kennedy concurrence than on the Scalia opinion. Is Justice Scalia's opinion in *Lujan* still good law after *EPA v. Mass.*?

2. *The Federalism Overlay on Standing Doctrine.* Justice Stevens makes much of the sovereign status of the state and its implication for the state's claim of standing. The result may be to empower the states to challenge federal actions that would otherwise be immune from suit by private parties. Is this a healthy reinforcement of the states' role in the federalist system, or is it an invitation to litigate questions that are essentially political disagreements rather than live controversies? Putting that question aside, to what extent is the state's status determinative of the outcome? Is the holding limited to state-initiated litigation, or has the Court relaxed standing requirements across the board?

3. *Counting to Five.* Justice Stevens seems to have done a remarkable job of corraling Justice Kennedy's vote — note how frequently he refers to Kennedy's *Lujan* performance as the gold standard in standing doctrine. If there is a retirement from the liberal side of the Court, however, the *Mass. v. EPA* majority may not hold up very long, depending on the next judicial appointment. Thus, Chief Justice Roberts' view could yet become the law. Could the Chief Justice's concerns be addressed by new scientific evidence, firming up the causal connections and demonstrating precisely how the EPA's actions (or refusal to act) affect the plaintiffs? Or under his view, are climate change claims inherently nonjusticiable, regardless of the specific factual showing made by plaintiffs?

Missouri v. Jenkins (Jenkins II), 495 U.S. 33 (1990). In 1977, the Kansas City, Missouri, School District (KCMSD) and a class of KCMSD students sued the state of Missouri for operating a segregated school system in Kansas City. The district judge realigned KCMSD as a party defendant and found in 1984 that the state and district had violated *Brown.* According to the judge, the state intentionally allowed the city school system to deteriorate; as a result, the district's "physical facilities have literally rotted" and educational services were substandard in an increasingly all-black system. In 1985, the district court ordered a far-reaching remedy, as summarized by the court of appeals:

> The magnet plan provided that by 1991-92 every high school and middle school in the KCMSD and about half the elementary schools would become magnet schools with one or more distinctive themes, such as foreign languages, performing arts, and math and science. The elementary magnets were to be located at selected sites throughout KCMSD, with at least one magnet in each area of the KCMSD.

> The district court also ordered a capital improvements program for KCMSD totaling some $260 million. The principal capital improvement plan called for the closing of some eighteen KCMSD school facilities, construction of seventeen new facilities and renovation of others.

One purpose of the remedy was to draw white students back into the public school system; another was to give minority students an educational experience of the same quality they would have received but for the results of segregation.

After some further proceedings, the case reached the Supreme Court, which did not pass on the validity of the remedy but only on the method of financing it. In an opinion by **Justice White**, the Court held that the district judge had erred in ordering an increase in the local property tax. The district judge had resorted to this extreme remedy because the school district was unable to afford the required actions, and under state law KCMSD was unable to increase the tax levy itself. The Supreme Court held that this was too intrusive a remedy; instead, the district court should have enjoined the operation of the state tax laws that interfered with the school district's efforts to raise taxes. Such an injunction would be proper under Article III and the Tenth Amendment, because the Court had repeatedly ruled that federal courts could issue writs of mandamus to compel local governments to levy taxes to satisfy their debt obligations. E.g., *Von Hoffman v. City of Quincy*, 4 Wall. 535 (1866).

Speaking for four Justices who concurred in the judgment, **Justice Kennedy** objected that "[t]oday's casual embrace of taxation imposed by the unelected, life-tenured Federal Judiciary disregards fundamental precepts for the democratic control of public institutions." He added that the expense was not surprising, given the scope of the remedy. "It comes as no surprise that the cost of this approach to the remedy far exceeded KCMSD's budget, or for that matter, its authority to tax. A few examples are illustrative. Programs such as a 'performing arts middle school,' a 'technical magnet high school' that 'will offer programs ranging from heating and air conditioning to cosmetology to robotics,' were approved. The plan also included a '25 acre farm and 25 acre wildlife area' for science study." The district court had rejected a renovation program proposed by the state because if would not achieve "suburban comparability or the visual attractiveness sought by the Court as it would result in floor coverings with unsightly sections of mismatched carpeting and tile, and individual walls possessing different shades of paint." Justice Kennedy objected to such a micromanaged approach.

NOTES ON THE KANSAS CITY SCHOOL DESEGREGATION CASE AND PROBLEMS WITH STRUCTURAL INJUNCTIONS

1. *Case or Controversy Problems.* Under *Warth v. Seldin* and *Allen v. Wright*, plaintiffs must show a concrete injury that can be remedied by a federal court, in order to meet the Article III requirements for Case or Controversy standing. What, precisely, was the injury suffered by the plaintiffs in *Jenkins*? Was it differentiated enough from that of others to satisfy *Allen*? Would a court order likely remedy the injury?

The foregoing questions can probably be answered in the affirmative; standing was not an issue in the case, so far as we can tell. Consider this twist, however. By the time the Supreme Court upheld the remedy, 1990, the original plaintiffs had all graduated from the KCMSD system. Presumably, they were replaced by fresh plaintiffs, to prevent the case from becoming moot, but given the accustomed time lag between lawsuit and remedy in these kinds of cases, the practical reality is that the original plaintiffs know that they will never benefit from any judicial remedy and that they are surrogates for future schoolchildren in the KCMSD. Does this reality create any Article III problems?

Justice Kennedy charged that the plaintiffs and the school district maintained a "friendly adversary" relationship (unsurprisingly, as they had originally been co-plaintiffs). This surely informed his objection that the remedy was unduly lavish, for it looked like the KCMSD officials were cooperating, at some level, with plaintiffs to achieve greater funding for their school system. It is not unusual in structural reform legislation for the interests of aggrieved plaintiffs (*e.g.*, prisoners) and institutional defendants (*e.g.*, prison administrators) to align against those of unnamed third parties — taxpayers or the legislature itself. Does this structural dilemma unduly threaten the integrity of Article III adjudication?

2. *Separation of Powers and Federalism Problems.* Related to the Article III problems are separation of powers and even federalism ones (*cf. Allen v. Wright*). First, was it appropriate for the *federal government* to intrude into the details of state decisionmaking? A central value of federalism is local autonomy in making decisions and policy affecting the community. While it is surely appropriate for the national government to enforce individuals' Fourteenth Amendment rights, it may not be appropriate for the national government to micromanage the state's response to a constitutional violation. In *Freeman v. Pitts* (Chapter 2, § 2C), Justice Kennedy's opinion for the Court said that *Brown II* remedies carried a heavy price in local official *accountability* for managerial decisions. See also the commandeering and Eleventh Amendment cases in Chapter 7.

Second, was it appropriate for a *federal court* to be making essentially "political" judgments in its remedial order? Justice Kennedy objected that taxation is not a judicial function. "In our system 'the legislative department alone has access to the pockets of the people,' *The Federalist* No. 48 (Madison), for it is the Legislature that is accountable to them and represents their will." In other cases, critics of structural injunctions attack federal courts for trying to solve polycentric problems, which are best left to the political process, which has the financial and factfinding resources to address them.[i]

Third, was it appropriate for a federal court to *concentrate in one institution* (itself) several constitutional functions? The trial judge in *Jenkins* was not only making big money decisions about how to structure the KCMSD, but was also directing the creation of a mini-bureaucracy to implement its program, including the hiring of a "public information specialist" to solicit community support for the district court desegregation plan. Is this the sort of concentration of governmental functions that Madison and Montesquieu warned were the very essence of tyranny? See *Federalist* No. 47 (App. 2).

3. *Practical Problems.* The district court program was carried into effect, paid for largely by the state of Missouri. Yet in the early years of the new program, only 200 suburban white students transferred into the district, even though the district was spending over 75% above the state average per pupil; test scores for KCMSD students remained steady or declined; and African-American

---

i. See Lon Fuller, *The Forms and Limits of Adjudication*, 92 Harv. L. Rev. 353 (1978), for an argument that courts are not appropriate institutions to resolve "polycentric" disputes, namely, disputes that involve interconnected social, economic, and political dimensions. Compare the response by Owen Fiss, *The Supreme Court, 1978 Term — Foreword: The Forms of Justice*, 93 Harv. L. Rev. 1 (1979).

parents became disgruntled by efforts to reserve places for white students.[j] See generally Chapter 2, § 2C3, which suggests that the most robust educational gains have come in programs where inner-city schoolchildren can attend suburban schools (a tactic federal courts usually cannot mandate because of *Milliken*).

SECTION 3: PRUDENTIAL CONCERNS WITH THE EXERCISE OF THE JUDICIAL POWER

Missouri v. Jenkins (Jenkins III), 515 U.S. 70 (1995). The Supreme Court evaluated two remedial issues not included in the grant of certiorari for *Jenkins II*. A narrow Court majority, in an opinion by **Chief Justice Rehnquist**, overturned several features of the district court's remedial orders. The district court's efforts to attract (white) students from outside the school district were beyond the scope of the constitutional violation. The Court in *Milliken v. Bradley*, 418 U.S. 717 (1974), had held that interdistrict relief could not be fashioned under *Brown II* unless there was a factual finding that surrounding school districts had been guilty of constitutional violations. For similar reasons, the Chief Justice ruled that the district court had erred in requiring across-the-board salary increases for teachers and staff in pursuit of the court's effort to attract white students from the suburbs. The Court also faulted the district court for requiring the state to continue to fund the magnet school programs so long as student achievement scores were below national norms at many grade levels. The Court remanded the case to the district court to reconsider the scope of its remedial jurisdiction under *Freeman v. Pitts* (Chapter 2, § 2C2): Has the effect of prior de jure segregation been remedied to the extent practicable? The Chief Justice sharply hinted that the district court should speed up the return of the school system to local authorities.

Writing also for **Justices Stevens**, **Ginsburg**, and **Breyer**, **Justice Souter** dissented. He objected to the Court's disinclination to defer to the district court's remedy (as the Court had generally done from *Swann* onward) and to its disregard of findings of fact made by the trial court. There was no interdistrict remedy of the sort disapproved in *Milliken*, where the trial court had ordered busing across districts, thereby imposing a direct judicial order on districts found not liable; in this case, there was only a candid effort to attract children from various districts. Accord, *Hills v. Gautreaux*, 425 U.S. 284 (1976). **Justice Ginsburg** also dissented separately: "The Court stresses that the present remedial programs have been in place for seven years. But compared to more than two centuries of firmly entrenched official discrimination, the experience with the desegregation remedies ordered by the District Court has been evanescent."

Justice Thomas wrote a concurring opinion that forcefully rejected the proposition that all-black school systems are constitutionally questionable.

---

j. Arlynn Leiber Presser, *Broken Dreams*, ABA Journal 60, 63 (May 1991). For an argument in favor of aggressive judicial efforts to enforce state educational standards that would advance the goals of *Brown*, see James Liebman, *Implementing Brown in the Nineties: Political Reconstruction, Liberal Recollection, and Litigatively Enforced Legislative Reform*, 76 Va. L. Rev. 349 (1990).

Under *Freeman*, trial courts cannot conflate voluntary white flight with state-imposed apartheid. Missouri had required school segregation until 1954. For a court to find that continuing school segregation 30 or 40 years later is a vestige of pre-1954 state law, the court must find more than continuing patterns of same-race schools. The district court had no basis for such a finding, and Justice Thomas charged that its opinion rested instead on racial stereotypes. "It never ceases to amaze me that the courts are so willing to assume that anything that is predominantly black must be inferior." Justice Thomas specifically scorned the social science data noted in footnote 11 of *Brown I* and insisted that the earlier decision rested upon sounder foundations:

"Segregation was not unconstitutional because it might have caused psychological feelings of inferiority. * * * Regardless of the relative quality of the schools, segregation violated the Constitution because the State classified students based on their race. * * * But neutral policies, such as local school assignments, do not offend the Constitution when individual private choices concerning work or residence produce schools with high black populations. *Keyes*. The Constitution does not prevent individuals from choosing to live together, to work together, or to send their children to school together, so long as the State does not interfere with their choices on the basis of race." Justice Thomas was confident that "there is no reason to think that black students cannot learn as well when surrounded by members of their own race as when they are in an integrated environment."

Justice Thomas continued by arguing that the district court not only violated the substantive limits of the Equal Protection Clause by its overly race-conscious approach to the case, but also violated the procedural limits of Articles I-III and the Tenth Amendment by its intrusive remedies. Here, Justice Thomas issued what amounted to a constitutional indictment of the structural injunction: (1) It is inconsistent with the Framers' intent to limit the reach of courts' equity powers. See *Federalist* No. 78 (Hamilton) (App. 2) (responding to Anti-Federalist attacks that federal courts would have potentially expansive equity powers, and insisting that the use of equitable remedies would be reserved for "extraordinary cases").[k] (2) When federal courts micromanage local school districts, they abridge the federalism precepts of the Tenth Amendment and, potentially, the Eleventh Amendment as well. (3) When federal courts direct managerial decisions, they are appropriating executive powers explicitly withheld from them in Article III (compare Article II).

As detailed in Chapter 8, in recent years a series of cases involving the War on Terror have refocused attention on the role of the Supreme Court in our system of governance. Returning to the *Boumediene* case provides us with a

---

k. Contrast, however, Theodore Eisenberg & Stephen Yeazell, *The Ordinary and the Extraordinary in Institutional Litigation*, 93 Harv. L. Rev. 465 (1980), showing that traditional judicial proceedings in the areas of wills and trusts, antitrust and monopoly, and so forth have required the judiciary to retain jurisdiction for long periods of time and to engage in ongoing compliance review. They maintain that these prior practices serve as a justifying parallel for the structural injunction. For a reply, see John Yoo, *Who Measures the Chancellor's Foot? The Inherent Remedial Authority of the Federal Courts*, 84 Calif. L. Rev. 1121, 1162-66 (1996).

final opportunity to examine prudential considerations in the exercise of judicial review.

BOUMEDIENE v. BUSH
___ U.S. ___, 128 S.Ct. 2229, ___ L.Ed.2d ___ (2008)

JUSTICE KENNEDY delivered the opinion for the Court.

[Striking down § 7 of the Military Commissions Act, which sought to bar habeas relief for accused terrorists detained at Guantanamo Bay, Justice Kennedy defended the Court's decision not to require the detainees to exhaust their remedies with the D.C. Circuit.]

[VI.A.] * * * The Government argues petitioners must seek review of their CSRT determinations in the Court of Appeals before they can proceed with their habeas corpus actions in the District Court. As noted earlier, in other contexts and for prudential reasons this Court has required exhaustion of alternative remedies before a prisoner can seek federal habeas relief. Most of these cases were brought by prisoners in state custody, and thus involved federalism concerns that are not relevant here. But we have extended this rule to require defendants in courts-martial to exhaust their military appeals before proceeding with a federal habeas corpus action.* * *

In cases involving foreign citizens detained abroad by the Executive, it likely would be both an impractical and unprecedented extension of judicial power to assume that habeas corpus would be available at the moment the prisoner is taken into custody. If and when habeas corpus jurisdiction applies, as it does in these cases, then proper deference can be accorded to reasonable procedures for screening and initial detention under lawful and proper conditions of confinement and treatment for a reasonable period of time. Domestic exigencies, furthermore, might also impose such onerous burdens on the Government that here, too, the Judicial Branch would be required to devise sensible rules for staying habeas corpus proceedings until the Government can comply with its requirements in a responsible way. Cf. *Ex parte Milligan*, 4 Wall., at 127 ("If, in foreign invasion or civil war, the courts are actually closed, and it is impossible to administer criminal justice according to law, *then*, on the theatre of active military operations, where war really prevails, there is a necessity to furnish a substitute for the civil authority, thus overthrown, to preserve the safety of the army and society; and as no power is left but the military, it is allowed to govern by martial rule until the laws can have their free course"). Here, as is true with detainees apprehended abroad, a relevant consideration in determining the courts' role is whether there are suitable alternative processes in place to protect against the arbitrary exercise of governmental power.

The cases before us, however, do not involve detainees who have been held for a short period of time while awaiting their CSRT determinations. Were that the case, or were it probable that the Court of Appeals could complete a prompt review of their applications, the case for requiring temporary abstention or exhaustion of alternative remedies would be much stronger. These qualifications no longer pertain here. In some of these cases six years have elapsed without the judicial oversight that habeas corpus or an adequate substitute demands. And there has been no showing that the Executive faces such onerous burdens that it cannot respond to habeas corpus actions. To require these detainees to complete DTA review before proceeding with their habeas corpus actions would be to require additional months, if not years, of delay. The first DTA review applications were filed over a year ago, but no decisions on the merits have been issued. While some delay in fashioning new procedures is unavoidable, the costs of delay can no longer be borne by those who are held in custody. The detainees in these cases are entitled to a prompt habeas corpus hearing.

* * * Our holding with regard to exhaustion should not be read to imply that a habeas court should intervene the moment an enemy combatant steps foot in a territory where the writ runs. The Executive is entitled to a reasonable period of time to determine a detainee's status before a court entertains that detainee's habeas corpus petition. The CSRT process is the mechanism Congress and the President set up to deal with these issues. Except in cases of undue delay, federal courts should refrain from entertaining an enemy combatant's habeas corpus petition at least until after the Department, acting via the CSRT, has had a chance to review his status.

[The Court remanded the cases to the District Court to determine whether the writ of habeas corpus should be granted.]

CHIEF JUSTICE ROBERTS, with whom JUSTICE SCALIA, JUSTICE THOMAS, and JUSTICE ALITO join, dissenting.

Today the Court strikes down as inadequate the most generous set of procedural protections ever afforded aliens detained by this country as enemy combatants. The political branches crafted these procedures amidst an ongoing military conflict, after much careful investigation and thorough debate. The Court rejects them today out of hand, without bothering to say what due process rights the detainees possess, without explaining how the statute fails to vindicate those rights, and before a single petitioner has even attempted to avail himself of the law's operation. And to what effect? The majority merely replaces a review system designed by the people's representatives with a set of shapeless procedures to be defined by federal courts at some future date. One cannot help but think, after surveying the modest practical results of the majority's ambitious opinion, that this decision is not really about the detainees at all, but about control of federal policy regarding enemy combatants.

* * * The critical threshold question in these cases * * * is whether the system the political branches designed protects whatever rights the detainees may possess. If so, there is no need for any additional process, whether called "habeas" or something else.

Congress entrusted that threshold question in the first instance to the Court of Appeals for the District of Columbia Circuit, as the Constitution surely allows Congress to do. See Detainee Treatment Act of 2005 (DTA), § 1005(e)(2)(A), 119 Stat. 2742. But before the D.C. Circuit has addressed the issue, the Court cashiers the statute, and without answering this critical threshold question itself. The Court does eventually get around to asking whether review under the DTA is, as the Court frames it, an "adequate substitute" for habeas, but even then its opinion fails to determine what rights the detainees possess and whether the

DTA system satisfies them. The majority instead compares the undefined DTA process to an equally undefined habeas right — one that is to be given shape only in the future by district courts on a case-by-case basis. This whole approach is misguided.

It is also fruitless. How the detainees' claims will be decided now that the DTA is gone is anybody's guess. But the habeas process the Court mandates will most likely end up looking a lot like the DTA system it replaces, as the district court judges shaping it will have to reconcile review of the prisoners' detention with the undoubted need to protect the American people from the terrorist threat — precisely the challenge Congress undertook in drafting the DTA. All that today's opinion has done is shift responsibility for those sensitive foreign policy and national security decisions from the elected branches to the Federal Judiciary.

I believe the system the political branches constructed adequately protects any constitutional rights aliens captured abroad and detained as enemy combatants may enjoy. I therefore would dismiss these cases on that ground.

NOTE ON CHIEF JUSTICE ROBERTS AND PRUDENTIAL LIMITS

The Chief Justice's dissent did not argue that the Court was violating Article III by deploying the "judicial Power" in something that was not a "Case or Controversy" under Article III. Instead, the Chief Justice was invoking the *prudential* feature of the Court's justiciability doctrines. The traditional defense of prudential justiciability is that best articulated by Alexander M. Bickel's *The Least Dangerous Branch: The Supreme Court at the Bar of Politics* (1962). Bickel's "passive virtues" theory defended judicial abstention from the perspective of the Court's own institutional limitations: the Court should typically not adjudicate complicated issues involving national policy when the Justices did not have sufficient information to make a confident decision, when they were unable to implement their will directly and were unwilling to invest years of judicial monitoring to do so, or when popular opinion was overwhelmingly aligned against them.

It is likely that the Chief Justice found much wisdom in such concerns, and his insistence that the legal issues were not ripe (and should first have been resolved by the D.C. Circuit) sounds highly Bickelian: good adjudication and careful resolution of thorny issues require complete procedural correctness, and no cutting of corners. On the other hand, the issues were "ripe" in a political sense: Congress in 2008 was controlled by Democrats highly critical of the Bush Administration's Iraq policies, and Republicans of all stripes joined Democrats in criticizing the Guantanamo Bay detentions, which had become something of an international embarrassment. So a Supreme Court that pounces on the procedural sloppiness of a lame-duck President (shackled with record low approval ratings) and wraps its opinion in The Great Writ and Liberty is not a Court that is sticking its neck way out and incurring big Bickelian risks.

It seems to us that the Chief Justice is making a broader point and is thinking outside of Article III. In the *Brown II* cases, the Supreme Court has invoked principles of federalism to require lower courts to trim back their desegregation activism. In the Guantanamo Cases, the dissenters are invoking principles of separation of powers to trim back habeas activism. The dissenters believe that the President (especially) and Congress are charged with plenary, and virtually unreviewable, authority to protect America against Terrorism. This is not only a legal requirement — it's Right There in the Constitution — but is also a pre-political requirement of necessity — The United States Cannot Survive Without Strong Executive Authority.

Chief Justice Roberts' plea is for the Court to look beyond the Bush 43 Administration and whatever exasperation some Justices might have about alleged mistreatment of these detainees and to remember that what the Court says in *Boumediene* will bind future Presidents and Congresses. Is this another *Bush v. Gore*, where a partisan majority announces a right to vote "principle" that is basically good just for that one case? Or *should* the Court's opinion in *Boumediene* be generalized? Would this undermine the President's options in the War on Terror?

By the way, where does the Court get the power to create prudential limits on standing? Is a power to go beyond Article III's restrictions on jurisdiction simply implicit in the Court's designation by Article III as the "Supreme Court"? Or is it an example of a broader power to create rules of common law that stem in a general sense from constitutional concerns but do not themselves have constitutional status?

CONCLUDING THOUGHTS ON THE SUPREME COURT AS PART OF THE POLITICAL SYSTEM

The cases in this chapter illustrate profound ambiguities of judicial review.[1] The Court is both reluctant to enter the political process openly (e.g., *Nixon v. United States* and *Allen v. Wright*) yet is itself an inevitable player in the political process by which public policy emerges in the United States (*Baker v. Carr* and the *Jenkins* decisions). The Court is both the "least dangerous branch" (*Federalist* No. 78) and the one subject to the fewest short-term constraints, both propositions evidenced in the Kansas City desegregation litigation. (Indeed, at times, the Court may seem to some to be the most powerful and *least* constrained political actor, see *Bush v. Gore*.) *Brown*, the case with which we began this casebook, may be evidence of these apparently contradictory propositions.

In *The Hollow Hope: Can Courts Bring About Social Change* (1991), Gerald Rosenberg argues that courts are able to produce significant social reform only when supported by ample legal precedent developed over time in a common-law-like way, by substantial backing and follow-up from Congress and the President, and by approval or at least acquiescence from the general public.

---

1. This theme is developed in Alexander Bickel, *The Least Dangerous Branch* (1962); William Eskridge, Jr. & Philip Frickey, *The Supreme Court, 1993 Term — Foreword: Law as Equilibrium*, 108 Harv. L. Rev. 26 (1994).

Specifically, he maintains that the desegregation decisions surveyed in Chapter 2 had little or no positive effect on actual school segregation until Congress and the President became actively engaged in the 1960s. Rosenberg's critics respond that the Court had great importance in signaling national support for civil rights activists and in putting desegregation on the national agenda through the *Brown* decision.[m] Both Rosenberg and some of his critics agree that *Brown* was a focal point for opposition in the South and may have hardened attitudes both for and against desegregation.

A similar story of agenda-setting, negative or positive feedback from the political process, and judicial retreat or accommodation can be told for most of the other big issues covered in this casebook: affirmative action (Chapter 3, § 3); equal rights for women and gay people (Chapter 4, §§ 2-3); freedom of contract (Chapter 5, § 2B); one person, one vote (Chapter 5, § 3A); the right of a woman to choose abortion (Chapter 5, § 4B); flagburning and other offensive or even hate speech (Chapter 6, §§ 1-2); school prayer (Chapter 6, § 6B); the reach of Congress' power under the Commerce Clause (Chapter 7, § 2) and limitations the dormant feature of that clause places on the states (Chapter 7, § 6); and executive privileges (Chapter 8, § 1C) as well as congressional power to delegate rulemaking but with strings attached (Chapter 8, § 2). We wonder how this interplay will work out in the context of new Supreme Court initiatives such as enforcement of the Second Amendment. As we have seen, there have also been important interactions between the Court and the other branches in the terrorism context.

Thus, to understand and appreciate the larger shifts in constitutional law — not just the formal amendments or major constitutional "moments" — the student needs to consider also the larger shifts in American politics and society, such as urbanization and the revolution in transportation and communications, the antislavery movement and reconstruction after the Civil War, the struggle between big business and organized labor, the pervasively regulatory state whose engine is agencies rather than courts, the civil rights revolution for people of color, the apparent worldwide dominance of market capitalism, the imperial presidency, the entry of fundamentalist sects into the political process, and the women's and later gay liberation movements. Many of these social and political changes are still in progress, and others are joining them. Constitutional law in the document's third century will have to account for developments such as the Internet and changes in the mass media, the nation's increasing racial heterogeneity, divided government, new issues raised by the changes in the roles of women and gay males and lesbians in public life, the growing political dominance of suburbs, revolutionary medical technologies such as cloning, and so forth.

Finally, think about how the law in general and the Supreme Court in particular influence these social and political developments, albeit often in ways

---

m. E.g., Neal Devins, Book Review, 80 Calif. L. Rev. 1027 (1992); David Garrow, *Hopelessly Hollow History: Revisionist Devaluing of* Brown v. Board of Education, 80 Va. L. Rev. 151 (1994); Michael Klarman, *Civil Rights Law: Who Made It and How Much Did It Matter?*, 83 Geo. L.J. 433 (1994).

that are not intended. Rosenberg argues that *Brown* itself created a new and hardened political dynamic, where resistance to "judicial activism" became a rallying cry. To what extent did the Court's Establishment Clause and abortion-rights activism fuel the creation of the "religious right" as a coherent and powerful political movement? Did *Bowers v. Hardwick* (Chapter 5, § 4C) help fuel a more aggressive gay rights movement? Has the Court's race and gender jurisprudence affected people's choices when they form families, make hiring decisions, and speak out in public discourse? Has the Court's new activism as to issues of federalism contributed to localism as a public value?

Appendix 1

THE CONSTITUTION OF
THE UNITED STATES

PREAMBLE

We the People of the United States, in Order to form a more perfect Union, establish Justice, insure domestic Tranquility, provide for the common defence, promote the general Welfare, and secure the Blessings of Liberty to ourselves and our Posterity, do ordain and establish this Constitution for the United States of America.

ARTICLE I

Section 1. All legislative Powers herein granted shall be vested in a Congress of the United States, which shall consist of a Senate and House of Representatives.

Section 2. [1] The House of Representatives shall be composed of Members chosen every second Year by the People of the several States, and the Electors in each State shall have the Qualifications requisite for Electors of the most numerous Branch of the State Legislature.

[2] No Person shall be a Representative who shall not have attained to the Age of twenty five Years, and been seven Years a Citizen of the United States, and who shall not, when elected, be an Inhabitant of that State in which he shall be chosen.

[3] Representatives and direct Taxes shall be apportioned among the several States which may be included within this Union, according to their respective Numbers, which shall be determined by adding to the whole Number of free Persons, including those bound to Service for a Term of Years, and excluding Indians not taxed, three fifths of all other Persons. The actual Enumeration shall be made within three Years after the first Meeting of the Congress of the United States, and within every subsequent Term of ten Years, in such Manner as they shall by Law direct. The Number of Representatives shall not exceed one for every thirty Thousand, but each State shall have at Least one Representative; and until such enumeration shall be made, the State of New Hampshire shall be entitled to chuse three, Massachusetts eight, Rhode Island and Providence Plantations one, Connecticut five, New York six, New Jersey four, Pennsylvania eight, Delaware one, Maryland six, Virginia ten, North Carolina five, South Carolina five, and Georgia three.

[4] When vacancies happen in the Representation from any State, the Executive Authority thereof shall issue Writs of Election to fill such Vacancies

[5] The House of Representatives shall chuse their Speaker and other Officers; and shall have the sole Power of Impeachment.

Section 3. [1] The Senate of the United States shall be composed of two Senators from each State, chosen by the Legislature thereof, for six Years; and each Senator shall have one Vote.

[2] Immediately after they shall be assembled in Consequence of the first Election, they shall be divided as equally as may be into three Classes. The Seats of the Senators of the first Class shall be vacated at the Expiration of the second Year, of the second Class at the Expiration of the fourth Year, and of the third Class at the Expiration of the sixth Year, so that one third may be chosen every second Year; and if Vacancies happen by Resignation, or otherwise, during the Recess of the Legislature of any State, the Executive thereof may make temporary Appointments until the next Meeting of the Legislature, which shall then fill such Vacancies.

[3] No Person shall be a Senator who shall not have attained to the Age of thirty Years, and been nine Years a Citizen of the United States, and who shall not, when elected, be an Inhabitant of that State for which he shall be chosen.

[4] The Vice President of the United States shall be President of the Senate, but shall have no Vote, unless they be equally divided.

[5] The Senate shall chuse their other Officers, and also a President pro tempore, in the Absence of the Vice President, or when he shall exercise the Office of President of the United States.

[6] The Senate shall have the sole Power to try all Impeachments. When sitting for that Purpose, they shall be on Oath or Affirmation. When the President of the United States is tried, the Chief Justice shall preside: And no Person shall be convicted without the Concurrence of two thirds of the Members present.

[7] Judgment in Cases of Impeachment shall not extend further than to removal from Office, and disqualification to hold and enjoy any Office of honor, Trust, or Profit under the United States: but the Party convicted shall nevertheless be liable and subject to Indictment, Trial, Judgment, and Punishment, according to Law.

Section 4. [1] The Times, Places and Manner of holding Elections for Senators and Representatives, shall be prescribed in each State by the Legislature thereof; but the Congress may at any time by Law make or alter such Regulations, except as to the Places of chusing Senators.

[2] The Congress shall assemble at least once in every Year, and such Meeting shall be on the first Monday in December, unless they shall by Law appoint a different Day.

Section 5. [1] Each House shall be the Judge of the Elections, Returns, and Qualifications of its own Members, and a Majority of each shall constitute a Quorum to do Business; but a smaller Number may adjourn from day to day, and may be authorized to compel the Attendance of absent Members, in such Manner, and under such Penalties as each House may provide.

[2] Each House may determine the Rules of its Proceedings, punish its Members for disorderly Behaviour, and, with the Concurrence of two thirds, expel a Member.

[3]   Each House shall keep a Journal of its Proceedings, and from time to time publish the same, excepting such Parts as may in their Judgment require Secrecy; and the Yeas and Nays of the Members of either House on any question shall, at the Desire of one fifth of those Present, be entered on the Journal.

[4]   Neither House, during the Session of Congress, shall without the Consent of the other, adjourn for more than three days, nor to any other Place than that in which the two Houses shall be sitting.

Section 6. [1] The Senators and Representatives shall receive a Compensation for their Services, to be ascertained by Law, and paid out of the Treasury of the United States. They shall in all Cases, except Treason, Felony, and Breach of the Peace, be privileged from Arrest during their Attendance at the Session of their respective Houses, and in going to and returning from the same; and for any Speech or Debate in either House, they shall not be questioned in any other Place.

[2]   No Senator or Representative shall, during the Time for which he was elected, be appointed to any civil Office under the Authority of the United States, which shall have been created, or the Emoluments whereof shall have been encreased during such time; and no Person holding any Office under the United States, shall be a Member of either House during his Continuance in Office.

Section 7. [1] All Bills for raising Revenue shall originate in the House of Representatives; but the Senate may propose or concur with Amendments as on other Bills.

[2]   Every Bill which shall have passed the House of Representatives and the Senate, shall, before it become a Law, be presented to the President of the United States; If he approve he shall sign it, but if not he shall return it, with his Objections to that House in which it shall have originated, who shall enter the Objections at large on their Journal, and proceed to reconsider it. If after such Reconsideration two thirds of that House shall agree to pass the Bill, it shall be sent, together with the Objections, to the other House, by which it shall likewise be reconsidered, and if approved by two thirds of that House, it shall become a Law. But in all such Cases the Votes of both Houses shall be determined by Yeas and Nays, and the Names of the Persons voting for and against the Bill shall be entered on the Journal of each House respectively. If any Bill shall not be returned by the President within ten Days (Sundays excepted) after it shall have been presented to him, the Same shall be a Law, in like Manner as if he had signed it, unless the Congress by their Adjournment prevent its Return, in which Case it shall not be a Law.

[3]   Every Order, Resolution, or Vote to which the Concurrence of the Senate and House of Representatives may be necessary (except on a question of Adjournment) shall be presented to the President of the United States; and before the Same shall take Effect, shall be approved by him, or being disapproved by him, shall be repassed by two thirds of the Senate and House of Representatives, according to the Rules and Limitations prescribed in the Case of a Bill.

Section 8. [1] The Congress shall have Power To lay and collect Taxes, Duties, Imposts and Excises, to pay the Debts and provide for the common Defence and general Welfare of the United States; but all Duties, Imposts and Excises shall be uniform throughout the United States;

[2]   To borrow Money on the credit of the United States;

[3]   To regulate Commerce with foreign Nations, and among the several States, and with the Indian Tribes;

[4]   To establish an uniform Rule of Naturalization, and uniform Laws on the subject of Bankruptcies throughout the United States;

[5]   To coin Money, regulate the Value thereof, and of foreign Coin, and fix the Standard of Weights and Measures;

[6]   To provide for the Punishment of counterfeiting the Securities and current Coin of the United States;

[7]   To establish Post Offices and Post Roads;

[8]   To promote the Progress of Science and useful Arts, by securing for limited Times to Authors and Inventors the exclusive Right to their respective Writings and Discoveries;

[9]   To constitute Tribunals inferior to the supreme Court;

[10] To define and punish Piracies and Felonies committed on the high Seas, and Offences against the Law of Nations;

[11] To declare War, grant Letters of Marque and Reprisal, and make Rules concerning Captures on Land and Water;

[12] To raise and support Armies, but no Appropriation of Money to that Use shall be for a longer Term than two Years;

[13] To provide and maintain a Navy;

[14] To make Rules for the Government and Regulation of the land and naval Forces;

[15] To provide for calling forth the Militia to execute the Laws of the Union, suppress Insurrections and repel Invasions;

[16] To provide for organizing, arming, and disciplining, the Militia, and for governing such Part of them as may be employed in the Service of the United States, reserving to the States respectively, the Appointment of the Officers, and the Authority of training the Militia according to the discipline prescribed by Congress;

[17] To exercise exclusive Legislation in all Cases whatsoever, over such District (not exceeding ten Miles square) as may, by Cession of particular States and the Acceptance of Congress, become the Seat of the Government of the United States, and to exercise like Authority over all Places purchased by the Consent of the Legislature of the State in which the Same shall be, for the Erection of Forts, Magazines, Arsenals, dock-Yards, and other needful Buildings;—And

[18] To make all Laws which shall be necessary and proper for carrying into Execution the foregoing Powers, and all other Powers vested by this Constitution in the Government of the United States, or in any Department or Officer thereof.

Section 9. [1] The Migration or Importation of such Persons as any of the States now existing shall think proper to admit, shall not be prohibited by the Congress prior to the Year one thousand eight hundred and eight, but a Tax or duty may be imposed on such Importation, not exceeding ten dollars for each Person.

[2]   The Privilege of the Writ of Habeas Corpus shall not be suspended, unless when in Cases of Rebellion or Invasion the public Safety may require it.

[3]   No Bill of Attainder or ex post facto Law shall be passed.

[4]   No Capitation, or other direct, Tax shall be laid, unless in Proportion to the Census or Enumeration herein before directed to be taken.

[5]   No Tax or Duty shall be laid on Articles exported from any State.

[6]   No Preference shall be given by any Regulation of Commerce or Revenue to the Ports of one State over those of another: nor shall Vessels bound to, or from, one State, be obliged to enter, clear, or pay Duties in another.

[7] No Money shall be drawn from the Treasury, but in Consequence of Appropriations made by Law; and a regular Statement and Account of the Receipts and Expenditures of all public Money shall be published from time to time.

[8] No Title of Nobility shall be granted by the United States: And no Person holding any Office of Profit or Trust under them, shall, without the Consent of the Congress, accept of any present, Emolument, Office, or Title, of any kind whatever, from any King, Prince, or foreign State.

Section 10. [1] No State shall enter into any Treaty, Alliance, or Confederation; grant Letters of Marque and Reprisal; coin Money; emit Bills of Credit; make any Thing but gold and silver Coin a Tender in Payment of Debts; pass any Bill of Attainder, ex post facto Law, or Law impairing the Obligation of Contracts, or grant any Title of Nobility.

[2] No State shall, without the Consent of the Congress, lay any Imposts or Duties on Imports or Exports, except what may be absolutely necessary for executing its inspection Laws: and the net Produce of all Duties and Imposts, laid by any State on Imports or Exports, shall be for the Use of the Treasury of the United States; and all such Laws shall be subject to the Revision and Controul of the Congress.

[3] No State shall, without the Consent of Congress, lay any Duty of Tonnage, keep Troops, or Ships of War in time of Peace, enter into any Agreement or Compact with another State, or with a foreign Power, or engage in War, unless actually invaded, or in such imminent Danger as will not admit of delay.

ARTICLE II

Section 1. [1] The executive Power shall be vested in a President of the United States of America. He shall hold his Office during the Term of four Years, and, together with the Vice President, chosen for the same Term, be elected, as follows:

[2] Each State shall appoint, in such Manner as the Legislature thereof may direct, a Number of Electors, equal to the whole Number of Senators and Representatives to which the State may be entitled in the Congress: but no Senator or Representative, or Person holding an Office of Trust or Profit under the United States, shall be appointed an Elector.

[3] The electors shall meet in their respective States, and vote by ballot for two Persons, of whom one at least shall not be an Inhabitant of the same State with themselves. And they shall make a List of all the Persons voted for, and of the Number of Votes for each; which List they shall sign and certify, and transmit sealed to the Seat of the Government of the United States, directed to the President of the Senate. The President of the Senate shall, in the Presence of the Senate and House of Representatives, open all the Certificates, and the Votes shall then be counted. The Person having the greatest Number of Votes shall be the President, if such Number be a Majority of the whole Number of Electors appointed; and if there be more than one who have such Majority, and have an equal Number of Votes, then the House of Representatives shall immediately chuse by Ballot one of them for President; and if no Person have a Majority, then from the five highest on the List the said House shall in like Manner chuse the President. But in chusing the President, the Votes shall be taken by States, the Representation from each State having one Vote; A quorum for this Purpose shall consist of a Member or Members from two thirds of the States, and a Majority of all the States shall be necessary to a Choice. In every Case, after the Choice of the President, the Person

having the greatest Number of Votes of the Electors shall be the Vice President. But if there should remain two or more who have equal Votes, the Senate shall chuse from them by Ballot the Vice-President.

[4] The Congress may determine the Time of chusing the Electors, and the Day on which they shall give their Votes; which Day shall be the same throughout the United States.

[5] No Person except a natural born Citizen, or a Citizen of the United States, at the time of the Adoption of this Constitution, shall be eligible to the Office of President; neither shall any Person be eligible to that Office who shall not have attained to the Age of thirty five Years, and been fourteen Years a Resident within the United States.

[6] In Case of the Removal of the President from Office, or of his Death, Resignation, or Inability to discharge the Powers and Duties of the said Office, the Same shall devolve on the Vice President, and the Congress may by Law provide for the Case of Removal, Death, Resignation or Inability, both of the President and Vice President, declaring what Officer shall then act as President, and such Officer shall act accordingly, until the Disability be removed, or a President shall be elected.

[7] The President shall, at stated Times, receive for his Services, a Compensation, which shall neither be encreased nor diminished during the Period for which he shall have been elected, and he shall not receive within that Period any other Emolument from the United States, or any of them.

[8] Before he enter on the Execution of his Office, he shall take the following Oath or Affirmation: "I do solemnly swear (or affirm) that I will faithfully execute the Office of President of the United States, and will to the best of my Ability, preserve, protect and defend the Constitution of the United States."

Section 2. [1] The President shall be Commander in Chief of the Army and Navy of the United States, and of the Militia of the several States, when called into the actual Service of the United States; he may require the Opinion, in writing, of the principal Officer in each of the executive Departments, upon any Subject relating to the Duties of their respective Offices, and he shall have Power to grant Reprieves and Pardons for Offenses against the United States, except in Cases of Impeachment.

[2] He shall have Power, by and with the Advice and Consent of the Senate, to make Treaties, provided two thirds of the Senators present concur; and he shall nominate, and by and with the Advice and Consent of the Senate, shall appoint Ambassadors, other public Ministers and Consuls, Judges of the supreme Court, and all other Officers of the United States, whose Appointments are not herein otherwise provided for, and which shall be established by Law: but the Congress may by Law vest the Appointment of such inferior Officers, as they think proper, in the President alone, in the Courts of Law, or in the Heads of Departments.

[3] The President shall have Power to fill up all Vacancies that may happen during the Recess of the Senate, by granting Commissions which shall expire at the End of their next Session.

Section 3. He shall from time to time give to the Congress Information of the State of the Union, and recommend to their Consideration such Measures as he shall judge necessary and expedient; he may, on extraordinary Occasions, convene both Houses, or either of them, and in Case of Disagreement between them, with Respect to the Time of Adjournment, he may adjourn them to such Time as he shall think proper; he shall receive Ambassadors and other public Ministers; he shall take Care that the Laws be faithfully executed, and shall Commission all the Officers of the United States.

Section 4. The President, Vice President and all civil Officers of the United States, shall be removed from Office on Impeachment for, and Conviction of, Treason, Bribery, or other high Crimes and Misdemeanors.

ARTICLE III

Section 1. The judicial Power of the United States, shall be vested in one supreme Court, and in such inferior Courts as the Congress may from time to time ordain and establish. The Judges, both of the supreme and inferior Courts, shall hold their Offices during good Behaviour, and shall, at stated Times, receive for their Services, a Compensation, which shall not be diminished during their Continuance in Office.

Section 2. [1] The judicial Power shall extend to all Cases, in Law and Equity, arising under this Constitution, the Laws of the United States, and Treaties made, or which shall be made, under their Authority;—to all Cases affecting Ambassadors, other public Ministers and Consuls;—to all Cases of admiralty and maritime Jurisdiction;—to Controversies to which the United States shall be a Party;—to Controversies between two or more States;—between a State and Citizens of another State;—between Citizens of different States;—between Citizens of the same State claiming Lands under Grants of different States, and between a State, or the Citizens thereof, and foreign States, Citizens or Subjects.

[2] In all Cases affecting Ambassadors, other public Ministers and Consuls, and those in which a State shall be Party, the supreme Court shall have original Jurisdiction. In all the other Cases before mentioned, the supreme Court shall have appellate Jurisdiction, both as to Law and Fact, with such Exceptions, and under such Regulations as the Congress shall make.

[3] The Trial of all Crimes, except in Cases of Impeachment, shall be by Jury; and such Trial shall be held in the State where the said Crimes shall have been committed; but when not committed within any State, the Trial shall be at such Place or Places as the Congress may by Law have directed.

Section 3. [1] Treason against the United States, shall consist only in levying War against them, or in adhering to their Enemies, giving them Aid and Comfort. No Person shall be convicted of Treason unless on the Testimony of two Witnesses to the same overt Act, or on Confession in open Court.

[2] The Congress shall have Power to declare the Punishment of Treason, but no Attainder of Treason shall work Corruption of Blood, or Forfeiture except during the Life of the Person attainted.

ARTICLE IV

Section 1. Full Faith and Credit shall be given in each State to the public Acts, Records, and judicial Proceedings of every other State. And the Congress may by general Laws prescribe the Manner in which such Acts, Records and Proceedings shall be proved, and the Effect thereof.

Section 2. [1] The Citizens of each State shall be entitled to all Privileges and Immunities of Citizens in the several States.

[2] A person charged in any State with Treason, Felony, or other Crime, who shall flee from Justice, and be found in another State, shall on Demand of the

executive Authority of the State from which he fled, be delivered up, to be removed to the State having Jurisdiction of the Crime.

[3]   No Person held to Service or Labour in one State, under the Laws thereof, escaping into another, shall, in Consequence of any Law or Regulation therein, be discharged from such Service or Labour, but shall be delivered up on Claim of the Party to whom such Service or Labour may be due.

Section 3. [1] New States may be admitted by the Congress into this Union; but no new State shall be formed or erected within the Jurisdiction of any other State; nor any State be formed by the Junction of two or more States, or Parts of States, without the Consent of the Legislatures of the States concerned as well as of the Congress.

[2]   The Congress shall have Power to dispose of and make all needful Rules and Regulations respecting the Territory or other Property belonging to the United States; and nothing in this Constitution shall be so construed as to Prejudice any Claims of the United States, or of any particular State.

Section 4. The United States shall guarantee to every State in this Union a Republican Form of Government, and shall protect each of them against Invasion; and on Application of the Legislature, or of the Executive (when the Legislature cannot be convened) against domestic Violence.

ARTICLE V

The Congress, whenever two thirds of both Houses shall deem it necessary, shall propose Amendments to this Constitution, or on the Application of the Legislatures of two thirds of the several States, shall call a Convention for proposing Amendments, which, in either Case, shall be valid to all Intents and Purposes, as Part of this Constitution, when ratified by the Legislatures of three fourths of the several States, or by Conventions in three fourths thereof, as the one or the other Mode of Ratification may be proposed by the Congress; Provided that no Amendment which may be made prior to the Year One thousand eight hundred and eight shall in any Manner affect the first and fourth Clauses in the Ninth Section of the first Article; and that no State, without its Consent, shall be deprived of its equal Suffrage in the Senate.

ARTICLE VI

[1]   All Debts contracted and Engagements entered into, before the Adoption of this Constitution, shall be as valid against the United States under this Constitution, as under the Confederation.

[2]   This Constitution, and the Laws of the United States which shall be made in Pursuance thereof; and all Treaties made, or which shall be made, under the Authority of the United States, shall be the supreme Law of the Land; and the Judges in every State shall be bound thereby, any Thing in the Constitution or Laws of any State to the Contrary notwithstanding.

[3]   The Senators and Representatives before mentioned, and the Members of the several State Legislatures, and all executive and judicial Officers, both of the United States and of the several States, shall be bound by Oath or Affirmation, to support this Constitution; but no religious Test shall ever be required as a Qualification to any Office or public Trust under the United States.

ARTICLE VII

The Ratification of the Conventions of nine States, shall be sufficient for the Establishment of this Constitution between the States so ratifying the Same.

ARTICLES IN ADDITION TO, AND AMENDMENT OF, THE CONSTITUTION OF THE UNITED STATES OF AMERICA, PROPOSED BY CONGRESS, AND RATIFIED BY THE LEGISLATURES OF THE SEVERAL STATES, PURSUANT TO THE FIFTH ARTICLE OF THE ORIGINAL CONSTITUTION.

AMENDMENT I [1791]

Congress shall make no law respecting an establishment of religion, or prohibiting the free exercise thereof; or abridging the freedom of speech, or of the press; or the right of the people peaceably to assemble, and to petition the Government for a redress of grievances.

AMENDMENT II [1791]

A well regulated Militia, being necessary to the security of a free State, the right of the people to keep and bear Arms, shall not be infringed.

AMENDMENT III [1791]

No Soldier shall, in time of peace be quartered in any house, without the consent of the Owner, nor in time of war, but in a manner to be prescribed by law.

AMENDMENT IV [1791]

The right of the people to be secure in their persons, houses, papers, and effects, against unreasonable searches and seizures, shall not be violated, and no Warrants shall issue, but upon probable cause, supported by Oath or affirmation, and particularly describing the place to be searched, and the persons or things to be seized.

AMENDMENT V [1791]

No person shall be held to answer for a capital, or otherwise infamous crime, unless on a presentment or indictment of a Grand Jury, except in cases arising in the land or naval forces, or in the Militia, when in actual service in time of War or public danger; nor shall any person be subject for the same offence to be twice put in jeopardy of life or limb; nor shall be compelled in any criminal case to be a witness against himself, nor be deprived of life, liberty, or property, without due process of law; nor shall private property be taken for public use, without just compensation.

AMENDMENT VI [1791]

In all criminal prosecutions, the accused shall enjoy the right to a speedy and public trial, by an impartial jury of the State and district wherein the crime shall have been committed, which district shall have been previously ascertained by law, and to be informed of the nature and cause of the accusation; to be confronted with the witnesses against him; to have compulsory process for obtaining witnesses in his favor, and to have the Assistance of Counsel for his defence.

AMENDMENT VII [1791]

In Suits at common law, where the value in controversy shall exceed twenty dollars, the right of trial by jury shall be preserved, and no fact tried by a jury, shall be otherwise re-examined in any Court of the United States, than according to the rules of the common law.

AMENDMENT VIII [1791]

Excessive bail shall not be required, nor excessive fines imposed, nor cruel and unusual punishments inflicted.

AMENDMENT IX [1791]

The enumeration in the Constitution, of certain rights, shall not be construed to deny or disparage others retained by the people.

AMENDMENT X [1791]

The powers not delegated to the United States by the Constitution, nor prohibited by it to the States, are reserved to the States respectively, or to the people.

AMENDMENT XI [1798]

The Judicial power of the United States shall not be construed to extend to any suit in law or equity, commenced or prosecuted against one of the United States by Citizens of another State, or by Citizens or Subjects of any Foreign State.

AMENDMENT XII [1804]

The Electors shall meet in their respective states and vote by ballot for President and Vice-President, one of whom, at least, shall not be an inhabitant of the same state with themselves; they shall name in their ballots the person voted for as President, and in distinct ballots the person voted for as Vice-President, and they shall make distinct lists of all persons voted for as President, and of all persons voted for as Vice-President, and of the number of votes for each, which lists they shall sign and certify, and transmit sealed to the seat of the government of the United States, directed to the President of the Senate;—The President of the Senate shall, in the presence of the Senate and House of Representatives, open all the certificates and the votes shall then be counted;—The person having the greatest number of votes for President, shall be the President, if such number be a majority of the whole number of Electors appointed; and if no person have such majority, then from the persons having the highest numbers not exceeding three on the list of those voted for as President, the House of Representatives shall choose immediately, by ballot, the President. But in choosing the President, the votes shall be taken by states, the representation from each state having one vote; a quorum for this purpose shall consist of a member or members from two-thirds of the states, and a majority of all the states shall be necessary to a choice. And if the House of Representatives shall not choose a President whenever the right of choice shall devolve upon them, before the fourth day of March next following, then the Vice-President shall act as President, as in the case of the death or other constitutional disability of the President. The person having the greatest number of votes as Vice-President, shall be the Vice-President, if such number be a majority of the whole number of Electors appointed, and if no person have a majority, then from the two highest numbers on the list, the Senate shall choose the Vice-President; a quorum for the purpose shall consist of two-thirds of the whole number of Senators, and a majority of the whole number shall be necessary to a choice. But no person constitutionally ineligible to the office of President shall be eligible to that of Vice-President of the United States.

AMENDMENT XIII [1865]

Section 1. Neither slavery nor involuntary servitude, except as a punishment for crime whereof the party shall have been duly convicted, shall exist within the United States, or any place subject to their jurisdiction.

Section 2. Congress shall have power to enforce this article by appropriate legislation.

AMENDMENT XIV [1868]

Section 1. All persons born or naturalized in the United States, and subject to the jurisdiction thereof, are citizens of the United States and of the State wherein they reside. No State shall make or enforce any law which shall abridge the privileges or immunities of citizens of the United States; nor shall any State deprive any person of life, liberty, or property, without due process of law; nor deny to any person within its jurisdiction the equal protection of the laws.

Section 2. Representatives shall be apportioned among the several States according to their respective numbers, counting the whole number of persons in each State, excluding Indians not taxed. But when the right to vote at any election for the choice of electors for President and Vice President of the United States, Representatives in Congress, the Executive and Judicial officers of a State, or the members of the Legislature thereof, is denied to any of the male inhabitants of such State, being twenty-one years of age, and citizens of the United States, or in any way abridged, except for participation in rebellion, or other crime, the basis of representation therein shall be reduced in the proportion which the number of such male citizens shall bear to the whole number of male citizens twenty-one years of age in such State.

Section 3. No person shall be a Senator or Representative in Congress, or elector of President and Vice President, or hold any office, civil or military, under the United States, or under any State, who, having previously taken an oath, as a member of Congress, or as an officer of the United States, or as a member of any State legislature, or as an executive or judicial officer of any State, to support the Constitution of the United States, shall have engaged in insurrection or rebellion against the same, or given aid or comfort to the enemies thereof. But Congress may by a vote of two-thirds of each House, remove such disability.

Section 4. The validity of the public debt of the United States, authorized by law, including debts incurred for payment of pensions and bounties for services in suppressing insurrection or rebellion, shall not be questioned. But neither the United States nor any State shall assume or pay any debt or obligation incurred in aid of insurrection or rebellion against the United States, or any claim for the loss or emancipation of any slave; but all such debts, obligations and claims shall be held illegal and void.

Section 5. The Congress shall have power to enforce, by appropriate legislation, the provisions of this article.

AMENDMENT XV [1870]

Section 1. The right of citizens of the United States to vote shall not be denied or abridged by the United States or by any State on account of race, color, or previous condition of servitude.

Section 2. The Congress shall have power to enforce this article by appropriate legislation.

AMENDMENT XVI [1913]

The Congress shall have power to lay and collect taxes on incomes, from whatever source derived, without apportionment among the several States, and without regard to any census or enumeration.

AMENDMENT XVII [1913]

[1]   The Senate of the United States shall be composed of two Senators from each State, elected by the people thereof, for six years; and each Senator shall have one vote.   The electors in each State shall have the qualifications requisite for electors of the most numerous branch of the State legislatures.

[2]   When vacancies happen in the representation of any State in the Senate, the executive authority of such State shall issue writs of election to fill such vacancies: *Provided*, That the legislature of any State may empower the executive thereof to make temporary appointments until the people fill the vacancies by election as the legislature may direct.

[3]   This amendment shall not be so construed as to affect the election or term of any Senator chosen before it becomes valid as part of the Constitution.

AMENDMENT XVIII [1919]

Section 1. After one year from the ratification of this article the manufacture, sale, or transportation of intoxicating liquors within, the importation thereof into, or the exportation thereof from the United States and all territory subject to the jurisdiction thereof for beverage purposes is hereby prohibited.

Section 2. The Congress and the several States shall have concurrent power to enforce this article by appropriate legislation.

Section 3. This article shall be inoperative unless it shall have been ratified as an amendment to the Constitution by the legislatures of the several States, as provided in the Constitution, within seven years from the date of the submission hereof to the States by the Congress.

AMENDMENT XIX [1920]

[1]   The right of citizens of the United States to vote shall not be denied or abridged by the United States or by any State on account of sex.

[2]   Congress shall have power to enforce this article by appropriate legislation.

AMENDMENT XX [1933]

Section 1. The terms of the President and Vice President shall end at noon on the 20th day of January, and the terms of Senators and Representatives at noon on the 3d day of January, of the years in which such terms would have ended if this article had not been ratified; and the terms of their successors shall then begin.

Section 2. The Congress shall assemble at least once in every year, and such meeting shall begin at noon on the 3d day of January, unless they shall by law appoint a different day.

Section 3. If, at the time fixed for the beginning of the term of the President, the President elect shall have died, the Vice President elect shall become President. If a President shall not have been chosen before the time fixed for the beginning of his term, or if the President elect shall have failed to qualify, then the Vice President elect shall act as President until a President shall have qualified; and the Congress may by law provide for the case wherein neither a President elect nor a Vice President elect shall have qualified, declaring who shall then act as President, or the manner in which one who is to act shall be selected, and such person shall act accordingly until a President or Vice President shall have qualified.

Section 4. The Congress may by law provide for the case of the death of any of the persons from whom the House of Representatives may choose a President whenever the right of choice shall have devolved upon them, and for the case of the death of any of the persons from whom the Senate may choose a Vice President whenever the right of choice shall have devolved upon them.

Section 5. Sections 1 and 2 shall take effect on the 15th day of October following the ratification of this article.

Section 6. This article shall be inoperative unless it shall have been ratified as an amendment to the Constitution by the legislatures of three-fourths of the several States within seven years from the date of its submission.

AMENDMENT XXI [1933]

Section 1. The eighteenth article of amendment to the Constitution of the United States is hereby repealed.

Section 2. The transportation or importation into any State, Territory, or possession of the United States for delivery or use therein of intoxicating liquors, in violation of the laws thereof, is hereby prohibited.

Section 3. This article shall be inoperative unless it shall have been ratified as an amendment to the Constitution by conventions in the several States, as provided in the Constitution, within seven years from the date of the submission hereof to the States by the Congress.

AMENDMENT XXII [1951]

Section 1. No person shall be elected to the office of the President more than twice, and no person who has held the office of President, or acted as President, for more than two years of a term to which some other person was elected President shall be elected to the office of the President more than once. But this Article shall not apply to any person holding the office of President when this Article was proposed by the Congress, and shall not prevent any person who may be holding the office of President, or acting as President, during the term within which this Article becomes operative from holding the office of President or acting as President during the remainder of such term.

Section 2. This article shall be inoperative unless it shall have been ratified as an amendment to the Constitution by the legislatures of three-fourths of the several States within seven years from the date of its submission to the States by the Congress.

AMENDMENT XXIII [1961]

Section 1. The District constituting the seat of Government of the United States shall appoint in such manner as the Congress may direct:

A number of electors of President and Vice President equal to the whole number of Senators and Representatives in Congress to which the District would be entitled if it were a State, but in no event more than the least populous State; they shall be in addition to those appointed by the States, but they shall be considered, for the purposes of the election of President and Vice President, to be electors appointed by a State; and they shall meet in the District and perform such duties as provided by the twelfth article of amendment.

Section 2. The Congress shall have power to enforce this article by appropriate legislation.

AMENDMENT XXIV [1964]

Section 1. The right of citizens of the United States to vote in any primary or other election for President or Vice President, for electors for President or Vice President, or for Senator or Representative in Congress, shall not be denied or abridged by the United States or any State by reason of failure to pay any poll tax or other tax.

Section 2. The Congress shall have power to enforce this article by appropriate legislation.

AMENDMENT XXV [1967]

Section 1. In case of the removal of the President from office or of his death or resignation, the Vice President shall become President.

Section 2. Whenever there is a vacancy in the office of the Vice President, the President shall nominate a Vice President who shall take office upon confirmation by a majority vote of both Houses of Congress.

Section 3. Whenever the President transmits to the President pro tempore of the Senate and the Speaker of the House of Representatives his written declaration that he is unable to discharge the powers and duties of his office, and until he transmits to them a written declaration to the contrary, such powers and duties shall be discharged by the Vice President as Acting President.

Section 4. Whenever the Vice President and a majority of either the principal officers of the executive departments or of such other body as Congress may by law provide, transmit to the President pro tempore of the Senate and the Speaker of the House of Representatives their written declaration that the President is unable to discharge the powers and duties of his office, the Vice President shall immediately assume the powers and duties of the office as Acting President.

Thereafter, when the President transmits to the President pro tempore of the Senate and the Speaker of the House of Representatives his written declaration that no inability exists, he shall resume the powers and duties of his office unless the Vice President and a majority of either the principal officers of the executive department or of such other body as Congress may by law provide, transmit within four days to the President pro tempore of the Senate and the Speaker of the House of Representatives their written declaration that the President is unable to discharge the powers and duties of his office. Thereupon Congress shall decide the issue, assembling within forty-eight hours for that purpose if not in session. If the Congress, within twenty-one days after receipt of the latter written declaration, or, if Congress is not in session, within twenty-one days after Congress is required to assemble, determines by two-thirds vote of both Houses that the President is unable to discharge the powers and duties of his office, the Vice President shall continue to discharge the same as Acting President; otherwise, the President shall resume the powers and duties of his office.

AMENDMENT XXVI [1971]

Section 1. The right of citizens of the United States, who are eighteen years of age or older, to vote shall not be denied or abridged by the United States or by any State on account of age.

Section 2. The Congress shall have power to enforce this article by appropriate legislation.

AMENDMENT XXVII [1992][a]

No law, varying the compensation for the services of the Senators and Representatives, shall take effect, until an election of Representatives shall have intervened.

---

a. *Editors' note:* For questions about the validity of the ratification of this amendment, see pp. 1267-68, *supra.*

Appendix 2

CONSTITUTIONAL RATIFICATION MATERIALS

Letter of George Washington, President of the Federal Convention, to the President of Congress, Transmitting the Constitution[a]

In Convention, September 17, 1787.

Sir,

We have now the honor to submit to the consideration of the United States in Congress assembled, that Constitution which has appeared to us the most adviseable.

The friends of our country have long seen and desired, that the power of making war, peace, and treaties, that of levying money and regulating commerce, and the correspondent executive and judicial authorities should be fully and effectually vested in the general government of the Union: But the impropriety of delegating such extensive trust to one body of men is evident — Hence results the necessity of a different organization.

It is obviously impracticable in the federal government of these states, to secure all rights of independent sovereignty to each, and yet provide for the interest and safety of all: Individuals entering into society, must give up a share of liberty to preserve the rest. The magnitude of the sacrifice must depend as well on situation and circumstance, as on the object to be obtained. It is at all times difficult to draw with precision the line between those rights which must be surrendered, and those which may be reserved; and on the present occasion this difficulty was increased by a difference among the several states as to their situation, extent, habits, and particular interests.

In all our deliberations on this subject we kept steadily in our view, that which appears to us the greatest interest of every true American, the consolidation of our Union, in which is involved our prosperity, felicity, safety, perhaps our national existence. This important consideration, seriously and deeply impressed on our

---

a. From Daniel Farber, *The Constitution's Forgotten Cover Letter: An Essay on the New Federalism and the Original Understanding*, 94 Mich. L. Rev. 615 (1995).

minds, led each state in the Convention to be less rigid on points of inferior magnitude, than might have been otherwise expected; and thus the Constitution, which we now present, is the result of a spirit of amity, and of that mutual deference and concession which the peculiarity of our political situation rendered indispensible.

That it will meet the full and entire approbation of every state is not perhaps to be expected; but each will doubtless consider, that had her interest been alone consulted, the consequences might have been particularly disagreeable or injurious to others; that it is liable to as few exceptions as could reasonably have been expected, we hope and believe; that it may promote the lasting welfare of that country so dear to us all, and secure her freedom and happiness, is our most ardent wish.

With great respect, We have the honor to be, Sir,

> Your Excellency's
>
> most obedient and humble servants,
>
> GEORGE WASHINGTON, *President*
>
> *By unanimous Order of the Convention.*

His Excellency the PRESIDENT OF CONGRESS.

Federalist No. 10[b]
Madison

Among the numerous advantages promised by a well-constructed Union, none deserves to be more accurately developed than its tendency to break and control the violence of faction. The friend of popular governments never finds himself so much alarmed for their character and fare, as when he contemplates their propensity to this dangerous vice.

By a faction, I understand a number of citizens, whether amounting to a majority or minority of the whole, who are united and actuated by some common impulse of passion, or of interest, adverse to the rights of other citizens, or to the permanent and aggregate interests of the community.

There are two methods of curing the mischiefs of faction: the one, by removing its causes; the other, by controlling its effects.

There are again two methods of removing the causes of faction: the one, by destroying the liberty which is essential to its existence; the other, by giving to every citizen the same opinions, the same passions, and the same interests.

It could never be more truly said than of the first remedy, that it was worse than the disease. Liberty is to faction what air is to fire, an aliment without which it

---

b. As excerpted in Daniel Farber & Suzanna Sherry, *A History of the American Constitution* (1990).

instantly expires. But it could not be less folly to abolish liberty, which is essential to political life, because it nourishes faction, than it would be to wish the annihilation of air, which is essential to animal life, because it imparts to fire its destructive agency.

The second expedient is as impracticable as the first would be unwise. As long as the reason of man continues fallible, and he is at liberty to exercise it, different opinions will be formed. As long as the connection subsists between his reason and his self-love, his opinions and his passions will have a reciprocal influence on each other; and the former will be objects to which the latter will attach themselves. The diversity in the faculties of men, from which the rights of property originate, is not less an insuperable obstacle to a uniformity of interests. The protection of these faculties is the first object of government. From the protection of different and unequal faculties of acquiring property, the possession of different degrees and kinds of property immediately results; and from the influence of these on the sentiments and views of the respective proprietors, ensues a division of the society into different interests and parties.

The latent causes of faction are thus sown in the nature of man; and we see them everywhere brought into different degrees of activity, according to the different circumstances of civil society. A zeal for different opinions concerning religion, concerning government, and many other points, as well of speculation as of practice; an attachment to different leaders ambitiously contending for pre-eminence and power; or to persons of other descriptions whose fortunes have been interesting to the human passions, have, in turn, divided mankind into parties, inflamed them with mutual animosity, and rendered them much more disposed to vex and oppress each other than to co-operate for their common good. So strong is this propensity of mankind to fall into mutual animosities, that where no substantial occasion presents itself, the most frivolous and fanciful distinctions have been sufficient to kindle their unfriendly passions and excite their most violent conflicts. But the most common and durable source of factions has been the various and unequal distribution of property. Those who hold and those who are without property have ever formed distinct interests in society. Those who are creditors, and those who are debtors, fall under a like discrimination. A landed interest, a manufacturing interest, a mercantile interest, a moneyed interest, with many lesser interests, grow up of necessity in civilized nations, and divide them into different classes, actuated by different sentiments and views. The regulation of these various and interfering interests forms the principal task of modern legislation, and involves the spirit of party and faction in the necessary and ordinary operations of the government.

No man is allowed to be a judge in his own cause, because his interest would certainly bias his judgment, and, not improbably, corrupt his integrity. With equal, nay with greater reason, a body of men are unfit to be both judges and parties at the same time; yet what are many of the most important acts of legislation, but so many judicial determinations, not indeed concerning the rights of single persons, but concerning the rights of large bodies of citizens? And what are the different classes of legislators but advocates and parties to the causes which they determine? Is a law proposed concerning private debts? It is a question to which the creditors are parties on one side and the debtors on the other. Justice ought to hold the balance between them. Yet the parties are, and must be, themselves the judges; and the most numerous party, or, in other words, the most powerful faction must be expected to prevail. Shall domestic manufactures be encouraged, and in what degree, by restrictions on foreign manufactures? are questions which would be differently decided by the landed and the manufacturing classes, and probably by neither with a sole regard to justice and the public good. The apportionment of taxes on the various descriptions of property is an act which seems to require the most exact impartiality; yet there is, perhaps, no legislative act in which greater opportunity and temptation are given to a predominant party to trample on the rules of justice. Every shilling with which they overburden the inferior number, is a shilling saved to their own pockets.

It is in vain to say that enlightened statesmen will be able to adjust these clashing interests, and render them all subservient to the public good. Enlightened statesmen will not always be at the helm. Nor, in many cases, can such an adjustment be made at all without taking into view indirect and remote consider- ations, which will rarely prevail over the immediate interest which one party may find in disregarding the rights of another or the good of the whole.

The inference to which we are brought is, that the *causes* of faction cannot be removed, and that relief is only to be sought in the means of controlling its *effects*.

If a faction consists of less than a majority, relief is supplied by the republican principle, which enables the majority to defeat its sinister views by regular vote. It may clog the administration, it may convulse the society; but it will be unable to execute and mask its violence under the forms of the Constitution. When a majority is included in a faction, the form of popular government, on the other hand, enables it to sacrifice to its ruling passion or interest both the public good and the rights of other citizens. To secure the public good and private rights against the danger of such a faction, and at the same time to preserve the spirit and the form of popular government, is then the great object to which our inquiries are directed. Let me add that it is the great desideratum by which this form of government can be rescued from the opprobrium under which it has so long labored, and be recommended to the esteem and adoption of mankind.

By what means is this object attainable? Evidently by one of two only. Either the existence of the same passion or interest in a majority at the same time must be prevented, or the majority, having such coexistent passion or interest, must be rendered, by their number and local situation, unable to concert and carry into effect schemes of oppression. If the impulse and the opportunity be suffered to coincide, we well know that neither moral nor religious motives can be relied on as an adequate control. They are not found to be such on the injustice and violence of individuals, and lose their efficacy in proportion to the number combined together, that is, in proportion as their efficacy becomes needful.

From this view of the subject it may be concluded that a pure democracy, by which I mean a society consisting of a small number of citizens, who assemble and administer the government in person, can admit of no cure for the mischiefs of faction. A common passion or interest will, in almost every case, be felt by a majority of the whole; a communication and concert result from the form of government itself; and there is nothing to check the inducements to sacrifice the weaker party or an obnoxious individual. Hence it is that such democracies have ever been spectacles of turbulence and contention; have ever been found incompatible with personal security or the rights of property; and have in general been as short in their lives as they have been violent in their deaths. Theoretic politicians, who have patronized this species of government, have erroneously supposed that by reducing mankind to a perfect equality in their political rights, they would, at the same time, be perfectly equalized and assimilated in their possessions, their opinions, and their passions.

A republic, by which I mean a government in which the scheme of representation takes place, opens a different prospect, and promises the cure for which we are seeking. Let us examine the points in which it varies from pure democracy, and we shall comprehend both the nature of the cure and the efficacy which it must derive from the Union.

The two great points of difference between a democracy and a republic are: first, the delegation of the government, in the latter, to a small number of citizens elected by the rest; secondly, the greater number of citizens, and greater sphere of country, over which the latter may be extended.

The effect of the first difference is, on the one hand, to refine and enlarge the public views, by passing them through the medium of a chosen body of citizens, whose wisdom may best discern the true interest of their country, and whose patriotism and love of justice will be least likely to sacrifice it to temporary or partial considerations.

On the other hand, the effect may be inverted. Men of factious tempers, of local prejudices, or of sinister designs, may, by intrigue, by corruption, or by other means, first obtain the suffrages, and then betray the interests, of the people. The question resulting is, whether small or extensive republics are more favorable to the election of proper guardians of the public weal; and it is clearly decided in favor of the latter[.]

[T]he greater number of citizens and extent of territory which may be brought within the compass of republican than of democratic government ... [is the] circumstance principally which renders factious combinations less to be dreaded in the former than in the latter. The smaller the society the fewer probably will be the distinct parties and interests composing it; the fewer the distinct parties and interests, the more frequently will a majority be found of the same party; and the smaller the number of individuals composing a majority, and the smaller the compass within which they are placed, the more easily will they concert and execute their plans of oppression. Extend the sphere, and you take in a greater variety of parties and interests; you make it less probable that a majority of the whole will have a common motive to invade the rights of other citizens; or if such a common motive exists, it will be more difficult for all who feel it to discover their own strength, and to act in unison with each other. Besides other impediments, it may be remarked that, where there is a consciousness of unjust or dishonorable purposes, communication is always checked by distrust in proportion to the number whose concurrence is necessary.

Hence, it clearly appears, that the same advantage which a republic has over a democracy, in controlling the effects of faction, is enjoyed by a large over a small republic,—is enjoyed by the Union over the States composing it. Does the advantage consist in the substitution of representatives whose enlightened views and virtuous sentiments render them superior to local prejudices and to schemes of injustice? It will not be denied that the representation of the Union will be most likely to possess these requisite endowments. Does it consist in the greater security afforded by a greater variety of parties, against the event of any one party being able to outnumber and oppress the rest? In an equal degree does the increased variety of parties comprised within the Union, increase this security. Does it, in fine, consist in the greater obstacles opposed to the concert and accomplishment of the secret wishes of an unjust and interested majority? Here, again, the extent of the Union gives it the most palpable advantage.

The influence of factious leaders may kindle a flame within their particular States, but will be unable to spread a general conflagration through the other States. A religious sect may degenerate into a political faction in a part of the Confederacy; but the variety of sects dispersed over the entire face of it must secure the national councils against any danger from that source. A rage for paper money, for an abolition of debts, for an equal division of property, or for any other improper or wicked project, will be less apt to pervade the whole body of the Union than a particular member of it; in the same proportion as such a malady is more likely to taint a particular county or district, than an entire State.

In the extent and proper structure of the Union, therefore, we behold a republican remedy for the diseases most incident to republican government. And according to the degree of pleasure and pride we feel in being republicans, ought to be our zeal in cherishing the spirit and supporting the character of Federalists.

Federalist No. 47[c]
Madison

One of the principal objections inculcated by the more respectable adversaries to the Constitution is its supposed violation of the political maxim that the legislative, executive, and judiciary departments ought to be separate and distinct. In the structure of the federal government no regard, it is said, seems to have been paid to this essential precaution in favor of liberty. The several departments of power are distributed and blended in such a manner as at once to destroy all symmetry and beauty of form, and to expose some of the essential parts of the edifice to the danger of being crushed by the disproportionate weight of other parts.

No political truth is certainly of greater intrinsic value, or is stamped with the authority of more enlightened patrons of liberty than that on which the objection is founded. The accumulation of all powers, legislative, executive, and judiciary, in the same hands, whether of one, a few, or many, and whether hereditary, self-appointed, or elective, may justly be pronounced the very definition of tyranny. Were the federal Constitution, therefore, really chargeable with this accumulation of power, or with a mixture of powers, having a dangerous tendency to such an accumulation, no further arguments would be necessary to inspire a universal

---

c. Edited for the present volume.

reprobation of the system. I persuade myself, however, that it will be made apparent to everyone that the charge cannot be supported, and that the maxim on which it relies has been totally misconceived and misapplied. In order to form correct ideas on this important subject it will be proper to investigate the sense in which the preservation of liberty requires that the three great departments of power should be separate and distinct.

The oracle who is always consulted and cited on this subject is the celebrated Montesquieu. If he be not the author of this invaluable precept in the science of politics, he has the merit at least of displaying and recommending it most effectually to the attention of mankind. Let us endeavor, in the first place, to ascertain his meaning on this point.

The British Constitution was to Montesquieu what Homer has been to the didactic writers on epic poetry. As the latter have considered the work of the immortal bard as the perfect model from which the principles and rules of the epic art were to be drawn, and by which all similar works were to be judged, so this great political critic appears to have viewed the Constitution of England as the standard, or to use his own expression, as the mirror of political liberty; and to have delivered, in the form of elementary truths, the several characteristic principles of that particular system. That we may be sure, then, not to mistake his meaning in this case, let us recur to the source from which the maxim was drawn.

On the slightest view of the British Constitution we must perceive that the legislative, executive, and judiciary departments are by no means totally separate and distinct from each other. The executive magistrate forms an integral part of the legislative authority. He alone has the prerogative of making treaties with foreign sovereigns which, when made, have, under certain limitations, the force of legislative acts. All the members of the judiciary department are appointed by him, can be removed by him on the address of the two Houses of Parliament, and form when he pleases to consult them, one of his constitutional councils. One branch of the legislative department forms also a great constitutional council to the executive chief, as, on another hand, it is the sole depositary of judicial power in cases of impeachment, and is invested with the supreme appellate jurisdiction in all other cases. The judges, again, are so far connected with the legislative department as often to attend and participate in its deliberations, though not admitted to a legislative vote.

From these facts, by which Montesquieu was guided, it may clearly be inferred that in saying "There can be no liberty where the legislative and executive powers are united in the same person, or body of magistrates," or, "if the power of judging be not separated from the legislative and executive powers," he did not mean that these departments ought to have no partial agency in, or no control over, the acts of each other. His meaning, as his own words import, and still more conclusively as illustrated by the example in his eye, can amount to no more than this, that where the whole power of one department is exercised by the same hands which possess the whole power of another department, the fundamental principles of a free constitution are subverted. This would have been the case in the constitution examined by him, if the king, who is the sole executive magistrate, had possessed also the complete legislative power, or the supreme administration of justice; or if the entire legislative body had possessed the supreme judiciary, or the supreme executive authority. This, however, is not among the vices of that constitution. * * *

If we look into the constitutions of the several States we find that, notwithstanding the emphatical and, in some instances, the unqualified terms in which this axiom has been laid down, there is not a single instance in which the several departments of power have been kept absolutely separate and distinct. New Hampshire, whose constitution was the last formed, seems to have been fully aware of the impossibility and inexpediency of avoiding any mixture whatever of these departments, and has qualified the doctrine by declaring "that the legislative, executive, and judiciary powers ought to be kept as separate from, and independent of, each other *as the nature of a free government will admit; or as is consistent with that chain of connection that binds the whole fabric of the constitution in one indissoluble bond of unity and amity.*" Her constitution accordingly mixes these departments in several respects. The Senate, which is a branch of the legislative department, is also a judicial tribunal for the trial of impeachments. The President, who is the head of the executive department, is the presiding member also of the Senate; and, besides an equal vote in all cases, has a casting vote in case of a tie. The executive head is himself eventually elective every year by the legislative department, and his council is every year chosen by and from the members of the same department. Several of the officers of state are also appointed by the legislature. And the members of the judiciary department are appointed by the executive department. [Madison discusses other state constitutions, all of which mix legislative, executive, and judicial power in this way.]

In citing these cases, in which the legislative, executive, and judiciary departments have not been kept totally separate and distinct, I wish not to be regarded as an advocate for the particular organizations of the several State governments. I am fully aware that among the many excellent principles which they exemplify they carry strong marks of the haste, and still stronger of the inexperience, under which they were framed. It is but too obvious that in some instances the fundamental principle under consideration has been violated by too great a mixture, and even an actual consolidation of the different powers; and that in no instance has a competent provision been made for maintaining in practice the separation delineated on paper. What I have wished to evince is that the charge brought against the proposed Constitution of violating a sacred maxim of free government is warranted neither by the real meaning annexed to that maxim by its author, nor by the sense in which it has hitherto been understood in America. * * *

Federalist No. 51[d]
Madison

In order to lay a due foundation for that separate and distinct exercise of the different powers of government, which to a certain extent is admitted on all hands to be essential to the preservation of liberty, it is evident that each department should have a will of its own; and consequently should be so constituted that the

---

d. As excerpted in Daniel Farber & Suzanna Sherry, *A History of the American Constitution* (1990).

members of each should have as little agency as possible in the appointment of the members of the others. Were this principle rigorously adhered to, it would require that all the appointments for the supreme executive, legislative, and judiciary magistracies should be drawn from the same fountain of authority, the people, through channels having no communication whatever with one another. Perhaps such a plan of constructing the several departments would be less difficult in practice than it may in contemplation appear. Some difficulties, however, and some additional expense would attend the execution of it. Some deviations, therefore, from the principle must be admitted. In the constitution of the judiciary department in particular, it might be inexpedient to insist rigorously on the principle: first, because peculiar qualifications being essential in the members, the primary consideration ought to be to select that mode of choice which best secures these qualifications; secondly, because the permanent tenure by which the appointments are held in that department, must soon destroy all sense of dependence on the authority conferring them.

It is equally evident, that the members of each department should be as little dependent as possible on those of the others, for the emoluments annexed to their offices. Were the executive magistrate, or the judges, not independent of the legislature in this particular, their independence in every other would be merely nominal.

But the great security against a gradual concentration of the several powers in the same department, consists in giving to those who administer each department the necessary constitutional means and personal motives to resist encroachments of the others. The provision for defence must in this, as in all other cases, be made commensurate to the danger of attack. Ambition must be made to counteract ambition. The interest of the man must be connected with the constitutional rights of the place. It may be a reflection on human nature, that such devices should be necessary to control the abuses of government. But what is government itself, but the greatest of all reflections on human nature? If men were angels, no government would be necessary. If angels were to govern men, neither external nor internal controls on government would be necessary. In framing a government which is to be administered by men over men, the great difficulty lies in this: you must first enable the government to control the governed; and in the next place oblige it to control itself. A dependence on the people is, no doubt, the primary control on the government; but experience has taught mankind the necessity of auxiliary precautions.

This policy of supplying, by opposite and rival interests, the defect of better motives, might be traced through the whole system of human affairs, private as well as public. We see it particularly displayed in all the subordinate distributions of power, where the constant aim is to divide and arrange the several offices in such a manner as that each may be a check on the other—that the private interest of every individual may be a sentinel over the public rights. These inventions of prudence cannot be less requisite in the distribution of the supreme powers of the State.

But it is not possible to give to each department an equal power of self-defence. In republican government, the legislative authority necessarily predominates. The remedy for this inconveniency is to divide the legislature into different branches;

and to render them, by different modes of election and different principles of action, as little connected with each other as the nature of their common functions and their common dependence on the society will admit. It may even be necessary to guard against dangerous encroachments by still further precautions. As the weight of the legislative authority requires that it should be thus divided, the weakness of the executive may require, on the other hand, that it should be fortified.

In a single republic, all the power surrendered by the people is submitted to the administration of a single government; and the usurpations are guarded against by a division of the government into distinct and separate departments. In the compound republic of America, the power surrendered by the people is first divided between two distinct governments, and then the portion allotted to each subdivided among distinct and separate departments. Hence a double security arises to the rights of the people. The different governments will control each other, at the same time that each will be controlled by itself.

Federalist No. 78[e]
Hamilton

Whoever attentively considers the different departments of power must perceive, that, in a government in which they are separated from each other, the judiciary, from the nature of its functions, will always be the least dangerous to the political rights of the Constitution; because it will be least in a capacity to annoy or injure them. The Executive not only dispenses the honors, but holds the sword of the community. The legislature not only commands the purse, but prescribes the rules by which the duties and rights of every citizen are to be regulated. The judiciary, on the contrary, has no influence over either the sword or the purse; no direction either of the strength or of the wealth of the society; and can take no active resolution whatever. It may truly be said to have neither FORCE nor WILL, but merely judgment; and must ultimately depend upon the aid of the executive arm even for the efficacy of its judgments.

This simple view of the matter suggests several important consequences. It proves incontestably, that the judiciary is beyond comparison the weakest of the three departments of power;[*] That it can never attack with success either of the other two; and that all possible care is requisite to enable it to defend itself against their attacks. It equally proves, that though individual oppression may now and then proceed from the courts of justice, the general liberty of the people can never be endangered from that quarter; I mean so long as the judiciary remains truly distinct from both the legislature and the Executive. For I agree, that "there is no liberty, if the power of judging be not separated from the legislative and executive powers."[**] And it proves, in the last place, that as liberty can have nothing to fear

---

e. As excerpted in Daniel Farber & Suzanna Sherry, *A History of the American Constitution* (1990).

*. The celebrated Montesquieu, speaking of them, says: "Of the three powers above mentioned, the judiciary is next to nothing."—"Spirit of Laws," vol. i., page 186.—PUBLIUS

**. *Idem.* page 181.—PUBLIUS.

from the judiciary alone, but would have every thing to fear from its union with either of the other departments; that as all the effects of such a union must ensue from a dependence of the former on the latter, notwithstanding a nominal and apparent separation; that as, from the natural feebleness of the judiciary, it is in continual jeopardy of being overpowered, awed, or influenced by its coordinate branches; and that as nothing can contribute so much to its firmness and independence as permanency in office, this quality may therefore be justly regarded as an indispensable ingredient in its constitution, and, in a great measure, as the citadel of the public justice and the public security.

The complete independence of the courts of justice is peculiarly essential in a limited Constitution. By a limited Constitution, I understand one which contains certain specified exceptions to the legislative authority; for instance, as that it shall pass no bills of attainder, no *ex-post-facto* laws, and the like. Limitations of this kind can be preserved in practice no other way than through the medium of courts of justice, whose duty it must be to declare all acts contrary to the manifest tenor of the Constitution void. Without this, all the reservations of particular rights or privileges would amount to nothing.

Some perplexity respecting the rights of the courts to pronounce legislative acts void, because contrary to the constitution, has arisen from an imagination that the doctrine would imply a superiority of the judiciary to the legislative power. It is urged that the authority which can declare the acts of another void, must necessarily be superior to the one whose acts may be declared void. As this doctrine is of great importance in all the American constitutions, a brief discussion of the ground on which it rests cannot be unacceptable.

There is no position which depends on clearer principles, than that every act of a delegated authority, contrary to the tenor of the commission under which it is exercised, is void. No legislative act, therefore, contrary to the Constitution, can be valid. To deny this, would be to affirm, that the deputy is greater than his principal; that the servant is above his master; that the representatives of the people are superior to the people themselves; that men acting by virtue of powers, may do not only what their powers do not authorize, but what they forbid.

If it be said that the legislative body are themselves the constitutional judges of their own powers, and that the construction they put upon them is conclusive upon the other departments, it may be answered, that this cannot be the natural presumption, where it is not to be collected from any particular provisions in the Constitution. It is not otherwise to be supposed, that the Constitution could intend to enable the representatives of the people to substitute their *will* to that of their constituents. It is far more rational to suppose, that the courts were designed to be an intermediate body between the people and the legislature, in order, among other things, to keep the latter within the limits assigned to their authority. The interpretation of the laws is the proper and peculiar province of the courts. A constitution is, in fact, and must be regarded by the judges, as a fundamental law. It therefore belongs to them to ascertain its meaning, as well as the meaning of any particular act proceeding from the legislative body. If there should happen to be an irreconcilable variance between the two, that which has the superior obligation and validity ought, of course, to be preferred; or, in other words, the Constitution ought to be preferred to the statute, the intention of the people to the intention of their agents.

Nor does this conclusion by any means suppose a superiority of the judicial to the legislative power. It only supposes that the power of the people is superior to both; and that where the will of the legislature, declared in its statutes, stands in opposition to that of the people, declared in the Constitution, the judges ought to be governed by the latter rather than the former. They ought to regulate their decisions by the fundamental laws, rather than by those which are not fundamental.

Appendix 3

JAMES MADISON'S SPEECH TO THE HOUSE OF REPRESENTATIVES PRESENTING THE PROPOSED BILL OF RIGHTS, JUNE 8, 1789[a]

Mr. Madison.—I am sorry to be accessary to the loss of a single moment of time by the House. If I had been indulged in my motion, and we had gone into a Committee of the Whole, I think we might have rose and resumed the consideration of other business before this time; that is, so far as it depended upon what I proposed to bring forward. As that mode seems not to give satisfaction, I will withdraw the motion, and move you, sir, that a select committee be appointed to consider and report such amendments as are proper for Congress to propose to the Legislatures of the several States, conformably to the fifth article of the Constitution.

It will be a desirable thing to extinguish from the bosom of every member of the community, any apprehensions that there are those among his countrymen who wish to deprive them of the liberty for which they valiantly fought and honorably bled. And if there are amendments desired of such a nature as will not injure the Constitution, and they can be ingrafted so as to give satisfaction to the doubting part of our fellow-citizens, the friends of the Federal Government will evince that spirit of deference and concession for which they have hitherto been distinguished.

It cannot be a secret to the gentlemen in this House, that, notwithstanding the ratification of this system of Government by eleven of the thirteen United States, in some cases unanimously, in others by large majorities; yet still there is a great number of our constituents who are dissatisfied with it; among whom are many respectable for their talents and patriotism, and respectable for the jealousy they have for their liberty, which, though mistaken in its object, is laudable in its motive. There is a great body of the people falling under this description, who at present feel much inclined to join their support to the cause of Federalism, if they were satisfied on this one point. We ought not to disregard their inclination, but, on principles of amity and moderation, conform to their wishes, and expressly declare the great rights of mankind secured under this Constitution.

---

a. As excerpted in Daniel Farber & Suzanna Sherry, *A History of the American Constitution* (1990).

But I will candidly acknowledge, that, over and above all these considerations, I do conceive that the Constitution may be amended; that is to say, if all power is subject to abuse, that then it is possible the abuse of the powers of the General Government may be guarded against in a more secure manner than is now done, while no one advantage arising from the exercise of that power shall be damaged or endangered by it. We have in this way something to gain, and, if we proceed with caution, nothing to lose.

I believe that the great mass of the people who opposed it, disliked it because it did not contain effectual provisions against the encroachments on particular rights, and those safeguards which they have been long accustomed to have interposed between them and the magistrate who exercises the sovereign power; nor ought we to consider them safe, while a great number of our fellow-citizens think these securities necessary.

It is a fortunate thing that the objection to the Government has been made on the ground I stated; because it will be practicable, on that ground, to obviate the objection, so far as to satisfy the public mind that their liberties will be perpetual, and this without endangering any part of the Constitution, which is considered as essential to the existence of the Government by those who promoted its adoption.

The amendments which have occurred to me, proper to be recommended by Congress to the State Legislatures, are these:

First. That there be prefixed to the Constitution a declaration, that all power is originally vested in, and consequently derived from, the people.

That Government is instituted and ought to be exercised for the benefit of the people; which consists in the enjoyment of life and liberty, with the right of acquiring and using property, and generally of pursuing and obtaining happiness and safety.

That the people have an indubitable, unalienable, and indefeasible right to reform or change their Government, whenever it be found adverse or inadequate to the purposes of its institution.

Secondly. That in article 1st, section 2, clause 3, these words be struck out, to wit: "The number of Representatives shall not exceed one for every thirty thousand, but each State shall have at least one Representative, and until such enumeration shall be made," and that in place thereof be inserted these words, to wit: "After the first actual enumeration, there shall be one Representative for every thirty thousand, until the number amounts to _____, after which the proportion shall be so regulated by Congress, that the number shall never be less than, nor more than _____, but each State shall, after the first enumeration, have at least two Representatives; and prior thereto."

Thirdly. That in article 1st, section 6, clause 1, there be added to the end of the first sentence, these words, to wit: "But no law varying the compensation last ascertained shall operate before the next ensuing election of Representatives."

Fourthly. That in article 1st, section 9, between clauses 3 and 4, be inserted these clauses, to wit: The civil rights of none shall be abridged on account of religious belief or worship, nor shall any national religion be established, nor shall the full and equal rights of conscience be in any manner, or on any pretext, infringed.

The people shall not be deprived or abridged of their right to speak, to write, or to publish their sentiments; and the freedom of the press, as one of the great bulwarks of liberty, shall be inviolable.

The people shall not be restrained from peaceably assembling and consulting for their common good; nor from applying to the Legislature by petitions, or remonstrances, for redress of their grievances.

The right of the people to keep and bear arms shall not be infringed; a well armed and well regulated militia being the best security of a free country: but no person religiously scrupulous of bearing arms shall be compelled to render military service in person.

No soldier shall in time of peace be quartered in any house without the consent of the owner; nor at any time, but in a manner warranted by law.

No person shall be subject, except in cases of impeachment, to more than one punishment or one trial for the same offence; nor shall be compelled to be a witness against himself; nor be deprived of life, liberty, or property without due process of law; nor be obliged to relinquish his property, where it may be necessary for public use, without a just compensation.

Excessive bail shall not be required, nor excessive fines imposed, nor cruel and unusual punishments inflicted.

The rights of the people to be secured in their persons, their houses, their papers, and their other property, from all unreasonable searches and seizures, shall not be violated by warrants issued without probable cause, supported by oath or affirmation, or not particularly describing the places to be searched, or the persons or things to be seized.

In all criminal prosecutions, the accused shall enjoy the right to a speedy and public trial, to be informed of the cause and nature of the accusation, to be confronted with his accusers, and the witnesses against him; to have a compulsory process for obtaining witnesses in his favor; and to have the assistance of counsel for his defence.

The exceptions here or elsewhere in the Constitution, made in favor of particular rights, shall not be so construed as to diminish the just importance of other rights retained by the people, or as to enlarge the powers delegated by the Constitution; but either as actual limitations of such powers, or as inserted merely for greater caution.

Fifthly. That in article 1st, section 10, between clauses 1 and 2, be inserted this clause, to wit:

No State shall violate the equal rights of conscience, or the freedom of the press, or the trial by jury in criminal cases.

Sixthly. That, in article 3d, section 2, be annexed to the end of clause 2d, these words, to wit:

But no appeal to such court shall be allowed where the value in controversy shall not amount to _____ dollars: nor shall any fact triable by jury, according to the course of common law, be otherwise re-examinable than may consist with the principles of common law.

Seventhly. That in article 3d, section 2, the third clause be struck out, and in its place be inserted the clauses following, to wit:

The trial of all crimes (except in cases of impeachments, and cases arising in the land or naval forces, or the militia when on actual service, in time of war or public danger) shall be by an impartial jury of freeholders of the vicinage, with the requisite of unanimity for conviction, of the right of challenge, and other accustomed requisites; and in all crimes punishable with loss of life or member, presentment or indictment by a grand jury shall be an essential preliminary, provided that in cases of crimes committed within any county which may be in possession of an enemy, or in which a general insurrection may prevail, the trial may by law be authorized in some other county of the same State, as near as may be to the seat of the offence.

In cases of crimes committed not within any county, the trial may by law be in such county as the laws shall have prescribed. In suits at common law, between man and man, the trial by jury, as one of the best securities to the rights of the people, ought to remain inviolate.

Eighthly. That immediately after article 6th, be inserted, as article 7th, the clauses following, to wit:

The powers delegated by this Constitution are appropriated to the departments to which they are respectively distributed: so that the Legislative Department shall never exercise powers vested in the Executive or Judicial, nor the Executive exercise the powers vested in the Legislative or Judicial, nor the Judicial exercise the powers vested in the Legislative or Executive Departments.

The powers not delegated by this Constitution, nor prohibited by it to the States, are reserved to the States respectively.

Ninthly. That article 7th be numbered as article 8th.

The people of many States have thought it necessary to raise barriers against power in all forms and departments of Government, and I am inclined to believe, if once bills of rights are established in all the States as well as the Federal Constitution, we shall find, that, although some of them are rather unimportant, yet, upon the whole, they will have a salutary tendency. It may be said, in some instances, they do no more than state the perfect equality of mankind. This, to be sure, is an absolute truth, yet it is not absolutely necessary to be inserted at the head of a Constitution.

In some instances they assert those rights which are exercised by the people in forming and establishing a plan of Government. In other instances, they specify those rights which are retained when particular powers are given up to be exercised by the Legislature. In other instances, they specify positive rights, which may seem to result from the nature of the compact. Trial by jury cannot be considered as a natural right, but a right resulting from a social compact, which regulates the action of the community, but is as essential to secure the liberty of the people as any one of the pre-existent right of nature. In other instances, they lay down dogmatic maxims with respect to the construction of the Government; declaring that the Legislative, Executive, and Judicial branches, shall be kept separate and distinct. Perhaps the best way of securing this in practice is, to provide such checks as will prevent the encroachment of the one upon the other.

But I confess that I do conceive, that in a Government modified like this of the United States, the great danger lies rather in the abuse of the community than in the Legislative body. The prescriptions in favor of liberty ought to be levelled against that quarter where the greatest danger lies, namely, that which possesses the highest prerogative of power. But this is not found in either the Executive or Legislative departments of Government, but in the body of the people, operating by the majority against the minority.

It is true, the powers of the General Government are circumscribed, they are directed to particular objects; but even if Government keeps within those limits, it has certain discretionary powers with respect to the means, which may admit of abuse to a certain extent, in the same manner as the powers of the State Governments under their constitutions may to an indefinite extent; because in the Constitution of the United States, there is a clause granting to Congress the power to make all laws which shall be necessary and proper for carrying into execution all the powers vested in the Government of the United States, or in any department or officer thereof; this enables them to fulfil every purpose for which the Government was established. Now, may not laws be considered necessary and proper by Congress, (for it is for them to judge of the necessity and propriety to accomplish those special purposes which they may have in contemplation,) which laws in themselves are neither necessary nor proper; as well as improper laws could be enacted by the State Legislatures, for fulfilling the more extended objects of those Governments? I will state an instance, which I think in point, and proves that this might be the case. The General Government has a right to pass all laws which shall be necessary to collect its revenue; the means for enforcing the collection are within the direction of the Legislature: may not general warrants be considered necessary for this purpose, as well as for some purposes which it was supposed at the framing of their constitutions the State Governments had in view? If there was reason for restraining the State Governments from exercising this power, there is like reason for restraining the Federal Government.

It may be said, indeed it has been said, that a bill of rights is not necessary, because the establishment of this Government has not repealed those declarations of rights which are added to the several State constitutions; that those rights of the people which had been established by the most solemn act, could not be annihilated by a subsequent act of that people, who meant and declared at the head of the instrument, that they ordained and established a new system, for the express purpose of securing to themselves and posterity the liberties they had gained by an arduous conflict.

I admit the force of this observation, but I do not look upon it to be conclusive. In the first place, it is too uncertain ground to leave this provision upon, if a provision is at all necessary to secure rights so important as many of those I have mentioned are conceived to be, by the public in general, as well as those in particular who opposed the adoption of this Constitution. Besides, some States have no bills of rights, there are others provided with very defective ones, and there are others whose bills of rights are not only defective, but absolutely improper; instead of securing some in the full extent which republican principles would require, they limit them too much to agree with the common ideas of liberty.

It has been objected also against a bill of rights, that, by enumerating particular exceptions to the grant of power, it would disparage those rights which were not placed in that enumeration; and it might follow by implication, that those rights which were not singled out, were intended to be assigned into the hands of the General Government, and were consequently insecure. This is one of the most plausible arguments I have ever heard urged against the admission of a bill of rights into this system; but, I conceive, that it may be guarded against. I have attempted it, as gentlemen may see by turning to the last clause of the fourth resolution.

It has been said that it is unnecessary to load the Constitution with this provision, because it was not found effectual in the constitution of the particular States. It is true, there are a few particular States in which some of the most valuable articles have not, at one time or other, been violated; but it does not follow but they may have to a certain degree, a salutary effect against the abuse of power. If they are incorporated into the Constitution, independent tribunals of justice will consider themselves in a peculiar manner the guardians of those rights; they will be an impenetrable bulwark against every assumption of power in the Legislative or Executive; they will be naturally led to resist every encroachment upon rights expressly stipulated for in the Constitution by the declaration of rights. Besides this security, there is a great probability that such a declaration in the federal system would be enforced; because the State Legislatures will jealously and closely watch the operations of this Government, and be able to resist with more effect every assumption of power, than any other power on earth can do; and the greatest opponents to a Federal Government admit the State Legislatures to be sure guardians of the people's liberty. I conclude, from this view of the subject, that it will be proper in itself, and highly politic, for the tranquillity of the public mind, and the stability of the Government, that we should offer something, in the form I have proposed, to be incorporated in the system of Government, as a declaration of the rights of the people.

I wish, also, in revising the Constitution, we may throw into that section, which interdicts the abuse of certain powers in the State Legislatures, some other provisions of equal, if not greater importance than those already made. The words, "No State shall pass any bill of attainder, *ex post facto* law," & c., were wise and proper restrictions in the Constitution. I think there is more danger of those powers being abused by the State Governments than by the Government of the United States. The same may be said of other powers which they possess, if not controlled by the general principle, that laws are unconstitutional which infringe the rights of the community. I should, therefore, wish to extend this interdiction, and add, as I have stated in the 5th resolution, that no State shall violate the equal right of conscience, freedom of the press, or trial by jury in criminal cases; because it is proper that every Government should be disarmed of powers which trench upon those particular rights.

[T]he State Governments are as liable to attack these invaluable privileges as the General Government is, and therefore ought to be as cautiously guarded against.

I think it will be proper, with respect to the judiciary powers, to satisfy the public mind on those points which I have mentioned. Great inconvenience has been apprehended to suitors from the distance they would be dragged to obtain justice in the Supreme Court of the United States, upon an appeal on an action for a small debt. To remedy this, declare that no appeal shall be made unless the matter in controversy amounts to a particular sum; this, with the regulations respecting jury trials in criminal cases, and suits at common law, it is to be hoped, will quiet and reconcile the minds of the people to that part of the Constitution.

I find, from looking into the amendments proposed by the State conventions, that several are particularly anxious that it should be declared in the Constitution, that the powers not therein delegated should be reserved to the several States. Perhaps other words may define this more precisely than the whole of the instrument now does. I admit they may be deemed unnecessary; but there can be no harm in making such a declaration, if gentlemen will allow that the fact is as stated. I am sure I understand it so, and do therefore propose it.

INDEX

References are to pages

[37]

References are to pages

†